Brill's
New Pauly

CLASSICAL TRADITION
VOLUME II

DEM-IUS

Brill's New Pauly

Brill's

Encyclopaedia of the Ancient World

New Pauly

Edited by
Manfred Landfester in cooperation with
Hubert Cancik and *Helmuth Schneider*

English Edition
Managing Editor *Francis G. Gentry*

Consulting Editors *Craig Kallendorf, Daniel C. Mack*

Assistant Editors *Michael Chase, Tina Chronopoulos,
Rebecca L. Garber, Edda Gentry, Susanne Hakenbeck,
Tina Jerke, Sebastiaan R. van der Mije, Joseph M. Sullivan,
Frank J. Tobin and James K. Walter*

CLASSICAL TRADITION
VOLUME II

DEM-IUS

LEIDEN - BOSTON
2007

BRILL

© Copyright 2007 by Koninklijke Brill NV,
Leiden, The Netherlands

Koninklijke Brill NV incorporates the imprints
Brill, Hotei Publishing, IDC Publishers, Martinus
Nijhoff Publishers and VSP.

Originally published in German as DER NEUE
PAULY. Enzyklopädie der Antike. In Verbindung
mit Hubert Cancik und Helmuth Schneider
herausgegeben von Manfred Landfester.
Copyright © J.B. Metzlersche Verlagsbuch-
handlung und Carl Ernst Poeschel Verlag
GmbH 1996ff./1999ff. Stuttgart/Weimar

Cover design: TopicA (Antoinette Hanekuyk)
Front: Delphi, temple area

Data structuring and typesetting:
pagina GmbH, Tübingen, Germany

ISBN 13 (volume) 978 90 04 14222 0
ISBN 13 (set) 978 90 04 12259 8
ISBN (volume) 90 04 14222 3
ISBN (set) 90 04 12259 1

Table of Contents

Preface

The NEW PAULY is a *Reallexikon* or encyclopaedia of the ancient world. It is supposed to be a practical reference work for everyday use, also to those, who like the classic German authors Herder, Goethe and Schiller "only know a very modest amount of Greek" (W. v. Humboldt, 1795). To remain readable and clear it offers simple paraphrases, quotes in translation, as well as numerous illustrations, survey maps and tables.

The NEW PAULY is intended as an aid for the study of Greek and Roman culture and its multifaceted presence in all periods of European and, since the Early Modern period, world history. Its entries and articles have been updated to the current state of scholarship while continuing the tradition which started with the old, but in its own day innovative 'Realencyclopädie der klassischen Altertumswissenschaft' of August Friedrich (von) Pauly and Georg Wissowa (1839ff., 1894ff.). Entries offer easy, direct access to basic information – names, places, dates, objects – from all areas of Greek and Roman culture as well as their predecessors, neighbours and heirs. The articles in the 'Antiquity' volumes are brief, usually factual, and closely related to persons and texts. By contrast, survey articles provide orientation in periods, social and economic structures, genres, and philosophical systems. There the inclination to monographic coverage or to write intellectual essays was also resisted. The 'encyclopaedia' is a genre of its own.

The *Sachlexikon* that August Friedrich (von) Pauly (1796–1845) had envisioned for the "concrete field of Classical Studies" was continued by Georg Wissowa (1859–1931) and Konrat Ziegler (1884–1974) and finally completed in 1980 with 86 volumes, 15 supplementary volumes and an index of additions, supplements and the names of the 1096 contributors.

The *Kleine Pauly* (1964–1975) a selection from the larger epynomous encyclopaedia as determined by modern academic interests, was edited by Konrat Ziegler, Walther Sontheimer and Hans Gärtner. Because of numerous new articles that not only incorporated the growth in material but also new methods and modern perspectives, the *Kleine Pauly* is more than an abbreviated edition of the large encyclopaedia. However, space and time for the development of new areas of emphasis was lacking.

Since Pauly and Wissowa an abundance of disciplines, schools and guiding theses in general, comparative and ancient cultural and literary studies has sprung up. Mass psychology, *histoire des mentalités*, historical anthropology, social history, history of technology, communication studies, aerial and underwater archaeology should be mentioned. Observations and fieldwork of modern trends in research, such as the *École des Annales*, resulted, first in research on the Middle Ages and the Early Modern period, in a discovery and awareness of facts that had not so far been considered or were forgotten: the study of *longue durée*, the history of the body and sexuality, daily life, mechanisms of communication, identification, distancing and psychological models of mass phenomena that examined the genesis of concepts of friend and foe. These themes also had their impact in Classical Studies. Particular mention should be made of specialisms such as religious aesthetics and ethno-psychoanalysis of Greek myths (Georges Devereux). Even this brief catalogue demonstrates that the possibilities and thematic breadth of a new encyclopaedia have not only grown but must also satisfy the demands on such a work.

In the NEW PAULY the decentralized organisation of work on more than 20 subjects should do justice to this increase in material and the diversity in methodology. The subject editors have developed the entries on their own account and in continuous mutual exchange. The editorial office, located in Tübingen for technical and historical reasons, co-ordinates the project and manages the scholarly work performed by the editors and authors independently. It should be noted that the first editors, August Friedrich Pauly, Christian Walz (1802–1857) and Wilhelm Sigmund Teuffel (1820–1878) worked in Stuttgart and Tübingen.

The NEW PAULY has, in contrast to the *Kleine Pauly*, two independent parts – 'Antiquity' (A-Z) and 'Classical Tradition' (A-Z) – and is doubled in volume, making it possible to include the most recent research results, to develop additional areas of emphasis and to add thematic articles, which complement the traditional subject-oriented perspective of the 'Pauly' with surveys.

Classical antiquity, i.e. Greek and Roman culture in all aspects – language and economics, family and politics, law and religion, literature and art, society and philosophy – constitutes the core of this encyclopaedia. Here (classical) antiquity is conceived of as an epoch of the cultural sphere of the Mediterranean, early Greek culture as a culture on the fringes of the ancient Near East, the 'End of Antiquity' as the separation of the Byzantine, Germanic and Islamic cultures from their Mediterranean connection. Therefore, the chronological scope of the 'Antiquity' volumes of the NEW PAULY ranges from the 'Aegean Koine' (middle of the 2nd millennium BC) to the formation of early medieval Europe (AD 600 to 800).

The following emphases are to be noted:
- the Oriental precursors of Greek and Roman culture, their foundations and their influence on the Celts, Germans, Slavs, Arabs as well as on Judaism and Christianity;

- the incorporation of Byzantine studies;
- a strengthening of economic and social history as well as the history of daily life;
- an expansion of the history of philosophical terminology;
- an equal treatment of verbal, visual and material sources.

The effects of ancient culture and the history of its study are further areas of emphasis in the NEW PAULY. That which is called 'antiquity' has always been the result of selection of and interpretation of ancient sources and phenomena subject to diverging interests. The various 'renaissances', the factual continuity, the repeatedly disrupted forms of continuity, and the layering of the phases of reception are discussed in the 'Antiquity' volumes (e.g. Astrology) or have their own entries (e.g. Alexandrinism, Greek Revival, Humanism) in the volumes on the Classical Tradition. For this purpose not only *belle lettrie* but also law and medicine, the revival of ancient architecture, the continuation of ancient spatial structures in medieval city centres, road systems and division of land are included. In contrast to the 'Antiquity' volumes, the articles on the Classical Tradition were conceived systematically, theoretically, and paradigmatically and problematized and in comprehensive surveys of countries and periods.

Culture is the state of its texts, whether acoustical, optical or 'motorial' – i.e., of music and in word, script and art, gestures, ritual and drama. All texts are defined by their context. The *Sitz im Leben*, the role of the observer, the user, the reader, the 'horizon of expectations' of the recipients must not only be sought for the primary audiences but also for audiences more remote in time and space.

The name 'antiquity' involves several languages, cultures and a history of one and a half millennium. Processes of reception can already be observed in antiquity itself. The history of reception within antiquity itself should go beyond the end of antiquity in the NEW PAULY, but so that no new myth of uninterrupted continuity, of an unchanged antiquity will be created. It is not antiquity *per se* but a select construct that itself was the result of multiple processes of reception. Each attempt to approach antiquity more or less deliberately starts with one's own position, contains imaginary components and, as a result, leads to more or less pronounced 'deformations'. Creative approaches are often 'leaps' from their own time over mediating tradition bearers and institutions 'to the sources themselves', contrary to authorities. Research into the history of influence not only registers these traditions and Renaissances but addresses deformations, the loss of meaning, abuse, ignorance and rejection.

The development of the arts, literature, philology and other academic disciplines has also been a process of familiarization and confrontation with antiquity since the early Middle Ages. Antiquity served as an ideal and model but was also criticized and fought against. The claim on antiquity, invoking an actual or pretended continuity, has been a political argument since the early Middle Ages both in the West and the Byzantine East. Modern Europe defined its self-understanding in a controversial discussion about antiquity (natural sciences, natural law and human rights, education).

An independent part of this history of reception is the history of science. It is not, as its opponents claim, a necrology of a discipline that has declared itself dead, closed and past. It is also not a fashionable invention but already since the 18th century a firm component of classical studies. The study of history of science arises from the necessity to account for the social, political and intellectual foundations of research and its outcomes.

History of science in the NEW PAULY examines the conditions that lead to the development of fields, themes and methods, the history of disciplines, of genres and forms in academia (commentary, footnote, index), the consequences for the field of the differentiation of the once all embracing Classical Studies into ancient history, archaeology, linguistics; how the division and attribution of individual areas has changed, how Latin philology became the study of Latin and allied itself with Middle and Neo-latin rather than with the study of Greek. In the NEW PAULY the history of reception and the history of science are advanced in special articles on countries. The history of science considers the present form of a discipline as a historical problem; it also functions as self-criticism and as the recollection of errors and blind alleys.

The editors express their gratitude to the publishing house J. B. Metzler, which in 1992 repurchased the rights to the *Pauly-Wissowa* and the *Kleine Pauly* and has recreated its old tradition of an encyclopaedia of classical studies with the planned publication of the large encyclopaedia and its commitment to a NEW PAULY.

The Philological Seminar and the University of Tübingen have supported the project in many ways.

Based on the established and fertile co-operation between the Centre for Data Processing (Professor Dr. Wilhelm Ort, Dirk G. Kottke) and the Philological Seminar, the electronic text and image processing were conceived as the foundation from the beginning. Dr. Matthias Kopp, who is equally qualified as an established historian and an expert in data processing, has converted these plans into concrete results.

Ms. Vera Sauer MA (Stuttgart) has performed the essential work in historical geography. The cartography was handled by Anne-Maria Wittke and Richard Szydlak, the images by Dr. Ingrid Hitzl and Günter Müller.

Researchers and research assistants have worked with great commitment in editing and in the individual subject areas. Cecilia Ames, Georg Dörr, Heike Kunz, Michael Mohr and Dorothea Sigel are named in place of many others. We are grateful to them all.

Hubert Cancik (University of Tübingen)
Helmuth Schneider (University of Kassel)
Summer 1996

Volumes 13–15

In contrast to the Antiquity section of this encyclopaedia, with its cornucopia of headwords and a majority of short entries, the lemmata in the section on The Classical Tradition are fewer but longer. Only in this way can the systematic structure of the subject-matter be properly accommodated within a lexical framework. In this respect, the Classical Tradition section resembles older encyclopaedias.

With its focus on the history of the reception of antiquity and on the history of classical studies, the Reception volumes enter new lexicographical territory. And yet, an orientation towards classical, i.e. Greco-Roman, antiquity prohibits an evenly-spread exploration of this new territory: the Near East, Judaism and Christianity can only be treated selectively, although in the Antiquity section they do constitute new points of emphasis.

Of course this encyclopaedia is primarily a repository for the fruits of scholarly research that are currently available to us. But by presenting this information in the individual articles in a methodical arrangement, the Reception History becomes itself a tool for research. Not all areas of reception have been explored to an equal degree, so that, for example, contributions on engineering and technology, natural science, social history and economic history have not been realised to the extent that might have been desirable.

The choice of headwords was guided by applying the following categories: (1) the various areas of reception (art and architecture, the educational system, everyday culture, law, literature, medicine, natural science, philosophy, political theories and symbols, religion, social and economic history), (2) individual countries and particular cultural regions (e.g. the Arabic-Islamic cultural sphere), (3) selected cultural movements and periods in European history, (4) the disciplines and methods of classical scholarship, (5) the institutions of reception and scholarship (academies, museums, schools, universities, scholarly societies) and (6) significant excavations and finds. In developing our headwords for the individual areas of reception and the history of scholarship, we were guided by the basic terms and conventions of the disciplines in question, while for cultural movements and periods, traditional designations such as, for instance, Baroque and Renaissance have been retained.

As the headwords do not fit into one conceptual grid, thematic overlaps are inevitable – they are even welcome inasfar as they enhance the accessibility of the individual articles. Especially between country articles and those on cultural movements and periods, there is a thematic overlap arising from differing scholarly perspectives: whereas country articles will primarily be concerned with national idiosyncrasies of reception, the other group of entries will emphasize the international character of the phenomenon.

In order to help the reader find his way despite the relatively small number of entries, a list of all entries comprising this volume is printed directly before its first article.

Manfred Landfester
(University of Giessen)
July 1999

Notes to the User

Arrangement of Entries

The entries are arranged alphabetically and, if applicable, placed in chronological order. In the case of alternative forms or sub-entries, cross-references will lead to the respective main entry. Composite entries can be found in more than one place (e.g. *a commentariis* refers to *commentariis, a*).
Identical entries are differentiated by numbering.

Spelling of Entries

Greek words and names are as a rule latinized, following the predominant practice of reference works in the English language, with the notable exception of technical terms. Institutions and places (cities, rivers, islands, countries etc.) often have their conventional English names (e.g. *Rome* not *Roma*). The latinized versions of Greek names and words are generally followed by the Greek and the literal transliteration in brackets, e.g. *Aeschylus* (Αἰσχύλος; *Aischýlos*).
Oriental proper names are usually spelled according to the 'Tübinger Atlas des Vorderen Orients' (TAVO), but again conventional names in English are also used. In the maps, the names of cities, rivers, islands, countries etc. follow ancient spelling and are transliterated fully to allow for differences in time, e.g. both Καππαδόκια and *Cappadocia* can be found. The transliteration of non-Latin scripts can be found in the 'List of Transliterations'.
Latin and transliterated Greek words are italicized in the article text. However, where Greek transliterations do not follow immediately upon a word written in Greek, they will generally appear in italics, but without accents or makra.

Abbreviations

All abbreviations can be found in the 'List of Abbreviations'. Collections of inscriptions, coins and papyri are listed under their *sigla*.

Bibliographies

Most entries have bibliographies, consisting of numbered and/or alphabetically organized references. References within the text to the numbered bibliographic items are in square brackets (e.g. [1.5 n.23] refers to the first title of the bibliography, page 5, note 23). The abbreviations within the bibliographies follow the rules of the 'List of Abbreviations'.

Cross-references

Articles are linked through a system of cross-references with an arrow → before the entry that is being referred to.
Cross-references to related entries are given at the end of an article, generally before the bibliographic notes. If reference is made to a homonymous entry, the respective number is also added.
Cross-references to entries within the *Classical Tradition* volumes are added in small capitals; cross-references to entries in the *Antiquity* volumes are added in regular type.
It can occur that in a cross-reference a name is spelled differently from the surrounding text: e.g., a cross-reference to Mark Antony has to be to Marcus → Antonius, as his name will be found in a list of other names containing the component 'Antonius'.

List of Transliterations

Transliteration of ancient Greek

α	a	alpha
αι	ai	
αυ	au	
β	b	beta
γ	g	gamma; γ before γ, κ, ξ, χ: n
δ	d	delta
ε	e	epsilon
ει	ei	
ευ	eu	
ζ	z	z(d)eta
η	ē	eta
ηυ	ēu	
θ	th	theta
ι	i	iota
κ	k	kappa
λ	l	la(m)bda
μ	m	mu
ν	n	nu
ξ	x	xi
ο	o	omicron
οι	oi	
ου	ou	
π	p	pi
ϱ	r	rho
σ, ς	s	sigma
τ	t	tau
υ	y	upsilon
φ	ph	phi
χ	ch	chi
ψ	ps	psi
ω	ō	omega
ʽ	h	spiritus asper
ᾳ	ai	iota subscriptum (similarly ῃ, ῳ)

In transliterated Greek the accents are retained (acute ´, grave `, and circumflex ˆ). Long vowels with the circumflex accent have no separate indication of vowel length (makron).

Transliteration and pronounciation of Modern Greek

Only those sounds and combinations of sounds are mentioned which are different from Ancient Greek.

Consonants

β	v	
γ	gh	before 'dark' vowels like Engl. 'go'
	j	before 'light' vowels
δ	dh	like Engl. 'the'
ζ	z	like Engl. 'zeal'
θ	th	like Engl. 'thing'

Combinations of consonants

γκ	ng	
	g	in initial position
μπ	mb	
	b	in initial position
ντ	nd	
	d	in initial position

Vowels

η	i
υ	i

Diphthongs

αι	e	
αυ	av	
	af	before hard consonants
ει	i	
ευ	ev	
	ef	before hard consonants
οι	i	
υι	ii	

Spiritus asper is not pronounced. The Ancient Greek accent normally retains its position, but the distinction between ´, ` and ˆ has disappeared.

Transliteration of Hebrew

א	a	alef
ב	b	bet
ג	g	gimel
ד	d	dalet
ה	h	he
ו	w	vav
ז	z	zayin
ח	ḥ	khet
ט	ṭ	tet
י	y	yod
כ	k	kaf

ל	l	lamed
מ	m	mem
נ	n	nun
ס	s	samek
ע	ʿ	ayin
פ	p/f	pe
צ	ṣ	tsade
ק	q	qof
ר	r	resh
שׂ	ś	sin
שׁ	š	shin
ת	t	tav

Pronunciation of Turkish

Turkish uses Latin script since 1928. Pronunciation and spelling generally follow the same rules as European languages. Phonology according to G. Lewis, Turkish Grammar, 2000.

A	a	French a in *avoir*
B	b	b
C	c	j in *jam*
Ç	ç	ch in *church*
D	d	d
E	e	French ê in *être*
F	f	f
G	g	g in *gate* or in *angular*
Ğ	ğ	lengthens preceding vowel
H	h	h in *have*
I	ı	i in *cousin*
İ	i	French i in *si*
J	j	French j
K	k	c in *cat* or in *cure*
L	l	l in *list* or in *wool*
M	m	m
N	n	n
O	o	French o in *note*
Ö	ö	German ö
P	p	p
R	r	r
S	s	s in *sit*
Ş	ş	sh in *shape*
T	t	t
U	u	u in *put*
Ü	ü	German ü
V	v	v
Y	y	y in *yet*
Z	z	z

Transliteration of Arabic, Persian, and Ottoman Turkish

ء, ا	ʾ, ā	ʾ	ʾ	hamza, alif
ب	b	b	b	bāʾ
پ	–	p	p	pe
ت	t	t	t	tāʾ
ث	ṯ	s	s	tāʾ
ج	ǧ	ǧ	ǧ	ǧīm
چ	–	č	č	čim
ح	ḥ	ḥ	ḥ	ḥāʾ
خ	ḫ	ḫ	ḫ	ḫāʾ
د	d	d	d	dāl
ذ	ḏ	z	z	dāl
ر	r	r	r	rāʾ
ز	z	z	z	zāy
ژ	–	ž	ž	že
س	s	s	s	sīn
ش	š	š	š	šīn
ص	ṣ	ṣ	ṣ	ṣād
ض	ḍ	ḍ	ḍ	ḍād
ط	ṭ	ṭ	ṭ	ṭāʾ
ظ	ẓ	ẓ	ẓ	ẓāʾ
ع	ʿ	ʿ	ʿ	ʿain
غ	ġ	ġ	ġ	ġain
ف	f	f	f	fāʾ
ق	q	q	q, k	qāf
ك	k	k	k, g, ñ	kāf
گ	–	g	g, ñ	gāf
ل	l	l	l	lām
م	m	m	m	mīm
ن	n	n	n	nūn
ه	h	h	h	hāʾ
و	w, ū	v	v	wāw
ى	y, ī	y	y	yāʾ

Transliteration of other languages

Akkadian (Assyrian-Babylonian), Hittite and Sumerian are transliterated according to the rules of RLA and TAVO. For Egyptian the rules of the Lexikon der Ägyptologie are used. The transliteration of Indo-European follows Rix, HGG. The transliteration of Old Indian is after M. Mayrhofer, Etymologisches Wörterbuch des Altindoarischen, 1992ff. Avestian is done according to K. Hoffmann, B. Forssman, Avestische Laut- und Flexionslehre, 1996. Old Persian follows R.G. Kent, Old Persian, ²1953 (additions from K. Hoffmann, Aufsätze zur Indoiranistik vol. 2, 1976, 622ff.); other Iranian languages are after R. Schmitt, Compendium linguarum Iranicarum, 1989, and after D.N. MacKenzie, A Concise Pahlavi Dictionary, ³1990. For Armenian the rules of R. Schmitt, Grammatik des Klassisch-Armenischen, 1981, and of the Revue des études arméniennes, apply. The languages of Asia Minor are transliterated according to HbdOr. For Mycenean, Cyprian see Heubeck and Masson; for Italic scripts and Etruscan see Vetter and ET.

List of Abbreviations

1. Special Characters

→	see (cross-reference)	i̯, u̯	consonantal i, u
<	originated from (ling.)	m̥, n̥	vocalized m, n
>	evolved into (ling.)	l̥, r̥	vocalized l, r
√	root	|	syllable end
*	born/reconstructed form (ling.)	#	word end
∞	married	⟨ ⟩	transliteration
ă	short vowel	/ /	phonemic representation
ā	long vowel	[ ]	apocryphal
†	deceased		

2. List of General Abbreviations

Common abbreviations (e.g., etc.) are not included in the list of general abbreviations.

abl.	ablative	contd.	continued
acc.	accusative	Copenhagen, NCG	Copenhagen, Ny Carlsberg Glyptothek
Athens, AM	Athens, Acropolis Museum	Copenhagen, NM	Copenhagen, National Museum
Athens, BM	Athens, Benaki Museum	Copenhagen, TM	Copenhagen, Thorvaldsen Museum
Athens, NM	Athens, National Museum	d.	died
Athens, NUM	Athens, Numismatic Museum	dat.	dative
b.	born	decret.	decretum, decreta
Baltimore, WAG	Baltimore, Walters Art Gallery	diss.	dissertation
Basle, AM	Basle, Antikenmuseum	ed.	edidit, editio, editor, edited (by)
Berlin, PM	Berlin, Pergamonmuseum	edd.	ediderunt
Berlin, SM	Berlin, Staatliche Museen	epist.	epistulae
bk(s).	book(s)	f.l.	falsa lectio
Bonn, RL	Bonn, Rheinisches Landesmuseum	fem.	feminine
Boston, MFA	Boston, Museum of Fine Arts	fig(s).	figure(s)
Bull.	Bulletin, Bullettino	Florence, MA	Florence, Museo Archeologico
c.	circa	Florence, UF	Florence, Uffizi
Cambridge, FM	Cambridge, Fitzwilliam Museum	fr.	fragment
carm.	carmen, carmina	Frankfurt, LH	Frankfurt, Liebighaus
Cat.	Catalogue, Catalogo	gen.	genitive
cent.	century	Geneva, MAH	Geneva, Musée d'Art et d'Histoire
ch.	chapter	Ger.	German
Cod.	Codex, Codices, Codizes	Gk.	Greek
col.	column	Hamburg, MKG	Hamburg, Museum für Kunst und Gewerbe
conc.	acta concilii	Hanover, KM	Hanover, Kestner-Museum
Cologne, RGM	Cologne, Römisch Germanisches Museum		
comm.	commentary		
Congr.	Congrss, Congrès, Congresso		

inventory no.	inventory number
Istanbul, AM	Istanbul, Archaeological Museum
itin.	itineraria
Kassel, SK	Kassel, Staatliche Kunstsammlungen
l.	lex
l.	line
L.	Lucius
l.c.	loco citato
Lat.	Latin
leg.	leges
lib.	liber, libri
ling.	linguistic(ally)
loc.	locative
London, BM	London, British Museum
Madrid, PR	Madrid, Prado
Malibu, GM	Malibu, Getty Museum
masc.	masculinum, masculine
Moscow, PM	Moscow, Pushkin Museum
MS(S)	manuscript(s)
Munich, GL	Munich, Glyptothek
Munich, SA	Munich, Staatliche Antikensammlung
Munich, SM	Munich, Staatliche Münzsammlung
Mus.	Museum, Musée, Museo
n.d.	no date
Naples, MAN	Naples, Museo Archeologico Nazionale
neutr.	neutrum, neuter, neutral
New York, MMA	New York, Metropolitan Museum of Arts
no.	number
nom.	nominative
N.S.	Neue Serie, New Series, Nouvelle Série, Nuova Seria
NT	New Testament
Op.	Opus, Opera
opt.	optative
OT	Old Testament
Oxford, AM	Oxford, Ashmolean Museum
p.	page
P	Papyrus
Palermo, MAN	Palermo, Museo Archeologico Nazionale
Paris, BN	Paris, Bibliothèque Nationale
Paris, CM	Paris, Cabinet des Médailles
Paris, LV	Paris, Louvre
pl.	plate
plur.	plural
pr(aef).	praefatio
Ps.-	Pseudo
rev.	revised

Rome, MC	Rome, Museo Capitolino
Rome, MN	Rome, Museo Nazionale
Rome, MV	Rome, Museo Vaticano
Rome, VA	Rome, Villa Albani
Rome, VG	Rome, Villa Giulia
Ser.	Serie, Series, Série, Seria
s.v.	sub voce
sc.	scilicet
schol.	scholion, scholia
serm.	sermo
s(in)g.	singular
Soc.	Society, Societé, Società
St.	Saint
St. Petersburg, HR	St. Petersburg, Hermitage
Stud.	Studia, Studien, Studies, Studi
The Hague, MK	The Hague, Muntenkabinet
Thessaloniki, NM	Thessaloniki, National Museum
tit.	titulus
trans.	translation, translated (by)
t.t.	terminus technicus
Univ.	Universität, University, Université, Università
v	verso
Vienna, KM	Vienna, Kunsthistorisches Museum
vol(s).	volume(s)

3. Bibliographic Abbreviations

A&A
Antike und Abendland
A&R
Atene e Roma
AA
Archäologischer Anzeiger
AAA
Annals of Archaeology and Anthropology
AAAlg
S. GSELL, Atlas archéologique de l'Algérie. Édition spéciale des cartes au 200.000 du Service Géographique de l' Armée, 1911, repr. 1973
AAHG
Anzeiger für die Altertumswissenschaften, publication of the Österreichische Humanistische Gesellschaft
AArch
Acta archeologica
AASO
The Annual of the American Schools of Oriental Research
AATun 050
E. BABELON, R. CAGNAT, S. REINACH (ed.), Atlas archéologique de la Tunisie (1 : 50.000), 1893
AATun 100
R. CAGNAT, A. MERLIN (ed.), Atlas archéologique de la Tunisie (1: 100.000), 1914

AAWG

Abhandlungen der Akademie der Wissenschaften in Göttingen. Philologisch-historische Klasse

AAWM

Abhandlungen der Akademie der Wissenschaften und Literatur in Mainz. Geistes- und sozialwissenschaftliche Klasse

AAWW

Anzeiger der Österreichischen Akademie der Wissenschaften in Wien. Philosophisch-historische Klasse

ABAW

Abhandlungen der Bayerischen Akademie der Wissenschaften. Philosophisch-historische Klasse

Abel

F.-M. ABEL, Géographie de la Palestine 2 vols., 1933–38

ABG,

Archiv für Begriffsgeschichte: Bausteine zu einem historischen Wörterbuch der Philosophie

ABr

P. ARNDT, F. BRUCKMANN (ed.), Griechische und römische Porträts, 1891 – 1912; E. LIPPOLD (ed.), Text vol., 1958

ABSA

Annual of the British School at Athens

AC

L'Antiquité Classique

Acta

Acta conventus neo-latini Lovaniensis, 1973

AD

Archaiologikon Deltion

ADAIK

Abhandlungen des Deutschen Archäologischen Instituts Kairo

Adam

J.P. ADAM, La construction romaine. Matériaux et techniques, 1984

ADAW

Abhandlungen der Deutschen Akademie der Wissenschaften zu Berlin. Klasse für Sprachen, Literatur und Kunst

ADB

Allgemeine Deutsche Biographie

AdI

Annali dell'Istituto di Corrispondenza Archeologica

AE

L'Année épigraphique

AEA

Archivo Espanol de Arqueología

AEM

Archäologisch-epigraphische Mitteilungen aus Österreich

AfO

Archiv für Orientforschung

AGD

Antike Gemmen in deutschen Sammlungen 4 vols., 1968–75

AGM

Archiv für Geschichte der Medizin

Agora

The Athenian Agora. Results of the Excavations by the American School of Classical Studies of Athens, 1953 ff.

AGPh

Archiv für Geschichte der Philosophie

AGR

Akten der Gesellschaft für griechische und hellenistische Rechtsgeschichte

AHAW

Abhandlungen der Heidelberger Akademie der Wissenschaften. Philosophisch-historische Klasse

AHES

Archive for History of Exact Sciences

AIHS

Archives internationales d'histoire des sciences

AION

Annali del Seminario di Studi del Mondo Classico, Sezione di Archeologia e Storia antica

AJ

The Archaeological Journal of the Royal Archaeological Institute of Great Britain and Ireland

AJA

American Journal of Archaeology

AJAH

American Journal of Ancient History

AJBA

Australian Journal of Biblical Archaeology

AJN

American Journal of Numismatics

AJPh

American Journal of Philology

AK

Antike Kunst

AKG

Archiv für Kulturgeschichte

AKL

G. MEISSNER (ed.), Allgemeines Künstlerlexikon: Die bildenden Künstler aller Zeiten und Völker, ²1991 ff.

AKM

Abhandlungen für die Kunde des Morgenlandes

Albrecht

M. v. ALBRECHT, Geschichte der römischen Literatur, ²1994

Alessio

G. ALESSIO, Lexicon etymologicum. Supplemento ai Dizionari etimologici latini e romanzi, 1976

Alexander

M.C. ALEXANDER, Trials in the Late Roman Republic: 149 BC to 50 BC (Phoenix Suppl. Vol. 26), 1990

Alföldi

A. ALFÖLDI, Die monarchische Repräsentation im römischen Kaiserreiche, 1970, repr. ³1980

Alföldy, FH

G. ALFÖLDY, Fasti Hispanienses. Senatorische Reichsbeamte und Offiziere in den spanischen Provinzen des römischen Reiches von Augustus bis Diokletian, 1969

Alföldy, Konsulat
  G. ALFÖLDY, Konsulat und Senatorenstand unter
  den Antoninen. Prosopographische Untersuchungen
  zur senatorischen Führungsschicht (Antiquitas 1,
  27), 1977
Alföldy, RG
  G. ALFÖLDY, Die römische Gesellschaft. Ausge-
  wählte Beiträge, 1986
Alföldy, RH
  G. ALFÖLDY, Römische Heeresgeschichte, 1987
Alföldy, RS
  G. ALFÖLDY, Römische Sozialgeschichte, ³1984
ALLG
  Archiv für lateinische Lexikographie und Gramma-
  tik
Altaner
  B. ALTANER, Patrologie. Leben, Schriften und Lehre
  der Kirchenväter, ⁹1980
AMI
  Archäologische Mitteilungen aus Iran
Amyx, Addenda
  C.W. NEEFT, Addenda et Corrigenda to D.A. Amyx,
  Corinthian Vase-Painting, 1991
Amyx, CVP
  D.A. AMYX, Corinthian Vase-Painting of the Ar-
  chaic Period 3 vols., 1988
Anadolu
  Anadolu (Anatolia)
Anatolica
  Anatolica
AncSoc
  Ancient Society
Anderson
  J.G. ANDERSON, A Journey of Exploration in Pontus
  (Studia pontica 1), 1903
Anderson Cumont/Grégoire
  J.G. ANDERSON, F. CUMONT, H. GRÉGOIRE, Recueil
  des inscriptions grecques et latines du Pont et de l'Ar-
  ménie (Studia pontica 3), 1910
André, botan.
  J. ANDRÉ, Lexique des termes de botanique en latin,
  1956
André, oiseaux
  J. ANDRÉ, Les noms d'oiseaux en latin, 1967
André, plantes
  J. ANDRÉ, Les noms de plantes dans la Rome an-
  tique, 1985
Andrews
  K. ANDREWS, The Castles of Morea, 1953
ANET
  J.B. PRITCHARD, Ancient Near Eastern Texts Relat-
  ing to the Old Testament, ³1969, repr. 1992
AnnSAAt
  Annuario della Scuola Archeologica di Atene
ANRW
  H. TEMPORINI, W. HAASE (ed.), Aufstieg und Nie-
  dergang der römischen Welt, 1972 ff.
ANSMusN
  Museum Notes. American Numismatic Society

AntAfr
  Antiquités africaines
AntChr
  Antike und Christentum
AntPl
  Antike Plastik
AO
  Der Alte Orient
AOAT
  Alter Orient und Altes Testament
APF
  Archiv für Papyrusforschung und verwandte Gebie-
  te
APh
  L'Année philologique
Arangio-Ruiz
  V. ARANGIO-RUIZ, Storia del diritto romano, ⁶1953
Arcadia
  Arcadia. Zeitschrift für vergleichende Literaturwis-
  senschaft
ArchCl
  Archeologia Classica
ArchE
  Archaiologike ephemeris
ArcheologijaSof
  Archeologija. Organ na Archeologiceskija institut i
  muzej pri B'lgarskata akademija na naukite
ArchHom
  Archaeologia Homerica, 1967ff.
ArtAntMod
  Arte antica e moderna
ARW
  Archiv für Religionswissenschaft
AS
  Anatolian Studies
ASAA
  Annuario della Scuola Archeologica di Atene e delle
  Missioni italiane in Oriente
ASL
  Archiv für das Studium der neueren Sprachen und
  Literaturen
ASNP
  Annali della Scuola Normale Superiore di Pisa, Clas-
  se di Lettere e Filosofia
ASpr
  Die Alten Sprachen
ASR
  B. ANDREAE (ed.), Die antiken Sarkophagreliefs,
  1952 ff.
Athenaeum
  Athenaeum
ATL
  B.D. MERITT, H.T. WADE-GERY, M.F. McGRECOR,
  Athenian Tribute Lists 4 vols., 1939–53
AU
  Der altsprachliche Unterricht
Aulock
  H. v. AULOCK, Münzen und Städte Pisidiens
  (MDAI(Ist) Suppl. 8) 2 vols., 1977–79

Austin

C. AUSTIN (ed.), Comicorum graecorum fragmenta in papyris reperta, 1973

BA

Bolletino d'Arte del Ministero della Publica Istruzione

BAB

Bulletin de l'Académie Royale de Belgique. Classe des Lettres

BABesch

Bulletin antieke beschaving. Annual Papers on Classical Archaeology

Badian, Clientelae

E. BADIAN, Foreign Clientelae, 1958

Badian, Imperialism

E. BADIAN, Roman Imperialism in the Late Republic, 1967

BaF

Baghdader Forschungen

Bagnall

R.S. BAGNALL ET AL., Consuls of the Later Roman Empire (Philological Monographs of the American Philological Association 36), 1987

BalkE

Balkansko ezikoznanie

BalkSt

Balkan Studies

BaM

Baghdader Mitteilungen

Bardenhewer, GAL

O. BARDENHEWER, Geschichte der altkirchlichen Literatur, Vols. 1–2, ²1913 f.; Vols. 3–5, 1912–32; repr. Vols. 1–5, 1962

Bardenhewer, Patr.

O. BARDENHEWER, Patrologie, ³1910

Bardon

H. BARDON, La littérature latine inconnue 2 vols., 1952 – 56

Baron

W. BARON (ed.), Beiträge zur Methode der Wissenschaftsgeschichte, 1967

BASO

Bulletin of the American Schools of Oriental Research

Bauer/Aland

W. BAUER, K. ALAND (ed.), Griechisch-deutsches Wörterbuch zu den Schriften des Neuen Testamentes und der frühchristlichen Literatur, ⁶1988

Baumann, LRRP

R.A. BAUMAN, Lawyers in Roman Republican Politics. A study of the Roman Jurists in their Political Setting, 316–82 BC (Münchener Beiträge zur Papyrusforschung und antiken Rechtsgeschichte), 1983

Baumann, LRTP

R.A. BAUMAN, Lawyers in Roman Transitional Politics. A Study of the Roman Jurists in their Political Setting in the Late Republic and Triumvirate (Münchener Beiträge zur Papyrusforschung und antiken Rechtsgeschichte), 1985

BB

Bezzenbergers Beiträge zur Kunde der indogermanischen Sprachen

BCAR

Bollettino della Commissione Archeologica Comunale di Roma

BCH

Bulletin de Correspondance Hellénique

BE

Bulletin épigraphique

Beazley, ABV

J.D. BEAZLEY, Attic Black-figure Vase-Painters, 1956

Beazley, Addenda²

TH.H. CARPENTER (ed.), Beazley Addenda, ²1989

Beazley, ARV²

J.D. BEAZLEY, Attic Red-figure Vase-Painters, ²1963

Beazley, EVP

J.D. BEAZLEY, Etruscan Vase Painting, 1947

Beazley, Paralipomena

J.D. BEAZLEY, Paralipomena. Additions to Attic Black-figure Vase-Painters and to Attic Red-figure Vase-Painters, ²1971

Bechtel, Dial.¹

F. BECHTEL, Die griechischen Dialekte 3 vols., 1921–24²

Bechtel, Dial.²

F. BECHTEL, Die griechischen Dialekte 3 vols., ⁴1963

Bechtel, HPN

F. BECHTEL, Die historischen Personennamen des Griechischen bis zur Kaiserzeit, 1917

Belke

K. BELKE, Galatien und Lykaonien (Denkschriften der Österreichischen Akademie der Wissenschaften, Philosophisch-Historische Klasse 172; TIB 4), 1984

Belke/Mersich

K. BELKE, N. MERSICH, Phrygien und Pisidien (Denkschriften der Österreichischen Akademie der Wissenschaften, Philosophisch-Historische Klasse 211; TIB 7), 1990

Bell

K.E. BELL, Place-Names in Classical Mythology, Greece, 1989

Beloch, Bevölkerung

K.J. BELOCH, Die Bevölkerung der griechisch-römischen Welt, 1886

Beloch, GG

K.J. BELOCH, Griechische Geschichte 4 vols., ²1912–27, repr. 1967

Beloch, RG

K.J. BELOCH, Römische Geschichte bis zum Beginn der Punischen Kriege, 1926

Bengtson

H. BENGTSON, Die Strategie in der hellenistischen Zeit. Ein Beitrag zum antiken Staatsrecht (Münchener Beiträge zur Papyrusforschung und antiken Rechtsgeschichte 26, 32, 36) 3 vols., 1937–52, ed. repr. 1964–67

Berger
  E.H. BERGER, Geschichte der wissenschaftlichen Erdkunde der Griechen, ²1903
Berve
  H. BERVE, Das Alexanderreich auf prosopographischer Grundlage, 1926
Beyen
  H. G. BEYEN, Die pompejanische Wanddekoration vom zweiten bis zum vierten Stil 2 vols., 1938–60
BFC
  Bolletino di filologia classica
BGU
  Ägyptische (Griechische) Urkunden aus den Kaiserlichen (from Vol. 6 on Staatlichen) Museen zu Berlin 13 vols., 1895–1976
BHM
  Bulletin of the History of Medicine
BIAO
  Bulletin de l'Institut français d'Archéologie Orientale
BiblH&R
  Bibliothèque d'Humanisme et Renaissance
BiblLing
  Bibliographie linguistique / Linguistic Bibliography
BIBR
  Bulletin de l'Institut Belge de Rome
Bickerman
  E. BICKERMANN, Chronologie (Einleitung in die Altertumswissenschaft III 5), 1933
BICS
  Bulletin of the Institute of Classical Studies of the University of London
BIES
  The Bulletin of the Israel Exploration Society
BiogJahr
  Biographisches Jahrbuch für Altertumskunde
Birley
  A.R. BIRLEY, The Fasti of Roman Britain, 1981
BJ
  Bonner Jahrbücher des Rheinischen Landesmuseums in Bonn und des Vereins von Altertumsfreunden im Rheinlande
BKT
  Berliner Klassikertexte 8 vols., 1904–39
BKV
  Bibliothek der Kirchenväter (Kempten ed.) 63 vols., ²1911–31
Blänsdorf
  J. BLÄNSDORF (ed.), Theater und Gesellschaft im Imperium Romanum, 1990
Blass
  F. BLASS, Die attische Beredsamkeit, 3 vols., ³1887–98, repr. 1979
Blass/Debrunner/Rehkopf
  F. BLASS, A. DEBRUNNER, F. REHKOPF, Grammatik des neutestamentlichen Griechisch, ¹⁵1979
Blümner, PrAlt.
  H. BLÜMNER, Die römischen Privataltertümer (HdbA IV 2, 2), ³1911

Blümner, Techn.
  H. BLÜMNER, Technologie und Terminologie der Gewerbe und Künste bei Griechen und Römern, Vol. 1, ²1912; Vols. 2–4, 1875–87, repr. 1969
BMC, Gr
  A Catalogue of the Greek Coins in the British Museum 29 vols., 1873–1965
BMCByz
  W. WROTH (ed.), Catalogue of the Imperial Byzantine Coins in the British Museum 2 vols., 1908, repr. 1966
BMCIR
  Bryn Mawr Classical Review
BMCRE
  H. MATTINGLY (ed.), Coins of the Roman Empire in the British Museum 6 vols., 1962–76
BMCRR
  H.A. GRUEBER (ed.), Coins of the Roman Republic in the British Museum 3 vols., 1970
BN
  Beiträge zur Namensforschung
Bolgar, Culture 1
  R. BOLGAR, Classical Influences on European Culture A.D. 500 – 1500, 1971
Bolgar, Culture 2
  R. BOLGAR, Classical Influences on European Culture A.D. 1500–1700, 1974
Bolgar, Thought
  R. BOLGAR, Classical Influences on Western Thought A.D. 1650–1870, 1977
Bon
  A. BON, La Morée franque 2 vols., 1969
Bonner
  S.F. BONNER, Education in Ancient Rome, 1977
Bopearachchi
  O. BOPEARACHCHI, Monnaies gréco-bactriennes et indo-grecques. Catalogue raisonné, 1991
Borinski
  K. BORINSKI, Die Antike in Poetik und Kunsttheorie vom Ausgang des klassischen Altertums bis auf Goethe und Wilhelm von Humboldt 2 vols., 1914–24, repr. 1965
Borza
  E.N. BORZA, In the shadow of Olympus. The emergence of Macedon, 1990
Bouché-Leclerq
  A. BOUCHÉ-LECLERQ, Histoire de la divination dans l'antiquité 3 vols., 1879–82, repr. 1978 in 4 vols.
BPhC
  Bibliotheca Philologica Classica
BrBr
  H. BRUNN, F. BRUCKMANN, Denkmäler griechischer und römischer Skulpturen, 1888–1947
BRGK
  Bericht der Römisch-Germanischen Kommission des Deutschen Archäologischen Instituts
Briggs/Calder
  W.W. BRIGGS, W.M. CALDER III, Classical Scholarship. A Biographical Encyclopedia, 1990

Bruchmann
  C.F.H. BRUCHMANN, Epitheta deorum quae apud poetas graecos leguntur, 1893
Brugmann/Delbrück
  K. BRUGMANN, B. DELBRÜCK, Grundriß der vergleichenden Grammatik der indogermanischen Sprachen, Vols. 1-2, 1897-1916; Vols. 3-5, 1893-1900
Brugmann /Thumb
  K. BRUGMANN, A. THUMB (ed.), Griechische Grammatik, ⁴1913
Brunhölzl
  F. BRUNHÖLZL, Geschichte der lateinischen Literatur des Mittelalters 2 vols., 1975-92
Brunt
  P.A. BRUNT, Italian Manpower 222 B. C. - A. D. 14, 1971
Bruun
  C. BRUUN, The Water Supply of Ancient Rome. A Study of Imperial Administration (Commentationes Humanarum Litterarum 93), 1991
Bryer/Winfield
  A. BRYER, D. WINFIELD, The Byzantine Monuments and Topography of Pontus (Dumbarton Oaks Studies 20) 2 vols., 1985
BSABR
  Bulletin de Liaison de la Société des Amis de la Bibliothèque Salomon Reinach
BSL
  Bulletin de la Société de Linguistique de Paris
BSO(A)S
  Bulletin of the School of Oriental (from Vol. 10 ff. and African) Studies
BTCGI
  G. NENCI (ed.), Bibliografia topografica della colonizzazione greca in Italia e nelle isole tirreniche, 1980 ff.
Buck
  A. BUCK (ed.), Die Rezeption der Antike, 1981
Burkert
  W. BURKERT, Griechische Religion der archaischen und klassischen Epoche, 1977
Busolt/Swoboda
  G. BUSOLT, H. SWOBODA, Griechische Staatskunde (HdbA IV 1, 1) 2 vols., ³1920-26, repr. 1972-79
BWG
  Berichte zur Wissenschaftsgeschichte
BWPr
  Winckelmanns-Programm der Archäologischen Gesellschaft zu Berlin
Byzantion
  Byzantion. Revue internationale des études byzantines
ByzF
  Byzantinische Forschungen. Internationale Zeitschrift für Byzantinistik
BYzZ
  Byzantinische Zeitschrift
Caballos
  A. CABALLOS, Los senadores hispanoromanos y la

romanización de Hispania (Siglos I al III p.C.), Vol. 1: Prosopografia (Monografias del Departamento de Historia Antigua de la Universidad de Sevilla 5), 1990
CAF
  T. KOCK (ed.), Comicorum Atticorum Fragmenta, 3 vols., 1880-88
CAG
  Commentaria in Aristotelem Graeca 18 vols., 1885-1909
CAH
  The Cambridge Ancient History 12 text- and 5 ill. vols., 1924-39 (Vol. 1 as 2nd ed.), vols. 1-2, ³1970-75; vols. 3,1 and 3,3 ff., ²1982 ff.; vol. 3,2, ¹1991
Carney
  T.F. CARNEY, Bureaucracy in Traditional Society. Romano-Byzantine Bureaucracies Viewed from Within, 1971
Cartledge/Millett/Todd
  P. CARTLEDGE, P. MILLETT, S. TODD (ed.), Nomos, Essays in Athenian Law, Politics and Society, 1990
Cary
  M. CARY, The Geographical Background of Greek and Roman History, 1949
Casson, Ships
  L. CASSON, Ships and Seamanship in the Ancient World, 1971
Casson, Trade
  L. CASSON, Ancient Trade and Society, 1984
CAT
  Catalogus Tragicorum et Tragoediarum (in TrGF Vol. 1)
CatLitPap
  H.J.M. MILNE (ed.), Catalogue of the Literary Papyri in the British Museum, 1927
CCAG
  F. CUMONT ET AL. (ed.), Catalogus Codicum Astrologorum Graecorum 12 vols. in 20 parts, 1898-1940
CCL
  Corpus Christianorum. Series Latina, 1954 ff.
CE
  Cronache Ercolanesi
CEG
  P.A. HANSEN (ed.), Carmina epigraphica Graeca (Texts and Commentary 12; 15), 1983 ff.
CeM
  Classica et Mediaevalia
CGF
  G. KAIBEL (ed.), Comicorum Graecorum Fragmenta, ²1958
CGL
  G. GÖTZ (ed.), Corpus glossariorum Latinorum, 7 vols., 1888-1923, repr. 1965
Chantraine
  P. CHANTRAINE, Dictionnaire étymologique de la langue grecque 4 vols., 1968-80

CHCL-G
E.J. KENNEY (ed.), The Cambridge History of Classical Literature. Greek Literature, 1985 ff.

CHCL-L
E.J. KENNEY (ed.), The Cambridge History of Classical Literature. Latin Literature, 1982 ff.

Chiron
Chiron. Mitteilungen der Kommission für alte Geschichte und Epigraphik des Deutschen Archäologischen Instituts

Christ
K. CHRIST, Geschichte der römischen Kaiserzeit von Augustus bis zu Konstantin, 1988

Christ, RGG
K. CHRIST, Römische Geschichte und deutsche Geschichtswissenschaft, 1982

Christ, RGW
K. CHRIST, Römische Geschichte und Wissenschaftsgeschichte 3 vols., 1982–83

Christ/Momigliano
K. CHRIST, A. MOMIGLIANO, Die Antike im 19. Jahrhundert in Italien und Deutschland, 1988

CIA
A. KIRCHHOFF ET AL. (ed.), Corpus Inscriptionum Atticarum, 1873; Suppl.: 1877–91

CIC
Corpus Iuris Canonici 2 vols., 1879–81, repr. 1959

CID
Corpus des inscriptions de Delphes 3 vols., 1977–92

CIE
C. PAULI (ed.), Corpus Inscriptionum Etruscarum, Vol. 1–2, 1893–1921; Vol. 3,1 ff., 1982 ff.

CIG
Corpus Inscriptionum Graecarum 4 vols., 1828–77

CIL
Corpus Inscriptionum Latinarum, 1863 ff.

CIL III Add.
M. SASEL-KOS, Inscriptiones latinae in Graecia repertae. Additamenta ad CIL III (Epigrafia e antichità 5), 1979

CIRB
Corpus Inscriptionum regni Bosporani, 1965

CIS
Corpus Inscriptionum Semiticarum 5 parts, 1881–1951

CJ
Classical Journal

CL
Cultura Neolatina

Clairmont
C.W. CLAIRMONT, Attic Classical Tombstones 7 vols., 1993

Clauss
M. CLAUSS, Der magister officiorum in der Spätantike (4.–6. Jahrhundert). Das Amt und sein Einfluß auf die kaiserliche Politik (Vestigia 32), 1981

CLE
F. BÜCHELER, E. LOMMATZSCH (ed.), Carmina Latina Epigraphica (Anthologia latina 2) 3 vols., 1895–1926

CM
Clio Medica. Acta Academiae historiae medicinae

CMA
Cahiers de l'Institut du Moyen Age grec et latin

CMB
W.M. CALDER III, D.J. KRAMER, An Introductory Bibliography to the History of Classical Scholarship, Chiefly in the XIXth and XXth Centuries, 1992

CMG
Corpus Medicorum Graecorum, 1908 ff.

CMIK
J. CHADWICK, Corpus of Mycenaean Inscriptions from Knossos (Incunabula Graeca 88), 1986 ff.

CML
Corpus Medicorum Latinorum, 1915 ff.

CMS
F. MATZ ET AL. (ed.), Corpus der minoischen und mykenischen Siegel, 1964 ff.

CodMan
Codices manuscripti. Zeitschrift für Handschriftenkunde

Coing
H. COING, Europäisches Privatrecht 2 vols., 1985–89

CollAlex
I.U. POWELL (ed.), Collectanea Alexandrina, 1925

CollRau
J. V. UNGERN-STERNBERG (ed.), Colloquia Raurica, 1988 ff.

Conway/Johnson/Whatmough
R.S. CONWAY, S.E. JOHNSON, J. WHATMOUGH, The Prae-Italic dialects of Italy 3 vols., 1933, repr. 1968

Conze
A. CONZE, Die attischen Grabreliefs 4 vols., 1893–1922

Courtney
E. COURTNEY, The Fragmentary Latin Poets, 1993

CPF
F. ADORNO (ed.), Corpus dei Papiri Filosofici greci e latini, 1989 ff.

CPG
M. GEERARD (Vols. 1–5), F. GLORIE, (Vol. 5), Clavis patrum graecorum 5 vols., 1974–87

CPh
Classical Philology

CPL
E. DEKKERS, A. GAAR, Clavis patrum latinorum (CCL), ³1995

CQ
Classical Quarterly

CR
Classical Review

CRAI
Comptes rendus des séances de l'Académie des inscriptions et belles-lettres

CRF
O. RIBBECK (ed.), Comicorum Romanorum Fragmenta, 1871, repr. 1962

CSCT
Columbia Studies in the Classical Tradition
CSE
Corpus Speculorum Etruscorum, 1990 ff.
CSEL
Corpus Scriptorum ecclesiasticorum Latinorum, 1866 ff.
SCIR
Corpus Signorum Imperii Romani, 1963 ff.
Cumont, Pont
F. Cumont, E. Cumont, Voyage d'exploration archéologique dans le Pont et la Petite Arménie (Studia pontica 2), 1906
Cumont, Religions
F. Cumont, Les Religions orientales dans le paganisme romain, ³1929, repr. 1981
Curtius
E.R. Curtius, Europäische Literatur und lateinisches Mittelalter, ¹¹1993
CVA
Corpus Vasorum Antiquorum, 1923 ff.
CW
The Classical World
D'Arms
J.H. D'Arms, Commerce and Social Standing in Ancient Rome, 1981
D'Arms/Kopff
J.H. D'Arms, E.C. Kopff (ed.), The Seaborne Commerce of Ancient Rome: Studies in Archaeology and History (Memoirs of the American Academy in Rome 36), 1980
Dacia
Dacia. Revue d'archéologie et d'histoire ancienne
Davies
J.K. Davies, Athenian Propertied Families 600–300 BC, 1971
DB
F. Vigouroux (ed.), Dictionnaire de la Bible, 1881 ff.
DCPP
E. Lipiński et al. (ed.), Dictionnaire de la Civilisation Phénicienne et Punique, 1992
Degrassi, FCap.
A. Degrassi, Fasti Capitolini (Corpus scriptorum Latinorum Paravianum), 1954
Degrassi, FCIR
A. Degrassi, I Fasti consolari dell'Impero Romano, 1952
Deichgräber
K. Deichgräber, Die griechische Empirikerschule, 1930
Delmaire
R. Delmaire, Les responsables des finances impériales au Bas-Empire romain (IVᵉ-VIᵉ s). Études prosopographiques (Collection Latomus 203), 1989
Demandt
A. Demandt, Der Fall Roms: die Auflösung des römischen Reiches im Urteil der Nachwelt, 1984

Demougin
S. Demougin, Prosopographie des Chevaliers romains Julio-Claudiens (43 av.J -C.–70 ap.J.-C.) (Collection de l'École Française de Rome 153), 1992
Deubner
L. Deubner, Attische Feste, 1932
Develin
R. Develin, Athenian Officials 684–321 B.C. 1949
Devijver
H. Devijver, Prosopographia militiarum equestrium quae fuerunt ab Augusto ad Gallienum (Symbolae Facultatis Litterarum et Philosophiae Lovaniensis Ser. A 3) 3 vols., 1976–80; 2 Suppl. Vols.: 1987–93
DHA
Dialogues d'histoire ancienne
DHGE
A. Baudrillart, R. Aubert (ed.), Dictionnaire d'Histoire et de Géographie Ecclésiastiques 1912 ff.
DID
Didascaliae Tragicae/Ludorum Tragicorum (in TrGF Vol. 1)
Diels, DG
H. Diels, Doxographi Graeci, 1879
Diels/Kranz
H. Diels, W. Kranz (ed.), Fragmente der Vorsokratiker 3 vols., ⁹1951 f., repr. Vol.1, 1992; Vol. 2, 1985; Vol. 3, 1993
Dierauer
U. Dierauer, Tier und Mensch im Denken der Antike, 1977
Dietz
K. Dietz, Senatus contra principem. Untersuchungen zur senatorischen Opposition gegen Kaiser Maximinus Thrax (Vestigia 29), 1980
Dihle
A. Dihle, Die griechische und lateinische Literatur der Kaiserzeit: von Augustus bis Justinian, 1989
DiskAB
Diskussionen zur archäologischen Bauforschung, 1974 ff.
Dixon
S. Dixon, The Roman Family, 1992
DJD
Discoveries in the Judaean Desert, 1955 ff.
DLZ
Deutsche Literaturzeitung für Kritik der internationalen Wissenschaft
DMA
J.R. Strayer et al. (ed.), Dictionary of the Middle Ages 13 vols., 1982–89
Dmic
F. Aura Jorro, Diccionario Micénico, 1985
Dörrie/Baltes
H. Dörrie, M. Baltes (ed.), Der Platonismus in der Antike, 1987 ff.
Domaszewski
A.V. Domaszewski, Aufsätze zur römischen Heeresgeschichte, 1972

Domaszewski /Dobson
  A.V. DOMASZEWSKI, B. DOBSON, Die Rangordnung des römischen Heeres, ²1967
Domergue
  C. DOMERGUE, Les mines de la péninsule Iberique dans l'Antiquité Romaine, 1990
Drumann /Groebe
  W. DRUMANN, P. GROEBE (ed.), Geschichte Roms in seinem Übergange von der republikanischen zur monarchischen Verfassung 6 vols., 1899–1929, repr. 1964
DS
  C. DAREMBERG, E. SAGLIO (ed.), Dictionnaire des antiquités grecques et romaines d'après les textes et les monuments 6 vols., 1877–1919, repr. 1969
Dulckeit /Schwarz /Waldstein
  G. DULCKEIT, F. SCHWARZ, W. WALDSTEIN, Römische Rechtsgeschichte. Ein Studienbuch (Juristische Kurz Lehrbücher), 1995
Dumézil
  G. DUMÉZIL, La religion romaine archaïque, suivi d'un appendice sur la religion des Etrusques, 1974
Duncan-Jones, Economy
  R. DUNCAN-JONES, The Economy of the Roman Empire. Quantitative Studies, 1974
Duncan-Jones, Structure
  R. DUNCAN-JONES, Structure and Scale in the Roman Economy, 1990
DVjS
  Deutsche Vierteljahrsschrift für Literaturwissenschaft und Geistesgeschichte
EA
  Epigraphica Anatolica. Zeitschrift für Epigraphik und historische Geographie Anatoliens
EAA
  R. BIANCHI BANDINELLI (ed.), Enciclopedia dell'arte antica classica e orientale, 1958 ff.
EB
  G. CAMPS, Encyclopédie Berbère 1984 ff.
Ebert
  F. EBERT, Fachausdrücke des griechischen Bauhandwerks, Vol. 1: Der Tempel, 1910
EC
  Essays in Criticism
Eck
  W. ECK, Die Statthalter der germanischen Provinzen vom 1.–3. Jahrhundert (Epigraphische Studien 14), 1985
Eckstein
  F.A. ECKSTEIN, Nomenclator philologorum, 1871
Edelstein, AM
  L. EDELSTEIN, Ancient medicine, 1967
Edelstein, Asclepius
  E.J. and L. EDELSTEIN, Asclepius. A Collection and Interpretation of the Testimonies, 1945
Eder, Demokratie
  W. EDER (ed.), Die athenische Demokratie im 4. Jahrhundert v. Chr. Vollendung oder Verfall einer Verfassungsform? Akten eines Symposiums, 3. – 7. August 1992, 1995

Eder, Staat
  W. EDER (ed.), Staat und Staatlichkeit in der frühen römischen Republik: Akten eines Symposiums, 12. – 15. Juli 1988, 1990
EDM
  K. RANKE, W. BREDNICH (ed.), Enzyklopädie des Märchens. Handwörterbuch zur historischen und vergleichenden Erzählforschung, 1977 ff.
EDRL
  A. BERGER, Encyclopedic Dictionary of Roman Law (TAPhA N.S. 43,2), 1953, repr. 1968
EEpigr
  Ephemeris Epigraphica
EI
  Encyclopaedia of Islam, 1960 ff.
Eissfeldt
  O. EISSFELDT (ed.), Handbuch zum Alten Testament, ³1964 ff.
Emerita
  Emerita. Revista de linguistica y filologia clasica
EncIr
  E. YARSHATER (ed.), Encyclopaedia Iranica, 1985
Entretiens
  Entretiens sur l'antiquité classique (Fondation Hardt)
EOS
  Atti del Colloquio Internazionale AIEGL su Epigrafia e Ordine Senatorio: Roma, 14–20 maggio 1981, 2 vols., 1982
EpGF
  M. DAVIES, Epicorum graecorum fragmenta, 1988
EpGr
  G. KAIBEL (ed.), Epigrammata Graeca ex lapidibus conlecta, 1878
Epicurea
  H. USENER (ed.), Epicurea, 1887, repr. 1963
EPRO
  Études préliminaires aux religions orientales dans l'Empire Romain, 1961 ff.
Eranos
  Eranos. Acta Philologica Suecana
Er-Jb
  Eranos-Jahrbuch
Erasmus
  Erasmus. Speculum Scientiarum. Internationales Literaturblatt der Geisteswissenschaften
Eretz Israel
  Eretz-Israel, Archaeological, Historical and Geographical Studies
Ernout/Meillet
  A. ERNOUT, A. MEILLET, Dictionnaire étymologique de la langue latine, ⁴1959
Errington
  R.M. ERRINGTON, Geschichte Makedoniens. Von den Anfängen bis zum Untergang des Königreiches, 1986
ESAR
  T. FRANK (ed.), An Economic Survey of Ancient Rome 6 vols., 1933–40

Espérandieu, Inscr.
  E. Espérandieu, Inscriptions latines de Gaule 2
  vols., 1929–36
Espérandieu, Rec.
  E. Espérandieu, Recueil généneral des bas-reliefs,
  statues et bustes de la Gaule Romaine 16 vols., 1907–
  81
ET
  H. Rix (ed.), Etruskische Texte (ScriptOralia 23, 24,
  Reihe A 6,7) 2 vols., 1991
ETAM
  Ergänzungsbände zu den Tituli Asiae minoris, 1966
  ff.
Euph.
  Euphorion
EV
  F. Della Corte et al. (ed.), Enciclopedia Virgili-
  ana 5 vols. in 6 parts, 1984–91
Evans
  D.E. Evans, Gaulish Personal names. A study of
  some continental Celtic formations, 1967
F&F
  Forschungen und Fortschritte
Farnell, Cults
  L.R. Farnell, The Cults of the Greek States 5 vols.,
  1896–1909
Farnell, GHC
  L.R. Farnell, Greek Hero Cults and Ideas of Im-
  mortality, 1921
FCG
  A. Meineke (ed.), Fragmenta Comicorum Graeco-
  rum 5 vols., 1839–57, repr. 1970
FCS
  Fifteenth-Century Studies
FdD
  Fouilles de Delphes, 1902 ff.
FGE
  D.L. Page, Further Greek Epigrams, 1981
FGrH
  F. Jacoby, Die Fragmente der griechischen Histori-
  ker, 3 parts in 14 vols., 1923–58, Part 1: ²1957
FHG
  C. Müller (ed.), Fragmenta Historicorum Graeco-
  rum 5 vols., 1841–1970
Fick/Bechtel
  A. Fick, F. Bechtel, Die griechischen Personenna-
  men, ²1894
FiE
  Forschungen in Ephesos, 1906 ff.
Filologia
  La Filologia Greca e Latina nel secolo XX, 1989
Finley, Ancient Economy
  M.I. Finley, The Ancient Economy, ²1984
Finley, Ancient Slavery
  M.I. Finley, Ancient Slavery and Modern Ideology,
  1980
Finley, Economy
  M.I. Finley, B.D. Shaw, R.P. Saller (ed.), Econo-
  my and Society in Ancient Greece, 1981

Finley, Property
  M.I. Finley (ed.), Studies in Roman Property, 1976
FIRA
  S. Riccobono, J. Baviera (ed.), Fontes iuris Ro-
  mani anteiustiniani 3 vols., ²1968
FIRBruns
  K.G. Bruns, Th. Mommsen, O. Gradenwitz (ed.),
  Fontes iuris Romani antiqui, 1909, repr. 1969
Fittschen/Zanker
  K. Fittschen, P. Zanker, Katalog der römischen
  Porträts in den capitolinischen Museen und den an-
  deren kommunalen Museen der Stadt Rom, 1983 ff.
Flach
  D. Flach, Römische Agrargeschichte (HdbA III 9),
  1990
Flashar
  H. Flashar, Inszenierung der Antike. Das griechi-
  sche Drama auf der Bühne der Neuzeit, 1991
Flashar, Medizin
  H. Flashar (ed.), Antike Medizin, 1971
FMS
  Frühmittelalterliche Studien, Jahrbuch des Instituts
  für   Frühmittelalter-Forschung   der   Universität
  Münster
Fossey
  J.M. Fossey, Topography and Population of An-
  cient Boiotia, Vol. 1, 1988
FOst
  L. Vidmann, Fasti Ostienses, 1982
Fowler
  W.W. Fowler, The Roman Festivals of the Period
  of the Republic. An Introduction to the Study of the
  Religion of the Romans, 1899
FPD
  I. Piso, Fasti Provinciae Daciae, Vol. 1: Die senato-
  rischen Amtsträger (Antiquitas 1,43), 1993
FPL
  W. Morel, C. Büchner (ed.), Fragmenta Poetarum
  Latinorum epicorum et lyricorum, ²1982
FPR
  A. Bährens (ed.), Fragmenta Poetarum Romano-
  rum, 1886
Frazer
  J.G. Frazer, The Golden Bough. A Study in Magic
  and Religion, 8 parts in 12 vols., Vols. 1–3, 5–9,
  ³1911–14; Vols. 4, 10–12, 1911–15
Frenzel
  E. Frenzel, Stoffe der Weltliteratur, ⁸1992
Friedländer
  L. Friedländer, G. Wissowa (ed.), Darstellungen
  aus der Sittengeschichte Roms 4 vols., ¹⁰1921–23
Frier, Landlords
  B.W. Frier, Landlords and Tenants in Imperial Ro-
  me, 1980
Frier, PontMax
  B.W. Frier, Libri annales pontificum maximorum.
  The origins of the Annalistic Tradition (Papers and
  Monographs of the American Academy in Rome
  27), 1979

Frisk
H. Frisk, Griechisches etymologisches Wörterbuch (Indogermanische Bibliothek: Reihe 2) 3 vols., 1960–72

FRLANT
Forschungen zur Religion und Literatur des Alten und Neuen Testaments

Fuchs/Floren
W. Fuchs, J. Floren, Die Griechische Plastik, Vol. 1: Die geometrische und archaische Plastik, 1987

Furtwängler
A. Furtwängler, Die antiken Gemmen. Geschichte der Steinschneidekunst im klassischen Altertum 3 vols., 1900

Furtwängler/Reichhold
A. Furtwängler, K. Reichhold, Griechische Vasenmalerei 3 vols., 1904–32

Fushöller
D. Fushöller, Tunesien und Ostalgerien in der Römerzeit, 1979

G&R
Greece and Rome

GA
A.S.F. Gow, D.L. Page, The Greek Anthology, Vol. 1: Hellenistic Epigrams, 1965; Vol. 2: The Garland of Philip, 1968

Gardner
P. Gardner, A History of Ancient Coinage, 700–300 B.C., 1918

Gardthausen
V. Gardthausen, Augustus und Seine Zeit, 2 parts in 6 vols., 1891–1904

Garnsey
P. Garnsey, Famine and Food Supply in the Graeco-Roman World. Responses to Risk and Crisis, 1988

Garnsey/Hopkins/Whittaker
P. Garnsey, K. Hopkins, C.R. Whittaker (ed.), Trade in the Ancient Economy, 1983

Garnsey/Saller
P. Garnsey, R. Saller, The Roman Empire, Economy, Society and Culture, 1987

GCS
Die griechischen christlichen Schriftsteller der ersten Jahrhunderte, 1897 ff.

Gehrke
H.-J. Gehrke, Jenseits von Athen und Sparta. Das Dritte Griechenland und seine Staatenwelt, 1986

Gentili/Prato
B. Gentili, C. Prato (ed.), Poetarum elegiacorum testimonia et fragmenta, Vol. 1, ²1988; Vol. 2, 1985

Georges
K.E. Georges, Ausführliches lateinisch-deutsches Handwörterbuch 2 vols., ⁸1912–18, repr. 1992

Gérard-Rousseau
M. Gérard-Rousseau, Les mentions religieuses dans les tablettes mycéniennes, 1968

Germania
Germania. Anzeiger der Römisch-Germanischen Kommission des Deutschen Archäologischen Instituts

Gernet
L. Gernet, Droit et société dans la Grèce ancienne (Institut de droit romain, Publication 13), 1955, repr. 1964

Geus
K. Geus, Prosopographie der literarisch bezeugten Karthager (Studia Phoenicia 13 Orientalia Lovaniensia analecta 59), 1994

GGA
Göttingische Gelehrte Anzeigen

GGM
C. Müller (ed.), Geographi Graeci Minores 2 vols., Tabulae, 1855–61

GGPh¹
F. Überweg (ed.), Grundriß der Geschichte der Philosophie; K, Prächter, Teil 1: Die Philosophie des Altertums, ¹²1926, repr. 1953

GGPh²
W. Otto, U. Hausmann (ed.), Grundriß der Geschichte der Philosophie; H. Flashar (ed.), vol. 3: Die Philosophie der Antike, 1983, vol. 4: Die hellenistische Philosophie, 1994

GHW 1
H. Bengtson, V. Milojcic et al., Großer Historischer Weltatlas des Bayrischen Schulbuchverlages 1. Vorgeschichte und Altertum, ⁶1978

GHW 2
J. Engel, W. Macer, A. Birken et al., Großer Historischer Weltatlas des Bayrischen Schulbuchverlages 2. Mittelalter, ²1979

GIBM
C.T. Newton et al. (ed.), The Collection of Ancient Greek Inscriptions in the British Museum 4 vols., 1874–1916

Gillispie
C.C. Gillispie (ed.), Dictionary of scientific biography 14 vols. and index, 1970–80, repr. 1981; 2 Suppl. Vols., 1978–90

GL
H. Keil (ed.), Grammatici Latini 7 vols., 1855–80

GLM
A. Riese (ed.), Geographi Latini Minores, 1878

Glotta
Glotta. Zeitschrift für griechische und lateinische Sprache

GMth
F. Zaminer (ed.), Geschichte der Musiktheorie, 1984 ff.

Gnomon
Gnomon. Kritische Zeitschrift für die gesamte klassische Altertumswissenschaft

Göbl
R. Göbl, Antike Numismatik 2 vols., 1978

Goleniščev
I.N. Goleniščev-Kutuzov, Il Rinascimento italiano e le letterature slave dei secoli XV e XVI, 1973

Gordon
A.E. Gordon, Album of Dated Latin Inscriptions 4 vols., 1958–65

Goulet
R. Goulet (ed.), Dictionnaire des philosophes anti-
ques, 1989 ff.
Graf
F. Graf, Nordionische Kulte. Religionsgeschichtli-
che und epigraphische Untersuchungen zu den Kul-
ten von Chios, Erythrai, Klazomenai und Phokaia,
1985
GRBS
Greek, Roman and Byzantine Studies
Grenier
A. Grenier, Manuel d'archéologie gallo-romaine 4
vols., 1931–60; vols. 1 and 2, repr. 1985
GRF
H. Funaioli (ed.), Grammaticae Romanae Frag-
menta, 1907
GRF(add)
A. Mazzarino, Grammaticae Romanae Fragmenta
aetatis Caesareae (accedunt volumini Funaioliano
addenda), 1955
GRLMA
Grundriß der romanischen Literaturen des Mittelal-
ters
Gruen, Last Gen.
E.S. Gruen, The Last Generation of the Roman Re-
public, 1974
Gruen, Rome
E.S. Gruen, The Hellenistic World and the Coming
of Rome, 1984, repr. 1986
Gruppe
O. Gruppe, Geschichte der klassischen Mythologie
und Religionsgeschichte während des Mittelalters
im Abendland und während der Neuzeit, 1921
Gundel
W. and H-G. Gundel, Astrologumena. Die astro-
logische Literatur in der Antike und ihre Geschichte,
1966
Guthrie
W.K.C. Guthrie, A History of Greek Philosophy 6
vols., 1962–81
GVI
W. Peek (ed.), Griechische Vers-Inschriften, Vol. I,
1955
Gymnasium
Gymnasium. Zeitschrift für Kultur der Antike und
humanistische Bildung
HABES
Heidelberger althistorische Beiträge und epigraphi-
sche Studien, 1986 ff.
Habicht
C. Habicht, Athen. Die Geschichte der Stadt in hel-
lenistischer Zeit, 1995
Hakkert
A.M. Hakkert (ed.), Lexicon of Greek and Roman
Cities and Place-Names in Antiquity c. 1500 B.C. –
c. A.D. 500, 1990 ff.
Halfmann
H. Halfmann, Die Senatoren aus dem östlichen Teil
des Imperium Romanum bis zum Ende des 2. Jahr-
hunderts n. Chr. (Hypomnemata 58), 1979

Hamburger
K. Hamburger, Von Sophokles zu Sartre. Griechi-
sche Dramenfiguren antik und modern, 1962
Hannestad
N. Hannestad, Roman Art and Imperial Policy,
1986
Hansen, Democracy
M.H. Hansen, The Athenian Democracy in the Age
of Demosthenes. Structure, Principles and Ideology,
1991, repr. 1993
Harris
W.V. Harris, War and Imperialism in Republican
Rome 327–70 B.C., 1979
Hasebroek
J. Hasebroek, Griechische Wirtschafts- und Gesell-
schaftsgeschichte bis zur Perserzeit, 1931
HbdOr
B. Spuler (ed.), Handbuch der Orientalistik, 1952
ff.
HbdrA
J. Marquardt, Th. Mommsen, Handbuch der rö-
mischen Alterthümer, vols. 1–3, ³1887 f.; vols. 4–7,
²1881–86
HBr
P. Herrmann, R. Herbig, (ed.), Denkmäler der
Malerei des Altertums 2 vols., 1904–50
HDA
H. Bächtold-Stäubli et al. (ed.), Handwörter-
buch des deutschen Aberglaubens 10 vols., 1927–42,
repr. 1987
HdArch
W. Otto, U. Hausmann (ed.), Handbuch der Ar-
chäologie. Im Rahmen des HdbA 7 vols., 1969–90
HdbA
I. v. Müller, H. Bengtson (ed.), Handbuch der
Altertumswissenschaft, 1977 ff.
Heckel
W. Heckel, Marshals of Alexander's Empire, 1978
Heinemann
K. Heinemann, Die tragischen Gestalten der Grie-
chen in der Weltliteratur, 1920
Helbig
W. Helbig, Führer durch die öffentlichen Sammlun-
gen klassischer Altertümer in Rom 4 vols., ⁴1963–72
Hephaistos
Hephaistos. Kritische Zeitschrift zu Theorie und
Praxis der Archäologie, Kunstwissenschaft und an-
grenzender Gebiete
Hermes
Hermes. Zeitschrift für klassische Philologie
Herrscherbild
Das römische Herrscherbild, 1939 ff.
Herzog, Staatsverfassung
E. v. Herzog, Geschichte und System der römi-
schen Staatsverfassung 2 vols., 1884–91, repr. 1965
Hesperia
Hesperia. Journal of the American School of Clas-
sical Studies at Athens

Heubeck
A. HEUBECK, Schrift (Archaeologia Homerica Chapter X Vol. 3), 1979
Heumann/Seckel
H.G. HEUMANN, E. SECKEL (ed.), Handlexikon zu den Quellen des römischen Rechts, ¹¹1971
Highet
G. HIGHET, The Classical Tradition: Greek and Roman Influences on Western literature, ⁴1968, repr. 1985
Hild
F. HILD, Kilikien und Isaurien (Denkschriften der Österreichischen Akademie der Wissenschaften, Philosophisch-Historische Klasse 215; TIB 5) 2 vols., 1990
Hild/Restle
F. HILD, M. RESTLE, Kappadokien (Kappadokia, Charsianon, Sebasteia und Lykandos) (Denkschriften der Österreichischen Akademie der Wissenschaften: Philosophisch-Historische Klasse 149; TIB 2), 1981
Hirschfeld
O. HIRSCHFELD, Die kaiserlichen Verwaltungsbeamten bis auf Diocletian, ²1905
Historia
Historia. Zeitschrift für Alte Geschichte
HJb
Historisches Jahrbuch
HLav
Humanistica Lavanensia
HLL
R. HERZOG, P.L. SCHMIDT (ed.), Handbuch der lateinischen Literatur der Antike, 1989 ff.
HM
A History of Macedonia, Vol. 1: N.G.L. HAMMOND, Historical geography and prehistory, 1972; Vol. 2: N.G.L. HAMMOND, G.T. GRIFFITH, 550–336 BC, 1979; Vol. 3: N.G.L. HAMMOND, F.W. WALBANK, 336–167 BC, 1988
HmT
H.H. EGGEBRECHT, Handwörterbuch der musikalischen Terminologie, 1972 ff.
HN
B.V. HEAD, Historia numorum. A manual of Greek numismatics, ²1911
Hodge
T.A. HODGE, Roman Aqueducts and Water Supply, 1992
Hölbl
G. HÖLBL, Geschichte des Ptolemäerreiches. Politik, Ideologie und religiöse Kultur von Alexander den Großen bis zur römischen Eroberung, 1994
Hölkeskamp
K.-J. HÖLKESKAMP, Die Entstehung der Nobilität. Studien zur sozialen und politischen Geschichte der Römischen Republik im 4.Jh. v. Chr., 1987
Hoffmann
D. HOFMANN, Das spätrömische Bewegungsheer und die Notitia dignitatum (Epigraphische Studien 7) 2 vols., 1969 f. = (Diss.), 1958

Holder
A. HOLDER, Alt-celtischer Sprachschatz 3 vols., 1896-1913, repr. 1961 f.
Honsell
H. HONSELL, Römisches Recht (Springer-Lehrbuch), ³1994
Hopfner
T. HOPFNER, Griechisch-ägyptischer Offenbarungszauber 2 vols. in 3 parts, 1921–24, repr. 1974–90
Hopkins, Conquerors
K. HOPKINS, Conquerors and Slaves. Sociological Studies in Roman History, Vol. 1, 1978
Hopkins, Death
K. HOPKINS, Death and Renewal. Sociological Studies in Roman History, Vol. 2, 1983
HR
History of Religions
HRR
H. PETER (ed.), Historicorum Romanorum Reliquiae, Vol. 1, 1914; Vol. 2, 1906, repr. 1967
HrwG
H. CANCIK, B. GLADIGOW, M. LAUBSCHER (from Vol. 2: K.-H. KOHL) (ed.), Handbuch religionswissenschaftlicher Grundbegriffe, 1988 ff.
HS
Historische Sprachforschung
HSM
Histoire des sciences médicales
HSPh
Harvard Studies in Classical Philology
Hülser
K. HÜLSER, Die Fragmente zur Dialektik der Stoiker. Neue Sammlung der Texte mit deutscher Übersetzung und Kommentaren 4 vols., 1987 f.
Humphrey
J.H. HUMPHREY, Roman Circuses. Arenas for Chariot Racing, 1986
Hunger, Literatur
H. HUNGER, Die hochsprachlich profane Literatur der Byzantiner (HdbA 12, 5) 2 vols., 1978
Hunger, Mythologie
H. HUNGER (ed.), Lexikon der griechischen und römischen Mythologie, ⁶1969
Huss
W. HUSS, Geschichte der Karthager (HdbA III 8), 1985
HWdPh
J. RITTER, K. GRÜNDER (ed.), Historisches Wörterbuch der Philosophie, 1971 ff.
HWdR
G. UEDING (ed.), Historisches Wörterbuch der Rhetorik, 1992 ff.
HZ
Historische Zeitschrift
IA
Iranica Antiqua
IconRel
T.P. v. BAAREN (ed.), Iconography of Religions, 1970 ff.

ICUR
  A. FERRUA, G.B. DE ROSSI, Inscriptiones christianae
  urbis Romae, 1922ff.
IDélos
  Inscriptions de Délos, 1926 ff.
IDidyma
  A. REHM (ed.), Didyma, Vol. 2: Die Inschriften,
  1958
IEG
  M. L. WEST (ed.), Iambi et elegi Graeci ante Alexan-
  drum cantati 2 vols., 1989–92
IEJ
  Israel Exploration Journal
IER
  Illustrierte Enzyklopädie der Renaissance
IEry
  H. ENGELMANN (ed.), Die Inschriften von Erythrai
  und Klazomenai 2 vols., 1972 f.
IF
  Indogermanische Forschungen
IG
  Inscriptiones Graecae, 1873 ff.
IGA
  H. ROEHL (ed.), Inscriptiones Graecae antiquissi-
  mae praeter Atticas in Attica repertas, 1882, repr.
  1977
IGBulg
  G. MIHAILOV (ed.), Inscriptiones Graecae in Bulga-
  ria repertae 5 vols., 1956–1996
IGLS
  Inscriptions grecques et latines de la Syrie, 1929 ff.
IGR
  R. CAGNAT ET AL. (ed.), Inscriptiones Graecae ad res
  Romanas pertinentes 4 vols., 1906–27
IGUR
  L. MORETTI, Inscriptiones Graecae urbis Romae 4
  vols., 1968–90
IJCT
  International Journal of the Classical Tradition
IJsewijn
  J. IJSEWIJN, Companion to Neo Latin Studies,
  ²1990 ff.
IK
  Die Inschriften griechischer Städte aus Kleinasien,
  1972 ff.
ILCV
  E. DIEHL (ed.), Inscriptiones Latinae Christianae
  Veteres orientis 3 vols., 1925–31, repr. 1961; J. MO-
  REAU, H.I. MARROU (ed.), Suppl., 1967
ILLRP
  A. DEGRASSI (ed.), Inscriptiones Latinae liberae rei
  publicae 2 vols., 1957–63, repr. 1972
ILS
  H. DESSAU (ed.), Inscriptiones Latinae Selectae 3
  vols. in 5 parts, 1892–1916, repr. ⁴1974
IMagn.
  O. KERN (ed.), Die Inschriften von Magnesia am
  Mäander, 1900, repr. 1967

IMU
  Italia medioevale e umanistica
Index
  Index. Quaderni camerti di studi romanistici
InscrIt
  A. DEGRASSI (ed.), Inscriptiones Italiae, 1931 ff.
IOSPE
  V. LATYSCHEW (ed.), Inscriptiones antiquae orae
  septentrionalis ponti Euxini Graecae et Latinae 3
  vols., 1885–1901, repr. 1965
IPNB
  M. MAYRHOFER, R. SCHMITT (ed.), Iranisches Per-
  sonennamenbuch, 1979 ff.
IPQ
  International Philosophical Quaterly
IPriene
  F. HILLER VON GÄRTRINGEN, Inschriften von Priene,
  1906
Irmscher
  J. IRMSCHER (ed.), Renaissance und Humanismus in
  Mittel- und Osteuropa, 1962
Isager/Skydsgaard
  S. ISAGER, J.E. SKYDSGAARD, Ancient Greek Agricul-
  ture, An Introduction, 1992
Isis
  Isis
IstForsch
  Istanbuler Forschungen des Deutschen Archäologi-
  schen Instituts
Iura
  IURA, Rivista internazionale di diritto romano e an-
  tico
IvOl
  W. DITTENBERGER, K. PURGOLD, Inschriften von
  Olympia, 1896, repr. 1966
Jaffé
  P. JAFFÉ, Regesta pontificum Romanorum ab con-
  dita ecclesia ad annum 1198 2 vols., ²1985–88
JBAA
  The Journal of the British Archaeological Associa-
  tion
JbAC
  Jahrbuch für Antike und Christentum
JCS
  Journal of Cuneiform Studies
JDAI
  Jahrbuch des Deutschen Archäologischen Instituts
JEA
  The Journal of Egyptian Archaeology
Jenkyns, DaD
  R. JENKYNS, Dignity and Decadence: Classicism and
  the Victorians, 1992
Jenkyns, Legacy
  R. JENKYNS, The Legacy of Rome: A New Appraisal,
  1992
JHAS
  Journal for the History of Arabic Science
JHB
  Journal of the History of Biology

JHM
Journal of the History of Medicine and Allied Sciences
JHPh
Journal of the History of Philosophy
JHS
Journal of Hellenic Studies
JLW
Jahrbuch für Liturgiewissenschaft
JMRS
Journal of Medieval and Renaissance Studies
JNES
Journal of Near Eastern Studies
JNG
Jahrbuch für Numismatik und Geldgeschichte
JÖAI
Jahreshefte des Österreichischen Archäologischen Instituts
Jones, Cities
A.H.M. JONES, The Cities of the Eastern Roman Provinces, ²1971
Jones, Economy
A.H.M. JONES, The Roman Economy. Studies in Ancient Economic and Administrative History, 1974
Jones, LRE
A.H.M. JONES, The Later Roman Empire 284–602. A Social, Economic and Administrative Survey, 1964
Jones, RGL
A.H.M. JONES, Studies in Roman Government and Law, 1968
Jost
M. JOST, Sanctuaires et cultes d'Arcadie, 1985
JPh
Journal of Philosophy
JRGZ
Jahrbuch des Römisch-Germanischen Zentralmuseums
JRS
Journal of Roman Studies
Justi
F. JUSTI, Iranisches Namenbuch, 1895
JWG
Jahrbuch für Wirtschaftsgeschichte
JWI
Journal of the Warburg and Courtauld Institutes
Kadmos
Kadmos. Zeitschrift für vor- und frühgriechische Epigraphik
KAI
H. DONNER, W. RÖLLIG, Kanaanaeische und aramaeische Inschriften 3 vols., ³1971–1976
Kajanto, Cognomina
I. KAJANTO, The Latin Cognomina, 1965
Kajanto, Supernomina
I. KAJANTO, Supernomina. A study in Latin epigraphy (Commentationes humanarum litterarum 40, 1), 1966

Kamptz
H. v. KAMPTZ, Homerische Personennamen. Sprachwissenschaftliche und historische Klassifikation, 1982 = H. v. KAMPTZ, Sprachwissenschaftliche und historische Klassifikation der homerischen Personennamen (Diss.), 1958
Karlowa
O. KARLOWA, Römische Rechtsgeschichte 2 vols., 1885–1901
Kaser, AJ
M. KASER, Das altrömische Jus. Studien zur Rechtsvorstellung und Rechtsgeschichte der Römer, 1949
Kaser, RPR
M. KASER, Das römische Privatrecht (Rechtsgeschichte des Altertums Part 3, Vol. 3; HbdA 10, 3, 3) 2 vols., ³1971–75
Kaser, RZ
M. KASER, Das römische Zivilprozessrecht (Rechtsgeschichte des Altertums Part 3, Vol. 4; HbdA 10, 3, 4), 1966
Kearns
E. KEARNS, The Heroes of Attica, 1989 (BICS Suppl. 57)
Keller
O. KELLER, Die antike Tierwelt 2 vols., 1909–20, repr. 1963
Kelnhofer
F. KELNHOFER, Die topographische Bezugsgrundlage der Tabula Imperii Byzantini (Denkschriften der Österreichischen Akademie der Wissenschaften: Philosophisch-Historische Klasse 125 Beih.; TIB 1, Beih.), 1976
Kienast
D. KIENAST, Römische Kaisertabelle. Grundzüge einer römischen Kaiserchronologie, 1990
Kindler
W. JENS (ed.), Kindlers Neues Literatur Lexikon 20 vols., 1988–92
Kinkel
G. KINKEL, (ed.), Epicorum Graecorum Fragmenta, 1877
Kirsten /Kraiker
E. KIRSTEN, W. KRAIKER, Griechenlandkunde. Ein Führer zu klassischen Stätten, ⁵1967
Kleberg
T. KLEBERG, Hôtels, restaurants et cabarets dans l'antiquité Romaine. Études historiques et philologiques, 1957
Klio
Klio. Beiträge zur Alten Geschichte
KlP
K. ZIEGLER (ed.), Der Kleine Pauly. Lexikon der Antike 5 vols., 1964–75, repr. 1979
Knobloch
J. KNOBLOCH ET AL. (ed.), Sprachwissenschaftliches Wörterbuch (Indogermanische Bibliothek 2), 1986 ff (1st installment 1961)
Koch/Sichtermann
G. KOCH, H. SICHTERMANN, Römische Sarkophage, 1982

Koder
  J. KODER, Der Lebensraum der Byzantiner. Histo-
risch-geographischer Abriß ihres mittelalterlichen
Staates im östlichen Mittelmeerraum, 1984
Koder/Hild
  J. KODER, F. HILD, Hellas und Thessalia (Denk-
schriften der Österreichischen Akademie der Wis-
senschaften, Philosophisch-Historische Klasse 125;
TIB 1), 1976
Kraft
  K. KRAFT, Gesammelte Aufsätze zur antiken Ge-
schichte und Militärgeschichte, 1973
Kromayer/Veith
  J. KROMAYER, G. VEITH, Heerwesen und Kriegfüh-
rung der Griechen und Römer, 1928, repr. 1963
Krumbacher
  K. KRUMBACHER, Geschichte der byzantinischen
Litteratur von Justinian bis zum Ende des oströmi-
schen Reiches (527–1453) (HdbA 9, 1), ²1897, repr.
1970
KSd
  J. FRIEDRICH (ed.), Kleinasiatische Sprachdenkmä-
ler (Kleine Texte für Vorlesungen und Übungen
163), 1932
KUB
  Keilschrifturkunden von Boghazköi
Kühner/Blass
  R. KÜHNER, F. BLASS, Ausführliche Grammatik der
griechischen Sprache. Teil 1: Elementar- und For-
menlehre 2 vols., ³1890–92
Kühner/Gerth
  R. KÜHNER, B. GERTH, Ausführliche Grammatik der
griechischen Sprache. Teil 2: Satzlehre 2 vols.,
³1898–1904; W. M. CALDER III, Index locorum,
1965
Kühner/Holzweißig
  R. KÜHNER, F. HOLZWEISSIG, Ausführliche Gram-
matik der lateinischen Sprache. Teil I: Elementar-,
Formen- und Wortlehre, ²1912
Kühner/Stegmann
  R. KÜHNER, C. STEGMANN, Ausführliche Gramma-
tik der lateinischen Sprache. Teil 2: Satzlehre, 2 vols.,
⁴1962 (revised by A. THIERFELDER); G.S. SCHWARZ,
R. L. WERTIS, Index locorum, 1980
Kullmann/Althoff
  W. KULLMANN, J. ALTHOFF (ed.), Vermittlung und
Tradierung von Wissen in der griechischen Kultur,
1993
Kunkel
  W. KUNKEL, Herkunft und soziale Stellung der rö-
mischen Juristen, ²1967
KWdH
  H.H. SCHMITT (ed.), Kleines Wörterbuch des Hel-
lenismus, ²1993
Lacey
  W.K. LACEY, The Family in Classical Greece, 1968
LÄ
  W. HELCK ET AL. (ed.), Lexikon der Ägyptologie 7
vols., 1975–92 (1st installment 1972)

LAK
  H. BRUNNER, K. FLESSEL, F. HILLER ET AL. (ed.),
Lexikon Alte Kulturen 3 vols., 1990–93
Lanciani
  R. LANCIANI, Forma urbis Romae, 1893–1901
Lange
  C.C.L. LANGE, Römische Altertümer, Vols. 1–2,
²1876–79; Vol. 3, 1876
Langosch
  K. LANGOSCH, Mittellatein und Europa, 1990
Latomus
  Latomus. Revue d'études latines
Latte
  K. LATTE, Römische Religionsgeschichte (HdbA 5,
4), 1960, repr. 1992
Lauffer, BL
  S. LAUFFER, Die Bergwerkssklaven von Laureion,
²1979
Lauffer, Griechenland
  S. LAUFFER (ed.), Griechenland. Lexikon der histo-
rischen Stätten von den Anfängen bis zur Gegen-
wart, 1989
Lausberg
  H. LAUSBERG, Handbuch der literarischen Rhetorik.
Eine Grundlegung der Literaturwissenschaft, ³1990
LAW
  C. ANDRESEN ET AL.(ed.), Lexikon der Alten Welt,
1965, repr. 1990
LCI
  Lexikon der christlichen Ikonographie
LdA
  J. IRMSCHER (ed.), Lexikon der Antike, ¹⁰1990
Le Bohec
  Y. LE BOHEC, L'armée romaine. Sous le Haut-Em-
pire, 1989
Leitner
  H. LEITNER, Zoologische Terminologie beim Älte-
ren Plinius (Diss.), 1972
Leo
  F. LEO, Geschichte der römischen Literatur. I. Die
archaische Literatur, 1913, repr. 1958
Lesky
  A. LESKY, Geschichte der griechischen Literatur,
³1971, repr. 1993
Leumann
  M. LEUMANN, Lateinische Laut- und Formenlehre
(HdbA II 2, 1), 1977
Leunissen
  P.M.M. LEUNISSEN, Konsuln und Konsulare in der
Zeit von Commodus bis zu Alexander Severus
(180–235 n. Chr.) (Dutch Monographs in Ancient
History and Archaeology 6), 1989
Lewis/Short
  C.T. LEWIS, C. SHORT, A Latin Dictionary, ²1980
LFE
  B. SNELL (ed.), Lexikon des frühgriechischen Epos,
1979 ff. (1st installment 1955)
LGPN
  P.M. FRASER ET AL. (ed.), A Lexicon of Greek Per-
sonal Names, 1987 ff.

Liebenam
W. LIEBENAM, Städteverwaltung im römischen Kaiserreich, 1900

Lietzmann
H. LIETZMANN, Geschichte der Alten Kirche, ⁴/⁵1975

LIMC
J. BOARDMAN ET AL. (ed.), Lexicon Iconographicum Mythologiae Classicae, 1981 ff.

Lippold
G. LIPPOLD, Die griechische Plastik (HdArch III), 1950

Lipsius
J.H. LIPSIUS, Das attische Recht und Rechtsverfahren. Mit Benutzung des Attischen Processes 3 vols., 1905–15, repr. 1984

Lloyd-Jones
H. LLOYD-JONES, Blood for the Ghosts – Classical Influences in the Nineteenth and Twentieth Centuries, 1982

LMA
R.-H. BAUTIER, R. AUTY (ed.), Lexikon des Mittelalters 7 vols., 1980–93 (1st installment 1977), 3rd vol. repr. 1995

Lobel/Page
E. LOBEL, D. PAGE (ed.), Poetarum lesbiorum fragmenta, 1955, repr. 1968

Loewy
E. LOEWY (ed.), Inschriften griechischer Bildhauer, 1885, repr. 1965

LPh
T. SCHNEIDER, Lexikon der Pharaonen. Die altägyptischen Könige von der Frühzeit bis zur Römerherrschaft, 1994

LRKA
Friedrich Lübkers Reallexikon des Klassischen Altertums, ⁸1914

LSAG
L.H. JEFFERY, The Local Scripts of Archaic Greece. A Study of the Origin of the Greek Alphabet and its Development from the Eighth to the Fifth Centuries B.C., ²1990

LSAM
F. SOKOLOWSKI, Lois sacrées de l'Asie mineure, 1955

LSCG
F. SOKOLOWSKI, Lois sacrées des cités grecques, 1969

LSCG, Suppl
F. SOKOLOWSKI, Lois sacrées des cités grecques, Supplément, 1962

LSJ
H.G. LIDDELL, R. SCOTT, H.S. JONES ET AL. (ed.), A Greek-English Lexicon, ⁹1940; Suppl.: 1968, repr. 1992

LThK²
J. HÖFER, K. RAHNER (ed.), Lexikon für Theologie und Kirche 14 vols., ²1957–86

LThK¹
W. KASPER ET AL. (ed.), Lexikon für Theologie und Kirche, ¹1993 ff.

LTUR
E.M. STEINBY (ed.), Lexicon Topographicum Urbis Romae, 1993 ff.

LUA
Lunds Universitets Arsskrift / Acta Universitatis Lundensis

Lugli, Fontes
G. LUGLI (ed.), Fontes ad topographiam veteris urbis Romae pertinentes, 6 of 8 vols. partially appeared, 1952–62

Lugli, Monumenti
G. LUGLI, I Monumenti antichi di Roma e suburbio, 3 vols., 1930–38; Suppl.: 1940

Lustrum
Lustrum. Internationale Forschungsberichte aus dem Bereich des klassischen Altertums

M&H
Mediaevalia et Humanistica. Studies in Medieval and Renaissance Society

MacDonald
G. MACDONALD, Catalogue of Greek Coins in the Hunterian Collection, University of Glasgow 3 vols., 1899–1905

MacDowell
D. M. MACDOWELL, The law in Classical Athens (Aspects of Greek and Roman life), 1978

MAev.
Medium Aevum

Magie
D. MAGIE, Roman Rule in Asia Minor to the End of the Third Century after Christ, 1950, repr. 1975

MAII
Mosaici Antichi in Italia, 1967 ff

MAMA
Monumenta Asiae minoris Antiqua, 1927ff.

Manitius
M. MANITIUS, Geschichte der lateinischen Literatur des Mittelalters (HdbA 9, 2) 3 vols., 1911–31, repr. 1973–76

MarbWPr
Marburger-Winckelmann-Programm

Marganne
M.H. MARGANNE, Inventaire analytique des papyrus grecs de médecine, 1981

Marrou
H.-I. MARROU, Geschichte der Erziehung im klassischen Altertum (translation of Histoire de l'éducation dans l'antiquité), ²1977

Martinelli
M. MARTINELLI (ed.), La ceramica degli Etruschi, 1987

Martino, SCR
F. DE MARTINO, Storia della costituzione romana 5 vols., ²1972–75; Indici 1990

Martino, WG
F. DE MARTINO, Wirtschaftsgeschichte des alten Rom, ²1991

Masson
O. MASSON, Les inscriptions chypriotes syllabiques. Recueil critique et commenté (Études chypriotes 1), ²1983

Matz/Duhn
F. MATZ, F. V. DUHN (ed.), Antike Bildwerke in Rom mit Ausschluß der größeren Sammlungen 3 vols., 1881 f.

MAVORS
M.P. SPEIDEL (ed.), Roman Army Researches 1984 ff.

MDAI(A)
Mitteilungen des Deutschen Archäologischen Instituts, Athenische Abteilung

MDAI(Dam)
Damaszener Mitteilungen des Deutschen Archäologischen Instituts

MDAI(Ist)
Istanbuler Mitteilungen des Deutschen Archäologischen Instituts

MDAI(K)
Mitteilungen des Deutschen Archäologischen Instituts (Abteilung Kairo)

MDAI(R)
Mitteilungen des Deutschen Archäologischen Instituts, Römische Abteilung

MDOG
Mitteilungen der Deutschen Orient-Gesellschaft zu Berlin

MededRom
Mededelingen van het Nederlands Historisch Instituut te Rome

Mediaevalia
Mediaevalia

Mediaevistik
Mediaevistik. Internationale Zeitschrift für interdisziplinäre Mittelalterforschung

MEFRA
Mélanges d'Archéologie et d'Histoire de l'École Française de Rome. Antiquité

Meiggs
R. MEIGGS, Trees and Timber in the Ancient Mediterranean World, 1982

Merkelbach/West
R. MERKELBACH, M.L. WEST (ed.), Fragmenta Hesiodea, 1967

Mette
H.J. METTE, Urkunden dramatischer Aufführungen in Griechenland, 1977

MG
Monuments Grecs

MGG¹
F. BLUME (ed.), Die Musik in Geschichte und Gegenwart. Allgemeine Enzyklopädie der Musik 17 vols., 1949–86, repr. 1989

MGG²
L. FINSCHER (ed.), Die Musik in Geschichte und Gegenwart 20 vols., ²1994 ff.

MGH
Monumenta Germaniae Historica inde ab anno Christi quingentesimo usque ad annum millesimum et quingentesimum, 1826 ff.

MGH AA
Monumenta Germaniae Historica: Auctores Antiquissimi

MGH DD
Monumenta Germaniae Historica: Diplomata

MGH Epp
Monumenta Germaniae Historica: Epistulae

MGH PL
Monumenta Germaniae Historica: Poetae Latini medii aevi

MGH SS
Monumenta Germaniae Historica: Scriptores

MGrecs
Monuments Grecs publiés par l'Association pour l'Encouragement des Etudes grecques en France 2 vols., 1872–97

MH
Museum Helveticum

MiB
Musikgeschichte in Bildern

Millar, Emperor
F.G.B. MILLAR, The Emperor in the Roman World, 1977

Millar, Near East
F.G.B. MILLAR, The Roman Near East, 1993

Miller
K. MILLER, Itineraria Romana. Römische Reisewege an der Hand der Tabula Peutingeriana, 1916, repr. 1988

Millett
P. MILLETT, Lending and Borrowing in Ancient Athens, 1991

Minos
Minos

MIO
Mitteilungen des Instituts für Orientforschung

MIR
Moneta Imperii Romani. Österreichische Akademie der Wissenschaften. Veröffentlichungen der Numismatischen Kommission

Mitchell
S. MITCHELL, Anatolia. Land, Men and Gods in Asia Minor 2 vols., 1993

Mitteis
L. MITTEIS, Reichsrecht und Volksrecht in den östlichen Provinzen des römischen Kaiserreichs. Mit Beiträgen zur Kenntnis des griechischen Rechts und der spätrömischen Rechtsentwicklung, 1891, repr. 1984

Mitteis/Wilcken
L. MITTEIS, U. WILCKEN, Grundzüge und Chrestomathie der Papyruskunde, 1912, repr. 1978

ML
R. MEIGGS, D. LEWIS (ed.), A Selection of Greek Historical Inscriptions to the End of the Fifth Century B.C., ²1988

MLatJb
Mittellateinisches Jahrbuch. Internationale Zeitschrift für Mediävistik
Mnemosyne
Mnemosyne. Bibliotheca Classica Batava
MNVP
Mitteilungen und Nachrichten des Deutschen Palästinavereins
MNW
H. Meier et al. (ed.), Kulturwissenschaftliche Bibliographie zum Nachleben der Antike 2 vols., 1931–38
Mollard-Besques
S. Mollard-Besques, Musée National du Louvre. Catalogue raisonné des figurines et reliefs en terrecuite grecs, étrusques et romains 4 vols., 1954–86
Momigliano
A. Momigliano, Contributi alla storia degli studi classici, 1955 ff.
Mommsen, Schriften
Th. Mommsen, Gesammelte Schriften 8 vols., 1904–13, repr. 1965
Mommsen, Staatsrecht
Th. Mommsen, Römisches Staatsrecht 3 vols., Vol. 1, ³1887; Vol. 2 f., 1887 f.
Mommsen Strafrecht
Th. Mommsen, Römisches Strafrecht, 1899, repr. 1955
Mon.Ant.ined.
Monumenti Antichi inediti
Moos
P. v. Moos, Geschichte als Topik, 1988
Moraux
P. Moraux, Der Aristotelismus bei den Griechen von Andronikos bis Alexander von Aphrodisias (Peripatoi 5 und 6) 2 vols., 1973–84
Moreau
J. Moreau, Dictionnaire de géographie historique de la Gaule et de la France, 1972; Suppl.: 1983
Moretti
L. Moretti (ed.), Iscrizioni storiche ellenistiche 2 vols., 1967–76
MP
Modern Philology
MPalerne
Mémoires du Centre Jean Palerne
MRR
T.R.S. Broughton, The Magistrates of the Roman Republic 2 vols., 1951–52; Suppl.: 1986
MSG
C. Jan (ed.), Musici scriptores Graeci, 1895; Suppl.: 1899, repr. 1962
Müller
D. Müller, Topographischer Bildkommentar zu den Historien Herodots: Griechenland im Umfang des heutigen griechischen Staatsgebiets, 1987
Müller-Wiener
W. Müller-Wiener, Bildlexikon zur Topographie Istanbuls, 1977

Münzer¹
F. Münzer, Römische Adelsparteien und Adelsfamilien, 1920
Münzer²
F. Münzer, Römische Adelsparteien und Adelsfamilien, ²1963
Murray/Price
O. Murray, S. Price (ed.), The Greek City: From Homer to Alexander, 1990
Muséon
Muséon Revue d'Études Orientales
MVAG
Mitteilungen der Vorderasiatischen (Ägyptischen) Gesellschaft
MVPhW
Mitteilungen des Vereins klassischer Philologen in Wien
MythGr
Mythographi Graeci 3 vols., 1894–1902; Vol. 1, ²1926
Nash
E. Nash, Bildlexikon zur Topographie des antiken Rom, 1961 f.
NC
Numismatic Chronicle
NClio
La Nouvelle Clio
NDB
Neue Deutsche Biographie, 1953 ff.; Vols. 1–6, repr. 1971
NEAEHL
E. Stern (ed.), The New Encyclopedia of Archaeological Excavations in the Holy Land 4 vols., 1993
Neoph.
Neophilologus
Newald
R. Newald, Nachleben des antiken Geistes im Abendland bis zum Beginn des Humanismus, 1960
NGrove
The New Grove Dictionary of Music and Musicians, ⁶1980
NGroveInst
The New Grove Dictionary of Musical Instruments, 1994
NHCod
Nag Hammadi Codex
NHS
Nag Hammadi Studies
Nicolet
C. Nicolet, L' Ordre équestre à l'époque républicaine 312–43 av. J.-C. 2 vols., 1966–74
Nilsson, Feste
M.P. Nilsson, Griechische Feste von religiöser Bedeutung mit Ausschluss der attischen, 1906
Nilsson, GGR,
M.P. Nilsson, Geschichte der griechischen Religion (HdbA 5, 2), Vol. 1, ³1967, repr. 1992; Vol. 2, ⁴1988
Nilsson, MMR
M.P. Nilsson, The Minoan-Mycenaean Religion and its Survival in Greek Religion, ²1950

Nissen
H. Nissen, Italische Landeskunde 2 vols., 1883–1902

Nock
A.D. Nock, Essays on Religion and the Ancient World, 1972

Noethlichs
K.L. Noethlichs, Beamtentum und Dienstvergehen. Zur Staatsverwaltung in der Spätantike, 1981

Norden, Kunstprosa
E. Norden, Die antike Kunstprosa vom 6. Jh. v. Chr. bis in die Zeit der Renaissance, ⁶1961

Norden, Literatur
E. Norden, Die römische Literatur, ⁶1961

NSA
Notizie degli scavi di antichità

NTM
Schriftenreihe für Geschichte der Naturwissenschaften, Technik und Medizin

Nutton
V. Nutton, From Democedes to Harvey. Studies in the History of Medicine (Collected Studies Series 277), 1988

NZ
Numismatische Zeitschrift

OA
J.G. Baiter, H. Sauppe (ed.), Oratores Attici 3 vols., 1839–43

OBO
Orbis Biblicus et Orientalis

OCD
N.G. Hammond, H.H. Scullard (ed.), The Oxford Classical Dictionary, ²1970, ³1996

ODB
A.P. Kazhdan et al. (ed.), The Oxford Dictionary of Byzantium, 1991 ff.

OF
O. Kern (ed.), Orphicorum Fragmenta, ³1972

OGIS
W. Dittenberger (ed.), Orientis Graeci Inscriptiones Selectae 2 vols., 1903–05, repr. 1960

OLD
P.G.W. Glare (ed.), Oxford Latin Dictionary, 1982 (1st installment 1968)

OIF
Olympische Forschungen, 1941 ff.

Oliver
J.H. Oliver, Greek Constitutions of Early Roman Emperors from Inscriptions and Papyri, 1989

Olivieri
D. Olivieri, Dizionario di toponomastica lombarda. Nomi di comuni, frazioni, casali, monti, corsi d'acqua, ecc. della regione lombarda, studiati in rapporto alle loro origine, ²1961

Olshausen/Biller/Wagner
E. Olshausen, J. Biller, J. Wagner, Historisch-geographische Aspekte der Geschichte des Pontischen und Armenischen Reiches. Untersuchungen Zur historischen Geographie von Pontos unter den Mithradatiden (TAVO 29), Vol.1, 1984

OLZ
Orientalistische Literaturzeitung

OpAth
Opuscula Atheniensia, 1953 ff.

OpRom
Opuscula Romana

ORF
E. Malcovati, Oratorum Romanorum Fragmenta (Corpus scriptorum Latinorum Paravianum 56–58); vols., 1930

Orientalia
Orientalia, Neue Folge

Osborne
R. Osborne, Classical Landscape with Figures: The Ancient Greek City and its Countryside, 1987

Overbeck
J. Overbeck, Die antiken Schriftquellen zur Geschichte der bildenden Künste bei den Griechen, 1868, repr. 1959

PA
J. Kirchner, Prosopographia Attica 2 vols., 1901–03, repr. 1966

Pack
R.A. Pack (ed.), The Greek and Latin Literary Texts from Greco-Roman Egypt, ²1965

Panofsky
E. Panofsky, Renaissance und Renaissancen in Western Art, 1960

Pape/Benseler
W. Pape, G.E. Benseler, Wörterbuch der griechischen Eigennamen 2 vols., 1863–1870

PAPhS
Proceedings of the American Philosophical Society

Parke
H.W. Parke, Festivals of the Athenians, 1977

Parke/Wormell
H.W. Parke, D.E.W. Wormell, The Delphic Oracle, 1956

PBSR
Papers of the British School at Rome

PCA
Proceedings of die Classical Association. London

PCG
R. Kassel, C. Austin (ed.), Poetae comici graeci, 1983 ff.

PCPhS
Proceedings of the Cambridge Philological Society

PdP
La Parola del Passato

PE
R. Stillwell et al. (ed.), The Princeton Encyclopedia of Classical Sites, 1976

Peacock
D.P.S. Peacock, Pottery in the Roman World: An Ethnoarchaeological Approach, 1982

PEG I
A. Bernabé (ed.), Poetae epici graeci. Testimonia et fragmenta. Pars I, 1987

Pfeiffer, KPI

    R. Pfeiffer, Geschichte der Klassischen Philologie. Von den Anfängen bis zum Ende des Hellenismus, 1978

Pfeiffer KPII

    R. Pfeiffer, Die Klassische Philologie von Petrarca bis Mommsen, 1982

Pfiffig

    A.J. Pfiffig, Religio Etrusca, 1975

Pflaum

    H.G.Pflaum, Les carrières procuratoriennes équestres sous le Haut-Empire Romain 3 vols. and figs., 1960 f.; Suppl.: 1982

Pfuhl

    E. Pfuhl, Malerei und Zeichnung der Griechen, 1923

Pfuhl/Möbius

    E. Pfuhl, H. Möbius, Die ostgriechischen Grabreliefs 2 vols., 1977–79

PG

    J.P. Migne (ed.), Patrologiae cursus completus, series Graeca 161 vols., 1857–1866; Conspectus auctorum: 1882; Indices 2 vols.: 1912–32

PGM

    K. Preisendanz, A. Henrichs (ed.), Papyri Graecae Magicae. Die griechischen Zauberpapyri 2 vols., ²1973 f. (1928–31)

Philippson /Kirsten

    A. Philippson, A. Lehmann, E. Kirsten (ed.), Die griechischen Landschaften. Eine Landeskunde 4 vols., 1950–59

Philologus

    Philologus. Zeitschrift für klassische Philologie

PhQ

    Philological Quarterly

Phronesis

    Phronesis

PhU

    Philologische Untersuchungen

PhW

    Berliner Philologische Wochenschrift

Picard

    Ch. Picard, Manuel d'archéologie grecque. La sculpture, 1935 ff.

Pickard-Cambridge/Gould/Lewis

    A.W. Pickard-Cambridge, J. Gould, D.M. Lewis, The Dramatic Festivals of Athens, ²1988

Pickard-Cambridge/Webster

    A.W. Pickard-Cambridge, T.B.L. Webster, Dithyramb, Tragedy and Comedy, ²1962

Pigler, I

    A. Pigler, Barockthermen. Eine Auswahl von Verzeichnissen zur lkonographie des 17. Und 1 8. Jahrhunderts. 2 vols., ²1974; Ill. Vol.: 1974

PIR

    Prosopographia imperii Romani saeculi, Vol. I-III, ²1933 ff.

PL

    J.P. Migni (ed.), Patrologiae cursus completus, se-

ries Latina 221 vols., 1844–65 partly repr. 5 Suppl. Vols., 1958–74; Index: 1965

PLM

    Ae. Baehrens (ed.), Poetae Latini Minores 5 vols., 1879–83

PLRE

    A.H.M. Jones, J.R. Martindale, J. Morris (ed.), The Prosopography of the Later Roman Empire 3 vols. in 4 parts, 1971–1992

PMG

    D.L. Page, Poetae melici graeci, 1962

PMGF

    M. Davies (ed.), Poetarum melicorum Graecorum fragmenta, 1991

PMGTr

    H.D. Betz (ed.), The Greek Magical Papyri in Translation, Including the Demotic Spells, ²1992

Poccetti

    D. Poccetti, Nuovi documenti italici a complemento del manuale di E. Vetter (Orientamenti linguistici 8), 1979

Pökel

    W. Pökel, Philologisches Schriftstellerlexikon, 1882, repr. ²1974

Poetica

    Poetica. Zeitschrift für Sprach- und Literaturwissenschaft

Pokorny

    J. Pokorny, Indogermanisches etymologisches Wörterbuch 2 vols., ²1989

Poulsen

    F. Poulsen, Catalogue of Ancient Sculpture in the Ny Carlsberg Glyptotek, 1951

PP

    W. Peremans (ed.), Prosopographia Ptolemaica (Studia hellenistica) 9 vols., 1950–81, repr. Vol. 1–3, 1977

PPM

    Pompei, Pitture e Mosaici, 1990 ff.

Praktika

    Πρακτικά της εν Αθήναις αρχαιολογικάς εταιρείας

Préaux

    C. Préaux, L'économie royale des Lagides, 1939, repr. 1980

Preller/Robert

    L. Preller, C. Robert, Griechische Mythologie, ⁵1964 ff.

Pritchett

    K. Pritchett, Studies in Ancient Greek Topography (University of California Publications, Classical Studies) 8 vols., 1969–92

PropKg

    K. Bittel et al. (ed.), Propyläen Kunstgeschichte 22 vols., 1966–80, repr. 1985

Prosdocimi

    A.L. Prosdocimi, M. Cristofani, Lingue dialetti dell'Italia antica, 1978; A. Marinetti, Aggiornamenti ed Indici, 1984

PrZ
  Prähistorische Zeitschrift
PSI
  G. Vitelli, M. Norsa, V. Bartoletti et al. (ed.),
  Papiri greci e latini (Pubblicazione della Soc. Italiana
  per la ricerca dei pap. greci e latini in Egitto), 1912 ff.
QSt
  Quellen und Studien zur Geschichte und Kultur des
  Altertums und des Mittelalters
Quasten
  J. Quasten, Patrology 2 vols., 1950–53
RA
  Revue Archéologique
RAC
  T. Klauser, E. Dassmann (ed.), Reallexikon für
  Antike und Christentum. Sachwörterbuch zur Aus-
  einandersetzung des Christentums mit der antiken
  Welt, 1950 ff. (1st installment 1941)
RACr
  Rivista di Archeologia Cristiana
Radermacher
  L. Radermacher, Artium Scriptores. Reste der vor-
  aristotelischen Rhetorik, 1951
Radke
  G. Radke, Die Götter Altitaliens, ²1979
Raepsaet-Charlier
  M-T. Raepsaet-Charlier, Prosopographie des
  femmes de l'ordre sénatorial (l. – II. siècles) (Fonds
  René Draguet 4) 2 vols., 1987
RÄRG
  H. Bonnet, Reallexikon der ägyptischen Religions-
  geschichte, ²1971
RAL
  Rendiconti della Classe di Scienze morali, storiche e
  filologiche dell'Academia dei Lincei
Ramsay
  W.M. Ramsay, The Cities and Bishoprics of Phrygia
  2 vols., 1895–97
RAssyr
  Revue d'assyriologie et d'archéologie orientale
Rawson, Culture
  E. Rawson, Roman Culture and Society. Collected
  Papers, 1991
Rawson, Family
  B. Rawson (ed.), The Family in Ancient Rome. New
  Perspectives, 1986
RB
  P. Wirth (ed.), Reallexikon der Byzantinistik, 1968
  ff.
RBA
  Revue Belge d'archéologie et d'histoire de l'art
RBi
  Revue biblique
RBK
  K. Wessel, M. Restle (ed.), Reallexikon zur byzan-
  tinischen Kunst, 1966 ff. (1st installment 1963)
RBN
  Revue Belge de numismatique

RBPh
  Revue Belge de philologie et d'histoire
RDAC
  Report of the Department of Antiquities, Cyprus
RDK
  O. Schmitt (ed.), Reallexikon zur deutschen Kunst-
  geschichte, 1937ff.
RE
  G. Wissowa et al., (ed.), Paulys Real-Encyclopädie
  der classischen Altertumswissenschaft, Neue Be-
  arbeitung, 1893–1980
REA
  Revue des études anciennes
REByz
  Revue des études byzantines
REG
  Revue des études grecques
Rehm
  W. Rehm, Griechentum und Goethezeit, ³1952,
  ⁴1968
Reinach, RP
  S. Reinach, Répertoire de peintures greques er ro-
  maines, 1922
Reinach, RR
  S. Reinach, Répertoire de reliefs grecs et romains 3
  vols., 1909–12
Reinach RSt
  S. Reinach, Répertoire de la statuaire greque et ro-
  maine 6 vols., 1897–1930, repr. 1965–69
REL
  Revue des études latines
Rer.nat.scr.Gr.min
  O. Keller (ed.), Rerum naturalium scriptores Gra-
  eci minores, 1877
Reynolds
  L.D. Reynolds (ed.), Texts and Transmission: A
  Survey of the Latin Classics, 1983
Reynolds/Wilson
  L.D. Reynolds, N.G. Wilson, Scribes and Schol-
  ars. A Guide to the Transmission of Greek and Latin
  Literature, ³1991
RFIC
  Rivista di filologia e di istruzione classica
RG
  W.H. Waddington, E. Babelon, Recueil général
  des monnaies grecques d'Asie mineure (Subsidia epi-
  graphica 5) 2 vols., 1908–1925, repr. 1976
RGA
  H. Beck et al. (ed.), Reallexikon der germanischen
  Altertumskunde, ²1973 ff. (1st installment 1968);
  Suppl.: 1986 ff.
RGG
  K. Galling (ed.), Die Religion in Geschichte und
  Gegenwart. Handwörterbuch für Theologie und Re-
  ligionswissenschaft 7 vols., ³1957–65, repr. 1980
RGRW
  Religion in the Graeco-Roman World
RGVV
  Religionsgeschichtliche Versuche und Vorarbeiten

RH
  Revue historique
RHA
  Revue hittite et asianique
RhM
  Rheinisches Museum für Philologie
Rhodes
  P.J. RHODES, A commentary on the Aristotelian
  Athenaion Politeia, ²1993
RHPhR
  Revue d'histoire et de philosophie religieuses
RHR
  Revue de l'histoire des religions
RHS
  Revue historique des Sciences et leurs applications
RIA
  Rivista dell'Istituto nazionale d'archeologia e storia
  dell'arte
RIC
  H. MATTINGLY, E.A. SYDENHAM, The Roman Im-
  perial Coinage 10 vols., 1923–94
Richardson
  L. RICHARDSON (Jr.), A New Topographical Dic-
  tionary of Ancient Rome, 1992
Richter, Furniture
  G.M.A. RICHTER, The Furniture of the Greeks,
  Etruscans and Romans, 1969
Richter, Korai
  G.M.A. RICHTER, Korai, Archaic Greek Maidens,
  1968
Richter, Kouroi
  G.M.A. RICHTER, Kouroi, Archaic Greek Youths,
  ³1970
Richter, Portraits
  G.M.A. RICHTER, The Portraits of the Greeks 3 vols.
  and suppl., 1965–72
RIDA
  Revue internationale des droits de l'antiquité
RIG
  P-M. DUVAL (ed.), Recueil des inscriptions gauloi-
  ses, 1985 ff.
RIL
  Rendiconti dell'Istituto Lombardo, classe di lettere,
  scienze morali e storiche
Rivet
  A.L.F. RIVET, Gallia Narbonensis with a Chapter on
  Alpes Maritimae. Southern France in Roman Times,
  1988
Rivet/Smith
  A.L.F. RIVET, C. SMITH, The Place-Names of Ro-
  man Britain, 1979
RLA
  E. EBELING ET AL. (ed.), Reallexikon der Assyriolo-
  gie und vorderasiatischen Archäologie, 1928 ff.
RLV
  M. EBERT (ed.), Reallexikon der Vorgeschichte 15
  vols., 1924–32
RMD
  M.M. ROXAN, Roman military diplomas (Occasion-

al Publications of the Institute of Archaeology of the
University of London 2 and 9), Vol. 1, (1954–77),
1978; Vol. 2, (1978–84), 1985; Vol. 3, (1985–94),
1994
RN
  Revue numismatique
Robert, OMS
  L. ROBERT, Opera minora selecta 7 vols., 1969–90
Robert, Villes
  L. ROBERT, Villes d'Asie Mineure. Etudes de géo-
  graphie ancienne, ²1902
Robertson
  A.S. ROBERTSON, Roman Imperial Coins in the
  Hunter Coin Cabinet, University of Glasgow 5 vols.,
  1962–82
Rohde
  E. ROHDE, Psyche. Seelenkult und Unsterblichkeits-
  glaube der Griechen, ²1898, repr. 1991
Roscher
  W.H. ROSCHER, Ausführliches Lexikon der grie-
  chischen und römischen Mythologie 6 vols.,
  ³1884–1937, repr. 1992 f.; 4 Suppl. Vols.: 1893–
  1921
Rostovtzeff, Hellenistic World
  M.I. ROSTOVTZEFF, The Social and Economic His-
  tory of the Hellenistic World, ²1953
Rostovtzeff, Roman Empire
  M.I. ROSTOVTZEFF, The Social and Economic His-
  tory of the Roman Empire, ²1957
Rotondi
  G. ROTONDI, Leges publicae populi Romani. Elenco
  cronologico con una introduzione sull' attività legis-
  lativa dei comizi romani, 1912, repr. 1990
RPAA
  Rendiconti della Pontificia Accademia di Archeolo-
  gia
RPC
  A. BURNETT, M. AMANDRY, P.P. RIPOLLÈS (ed.), Ro-
  man Provincial Coinage, 1992 ff.
RPh
  Revue de philologie
RQ
  Renaissance Quarterly
RQA
  Römische Quartalsschrift für christliche Altertums-
  kunde und für Kirchengeschichte
RRC
  M. CRAWFORD, Roman Republican Coinage, 1974,
  repr. 1991
RSC
  Rivista di Studi Classici
Rubin
  B. RUBIN, Das Zeitalter Iustinians, 1960
Ruggiero
  E. DE RUGGIERO, Dizionario epigrafico di antichità
  romana, 1895 ff., Vols. 1–3: repr. 1961 f.
Saeculum
  Saeculum. Jahrbuch für Universalgeschichte

Saller
R. SALLER, Personal Patronage Under the Early Empire, 1982
Salomies
O. SALOMIES, Die römischen Vornamen. Studien zur römischen Namengebung (Commentationes humanarum litterarum 82), 1987
Samuel
A.E. SAMUEL, Greek and Roman Chronology. Calendars and Years in Classical Antiquity (HdbA I 7), 1972
Sandys
J.E. SANDYS, A History of Classical Scholarship 3 vols., ²1906–21, repr. 1964
SAWW
Sitzungsberichte der Österreichischen Akademie der Wissenschaften in Wien
SB
Sammelbuch griechischer Urkunden aus Ägypten (Inschriften und Papyri), Vols. 1–2: F. PREISIGKE (ed.), 1913–22; Vols. 3–5: F. BILABEL (ed.), 1926–34
SBAW
Sitzungsberichte der Bayerischen Akademie der Wissenschaften
SCCGF
J. DEMIAŃCZUK (ed.), Supplementum comicum comoediae Graecae fragmenta, 1912
Schachter
A. SCHACHTER, The Cults of Boiotia 4 vols., 1981–94
Schäfer
A. SCHÄFER, Demosthenes und seine Zeit 3 vols., ²1885–87, repr. 1967
Schanz/Hosius
M. SCHANZ, C. HOSIUS, G. KRÜGER, Geschichte der römischen Literatur bis zum Gesetzgebungswerk des Kaisers Justinian (HdbA 8), Vol. 1, ⁴1927, repr. 1979; Vol. 2, ⁴1935, repr. 1980; Vol. 3, ³1922, repr. 1969; Vol. 4,1, ²1914, repr. 1970; Vol. 4,2, 1920, repr. 1971
Scheid, Collège
J. SCHEID, Le collège des frères arvales. Étude prosopographique du recrutement (69 –304) (Saggi di storia antica 1), 1990
Scheid, Recrutement
J. SCHEID, Les frères arvales. Recrutement et origine sociale sous les empereurs julio-claudiens (Bibliothèque de l'École des Hautes Études, Section des Sciences Religieuses 77), 1975
Schlesier
R. SCHLESIER, Kulte, Mythen und Gelehrte – Anthropologie der Antike seit 1800, 1994
Schmid/Stählin I
W. SCHMID, O. STÄHLIN, Geschichte der griechischen Literatur. Erster Theil: Die klassische Periode der griechische Literatur VII 1) 5 vols., 1929–48, repr. 1961–80
Schmid/Stählin II
W. CHRIST, W. SCHMID, O. STÄHLIN, Geschichte

der griechischen Litteratur bis auf die Zeit Justinians. Zweiter Theil: Die nachklassische Periode der griechischen Litteratur (HdbA VII 2) 2 vols., ⁶1920–24, repr. 1961–81
Schmidt
K.H. SCHMIDT, Die Komposition in gallischen Personennamen in: Zeitschrift für celtische Philologie 26, 1957, 33–301 = (Diss.), 1954
Schönfeld
M. SCHÖNFELD, Wörterbuch der altgermanischen Personen- und Völkernamen (Germanische Bibliothek Abt. 1, Reihe 4, 2), 1911, repr. ²1965)
Scholiall
H. ERBSE (ed.), Scholia Graeca in Homeri Iliadem (Scholia vetera) 7 vols., 1969–88
SChr
Sources Chrétiennes 300 vols., 1942 ff.
Schrötter
F. v. SCHRÖTTER (ed.), Wörterbuch der Münzkunde, ²1970
Schürer
E. SCHÜRER, G. VERMÈS, The history of the Jewish people in the age of Jesus Christ (175 B.C. – A.D. 135) 3 vols., 1973–87
Schulten, Landeskunde
A. SCHULTEN, Iberische Landeskunde. Geographie des antiken Spanien 2 vols., 1955–57 (translation of the Spanish edition of 1952)
Schulz
F. SCHULZ, Geschichte der römischen Rechtswissenschaft, 1961, repr. 1975
Schulze
W. SCHULZE, Zur Geschichte lateinischer Eigennamen, 1904
Schwyzer, Dial.
E. SCHWYZER (ed.), Dialectorum Graecarum exempla epigraphica potiora, ³1923
Schwyzer, Gramm.
E. SCHWYZER, Griechische Grammatik, Vol. 1: Allgemeiner Teil. Lautlehre Wortbildung, Flexion (HdbA II 1, 1), 1939
Schwyzer/Debrunner
E. SCHWYZER, A. DEBRUNNER, Griechische Grammatik, Vol. 2: Syntax und syntaktische Stilistik (HdbA II 1,2), 1950; D. J. GEORGACAS, Register zu beiden Bänden, 1953; F. RADT, S. RADT, Stellenregister, 1971
Scullard
H. H. SCULLARD, Festivals and Ceremonies of the Roman Republic, 1981
SDAW
Sitzungsberichte der Deutschen Akademie der Wissenschaften zu Berlin
SDHI
Studia et documenta historiae et iuris
SE
Studi Etruschi
Seeck
O. SEECK, Regesten der Kaiser und Päpste für die

Jahre 311 bis 470 n. Chr. Vorarbeiten zu einer Prosopographie der christlichen Kaiserzeit, 1919, repr. 1964

SEG
Supplementum epigraphicum Graecum, 1923 ff.

Seltman
C. SELTMAN, Greek Coins. A History of Metallic Currency and Coinage down to the Fall of the Hellenistic Kingdoms, ²1905

Sezgin
F. SEZGIN, Geschichte des arabischen Schrifttums, Vol.3: Medizin, Pharmazie, Zoologie, Tierheilkunde bis ca. 430 H., 1970

SGAW
Sitzungsberichte der Göttinger Akademie der Wissenschaften

SGDI
H. COLLITZ ET AL. (ed.), Sammlung der griechischen Dialekt-Inschriften 4 vols., 1884–1915

SGLG
K. ALPERS, H. ERBSE, A. KLEINLOGEL (ed.), Sammlung griechischer und lateinischer Grammatiker 7 vols., 1974–88

SH
H. LLOYD-JONES, P. PARSONS (ed.), Supplementum Hellenisticum, 1983

SHAW
Sitzungsberichte der Heidelberger Akademie der Wissenschaften

Sherk
R.K. SHERK, Roman Documents from the Greek East: Senatus Consulta and Epistulae to the Age of Augustus, 1969

SicA
Sicilia archeologica

SIFC
Studi italiani di filologia classica

SiH
Studies in the Humanities

Simon, GG
E. SIMON, Die Götter der Griechen, ⁴1992

Simon, GR
E. SIMON, 1 Die Götter der Römer, 1990

SLG
D. PAGE (ed.), Supplementum lyricis graecis, 1974

SM
Schweizer Münzblatter

SMEA
Studi Micenei ed Egeo-Anatolici

Smith
W.D. SMITH, The Hippocratic tradition (Cornell publications in the history of science), 1979

SMSR
Studi e materiali di storia delle religioni

SMV
Studi mediolatini e volgari

SNG
Sylloge Nummorum Graecorum

SNR
Schweizerische Numismatische Rundschau

Solin/Salomies
H. SOLIN, O. SALOMIES, Repertorium nominum gentilium et cognominum Latinorum (Alpha – Omega: Reihe A 80), ²1994

Sommer
F. SOMMER, Handbuch der lateinischen Laut- und Formenlehre. Eine Einführung in das sprachwissenschaftliche Studium des Latein (Indogermanische Bibliothek 1, 1, 3, 1), ³1914

Soustal, Nikopolis
P. SOUSTAL, Nikopolis und Kephallenia (Denkschriften der Akademie der Wissenschaften, Philosophisch-Historische Klasse I 50; TIB 3), 1981

Soustal, Thrakien
P. SOUSTAL, Thrakien. Thrake, Rodope und Haimimontos (Denkschriften der Österreichischen Akademie der Wissenschaften, Philosophisch-Historische Klasse 221; TIB 6), 1991

Sovoronos
J.N. SOVORONOS, Das Athener Nationalmuseum 3 vols., 1908–37

Spec.
Speculum

Spengel
L. SPENGEL, (ed.), Rhetores Graeci 3 vols., 1853–56, repr. 1966

SPrAW
Sitzungsberichte der Preußischen Akademie der Wissenschaften

SSAC
Studi storici per l'antichità classica

SSR
G. GIANNANTONI (ed.), Socratis et Socraticorum Reliquiae 4 vols., 1990

Staden
H. V. STADEN, Herophilus, The Art of Medicine in Early Alexandria, 1989

Stein, Präfekten
A. STEIN, Die Präfekten von Ägypten in der römischen Kaiserzeit (Dissertationes Bernenses Series 1, 1), 1950

Stein, Spätröm.R.
E. STEIN, Geschichte des spätrömischen Reiches, Vol. 1, 1928; French version, 1959; Vol. 2, French only, 1949

Stewart
A. STEWART, Greek sculpture. An exploration 2 vols., 1990

StM
Studi Medievali

Strong/Brown
D. STRONG, D. BROWN (ed.), Roman Crafts, 1976

Stv
Die Staatsverträge des Altertums, Vol. 2: H. BENGTSON, R. WERNER (ed.), Die Verträge der griechisch-römischen Welt von 700 bis 338, ²1975; Vol. 3: H.H. SCHMITT (ed.), Die Verträge der griechisch-römischen Welt 338 bis 200 v. Chr., 1969

SVF
  J. v. ARNIM (ed.), Stoicorum veterum fragmenta 3
  vols., 1903–05; Index: 1924, repr. 1964
Syll.²
  W. DITTENBERGER, Sylloge inscriptionum Graeca-
  rum 3 vols., ²1898–1909
Syll.³
  F. HILLER VON GAERTRINGEN ET AL. (ed.), Sylloge
  inscriptionum Graecarum 4 vols., ³1915–24, repr.
  1960
Syme, AA
  R. SYME, The Augustan Aristocracy, 1986
Syme, RP
  E. BADIAN (Vols. 1,2), A.R. BIRLEY (Vols. 3–7) (ed.)
  R. SYME, Roman Papers 7 vols., 1979–91
Syme, RR
  K. SYME, The Roman Revolution, 1939
Syme, Tacitus
  R. SYME, Tacitus 2 vols., 1958
Symposion
  Symposion, Akten der Gesellschaft für Griechische
  und Hellenistische Rechtsgeschichte
Syria
  Syria. Revue d'art oriental et d'archéologie
TAM
  Tituli Asiae minoris, 1901 ff.
TAPhA
  Transactions and Proceedings of the American
  Philological Association
Taubenschlag
  R. TAUBENSCHLAG, The law of Greco-Roman Egypt
  in the light of the Papyri: 332 B. C. – 640 A. D.,
  ²1955
TAVO
  H. BRUNNER, W. RÖLLIG (ed.), Tübinger Atlas des
  Vorderen Orients, Beihefte, Teil B: Geschichte, 1969
  ff.
TeherF
  Teheraner Forschungen
TGF
  A. NAUCK (ed.), Tragicorum Graecorum Fragmenta,
  ²1889, 2nd repr. 1983
ThGL
  H. STEPHANUS, C. B. HASE, W. UND L. DINDORF ET
  AL. (ed.), Thesaurus graecae linguae, 1831 ff., repr.
  1954
ThlL
  Thesaurus linguae Latinae, 1900 ff.
ThlL, Onom.
  Thesaurus linguae Latinae, Supplementum onoma-
  sticon. Nomina propria Latina, Vol. 2 (C – Cyzistra),
  1907–1913; Vol. 3 (D – Donusa), 1918–1923
ThLZ
  Theologische Literaturzeitung Monatsschrift für das
  gesamte Gebiet der Theologie und Religionswissen-
  schaft
Thomasson
  B.E. THOMASSON, Laterculi Praesidum 3 vols. in 5
  parts, 1972–1990

Thumb/Kieckers
  A. THUMB, E. KIECKERS, Handbuch der griechi-
  schen Dialekte (Indogermanische Bibliothek 1, 1, 1),
  ²1932
Thumb/Scherer
  A. THUMB, A. SCHERER, Handbuch der griechischen
  Dialekte (Indogermanische Bibliothek, 1, 1, 2),
  ²1959
ThWAT
  G.J. BOTTERWECK, H.-J. FABRY (ed.), Theologisches
  Wörterbuch zum Alten Testament, 1973 ff.
ThWB
  G. KITTEL, G. FRIEDRICH (ed.), Theologisches Wör-
  terbuch zum Neuen Testament 11 vols., 1933–79,
  repr. 1990
TIB
  H. HUNGER (ed.). Tabula Imperii Byzantini 7 vols.,
  1976–1990
Timm
  S. TIMM, Das christlich-koptische Ägypten in ara-
  bischer Zeit. Eine Sammlung christlicher Stätten in
  Ägypten in arabischer Zeit, unter Ausschluß von
  Alexandria, Kairo, des Apa-Mena-Klosters (Der
  Abu Mina), des Sketis (Wadi n-Natrun) und der Si-
  nai-Region (TAVO 41) 6 parts, 1984–92
TIR
  Tabula Imperii Romani, 1934 ff.
TIR/IP
  Y. TSAFRIR, L. DI SEGNI, J. GREEN, Tabula Imperii
  Romani. Iudaea – Palaestina. Eretz Israel in the Hel-
  lenistic, Roman and Byzantine Periods, 1994
Tod
  M.N. TOD (ed.), A Selection of Greek Historical In-
  scriptions to the End of the Fifth Century BC, Vol. 1:
  ²1951, repr. 1985; Vol. 2: ²1950
Tovar
  A. TOVAR, Iberische Landeskunde 2: Die Völker und
  Städte des antiken Hispanien, Vol. 1 Baetica, 1974;
  Vol. 2: Lusitanien, 1976; Vol. 3: Tarraconensis, 1989
Toynbee, Hannibal
  A.J. TOYNBEE, Hannibal's legacy. The Hannibalic
  war's effects on Roman life 2 vols., 1965
Toynbee, Tierwelt
  J.M.C. TOYNBEE, Tierwelt der Antike, 1983
TPhS
  Transactions of the Philological Society Oxford
Traill, Attica
  J. S. TRAILL, The Political Organization of Attica,
  1975
Traill, PAA
  J. S. TRAILL, Persons of Ancient Athens, 1994 ff.
Travlos, Athen
  J. TRAVLOS, Bildlexikon zur Topographie des anti-
  ken Athen, 1971
Travlos, Attika
  J. TRAVLOS, Bildlexikon zur Topographie des anti-
  ken Attika, 1988
TRE
  G. KRAUSE, G. MÜLLER (ed.), Theologische Realen-
  zyklopädie, 1977 ff. (1st installment 1976)

Treggiari
S. TREGGIARI, Roman Marriage. Iusti Coniuges from the Time of Cicero to the Time of Ulpian, 1991
Treitinger
O. TREITINGER, Die Oströmische Kaiser- und Reichsidee nach ihrer Gestaltung im höfischen Zeremoniell, 1938, repr. 1969
Trendall, Lucania
A.D. TRENDALL, The Red-figured Vases of Lucania, Campania and Sicily, 1967
Trendall, Paestum
A.D. TRENDALL, The Red-figured Vases of Paestum, 1987
Trendall/Cambitoglou
A.D. TRENDALL, The Red-figured Vases of Apulia 2 vols., 1978–82
TRF
O. RIBBECK (ed.), Tragicorum Romanorum Fragmenta, ²1871, repr. 1962
TRG
Tijdschrift voor rechtsgeschiedenis
TrGF
B. SNELL, R. KANNICHT, S. RADT (ed.), Tragicorum graecorum fragmenta, Vol. 1, ²1986; Vols. 2–4, 1977–85
Trombley
F.R. TROMBLEY, Hellenic Religion and Christianization c. 370–529 (Religions in the Graeco-Roman World 115) 2 vols., 1993 f.
TU
Texte und Untersuchungen zur Geschichte der altchristlichen Literatur
TUAT
O. KAISER (ed.), Texte aus der Umwelt des Alten Testaments, 1985 ff. (1st installment 1982)
TürkAD
Türk arkeoloji dergisi
Ullmann
M. ULLMANN, Die Medizin im Islam, 1970
UPZ
U. WILCKEN (ed.), Urkunden der Ptolemäerzeit (Ältere Funde) 2 vols., 1927–57
v. Haehling
R. v. HAEHLING, Die Religionszugehörigkeit der hohen Amtsträger des Römischen Reiches seit Constantins I. Alleinherrschaft bis zum Ende der Theodosianischen Dynastie (324–450 bzw. 455 n. Chr.) (Antiquitas 3, 23), 1978
VDI
Vestnik Drevnej Istorii
Ventris/Chadwick
M. VENTRIS, J. CHADWICK, Documents in Mycenean Greek, ²1973
Vetter
E. VETTER, Handbuch der italischen Dialekte, 1953
VIR
Vocabularium iurisprudentiae Romanae 5 vols., 1903–39

VisRel
Visible Religion
Vittinghoff
F. VITTINGHOFF (ed.), Europäische Wirtschafts- und Sozialgeschichte in der römischen Kaiserzeit, 1990
VL
W. STAMMLER, K. LANGOSCH, K. RUH ET AL. (ed.), Die deutsche Literatur des Mittelalters. Verfasserslexikon, ²1978 ff.
Vogel-Weidemann
U. VOGEL-WEIDEMANN, Die Statthalter von Africa und Asia in den Jahren 14–68 n.Chr. Eine Untersuchung zum Verhältnis von Princeps und Senat (Antiquitas 1, 31), 1982
VT
Vetus Testamentum. Quarterly Published by the International Organization of Old Testament Scholars
Wacher
R. WACHER (ed.), The Roman World 2 vols., 1987
Walde/Hofmann
A. WALDE, J.B. HOFMANN, Lateinisches etymologisches Wörterbuch 3 vols., ³1938–56
Walde/Pokorny
A. WALDE, J. POKORNY (ed.), Vergleichendes Wörterbuch der indogermanischen Sprachen 3 vols., 1927–32, repr. 1973
Walz
C. WALZ (ed.), Rhetores Graeci 9 vols., 1832–36, repr. 1968
WbMyth
H.W. HAUSSIG (ed.), Wörterbuch der Mythologie, Teil 1: Die alten Kulturvölker, 1965 ff.
Weber
W. WEBER, Biographisches Lexikon zur Geschichtswissenschaft in Deutschland, Österreich und der Schweiz, ²1987
Wehrli, Erbe
F. WEHRLI (ed.), Das Erbe der Antike, 1963
Wehrli, Schule
F. WEHRLI (ed.), Die Schule des Aristoteles 10 vols., 1967–69; 2 Suppl. Vols.: 1974–78
Welles
C.B. WELLES, Royal Correspondence in the Hellenistic Period: A Study in Greek Epigraphy, 1934
Wenger
L. WENGER, Die Quellen des römischen Rechts (Denkschriften der Österreichischen Akademie der Wissenschaften. Philosophisch-Historische Klasse 2), 1953
Wernicke
I. WERNICKE, Die Kelten in Italien. Die Einwanderung und die frühen Handelsbeziehungen zu den Etruskern (Diss.), 1989 = (Palingenesia), 1991
Whatmough
J. WHATMOUGH, The dialects of Ancient Gaul. Prolegomena and records of the dialects 5 vols., 1949–51, repr. in 1 vol., 1970

White, Farming
   K.D. WHITE, Roman Farming, 1970
White, Technology
   K.D. WHITE, Greek and Roman Technology, 1983,
   repr. 1986
Whitehead
   D. WHITEHEAD, The demes of Attica, 1986
Whittaker
   C.R. WHITTAKER (ed.), Pastoral Economies in Clas-
   sical Antiquity, 1988
Wide
   S. WIDE, Lakonische Kulte, 1893
Wieacker, PGN
   F. WIEACKER, Privatrechtsgeschichte der Neuzeit,
   ²1967
Wieacker, RRG
   F. WIEACKER, Römische Rechtsgeschichte, Vol. 1,
   1988
Wilamowitz
   U. v. WILAMOWITZ-MOELLENDORFF, Der Glaube
   der Hellenen 2 vols., ²1955, repr. 1994
Will
   E. WILL, Histoire politique du monde hellénistique
   (323–30 av. J. C.) 2 vols., ²1979–82
Winter
   R. KEKULÉ (ed.), Die antiken Terrakotten, III 1, 2: F.
   WINTER, Die Typen der figürlichen Terrakotten,
   1903
WJA
   Würzburger Jahrbücher für die Altertumswissen-
   schaft
WMT
   L.I. CONRAD ET AL., The Western medical tradition.
   800 BC to A.D. 1800, 1995
WO
   Die Welt des Orients. Wissenschaftliche Beiträge zur
   Kunde des Morgenlandes
Wolff
   H.J. WOLFF, Das Recht der griechischen Papyri
   Ägyptens in der Zeit der Ptolemaeer und des Prinzi-
   pats (Rechtsgeschichte des Altertums Part 5; HbdA
   10, 5), 1978
WS
   Wiener Studien, Zeitschrift für klassische Philologie
   und Patristik
WUNT
   Wissenschaftliche Untersuchungen zum Neuen Tes-
   tament
WVDOG
   Wissenschaftliche Veröffentlichungen der Deut-
   schen Orient-Gesellschaft
WZKM
   Wiener Zeitschrift für die Kunde des Morgenlandes
YCIS
   Yale Classical Studies
ZA
   Zeitschrift für Assyriologie und Vorderasiatische
   Archäologie

ZÄS
   Zeitschrift für ägyptische Sprache und Altertums-
   kunde
ZATW
   Zeitschrift für die Alttestamentliche Wissenschaft
Zazoff, AG
   P. ZAZOFF, Die antiken Gemmen, 1983
Zazoff, GuG
   P. ZAZOFF, H. ZAZOFF, Gemmensammler und
   Gemmenforscher. Von einer noblen Passion zur
   Wissenschaft, 1983
ZDMG
   Zeitschrift der Deutschen Morgenländischen Gesell-
   schaft
ZDP
   Zeitschrift für deutsche Philologie
Zeller
   E. ZELLER, Die Philosophie der Griechen in ihrer ge-
   schichtlichen Entwicklung 4 vols., 1844–52, repr.
   1963
Zeller/Mondolfo
   E. ZELLER, R. MONDOLFO, La filosofia dei Greci nel
   suo sviluppo storico, Vol. 3, 1961
ZfN
   Zeitschrift für Numismatik
Zgusta
   L. ZGUSTA, Kleinasiatische Ortsnamen, 1984
Zimmer
   G. ZIMMER, Römische Berufsdarstellungen, 1982
ZKG,
   Zeitschrift für Kirchengeschichte
ZNTW
   Zeitschrift für die Neutestamentfiche Wissenschaft
   und die Kunde der älteren Kirche
ZpalV
   Zeitschrift des Deutschen Palästina-Vereins
ZPE
   Zeitschrift für Papyrologie und Epigraphik
ZKG
   Zeitschrift der Savigny-Stiftung für Rechtsgeschich-
   te. Romanistische Abteilung
ZRG
   Zeitschrift der Savigny-Stiftung für Rechtsgeschich-
   te
ZRGG
   Zeitschrift für Religions- und Geistesgeschichte
ZVRW
   Zeitschrift für vergleichende Rechtswissenschaft
ZVS
   Zeitschrift für Vergleichende Sprachforschung

4. Ancient Authors and Titles of Works

Abd	Abdias
Acc.	Accius
Ach.Tat.	Achilles Tatius
Act. Arv.	Acta fratrum Arvalium
Act. lud. saec.	Acta ludorum saecularium

Acts	Acts of the Apostles		Mac.	Macedonica
Aet.	Aetius		Mith.	Mithridatius
Aeth.	Aetheriae peregrinatio		Num.	Numidica
Ael. Ep.	Aelianus, Epistulae		Reg.	Regia
NA	De natura animalium		Sam.	Samnitica
VH	Varia historia		Sic.	Sicula
Aen. Tact.	Aeneas Tacticus		Syr.	Syriaca
Aesch. Ag.	Aeschylus, Agamemnon		App. Verg.	Appendix Vergiliana
Cho.	Choephori		Apul. Apol.	Apuleius, Apologia
Eum.	Eumenides		Flor.	Florida
Pers.	Persae		Met.	Metamorphoses
PV	Prometheus		Arat.	Aratus
Sept.	Septem adversus Thebas		Archil.	Archilochus
Supp.	Supplices		Archim.	Archimedes
Aeschin. In Ctes.	Aeschines, In Ctesiphontem		Archyt.	Archytas
Leg.	De falsa legatione		Arist. Quint.	Aristides Quintilianus
In Tim.	In Timarchum		Aristaen.	Aristaenetus
Aesop.	Aesopus		Aristid.	Aelius Aristides
Alc.	Alcaeus		Aristob.	Aristoboulus
Alc. Avit.	Alcimus Ecdicius Avitus		Aristoph. Ach.	Aristophanes, Acharnenses
Alex. Aphr.	Alexander of Aphrodisias		Av.	Aves
Alci.	Alciphron		Eccl.	Ecclesiazusae
Alcm.	Alcman		Equ.	Equites
Alex. Polyh.	Alexander Polyhistor		Lys.	Lysistrata
Am	Amos		Nub.	Nubes
Ambr. Epist.	Ambrosius, Epistulae		Pax	Pax
Exc. Sat.	De excessu Fratris (Satyri)		Plut.	Plutus
Obit. Theod.	De obitu Theodosii		Ran.	Ranae
Obit. Valent.	De obitu Valentiniani (iunioris)		Thesm.	Thesmophoriazusae
Off.	De officiis ministrorum		Vesp.	Vespae
Paenit.	De paenitentia		Aristot. An.	Aristotle, De anima (Becker 1831–
Amm. Marc.	Ammianus Marcellinus			70)
Anac.	Anacreon		An. post.	Analytica posteriora
Anaxag.	Anaxagoras		An. pr.	Analytica priora
Anaximand.	Anaximander		Ath. Pol.	Athenaion Politeia
Anaximen.	Anaximenes		Aud.	De audibilibus
And.	Andocides		Cael.	De caelo
Anecd. Bekk.	Anecdota Graeca ed. I. Bekker		Cat.	Categoriae
Anecd. Par.	Anecdota Graeca ed. J.A. Kramer		Col.	De coloribus
Anon. De rebus	Anonymus de rebus bellicis (Ireland		Div.	De divinatione
bell.	1984)		Eth. Eud.	Ethica Eudemia
Anth. Gr.	Anthologia Graeca		Eth. Nic.	Ethica Nicomachea
Anth. Lat.	Anthologia Latina (Riese		Gen. an.	De generatione animalium
	²1894/1906)		Gen. corr.	De generatione et corruptione
Anth. Pal.	Anthologia Palatina		Hist. an.	Historia animalium
Anth. Plan.	Anthologia Planudea		Mag. mor.	Magna moralia
Antiph.	Antiphon		Metaph.	Metaphysica
Antisth.	Antisthenes		Mete.	Meteorologica
Apc	Apocalypse		Mir.	Mirabilia
Apoll. Rhod.	Apollonius Rhodius		Mot. an.	De motu animalium
Apollod.	Apollodorus, Library		Mund.	De mundo
App. B Civ.	Appianus, Bella civilia		Oec.	Oeconomica
Celt.	Celtica		Part. an.	De partibus animalium
Hann.	Hannibalica		Phgn.	Physiognomica
Hisp.	Iberica		Ph.	Physica
Ill.	Illyrica		Poet.	Poetica
It.	Italica		Pol.	Politica
Lib.	Libyca		Pr.	Problemata

Rh.	Rhetorica	Cato Agr.	Cato, De agri cultura
Rh. Al.	Rhetorica ad Alexandrum	Orig.	Origines (HRR)
Sens.	De sensu	Catull.	Catullus, Carmina
Somn.	De somno et vigilia	Celsus, Med.	Cornelius Celsus, De medicina
Soph. el.	Sophistici elenchi	Celsus, Dig.	Iuventius Celsus, Digesta
Spir.	De spiritu	Censorinus, DN	Censorinus, De die natali
Top.	Topica	Chalcid.	Chalcidius
Aristox. Harm.	Aristoxenus, Harmonica	Charisius,	Charisius, Ars grammatica (Bar-
Arnob.	Arnobius, Adversus nationes	Gramm.	wick 1964)
Arr. Anab.	Arrianus, Anabasis	1 Chr, 2 Chr	Chronicle
Cyn.	Cynegeticus	Chron. pasch.	Chronicon paschale
Ind.	Indica	Chron. min.	Chronica minora
Peripl. p. eux.	Periplus ponti Euxini	Cic. Acad. 1	Cicero, Academicorum posterio-
Succ.	Historia successorum Alexandri		rum liber 1
Tact.	Tactica	Acad. 2	Lucullus sive Academicorum pri-
Artem.	Artemidorus		orum liber 2
Ascon.	Asconius (Stangl Vol. 2, 1912)	Ad Q. Fr.	Epistulae ad Quintum fratrem
Athan. ad Const.	Athanasius, Apologia ad Constan-	Arat.	Aratea (Soubiran 1972)
	tium	Arch.	Pro Archia poeta
c. Ar.	Apologia contra Arianos	Att.	Epistulae ad Atticum
Fuga	Apologia de fuga sua	Balb.	Pro L. Balbo
Hist. Ar.	Historia Arianorum ad mona-	Brut.	Brutus
	chos	Caecin.	Pro A. Caecina
Ath.	Athenaeus (Casaubon 1597) (List	Cael.	Pro M. Caelio
	of books, pages, letters)	Cat.	In Catilinam
Aug. Civ.	Augustinus, De civitate dei	Cato	Cato maior de senectute
Conf.	Confessiones	Clu.	Pro A. Cluentio
Doctr. christ.	De doctrina christiana	De or.	De oratore
Epist.	Epistulae	Deiot.	Pro rege Deiotaro
Retract.	Retractationes	Div.	De divinatione
Serm.	Sermones	Div. Caec.	Divinatio in Q. Caecilium
Soliloq.	Soliloquia	Dom.	De domo sua
Trin.	De trinitate	Fam.	Epistulae ad familiares
Aur. Vict.	Aurelius Victor	Fat.	De fato
Auson. Mos.	Ausonius, Mosella (Peiper 1976)	Fin.	De finibus bonorum et malorum
Urb.	Ordo nobilium urbium	Flac.	Pro L. Valerio Flacco
Avell.	Collectio Avellana	Font.	Pro M. Fonteio
Avien.	Avienus	Har. resp.	De haruspicum responso
Babr.	Babrius	Inv.	De inventione
Bacchyl.	Bacchylides	Lael.	Laelius de amicitia
Bar	Baruch	Leg.	De legibus
Bas.	Basilicorum libri LX (Heimbach)	Leg. agr.	De lege agraria
Basil.	Basilius	Lig.	Pro Q. Ligario
Batr.	Batrachomyomachia	Leg. Man.	Pro lege Manilia (de imperio Cn.
Bell. Afr.	Bellum Africum		Pompei)
Bell. Alex.	Bellum Alexandrinum	Marcell.	Pro M. Marcello
Bell. Hisp.	Bellum Hispaniense	Mil.	Pro T. Annio Milone
Boeth.	Boethius	Mur.	Pro L. Murena
Caes. B Civ.	Caesar, De bello civili	Nat. D.	De natura deorum
B Gall.	De bello Gallico	Off.	De officiis
Callim. Epigr.	Callimachus, Epigrammata	Opt. Gen.	De optimo genere oratorum
Fr.	Fragmentum (Pfeiffer)	Orat.	Orator
H.	Hymni	P. Red. Quir.	Oratio post reditum ad Quirites
Calp. Ecl.	Calpurnius Siculus, Eclogae	P. Red. Sen.	Oratio post reditum in senatu
Cass. Dio	Cassius Dio	Parad.	Paradoxa
Cassian.	Iohannes Cassianus	Part. or.	Partitiones oratoriae
Cassiod. Inst.	Cassiodorus, Institutiones	Phil.	In M. Antonium orationes Phi-
Var.	Variae		lippicae

Philo.	Libri philosophici	Dionys. Per.	Dionysius Periegeta
Pis.	In L. Pisonem	Dion. Thrax	Dionysius Thrax
Planc.	Pro Cn. Plancio	DK	Diels /Kranz (preceded by fragment number)
Prov. cons.	De provinciis consularibus		
Q. Rosc.	Pro Q. Roscio comoedo	Donat.	Donatus grammaticus
Quinct.	Pro P. Quinctio	Drac.	Dracontius
Rab. perd.	Pro C. Rabirio perduellionis reo	Dt	Deuteronomy = 5. Moses
Rab. Post.	Pro C. Rabirio Postumo	Edict. praet. dig.	Edictum perpetuum in Dig.
Rep.	De re publica	Emp.	Empedocles
Rosc. Am.	Pro Sex. Roscio Amerino	Enn. Ann.	Ennius, Annales (Skutsch 1985)
Scaur.	Pro M. Aemilio Scauro	Sat.	Saturae (Vahlen ²1928)
Sest.	Pro P. Sestio	Scaen.	Fragmenta scaenica (Vahlen ²1928)
Sull.	Pro P. Sulla		
Tim.	Timaeus	Ennod.	Ennodius
Top.	Topica	Eph	Letter to the Ephesians
Tull.	Pro M. Tullio	Ephor.	Ephorus of Cyme (FGrH 70)
Tusc.	Tusculanae disputationes	Epicurus	Epicurus
Vatin.	In P. Vatinium testem interrogatio	Epict.	Epictetus
		Eratosth.	Eratosthenes
Verr. 1, 2	In Verrem actio prima, secunda	Esr	Esra
Claud. Carm.	Claudius Claudianus, Carmina (Hall 1985)	Est	Esther
		Et. Gen.	Etymologicum genuinum
Rapt. Pros.	De raptu Proserpinae	Et. Gud.	Etymologicum Gudianum
Clem. Al.	Clemens Alexandrinus	EM	Etymologicum magnum
Cod. Greg.	Codex Gregorianus	Euc.	Euclides, Elementa
Cod. Herm.	Codex Hermogenianus	Eunap. VS	Eunapius, Vitae sophistarum
Cod. Iust.	Corpus Iuris Civilis, Codex Iustinianus (Krueger 1900)	Eur. Alc.	Euripides, Alcestis
		Andr.	Andromache
Cod. Theod.	Codex Theodosianus	Bacch.	Bacchae
Col	Letter to the Colossians	Beller.	Bellerophon
Coll.	Mosaicarum et Romanarum legum collatio	Cyc.	Cyclops
		El.	Electra
Colum.	Columella	Hec.	Hecuba
Comm.	Commodianus	Hel.	Helena
Cons.	Consultatio veteris cuiusdam iurisconsulti	Heracl.	Heraclidae
		HF	Hercules Furens
Const.	Constitutio Sirmondiana	Hipp.	Hippolytus
1 Cor, 2 Cor	Letters to the Corinthians	Hyps.	Hypsipyle
Coripp.	Corippus	Ion	Ion
Curt.	Curtius Rufus, Historiae Alexandri Magni	IA	Iphigenia Aulidensis
		IT	Iphigenia Taurica
Cypr.	Cyprianus	Med.	Medea
Dan	Daniel	Or.	Orestes
Din.	Dinarchus	Phoen.	Phoenissae
Demad.	Demades	Rhes.	Rhesus
Democr.	Democritus	Supp.	Supplices
Dem. Or.	Demosthenes, Orationes	Tro.	Troades
Dig.	Corpus Iuris Civilis, Digesta (Mommsen 1905, author presented where applicable)	Euseb. Dem. evang.	Eusebios, Demonstratio Evangelica
		Hist. eccl.	Historia Ecclesiastica
		On.	Onomasticon (Klostermann 1904)
Diod. Sic.	Diodorus Siculus		
Diog. Laert.	Diogenes Laertius	Praep. evang.	Praeparatio Evangelica
Diom.	Diomedes, Ars grammatica	Eust.	Eustathius
Dion. Chrys.	Dion Chrysostomus	Eutr.	Eutropius
Dion. Hal. Ant. Rom.	Dionysius Halicarnasseus, Antiquitates Romanae	Ev. Ver.	Evangelium Veritatis
		Ex	Exodus = 2. Moses
Comp.	De compositione verborum	Ez	Ezechiel
Rhet.	Ars rhetorica		

Fast.	Fasti
Fest.	Festus (Lindsay 1913)
Firm. Mat.	Firmicus Maternus
Flor. Epit.	Florus, Epitoma de Tito Livio
Florent.	Florentinus
Frontin. Aq.	Frontinus, De aquae ductu urbis Romae
Str.	Strategemata
Fulg.	Fulgentius Afer
Fulg. Rusp.	Fulgentius Ruspensis
Gai. Inst.	Gaius, Institutiones
Gal	Letter to the Galatians
Gal.	Galenus
Gell. NA	Gellius, Noctes Atticae
Geogr. Rav	Geographus Ravennas (Schnetz 1940)
Gp.	Geoponica
Gn	Genesis = 1. Moses
Gorg.	Gorgias
Greg. M. Dial.	Gregorius Magnus, Dialogi (de miraculis patrum Italicorum)
Epist.	Epistulae
Past.	Regula pastoralis
Greg. Naz. Epist.	Gregorius Nazianzenus, Epistulae
Or.	Orationes
Greg. Nyss.	Gregorius Nyssenus
Greg. Tur. Franc.	Gregorius of Tours, Historia Francorum
Mart.	De virtutibus Martini
Vit. patr.	De vita patrum
Hab	Habakkuk
Hagg	Haggai
Harpocr.	Harpocrates
Hdt.	Herodotus
Hebr	Letter to the Hebrews
Hegesipp.	Hegesippus (= Flavius Josephus)
Hecat.	Hecataeus
Hell. Oxy.	Hellennica Oxyrhynchia
Hen	Henoch
Heph.	Hephaestio grammaticus (Alexandrinus)
Heracl.	Heraclitus
Heraclid. Pont.	Heraclides Ponticus
Herc. O.	Hercules Oetaeus
Herm.	Hermes Trismegistus
Herm. Mand.	Hermas, Mandata
Sim.	Similitudines
Vis.	Visiones
Hermog.	Hermogenes
Hdn.	Herodianus
Hes. Cat.	Hesiodus, Catalogus feminarum (Merkelbach /West 1967)
Op.	Opera et dies
Sc.	Scutum (Merkelbach /West1967)
Theog.	Theogonia
Hsch.	Hesychius
Hil.	Hilarius

Hippoc.	Hippocrates
H. Hom.	Hymni Homerici
Hom. Il.	Homerus, Ilias
Od.	Odyssea
Hor. Ars P.	Horatius, Ars poetica
Carm.	Carmina
Carm. saec.	Carmen saeculare
Epist.	Epistulae
Epod.	Epodi
Sat.	Satirae (sermones)
Hos	Hosea
Hyg. Astr.	Hyginus, Astronomica (Le Bœuffle 1983)
Fab.	Fabulae
Hyp.	Hypereides
Iambl. Myst.	Iamblichus, De mysteriis
Protr.	Protrepticus in philosophiam
VP	De vita Pythagorica
Iav.	Iavolenus Priscus
Inst. Iust.	Corpus Juris Civilis, Institutiones (Krueger 1905)
Ioh. Chrys. Epist.	Iohannes Chrysostomus, Epistulae
Hom. ...	Homiliae in ...
Ioh. Mal.	Iohannes Malalas, Chronographia
Iord. Get.	Iordanes, De origine actibusque Getarum
Iren.	Irenaeus (Rousseau/Doutreleau 1965–82)
Is	Isaiah
Isid. Nat.	Isidorus, De natura rerum
Orig.	Origines
Isoc. Or.	Isocrates, Orationes
It. Ant.	Itinerarium, Antonini
Aug.	Augusti
Burd.	Burdigalense vel Hierosolymitanum
Plac.	Placentini
Iul. Vict. Rhet.	C. Iulius Victor, Ars rhetorica
Iuvenc.	Iuvencus, Evangelia (Huemer 1891)
Jac	Letter of James
Jdg	Judges
Jdt	Judith
Jer	Jeremiah
Jer. Chron.	Jerome, Chronicon
Comm. in Ez.	Commentaria in Ezechielem (PL 25)
Ep.	Epistulae
On.	Onomasticon (Klostermann 1904)
Vir. ill.	De viris illustribus
1 – 3 Jo	1st – 3rd letters of John
Jo	John
Jon	Jona
Jos. Ant. Iud.	Josephus, Antiquitates Iudaicae
BI	Bellum Iudaicum
Ap.	Contra Apionem
Vit.	De sua vita

Jos	Joshua
Jud	Letter of Judas
Julian. Ep.	Julianus, Epistulae
In Gal.	In Galilaeos
Mis.	Misopogon
Or.	Orationes
Symp.	Symposium
Just. Epit.	Justinus, Epitoma historiarum Philippicarum
Justin. Apol.	Justinus Martyr, Apologia
Dial.	Dialogus cum Tryphone
Juv.	Juvenalis, Saturae
1 Kg, 2 Kg	1, 2 Kings
KH	Khania (place where Linear B tables were discovered)
KN	Knossos (place where Linear B tables were discovered)
Lactant. Div. inst.	Lactantius, Divinae institutiones
Ira	De ira dei
De mort. pers.	De mortibus persecutorum
Opif.	De opificio dei
Lam	Lamentations
Lex Irnit.	Lex Irnitana
Lex Malac.	Lex municipii Malacitani
Lex Rubr.	Lex Rubria de Gallia cisalpina
Lex Salpens.	Lex municipii Salpensani
Lex Urson.	Lex coloniae Iuliae Genetivae Ursonensis
Lex Visig.	Leges Visigothorum
Lex XII tab.	Lex duodecim tabularum
Lib. Ep.	Libanius, Epistulae
Or.	Orationes
Liv.	Livius, Ab urbe condita
Lc	Luke
Luc.	Lucanus, Bellum civile
Lucil.	Lucilius, Saturae (Marx 1904)
Lucr.	Lucretius, De rerum natura
Lucian. Alex.	Lucianus, Alexander
Anach.	Anacharsis
Cal.	Calumniae non temere credendum
Catapl.	Cataplus
Demon.	Demonax
Dial. D.	Dialogi deorum
Dial. meret.	Dialogi meretricium
Dial. mort.	Dialogi mortuorum
Her.	Herodotus
Hermot.	Hermotimus
Hist. conscr.	Quomodo historia conscribenda sit
Ind.	Adversus indoctum
Iupp. trag.	Iuppiter tragoedus
Luct.	De luctu
Macr.	Macrobii
Nigr.	Nigrinus
Philops.	Philopseudes
Pseudol.	Pseudologista

Salt.	De saltatione
Somn.	Somnium
Symp.	Symposium
Syr. D.	De Syria dea
Trag.	Tragodopodagra
Ver. hist.	Verae historiae, 1, 2
Vit. auct.	Vitarum auctio
Lv	Leviticus = 3. Moses
LXX	Septuaginta
Lydus, Mag.	Lydus, De magistratibus
Mens.	De mensibus
Lycoph.	Lycophron
Lycurg.	Lycurgus
Lys.	Lysias
M. Aur.	Marcus Aurelius Antoninus Augustus
Macrob. Sat.	Macrobius, Saturnalia
In Somn.	Commentarii in Ciceronis somnium Scipionis
1 Macc, 2 Macc	Maccabees
Mal	Malachi
Manil.	Manilius, Astronomica (Goold 1985)
Mar. Vict.	Marius Victorinus
Mart.	Martialis
Mart. Cap.	Martianus Capella
Max. Tyr.	Maximus Tyrius (Trapp 1994)
Mela	Pomponius Mela
Melanipp.	Melanippides
Men. Dys.	Menander, Dyskolos
Epit.	Epitrepontes
Fr.	Fragmentum (Körte)
Pk.	Perikeiromene
Sam.	Samia
Mi	Micha
Mimn.	Mimnermus
Min. Fel.	Minucius Felix, Octavius (Kytzler 1982,²1992)
Mk	Mark
Mod.	Herennius Modestinus
Mosch.	Moschus
Mt	Matthew
MY	Mycenae (place where Linear B tables were discovered)
Naev.	Naevius (carmina according to FPL)
Nah	Nahum
Neh	Nehemia
Nemes.	Nemesianus
Nep. Att.	Cornelius Nepos, Atticus
Hann.	Hannibal
Nic. Alex.	Nicander, Alexipharmaca
Ther.	Theriaca
Nicom.	Nicomachus
Nm	Numbers = 4. Moses
Non.	Nonius Marcellus (L. Mueller 1888)
Nonnus, Dion.	Nonnus, Dionysiaca

Not. Dign. Occ.	Notitia dignitatum occidentis		Pall. Agric.	Palladius, Opus agriculturae
Not. Dign. Or.	Notitia dignitatum orientis		Laus.	Historia Lausiaca
Not. Episc.	Notitia dignitatum et episcoporum		Pan. Lat.	Panegyrici Latini
Nov.	Corpus Iuris Civilis, Leges Novellae (Schoell/Kroll 1904)		Papin.	Aemilius Papinianus
			Paroemiogr.	Paroemiographi Graeci
Obseq.	Julius Obsequens, Prodigia (Rossbach 1910)		Pass. mart.	Passiones martyrum
			Paul Fest.	Paulus Diaconus, Epitoma Festi
Opp. Hal.	Oppianus, Halieutica		Paul Nol.	Paulinus Nolanus
Cyn.	Cynegetica		Paulus, Sent.	Julius Paulus, Sententiae
Or. Sib.	Oracula Sibyllina		Paus.	Pausanias
Orib.	Oribasius		Pelag.	Pelagius
Orig.	Origenes		Peripl. m. eux.	Periplus maris Euxini
OrMan	Prayer to Manasseh		Peripl. m.m.	Periplus maris magni
Oros.	Orosius		Peripl. m.r.	Periplus maris rubri
Orph. A.	Orpheus, Argonautica		Pers.	Persius, Saturae
Fr.	Fragmentum (Kern)		1 Petr, 2 Petr	Letters of Peter
H.	Hymni		Petron. Sat.	Petronius, Satyrica (Müller 1961)
Ov. Am.	Ovidius, Amores		Phaedr.	Phaedrus, Fabulae (Guaglianone 1969)
Ars am.	Ars amatoria			
Epist.	Epistulae (Heroides)		Phil	Letter to the Philippians
Fast.	Fasti		Phil.	Philo
Ib.	Ibis		Philarg. Verg. ecl.	Philargyrius grammaticus, Explanatio in eclogas Vergilii
Medic.	Medicamina faciei femineae			
Met.	Metamorphoses		Philod.	Philodemus
Pont.	Epistulae ex Ponto		Phlp.	Philoponus
Rem. am.	Remedia amoris		Philostr. VA	Philostratus, Vita Apollonii
Tr.	Tristia		Imag.	Imagines
P	Papyrus editions according to E.G. Turner, Greek Papyri. An Introduction, 159–178		VS	Vitae sophistarum
			Phm	Letter to Philemon
			Phot.	Photius (Bekker 1824)
P Abinn.	Papyrus editions according to H.I. Bell et al. (ed.), The Abinnaeus Archive papers of a Roman officer in the reign of Constantius II, 1962		Phryn.	Phrynichus
			Pind. Fr.	Pindar, Fragments (Snell/Maehler)
			Isthm.	Isthmian Odes
			Nem.	Nemean Odes
P Bodmer	Papyrus editions according to V. Martin, R. Kasser et al. (ed.), Papyrus Bodmer 1954ff.		Ol.	Olympian Odes
			Pae.	Paeanes
			Pyth.	Pythian Odes
P CZ	Papyrus editions according to C.C. Edgar (ed.), Zenon Papyri (Catalogue général des Antiquités égyptiennes du Musée du Caire) 4 vols., 1925ff.		Pl. Alc. 1	Plato, Alcibiades 1 (Stephanus)
			Alc. 2	Alcibiades 2
			Ap.	Apologia
			Ax.	Axiochus
			Chrm.	Charmides
			Clit.	Clitopho
P Hercul.	Papyrus editions according to Papyri aus Herculaneum		Crat.	Cratylus
			Crit.	Crito
P Lond.	Papyrus editions according to F.G. Kenyon et al. (ed.), Greek Papyri in the British Museum 7 vols., 1893–1974		Criti.	Critias
			Def.	Definitiones
			Demod.	Demodocus
			Epin.	Epinomis
P Mich	Papyrus editions according to C.C. Edgar, A.E.R. Boak, J.G. Winter et al. (ed.), Papyri in the University of Michigan Collection 13 vols., 1931–1977		Ep.	Epistulae
			Erast.	Erastae
			Eryx.	Eryxias
			Euthd.	Euthydemus
			Euthphr.	Euthyphro
P Oxy.	Papyrus editions according to B.P. Grenfell, A.S. Hunt et al. (ed.), The Oxyrhynchus Papyri, 1898 ff.		Grg.	Gorgias
			Hp. mai.	Hippias maior
			Hp. mi.	Hippias minor
			Hipparch.	Hipparchus

Ion	Ion
La.	Laches
Leg.	Leges
Ly.	Lysis
Men.	Menon
Min.	Minos
Menex.	Menexenus
Prm.	Parmenides
Phd.	Phaedo
Phdr.	Phaedrus
Phlb.	Philebus
Plt.	Politicus
Prt.	Protagoras
Resp.	Res publica
Sis.	Sisyphus
Soph.	Sophista
Symp.	Symposium
Thg.	Theages
Tht.	Theaetetus
Ti.	Timaeus
Plaut. Amph.	Plautus, Amphitruo (fr.according to Leo 1895 f.)
Asin.	Asinaria
Aul.	Aulularia
Bacch.	Bacchides
Capt.	Captivi
Cas.	Casina
Cist.	Cistellaria
Curc.	Curculio
Epid.	Epidicus
Men.	Menaechmi
Merc.	Mercator
Mil.	Miles gloriosus
Mostell.	Mostellaria
Poen.	Poenulus
Pseud.	Pseudolus
Rud.	Rudens
Stich.	Stichus
Trin.	Trinummus
Truc.	Truculentus
Vid.	Vidularia
Plin. HN	Plinius maior, Naturalis historia
Plin. Ep.	Plinius minor, Epistulae
Pan.	Panegyricus
Plot.	Plotinus
Plut.	Plutarchus, Vitae parallelae (with the respective name)
Amat.	Amatorius (chapter and page numbers)
De def. or.	De defectu oraculorum
De E	De E apud Delphos
De Pyth. or.	De Pythiae oraculis
De sera	De sera numinis vindicta
De Is. et Os.	De Iside et Osiride (with chapter and page numbers)
Mor.	Moralia (apart from the separately mentioned works; with p. numbers)

Quaest. Graec.	Quaestiones Graecae (with chapter numbers)
Quaest. Rom.	Quaestiones Romanae (with ch. numbers)
Symp.	Quaestiones convivales (book, chapter, page number)
Pol.	Polybius
Pol. Silv.	Polemius Silvius
Poll.	Pollux
Polyaenus, Strat.	Polyaenus, Strategemata
Polyc.	Polycarpus, Letter
Pompon.	Sextus Pomponius
Pomp. Trog.	Pompeius Trogus
Porph.	Porphyrius
Porph. Hor. comm.	Porphyrio, Commentum in Horatii carmina
Posidon.	Posidonius
Priap.	Priapea
Prisc.	Priscianus
Prob.	Pseudo-Probian writings
Procop. Aed.	Procopius, De aedificiis
Goth.	Bellum Gothicum
Pers.	Bellum Persicum
Vand.	Bellum Vandalicum
Arc.	Historia arcana
Procl.	Proclus
Prop.	Propertius, Elegiae
Prosp.	Prosper Tiro
Prov.	Proverbs
Prudent.	Prudentius
Ps (Pss)	Psalm(s)
Ps.-Acro	Ps.-Acro in Horatium
Ps.-Aristot. Lin. insec.	Pseudo-Aristotle, De lineis insecabilibus
Mech.	Mechanica
Ps.-Sall. In Tull.	Pseudo-Sallustius, In M.Tullium Ciceronem invectiva
Rep.	Epistulae ad Caesarem senem de re publica
Ptol. Alm.	Ptolemy, Almagest
Geog.	Geographia
Harm.	Harmonica
Tetr.	Tetrabiblos
PY	Pylos (place where Linear B tablets were discovered)
4 Q Flor	Florilegium, Cave 4
4 Q Patr	Patriarch's blessing, Cave 4
1 Q pHab	Habakuk-Midrash, Cave 1
4 Q pNah	Nahum-Midrash, Cave 4
4 Q test	Testimonia, Cave 4
1 QH	Songs of Praise, Cave 1
1 QM	War list, Cave 1
1 QS	Comunal rule, Cave 1
1 QSa	Community rule, Cave 1
1 QSb	Blessings, Cave 1
Quint. Smyrn.	Quintus Smyrnaeus
Quint. Decl.	Quintilianus, Declamationes minores (Shackleton Bailey 1989)

Inst.	Institutio oratoria
R. Gest. div. Aug.	Res gestae divi Augusti
Rhet. Her.	Rhetorica ad C. Herennium
Rom	Letter to the Romans
Rt	Ruth
Rufin.	Tyrannius Rufinus
Rut. Namat.	Rutilius Claudius Namatianus, De reditu suo
S. Sol.	Song of Solomon
Sext. Emp.	Sextus Empiricus
Sach	Sacharia
Sall. Catil.	Sallustius, De coniuratione Catilinae
Hist.	Historiae
Iug.	De bello Iugurthino
Salv. Gub.	Salvianus, De gubernatione dei
1 Sam, 2 Sam	Samuel
Schol. (before an author's name)	Scholia to the author in question
Sedul.	Sedulius
Sen. Controv.	Seneca maior, Controversiae
Suas.	Suasoriae
Sen. Ag.	Seneca minor, Agamemno
Apocol.	Divi Claudii apocolocyntosis
Ben.	De beneficiis
Clem.	De clementia (Hosius ²1914)
Dial.	Dialogi
Ep.	Epistulae morales ad Lucilium
Herc. f.	Hercules furens
Med.	Medea
Q Nat.	Naturales quaestiones
Oed.	Oedipus
Phaedr.	Phaedra
Phoen.	Phoenissae
Thy.	Thyestes
Tranq.	De tranquillitate animi
Tro.	Troades
Serv. auct.	Servius auctus Danielis
Serv. Aen.	Servius, Commentarius in Vergilii Aeneida
Ecl.	Commentarius in Vergilii eclogas
Georg.	Commentarius in Vergilii georgica
Sext. Emp.	Sextus Empiricus
SHA Ael.	Scriptores Historiae Augustae, Aelius
Alb.	Clodius Albinus
Alex. Sev.	Alexander Severus
Aur.	M. Aurelius
Aurel.	Aurelianus
Avid. Cass.	Avidius Cassius
Car.	Carus et Carinus et Numerianus
Carac.	Antoninus Caracalla
Clod.	Claudius
Comm.	Commodus
Diad.	Diadumenus Antoninus
Did. Iul.	Didius Iulianus

Gall.	Gallieni duo
Gord.	Gordiani tres
Hadr.	Hadrianus
Heliogab.	Heliogabalus
Max. Balb.	Maximus et Balbus
Opil.	Opilius Macrinus
Pert.	Helvius Pertinax
Pesc. Nig.	Pescennius Niger
Pius	Antoninus Pius
Quadr. tyr.	Quadraginta tyranni
Sev.	Severus
Tac.	Tacitus
Tyr. Trig.	Triginta Tyranni
Valer.	Valeriani duo
Sid. Apoll. Carm.	Apollinaris Sidonius, Carmina
Epist.	Epistulae
Sil. Pun.	Silius Italicus, Punica
Simon.	Simonides
Simpl.	Simplicius
Sir	Jesus Sirach
Scyl.	Scylax, Periplus
Scymn.	Scymnus, Periegesis
Socr.	Socrates, Historia ecclesiastica
Sol.	Solon
Solin.	Solinus
Soph. Aj.	Sophocles, Ajax
Ant.	Antigone
El.	Electra
Ichn.	Ichneutae
OC	Oedipus Coloneus
OT	Oedipus Tyrannus
Phil.	Philoctetes
Trach.	Trachiniae
Sor. Gyn.	Soranus, Gynaecia
Sozom. Hist. eccl.	Sozomenus, Historia ecclesiastica
Stat. Achil.	Statius, Achilleis
Silv.	Silvae
Theb.	Thebais
Steph. Byz.	Stephanus Byzantius
Stesich.	Stesichorus
Stob.	Stobaeus
Str.	Strabo (books, chapters)
Suda	Suda = Suidas
Suet. Aug.	Suetonius, Divus Augustus (Ihm 1907)
Calig.	Caligula
Claud.	Divus Claudius
Dom.	Domitianus
Gram.	De grammaticis (Kaster 1995)
Iul.	Divus Iulius
Tib.	Divus Tiberius
Tit.	Divus Titus
Vesp.	Divus Vespasianus
Vit.	Vitellius
Sulp. Sev.	Sulpicius Severus
Symmachus, Ep.	Symmachus, Epistulae
Or.	Orationes

Relat.	Relationes	Val. Fl.	Valerius Flaccus, Argonautica
Synes. epist.	Synesius, Epistulae	Val. Max.	Valerius Maximus, Facta et dicta
Sync.	Syncellus		memorabilia
Tab. Peut.	Tabula Peutingeriana	Varro, Ling.	Varro, De lingua Latina
Tac. Agr.	Tacitus, Agricola	Rust.	Res rusticae
Ann.	Annales	Sat. Men.	Saturae Menippeae (Astbury
Dial.	Dialogus de oratoribus		1985)
Germ.	Germania	Vat.	Fragmenta Vaticana
Hist.	Historiae	Veg. Mil.	Vegetius, Epitoma rei militaris
Ter. Maur.	Terentianus Maurus	Vell. Pat.	Velleius Paterculus, Historiae
Ter. Ad.	Terentius, Adelphoe		Romanae
An.	Andria	Ven. Fort.	Venantius Fortunatus
Eun.	Eunuchus	Verg. Aen.	Vergilius, Aeneis
Haut.	H(e)autontimorumenos	Catal.	Catalepton
Hec.	Hecyra	Ecl.	Eclogae
Phorm.	Phormio	G.	Georgica
Tert. Apol.	Tertullianus, Apologeticum	Vir. ill.	De viris illustribus
Ad nat.	Ad nationes (Borleffs 1954)	Vitr. De arch.	Vitruvius, De architectura
TH	Thebes (place where Linear B tables	Vulg.	Vulgate
	were discovered)	Wisd	Wisdom
Them. Or.	Themistius, Orationes	Xen. Ages.	Xenophon, Agesilaus
Theoc.	Theocritus	An.	Anabasis
Theod. Epist.	Theodoretus, Epistulae	Ap.	Apologia
Gr. aff. Cur.	Graecarum affectionum curatio	Ath. pol.	Athenaion politeia
Hist. eccl.	Historia ecclesiastica	Cyn.	Cynegeticus
Theopomp.	Theopompus	Cyr.	Cyropaedia
Theophr. Caus.	Theophrastus, De causis plantarum	Eq.	De equitandi ratione
pl.		Eq. mag.	De equitum magistro
Char.	Characteres	Hell.	Hellenica
Hist. pl.	Historia plantarum	Hier.	Hiero
1 Thess, 2 Thess	Letters to the Thessalonians	Lac.	Respublica Lacedaemoniorum
Thgn.	Theognis	Mem.	Memorabilia
Thuc.	Thucydides	Oec.	Oeconomicus
TI	Tiryns (place where Linear B tablets	Symp.	Symposium
	were discovered)	Vect.	De vectigalibus
Tib.	Tibullus, Elegiae	Xenoph.	Xenophanes
1 Tim, 2 Tim	Letters to Timothy	Zen.	Zeno
Tit	Letter to Titus	Zenob.	Zenobius
Tob	Tobit	Zenod.	Zenodotus
Tzetz. Anteh.	Tzetzes, Antehomerica	Zeph	Zephania
Chil.	Chiliades	Zon.	Zonaras
Posth.	Posthomerica	Zos.	Zosimus
Ulp.	Ulpianus (Ulpiani regulae)		

List of Authors

Albrecht, Ruth
Alonso-Núñez, José Miguel
Apel, Hans Jürgen
Aurnhammer, Achim
Backhaus, Ralph
Bartels, Jens
Bartels, Klaus
Barth, Andreas
Baumbach, Manuel
Baumgartner, Marcel
Berschin, Walter
Bertoni, Clotilde
Borzsák, István
Bräunl, Christoph
Bulitta, Brigitte
Burmeister, Karl Heinz
Cagnetta (†), Mariella
Chiesa, Paolo
Christof, Eva
Corsten, Thomas
Dassmann, Ernst
Davies, John K.
Demandt, Alexander
Dithmar, Reinhard
Dolezalek, Gero
Dummer, Jürgen
Eberle, Martin
Eberlein, Johann Konrad
Egger, Brigitte
Erdmann, Elisabeth
Ernst, Ulrich
Étienne, Roland
Feichtinger, Barbara
Fittschen, Klaus
Föllinger, Sabine
Fornaro, Sotera
Friedrich, Leonhard
Fritscher, Bernhard
Fusillo, Massimo
Gehrke, Hans-Joachim
Goesch, Andrea
Gordesiani, Rismag
Grosse, Max
Habermann, Mechthild
Habermehl, Peter
Hager (†), Fritz-Peter
Hammer-Schenk, Harold
Harth, Dietrich
Hazenbos, Joost
Helas, Philine
Hess, Peter

Hickey, Todd M.
Hinz, Berthold
Hinz, Manfred
Höcker, Christoph
Hölter, Achim
Holtermann, Martin
Huber, Gabriele
Hübner, Wolfgang
Huss, Bernhard
Huyse, Philip
Jäger, Jürgen
Jeppesen, Kristian
Job, Michael
Johne, Renate
Kaiser, Wolfgang
Kammasch, Tim
Kimmich, Dorothee
King, Helen
Knape, Joachim
Kockel, Valentin
Köhler, Jens
Kranz, Margarita
Krasser, Helmut
Kreikenbom, Detlev
Kreutzer, Gert
Kreyszig, Walter
Kuhlmann, Peter
Kunst, Christiane
Kurz, Gerhard
Kyrieleis, Helmut
Landfester, Manfred
Latacz, Joachim
Leonhardt, Jürgen
Lill, Anne
Llanque, Marcus
Lück, Heiner
Michel, Simone
Mohnhaupt, Heinz
Müller-Karpe, Michael
Müller-Richter, Klaus
Münkler, Herfried
Nagel, Olev
Niehoff, Johannes
Nutton, Vivian
Oestmann, Günther
Olshausen, Eckhart
Penzenstadler, Franz
Pisani, Salvatore
Poppe, Erich
Prayon, Friedhelm
Ränsch-Trill, Barbara

Ratkowitsch, Christine
Rebenich, Stefan
Reichel, Andrea
Ritoók, Zsigmond
Ritoók-Szalay, Ágnes
Rölleke, Heinz
Rommel, Bettina
Rückert, Joachim
Rudolph, Wolf
Schäfer, Daniel
Scharf, Friedhelm
Schefold, Bertram
Schenkel, Wolfgang
Schiano, Claudio
Schier, Volker
Schmitz, Thomas A.
Schneider-Seidel, Kerstin M.
Scholz, Bernhard
Schwarz, Stefan
Schweizer, Stefan
Seebold, Elmar
Seidensticker, Bernd
Skafte Jensen, Minna
Spikermann, Wolfgang
Steiger, Heinhard

Strothmann, Jürgen
Stuckrad, Kocku von
Taddei (†), Maurizio
Tichy, Susanne
Torresin, Giuseppe
Tsakmakis, Antonis
Usener, Sylvia
Vainio, Raija
Virlouvet, Catherine
Visser, Romke
Vogt-Spira, Gregor
Vöhler, Martin
Wacke, Andreas
Walde, Christine
Wallenstein, Uta
Walther, Gerrit
Waquet, Françoise
Widmer, Anna
Wieber-Scariot, Anja
Wild, Gerhard
Wilhelm, Gernot
Wiplinger, Gilbert
Youkhanna, Donny George
Zimmermann, Bernhard

Classical Tradition translators

List of Entries

Democracy

A. Introduction   B. England and America in the 17th and 18th Centuries   C. French Revolution   D. The Critical Examination of the French Revolution   E. England, France and the United States in the 19th Century   F. Democracy and Social Dimensions: Discussions in the 19th and at the Beginning of the 20th Century   G. Outlook: 20th Century

A. Introduction

The reception of the ancient concept of democracy took place under the influence of varying notions of Antiquity, which were used repeatedly in the history of ideas to evaluate contemporary political conditions and as paradigms for a democratic political order. How have these ideas of democracy in Classical Antiquity shaped the modern concept of democracy? Viewed as in a system of political concepts, democracy stands in a reciprocal relationship with neighbouring or competing concepts, such as → MIXED CONSTITUTION and → REPUBLIC. Compared to the republic, democracy does not indicate the rule of law or good government vis-à-vis despotism, but rather political self-determination by including the mass of the people together with the associated risks of despotic rule. Thus, democracy and republic can compete or be positioned as competitors with respect to the concept of freedom and to the concept of good order. In competition with the concept of republic, the political order of → ATHENS was usually understood as the alternative to that of → Sparta [64]. Where democracy was used to characterize the political order as a whole, it did not usually refer to individual aspects of the theory of government; and the concept did then not occur in discussions of the mixed-constitutions theory. Outside of the theory of mixed constitutions, the concept of democracy only attained independent relevance in connection with the great revolutionary epochs.

Reception processes start in Antiquity itself. A well-known example occurred when Demosthenes emphasised the model character of the democracy of the forefathers. Typical for post-Classical times is the lively reception of Athenian democracy in periods when a political order was to be established or re-established. The Italian Renaissance, the English Revolution, the Dutch struggle for independence, the American and, finally, the French Revolution are the classic fields for the reception of ancient concepts of democracy. In the 19th cent., reception branched out, the strands initially proceeding concurrently, but then separating until, in reaction to Bolshevism and National Socialism and the total reduction of the individual to a political entity observable there, one finds a complete rejection of 'pure' democracy understood as a particular interpretation of Athenian democracy.

It can be said that in the entire history of political ideas, the concept of democracy, aside from its use in connection with the theory of mixed constitutions, repeatedly encounters antagonism [58; 66]. In such situations, in order to prove the reprehensible nature of democracy overall, stereotypical accusations were often leveled against individual aspects of Athenian democracy, such as the people's courts, how rapidly legislation could be passed and how susceptible the people's assembly was to demagogic influence. In what follows, the intention is mainly to highlight deviations from and exceptions to this prevalent manner of reception.

B. England and America in the 17th and 18th Centuries

[63; 66; 72; 73] As a rule, the argument of the non-transferability of ancient theories and concepts to modern conditions served the critics of an autonomous legislative political order as a weapon in the struggle against the legitimacy of democratic claims. For Thomas Hobbes, Aristotle (he refers to Pol. 6,2) was responsible both for the mixed constitution theory as well as the widely held belief that true freedom could only be assured in democracy. Thus, according to Hobbes, Aristotle had promoted the presumptuous idea among the citizenry that claims for personal freedom could be put forward against a system of rule guaranteed by a sovereign. According to Hobbes's theory, however, freedom was only ensured at all by having this order. In Hobbes's mind, the reception of ancient political literature had caused nothing but revolts and civil war since the foundation of universities in Western Europe (cf. [1], as well as *Behemoth or The Long Parliament*, 1682). Therefore, the analytical concept of democracy used by Hobbes himself is not aimed at political participation by the people, but at the sovereignty of an assembly as a permissible alternative to the sovereignty of a single individual.

But with the heightened consciousness that a political order could be created in a self- responsible way against the interests of far greater powers, the Athenian democracy was no longer exclusively seen as a cautionary historical example, but also as an example of the fact that, in establishing a new political order, not only cleverly crafted institutions were important; most important was the appropriate inner attitude of the citizens. For the Netherlands, this was demonstrated by Hugo Grotius, who compared the customs of the Athenians, Romans and Dutch and who, in spite of all the institutional differences and all the skepticism in relation to democratic government, nevertheless emphasised the exemplary ability of ancient democracy to engage citizens in politics ([2]. On the themes of socio-moral attitudes in relation to political-institutional matters, cf. [57. 210ff.]).

Already at the time of the English Revolution, democracy was regarded as the root of chaos and anarchy. The radical ideas of the Levellers, who espoused equality, were pejoratively equated with democracy [47. 295f.]. David Hume continued this tradition of equating tumults and chaos with democracy to great effect [3]. Nevertheless, numerous treatises on political conditions in Antiquity, despite all the stereotypical criticisms of Athens, also served as criticism of contemporary, non-democratic conditions. Jonathan Swift, for example, did collect all reservations against Athenian democracy; but at the same time he praised the Athenian people's assembly, noting that it had not been vain and had not, out of fear of losing face, upheld resolutions it had passed if they proved to be wrong. Swift expressly uttered this as a pointed remark against the English House of Commons [4]. His remarks were, of course, aimed less at the principle of representation itself, but rather at the manner of its execution. David Hume, with an eye on ancient conditions, advocated a representative democracy and thus gave expression to a fundamental conviction maintained in the Anglo-American tradition until well into the 19th cent. and beyond [5]. For instance, for Thomas Paine, who successfully supported the American as well as the French Revolution with his publications, Athens was not regarded as an example of anarchic terror; Paine, too, clearly belonged to the tradition of the idea of a representative democracy. For him, with an eye on Athens, democracy meant that political order which could most readily bring out and promote the talents and abilities of a population. However, as a form of government for large countries with a sizable population, he thought democracy unsuitable. This did not mean, of course, that it had no place there at all. Paine made the point that democracy should be ennobled by way of representation in order to make it practicable for the present as well. He saw no fundamental contradiction between the two ideas and wanted to have representation understood as coming out of the spirit of democracy [6].

In general, Antiquity was seen by the founding fathers of the USA as the crucial site where republican freedoms were developed. Also, in the pamphlet disputes about the requirement of a strong and unitary executive power, Antiquity provided the model giving writers common ground. Instead of referring to Athens, however, they preferred to point to Sparta ([72. 97]; cf. also [63; 65]). Athenian democracy, on the other hand, was the spectre of a political order inclined to anarchy. Only the republic was regarded as the quintessence of a balance between rule of law and freedom, stability and participation, and thus as the appropriate political goal [7]. A similar attitude can also be found in some of the articles of the *Federalist Papers* [8] written by James Madison. The intellectual-historical transmission to the New World of the Florentine Republic, as it was perceived in 16th and 17th cent. England, had sharpened the awareness of the fact that, with the establishment of an autonomous political order, the problem of the

socio-moral fiber of the citizens became paramount. Thus, institutional arrangements had to anticipate the problem of citizens with decreasing virtue and an inclination towards corruption [61. 506ff.]. In France, the revolutionaries did not consciously reflect on this problem to the same extent at the time of the founding of the republic. As they were gaining experience, they had to react theoretically and frequently did so too late. Here, too, the model of Antiquity and its reception played an important role.

C. FRENCH REVOLUTION

[49; 56; 60; 74] With the French Revolution, Greek democracy assumed a new and definitively changed meaning. The French Enlightenment preceding the revolution, with its concentration on such themes in the works of the Encyclopaedists [9] as well as by Montesquieu and Rousseau, structured the revolutionary debate. Montesquieu developed his central theme, namely, that virtue was the principle of democracy, on the basis of the Greek example: The Greeks had only tolerated the rule of virtue and had not determined a person's rank in society, as Montesquieu's contemporaries did, according to his wealth (Montesquieu, *De l'esprit des lois*, Geneva 21749, 3,3). This was intended as a criticism of the times and was by no means a call for a democratic style of government. The philosophers of the Enlightenment could not be won over to democracy. If they were not already aherents of an enlightened monarchy, then a republic was as far as they would go in defending ideas concerning participatory politics. For them, too, democracy remained the spectre of political disorder or even of the partisan dictatorship of the mob. Voltaire presented democracy as the 'gouvernement de la canaille: Quand je vous suppliais d'être le restaurateur des beaux-artes de la Grèce, ma prière n'allait pas jusqu' á vous conjurer de rétablir la démocratie athènienne: je n'aime point le gouvernement de la canaille' [10] ("If I were to beg you to be the restorer of the fine arts of Greece, my request would not go as far as entreating you to re-establish Athenian democracy. I care not at all for the government of the rabble"). Rousseau, despite all his sympathy for democracy, removed it from reality by referring to it as a form of government for gods, but not for human beings [11]. At the same time, he broke with both the traditional concept of the republic as well as that of democracy when he did not equate the republic with obedience before the law. Rather, he postulates legislation for the general public and its primacy *vis-à-vis* the claims of an individual will. On the other hand, he wanted democracy to be understood in the sense of a genuine direct democracy which he could not see as having been achieved at all in Antiquity: 'Qu'on ne m'oppose donc point la démocratie d'Athenes, parce qu'Athenes n'étoit point en effet une démocratie, mais une aristocratie trés-tyrannique, gouvernée par des savans et des orateurs' [12] ("One should not in the least be opposed to the democracy in Athens because Athens never really had a democracy, but rather a very tyrannical aristocracy, governed by the learned and orators"). However, he was of the opinion that Switzerland could be a model for this type of democracy. In his plans of a constitution for Corsica, he contemplated the possibilities and limits of such a direct and non-representative people's government.

It was Camille Desmoulins who attempted most frequently and comprehensively to apply the model of ancient democracy directly to the events of the French Revolution. For him, political self-determination according to the Athenian model was the form of government appropriate for humankind. Therefore, it should also be the model for France [13]. His Vieux Cordelier was abundantly full of ancient analogies and parables; but he lacked a systematic way of working. Desmoulins was a publicist first and foremost, not a theoretician or politician.

When Sieyès, on the other hand, started from the assumption that France could not become a democracy, he was thinking, probably also influenced on this point by Rousseau, of the size of the country in comparison to that of the city state in Antiquity. At the same time, he considered it essential to assume that the nation had a common will, and he therefore saw in the representative system the only possibility for forming a unified will within the nation. Permanent elections were to uphold the 'democratic spirit' in order to prevent the development of an aristocracy among the representatives, who would normally vote on matters in a free and independent manner [14]. Overall, Sieyès has a tendency to enhance the status of a 'federalist' Athens compared to a 'centralist' Rome – a tendency, however, that never gained any footing in constitutional politics because of the revolutionary wars [50. 268f.].

This form of autonomous self-determination, not fundamentally bound by the barriers of personal rights, did not become associated with the concept of democracy until the second phase of the French Revolution, namely, in the works of Saint-Just [15]. For Saint-Just, the advantage of democracy was the fact that it legitimised infringement on property and freedom in order to give validity to the will of the people against its enemies. Therefore, even terror could be postulated as a democratic form of government. Of course it was not to be equated with an arbitrary regime of tyranny. As an instrument of democracy, terror would serve both the legitimate struggle of the people against a minority as well as the renewal and maintenance of virtue, which was one of the characteristics of the people necessary for democracy. The first idea was borrowed from the Aristotelian description of democracy. The second is a further development of the Classical concept of virtue, although this, in the political theory of Antiquity, is connected with the concept of republic.

The political struggles between the revolutionaries themselves also influenced the way the concept of democracy was used as a political model. While it was the model to be emulated, it was also pointed out that, in its function as a model, it should not be overrated.

Robespierre serves as a good example of this way of thinking. He advocated both points of view, depending on whom he debated. In his speech at the convention on 10 May 1793, he argued against a Girondist majority and their claim of being the only legitimate parliamentary representatives. His understanding of democracy called for the independent legitimacy of the people's assemblies below the parliamentary threshold (by which he meant the Paris Commune in particular). Furthermore, with the Athenian model in mind, he demanded per diem allowances for ordinary people who, in these assemblies, were in charge of the public welfare [16]. But, when he himself was in political office, he declared the Roman Republic and the Athenian democracy to be a common model to the extent that both had determined virtue to be the essential prerequisite for a political order that made laws for itself. For Robespierre, of course, virtue in this context first meant that the people did all those things they could do, and those things they could not do they left to their deputies [17. 586]. The background to Robespierre's way of arguing here is his beginning struggle against the extreme wings of the revolutionary party; in this case, the Hébertists. With them in mind, Robespierre had declared shortly before, that revolutionary politics was based on a new theory and could not simply adapt ancient models. In particular, Robespierre rejected a straight transfer of direct democracy to French conditions, and he considered both the extremists and the reactionary forces as enemies of the revolution: "The theory of the revolutionary government is just as new as the revolution this government has emerged from. One should neither look for it in the books of political writers, who did not foresee this revolution, nor in the law books of tyrants, who are satisfied with the abuse of their power" [17. 563f.].

D. The Critical Examination of the French Revolution

While in France itself it can be observed that, with the establishment of the bourgeois concept of property, democratic Athens as a prospering trading state gained a new reputation in contrast to an immobile Sparta [74], outside France the criticism of the French Revolution continued to concentrate on the spectre of Athens. In principle, Edmund Burke did not reject democracy, but he insisted that there had never been a democratic government in history worthy of emulation, neither in Antiquity nor in the present. In agreement with Aristotle, Burke rejected pure democracy as a degenerate form of government. He emphasised its proximity to despotism and, in particular, pointed out the danger of an arbitrary rule of the majority over minorities, which was the worst tyranny of all conceivable forms. In particular, the peculiarity of the Athenian democracy to govern by way of "occasional decrees", the *psephismta*, had driven Greek democracy to ruin. Burke dared to make an equivalent prophecy for France as well [18].

Not least under the impression of the events in France and with the aid of Antiquity as the teacher of political history, Kant emphasised the primacy of the republic over the self-determination by the people in democracy, especially since, in his concept of democracy, he does not underscore the source of power, but rather the form of rule, with democracy (as also demonstrated by the Greek example) being regarded as a form of despotism. A republic should not be confused with democracy; rather, democracy should be considered in light of the far more fundamental contrast between republicanism and despotism. Despotism is the congruence of the private will with the public will due to the autocratic nature of law enforcement, which becomes possible where there is no distinction between executive and legislative powers. In this sense, Kant declared democracy to be a despotic form of government [19].

Kant's pupil Johann Benjamin Erhard refined his master's work, but he politicised it as well. For him, too, democracy is a form of despotism, and the Athenian model, in particular, is an example of a political order that served the passions of a dependent and immature people. Thus it makes a regime possible that appears even more wicked to him than the respect shown towards a supremacy of the aristocracy [20]. But for Erhard this was not the end of the matter. For him to restrict oneself to the demand for political freedom while remaining intellectually dependent is an outrage. This is why the Enlightenment for him represents the decisive vehicle for elevating a dependent population to the status of political self-determination. It is precisely the struggle for the Enlightenment against a regime suppressing it, which expressly grants a legal entitlement to revolution.

If one considered the French Revolution from the point of view of political theory and, in particular, from a predominantly institutional perspective, and if one understood the function of government to be the realisation of a particular purpose which, by consensus, was formulated as a realisation of freedom, then the Athenian democracy served as a negative example, because it was personal freedom in particular which it was unable to value or bring about. Thus, from Kant to Constant we see, in the discussion of the French Revolution, the concept of modern personal freedom move to the centre of political theory; and therein lies a clear distancing from the ancient model. What was still intended as an implicit criticism of Antiquity in Kant's work, was elevated to the main matter of reflection by Constant.

After the Restoration, Benjamin Constant adopted a clear position against the analogies between the present and Antiquity, as they had been drawn during the French Revolution. In doing so, he not only criticised the failed attempt of the revolution to establish a political order modelled on the Athenian democracy or the Roman Republic by contrasting these models with Sparta as an alternative political paradigm; he also at-

tacked the notion that such analogies were in principle allowable. Against such thinking he emphasised the independence of modernity, whose contrast to Antiquity he demonstrated on the concept of freedom. In this respect, he rejected the Athenian democracy as a particularly obsolete model. Of course, his reasoning was problematic to the extent that he explained modern freedom by way of the developed personality and its pursuit of happiness and that he considered the decisive difference to Antiquity to be found in commerce. For it was in commerce that the closeness of European countries to each other became evident, countries that were no longer 'intimate enemies'. Here, there was also the opportunity of a new field of activity for the individual, who was no longer exclusively dependent on politics to prove himself. But precisely these characteristics could also be found in the Athenian democracy, at least in part. Therefore, Constant claimed for Classical democracy, as well as for Antiquity in general, the complete dependence of the individual on the body politic and its unfettered ability to determine all aspects of an individual's life. He attempted to explain this especially through the example of ostracism [21]. The thesis formulated in detail by Constant, i.e. the fundamentally different, basic political ideas of Antiquity and modernity and the resulting rejection of Antiquity as an obligatory reference for political theory, triggered a controversy lasting for the whole of the 19th cent. Numa Denis Fustel de Coulanges endorsed Constant's basic thesis and expressly opposed George Grote who, in the middle of the 19th cent., once more proposed the idea of the model character of the Athenian democracy. Friedrich Julius Stahl, Robert von Mohl and Johann Caspar Bluntschli endorsed Fustel, while Jacob Burckhardt formulated the thesis in an even more fundamental manner; but Georg von Jellinek was critical of it [67. 274ff.].

This was the tradition that saw the condemnation of democracy in the light of a political order that had condemned to death one of the greatest individuals of world history. Wilhelm Gottlieb Tennemann had written the following about the death sentence against Socrates: "It is outrageous for humankind that this excellent man had to drink out of the poisoned chalice as a victim of cabals which occur so frequently in democracies" [22]. Hegel, with reference to Tennemann, emphatically protested against such an interpretation. Namely, if one did not superimpose the modern understanding of freedom onto Classical democracy and if one did not reduce the problem of the 'conveyance' of personal freedom to the mechanics of an institutional system of regulations, but if one rather concentrated the question of political order at a level where it had been dealt with in Hegel's substantial morality or Robespierre's virtue, then one could still see a great political model in Greek democracy or attach to its epoch a central importance for the development of the understanding of human freedom. Thus, Hegel protested against the moralising criticism of Socrates' sentencing by the

Athenian democracy; rather, he granted it the right to make a decision about the fate of an individual at the moment when a type of freedom irreconcilable with it [i.e., democracy] began to develop that was understood to be personal and resting on one's own rights. The background to this are Hegel's earlier reflections on the basic morality of the Greeks, the attempt of its revitalisation through the Christian religion, as well as Hegel's concept of the state as the carrier of a new understanding of morality, whose historical task should not be allowed to fail because of the personal rights of the individual and Constant's understanding of freedom [23].

E. England, France and the United States in the 19th Century

The reception of Greek democracy in England was ambivalent. Here, as everywhere else, the determining factor was: which aspect was especially emphasised and claimed to be characteristic of democracy. Among his contemporaries, George Grote was the strongest spokesperson who continued to hold to the model character of Athenian democracy. Grote had to struggle against Burke's verdict and, in this context, pointed out two essential aspects: Even though he, too, saw a risk for personal freedom from political decisions which were made in people's assemblies, he nevertheless highlighted the educational effect of political debate and decision-making for the population, and he emphasised a point left out by Burke: the similarity of the jury courts in the Anglo-Saxon world to the courts of Athens and the concomitant avoidance of a professional oligarchy. Here, too, Grote highlighted the educational effect of broad participation in legal decision-making [24]. Lord Acton, on the other hand, spoke for a whole generation of skeptics who had abandoned hopes for the educative effect of democratic institutions and, with the growing importance of the British Empire and its political and administrative tasks, regarded a democratic solution as impractical. Such critics stressed less the normative legitimacy but rather the quality of the content of political decisions. Therefore, Lord Acton could emphasise that the Athenians, under their democracy, had steadily grown to unimaginable greatness but that they had achieved this only under this form of government. Even strong religious attachments had not been able, in the end, to stop the corruption of democracy: 'But the possession of unlimited power, which corrodes the conscience, hardens the heart, and confounds the understanding of monarchs, exercised its demoralising influence on the illustrious democracy of Athens'. Just as the French Republic of the revolutionary period did later, the Athenians had plundered the rich for so long that the rich finally collaborated with the enemy [25]. The change of perspective embraced by Acton in his theory of government is comparable to the change in the discussion about democracy in all imperial powers, where reference to ancient democracy is made, more and more, in academic and cultural circles only, but no longer in political discussions.

These reservations, which could be called classic, about the Athenian democracy from the perspective of a liberal understanding of freedom, as well as the growing demand for political decision-making competency as a result of imperial expansion, could only be undermined by other ideas of freedom. In the United States, whose political theoreticians had vigorously argued against Classical democracy and for the Classical republic during the foundation and consolidating phase of the revolution, there developed such a changed understanding of freedom and, thus, also a changing regard for democracy. Here, we can observe a gradual emancipation of the modern concept of democracy from its models in Antiquity. This took place, however, with a clear look at Antiquity and not by simple denial or forgetting. While Constant, through the claim of a changed concept of freedom, promoted a liberal, undemanding attitude and proposed to come to an arrangement with the monarchy, which does "not rule" (Guizot), critics of this system began to look to the land of modern democracy, namely to the United States in the era of Jacksonian democracy. Here, Tocqueville saw a field of observation, opening up to him, which presented him an entirely new kind of freedom – that of the self-confident petit bourgeois. The ensuing analyses founded a new branch of the analyses of democracy, one which no longer had any connection to the ancient or Athenian model. Still, Tocqueville appreciated the value of ancient literature for the development of a democratically inspired and theoretically demanding political literature because of its high educational content in terms of politics. However, as a disadvantage, he pointed out the effect of this literature on the uneducated population: disorder and dissatisfaction [26]. In this, Tocqueville followed in the footsteps of Thomas Hobbes. On this point, Tocqueville was supported by John Stuart Mill, his most important English-speaking interpreter. It was Mill's aim to produce political elites that would not reinforce their position in an aristocratic or repressive manner and would close themselves off from the democratic tendencies of the time [45. 7–42], which he considered unstoppable and whose moulding and shaping he declared to be the overarching task of political theory. Precisely in this respect, Mill recognised the superiority of ancient democracy, which he always saw as an Athenian one. There talent had been able to flourish without institutional obstacles, while representative governments and also representative democracy had failings, precisely in this area. Under contemporary conditions, Themistocles or Demosthenes would hardly have gained a seat in parliament. In contrast to that, he saw the advantages of the representative system in the fact that the rise of talented politicians, even if they were in the minority, would occur more quickly and with more certainty in parliaments; and their influence on the political decision-making process would be greater, whereas the Athenian democracy quite often excluded its great talents but instead promoted politicians, who were avowed opponents of democracy or who were, at any rate, not its supporters, such as Nicias, Theramenes and Alcibiades [27].

F. Democracy and Social Dimensions: Discussions in the 19th and at the Beginning of the 20th Century

Ultimately, it was a third strand of the understanding of freedom that disengaged the modern debate completely from the predetermined conceptions of the ancient paradigm. The problem of social freedom, and thus that of social democracy, pushed into the background purely institutional questions of political constitutionality. Responsible for this was, in particular, the detaching of the modern understanding of democracy from the ancient model and the advancement beyond the ancient theories of forms of government which were reduced to either the form of the democratic monarchy (king or emperor) or the dictatorship of the proletariat as the only political alternatives for the realisation of a revolutionary democracy. This strand of the thematizing of freedom understood the political-institutional problems predominantly from the point of view of the social question, which, it is true, had already been present earlier, but had never been put centre-stage to a similar extent as it was by Lorenz von Stein or Karl Marx.

In a "critical battle against the French Revolution", Karl Marx and Friedrich Engels wanted to make a clean break with the imitation of ancient forms of state. Because of the fundamentally different structures of the modern world, this had been a cause of the hubris of the Jacobins and therefore presented a "colossal delusion", which further revolutions should no longer succumb to: "Robespierre, Saint-Just and their party went under because they confused the ancient, realistic-democratic community, which was based on real slavery, with the modern spiritualistic-democratic representative state, which is founded on an emancipated slavery, namely bourgeois society" [28]. Just as for Marx, the true characteristic of Antiquity for Lorenz von Stein was slavery as an economic system. In relation to this characteristic, decisive for the shape of the rest of society, the differences in the constitutional institutions and forms of government in Athens, Sparta or Rome were of subordinate and, to that extent, minor importance. For the struggle there about the appropriate establishment of freedom could only find an appropriate solution through the recognition of the value of a gainful occupation, which did not happen prior to the Christian-Germanic world view [29. vol. 3, 147ff.]. Thus, Stein saw two separate strands of reception of ancient political thinking clash during the French Revolution: on the one hand, the ancient theory of government as well as doctrinaire ideas about the republic and democracy and, on the other hand, the increasing awareness of the decisive importance of economic conditions for political structures and developments. The first strand of reception, by not considering social conditions, necessarily had to remain doctrinaire and ideological [29. vol. 1, 290f.].

Considering the social question as a theme allowed Stein to gain a different perception of the theory of government. The concept of the pre-eminence of social over political conditions opened up new combinations which Stein generally saw in the conception of a "social democracy" and concretely in the institutions of a "social monarchy". In view of these modern problems, the models of Antiquity were no longer sufficient [29. vol. 1, 120ff.].

Although he strongly accented the social question, Stein's own political ideas tended to be conservative. This connects him with Jacob Burckhardt who, similar to Grote, saw the most effective form for the development of the individual to be democracy. In contrast to Grote, however, he put a more negative emphasis on it. In Burckhardt's view, the effect of democracy was really only a reaction against the total subjugation of the individual under the polis. Since talented individuals could not extricate themselves from the polis, they had to make the polis into a means of its own power and rise to the top in order not to go under themselves [30. 8off.]. For Burckhardt, however, complete democracy was a "permanent desire for revolution" [30. 80], a view of Greek democracy that emerged against the background of the continuing revolutionary effect of the French Revolution in the 19th cent. and the decline of the educated bourgeoisie (Bildungsbürgertum).

In the *Birth of Tragedy*, Nietzsche, going far beyond Burckhardt, tried to free the concept of culture from the classicistic reduction to its Apollonian side and to emphasise the Dionysian aspect. Therefore, he rejected an interpretation of the chorus in the Attic tragedy as a symbolic representation of the demos, as the voice of the democratic conscience or as the original image of a constitutional representation of the people [31]; and he made democracy responsible for the one-sidedness and thus the decadence of the concept of culture, a process reaching into his own time. It is true that this fundamental critique in the early phase of his work was followed, in the middle phase, by a more differentiated way of viewing democracy, but Nietzsche's thesis of an immanent connection between democratisation and cultural decline remained his chief legacy in this area. This idea rapidly became detached from the discourse about the ancient model and assumed a life of its own, particularly in sociological discussions about 'mass democracy'.

For the action directe in France, the comparison of the Third Republic with the Athenian democracy served as proof that the Republic was an anachronism, and only someone who misunderstood the foundations of Classical democracy would not recognize this. To the extent that the Athenian democracy had indeed been the political order of a slave-owning society, it had also been the political order of an elite and not an order of equality. Consequently, one would have to accept the naked truth that it had been an elitist political order (and here the influence of Nietzsche and his judgments on the Athenian democracy come through loud and clear), and, against this background, the criterion of assessment, when comparing the aristocracy with democracy, would not be equality but usefulness. Here, the Athenian democracy, in common with all later versions of this form of government, had shown that an aristocracy would be productive and remain healthy, while democracy, on the other hand, would consume and destroy [32]. The phrase morbus democraticus (democratic disease), which had befallen the nation, was here, as it was in Maurras's later political writings, the major concept of his fundamental critique of parliamentary democracy.

With the challenge of → SOCIALISM, a theory of society which saw itself connected to democracy as a form of politics complementary to itself, examination of the Athenian democracy at the end of the 19th cent. became a foil for criticism and discussion of one's own times. However, nowhere was this connection as explicit as in Robert von Pöhlmann's work. His verdict is that the democracy of the Hellenic city state had developed socialism as a necessary counterpart [33. 126]. Constantly drawing on ancient and modern discussions, Pöhlmann carries on parallel discourses dealing with the politics of social democrats and the middle-class parties, as well as with the beginnings of a coalition strategy between bourgeoisie and the workers' movement. In this context, the history of Antiquity in general and of the Athenian democracy in particular serves him as an indication of the dangers and risks of such an undertaking. Pöhlmann objected, for example to the ideas of Friedrich von Payer regarding political concessions made to the masses – that these measures, conceived as a "precaution against social democracy", would lead politically in the wrong direction, as the ancient example of the connection between democracy and socialism demonstrated. He then supports this statement with an extensive theory, according to which the Athenian democracy had been the political government of the masses; and this is the reason why democracy can only be explained by mass psychology. Hence any coalition policies on the part of the bourgeoisie should be rejected. In this, Pöhlmann was mainly fighting against Grote and his school [33. 272ff.]. 'Democratic actions by the masses in a way resemble a phenomenon of nature' [33. 274]; the masses are a large animal, as Plato said, and the theory for explaining this natural phenomenon was mass psychology, whose rise as a science was just starting at about this time. From this perspective then, the Athenian democracy and therefore any democracy is regarded, from a liberal perspective, as impervious to learning. Proof of this for Pöhlmann is, once again, the trial of Socrates. In Sokrates und sein Volk (Munich 1899), Pöhlmann declares Socrates to be the victim of the soul of the masses expressing itself in the people's court, which did not want to tolerate the outstanding personality of the philosopher in their midst and therefore convicted him out of a feeling of inferiority. Democracy could not tolerate a non-conforming opinion and, thus, the conviction of Socrates was also a refutation of the claim that academic freedom and freedom of expression were best protected in a democracy. Opposing voices against this were quickly raised, of which only Adolf Menzel's Untersuchung zum Sokrates-Processe (1903) shall be mentioned here. Menzel expressly defends democracy against the accusation that it was responsible for the conviction of Socrates. Against Hegel, who equated the spirit of the people with the vote in court, Menzel responded that the majority against Socrates had been too slim to represent the spirit of the people in the Athenian democracy; but he emphasized most of all that it had been the religious piety of the Athenians that had led them, independently of their democracy, to conduct the trial against Socrates for impiety. Precisely the variety of opinions in the Athenian as well as in a modern democracy indicated that a democracy more so than non-democratic organisations, such as the Church or feudal state, was a refuge for academic freedom and freedom of expression – a statement that was expressly directed against Pöhlmann [34].

G. OUTLOOK: 20TH CENTURY

This point of view, however, did not prevail among German-speaking scholars of Antiquity. Thus, after World War I, for Eduard Meyer dealing with the Athenian democracy served both as an opportunity to analyse the essence of Western democracy and, at the same time, led him to condemn it. One recognises that political wishful thinking was the 'father' of scholarly thought when Meyer reproaches the Athenian democracy by saying that anarchic turmoil and decline in political power were a result of the form of government and simultaneously brands Lloyd George and Woodrow Wilson as demagogues comparable to the Athenian warmongers, the only difference being that the latter had won the war [35].

With → NATIONAL SOCIALISM a change of perspective began to occur among German scholars, which, as a result of the problems of the time, approached ancient democracy with new questions in the hope of obtaining answers for the present from their treatment. Now, a possible inner connection between democracy and totalitarianism stood in the foreground, and a deep skepticism as to the consequences spread, especially among those who were open to democracy, as the examples of Carl Joachim Friedrich and Kurt von Fritz indicate [36; 37]. This view culminated ultimately in the positing of a totalitarian democracy, as it had been developed by Jacob L. Talmon; in his case, of course, without harking back to Classical democracy [38].

In the fields of political science and political philosophy after World War II, discussions of the ancient model of democracy were more productive. Leo Strauss was at pains to show the timeless validity of Plato's and Aristotle's "classical political philosophy". Against the accusation that their anti-democratic bias no longer permitted their reception in modern democracy, Strauss retorts that the fundamental problems of democracy had not changed since Antiquity, namely that the uneducated had a legitimate claim to rule. Plato's and Aristotle's criticism of democracy therefore continues to be topical and their critical stance towards democracy remains relevant [39]. Hannah Arendt, on the other hand, used the Greek polis to explain central political institutions, such as the 'theory of action' (Handlungslehre) and the theory of public life which, as a whole, can no longer be adapted to modernity because of the novel emergence of 'society'. Nevertheless, there are strands of argumentation, particularly those that are critical of democracy, which can be followed down to the present. Here, Arendt emphasised attempts to replace political practice with mechanisms for the establishment of political order. The plurality and openness of the ancient polis and democracy, but at the same time the risk of its fragility and unpredictability as well as the precarious position of the individual vis-à-vis the concentration of power in a democracy without barriers, according to her analysis, are giving way more and more to attempts to achieve a technical and competent establishment of security and order; and thus undermine the political civic character of the human being, whose normative model can still be found in Antiquity [40].

→ ATHENS; → MIXED CONSTITUTION; → REPUBLIC; → REVOLUTION; → SPARTA; → TYRANNIS

SOURCES 1 TH. HOBBES, Leviathan oder Stoff, Form und Gewalt eines kirchlichen und bürgerlichen Staates, 1651, edited and with an introduction by I. FETSCHER, 1966, (Leviathan, or The Matter, Forme and Power of a Commonwealth Ecclesiasticall and Civil, 1651, J. C. A. GASKIN (ed.), 1998) 2 H. GROTIUS, Batavi – Parallelon rerumpublicarum liber tertius: de moribus ingenioque populorum Athenensium, Romanorum, Batavorum, J. MEERMAN (ed.), 4 vols., Haarlem 1801 (Engl. L. WASZINK (ed.), The Antiquity of the Batavian Republic, 2000) 3 D. HUME, On Some Remarkable Customs, 1752, in: Id., Essays Moral, Political and Literary E. F. MILLER (ed.), 1987, 14–31 4 J. SWIFT, Discourse of the Contests and Dissensions between the Noble and Commons in Athens and Rome, 1701 5 D. HUME, That Politics may be reduced to a Science, 1741, in: Id., Essays Moral, Political and Literary, E. F. MILLER (ed.),1987, 14–31 6 TH. PAINE, Die Rechte des Menschen 1791/1792, in contemporary translation by D. M. FORKEL, revised and with an introduction by TH. STEMMLER, 1973, 203ff. (E. FONER (ed.) The Rights of Man, 1792/1792, 1984) 7 J. ADAMS, Defence of the Constitutions of Government of the United States of America, 3 vols., 1, 1787 (in: Works, 10 vols., Boston 1850–1856, vol. 4, 287) 8 A. HAMILTON, J. MADISON, J. JAY, Federalist Papers, 1787/1788, with an introduction by C. ROSSITER, 1961, see especially Nos. 1, 9, 10, 37 und 70 9 CH. DE JAUCOURT, Démocratie, in: Encyclopédie ou Dictionnaire raisonné des sciences, des arts et des métiers, vol. 4, Paris 1754, 816–818 10 VOLTAIRE, Brief an den Preußenkönig von 28.10. 1773, in: Œuvres complètes de Voltaire, Voltaire Foundation, eds.,1975, vol. 124: Correspondence June 1773–May 1774, 159f. (Engl. R. ALDINGTON (trans.), Letters of Voltaire and Frederick the Great, 1927) 11 J.-J. ROUSSEAU, Du Contrat Social ou principes de droit politique, Amsterdam 1762, 3, 4 (Engl. S. DUNN (trans.), The Social Contract; and The First and Second Discourses, 2002)

12 Id., Discours sur l'économie politique, 1755, in: Id., Contrat social. Écrits politiques, ed. Pléiade 1966, 246 (Engl. S. DUNN (trans.), The Social Contract; and The First and Second Discourses, 2002) 13 C. DESMOULINS, La france libre, in: Id., Œuvres, 3 vols., 1866, vol. 1, 123–188, 176 (Engl. J. OWEN (printer), The History of the Brissotins, ²1794) 14 E. J. SIEYÈS, Rede von. 7.9. 1789, in: Politische Schriften, E. SCHMITT, R. REICHARDT (eds.), ²1981, 269 (Engl. M. SONENSCHER (trans.), Political Writings, 2003) 15 L.-A.-L. SAINT-JUST, Rapport sur la nécessité de déclarer le gouvernement révolutionaire, 10. Okt. 1793, in: Id., Œuvres complètes, M. DUVAL (ed.), 1984, 520–530 16 M. ROBESPIERRE, Über die repräsentative Regierung, in: Id., Ausgewählte Texte, deutsch von M. UNRUH (trans.), Introduction by C. SCHMID, ²1989, 429ff. 17 Id., Über die Grundsätze der revolutionären Regierung, in: Id., Ausgewählte Texte, M. UNRUH (trans.), Introduction by C. SCHMID, ²1989 18 E. BURKE, Reflections on the Revolution in France, 1790, in: Id., Works in 12 vols., vol. 3, 1899, 508 19 I. KANT, Zum ewigen Frieden. Ein philosophischer Entwurf, 1795, in: Id., Werke in 10 vols., W. WEISCHEDEL (ed.), vol. 9, 1970, 191–251, 206f (Engl. W, SCHWARZ (trans.), Principles of Lawful Politics: Immanuel Kant's Philosophic Draft toward Eternal Peace, 1988) 20 J. B. ERHARD, Über das Recht des Volks zu einer Revolution, Jena and Leipzig 1795, 90 21 B. CONSTANT, Cours de politique constitutionelle, 1820, vol. 4 22 W. G. TENNEMANN, Geschichte der Philosophie in 11 Teilen, Leipzig 1798–1819, 2, 39ff. (A. JOHNSON (trans.), A Manual of the History of Philosophy, 1932) 23 G. W. F. HEGEL, Vorlesungen über die Geschichte der Philosophie I, in: Id., Werke, E. MOLDENHAUER, K. M. MICHEL (eds.), vol. 18, 1971, 497 (Engl. R. S. HARTMAN (trans.), Reason in History: A General Introduction to the History of Philosophy, 1953) 24 G. GROTE, A History of Greece, 12 vols., London 1846–1856 25 J. E. E. DALBERG-ACTON, The History of Freedom in Antiquity (1877), in: Id., Essays in the History of Liberty. Selected Writings of Lord Acton, 1985, vol. 1, 5–29, 13f. 26 A. DE TOCQUEVILLE, Über die Democratie in Amerika, 1835/1840, H. ZBINDEN (trans.), 1987, II, 1, 15 (= S. 92ff.) (De la démocratie en Amérique, Engl. A. GOLDHAMMER (trans.), Democracy in America, 2004) 27 J. ST. MILL, Considerations on Representative Government, 1861, R. B. MCCALLUM (ed.), 1948, 199ff. 28 K. MARX, Die Heilige Familie 1844/45, in: MARX/ENGELS-Werke, vol. 2, 1960, 125ff., 129 (Engl. R. DIXON (trans.), The Holy Family, 1956) 29 L. VON STEIN, Geschichte der sozialen Bewegung in Frankreich von 1789 bis auf unsere Tage, 1842/1850, G. SALOMON (ed.), 3 vols., 1921 (K. MENGELBERG (trans.), History of the Social Movement in France, 1959–1850, 1964 30 J. BURCKHARDT, Griechische Kulturgeschichte, 4 vols., 1898ff., repr. 1956ff., vol. 1 (Engl. P. HILTY (trans.), History of Greek Culture, 1963) 31 F. NIETZSCHE, Die Geburt der Tragödie aus dem Geiste der Musik, 1872, Stück 7, M. LANDFESTER (ed.), 1994 (Engl. D. SMITH (trans.), The Birth of Tragedy, 2000) 32 CH. MAURRAS, Forward to: P. LASSERRE, La science officielle. M. Alfred Croiset historien de la démocratie athénienne, 1909 (repr. by B. HEMMERDINGER, in: Quaderni di Storia 4, 1976, 13–18) 33 R. VON PÖHLMANN, Geschichte der sozialen Frage und des Sozialismus in der antiken Welt, 2 vols., ²1912, vol. 1 34 A. MENZEL, Untersuchungen zum Sokrates-Processe, Sitzungsberichte der Kaiserlichen Akademie der Wissenschaften, Philosophisch-historische

Classe, vol. 145, 1903, 58ff.   35 ED. MEYER, Caesars Monarchie und das Principat des Pompejus. Zur inneren Geschichte Roms von 66–44 n.Chr., ³1922, 185f. 36 C. J. FRIEDRICH, Greek Political Heritage and Totalitarianism, in: Review of Politics 2, 1940, 218–225   37 K. VON FRITZ, Totalitarismus und Demokratie im alten Griechenland, in: A&A 3, 1948, 47–74   38 J. L. TALMON, The Origins of Totalitarian Democracy, 1952, 1970 39 L. STRAUSS, What is Political Philosophy?, in: Id., What is Political Philosophy and other Studies, 1959, 9–55, 36–38   40 H. ARENDT, Vita activa, oder, vom tätigen Leben, 1958, 214f.

LITERATURE   41 H. VON BOSE, Republik und Mischverfassung. Zur Staatsformenlehre der Federalist Papers, 1989   42 W. BREIL, Republik ohne Demagogie. Ein Vergleich der soziopolitischen Anschauungen von Polybios, Cicero und Alexander Hamilton, 1983   43 R. BREITLING, Zur Renaissance des Demokratiebegriffs im 18. Jahrhundert, in: P. HAUNGS (ed.), Res Publica: Studien zum Verfassungswesen: Dolf Sternberger zum 70. Geburtstag, 1977, 37–52 1977, 37–52   44 G. DIETZE, Das Problem der Demokratie bei den amerikanischen Verfassungsvätern, in: Zeitschrift für die gesamte Staatswissenschaft 113, 1957, 301–313   45 M. I. FINLEY, Antike und moderne Demokratie, 1980 (Democracy Ancient and Modern, 1973)   46 E. GOTHEIN, Platos Staatslehre in der Renaissance, 1912. Sitzungsberichte der Heidelberger Akademie der Wissenschaften, philosopsch-historische Klasse, 5. Abhandlung   47 M. GRALHER, Demokratie und Repräsentation in der Englischen Revolution, 1973 48 L. GUERCI, L'Immagine di Sparta e Athene in Mably e nei fisiocratici, in: Quaderni di Storia 9, 1979, 71–108 49 Id., Libertà degli antici e libertà dei moderni, 1979 50 TH. HAFEN, Staat, Gesellschaft und Bürger im Denken von Sieyès, 1994   51 B. HEMMERDINGER, La démocratie athénienne vue par le comte de Montlosier et Maurras, in: Quaderni di Storia 14, 1981, 227–229   52 P. JOACHIMSEN, Die Bedeutung des antiken Elements für die Staatsauffassung der Renaissance, in: Id., Gesammelte Aufsätze, N. HAMMERSTEIN (ed.), 1970   53 K. H. KINZL (ed.), Demokratia. Wege zur Demokratie bei den Griechen, 1995   54 E. KÜCHENHOFF, Möglichkeiten und Grenzen begrifflicher Klarheit in der Staatsformenlehre, vol. 2, 1967   55 J. S. MCCLELLAND, The Crowd and the Mob – from Plato to Canetti, 1989   56 C. MOSSÉ, L'Antiquité dans la révolution française, 1989   57 H. MÜNKLER, H. GRÜNBERGER, K. MAYER, Nationenbildung. Die Nationalisierung Europas im Diskurs humanistischer Intellektueller, 1998   58 B. NÄF, Von Perikles zu Hitler? Die athenische Democratie und die deutsche Althistorie bis 1945, 1986   59 C. NICOLET, L'Idee républicaine en France (1789–1924). Essai d'histoire critique, 1982 60 H. T. PARKER, The Culture of Antiquity and the French Revolutionaries, 1937   61 J. G. A. POCOCK, The Machiavellian Moment. Florentine Political Thought and the Atlantic Republican Tradition, 1975   62 E. RADNITZKY, Der moderne Freiheitsbegriff und die attische Demokratie, in: Zeitschrift für Öffentliches Recht 3, 1922, 287–351 63 P. A. RAHE, Republics Ancient and Modern. Classical Republicanism and the American Revolution, 1992 64 E. RAWSON, The Spartan Tradition in European Thought, 1966, repr. 1991   65 C. J. RICHARD, The Founders and the Classics. Greece, Rome, and the American Enlightenment, 1994   66 J. T. ROBERTS, Athens on Trial. The Antidemocratic Tradition in Western Thought, 1994   67 G. SARTORI, The Theory of Democracy Revisited, 1987   68 U. SCHINDEL, Demosthenes im 18. Jahrhundert. 10 Kapitel zum Nachleben des Demosthenes in Deutschland, Frankreich, England, 1963   69 V. VON SCHOEFFER, Demokratia, RE Supplement vol. 1, 346–374 70 G. SPRIGATH, Themen aus der Geschichte der römischen- Republik in der französichen Malerei des 18. Jahrhunderts, 1968   71 O. STAMMER, Demokratie und Diktatur, 1955   72 M. REINHOLD, Classica Americana. The Greek and Roman Heritage in the United States, 1984 73 J. URZIDIL, Amerika und die Antike, 1964   74 P. VIDAL-NAQUET, Die Entstehung des bürgerlichen Athens, in: Id., Athen-Sparta-Atlantis. Die griechische Demokratie von außen gesehen, vol. 1, 1993, 95–169   75 V. WEMBER, Verfassungsmischung und Verfassungsmitte – moderne Formen gemischter Verfassung in der politischen Theorie des beginnenden Zeitalters der Gleichheit, 1977.

HERFRIED MÜNKLER, MARCUS LLANQUE

Denmark
I. CULTURE   II. HISTORY OF CLASSICAL SCHOLARSHIP

I. CULTURE
A. MIDDLE AGES   B. RENAISSANCE AND BAROQUE C. RATIONALISM AND NEO-CLASSICISM   D. NINETEENTH CENTURY   E. TWENTIETH CENTURY

A. MIDDLE AGES
Classical Antiquity first arrived in Denmark (D.) in the 10th cent. AD with Christianity, which considered itself the legitimate heir of the Latin language and culture. The first great churches in Romanesque style, which were built during the 11th cent., are manifestations of a tradition of architecture which, like an unbroken chain, links the Middle Ages to Antiquity. Latin learning was international, and those who held key positions in the Danish Church had received their higher education abroad. Saxo Grammaticus' Latin *Gesta Danorum* (ca. 1186–1200) and the contribution to Scholastic linguistic philosophy, the *Modi significandi* of Martinus de Dacia (d. 1304), can be singled out as a noteworthy indications of a 12th cent. Renaissance. Stories about Troy appear to have been part of the popular oral tradition during the Middle Ages in D.

B. RENAISSANCE AND BAROQUE
The Renaissance reached D. ca. 1500. Whereas in medieval learned culture, Latin Antiquity had been the natural model that was followed even unconsciously, the 16th cent. criticism of medieval Latinity brought a new start which was also a return to ancient origins – in language, culture, and Christianity. A certain secularism made itself felt, as patronage became characteristic for king and nobility. King Christian II (1513–1523) was interested in modern culture and invited Dutch painters to his court. The scholar Christiern Pedersen (ca. 1480–1554), who published Saxo's history in Paris in 1514, set the trend for subsequent generations of intellectuals by means of his enthusiasm for indigenous culture and for Classical learning,.

The flowering of Latin culture during the reign of Frederik II (1559–1588) was strongly influenced by Philip Melanchthon. Supported by royal funding, young scholars of burgher stock were sent to leading Protestant universities in the German lands, first and foremost Wittenberg. An important amount of Neo-Latin poetry was composed by ambitious scholar-poets such as the imitator of Virgil, Erasmus Laetus (1526–1582), and the lyrical poet and epigrammatist Hans Jørgensen Sadolin (1528– ca. 1600). The pattern consisting of burgher poets working for noble patrons was broken by the astronomer and imitator of Ovid, Tycho Brahe (1546–1601), who belonged to the nobility. In medicine, Galen reigned in the university, while the Paracelsist Peder Sørensen (1540–1602) enjoyed a career as court physician.

This was also a period of great building activity, and noblemen as well as kings had castles constructed in the Renaissance style, decorated with sculpture, fountains, paintings and tapestries. Whereas the Latin poets were mainly Danes educated abroad, artists and architects were most often foreigners, or works of art were commissioned by Danish patrons in, for example, Dutch workshops.

During the reign of Christian IV (1588–1648), his court developed into one of the most elegant in Europe. His lavish festivals, especially the princely marriage of 1634, attracted musicians, poets and other artists, and the various entertainments were expressed in ancient imagery. His building activity was on a grand scale and has left its mark on Copenhagen. In 1658 Sweden conquered some of the richest regions (from then on, southernmost Sweden), and D. lost its Nordic supremacy. With absolutism introduced in 1660, however, the kings were still in a position to act as patrons.

Baroque poetry was characterized by the dynamics gradually shifting from Latin to the vernacular. Latin Literary forms were imitated in Danish, while the mental framework remained Roman – until Thomas Kingo (1634–1703) and other poets who composed in Danish began to favour German and Dutch models over Roman ones. However, the German poet Martin Opitz, who was very influential in D., was still, in both his Latin and German poetry, influenced by an ancient way of thinking, and so were his Danish adherents.

C. Rationalism and Neo-Classicism

Rationalism to some degree broke with the dominance of Classical Roman models, but not entirely; the great scholar and poet Ludvig Holberg (1684–1754) composed Latin epigrams in the tradition of John Owen, a satirical Latin novel, *Niels Klim* (*The Journey of Niels Klim to the World Underground*, 1741; trans. 2004), after the fashion of Thomas More and Jonathan Swift, and an impressive series of Danish-language comedies, which among their many models also count Plautus and Terence. The architect Nicolai Eigtved (1701–1754) built the royal palace of Amalienborg in Copenhagen in a rococo version of Antiquity, and

French sculptors and architects were invited to embellish this new residential area of the city.

Neo-Classicism brought a renewed interest in ancient Greek culture. Greek authors had been studied in D. since the 16th cent., but in general they had been considered inferior to their Roman successors. This picture began to change towards the end of the 18th cent.; the rising bourgeois class found their intellectual predecessors in → Athens rather than in → Rome. The sculptor Johannes Wiedewelt (1731–1802), a personal friend of Winckelmann, was instrumental in transmitting this scholar's enthusiasm for Greek art and architecture to D., and the architect C.F. Harsdorff (1735–1799) preferred Greek to Roman models; after a big fire in 1795 he led the rebuilding activities which transformed central Copenhagen into a mainly classicizing environment. Painters of the period, like the portrait painter Jens Juel (1745–1802), were also guided by Greek art. Nicolai Abildgaard (1743–1809) was employed by the king, but fascinated by the French Revolution, and an analysis of his favourite Classical motifs reveals a tacit subversiveness.

The sculptor Bertil Thorvaldsen (1768–1844) was the most important Danish classicist. As a young artist he preferred ancient Greek themes and represented them in an idealized style, such as his statue of Jason with the Golden Fleece, made in Rome in 1803. After the fall of Napoleon he changed his motifs to some degree, preferring themes from national history or the Bible; even these, however, were expressed in an artistic expressiveness modelled on ancient Greek sculpture. A museum was built for him in Copenhagen, and the architect Gottlieb Bindesbøll (1800–1856) demonstrated in this building a new understanding of ancient Greek architecture as having been richly coloured.

D. Nineteenth Century

In the middle of the 19th cent., Antiquity as an idealized vision of the past came to be replaced by the Nordic heritage. The leading Romanticist Adam Oehlenschläger (1779–1850) as well as the theologian and poet N.F.S. Grundtvig (1783–1872) were programmatic in their substitution of Nordic for ancient mythology, and for H.C. Andersen (1805–1875), the author of fairy-tales, Classical culture was of little importance. The philosopher Søren Kierkegaard (1813–1855), however, was fundamentally influenced by Classical Greek philosophy, not least by Socrates, whom he positioned within his intellectual system as the pagan counterpart to Christ.

The Greek war of independence had a great impact on Danish intellectuals. Close relations with Greece manifest themselves in the work of the architect brothers Christian (1803–1883) and Theophilus Hansen (1813–1891), who in their contributions to the embellishment of Athens as the new metropolis saw ancient and contemporary Greece as a united whole. The painter Constantin Hansen (1804–1880), in his fresco decoration of the entrance hall of the University of

Copenhagen, celebrated the freedom of science and scholarship through depictions of ancient Greek myths such as Prometheus forming human figures out of clay.

Two leading spirits in the breakthrough of modernism were both profoundly indebted to the study of Antiquity: the art historian Julius Lange (1830–1896) saw Periclean Athens as the ideal never surpassed, and his friend, the literary critic Georg Brandes (1842–1927), drew inspiration from Hellas for his programmatic demand that literature should be a vehicle of the free mind. His powerful biography of Caesar (1918) paints the portrait of a remarkable genius. At the same time, the two great patrons of art, the brewer I.C. Jacobsen (1811–1887) and his son Carl Jacobsen (1842–1914), invested unending energy and money in making ancient Greek and Roman sculpture accessible to the Danish public through their generous import of original works, supplemented by plaster casts of the most famous masterpieces. However, in the meantime the 'golden age' of Danish painters was turning from idealized Antiquity to Danish realism. The composer Carl Nielsen (1865–1931) mainly drew on national themes and folk traditions. A painting by Harald Giersing (1881–1927), *Paris' Dom* (allegedly representing the Judgment of Paris), might be seen as a memorial to the rejection of Antiquity, for it is the painter himself, his back turned to the onlooker, who is surveying three female models in his atelier (1909).

E. Twentieth Century

Even though in the course of the 20th cent. Antiquity became the object of study rather than a 'source of inspiration', the sculptor Rudolph Tegner (1873–1950) gave form to ancient figures such as Oedipus, and in many of his other works elaborated on ancient patterns. At the opposite end of the political spectrum, the communist intellectual Otto Gelsted (1888–1968) devoted a large part of his life to making Greek literature accessible to the Danish working class through translations of Attic drama and paraphrases of Homer; in his own poetry he made extensive use of Greek thought. Nis Petersen (1897–1943) wrote a historical novel set in the time of Marcus Aurelius, *Sandelmagernes Gade* (1931). Antiquity also plays an important role in the works of Karen Blixen (1885–1962).

The most eminent classicist of recent times was Villy Sørensen (1929–2001). Ebbe Kløvedal Reich (1940–2005) depicts in his historical novels many scenes from ancient Rome that are mainly interpreted as metaphors for the EU of modern times. In the graphic art of Palle Nielsen (1920–2000) Orpheus and Eurydice have been guiding figures, and Per Kirkeby (b. 1938) borrowed some of his themes in ancient Greece. The film-maker Lars von Trier (b. 1956) based his first television production on the myth of *Medea* (1987).

These examples do not alter the fact that ancient culture has little relevance in present-day D., even though classics in translation continue to be sold and read, and Greek drama is often performed, drawing considerable audiences.

→ Antiquities collections; → Baroque; → Cast; Cast collections; → Classicism; → Renaissance

1 J. P. Christianson, On Tycho's Island. Tycho Brahe and his Assistants, 1570–1601, 2000   2 K. Friis-Jensen, Saxo Grammaticus as Latin Poet, 1987   3 I. Haugsted, The Architect Christian Hansen, in: Analecta Romana Instituti Danici 10, 1982, 53–96   4 M. Skafte Jensen (ed.), A History of Nordic Neo-Latin Literature, 1995   5 M. Skafte Jensen, Friendship and Poetry. Sudies in Danish Neo-Latin Literature, M. Pade, K. Skovgaard-Petersen, P. Zeeberg (eds.), 2004 (Renaessancestudier 11.)   6 P. Kragelund, The Church, the Revolution, and the 'Peintre Philosophe'. A Study in the Art of Nicolai Abildgaard, in: Hafnia 9, 1983, 25–65   7 M. Leisner-Jensen, Holberg et le Latin, in: Analecta Romana Instituti Danici 15, 1986, 151–180   8 H. Raabyemagle, C. M. Smidt (eds.), Classicism in Copenhagen: Architecture in the age of C.F. Hansen, J. Lundskaer-Nielsen (trans.), photographs by J. Lindhe, 1998   9 S. H. Rossel, A History of Danish Literature, 1992   10 K. Skovgaard-Petersen, Historiography at the court of Christian IV (1588–1648). Studies in the Latin Histories of Denmark by Johannes Pontanus and Johannes Meursius, 2002 (Renaessancestudier 12.)   11 H. M. Svendsen, W. Svendsen, Geschichte der dänischen Literatur, 1964 (trans. of the original Danish edition)   12 M. Wade, Heinrich Schütz and 'det Store Bilager' in Copenhagen (1634), in: Schütz-Jahrbuch 11, 1989, 32–52   13 Id., Festival Books as Historical Literature: The Reign of Christian IV of Denmark (1596–1648), in: The Seventeenth Century 7, 1992, 14   14 P. Zeeberg, Tycho Brahes 'Urania Titani' – et digt om Sophie Brahe, 1994.

MINNA SKAFTE JENSEN

II. History of Classical Scholarship
A. Up to 1750   B. After 1750   C. Periodicals

A. Up to 1750

Regular instruction in the Latin and Greek languages on a higher level began in the Kingdom of D. with the reopening of the University of Copenhagen after the Reformation in 1537; the aim was to provide an adequate education for theologians. Up until the 19th cent., many students, doctoral candidates and professors, often supported by royal grants, went on extended study visits abroad. The resulting international relations helped Danish scholarly and scientific institutions stay abreast of the latest developments even in fields where they did not do primary research work. Aside from producing text books for schools and universities, Danish philologists explored antiquarian subjects and the history of the Latin language (Ole Borch, 1636–1690) as well as early Danish history and the runes. The considerable interest shown by European scholars in this expansion of European pre-history is reflected in the correspondence of Ole Worm (1588–1654) and the relations entertained by Joh. Rhodius during his 37-year stay in Padua. These scholarly studies culminated in the systematic edition of the medieval sources on Danish history (1772ff.).

B. After 1750

In the middle of the 18th cent., the Danish Crown sent two scientific expeditions to Egypt and the Middle East, the second of which was led by Carsten Niebuhr (1733–1815). Based on the manuscripts and transcripts collected during these and later travels, Danish Oriental studies delivered impressive yields in the decipherment efforts of Fr. Münter (1761–1830), Rasmus Rask (1787–1832) and N.L. Westergaard (1815–1878). In 1818 R. Rask published his theory positing the interrelatedness of certain Indo-European languages. Even though he lived his entire life in Rome, G. Zoega (1755–1809), a former pupil of Heyne in Göttingen, exercised considerable influence on Classical scholarship in D. P.O. Brønsted (1780–1842) travelled in Greece (1810–1814) and wrote descriptions of the Parthenon.

In a series of tracts on Cicero and Lucretius from 1825 until the publication of Cicero's *De finibus* in 1839, J.N. Madvig, given to polemic at times, but also working with colleagues in German-speaking countries (esp. Orelli, Zumpt and Lachmann), developed fundamental principles of textual criticism: the genealogical relationship between manuscripts (stemmatics) and the definition of the archetype [1]. J.N. Madvig's (1804–1886) philological activities included textual and conjectural criticism of Greek and Latin (prose) authors, books on Latin (1841) and Greek (1846) grammar (both translated into all major European languages), writings on general grammar with polemic tendencies against the Romantic philosophy of language, as well as a work on the Roman constitution and administration. He also left his mark on Danish → SCHOOLS as a cultural organizer and politician, and he fostered a generation of Danish philologists whose editions and text-critical studies were widely influential, e.g. J.L. Ussing (1820–1905, commentary on Plautus), M.Cl. Gertz (1844–1929, Seneca), J.L. Heiberg (1854–1928, Archimedes, Greek commentators on Aristotle, Euclid, Hippocrates, Greek mathematicians), K. Hude (1860–1936, Herodotus, Thucydides, Lysias), A.B. Drachmann (1860–1935, Scholia vetera in Pindari carmina, Diodorus), Ada Adler (1878–1946, Suidas), J. Ræder (1869–1959, Oribasius, Theodoretus), W. Norvin (1878–1940, Olympiodorus). Heiberg initiated the international cooperation in the publication of the *Corpus Medicorum Graecorum*, to which he and other Danish philologists contributed several issues. Similiarly, Carsten Høeg (1896–1961) initiated the international edition of the *Monumenta Musicae Byzantinae* (begun in 1935).

From the end of the 19th cent. onwards, there was a growing desire to expound in detail problems of cultural history and the interpretation of ancient works in the form of tracts, articles and handbooks. New fields of study were embraced in the process: philosophy, esp. Plato and → NEO- PLATONISM, the lexicography of → MIDDLE LATIN (Fr. Blatt, 1903–1979), Roman history (A. Afzelius, 1905–1957), the history of technology (A.G. Drachmann, 1891–1980); aspects of intellec-

tual history were also investigated (above all by the religious historians V. Grønbech, 1873–1948, and H. Frisch, 1893–1950). Chr. Blinkenberg (1863–1948) directed and published (1941) the excavations at Lindos (1902–1905); Knud Friis Johansen (1887–1971) confirmed the Early Archaic chronology in his examination of proto-Corinthian vases. Frederik Poulsen (1876–1950) made outstanding contributions to the study of Greek and Roman portraiture.

Research in recent decades (cf. the near-complete list of currently active scholars and the bibliography in [2]) has shown a particular interest in methodology. Without diminishing the achievements in traditional fields, especially epic, drama and philosophy, Hellenistic culture, Byzantine studies, the Latin Middle Ages and reception history are major areas of specialization. Numerous classical authors are made accessible to wider audiences through modern translations. Some of the latest cooperative projects have focused on the political structures in Greece, the *Corpus Philosophorum Danicorum Medii Aevi* and Nordic Neo-Latin literature.

Classical Studies are taught at three of the five Danish universities: Copenhagen, Aarhus (since 1930) and Odense (since 1966).

C. Periodicals

Nordisk Tidskrift for Filologi, København 1859–1919. *Museum Tusculanum* 1967–1987; contributions to both these publications were in Scandinavian languages only. *Classica et Mediaevalia*, 1938ff., with contributions in English, French and German.

→ ANCIENT LANGUAGES, TEACHING OF; → ANCIENT NEAR EASTERN PHILOLOGY AND HISTORY (ASSYRIOLOGY); → DECIPHERMENT; → DIGESTA; TEXTUAL TRANSMISSION; → LINGUISTICS; → MUSIC; → SCHOOL TEXTBOOKS

SOURCES 1 S. TIMPANARO, La genesi del Metodo del Lachmann, 31985, 49–62 (Engl. G. W. MOST, (ed. and trans.), The Genesis of Lachmann's Method, 2005) 2 C. G. TORTZEN, A. BÜLOW-JACOBSEN, Græsk, latin-og sidenhen. Tolv års forskning ved de klassiske institutter (1978–1989). Et flyveskrift og en bibliografi, 1989

LITERATURE 3 FL. G. ANDERSEN, Danmark og Antikken 1980–1991. En bibliografi over 12 års dansksproget litteratur om den klassiske oldtid, 1994 4 Id., Danish Contributions to Classical Scholarship 1971–1991. A Bibliography, 2004 5 K. ELKJÆR, P. KRARUP, G. MONDRUP, Danmark og Antiken ²1968 (bibliography 1836–1968) 6 B. J. KRISTENSEN, J. M. KRISTENSEN, Danmark og Antikken 1968–1979, 1982 7 P. A. HANSEN, A Bibliography of Danish Contributions to Classical Scholarship from the Sixteenth Century to 1970, 1977 8 P. J. JENSEN et al., Københavns Universitet 1479–1979, 1979–1990, vol. 8, 69–474; vol. 11, 121–157 9 Id., J.N. Madvig. Avec une esquisse de l'histoire de la philologie classique au Danemark, 1981 10 Johan Nicolai Madvig. Et Mindeskrift, 2 vols., 1955–1963. GIUSEPPE TORRESIN

Deutsche Orient-Gesellschaft A scholarly society, founded Jan. 1, 1898, with the task "of promoting the study of Oriental Antiquity ... to support ... the efforts of the Royal Berlin Museum toward the acquisition of Oriental antiquities and monuments of art and general culture and to disseminate ... the knowledge of the results of research on Oriental Antiquity" (session of 1902). The moving force behind the society was the textile wholesaler, patron of the arts and philanthropist James Simon (1851–1932). The rapid success of the Deutsche Orient-Gesellschaft (DOG) was due to the cooperation between scholars and representatives of the haute bourgeoisie, the aristocracy, the political and administrative class; to encouragement by Emperor Wilhelm II (declared 'Protector' of the DOG in 1901), and to the great public interest in the newly discovered connections between the OT and ancient Mesopotamia (beginning in 1902, the so-called *Babel-Bible controversy*, following public lectures at the DOG by F. Delitzsch; see → BABYLON). The first president was Prince H. zu Schoenaich-Carolath (1852–1920), and his lieutenant and successor Admiral F. von Hollmann (1842–1913), who belonged to the emperor's inner circle and used this influence for the benefit of the DOG. In 1901, B. Güterbock (1858–1940) became Secretary, and in this capacity participated decisively in the activity of the DOG until 1936. The DOG achieved its highest membership in 1913, with 1510 members.

The DOG's first excavation took place from 1899–1917, under the direction of R. Koldewey (1855–1925) at Babylon. The excavation of Assur began in 1903, under the direction of W. Andrae (1875–1956); it was completed in 1914. New excavation techniques (structural history, town planning, the preparation of clay bricks) and of documentation were developed at Babylon and Assur, which were fundamental for the subsequent development of → NEAR EASTERN ARCHAEOLOGY. In Babylon, it was above all the public buildings of the time of Nebuchadnezzar II (6th cent. BC) that were investigated (including the Ištar-gate with the processional street; reconstruction with original enamel reliefs in the Near Eastern Museum at Berlin; and the palaces, especially the 'south citadel', the main Esagil temple and the Etemenanki temple tower). In Assur, the question of the ancient history of Assyria, still little known at the time, stood in the foreground. Excavations focused above all on the temple and palace areas (including the temple of Aššur, the archaic and more recent temple of Ištar, the temple of Anu-Adad, and the temple of Sin-Šamaš); however, living quarters were also uncovered in extensive exploratory digs.

On the margins of the two long-term projects at Babylon and Assur, shorter-term investigations were carried out at nearby ruins (Borsippa, Kisurra: Abū Hatab, Šuruppak: Farā, Hatra, Kar-Tukulti-Ninurta). Beginning in 1902, the DOG broadened its activities to areas outside of Mesopotamia (Egypt: Abusir, Abusir el-Meleq, Amarna: find of the bust of Nefertiti; Palestine: participation in the excavation at Megiddo, surveys of Galilean synagogues, Jericho; Turkey: Hattuša/Boğazköy). In 1913, the DOG included a further great Mesopotamian urban ruin in its excavation program with Uruk (Warka). Finds from the DOG's Mesopotamian excavations have moulded the Near Eastern Museum at Berlin until today.

World War I put an end to the heyday of the DOG. Membership shrank to approximately 900, and state subsidies dwindled appreciably. Since excavations in the Near East were initially no longer feasible for political and financial reasons, the DOG concentrated on the publication of its excavation results. By the end of the 1920s it set excavations in motion once again, although they were limited in extent. The most important was the excavation at Hattusa, which was taken up once again in 1931, in honour of James Simon on the occasion of his 80th birthday.

For the DOG, which was supported precisely by the cultural interest and personal and financial commitment of its numerous members of Jewish descent, the era of National Socialism spelled a decline into insignificance. The high reputation of its president F. Schmidt-Ott (1860–1956), who had been Prussian Minister of Education in the Weimar Republic and co-founder of the future Deutsche Forschungsgemeinschaft (DFG), enabled the DOG to be re-founded as early as 1947. Walter Andrae, the excavator of Assur and Director of the Near Eastern Museum, became president in 1949.

The excavations at Hattusa (1952) and Uruk (1954) were taken up once again, in cooperation between the → DEUTSCHES ARCHÄOLOGISCHES INSTITUT and the DOG, with financing by the DFG. On the initiative of its President Ernst Heinrich (1899–1984), the DOG inaugurated two excavations in Syria in 1969, in the area of the future Lake Assad on the middle Euphrates (1969–1975: Habūaba Kabīra, under the direction of E. Strommenger; 1969–1995: Ekalte/Tall Munbāqa, directed since 1979 by D. Machule). A further dig in Syria was devoted to Tall Bīʿa near Raqqa, where, under the leadership of E. Strommenger from 1980–1995, parts of the ancient oriental city Tuttul were uncovered. Since 1995, the DOG has supported excavations at the Hittite city of Šarišša (Kušakli) near Sivas (under the leadership of A. Müller-Karpe), and since 1996–1998 it has promoted a systematic surface survey of the environs of Hattusa (under the leadership of R. Czichon). With excavations further on (a.o. Tell Mozan/Urkes, Qatra) relations were set about for cooperation since 1998. Immediately following German reunification, the DOG, in collaboration with the Near Eastern Museum, set in motion a longer-term project for the processing and publication of the numerous unpublished finds from the excavations at Assur. In 2004 the DOG counted 1036 members. Since its foundation, the publishing organs of the DOG have been the *Mitteilungen* (MDOG; volume 130 appeared in 1998), the *Wissenschaftliche Veröffentlichungen* (WVDOG; 97 volumes as of 1998), and the *Sendschriften der DOG*.

They were joined in 1953 by the *Abhandlungen* (ADOG, 23 volumes as of 1998) and, since 1997, *Colloquien* (CDOG) and the *Studien zu den Assur-Texten* (StAT).

→ Amarna; → Assur; → Babylon; → Esagil; → Ḫattusa; → Jericho; → Uruk

→ BERLIN, VORDERASIATISCHES MUSEUM

> E. v. SCHULER, 70 Jahre Deutsche Orient-Gesellschaft, in: MDOG 100, 1968, 6–21; G. WILHELM (ed.), Zwischen Tigris und Nil, 1998
> URL http://www.orientgesellschaft.de/

GERNOT WILHELM

Deutsches Archäologisches Institut

A. GENERAL   B. STRUCTURE UND ORGANISATION
C. HISTORY   D. TASKS AND OBJECTIVES

A. GENERAL

The Deutsches Archäologisches Institut (DAI) is one of the oldest German research institutions and is currently the most important establishment in Germany in the field of international archaeological research. Its origins go back to 1829. The DAI is a scholarly corporation with its own charter; it is under the authority of the Foreign Office, and has its head office in Berlin. The focus of its activity lies on the Mediterranean region and the Near East.

B. STRUCTURE UND ORGANISATION

The head office of the DAI, with the seat of the president, its scholarly department with library, and its administration, is in Berlin, while foreign departments are located at Rome, Athens, Cairo, Istanbul and Madrid. Based in Germany are the → RÖMISCH-GERMANISCHE KOMMISSION in Frankfurt, the *Kommission für Alte Geschichte und Epigraphik* in Munich, the *Kommission für Allgemeine und Vergleichende Archäologie* in Bonn, the Orient Department in Berlin, with field offices in Baghdad, Sanaa and Damascus, and the Eurasia Department, also in Berlin, with a field office in Tehran. The highest supervisory and executive board is the Central Directorate, which determines the budget, the scientific programme and the acceptance of publications; it also elects the president and the directors of departments and commissions. It consists of the president, a representative of the Foreign Office, the directors of departments and commissions, the General Director of the *Römisch-Germanisches Zentralmuseum* in Mainz, a representative of the museums of antiquities, ten university professors in Classical archaeology from the various federal states, as well as one representative each from the fields of → EGYPTOLOGY, ANCIENT HISTORY, → ARCHAEOLOGICAL STRUCTURAL RESEARCH, → CHRISTIAN ARCHAEOLOGY, → CLASSICAL PHILOLOGY, → NEAR EASTERN ARCHAEOLOGY, Prehistory and Protohistory. The commissions of the DAI have their own charters and executive boards. The subject area committees of the departments in Cairo, Istanbul and Madrid, as well as of the Orient and Eurasia de-

partments, have an advisory function. They are made up of researchers from the various sub-disciplines covered in the research areas of these departments.

C. HISTORY

The history of the DAI reflects its purpose as an internationally-oriented research institute. Its foundation falls into the period when archaeology was being established as a scholarly discipline, and it has contributed decisively to the development of archaeology.

The idea of founding an archaeological institution arose among the 'Roman Hyperboreans', a private group of friends composed of European scholars, artists and diplomats in Rome, who were firmly committed to the promotion of archaeological research. The intentions and aims surrounding the foundation of the Institute had already been expressed in the drafts of the statutes for a Hyperborean Roman Society. It was recognized that a scientific understanding of the rapidly increasing archaeological material required organized international collaboration, as well as the systematic publication of monuments. An organizational framework was to be provided by the *Istituto di Corrispondenza Archeologica* . The archaeologist Eduard Gerhard, the Prussian envoy Christian Carl Josias von Bunsen, the Hanoverian chargé d'affaires at Rome August Kestner, the Commissario delle antichità di Roma Carlo Fea and the great Danish sculptor Bertel Thorvaldsen called for its foundation on 2 January 1829. The constitutive session took place on 21 April, the mythical anniversary of the foundation of Rome, in the Palazzo Caffarelli, the seat of the Prussian embassy on the Capitol. The Prussian crown prince, who later became King Friedrich Wilhelm IV, took on the role of patron, while the Duke de Blacas d'Aulps, an influential French envoy at the court of Naples, was persuaded to assume the presidency, a position which was intended for political and social representation. From 1841 it was held by the Austrian chancellor Prince Clemens of Metternich, after whose death in 1859 it was abolished. The management of affairs was the responsibility of the secretaries (now the directors), lead by the secretary-general (now the president).

The aim of the newly founded Institute was to collect and disseminate all archaeological discoveries and materials in the field of Classical Antiquity; the emphasis was on Italy and Greece, though Egypt and the Near East were also included. Collection of information and drawings was to take place by means of a system of corresponding members (*socii ordinarii*), which was distributed across the whole of Europe, while the regular members (*membri*) were responsible for delivering scientific contributions and accepting publications. The European organization of archaeological correspondence was assisted by sections of the Institute in Italy, France, Germany and England; the Parisian section in particular, under its secretary the Duc de Luynes, a noted patron of the arts, intermittently displayed energetic activity. The journals *Bulletino* and *Annali dell'*

Instituto di Corrispondenza Archeologica, as well as the *Serie Monumenti Inediti* were used for publications.

The idea and concept of the Institute mainly go back to Gerhard. With his academic appointment to Berlin in 1833 a development began, over the course of which the management increasingly shifted to Berlin. At the same time, the pan-European structure of the Institute declined because of the diverging nationalist tendencies of the participating countries. 1836 saw the construction of the first of the Institute's buildings, still modest, in the area of the Prussian embassy on the Capitol; from 1842 the Secretaries and from 1859 the all expenses were paid by the Prussian Ministry of Culture. After the revolutionary year of 1848, the central directorate, originally made up of scholars from various European countries, only consisted of German members. The formal transformation of the Institute into an institution of the Prussian state took place in 1871, and in 1874 it was named the *Kaiserlich-Deutsches Archäologisches Institut*. This development "from an international private association into a Prussian state institution" (Deichmann) was not the result of a deliberate 'usurpation' of the Institute by Prussia, but reflects the political developments of the time. Such an early attempt to create a lasting international institution was as yet destined to fail.

The foundation of the Institute at Rome in many respects indicated the direction that the organization of scholarly archaeology would take. Here the idea that the evidence base of archaeological research could only be developed through the systematic collection and publication of all monuments, even the most humble, was first realised. Up-to-date publication of discoveries and research results for the first time took a continuous, internationally-oriented form in the *Bulletino* and the *Annali dell'Istituto*, the earliest specialized archaeological journals.

The creation of a permanent, cosmopolitan research facility in the centre of the ancient world was decisive and provided direction. The establishment of an archaeological reference library, open to all researchers, was a novelty in Classical Studies. This library, together with the regular public lectures and debates (the so-called *adunanze*), soon made the Institute at Rome a centre of scholarly archaeology, which at that time was flourishing throughout Europe. In addition to its significant research and publication activity, the Institute gave both established and junior scholars from Germany the opportunity for long research stays in Rome, especially after 1874, when it was able to move into a considerably larger building on the Capitol. This enabled them to encounter the original monuments of Antiquity and the people and culture of Italy, as well as colleagues from many European countries.

Just how forward-looking the concept of the Institute was can be measured by the fact that it became a model for other nations who subsequently founded similar institutes in Athens (the → ÉCOLE FRANÇAISE D'ATHÈNES, since 1846) and Rome and later also in other countries of the Mediterranean and the Near East. As a base for research and exchange with the host countries these have become an indispensable element of world-wide archaeological collaboration. In keeping with its original objectives, the scholarly work of the Roman Institute focused on the discovery and publication of monuments by editing fundamental museum catalogues and collective volumes, as well as by undertaking local cultural, historical and geographical research. The DAI first took part in archaeological fieldwork and investigations of standing buildings only after the second World War. Initially these were smaller projects with limited aims, such as the excavations at Policoro, Rusellae, → POMPEII and Santa Maria d'Anglona near Policoro or structural research of the city walls at Pompeii and of the buildings complex in the Villa Hadriana near Tivoli. Since the 1960s these research activities have been extended considerably and have led to long-term research enterprises in greater Greece (Metapontum, Sybaris, Syracuse, Segesta, Selinunte) and Tunisia (Chemtou, Carthage). In the field of → CHRISTIAN ARCHAEOLOGY, the Institute participated in such projects as the survey of the catacombs and the publication of their paintings in Rome.

At the same time as the *Institut für archäologische Korrespondenz* was transformed into the *Deutsches Archäologisches Institut*, a regional branch was founded at Athens. Research activity in Greece had been lively since the Greek War of Independence, supported by the *Griechische Archäologische Gesellschaft*, which was founded in 1837. German archaeologists and architects were involved in it alongside other European scholars. A French Archaeological Institute existed in Athens from 1846, followed by the foundation of similar Institutes by America and Britain in 1882 and 1895. From the beginning, the emphasis of the work of the Athens Institute was on local archaeological history, topographical surveys and excavations, unlike the situation in Rome. In addition to numerous smaller excavations carried out by the Athenian Institute in many parts of Greece, four large-scale, long-term research projects in particular have been maintained until today. As 'Imperial excavations', the excavations in → OLYMPIA were directed from Berlin, and were not transferred to the responsibility of the DAI until 1937, but from the outset they were closely linked to the Athenian department of the DAI. Archaeological excavation derived decisive methodological impulses from this first systematic large-scale excavation within classical archaeology, which focused not merely on individual monuments but investigated the totality of buildings and finds in their historical context. The excavations begun by Schliemann at Tiryns were continued by the DAI from 1905, while the excavations on Samos, begun under the auspices of the Berlin Museum, became the responsibility of the DAI from 1925, and the excavations begun at the Kerameikos in Athens by the *Griechische Archäologische Gesellschaft* were continued by the DAI from 1913. The DAI Athens also supports the projects of German universities and of researchers in Greece and carries out standing buildings research and regional studies.

At the turn of the century and under the growing influence of → HISTORICISM, the interests and aims of archaeological research had moved away from the Classicistic view of Antiquity and the methodology of its origins, which had been determined primarily by philology and art history, towards empirical knowledge, which focused on the results of field research. In this context, the foundation in 1902 of the *Römisch-Germanische Kommission* (RGK) in Frankfurt signified a decisive and timely expansion of the DAI's field of activities. This new branch was to be an institutional focal point for research into prehistory and Roman provincial archaeology (→ PROVINCIAL ARCHAEOLOGY), which until then had been carried out primarily by regional establishments for the preservation of monuments and by antiquarian societies, as well as by the *Reichslimeskommission*.

The RGK did not initially undertake its own excavations, but participated in pre-existing projects, e.g. at Haltern or Trier. The emphasis of its activity lay on promoting systematic studies and on the publication of research results–in summary form–in journals, series and monographs. Because of its research and its constantly growing specialist library, the RGK has developed into an important research centre for the pre- and protohistoric archaeology of Europe and the archaeology of the Roman provinces, and its sphere of influence extends far beyond national borders. In the decades of the political division of Europe following the Second World War, the RGK thus became the most important point of connection between 'Western' archaeology and the scholars and institutions of the countries of Eastern and Southeastern Europe. Only in more recent times has the RGK also carried out its own excavations. The most extensive investigation of this kind has been that of the Celtic oppidum of Manching, which has been ongoing since 1955. There have also been problem-oriented investigations of Roman fortifications and settlements, as well as, recently, excavations of the extensive offensive and defensive installations at Alesia (in Burgundy) from the time of its siege by Caesar, of the Iron Age hillfort at Soto de Bureba in Spain, and of prehistoric settlement sites at Kirklareli in Turkish Thrace. These were partly undertaken in collaboration with local researchers. After German reunification, as a result of which the RGK was able to take on the personnel and projects of the *Zentralinstitut für Alte Geschichte und Archäologie der Akademie der Wissenschaften der DDR* (ZIAGA), work began on the German-Bulgarian excavation of the Late Roman military base at Iatrus/Krivina, and on the German-Polish research project *Mensch und Umwelt im Odergebiet in ur- und frühgeschichtlicher Zeit* (humans and the environment in the Oder area in pre- and protohistory). A further example, typical of the RGK's aims and international orientation, is the coordination and publication of Roman finds in barbarian Europe (*Corpus der römi-*

schen Funde im europäischen Barbaricum), which involves scholars from all over Northern, Central, and Eastern Europe.

The subsequent growth of the DAI was also determined by the dramatic development of archaeology since the late 19th cent. in the area of excavations and new discoveries, far beyond Italy and Greece. This development found visible expression in the opening of departments of the Institute at Cairo and Istanbul in 1929, the centennial of the DAI. In both cases pre-existing German research institutions were continued or taken over.

The precursor of the DAI in Cairo was the *Deutsche Institut für ägyptische Altertumskunde*, founded in 1907. In conjunction with the → DEUTSCHE ORIENT-GESELLSCHAFT, the Berlin Museums and the Berlin Academy, this Institute had already developed extensive research and excavation activities in Egypt (Abusir, Amarna, etc.), which were then continued and expanded by the DAI. The Institute was responsible for all cultures of Egypt, from the Neolithic to the Islamic Middle Ages, with particular emphasis on ancient Egyptian civilizations. From the outset, the emphasis of the department's research activity lay on field research and its publication. Particularly since its re-opening in 1955, after the Second World War, excavation activities have been expanded to many areas: e.g. the methodical excavation and investigation of the city of Elephantine on southern border and its history of more than 3000 years; long-term investigations of the necropoleis and the funeray temple of Sethos I west of Thebes, of the pyramids and necropoleis of Dashur and of Buto, the prehistoric capital of Lower Egypt; re-excavations in the royal necropolis of Abydos, with results important for the early history of Egypt; urban excavation and investigation of the oracle temple in the Oasis of Siwa; large-scale investigation of the early Christian town and pilgrimage site of St. Menas (Abu Mina), as well as standing buildings research and restorations of Islamic buildings in the old city of Cairo.

In Istanbul, the foundation of a department of the DAI in 1929 followed on from a research station which the Königlich-Preußisches Museum at Berlin had maintained there from the end of the 19th cent. for excavations in Pergamum, Magnesia, Priene, Miletus, and Didyma. Even before it was established on the Bosphorus the DAI had increasingly engaged in archaeological field research in Anatolia and all of Asia Minor, partly through the Athens department (Troy, Gordion, Pergamum) and partly also from Berlin (Boğazköy). In addition to the prehistory of Anatolia and Classical Antiquity, the area of responsibility of the DAI Istanbul also included Christian archaeology, → BYZANTINE STUDIES and Oriental studies. The department's research programme was correspondingly varied: it continued and resumed older large-scale excavations in western Turkey, but it also focused on the excavation, standing buildings research and topographical survey of Late Antique, Byzantine and Islamic buildings in Istanbul and Iznik. The long-term systematic excavations at Boğazköy led to the discovery of Hittite culture and history, which had hitherto been virtually unknown. These older research projects are still continuing. After the Second World War, excavations at → AEZANI were began again and, more recently, the investigation of Neolithic settlements in southeast Anatolia.

The establishment of a branch in Madrid, which had been planned since 1929, was realized in 1943, but until the end of the war it was not able to transcend its modest beginnings. Only after its reopening in 1957 did it develop intense research activities in many areas of pre- and protohistoric, Roman, Visigothic and Islamic periods of the Iberian peninsula, and to some extent also in Morocco. Important excavation and research projects are, i.a.: the early Bronze Age settlements of Zambujal (Portugal) and Fuente Alamo, Phoenician trading stations near Torre del Mar, the terraced shrine and urban site of Roman Munigua, and the monumental late Antique mausoleum (possibly of the emperor Constans) at Centcelles near Tarragona. In 1971, a branch of the Madrid division was opened at Lisbon, which carried out smaller-scale research on the prehistory and Roman period of Portugal.

The incorporation in 1967 of the *Kommission für Alte Geschichte und Epigraphik* in Munich, which had been founded in 1951, signified an important extension of the spectrum of the disciplines covered by the DAI. The emphasis of its activities lies on epigraphy and numismatics, which are particularly closely connected with archaeology. Its activities include the work on and publication of inscriptions and coins from the DAI's excavations, the publication of Latin inscriptions of the Iberian peninsula in the context of the CIL, the publication of the *Sylloge nummorum graecorum Deutschland* and monograph series on ancient history.

In the Near East pioneering excavations and discoveries had already been made by German archaeologists (Babylon, Assur) since the late 19th cent., primarily through the *Deutsche Orient-Gesellschaft*. However, the DAI did not manage to secure its position there until after the Second World War. With the emergence of independent states the preconditions had arisen for the establishment of permanent branches of the Institute, which were in the mutual interest of German and local research. The Baghdad department, which opened in 1955, devoted itself primarily to the intensive and large-scale excavation of Uruk, which shed light on the history and nature of this city from the early Sumerian to the Hellenistic-Parthian period. In addition, the excavations in Babylon were continued in a limited way. As a result of the war that began in Iraq in 1980, the Baghdad department was so restricted in its ability to work that its library and personnel initially had to be evacuated to Berlin. In 1996, the division was integrated into the newly-founded Oriental department of the DAI as a foreign branch.

With the foundation of a department at Teheran in 1961, the DAI linked up with significant German schol-

arship and publications on the archaeology and the history of Islamic art in Iran and soon developed extensive research activities in the country. Excavations were carried out above all in the main Sassanid capital Takht-i Suleiman, as well as near Bistum and in the Urartian provincial town of Bastam (Azerbaidjan). Standing buildings and art historical investigations of Achaemenid and Sassanid monuments (Persepolis, Firuzabad, Qaleh Dukhtar) were also undertaken, as well as extensive field research on Islamic caravanserais. The Islamic revolution of 1979 forced scholars to withdraw from Teheran to Berlin. Since then only research trips for local-historical and standing buildings investigations have been possible. Since 1995 the department has been a foreign branch of the Eurasia department of the DAI.

The DAI's research in the Near East was considerably strengthened and enriched by the establishment of smaller foreign branches in Yemen and in Syria. The branch in Sanaa, which opened in 1978, focuses on the ancient South Arabian civilisation: e.g. excavations and research in Marib, the capital of the kingdom of the Sabaeans, in Sirwah, as well as of the Bronze Age settlement of Sabir near Aden. The branch in Damascus, which opened in 1980, focuses its research activities above all on the Roman, early Christian and Islamic monuments of Syria: excavation of the caliphal city of Raqqa and the early Christian pilgrimage town of Resafa; research into the architecture and urban development in the ancient cities of the Hauran, and other Imperial period monuments of the country; and the history of Islamic architecture. Since 1996, the DAI's archaeological research in the Near East has been centralized in the Orient department, which has its seat in Berlin and maintains foreign branches in Baghdad, Sanaa and Damascus.

In 1979, on the occasion of the DAI's 150th anniversary, the *Kommission für Allgemeine und Vergleichende Archäologie* (KAVA) was founded, with its head office in Bonn. The DAI thereby took account of the wider development of archaeology, which had long transcended the boundaries of the ancient world and now enabled basic research on all past cultures of the world. The aim of the Bonn branch was to contribute to the study of the culture and history of other parts of the world through clearly defined field research projects, and to investigate characteristic intercultural phenomena through comprehensive studies, conferences and publications. The KAVA's research currently focuses on Guatemala, Sri Lanka, Nepal, Morocco and Vietnam.

The most recent expansion of the Institute was a consequence of German reunification. In 1992, the DAI took on a number of the personnel and archaeological institutions of the former *Zentralinstitut für Alte Geschichte und Archäologie der Akademie der Wissenschaften der DDR*. Initially they were affiliated as *Arbeitsbereich für Ur- und Frühgeschichte* of the *Römisch-Germanische Kommission*, as a Berlin branch. With this enlargement, the archaeological sciences also made their entry in the DAI (archaeobotany, zooarchaelogy, dendrochronology and radiocarbon dating). In 1995, the expansion led to the formation of the Eurasia department, whose field of activity lies in Eastern Europe and Central Asia. Thus it has become possible to react appropriately to a political situation which has completely changed after the breakup of the Soviet Union and to renew relations with the countries of this region, which had largely come to a halt for decades. In the few years since its foundation, the Eurasia department has already developed an extensive programme of excavation, research and publications: including excavations of the Greek colony of Tanais on the Don; in the late Bronze Age urban site at Jarkutan in Uzbekistan; in various cemeteries and kurgans in southern Siberia and Kazakhstan; and further research projects in Georgia and Tadjikistan.

D. TASKS AND OBJECTIVES

The research mandate of the DAI embraces all areas of archaeology and its auxiliary disciplines, with particular emphasis on basic research and making source material accessible. This is primarily pursued through excavations and archaeological and regional studies, as well as through standing buildings research, the systematic photographic documentation of monuments and collections and the editing of publications. Excavations are carried out in close collaboration with the archaeological authorities and institutions of the host countries. Typical of the DAI's work are its long-term projects and interdisciplinarity, through which sites of particular historical importance can be investigated systematically and comprehensively over a fairly long period. A traditional focus of the Institute's work, and closely connected with its excavation activity, is standing buildings research, i.e. recording and making scientifically accessible the structural monuments of Greco-Roman Antiquity, the Near East and Egypt, of early Christianity and of Islam. Connections within architectural history, and in particular with the technical universities, are maintained by the architectural department of the central office. A sub-field of → ARCHAEOLOGICAL STRUCTURAL RESEARCH (standing buildings archaeology) that is increasingly gaining in importance is the conservation and restoration of ancient architecture. In contrast to the 19th cent., researchers now have the responsibility not to abandon historical monuments and excavation sites after they have been exposed, but to secure the original inventory against further decay, and, within reasonable limits, to make the sites accessible for visitors by means of cautious additions. The DAI complies with this obligation within its own projects and also takes on the scientific planning and direction of restoration projects that are financed and carried out by other institutions.

One of the DAI's most important tasks is the dissemination of research results through publications. Every branch publishes an annual journal and at least one monograph series; the head office publishes the *Jahrbuch des DAI* and the quarterly *Archäologischer Anzeiger*, as well as most book publications. These periodicals and monographs not only publish research of the staff of the DAI, but also to a great extent the work of other scholars, both at home and abroad. A large proportion of German research literature in the fields of archaeology and architectural history has appeared in publications of the DAI. The final results of large-scale and long-term excavations are published in monograph series. Systematic editions of material culture or monuments represent another kind of ongoing publications. They are edited by the DAI, sometimes in collaboration with foreign and domestic institutions. As is laid down in the charter as one of the tasks of the DAI, future generations of researchers are supported and promoted by the giving of travel and research grants and by students and young archaeologists contributing to the DAI's research and publication projects.

International collaboration is a necessary condition if archaeology is to provide basic historical research. Characteristically, the DAI's structure and *modus operandi* are oriented towards the cultivation of international relations. The establishment of foreign departments is not only motivated by German interest in archaeology, but also by the desire of researchers and institutions of other nations for a lasting and responsible presence of the DAI in their countries. Like the corresponding institutions of other countries, the foreign departments are integrated into the scientific and cultural life of the host countries. Their libraries are among the most important specialist libraries in these countries and provide local researchers with access to international research literature. The photographic archives constitute an important component of local archaeological records and they fulfil the need of local and international researchers for high-quality scientific images, far beyond the interest of the DAI.

For archaeologists from Germany and other countries the departments of the DAI serve as bases and intermediaries with the authorities and institutions of the host country. The commissions and departments located in Germany are also internationally oriented, corresponding with the interdisciplinary and transnational spectrum of their research. Common research projects with foreign partners, participation in international publication projects and the publication of the research results of scholars from other countries play an important role in their work. The DAI's foreign relations are fundamentally supported by a scholarship programme which invites foreign researchers and by the Lepsius College in Berlin. As the DAI's guest-house it represents a unique place for meetings between archaeologists from across the world.

→ GERMANY

1 F. W. DEICHMANN, Vom internationalen Privatverein zur preußischen Staatsanstalt. Zur Geschichte des Istituto di Corrispondenza Archeologica = Das DAI, Geschichte und Dokumente 9, 1986   2 K. JUNKER, Das Archäologische Institut des Deutschen Reiches zwischen Forschung und Politik. Die Jahre 1929 bis 1945, 1997   3 A. RIECHE (ed.), Die Satzungen des DAI 1828 bis 1972 = Das DAI,

Geschichte und Dokumente 1, 1979　　4 G. Roden-waldt, Archäologisches Institut des Deutschen Reiches 1829–1929, 1929　5 V. M. Strocka, H.-G. Kolbe, 150 Jahre DAI, in: W. Arenhövel (ed.), Berlin und die Antike, Exhibition catalogue, Berlin, 1979, 419–429 6 C. Weickert, Das DAI: Geschichte, Verfassung, Aufgaben, 1950²　7 L. Wickert, Beiträge zur Geschichte des DAI 1879 bis 1929 = Das DAI, Geschichte und Dokumente 2, 1979
Departments: 8 F. W. Deichmann, T. Kraus, Abteilung Rom, in: K. Bittel et al., Beiträge zur Geschichte des DAI 1929 bis 1979, Teil 1 = Das DAI, Geschichte und Dokumente 3, 1979, 1–39　9 A. Rieche, 150 Jahre DAI Rom. Exhibition catalogue, Bonn, 1979　10 L. Wickert, Beiträge zur Geschichte des DAI 1878 bis 1929 = Das DAI, Geschichte und Dokumente 2, 1979, 27–82　11 U. Jantzen, 100 Jahre Athener Instituts 1874–1974 = Das DAI, Geschichte und Dokumente 10, 1986　12 H. Kyrieleis, Abteilung Athen, in: K. Bittel et al., Beiträge zur Geschichte des DAI 1929 bis 1979, Teil 1 = Das DAI, Geschichte und Dokumente 3, 1979, 41–64　13 L. Wik-kert, Beiträge zur Geschichte des DAI 1879 bis 1929 = Das DAI, Geschichte und Dokumente 2, 1979, 83–99 14 K. Bittel, Beiträge zur Geschichte des DAI 1929 bis 1979, Teil 1. Das DAI, Geschichte und Dokumente 3, 1979, 65–91 (Istanbul)　15 W. Grünhagen, Abteilung Madrid, in: K. Bittel et al., Beiträge zur Geschichte des DAI 1929 bis 1979, Teil 1 = Das DAI, Geschichte und Dokumente 3, 1979, 117–165　16 W. Kaiser, Abteilung Kairo, in: K. Bittel et al., Beiträge zur Geschichte des DAI 1929 bis 1979, Teil 1 = Das DAI, Geschichte und Dokumente 3, 1979, 93–116　17 Id., 75 Jahre DAI Kairo 1907–1982 (DAI / Abteilung Kairo, Sonderschrift 12, 1982)　18 Festschrift zum 75jährigen Bestehen der RGK. Beiheft zum 58. Bericht der RGK, 1977 (1979)　19 25 Jahre RGK. Zur Erinnerung an die Feier des 9.–11. Dezember 1927, 1930　20 W. Wurster, Was macht die KAVA in Bonn?, in: Antike Welt 25/3, 1994, 226–236 21 H. Parzinger, H. Kyrieleis, G. Kossack, Gründungsveranstaltung der Eurasien-Abteilung des DAI am 8. Februar 1995, in: Eurasia Antiqua 1, 1995, 1–43 22 H. Parzinger, Archäologie am Rande der Steppe. Die Eurasien-Abteilung des DAI, in: Antike Welt 29/2, 1998, 97–108　23 Deutsches Archäologisches Institut on the World Wide Web: http://www.dainst.org/　24 Some of the DAI's publications, including the Subject Catalogue of the DAI in Rome, the Acquisition List of DAI in Madrid, and the Eurasia Bibliography of the DAI, are available on the World Wide Web for a fee at http:// www.dyabola.de.

HELMUT KYRIELEIS

Dialectics
A. Logic und Rhetoric　B. Speculative Philosophy: Hegel and After　C. The Socratic Dialogue

A. Logic und Rhetoric
From late Classical times to the present the word *dialectics* stands for a variety of sometimes sharply differentiated concepts. They are all derived more or less directly from Classical definitions. In Classical Antiquity dialectics can mean thinking in antitheses, something which may be traced back to Zeno or Heraclitus, a

methodological questioning process, the art of a well-balanced discourse, as we find it in Plato's dialogues, or in philosophy or science in general. Going beyond the Aristotelean topics, with its syllogistic systematisation of testing and justifying theses, dialectics has provided the basic framework for every → argumentation theory since that time. It becomes part of → Logic or is equated with it [12] and is one of the set components of the *trivium* in the → Artes liberales in university education.

With the *Topics* of Aristotle dialectics, or rather the dialectic conclusion, is reserved for those questions and problems whose premises are not in the strictest sense provable but are merely generally accepted opinions (*éndoxa*), whose results are therefore only probable. Cicero's rhetoricising of the topics makes dialectics a part of → Rhetoric. The basic question of whether dialectics is to be applied formally or in terms of content, that is, whether it serves to provide for the victory of truth or of rhetoric, not only divides the tradition of formal dialectics into basically Aristotelean or Ciceronian directions, but also within philosophy separates dialecticians from anti-dialecticians. The criticism that dialectics leads to mere sham-fighting, to logic-chopping rather than to the truth, essentially takes up once more the criticism that Plato leveled at the Sophists–that it is purely the art of argument (eristics), concerned with mere appearance and opposed to his concept of dialectics, which is bound up metaphysically with the knowledge of the idea of goodness. Even though the history of dialectics in its first phase down to modern times very largely draws upon the methodological aspect of the doctrine of argument, nevertheless Plato's metaphysical-contemplative force also turns up once more in the Platonic tradition when dialectics is defined as 'vera rerum contemplatio' (Iohannes Scotus Eriugena, *De divisione naturae* 1,44).

With the restriction of logic to purely formal operations, the description of dialectics as logic is abandoned in the 17th cent. On the other hand, rhetorical dialectic and the use of the → loci communes blossoms forth again with the rhetoric of the Humanists. However, faced with the modern criticism of dialectics, that it promotes no new knowledge and is therefore useless to science (Bacon), dialectics as the one-time 'science of sciences' (*scientia scientiarum*) has run its course and can, according to I. Kant, be given a quite different significance. Kant develops from logical dialectics a transcendental dialectics, which assumes the task of a critique of appearance, which is 'ineluctably' associated with human reason [4. B 354].

B. Speculative Philosophy: Hegel and After
A turning-point in the history of dialectics as a concept is provided by G. W. F. Hegel's genetic logic, which considers contradictions as being productive not only in thought or concept, but in reality itself. In terms of the development of this theory, dialectics is concei-

ved as the effort to represent the achieving of knowledge to be the same as the course of events itself, and to equate reality with reason.

The concept of pragmatic dialectics becomes, for all the distancing from Hegel, determinative also for the social theory of dialectical and historical materialism in the thought of K. Marx und F. Engels. This materialistically oriented dialectics undertakes an ideologically critical analysis of bourgeois economics and society. Engels defines dialectics in the broadest possible terms as the "science of the laws of general movement and development of nature, human society and thought" [3. 132]. As a means of stirring the inflexibility of an existing order into movement, dialectics can become a basic tenet of Marxist self-awareness, as 'subversive' (Marx), or as "the algebra of revolution" (A. Herzen), even in critical modifications or in adaptations [10].

The Hegelian concept of dialectics remains, in spite of deliberate distancing from it, an essential reference point right down to the Critical Theorists and to the French Philosophy of Difference. Setting Hegel aside, Th.W. Adorno perceives 'negative dialectics' as a consistent awareness of non-identity [1. 17]. The critical function of dialectical awareness is evident not only in the criticism of the premises for the establishment of philosophical systems. Even the "negative Dialectics" of Adorno intends social criticism as a critique of the "historically efficacious form of the collective context of delusions" ('Verblendungszusammenhänge').

Others refer back to the dialectics of the Greeks themselves, to its eristic character, as does A. Schopenhauer's manual on dogmatism [8], or to the logic of Neo-Kantianism in the early 20th cent. [2], which is strongly oriented to Greek logic throughout. K. R. Popper sees in dialectics an early form of the scientific method of 'trial and error' [8]. The later Schelling and Schleiermacher [6] as critics of Hegel emphasise the dialogical aspects of dialectics with reference back to Plato[7].

C. The Socratic Dialogue

Dialectics has its origins in the Socratic discussions of the Platonic dialogue, but for all that, the actual conversation aspect remains initially subordinate in the further development of the concept of dialectics. Aside from literary imitators in all centuries (→ DIALOGUE), conversation is not revived as a means of philosophising in the 'colloquy' until Schleiermacher. In the 20th cent., the Socratic dialogue is picked up again for an ethical-moral orientation as a means of "teaching the art of philosophising" and not of transmitting philosophy as a technical subject [5. 271]. Down to the present, following Leonard Nelson, the 'Socratic dialogue' has been maintained, with explicit reference to Plato and Socrates, within everyday behaviour for practice in 'communication' [11. 7] and for the development of a 'moral attitude'.

→ Dialectics; → Elenchus

→ Philosophy

Sources 1 Th. W. Adorno, Negative Dialektik, (= Gesammelte Werke, R. Tiedemann (ed.), vol. 6, 1973; (Engl. E. B. Ashton (trans.), Negative Dialectics, 1973) 2 J. Cohn, Theorie der Dialektik, 1923 3 F. Engels, Anti-Dühring (= Marx-Engels Werke (MEW), vol. 20), 1975; (Engl. E. Burns (trans.), Herr Eugen Dühring's Revolution in Science (anti-Dühring), 1939) 4 I. Kant, Kritik der reinen Vernunft, Berlin ²1787; (Engl. P. Guyer, A. W. Wood (trans.), The Critique of Pure Reason, 1992) 5 L. Nelson, Die sokratische Methode (1922), in: Id., Gesammelte Schriften, 1970 ff., vol. 1, 269–316 6 F. D. E. Schleiermacher, Vorlesungen über Dialektik, A. Arndt (ed.), (= Kritische Gesamtausgabe II/10), 2002 7 Id., Einleitung in die Übersetzungen der Dialoge Platons, repr. in: Das Platonbild: Zehn Beiträge zum Platonverständnis, K. Gaiser (ed.), 1969, 1–32; (Engl. W. Dobson (trans.), Schleiermacher's Introductions to the Dialogues of Plato, 1973) 8 A. Schopenhauer, Eristische Dialektik oder die Kunst, Recht zu behalten, in: Id., Handschriftlicher Nachlaß, A. Hübscher (ed.), 1970, 3, 666–700 9 K. R. Popper, What is Dialectic (1940), in: Id., Conjectures and Refutations, ⁴1972, 312–335
Literature 10 W. F. Haug, in: Historisch-Kritisches Wörterbuch des Marxismus, vol. 2, 1995, 657–693 11 D. Horster, Das Sokratische Gespräch in Theorie und Praxis, 1994 12 L. Oeing-Hanhoff, in: Dialektik III., in: HWdPh 2, 175–184 13 N. Rescher, Dialetics. A Controversy-Oriented Approach to the Theory of Knowledge, 1977 14 M. Riedel (ed.), Hegel und die antike Dialektik, 1990 15 N. Waszek, Bibliographie zu Hegel und die antike Dialektik, in: [14. 275–283]
Additional Bibliography M. Rosen, Problems of the Hegelian Dialectic: Dialectic Reconstructed as a Logic of Human Reality, 1992 T. Smith, Dialectical Social Theory and its Critics: From Hegel to Analytical Marxism and Postmodernism, 1993.   MARGARITA KRANZ

Dialogue

A. Introduction B. The Middle Ages C. Renaissance D. Modern Times

A. Introduction

In the medium of written literary prose, the ancient genre of dialogue imitates oral conversation between at least two speakers, who discuss with one another themes that deal in particular with philosophical, rhetorical or religious topics. In contrast to drama, dialogue is not intended for performance on stage, but for individual reading. The unity of a dialogue is constituted by the conversational situation and its respective thematic guidelines, rather than the representation of action as in dramatic dialogues. In addition, the dialogue as an independent genre is to be distinguished from the dialogue as a form that can be incorporated into narrative texts of very different genres, without, however, characterizing them as a whole. The decisive factor remains that a subject (the soul, love, the perfect orator) is discussed controversially in speeches and counter-speeches from the various standpoints of the speakers involved. In this process, individual replies are either counterposed immediately (as in Plato's Phaedo), or introduced by the author and linked to one another by means of transitions, so that the figure of the narrator assumes the role of an intermediary (for instance in Cic., Orat.). In Cicero, the participants' speeches often grow into rather lengthy declamations. Since the Middle Ages, the ancient term 'dialogue' has found its way into the modern languages; in addition, since the Renaissance such synonyms as *conversazione*, *ragionamenti*, *entretien*, *colloquio* or *Gespräch*, which designate both the literary genre and everyday conversation, have more and more come into use. From dialogue, the Russian literary theorist Mikhail Bakhtin derives the concept of the dialogical, to characterize the stylistic relation of tension between one's own discourse and foreign discourse, narrative discourse and directly or indirectly quoted personal discourse, especially in the post-Renaissance novel (Rabelais, Sterne, Dostoevsky) [22. 95–115]. A work that is dialogical in this sense need not be a dialogue with regard to genre; on the other hand, a dialogue such as Cic. Lael., because of the largely unitary Ciceronian literary prose in the contributions of all the participants in the conversation, is only then dialogical in Bakhtin's sense when verses from such older authors as Ennius or Terence are quoted. Ancient poetic theory does not deal with dialogue as an independent genre, but only in the context of the Platonic distinction between narration and depiction (Plat. Resp. 392), which precedes every more precise determination of genre, and was subsequently taken up again in the 4th cent. AD by the grammarian Diomedes (Grammatici latini 1,482 Keil). Here, dialogue, like drama, falls under the category of representative speech by the characters. The maieutic dialogues of the Platonic Socrates, who wrestles with the truth in the circle of his students, Xenophon's presentation of the symposiums, Cicero's elegant didactic conversations, which show the Roman upper classes in their leisure hours, and Lucian's satiric-parodistic dialogues, interspersed with mythic and comedic elements, all decisively influenced the subsequent development of the genre, both in Latin and in the modern languages since the rediscovery and dissemination of these ancient models in the Renaissance. Boethius' work *De consolatione philosophiae*, in which the author is engaged in a dialogue with personified Philosophy, had already been absorbed in the Middle Ages, as had Augustine's *Soliloquies*, with their striving for inner contemplation and the knowledge of God, and in which the author debates with reason as his higher self.

B. THE MIDDLE AGES

Most of the masterworks of the dialogue tradition of Classical Antiquity were largely unknown in the Western European Middle Ages. All that was read of Plato down to the 12th cent. was the *Timaeus*, in the partial Latin translation of Chalcidius; but it was studied from a cosmological viewpoint, without attention to the dialogue form. In contrast, didactic dialogues enjoyed a great popularity. They were played out between a typified student and a teacher representing the person of the author, and adopted the question-and-answer scheme used by the grammarian Donatus in his *Ars minor* (4th cent.). Here, the dialogue form is used for the organization and presentation of a given field of knowledge, which could be understood as a written reflex of the dominant oral transmission of knowledge; however, it does not demonstrate any cognitive process in the conversation. In the course of the Carolingian educational reform (→ CAROLINGIAN RENAISSANCE), Alcuin composed such dialogues near the end of the 8th cent. on grammar, rhetoric and dialectics. Charlemagne assumes the role of the student in the last two, but is not vividly characterized. With his *Elucidarium*, around 1100, Honorius Augustodunensis brought the fundamental tenets of the Christian faith to the form of a catechism, which was soon disseminated in numerous vernacular translations and adaptations, even among the lay public. In contrast, theologians such as Anselm of Canterbury and Peter Abelard, who strove for a rational foundation of revealed Truth, reinforced the position of the questioner and transformed the philosophical-theological dialogue into an ambitious dialectical medium for intellectual debates and persuasion. In the dream vision of the *Collationes*, datable to 1125/26, Peter Abelard adapted the Christian controversy-dialogue of Late Antiquity, depicting a heathen philosopher, a Christian and a Jew who argue over the question of the highest good. However, the attitude of the interlocutors, who are no further individualized, is highly respectful, and the controversy is ultimately decided by a not-unequivocal judgment in favour of the Christian. The *Dialogus Ratii* of Eberhard of Ypern, which originated after 1190, can also be considered a "testimony of a new culture of the problematizing dialogue" [17. 199]; the author deals with the conflict between his teacher Gilbert of Poitiers and Bernhard of Clairvaux on the status of such universal concepts as 'divinity', while the appearance of the serfs, who derive from the ancient comedy tradition, lighten up the linguistic-philosophical debate with their jokes. In the *De secreto conflictu curarum mearum* (1347–1353) by Francesco Petrarca, a conversation entirely devoted to self-examination and self-dramatization unfolds over three days and as many books, between his alter ego Franciscus and his admired model Augustine, who as the author of the *Confessiones* defends the highest moral demands addressed to an ego. Franciscus seeks advice more from Augustine the autobiographer than from the Doctor of the Church. While Petrarch draws up the balance sheet of his life in a period of crisis, he vacillates between dejection, humble contrition over his own sinfulness, and pride in his poetical achievements, from which he expects to achieve glory. The glorious personification of wisdom, reminiscent of the allegory of philosophy in Boethius, remains mute after the prologue, and is thereby, to some extent, both the presupposition and the goal of the monologue. With the dialogue *De remediis utriusque fortunae* of 1366, Petrarch completed his most widely-read Latin work of the late Middle Ages and the Early Modern period, in which only allegorical personifications appear. Ratio ('Reason') finds herself in conflict with Gaudium ('Pleasure'), Spes ('Hope'), Dolor ('Pain'), and Metus ('Fear'); the dialogue, which consists of a multitude of brief verbal skirmishes, depicts a world internally torn and ruled by strife and recommends Stoic principles, gleaned from readings of Cicero and Seneca, as a remedy against the passions and the machinations of Fortune (→ STOICISM).

C. RENAISSANCE

From the beginning of the 15th cent., starting in Italy, the ancient dialogues of Cicero, Plato, Plutarch and Lucian gradually became available once again in their full extent. Study of these newly discovered ancient models contributed to an unprecedented flourishing of the dialogue, first in Latin, and then also in the vernacular. In the dialogue, the humanistic culture of conversation sets itself apart from the ritualized disputes of the medieval university and from Augustinian introspection, to create its own ideal image of communication. Courtly sociability is represented in the dialogue, and women are also included in the conversation. The dialogue confronts and reconciles the newly-experienced multiplicity of diverse opinions, viewpoints and perspectives [2. 126]. It was disseminated through printing, whereby the loss of oral proximity was simultaneously compensated for by the new medium, and in this medium itself. With Leonardo Bruni's *Dialogi ad Petrum Paulum Histrum* (1406) the Humanistic dialogue took the path of Cicero-imitation and adopted the *De orat.* as a model, so that, in contrast to the medieval dialogue, the representations of the interlocutors, and thus of the author himself and other historically attested protagonists of early Florentine Humanism, observe decorum, and the configuration of the context, with its reference to civic society, receives greater emphasis. The debate over the value of the work of Dante, Petrarch and Boccaccio is expressly characterized as a playfully elegant 'disputatio in utramque partem', distinguishing itself from scholastic disputation in its Classical stylistic form, secular contents and critical confrontation with authorities [16. 35]. In his *De avaritia* (1428), Poggio Bracciolini transfers this approach to the moral-philosophical treatment of greed. For the sake of rhetorical practice, the interlocutors defend positions that do not coincide with their genuine, historically attested views, a procedure adopted by Lorenzo Valla in his *De vero falsoque bono* (1431–1441). The figure of the arbiter who creates agreement, appearing in both Poggio and Valla, goes back to Augustine (*Contra Academicos*). With his *Cortegiano* (1528), Baldesar Castiglione integrates Ciceronian dialogue within the vernacular and sketches a 'portrait', from a refracted perspective, of the court at Urbino in 1506, where, as in the *De orat.*, the urbane manners of the recently dead are stylized into a model [4]. The ideal of the courtier and the lady-in-waiting gradually emerge in the conversational game led by the

duchess Elisabetta Gonzaga. The skillfully casual conversation not only exemplifies in itself the qualities demanded of the courtier, of charm and nonchalance (*sprezzatura*), but it also attributes a positive, independent value to differences of opinion, thereby subjectivizing the access to truth [12. 108f.]. Compared to *De orat.*, there is a correspondingly greater stylistic and thematic variation in Castiglione, extending from the ribald pranks of Italian novellas (building on Cic. Orat. 22,216–290) to the Neoplatonic theory of love, which evokes cosmic harmony (following Plat., Symp. 201d–212c, Marsilio Ficino's Commentary thereon and Pietro Bembo's *Asola*). The *Cortegiano* left its mark on the norms of interaction of European upper classes until well into the 17th cent. and exerted particular influence on the French culture of conversation [3]. In contrast, Torquato Tasso's dialogues, oriented rather towards the Platonic model in the style of their conversation (e.g., *La Molza overo De l'Amore* of 1586), confronted their courtly audience more intensely with philosophical conceptual distinctions and quotations from ancient authors.

With his *De dialogo liber* (1562), Carlo Sigonio produced the first comprehensive theoretical work on the dialogue in general [21. 39–86; 18; 10]; his reflections focus on the potential of the applicability of the Aristotelian concept of → MIMESIS (the imitation both of spoken discourse and of canonical ancient texts used as examples) and the doctrine of decorum in Ciceronian rhetoric. The Italian Humanists of the 15th cent. saw in Lucian primarily a moral philosopher [20. 84]; such works as the brief *Intercoenales* (from 1436) by Leon Battista Alberti denounce human weaknesses and vices in general. With the translations of Lucian (1506) and the *Colloquia familiaria* (1522–1533), partially developed from it, of Erasmus of Rotterdam, → SATIRE increased in both popularity and in acuity, since the critique of philosophical schools was henceforth directed at contemporary clerics. Lucianic dialogue thereby entered the service of the political and religious debates of the age of the Reformation [15], for instance in Ulrich von Hutten, who spoke up for German independence from the Roman curia and for Luther (e.g., in the *Bulla vel Bullicida*, 1521, with its linguistic borrowings from Plautus), or Alfonso de Valdés, who defended the policies of Emperor Charles V in his *Diálogo de Mercurio y Carón* (1528). The form of dialogue with the gods or the dead represented everyday earthly life from an ironically superior distance. The dialogues of Lucian and his imitators scandalized the learned advocates of seemliness (cf. Iulius Caesar Scaliger, *Poetices libri septem* 1,3). One encounters a highly complex reworking of Lucianic models in *El Crótalon* (ca. 1552), attributed to Cristóbal de Villalón, who in imitation of Lucian's *Gallus* presents a philosophical rooster in conversation with a poor shoemaker. Largely independent episodes, partially configured after other dialogues of Lucian and Plutarch, are added onto this framework, which, by means of the motif of transmigration of souls, enable various social types to be set on stage in the manner of a picaresque novel, and thereby subject them to satirical critique [19. 100–128].

D. Modern Times

Toward the end of the 16th cent., the dialogue seemed to be threatened by a crisis, insofar as Lucianic satire was increasingly exposed to counter-reformation censorship and the Ciceronian rhetoric of the critique of knowledge (for instance, in Montaigne and Descartes). The gradually emerging mathematical-experimental natural sciences gave preference to discursive forms of presentation; nevertheless, they used dialogue to disseminate their discoveries. Thus, for instance, Galileo Galilei cleverly uses the dialogue form to refute Aristotelian natural philosophy, and yet, because of Church censorship, also to refrain from openly stating his agreement with the Copernican world view. Since the arguments pro and contra are delegated to the characters of the dialogue, judgment is left up to the reader (*Dialogo sopra i due massimi sistemi del mondo*, 1632). Descartes popularized themes from his *Meditationes metaphysicae* in his posthumous dialogue *La Recherche de la vérité par la lumière naturelle*. When the *Dialogus de arte computandi* (ca. 1676) by Gottfried Wilhelm Leibniz, which grew directly from his readings of Plato, transmitted the foundations of arithmetic and algebra, it simultaneously exemplifies through its form the Platonic doctrine of reminiscence, since an ignorant child can be led to mathematical insights through maieutic questioning. In his *Conversations chrétiennes* (1677), reminiscent of the controversy dialogues of Late Antiquity and of the model of Augustine, Nicolas Malebranche laid the foundations of Christian faith for a rationalistically influenced public, whereby the thematic sequence of the individual dialogues delineates a comprehensive systematics, mediating between treatise and dialogue. Even purely philosophical dialogues often transformed the interlocutors into de-individualized bearers of specific positions, as is already indicated by meaningful names. Thus, in his *Three Dialogues between Hylas and Philonous* (1713), George Berkeley has a materialist compete against the idealist who ultimately ensures the triumph of the author's view. The imitation of Lucian's *Dialogues of the Dead* produced its own subgenre, at the latest with Bernard de Fontenelle's *Nouveaux dialogues des morts* (1683). With paradoxical virtuosity, Fontenelle used the ancient form specifically to cast the superiority of Antiquity over the modern age in doubt. On the one hand, the European → Enlightenment, like the Renaissance, can be characterized as an era of dialogue, in which the genre enjoyed particular popularity from a purely quantitative viewpoint [1], and was also promoted by the culture of the salon. On the other hand, as had already occurred in the Reformation, the dialogue was often used as a monological vehicle of doctrine or satire, without two viewpoints really coming into conflict. Thus, Voltaire's ironically pointed *Dialogues chrétiens*

ou préservatif contre l'Encyclopédie (1760) merely expose the clergy to ridicule. In contrast, the dialogue is given its own epistemological function in Christoph Martin Wieland [14. 201–226] and Denis Diderot [8]. As an ingenious translator of and commentator on Xenophon, Lucian, Cicero and Horace, Wieland passed on the ancient culture of conversation to his time, whereby he explicitly preferred the *sermo urbanus* to Platonic maieutics, which was felt to be presumptuous. Truth is not provided in a manner that is valid once and for all, but becomes gradually crystallized through amicable and convivial dispute, as is represented in the *Göttergespräche* (1796), which are only at first glance Lucianic. Here, satire recedes into the background, behind the perspectivist discussion of various forms of government. Diderot's dialogical writing, however, has freed itself completely from the imitation of ancient models and obeys a poetics of digression, which undermines any hierarchization among main and ancillary themes. It thereby exemplifies the movement of thought and enables the experience of the "alienation" (Hegel) of a modern consciousness in the split between the two persons 'I' and 'He' (*Le neveu de Rameau*, 1761–1773). Around 1800, the possibilities of the dialogue were thereby exhausted; the sovereign, reflexive 'I' seems to pull its own literary genre out from under polite conversation [23. 201; 11. 240]. The 'post-history' of the dialogue in the 19th and 20th cents. can confirm this thesis precisely by the evidence of the outstanding works one might be inclined to cite against it: Giacomo Leopardi articulates his profound pessimism in his Lucianesque *Operette morali* (1824), where the ancient gods and heroes represent the opposite distance between the ego and the world, while Oscar Wilde (*The Decay of Lying*, 1889), Rudolf Borchardt (*Das Gespräch über Formen*, 1905) and Paul Valéry (*Eupalinos ou L'architecte*, 1923) give their dialogues an aestheticist turn. Here, the Platonic dialogue, quite unplatonically, has become a means for artistic self-reflection, alongside the essay and the notebook.

→ Dialogue

→ Genre theory; → Imitatio; → Platonism

1 D. J. Adams, Bibliographie d'ouvrages français en forme de dialogue 1700–1750, 1992   2 M. L. Batkin, Gli umanisti italiani. Stile di vita e di pensiero, 1990, 123–176   3 P. Burke, The Fortunes of the 'Courtier'. The European Reception of Castiglione's Cortegiano, 1995 4 A. Carella, Il libro del Cortegiano di Baldassare Castiglione, in: A. Asor Rosa (ed.), Letteratura italiana. Le opere, vol. I, 1992, 1089–1126   5 V. Cox, The Renaissance Dialogue. Literary Dialogue in its Social and Political Contexts, Castiglione to Galileo, 1992   6 C. Forno, Il 'Libro animato': Teoria e scrittura del dialogo nel Cinquecento, 1992   7 Th. Fries, Dialog der Aufklärung. Shaftesbury, Rousseau, Solger, 1993   8 R. Galle, Diderot oder die Dialogisierung der Aufklärung, in: J. v. Stackelberg (ed.), Europäische Aufklärung III, 1980, 209–247   9 J. Gómez, El diálogo en el Renacimiento español, 1988   10 M. Grosse, Kanon ohne Theorie? – Der Dialog als Problem der Renaissance-Poetik, in: M. Moog-Grünewald (ed.), Kanon und Theorie,

1997, 153–179   11 S. Guellouz, Le Dialogue, 1992
12 D. Heitsch, J.-F. Vallee (eds.), Printed Voices. The
Renaissance Culture of Dialogue, 2004   13 K. W. Hempfer, Rhetorik als Gesellschaftstheorie: Castigliones *Il
libro del Cortegiano*, in: Festschrift B. König, 1993, 103–
121   14 R. Hirzel, Der Dialog. Ein literaturhistorischer
Versuch, 2 vols., Leipzig 1895   15 G. Kalmbach, Der
Dialog im Spannungsfeld von Schriftlichkeit und Mündlichkeit, 1996   16 J. Kampe, Problem 'Reformations-
Dialog. 'Untersuchungen zu einer Gattung im reformato-
rischen Medienwettstreit, 1997   17 D. Marsh, The
Quattrocento Dialogue. Classical Tradition and Humanist Innovation, 1980   18 D. Marsh, Lucian and the
Latins: Humor and Humanism in the Early Renaissance,
1998 (Recentiores)   19 P. v. Moos, Literatur- und bil-
dungsgeschichtliche Aspekte der Dialog-Form im lateinischen Mittelalter. Der *Dialogus Ratii* des Eberhard von
Ypern zwischen theologischer disputatio und Scholaren-
Komödie, in: Festschrift Brunhölzl, 1989, 165–209
20 Id., Gespräch. Dialog-Form und Dialog nach älterer
Theorie, in: B. Frank, T. Haye, D. Tophinke (eds.), Gattungen mittelalterlicher Schriftlichkeit, 1997, 235–259
21 A. Rallo Gruss, La escritura dialéctica: Estudios
sobre el diálogo renacentista, 1996   21 Chr. Robinson,
Lucian and his Influence in Europe, 1979   22 J. R. Snyder, Writing the Scene of Speaking. Theories of Dialogue
in the Late Italian Renaissance, 1989   23 T. Todorov,
Mikhaïl Bakhtine. Le principe dialogique, suivi de Écrits
du cercle de Bakhtine, 1981   24 J. Wertheimer, 'Der
Güter Gefährlichstes, die Sprache': Zur Krise des Dialogs
zwischen Aufklärung und Romantik, 1990   25 C. H.
Winn (ed.), The Dialogue in Early Modern France, 1547–
1630. Art and Argument, 1993.   MAX GROSSE

Dialogue of the Dead

A. Creation of the Genre   B. Renaissance
C. Enlightenment   D. 19th/20th Century

A. Creation of the Genre

'How much would a person possibly give (...) for
questioning him who led the great army against Troy, or
Odysseus, or Sisyphus, or the countless other men and
women that could be named and for the eternal bliss of
talking to them, of being with them and asking them
questions?' (Pl. Ap. 41b-c). Socrates' vision of continuing the 'Socratic' dialogues in the underworld where he
imagines a temporarily and spatially unlimited dialogue
with the shadows of the dead can be regarded as the
impetus for the genre 'dialogue of the dead' (DD) as it
was established in the form of a comical dialogue [5. 73]
by Lucian of Samosata (ca. AD 120–180): his thirty
short Νεϰριϰοὶ Διάλογοι present fictitious conversational situations that not only take place in a space faraway
from the earthly realm but are also held exclusively by
deceased persons (thus, Lucian goes beyond the theme
of katabasis used frequently beginning with Homer's
Odyssey (bk. 12)). The fact that these dialogues are
staged between typified characters as representatives of
certain human behaviours shows that the DD were conceived as social rather than personal satires aimed at
mocking the triviality of earthly life and its ideas of
happiness. Lucian wrote no literary satires in the style

of Aristophanes' *Frogs*. In more than a third of the dialogues, Menippus functions as the mouthpiece of the
Cynic thoughts characteristic of DD, suggesting an
intended reference to the Cynic Menippus of Gadara
(3rd cent. BC) [13] whose lost works include a
'Nekyia' that might have served Lucian as a model for
the genre [6. 191–214]. Within the Lucianic œuvre, the
DD formally belong to the collections of dialogues of
gods, sea gods and hetaerae, and, with regard to content, belong to the underworld dialogues *Nekyomanteía* and *Katáplous*.

B. Renaissance

While Lucian's works had received hardly any attention in Late Antiquity, the first traces of a creative
reception of the DD can be found in the Byzantine journeys to Hades, *Timarion* (12th cent.) and *Mazaris* (14th
cent.), modelled after the *Nekyomanteía* [14. 21–22;
15. 76–81]. The genre reached new heights in the course
of the general renaissance of Lucian in the era of → Humanism [11; 10; 1. 27–51], when, after many translations into Latin and Greek, under the influence of
Melanchthon, the DD and other Lucianic works were
added to the educational canon and became recommended school reading. Essential for the popularity of
the genre were, along with the brevity of the dialogues
and the exemplary Attic language, its moralizing content and its satirical potential; in creative receptions
(such as Ulrich von Hutten's *Phalarismus*, 1517) this
potential could increasingly be exploited for personal
satires. DD were used, especially frequently, to criticize
the prevailing deplorable state of affairs in the Church,
which became even more clearly evident under the veil
of a pagan scenario [1. 49–50]. Thus, many anonymously published DD transported popes into the
underworld in order to parody their unChristian attitudes [14. 24], and Erasmus drew upon Lucian's 14th
and 20th DD [15. 174–177] in *Charon* (*Colloquia
familiaria* XLV, 1518) in order to criticize the indulgence preachers and the contemporary heresy trials.
Further important testimonies of reception are the use
of Lucian's 12th DD for patriotic purposes in Hutten's
Arminius (1529), where the German commander
claims and is granted pre-eminence among his colleagues, as well as Hans Sachs's tragedy *Charon mit den
abgeschiednen Geistern* (1531), modelled after
Lucian's 20th DD. In painting, Lucian's DD provided
the impetus for Hans Holbein's *Dances of Death*.

C. Enlightenment

1. France   2. Germany   3. England

1. France

In the 17th cent., DD were among the most popular
Lucianic works [1. 59–60], with Fontenelle and Féne-
lon as the most influential followers during the early
French Enlightenment [18. 52–64; 4. 33–113]: in his 36
Nouveaux dialogues des morts (1683/84), Fontenelle
modernized the Lucianic form by renouncing the

ancient inventory of the Underworld and by engaging famous personalities from recent history in conversation. Characteristic of his collection is the schematic tripartite division into *Dialogues des morts anciens*, *Dialogues des morts anciens avec des modernes* and *Dialogues des morts modernes*. Here, Fontenelle retains the moral orientation which he regards as typically Lucianic and which he summarizes at the end of his dialogues in an aphorism. Fénelon's *Dialogues des morts composez pour l'éducation d'un prince*, published beginning in 1690 and written when he was tutor of the Duc de Bourgogne, completely separate the form from pagan concepts of the Underworld in an effort to systematically christianize the DD [18. 64–83]. The popularity of both collections of dialogues, especially Fontenelle's, made possible the tremendous success of the genre all over Europe.

2. GERMANY

In Germany, David Faßmann – following Fontenelle – published the journal *Gespräche im Reiche derer Todten* between 1718 and 1739, in which a total of 240 DD were published [7; 9]. However, instead of moralizing like his model, Faßmann used the form for describing the lives of famous personalities and for presenting historical events which he enriched with his own political observations. The popularity of Faßmann's dialogues, which embraced Lucian only indirectly through the genre, contributed also to an increased reference to the Greek satirists: in an effort to find a standard of quality for the 'flood' of DD in the wake of Faßmann, Johann Christoph Gottsched developed his theory of the dialogue based on Lucian after his translation of Fontenelle's DD (1725) [1. 75–81] and published his own DD in Lucianic style in his journal *Die Vernünftigen Tadlerinnen* (1725–1726). In the period following, Lucian again became the model for the genre he had created; this is particularly apparent in the preface to the anonymously published *Ausserordentliches Gespräch im Reiche der Todten zw. dem ersten Menschen Adam und Joseph dem Pflege-Vater des Herrn Christi* (1735): 'Das gute Absehen, welches der Erfinder oder Anfänger solcher Todtengespräche gehabt, ist nachgehends von andern, die nur lauter abgeschmackte Sachen um eines schnöden und schlechten Gewinns willen vorgetragen haben, sehr gemißbrauchet worden, also, daß manchem Gelehrten anjetzo dieser Titel gantz eckel vorkommet. Gleichwohl ist es auch gewiß, daß man eines bösen Mißbrauchs halber einen guten Gebrauch nicht wegwerfen sondern solchen immer mehr und mehr zu erheben suchen soll' ("The good intention of the inventor or instigator of such dialogues was later misused by others who presented only fatuous material for vile or bad profits with the result that the title itself disgusts many a scholar today. At the same time it is also true that bad misuse should not lead one to dismiss a good use, but that the latter should always be encouraged and elevated") [1. 71]. The thematic potential of the more than 500 instances of a creative reception of DD that appeared in 18th-cent. Germany

[16. 134–163] pertains to religious, historical and political questions as well as to discourses on literary criticism. Goethe used the form in his farce *Götter, Helden und Wieland* (1773/74) in order to stage a polemical attack against a sentimentally distorted reception of Antiquity [12]; Klopstock alias Kostpolk had to part with his overly shallow literary outpourings in Georg Karl Claudius' *Zweyten Transport der Schatten in die Unterwelt* and David Christoph Seybold had Gottsched and Klotz lament the decay of their 'paper thrones' in his *Gespräche im Reiche der Toten in Lucianischer Manier* (1780). The reception of this genre was an essential factor in the rediscovery of Lucian's works in general, culminating in Wieland's enthusiasm for Lucian [1. 89–113]. Wieland himself contributed two further testimonies of reception with his *Gespräche im Elysium* and the *Peregrinus Proteus*.

3. ENGLAND

In England, where numerous receptions of DD are attested as early as the mid 17th cent. [8. 279–280], the influence of Fontenelle's dialogues–available in separate English translations as early as the year of publication (1683)–is apparent as well [3. 149]. Although the first large collection of ten DD by William King (1699), written as a literary critique of Richard Bentley's positions in the → QUERELLE DES ANCIENS ET DES MODERNES [8. 38–48], contains no direct references to Fontenelle [8. 25–27], authors such as John Hughes (1708), Matthew Prior (ca. 1721) and George Lyttelton (1760) expressly place themselves in the tradition of Fontenelle. Characteristic of Lyttelton's *Dialogues of the Dead*, conceived as a dramatic presentation of a 'history of all times and all nations' and highly popular [8. 75 f.], is the varied mixture of the three groups of dialogues known from Fontenelle as well as the 'openness' of his collection. By including three dialogues written by Elisabeth Montagu, he expanded the dialogues thematically by including the voice of 'bluestockings', and he invites his audience symbolically to add their own DD–with success: along with a broad reception of his collection in France and Germany, a large part of English DD reception of the late 18th and 19th cents. can be traced back to Lyttelton [8. 104–126].

D. 19TH/20TH CENTURY

In the 19th cent., the popularity of the DD declined, particularly in Germany. Reasons can be found in a gradual turning away from satire and dialogue as literary forms as well as in an increasingly critical evaluation of the entire Lucianic œuvre [1. 201–239]. The genre's strong ties to its founder that were still propagated successfully in the 18th cent. proved counterproductive, and it is revealing that the general critique of Lucian's satire and of his followers becomes the theme of a 'Lucianic' DD in Luise Hoffmann's *Heine's Ankunft im Schattenreich* (1857) [1. 215–216]. In the 20th cent., DD can be found in the form of satires critical of the times in Fritz Mauthner (*Totengespräche*, 1906), Paul Ernst (*Erdachte Gespräche*, 1934), Arno

Schmidt (*Dichtergespräche im Elysium*, 1941) and Bertolt Brecht (*Verurteilung des Lukullus*, 1939), among others [17]. Jean-Paul Sartre transports three persons into hell in his play *Huis clos* (*No Exit*, 1944); there they become aware of their earthly dependence on the judgement of others and, in retrospect, of their self-induced 'living death' [2]. A 'mediated' afterlife is offered by Hans Magnus Enzensberger in his radio play *Ohne uns. Ein Totengespäch* (1999), in which he brings together two former rivals hiding in Malaysia as 'dead persons on vacation' cut off from the world. In the most recent reception of DD, Walter Jens stages again a debate between writers in the underworld–now Lessing Heine and Brecht–who discuss the value and transitoriness of their works (*Der Teufel lebt nicht mehr, mein Herr! Erdachte Monologe – imaginäre Gespräche*, 2001).

→ Katabasis; → Lucianus [1] of Samosata; → Menippus [4] of Gadara

BIBLIOGRAPHY   1 M. BAUMBACH, Lukian in Deutschland, 2002   2 M. BEYERLE, Die Modernisierung der Hölle in Sartres 'Huis clos', in: Aufsätze zur Themen- und Motivgeschichte Festschrift H. Petriconi, 1965, 171–188   3 H. CRAIG, Dryden's Lucian, in: Classical Philology 16, 1921, 141–163   4 J. S. EGILSRUD, Le dialogue des morts, 1934   5 J. HALL, Lucian's Satire, 1981   6 R. HELM, Lucian und Menipp, 1906
ADDITIONAL BIBLIOGRAPHY D. MARSH, Lucian and the Latins: Humor and Humanism in the Early Renaissance, 1998.   MANUEL BAUMBACH

Fig. 1: Diana of Ephesus as Isis in the *Imagini Vincenzo Cartaris*, Venice 1647

Diana of Ephesus

A. INTRODUCTION   B. DIANA OF EPHESUS AS DECORATIVE ELEMENT   C. NATURA AND MAN D. DIANA OF EPHESUS AS ISIS   E. NATURA AND ARS   F. NATURA AS POLITICAL ALLEGORY G. NATURA AS OBJECT OF SCHOLARLY STUDIES

A. INTRODUCTION

Although Diana of Ephesus (DoE)–in Greek properly 'Artemis'–, the fertility goddess of Asia Minor, was known in the Middle Ages through Paul's *Acts of the Apostles* (19:27), neither artistic representations nor descriptions can be shown to have existed. Humanists, artists and antiquarians did not discover their interest in the goddess until the 16th cent., after several statues of Ephesia were brought to light during archaeological excavations in Italy [4]. Citing authors of Antiquity (S. Eusebii Hieronymi, Comm. in Epist. Ad Ephesios, PL 26, 540f.; Macr. Sat. 1,20,18), Vincenzo Cartari (*Imagini de i dei degli antichi*, Venice 1548 and Padua 1647), interpreted her allegorically as earth and nature and equated her with the Egyptian goddess Isis (fig.1). Mythographers and emblematists like Pierio Valeriano (*Les Hieroglyphiques*, Lyons 1615), Sambucus (*Emblemata*, 1564), Johannes Mercerius (*Emblemata*, Avarici Biturigum 1592), Claudio Menetreius (*Symbolica Dianae Ephesiae Statua*, Rome 1657 and 1688), Laurentius Beger (*Thesaurus Brandenburgicus*,

1696), Bernard de Montfaucon (*Antiquité expliquée*, London 1719ff.), Comte de Caylus (*Recueil d'Antiquités*, Paris 1752–68), Romeyn de Hooghe (*Hieroglyphica*, Amsterdam 1744), Jean Baptiste Boudard (*Iconologie*, Vienne 1766), H.F. Gravelot/ C.N. Cochin (*Iconologie*, 1791) and others disseminated knowledge about the goddess as the universal nurturing mother across the whole of Europe. Due to the wide field of influence of the *Natura*, which equally covers aspects of biology, philosophy and art, DoE was integrated into various allegorical visual contexts well into the 19th cent. where she often appeared as an iconographic variant of the many-breasted woman. To emphasise the aspect of fertility, the breasts of the figure are sometimes turned into water spouts, as for example in the Villa d'Este in Tivoli, in the *Fontana della Dea Natura* by Gillis van den Vlietes (around 1568, fig.2), and in *Oedipus Aegyptiacus* (Rome 1652, In ara magnae deorum multimammae) by Athanasius Kircher.

B. DIANA OF EPHESUS AS DECORATIVE ELEMENT

The first artistic representation of the modern period is found in Raphael's *Stanza della Segnatura* in the Vatican, where DoE appears as throne herm in the ceiling tondo of Philosophy. In around 1516 the figure for the first time is used as a grotesque motif in the loggias of the Vatican. Particularly in the second half of the 16th

Fig. 2: Gillis van den Vliete, Fontana della Dea Natura in the Villa d'Este in Tivoli, 1568

Fig. 3: Raphael, ceiling medallion of Philosophy in the *Stanza della Segnatura* in the Vatican, ca. 1509

cent. she is frequently found in the decoration schemes of Italian palaces, as for example in the Palazzo de Tè in Mantua, the Villa Madama in Rome, Castel Sant'Angelo, in the Palazzo Farnese in Caprarola and the Villa of Andrea Doria in Genoa. During the period of → CLASSICISM interest in the decorative aspect of the statue is rekindled, as for example with Piranesi (*Diverse maniere d'adornare i camini*, 1769), Tischbein (*Dekorationsentwürfe im Pompeianischen Stil*, 1787–99) and Semper (*Japanisches Palais*, Dresden, 1834–36).

C. NATURA AND MAN

In her function as Mother Nature, DoE has been integrated since the 16th cent. into pictorial contexts that thematise the entrance of humans into life. Giulio Romano represented her as midwife and divine wet-nurse in the *Loggia del Giardino segreto* in the Palazzo del Tè in Mantua (*Loggia del Giardino segreto*, after 1524), as did Sodoma in his oil painting *The Three Fates* (Galleria d'Arte Antica, Rome, ca. 1530), Philips Galle in his series of engravings *De allende van het menselijk bestaan* (1563) and Marten van Heemskerck in his engraving *Natura* (1572). Cornelis Ketel (Deughtspiegel, Rijkskabinet, Rijksmuseum Amsterdam, inv. A 1423, ca. 1590), Otho van Veen (*Emblemata Horatiana*, 1607) [13] and Jacob Jordaens in his drawing

Diliget (ca. 1640) [5] elevated her to the rank of a moral authority and a power that determines destiny. Dutch depictions of the 17th cent. are influenced by neo-Stoic moral doctrine, the motto of which – *sequere naturam* – sees nature as the inner guide to a virtuous life. Until well into the 18th cent., DoE appears in the first phase of human life, as for example in William Hogarth's draft for an escutcheon for the London Home for Foundlings (1747) or Heinrich Meyer's frieze in Queen Luise's round room in the Weimar Palace (1799).

D. DIANA OF EPHESUS AS ISIS

Against the background of the interest in and appreciation of Egyptian art and culture in Italy beginning in the Quattrocento, the syncretistic fusion of DoE and Isis gains special significance. Giulio Clovia portrays a dark-skinned Isis-Diana amid Egyptianising motifs taken from the *Tabula Bembi* on the frontispiece engraving of his missal for Pompeo Colonna (1532, John Rylands Library, Manchester, Latin ms. I, fol. 79). Among contemporary writers who glorify the land on the Nile as the cradle of culture, wisdom and *prisca theologia* the Dominican friar Annio da Viterbo has a prominent place. With the help of manipulated sources, he declares Isis to be the first ancestress of Italy in his *Commentaria super opera diversorum auctorum ab antiquatibus loquentium* (Rome 1498) and has her carrying out a civilisation campaign across Europe, together with her spouse Osiris. In France, where the *Commentaria* appear in 1512 and 1515, legends soon begin to grow around alleged Isis sanctuaries [1]. The example of the *Virgo Paritura* of Chartres shows the curious typologies that arise between the pagan and Christian religion in this context. Originally she represented a Madonna and child. However, in his *L'Histoire de*

Fig. 4: Diana of Ephesus as Isis in *L'Histoire de l'origine et des progrez de la monarchie française* by Guillaume Marcel

l'origine et des progrez de la Monarchie francaise (Paris 1686, I.l37ff.) the French chronicler Guillaume Marcel portrays her in the likeness of DoE (fig. 4) and thus alludes to an old legend according to which the figure had once been revered as an idol of Isis by the → DRU-IDS. In his mythographic work *Atlantica sine Manheim* (Uppsala, 1675), Olaf Rudeck has the civilisation campaign of the Egyptian goddess beginning in Scandinavia and represents her repeatedly as the many-breasted Diana (vol. 2, 350, illust. vol. pl. X, vol. 2, 519, vol. 2, pl. XIV, Ill. 50, pl. XI, Ill. 35, vol. 3, 102, pl. XV, Ill. 63)

E. NATURA AND ARS

The interplay between art and nature that is reflected in the cabinets of art and curiosities inspired artists of the 16th to the 18th cents. to include DoE in this thematic area, as for example on the ceiling frescoes in the studiolos of Francesco I. de'Medici in the Palazzo Vecchio in Florence (1570–75) or on the frontispiece engravings to Abraham Gorlaeus' *Dactyliotheca* (Delft, 1601–04) and Michele Mercatis' *Metallotheca* (Rome 1717). The goddess makes her entry into alchemy in Athanasius Kircher's *Mundus subterraneus* (Amsterdam 1664, vol. 2, frontispiece) and Hierne Urbani's *Actorum chymicorum holmiensium* (Stockholm 1712). Around 1800 Friedrich Gilly returns to the idea of the transformation of nature into art with the image of DoE in his relief frieze for the *Alte Münze* in Berlin. Here she is present at the processing of metal chunks into coins.

Against the background of the discussion surrounding the concept of imitation of nature (*imitazione della natura*), DoE acquires a central significance in the theory of art. In Giorgio Vasari's residences in Arezzo (Sala del camino, 1548) and Florence (Sala delle Arti, bet. 1569 and 1573), the goddess directly refers to scenes from the lives of famous artists from Antiquity, for which the empirical study of nature is of central importance for creative work. The idea that nature is the most important teacher of the artist is expressed in the image of DoE in Benvenuto Cellini's designs for a seal for the *Accademia del Disegno* in Florence (*Staatliche Graphische Sammlungen* Munich, Inv. 2264 and 1147; *Archivio Calamadrei*, Florence; London, BM; Paris, LV: *Cabinet des Dessins*, Inv. 2752), as well as in Joachim Sandrart's frontispiece for the *Teutsche Akademie der edlen Bau-, Bild- und Mahlerey-Künste* (Nuremberg 1675). In Carlo Maratta's copper engraving *Die trauernden Künste am Grabe Raffaels* (1675) the representation of Painting gazes at the image of DoE. This is a reference to Pietro Bembo's distich ('Ille hic est Raphael timuit qui sospite vinci / Rerum magna parens et moriente moris') for the grave of Raphael in the → PANTHEON, praising him as the one who surpassed his teacher, Nature. Two drawings by Federico Zuccari, one with the portrait of Raphael (Florence, UF: Gab. Disegni e stampe, Inv. 1341 F), the other with that of his brother Taddeo Zuccari (Florence, UF: Gab. Disegni e stampe, Inv. 11025 F), belong to the same tradition of the cult of genius that developed around Raphael. Each of the two painters holds out a drawing of DoE to the viewer, in the pose of the prophet Isaiah which was created by Raphael in Sant'Agostino in Rome. Similarly, Pelagio Palagi's drawing *Le bell'arti alla tomba die Rafaelle* (1802) [10] is to be understood as the apotheosis of Raphael. In the middle of a Pantheon-like round temple the bust of the Renaissance master is shown on an altar, with a relief of the nature goddess carved into its base. Tommaso Minardi, a disciple of Canova, adopts Palagi's compositional scheme in his drawing *Canova L'Arti belle incoronano divotamente* [2], but places the statue of DoE in the centre. In a drawing by Francesco Bosa from 1824 (Gab. Disegni e Stampe, Museo Correr, Venice, A XIII. F. 16) Canova, represented as a master of the study of Antiquity and nature, strides towards a temple and an Ephesia statue, accompanied by Painting, Architecture and Sculpture. As an expression of their personal commitment to the study of nature, Daniel Chodowiecki (Exlibris, 1777), Felice Giani (Self portrait, 1789, Turin, Museo Civico) and Heinrich Keller (Sketchbook, Züricher Kunsthalle, Inv. 1924/23, fol. 2r.) show the artist engaged in dialogue with the image of DoE.

From the middle of the 18th into the 19th cent., DoE is portrayed as the *Mater Artium*, as for example in a drawing by Tommaso Minardi from 1808 (Gall. d'Arte Mod., Rome, Inv. 5331/100/24). A sketch by Johann Gottlieb Schadow (Kupferstich-Kabinett, Berlin, Schadow-Album, fol. 24/2), executed in the 1830s, shows the goddess between representatives of several artistic and scientific professional groups. She appears as an

Fig. 5: *La Liberté et l'Égalité unies par la Nature*, etching by Ruotte

attribute of *Pictura* in Johann Georg Hertel's *Iconologia* of 1758/60 under the heading *Ars*, on the title page of the monthly publication of the Akademie der Künste und mechanischen Wissenschaften zu Berlin (1788, vol. 1, 245) and as an acroterium figure of the former building of the Akademie on Unter den Linden in Berlin. William Hogarth's vignette *Boys Peeping at Nature* (1730/31, Windsor Castle, Royal Library) parodies this iconographic type: it shows a putto and a satyr lifting the skirt of the nature goddess while another putto captures her image on canvas.

F. NATURA AS POLITICAL ALLEGORY

During the French Revolution, DoE is placed in the service of a visual propaganda that manifests itself above all in printed graphics. As the basis of society's laws and power of protection, she frequently appears in the company of *Égalité*, *Liberté* and *Raison* or as their attribute, for example in Ruotte's etching *La liberté et l'Égalité unies par la Nature* (1795/96, Paris, BN, Cab. Des Est., Hennin T. 139) (fig. 5), Armand-Charles Caraffe's *Thermomètre du Sans culotte* (Paris, BN, Cab. Des Est., de Vinck T 25), as well as the representations of *Égalité* by Alexandre Evariste Fragonard/Allais (1794, Paris, BN, Cab. Des Est., De Vinck T. 44) and Quéverdo/Guyot (Paris, BN, Cab. Des Est., Qb 1 1793). Pézant, in his *L'espoir du bonheur dédié à la Nation* (1789, Paris, BN, Cab. Des Est., de Vinck 1390), and Villeneuve, in his *Les Crimes des Rois* (1792, Paris, BN, Cab. Des Est., de Vinck, T. 19), represent the time before the Revolution as a time of violent suppression of nature.

The phenomenon of a pseudo-religious veneration of reason and nature leads to the establishment of new cult sites. On an anonymous engraving of 1793 (fig. 6), Strasbourg Cathedral appears as a 'temple of nature' with a statue of DoE in the choir. Etienne-Louis Boullée's designs for a tomb for Isaac Newton (Florence, UF: Gab. Delle stampe e dei disegni, 6593 A and 6594 A) also appear as sanctuaries of the nature goddess.

The intention of a spiritual renewal of the people is expressed in numerous allegorical frontispiece engravings and illustrations in pedagogical treatises and educational edicts that show the image of Diana of Ephesus. Among them is an anonymous copperplate engraving from 1793 with the herm of the goddess on the throne of *Publique Instruction* (Bibliothèque Municipale, Rouen, Inv. Leber 6076/6). Natura is also described and visually represented as a moral authority in Pierre-Platon Blanchard's *Catéchisme de la Nature* (Paris 1794), L.M. Henriquez' *Histoires et morales choisies* (Paris 1795), François Jean Dusausoir's *Livre indispensable aux enfants de la liberté* (1793) and Chemin-Dupontès' *Alphabet républicain* (Paris 1794). There is a close connection between the veneration of Jean Jacques Rousseau, as 'homme de la nature', and the writings on education cited above. In 1781 Hubert Robert created an allegorical relief for the philosopher's sarcophagus in Ermenonville, showing young mothers worshipping the cult image of DoE [7].

G. NATURA AS OBJECT OF SCHOLARLY STUDIES

From the second half of the 17th cent. into the 19th cent., DoE appears as the symbol of philosophical and scientific striving for knowledge, as for example in Charles Monnet's frontispiece to Francois Peyrard's *De la Nature et ses lois* (Paris 1793) or Prudhon's *Le Séjour de l'Immortalité* (beginning of 19th cent., Legs Winthrop, Fogg Museum, Harvard Univ.). The motif of the unveiling of the goddess as the symbolic revelation of nature's secrets, which appears frequently in this context, has its origin in Plutarch's account of the veiled image of Isis in the temple at Sais (Is. 9). DoE appears frequently as the attribute of the naturalist, as for example in Gravelot/Cochin, *Iconologie* (1791, s.v. Medicine), or Ernst Herter, monument to the physicist Hermann von Helmholtz in Berlin (1899). Numerous scientific works bear her image on the frontispiece, among them Gerardus Blasius' *Anatome Animalium* (1681), Erasmus Darwin's *Temple of Nature* (1808), Carl von Linné's *Fauna Svecica* (1746), F.H.W. Martini's *Geschichte der Natur* (1771) as well as Büffon's *Naturgeschichte* (1774). The late 19th cent. marks the end of the iconographic development of DoE. In the few cases in which the goddess appears in the post-classical period, she is already frozen as a visual formula and is referred to only marginally.

→ Artemis; → Diana; → Isis
→ EPHESUS; → STOICISM

1 J. BALTRUSAITIS, La quete d'Isis, 1967, ch. 3–4
2 Disegni di Tommaso Minardi, Exhibition catalogue of

Monument élevé à la Nature dans le Temple de la Raison à Strasbourg la 3.me décade

Fig. 6: Allegoric picture of Strasbourg Minster based on an anonymous engraving in the Strasbourg Musée de l'Œuvre Notre-Dame, 1793

the Galleria Nazionale d'Arte moderna di Roma, 1982, Cat. 31–32   3 R. FLEISCHER, Artemis von Ephesos, 1973 4 A. GOESCH, Diana Ephesia, Ikonographische Studien zur Allegorie der Natur in der Kunst vom 16. bis 19. Jahrhundert, 1996   5 J. S. HELD, Tekeningen von Jacob Jordaens, in: Kunstchronik 1967, H. 4, 94–110   6 K. HERDING, R. REICHARD, Die Bildpublizistik der französischen Revolution, 1989   7 C. C. L. HIRSCHFELD, Théorie de l'art des jardins, Leipzig 1785, vol. V, fig. on p. 305 (Engl. L. B. PARSHALL (trans.), Theory of Garden Art, 2001) 8 Images de la Révolution française, Catalogue du vidéodisque coproduit par la Bibliothèque National et Pergamon Press, 3 vols., 1990   9 W. KEMP, Natura. Ikonographische Studien zur Geschichte und Verbreitung einer Allegorie, 1973   10 L'ombra di Core, exhibition catalogue of the Galleria Comunale d'arte moderna Giorgio Morandi, 1988, 83   11 H. THIERSCH, Artemis Ephesia, 1935   12 M. VOVELLE, La Révolution française. Images et récit. 1789–1799, 5 vols., 1986   13 P. VAN ZESEN, Moralia Horatiana, (repr. 1963), vol. I, no. 1, no. 11, no. 16, vol. 2, no. 31).

ANDREA GOESCH

Diatribe see→ SATIRE

Dicta
JENS BARTELS

A. GENERIC CONCEPT   B. CHARACTERISTIC FEATURES   C. EDUCATIONAL AND CULTURAL BACKGROUND   D. INDEPENDENT DISSEMINATION E. CHANGES OF MEANING   F. LANGUAGE AND FORM   G. GENERAL APPLICABILITY   H. THE CONTEMPORARY SITUATION   I. RECOGNISABILITY

A. GENERIC CONCEPT

Long before Büchmann there existed a body of familiar 'famous quotations' from the ancient languages. Vast numbers of such quotations from lost works fill our collections of fragments: Solon's 'γηράσκω δ' αἰεὶ πολλὰ διδασκόμενος', "I grow old and ever go on learning" may stand as one example for hundreds of others. Macrobius in the Saturnalia 5,16,7, gives a series of quotations from Virgil "which are used proverbially by all" ('vice proverbiorum in omnium ore funguntur'). However, it was not until the appearance of Georg Büchmann's collection, first published in 1864 in Berlin and very soon afforded the status of a classic work, that this wealth of quotations developed into a genre as such; his title, *Geflügelte Worte* ('Winged Words', after the Homeric verse '...ἔπεα πτερόεντα προσηύδα', "... and uttered the winged words", *Iliad* 1, 201 and elsewhere) has quite properly become a generic concept. The *Adagia*, which Erasmus first edited in 1500 in a relatively small collection, and ultimately in more than four *Chiliades* in 1533 do indeed contain a number of dicta in the sense that we would understand the word, but as a whole they are to be seen rather as graphic turns of phrase, and the difference of epochs alone means that it is perhaps better to keep *adagia* and dicta separate.

B. CHARACTERISTIC FEATURES

One of the principal characteristics of dicta is that of familiarity within the relevant cultural group, and also of separation from literary sources and historical connections. Dicta are usually words that have, therefore, used their winged nature to fly away; they are usually introduced without reference to the author or to the work from which they come. Frequently neither the person quoting nor the audience know what author or what kind of work is being cited, which period the phrase comes from and to what it refers. Georg Büchmann wanted only those phrases to be considered 'winged words' which "derive from known and noted writers". Phrases for which there is no demonstrable author, even such much-quoted ones as 'In dubio pro reo' or 'De gustibus non est disputandum', are not listed even in the most recent editions of Büchmann's collection. Of course, modern linguistic usage has taken on board phrases like those – ones which have broken away completely from their origins, especially those from the Classical languages. It has thus been undoubtedly rather kinder to these stray birds of passage, even if they are not clearly and officially ringed with details of author and work, chapter and verse.

C. Educational and Cultural Background

An appropriate educational and cultural background is a necessary prerequisite for any compilation of quotations. Anyone citing one of these dicta presupposes that the recipient will not only understand the words without difficulty, even when they are Latin or Greek and even in the form of a fairly free allusion ('Si tacuisses ...'), but also that the recipient will accept it as a familiar quotation. The use of dicta brings the speaker and the listener together in a comfortable complicity. The "compilation of quotations" from the Classical languages documented by Büchmann since 1864 (the centenary edition of 1964 includes 66 Greek and 480 Latin dicta) reflects the general education of the middle classes in the late 19th and early 20th cents. and also the canon of texts read in the Classical grammar schools of the period. In line with this is the large proportion of quotations from Greek and Latin school texts. A series of quotations from the comedies, like 'Sapienti sat' and 'Homo sum; humani nil a me alienum puto' still point to the reading of Terence by younger pupils, which was usual before the reading of Caesar became obligatory later on. A body of quotations from Horace bears witness to the reading – in earlier periods far more widespread than it later became – of the *Satires* as well, giving us, for example, 'Quot capita, tot sensus', and the *Ars poetica* providing 'In medias res'. As far as the Classical languages are concerned, in the century between 1864 and 1964 the 'school' and 'Büchmann' enjoyed a fruitful symbiotic relationship on the fertile soil of a widespread classical education. Classroom texts provided and supported the body of dicta; 'Büchmann's' thesaurus in its turn provided first class material for practice and as examples. The spread of dicta by way of exercises and examples should not be underestimated; the celebrated 'De gustibus ... ' may even have its obscure origins in such an 'example of usage', in this case, of a negated gerundive.

D. Independent Dissemination

Generally speaking, the reception of dicta, once a phrase has actually taken flight, is already pretty well completely separate from the reception of the original author or work. The familiar tag 'Habent sua fata libelli' is true for dicta as such, just as it is for the original works that they come from; and it provides in itself an ideal illustration: the much-cited phrase (since 1825 it has also been the heraldic motto of the *Börsenverein des Deutschen Buchhandels*) comes from a long-forgotten little book by Terentianus Maurus, *De litteris, syllabis et metris*. Three examples may suffice to illustrate the many dicta that have winged their way successfully from the oblivion of their original sources: 'Homo homini lupus comes' from a comedy by Plautus that is now hardly ever read, 'Mens sana in corpore sano' and 'Panem et circenses' are from Juvenal's satires, now also rarely read. Vita brevis, ars longa, found in its Greek original at the beginning of the Hippocratic *Aphorisms*, acquired new and much-cited sources first at the start of Seneca's tract *On the Brevity of Life*, and then in Goethe's *Faust* in Wagner's despairing sigh 'Ach Gott, die Kunst ist lang ....' More recently, drug-dealing and money-laundering have provided for a considerable rise for Vespasian's 'Non olet' on the 'citation index', and in view of our most recent equivalents to Prometheus's theft of fire from the gods, namely the unleashing of nuclear power and the decipherment of the human gene-code, the Sophoclean 'Πολλα τα δεινα κ'ουδεν ανθρώπου δεινότερον πέλει', "much is monstrous, but nothing is more monstrous than man", has taken on a new and urgent topicality.

E. Changes of Meaning

Once removed from their literary or historical contexts, dicta from Greek or Latin in particular have in the course of the centuries regularly changed and have assumed more or less well understood meanings. The last words of Archimedes 'Noli turbare circulos meos' referred quite literally to the lines drawn in the fine sand on his drawing-board, and not, as the usual translation "Do not disturb my circles!" suggests, some kind of personal sphere. Caesar's 'Alea iacta est(o)', regularly misconstrued as "the die is cast", is more correctly translated as: "the die is (or is to be) thrown". This phrase, a verse of Menander's that was already proverbial, does not refer to the decision made by the fall of the die, but the decision for the boldness of casting it in the first place. Vergil's 'Labor omnia vicit/improbus' refers to the unstoppable displacement of the Golden Age by the Iron Age. Following what was clearly already a misunderstanding in the Classical world, Büchmann cites it as 'Labor omnia vincit' and translates "work unceasing conquers all". The 'schoolroom' makes itself felt here. The key role of the Classical grammar school for the reception of these dicta is clear also in the crass reversal of the bitter reproach to the school 'Non vitae, sed scholae discimus' from Seneca's letters to give the wonderful programmatic motto 'Non scholae, sed vitae discimus' over the gates of the school itself.

F. Language and Form

A number of dicta owe their status as 'winged words' to their firm and memorable language and form. The classic illustration of this is Caesar's brilliant 'Veni vidi vici', "I came, I saw, I conquered", with its three ordered and equivalent verb forms, anaphoric and with identical end-vowels as well – to say nothing of the gradual build-up to that thundering final *vici*. Extreme conciseness of expression, anaphora and rhymes are also found in dicta, such as 'Amantes amentes, Fortes Fortuna adiuvat, Multum, non multa' and 'Nomen est omen'. Equivalence and antithesis, spread in each case over four words, are the distinguishing features of phrases like 'Qualis rex, talis grex', 'Quot capita, tot sensus', 'Hic Rhodus, hic salta!', 'Aut Caesar aut nihil', 'Vita brevis, ars longa'. In 'Summum ius, summa iniuria' there is, in addition, a challenging paradox. In such dicta the characteristically pregnant conciseness of the Latin language is especially clear.

G. General Applicability

The deciding factor for whether or not a quotation will take on a life of its own is not, however, its visually or acoustically pleasing language, nor the pregnant form of the words, but rather the breadth of general applicability of the phrase. The more often dicta provide a suitable, striking and illuminating quotation to sum things up in different everyday situations, the more likely they are to be cited and cited again. This accounts for the familiarity of phrases like 'Errare humanum est' or 'Quot capita, tot sensus'. In the case of Greek and Latin dicta there is often the additional effect of an enhanced tone and quality. 'Alea iacta est' transports any everyday situation in which a decision has to be made straight to the Rubicon, while 'Veni vidi vici' confers on any rapidly concluded business success a little of the glory of Caesar. And plenty of people would rather be told in Latin 'Si tacuisses ...' than have things spelled out more bluntly in the vernacular.

H. The Contemporary Situation

With the constant recession in the teaching of Classical languages in grammar schools over the last few decades, Greek and Latin dicta have lost their natural vitality. There is no longer a level of society with a thoroughgoing Classical education, no more Classically oriented groups within society in which these dicta are current and 'natural'. Among the circumscribed group of 'Classical Greek' and 'Latin' students, Büchmann's flock of quotations, many hundred strong, may perhaps still be tended and nurtured; in the wild, however, in society as a whole, dicta cited in Latin or Greek would be seen as a 'rara avis' – or perhaps we had better now say, as a 'rare bird'. The only ones that are still in the original language and likely to remain so are the most commonly used dicta, which over time have become familiar even to those with no Greek or Latin – words and phrases like the Greek 'Eureka!' and 'Πάντα ρεῖ', or Latin 'Carpe diem!', 'Ceterum censeo ...', 'In dubio pro reo', 'In medias res', 'Nomen est omen', 'Non olet', 'Veni vidi vici' and other similar pithy expressions. The rest will have to be presented, if at all, then, sit venia verbo, with a translation and commentary; and if this is the case the whole charm of the 'words with wings', that knowing complicity between speaker and listener, the ironic allusion to a shared background – all that will be lost. In the remarkably small number of cases in which the vernacular translations of dicta originally in Classical languages have become recognised quotations in their own right, those versions have to a large extent supplanted the original. We may note here in passing that the habit of quotation as a means of showing-off – wearing the Classics on one's sleeve – 'sapienti sat' – has helped to bring discredit to dicta in the Classical languages.

I. Recognisability

In spite of these developments, the high level of familiarity of many Greek and Latin dicta, together with the general prestige value of the Classical world seems to have commended them to the world of advertising. Here it is principally a matter of simple recognisability. Archimedes' cry of discovery, 'Eureka!', has often been used as a brand name, for example, as the name of a hay-spreader (playing on the more correct form *Heureka* and the German word *Heu*, 'hay'), and also for Swiss 'Reka' (traveller'–') cheques; 'Veni vidi vici' has served as an advertising tag in all sorts of marketing campaigns, from the cigarette advertisement "Veni vidi fumi" down to the mock-campaign to elect the cartoonist-comedian Loriot as president, with the slogan "Veni vidi Vicco". In a full-page advertisement in the now-defunct magazine *Punch*, Julius Caesar, resplendent in his toga, offers a similarly draped gentleman a box of chocolates with the words: 'Et tu, Brute? De gustibus non est disputandum'.

1 G. Büchmann (ed.), Geflügelte Worte, Der Zitatenschatz des deutschen Volkes, collected and explained by G. Büchmann, continued by W. Robert-Tornow et alii, ³¹1964 (with a preface on the history of the collection), revised by W. Hofmann, ⁴¹1998   2 K. Bartels, VENI VIDI VICI. Geflügelte Worte aus dem Griechischen und Lateinischen, selected and explained by K. Bartels, ⁹1992, pocket book edition: ⁵2000   3 E. Knowles (ed.), Oxford Dictionary of Quotations, 2004   4 K. Noble, Classic Quotes, 1998.   Klaus Bartels

Dictatorship

A. Introduction   B. Early Modern Discussion   C. Enlightenment and French Revolution   D. 19th Century   E. Pathways into the 20th Century

A. Introduction

The reception of dictatorship as an ancient political model was focused almost entirely on the Roman example. Well into the 20th cent., it was seen as a laudable republican institution, or at least as one worth considering. Dictatorship and → democracy were not at all seen as conceptual opposites; on the contrary, under certain circumstances, dictatorship was seen as the enabling condition for democracy. Tyranny or despotism were the terms used to describe illegal forms of government. It was only in the course of the 20th century, under the impression of → National Socialism, → Fascism and Stalinism, that the concept of dictatorship assumed all the negative connotations of an illegitimate reign of terror. Against this backdrop, the view of the Antiquity also changed, and ancient dictatorship was now studied as a model or precursor of modern tyranny.

B. Early Modern Discussion

In theoretical deliberations on the modern state, the Roman institution of dictatorship gained paradigmatic importance; very early it was discussed as an ideal type, and not with the ancient model as a point of comparison. Two groups of questions dominated the discussion.

On the one hand, the emphasis was on the modern state in its specific governmental activity, particularly with regard to continuity and stability. In this context, dictatorship was seen as a subsumption of the *arcana imperii*. Arnold Clapmarius drew a distinction between dictatorship as *arcanum dominationis* [I. lib. 3, 19] and tyranny [I. lib. 5, 1]; he saw the problem of domination and pacification of the subject peoples even under the guise of legitimate violence not as tyrannical rule, but as a technical problem of *raison d'état*. With this notion of dictatorship and its concern with problems of internal stability, this modern academic debate on constitutional law had already greatly distanced itself from the Roman notion of dictatorship, particularly as shaped by Livy. On the other hand, dictatorship was seen as a touchstone for the growing theoretical interest in the problem of the longevity of the power of the state. Once political order was no longer exclusively seen in relation to the people who constituted it, but rather with the focus shifted to the state as an institutional order, the question of its continuity arose anew, especially as sovereignty had become the key aspect in the concept of the state. Discussing dictatorship provided the opportunity to include within this concept even situations where sovereignty was to be only temporary. From Jean Bodin [2] to Hugo Grotius [3], from Thomas Hobbes [4] to Samuel Pufendorf [5], dictatorship became the solution to the problem of a sovereignty requiring time limitations. This debate was also of importance to the republican strand of political thinking, as is evident, for example, in Algernon Sidney's [6] entering into this controversy. He recognized the sovereignty of the Roman dictator only in relation to the rest of the governing body, and not with respect to the people of Rome. This republican line of argument was largely rooted in the theoretical debates of the Italian Renaissance.

Real innovation, however, in the reception of dictatorship in modern history – and thus the opening of an entirely new strand in the debate – did not arise in the literature on constitutional law, but rather in the republican literature, particularly in the writings of Niccolò Machiavelli, who rediscovered the Roman institution of dictatorship for the modern history of political ideas and greatly influenced its debate with his interpretations [7. lib. 1, 33f.]. Central was his distinction between dictatorship for the protection of freedom (republic) and dictatorship in the sense of tyranny [7. lib. 1, 34]. The cause for this distinction were competing interpretations that saw dictatorship always as a forerunner of tyranny. This was the view to which Machiavelli objected with his typical focus on the analysis of power. He argued that dictatorship as a constitutional institution could be useful in defending against internal and external threats to the order of a free society, because the absence of such a pre-defined instrument of defence might force the political order to violate its own constitution, if it did not wish surrender itself completely. If this became common practice, as it potentially could, it might develop into a lever for anti-constitutional intentions.

In contrast, regulating the use of exceptional powers, especially through time limitations, posed no threat to the constitutional government and could ensure its continued existence in emergency situations. The danger that a dictatorship might pose a risk to the republican order only arose if it fell into the hands of a person already possessing superior powers. However, since the dictator was elected, it was hardly likely that the vote would fall to a candidate who would turn his dictatorial powers into a threat to the republic. In Machiavelli's view, the viability of a republic showed itself in its very ability to suppress the rise of overly powerful individuals. In this way, he linked the debate on dictatorship with his central focus on the self-preservation of a political order, whose security he saw more ensured by the inner attitude of its citizens than by its constitutional institutions. This already shows the germ of the problem which, in the subsequent revolutionary age, would lead to a departure from the classical model. At the centre was not the preservation of an already established republic, but founding one. Machiavelli's proximity to the ancient model is also evident in his view, in contrast to most later authors, that the significant feature of Roman dictatorship as a republican constitutional institution was the suspension of compulsory consultation prior to a making a binding decision. Hardly anyone after Machiavelli discussed this very important and characteristic constant in the Roman constitution, namely, the relationship between decision and deliberation or *consilium*, whose suspension in the case of a dictatorship was an exception and only for a limited time. In his description of dictatorship, which was to prove seminal in the modern history of ideas, Carl Schmitt saw dictatorship almost exclusively as an executive institution and thus shifted the focus to the decision and its generally self-referential legitimacy. Constantly referring to the example of Rome, Machiavelli understood dictatorship as an institution for the internal reform of the republic. For him dictatorship drew possibly its only legitimisation from this recourse to its roots. Dictatorship eradicated the dangerous political changes that had occurred over time and attempted to restore the constellations of the early years of the republic.

Baruch de Spinoza also discussed dictatorship as the ultimate means of maintaining order in a free society and of warding off any associated threats. However, his solution was somewhat different from Machiavelli's. He recommended awarding the office of dictator not to an individual, but to a group whose members should be too numerous to be able to divide the state amongst themselves [8. 210]. In contrast, James Harrington modelled his *Dictator Oceanae* entirely on the example typified by Livy and understood dictatorship solely as an office in times of war ([9. 177ff.], 19th order). However, though completely Roman in form, in purpose it was seen by Harrington, too, just as by Machiavelli, as an instrument in the foundation or reform of republics. In principle, Harrington saw dictatorship less as a means for the establishment of a monarchy than for preventing it. In times of crisis, when it would be all too easy to resort to a *de facto* monarchy without being able to contain its inherent risks, it would be much wiser to learn from ancient examples and to create in a timely manner an institution like a dictatorship, thus curbing the uncontrolled expansion of power of an individual. In contrast to Machiavelli, Harrington also took guidance from the Venetian example of instituting a dictatorship ([9. 180ff.], 23. order). In particular, a dictator must not have the right to appeal directly to the people, and his office, created to preserve the republic and indispensable, must not be allowed to degenerate into an autocracy on the basis of popular rule ([9. 238], 23rd order). Aware of the debates among English speaking thinkers, Thomas Jefferson argued against the Machiavellian interpretation of dictatorship as a republican principle and saw in it the inherent danger of tyranny. He maintained that even well-meaning supporters of a motion presented to the Virginia chamber of representatives in 1781, who, in suggesting the establishment of a dictatorship in light of the imminent British military threat, were seduced by the apparent example of the Roman Republic, where dictatorship was repeatedly introduced to repress a populace with a tendency towards tumult and unrest, thus directing its effectiveness towards internal strife. The American people, in contrast, tended towards mildness, and the historical example was thus not applicable [10].

C. ENLIGHTENMENT AND FRENCH REVOLUTION

Jean-Jacques Rousseau, too, suggested in his *Contrat Social* (1762) – expressly influenced by Machiavelli – that dictatorship was an office whose purpose was to preserve the political order. In addition, he found himself confronted with an entirely new problem, namely, how initially to create the republican constitution that was then to take dictatorship into account to secure its own continued existence. With this gradual change in perspective, the classical model lost importance until it faded almost entirely. Though Rousseau took as his point of departure the institution of dictatorship in the classical sense, he transcended this tradition by introducing the notion of a *législateur*. Whereas the dictator has the task of safeguarding the republic and was only prevented by a time restriction from establishing a tyranny (which is why he makes no reference at all to Sulla's extended dictatorship), the *législateur* has to create the laws and establish the order necessary to transform a people into a republic. However, in order not to violate the basic principle of a republic, the people have to agree to the constitution proposed by the *législateur;* the *législateur* thus had no legislative competence, but only the right of proposal. In this way, Rousseau tackled, quite along Machiavellian lines, the difficult problem that a republican constitution presupposes a sense of common purpose within the population, which in turn could really only be the result of such a constitution. Rousseau still shied away from a solution in which the executive power could legitimise itself by creating such a constitution.

Even though the Enlightenment upheld the distinction between a dictator as the one who safeguards freedom and a tyrant as the one who endangers it [11] (a view which contrasted the classical Republican dictatorship with the dictatorship of a Sulla, Caesar, or Augustus, who all as *dictator perpetuus* changed over to tyranny), revolutionaries who used this term soon met with fierce resistance, as, for example, Robespierre, who had to defend himself in his speech of 13 Messidor against the accusation that he was aspiring to a dictatorship.

It was this narrowing of dictatorship, however, to an instrument of the executive power that was to become a problem for the revolutionaries in view of the problems of implementing the 1791 constitution. Jacobins with political responsibility, such as Robespierre or Saint-Just, were reluctant to use the term *dictature* [12].

This reluctance was not least caused by Marat's aggressive use of the term with deliberate recourse to the ancient example. Marat, as spokesman for the Paris section, had a much clearer focus on the problem of popular violence and its legitimisation, most obvious after the September killings of 1792. Even in the run-up to these events, he had denounced the stagnating revolution in his paper *Ami du Peuple* and tried to win the increasingly passive population for institutions, such as a people's tribunal or a dictatorship, in order to break the impasse between the revolutionary aim and the shackles of the 1791 constitution. In the *Ami du peuple* no. 177 of 30 July 1790, he suggested the appointment of an elected dictator for a three-day period of office [13. 113] who was to eliminate potential tyrants from the populace in order to safeguard the revolution. Marat thus opposed the view that, as a result of the freedom achieved and institutionally secured by the revolution, the enemies of the revolution could only be fought using these very powers. He reminded his readers that even the Roman Republic had known an institution that permitted fundamental actions to secure freedom within the limits of the law. Soon thereafter, Marat specified his demands just as if the constitution were both modifiable and fixed at the same time. Instead of a dictator, he demanded a tribune of the poor. He was no longer concerned with the defence of the revolution, but with the protection of the poor, who had been cheated by the non-implementation of equality but also prevented from alleviating their poverty because of the property rights protected in the constitution (Ami du Peuple No. 223, 17.9.1790, 117). It became increasingly clear that the task was not only to save an existing constitution by its extraordinary suspension, but to suspend an existing constitution in order to achieve the very goals and principles at the root of this constitution in the first place – albeit in a very individual interpretation. For that reason, in justifying the September killings, Marat spoke of the dictatorship of the people that had manifested itself in those exceptional days, and of the axe of the people that had to fall because the sword of justice had not struck. He claimed that a timely blood toll among the enemies of the revolution would have prevented the flood of blood spilled later. Furthermore, he suggested the establishment of a dictatorship for as long as there were still Girondists at the Convention, namely, for as long as it was not under the leadership of the true revolutionary forces [13. 183ff.].

For this perspective, Rousseau could no longer serve as a model, but perhaps Gabriel Bonnot de Mably could. In his studies on Roman history in [14. 296, 338], he described dictatorship not as part of the usual government whose competency was only suspended for a certain period of time, but as replacing the normal government for the purpose of preserving the state, which the institution of *videant consules* could not achieve. Mably claimed that this was obvious in the case of Cicero, who was held to account for his conduct in office because he had ordered the execution of conspirators. A dictatorship would have spared him this ordeal and thus could have preserved the republic more securely and reliably. In such a situation, dictatorship is already no longer understood as governed by the needs of the constitution which is to be preserved, but is subordinated to the demands of political considerations outside of possible constitutional control.

D. 19TH CENTURY

These political-constitutional problems also influenced Fichte in his thoughts on the *Zwingherr,* the masterly leader, as the solution in establishing a political order which in turn would render such leader superfluous [15. 564]. Fichte deliberately avoided the term dictator because he no longer considered the ancient example exemplary, but outdated due to the essentially Germanic and Christian stamp put on the modern world. For that reason, he did not use terminology, even though in content he did indeed deal with the programme of self-reliance and dictatorship in its Machiavellian reception. In contrast, Friedrich Schlegel treated dictatorship as an institution of republican emergency law, as a transitory exception to the separation of powers, which is why *dictatura perpetua* was a self-contradictory term [16]. This view from Schlegel's more strongly republican period stands in sharp contrast to his later views, such as those voiced in 1828: "The normal and natural ... transition from popular anarchy, once it has ... exhausted itself, is that to absolute rule or perpetual dictatorship, in whatever form, but without ... divine sanction" [17. 408].

Theodor Mommsen's portrait of Caesar as *dictator perpetuus,* striving to incorporate this function into Rome's reformed political order, culminated in the assumption that Caesar had *de facto* wanted to reestablish the ancient monarchy. However, it had not been his aim to abolish the freedom of the citizens, but to establish this very freedom properly in the first place, against the "unbearable yoke of the aristocracy"

[18. 149]. This is an early reflection of the special situation of the politically active German intellectual middle class, who saw that achieving national unity would require the overthrow of the duodecimo princedoms (some of whose sovereigns called themselves kings) and who saw the Prussian monarchy as the executor of the historic mission of creating such unity and a political order that met contemporary expectations.

Much more outspoken were the political publicists of Borussian historiography, foremost among them Heinrich von Treitschke. After Bismarck had called upon the king during the Prussian constitutional conflict to endure a "period of dictatorship" in the battle with the parliamentary majority [19. 247], Treitschke became a staunch advocate of the Prussian policy of a kleindeutsch solution and supported this policy vociferously in his publications [20]. In doing so, he attempted to repudiate the allegation of Caesarism raised against Prussia by focusing his criticism only on the French version of Caesarism under Napoleon III which, with its Roman roots, he characterized as despotic and a danger to freedom. In contrast, Treitschke claimed that the German version stemmed from completely different, independent roots and thus could not be evaluated using the terminology and concepts of Roman political thinking. Treitschke considered the essential characteristic of the Romance tradition of autocracy to be the special role of Paris – the "dictatorship of this city" [20. 50], which had become the successor of Rome. Napoleon I, more than anyone else, had understood how to tie in with this tradition and to establish a democratically legitimised autocracy on its basis: "how masterly he was able to revive from Roman history most of all those images that spoke straight to the heart of 'the armed democracy' of the new French Empire. To his regiments he presented the same eagles that had once been awarded by the democratic general Marius to his Roman legions and that had spread Caesar's democratic monarchy across the world. With disastrous zeal, the nation assumed the deplorable habits of the Roman imperial age" [20. 79].

The French Revolution had gradually shifted the focus from the classic problem of how to restore a republican constitution through dictatorship towards how initially to establish such a constitution. With that shift, the ancient example also lost its paradigmatic character, and in its place stepped the French Revolution itself. However, ancient history remained the backdrop to the debate for as long as a distinction was made between revolutionaries using contemporary arguments and those using antiquarian ones. This is particularly true for the dispute between Marx and Engels, on one side, and Ferdinand Lassalle, on the other, about the future strategy of German social democracy.

In his famous Rhonsdorf speech, Lassalle had distinguished between a liberal concept of freedom and that of the working classes. The former he associated with individual opinionating and whining, the latter with the ability to give free consent to a judicious dictatorship in order to acquire the necessary political clout needed in that period of transition [21. 420]. Lassalle aimed for a republican concept of freedom, in contrast to a liberal-burgeois concept, and he propounded his arguments against the backdrop of a political strategy of conquering the state; not, however, to overthrow it in its structure, but to lead it to its real cultural mission in which it had so far been hampered by the powers of the middle class and the aristocracy. Marx and Engels polemicised continually against this adherence to the traditional concept of the state and its associated republican concept of freedom, as well as the advocacy of general suffrage for its own sake. They rejected this doctrine of the "state as the ancient vestal fire of civilization" in the same way that they rejected the model of ancient democracy, as perceived by the French Jacobins, or any talk of a free state [22]. Against the judicious dictatorship, as propagated by Lasalle, Marx put forward the dictatorship of the proletariat. Instead of the institutional culmination of executive power in a single person, Marx proposed the dictatorship of a collective; and he was not interested in its institutional form or its justification, but only its character as a transitory stage which was beyond constitutional or normative regulation.

Marx understood dictatorship as depersonalised class rule and was ill-disposed towards any orientation based on ancient models. In contrast, Karl Kautsky, referring to the classical concept of dictatorship, pointed out that, particularly in view of the contents and possibilities of a political dictatorship, the developments in Bolshevist Russia, though described as the dictatorship of the proletariat, were in reality neither the dictatorship of a class nor a party, but rather that of individuals, namely, the leaders [23. 136f.]. The socialist discourse distanced itself further and further from the ancient paradigm which was, in any case, viewed with mistrust by the workers' movement because of its association with the middle-class educational canon.

The reply of the opponents of the revolution to this absorption of the notion of dictatorship into revolutionary thought was to reinvent it as a counter-revolutionary strategy. While there was now the choice between dictatorship from the bottom up or from the top down, dictatorship of the dagger or the sword (Donoso Cortés), the traditional conservative choice, namely, that of preserving an order whose only legitimacy was that it was part of natural evolution was no longer an option. For that reason, Donoso chose active counter-revolution and demanded a dictatorship of the government. Dictatorship was thus neither an institutional tool to maintain an established order nor a tool to create a new one, but rather a means for the active restoration of an already declining or vanished order, in particular, the authority of Roman Catholic Church [24. 48f.].

E. PATHWAYS INTO THE 20TH CENTURY

In both revolutionary and counter-revolutionary reasoning, dictatorship had thus departed from the ancient model and moved forward into an area conceived of as modern and thus not able to be illumined by comparison. The ancient example only reappeared in the context of the phenomenon of Bonapartism, or → CAESARISM. Initially, it was measured against the benchmarks of classical dictatorship, for example, by Constantin Frantz [25]. He saw dictatorship as the essential feature of the Napoleonic state, particularly because of its *de facto* republican orientation. By its very nature, dictatorship was only conceivable in a republic and not a monarchy; however, in contrast to the ancient model of republican dictatorship, its modern variant was not based on 'exception', but on 'principle', and thus, as Frantz argued, the modern form of the French Republic was for its part an exceptional form of government [25. 77]. Dictatorship was defined as the rule of one man who did not prevail due to his legitimacy or the strength of a moral idea, but under the guise of physical necessity and by violent means.

In the further analysis of this democratically legitimised, but still anti-republican phenomenon of executive power, the other ancient model prevailed – that of Caesarism, which for some time displaced the notion of dictatorship from political discourse [26]. Caesarism came to epitomize the assumption of political power by force pure and simple, without the bother of concerning itself with the appearance of legitimacy associated with a traditional republican term like dictatorship. Oswald Spengler can be seen as representative for this process. In his view [27. 1004ff., 1101ff.], the age of Caesarism had dawned. Although he constantly drew analogies to historical events and structural changes in ancient times as proof for his theories, Spengler perceived the constitutional structures of the political order as a mere façade masking the power struggle behind it. This made such traditional concepts as dictatorship the playthings of political self-legitimisation. To prove this thesis, Spengler pointed to the description by Diodorus Siculus 19,6ff. of mob rule in Syracuse and the solemn bestowal of the dictatorship on Agathocles in gratitude for his 'butchery' of the upper classes [27. 1066 fn. 1].

Against this backdrop, the attempt to discuss the fundamental principles of the Weimar constitution with the aid of the classical notion of dictatorship is even more surprising. Quite early on and almost as a matter of convention, the exceptional powers granted to the president by the Weimar constitution were referred to as constitutional dictatorship. One, but not the only source for this, was Carl Schmitt, probably the most important theoretician on dictatorship. In an extensive study on the history of ideas written during the First World War, Schmitt had arrived at a systematic distinction between provisional and sovereign dictatorship after a careful analysis of the various tangled strands of the notion of dictatorship in the reception of both the classical and the revolutionary models. The anti-democratic use, so unmistakable later on, was not so clear then, because Schmitt cites as his main examples for sovereign dictatorship the French Convention of 1793 and its Committee of Public Welfare, thus bestowing the term dictator on an explicitly non-executive, but rather legislative power. Consequently Schmitt initially saw the *Reichstag* as the sovereign dictator, because of its legislative competency to establish the legal framework for the (therefore only provisional, i.e. secondary) dictatorship of the president. Only when this regulation was omitted, did Schmitt turn his attention to the president and successfully looked for non-legislative foundations to legitimise the executive power, particularly in the distinction between constitutional law and the constitution (as the legislatively available, essentially normative basis of the political order). In this discussion of constitutional law, the ancient model, however, became little more than a rough overlay for the initial terminological clarification [28]. Thus Hermann Heller mentioned the differences between a republican dictatorship preserving the constitution and a dictatorship with a legitimisation *sui generis* and its anti-republican connotations [29]. However, the term had already acquired a life of its own, and even a politically active ancient historian such as Arthur Rosenberg failed to clarify the current understanding of dictatorship through recourse to the ancient model. The same also applies to Arkadij Gurland's distinction between a legal and a sociological concept of dictatorship [30. 101ff.], which makes almost no reference at all to ancient history. In contrast, Franz Neumann, in his posthumously published *Notes on the Theory of Dictatorship*, claimed of the Roman dictatorship before Sulla that "strictly speaking... it had been not a dictatorship, but a form of emergency rule" [31. 147]. Leo Strauss, too, may have had the classical notion of dictatorship in mind when he objected to the term 'Age of Dictatorships', which came into fashion after 1945, by maintaining that "a number of currently existing regimes were tyrannies in the guise of dictatorships" [32. 197].

→ Tyranny

Sources 1 A. Clapmar, De Arcanis rerumpublicarum libri VI, Bremen 1605, vol. III   2 J. Bodin, Les six livres de la République, 1583, repr. 1961 (Engl. K. D. McRae (ed.), The six books of a commonweale. A facsimile reprint of the English translation of 1606, corrected and supplemented in the light of a new comparison with the French and Latin texts, 1962, repr.1979)   3 H. Grotius, De jure belli ac pacis libri III, 1625, I,3,8,12 und I,3,11,1 und 2 (Engl. R. Tuck (ed.), The Rights of War and Peace, 2005)   4 Th. Hobbes, De Cive, G. Gawlick (ed.), 1994, Ch. 7, 155f.   5 S. Pufendorf, De jure naturae et gentium libri VIII, J. K. Hertius (ed.), Frankfurt 1704, Book VII, 6 § 15; VIII, 6 § 14 (Engl. B. Kennett (trans.), Of the Law of Nature and Nations: Eight Books, 1729, repr., 2005)   6 A. Sidney, Discourses concerning Government 1698, Th. G. West (ed.), 1996, Ch. II, sect. 13   7 N. Machiavelli, Discorsi sopra la prima deca di Tito Livio (Engl. H. C. Mansfield, N. Tarcov (trans.), Discourses on Livy, 1996)   8 B. de Spinoza, Politische Traktate, latein-deutsch, W. Bartuschat (trans. and ed.),1994 (Engl. S. Shirley (trans.), Political Treatise by Spinoza, Introduction and notes S. Barbone, L. Rice, 2000)   9 J. Harrington, Oceana (1656), H. Klenner, K. U. Szudra (eds.),

1991   10 Th. Jefferson, Notes on the State of Virginia: With Related Documents, D. Waldstreicher (ed.), 2002   11 Ch. de Jaucourt, Dictateur, in: Encyclopédie ou Dictionnaire raisonné des sciences, des arts et des métiers, IV, Paris 1754, 956–958 (Engl. N. S. Hoyt, T. Cassirer (trans.), Encyclopedia: Selections, Diderot, D'Alembert, and a Society of Men of Letters, 1965)   12 M. Robespierre, Rapport sur les principes du Gouvernement révolutionnaire vom 25.12.1793, in: Id., Oeuvres, 10, 1967, 273ff.   13 J.-P. Marat, Marat textes choisis, C. Mossé (ed.), 1950   14 G. B. de Mably, Observations sur les Romains, in: Collection complète des Oeuvres, G. Arnoux (ed.), 1794–1795, repr. 1977, Vol. 4 (Engl.: Observations on the Romans, London, 1751)   15 G. Fichte, Aus dem Entwurf zu einer politischen Schrift 1813, in: Sämmtliche Werke, 7, Berlin/Bonn 1846, 546–573 (Engl. W. Smith (ed.), The Popular Works of Johann Gottlieb Fichte, 1999 (repr. of 1889 edition)   16 F. Schlegel, Versuch über den Begriff des Republikanismus, 1796, in: Kritische Friedrich-Schlegel-Ausgabe, 7, E. Behler (ed.), 1966, 11–25 (Engl. E. J. Millington (trans.), The Aesthetic and Miscellaneous Works of Frederick von Schlegel, 1849)   17 Id., Philosophie des Lebens, Wien 1828 (Engl. A. J. W. Morrison (trans.), The Philosophy of Life and Philosophy of language, 1847)   18 Th. Mommsen, Römische Geschichte, 1854–1885, ⁹1902, vol. 5 (Engl. The History of Rome, 1894; repr. 1986)   19 O. von Bismarck, Gedanken und Erinnerungen, 1928 (Engl. A. J. Butler (trans.), The Memoirs: Being the Reflections and Reminiscences of Otto, Prince von Bismarck, 1966)   20 H. von Treitschke, Frankreichs Staatsleben und der Bonapartismus, 1865/69, in: Id., Historische und politische Aufsätze, Leipzig 1886, vol. 3, 44–426   21 F. Lassalle, Die Agitation des Allgemeinen Deutschen Arbeiter-Vereins und das Versprechen des Königs von Preußen. Rede am Stiftungsfest des ADAV, Rhonsdorfer Rede, vom 22. Mai 1864, in: Id., Rede und Schriften, F. Jenaczek (ed.), 1970, 392–421   22 A. Bebel, Aus meinem Leben, 1911, 221f. (F. Engels to A. Bebel) (Engl. My Life, London, 1912; repr. 1983)   23 K. Kautsky, Die proletarische Revolution und ihr Programm, 1922 (Engl. H. J. Stenning (ed.), The Labour Revolution, 1925)   24 J. Donoso Cortéz, Drei Reden: Über die Diktatur. Über Europa. Über die Lage Spaniens, J. Langenegger (trans.), 1948 (Engl. J. P. Johnson (trans.), Selected works of Juan Donoso Cortés, 2000)   25 C. Frantz, Louis Napoleon, ²1852, repr. 1960   26 A. Romieu, L'ère des Césars, 1850 (Der Cäsarismus oder die Notwendigkeit der Säbelherrschaft, dargetan durch geschichtliche Beispiele von den Zeiten der Caesaren bis auf die Gegenwart, Leipzig 1851)   27 O. Spengler, Der Untergang des Abendlandes. Umrisse einer Morphologie der Weltgeschichte, ²1922 (Engl. C. F. Atkinson (trans.), The Decline of the West, 1991)   28 C. Schmitt, Die Diktatur von den Anfängen des modernen Souveränitätsgedankens bis zum proletarischen Klassenkampf, ²1928, repr. 1989   29 H. Heller, Rechtsstaat oder Diktatur?, 1930, in: Id., Gesammelte Schriften, 1971, vol. 2, 443–462   30 A. Gurland, Marxismus und Diktatur, 1928, D. Emig (ed.), 1981   31 F. L. Neumann, Notizen zur Theorie der Diktatur, 1957, in: Id., Demokratischer und autoritärer Staat. Beiträge zur Soziologie der Politik, 1967, 147–1(Engl. H. Marcuse (ed.), The Democratic and the Authoritarian State; Essays in Political and Legal Theory, 1957)   32 L. Strauss, Über Tyrannis, 1963 (Engl.: On Tyranny, V. Gourevitch, M. S. Roth (eds.), rev. and expanded ed. including the Strauss-Kojève correspondence, 1991)

LITERATURE 33 D. GROH, Cäsarismus, Geschichtliche Grundbegriffe 1, 726–71 34 F. HINARD, (ed.), Dictatures, 1988 35 H. HOFMANN, Diktatur – eine begriffsgeschichtliche Miniatur, in: Id., Recht-Politik-Verfassung – Studien zur Geschichte der politischen Philosophie, 1986, 122–126 36 P. JOACHIMSEN, Die Bedeutung des antiken Elements für die Staatsauffassung der Renaissance, in: Id., Gesammelte Aufsätze, N. HAMMERSTEIN (ed.), 1970 37 E. E. KELLETT, The Story of Dictatorship – from the Earliest Times till To-Day, 1937 38 H. KOHN, Revolutions and Dictatorship, ²1941 39 J. A. R. MARRIOTT, Dictatorship and Democracy, 1935 40 F. MEHMEL, Machiavelli und die Antike, in: A&A 3, 1948, 152–186 41 E. NOLTE, Diktatur, Geschichtliche Grundbegriffe 1, 900–25 42 C. L. ROSSITER, Constitutional Dictatorship. Crisis Government in the Modern Democracies, 1941 (repr. 1963) 43 G. SPRIGATH, Themen aus der Geschichte der römischen Republik in der französischen Malerei des 18. Jahrhunderts, 1968 44 O. STAMMER, Demokratie und Diktatur, 1955

HERFRIED LLANQUE, MARCUS MÜNKLER

Didactic literature see→ DIDACTIC POEM

Didactic Poem
A. CONCEPT B. THEORETICAL PROBLEMATIC
C. POETIC PRACTICE

A. CONCEPT
The term *Lehrgedicht* ('didactic poem'/DP), used in Germany since 1646 and disputed thereafter [1. 10–29], particularly in the 18th cent., is even today not clearly defined. It is frequently not distinguished from 'didactic literature' and 'didactic poetry' and is also extended to cover poetry that has only implicitly didactic intentions (so-called 'indirect didactic poetry' [5. 11]). Its definability as a genre was disputed for example in the Middle Ages [3. 9]. Such a broad term [survey of scholarship: 7. 19–38] requires the inclusion of almost the whole spectrum of literature of an epoch like that of the Middle Ages (including fables, animal poetry, riddles; cf. [14]) that has a predominantly didactic focus. In view of this, a narrower term commends itself: DPs are versified texts, mainly cast in the present tense, with the primary intention of imparting an item of knowledge, however formulated. This requires a presupposed or explicit teacher-student relationship between the author and the addressee [7. 38]. Pleasure in subject-matter innovation is a constant feature of the genre. These texts are particularly strongly represented in those eras that value highly the imparting of 'knowledge' and mostly see no problem with a poetic mode of transmission (Middle Ages, Enlightenment). The most important ancient authors serving as models are Lucretius (*De rerum natura*), Virgil (*Georgics*) and Ovid (*Ars amatoria*, *Remedia amoris*, *Medicamina faciei femineae*).

B. THEORETICAL PROBLEMATIC
Besides the problem of defining the term there is the question of whether it is possible to define a poetic genre of didactic poetry [6]; it is characterized by the constitutive tension between *didaxis* and *poiesis*. Under the pressure of the mimesis theory as the fundamental criterion of poetic literature, Aristotle (Poet. 1) excludes didactic literature from the realm of poetic literature but at the same time introduces the theoretical conception of the DP. Later theory bypasses the Aristotelian judgement [2; 10]: the *Tractatus Coislinianus* (1st cent. BC) differentiates between mimetic and amimetic poetic literature: the latter is divided into *historiké* and *paideutiké*, which, in turn, are divided into *hyphegetiké* (instructive) and *theoretiké*. In that way the DP was rescued, just as it was with Diomedes (4th cent. AD), who was extremely influential in the following period. He distinguishes between three flexible main forms: *genus activum* (*imitativum*, *dramaticon*, *mimeticon*), *genus enarrativum* (*enuntiativum*, *exegeticon*, *apangelticon*), *genus commune* (*mixtum*, *koinon*, *micton*). Under the *genus enarrativum*, which is characterized by a uniform author-narrator, comes aphoristic literature (*angeltice*) and narrative-genealogical literature (*historice*), as well as the DP (*didascalice*).

The Middle Ages extended this tripartite schema in modified form further with Bede (673–735), who repeated it verbatim in places, by elevating the *didascalicum* in the poetological hierarchy (without making an explicit distinction between verse and prose in the process) [7. 39–44]: in Eberhard of Béthune's (ca. 1200) *Grecismus*, the three principal genres are *dragmaticon*, *hermeneticon*, *didascalicon*, and in John of Garlandia (*Poetria*, 1252), the *genus commune*, which in Diomedes was still supposed to describe the epic, is called *didascalicon*, *idest doctrinale*. In the dominant key of the Horatian dual definition of literature (Ars 333: 'aut prodesse volunt aut delectare poetae', a dichotomy which the DP seemed to form impeccably into a synthesis), the Renaissance initially adopted the medieval concepts, but 'rediscovery' of Aristotle's *Poetica* from the middle of the 16th cent. led to a confrontation with his determination outlined above (→ GENRE/GENRE THEORY). The resulting diversity of learned views ranged from acceptance of the determination (e.g. by the Horace commentator F. Luisinus and by A. Riccoboni) to its categorical rejection by J. C. Scaliger, who supported DPs against the background of a markedly didactic concept of literature and by resorting to the old criterion of verse for a definition of poetry [6. 74–81]. Certainly an attempt was made to advance beyond Aristotle while maintaining his concept of mimesis. Thus G. Fracastoro (*Naugerius*, 1540) defines the (Aristotelian-confirmed) universal instead of the particular as an object of poetic imitation, with the poet becoming the mediator of the real nature of things. The gradual distancing from Aristotle becomes rejection with later theoreticians: F. Bacon (*Advancement of learning*, 1608/23) attributes empirical reality to philosophy as object and by contrast, attributes the world of imagination to literature. Following in the same direction, the theories during the English Restoration (1660–1700) endow literature with the capacity of representing psychologically motivated models, of *beings in nature* at most still loosely connected to the empirical world, including universal and abstract concepts. That took away from DPs the Aristotelian stigma of their amimetic character and provided a theoretical basis for their revival in the 18th cent. [6. 84–88]. A little later, efforts to establish a didactic main genre reached their climax with Ch. Batteux [13. 26–29]. Thereafter, the DP lost ground in a theoretical and practical sense. In Germany, that was due, among other things, to Lessing's Aristotelian-based disparagement of the DP [13. 29 f.].

C. POETIC PRACTICE

The Middle Ages inherited the predominantly pagan tradition of the ancient DP, which was flanked, however, by Christian instructive literature (e. g. Commodian, Orientius, Prudentius [14. 20]). The dominant language of the medieval DP was Latin, nourished by a) language of specialization, and b) the Virgilian-Horatian-Ovidian tradition. Vernacular DPs [7. 212–216] were rare. The extremely numerous (Index: [7. 430–444]) medieval Latin DPs mostly serve a practical instructive purpose, are strongly issue-related and are clearly sub-divided on a rhetorical-didactic basis. Thematically they concentrate on three areas: grammar/rhetoric/poetics, medicine/botany and astronomy/mathematics/arithmetic. The early medieval works of W. Strabo (*De cultura hortorum*) and W. von Prüm (*De mensium duodecim nominibus*) are examples of a particularly successful adoption of ancient models [9. 173–177]. In the Renaissance, a development took place that ran the range from the medieval version of versified manual to the polished literary classical version of the DP in the ancient mould [11. 24]. However, even in innovative Italy, this is a gradual and not abrupt process ([7. 28–31, 373], a contrary view in [11]). The persistence of the categories of DPs in the Middle Ages continued, especially in the Humanistic domain [7. 374–397], and just as firmly did the use of Latin: about one half of the DPs of the Italian Renaissance are in Latin [11. 8]. Thematically, Renaissance DPs are not substantially different from those of the Middle Ages. 'Weightier' themes are generally treated in Latin [11. 10]. Under the influence of the Humanistic *imitatio*-theory [11. 91], among other things, interest slowly shifted away from the handling of the *res* (archaically still in the foreground e.g. in Dati, *Sfera*, early 15th cent. [11. 27–35]) to the shaping of the *carmen* (virtuoso: G. Pontano, *Urania*, end of the 15th cent.; G. Vida, *Scacchia, ludus*, ca. 1520; G. Fracastoro, *Syphilis*, 1530), down to the explicit rejection in B. Baldi's *Nautica* (ca. 1590) of there being any possibility of transmitting knowledge through didactic literature [11. 236–239]. After a low-point during the Baroque era [1. 108–131],

the DP enjoyed one last upswing in the Enlightenment. Highly Influential in that were A. Pope's *Essay on criticism* (1709), influenced by Horace, his fragment *Essay on man* (1733 ff.), as well as J. Thomson's *Seasons* (1726/30), inspired by Virgil and Lucretius [15]. While French didactic literature (L. Racine, *De la grâce, La religion*, 1742; A. Chénier, *Hermès*, fragmentary, 2nd half of the 18th cent.) is firmly rooted in the aristocratic milieu, the German DP of the 18th cent. is a phenomenon of the bourgeoisie Enlightenment. Thematically, moral-philosophical problems predominate, while specialist DPs are in the minority and are especially concerned with poetics [13. 53–68]. The Enlightenment concept 'humanities' implies a favouring of the *res* over the *carmen* [13. 12 f.]. Amongst the most important authors are B. H. Brockes, A. v. Haller, J. J. Bodmer. The literary attachment to ancient *auctores*, especially Lucretius, continued; in terms of content, however, modern authorities (Newton, Leibniz) strongly gained influence [13. 142–144]. Indebted to traditional rhetorical poetics, the DP lost its status at the end of the 18th cent., due to the increasingly stronger emphasis on poetic subjectivity (symptomatic was the influence of E. Young's *Night thoughts*, 1742–45) and to immanent-aesthetic justification of poetic creativity [13. 4, 248 f.]. Moreover, at this time, Latin, its longtime, steady support, became weakened [7. 394–397].

→ Didactic poetry

1 L. L. ALBERTSEN, Das Lehrgedicht, 1967   2 I. BEHRENS, Die Lehre von der Einteilung der Dichtkunst, 1940   3 B. BOESCH, Lehrhafte Literatur, 1977   4 U. BROICH, Das Lehrgedicht als Teil der epischen Tradition des englischen Klassizismus, in: Germanisch-romanische Monatsschrift 13, 1963, 147–163   5 L. DANZI, Prime note sulla poesia didascalia e scientifica tra XVIII e XIX secolo, in: BARDAZZI, GIOVANNI/GROSRICHARD, ALAIN (eds.), Dénouement des Lumières et invention romantique. Actes du Colloque de Genève, 24–25 novembre 2000, 2004, 143–60   6 B. EFFE, Dichtung und Lehre, 1977   7 B. FABIAN, Das Lehrgedicht als Problem der Poetik, in: H. R. JAUSS (ed.), Die nicht mehr schönen Künste, 1968, 67–89   8 T. HAYE, Das lateinische Lehrgedicht im Mittelalter, 1997   9 E. LEIBFRIED, Philosophisches Lehrgedicht und Fabel, in: NHL 11, 1974, 75–90   10 A. ÖNNERFORS, Die lateinische Literatur der Karolingerzeit, in: NHL 6, 1985, 151–187   11 E. PÖHLMANN, Charakteristika des römischen Lehrgedichts, in: ANRW 1.3, 813–901   12 G. ROELLENBLECK, Das epische Lehrgedicht Italiens im 15. und 16. Jahrhundert, 1975   13 A.-M. SCHMIDT, La poésie scientifique en France au seizième siècle, 1938   14 C. SIEGRIST, Das Lehrgedicht der Aufklärung, 1974   15 B. SOWINSKI, Lehrhafte Dichtung des Mittelalters 1971   16 E. WOLFF, Dichtung und Prosa im Dienste der Philosophie, in: NHL 12, 1984, 155–204.

ADDITIONAL BIBLIOGRAPHY Y. A. HASKELL, Loyola's Bees: Ideology and Industry in Jesuit Latin Didactic Poetry, 2003. Y. A. HASKELL, P. R. HARDIE (eds.), Poets and Teachers: Latin Didactic Poetry and the Didactic Authority of the Latin Poet from the Renaissance to the Present, 1999.   BERNHARD HUSS

Dietetics Classical ideas of dietetics, based on the Hippocratic and Galenic notions of a balance between the four humours, continued to play an important role in medicine into the 20th cent. (→ HUMORAL THEORY). In → ARABIC MEDICINE, all substances taken into the body had properties that could affect its health, for good or ill, and hence it was the doctor's duty to prescribe diets for health, as well as for disease, and equally that of his patient to understand the rules for a healthy lifestyle. Thus a long chapter on diet could form part of a tract on government written for an emir by al-Muradi (d. 1095). The most important Arabic tract on dietetics, by Ibn Butlan (d. ca. 1068), was a comprehensive guide to foodstuffs which, in Latin translation as *Tacuinum Sanitatis*, continued to be followed well into the 16th cent. The Latin High Middle Ages followed the Arabic synthesis of → GALENISM. The Medical Humanists, like Manuel Brudus, author of a tract on Hippocratic dietetics, 1544, while correcting identifications of plants, and modifying a few usages, kept the general scheme. Diet, as one of the six non-naturals, was universally seen as an essential control of health, and was widely discussed in medical tracts as well as in popular handbooks for the layman, e.g. Sir Thomas Elyot's *Castell of helth*, 1541. Changes in dominant medical theory, from Paracelsianism in the 16th cent. to Brunonianism in the 19th, did not dislodge dietetics from a central place in medical practice, although the meaning of dietetics in medical speech tended to reduce dietetics from the ancient concept of a lifestyle merely to food and drink. Patients, however, took a wider view. Sociological studies in the 1970s and 1980s revealed the persistence of this ancient concept among patients. At the same time, just as many foodstuffs originally recommended as dietetic medicines by fringe practitioners, e.g. cornflakes and muesli, had become part of everyday Western diet, so that in the last third of the 20th cent. emphasis on the role of healthy eating and healthy lifestyle could be found in orthodox medicine, and was being advocated once again as a prophylaxis.

→ Dietetics

→ HIPPOCRATISM; → HUMANISM III. MEDICAL; → MEDICINE

1 M. WEISS ADAMSON, Medieval Dietetics: Food and Drink in *regimen sanitatis* Literature from 800 to 1400, 1995 VIVIAN NUTTON

Digesta; Textual Transmission
A. LATE ANTIQUITY B. EARLY MIDDLE AGES C. HIGH MIDDLE AGES D. HUMANISM E. FROM THE 17TH TO THE 20TH CENTURY

A. LATE ANTIQUITY
1. CODEX FLORENTINUS 2. FURTHER TEXTUAL RECORDS FROM LATE ANTIQUITY 3. BASILICA

1. CODEX FLORENTINUS
The parchment manuscript in Florence from Late Antiquity–Biblioteca Medicea Laurenziana (Codex

Florentinus; Codices latini antiquiores III 295)–constitutes the authoritative textual record of Digesta transmission [1; 4; 5; 6; 7]. Along with the text of the Digesta, it contains the accompanying constitutions of Justinianus, the *index auctorum* and *index titulorum* (with a Greek epigram). At present, the manuscript (366 x 320 mm) is divided into two volumes (translations of Greek texts by Leonzio Pilato are bound in), the text appearing in two columns except for the Latin introductory constitutions. The BR-uncial serves as the text, older half-uncials contain the Latin constitutions and the *index auctorum* [8]. It was produced by more than ten scribes and revised by at least two proofreaders. The rubrics and (most) of the jurists' names are in red, as are the majority of the explicits/incipits. The Justinian division of the Digesta into seven *partes* (e.g. Dig. 5 expl.) is only rarely observed. The inscriptions and Graeca are complete; literal quotations often appear in quotation marks (Diple). The rubrics were later numbered in Greek or in Latin by the proofreaders. They corrected not only the errors made by the scribes but supplemented jurists' fragments and individual sections as well. They therefore must have had access to a further manuscript of the Digesta that differed from the model of the Codex Florentinus (Cod. Flor.). In Dig. 37,8.9, they corrected a reversal of titles in the original source through a commentary in Greek (Dig. 37,9.8). The supplement of Dig. 35,2,50–52 pr. by the proofreaders reflects a scholium on basilica 41,1,51 which points out a difference in the length of the text compared to the manuscripts. The manuscripts from Late Antiquity therefore were not completely uniform [9]. The Cod. Flor. also shows gaps in its proofreading, as in Dig. 17 and Dig. 36 (for instance, the names of the jurists are missing in Dig. 17,1,33–36). A loss of certain texts is due partially to missing pages in the manuscript (beginning of the Const. Dedoca, end of Dig. 19,5 and Dig. 46,8), in Dig. 48 to a gap in the model. In the latter, the end of Dig. 48,20,7,5 was missing as well as four fragments, and nine to ten fragments after Dig. 48,22,9. A paper misplacement in Dig. 50,17 led to a serious text interruption (Dig. 50,17,117; 158–199; 118–157; 200). The manuscript still shows traces of the compilation process [10]. Neither its date nor its location are indicated. Its origin in the east is evidenced by Greek corrections, by the partially Greek rubric narrative, the Greek explicit of a scribe after Dig. 11 as well as by particularities of the quire count and the script [8]. The dating of the manuscript is hampered by the lack of other evidence of the BR-uncial. The composition and design of the Cod. Flor. shows similarities with the Veronese Codex palimpsest (Ms. Verona, Bibl. cap. LXII pp. 481; CLA IV 511) which must have been produced under Justinianus still based on the references to novellas in the supplementary Greek body of scholia. The Cod. Flor. probably found its way to Italy in the 6th cent. during the Justinian recapture (according to [11], it was still located in Byzantium in the 9th cent.; differing: [12]). For the early 10th cent., notes in the margins in Beneventana document that Southern Italy was the location of the time [12]. In the mid 12th cent., the Cod. Flor. was located in Pisa, where it was revered and consulted for the determination of correct versions (which thereby entered into the manuscripts of the Middle Ages). In 1406, the Florentines seized the manuscript during the capture of Pisa.

2. FURTHER TEXTUAL RECORDS FROM LATE ANTIQUITY

The remaining records from Late Antiquity consist of fragments of individual Digesta titles, thus P. Pomm. Lat. 1–6 (Dig. 45,1,35–49. 72–73; CLA IX 1351), P. Ryl. 479 (Dig. 30,11–26; CLA Suppl. 1723), P. Heid. Lat. 4 (Dig. 5,2,17–19; CLA VIII 1221), all in BR-uncial, as well as P. Sorb. Reinach 2173 (Dig. 19,2,54; CLA Add. 1858) in a leaning uncial. All of the single-column fragments show no colour variations and appear to be unadorned copies for everyday use (in contrast to the Cod. Flor.). In P. Pomm. Lat. 1–6 and P. Ryl. 479, the fragments are counted in Greek. Section markers (without numbers) appear in P. Pomm. Lat. 1–6. In general, the fragments date back to the eastern 6th cent., although the same uncertainties as those mentioned for the Cod. Flor. remain. Here and there, the fragments have marginalia, for instance the reference *regula* in P. Pomm. Lat. 5 to Dig. 45,1,41,1 as well as Greek scholia in P. Heid. 4 and P. Sorb. Reinach 2173. These contribute little to the structure of the text. The *fragmenta Neapolitana*, Ms. Neapel, Biblioteca nazionale IV A 8, fol. 36–39 (CLA III 402) are written in a western uncial (s. VI²) and belong to the palimpsest of a grammarian's manuscript that was created in Bobbio s. VIII ineunte. The single-column text without colour variations comprises Dig. 10,2,3–10,4,19 and counts rubrics and fragments in Latin. It shows several corrections compared to the Cod. Flor. Some of the fragments are accompanied by brief marginal summaries.

3. BASILICA

Indirectly, the Digesta transmit the Basilica as well. The Basilica are a compilation of Digesta, codex and novellas (incomplete) produced in the early years of Leon VI's reign (886–912) in 60 books. In the text as well as in many of the scholia that accompany some of the manuscripts, they draw from the Greek didactic works by Justinian jurists which, in their faithfulness to the Latin original, vary between strong abbreviations to the core message on the one hand and almost verbatim repetitions on the other hand. The scholia cite the Digesta numerically by referring to the book, title, fragment (*digestum*) and section (*thema*). In the west, the title Dig. 10,1 *finium regundorum* was still used in Late Antiquity in some of the Agrimensor manuscripts [13], a fact that made various textual improvements possible. Among other law sources, Dig. 48,4,7,3 cites Gregory the Great Reg. XIII 49 (a. 603). The manuscript of the *epitome Juliani* Vienna, NB 2180 (s. IX¹), contains, among other things Dig. 22,5,12 [14] at the end.

B. EARLY MIDDLE AGES

The Berlin fragment of Institutions and Digesta, Ms. Berlin, Staatsbibl. fol. Lat. 269ff. 183–190 [15; 14], a quaternio bound in a manuscript of the *epitome Juliani* containing the closing parts of the Institutions (Inst. 4,18,5 [vel] eos qui – fin.) and the beginning of the Digesta without any introductory passages (Dig. 1,1–1,7,3) originated in the Early Middle Ages. The complete manuscript probably began with the *Institutiones* but it is unknown how far the Digesta reached. The immediate model was a manuscript from Late Antiquity of Eastern provenance; the connection between Institutions and Digesta is disputed already there (opposing [15], in favour [14]). The copy is of poor quality–the Greek passages and the Greek count of fragments were simply depicted. The fragment shows several corrections compared to the Cod. Flor. (e.g. Dig. 1,2,2,43). The quaternio (and the epitome manuscript) were probably produced in the early 9th cent. in Burgundy; P. Pithou (Pithoeus; 1539–1596) discovered it, probably in the monastery of Flavigny, before 1570 [14]. The occasion and purpose of the copy are still unknown. No clear *testimonia* exist from this period. The phrase *vi vim repellere* in the files from the Roman synod of 679 may refer to Dig. 4,2,12,1 or Dig. 43,16,1,27 [16].

C. HIGH MIDDLE AGES

[2; 17]. At present, the earliest known manuscripts of Digesta are Vat. Lat. 1406 (ca. 1050–1075) and Paris BN Lat. 4450 (ca. 1075–1100) [18]. They only contain Digesta through Dig. 24,3,2 *inscr.: Paulus libro trigensimo*. Other early manuscripts such as Padua, BU 941 (s. XII), Leipzig, UB 873 (s. XII) end with Dig. 24,3,1. manuscripts containing the full textual passages (from s. XII¹) already begin with Dig. 24,3 rubr. only to break off abruptly in Dig. 35,2,82 with *quattuor partes dividantur*. Evidence that an original continuation existed in a third volume with *tres partes ferant legatarii* can be found in the fragmentary beginning of many manuscriptS with Dig. 38,17 as well as in other literary sources [19]. The three volumes are documented from ca. s. XII medio as *Digestum(-a) vetus(-era)*, *Infortiatum(-a)*, *Digestum(-a) novum(-a)* [19]. The body of texts changed to such an extent that *D. vetus* Dig. 1–24,2 ended up containing the *Infortiatum* Dig. 24,3–38 and the *D. novum* Dig. 39–50. The names *D. vetus* and *D. novum* were explained by the → GLOSSATORS as the result of the successive finds of the individual parts, but the name *Infortiatum* was already incomprehensible to them. To this day, no satisfactory explanation has been found [4]. The manuscripts of the *D. vetus* have no introductory parts, only the ms. Paris, BN Lat. 4450 has a list of titles following Dig. 9. The Const. Omnem was included in the manuscripts at a later point and is glossed as the *prooemium* of the Digesta. The medieval manuscripts refer in their entirety to a copy of the Cod. Flor. whose location and time of origin are debated [18]. The gaps in Dig. 19,5 a.E. and in Dig. 48,20. 22 reappear; Dig. 37,8. 9 appear in inverse order; the fragments in

Dig. 50,17 are shifted as in the Cod. Flor. Furthermore, there are many other *errores coniunctivi*. However, many of the textual corruptions of the Cod. Flor. are removed–in Dig. 17,1,33–36, for instance, the names of jurists were added. This means that the copy of the Cod. Flor. had been corrected with the aid of a second manuscript. The scope and the intensity of the corrections are debated [7]. The copy showed a gap in the text in the area of Dig. 23,3–23,4 which was probably caused by the displacement of the quire [20]. The early manuscripts of the *D. vetus* follow the Graeca more or less completely even in long passages. In the course of the development, they have gradually replaced Latin translations (partially in the text, partially in the margins) that go back to Burgundio of Pisa (d. in 1193) (contested regarding the Graeca in Dig. 26,3.5.6 and 27,1 [4]). The inscriptions gradually shrink down to the plain names of the jurists. Sporadically, readings from the Cod. Flor. based on later comparisons are included in the text. Beginning with the Humanists, the (never completed) medieval version is referred to as a vulgate, that is, an older and a newer vulgate depending on its reference to the Cod. Flor. The earliest documented record of the Digesta is a Placitum from Marturi (1076) which quotes Dig. 4,6,26,4 with reference to the law book [27]. The Digesta excerpts used by Ivo of Chartres and the two manuscripts of Church Law, mss. London, British Mus. add. 8873 (Collectio Britannica) and Paris, Bibl. Arsenal 713, are based on the same model. The Digesta are quoted as *liber pandectarum*, the texts are based on the *D. vetus*, only one Digesta in each is based on the *Infortiatum* (Dig. 30,39,6) and the *D. novum* (Dig. 41,3,15,1) [21].

D. HUMANISM

During → HUMANISM [22], the Cod. Flor. was regarded as essential for the recovery of the correct (Justinian) text. The latter was often regarded as the progenitor of the medieval transmission. A. Poliziano (1454–1494) collated the manuscript in 1492 by integrating the Graeca as well as the inscriptions up to Dig. 4 into a printed edition (in a separate text, he created a continuous list of the complete inscriptions). His records were a useful source for L. Bolognini (1446–1508). The prints [3], which at first preserved the division into three volumes along with their titles, began in the year 1475. Printing centres were Venice and later Lyon and Paris. Literal quotations were not marked. The text corresponded to the medieval manuscripts and included the *Glossa ordinaria*. Rubric tables, lists of the initials and subject indexes (the latter for the glosses as well) etc. made it easier to use. Of the introductory parts, only the *Const. Omnem* and the epigram (known since 1486 through Ch. Landino and M. Ficino) were included. Rubrics and fragments were first counted in ca. 1510 in the editions by N. de Benedictis, Lyon ³1509 (2°) and F. Fradin, Lyon 1510–1511 (2°). Improvements in recovering the text began with the above mentioned edition by F. Fradin which incorporated

Bolognini's corrections. L. Blaublom, who through an intermediary source, had access to Politian's comparisons to the *D. vetus* supplemeted the Graeca in parts in the edition by C. Chevallon, Paris 1523 (2°). The inscriptions for the *D. vetus* are complete with few exceptions; Blaublom acquired them from an old manuscript. The edition by R. Etienne (Stephanus), Paris 1527–1528 in five volumes (8°) was the first to abandon the traditional tripartite division in the title and volume number (*Digestorum seu Pandectarum iuris civilis volumen primum* etc.) without the volume divisions corresponding to the Justinian division into *partes* (which are not mentioned in the text either); glosses were also done away with. This edition used quotation marks to set off literal quotes (except in documents). The *Constt. Deo auct.* and *Tanta* (each drawn from the Codex Justinianus) as well as the *index auctorum* (revised) were placed at the end (after Dig. 50). G. Meltzer (Haloander; 1501–1531) finally divided the text into the Justinian *partes* in his Nürnberg edition from 1529 (4°, 2°). He marked the beginning and the end of the *partes* in the text, however, the explicits/incipits of the book transitions were left out. Rubrics and fragments were counted, and literal quotations were printed in capital letters for the first time. For his edition, Haloander was able to use the work by Politian (as he stated in the preface) or only that by Bolognini (as A. Agustin claimed, s. [23]), while drawing from yet other manuscriptS. The work opens with Justinian's Latin constitutions (the *Constt. Deo auct.* and *Tanta* correspond to Cod. Iust. 1,17,1.2), also with the *index auctorum* (revised) as well as a general index of all the titles of the Digesta (not the *Ind. titulorum* of the Cod. Flor.). The inscriptions that had been complete in the *D. vetus* were increasingly reduced after Dig. 24,3 to only the jurists' names. The Graeca were included with the exception of Dig. 26,3.5.6 and Dig. 27,1. In the case of the title displacement of Dig. 37,8.9, Haloander at least mentions the reference made by the proofreader (from Late Antiquity), otherwise the medieval gaps and corruptions of the text are still present. Haloander did not regard the Cod. Flor. as the origin of the medieval manuscripts; he therefore subjected the latter to his own textual criticism. His text was often adopted despite the fact that A. Agustin (1517–1586) soon criticised it. A new edition by J. Hervagen, Basel 1541, contained the Graeca in Dig. 27,1 (with complete inscriptions) thanks to the assistance of A. Alciat (1492–1550), and the edition by Hugo a Porta, Lyon ⁵1547 (2°) contained those in Dig. 26,3.5.6 as well. The Const. Dedoca first appeared in the Edition Hugo a Porta, Lyon ⁷1551 (4°). This edition contains an *index titulorum* comparable to that of the Cod. Flor. as well as continuously complete inscriptions. It refers to many different versions of the Cod. Flor. in the margins. Also, it refers to the textual gaps in Dig. 48,20,7,5 and after Dig. 48,22,9, and to the title displacement in Dig. 37,8.9 and the transposition in Dig. 50,17. Hugo a Porta owed this textual richness to the betrayal of a friend of L. Torelli's (J. Matal? [24]) who supplied him with the material. After many difficulties, the much awaited printed version of the Cod. Flor. appeared in Florence (2°) in three volumes by L. Torelli (1489–1569). Torelli named the Justinian *partes* and was the first to count the sections. Majuscules mark the literal quotes, while quotation marks are used only for the imperial rescripts. Torelli corrected the title displacement in Dig. 37,8.9 as well as the transposition of the text in Dig. 50,17. He largely reproduced the Cod. Flor. *ad litteram* (including obvious text corruptions), but amended it in certain places with the aid of the vulgates (usually marked by round parentheses, e.g. in Dig. 9,2,36, but at times unmarked, e.g. the jurists' names in Dig. 17,1,33–36). Otherwise, he preserved the text of the Cod. Flor. (e.g. in Dig. 1,2,2,43). The gaps in Dig. 48,20 and Dig. 48,22 remained. They were supplemented by A. Le Conte (Contius; 1517–1586) in his edition Lyon 1571 in Latin based on the Basilica. In his edition of Justinian law sources (Lyon-Geneva 1583) (4°), D. Godefroy (Gothofredus, 1549–1622) was the first to introduce the title *Corpus iuris civilis* (the phrase was already known to the glossators). He combined the Institutiones and Digesta in one volume. In the text, he looked for a balance between the interpretations of the Cod. Flor. and the medieval manuscripts. The Graeca in Dig. 26,3.5.6 and Dig. 27,1, however, only appear in Latin. Gothofredus added his own notes to his edition; later, he published editions that included the glosses (the last in 1627) or that had no notes at all. The editions by Gothofredus were very successful already during his lifetime.

E. From the 17th to the 20th Century

In the late 17th and early 18th cent., L. Gronovius (1648–1724) [25] and H. Brenkman (1681–1736) [26] worked on improving the text of the Digesta. Gronovius collated the Cod. Flor. from the end of 1679 to early April 1680. He published observations about the *Constt. Deo auctore, Omnem, Tanta* and the *index auctorum* in the *Emendationes pandectarum*, Leiden 1685. Since his otherwise unpublished collation was not accessible to other scholars, it had no influence on the textual criticism to follow. In 1711–1712, Brenkman compared the manuscript twice and recorded his results in various notebooks. His *Historia Pandectarum seu fatum exemplaris Florentini*, Utrecht 1722, presents a description of the Cod. Flor., but he did not get around to publishing his own edition. Since Brenkman's papers ended up in the university library of Göttingen in 1745, G.C. Gebauer (1690–1773) was able to use them for a new edition of the Digesta which was completed after his death by G.A. Spangenberg (1738–1806) and appeared in Göttingen in 1776. The Göttingen edition is based on the Torelli edition but contains a large body of textual criticism including differing interpretations of the medieval manuscripts, earlier editions and conjectures (many from Brenkman's unpublished works). The Basilica were used as a source as well, although not consistently. The entries about the vulgate are largely

based on Brenkman. In the years from 1825 and again from 1829, an edition appeared by J.L. Beck (1786–1869) [23] who primarily used the edition by Gebauer as his source. H.E. Schrader's (1779–1860) [23] plan to produce a critical edition with a large body of variants failed due to the enormity of the material and the lack of selection criteria. Only the Institutions were completed (Leipzig 1832). In 1833, the edition of the brothers K.A. and K.M. Kriegel (17 editions up to 1887) appeared in Leipzig, an edition based on the text of Torelli and the critical apparatus of Gebauer. For each fragment, the Basilica as well as the textual classification is marked according to F. Bluhme's method (along with an overview of textual classifications at the end of the edition). Th. Mommsen (1817–1903) finally produced the edition of the Digesta that has remained authoritative until today (Berlin 1870, so-called *ed. maior*). Two assistants again compared the Cod. Flor. for him. In his work, Mommsen made use of the advanced philological methods of his time (Lachmann Method). He proceeded from the idea that the medieval manuscripts were based on the Cod. Flor. but recognised the fact that the corrections came from a second manuscript. Wherever the text of the vulgate corresponded to the transmission of Basilica, he edited the text by referring to the Cod. Flor. Otherwise, he only gave special significance to the oldest manuscripts of the *D. vetus*. He gave up the division into *partes* as well as the explicits/incipits; Basilica and Bluhme's classifications are marked in all fragments. As early as in 1872, an *ed. minor* appeared with a limited critical apparatus along with a critical edition of the Institutions by P. Krüger (1840–1926). Beginning with the 11th edition (1908), Krüger published the *ed. minor*. He integrated the results of the palingenetic research by O. Lenel and expanded the apparatus of notes. In 1908, the first volume of a new edition by P. Bonfante, C. Fadda, C. Ferrini, S. Riccobono and V. Scialoja appeared in Milan, volume 2 (ed. by P. Bonfante, V. Scialoja) followed in 1931. The editors took the *ed. maior* by Mommsen as a basis, but, influenced by Ferrini, regarded the Basilica more comprehensively than Mommsen in the constitution of the text up to Dig. 20,3 (e.g., v. Bas. 20,1,44 as Dig. 19,2,56). A concordance of the three latter editions does not exist. More recent criticism was aimed primarily against Mommsen's reluctant reference to the vulgate manuscripts. These manuscripts are supposed to have contained a greater wealth of variants and genuine interpretations than Mommsen had suspected (bibliography in [17]).

→ Digesta; → Iustinianus

→ Roman Law

1 Iustiniani Augusti Digestorum seu Pandectarum codex Florentinus olim Pisanus, 10 vols. 1902–10; Justiniani Augusti pandectarum codex Florentinus, A. Corbino, B. Santalucia (eds.), 1988 (facsimile)   2 G. Dolezalek et al, Verzeichnis der Handschriften zum römischen Recht bis 1600, 1972   3 E. Spangenberg, Einleitung in das Römisch-Justinianeische Rechtsbuch, Hannover 1817, 650–929   4 H. Lange, Römisches Recht im Mittelalter 1, 1997   5 Wieacker, RRG   6 F. Schulz, Einführung

in das Studium der Digesten, 1916   7 H. KANTOROWICZ, Über die Entstehung der Digestenvulgata, 1910   8 E. A. LOWE, Greek Symptoms in a Sixth-Century Manuscript of St. Augustine and in a Group of Latin Legal Manuscripts in: L. BIELER (ed.), E.A. Lowe. Palaeographical Papers 1907 – 1965, II, 1972, 466–474   9 J. MIQUEL, Mechanische Fehler in der Überlieferung der Digesten, in: ZRG 80, 1963, 233–286   10 W. KAISER, Digestenentstehung und Digestenüberlieferung, in: ZRG 108, 1991, 330–350   11 N. WILSON, A Greek Paleographer looks at the Florentine Pandects, in: Subseciva Groningana 5, 1992, 1–6   12 W. KAISER, Zum Aufbewahrungsort des Codex Florentinus in Süditalien, in: W. E. VOSS, F. THEISEN (eds.), Summe – Glosse – Kommentar: Juristisches und Rhetorisches in Kanonistik und Legistik, 2000   13 B. STOLTE, Finium regundorum and the Agrimensores, in: Subseciva Groningana 5, 1992, 61–76   14 W. KAISER, Die Epitome Iuliani: Beiträge zum römischen Recht im frühen Mittelalter und zum byzantinischen Rechtsunterricht, 2004   15 R. RÖHLE, Das Berliner Institutionen- und Digestenfragment Ms. lat. fol. n. 269, in: Bullettino dell'Istituto di diritto romano 71, 1968, 128–173   16 S. KUTTNER, An Implied Reference to the Digest in Pope Agatho's Roman Synod of 679, in: ZRG (kanonistische Abteilung) 107, 1990, 382–384   17 E. RICART, La tradicion manuscrita del Digesto en el occidente medieval, in: Annuario de historia del derecho español 57, 1987, 5–206   18 C. RADDING, Vatican Latin 1406, Mommsen's Ms. S, and the Reception of the Digest in the Middle Ages, in: ZRG 110, 1993, 501–551   19 H. V. DER WOUW, Zur Textgeschichte des Infortiatum und zu seiner Glossierung durch die frühen Bologneser Glossatoren, in: Ius commune 11, 1984, 231–280   20 TH. MOMMSEN, Schriften II, 107–140   21 C. G. MOR, Il digesto nell'età preirneriana, in: Scritti di storia giuridica altomedievale, 1977, 832–34   22 H. TROJE in: H. COING (ed.) Handbuch der Quellen und Literatur der neueren europäischen Privatrechtsgeschichte, 1977, 615–795   23 R. STINTZING, E. LANDSBERG, Geschichte der Deutschen Rechtswissenschaft, 1880–1910   24 G. GUALANDI, Per la storia della editio princeps delle pandette fiorentine di Lelio Torelli, in: Le pandette di Giustiniano, 1986, 143–198   25 T. WALLINGA, Laurentius Theodorus Gronovius, in: Tijdschrift voor Rechtsgeschiedenis 65, 1997, 459–495   26 B. STOLTE, Henrik Brenkman, 1981   27 B. PARADISI, Il giudizio di Márturi, in: Rendiconti della accademia nazionale dei lincei, classe di scienze morali, storiche e filologiche, 9. ser., 5, 1994, 3–21.   WOLFGANG KAISER

Dithyramb see → LYRIC POETRY

Dog Latin. A pejorative term for faulty Latin interspersed with 'barbarisms' and nonstandard or ungrammatical forms. The oldest known evidence for the origin of the term Dog Latin (DL) (aka *Kitchen Latin*/German *Küchenlatein*) is found in Lorenzo Valla's *Apologus* (1452/1453) in the context of a debate about correct Latin. Guarino da Verona, his cook Parmeno, and stableman Dromo engage in a biting critique of the language of certain passages in a letter by Poggio Bracciolini; Poggio is accused of having learned Latin from his cook, and of using *culinaria vocabula;* as a result he could start working as a cook's helper and give a

beating to grammatically correct Latin just as a cook might do to his pots [2. 486–488]. In Plautus and Terence, whose comedies served as the model for the first act of the *Apologus,* the names Parmeno and Dromo are common slave names. Since Antiquity, among slaves precisely those from the kitchen were held in very low regard (cf. Liv. 39,6; [6. 210f.]), a fact that may have suggested a derogatory connection between the kitchen and faulty Latin to Valla, for whom only the use of 'Classical Latin' was defensible.

In Germany, the term seems to have been transmitted [8. 290] by P. Luder and S. Karoch, both of whom had formerly studied in Italy. [6. 210] There are references by them to this faulty Latin as *culinarium Latinum* and *culinaria lingua* in the years 1462 and 1472 [3. 6, 14]. In 1485, J. Kerckmeister offered the following in his *Codrus* about schoolmaster Codrus' knowledge of Latin: *In coquina, ceu sit, apud coquos forte Latinum didicit* [1. 78]. The Latin which had been extensively corrupted through vernacular elements was often mocked in the *Epistulae obscurorum virorum* (1515/1517) as DL as well [7. 455]. Likewise, the term DL is sometimes mistakenly equated with the term 'Monk's Latin' [5]. By far the greatest contemporary use of DL in literature is to be encountered with the magic spells in J. K. Rowling's *Harry Potter* novels.

→ Comedy

→ NEO-LATIN

SOURCES 1 J. KERCKMEISTER, Codrus, L. MUNDT (ed.), 1969   2 L. VALLA, Apologus, S. CAMPOREALE (ed.) in: Id., Lorenzo Valla, Umanesimo e Teologia, 1972, 469–534

LITERATURE   3 L. BERTALOT, Humanistische Vorlesungsankündigungen in Deutschland im 15. Jahrhundert, in: Zschr. für Gesch. der Erziehung und des Unterrichts 5, 1915, 1–24   4 E. R. CURTIUS, Europäische Literatur und lateinisches Mittelalter, ²1954, 431ff. (Engl. W. TRASK (trans.), European Literature and the Latin Middle Ages, 1953)   5 J. AND W. GRIMM, Deutsches Wörterbuch, vol. 5, 2504f. (1873 edition)   6 P. LEHMANN, Mittelalter und Küchenlatein, in: HZ 137, 1928, 197–213   7 R. PFEIFFER, Küchenlatein, in: Philologus 86, 1931, 455–459   8 E. WEISSBRODT, Niederdeutsch-lateinische Glossen um 1500, in: Zschr. für dt. Wortforsch. 15, 1914, 278–310.
                                                CHRISTOPH BRÄUNL

Dome construction see → PANTHEON

Doric revival see→ GREEK REVIVAL

Drama see→ COMEDY

Dream interpretation. The multi-voiced discourse conducted within Graeco-Roman Antiquity regarding dreams and dream interpretation in religion, literature, everyday life, philosophy, divination/mantic art and medicine shows clear signs of cultural determination [19]. Despite striking breaks with tradition – above all through Christianity – a relatively high degree of continuity in dream discourses can be observed since Antiquity [18]. Among other things, this is probably owing to the fact that the ancient pagan tradition, which had raised existential questions as to whether dreams could be interpreted, remained alive in the key texts on the subject (with two separate strands of tradition in the Greek and Latin Middle Ages) [17], and that the interpretation of dreams as a means of ascribing meaning to the nightly counter-world of dreams was impossible to suppress. Consequently, we must differentiate between a (little attested) popular dream interpretation on the one hand and one that lays claim to scientific standards on the other.

Christianity, with its idea of a cosmos determined by the creator God, had no space left for the arts of prediction [6; 21; 15] (cf. the loathing of the mantics in Dante, *Inferno* 20,10ff.), even though the dream as a medium of personal communication between the individual and God could still be regarded in a positive light. Mantic dream interpretation was strongly marginalized by the authorities, yet its popular forms were never lost. The great continuing need for dream interpretation is demonstrated for instance by dream-books like the *Somnium Danielis*, which can ultimately be traced back to Artemidorus' *Oneirocritica* [17], and from which it differs in its lack of a theoretical basis detailing the origin and interpretation of dreams and its attempts to harmonize pagan dream interpretation with Christian belief, e.g. by attributing it to the prophet Daniel.

In the Latin Middle Ages, no trace of a direct reception of Artemidorus can be found, but as the most important exponent of pagan, secular dream interpretation he enjoyed an uninterrupted presence in the Greek-speaking regions and in one Arabic strand of the tradition. The great scientific curiosity of the Renaissance, which did not shy away from the occult and borderline experiences of human rationality, led to a lively interest in all the mantic arts and, as a result, a surge in the study of the Graeco-Roman reference texts – apart from Artemidorus in particular Synesius' *Perì enhypníôn* and *Perì tēs kath' hýpnou mantikês*. Artemidorus' *Oneirocritica* quickly became very popular, as the numerous editions (first edition Venice 1518) and translations show [11]. The humanist Philipp Melanchthon even wrote a treatise on the occasion of a Basel edition (1597), in which he sought to harmonize the Christian view of the world with pagan dream interpretation through their shared contempt for the Epicureans. A milestone in the reception and transformation of ancient dream discourse was the almost pre-psychoanalytical text *Synesiorum somniorum omnis generis insomnia explicantes* (1562) by the polymathic scholar Hieronymus Cardanus [4], who regarded the image production of the dream as an inexhaustible source of allegories and meaning. In his view they offered material for self-analysis by the dreamer as to the inner workings of his soul and imagination.

Epitomized, Artemidorus' basic work found many followers in popular dream interpretation, while others who continued the discourse in what would still be considered a valid form today, took their inspiration from the theory and interpretative hypotheses of the complete version. It was only through the scientific approaches of the 18th/19th cents. that the *Oneirocritica* finally came to be viewed as 'outdated' or as 'superstition'. Even though, strictly speaking, the exploration of the basic neurological conditions for the occurrence of dreams concerns itself with a different aspect of the dream phenomenon and does not consider the question – raised by the ancient dream interpretation discourses – as to whether dreams can be interpreted, it was because of these investigations that the extremely persistent prejudice against the legitimacy of dream interpretation gained the upper hand. In doing so it caused an important treasure-house of experience in dealing with dreams to be lost. Against this 'rational' background, genuine 19th cent. works in the field of Classical studies – e.g. by Gomperz [10] or Büchsenschütz [3] – also looked at ancient dream interpretation as a primitive phase in human thinking that has been overcome.

In Romanticism the dream was associated with the counter-movement to the rationality dispositive of the → ENLIGHTENMENT, and to this extent it did not draw upon the ancient tradition of dream interpretation. Only Freud, whose understanding of dreams was anti-Romantic and hence methodological in its orientation, returned to the ancient discourse on the interpretability of dreams in his epoch-making *Die Traumdeutung* (1900) [9], the founding manifesto of → PSYCHOANALYSIS: 'Bezeichnenderweise im alles entscheidenden zweiten Kapitel der Traumdeutung, 'Die Methode der Traumdeutung: Die Analyse eines Traummusters' setzt sich Freud vergleichsweise ausführlich mit Artemidor auseinander, dem er eine 'interessante Abänderung' [9. 119] des 'Chiffrierverfahrens' bescheinigt, das er von der 'symbolischen Traumdeutung' unterscheidet, welche im Gegensatz zu einem modifizierten, auf die Assoziationen des Träumers gestützten Chiffrierverfahren ihm gänzlich verfehlt zu sein scheint. [...] Für Artemidor wie für Freud selber ist der Traum ein typisches 'Kontextphänomen'. Vorbildlich erscheint ihm an den *Oneirokritiká*, daß sich die Deutung nicht auf das Ganze des Traumes richtet, was die symbolische Deutung ausmacht, sondern 'auf jedes Stück des Trauminhalts für sich'. Und 1914 fügt er an dieser Stelle hinzu, daß seine Deutetechnik sich nur darin von der ant., d.h. Artemidors, unterscheide, 'daß sie dem Träumer selbst die Deutungsarbeit auferlegt" [12. 226] ("Characteristically, in the all-deciding second chapter of *Die Traumdeutung*, 'The Method of Interpreting Dreams: An Analysis of a Specimen Dream', Freud discusses Artemidorus in relative detail, and he credits him with an 'interesting modification' of the 'process of decoding', which he distinguishes from 'symbolic dream-interpreting'. Freud thought the latter to be wholly misguided, while he favoured a modified decoding procedure that was based on the associations of the dreamer. [...] For Artemidorus, as for Freud himself, the dream was a typical 'contextual phenomenon'. Freud thought the *Oneiro-critica* to be exemplary in that it did not bring to bear the work of interpretation on the dream as a whole – which constitutes the symbolic interpretation – but 'on each portion of the dream's content independently'. And in 1914 he added at this point that his interpretation technique only differed from the ancient one, i.e. that of Artemidorus, in that it imposes the task of interpretation upon the dreamer himself"). This leads one to suspect Freud could no longer sustain his earlier assertion that the *Oneirocritica* was an example of the "pre-scientific view of dreams adopted by the peoples of Antiquity" ('vorwissenschaftliche Traumauffassung der Alten' [9. 32]) – a typical "lay opinion" ('Laienmeinung' [9. 117]).

The prominent position of ancient dream interpretation in Freud's *Traumdeutung* meant that it received a certain amount of attention which was entirely unproblematic. It not only manifested itself in the shape of overview studies e.g. by L. Binswanger [1], whose work approached psychoanalysis, but also in an association – both in positive and negative terms – with the criticism of psychoanalytical dream interpretation [12; 14; 19]: Freud's ambivalent attitude of recognition and disparagement towards his 'pre-scientific' fellow proponents of dream interpretation was even reproduced by those who positioned themselves as opponents and critics of Freud.

Over the last 30 years, with the emergence of cultural studies, interest in dreams and dream interpretation has grown across a variety of disciplines (classical studies, ethnology, psychoanalysis), not least because of E.R. Dodd's influential study *The Greeks and the Irrational*. Artemidorus' *Oneirocritica* has in this context become a source of sociological information and is being examined for its content relating to the history of mentalities (e.g. [7]). The most important impulses in this regard were provided by M. Foucault, especially in his 1954 'Introduction' to Binswanger's *Traum und Existenz* [8], the significance of which was not re-appraised until the 1990s. In it he notes the considerable heuristic potential of ancient dream interpretation which – unlike Freud – also recognized dreams as a phenomenon shaped by socio-cultural factors.

The 100th anniversary of Freud's *Traumdeutung* (2000) has led in the last few years to a further boost in research work: historical studies that are also concerned with the history of mentalities [19] and psychoanalytical-clinical [2] studies sit side by side with those examining ancient (and Freudian) dream interpretation by contrasting it with corresponding practices in other cultures and eras [16]. One aim of modern dream research is to combine cognitivistic, neurological and (deep) hermeneutic approaches. In this endeavour, ancient dream interpretation will continue to play a key role insofar as we will never be able to define dreams conclusively and exclusively as a neurophysiological phenomenon.

→ Artemidorus [6] of Daldis; → Divination; → Dreams; Interpretation of dreams; → Synesius [1] of Cyrene

1 L. BINSWANGER, Wandlungen in der Auffassung und Deutung des Traumes: Von den Griechen bis zur Gegenwart, 1928　2 S. BOLOGNINI (ed.), Il sogno cento anni dopo, 2000　3 B. BÜCHSENSCHÜTZ, Traum und Traumdeutung im Alterthume, Berlin 1868　4 HIERONYMUS CARDANUS, Synesiorum somniorum omnis generis insomnia explicantes, Basel 1562, (Ital. S. MONTIGLIO, A. GRIECO (trans.), Sogni, 1989–1993)　5 E. R. DODDS, The Greeks and the Irrational, 1966　6 TH. FÖGEN, Die Enteignung der Wahrsager, 1993　7 M. FOUCAULT, Sexualität und Wahrheit, vol. 2, 1991 (original French edition: Histoire de la sexualité, vol. 2, L'usage des plaisirs, 1984; Engl. The History of Sexuality, vol. 2, The Use of Pleasure, 1985)　8 Id., Introduction to L. BINSWANGER, Traum und Existenz, 1992 (originally in French, 1954; Engl. M. Foucault, Dream, Imagination, and Existence, in: M. FOUCAULT, L. BINSWANGER, Dream and Existence, K. HOELLER (ed.), 1993)　9 S. FREUD, Die Traumdeutung (1899/1900), Studienausgabe, vol. 2, 1972 (Engl. quotations taken from J. STRACHEY (trans. & ed.), S. Freud. The Interpretation of Dreams, 1953)　10 TH. GOMPERZ, Traumdeutung und Zauberei, Wien 1866　11 L. GRENZMANN, Traumbuch Artemidori. Zur Tradition der ersten Übersetzungen ins Deutsche durch W.H. Ryff, 1980　12 A. KROVOZA, Die Stellung Freuds zur Vorgeschichte der Traumdeutung, in: [19. 223–233]　13 R. A. PACK, On Artemidorus and his Arabic Translator, in: TAPhA 98, 1967, 313–326　14 S. R. F. PRICE, The Future of Dreams. From Freud to Artemidoros, in: Past and Present 113, 1986, 3–37　15 J.-C. SCHMITT, The Liminality and Centrality of Dreams in the Medieval West, in: [16. 274–287]　16 D. SHULMAN, G. G. STROUMSA (eds.), Dream Cultures. Explorations in the Comparative History of Dreaming, 1999　17 L. THORNDIKE, Ancient and Medieval Dream-books, in: Id., A History of Magic and Experimental Science during the First Thirteen Centuries of our Era, vol. 2, 1923, 290–302　18 O. VEDFELT, Dimensionen der Träume, 1999, (Engl. K. TINDALL (trans.), The Dimensions of Dreams: The Nature, Function, and Interpretation of Dreams, 1999; orig. Drommenes dimensioner)　19 C. WALDE, Antike Traumdeutung und moderne Traumforschung, 2001　20 Id., Von Artemidor und anderen Traumdeutern, in: Zeitschrift für psychoanalytische Theorie und Praxis 16, 2001, 209–231　21 M. E. WITTMER-BUTSCH, Zur Bedeutung von Schlaf und Traum im Mittelalter, 1990.

CHRISTINE WALDE

Dresden, Staatliche Kunstsammlungen, Sculpture Collection

A. INTRODUCTION　B. THE COLLECTION IN THE EIGHTEENTH CENTURY　C. THE JAPANISCHES PALAIS AS MUSEUM　D. THE ALBERTINUM

A. INTRODUCTION

Founded on the initiative of the Saxon court and thus originally an expression of the absolutist desire for representation, the Dresden *Kunstsammlungen* in general and the *Antikensammlung* in particular played a leading role in the establishment of civic museums in Germany. Even though the plans led to a suitable presentation only toward the end of the 18th cent. and – with regard to the actual building – were only realized with limited aspirations, earlier Dresden projects had

Fig. 1: Dresden, Albertinum,
Mosaic Hall (Photograph
by K. Klemm 1905),
*Sculpture Collection, Staatliche
Kunstsammlungen Dresden*

already given momentum to the museum idea elsewhere, e.g. in the form of the Antique Temple in Sans-
souci Park, Potsdam (→ BERLIN I. STAATLICHE
MUSEEN). In the late 19th cent., it was the *Albertinum*
which then led the way towards the functional determination of a sculpture museum.

B. THE COLLECTION IN THE EIGHTEENTH CENTURY

From the time it was established in the 16th cent.,
antiquities had not play a significant role in the electoral
art chamber at the Saxon residence. This changed with
August the Strong (reigned 1694–1733; from 1697
King of Poland), who is credited with building a sculpture collection that reached a considerable size within a
short time. The initial core collection consisted of
roughly 50 terra-cottas and marble sculptures which
had reached Dresden between 1723 and 1726 as a 'gift'
from the royal collection in Berlin. These were followed
immediately by substantial acquisitions in Rome (Chigi
and Albani collections). As early as 1733 Leplat published detailed engravings of the Dresden sculptures
(*Recueil des marbres antiques qui se trouvent dans la
galerie du Roy de Pologne à Dresden*). Under August III
(reigned 1733–1763), who was more interested in
expanding his collection of paintings, patronage for the
antiquities collection was effectively cut off. Fortunately, this did not prevent the important new addition in
1736 of three female statues excavated in → HERCU-
LANEUM. Documents for 1742 list a total of about 400
ancient sculptures; their presentation, however, was inadequate. Ambitious museum projects by Longuelune
and Algarotti were not realised, instead the objects were
given a makeshift home in a building of the Great
Garden outside the city.

During the Seven-Year War, the sculptures were temporarily sheltered in the basement of the armoury, thus
escaping Prussian shelling. After their return to the area
of the Great Garden, Johann Friedrich Wacker oversaw
their new arrangement.

C. THE JAPANISCHES PALAIS AS MUSEUM

In 1785/86 the sculptures were relocated to the Japanisches Palais (built in 1715–1717, with an extension in
1730) on the Neustadt side of the river, where sufficient
space was available for the new assembly, in accordance with contemporary ideas. The structuring principle of the exhibition repeated Johann Friedrich Wak-
ker's conventional organisation according to themes
rather than periods of Greek and Roman art. In ten
rooms altogether the statues and busts were lined up
evenly along the walls, with major works moved into a
more prominent position towards the centre of the
room. Before the opening of the antiquities museums in
Munich and Berlin, this *museum usui publico patens*
('museum, open for public use'), which also contained
other sections and the royal library, was regarded as the
most important public collection of antiquities (→ AN-
TIQUITIES COLLECTIONS) in Germany, notwithstanding
the occasional criticism regarding on the presentation
of its material (Carl August Böttiger). Gottfried Semper
introduced a markedly classicistic character with his
re-design of the rooms in 1835 that included wall decorations in the 'Pompeian style'.

As early as 1798 Johann Gottfried Lipsius published
the first descriptive catalogue. It was followed, beginning in 1804, by the publication of Wilhelm Gottlieb
Becker's *Augusteum* in three volumes and one supplement. Compared to the latter authoritative work, other
19th cent. inventories that were compiled by Heinrich
Hase and Hermann Hettner seem rather modest.

For more than 100 years, the *Japanisches Palais*
remained the home of the ancient (and a number of
modern) sculptures. During that time, the range of

Fig. 2: Replica of the head
of Myron's Athena,
*Sculpture Collection, Staatliche
Kunstsammlungen Dresden*

Fig. 3: Statuette of the
'Frenzied Maenad',
*Sculpture Collection, Staatliche
Kunstsammlungen Dresden*

ancient sculpture on display was complemented by numerous casts. The original collection of 833 items from the estate of the painter Anton Raphael Mengs was purchased in 1783/84. First housed from 1794 in the *Brühlsche Galerie* and shortly afterwards in the stables on the other side of the Elbe, the fast-growing collection, which increasingly included casts of modern works as well, then moved into the Semper Gallery building and into the adjoining wings of the *Zwinger* in 1857. The cast collection (→ CAST; CAST COLLECTIONS) was continually expanded into the 20th cent.

D. THE ALBERTINUM

In 1879, it became apparent that the rooms of the *Japanisches Palais* used for the stone sculptures were needed for the library. The cast collection, too, had grown to such an extent (additions included, for instance, casts of the freshly excavated finds from → OLYMPIA) that finding a new location became imperative. Thus, from 1884 to 1889, the late 16th cent. armoury was converted into a museum space large enough to house both collections. In this museum, opened in 1894 and named *Albertinum* after its royal builder, the casts were set up on the second floor, while the main floor was reserved for the marble sculptures. Georg Treu, the director from 1882 to 1915, steered a clear course: within the context of archaeological research, he had the Baroque 'completions' removed from the older sculptures in the collection and instead preferred to conduct his own reconstruction attempts on the casts. His acquisition policy aimed to create a comprehensive sculpture museum: among his purchases were items of Egyptian and Ancient Oriental art as well as original Greek monuments from the Archaic and later periods – in this regard he did follow his predecessors Heinrich Hase and Hermann Hettner rather more closely. At the same time he also turned his attention to

contemporary works (Rodin, Meunier, Klinger) and, lastly, from around 1910, tried – but failed – to integrate medieval works into the Albertinum. Among the objects acquired by Treu, a replica head of Myron's Athena (fig. 2) and the statuette of a Raging Maenad ascribed to Scopas (fig. 3) are particularly noteworthy. While in Treu's time restrictions on new acquisitions were due to limited funds, this was all the more true for the decades after the First World War. Nevertheless, the collection continued to grow: small-scale objects in particular were still being added in the 1930s.

The presentation of the objects devised by Treu, however, remained conventional (fig. 1). The arrangement in rows along the sides of the room, with 'masterpieces' moved into the centre, reveals an older conceptual origin. A new feature was the addition of small-scale objects on stepped wall ledges. Individual statues in both the cast and the original collections were placed on wall consoles to raise them above eye-level.

While the cast collection suffered damage in 1945, the original collection survived World War II without major losses. It was transferred to the Soviet Union and returned in 1958/59. After several years of building work, the antiquities collection was reopened in 1969 on the ground floor of the *Albertinum*, formerly the museum's repository. The limited space available meant that only a selection of the items in the collection could be put on display. Today, the double-nave, late Renaissance hall, having been restored with deliberate simplicity, accommodates the objects in an unobtrusive arrangement that is essentially chronological. The intrinsic value of the individual works of art can thus be fully appreciated. Small art objects associated with the sculptures are displayed in nearby cabinets, which help divide the room into different segments without creating unnecessary barriers.

Under conditions in the → GDR, new acquisitions were largely out of the question. Worth mentioning, though, is a gift comprising several hundred small art objects from West Berlin resident Curt Luckow (1976). What is missing is an exhibition space for the cast collection.

1 Das Albertinum vor 100 Jahren – die Skulpturensammlung Georg Treus. K. KNOLL (ed.), Exhibition catalogue, Staatliche Kunstsammlungen Dresden, 1994   2 H. HASE, Verzeichnis der alten und neuen Bildwerke und übrigen Alterthümer in den Sälen der Königlichen Antikensammlung zu Dresden, Dresden 1826, ⁵1839   3 G. HERES, Dresdener Kunstsammlungen im 18. Jahrhundert, 1991   4 P. HERRMANN, Verzeichnis der Originalbildwerke der Staatlichen Skulpturensammlung Dresden, 1915, ²1925   5 H. HETTNER, Die Bildwerke der Königlichen Antikensammlung zu Dresden, Dresden 1856, ⁴1881   6 Id., Das Königliche Museum der Gypsabgüsse zu Dresden, Dresden 1857, ⁴1881   7 K. KNOLL, Die Geschichte der Dresdener Antiken- und Abgußsammlung von 1785–1915 und ihre Erweiterung zur Skulpturensammlung unter Georg Treu, Diss. Dresden 1993   8 Id. et al., Die Antiken im Albertinum. Staatliche Kunstsammlungen Dresden, Skulpturensammlung, 1993   9 H. PROTZMANN, Griechische Skulpturen und Fragmente. Staatliche Kunstsammlungen Dresden, Skulpturensammlung, 1989   10 M. RAUMSCHÜSSEL, Die Antikensammlung August des Starken, in: H. BECK et al. (eds.), Antikensammlungen im 18. Jahrhundert (= Frankfurter Forschungen zur Kunst 9), 1981   11 K. ZIMMERMANN, Vorgeschichte und Anfänge der Dresdener Skulpturensammlung, in: Id. (ed.), Die Dresdener Antiken und Winckelmann (= Schriften der Winckelmann-Gesellschaft 4), 1977, 9–32.

DETLEV KREIKENBOM

Druids

A. DRUIDS IN HISTORY   B. DRUIDS IN LITERATURE AND MUSIC   C. DRUIDS IN ART

A. DRUIDS IN HISTORY

The druid figure best known at present, Getafix (Fr. Panoramix; Ger. Miraculix), is distinguished by the fact that he does not divulge any of his secret teachings. And not only that – apart from the traditional cutting of mistletoe with a golden sickle passed down to us in Pliny (nat. 16,95) – Getafix is never observed indirectly or directly during a cult activity, nor does he function as a judge in his village. Clad in white and with a long white beard, he embodies the cliché based on Pliny of the wise, old, somewhat remote magician whose most notable task is the brewing of magic potions and sometimes the supply of medicines to the inhabitants of the village. Getafix's colleagues are depicted in a similar manner by the authors of the famous Asterix tales, René Goscinny and Albert Uderzo: the volume *Asterix and the Goths* describes the meeting attested in Caesar (Gall. 6,13) of the druids in Carnute Forest; there it is,however, not a matter of legal disputes but of the best magic. Thus exaggerated, in the comic character (→ COMICS) of Getafix – as is also the case with most of the other characters – the authors forego too great a

closeness to the historical original. Rather Getafix tends to resemble a French country parson.

The secret teachings and skills attributed to the druids inspired the imagination of people already in Antiquity, especially since nothing of them had been passed down in writing. Even after they had almost vanished completely from the continent towards the end of the 1st cent. AD at the latest, they were not forgotten. Ausonius speaks of them as something vanished (Auson. profess. 4,7; Phoeb. 10,27), but the SHA mention wise women (Alex. 60; Car. 14,14; Aurelian. 44) who are called druids although this title only alludes to their prophetic roles. In Britain and also in ancient Ireland, the druids appear to have salvaged their priestly function in a changed form. Ancient Irish texts from the 6th and 7th cents. AD concentrate above all on the magical abilities of the druids, *magi* and *filid*, who are stylized by the Christian authors as a heathen contrast to the Christian saints. There is however a dearth of sources with regard to their concrete significance in the tribes. They possibly retained their role of seers or prophets. Until the end of the Gaelic culture, Irish legends and literary traditions passed down primarily archaic ideas with regard to the connection of the druids with the sacred royal cults and the holy trees venerated by the ancient Irish tribes. Worthy of particular mention here are the mythological texts of the *Ulster Cycle* and the *Mythological Cycle* written in the 12th cent. Before 1500 the *filid* then appear to have assumed the roles of the druids and bards until they too, under English influence, disappeared in the 17th cent.

With the rediscovery of the Classical texts in the Renaissance and Humanism, interest in the teachings of the druids also grew. In 1532 Jean le Fèvre wrote *Les Fleurs et Antiquitez des Gaules, où il est traité des anciens Philosophes appelez Druides*, and in Germany Esaias Puffendorf wrote his *Dissertatio de Druidibus* in 1650. More significant were the *Monumenta Britannica* by the English antiquarian John Aubrey, written around 1690, who linked the druids with the megalithic monument, Stonehenge. This directly influenced John Stukeley who regarded himself as a new archdruid and attempted to create a connection between Christianity and the druid religion by tracing the druids back to the Biblical Noah. His works *Itinerarium curiosum* (1724) and *The History of the Religion and Temples of the Druids* (1733) positioned Stonehenge at the centre of the cult and decisively influenced the establishment of the neo-pagan druid associations of the 18th cent. The first larger group went back to the Irish Catholic John Tolland who founded a *Druid Order* in 1717 as a non-Christian protest movement. This group was especially influenced by the painter and poet William Blake (1757–1827) in an esoteric sense. In the 18th cent. in Wales, Edward Wilkins, under the pseudonym of the bard Iolo Morgannwg, associated the druids with the ceremony of the Gorsedd for the ceremonial enthronement of the king and the National Eisteddfod – the competition for bards and musicians held since the 12th cent. British druids have been attempting up to the present to hold a National Eisteddfod in Stonehenge, although this is always rejected for conservative reasons. In 1781 Henry Hurle founded the *Ancient Order of Druids* in London; which, influenced by Celtic models, has, as an ideologically compatible, fraternal society, has aimed, to the present, to be politically and religiously engaged. In the course of time, numerous offshoots of it developed that operated independently of each other. The order spread throughout North America (1824), Australia (1850), France (1869) and New Zealand (1879). In 1908 even Winston Churchill was accepted into the Albion Lodge of the *Ancient Order of the Druids*. The order reached Germany in 1872, and a national grand lodge has existed with several regional grand lodges and individual lodges since 1874; today these are divided into the Präsidium (headquarters), regional Grand Lodges and local Lodges. During the National Socialist period and in the GDR, the druid order was prohibited. After reunification new groups were also founded there (e.g. Grand Lodge – Saxonia 1991).

Recently it has been possible to discern among druid associations a neo-pagan or esoteric strand of reception on the one hand and an ethical-humanitarian faction following the Free Mason lodges on the other. To the former faction belong numerous alliances, brotherhoods, groups and sects worldwide which are distinguished from each other. Common to all of them is their reference to the secret teachings of the druids which are then often blended with other esoteric and/or Far Eastern elements. Modern groups are also influenced by similar ideas; these use phantasy role-playing games (e.g. the venerable *Dungeons and Dragons*) to adopt the identity of druids whose functions are essentially restricted to those of magicians.

The druid orders primarily belong to the ethical-humanitarian faction. Three levels of initiation can be differentiated (1. Ovate, 2. Bard, 3. Druid) which teach insight and knowledge, aesthetic understanding and commitment, decision-making and action. In addition there are honorary levels of Honorary and Ancient Noble Archdruid. The main body of the order in Germany is the *Druidenzeitung*, and current publications are also to be found on the internet. The order, amalgamated worldwide in the *International Grand Lodge of Druids,* regards itself as the sole legitimate representative of druidism and distances itself from other druid groups. Like the druid order, the Celtic Reformed Church also aims at a synthesis between orthodox Christianity and the teachings of the druids.

B. DRUIDS IN LITERATURE AND MUSIC

Around 1148 Geoffrey of Monmouth, taking up older traditions, wrote the *Vita Merlini* of the magician and seer Merlin. As early as the beginning of the 12th cent., Robert de Boron linked the myth of Merlin with that of the Holy Grail, in other words also with the Arthurian cycle. In this way Merlin stands between Christianity and the druid religion. In Germany, the version of Boron in particular was subsequently adapted several times, first of all, for example, by Albrecht von Scharfenberg (12th cent.). Worthy of mention with respect to the modern period is the drama *Merlin* (1832) by Karl Leberecht Immermann that represented the start of the modern reception of this character in literature, theatre and later also in film. (Also worthy of note in this context is a more recent example of productive Merlin reception, *Merlin oder das wüste Land* by Tankred Dorst [1981].) The basic theme of the Irish and Welsh stories and also of the novels of Arthur is the 'Other World', the place, the 'somewhere else', a place where there is no time and space, where the world of the imagination has become reality according to the Divine plan. The 'somewhere else' determines the state of being after death. These ideas also called up paradisiacal images of the Isle of Avalon or Emain Ablach. The Gaelic tradition and Celtism, as they gathered strength again in the 18th cent. also greatly influenced the northern European Storm and Stress movement via Herder and Goethe through the literary forgery by James MacPherson (1736–1796) of the songs of the mythical Irish singer Ossian,. Ultimately they left their mark on the melancholic, emotionally passionate overture *Nachklänge aus Ossian* (1840) by Niels Wilhelm Gade. The Romantically-imbued story *Der Druide* (1842) by the Swiss storyteller Jeremias Gotthelf that was published at the same time is a peculiarity. Actually linked with narrative realism, the author attempts, using the figure of the Helvetian druid Schwito to depict the religiosity already inherent in his people in the pre-Christian period and their love of freedom. The ancient Irish conception of the power of the druids is also to be found in the drama *The Shadowy Waters* (1900) by the well known Irish poet William Butler Yeats. Worthy of mention in this context at the present time, aside from purely esoteric literature, are also the numerous publications of the 'New Age' wave that repeatedly keenly adopt the druid theme within the framework of crime thrillers and historical novels etc. (e.g. Wolfgang Hohlbein, especially 1995–1998 and Marion Zimmer Bradley, particularly 1990–1998).

C. DRUIDS IN ART

In addition to numerous book illustrations (the first German depiction of a druid appeared in 1648 on the title page of *De Dis Germanis* by Elias Schedius) can be found 18th and 19th cent. works, which were influenced above all by Romanticism. Worthy of particular mention is the oil painting *The Bard* by Thomas Jones (1774) based on the Romantic poem of the same name by Thomas Grey, which tells of the last Welsh bard who, while being persecuted by Edward I, falls from a cliff into the River Convey (also: William Holman Hunt (1850) *Converted British Family Sheltering a Christian Missionary from the Druids*; George Henry, Edward Atkinson Hornel (1890) *The Druids: Bringing the*

Misteltoe; Sir Hubert von Herkomer (1896): *The Druid*).

→ Druids
→ FRANCE; → CELTIC-GERMAN ARCHAEOLOGY; → MYSTERIES

1 G. ASHE, Mythology of the British Isles, 1990   2 M. GREEN, Exploring the World of the Druids, 1997   3 J. MARKALE, Le druidisme: traditions et dieux des Celtes, 1985 (Engl. J. GRAHAM (trans.), The Druids: Celtic Priests of Nature, 1999)   4 H. E. MIERS, Lexikon des Geheimwissens, 1993, 173   5 H. WIESE/H. FRICKE, Handbuch des Druidenordens ³1931
ADDITIONAL BIBLIOGRAPHY H. BIRKAN, Kelten. Bilder ihrer Kultur, German-English edition, 1999 P. CARR-GOMM, The Druid Renaissance: The Voice of Druidry Today, 1996 CHR.-J. GUYONVARC'H, F. LE ROUX, Mythos, Magie und Wirklichkeit der Kelten, 1996
WOLFGANG SPIKERMANN

Dumbarton Oaks

A. INTRODUCTION B. INSTITUTIONAL HISTORY
C. SCHOLARSHIP D. THE BYZANTINE
COLLECTION

A. INTRODUCTION

Dumbarton Oaks (DO), which is located in the Georgetown district of Washington, DC, is one of the world's foremost institutions for the study of Byzantine civilization (loosely construed and including Late Antiquity, early Christianity, the medieval Balkans, the Latin West, and the Islamic Near East). It also possesses a collection of Byzantine (*sensu strictiore*) art of great importance, as well as a number of objects from earlier periods and neighboring cultures.

B. INSTITUTIONAL HISTORY

DO owes its existence to Ambassador and Mrs. Robert Woods Bliss, who purchased the Federal-style house and its grounds in 1920. Twenty years later, in an effort to ensure the vitality of their scholarly interests, the Blisses deeded the house, its formal gardens, their collection of Byzantine art, and a reference library of 14,000 volumes to Mr. Bliss' alma mater Harvard University. Perpetuation of the library and collection had long been the intent of the couple, but their conveyance to Harvard was hastened by the realization that the US would soon become embroiled in WW II [14. 78]. The first Senior Research Fellows (Henri Foçillon and Charles Rufus Morey) were appointed shortly after the transfer [14. 81–82]. At the urging of Director of Studies Albert M. Friend (1944–1956), Senior Fellows were given academic rank as members of the Faculty of Arts and Sciences; there were DO professorships in Byzantine art, architecture, history, literature, and theology [1. 7–8]. Significant changes occurred in the 1970s, especially under Director Giles Constable (1977–1984). The research faculty was phased out as vacancies occurred, and Constable emphasized increasing both DO's interaction with the learned world at large and the number of scholars who benefited from its resources [1. 9; 7].

C. SCHOLARSHIP

DO publishes several important series and has sustained large-scale research projects like the *Oxford Dictionary of Byzantium* and the DO Hagiography Database. Through its residential fellowships, it directly supports scholars from around the world; fellows' research profits not only from access to the excellent Byzantine Library (now housing over 123,000 volumes and receiving over 900 journals), but also from research resources like the Byzantine Photograph and Fieldwork Archives. DO's involvement in fieldwork began after the death (in 1950) of Thomas Whittemore, the founder of the Byzantine Institute. Initially DO scholars directed the work of the Byzantine Institute in Istanbul, but in 1963 DO started to conduct fieldwork of its own. In the 1960s and 1970s, DO supported (in whole or in part) numerous projects (in Turkey, Greece, Cyprus, Syria, the former Yugoslavia, Italy and Tunisia), but under Director Constable there was a shift to smaller and more cooperative endeavors (including surveys and conservation) [6].

D. THE BYZANTINE COLLECTION

Mrs. Bliss had an early interest in the Middle Ages and had begun collecting as a young woman; her husband made his first serious purchase (an object of pre-Columbian art) in 1912 [14. 59–60]. Though the couple made significant acquisitions of early Christian and Byzantine art in the 1920s, it was not until the early 1930s that they decided to focus upon it. Royall Tyler, a longtime friend, greatly influenced this decision, and the 1931 Louvre exhibition that Tyler helped organize, the *Exposition internationale d'art byzantin*, may be seen as its pivotal event [5. vii; 14. 61, 68–70]. Between its transfer to Harvard in 1940 and the late 1970s, the Collection more than doubled in size, largely due to the continued generosity of its former owners and the acquisitions made by Director John S. Thacher (1940–1969). Its strength is in the 'minor arts', i.e., objects of gold, silver and ivory, as well as jewelry, *cloisonné* enamels, illuminated manuscripts and textiles. Most of these were luxury items intended for the highest strata of society. The collection also includes some monumental pieces (e.g., pavement mosaics from Antioch), as well as several study collections (e.g., potsherds collected by David Talbot Rice and samples of tesserae, nails, glass, and bricks and mortar collected by the Byzantine Institute from monuments in Istanbul). Most of the Collection has been published in a series of *catalogues raisonnés* [11; 12; 13]. DO also possesses one of the greatest collections of late antique and Byzantine coins [2; 3; 4; 8], as well as the largest and most comprehensive collection of lead seals in the world [10].

→ Antioch [1] on the Orontes; → Byzantium
→ BYZANTINE STUDIES; → BYZANTIUM

1 M. V. ANASTOS, Dumbarton Oaks and Byzantine Studies. A Personal Account, in: A. E. LAIOU, H. MAGUIRE (eds.), Byzantium. A World Civilization, 1992, 5–18
2 A. R. BELLINGER, Roman and Byzantine Medallions in

Fig. 1: The 'Riha paten', depicting the Apostles' Communion (ca. 565-578)

Fig. 2: Pyxis from Moggio: Moses receiving the tablets

Fig. 3: Tapestry with two Nereids (5th–6th. cent.)

Fig. 4: Necklace with Aphrodite Anadyomene
(late 5th–6th. cent.)

the Dumbarton Oaks Collection, in: Dumbarton Oaks
Papers 12, 1958, 127–156   3 Id. et al., Late Roman Gold
and Silver Coins at Dumbarton Oaks, in: Dumbarton
Oaks Papers 18, 1964, 161–236   4 Id., P. GRIERSON,
Catalogue of the Byzantine Coins in the Dumbarton Oaks
Collection and in the Whittemore Collection, 3 vols.,
1968–1973   5 S. A. BOYD, Byzantine Art, 1979   6 G.
CONSTABLE, Dumbarton Oaks and Byzantine Field Work,
in: Dumbarton Oaks Papers 37, 1983, 171–176   7 Id.,
Dumbarton Oaks and the Future of Byzantine Studies,
1979   8 P. GRIERSON, M. MAYS, Catalogue of Late
Roman Coins in the Dumbarton Oaks Collection and in
the Whittemore Collection, 1992   9 Handbook of the
Byzantine Collection, 1967   10 J. NESBITT, N. OIKONO-
MIDES, Catalogue of Byzantine Seals at Dumbarton Oaks
and in the Fogg Museum of Art, 3 vols., 1991
11 G. M. A. RICHTER, Catalogue of Greek and Roman
Antiquities in the Dumbarton Oaks Collection, 1956
12 M. C. ROSS, K. WEITZMANN, Catalogue of the Byzantine and Early Mediaeval Antiquities in the Dumbarton
Oaks Collection, 3 vols., 1962–1972   13 G. VIKAN,
Catalogue of the Sculptures in the Dumbarton Oaks Collection from the Ptolemaic Period to the Renaissance,
1995   14 W. M. WHITEHILL, Dumbarton Oaks: The
History of a Georgetown House and Garden, 1967
15 http://www.doaks.org   TODD M. HICKEY

Dynamics see → NATURAL SCIENCES

E

Eclecticism. The term eclecticism, widely used today in a negative sense to denote an imitative, dependent, combinative mode of philosophising, stands from Antiquity on for a model of philosophical reflection that, eschewing connection with a particular school (or sect), instead selects the best from all teachings. At the turn of the 15th cent., Gianfrancesco Pico della Mirandola recalled the 'selective philosophers' (Diog. Laert. 1.21), who, like bees, chose everywhere the things that pleased them, to produce from them their honey; a way of proceeding that was also recommended by the Apostle Paul: "Think before you do anything; hold on to what is good!" (1 Thess. 5:21). Gianfrancesco holds to this approach – alongside scepticism – in critical opposition to the unifying philosophy of his uncle; thus from the beginning syncretism and eclecticism are distinguished one from the other (Leibniz for example was rightly regarded by Jakob Thomasius as a syncretist, not an eclectic). But eclecticism comprised more than mere selection from the teachings of the various philosophical sects, for this selective attitude promised freedom from being bound to a particular sect, and thus freedom for the independent judgment, owing allegiance only to the love of and the search for truth. Thus the keyword of 'philosophical freedom' found concrete expression in the idea of eclecticism.

According to Petrus Ramus in ca.1550 Galen had been an eclectic, on account of his free judgment. Subsequently, an increasing number of philosophers was referred to as eclectic (e.g., apart from Potamon, who had been mentioned by Diog. Laert., not only Cicero, Giovanni Pico della Mirandola (!), Ramus and Lipsius, but also Clement of Alexandria, Origen and the Neoplatonists), until finally Johann Christoph Sturm towards the end of the 17th cent. declared all founders of philosophical sects (e.g. Plato, Aristotle, Descartes) to be eclectics, as by definition belonging to no sect, and therefore, as non-'sectarians', owing allegiance to none. For them it was true that they "swore by no master's words" (Hor. Epist. 1.14) – a quotation popular beyond the confines of eclecticism. The separation of philosophers into eclectics and sectarians goes back to Francesco Redi (1664); it was he too who (always with reference to Diog. Laert. 1.21) made the selective procedure the basis of his groundbreaking biological experiments, as a kind of theory of science. Sturm not only elaborated upon this initiative theoretically, but also put it into actual practice in the context of physics (in the broader sense), in that he selected the most probable hypotheses in any particular case, from whomever they might come. Because physics was understood as a central discipline of philosophy, it could not be perceived that this process of all-round, gradual acquisition of knowledge, successful though it can be and actually proves to be in the natural sciences (and medicine), is impracticable in philosophy (in the narrower sense, e.g. in metaphysics or ethics).

From ca.1650 anyone who wished to be seen as a free, progressive thinker gladly chose to describe himself as an eclectic, the first being several Dutch professors. But it was also in the Netherlands that a powerful adversary of eclecticism arose owing to the successes of Cartesianism. The Cartesians declared themselves (again) to be a sect, swore by the words of their master, and demanded philosophical freedom only insofar as it applied to the acknowledgement of (Cartesian) truth. In Germany, Christian Wolff was able to exploit the tools of systematic thought against eclecticism. Although many philosophers of the German Enlightenment, beginning with Christian Thomasius, saw themselves as eclectics, in them the term eclecticism became a fashionable label denoting a vague notion of independence, but lost the aspect of (rigorous) selection. As a consequence, under the pressure of systematic thought during the course of the 18th cent. the term came to denote the unsystematic and derivative mingling of concepts for mingling's sake, so that in the end eclecticism and syncretism were seen as being synonymous.
→ Eclecticism; → Hairesis

1 M. ALBRECHT, Eklektik. Eine Begriffsgeschichte, 1994
2 H. DREITZEL, Zur Entwicklung und Eigenart der 'eklektischen Philosophie', in: Zschr. für Histor. Forsch. 18, 1991, 281–343   3 H. HOLZHEY, Philosophie als Eklektik, in: Studia Leibnitiana 15, 1983, 19–29.
RUTH ALBRECHT

École Française d'Athènes
A. HISTORY   B. EFA PERSONNEL   C. SCHOLARLY ACTIVITIES   D. LIBRARIES AND ARCHIVES
E. PUBLICATIONS

A. HISTORY
France's oldest scholarly institute abroad, the École Française d'Athènes (EFA) came into being in 1846 against the double backdrop of the Greek and Romantic revolutions. → FRANCE had actively participated in the Greek Revolution by dispatching an expeditionary corps to free the Peloponnese in 1825. The Romantic movement was based on the great cultural significance attributed to → GREECE and its occupation was felt in France to threaten this cultural heritage.

In order to maintain France's standing in Greece – especially in view of competition with the United Kingdom – the government of King Louis-Philippe (1830–1848) decided to found a cultural institute on the model of the Villa Medici in Rome, where artists had been trained since the time of Louis XIV. The EFA's decree of foundation assigned quite varied duties: on the one hand, it was to be a centre in Athens for advanced study of Greek language and history as well as of the monuments of Greece's ancient culture and, on the other hand, the members were obliged to teach the French language and to administer examinations in the French

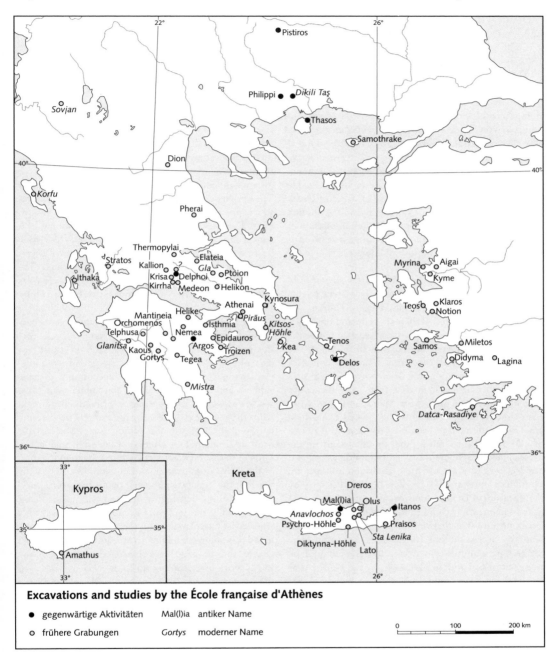

Excavations and studies by the École française d'Athènes

- • gegenwärtige Aktivitäten   Mal(l)ia   antiker Name
- ○ frühere Grabungen   *Gortys*   moderner Name

schools of the Orient. The obligation to teach, however, was abolished within two years.

In the first thirty years of its existence, many EFA members followed the advice of French writer Sainte-Beuve (1804–1869), "in Colonus to read the choruses of Oedipus and in Delphi those of Ion". For these first generations of visitors to Greece, physical contact with the homeland of Homer, Sophocles and Euripides was sufficient. Gradually, however, the EFA's activities became more extensive. For instance, Ernest Beulé excavated below the Acropolis, Paul Foucart exposed a

part of the supporting walls of the Temple of → DELPHI, and Léon Heuzet led an expedition to Macedonia financed by Napoleon III (1852–1870). The → LOUVRE, in accordance with common practice of the time, expanded its collection with artifacts that the enterprise had found.

After France's loss to Germany in 1871, French intellectuals sought to redress the lead taken by a Germany that also rivaled France on Greek soil. (The → DEUTSCHES ARCHÄOLOGISCHES INSTITUT was founded in Athens in 1873, and German excavations of

→ OLYMPIA began in 1875.) From 1871 to 1874, the EFA erected its buildings on the Lycabettus hill, where it is still housed today. And, with its new statutes of 1874, the EFA was transformed into a research centre.

The 1874 reform proved very advantageous to the EFA. For instance, the role of the *Académie des Inscriptions et Belles-Lettres* as custodian of scholarship was strengthened, with the EFA members now able to report to it on their research activities. Furthermore, the new director, Albert Dumont (1875–1878), founded both the journal *Bulletin de Correspondance hellénique* for the dissemination of information as well as a monograph series; both periodical and series still exist. He encouraged the 'Athéniens' to study all areas of Greek culture and promoted, for example, Byzantine Studies, the study of the Greek languages and the compilation of catalogues of objects. Additionally, during his period of office there occurred an important intensification of the excavations on → DELOS.

The period of great excavations that systematically exposed ancient cities and sacred places had begun. Digs on Delos, at Delphi, Argus, Thasus, Philippi and Malia started at the end of the 19th cent. and the beginning of the 20th, with extensive work carried out on the Delos, Delphi, and Argus sites before World War I. The EFA still works on all these sites today, though with new methods and emphases. The choice of these sites makes particular sense in that they span the entire ancient period from prehistory (Malia) until early Christian times (Philippi). The insights gained from these great excavations have been in every respect of fundamental significance. While the abundance of monuments, including numerous original buildings, several hundred works of art and many thousand inscriptions, prohibits a summary of the results here, suffice it to say that the finds at Delphi alone (excavations 1893–1902) have fundamentally changed modern understanding of Greek art and that their influence extends far beyond scholarly circles. Matisse, for example, was inspired by the archaic sculptures discovered in these comprehensive excavations and, in particular, by the *kouroi*, that is, the large representations, albeit in rather simple forms, of naked young men. As it had in previous periods, Greek art brought about a change in the canon of contemporary art.

Today as in its previous phases, EFA activity revolves around establishing great excavation sites and making them accessible. And as in its earlier periods, the EFA conducts smaller campaigns both inside and outside Greece on a continuous basis.

Starting in 1923 conditions favouring an extension of EFA activities worsened. With the Greco-Turkish War of 1922, Asia Minor ceased to be an area available for excavations. In 1924, the Greek government's more restrictive policies also limited the number of excavations in Greece. Furthermore, financial difficulties related to the crises between the World Wars set limitations on EFA activities. And, finally, during the Second World War and the Greek Civil War, which lasted until 1949, little work in the field could be conducted.

In the 1950s, the necessity arose to modernise both the EFA's infrastructure, which had since become out of date, and its working methods, which had remained largely unchanged since the beginning of excavations. The EFA established technical departments administered by specialist personnel including a manuscript archive, a library, a drawings department, a photograph library and a map library, and thereby adapted to the demands of a modern research centre. With the adoption and dissemination from 1956 onward of methods developed by British scholars, the excavations became scholarly undertakings. The areas of research also expanded, both in the spatial and temporal senses. Thus prehistoric excavation sites have, in the last forty years, produced probably the most important discoveries. These locations include both the traditional EFA sites such as Argos and Malia and newer ones like Dikili Tash, where excavations were resumed in 1961 after a first campaign there between 1920 and 1922. The beginning of excavations in Amathus in Cyprus in 1975 demonstrates the EFA's new interest in Greek culture outside Greece.

The EFA has also implemented the most recent changes in the field of archaeology. For example, in the production of archaeological maps such as those for Thasus and Malia, there is less digging and more non-evasive observation involved. Collaboration with geographers and scientists studying the animal and plant worlds as well as the application of methods adopted from the more exact sciences for the precise determination of the age, origin or production of objects have profoundly altered the content of research. Such development in scholarly activity corresponds to innovation in the EFA's organization and mission. Until 1985 the work of the EFA was governed by more than century-old regulations that had undergone only insignificant change. While the new 1985 statutes retain as the EFA's chief tasks "scholarship and the teaching of research" in all disciplines relating to ancient and Byzantine Greece, they nevertheless also broaden the scope of the EFA's work by opening it up to the various aspects of the ancient, mediaeval, modern and contemporary Greek world. Today the more than century-and-a-half-old EFA is an international research centre studying all areas of Greek culture.

B. EFA PERSONNEL

The quality of its personnel has earned the EFA its status as an international scholarly institute. The EFA consists of French members, overseas members and stipendiaries (i.e., grant recipients). Traditionally, all French members were selected by an admission competition. Those admitted were often, but not always, former pupils of the elite *École Normale Supérieure* and generally possessed an *agrégation* – that is, a diploma certifying advanced proficiency and issued by the French state upon completion of a final university examination – in a philological discipline and sometimes also in history. The length of their stay at the EFA could vary but amounted to at most three years. Until the beginning of the 20th cent. the members were bound to celibacy, with the first female member, a French woman, not being admitted until 1956.

According to the 1985 statutes, applicants must possess both an *agrégation* and the D.E.A. (that is, the *Diplôme d'Études Approfondies*, a one-year degree that is earned after the completion of studies and which leads to a dissertation) or a degree deemed equivalent by a commission appointed annually by the education ministry. The appointments of the members, who presently number nine individuals, is for one year initially but can be renewed three times. The members are obligated both to participate in the common work of the EFA as well as to pursue their own research. Before 1996 all members had been French citizens. The statutes, however, provide for the admission of foreigners, and, in the application competition of July 1996, the first member without French citizenship – a Greek national – was accepted. Previously, admission of members without French citizenship was considered unnecessary since the EFA has also had a foreign department since 1900. The responsibility of the foreign department, which was conceived of as early as 1846 and originally for Belgians, is to accommodate stipendiaries from friendly countries that do not have access to permanent establishments in Greece. These stipendiaries are paid by their country of origin and have the same rights and duties as the French members. The foreign department regularly has Belgian and Swiss members and, in recent years, has also admitted three Brazilians and a Canadian. The foreign department plays an important role in the scholarly life of the EFA.

Since 1985, admission of doctoral students as stipendiaries has been firmly anchored in the statutes. In addition, the EFA also takes on guest scholars of any nationality for working visits of various lengths. Stipendiaries and visiting scholars pursue their own research projects or participate in the various programmes of the EFA. Between 1991 and 1994, the EFA's guests included individuals from thirty-three different countries, indicating its attractiveness and significance on the international stage.

C. SCHOLARLY ACTIVITIES

The history of the EFA is closely connected to the emergence and development of Greek architecture. Nevertheless, the EFA did not, even in its earlier phases, see this as its only area of responsibility. Thus the 1985 statutes extended the scope of scholarly inquiry to encompass also modern and contemporary Greek culture. Since 1990 the EFA has reserved a membership position for modern studies and since 1995 a position for an associated professor for studies in Modern Greek. And in addition to young Antiquity researchers, there are also stipendiaries who specialise in modern and contemporary Greece. Nevertheless, archaeology remains the chief area of EFA scholarly inquiry.

As mentioned above, the EFA does not conduct archaeological work in the traditional excavation sites alone. Although some of those sites, including Argos, Delos, Delphi, Malia, and Thasus, were established as early as the end of the 19th and beginning of the 20th cent., they remain of great academic interest and are still rich sources for discoveries of the greatest significance. At the moment there are some one-hundred scholars working on the excavation sites within the larger framework of the EFA's academic programs. These scholars are either at a university or at the CNRS (i.e., the *Centre national de la recherche scientifique*), which have formal agreements with the EFA. In the context of this extension of contractually regulated relationships, it is also noteworthy that the Ministry of Foreign Affairs is contributing financially to the excavations in Amathus, Dikili Tash and Sovjan and that the number of projects conducted in partnership with other French or foreign institutes, such as those projects at Dikili Tash, Itanos and Sovjan, is growing. Thus the EFA is at the centre of an international network of research on Greek culture.

The EFA has always maintained an additional interest for Greek culture outside Greece proper. Whereas until 1923 Turkey was a favourite location for its scholarly activity, the EFA has more recently turned its attention to the Balkan countries – with excavations, for example, in Albania – and to the Black Sea. Furthermore, it is supporting excavations in → ALEXANDRIA.

D. LIBRARIES AND ARCHIVES

The EFA possesses extraordinarily rich library and archival resources. The main library, assembled over the space of more than 160 years, boasts an exhaustive Greek archaeology collection as well as comprehensive coverage of all aspects of Greek culture from prehistory to → BYZANTIUM. Currently comprising 90,000 volumes and subscribing to 600 periodicals, it is a reference library to which researchers and doctoral students have free access. Open year round without interruption, it offers day and night access to members as well as the EFA's visiting scholars and stipendiaries.

The academic archive principally holds materials relating to EFA excavations in Greece, Cyprus and Turkey as well as the museum collections published by the EFA. It comprises photographs, drawings and manuscript sources including, most notably, the excavation notebooks.

The photograph library contains 400,000 photos in various photographic media, and the drawings library (i.e., *Planothèque*) maintains 20,000 plans and drawings and a collection of 6,000 prints.

E. PUBLICATIONS

The EFA's many publications serve to disseminate the results of its scholarship. Six of its current ten serials, that is, *Fouilles de Delphes*, *Exploration archéologique de Délos*, *Études crétoises*, *Études thasiennes*, *Études péloponnésiennes* and *Études chypriotes* (listed here in the order of their founding), are dedicated to the traditional excavation sites. *Bulletin de Correspondance héllenique* (BCH), founded in 1876, appears biannually. Two regular sections of the BCH, namely the *Chronique des fouilles en Grèce* and *Chronique des fouilles de Chypre*, are indispensable research tools and guarantee the journal's wide circulation. In the supplemental volumes of BCH both monographs on sites that are not researched by the EFA as well as conference proceedings are published. With the founding of those supplemental volumes, the EFA discontinued publication of *Travaux et Mémoires des anciens membres étrangers de l'École et de divers savants*, of which 21 volumes had appeared between 1929 and 1978. *Bibliothèque des Écoles françaises d'Athènes et de Rome* continues to publish the doctoral dissertations and postdoctoral theses (i.e., *habilitations*) of the members. The serial *Sites et monuments* comprises guides to the excavations as well translations of those guides into other languages. *Recherches franco-helléniques*, founded in 1990, publishes in Greek and French collaborative works of the EFA and the Greek Department of Antiquities. A new collection, the *Études Épigraphiques*, was founded in 1992 for the study of the corpus of those inscriptions with no direct connection to traditional EFA excavation sites.

With its more than 160–year history, its presence in all areas of contemporary archaeology and its openness to the modern world, the EFA occupies an important place in national and international scholarship in the service of Greek culture.

1 *Bulletin de Correspondance héllenique* 120 (1), 1996, Numéro spécial, Cent cinquantenaire de l'École française d'Athènes   2 G. RADET, L'histoire et l'oeuvre de'École française d'Athènes, 1901   3 La redécouverte de Delphes, published by the EFA, 1992.   4 L'espace grec: 150 ans de fouilles de l'Ecole française d'Athènes, published by the EFA, 1996.   5 École française d'Athènes URL: http://www.efa.gr/   ROLAND ÉTIENNE

École Française de Rome
A. FOUNDATION B. LOCATION C. ACTIVITIES AND SCHOLARSHIP D. PUBLICATIONS

A. FOUNDATION
The founding of the *École Française de Rome* (EFR) in 1875 is associated with France's defeat by Germany four years earlier. The *Istituto di Corrispondenza Archeologica*, where intellectuals from all countries researching ancient Rome had met since 1829, ceased to exist in the aftermath of the Franco-Prussian War of 1870–1871. While French researchers had played an important role in the Institute, German scholars nevertheless had been its driving force and had continued the Institute. In reaction, at the beginning of the EFR, there existed a clear wish for requital. One of the basic ideas of the first members of the *École* was that of reinvigorating in the scholarly sphere the self-confidence that had been damaged in the political and to do this by engaging in a field in which German scholarship occupied a preeminent position. A good example of this ambivalent stance, in which admiration was mixed with the need to measure oneself against German scholars, was the historian Camille Jullian. Rather than spending a third year in Rome, in 1882 he applied for a one year residency in Berlin where he wanted to study under Th. Mommsen and other great German scholars. "It is a matter of going to Germany not only as an admirer and a student but, if you will forgive the expression, also as a spy", he wrote to the historian N.D. Fustel de Coulanges. Thus, the EFR almost became just an archaeological institute, a French counterpart to the → DEUTSCHES ARCHÄOLOGISCHES INSTITUT. Thus, the original intention was to admit the young members of the → *École Française d'Athènes* for a year in advance of their stay in Greece. From the time of the founding of the *École Française d'Athènes* in 1846, it had become customary for many of its members to spend time in the Villa Medici in Rome before their study of ancient Greece, which at the time was considered 'the' cultural point of reference. In 1873, a presidential decree named a former member of the *École Française d'Athènes*, Albert Dumont – who had himself made use of such an interim stay in the Villa Medici and who had supported the project – "deputy director of the École d'Athènes with responsibility for teaching archaeology in Rome". The following year he was appointed by a further decree director of the *École Archéologique de Rome*.

Still, "to visit Rome before Athens is to place the cart before the horse", as the then president Thiers put it. Regardless of whether or not H. Wallon – from 1875 onward Minister of Education and a specialist on slavery in Antiquity – gave any credence to this sentiment, he was responsible in 1875 for a decree that called the EFR into existence and established its mission, which remains the same today; that is, the admission of six (today eighteen) members who are to occupy themselves with the combined history of Rome and Italy. The preamble to the statutes from that time assigns the *École* this very area of scholarship: "it is the duty of the EFR to promote research and the teaching of research in all cultures indigenous to Italy or derived from Rome from pre-history until today". It is within the context of this historical ambition, present since the beginning of the EFR, that the exceptional nature and great diversity of its activities lie.

B. LOCATION
In 1875 the EFR moved into the rooms on the second floor of the Palazzo Farnese, where it is still located today. Shortly before that date, the French embassy had been offered the distinguished site by the still young Italian state and was looking for an institution with which it might share the rooms. The *École* needed space for a library, which, in view of the tasks it had set for itself, was indispensable. Thus, it established itself in the generous rooms that had previously housed the library of the Duke of Parma. Today, over 125 years later,

the library contains 180,000 monographs and 1,600 periodicals. Over time, it became necessary to extend the library, first to the attic, then to the third floor of the Palazzo, and, finally, also to the basement, where sliding stacks were installed in 1996. From its inception, the library has not only been open to members but also to established scholars of all nationalities, who continue to make use of it in ever increasing numbers. A desire to accommodate this dual public helps to explain the diverse nature of the library, whose resources must satisfy both the demands of members and French scholars who work on the history of Italy from Antiquity to the present as well as the demands of Italian scholars and those of other nationalities, many of whom consult the large collections of French historical texts. Since the library is not able to meet fully these manifold demands, it concentrates on ancient and mediaeval history, on Classical and mediaeval archaeology and on those areas that are poorly represented in other libraries in Rome, for example, Antiquity in Africa and Gaul. Since 1989, Eduardo Volterra's important and unique collection of material on Roman and mediaeval law has been part of the library, which is working on its conservation and expansion.

C. Activities and Scholarship
1. Until 1945 2. Developments since 1945

1. Until 1945

The continuity of the *École's* activities during its more than 125 years should not be mistaken for stagnation. The development of the *École* can be divided into several phases, the first of which stretches from its foundation until the Second World War. In this period, the *École* worked chiefly in the area of ancient history and Classical archaeology. Since the Italian state did not grant excavation permits to foreign institutes at that time, members of the *École* concentrated on already known ancient sites and monuments. From these studies there resulted numerous monographs that are still considered standard works: e.g., on the Tiber Island, the Aventine and the Temple of Apollo in Rome during the reign of Augustus, Praeneste, Terracina and the Pontine Marshes in Latium, Pozzuoli in Campania etc. In northern Africa, by contrast, the members of the EFR had the opportunity to make field excavations. The close scholarly relationships that came into being in this period between the *École* and the countries of the Maghreb still exist today. Among the EFR's excavation sites are Mactaris in Tunisia, Cherchell and Tipasa in Algeria and Volubilis in Morocco. Also in the more narrow sense of historical scholarship, the *École's* Antiquity scholars have done significant work. Here, for example, it is possible to cite – mentioning only the work of directors – an edition of the *Liber Pontificalis* by Louis Duchesne, which marks the resumption of scholarship on the history of ancient Christianity, and Jérôme Carcopinos's scholarship on Vergil, the origins of Ostia, and the *Lex Hieronica*.

Furthermore, the *École's* scholarship before the Second World War also dealt with the Middle Ages. As early as 1877, Élie Berger, a rather young and, moreover, Protestant member, had received permission to work in the then still private archives of the Vatican. His scholarly activity led to the eventual opening up of the Vatican archives (1880/1881) and paved the way for the grand project of publishing the papal registers (also known as papal letters), on which generations of *École* members – most of whom were graduates of the *École Nationale des Chartes*, which taught historical subjects – worked. The series containing papal registers from the 13th cent. was finished in 1959, while the publication of registers from the 14th cent. is still in progress. The *École* is also preparing a CD-ROM that is to hold all 78 of the volumes that have appeared so far. In addition to this undertaking, the *École* is conducting scholarship not only on Church history and on the history of the Papal States but also on Venice, southern Italy and the relationships between Italy and the kingdom of France. Most of this research deals with the Late Middle Ages (13th–15th cents.). Mediaeval art historical scholarship is also well represented. Here there is sufficient space to name only the outstanding Émile Mâles, who followed Louis Duchesne in 1922 as director of the *École*.

Whereas scholars of the Early Modern and modern periods were relatively well represented among *École* members until the beginning of the 1920s, their numbers subsequently decreased considerably; from 1922 to 1945, there were only seven. Their scholarship at that time was primarily concerned with the 16th cent. and, indeed, exclusively in the areas of art history and political history, whereas earlier it had extended as far forward as the beginning of the 19th cent..

2. Developments since 1945

One may divide the period from the end of the Second World War until today into two phases: From 1945 to 1970 the *École* underwent a number of changes under the direction of Albert Grenier, Jean Bayet and Pierre Boyancé, and since 1972 it has gradually taken on its current form under the direction of Georges Vallet, Charles Pietri, Claude Nicolet and André Vauchez.

The changes referred to concern, first, the administration. Over time, the director came to be supported in his work by a number of close collaborators: from 1953 by a general secretary, whose post was abolished in 1972 in favour of a trio of directors of studies with competencies corresponding to the three newly created departments of the *École* (Archaeology and Ancient History, Mediaeval History, Modern and Recent History); from 1959 by a librarian and a deputy librarian; from 1966, when the institute became financially independent, by an accountant; and from 1981 by a secretary (later director) responsible for publications, whose post became necessary when the *École* took over publication of its own research (in 1972).

The *École* also expanded spatially. In 1966, it acquired a building at 62 Piazza Navona, where the bookkeeping and the publications divisions have been housed since 1975 and where an archaeological laboratory, an architecture bureau, an exhibition hall, a conference room and fourteen rooms for visiting scholars and grant recipients were established.

The number of members doubled between 1945 and 1975 from eight to sixteen, with eight members in the department for Ancient History, four in the department for Mediaeval History and four in the department for Modern and Recent History. The greatest innovation began in 1978 with the systematic admission of young scholars who worked on 19th- and 20th-cent. Italy. It had become clear that the earlier work of those researching modern times had hardly extended past the Napoleonic period. However, with the foundation in 1991 of a department for Social History under the director of studies in Modern and Recent History, the *École* confirmed its commitment to the study of very recent history. This department currently counts two members, who generally hold degrees in political science, or are geographers or lawyers, and whose research focuses on contemporary Italy. In addition to housing its own members, since the 1970s the *École* has also admitted grant recipients for short stays. The *École* today has at its disposal 130 monthly stipendiary payments. These allow it to support the work of a significant number of French and non-French scholars, who, in turn, represent a valuable addition to the *École*.

After the Second World War, the foreign institute received excavation concessions from Italy, which meant that Classical archaeologists were now able to conduct further research in the Apennine peninsula. In this work, there has existed constant and close collaboration with Italian surintendances (*soprintendenze*) and universities. Bolsena in former Etruria, where excavations began in 1946, and Megara Hyblaia in Sicily, where excavations started in 1948, became the 'classical' excavation sites of the *École*. The findings from these sites, which already fill several volumes, have still not been completely published. In 1971, Marzabotto near Bologna followed. After an interruption, and under an arrangement with the site's surintendance and the University of Bologna, there is again research there today. A further agreement with French and Italian partners regulates the more than quarter-century-long investigation of Paestum's urban architecture. Since the end of the 1970s and the beginning of the 1980s, the *École* has conducted excavations on a number of important sites in Rome and its suburbs; for example, in the suburb of Magliana, on the Pincio (land belonging to the monastery of *Trinità dei Monti* and to the *Villa Medici*) and on the Palatine Hill (*Vigna Barberini*). Among current excavations outside Rome are those in Musarna/Etruria begun in 1983 and in the district of the river port of Aquileia in Friuli that started in 1990.

Outside Italy there are projects, for example, in Sirmium in collaboration with the archaeological institute in Belgrade and, particularly, the continuing collaboration with the countries of the Maghreb, especially with the Tunisian state institute for cultural heritage and at the excavation sites of Sbeitla, Haïdra, Bulla Regia and Jedidi. Furthermore, since the 1970s mediaeval archaeology has also been represented at the *École*, with investigations building upon the innovative work of historians and focusing on fortifications – particularly of villages – and on everyday culture. The department for Mediaeval History's first two excavation sites were Brucato in Sicily and Scribla in Calabria. Tabarka in Tunisia and Caricin Grad in Serbia followed. Currently the *École*'s mediaeval archaeologists are working on two sites in southern Italy, Squillace in Calabria and Vaccarizza in Apulia, as well as on two in Latium, Valle del Turano and Cencelle.

The increase in archaeological activity during the most recent phase of the *École*'s history has not been at the expense of more strictly historical scholarship. The *École*'s Antiquity historians have worked, as did their predecessors, in quite varied areas. These include, for instance, not only literary and intellectual history, the history of religion and mentalities and the history of early Christianity but also legal history and the history of institutions as well as economic and social history. Although the interests of the school's mediaevalists, like those of the philologists of earlier generations, include diplomacy and the history of the Papacy, those interests – encouraged by the resurgence of Medieval Studies in France – have grown to include also religious and cultural history as well as the political, social and economic structures of mediaeval Italy. While traditionally the history of the Papacy and religious history in general have also been important areas of research for the historians of the department for Modern and Recent History, that department has also done important scholarship both in the area of political and intellectual history as well as in those of population, economic and social history. In the last quarter-century, the department has initiated a series of joint projects that have produced numerous stimulating findings and which, on occasion, have also involved the disciplines of anthropology and religious and political history. Examples of such studies include that on kinship relationships in the kingdom of Naples, a qualitative study on pilgrimages in early modern times, a study of monuments to honour the dead of the First World War in Latium, and a research project on capital cities from the 16th to 20th cents..

In conjunction with many of these historical and archaeological investigations, the École has held – in the conference room on the Piazza Navona – international scholarly meetings on topics specific to the individual departments as well as colloquia on topics of common interest to scholars of all the historical periods represented at the school. Among the latter are, for example, the investigation of the great cities of the Mediterranean initiated by Claude Nicolet and the more recent study "on space, the human being and the sacred" led by André Vauchez. Through such activities, the École distinguishes itself today by the same openness to the whole area of history that has constituted its originality from its foundation.

D. Publications

The abovementioned activities of the École such as excavations, projects for making archives accessible and academic congresses have resulted in a number of publications on which future research can orient itself. As early as 1876, the École, together with the École Française d'Athènes, published the Bibliothèque des Écoles Françaises d'Athènes et de Rome (BEFAR) with its various series, especially that of the dissertations of present and former members. From 1881, the École published a journal, Mélanges d'Archéologie et d'Histoire. Initially, this was intended only for the work of École members, but gradually it became open also to external authors. The decisive step was taken in 1971, when the journal, now divided into two series and renamed Mélanges de l'École Française de Rome, was placed at the disposal of the whole international, primarily Francophone and Italian, scientific community. Today, the Mélanges encompass three series (Antiquity: MEFRA; Middle Ages: MEFRM; Italy and the Mediterranean: MEFRIM), of which volumes of each appear biannually. In 1964, a further series, Suppléments aux Mélanges d'Archéologie et d'Histoire, which in 1972 was renamed Collection de l'École Française de Rome, was added to BEFAR. In this series, which today comprises more than 300 volumes, most of the findings of the École's research activities (excavations, conferences, colloquia, joint projects) as well as monographs – whose writing is frequently enabled by residences at the EFR – are published. Research conducted in collaboration with partner institutes is published in further series: Acta Nuntiaturae Gallicae (starting 1961) with the Università Gregoriana (in Rome), Images à l'Appui (starting 1986) with the Centre Louis Gernet (in Paris), and Roma Antica (starting 1987) with the archaeological Soprintendenza of Rome. With some thirty volumes a year and almost 3,000 journal pages, the EFR plays a significant role in French academic publishing.

→ France; → Italy

1 L'histoire et l'oeuvre de l'EFR, 1931   2 L'EFR 1875–1975: catalogue de l'exposition organisée à l'occasion de son centenaire, 1975   3 J. Carcopino, Souvenirs romains, 1968   4 M. R. de La Blanchère, Lettere dalle terre pontine, (Letters from the years 1879–1881 by Marie-René de La Blanchère, member of the EFR, to the director Auguste Geffroy, ed. and trans. into Italian by G. R. Rocci), 1998   5 O. Motte, Camille Jullian, élève de Mommsen à l'Université de Berlin, in: Ius Commune 9, 1980, 315–453   6 Id., Camille Jullian. Les années de formation, 1990   7 C. Nicolet, Avant-propos, in: F. Bérard, G. Di Vita-Evrard (eds.), L'épigraphie dans les Mélanges d'Archéologie et d'Histoire (1881–1970), 1997   8 Ch. Pietri and Ph. Boutry, with the assistance of F.-Ch. Uginet, La Scuola francese di Roma, in: Speculum Mundi: Roma centro internazionale degli istituti di archeologia, storia e storia dell'arte in Roma (1991)   9 C. Virlouvet, J. Dalarun, La scuola francese di Roma, in: Forma Urbis I/11, 1996, 31–35   10 B. Waché, Monseigneur Louis Duchesne (1843–1922): historien de l'Eglise, directeur de l'EFR, 1992.   11 École française de Rome URL: http://www.ecole-francaise.it/

CATHERINE VIRLOUVET

Economic Theory
I. Antiquity   II. Early Modern Period

I. Antiquity
A. Economic Life in Antiquity   B. Domestic Economy   C. Economic Ethics in Antiquity   D. Exchange   E. Chrematistics   F. Conceptions of Order and Associated Virtues

A. Economic Life in Antiquity

In spite of the political disputes due to the changing forms of government in Antiquity, there was a surprising uniformity in the use of basic economic terms in philosophical, literary and historiographic texts. From Homer to Late Antiquity, the notion that the good life is to be achieved through a well-ordered household prevailed. In such a household, there existed a unity of consumption and production, with the excess products to be exchanged in the town market (Agora). Division of labor did exist, but there was no conceptual division between the household as a place of consumption and the firm as the place of production. Even the spread of → coins (7th cent.) and the development of the banking industry (4th cent.) caused no changes in this thinking. When the cities were incorporated into the Hellenic states, and later the Roman Empire, the new duties and responsibilities of public administration were seen as the ordering of the royal or imperial household. Ptolemaic Egypt has been interpreted as a planned economy. The Oikonómos was in charge of management of the agricultural plans in the king's name [23. 279]. This title is assigned to the housewife in Phocylides (6th cent.) [9.174]. Even the Roman latifundia were still considered to be households; only in modern times did firms enter the scene independent of households [31. 226 ff.]. It was then legitimate for firms to arrange their activity to the acquisition of profit, which had formerly been denied to the household.

Different economic functions were assigned to citizens and non-citizens. There were nuances in the stratification of wealth, in which wage labor enjoyed little prestige, while → slavery exhibited a complicated spectrum: there was the unfree domestic staff in houses; there were slaves with more responsible duties such as the management of banks; there were those with the prospect of emancipation or the possibility to buy their freedom through their own business dealings; and there were the more miserable forms of slavery such as work in the mines. In addition to agriculture, there were urban handicrafts; already in Classical Athens, there were manufactories (ergasteria) of decent size. The polis furnished social events such as public meals. The ancient states differentiated themselves through combinations of such elements. In the hellenistic period, the concepts of social cohesion transcended the boundaries of the cities. Cosmopolitanism arose, and also eventually new social movements that at times have been interpreted as → Socialism [5. 116]. It is said about the first

Christian commune in the Acts of the Apostles: "The faithful all lived together and owned everything in common; they sold their goods and possessions and shared out the proceeds among themselves according to what each one needed" (Acts 2: 44–45, New Jerusalem Bible).

At the beginning of the Classical period, at the latest, there existed already a literature on economics. Of those. writings about agricultural cultivation are preserved (Columella). Attempts toward a comprehensive explanatory theory seem to have been only sporadically pursued, in particular by Xenophon [27] and in the attempt by Aristotle to ascribe the boundless pursuit of wealth to the false use of money.

Because the Greeks founded the canon of Western science with descriptive and explanatory approaches, and because the Roman economy spanned the entire Mediterranean world, the lack of an independent economic science in Antiquity can be traced neither to a poor state of general scientific knowledge nor to insufficient practical knowledge. Economic actions remained embedded in more general societal concerns [22]. The literature, even the myths, described growing tensions resulting from this, and affirmed the presence of a traditional set of values, as can be found in ancient epics and didactic poems. Classical philosophy reached the same conclusions; with the new tool of deductive reasoning from basic principles, without fundamentally altering the objectives [26. 13–89]. Hence, ancient economic thinking must be understood as a relatively certain element of an ethical philosophy that dealt with non-economic questions, on a more varied scale, and, in contrast to modern theory, not as an attempt to understand the functional mechanisms of an economy in a value-free manner.

B. DOMESTIC ECONOMY

The original unity of household and production on a farm found its equivalent in the skilled trades carried out at home, and even in noble households, which were also simultaneously producing and consuming entities. The appointment of slaves as overseers over parts of estates (including *ergasteria*) certainly had to lead to comparisons of their relative cost-effectiveness, which is described in the sources, but this consideration did not lead to an independent theory of managerial economics. For the domestic businesses of Antiquity that had slaves, different criteria for the allocation of resources arose than in modern economic theory, because the employment of labor was not determined by the balance of real wages and marginal disutility of work, and wealth was seen seen in social display so that – in modern terms – extravagant luxury could imply greater prestige and power and was, thus, an investment *sui generis*. While Solon regretted that no clearly defined goal was set by the gods for man in his striving for wealth, Aristotle and most of the later philosophers maintained that the good life, corresponding to the nature of man as focused on knowledge, required only a

limited amount of possessions, which, of course, had to be of sufficient abundance in his striving toward these higher goals. (To be sure, Epicurean philosophy built on the assumption that attainment of pleasure was the primary purpose; however, Hedonism, correctly understood, limited the appetites and thereby also the needs. The cynics stood for radical restriction of needs. Of special interest is the work of the late Epicurean Philodemus [13] about household management, because he asks only what the correct management of the household is for philosophers, thereby restricting the validity of his norms with the tolerance of the Epicureans.)

A household requires guidance. For Plato, Aristotle and Philodemus it is provided by one person, but with conditions. Of the three texts about households transmitted under the name of Aristotle, according to Philodemus the first stems from Theophrastus, Aristotle's successor. The second, certainly not genuine but rich in factual information, concerns the household financing of the state. The third, only preserved in a Latin translation from the Middle Ages, addresses primarily the theme of married life, the introductory topic of household management following the *Politics* of Aristotle. The wife is entitled to the mastery of affairs within the house; she spends what the husband earns. Faithfulness and progeny are lauded.

Slaves: Confronted with the task of justifying the sufferings of servitude, the philosophers support their view that a worthy life is impossible without slavery – only mechanised production, says Aristotle (Pol. 1253 b 38), could make slavery dispensable, and in fact in the *Iliad* (18,417–420) the god Hephaistos forges 'artificial virgins' for his own personal use. Aristotle asks who is born to rule by nature, and he stipulates that slave labor should be performed by non-Greeks. But the person who is best designed for the task by nature does not always rule – the philosophical problem cannot be solved satisfactorily (Arist. Pol. 1255 b 5). On the other hand, slaves can be assigned different tasks, some honorable and others less so (Arist. Pol. 1255 b 28), and finally slaves do receive payment, at least in the form of subsistence (Arist. Oec. 1 1344 b 4). They should be freed within a foreseeable time period (Aristot. Oec. 1 1344 b 15), and they should be allowed to have families.

The household texts mostly take agricultural earnings as their starting point. Philodemus, however, considered it not unworthy for the philosopher to live from the renting out of slaves, just as he also approved of the renting out of houses – it was, however, better for a philosophically-inclined person to own land, and even better when like Epicurus he could live as a philosopher from the fees of his students for his teaching in "non-slanderous, sincere words that do not cause trouble" [13.54].

Home economics was based originally on the so-called natural forms of acquisition like hunting, fishing and agriculture. There is a large distance between Hesiod, who describes the meager life of the peasant who lives in fear of the elements but is supported by the help of his neighbors, and Columella, who gives instructions about the best use of large agrarian holdings in Rome; some principles, however, remain the same in all areas, such as the avoidance of risk. Xenophon gives a picture of household handicrafts in his *Memorabilia*, where Socrates advises a landlord suffering a financial emergency that he should draw on the freeborn, the relatives and the slaves in his household in order to get by with home-made crafts. In the administration of the household, a development emerged which in Columella included an investment calculation that factored in interest charges. In the text now accredited to Theophrastus but was transmitted under the name of Aristotle, various systems of administration are described; according to that text, for example, the poor Athenian peasants – unlike the farmers in a barter economy who guarded against harvest fluctuations (Arist. Oec. 1 1344 b 34) – sold their output without a backup inventory for money and were integrated into the market.

C. Economic Ethics in Antiquity

Despite the emergence of comprehensive market relations, societal ideals from the aristocratic times carried over into the democratic period. Although the citizens of the numerous Greek cities, overwhelmingly from the class of independent farmers, traded with one another, the goal was still an economic independence (autarchy) which with limited means could only be achieved through a modest lifestyle. Painstaking workmanship was also a part of the good life, in which for instance free workers and slaves work next to one another and with one another in the construction of temples. The devotion to a good handiwork is substantiated in myth and literature. It is reflected in the philosophical thinking about economics when Plato draws on the image of the good shepherd who dedicates himself to his sheep and does not think about selling or enjoying them as food; or when Aristotle stresses that a shoe is made in order to be used and not to be sold; that the general is to think about war and not about honor; and the doctor about health and not about his earnings. The philosophers did indeed realize – according to Plato – that the division of labor increases productivity, and Xenophon knew that the degree depended on the size of the market – there is more room for specialization in the Persian metropolis than in the smaller cities of Greece (Kýru paideía 8,22,5) – but it was always stressed that the division of labor was primarily for the purpose of higher quality of products.

In their history, the Greeks avoided overpopulation by means of the formation of colonies. They saw the polis as a self-sustaining entity, in which the households interacted with the exchange of their surpluses. In the *Politeía* Plato wanted to confront the danger of market interactions disturbing societal stability in the city by means of strict legislation. He feared more than anything that disparities of wealth that were too large could lead the city into tyranny, mob rule or oligarchy. The recommended rules in the *Nómoi* tolerate the market, to be sure, but also provide that exchanges be supervised so that they can be corrected through redistribution should inequalities become too great. Aristotle also searched for theoretical rules of exchange that were not to damage the presumed justice of distribution. In light of the proletarization in the larger cities during the Hellenistic and Roman periods, demands arose for reallocation (e.g. the distribution of grain) that were based on general philanthropy.

D. Exchange

First, the exchange of goods and the exchange of gifts must be differentiated. Aristotle starts with the assumption of reciprocity (ἀντιπεπονθός, Eth. Nic. 1132 b 24) as an independent category; it is connected to neither distributive nor compensatory justice, because of its capacity to be unjust. Reciprocally fair and just action is what actually holds the polis together, where the freeman pays like with like; for example, a gift is answered with a gift, and – this is vital – everyone demonstrates his readiness to lead the way with a contribution, also to the state. Altars were erected according to Aristotle to the Charites, the goddesses of grace and thanks: so that one learned to take thankfully, but also to always be the first to give again.

Gifts and gifts in return generally play an important role in the lives of primitive peoples [18;19]. The exchange of gifts differs from the exchange of goods in that for a gift, a gift is to be given in return, which is not of equal value, but of the same kind, or even better a gift of the exact same importance – often after a period of time – with which the obligation incurred with the acceptance of the gift is fulfilled. In Homer, numerous examples of exchanges of gifts are to be found: a hero can boast that he will receive gifts from his followers (Menelaus, Od. 15,79–84); the laws of hospitality are bound to the obligations of the giving and receiving of gifts (Glaukon und Diomedes, Il. 6,234); and in linguistic research it has been demonstrated that in the Homeric epics a rich vocabulary for the exchange of gifts is used that is related to even older Indo-European traditions and customs. Thus, Aristotle thought in traditional categories.

The donation (μετάδοσις) in the exchange of gifts is followed by the exchange of goods without clear delineation: more precisely, a law of the exchange of gifts is described, which is then interpreted as an exchange of goods. Aristotle says that for a contribution, "a gift in return" takes place "corresponding in proportion" that is "brought about" by "cross allocation" (ποιεῖ δὲ τὴν ἀντίδοσιν τὴν κατ' ἀναλογίαν ἡ κατὰ διάμετρον σύζευξις, Eth. Nic. 1133 a 6–7). In Aristotle's example, A is a builder and B a shoemaker, a is a house and b a shoe. So the direct allocation is A to a and B to b. Aristotle says then: "When there was proportional equality, then reciprocity takes place" (1133 a 10–12). An illustration of this somewhat enigmatic passage can be gathered from the *Eudemian Ethics* of Aristotle, where likewise a cross allocation is discussed (1242 b 17). Something shall be granted to friends, one of whom is superior. Suitability or proportionality – ἀναλογία – exists when the superior one receives more, so that the allocation A to a, B to b takes place, with A > B and a > b. The cross allocation means that A receives b and B a – but then, says Aristotle, friendship leads in the presence of such proportions to the rendering of services (λειτουργία, 1242 b 18).

But what proportion is meant in a reciprocal exchange? In summary, one can establish (more extensively in [25]) that Aristotle, to start with, symbolically applies the arithmetic mean (which also means 'proportion' in Greek) to the compensatory justice that a judge carries out when he searches for a compromise in matters of civil law; then applies the usual proportionality, as is indicated in the example of friends above, to the dispensing justice, by which resources are assigned to everyone according to rank, so that the superior one receives more. It holds then that A : B = a : b. One can therefore also say after the allocation that A : B = (A + a) : (B + b) = a : b; that persons, when combined with their allocations, are in the same proportion as they were previously and the items likewise (the intercept theorems). We deal here with symbolic comparisons as they appeared frequently not only in philosophy, but also in Greek literature (Aristotle provides in his *Poetics* examples of the model: old age is related to life as the evening to the day; Poet. 1457 b). In the mathematical-physical sense, the proportions do not hold, for people and the goods allocated to them are not commensurable. In the exchange of goods, however, there exists not only a commensurability of the goods, but they are also, as we know, the same even as values, which cannot be claimed by the bartering people. In order to explain the exchange in Aristotle, it was therefore suggested, to draw on a proportion of proportions used by Euclid [28] in the case of reciprocity present in the exchange of goods. The relationship of the persons to their allocated items in a case of reciprocity is the same before and after the exchange, thus: (A : a) : (B : b) = (A : b) : (B : a). In this case, this proportion of proportions is only fulfilled for any arbitrary A and B when a = b; the reciprocity became the exchange of equivalences. This interpretation would therefore be all the more elegant, because Aristotle only speaks of reciprocity when, 'in the first place', the exchanged objects are 'equal' (Eth. Nic. 1133 a 10). It is, however, questionable whether something other than a normal proportion may be assumed to underlie the Aristotelian text.

There are unequal people like the above-mentioned builder and shoemaker who through trade "become equally positioned" (Eth. Nic. 1133 a 19). But how can one speak of the preceding equality of the things? Aristotle confronts the problem explicitly when he says that everything must be measured through a definite entity (ἑνί τινι πάντα μετρεῖσθαι, Eth. Nic. 1133 a 26). This entity is for him "in truth the need" (χρεία, 1133 a 28). Thus, reciprocity, which we first connected with

gifts and gifts in return, suddenly has become the economic exchange of goods, and Aristotle continues correctly when he speaks of money as a measure that arose out of convention and agreement with a hint at a nominalistic understanding of money as it could be applied to fractional money.

There have been attempts to interpret the suggested equivalence of Aristotle in terms of the theory of the value of labor, because the people are included in the proportions; however, there is no mention of work in the wider context of the discussed situation; for others, the 'need' points to utility theory, though the term utility, which Aristotle extensively discusses in other places for different purposes, is completely missing in this particular context. It would fit best into his concept to imagine here an exchange of household surpluses, which are set up precisely as being equivalent because of the need, when the latter really exists mutually. It is certain is that Aristotle does not bring up this topic with the goal of building an economic theory, in the sense of a causal explanation of the relationships in an exchange; rather, the discussion is explicitly about special examples of his theory of justice, i.e. the search for an ethical rule for exchange. His goal is to illustrate the principle of reciprocity with the exchange of equivalent objects, which is to him self explanatory; and not to explain equivalent exchange with the idea of reciprocity. Exchange based on reciprocity conforms to his image of the polis.

E. CHREMATISTICS

Admittedly, Aristotle also describes the unnatural art of acquisition, 'chrematistics' – an acquisition that transgresses the boundaries of the natural, which became possible through the invention of money. Originally precious metals were used only by weight as means of exchange; then they were stamped and became money; in this point, his theory of money sounds dependent on metal and is suitable for foreign trade with coins made from precious metals (Pol. 1257 a 40). It is here that the misunderstanding arose that money is to be considered wealth. This type of wealth does not have a boundary in itself. Hence those concerned with chrematistic acquisition are tempted to increase their holdings of money without limit (Pol. 1257 b 35). Chrematistics, which is different from the natural art of acquisition, including exchange, is not necessary as long as it enables the natural intercourse between households. Aristotle systematically presents the forms of unnatural acquisition. Mining stands on the border between natural and unnatural acquisition; specifically unnatural are retail trade, wholesale trade, usury and wage labor. Although these are all in principle unnecessary, he does not speak of their abolition – rather, the state absolutely requires the acquisition of money (Pol. 1259 a 35). The practical studies on this, for which he recommends works–no longer extant, nevertheless did not enjoy a good reputation. And in fact with this negative judgment and with philosophical reasoning, he repeats the old established aristocratic values that were adopted by the citizens of the democracy; they are widespread preconceptions in agrarian societies (thus he says that usury is "most commendably hated", Pol. 1258 b 4).

The philosophers expressed valuations, which only the fewest could consistently follow. Roman philosophy was perhaps not as original as Greek, but it did on occasion give morality a practical perspective that allows insight into compromises compelled by reality. For example, Cicero speaks in *De officiis* of possible conflicts between honor and benefit. He mentions a good merchant who brings grain from Alexandria to Rhodes and who knows that hunger is widespread there as a result of a bad harvest, and knows also that more merchant vessels with cargoes of grain are following him from Alexandria. Should he explain to the Rhodians that their shortage will soon change to an excess supply, or should he quickly sell his own cargo for high prices (Off. 3,12,50)? Cicero has two Stoics discuss the case. The first holds that, speaking modernly, it would result in the abolition of private property if the merchant were not allowed to sell by exploiting his informational advantage; the other maintains that such behavior is a renunciation of human society. Eventually Cicero decides that hiding such knowledge is certainly not the quality of an open, simple and just man, but rather that of a devious and crooked knave, and he adds a common phrase: 'haec tot et alia plura nonne inutile est vitiorum subire nomina?' ("Is it not inexpedient to subject oneself to all these terms of reproach and many more besides?", Off. 3,13,57, trans: Walter Miller, 1961 ['1913 = Loeb Library]). That which is good and usefulness are in harmony because honest dealing with asymmetric information is supported by reputation.

F. Conceptions of Order and Associated Virtues

The democratic phase is just one step in the succession of state structures discussed in Greek philosophy; their change contributed to the relativizing of values. A basic understanding of life rooted in the tragic and also religious timidity stood in opposition to the progressive thinking that could have otherwise resulted from the development of technology, economic integration and the conquest of new regions. The rival city-states showed through their orators strong individual identities, and the historians indulged themselves with the depictions of the conflicts between the states in elaborate polar comparisons of their life styles, which one can also read as comparisons of economic styles (for example, Herodotus in the comparison of oriental despotism of Persia and Greek democracy, and Thucydides in the comparison of Athens and Sparta). From the change in governmental structure, the question arose which ethical principles possess transhistorical validity and which ones should be considered conditional. Plato leans toward economic equality and political privileges for the intellectual elite, Aristotle toward political equa-

lity and greater tolerance for polarities of wealth. Aristotelian ethics turns from the Platonic designation of the good to that of the good life or happiness (εὐδαιμονία, Eth. Nic. 1095 a 21). It is in the nature of man to strive toward insight and to protect the necessary means of reaching that goal. The useful is not considered by Aristotle to be a goal in itself; it is not a good that is good in and of itself, but rather one that serves another good. That which is useful is thus determined by higher principles; it is however not as easy to find in humans as it is in an animal, for instance, whose nature requires quite specific nourishment. Hedonism, which Plato criticizes in *Protagoras* and in *Philebus*, is dealt with by Aristotle in the tenth book of the *Nicomachean Ethics*. Indeed, a well managed life is also satisfying; satisfaction is nevertheless not the cause or the hallmark of the correct orientation of life (Eth. Nic. 1099 a 8). The good man becomes the criterion (1176 a 18). He comes into his own by actualizing the greatest human potential. For him, pleasure is not a goal, but rather a means: a sort of repose in order to gain strength for greater efforts (Eth. Nic. 1176 b 34).

The good man distinguishes himself by his virtues. In ethics, the economic dimension also appears, relating to the way of life suitable to the city-state. Indeed, in Aristotle's sense, a preferred order for material goods can be imagined, one that is structured by the good – if one wants, this order can be seen as a finite maximization of utility with the best furnishing of the household, neither too poor nor too rich (Kraus saw in Aristotle a precursor of the theory of utility [16]; for a suggestion of the paradox of values in Aristotle cf. [26. 74]), but it is more interesting with regard to the economical and ethical questions to relate concrete virtues to concrete institutions.

In the real Athenian democracy, the hierarchy that resulted from status, wealth or earnings stood opposite the demand for the formal equality of the citizens (for which they strove by the lottery for official offices instead of an election of the best, and also by ostracism – cf. Aristot. pol. 1284 a 18). The polis made demands upon its citizens for services (liturgy system) to the state usually according to their wealth. Such services were originally voluntary and provided the contributor nothing other than prestige. Later they took on a coercive nature. Visible wealth was differentiated from unseen wealth. Visible wealth, e.g. a manor, became cause for the other citizens to call upon the owner to make a contribution. From that, there arose the incentive to invest wealth in 'unseen' forms, e.g. to lend it out in order to avoid the obligation – this was also a reason for the philosophers' firmly grounded mistrust of the business of lending (for this and for the swap of property as a sanction, c.f. the conflicting analyses in [7; 20]). The liturgies were supported by corresponding concepts of virtue.

Virtue is a mean between extremes. Theophrastus (*Characters*) hints at it through caricatures of the extremes; he depicts for example how a stingy rich man in the people's assembly stands up and quietly leaves when he feels that the debate could soon bring up the necessity of additional contributions (ἐπίδοσις, Char. 22). In this way, the Attic → COMEDY also brought misers and prodigals to the stage. An index of the virtues is to be found in the *Eudemean Ethics* of Aristotle (1220 b 40), where e.g. the just is ordered as the middle between profit and loss, courage between haste and cowardice, munificence between prodigality and miserliness, magnanimity between vanity and narrow-mindedness. Because the munificent person gladly gives, he is easily deceived, and it is difficult for him to preserve his wealth (Eth. Nic. 1120 b 16, 1121 a 6). An escalation of munificence is generosity, the high sense or the love of splendour (μεγαλοπρέπεια). He who has this virtue at his disposal is an artist in spending great sums of money in good taste, willing to contribute for public purposes – Aristotle mentions worship and public buildings (Eth. Nic. 1122 b 20) – this person knows to give the right gifts and to practice hospitality, and he is certain to have honour. Finally, the great soul demands much and is worthy of much. He who possesses this virtue must be a good man; it becomes apparent insofar as there is greatness in virtue at all (Eth. Nic. 1123 b 30). Aristotle supposes that the virtues of munificence and the display of splendour are to be found mostly in the generation of children and grandchildren of the businessman who has earned a fortune. He is thus familiar with generational theory; but where the early modern period sees virtue on the side of the founders' generation where parsimony is practiced, Aristotle sees the virtue in the descendents, for their generosity facilitates urban co-existence.

In the economic thinking of Stoicism, the pursuit of a correctly understood self-interest supports the whole, because the world is to be found so ordered; also in the combat against evil can man grow. "He (Zeus) has made the nature of the rational animal such that it cannot obtain any one of its own proper interests, if it does not contribute something to the common interest" (Epictetus, Discourses 1, 19; trans: George Long, London 1888) In particular, the scope of economic activity under private law was more securely connected and justified with natural rights by the Romans.

→ Agora; → Banks; → Columella; → Epicurus; → Hesiodus; → CYNICISM; → Philodemus; → Phocylides; → Polis; → Solon [1] S. von Athen; → Theophrastus; → Economy; → Economical Ethics; → Xenophon [2] X. from Athens

1 M. AUSTIN, P. VIDAL-NAQUET, Économies et sociétés en Grèce ancienne, 1972 2 CH. BALOGLOU, Η οικονομική σκέψη των αρχαίων Ελλήνων, 1995 3 Id., H. PEUKERT, Zum antiken ökonomischen Denken der Griechen. Eine kommentierte Bibliographie, 1992 4 W. BRAEUER, Urahnen der Ökonomie, 1981 5 K. BÜCHER, Die Aufstände der unfreien Arbeiter 143–129 v. Chr., Frankfurt 1874 6 A. BÜRGIN, Zur Soziogenese der polititschen Ökonomie. Wirtschaftsgeschichtliche und dogmenhistorische Betrachtungen, 1993 7 E. E. COHEN, Athenian Economy and Society. A Banking Perspective, 1992 8 A.

DEMANDT, Antike Staatsformen, 1995 9 J. H. EDMONDS (ed.), Greek Elegy and Iambus, vol. I, 1982 (1931) 10 E. EGNER, Der Verlust der alten Ökonomik, 1985 11 M. I. FINLEY, The Ancient Economy, ²1975 12 Id. (ed.), The Bücher-Meyer Controversy, 1979 13 J. A. HARTUNG, Philodems Abhandlungen Über die Haushaltung und Über den Hochmuth, und Theophrast's Haushaltung und Charakterbilder, Griechisch und Deutsch, Leipzig 1857 14 H. KLOFT, Die Wirtschaft der griechisch-römischen Welt, 1992 15 J. X. KRAUS, Die Stoa und ihr Einfluß auf die Nationalökonomie, 2000 16 O. KRAUS, Die aristotelische Werttheorie in ihren Beziehungen zu den Lehren der modernen Psychologenschulen, in: Zschr. für die gesamte Staatswiss. 61, 1905, 573–592 17 S. TODD LOWRY, Archaeology of Economic Ideas, 1987 18 B. MALINOWSKI, Argonauts of the Western Pacific, 1972 (1922) 19 M. MAUSS, Sociologie et anthropologie, 1983 (1950) 20 P. MILLETT, Lending and Borrowing in Ancient Athens, ²1994 21 W. NIPPEL, Griechen, Barbaren und 'Wilde', 1990 22 K. POLANYI, The Livelihood of Man, 1977 23 M. ROSTOVTZEFF, The Social and Economic History of the Hellenistic World, 1972 (1941) 24 E. SALIN, Politische Ökonomie. Geschichte der wirtschaftspolitischen Ideen von Platon bis zur Gegenwart, 1967 25 B. SCHEFOLD, Platon und Aristoteles, in: J. STARBATTY (ed.), Klassiker des ökonomischen Denkens, 1989, 15–55 26 Id., Spiegelungen des antiken Wirtschaftsdenkens in der griechischen Dichtung, in: Id. (ed.), Studien zur Entwicklung der ökonomischen Theorie XI. Schriften des Vereins für Socialpolitik, Neue Folge 115/XI, 1989, 13–89 27 Id., Xenophons Oikonomikos: der Anfang welcher Wirtschaftslehre?, in: Id. et al. (eds.), Vademecum zu einem Klassiker der Haushaltsökonomie. Kommentarband zum Ndr. von 1734 in der Reihe Klassiker der Nationalökonomie, 1998, 5–43 28 J. SOUDEK, Aristotle's Theory of Exchange, in: Proceedings of the American Philosophical Society 96, 1952, 45–75 29 G. VIVENZA, Benevolenza pubblica, benevolenza privata e benevolenza reciproca: la virtù del dono e dello scambio dall' antichità al settecento, in: Studi Storici Luigi Simeoni 46, 1996, 15–37 30 F. WAGNER, Das Bild der frühen Ökonomik, 1969 31 M. WEBER, Wirtschaft und Gesellschaft, ⁵1976.

ADDITIONAL BIBLIOGRAPHY M. S. PEACOCK, The Origins of Money in Ancient Greece: The Political Economy of Coinage and Exchange in: Cambridge Journal of Economics 30, 2006, 637–650 BERTRAM SCHEFOLD

II. EARLY MODERN PERIOD
A. GENERAL B. HOUSEHOLD ECONOMY IN THE MIDDLE AGES AND THE EARLY MODERN PERIOD C. ADAM SMITH AND THE DEVELOPMENT OF ECONOMICS D. OUTLOOK: ARISTOTELIANISM IN GERMAN NATIONAL ECONOMY OF THE 19TH CENTURY

A. GENERAL

As economics did not exist in Antiquity as an independent science, being instead a part of philosophy and in particular was treated within the scope of ethical questions, it was taught in the Middle Ages as a branch of → PRACTICAL PHILOSOPHY, to which also belonged ethics and politics, following the Aristotelian division of sciences. Only with the emergence of the political economy in the 18th cent. did economics develop as an independent discipline by freeing itself from ethical and philosophical questions and focusing on questions of the market, allocations and acquisition. Crucial in this development was also the fact that the Aristotelian condemnation of the chrematistics had some validity until the beginning of the modern period. Only then were the accumulation of money and the gathering of wealth, even on the 'national' level, seen as something positive in themselves. Until this time of the revaluation of basic principles, the Old European economy was characterized by the art of the management of household economy [4; 10. 50]).

B. Household Economy in the Middle Ages and the Early Modern Period

Household economy is the science that views the household itself as a 'business unit'; it presents therefore a type of 'microeconomic' theory for a subsistence economy. However, the significance of the household for the market economy, characterized by the division of labor – now seen as going beyond the households' purported function as a self-supporting entity – has been more clearly discovered and expanded upon in research in the last decades [1; 11; 12]. There is a correspondence between its significance and the relevance of the theory applied to it; for an appropriate appraisal the term 'household economy' is preferable to the synonymous designation *Hausväterliteratur* which evokes a too narrow perception of this discipline [12. 11 f.]. Household economy was an important area for the influence of ancient teachings about the economy of the óikos ('house') to which most notably Xenophon's *Oikonomikós*, the Aristotelian concepts of the óikos, the pseudo-Aristotelian *Oikonomiken* and the Hellenistic pseudo-Pythagorian *Oikonomiken* belonged. They were transmitted to the Middle Ages through the Latin agricultural writers like Cato the Elder (234–149 BC), Varro (118–27 BC), Columella (1st cent. AD), through medieval encyclopedias like that of Isidore of Seville (ca. 550–636) as well as through medieval translations into Latin [9. 546f.], and arguably also through the Islamic *Oikonomiken* [12. 30 f] preserved in the Middle Ages. The texts of household economy adopted the division of the house, inherited from Antiquity, into personal relations on one side and property of the master of the house on the other, and address – with Christian orientations and in each case with different main focuses – all aspects of economically and ethically perfect household management. The late medieval text *Yconomica* of Konrad von Megenberg (1309–1374) is one of the first of these texts that arose in and around the university of Paris; in this text, he amply uses, in addition to many other ancient and early medieval authors [1. XXXIIff.], also the 'outstanding' (I, 1. Traktat, 1. Kap.: 1,23 f.) philosopher Aristotle, whose *Politics* had been available since the the middle of the 13th cent. in Latin translation and commentary by Albertus

Magnus and Thomas Aquinas. Konrad's view of the personal relations and forms of household management are obviously influenced above all by the Aristotelian and pseudo-Aristotelian treatments of the óikos, in that, however, he integrates contemporary practices (feudal relations, paid servants). He expands the Aristotelian concept of óikos, insofar as he distinguishes between the house of the simple man and the noble and religious house [5. 17 ff.]. Going beyond Aristotle, he mentions the exchange of service or work for goods or money, as well as the exchange of material things for spiritual (I, Treatise 4, ch. 14 : 1,338). Compared with Aristotle's negative valuation of chrematistics, Konrad values commerce more positively [12. 57].

From the 16th–18th cents., the works of modern German household economy were produced, which on the one hand remained in the tradition of the Old European economy, and on the other revealed new thoughts of the → Enlightenment and new social theories [12. 161 ff.]. Among these are the benchmarks *Oeconomia oder Hausbuch* by M. Johann Coler (1566–1639), *Georgica Curiosa* (1682) by Wolff Helmhard von Hohberg and *Oeconomus prudens et legalis* by Franz Philipp Florin (1699).

C. Adam Smith and the Development of Economics

Adam Smith (1723–1790), recognized as the founder of economics, developed his economic theory in the intellectual environment of the Scottish Enlightenment. Preceding this, in rejection of Aristotelian concepts, was the mercantilist appreciation of chrematistics so that now the greatest possible national affluence could be considered the highest goal [7. 163 ff.]. Researchers began to discover systematically only in the last two decades the ancient roots of Smith's economic theory. These are to be found in philosophy, corresponding to the status of economics as a part of moral philosophy. Here the Stoic moral philosophy plays a special role [8. 174ff.; 14. 158 ff.]. This is due to the general significance of Stoic philosophy in the Early Modern period [7. 245 ff.]. Smith was, for instance, influenced by Hugo Grotius (1583–1645), who based his theory of a universal legal system underlying all rights on the Stoic concept of reason common to all men, and who saw → Natural law as the basis of → International law, and on the basis of that proposed freedom of commerce and trade [8. 138f.]. Smith, who owed to his Glasgow teacher Francis Hutchinson a comprehensive Classical education [13. 102 f.], fostered an individual interest in the philosophy of the Stoics, whose views he quoted at length (for example in *The Theory of Moral Sentiments*, Part VII). His version of a harmonic universe, controlled by natural laws, – together with the Newtonian concept of scientific law – formed the basis of his view of the functioning of the free market economy which he develops in *An Inquiry into the Nature and Causes of the Wealth of Nations* (1776) [13. 166]; as a result, basic factors to natural laws are to be found in the market economy. Smith [3. VII. ii.1.15, VI. ii.1.1, II. ii.2.1] especially adopted as the basis of his economic theory the Stoic view of human self-love, *Oikeiosis* theory [7. 272 ff.; 8. 174 ff.; 15. 61 ff.], and arguably also the view that human actions motivated by self-interest serve the common good [8. 175; 15. 61 ff.]. This is compressed in the famous phrase [2. i.ii.2]: 'It is not from the benevolence of the butcher, the brewer, or the baker, that we expect our dinner, but from their regard to their own interest'. This view also forms the basis of Smith's theory of the 'invisible hand' that says that man, by following his own interests, also (unintentionally) furthers the common good [2. IV. ii.9; 3. IV. i.10]. This view forms the intellectual foundation of his concept of the "free market economy".

In the field of the theory of value, it is one of the controversial questions in modern research whether Smith's theory of labor value can be traced back to Aristotle [6. 109 ff.; 15. 146 ff.]; it seems rather unlikely that Aristotle was already thinking of labor value [15. 147].

D. Outlook: Aristotelianism in German National Economy of the 19th Century

A return to Aristotle is to be found in one branch of German economics of the 19th cent. Its goal was to redesign economics from a theory of production, market and exchange to a discipline that made people the focus and thus to put them in the service of higher moral goals [10]. In critical debate with the 'individualistic' theory of market economics of Smithian origin and in a return to Aristotle's criticism of chrematistics, 'virtue' was stipulated as a national ethos in order to enable a constant state welfare [10. 47 ff.].

→ Aristotele [6] Aristotle, son of Nicomachus, of Stagira; → Cato [1] Porcius C., M.; → Chrematistics; → Cicero; → Columella; → Isidorus [9] Isidorus]; → Oikeiosis; → Oikos economy; → Stoicism; → Varro [2] V. Terentius, M. (Reatinus); → Economy; → Economical Ethics; → Xenophon [2] X of Athens

SOURCES 1 K. v. MEGENBERG, Werke: Ökonomik (vol. I), S. KRÜGER (ed.), 1973 2 A. SMITH, An Inquiry into the Nature and Causes of the Wealth of Nations, R. H. CAMPBELL, A. S. SKINNER, W. B. TODD (eds.), 1976 3 Id., The Theory of Moral Sentiments, D. D. RAPHAEL, A. L. MACFIE (eds.), 1976

LITERATURE 4 O. BRUNNER, Das 'ganze Haus' und die alteuropäische 'Ökonomik', in: Id., Neue Wege der Verfassungs- und Sozialgeschichte, 1956, 33–61 5 G. DROSSBACH, Die *Yconomica* des Konrad von Megenberg, 1997 6 O. ISSING, Aristoteles – (auch) ein Nationalökonom?, in: B. SCHEFOLD (ed.), Aristoteles. Der Klassiker des antiken Wirtschaftsdenkens, 1992, 95–125 7 T. KOPP, Die Entdeckung der Nationalökonomie in der schottischen Aufklärung – Natur- und sozialphilosophische Grundlagen der klassischen Wirtschaftslehre, Diss. St. Gallen 1995 8 J. X. KRAUS, Die Stoa und ihr Einfluß auf die Nationalökonomie, Diss. St. Gallen 2000 9 S. KRÜGER, Zum Verständnis der *Oeconomica* Konrads von Megenberg. Griechische Ursprünge der spätmittelalterlichen Lehre vom Haus, in: Dt. Archiv für Erforsch. des MA 20, 1964, 475–561 10 B. P. PRIDDAT, Der ethische Ton

der Allokation, 1991 11 I. RICHARZ, Herrschaftliche Haushalte in vorindustrieller Zeit im Weserraum, 1971 12 Id., Oikos, Haus und Haushalt. Ursprung und Geschichte der Haushaltsökonomik, 1991 13 I. S. ROSS, The Life of Adam Smith, 1998 14 A. RÜSTOW, Das Versagen des Wirtschaftsliberalismus, ³2001 15 G. VIVENZA, Adam Smith and the Classics: The Classical Heritage in Adams Smith's Thought, 2001 (It. Original: Adam Smith e la cultura classica, 1984).

SABINE FÖLLINGER

Education/Culture
A. TERM   B. HISTORY

A. TERM
With respect to the influence and reception of ancient education/culture (E/C) on the post-Classical history of E/C in the sense of a very general framework concept, E/C is regarded as meaning any kind of intellectual formative process (and its results), whether or not this is initiated or caused by the individual himself or by his fellow human beings, by the divine or by people and whether or not it is co-determined by external (e.g. social) circumstances or historical tradition. Terms and concepts with regard to E/C, ideals of E/C and ideas of humanity from which they emanate as well as E/C content and → CURRICULA (syllabi) are central to the discussion.

B. HISTORY
1. THE MIDDLE AGES

1. THE MIDDLE AGES
Ancient E/C was transmitted to the Middle Ages by a number of late Classical Christian authors who all adapted the philosophical and rhetorical traditions of ancient E/C in a reduced form, tailor-made to fit the needs of the Christian faith and Christian theology, e.g. Jerome, Boethius, Cassiodorus, Isidore of Seville, Benedict of Nursia, Gregory the Great and Bede [1. 315–342]. Augustine is regarded as exceptionally important in the transmission of Classical E/C to the Latin West (especially De magistro, De catechizandis rudibus, De doctrina christiana II [1. 293–303], cf. [2]).

1.1. THE CAROLINGIAN REFORM OF EDUCATION/CULTURE

1.1 THE CAROLINGIAN REFORM OF EDUCATION/CULTURE
Charlemagne gathered together at his court a number of significant scholars, like the Anglo-Saxon Alcuin (ca. 730–804), adviser to the emperor and principal director of education. Their role was to reform E/C and knowledge on behalf of the emperor and, according to a formulation of Heiric of Auxerre, to supplement the *Translatio imperii* completed by Charlemagne with a *Translatio studii* – a transplanting of ancient E/C to the new empire (→ CAROLINGIAN RENAISSANCE). Alcuin's student Hrabanus Maurus (d. 856), Abbot of Fulda and Archbishop of Mainz, had an important

function as an author and propagandist for the new educational/cultural movement, and this role extended to his position as *Praeceptor Germaniae*.

The Classical educational/cultural tradition had a particularly profound effect in the organization of the teaching of the seven liberal arts which – already known as a canon of E/C in Hellenism (*enkyklios paideia*, cf. the beginnings among the Sophists and in Plato) and in the Roman imperial period (Quint. Inst. 1,10,1; cf. Cic. De or. 3,21; Varro) – constituted after the Carolingian educational/cultural reforms the general basis for the study of theology in the Middle Ages. They were first identified with philosophical E/C but then made subordinate to it (→ ARTES LIBERALES). Alcuin and Hrabanus Maurus wrote about the seven liberal arts (*septem artes liberales*) (Alcuin in various textbooks on the individual *artes*; Hrabanus in his *De institutione clericorum* 3). Alcuin, in his depiction of the *trivium* (the three verbal disciplines of grammar, dialectic and rhetoric) took his direction from Donatus, Priscian, Cassiodorus, Isidore and Bede, while Hrabanus, in his discussion of the liberal arts, followed Cassiodorus but also in his concept of E/C adopted much from Augustine. A well-known early medieval philosophical-theological interpretation of the educational/cultural meaning of the seven liberal arts is also to be found in the commentary of Remigius of Auxerre (841–908) on the work of the late Roman (5th cent.) encyclopaedist Martianus Capella, *De nuptiis philologiae et mercurii*, which, couched in allegory and in the spirit of Neo-Platonism, deals with the *septem artes* [1. 343–387; 3. 99–106].

1.2. EDUCATIONAL/CULTURAL THINKERS OF THE HIGH MIDDLE AGES 2.1 RENAISSANCE HUMANISM 2.2. THE REFORMATION 2.3. RATIONALISM AND THE ENLIGHTENMENT 2.4. NEO-HUMANISM 2.5. GERMAN CLASSICISM AND GERMAN IDEALISM 3. 19TH–20TH CENTURIES

1.2 EDUCATIONAL/CULTURAL THINKERS OF THE HIGH MIDDLE AGES

The High Middle Ages produced a series of systems of knowledge and E/C (mostly in the form of encyclopaedias) which – in individual prominent forms of intellectual adaptation – represented in various ways the relationships between the seven liberal arts, philosophy and Christian theology. The recourse to Classical philosophy and its theory of E/C played a significant role in determining the relationship between these three fields. Thus Hugh of St. Victor (1096–1141), for example, designed in his *Didascalicon* a system for all knowledge in the form of an encyclopaedia, classifying all knowledge into four general fields ('theory', 'practice', 'mechanics' and 'logic'). For the first of these categories, Hugh referred explicitly to Boethius, although the philosophical concept of Aristotle shines through clearly, at least in the areas of theory, practice and logic (dialectic). John of Salisbury, (1115–1180) in his work known as

the *Metalogicon*, defended the *trivium* but particularly grammar and dialectic (→ LOGIC) against theological opponents as the basis of higher general E/C and as a propaedeutic for the study of theology, referring here to authorities like Plato and Aristotle, Cicero and Martianus Capella and, for the first time, taking into account all the writings on logic by Aristotle brought together in the *Organon*. Alain de Lille (Alanus ab Insulis, 1128–1203), in his philosophical-theological epic *Anticlaudianus*, in which he referred to the late Roman writer Claudius Claudianus (around AD 400), summed up the seven *artes*, discussing in the Neo-Platonic spirit of the School of Chartres topics ranging from the arts and science to natural philosophy, and even ranging higher to ethereal philosophy, i.e. theology as the crowning glory of all knowledge. The all-embracing reception of the philosophy of Aristotle in the 13th cent. by Albert the Great and Thomas Aquinas led in reflections on E/C to a strict separation of the *artes* from philosophy and of the latter (together with its natural theology) from the theology of revelation. According to Thomas Aquinas (Expositio in Boethii de trinitate qu. 5, Art. 1, ad 3), the *artes liberales*, although still superior to the *artes mechanicae*, are only a preliminary step – closer to experience – to philosophy as pure knowledge and do not come into question as a principle for classifying theoretical philosophy. For educational/cultural theory, Thomas was also important in that – taking issue with Augustine's *De magistro* and its doctrine of God as the sole teacher – he also accorded to man a co-role in the imparting of truth through teaching (Quaestiones disputatae de veritate qu. 11, art. 1) [1. 388–432; 4. bk. 1].

2. The Modern Period: 14th–18th Centuries

2.1 RENAISSANCE HUMANISM

The E/C ideal and E/C concepts of Renaissance Humanism proved to be the basis for the encounter between the modern image of man developing from these origins and the E/C world of Antiquity. The nexus was to be highly influential. The new man is interested in himself as an individual personality and gradually emerges from the political and Church-religious ties of the Middle Ages. "He is imbued with the unique dignity of the human being, who as a kind of second Prometheus repeats God's act of creation and is called through education to reshape himself repeatedly" (Boccaccio). "As man is no mere likeness of a divine archetype, he has a duty to reproduce the whole world and all the creatures in himself" (Pico della Mirandola). From this initial position the relationship between Renaissance Humanism and Antiquity was also moulded. In Antiquity, especially in ancient art and science, the true humanity of man shaping himself in freedom was realized in an exemplary manner. For the Middle Ages, the ancient world of E/C was an instrument of faith and, in questions of secular knowledge, authority. For the → HUMANISM of the → RENAISSANCE it is a matter of discovering, from individual experience and self-education, Antiquity as a model of a humanity liberated from the preconditions of theology and the Church.

The ancient authors ought not to be transmitted merely in a fragmentary, second-hand manner in compendia, but their original texts were to be studied in a philological-critical sense and in the historical context.

Antiquity was a model for Humanism, especially from the point of view of its culture of language, writing and rhetoric, which is where the humanity of Antiquity was expressed with particular clarity. These premises also determined the priorities set by the Humanists with regard to the educational content and syllabus of higher general education. Of the seven liberal arts, Renaissance Humanism, emphasized – because of its predilection for education in language and literature – the *trivium*, foregrounding → GRAMMAR including the art of interpretation of texts and → RHETORIC, as opposed to more abstract dialectics (which was often linked with what was dismissed as scholastic quibbling). In Renaissance Humanism, however, it was not only a matter of the philological-historical appropriation of Classical civilisation, but also of the creative revival of ancient artistic forms of linguistic expression. Characteristic of this were the blossoming of a new rhetoric, the writing of Latin treatises and letters as well as a new high regard for all forms of poetry, which the likes of Thomas Aquinas (following Augustine and others) had still been able to designate as the lowest of the arts. In this way Petrarch positioned grammar and rhetoric as well as creative writing in the centre of Humanist endeavours in E/C. And, according to Pope Nicholas V, grammar, rhetoric, history and poetry were also essential for moral character-building. Polished Humanist syllabi are extant, e.g. from Battista Guarino the Younger (De modo et ordine docendi ac discendi, 1459) and Aeneas Sylvius Piccolomini (De liberorum educatione, 1450). In the writings of Erasmus, the sequence of Humanistic subjects for study was formulated particularly clearly (cf. e.g. De ratione studii, 1511). For Erasmus a basic education in grammar and rhetoric prepared the way for a philosophical education. This in its turn formed the transition to an education in theology which, even for a Christian Humanist, was the crowning glory of the entire course of E/C. Philosophical and theological E/C were inconceivable, for the Humanist concept of E/C, without fundamental linguistic training; the budding philosopher and theologian was obligated by Humanism to take his direction from the standard source texts [1. 507–631; 3. 176–193; 4. bk. 2].

2.2 THE REFORMATION

The renewal of the Christian faith and of the Christian Church by Martin Luther (1483–1546) would not have been possible without the Humanist E/C movement with its rediscovery of Antiquity and its tendency, through the appropriation of the ancient languages of Latin, Greek and Hebrew, to gain direct, unadulterated and critical access to the source texts of Classical civilisation. Luther himself regarded the study of ancient languages as useful and important for access to the Holy Scriptures and even fended off attacks on Humanist E/C (e.g. in his open letter to the mayors and councilors of

German cities regarding the need to build Christian schools, Wittenberg 1524). However, it was not until Philipp Melanchthon (1497–1560), the great-nephew of the Humanist and Hebrew scholar Reuchlin and Professor of Greek Language in Wittenberg from 1518 as well as a close colleague of Luther from 1519, that a comprehensive synthesis of the thought of the Reformation and the new achievements of Humanist E/C was realized. Already in his inaugural lecture at Wittenberg he outlined enthusiastically the path for the revival of studies and rediscovery of the ancient authors in Humanism, and he also expressed his regret at the contrasting darkness of the Middle Ages and → SCHOLASTICISM, a period when Humanistic studies were in a wretched state (De corrigendis adulescentiae studiis, 1518). In the spirit of Humanism and on the basis of a Christian Platonic image of man, Melanchthon also designed his Humanist-Reformation syllabus. It encompassed the study of the ancient languages, with the *trivium* of grammar, rhetoric and dialectic, but also included mathematics, history and philosophy [4 vol. 3. 7–20; 5. 15–101].

2.3 RATIONALISM AND THE ENLIGHTENMENT

The spirit of the Modern Age, which developed through the thoughts and doubts of individuals, gradually broke free of the fetters of admiration for Antiquity and its authority, and scholars came to believe that, with the powers of their own thought and particularly through an empirical exploration of the external world, they could create a new system of knowledge and E/C independent of Antiquity. The rationalism of the 17th cent. and the philosophy of the → ENLIGHTENMENT of the 18th cent. also created a distance between their philosophy of E/C and the fundamental Humanist attitude to E/C. The new view of E/C was no longer primarily interested in language and words but in things and in coming to terms with them intellectually and making practical use of them through reason. Nonetheless, in this era too, the influence of Antiquity on various aspects of intellectual life is also demonstrable. This is already clear in Montaigne (1533–1592), who, in spite of the realist orientation of his thought on E/C, was an admirer of and expert on ancient philosophy (Socrates, Plato, Cicero, Seneca and Plutarch) and implemented its ideas in education as an art of living (cf. Essais 1,25 and 1,26). It is equally obvious in Descartes (1596–1650) who, despite his rejection of scholastic thinking (e.g. the methods that went back to Aristotle), was nevertheless inspired by the spirit of Augustine and by a scholasticism influenced by Antiquity (Anselm) (cf. Discours de la méthode 1 and Meditationes 2,3 and 5). It is also apparent in the Baroque rationalism of the didact Ratke, and especially in that of the pedagogue Comenius, for whom secondary school as preparation for university should still be a → LATIN SCHOOL. He recommended not just modern disciplines but also the liberal arts (Didactica magna 20–21) and, despite moralising warnings against heathen authors (ibid. 25), he also always wrote in Latin, with his *pansophia* influenced by Neo-Platonism (cf. Prodromus pansophiae). The father of English Enlightenment philosophy, Locke (1632–1704), certainly also positioned Humanistic E/C in the background but still retained Latin (in contrast to Greek) for the E/C of a gentleman (cf. Some Thoughts Concerning Education, 162ff., 168ff.). Even Rousseau (1712–1778), who gave French Enlightenment philosophy its finishing touches, allowed his model pupil Emile, in other respects thoroughly raised according to naturalistic and realistic principles, to continue pursuing Classical studies (cf. Emile 4). The founder of German Enlightenment philosophy, Christian Thomasius (1655–1728), viewed Socrates as the origin of the European Enlightenment and was drawn to Humanism, while Trapp, for example, in Campe's work of revision, discussed the value of Humanistic E/C very critically (Part 7, Vienna/Braunschweig 1787, p. 309ff.) [4 Vol. 3. 21–55; 5. 115–375].

2.4 NEO-HUMANISM

The high point in German intellectual life (1770–1830) in writing and philosophy occurred simultaneously with the flourishing of a new humanism that was now first and foremost orientated towards Greek art, the Greek mentality, philosophy and literature (Hellenism); but just like Renaissance Humanism, which primarily took its direction from Latin, it promoted the return to the sources of European culture in Antiquity and focused on the idea of humanization through E/C by means of the mastery of language. The most brilliant exponent of the concept of E/C in → NEO-HUMANISM was the language scholar, educational theoretician and educational policymaker W. v. Humboldt. Humboldt's Neo-Humanism was aided particularly through the increased philological-historical interest in Classical Antiquity that initially found expression in a reform of the → TEACHING OF ANCIENT LANGUAGES and Humanistic studies by philologists and school teachers like J.M. Gesner (1691–1761) and J.A. Ernesti (1707–1781). Classes in ancient literature were to move beyond verbalism and grammatical-rhetorical formalism to an ethically relevant concern with the content of classical literature. This ultimately led to a comprehensive new concept of academic exploration of classical Antiquity by C. G. Heyne (1729–1812) and F. A. Wolf (1759–1824) (cf. his Darstellung der Alter-tumswissenschaft, Berlin 1807). If F. A. Wolf also in fact expected that engrossing the soul in the world of Antiquity would boost all powers of the mind so that a beautiful harmony between the inner and outer man would be achieved, J. J. Winckelmann (1717–1768) in his Geschichte der Kunst des Altertums (Dresden 1764) had already conceived of an ideal image of the art of the Greeks which through the idea of "noble simplicity and quiet greatness" lent great impetus to the general enthusiasm for Antiquity (cf. also his Gedanken über die Nachahmung der griechischen Werke, Dresden 1755).

Neo-Humanism in W. v. Humboldt (1767–1835) now demonstrated a new philosophical-anthropological basis for the Humanistic concept of E/C that was oriented towards the intellectual world of Antiquity. Humboldt, influenced by Leibniz's metaphysics, to a certain extent also carries to extremes the modern individualism that had already first suggested itself in the concept of E/C in Renaissance Humanism. The sole true purpose of the universe, according to Humboldt, was the E/C of individuality. However, it was because of this modern point of departure itself that W. v. Humboldt felt called upon to emphasize particularly the ideal and exemplary nature of the intellectual world of Classical Antiquity. The Greek poets, philosophers and historians (like Homer, Pindar, Aeschylus, Sophocles, Aristophanes, Herodotus, Thucydides and Plato) revealed to him a "pure humanity of mankind, realized for its own sake" (On the Character of the Greeks ... = Collected Writings, vol. 7, 609–616). Humboldt's ideal of E/C itself also took its direction, therefore, from the model of ancient culture. He was concerned with the "highest and best proportioned" education to harness all the powers of man "into one whole". Freedom (from political interference by the state) was the indispensable prerequisite for this education that should be a purely humane education, beyond all vocational utility and beyond all differences in rank and class (Ideas for an Attempt to Determine the Limits of State Effectiveness = Collected Writings, vol. 1, 107). In language and art, in which the culture and education of man were realized, Greek culture was highly significant. In the Greek language there was an ideal fusing of the sensual with the spiritual, of the object with the subject, of the world with the soul; and Greek art attested to a superb training in the sense of beauty and taste among the Greeks. This ideal of education and its ancient preconditions also served to determine Humboldt's curricular ideas, which he introduced into his organizational concepts for secondary schooling. His concept of general education comprised a gymnastic, aesthetic and didactic component, the last of which was divided again into mathematical, philosophical and historical aspects. He was concerned with physical, musical and intellectual education. Language mastery, historical consciousness and morality were the educational goals of this general education (cf. the Lithuanian School Plan, Collected Writings 13, 277f.) [5. 490–523; 6. 177–179, 185–189].

2.5 GERMAN CLASSICISM AND GERMAN IDEALISM

Neo-Humanism as an E/C movement was both framed and borne by intellectual forces and currents which developed their concept of E/C by admiring and coming to terms with Classical civilisation in the same way as Neo-Humanism itself had done. This came about in the E/C concepts and E/C theories of German → CLASSICISM, e.g. of J. G. Herder (1744–1803), who called the studia humanitatis with Antiquity (Cicero) beautiful disciplines that developed mankind into mankind in terms of language, reason and sociability (cf. e.g. Herder's Schulreden, 1763–1802, and his Briefe zu (sic!) Beförderung der Humanität, 1793–95); of Goethe

(1749–1832), who in the classical period of his artistic creativity was shaped completely by the Neo-Humanist ideal of an aesthetically transfigured Hellenism (*Iphigenie* 1787, *Torquato Tasso* 1790) and who in his novel of development (*Bildungsroman*) *Wilhelm Meisters Lehrjahre* (1796), subscribed to an educational ideal of the self-education of man through the substance of the world, something which is comparable with the educational concept of Humboldt; as well as of Schiller (1759–1805) who, in his *Briefe über die ästhetische Erziehung des Menschen* (1793/94), inspired by Classical art and poetry, attributed to aesthetics and to art as well as to the 'play drive' effective in these as a synthesis of the 'formal' and the 'sensuous drives' an importance for the education of man into man of such significance as would not have been conceivable since Plato, either in ancient aesthetics or in ancient metaphysics.

The link between the E/C theories of speculative German Idealism in Fichte and Hegel and Classical Antiquity is present insofar as Antiquity itself as a cultural era and Humanistic E/C are held in high esteem, and in that the concepts of E/C themselves were inspired by Platonic/Neo-Platonic intellectual constructs. Thus J. G. Fichte (1762–1814) started with Antiquity as the golden age of the rule of reason through instinct, to which – by way of the superficial rationalism of the Enlightenment – it would be necessary to return again in a conscious science and art of reason (*Grundzüge des gegenwärtigen Zeitalters* 1804/05). Thus one could take one's direction in one's educational ideal of the scholar, completely in the spirit of Platonism/Neo-Platonism, from the ideas as the manifestation of the absolute (cf. e.g. *Fünf Vorlesungen über die Bestimmung des Gelehrten* 1811). Similarly, G. F. W. Hegel (1770–1831) in his *Gymnasialreden* (1809–1815) regarded the culture of the Greeks and Romans as the basis upon which all further development of Europe had occurred, and he saw the nature of true E/C in finding one's true self in the ancient cultural legacy as in another person (cf. Hegel's *Philosophische Propädeutik* 1809/11) [5. 403–528; 6. 167–242].

3. 19TH–20TH CENTURIES

The E/C terms connected with the history of the discipline of pedagogics, which developed around 1800 (e.g. with Schleiermacher, Herbart, Dilthey and in humane sciences pedagogy in the 20th cent.) and associated with Antiquity are treated under the keyword → PEDAGOGY. Conditions for a comprehensive reception of Classical E/C and the intellectual world in the philosophy and pedagogics of the 19th and 20th cents. were not favourable. The major upturn in science and in technology in the 19th and 20th cents., which was also of great importance for economic progress and the positivism at a philosophical level that went hand in hand with it, both gave rise to E/C theories and E/C concepts characterized by a decisive pushing back of Humanistic studies and of the historical-philological appropriation of Classical Antiquity in favour of scientific and mathematical subjects. This often resulted in full-blown polemics against Classical Studies (cf. H. Spencer, *What Knowledge is of Most Worth?* 1861; A. Comte, *Cours de philosophie positive* vol. 1, 1830, 1. Lecture and *Discours sur l'ensemble du positivisme* 1848). In the German linguistic and cultural area the development of the disciplines of natural science and sociology was matched to an almost equally great extent by comprehensive advances in the so-called humanities, particularly history, literature and philology. As a historical discipline, the study of Classical Antiquity also continued to develop up into the 20th cent., and it covered the most varied of sub-fields. So even in the 19th cent., after the discipline had been founded by Melanchthon and reinvigorated with new ideas by Humboldt, nothing stood in the way of a certain dominance of the → HUMANIST GYMNASIUM in Germany.

Because of this particular method of acquisition of ancient culture and education through the study of Antiquity at the Humanist gymnasiums on the basis of the historical-philological exploration of Antiquity, Friedrich Nietzsche (1844–1900), turned away from its *Lebensphilosophie* ('philosophy of life') and its concept of E/C. The Classical philologist presented already in his first major publication, *Die Geburt der Tragödie aus dem Geiste der Musik* (Leipzig ¹1872, ²1874), a comprehensive historical- and cultural-philosophical reflection in which he interpreted the further development of European cultural history essentially on the basis of fundamental events, conflicts and antitheses in the art and philosophy of Antiquity. Nietzsche's lectures *Über die Zukunft unserer Bildungsanstalten* ('On the Future of our Schools', 1872) demonstrate the fundamental concern of his theory of E/C: the teachers at Humanist gymnasiums should not pass on their own specialized knowledge of the subject acquired at university as philologists and historians but should take as their starting-point training in the native language and the study of the German literary classics. From this they should proceed to an encounter with the "general questions of a serious nature" to be found in the great writers and thinkers of Antiquity and, with the aid of the two ancient languages, Greek and Latin, help their students master a properly defined language by means of grammar and lexicography.

Critical comment on contemporary issues and culture, on the one hand, and concerns with regard to a classical philology operating on the basis of a positivist-historicist spirit, on the other, led to the so-called → THIRD HUMANISM of Werner Jaeger (1888–1961) who, by examining the historical origin of the presence of Antiquity in Greek culture, demonstrated the eternally valid models that should help the present orient itself, and in view of which the necessity for a revival of Classical Studies arises (cf. *Die geistige Gegenwart der Antike*, 1929; *Paideia, die Formung des griechischen Menschen* I, 1933; II, 1944; III, 1947; *Humanistische Reden und Vorträge*, 1937).

In the 20th cent. it was only isolated thinkers and theoreticians of E/C (mostly those still concerned with the study of pedagogical theory) who continued in their theory of or reflections upon E/C to refer to Antiquity, to discuss it, or even to be inspired by it. The discussion of E/C in the 20th cent. – if it related to Antiquity – essentially pivoted around the problem of Humanism. This becomes clear in the influential work by Theodor Litt (1880–1962) on *Das Bildungsideal der deutschen Klassik und die moderne Arbeitswelt* (1955) in which the ideal – oriented towards Antiquity and its social conditions – of pure E/C as a value in itself, as developed by Humboldt, is confronted by the world of technology as a product of modernity and its knowledge. This is, however, also shown in Theodor Ballauff (1911–1995) in the extensive, problematizing discussion of the concept and reality of E/C as an attempt by man to achieve self-empowerment and come to terms with the world. Following Martin Heidegger (1889–1976), Ballauff analysed Humanism and its E/C intentions, considering it a result of the existential oblivion of man which started in European thought with the ontotheology of Plato and Aristotle. Ballauff sought to educate man to a new thinking with regard to being which allows things and fellow humans to be themselves (cf. Heidegger's *Platons Lehre von der Wahrheit* and *Humanismusbrief*, 1947, and Ballauff's *Die Idee der Paideia*, 1952 as well as *Systematische Pädagogik*, 1962, ²1966 and *Philosophische Begründungen der Pädagogik*, 1966). Josef Derbolav (1912–1987), who also produced various works on ancient philosophy (cf. his books on Plato 1953, 1954, 1972 as well as on Plato and Aristotle, 1979), adopted as his particular topic the problem of the search for a new humanity (1988), and has further developed – also following Theodor Litt (cf. *Das Selbstverständnis der Erziehungswisssschaft*, 1966) – in his concept of E/C the Hegelian idea developed through the Humanistic encounter with Antiquity of "finding oneself in another". He took up in his praxeological refounding of pedagogics, like Dietrich Benner (born 1941, cf. his *Allgemeine Pädagogik*, 1987), the theory-practice discussion (→ THEORY/PRACTICE) of Plato and Aristotle (cf. Derbolav's *Grundriß einer Gesamtpädagogik*, 1987). Hartmut von Hentig (born 1925) presented in his book *Platonisches Lehren* (1966) – taking as his starting-point the problems with teaching methods in ancient languages and expressing his support for rescuing the Humanist gymnasium – a theory of E/C directed towards the philosophical questions of Plato and using Humanism as a method (so far vol. 1 has appeared) [6. 244–369; 7].

→ Artes liberales; → Education/Culture; → Enkyklios paideia

→ Schools; → university

Sources   1 T. Ballauff with the cooperation of G. Plamböck, Pädagogik. Eine Geschichte der Bildung und Erziehung, vol. 1: Von der Antike bis zum Humanismus, 1969   2 H. Marrou, Histoire de l'education dans l'antiquité, 1948 (G. Lamb (trans.), A History of Education in Antiquity, 1956)   3 J. Dolch, Lehrplan des Abendlandes. Zweieinhalb Jahrtausende seiner Geschichte, 1959   4 E. Garin, Geschichte und Dokumente der abendländischen Pädagogik, vol. 1: Mittelalter, 1964, vol. 2: Humanismus, 1966, vol. 3: Von der Reformation bis John Locke, 1967   5 T. Ballauff, K. Schaller, Pädagogik. Eine Geschichte der Bildung und Erziehung, vol. 2: Vom 16. bis zum 19. Jahrhundert, 1970   6 A. Reble, Geschichte der Pädagogik, 1951, ¹¹1971   7 T. Ballauff, K. Schaller, Pädagogik. Eine Geschichte der Bildung und Erziehung, vol. 3: 19./20. Jahrhundert, 1973
Literature   8 G. Böhme, Bildungsgeschichte des frühen Humanismus, 1984   9 Id., Der historische-systematische Zugang zur Historischen Pädagogik, in: Id., H.-E. Tenorth, ed., Einführung in die Historische Pädagogik, 1990, 47–116   10 F.-P. Hager, Plato Paedagogus. Aufsätze zur Geschichte und Aktualität des pädagogischen Platonismus, 1981   11 Id., Wesen, Freiheit und Bildung des Menschen. Philosophie und Erziehung in Antike, Aufklärung und Gegenwart, 1989   12 Id., Aufklärung, Platonismus und Bildung bei Shaftesbury, 1993   13 E. Lichtenstein, Bildung, in: HWdPh 1, 921–937   14 Id., Zur Entwicklung des Bildungsbegriffs von Meister Eckhardt bis Hegel, Pädagogische Forschung des Comenius-Instituts 34, 1966   15 C. Menze, Humanismus., in: HWdPh 3, 1217–1219   16 Id., Das griechische Altertum und die deutsche Bildung aus der Sicht Wilhelm von Humboldts, in: F.-P. Hager (ed.), Aspects of Antiquity in the History of Education, 1992, 45–60   17 G. Müller, Bildung und Erziehung im Humanismus der italienischen Renaissance, 1969   18 F. Paulsen, Geschichte des gelehrten Unterrichts auf den deutschen Schulen und Universitäten vom Ausgang des Mittelalters bis zur Gegenwart. Mit besonderer Rücksicht auf den klassischen Unterricht, 2 vols., Leipzig 1885, ²1896   19 R. Pfeiffer, History of Classical Scholarship from 1300 to 1850, 1976   20 W. Ritzel, Philosophie und Pädagogik im 20. Jahrhundert, 1980   21 W. Rüegg, Cicero und der Humanismus, 1946   22 H. Weil, Die Entstehung des deutschen Bildungsprinzips, 1930
Additional Bibliogaphy   R. Black, Humanism and Education in Medieval and Renaissance Italy, 2001   E. Garin, Il pensiero pedagogico dello Umanesimo, 1958   A. Grafton, L. Jardine, From Humanism to the Humanities: Education and the Liberal Arts in Fifteenth- and Sixteenth-Century Europe, 1986   C. W. Kallendorf, Humanist Educational Treatises, 2002   F. Waquet, Le latin, ou, L'empire d'un signe: XVIe-XXe siècle, 1998, (Engl. J. Howe (trans.), Latin, or the Empire of a Sign: From the Sixteenth to the Twentieth Centuries, 2001)   C. Winterer, The Culture of Classicism: Ancient Greece and Rome in American Intellectual Life 1780–1910, 2002

FRITZ-PETER HAGER (†)

Egyptology

A. Origins   B. Accessing the Text Material
C. Documentation of Monuments in Egypt
D. Excavations   E. Reasons for the Interest in Ancient Egypt   F. Institutionalization

A. Origins

Egyptology is the academic study of Pharaonic Egypt, i.e. Ancient Egyptology, as it ought to be called more correctly. Its origins date back to 1822, when the Frenchman Jean François Champollion (1790–1832) achieved a breakthrough in the → DECIPHERMENT of the hieroglyphic script. Egyptology owes its origins and further development to the modern desire of subjecting the traditions regarding Ancient Egypt to a critical-rational discussion, with the aim of confirming or contradicting them – depending on the observer's standpoint. The traditions in question are the ancient Classical and the biblical sources. In the ancient Classical tradition Ancient Egypt was seen as a source of wisdom and profundity, but also as a treasure trove of interesting curiosities. In the biblical tradition, the interest in Ancient Egypt mainly focused on its role as the location of salvatory events: in the OT the servitude of the people of Israel and in the NT the flight of the Holy Family to Egypt.

Until the end of the 18th cent. an insufficient amount of independent records was available to verify either of these traditions. The systematic exploration of monuments in Egypt itself only began with the French expedition to Egypt under Bonaparte (1798–1801), which was accompanied by a high-ranking scientific commission. Only this increase in material evidence made the breakthrough in the decipherment of the hieroglyphics possible, and this in turn opened up the richest group of source material – written texts.

B. Accessing the Text Material

The ongoing accessing of the text material has actively been tackled since the middle of the 19th cent.; at that time scholars progressed beyond the reading of shorter → inscriptions and text excerpts and began to interpret longer texts in their entirety (Émanuel de Rougé 1849 and 1851). From the last quarter of the 19th cent. grammars and dictionaries were put on an academically sound basis; they were developed from the original texts themselves, under observation of fundamental methodological principles. This is the achievement of the Berlin School, i.e. of Adolf Erman (1854–1937) and his pupils. Two scholars subsequently were of outstanding importance: the Englishman (Sir) Alan H. Gardiner (1879–1963), who worked within the Berlin tradition and whose *Egyptian Grammar* of 1927 is still the best reference grammar of the Egyptian hieroglyphic language, and the Egyptologist Hans Jakob Polotsky (1905–1991) from Jerusalem, who was also influenced by the Berlin School and who provided new and strong impulses to the study of Egyptological linguistics since the 1940s which fundamentally determine the arguments on both sides in the current debate on grammar. As far as the texts themselves are concerned, investigations in museums and other collections have recently unexpectedly opened up a new horizon. Masses of papyrus fragments, which had remained largely unprocessed because of their state of preservation but also because of their textual difficulties, now prove to be immensely fruitful. They include relatively late but fairly reliable copies which provide access to much older libraries and thus to bodies of knowledge such as had been recorded and transmitted in the temples.

C. Documentation of Monuments in Egypt

Whereas older European travel journals only provide somewhat vague information about the monuments, the antiquarian interests of travellers since the 18th cent. resulted in an ever increasing documentary accuracy. The reports by the Englishman Richard Pococke (1704–1765) and the Dane Frederik Ludwig Norden (1708–1742) particularly deserve to be mentioned. Documentary material was crucially increased by the activities of the scientific commission which accompanied Bonaparte to Egypt. However, since it was not yet possible to read hieroglyphics, the reproductions are still quite imprecise. Fortification works in ar-Rashid, located east of Alexandria on the Mediterranean coast, led to the discovery of the Rosetta stone, which was to play a part in the decipherment of the hieroglyphics.

Once hieroglyphics had been deciphered, scientific expeditions to Egypt were undertaken. The decipherer himself, Champollion, undertook a first systematic survey together with the Italian Ippolito Rosellini (1800–1843) as part of a French-Tuscan expedition in 1828–1829. The most important expedition was the Prussian one to Egypt and the northern Sudan from 1842 to 1845, led by Richard Lepsius (1810–1884). His work on the *Denkmäler aus Aegypten und Aethiopien*, published between 1849 and 1859 in 12 large folio volumes, is now itself considered a monument of 19th cent. scholarship. Later documentation projects never again achieved the global scope and outstanding success of these great expeditions. A complete *Catalogue des monuments et inscriptions de l'Égypte antique*, which the Egyptian *Service des antiquités* had begun to publish in 1894, faltered even in its very beginnings. In contrast, the aims of the *Archaeological Survey of Egypt* were more realistic. Under the aegis of the British *Egypt Exploration Fund* it completely recorded a large number of individual monuments that were visible above ground – predominantly decorated graves. The *Institut français d'archéologie orientale* concerned itself with recording the very extensive imagery and text material from the Ptolomaic-Roman temples. Finally, the repeated campaigns to save the Nubian monuments from inundation, following the building of the Aswan dams, deserve to be mentioned [8]. As far as the accuracy of the records is concerned, the work of the Oriental Institute of the University of → Chicago, initiated by the American James H. Breasted (1865–1935) and financed by John D. Rockefeller Jr., set new standards in the 1920s and 1930s. The main focus of this research was on Luxor, particularly on the temple of Madinat Habu; to this end, the *Chicago House* was set up on location, a research centre provided with an extensive library and all other necessities. The documentation of monuments has not yet been completed and is still the objective of ongoing projects undertaken by many different nations.

D. Excavations

From a modern perspective the earliest excavations in Egypt can be described as little more than looting. The primary concern of the European excavators was to obtain individual objects in order to enrich their own collections, often for financial gain, or those of museums, often for national aggrandisement. In the second half of the 19th cent., partly under French, party under Egyptian patronage, Auguste Mariette (1821–1881) had an almost complete monopoly on excavations in Egypt.

A new era began with the British archaeologist W.M. Flinders Petrie (1853–1942). Without specific academic education, but with the skills of a field archaeologist, acquired through practical experience, and, in particular, with a sound knowledge of surveying techniques, he went to Egypt in 1880–1882. He was fascinated by the hypotheses of the astronomer Piazzi Smith (1819–1900) regarding the pyramids and intended to undertake a new survey of the pyramids of Giza. After that he worked for a short period (1884–1886) for the *Egypt Exploration Fund* in the Eastern Delta (Tanis), the region where the sites of the Israelites' servitude in Egypt were believed to be found. He then spent decades working independently on extensive excavation projects across the whole of Egypt, partly funded by his own excavation finds, every year in a different location and often running excavations in parallel. To this day, his excavation results still represent a major part of the fundamental knowledge of Egyptian archaeology. One of his greatest achievements is the development of a procedure for creating a chronological seriation of Predynastic finds that cannot be dated with the help of textual evidence, i.e. sequence dating.

New standards were set by the American George A. Reisner (1867–1942), who systematised excavation and recording techniques, but who was ultimately barely able to publish his results because of his own heightened standards. In more recent times, processual archaeology with its interest in socio-economic questions, its result-oriented sondage trenches and sampling techniques and its particular interest in settlement archaeology has left its mark. Alongside this, however, an archaeology continues to this day which hardly deserves to be called anything other than looting or digging for treasure; it is unfortunate that the urgently necessary rescue archaeology of salvage excavations also at times falls into this category.

E. Reasons for the Interest in Ancient Egypt

A strong – and these days probably the strongest – impulse for the preoccupation with Ancient Egypt is the fascination of the impressive, almost exotic, imagery of the heritage of Ancient Egypt, ranging from the pictographic hieroglyphic script to works of visual art all the way to monumental architecture. Outstanding individual finds such as the discovery in 1922 by Howard Carter (1874–1939) of the almost untouched grave of

Tut-Ankh-Amun with its rich furnishings, and spectacular displays of art objects in the great exhibitions of recent decades are crowd pullers. No less impressive are the artifacts and monuments on display in Egypt itself: while in the 19th cent. only adventurers, wealthy members of high society and specialist scholars could afford to admire them, the growth in tourism has now made them accessible to anyone interested, at least anyone comfortably off in the developed world. Even though this does not play a major role within the scholarly discipline of Egyptology, which is an association of varied, specialized scholars whose everyday business is the clarification of specific problems, it is of great importance for the discipline as a whole, because the new generation of scholars is often recruited among enthusiasts of Egypt and also because research has the responsibility to satisfy public interest with sound scholarly information and to direct it towards interesting artifacts. However, the dominance of visual representations should not create the – wrong – impression that there are no other things of interest, such as e.g. the religion of Ancient Egypt – as a religion and not just in its curious visual manifestations – or the study of Ancient Egyptian literature.

Cultural history is another important dimension in dealing with Ancient Egypt. The most important question in this context is that of the connections between European culture with that of Ancient Egypt, the question regarding the roots of European culture and the continued existence of Ancient Egyptian cultural achievements [4], not least in the context of the history of science and medicine. Egyptologists also examine the links of Ancient Egypt with its neighbouring countries and cultures. In contrast, attempts to establish a typological ordering of civilizations or other comparative approaches have to date rarely been topics of research among Egyptologists.

These days, the instrumentalization of Egyptology for political purposes (colonialism, imperialism, orientalism [6]) is fairly limited. However, undeniably cultural policy does play a part in questions of financial support for Egyptological research institutions in countries outside Egypt and in decisions about the expediency of diplomatic measures to support fieldwork in Egypt by non-Egyptian nationals.

F. Institutionalization

Museums with extensive Egyptian collections have been and continue to be centres of Egyptological research. The oldest and/or most important is the Egyptian Museum (Antikhana) in Cairo, the → Louvre in Paris, the Museo Egizio in Turin, the British Museum in → London, the → Ägyptisches Museum in Berlin and the Metropolitan Museum in New York. The first ever chair for Egyptology was established for Champollion at the Collège de France in Paris in 1831, the second for Lepsius in Berlin in 1846. These days, Egyptology is taught all over the world, especially in central and western Europe and in North America. Field research in Egypt is carried out by archaeological institutes and associations from many different nations, and also by museums and universities. Important research institutions worth mentioning are the extensive specialist libraries of the Wilbour Library in New York (Brooklyn), the Griffith Institute in Oxford, the Collège de France in Paris and the Fondation Égyptologique Reine Élisabeth in Brussels. A bibliographical basis is provided by the annual bibliography published in Leiden [3] and the topographical bibliography compiled in Oxford [5].

→ Egypt; → Horapollo

1 C. BEINLICH-SEEBER, Bibliographie Altägyptens 1822–1946, 1998   2 W. R. DAWSON et al., Who was Who in Egyptology, 1995   3 International Association of Egyptologists, Annual Egyptological Bibliography, 1948ff. 3a E. HORNUNG, The Secret Love of Egypt: Its Impact on the West, 2001   4 S. MORENZ, Die Begegnung Europas mit Ägypten, 1968   5 B. PORTER, R. B. MOSS, Topographical Bibliography of Ancient Egyptian Hieroglyphic Texts, Reliefs and Paintings, 1927ff.   5a D. M. REID, Whose Pharaohs? Archaeology, Museums and Egyptian National Identity from Napoleon to World War I, 2002 6 E. W. SAID, Orientalism, 1978   7 S. SAUNERON, L'égyptologie, 1968   8 T. SÄVE-SÖDERBERGH, Temples and Tombs of Ancient Nubia, 1987   8a U. SCHIPPER (ed.), Aegyptologie als Wissenschaft, Adolf Erman (1854–1937) in seiner Zeit, 2006
The Bibliographie Altägyptens and the Annual Egyptological Bibliography are also available on CD-ROM and on the World Wide Web (http://www.leidenuniv.nl/nino/aeb.html) as the Egyptological Bibliography, 1822–1997.   WOLFGANG SCHENKEL

Egyptomania see → Orient, reception in the West

Ekphrasis

A. CONCEPT   B. PRACTICE

A. CONCEPT

In ancient (Greek) rhetoric (Dionysius of Halicarnassus, Rhet. 10,17), the term *ekphrasis* describes a mode of epideictic speech, specifically a form of description that aims at depicting the subject so clearly (i.e., in such detail) that listeners or readers would have the impression of seeing the subject before their own eyes. *Descriptio*, the equivalent Latin rhetorical term, preserves this speech-related meaning, for example, in Quintilian, who presents the visualization evoked by a successful *descriptio* in the context of *figurae in mente* as *sub oculos subiectio* (to place before one's eyes, visualization) (Quint. Inst. 9,2,40–44; 9,1,27 and 45). By contrast, in the Greek rhetorical tradition of the imperial period, the ekphrasis described a rhetorical school exercise through which the apprentice orator learned the ekphrastic mode of speaking and its intended effect (Theon, 1st/2nd cent. AD). Thus, ekphrasis secondarily became the name for a subgroup of school exercises in addition to being a genre name.

Initially, living creatures, events, places and times were considered possible subjects of rhetorical ekphrasis, but in Nicolaus Sophistes' *Progymnasma* (5th cent. BC), the tendency to restrict the generic name of ekphrasis to works of fine art is found for the first time. This had significant consequences in the history of the term [7]. Essentially, this would have been an opportunity to separate the term ekphrasis as image description from *descriptio* in its rhetorical meaning and to link the former with reflections on the relationship of word to image derived from various traditions, such as the saying ascribed to Simonides (late 6th cent. BC) that an image is silent poetry or the dictum *ut pictura poesis* of Horatian poetry (Ars 361) [12]. However, this did not happen. Ekphrasis became an equivocal term for describing works of fine art and, as a rhetorical term without this specific meaning, the Greek equivalent of the Latin *descriptio*. In the Renaissance, an amalgam of terms was formed from this heterogeneous tradition of linguistic reference to the visual and images (ekphrasis as an image description, ekphrasis as *sub oculos subiectio*, image as silent poetry – poetry as a speaking image, *ut pictura poesis*) with the result that, until it was put in doubt in Lessing's *Laocoon* (1766), ekphrasis seems not only to confirm the similarity, and thus the comparability, of poetry and fine art, but to demand it [13]. During the Renaissance, the idea of a competition between the arts was added to this terminological amalgamation (*paragone*; Leonardo da Vinci, *Libro di Pittura*, ca. 1490), in which the question of the relationship between fine arts and poetry and between the rank of poet and artist was discussed [5]. In as much as the relationship between word and picture became a topic for discussion and elements of the amalgamated term were used, the attention of historians of art and literature who were interested in these 'sister arts' [8] focused exclusively up to the 18th cent. on the *historia* shared by the two arts, i.e., what they had in common as to what they depicted, but not as to how they depicted it. Again, Lessing's *Laocoon* marked a turning point in the history of the term because Lessing differentiated the successive process of language from the simultaneous process of the image. From then on, the terminological formation of ekphrasis as well as other elements of the theoretical complex of the word-and-image issue included both the similarities and differences in linguistic and visual means of representation [6]. To the extent that modern literary and artistic studies have incorporated reflections from the theory of signs, the difference between image and text [1. 15] and the tension between the two are emphasized in the ekphrastic representation of images [3].

B. PRACTICE

The *loci classici* of ekphrasis in the meaning of a (literary) description of a work of fine art are: Homer's description of the shield of Achilles (Il. 18,483–608), Virgil's description of the shield of Aeneas (Aen. 8,626–731), the description of a beaker by Theocritus (Idylls

1,27–56), Europa's basket by Moschus (Europa 43–62) and, finally, the images (εἰκόνες) of Philostratus. Also, certain epigrams in the *Anthologia Graeca*, originally conceived as inscriptions on statues and grave monuments, have been considered since the Renaissance to be classical models of ekphrasis and to provide, similar to the *loci classici*, models in form and content for the lesser ekphrastic genres of the Renaissance and the Baroque, such as the device, → EMBLEMS and blazon. The descriptions in Vasari's *Vita* (*Le Vite de' più eccellenti Pittori Scultori ed Architettori*, 1550/1568) are linked to the image description of the ancient *progymnasma* without mentioning its use in the teaching of rhetoric. The 18th-cent. fashion of poetic painting (*poetische Malerey*) as well as poetry that paints pictures [4] was primarily guided by the Horatian tradition of *ut pictura poesis*: It had a metaphorical understanding of the demand that poetic representation should resemble pictorial representation, but put little value on the description of individual works of art. With the emphasis on aesthetics and on autonomy of beauty around the mid–18th cent., the aim of ekphrastic representation shifted from the *historia* shared by image and text to the linguistic representation of the perception or experience of a work of art, and this was often considered problematic (e.g., J.J. Winckelmann, *Beschreibung des Torso im Belvedere zu Rom* ('Description of the Torso in the Belvedere in Rome'), 1759). The modern image poem (→ FIGURED POEM, e.g., R.M. Rilke, *Früher Apollo*, 1907; *Archäischer Torso Apollos*, 1908) for the most part belongs in this tradition of an ekphrastic representation of works of art [10; 14], which is occasionally described as 'paragonal' [9].

→ Ekphrasis
→ UT PICTURA POESIS

1 O. BÄTSCHMANN, Bild-Diskurs. Die Schwierigkeit des Parler Peinture, 1977 2 G. BOEHM, H. PFOTENHAUER (eds.), Beschreibungskunst – Kunstbeschreibung. Ekphrasis von der Antike bis zur Gegenwart (with bibliography), 1995 3 G. BOEHM, Bildbeschreibung. Über die Grenzen von Bild und Sprache, in: Beschreibungskunst – Kunstbeschreibung (in 2), 23–40 4 H. C. BUCH, Ut pictura poesis. Die Beschreibungsliteratur und ihre Kritiker von Lessing bis Lukács, 1972 5 C. J. FARAGO, Leonardo da Vinci's Paragone. A Critical Interpretation with a New Edition of the Text in the Codex Urbinas, 1992 6 G. GEBAUER (ed.), Das Laokoon-Projekt: Pläne einer semiotischen Ästhetik, 1984 7 F. GRAF, Ekphrasis: Die Entstehung der Gattung in der Antike, in: Beschreibungskunst – Kunstbeschreibung (in 2), 143–155 8 J. H. HAGSTRUM, The Sister Arts: The Tradition of Literary Pictorialism and English Poetry from Dryden to Gray, ²1965 9 J. H. HEFFERNAN, Music of Words. The Poetics of Ekphrasis from Homer to Ashberry, 1993 10 G. KRANZ, Das Bildgedicht, 3 vols., 1981–1987 11 G. M. KRIEGER, Ekphrasis. The Illusion of the Natural Sign, 1992 12 R. W. LEE, Ut pictura poesis. The Humanistic Theory of Painting, 1967 13 M. PRAZ, Mnemosyne: The Parallel between Literature and the Visual Arts, 1970 14 H. ROSENFELD, Das deutsche Bildgedicht. Seine antiken Vorbilder und seine Entwicklung bis zur Gegenwart, 1935 (repr. 1967) 15 B. F. SCHOLZ, Sub oculos subiectio:

Quintilian on Ekphrasis and Energeia, in: V. ROBILLARD et al. (eds.), Pictures into Words, 1998, 71–97 16 L. SPITZER, The Ode on a Grecian Urn, or Content vs. Metagrammar, in: Comparative Literature 7, 1955, 203–225 17 P. WAGNER (ed.), Icon – Texts – Iconotexts: Essays on Ekphrasis and Intermediality, 1996 18 C.-P. WARNCKE, Sprechende Bilder – Sichtbare Worte: Das Bildverständnis in der frühen Neuzeit, 1987 19 U. WEISSTEIN (ed.), Literatur und bildende Kunst. Ein Handbuch zur Theorie und Praxis eines komparatistischen Grenzgebietes (with bibliography), 1992.   BERNHARD F. SCHOLZ

Eleatism see → PRE-SOCRATICS

Elegy
A. INTRODUCTION   B. MIDDLE LATIN ELEGY
C. NEO-LATIN ELEGY (ITALY)   D. FRENCH ELEGY
E. ENGLISH ELEGY   F. GERMAN ELEGY

A. INTRODUCTION
The subject matter of ancient elegy vacillated between grief and desire, covering topics ranging from the sympotic (drinking songs), through threnetic (lament) and parenetic (persuasion) to the erotic. Through its structural use of the distich, elegy extends itself to the → EPIGRAM, epistolary works (→ LETTER) and didactics (→ DIDACTIC POEM). Many of the aspects of ancient elegy are present in the modern revival of the genre as well, which, almost without exception, draws on the Roman elegy. The definition of elegy remains imprecise, as modern elegy is defined by content rather than metre. This confusion has been compounded by ancient definitions that are still valid, but have no current practical impact (Horace denounced erotic elegy in Ars P. 75ff.; in Ars am. 3,9,3f. Ovid, misled by etymology, assumed elegy consisted solely of lament). The ancient texts survived in the form of translations and examinations of complete (books of) elegies, or were integrated as quotations and motifs – e.g., the *recusatio* of epic in favour of elegiac poetry in Pierre de Ronsard (*Elégie à Cassandre*, 1554).

The significance of the various elegiac poets changed over time: From the Middle Ages to the 14th cent., when the works of Tibullus (ca. 55 BC- ca. 19 BC) and Propertius (ca. 50 BC – ca. 16 BC) only survived in rare manuscripts, the form and content of elegy were shaped by Ovid. The influence of Ovid's *Amores* is evident in the lyric love poetry of Marbod of Rennes (ca. 1035–1123) as well as in the bawdiness of the *Carmina Burana* (13th. cent.) by the Archipoeta. Petrarch's (1304-1374) *Trionfi* as well as Boccaccio's (1313–1375) *Fiammetta* attest to their authors' thorough knowledge of Ovid. Boethius (ca. 480–524/525), who opened his *De consolatione philosophiae* in distichs, helped spread elegiac poetry of exile, eventually influencing the *De exilio* by Hildebert of Lavardin (ca. 1056–1133/1134). Early medieval examples of the heroine epistle as a productive offshoot, if not indeed the basis, of the modern elegy, are Venantius Fortunatus' (ca. 530–609) epistle from a nun to God, and also in Baudri de Bourgueil's (1046–1130) platonic love sentiments. This genre, with its pagan and Christian motifs, continued to reverberate into the Baroque Period (Second Silesian School).

In contrast, Tibullus was appreciated in the 18th cent., as is evident from the Tibullus novel by Jean de La Chapelle (1688–1723), which contains passages from ancient elegies, and as the elegies by Louis-Jules Mancini-Mazarini, duc de Nivernais (1716–1798) or those by Pierre Le Brun (1661–1729) demonstrate. Propertius had a modest presence, aside from highlights in the works of Johannes Secundus (1511–1536) (*Propertii Manes invocat*) and Johann Wolfgang von Goethe (1749–1832), until his provocative re-evaluation by Ezra Pound (1885–1972) in *Homage to Propertius*.

B. MIDDLE LATIN ELEGY

The Middle Ages deserves credit for having preserved the appreciation of the distich through non-elegiac times. Giraldus de Barri (Giraldus Cambrensis (ca. 1146 – ca. 1223)), who suffered from gout, displayed a good sense of form and Ovidian self-mockery: He responds to a poem written in distichs with his *Musa morbida*, composed in rhyming hexameter! Motifs of mourning and consolation in Christian guise can be found in the poetry by St. Eugenius III, Archbishop of Toledo(† 657), and Alcuin (735–804). By the end of the Middle Ages, the genre was in danger of drowning in a flood of elegiac distichs, which included epic poetry and comic verse. Elegy, as presented in Matthew of Vendôme's (late 12th cent.) *Ars versificatoria* and the *Laborintus* by Eberhard the German (Everardus Alemannus, 13th. cent.), remained secular and erotic.

C. NEO-LATIN ELEGY (ITALY)

The works of the Humanists are characterised by their imitation of Roman elegy; thus the Humanist influence on vernacular poets is inseparably tied to the ancient models. The erotic elegy gained ground again after it had gone silent with Maximus in Late Antiquity. In addition to Jovianus Pontanus' (Giovanni Gioviano Pontano, 1426–1503) praise of marital love and the lascivious tone of Antonio Beccadelli (1394–1471, called Il Panormita), there were love elegies by Baptista Mantuano, Poliziano (Angelo Ambrogini, 1454–1494), Filippo Beroaldo (1453–1505), Conrad Celtes (1459–1508), Petrus Lotichius Secundus (1528–1560) and Jacopo Sannazaro (1458–1530). Secundus wrote *Basia* as well as three books of 'Elegies'. Fausto Andrelini (1462–1518) formed a bridge between Italy and France where elegy was moralising in character (e.g. Robert Gaguin, 1433–1501). An exception appears in the form of R. d'Ardennes' *Amores*, which inspired successors after the establishment of French elegy post-1540 (Jean de Boyssonné, George Buchanan (1506–1582)).

D. FRENCH ELEGY

For the French elegiasts in the 16th cent. – Clément Marot (1496–1544), Jean Bouchet (1476–1557), Fran-

çois Sagon (d. 1544?) – the medieval poems of *fin amor*, the lyric poetry of the troubadours, the *Roman de la Rose*, the works of François Villon (ca. 1431–ca. 1474) and a number of the *Epîtres Amoureuses* modeled after Ovid's *Heroides* were of greater significance than Roman elegies. Only the selection of the title preserved the genre: 'Pren donc l'elegie pour epistre amoureuse' [17]. The 'élegie déplorative' was thus associated, along with the poetry of lament composed by the *Rhétoriqueurs*, the dirge of the Roman elegy, and Horace's *Poetics*, with the elegiac topic of love.

In the elegies of Charles de Sainte-Marthe (1512–1555), reflexive philosophy reappears. The influence of the Roman elegies is more concrete in the case of Charles Fontaine (1515–1590), as is evident from his apology for lascivious poetry modelled after Catullus and Ovid [18. 7f.]. Far removed from ancient subjectivity, the *élegie marotique* lived on in the works of Pernette du Guillet (1520? – 1545), Victor Brodeau (1502? – 1540) and Gilles d'Aurigny († 1553), who established the form of the ten-syllabic verse in *rimes plates*. In their theoretical writings on poetry (e.g., *Déffense et Illustration de la Langue Françoyse*) as well as in Latin elegies written in distich, the poets of the → PLÉIADE (Joachim Du Bellay, Pierre de Ronsard, Jean-Antoine de Baïf, Remy [Rémi] Belleau) deliberately returned to Antiquity. However, their early intense reception of Roman elegy (including Catullus) notwithstanding, in their literary practice they adhered to love epistles in the vein of Marot. The generalized 'role elegies' were as (mis)adapted in their autobiographical use as were the other ancient models.

Around 1550, Louise Labé liberated the elegy from its medieval tradition, returning to the Propertian concept of love as physical desire, and thus prepared the way for Ronsard's love elegy 'proper', which distinguished itself through subjectivity and integration of classical motifs. Jean Doublet (ca. 1528–ca. 1560) provided an example of reception through paraphrase. For a brief time period, religious struggles produced (anonymous) pamphlets containing a bizarre variant of elegy.

In the 18th cent., the motif of mourning and dirge took on a life of its own. Elegy, eclogue and the Anacreontic ode achieved a closer resemblance: content and form no longer defined the genres, with this defining role being determined instead by sentiment and tone. As long as elegy was considered to be gallant poetry, authenticity of feeling, *passion*, received increasing emphasis as the defining point. The immediacy of the tone of the elegiac "I" became a characteristic of the genre; on a stylistic level, *beau désordre* expressed sensual passion. Melancholy, *tristesse*, appears in the the works of the Neoclassical admirers of Tibullus: Évariste de Forges de Parny (1753–1814), Antoine de Bertin (1752–1790) and André Marie Chénier (1762–1794). Charles-Hubert Millevoye (1782–1816) rings in the final period of French elegy, with Alphonse de Lamartine (1790–1869), Victor Hugo (1802–1885) and Charles Baudelaire (1821–1867) as its highlights.

E. ENGLISH ELEGY

English Elegy is characterised by a disengagement of elements of elegiac sentiment, a limitation of its scope to dirge (similar to Spanish (romantic) elegy) and a merger of the genre with bucolic poetry (Theocritus' *Idyls*, Virgil's *Eclogues*). Ovid's lament for Tibullus (Am. 3,9) had an enormous impact at the end of the 16th cent.: Edmund Spenser's (1552–1599) *Astrophel* and John Milton's (1608–1674) *Lycidas* connect lament and *consolatio* (including pastoral elements) with the motifs of self-reflexive and self-conscious poetic lineage. The chain of elegiac sorrow and lineage, found in the works of John Dryden (1631–1700), William Wordsworth (1770–1850), Percy Bysshe Shelley (1792–1822), John Keats (1795–1821), Alfred Tennyson (1809–1892) and A. C. Swinburne (1837–1909), reinvigorated the ancient branch of the elegiac canon. Along with genre parodies, such as those by John Gay (1685–1732) and Jonathan Swift (1667–1745), the Neoclassical Romantic *pastoral elegy* (funeral elegy) continued to be productive into the 20th cent. (cf. Thomas Gray's (1716–1771) *Elegy Written in a Country Churchyard*).

Due to the experiences of the First World War, which rendered the Classical motifs of consolation obsolete, the generic strictures shattered (William Butler Yeats (1865–1939), *In Memory of Major Robert Gregory*). The seemingly shapeless lyric poetry of the Modern Period (in the United States), sometimes motivated by feminist, gay and anti-racist concerns, was often deliberately and radically written against the elegiac norm. It rediscovered itself in conflict-ridden, aggressive and destructive fragments and became *anti-elegy, mock elegy, self elegy* and *the blues* in works by Ezra Pound (1885–1972), T.S. Eliot (1888–1965), Thomas Hardy (1840–1928), Wilfred Owen (1893–1918), Wallace Stevens (1879–1955), Langston Hughes (1902–1967), and W. H. Auden (1907–1973). In the middle of the 20th cent., Sylvia Plath (1932–1963), Robert Lowell (1917–1977), John Berryman (1914–1972), Anne Sexton (1928–1974), Allen Ginsberg (1926–1997) and Michael S. Harper (1938–) wrought havoc with the (en-comiastic) tradition of *family elegy*, which, from the time of Propertius' *Cornelia Elegy* had paid homage to (deceased) relatives (e. g. Plath's *Daddy, I Have Had To Kill You*).

F. GERMAN ELEGY

Although the term 'elegiac' is restrictive in terms of content, it truthfully reflects the complexity of the ancient genre. Martin Opitz (1597–1639) started his canon of topics with "affairs of love and sad things" and tried to imitate the distich by using alexandrines in alternate rhyme. Johann Rist (1607–1667) revived the parenetic elegy; Paul Fleming (1609–1640), Daniel Heinsius (1580–1655), Caspar Ziegler (1621–1690) and Christian Hofmann von Hofmannswaldau (1617–1679) treated mixed (humorous) topics.

In the 18th cent., in a tribute to Catullus, the *Anacreontic poets* introduced a new type of dirge, the (ani-mal) epicedium; in the context of the *Göttinger Hainbund* (founded 1772), this new form contributed to a deepened elegiac sentiment. The poets of *Empfindsamkeit* (Thomas Abbt (1738–1766), Johann Georg Jacobi (1740–1814), Ludwig Christoph Heinrich Hölty (1748–1776)) struggled with the contrast between the mundane reality and a longing for an idyllic life (→ BUCOLIC). Friedrich Gottlob Klopstock (1724–1803) combined this subject matter with the ancient form of the distich and thus paved the way for the classical harmony of form and content. Johann Wolfgang von Goethe's (1749–1832) *Römische Elegien* (*Erotica Romana*, 1788–90, published 1795) expanded the content of the genre by explicitly returning to Propertius. As foreshadowed by Propertius and Ovid, the immediate experience could be softened by reflective and self-mocking distance, e. g., when the elegiac "I" counted the hexameter on his lover's back (5,15–17).

Influenced by Friedrich Schiller's (1759–1805) theoretical discourses and elegies, Goethe, in his second collection of elegies, tended to restrict the genre again to the 'mixed sentiments' of a lost idyll (cf. August Wilhelm von Schlegel (1767–1845), Karl Wilhelm Friedrich von Schlegel (1772–1829), Wilhelm von Humboldt (1767–1835)). Goethe himself formally dissolved the distich in the stanzas of the *Marienbader Elegien* (1823). Friedrich Hölderlin (1770–1843) thereafter used hexameter; Franz Grillparzer (1791–1872) followed Ovid by using alternate rhyme; Rainer Maria Rilke (1875–1926) composed his *Eighth Duino Elegy* in blank verse; Hugo von Hofmannsthal (1874–1929) and Rudolf Borchardt (1877–1945) chose the tercet; and Gottfried Benn (1886–1956) found the song strophe. Eduard Mörike (1804–1875), Stefan George (1868–1933), Georg Trakl (1887–1914), Franz Werfel (1890–1945), Gottfried Benn, Nelly Sachs (1891–1970), Paul Celan (1920–1970) and Ingeborg Bachmann (1926–1973) replaced the fixed meter with free rhythm.

But the principle of antithesis, encouraged by the epigrammatic structure of the distich, remained, as demonstrated by Bertolt Brecht's (1898–1956) *Hollywood-Elegien* and *Buckower Elegien* as well as by the 'classical attempts' of authors from the former GDR, for example, Peter Hacks (1928–2003) and Christa Wolf (1929–). Thus elegy and epigram, in Antiquity two branches that had grown on the same tree, came full circle.

→ Elegy

→ ANACREONTIC POETRY

1 L. ALFONSI, W. SCHMID, 'Elegie', Reallexikon für Antike und Christentum 4, 1026–1061, 1959   2 M. BAIER, Tibull in der französischen Versdichtung, 1955   3 F. BEISSNER, Geschichte der deutschen Elegie, 1965   4 D. FREY, Bissige Tränen. Eine Untersuchung über Elegie und Epigramm von den Anfängen bis Bertolt Brecht und Peter Huchel, 1995   5 R. E. HALLOWELL, Ronsard and the Conventional Roman Elegy, 1954   6 G. S. HANISCH, Love Elegies of the Renaissance: Marot, Louise Labé and Ronsard, 1979   7 D. KAY, Melodious Tears: The English

Funeral Elegy from Spenser to Milton, 1990   8 K.-W.
KIRCHMEIR, Romantische Lyrik und neoklassizistische
Elegie: Studien zur Theorie der Lyrik in Frankreich im 18.
Jahrhundert und in der Romantik, 1976   9 B. KRONE-
BERG, Studien zur Geschichte der russischen klassizisti-
schen Elegie, 1972   10 M. PAZ DÍEZ TABOADA, La Eligía
romántica española: estudio y antología, 1977   11 H.
POTEZ, L'élégie en France avant le romantisme (de Parny à
Lamartine) 1778–1820, 1898   12 J. RAMAZANI, Poetry
of Mourning. The Modern Elegy from Hardy to Heaney,
1994   13 P. M. SACKS, The English Elegy. Studies in the
Genre from Spenser to Yeats, 1985   14 J. SCODEL, The
English Poetic Epitaph: Commemoration and Conflict
from Jonson to Wordsworth, 1991   15 CH. M. SCOLLEN-
JIMACK, The Birth of the Elegy in France (1500–1550),
1967   16 J. P. SULLIVAN, Ezra Pound and Sextus Proper-
tius. A Study in Creative Translation, 1964   17 TH. SÉBIL-
LET, Art Poétique françoys (1548), F. GAIFFE (ed.), 1932,
F. GOYET (ed.),1988   18 CH. FONTAINE, La Fontaine
d'Amour, Lyon 1545   19 K. WEISSENBERGER, Formen
der Elegie von Goethe bis Celan, 1969
ADDITIONAL BIBLIOGRAPHY E. Z. LAMBERT, Placing
Sorrow, 1976 G. PIGMAN, III, Grief and English Renais-
sance Elegy, 1985 T. ZIOLKOWSKI, The Classical German
Elegy 1795–1950, 1980   BARBARA FEICHTINGER

Elements, theory of see→ NATURAL SCIENCES

Eleusis The first indications of the shrine of Demeter at
Eleusis (E.) were provided by the surveying work commissioned by the → SOCIETY OF DILETTANTI and undertaken by R. Chandler, N. Revett and W. Pars in 1776,
(published in 1797 [2]) in the ruins, which were at that
stage still covered by the huts of a village whose name –
Lefsina or similar – still preserved the ancient name. Far
more precise and detailed were the investigations, also
commissioned by the Dilettanti, undertaken by W. Gell,
J.P. Gandy and F. Bedford in 1812/13, and presented in
1817 (fig. 1 [23]). The remains of the Telesterion which
were still visible at that time were interpreted as a crypt
on the basis of the non-fluted columns and the lower
level vis-a-vis the porch., an opinion that was taken
over by K.O. Müller among others, in his extensive article about the Eleusinian mysteries in 1840 [10].

A beginning was made on the excavation of the
shrine in 1882 by D. Philios, assisted by W. Dörpfeld,
under the aegis of the Greek Archaeological Society
after the inhabitants of the village had been re-settled
(unfortunately, as it later

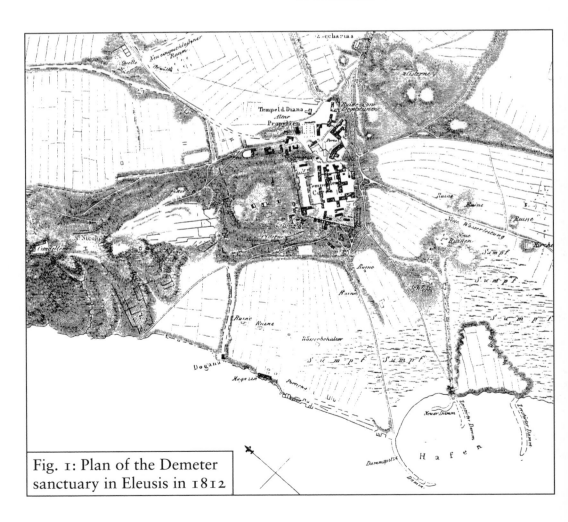

Fig. 1: Plan of the Demeter
sanctuary in Eleusis in 1812

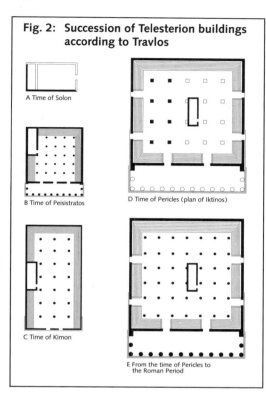

Fig. 2: Succession of Telesterion buildings according to Travlos

A Time of Solon

B Time of Peisistratos

C Time of Kimon

D Time of Pericles (plan of Iktinos)

E From the time of Pericles to the Roman Period

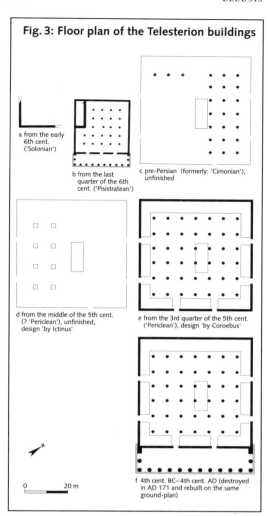

Fig. 3: Floor plan of the Telesterion buildings

a from the early 6th cent. ('Solonian')

b from the last quarter of the 6th cent. ('Pisistratean')

c pre-Persian (formerly: 'Cimonian'), unfinished

d from the middle of the 5th cent. (? 'Periclean'), unfinished, design 'by Ictinus'

e from the 3rd quarter of the 5th cent. ('Periclean'), design 'by Coroebus'

f 4th cent. BC–4th cent. AD (destroyed in AD 171 and rebuilt on the same ground-plan)

0 20 m

turned out, not far enough away from the nucleus of the classical settlement; this error was avoided when the excavations at Delphi began ten years later). In a mere five years the entire shrine was exposed, so that the development of its construction was clearly discernible from the 6th cent. BC down to Roman times [11; 15; 22]. In 1906 and 1921 F. Noack carried out structural investigations which constitute, in view of the most detailed plan thus far of the *telesterion* building and numerous carefully documented observations of details, a basis for the study of the ruins which has not yet been surpassed.[13]. In the 1930s the excavations were resumed by K. Kourouniotis, assisted by G. Mylonas and J. Travlos [8; 9]. These led to the discovery of the prehistoric beginnings of the shrine, but brought to light also finds which demanded a correction of existing views on the structural development in historical times. An anastylosis of individual well-preserved edifices begun in the 1960s did not get past the initial stages [25].

The progressive enlargement of the central cult building, which corresponds with enlargement of the perimeter walls belonging to each stage is visible at E. in an exemplary form. At the beginning is the late Mycenean Megaron, which remained in use until the geometric period, and thus is one of the most important pieces of evidence for the continuity between Bronze and Iron-Age Greece [8; 9]. The dating of the succeeding building phases is a matter of debate, its connection with historical names seeming to offer a degree of cer-

tainty which can very seldom be supported by archaeological finds (which have themselves, unfortunately, insufficiently been taken into account) [6; 19]. In the early 6th cent. BC there arose the rectangular 'solonian' building, which was replaced in the later 6th cent. BC by a hypostyle building which was twice the size and had a porch ('Pisistratan', more recently and probably correctly seen as 'quasi-Pisistratan' [1; 5]). According to a view which is still current, this would have been the building burned by the Persians in 480 BC (Hdt. 9,65,2). On that site a new *telesterion* appears to have been erected, which was to be made twice the size through quarrying the rock-faces towards the west. This 'Cimonian' building was certainly never completed, as is clear simply from the absence of any support foundations for the western part of the southern wall. Since L. Shear [17] was able to demonstrate by reference to the inscriptions IG I² 81 und 313/4 that the late archaic cult building had not been burned, but had been dismantled, and that the materials, including roof-beams and tiles, were stored so that they could be used again, and that the Persians could only have been able to burn the sanctuary (the *anaktoron* [19]), which had been left standing, it is evident that the 'Cimonian' *telesterion* must have been begun already in the pre-Persian period [1]. Since, as Noack in particular has shown [4; 7; 13. 93], the system of 'Cimonian' column-setting is also attested elsewhere, other than in buildings thus far deemed to be 'Cimonian', there is also a compelling argument that the pre-Persian building was the same size as the later 'Periclean' one. Since the pre-Persian origin of a proto-Parthenon in Athens can now no longer be doubted, the parallels with the building of the Acropolis which have always been noted, are now particularly clear [7; 17], For the succeeding 'Periclean' construction there is evidence of two different plans: one, not completed, with a further development of the inner supports (usually associated with the architect Ictinus), and another, with a narrower positioning of the columns (and in that corresponding to the 'Cimonian' plan, so that it has been taken back to the architects Koroibos and Metagenes [11; 19; 22]). This building existed – extended by the addition of a huge porch erected in the 4th cent. BC and named after the architect Philo [6; 19] – down to the destruction by the Costoboci in 170/1 AD, [14]. Thereafter it was completely rebuilt from the foundations, exactly like the original, with only minor modifications, by the Emperor Marcus Aurelius. [20] and presumably completed in 176 AD (and is one of many examples of architectural copying of which there are many to be found in E. [3]). How the celebrations of the annual mysteries were contrived during the extensive building interruptions in the 5th cent. BC and in the 2nd cent. AD is an unresolved problem.

Unclear, too, is the meaning of the two arrow-shaped foundations on the south-east and north-east corners of the *telesterion*. While earlier researchers considered these to be evidence that the *telesterion* was to be provided with a massive *peristasis*, and of course linked this idea with Ictinus [4; 13; 16], the excavations of the 1930s have shown that those foundations must be post-Periclean [9]. Since the publication of details of these excavations did not appear until the start of the Second World War, and were thus unknown in Germany, German research adhered for a particularly long time to the rejected view [4; 16] and only recently – and clearly with some reluctance – has it accepted the more recent findings [4].

The area where the processional route from Athens meets the enclosed shrine of the mysteries was developed in the 2nd cent. AD into a monumental square [25; 26]: in the centre was erected the temple of Artemis Propylaia as a doric *amphiprostylos* (based on an unidentified classical model); hypostyle buildings, a *nymphaeum* and two triumphal arches (copies based on Hadrian's arch in Athens) enclose the square; the Great Propylaia, an exact, slightly adapted copy of the Propylaia on the Acropolis in Athens [26], form the entrance to the outer precincts of the shrine. In the inner areas, too, two (badly preserved) temples were erected, perhaps for deified female members of the imperial family; the pediment of one was decorated with copies of those on the western pediment of the Parthenon [24]. The program of building was completed at the latest under Marcus Aurelius, probably in 176 AD. Scholarship is divided on the question of whether the renovation of the entrance square was begun already under Hadrian [26] or only under his successors [25].

While little is known of the ancient settlement, the necropoles have provided important finds (the so-called Isis-grave from the 8th cent. BC [18]; proto-attic Gorgon-amphora [12]).For the question – much discussed in historical research – of when the area of E. became attached to the attic state there are thus far no absolutely clear indications.

→ Athenai; → Eleusis

1 S. ANGIOLILLO, Arte e cultura nell' Atene di Peisistrato e dei Pisistratidi, 1997, 87–90   2 Antiquities of Ionia, Published by the Society of Dilettanti II, London 1797   3 F. FELTEN, Antike Architekturkopien, in: Komos. Festschrift für Th. Lorenz, 1997, 61–69   4 G. GRUBEN, Die Tempel der Griechen, 1966 (^{2}1976, ^{4}1986)   5 T. HAYASHI, Bedeutung und Wandel der Triptolemosbilder vom 6.–4. Jahrhundert vor Christus, 1992, 20–29   6 K. JEPPESEN, Paradeigmata, 1958, 103–149   7 TH. KALPAXIS, Hemiteles, 1986, 97–102   8 K. KOUROUNIOTIS, G. MYLONAS, Excavations at Eleusis, in: AJA 37, 1933, 271–286   9 Id., J. TRAVLOS, Συμβολὴ εἰς τὴν οἰκοδομικὴν ἱστορίαν τοῦ ἐλευσινιακοῦ τελεστηρίου, in: AD 1935–1936, 1–42   10 K. O. MÜLLER, Eleusinien, in: Kleine deutsche Schriften II, Breslau 1848, 242–311, esp. 284–287   11 G. MYLONAS, Eleusis and the Eleusinian Mysteries, 1961   12 Id., Τὸ δυτικὸν νεκροταφεῖον τῆς Ἐλευσῖνος I–II, 1975   13 F. NOACK, Eleusis. Die baugeschichtliche Entwicklung des Heiligtums I–II, 1927   14 D. PHILIOS, Τὸ ἐν Ἐλευσῖνι Τελεστήριον καὶ Ἀριστείδης ὁ Σοφιστής, in: MDAI(A) 21, 1896, 242–245   15 O. RUBENSOHN, Die Mysterienheiligtümer in Eleusis und Samothrake, 1892, 13ff.   16 Id., Das Weihehaus von Eleusis und Allerheiligstes, in: JDAI 70, 1955, 1–49   17 T. L. SHEAR JR., The Demolished Temple at Eleusis, in: Festschrift H. Thompson (Hesperia Suppl. XX, 1982), 128–140   18 A. SKIAS, Παναρχαία ἐλευσινιακὴ νεκρόπολις, in: ArchE 1898, 29–122   19 H. SVENSON-EVERS, Die griechischen Architekten archa. und klassischen Zeit, 1996, 157–196; 237–251; 284–315   20 R. TOWNSEND, The Roman Rebuilding of Philon's Porch and the Telesterion at Eleusis, in: Boreas 10, 1987, 97–106   21 J. N. TRAVLOS, Τὸ ἀνάκτορον τῆς Ἐλευσῖνος, in: ArchE 1951, 1–16   22 Id., Attika, 91–169 (complete bibliography up to 1985)   23 The Unedited Antiquities of Attica, Comprising the Architectural Remains of Eleusis, Rhamnus, Sunium and Thoricus. Published by the Society of Dilettanti, London 1817   24 L. WEIDAUER, I. KRAUSKOPF, Urkönige in Athen und Eleusis, in: JDAI 107, 1992, 1–16   25 D. WILLERS, Der Vorplatz des Heiligtums von Eleusis – Überlegungen zur Neugestaltung im 2. Jahrhundert nach Christus, in: M. FLASHAR, H. J. GEHRKE, E. HEINRICH (eds.), Retrospektive. Konzepte von Vergangenheit in der griechischen Antike, 1996, 179–191   26 D. ZIRO, Ἐλευσίς: Ἡ κύρια εἴσοδος τοῦ ἱεροῦ τῆς Ἐλευσῖνος, 1991 Ἡ κύρια εἴσοδος τοῦ ἱεροῦ τῆς Ἐλευσῖνος, 1991

ADDITIONAL BIBLIOGRAPHY K. CLINTON, Eleusis. The Inscriptions on Stone: Documents of the Sanctuary of the Two Goddesses and the Public Documents of the Deme, 2 vols., 2005   KLAUS FITTSCHEN

Emblems

A. DEFINITION   B. HISTORY OF THE CONCEPT
C. SOURCES   D. POETICS   E. APPLIED
EMBLEMATICS

A. DEFINITION

Term for a didactic literary genre prevalent from the 16th to the 18th cents. Typically, the emblem consists of three elements, which are differentiated textually as well as typographically. The first element is the motto, which is also termed the *inscriptio* or lemma. It is often in Latin and remains so even after the transition from the Latin of the Humanists to the vernacular languages. This is followed by a visual image–the *pictura, icon,* or *symbolon*–that depicts a subject or theme, the *res picta,* in a symbolic way and which thus lends itself to an interpretation of its allegorical meaning, or *sensus spiritualis.* The theme is then described and interpreted, initially in Latin but later increasingly in the vernacular in the *subscriptio,* which is traditionally presented in verse as a piece of → EPIGRAMMATIC POETRY. Particularly in the 17th cent., these three parts of the emblem itself are frequently followed by a commentary, the function of which is to establish the origin of the emblem parts by means of references to the *auctores* and in this way to clarify the behavioural norms, maxims and general truths contained in the emblem. The author's own commentary on the individual emblems of an emblem book is an optional, never obligatory, characteristic of the genre that may be seen as a continuation of the commentaries added by Claudius Minos to his *Emblemata* editions (Paris 1571,1583; Antwerp 1574,1577,1581).

B. HISTORY OF THE CONCEPT

In its original Greek and Latin usage, *emblema* refers to a craft artifact and specifically to inlaid work or intarsia, that is, mosaic [8]. In association with the *theoremata* literature of the 12th cent., it also describes a particular form of theological discourse (Alain de Lille, *Regulae celestis iuris,* printed Basel 1492, Strasbourg 1497) that distances itself from, for example, paradox and enigma and is instead characterised by its "intrinsic clarity of reason", that is, by its *interna intelligentiae splendor* [6].

It was from the dedicatory poem to the Humanist Conrad Peutinger that the Milan jurist Andrea Alciato (1492–1555) chose the title *Emblemata* for his epigrams (*Emblematum liber,* written ca.1520, first printed Augsburg 1531), because they were to serve as models and inspiration for craftsmen. It is possible, however, that the use of *emblema* to describe a form of discourse also played a part in this title choice. Thus, the epigrams contained in the *Emblematum liber* are inten-

ded to represent the meaning of the objects described. In the 16th cent. and starting in France, 'emblem' is used to describe a genre of text and image, distinguished from the *devise* or impresa by the general character of the didactic reference–as opposed to reference to the particular object–and from the fable by the obligatory image. For a time in Germany, the term *Sinnbild,* a loan translation probably modelled on the Dutch *zinnebeeld,* was in use.

C. SOURCES

Although Andrea Alciato with his *Emblematum liber* (Augsburg 1531) is rightly regarded as the founder of the genre–that is, as the *emblematum pater et princeps*–and while the emblem is thus to be seen as a → RENAISSANCE creation, Alciato's initiative does not represent an entirely new beginning. A distinction must be made between genre-specific sources, that is, those sources calculated to contribute to the emblem's textual form, and content-specific sources, that is, those calculated to have a role in the emblem's semantic or didactic aspect. The most important of the first type of sources are ancient epigrams, particularly those of the *Anthologia Graeca.* Indeed, Alciato himself saw his poems published under the title *Emblemata* as epigrams in the tradition of the *Anthologia Graeca,* that is to say, as notes and comments on works of art. Alciato's *Emblemata* were in part translations from the original Greek into Latin and in part his own imitations of epigrams from that collection [5]. The illustration, at the urging of the Augsburg printer Heinrich Steiner, of each of the *Emblematum liber*'s epigrams by a Jörg Breu woodcut representing the *res* depicted in the epigram did not at first meet with Alciato's approval. The first edition to find his favour was Christian Wechel's Paris edition of 1534, the *Emblematum libellus.* The distinctive page format of this edition, namely the vertical arrangement of the emblem's three parts and the printing of only one emblem per page, subsequently became a basic genre characteristic for the emblem's general layout [13] (although it should be noted that in the edition of 1531 there is still continuous text). The 'impresa' or 'devise' of the Late Middle Ages and Renaissance must be regarded as the second genre-specific source. Starting in the last third of the 14th cent., this fashion spread from the Burgundian courts, first to France and then, in the 15th cent., to Italy, and consisted of writing mottos on helmets, shields, and other items of clothing and weaponry. To this, a pictorial element was added. Initial attempts to describe in generic terms the genre of text and image that was developing in the wake of Alciato's *Emblematum libellus* were modelled on the normative description of the 'devise' that Paolo Giovio proposed in his *Dialogo dell'imprese* (Rom 1555) [3; 7; 14]. Further sources for the emblem's textual and graphic elements were proverb collections such as Erasmus of Rotterdam's *Adagia* (Venice 1508), medallions and engraved gems, mythological compilations, bestiaries, herbaria and the *Physiologus.* Among content-specific sources is also the epigram in the tradition of the *Anthologia Graeca*, insofar as in the epigrams that Alciato translated or drew upon for imitation, an element describing a particular artwork, that is, a descriptive element, is followed in the anthology by an element interpreting the same artwork. A prerequisite was thus the association of description and interpretation, and, indeed, this later becomes characteristic of the emblem as a genre. Additional defining influences on the form of description specific to the emblem were medieval → AL-LEGORISM (four-fold method of scriptural interpretation); the doctrine of nature as a second *Book of Revelation* (*liber naturae*), that is, the world as a *mundus symbolicus*; the illustrated → FABLE; the *Pauper's Bible* (*Biblia pauperum*); and Renaissance hieroglyphics (Horapollo, *Hieroglyphica*, 4th cent. (?), rediscovered in 1419, printed in Basel 1518; Valerianus, *Hieroglyphica*, first edition 1556; Fra Francesco Colonna, *Hypnerotomachia Poliphili*, first printed Venice 1499). With these latter, the attempt was made to revive ancient Egyptian hieroglyphics as a form of ancient occult knowledge, that is, of *sapientia veterum*. On the one hand, it was in these references and sources that the association of word and image typical of the emblem had its genesis. On the other, the frequent reference to ancient Egyptian hieroglyphics in the then-current emblem theory as first set out in Alciato's *De verborum significatione* (Lyon 1530), together with reference to the decipherable book of nature and, thus, to God as the first emblem maker, offered the possibility of grasping the *sensus spiritualis* of a *res picta*. More specifically, the *sensus spiritualis* as represented in the emblematic description and interpretation could be understood as inherently and properly belonging to the *res picta* and not merely arbitrarily chosen and assigned. This possibility became especially important for the 17th-cent. religious and didactic emblem. For the Humanist emblem of the 16th cent., where witty intellectual invention predominated, there was less need of such legitimisation.

D. POETICS

The unresolved question in the poetics of the time about the relationship of image and epigram in the emblem resonated in mutually contradictory attempts at classifying the emblem as a genre: Was the emblem an illustration of an epigram, thus giving priority to the word, or was the emblem the interpretation of a theme, thus giving priority to the image? If the epigram was to be seen as interpreting the image, so that, of the three parts of the emblem, the latter–that is, the image– therefore had priority, then a generically systematic definition of the emblem, which set the latter off from other genres of word and image such as the hieroglyphic, the impresa, the medallion or the rebus, suggested itself. If, on the other hand, the emblematic image was to be seen as illustrating the epigram, then the group of characteristics *brevitas, suavitas* and *argutia* offered itself to attempts at definition. The emblem accordingly might then be regarded as an illustrated variant of the epigram, as Alciato perhaps intended [12].

E. APPLIED EMBLEMATICS

In addition to the emblem in book form, which developments in printing and book illustration had especially favoured, there arose, beginning in the 16th cent. and then increasingly in the 17th and 18th cents., what is today termed 'applied emblematics' in the form of decorative programs for sacred and secular buildings and decorations on products from the various handicrafts such as goldsmithing, cabinet-making, glassblowing, silk embroidery and weaving. This was especially true for products created for a particular, often ceremonial purpose but was also the case for products of the cannon foundry and the shipyard, which produced artifacts with a distinct representational function [1; 2. 193–221]. It is, however, not entirely valid to view applied emblematics as a later development, wholly separate from emblematics in book form, since even Alciato's *Emblematum liber* (Augsburg 1531) was expressly designed as a pattern book for craftsmen [4. 39–66]. It is probably also warranted to assign to the area of applied emblematics the widespread tendency during the 17th cent. to endow cultural phenomena such as drama and the theatre, opera, ecclesiastical and secular ceremonies, parades and processions with possibilities of interpretation on a spiritual level by means of emblems [10; 11]. The requisite material in the form of words and images was taken either directly from emblems in books, thus using the emblem book as kind of art manual [4], or from systematised encyclopedic compendia of collected word and image combinations in the tradition of C. Ripa's *Iconologia* (Rome 1593, without illustrations in its first edition).

→ Anthologia Graeca

→ EPIGRAMMATIC POETRY; → COMMENTARY; → DIDACTIC POEM

1 H. FREYTAG, W. HARMS (eds.), Außerliterarische Wirkungen barocker Emblem-Bücher, 1975   2 W. S. HECKSCHER, K.-A. WIRTH, Emblem, Emblem-Buch, Reallexikon zur deutschen Kunstgeschichte, vol. 5, 85–228   3 A. HENKEL, A. SCHÖNE (eds.), Emblemata. Handbuch zur Sinnbildkunst des XVI. und XVII. Jahrhunderts, 1967   4 I. HÖPEL, Emblem und Sinnbild. Vom Kunstbuch zum Erbauungsbuch, 1987   5 J. HUTTON, The Greek Anthology in Italy to the Year 1800, 1935   6 J. KÖHLER, 'Theophanie celestis emblema'. Zu einem Theorematabegriff bei Alain de Lille, in: Miscellanea Mediaevalia 22, 1994, 158–170   7 R. KLEIN, La Théorie de l'expression figurée dans les traités italiens sur les imprese, 1555–1612, in: Bibliothèque d'Humanisme et Renaissance 19, 1957, 320–342   8 H. MIEDEMA, The Term Emblema in Alciati, in: Journal of the Warburg and Courtauld Institutes 31, 1968, 234–259   9 M. PRAZ, Studies in Seventeenth-Century Imagery, 1939   10 D. RUSSELL, Emblematic Structures in Renaissance French Culture, 1995   11 A. SCHÖNE, Emblematik und Drama im Zeitalter des Barock, 1964   12 B. F. SCHOLZ, Emblematik: Entstehung und Erscheinungsweisen, in: U. WEISSTEIN (ed.), Literatur und Bildende Kunst, 1992, 113–137   13 Id., From Illustrated

Epigram to Emblem, in: W. S. HILL (ed.), New Ways of Looking at Old Texts, 1993, 149–57   14 D. SULZER, Traktate zur Emblematik, 1992
ADDITIONAL BIBLIOGRAPHY P. M. DALY, Emblem Scholarship: Directions and Developments. A Tribute to Gabriel Hornstein, 2005; Id., Literature in the Light of the Emblem: Structural Parallels between the Emblem and Literature in the Sixteenth and Seventeenth Centuries, ²1998; Id., D. RUSSELL (eds.), Emblematic Perceptions: Essays in Honor of William S. Heckscher, 1997; Id., M. SILCOX (eds.), The English Emblem: Bibliography of Secondary Literature, 1990; Id. (ed.), The English Emblem and the Continental Tradition, 1988; Id. (ed.), The European Emblem: Towards an Index Emblematicus. 1980; Id., Emblem Theory: Recent German Contributions to the Characterization of the Emblem Genre, 1979; A. SAUNDERS, Alciati and the Greek Anthology, Journal of Medieval and Renaissance Studies 12, 1982, 1–18; B. WESTERWEEL (ed.), Anglo-Dutch Relations in the Field of the Emblem, 1997;
URLs http://www.mun.ca/alciato/index.html; http://www.emblems.arts.gla.ac.uk/french/

BERNHARD F. SCHOLZ

Encyclopaedia

A. INTRODUCTION   B. MIDDLE AGES AND HUMANISM   C. ENLIGHTENMENT   D. NINE-TEENTH AND TWENTIETH CENTURIES   E. SPECIAL-ISED ENCYCLOPAEDIAS

A. INTRODUCTION
1. DEFINITION   2. ETYMOLOGY   3. HISTORY OF THE CONCEPT

1. DEFINITION

'Encyclopaedia' here refers to a compilatory work which intends to summarise comprehensively the entire body of knowledge (general encyclopaedia, universal encyclopaedia) or the knowledge in a specific field (subject encyclopaedia) in a systematic or alphabetical order. This article focuses on general encyclopaedias and on specialised encyclopaedias in the field of Classical studies. Distinctions between encyclopaedias and lexica (= alphabetical) or handbooks (= systematic) cannot be drawn clearly and are roughly determined by size and purpose (as in: a practical reference book as opposed to a comprehensive survey) and, if at all, are not applied too strictly here for practical reasons, e.g. in the case of modern large-scale *Lexika* or the *Handbuch der Altertumswissenschaft*. Works presenting a systematic overview of various sciences (e.g. Hegel's *Enzyklopädie der philosophischen Wissenschaften*, Engl. *Encyclopedia of the Philosophical Sciences*), however, are not the subject of this article.

2. ETYMOLOGY

The term encyclopaedia (Middle Latin and New Latin *encyclopaedia*; sometimes *cyclopaedia*) is a reference to the Greek term *enkýklios paideía,* first made during → HUMANISM. Already misunderstood in Antiquity, probably through the influence of *orbis doctrinae* (Quintilian 1,10,1; roughly: 'circle of scholarly disci-

plines', 'education as a circle formed by items of knowledge'), it was not used in Antiquity or during the Middle Ages (first evidence: late 15th cent.) for works in the sense of this article.

3. HISTORY OF THE CONCEPT

Despite the commonalities in genre and tradition, ancient efforts to create comprehensive collections of knowledge failed to bring about a consistent set of concepts comparable to the comprehensive educational concepts emerging at the same time (cf. *enkýklios paideía* and *artes liberales*), and this trend continued throughout the Middle Ages (*summa* was limited to works of theological purpose). Even in the modern period, 'encyclopaedia' was slow to win acceptance among a multitude of competing terms; early examples included J.H. Alsted's still-systematic *Encyclopaedia septem tomis distincta* (1630), E. Chambers' *Cyclopaedia* (1728) and the French *Encyclopédie* (1751–1780). Since then, answers to the question as to what constitutes an encyclopaedia have been strongly guided by considerations relating to the philosophy of science, to pedagogy and the needs of the users. The economics of publishing have also played a role (cf. *Kleine Enzyklopädie der antiken Autoren*).

B. MIDDLE AGES AND HUMANISM
1. LATE ANTIQUITY   2. EARLY MIDDLE AGES
3. HIGH MIDDLE AGES/SCHOLASTICISM
4. HUMANISM

1. LATE ANTIQUITY

Looking back at the history of the genre, a break clearly occurred in Late Antiquity; encyclopaedias from that period resemble more closely those of the Middle Ages rather than their predecessors from Antiquity, both in their form and in their propaedeutic and paedagogic intent within the framework of the *artes liberales*. Three of these works were particularly influential during the Middle Ages: the first is an allegorising encyclopaedia composed in a popular alternating rhythm of prose and poetry (*De nuptiis Philologiae et Mercurii*, 4th/5th cent.?) by Martianus Capella, who handed the pedagogical concept of the seven liberal arts down to the Middle Ages. The fact that he was highly valued is evidenced in many manuscripts and commentaries and in an Old High German translation by Notker III of St Gall (10th cent.; → Ottonian Renaissance). The second is the *Institutiones divinarum et saecularium litterarum* (AD 551–556) by Cassiodorus. The encyclopaedic section, above all, shaped the monastic educational ideal through its inclusion of theology, for which it also functioned as a propaedeutic. The third, the *Etymologiae* by Isidore of Seville (ca. AD 560–636), is concerned with the equally popular search for the 'true meaning' of words, also from a strictly religious perspective. It achieved an early (7th cent. in → IRELAND) and very wide dissemination (ca. 1,000 manuscripts; it served, e.g., as the model for the largest German collection of glosses, the *Summarium Heinrici*, ca. 11th cent.).

Warum follten auch die Regenten und Helden diefes hiftorifch-critifche Werf verächtlich halten, da es ja von den größeften Beyfpielen der Staatskunft und Tapferkeit, in alten und neuern Zeiten, wohlgegründete Nachrichten in fich hält? Der einzige Buchftab A, der in diefem erften Bande deffelben enthalten ift, befchreibt uns ja fchon den unüberwindlichen Heldenmuth Achills, die kluge Staatskunft des Agefilaus, den patriotifchen Eifer des Agis, den trotzigen Uebermuth des Ajar, die Gaftfreyheit und Freygebigkeit des Alcinous, die ftrenge Redlichkeit des Amphiaraus, den großen Verftand und die Glückfeligkeit Antipaters, das unfelige Ende des Unterdrückers der römifchen Freyheit Antonius, die Gnade gegen die Gelehrten bey dem Archelaus, das vollkommenfte Mufter der Gerechtigkeit an dem Ariftides, und die abfcheuliche Graufamkeit des hunnifchen Wüterichs, Attila; unzähliger andern, die minder berühmt geworden, zu gefchweigen.

Dedication to the Elector of Saxony

Beyond these, Boethius' great unfinished encyclopaedic project was also of significance.

2. EARLY MIDDLE AGES

On the basis of these works, the Early Middle Ages, by combining faith and knowledge, sought to order the details of the world (= Creation) towards a universal core of Christian theological ideas. While this purpose was served by an uncritical compilation of factual information, greater originality can be observed in the use of encyclopaedic methods such as allegoresis and → ETYMOLOGY, which constitute the link between the individual matter and its provider of meaning, the divine world order. This is the case, for instance, with De rerum naturis by Hrabanus Maurus (9th cent.), a work organised according to the principles of pastoral ministry. Both elements – the (rather meager) factual information and the method of interpretation – were encountered in the above-mentioned works of Late Antiquity, and consequently their systematic ordering principle was often copied along with everything else. Not only were alphabetical models from Antiquity rare and virtually inaccessible, they were also unsuitable for medieval purposes. With its alphabetical, factual lexicon style clearly standing in the ancient dictionary tradition, the Byzantine Suda (ca. 1000; approx. 31,000 headwords) remained an exception even in its own cultural sphere.

3. HIGH MIDDLE AGES/SCHOLASTICISM

The High Middle Ages applied a stricter separation between encyclopaedic works with a propaedeutic character (e.g. Specula) and those presenting a universal theological concept. An enormous increase in knowledge and in the number of theological and philosophical tools was the result, for which Aristotle and his school provided the original model. Their appreciation especially of factual knowledge now seemed an ideal attitude to adopt as factual knowledge itself was growing rapidly through new translations and precisely through the Arabic-Jewish transmission of Aristotle in the 12th/13th cents. (→ ARISTOTELIANISM). The theological context obviously remained all-important, as is evident in the summa literature, especially of Albertus Magnus and Thomas Aquinas, which reached a higher intellectual level than encyclopaedic literature. At this point, though, compilations began to emerge with

looser theological ties: the Compilatio de libris naturalibus (ca. 1240) drew from Aristotle and Arabic writers, and the curious Secretum secretorum was a widely-read Greek-Oriental pseudo-Aristotelian text. A similarly expanded range of material is presented in De proprietatibus rerum by Bartholomäus Anglicus (d. after 1250). Following the example of Albertus Magnus, Bartholomäus' work referred directly – not through the usual Late Antique Christian authors – to one of their main sources, the Naturalis historia by Pliny the Elder (d. in AD 79). It was still popular in the 16th cent. The development reached its peak in the Speculum maius by Vincent of Beauvais (ca. 1190–1264), with its large number of sources (ca. 2,000) and its broad scope. Divided into a speculum naturale, speculum doctrinale and speculum historiale (the authenticity of the speculum morale is disputed), its use continued far into the Early Modern period. This encyclopaedia was new, for instance, in that it 'no longer merely [served] the purpose of understanding, [but] its pragmatic use [became] itself the purpose of the work' ('nicht mehr nur dem Erkennen [diente, sondern] ihre pragmatische Nutzung – zum Gegenstand des Werkes [wurde]') [11].

In keeping with the general medieval tradition, however, the work failed to grasp Antiquity in its entirety while presenting a series of isolated phenomena. The Middle Ages engaged, above all, with biblical texts and – within the boundaries imposed by the theological and systematic focus of the work – with patristic and at times with pagan philosophical texts and ideas as well. In all other instances, the adoption of ancient knowledge was preferred over the gathering of empirical knowledge, which was as yet in its fledgling stages. Even though it was limited to the natural world, the search for empirical knowledge nevertheless gained a first foothold in the great encyclopaedic and scientific-methodological works (Opus maius, Opus minus, Opus tertium) of Roger Bacon (ca. 1219 – ca. 1292).

4. HUMANISM

Humanism, in its appreciation of (even pagan) Antiquity as much more than just a quarry of knowledge and an authority on factual knowledge but as a model for individual thought and action, did not produce a universal encyclopaedic work, a fact which may explain the long-standing and ever-more-anachronistic success of the Speculum maius. Admittedly, a new approach for criticising the traditional didactic institutions had to be developed first, and the time for major new collections of knowledge would not arrive until the → BAROQUE and the → ENLIGHTENMENT eras. Inititally there was a tendency to eschew the dead weight of abstract knowledge amassed in the Middle Ages and to seek instead the essential and the methodical, for example in the immediate, systematic treatment of ancient texts in the great linguistic thesauri. Robertus Stephanus' Thesaurus linguae latinae (1536; → THESAURUS LINGUAE LATINAE) and the Thesaurus linguae graecae by Henricus Stephanus (1575) were two important stepping stones on the way to the the alphabetical encyclopaedias of the future [12]. As early as the 14th/15th cents., a number of otherwise-conservative encyclopaedic works in Italy had already pointed in a new direction through their more pronounced, critical treatment of ancient history and myth. One example was Guglielmo da Pastrengo (ca. 1290–1362), a close associate of Petrarca; another was Domenico Bandini (between 1374 and 1418) [15].

C. Enlightenment

The old encyclopaedia reflected the theological goals of → Scholasticism; it was usually systematic, written in Latin and characterised by biblical and ancient content. Following the efforts of Francis Bacon (1561–1626), the new encyclopaedia of the → Enlightenment was supposed to realise practical as well as secular and emancipatory goals; its structuring principle was usually alphabetical; it was written in the vernacular and its content dominated by modern topics. This shift occurred in both the more academic sector (with precursors such as L. Moréri, *Grand dictionnaire historique ...*, 2 vols., 1674, many new editions; Bayle; Zedler) and in the fields of natural science and technology, which had seen a surge in interest following the rise of empiricism and rationalism in the 17th cent. The founding work of the French Enlightenment, Diderot's and d'Alembert's *Encyclopédie ou Dictionnaire raisonné des sciences, des arts et des métiers* (17 vols., 11 plate vols., 5 supplementary vols., 1751–1777), in its indebtedness to E. Chambers' *Cyclopedia, or an universal dictionary of arts and sciences* (2 vols., 1728), is a prime example of this modern type of encylopaedia. The new orientation is particularly apparent in the very carefully crafted vols. of plates.

While this change resulted in a much decreased amount of knowledge from and about Antiquity, it also signalled a change in the function of ancient material. An important forerunner of Enlightenment encyclopaedias – aside from the Alsted (see above) [8], which dissolved the medieval hierarchy of disciplines – was P. Bayle's *Dictionnaire historique et critique* (2 vols., 1695–1697, several new editions and translations). It broke with the tradition of an uncritical collection of material in favour of brief and critical articles with a programmatic, enlightened agenda. Unlike the humanists, Bayle no longer regarded the ancient authors simply as role models. Rather, he adopted their skepticism in his treatment of the modern world, and in doing so displayed his extraordinary familiarity with them [13. 280ff.]. The 18th cent., esp. Diderot and d'Alembert, found this skeptical and critical world view e.g. in Tacitus. Both Bayle's *Dictionnaire* and the *Encyclopédie* offer a 'dark' analysis of – in particular – contemporary politics in the spirit of the ancients (cf. [13. 362ff.]). Compared to Tacitus and Bayle, however, the *Encyclopédie* displays a much more positive, forward-looking perspective in line with the enlightened idea of progress. The perception of ancient figures had thus been changed from quarries of knowledge and Humanist role models to catalysts of thinking. This change

was later to be reflected more in pedagogical concepts than in encyclopaedias. Consequently, Antiquity remained a strong presence in these works, e.g. as a reservoir of examples or as an intellectual training ground, but in light of the economic and political situation at the time, it is hardly surprising that England – its philosophy, view of society and social architecture – became the real paradigm with its enlightened combination of practical and pedagogical elements for the progressive advancement of mankind. Direct discussion of ancient subjects was pushed into the background; the *Encyclopédie* offers only a selection of headwords dealing with Antiquity rather briefly while entries on people are usually lacking altogether (exceptions: e.g. Alexander the Great, Augustus).

In Germany, Zedler's *Großes vollständiges Universal-Lexicon aller Wissenschaften und Künste* (64 vols., 1732–1754) marked the beginning of the new age even prior to the *Encyclopédie*. It differed from the *Encyclopédie* not so much in its didactic intentions but rather in the exact, concise and objective presentation of the enormous amount of information on contemporary topics. Unlike the *Encyclopédie*, it is still usable today thanks to its inventory-like character [9]. In addition to the already low rate of straightforward articles on ancient subjects, this inventorising tendency reduced the significance of Antiquity as a thought and argumentational scheme even further in comparison with its French competitors. In the dedication to the 5th edition of the German translation of Bayle's *Dictionnaire*, published by J.Chr. Gottsched in 1741, the work is recommended to the Elector of Saxony especially on the merits of its articles on Antiquity, and Bayle's knowledge of ancient authors receives immediate praise in the introduction (fig. 1). The larger share of Gottsched's admiration, however, was reserved for the qualities outlined above: the leading scholars seem to have turned away from Antiquity to a greater degree than the educated classes in general, notwithstanding Gottsched's favourable view of of Antiquity as opposed to the 'barbarism of the middle centuries' ('Barbarei der mittleren Jahrhunderte').

D. Nineteenth and Twentieth Centuries
1. General 2. Academic Encyclopaedias
3. Conversation Lexica
4. Ideologically-Slanted Ecyclopaedias of the Twentieth Century 2. France

1. General

Two developments coincided at the end of the 19th cent.: a) the rise of the sciences and the corresponding explosion of knowledge put an end to the notion of a universal academic encyclopaedia; and b) the practical educational needs of the rising bourgeoisie led to the creation of the *Konversationslexikon*, the original prototype of most modern encyclopaedic dictionaries. In both instances, the occupation with Antiquity became once more a presentation of more or less self-evident knowledge, although to varying degrees.

2. ACADEMIC ENCYCLOPAEDIAS

Owing to the important role of Classical studies in the development of modern critical scholarship and certainly not least through the lasting influence of Humboldtian → NEO-HUMANISM, Antiquity filled a large amount of space in the most ambitious encyclopaedic project attempted by and for the academic world of the 19th cent., the *Allgemeine Enzyklopädie der Wissenschaften und Künste* (J.S. Ersch and J.G. Gruber (eds.), 167 vols., 1818–1889, unfinished), which contained contributions from the leading scholars of the time. The articles on Antiquity are often of a very high quality and they, too, allow insights into the academic developments of the period: one can detect an increasing trend from at first almost narrative and didactic entries towards major scholarly monographs, and towards a rather positivist accumulation of knowledge in a grand if not always consistent style. The article on Greece comprises eight volumes and is further enhanced by separate, substantial articles on individual phenomena of Greek Antiquity, e.g. a long article on Homer (again in a rather emphatic style) and another generous entry on the *Odyssey* – all this indicating more than anything a lack of moderation. The fact that the knowledge explosion and increasing positivism of the age defeated the ambition of the *Ersch und Gruber* may have contributed to the emergence of the great new specialised encyclopaedias. In the field of Classical Studies, for instance, the first edition of *Pauly's Realencylopädie* (see below) probably did not even match the length of the Antiquity section in *Ersch und Gruber*. It is interesting to observe that even medieval and modern Greece received the utmost attention, far exceeding that bestowed upon England and France. This avid interest may be explained by the contemporary climate of → PHIL-HELLENISM following the Greek war of independence. Although the work broke off with the letters L (section 2) and P (section 3) after the publication of 167 volumes – thus excluding Rome – *Ersch und Gruber* has remained an impressive and useful torso.

Greater success was reserved for academic encyclopaedias which sought to demonstrate their integrity by a solid academic stance and manner of presentation rather than exhaustive thoroughness. In the 19th cent. this holds true for several editions of the *Encyclopaedia Britannica* (the first appeared in 1768–1771; its scholarly character was maintained above all until the 11th edition of 1911) and the non-commercial *La grande ecyclopédie* (31 vols., 1886–1902), which differs from German works in its much stronger focus on Roman Antiquity (as is the case with the similarly voluminous but less academic *Grand dictionnaire universel du XIXe siècle*, published by P. Larousse in 15 vols., 1866–1888). In the 20th cent., this standard was met once more by the *Enciclopedia italiana* (see below).

3. CONVERSATION LEXICA

While the production of academic encyclopaedias with their broad presentation of material was henceforth confined to specialised fields, conversation lexica for the educated middle classes in the mould of the *Brockhaus* led the way to the practical reference work of the 20th cent. (*Brockhaus*: first edition under the title *Conversationslexikon mit vorzüglicher Rücksicht auf die gegenwärtigen Zeiten*, 6 vols., 1796–1811, 14 editions by the end of the 19th cent., six more in the 20th cent., varying titles, some including the term encyclopaedia from the 4th edition in 1918/19). As early as the middle of the century the still-lengthy sections on Antiquity had to yield more and more to other areas of public interest, as can be gleaned from the direction taken by progressive *Brockhaus* editions: the encyclopaedias grew in size but the sections on Antiquity did not grow proportionally or were even reduced. The strong surge in the demand for information especially on England (already apparent in the supplements to the first editions, vols. 1–4, 1819/1820) demonstrates that other concepts besides Neo-Humanism were now relevant – for obvious political and economic reasons. The decline in the share of ancient subjects slowed down in the second half of the 19th cent. The new competitor, *Meyers Konversations-Lexikon* (first edition with the title *Das große Conversationslexikon*, 46 vols., 1840–1855, further editions were reduced approximately by half), at first paid slightly more attention to Antiquity than the *Brockhaus* especially in the areas of history and myth, only to match the latter at the end of the century at a quantitative level comparable to that of late 20th-cent. editions – perhaps as a result of the Wilhelminian climate that was less friendly toward Antiquity. This is a surprising fact considering the development of schools in the last 100 years. It was accompanied by a trend towards objectification that anticipated the style of present-day encyclopaedias: clear factual information about everything including Antiquity. Among those who lost out as a result of these developments in the last ca. 130 years were Pericles, Alexander the Great, Aeneas, Cicero and Tacitus, while Zeus – who does not appear independently from 'Juppiter' until after 1850 –, Apollo, Achilles, Sophocles, Caesar, Augustus, Virgil and Justinian have held on to their positions quite comfortably, with Augustine even gaining ground. The modern German large-scale encyclopaedia (e.g. *Meyers enzyklopädisches Lexikon*, 25 vols., 1971–1979; *Brockhaus Enzyklopädie*, 24 vols., 1986–1994) thus pays no less attention to Antiquity than its precursors from 100 years ago, although this is not the case for similar works in the GDR.

4. IDEOLOGICALLY-SLANTED ECYCLOPAEDIAS OF THE TWENTIETH CENTURY

The era of totalitarian ideologies in the first half of the 20th cent. gave rise to a number of highly significant encyclopaedic works; pre-eminent among them were the *Great Soviet Encyclopaedia* (65 vols., 1926–1947) and especially the *Enciclopedia Italiana di Scienze, Lettere ed Arti* (35 vols., 1929–1949). Backed by the Italian government and the industrialist Giovanni Treccani, it marked the last successful attempt at a universal academic encyclopaedia. The tendency to emphasise

Italy's superiority is here revealed not so much in a clear ideological classification of the material as in a high standard of scholarship. The same is true for the at times exceedingly long articles on Antiquity. The ancient past presented a natural object of identification for the fascist state, whose 'greatness' it sought to emulate, above all, in its definition of the *Impero*. Surprisingly, this applied not only to Roman Antiquity but to Greek Antiquity as well (see, for instance, the major article 'Omero').

National Socialist Germany did not produce works of similar stature. While the 15th edition of *Der Große Brockhaus* (20 vols., 1928–1937) largely refused to surrender to the influence of → NATIONAL SOCIALISM, the 8th edition of *Meyers Lexikon* (8 vols., 1936–1942, unfinished) presents its material filtered through an ideology of race, which particularly dominates the major survey articles. In these, much is made of the negative influence of Roman Christian culture on Germany (vol. 2, 991f.) while, on the other hand, the exemplary (vol. 5, 627) character of the Greek development is stressed because it serves to illustrate the cultural rise of a closed 'Aryan' society; its decline is attributed to racial mixing (vol. 5, 227 and 331). However, Greek civilisation no longer provides a meaningful model here, least of all in its vast array of cultural achievements. This is apparent in the much-reduced articles on sub-items, with the tell-tale exception of the article on Alexander the Great. The presentation of Antiquity in the 8th edition of *Meyers Lexikon* offers a clear picture of the National Socialist view of humanity, society and history.

E. SPECIALISED ENCYCLOPAEDIAS

In Germany, from the middle of the 19th cent., the need for documentation and utilisation of the rapidly growing amount of material compiled by Classical scholars led to the creation of comprehensive specialised encyclopaedias – products of the expanding field of cultural-historical studies. The great language thesauri of the Renaissance can, in a certain sense, be regarded as their precursors (see above): provided with new explanations, these had been re-published again and again but could no longer satisfy the modern demands for exhaustive factual information. A major effort to produce a specialised encyclopaedia had met with failure in the 18th cent.: J.A.B. Bergsträsser, *Gesammeltes, vermehrtes und berichtigtes Realwörterbuch* ... (7 vols., 1772–1781; only A-equus). In France, a work of 37 vols. by F. Sabbathier (1766–1815) was completed, although there was a pronounced unevenness in its treatment of subjects: *Dictionnaire pour l'intelligence des auteurs classiques, grecs et latins*. The *Realencyclopädie der classischen Alterthumswissenschaft in alphabetischer Ordnung* (6 vols., in 9 parts), founded by August Pauly and completed by W.S. Teuffel between 1839 and 1852, was to become a seminal work. Pauly placed his work in the tradition of the great school encyclopaedias (e.g. B. Hederich's *Reales Schul-Lexicon*,

1717; C.Ph. Funke's *Neues Real-Schullexicon*, 5 vols., 1800–1805), but he also stressed the scholarly usefulness of the project in his 1837 preface. Because of this ambition and the advances made in Classical scholarship, the size of the work grew so quickly that it became seriously unbalanced, resulting in a second edition of vols. A and B as early as 1862. Pauly was probably encouraged in his undertaking by his friend August Memminger, who had worked on the *Ersch und Gruber* [1].

The first *Pauly* was clearly surpassed by the *Dictionnaire des Antiquités Grecques et Romaines* by Ch. Daremberg and E. Saglio (5 vols., in 10 parts 1873–1919) – its wealth of information in the areas covered is still useful today. But the topographical, literary and biographical articles missing in this work are a particular strength of the revised *Pauly*, begun by Georg Wissowa, continued by Wilhelm Kroll and Karl Mittelhaus and completed by Konrat Ziegler under the title *Paulys Real-Encyclopädie der classischen Altertumswissenschaft* (RE). It was published in 84 vols. between 1893 and 1980. In the preface, Wissowa spoke of the 'reproductive, summarising character' of the work which nevertheless 'creates something new in the summary' ('einen reproductiven, zusammenfassenden Charakter [des Werkes, der allerdings durch die] Zusammenfassung – etwas Neues schafft', p. III). The articles were to 'present and utilise all of the source material on a given subject, under careful consideration of the newer literature' ('das ganze für den Gegenstand vorliegende Quellenmaterial unter gewissenhafter Berücksichtigung der neueren Litteratur vorführen und verwerten', p. v), so as to record the expert knowledge accumulated in all areas of Classical scholarship. The decision to 'sacrifice balance of execution for the sake of quality' ('lieber die Gleichmässigkeit der Ausführung als ihre Güte preisgegeben', p. iv) was confirmed, in the end, in a negative but above all in a positive sense, even though the scope of the work grew four times larger than the promised 20 half-volumes, and it took eight times longer to complete than projected. As a result, this encyclopaedia forms a unique store of knowledge even when compared to specialised encyclopaedias in other disciplines, and it remains an indispensable academic tool to this day – a legacy from the peak of German Classical scholarship at the turn of the last century that will in all likelihood never be repeated. And yet it is also a veritable 'cathedral of positivism': in its deliberate atomisation of knowledge and the overall absence of framework articles (which had originally been envisioned), it displays an almost anti-encyclopaedic attitude. (A partially modernised and abridged version appeared 1964–1975 in five vols. as *Der kleine Pauly*.) The systematic *Handbuch der Altertumswissenschaft*, appearing since 1886, emerged from a similar concept of an 'encyclopaedic character', as the editor I. v. Müller states in his preface to the first volume(p. v). Originally planned and largely realised as a collection of handbooks, this corpus has managed – e.g. through revisions of individual parts –

to preserve its rank as a standard academic work to the present day.

The *Reallexikon für Antike und Christentum* (20 vols. as of 2004) has embraced a somewhat different approach. Founded by F.J. Dölger and from 1941 published by Th. Klauser, it is more than the fruit of a heightened interest in Christian Late Antiquity: although it refers to itself modestly as a non-judgemental collection of material and a scholarly tool, it forges bold paths into an expansive horizon of knowledge by means of frequently overlapping lines of inquiry, the use of modern terms as lemmata and a broad frame of reference.

The permeation of the material with modern terms (in survey articles) in conjunction with the presentation of traditional factual information is also the declared aim of *Der Neue Pauly. Enzyklopädie der Antike* (15 vols., 1996ff.). Volumes 13 to 15 attempt, for the first time, to cover lexically the reception-history of Antiquity as well as the history of Classical scholarship in response to an ever-growing interest expressed in recent years towards those aspects. Both signal a new orientation towards interdisciplinarity and a more widespread appeal of Classical scholarship, which in the past has all too often indulged in self-absorption during its most prolific periods.

→ Allegoresis; → Artes liberales; → Boethius; → Cassiodorus; → Encyclopaedia; → Enkyklios paideia; → Etymologica; → Isidorus [9]; → Plinius; → Quintilianus; → Suda; → Tacitus

→ EDUCATION/CULTURE; → FASCISM; → LEXICOGRAPHY

1 M. BALZERT, August von Pauly – Professor am Gymnasium illustre, in: Das Jahrbuch Ebelu 1996 (= Jahrbuch des Eberhard-Ludwigs-Gymnasiums Stuttgart), 123–125 2 H. CANCIK, Altertum und Antikerezeption im Spiegel der Geschichte der Realencyclopädie (1839–1993), in: Id., Antik – Modern. Beiträge zur römischen und deutschen Kulturgeschichte, 1998, 7–22   3 R. COLLISON, Encyclopaedias: Their History throughout the Ages, 1964 4 V. DIERSE, Enzyklopädie. Zur Geschichte eines philosophischen und wissenschaftstheoretischen Begriffs, 1977 5 F. M. EYBL et al. (eds.), Enzyklopädien der frühen Neuzeit, 1995   6 J. FONTAINE, s.v. Isidor von Sevilla, LMA 5, 677–680   7 J. HENNINGSEN, s.v. Enzyklopädie, in: Archiv für Begriffsgeschichte 10, 1996, 271–362   8 G. HUMMEL, s.v. Enzyklopädie, TRE 9, 716–742 9 B. KOSSMANN, Deutsche Universallexika des 18. Jahrhunderts, in: Archiv für Geschichte des Buchwesens 9, 1969, 1553–1596   10 CHR. MEIER, Grundzüge der mittelalterlichen Enzyklopädik, in: L. GRENZMANN, K. STACKMANN (eds.), Literatur und Laienbildung im Spätmittelalter und in der Reformationszeit, 1984, 467–500   11 Id., Vom homo caelestis zum homo faber, in: H. KELLER et al. (eds.), Pragmatische Schriftlichkeit im Mittelalter, 157–175   12 F. SCHALK, Einleitung in die Enzyklopädie der französischen Aufklärung, 1936   13 Id., Studien zur französischen Aufklärung, ²1977   14 W. SCHMIDT-BIGGEMANN, Topica universalis. Eine Modellgeschichte humanistischer und barocker Wissenschaft, 1983   15 J. VERGER et al., s.v. Enzyklopädie, Enzyklopädik, LMA 3, 2031–2039 16 G. A. ZISCHKA, Index Lexicorum, 1959

ADDITIONAL BIBLIOGRAPHY P. BINKLEY (ed.), Pre-Modern Encyclopaedic Texts: Proceedings of the Second COMERS Congress, Groningen, 1–4 July 1996, 1997 R. DARNTON, The Business of Enlightenment: A Publishing History of the Encyclopedie, 1775–1800, 1979 F. G. GENTRY, Renatus Gotthelf Löbel and the Conversationslexikon, in: K-H. J. SCHOEPS, C. J. WICKHAM (eds.), 'Was in den alten Büchern steht...': Neue Interpretationen von der Aufklärung zur Moderne. Festschrift für Reinhold Grimm, 1991, 99–123 R. YEO, Encyclopaedic Visions: Scientific Dictionaries and Enlightenment Culture, 2001
                                        JÜRGEN JÄGER

Enlightenment

A. ENLIGHTENMENT AS A EUROPEAN MOVEMENT
B. ENLIGHTENMENT AND THE RECEPTION OF ANTIQUITY   C. BASIC IDEAS AND PRINCIPLES

A. ENLIGHTENMENT AS A EUROPEAN MOVEMENT

The German word *Aufklärung* is a metaphor [33] that has equivalents in most European languages: in English, 'Enlightenment' has become customary, in French, *lumières*, in Italian, *illuminismo*, in Spanish, *ilustración*, in Dutch, *verlichting*. However, only in France and Germany were the terms *Aufklärung* and *lumières* actually used at the time. The terms in the other languages were later translations. In France the → QUERELLE DES ANCIENS ET DES MODERNES marked the beginning of the Enlightenment, set off by C. Perrault's poem *Le Siècle de Louis XIV* (1687) and the four books *Parallèle des Anciens et des Modernes* (Paris 1688, 1690, 1692, 1697). In England, the Enlightenment arrived with the 'Glorious Revolution' of 1688 and the Bill of Rights of 1689, the Toleration Act of 1689, and the *Epistola de tolerantia* by J. Locke (Gouda 1689), and in Germany with the influence of Chr. Thomasius around 1690; it ended with the French Revolution of 1789, which effectively spread the Enlightenment through the European political sphere after having determined the political reality in America in 1776 with the Declaration of Independence.

The Enlightenment can be divided into three phases: 1st phase (early Enlightenment, rationalism): J. Locke (1632–1704), P. Bayle (1647–1706), Chr. Thomasius (1655–1728), B. Le Bovier de Fontenelle (1657–1757), Chr. Wolff (1679–1754), C. de Montesquieu (1689–1755), esp. with *De l'esprit des lois* (Geneva 1748), Voltaire (1694–1778); 2nd phase (esp. empiricism, sensualism): J.J. Bodmer (1698–1783), J.Chr. Gottsched (1700–1766), J.J. Breitinger (1701–1776), G.L.L. Buffon (1707–1788), D. Hume (1711–1776), J.-J. Rousseau (1712–1778), D. Diderot (1713–1784), esp. with the *Encyclopédie* published jointly with d'Alembert from 1751, A.G. Baumgarten (1714–1762), É.B. Abbé de Condillac (1715–1780), J. le Rond d'Alembert (1717–1783), M. Mendelssohn (1729–1786); 3rd phase (late Enlightenment): P.H.T. d'Holbach (1723–1789), G.E. Lessing (1729–1781), I. Kant (1724–1804), A.R.J. Turgot (1727–1781), esp. with the *Discours sur les progrès successifs de l'esprit humain* of 1751–1753 (Paris 1808), Chr.M. Wieland (1733–1813), A. de Condorcet (1743–1794), e.g. with *Esquisse d'un tableau historique des progrès de l'esprit humain* (Paris 1795).

As a movement in cultural history, the Enlightenment was a phenomenon occurring throughout Europe [11; 13; 27] and spanning almost exactly the entire 18th cent. Although concentrated in England,→ FRANCE and → GERMANY, it also reached North America (American Declaration of Independence, 1776) as well as southern and eastern Europe. Since it became the dominant movement of the 18th cent., that century is rightfully called the era of the Enlightenment. And while it provided the signature ideas of the century, a number of simultaneous cultural trends stood in polar opposition to the Enlightenment or became its adversaries: Rococo, late Baroque traditions in music, art and architecture, but also – in Germany – → CLASSICISM, early Romanticism, idealism and → NEO-HUMANISM and, finally, religious, pseudo-religious and anti-rationalist movements such as Pietism, occultism, Storm and Stress and sentimentalism. Some of these, e.g. Storm and Stress or sentimentalism may very well be understood as emotional undercurrents or radicalised varieties of the Enlightenment.

B. ENLIGHTENMENT AND THE RECEPTION OF ANTIQUITY

As a philosophy, the Enlightenment did not construct a closed system; instead it developed an ensemble of ideas [14; 19; 23] which could vary between the individual phases and countries. Nevertheless, the representatives of the Enlightenment were conscious of the unity of their movement because they all shared a belief in reason as the founding principle in the development and perfection of the individual, society, the state and humanity. For one century, this optimism of reason had a strong mobilising effect. It opposed the social and political system out of strength, not weakness; it was decidedly eclectic [16] in its adherence to a method espoused by the philosophers of the early Imperial period such as Seneca und Plutarch: 'Wahre Aufklärung ist eklektisch. Sie prüft alles, und das Gute behält sie' ("True Enlightenment is eclectic. It examines everything and keeps the good") [28]. The article 'Eclecticisme' by D. Diderot in the *Encyclopédie* praises → ECLECTICISM: 'L'éclectique est un philosophe qui foulant aux piés le préjugé, la tradition, l'ancienneté, le consentement universel, l'autorité, en un mot tout ce qui subjuge la foule des esprits, ose penser de lui – même, remonter aux principes généraux les plus clairs, les examiner, les discuter, n'admettre rien que sur le témoignage de son expérience & de sa raison; & de toutes les philosophies, qu'il a analysées sans égard & sans partialité, s'en faire une particuliere & domestique qui lui appartienne: je dis une philosophie particuliere & domestique' ("The eclectic is a philosopher who stomps on prejudice, on tradition, on old customs, on general agreement, on authority, yes, on everything that subjugates most intellects, and who dares, therefore, to think independently, to refer to the clearest general principles, to examine them and to debate them, not to accept anything without consulting his experience and his reason, and to create a special philosophy uniquely his own from all philosophies which he has subjected to ruthless and unbiased analysis")[1; 5]. This eclecticism also guided the reception of Antiquity. As a result, Enlightenment views of Antiquity differed from those held during the → RENAISSANCE and → BAROQUE periods. While representatives of the latter regarded the authors and texts of Greco-Roman Antiquity as models to be revered without reservation, the Enlightenment did not hesitate to apply its fundamental principle of rational criticism [17. XI; 29] to appraising the value and validity of Antiquity [32]. Even though this criticism marked its incipient relativisation and historisation, it did not deprive Antiquity of its pre-eminent position over all other epochs in regard to the present, as it had shown the greatest progress on the way towards Enlightenment (Voltaire, *Le siècle de Louis XIV*, Berlin 1751; id., *Essay sur l'histoire génerale sur le moeurs*, Geneva 1756) [24. 356f.]. Similarly, in his *Journal meiner Reise aus dem Jahre 1769*, J.G. Herder granted Greek history a privileged status in the history of humanity. The justification for this privileged position, formulated to a large extent during the later stages of the German Enlightenment, then gave rise to a momentous construct in the philosophy of history: modern man is caught in a process of development which will lead him from the fragmentation of his powers in the present time to regain that wholeness once enjoyed in Antiquity, especially that of Greece (J.G. Herder, *Ideen zur Philosophie der Geschichte der Menschheit*, Riga 1784–1791; G.E. Lessing, *Die Erziehung des Menschengeschlechts*, Berlin 1780; in a similar vein, F. Schiller, *Über die ästhetische Erziehung des Menschen* in *Die Horen*, Tübingen 1795) [2. 316–319]. Although the Enlightenment thinkers presented themselves as innovators and, because of their criticism of tradition as the epitome of prejudice, assumed the role of the 'moderns' in the *Querelle*, they did not dismiss Antiquity in its entirety. Rather, they appreciated it from a critical perspective and made use of it for their own productivity. Even enlightened thinkers as radical as D. Diderot and G.E. Lessing still derived their arguments primarily from Greek models. In doing so, they often employed Antiquity provocatively as an antithesis to the civil and religious authorities of the time. In any case, the knowledge of the ancients had a stimulating effect. The study of the ancients did not result in the adoption of norms but it provided inspiration: 'Kurz! als Poetische Heuristik wollen wir die Mythologie der Alten studiren, um selbst Erfinder zu werden' ("In short! we will study the mythology of the ancients as poetic heuristics so that we can become inventors ourselves") [12. 444]. Most ideas and themes of the Enlightenment can therefore be traced back to Antiquity. The ancient system of poetic genres, for instance, still exerted a powerful influence on Enlightenment poetics. New literary forms such as the short narrative or the novel were adopted only reluctantly, as evidenced by J.Chr. Gottsched's *Versuch einer Critischen Dichtkunst* from the first edition (Leipzig 1730) to the fourth edition (Leipzig 1751).

However, the Enlightenment was not the only phenomenon in the history of ideas to remain under the spell of Antiquity – the same holds true for concurrent anti-rationalist movements. For the most part, the reception of Antiquity has always been characterised by ambivalence. It is therefore not surprising to find Socrates being hailed as the 'forefather' of all Enlightenment thinkers because of his unconditional employment of reason, and claimed by the Counter-Enlightenment for confessing his own ignorance (example: J.G. Hamann) [8].

C. Basic Ideas and Principles

The basic ideas and principles of the Enlightenment quickly exerted a great power of suggestion in the everyday world as well as in religious, scientific, literary/poetic and artistic environments. The term 'Enlightenment' became a buzzword lacking in conceptual clarity. At the end of the epoch, K.F. Bahrdt [3] was able to state: 'Das Wort Aufklärung ist jetzt in dem Munde so vieler Menschen, und wir haben gleichwohl noch nirgends einen Begriff gefunden, der ganz bestimmt und gehörig begrenzt gewesen wäre' ("the word Enlightenment is spoken by so many people today, but we have yet to find a concept that would be quite definite and properly defined").

The most important basic ideas and principles: 1) The idea of the Enlightenment. It is determined by the principle of reason. Although the concepts of Enlightenment and reason were understood differently and inconsistently – cf. G.E. Lessing, *Minna von Barnhelm* 2,9: 'Aber lassen Sie doch hören, wie vernünftig diese Vernunft' ("But let us hear how reasonable this reason") – the unity of Enlightenment and reason was undisputed. Enlightenment was understood as the correct use of intellect or reason [31]. At the end of the Enlightenment, the most conclusive definition of the term was provided by I. Kant (*Was ist Aufklärung?*, *Berlinische Monatsschrift* 1784): 'Aufklärung ist der Ausgang des Menschen aus seiner selbstverschuldeten Unmündigkeit. Unmündigkeit ist das Unvermögen, sich seines Verstandes ohne Leitung eines anderen zu bedienen. Selbstverschuldet ist diese Unmündigkeit, wenn die Ursache derselben nicht am Mangel des Verstandes, sondern der Entschließung und des Mutes liegt, sich seiner ohne Leitung eines anderen zu bedienen. Sapere aude! Habe den Mut, dich deines eigenen Verstandes zu bedienen! ist also der Wahlspruch der Aufklärung '("Enlightenment is man's emergence from his self-imposed tutelage. Tutelage is the inability to use one's reason without the guidance of another. This tutelage is self-imposed when its cause does not lie in a lack of reason but in a lack of resolution and courage to use it

without the guidance of another. Sapere aude! Have the courage to use your own reason is therefore the motto of the Enlightenment") [15. 444]. Through the Early Modern philosophy of reason, radicalised by Descartes, the Enlightenment concept of reason harks back to the Classical Greek philosophy of reason that had reached its first peak in Plato and in the figure of the Platonic Socrates. The Enlightenment philosophers regarded this Platonic Socrates as their ancestor; he was seen as the first to have endeavoured and achieved the validation of certain categories of knowledge and standards of behaviour through reason alone. Thus, the era of the Enlightenment was commonly referred to not only as a 'siècle philosophique' but also as a 'Socratic century'. [4; 9].

The concept of reason was implemented as a structural principle in every possible realm: from literature, art, science, religion, law and politics to social and everyday matters. The subsequent discovery of this concept in Antiquity created new contexts for its reception, giving rise to further ideas and principles.

2) The idea of a rational and natural religion. It was first developed in England under the term deism and became the basis of the religious articles in the *Encyclopédie*, most of which were written by D. Diderot; the following, however, by E.-F. Mallet: 'Le nom de Déistes est donné ... à ces sortes de personnes qui ... rejettent toute révélation comme une pure fiction, & ne croyent que ce qu'ils reconnoissent par les lumieres naturelles, & que ce qui est crû dans toute religion, un Dieu, une providence, une vie future, des récompenses & des châtimens pour les bons & pour les méchans' ("The name deists applies primarily to persons ... who ... dismiss any kind of revelation as mere fiction and who only believe in that which they can recognise based on natural insights and what every religion believes, and that is in a God, a destiny, an afterlife, rewards and punishments for the good and the bad", see 'Déistes': [1. vol. 4]). In contrast to England and France, deism found few outspoken proponents in Germany (H.S. Reimarus). As a religion of reason, it became a more or less explicit adversary of Christianity as a religion of revelation and came under suspicion of heresy; at the very least, its adherents were defamed as 'freethinkers'. Essentially, the idea of deism (as defined above) is a selective reformulation of Plutarch's (ca. 46 – after 120) philosophy of religion, which is characterised by Middle Platonic and Stoic elements [25]. The enemy of a rational religion is superstition because it is an exaggeration of religion (with phenomena such as church rites, magic, astrology, belief in witches or ghosts). Diderot's explanation relies heavily on Plutarch's term δεισιδαιμονία (*deisidaimonía*), from his Περὶ δεισιδαιμονίας (*Perí deisidaimonías*) [25. 411f.]. And just as the Greek philosopher of religion regarded superstition as worse than atheism, L. de Jaucourt writes in the *Encyclopédie* article on 'Superstition' [1. vol. 15]: 'c'est le plus terrible fléau de l'humanité. L'athéisme même (c'est tout dire) ne détruit point cependant les sentimens naturels, ne

porte aucune atteinte aux lois, ni aux mœurs du peuple; mais la superstition est un tyran despotique qui fait tout céder à ses chimères' ("It is the most terrible plague of humanity. Not even atheism (this says it all) destroys natural feelings, nor does it offend the laws and customs of the people; but superstition is a despotic tyrant capable of imposing its delusions on everything").

Although the deists among the Enlightenment thinkers emphatically distanced themselves from atheism, deism had gained many footholds in the religious criticism of the time. It was P.H.T. d'Holbach who, in his *Système de la nature* (Amsterdam 1770), finally combined the various approaches in a consistently materialistic atheism, supported by the example of ancient materialism (Epicurus and Lucretius).

3) The idea that rational knowledge is empirical knowledge. Since the world was created according to the principles of reason, Enlightenment holds that it can be understood through an empirical and experimental science based on the rules of reason. While this insight in the name of progress clearly identified the Enlightenment thinkers as 'moderns', they remained open to the achievements of the 'ancients'', as these had been gained in accordance with modern rules and could be played off against faulty modern methods: "The ancients, to whom we deem ourselves superior in the sciences because we find it easier and more convenient to claim our advantage than to read them, have by no means neglected experimental physics as we commonly like to imagine; instead, they have realised early on that observation and experience are the only means of understanding nature. The works of Hippocrates alone would suffice to show what type of spirit guided the philosophers of old. In place of the ridiculous, if not murderous systems that have been brought forth by modern medicine only to be condemned later we find in Hippocrates splendidly observed facts that he brought in accord with one another; one also finds a system of observations that has been the foundation of medicine to this day and will probably continue to be its foundation forever" (see 'Experimentel': [1. vol. 6]).

4) The idea of the usefulness of knowledge. The goal of science should not be theory but practice and usefulness: 'Der Mensch ward zum Thun und nicht zum Vernünfteln erschaffen' ("Man was created for action, not theorising") [20. 155]. Philosophy is therefore not an end in itself but is supposed to be useful for – individual, social, and political – life. In stressing practical usefulness, the early Enlightenment distanced itself from the philosophy of reason, thus initiating the turn from metaphysics and theology towards anthropology. In Germany, it was mainly Chr. Thomasius who advocated the primacy of action over insight, e.g. in his *Einleitung zur Sittenlehre* (Halle 1692). Early Enlightenment thinkers – such as Thomasius – regarded the Athenian philosopher Socrates as their ancestor because he had initiated the transition from pre-Socratic theoretical philosophy to practical philosophy. And they sought to bolster their assessment with the now-classic

characterisation from Cicero's *Tusculanae disputationes* (5,4,10): 'Socrates ... primus philosophiam devocavit e caelo et in urbibus conlocavit et in domus etiam introduxit et coegit de vita et moribus rebusque bonis et malis quaerere' ("Socrates was the first to call philosophy down from the heavens; he placed it in the cities and introduced it into homes, and he compelled man to enquire about life and ethics, as well as good and evil"). While the new philosophers felt at one with Socrates in their philosophical method, in terms of content they were more in tune with the moral teachings of Plato [30], Seneca and Plutarch. Perfectly suited to the new age, these were rational and at the same time – like Plutarch and Seneca themselves – eclectic; yet they attacked the idea of learnedness for its own sake. They approved only of knowledge that "nourished" *virtus* (Sen. Ep. 88).

For the philosophers, books and journals in addition to university instruction became the most important media for the dissemination of enlightened ideas. Popularisation was the declared goal. First appearing in 1751, one factor not to be underestimated in the communication of Enlightenment ideas was the *Encyclopédie*. Its publication history reveals the more or less honourable means with which Enlightenment thinkers pursued their ambitions [6]. A new type of man of letters emerged who worked from the 'underground' to liaise between philosophy and the unrest on the streets [7]. The philosophers received support from the writers of fiction, who in many ways adopted the cause of the Enlightenment and openly propagated enlightened ideas. Some philosophers like Voltaire and D. Diderot even became literary authors themselves. Literature was devised programmatically for those without a philosophical education, in a marked departure from the exclusive character it had enjoyed during the Baroque era: 'Die gründliche Sittenlehre ist für den großen Haufen der Menschen viel zu mager und zu trocken. Denn die rechte Schärfe in Vernunftschlüssen ist nicht für den gemeinen Verstand unstudirter Leute. Die nackte Wahrheit gefällt ihnen nicht: es müssen schon philosophische Köpfe seyn, die sich daran vergnügen sollen. Die Historie aber, so angenehm sie selbst den Ungelehrten zu lesen ist, so wenig ist sie ihm erbaulich. Die Poesie hergegen ist so erbaulich, als die Morale, und so angenehm, als die Historie; sie lehret und belustiget, und schicket sich für Gelehrte und Ungelehrte: darunter jene die besondere Geschicklichkeit der Poeten als eines künstlichen Nachahmers der Natur bewundern, diese hergegen einen beliebten und lehrreichen Zeitvertreib in seinen Gedichten finden' ("An exhaustive ethics is much too dry and meagre for the large mass of humanity. The proper clarity of rational conclusions is not for the common mind of unlearned people. They do not like the naked truth: it takes a philosophical mind to find pleasure in it. History, on the other hand, is as pleasant to read for the unlearned as it is un-edifying. Poetry, however, is as edifying as moral instruction and as pleasant as history; it educates and entertains, and is proper for the learned and unlearned alike: the former admiring the special skill of the poet as an artistic imitator of nature, the latter finding a beloved and instructive pastime in his poems") [10. 167]. Regarding the intended effect of literature, the preferred stance was to invoke Horace's phrase from his *Ars poetica* (333f.): 'aut prodesse volunt aut delectare poetae/aut simul et iucunda et idonea dicere vitae' ("poets want either to be useful or delightful or want to say something pleasant and appropriate for life"), although *prodesse* was usually preferred, or *delectare* became a tool for *prodesse*. It is therefore no coincidence that J.Chr. Gottsched begins his *Critische Dichtkunst* not with an introduction but with a translation and explanation of the *Ars poetica*.

Notwithstanding the fact that new genres grew more important, it was primarily the old genres which, in the service of the Enlightenment, made education according to the rules of reason their central concern [2]. In practice as much as in theory, ancient traditions remained largely in place. In the realm of theory, the *Critische Dichtkunst* by Gottsched (Leipzig 1730, ⁴1751) was the most decisive attempt to measure the ancient genres against Enlightenment ideas [2. 70f.], with the aim to preserve their usefulness for the present. The biggest challenge both in theory and practice was posed by → TRAGEDY: its specific task of evoking fear (*phóbos*) and pity or sorrow (*éleos*), stated again and again since Aristotle (Aristot. Poet. 1449 b24–27), stood at odds with the rational thinking of the Enlightenment [21], and it dominated the contemporary debate in the theory of drama. While Gottsched regarded affects as components to further the educational purpose of tragedy, Lessing developed an aesthetic of pity, which defined the function of tragedy: 'Verwandlung der Leidenschaften in tugendhafte Fertigkeiten' ("transformation of the passions into virtuous skills", *Hamburgische Dramaturgie*, 78. Stück) [22].

5) The idea of natural rights. Enlightenment thinking was governed by the idea of natural rights as rights of reason. It influenced the American (1776) and French Revolutions (1789) in equal measure. One particular notion – the freedom and equality of all people – was the central element of these natural rights. As human rights or basic rights, they have been incorporated into modern constitutional texts.

The philosophical discourse of the Enlightenment received most of its impulses from Neo-Stoicism (e.g. Pufendorf, *De iure naturae et gentium*, Lund 1672, Frankfurt 1684) and thus, whether directly or indirectly, ancient Stoicism played a part as well [26]. In Germany, efforts to propagate the political implications of the doctrine of natural rights were led by Chr. Thomasius (*Fundamenta juris naturae et gentium*, Halle/Leipzig ⁴1718) [18]. The *Encyclopédie* introduced the notion of natural rights in France (explicitly in the articles 'Droit naturel', 'Egalité naturelle', 'Esclavage', all in vol. 5; 'Homme', 'Intolérance', both in vol. 8; and 'Liberté naturelle', vol. 9). Against the backdrop

of the philosophical debate and British constitutional reality (Bill of Rights, 1689), natural rights played a key part in the drafting of the Virginia Declaration of Rights (12.6.1776). It, in turn, became the model for civil and human rights catalogues in the United States and for the *Déclaration des droits de l'homme et du citoyen* (26.8.1789) at the beginning of the French Revolution. While the Virginia Declaration of Rights states that 'all men are by nature equally free and independent', the French declaration opens with (art. 1):' Les hommes naissent et demeurent libres et égaux en droits'. With these declarations natural rights, formerly a matter of philosophical discourse, gained the status of positive law.

These human rights are not founded in Christianity but are based on ancient Stoicism in particular and on Roman law [5]. They were mediated through Neo-Stoicism and modern Roman law as the law of the land. According to Stoic anthropology, all humans are equal because they partake of the rationality of the universe; this makes all humans related to each other. At the beginning of history, this equality did exist – an expression of the natural state of man, in which human beings were happy: 'in commune rerum natura fruebantur: sufficiebat illa ut parens ita tutela omnium, haec erat publicarum opum secura possessio. Quidni ego illud locupletissimum mortalium genus dixerim, in quo pauperem invenire non posses' ("The gifts of nature were enjoyed together: like a mother, nature cared for the protection of all, she was the guarantor for the assured possession by all of the common resources. Am I wrong to call that race the richest on earth, since no poverty could be seen among them", Sen. Ep. 90,38). This idea of a natural state became productive in J.-J. Rousseau. The justification of freedom and equality based on natural rights was adopted into Roman law (Dig. 1,1,9), so that it could declare that slavery was 'contra naturam' ("against nature", Dig. 1,5,4). Elsewhere, more positive statements confirm this assessment: 'Iure enim naturali ab initio omnes homines liberi nascebantur' ("because all humans are born free from the beginning according to natural law", Inst. 1,2,2) and 'quod ad ius naturale attinet, omnes homines aequales sunt' ("concerning natural law, all humans are equal", Dig. 50,17,32). The exact same phraseology was chosen for the French *Déclaration*. Due to the fact that these natural rights principles shaped positive law, the Enlightenment became extraordinarily significant in social and political terms, thus fulfilling its own requirement of practical applicability.

→ Superstitio

→ HUMAN RIGHTS; → PHILHELLENISM; → REVOLUTION; → ROMAN LAW; → STOICISM

SOURCES 1 D. DIDEROT, J. LE ROND D'ALEMBERT (eds.), Encyclopédie ou dictionnaire raisonné des sciences, des arts e des métiers, par une société de gens de lettres, 17 vols., Paris 1751–1772, ²1985 (German trans. of selected articles in: TH. LÜCKE, Artikel der von Diderot und d'Alembert herausgegebenen Enzyklopädie, ²1985 (Engl. trans. Encyclopedia: Selections, N. S. HOYT, TH. CASSI-

RER (eds.), 1965. Also: S. J. GENDZIER (ed. and trans.), Denis Diderot's The Encyclopedia: Selections, 1967) URL http://portail.atilf.fr/encyclopedie/Formulaire-de-recherche.htm

LITERATURE   2 P.-A. ALT, Aufklärung, 1996   3 K. F. BAHRDT, Über Aufklärung und die Beförderungsmittel derselben, Leipzig 1789, 3 (response to a footnote by J.F. Zöllner in: Berlinische Monatsschrift, vol. 2, 1783: 'Was ist Aufklärung?')   4 B. BÖHM, Sokrates im 18. Jahrhundert. Studien zum Werdegang des modernen Persönlichkeitsbewußtseins, 1929   5 H. CANCIK, Gleichheit und Freiheit. Die antiken Grundlagen der Menschenrechte (1983), in: Id. (ed.), Antik – Modern. Beiträge zur römischen und deutschen Kulturgeschichte, 1998, 293–316   6 R. DARNTON, The Business of the Enlightenment, 1979   7 Id., The Literary Underground of the Old Regime, 1982   8 K. DÖRING, Sokrates, die Sokratiker und die von ihnen begründeten Traditionen, GGPh2, vol. 2/1, 1998, 172–174   9 G. FUNCKE, Einleitung, in: Id. (ed.), Aufklärung. In ausgewählten Texten dargestellt, 1963, 10ff.   10 J. CHR. GOTTSCHED, Versuch einer Critischen Dichtkunst, Leipzig ⁴1751 (facsimile reprint 1962)   11 N. HAMPSON, The Enlightenment, 1968   12 J. G. HERDER, Kritische Wälder, in: B. SUPHAN (ed.), Sämmtliche Werke 1, Berlin 1877   13 W. HINCK, Europäische Aufklärung, vol. 1, 1974   14 N. HINSKE, Die tragenden Grundideen der deutschen Aufklärung. Versuch einer Typologie, in: R. CIAFARDONE (ed.), Die Philosophie der deutschen Aufklärung. Texte und Darstellung. Deutsche Bearbeitung von N. HINSKE und R. SPECHT, 1990, 407–458 (orig. L'illuminismo tedesco)   15 Id. (ed.), Was ist Aufklärung? Beiträge aus der Berlinischen Monatsschrift, ⁴1990   16 H. HOLZHEY, Philosophie als Eklektik, in: Studia Leibnitiana 15, 1983, 19–29   17 I. KANT, Unser Zeitalter ist das eigentliche Zeitalter der Kritik, in: Id., Kritik der reinen Vernunft, Riga 1781 (⁵1975)   18 D. KLIPPEL, Politische Freiheit und Freiheitsrechte im deutschen Naturrecht des 18. Jahrhunderts, 1976   19 G. KURZ, 'Aber lassen Sie doch hören, wie vernünftig diese Vernunft...' Perspektiven der Aufklärung in Deutschland, in: A. MALER, A. SAN MIGUEL, R. SCHWADERER (eds.), Europäische Aspekte der Aufklärung, 1998, 13–23   20 G. E. LESSING, Gedanken über die Herrenhuter (1750), in: Id., Sämtliche Werke, K. LACHMANN, F. MUNCKER (eds.), vol. 14, Leipzig ³1898   21 M. LUSERKE, Die Bändigung der wilden Seele. Literatur und Leidenschaft in der Aufklärung, 1995   22 Id. (ed.), Die Aristotelische Katharsis. Dokumente ihrer Deutung im 19. und 20. Jahrhundert, 1991   23 R. MORTIER, Varianten der europäischen Aufklärung, in: A. MALER, A. SAN MIGUEL, R. SCHWADERER (eds.), Europäische Aspekte der Aufklärung, 1998, 25–36   24 U. MUHLACK, Geschichtswissenschaft im Humanismus und in der Aufklärung. Die Vorgeschichte des Historismus, 1991   25 NILSSON, GGR, vol. 2, 402–413   26 G. OESTREICH, Antiker Geist und moderner Staat bei Justus Lipsius (1547–1606). Der Neustoizismus als politische Bewegung, 1989   27 R. POMEAU, L'Europe des Lumières, 1966, ²1982   28 J. W. RECHE, Vermischte Papiere. Für Westphalens Leser. Zur Beförderung wahrer Aufklärung und Menschlichkeit, vol. 1, Düsseldorf 1790, 188f.   29 F. SCHALK, s.v. Aufklärung, HWdPh 1, 622f.   30 J. SCHAPP, Moral und Recht. Grundzüge einer Philosophie des Rechts, 1994   31 W. SCHNEIDERS, Die wahre Aufklärung. Zum Selbstverständnis der deutschen Aufklärung, 1974   32 A. WETTERER, Publikumsbezug und Wahrheitsanspruch. Der Widerspruch zwischen rhetori-

schem Ansatz und philosophischem Anspruch bei Gottsched und den Schweizern, 1981, 24f.   33 F. WOLFZETTEL, Zur Metaphorik der Renaissance in der französischen Literaturgeschichtsschreibung der Romantik, in: H. KRAUSS (ed.), Offene Gefüge. Festschrift F. Nies, 1994, 101–116

ADDITIONAL BIBLIOGRAPHY H. S. COMMAGER, The Empire of Reason: How Europe Imagined and America Realized the Enlightenment, 1977; P. GAY, Age of Enlightenment, 1966; Id., The Enlightenment, an Interpretation, 1966–1969; A. C. KORS (ed.), Encyclopedia of the Enlightenment, 2003; H. F. MAY, The Enlightenment in America, 1976; E. VOEGELIN, From Enlightenment to Revolution, 1975   MANFRED LANDFESTER

Ephesus

A. 19TH CENTURY UNTIL 1918   B. THE PERIOD BETWEEN THE WARS UNTIL THE END OF THE 1950S C. 1960 TO 1986   D. 1987 TO 1997   E. MOST RECENT ACTIVITIES

A. 19TH CENTURY UNTIL 1918

In 1893 O. Benndorf received the commission from the Imperial Austro-Hungarian Ministry of Education to propose an excavation project abroad. Austria-Hungary thereby joined, if only belatedly, the group of European major powers who were competing with each other in archaeological investigations of the Mediterranean area. Benndorf's choice was Ephesus (E.) in the territory of the neighbouring Ottoman Empire, which as the capital of the Roman province of Asia had never sunk into complete obscurity. E. had become a focus of research interest primarily through the investigations of E. Falkener around the middle of the 19th cent., and through the excavations of J. T. Wood, who had uncovered a series of buildings during his seven-year search (ending in 1869) for the Temple of Artemis (→ DIANA OF EPHESUS), one of the Seven Wonders of the World.

As an initial project, a follow-up investigation into the Artemesium was carried out in 1895. Until 1913 excavations and investigations of a series of projects in the area which had been purchased between the harbour and the agora (figs. 1 and 2) were carried out under the direction of Otto Benndorf and Rudolf Heberdey. G. Niemann, along with W. Wilberg, completed a large number of extremely valuable drawings, from an artistic viewpoint, of reconstructions for nearly all the exposed buildings. A. Schindler produced a map of E. and surrounding areas, J. Keil and F. Knoll attempted to clarify the periods of construction for the Church of the Virgin, and P. Forchheimer investigated the ancient water-supply system. Further examples are the three harbour gates, the harbour gymnasium, the agora and Celsus Library on the south side, and the theatre.

B. THE PERIOD BETWEEN THE WARS UNTIL THE END OF THE 1950S

The collapse of the monarchy and national economy, as well as the international Depression, were the

Fig. 1: Site in the level port area in 1906 after the discovery of the Celsus library (1903) and before the excavations of the Agora

Fig. 2: Heroon and Octagon after their discovery in 1904

Fig. 3:
Excavation
of the Temple
of Hadrian on
Curetes Street
in 1956

worst possible conditions for the continuation of re-search activity between the wars under the direction of Josef Keil (1926–35). At the same time, the excavation of large sites such as the great gymnasia had begun. Driven by those providing the funding, the Christian sites of the Cemetery of the Seven Sleepers and the Basi-lica of St. John were studied. The search for the ancient Ionian town and the Parthian Monument had led by chance to the uncovering of several buildings such as the temple of Domitian. M. Theuer and F. Miltner led a series of excavation projects, while H. Hörmann worked at the Basilica of St. John, and with the exami-nation of the Belevi Mausoleum, another monument in the broader vicinity of E. was included.

Following the Second World War, after an interrup-tion of 19 years, Curetes Street, which led uphill, was chosen for the resumption of the work. Under the direc-tion of Franz Miltner (1954–58), a vigorous start was made on the first anastyloses, notably of the temple of Hadrian (fig. 3) and the Basilica of St. John. With these exemplary reconstructions and with Curetes Street, which made clear the urbanistic connexion between the agora and the public marketplace, tourists could now obtain a new, three-dimensional impression of the buildings and of an important arterial road.

A focus of the operations was the investigation of the Byzantine town. The huge complex of the Scholasticia Thermae (Varius Baths) had remained in use until Byzantine times and was probably restored after an earthquake in the 4th cent. by the Christian woman Scholasticia. Since 1956 an *insula* on the northern slope of Bülbül Dağ, known as *Hanghaus* 1 (house on the slope), was uncovered. On the northern side of this fre-quently rebuilt four-storey house, a broad colonnade extends along Curetes Street, to the rear of which are barrel-vaulted taverns. Further excavation on the upper

part of the marketplace has revealed the prytaneion, the town's religious centre, in which three statues of Arte-mis have been found.

C. 1960 TO 1986

The director of excavations Fritz Eichler (1960–68), while not an excavator himself, did establish several long-term digging projects. Those already begun on Domitian's square and road were completed. A. Bammer provided architectural models of the Mem-mium and Pollio buildings and the Pollio Nymphaeum, all strongly influenced by Bammer's personal creative will in the style of the period. Once the work in the Artemesium had been resumed after a 70–year inter-ruption, Bammer succeeded in discovering the long sought-after altar. W. Alzinger concentrated his re-search on the public marketplace and the prytaneion. On the southwestern side of the square G. Langmann excavated the moated palace of Laecanius Bassus. H. Vetters continued the excavation of *Hanghaus* 1, and unearthed the entire *insula* with its large, magnificently appointed banqueting hall and other smaller dwellings either with a peristyle courtyard or with simple open courts.

Under the directorship of Hermann Vetters (1969–86), the excavations became a large-scale undertaking. At the same time, together with two major projects in the conservation of ancient monuments, there was a new emphasis on providing visual objects for the pub-lic. V. M. Strocka led the archaeological research on the anastylosis of the Celsus Library, the reconstruction of which was undertaken by F. Hueber, and G. Wiplinger erected a protective roof over the first and second apart-ments in *Hanghaus* 2. Alzinger continued to investigate the marketplace, and supervised another project with the Belevi Mausoleum. In the Artemesium Bammer uncovered a hekatompedos between the altar and the temple. In *Hanghaus* 2 the connexion to Curetes Street was established in 1983, and on three terraces a total of seven large apartments were excavated, the largest portion being the richly furnished ceremonial dwelling of G. Fl. Furius Aptus, the priest of Dionysus. Since 1978 K. Herold has directed the restoration of the murals and mosaics, published by Strocka and W. Jobst.

S. Karwiese directed a whole series of investigations in the Rock Temple, on the acropolis and in the Olympieion. Jobst examined the Byzantine church in the eastern gymnasium and the so-called auditorium on Library Square. G. Langmann began deeper excavations on the agora and unearthed the archaic processional road with its graves. G. Seiterle conducted excavations at the Magnesian Gate, D. Knibbe continued to examine all the inscriptions, and H. Thür worked on the architectural history of Hadrian's Gate. In addition, several projects were initiated to examine individual groups of materials.

D. 1987 TO 1997

The large team led by excavation directors Gerhard Langmann (1987–92) and Stefan Karwiese (1993–97) was able to work using modern methods and thus could formulate old questions in a new manner. To a far greater extent emphasis was now on interdisciplinary research. Bammer continued his research in the Artemesium, where he concentrated above all on the central section in the middle of the temple, while U. Muss worked on the altar. Karwiese directed excavations in the Church of the Virgin and in the Episcopium. He also carried out work on two new major projects: in the stadium two stairways were uncovered to the north, as well as a Byzantine church in the north side's barrel-vaulted area, while in the case of the theatre's staircases, it was now evident that they had originally been vaulted. Langmann investigated ancient Smyrna with deeper excavations under the agora, and carried out additional investigations in the temenos of the Serapeion. Both projects were continued by P. Scherer. A smaller project was the examination of the quayside wall in the harbour. C. Lang directed further investigations in *Hanghaus* 1 and R. Meric unearthed a fountain in the public marketplace. Knibbe completed examination of the Stoa of Damianus. W. Oberleitner resumed research into the Parthian Monument. Having completed the Gate of Macaeus and Mithridates, Hueber took up work on further anastyloses with the Neronian hall and Hadrian's Gate. Thür undertook an architectural-historical investigation of the Heroon and the Octagon. The systematic evaluation of the finds at the various excavation sites was intensified.

E. MOST RECENT ACTIVITIES

Under the Institute's current director, Fritz Krinzinger, who has also been director of excavations since 1998, the emphasis, since 1995, has been upon the scientific evaluation of finds in the E. excavations. At present, with the support of the *Fonds zur Förderung der Wissenschaftlichen Forschung*, seven projects are in progress. The aim of these investigations is to complete the publication of materials relating to earlier excavations. In the process, through intensive examination of what remains of the buildings, and by use of probes, it has been possible, especially in the case of the previously studied apartments of *Hanghaus* 2, to clarify the sequence of construction in individual periods and to propose new dates. A further focus is the roofing over of *Hanghaus* 2, the detailed planning for which is nearly complete. The guiding idea for this protective covering was the development of a lightweight construction in the spirit of contemporary design. The project's construction (by O. Häuselmayer and W. Ziesel) consists of only three materials: a pre-fabricated support structure made of stainless Nirosta steel, a translucent and extremely lightweight roof, and an outer facade made of Lexan ribbing Greatest consideration was given to climate control in the covered space.

→ AUSTRIA

1 G. WIPLINGER, G. WLACH, 100 Jahre Österreichische Forschungen in Ephesus, 1995   2 T. WOHLERS-SCHARF, Die Forschungsgeschichte von Ephesus, 1995
3 Ongoing annual excavation reports in: JÖAI 1 (1898)–66 (1997) and AAWW 34 (1897)–125 (1989)
4 Publications and monographs relating to excavation in: FiE 1–12, 1906–1996.   GILBERT WIPLINGER

Epic
I. ITALY AND FRANCE

I. ITALY AND FRANCE
A. THE MIDDLE AGES   B. THE RENAISSANCE
C. FROM THE BAROQUE TO NEOCLASSICISM
D. FROM ROMANTIC TO (POST-)MODERN

A. THE MIDDLE AGES
Of the Classical epic poets the Middle Ages knew Homer by name, but his work was unknown. Virgil, on the other hand, was studied in the schools, as were Statius and Lucan [17. 27ff.]. Ovid's *Metamorphoses*, still viewed in the Renaissance to an extent as an epic, enjoyed a broadly based reception.

The Classical genres did not represent any system of valid norms of discourse for medieval Romance literature. Even if the author(s) of the Old French *Song of Roland* had read Virgil as a 'school text', the work follows the constitutive rules of the Classical epic just as little as does the genre of the *chanson de geste* as a whole [16. 281 and 272f.]. The same applies to the courtly romance, including the so-called Classical romance, which in terms of content draws exclusively upon Classical literature (and not just the epic). And even in the *Divina Commedia*, in which Virgil serves as Dante's 'maestro", 'and where the other-world journey constitutes an explicit intertextual reference to the sixth book of the *Aeneid*, the Classical epic is not used as a systematic point of reference. There are, however, formal links to the Classical tradition in the Biblical Epic after Juvencus (4th cent. AD).

B. The Renaissance
I. Italy II. Ibero-Romania III. Germany IV. The Anglo-Saxon Nations

I. Italy

From the time of Boccaccio and Petrarch, Homer was read once again in the Latin translation of Leonzio Pilato (d. 1365). Partial translations of the *Iliad* into Latin were provided in the 15th cent. by Lorenzo Valla (in prose) and by Angelo Poliziano (in hexameters). In 1488 the first printed edition of the Greek text appeared in Florence (and it included the *Batrachomyomachia*, which was ascribed to Homer, the *Homeric Hymns* and the *Lives of Homer*). The reestablishment of the Classical system of genres, which is characteristic of the Renaissance [21. 12ff.], determined first of all the Latin Humanism of the 14th and 15th cents., starting with Petrarch's restoration of a Virgilian model in his fragment *Africa* (begun 1338/39). Down to the likewise-fragmentary *Borsias* (begun 1460) of Tito Vespasiano Strozzi, there arose a number of neo-Latin epics, which were based as a rule on Virgil and only in odd instances (such as the *Hesperis* of Basinio Basini) [12. 159ff.] upon Homer.

The poetics of the epic is, in the late 15th and early 16th cent., still appreciably more open than it became after the large-scale reception of Aristotle's *Poetics* after the mid–16th cent. Thus Della Fonte, in his *Poetics* (written ca. 1490–1492), defined the epic on the one hand, following Diomedes, as 'heroum et fortium virorum gesta' ("the deeds of heroes and brave men") [29. 115], but demanded on the other hand of every poet (and thus precisely of epic poets) that they should take account of rhetorical *varietas*, which included changes in the *genera dicendi* ('styles'), and of the basic effects of pathos/seriousness and ethos/comedy, which presumably derives ultimately from Quintilian's characterisation of Homer (inst. 10,1,46–48) [26. 72ff.]. And then again there are writers like Landino or Daniello, who expressly forbade a mixed style [30. 1,81; 250]. If poetics as such were, at the start of the 16th cent., still characterised by an absence of any explicitly normative restrictions on the one hand, on the other Virgil was viewed from Petrarch's time onward as the most respected Latin epic poet, albeit not as the only one worthy of imitation; that is, it was impossible to derive a binding poetic of the epic even from – divergent – practice, and this was even less possible since writers such as Della Fonte included Lucretius or the *Metamorphoses* of Ovid under the heading of epic [26. 75f.].

The modalities of reestablishing the Classical epic in the course of the 16th cent. and the poetic discussion that went along with them have to be viewed against the initially somewhat 'open' concept of the epic among the Humanists. While with Pulci's *Morgante* (1478 in 23 cantos, 1483 in 28 cantos) and Boiardo's *Orlando inna-morato* (1483 in two books, 1495 in three) the artistic *romanzo* established itself in various forms [26. 76ff.], even in Boiardo's case recourse to the Classical epic is restricted to the → adaptation of individual episodes and to intertextual references without any specifically systematic function. Not until Ariosto's *Orlando furioso*, which appeared in three versions, each one reworked, in 1516, 1521 and 1532, does the Classical epic become an explicit reference system, which is signaled already with the *canto*-formula of the second line ("Le donne, i cavallier, l'arme, gli amori,/le cortesie, l'audaci imprese io canto" [1. 1,1f.]) and is underlined again at the end by the imitation of the duel between Aeneas and Turnus in that between Rodomonte and Ruggiero. The text as a whole is based upon a large number of varying allusions to the Classical epic from Homer to Lucan, ranging from metaphors down to the modified adoption of entire episodes, which repeatedly allude to several Classical texts in one and the same intertextual reference (the Cloridano-Medoro-episode, for example, depends at the same time upon the Nisus-Euryalus-episode in the *Aeneid* and its imitation in the *Thebaid* of Statius [13. 17ff.]). While the *Orlando furioso* clearly calls upon the Classical epic as a generic referent, it deconstructs the act as it does so. This comes about on the one hand through a partly humorous means of reference, and on the other (and most importantly) by the juxtaposing of different and opaque generic references: Virgil's 'Arma virumque cano' ("Of arms and the man I sing") becomes a poetic celebration of arms and love, in which not only the Classical epic and the native *romanzi*-traditions, but also the quite different norms and configurations of the *chanson de geste* ('matière de France') and of the courtly romance ('matière de Bretagne') are set off one against the other [19; 28]. Although *Orlando furioso* was probably the most widely-read text in Italy in the 16th cent. [20. 48ff.], it attracted numerous imitations and continuations [18] and was also rapidly disseminated outside Italy through translations [14; 15]. Already before the renewed reception of Aristotle's *Poetics*, *Orlando furioso* was a much debated text poetologically and a protagonist in the battle of the epics in the 16th cent. [30. 954ff.]. What was debated was precisely the relationship between the Classical epic and the norms, now viewed as prescriptive poetics, which derived above all from the rhetoric of Horace and from Aristotle. By the use of the most varied arguments, the *Orlando furioso* was seen both as a genuine epic and as a genuine vernacular *romanzo*, continuing the medieval tradition, and also as a mixture of various genres [20]. Differentiation criteria for the epic included above all the unity of action, its 'high' level of content and style, truth in the sense of an historical or literary guarantee of the basic action, and the fading into the background of the narrator [20. 98ff.].

In contrast with the huge success of the much-debated *Orlando furioso*, the first thoroughly Classical vernacular epic, Trissino's *L'Italia liberata dai Goti*

(1547/48) enjoyed no success at all. Even Tasso in his *Discorsi dell'Arte poetica* (1587, composed in the 1560s), is critical of the fact that Trissino imitates Homer too slavishly and offers us *costumi* which no longer accord with contemporary decorum [4. 384]. With his *Rinaldo* (1562, ²1570) Tasso published first a *romanzo*, the heterogeneity of which he did, to be fair, reduce to the deeds of a single hero [27]. With his *Gerusalemme liberata* (1581), later reworked to become *Gerusalemme conquistata* (1593), Tasso laid down a model for the epic, not just as far as the debate at the end of the 16th cent. was concerned, but also for the theory and practice of the epic in French classicism [11. 336f.], which has recourse not only to Castelvetro, Scaliger and others, but also to Tasso's theory of the epic in the early *Discorsi* and in the later expanded *Discorsi del poema eroico* (1594) [11. 34ff.]. The distance from Ariosto and the connection to Virgil is signalled in the two opening lines ('Canto l'arme pietose e 'l capitano/che 'l gran sepolcro liberò di Cristo' [7. 1,1f.]). Although Tasso in the Armida-Rinaldo-episode adopts completely the love-themes of the *romanzi*-tradition, their suppression in the proem signals their intended episodic function in a way analogous to Virgil. On the other hand the explicitly formulated theme puts into action in paradigmatic form the proposition of the early and the later *Discorsi*, according to which an epic must have a true theme as its subject, which must however be at the same time historically as far from the present as possible, to allow for elaboration and the inventive powers of the poet.

2. FRANCE

In contrast with Italy, the renewed reception of Homer began in France with a partial vernacular translation by Hugues Salel, who translated the first 12 books of the *Iliad* (1545). The translation was completed by Amadís Jamyn. In 1566 there appeared at the press of Henri Estienne the Greek text of the works ascribed to Homer, which became the basis for later editions. For Du Bellay epic is the highest form of poetry (*Défense et illustration de la langue française* 2,5), but he recommends that young poets (against his customary rejection of native traditions) go back to materials from the *romanzi*, following Ariosto, whom he sees as the equal of Homer and Virgil. While Du Bellay himself wrote no epics, Ronsard published (1572) the first four books of his Homer-imitation, the intended 24-book *Franciade*, with a preface *Au lecteur*, which is missing from the second edition of 1573 on and was replaced only in the posthumous edition of 1587 by an extensive *Préface sur la Franciade, touchant le Poème Heroïque*, which is partly by Claude Binet. Ronsard does not follow Du Bellay, but names explicitly as model authors Homer and Virgil, claiming to have followed more the 'naïve facilité d'Homere' than the 'curieuse diligence de Virgile' (*Au lecteur* [3. 1,5]). The thematic subject of the *Franciade*, which is composed in decasyllabic rhymed couplets, is the 'history' of Francion, the son of Hector (who appears in Boiardo and Ariosto as Astyanax), who had escaped from the burning of Troy and became the founder of the French royal house. Into the story of Francion, by means of the device of historical prophecy, which is used in Virgil and also in the vernacular *romanzi*-tradition before Boiardo und Ariosto, was to be built the history of the subsequent 63 kings ('j'ay le faix de soixante & trois Rois sur les bras' (*Au lecteur* [3. 1,5]), so that the 'history' of Francion was not only to contain a genealogical and dynastic component, but one which was conceived as the basis for a veritable national epic.

While Ronsard, having reached the death of Charles IX. (1574), who had provided particular support for the undertaking, gave up his project, there was in the late 16th and early 17th cent. a series of writers who further pursued Ronsard's planned national epic (Jacques Guillot, Pierre Delaudin, Nicolas Geuffrin). But beside this, contemporary epics were produced based on the figure of Henri IV. and his role in the wars of religion, or as a new founding father of national unity (Sébastien Garnier, Jean Godard, Alexandre de Pontaymeri and others [9]).

Deliberately distanced from the norms of the Classical-style epic are the Biblical epics of writers like Du Bartas (*Judit*, 1574, *La Sepmaine*, 1578 and *La seconde Sepmaine*, 1584), who, as evidenced by the numerous editions of their works, were very successful down to the 17th cent., and also Agrippa d'Aubigné's *Les Tragiques* (written 1577–89, first printed 1616), which treated the wars of religion in an expressly satirical manner. The real century of the epic in French is, however – in spite of the usual assumptions – the 17th cent.

C. FROM THE BAROQUE TO NEOCLASSICISM
1. ITALY 2. FRANCE

1. ITALY

While Marino with his mythological epic *Adone* (written 1593–1622, first edition 1623) explicitly moves away from the classicising epic tradition in his concept of a 'poema fantastico e fuor di regola', the new rules for which consist in 'rompere le regole' [2. 31f.], there exists at the same time a quasi-Classical theory and practice of the epic which is, however, characterised in particular by its reference to Tasso. The exemplary nature of Tasso's epics together with and also in contradistinction to the Classical epic is reflected for example in Paolo Beni's *Comparazione di Omero, Virgilio e Torquato* (1607, ²1616), and in the *Tancredi* (1636) of Ascanio Grandi: the *Gerusalemme liberata* is the model, whose plot is continued in the same way as that of the *Iliad* in the *Odyssey*. Writers like Francesco Bracciolini with his *La Croce racquistata* (first 15 books, 1605, complete edition in 35 books, 1611) place themselves clearly in the tradition of Tasso; Marguerita Sarrocchi, an opponent of Marino, composed a *Scanderbeide* (1623); Gabriele Zinano an *Eracleide* (1623); Giulio Strozzi a *Venezia edificata* (1624) and so on.

The theme of a New World is treated by another opponent of Marino, Tommaso Stigliani, in his epic *Il Mondo nuovo* (1617 in 20 cantos, complete edition in 34 cantos, 1634), who introduces as a novelty in the high-style epic the element of personal satire (against Marino in 14, 34f.). The first epic about the New World appeared in Latin from the pen of Lorenzo Gambara (*De navigatione Christophori Columbi*, 1581), followed by *Mondo nuovo* (1596) of Giovanni Giorgini. In thematic terms the range of an extremely extensive number of works reaches from the period of the Germanic migrations (Gabriello Chiabrera, *Delle Guerre de' Goti*, 1582) through and beyond the period of the crusades down to – against the recommendations of Tasso – contemporary history (Francesco Bracciolini, *Roccella espugnata*, 1630). Furthermore it still remains a possibility in the 17th cent. to opt not for the epic of Tasso but for Ariosto's *romanzo*, as does Gabriello Chiabrera in his *Ruggero* (1653) [8].

The tendency, typical of Baroque literature, to mix genres manifests itself in the creation of a genuine *poema eroicomico* with a programmatic rejection of the parodistic elements in the context of the *romanzo*. There was a conflict about the invention of this new genre between Francesco Bracciolini, whose *Scherno degli dei* (1618 in 14 cantos, 1626 in 20) is a parody of the mythological epic, and Alessandro Tassoni, whose *Secchia rapita* was already in circulation in manuscript form before 1618 (first edition 1622, final life-time edition 1630). Where Tassoni insists precisely upon the mixed nature of his text, which is not to be reduced to the treatment of a low theme in high style or its opposite, the low-style treatment of a high theme (*A chi legge*), Giovan Battista Lalli brings in precisely these two forms of epic parody with his *Moscheide* (1624) on the one hand, which takes up the tradition of the *Batrachomyomachia*, and on the other with his *Eneide travestita* (1633). Both of these had numerous followers in Italy (for example Giovan Francesco Loredano, *L'Iliade giocosa*, 1653, Loreto Vittori, *La troia rapita*, 1662, etc.) [8].

In 18th-cent. Italy the tradition of the Classical epic no longer played a significant part [10. 297], but towards the end of the century and at the beginning of the 19th there were important new translations of the *Iliad* (by Alessandro Verri, Melchiorre Cesarotti, Vincenzo Monti, Ugo Foscolo), the *Odyssey* (by Ippolito Pindemonte) and the *Aeneid* (by Clemente Bondi and Alfieri).

Among the many and very different *poemi giocosi* there are, beside epic parodies like the *Bajamonte Tiepolo in Schiavonia, poema eroicomico* (1770) of Zaccaria Valaresso, still parodies of the *romanzo*, such as the *Ricciardetto* (published posthumously, 1738) of Niccolò Forteguerri [25. 362ff.]. Most *poemi giocosi* are characterised by a more or less clearly satirical tendency introduced already in Tassoni's *Secchia rapita*, and which became a dominant structural feature in Carlo Gozzi's *Marfisa bizzarra* (1772). A decisive

factor here is that even at the end of the 18th cent. the *romanzo* as well as the epic was still available as an object for parody in generic terms.

2. FRANCE

The 17th cent. French verse epic in alexandrine rhymed couplets has largely been banished from literary memory. From the middle of the century views were voiced about the impossibility of a verse epic in French [23. 2]. Nevertheless, at least 115 epics are bibliographically known, and they had a readership in their own times: thus there appeared within the first year of publication of the first twelve cantos of Chapelain's *Pucelle* (1656) no fewer than five editions. *Clovis* (1657) of Desmarets de Saint-Sorlin was reprinted six times within a few years. Saint-Amant's *Moyse sauvé* (1653) and Scudéry's *Alaric* (1654) got up to eight editions, and Brébeuf's translation of the *Pharsalia* even made it to 14 [23. 15]. At the same time, critical discourse on the epic was at least as lively as the production of the epics themselves, and the great majority of theorists placed the epic above tragedy at the very top of the hierarchy of genres, even though in practice, after the 1630s, the dramatic genres came to establish themselves as dominant [23. 57ff.]. The discussion takes its guidance from the Classical writers on theory and practice, but at the same time refers back to the comprehensive discussions in the Italian Renaissance since Vida's *Poetics* (1528), and to Tasso's *Gerusalemme liberata* as the paradigm of a Christian epic. In a majority of texts such as, for example, *Clovis*, the genealogical and dynastic components of the *Aeneid* remain of central importance. Alongside more or less binding concepts of high style or of high themes, the dominance of deeds of arms, the unity of action, the historical-literary genuineness of the basic plot, the special significance, proper to the genre, of the marvelous and other features, there are also divergences, which are still included in Boileau's *Art poétique* (1674), such as the dispute about the Christian marvelous and whether it can or cannot be mediated with the pagan, the acceptability of the theme of love and so on. When a poetology of the epic such as the *Traité du poëme epique* of René Le Bossu could appear in six editions between 1675 and 1714 and another leader of the *modernes*, Charles Perrault, published a Christian epic (*Saint Paulin*, 1686) as well as a cosmological poem (*La Création du monde*, 1692), it seems anachronistic to want to go on describing the epic of the 17th cent. as an 'anachronistic form' [23. 263ff.] and as a result of the crisis in Renaissance poetics [23. 306]. Equally unconvincing are views which claim the texts in an undifferentiated manner as a basis for a Baroque aesthetic because they take up genre-specific elements such as the marvelous, or an increase in rhetorical usage, as defining the period [22. 225ff.]. It must certainly be asked to what extent texts like Saint-Amant's *Moyse sauvé* depend rather upon Marino than upon the tradition of the Classical epic. The theory and practice of epic in France in the 17th cent. have, however, their major point of contact in the theory and practice of the

Classical epic and their reception, with modifications, in the Italian Renaissance.

As in Italy a comic epic also develops in 17th-cent. France in the context of burlesque writing, which goes beyond the genre of epic. The 'burlesque' epic appears either in the form of an epic travesty, that is, a treatment in low style of a high theme (in texts like Scarron's *Virgile travesti en vers burlesques*, 1648–53) or of the high burlesque, that is, the realisation of a low theme in high style, as in Boileau's *Le Lutrin* (1674 in four cantos, in 1683 increased to six). In the preface to the first edition, Boileau explains the distinction between these two types, while attributing aesthetic dignity only to his own *burlesque nouveau* (on the rejection of low burlesque, see *Art poétique*, Canto I, V. 79ff.).

Even though Voltaire is the first (and for literary history to the present definitive) commentator upon the basic collapse of epic ambitions in the 17th cent. (in his *Essai de la poésie épique*, 1733, first in English in 1727), this does not at all imply a rejection of the epic genre as such; quite the reverse. Voltaire's reputation in the 18th cent. rests essentially upon his *Henriade* (1728) – which appeared originally with the title *La Ligue ou Henry le Grand* (1723) –, one of the great literary successes of the 18th cent., with a good 60 editions in Voltaire's own lifetime. The text is about the battle of Henri IV against the Catholic League down to the triumphant entry of the king into Paris (1594); on the one hand the tradition of the national epic is continued in this, but at the same time it is radically refunctionalised in the spirit of the Enlightenment: by its anti-Catholic and anti-Christian thrust, by the pleas for tolerance or the ideal, embodied in Henri IV, of an 'enlightened' ruler. Beyond that, the text is also highly political in contemporary terms in that it sets up an implicit parallel to the succession problems of the regency. In aesthetic terms, however, the principle of the *imitatio auctorum* and the basic norms for the epic as developed in the Italian Renaissance and in the poetics of the 17th cent. remain valid. Among the Classical epic poets Voltaire, in line with tradition, prefers Virgil to Homer, something which manifests itself textually by a plethora of references to the *Aeneid*.

Voltaire's enormous success soon encouraged imitators. Only towards the middle of the century was there a certain renaissance in the genre, in the course of which not only Christian-nationalistic and 'exotic' texts (N.L.Bourgeois, *Christophe Colomb, ou l'Amérique découverte*, 1773) but also genuine Enlightenment works were written. Overall the production of 35 epics for the whole century is insignificant.

Against this, the numerous (new) translations of Homer are striking, these appearing in the context of the Homer-debate initiated by Anne Dacier (13 *Iliad*-(partial) translations, four translations of the *Odyssey*). Of the *Aeneid*, however, there appeared only three translations, with two of the *Pharsalia* and one of the *Thebaid* [6. 214ff. und 682ff.].

That the epic was by no means viewed as an anachronistic form to the end of the 18th cent. is shown by Chénier's fragmentary epic project *L'Amérique*, which was intended to realise his fundamental poetic concept in an ideal way: 'Sur des pensers nouveaux faisons des vers antiques' (*L'Invention*, V. 184). That verse formulates in a paradigmatic manner the joining of Enlightenment ideas and neo-Classical aesthetics, which is typical for the 18th cent. as a whole.

In the tradition of the comic epic, Marivaux' *Homère travesti ou l'Iliade en vers burlesques* (1716) is one of the last examples of a travesty-epic, while Voltaire, with his *Pucelle d'Orléans* (pirated editions from 1755, first authorised edition 1762), of which 31 manuscripts and over 100 editions are known to us down to the end of the 18th cent., provides a comic epic which is explicitly linked with the comic tendencies of the Italian artistic *romanzo*. This poem operates as a parody of the epic in general and of the *Pucelle* of Chapelain in particular, but in a typically Enlightenment manner insofar as the comic elements of that parody are set up to ridicule above all the institution of the Church and the foundations of Christian belief [24]. By the end of the century, Voltaire had found several less significant followers [7. 221ff.], which brought the comic epic necessarily to an end just at the point at which the serious epic de facto became an anachronistic genre.

D. FROM ROMANTIC TO (POST-)MODERN

Because of the stronger ongoing effect of the neo-Classical tradition, there is in Italy (in contrast to France) in the first half of the 19th cent. a final 'florescence' of the Classical epic with ca. 50 new texts [10. 297ff.]. With the loss of the *imitatio-auctorum*-principle, as formulated especially by the Romantics from the 1820s on, the Classical epic loses, like the other Classical genres, its normative validity, and new forms of the Christian epic, such as Lamartine's *La Chute d'un ange* (1838) or Hugo's *La Fin de Satan* (posthumous, 1886), arise. When any recourse is taken to the Classical epic, then this is no longer done to realise a specific system of generically constitutive rules, but it happens in the shape of intertextual connections with a wide variety of functions, and they are especially frequent in modern literature, from Giraudoux's *La Guerre de Troie n'aura pas lieu* (1935) to Claude Simon's *La Bataille de Pharsale* (1969). For the modern world the Classical epic is a repertory of themes, motifs and stylistic elements which may, in a whole variety of ways, become the ingredients of, or the starting point for new texts, whose structure and function are nevertheless radically new, so that the use of this material sets up something that is different from, rather than similar to it.

→ Discourses; → Genera dicendi
→ METAPHOR; → NEO-LATIN LITERATURE

SOURCES 1 L. ARIOSTO, Orlando furioso, (ed.) E. BIGI, 2 vols., 1982   2 Marino e i Marinisti, (ed.) G. G. FERRERO, 1954   3 P. DE RONSARD, La Franciade, (ed.) P. LAUMO-

NIER (Œuvres complètes, 16), 2 vols., 1950/52   4 T. TASSO, Prose, (ed.) E. MAZZALI, 1959   5 Id., Gerusalemme liberata, (ed.) F. CHIAPPELLI, 1982   6 VOLTAIRE, La Henriade, (ed.) O. R. TAYLOR (Les Œuvres complètes de Voltaire, 2), 1970   7 Id., La Pucelle d'Orléans, (ed.) J. VERCRUYSSE (Les Œuvres complètes de Voltaire, 7), 1970 LITERATURE   8 G. ARBIZZONI, Poesia epica, eroicomica, satirica, burlesca. La poesia rusticale toscana. La 'poesia figurata', in: E. MALATO (ed.), Storia della letteratura italiana, 14 vols., 1997, vol. 5, 727–770   9 A. BECHERER, Das Bild Heinrichs IV. (Henri Quatre) in der französischen Versepik (1593–1613), 1996   10 A. BELLONI, Il poema epico e mitologico, 1912   11 R. BRAY, Formation de la doctrine classique en France, 1978 (¹1927)   12 A. BUCK, Die Rezeption der Antike in den romanischen Literaturen der Renaissance, 1976   13 M. C. CABANI, Gli amici amanti. Coppie eroiche e sortite notturne nell'epica italiana, 1995   14 M. CHEVALIER, L'Arioste en Espagne (1530–1650). Recherches sur l'influence du 'Roland Furieux', 1966   15 A. CIORANESCU, L'Arioste en France. Des Origines à la fin du 18ᵉ siècle, 2 vols., 1939   16 E. R. CURTIUS, Über die altfranzösische Epik, in: Zschr. für Romanische Philol. 64, 1944, 233–320   17 Id., Europäische Literatur und lateinisches Mittelalter, ⁴1963   18 G. FUMAGALLI, La fortuna dell''Orlando furioso' in Italia, 1910   19 K. W. HEMPFER, Textkonstitution und Rezeption: zum dominant komisch-parodistischen Charakter von Pulcis 'Morgante', Boiardos 'Orlando Innamorato' und Ariosts 'Orlando Furioso', in: Romanistisches Jb. 27, 1976, 1–26   20 Id., Diskrepante Lektüren: Die Orlando-Furioso-Rezeption im Cinquecento, 1987   21 Id., Probleme traditioneller Bestimmungen des Renaissancebegriffs und die epistemologische 'Wende', in: Id. (ed.), Renaissance – Diskursstrukturen und epistemologische Voraussetzungen, 1993, 9–45   22 M. JARRETY (ed.), La Poésie française du Moyen Age jusqu'à nos jours, 1997   23 R. KRÜGER, Zwischen Wunder und Wahrscheinlichkeit. Die Krise des französischen Versepos im 17. Jahrhundert, 1986   24 M. LINDNER, Voltaire und die Poetik des Epos, 1980   25 G. NATALI, Il Settecento, 2 vols. (Storia letteraria d'Italia, 8), ⁶1964, vol. 2, chap. 12   26 F. PENZENSTADLER, Der 'Mambriano' von Francesco Cieco da Ferrara als Beispiel für Subjektivierungstendenzen im Romanzo vor Ariost, 1987   27 G. REGN, Restituierte Idealität. Einheitspoetik und Pragmatisierung der Geschichtsebene in Torquato Tassos 'Rinaldo', in: K. W. HEMPFER (ed.), Ritterepik der Renaissance, 1987   28 K. STIERLE, Die Verwilderung des Romans als Ursprung seiner Möglichkeit, in: H. U. GUMBRECHT (ed.), Literatur in der Gesellschaft des Spätmittelalters, 1980, 253–313   29 C. TRINKAUS, The Unknown Quattrocento Poetics of Bartolomeo della Fonte, in: Stud. in the Ren. 13, 1966, 40–122   30 B. WEINBERG, A History of Literary Criticism in the Italian Renaissance, 2 vols., 1961 (repr. 1974). ADDITIONAL BIBLIOGRAPHY C. KALLENDORF, In Praise of Aeneas: Virgil and Epideictic Rhetoric in the Early Italian Renaissance, 1989 F. LETOUBLON, C. VOLPILHAC-AUGE R (eds.), Homère en France après la querelle (1715–1900), 1999 J. K. NEWMAN, The Classical Epic Tradition, 1986 D. QUINT, Epic and Empire: Politics and Generic Form from Virgil to Milton, 1993 V. ZABUGHIN, Vergilio nel Rinascimento italiano da Dante a Torquato Tasso, 2 vols., 1921

II. IBERO-ROMANIA
A. THE MIDDLE AGES   B. THE RECEPTION OF THE ITALIAN EPIC IN THE 16TH CENTURY   C. EPIC CRITICISM AND EPIC THEORY IN THE 16TH CENTURY   D. SIGLO DE ORO   E. THE FLOURISHING OF THE PORTUGUESE EPIC

A. THE MIDDLE AGES
Classical themes reached Spain through the filter of a clerical monopoly on education (world chronicles) and were used in the service of the *reconquista*. Independent of this, there appeared in the 12th cent. a vernacular epic performed by *juglares* (*Cantar de Mío Cid*). The precise inventory of the epic is hard to estimate, since nearly all Spanish and all Portuguese epics have been reconstructed from late medieval prose redactions in chronicles, which guarantee a modern transmission of the epic.

B. THE RECEPTION OF THE ITALIAN EPIC IN THE 16TH CENTURY
On the basis of the prose redactions of the medieval epic, the genre renewed itself initially by recourse to the Italian *romanzo*, which was much read in the zenith of the prose chivalric romance (*Amadís*, 1504ff., *Palmerín*, 1511ff.). Pulci (1533), Boiardo (1555), Ariosto (1550) and Folengo's *Baldus* (1542) were translated into prose versions. Their predominantly ironic feel was lost under the influence of the Inquisition, which subjected the works to a rigid text-based commentary in line with the moral norms of the time. Later verse translations of Ariosto (1578) and of Boiardo (1581), which even Cervantes (*Don Quixote*, 1,6) mocks, are imitated by, among others, Luis Barahona de Soto (*Angélica*, 1586) and Lope de Vega (*La hermosura de Angélica*, 1609). In Castilian prose the *romanzo*, the French *chanson de geste* (*Renaldos de Montalván*, 1523), the older Spanish (*Fernán González*, 1516) and the Classical epic (*Historia troyana*, 1502; *Pharsalia*, 1541) all merge into a commercial literary system, which is focused without differentiation of genre or epoch upon the great fascination with 'heroic deeds and love'. Where with the epic reception of the early 16th cent. we are concerned with the disappearance of formal aspects of the Classical epic, Classical Antiquity still exerts a significant influence on the emerging Spanish narrative literature by providing a fund of picturesque and romanesque situations. For the chivalric romance Classical epics serve as an arsenal in terms of rhetoric and in the shaping of individual episodes.

C. EPIC CRITICISM AND EPIC THEORY IN THE 16TH CENTURY
Spanish Humanism reacted with some reluctance to the Classical epic. Antonio Nebrija's Virgil-commentary appeared after a 50–year delay in 1550; Juan de Arjona's translation of the *Thebaid*, composed at the end of the 16th cent., did not appear until 1855. The theoreticians were dismissive not only of the contempo-

rary epic but also of its Classical models as simply a literature of entertainment. The Inquisition and Spanish Humanism criticise the Classical and the Italian epics on grounds of alleged immorality and a lack of historicity. According to Juan Luis Vives (*De causis corruptarum artium* 4) the Classical epic is concerned with 'the triumph of the passions'; both the Classical and the modern epic, he claims, fail to distinguish between historically verifiable and invented subjects [1]. Alonso López 'el Pinciano' (1547–1627), who imitates Tasso and Virgil in his epic *El Pelayo* (1605), created on the model of Aristotle's *Poetics* his own *Philosophia antigua poética* (1596). Not only is the blending of the tragic, the heroic and the comic in one work (following the pattern of Ariosto) possible; the Classical models supposedly support the theoretical demand for the combining of historical truth and fiction. In Counter-Reformation Spain, Tasso becomes the model for an epic that is in line with the aesthetic rules of the Council of Trent, which finds exemplary expression in Lope de Vega's spiritual epic *Jerusalén conquistada* (1609) [2]. Pinciano's theory of epic provides at the same time the guidelines for the fictionality of the modern novel as represented by Cervantes.

D. SIGLO DE ORO

Alonso de Ercilla y Zuñiga's (1533–1594) *La Araucana* (1569–1578) becomes the model of a modern epic based upon the Classical epic; it glorifies the battle of the conquistadors in Chile. Ercilla's model is Lucan's *Pharsalia* [8] when he casts into epic form the events of the recent national past. Classical references are most frequent in the freely invented episodes in the work. Ercilla had numerous imitators, who used the epic of the mythical foundation of the existing nation as a means of current political propaganda. Under the influence of the Counter-Reformation, the epic moves closer to earlier forms of religious discourse: when Cristóbal de Virués' (1550–1609) in *El Monserrate* (1587) sends a hermit off on a Catholic odyssey, he is turning around the medieval typological interpretation of myth; in turn Lope de Vega usurps allegorical models when in *La Dragontea* (1598) the Protestant 'enemy of the state' Francis Drake becomes a dragon – and thereby an image of Satan. The heroic-comic epic is a special development which reaches Spain at first via Teofilo Folengo's *La Moschea* (1521). José de Villaviciosa's *La Mosquea* (1615) and Lope de Vega's *La Gatomaquía* (1634) together consciously fall back on the pseudo-Homeric *Batrachomyomachia*.

1. SPANISH COLONIAL WRITING

1. SPANISH COLONIAL WRITING

With *La Araucana* not only does the *conquista* of America become a theme for the epic, but the Classical genre is thereby established in the New World. In the Baroque writings of the Peruvian *Academia antártica* features of the beginning of the bucolic tradition (Pedro de Oñas *Arauco domada*, 1596) are visible. The reforms of the Council of Trent also effected in South America a turn towards religious poetry (Diego de Hojeda, *Christiada*, 1611).

E. THE FLOURISHING OF THE PORTUGUESE EPIC

Luís de Camões (1524?–1580) re-established the Portuguese epic with *Os Lusíadas* (1572), in which Classical models (Homer, Virgil) are combined with national myth and history. In the context of the *translatio imperii* this was intended to legitimise in literature Portugal's claims to world power [3]. The fact that the action covers the period from Roman times down to Vasco da Gama, was attacked by contemporaries as *diversitas* (a plurality of strands in the action, which went against Aristotelean norms). The merging of Classical education with the Portuguese Humanist and medieval Christian traditions was criticised by the Jesuits as *contaminatio* (as a non-permissible mixture of cultures). In spite of that, Camões has an influence not only on the next generation of Baroque epic writers in Portugal, but also those in Brazil (Bento Texeiras, *Prosopopéia*, 1601), where, in the course of the Enlightenment, epic acquires significance as an early expression of American 'otherness' (José Basílio da Gama, *Urugay*, 1769).

→ Aristotle [6]; → Batrachomyomachie; → Lucan
→ SACRUM IMPERIUM ROMANUM

1 M. BATAILLON, Erasme et l'Espagne, 1937   2 M. CHEVALIER, L'Arioste en Espagne, 1966   3 A. DA COSTA RAMALHO, Estudios Camonianos, 1980, 2–26   5 G. HIGHET, The Classical Tradition: Greek and Roman Influences on Western Literature, 1985 (¹1949)   6 M. R. LIDA DE MALKIEL, La tradición clásica en España, 1975   7 F. PIERCE, La poesía épica del Siglo de Oro, 1961   8 C. SCHLAYER, Spuren Lukans in der spanischen Dichtung, 1927
ADDITIONAL LITERATURE C. KALLENDORF, Representing the Other: Ercilla's La Araucana, Virgil's Aeneid, and the New World Encounter, Comparative Literature Studies, 40, 2003, 394–414 N. NICOLOPULOS, The Poetics of Empire in the Indies: Prophecy and Imitation in La Araucana and Os Lusiadas, 2000   GERHARD WILD

III. GERMANY
A. INTRODUCTION B. MEDIEVAL LATIN AND NEO-LATIN LITERATURE C. LITERATURE IN GERMAN

A. INTRODUCTION

The reception of the Classical model of the verse epic provided in particular by the works of Homer and by Virgils *Aeneid* developed in German literature from its beginnings in the 9th cent. under the same specific conditions which obtain for the German reception of the Classical world in general. On the one hand, a Latin-based higher education system provided for a continued knowledge of Virgil to the 19th cent., strengthened in each of the various periods of renaissance (→ THE CAROLINGIAN, → the Ottonian, the Cluniac and so on). Other writers of Latin metrical epics, too, such as Lucan, play an important role in the history of reception (overview for the Middle Ages in [5. 9–36]); Homer is added from the 16th cent. on in connection with the new Humanist studies of Greek. On the other hand, the Classical model comes into competition with the newer European or autochthonic epic traditions of form and content, especially in the case of narratives in the German language. Thus in the reception context of the courtly-aristocratic classes, for example, Germanic, Celtic or the more recent Romance narrative traditions are regularly considered to be equally, or indeed more, interesting as literary sources. It is true in general that school knowledge of Latin does not automatically lead in the literary life of Germany to a reflective discourse with the Classical models or to a necessary and productive appropriation of Classical material. For that, a particular motivation is always required, such as a political impetus (recourse to Classical traditions as a means towards the legitimisation and representation of the concept of a Holy Roman Empire, the → TRANSLATIO IMPERII), the idea of a genealogical tradition based on the establishment of a lineage of fame (narrative as a link with the past and the memorialising of life-stories, or the stories of the development of particular families), and also ideals in humanistic discourse (using Classical models for normative purposes because of the higher value afforded to Classical aesthetic standards). The power of motivating forces of this kind was, however, never great enough in Germany to provide for a continuous and vital tradition of verse epics in Classical style. Native traditions or the influences of contemporary European literature and the epic narrative models associated with it were always stronger, and from the start of the Early Modern period pushed the new prose novel as the principal narrative genre into the foreground, thereby contributing to the ultimate demise of the epic in Germany.

B. MEDIEVAL LATIN AND NEO-LATIN LITERATURE

The dominant position of Latin scholarship was widely accepted in the Middle Ages as an epistemological fact. The discrepancy in esteem associated with this usually prevented works in the less highly esteemed German vernacular from being transposed into Latin. Nonetheless, we may point to a number of special cases where the polarity of the reception has been reversed. First we have in the 9/10th cent. the Germanic heroic saga of Waltharius, which was reworked as a Latin epic; secondly there are two Middle High German epic works of the period around 1200 which were translated into Latin verse, namely the Reiseroman (travel romance) of Herzog Ernst and the papal legend, originally from a French source, the Gregorius of Hartmann von Aue. The case of Waltharius, in some senses unique, is linked in terms of content to a well-known Germanic cycle of material known from the German Nibelungenlied. The protagonist, Walther of Aquitaine, lives with Hagen and others at the court of Attila, King of the Huns; after King Gunther cancels the treaty with the Huns, Walther flees. In what follows he comes into armed conflict with Gunther and others for the sake of a hoard of gold. In the end, Walther is victorious and is able, after his marriage to Hiltgunt, to assume the sovereignty of his own land. The clerical poet modifies the heroic aspect in favour of Christian reflection on the part of the hero, but still adheres to the formal Classical model in the 1456 hexameters of the work. Through the use of Virgilian stylistic features not only does the language retain a Classical veneer, but the inner approach to the material is also often Classical [3. 392]. As far as the two translations from Middle High German into Latin are concerned, the one case tells the story of the Bavarian Duke Ernst, who escapes from a military conflict with Emperor Otto into the fabulous world of the Orient, while the other has at its center the sinner Gregorius, born of an incestuous relationship, who in his turn becomes incestuously involved with his mother, and, as a penitent, is at the end even elevated to the papacy. Between 1212 and 1218 Odo von Magdeburg produced his Latin epic in hexameters, Ernestus, in 3600 partly rhymed verses, and in so doing adapted the German saga in Classical style without disturbing its Christian core, giving it a dazzling scholarly external form. Gregorius was translated by Arnold von Lübeck around 1210 in 4210 mostly rhythmic lines in which he imitated Hartmann's four-stress German lines, which, however, he sometimes made longer or shorter, with an admixture of Leonine hexameters [17. 186f.].

In the large-scale medieval and neo-Latin epics in Germany, Classical models always exerted, as might be expected, a more or less strong influence. Intertextual connections with the Classical epic were pretty well unavoidable. Here too, however, a distinction has to be made between use of theme and use of form. Already in the Carolingian period the writers of verse epics in what would become the German empire, while influenced by Virgil, drew their politically motivated themes from the lives of contemporary rulers and did not, for example, rework Classical themes. In putting things into verse epic form, however, some narrators strive for a particular closeness to their Classical models, especially to Virgil. An example of this is the Paderborn Epic, originally in four books, which is formally very much influenced by Virgil. Of this text only 536 hexameters of the third book have survived. The anonymous writer describes how Charlemagne, immediately after his imperial coronation in Aachen, builds up a second → ATHENS, goes off on a hunt with his court and meets with Pope Leo in Paderborn in 799. Also in the Carolingian period the Poeta Saxo composed ca. 2,700 lines of his Gesta Caroli metrica, presenting Charlemagne's life in epic verse based upon the writing of the emperor's biographer, Einhard. In the Ottonian period Hrotsvitha von Gandersheim wrote two historical epics in hexameters, of which her Gesta Oddonis I. imperatoris (before 968) belongs among the epics about rulers. Centuries later German Renaissance Humanists like Heinrich Bebel

(1472–1518) and Konrad Celtis (1459–1508) saw in Hrotsvitha the first great female poet, and their own predecessor. Celtis not only edited her works in 1501, but in 1507 he also published the Latin verse epic *Ligurinus,* written in 1207/1208 by Gunther von Pairis, from the Alsace. What assured the fame of this work in the Early Modern period was the combination of 'patriotic' content with a language of almost Classical purity, which in its simplicity and sublimity seemed to derive directly from Virgil; and even in → meter Gunther strove for an immediate association with the Classical epic in hexameters [15. V]. On the other hand, the content is once again completely contemporary, characterised by a political desire to lay stress upon the Hohenstaufen imperial idea. Gunther reworked in 10 books with an unmistakably panegyric tendency Otto von Freising's imperial biography *Gesta Friderici I. imperatoris,* concentrating on the first years of Barbarossa's rule.

The German 'Archhumanist' Celtis probably had thoughts himself of creating a kind of German national epic, but he made little progress beyond the initial ideas and plans for a *Theodericeid* (on Theoderich, king of the Goths) and a *Maximilianeid* (on the Emperor Maximilian I). These projects are linked with the Humanistic and political interests in the epic as a genre, an interest which existed among the scholars, artists and writers in the circle of Emperor Maximilian I (1459–1519). Maximilian himself had epics from the Middle High German period copied, and wrote with his *Theuerdank* and other works his own autobiographical epic in German verse, with which he wanted to set up a literary monument to himself. It is characteristic of Humanist thought in the 16th cent. that Richardus Sbrulius should have made the attempt to turn the *Theuerdank* into a neo-Latin epic. But this plan, too, came to nothing, and thus it was left to Maximilian's Italian court poet, Richardo Bartolini, to compose the requested *summum opus* of the courtly → PANEGYRIC, and to provide therewith the sole Renaissance epic for a significant sovereign north of the Alps [7. 144]. In 1516 the work was printed with the title *Austrias.* As a theme, Bartolini wrote up over a period of eight years the military successes of the emperor in the Bavarian-Palatine war of succession of 1504/05. In composition the 9,546 hexameters of the 12 books remain close to Virgil as a model not only formally, but also in the humanistically-inspired reworking of Classical themes (as in the mythological apparatus).

In the period of Renaissance Humanism in Germany and in the → BAROQUE there arose a rich neo-Latin literature, but in terms of imposing forcefulness the epics of the neo-Latin writers cannot compete with the lyric [4. 485]. The only German neo-Latin short epic that attempted to preserve the unity of the chosen Classical material and form was the work first performed in 1571, the *Kampf der Horatier und Kuratier* by Peter Dorfheilige (Petrus Paganus: *Historia tergeminorum Romanorum et Albanorum*). Several new Greek epics,

too, were composed in Germany. Laurenz Rhodomannus, for example, a professor who died in Wittenberg in 1606, wrote a brief *Iliad,* an *Argonautika* and a *Thebaika,* which were taken for Classical works and translated into Latin. Five main sub-genres have been distinguished for the Neo-Latin epic: 1. religious, 2. historical, 3. biographical, 4. allegorical and 5. comic [4. 485–490; 8. 695–702; 20. 207–212]. Of these, it is above all the religious epic of the post-Reformation period which introduced new tones. Nikodemus Frischlin composed in 1590 a biblical *Aeneid* with the title *Hebraeid* in 12,500 lines, narrating the history of the kings of Israel, and the aforementioned Laurenz Rhodomannus even wrote an epic on the life and works of Luther. Even the messiad in hexameters, *Olivetum* (Mount of Olives), which Andreas Gryphius presented in 1646 to the Venetian senate, belongs in this category.

C. LITERATURE IN GERMAN

The reception of the Classical epic, or the reaction to the Classical epic model, comes about for literature in the German language in the context of the medieval Latin and neo-Latin receptive processes already noted, as well as against a background of Latin education. In all cases writers in the German language had to come to terms with the question of the rationale for the appropriation of Classical epic, which elements of the Classical models were to be adopted, and how the adaptation into German might come about. For vernacular writers in the Middle Ages we must note in this respect considerable reserve. Even questions about the sense and the usefulness of the appropriation of the Classical epic were clearly viewed negatively by those who were completely rooted in the German-language literature system of their time. In the Middle Ages there was not even one German translation of a Classical epic, such as those of Homer or Virgil.

The longer type of German epic in the Middle Ages, most notably the heroic epic and the courtly Arthurian and courtly love romances, had their own traditional contexts. The influence of France was for a long time the standard for elevated literature in Middle High German. This applies too to those German verse-epics (usually also termed romances), the themes of which were in origin from Classical Antiquity (romances of Troy or of Alexander the Great), and it is also true for the single exception of a German adaptation of Virgils *Aeneid,* written between 1184 and 1190. This is the *Eneasroman* of Heinrich von Veldeke. The 13,528 lines of Middle High German verse are indeed based on knowledge of the Latin *Aeneid* (Veldeke calls it the 'Eneide'), but they represent in essence a faithful rendering of the Anglo-Norman *Roman d'Eneas,* written ca. 1160, which, in turn, is based directly on Virgil's *Aeneid.* Veldeke's adaptation is in line with the standard medieval principles of assimilation, by which Classical themes can be adapted to contemporary expectations and assumptions without difficulty (such as the re-interpretation, reduction or elimination of the mythological apparatus; the abbreviation and poeticising of the entire material in line with medieval courtly aesthetics etc.). The French Classical romance, influenced by chivalry, belongs with the romances of Thebes, Troy and Alexander to the group of *romans d'antiquité*, which for their contemporaries in the 12th cent. were viewed as the most modern of French works. In formal terms they are characterised by short rhymed couplets, and by pure rhyme rather than assonance, while in terms of content they stress the chivalric ethos, courtly behaviour and the theme of courtly love (*Minne*). The present border area between Germany, France and Belgium was in the Middle Ages a significant gateway for French culture. With the *Alexanderroman* of Lamprecht or the *Straßburger Alexander* and also the above-mentioned *Eneasroman* of Heinrich von Veldeke there arose here under French influence the first German romances of Antiquity from the hands of clerics, and initially they were doubtless also intended to be linked to French literary standards. In the course of its history of production and of later effect, however, the *Eneasroman* found itself in a context which makes it into a special case. As a by-product of the marriage policies of the Thuringian landgraves, the final version of Veldeke's *Eneasroman* became a factor in the literary pretensions of the Thuringian 'court of the muses' gathered around Landgrave Hermann I (ruled 1190–1217). Even as it was being written, the *Eneasroman* must have been a sensation [10. 848]. And in the following decades something like a Thuringian antiquities project was pursued at the court of the landgrave. Among other things there appeared here around 1200 the first and only Middle High German adaptation of Ovid's *Metamorphoses* by Albrecht von Halberstadt; but above all there was an epic German Classical trilogy. With express reference back to his predecessor Veldeke, a cleric associated with the court named Herbort von Fritzlar wrote an epic of Troy, and then, it is presumed, also a Jerusalem-epic. Just as we have only a fragment of the *Metamorphoses* adaptation from the Middle High German period, so too we possess only a few hundred lines of Middle High German verse from the start of the Jerusalem epic (now known under the name of *Pilatus*), the Latin and French sources of which are known. The background concept which links the three works in terms of content is the combination of the Christian concept of salvation with the Roman imperial idea as promoted by the Hohenstaufens, who were related to the Thuringians [13]. The three works allow for the development of a transmission of a ruling authority into a Christian empire (*translatio imperii*): from ancient Troy (Herbort's *Trojaroman*) sovereignty moves to ancient Rome (Veldeke's *Eneasroman*) and then to the Jerusalem of the New Testament, which, however, throws away its opportunity, is destroyed by the converted Roman emperors and then eventually has to surrender imperial power to the new, Christian Rome (*Jerusalemroman*). Veldeke's *Eneasroman* was well known in the Middle Ages, frequently copied and

transmitted, but never reworked or replaced by new versions.

In the 15th and 16th cents. a new literature of German prose novels began to establish itself. In the long term these became the most decisive competition for the genre of the verse epic. Many of the older German verse epics were put into prose, but not Veldeke's *Eneasroman*. Meanwhile the Humanists had set new parameters, and had even surrounded Virgil with a particular aura. First on the agenda now was the philological establishing and dissemination of the original text before setting about to provide for the first time a genuine, complete translation. In Germany it was the Strasbourg Town Clerk and author of the *Narrenschiff*, Sebastian Brant (1457–1521) who took the most important step. He, too was part of the circle of Maximilian I., and had already emerged at the end of the 15th cent. as the editor of Latin → PRINTED WORKS . In 1502 he set up, together with the Strasbourg printer Johann Grüninger a Virgil-edition which has rightly been described as epoch-making [27. 271]. It was the first illustrated Virgil-edition, with 214 woodcuts, which remained an iconographical standard for a long time. The *Aeneid* achieved with this edition a great rise in esteem and an entirely new status.

From here there is a direct line to the first early New High German translation of the *Aeneid* by Thomas Murner (1475–1536) of Strasbourg. Murner based himself upon Brant's edition and had his text, in a good 20, 000 freely-done, rhymed couplets, printed also by Grüninger in 1515. His dedication to Emperor Maximilian I underscores in this case quite explicitly the programmatic recourse, always to be kept in mind too for earlier centuries, to the Classical combination of epic and sovereignty and its application to German circumstances. Virgil is to be brought, in honour of Emperor Maximilian as a German version of the Augustan literary cult of the ruler, from 'latynschem todt in tütsches leben' ("Latin death into German life"). While the 'German re-birth' of Virgil made clear the new precedence given to the vernacular, the German version in Maximilian's honour of the Augustan *Aeneid* demonstrates at the same time the connection, also spread in imperial propaganda, of Maximilian and Augustus [27. 273]. Only in 1610 did there appear the second German Virgil translation in rhymed couplets, from the pen of Johann Spreng (1524–1601); up to that point Murner's translation, with its seven later re-workings, remained the standard 'German Aeneid'. In the mid–17th cent. there followed then the *Aeneid* translation of Daniel Symonis (1637–1685) from Pomerania, and the first complete German Virgil in prose by Johann Valentin (1601–1684), long-serving rector of the Frankfurt Gymnasium. Lucan's *Pharsalia*, on the other hand, was not translated until 1695.

Homer was only really discovered in Germany in the period of Renaissance Humanism in the 16th cent. The first printed editions of the original texts appeared at this time (Strasbourg 1525 and Basle 1535). At that time, too, a Munich city clerk, Simon Schaidenreißer, took it upon himself to present to the Germans the first translation of Homer, the *Odyssey* in prose (1537), admittedly based essentially on Latin prose redactions. At all events, there is little evidence of the Classical spirit. The Greeks are transmitted into 16th cent. Germany: the siege by the suitors is rather like the scene in a Munich Beer Hall during a festival, Odysseus curses and fights like a sixteenth-cent. mercenary. The gods are either indicated symbolically or provided with a Christian veneer: Circe is voluptuousness personified, and Minerva is referred to as the 'heavenly helper' of Telemachus. All this makes Schaidenreißer stand out among his fellow-translators as a personality in his own right, and one who did not undeservedly acquire the nickname Minervus [22. 374]. The first prose translation of the *Iliad* was written in 1584 by the Austrian Johann Baptist Rexius, and it was followed in 1610 by the posthumous edition of the verse adaptation by Johannes Spreng, already named as a Virgil translator. What is still the standard Homer translation in Classical dress was, however, first provided by Johann Heinrich Voß (1751–1826) in the course of a renewed enthusiasm for the epic in the 18th cent. In 1778/79 appeared his translation of the *Iliad* and in 1781 that of the *Odyssey*, and in them he strove to match the syllables and the caesuras of the original, and in that way to achieve an imitation and echo of the sound of Homeric verse.

All these early modern efforts with the Classical tradition of the verse epic, the attempts to revive the genre by the Neo-Latin writers, the striving for an integration of the Classics into German literature by means of translation, the model of Italian masters such as Dante and Ariosto or Tasso, and even the continued study of Virgil and Homer in schools, all these things were powerless to resist the marginalisation and eventually the abandonment of the genre in the long term. The new, freer and more open genre of the prose novel attracted the interest of modern narrators like magic, and led in the 19th cent. to the de facto end of of verse epics in Germany. Carl Leo Cholevius notes in 1854 with surprise that not even Baroque literature, which was well-disposed towards Classical Antiquity, was inclined toward the epic, and in Germany readers had to wait for a long time for Klopstock's Milton-influenced *Messias* as a kind of national epic without a national theme: 'Das eigentliche Epos wird im 17. Jahrhundert nur vorbereitet (...) Es ist merkwürdig, daß diese Zeit, welche sich in die mannichfachsten Dichtungszweigen versuchte, vor dem Epos eine unüberwindliche Scheu hatte. Opitz meinte, heroische Gedichte seien leichter zu wünschen als zu hoffen. Zwar mußte, seitdem man an der Herstellung der strengen Kunstform arbeitete, nothwendigerweise auch einmal das Epos an die Reihe kommen. Indessen gehörte die nächste Zukunft noch dem Romane' ("in the 17th cent. the epic as such is really only in preparation (...) it is noteworthy that this period, in which experiments were made in the broadest range of poetic forms, had a fear

of the epic that could not be overcome. Opitz voiced the opinion that it was easier to wish for heroic poems than to hope for them. To be sure, when writers were working on the establishment of strict forms for artistic production, inevitably the epic, too, would have its turn. But for the moment, the immediate future belonged to the novel") [2. 337]. In the course of the centuries there did appear, however, beside the great novels also a whole series of significant verse-epics which are worthy of mention: the major satiric-comic beast epic *Froschmeuseler* by Georg Rollenhagen (1542–1609); the first Christian epic in the German language, with the title *Deutscher Phönix* by Kaspar von Barth (1587–1658); the *Habsburgische Ottobert* (1664) of Freiherr von Hohberg as the sole clear example of a large-scale epic in the Baroque period which has as its theme the glorification of a hero from an earlier age; then Klopstock's undeniably important epic of the 18th cent. *Der Messias* (1748–73); Goethe's model epic *Hermann und Dorothea* (1797); and finally the romantic-ironic swansong of the genre in Heine's *Atta Troll* (1843). A passing reference alone may be made to numerous further, but less significant attempts down to and into the 20th cent. [18. 718–746].

The fall of the genre of verse-epic and the de facto rise of the → NOVEL has long stood alongside a theoretical consideration of the epic as of major and of the novel as of minor value. Where an early theorist of the novel like Friedrich von Blankenburg could in his *Versuch über den Roman* (1774) still assume that the novel was the more or less natural continuation of the Classical epic, and could therefore legitimise the claims of the novel and place it on the same level as the epic, this changed in the period of German → CLASSICISM. "Schiller's judgments on the novel are thoroughly disapproving" [16. 16]. It is true that an explicit orientation towards the Classical epic as a poetological norm is no longer demanded in the modern period, and of course it was always accepted that things can be narrated well in both genres, but a fundamental difference of level is still assumed down to the 20th cent. In 1949 Paul Böckmann saw Klopstock's *Messias* as the last attempt in Germany to realise fully the genre of epic. He claims that already the subjective elements in Klopstock permit one to see: '...daß fortan die Zeit für das Epos vorbei ist, weil es sich auf eine vorgegebene Sagen- und Glaubensüberlieferung angewiesen sieht, während der Roman künftig gerade dadurch sein Leben gewinnt, daß er von einer persönlichen Erfahrungswelt erzählt' ("that from now on the time for the epic is past, because it sees itself as bound to a prescribed tradition in narrative theme and beliefs, whereas the novel will take its vitality from the fact that it tells of the world of personal experience") [1. 592]. Wolfgang Kayser spoke even more strongly in 1948 when he determined that in the novel the characters are: 'nicht mehr so welthaltig wie Odysseus, der König, der Götterliebling, der griechische Heimkehrer, – es sind persönliche private Figuren: Tom Jones, Madame Bovary oder Wilhelm Meister' ("no longer on such a grand scale as Odysseus, the king, the favourite of the gods, the Greek returning home – they are personal private figures: Tom Jones, Madame Bovary or Wilhelm Meister") [11. 359]. Helmut Koopmann rightly protested in 1983 against such prejudices with the comment: 'Diese Unterscheidung ist so antiquiert wie willkürlich. Käme heute tatsächlich noch jemand auf die Idee, Thomas Manns *Zauberberg* als Erzählung von einer privaten Welt in privatem Ton zu kennzeichnen, die *Odyssee* aber als Bericht von einer totalen Welt? Haben sich die Verhältnisse nicht umgekehrt – zumindest in dem Sinne, daß in der eine zwar charakteristische, aber letztlich doch auf einen einzelnen bezogene Weltfahrt dargestellt ist, im *Zauberberg* aber die Lebensstimmung und die Untergangsangst einer ganzen europäischen Generation, einbezogen in Versuche, den Untergang dennoch zu überwinden? Es geht hier weniger um das Verhältnis der erzählenden Dichtung zur Wirklichkeit und zum Leben als vielmehr um die Frage, in welchem Ausmaß das erzählte Geschehen repräsentativ ist' ("that distinction is as antiquated as it is capricious. Would anyone really think nowadays of saying that Thomas Mann's *Zauberberg* is a narrative of a private world in private terms, but see the *Odyssey* as presenting a total world? Have the relationships rather not been reversed, – at least in the sense that in the *Odyssey* a journey is being portrayed which is indeed characteristic, but which is in the last analysis dependent upon a single individual, whereas in the *Zauberberg* we have the mood and the apocalyptic angst of an entire generation in Europe bound up in the attempt to overcome the apocalypse in spite of everything? It is less about the relationship of narrative writing to reality and life than the question of to what extent the narrated material is representative") [16.12].

In the context of the category of privacy, as discussed here, it is worth considering, beside the interpretative also the receptions-aesthetic aspect. The verse epic had its starting point as a major narrative form in the period of orality. Even if an epic like the *Aeneid* arose with much rewriting over a period of years, it was still intended for oral delivery. The change to essentially written literature, which has come about on a large scale since the 14th cent., and above all the possibilities opened up by the 'Gutenberg galaxy' demanded in the modern period different conditions of reception, most notably the privacy of the actual act of reading. In earlier periods, large-scale epics had to be recited over a period of days. Now portions of large-scale narratives could be read whenever desired. The older aesthetic of a metrical offering intended to be listened to, which depended upon an original *aísthēsis*, on theatrical performance, on the experience of sounds and rhythms, were now functionally obsolete, and could only be maintained as a norm down to the 20th cent. in short forms (lyric poems) which could be performed in a short time. All forms of verse epic, even those that were autochthonic, were no longer fashionable. In the 15th cent., therefore, many of the old epics were put into prose; in the 16th

cent. people began to write original prose novels as well. The inclusion as a living form of the major Classical epic into the context of German literature was, apart from individual borrowings, always a problem on grounds of content, because in thematic terms there was mostly not enough potential for identification, and they exerted in literary terms clearly too little fascination. As part of the cultural heritage they were clearly appreciated, on the other hand, and were essential as the starting point for aesthetic debate. But it is indicative that the late German national epic on a large scale, Klopstock's *Messias*, is a biblical poem which no one really ever tried to surpass, which did not point on to new directions, and whose 'readability' was so limited that even many contemporaries freely reported that they had not been able to read it to the end.

→ Alexander Romance
→ GERMANY; → NEO-LATIN

1 P. BÖCKMANN, Formgeschichte der deutschen Dichtung, vol. 1, Von der Sinnbildsprache zur Ausdruckssprache, 1949   2 C. L. CHOLEVIUS, Geschichte der deutschen Poesie nach ihren antiken Elementen: I, Von der christlich-römischen Cultur des Mittelalters bis zu Wieland's französischer Gräcität, Leipzig 1854 (repr. 1968)   3 G. EHRISMANN, Geschichte der deutschen Literatur bis zum Ausgang des Mittelalters, I, 1918   4 G. ELLINGER, s.v. Neulateinische Dichtung Deutschlands im 16. Jahrhundert, in: P. MERKER, W. STAMMLER (eds.), Reallexikon der deutschen Literaturgeschichte, vol. 2, 1926/28, 469–495   5 W. FECHTER, Lateinische Dichtkunst und deutsches Mittelalter. Forschungen über Ausdrucksmittel, poetische Technik und Stil mittelhochdeutscher Dichtungen, 1964 (= Philol. Stud. und Quellen 23)   6 H. FROMM, s.v. Epos., Narrative Großform in Versen, in: K. WEIMAR (ed.), Reallexikon der deutschen Literaturwissenschaft, vol. 1, rev. ed., 1997, 480–484   7 S. FÜSSEL, Riccardus Bartolinus Perusinus, Humanistische Panegyrik am Hofe Kaiser Maximilians I., 1987 (= SAECVLA SPIRITALIA 16)   8 K. H. HALBACH, s.v. Epik des Mittelalters in: W. STAMMLER (ed.), Deutsche Philologie im Aufriß, vol. 2, ²1960, 397–684   9 G. FINSLER, Homer in der Neuzeit, 1912   10 D. KARTSCHOKE (ed.), Heinrich von Veldeke, Eneasroman, mittelhochdeutsch/neuhochdeutsch, 1986   11 W. KAYSER, Das sprachliche Kunstwerk, Eine Einführung in die Literaturwissenschaft, 1948   12 J. KNAPE, Die mittelhochdeutsche Pilatus-Dichtung und die Literatur im Umfeld des Thüringerhofs 1190–1227, in: Jb. der Oswald von Wolkenstein Ges. 6, 1990/91, 45–57   13 Id., Hochmittelalterliche Vergangenheitsdeutung in mittelhochdeutscher Antikeliteratur, in: H.-W. GOETZ (ed.), Hochmittelalterliches Geschichtsbewußtsein im Spiegel nichthistoriographischer Quellen, 1998, 317–329   14 Id., War Herbort von Fritzlar der Verfasser des Vers-Pilatus?, in: Zschr. für dt. Alt. 115, 1986, 181–206   15 F. P. KNAPP (ed.), Der Ligurinus des Gunther von Pairis in Abbildungen des Erstdrucks von 1507, 1982 (= Litterae 76)   16 H. KOOPMANN, s.v. Vom Epos zum Roman, in: Id. (ed.), Handbuch des deutschen Romans, 1983, 11–30   17 K. LANGOSCH, Die deutsche Literatur des lateinischen Mittelalters, 1964   18 H. MAIWORM, Epos der Neuzeit, in: W. STAMMLER (ed.), Deutsche Philologie im Aufriß, vol. 2, ²1960, 685–748   19 J.-D. MÜLLER, Gedechtnus. Literatur und Hofgesellschaft um Maximilian I., 1982 (= Forsch. zur Gesch. der älteren dt. Lit. 2)   20 H. RUP-

PRICH, Vom späten Mittelalter bis zum Barock, 1970–73 (= DE BOOR/NEWALD: Geschichte der deutschen Literatur IV, 1 und 2)   21 W. J. SCHRÖDER, s.v. Epos (Theorie), in: W. KOHLSCHMIDT, W. MOHR (eds.), Reallexikon der deutschen Literaturgeschichte, vol. 1, ²1958, 381–388   22 W. STAMMLER, Von der Mystik zum Barock, 1927   23 H. STECKNER, s.v. Epos: Theorie, in: P. MERKER, W. STAMMLER (eds.), Reallexikon der deutschen Literaturgeschichte, vol. 4, 1931, 28–39   24 Vergil 2000 Jahre. Rezeption in Literatur, Musik und Kunst. Katalog zur Ausstellung der Universitätsbibliothek, Bamberg und der Staatsbibliothek Bamberg 1982–1983, 1982   25 J. WIEGAND, s.v. Epos, in: P. MERKER, W. STAMMLER (eds.), Reallexikon der deutschen Literaturgeschichte, vol. 1., 1925/26, 318–328   26 Id., s.v. Epos: Neuhoch-dt., in: RealLexikon, ²1958, 388–393   27 F. J. WORSTBROCK, Zur Einbürgerung der Übersetzungen antiker Autoren im deutschen Humanismus, in: Zschr. für dt. Alt. 99, 1970, 45–81   28 Id., s.v. Vergil, in: B. WACHINGER et al. (eds.), Verfasserlexikon, 10, 1998, 247–284.   JOACHIM KNAPE

IV. THE ANGLO-SAXON NATIONS
V. → CLASSICISM AFTER CLASSICAL ANTIQUITY

Epicureanism

A. INTRODUCTION   B. ANTIQUITY   C. MIDDLE AGES AND RENAISSANCE   D. THE 17TH CENTURY   E. THE 18TH CENTURY   F. THE 19TH CENTURY   G. THE 20TH CENTURY

A. INTRODUCTION

The reception history of Epicureanism displays some peculiarities when compared with the rest of ancient philosophy. The theses and ideas that go to make up Epicureanism are to be found not only in philosophical texts, but also and primarily in literature and poetry. Poems, treatises, articles from journals, novels, dramas, and essays make up a large part of the tradition. Epicureanism was rarely received as a closed system. Works of natural philosophy, ethics and popular philosophy crop up independently of one another. Already in Antiquity, but particularly during the period of the Church Fathers (→ PATRISTIC THEOLOGY/PATRISTICS) and the Christian Middle Ages, Epicureanism was exposed to polemic criticism. The axioms of Epicureanism are therefore often presented only indirectly or in a hidden fashion. For this reason the Epicurean tradition appears to be exceptionally disparate in character. This does not mean, however, that its influence was less robust than that of the other ancient philosophies. On the contrary, thanks to this kind of reception the axioms of Epicureanism enjoyed a certain degree of popularity.

B. ANTIQUITY
1. GENERAL   2. THE ROMAN POETS   3. SENECA

1. GENERAL
From the 3rd to the 1st cent. BC Epicurean theory exhibits no substantial changes in either content or form [23]. Not until the 1st cent. BC with the Roman reception of Epicureanism does a new phase set in. Philodemus, Piso, Caesar, Lucretius, Virgil, and Horace were all, at least in part and on occasion, adherents of Epicureanism. Even Cicero had a detailed though hostile interest in Epicureanism and thus became an important source. Seneca, actually known as an adherent of Stoicism, was an advocate of some elements of Epicurean theory and was instrumental in gaining for them authority and popularity, above all in the Middle Ages and the Modern Period.

Against the background of Roman expansion in the Mediterranean world and the growing influence of Hellenistic culture on Rome, Epicureanism attained new significance in the 1st cent. BC. An important advocate of Epicurean ideas was Philodemus of Gadara [27]. Unlike other Epicurean schools, those on Rhodes and Kos for example, his Epicurean circle in Herculaneum turned its attention also to the theory of art and aesthetics.

2. THE ROMAN POETS
In the Roman period it is the poets, especially Virgil, Horace, and Lucretius, who define the reception of Epicureanism. The links between Virgil and Epicureanism are a matter of debate [24. 370f.], but, in any case, he did study in his youth under the Epicurean Siron in Naples. The influence of Lucretius's De rerum natura is obvious, although more in respect to form and a general reverence for nature than to → NATURAL PHILOSOPHY itself. The influence of Epicureanism is clearer in Horace [24. 372f.]. Although he does not share Epicurus's principles of theology and natural philosophy, he does adopt some important aspects of his philosophy of happiness. His 'carpe diem' and 'frui paratis' are elements of a philosophy of life inspired by Epicureanism, with the particular aim of coming to terms with the exposure of human beings to an uncertain fate. Hedonism and aesthetics are very closely associated in the life and art of this poet (Carm. 1.11; Epist. 1.4). The writings of Horace became especially important to the tradition of Epicureanism. The same applies to Lucretius, whose influence is based not least on the fact that his didactic poem De rerum natura was capable of reception as poetry, independent of content [24. 383 ff.]. Despite all subsequent attempts to separate the poetry from the philosophy, it is this very proximity to both areas that constitutes the special character of De rerum natura. The aesthetic enjoyment experienced in reading it is a first step in implementing the Epicurean programme and making voluptas into dux vitae.

3. SENECA
In the case of Seneca it is not any systematic doctrinal edifice that conveys the spirit of Epicureanism, but rather his eclectic style. Although Epicurus's philosophy has fundamental flaws in Seneca's eyes, he has sympathy for its maxims, giving as they do a view of humanity as a whole, as body and soul at the same time. The Epicurean style of self-concern, preferring all-round, meaningful and methodical observation and nurturing of all needs and capacities as against the rigorous as-

ceticism deriving from Stoicism, comes very close to the ethics of Seneca the humanist. The Roman reception of Epicurean doctrines [24. 363 ff.] also clearly brings out their characteristic traits: polemical rejection of received tradition, criticism of all forms of religious and metaphysical prejudice liable to restrict human autonomy and, in a positive sense, self-concern oriented towards a refined experience of happiness that is both sensual and intellectual. Political and social aspects of Moral philosophy, on the other hand, are almost completely absent.

C. MIDDLE AGES AND RENAISSANCE
1. CHRISTIAN POLEMICS   2. REDISCOVERY IN THE RENAISSANCE

1. CHRISTIAN POLEMICS
Whereas in the → RENAISSANCE a number of important authors devoted their efforts to the rediscovery and rehabilitation of Epicureanism, Patristic and medieval reception was almost exclusively negative [25]. Christian rejection of Epicureanism was directed against atomism (→ ATOMISM), so-called atheism (→ RELIGION, CRITIQUE OF), the doctrine of the mortality of the soul, the denial of Providence and a misunderstood notion of Epicurean sensuality. The pig had now definitively become Epicurus' trademark. More interesting than the superficial polemics of the Church Fathers Arnobius, Lactantius and Jerome is the examination of Epicurean theory that Augustine undertakes in his *Confessiones* (6.16). Only fear of death, apparently, had prevented him from choosing Epicurus as his saviour. But the explicit and polemical rejection of Epicurean theories by Christian writers does not exclude the possibility that Christian psychagogics and pastoral care owe more to Hellenistic thinking than is initially apparent. It must also perhaps be assumed that the routes by which Epicureanism was received were various. Whereas Lucretius's *De rerum natura* is no longer mentioned after the 9th cent., the biography of Epicurus contained in Diogenes Laertius (*Vitae philosophorum*, B. 10) continued to circulate. It is thus entirely possible that, alongside the commonly held image of Epicurus created by early Christian polemicists, a more benevolent tradition persisted. Epicurus as a good person and Epicureanism as a dangerous philosophy obviously had a simultaneous influence on the medieval image of the Epicurean tradition [36]. Contradictory judgments of Epicureanism, as found in Petrarch, Dante, and Boccaccio, may evidently be ascribed to these diverging traditions. Typical is the juxtaposition in Boccaccio (Il commento alla Divina Commedia, ed. D. Guerri, 1981, bk. 3.45) of the person, the 'molto morale e venerabile uomo', and his perverse 'e detestabili opinioni'. Such statements attest to a rather superficial awareness of Epicurean philosophy. Comprehensive theoretical examination of the hedonism and radical moral autonomy of Epicurean teaching does not begin until the Renaissance with the works of Cosma

Raimondi, Lorenzo Valla, Marsilio Ficino, Erasmus of Rotterdam, Thomas More, Rabelais, and Montaigne [15].

2. REDISCOVERY IN THE RENAISSANCE
For the first time since Antiquity, in Lorenzo Valla's dialogue *De voluptate* (1428–1431) [8] Epicurean hedonism is fully discussed and placed in context [37]. The picture he gives turns out to be extremely favourable. It appears that the conflict between Christianity and ancient hedonism is reconcilable. Similar attempts at a reconciliation between Christianity and hedonism are to be found in the *Colloquia familiaria* of Erasmus of Rotterdam and in Thomas More's *Utopia* (1516). It is above all conceptions of an inner eudaimonism that are adopted from ancient Epicureanism. For Renaissance Christian Epicureans, realisation of the greatest possible happiness on earth does not represent any conflict with Christian doctrine, but rather the fulfillment of God's commandments. The re-evaluation of material things, the world, nature, humanity, sensuality, and aesthetics always remains in the context of Christian belief. Only in retrospect can such reflections and re-evaluations on the part of the Humanists be discerned as the beginning of the general secularisation of European thought. The Epicurean is also to be found in Rabelais's grotesque novel *Gargantua and Pantagruel* (1532–1564). Laughter, pleasure, eating, zest for life and enjoyment are associated here with a specific worldly knowledge that encompasses the entire human condition and ridicules the separation of the physical and the spiritual, body and soul. In the Abbey of Thélème, a kind of 'anti-monastery', the elite among life's artists lead a free, autonomous life devoted to enjoyment, where self-interest and the common good easily converge. There is as little contradiction here between happiness and morality as between sensuality and rationality, and poetry and truth are no longer mutually exclusive.

As in Rabelais, in Montaigne's anthropology too the physicality and sensuality of human beings, the *condicio humana*, is a central theme, but more from the aspect of pain and suffering than of pleasure and enjoyment [32]. For Montaigne, too, asceticism in the sense of Hellenistic self-concern is the most appropriate means of leading a life that is as far as possible free of care and therefore happy. But what mainly interests Montaigne is coping with death; in this, in common with Epicurus, he sees the decisive element of a happy and successful life. He, however, recognises that what is vital is to cope with the fear of death in life, and not, as Epicurus suggests, to banish death from life. For the sake of *volupté* the fear of death must be kept in check. In this respect, Montaigne succeeds in improving on Epicurean teaching by its own means and equipping it with a differentiated psychology *(Essais* 1.20). A similar process applies to the link between sensualism and aesthetics. In the sensual enjoyment of aesthetic experience, humanity transcends reality with the aid of the imagination and in this way gains a creative and free relationship with its world. For Montaigne, morals and aesthetics are related to one another in a manner that is typical of Epicurean thinking. The period of the Renaissance is of central significance for the history of the influence of Epicureanism in subsequent centuries. The characteristic traits of a tradition that exists, above all, in the areas of transition between literature and philosophy, where it proceeds to establish a further influential web of discourse, are to be found less in established philosophical discussion than in often-obscure traces of Epicurean motifs. Here one can already discern in form and content that productive model, characteristic of the reception of Epicurus, to which 'Epicureans' remain obligated right through to the 20th cent.

D. The 17th Century
1. The Erudite Libertines and Hobbes
2. Reflections on Morals and Manners

1. The Erudite Libertines and Hobbes

It is almost possible to speak of an Epicurean 'fashion' in the 17th cent.; in France in particular, both the doctrine on nature, i.e., atomistic theories in particular, and its thoughts on philosophy were highly successful [19]. Especially in so-called 'libertine' circles, Epicureanism was enthusiastically received. Towards the end of the Renaissance the concern with nature underwent enormous re-evaluation, and it can certainly be said that neither Aristotelian physics nor Christian theology served as a basis for this new scholarship. In the 17th cent. → Scepticism and Epicureanism enter into alliance against scholastic Aristotelianism and Christian theology, forming the basis for the ideal of a happy inner life that is, in contrast to the Renaissance, to a large extent detached from religious guidelines, and is even capable of assuming a polemically anti-religious character. Elie Diodati, Gabriel Naudé, François de la Mothe le Vayer, and Pierre Gassendi are regarded as the most important representatives of erudite libertinism (*libertinage érudit*). For Gassendi the rehabilitation of Epicurean philosophy stands at the focal point of his philosophical oeuvre [40], from his anti-Aristotelian *Exercitationes paradoxicae adversus aristoteleos* and his *De vita et moribus epicuri* (1647), where in books three to eight he defends Epicurus against accusations and slanders [2. Vol. 5: 192–236], to the posthumously published *Syntagma philosophicum* ([2] Vols. 1 and 2). He speaks of 'ma philosophie d'Épicure', details of which he wishes to change, so as to 'y interposer encore quelques nouveaux raisonnemens avec des responses et adoucissemens convenables aux points qui touchent nostre foi' ("to interject here some new arguments with responses and qualifications suitable on points which touch our faith"; *Lettres de Peiresc* 4, 1893: 249). The *adoucissemens* relate to the immortality of the soul and the Christian doctrine of creation, which he expressly acknowledges. Although Gassendi thus distanced himself from core elements of Epicurean theory and funda-

mentally rejected its materialism, he contributed significantly to the dissemination of Epicureanism, not only in France, but also, through Walter Charleton [3], in England [19.227].

Cartesian philosophy was discussed in the Parisian circles around Marin Mersenne, also frequented by Hobbes on his journeys [35]. The central problem was the question as to whether and to what extent it was possible for humanity to achieve certain knowledge. In this connection, Hobbes returned to the 'eidola' concept and hence to Epicurus' theory of perception. [31] Epicurean moral philosophy was of lesser importance.

2. Reflections on Morals and Manners

On the other hand, it was precisely the implications of Epicureanism at the level of personal ethics that interested the moralists of the 17th and 18th cents. [16]. Salon culture formed the basis of morals and manners in the second half of the 17th cent. This was where the ideal of the *honnête homme* was molded and the unmasking of the love of self, *amour-propre*, carried on. The moralists too were skeptics, less with respect to human potential for knowledge than to the capacity for moral action. In La Rochefoucauld, it is the critical and self-critical function of Epicurean philosophy that is received; in Saint-Evremont, cultivated hedonism. La Fontaine too values the critical and educational potential of Epicurean moral teaching. Unconditional faith in the power of reason is as foreign to these thinkers as is theology's disdain for human autonomy.

E. The 18th Century
1. General 2. Empiricism and Early Enlightenment Eclecticism 3. Moralist Weeklies and the Rococo 4. Christoph Martin Wieland 5. Radicalism and Popular Philosophy

1. General

In the 18th cent. the reception of Epicurean axioms enjoyed a sharp upsurge. The European Enlightenment appropriated to itself a whole series of Epicurean arguments. These included an emphasis on human autonomy in matters concerning the shaping of the inner life, atomistic and mechanistic positions in natural philosophy, the re-evaluation of sensuality and aesthetics and, above all, eudaimonism and the philosophy of happiness. Everywhere private happiness became a publicly discussed topic because, in the context of an increasingly differentiated bourgeoisie, its realisation was seen as fundamental to the overall design of a happy life. Family, marriage, and friendships were not pre-existent structures. They had to be shaped. They were the challenge, the task and the touchstone of a successful life. The essentially eudaimonistic character of the related patterns of thinking pointed up the universal validity of the premises involved but, at the same time, relegated to the individual the task of shaping his or her own destiny. This concept entailed a gradually increased emphasis on the affective aspects of the human person. This is attested to as much by the new disciplines of psychology, pedagogy, and aesthetics, as by the literary styles of Sentimentalism and Storm and Stress. Reason without the corrective of experience and sensuality was increasingly regarded as inadequate and futile. The conditions for the possibility of experience and knowledge in the area of nature were the concern of English empiricism; the early Enlightenment eclectics around Thomasius, the authors of lexica and philosophical histories, sought to make the significance and function of historical experiential knowledge a fertile source for the practically-oriented thinking of the Enlightenment.

2. Empiricism and Early Enlightenment Eclecticism

Locke joined the critics of Cartesianism. He had read Gassendi's works and become acquainted with his successful student François Bernier in Paris [34]. His atomistic physics and hedonistic 'fundamental ethics' are in the Epicurean tradition. The analogies between the philosophy of Locke and early German Enlightenment thinking are obvious. Christian Thomasius, who is seen in Germany as the "saviour of Epicurus" (Ernst Bloch,) was also influenced by the corresponding French tradition. Besides Pierre Bayle's *Dictionnaire historique et critique* (1697), which contains an article on Epicurus that built on Gassendi's mediation between Christianity and hedonism [1 Vol. 1. 364–376], Thomasius recommends that his readers read the French libertines. The rules of discretion advocated by Thomasius in his doctrine of practical philosophy are modelled on Epicurean conceptions of eudaimonism. Accordingly, for him the highest form of happiness is "peace of mind" (*Einleitung zur Sittenlehre*, 1692, repr. 1968, sections 63, 85). Thomasius used every opportunity to defend Epicurus against polemical attacks. His students and followers, such as Johann Franz Budde, Gottlieb Stolle and Christoph Heumann (editor of *Acta philosophorum*, the first German periodical on the history of philosophy) and, above all, Nikolaus Hieronymus Gundling continued these endeavours. Influential lexica and philosophical histories, such as those of Johann Georg Walch and Jakob Brucker, devoted detailed and, for the most part, balanced articles on Epicurus, some of them even favourable. Scattered but nonetheless extremely effective, this eclectic evolution of Epicurus' image went to make up that fund of material which provided, virtually of necessity, the literature and poetry of the time with numerous motifs of an enlightened Epicureanism.

3. Moralist Weeklies and the Rococo

Around the middle of the century, so-called *Moral Weeklies* arose in Germany based on English and French models. These had set themselves the goal of providing for their readers an appealing and entertaining education in leading the good life [33]. Reason and emotion in correct balance were to be the guarantee of a happy and virtuous life. Besides other wise men from cultural history, for example, Seneca, Marcus Aurelius, Luther, and Saint Paul, they also included Epicurus among those models they deemed worthy of imitation. The heretic and sensualist had thus become a *Biedermann* ('normal person'), his maxims recommended without reservation. The bright, conversational tone struck up in many of these weeklies already bears the hallmarks of the literary Rococo. Here too there is much that is Epicurean, Horace now being the preferred source – or allusion has to suffice, in order to avoid any hint of a scorned erudition. Peaceful rural life and a happy equanimity in the enjoyment of simple and innocent pleasures shared with friends or a lover: this is the Rococo poet's encounter with the ideal. Harmless dalliance also has its serious sides: the demand is for distance from deceitful (courtly) city life, and freedom with regard to way of life and poetry, as stipulated, for example, in Johann Wilhelm Ludwig Gleim and Johann Peter Uz or, too, in Johann Arnold Ebert, Friedrich von Hagedorn and Johann Nikolaus Götz. And, in an early poem by Albrecht von Haller, Epicurus is addressed as the "favoured child" of fate and guarantor of a happy life (Albrecht von Haller, *Gedichte*, L. Hirzel, (ed), n.p. 1882, 315). The Rococo search for happiness, striving for success in life, for protection from threat and from fear and its concern for physical well-being may indeed include human sensuality in its 'calculation of happiness' (*Glückskalkül*); the difficulties normally encountered by humanity in dealing with its sensuality are thematised as, at most, easily remediable defects [30]. The great novels of Christoph Martin Wieland are the first to successfully 'psychologize' the problem.

4. Christoph Martin Wieland

Wieland's concern with Epicureanism began with his didactic poem *Die Natur der Dinge* (1751), in which he sought to create a German 'anti-Lucretius' of the kind that had been produced with great success by Cardinal Polignac in France in 1747. Not until 15 years later, in 176,6 had he freed himself from the opinions expressed there, and in *Musarion* he offered a new world vision. In his novels *Agathon* (the three versions were published in 1766/67; 1773; 1794) [9] and *Aristipp* (1800/1802) [10] he embarked upon a substantial examination of Epicureanism. The *Commentaries on Horace* and the conversations with the dead, *Euthanasia*, expand on this. The philosophical discussions between Agathon and Aristipp constitute the core elements of the novel *Agathon*. Hippias, as the representative of Epicurean materialism, Epicurean theology and self-concern, sets out to purge Agathon of his wildly exuberant ideas. The ambitions of both characters meet with failure. In the complex interplay of different ways of life proposed, it is the subsidiary character Aristipp who seems most to represent an exemplary lifestyle. He adheres to a moderate, highly cultivated Epicureanism. Also in the novel named after him, Aristipp embodies the ideal of a cultivated man living happily according to Epicurean rules [9. 355]. The pipe-dreams of the idealistic popular rationalists (*Volksaufklärer*) and fanatical utopians have long been consigned to oblivion. Neither does Aristipp espouse the self-seeking goals of a Hippias. In the *Commentaries on Horace* and *Euthanasia* various aspects of Epicurean doctrine are again explained and discussed from aesthetic and ethical points of view. In an extraordinarily diverse approach, Wieland presents the entire tradition of Epicurean argument and theory, in order to expound in literary form its potential significance, but also to point out its deficiencies and the risks for the philosophers of the European Enlightenment.

5. RADICALISM AND POPULAR PHILOSOPHY

Wieland was an attentive observer of political and intellectual developments in France. He often stressed how important the influence of Diderot, La Mettrie, and above all Helvétius was for him. All were advocates of Epicurean materialism. In Germany too some publications existed in the area of radical materialism. Many of the relevant texts appeared anonymously. More frequent than such a radical tendency in popular philosophical discussion during the last years of the 18th cent. is a toned-down version of Epicureanism, as advocated, for example, by Karl Ludwig von Knebel, translator of *De rerum natura*, by Christoph Meiners, or even by Georg Friedrich Meier in his *Sittenlehre* (1758ff.). Even Frederick II expressed marked approval, especially with respect to the critique of religion. But critics remarked time and again that Epicureanism was not a suitable basis for a political philosophy, and that it denied all the problems entailed in the organisation of life in society. Liberation from all forms of political exclusion, liberation for a life free of care in the spirit of the Enlightenment, was one of the most important attractions of Epicurean philosophy for the 18th cent.

F. THE 19TH CENTURY

In the 19th cent. reception is dominated by polemical and radical elements of the Epicurean doctrine of the autonomy of humanity and, more than ever, by the materialistic foundations of this philosophy. Even here, though, it is the case that Epicureanism occurs less systematically and frequently in marginal areas of literature and philosophy. In Schopenhauer's philosophy, atomistic and eudaimonistic concepts are no longer referred to except critically. Ancient materialism and contemporary materialism alike are revealed to be idealism disguised (*The World as Will and Representation* 2.1, Ch. 24, *On Matter*). On the other hand, Ludwig Feuerbach's work can be interpreted as a comprehensive adaptation of Epicurean axioms. His critique of religion and his demand that humanity be seen as a spiritual and physical whole, his sensualist theory of knowledge and his approaches to a eudaimonistic ethics, refer to the Epicurean tradition, although the latter plays no explicit part.

In the same year as Ludwig Feuerbach's *Wesen des Christentums*, the dissertation by the 23–year-old Karl Marx on *Die Differenz der demokratischen und epikureischen Naturphilosophien* (1841) appeared. Marx quotes extensively from the writings of Epicurus and

compares the depictions of Epicurus in Plutarch, Lucretius, and Diogenes Laertius [6]. He is concerned to differentiate clearly between the materialistic positions of Epicurus and Democritus, for example, with respect to the theory of liberty. For Marx, Epicurus' real achievement is his recognition of the fictional character of all speculation, which opens the way to unmasking true knowledge as myth. Marx's re-evaluation of Epicurean philosophy in the face of contemporary historical/philosophical classification concentrates in particular on the diagnosis that there is a radical difference between idea and world. This demonstrates its decidedly anti-Hegelian character. After Marx's text and the notebooks containing his Epicurus excerpts were published in the 1920s, they were translated into many languages and contributed considerably to the dissemination of the philosophy of Epicurus as an early form of materialism.

After initial sympathy for the Epicurean philosophy of happiness, F. Nietzsche concluded that it was merely another manifestation of weakness. For him, to despair of the feasibility of human happiness does not lead to melancholic resignation, but rather provokes "pleasure at causing suffering" and "Dionysian pessimism" [7. Vol. IV.2. 342; Vol. V.2. 304].

G. THE 20TH CENTURY

S. Freud developed a theory of culture essentially based on an anthropology grounded in hedonism. He held that it is the "programme of the pleasure principle that sets the purpose of life" [5. 207f.]. Besides the use of narcotics and sublimation through intellectual or artistic activity, he included ancient → DIETETICS as one of the various forms of a necessary 'economy' of frustrations. To supplement the Kantian ethic of duty, but also in rejection of it, more recent → PRACTICAL PHILOSOPHY increasingly referred back once more to ancient approaches; in particular, to projects for a happy life, and thus also returned to Epicurus, as, for example, among others, Hans Krämer in his *Individualethik* (1992). Michel Foucault, too, in his later work [4] returned to the ancient practice of "self-concern" as a form of individual ethics or non-idealistic method of formation of the subject.

→ Epicurus; → Epicurean School; → Lucretius,III. Poet [III 1] L. Carus, T.

SOURCES 1 P. BAYLE, Dictionnaire historique et critique, Amsterdam ⁵1740 (Engl. The Dictionary Historical and Critical of Mr. Peter Bayle, 1734, 1984) 2 P. GASSENDI, Opera Omnia, Lyon 1658 (repr. 1964, Introduction by T. GREGORY) 3 W. CHARLTON, Physiologia Epicuro-Gassendo-Charltoniana: or a fabrick of science natural upon the hypothesis of atoms, founded by Epicurus, repaired by Petrus Gassendus, augmented by Walter Charlton, London 1654 (repr. R. H. KARGON (ed.), 1966) 4 M. FOUCAULT, Histoire de la sexualité, 1976ff., (German: Sexualität und Wahrheit, 3 vols., 1976ff., Engl. R. HURLEY (trans.), The History of Sexuality, 1984ff.) 5 S. FREUD, Das Unbehagen in der Kultur, in: Id., Studienausgabe, A. MITSCHERLICH et al. (eds.), 11 vols., 1967ff., vol.

9 (Engl. J. STRACHEY (trans.), Civilization and its Discontents, 1961) 6 K. MARX, Über die Differenz der epikureischen und demokritischen Philos., in: Id., F. ENGELS, Werke (MEW), Berlin 1967ff., Supplement 40, 1973, 257–374 (also in: Karl Marx, Friedrich Engels, Gesamtausgabe (MEGA), 1975ff, vol. 1.1, 5–91, Engl. The Difference between the Democritean and Epicurean Philosophy of Nature, 2000) 7 F. NIETZSCHE, Kritische Gesamtausgabe (KGW), G. COLLI, M. MONTINARI (eds.), 1967ff. (Engl. R. GUPPY (trans.), The Early Greek Philosophers and Other Essays, vol. 2 of Complete Works, 1964, 1909) 8 L. VALLA, De voluptate, revised with title: De falsoque bono, M. DE PANIZZA LORCH (ed.), 1970 (Engl. A. K. HIEATT, M. LORCH (trans.), On Pleasure, 1977) 9 CH. M. WIELAND, Geschichte des Agathon, in: Id., Sämmtliche Werke, 39 vols., Leipzig 1794–1811, reprint 1984, vol. 1.1 (Engl. The History of Agathon, 1773) 10 Id., Aristipp und einige seiner Zeitgenossen, Sämmtliche Werke, vol. XI

LITERATURE 11 M. OSLER, (ed.), Atoms, Pneuma, and Tranquility: Epicurean and Stoic themes in European Thought, 1991 12 Actes du VIIIe congrès de l'Association Guillaume Budé, Paris 1968, 639–727: épicurisme au XVIe siècle 13 Spinoza, Épicure, Gassendi, Actes d'un Colloque de la Sorbonne, 1993, Archives de Philosophie 57, 1994, 457–604 (cf. especially: P.-F. MOREAU, Epicure et Spinoza; L. BOVE, Epicurisme et Spinozisme; P. LURBE, J. Toland et épicurisme) 14 A. ALBERTI, Sensazione e realtà: Epicuro e Gassendi, 1988 15 D. C. ALLEN, The Rehabilitation of Epicurus and His Theory of Pleasure in the Early Renaissance, in: Studies in Philology 41, 1944, 1–15 16 H. P. BALMER, Philosophie der menschlichen Dinge. Die europäische Moralistik, 1981 17 E. BIELOWSKI, Lukrez in der französischen Literatur der Renaissance, 1967 18 O. BLOCH, La philosophie de Gassendi, 1971 19 Id., Pierre Gassendi, in: GGPh2. Die Philosophie des 17. Jahrhunderts, vol. 2: Frankreich und Niederlande, J.-P. SCHOBINGER, (ed.), 1993, § 8; Vol. 2.1, 202–27 20 P. BOYANCÉ, Lucrèce et l'épicurisme, 1963 21 B. BRUNDELL, PIERRE GASSENDI, From Aristotelianism to a New Natural Philosophy, 1987 22 W. DETEL, Scientia rerum natura occultarum. Methodologische Studien zur Physik Pierre Gassendis, 1978 23 J.- F. DUVERNOY, L'épicurisme et sa tradition antique, 1990 24 M. ERLER, Epikur – Die Schule Epikurs – Lukrez, especially § 8 und § 32 Reception, in: GGPh2 Vol. 4.1, 188–202; 477–490 (with bibliography) 25 W. B. FLEISCHMAN N, Christ and Epicurus, in: S. G. NICHOLS, R. B. VOWLES, (eds.), Comparatists at Work, 1968, 235–246 26 M. FORSCHNER, Über das Glück des Menschen: Aristoteles, Epikur, Stoa, Thomas von Aquin, Kant, 1993 27 M. GIGANTE, La bibliothèque de Philodème et l'épicurisme romain, 1987 28 J.-M. GUYAU, La morale d'Épicure et ses rapports avec des doctrines contemporaines, 1927 29 H. JONES, The Epicurean Tradition, 1989 30 D. KIMMICH, Epikureische Aufklärungen, 1993 31 H. KRÄMER, Epikur und die hedonistische Tradition, in: Gymnasium 87, 1989, 294–326 32 B. MÄCHLER, Montaignes Essais und das philosophische System von Epikur und Lukrez, 1985 33 W. MARTENS, Die Botschaft der Tugend. Die Aufklärung im Spiegel der deutschen Moralischen Wochenschriften, 1968 34 T. F. MAYO, Epicurus in England, 1650–1725, 1934 35 S. MURR (ed.), Gassendi et l'Europe, 1592–1792, 1997 36 M. R. PAGNONI, Prime note sulla tradizione medievale ed umanistica di Epicuro, in: Annali della scuola Normale superiore di Pisa, classe di letteratura 4, 1974, 1443–1477 37 M. DE PANIZZA LORCH, A Defense of Life. L. Valla's Theory of Pleasure, 1985 38 M. PLANIC, Marx on Epicurus. Much Ado about Nothing, in: Dionysius 11, 1987, 111–145 39 P. PREUSS, Epicurean Ethics: Katastematic Hedonism, 1994 40 B. ROCHOT, Les travaux de Gassendi sur Epicure et l'atomisme, 1619–1658, 194.

ADDITIONAL BIBLIOGRAPHY D. CLAY, Paradosis and Survival: Three Chapters in the History of Epicurean Philosophy, 1998; J.-C. DARMON, Philosophie épicurienne et littérature: Propositions pour l'étude de leurs relations de Gassendi à l'Encyclopédie, in: J. DAGEN, PH. ROGER (eds.), Un Siècle de deux cents ans?: Les XVIIe et XVIIIe Siècles: Continuités et discontinuités, 2004, 19–55; C.-F. GEYER, Epikur zur Einführung, 2000; D. R. GORDON, D. B. SUITS (eds.), Epicurus: His Continuing Influence and Contemporary Relevance, 2003; M. HOSSENFELDER, Epikur, 1991; H, JONES, The Epicurean Tradition, 1992; M. J. OSLER, Atoms, Pneuma, and Tranquility: Epicurean and Stoic Themes in European Thought, 1991; D. N. SEDLEY, Lucretius and the Transformation of Greek Wisdom, 1998; J. WARREN, Epicurus and Democritean Ethics: An Archaeology of Ataraxia, 2002; J. WARREN, Facing Death: Epicurus and his Critics, 2004 DOROTHEE KIMMICH

Epigrammatic Poetry

A. DEFINITION B. GREEK AND LATIN EPIGRAMMATIC POETRY C. THE EPIGRAM IN NATIONAL LITERATURES

A. DEFINITION

The epigram is today considered to be exclusively a written, self-contained short poem that tries to reach a climax and conclusion in the shortest space possible and makes apodictic statements about a particular subject or thought in an often-fictionalized setting. Conceptual vagueness and a complex historical development of the genre do not permit a precise definition of the latter or a general typology. Antiquity knows no coherent theory of the epigram but offers rather a conceptual polyvalence. Greek *epigramma* means inscription, title (legend), in prose first of all, and then later in verse. The term is also applied to elegiac forms or to short poems in general. Latin *epigramma* is attested since Varro and Cicero and denotes not just inscriptions but little poems of all kinds. Even medieval Latin has no precise definition of an epigram. Not until Humanistic poetics was there any interest in a genre-related theory of the epigram. The epigram was regarded as a short, pointed and generally satirical poem. Since that time, the epigram has been a fixed component of the genre-canon as a short poem of satirical, elegiac, gnomic or panegyric character.

B. GREEK AND LATIN EPIGRAMMATIC POETRY

1. ANTIQUITY 2. MEDIEVAL AND LATE LATIN EPIGRAMMATIC POETRY

1. ANTIQUITY

Archaic prototypes and epigrams from the Greek Classical period have scarcely any role to play in post-

Antiquity reception. Among the many ancient writers of epigrams, Martial and Catullus in particular, and the poets of the *Anthologia Graeca* were to exercise an influence on the epigram's later history. Of much lesser influence were such poets as Asclepiades, Meleager, Lucillius, Nicarchus, Ausonius and Ennius. Martial, the outstanding figure for Roman epigrams, is of unique importance for the European reception of the epigram until the Enlightenment. Despite lyrical and elegiac elements in his work, Martial is regarded as the doyen of the satirical epigram.

2. MEDIEVAL AND LATE LATIN EPIGRAMMATIC POETRY

The Latin epigram continued throughout the Middle Ages without being given any special attention, although with a clear tendency towards the aphoristic [2. 312–317]. The medieval epigram is not regarded as satirical; nonetheless the satirical epigram does recur from the 11th cent. on [12. 103]. Although Martial was well-known and imitated, he was generally rejected as immoral or un-Christian [16. 557f.]. That changed with Martial's rediscovery by Giovanni Boccaccio and with the appearance of the *editio princeps* in 1471 [16. 561]. Through the renewed reception of Martial, and of Antiquity in general, the epigram, and quite specifically the satiric epigram, became a widely popular genre in the Renaissance. It proved to be an ideal vehicle for the positions of → HUMANISM vis-a-vis scholasticism [16. 562]. Humanism also opened up the epigram to religious themes. It was not until this period that a theory of the epigram was formulated [7. 27–47], at first tentatively with Celtis (1486), and then more systematically in the poetics of Robortello (1548), Sebillet (1548) and Minturno (1559). The definition of the epigram in J.C. Scaliger's *Poetices libri septem* (1561), following Martial and Scaliger's Humanistic predecessors, held sway until the 18th cent., and also the first work devoted solely to the epigram, that of Tommaso Correa (1569), relied on them. For Scaliger, brevity (*brevitas*) and astuteness (*argutia*) are essential features of the genre. The first printed publication, in Florence in 1494, of the *Anthologia Planudea*, as it was known then, introduced the reception of the *Anthologia Graeca*, a collection of 3,700 Greek epigrams deriving from the 6th cent. BC to the 10th cent. AD. The anthology is mostly representative of a Catullus-oriented, lyrical-elegiac form of epigram that Scaliger identified as *epigramma simplex* (*brevitas* and *lepos*) but that, in European reception until Herder, played only a secondary role, with the exception of French classicism. Late Latin epigrammatic poetry was already very popular in Italy in the 15th cent. (Beccadelli, Landino, Campano) and achieved an impressive scope in the whole of Europe until the 16th cent. Almost all important Humanists like Erasmus, More or Celtis tried their hand at epigrams. Epigrams are found scattered as occasional texts or as part of larger textual editions, but only rarely as collections. The pre-eminent figure of Late Latin epigrams is the Englishman Owen. Together with Martial, he is one of the fixed points of European epigram-reception in the 17th cent. [18].

C. THE EPIGRAM IN NATIONAL LITERATURES

Before the 16th cent., epigrammatic poetry in national languages existed only to a limited extent. It developed from familiarity with Late Latin epigrams, although there have been attempts to explain its origins from medieval vernacular didactic forms (e.g. Freidank in the early 13th cent.). Epigrams in the vernacular were to co-exist with those in Late Latin until the late 17th cent.

1. 16TH AND 17TH CENTURIES 2. 18TH CENTURY 3. 19TH AND 20TH CENTURIES

1. 16TH AND 17TH CENTURIES

The *Épigrammes* (1538) of Marot are considered to be the first collection of epigrams in a national language. They were inspired by Late Latin epigrams, by Martial and also the Italian Strambotto [8. 58f.; 9. 301]. Marot introduced the *causerie* style into French poetry, which enabled the epigram's passage into the French courtly tradition. Consequently, epigrams became popular with poets of the → PLÉIADE like Ronsard and Du Bellay. Alamanni published his Italian epigrams even before 1546 [8. 58f.], and Heywood's six books of epigrams in English appeared in 1562. German epigrams from this period, among others those of Hunger and Rittershausen, are known to us mainly as translations. The first German-language collection came from Lobwasser (posthumously, in 1611). The mannerist *argutia*-, *agudeza*- and *argutezza*-theories of Gracián, Tesauro, Pellegrini and Masen develop astuteness as the poetic ideal *per se* [13. 146–155]. The Martial-like epigram in the 17th cent. thus acquired a central place in the genre structure of the time and experienced a widespread reception throughout Europe. Its essential stylistic means are the *concetto* and *acumen*; playful punning is prized more highly than jokes of substance. In the 17th cent., the epigram flourished in the whole of Europe and reached the peak of its popularity. Even in the early 17th cent. it was the most widely disseminated literary genre in England and was used by virtually all poets of importance (Harington, Jonson, Donne, Crashaw, Benlowes, Herrick). For poetics written in the vernacular, especially in Germany (Opitz 1624, Birken 1679, Morhof 1682, Meister 1698, Gottsched 1740), as well as for the praxis of writing epigrams in German (Opitz, Weckherlin, Logau, Grob, Wernicke), Scaliger remained the principal authority, even if a large quantity of gnomic and panegyric epigrams can also be found [20. 80–127].

The mystical epigram, with its ascetic view of language (Czepko, Scheffler), exploited the possibilities of the *argutia*-aesthetics for the purposes of a mystical vision of God and distinguished itself by its delight in experimenting with forms. It is precisely this spiritual epigrammatic poetry that achieved a perfection of literary style and epigram form. In the later 17th cent., *argutia* was more and more regarded as helping clarity of expression (*perspicuitas*), as practised by Wernicke, for example. A subtly different practice and discussion of the epigram took place, however, mainly in France in the 17th cent. Poets like Maynard took up the epigram again after 1600, and it was used by the poets of the Rambouillet salon, among others, to express *préciosité*. In the *Traitté de l'epigramme* (1658), Colletet went beyond the usual discussion of brevity, pointedness and aesthetics of effect and took the epigram, through its qualities of *subtilité* and *argutie*, towards the *esprit*-ideal. Brevity was understood as economy of linguistic means, and the subject was an individual person or thing. Following him, the theory of the epigram, e.g. that of Vavasseur (1669) and of Boileau (1674), was built directly upon it. The representatives of French → CLASSICISM, on the other hand (Rapin, Montaigne, Nicole) devalued the *pointe* in favour of the Catullan model, and as a result the epigram all but disappeared from the French canon of genres.

2. 18TH CENTURY

Until late in the 18th cent., the theory and reception of the epigram throughout Europe remained attached to the old models of Martial and Catullus, with the pointed and occasionally satirical epigram *à la* Martial being the dominant model. For the newly-flourishing French epigram in the 18th cent., the blending of *pointe* with *esprit* was all-important. Representatives of the lightly satirical epigram of the 18th cent. are Lebrun, J.-B. Rousseau, Piron, Destouches and Voltaire. Du Bos and Saint-Mard are some of the few adherents of Catullus. After 1760, the epigram re-assumed the tradition of the Greek Anthology, which was emulated even by Voltaire [6. 17]. In England the satirical epigram as written by poets like Prior, Pope and Swift also lost ground after 1750.

Lessing (1771) constitutes the apogee and end-point of the Martial-influenced theory of the two-part epigram. 'Anticipation' depicts the object and creates the pointe that is resolved in the succinctly shaped 'dénouement'. Most poets of the 18th cent. (e.g. Lessing, Kästner, Goeckingk, Haug, Weisser) composed epigrams in this spirit, even though only a few epigrams were produced in the period from Wernicke's death (1704) until 1740. After 1740 the epigram proved to be more expressive and at times more frivolous and dramatic, with a more refined *pointe* (Hagedorn, Gleim, Klopstock). It is only with Herder (1786), who relied on the original elegiac and hymnal tradition of Greek Antiquity, that the *pointe* lost its dominant role in Germany, very late in comparison with the rest of Europe. Like other poets of the late 18th cent., Goethe, in his Venetian Epigrams (1796), sought to balance the satirical, erotic and elegiac. The *Xenien* (1797) of Goethe and Schiller occupy a special position, in that the traditional satirical distich is used in the service of literary retaliation. The Xenien battle that it launched had its effect on the 19th-cent. epigram.

3. 19TH AND 20TH CENTURIES

With the process of subjectivization and autonomization in literature of the late 18th cent., the epigram became a marginal genre, especially as the areas of the personal, subjective and experiential were closed to it as an object-focused genre. After 1800, the lines of reception disappear; the epigram – mostly atmospheric and emotional, rather than pointed, sagacious and ambiguous – is used only by individual writers like Grillparzer, Mörike, Hebbel, George and Kraus, in England by poets like Blake, Coleridge, Byron, Landor and later by Kipling, Pound and Graves. By some poets of the 20th cent., it is mainly used for social criticism (Brecht, Braun).

→ Anthology; → Catullus; → Epigram; → Martial
→ BAROQUE; → ELEGY; → LYRIC POETRY; → POETICS

1 T. ALTHAUS, Epigrammatisches Barock, 1996   2 G. BERNT, Das lateinische Epigramm im Übergang von der Spätantike zum frühen Mittelalter, 1968   3 W. DIETZE, Abriß einer Geschichte des deutschen Epigramms, in: Erbe und Gegenwart, 1972, 247–391   4 P. ERLEBACH, Formgeschichte des englischen Epigramms von der Renaissance bis zur Romantik, 1979   5 D. FREY, Bissige Tränen. Eine Untersuchung über Elegie und Epigramm seit den Anfängen bis Bertolt Brecht und Peter Huchel, 1995   6 K. HEKKER, Die satirische Epigrammatik im Frankreich des 18. Jahrhunderts, 1979   7 P. HESS, Epigramm, 1989   8 J. HUTTON, The Greek Anthology in Italy to the Year 1800, 1935   9 Id., The Greek Anthology in France and the Latin Writers of the Netherlands to the Year 1800, 1946   10 P. LAURENS, L'abeille dans l'ambre. Célébration de l'épigramme de l'époque alexandrine à la fin de la Renaissance, 1989   11 M. LAUSBERG, Das Einzeldistichon. Studien zum antiken Epigramm, 1982   12 W. MAAZ, Lateinische Epigrammatik im hohen Mittelalter, 1992   13 K.-H. MEHNERT, Sal Romanus und Esprit Français. Studien zur Martialrezeption im Frankreich des 16. und 17. Jahrhunderts, 1970   14 J. NOWICKI, Die Epigramm-Theorie in Spanien vom 16. bis 18. Jahrhundert, 1974   15 G. PFOHL (ed.), Das Epigramm. Zur Geschichte einer inschriftlichen Gattung, 1969   16 H. C. SCHNUR, The Humanist Epigram and its Influence on the German Epigram, in: J. IJSEWIJN (ed.), Acta Conventus Neo-Latini Lovaniensis, 1973, 557–576   17 Z. SKREB, Das Epigramm in den deutschen Musenalmanachen und Taschenbüchern um 1800, 1977   18 E. URBAN, Owenus und die deutschen Epigrammatiker des XVII. Jahrhunderts, 1900   19 TH. VERWEYEN, G. WITTING, Das Epigramm. Beschreibungsprobleme einer Gattung, in: Simpliciana 11, 1989, 161–180   20 J. WEISZ, Das Epigramm in der deutschen Literatur des 17. Jahrhunderts, 1979

ADDITIONAL BIBLIOGRAPHY T. ALTHAUS, S. SEELBACH (eds.), Salomo in Schlesien: Beiträge zum 400. Geburtstag Friedrich von Logaus (1605–2005), 2006; J. DOELMAN, The Religious Epigram in Early Stuart England, in: Christianity and Literature 54, 2005, 497–520; T. SCHÄFER, The Early Seventeenth-Century Epigram in England, Germany, and Spain: A Comparative Study, 2004

PETER HESS

Epigraphy, Greek
I. History of Finds   II. History of Epigraphical Studies

I. History of Finds
A. Historical Overview   B. Selection of Significant Individual Finds and Groups of Finds

A. Historical Overview

Inscriptions have been and are still found by various means and by employing various methods; chance often plays a fairly significant role as well. That is especially true of the early phase in the study of inscriptions (15th–17th cents.), as the first finds were not the result of targeted and systematic searches but were by-products, as it were, of the finders' real work; in most cases the finders were travellers and diplomats. Even later on, when research expeditions were undertaken with the express and solitary purpose of finding inscriptions, epigraphers gladly took on additional commitments that had other objectives but that nevertheless provided an opportunity to enter hitherto inaccessible territories. Thus, after construction of the Anatolian railway at the end of the 19th cent., the railroad company financed a research expedition into the Turkish interior which also brought inscription finds to light. Even military campaigns were used for this purpose, as for example Napoleon I's Egyptian campaign (1798–1799) and the French campaign in Greece against Ibrahim Pasha (1828) [27. 58, 81].

Study of Greek inscriptions began in the late Middle Ages. What was novel here becomes clear especially when compared to the situation with Latin epigraphy. For interest in Latin inscriptions had never completely evaporated with the onset of the medieval era, especially as the Italian population was virtually surrounded by Latin inscriptions. Moreover, the language provided them easier access compared with Greek inscriptions. By contrast, Greek inscriptions had, with the passage of time, become incomprehensible outside the area of Byzantine culture. Renewed interest in Greek inscriptions can be included among the characteristic phenomena of the Renaissance. Consequently, it was people from Western European countries who first began to study Greek inscriptions. Only later were they joined by Greeks themselves (around the middle of the 19th cent.), then by Russians and, towards the end of the 19th cent., by Turks and Americans as well.

The merchant Cyriacus of Ancona (or Ciriaco de' Pizzicolli, 1392–1457) can be regarded as the founder of the interest in Greek inscriptions that began in the 15th cent. [19]. Initially, it was business travel that took Cyriacus as far as Asia Minor and Egypt, where he copied inscriptions in every locality to which his dealings led him; in the course of time, his interest in epigraphical study took on a life of its own, to the point that he undertook extensive journeys just for that purpose. Much of what was lost after his time has at least been saved in his (generally reliable) copies, and Cyriacus is our only source for countless texts. Unfortunately, he never managed to publish his finds; it is only through his incompletely preserved diary records and his letters to friends and acquaintances that numerous Greek inscriptions have been passed down.

Only a few years after Cyriacus' travels, the situation changed with the Ottoman conquest of almost the entire area of Greek cultural influence (except southern Italy). Travel was then severely restricted. Among the rare finds in the period that followed was a major discovery for epigraphy about 100 years later in the modern Turkish capital Ankara, that of the *Monumentum Ancyranum*, a bilingual version of the achievements of Emperor Augustus.

At the end of the 16th cent., the number of scattered published Greek inscriptions had grown so large that the first published compilations were tackled; first of all a collection of selected readings by M. Smetius and finally the first complete 'thesaurus' by J. Gruter. They both have long remained an indispensable basis for study, even if they were soon overtaken by a flood of new finds, as greater opportunities for travel in the eastern Mediterranean expanded again in the second half of the 17th cent. In that period, a large number of books were produced with publications of Greek inscriptions, either as a collection pure and simple or in association with travel accounts (in the text or as an appendix). Some of the journeys in question extended over quite considerable distances and territories, but most were confined to a limited geographic area. Noteworthy among several such reports are those of Spon and Wheler [14; 15; 17]), Smith [13], Chishull [4], Pococke [12] and Vidua [16]. Their quality in terms of publication and occasionally also in terms of explanation of the inscriptions is highly variable.

Along with continuing activity by individuals, from the 18th cent. on there appear collective efforts in research into Antiquity by societies established specifically for this purpose and consisting of or involving those with professional expertise. Among the earliest of these was the → Society of Dilettanti, founded in London in 1733. After the successful completion of the expedition of J. Stuart and N. Revett to Greece, undertaken with the Society's support in 1751–1753 as a result of an association with an excavation, a second expedition, this time with the participation of R. Chandler, yielded a rich harvest of epigraphical material that was published *inter alia* in [3]. A little later, the French student of Antiquity and envoy in Istanbul, M. G. A.L. de Choiseul-Gouffier, used his travels and diplomatic activity to acquire a considerable number of Greek inscriptions that he bequeathed to the Louvre. A large increase in material was also the result of the residence of English architect and archaeologist Ch. R. Cockerell in Italy, Greece and Turkey for several years. To be sure, he did not publish his finds himself, but rather passed them on to a friend for publication, which was, however, never realised.

The 19th cent. introduced virtually a new era for epigraphy. Not only did the *CIG* appear then but, from that time on, epigraphical research was carried out by researchers of those countries where Greek inscriptions were found. Moreover, excavation activity that was getting underway increased the epigraphical inventory in an until then unknown way. Russia was one of the first nations to dedicate itself to epigraphy on the basis of finds in its own country: beginning in the early 19th cent., inscriptions from the Crimea and the northern coast of the Black Sea were published. On obtaining independence, the Greeks turned to their past, founded the *Archaeological Society* and conducted excavations in grand style (Athens, Eleusis, Epidaurus, Thebes, Sparta, Messene, Thermos, Dodona, among others). At the same time, excavations by foreigners continued; their epigraphical finds were published primarily in series (*inter alia* [6; 9; 10]). The Greek inscriptions discovered on Crete were compiled by M. Guarducci [7].

In Turkey, it was initially Greek societies (the Protestant school in Smyrna was founded as early as 1743), and then finally Turkish scholars who saw to the safeguarding of archaeological finds, while excavations were mainly carried out by foreigners and epigraphical finds were published in local journals by Greeks and other Westerners resident in the country. In more recent times, inscriptions found in Asia Minor have appeared in the series [8] (50 volumes to date), organized according to towns and cities. On the Turkish side, more and more epigraphic surveys are being conducted.

The study of inscriptions has thus proceeded in an increasingly close relationship with archaeology, and so it is only logical that epigraphers have been collaborating with the foreign archaeological institutes that have appeared in Greece and Turkey since the 19th cent. These institutes' excavation teams have generally also included an epigrapher responsible for the publication of epigraphical finds. In the meantime, along with excavations, a second archaeological-historical method has taken root and led to the discovery of Greek inscriptions, namely the so-called (archaeological, historical, topographical and/or epigraphical) survey: while inscription finds in an excavation represent only one of several groups of finds, a large number of surveys are conducted with the express purpose of recording inscriptions, without, however, neglecting the links with excavation finds in the process.

Grave-robbing has been and still is a dark side of the increased interest in inscriptions and their supposed material worth. Admittedly, it has helped bring many texts to light but they disappear very quickly into private collections, where they are rarely accessible for academic research. What is more, should such an item come to an expert's attention, all details of the location and circumstances of its finding are missing, which has a serious negative impact on its evaluation and considerably diminishes its scientific value.

B. SELECTION OF SIGNIFICANT INDIVIDUAL FINDS AND GROUPS OF FINDS

Although all Greek inscriptions are historical documents, their significance is quite variable, and it is often individual texts or groups of texts that dramatically extend our knowledge. The following offers a selection of the most important of these, in roughly chronological order (according to their dates of discovery).

In first place is the 1555 discovery of the so-called *Monumentum Ancyranum*. Chiselled into a wall of the temple of Roma and Augustus in the modern Turkish capital of Ankara, it consists of a Latin and Greek version (fig. 1) of the achievements (*Res gestae*) of the first Roman emperor. It is indicative of the period that this find occurred during the travels of an envoy, the scholar from Flanders, Augier Ghislain de Busbecq (1522–1592). The text was written down by his companion, H. Dernschwam (also written as Dornschwamm), but not published right away. The Latin version of this document is a copy of the report set out on bronze plates that Augustus had had installed in front of his mausoleum in Rome. A Greek translation, which must have been distributed (sometimes alone, sometimes together with the Latin original) throughout the eastern half of the Empire, was prepared for the Empire's Greek-speaking subjects. In any event, other fragments of the *Res gestae* have been found in Apollonia/Pisidia (in Greek only), while, significantly, in the Roman colony Antiochia/Pisidia, fragments only of a Latin version were only discovered at the beginning of the 20th cent [34].

The beginning of the 17th cent. saw an important find for Greek chronology, when a block of Parian marble obtained from Smyrna found its way into the Earl of Arundel's collection. This was a piece of the so-called Parian Marble (Marmor Parium), which originally contained a list of mythical and historical dates up to the year 264/3 BC, beginning with the Athenian King Cecrops dated to 1581/80. At the same time, the inscription is an example of the accidental nature of the circumstances surrounding epigraphical finds: the stone from Smyrna held lines 1–93, and it was not until 1897 that a second fragment was found on Paros itself with the lines 101–132 [24].

Just like the account of Augustus' achievements, another significant bilingual inscription was posted in the eastern Roman Empire, Diocletian's Price Edict, with which the emperor sought to put a cap on prices. No bilingual texts have been found, however, and the only Greek versions come from the province of Achaea. The first fragments were found by W. Sherard (British Consul in Smyrna) in 1709 in the Carian city of Stratoniceia; others have turned up since [28].

Found during Napoleon I's Egyptian campaign of 1798/99, the so-called Rosetta Stone was crucial for the decipherment of Egyptian hieroglyphs. It carries a decree of King Ptolemy V Epiphanes in Greek, to which translations in hieroglyphs and Demotic were added. It provided J. F. Champollion with the basis for deciphering hieroglyphs. His decipherment was confirmed by another find (decree in honour of Ptolemy III Euergetes) in the same three languages by K. R. Lepsius in 1866 [1. No. 8, 16].

Of similar importance to that of the 'Rosetta Stone' are a large number of bilinguals (Greek, Lycian) in Lycia in Asia Minor. The first of these were discovered and published in the middle of the 19th cent. A trilingual, found in 1973, contains a text (also of great historical interest) in Greek, Lycian and Aramaic, on which the decipherment of Lycian is based [30].

Excavations in the Cretan city of Gortyn in 1884 produced one of the most important finds for the history of early Greek law: the so-called Gortyn town charter from the 5th cent. BC. It contains a collection of juristic regulations in twelve columns [11. No. 163–181]. In addition, a large number of other legal texts, some of which go back to the 7th cent. BC, were unearthed there [11. No. 116–162].

Excavations in Athens have yielded a multitude of inscriptions that enable a deeper understanding of the Delian League's financial organisation. The texts can be divided into two groups, the 'tribute lists', in which the sixtieth part of the tribute of 'league members', earmarked for Athena, was recorded, and the 'appraisal documents', in which Athens' claims for tribute from 'league members', revised every four years [29], were drawn up.

The area of modern Turkey has proven to be extremely productive for significant finds in the last half of the 20th cent. The trilingual of Xanthos [30], which played a major role in the decipherment of the Lycian language, was mentioned above. Playing a comparable role for Carian was a bilingual, found in Caunus as recently as 1996 and published a year later. The value of its many layers of information, not only for Carian itself but also for the history of the period (possibly during the Lamian War), led immediately after its publication to a specially summoned interdisciplinary conference [18]. This inscription is thus a perfect example of the speedy publication and thorough and comprehensive study of an epigraphical find. The text, a proxeny decree of the Caunians for two Athenians, in Carian and Greek, confirms the readings of many letters of the alphabet that had been in contention up until then, makes possible both the decipherment of other symbols and the clarification of grammatical problems, and throws new light on political events in the second half of the 4th cent. BC (fig. 2).

An inscription from Macedonian Beroea, excavated as early as 1949 but published only in 1993, details the duties of the city gymnasiarch and thus offers a glimpse into the education of young men in the late period of the Macedonian kingdom [21]. Likewise from Beroea, there comes an honours decree of around 100 BC for a certain Harpalus who came from a family for which there are references back to the 3rd cent. BC [22]. Apart from the detailed account of the honoree's good deeds, in areas both military and religious, during difficult

times for the city, the nature of the honours given to Harpalus is especially interesting; he received not only a wreath but also a bronze statue (a singular honour at that time), and the honours decree was to be read in public annually at the election of officials.

During the excavations in Ephesus in 1976, a large marble sheet was found with most of the Customs Law for the province of Asia (*Monumentum Ephesenum*). The inscription consists of an original law from 75 BC and several addenda extending into the period of Nero's reign. The document's value for the early history of the province and Roman administration should thus not be underrated [5]. Two inscriptions throw light on the administrative development of the interior of Asia Minor during the Hellenistic period. Both texts, in which the issue is the status of localities as Greek πόλεις, contain letters of kings of Pergamon. The first was found in the 70s in Olbasa/Pisidia [26], the second, in 1997 in Tyriaion/Phrygia [25]. The inscription from Olbasa dates from 159 BC and points to the city being a Greek *polis*, with its characteristic institutions of council, popular assembly, city *strategoi* and a scribe, even before Attalid rule (from 188 BC). As well, many of the named officials bear Greek personal names. The text from Tyriaion, on the other hand, contains letters of King Eumenes II, one of which confers the status of *polis* upon the town; the king likewise refers to the necessary features of a Greek town: constitution, its own laws, council, officials and gymnasium. In connection with the latter, he provided for the distribution of oil and offered to send experts to help organise city administration and divide of the population into phyles (administrative districts). In exchange, he expected political loyalty from the citizens. Rome's dominant influence, too, is documented in the royal letter, in that Eumenes leaves no doubt that he has only Rome to thank for the land acquired through the peace of Apameia.

New information about the organisation of the Nemean Games, and their significance for the policies of Macedonian kings, as well as the furnishing of the *theorodokia* can be had from a list of *theorodokoi* that was excavated in 1978 in Nemea [31].

In recent decades the territory of Lycia in southwestern Asia Minor has alone yielded three historically very informative documents. In Oenoanda (north Lycia) provisions for founding a festival were set out in detail in a long inscription. In addition, repeated reference to the political, social and economic circumstances of the town and its environs offers insight into the region's administration and life in the middle of the Imperial period [35].

The well-known fact that in Antiquity towns and peoples were viewed as having an affinity through their descent from the same or at least related mythical founders, and could claim mutual assistance on this basis, is illustrated – with all possible consequences and attendant phenomena – by a revealing inscription, from shortly before 200 BC, that was found in Lycian Xanthus. The little town of Cytinium in Doris (Central Greece) turned to Xanthus for assistance in rebuilding walls destroyed by earthquake and the effects of war, basing its appeal on the affinity between the two towns. The text is an instructive example of how, on one hand, the myth gets 'shaped' by the petitioner in order to create the closest possible connection between the two parties, while on the other hand, the second party does not wish to decide to give generous assistance and can get out of the expected – and morally quite justified – assistance only through the pretext of financial strain.

One of the most recent sensational finds (1993) is the *Stadiasmus Lyciae* from Patara, a list, which was drawn up at the time of Lycia's adoption into the Roman Empire as a province, of all Lycian localities, showing connecting routes and distances. This monument not only helped clear up many questions of the country's historical topography but also shed light on the processes by which a region was reorganised as a Roman province (Preliminary Report SEG 44, 1994, 1205).

An inscription from Rhamnus (Attica, middle of the 3rd cent. BC) offers new insights into the cult of the ruler and the history of Athens in the Hellenistic period. It shows that the deme adopted the cult veneration of the Macedonian king Antigonus Gonatas, following a decision agreed upon by the entire Athenian community. Other information in the text confirms in particular the view that cult honours always depended on previously performed charitable deeds on the part of the honoree and were not, for instance, a sign of subservience (SEG 41, 1991, 75).

The consequences of rampant piracy in the Hellenistic period are given clear expression in an inscription, unfortunately badly damaged, of over 100 lines from Teos (Ionia) [32]. The town had been occupied in the second half of the 3rd cent. BC by pirates who demanded such a high ransom that the inhabitants of Teos were apparently obliged to take out a form of compulsory loan; the money collected in this way is documented in the inscription.

An inscription from Caria offers an instructive example of the involuntary sympoliteia, evidently on the orders of the satrap Asander (323–313 BC), between the localities of Latmus (later 'Heraclea on Latmus') and Pidasa. (It is not known, however, whether this measure ever became a reality.) An unusual element of the contract is the proviso, aiming at a quicker merger of the localities, that, for a six-year period, only mixed-marriages (ones between citizens of the two communities) could be entered into. [2].

Also from Caria, from → HALICARNASSUS, is a long Hellenistic poem in 30 distichs, which its editor entitled *The Pride of Halikarnassos* [23]. The first part deals with the founding of the town by a whole range of divine and mystic forebears of diverse origin who are brought together in a complex textual structure and linked through topographical references and allusions to local legends; *inter alia*, the birth of Zeus is shifted to Halicarnassus, and the city thus joins the ranks of the numerous locations claiming to be the divine father's birthplace. The second part of the epigram proudly enumerates famous writers who reputedly or actually came from Halicarnassus, such as Herodotus.

From Athens we have a most interesting law from 374/3 BC concerning the taxation and sale of grain [33]. In order to provide the population with adequate food supplies in winter, a 12 per cent tax paid in kind on grain was introduced by the Athenian cleruchies of Lemnos, Imbros and Scyros. Grain acquired in that way was to be sold in the agora on a day determined by the Popular Assembly at a price fixed by it. As well, the procedure for the delivering, storing and weighing, etc. of the grain was set down with great precision, with the names of those responsible as well as the deadlines to be met.

SOURCES   1 A. BERNAND, La prose sur pierre, 1992 2 W. BLÜMEL, Vertrag zwischen Latmos und Pidasa, in: EA 29, 1997, 135–142   3 R. CHANDLER, Inscriptiones antiquae pleraeque nondum editae, in Asia Minori et Graecia, praesertim Athenis collectae, Oxford 1774   4 E. CHISHULL, Antiquitates Asiaticae christianam aeram antecedentes ..., London 1728   5 H. ENGELMANN, D. KNIBBE, Das Zollgesetz der Provinz Asia, in: EA 14, 1989 6 FdD III, Épigraphie, 1909 ff.   7 M. GUARDUCCI, Inscriptiones Creticae, 4 vols., 1935–1950   8 G. PETZEL, Inschriften griechischer Städte aus Kleinasien, 1972 ff.   9 F. DÜRRBACH, Inscriptions de Délos, 1926 ff. 10 L. JALABERT, R. MOUTERDE, Inscriptions grecques et latines de la Syrie, 1929 ff.   11 R. KOERNER, Inschriftliche Gesetzestexte der frühen griechischen Polis, 1993 12 R. POCOCKE, Inscriptionum antiquarum Graecarum et Latinarum liber, London 1752   13 TH. SMITH, Septem Asiæ ecclesiarum et Constantinopoleos notitia, Utrecht 1694   14 J. SPON, Itinerarium in Italiam, Illyricum, Graeciam et Orientem, Lyon 1678   15 Id., G. WHELER, Voyage d'Italie, de Dalmatie, de Grèce et du Levant fait aux années 1675 et 1676, Lyon 1678   16 C. VIDUA, Inscriptiones antiquae a comite C. V. in itinere Turcico collectae, Paris 1826   17 G. WHELER, Journey into Dalmatia, Greece and Levant, London 1682

LITERATURE   18 W. BLÜMEL, P. FREI, CHR. MAREK, Colloquium Caricum, in: Kadmos 37, 1998   19 E. W. BODNAR, Cyriacus of Ancona and Athens, 1960   20 J. BOUSQUET, La stèle des Kyténiens au Létôon de Xanthos, in: REG 101, 1988, 12–53   21 PH. GAUTHIER, M. B. HATZOPOULOS, La loi gymnasiarchique de Beroia, 1993 22 D. A. HARDY, J. TOURATSOGLOU, The Harpalos Decree at Beroia, in: Tekmeria 3, 1997, 46–54   23 S. ISAGER, The Pride of Halikarnassos, in: ZPE 123, 1998, 1–23   24 F. JACOBY, Das Marmor Parium, 1904   25 L. JONNES, M. RICL, A New Royal Letter from Phrygia Paroreios: Eumenes II grants Tyriaion the Status of a Polis, in: EA 29, 1997, 1–30   26 R. A. KEARSLEY, The Milyas and the Attalids: A Decree of the City of Olbasa and a New Royal Letter of the Second Century B.C., in: AS 44, 1994, 47–57   27 W. LARFELD, Handbuch der griechischen Epigraphik I, 1902   28 S. LAUFFER, Diokletians Preisedikt, 1971   29 B. D. MERRITT, H. T. WADE-GERY, M. F. MACGREGOR, The Athenian Tribute Lists, 1939–1953 30 H. METZGER, E. LAROCHE, A. DUPONT-SOMMER, M. MAYRHOFER, La stèle trilingue du Létôon, 1979   31 ST. G. MILLER, The Theorodokoi of the Nemean Games, in: Hesperia 57, 1988, 147–163   32 S. ŞAHIN, Piratenüberfall auf Teos, in: EA 23, 1994, 1–36 33 R. STROUD, The Athenian Grain-Tax Law of 374/3 B.C., Hesperia Suppl. 29, 1998 34 E. WEBER, Augustus. Meine Taten (Res gestae divi Augusti, Latin, Greek, German), ³1975 35 M. WÖRRLE, Stadt und Fest im kaiserzeitlichen Kleinasien, 1988 36 ST. YERASIMOS, Les voyageurs dans l'empire ottoman, 1991.

II. HISTORY OF EPIGRAPHICAL STUDIES
A. INTRODUCTION B. HISTORY C. TASKS AND ACHIEVEMENTS

A. INTRODUCTION
Epigraphy is the branch of Classical archaeology that concerns itself with texts written on stone (freestanding monuments, walls, cliff-faces) and metal, alongside those on wood and ceramics. Inscriptions are valuable for research in that they (like coins and papyri) constitute direct evidence from Antiquity, without having been subject to an often distorting textual transmission of several centuries.

B. HISTORY
Even ancient authors used inscriptions as sources for their works, either by copying them off the stone or from a text preserved in an archive. Thus, for example, Herodotus (5,77,4) quoted an epigram from the Acropolis of the Athenian victory over the Boeotians and Chalcidians [53. 35]. Thucydides made use of nine inscriptions [50]; and also in Pausanias we find many which have for the most part been lost in the original but which are absolutely necessary for understanding mythical stories and historical events [37. 64–94]. While Arrian does not pass down any inscriptions, he is, however, an early witness to the inability in broad areas of the Hellenised world to compose inscriptions in correct Greek [4] (Trapezus on the Pontus), something which has also been observed by modern epigraphers.

Along with this use of individual inscriptions, more systematic collections of texts hewn in stone appear quite early. They have all been lost and at best are known in a few isolated quotations. Thus, we know that the Athenian Philochorus, the Macedonian Craterus and Polemon from Ilion in Asia Minor copied down (either from archives or from stone) and published inscriptions, while other works have been transmitted without authors' names; they bore general titles such as περὶ ἐπιγραμμάτων or specific ones like περὶ τῶν ἐν Δελφοῖς ἀναθημάτων [39. 12–13].

Interest in inscriptions was not rekindled until the end of the Middle Ages (for the following [39. 13–20]); inscriptions seen while on journeys were copied down, and collections of stones with writing on them were assembled in the houses, castles and palaces of the wealthy upper class. This revival in epigraphical studies can be ascribed to the merchant Cyriacus of Ancona, who undertook extensive journeys in the Mediterranean in the 15th cent. and copied down innumerable texts (but never published them). Only excerpts from his diaries have come down to us and constitute a

source which cannot be disregarded, especially for inscriptions that are otherwise lost to us today. That applies all the more so for the large number of travellers, especially diplomats, who published their finds subsequently and to whom we are often indebted for our only knowledge of many epigraphical documents. In the process the building up of collections shifted from a purely geographic arrangement, according to the location of the find, to a sequence based on the inscriptions' genres. The Dutchman M. Smetius (16th cent.) stands out, as he also placed value on obtaining an exact copy of the inscription, realizing that the form of a letter of the alphabet can be an important dating criterion. The first corpus of all inscriptions then known was produced by J. Gruter, who was active in Heidelberg, (Inscriptiones antiquae totius orbis romani in corpus absolutissimum redactae cum indicibus XXV, ingenio ac cura Iani Gruteri, auspiciis Ios. Scaliger ac M. Velseri, Heidelberg, 1603; reprinted in 1616 under a different title, Amsterdam ²1707), which long remained a standard work.

Because of increased travel by citizens of various countries (above all the English and French), the material was constantly growing in size even by the end of the 17th cent. but especially in the 18th cent., and Gruter's corpus was soon out of date. As early as the first half of the 18th cent., F. S. di Maffei planned a new publication of all inscriptions, envisioning for the first time the separation of Greek and Latin inscriptions. He wanted to publish, in a single volume, the ca. 2000 Greek texts then known. Maffei was, however, unable to carry out his plan, and the collections of inscriptions that were prepared (inter alia by Muratori, Donatus) [42. 40–66], contain only a few Greek texts in comparison with those in Latin and could not supplant Gruter's corpus.

In 1828 Volume 1 of the C(orpus) I(nscriptionum) G(raecarum) appeared (II in 1843, III in 1853, IV in 1859, Indices in 1877); it was created in 1815 by the Königlich- Preussische Akademie der Wissenschaften (Royal Prussian Academy of Science) at the initiative of A. Böckh and contained all Greek inscriptions known at that time, sorted geographically. While epigraphy was launched in modern times with the critical analysis of stones, the texts reproduced in the CIG, on the other hand, were not subjected to any checking of the stone, which would have been quite impossible anyway (even in the case of those stones that were still available). Before further treatment of the material, it was more important at that time to bring order to the unruly mass of known epigraphical resources. Even before the second volume was ready, however, conditions for travel in Greece itself had improved with its independence from the Ottomans, to the extent that, at the same time, a fresh increase in material had to be recorded. The original intention to keep the CIG updated with supplementary volumes was therefore not pursued but rather replaced with a regional approach, in keeping with which first the Attic inscriptions were published in a new revision (*C(orpus) I(nscriptionum) A(tticarum)*), 1873–1888), with other regions of Greece following. Critical analysis was once again an important methodological principle of this work.

While the *CIG* was in production, J. A. Letronne in France performed a fundamental service for epigraphical methodology by placing evaluation of inscriptions into a broader historical framework [45].

At the end of the 19th cent. the *Österreichische Akademie* (Austrian Academy) began a treatment of the entire corpus of all inscriptions (indigenous, Greek and Latin) found in Asia Minor, calling it *T(ituli) A(siae) M(inoris)* [31. 9–13]. Consequently, the work of a Berlin epigraphical project (named *I(nscriptiones) G(raecae)*), under the direction of U. v. Wilamowitz-Moellendorff since 1902, was limited to the Greek mainland and the islands and thus excluded those areas where inscriptions were to be published by archaeologists working there (e. g. Delphi, Olympia). In addition, the concept was further modified in that numbered geographical individual volumes (I–XV) were published, incorporating the *CIG* successor volumes that had appeared in the meantime (the *CIA* thus became *IG* I–III) and enlarging them with historical introductions and more detailed indices. Moreover, it had been intended from the very start to publish any new editions of these corpora under the title *IG Editio minor* in a modified, more easily accessible form that, however, soon became mandatory for all volumes. During this period, epigraphy had gained a foothold in Greece as well; by contrast, Turkish epigraphers did not appear on the scene until the 20th cent.

While the above named corpora make geographically-ordered inscriptions of all kinds accessible, a large number of thematic collections pursue the objective of making material in their subject area available to specialists, who generally lack any epigraphical training – either in entirety or arranged in selections. As representative examples only, we might name collections of epigrams [5; 6; 10; 13], 'historical' inscriptions, for example [11; 20], texts composed in Greek dialects [2], inscriptions on art history [8] and on religion [16–18].

Of the great number of Greek epigraphers in the modern period one may name the following scholars as representative: A. Wilhelm (1864–1950) (works: Österreichische Akademie der Wissenschaften (ed.), Adolf Wilhelm. Zum Gedenken an die 100. Wiederkehr seines Geburtstags am 10 September 1964, 1964) and, in particular, L. Robert (1904–1985), whose enormous power of creativity is just as impossible to emulate successfully as is the standard that he set for the publication of and commentary on inscriptions (works: L. Robert, *Opera minora* IV 1–52, V 11–23).

Two partially annotated annual surveys provide information on new finds and new treatments of published inscriptions: *Supplementum Epigraphicum Graecum* and *Bulletin épigraphique* (in *Revue des Études grecques*).

C. TASKS AND ACHIEVEMENTS

For almost all branches of the study of Antiquity, epigraphy offers essential material without which much of our knowledge would not be possible [56, especially 18–31], and it is the task of the field to secure the existing material, publish it and increase it. Securing inscriptions consists primarily of preserving for posterity, and making accessible to researchers, the text, the appearance of the inscribed surface and the context of its discovery, by means of notes, transcriptions, photographs and squeezes. Squeezes are paper or latex impressions of the original; a sheet of absorbent paper is moistened and applied to the stone, the paper is then cast over the surface and the indented letters with a brush, so that when dried one obtains a mirror image that can be easily read and transported. A latex squeeze is obtained by applying liquid rubber with a brush or roller onto the stone in several layers. Inscriptions documented in this way should be made public (and verifiable, if possible, by the provision of photos) in a manner that is comprehensible also to non-specialists, i.e. with translations as well as commentaries in a modern language. For larger collections, indices and concordances to help grasp the meaning of the material are indispensable. Study of inscriptions in isolation, however, offer scarcely any promise of an increase in knowledge, for the mutual dependence of the various types of source material (literature, papyri, coins, objects of archaeological research) means that they always have to be placed in an interpretative context.

Sometimes, identification of the original site of installation must first precede analysis and evaluation of the inscription, for even in Antiquity stones can be removed from their first location for a secondary purpose, e.g. construction of a wall. Thus, countless older monuments are found used in city walls that were constructed in Asia Minor as protection against invading Goths in the 3rd cent. AD. In not a few instances in the modern period, even relatively large stones were dragged over long distances, in particular for use as ship's ballast. In such cases it is, where possible, the task of the epigrapher to discover the original site of installation of the particular inscription, on the basis of the wording used, for example, or a relief depiction linked to the text, or the mention of particular terms (e.g. titles of officials) and other clues.

Greek inscriptions are indispensable, especially for historical research (political, economic and social history) and indeed not just for Greek but also for Roman history, as Latin never took hold in the eastern provinces of the Roman Empire. For that reason, only relatively few inscriptions in Latin are to be found there and they are largely limited to administrative matters carried out by Roman office holders. Epigraphically preserved texts are thus all the more significant for all areas of the ancient world, as the most commonly used writing materials, paper and parchment have not survived, except in Egypt. For the documents were generally kept in archives and, when the occasion arose, published on

whitewashed wooden panels (*leukomata*). Less frequently, by contrast, was the (costly) recording on more
durable stone – they are the texts available to us today,
giving an insight into the richness of official documents
that there must once have been in priestly, municipal
and state archives. It should at the same time be noted
that the documents stored in the archives were the officially valid originals, while the versions on stone are
only copies and do not necessarily reproduce the entire
text of the document. Even inscriptions of an unofficial
character, however – even 'unproductive' grave inscriptions – offer valuable information, especially as the
copious material often allows us, through the stringing
together of a large number of similar texts, to arrive at
more far-reaching interpretations than is, as a rule, possible with a single text.

While the authors do indeed offer information
about, and sometimes even quote important passages
from agreements concluded between cities, federations
and kingdoms, they do not generally transmit the complete wording of the agreements. In a large number of
cases, this is known to us only through epigraphical
finds that allow us to draw historical conclusions [1].
Other inscriptions permit insights into other areas of
ancient law; collections of laws are known to us, even
from the earliest period, e.g. through the municipal law
of the Cretan city of Gortyn (5th cent. BC) [7. No. 163–
181].

The organization of various forms of state as well as
institutions of state administration, rule and government are clear, or in many cases comprehensible or possible to reconstruct, only from the decrees and other
documents preserved on stone [15]. Thus, the functioning of (Attic) democracy, for example, is better understood through the process of passing resolutions which
is reflected in the inscriptions. The responsible officials
and the bodies taking part in the decision-making process are detailed there, and the motives and intentions
behind the decisions are given. The adoption of forms
of state and government is also reflected in inscriptions
by references to democratic or oligarchic institutions.
Epigraphical evidence offers important clues to help
distinguish between different states in terms of their organizational structure. Thus, inscriptions throw light,
for example, on the organization of alliances like that of
the Delian League [48], and, through certain formulae
used in inscriptions, confirm the development of Greek
federations of states and their departure from other
state forms [29]. In this context belong also the decrees
of rulers that led to the founding of a town, e.g. through
the merger of several settlements (synoecism) [27], as
well as contracts between cities to form a common
entity (e.g. Melitaea and Peraea in Aetolia, IG IX I² 1,
188).

Of utmost historical interest, and significant for the
study of self-representation and the ideology of rule, are
accounts of the deeds of the ruler that were set up in a
large number of places for all to see. Certainly the most
important of these, preserved in partly complementary

fragments, are the "Deeds" (*Res gestae*) of Augustus
[21], but also worthy of mention here are those of the
Sassanid ruler Shapur in Persia, who had a Greek version chiseled next to a Middle Persian one [47]. Numerous letters of Hellenistic kings and Roman emperors are
preserved on stone, which not only transmit their official titles with endless variants and honorifics but also
especially letters that refer in particular to historical
events, economic and social conditions and the relations between the central government and the towns
[12; 22]. The prosopography of the ruling classes in the
Hellenistic world and the Roman Empire, as well as the
chronology of Roman governors and their names
would be almost unknown without inscriptions [60].

Inscriptions are one of the most important types of
source material for economic and social conditions and
relations between town and country [40. 54–62]. They
provide information about the economic power of states, as in the previously mentioned example of the
Delian Leagues' tribute lists; they relate to trade in its
various aspects, among other things, by means of laws,
including the attempt by Athens to standardize the
systems of weights, measures and coins within the zone
of the League [9. No. 45]. Other laws regulate the
amount of customs duties and the process of collecting
them, e.g. the customs laws from Ephesus [3], or the
provision of grain (Samos, 2nd cent. BC, Syll.³ 976);
building inscriptions indicate *inter alia* wages and
prices [46]. Likewise, private documents, e.g. endowments to the home town [44], written mortgage stones
[33], and lease documents [23] (cf. inscriptions from
Mylasa II 801–854) must be included. By giving the
deceased's occupation and/or by depicting the tools of
his trade, grave inscriptions can offer insights into the
working life of ordinary people (fig. 1).

We have available to us a large quantity of inscriptions on the administration of properties in the east of
the Roman Empire. Titles are given of the men who
were entrusted with administrative responsibilities, as
well as the names of the property owners, slaves and
freedmen, with their tasks and status; villages on the
estates' territory are mentioned (for Asia Minor e.g.
[25]). "Documents of manumission" found in shrines
provide information about the freeing of slaves [54].
Another aspect of everyday life clarified by inscriptions
is the supply of goods; the organization of market days,
the observation of which was connected with a privilege, depended on upper echelons of the administration,
and the relevant regulations are preserved on large
steles [51]. The period of crisis in the 3rd cent. AD
caused Diocletian to prescribe maximum prices and
have them set down in a "Price Edict", which was able
to be reconstructed in large part from fragments,
among them Greek ones, found in many locations [43].

From the multitude of other objects of historical
study we might single out the institution of the 'Foreign
Judges', the nature of festivals, and Hellenization or
Romanization. The custom of calling upon judges from
other cities to arbitrate internal disputes is known only

through the relevant honours decrees [57. 137–154], and inscriptions offer a great deal of information on the nature of festivals e.g. through texts on the arrangement, organization and financing of festivals [64], through lists of victors and *theorodokia* [52], and through the mention of competition prizes etc. Processes and progress in Hellenization and Romanization or 'acculturation' in the eastern Mediterranean and beyond can be traced with the help of epigraphically preserved evidence that illustrates reciprocal influence in, for example, the areas of cult and ritual, philosophy, administration, nomenclature and lifestyle in general. Thus, on the one hand, for example, a wealthy private individual in the city of Oenoanda in Lycia in Asia Minor had texts of Epicurean philosophy carved onto the walls of a stoa [59], and on the other hand, the Indian king Aşoka had long inscriptions, also in Greek, displayed on cliff faces in Kandahar (Afghanistan) to bear witness to, among other things, his efforts to propagate Buddhist philosophy [24].

Epigraphy offers a wealth of information for religious history and helps clarify many questions relating both to Greek and, in particular, to indigenous religions in regions of Greek settlement. Many epithets of the gods are known only through inscriptions; dedications give not only the names of the deity/deities but also the reasons for erecting the monument and the names of those making the dedication. A great number of cult laws are preserved on stone [16–18]; hymns, aretalogies and accounts of cures from shrines (especially of Asclepius, e.g. Syll.³ 1168–1173) complete our picture of the conceptions of gods and their influence held by people in Antiquity. 'Popular belief' is discernible in, for example, oracles, formulaic oaths on grave-stones [19] and in the so-called confessional inscriptions of Asia Minor (fig. 3), in which sinners admit their transgressions [14] – these are all categories of which we would know nothing from literature and other sources alone.

Classical philology benefits in many ways from epigraphical scholarship, beginning with the production of texts and extending to their comprehension [63]. Along with poetry and prose transmitted in literature, epigraphical examples (often no less artistic) appear in epigrams chiseled on stone [5; 6; 10; 13]. King Antiochus of Commagene had inscriptions in literary prose displayed on his mausoleum [32]. Consolation decrees supplement the consolation literature of Antiquity [35], and, in the form of lists of winners, fasting inscriptions and didascalic inscriptions, epigraphical transmission offers valuable testimony for the production of comedies and tragedies [49].

Linguistic scholarship draws crucial insights from epigraphically transmitted evidence, both for Greek [30; 61] (particularly for the development of its dialects [2]), and for many indigenous languages in those areas of the Mediterranean that became more thoroughly Hellenized with the passage of time, whether through bilinguals or through the influence of foreign languages on Greek [26]. In this context, onomastics may be coun-

ted among the beneficiaries of epigraphy [34]. Through progressive orthographical changes detectable in inscriptions, it is possible to identify the shift in the pronunciation of individual sounds in the transition from ancient to modern Greek pronunciation [58. 169–289]. The origin and development of Greek script from the beginnings onwards can be traced in a similar manner [38] (fig. 2).

Epigraphy can even further the study of philosophy in Antiquity [62]. Thus, it is through inscriptions that we know of the role of philosophy in the education of Athenian youth (IG II² 1006). Inscriptions are the only sources for the existence of philosophical schools, present even in small cities (e.g. inscriptions of Prusa ad Olympum 17–18), and extensive texts of philosophical content are, for example, found chiseled in stone in the Lycian city of Oenoanda (see above). Sayings of the "Seven Sages" are attested not only within the Greek world, namely in the small town of Miletupolis near Cyzicus in Asia Minor and on the Aegean island of Thera (inscriptions from Miletupolis 2; IG XII 3 No. 1020), but were even conveyed to Bactria (modern Afghanistan) [57. 510–551].

A reciprocal and productive relationship of dependence likewise exists with archaeology. Thus, inscriptions help identify people and objects depicted in relief (fig. 4); building inscriptions name the construction project on which they were placed; in describing the grave layout, grave inscriptions provide detailed information on the construction and the identification of individual elements [41]; many artists are known to us only through their autographs [8]. Even in the context of finds, inscriptions can help, among other things, with questions of date and of the identification of objects and their functions. However, the difficulties in dating an artwork through an inscription belonging to it should not be overlooked; a date obtained on the basis of alphabetical forms is just as uncertain as one based on the arrangement of folds on a statue and even a date preserved in an inscription by allusion to a historical event or an era still often brings no clarity [28].

The same holds true for the connection between epigraphy and numismatics; in addition to the names of emperors and kings, the names and offices of leading municipal or provincial personalities, as well as the title of towns and cities are mentioned both in inscriptions and on coins; festivals and competitions are mentioned on specimens of both types; allusions to mythical and historical events are mutually complementary, and information on coins and currency can be found on a great number of inscriptions [55].

The field of medicine in Antiquity is represented for example through the abovementioned accounts of healing (Syll.³ 1168–1173) and through a large number of honorary and grave inscriptions for doctors [36].

SOURCES 1 H. BENGTSON, H. H. SCHMITT, Die Staatsverträge des Altertums, 1962–1969   2 H. COLLITZ, F. BECHTEL, Sammlung der griechischen Dialektinschriften, 1884–1915   3 H. ENGELMANN, D. KNIBBE, Das Zollge-

setz der Provinz Asia. EA 14, 1989 4 GGM 1,370 (Periplus Ponti Euxini 2) 5 P. A. HANSEN, Carmina epigraphica Graeca, 1983–1989 6 G. KAIBEL, Epigrammata Graeca ex lapidibus conlecta, 1878 7 R. KOERNER, Inschriftliche Gesetzestexte der frühen griechischen Polis, 1993 8 E. LOEWY, Inschriften griechischer Bildhauer, 1885 9 R. MEIGGS, D. LEWIS, A Selection of Greek Historical Inscriptions I, ²1988 10 R. MERKELBACH, J. STAUBER, Steinepigramme aus dem griechischen Osten, 1998ff. 11 L. MORETTI, Iscrizioni storiche ellenistiche, 1967–1976 12 J. H. OLIVER, Greek Constitutions of Early Roman Emperors from Inscriptions and Papyri, 1989 13 W. PEEK, Griechische Versinschriften I, 1955 14 G. PETZL, Die Beichtinschriften Westkleinasiens, 1994 15 P. J. RHODES, D. M. LEWIS, The Decrees of the Greek States, 1997 16 F. SOKOLOWSKI, Lois sacrées de l'Asie Mineure, 1955 17 Id., Lois sacrées des cités grecques, Suppl., 1962 18 Id., Lois sacrées des cités grecques, 1969 19 J. STRUBBE, ΑΡΑΙ ΕΠΙΤΥΜΒΙΟΙ (Arai epitymbioi: Imprecations against Desecrators of the Grave in the Greek Epitaphs of Asia Minor: A Catalogue), 1997 20 M. N. TOD, A Selection of Greek Historical Inscriptions, 1933–1948 21 E. WEBER, Augustus. Meine Taten (Res gestae divi Augusti, Latin, Greek, German), ³1975 22 C. B. WELLES, Royal Correspondence in the Hellenistic Period, 1934
LITERATURE 23 D. BEHREND, Attische Pachturkunden, 1970 24 É. BENVENISTE, Édits d'Asoka en traduction grecque, in: Journal asiatique 252, 1964, 137–157 25 H. BRANDT, Gesellschaft und Wirtschaft Pamphyliens und Pisidiens im Altertum, 1992 26 CL. BRIXHE, Essai sur le grec anatolien: au début de notre ère,² 1987 27 G. M. COHEN, The Hellenistic Settlements in Europe, the Islands, and Asia Minor, 1995 28 TH. CORSTEN, Über die Schwierigkeit, Reliefs nach Inschriften zu datieren, in: Istanbuler Mitteilungen 37, 1987, 187–199 29 Id., Vom Stamm zum Bund, 1999 30 K. DIETERICH, Untersuchungen zur Geschichte der griechischen Sprache, Leipzig 1898 31 G. DOBESCH, Hundert Jahre Kleinasiatische Kommission – Rückblick und Ausblick, in: Id., G. REHRENBÖCK (eds.), 100 Jahre Kleinasiatische Kommission der Österreichischen Akademie der Wissenschaften, 1993 32 H. DÖRRIE, Der Königskult des Antiochos von Kommagene im Lichte neuer Inschriften-Funde, 1964 33 M. I. FINLEY, Studies in Land and Credit in Ancient Athens, 500–200 B. C. The Horos-Inscriptions, 1952 34 P. M. FRASER, E. MATTHEWS (eds.), A Lexicon of Greek Personal Names, 1987ff. 35 E. GRIESSMAIR, Das Motiv der mors immatura in den griechischen metrischen Grabinschriften, 1966 36 H. GUMMERUS, Der Ärztestand im Römischen Reich nach den Inschriften, 1932 37 CHR. HABICHT, Pausanias' Guide to Ancient Greece, 1985 38 L. H. JEFFERY, The Local Scripts of Archaic Greece, ²1990 39 G. KLAFFENBACH, Griechische Epigraphik, ²1966 40 H. KLOFT, Die Wirtschaft der griechisch-römischen Welt, 1992 41 J. KUBINSKA, Les monuments funéraires dans les inscriptions grecques de l'Asie Mineure, 1968 42 W. LARFELD, Handbuch der griechischen Epigraphik I, 1902 43 S. LAUFFER, Diokletians Preisedikt, 1971 44 B. LAUM, Stiftungen in der griechischen und römischen Antike, 1914 45 J. A. LETRONNE, Recueil des inscriptions grecques et latines de l'Égypte, étudiées dans leur rapport avec l'histoire politique, l'administration intérieure, les institutions civiles et religieuses de ce pays depuis la conquête d'Alexandre jusqu'à celle des Arabes, Paris 1842 and 1848 46 F. G. MAIER, Griechische Mauerbauinschriften, 1959–1961 47 A. MARICQ, Syria 35, 1958, 295–360 48 B. D. MERRITT, H. T. WADE-GERY, M. F. MACGREGOR, The Athenian Tribute Lists, 1939–1953 49 H. J. METTE, Urkunden dramatischer Aufführungen in Griechenland, 1977 50 F. L. MÜLLER, Das Problem der Urkunden bei Thukydides, 1997 51 J. NOLLÉ, Nundinas instituere et habere, 1982 52 P. PERLMAN, City and Sanctuary in Ancient Greece, 2000 53 G. PETZL, Vom Wert alter Inschriften-Kopien, in: J. H. M. STRUBBE, R. A. TYBOUT, H. S. VERSNEL (eds.), ΕΝΕΡΓΕΙΑ – Energeia: Studies on Ancient History and Epigraphy presented to H.W. Pleket, 1996 54 H. RÄDLE, Untersuchungen zum griechischen Freilassungswesen, 1969 55 L. ROBERT, Études de numismatique grecque, 1951 56 Id., L'épigraphie in: Encyclopédie de la Pléiade. L'histoire et ses méthodes, 1961, 453–497 57 Id., Opera minora V 58 E. SCHWYZER, Griechische Grammatik I, ³1959 59 M. F. SMITH, Diogenes of Oinoanda: The Epicurean Inscription, 1993 60 B. E. THOMASSON, Laterculi Praesidum, 1972–1980 61 L. THREATTE, The Grammar of Attic Inscriptions, 1980ff. 62 M. N. TOD, Sidelights on Greek Philosophers, in: JHS 77, 1957, 132–141 63 H. WANKEL, Die Rolle der griechischen und lateinischen Epigraphik bei der Erklärung literarischer Texte, in: ZPE 15, 1974, 79–97 64 M. WÖRRLE, Stadt und Fest im kaiserzeitlichen Kleinasien, 1988 65 F. BÉRARD, D. FEISSEL, P. PETITMENGIN, M. SÈVE, Guide de l'épigraphiste, ²1989.

ADDITIONAL BIBLIOGRAPHY R. W. BAGNALL, P. DEROW, The Hellenistic Period: Historical Sources in Translation, 2004; J. BODEL (ed.), Epigraphic Evidence: Ancient History from Inscriptions, 2001; B. McLEAN, An Introduction to Greek Epigraphy of the Hellenistic and Roman Periods from Alexander the Great down to the Reign of Constantine (323 BC-AD 337), 2002; E. LUPU, Greek Sacred Law: A Collection of New Documents, 2005; P. J. RHODES, R. OSBORNE, Greek Historical Inscriptions 404–323 BC, 2003 THOMAS CORSTEN

Epigraphy, Latin see → LATIN EPIGRAPHY

Epistle, Epistolography see → LETTERS, EPISTOLARY LITERATURE

Epochs, Concept of
I. ANCIENT HISTORY II. ARCHAEOLOGY III. CLASSICAL PHILOLOGY IV. ART HISTORY-ARCHITECTURE

I. ANCIENT HISTORY
A. DEFINITIONS AND SCOPE B. CHARACTERISATIONS OF THE EPOCH OF ANTIQUITY C. INTERNAL DIVISIONS

A. DEFINITIONS AND SCOPE
By *Altertum* ('Antiquity")', *Paulys Realencyclopädie der classischen Altertumswissenschaft*, newly revised since 1890 by Georg Wissowa, understands the culture of the 'Classical' peoples of the Greeks and Romans, with the additions of the Ancient Orient, inclusive of Egypt, insofar as it has connecting links to the former; of the ancient peripheral cultures (Arabs,

Germanic tribes, Jews, Carthaginians, Celts, Numidians, Scythians); and of early Christianity, down to the time of Justinian. In other words, what is at issue is the history of the Mediterranean area in the broad sense, from approximately 1200 BC to approximately 600 AD. Both the preceding non-literate prehistory and the successive Byzantine-Latin-Arab Middle Ages are excluded from consideration.

In the 18th cent., the words *Altertum* ('Antiquity') and *Antike* ('Ancient world') were used predominantly in the sense of 'antique', as is shown by such plural formations as 'Roman antiquities' and 'antiquities collection'. In the works of Winckelmann (1755), Fr. Schlegel (1798) and Novalis (1798), 'Ancient world' denotes the spirit of Antiquity, while 'Antiquity' denotes the time period of the Ancient world. As an epoch, 'Ancient world' occurs as objectively synonymous with Antiquity around 1900, while until then the humanistic idealization of the 'Classical' peoples and their works was dominant (W. Rüegg, 1959 in: [10. 322–35]). Cognitive discourse about 'Antiquity' is preceded by a normative view of the Ancient world, which became determing element in Renaissance Humanism.

The Middle Ages lacked a term for Antiquity, since it lacked its own self-awareness as an epoch. People saw themselves in a continuity that began with Christ and Augustus, which popes and emperors used to legitimise their rule; or in a kind of extended late Antiquity, at the end of which the Last Judgment was expected. In his *Weltchronik*, Otto von Freising enumerates the emperors: Augustus was the first emperor, Barbarossa the 94th. Augustine's world-week, modelled after the days of creation, was used as a periodisation scheme: this was still the case in Schedel's *Weltchronik*, which ends in 1492 with the sixth age of the world. Alternatively, one finds, following the Book of Daniel, which originated during the Maccabaean war, a series of four world empires, the last of which was originally considered the reign of Alexander and his successors, and later, for instance in the Gospels, the Roman Empire. This was still the view of Bossuet (1681), for whom Louis XIV continues the series of rulers initiated by Augustus.

One conception of the Ancient world as an epoch begins with admiration for its culture. In the 11th cent., the Byzantine humanist Michael Psellos lamented the dark night that had fallen over Classical Hellas. This led to the concept of the intermediate 'Dark Ages' in Petrarch, Boccaccio, Hutten, Melanchthon and others. People saw themselves at the dawn of a reawakened culture, and thus simultaneously arrived at the idea of the Middle Ages, which was thought to have been overcome. Papacy and Empire receded into the background, in favour of the cultivated urban bourgeoisie, which found itself as being back in → ATHENS and → ROME. The sense of optimism about the future among intellectuals since the 15th cent., with its will to a renewal in literature, art and religion, awakened an awareness of two cultural thresholds: the 'dawn' of modern times

and the 'twilight' of Antiquity, with the 'night' of the Middle Ages in between. The idea of a rebirth presupposes the notion of a previous extinction, making possible the concept of the Ancient world, as well as the three-period scheme of ancient, middle and modern history.

Beginning with the 17th cent., this division supplanted the older classifications. The textbooks by the Halle historian Christoph Cellarius (1638–1707) played an important role. His *Historia Antiqua* of 1685 begins with the legendary Assyrian king Nimrod, and ends with the abdication of Diocletian; while Constantine ushers in the *Historia medii aevi* in 306. However, Cellarius also used later dates for the end of Antiquity, such as 330 (foundation of Constantinople), 454 (death of Aetius, the "last Roman"), and 476 (deposition of Romulus Augustulus). In subsequent times, other authors added to this series of end dates: for instance, the year 375, with the emergence of the Huns (erroneously deduced from the appearance of the Visigoths, whom they supplanted, on the Lower Danube in 376 AD); the battle of Hadrianopolis in 378; the settlement of the Visigoths, who lived according to their own law, in 382; the division of rule after the death of Theodosius in 395 among his sons, Arcadius in the East and Honorius in the West; the occupation of Rome by the Gothic king Alaric in 410. Most widely accepted was the caesura in 476, already referred to by Marcellinus Comes (Monumenta Germaniae, Auctores Antiquissimi 11, p. 91) in the 6th cent. as the end of the *Hesperium Romanae gentis imperium*, and adopted as such by Procopius, Jordanes, Bede, Paulus Diaconus, and others. It has been dominant since the 16th cent. (Machiavelli, Melanchthon, Sigonius, Conring, Montesquieu, Gatterer, Gibbon, Heeren, Luden, Niebuhr, Seeck, Momigliano).

Among later dates for the end of Antiquity in the literature are the following: Theoderic's invasion of Italy in 488 (Demougeot 1978); the closing of the Platonic Academy in 529 (De Sanctis 1932); the death of Justinian in 565 (Demandt 1989); the appearance of the Langobardi in Italy in 568 (Gutschmid 1863); the founding of Islam in 622 (Pirenne 1922); the death of Heraclius in 641 (Ernst Stein 1949); and the coronation of Charlemagne in 800 (Eduard Meyer 1884). These various approaches are based on different emphases. There is wide agreement that for the transition from Antiquity to the Middle Ages, we must assume "broad swaths of gradual transformations" (Aubin 1948: [9. 204]). The same holds true for the beginning of the Ancient World. According to the dominant conception, it is identical with the beginning of history *per se*, or, more precisely, with the written tradition. "The first page of Thucydides (said Hume) is the only beginning of all true history", according to Kant 1784 (footnote to paragraph 9 of his *Idee zu einer allgemeinen Geschichte in weltbürgerlicher Absicht*); beyond him, all is *terra incognita*. In his *Vorlesungen über die Philosophie der Geschichte* 1831 [7. 115], Hegel identified the beginning of historical writing with awakening consciousness, thereby enabling a retrospective extension of history to the ancient Orient. With his universal-historical approach and comprehensive language competence, Eduard Meyer (1855–1930) began his *Geschichte des Altertums* (1884ff.) with the most ancient Orient, while inserting a caesura between the ancient Oriental and the Greco-Roman age.

B. Characterisations of the Epoch of Antiquity

The attempt has often been made to describe the Ancient World by means of essential characteristics. Here, following Renaissance Humanism, cultural achievements initially stood in the foreground. This was questioned by Charles Perrault, who in his four-volume work *Le parallèle des Anciens et des Modernes* (1688 to 1698) declared that the artists and poets under Louis XIV had eclipsed their ancient predecessors. Nicolas Boileau-Despraux's riposte, *Réflexions sur Longin* (1693), unleashed the → QUERELLE DES ANCIENS ET DES MODERNES, which made an essential contribution to the historicisation of the concept of Antiquity. Bernard de Fontenelle questioned the terminology in his *Digression sur les anciens et les modernes* (1688) insofar as he explained, as Giordano Bruno had already done in 1584 and Francis Bacon in 1620, that the 'Ancients', since they lived earlier in history, are really the 'younger' generation, while the Moderns are really the elders, since they came later. Ancient World and modernity – here, the Middle Ages were left out of consideration – were no longer viewed as two cultures alongside one another, but as two phases of one and the same process. The underlying metaphor of the ages of life, known for Roman history from Ammianus Marcellinus (14,6,3–6), was used in the Enlightenment for human history as a whole, for instance by Herder in 1774 and Lessing in 1780. They were concerned with the significance of the Ancient World for the moral development of mankind, which in its youth learned 'civic morality' through Greek philanthropy, Roman humanity and Christian charity.

The same image, here transferred to politics, was offered by Hegel in his lecture on the history of philosophy from 1831. Hegel declared that only one person is free in the Orient, the despot; among the classical peoples it is the citizen, whereas in the Christian-Germanic world, everyone is free. He also divides world history according to the four world ages of mankind, attributing childhood to the ancient Orient, ending with boyhood, which "spends its time fighting and kicking", followed by the adolescence of the Greek world, from Achilles to Alexander. To the Romans he attributes the "bitter work of the adulthood of history", while the 'Germanic empire' corresponds to old age, which however displays not feebleness but "perfect maturity" [7. 171ff.].

Following Hegel, Marxist literature spoke of the ancient 'slaveholder society' or 'slaveholder structure'.

In his inaugural lecture at the University of Freiburg in 1896, Max Weber emphasised the urban nature of the ancient 'coastal culture', which was determined by the Mediterranean. Oswald Spengler, in his *Untergang des Abendlandes* (1918), identified the inner unity of the Ancient World in its underlying "Apollonian cultural soul". In 1926, Kurt Breysig separated "ancient and modern European history" by the end of the West Roman Empire. In 1949, Karl Jaspers, following Ernst von Lasaulx (1856) and Jacob Burckhardt (1868), saw the world-historical significance of the Ancient World in the 'Axial period' between 800 and 200 BC, when reason and personality were formed. It was here that Jaspers found the "intellectual summit of history to date".

Greeks and Romans were not always characterised together. In German intellectual history, a special proximity to the Greek world has been felt since the Humanists of the 16th century. Insofar as they belonged to Protestantism, this could be explained by the aversion to papist Rome, which was sensed as a continuation of Imperial Rome, together with its immorality. Insofar as there was an undertow of opposition to France, it had to be granted a closer connection with Rome, on the basis of its Romance language, its past as a province and its Catholic confession. The enthusiasm for Rome of the French revolutionaries and Napoleon explains the imitation of the Arch of Titus from the Forum in the Arc de Triomphe du Carrousel (1805), in contrast to the quotation of the Propylaea on the Acropolis in the (Berlin) Brandenburg Gate (1792). French proximity to Rome confirmed and strengthened the turn to Greece on the right bank of the Rhine. Winckelmann sought Hellenic genius in the antiquities of Rome, while Herder had harsh words for Roman imperialism, which had trampled on nations and their cultures. Wilhelm von Humboldt simply identified culture and Hellas. Germans and Greeks were considered nations of culture. Not until the time of Bismarck did Rome regain some sympathy in Germany. Mommsen's *Römische Geschichte* (1854ff.) celebrated the unification of Italy by Rome, as that of Germany by Prussia was hoped for, and indeed experienced.

C. Internal Divisions

The beginning, end and essential characteristics of Antiquity are more controversial than its internal divisions, about which there is widespread agreement. The Minoan-Mycenaean phase of Greek history was followed, after the dark ages before Homer (ca. 700), by the archaic period, in which writing came into existence, the polis developed and the great colonization on the coasts of the Mediterranean and the Black Sea took place. The classical period usually extends from the Persian Wars until Alexander, that is, from 500 to 300 BC. Here, Athens, as the city of democracy and culture, stood at the center of interest. There followed the period defined by Droysen as Hellenistic, which ended politically with the incorporation of Egypt into the

Roman Empire by Octavian in 30 BC, but continues to last on a cultural level. It was characterized by the diffusion of Greek culture to non-Greek peoples, through civilizing technical progress and the emergence of monarchic territorial states on the model of the Achaemenid kingdom.

Roman history is preceded by that of the Etruscans, an urban network in Tuscany that emerged under Oriental and Greek influence. The Roman age of the kings is obscure, and becomes clearer only with the Law of the Twelve Tables in 450, the class struggles between plebeians and patricians, and the unification of Italy in the 4th cent. Carthage was defeated in the 3rd cent., and Rome became mistress of the western Mediterranean. The Hellenistic east was conquered in the 2nd cent., and Rome itself fell increasingly under Greek cultural influence. The civil wars of the 1st cent., conditioned by the power of the proconsuls in the provinces, ended with the Principate. Caesar and Augustus established the borders of the Empire at the Rhine, the Danube and the Euphrates. The High Empire and the *Pax Romana* (according to Gibbon the happiest period of mankind), in which Roman law developed, was followed in the 3rd cent. by the crisis of the Empire under the soldier-emperors. Borders became insecure on every side. Around 300, Diocletian and Constantine ushered in Late Antiquity, characterized by bureaucratisation, Christianisation and Germanification. By taking over military service for the empire, the Germanic people also gained the upper hand politically, and in the period of the 'Great Migrations' they divided the Empire into several successor states, with the remainder of the Empire around Byzantium.

1 K. Breysig, Der Stufenbau und die Gesetze der Weltgeschichte, 1927   2 J. Burckhardt, Weltgeschichtliche Betrachtungen, 1868/1905 (In English: Force and Freedom: Reflections on History, 1964)   3 W. Dahlheim, Die Antike. Griechenland und Rom von den Anfängen bis zur Expansion des Islam, 1994   4 A. Demandt, Der Fall Roms. Die Auflösung des römischen Reiches im Urteil der Nachwelt, 1984   5 Id., Die Spät-Antike. Römische Geschichte von Diocletian bis Justinian (284–565 n.Chr.), 1989   6 Id., Antike Staatsformen, 1995   7 G. W. F. Hegel, Vorlesungen über die Philosophie der Geschichte, 1831 (repr. 1961. Engl.: The Philosophy of History, 2001)   8 J. G. Herder, Auch eine Philosophie der Geschichte zur Bildung der Menschheit, 1774 (repr. ed. H. D. Irmscher, 1990)   9 P. E. Hübinger (ed.), Kulturbruch oder Kulturkontinuität im Übergang von der Antike zum Mittelalter (= Wege der Forsch. 201), 1968   10 Id., Zur Frage der Periodengrenze zwischen Altertum und Mittelalter (= Wege der Forsch. 51), 1969   11 K. Jaspers, Vom Ursprung und Ziel der Geschichte, 1949 (Engl. M. Bullock (trans.), The Origin and Goal of History, 1953)   12 G. E. Lessing, Die Erziehung des Menschengeschlechts, Berlin 1777/1790 (Zürich 1840)   13 E. v. Lasaulx, Neuer Versuch einer alten auf die Wahrheit der Thatsachen gegründeten Philosophie der Geschichte, München 1856   14 W. Müri, Die Antike. Untersuchungen über den Ursprung und die Entwicklung der Bezeichnung einer geschichtlichen Epoche, in: A&A 7, 1958, 7–45   15 J. H. J.van der Pot, De periodisering der geschiedenis.

Een overzicht der theorien, 1951   16 M. Weber, Die sozialen Gründe des Untergangs der antiken Kultur (1896) in: Id., Soziologie. Weltgeschichtliche Analysen. Politik (1968), 1ff.

II. Archaeology
A. General Overview of the Development of Epochal Arrangement since the Ancient World B. Concepts of Individual Epochs

A. General Overview of the Development of Epochal Arrangement since the Ancient World

Awareness of the development of art and a notion of individual epochs began early: Democritus was apparently the first to already connect the reflection on art with a concept of development; the comparative method and the scheme of a gradual increase in artistic ability and means of presentation were also known in the circle of the Academy [26. 24f.]. To be sure, Attic philosophy of the 4th cent. BC recognised art as a discipline in its own right, determined by the mind rather than by technique, but judged it rather according to ethical standards. Not until the theory of art transmitted by Varro and Pliny the Elder [15. 118–126; 21. 73–80], which is perhaps to be linked to Xenocrates of Athens, was attention directed once again to formal problems of the work of art, and a developmental scheme constructed for Greek art, which extended from crude and deficient attempts to solve artistic problems (*rudis antiquitas*) to their competent mastering by Lysippus and Apelles.

A different periodization, based on a classicistic theory from the 2nd half of the 2nd cent. BC, but whose effects also persist down to modern times, is transmitted by Cicero's *Brut.* 70, Quintilian's *inst.* 12,10,7–9 and Pliny's *nat.* 34, 51f. According to this view, after difficult beginnings an exemplary level was quickly reached in Polyclitus and above all Pheidias, with the decline beginning immediately thereafter. Here, formal criteria scarcely played a part, but rather such abstract valuations as *decor*, *auctoritas*, and *pulchritudo*. The vertical scheme is superposed here by the canonisation of obligatory examples in individual genres (on this, see [11. 21f.; 15. 126–140; 21. 81–84; 22. 273–277; 23; 26. 32–46]).

In modern treatments of the Ancient World, it was chiefly a 'biological' scheme (youth-maturity-old age-decrepitude) that was developed, formulated with some modifications for ancient literature by J. J. Scaliger (cf. below, the article by Kuhlmann). Winckelmann (1717–1768) then refers explictly to Scaliger in his *Geschichte der Kunst des Altertums*, published in 1764 [5. 166 with n. 32]; (cf. the article by Kuhlmann) corresponding to Scaliger's 'four principal ages', he was the first to divide Greek art into epochs: 1. straightforward and severe style, 2. high style (460–400), 3. 'beautiful style' (400–320), 4. 'decline of art' after Alexander the Great. This periodisation of styles remained a methodological principle in all of Winckelmann's works, with the characterisation of stylistic epochs taking place according to Pliny, Quintilian and Cicero. Winckelmann was already aware of the problem of distinguishing between Greek originals and Roman copies, as he was of the inadequate material basis for early epochs [5. 17f.]. Decisive for Winckelmann's system was his absolute concept of beauty, whose realization in classical Greek art was the immanent telos of its development [12. 18f.]. A model of growth-blossoming-decline had also already been proposed by J.F. Christ (1701–1756). Highly esteemed by Winckelmann, he was the first to deal with art in his lectures, but he had not yet undertaken a separation between the Greek and Roman epochs. Christ's student Chr. G. Heyne (1729–1812), the founder of the discipline of the scholarly study of Antiquity at the university, undertook, in steady critical engagement with Winckelmann's work, a systematic treatment of ancient art, but remained highly critical in particular of Winckelmann's stylistic periodisations, and reproached him with taking over Pliny's division of epochs with excessive naiveté. Heyne himself, however, scarcely offered an alternative division of epochs: he saw Antiquity more as a closed unit, whose art he divided according to genres [5. 26ff.]. Great influence was exerted on archaeological research, particularly in Italy and France, by E. Q. Visconti (1751–1818), who studied Winckelmann's method attentively. Rejecting the model of blossoming and decline, however, he defended the opinion that art had remained on the same level from Pericles to the 'Adoptive Emperors'. He thereby exerted an essential influence on Heyne's student F. Thiersch (1784–1860), who likewise did not place the decline of art until the period after Hadrian, and was the first German Classical scholar explicitly to turn against Winckelmann's stylistic periodisation. His own model (*Über die Epochen der bildenden Kunst bei den Griechen*, 1829) envisaged two epochs of Greek art, each comprising 500 years (the 'symbolic-sacred' and 'perfect-ideal' style), with a 100 year-long period of development from Archaic to High Classical art in between. Here, the influence of → ROMANTICISM became visible, which shifted interest to the symbolic and religious interpretation of ancient myth ('ur-religion') and abstracted art increasingly from its historical preconditions (which had still constituted a unity in Winckelmann). This opinion was quite evident in the case of G.F. Creuzer (1771–1858), who reviewed Thiersch's book in 1830 and for whom the monumental tradition was merely a source for the interpretation of myths [5. 34ff.].

Research in the 19th cent. was strongly marked by an approach to ancient art determined by Boeckh's historicism. However, K. O. Müller (1797–1849) and O. Jahn (1813–1869) also attributed very high importance to the artist's individual personality so that a genuine stylistic periodisation became impossible. E. Gerhard (1795–1844, like Jahn a student of Boeckh) undertook a higher evaluation of the Hellenistic epoch (in which

interest had increased since Droysen, see below). As for Visconti, so also for Gerhard the decline of art did not begin until post-Hadrianic times [5. 101ff.]. The positivism of the 19th cent. made the exact grasp of 'reality' an absolute criterion, a goal that Wickhoff did not consider fulfilled until Roman Impressionism [12. 16]. It was only the scholarship of the 20th cent. that granted each epoch its own worth, abandoning the concept of the entelechy of a developmental scheme [12. 15ff.]. However, the problems of the beginning and end of individual epochs have remained unsolved [12. 20].

B. Concepts of Individual Epochs
1. The Ancient World 2. The Archaic Period 3. The Classical Period 4. Hellenism 5. The Empire and Late Antiquity

1. The Ancient World
The term *Antike* ('Ancient world') does not appear as an all-encompassing designation for the epoch of Greco-Roman Antiquity until relatively late, and not in general language usage until the 1920s. For Winckelmann, the Greco-Roman world was still *Das Altertum* ('Antiquity'), or *Die Alten* ('the Ancients'); under the influence of such French models as de Piles and Caylus, monuments were also called 'antiques' (only in the plural for statues), while from 1760 sculptures were also called 'the Antique' (from the French *l'antique*). At the same time, and also inspired by the French, Chr.L. v. Hagedorn used *Die Antike* both as a designation for individual statues and as the essence of the fine arts of Antiquity. It is not quite clear why it was precisely this term that became accepted; in any case, by the second half of the 19th cent. the competing expression *Klassisches Altertum* ('Classical Antiquity'), coined by Fr. Schlegel, seems no longer to have found approval, owing to the claim to pedagogic exemplarity that was inherent in it. Even the more neutral designation *Antike* was sometimes used more normatively than as the delimitation of a historical period; it was further developed by the works of Burckhardt, Grimm and Wölfflin. After the First World War, the term had become definitively transformed into a term for an epoch in intellectual history, which henceforth also included the 'non-Classical, non-exemplary' aspects of Antiquity.

2. The Archaic Period
The term 'Archaic period' was coined in archaeology; it remains problematic whether there is a genuine historical epoch that runs parallel to this phase in the fine arts [10. 26]. Winckelmann himself knew scarcely any works of art from this period; his image of the Archaic style relied primarily on supposed Egyptian and 'Etrurian' parallels. In the first half of the 19th cent., the pediment sculptures from the Temple of Aphaea at → AEGINA, discovered in 1811 and brought in 1828 to the specially constructed Aeginetan room in the Munich Glyptothek, which today are considered an example of the transition to the Severe style, shaped the image of the beginnings of Greek art. In Germany, the

Apollo of Tenea (also in the Glyptothek since 1854) was acknowledged as the first genuinely Archaic work. The technical term 'Archaic' appears for the first time in the description of that statue in J. Overbeck's *Kunstarchäologische Vorlesungen*, published in 1853, but Overbeck's negative judgment [19. 6] remained authoritative until the 1870s. This changed through the work of H. Brunn (Professor at Munich since 1865 and curator of the numismatic department and the antiquities collection), who for the first time exhibited a series of comparable monuments that enabled reflections on stylistic development (whereas his predecessors Hirt and Müller had to some extent not yet distinguished between Archaic and archaistic works). Beginning in 1867, the technical term 'Archaic' occurs more frequently in Brunn, not only as a style, but also as an epoch. In 1872–1873, he wrote a comprehensive account of Archaic sculpture and architecture (edited from his posthumous papers in 1897 [27. 8]), a first attempt to conceive of the Archaic period as an epoch in its own right, and not just as a forerunner of the Classical epoch. The transfer of the term from a style to the period in which it emerged presupposed a parallelisation of the various contemporaneous phenomena occurring at the time (art, literature, politics, economics), as was probably first attempted by J. Burckhardt in his lecture on Greek cultural history of 1872 (edited from the manuscript and transcriptions of his posthumous papers in 1902 [19. 11]). The cultural pessimism of the late 19th and early 20th cents. (Nietzsche, Spengler) brought about a re-evaluation of the concept of the Archaic; enthusiasm for this epoch, which was now felt to be original, vital and powerful, reached its height in the 1920s. Yet another change has occurred since the 1970s, when the material tradition was placed at the center of the interpretation of epochs, and the literary tradition was approached with greater skepticism [7. 200ff.; 27]; this also led to a questioning of the separation between the Archaic and the Classical [27]. This problem of periodisation and the limits of epochs [13. 159ff.] is today as current as it was previously, and also finds expression in inconsistent terminology: The epoch called Archaic as a whole is divided into the Geometric (1050–700 BC, itself further subdivided) and the Archaic (700–480 BC) epoch, yet their succession of styles is not consistent; on this point, and for a better understanding of the stylistic plurality: [17. 586].

3. THE CLASSICAL PERIOD

Chronologically, this epoch is understood as the high point and transition from the archaic polis to the bourgeois society of the Hellenistic monarchies [4. 609]. Winckelmann, too, whose theories were typified by the masterpieces in the Belvedere and who defended the thesis of the exemplary nature of classical Greek art (as Caylus [1692–1765] had already done before him), had considered this period as a 'flowering'. In Winckelmann's view of art, the freedom and democracy of the Periclean age played a central role in the development of this flowering, but the distortion of

his theory by the → CLASSICISM of the 19th cent. brought about an increasing dissociation from historical preconditions. The Greek Classical period was received in conscious rejection of the courtly Baroque, and was experienced exclusively as an ideal, not as a historical phenomenon. Although there was some criticism of Winckelmann's scheme, his conception of the flowering of art in the 5th–4th cent. BC was nevertheless "institutionalised" at the end of the 19th cent. [5. 9ff.]. There followed an intensive discussion of the Classical period in the first 30 years of the 20th cent. ([3]; on the attempts to define the essence and content of the Classical [11. 16f.]), which was not to be taken up again until recently (above all in connection with the questions surrounding the Classical vs. classicism, cf. [11. 14ff., 56ff.]). The formal analyses of Wickhoff, Riegl and von Salis led to a new evaluation of Roman art and to the first attempts to grasp the particular character of the Hellenistic as distinct from the Classical style [3. 207–211]. In response to the research of Wölfflin (1916), Rodenwaldt defended the view that classical periods appear cyclically, with, however, the Greek Classical period being the foundation of all classical styles [3. 212–217]. Rodenwaldt's thoughts were taken up by the structural research of → CLASSICAL ARCHAEOLOGY, which, to be sure, utilized 'Classical' as a value concept, but avoided Winckelmann's scheme and no longer made pronouncements about the artistic quality of individual works. The first decades of the 20th cent. also witnessed the re-evaluation and increasing appreciation of the Archaic style, which led to the 4th cent. BC being viewed as the epoch of decline.

So far, there is no consensus with regard to the beginning and end of the Classical period, except for the years 450–430 BC, which roughly encompass the period of construction of the → PARTHENON [3. 219]. The 5th century is wholly or partially included in this span, and to some extent even the 4th cent. ([3. 219]: Schefold). However, this last viewpoint is most likely untenable, since Greek artists of the 4th cent. already sensed those of the 5th cent. as 'Classical' and exemplary, and therefore assimilated their art selectively and consciously ([2]; on the Classical style and Classicism of the Augustan period: [2. 305ff.]).

4. HELLENISM

The term was first used by Droysen in 1833, in the sense of a blending of Greek and Oriental culture through the policies of Alexander the Great, whence it was also adopted in archaeology. However, archaeology long lacked the material basis that would have enabled knowledge of the artistic work of this epoch, which had been stricken from the history of art without further ado by Pliny the Elder. According to nat. 34,51f., art had ceased around 295 BC, and had not returned to life until 156 BC (the so-called *cessavit-revixit* judgment). To be sure, works such as the → LAOCOON GROUP and the Farnese bull had long been known in Rome; yet since Winckelmann these and other works had been attributed to the epoch of 'decline'. "A broad gap in our knowledge" (i.e. of the Hellenistic epoch) still existed around 1860 [18. 109], to which the sparse literary tradition also contributed. This first changed with W. Helbig's studies of the wall-paintings of → POMPEII and → HERCULANEUM [9; 16. 154, 164f.]. Helbig demonstrated the Hellenistic origin of these paintings, and, in the second half of his book [9], with its chapters on the external conditions of Hellenistic art, society, feeling for nature, etc., wrote the first cultural history of the Hellenistic age [18. 110; 9. 140ff.]. Burckhardt took over entire sections of this work, sometimes word for word, in his *Griechische Kulturgeschichte* [16. 169f. with n. 39]. Later, the concept of Hellenism as an epoch was suddenly filled with further content by the sensational find of the → PERGAMUM ALTAR 1878–80, about which the excavator C. Humann rightly judged that it represented the find of an entire period of art [30. 5ff.]. However, the first reactions of 19th-cent. research, still under the influence of Classicism, were negative. Brunn ("materialism, formalism of the purely material"), Conze ("a desperate grasping after effects") and Furtwängler ("the disorderly excesses of Hellenistic art") all made deprecating pronouncements on the work [30. 6f.]. Kekulé was the first who was able to comprehend the sculptures adequately and to appreciate them in their special character, urging (1908) that works of art be explained independently and on the basis of the conditions of their origin. A true investigation of Hellenistic art did not begin until the 1920s, once the inscriptions, sculptures and the altar had been presented in the multi-volume *Altertümer von Pergamon* (1890–1910) [30. 7]. Here too, however, the problems of delimiting epochs have remained unsolved until today [1. 182–188]. There are divergences in the archaeological literature in estimates both of the beginning of this period (death of Alexander; around 300 BC; beginning of the 3rd cent. BC) and of the end (Battle of Actium; before or after the 1st cent. BC). A chronological framework obtained through historical events cannot be brought into precise agreement with its fundamental cultural content; therefore, one is often defined by means of the other. Thus, in the archaeological literature Alexander and/or his death are often designated as a 'time marker', while in the same works stylistic epoch-boundaries with different dates are drawn on the basis of art-historical criteria, as for instance in Schuchhardt [1. 186]. There are no sharp delimitations, manifesting themselves simultaneously in every domain (art, politics, etc.) and at all places; on the latter point (early comparable phenomena in the realm of the Greek colonies; 'pre-Hellenism' in Phoenicia), cf. [8. 635].

5. THE EMPIRE AND LATE ANTIQUITY

The problem of the beginning of the Roman empire is inextricably bound up with that of the end of the Hellenistic epoch. The beginning is most often fixed with the Battle of Actium, which spelled the end of the last great Hellenistic empire. Since Augustus, one may speak of 'Imperial art' [28. 659].

The term 'Late Antiquity' is archaeological and art-historical in origin, and was later adopted by historians [29. 678]. Whereas, following Winckelmann, the time of Constantine the Great and the early Middle Ages had been seen only as the decline of the ancient world, Riegl was the first at the end of the 19th cent. to relativise this evaluation with his concept of the 'conscious creation of art'. He used the expression 'Late Roman', which was only gradually replaced by 'Late Antique'. The content of this epoch is still controversial today: a point in time for the change from the Empire to late Antiquity cannot be defined with certainty [24. 85]. Whereas some see a continuity of the ancient habitus until the Byzantine iconoclastic controversy of the 8th cent., for others Late Antiquity begins in the Severan period, and the ancient world overall ends at the beginning of the 4th cent. with the conversion of Constantine. Today, most scholars place the beginning of this epoch in the time of the Diocletian tetrarchy, the preliminary stage for which was the crisis of the Empire under the soldier-emperors [6.1. 23; 24. 88; 29. 678f.]. The transition from Late Antiquity to the Middle Ages is still the subject of debate (cf. in general [14]). For Rodenwaldt, a sudden cultural break in the West occurred with the invasion of the Lombards (568), and in the East with the almost contemporaneous death of Justinian (565) [24. 86]. Other researchers see the end of Late Antiquity in the dissolution of the imperial union into the successor states [6. 24], with the penetration of the Arabs into the Mediterranean region (mid–7th cent.), or, as mentioned, with the Iconoclastic crisis of the 8th cent. ([29. 678f.] in general [14]).

→ NIETZSCHE-WILAMOWITZ CONTROVERSY; → CLASSICAL ARCHAEOLOGY

1 R. BICHLER, Hellenismus. Geschichte und Problematik eines Epochenbegriffs, 1983 2 A. H. BORBEIN, Die klassische Kunst der Antike, in: W. VOSSKAMP (ed.), Klassik im Vergleich. Normativität und Historizität europäischer Klassiken. DFG-Symposium 1990, 1993, 281–316 3 Id., Die Klassik-Diskussion in der klassischen Archäologie, in: H. FLASHAR (ed.), Altertumswissenschaft in den 20er Jahren. Neue Fragen und Impulse, 1996, 205–245 4 Id., Griechische Kunst. Klassik, in: H.-G. NESSELRATH (ed.), Einleitung in die griechische Philologie, 1997, 609–634 5 ST.-G. BRUER, Die Wirkung Winckelmanns in der deutschen Klassischen Archäologie des 19. Jahrhunderts (AAWM 3) 1994 6 A. DEMANDT, Die Spät-Antike als Epoche, in: L. J. ENGELS, H. HOFMANN (eds.), Spät-Antike. Mit einem Panorama der byzantinischen Literatur, 1997, 1–28 7 N. FISHER, H. VAN WEES (eds.), Archaic Greece: New Approaches and New Evidence, 1998 8 R. FLEISCHER, Griechische Kunst. Hellenismus, in: H.-G. NESSELRATH (ed.), Einleitung in die griechische Philologie, 1997, 635–658 9 W. HELBIG, Untersuchungen über die campanische Wandmalerei, Leipzig, 1873 10 A. HEUSS, Die archaische Zeit Griechenlands als geschichtliche Epoche, in: A&A 2, 1946, 26–62 11 TH. HIDBER, Das klassizistische Manifest des Dionys von Halikarnass, 1996 12 N. HIMMELMANN, Der Entwicklungsbegriff der modernen Archäologie, in: MarbWPr 1960, 13–40 13 W. HORNBOSTEL, review of J. Kleine, Untersuchungen zur Chronologie der attischen Kunst von Peisistratos bis

Themistokles (= MDAI (Ist.) fasc. 8, 1973) in: GGA 230, 1978, 153–166   14 P. E. HÜBINGER (ed.), Zur Frage der Periodengrenze zwischen Altertum und Mittelalter, 1969   15 H. JUCKER, Vom Verhältnis der Römer zur bildenden Kunst der Griechen, 1950   16 R. KASSEL, Die Abgrenzung des Hellenismus in der griechischen Literaturgeschichte, KS 1991, 154–173   17 W. MARTINI, Griechische Kunst. Archaische Zeit, in: H.-G. NESSELRATH (ed.), Einleitung in die griechische Philologie, 1997, 585–608   18 A. MICHAELIS, Ein Jahrhundert kunstarchäologischer Entdeckungen, 1908   19 G. W. MOST, Zur Archäologie der Archaik, in: A&A 35, 1989, 1–23   20 W. MÜRI, Untersuchungen über den Ursprung und die Entwicklung der Bezeichnung einer geschichtlichen Epoche, Beil. zum Jahresber. über das städtische Gymnasium in Bern 1957 = A&A 7, 1958, 7–45   21 J. J. POLLITT, The Ancient View of Greek Art: Criticism, History and Terminology, 1974   22 F. PREISSHOFEN, Kunsttheorie und Kunstbetrachtung, in: Le classicisme à Rome aux 1ers siècles avant et après J.-C., Entretiens 25, 1978, 261–282   23 Id., P. ZANKER, Reflex einer eklektischen Kunstanschauung beim Auctor ad Herennium, in: Dialoghi di Archeologia 4, 1970/1, 100–119   24 G. RODENWALDT, Zur Begrenzung und Gliederung der Spät-Antike, in: JDAI 59/60, 1944/45, 81–87 (repr. in: 14, 83–92)   25 W. RÜEGG, Antike als Epoche, in: MH 16, 1959, 309–318 (repr. in: 14. 322–335)   26 B. SCHWEITZER, Xenokrates von Athen, 1932   27 A. SNODGRASS, Archaic Greece. The Age of Experiment, 1980   28 D. WILLERS, Griechische Kunst. Kaiserzeit, in: H.-G. NESSELRATH, Einleitung in die griechische Philologie, 1997, 659–677   29 Id., Spät-Antike, in: H.-G. NESSELRATH, Einleitung in die griechische Philologie, 1997, 678–693   30 'Wir haben eine ganze Kunstepoche gefunden!' Ein Jahrhundert Forschungen zum Pergamonaltar, Exhibition Catalogue (Berlin), 1986/87.

III. CLASSICAL PHILOLOGY

A. CONCEPTUAL SYSTEMS   B. HISTORY OF THE TERMINOLOGY DESIGNATING EPOCHS   C. PROBLEMS IN EPOCHAL STRUCTURING

A. CONCEPTUAL SYSTEMS

The Ancient world and the Middle Ages were not clearly aware of literary epochs [27]. Such an awareness appeared only gradually in the age of Humanism, beginning with the 16th cent., and even then, at first only for Latin literature. Neither the history of literature by Sicco Polentone (1437) nor that by Lorenzo Valla (1471) divided Latin literature into epochs [4]. The Humanists of the following period had recourse to basically two competing schemes of division already known to ancient authors, which were now transferred to the development of Latin style: 1) the biological model of rise and fall, with its epochs of 'childhood', 'youth', 'maturity' and 'old age', with a peak in the middle, and 2) the theory of the ages of the world: 'gold', 'silver', 'bronze' and 'iron' ages (and to some extent 'lead' and 'clay' as well), as a pure model of decadence. These evaluative schemes were mainly arrived at by normative stylistic criticism (for instance, the Antibarbarus literature) [4]. The Humanists started out from an epoch felt to be exemplary as the center,

around which a kind of inchoate 'pre-Classical' and a decadent 'post-Classical' period were grouped. The first attested division into epochs stems from Adriano Castello, who distinguished four epochs in his *Antibarbarus* (1505): 1. From the foundation of the urbs to Livius Andronicus, as the *tempus antiquissimum*, 2. from Livy to Cicero, the *tempus antiquum*, 3. the time of Cicero himself, and the Augustan epoch, as the *tempus perfectum*, and 4. the remaining period of the ancient world, as the *tempus imperfectum*. The combination of the theory of the ages of the world and of Ciceronianism is first found in Erasmus of Rotterdam, in the *Praefatio* of his edition of Seneca (²1529): here, Erasmus defines Cicero's epoch as the 'Golden Age' of exemplary Latin usage. It was followed by the time of Seneca, against whose usage Erasmus admonishes the reader, as the 'Silver Age'. In 1561 in his *Poetices* [Book 2, 6, 294ff.], Julius Caesar Scaliger undertook an assessment of this model of the ages of life and the world, which was apparently a subject of discussion at the time. He chose a modified five-stage model of the ages of life, encompassing the Ancient world and his own period: 1. Early period (*rudimenta*), with the Old Latin poets, 2. the flawless zenith (*florens robur*), from Terence to Ovid and Virgil, absolute summit of literature overall, 3. time of fading (*ad … devergens … efflorescit*), with the poets of the early Empire, from Seneca and Lucan to Juvenal, 4. old age (*senium*), with the other authors down to Late Antiquity, 5. modern times of the 15th–16th cent., as the rebirth of literature (*nova pueritia*) after the Middle Ages, which was left aside. The division of the history of Latin language and style according to the metallic scale gained broad acceptance in philology and lexicography, beginning in the 17th cent.: Scioppius' *Consultationes* (1616), Vossius' *Rhetoric* (1630), Cellarius' *Antibarbarus* (1668), Borrichius' *Cogitationes de variis linguae Latinae aetatibus* (1675), Walchius' *Historia critica Latinae linguae* (1716). Golden Latin was defined more and more precisely, and, since Borrichius, limited to the language of Cicero and Virgil. There was no unanimity regarding the delimitation of the subsequent epochs. Sometimes AD 68 was proposed as the end of Silver Latin (Scioppius), sometimes AD 117 (Borrichius) or even AD 161 (Cellarius). The Age of Justinian was usually considered the end of ancient literature, although in Cellarius it was the Age of Charlemagne. With the 17th cent., the periodisation of the history of Greek literature also began. In a letter to C. Salmasius of 1607 (published at Leiden 1627, no. 247), J. J. Scaliger subdivided Greek poetry modelled on the seasons, into: 1. Spring or youth (early Greek epic), 2. Summer (lyric poetry), 3. Fall (the Hellenistic period), and 4. Winter (the Empire). It was precisely 'classical' drama that remained unmentioned.

In Neo-Humanism, criteria of division oriented toward Classicism and aestheticism took the place of normative stylistic criticism. Winckelmann's *Geschichte der Kunst des Altertums* (Vienna, et al., 1776) was of decisive influence which, inspired by J. J.

Scaliger's Letter to Salmasius, undertook a division of Greek art into four epochs: 1. 'straightforward and 'severe style' (Archaic age), 2. 'high style' (460–400 BC), 3. 'beautiful style' (400–320 BC), 4. 'decline of art' following the upheaval caused by Alexander the Great. The second and third period represent the acme, corresponding to what would later be called the Classical style. Herder and F. A. Wolf called for the transfer of this periodisation to ancient literature as well, which was undertaken by F. Schlegel in 1795–97 and 1812 [25]. Schlegel divided Greek literature into a pre-literary 'Heroic Age', an 'Epic age' (Homer), and the 'genuine epoch', from Solon (594 BC) to Alexander the Great, within which he in turn distinguished a 'Lyric age' down to the Persian Wars, and a 'Golden age' under Pericles and down to the Peloponnesian War. This was followed, without any definite demarcation by the 'Alexandrian age', while the conclusion was represented by the 'Late Bloom' from Hadrian to Julian (117–363 AD).

Roman literature was subdivided into the (pre-literary) 'Heroic Age', the 'Republican Age' from ca. 250 BC, and a 'Classical Age' from Cicero to AD 117, with four subsections: 1: the time of Caesar, Cicero and Sallust, 2. the 'Age of Augustus', 3. the early Empire as the first age of decline (Seneca, Lucan), and 4. the Age of Trajan (Tacitus, Pliny). Following Hadrian, and after a brief flowering, the decline of Roman literature began.

Schlegel's model of epochs was differentiated and elaborated in Classical philology, which emerged as an independent discipline since the 19th cent. In his *Grundriß der griechischen Litteratur* [1], G. Bernhardy called the time from the Persian Wars in 490–480 to 336 BC the 'Classical age', made the Alexandrian epoch end with Augustus (30 BC), and did not see the end of ancient Greek literature until Justinian (AD 529). This classification gained acceptance in subsequent times.

In the field of Latin literature, the delimitation of an Old Latin-Archaic epoch from ca. 250 BC to the 1st cent. BC was consolidated, a flowering initially still called 'Golden Latin' or 'Classicism' (that is, the Classical style; A. Draeger, *Historische Syntax der lateinischen Sprache*, Leipzig 1874–78 and E. Norden, *Antike Kunstprosa*, Berlin 1898), beginning with Cicero and Caesar and usually including the so-called 'Augustan age'. Already according to J. J. Eschenburg's *Handbuch der klassischen Literatur* (1783ff.), the following epoch, as 'Silver Latin', extended down to Trajan's death in AD 117, which was adopted by most literary histories as the boundary of the period (for instance, W. S. Teuffel, *Geschichte der römischen Literatur*, Leipzig 1870, E. Norden, *Kunstprosa*, 1898). The age that began with Hadrian after the caesura was seen either as a unit and the last ancient epoch, or, as in Teuffel, was further subdivided by centuries, without any particular designation of epochs (e.g., 'literature of the 2nd cent.', etc.).

The most important change in periodisation to occur in the 20th cent. was the discovery, emanating from art history (A. Riegl, *Spätrömische Kunstindustrie*, 1901) of 'Late Antiquity' as a literary epoch in its own right, no longer condemned as an age of decline but seen as a bridge between the ancient world and the Middle Ages, above all in the field of Latin studies. It is widely agreed that the beginning of 'Late Antiquity' is to be situated around AD 284 (beginning of the tetrarchy), and designates the revival of (Latin) literature, after its almost complete extinction in the 3rd cent. In contrast, Greek literature manifests a rich production from the 2nd to the 3rd cent. We also witness the overcoming of the negative image of Christian literature, which had prevailed in the 19th cent.

In Greek studies, the → DECIPHERMENT of the Linear B script by M. Ventris and J. Chadwick in 1952 resulted in discovery of the Mycenaean age from the 15th to the 13th cent. BC as a new epoch. The term Dark ages or 'Dark centuries' was coined for the following non-literate, pre-Homeric period. In general, 20th-cent. philology clearly displays terminological changes, without new boundaries of epochs being thereby defined. For the time from Homer until approximately 500 BC, the terms 'Early Greek' and 'Archaic' (from archaeology) are becoming customary; for the 'Classical' or 'Golden Age' the substantive Classic (analogous to Germanic studies and archaeology). Not until until Wilamowitz and Körte does 'Hellenism' appear alongside the 'Alexandrian Age' as a term for an epoch, following Droysen.

In the history of Latin literature, the evaluative metallic scale is increasingly avoided, in favour of terms that are more neutral, but less unified: 'literature of the Republic', 'Augustan Age', 'literature of the Empire', for instance, in M. v. Albrecht (*Geschichte der römischen Literatur*, 1992), alongside 'Archaic Age', 'Classical Age', 'Post-Classical Age' and 'Late Antiquity' in F. Graf (*Einleitung in die lateinische Philologie*, 1997).

B. HISTORY OF THE TERMINOLOGY DESIGNATING EPOCHS

1. ARCHAIC 2. CLASSICAL 3. HELLENISM
4. GOLDEN AND SILVER LATIN 5. LATE ANTIQUITY

1. ARCHAIC

In German, the adjective *archaisch* was formed at the end of the 19th cent., under the influence of the French *archaïque* (archaic), from the Greek *archaîos* (old). The substantive *Archaismus* (archaism) had aleady been in use since the 18th cent., and the adjective *archaistisch* (archai(isti)c) had been used for antiquated speech since the 19th cent. In art history, 'archaic' was used with a negative connotation at the end of the 19th cent. for pre-Classical, still unformed art styles, and then in a narrower sense, for the pre-Classical art of Greece. This Archaic epoch was called 'older Greek art' until the end of the 19th cent., and from about 1900 on 'Early Greek' or 'Archaic' art [20.6]. In subsequent times, both these terms for epochs were adopted by Greek philology. In the 19th cent., the designations Alt latein (Old Latin) and 'archaistic language' were in use for pre-Classical Latin. In his *Geschichte der römischen Literatur* (1913), F. Leo used the term 'Archaic literature' for it. Nevertheless, the usual designation for the period became 'Old Latin'.

2. CLASSICAL

The designation ultimately derives from Latin *classicus*, "belonging to a taxation bracket (classis)". In Aulus Gellius (2nd cent. AD), it designates, with a narrowing of meaning, in one text passage (noctes Atticae 19,8,15: 'classicus assiduusque scriptor, non proletarius', "an author of the first rank and by no means subordinate"), an "(author) who belongs to the first class", that is, "first-class; of the first rank", in contrast to "belonging to the lowest class", that is, "common". Apart from this isolated attestation, the adjective does not appear again with this meaning until 1548, in French. In his *Art poétique*, Sébillet speaks of 'les bons et classiques poètes françois', thereby meaning a few 'exemplary' authors of the Middle Ages [28. 157]. Since only ancient authors were considered exemplary in the humanistic curriculum, and were the only profane authors allowed to be read, a broadening of the adjective's meaning occurred to the 18th cent., from 'exemplary' to ancient. In particular, it meant pagan authors. Similarly, classic (from ca. 1770 on) initially designated ancient, pagan authors. Relics of this meaning are such formations as 'classical (that is, Greco-Roman) Antiquity' or 'classical philology' (both from the turn of the 19th–20th cent.). In the 18th cent., based on the meaning ancient, the adjective *klassisch* (classical), attested in German since 1748, was also used for modern authors, with the meaning 'antiquarianizing' (and hence 'exemplary') (Lessing, Herder, Schiller). By the end of the 18th cent., 'classical', or the French *classique*, were increasingly limited to those modern and ancient authors and works of art "in whom reason has developed a particularly high level" [3. 475ff.]. The nominal formulations 'the Classical' and 'classicality' arose with this meaning. Voltaire, who assigned 'Classical' authors to various golden ages (Augustan Age, Age of Alexander the Great, Age of Louis XIV, later also the Periclean Age) comes close to using the adjective as the term for an epoch. In 19th-cent. Classical philology, its use as a term designating an epoch of authors of the 'Golden Ages' of Greek and Roman literature gradually became current, as did the expressions 'Classical prose', 'Classical Latin', and the equivalents for Attic language in the 5th–4th cents. BC, and the Latin of Caesar and Cicero (e.g. [1. 173f.]). As a noun for the respective 'Classical' period or 'period of flourishing' of literature, 'Classicism' (e.g. A. Draeger, *Historische Syntax der lateinischen Sprache*; E. Norden, *Antike Kunstprosa*) first appeared in the second half of the 19th cent.; it was replaced by the newly coined term *Klassik* (Classics) in German studies since 1887, and in Classical philology in the 20th cent. (isolated attestations already in Schlegel, 1797: [28. 163] and Laube, 1839: [5. 360]).

3. HELLENISM

The term derives from the Greek *hellēnízein*, a) to speak Greek, b) 'to hellenise', as well as from *hellēnismós*, which was formed from it probably in Alexandrian times, with the meanings of 1. 'Greek culture' (LXX 2 Macc 4,13; Iul. epist. 39); 2. '(correct) Greek language usage' (Diog. Laert. 7,59); 3. beginning in Christian times, and with a semantic shift, 'paganism' (Cod. Iust. 1,11,9,1). In addition, the deverbative nominal formation *hellenistés* (hellenised Jew) is attested in Biblical Greek. The Latin adjective *hellenisticus*, formed from this Greek term, served from the 17th cent. on in specialised philological literature (Salmasius, *De lingua Hellenistica commentarius*, Lugduni Batavorum 1643) to designate Biblical Greek, as it was influenced by Hebrew elements (*lingua* or *dialectus hellenistica*). The noun *Hellenismus* is found in German since the 18th cent. (in Hamann and Herder), with the following meanings: a) 'Greek culture and intellectual world' (as in *hellēnismós*), and b) 'Graecism, a Greek linguistic peculiarity' (formed like 'Latin-ism'). Both these meanings maintained general validity down to the end of the 19th cent. in encyclopaedias, dictionaries of foreign words and specialised literature. As early as 1833, J. G. Droysen in his *Geschichte Alexanders des Großen* (Berlin) and his *Geschichte des Hellenismus* (Hamburg 1836) used 'Hellenism' in the sense of a productive blending of Greek and Oriental culture through Alexander the Great's program of hellenisation. Locally, Hellenism referred to the Hellenised East, not to Greece and the Roman area. The Battle of Actium in 31 BC did not yet spell the end of Hellenism. Droysen's goal was the revaluation of this culture of blending, which had hitherto been judged negatively. His contemporaries criticised this unusual use of the term, and to some extent denied the factual basis of cultural blending; consequently, Hellenism continued to be used exclusively in its old meaning in the specialised literature. It did not develop into the term for an epoch until J. Kaerst's *Geschichte des hellenistischen Zeitalters* (1901–09), although here too its meaning as a cultural term was still dominant. Hellenism first appeared as a firmly defined term for the age from Alexander the Great to 31–30 BC around 1910 in E. Meyer and Wilamowitz, and in 1926 in Geffcken's *Griechische Literaturgeschichte*. Here, the aspect of cultural blending disappears almost completely. Hellenism thus entered literary studies as a literary epoch that was no longer judged negatively, alongside the already-existing term 'Alexandrian Age' (evaluated as an age of decline until the 19th cent.), or else it replaced the latter.

4. GOLDEN AND SILVER LATIN

This terminological pair, which served to delimit the exemplary Latin of the Classical age from that of the post-Classical, is first attested in Erasmus of Rotterdam, in the *Praefatio* to his edition of Seneca (second edition). Here, Erasmus calls the age of Cicero 'aureum saeculum', and cautions against the linguistic usage of Seneca, as the 'argenteum saeculum'. These terms are to be placed within the context of the theory of the Ages of the World, transferred to Latin stylistic history, as transmitted in the ancient world above all in Hes. erg. 109–201 and Ov. met. 1,89–150, but also in the OT (Dan 2: 32–35: The ages of the world are presented metaphorically as a statue). Golden, silver, bronze, and iron (in Daniel: clay) ages follow one another in this model, which correspondingly characterises the history of Latin rhetorical style as one of progressive decline. It is not known who, among Erasmus' predecessors, introduced this kind of periodisation into the history of literature. The division of Latin authors according to the four metals gold, silver, tin (*stagnum*), and lead, already found with Aimericus in 1086, does not refer to epochs, but offers an evaluation according to viewpoints that are genre-specific and related to content. From the 17th cent. to the threshold of the 18th cent., the metallic scale, usually with four metals, belongs to the favourite methods of periodisation in histories of literature and dictionaries, in which either the scale from Ovid's *Metamorphoses* or the one known from Daniel serves as the foundation. The attribution of specific epochs to the metals is not constant. Only the Ciceronian and Augustan eras are most often designated as the Golden Age. In the history of literature, the metallic scheme, already criticised by Herder in 1775, was replaced beginning in the 19th cent. by new terms, such as the 'Imperial Age', for Silver and Bronze Latin. Only the terms of Silver and above all Golden Latin have survived as stylistic terms In philological scholarship and the curriculum.

5. LATE ANTIQUITY

The designation Late Antiquity is first attested in Jacob Burckhardt [8; 15. 39f.], albeit not yet as a firmly defined term for an epoch. As such, it was introduced into art history for the time from 313 (Edict of Milan) to 768 (accession of Charlemagne) only after 1900, by Riegl [23]. The concept of a 'transitional period', at first judged negatively as a decline, between Antiquity and the Middle Ages, had already existed at least since the 16th cent. (Carolus Sigonius, *Historia de occidentali imperio a Diocletiano ad Iustiniani mortem*, 1579; the 'Bas-Empire' in Ch. Lebeau's *Histoire du Bas-Empire*, 1752) and was designated as such by E. Meyer in his *Geschichte des Alterthums* in the editions following 1884 for the period from Diocletian to Charlemagne [15. 39f.]. It was above all M. Fuhrmann who made Late Antiquity a focal point of interest of Classical philology, as an independent epoch to be dealt with in an unprejudiced manner. He pointed to the lack of literary production in Latin between ca. AD 240 and 280, and saw here a clear boundary of an epoch immanent within literature [13; 14]. The transition from Late Antiquity to the Middle Ages is variously fixed: for the ancient historian Demandt it lies in the 6th cent. (Justinian) [9]; for the Latinists Fuhrmann [10; 29. 17] and Herzog [15. 1] in the 8th cent. (735: death of Beda Venerabilis).

C. PROBLEMS IN EPOCHAL STRUCTURING

The criteria used for the determination of literary-historical epochs are heterogeneous. Alongside factors that are intrinsic to literature, such as common stylistic tendencies, dialect, preferences for specific contents or genres, one encounters external historical factors, such as time, political conditions ('Age of the polis', 'Roman' instead of Latin, 'Imperial Age') or place of origin (Athens, Alexandria). Overlaps result from the partially lacking coincidence of the factors of this diasystem, which are only seldom reflected in presentations of literary histories. Thus, as a consequence of the history of their transmission, genuine literary groups are indeed recognizable in Greek literature, according to time, genre and place of origin, which, in turn, are differentiated by historically far-reaching events: epic and lyric before the Persian Wars, Attic literature to Alexander the Great; Alexandrian literature to the 1st cent. BC; the continuum of imperial literature under Roman rule. However, the lyric poet Pindar is situated in the 5th cent. BC; Herodotus, contemporary of the 'Classical' 'authors', exhibits archaic features; and the genre of Attic comedy stretches from Archaic to Hellenistic times. Thus, for instance, in the middle of the uninterrupted literary production of the 1st cent. BC, the so-called 'Classical' period, a clear political upheaval occurs with the end of the Republic, which takes place precisely in the creative period of Horace, Virgil and Tibullus; while Christian and pagan literature exist alongside one another in Late Antiquity. On the other hand, the factually attested upheaval of the 3rd cent. AD, caused by the extinction of literary production, was long taken insufficiently into consideration in periodisations. On the whole, histories of Latin literature, even of more recent date, are oriented more towards external turning points of event-based history than according to criteria intrinsic to literature.

→ Dark Ages

→ ANTIQUITY;

SOURCES 1 G. BERNHARDY, Grundriß der Griechischen Litteratur, Halle ²1852   2 J. C. SCALIGER, Poetices libri septem (facsimile repr. of the Lyon ed. 1561), 1987   3 J. G. SULZER, Allgemeine Theorie der schönen Künste I, Leipzig ²1792

LITERATURE 4 W. AX, Quattuor Linguae Latinae Aetates, in: Hermes 124, 1996, 220–240   5 E. D. BECKER, 'Klassiker' in der deutschen Literaturgeschichtsschreibung, in: J. HERMAND (ed.), Zur Literatur der Restaurationsepoche 1815–1848, 1970, 349–370   6 R. BICHLER, Hellenismus: Geschichte und Problematik eines Epochenbegriffs, 1983   7 H. BLUMENBERG, Aspekte der Epochenschwelle, 1976   8 J. BURCKHARDT, Die Zeit Constantins des Großen, (= Gesammelte Werke vol. 1, 1978, repr. 1982)   9 A. DEMANDT, Die Spät-Antike. Römische Geschichte von Diocletian bis Justinian 284–565, 1989   10 M. FUHRMANN, Die lateinische Literatur in der Spät-Antike, in: A&A 13, 1967, 56–79   11 Id., Die Geschichte der Literaturgeschichtsschreibung von den Anfängen bis zum 19. Jahrhundert, in: B. CERQUIGLINI, H. U. GUMBRECHT (eds.), Der Diskurs der Literatur- und Sprachhistorie, 1983, 49–72   12 Id., Die Epochen der griechi-

schen und der römischen Literatur, in: 11, 537–555
13 Id., Der neue Kanon lateinischer Autoren, in: W. Vosskamp (ed.), Klassik im Vergleich, 1993, 389–402   14 Id.,
Rom in der Spät-Antike, 1994   15 R. Herzog, Restauration und Erneuerung. Die lateinische Literatur von 284
bis 374 n.Chr., 1989   16 W. Jaeger (ed.), Das Problem
des Klassischen und die Antike, 1933 (repr. 1961)
17 H. R. Jauss, Il faut commencer par le commencement,
in: R. Herzog, R. Koselleck (eds.), Epochenschwelle
und Epochenbewußtsein (Poetik und Hermeneutik 12),
1987, 563–570   18 R. Kassel, Die Abgrenzung des Hellenismus in der griechischen Literaturgeschichte, 1987
19 U. Klein, Gold- und Silber-Latein, in: Arcadia 2, 1967,
248–256   20 G. Lippold, Die griechische Plastik, ⁷1950
21 R. M. Meyer, Principien der wissenschaftlichen Peri-
odenbildung, in: Euphorion 8, 1901, 1–42   22 R. Pfeiffer, Die klassische Philologie von Petrarca bis Mommsen,
1982   23 A. Riegl, Spätrömische Kunstindustrie, 1901
24 U. Schindel, Archaismus als Epochenbegriff, in:
Hermes 122, 1994, 327–341   25 F. Schlegel, Über das
Studium der griechischen Poesie, 1795–97 (repr. 1981)
26 Id, Vorlesungen zur Geschichte der alten und neuen
Literatur, 1812 (critical new edition: (ed.) E. Behler,
1989)   27 P. Steinmetz, Gattungen und Epochen der
griechischen Literatur, in: Hermes 92, 1964, 454–466
28 R. Wellek, Das Wort und der Begriff Klassizismus, in:
Schweizer Monatshefte 45, 1965/66, 154–173   29 M.
Windfuhr, Kritik des Klassikbegriffs, in: Études Germaniques 29, 1974, 302–318.   PETER KUHLMANN

IV. Art History-Architecture

see → Baroque; → Gothic; → Classical period;
→ Classicism; → Modern age; → Renaissance;
→ Romanesque style

Equestrian Statues

A. Middle Ages   B. Late Middle Ages, Early
Modern Age   C. Baroque   D. Modern Times

A. Middle Ages

The history of the reception of the ancient Equestrian Statue (ES) begins with the bronze statue of the
mounted Marcus Aurelius (erected ca. AD 173); it is the
sole survivor among numerous – even bigger and more
aesthetically attractive – Roman monuments of this
nature, having been separated and turned into Constantine the Great as the embodiment of a Christian
hero. Since the statue was clearly respected – even in the
darkest times of Late Antiquity, the reinterpretation,
not attested until the 10th cent., may date to an earlier
period.

Probably erected on the Lateran Square during the
reign of Pope Hadrian I (772–795), the *Caballus Constantini* came to manifest secular papal power, founded
as this was on the supposed → Donation of Constantine, and during the Middle Ages it was used as the
location for dealing with papal legal affairs [7]. Having
become unsuitable for this purpose in the 15th cent.
after its identification as Marcus Aurelius, the rider
(after being restored under Popes Paul II and Sixtus IV,
in the 1460s and 1470s) was donated to the Capitol, the

seat of Roman government. Transported there under
Pope Paul III in 1538 [4], it has remained to this day at
the centre of the Square of the Capitol, erected after
Michelangelo's conception on the plinth designed by
him (today a copy; the original is in the Capitoline
Museums; → Rome VI. Museums).

A comparable example is Charlemagne's transfer of
the bronze ES of Theodoric the Great from the latter's
palace in Ravenna to a place in front of the imperial
palace in Aachen in 801. It was intended to symbolize
the legitimisation of the empire of the Franks, which
had been recently revived on the model of Constantine.
The sculpture nevertheless aroused strong hostility (as a
symbol of *superbia*: Walahfried Strabo, *De imagine
Tetrici*), and was soon removed [18]. The equestrian
statuette of Charlemagne (?) from Metz (Paris, Louvre),
the first copy of the *Constantine*, can probably be attributed to the same concern for legitimisation.

Marcus Aurelius' horse is characterised by three
hooves set on the ground and an outstretched (right)
fore-hoof and its rider by the (likewise right) arm held
out in salute. The (disputed) surmise of archaeologists
that originally a defeated barbarian cowered beneath
the raised fore-hoof is reinforced by the tradition of the
Constantine horsemen in Romanesque sculpture. These
are usually placed in a prominent position on the facades of churches in 'Constantine niches' and are characteristically depicted vigorously crushing a fallen figure –
the personification of heathenism – under their hoof (in
France: Châteauneuf-sur-Charente, Melle, Parthenay-
le-Vieux, Surgères, Benet [16. 246–251]). On the capitals of the two eastern pillars in the choir of St. Lazare in
Autun, such ascendancy over heathenism is presented
in graphic parallel with the theme of idolatry: a naked
heathen stumbles, struck down by the hoof of the
emperor's horse (fig. 1); opposite is the figurative antithesis: a naked heathen woman (an idol?), worshipped
by a bedazzled youth, who is in turn struck dead by a
devil.

Other large-format (stone) equestrian sculptures of
the Middle Ages may have been produced in knowledge
of the triumphantly striding *Constantine*, but at a visible (and intentional?) distance from it, as for example
the Bamberg and Magdeburg riders: these are not triumphant, but stand accepting homage [5].

B. Late Middle Ages, Early Modern Age

Since the 15th cent., the ES of Marcus Aurelius has
been counted among the most distinguished examples
of the art of Antiquity; it was regarded as an exemplary
model for the depiction of horse and rider, as the incarnation of an art that is true to nature (as cited with
respect to Michelangelo, Pietro da Cortona and Bernini
[11. no. 49]). A first copy was in the form of a statuette
by Filarete, dedicated in 1465 to Piero de' Medici, in
Dresden (fig. 2); other (for the most part small-scale)
copies were produced to the 18th cent. Numerous drawings and engravings have been made since the 15th
cent. [11. no. 49; 2. no. 176].

Fig. 1: Filarete (Antonio Averlino),
Statuette of Marcus Aurelius. Bronze, 1465.
*Sculpture Collection, Staatliche
Kunstsammlungen Dresden*

Fig. 2: René Antoine Houasse, Transporting the
Equestrian Statue of Louis XIV from Girardon
to the Place Vendome, 1699. Painting, about 1700.
Paris, Musée Carnavalet, © *Phototèque des Musées
de la Ville Paris*

The interest in the ES as representing a specific individual, which began in the Late Middle Ages, could not, during the course of its history to the present, entirely ignore the Roman original, even if in their iconography artists often forged their own path or looked to a small number of other ancient models, such as the *Regisole* in Pavia (presumed ES of Theodoric the Great, destroyed in 1796) or the → HORSES OF SAN MARCO (*quadriga* from Constantinople) in Venice [17; 3. no. 177]).

The revival of the ES in Italy from about the 14th cent. was evidently associated with a change of meaning, perhaps representing folkloric reinterpretations of the rider as a popular liberating hero (*Mirabilia*, ca. 1140 [9. 57 ff.]), or Cola di Rienzo's usurpation of the *Caballus Constantini* in 1347 [10. 155 f.]. In any event, the riders depicted during this period were no longer kings or emperors, but usurpers, mercenary leaders and defenders of the homeland. The occasions for and locations of their installation were sepulchres; thus they adorned the Della Scala tombs in Verona: Cangrande I (d. 1329), Mastino II (d. 1351), and Cansignorio (d. 1375) in the posture of tournament riders. There are numerous wooden monuments in churches, the most artistically notable being the ES of Paolo Savelli (Jacopo della Quercia?, ca..1406, Venice, Frari Church); a late example in Germany: the equestrian tomb of the Mecklenburg Chancellor Samuel von Behr (d. 1621) in the monastery church in Bad Doberan. A wall tomb of the *condottiere* John Hawkwood in the Florence Cathe-

dral, painted *al fresco* in perspective by Paolo Uccello (1436), imitates a 'real' ES and sets the model for future representations. On the wall nearby there is a similar tomb for Nicolò da Tolentino of Castagno, 1456.

The free-standing bronze monuments of the 15th cent., whether oriented towards the horses of San Marco or towards Marcus Aurelius, were, even from a technical point of view, the first comparable equestrian statues of the Modern Age. Examples are the ES of Niccolò III d'Este in Ferrara (1451), destroyed in 1796; Donatello's Gattamelata in Padua (1453), whose plinth alludes to Roman tombs; or the Colleoni, erected in Venice in 1496 based on a model by Verrocchio. The Colleoni statue departs furthest from the ancient model, replacing the latter's dignity and repose with that gesture of concentrated power, which became the hallmark of military and mercenary leaders when they had themselves honoured with an ES. It also departs from the equestrian tomb tradition, which is nevertheless maintained in Colleoni's funeral chapel in Bergamo.

The most celebrated project for an ES during the Renaissance, Leonardo's Sforza monument in Milan (1483–1495), was never completed (as was also the case with the later Trivulzio project), but the surviving abundance of studies and sketches indicates experimentation with various new techniques. The artistically and technically most ambitious variants of these, the leap and levade of the mount, complement the ancient tradition. Whether the Hellenistic variant of the rearing horse was available at that time is uncertain (cf. the statuette [15. 66]). The first monument with a rearing horse to be completed was modelled on Leonardo (probably after a painting by Rubens) and completed by Pietro Tacca for Philip IV in Madrid (1636–1640, with technical and physical advice from Galileo).

During the 16th cent. monarchs began to show interest in the new form of representation, but most projects came to naught, as happened in the case of Maximilian I (Gregor Erhart), Francis I (Giovanni Francesco Rustici), Henry II of France (Michelangelo or Daniele da Volterra) and Emperor Charles V (Leone Leoni). The first ES of a prince (significantly–a usurper) is that of Grand Duke Cosimo I in Florence, by Giovanni da Bologna (1594), who is not represented as a military commander, but rather in contemporary, more or less civilian dress, as a self-restrained prince, thus embodying a model for the absolutist ES and its conceit: skillful in leading his horse and thus also in leading the state. At about the same time the volume of copperplate engravings *XII Caesares in equestri forma* (...) by Antonio Testa (Rome 1596) appeared, a veritable catalogue of variants for paintings and statues of mounted monarchs.

C. Baroque

The two expressive ES of Ranuccio and Alessandro Farnese by Francesco Mocchi in Piacenza (1620 and 1625) derive from the triumphant models à la Colleoni, while at the same time in France the dignified absolutist model is preferred. These statues were, of course, without exception destroyed in the French Revolution, but regarding the greatest and most representative, that of Louis-le-Grand on the Parisian square named for him (the modern Place Vendôme) by François Girardon (erected in 1699), we have sufficient illustrative material to recognise its epochal stature (fig. 3). The statue is some 7 metres high and expresses in equal measure calm and energy, lightness and gravity and thus royal sovereignty The rider is represented in Roman imperial dress, without stirrups but wearing a full wig. Characteristically for the dominant spirit, the marble ES of Louis XIV by Bernini (1685), showing the monarch as a pathetic hero, was rejected, remodelled by Girardon himself, and relegated to Versailles as a garden statue.

Girardon's Louis XIV is followed by the ES of the Great Elector, Frederick the Great of Prussia, by Andreas Schlüter in Berlin (erected 1703). It is, however, more baroque and dynamic in form, and, unlike its model, portrays two different aspects (commander and statesman). The monument is effectively enhanced by four slaves chained to its plinth, as previously featured on the ES of Henry IV of France on the Pont Neuf in Paris by Pietro Tacca (unveiled 1614, destroyed 1792). The last examples of the absolutist ES – among others, the monuments to King Frederick V of Denmark by Jacques Saly in Copenhagen (1754–1764), Emperor Joseph II by Franz Anton Zauner in Vienna (1795–

1806), and Prince Poniatowski by Bertel Thorwaldsen in Warsaw (1826/27; destroyed; today a copy), all take their orientation from the ancient model (Marcus Aurelius).

In stark contrast and even declared hostility to the ancient model is the ES of Peter the Great in St. Petersburg (1766–1782) by Étienne Falconet, who in *Observations sur la statue de Marc-Aurèle* (...) (Amsterdam 1771), written in the context of the → QUERELLE DES ANCIENS ET DES MODERNES, denounced the ancient work as a flawed monstrosity. In the spirit of explicit naturalism, horse and rider are placed on a massive block of natural rock (rock = *petros* = Peter), before whose steep edge the horse, trampling a snake (which functions as an anchor), rears up in a dressage courbette, giving its rider a triumphal pose (ultimately in the tradition of Leonardo, Tacca and Bernini).

D. Modern Times

During the 19th cent. the ES is ubiquitous, countless examples appearing in the Old and the New World (notably in South America: Simón Bolívar). As regards Germany, mention may be made *pars pro toto* of the early historical ES of Friedrich the Great by Christian Daniel Rauch in Berlin (1840–1851) and the statues of the four last Hohenzollerns on the *Hohenzollernbrücke* in Cologne: Friedrich Wilhelm IV by Gustav Bläser (1861–1863), Wilhelm I by Friedrich Drake (1867), Friedrich III and Wilhelm II by Louis Tuaillon (1909). Tuaillon's earlier statue of Emperor Friedrich III in Bremen (1905) was much celebrated in its day as an ES worthy of the modern era.

In the 20th cent., once the mounted figure had lost its triumphal aura and its status as a symbol of power to rule, the ES generally went into marked decline. It repeatedly crops up in countries where there is a need to 'catch up'. It is not only in the so-called Third World that it was adopted to portray a new iconography of leadership; in Turkey, too, where images had hitherto been forbidden, numerous ES of Kemal Atatürk came into being. In Spain, too, notably during the Franco period, a late boom in ES arose, considerable numbers of them being erected for various generals (in particular the Caudillo himself). The most prominent and imposing of them (6 metres high) is the Franco Monument by Federico Coullat-Valera (1967) in Franco's Galician home town of El Ferrol. Even in an established democracy such as Finland, as late as 1960 Marshal Mannerheim was honoured by the erection of a monumental ES by Aimo Tukiainen (Helsinki).

Famous artists are no longer numbered among its sculptors. Only Émile Bourdelle, the renowned pupil of Rodin, still contributed such a work: the ES of General Alvear in Buenos Aires (1926). The artistic challenge that the image of horse and rider always posed was then taken up repeatedly in the works of Marino Marini (1901–1980); but, in contrast to the ES, his works do not represent real persons, concentrating as it does in many variants on the different formal aspects and motifs of the genre.

1 CH. AVERY, Equestrian Monument, in: J. TURNER (ed.), The Dictionary of Art, vol. 10, 1996, 440–442   2 Id., Giambologna, 1987, 157–165   3 PH. BOBER, R. RUBIN-STEIN, Renaissance Artists and Antique Sculpture, 1986 4 T. BUDDENSIEG, Zum Statuenprogramm im Kapitols-plan Pauls III., in: Zeitschrift für Kunstgeschichte 32, 1969, 177–228   5 P. C. CLAUSSEN, Kompensation und Innovation. Zur Denkmalproblematik im 13. Jahrhun-dert am Beispiel der Reitermonumente in Magdeburg und Bamberg, in: H. BECK, K. HENGEVOSS-DÜRKOP (eds.), Studien zur Geschichte der europäischen Skulptur im 12./13. Jahrhundert, 1994, 565–585   6 D. ERBEN, Bar-tolomeo Colleoni. Die künstlerische Repräsentation eines Condottiere im Quattrocento, 1996   7 PH. FEHL, The Placement of the Equestrian Statue of Marcus Aurelius in the Middle Ages, in: JWI 37, 1974, 362–367   8 H. FRIIS, Rytterstatuens historie i Europa, 1932   9 N. GRAMAC-CINI, Die Umwertung der Antike – Zur Rezeption des Marc Aurel in Mittelalter und Renaissance, in: H. BECK, P. C. BOL (eds.), Natur und Antike in der Renaissance, Austellung im Liebieghaus Museum alter Plastik, 1985, 51–83 (Exhibition catalogue)   10 Id., Mirabilia. Das Nachleben antiker Statuen vor der Renaissance, 1996 11 FR. HASKELL, N. PENNY, Taste and the Antique, 1981 12 H. W. JANSON, The Equestrian Monument from Can-grande della Scala to Peter the Great, in: Id., Sixteen Stu-dies, 1973, 159–169   13 U. KELLER, Reitermonumente absolutistischer Fürsten, 1971   14 W. LIEDTKE, The Royal Horse and Rider, 1989   15 D. VON DER BURG (ed.), Marc Aurel. Der Reiter auf dem Kapitol, 1999 16 E. MÂLE, Religious Art in France. The Twelfth Cen-tury, 1978 (Orig. L'Art religieux du XIIe siécle en France. Etude sur l'origine de l'iconographie du Moyen Age, 1953)   17 Die Pferde von San Marco, Staatliche Musseen Preussicher Kusturbesitz, Berlin 1982 (Exhibition catalo-gue)   18 F. THÜRLEMANN, Die Bedeutung der Theode-rich-Statue für Karl den Großen und bei Walahfried Strabo, in: AKG, 59, 25–65.   BERTHOLD HINZ

Erechtheion see → SUPPORTING FIGURES

Erotica
A. MIDDLE AGES   B. MODERN ERA

A. MIDDLE AGES
Both Greek and Roman art is rich in erotic themes and objects of all kinds. They are found in a multitude of genres and modes of expression, from large-scale sculpture, painting and mosaics to craft products and finally small art objects (e.g. gems and cameos). When the triumph of Christianity brought an end to the ero-ticism of ancient art, the world of erotic imagery also disappeared from the light of day. Objects of this kind were, of course, collected and appreciated by connois-seurs in secret during the entire Middle Ages [1]. More importantly, however, a collective memory of those images remained, condemned now as idols and the seat of demons, and was kept alive initially by the pro-nouncements of many Church Fathers hostile to sexua-lity and images alike. It was their habit, while warning against heathen images, to allude to their seductive but pernicious qualities. Particular reference was made to

the case of Praxiteles' Aphrodite of Cnidus, who by her nakedness and artistic perfection had ensnared a youth and caused him to attempt sexual intercourse with her [6].

The assumed erotic power of (naked) statuary re-emerged in distorted and negative form during the Ro-manesque period in two ways: 1. in words and writing, for example, in the legends of diabolically instigated betrothals to statues of Venus (William of Malmesbury, 1125, German *Kaiserchronik*, ca.1150); 2. artistically, in the architecture of the pilgrim churches of southern France and northern Spain of ca.1100, in which the sculpture, scorned until then, reappeared in the form of obscene antitypes. Resistance to the assumed seductive power expressed itself in monstrously perverted ima-gery. Thus, for example, the motif of the *Spinario* (thorn-puller) was interpreted as an incarnation of heathen-priapic nature (Magister Gregorius) and circu-lated in countless male and female variants, sculptural and otherwise [3; 5] (fig. 1). The image of Venus muta-ted into that of Luxuria, the snake- and toad-covered personification of lust (Moissac).

B. MODERN ERA
Gradually rehabilitated since the → RENAISSANCE, ancient subjects and artworks now became catalysts for contemporary erotic desires. Thus erotic themes from Antiquity with intent to arouse ('Amor and Psyche', 'Judgement of Paris', 'Rape of Helena', etc.) were first popularised on Florentine marriage chests (15th cent.). In the *Hypnerotomachia Poliphili* (Venice 1499) the dream of sexual fulfillment in word and image is trans-ported to an ancient Utopia.

Now there began a stream of related ancient subjects in the art and imagery of the New and Old World that continues unabated to this day. No style, and scarcely an artist, has failed to contribute to it [4]. The most widely distributed personifications of male and female eroticism continue to be of ancient origin: Aphrodite/ Venus, Eros/ Amor, satyr, Pan/faun, maenad, centaur (Picasso!), etc. The gods, especially the amours of Venus and Jupiter, were models available for the repre-sentation of loving couples and couplings (cf. Carag-lio's cycle of engravings *Lascivie* or *Amours of the Gods* after drawings by P. del Vaga, ca.1530); the preferred iconic models for women as the recipients of sexual attentions were Danaë (Titian, Rembrandt, Klimt) and Io (Correggio). Even more than in the case of 'standard eroticism",' ancient models were used in the cultivation of deviant erotic inclinations. Hyacinth (Cellini) and Ganymede (Correggio, Rubens), and Antinous, for example, were encoded homosexually, while the Venus Callipygus and the reclining Hermaphrodite were favourite subjects where the aim was for fetishistic effect (cf. the adaptation of the Louvre Hermaphrodite by Bernini). The motif of *Leda and the Swan* was used to serve bizarre fantasies (Michelangelo, Leonardo da Vinci, Correggio). And Narcissus (Caravaggio, Pous-sin, Dali) became a synonym for pathological autoero-

Fig. 1: 'Spinario' on the tomb of
Archbishop Friedrich von Wettin, 1152,
Magdeburg Cathedral

Fig. 2: *The lecherous female faun*. Anonymous
engraving after Marcanton Raimondi,
based on a motif from a Dionysian sarcophagus
in the Museo Nazionale, Naples

Fig. 3: Rezsö Balászfy, Exlibris

Fig. 4: Aubrey Beardsley, Frontispiece to the
Lysistrata illustrations, 1896

Fig. 5: Bonaventura Genelli, *Who will buy love
gods?*, watercolour, about 1830

ticism (Freud). With the turn of the 19th cent., new icons of eroticism (e.g. 'Femme fatale', 'Pin-up girl') broke the dominance of ancient models, though without causing their demise (cf. the *Lysistrata* illustrations by A. Beardsley, 1896, fig. 4).

Alongside these themes, particular motifs of ancient eroticism, such as coupling fauns, after a Roman sarcophagus (Marcanton Raimondi, fig. 2), have been popular over the centuries. The excavations of → POMPEII (from 1748) and → HERCULANEUM brought a breakthrough as regards motifs. Here small-scale and everyday art, often of a crudely pornographic nature, came particularly to light: copulating couples in many varying configurations on murals, graffiti, *terra sigillata* vessels, mirrors, clay lamps; and numerous phallic/priapic motifs, including winged penises (lamps, *tintinnabula*, amulets), which from then on became a favourite motif in classicistic graphics (B. Genelli, *Wer kauft Liebesgötter?*, ca.1830, fig. 5). The finds were brought together into the *Gabinetto segreto* collection of the King of Naples (now Museo Nazionale), to which only selected visitors were allowed access [8]. The cloak of secrecy (still existing) around the collection, which was later called the *Raccolta Pornografica (RP)*, gave rise to all kinds of erotic publications (e.g. Baron d'Hancarville, *Monuments du culte secret des Dames Romaines*, Capri 1784) and unauthorised connoisseurs' editions (e.g. Marie-César Famin, *Musée Royal de Naples. Peintures, Bronces et Statues Erotiques*, Paris 1832; Gaston Vorberg, *Museum eroticum Neapolitanum*, 1910). Numerous private collections came into existence in this context, among them Goethe's *Priapeia* and *Erotika* (for the most part impressions from antique intaglios). There was a late blossoming of 'priapism' in the *exlibris* art of the 19th and 20th cents. (R. Balázsfy – after the Delian marble *phalloi*, fig. 3).

Antique erotica, in their artistic reception and in collections and publications, long continued to play a role as a semi-sanctioned reserve for the articulation and satisfaction of erotic needs (especially erotic images), which was otherwise condemned. Even more recent scholarly publications, such as H. Licht's *Sittengeschichte Griechenlands* [7], cannot deny this continuing impetus.

→ Aphrodite; → Danae; → Eros; → Ganymed; → Hermaphroditus; → Hyacinthus; → Narcissus I. Mythical character; → Pan; → Satyrus

1 H. G. BECK, Byzantinisches Eroticon, 1986 2 A. DIERICHS, Erotik in der römischen Kunst, 1997 3 R. HAMANN, Kunst und Askese, 1987, 45–64 4 E. FUCHS, Geschichte der erotischen Kunst, 3 vols., 1908–26 5 W. S. HECKSCHER, Dornauszieher, in: RDK 4, 1958, 289–299 6 B. HINZ, Aphrodite. Geschichte einer abendländischen Passion, 1998 7 H. LICHT, Sittengeschichte Griechenlands, 3 vols., 1925–28 (Engl. J. FREESE (trans.), Sexual Life in Ancient Greece, 2000, ¹1931). 8 G. L. MARINI, Il Gabinetto Segreto del Museo Nazionale di Napoli, 1971.   BERTHOLD HINZ

Estate register see → LAND SURVEYING; → WEIGHTS AND MEASURES

Estonia

I. LATIN LANGUAGES II. CLASSICAL LANGUAGES AT THE UNIVERSITY OF DORPAT (TARTU) III. CLASSICAL MOTIFS IN LITERATURE AND TRANSLATIONS

I. LATIN LANGUAGES

The influence of Antiquity in Estomia (E.), mediated through Christianity in the Middle Ages, can only be traced with relative precision since the end of the 11th cent. The first documents pertaining to Estonian history date from this time. In the chronicles (Adam of Bremen, Saxo Grammaticus), the inhabitants of present-day E. are referred to as *Aisti* and *Estones;* the encyclopedia of Bartholomaeus Anglicus, *De proprietatibus rerum*, contains rather precise descriptions of individual localities (*de Rivalia, de Vironia*). Direct relationships and contacts between E. and the ancient world cannot be documented. Although the term *gentes Aistiorum* does indeed appear in the *Germania* (45) of Tacitus, he was using it to denote the Indo-Germanic ancestors of the Baltic peoples (Old Prussians, Lithuanians and Latvians). At the beginning of the 13th cent., E. became part of the lands of the Teutonic Order and the European cultural sphere where Latin was regarded as the general language of science and culture until the 17th cent. The oldest work in the Latin language and the most important source regarding Livonia and E. is the *Chronicon Livoniae* of Henry of Latvia (written ca. 1225, first edition 1740). Of other Baltic history books the most important are the *Chronicon Livoniae* of Hermann von Wartberge (written in 14th cent., first edition 1863), the *Livoniae historia* of Thomas Horner (first edition 1551), the *Belli Livonici historia* of Tillmann Bredenbach (first edition 1564), and the *Livonicae historiae compendiosa* series of Dionysius Fabricius (written ca. 1610, first edition 1795). In addition to the specifically Baltic chronicles, information about E. is found in many Latin-language books of the time, as for example in the works of H. Schedel, S. Münster, S. von Herberstain, and in the famous Elzevier editions of *Respublica sive status regni Poloniae, Lituaniae, Prussiae, Livoniae diversorum auctorum*.

In E., the first information about → CATHEDRAL SCHOOLS and → MONASTERY SCHOOLS, in which the Classical languages were taught, dates from the middle of the 13th cent. Usually instruction consisted only of the subjects of the trivium, and the pupils read mainly Donatus, Cassiodorus and Capella. Of the monastery schools, the one at the Dominican monastery in Tallinn played the most important role. After the Reformation and Melanchthon's school reforms, new schools were founded in which Greek and Hebrew were taught alongside Latin, and the works of authors of Antiquity were read (there is at least evidence for Aesop and Terence) (→ SCHOOL SYSTEM). At the turn of 15th to the

16th cent. there existed a Jesuit Gymnasium (→ JESUIT SCHOOLS), in Tartu in which the study of Latin encompassed all levels (after 1593, also rhetoric) of the *studia inferiora*. Study of the Classical languages attained a higher level in the Reval Gymnasium (opened in 1631; → HUMANIST GYMNASIUM) where there were professorships for Greek language, poetry and rhetoric. Latin as a major subject was taught by the rector and the professors of poetry and rhetoric. At the end of the 17th cent., and especially during the 18th cent. when the university in Tartu was closed, the Reval Gymnasium, as an academic Protestant teaching establishment, was an important institution at which the Classical languages were cultivated, the works of most writers of Antiquity were available and the most significant of them were studied.

→ ARTES LIBERALES

1 Eesti kooli ajalugu 1, 1989   2 G. v. RAUCH, Geschichte der deutschbaltischen Geschichtsschreiber, 1986.

OLEV NAGEL

II. CLASSICAL LANGUAGES AT THE UNIVERSITY OF DORPAT (TARTU)

At the University of Dorpat, opened in 1632, it was primarily the professors of Greek language, rhetoric and poetics who worked with Latin and Greek as well as with the writers of Antiquity. In addition, the Classical authors formed the basis of the study of mathematics (Euclid, Aristotle, Archimedes, Ptolemy), philosophy (*methodus Socratica*) and jurisprudence. In accordance with the statutes of the university, the principles of instruction required that the professor of poetry should derive his *praecepta* from the works of Aristotle in addition to those of authorities of more recent times, and select his examples from the writings of Homer, Hesiod, Theocritus, Pindar, Euripides, Sophocles, Vergil, Horace, Ovid and Juvenal. Professors of Greek were supposed to teach in the manner of Socrates. For the professor of rhetoric, the rules of Ramus and Thaleus were obligatory, together with the principles of Ciceronian eloquence (especially from *De oratore*). Speeches and epigrams were composed according to the model provided by the works of Demosthenes, Thucydides, Herodotus, Plutarch, and Livy as well as the speeches and letters of Cicero. The subject of many disputations was the justification of 'good speech in the manner of Cicero' (e.g. *De oratore*, Dorpat 1641 and *De elocutione*, Dorpat 1645, by Laurentius Ludenius; → RHETORIC). Encomiastic speeches (panegyrics) contained numerous comparisons with Antiquity and used Classical mythological motifs for ornamental figures of speech. The Swedish professor of rhetoric and poetics Olaus Hermelin, who wrote about Classical culture and frequently referred to Cicero, Livy, Tacitus, Virgil and Suetonius (e.g. in his *De studio honoris, De varietate ingeniorum, De columnis Herculis* i.a.), used the most citations from Classical Antiquity.

Works from later periods and of local significance occasionally drew parallels to Antiquity, as for example the speech *De civitate Dorpatensi* (Dorpat 1637), in which the author compared his native city, which had suffered greatly during the war, with Troy and Carthage. In the disputation *Templa non templa*, the eradication of superstition in E. is compared with the heroic deeds of Hercules, in this case, the cleaning of the Augean stables. Latin occasional poems were an element of the disputations, which in part were written in Alcaic and Sapphic strophes. Stylistic ornamentation in wedding and inaugural poems can be traced back to Antiquity in many ways. The second-oldest Estonian grammar, the *Observationes criticae circa linguam Esthonicam*, written in Latin by Johann Gutslaff (Dorpat 1660), was an important step in the development of the literary language. Description of the grammatical system of Estonian was based mainly on the principles of Latin and German (→ LINGUISTICS).

Of special significance for the expansion of the influence of Classical Antiquity was the reopening of the University of Dorpat in 1802. Karl Morgenstern, in particular, a student of F.A. Wolf, was active in this respect: for him, study of the Classical languages was the basis of all knowledge. He is the author of the works *De litteris humanioribus* (1798, published in Leipzig and Danzig 1800), *Über den Einfluß des Studiums der griechischen und römischen Klassiker* (1802, published in Leipzig 1805), and *Vom Sprachenstudium* (1816, published in Dorpat 1821). He was guided by the idea that one can develop reason and come to know all the other branches of learning, e.g. history and philosophy, through the literature of Antiquity. All genres of Classical literature should serve as 'teacher' for later times. He repeatedly emphasised the significance of Antiquity in the collection that he edited, *Dörptische Beyträge für Freunde der Philosophie, Litteratur und Kunst* (3 volumes, Dorpat 1813, 1815, 1816). Through Morgenstern's efforts, Latin came to life in academic circles (e.g. through his speeches and correspondence in Latin). Instruction at the university and, even more, at the Philological Seminar that Morgenstern founded in 1821 laid the foundation for Classical studies in the gymnasia (→ HUMANIST GYMNASIUM). Although the position of most important external cultural influence in E. was occupied by German, these schools also transmitted an essential part of Classical culture. Instruction in the Classics was continued by Morgenstern's successors. Ludwig Schwabe, Ludwig Preller, Ludwig Mercklin and others taught in Dorpat. After the First World War, Wilhelm Süß taught for a lengthy period of time (1923–34), after which the first Estonian Classical philologists (Pärtel Haliste, Ervin Roos and others) were trained. Following the Second World War, during the Soviet period (1945–1990), Classical philology steadily lost ground; in 1954, the academic chair was abolished. Its re-establishment in 1990 coincided with the attainment of political independence. In 1992, a professorship was established for the first time in the post-war

period, and study of the Classical languages was resumed under the direction of A. Lill.
→ COURSE OF INSTRUCTION; → SCHOOLS; → UNIVERSITY

1 Acta et commentationes universitatis Tartuensis (Dorpatensis). Annales XIV. Quellen zur Geschichte der Universität Tartu (Dorpat), I Academia Gustaviana, 1932 2 W. Süss, Karl Morgenstern, 1928 3 Tartu Ülikooli ajalugu I, II, III, 1982.

III. CLASSICAL MOTIFS IN LITERATURE AND TRANSLATIONS

Classical motifs were also used in the narrative literature of the 18th and 19th cents. within the context of pietistic stories told following the German model and most often with a devoutly religious manner of presentation. Especially significant is Friedrich Wilhelm Willmann's book *Juttud ja Teggud* ('Fables and Stories', Tallinn 1782, with three later reprints), in which several familiar themes from the prose of Petronius (*Matron of Ephesus*) and the fables of Aesop and Phaedrus can be found. In general, though, contact with Antiquity remained slight until the 19th cent. After that, numerous different Classical influences can be discerned in the cultural life of E. as expressed in translations of Classical writers, use of Classical verse meter, retellings of Greek myth, and interpretations of ancient history and literature. One of the first Estonian writers to work with Classical models was Kristjan Jaak Peterson. In his odes one finds free adaptations of Pindar's *Epinikia*: he used the strophic structure of the model and gave Estonian designations to the odes. Following the *Finnische Mythologie* of Ganander, he tried to compose an Estonian mythology after the Greek model, thereby introducing pseudo-mythologizing tendencies into Estonian literature. In his ode *Innimenne* ('Man') Peterson treated the motif of Antigone (V. 332–375); he also wrote bucolic and anacreontic poems.

Attempts were made in the mid–19th cent. to write poems in Estonian in Classical verse meter in order to demonstrate the flexibility and usability of the language (among others, the elegiac distichs and Alcaic strophes, as well as the iambic verse of F.R. Faehlmann and the Sapphic strophes and hexameters of Jaan Bergmann). Themes from Classical literature were reproduced in several works of this period, as for example Arion as the image of life (ship at sea) or allegorical animal stories in→ FABLE (some mediated through German, others through Russian). Jakob Tamm treated the mythic motifs of Tantalus, the Sirens and Antiochus. Toward the end of the 19th cent., → TRANSLATION of Classical poetry gained significance

The influence of Antiquity increased as part of the rapprochement between E. and western Europe. Thanks to translations from the German (books by J.C. Andrae, R. Schneider and G. Schwab), Greek myths were well known in E. at the beginning of the 20th cent. Translations of the *Iliad* (Book 1, Eesti 1917) and of the first 12 Books of the *Odyssey* (Kirjandus 1938) were published. The Homeric epic in its entirety was translated into Estonian by August Annist (*Iliad*, Tallinn 1960, *Odyssey*, Tallinn 1963). Greek → TRAGEDY became known in E. later than the epic (the Prometheus tragedy of Aeschylus, Tartu 1908). In 1924 the adapted translation of *Oedipus Rex* by Anna Haava was published in Tallinn, based not only on the work of Sophocles but also on the version by H. v. Hofmannsthal. A more comprehensive view of Classical literature became possible only after the publication of anthologies of Greek and Roman literature (Tallinn 1964 and 1971) in which excerpts from the works of Classical writers (Hesiod, Herodotus, Thucydides, Xenophon, Demosthenes; Cicero, Caesar, Sallust, Livy, Lucretius, Ovid, Seneca) appeared in translation. These anthologies also contain complete tragedies and comedies; in them, comedies of Aristophanes (*The Knights, The Clouds*), Plautus (*Pseudolus*) and Terence (*Adelphoe*) appeared in Estonian for the first time. In the theatre, *Oedipus Rex, Antigone,* and *The Bacchae* were staged.

Other translations: a) Greek: Herodotus, *Historia* (excerpts, Tallinn 1983); Longos, *Daphnis ja Chloe* (Tallinn 1972); Plato, *Pidusöök, Sokratese apoloogia* ('Symposium', 'Apology', Tallinn 1985); Lucian, *Timon* (Tallinn 1970), Marcus Aurelius, *Iseendale* ('Meditations', Tallinn 1983); Aristotle, *Luulekunst* ('Poetics', Keelja 1982); *Nikomachose eetika* ('Nicomachean Ethics' Tartu 1966). b) Latin: Virgil, *Bucolica, Aeneis* (Tallinn 1992); Petronius, *Trimalchio pidusöök* ('The Banquet of Trimalchio',Tallinn 1974); Augustine, *Pihtimused* ('Confessions', n.p. 1993); Apuleius, *Metamorfoosid* ('Metamorphoses', Tallinn 1994); Seneca, *Moraalikirjad Luciliusele* ('Letters to Lucilius', n.p., n.d.). Among the works by Estonian writers using Classical material, the following merit attention: Mati Unt, *Phaeton, päikese poeg* ('Phaeton, The Son of the Sun', Tallinn 1966); Leo Metsar, *Keiser Julianus* (Tallinn 1978). The poems of Ain Kaalep are likewise closely linked to Classical motifs and Classical stanzaic structure, as for example *Paani surm* ('The Death of Pan', Tallinn 1976), *Kuldne Aphrodite* ('Golden Aphrodite', Tallinn 1986). Numerous other Estonian poets of the 20th cent. (G. Suits, B. Alver, V. Ridala, J. Kross and others) have also incorporated Classical themes into their poetry.   ANNE LILL

Ethics see → PRACTICAL PHILOSOPHY

Etruscans: Later Reception
A. INTRODUCTION B. FROM THE RENAISSANCE TO THE 17TH CENTURY C. FROM THE 18TH TO THE 20TH CENTURY

A. INTRODUCTION
In contrast to the reception of Greek and Roman cultures, the reception of Etruscan culture can be considered peripheral and largely indirect. However, during the → RENAISSANCE and in the 18th cent. (as a result of a 'misinterpretation', particularly in the field

Fig. 1: Tuscan column, anthropomorphic Tuscan column and Tuscan column with bosses from the *Architectura* by Wendel Dietherlin (1598 edition), pl. VI; Paris, Ecole Nationale Supérieure des Beaux-Arts Cat. 432

Fig. 2: John Flaxman, Vase depicting the Apotheosis of Homer, maunfactured at the Etruria pottery works of Josiah Wedgwood, late 18th cent.; Barlaston (Staffordshire), *by courtesy of the Wedgwood Museum Trust, Barlaston, Staffordshire (England)*

of architecture) it was of some importance, as well as in the modern era.

B. FROM THE RENAISSANCE TO THE 17TH CENTURY

Even though individual monuments and literary reports of the Etruscans were known in the Middle Ages and the iconography of demons in particular was frequently associated with Etruscan wall paintings [3. 240ff.], a reception of Etruscan culture as such only became apparent with the onset of the Renaissance. It was characterized on the one hand by an improved knowledge of the works of ancient authors such as Vitruvius, Pliny, Livy and Dionysius of Halicarnassus and on the other by a striving for Humanist education and spiritual reorientation. Because of a special interest in cultures that predated the 'standard' Classical periods like the Etruscan culture or that of Ancient Egypt and assisted by spectacular new discoveries, which led

to the creation of myths regarding the central importance of the Etruscans in the earliest history of Italy, the reception of Etruscan culture had a strong local, i.e. Tuscan, character (→ ETRUSCOLOGY). Initially, the central focus was on Etruscan architecture, the rudimentary knowledge of which was derived from extant fortifications, city gates and funerary monuments, as well as from information provided by ancient authors. Numerous attempts were made to discover the monumental tomb of king Porsenna of Chiusi as described by Pliny (HN 36,91) and to reconstruct it in drawings (esp. B. Peruzzi and A. Sangallo the Younger) [1. 36ff.]. The draft design of a mausoleum, whose internal structure and external appearance were based on the then recently discovered tumulus in Castellina-in-Chianti, is attributed to Leonardo da Vinci (fig.: [3. 276]). However, learned debate (L.B. Alberti) initially focused on the Etruscan temple, as described by Vitruvius (4,7). It was admired as a precursor to the Greek temple and also for its primitive qualities and its special architectural features, in particular its wooden construction. The Etruscan temple met not only with lively interest in the theoretical debate, but was also transformed into actual architectural projects, albeit with a large degree of alienation (church of Sant'Andrea in Mantua, 1470) [3. 292ff.]. The Tuscan column (fig.1) was also of great significance in the reception of Etruscan culture. It differed from the Doric column by the addition of a moulded ring below the echinus, by its smooth shaft which was thickened at the centre and by its profiled round base. Until early 19th-cent. → CLASSICISM, this type of column was used as part of a distinct Tuscan order, mainly in the form of a lesene, in which the profiling of column and capital was being used as a continuous structuring element of exterior façades and interior courtyards, sometimes across several stories (e.g. → UFFIZI GALLERY by Giorgio Vasari; Escorial near Madrid) [1. 44ff.; 3. 224ff., 292ff.]. Other individual architectural components, albeit of only regional importance, are the 'Doric' doors (with owner inscriptions) of residential buildings and palaces in northern Latium and Tuscany, and also the predilection for quarry-faced masonry, probably inspired by the entrances to Etruscan tombs (Orvieto) or by city gates. It is likely that Etruscan urns and sarcophagi were already known in the Middle Ages and then further disseminated in the wake of excavations; the characteristic feature of the latter is the complete plastic representation of the figure of the deceased on the lid, either supine or propped up on his/her arms. Towards the end of the 15th cent. this form of burial was adopted in western central Italy by the local aristocracy and clergy, and from there it spread to Spain as well as to central and northern Europe, enriched with Roman sepulchral symbolism [3. 232ff.].

C. FROM THE 18TH TO THE 20TH CENTURY

Originating with the 'false assumption' that the Greek vases found in Etruscan chamber tombs were indigenous, a distinctive artistic fashion developed in 18th-cent. Europe. It was considered 'Etruscan' and seen as an indication that Etruscan culture predated Greek and Roman art. Influenced also by the newly discovered Roman wall paintings in → POMPEII and → HERCULANEUM, in particular by the Third Style, a specifically 'Etruscan' style of interior decoration was developed, initially in Britain and France. Entire rooms were painted in this style, such as at Derby House in London (1773/74), the Etruskisches Kabinett in the Kronprinzenpalais in Berlin (1830) or the Gabinetto Etrusco in Racconigi (1834). Not only were walls and ceilings decorated 'all'etrusca', but the furnishings, including the ceramics, also coordinated. The output of J. Wedgewood's ceramic works 'Etruria' in England enjoyed international recognition from 1769 onwards. Its vases, which were not only artistically sophisticated and – since the invention of stoneware – of exceptional quality, were widely distributed and had a profound

Fig. 3: R. Calligano, *I turisti ci guardano*, 1984

and enduring influence on the interest in the Etruscans [3. 300ff.] (fig. 2). The interest in all things 'Etruscan' is also evident in the flourishing forgery workshops of the 19th cent., whose products were of remarkable quality and artistic skill [3. 432ff.], particularly in the case of gold jewellery. Beyond the imitation of Etruscan jewellery the rediscovery of the ancient technique of granulation was of wider significance for the contemporary craft industry [3. 440]. In addition, this period saw the large scale excavations of the chamber tombs at Tarquinia, whose genuine Etruscan imagery attracted not only those on an educational 'Grand Tour', but also artists, painters and travel writers, whose yearning for adventure and unspoiled nature created a fruitful synthesis of science and art in Etruria, such as in the sophisticated 'travel guides' by E.C. Hamilton Gray (*A Tour to the Sepulchres of Etruria*, 1839) and G. Dennis (*The Cities and Cemeteries of Etruria*, 1848). Against the backdrop of increasing industrialization, the 'unspoiled' mysticism of the Etrurian funerary landscape brought forth paintings such as A. Böcklin's *Island of the Dead* (1880), which reflected the mood of the German bourgeoisie of the late 19th cent. Nostalgia, but with a greater degree of euphoria, also characterizes the influence of the Etruscan grave paintings on English writers, such as D.H. Lawrence (*Etruscan Places*, 1932) and A. Huxley (*Those Barren Leaves*, 1925, and *Point Counter Point*, 1928): glorified, the Etruscans become part of the myth of a lost world, in which the individual could live freely and was not yet subjected to the rigours of a standardized and mechanized environment [3. 450ff.]. Figurative art of the early 20th cent. was equally inspired by the 'unstandardized' nature of Etruscan art, such as the extremely elongated bronze statuette of a young man found in Volterra (*Ombra della sera*) or the archaizing stern figure of the *Lupa Capitolina*, which inspired artists such as A. Giacometti, A. Martini or M. Marini to use similar styles and motives in their sculptures and paintings [1. 151ff.]. The current reception of Etruscan culture finds expression in a vibrant production of → FILMS, → COMICS, advertising posters, and 'art works' of a wide variety of genres and qualities, mainly boosted by modern tourism (fig. 3). Alongside actual Etruscan imagery, a mysticism rooted in the sepulchral context (death and afterlife) as well as various popular 'myths', such as the Etruscans' alleged Oriental origins, the 'riddle' of their language or the destruction of Etruscan culture by the Romans are also significant. There are also political implications; anti-Roman feelings, which have been evident since the Renaissance, are reviving in Tuscany, partly supported by ethnic and linguistic arguments and with links to the separatist movements in northern Italy [1. 139ff., 151ff.].

→ Etrusci, Etruria
→ FORGERY

1 F. BORSI (ed.), Fortuna degli Etruschi, Florence, 1985 (Exhibition catalogue)   2 M. CRISTOFANI, La scoperta degli Etruschi. Archeologia e antiquaria nel '700, 1983 3 Die Etrusker und Europa, Berlin, 1993, 273ff. (Exhibition catalogue)

ADDITIONAL BIBILIOGRAPHY E. GORING, Treasures from Tuscany: The Etruscan Legacy, 2004; J. F. HALL, Etruscan Italy: Etruscan Influences on the Civilizations of Italy from Antiquity to the Modern Era, 1996; R. T. RIDLEY, The Discovery of the Etruscans in the Early Nineteenth Century, in: I. BIGNAMINI (ed.), Archives and Excavations, 2004   FRIEDHELM PRAYON

Etruscology

A. INTRODUCTION B. MIDDLE AGES AND RENAISSANCE C. ETRUSCOMANIA IN THE 18TH CENTURY D. SCHOLARSHIP IN THE 19TH CENTURY E. OUTLOOK: STRUCTURE AND ACHIEVEMENT

A. INTRODUCTION

Research on the Etruscans as a people and culture did not follow a linear progression, nor was it initially guided by scholarly considerations. Instead it was full of speculation (Etruscheria) and theories of art. However, since the 19th cent. Etruscology has been a significant element in the development of the methodology and modern questions of Classical Studies.

B. MIDDLE AGES AND RENAISSANCE

Apart from occasional references in the Tuscan chronicles of the late Middle Ages and in Humanist literature, general interest in the Etruscans arose only during the → RENAISSANCE, inspired by the discovery of burial complexes, written records and grave paintings as well as by significant chance finds such as the bronze *Chimaera of Arezzo* (1507) or the life-size bronze statue of the *Arringatore* (orator) in Lake Trasimene (1566). The Dominican Annio of Viterbo (1432?–1502) was of central importance in the development of Etruscology. He was an astrologer, excavator and antiquarian, author of the 16–volume *Antiquitates* that included 3 volumes on the history of Viterbo and the Etruscans. His expositions, such as the descent of the Etruscans

from Noah and Vertumnus [1. 12; 6. 282], were mostly fantastic and did not shy away from the falsification of ancient literary sources. Nevertheless they had a far-reaching impact, not least at the court of the Medici. They (especially Cosimo I) not only sponsored Etruscan studies, developed private collections of Etruscan finds, among them the *Chimaera* and the *Arringatore*, but they also identified themselves as the political and moral successors of the Etruscans (Cosimo I: *Dux Magnus Hetruscus*). With reference to ancient authors such as Livy and Pliny the Elder, the Etruscans were considered as a model for social renewal. This allowed the Medici to distance themselves ideologically from Rome [2. 18ff.]. During the 16th cent., the interest in the Etruscans therefore increasingly shifted from Rome and southern Etruria (*Tuscia*) to Florence and Tuscany. Artists like Leon Battista Alberti and Giorgio Vasari were concerned with the reconstruction of Etruscan monuments such as the tomb of king Porsenna of Chiusi and with the development of early theories of Etruscan architecture [4. 7ff.]. The crowning achievement of this first phase of Etruscology was the 7–volume work *De Etruria regali* by the Scotsman Thomas Dempster (1579–1625), which included a complete collection of the literary and antiquarian sources and the attempt at a comprehensive presentation of the history and culture of the Etruscans and of the topography of their towns.

C. ETRUSCOMANIA IN THE 18TH CENTURY

Dempster's *De Etruria regali* was only printed in 1726. However, it affected a whole epoch and triggered an enthusiasm for all things Etruscan among Italian historians and artists of later decades that became known as 'Etruscheria' or Etruscomania [2. 89ff.]. Two strands, which had a patriotic, largely uncritical or one-sided interpretation of the ancient tradition in common, can be differentiated. One strand, led by Mario Guarnacci, Giovan Battista Passeri and Giovan Battista Piranesi, attributed basic inventions in the art and architecture of Antiquity to the Etruscans, including central components of Roman construction design and technology as well as the multitude of painted Greek vases, which had been found in Etruscan chamber tombs but were in fact produced in Corinth and Athens. The other strand, represented by Anton Francesco Gori and Scipione Maffei, initiated a controversial discussion regarding the origins of the Etruscan alphabet and the 'genealogical' classification of the Etruscan language, which burdened rather than enlivened research. However, Etruscomania also had a positive effect on the collection of available documents and finds, the foundation of private collections and public museums (Cortona, Florence, Siena, Volterra) and scientific associations such as the still active *Accademia Etrusca* in Cortona (1726), the centre of scholarship at the time. The end of Etruscomania came with a better knowledge of the Greek originals through the publications of the → *Society of Dilettanti* in London (esp. J. Stuart, N.

Revett, R. Dalton and A. Ramsay), publications such as the *Geschichte der Kunst des Altertums* by Johann Joachim Winckelmann, which established the priority of Greek over Etruscan art (1766), and works by Luigi Lanzi (1732–1810), whose *Saggio di Lingua etrusca e di altre d'Italia* (1789, printed 1824) not only laid the scientific foundations for Etruscan linguistics but – under the influence of Winckelmann – also was an early attempt at dividing Etruscan art into periods and finally did away with the classification of Greek vases as Etruscan [2. 167ff.; 4, 9].

D. Scholarship in the 19th Century

The insights of Winckelmann and Lanzi resulted in a renewal of Etruscology through the use of more nuanced historical, philological, linguistic and archaeological methods. It was associated with scholars such as E.Q. Visconti, C. Fea, W. Corssen, W. Deeke, K.O. Müller and E. Gerhard. On the latter's initiative the *Istituto di Corrispondenza Archeologica was* formed in Rome in 1829 as an association of mostly German and North European artists and scholars, architects and educational travellers (the 'Hyperboreans'), which came to be of fundamental importance in the study of Italian antiquity [3; 4. 10; 6. 362ff.]. Thus, it was primarily scholars and guests of the *Istituto di Corrispondenza*, such as W. Helbig, C. Ruspi and J. Byres, who visited and recorded the large scale excavations such as those by L. Bonaparte, prince of Canino, in Vulci and by the banker G.P. Campana in Cerveteri and Veii. They published the results, including facsimiles of the wall paintings from the graves in Tarquinia, in the newly founded journals of the Institute (*Bollettino, Annali, Monumenti Inediti*) and thus made them available to a wider public. The newly discovered monuments and necropoleis aroused interest in the topography of Etruria, which is reflected in the monographs of W. Gell, L. Canina and A. Noel des Vergers, but especially in those of G. Dennis, whose *The Cities and Cemeteries of Etruria* (1848) continues to be in print. The first corpora of systematically documented types of finds such as *Select Vase Images* (1840–58) and *Etruscan Mirrors* (1839–67) were created by Gerhard either alone or in collaboration with G. Körte, while *I rilievi delle urne etrusche* (1870–1916) was produced by H. Brunn and Körte. The increased engagement with comparing iconographic and mythological themes with representations in Greek art in the late 19th cent. brought about an enduring negative assessment of Etruscan art and culture, beginning with J. Martha's *L'art étrusque* (1889) [4. 11].

E. Outlook: Structure and Achievement

In the 20th cent. research became interdisciplinary and expanded to cover Etruscan culture in its broadest sense, including political and societal factors (cf. J. Heurgon, *La vie quotidienne chez les Étrusques*, 1961 and Pallottino [4]). In Italy, Etruscology developed into an independent field of study with a central research institute (*Istituto Nazionale di Studi Etruschi ed Italici*, Florence, since 1927) and its own series of publications such as the journal *Studi Etruschi*. Outside Italy, Etruscology is integrated into several disciplines, especially Classical Archaeology and Comparative Linguistics, but also Ancient History, Classical Philology and Prehistory [5]. Since its origins in the Renaissance, Etruscology has not only made a lively contribution to the development of the study of Antiquity but it has even decisively shaped it, for example, in the sponsorship of research (Medici) and research organization (academies, institutes), fieldwork and excavation techniques, the presentation of monuments and the systematic collection of material (museums, corpora) and not least in the formation of art theory and the methodological foundations of linguistic research. [5. 11ff.].

→ Etrusci, Etruria

1 M. Cristofani (ed.), Dizionario della civiltà etrusca, 1985   2 Id., La scoperta degli Etruschi. Archeologia e antiquaria nel '700, 1983   3 J. Heurgon, La découverte des Étrusques au début du XIXe siècle, 1973   4 M. Pallottino, Die Etrusker, 1988, 6–27   5 A. J. Pfiffig, Einführung in die Etruskologie, 1972   6 Die Etrusker und Europa, Berlin, 1993 (Exhibition catalogue)

Additional Bibliography S. Haynes, Etruscan Civilization: A Cultural History, 2005; M. Torelli, The Etruscans, 2001   FRIEDHELM PRAYON

Etymology The object of modern etymology is the study of the history of words (and their components) and of their attested or deduced origin. It primarily examines an individual word, which, however, is treated within the structural context of word fields and word families. The historical linguistic perspective of etymology requires the study of the rule-driven processes of sound shifts (sound laws) and of the mechanisms of word formation operative in the language at hand: for example, the Greek word πέντε 'five' can be derived in terms of sound laws from Indo-European $*penk^we$, while Latin *quīnque* shows rule-driven assimilation of the initial consonant sound to the labiovelar of the second syllable and the analogous adoption of *ī* from the ordinal number *quīntus* (with *ī* based on sound laws); thus the Latin word as well can be derived from the Indo-European base form. More extensive changes in the form of the word result from the deletion of vowels (apocope, syncope); syncope often reduces the etymological transparency of composites, e.g. Lat. *princeps* < **prīmo-kap-s* 'first one to take (from the spoils)' [1. 97], with the regular change **a> e* in a closed final syllable and syncope of **o*, assimilation of the nasal and regular shortening of **ī* before a nasal and plosive. Thus *princeps* can be connected to *prīmus* and *capiō*. The number of rule-bound etymological connections was increased considerably by the discovery that three sounds could be attributed to the original Indo-European language (the so-called laryngeals, represented as $*h_1$, $*h_2$, $*h_3$) whose modern reflexes appear syllabically as Greek ε, α, o, and which, if non-syllabic, partially 'color' the surrounding vowels or (for instance as an initial sound before consonants in most Indo-European languages) disappear without a trace, cf. Greek ἀμέλγω < '(I) milk'< *$h_2melǵ$-, German *melken*, Lat. *mulgeō* < *$h_2molǵ$- (with *e/o*-ablaut).

Also of significance are ablaut conditions and the intonation patterns of inflectional classes. Furthermore, semantic changes and object references (reasons behind a name) must be considered as well: the etymological explanation of Lat. *augur* < *$av(i)$-gus* 'assessor of birds or their signs' [2. 228] as a verbal compound whose first segment belongs to *avis* and whose second segment is connected to a basic verb which can be posited for *gustare* [2. 227f.] among others, and which is based, not only on its formal derivation, but also on a rather precise identification of the augur's function.

The etymological study of vocabulary also leads to the discovery of lexical layers (inherited vocabulary, innovations in the branch of a language family or in an individual language, loan vocabulary): for reasons of phonetics, Latin *lupus* and *bōs* cannot be the Latin reflexes of Indo-European *ulk^wos 'wolf' and *g^weh_3us 'cow', instead, they must have been loaned from neighbouring Italic dialects where the Indo-European labiovelars were realized as labials. The assessment of a particular etymological explanation's plausibility is based on a process that, beyond the above criteria, must take numerous points of view into consideration [3]; for instance, the circumstances surrounding an item's attestation, a detailed philological determination of meaning, and if necessary, the phonetically and functionally based derivation from a reconstructed (prehistoric) state of the language. The etymological connection to words of similar origin in the same language or in related languages allows–based on rules of sound correspondence and word formation–the identification of etymologically related word elements (roots, stems, affixes); thus, for *augur*, a connection can be made to OHG *kiosan* 'choose, perceive, recognise'. Several etymological dictionaries exist for the Classical languages [4; 5]; these are constantly supplemented through new studies (cf. e.g. [6; 7]).

→ LINGUISTICS

1 LEUMANN   2 G. NEUMANN, Zur Etymologie von lateinischem *augur*. Würzburger Jahrbücher für die Altertumswissenschaft, Neue Folge vol. 2, 1976, 219–230   3 K. HOFFMANN, E. TICHY, Checkliste zur Aufstellung bzw. Beurteilung etymologischer Deutungen, Anhang II, in: M. MAYRHOFER (ed.), Zur Gestaltung des etymologischen Wörterbuchs einer Großkorpussprache, 1980, 47–52   4 FRISK   5 WALDE/HOFMANN   6 RIX, HGG   7 P. SCHRIJVER, The Reflexes of the Proto-Indo-European Laryngeals in Latin, 1991.   MICHAEL JOB

Euhemerism see → MYTH

Europe

A. ANCIENT REFERENCES AND CONCEPTIONS
B. LATE-ROMAN IMPULSES AND DEVELOPMENTS IN THE MIDDLE AGES   C. THE RISE OF THE EUROPEAN IDEA AND CONSCIOUSNESS OF EUROPE SINCE THE 15TH CENTURY   D. THE MYTH IN MUSIC, LITERATURE AND THE VISUAL ARTS

A. ANCIENT REFERENCES AND CONCEPTIONS

The etymology of the word 'Europa' is controversial (Pre-Greek, Indo-Germanic, Semitic). The designation 'Europa' has a geographical as well as a mythical root, both going back to the 7th cent. BC. Europe (E.) is first mentioned by name in the Apollo hymn (Hom. H. Apollo 251, 291), where, however, it denotes only Central Greece. Herodotus frequently mentioned E. in connection with the Hellespont. In addition, E. was simultaneously the name for a part of Thrace, a river, and several cities. According to Hecataeus of Miletus, ca. 500 BC, the world was divided into E. and Asia (FGrH 1, 36ff.). Herodotus had already mentioned a third continent, Libya, which later would be called Africa. In the course of Greek explorations, the geographical scope of the name 'Europa' was expanded to the Atlantic in the west and, in the north, as far as Scandinavia, which was thought to be an island. Herodotus (4,42–45) mentioned the Rion or the Don as the border between E. and Asia north of the Black Sea. The geographical concept of E. shifted farther to the west as a result of Roman conquests. According to myth, Europa was the daughter of King Agenor of Sidon (older version Hom. Il. 14,321: Phoenix). Zeus transformed himself into a young white steer, had the flower-picking Europa climb on his back, and carried her across the sea to Crete. There he assumed human shape (Ov. Met. 2,846ff.). In Pliny's time (Nat. 12,11), the site of their sexual congress was said to be located in the vicinity of Gortyn. Europa bore Zeus three sons: Minos, Rhadamantys and Sarpedon. Europa also appears as an epithet for Demeter and other earth goddesses in Crete and Boeotia (Paus. 9,39,4). A list of sea goddesses in the works of Hesiod (Theog. 357,359), around 700 BC, contains among others the names Asia and Europa. Why the continent bore the name E. was unclear to Herodotus. For Sextus Pompey Festus (2nd cent. AD) it was a certainty that the continent E. was named after the daughter of Agenor. Mythical person and geographical concept became fused in the writings of Claudius Claudianus (Carm. 21,88), around AD 400.

Whether or not E. existed in Antiquity as a concept, i.e. as a political-cultural idea, is disputed. To be sure, one finds an operationalization of the concept of E. in Herodotus. It is, however, not a European perception but rather a Persian one and alien to E., which views E. only as an object of domination [7.11f.]. The other sources that are cited to support the existence of a European consciousness, as for example Isocrates, Strabo, Manilius and the Hippocratic text *Air, Water and Localities*, have also been interpreted in different ways

Fig. 1: Mirko Szewczuk, Europe and the Bull, 1949,
ink on paper, published in DIE ZEIT, 3. February 1949

Fig. 2: Eres, nom de plum of Rudolf J. Schummer,
'Oh, der ist ja viel temperamentvoller...!'
(Oh, he so is so much more temperamental...!),
1949/50 (?), ink on paper

Fig. 3: Max Beckmann, *The Rape of Europe*
1933, in private ownership

with regard to E. as an idea (according to [5.31,41; 7.12; 16.19], E. as an idea was unknown in Antiquity, while according to [13.489ff.; 3.407ff.; 11.167] it can be shown that the idea of E. did exist). Demandt [4.148] comes to the conclusion, after citing further instances in which E. is mentioned, that there were tendencies in Antiquity to ideologize the concept of E., but only among a few writers. In politics, he maintains, the idea of E. played only an occasional role at best.

B. LATE-ROMAN IMPULSES AND DEVELOPMENTS IN THE MIDDLE AGES

In Late Antiquity, E. was given a biblical basis: the three sons of Noah were put in relation to the system of the three continents, so that the descendants of Japhet were equated with the inhabitants of E. (Historia Brittonum, 7th cent., MGH AA1 3,159). Not until the time of the Migration of Peoples did the idea of E. first appear as the expression of a common fate (since the 6th cent., according to [6.41f.; 7.18; 16.12]). Early signs of an ecclesiastical idea of E. can be discerned (the saint as a representative of early medieval society, the bishop of Rome as the highest authority in Christendom), but these beginnings were superseded by the Carolingian idea of E., in accordance with which Charlemagne was characterized as *pater Europae*. It must be emphasized that Charlemagne's empire did not encompass 'Europe'. Rather, the Franks tried to avoid an identification of their domain with the Occident, since this term was religiously loaded as a geographical designation [6.76ff.]. The terms *oriens – occidens* have their origin in the Roman administrative partitioning of the Empire in 395 AD, which then became codified at the beginning of the 5th cent. in the *Notitia dignitatum*. The terms can also mean the two realms within the one *ecclesia*. The Carolingian idea of E., which emphasized unity and at the same time was directed against → BYZANTIUM and → ROME [6.78ff] but did not encompass programmatic demands or projection onto the future [7.25], ceased to exist with the collapse of the Carolingian Empire. In the Middle Ages *Christianitas*, not E., was a unifying idea that could also be used politically.

Only the external threat posed by the Turks brought the term E. back into play. It no longer stood for a unified, single entity, however, but rather for plurality. A forerunner of this idea of E. is Alexander von Roes (toward the end of the 13th cent.), who already assigned certain roles to the most important powers and used the name E. as a political category [7.25ff.].

C. THE RISE OF THE EUROPEAN IDEA AND CONSCIOUSNESS OF EUROPE SINCE THE 15TH CENTURY

The name E.. did not acquire general validity until the middle of the 15th cent. In view of the conquest of Constantinople by the Turks, Enea Silvio Piccolomini as Pope Pius II referred to E. as the embodiment of many peoples, all of them partaking of the same culture, and as a fatherland. Since the beginning of European expansion into the 'New World', E. acquired hegemonic status. Gollwitzer [9.169] names Erasmus, Bodin, Comenius, Grotius, Leibniz, Shaftesbury, Bolingbroke, Montesquieu, Locke, Hume, Voltaire and Rousseau as proof that a European consciousness had been preserved amidst all the centrifugal tendencies operating among the European states, and that even a "European patriotism" had been newly formed. E. has developed as a modern secular entity out of–and alongside–a denominationally divided western Christianity. The most important topic of lively debate from the 15th to the 18th cent., as well as later, has been the European balance of power. To be sure, the debate has varied, ranging from Christian wake-up calls to decided hostility to the Church to an awareness of decline. In the 18th and 19th cents., it was especially the three revolutions of 1789, 1830 and 1848, with their modernisation impulses, that led writers to publish essays on the upheavals. In the 20th cent. it has been mainly the two World Wars and, since the end of the 1980s, the upheavals in Central E. The idea of E. has offered Germany and France an alternative orientation to nationalism, whether as a cultural concept or as a political utopia [12.29]. In most recent times, E. is being faulted with accusations of a 'myth deficit' [17.76].

D. The Myth in Music, Literature and the Visual Arts

The Europa myth has been treated far less often in music and literature than in the visual arts, even before the Enlightenment. Still, in the 20th cent. one can cite the opera *The Abduction of Europe* by D. Milhaud (1927), also the dramatisation *Europa* by G. Kaiser (1915), the novel *Viaggio d'Europa* by M. Bontempelli (1942), and the novella *Er kam als Bierfahrer* by H. Böll (1969).

In the visual arts the situation is different. From Antiquity to the present time, portrayals of Europa can be found throughout all periods. In Antiquity, since the archaic period, she has been frequently portrayed as the rider on the bull. This motif can also be found on numerous vases from the 5th cent. BC. Beginning with the 4th cent. BC, the depiction changes. The erotic element dominates. Europa is represented with her female companions, and marginal figures begin to appear. In the Hellenistic period, the number of representations of Europa decreases, and types from the 4th cent. are developed further. New is the motif of the billowing veil over Europa's head. During the time of the Roman Empire, Europa is again depicted frequently. Paintings and mosaics predominate [2]. Only a few depictions of the Europa myth have been preserved from the Middle Ages. Apart from a few examplars, they do not follow the tradition of Classical Antiquity. In accordance with the christocentric thinking of the Middle Ages, the myth was reinterpreted. Thus the bull, borrowing from the *Ovidius moralizatus* (1342) of Petrus Berchorius, is interpreted as Christ who would save the soul, peronified by Europa. At the turn of the 16th to 17th cent.,

these presentations undergo a Platonic reinterpretation [18.61ff.]. At the same time, Boccaccio interprets the myth in a rationalist manner, as was already done by Herodotus. In the connection between Jupiter and Europa, appropriateness of social rank is frequently emphasised, but also the power of love. Europa is also shown in emotionally charged situations (Titian). The depiction of an angry Europa, as based on Horace (Odes 3,27ff.) (attributed to Andrea Riccio, beginning of the 16th cent.), is a rarity. As the personification of the continent, Europa is represented as being far superior culturally to all others, e. g. as painted by Tiepolo (1752) in the grand staircase of the Würzburg Residence. The figure of Europa rests on a stone pedestal and leans against the bull. In her right hand she holds a scepter, and beside her on the floor lies a globe. Here the Eurocentric view of the world is plain to see. Europa was depicted less frequently in the 19th cent., but at the beginning of the 20th cent. the number of representations again increased. The myth became topical once more as depictions of women are eroticised. The traditional roles of the sexes break down (Valloton 1908). In the course of the 20th cent., the Europa-myth has also been used to thematise the disastrous course of history (Beckmann 1933: Ill.3; Trökes 1947). A special form is the caricature, which uses Europa almost exclusively as the personification of the continent or the European Community [15;18] (figs. 1 and 2).

1 J. Assmann, Das kulturelle Gedächtnis, ²1997   2 W. Bühler, Europa, 1968   3 J. Cobet, Europa und Asien – Griechen und Barbaren – Osten und Westen, in: Gesch. in Wiss. und Unterricht 47, 1996, 405–419   4 A. Demandt, Europa: Begriff und Gedanke in der Antike, in: P. Kneisel, V. Losemann (eds.), Imperium Romanum. Studien zur Geschichte und Rezeption. Festschrift für Karl Christ zum 75. Geburtstag, 1998, 137–157   5 J. B. Duroselle, L'Idée d'Europe dans l'histoire, 1965   6 J. Fischer, Oriens-Occidens-Europa, 1957   7 M. Fuhrmann, Alexander von Roes, Sitzungs-Ber. der Heidelberger Akad. der Wiss., philos.-histor. Kl., 1994, 4   8 Id, Der Name Europa als kulturelle und politische Idee, in: Europa Verstehen, 1997, 19–37   9 H. Gollwitzer, Zur Wortgeschichte und Sinndeutung von 'Europa', in: Saeculum 2, 161–172   10 Id, Europa-Bild und Europa-Gedanke, ²1964   11 K. Koch, Europa, Rom und der Kaiser, 1997   12 P. M. Lützeler, Die Schriftsteller und Europa, 1992   13 A. Momigliano, L'Europa come concetto politico (1933), in: Terzo contributo, Bd. 1, 1966, 489–487   14 P. Nora, Zwischen Geschichte und Gedächtnis, 1990   15 S. Salzmann (ed.), Mythos Europa, 1988   16 J. A. Schlumberger, Europas antikes Erbe, in: Id., P. Segl, Europa – aber was ist es?, 1994, 1–19   17 W. Schmale, Scheitert Europa an seinem Mythendefizit?, 1997   18 Staatliche Museen Preußischer Kulturbesitz (ed.), Die Verführung der Europa, 1988.

Additional Bibliography N. Davies, Europe: A History, 1996; R. Guerrina, Europe: History, Ideas, Ideologies, 2002; J. Laughland, Fascists and Federalists, in: Id. The Tainted Source: The Undemocratic Origins of the European Idea, 1997, 9–70   ELISABETH ERDMANN

Exam Guidelines
A. CONCEPT B. HISTORY C. PRESENT

A. CONCEPT

Exam Guidelines (EG) are statutory provisions in which prerequisites and methods for admission to and conduct of the examination are stipulated, as are the content requirements of the examination and the guidelines for its assessment. These contain, both as to content and form, the prerequisites by which candidates are admitted to the exam as well as the conditions under which the examination may be passed and a specific qualification awarded. EG are closely related to → SYLLABI for schools and curricula for → UNIVERSITIES as well as teachers' colleges, universities of applied technology and training regulations for seminaries. The prerequisite for practicing a given career is holding publicly and legally recognised qualifications. EG provide for both the candidates and for the examiners the necessary legal security in the implementation of the examination procedure, and they also facilitate its legal supervision. They include (1) school-leaving certificates (diplomas) of every kind in both public and private schools, particularly the *Abitur* (a kind of school-leaving examination which qualifies a student for university entrance), (2) final examinations for vocational training, (3) state examinations as entry qualifications to seminaries or for practical training and later the legally recognised practice of the career concerned; and (4) academic qualifications like the M. A. degree, the doctoral degree and the higher doctorate (*Habilitation*) required for advancement as a university instructor (above all in Germany; not in the United States, for example). In this way the EG establish prerequisites for the acquisition of entitlements: the EG for the *Abitur*, the EG for the teachers' examination for the practice of the teaching profession in schools, the EG for degree examinations for research and teaching, the EG for vocational examinations for the independent practice of a given trade.

B. HISTORY

From the time of the institutionalization of education at the end of the Enlightenment onwards, school regulations came to be established for the holding of final and entrance examinations. With the establishment of public education around and after 1800, various examination and training regulations were introduced in the German states. At the same time, administrative educational authorities were established and these were controlled by official rules and laws. School regulations served as guidelines for regulated educational conditions. Regulations regarding the obligation to attend school, about being kept back or being promoted to the next year level and about school discipline formed the basis of the gradually evolving legal provisions in → SCHOOLS as a whole. In this social context the EG for the *Abitur* to qualify for university entrance and the teachers' examinations were stipulated.

In the EG for the *Abitur* examination (Bavaria 1809, Prussia 1788/1812), provision was made for testing the general education of those leaving school in the school subjects of their highest year level. In Prussian *Gymnasien* (secondary schools leading to university acceptance) this meant that for Latin the candidate should "understand Cicero, Livy, Horace and Virgil in their entirety and with ease". He should, "after the time allowed for reflection", be able to explain Tacitus correctly without making any basic grammatical errors. In Greek he should understand Attic prose and Homer without further explanatory notes and be able to interpret a fairly difficult chorus from a tragedy. In 1834 the awarding of entitlements for students to study at a university in Prussia was finally linked to the completion of the *Abitur* qualifying for university entrance. This regulation then became the general standard in the German states. In the course of the 19th cent., the EG were adapted on many occasions by revisions to match syllabus changes and indeed to match new social requirements. In the process, the original obligatory examination in the ancient languages continually lost its importance. From 1900 students could also qualify for the *Abitur* without being examined in the ancient languages. Since their introduction the EG have been adjusted at irregular intervals to fit in with social trends.

The EG for the examinations for teachers were likewise introduced at the beginning of the 19th cent. They became necessary in order to stop large numbers of unqualified people from entering the teaching profession.

EG for academic examinations were redesigned with the development and expansion of modern universities from the beginning of the 19th cent. within the various faculties. They regulated the conditions under which an academic degree, a first degree, a Master of Arts or a doctorate could be awarded. In this way, right from the outset the faculties had a certain amount of autonomy in stipulating conditions but were at the same time subject to monitoring by the committees of the universities and the supervision of the Ministry of Education. EG for academic examinations not only serve to regulate a procedure but, at the same time, to make its implementation subject to legal scrutiny.

C. PRESENT

The most important change in the content of the EG for the *Abitur* in the Federal Republic of Germany occurred through the reform of the upper levels of the *Gymnasium* in 1972. The current German *Abitur* regulates the procedure and contains details regarding special qualifications like the Latin, Greek and Hebrew qualifying examinations that may only be awarded after the candidate has passed the *Abitur* examination. Agreements by the Conference of the Ministers for Education and the Arts ensure extensive conformity between the formal and syllabus standards for the *Abitur* qualifying for university entrance in the various states of the Federal Republic of Germany. The norm at present is for the written *Abitur* in Greek and Latin to consist of a translation and an interpretation.

In the university sector, discussion is currently centred both on the content of the EG for academic examinations and on whether courses with simpler EG suitable for shorter degree programs (Bachelor's/Master's degree) should be introduced for early completion of university studies.

→ Humanist gymnasium; → teachers

Sources 1 H. J. Apel, Die Ausbildung zum Gymnasiallehrer im 19. Jahrhundert, in: J. G. Prinz v. Hohenzollern, M. Liedtke (eds.), Schreiber, Magister, Lehrer, 1989, 291 – 306   2 M. Liedtke, Gesamtdarstellung, in: Handbuch der Geschichte des Bayerischen Bildungswesens, vol. 2, 1993, 11 – 133
Literature   3 Abitur- und Lehrerprüfungen der Bundesländer   4 N. Niehues, Prüfungsrecht, 1994   5 F. Paulsen, Die Geschichte des gelehrten Unterrichts, vol. 2, 1921.   HANS JÜRGEN APEL

F

Fable
A. Concept B. Definition C. Boundaries between Fable and Other Narrative Forms D. Origin E. History

A. Concept
Fable (Lat. *fabula*, 'that which is made up'), with the addition 'Aesopic' already used by Phaedrus as a generic term for exemplary animal stories and the like, was introduced into German by H. Steinhöwel (*Der Ulmer Aesop* of 1476/77, ed. O. Schäfer, 1992). The oldest fables appear in Ionic poetry and are called *ainos*, a term that embraces parable as well as proverb and riddle. The terms most often used are *mythos* and *logos*, stressing respectively the fantastic/magical and the rational element of fables. Since the 18th cent., the term has also been used for the plot of an epic or a drama.

B. Definition
The briefest definition stems from Theon of Alexandria (1st cent. AD): 'lógos pseudès eikonízōn alétheian' ("an invented story illustrative of truth"). B.E. Perry, one of the finest experts on the ancient fable, quotes it with the comment: 'This is the best definition of Aesopic fable that can be given, provided we understand its implication. It applies to the Greek fable in all periods as well as to the ancient Oriental fable'.

A factual message is forcefully and convincingly presented in a vivid story. By aid of analogy, the listener or reader conveys the content of the story through the intended message (transfer). What is critical to the understanding is less the detail than the central statement, the single point of reference (*tertium comparationis*). The fable's didactic intent defines its textual structure and sets limits to its narrative impulse. The effective fable is predicated upon its ending, and aims toward a pointed conclusion.

In the Middle Ages the (German) term 'bispel' or 'bischaft' is often used. Both designations make evident that it is a question of a didactic narrative. Furthermore, the word 'bispel' points to the connection between fable, parable and proverb. It indicates a narrative that stands not for itself but for something else whose meaning does not lie in the story itself. Already in the 13th cent. the term 'spel' ("tale", "account") is devalued to mean a narrative that is not vouched for, and therefore untrue or even mendacious, while 'bispel' appears as the truth (clad in an entertaining wrapping, i.e. narrative). Even the biblical parable is called 'bispel' (e.g. Hugo von Trimberg). Thomasin von Zerklaere translates *fabula* as 'bispel'. In German medieval didactic poetry Aesopic fables are designated as 'bispel' (e.g. Der Marner, Bruder Wernher, Reinmar von Zweter).

C. Boundaries between Fable and Other Narrative Forms
Adolf Jülicher (1888ff.) in his examination of NT parables compared them with Aesop's fables, and came to the conclusion that most of Jesus' narrated parables are "fables like those of Stesichorus and Aesop" ('Fabeln ... wie die des Stesichoros und des Äsop', [8. 98]). Its three basic elements are: a complete thought and a narrative of metaphorical character with a deeper meaning. Jülicher bases his definition of the fable on Aristotle (Rh. 2,20): 'die Redefigur, in welcher die Wirkung eines Satzes (Gedankens) gesichert werden soll durch Nebenstellung einer auf anderm Gebiet ablaufenden, ihrer Wirkung gewissen erdichteten Geschichte, deren Gedankengerippe dem jenes Satzes ähnlich ist' ("that figure of speech in which the effect of an axiom (a thought) is to be assured by the juxtaposition of an invented narrative, certain in its effect, and set in another sphere, but whose rational framework is similar to that of the original axiom", [8. 98]). Despite the Aristotelian approach, which is disputed in theological circles, Jülicher's two-volume work is fundamental to interdisciplinary research on fables and parables. Fable and *exemplum* as 'minimal narrative forms' [10. 354] are distinct in intention. The *exemplum*, as "the narrative transposition of a moral axiom" [10. 365], is paradigmatic; the fable, on the other hand, is parabolic.

G. Couton, who edited the fables of La Fontaine, pointed to the 'liens de cousinage' [3. 8] between fable and → Emblems. This affinity becomes evident in the 17th cent. (e.g. in Jean Baudoin, 1659), but, notably, already during the century before La Fontaine. In 1540 Gilles Corrozet published a collection of emblems, and two years later one of fables, both of them structured according to the *Centurio* principle, and influenced by each other (cf. [6.10]). In the *emblem*, with its three parts *inscriptio, pictura, subscriptio*, the pictorial illustration has priority and is an inseparable component. In the fable, on the other hand, with its two parts, the picture, while sometimes a well-loved addition, is by no means a necessary enhancement of the narrative. Thus the *emblem* is central to *pictura-poesis* literature, while the fable is only marginally so (→ *ut pictura poesis*).

It is not by its inventory but by its intention that the fable differs from the → Fairy tale. Its intention is to instruct as it entertains. La Fontaine, reviled in Germany by writers from Lessing to Vossler on account of his 'loquaciousness', writes in a section of his poem *Le Pâtre et le Lion* something that is fundamental to his theory of the fable: 'En ces sortes de feinte il faut instruire et plaire,/Et conter pour conter me semble peu d'affaire'. Whereas the fairy tale portrays "an event subject to the principle of the miraculous" [7. 47], the fable wishes to convince and tends towards the rational. To its "world of purposive action" the fairy tale opposes a "world of fantastic wish-fulfilment" (cf. the tabular overview in [7. 47]). Above all, however, it is the allegorical character of the fable that distinguishes it from the fairy tale and the aetiological animal story. Of the three essential characteristics of the folk animal story (cf. [4; 5]) – animal characters, anthropomorphizing and a form of experience based on the observation of animals – only the first of them, at most, applies to the fable (i.e. to the special genre of animal fable). For the animals that feature in fables have been created by humans for the instruction of humans. They are "animal skins" (Luther); any similarity between them and nature is contingent upon their didactic purpose.

D. Origin

The controversy that flared up as early as 1860 as to the country of origin of the fable has not been settled, and whether the Greek or the Indian fable is the original one remains a matter of dispute. After the discovery of the Mesopotamian fable, the parallels with the Greek and Indian form led many to believe that a Mesopotamian origin could be established, and ancient Mesopotamia was seen as the source of the fable. Although the literature of Egypt exerted its influence on Babylonia, Greece and India, it is difficult to determine to what extent Greek fables are secularised Egyptian myths, especially as the Egyptian finds comprise images without texts (the associated stories having to be deduced from the images), or only fragmentary texts.

On the other hand, if we understand the fable as a primal expression of our spiritual being, the search for the fable's homeland makes little sense. It is possible, at best, to establish the origin of individual motifs. One of the best-known of these might (in its early form) originate in Egypt: the dispute between head and body (ca. 1100 BC) as an allegory of the stomach and the limbs became famous through Titus Livius' *Roman History*. Perhaps the oldest literary instance survives only in fragmentary form on a student's tablet (significant for the importance of the fable in schools).

E. History

The two most important Oriental books of fables, *Pancatantra* and *Kalila and Dimna*, are based on an Indian original that already existed around AD 500 at the latest and whose author professed the Buddhist faith. The work is written as a → Princes' mirror, and, for reasons of safety, makes use of the fable form.

The *Romulus Nilatinus* (*RN*), an 11th-cent. Latin adaptation of the Romulus story, formed the model for the *Esope* of Marie de France, the first medieval collection of fables in the vernacular. In contrast to the *RN*, Marie de France wrote not in prose but in octosyllabic couplets, the classic meter for court poetry. The *RN* also forms the most important basis for the *Misle sualim* (fox fable) of Rabbi Berechja ha-Nakdan (end of the 12th/beginning of the 13th cent.). With his fables he is predominantly aiming at Jewish readers, and has, in spite of the common source, a fundamentally different intention than that of Marie de France. The preacher-

monk Ulrich Boner took his fables among others from Avianus. *Der Edelstein*, a collection of 100 fables in verse (iambic tetrameters, in rhymed couplets), appeared in 1461; it was the first German book of fables and one of the first printed works in the German language. In 1480 Anton von Pforr translated the Oriental fable into German for Count Eberhard of Württemberg. The translator describes his work as a book of exemplary tales from the 'ancient heathen' – as opposed to Jewish – sages. Four years earlier the German translation of the Graeco-Roman fables had appeared: the *Esopus* of the Ulm medical doctor Heinrich Steinhöwel was published in 1476 by J. Zainer in Ulm in a bilingual edition illustrated with woodcuts; it caused a great sensation beyond Germany's borders and was repeatedly reprinted.

Martin Luther became familiar with Aesop's fables as a schoolboy and had to learn them by heart along with Cato's *Disticha moralia*. His interest in fables was lifelong and he wove them as well as proverbs into his writings and sermons. Steinhöwel's *Esopus*, esteemed by Luther as the 'German Aesop', and at the same time criticised by him for its supposed obscenities, inspired him to work on a revised edition. His Aesop revision, which was produced in the Coburg fortress during the Diet of Augsburg in 1530, remained a fragment, as did the collection of proverbs. The new translations of 13 fables did not appear during Luther's lifetime; rather they were first published by Johannes Mathesius in 1557. Philipp Melanchthon in his work *De utilitate fabularum* (1526) followed Luther in judging that, apart from the Bible, there are no better schoolbooks than Cato's writings and Aesop's fables, and in the *Unterricht der Visitatoren* (1528) he accords them favoured status. In the Schulordnungen, regulations for schools in Eisleben and Herzberg (1525 and 1538), the Praeceptor Germaniae lists three reasons for the necessity of according fables a place in the curriculum: they are character-building, they sharpen the pupils' powers of judgment, and they promote understanding of the Bible. Two of the most famous books of fables come from Luther's time: the *Esopus* (1548) of Burkard Waldis with its 400 fables is the most extensive 16th-cent. collection. In the *Buch von der Tugent und Weißheit* (1550) of Erasmus Alberus, the enthusiasm of the storyteller is evident not only in the length of the fables (between 50 and 300 lines, mostly more than 100 lines) but also in the geographical details. Many of the fables are set in the Wetterau, Alberus' home region. In the case of Hans Sachs (1558), the fable approaches the genre of the farce (*Schwank*), with the boundaries between the two types of text becoming fluid. The effect of this on the fable's intention and content can be seen, for example, in the motif of the 'wolf and the lamb'.

Despite the criticism of the 'Fabul-Hannsen', the fable flourished in the sermons of the Baroque period. It already had a firm place for itself in the vernacular sermons of the Middle Ages, a tradition also picked up by the Counter-Reformation, and it accommodated the narrative impetus that grew in the second half of the 17th cent. There is substantial documentary evidence to show that the fable drew people into the church and kept sleep at bay during sermons. Just as during the Reformation, in the Baroque period, too, reference to the Bible and to ecclesiastical authority was one of the most popular arguments for the use of fables in sermons, particularly the Easter sermons. Abraham a Sancta Clara, the most popular Church preacher of the Baroque period, referred among others to the Church Fathers in the foreword to his four-volume work *Judas der Ertzschelm* (1688–95). That 'Pater Fabel-Hanns' and Johann Balthasar Schupp, the most famous Protestant preacher (who was fiercely attacked by the orthodox on account of his fables), were not the only Baroque preachers to weave fables into the fabric of their sermons is shown by the 'Predigtmärlein' of the lesser-known preachers like Ignatius Ertl, Wolfgang Rauscher, Andreas Strobl and others. Special significance has to be accorded the use of fable in sermons, though its frequency was disputed in Catholic homiletics, insofar as then -often in highly stylised rhetoric and with a highly vivid mode of delivery – literary tradition was translated into the spoken word and thus transmitted to the illiterate population. The occasional casual mention of fable motifs speaks for the level of familiarity with the genre.

The twelve books by the fable author Jean de La Fontaine, containing in all 240 fables, appeared in 1668 (1–6), 1678 (7–11) and 1694 (12). These fables distinguish themselves particularly by their accomplished form and humorous tone. In Germany, La Fontaine was often falsely called a non-political writer, although his fables hold up a critical mirror to the period of Louis XIV. Many of his fables relate to wars, external and internal politics, social problems, the abuse of power, the plundering of the provinces, relationships of the classes, etc. A century after La Fontaine, and influenced by him, Jean-Pierre Claris de Florian published his 'pleasant fables' (1792). Also influenced by La Fontaine are the fables of the Italians Tommaso Crudeli (1798), Gian Carlo Passeroni (1779–88), Lorenzo Pignotti (1782), Aurelio Bertola de Giorgi (1788) and Luigi Fiacchi (1795, 1802, 1807), while the Spaniards Félix María de Samaniego (1781–84) and Tomás de Iriarte (1782) were influenced in addition by the English poet John Gay (1727–38).

During the age of the Enlightenment the fable attains its second, and real, zenith. In *Dichtung und Wahrheit*, Goethe noted with astonishment that the 'best brains' of this period declared Aesop's fables to be the 'foremost and greatest literary genre'. During the three decades between Gottsched's *Critische Dichtkunst* (1730) and Lessing's *Fabeln. Drei Bücher. Nebst Abhandlungen mit dieser Dichtung verwandten Inhalts* (1759) there appeared, among others, the fable collections and theories of Breitinger, Bodmer, Triller, Stoppe, Hagedorn, Gleim, Lichtwer, and Pfeffel. Lessing sees the fable as 'an example of practical ethics'.

The intention of the writer of fables is to vividly convince the reader of a moral truth, by referring a general moral axiom to a particular case and presenting it in the form of a plot. It is not the allegorical theme alone, but its narration, that constitutes a fable. The referral to the particular is necessary, because the general achieves recognition in the particular. The more vivid that recognition, the greater both the power to convince and the influence on the will. In the story of the owner of the bow, Lessing illustrated his conception that the fable must be concise, specific, and pointed. To him, brevity was 'the soul of fable', and the absence of decoration its 'finest embellishment'. Embellishments as 'empty prolongations' detract from the fable's intention. – Among these 'empty prolongations' are the details of time and place particularly esteemed by Jacob Grimm and found, for example, in the 16th cent. in Erasmus Alberus and Hans Sachs. It is this epic tendency that brings the fable close to the animal epic and the farce, or *Schwank*. The way in which the joy of narrating, in particular the loving embellishment of details not central to the fable's intention, has transformed the fable into the fairy tale can be seen, for exampl,e in many Oriental texts (e.g., The Lion and the Mouse). The masterly fables of Gellert, Gleim and Hagedorn show that, in spite of Lessing, the fable's narrative element predominates during the German Enlightenment.

During the century of the → ENLIGHTENMENT Horace's maxim 'aut prodesse volunt aut delectare poetae/aut simul et iucunda et idonea dicere vitae' (Ars P. 5,333ff.), usually abbreviated as *docere et delectare* ("to instruct and to entertain"), and already adopted in modified form by Phaedrus, becomes a ruling principle and at the same time the basis for the esteem in which the fable was held at the time. The appeal to Horace's *Ars poetica* in Breitinger's *Critische Dichtkunst* is followed immediately by a reference to Aesop. For Gellert, for whom the fable is "the oldest form of human wit", its 'double purpose' to amuse and to be of use demands that it display something "rare, new and marvelous". The very titles of their collections show that for Hagedorn and for Gellert the narrative predominates, as does their interest in unusual things, foreign lands etc. Narrating a story counts for more than the parabolic statement.

During the periods of Storm and Stress, Classicism and Romanticism, the Vormärz and Biedermeier, the fable as an autonomous genre is of little importance. The texts scarcely appear any longer in collected form, but are, for the most part, inserted in other works, such as the famous fable of the animals' election of a king in Schiller's drama *Fiesco*. Intention and relationship to the audience both change. The original intention of social criticism is replaced by moralising tendencies, and the audience narrowed to children (→ CHILDREN AND YOUNG ADULTS' LITERATURE). Books of fables for children, such as those of Friedrich Haug in the tradition of Stoppe and Lichtwer and the anthropomorphic animal poems of Wilhelm Hey, increasingly make their appearance and gain in interest.

During the 20th cent. the fable regains its dimension of existential and social criticism. That the Graeco-Roman fables have survived to the present day is shown among others by the reception of classical motifs in modern fable-writing. Besides its frequent traits of satire and caricature, it is epigrammatically concise and pointed, and approaches the format of the → APHO-RISM (e.g. Schnurre, Arntzen). In addition to its appearance in traditional form (Kirsten) and with social perspective (Branstner), we now see a dialectic with the tradition of the fable incorporated in the texts themselves: the animals refer to their own tradition, question the axioms of the old fables, comment on them or have learned from them. In the epimyth – which in this way acquires new significance – the American caricaturist James Thurber questions the past by means of the present, and adds the ironic question mark of the modern reader, who knows the tradition of the fable and is testing it critically, to the proverbial wisdom of the past.
→ Aesopus; → Fable; → Myth
→ ANIMAL STORIES; → DIDACTIC POEM

SOURCES   1 R. DITHMAR, Fabeln, Parabeln und Gleichnisse, 1995 (Texts and commentary)
LITERATURE   2 Id., Die Fabel, 1997 (with extensive bibliography)   3 G. COUTON, La poétique de La Fontaine, 1957   4 F. HARKORT, Tiergeschichten in der Volksüberlieferung, in: U. SCHWAB (ed.), Das Tier in der Dichtung, 1970   5 Id., Tiervolkserzählungen, in: Fabula 9, 1967, 87–99   6 M. HUECK, Textstruktur und Gattungssystem, Studien zum Verhältnis von Emblem und Fabel im 16. und 17. Jahrhundert, 1975   7 H. R. JAUSS, Alterität und Modernität in der mittelalterlichen Literatur, 1977   8 A. JÜLICHER, Die Gleichnisreden Jesu, 1888ff. (repr. 1963)   9 B. E. PERRY, Fable, in: Studium generale 12, 1959, 17–37   10 K. STIERLE, Geschichte als Exemplum – Exemplum als Geschichte, in: R. KOSELLECK, W.-D. STEMPEL (eds.), Geschichte – Ereignis und Erzählung, vol. 3, 1973, 347–375   11 Id., Poesie des Unpoetischen. Über La Fontaines Umgang mit der Fabel, in: Poetica 1, 1967, 508–533   12 B. TIEMANN, Fabel und Emblem. Gilles Corrozet und die französische Renaissance-Fabel, 1974

ADDITIONAL BIBLIOGRAPHY D. MARSH, Renaissance Fables. Aesopic Prose by Leon Battista Alberti, Bartolomeo Scala, Leonardo da Vinci, and Bernardino Baldi, 2004; E. WHEATLEY, Mastering Aesop. Medieval Education, Chaucer, and His Followers, 2000.
REINHARD DITHMAR

Fairy-Tale.

Jacob Grimm [1. 194] stated that a valuable addition to scholarship in the field of the fairy-tale (FT) would be "to track down in the Latin and Greek classical authors any anilis fabula, any graódēs mýthos mentioned by them" ('bei den lateinischen und griechischen classikern jede anilis fabula, jeden graódēs mýthos aufzuspüren, deren sie erwähnen'). This demand has been met: a wealth of ancient FT motifemes has been discovered and catalogued [5]. There is no evidence from Antiquity for entire FTs that would adhere to the laws of the genre, just as there is none from the Middle Ages. Consequently, the history of

their reception can only inquire into motif filiations and the paths by which these were passed down, the reasons for modifications, as well as their scope and nature. Results to date have been few, and even these are not always conclusive [3], especially if we leave aside the straightforward adoption of ancient motifs in modern FT collections (for instance, the Grimm FTs *Das Unglück* or *Der Räuber und seine Söhne* are descended – via intermediate German language stages of the 15th and 16th cent. – from the *Bidbai* and the *Odyssey* respectively [3. 541f.]). J. Grimm made reference to the relationship between two tales by G.B. Basile (1634) and a motif (the picking apart of grain by helpful animals) in Apuleius' *Asinus aureus*, which then reappeared in the FT of the *Cinderella* type. The paths of tradition are unclear and a matter for debate, as are those of the central motif of *Sleeping Beauty*: there may be a bridge leading from the 57–year sleep of Epimenides to Basile [4. 134f.] (who, in addition, interwove it with the myth of the Palici – probably from the oral Neapolitan tradition); however, it is nearly impossible to determine whether Ch. Perrault (*Contes*, 1697) drew on Basile or an independent oral tradition. The Grimm version, meanwhile, goes back to Perrault [3. 463f.]. Common to all, and perhaps more plausible, may be the presence of a hero pattern: a largely identical basic motif structure that is re-told again and again in countless genre-specific variations. An exception to this rule is the FT of the *Juniper Tree* type, where the basic motif of the boy killed by his mother, devoured by his father and transformed into a bird can, with some stringency, be traced to the aetiological myth of Tereus and Procne, as told by Virgil (Verg. Ecl. 78–81). Disseminated by students begging for alms throughout the Middle Ages, it led in turn to the invention of an aitiological FT ("Who is the bird carried along on a stick, and how did his song come about?" [4. 113–125]). Without the discovery of such bridges in the tradition, most assumptions about the underlying reception processes must remain speculation.
→ Folk-tales

1 J. GRIMM, Vorrede zu Basiles Pentamerone, 1846, in: Id., Kleinere Schriften, vol. 8, Gütersloh 1890   2 M. LÜTHI, Märchen, H. RÖLLEKE (ed.), ⁹1996, 40–43   3 H. RÖLLEKE (ed.), Kinder- und Hausmärchen, 1994   4 W. SIEGMUND (ed.), Antiker Mythos in unseren Märchen, 1984   5 S. THOMPSON, Motif-Index of Folk-Literature, ²1956–1958

ADDITIONAL BIBLIOGRAPHY J. ZIOLKOWSKI, Fairy Tales before Fairy Tales. The Medieval Latin Past of Wonderful Lies, (forthcoming)
HEINZ RÖLLEKE

Family see → MARRIAGE

Fascism
I. ART AND ARCHITECTURE   II. POLITICS AND
SOCIETY

I. ART AND ARCHITECTURE
A. INTRODUCTION   B. ARCHAEOLOGY IN THE
SERVICE OF POLITICS   C. ART AND STATE

A. INTRODUCTION
The Italian Fascist image of Antiquity between 1922 and 1943 was first and foremost characterized by its use as a propaganda tool. The focus was almost entirely on the Rome of the Imperial Age and, most particularly, Rome under Augustus, who as a person and in his work was stylized and idolized in every imaginable way. An important reason for this lay in the apparent analogy of the historical situation. In the same way as Augustus ended the crisis in the Republic by establishing the Principate, so Mussolini put an end to the years of crisis following the First World War with his Fascist 'revolution' (or dictatorship). After his march on Rome on 28 October 1922, *Romanità* was both an ideological constant and a striking vehicle for Fascist propaganda [18]. The Rome ideology was used massively during the period of consolidation and ideological development after 1933 with the establishment of the *Comitato d'Azione per l'Universalità di Roma* (CAUR). The coincidence of the 2000th anniversary of Augustus's birth on 23 September 1937, the *Bimillenario Augusteo,* with the Fascist era was exploited propagandistically for drawing exact parallels between Mussolini and Augustus. Lavish celebrations marked the jubilee, at whose centre was the extensive Augustus exhibition, the *Mostra Augustea della Romanità.* The entire academic programme of symposia and publications accompanying it took place under ideological auspices and created an academically certified legitimization for drawing these parallels [20. 12–15]. The regime's insistent recourse to Antiquity followed a basic nationalistic pattern rooted in the Italian colonial policy of 1911–12. Italy assumed the Roman inheritance in order to fulfil once again its imperial mission: the establishment of a Mediterranean empire [20. 7f.].

B. ARCHAEOLOGY IN THE SERVICE OF POLITICS
1. GENERAL   2. IMPERIAL FORUMS AND VIA
DELL'IMPERO   3. THE PIAZZA AUGUSTO
IMPERATORE   4. THE AUGUSTUS EXHIBITION

1. GENERAL
Archaeology took centre stage within the regime's ideology of ruler and its focus on ancient Rome. Through discoveries and restorations, it accomplished the visual realization of the ancient world and thus the visual transference of Fascist values onto the face of the city of Rome. Extensive archaeological excavation and restoration projects in Rome between 1924 and 1938 (Largo Argentina, Theatre of Marcellus, Capitol, Circus Maximus, Pantheon, Mausoleum of Augustus,

Imperial Forums) was accomplished by relentlessly abandoning historic city districts. The cleared archaeological spaces bear witness to the despotism of the regime, because only Fascism could make such sovereign decisions on expropriation, demolition and land use. The clearance of the densely built-up residential quarter over the Imperial Forums in 1930 destroyed 5500 residential units, caused the resettlement of 1886 people into suburban areas and forced a cut through the Velian Hill toward the Colosseum. The excavated remains were given a major role in the regime's dramatic display of its power, with the aim of appealing to the broad masses. Mussolini's speeches, as well as political marches and assemblies, were recorded on film and in photographs in such a way as to present the public with an image of stately power that was iconically linked with ancient history. Of ultimately far-reaching consequences for town planning and the presentation of the ancient monuments was a concept introduced by Mussolini in 1925 during an official address in the Capitol Palace: "The millennia-old monuments of our history need to appear monumental in essential isolation" [8. 49, 51].

2. IMPERIAL FORUMS AND VIA DELL'IMPERO
The excavation of the Imperial Forums and the construction of the Via dell'Impero in the centre of ancient and modern Rome was of strong symbolic importance for the then emerging Fascist Italy. At lavish cost and with great speed, the excavation of the Forum of Augustus (1924–28) was followed in quick succession by Trajan's Market (1926–29) and the Forum of Caesar (1927–28) [8. 58]. As part of the redrawing of the general development plan for the city of Rome in 1930/31, the Via dell'Impero was designed as a completely straight processional boulevard with a length of 900 metres and a width of 30 metres [10. 53–56; 15, 50]. It links the Piazza Venezia with the Colosseum, the solitary building and dominant feature at the end of this axis. This processional avenue turned the Colosseum into the counterpart of the colossal Vittoriano (1884–1910), the symbolic monument of Terza Roma, the capital of united Italy after 1870. The Fascist thoroughfare thus placed Antiquity and Modernity into a new and deeply symbolic context. Mussolini conducted the official inauguration of Rome's new political and spatial spine on 28 October 1932, the tenth anniversary of his march on Rome.

According to one calculation, the construction of the Via dell'Impero resulted in 84 per cent of the excavated terrain in the area of the Imperial Forums being filled in again [13. 136]. Along the central section of the boulevard, raised promenades and terraces were built to afford a view of the excavated area. The strolling visitor is presented with the remains of Roman Antiquity in a kind of continuous succession of top architectural achievements. In accordance with this understanding, the visible remains of the Imperial Forums of Trajan, Augustus, Nerva, and Caesar were didactically prepared like decorative artificial ruins. The steps leading up

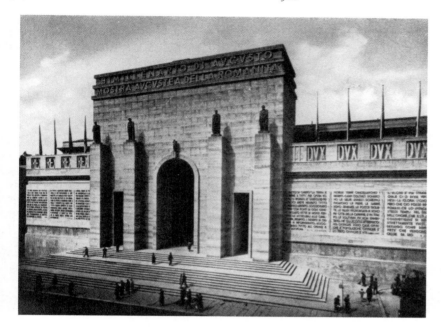

Fig. 1: Alfredo Scalpelli; Façade of the Palazzo delle Esposizioni in Rome for the Mostra Augustea della Romanità 1937–38

Fig. 2: Mario Paniconi and Giulio Pediconi; Sala dell'Impero at the Mostra Augustea della Romanità 1937–38

to the Temple of Mars Ultor in the Forum of Augustus were largely made up from new travertine, and the portico columns were reconstructed from unconnected pieces. The documentation on the excavation findings, largely unpublished to this day, does not stand up to scholarly scrutiny. The plans of the Forum of Augustus, drawn up in 1930 by the architect Italo Gismondi, are schematic and incomplete. Together with his reconstruction drawings, they were used for the model built for the Augustus Exhibition of 1937 [12. 157f.].

3. The Piazza Augusto Imperatore

With a view to the Bimillenario Augusteo, the excavation of the Mausoleum of Augustus was actively pursued after 1934. The overall management of the project was shared by the archaeologist Antonio Muñoz and the architect Vittorio Ballio Morpurgo. An essential part of the building programme was the construction project carried out on three sides of the square, with administration buildings for social welfare, the preservation of the churches of St. Carlo, St. Rocco, and St. Girolamo and also, after February 1937, the *Ara pacis*. By special request of Mussolini this altar was to be reconstructed on the Tiber side of the square, not on its original location. Here, too, the primary concerns were not urban concepts, but the creation of a deeply symbolic political space through the juxtaposition and pairing of monuments from ancient, papal and Fascist Rome. Here memorial sites and modern social institutions were to be joined in a grand identity-creating synthesis. The most obvious hallmark of this falsification of history is the forced architectural combination of heterogeneous styles. The imagery, both sculptural and mosaic, of the buildings, expressing Fascist prosperity and social security, the planting of cypresses around the mausoleum in accordance with a reference found in Strabo, and the mounting of the *Res gestae* as a huge frieze of letters on the exhibition building housing the *Ara pacis* clearly document the contrived, collage-like character of the Fascist image of Antiquity [2. 497, 502; 16. 303f., 309].

4. THE AUGUSTUS EXHIBITION

On 23 September 1937, the exhibition marking the 2000th anniversary of the birth of the first Roman Emperor was ceremoniously opened by Mussolini. The exhibition in the specially reconstructed *Palazzo delle Esposizioni* remained open in Rome for an entire year [1; 21]. The organization and scientific management of the exhibition was taken on by the *Istituto di Studi Romani*, established in 1925 by Carlo Galassi Paluzzi [20. 10f.], under the particular auspices of Giulio Quirino Giglioli, who was both a member of parliament and an archaeologist. He had personally presented the idea to Mussolini in 1932 [7. 160–167]. The historical span of the exhibition programme ranged from the foundation of Rome to the fall of the Roman Empire. Ordered according to individual themes, the sixty-eight sections of the exhibition presented as a pictorial panegyric for the ancient empire its achievements in the military field, in administration, engineering, education, law, craftsmanship and other areas. The exhibition of 200 sculptures and 2000 plaster casts from Italian and European collections, as well as the manufacture of a large number of town, architectural and street models, was seen as an outstanding organizational achievement of the Fascist regime and was widely celebrated in the media. The first impression of any visitor was most memorable and striking: ancient symbols, references and quotations on the façade of the exhibition building based on designs by Alfredo Scalpelli (fig.1). The main motif on the street front was a triumphal arch, reduced to its basic form and decorated with copies of ancient images of captured barbarians and a statue of Victoria. The lower side wings bore imposing letter friezes with quotations from ancient authors in praise of Italy (Livy, Pliny, Cicero and others). The terse impact of the façade reflected the regime's ideologically filtered view of Antiquity, which also pervaded the entire interior space and design. The gaze of entering visitors was drawn from the atrium through the Sala dell'Impero – with its display of scenes of sacrifices, battles and triumphs, together with inscriptions – to the centrally placed statue of Augustus, where, according to Giglioli, "the imperator appeared as the spiritual force protecting the Roman people" (fig.2) [1. 655]. The immediate propagandistic purpose and contemporary reference of this selective view of history and the pictorial declamation of Augustus and the Roman

Empire was clearly demonstrated in the hall entitled "Rome's Immortality. The Empire reborn in Fascist Italy". The exhibits in this hall celebrated the victorious campaign in Abyssinia and the subsequent proclamation of the empire on 9 May 1936, when Mussolini had hailed: "after fifteen centuries the reappearance of the Roman Empire ... upon these fateful hills of Rome" [18. 312]. The centre piece of the hall was a statue of Victory, whose high pedestal bore excerpts of this proclamation, flanked by busts of Victor Emanuel III and Mussolini. While photographic montages on the lower register of the side walls showed images of ancient history and their tradition from the Renaissance to Fascism, above them were columns of letters modelled on ancient epigraphs with quotations ranging in a triumphal arch from Dante to Mussolini. With memorable symbols and formulas along with their connotations, the imagery used the familiar tools of modern product advertising to ensure a wide popular impact of the statements made [11. 29].

C. ART AND STATE
1. GENERAL   2. THE ANCIENT FORUM CONCEPT
3. LATINITY VERSUS MODERNITY   4. FINE ARTS

1. GENERAL

Within the multifaceted interrelations between state-directed patronage of the arts and the self-representation of the regime, the return to the values of Roman Antiquity took centre stage. Nevertheless, Mussolini did not implement a cultural policy comparable to that of enforced conformity (*Gleichschaltung*) fostered by the National Socialists. On the contrary, the art of Fascist Italy is characterized by a plurality of movements that even developed completely opposing positions, such as the extreme traditionalism (the *Premio Cremona* sculpture and painting competition) and second futurism (Aeropainting) [5. 133–135]. The artistic situation in Italy was characterized by the lack of a clear directive from the state. Mussolini's statements on Fascist art remained unspecific [11. 26]. In the field of state architecture, a fierce controversy developed between classicists and rationalists. In a 1941 article in the architectural journal *Casabella*, its editor Giuseppe Pagano publicly decried Marcello Piacentini's recourse to Antiquity as a masquerade and denounced him as a 'Pseudo-Vitruvius' [3. 4]. This led to the seizure of the journal. In this instance, architectural criticism was synonymous with criticism of the regime; however, as far as Pagano was concerned, it was self-criticism, since he himself was a fervent Fascist. The cult of Antiquity and its fictional character had already dominated public criticism in the 1930s, especially by the art critic Margherita Sarfatti, the spokeswomen for the avant-garde Milan movement *Novecento Italiano*, and also by Giuseppe Bottai, the Minister for Education [5. 178–181; 6. 349]. Both made clear that the boldly simplified Fascist image of Antiquity did not live up to the standards and expectations of the intellectual elite and of active

Fig. 3:
Enrico Del Debbio,
Architectural model
of the Foro Mussolini
in Rome

Fig. 4:
View of the Stadio
dei Marmi in the
Foro Mussolini,
Rome

Fig. 5:
Giovanni Guerrini,
Ernesto La Padula and
Mario Romano,
Palazzo della Civiltà
Italiana in E 42

artists, and they supported the establishment of modernity as the official art of the Fascist state.

2. The Ancient Forum Concept

This concept was largely arbitrarily reactivated in two large-scale urban development projects: the Foro Fascista and the Foro Mussolini. The Foro Fascista, designed in 1932 as a counterpart to the Forum Romanum opposite the Basilica Maxenti within the context of building a new party headquarters (the Palazzo Littorio, never built) was, in the view of the popular reactionary ideology, to symbolize a symbioses of Roman classicism and the political renewal of the state. The Fascist notion of the rebirth of a new Italy from the spirit of Antiquity was based on a purely propagandistic matrix and thus clearly to be differentiated from the parallel notion in Renaissance Humanism and its deliberately open, dynamic and human concept of culture. Particularly illuminating for the Fascist adoption of this concept is the Foro Mussolini (the modern Foro Italico, fig.3). This complex in northern Rome, originally designed as a sports forum for the Opera Nazionale Balilla, the Fascist youth organization, and from 1927 on built under the overall direction of the architect Enrico Del Debbio, was declared a reconstitution of the ancient gymnasium with a new purpose [4. 65]. Through physical exercise, youngsters should learn disciplined conformity, faith in the Duce, respect for national values and contempt for democracy. The creation of a new type of human being was a fundamental component in Mussolini's plans for a cultural revolution. The Foro Mussolini was used as an elite training facility for coaches and athletes. To this end, the choice was not for a restrained architecture and imagery, but rather a rhetorical, grandiose one. The first and most significant building of the forum was the marble stadium, modelled on ancient examples (→ Delphi) with a circle of 60 athletes in classical → nudity (figs. 4, 6). As symbols of a superhuman ascetic ideal, they are the most eloquent expression of the intention of making society Fascist under the banner of a reinterpreted Antiquity.

3. Latinity versus Modernity

The state-directed art production, predominantly conditioned by the Fascist image of Antiquity, on the one hand, and the strong orientation of Italian artists toward modern movements, on the other, resulted in an explosive conflict. This tension between Latinity and Modernity characterizes the development and history of the most important Fascist building project, the E 42 (the modern EUR) [17]. This urban development in the south of Rome towards Ostia was to house the 1942 World Exhibition, which was to have opened on the 20th anniversary of the march on Rome as an 'Olympiad of Cultures'. (As a consequence of Italy's entry into the war, it never opened.) The drawing up of the overall plan in 1937 was mainly the work of Marcello Piacentini. The planning concept was, as usual, ideologically coloured in its expression of the regime's imperialistic ambitions. The ensembles of representative buildings within this development are authoritative and com-

Fig. 6:
Carlo De Veroli, Football player,
Stadio dei Marmi, Rome

manding; the layout is dominated by generous axes and triumphal urban squares – reminiscent of Hellenistic peristyle courtyards and Roman forums, together with an inflationary distribution of obelisks. As in the Foro Mussolini, there was no call for a more subtle visualization of the Fascist state by way of a more sensible and constructive organization of urban space. In 1938, Piacentini pressured the more avant-garde building designers to conform by preferentially awarding designs for individual buildings to architects subscribing to *Razionalismo*. One of the architecturally most contradictory solutions is Adalberto Libera's *Palazzo dei Ricevimenti e Congressi*, whose core building is a product of rationalistic design, but whose entrance is adorned with a Classical portico. Libera's intention of expressing the building's character as an assembly place through its open display of rationality and modernity was thwarted by the addition of a style element expressing power and dignity. On a prominent spot, the most deeply symbolic and, at the same time, most controversial project of E42 was realized: the Palazzo della Civiltà Italiana (fig. 5). The bid of the architectural group Giovanni Guerrini, Ernesto La Padula and Mario Romano was successful. Their chosen style represents a form of → Classicism that is reduced to its most basic design elements. The archaizing horse tamer on the stair stringers as well as the epithet *Colosseo quadrato* were a clear indication of Fascism's nationalist credo: Italian art once again spoke Latin [9. 481ff.].

Fig. 7: Mario Sironi, *Justice between Law and Power*, 1936, wall mosaic, Law Courts (Palazzo di Giustizia), Milan © *Beeldrecht Amsterdam 2006*

4. FINE ARTS

The images and sculptures adorning public buildings and public spaces generally followed the architecture's stylistic and thematic leads. Correspondingly, Fascist fine art is also characterized by a static monumentalism and numerous archaisms. The total embodiment of both of these elements is found in the monumental statue of the soccer player by Carlo De Veroli in the marble stadium of the Foro Mussolini (fig. 6), who, in step as well as in the formation of the head and body, continues the tradition of Greek *kouroi*. In monumental sculptures in general, recourse was taken to examples from Classical Antiquity, which were then archaized, as in the case of the horse tamers of the Palazzo della Civiltà Italiana. In addition to monumental sculptures, another prominent element of the revived ancient decorative art was the art of wall or floor mosaics, especially in the bi-chromatic black and white technique, emulating Roman examples. On a large scale, mosaics were used in the Foro Mussolini (in Mussolini's gymnasium, indoor pool and the Piazzale dell'Impero) and in E 42 (forecourt of the Palazzo dell'Ente autonomo). A dominant figure in the field of official paintings was Mario Sironi. With his programmatic renunciation of easel painting and his move towards wall paintings and wall mosaics, he also turned towards a monumental, archaizing Classicism. With his deliberate disregard of scale and perspective – the artistic achievement of Renaissance art – as well as the blockiness of his figurative style, he wanted to connect to the originality and essence of Italian art – and thus to the politically invoked *Italianità*. Ancient Roman tradition is also recalled in the regressive choice of topics for the wall decorations themselves (fig. 7; [6. 348, 353]). A telling example for the split artistic awareness in the Fascist era was Lucio Fontana. While he conformed with the official demands for a Classical style in his public commissions (for example, in the sculpture ensemble Heroic Italy, now in the Sala della Vittoria of the 6th Milan Triennale of 1936, on the occasion of the Ethiopian victory), in his private work he tended toward abstract art [9. 487; 11. 28]. In this field he gained fame and recognition in the post-war period after 1945.

→ FORUM; → ROME

SOURCES 1 G. Q. GIGLIOLI, La Mostra Augustea della Romanità, in: Architettura 17, 1938, 655–666 2 A. MUÑOZ, La sistemazione del Mausoleo di Augusto, in: Capitolium 13, 1938, 491–508 3 G. PAGANO, Potremo salvarci dalle false tradizioni e dalle ossessioni monumentali?, in: Costruzioni-Casabella 19, 157, 1941, 2–7 4 M. PIACENTINI, Il Foro Mussolini in Roma, in: Architettura 12, 1933, 65–74

LITERATURE 5 Articles by T. BENTON, S. FRAQUELLI, L. BECKER, E. COEN, in: Kunst und Macht im Europa der Diktatoren 1930 bis 1945, 1996, 120–181 6 E. BRAUN, Political Rhetoric and Poetic Irony. The Uses of Classicism in the Art of Fascist Italy, in: E. COWLING, J. MUNDY (eds.), On Classic Ground. Picasso, Léger, de Chirico and the New Classicism 1910–1930, 1990, 345–358 7 M. CAGNETTA, Il mito di Augusto e la 'rivoluzione' fascista, in: Matrici culturali del fascismo. Kongress-Akten Bari 1977, 153–184 8 A. CEDERNA, Mussolini Urbanista. Lo sventramento di Roma negli anni del consenso, 1980 9 R. A. ELTIN, Modernism in Italian Architecture: 1890–1940, 1991 10 M. ESTERMANN-JUCHLER, Faschistische Staatsbaukunst. Zur ideologischen Funktion der öffentlichen Architektur im faschistischen Italien, 1982 11 S. VON FALKENHAUSEN, Die Moderne in Italien: Avantgarde-

Faschismus-Rezeption, in: S. GERMER, A. PREISS (eds.), Giuseppe Terragni. Moderne und Faschismus in Italien, 1991, 21–38   12 J. GANZERT, V. KOCKEL, Augustusforum und Mars-Ultor-Tempel, in: Kaiser Augustus und die verlorene Republik, 1988, 149–163 (Exhibition catalogue)   13 I. INSOLERA, Roma moderna. Un secolo di storia urbanistica, 1962   14 Id., F. PEREGO, Archeologia e città. Storia moderna dei Fori di Roma, 1983   15 S. KOSTOF, The Third Rome. 1870–1950: Traffic and Glory, 1973   16 Id., The Emperor and the Duce: The Planning of Piazzale Augusto Imperatore in Rome, in: H. A. MILLON, L. NOCHLIN (eds.), Art and Architecture in the Service of Politics, 1978, 270–325   17 R. MARIANI, E 42. Un progetto per l'Ordine Nuovo, 1987   18 L. SCHUMACHER, Augusteische Propaganda und faschistische Rezeption, in: Zeitschrift für Religions- und Geistesgeschichte 40, 1988, 307–330   19 W. VANNELLI, Economia dell'architettura in Roma fascista, 1981   20 R. VISSER, Fascist Doctrine and the Cult of the Romanità, in: Journal of Contemporary History 27, 1992, 5–22   21 F. SCRIBA, Augustus im Schwarzhemd? Die Mostra Augustea della Romanità in Rom 1937/38, 1995   22 Articles by C. LAZZARO, C. FOGU, A. T. WILKINS, J. WELGE, J. T. SCHNAPP, in: C. LAZZARO, R. J. CRUM (eds.), Donatello among the Blackshirts. History and Modernity in the Visual Culture of Fascist Italy, 2005   SALVATORE PISANI

II. POLITICS AND SOCIETY
A. INTRODUCTION   B. THE ROME IDEAL   C. NATIONALIZATION FROM ABOVE   D. THE REACTIONARY CULTURAL MODEL   E. THE EXPANSION OF THE FASCIST MODEL

A. INTRODUCTION
Fascism, the political movement and party ruling Italy from October 1922 to July 1943, was by no means a homogenous phenomenon and did not have any coherent ideology. Rather, it presents itself as a conglomerate of different schools of thought, personalities and interests, unified only in their totalitarian dimension. Fascism was a "reactionary mass movement" (P. Togliatti). Its aim was the integration of broad sectors of society around a model of nationhood based on the principles of elitism, hierarchy, anti-democracy and a culture of power. The militaristic and centralized organization of the state culminated in the figure of its leader, Benito Mussolini; it was modelled on myths dominant in Europe between the end of the 18th and the early decades of the 20th cent. In addition to a break with the most recent past, the Fascist regime attempted to integrate the masses through their faith in the construction of a modern nation. All the mass media available at the time were harnessed into achieving this purpose.

In recent decades, the research into Fascism has been dominated by the studies of R. De Felice, who emphasized the consent of the masses to the regime. The historiography of the political left (C. Pavone, N. Tranfaglia, G. Vacca, G. De Luna, et. al.) has challenged the revisionist aspects of this approach, which gives no consideration to sanctions against the forces of political and cultural resistance. Indeed, while it was still possible in 1925 for a group of intellectuals (G. De Sanctis, G. Pasquali, P. Fraccaro, M. Valgimigli, N. Festa et. al.) to unite under the leadership of B. Croce in response to the Fascist Manifesto of G. Gentile, six years later all academics were forced to swear an oath of allegiance to the regime. Only a few resisted (of the ancient history scholars only G. De Sanctis and G. Levi Della Vida), and in consequence were dismissed from their university positions. The Fascists perceived the necessity of an integration of the masses as part of a collective ideological project embodied in the myth of an unbroken Italian history culminating in Fascism. The memory of Rome's imperial greatness thus played a significant part in the attempt to recreate such an empire in the present.

B. THE ROME IDEAL
The research of the last two decades into the regime and the intellectual class has shed light on a certain continuity between liberal and Fascist Italy, at least as far as the influence of authoritarian thinking and chauvinistic pressure on the academic discipline of history are concerned. The first decade of the regime, in particular, saw the continuation of old debates between various historical schools. The followers of the positivistic method, the intellectual heirs of the late 19th cent. German philologists, opposed those proposing a contemporizing of Classical history in conformity with the dominant nationalistic ideology. The crisis of 1914, the conflict between the proponents of neutrality and those of intervention, drew attention to the problem of integrating Classical studies into the conceptual beginnings of the idea of nationhood. This is typified in the stance taken by the historian Ettore Pais (1856–1939), a specialist in the history of ancient Rome. Even though he himself was moulded by the strict tenets of Th. Mommsen, he realized, not least in consequence of the defeat of the Italian army at Adua (1896), the need to be liberated from positivism with its German roots. He entered into a polemic controversy with Karl Julius Beloch in particular, the influential German ancient historian who lived in Italy. According to Pais, the study of the Classics had a role to play in historical and political education. Equally dismissive of the postulate of pure philology was Ettore Romagnoli (1871–1938), who first accused G. Vitelli, then Pasquali, of 'Germanophilia'. He extolled the Italian ability to revive life that had materially disappeared. There is a clear influence of irrational theories, such as those by O. Spengler, who enjoyed great popularity at the time. His rhetoric is echoed in Fascist propaganda. Romagnoli and Pais and their philosophical school were among the most vociferous supporters of the claim of Fascist Nationalism as the natural conclusion of Rome's historical purpose.

The idea of Rome with its political function of integrating the various social classes into a state project was already well along at the time of the Risorgimento and had simultaneously acquired both liberal as well as nationalistic connotations. The expansionist pressure of liberal Italy with the aim of conquering Libya and Eritrea also resulted in an immediate resurrection of the myth of the Roman Empire, with particular emphasis on the aggressive aspect of Roman power. Furthermore, the war and the ideological crisis of the 19th cent. (Christian-social, liberal and socialist ideology) had resulted in a loosening of social bonds and raised the demand for a new basis for legitimacy. In this context, the resurrection of the Roman model was the Italian reply to the 'Crisis of Western Civilization' and, at the same time, a revolt against the modern world. It claimed to be of importance for the political community as well as for the civilized world as a whole by suggesting an entirely new solution to the problems of human society (Rome as a new solution between the opposing models of London and Moscow). The construction of a historical narrative that would lay the foundation for a new national myth demanded values which were to be represented by Rome. The selection of such values was in turn determined by the new requirements of the present times. Ancient Rome was thus seen as the predecessor of an organization of the state in which the principles of hierarchy, realism, balance, and stability of power not only guaranteed survival but, even more, the greatness of the nation. The ideas of the priority of the body politic, the submission of individual interests to the requirements of the organized collective – the expression of an ethical state – immediately harmonized with the cultural model of Rome. In this way, elevated to a meta-historical level, the 'idea of Rome' presented itself as an antidemocratic and anti-parliamentarian myth.

C. Nationalization from Above

One of the theoretical founders of a new authoritarian humanism was Giuseppe Bottai (1895–1959). He spoke out against a neglect of cultural and educational policy. Even though he inclined more towards modernism and the avant-garde, he did not at all underestimate the importance of → Classicism for the ideological legitimization of an Italian predominance in Europe.

The mobilization of culture and with it its bureaucratization was shaped by the establishment of important institutions. The year 1925 saw the foundation of the *Istituto di Studi Romani* and the *Istituto Nazionale Fascista di Cultura*. Beyond the promotion of propaganda and cultural events, they operated as centres of power, not least with their remarkable readiness to supply public funds to facilitate the organization of academic congresses and excavation programmes. They were always ready to support the regime's political directives. Nor should the extensive archaeological campaigns be forgotten, whether in Italy itself or on African soil. Propagandistically, these were hailed as accomplishments of the regime. However, at the government's initiative, they were followed by the 'reorganization' (more correctly: the destruction) of Rome's urban structure.

Because it was continually adapted to the political atmosphere of the day, the myth of Rome was not without inherent contradictions. Whereas until the mid-1930s, *Italianità* and *Romanità* were perceived as alternatives to German National-Socialist racism and to German Classicism with its focus on Hellas, and although elements of anti-German polemics dating back to 1914 were still present in Italy, such positions had to be abandoned with the constitution of the axis Rome-Berlin in 1936. Rather, a common denominator then had to be found for the equally difficult reconciliation with the intrinsically anti-Roman German national mythology (Arminius legend). Fundamentally important for propagandizing Rome as an ideology were the celebrations of the 2000th anniversary of the births of Virgil (1930–31), Horace (1935–36), and Augustus (1937–38). Fascism found an appropriate point of reference in the rule of Augustus. This was particularly suited to ideological borrowings because of its authoritarian and autocratic features. Virgil's *Georgics* and *Aeneid*, for example, were seen to represent perfectly the cultural and civic values propagated by Augustus. Fascism saw itself as well on the way to recapture these values: imperialism as a mission, supremacy of the Occident over the Orient, a life close to nature and the soil. In those years, the regime had just achieved great success in the 'grain battle', portrayed as the antidote to the devastating crisis of global capitalism from 1929 to 1933. Anti-modernism, one of the features of Fascist ideology, banded together with a pacifistic ideology of Rome, with the ultimate aim of a restoration of *mores*. Virgil's poetry, with its prophetic and mystical undertones – a favourite of many of the regime's leaders – became an instrument for the glorification of Rome's greatness, which could be used and exploited educationally in everyday life at school.

The *Bimillennial Celebrations* in honour of Augustus took place in a different climate. Ethopia had been conquered just a few years earlier and, as a result, the *Imperium* proclaimed. The image of a rural and peaceful power was discarded. Fascist Italy now invoked the martial side of the Roman myth. The *Bimillennial Celebrations* signified, among other things, the zenith of Mussolini's identification with Ocatavian, which had long been in the offing. In September 1937, the *Mostra Augustea della Romanità* was opened, timed to coincide with the reopening of the *Mostra della Rivoluzione Fascista*. The parallels between these historical periods were intended to point to the desired interpretation of Fascism: Mussolini's revolution, seen as pacification inasmuch as it had taken place without resorting to terror, had resulted in a regime which, though formally respecting existing institutions, really had at its aim their ultimate destruction. Furthermore, the Augustan model provided a historical comparison that could be exploited under a variety of aspects: the abolition of parliamentary debate in favour of the *auctoritas* of the leader, the unification of Italy as a national process under leadership from above, the need for demographic growth ('strength in numbers'), as well as the development of an economy based on agriculture.

The historical analogy was plainly obvious in Bottai's statements regarding the opportune nature of Augustus's policy of 'cleansing' the Senate. The numerous historical studies written at that time focused on the figure of Augustus, and he reflected a resolutely reactionary image inspired by Fascist demagogy. The Roman people placed their trust in their leader because he was a peacemaker as well as a conqueror. It was tacitly ignored that Octavian was very cautious in his foreign policy and refrained from any potentially disastrous adventures. Augustus was portrayed as a synthesis of the present with the past, because it was thanks to him that the Roman revolution became consolidated as a regime or as a 'permanent revolution'–the embodiment of Fascism's most genuine aim. Drawing parallels between Augustus and Mussolini was further favoured by a wave of mysticism. This is particularly obvious in the works of the *Scuola di Mistica Fascista*. The Rome ideology was also given a major part there.

The bimillennium of Horace's birth was a far more muted affair, most likely because of the difficulty of fitting this poet, with his outspoken resistance to public roles, into the regime's cultural directives. He was portrayed as an example of the intellectual who overcame his initial skepticism towards the new direction, but who in the end found his place in the new order. However, it was hard to ignore that the notion of individualism and freedom, the basis of such a large part of Horatian poetry, was irreconcilable with the values of the Fascist ethical state. For that reason, the main focus was on his Odes (3,1–6) and the *Carmen Saeculare*, Italy's first national anthem. Many motifs that were not in line with the new Fascist ideology, such as that of the discarded shield (carm. 2,7,10), either had to be suppressed or laboriously forced into a uniform interpretation.

Horace's poetry was the subject of a dispute about the originality of Latin literature. This had long been denied, in particular, by the 19th-cent.German philology with its deep roots in the myth of Greece, but it finally was recognized by F. Leo and later U. von Wilamowitz-Moellendorff. The glorification of Rome in its most extreme forms implied a certain devaluation of the study of Greek, whereas the study of Latin rose to ever higher recognition in the organization of academic knowledge. Authors such as E. Bignone, A. Rostagni and L. Castiglioni attempted to separate Latin culture from its dependence on Greek culture. Those who still insisted on analysing the Greek sources of Horace's poetry (without denying the Roman influence), as, for example, G. Pasquali, could find themselves under attack from the supporters of the regime (E. Romagnoli et.al.). Once again, this resulted in the rejection of a philology and a study of source material that was entirely focused on technical aspects.

The conquest of Ethiopia and the proclamation of the empire in 1936 played an important role in changing the relationship between the regime and the intellectu-

als. The notion of having colonies as part of the 'will to power', as the Fascists referred to it bluntly from the very beginning and whose organic form they quickly worked out in detail when the conflict actually happened, appeared just in time to counteract the lack of legitimization at a period when the ability of the Fascist state to achieve social integration was waning. On a moral level, the *Imperium* was seen as the mission of a civilization based on the values of discipline, authority and duty. The perception of a natural inferiority of other peoples provided the justification for armed conquest. The conflict between Rome and other nations was seen as a battle between civilization and barbarism. This interpretation of a 'Roman' colonialism was polemically directed against British and French colonialism, both of which were portrayed as purely mercantilistic, i.e., based on the economic exploitation of subordinate peoples. The press referred to the latter as 'Carthaginian colonialism'. The Punic state was turned into a negative myth, its conflict with Rome into a battle of opposite cultural models: one based on ideals, the other on interest. When racist laws were passed in 1938 against the background of an anti-Semitic climate and the increasing recognition of → NATIONAL SOCIALISM, the anti-Carthaginian polemics assumed an anti-Semitic tone. The 'Carthaginian destiny of defeat' no longer depended solely on the interpretation of Rome as the power of progress, but was justified by the 'racial superiority' of an Aryan Rome. Incidentally, Classical studies had for years been dominated by an anti-Semitic climate; and the situation of Jews became increasingly difficult after the Concordat of 1929, when Roman Catholicism became the state religion.

Roman imperialism offered a great deal of ambivalence. The myth of Rome appeared, on the one hand, as a factor in the nation-building and cultural unification of Italy and, on the other, as the link between different peoples under the name of Rome, representing, in this latter form, a movement towards cosmopolitanism. Only the most sharp-minded of historians, such as M.A Levi and P. De Francisci, realized the problem inherent in the contradictory nature of such visions. They criticized the policies of those Roman emperors who were accused of attacking the Italian nation's claim to supremacy, as, for example, Caracalla because of his extension of Roman citizenship. Furthermore, they placed great emphasis on the importance of Augustus' achievements, who, though bringing peace to all nations, increased the predominance of the Italian tribes with a policy of demographic growth. In this way, the selection of Augustus as the regime's preferred model also indicated the solution to a problem that presented itself, at least subliminally, in the interpretation of Caesar's role. As a pioneer and active proponent of Rome's will to power, Caesar fitted in well with the militaristic spirit of Fascism (in 1926, G. Polverelli, then Mussolini's press attaché, had suggested parallels between Caesar and the Duce), but the political interpretation of the Roman dictator was soon characterized by Oriental elements–a 'Levantine attitude' that seemed alien to true Roman tradition and open to ideological double entendre. Though never officially repudiated by the regime, the character of Caesar remained in shadow.

D. THE REACTIONARY CULTURAL MODEL

After the signing of the Concordat, Roman Catholics played an increasingly important political and cultural role, not least because of agreement between some aspects of Fascist ideology and the teachings of the Church. Where the Church had influence, the Rome ideology became an integrating element of journalism as well as science. The Church claimed that during the Middle Ages it and only it had guaranteed a continuity of values from the Rome of the imperial age; conversely, from a providential point of view, the Roman Empire was seen as an instrument that made Christ's birth possible. In Fascism, this ideological aspect became a political instrument. Modern civilization thus appeared as the product of two different, but converging factors: *Romanitas* and *Christianitas*. The former guaranteed political unity to the state, the latter the unity in ideas and morals. This synthesis found its true organic expression in the *Scuola di Mistica Fascista*, in the balance between anti-rationalism and a spiritualism influenced by the Roman Catholic Church. Such 'militant mysticism' as practised by high-ranking prelates as Ildefonso Schuster, Cardinal of Milan, was not contemplation, but a philosophy aimed at action. Roman Catholics, for example, supported the policy of expansion with the argument that it was imperative to evangelize people suffering from 'spiritual poverty'. This theological reason was equated with that of the cultural inferiority of peoples conquered by Rome. The Church also endorsed the regime's anti-Semitic propaganda, even if it distanced itself when the race laws were passed. Even though Roman Catholics were seldom openly polemical, they tended to emphasize that Rome's superiority was spiritual, and not based on race. Hostility towards the (Semitic) Carthage was synonymous with the hostility toward British and French mercantilism (also seen as Semitic, because of its plutocracy).The latter was inherently materialistic, whereas Roman colonialism was idealistic and catholic.

Not even a historian with basically anti-Fascist views such as Gaetano De Sanctis (1870–1957) was immune from such philo-aryan racism. He was expert at using German historiography for a renewal of the study of ancient history in Italy. He combined the critical assessment of sources with the interest in political-institutional topics within ancient societies and an awareness of the spiritual aspects in the life of a people. Together with Pasquali, De Sanctis was one of the less opportunistic voices in Italian academia under Fascist rule. Nonetheless, he considered the disappearance of the Carthaginians as a historical necessity. In his view, the African city had no will of its own in the history of civilization, but was only 'peso morto' ("dead weight"; *Storia dei Romani* IV 3, 1964, 75). It may be that De

Sanctis was influenced in this statement by his strict Roman Catholicism.

The relationship between the Roman-Catholicism and Classical Antiquity was one of the most consistent elements in the continuity between the Fascist period and Republican Italy because, after the fall of the regime, many academics sought a new intellectual innocence by stressing their own Catholic descent, as in the case of the entire *Istituto di Studi Romani*. The Catholic inclination towards conservatism was a guarantor of continuity for those who had openly supported the demands of an authoritarian culture. In that way, the idea of Rome, devoid of its aggressive and imperialist forms, was confirmed as the emblem of a peace built on justice, a concept clearly moulded by the Christian-Latin tradition.

Within the larger programme of placing Classical Studies in the service of constructing a modern national culture, the reform of school education played a pivotal role. The process was started in 1923 by the philosopher Giovanni Gentile (1875–1944). The purpose of studying the world of Classical Antiquity was not only to master grammar and rhetoric. The aim of the school reform was to plant and strengthen a sense of identity and national pride in the future elite. This aim was pursued by an approach that was both aesthetic and historicist and by a careful selection of topics in which the Rome myth prevailed. The new orientation of school education displayed a remarkable openness towards the demands of philology and historicism, which brought it Pasquali's approval. Giorgio Pasquali (1885–1952) renewed Italian philology. The academic heir to Leo, Schwartz, Wilamowitz and their school, he embodied German philology and Italian culture. He taught one to transcend the boundaries of academic disciplines and to interpret every philological problem in terms of its history of transmission. Endowed with an almost Greek spirit, by his very nature distant to the then prevailing anti-rationalism, he managed to find a way of living under the regime. It has to be said, though, that his initially strong rejection of it turned into considerable rapprochement. His interest in the Rome ideology is manifest in his works on the images of the Roman Empire, as transmitted by the Greeks (*La nascita dell'idea di Roma nel mondo greco*, Nuova Antologia, 1940, 149–155).

One of the most enduring and less ideologically affected achievements was the extensive series of publications on Classical Antiquity by the *Enciclopedia Italiana*. Under the scholarly direction of G. De Sanctis, it united the most important names in academic culture, independent of their political orientation. Based on an idea by Gentile, the *Enciclopedia Italiana* was to offer a critical and scholarly investigation of the myths presented to the general public. In reality, the encyclopedia was a compendium of everything that represented superior quality in Italian culture, because it offered academic autonomy even to those who had quite considerably distanced themselves from the regime. The new policies in education and culture also boosted educational publishing with several new series of school books and translations.

E. The Expansion of the Fascist Model

The myth of Rome, mediated by Fascism, spread internationally, but until now this phenomenon has been little investigated. With the exception of the role played by the reception of Classical Antiquity in Germany under National-Socialist rule, it should be pointed out that several volumes of the *Studi Romani nel Mondo* were published between 1934 and 1939 with contributions by A. Alföldi, L. Constans, P. Faider, J. Gagé, E. Kornemann et.al. After the end of the Spanish Civil War in 1939, the Franco regime celebrated – belatedly – the bimillennium of Augustus' birth, using elements from the Italian propaganda. The exploitation of Classical Antiquity for an authoritarian ideology is also evident in France. Among other things, the myth of Vercingetorix, the Francophone counterpart of the German Arminius, was used by the collaborationist Vichy government of Marshal Pétain because of his nationalistic idea; but it was also claimed by the *Résistance* inasmuch as the myth takes up a familiar theme of resistance against a tyrant. Incidentally, as early as the beginning of the 20th cent., the *Action Française* had listed among its models Athenian democracy, with particular focus on the topic of slavery. Even today, questions regarding the Fascist tendencies of scholars such as J. Carcopino and G. Duémzil, and in which way such tendencies influenced their academic work remain unanswered.

1 G. Bandelli, Le letture mirate, in: Lo spazio letterario di Roma antica, 4, 1991, 361–397 (survey of research) 2 M. Cagnetta, Antichisti e impero fascista, 1979   3 Id., Antichità classicha nell'Enciclopedia Italiana, 1990 4 Id., Bimillenario della nascita, Enciclopedia oraziana, III, 1988   5 L. Canfora, Ideologie del classicismo, 1980 6 Id., Fascismo e bimillenario della nascita di Virgilio, EV 2, 469–472   7 Id., Polititische Philologische Altertumswissenschaft und moderne Staatsideologien, 1995 (Italian: Le vie del classicismo, 1989)   8 Ph. V. Cannistraro, La fabbrica del consenso, 1975   9 E. Gabba, K. Christ (eds.), Römische Geschichte und Zeitgeschichte in der deutschen und italienischen Altertumswissenschaft während des 19. und 20. Jahrhunderts, I–II, 1989–1991 10 E. Gabba, Cultura classica e storiografia moderna, 1995   11 F. Giordano, Filologi e fascismo. Gli studi di Letteratura latina nell'Enciclopedia Italiana, 1993   12 F. Scriba, Augustus im Schwarzhemd. Die Mostra Augustea della Romanità in Rom 1937/38, 1995.

MARIELLA SCHIANO, CLAUDIO CAGNETTA (†)

Fashion
A. Introduction B. Middle Ages C. Renaissance D. Classicism E. Late Nineteenth and Twentieth Centuries

A. Introduction
The reception of ancient fashion is inextricably linked with the reception of ancient art. It is examples of that art – sculptures, frescoes, mosaics, terracottas and vase paintings – that shape our image of clothing fashions in Greek and Roman Antiquity. Since only few original pieces have been preserved, the study of clothing styles up to the Middle Ages and beyond largely depends on art history in order to reconstruct the materials used for clothing during those periods and to determine how it was worn. However, the question is just how accurate such pictures are. The appropriation and adaptation of older (including ancient) models in the history of fashion is a multi-layered process: an independent development that nevertheless allowed for a relationship of mutual inspiration with the visual and theatrical arts. Clothing styles derived from ancient patterns reflect shifting perspectives and motives that change along with the ideas they are designed to convey. An item of clothing or detail of it can be a significant factor in expressing a new body ideal or role model, a longing for nature or a political consciousness.

In the reception history of ancient clothing, the focus has been on giving concrete form to the idea of Antiquity rather than on authenticity. This idea manifests itself primarily in the folds of a garment and the way it is draped – the central features of ancient clothing that also represent the fundamental difference between it and the clothing of later periods, which is cut and sewn to fit

B. Middle Ages
The issue of a change in perspective outlined above is most apparent in the Middle Ages, a period that still saw itself in cultural continuity with the Ancient world (Carolingian 'renovatio') and for which Antiquity primarily meant Late Antiquity. However, it was mainly the models of this latter period that were handed down, influencing the clothing of the common people as well as that of secular and religious leaders. Up to the high Middle Ages, the basic article of clothing worn by both sexes and all segments of society was still the tunic, albeit in the style of the dalmatica: a cross-shaped robe with attached long sleeves (*tunica manicata*) – a style that did not appear in Roman fashion until the 3rd cent. Ankle-length for women, knee-length for men, the belted tunic was worn by working people until the late Middle Ages and survived in the form of smocks worn by tradespeople and farmers in the modern era. During the early Middle Ages, men's clothing also included the knee- or ankle-length trousers (*braccae*), complete with leg-wrappers, that were commonly worn by Roman men since the 2nd cent. The cloaks worn during the Middle Ages were also traditional in style; up until the

Fig. 1: Emperor Justinian with retinue, *Justinian Court* wall mosaic, S. Vitale, Ravenna, mid-6th cent.
Digital Image © 2007, The Museum of Modern Art, NY/Scala, Florence.

12th cent., these were knee-length capes fastened with a fibula, usually at the right shoulder, sometimes rectangular, like the pallium, and sometimes semi-circular, like the sagum. Members of the upper classes depicted in mediaeval illuminated manuscripts are usually wearing precious silk fabrics from Byzantine workshops. Byzantine courtly clothing, which incorporated 'stiffening' gold fibres into garments that were based on ancient models, inspired the development particularly of the regalia worn by Frankish rulers. As a sign of his imperial power, Charlemagne adopted the paludamentum worn by Byzantine dignitaries, now floor-length, in which Justinian was immortalized at San Vitale in Ravenna (fig. 1). The purple cloak and purple shoes also remained obligatory as a sign of royal standing for the successors of the Frankish emperors, but with a difference in cut. As styles changed in the 12th cent., the general fit becoming tighter and men's clothing longer, the semi-circular cloak fastened over the chest with strings or tassels became popular, and in the 13th cent. it was adopted as part of the coronation vestments. Also related to the clothing worn by mediaeval rulers are the liturgical vestments of the clergy, which recall in their basic elements clothing worn during the late Roman period. Liturgical dress, essentially established by the

6th cent., took on such elements as the paenula and the tunic, which became the chasuble and the alb; the dalmatica, the traditional early Christian form of dress, was adopted as early as the 4th cent. – signifying the authority of both emperor and bishops alike. In the visual arts, the standard costume worn by saints and Biblical figures was a combination of the dalmatica, a tunic (sometimes long) and a simple pallium; this remained the characteristic attire in which Christ and the apostles were depicted until long after the Middle Ages had come to an end (fig. 2)

C. RENAISSANCE

Significant for the reception of Antiquity during the Renaissance is that period's sense of caesura, as it sought to distinguish itself from the preceding period, the Middle Ages, by harking back to the typical forms of Classical Antiquity. However, the focus of interest was not ancient clothing itself, but the body underneath and its expressive quality.

This is difficult to document in the history of clothing, but it is a prominent feature in art history. Particularly in Italian art, the reception of ancient models manifests itself in a new kind of interplay between clothing and the body, both in repose and in motion. This

Fig. 2: Two Apostles, eastern quire, Bamberg Cathedral, ca. 1220/1230

applies mainly to female figures, since male figures are more frequently depicted nude or wearing only a brief tunic or similar attire, as in Classical sculpture. Gone are heavy folds of fabric obscuring the body that were seen in late → GOTHIC sculptures; instead clothing is animated by a body (particularly a female body), both in religious and secular works of art; cf. Ghiberti, Donatello, Ghirlandaio, Filippo and Filippino Lippi, Botticelli. The latter's characteristic thin, light-coloured fab-rics are well known; sometimes they are pleated in the manner of a chiton, reminiscent of the folds and draped fabrics displayed by ancient statues and some Roman-esque monumental statues as well – fabrics that give the illusion of wet cloth clinging to the body. The fanciful costumes created by Renaissance artists, combining ele-ments of contemporary fashion, such as slit and puffed sleeves, with forms borrowed from Antiquity, like the gathered cloth of the kolpos, toga or pallium, enhance

Fig. 3: Sandro Botticelli, The Birth of Venus (detail), Uffizi, Florence, 1482/1483 (*Photo Artothek*)

the movement of their wearers and dramatize their figuration. Floating cloaks and ballooning cloth panels, fluttering skirts and flying hair, described by Aby Warburg as 'pathos formulae', appear to reflect internal states of excitement (fig. 3).

D. CLASSICISM

Like no other, this period is characterized by its affinity for Classical Antiquity; it is also a counter-movement, this time – against the backdrop of the Enlightenment – rejecting the forms of the Baroque and Rococo styles, which it viewed as artificial and overly ornate. Ancient dress was seen as natural and moderate. Increasingly well-documented discoveries were very influential, particularly the excavation of the cities buried by the eruption of Mount Vesuvius. The socio-political dimension of Winckelmann's call to emulate Antiquity found direct expression in the clothes that Jacques-Louis David made into an emblem of republican sympathies, not only in paintings (such as *The Oath of the Horatii*, 1784; → PAINTINGS ON HISTORICAL SUBJECTS, fig. 9), but most of all in his designs for a national costume for the Directorate during the 1790s. While the Phrygian cap was adopted by the Jacobins as a revolutionary symbol of liberty, fashion in the ancient style, particularly for men, failed to win widespread acceptance. It manifested itself mostly in details such as the post-revolutionary hairstyle drawn from portraits of the Roman emperors: the short curls of Titus and the straight-haired style of Caesar favoured by Napoleon.

Fashionable items most affected by the Neo-Classical enthusiasm for Antiquity were women's dresses and accessories. In the course of the reform efforts emanating from England, which led to a simplification of clothing styles, the late 18th cent. saw the emergence of a *mode à la grecque* in the form of the chiton-like chemise dress. Until the 1820s, European women's fashions were characterized by a simple, usually short-sleeved, high-waisted garment cut straight, like a shirt, with a soft skirt made of thin cotton, muslin or cambric. While they were affordable and simple in style, it would appear that these low-cut dresses from the turn of the century – sometimes disparagingly referred to as 'nude fashion' because of their transparency and because they were worn over a leotard resembling a ballerina's costume, and without a chemise underneath – were designed primarily for women of the French salons like Madame Récamier (fig. 4). Along with a pinafore-like drape in the style of a tunic, a scarf, preferably of patterned cashmere, was the most important component of this Classically-inspired costume. As in the ancient world, its draping was considered an art that was now learned under the direction of a dance teacher and demonstrated in the performance of *tableaux vivants*. Fashion had turned into a staged art, closely tied to the theatre. Like the dancers in Vigano's tragic ballets, elegant women appeared in sandals or ribbon-tied shoes, their hair done *à la Sappho*, inspired by Grillparzer's stage play of the same name. In addition to 'Grecian' hairstyles, which combined curls at the forehead and temples with a chignon at the back of the head, the short

Fig. 4: François Gérard, Madame Récamier,
Musée Carnavalet, Paris, 1802
© Photothèque des Musées de la Ville de Paris

'Titus' was also very popular. Ribbons and tiaras, in addition to feathers and pearls, also decorated women's wigs. Particularly in the evening, women wore light-blond wigs, a colour that was favoured during the late Roman era as well as the Italian Renaissance.

It was characteristic of this period for there to be mixtures and incongruities of style, not only in hair and hat fashions, which ranged from brimless toques and bonnets to helmet-shaped hats and turbans. But it was precisely the fashionable accessory items that highlighted the fanciful nature of the references to Antiquity during the Empire and Directoire periods. Wedgwood buttons depicting scenes from Classical mythology, fans showing pictures of Roman monuments and handbags in the shape of ancient urns were typical of the 'Antiquity craze', whose dissemination was both encouraged and parodied by fashion magazines. The high-waisted, straight-cut dress continued to be popular in women's fashions of the Restoration period (after 1815). However, the use of heavy, stiff materials and a fondness for puff sleeves and opulent decorations with rouching, lace and flounces thoroughly disguised the ancient patterns on which these clothes were based. So-called Greek fashion was now confined to evening clothes and, ultimately, women's ball gowns.

E. Late Nineteenth and Twentieth Centuries

The reception history of ancient fashion as it relates to more recent times is difficult to grasp within conventional chronological classifications. The complex inter-relationships among various – often contradictory – currents culminated around the turn of the 20th cent. in social and artistic renewal movements. Again there was a striving for naturalness in opposition to fashionable but unhealthy foolishness, in particular the return of the corset style. And again the trend was set by England. It was above all the social-reformist Pre-Raphaelites who sought to modernize fashion with designs incorporating both aesthetic and functional aspects. A characteristic feature was the 'Classical waistline' of their loose, heavily pleated shirtwaist dresses which, in the spirit of the Renaissance, evoked a sense of freedom of movement. This also applied to their artistic creations, e.g. Edward Burne-Jones' Mantegnesque draperies, as well as the designs of William Morris and Dante Gabriel Rossetti that were worn by the artists' models and wives, styles with gathered sleeves and voluminous skirts that recalled Raphael's portraits of women.

While Pre-Raphaelite designs underscored the femininity of the women who wore them, the fashions designed by artists of the Art Nouveau movement (e.g. Henry van de Velde, Peter Behrens and Alfred Mohrbutter) tended to reflect moral influences that were critical of the prevailing styles' eroticization of the body. Accordingly, the loose-fitting dress referred to as a *Reformkleid*, which falls loosely from the shoulder and is cut with the high waist of the Empire style, was an attempt to accommodate a more 'natural' body ideal developed from ancient sculptures.

More directly than in reform fashion, the desire for freedom found expression in the complete removal of all clothing, i.e. in the body culture and nudism movements which, unlike the exclusive artistic reform efforts, were able to mobilize large groups of people. The goal was to discover the true nature of the body, formed and strengthened in accordance with the ancient ideal, seeking to achieve unity between the soul and the cosmos in the rhythmic movement of exercise and expressive dance. Performed in the appropriate costume, dance was the medium through which the mythical quality of Antiquity was thought to take on concrete form. Lay choirs draped in Classicizing robes performed their rhythmic and demonstrative physical routines *à la grecque*. Barefoot, wearing a peplos or a light tunic with a veil or scarf, a star of the stage like Isadora Duncan would in the first decade of the 20th cent. present to European audiences her visions of Antiquity through dance. This pioneer of modern dance, who came to ancient art through Pre-Raphaelite images and Botticelli's *Primavera*, was particularly inspired by Greek vase paintings and the dance of the maenads, with its ecstatic movements, swaying folds of fabric and translucent chitons. Soft, flowing chiton-like garments were also created by fashion designers like Paul Poiret

Fig. 5: Afternoon dress
'Medieval Gown' (front) and
afternoon dresses 'Delphos',
Mariano Fortuny, Venice,
ca. 1910 and 1930,
© *Museum für Kunst und
Gewerbe, Hamburg*

and especially Mariano Fortuny. Influenced both by his study of ancient sculpture and by the theatricality of dance, the former stage designer Fortuny created his famous 'Delphos' gown, a simple, chiton-shaped silk dress with narrow pleats that was styled after the Delphic charioteer and sometimes included an overfold resembling the Greek apoptygma (fig. 5); this dress was manufactured up until the 1950s. The designs of Alix Barton (Madame Grès) were also draped in a Classicizing style, albeit using different materials. Almost like a sculptor, Barton moulded her creations directly to the bodies of her models. Her elaborately wrapped and gathered, voluminous flowing designs, usually of flexible, shimmering silk jersey, made film history as early as the 1930s, when they were worn by Hollywood 'goddesses'. Along with the pleated designs reminiscent of Fortuny's that were developed by Issey Miyake in the 1980s and 1990s for the choreographer William Forsythe and others (known as 'dancing dresses'), sophisticated draping along the lines of the Grès designs is still seen in gowns by couturiers such as Thierry Mugler and Karl Lagerfeld, but these are intended for special occasions rather than everyday wear.

Antiquity continues to be ubiquitous in the beauty ideal widely promoted through advertising, particularly for cosmetics, as well as in photography and films. Its present-day incarnation is still based largely on images from the 1930s and 1940s, as in the glamorous Classicistic arrangements of the fashion photographer Horst P. Horst. His photographic compositions, e.g. a perfume advertisement from 1982, would seem to suggest that all we need today to activate our visual memory of ancient fashion is a few sparingly placed references – for example, a veil, together with a certain physical bearing, reminds us of Nike, the winged statue of Samothrace that took on kinetic form in the serpentine dances of Loie Fuller and came to be the personification of modern progressive thinking as the Rolls Royce hood emblem.

→ Dalmatica; → Maenads; → Paenula; → Pallium;
→ Paludamentum; → Sagum; → Sandals; → Tunica

1 G. Barmeyer, Die Gewandung der monumentalen Skulptur des 12. Jahrhunderts in Frankreich, 1933 2 E. Birbari, Dress in Italian painting 1460–1500, 1975 3 G. Brandstetter, Spiel der Falten. Inszeniertes Plissee bei Mariano Fortuny und Issey Miyake, in: G. Lehnert (ed.), Mode, Weiblichkeit und Modernität, 1998, 165–193 4 Id., Tanz-Lektüren. Körperbilder und Raumfi-

guren der Avantgarde, 1995 5 J. Braun, Die liturgische Gewandung im Occident und Orient nach Ursprung und Entwicklung, Verwendung und Symbolik, 1907 6 B. Doering (ed.) Pompeji an der Alster. Nachleben der Antike um 1800, Hamburg 1995, (Exhibition catalogue) 7 A. Hollander, Seeing through Clothes, 1993 8 R. Kinzel, Die Modemacher. Die Geschichte der Haute Couture, 1990 9 H. Kühnel, Bildwörterbuch der Kleidung und Rüstung, 1992 10 A. Meyer-Winschel, Renaissance und Antike. Beobachtungen über das Aufkommen der antikisierenden Gewandgebung in der Kunst der italienischen Renaissance, 1933 11 St. M. Newton, Fashion in the Age of the Black Prince. A Study of the Years 1340–1365, 1980 12 P. E. Schramm, Herrschaftszeichen und Staatssymbolik. Beiträge zu ihrer Geschichte vom 3. bis zum 16. Jahrhundert, 3 vols., 1954–1956 14 B. Stamm, Das Reformkleid in Deutschland, 1976 15 E. Thiel, Geschichte des Kostüms, 1989 16 A. Warburg, Sandro Botticellis 'Geburt der Venus' und 'Frühling' (1893), in: Id., Ausgewählte Schriften und Würdigungen, D. Wuttke (ed.), 1992, 11–63 17 J. Wilpert, Die Gewandung der Christen der ersten Jahrhunderte, Cologne 1898 18 J. Wirsching, Die Manteltracht im Mittelalter, 1915 19 G. Wittkop-Ménardeau, Unsere Kleidung. Aus der Geschichte der Mode bis zum Jahr 1939, 1985.

ANDREA REICHEL

Fatum see → Fate

Federation

A. Introduction B. Antiquity C. Middle Ages and Early Modern Period D. Religious Federation and Federal Theology E. Theoretical Approaches to a Federal State F. The Federal State and Antiquity-related Argumentation in the 19th Century

A. Introduction

As reflected in this concept's multi-faceted historical breadth, Federation is a many-layered institution. As a basic concept in the history of human socialization, and in legal constitutional history as well, federation is able to represent both social and political organizations [10. 582f.] Federation came about through the 'binding together' of socially or politically definable groups of individuals or organizational units striving for the effective pursuit of common interests by means of such a union. This union can, on the one hand, take place with the preservation of group individualities and organizational autonomy, or, on the other, with a partial surrender of autonomous positions "with recognition of the necessity of greater connections" [15. 7f.]. In modern times this dominant rationale contained in the idea of federation has taken the form of constitutional federalism. In this respect the current common understanding of federation has been derived from its relation to the state. From Antiquity onward, the differentiation of "philosophical and sociological federalism" [5. 13] and federal theology has been based upon the historical development of federative institutions and upon the multiplicity of their conceptual and institutional vari-

ants [7. 462; 10. 584]. This differentiation has also been connected with emerging legal forms that have always made the tradition and action line of federation dependent upon context and difficult to follow in a linear fashion.

B. Antiquity

1. The Greek Poleis 2. Rome

1. The Greek Poleis

For the Greek poleis, federations had great significance for cooperation between states and for purposeful alliances among the city-states. In the most recent scholarship these forms are often understood with reference to the ideas of modern 'federal states' or 'confederations of states' [5. 14ff.; 6. 103–131]. This terminology is only valid to a limited extent since no Greek expression existed for 'federation' in this sense. The connections and unions of the Greek poleis or city-states were highly differentiated according to origin, purpose and form so that appropriate classifications for reception were difficult and the terminology varied widely. Understandably, a unifying collective term for federation was therefore lacking. One can nonetheless speak of functional equivalents. The most important institutions were the *symmachía*, functioning as military defense and war alliances among two or more city-states [2. 191], most probably with a genetic connection to the idea of a [Swiss-style] 'confederation' [28. 149ff.]. The *koiné eiréne* was a peace treaty, usually between two city-states, for the purpose of preserving peace; the *sympoliteía* represented the merger of two or more city-states (*póleis*) into a new governmental unit (*politeía*; *koinón políteuma* – thus in Pol. 2, 41, 6) with civil rights in each state. The legal foundation of this federation was usually a contract. By this means, the *koiné eiréne* and the *symmachía* could also be fused into a single instrument, as in the League of Corinth of 338–337 [21. 3–14]. Independent of the type of merged alliance, there was a structural and legal problem that regularly arose between the individual city-state and the superior federal organs with reference to the federation's scope of authority. This problem had to do with the following: the composition of the allied council's organs and assemblies, the binding nature of their decisions, their executive power, the authority of the federal head, that of the federal military commander and that of the *synedrion* in its role as federal court [21. 12f.; 6. 126–131]. The contracts attempted to govern expressly those items essential to the functioning of the federation, namely, in declarations of autonomy and in the obligation to seek reconciliation by means of an arbitrative court [2.75, 118]. For Aristotle, a new unified polis, i. e., a composite state, could not arise from such alliance contracts if the polis's typical elements of shared superior ruling organs for the creation of a superior and inferior relationship were not present [Aristot. Pol. 1280 a 38]. The contractual nature of a federation pointed in the direction of equal rights and preservation of independence, which, under the influence of prevailing political power relationships, could, nonetheless, also lead to concrete, legal hierarchical structures based on a staged ordering of superior and inferior – in each case according to the type of federation. In scholarly literature, legal and actual equality of federation members has often been used as an indication of the quality of a federal state or confederation [17. 1102ff.; 6. 127]. The various central and federated organizational forms did not possess the ability to bring about uniformity within the corresponding institutions of the federation's individual city-states [11. 45f.]. Their constitutions also remained in force within the federation [5. 17].

2. ROME

The Roman term *foedus* denoted a federative contract with the quality of international law, by means of which a friendly relationship (*amicitia*), peace (*pax*) or a federation (*societas*) could be established [21. 258–266]. The Latin root *foedus* became the basis for the modern federal state's concept of 'federalism', but without displaying its typical structural characteristics. *Foedera* and political alliances were the legal instruments with the help of which Rome established its empire under recognition of the rights and obligations of international law. The *foedus aequum* [21. 46ff.] proceeded from the equal rights of the *civitates foederati* that were bound to Rome in this manner. According to the particular shape of their contract, each of the *civitates foederati* maintained its own institutions (administration, courts, taxes). In contrast, the *foedus iniquum*, in the way of a contract with a client [state], was geared to the recognition of Rome's domination ('... foedere comprehensum est, ut is populus alterius populi maiestatem comiter conservaret ... ut intellegatur alterum populum superiorem esse', Dig. 49,15,7,1). Nonetheless, when shaped by the power-conscious, "softstyle" of Roman officialdom, even the *foedus aequum* could stipulate a dependency for the *foederati*. These sorts of contractual relationships were typical for Latin and Italian city federations to the time of their dissolution. Outside of Italy these federations still remained common until the first century BC; however, they were increasingly replaced by a status of the cities that rested on a *senatus consultum*. This configuration offered Rome legally strengthened possibilities for manipulation. The goal of the *foedora*, pursued by these instruments, was oriented toward peace and/or the military assistance of the *foederati* and command of the foreign policy field [23. 158ff.]. Viewed in light of Rome's dominance, shared 'federative' institutions (federation assemblies, courts, etc.) were unnecessary. Their typical problems of rivalry at various levels of authority and of decision-making did not belong to the core of Roman governmental practice and policy.

C. MIDDLE AGES AND EARLY MODERN PERIOD

In the semantic field of *Bund* ('federation'), the term *Einung* (*Aynung, verpuntnus*) ['unification', 10. 583–586] constituted the dominant German-language equivalent of *foedus* and *confederatio*. This unification was a consensual agreement empowered to make law or to establish constitutionally federated organizations in both the state and societal spheres. Within the empire, unification determined the constitutional relationship between the empire's monarchic head and the estates. Empire and federal organizations did not stand in opposition. Instead, federative agreements constituted an element of the imperial constitution itself within the imperial alliance's complex system, even when they, corresponding to differing federal goals, could produce oppositional or separatist positions. Reflecting the view of the 19th cent., Gierke even went so far as to confer on the unity of the Middle Ages, the – missed – chance to "recapture the lost unity by following the federative path" [7. I 299, 458]. Federation was an ambivalent instrument of legal and political structural possibilities, and often subject to imperial or, alternatively, electoral/feudal agreement [29. 310 § 6, 7]. Unification's many forms included associations bound by oath, coalitions, federations, confederations, etc., all based on the treaty principle. For the most part they display the characteristics of the *foedus aequale* and the federal aims of Antiquity: peace, military assistance, protection, trade, preservation of the legal and other interests of the parties involved. City leagues, aristocratic federations, chivalric societies, clerical unions, religious federations, peasant unions, associations – all belonged to the major forms of unification containing federal organizational forms. Some of these included the regional beginnings of a federal state (Swiss Confederation, the United Netherlands) [27. 108; 7. 514ff.]. The institutionalization and development of solid organizational and decision-making structures remained uneven. Arbitration tribunals, joint council assemblies, executive procedures, tax systems and organizational subdivisions have been documented and have substantiated the general analogous, structural problematic of federations, albeit without specific reference to ancient models. In those imperial circles that had been expanded to constitutional institutions, the problem of a multi-leveled structure became clear, especially so in the "special foedus und Association" (1691), which was conceived as a defensive league, and whose basic federative traits corresponded to the empire's constitutional structure [13. 23ff.]. The *Partikular Kreistage* ('regional parliaments') retained the right of final decision before their superior body, the association convention, was allowed to pass the association recess. The parliaments possessed both embassy rights and the 'ius foederis et armorum '("the right to form alliances and to be armed") neither of which conferred on them the quality of a state or a federation of states since they did not have their own independent legal authority. Beginning in 1648, the 'ius faciendi inter se et cum exteris foedera' ("the right to form alliances among themselves and with others") was granted to the imperial estates as part of the imperial constitution (*Instrumentum pacis*

Osnabrugense, Art. VIII § 2). This law also established sovereignty within the imperial coalition.

D. RELIGIOUS FEDERATION AND FEDERAL THEOLOGY

In Calvinistic Protestantism of the 16th and 17th cents., the idea of the relationship between God and man attained great significance for the political theory of treaties, both for the social contract and for the contract between ruler and ruled. Thomas Aquinas spoke of the 'foedus amicitiae hominis ad Deum' ("the bond of friendship between Man and God": Tertia pars Summae Theologiae, Suppl.: quaestio 65, art. 4). Accordingly, the political community could be understood in analogy to the religious community as a bond between God and man [16. 177]. The members of this bond of grace–the *confoederati*–were, according to Olevianus (1585), the 'veri regni Christi cives' ("the true citizens of Christ's Kingdom") [16. 166]. A further analogy in the relationship between God and man, and in that between ruler and people as well, existed in Roman Law's common contractual characteristic, the 'mutua obligatio' ("the mutual obligation") [16. 165]. This secularized bond concept was seen as an expansion of the Greek theory of state that promoted the "recognition of composite systems of order" [5.33]. This theory of contracts played a central role in the social theory (*consociatio*) of Johannes Althusius (*Politica methodice digesta*, 1603).

E. THEORETICAL APPROACHES TO A FEDERAL STATE

With regard to higher and lower positions within a hierarchy, that is the formation of a federal state with a main government and member states, the Roman legal concepts of *foedera aequalia* and *inaequalia* served as a starting point. For Bodin, the first item was the impossibility of abandoning sovereignty on account of the foedus aequale, as he documented with Greek examples: 'In omni ... foedere ... iura maiestatis cuique principi populove salva sint, oportet' [3. 110]. This position does not exclude the possibility that an identical total state could be created from all individual states ('ex omnibus civitatibus eadem respublica') if, using the example of the Achaic League, the *foederatae civitates* joined in a unified sovereignty [3. 116]. Even the creation of joint public organs, as in the Ionic League of cities, did not lead to a loss of sovereignty. For Bodin, the federation had absolutely no character as a state but rather merely confederated sovereign states or city-states. For Althusius the state was created by means of the contractual 'vinculum consensus' ("bond of agreement") [1. Cap. IX, 88f.]. No particular concept of a federal state follows from this bond, but the possibility nonetheless exists for a 'plena or non-plena confederatio' (a "total or partial confederation"). In the *plena confederatio* or *consociatio* the members are quasi-united in one and the same body ('quasi in unum idemque corpus') while in the *non-plena confederatio* the

members maintain their sovereignty. The Greek *symmachia* is an example of the latter. It is divided, based on the Roman model. into *foedus eaquum* and *impar* with a ranking hierarchy that under the auspices of Cod. Iust. 5,59,5,2 ('quod omnes similiter tangit') [1.133 f.] allows binding conclusions to be reached at the federation members' own meetings (conventibus confederatorum sociorum) [1. 337–342]. Even if the "model of the Greek polis" is still perceptible, a more highly differentiated interpretation of internally-structured state entities becomes evident [5. 37]. The Greek city leagues repeatedly provided historical models for analyzing Roman law's 'conventiones aequales aut inaequales' (Grotius, De iure belli ac pacis, Lib. II, cap. 15, VI; Lib. I, cap. 3, XXI). Here the *symmachia* often appears as the reference for the *foedus offensivum* by means of which Athenians and Spartans united their federated allies 'sub ipsorum ducatu' ("under their own leadership") (U. Huber, Institutionis respublicae liber singularis, Franequerae 1698, 190f.).

In Besold's case, efforts to explain the phenomenon of the Old Empire's 'composite state' by using the 'federalist idea' (Hoenius, Ludolph Hugo) lead to the *civitas composita* [8. 226–263, 245f.; 10. 629–635; 5. 37–46]. In this instance Besold employed the aims of Roman law's *foedera* and their categories *amicitia*, *pacificatio* and *societas* [10.630]. As a defining concept, the Old Empire was problematic when discussing the development of federal-state structures. 'Experience and history' constituted the test criterium [18. 21]. The traditional structure problematic of higher and lower ranking–as well as that of "allied states" shared and limited *majestas* ('sovereignty') [18. 25]–is therefore treated more on the basis of contemporary constitutional examples than according to ancient models (Corpus Helveticum, Respublica Belgarum unita etc.). On the basis of empirical evidence, however, the Artistotelian theory of government is rejected as irrelevant for the purpose of defining the quality of the Old Empire's government (Leibniz: 'nudum foedus, unio, systema foederatorum; Pufendorf: foedus systema producens'; Pütter: 'systema foederatorum civitatum') [10. 630–633].

F. THE FEDERAL STATE AND ANTIQUITY-RELATED ARGUMENTATION IN THE 19TH CENTURY

As Gierke noted (1902), for the developmental history of state and federation – in the face of a contemporary battle about a federal re-organization of the Empire –, it depended "less upon that which the Greeks and Romans had thought about state and law and more upon those of their thoughts that lived on in transmitted tradition and those that they were believed to have thought" [8. 327]. Political and constitutional discussions about the advantages of a federation of states versus a federal state and also about the precise description of both forms were carried on with only peripheral reference to ancient models. In connection with discussions before the Congress of Vienna in 1814, Schleiermacher took up once again the Aristotelian theory of government, a theory that he described as a gradual development leading to monarchy. He called for a 'federative state' and at the same time he regarded the mergers of the Greek poleis into state federations as exemplary but deficient federative forms [5.68f.; 10. 649f.]. With a philo-Hellenistic emphasis, Welcker championed in 1834 the Achaic League as a "national federal state" with "sovereign leadership and the decision-making power in all the most important national affairs" [26. 195]. Waitz (1852) and Swoboda (1914) employed the Greek city-states and their allies as illustrations of federative order in connection with the question as to the extent that these (*Sympoliteia, Koinon*) could be untilized as models for a modern federal state [15.18–22]. Swoboda emphasized not only the analogies between the Greek leagues and the modern federal republic but also the partial identity of their criteria for a federal state. In light, however, of the Roman Empire's centralized structure, the Roman *foedera* were unsuitable for such an interpretation and appropriation of ancient institutions.

→ Amicitia; → Foedus; → Koine Eirene; → Pax; → Polis; → Societas; → Symmachia; → Sympoliteia
→ Citizen; → Sacrum Imperium

1 J. Althusius, Politica methodice digesta, C. J. Friedrich (ed.), 1932　2 H. Bengtson (ed.), Die Verträge der griechisch-römischen Welt von 700 bis 338 v.Chr. (= Die Staatsverträge des Altertums II), 1962　3 J. Bodin, De republica libri sex, Lib. I, Cap. VII, Francofurti 1622　4 S. Brie, Der Bundesstaat I, 1874　5 E. Deuerlein, Föderalismus. Die historischen und philosophischen Grundlagen des föderativen Prinzips, 1972　6 V. Ehrenberg, The Greek State, ²1974　7 O. v. Gierke, Das deutsche Genossenschaftsrecht I: Rechtsgeschichte der deutschen Genossenschaft, 1868 (repr. 1954)　8 Id., Johannes Althusius, ⁵1958　9 H. H. Horn, Foederati, 1930　10 R. Koselleck, s.v. Bund, Bündnis, Föderalismus, Bundesstaat, in: Geschichtliche Grundbegriffe, Bd. 1, 582–671　11 J. A. O. Larsen, Representative Government in Greek and Roman History, 1966　12 A. Laufs, Der Schwäbische Kreis, 1971　13 H. Mohnhaupt, Die verfassungsrechtliche Einordnung der Reichskreise in die Reichsorganisation, in: K. O. Frhr. v. Aretin (ed.), Der Kurfürst von Mainz und die Kreisassoziationen 1648–1746, 1975, 1–29　14 Mommsen, Staatsrecht　15 H. Nawiasky, Note sur le concept Foedéralisme, in: Politeia I, 1948/49　16 G. Oestreich, Die Idee des religiösen Bundes und die Lehre vom Staatsvertrag, in: Id., Geist und Gestalt des frühmodernen Staates, 1969　17 W. Schwahn, s.v. Symmachia, RE 4 A, 1102–1134　18 J. St. Pütter, Beyträge zum Teutschen Staats- und Fürsten-Rechte I, Göttingen 1777　19 A. Randelzhofer, Völkerrechtliche Aspekte des Heiligen Römischen Reiches nach 1648, 1967　20 F. Schleiermacher, Über die Begriffe der verschiedenen Staatsformen (1814), in: Sämtliche Werke, III. Abt., Bd. 2, Berlin 1838, 246–286　21 H. H. Schmitt (ed.), Die Verträge der griechisch-römischen Welt von 338 bis 200 v.Chr. (= Die Staatsverträge des Alt. III), 1969　22 G. Schrenk, Gottesreich und Bund im Älteren Protestantismus, vornehmlich bei Johannes Coccejus, 1923　23 R. Schulz, Die Entwicklung des römischen Völkerrechts im 4. und 5. Jahrhundert n.Chr., 1993　24 H. Swoboda, Die griechischen Bünde und der moderne Bundesstaat. Prager Rektoratsrede vom 20. Oktober 1914, in: Die feierliche Inauguration der K.K. Dt. Karl-Ferdinands-Univ. in Prag ... 1914/15 ..., 30–62　25 G. Waitz, Das Wesen des Bundesstaates. Reden und Betrachtungen von J. v. Radowitz (GS II), Berlin 1852, Rezension, in: Allg. Monatsschrift für Wiss. und Lit. 1853, 494–530　26 C. Welcker, s.v. Achaiischer Bund, in: Staats-Lex. I, 1834, 185–199　27 D. Willoweit, Deutsche Verfassungsgeschichte, 1997　28 F. R. Wüst, Amphiktyonie, Eidgenossenschaft, Symmachie, in: Historia 3, 1954/55, 149ff.　29 K. Zeumer, Quellensammlung zur Geschichte der deutschen Reichsverfassung in Mittelalter und Neuzeit (Wahlkapitulation 1519), ²1913.　HEINZ MOHNHAUPT

Festive Processions/Trionfi

A. Introduction　B. Renaissance　C. Baroque
D. Around 1800　E. 19th and 20th Centuries

A. Introduction

Festive Processions or *trionfi* are processions of vehicles, based upon the Classical triumph, bearing representations of allegorical, historical, mythological or religious themes or figures in a visual, literary or staged form. The triumph of the god Dionysus in India, recorded in mythology, was the model for the honouring of victorious generals, as was carried out in the triumphs of the Roman emperors [7.90–116]. The *carrus navalis*, part of the festivals of Dionysus, may be seen as the root of later triumphs, and the Dionysian triumph lives on in the present in carnival celebrations and wine festivals. The military aspects of the ceremony survived in fragmentary form into the Christian Middle Ages either as ceremonials associated with a ruler, or re-directed toward Christ [10]. There were increased appearances in times when there was either an interest in the Classical period, or when a political power-base wished to draw a connection between itself and the Roman Empire. Thus Frederick II made triumphal entries with explicitly Classical allusions into Jerusalem in 1229 on the occasion of his self-coronation, and into Cremona after his victory in 1237.

B. Renaissance

The Italian designation *trionfi,* which spread from the 15th cent. onward and was used mostly in the plural form, implies an increase in art, literature and festival staging, and also indicates Italy as the starting point for this popularisation.

The idea of a triumph first spread in Italy through the medium of poetry. Dante describes the triumph of the Church (*Purgatorio* 29) as well as the triumphal procession of Christ and the Virgin (*Paradiso* 23). However, Petrarch's allegorical vision *Triumphi* (1348–1356), in which, in a clear evocation of the Roman ceremony, Amor initially celebrates a triumph, had a greater effect. But Amor is overcome by *Castità* ('purity'), which is in turn defeated by *Morte* ('death'), which is overcome by *Fama*, which itself is subject to *Tempo*;

Fig. 1: *Alfonso d'Aragonas' entry into Naples in 1443*; Florentine cassone, 1452, *in private ownership*

over all of these triumphs the Christian *Eternità*. Although Petrarch only describes Amor as progressing on a chariot, the many illustrations from the 15th and 16th cents. (book illumination, prints, cassoni-decorations, tapestries) show virtually all of the personifications on vehicles of some sort, which seems at least in part to reflect a genuine performance practice [13]. In addition to the literary adaptation of the idea we may note among other works Flavio Biondo's *Roma triumphans* (1457–59, Venice 1511) [5. 90–112] and later Onofrio Panvinio's *De triumpho commentarius* (Venice 1571) as examples of antiquarian examination of the Classical heritage.

The first Classical triumph of a ruler in this period was staged with the entry of Alfonso of Aragon into Naples in 1443. The king rode on a ceremonial chariot drawn by four horses into the city through a breach in the walls, but dispensed with the laurel crown and the escort of prisoners. The members of the Florentine merchant community honoured the king with a procession of *tableaux vivants*, in which, among others, Caesar and Fortuna-Occasio appeared [9]. The event was preserved in idealised form on the triumphal arch of the Castel Nuovo in Naples. A Florentine *cassone* (1452), on which the *tableaux vivants* push the actual recipient of the triumph to the image border, offers us another view of the events (fig. 1).

The reception of the Classical triumph operates on two levels: in the adoption of elements of the ceremonies of the triumph; and in the introduction of Classical figures in *tableaux vivants* or portrayed by actors, mostly placed upon wagons or portable stages. Both elements were customary in later triumphs, although the emphasis varies, and towards the end of the 15th cent. it is the erection of temporary triumphal architecture which increases in importance. All aspects of the triumphal procession are affected: the entry of rulers, wedding ceremonies, tournaments, city celebrations, religious processions, the *Possesso* of the Pope in Rome, and carnival processions. Special forms develop in different regions, such as the water-trionfi in Venice. Further, the catafalques erected for funerals also show a relationship with the triumph, and ceremonies as such could also take on a triumphal character. In the exequies for Ferdinand the Catholic in 1516 an empty triumphal chariot was part of the procession, and after his death in battle Guido Villa was brought back to Ferrara in 1648 in a triumphal procession set up as if for a living person [15. 84–91]. In the context of court banquets, displayed table decorations found application as *trionfi*, the material either made to last, or edible (mostly confectionery), or ephemeral (serviettes). Depending upon the context, the *trionfi* thematised subjects or figures from Classical myth and history, as with the procession for Paul II into Rome in 1466 [5. 126–131]; allegories, as for the victorious return of Julius II to Rome in 1507 [5. 320–326]; but also religious themes, as in Crema in 1469 when the Madonna and Child were carried by apostles in an Offerta-procession [9]. Makers of the materials sometimes included important artists like Pontormo, who designed the carriages for the Florence carnival in 1513 [11].

Trionfi are encountered in literature and the plastic arts with the same range of themes, being both influenced by and influencing aspects of the public performances. Songs like the *canzone* " *Trionfo di Bacco e Arianna* " of Lorenzo de Medici served to accompany Florentine carnival processions. In the *Hypnerotomacchia Poliphili* (Venice, 1499), which is illustrated with woodcuts, six triumphal processions are described, the substance of which is in each case influenced by antiquarian knowledge and by contemporary festival practice. Four triumphs represent loves of Jupiter, with the fifth being the triumph of Vertumnus and Pomona. The high point is the triumph of Amor, who appears – in an inversion of Petrarch's version – as the real triumphant (fig 2). The triumph as a theme is of course frequent in panegyric writing, as in Giovanni Santi's *La vita e le gesta di Federico di Montefeltro* (1474–1488) [14. 329]. The Dominican monk Savonarola, however, sketched out a *Triumphus Crucis*, in which Christ appears with the tokens of the Passion on a triumphal chariot accompanied by apostles, prophets, martyrs and so on.

For the plastic arts the following may stand as representatives for the adaptation of different subjects: the triumphs by Piero della Francesca on the versos of the portraits of Federico da Montefeltro and Battista Sforza (ca. 1474); the planetary deities in the depictions of the months in the frescos of the Schifanoia-palace in Ferrara (1469–1471); Mantegna's nine-part *Triumph of Caesar* (after 1486), which was used as a festival decoration in 1501; and the monumental woodcut by

Fig. 2: *Hypnerotomachia Poliphili*: The Triumph of Amor, 1499

Fig. 3: *Maximilian's chariot* by Albrecht Dürer

Fig. 4: A centrepiece with trionfi by Pierre Paul Sevin, 1667

Fig. 5: *Triomphe de Voltaire le 11 Juillet 1791*,
copperplate engraving by Berthault based on Prieur

Fig. 6: Trotsky on the chariot of Imperialism, Leningrad 1930

Titian, *Trionfo della Fede* (1510), which was probably produced under the influence of Savonarola's work.

The festival procession in Italy aided the popularisation both of Classical gods and other important figures, and also architectonic elements and decorative forms. This mediatory role was also instrumental north of the Alps with the start of the 16th cent. in the spread of the→ RENAISSANCE. There A. Dürer's monumental series of woodcuts *Der Triumphzug Kaiser Maximilians* (1515–1518), and in particular the triumphal chariot of Maximilian, was inspired by the Italian *trionfi* (fig. 3)[1. 292–331]. In France, in the Netherlands and in England, too, 16th- cent. festivals were modelled on the Italian *trionfi*, and in each case locally available elements were combined with the imported ideas. Thus in the Netherlands in 1549 with the entry of Philip II into Antwerp, the traditional *tableaux vivants* were combined with triumphal arches, and the *ommegang* was presented in Heemskerk's 1561 etchings as *Trionfi all'antica* [6 vol. 2. 359–388].

C. BAROQUE
The extravagance in the development of the triumphal procession reached a new dimension with the absolutist monarchs, notably at the *entrée solennelle* of Louis XIV into Paris in 1660. At the head of a series of imposing examples of triumphal architecture, reproduced in Troncon's report of the festival, stood a triumphal arch as a quotation of the arch of Constantine in Rome in proportions and decoration, providing a link also with its metaphor of a national cult of the sun. Following this, the first permanent triumphal arches would be erected in Paris under Louis XIV [12].

Baroque festival celebrations made use of the triumph in all the variations seen already in the Renaissance. The increased expenditure is reflected in the designs by Pierre Paul Sevin for table decorations (fig. 4). Triumphs play a part too in performances, mostly with music and ballets, like the Italian *intermezzi* [17. 126–152] or the English *masques*, with which, as with the *Coelum Britannicum* in 1634, the Stuart monarchy celebrated itself. In these performances, in contrast with those of the Renaissance, the rulers themselves could assume roles. Thus in Dresden in 1695 Augustus the Strong appeared in the procession of the gods on a triumphal chariot as Mercury [18. 128].

As in the Renaissance, important artists were called upon as designers: Rubens, in whose paintings several triumphs can be found, designed in 1635 the *Introitus Ferdinandi* [6 vol. 3. 173–186].

D. AROUND 1800
The French Revolution afforded considerable significance to festival productions which were deliberately disseminated through reports, decretals and graphic media. Jacques Louis David was responsible for the design, and he drew his inspiration from the description of Classical celebrations. The *Triomphe de Voltaire* of 1791 brought the ashes of the poet, who had been buried outside Paris in 1778, in a triumphal procession to his acceptance into the Pantheon (fig. 5). Voltaire appeared not only lying in state on a bier above which a Victoria held a victor's crown, but also as a seated statue, surrounded by standards bearing the titles of his works, accompanied by delegates from all classes and levels of education [3. 35–44].

With later festivals, people seemed to have tried to move explicitly away from ceremonials of the ruler, although the structure of the triumph nevertheless confirmed in this inversion some elements of its significance.

In the celebration of the constitution on 10 August, 1793, choreographed by David, the procession passed through six stages. The second was a triumphal arch decorated with a relief of guillotined heads, in honour of those women who had forced the king to leave Versailles and make a shameful *entrée* into Paris [3. 57–84]. Under Napoleon the relationship to Classical Antiquity gained a new dimension in 1798 when looted Italian works of art were put on show in a triumphal entry procession [3. 126–128].

E. 19TH AND 20TH CENTURIES

In the 19th and early 20th cents. triumphs are encountered in the context of historical processions which, in contradistinction to the courtly festivals, had the stamp of the bourgeoisie in their makeup and were characterised by nationalism. An impetus was provided by jubilees (of the founding of towns or universities, shooting-matches and so on), carnivals or artists' processions. The theme was usually an historical one matching the occasion: political events, the honouring of 'national heroes' such as Gutenberg or Dürer, or of self-representation of societies or professional/trade groups. Allegory and myth are rare, as in the case of the festival 'railway-carriage' decorated by Hans Markat in 1879 for the silver wedding anniversary of the Emperor and Empress in Vienna, in which the couple is represented as a fire-god and a water-nymph [8. 34].

In the wake of the colonisation and conversion to Christianity of lands beyond Europe, new festive and ceremonial structures were imported. In 1971 an historical procession was organised in Persepolis in honour of 2500 years of the Persian empire [8. 164]. Echoes of the *trionfi* are found in South American carnival processions, but also in the reception of Miss Universe in 1998 in her homeland of Venezuela, when she travelled through the city on a triumphal carriage escorted by the National Guard. The medium of the triumph is found in the 20th cent. in the most heterogeneous ideological and artistic contexts: as part of the propaganda for the Russian revolution in 1930 there is a carriage representing the triumph of imperialism upon which Trotzky is leaping [16. fig. 186] (fig. 6); so too in the service of German → NATIONAL SOCIALISM with the day of German art and the Amazon festival in Munich [8. 50–56]; or as part of a political ceremony at the inauguration of an American president with the procession of representatives of all the states of the union in their ceremonial cars; and in popular culture, as with the Berlin love-parade, in which the loudspeaker has taken on the role of the triumphant himself. → Dionysus; → Triumph, Triumphal procession

1 B. WISCH, S. SCOTT MUNSHOWER (eds.), 'All the World's a Stage ...', Art and Pageantry in the Renaissance and Baroque, Papers in Art History from The Pennsylvania State University VI, 2 vols., 1990 (vol. 1, 359–385 Bibliography on the Triumph from Antiquity to the Early Modern Period)   2 J. BERNS, Die Herkunft des Automobils aus Himmelstrionfo und Höllenmaschine, 1996   3 M.-L. BIVER, Fêtes révolutionaires à Paris, 1979   4 G.

CARANDENTE, I trionfi del primo rinascimento, 1963   5 F. CRUCIANI, Teatro nel Rinascimento. Roma 1450–1550, 1983   6 J. JACQUOT (ed.), Les fêtes de la Renaissance, 3 vols., 1956, 1960, 1975, (conference proceedings)   7 M. GESING, Triumph des Bacchus. Triumphidee und bacchische Darstellungen in der italienischen Renaissance im Spiegel der Antikenrezeption, 1988   8 W. HARTMANN, Der historische Festzug. Seine Entstehung und Entwicklung im 19. und 20. Jahrhundert, 1976   9 PH. HELAS, Lebende Bilder in der italienischen Festkultur des 15. Jahrhunderts, 1999   10 M. McCORMICK, Eternal Victory. Triumphal Rulership in Late Antiquity, Byzantium, and the Late Medieval West, 1986   11 B. MITCHELL, Italian Civic Pageantry in the High Renaissance. A Descriptive Bibliography of Triumphal Entries and Selected other Festivals for State Occasions, 1979   12 K. MÖSENEDER, Zeremoniell und monumentale Poesie. Die 'Entreé solennelle' Ludwig XIV. 1660 in Paris, 1983   13 K. EISENBICHLER, A. JANNUCI (eds.), Petrarch's Triumphs. Allegory and Spectacle, 1990   14 A. PINELLI, Feste e Trionfi: Continuità e metamorfosi di un tema, in: S. SETTIS (ed.), Memoria dell'antico nell'arte italiana, vol. 2: I generi e i temi ritrovati, 1985, 281–352   15 L. POPELKA, Castrum doloris oder 'trauriger Schauplatz'. Untersuchungen zu Entstehung und Wesen ephemerer Architektur, 1994   16 V. TOLSTOY, I. BIBIKOVA, C. COOKE (eds.), Streetart of the Revolution. Festivals and Celebrations in Russia 1918–1933, 1990   17 R. STRONG, Art and Power. Renaissance Festivals 1450–1650, 1973, ²1984   18 H. WATANABE-O'KELLY, Triumphal Shews. Tournaments at German-speaking Courts in their European Context 1560–1730, 1992   19 W. WEISBACH, Trionfi, 1919.

PHILINE HELAS

Feudal Law

A. TERMS   B. THE EARLY MIDDLE AGES   C. THE HIGH MIDDLE AGES   D. SOURCES   E. LATE MIDDLE AGES/EARLY MODERN PERIOD

A. TERMS

Feudal law (*ius feodale*) (FL) describes legal norms relating to the medieval feudal system in general and, more specifically, the feudal relationship between lord and vassal. The German word *Lehen* ('fief') is derived from Old High German *lehan* ('loan', 'lend') and describes the transfer of economically useful land (property law, office, etc.,) against the performance of services. From the late 9th cent., the Middle Latin term *feodum/feudum* was also used. In Latin texts *lehan*, *lehen*, *len* is routinely called *beneficium*. The two terms existed side-by-side for centuries with meanings that cannot be precisely delimited. The legal concept of the feudal relationship was created from Roman legal and Germanic components. Roman law provided a technical term with *beneficium* (e.g., for transferring public land to be used by a municipality). Furthermore, there was the *commendatio*, which meant the transfer of a client's affairs for settlement to a patron against a service of gratitude. Another source is seen in 'vassaldom' (from Middle Latin *vassus*, *vasallus*; Celtic *gwas* – 'servant'). However, a characteristic of the Middle Latin feudal relationship is that the vassal kept his free status

A special form of land rent (*precaria*) is known from Late Antiquity. In this legal form, Church property was bestowed against rent payments to the Church. Finally, a root of Germanic provenance is assumed to be the lord's following, as it developed in the Gallo-Roman region (*antrustiones* or 'followers'). The associated oath (of fidelity) would be typical of the close personal bond between lord and vassal in the Middle Ages.

B. THE EARLY MIDDLE AGES

Medieval feudalism arose during the 6th to 8th cents. in the Frankish empire from the close association of these elements. The first legal principles that developed in tandem were the return of the benefice, the end of the vassal status with the lord's death (*Herrenfall*), and the withdrawal of the fief (*Felonie*) if the duty of service was violated (contumacious vassal). In the Carolingian period, the heredity of fiefs, multiple vassalage and the linkage of fiefs to sovereign offices can be identified. The feudal system spread from the Franconian empire to its successor states and beyond these to all of Europe.

C. THE HIGH MIDDLE AGES

In the course of the Middle Ages, a multitude of regional and local FLs developed. Feudalism and FL flowered in the 12th cent. The inclusion of the Church and the tribal duchies in the imperial feudal association was critical. The closing of the status of the imperial princes to outsiders and the military ranking (*Heerschildordnung*) are also products of the FL policies of the Hohenstaufen dynasty. More recent research disputes the existence of a requirement to surrender a fief (the king's duty to surrender a prince's fief a year and a day after it had fallen to him) in favour of a hereditary and contractual duty to surrender the fief [5]. The tendency towards a completely feudal state is unmistakable under Emperor Frederick I Barbarossa, but was not able to completely impose itself. By contrast, in France and England a complete feudalization with the king as supreme feudal lord (*Nulle terre sans seigneur*; *homo ligius*) succeeded. While in the German empire the personal bond was initially important, the emphasis shifted in the High Middle Ages to the material aspect of feudalism. The vassal no longer served because of the fief but for the fief or from the fief. Refusal of the service requirement could result in a withdrawal of the fief but not separate punishment (as, for example, in France).

D. SOURCES

Initially, FL only existed as unwritten customary law. Probably still in the 11th cent., the *consuetudines feudorum* were fixed in writing in the Lombard kingdom, which became part of the *Regnum Francorum* in 774. These were the private legal records of legal scholars that, as part of Lombard law, were treated with the scientific methodology and terminology of Roman law. Under the title of *Libri feudorum*, they had become the most important source of FL in the Middle Ages. Their textual development was completed about 1250 after several editions and amendments as the *Recensio vulgata* or the *Accursian gloss*. Even earlier (early 13th cent.) the *Libri feudorum* had been inserted as the tenth *Collatio* of the *Authenticum* into the *Corpus Iuris*. The law schools of Pavia and Bologna (since the 12th cent.) profiled themselves as early European centres of learned FL. The jurists there succeeded in tying the construct of the fief, which was unknown in Antiquity, to Roman law although the latter had no parallel because of the notion of undivided → PROPERTY (*dominium*). The legal institution of hereditary land leases appeared comparable (*emphyteusis*). Medieval jurists saw two types of property in the fief (Dig. 6, 3, 1, 1): a *dominium utile* of the vassal and a *dominium directum* of the lord. In the course of the reception of foreign laws, Lombard law and the doctrine of divided property entered the medieval laws of Europe and became the subject of further teaching and scientific treatment at the universities. The earliest version of the *Libri feudorum* already linked to a FL of emperor Conrad II of 1037 (MGH DD Ko. II., 244) that had been passed for Upper Italy but soon was generally recognized. It strengthened the position of vassals by making the withdrawal of the fief dependent on a violation of duties and a court judgement that was appealable to the emperor. Also, the inheritance of the fief by the son, grandson or brother of the vassal was fixed. Additional imperial FLs were issued in 1136 (MGH DD L.III., 105), 1154 and 1158 (MGH Const. I, 148, 177). They pursued securing imperial service, suppression of the sale of fiefs, a prohibition of the division of duchies and counties (and marches), and exclusion of the emperor as the addressee of the oath of fidelity. In Germany, private legal collections relating to FL were created during the High Middle Ages (FL Books). The earliest and most important that were largely uninfluenced by Roman Law was the FL of the *Sachsenspiegel*, which probably was preceded by the Latin *auctor vetus de beneficiis* (1221/1224). About the middle of the 14th cent., the *Sachsenspiegel*'s FL was provided with a gloss to harmonize it with the received Roman and canon law. Special feudal courts staffed with vassals decided in FL disputes. Their judgements supplemented the regulations of FL. Although Lombard FL was initially only intended as a supplement, it became dominant in the German empire with its vassal-friendly provisions.

E. LATE MIDDLE AGES/EARLY MODERN PERIOD

The study of FL (German: *Feudistik*) is considered to be the root of public law. Already in the High Middle Ages, the doctrine of *regalia* was derived from a passage of the *Libri feudorum* [10. 167]. The territorialization of FL recognizable in the Late Middle Ages contributed to the formation of territorial states. From that time, imperial and territorial FLs must be distinguished. By linking the feudal systems with the internal condition of the territories, important elements of early modern states (organization of bureaucracies and court, parliaments and diets) formed. The development of the authoritarian state in the 17th/18th century finally displaced FL. As a result, FL lost in significance for the territorial states and with emphasis on its material component became considered part of private law. However, FL remained relevant to the German empire until its end in 1806.

→ Beneficium; → Cliens, clientes; → Commendatio; → Corpus iuris; → Emphyteusis; → Precarium

SOURCES   1 K. LEHMANN (ed.), Das langobardische Lehnrecht, 1896 (repr. 1971)   2 K. A. ECKHARDT (ed.), Sachsenspiegel: Lehnrecht. (MGH Fontes iur. Germanici antiqui N. S. I/2) ³1973 (Engl. MARIA DOBOZY (trans.), The Saxon Mirror: A Sachsenspiegel of the Fourteenth Century, 1999)   3 K. A. ECKHARDT (ed.), Auctor vetus de beneficiis (MGH Fontes iur. Germanici antiqui N. S. II), 1964/1966
LITERATURE   4 F. L. GANSHOF, Qu'est-ce que la féodalité, ⁵1972 (Engl. P. GRIERSON (trans.), Feudalism, ³1964)   5 W. GOEZ, Der Leihezwang. Eine Untersuchung zur Geschichte des deutschen Lehnrechtes, 1962   6 K. F. KRIEGER, Die Lehnshoheit der deutschen Könige im Spätmittelalter (ca. 1200–1437), 1979   7 H. MITTEIS, Lehnrecht und Staatsgewalt, 1933 (repr. 1971)   8 Id., Der Staat des hohen Mittelalters, ⁹1974 (Engl. H. F. ORTON (trans.), The State in the Middle Ages, 1975)   9 S. REYNOLDS, Fiefs and Vassals. The Medieval Evidence Reinterpreted, 1994   10 M. STOLLEIS, Geschichte des öffentlichen Rechts in Deutschland I, 1988   11 P. WEIMAR, Legistische Literatur der Glossatorenzeit, in: Hdb. der Quellen und Lit. der neueren europ. PrRG I, 1973, 155 ff.

ADDITIONAL BIBLIOGRAPHY S. PAINTER, Feudalism and Liberty, 1988 (1961); Id., The Rise of the Feudal Monarchies, 1982 (1951); Id., Studies in the History of the English Feudal Barony, 1980 (1964); C. STEPHENSON, Mediaeval Feudalism, 1993 (1942)   HEINER LÜCK

Figured Poem
A. INTRODUCTION   B. MIDDLE AGES   C. EARLY MODERN PERIOD   D. CONCRETE POETRY

A. INTRODUCTION
In Antiquity, three forms of the Figured Poem (FP) were developed: 1. the mimetic acrostic poem invented by members of the Koian Writers' League around or after 300 BC: Simias of Rhodes in the form of wings, an egg and a hatchet; Theocritus in the verse measures of a syrinx; and Dosiadas of Crete in the contours of two altars [4]. Evidence of correlations with figurative epigraphics, magical words, griphos poetry and verse experiments can be found just as much as the influence of orphism; 2. the reading permutative crossword labyrinth (Cubus) encountered on *tabulae iliacae* of the Roman Imperial period, on the Stele of Moschion and in a floor labyrinth in the Reparatus Basilica in Orléansville; 3. the steganographic grid poem that was invented by Optatianus Porfyrius at the court of Constantine the Great and characterized by a quadratic base text of isogrammatic hexameters in which are recorded *versus intexti* in the form of geometric figures

(e.g. rhombus, coordinate system), oversized letters (e.g. monogram of Christ, names of emperors) and stylized objects (e.g. palms, ship); the poet also wrote acrostic poems in the form of a flute of Pan, altar and water organ [2].

B. MIDDLE AGES
In the Middle Ages, Greek acrostic poems were handed down in the *Anthologia Palatina* and in manuscripts of the Bucolic writers; the Byzantine edition of Manuel Holobolos (ca. 1240–1284) has pictorial ornamentation. The crossword labyrinth type is to be found in manuscripts of the Merovingian period (e.g. ms. 219, Bern, Burgar Library, fol. 76v). A tablet at the Church of San Juan de Pravia in Oviedo also presents a cubus whose text 'Silo Princeps fecit' – that can be read in many different ways – identifies King Silo of Asturia (774–783) as its founder. Letter labyrinths as a copyist signature and *ex libris* are frequently encountered in codices of the Spanish commentary on the apocalypse by Beatus of Liébana (e.g. Cod. 8878, Paris, BN, fol. 1r). Written in the cubus form and adapted to a cross graphic right through to the early modern period were the *Versus sanctae crucis* of the grammarian Calbulus (5th cent.). The Porfyrian *carmina cancellata* with geometric figures, among these the cross, were often imitated in the early Middle Ages by Venantius Fortunatus (MGH AA 4,1,30; 32; 116), Ansbert of Rouen (Cod. CLXIV, inter Augienses, Karlsruhe, University Library, fol. 2v), Boniface (M.p. th. f. 29, Würzburg, University Library, fol. 44r) and the authors of the court school of Charlemagne like Alcuin (MGH PL 1,225 und 227), Josephus Scottus (MGH PL 1,153; 155; 157; 159) and Theodulf of Orléans (MGH PL 1,482), and finally by Hrabanus Maurus, who in his *Liber de laudibus sanctae crucis* that glorifies the cross as a cosmic symbol of salvation mentions Porfyrius explicitly (MGH PL 107, 146). In the 9th cent. the monk Gosbert (MGH PL 1,622) and Milo of St. Amand (MGH PL 3,563; 565) also designed grid poems, and at the beginning of the 10th cent. Eugenius Vulgarius dedicated to Pope Sergius III. (904–911) a *carmen quadratum* with cross-shaped intexts, as well as an acrostic poem in the textual graphic of a psalterium that resembles the syrinx poem of Porfyrius (MGH PL 4,1, 436, 438). Abbo of Fleury (940–1004) wrote two grid poems to E. Dunstan of Canterbury (died in 988) and one to Otto III. (MGH PL 5,1,469–471). Other *carmina cancellata* from the 10th cent. are by Vigilán of Albeld, who in the context of the Reconquista dedicated them to the Christian minor kings of northern Spain [8].

C. EARLY MODERN PERIOD
In the Renaissance, the ancient acrostic poem became extremely influential, a development triggered by the dissemination of the *Anthologia Graeca* and editions of Theocritus. Early imitations of the technopaegnia are attested since the 16th cent.: for instance in

R. WILLEII
Neapolioni Comitolo.
A L A E.

ἀντιστρωφη

9.

Summa colentes iuga Parnaſsia Nymphæ tenera, Caſtalides puellæ,
Si latices haurio ſuaues, Helicon vertice quos ab alto
Murmure agit dulciſono, ſi colui ſacratam
Aoniam paruulus, & repoſta
Munera ſi quid a me
valebunt,

Hyblæam
Candidula tyaram
Ferte manu, lilia ferte pulchra,
Neapoleonem decorate, O, violis roſiſquè
Neapoleonem Peruſinæ decus vrbis, cui nomen æuo
Par celebris fama dedit, perpeti agendum ſtudio cum pietate nomen.

Fig. 1: Figured poem in the shape of a wing. Richard Willis: *Poematum liber*, 1573, 8

P Ö E M A T A.

στρωφη ωδ' η

13

11

Triſte mari velivolo, dum Notus atque Eurus, & horrens Aquilo pcellis
Conſpicere praecipitatum in ſcopulos & breuia innatantem,
Plurimus illi ſit honos, plurima ſit beatitas,
Sit celebris perpetuo Bipennis
Per Vada feruida
Camoenae

In reditu Moecenatis ſui e Gallia. Securis.

Decus meae.
Quà vehitur dominum
Carmine, quæ prima ratim poluit,
In patria, qui prior almam pelago ratim dedit,
Luctiferum diſperenti: geminam remigis aurecondi,
Turbine verſant violento pelagus, littora dum fluctibus alma ſpumans,

Fig. 2: Figured poem in the shape of an axe. Richard Willis: *Poematum liber*, 1573, 11

Allgemeine Altars-Trauer.

Ach!
Der Noht /
Daß /
Der Tod /
Seine Pfeile /
Mörders- Keule /
So wild / ergrimmt /
Auff heute nimmt /
Ach daß der Menschen-Haſſer /
So manches Leibs Verpraſſer /
Auff unſre kurtze Freud' entrüſt /
Deß Schonens also gar vergiſſt /
Ach daß der Hirt in Iſrael gefallen!
Der ſeine Stimm ließ frü unnd ſpat erſchallen /
Für ſeine Schaf / die Er als ſich geliebt /
Mit den Er ſich erfreuet und betrübt.
Ach! daß der Hirt in Iſrael geſtorben!
Der / wann er ſah das Einfaltsſchaf verdorben /
Vnd irrend gehn / mit Thrennen es geſucht /
Daß es nicht werd zu Theil der Wölfe Zucht.
Ach! daß der Hirt in Iſrael verblichen!
Der / wann Er ſah die Mord-Wölf' eingeſchlichen /
Sie mit dem Stab deß Wortes außgejagt.
Trutz jenem Feind'! ob dem Er wer verzagt.
Ach! daß der Hirt in Iſrael verſchieden!
Der ſeiner Herd' hat Ruh' und Weid' und Frieden
Von GOTT erlangt / der ſie auff grüner Heid /
Nechſt friſcher Quellen / geweidet alle Zeit.

Ach!
GOTT /
Zebaoth /
Vnſer Güter
Treuer Hüter /
Fürſt der greiſen Ewigkeit /
Herrſcher dieſer letzten Zeiten /
Suche deinen Weinſtock heim /
Welchen du dir ſelbſt gepflantzet
Vñ mit ſtarke Zaun umſchätzet /
Daß der gallen-grüne Schleim /
Den die Spinnen - arge Feind /
So für Gutes Böſes günnen /
Anzukletten fertig ſeynd /
Seiner edlen Auge - Rinnen /
Kein vergälltes Heuchl - Gifft
Möge ſchmeichlend untermiſché.
Vielmehr wölleſt ihn erfriſchen
Mit dé lautern Tau der ſchrifft /
Welcher Himel-rein entſpringet
Vñ uns in die Wolfé ſchwinger.

Ach!
GOTT /
Zebaoth /
Sonder Alter /
Zeit-Verwalter /
Der du über Cherubinen
Jakobs fromer Herd' erſchienê /
Warum läſt du doch den Bau
Deines reiffé Stotts zerbreché?
Wilt du den nicht widerſprechen
Dieſer wütend - wilden Sau?
Sihe doch / Ach! ſihe drein /
Der hätt ſollen ewig ſeyn /
Ligt / Ach! itzund umgeſchmiſſen
Sihe drein und machs ein End /
Schütze deine werthe Reben /
Die uns Moſt des Lebens geben /
uñ wie du dich ſelbſt verpfändt /
Alſo bleibe bey uns Allen /
Biß diß Gantze ſoll hinfallen.

Ach! daß den Hirten / der ſich / Nürnberg / ſo befliſſen /
Vm deiner Seelen Heil / der Tod dir weggeriſſen /
So beweinen   folgt ihr andern
Wir Altár   Vnſerm Klang
Nach Begehr   Sonder Zwang
Die Gemeinen   Nachzuwandern.
Ach! weint / beweint den / den man nit gnug beweint /
So lang der blaſſe Mond am blaum Himmel ſcheint!
Aber / Ach! du Güte ſelbſt / Güte = reicher Himmels = König /
Wie? Daß du heut' unter uns machſt der Hirten alſo wenig /
Die uns doch zu dir gewieſen / in erpreſſtem Arbeit=Schweiß?
Wilt du denn in Ewigkeit deines Zornes grimme Flammen
Vber deine kleine Herd / ſonder alle Gnad / zuſammen
Laſſe ſchlagé? ſtekk das Schwert / dz auf unſerm Teutſchen Kreiß
Flinkert voller Grimmes = Loh' / eins in ſeine Scheiden wieder;
Mach deß Würgens doch ein End; ſchone / Haubt / Ach! deiner Glieder!

AVs VnterthänIgſt; fChVLDIger GebVr / Wegen
ertheILter GVt; VnD WoLthaten / WIe aVCh
zVr BezeVgVng ſelner betrVbten
SeeLen / VerfertIgte ſoLCheſ

Quirinus Moſcheroſch.

Fig. 3: Figured poem imitating the shape of an altar. Quirin Moscherosch, Allgemeine Altars-Trauer, 1647

<pre>
          o v o
       n o v e l o
    novo   no   velho
   o filho em folhos
  na jaula dos joelhos
   infante   em   fonte
    f e t o   f e i t o
      d e n t r o   d o
          centro
</pre>

<pre>
             o
          p o n t o
       onde se esconde
      lenda ainda antes
     e n t r e v e n t r e s
      quando   queimando
        os   seios   são
          p e i t o s   n o s
             dedos
</pre>

<pre>
          nu
       des   do   nada
     a t e   o   h u m
    a n o m e r o n u
   m e r o   d o   z e r o
    crua criança incru
    stada no cerne da
      carne viva en
         fim nada
</pre>

<pre>
             n o
          turna noite
       em tôrno em treva
      turva sem contôrno
     morte negro nó cego
     sono do morcego nu
     ma sombra que o pren
     dia preta letra que
         se torna
             sol
</pre>

Fig. 4: Augusto de Campos: *ovo novelo*. Figured poem in the shape of an egg.

Mellin de Saint-Gelais (1506; Œuvres II, Paris 1873 ed. P. Blanchemain, 130: wings), Giovanni Battista Pigna (Carminum libri quattuor, Venetia 1553, 97f.: syrinx), Jean Grisel (Premières Œuvres poétiques, Rouen 1599, 96: wings, 76f.: Easter eggs) and Robert Angot de l'Eperonnière (Chef-d'Œuvre poétique, Caen 1634, 16: Easter eggs). Copies in the Greek and Latin languages are encountered in 1592 in a collection by students of the Jesuit School in Dôle with the title Sylvae (altar, hatchet, wings), in Mannerist cycles by Richard Willis (Poematum liber, London 1573, 4: altar, 6: egg, 7: shepherd flute, 8: wings, cf. fig.1, 11: hatchet, cf. fig. 2) and Baldissare Bonifacio (Musarum libri XXV, Venetia 1628, No. VIII: organ, No. IX: hatchet, No. XXI: altar) as well as in the pastoral writings of the Pegnitz Shepherds, in Johann Helwig (Die Nymphe Noris, Nürnberg 1650, 7: organ) and Johann Geuder (Der Fried-Seligen Irenen Lustgarten, in: Johannes Praetorius: Satyrus etymologicus, n.p. 1672, 225: wings, 248: Irene altar, 249: syrinx, 271: ship of peace). In the poetics of Iulius Caesar Scaliger (Poetices libri septem, 1561, ed. L. Deitz, 1994, I., 558: nightingale and swan motifs), Paschasius a. S. Iohanne Evangelista (Poesis artificiosa, Würzburg 1674; various crossword labyrinths) and Theodor Kornfeld (Selbst-lehrende alt-neue Poesie, Bremen 1685, 81f.: two Easter eggs), the ancient paradigmata enter the literary canon. Acrostic poems also appear in the Baroque as Casualcarmina in funeral sermons, as shown by the Alae of Samuel Gloner of 1638 (Wolfenbüttel, Herzog-August Library: 48.7 Poet., 38) and a Triptychon altar of Quirin Moscherosch from 1647 (Herzog-August Library, Stolberg Collection 19673; cf. fig.3). Especially popular with the English in the 17th cent. were altar poems like Robert Herrick's "The Pillar of Fame" (Hesperides, London 1648, 398). Many poems, e.g. George Herbert's "Easter Wings" (The Temple, Cambridge 1641, 34f.), still occupy an important place today in the literary canon. Fortunio Liceti wrote encyclopaedic treatises about the ancient acrostic poems with textual variations, translations, copies, commentaries and interpretations (e.g. Encyclopaedia ad aram Pythiam Publilii Optatiani Porphirii, 1630; Ad alas Amoris divini Simmia Rhodio ..., 1640). The carmina figurata are also encountered in Johann Heinrich Alsted's Encyclopaedia (facsimile repr., bk. 1, 1989, 542, 549f.) published in 1630, in the hymn book of Georg Weber (Sieben Theile Wohlriechender Lebens = Früchte eines recht Gottes = ergebenen Herzen, Danzig 1649, 190f., 242, 376) and in the cryptographic handbook by Duke August of Brunswick, in which, aside from letter labyrinths, a poem by Porfyrius and the Praefatio of Hraban's cross poems were included (Cryptomenytices et Cryptographiae Libri IX, Lüneburg 1624). The Greek acrostic poems were also partly analysed from a critical standpoint, for instance by Michel de Montaigne, who viewed them as 'subtilitez frivoles et vaines' (Essais I, 54, Leyden 1602, 266f.), and by John Addison, who discredited them in the *Spectator* on 7th May 1711 (No. 58) as 'Species of false Wit'.

D. CONCRETE POETRY

Although the tradition of the FP gradually declined in the 18th cent., the reception of ancient models, still seen e.g. in Guillaume Appollinaire, creator of the *Calligrammes*, never came to an end, as its survival in concrete poetry shows. Even the Swede Öyvind Fahlström referred in his manifesto of 1953 to the Greeks, while Ferdinand Kriwet established a pattern of evolution from the technopaegnia to modern advertising posters (*Com.Mix., Die Welt der Bild- und Zeichensprache*, 1972), and Franz Mon was also conscious of historicity when he made reference to the fact 'daß seit dem Hellenismus eine Tradition besteht, Texte auf der Fläche bildlich-figurativ zu organisieren' ("a tradition exists since Hellenism to organise texts in a visual-figurative manner on a surface")[16. 116]. The Brazilian Augusto de Campos, in a work titled *ovo* (1955), wrote a poem in the shape of an egg that was included by Emmett Williams, with a commentary by Haroldo de Campos ('Greek technopaegnis revisited with a concrete sensibility for synthesis') in his *Anthology of Concrete Poetry* (1967) (cf. fig.4). Michel Butor in his discourses on the book as an object made reference to Classical FP [6. 47].

→ Anthology; → Orphism, Orphic poetry
→ TRANSMISSION

SOURCES 1 K. P. DENCKER, Text-Bilder, 1972 2 G. POLARA (ed.), Pvblilii Optatiani Porfyrii Carmina, I–II, 1972
LITERATURE 3 J. ADLER, U. ERNST, Text als Figur, ³1990 4 H. BECKBY, Anthologia Graeca, I–IV, ²1966, XV, 21–26 5 B. BOWLER, The Word as Image, 1970 6 M. BUTOR, Die Alchimie und ihre Sprache, 1990, 47 7 M. CHURCH, The Pattern Poem (diss. typescript) 1944 8 M. C. DÍAZ Y DÍAZ, Vigilán y Sarracino, in: W. BERSCHIN, R. DÜCHTING (eds.), Lateinische Dichtungen des X. und XI. Jahrhunderts, 1981, 60–92 9 F. DORNSEIFF, Das Alphabet in Mystik und Magie, 2 1925 10 U. ERNST, Carmen figuratum, 1991 11 A. HATHERLY, A Experiência do prodígio, 1983 12 D. HIGGINS, Pattern Poetry, 1987 13 D. KESSLER, Untersuchungen zur Konkreten Dichtung, 1976 14 A. LIEDE, Dichtung als Spiel, I–II, ²1992 15 R. MASSIN, Letter and Image, 1970 16 F. MON, Essays, in: Gesammelte Texte 1, 1994, 116 17 J. PEIGNOT, Du Calligramme, 1967 18 G. POZZI, La parola dipinta, 1981 19 P. RYPSON, Obraz słowa historia poezji wizualnej, 1989 20 J. SALLOIS (ed.), Poésure et Peintrie, 1993 21 D. W. SEAMAN, Concrete Poetry in France, 1981 22 G. WOJACZEK, Daphnis, 1969.

ULRICH ERNST

Figures, Theory of
A. DEFINITION B. ANCIENT RHETORIC
C. HISTORY OF INFLUENCE

A. DEFINITION

The rhetorical and stylistic theory of figures (ToF) addresses the form, function and origin as well as the classification of figures of speech. According to the ancient (and still generally valid) definition, figures are intentional deviations from normal usage or elaborations of 'normal language' aimed at achieving different stylistic or argumentative effects. The rhetorical ToF, as a prose style, differs from the poetic ToF in terms of function and intention rather than in content and structure, since there are extensive areas of overlap between their respective inventories. No authoritative system of figure theory emerged as rhetoric and poetics developed, since the use of figures is always dependent on variable historical and cultural conditions.

As a component of stylistic theory, in the system of ancient rhetoric the ToF was part of *elocutio*, the linguistic expression (*verba*) of thoughts that have already been found and ordered (*res*). This successivity view is no longer shared by modern rhetoric, but it makes clear the function of providing 'clothing' or decoration (*ornatus*) for a thought. This was seen as the main function of figures during Antiquity. The concept of the figure did not become firmly established in Roman rhetoric until the time of Quintilian (1st cent. AD) (inst. 9,1,11: definition of *figura* as an "intentional change in meaning or expression from the normal and simple version"); the older term is *exornatio*. The Greek word *schéma* was not commonly used until the Hellenic period; during Roman and Latin Antiquity and in the Middle Ages both concepts were used interchangeably. Even today, both Greek and Latin terms are used for rhetorical figures. Latin terminology, first found in the *Rhetoric to Herennius* (ca. 84 BC), which lists 65 figures (*verborum/sententiarum exornationes*) along with text examples, was rediscovered and made accessible to literary scholars by H. Lausberg.

B. ANCIENT RHETORIC

While the ToF was already part of rhetoric during the early 5th cent. BC (the 'Gorgian figures' are well known; Dion. Hal., Demosthenes 5,25), a comprehensive systematic stylistics was first found in Theophrastus (371–287 BC), in the lost document *Péri léxeos*. His teacher, Aristotle, was primarily interested in metaphor, which he generally viewed as a type of non-literal speech (rhet. 3,2,1404 b 31ff.); he discusses the use of metaphorical expression from a stylistic-critical perspective, but without developing an actual ToF, in his *Rhetoric* and *Poetics* (Cap. 22). The close links between the two spheres that became apparent at that time (Cicero mentions as areas of linguistic embellishment *vel poesis vel oratio*: de orat. 3,100) have been maintained to the present.

In terms of function, the ancient ToF was determined by the rules of appropriateness (*aptum*; Greek *prépon*) and clear expression (*perspicuitas*; Greek *saphéneia*) associated with *elocutio* – this is expressed as far back as Aristotle (rhet. 3,2) – as well as by the levels of style (lower, middle, elevated style) and the intended effect (*docere* 'to instruct', *movere* 'to move', *delectare* 'to delight') of a speech (Cic. orat. 21,69; de orat. 3,210ff.). Even if, from the ancient perspective, the function of figures is primarily to embellish (Cic. orat. 39,134), making them a 'bonus' in addition to the information that is provided (Quint. inst. 8,3,61), because they serve to impress or delight the audience (Aristot. rhet. 3,11), their function in enhancing insight was also recognized (Aristot. poet. 22,1458 b 4f., 1459 a 5ff.; Cic. orat. 39,134; Quint. inst. 8,2,11).

The ancient world devoted a great deal of attention to the problem of classifying figures. While no taxonomy had been developed in Aristotle's work, during the subsequent period a division emerged between figures of word and those of thought (*figurae/exornationes verborum* or *sententiarum*; Greek *schémata léxeos* or *diánoias*) (Rhet. Her. 4,13; Cic. de orat. 3,200); that is, a division was undertaken into figures at the lexical and grammatical level (determined, for example, by the choice or placement of a word) and figures at the semantic level (determined by the meaning of their content). An expansion or modification of this dichotomy, which is often the basis of a definition even today, is found in the three-part classification model, which treats the trope (the substitution of another concept for what is literally meant) as a separate class. Tropes were already identified by Theophrastus as a special group of figures [31. 277]; the author of the *Rhetoric to Herennius* also discusses figures considered to be tropes in his catalogue of figures, although he does not use the term (4,42–46). Quintilian's definition became standard (inst. 8,6,1: 'tropus est verbi vel sermonis a propria significatione in aliam cum virtute mutatio', "the artful change of a word or expression from its literal meaning to another": e.g., metaphor, metonymy, antonomasia, allegory). In his view, *tropus* is the substitution of one concept for another, while *figura* is a special forming of an expression (*conformatio*; inst. 9,1,4). Word figures (figures of repetition, omission, transposition) are divided by Quintilian (inst. 9,3,1f.) into those that are grammatical in nature (a modification of normal grammar) and those that are rhetorical (a change in the position of words). Figures of thought further the semantic effect of a statement ('ab simplici modo indicandi recedunt'; Quint. inst. 9,2,1) by means of enhancement, emphasis, rhetorical questions, etc. (Cic. de orat. 3,200ff.; orat. 39,136ff.). The basic features of this classification model shaped further reception history, although variations occurred as time went by.

Quintilian also established an important foundation for the modern ToF, which studies the conditions and mechanisms governing the emergence of figurative speech, with his doctrine of the 'categories of change'

(inst. 1,5,38ff.): [35. § 462]. Linguistic changes occur in four possible ways (*quadripertita ratio*): by addition (*adiectio*) or subtraction (*detractio*) of elements or by rearranging (*transmutatio*) or replacing (*immutatio*) them. During Late Antiquity, the categories of change once again served as a starting point for the treatise on figures of speech by Phoibammon (5th/6th cent. AD). Excerpts of this treatise have been preserved, with these categories referred to as *pleonasmós, éndeia, metáthesis, enallage* (Phoibammon, ed. Spengel 3,41ff.); otherwise, they have been of little significance in the ToF up to the modern era.

The ToF was a subject taught until Late Antiquity, modelled after the textbooks of the Hellenistic-imperial periods and their Roman reception. It focused in part on fundamental grammar instruction (beginning in the 3rd cent. AD, the ToF frequently appeared as an addendum to grammar textbooks: Marius Plotius Sacerdos, Charisius, Diomedes, Donatus; regarding the link between rhetoric and grammar: Isid. orig. 2,1), and in part on 'advanced studies' using special treatises (Rutilius Lupus, Aquila Romanus, Iulius Rufinianus; also in the form of a didactic poem, such as the anonymous *Carmen de figuris*, 4th/5th cent. AD) [41. 12f.]. The inventory of figures expanded: Aquila Romanus (3rd cent. AD) dealt with 200 figures in his treatise *De figuris sententiarum et elocutionis*. With Donatus' addendum on figures in his *Ars grammatica maior* (later also disseminated separately under the title *Barbarismus*), a separate tradition of grammatical figures began in the 4th cent. AD that proved to be of importance for the Middle Ages, once the boundary between the roles of grammar and rhetoric in the ToF had already become the subject of discussion (Quint. inst. 9,3,2). In addition, there was a rhetorical tradition that was based primarily on the *Rhetoric to Herennius*.

C. HISTORY OF INFLUENCE
1. MIDDLE AGES 2. RENAISSANCE AND THE MODERN ERA 3. MORE RECENT TIMES

1. MIDDLE AGES
Definitive for the reception of Roman rhetoric during the Middle Ages and the early modern era were, above all, Cicero's *De inventione* and the *Rhetoric to Herennius*, which was attributed to Cicero during the mediaeval period; in addition, Donatus, Priscian and Horace (*Ars poetica*) were of great importance in questions of grammar and style. In contrast, Quintilian, whose *Institutio oratoria* was not rediscovered in complete form until 1416 by Poggio Bracciolini, played only a secondary role. However, mention should be made of the *Epitome rhetoricae* of Ulrich of Bamberg (d. 1127), whose ToF was based on Quintilian, but who also made reference to the *Rhetoric to Herennius* [36].

The mediaeval ToF is not only part of rhetorical and grammatical doctrine, but also an essential element in the theory of poetry. Since mediaeval grammar was understood not only as the science of correct speech but also claimed to teach the basics of understanding language and literature, the ToF became an integral component of it. This led to a decline in the importance of rhetoric in its comprehensive ancient sense. The study of rhetorical argumentation often became a subject of dialectics; stylistics and the ToF were also dealt with by grammar, which poetics also fell back on. Numerous authors of mediaeval *artes poetriae* were teachers of grammar but not of rhetoric [37. 135f.]. The ToF was chosen as a theme both as a component of *artes* treatises and in individual treatises (often in the form of didactic poems written in hexameter) whose prescriptive character clearly demonstrated their function as guidelines for authors. Separate ToFs (some of which might rather be described as catalogues) began to appear in larger numbers from the 5th cent. AD, such as the *Liber de schematibus et tropis* of Bede (673–735), which presented Donatus' ToF. A model for the mediaeval tradition of this genre, which demonstrates the importance of ToFs as 'handbooks for authors', was the treatise entitled *De ornamentis verborum* by Marbod of Rennes (1035–1123; PL 171, 1687–1692).

Fundamental works that set down the ToF for grammar instruction during the Middle Ages included the *Doctrinale* of Alexander de Villa Dei (1199) and the *Graecismus* of Eberhard of Béthune (1212), two didactic poems, both of which refer back to Donatus and Priscian [2; 3]. The *Doctrinale* deals not only with syntax, etymology, quantities and accents, but at the end in some 300 verses, with the *figurae loquelae*, divided into 25 tropes, 16 schemata, 16 metaplasms and 23 figures with no general heading; the *Graecismus* begins with a ToF that is organized in categories containing a total of some 100 figures: 'permitted' (*permissiva*: metaplasms, schemata, tropes), 'prohibited' (*prohibitiva*: barbarisms, solecisms) and 'prescribed' (*preceptiva*: the so-called *colores rhetorici*). The problem of terminology and taxonomy is clearly evident, a problem that was not conclusively solved even in the Middle Ages. Assignment of figures to certain categories varied and often appeared less than convincing.

Behind the various concepts are two traditional strains: the grammatical tradition of Donatus, which retains the Greek terms (*schéma = figura*; cf. Isid. orig. 1,36), and the tradition of the *Rhetoric to Herennius*, with Latin terminology. The decorative function emphasized in the ToF of Roman rhetoric is reflected in the mediaeval term col ores rhetorici, coined by Onulf of Speyer (ca. 1050) [8], used in reference particularly to poetic figures, although no uniform and precise use emerged. Also in connection with the structure of poetic language, the figure category of metaplasm appeared, defined by Isidore (570–636) as a change in a word undertaken for metrical reasons (orig. 1,35). The term *figura* itself is rather uncommon.

Among the mediaeval genres of rhetorical and literary theory (*ars poetriae, ars dictaminis, ars praedicandi*), it was primarily poetics that dealt with the ToF, but poetics also played an important role in epistolary and sermon theory, in which levels of style (along with their implications for the ToF) were increasingly linked with the social status of the targeted audience. The *artes poetriae* that emerged during the 12th and 13th cents. dealt with the function and effect of figures, and presented figure catalogues.

Matthew of Vendôme wrote his *Ars versificatoria* (ca. 1175) with the goal of providing instruction in the art of poetry [6]. Tropes, schemata and *colores rhetorici* determined the *modus dicendi*, and were necessary for the artful arrangement (*appositio artificialis*) of the words on which their poetic effect was based. In accordance with tradition, poetological considerations were associated with a listing of the individual figures (organized according to general categories). The decorative function of figures was particularly emphasized in Geoffrey of Vinsauf's *Poetria nova* (1208–1213), which documents the difficulty of distinguishing among mediaeval grammar, rhetoric and poetics, since topics from all three areas are dealt with [4]. It contains suggestions for amplification, abbreviation and other effects intended to have an impact on both the aesthetic sense and the intellect of the audience. Indeed, Geoffrey referred to figures as *flores verborum*, like Cicero, who also underscored the *ornatus* function by using terms like *flores verborum sententiarumque* (de orat. 3,96) or *lumen orationis* (orat. 39,135; also Quint. inst. 9,1,1). Joannes de Garlandia, in his three-part poetics (*De arte prosayca, metrica et rithmica*, after 1229), which played an important role in the history of style theory (*rota Virgili*), declared figurative ornamentation to be equally meaningful in poetry and prose with respect to phonetic or expressive effects. Ancient models are alluded to by other authors as well, such as Gervasius of Melkley (*Ars versificaria*, ca. 1215), who dealt with the genres of 'general speech', poetry and *dictamen prosaicum*; he refers authors seeking help to Cicero, Horace and Donatus, or Evrardus Allemannus, whose didactic poem *Laborintus* (between 1213 and 1280) lists almost all the figures in the *Rhetoric to Herennius* (with examples).

During the 11th cent., Alberic of Monte Cassino added a rhetorical and grammatical foundation (and hence the ToF) to mediaeval epistolary theory. The most important treatises concerning letter writing appeared during the 12th and 13th cents., at approximately the same time as the main works on poetics. In his seminal work *Dictaminum radii* or *Flores rhetorici* (as it is called in the edition's title), the ToF takes up more than half the chapters; Alberic asserts that knowledge of these matters determines whether or not a person can even be called an author: '... utillimi dictandi colores, quos si quis notat, scriptores accedere praesumat, qui nescit, nomen non usurpet scriptoris' ("Those who are familiar with the most useful decorative figures of the epistolary art may regard themselves as authors; those who do not should not claim the name of author") [1. 59].

Among the authors of books of mediaeval sermon rhetoric, particular mention should be made of Robert of Basevorn (*Forma praedicandi*, 1322), who recommended the catalogue of figures contained in the *Rhetoric to Herennius* as an inventory to be used by preachers (Cap. 50) [9], or Thomas of Todi, in whose *Ars sermocinandi* the use of figures is a form of argumentation (*probatio*) along with the topos of authority, logical argument, illustration and historical documentation.

2. RENAISSANCE AND THE MODERN ERA

Against the backdrop of the humanists' ideal of *elegantia*, the Renaissance produced an abundance of treatises on the ToF. Antoine Haneron wrote his work *De coloribus verborum et sententiarum* (ca. 1475) in the tradition of Alexander de Villa Dei's *Doctrinale* and the *Rhetoric to Herennius*. He was followed in the 16th cent. by authors like Erasmus of Rotterdam (*De copia verborum ac rerum*, 1512), Joannes Susenbrotus (*Epitome Troporum ac Schematum*, ca. 1541), Petrus Ramus and Audomarus Talaeus (*Rhetorica*, 1548, one of the most widely disseminated rhetoric textbooks), among many others. Works on the ToF written in the vernacular appeared as well, such as Caspar Goldtwurm's *Schemata Rhetorica. Teutsch* (1535), which was intended for use in training preachers.

A trend emerged to expand the stock of figures (H. Peacham's *Garden of Eloquence*, 1593, lists more than 200 figures) and efforts were made to facilitate learning the material by providing charts and figure stemmata. An example of the latter is appended to the edition of the *Rhetoric* of Ramus/Talaeus edited by C. Mignault. It divides rhetoric into *elocutio* and *pronuntiatio,* then *elocutio* (following the model of Quintilian) into *tropus* and *figura, tropus* into *metonymia, ironia, metaphora* and *synecdoche; figura* into *figurae dictionis* and *figurae sententiae* (each of these with further subcategories) [12. 1291f.].

The *Rhetoric* of Ramus/Talaeus is significant in terms of its influence as a consistent rhetoric of style that excludes → THEORY OF ARGUMENTATION, since Ramus assigned this area of rhetoric solely to dialectics. This view of rhetoric, which reduced it to the structure of language and recitation and devoted particular attention to the ToF, established the tradition of the 'Ramists', which took hold particularly in England, Germany (especially in Baroque rhetoric: Johann Matthaeus Meyfarth, *Teutsche Rhetorica*, 1634) and France (C.C.Du Marsais, *Les Tropes*, 1730; P. Fontanier, *Manuel Classique pour l'étude des Tropes*, 1821; J. Dubois and others, the so-called 'groupe μ', *Rhétorique générale*, 1970) and has continued to exist to the present.

Classification systems contained in Renaissance and Baroque treatises are largely shaped by ancient models of figure classification—for example, the distinction between rhetorical and grammatical figures in the *Tabula de elocutione et de figuris* of David Chytraeus (ca. 1570) [13. 1053f.]–but they also expand and modify

these models, for example, by deriving figures from certain *topoi* found in Melanchthon (*Elementa rhetorices*, 1531) [7. 103ff.].

The 'poetics of rhetoric' of Julius Caesar Scaliger (*Poetices libri septem*, 1561), which was pioneering for the theory of poetry (particularly vernacular poetry) of the subsequent period, dealt in two books with material figures and figures of speech (*figurae rerum* and *verborum*) that refer back to the ancient distinction between *figurae sententiarum* (as well as tropes) and *figurae verborum*. Material figures are determined according to their relationship to the content of their subject, while figures of speech are determined by the categories *natura/essentia, situs, quantitas, qualitas*, which are related to the word material and by which amplification, positional or sound figures, for example, can be explained [10]. Scaliger is a model for the ToF contained in the *Commentariorum rhetoricorum libri sex* of Gerhard Johannes Vossius (1609), who, in turn, had a profound influence on the Baroque view of rhetoric. In connection with the ToF, Martin Opitz (*Buch von der Deutschen Poeterey*, 1624) refers to Scaliger as well as to the Latin tradition and (like Georg Philipp Harsdörffer's *Poetischer Trichter*, 1647–1653) shows the close links between rhetoric and the art of poetry. In France poetry was regarded as a 'second rhetoric' during the 17th cent. [28].

Particular emphasis was placed in baroque rhetoric on the emotional effect of figures and the ways in which they might be used in the realm of virtuoso word play ('argutia movement'), for example, in Emanuele Tesauro's *Cannocchiale Aristotelico* (1655), which is characterized by a trichotomy of *figure harmoniche, patetiche* and *ingeniose*.

Against the intellectual backdrop of the Enlightenment, there was a change in the perception of language and the related aesthetic and poetological concepts that also relate to the ToF. Language was increasingly seen as an expression of the individual; individual style and the ideal of the natural (expression of 'genuine' emotion), rather than normative poetic and rhetorical stylistics, were promoted by the tradition of effects contained in A.G. Baumgarten's *Aesthetica* (1750/1758) (J. G. Hamann, J. G. Herder, K. P. Moritz), which made the ToF in the traditional prescriptive sense appear useless. A changed understanding of figures was manifested in the new impetus gained by the theory of figuration during the 17th and 18th cents. The *ornatus* theory of Antiquity and the early modern era was no longer regarded as a satisfactory explanation for figurative expression. Du Marsais, who was a major influence on the further development of the ToF in France, regarded figures not as ornamental, but as having the function of indicating affiliation (*Les Tropes*, 1730). The perception of an emotional and affective origin of figurative speech was widespread in German theories of rhetoric during the 18th cent. (J. A. Fabrizius, F. A. Hallbauer, K. P. Moritz, J. A. Adelung). Bernard Lamy's (*L'art de parler*, 1675) psychological view of figures (attributing certain emotions to corresponding figures) already pointed toward this development [5. 111ff.]. Thus J. J. Bodmer (*Critische Betrachtungen über die poetischen Gemählde der Dichter*, 1741) and J. J. Breitinger (*Critische Dichtkunst*, 1740) came to the inverse conclusion that it was not the schematic use of figures that evoked emotion (rather, this produced an unnatural style), but emotions determined the form of expression. J. G. Sulzer (*Allgemeine Theorie der schönen Künste*, 1792) even feared that "the desperate names and explanations of all figures" might produce "revulsion to eloquence" [11. 232]. Even a proponent of the use of the ToF in instruction like J. C. Gottsched (*Versuch einer Critischen Dichtkunst* [4]1751) criticized overtaxing pupils by using Greek terminology and attaching too much importance to the ToF as an educational discipline. Following the general decline of rhetoric that began in the mid–18th cent., the ToF, used for pragmatic purposes rather than as a matter for theoretical consideration, was preserved primarily in its function in school instruction; or it became a subject for stylistics as a separate discipline. It was here that the ancient tradition remained most alive.

3. More Recent Times

It was not until the 20th cent., in the wake of the rediscovery of rhetoric in the 1930s (United States) and after World War II (Europe), that the ToF again attracted the attention of theoreticians and was taken up by various modern disciplines (primarily linguistics, but also cognition and communication research or semiotics, which seeks to apply the model of figures of speech to other sign systems). In modern rhetoric and literary studies, the ToF is viewed as a conceptually variable system of analysis, in contrast to the prescriptive, instructional character of the ToF during the Middle Ages and the early modern period. The ancient inventory of figures, system of classification and terminology were frequently utilized, as in H. Lausberg's basic work of modern text analysis *Handbuch der literarischen Rhetorik* (1960), which reestablished the ancient world's ToF. The argumentative function of figures, which was recognized during Antiquity and subsequent eras, but was generally regarded as secondary to the *ornatus* function, was given a more prominent position in modern theory in accordance with the view that not only do words express a thought, but cognitive and linguistic acts are closely interwoven. Thus it is possible to distinguish amplification and argumentation figures as well as, following the ancient trichotomy model, substitution figures (= tropes), which are used for decorative as well as argumentative purposes [38. 155ff.]. A separate focus is the study of metaphors, in which the Aristotelian approach to metaphorical thought and speech (creative performance, formation of analogies, control of insights; cf. Aristot. poet. 22; rhet. 3,2) is developed further.

Modern classification models contain the ancient categories as well as a broad range of new classes of figures in which structure and/or function are differentiated to a greater degree; this, however, tends to exacerbate rather than solve the problem of taxonomy that has existed since ancient times. There is frequently no longer an explicit distinction between figures of word and thought, for example, although the distinction is maintained in new (linguistic) terminology. Moreover, the separation of tropes and figures that became the norm as a result of the school tradition of teaching rhetoric, although it was not shared by all ancient theoreticians (see Quint. inst. 9,1,2), remains controversial. During the 1960s and 1970s, triggered by the problem of classification and by criticism of a ToF that focused on lists (B. Croce, R. Barthes) [20. 446; 17. 218], new theories of figuration emerged that were shaped mainly by linguistic approaches. In efforts to avoid cataloging figures according to their form and function, but instead to construct model schemata for their development, Quintilian's long-ignored doctrine of change categories (inst. 1,5,38) is again gaining recognition. The Liège 'groupe μ' (main proponents: J. Dubois, J.-M. Klinkenberg) proceed on the assumption of a linguistic zero stage (*degré zero*) that was figurized by the operations (or change categories) *suppression, adjonction, suppression-adjonction* and *permutation* (*Rhétorique générale*, 1970). Classes of figures are further divided according to operational level (word, sentence, meaning) into metaplasms, metataxes and metasemes.

A new aspect of schematic and graphic presentation is the location of figures in a biaxial system of coordinates ('figure matrix') that defines each figure in terms of two different criteria at the systematic level, replacing the primary and subordinate classes of the hierarchically structured figure stemmata. T. Todorov's *Essai de classification* (in: [43]) locates figures on a vertical axis according to the criteria of *anomalies* (violations of grammatical rules) and *figures* (deviations from 'normal speech' without violating rules), thus following the ancient distinction between grammatical and rhetorical figures; and on the horizontal axis according to linguistic descriptive criteria (*son-sens, syntaxe, sémantique, signe-référent*). J. Durand (*Classement général des figures*) [21. 75] locates figures on one axis by the type of relationship (*relation*) they have to what is meant (*identité, similarité de forme/contenu, différence, opposition de forme/contenu, fausse homologies/double sens/paradoxe*), and on the other by the method (*opération*) by which they are formed (*adjonction, suppression, substitution, échange*; cf. Quintilian). H.F. Plett (*Die Rhetorik der Figuren*, 1975, in: [39]) distinguishes in a similar manner between linguistic operations (addition, subtraction, substitution, permutation as violating rules and equivalence as reinforcing rules) and linguistic levels (phonological, morphological, syntactic, semantic, graphemic) as a means of identifying figures.

While these approaches can be regarded as examples of modern theory formation, in terms of the ToF in actual 'use' (school instruction, especially in the ancient languages; popular stylistics) the ancient classification

and descriptive categories have largely been preserved.
→ Figures

→ Argumentation; → Baroque; → Ciceronianism;
→ Grammar; → Rhetoric textbooks; → Rhetoric

Sources 1 Albericus v. Monte Cassino, Flores rhetorici, D. M. Inguanez, H. M. Willard (eds.), Miscellanea Cassinese 14, 1938   2 Alexander v. Villa Dei, Doctrinale, D. Reichling (ed.), Berlin 1893 (= Monumenta Germanicae paedagogica 12)   3 Eberhard v. Béthune, Graecismus, I. Wrobel (ed.), Breslau 1887 (= Corpus grammaticorum medii aevi Vol. 1), repr. 1987   4 Galfried v. Vinsauf, Poetria nova, E. Gallo (ed.), (with English translation), 1971   5 B. Lamy, l'art de parler, E. Ruhe (ed.), 1980   6 Matthias v. Vendôme, Ars versificatoria, E. Faral (ed.), Les arts poétiques du XIIᵉ et du XIIIᵉ siècles, 1924   7 Ph. Melanchton, Rhetorik, J. Knape (ed.), 1993   8 Onulf v. Speyer, Colores rhetorici, W. Wattenbach (ed.), = SPrAW 1894, 361–386   9 Robert v. Basevorn, Forma praedicandi, Th.-M. Charland (ed.), 1936   10 J. C. Scaliger, Poetices libri septem, Vol. 2 (with an index of figures), L. Deitz (ed.), 1994   11 J. G. Sulzer, Allgemeine Theorie der schönen Künste, vol. 2, repr. 1967
Illustrations 12 see Barock, HWdR 1   13 see elocutio, HWdR 2
Literature 14 L. Arbusov, Colores rhetorici. Eine Auswahl rhetorischer Figuren und Gemeinplätze als Hilfsmittel für akademische Übungen an mittelalterlichen Texten, ³1963   15 W. Ax, Quadripertita ratio. Bemerkungen zur Geschichte eines aktuellen Kategoriensystems, in: Historiographia Linguistica 13, 1986, 191–214   16 W. Barner, Barockrhetorik, 1970   17 R. Barthes, L'ancienne rhétorique. Aide-mémoire, in: Communications 16, 1970 172–229   18 D. Breuer, Rhetorische Figur, in: Ch. Wagenknecht (ed.), Zur Terminologie der Literaturwissenschaft., 1989   19 A. Buck et al. (eds.), Dichtungslehren der Romania aus der Zeit der Renaissance und des Barock, 1972   20 B. Croce, Ästhetik als Wissenschaft vom Ausdruck und allgemeiner Sprachwissenschaft (Ger. H. Feist, R. Peters (trans.), 1930; Engl. C. Lyas (trans.), The Aesthetic as the Science of Expression and of the Linguistic in General, 1953; Trans. of: Estetica come scienza dell'espressione e linguistica generale, ⁵1922)   21 J. Durand, Rhétorique et image publicitaire, in: Communications 15, 1970, 70–95   22 J. Dyck, Ticht-Kunst. Deutsche Barockpoetik und rhetorische Tradition, ³1991   23 D. Fehling, Die Wiederholungsfiguren und ihr Gebrauch bei den Griechen vor Gorgias, 1969   24 G. Fey, Das Antike an der modernen Rhetorik, 1979   25 J. P. Fruit, The Evolution of Figures of Speech, in: Mod. Language Notes 111, 1988, 501–505   26 M. Fuhrmann, Die antike Rhetorik, 1984   27 G. Genette, Figures, 1966   28 F.-R. Hausmann, Französische Renaissance-Rhetorik, in: H. Plett (ed.), Renaissance-Rhetorik, 1993, 59–71   29 A. Haverkamp (ed.), Theorie der Metapher, 1983   30 R. Hildebrandt-Günther, Antike Rhetorik und deutsche literarische Theorie im 17. Jahrhundert, 1966   31 G. Kennedy, The Art of Persuasion in Greece, 1963   32 J. Knape, see Figurenlehre, HWdR 2, 289–342   33 J. Kozy, The Argumentative Use of Figures, in: Philosophy and Rhetoric 3, 1970, 141–151   34 U. Krewitt, Metapher und tropische Rede in der Auffassung des Mittelalters, 1971   35 H. Lausberg, Handbuch der literarischen Rhetorik. 1960, Engl. trans. M.T. Bliss, A. Jansen, & D.E. Orton, ed. D.E. Orton & R.D. Anderson, 1998.   36 P.

Lehmann, Die institutiones des Quintilian im Mittelalter, in: Id., Erforschungen des Mittlelaters 2, 1959, 1–28   37 J. J. Murphy, Rhetoric in the Middle Ages, 1974   38 C. Ottmers, Rhetorik, 1996 (with more bibliography)   39 H. F. Plett (ed.), Rhetorik, 1977   40 Id., Textwissenschaft und Textanalyse, 1975   41 U. Schindel, Die lateinischen Figuren des 5. bis 7. Jahrhunderts und Donats Vergilkommentar, 1975   42 W. Taylor, Tudor Figures of Rhetoric, 1972   43 T. Todorov, Littérature et signification, 1967   44 W. Welte (ed.), Sprachtheorie und angewandte Linguistik, Festschrift A. Wollmann, 1982   45 F. J. Worstbrock et al., Repertorium der artes dictandi im Mittelalter, vol. 1, Von den Anfängen bis um 1200, 1992

Additional Bibliography J. Dubois et al, Rhétorique générale, 1970 (Engl. P. B. Burrell, E. M. Slotkin (trans.), A General Rhetoric by Group Mu, 1981); R. A. Lanham, Handlist of Rhetorical Terms, ²1991; L. A. Sonnino, A Handbook to 16th-Century Rhetoric, 1968

SYLVIA USENER

Film

A. History   B. Typology   C. Effect

A. History

The beginning of the silent film era at the end of the 19th cent. opened up a new venue for communicating information about the ancient world. The medium of film addresses Antiquity in two ways, first in the form of citations [30; 36], i.e. references to ancient names, motifs and objects. For example, ancient tragedy and its chorus provided the framework plot for Woody Allen's *Mighty Aphrodite* (USA 1995), while the comedy *9 to 5* (USA 1980), in which three secretaries stage a revolt against their boss, echoes Aristophanes [1]. Particularly in the science fiction film genre, the ancient world, as a setting that is simultaneously familiar and distant, becomes the model for an unknown future where the inhabitants may be dressed in Greek garb and their forms of government resemble an Amazon state or a gerontocracy [23]. Second, the plot of these films may take place in the ancient world itself. A cinematic adaptation of ancient subject matter is multi-dimensional in a way previously unknown in reception history. It shares its visual presence with the fine arts; its narrative continuity with literature, especially modern novels; and beginning in the sound era, its acoustic presence with music and theatrical plays. Since there is much that we do not know about ancient life, owing to gaps in the fragmentary materials that have been handed down, it has been necessary to fill in these gaps with assumptions and opinions in order to arrive at a coherent picture [34. 73–74]. This applies to the plot as well as to all aspects of the backdrop and acting, such as gestures. However, these additions have frequently taken on a dynamic of their own, resulting in a new version of Antiquity being created in people's minds by the cinema. Thus well-known actors (particularly in the numerous cinematic versions of Nero and Cleopatra) have shaped our conception of historic figures and are ever-present associations [27. 35–36]. The portrayal of Imperial Rome in the film *The Fall of the Roman Empire* (USA 1963) was regarded as so accurate that it was used to depict Rome in a non-fiction book series [37. 147]. This reception process was enhanced as film became a mass medium in the first third of the 20th cent., and underwent a further increase and popularization in the television era, as famous films with ancient themes were rebroadcast and television productions took on these topics as well [30].

The genre of Antiquity films had already emerged during the silent film era, beginning in Italy [17; 11. 14–16; 31. 403–404], which was soon to be overtaken by the United States in this genre. Among the pioneers, as directors and often producers as well, were Giovanni Pastrone, D.W. Griffith and Cecil B. de Mille [2. 916–917, 1020–1024, 1253]. After World War I, as the sound era began, Hollywood took the lead [7; 11] in this area; these films were generally also costume dramas, and the American studios had greater economic resources than the Italian film industry. This did not put an end to the popularity of the genre in Italy, however, even if Italian productions were often much less lavish than those of their American competitors. For a long time the United States and Italy maintained their position as market leaders in this genre, followed by England.

During the 1950s and 1960s, in the era of widescreen films, films set in Antiquity experienced a real boom [7; 11; 14; 31], which came to an end under the influence of the modernization movement of the 1970s. However, as the number of private broadcasting stations increased in the 1990s, and old productions have been shown more and more often on television as well as released on video, these films have not been forgotten, but, in terms of numbers, are reaching larger audiences. Toward the end of the 20th cent. there was clearly renewed interest, especially in the area of television productions, in making films particularly of mythological matter of Greek origin such as the ambitious filming of the myth of Odysseus (*Homer's Odyssey*, 1996) as a joint English, Turkish and Maltese production under the direction of Andrei Konchalovsky and with a cast of well-known actors.

Academic treatment of the genre was originally limited to film studies [7; 11; 14; 31]. While the study of the ancient world was long linked to the idea of a normative → CLASSICISM which the genre of film as popularly understand did not satisfy, perspectives have since changed. Particularly in Anglo-American ancient studies, and specifically in the field of philology, films have become more prominent in modern research as a medium for the reception of information about the ancient world [19; 20; 21; 36; 38], and are also finding application in the framework of teaching the subject matter. [5; 6]. The question is often formulated in a dual manner, that is, what information the cinematic version of Antiquity gives us about the present of that time and its social, economic and political interests, as well as what it contributes to our current picture of the ancient world [38].

WIEBER-SCARIOT, ANJA

B. TYPOLOGY

Since there is no uniform and all-encompassing term for films that deal with the ancient world, we shall in the present article use the term Antiquity films [24]. In the Anglo-American world, most Antiquity films are considered to be part of the epic genre [7; 11]. Following the ancient concept of the epic, this refers to monumental films that treat, on an epic scale, heroic deeds performed in mythic and historical periods, not only ancient but also more recent ones, as well as themes drawn from the Bible [7. 1–24; 11. 29–46]. As such, the demands made by the *genus grande* are apparent in the decor and staging of the films (crowd scenes, costuming and sets, pathos-laden music and, in Anglo-American films, the use of Shakespearean language) and also in their presentation at the cinema (unusual length, intermissions, special premieres, high ticket prices, operatic overtures and intermission music, operatic length [38. 120]), as well as the descriptions used in the advertising of such films: 'The Mightiest Story of Tyranny and Temptation Ever Written – Ever Lived – Ever Produced' for the film *The Silver Chalice*, 1954 [27. 27; 14. 47–48]; similarly, German television advertising for *Homer's Odyssey* called it "a TV production of superlatives".

Progress in cinematic technology, such as the development of the dolly and the wide screen [11. 22], made such a monumental endeavour possible, and the production phase was often epic as well. The Cleopatra production with Richard Burton and Elizabeth Taylor, for example, had to cope with epic demands in its lengthy filming process, ruinous expense for 20th Century-Fox and spectacular scandals involving the cast, with hitherto undreamt-of interest shown by radio, television and the print media. The affair between Burton and Taylor seemed to blur the distinction between the modern-day actors and the historical figures they portrayed [3; 4; 33; 38. 100–105].

Just as Antiquity films are sometimes classified according to characteristics of their style, they are also referred to in terms of their costumes. Thus in German-speaking countries the term *Sandalenfilme* [24], ('sandal films'), is used; in the Anglo-American world, reference is sometimes made to 'peplum films', derived from the Latinized form of the Greek word for the women's upper garment (*péplos*) [7. 21]–more commonly called (in the United States, at any rate) "sword and sandal" or "sandal and toga" films. Common classifications of epics include the following: moral and religious, particularly Biblical films; national epics, such as typically American films like *Birth of a Nation* (USA 1915) and *Gone With the Wind* (USA 1939); as well as historical epics, including not only Antiquity films such as *Alexander the Great* (USA 1956), *Spartacus* (USA 1960) and the various Cleopatra films, but also historical films from more recent periods, like

Lawrence of Arabia (GB 1962) and *El Cid* (USA/Spain 1961) [7; 11].

Biblical films draw on motifs and stories from the Old and New Testaments (*The Ten Commandments* USA 1957; *Samson and Delilah* USA 1950; *The Prodigal* USA 1955; *King of Kings* USA 1960) [16; 28. 80–126], while historical Antiquity films often base their scripts on 19th cent. novels, for example *Quo Vadis*, by Henryk Sienkiewicz (1894–1896), Edward Bulwer-Lytton's *The Last Days of Pompeii* (1834) and Lewis Wallace's *Ben Hur* (1880) [38. 28, 112–140, 150–173]. Along with periods in Near Eastern history (*Io, Semiramide* It. 1962; *Land of the Pharaohs* USA 1955; *The Egyptian* USA 1954), these films are set mainly in the Greek and Roman eras [28. 141–165], and in the case of Roman history the focus is largely on the conflict between the Roman state and early Christians (*The Sign of the Cross* USA 1932; *Ben Hur* USA 1959; *Quo vadis* USA 1951; *The Robe* USA 1953; *Silver Chalice* USA 1954) [28. 126–140].

The genre of Antiquity films also includes works under the general heading of neo-mythologizing [24. 83–90; 31] that present ancient myths and legends of Greece and Rome in a manner that is often only very loosely based on the source material; thus the Greek hero Hercules, the fictional character Maciste or Samson are depicted in Italian films of the 1950s and 1960s as popular heroes in a constant battle against evil in a setting somewhere to the east of Greece, and in periods other than Antiquity (e.g. *Maciste alla Corte dello Zar* It. 1964) [7. 81–84; 17. 174–175; 28. 191–201]. During the 1980s, Hercules became almost a fantasy figure (*Hercules in New York* USA/It. 1982), showing up again in the 1990s as a Disney Studios cartoon character (*Hercules* USA 1997).

Early Roman history during the time of Punic War was made into a musical with aquatic numbers in *Jupiter's Darling* (USA 1955), with Esther Williams in the lead role as Amytis, the betrothed of Fabius Maximus who falls in love with Hannibal. The genre of the Antiquity film was parodied in the idiosyncratic version of the story of Jesus by the English comedy group Monty Python (*The Life of Brian* GB 1979) as well as in the story of Cleopatra presented in the Carry On film series, also a British production (*Carry on Cleo* GB 1965) [28. 180–190].

Quite different from the films mentioned above are Antiquity films based on ancient literature (tragedy, epic, novel, history) [28. 166–179] or more recent treatments of ancient motifs, such as the plays of Shakespeare or Shaw [7. 89–93, 99–102]. Particular mention should be made in this context of the filming of the Euripides trilogy (*Elektra/The Trojan Women/Iphigenia*) by Michael Cacoyannis [19; 20; 21] and the works of Pier Paolo Pasolini, *Medea* (1970) and *Edipo Re* (1967), as well as Federico Fellini's *Satyricon* (1969) [32], in which the ancient world is presented not in its popularised, classicistic image, but as strange, threatening, ugly and often obscene.

The main plot of Antiquity films based on modern works is generally a love story with a happy ending, whatever the actual historical facts. The epic hero and heroine are thus depicted according to strict gender-specific conventions. The male protagonist is generally courageous and able to master difficult challenges and tests; the virtuous heroine tends to be noble and to require protection. Female figures such as ancient ruling women who break with these gender-specific conventions are often portrayed in a very ambivalent manner, often as a *femme fatale*, and by the end of the film they are usually reduced to the role of a loving wife or required to heroically renounce love or even their lives [11. 103–112; 12; 34. 84–89].

Like the depiction of role-defined behaviour, physical depictions in such films adhere to traditional gender-specific expectations. Most of the male actors are muscular and even, in the case of some "B movies", former winners of the Mr. Universe title [12. 70], while the actresses portraying ancient women, particularly in Italian films, have come to the cinema by way of beauty contests [2. 313]. The women's costumes and hair styles tend to present a version of ancient fashion that is adapted to suit modern tastes, and eroticism is a marked characteristic [8. 235; 25; 26; 34. 83]. Thus standard motifs of this genre include belly dancing performed by the main or by secondary female characters, usually dressed in bikini tops and harem trousers or slit skirts (*The Prodigal* USA 1955; *Cleopatra* USA 1934; *The Serpent from the Nile* USA 1953; *Le Legioni di Cleopatra* It./France 1959; *Cleopatra* USA 1963; *Quo vadis* USA 1951; *Nel segno di Roma* It./France/West Germany 1958; *La vendetta dei barbari* It. 1960; *Teodora, imperatrice di Bisanzio* It. 1954) [34. 80].

This type of erotic emphasis also points to another characteristic of the reception of Antiquity in film: orientalization. It is of little significance in this context whether the action of a given film takes place in the Near East or in the Eastern hemisphere of the Roman Empire. Rather, a certain contemporary image of a Turkish or Arabian Orient acts here as a code for decadence that can be portrayed at any time or place in ancient history [34. 77–83]. The lavish and detailed picture of the Orient presented in 19th cent. painting, in particular, was the inspiration for the sets and costumes of these films [13]. The exoticism typical of the oriental style of certain → OPERAS of the 19th cent. with subjects like 'Aida' also made its way into the film industry [9]. In the absence of ancient musical themes, and owing to the fact that ancient instruments are largely familiar only as images, ancient music is presented in modern films in the style of Janissary music, romantic themes or pompous march music, a tradition broken only when Pasolini and Fellini began to try ethnomusic [29].

Along with an emphasis on physicality, there is a striking degree of brutality in the action depicted in these films. Hidden among the themes of Antiquity films, this satisfies the demands of a contemporary audience for scenes of violence and cruelty, as in the gladiator scenes in *Spartacus* (USA 1960); in some cases, a display of the male body plays to homoerotic voyeurism [12; 14. 49–50; 31. 407]. The topical elements of Antiquity films also include chariot races (*Cleopatra* 1934; various versions of the Ben Hur subject matter, *Teodora, imperatrice di Bisanzio* It. 1954; a parody in the film *A Funny Thing Happened on the Way to the Forum* (USA 1966), based on plays by Plautus) and the 'Voice of God', the resonant masculine voice of a quasi-omniscient commentator from offstage, who introduces the action and offers final comments at the end, lending authority to the film's content [27. 25, 34–35].

C. EFFECT

The success of the Antiquity film genre during the period between the two World Wars and after World War II can be explained in terms of two effects: escapism and identification. By transporting the audience to another time and another, more colourful place, they provided distraction from everyday problems. Furthermore, the eroticization of the main female roles in particular made it possible to get around strict censorship in Italy and the United States, where most Antiquity films were produced. In Italy, it was especially the Catholic Church that monitored sexual morality in films, simultaneously acting as moral censor and as cinema owner, particularly in rural areas [15. 13–14; 24. 84]. In Hollywood, meanwhile, agreement had been reached in the 1930s on the so-called 'production code', a system of self-censorship by the film studios set up in response to pressure from social interest groups (the Catholic Church and other religious groups) [2. 775–776] that remained in force until the 1960s. Under this code it was prohibited to show explicit sexual acts; nor were films permitted to show double beds [22. 276–277]. Moreover, films were expected to portray intact families and marriages in a favourable light. Ancient female figures like Cleopatra, who since Antiquity had been associated with seduction and adultery in literature and the fine arts, offered an excellent opportunity for projecting erotic fantasies without endangering contemporary morals, since such figures were, after all, from a long-ago era [10; 35]. The same was true of the motif of decadence (e.g. scenes of sumptuous banquets and court revelry) or the well-known female sinners in the Bible (such as the temple priestess Samarra in *The Prodigal* or *Delilah*).

In southern Europe, Antiquity films served to strengthen national and cultural identity, apparent for example through the leading role played by Italy in this film sector, and also through the success during the silent-film era of *Cabiria*, a cinematic depiction of the confrontation between Rome and Carthage [7. 81–84]. The Romanian productions depicting the Dacians as proto-Romanians (*Battle of the Titans against Rome* 1966; *The Tyrant* 1968) demonstrate this national tradition, which is analogous to the preference for medieval sagas in English and German epic films about the

exploits of knighthood [7. 136–159; 24. 94–96]. Although its second part was an international co-production, the filming of the Euripides trilogy (*Elektra/The Trojan Women/Iphigenia*) was in Greek hands: it was directed by the Cypriot Michael Cacoyannis, most of the cast was Greek, and the music for *Elektra* was written by Mikis Theodorakis [28. 168–170; 18. 844]. In the United States, Biblical films and epics showing Christians doing battle against the Roman Empire contributed to the creation of a cultural identity based on Christianity and democracy [14. 49; 16; 24. 78–79; 37. 140]. The interest shown by both the United States and England in the subject of the Roman Empire reflects a fascination with the development of empires and the forces that threaten their existence that is rooted in those countries' own history [38]. Such films also contain hidden messages, as when the cinematic Marcus Aurelius speaks of a multi-cultural Roman society in the film *The Fall of the Roman Empire*, echoing the American concept of the 'Great Society' during the Johnson administration in the context of the civil-rights movement, or in the case of references to the Cold War [37. 145f.]. The vision of a united world following Alexander the Great contained in the uncut version of *Cleopatra* 1963 hints at American hopes for a solution to the enmity between NATO and the Warsaw Pact [38. 100], while the idea of a corrupt Eastern Bloc is reflected in numerous films when the ancient Orient is transformed and reinterpreted in terms of contemporary Turkish/Arabian circumstances. Antiquity films of the post-war period sought to convey to the female audience in particular the importance of the role of 'wife' (less frequently that of 'mother'), thus imposing social discipline on women while offering them a character with whom they might identify (the woman who conforms to norms) [34. 84–89].

The economic interests behind these Antiquity films should not be underestimated. Compared with the reception and reproduction of ancient content in the media of other eras, the film industry is a far more effective multiplier. *Cleopatra* 1934 initiated quite an advertising campaign: department stores established separate departments and display windows advertising for clothing and cosmetic articles in the style of the film. This advertising was aimed at the female half of the population, with the goal of inducing them to see the film as well as to purchase goods. The same method was revived for *Cleopatra* 1963: the print media in particular, most prominently *Vogue* [10. 121–124; 38. 102], set the standard for fashion à la Cleopatra, as portrayed by Elizabeth Taylor, and the actress reinforced the message by commissioning her costume designer to recreate her film costume for her wedding to Richard Burton [26. 44]. After films are shown in the cinema, the ancient world is used by other industries in → ADVERTISING for their own purposes, and female figures are eroticized as a part of marketing strategy. Even low-budget Italian films have made a great deal of money, not least as a result of their many showings at home and abroad (cf. the contemporary German film magazines *Illustrierte Film-Bühne* and *Das Neue Film-Programm*) [31. 403]. The fact that the modern protagonist in the film *The English Patient* (USA 1996) carried a copy of Herodotus' *Histories* around with him, in which he kept letters and from which he quoted, actually led to a dramatic rise in demand for that ancient historian's work.

1 J. Baron, 9 to 5 as Aristophanic Comedy, in: M. M. Winkler (ed.) Classics and Cinema, 1991, 232–250 2 L.-A. Bawden (ed.), The Oxford Companion to Film, 1976 3 J. Beuselink, Mankiewicz's Cleopatra, in: Films in Review 39, 1989, 2–17 4 J. Brodsky, N. Weiss, The Cleopatra-Papers: A Private Correspondence, New York 1963 5 J. Clauss, A Course on Classical Mythology in Film, in: CJ 91, 1996, 287–295 6 A. Collognat, L'antiquité au cinéma, in: Bulletin de l'Association Guillaume Budé 1994/1995, 332–351 7 P. Drexler, Zur Funktion des Chors und chorischer Elemente in den Filmen Woody Allens, in: P. Riemer, B. Zimmermann (eds.), Der Chor im antiken und modernen Drama, 1998, 247–270 8 D. Elley, The Epic Film. Myth and History, 1984 9 P. W. Engelmeier, R. Engelmeier (eds.), Fashion in Film, 1997 10 Ch. Fritze, G. Seesslen, C. Weil (eds.), Der Abenteurer: Geschichte und Mythologie des Abenteuer-Films, 1983 (especially: Sandalen und Muskeln: Der Antikfilm, 66–97). 11 R. Gulrich, Exotismus in der Oper und seine szenische Realisation (1850–1910): unter besonderer Berücksichtigung der Münchener Oper, 1993 12 M. Hamer, Signs of Cleopatra: History, Politics, Representation, 1993 13 F. Hirsch, The Hollywood Epic, 1978 14 L. Hunt, What Are Big Boys Made Of? Spartacus, El Cid and the Male Epic, in: You Tarzan: Masculinity, Movies and Man, P. Kirkham, J. Thumin (eds.), 1993, 65–83 15 R. Kabbani, Europe's Myths of Orient, 1986 16 H. P. Kochenrath, Von Quo Vadis bis Kleopatra, in: Filmstudio (März) 1964, 46–56 17 H. Koppel, Film in Italien – Italien im Film, 1970 18 Th. Kuchenbuch, Bibel und Geschichte – Zum religiösen Film: Die Zehn Gebote (The Ten Commandments, 1957), in: Fischer Filmgeschichte Vol. 3, W. Faulstich, H. Korte (eds.), Auf der Suche nach den Werten 1945–1960, 1990, 299–330 19 P. Leprohon, Le cinéma italien, rev. ed. 1966 (Engl. R. Greaves, O. Stallybrass (trans), The Italian Cinema, 1972) 20 Lexikon des Internationalen Films: das komplette Angebot in Kino und Fernsehen seit 1945: 21 000 Kurzkritiken und Filmographien, rev. by K. Brüne, 10 vols., 1987. 21 K. MacKinnon, Greek Tragedy into Film, 1986 22 M. McDonald, Cacoyannis vs. Euripides: From Tragedy to Melodrama, in: Drama, Beiträge zum antiken Drama und seiner Rezeption 2, 1993, 222–234 23 Id., Euripides in Cinema: The Heart made Visible, 1983 24 J. Monaco, H.-M. Bock, R. Wolleben, Film verstehen: Kunst, Technik, Sprache: Geschichte und Theorie des Films und der Medien; mit einer Einführung in Multimedia, 2000 25 K. M. Passman, The Classical Amazon in Contemporary Cinema, in: Classics and Cinema, M. M. Winkler (ed.), 1991, 81–105 26 H. Schlüpmann, Politik als Schuld, Zur Funktion des historischen Kostüms in Weiblichkeitsbildern der Filme Maria Ilona (1939) und Königin Luise (1956), in: Frauen und Film 38, 1985, 46–57 27 I. Sharaff, Les costumes de Cléopâtre, in: Positif 193 (May edition), 1977, 42–47 28 V. Sobchak, Surge and Splendor: A Phenomenology of the Hollywood Historical Epic, in: Representations 29, 1990, 24–49 29 J. Solomon, The Ancient World in the Cinema, 2001 30 Id., The Sounds of Cinematic Antiquity, in: Classics and Cinema, M. M. Winkler (ed.), 1991, 264–281 31 Id., In the Wake of Cleopatra: The Ancient World in the Cinema since 1963, in: CJ 91, 1996, 113–140 32 V. Spinazzola, Herkules erobert die Leinwand, in: Filmkritik 8, 1964, 402–408 33 J. P. Sullivan, The Social Ambience of Petronius' Satyricon and Fellini's Satyricon, in: Classics and Cinema, M. M. Winkler (ed.) 1991, 264–281 34 W. Wanger, J. Hyams, My Life with Cleopatra, 1963 35 A. Wieber-Scariot, Herrscherin und doch ganz Frau – Zur Darstellung antiker Herrscherinnen im Film der 50er und 60er Jahre, in: metis 7, 1998, 73–89 36 D. Wildung, Mythos Kleopatra, in: Kleopatra. Ägypten um die Zeitenwende, Kunsthalle der Hypo-Kulturstiftung, 16. Juni – 10. September 1989, 1989, 13–18 37 M. M. Winkler (ed.), Classics and Cinema, 1991 38 Id., Cinema and the Fall of Rome, in: TAPhA 125, 1995, 135–154 39 M. Wyke, Projecting The Past: Ancient Rome, Cinema and History, 1997

Additional Bibliography I. Blom, Quo Vadis? From Painting to Cinema and Everything in between, in: L. Quaresima, L. Vinchi (eds.), La decima Musa. Il cinema e le altri arti / The tenth Muse. Cinema and the other arts, 2001, 281–292; A. Boschi, A. Bozzato, I greci al cinema. Dal peplum 'd'autore' alla grafica computerizzata, 2005; M. S. Cyrino, Big Screen Rome, 2005; S. R. Joshel, M. Malamud, D. T. McGuire Jr. (eds.), Imperial Projections. Ancient Rome in Modern Popular Culture, 2001, 23–49; M. Junkelmann, Hollywoods Traum von Rom. Gladiator und die Tradition des 'Monumentalfilms', 2004; M. Korenjak, K. Töchterle (eds.), Pontes II: Antike im Film, 2002; M. Lindner (ed.), Drehbuch Geschichte. Die Antike Welt im Film, 2005; Ll. Llewellyn-Jones, Celluloid Cleopatras or Did the Greeks ever Get to Egypt?, in: D. Ogden (ed.), The Hellenistic World. New Perspectives, 2002, 275–304; Ll. Llewellyn-Jones, The Fashioning of Delilah. Costume Design, Historicism and Fantasy in Cecil B. DeMille's Samson and Delilah (1949), in: Ll. Llewellyn-Jones, L. Cleland, M. Harlow (eds.), The Clothed Body in the Ancient World, 2005, 14–29; F. Martin, L'Antiquité au Cinéma, 2002; M. Meier, S. Slanicka (eds.), Antike und Mittelalter im Film. Konstruktion – Dokumentation – Projektion (forthcoming); P. Michelakis, Greek Tragedy in Cinema: Theatre, Politics, History, in: E. Hall, F. Macintosh, A. Wringley (eds.), Dionysus Since '69: Greek Tragedy and Public Imagination at the End of the 2nd Millenium, 2004, 199–217; G. Nisbet, Ancient Greece in Film and Popular Culture (forthcoming); S. Schulze-Gattermann, Das Erbe des Odysseus: antike Tragödie und mainstream-Film, 2000; J. Solomon, The Ancient World in the Cinema. Revised and expanded edition, 2001; E. Theodorakopoulos, Story and Spectacle: Rome at the Cinema (forthcoming); D. Wenzel, Kleopatra im Film. Eine Königin Ägyptens als Sinnbild für orientalische Kultur, 2005; A. Wieber (ed.), "Antike im Film", thematic issue of the Journal "Der Altsprachliche Unterricht", 2005; A. Wieber, Von der Völkerwanderung zum Kalten Krieg: Sign of the Pagan zwischen antikem Topos und Mentalitäten der 50er Jahre, in: S. Machura, R. Voigt (eds.), Krieg im Film, 2005, 59–101; M. M. Winkler (ed), Classical Myth and Culture in the Cinema, 2001; M. M. Winkler (ed), Gladiator. Film and History,

2004; M. M. WINKLER (ed.), Spartacus: Film and History (forthcoming); M. M. WINKLER (ed.), Troy: From Homer's Iliad to Hollywood Epic, 2006; M. M. WINKLER, Dulce et decorum est pro patria mori? Classical Literature in the War Film, in: International Journal of the Classical Tradition 7, 2, 2000, 177–214   ANJA WIEBER-SCARIOT

Fin de siècle
A. INTRODUCTION   B. FUNCTIONS AND IMAGES OF ANTIQUITY   C. PHILOSOPHY AND PSYCHOLOGICAL SCHOOLS

A. INTRODUCTION
A phenomenon of the second half of the 19th cent. that followed out of the aesthetic re-orientation of the French → DÉCADENCE movement, the *Fin de siècle* (FdS) literary period encompassed a paradigmatic re-evaluation of the largely uniform conception of Antiquity that practitioners of French and German Classicism, and most notably among them Goethe and Winckelmann, had established and which had continued to persist in broad sections of established, official European culture. By the FdS period, however, the general reception of Antiquity had departed in the most fundamental ways from that which had prevailed in the last years of the 18th cent. Creating a greater cultural awareness of ancient mythological themes and characters as well as a more widespread and more detailed historical knowledge of Antiquity among broader strata of the population than ever before were developments such as the following: access to an education in a → HUMANIST GYMNASIUM; the establishment of a public → MUSEUM system; the publishing of archaeological accounts by H. Schliemann and W. Dörpfeld about their excavations at → TROY, Tiryns, → Orchomenus and → KNOSSUS; the growth of the historically positivistic fields of Religious Studies and of Ancient Philology, with its own related associations of gymnasium teachers; an idealised association of the Hohenzollern imperial house with the Ancient Imperium that manifested itself in Wilhelmine city planning, architecture and public monument design and in a historically inspired pageantry that is visible, for instance, in the reconstructed → SAALBURG [9]); the popularity of historical novels such as F. Dahn's *Kampf um Rom*, L. Wallace's *Ben Hur* (1880) and H. Sienkiewicz's *Quo vadis?* (1895/96) and of historical dramas like H. Ibsen's *Emperor and Galilean* (1883), R. Specht's *Das Gastmahl des Plato* (1893) and L. Ebermann's *Die Athenerin* (1896); the publication of numerous studies by academics and professors; and the staging of scenes from ancient myth in the booths of annual markets and fairs (cf. [8]) [11]. Antiquity can, therefore, serve as a point of reference and as background knowledge for understanding the FdS.

B. FUNCTIONS AND IMAGES OF ANTIQUITY
The great variety both of 'archives' from Antiquity as well as of media in which they are transmitted found a correspondence in the FdS in the manifold ways in which Antiquity was 'encoded' and used. Thus, Antiquity served as a stock of mythological stories and materials, as a mythologically configured narrative space in which lyric, dramatic or narrative action might unfold, as a historical arsenal of real or semi-real ancient figures and characters, as a historical space, as a literary archive and, finally, as a stylistic category and literary process. But the omnipresence of the ancient by no means implied a homogeneity in that which was drawn upon from Antiquity or in that which was called ancient. Indeed, for the artistic and cultural establishment, Antiquity represented a refuge from the oppressive middle-class civilisation of the French Second Empire and the Second German Reich, from Josephinism and Victorianism, and thus had a compensatory and identificatory function. For others, however, Antiquity served to legitimise monarchical empire and claims of imperial power, and, for some, even to reflect moral doctrine. In such respects, Modernity gained an ancient face.

At the same time, Décadence and FdS literature, in alliance with mostly non-academic philosophy as represented by names such as J.J.Bachofen, J. Burckhardt, F. Nietzsche, E. Rohde and W. Pater and with psychology as propounded, for example, by P. Bourget, S. Freud and J. Breuer, proposed a new and different picture of Antiquity. More specifically, with that new conception of the ancient, radical Modernism–with the notable exception of Naturalism–avoided setting itself up in opposition to Antiquity in a renewed → QUERELLE DES ANCIENS ET DES MODERNES. Instead, Antiquity took on the appearance of Modernity. Among members of the FdS avant-garde, those who chose to make use of Antiquity–and not all members did–demonstrated great heterogeneity in how they employed it.

The first of two basic FdS conceptions of Antiquity, and a conception that was particularly important in France and England, considered the Roman Imperium within the decadent context of an Antiquity characterized by its 'sinister' nature. Specifically, the Empire became the mythic setting for terrible crimes such as those of Tiberius, Messalina, Caligula, Nero, Elagabalus, the mother-daughter dyad Herodias and Salome and the tetrarch Herod Antipas. Furthermore, it became the locus of an aesthetically exaggerated sensuality and sexual mystery. The FdS was thus able to exploit the Roman Imperium as an allegory for a present that regarded itself as decadent. Additionally, the FdS used the Imperium as a poetological Allegoresis of the literary process, a process it viewed critically at first but then–pointing positively to post-Republican authors like Petronius, Juvenal, Apuleius, Lucian, Tacitus, Martial and Suetonius and with an eye to ennobling its own literary position–it began to view affirmatively.

Alongside this conception of a decadent Antiquity–a conception that quickly established itself as an object of academic research–we must by no means overlook a second conception. Specifically, in laying bare or stylising those aspects of Antiquity suppressed in the Classical conception, such as the 'wild' and subversive as represented in G. Flaubert, the intoxicatingly Dionysian as expounded by Nietzsche and Rohde, the Heraclitic of W. Pater and A. Symons, the 'hysterical' of H. Bahr and H. von Hofmannsthal and the cultic pagan of St. George and the Munich *Kosmiker*, artists activated Antiquity as Modernism's Other, with the aim of obtaining renewal from contact with that Other.

One might cite Flaubert's novel *Salammbô* (1862) about Carthage's Mercenary war, which emancipated itself from the contemporary reader's store of myth by tapping into a marginal zone of Antiquity erased from historical as well as poetic memory. With its mass scenes of unleashed decadence and its depiction of cruel perversions and rituals, it created an epic counterpart to the artificial paradises of Baudelaire. But at the same time, in the figure of Salammbô, rendered neurotic by the contradiction between her sensuality and her idealised priestly status, Flaubert created a female type that in countless variants (e.g., in St. Mallarmé's *Hérodiade*, 1864, Flaubert's *Hérodias*, 1877, J.-K. Huysmans' description of Moreau's painting *Salomé* and *Die Erscheinung*, 1878, in *À Rebour* 1884, P. Hille's *Herodias*, 1893, R. Schaukal's *Herodes und Salome*, 1897) and after many metamorphoses led typologically to O. Wilde's cruel, nymphomaniac child-woman *Salome* (1892).

Nietzsche's *Geburt der Tragödie* (1872) continued the preoccupation with an Antiquity that was more Archaic–it promoted, for instance, the tragedies of Sophocles over those of Euripedes–more ecstatic and, therefore, more subversive. On the one hand, Nietzsche reformulated the opposition between Dionysus and Apollo earlier emphasised in Romanticism and then by Bachofen as an aesthetic opposition of two fundamental formal principles, decomposition and re-composition, a duality characteristic of the FdS. On the other hand, for Nietzsche the Dionysian aspect stands is opposition both to the moralising tendency of a Judaeo-Christian tradition anchored in the Apollonian and to the overvaluation of reason. Rohde's religious-historical *Psyche, Seelenkult und Unsterblichkeitsglaube bei den Griechen* (1890–1894) defended Nietzsche's intuition against the harsh criticism coming from the camp of the university-based Ancient Philologists, most notable among them, U. von Wilamowitz-Moellendorf. His portrayal of the Mysteries of Eleusis and Dionysus remained a fundamental influence for the next generation of writers (cf., for example, Th. Mann's *Tod in Venedig*, 1911/12).

C. Philosophy and Psychological Schools

Reference to Greek and Roman Antiquity was as fundamental to the pan-dynamism of Pater's philosophy of life as it had been to Nietzsche's early work. Drawing both on the pre-Socratic physics of Empedocles and Heraclitus as well as on the teachings of Epi-

curus and Lucretius, Pater, in the *Conclusion* to his *Studies in the History of the Renaissance* (1873, first published as the final part of a review of W. Morris) [7], developed the hedonistic aesthetic and ethics of a purely subjective foundation for perception and action "for the moment's sake". (Cf. his novel *Marius the Epicurean*, 1885; the figure of Denys l'Auxerrois, the descriptive name given to a combination Dionysus-Zagreus figure that is transplanted into the Middle Ages in *Imaginary Portraits*, 1887; *Plato and Platonism*, 1893; from his *Greek Studies*, 1895, especially *A Study of Dionysos. The Spiritual Form of Fire and Dew*). Symons tested out the impressionistic aesthetic of *mood*–which oriented itself both on Pater's philosophy of the moment and on French Decadent literature (esp. Huysmans) [12]–in dramatic and lyric form, again using familiar ancient themes (e.g., the loose series of scenes *Images of Good and Evil*, 1900; the Nero drama *The Death of Agrippina*, 1916). And Wilde derived his justification of an amoral aestheticism from Pater's position.

In Viennese Modernism, Antiquity moved into the context of dreams and their interpretation, psychoanalysis of the unconscious, nervous pathology (*Nervenkunst*) and hysteria. A striking example of the fantastical conception of Antiquity was R. Beer-Hofmann's extravagant vision of cultic temple-prostitution in *Der Tod Georgs* (1900). With Freud and Breuer's *Studien über Hysterie* (1895), in which Freud's developed a 'cathartic' therapy using the terminology of ancient myth, and with A. von Berger's critique of Aristotle's 'moral' doctrine of catharsis (1897) [2], the ground was prepared for the association of dramatic theory with psychopathology. Bahr's *Dialog vom Tragischen* [1] saw in modern drama the possibility of abreacting the hysteria caused by the renunciation of instincts in civilised humanity. Hofmannsthal's drama *Elektra* (1904), which differs notably from its prototype by Sophocles in replacing the *agon* over the guilt or innocence of Clytaemnestra with Electra's raging vision of the murder, is generally regarded as the most radical instance of this 'Hysterisierung der Griechen', or "hystericalizing of the Greeks" (Fr. Gundolf).

Gundolf's critique of the Viennese conception of Antiquity–a critique that would serve as an example for the Munich Modernists–rested upon a conception of Antiquity that, not unlike that of German Classicism, reinterpreted Greek civilisation as a valid historical manifestation of, and model for, one's own aesthetic lifestyle. As early as 1892, George's *Algabal* presented the Roman emperor more as a hyper-refined, sensitive poet-seer and high priest of art than as an unbridled *décadent* (cf. also the translations of ancient authors by members of George's circle and the poetological program and dramas in imitation of ancient precedents in *Blätter für die Kunst*). In the same vein are George's para-Christianity with its neo-pagan characteristics and both A. Schuler's defence of Nero as a great aesthete, artist and town-planner [6] and his idea of a neo-pagan restoration and an activation of the 'pagan heritage'.

→ ADAPTATION; → PAGANISM

1 H. BAHR, Neue Rundschau 14, 1903, 716–736   2 A. V.
BERGER, Wahrheit und Irrtum in der Katharsislehre des
Aristoteles, in: TH. GOMPERZ (ed.), Aristoteles Poetik,
Leipzig 1897, 71–98   3 M. BOSSE, A. STOLL, Die Agonie
des archaischen Orients. Eine verschlüsselte Vision des
Revolutionszeitalters, in Id. (eds.), G. Flaubert,
Salammbô, 1979, 401–448   4 R. JENKYNS, The Victorians and Ancient Greece, 1980   5 N. KOHL, memento
vivere: Walter Paters Philosophie des Augenblicks in der
Conclusion, in: Antike und Abendland 20, 1974, 135–150
6 A. SCHULER, Nero-Vortrag (1889), in: B. MÜLLER (ed.),
A. Schuler, Cosmogonische Augen: Gesammelte Schriften, 1997, 198–213   7 W. PATER, Review of the 'Poems',
in: The Westminster Review 34, October 1868, 300–312
8 F. SALTEN, Wurstelprater, 1911   9 E. SCHALLMEYER
(ed.), Hundert Jahre Saalburg. Vom römischen Grenzposten zum europäischen Museum, 1997   10 E. STÄRK,
Hermann Nitschs 'Orgien Mysterien Theater' und die
'Hysterie der Griechen'. Quellen und Traditionen im
Wiener Antikebild seit 1900, 1987, 67–108   11 A.
SYMONS, The Decadent Movement in Literature, in: Harpers New Monthly Magazine, September 1893, 858–867
12 G. WUNBERG, Chiffrierung und Selbstversicherung des
Ich. Antikefiguration um 1900, in: M. PFISTER (ed.), Die
Modernisierung des Ich, 1989, 190–201
ADDITIONAL BIBLIOGRAPHY M. GUBSER, Time's Visible Surface: Alois Riegl and the Discourse on History and
Temporality in fin-de-siècle Vienna, 2006 S. L. MARCHAND, Germany at the fin de siecle: Culture, Politics, and
Ideas, 2004 M. S. MICALE, The Mind of Modernism:
Medicine, Psychology, and the Cultural Arts in Europe
and America, 1880–1940, 2004   KLAUS MÜLLER-RICHTER

Finland

A. GENERAL   B. THE RECEPTION OF CLASSICAL
ANTIQUITY   C. CLASSICAL PHILOLOGY

A. GENERAL

Until 1809 Finland (F.) was part of the Swedish
Kingdom. It was then incorporated into Czarist Russia
as an autonomous state until it gained its independence
in 1917.

B. THE RECEPTION OF CLASSICAL ANTIQUITY
1. LITERATURE   2. FINE ARTS

1. LITERATURE

With the exception of the work being conducted on
Antiquity in universities, the Finnish culture, in comparison with many other European countries, has been
far less influenced by the ancient world. German Romanticism, however, has left its mark on F. The oldest
texts found in F. were of a religious nature, and the peak
of Latin literature in the Middle Ages can be seen in a
collection of songs, some of them secular, which was
compiled in the Piae Cantiones. The Finnish national
poet J.L. Runeberg is closest to ancient thought in his
drama Kungarne på Salamis ('The Kings of Salamis',

1863), in which he focuses on the theme of power and
justice. In several poems written in hexameters, the
Homeric style and tone are also discernible and are
demonstrated particularly in the use of metaphors.
Later another representative of Swedish literature, R.
Enckell, incorporated themes from Classical Antiquity
into a number of lyrical dramas to reflect in them his
own experiences, for instance Orpheus och Eurydike
('Orpheus and Eurydice', 1938), Agamemnon (1949)
and Hecuba (1952). Among the greatest Finnish writers, E. Leino (1878–1926) transported the dramatic
action of some of his plays into the ancient world. Even
V.A. Koskenniemi (1885–1962) drew his inspiration
from Antiquity: he composed poems in elegiac couplets,
in which he showed that man ultimately depends on the
mercy of fate. Ancient images are expressed most clearly in two of his collections: Elegioja ynnä muita runoja
('Elegies', 1917) and Sydän ja kuolema ('The Heart and
Death', 1920). P. Mustapää (1899–1973) may be regarded as a poeta doctus because he rendered ancient
mythology in lyric verse. O. Manninen (1872–1950)
gained prominence above all as a translator; his verse
translations of the Iliad and the Odyssey are particularly noteworthy. P. Saarikoski (1937–1983) translated
Hipponax and Sappho, among others, into free verse.
The mockery of Hipponax even shines through in Saarikoski's own modern poems, which display an ironic
attitude towards the image of the ancient ideal. T.
Vaaskivi and M. Waltari have written historical narratives set in the world of Antiquity. The main work of the
first author, Yksinvaltias ('The Autocrat', 1942) is a
novel about the emperor Tiberius – a sophisticated
work full of brilliant character drawings. Waltari is the
Finnish writer best known in foreign countries; a Hollywood film has even been made of his novel Sinuhe,
egyptiläinen (Engl. The Egyptian, 1945). Its essential
feature, the synthesis of idealism and realism, is the leitmotif of many of his works (e.g. Turms kuolematon,
Engl. The Etruscan, 1955; Valtakunnan salaisuus,
Engl. The Secret of the Kingdom, 1959; Ihmiskunnan
viholliset, Engl. The Roman, 1964). In recent years, two
essayists, K. Simonsuuri and P. Suhonen, have been
exploring Ancient themes, and of the translators M.
Itkonen-Kaila is particularly worthy of mention.

2. FINE ARTS

In the fine arts, the motifs have been taken more
from the Kalevala than from the ancient world but
sculpture has in several instances been influenced by
Neo-Classicism. C.E. Sjöstrand depicted characters
from the Kalevala but behind the sculpture Kullervo
katkoo kapalonsa ('Kullervo removing his swaddling
clothes', 1858), for example, stands the motif of 'Hercules strangling the snakes'. Classical themes have been
embraced, above all, by W. Runeberg (1838–1920),
e.g. in three Psyche groups, as well as in Apollon ja
Marsyas ('Apollon and Marsyas'), Nukkuva Amor
('Sleeping Amor') and Amor ja Bacchus lapsina ('Amor
and Bacchus as Children'), and by J. Takanen (1849–
1885) in Venus ja Amor ('Venus and Amor') and

Andromeda. 'The Shipwrecked' (*Haaksirikkoiset*, 1898) by R. Stigell is reminiscent in its composition of the → LAOCOON GROUP; Classical influences can also be traced in the sculptures of W. Aaltonen (1894–1966). In the field of architecture, Neo-Classicism reached F. in the late 18th cent.: the church in Hämeenlinna (built by L.J. Desprez between 1792 and 1798) was in its original form a successful imitation of the → PANTHEON in Rome. However, the most important example is the centre of the new capital Helsinki, designed in a monumental style by C.L. Engel (1778–1840), and in particular Senate Square with its surrounding buildings. The ground plan of the university library reflects that of the thermal baths of Diocletian in Rome. G. Nyström (1856–1917) incorporated the state archives and the House of the Estates into this centre, and in the early 20th cent. E. Bryggman and J.S. Sirén integrated Classical themes into their architecture (the latter in the design of the parliament building). Classical influences are also present particularly in the earlier buildings of A. Aalto (1898–1976). Worth mentioning as curiosities are the Latin → OPERA *Laurentius* by H. Rechberger (1994) and the news in Latin produced by T. Pekkanen and R. Pitkäranta – *Nuntii Latini* – that can be heard on the radio every week.

C. CLASSICAL PHILOLOGY

During the period of Swedish rule and under the palpable influence of Western culture, Latin became the dominant language in the Church and partly also in the administration. With Protestantism at the time of the Reformation (1523–1617) and the Finnish translation of the Bible by Agricola, Latin then suffered increasingly from a loss of influence in public life, but it remained the language of science and scholarship. The first → UNIVERSITY was founded in Turku in 1640; it was destroyed after the fire of 1828 and rebuilt in Helsinki. Up until that year, lectures at the university were held in Latin, and academic papers were for the most part written in Latin. Despite the presence of orthodox Protestantism, the central ideas of → HUMANISM came to be spread in F., although this did not occur until late in the 17th cent. The ideals derived from Aristotle, Cicero and Seneca were expressed primarily in public lectures and in poetry. Even more significant was the arrival of German → NEW HUMANISM in the late 18th cent. – at a time when the Swedish language gradually began to replace Latin, prompting discussions as to whether Latin should be retained. New Humanism again declared its faith in Latin, and the first person to emphatically support these ideas was H.G. Porthan (*p rofessor eloquentiae* 1777–1804); his pre-eminence as a Classical philologist is founded not so much in his research as in the fact that he had a formative effect on the academic style of his time. New Humanism also played a significant role in the national awakening. Not surprisingly, therefore, E. Lönnrot modelled the Finnish national epic *Kalevala* on Homer.

At the universities there were two professorships in Latin: *professor eloquentiae* and *professor poesis*; the latter was rescinded as being as anachronistic in 1747. Greek and Hebrew were combined under one professorial chair (*professor linguarum*), with the reading of Biblical texts taking centre stage. Towards the end of the 18th cent., secular authors like Homer were also treated in lectures, until a separate chair of Greek was finally established in 1812. From 1852 Latin only remained compulsory as the language for doctoral theses in Classical and Oriental studies. However, all students still had to acquire a basic knowledge of Latin right through to the 1960s, and in the modern languages this requirement was upheld even longer. Today Latin and Greek literature can be studied at six universities in Finland. There are professorships in Helsinki, Jyväskylä and Turku (Chair of Classical Languages and Culture); at the Swedish University in Turku – the so-called Åbo Akademi – the chair has been in a state of reorganization since 1993; in Tampere and Oulu there are lectureships in Latin; Greek as a major subject can only be studied in Helsinki and Turku. In the 18th cent., a limited selection of Latin authors were studied (e.g. Cicero, Livy or Virgil) in secondary schools, with the addition of various Greek authors in the *gymnasium* (e.g. Plutarch and Isocrates, occasionally Homer). The curriculum was then radically reshaped: in the 19th cent., Latin was still the most important language in the *gymnasium* but with the restructuring of the school system, the old-style *gymnasium* practically died out; today are only five left. Latin, which used to be part even of the lower secondary school curriculum, has now become a rare commodity at Finnish schools, Greek is no longer being taught there at all.

In the field of academic research, Classical philology in F. initially continued along the conventional paths of its tradition. The first Finnish Latinist to acquire international fame was E.J.W. af Brunér (Professor 1848–1871). His work set the trend in three disciplines and so outlined the areas of emphasis for future generations: → LINGUISTICS, textual criticism and Classical studies in general. Three of Brunér's successors also worked in textual criticism, even though the discipline was later neglected to some extent; recently interest has again intensified. One of Brunér's successors was I.A. Heikel (Professor of Greek, 1888–1926), who published an edition of two books by Eusebius. Around the same time, at the end of the 19th cent., J. Sundwall emerged as a leading expert in epigraphy, onomastics and archaeology; his achievements in the decoding of Linear B MSS are particularly noteworthy (→ DECIPHERMENT). H. Gummerus specialized in the social and economic history of Imperial Rome. Linguistics, esp. Latin syntax, has always been the most important field of research for Finnish scholars. A.H. Salonius pursued this aspect beyond the borders of Classical Latin in his book *Vitae patrum* (1920), and Y.M. Biese examined the phenomenon in his 1928 book about the absolute accusative – which in turn was the subject of a study by E.

Linkomies. V. Väänänen, a Romance languages scholar, became known internationally because of his epoch-making research into Vulgar Latin. Salonius had conducted papyrological studies in Berlin, and papyrology was also the main interest of his successor H. Zilliacus (Professor of Greek, 1944–1974). As the Director of the Finnish Institute in Rome, he focused on epigraphy which is methodologically related to papyrology. Sundvall and Väänänen, too, had been active in the field. Today the investigation and publication of inscriptions are still among the principal activities of the Institute in Rome. In the field of – Roman – numismatics, P. Bruun has been a prolific contributor, while E. Mikkola has explored the philosophy of Isocrates. L. Routila found international recognition with her seminal work on Aristotle.

Because the Classical Institutes at Finnish universities are fairly small – to this day only Helsinki has had more than one chair –, research has inevitably concentrated on a relatively narrow range of subjects. A primary focus at the University of Helsinki is the study of ancient literature, especially Greek drama under M. Kaimio; an important epigraphical and onomastic school has been represented by I. Kajanto, H. Solin and O. Salomies among others, papyrology after Zilliacus is represented by J. Frösén and Late Antiquity by P. Castrén, Neolatin scholars have included I. Kajanto and R. Pitkäranta, Byzantine studies has been the speciality of P. Hohti and ancient philosophy that of H. Thesleff, who has worked extensively on Plato. Classical Archaeology is the realm of L. Pietilä-Castrén; E.M. Steinby is another well-known representative of the discipline. In Turku H. Koskenniemi has conducted papyrological studies. The research of T. Viljamaa ranges from Greek literature to Latin grammar, and aside from semantic investigations into Greek tragedy, S. Jäkel has published a collection of maxims attributed to Menander. At the Åbo Akademi, aside from engaging in textual criticism of Cicero, R. Westman has conducted syntactical research and explored the field of Greek philosophy. Jyväskylä is a centre of Neolatin studies; T. Pekkanen has for instance translated the *Kalevala* into Latin, and O. Merisalo, a Romance languages scholar, has made Renaissance Latin the subject of her research. At the University of Tampere, T. Oksala has specialised in the study of ancient literature and the issues surrounding Humanism; H. Riikonen in Helsinki is well-known for his work his work on the same subject. At the University of Oulu, the political history of Rome is the research topic of U. Paananen, whilst Classical Archaeology is represented by E. Jarva. There is no chair of Ancient History in F., but occasionally general historians have nurtured an interest in Antiquity: e.g. J. Soulahti, an expert in prosopography and founder of the Finnish brick stamp research tradition, and P. Setäla, who has above all been engaged in Women's studies. Finnish Institutes exist in Rome (since 1954) and in Athens (since 1985); many junior scholars have been able to develop research projects based on the working groups forged at

these Institutes, which are also important from an interdisciplinary perspective.

→ NATIONAL RESEARCH INSTITUTES VI. THE FINNISH INSTISTUTE AT ATHENS; → SCHOOLS

1 P. Aalto, Classical Studies in Finland 1828–1918, 1980 2 I. Kajanto, The Classics in Finland, in: Arethusa 3, 1970, 205–226 3 Id., Porthan and Classical Scholarship: A Study of Classical Influences in Eighteenth Century Finland, 1984 4 Id., Humanism in a Christian Society I–II, 1989–1990 5 Id., Studi di filologia classica in Finlandia, in: Settentrione, Rivista di studi italo-finlandesi 6, 1994, 153–161 6 Id., s.v. Finland, in M. Skafte Jensen (ed.), A History of Nordic Neo-Latin Literature, 1995, 159–200 7 N. Kent, The Triumph of Light and Nature: Nordic Art 1740–1940, 1987 8 K. Laitinen, Finnish Literature: An Outline, 1989 9 Id., Suomen kirjallisuuden historia, ³1991 10 T. Oksala, Homeroksesta Alvar Aaltoon, 1985 11 A. Salokorpi, Modern Architecture in Finland, 1970 12 S. Sarajas-Korte et al. (eds.), Ars: Suomen taide 1–6, 1987–1990 13 G. Schildt, Alvar Aalto: A Life's Work – Architecture, Design and Art, 1994 14 J. B. Smith, The Golden Age of Finnish Art, ²1985 15 R. Westman, History of Classical Scholarship in Finland: A Bibliography, in: Arctos 30, 1996, 7–20 16 N. E. Wickberg, The Senate Square Helsinki, 1981.
RAIJA VAINIO

Finno-Ugric Languages
I. BALTO-FINNIC II. HUNGARIAN

I. BALTO-FINNIC
Of the contemporary Balto-Finnic languages, only Estonian and Finnish enjoy official state status as developed, standardized written languages. The sphere of use for Ingrian, Karelian, Livonian, Vepsian and Votian, where the speakers number from a few dozen (Livonian) to well over 100,000 (Karelian), is very restricted. Estonian and Finnish were considerably influenced by Germanic languages at the time of the creation of the standard written languages in the 15th–16th cents.: Finnish by Swedish, and Estonian, to a greater extent, by German (more precisely Low German), so that Latin and Greek lexemes were initially and almost without exception borrowed through these mediator languages. Finnish *r aamattu* 'Bible' and Estonian *raamat* 'book' came through Russian (< Old Russian *gramata* < Gr. γράμματα/*grámmata*).

The first documentation for such borrowings comes from the 16th cent. (e.g. Finnish *elementti*, attested in 1544); however, most borrowings did not find their way into these languages until the end of the 19th cent., when use of them was no longer restricted to the peasant class. The orthography of both languages (especially of Finnish) is very phonemic, which is why foreign phonemes and graphemes are predominantly rendered by means of native material: *kv* instead of *qu*, *ts* instead of *c* or *z*, *ks* instead of *x* etc. (cf. Finnish *kvaliteetti*, Estonian *kvaliteet* 'quality'). Both languages have a fixed accent on the initial syllable, which is consistently applied in Finnish even to foreign words. The accent of the donor language is often reflected in Finnish by the lengthening of the respective vowels: *pólitiikka* < Swedish *politík* 'politics' in contrast to *póliitikko* < Swedish *politíker* 'politician' similarly *póliittinen* < Swedish *politísk* 'political'. Estonian generally follows the accent pattern of the donor language; the lengthening is marked by reduplication according to the Estonian orthography: *situatsióon, süstéem*. A consonant in word-final position is unusual in Finnish and is remedied in foreign words by vowel epenthesis – usually by *i* (irrelevant for vowel harmony) but also, as in the example above, with other vowels by analogy to a native morpheme (here *-kka/-kkä*). Similarly, initial consonant clusters that are possible in Estonian are avoided in Finnish: Finnish *selluloidi*, Estonian *tselluloid* 'celluloid'. Some of the many productive Greek and Latin prefixes and suffixes [3. 76–80] such as *makro-, maksi-* can also be used in compounds with native word material [1. 484–489]. Adjectives are given the native suffix, Finnish *-inen*, Estonian *–(li)ne*, while verbs are given special suffixes reserved for foreign words: *-eerima* (Estonian) and *-oida* (Finnish), which can also be made intransitive: Estonian *-eeruma*, Finnish *-oitua*: Estonian *konkretiseeruma*, Finnish *konkretisoitua* 'to concretise'. Of the three major Finno-Ugric written languages, Estonian is by far the most amenable to assimilating foreign words [2].

1 M. ERELT, T. ERELT, K. ROSS, Eesti keele käsiraamat, 1997   2 J. KISS, P. KOKLA, W. SCHLACHTER, Kontrastive Untersuchungen zur Übernahme internationaler Wörter im Estnischen, Finnischen und Ungarischen, in: Nyelvtudományi Közlemények 77, 1975, 5–30   3 P. SAJAVAARA, Vierassanat, in: J. VESIKANSA (ed.), Nykysuomen sanavarat, 1989, 64–109

ADDITIONAL BIBLIOGRAPHY A. LILL, Words in Contact: German, Latin and early Estonian Literary Languages, in: Jahrbuch der Estnischen Goethe-Gesellschaft, 1991, 25–44

II. HUNGARIAN
A. GREEK B. LATIN

A. GREEK
The contacts between Hungary and the Byzantine Greeks (before the Hungarian settlement in 896; peaking from the second half of the 11th cent. to the end of the 12th cent.) left no unambiguous linguistic traces in Hungarian. No layer of 'borrowing' can be ascertained; borrowings are mostly restricted to the so called travelling words such as, e.g. Hungarian *fátyol* 'veil' (cf. Modern Gr. φακιόλι/*fakioli*), Hungarian *iszák* 'knapsack, satchel' (Modern Gr. βισάκκιν *isakki*).

B. LATIN
After the general conversion of the Hungarians to Christianity under King Stephen, Medieval Latin first permeated the language of the clergy, transmitted by German, Italian, and Slavic speaking churchmen in various forms. Because of the spiritual and economic power of the Church and the high prestige of the Latin-schooled educated class, Latin exerted strong influence on the entire society.

With Humanism, Classical Latin entered secular life. From the middle of the 17th cent., one can speak, from a lexical point of view, of a Latin-Hungarian 'mixed language' used by the upper classes (with contractions such as *judlium* < *judex nobilium* 'noble judge'). Until the introduction of Hungarian as the official language in 1844, Latin was the language of the establishment (law, politics, religion, education, etc.) and also shaped the Hungarian literary language.

1. PHONOLOGY AND SUBSTITUTION 2. MORPHOLOGY

1. PHONOLOGY AND SUBSTITUTION
Phonetic features of old borrowings are Latin *s* > Hungarian /ž/ / V_V, otherwise /š/; Latin dentals as well as *g* Hungarian palatalized dental/dʲ/ /_i; e: Lat. *sacramentum*, Hungarian *sákrámentum* (/ˈša:kra:mɛntum/) 'sacrament' (always with initial stress); Lat. *legenda*, Hungarian *legyenda* (/ˈlɛdʲɛå/) 'legend'. Because of the use of Classical pronunciation beginning in the 16th cent., new substitutions have appeared: Lat. *s* > Hungarian /z/ / V_V, otherwise /s/; Lat. dentals and *g* are preserved unchanged in all positions. Therefore doublets such as *szakramentum* (/ˈsåkråmɛntum/); *legenda* (/ˈlɛgɛndå/) have arisen. In part, one or the other form is used depending on the religious confession of the speaker.

2. MORPHOLOGY
Nouns are always borrowed with the nominative singular ending: *kórus* < *chorus* 'choir', *tégla* < *tegula* 'brick', etc. (Borrowings without a reflex of the ending are considered indirect borrowings: *kar* Middle High German *kōr* < *chorus* 'choir'). Adjectives are mostly taken over in the nominative singular masculine form; verbs, independent from the Latin stem type, always with *-ál*: *prédikál* < *praedicare* 'to preach', *konveniál* < *convenire* 'to convene', etc.

The influence of Latin also becomes clear in light of borrowed derivational suffixes, the productivity of which is attested since the 17th cent., as e.g. *-ista*: *egyetemista* 'student' (from *egyetem* 'university'), *–tórium*: *pipatórium* 'smoking room' (from *pipa* 'pipe'), *-ikus*: *bolondikus* 'foolish' (from *bolond*, same meaning), *-izál* (< Lat. °*isare*) and *-fikál* (< Lat. °*ficare*).

In the area of syntax, the influence of Latin is especially apparent in the use of tense.

1 J. BALÁZS, A latin a Duna-tájon ('Latin in the Danube Region'), in: Id. (ed.), Nyelvünk a Duna-tájon ('Our Language in the Donau Region'), 1989, 95–140   2 G. BÁRCZI, A magyar szókincs eredete ('The Origins of Hungarian Vocabulary'), 1958   3 K. BARTHA, A magyar szóképzés története ('History of Hungarian Word Formation'), 1958   4 L. BENKŐ, A latin jövevényszavak (Latin Loanwords), in: G. BÁRCZI, L. BENKŐ, J. BERRÁR, A magyar nyelv története ('The History of the Hungarian Language'), 1987, 293–296   5 Id. (ed.), A magyar nyelv történeti-etimoló-

giai szótára ('The Historical-Etymological Dictionary of Hungarian'), vol. I, 1967, vol. II, 1970, vol. III, 1976.

ANNA WIDMER

Florence, Archaeological Museum see→ ITALY VI Museums

Florence, Uffizi Gallery see → UFFIZI GALLERY, FLO-RENCE

Forgery
I. IN ART HISTORY II. IN LITERATURE

I. IN ART HISTORY
A. PARAMETERS OF THE PROBLEM B. RENAIS-SANCE C. THE BAROQUE AND CLASSICISM
D. 19TH AND 20TH CENTURIES

A. PARAMETERS OF THE PROBLEM
Forgery constitutes a subcategory within the field of reproductions of artworks by hand, where forgery itself, however, in the form of an ultimate (deceitful) intention, need not be involved. The gap between authentic and non-authentic products depends to a large extent upon the attitude of the possessor or the recipient [10. 416–418]. Indications of intent to deceive on the part of the originator, in the form of manipulated ageing or circumstances of discovery, can only rarely be proved. The fact that the overwhelming majority of ancient (representational) art has come down to us only in the form of ancient copies (or 'forgeries') puts the problem in perspective, reducing it to the question: ancient or not ancient.

The validation of doubtful pieces is today the province of stylistic criticism. The catalogues by Matz and Duhn of Roman private collections (1867–1881) created a basis in this respect. Among approximately 4,000 objects investigated they found 123 non-authentic statues, busts and reliefs, and 44 portraits [9]. A survey carried out on behalf of the *Deutsche Forschungsgemeinschaft* in 1978 (2,000 objects) also conveyed the impression of forgery on an enormous scale [3]. The overwhelming majority of the objects produced between the 15th and the first half of the 20th cent. come from Italy. Much remains to be accomplished here in the areas of classification, attribution, and provenance. Furthermore, recent research has addressed itself to the concept of forgery from the aspect of artistic and cultural theory [7. 235].

B. RENAISSANCE
There have been accounts of forgeries since the 15th cent. Their occurrence is a consequence of the enthusiasm for collecting and the increasing imbalance between supply and demand, despite numerous finds. Poggio Bracciolini already mentioned those traders in so-called 'Greek' curiosities who freely misused the names of such artists as Phidias, Polyclitus, and Praxiteles to validate their wares [7. 238].

The lives of Michelangelo by Vasari and Condivi contain accounts of the most prominent case of a Renaissance forgery. In 1495 Michelangelo made a sleeping *Cupido all'antica*. Pierfrancesco de' Medici's praise of the sculpture encouraged Baldassare Milanese to sell it in the guise of an object from Antiquity to Cardinal Riario in Rome, without Michelangelo's knowledge. When the deception was discovered Milanese had to return the purchase price and take back the *Cupido*. This became a sought-after piece, coming into the collection of Isabella d'Este in Mantua; today it has disappeared [12]. The affair redounded to the fame of the young artist. Comparable capabilities, which according to Vasari did no discredit to the artist but increased his standing, were imputed to the sculptor Tommaso della Porta, who specialised in 'forging' ancient marble heads, a large number of which subsequently found a ready sale [1. 550].

The majority of pseudo-ancient portraits, perhaps the most successful genre of forgery (e.g. [10. 436]), probably originated in the region of Venice and northern Italy. In the process, for example in the numerous busts of Caesar, it was the forgers' manifest intention to accommodate the Classical imperial type to Renaissance taste, that is to say to the image of Renaissance rulers (cf. Cristofero Romano's piece in the Museo Archeologico, Venice). Exemplary for the Renaissance in Padua is the discussion of the portrait bust of Livy (Kunsthistorisches Museum, Vienna), which was believed to be authentic until the beginning of the 20th cent. (fig. 1). It was evidently created for the memorial to the Roman historian erected in Padua in 1547. Attributions vary between the school of Donatello and Agostino Zoppo [10. 428]. A selection typical of the epoch and genre can also be seen in the many attested bronze and marble busts of Antinous from the first half of the 16th cent. (Museo Archeologico, Venice; Paris LV), of which the sculpture in the Louvre by Primaticcio is possibly one [6. 45].

The extensive trade in ancient or pseudo-ancient objects (gems, coins, small bronzes) in 15th- and 16th-cent. Venice reflects the antiquarian interest that prevailed in the city on the lagoon. The collection of Giovanni Grimani is especially significant in this respect. Of the 22 pieces that passed into the Republic's possession (now in the Museo Archeologico there) as a result of his will of 1586, not until the 20th cent. were 15 objects found to be pseudo-Antiquities [11. 101–110]. In the case of some pieces, for example the small bronze of the *Praying Youth*, a fragmentary provenance is simulated. All in all, for the Renaissance no clear dividing line can be drawn "between copies, imitations and original creations" [7. 241]. What can be said is that in Rome a number of workshops were established, such as that of the Della Portas, where counterfeiting was carried out on a commercial basis [7. 248]. A papal decree of Pius IV in 1562 sought to regulate the ancient patrimony of Rome, defining forgery as a crime on a par with art theft [7. 448].

Fig. 1: Bust of Livy, marble;
Este Collection, *Kunsthistorisches
Museum Vienna*

Fig. 2: Anton Raffael Mengs,
Jupiter and Ganymed, fresco,
1758/59; Galleria Nazionale
dell'Arte Antica, Rome

C. The Baroque and Classicism

During the 17th cent. contemporary art underwent a pronounced positive revaluation with respect to Antiquity, with corresponding repercussions for the princely collections. Symptomatic of this development are the copies and originals from Italy ordered by Louis XIV to be installed in the park at Versailles. The preference was for Baroque interpretations of Classical models such as the *Meleager* of Scopas in the Vatican, and this to some extent cut the ground from under the antiquarian imitations [10. 438]. Forgery found favor again from the middle of the 18th cent. with the rise of archaeology as a science and the → Classical period. It was aided by the boost in demand caused by the 'Grand Tour' of the English aristocracy, while at the same time restrictions on exports implemented by the Italian states led to reductions in supply.

Classical painting first entered the purview of the forger's craft with the discovery of the cities of Vesuvius. In around 1750 Giuseppe Guerra, a pupil of Solimena, placed great expectations in the sale of frescoes allegedly removed from → Herculaneum. His forgeries, which were shown in English salons as rarities and even entered the collections of Roman museums, included simulated traces of their removal (from the wall), and sought to imitate the then keenly discussed technique of ancient wax painting (encaustic) [5. 84–88]. J.J. Winckelmann was involved in two cases in which archaeological scholarship was itself both the instigator and the test-bed of forgeries. On the occasion of the first edition of *Geschichte der Kunst des Alterthums* (1764), Giovanni Battista Casanova's fake report of the discovery of ancient paintings encouraged him to have the drawings engraved that had been created purposely for the deception of the scholar. Another ancient work discussed by Winckelmann was a forgery by A.R. Mengs: the fresco of Jupiter and Ganymede (Galleria Corsini, Rome; fig. 2). The artist's purpose in painting the picture was to demonstrate his qualification for Classical greatness; out of respect for Winckelmann, he only revealed his secret on his deathbed, after the former's death [7. 271]. During the 2nd half of the 18th cent. forgery entered into a close relationship with restoration. Orfeo Borelli integrated into his reliefs (Palazzo Cardelli, Rome) entirely disassociated but genuine fragments, in a way that they were accepted into contemporary collections as intact pieces [7. 275]. Winckelmann's artist friend Bartolomeo Cavaceppi worked in a similar way, being fond of giving his ancient restorations the Late Classical flavour of the Hadrianic period (bust of Otho, Merseyside County Art Galleries, Liverpool). This contrasts with the responsible attitude of Antonio Canova, who refused to work on the so-called Elgin Marbles (from the → Parthenon) out of respect for Antiquity.

D. 19th and 20th Centuries

The rise of → Etruscology during the course of the 18th cent. brought corresponding forgeries along with it. Sensational archaeological finds at the Etruscan cities of Vulci and Cerveteri inspired a forging activity of well-nigh criminal proportions from the 1820s on (small bronzes and jewellery). This led at the beginning of the 20th cent. to the scandal around Alceo Dossena, who, besides Etruscan and Classical sculptures, also counterfeited works of the Gothic and Renaissance periods [7. 299]. The discovery of the Apollo of the Portonaccio sanctuary in 1916 near Veji (ca. 530 BC, Rome, VG) – one of the most astounding sculptural achievements of Archaic Etruria – misled the Metropolitan Museum of New York into purchasing a monumental warrior figure and a warrior head in the same style. These masterly imitations of the Etruscan artist Vulco, made by Alfredo Fioravanti shortly after the discovery of the above-mentioned Apollo, are at the same time indebted to the contemporary avant-garde [16. 97. 105]. Otherwise in the 20th cent., however, cheap, smaller-scale, mass-produced articles such as the Tanagra figures, so admired around the turn of the century, have predominated. The Berlin museums had to remove around 20% of their holdings as false [14. 185–196]. As late as 1983 the Getty Museum in Malibu bought the Late Archaic *kouros* (originating from a Swiss private collection) concerning the authenticity of which justified doubts were soon afterwards raised [16]. Probably the most spectacular art forgery of the 20th cent. on the political level were the (pseudo-Roman) medallion images from Centuripe (Naples, NM), presented to Mussolini in a solemn act of 'Imperial' pomp; they were discovered in 1942 by the archaeologist Carlo Albizzati, who only barely escaped prosecution [2; 7. 300].

1 G. Vasari, Le vite dei più eccelenti pittori, scultori et architetti, G. Milanesi (ed.), vol. II, Firenze 1878 2 C. Albizzati, Come si fabbrica una scoltura antica, in: Primato artistico italiano III, Nr. 12 3 P. Bloch, Typologie der Fälschung in der bildenden Kunst, in: Mitt. der Dt. Forschungsgemeinschaft, No. 3, 1978 4 M. Cagiano De Azevedo, La 'Polimnia' di Cortona, in: Storia dell'Arte, 38–40, 1980 5 G. Consoli Fiego, False pitture di Ercolano, in: Napoli Nobilissima II, 1921 6 H. Dütschke, Antike Bildwerke, Leipzig 1882 7 M. Feretti, Fälschung und künstlerische Tradition, in: G. Previtali, F. Zeri (eds.), Italienische Kunst. Eine neue Sicht auf ihre Geschichte, vol. II, 1987 8 S. Howard, B. Cavaceppi and the Origin of Neoclassic Sculptures, in: The Art Quarterly 33, 1982 9 F. Matz, F. von Duhn, Antike Bildwerke in Rom, vols. I–III, Leipzig 1881–82 10 E. Paul, Falsificazioni di antichità in Italia dal Rinascimento alla fine del XVIII secolo, in: S. Settis (ed.), Memoria dell'antico nell'arte italiana, vol. II, 1985, 413–439. 11 G. Traversari, Museo Archeologico di Venezia. I ritratti, 1968 12 W. R. Valentiner, Il Cupido Dormiente di Michelangelo, in: Commentari, VII, 1956, 236–48 13 Fälschung und Forschung, Museum Folkwang Essen, Skulpturengalerie Staatliche Museen Berlin (Essen), Exhibition Catalogue. 1977 14 Hauch des Prometheus. Meisterwerke in Ton, Staatliche Antikensammlungen und Glyptothek, München 1996 (Exhibition Catalogue) 15 K. Tür, Fälschungen antiker Plastik, 1984 16 The Getty Kouros Colloquium, The Pauly Getty

Museum (Nicholas Gounadris Foundation, 25–27 May 1993, Athens), 1993.

ADDITIONAL BIBLIOGRAPHY I. ROWLAND, The Scarith of Scornello: A Tale of Renaissance Forgery, 2004.
FRIEDHELM SCHARF

II. IN LITERATURE
A. INTRODUCTION AND DEFINITION   B. DEVELOPMENT AND FUNCTIONAL CHANGE BETWEEN THE MIDDLE AGES AND THE POST-MODERN
C. HISTORY OF FORGERIES AND PSEUDEPIGRAPHA
D. A SURVEY OF THE MOST INFLUENTIAL FALSE ATTRIBUTIONS   E. THE HISTORY OF INTERPOLATIONIST CRITICISM (ECHTHEITSKRITIK)   F. SUPPLEMENTS TO ANCIENT AUTHORS

A. INTRODUCTION AND DEFINITION
Forgeries are works ascribed by their originators to a more celebrated or invented author or to a different historical context, with the intention to deceive (not as e.g. in the case of fiction based on invented sources for artistic reasons). It is the opposite of plagiarism. The legitimate procedures of imitation and citation correspond to this antithesis. A distinction must be drawn between forgery of a text, an analytic procedure that presupposes an intimate knowledge of the author or the medium (document, attestation) to be counterfeited, and a craft based on knowledge of writing materials and implements. The latter is uncovered by the criminal investigator, the former by the literary historian.

B. DEVELOPMENT AND FUNCTIONAL CHANGE BETWEEN THE MIDDLE AGES AND THE POST-MODERN
The popularity of the Roman original authors is reflected e.g. in pseudo-Ovidian poetry. Furthermore, actual forgeries were tolerated, cited, and often responded to in 'Counter-forgeries' [19. 120]. Complex mythical traditions were devised, as for example in the case of the 8th-cent. cosmography by a supposed philosopher called Aethicus [13]. Medieval imitations and textual completions, explicable in terms of a poetic authority, were perceived as forgeries only upon their appearance in the tradition. The printing press made it possible to use counterfeit letters or documents not only in the immediate term, but also in the service of purported political and confessional claims. Generally speaking, forgery was used as a weapon of literary polemics (W. Hauff, who published in 1826 under the name H. Claurens). Commercial motives play a minor role in literary forgery. On the other hand, while forgery is a hermeneutic act, like parody or pastiche constructing preternaturally sharp images of authors in the context of a horizon of expectation, and at the same time highlighting the mind-set of the believing public, at its basis lies a longing for lost or hypothetical texts; and this is also true of the figure of the forger, who, while fearing discovery, also hopes for it, projecting a contrived figure, the putative writer, as a personal mask, in a manner analogous to a pseudonym. Forgeries attack the concept of the demonstrable identity of the author, the 'aesthetic fingerprint'. Italian Humanists in particular succeeded in unmasking numerous pseudo-epigraphs or forgeries such as the notorious so-called Donation of Constantine [20; 21]. While controversies such as that regarding the authenticity of the *Phalaris Letters* led to the → QUERELLE DES ANCIENS ET DES MODERNES, debates on the most celebrated mystifications, as e.g. B. J. MacPherson's 'discovery' from 1760 of the works of the Gaelic writer Ossian, and the alleged writings of a Late Medieval monk by Th. Chatterton, whose suicide in 1770 has made him a literary protagonist himself since the Romantic era (W. Wordsworth, A. de Musset, P. Ackroyd), have enhanced the philological apparatus. But it is only today, with computer-aided stylistic analysis, that 'higher criticism', once based on conjecture, comes close to the reliable verification of forgeries. But it was the unmasking of successful forgeries in the 1770s that turned critical attention upon inventive forgers and the notion that the concepts 'correct', 'true', and 'authentic' delineate metaphysical as well as artistic parameters: can an inauthentic text be true art? Forgeries thus accentuate that which has been made (*das Gemachte*) in art and that which can be made (*das Machbare*), but negate 'that which has become' (*das Gewordene*) and the unique.

In contrast to the ancient and medieval tendency, when filling in gaps in the historical, juridical, or diplomatic record, to proceed on the basis that greater complexity brings greater credibility (a principle demonstrated by the 20th-cent. fictional biographies of M. Aub or W. Hildesheimer), since the Early Modern Age the motivation of forgeries has become increasingly secular and aesthetic. They are fruits of the professionalisation of literary history, historical benchmarks for the degrees of appropriation of distant epochs achieved at a given time; extreme instances of "creative identification with the past" [14. 85], and yet genuine witnesses of their period of origin. The secondary literature catalogues innumerable literary scandals revolving around the question of forgery, from false sequels such as Avellaneda's second part of *Don Quixote* to Sholokhov's Nobel prize.

At least since A. Gide's *Faux-monnayeurs*, forgeries have been a modern "challenge to authenticity" [1. 44]. The material aspect of texts, the grounding of authors in the minutiae of literary history, the axiom of an intertextual universe, and the change in perspective from invention to combination, make the idea of forgery symptomatic of Post-Modernity. A distinction must be drawn between literary forgeries and those literary texts that, whether modelled on the example of forgeries in literature, representational arts, or on documentary forgeries, thematise the phenomenon self-referentially. Moreover, in respect of such allegorical positioning on the part of authors, the accent is on moral parallels in the sense of counterfeit lives (H. Kasack), on the involvement in the unending text (P. Ackroyd), on a playful handling of the cultural heritage, pointed up by the elimination of difference (G. Perec, J. Banville), on the premise that the recipient decides as to authenticity (U. Eco).

Just as, according to W. Benjamin, the reproducible artwork loses the aura of truth, which is the sole prerogative of the unique, so imitation avoids the odium of forgery, and the latter in turn the aura of malicious negation of the authentic. The cult value of the commodity as such then comes to cap the destruction of mystique. The age of digital media brings with it universal falsifiability (cf. the Orson Welles film *F for Fake*, 1973/75), which, while vindicating mistrust as a guiding literary principle, at the same time removes all inhibitions, for, as J.L. Borges anticipates, the "death of the author-subject" makes forgery meaningless. In this way, forgery becomes a metaphor for intertextuality, which promises to convert to a second grade of authenticity/truth. With the loss of the key distinction between the authentic and the false, aesthetics as a Luhmannist social system would become instable; but the increasing relevance of forgery/plagiarism in the field of litigation conserves that dualism, so that now it is less as a morally reprehensible phenomenon that forgeries pose their challenge to the commodity value of art, than as an actionable one. Insofar as the unique original has been displaced by any number of versions, literature at the turn of the 21st cent. openly creates "Coversions" (H. Krausser). In the absence of any taboo, from being the opposite of true art, forgeries become a kind of art in themselves.

→ Forgeries; → Pseudepigraphy

→ Imitatio; → Mimesis

1 K. Ackermann, Fälschung und Plagiat als Motiv in der zeitgenössischen Literatur, 1992   2 G. Constable, Forgery and Plagiarism in the Middle Ages, in: Archiv für Diplomatik 29, 1983, 1–41   3 K. Corino (ed.), Gefälscht! Betrug in Politik, Literatur, Wissenschaft, Kunst und Musik, 1990   4 D. Dutton, Artistic Crimes. The Problem of Forgery in the Arts, in: British Journal of Aesthetics 19, 1979, 302–314   5 H. Eich, G. Matthias (Dr. Matthias Quercu), Falsch aus der Feder geflossen. Lug, Trug und Versteckspiel in der Weltliteratur, 1964   6 Fälschungen im Mittelalter: Internationaler Kongress der Monumenta Germaniae Historica, München, 16.–19. September 1986   7 P. Eudel, Le Truquage, 1880   8 J. A. Farrer, Literary Forgeries, 1907   9 E. Frenzel, s.v. Fälschung, literarisch, Reallex. der dt. Literaturgesch. 1, 444–450   10 H. Fuhrmann, Die Fälschungen im Mittelalter, in: HZ 197, 1963, 529–601   11 A. Grafton, Fälscher und Kritiker. Der Betrug in der Wissenschaft, 1991   12 I. Haywood, Faking it. Art and the Politics of Forgery, 1987   13 M. W. Herren, Wozu diente die Fälschung der Kosmographie des Aethicus?, in: A. Lehner, W. Berschin (eds.), Lateinische Kultur im VIII. Jahrhundert, Traube-Gedenkschrift, 1990, 145–159   14 A. Höfele, Die Originalität der Fälschung. Zur Funktion des literarischen Betrugs in England 1750–1780, in: Poetica 18, 1986, 75–95   15 P. Lehmann, Pseudo-antike Literatur des Mittelalters, 1927   16 Literarische Fälschungen der Neuzeit: Bayerische Staatsbibliothek, Monumenta Germaniae Historica (G. Hooffacker, Exhibition and Catalogue), 16. September – 14. November 1986   17 C. G.v. Maassen, Literarische Fälschungen, in: Süddt. Monatshefte 33, 1936, 649–660   18 H. Rogge, Fingierte Briefe als Mittel politischer Satire, 1964   19 P. G. Schmidt, Kritische Philologie und pseudo-antike Literatur, in: A. Buck, K. Heitmann (eds.), Die Antike-Rezeption in den Wissenschaften während der Renaissance, 1983, 117–128   20 W. Speyer, Literarische Fälschungen, in: RAC 7, 1969, 236–277   21 Id., Italienische Humanisten als Kritiker der Echtheit antiker und christlicher Literatur, Akad. der Wiss. und der Lit. zu Mainz, Abh. der geistes- und sozialwiss. Kl., 1993, No. 3   22 Id., Die literarische Fälschung im heidnischen und christlichen Altertum. Ein Versuch ihrer Deutung, 1971   23 H. Tietze, Zur Psychologie und Ästhetik der Kunstfälschung in: Zschr. für Ästhetik und allg. Kunstwiss. 27, 1933, 209–240   24 J. Whitehead, This Solemn Mockery. The Art of Literary Forgery, 1973.

Additional Bibliography N. Groom, The Forger's Shadow: How Forgery Changed the Course of Literature, 2002 (Rev. by T. Eagleton, Thursday June 6, 2002; Guardian Unlimited; URL: http://books.guardian.co.uk/lrb/articles/0,6109,728520,00.html)

Achim Hölter

C. History of Forgeries and Pseudepigrapha

Works transmitted under a false name have played a conspicuous and disproportionate role in the reception of ancient literature from Late Antiquity to the 16th cent., and even far beyond. The works concerned belong for the most part to the categories of school or specialist literature. The common factor is almost always that unknown or new works are associated with an illustrious name from Antiquity. The original cause of the false attribution, whether conscious forgery, inadvertent false attribution, use of a philosopher as a source for a corpus of traditional learning, or the uncritical adoption of a literary fiction, plays no part insofar as the reception of individual cases is concerned. The popularity of such pseudepigrapha usually indicates a particular expectation with respect to its intellectual dimension. Therefore these texts, which were completely forgotten after their removal from the literary canon, were in need of reappraisal. Most forgeries or false attributions have their origin in Late Antiquity or earlier; few texts, mainly the pseudo-Ovidiana and -Aristotelica, arose in the High Middle Ages. As early as the Late Middle Ages the amount of newly-produced pseudo-literature went into an appreciable decline, while those pseudo texts that had already achieved canonical status continued to enjoy a brisk reception. A new situation arose after the Early Renaissance. It was only then that some Greek pseudepigrapha, e.g., the *Phalaris Letters* and the *Corpus Hermeticum* (see below), became known and celebrated in the West. Some few forgeries were presented as rediscoveries of ancient works ([8 Vol. I.172ff; II.199ff; 14.318ff.], e.g. Apuleius' *De orthographia*). The widely circulated 15th-cent. text of Fiocchi's *De magistratibus et sacerdotiis Romanorum* went, unintended by its author, under the ancient name of Fenestella; the background to the *Consolatio* of Cicero (1583), written by C. Sigonius, is yet to be investigated. A late, prominent case is the forgery of the complete text of Petronius by Nodot [10]. After the development of a critically secured corpus of ancient literature during the 18th and 19th cents. new forgeries occurred only as literary fiction or humorous mystification; there are individual instances where the authenticity of newly discovered writings, e.g. the *Fibula Praenestina*, known since the 19th cent., or the (probably genuine) Gallus papyrus, published in 1979, is disputed. A particular case for examination is Christian literature, where, until the final triumph of Christianity, false attributions were for the most part conscious forgeries arising in the course of conflict with non-Christians or between Christians [14. 176f.]. The early appearance of false texts (even Paul, in 2 Thess 2: 2, was aware of false letters in his name) promoted the critical development of the New Testament canon. Especially in the Greek East, the number of Christian forgeries was enormous. Only a few, however, have achieved significance beyond the circle of their primary reception. The Acts of the Martyrs and Lives of the Saints contain evolved legends as well as texts produced for a particular purpose, and it is not possible to separate the two categories. The apocryphal texts among the writings of the Church Fathers for the most part exerted no great influence.

D. A Survey of the Most Influential False Attributions

While the majority of ancient Latin epistolary corpora are authentic, almost all collections of the letters of famous Greek personages (e.g. Themistocles, Socrates, Anacharsis, the Socratics, the tyrant Phalaris) are fictions from the Hellenistic or the Imperial Period, in part conceived in the form of epistolary novels (bibliography in [4]); today the authenticity of only some of Plato's 13 letters and some of the letters of Brutus is controversial. The Phalaris letters, known in the West since 1427 and also widely read in Byzantium, were, in the new Latin edition by Francesco Griffelini, one of the most important school texts from the early 15th to late 16th cent. Some of the other collections of letters were not printed until late, and had a modest but by no means marginal readership. Comparable instances in pagan Latin literature are a few letters by Cicero (in particular the letter to Octavian, which impressed Petrarch), but above all the fake correspondence between Seneca and St. Paul and some letters on the life of Jerome [13]. In philosophy, the significance of the writings of Pseudo-Dionysius Areopagita are scarcely to be overestimated; via Johannes Scotus Eriugena and other philosophers they exerted an influence throughout the Middle Ages and beyond. The *Corpus Aristotelicum* as it came down from Antiquity was supplemented with numerous pseudepigrapha during the Middle Ages [9], the most widely known being the *Secretum secretorum* (*de regimine sanitatis*), a collection of teachings, originally Syrian, of a hermetic bent, which came down into many eastern and western languages in various textual versions (in part also under various authors' names), and were very influential also during the Italian Renaissance (e.g. in the work of Brunetto Latini) [7]; more significant philosophically are the *Liber de causis* and the *Liber de pomo*, which were probably written in the Arab world on the basis of texts by Proclus. Of individual works from the actual, ancient *Corpus Aristotelicum*, precisely some inauthentic writings have achieved major significance, in particular the text *De mundo*, already revised in Latin by Apuleius, also the *Problemata physica* and *De coloribus*. The written corpora of Apuleius and Boethius also contained influential pseudepigrapha, in particular Pseudo-Apuleius *De virtutibus herbarum* and Pseudo-Boethius *De disciplina scholarium*. The *Corpus Hermeticum* (known since the 15th cent.), the *Orphica*, and the *Tabula Cebetis* were read as original philosophical texts into the modern period. Comparable is the tradition of the *Corpus Hippocraticum*, which contains both authentic and inauthentic texts. Martinus von Bracara's treatise *De quattuor virtutibus* (*Formula honestae vitae*), drawing on Seneca, often went under Seneca's name into the 16th cent., and has come down to us in over 600 manuscripts. Of even more importance as a textbook on morals in Latin and numerous translations were the *Disticha Catonis*, which date from the 3rd cent. Ovid occupied a particularly conspicuous position in the field of poetry. The pseudo-Ovidian canon (the most widely disseminated of which were the *Ovidius puellarum* = *De nuntio sagaci*, probably 11th cent., and the epic *De vetula*, 13th cent.) originated in its entirety in the Middle Ages, and thematically reflected the specific conditions pertaining to the reception of the ancient writer, who had been widely read since the 11th/12th cents. Also authentic poems by Ovid or sections thereof were given a special transmission under its own name (e.g. am. 1.5 under the title *De meridie*). Besides Ovid, virtually the only name to be used for new poems was Martial, in part owing to confusion with Godfrey of Winchester (11th cent.). As to Virgil, Horace, Terence, Plautus, and others, only those poems still ascribed to them today (including the partially inauthentic *Appendix Vergiliana*) have ever circulated under their names. A special case is the *Anacreontea*, not printed until 1554, whose great influence on European poetry under the name of Anacreon came only during the 17th to 19th cents.

There were no false attributions of historical works to Classical authors in the Middle Ages; the *Corpus Caesarianum*, which embraces the works of various authors, and the collection *Historia Augusta*, widely disseminated under false authors' names, are already from Antiquity. The fictional stories of Dares Phrygius (which Cornelius Nepos was supposed to have translated into Latin) and Dictys Cretensis, the Alexander Romance and associated texts, especially Alexander's letter to Aristotle about India, the *Historia Apollonii* regis Tyri, and the *Gesta Romanorum* were in any case in the Middle Ages believed to be historical accounts. In rhetoric, the most influential false attributions are the *Rhetoric* probably written by Anaximenes and ascribed to Aristotle and the *Rhetorica ad Herennium*, transmitted as a work by Cicero. The *Synonyma Ciceronis* from Late Antiquity and a text *De differentiis* also ascribed to him achieved considerable influence in the Early Renaissance. The most influential Jewish false attribution outside the Old Testament is the Aristeas letter; of Christian forgeries, the Donation of Constantine (probably 8th cent.) and the Pseudo-Isidoran Decretals designed to reinforce papal claims, and the Pseudo-Clementine homilies developed the greatest influence.

E. The History of Interpolationist Criticism (Echtheitskritik)

Interpolationist criticism (IC) was from early on a major concern of literary history, and was practised systematically in Alexandria. Through the development of canons (in Alexandria for poets, tragedians, orators; in Rome by Varro for the comedies of Plautus) ancient IC regarding text tradition has become of critical importance for our concept of ancient literature. In Late Antiquity, as shown by the many pseudepigrapha and false attributions, no such effective examination appears to have been the norm outside the field of Christian theology, or it may have been that no conception of authenticity existed. Systematic, methodically-based IC did not resume until the time of the Italian Humanists, in particular Petrarch, Salutati, Valla, and Bruni. Characteristic, however, of the reception of the pseudepigrapha circulating in the Middle Ages appears to have been that its dissemination was not necessarily linked to conviction as to its authenticity. In the case of nearly all of the pseudepigrapha listed above – including the Donation of Constantine – their authenticity was more or less in doubt early on; the merit of Lorenzo Valla's celebrated text *De falso credita et ementita Constantini donatione* lies in its philological methodology and finally conclusive effect rather than in the originality of its thesis. By about 1500 all of the more important pseudepigrapha circulating in the Late Middle Ages had been recognised and rejected by the Humanists, but the elimination of these texts from the canon of widely-read works essentially occurred in the first half of the 16th cent., and to some extent the process extended into the 19th cent. (as in the case of the Pseudo-Dionysius). Bentley's text [1], which has become celebrated in the history of IC, originated more or less by chance at a time when the popularity of the Phalaris letters repudiated by him was long past. Besides indisputable pseudepigrapha, however, there are also some instances whose authenticity is a matter of dispute to the present day, as in the case of the letters of Plato and Sallust, the *Appendix Vergiliana*, the *Consolatio ad Liviam*, and *Hercules Oetaeus*, which has come down to us as one of the tragedies of Seneca. The attribution of the *Corpus Caesarianum* and *Corpus Tibullianum* to various authors was for the

most part discussed between the 17th and 19th cents. In the 19th cent. some authentic ancient texts were also wrongly suspected of being forgeries [14. 318].

F. Supplements to Ancient Authors

From the 15th cent. on, supplements to texts that had come down in an incomplete form were provided, for practical reasons, without dishonest intent (on the Petronius forgeries and on Cicero's *Consolatio* see above). The following categories can be distinguished. The 15th- and 16th-cent. Humanists wrote passages to fill in gaps in the comedies of Plautus so as to make the plays performable: these texts were left in the Plautus editions for centuries (sometimes in supplements), and so were still able to influence the treatment of the Amphitryon material by Molière and Kleist [2. 28ff.]. The supplements to Virgil's Aeneid (P.C.Decembrio 1419, M. Vegio 1427, Foreest 1650), to Ovid's *Fasti* (1649) and to Lucan (May 1639) provide what, in the opinion of the author of the supplement, the ancient writer wanted to write or should have written. The supplements to the historical writings of Julius Obsequens, Livy, Curtius Rufus, Tacitus and Velleius Paterculus, written between the 16th and 18th cents., fill in gaps in the tradition; of these, the supplements to Tacitus by J. Lipsius, J. Freinsheim, and Ch. Brotier are especially notable, as they adhere closely to the original in style and external form. The historical fragments appear to reflect a situation in which readers had given up hope of rediscovering the lost original passages, while at the same time the reading of primary literature (as opposed to recently written secondary literature) was still seen as vital to an understanding of ancient history.

→ Alciphron; → Alexander Romance; → Anacreontea; → Apopudobalia; → Appendix Vergiliana; → Aristeas [2] Letter of Aristeas; → Consolatio ad Liviam (Epicedion Drusi); → Cornelius,II. Imperial period [II 18] C. Gallus; → Corpus Caesarianum; → Corpus Hermeticum; → Dicta Catonis; → Dictys Cretensis; → Dionysius Areopagites; → Epistolography; → Hermetic writings; → Historia Apollonii regis Tyri; → Historia Augusta; → Rhetorica ad Herennium

1 R. Bentley, Dissertations upon the epistles of Phalaris, Themistocles, Socrates, Euripides, and upon the fables of Aesop, London, 1699   2 L. Braun, Scenae suppositiciae, 1980   3 Fälschungen im Mittelalter: Internationaler Kongress der Monumenta Germaniae Historica, München, 16.–19. September 1986, I and V   4 N. Holzberg (ed.), Der griechische Briefroman, 1994   5 P. Lehmann, Pseudo-antike Literatur des Mittelalters, 1927 (repr. 1964)   6 G. Bernt et al., s.v. Disticha Catonis, LMA 3, 1123–1127   7 W. F. Ryan, Ch. B. Schmitt, Pseudo-Aristotle. The Secrets of Secrets. Sources and Influences, 1982   8 R. Sabbadini, Le scoperte dei codici, 1905, (repr. 1996)   9 Ch. B. Schmitt, D. Knox, Pseudo-Aristoteles Latinus. A Guide to Latin Works Falsely Attributed to Aristotle before 1500, 1985   10 W. Stolz, Petrons Satyricon und François Nodot. Ein Beitrag zur Geschichte literarischer Fälschungen, 1987   11 P. G. Schmidt, Kritische Philologie und pseudo-antike Litera-

tur, in: A. Buch, K. Heitmann (eds.), Die Antike-Rezeption in den Wissenschaften während der Renaissance, 1983, 117–128   12 Id., Supplemente lateinischer Prosa in der Neuzeit, 1964   13 Id., Pseudo-antike Literatur als philologisches Problem in Mittelalter und Renaissance, in: N. Mann, B. Munk Olsen (eds.), Medieval and Renaissance Scholarship, 1997, 186–195   14 W. Speyer, Die literarischen Fälschungen im heidnischen und christlichen Altertum, 1971   15 Id., Italienische Humanisten als Kritiker der Echtheit antiker und christlicher Literatur, 1993

Additional Bibliography A. Grafton, Forgers and Critics: Creativity and Duplicity in Western Scholarship, 1990; M. Vegio, Short Epics, M. C. J. Putnam (ed. and trans.), 2004, 2–41.   Jürgen Leonhardt

Forum/Square

A. The Forum as an Idealized Square   B. The Place Royale Type   C. Forum Designs in Revolutionary Architecture   D. Fora in Modern Urban Development

A. The Forum as an Idealized Square

The actual structural shape of an ancient Roman forum was no longer known in the Middle Ages. The various editions of the *Mirabilia Romae* treat the forum merely as a topos, while the medieval *Städtelob* ('Praise of Towns') mentions the lost fora only to evoke the glorious past of certain cities (Milan and Verona among others).

It is not even possible to reconstruct the architecture of the Roman imperial fora and the Forum Romanum from the topical 15th cent. descriptions that were based on ancient sources (Poggio Bracciolini, *De varietate fortunae*, 1447/48 and Flavio Biondo, *Roma instaurata*, 1448, among others). Although a topical and at times functional continuity between the ancient forum and the medieval market square can be observed in some Italian cities (Verona: Piazza Erbe, Fermo: Piazza del Popolo), the ancient structural shape had been lost. Not until the reception of Vitruvius' treatise on architecture (15th cent.), containing descriptions of a Greek and a Roman forum, did one have access to depictions of the ancient town square [16]. Vitruvius describes the Roman forum–here a provincial forum–as a rectangle enclosed by porticos, a description which was adopted by most Renaissance treatises on architecture (primarily by Alberti, F. di Giorgio, Filarete and Palladio). Vitruvius presents the ancient forum as a clearly delineated square that functioned as the administrative, economic, and religious centre of the city. The Piazza Ducale in Vigevano near Milan (fig. 1), which was presumably designed by Bramante for Lodovico il Moro, is regarded as the first example of a square in the ancient style. The square, begun in 1490 and referred to as a forum in its inscriptions, was enclosed on three sides by uniformly structured facades that open up onto ground-level porticos. This design principle also guided other squares modelled after Vitruvius's example, such as those in Ascoli Piceno (Piazza del Popolo), Florence

(Piazza SS. Annunziata) and Bologna (Piazza Maggiore) as well as in Freudenstadt [7]. The Renaissance squares modelled after fora can be distinguished from medieval market loggias by their uniform facades and a largely symmetrical ground plan. The portico in particular characterises the forum as public architecture, since it was regarded as the architectural symbol of the contemporary *res publica* [11].

Based on archeological finds, early 16th cent. architects and experts of antiquities, such as A. da Sangallo, B. Peruzzi and A. Palladio, reconstructed imperial fora. Their representation of fora as column-lined forecourts of temples determined Bernini's design of St. Peter's Square. With the Piazza S. Marco, the Venetian Republic created a state forum that structurally derived from ancient fora, while functionally corresponding to Vitruvius's description. The newly constructed structures of the 15th and 16th cents. especially contributed to the standardization of the facades and the concentration of important institutions around the Piazza S. Marco. The impression of an ancient forum was further enhanced by the square's sculptures (column monuments, spolia, etc.). While the Piazza S. Marco illustrates a type of square that interprets the ancient forum as an urban centre, the Roman Capitol Square can be regarded as the model of its monumental counterpart (fig.2). The installation of the equestrian statue of Marcus Aurelius in 1538 marked the beginning of the new construction project–at times referred to as the forum project–which was assigned to Michelangelo by Pope Paul III. The square, surrounded by palaces for conservators, senators and the new palace, was influenced, in part, by Trajan's forum, which had been transmitted on coins [2]. This square served as a connecting link for later forum designs, since the dimensions and uniform facades of the Capitol Square form an excellent backdrop for monuments. Thus an ancient-style square emerged that recreated the function of the forum through its use as a centre for administration, law, culture and museums [5].

B. The Place Royale Type

The Place Dauphine and the Place Royale (present-day Place des Vosges, fig.3), created in Paris shortly after 1600 under Henry IV, were directly modelled on the idealized notion of an ancient forum. While the triangular Place Dauphine was designed more for commerce, the Place des Vosges served primarily as a public arena for courtly life. The buildings around the square were uniformly four-winged residences, interrupted only by two slightly elevated royal palaces facing each other. With the installation of the equestrian statue of Louis XIII in 1639 (later destroyed), the Place Royale became the model for many new European squares of the 17th and 18th cents.

The Plaza Mayor in Madrid (1617–1619) also combined the public nature of the square with a temporary royal residence and an → equestrian statue. In contrast to the Place des Vosges which served as an

Fig. 1: Vigevano, Piazza Ducale, photographed in 1973, © *Bildarchiv Foto Marburg*

Fig. 2: Rome, Capitol Square, engraving based on Duperac, © *Bildarchiv Foto Marburg*

Fig. 3: Paris, Place des Vosges, engraving based on Perelle, © *Bildarchiv Foto Marburg*

Fig. 4: Nancy, Place Stanislas, photographed in 1940/44, © *Bildarchiv Foto Marburg*

aristocratic residence, the Plaza Mayor became an urban city centre. The urban development of feudal absolutism was characterised by the transfer of social hierarchies onto the design of squares, a principle perfectly realised in the present-day Place Vendôme in Paris (formerly Place Louis-le-Grand). The original design by J. Hardouin-Mansarts allowed for a concentration of royal institutions at the square (mint, library, academy). The buildings with their uniform facades–erected from 1699–1725 after the installation of the royal equestrian monument (since 1810 Austerlitz Column)–exemplify the Place Royale type [14]. In the course of the 18th cent., urban building projects were developed that reveal the broad influence of ancient fora. Their similarity to ancient fora is apparent in an imaginative reconstruction of Trajan's Forum created by J. Fischer von Erlach in his *Entwurf einer historischen Architektur* (Sketch of Historical Architecture) published in 1721.

The name *Forum Friderizianum* refers to a partially completed project by Frederick II in Berlin, which he designed together with G.W. von Knobelsdorff. The term *forum* for the square that runs perpendicular to the *Lindenallee* was employed by F. Algarotti, who designed the inscriptions for the planned buildings: opera, royal palace and academy. From 1741 to 1743 Knobelsdorff built the royal opera, then, in 1746 the Hedwig Church, while his royal palace (1747–66) came into use as the Prinz-Heinrich-Palais with a courtyard opening onto the forum. Thus, all institutions that architecturally express a royal identity are concentrated around the square [8]. An impressive continuation of the Place Royale type is embodied in the ensemble of the Place Stanislas in Nancy (fig. 4). A rhythmic arrangement of spaces was achieved by E. Héré de Corny 1751–55 for the Duke of Lorrain, Stanislas Lescinski. The almost perfectly square Place Royale extends to a promenade that ends at a triumphal gate. Its narrow side opens onto a square surrounded by colonnades in front of the office of the director of the royal governor's theatre in such a way that the administrative buildings–city hall and provincial government–dominate the public space [12]. The urban complex of the Place Stanislas bears a much stronger resemblance to an ancient forum than the present-day Piazza Dante in Naples, which was called the *Foro Carolino*. The square, designed by L. Vanvitelli after 1760 and commissioned by Charles III, King of Naples and Sicily, can be regarded as an architectural example of a 'representative publicness' (Habermas), since the concave main building of the forum only exists to accentuate the royal equestrian statue located in front of an alcove within a triumphal arch [12].

C. FORUM DESIGNS IN REVOLUTIONARY ARCHITECTURE

Urban designs dedicated to the glorification of the French Revolution and later of Napoleon Bonaparte derive from ancient fora only in their character as

monuments. One of the most outstanding plans can be found in the *Foro Bonaparte* in Milan, designed by G.A. Antolini 1801–03, which is a republican monument dedicated to the Cisalpine Republic. In a circle with a diameter of 633 metres, public buildings, such as the stock exchange, pantheon, theatre, museum and thermal baths, were intended to form a group around the Castello Sforzesco, joined together by a colonnade ring. Although Antolini's forum plans could not be realised, they influenced the later design of the area [13]. Even plans of a much more modest nature, such as F. Weinbrenner's plan of a monument to the French Republic in Bordeaux (1797) failed to be carried out. Designs modelled on ancient imperial fora clearly reveal that these were interpreted as memorials. The enormous scope envisioned for forum projects within revolutionary architecture became apparent in the plans for a *Forum Napoleone* by S. Perosini, which was to reconfigure the Roman Capitol and the Forum Romanum into a megalomaniac imperial residence [6].

D. FORA IN MODERN URBAN DEVELOPMENT

Modern urban development continues to use the architectonic ensemble of the square as some sort of space of public display. Guided by the model of the Capitol, which was the prototype of an architectural symbiosis between political power and culture through the establishment of a museum (1734), several squares were created in the 19th cent. that derive from ancient fora.

In 1830, the *Altes Museum* was opened in Berlin and the *Glyptothek* in Munich, both situated directly on public squares. While Schinkel's museum in Berlin resulted in a renewal of the city centre, whose buildings (castle, cathedral, Museum of Antiquity) symbolized the joining of the pillars of royal power, the *Königsplatz* in Munich, with Klenze's *Glyptothek*, an exhibition hall and a gate, was meant to be perceived as a monument to a politically motivated Bavarian → PHILHELLENISM [2]. Beginning in 1837 in Dresden, G. Semper included the opera and the picture gallery in his design of the 'Zwingerforum' between the *Zwinger* and the banks of the Elbe. However, the gallery, built from 1847 to 1856, cut off the *Zwinger* courtyard from the square between opera and cathedral, with the result that a loose arrangement of buildings from different epochs around the square and a conscious reference to the Forum Romanum could not be carried out [5]. Later Semper designed a *Kaiserforum* in Vienna, for which he envisioned an area separated from the *Ringstraße* by triumphal arches and by the walls of the museum and the castle wings that ran along both sides of *Ringstraße*. Here, the forum again had the character of an overly glorified museum for royal display. An important attempt to combine historical squares of a highly uniform style with modern urban development can be found in C. Sitte's work *Der Städtebau nach künstlerischen Grundsätzen* ('Urban Development according to Artistic Principles', 1899). Sitte regarded Semper's concepts of fora as exemplary and advocated a 'public life' on such squares, removed from functionalist theories.

Twentieth-cent. urban development looked to the model of ancient fora in its concentration of impressive state and government buildings in city centres. Independent thereof, the term *forum* developed into a synonym for the public realm beyond urban development (trade forum, film forum etc.), thus taking on connotations which were unknown in the 19th cent.

American urban development was influenced by the idea of ancient fora only for a short time; that is, on the occasion of the 'World Columbian Exposition' in Chicago in 1893, when D.H. Burnham directed the construction of an exhibition area modelled after ancient fora. The so-called *White City*, a square with an artificial lake, its core surrounded by pavillons, served for two more decades as a model for an American city with administration buildings arranged around a forum [17].

Between 1900 and 1930, competitions were held for the construction of a state forum (or *Deutsches Forum*) at the bend of the Spree River in Berlin. The occasion for these designs, which were continued into the Weimar Republic, was the building of the *Reichstag* on the *Platz der Republik* (*Königsplatz*), which was to form a central ensemble of buildings along with the opera house, *Reichshaus*, ministries etc. The urban development under Italian → FASCISM and German → NATIONAL SOCIALISM again moved the forum into the limelight. In 1925, Mussolini initiated the building of the *Foro Italico* (or *Forum Mussolini*) in Rome, which had the character of a sports forum with its sport academy and sports fields (a similar one was begun in Berlin in 1926). Plans by M. Piacentini were meant to redesign the Piazza Venezia into a *Foro dell' Impero Fascista* in the centre of Rome, primarily to serve the purpose of parades marching by. The same idea informed the *Gau Fora* (*Gau*= administrative district) that Hitler had planned for the German *Gau* cities: party buildings, a *Gau* hall, bell tower and state offices were to form a National Socialist city centre [11].

The urban centres of the German Democratic Republic were modelled on the example of Moscow, which was to receive a central square at the Palace of Soviets from 1935 on (never carried out). The corresponding designs were guided by the spatial needs of mass demonstrations. The result in Berlin was the establishment of the *Marx-Engles-Platz* above the ruins of the city castle, originally referred to as the *Marx-Engles-Forum*.

After 1970, postmodern architecture attempted here and there to exploit ancient fora in an ironic way. One of the most famous examples is Ch. Moore's *Piazza d'Italia* in New Orleans (1977/78) [15]. Inspired by the public symbolism of ancient fora, the architect A. Schulte attempted to create a 'citizen's forum' as a meeting place at the bend of the Spree River in Berlin between the chancellor's office and the parliament (given up after a change of plans in 1997). A decade

earlier, a project by H. Hollein intended to give the area of the *Kemperplatz* in Berlin–referred to as the *Kulturforum*–the architectural shape of an ancient forum, although in a more abstract form.

→ Forum; → Vitruvius

→ ARCHITECTURAL THEORY/VITRUVIANISM

1 L. B. ALBERTI, Zehn Bücher über Architektur (De re aedificatoria), M. THEUER (ed.), 1912   2 A. BALFOUR, Berlin: The Politics of Order, 1737–1989, 1990   3 T. BUDDENSIEG, Zum Statuenprogramm Paul III., in: Zeitschrift für Kunstgeschichte 32, 1969, 177–228   4 C. CRESTI, Architettura e fascismo, 1986   5 M. FRÖHLICH, G. Semper, 1974   6 W. D. GARRETT, Classic America: The Federal Style and Beyond, 1992   7 Glyptothek München 1830–1980, 1980 (Exhibition Catalogue)   8 A. LA PADULA, Roma nell'Epoca Napoleonica, 1969   9 W. LOTZ, Italienische Plätze, in: Jahrbuch der Max-Planck-Gesellschaft, 1968, 41–60   10 H. MACKOWSKY, Das Friedrichsforum, in: Zeitschrift für bildende Kunst, Neue Folge 21, 1910, 15–21   11 R. SCHNEIDER, W. WANG, Moderne Architektur in Deutschland 1900 bis 2000, 1998   12 A. E. J. MORRIS, History of Urban Form, 1972   13 W. OECHSLIN, Der Portikus, in: Daidalos 24, 1987, 44–49   14 J. RAU GRÄFIN VON DER SCHULENBURG, E. Héré, 1970   15 A. SCOTTI, Foro Bonaparte, 1989   16 H. SPECKTER, Paris. Städtebau, 1964   17 R. A. M. STERN, Moderner Klassizismus, 1990   18 VITRUVIUS, De architectura libri decem, FENSTERBUSCH (ed.), 1964 (Engl. I. D. ROWLAND (trans.), Vitruvius: Ten Books on Architecture, 1999).   19 J. ZUCKOWSKY, Chicago Architecture, 1987.

STEFAN SCHWEIZER

France

I. TO THE 12TH CENTURY   II. 13TH–15TH CENTURY   III. 16TH–18TH CENTURY   IV. 19TH AND 20TH CENTURIES   V. HISTORY OF THE TEACHING OF LATIN

I. TO THE 12TH CENTURY

A. THE FRANKISH KINGDOM UNDER THE MEROVINGIANS   B. THE FRANKISH KINGDOM UNDER THE CAROLINGIANS   C. FRANCE UNDER THE CAPETIANS

A. THE FRANKISH KINGDOM UNDER THE MEROVINGIANS

1. HISTORY AND SOCIAL DEVELOPMENT   2. LITERATURE   3. FINE ARTS AND ARCHITECTURE

1. HISTORY AND SOCIAL DEVELOPMENT

The Franks were initially integrated into the Roman empire as allies (*foederati*). With his victory over Syagrius (486/87), Clovis (466–511) shattered what was left of Roman rule. He is considered the founder of the dynasty of the Merovingians and the great Frankish kingdom, whose area on the Seine and the Loire he increased by the addition of Aquitaine. He had himself baptized at Reims in 498/99. These decisive transformations in Gaul justify beginning this presentation as early as the reign of Clovis. After a quartering of the kingdom upon Clovis' death into regions corresponding to the Roman *civitates* Reims, Orléans, Paris and Soissons and after the integration of Burgundy and Provence, a tripartition, beginning in 567, into Austrasia (the eastern section of the empire, on the Rhine and the Maas), Neustria (the western section, around Soissons and Paris) and Burgundy (Burgundy and Orléans) took place. Reunited in 629, the empire reached its apogee under Dagobert I (629–638/9). After this, decline set in: To be sure, Merovingians continued to rule, but governance lay with the majordomos, who came primarily from the house of Pippin. Pippin the Younger drove the Merovingians out of power once and for all in 751.

The Franks took over the walled, Late-Roman towns and *castellum* sites; in rural areas, however, *vici* 'villages' and *villae* 'estates' were replaced by homesteads on stream banks built on stilts. In contrast, continuity was preserved in administration (upper-level civil service, public offices and registries) and in social institutions (→ TOWN). The → SCHOOLS of late Antiquity, established in the towns and run by laymen paid by the state, collapsed with the end of the Roman empire. Schooling was taken over by the Church through the establishment of the → CATHEDRAL SCHOOL. These were open to laymen and clergy; however, the nobility usually contented itself with tutors and training in the martial arts. This led to an increasing lack of education among the nobility.

2. LITERATURE

Because of the break with Roman tradition, only a few personalities achieved literary prominence. Gregory of Tours (538/9–593/4) should be mentioned in the field of → HISTORIOGRAPHY; he was the author of the *Historiae Francorum*, which, riddled with vulgarisms, focused on Gaul and a history of the times. In the 7th cent., a satirical parody on grammatical education was written under the pseudonym Virgilius Maro. The author probably lived in south Gaul and claimed to be a student of the grammarian Aeneas and classmate of a certain Donatus. (Virgil was still the most important poet in the grammar schools, where he was read in conjunction with the commentaries of Servius and Donatus.) Besides the poet Alcimus Avitius (460–518), author of biblical narratives, who still belonged fully to Late Antiquity as far as his intellectual attitude was concerned, Venantius Fortunatus (ca. 540–ca. 600, bishop of Poitiers) was outstanding in poetry. He left behind numerous poems, as well as a *Vita S. Martini* in hexameters based on Sulpicius Severus. It was oriented linguistically toward Virgil, but intellectually can already be fully attributed to the Middle Ages.

3. FINE ARTS AND ARCHITECTURE

In manuscript illumination, decorative elements conformed to those of late Antiquity, as did the depiction of the *maiestas Domini* and the full-page-sized images of the evangelists in the Gundohinus Gospels of 754. Important → Scriptoria were to be found at Luxeuil and Corbie, the latter of which developed its own style. Small hall churches predominated in church architecture; preserved examples include the baptistery of St. Jean at Poitiers (5th cent.), and the annex to the church of Jouarre (late 7th cent.).

B. THE FRANKISH KINGDOM UNDER THE CAROLINGIANS

1. HISTORY   2. EDUCATION AND LEARNING
3. POETRY   4. FINE ARTS AND ARCHITECTURE

1. HISTORY

Charles Martel, who prevented the Arabs from penetrating more deeply into Europe by his victory at Poitiers (732), subsequently reigned alone from 737 in the name of the dead Merovingian without taking on the royal title for himself. It is from him that the dynasty of the Carolingians derives its name. His son Pippin III 'the Younger' was the first to depose the Merovingians once and for all; he had himself confirmed as king by the pope in 751 and, following the Old Testament model, anointed (divine right). Intellectual life, which had already experienced a great upsurge under Pippin (establishment of the court chapel and ministries, reform of the liturgy) was brought by his son Charlemagne (747–814), through comprehensive educational reform, to the first Golden Age of the Middle Ages. Charlemagne began by turning the Frankish kingdom into the leading power of Europe by assimilating the kingdom of the Lombards, Saxony, Bavaria and the kingdom of the Avars. On Christmas Eve of the year 800, he had himself crowned at Rome, in competition with the Byzantine emperor, as *imperator Romanum gubernans imperium*. While Charlemagne's reforms were of a cultural-political nature (see below), his son Louis the Pious (778–840) concentrated on ecclesiastical reforms. He also laid the foundation for the later emergence of Germany and France (F.), insofar as he divided the kingdom among his three sons: Lothair (795–855) received the title of emperor and the central empire (the area from the North Sea to southern Italy, including what would later be Lorraine); Louis the German (ca. 805–876) received the eastern empire, and Charles the Bald (823–877) the western empire. Once the West-Frankish line of the Carolingians had died out and Charles the Fat (839–888), who had reunited it once again as emperor, was deposed, the empire collapsed in 887 into five successor states. A Carolingian once again came to power in western Francia from 936–954, in the person of Louis IV Transmarinus, until power went over once and for all to the Capetians in 987, after the death of Louis's successors.

2. EDUCATION AND LEARNING

Charlemagne's court at Aachen (Aix-la-CHapelle) was the political and intellectual centre of the kingdom; it was from here that the great educational reform also known as the → CAROLINGIAN RENAISSANCE arose. In an attempt to combine Christian and ancient cultural heritage, Charlemagne summoned leading scholars to his court from Italy, Spain, England and Ireland. They were led by the Anglo-Saxon Alcuin of York, director of the court school from 781 and from 796 abbot of St. Martin of Tours, which he made into an important cultural centre. His interests centred primarily on reviving in school curricula the → Artes liberales, which he considered the road to wisdom. With this plan, he exercised great influence on the cathedral schools, whose expansion was also promoted. Centres were located at Reims–where a library and scriptorium were established by Archbishop Hincmar–, Metz and Laon. Even more important than the cathedral schools at the time were the → Monastery schools, particularly that of St. Martin in Tours. Others included St. Germain in Auxerre, under the direction of Heiric (841–875, the student of Lupus of Ferrière, who edited texts of Cicero and Boethius), Remigius (ca. 841–908, author of commentaries on ancient authors) and Fleury, under the direction of the West Goth Theodulf (ca. 760–821, bishop of Orléans and abbot of Fleury). The Irishman Dungal, who concerned himself with scientific questions, was active at the abbey of St. Denis around 784. It was here, under the abbot Hilduin around 832, that the first Latin translations of the Neoplatonic-Christian writings of pseudo-Dionysius (5th–6th cent.) emerged. Louis the Pious had received them as a gift from the Byzantine emperor. Hilduin also composed a *vita* of Saint Dionysius (St. Denis), who was falsely identified with the Areopagite. Because of the numerous errors in this version, the Irish scholar Johannes Scotus Eriugena, director of the court school of Charles the Bald, was entrusted with the task of a new translation, to which he added a commentary. He presented the fruits of his philosophical studies in his work *De divisione naturae*, which made him an important transmitter of Neoplatonic thought to the School of Chartres in the 12th cent. Eriugena's commentary on Martianus Capella was the basis of Capella's importance for the *quadrivium*.

3. Poetry

Charlemagne gathered a circle of poets around him, who, through the study of Roman authors (Virgil, Ovid), revived ancient quantitative meters (hexameter, elegiac distichs). In addition to Alcuin, mention must be made above all of Theodulf, who in one of his poems justified the reading of heathen poems by interpreting them allegorically. Exiled by Louis, he sent a plaintive elegy in the style of Ovid's exile poetry to his friend Modoin (d. 840, bishop of Autun from 815). Modoin replied with a similar elegy; in his youth he had also composed two panegyrical eclogues on Charlemagne, based on Virgil and Calpurnius (a revivial of → Bucolics). Finally, Ermoldus Nigellus, also exiled under Louis, wrote a panegyric epic on the emperor, not in hexameters but rather, for the first time in the history of the epic, in elegiac distichs, since he took up Ovid's exile poetry with a view to its aiding his return from exile. These achievements were made possible by the intense collecting and editing of ancient texts in all the important monasteries of the empire, to which the texts were handed over by the court library for copying.

4. Fine Arts and Architecture

The development of the Carolingian minuscule led to a flourishing of scriptoria where manuscripts were often magnificently illuminated. Illustrators followed ancient models in their pictorial representations with regard to corporeality and three-dimensionality. One centre was the monastery at Corbie, where an early form of minuscule script was developed around 780 under abbot Maurdramnus. Corbie received a fresh impetus in the 9th cent., under abbots Adalhard (founder of the daughter monastery Corvey) and Paschasius Radbert. Here, around the middle of the century, Hadoard compiled a collection of excerpts from Cicero's philosophical works and *De oratore*. In addition to the court scriptorium (Soissons Gospel, beginning of the 9th cent.), centres of manuscript illumination included St. Martin at Tours (the Alcuin Bible), Metz, and Reims (the Utrecht Psalter, mid–9th cent.). In the minor arts, the bronze equestrian statuette of Charlemagne (in the Louvre) represented a return to Roman → Equestrian statues, while classicizing capitals were used in architectural sculpture. Architecture took the form of palace complexes and churches. The cathedral of St. Denis, consecrated in 775, went back to the traditional ancient pillared basilica; in contrast, the cathedral of St. Riquier, consecrated in 779, cruciform and with transept-tower, was influential for the future. The domed cruciform cathedral built in 806 by Theodulf at Germigny-des-Prés, displays Byzantine influence with its apse mosaic

C. France under the Capetians

1. History   2. Education and Learning
3. Poetry   4. Fine Arts and Architecture

1. History

The period of the early Capetians, down to Louis VI (1101/1108–1137), was marked by the consolidation of their sovereignty. The borders of the kingdom did not change, but Paris became its political, economic and cultural centre. Numerous abbeys (St. Denis, St. Germain-des-Prés in Paris, Fleury) and archbishoprics (Reims, Sens, Bourges, Tours), were supported by the Capetians. F. included several great principalities with their own dynasties, all of which were bound to the king by oath of fealty. The duchy of Normandy emerged in the area around Rouen, which the Carolingians had ceded to the Normans in 911. With the victory of William the Conqueror at Hastings in 1066, the Normans became kings of England, but as dukes of Normandy remained vassals of the French king. The earldom of Anjou arose in the 11th cent., by absorbing the counties of Touraine and Maine, while Henry II Plantagenêt became king of England in 1154. The earldom of Blois-Champagne lost Touraine to Anjou in 1044, while the earldom of Flanders, which extended as far as the borders of Normandy, enjoyed its heyday from 1035–1127. The duchy of Aquitaine had been under the suzerainty of the House of Poitou since the mid–10th cent.

Under Louis VII (1137–1180) two developments became evident that were to be influential down to the mid-13th cent.: the increasing ties of the Capetians to the reformist papacy (Louis as leader of the Second Crusade, 1147–1149) and the growing rivalry with the house of Anjou-Plantagenêt. These tensions persisted under Philip II Augustus (1180–1223), who tore Normandy, Anjou and Touraine away from the English king and established the supremacy of the Capetians, which continued until the outbreak of the Hundred Years War (1337–1453).

2. EDUCATION AND LEARNING

At the beginning of the 12th cent., F. was marked, on the one hand, by increasing spirituality (Congregation of St. Victor in Paris, Bernard of Clairvaux) and, on the other, by a great intellectual upsurge, which had already begun in the 11th cent. There were manifold causes of this renaissance: ancient writings in the natural sciences and medicine, preserved by the Arabs, were first made available to the West through translations from the Arabic in the second half of the 12th cent., and then directly from the Greek. This led to a strong increase in the study especially of the *quadrivium* and dialectics, which penetrated the other disciplines as a method, leading to the transformation of grammar into the science of logic under the influence of Aristotle's *Organon*. The most important representative of dialectic was Peter Abelard (1079–1142), who saw logic as a means toward partial knowledge of God. Even before Abelard, early scholasticism had been founded on the basis of Aristotle's theory of the acquisition of knowledge. One of its first representatives, Anselm of Canterbury (1033–1109, abbot and teacher in Bec in Normandy, then archbishop of Canterbury), demonstrated his method of deepening one's faith by examining it in the light of reason (*fides quaerens intellectum*). He illustrates this in his *Proslogion* by the example of the ontological proof of God's existence, combining logic based on Aristotle and Boethius with the Augustinian concept of love. A further cause lay in the school system: the monastic schools lost importance compared to the cathedral schools, over which the bishops' power to grant permission to teach (*licentia docendi*) once again fell into uncertainty. This led to an increase in the number of free masters, who taught in cathedral and monastic schools but lived off their students' tuition. In addition, private state schools also emerged. Alongside the *artes liberales* and the the usual reading canon (Virgil, Lucan, Statius, *Ilias latina*, Horace, Persius, Juvenal, Terence, Ovid, Maximian, Boethius, Martianus Capella, late Latin Christian poets), logic, Roman law and medicine were henceforth also taught. The new educational method of *quaestio* and *disputatio* led to the development of the scholastic analysis of problems. Tensions between the teaching body and the bishops culminated around 1200 in the union of the masters and scholars of Paris into a *univeristas magistorum et scholarium*. The main emphasis at this university, the oldest in Europe together with Bologna, was on phi-

losophy and theology. There followed, still before 1220, the university of Montpellier as a medical centre.

Paris was one of the most important places of study in the first half of the 12th cent. In addition to Abelard (dialectic), teachers working here included Petrus Helie (grammar and rhetoric, commentary on Priscian), Peter Lombard (author of the theological textbook known as the *Sententiae*, which remained in use until Luther's time), and Hugh of St. Victor, who, in his *Didascalicon de studio legendi*, produced an independent presentation of the doctrine of learning in which the *artes mechanicae* found a place alongside the *artes liberales*. Other centres included the cathedral schools at Laon, where Anselm of Laon (d. 1117) was the co-founder of early scholasticism with emphasis on theology; and Reims, where Gerbert of Aurillac (Pope Silvester II after 999) cultivated the *quadrivium*, especially mathematics and astronomy. Gerbert's student Fulbert, bishop of Chartres from 1006, was the first important teacher of the School of Chartres, whose influence extended far beyond that locality. Taking as its starting point the Christianizing translation and commentary of Plato's *Timaeus* by Chalcidius and the works of Eriugena, the School of Chartres attempted, with a view to creating a theodicy, to explain the cosmogony of *Genesis* from a natural-scientific and philosophical viewpoint by combining it with the *Timaeus*. In their efforts some scholars of Chartres came dangerously close to heretical statements. Its most outstanding teachers were Bernhard of Chartres (ca. 1114–1126, teacher and chancellor at Chartres, author of a commentary on the *Timaeus*); Thierry (ca. 1100–1155/56, teacher at Chartres, author of a commentary on the *Hexaemeron* with scientific explanations and of a textbook on the *artes liberales*–the *Heptateuchon*); William of Conches (ca. 1080–1154, teacher at Paris and Chartres, commentator on the *Timaeus* and on Boethius, author of such works on the philosophy of nature as the *Philosophia mundi*); Gilbert of Poitiers (ca. 1080–1154, teacher at Chartres and Paris, commentator on the *Opuscula sacra* of Boethius); and finally Bernard Silvestris, the most original thinker of this school (d. after 1159, a student of Thierry and a teacher at Tours). In his prosimetrum *Cosmographia*, Bernard created a new myth of creation according to which the transcendental Tugaton (God) does not take an active part in creation and is therefore not responsible for its degeneration. In his place, a series of increasingly subordinate feminine powers create the world and man. An allegorizing commentary on Virgil's *Aeneid*, based on Fulgentius, is also attributed to Bernard.

3. POETRY

Among other factors, the flowering of poetry was a result of the strong reception of Ovid. Around 1100, several poets of the so-called Loire Circle composed minor poetry stylistically polished after the model of Ovid, primarily in elegiac distichs. They included Hildebert of Lavardin, Marbode of Rennes and Baudri (Baldricus) of Bourgueil (author of a Christianizing adaptation of the correspondence between Paris and Helen in Ovid's *Heroides*). The great epic poems, all of which dealt with ancient material, arose approximately between 1180 and 1185. Walter of Châtillon wrote a historical epic on Alexander the Great (*Alexandreis*), in which the crusades were reflected. The external plot follows the 'History of Alexander' by Q. Curtius; for the internal plot, however, Walter combined Lucan's concept of *Fatum-Fortuna* with that of Boethius. Alexander's fall at the end is a justified punishment for his *superbia*, in that he associated himself ever more closely with Christ. Alan of Lille's allegorical epic *Anticlaudianus* was a response to the *Alexandreis*. Here, Natura, who as the *vicaria Dei* is responsible for the maintenance of the world created by God, wishes to counteract the degeneration of creation, caused by her own imperfection, by a *homo novus*. Prudentia, in the course of a heavenly journey, prays successfully on behalf of his soul. In a battle modelled after Prudentius's *Psychomachia*, he overcomes all obstacles and ushers in a new golden age. The epic shows the human soul the way to a genuine knowledge of God through the arts, theology and faith (represented as Prudentia's three escorts). This represents a critical confrontation with the Neoplatonic concept in the *Cosmographia* of Bernard Silvestris, and with Virgil's *Aeneid* in the interpretation ascribed to Bernard. Finally, John of Hauvilla alludes to Alan in his great satirical-didactic poem *Architrenius*. Here, the 'arch-mourner' finds the path from degeneration to salvation no longer through a heavenly journey, but through intellectual wandering on earth (instruction through the ancient philosophers and nature) and through his wedding with Moderantia. The genre of → COMEDY was not received in the form of the ancient *palliata*, but in the style and meter of Ovid's elegiac poetry. The main representative of this *Comoediae elegiacae* in the first half of the 12th cent. was Vitalis of Blois, whose comedies *Amphitryon* and *Aulularia* did not not go back directly to Plautus, but were mediated by late Latin prose comedies (*Querolus*). The → DIDACTIC POEM also experienced a renaissance at the end of the 12th and the first half of the 13th cent. It consisted above all in metrical poetics modelled after Horace's *Ars poetica*, which subsequently provided the theoretical foundation for poems (Matthaeus of Vendôme, Geoffroi of Vincauf, John de Garlandia). Added to these were didactic poems on grammar inspired by Donatus and Priscian. (Eberhard of Béthune, Alexander of Villa Dei).

4. FINE ARTS AND ARCHITECTURE

The scriptoria of St. Denis and St. Germain-des-Prés were already leading centres of manuscript illumination in the mid–11th cent. (*St. Denis Missal*). In the 12th cent., they were joined by Cluny (*Parma Ildefonsus* manuscript, early 12th cent.), Cîteaux (the four-volume bible in Dijon) and St. Amand (*vita* of Amandus at Valenciennes, ca. 1140). The greatest accomplishments were achieved in architecture. The → ROMANESQUE STYLE, whose name derives from its adoption of

Roman elements (vaults, round arches, columns and pillars), developed independently in F. (Early Romanesque 1000–1080, High Romanesque 1080–ca.1150). Characteristics of the cathedral buildings include vaults, verticality of space, the division and gradual elimination of the walls of the central nave (for instance, triforia). This tendency is particularly evident in Norman Church architecture of the 11th cent. (Jumièges, St. Étienne and Sainte Trinité in Caen, Mont St. Michel). In Provence, simple single-naved churches arose in the first half of the 12th cent. (St. Trophime in Arles), while in Poitou steep triple-naved hall churches arose with transept, ambulatory and chevet chapels (St. Martin in Tours, late 11th cent.). The culmination was represented by the vaulted → BASILICA churches of Burgundy, with their pointed-arched arcades, round-arched decorative triforia, ambulatory and chevet chapels (reconstruction of the church at Cluny, 1088–1130). Capitals and tympana began to be decorated with sculptures (capitals of the porch of St. Benoît-sur-Loire, second quarter of the 11th cent.; main porch at Vézelay, ca. 1125–1130). The → GOTHIC, in which Norman and Burgundian elements were combined, began around 1140 in the Ile-de-France (St. Denis, Sens). Unlike the Romanesque style, ambulatory and chevet chapels were unified in the cathedral of St. Denis (1040–1044), a work commissioned by abbot Suger, which he also documented in writing (*Libellus de consecratione ecclesiae sancti Dionysii*). The double-towered façades of St. Denis, Sens (1164), Chartres (1145–1175), and Laon (1190–1205) derive from Norman buildings, while the steep verticality is already present at Cluny. Typically Gothic, in contrast, is the concept of light, which Suger, influenced by the Neoplatonic metaphorics of light of Dionysius the Areopagite, saw as a means for the elevation of the soul. These ideas led to the replacement of solid walls by large windows decorated with stained glass paintings in the place of Romanesque frescoes (Chartres, ca. 1180). Also without Romanesque antecedents was the unity of architecture and illusion (the cathedral as Heavenly Jerusalem). The transition from Early to High Gothic took place around 1180–1190 (new construction at Chartres 1194, Reims 1211, Amiens 1220); the rich decoration of portals, porches, entire façades and towers with sculptural motifs continued to develop.

→ Aristotle; → Artes Liberales; → Basilica; → Boethius; → Ovid(ius)

1 H. AMENT, H. H. ANTON, J. FLECKENSTEIN, R. SCHIEFFER, A. VERHULST, A. PATSCHOVSKY, see Franken/Frankreich, in: LMA 4, 689–728 2 B. BISCHOFF (ed.), Karl der Grosse – Lebenswerk und Nachleben, vol. 2: Das geistige Leben, ²1966 3 Id., Paläographie des römischen Altertums und des abendländischen Mittelalters, ²1986 4 PH. CONTAMINE, J. EHLERS, N. BULST, B. BLUMENKRANZ, see Frankreich, in: LMA 4, 747–798 5 F. C. COPLESTON, A History of Medieval Philosophy, 1972 6 P. DRONKE (ed.), A History of 12th-Century Western Philosophy, 1988 7 P. GODMAN, Poets and Emperors. Frankish Politics and Carolingian Poetry, 1987 8 J. LE GOFF, Les

intellectuels au Moyen Age, 1985 (Engl.: Intellectuals in the Middle Ages, 1993)   9 O. MAZAL, Buchkunst der Romanik, 1978   10 W. MESSERER, Karolingische Kunst, 1973   11 F. MÜTHERICH, J. E. GAEHDE, Karolingische Buchmalerei, 1976/79   12 J. J. O'MEARA, Eriugena, 1988   13 CH. RATKOWITSCH, Platonisch-kosmogonische Spekulation im 12. Jahrhundert, in: Wiener Humanistische Blätter, Sonderheft: Zur Philosophie der Antike, 1995, 135–158   14 P. RICHÉ, Les écoles et l'enseignement dans l'Occident chrétien de la fin du Vᵉ siècle au milieu du XIᵉ siècle, 1979   15 B. RUPPRECHT, Romanische Skulptur in Frankreich, 1975   16 W. SCHÄFKE, Frankreichs gotische Kathedralen, 1979   17 W. SCHLINK, Die Kathedralen Frankreichs, 1978   18 R. SCHNEIDER, Das Frankenreich, 1982   19 J. VERGER, Les universités françaises au moyen âge, 1995.

CHRISTINE RATKOWITSCH

II. 13TH–15TH CENTURY
A. ON THE RELATION OF VERNACULAR POETRY AND LATIN TRADITION IN THE 12TH AND EARLY 13TH CENTURY   B. THE ZENITH OF CAPETIAN RULE   C. THE HOUSE OF VALOIS AND THE HUNDRED YEARS' WAR

A. ON THE RELATION OF VERNACULAR POETRY AND LATIN TRADITION IN THE 12TH AND EARLY 13TH CENTURY

Although individual documents in French (*langue d'oïl*) or Occitan (*langue d'oc*) had already existed earlier, such as the *Oaths of Strasbourg* from 842, cited by Nithart, the *Eulalia* sequence (transmitted together with its Latin model, late 9th cent.) or the fragment of an Old Provençal version of Boethius from the 11th cent., it was basically not until the 12th cent. that a continuity of the literary tradition in both vernaculars, clearly independent of liturgical or juristic motives, came into existence. The first narrative poems with a secular theme, composed in French octosyllabic rhyme pairs, were free versions of ancient epics for a courtly public. Like many early works of French literature, they stem from the Anglo-Norman area, since French had been the preferred speech of the aristocracy in England since the Norman conquest of 1066. The *Roman de Thèbes* (ca. 1150/1155) takes Statius's *Thebaid* as its model, yet scarcely has the gods themselves intervene in the plot, while it introduces ekphrastic passages (description of the chariot of Amphiares) alongside mythological digressions (the myth of Oedipus as the prehistory of the Theban War), a technique which was to have a formative influence on the style of later ancient romances. While Thebes served as a grave example of the consequences of incest and fraternal strife in the ruling house, the author of the *Roman d'Eneas* (ca. 1160) adapted from Virgil's *Aeneid* the founding myth of the vast Roman empire, in whose splendour the House of Plantagenêt also had an indirect share, insofar as, like the Frankish Merovingians, it strove to trace its genealogy back to the Trojans. In comparison to the *Aeneid*, one observes the omission of many mythologi-

cal allusions, while the love story between Aeneas and Lavinia was expanded with the help of Ovid's *Metamorphoses*. The close connection between ancient romance and (pseudo-) historical literature is clearly apparent in the *Roman de Troie* (ca. 1165) by Benoît de Sainte-Maure. Here, the court historian of Henry II Plantagenêt does not refer to the 'untruthful' Homer, who sent the gods into battle and who, in any event, was known only second-hand in the 12th cent. Rather, he calls upon Dictys Cretensis (*Ephemeris Belli Troiani*, 4th cent.) and Dares Phrygius (*Historia de excidio Troiae*, 6th cent.), since they had the authority of immediately trustworthy eye-witnesses. The amplification of both these meagre source texts, rich in amorous adventures and containing some 30,000 verses, begins with Jason's voyage with the Argonauts and is intended to transmit knowledge of Antiquity to a lay public, an Antiquity which–as usual in the vernacular poetry of the Middle Ages–was adapted largely anachronistically to the life familiar to the medieval aristocracy, so that Hector and Achilles fight out their tourneys in full knight's armor on horseback, and Achilles delivers long monologues on the pangs of love that Polyxena has caused him. Ancient romances combined the learning of the clerics (*clergie*), which had been nourished by the Latin tradition and which manifested itself in the form of appeals to ancient sources or recourse to such rhetorical techniques as → EKPHRASIS, with chivalric norms (*chevalerie*) and the love between the portrayed characters [4. 50]. They thereby marked the further development of the courtly romance that, with Chrétien de Troyes, freed itself from ancient models and turned to the fictional Arthurian world of Celtic legendary cycles. In the prologue to his Byzantine romance *Cligès* (1176), Chrétien characteristically develops the theory of the *translatio studii*, or the transmission of knowledge and chivalry from Greece to F. by way of Rome. This concept of cultural migration, analogous to the *translatio imperii*, also surfaces in Giraldus Cambrensis and Alexander Neckham; it was the common property of the Parisian schools since the 1160s and promoted the self-awareness of the intellectuals active there [31]. The *Roman d'Alexandre* (1177–1180) by Lambert le Tort and Alexandre de Bernay goes back by way of the epitome of Julius Valerius (9th cent.) to pseudo-Callisthenes (2nd cent.), and was the first French poem to be written in twelve-syllable verse, called *alexandrins*. Here, on the one hand, the Macedonian ruler was stylised into an exemplary prince while, on the other, the medieval audience's interest in the marvelous was also satisfied (for instance, by fountains of youth or automata). In the redemptive-historical animal allegories in the *Physiologus*, too, that which was worth knowing was paired with the marvelous. In this context, Philippe de Thaon (1130) or Guillaume le Clerc de Normandie (1210/1211) explicitly based their bestiaries on the authority of a Latin model expressly called a 'book' (*livre*) [14]. In the Occitan love-poetry of the troubadours Wilhelm IX of Aquitaine (1071–1126), Jaufré

Rudel (ca. 1130–1170), Bernart de Ventadorn (2nd half of the 12th cent.) and Arnaut Daniel (ca. 1150–1200), the concept emerged–perhaps through contact with Arabic poetry coming over the Pyrenees from the Iberian peninsula–of a refined love (*fin'amors*), which demanded the unconditional veneration of the lady by the amorous male first-person narrator. Here, the poets also made use of religious connotations (e. g., veneration of Mary) and used concepts from feudal law, so that the lady appears in place of the liege lord; to her the lover pledges his troth. Ovid's love poetry was widely received in F. from the 12th to the 14th cent.; in particular the *Ars Amatoria* was translated and adapted many times [11. 218]. However, what is most striking is the rift separating ancient and medieval vernacular love poetry. Ovid's ironic advice was distorted into earnest precepts, and the unapproachable, perfect Lady replaced the fun-loving girls and capricious *hetairai* of the Roman love elegy. Innovative strophic poems such as *canzone* or *sestinas* were performed to musical accompaniment and were distinguished by highly complex patterns of verse and rhyme. Vernacular lyric poetry also naturally made much more sparing use of mythological allusions than its Latin counterpart: at most, the figure of Narcissus was cited as the embodiment of the courtly lover. In northern F., such poets as Conon de Béthune (ca. 1150–1220), Gace Brulé (ca. 1159–1213) and Thibaut de Champagne (1201–1253) continued Occitan love poetry, which also had a lasting influence on Middle High German and Italian lyric poetry. Troubadours such as Sordello (1200–1269) or Lanfranco Cigala (d. 1257/1258) even wrote poetry in Occitan.

B. The Zenith of Capetian Rule
1. History 2. Education and Learning 3. Literature 4. Fine Arts and Architecture

1. History

The Capetian Royal House reached the height of its power in the 13th cent., although the king's influence was at first still limited by the great feudal lords, who contributed little to the kingdom's tax revenue. Even before his ascent to the throne, Louis VIII (1223–1226) commanded the Albigensian Crusade, in which the Cathar heretics of southern F. were annihilated. Following the turbulent regency of his wife Blanche of Castille, a 'foreigner' whose authority was contested by the great barons, Louis IX (1226–1270) secured the stability of his rule, which was not jeopardized even by participation in the Sixth and Seventh Crusades. He was soon recognized as the embodiment of all the virtues of a ruler and was canonized as early as 1297. From the mid–13th to the mid–14th cent., F. was the leading European power. This ensured the French king his complete independence from the Holy Roman emperor. The gradually developing French national consciousness manifested itself in such symbols of the sovereignty of the royal house as the lily, the oriflamme (banner of St. Dionysius, whose relics were venerated in the abbey

of St. Denis), the holy vial (believed to have fallen from heaven, with whose oil the king was anointed) and the ability ascribed to the French kings to heal scrofula by the laying on of hands. The high point of national unity was achieved under Philip IV 'The Fair' (1285–1314), although resentment arose against him among all classes because of excessive taxation, which led to regional unrest under Louis X ('le Hutin'–the quarreller, the quarrelsome, the stubborn, 1314–1316). After Louis's death, succession to the throne proved markedly difficult, since he, like his successors, died without male descendants. Philip V ('le Long'–the tall, 1316–1322), brother of Louis X, was followed by Charles IV (1322–1328), youngest son of Philip the Fair, and Charles's cousin Philip VI (1328–1350), whereby power was transferred to the House of Valois. Despite the resistance of the feudal lords, the Capetians were able to set up an efficient administration, impose taxation, and consolidate the kingdom's military might.

2. Education and Learning

Of particular importance for the cultural development of F. was the prosperity of the towns. Here, the division of labour clearly emerged; the universities produced a new type of independent critical intellectual who was no longer obligated to his religious community alone; such laymen as merchants and tradesmen became literate and therefore gradually obtained access to learning; and the mendicant orders developed their preaching activity geared specifically to urban populations [16]. Solidarity among 'secular' teachers prevailed against the bishop of Paris and, in 1215, brought about the foundation of the university, that is, the amalgamation into a community, divided guild-style into four 'nations' (French, Normans, Picards, English) and as many faculties (Arts, Medicine, Law, Theology), which was immediately ratified, so to speak, on April 13, 1231 by Pope Gregory IX in the bull *Parens scientiarum* [29. 30]. The ensuing conflict between 'seculars' and the representatives of the Dominicans and the Franciscans, ignited around the person of Guillaume de Saint-Amour, ended in 1257 with the victory of the mendicants, thereby clarifying, on the one hand, the limits of university autonomy and, on the other hand, integrating the representatives of the mendicant orders into the university. In the same year, Robert de Sorbon founded the first college for poor theology students, whence comes the name *Sorbonne* for the oldest Parisian institution of higher learning. Through the bequests of its teachers, the college gradually acquired a superb library where the students could read folio volumes, fastened by chains [30. 112–123]. Primarily because of the university, Paris became the intellectual centre of Christianity and the cultural hub of F. at the beginning of the 13th cent., although the foundation of other universities in other cities soon followed. Orléans, which had already been a centre for the study of authors and epistolary rhetoric in the 12th cent. (→ Letter-writing/ Ars dictaminis), was recognized as a university in 1306 by Pope Clement V. Angers did not achieve the status of a university until the 14th cent., while Montpellier possessed statutes for the study of medicine since 1220 and then, from 1300 on, also developed into a centre for jurisprudence, whereby it competed with the university at Toulouse, founded in 1229. The core of university instruction comprised the *lectio* and *disputatio* on a canonical text. On the basis of the presentation and explanation of a section of text, a systematic question was formulated, which was to be discussed in a controversial and public way. These *quaestiones disputatae* marked the scholarly culture of the 13th and 14th cent. in an essential way and lent it an agonistic nature. Thus the simple transmission of knowledge was replaced by the innovative production thereof [24; 18. 368 f.]. The reading of the Roman classics, above all of the poets, remained basically stagnant in the 13th cent., although they often still appeared on the program of the faculties of arts. The so-called → HUMANISM of the 12th cent. was over [26. 82; 12. 127]. Aristotle, together with the Neoplatonically-influenced Arabic commentators Avicenna (Ibn Sīna) and Averroes (Ibn Rušd), therefore stepped into the limelight. This situation did not change substantially despite all kinds of ecclesiastical obstacles, from the banning of Aristotelian → NATURAL PHILOSOPHY at the Council of Sens (1210) to the condemnation of 219 Averroist theses by the Parisian bishop Étienne Tempier (1277). The Stagirite's work was known to the West in its totality by the end of the 12th cent., often by way of Latin translations from the Arabic. From Spanish Toledo, where Muslim, Jewish and Christian scholars worked together, the works of Averroes also reached F. in the 1st half of the 13th cent., where they soon became a bone of contention. For instance, around 1275, Boethius of Dacia, following the Cordovan philosopher, sought to delimit the respective claims to validity of philosophy and faith, while Saint Bonaventure (ca. 1217–1274) saw Averroes primarily as a heretic. Under the influence of Aristotelian thought as it was developed by Albert the Great (ca. 1200–1280) and Thomas Aquinas (ca. 1225–1274) in their great summas, theology evolved into a refined academic discipline. Albert dedicated himself to the natural sciences and saw the highest form of life in the *vita contemplativa*, while his student Thomas strove to combat both pagan and Muslim philosophers with their own weapons and to expose the inner logical contradictions in the doctrine of the 'double truth'–the truth of reason and the truth of belief–, which was ascribed to the Averroists. The reception of Islamic-Greek philosophy was responsible for new standards of rational argumentation and the development of philosophy into an autonomous discipline [17].

The operation of the universities also led to an increase in the need for books. In response, the system of *peciae* was introduced, in which parts of extensive works could be borrowed and copied out. A clear layout, placing the text to be commented on in the middle and the 'glosses' in the margin, articulated the text through headings and coloured initials and also provided it with indices and running lemmas, thereby helping to orient the reader in these corpulent summas. Paris also became the centre of the book trade and book production, which was transferred from the monastery scriptoria into the hands of laymen. In general, 13th-cent. culture was characterized by new forms of collecting and organizing knowledge. Thus, the Dominican Vincent of Beauvais (d. 1264) compiled the most comprehensive encyclopedia of his time from ancient and Christian authors, as well as from medieval compilations. It consisted of three parts: the *Speculum naturae* on nature, the *Speculum doctrinae* on the branches of learning, and the *Speculum historiae* on history, to which a further apocryphal *Speculum morale*, by an unknown author, was added near the end of the 13th cent. With his *Livres dou Tresor*, Brunetto Latini (ca. 1220–1294), the Florence-born teacher of Dante, wrote a successful encyclopedia for laymen in French (transmitted in more than 70 manuscripts), whose articulation was modelled after that of Eustratius's commentary on Aristotle's *Nicomachean Ethics*. Here, the treatment of theology, history and natural science in the first book was followed by ethics, rhetoric (following Cicero's *De inventione*) and politics. On the basis of his experience with Italian civil politics, Brunetto was the first to bring the public-political function of eloquence once again to general awareness. He chose French as a means of reaching a broader audience.

3. LITERATURE

The most important innovations in French literature of the 13th cent., such as the extensive prose romance cycles on Tristan or King Arthur and his Knights of the Round Table, the development of a vernacular prose chronicle literature in connection with the Fourth Crusade in Robert de Clari and Geoffroi de Villehardouin, the emergence of a secular theatre, independent of liturgical occasions in Arras (Jean Bodel and Adam de la Halle) or the staging of literary subjectivity in Rutebeuf occurred in a manner largely independent from the reception of ancient models. Ancient influence can be discerned, above all, in allegorical poetry. Thus, in the gallery of exemplary lovers in the *Roman de la Poire* by Thibault (mid–13th cent.), Pyramis and Thisbe appear alongside Tristan and Isolde, as do Paris and Helen, entirely in the tradition of the courtly interpretation of Classical mythology. With the *Roman de la Rose* by Guillaume de Lorris and Jean de Meun (first part ca. 1230, continued by Jean de Meun around 1270), allegorical poetry in F. reaches its zenith. This romance, which consists of nearly 22,000 verses, was the most successful work of the later French Middle Ages. Transmitted in some 300 manuscripts, often richly illustrated, it played a quite intrinsic role, by means of the commentaries and imitations it inspired, in the emergence of a self-aware French literature basing itself in its own canon. The first-person narrator presents his experiences as a lover in the context of a dream-vision: he must defend himself against personifications that attempt to bar his way, such as Danger (*dangier*) or Reason (*raison*), in order to finally pluck the rose, that is, to be united with his beloved. In the process, he is supported by Amor and Venus. The doctrines proclaimed by the god of love are based in the courtly reinterpretation of Ovid's *Ars Amatoria* as a serious didactic poem. Both parts of the romance, moreover, adapt myths from Ovid's *Metamorphoses* (Narcissus, the Golden Age and the Castration of Saturn, Pygmalion), which, while they are not interpreted allegorically, nevertheless give the reader hints for interpreting the romance. The learned cleric Jean de Meun, who had gained his reputation as a translator of Boethius and Vegetius, placed the erotic allegory of his predecessor Guillaume within a broader cosmological framework, taking Boethius (*De consolatione philosophiae*) and Alan of Lille (*De planctu naturae*) as his models, whereby he was obliged to develop a philosophical terminology in the vernacular. Here, the praise of sexuality, understood to be in the service of procreation, takes the place of unfulfilled, ever-deferred courtly desire. Like Rutebeuf, Jean de Meun became involved in the quarrel between the mendicant orders and the university of Paris. He took up a vehement position against the mendicants in order retrospectively to defend Guillaume de Saint-Amour, who had already been condemned. The echo of the university quarrels in the vernacular literature written for laymen can be taken as a proof of the connection between university and civic identity. The striving for totality that was peculiar to the 13th cent. also manifests itself in the *Ovide moralisé*, written in 72,000 octosyllables by an anonymous author from Burgundy between 1291 and 1328. In this gigantic adaptation of Ovid's *Metamorphoses*, each transformation myth is interpreted from the viewpoint of natural philosophy, morality or sacred history so that, for instance, Pygmalion could become the *figura* of God the Creator. Other Ovidian works (*Heroides*, *Fasti*) were also incorporated into this process, and older vernacular adaptations of Ovid were used.

4. Fine Arts and Architecture

From the 13th to the 15th cent., the influence of ancient art, as well as interest therein, decreased considerably as compared to the preceding era of the → Romanesque style. In the 13th cent., for instance, ancient ruins were connected with Charlemagne, or even considered to be 'Saracen' monuments [1. 112ff.]. The Romanesque fabled animals and Corinthian columns disappeared from the churches of the Cistercian order.

Manuscripts of Terence were still copied and illustrated down to 1200, but then not again until 1407, while the last illustrated Prudentius manuscript stems from 1289. The connection between the images and texts of Antiquity, and between form and meaning broke down completely [22. 92].

In the → Gothic, borrowings from ancient models are perceptible, above all, in the cathedral in Reims, begun in 1211, that is, in a city in which ancient statues and monuments stood right before the eyes of the master-builders of the cathedral. Thus, in the staggered gables of the porch structure, the model of a → Triumphal arch can be discerned–that of the Gate of Mars, not far from the cathedral [15. 32]. The head of the apostle Paul resembles that of the emperor Antonius Pius, while the features of the resurrected dead were influenced by a sarcophagus relief [22. 74]. In addition to a few sketches of nudes, designs, in an Antique-like style, of garment drapery are present in the *Bauhüttenbuch* of Villard de Honnecourt (early 13th cent.), who long worked at Reims. Most artists, however, obtained their direct knowledge of ancient art at best from works of the minor arts, such as → Gems. Thus, around 1200, an ancient cameo was used as a pagan idol on the cathedral of Notre Dame in Paris. The legacy of the ancient world was a 'treasure-house', from which the master-builders helped themselves as naturally as did the encyclopedists, without regard for the meaning the → Spolia may once have had in their original context. Finally, ancient forms were also seen in the Middle Ages as a dangerous temptation to idolatry. The pagan gods were reinterpreted as personifications of vices: Pan's horns were those of the devil, and Diana became a witch. The second method for domesticating the ancient divinities consisted in resettling them in the contemporary courtly environment. Thus, in the illustrated manuscripts of the *Roman de la Rose*, Venus appears as a lady in fashionable dress, while only the angel's wings of the god of love remind us that the elegant young courtier is ancient Amor. Not until the Italian Renaissance did aesthetization and historical distancing put an end to the threat represented by the ancient gods [5].

C. The House of Valois and the Hundred Years' War

1. History   2. Education and Learning
3. Poetry   4. Fine Arts

1. History

From the second third of the 14th to the mid–15th cent., F. went through a difficult period of crises, in which the nation was shaken by war, social unrest and, beginning in 1348, the Black Death (plague). The impact on the demographic and economic development of the kingdom were catastrophic. The Hundred Years' War between F. and England, which lasted from 1337 to 1453, with occasional interruptions, began with a dynastic dispute and ended with the development of a French national consciousness. Edward III of England, who as recently as 1331 had sworn an oath of fealty to the French king for the Duchy of Guyenne, contested the legitimacy of the accession to the throne of Philip VI of the House of Valois and asserted his own claim to the French throne as the grandson of Philip IV (the Fair). He invaded F. with his army, inflicted a series of crushing defeats on the French troops (especially at Crécy in 1346) and in 1347 won a valuable bridgehead on the continent at Calais, while his son, the Black Prince, fought in southern F. The situation deteriorated still further under Jean II 'le Bon' (the Good) (1350–1364), who was forced to take the field simultaneously against the English and his renegade son-in-law Charles II 'le Mal' (the Bad) of Navarre, supported for his part by disgruntled cities and clerics. When Jean II was taken prisoner by the English at Poitiers in 1356, the peasants, oppressed by war taxes, also rose in revolt in 1358. After the suppression of this revolt by the aristocracy, the prince regent, the later King Charles V (1364–1380), succeeded in calming the situation. He purchased his father's freedom by the Treaty of Brétigny-Calais (1360), but his father was obliged to cede a third of the domains of the French crown to England. After the death of Jean II, Charles V raised a powerful army, drove the English back and gave new lustre to the French crown through his well-considered cultural policies. After Pope Gregory XI returned from Avignon to Rome, thereby escaping the influence of the French king, Charles V acknowledged the antipope Clement VII in 1378, so that the Great Western Schism, which was to last until 1417, became confirmed. The French king's independence from Rome was thereby underscored, and the Gallicanism that had determined the policies of the French crown with regard to the Roman Curia since at least the time of the confrontation between Philip IV and Pope Boniface VIII, was continued. Charles's brother Philip II 'the Bold' became Duke of Burgundy in 1363, which marked the beginning of the duchy's rise to the status of the third great continental power. Under Charles VI (1380–1422), who had been mentally ill since 1392, the legacy of Charles V soon declined. The kingdom was torn by the rivalries between the Armagnacs, supporters of Louis of Orléans, and the Burgundian followers of Philip the Bold, both of whom sought control of the state apparatus. This civil war favoured a renewed English invasion in 1415, leading to the French defeat at Agincourt at the hands of Henry V of Lancaster. Charles VII (1423–1461) resisted the attempts of Philip the Good of Burgundy to achieve peace with England at the cost of maintaining English claims to the French throne, while Joan of Arc became the symbol of French resistance against the English occupation and brought about the crowning of the Dauphin at Reims, the traditional memorial site of the French monarchy. With the help of a standing army and continuous taxation, Charles VII was able to win back the French territory and reinforce the position of the monarchy. The English defeat at Castillon ended the Hundred Years' War in 1453 and strengthened the position of the French king. When Louis XI (1461–1483) extended the central power still further, he encountered the resistance both of the nobility and the bourgeoisie, who were able to ally themselves with Charles the Bold (1467–1477) of Burgundy. The confrontation between F. and Burgundy came to an end in 1477 with the death of Charles the Bold before Nancy and the annexation of the Duchy of Burgundy, as well as the towns of the Somme. Through marriage,

Louis's successor, Charles VIII (1483–1498), also acquired Bretagne, and in 1494 he marched at the head of his army into Italy. The expedition was a military fiasco, but it strengthened contact with the rich Italian culture of the Renaissance.

2. EDUCATION AND LEARNING

The series of university foundations continued in the 14th and 15th cents. (Cahors 1332, Grenoble 1339, Orange 1365, Aix-en-Provence 1409, Dôle 1422, Poitiers 1431, Caen 1432–36, Bordeaux 1441, Valence 1452–59, Nantes 1460, Bourges 1464) and brought with it a clear regionalization of the various student bodies [29. 79]. With the exception of Avignon, which as the seat of the Curia from 1309 to 1377 developed a particular force of attraction, the founding of new institutions of higher learning throughout Europe, together with the confusion caused by war, led to a clear decrease in the percentage of foreigners in the student body compared to the 13th cent., even in Paris, and to lower student mobility within the country itself. Since most of the popes residing in Avignon had attended a French institution of higher learning, fewer conflicts arose between university and Church in the Late Middle Ages than in the 13th cent., while the increasing influence of royal power became ever more noticeable. In any case, the University of Paris forfeited its intellectual predominance in the 14th cent. Thus, the genuinely innovative philosophical trend of nominalism came from Oxford, where the Franciscan William of Ockham (ca. 1285–1349) taught. He denied the reality of essences beyond sensibly perceptible individual things, as, for instance, John Duns Scotus (1265–1308) had maintained. Instead, he conceived universals from an ontological viewpoint as concepts and, with a glance at epistemology, promoted empiricism. John Buridan (before 1300–1358) adopted Ockham's ideas in his linguistic-philosophical theory of reference and also devoted himself to the philosophy of nature; of course, he remained his entire life a member of the faculty of arts in Paris and did not teach theology. It was not by chance that Buridan was connected with the *Collège de Navarre* (founded in 1305), the nodal point of early French Humanism. Humanists trained at the *Collège de Navarre* often turned up as notaries or secretaries in the service of the crown; they took part in politics and had contacts with Italy by way of Avignon [28. 37–38]. In southern F., the Curia had become an important cultural centre since the pontificate of John XXII (1316–1334). The papal palace sheltered a rich library, which had been used by Petrarch (1304–1374); theological works were predominant in it, but the popes also acquired the Latin Classics. At the *Collège de Navarre*, Jean de Montreuil (1354–1418) impressed Petrarch, corresponded with Coluccio Salutati and polemicized against the English occupation of F., while Nicolas de Clamanges (1363–1437) strove for the improvement of Latin style, composing speeches and an eclogue (1394) and carrying out a critical revision of the text of Cicero's orations. The theologian Jean Gerson (1363–

1429), who became chancellor of the University of Paris in 1396 and was an active participant at the Council of Constance from 1415–1418, was deeply influenced by Petrarch's Latin works but, like Nicolas de Clamanges, defended the Paris university teachers against the mockery of the Italian, who had taken aim at the lack of dexterity displayed by the French in Latin stylistics [30.267]. Sermons for the laity can be found in Gerson's extensive work alongside treatises on mystical theology, but he wrote his Petrarchan Latin poetry like the *Pastorium carmen* (ca. 1382) only for a limited circle of Humanist friends. This slight public impact is characteristic of early French Humanism. At the University of Paris, the study of the Roman Classics had a primarily propaedeutic character, and there was no genuine instruction in rhetoric [26. 357f.]. This did not change until Guillaume Fichet (ca. 1433–1480). He knew Cardinal Bessarion, established, together with Jean Heylin, the first printing press in F. at the Collège de Sorbonne in 1470 and in 1470–1471 composed a *Rhetorica* based on his Paris lectures. Overall, French university teaching became markedly ossified in the 15th cent. It is true that Gregorio da Città di Castello taught Greek for the first time in Paris in 1458, but he was still unable to establish a genuine tradition. An early vernacular humanism developed at the courts of the king and such great princes as Jean de Berry or the dukes of Burgundy, and a series of French translations were written, primarily of ancient philosophers and historians. Jean le Bon had already commissioned the Benedictine priest Pierre Bersuire, who had been inspired by the *Ovide moralisé* for the allegorical interpretation of ancient myths in his *Repertorium morale* (1320–1350), with the translation of the first, third and fourth decades of Livy. This was possible only because the commentary on Livy by the English Dominican Nicolas Trevet (1265–1334) was available to Bersuire, and Petrarch, whom he had met at Avignon, allowed him access to his collection of manuscripts [11. 227f.]. After his prologue, Bersuire added his own chapter with an explanation of technical terms, Roman institutions and religious customs of the pagans [3. 118]. Livy's value for the ruler consisted above all in his exemplary narratives, and the *Ab urbe condita* was read as a kind of → PRINCES' MIRROR. Charles V intensified the patronage carried out by his father and had Augustine's *De civitate dei* translated by Raoul de Presle (1371–1375); the preface offers a defense of the French monarchy and the House of Valois, whereby it precisely fulfilled the purposes of the monarchy's cultural policy. Charles V was the first French king to systematically compile an entire library, which he had housed in the Louvre. He was particularly interested in such astrological-cosmological and historical works as Ptolemy's *Quadripartitum* and Flavius Josephus *Jewish War*. Nicolas Oresme (ca. 1322–1382), author of an essay on money (*De moneta*, 1356–1357) and head of the Collège de Navarre in 1356, was probably the most important translator of the 14th cent. He was the first to make

Aristotle's ethics, politics, economics and a part of his natural philosophy (*De caelo et mundo*) available to the lay public, whereby he simultaneously created a French scholarly language. All translators had the greatest difficulties with the *brevitas* of Latin and had recourse to periphrase or the accumulation of synonyms when an equivalent term was lacking. Laurent de Premierfait, who in 1405 translated Cicero's *De senectute* for Louis of Bourbon and the *De amicitia* for the bibliophile Jean de Berry (1340–1416) in 1411, and also commented on Terence and Statius, wanted to see his translation placed alongside the original text so that each reader might choose the version he found most comprehensible [11. 235]. The first half of the 15th cent. was relatively poor in new translations. Under Philip the Good, Antiquity served primarily as an exotic backdrop for courtly celebrations in Burgundy. Under Charles the Bold, the ancient historians once again functioned as educators of princes, like Xenophon in his *Education of Cyrus*, which Vasque de Lucène (1435–1512) translated from Poggio's Latin version in 1470. The reception of ancient literature served primarily moral edification and the acquisition of knowledge; not until near the very end of the 15th cent., under Charles VIII, was there an accumulation of translations of purely literary works, such as Ovid's *Heroides* or Virgil's *Aeneid*. Antiquity, henceforth experienced as something distant, could now become the *locus* of aesthetic nostalgia [22. 116f.].

3. POETRY

French poetry achieved self-awareness in the 14th and 15th cents. Not only did vernacular poetics and rhetorics emerge (for instance, Eustache Deschamps, *Art de dictier*, 1393), which led to the composition of new lyric forms such as the *rondeau*, the *ballade* or *chant royal*, but individual poetic works also reflected, to an increasing degree, on themselves and their formal possibilities, which were then speculated upon exhaustively by the Burgundian *Grands Rhétoriqueurs* of the 15th cent. The staging of the poetic and even authorial first-person was constitutive for the beloved narrative form of the *dit*, in which lyric poems or prose letters were often inserted [23. 86–94]. By the end of the 14th cent., poetry was no longer sung but was restricted to the 'natural music' of the words. As nominalism sharpened philosophers' attention to the empirical world and the early Dutch-Burgundian painting of the van Eyck brothers sought to capture the fullness of phenomena in images, so poetry now absorbed within itself, alongside the idealized courtly world, the contradictory experiential multiplicity of daily life. All these new tendencies culminated in the testament of François Villon (1431–ca. 1463), who posed as a vagrant and layabout. His work owed Antiquity at most a few exemplary figures transformed into ironic form and the legal fiction of a poetic last will. Significantly, the two most often received texts in French poetry of the Late Middle Ages were Ovid's *Metamorphoses* and Boethius's *De consolatione philosophiae*, since the former shows a world in constant transformation, while the latter dispenses consolation to a victim of adverse circumstances through the allegory of philosophy (as well as through poetry). Likewise, in Guillaume de Machaut (1300–1377), Jean Froissart (ca. 1337–1404), Eustache Deschamps (ca. 1346–1406) and Christine de Pizan (ca. 1364–1430), Classical mythology, and even terse allusions to individual myths, such as the description of the goddess of luck Fortuna, became an established a component of French poetry. This can be understood as an attempt to reconcile, at least metaphorically, experiences of contingency and crisis with the order of the world. In his *Confort d'Ami* (1357), Guillaume de Machaut consoled his addressee Charles II 'the Bad' of Navarre with mythological examples from the *Ovide moralisé*, whereby religious → ALLEGORISM naturally fell by the wayside. The increasingly free and creative approach towards ancient mythology led to the invention of new myths. Froissart inserted the pseudo-Ovidian myth of Pynoteus and Neptisphele, reminiscent of the story of Pyramus and Thisbe, into his *Prison amoureuse* (1372–1373). In Christine de Pizan, the first self-aware female author in French literary history, the goddess Othea instructs the young Hector with mythological examples (*Epistre d'Othéa*, 1400–1401); this can probably be correlated with the instruction–unfortunately in vain–that the protohumanist gave to Charles VI.

4. FINE ARTS

The sons of John the Good–Charles V, Jean de Berry and Philip the Good of Burgundy–were passionate collectors not only of books but also of works of art, including the ancient minor arts. Thus, the Duke of Berry possessed more ancient cameos than Piero de' Medici, for which the Italians envied him. Even magical properties were ascribed to precious cut stones. Charles V donated a particularly fine cameo of Jupiter to the cathedral at Chartres as a votive gift for the birth of a son [10. 208]. Some of the coins and medals in the collection of Jean de Berry were also ancient [20. 52–60]. However, they remained unnoticed, and antiquarian erudition did not begin in F. until the time of Guillaume Budé (1468–1540).

In the fine arts, the French reception of Antiquity in the Late Middle Ages took place primarily in the area of manuscript illumination, which nowhere developed so exuberantly as in F. and the Burgundian Netherlands. Still in the 12th cent., it was particularly those ancient works for which, as in the case of Virgil, Terence or Prudentius, an iconography from late Antiquity already existed that were illustrated. However, the continuity of this tradition, transmitted via Carolingian models, was largely interrupted in the course of the 13th cent., so that illuminators were forced to improvise and invent. At the zenith of the University of Paris in the 13th cent., it was primarily texts for instruction, such as the works of Galen or Ptolemy, that were illustrated. Allegories made abstract material perceptible; thus, in the illustrated commentary to Aristotle's *De sensu et*

sensato, the five senses were represented by people engaged in characteristic activities (for instance, harp playing for hearing). Nicolas Oresme himself specified the program of images for the illustration of his translations of Aristotle in order effectively to impress the concepts on his readers in the manner of the medieval art of memorisation [2]. Christine de Pizan collaborated on the illustrations of myths in the *Epistre Othea*. The frontispiece illustrations of two Terence manuscripts from the collection of Jean de Berry (Paris, BN lat. 7907 A, dating from 1407, and the *Térence des Ducs*, Arsenal, ms. 494 from ca. 1412) are the first in the late Middle Ages and the Renaissance to feature the reconstruction of a Roman theatre, which is presented as round but contains no tribunes and, like the setting for the medieval mystery plays, has no clear line of separation between stage and spectators' area. The masks of the violently gesticulating actors are striking, since the usual tendency was to see masks as something demonic or to fail utterly to understand their function [21. 50–54]. Also striking is the occasional use of Byzantine costumes or architectural elements to indicate a difference between medieval society and that of ancient Rome. Finally, it was customary throughout the Middle Ages to dress ancient gods and heroes in the garb of contemporary court society.

1 J. ADHÉMAR, Influences antiques dans l'art du Moyen Âge français. Recherches sur les sources et les thèmes d'inspiration, 1939   2 F. AVRIL, Gli autori classici illustrati in Francia dal XIII al XV secolo, in: M. BUONOCORE (ed.), Vedere i Classici. L'illustrazione libraria dei testi antichi dall'età romana al tardo medioevo, 1996, 87–98   3 F. BERRIOT, Langue, nation et pouvoir: les traducteurs du XIVe siècle précurseurs des humanistes de la Renaissance., in: M. T. JONES-DAVIES (ed.), Langues et nations au temps de la Renaissance, 1991, 113–135   4 R. BLUMENFELD-KOSINSKI, Classical Mythology and Its Interpretations in Medieval French Literature, 1998   5 M. CAMILLE, The Gothic Idol. Ideology and Image-Making in Medieval Art, 1989   6 J. CHANCE, The Mythographic Art: Classical Fable and the Rise of the Vernacular in Early France and England, 1990   7 PH. CONTAMINE, J. EHLERS, N. BULST, B. BLUMENKRANZ, see Frankreich, LMA 4, 747–798   8 CURTIUS, E. R., European Literature and the Latin Middle Ages, 1990   9 E. FARAL, Recherches sur les sources latines des contes et romans courtois du moyen âge, 1913   10 Les Fastes du Gothique. Le siècle de Charles V, 1981   11 A. FOURIER (ed.), L'Humanisme médiéval dans les littératures romanes du XIIe au XIVe siècle, 1964   12 G. GLAUCHE, Schullektüre im Mittelalter. Entstehung und Wandlungen des Lektürekanons bis 1200 nach den Quellen dargestellt, 1970   13 G. GRENTE (ed.), Dictionnaire des lettres françaises. Le Moyen Âge. Édition entièrement revue et mise à jour sous la direction de G. HASENOHR et M. ZINK, 1992   14 M. GROSSE, Das Buch im Roman. Studien zu Buchverweis und Autoritätszitat in altfranzözischen Texten, 1994   15 H.-J. KUNST, W. SCHENKLUHN, Die Kathedrale in Reims. Architektur als Schauplatz politischer Bedeutungen, 1987   16 J. LE GOFF, Les intellectuels au Moyen Âge, 1985 (1957)   17 A. DE LIBERA, Penser au Moyen Âge, 1991   18 Id., La philosophie médiévale, 1993   19 R. H. LUCAS, Medieval French Translations of the Latin Classics to 1500, in: Spe-

culum 45, 1970, 225–253   20 M. MEISS, French Painting
in the Time of Jean de Berry. The Late Fourteenth Century
and the Patronage of the Duke, 1967   21 Id., French
Painting in the Time of Jean de Berry. The Limbourgs and
their Contemporaries, 1974   22 E. PANOFSKY, Renaissance and Renascences in Western Art, 1960   23 D. POI-
RION (ed.), La littérature française aux XIVe et XVe siècles,
1988 (Grundriß der romanischen Literaturen des Mittelalters VIII/1)   24 TH. RENTSCH, Die Kultur der quaestio.
Zur literarischen Formgeschichte der Philosophie im Mittelalter, in: G. GABRIEL, CH. SCHILDKNECHT (eds.), Literarische Formen der Philosophie, 1990, 73–91   25 P.
RENUCCI, L'Aventure de l'humanisme européen au
moyen-âge (IVe – XIVe siècle), 1953   26 A. SCAGLIONE,
The Classics in Medieval Education, in: A. S. BERNARDO,
S. LEVIN (eds.), The Classics in the Middle Ages, 1990,
343–362   27 J. SEZNEC, La survivance des dieux antiques, 1993 (1940)   28 F. SIMONE, The French Renaissance, Medieval Tradition and Italian Influence in Shaping
the Renaissance in France, 1961   29 J. VERGER (ed.),
Histoire des universités en France, 1986   30 A. VERNET
(ed.), Histoire des bibliothèques françaises. Les bibliothèques médiévales. Du VIe siècle à 1530, 1989   31 F. J.
WORSTBROCK, Translatio artium. Über die Herkunft und
Entwicklung einer kulturhistorischen Theorie, in: Archiv
für Kulturgeschichte 47, 1965, 1–22   32 M. ZINK, Littérature française du moyen âge, 1992.

ADDITIONAL BIBLIOGRAPHY R. L. BENSON AND G.
CONSTABLE, Renaissance and Renewal in the Twelfth
Century, 1984; M.-R. JUNG, La légende de Troie en France
au Moyen Age: analyse des versions françaises et bibliographie raisonnée des manuscrits, 1996 (Romanica Hel-
vetica 114); A. WELKENHUYSEN, H. BRAET, W. VERBEKE
(eds.), Medieval Antiquity, 1995 (Mediaevalia Lovanen-
sia)   MAX GROSSE

III. 16TH–18TH CENTURY
A. 16TH CENTURY   B. 17TH CENTURY   C. 18TH CENTURY

A. 16TH CENTURY
1. HISTORY, POLITICAL, SOCIAL, AND CULTURAL
CONDITIONS   2. EDUCATION AND LEARNING
3. POETRY AND LITERATURE   4. FINE ARTS, ARCHI-
TECTURE, AND OTHER ARTS

1. HISTORY, POLITICAL, SOCIAL, AND
CULTURAL CONDITIONS
In the first half of the century, the foreign policy of
the French kings was determined by the conflict with
the Habsburgs, against whose geopolitical superiority
the monarchy struggled until the peace treaty between
Henry II and Philip II in 1559. F.'s actions were initially
not lacking in strategic skill, insofar as the king used the
vacant succession to the kingdom of Naples as a pretext
to shift the theatre of war onto Italian soil, which was
equivalent to a coup. This campaign, begun in 1494
under Charles VIII, was continued by Louis XII from
1497 to 1507. Between 1515 and 1544, alleged claims
to succession gave François I the opportunity for five
more campaigns, yet he too was unable to achieve
lasting control over upper Italy. This military invasion

of Italian territory can be interpreted as an act of symbolic politics [30]: through the Italian wars, F. articulated a claim to empire. The goal was → ROME as the
centre of secular and spiritual rule over Western
Europe. This claim determined the ideological horizon
from which F.'s relations with Italy were shaped both
politically and culturally. Since the end of the Hundred
Years' War, the internal policy of French rulers had
been constantly oriented towards the further consolidation of the kingdom. By a skillful marriage policy, the
monarchy finally achieved territorial hegemony
through the union of François I and Claude de France.
Under the reign of this 'Renaissance King' (1515–1547)
and his successor Henry II (1547–1559), the monarchical state established itself as a stable form of government [61]. The Wars of Religion (1562–1598), which
the ruling feudal dynasties employed against the monarchy, halted the advance of the centralized state only
temporarily. It was above all François I who succeeded
in strengthening royal power. He thereby continued the
policies of his predecessors, which sought to promote
the unification of the territorial state through measures
in the fields of administration, finance, and jurisdiction.
F. entered a phase of solid prosperity under this ruler.
Structural improvements, such as the securing of transport routes and the promotion of the movement of
goods, provided for the economic progress of the
towns. The expansion of the new profit-oriented publishing trade promoted cultural change, while the rapid
diffusion of new communication technologies led to the
replacement of the literary culture of the late Middle
Ages and its high standards of craftsmanship. In addition to Paris, site of the publication of Humanistic editions of ancient texts, Lyon, situated in a region of
transfer between northern and southern Europe,
became a trade centre for Italian cultural goods and the
most important centre of book production and the printing of many translations of Greek, Latin and Italian
texts. The large numbers of copies printed and widespread writing in the vernacular point to a rapid expansion of the culture of reading, beyond the old centres of
learned written tradition [45].

2. EDUCATION AND LEARNING
At the beginning of the century, proto-Humanistic
educational activity could be increasingly observed in
the towns. Its initiators came primarily from the ranks
of the juristically-trained urban bourgeoisie and the bureaucratic aristocracy, that is, the bearers of traditional,
secular written culture. The fact that this cultural elite
was anchored in the rhetorical-literary tradition of the
14th and 15th cents. [32] had as its consequence that
the change in the perception of Antiquity did not take
place abruptly in France. In fact, it was initially often
the old subjects that were transmitted by the communication technology of book printing. A similar phenomenon can be observed in the establishment of colleges, which arose in the towns with increasing frequency beginning in the 1520s [38]. The laicization of
education did not initially pursue any anticlerical goal,

and it was not until the second half of the century that Humanistic → PEDAGOGY became increasingly confessionalized. From an organizational viewpoint, the new type of school was based on the (*septem*) → ARTES LIBERALES; however, the *trivium* in the colleges was no longer intended just as preparation for theology. Meanwhile, a consistent orientation of schooling toward the acquisition of linguistic-literary competence in the Humanistic sense remained up to the initiative of individuals. For example, Mathurin Cordier (1479–1564) at the Parisian Collège de Sainte-Barbe placed the emphasis of instruction on rhetorical exercises in addition to grammatical rules and the elucidation of authors [49. 159]. Most of the colleges attended by foreign students in Paris, however, kept with the arts curriculum. Even in the colleges of provincial towns, instruction initially remained under the influence of late scholastic grammar, especially in the *classes grammaticae*. There can therefore be no question of a unified or even region-wide penetration of the Humanistic *trivium* in the first half of the century [31]. Starting in the 1540s, however, reading lists indicate that a canon of school classics was beginning to form: Terence, Virgil, Horace, Catullus and Cicero figured among the standard inventory, while among Greek authors Homer, Pindar and Demosthenes were ranked at the top.

For the diffusion of ancient educational material, Humanist educational work, for its part, played on the reception habits of the lay public with great success. Erasmus's *Adagiorum Chiliades* (1500) anticipated the success of French collections of apophthegms, which familiarized the urban bourgeois public with the repertoire of mythological and moral-philosophical lore of Antiquity in the form of exemplary instruction. Predominant here, as is shown by the example of the little handbook *Le Cathon en françois* (1492), reprinted again and again until well into the first half of the century, was the attempt to embed ancient wisdom in one's own cultural tradition. The reception of Lucian also fits in here: typical was the translation of the *Dialogues of the Dead* as *Trente dialogues moraulx de Lucien* (1529). Such florilegia remained in use until the end of the century and were supposed, like the *Sentences illustres de M. T. Cicero* (1582) and the *Œuvres morales et meslées de Sénèque* (1595), to facilitate access to '*philosophie morale*'. The translation of ancient authors was also often given a national justification, as was affirmed by Claude de Seyssel (1450–1520), professor, diplomat and theologian in the service of Louis XII in his *Exorde à la Translation de l'histoire de Justin* (1510). Likewise, Lefèvre d'Etaples (ca. 1455–1536) believed he could adapt the doctrines of the Florentine Neoplatonists to the scholastic philosophy of the Sorbonne, thus reconciling Antiquity and Christianity.

In the first half of the century, Guillaume Budé (1468–1540), the most influential representative of French Humanism, also presupposed the learned adaptation of the ancient tradition of *eruditio moralis*. This moral-practical conception of Antiquity, which had its roots in the rhetorical-literary tradition of the Paris Parliament, was echoed not least in the areas that attracted his philosophical erudition. In his *Annotationes ad pandectas* (1508), that is, commentary on the civil code of → ROMAN LAW, he laid the foundations for overcoming the scholastic method of the *mos italicus*. Budé read the *Corpus Iuris Civilis* in the original and, by means of it, reached the oldest sources of French law. Following in his footsteps, jurisprudence–here the role played by Jacques Cujas (1520–1590) should be mentioned–found access to the classical Roman legal system from a historical perspective as well. In his treatise *De Asse eiusque partibus* (1514), Budé placed the investigation of the material documents of Antiquity on a wholly new foundation. He turned to Greek in the following years, and the fruits of his labours were the *Commentarii linguae graecae* (1529). His works entitled *De philologia* and *De studio litterarum* (both from 1532) developed a concept of philological activity in which the philologist is characterized not by eloquence, but by encyclopedic knowledge. With the programmatic revaluation of philology to the status of leading discipline of Humanistic education, as had already been accomplished by Politian, Budé was reacting to a cultural-political measure enacted by the king. In 1530, at the behest of François I and against the resistance of the Sorbonne, royal chairs were established at Paris for Greek, Hebrew, and mathematics, to which outstanding representatives of the Humanist movement were called. The foundation of these chairs functioned as a signal that Humanism had penetrated into F. [25]. The initiative made it clear that the traditionalism of the Parisian universities was everywhere being called into question. The teaching of the *lecteurs royaux* did not fall under the supervision of the Sorbonne. The scholarly organization of the scholastic educational institutions was increasingly subject to criticism in the 1530s. This criticism found its literary echo above all in the famous satirical passages of *Pantagruel* (1532) and *Gargantua* (1535) by François Rabelais (ca. 1494–1553).

The model of what would later become the Collège Royal (now the Collège de France) was the Alexandrian Museion rather than the Platonic Academy, which had served as model for the Florentine Humanists. The philological-methodological orientation of the teaching, together with the emphasis on Greek, represented a novelty in F. [47. 127–178]. This combination had a tremendous effect on the Parisian intellectual milieu, especially through the discovery of previously little-known Greek authors. Jean Dorat (1508–1588), who taught at the Collège de Coqueret before being named in 1556, together with Adrien Turnèbe (1512–1565), as *lecteur royal* for Greek, lectured on the totality of Greek poetry. Extraordinary here were his reading of Aeschylus and his lecture on Pindar and the Alexandrians, particularly Callimachus [29]. Beginning in the 1540s, the foundations were laid, in collaboration with Parisian printers, for making Greek and Latin original texts accessible in a comprehensive way. Turnèbe, who was simultaneously in charge of the Presse Royale founded by François I, initiated the printing of critical editions. Outstanding among the works he edited was his edition of Homer, which formed the first volume of the *Poetae Graeci principes heroici carminis* (1566). Turnèbe was, of course, surpassed by Henri Estienne (1531–1598), who, upon taking over the directorship of the press in 1551, continued the pioneering editorial and philological work of his father Robert, who had completed the first *Latinae Linguae Thesaurus* in 1543, despite all manner of difficulties of a confessional nature, as a result of which the members of the printing dynasty supporting the Reformation were forced to open a branch in Geneva. Among the large number of Latin and Greek text editions (74 in Greek alone, 18 of which were first editions) which Estienne published and often provided with a commentary, the *Anacreontea* (1554), which he discovered, and the collection of all fragments of Greek lyric poets (first appearing in 1560, then definitively in 1586) are particularly worthy of mention. Plato is still cited after the pagination of his Plato edition of 1578. A no less significant philological accomplishment was the monumental *Thesaurus Graecae Linguae* (1572).

The evolution of learned reception into historical-scholarly critique characteristic of the first half of the century stood in a tense relationship to the prestige-driven attitude of the court towards the ancient tradition. For the first time, the Académie du Palais (1576), brought to life by Henry III (1574–1589), sought to join up with the new encyclopedism, whereby it obviously pursued national goals, concentrating on the antiquarian publication of 'Gallic' antiquities. Important here were Étienne Pasquier's (1529–1615) *Recherches de la France* [14]. Blaise de Vigenère (1523–1596) translated, in addition to Caesar, the fourth book of Tacitus's *Histories*, which treated Gaul. The turn on the part of the Humanistic cultural elite to the ancient philosophy of life at the end of the century was a reaction to the confessional wars. An important representative of Neo-Stoic humanism was Guillaume du Vair (1556–1621), who translated Epictetus and in 1599 published *La Philosophie morale des Stoïques*.

3. POETRY AND LITERATURE

The comprehensive learned publication of original texts provided, in addition, the precondition for their translation into French. This resulted in an acculturation of vernacular poetry and literature to the ancient models. The acquisition of generic-poetic knowledge can already be observed in the books of rhetoric of the first half of the century; the Horace-reception of the 1540s provided the model for an independent poetics [16]. Jacques Peletier (1517–1582) translated Horace's *Letter to Piso* into French in 1541, while his *Art poétique* appeared in 1555. The step toward a theory of poetry focusing on *inventio* had already been taken before him by Thomas Sébillet (1512–1589) in his *Art poétique françois* (1548). This approach to poetry replaced the late medieval metrical catalogues, which

aimed at practical instruction in rhyme. Sébillet calls the poet '*poète*' instead of '*rhimeur*'. The *Ion*, in which the Platonic doctrine of enthusiasm was formulated, was translated into French in 1546. Joachim Du Bellay's (1522–1560) programmatic work *La Deffence et illustration de la langue françoyse* (1549) was, however, the first to call the autonomous rhetorical tradition of 15th-cent. poetry completely into question. The goal here was the total reorganization of literature through a new orientation toward the canonical authors, as well as the determination of form on the basis of linguistic and literary ideals of Antiquity. The broad range of late medieval kinds of text was reduced, and vernacular poetry was adapted to the Classical genres.

Du Bellay pleaded for the discovery of an independent style, for which purpose he recommended to French poets the procedure of → IMITATIO, which the Romans, for their part, had used in the reception of Greek culture:' Ly donc & rely premierement (ò Poëte futur), feuillete de main nocturne & journelle les exemplaires Grecz & Latins: puis me laisse toutes ces vieilles poësies Francoyses [...] qui corrumpent le goust de nostre Langue [...]. Jéte toy à ces plaisans epigrammes [...] à l'imitation d'un Martial [...]. Distile avecques un style coulant & non scabreux ces pitoyables elegies, à l'exemple d'un Ovide, d'un Tibule & d'un Properce [...]. Chante moy ces odes incognues encores de la Muse Francoyse, d'un luc, bien accordé au son de la lyre Grecque & Romaine & qu'il n'y ait vers ou n'aparoisse quelque vestige de rare et antique erudition' ("O future poet, read therefore and re-read primarily, page through by hand, night and day Greek and Latin models; then abandon all the old French poems [...] that have corrupted good taste in our language [...]. Devote yourself to the playful epigrams, to imitating Martial [...]. Distill in a flowing and not coarse style those mournful elegies after the example of an Ovid, a Tibullus and a Propertius. Sing for me odes still unknown to the French muse, on a lute well in tune with the sound of the Greek and Roman lyre; and let all verses bear some trace of rare and ancient learning" [3. 74–75]).

The basic principles sketched by Du Bellay of *imitatio* as a transposition, transcending pure translation, and as an internal assimilation of ancient structures and materials was implemented by the poets of the so-called → PLÉIADE, which formed in Paris from 1550–1555 in proximity to the royal court [64]. Here they were able to fall back on contemporary Neo-Latin poetry [46]. Pierre de Ronsard (1524–1585) published *Les Quatres premiers livres des odes* (1550), which were based on Pindar's *Victory Odes*, as well as Horace's *Odes*, as their models. The first book contains twelve '*odes pindariques*', constructed in the metrical form of a triadic ode [57]. The parallels between the poetic and philological reception of Greek model authors, first and foremost that of the Hellenist Jean Dorat (see above) who was linked with the Pléiade, is also evident in the *Odelettes*, composed in 1554–1555 on the model of the *Carmina anacreontea*. Whereas the development of a new type of text in French poetry was successful in the case of poetry in the form of odes, Ronsard's adaptation of the → EPIC *Franciade* (1576), a myth about the foundation of the kingdom originally destined for Henry II, remained without lasting influence. The intended appropriation of prestigious genres and lofty stylistic models–Pindar and Horace, Homer and Virgil–shows that Ronsard's reconfiguration of French poetry on the basis of the Classical tradition was tailored to the court; the younger members followed his lead. The Pléiade carried forward linguistic traditions of the late medieval courtly culture of praise; under the catchword 'pindariser', Ronsard's establishment of poetry at a lofty stylistic level became the subject of later criticism. Of course, there was a correspondence in the antique-like grandiosity of this poetry between the national project (promoted by the monarchy) of raising French to the status of a classical literary language and Humanistic erudition. The most famous example of a downright aggressive annexation of Antiquity as a monument of French poetry [53] was *Le Premier Livre des Antiquitez de Rome, contenant une generale description de sa grandeur et comme une deploration de sa ruine plus un Songe ou vision* (1558) by Joachim Du Bellay, a sonnet cycle that became a model for European poetry about Rome.

In the renewal of the theatre, the Pléiade also provided the impulse to bring the Classical forms of theatre to the stage, alongside the firmly-rooted dramatic tradition of the late Middle Ages. Once again, Humanistic editorial activity, together with Neo-Latin poetry, supplied the decisive preconditions. Despite knowledge of the Greek tragedians, contemporary drama continued to model itself after Seneca, widely read since the late 15th cent., who had won a solid place in Humanistic school theatre [62]. Étienne Jodelle (1532–1573) experienced a great success with his tragedy in five acts entitled *Cléôpatre captive* (1553), dedicated to Henry II. Jacques Grévin (1538–1570), author of *La mort de César* (1558), the first French drama set in Rome, was at the same time the first to establish formal criteria for tragedy. In the 1570s, these were then declared, with reference to Aristotle, to be the set of rules in theatrical poetics. Above all, it was Robert Garnier (1544–1590) who anticipated the classical theatre of the 17th cent. with such tragedies as *Hippolyte* (1573), *Troade* (1579) and *Antigone* (1580).

In the field of prose, the rhetorical forms of public discourse initially followed the usages of epideictic and deliberative speech that had been customary since the 15th cent. A wide variety of styles predominated in 16th-cent. rhetoric. This eclecticism, particularly characteristic of the second half of the century, was not replaced until the deliberate re-introduction of Classical Rome as the model for a national French style in the 17th cent. The everyday political and juridical rhetoric of the magistrates, who were closely connected with the monarchy, was based on Cicero's ethical ideal of the orator as expressed first and foremost in the *De oratore*,

as well as on Seneca the Elder and, at the same time, made explicit reference to Demosthenes as a model. Louis le Roy's translation of the *Olynthian Discourses* (1551), followed by the *Philippics* (1575), arose in the environment of parliament as models of agitprop discourse. In the field of literary prose, such textual varieties as the dialogue and the letter were cultivated. It is striking that here, too, Cicero did not prevail as a stylistic model: the → CICERONIANISM defended by Etienne Dolet in *De imitatione Ciceroniana* (1535) remained an exception to the widespread tendency to laconicism. Through the intermediary of Erasmus, Lucian became an important author of reference for satirical writings, particularly for Bonaventure Des Périers (ca. 1510–1542) and François Rabelais (see above). The *Satire Ménippée* (1594) used the more informal form of the *menippea* as the model for a political flier written communally [41].

The translation of Plutarch, begun by Jacques Amyot (1513–1593) at the request of François I, pointed toward future developments as opposed to the highly rhetorical prose that emerged in the context of the religious wars: *Les Vies des hommes illustres grecs et romains, comparées l'une avec l'autre par Plutarche* (1542–1559) was still regarded as exemplary in the 17th cent. and decisively advanced the development of a French prose style. A translation of the *Moralia* followed in 1574. Together with the Humanistic compilation literature of the beginning of the century, Amyot's translations represented an important point of reference for Michel de Montaigne (1533–1592), whose *Essais* (1580) inaugurated French moralism. Finally, in his *Six Livres de la république* (1576, translated by the author himself into Latin in 1586), Jean Bodin (1530–1596) anticipated a historically relativizing treatment of Antiquity.

4. FINE ARTS, ARCHITECTURE, AND OTHER ARTS

In architecture, the delayed reception of Antiquity specific to F. is particularly noticeable in the use of late Gothic architectural forms. A reorientation did not occur until the reign of Henry II. Such master builders as Pierre Lescot (1515–1578) and Philibert de L'Orme (ca. 1510–1570) created a new style. De L'Orme's treatise *L'Architecture françoise* (1567) illustrates the adaptation of Classical models. A sign of the transformation was the famous Parisian Entrée Royale (1549), in which triumphal structures were erected for the first time after ancient models. The new style was employed in the part known as the Fontaine des Innocents, with its decoration by Jean Goujon (ca. 1510–ca. 1569). Together with Lescot, this sculptor designed the antique-style façade of the Cour Carrée of the Louvre, which was expanded beginning in 1549. The strictly symmetrical façade was immediately seen as exemplary and was considered by contemporaries to be a model of the classical style [20]. A famous detail of the interior decoration of this extension is the four caryatids, probably designed by Goujon after those of the Erechtheium. The sculptor also illustrated Jean Martin's translation of Vitruvius (1547).

The royal house of Valois introduced the prestige value of Antiquity for the development of new forms displaying sovereignity. Exemplary here was the configuration of the castle complex at Fontainebleau [54]. François I sent artists to hunt for antiquities in Italy in order to purchase sculptures. This, on the one hand, was how such originals as the *Venus genetrix* reached F.. At the same time, use was made of the flourishing contemporary practice of copying. In 1540, Francesco Primaticcio (1504–1570) returned from a stay in Rome with a series of casting molds. The bronzes (including the→ BELVEDERE APOLLO, the → CNIDIAN APHRODITE and *Tiber, the River God*) were exhibited by Henry II in the castle gardens. In addition to majestic buildings and triumphal architecture, the Valois also made use of other media of political propaganda from the Roman imperial age. During his stay in F., Benvenuto Cellini designed a coin showing François I as a Roman emperor [42]. François Clouet (ca. 1505–ca. 1572) inaugurated a type of → EQUESTRIAN STATUE, on the model of the statue of Marcus Aurelius, which henceforth became standard in the 16th cent. There were also countless designs for portraits and busts of rulers showing the Valois as Caesars. The conception of ancient myth was transformed in a complementary way. As is attested by the pictorial program at Fontainebleau, with its interplay of frescos, stuccos, and tapestries, the didactic-moral conception of mythological material was increasingly overlaid by a symbolism tailored to the sovereign.

B. 17TH CENTURY
1. HISTORY, POLITICAL, SOCIAL, AND CULTURAL CONDITIONS 2. EDUCATION AND LEARNING 3. POETRY AND LITERATURE 4. FINE ARTS, ARCHITECTURE AND OTHER ARTS

1. HISTORY, POLITICAL, SOCIAL, AND CULTURAL CONDITIONS
In order to safeguard internal peace, Henry IV (1589–1610) built a coalition of interests among the warring confessional and political groups after the end of the religious wars in the kingdom (Edict of Nantes, 1598). The success of his politics of appeasement was once again in doubt after his assassination. With the help of the cunning policies of Cardinal Richelieu (1624–1642), Louis XIII (1610–1643), once he had shaken off the regency of his mother Maria de Medici in 1617, was the first to succeed in implementing absolutist centralization against the divergent interests of the old elites, the feudal families and parliament (that is, the bureaucratic aristocracy). There were renewed uprisings under the regency of Anne of Austria and Cardinal Mazarin, and the suppression of the so-called Fronde (1648 and 1650–51) spelled a political interruption in the further development of the monarchic state. Louis XIV (1643–1715) set new benchmarks for the

unfolding of absolutist power. In the first decade of his reign, the protectionist measures of his middle-class finance minister Jean Baptiste Colbert (1619–1683) led to a fundamental reorganization of state finances. Colbert promoted manufacturing; initiated measures for social welfare, the reform of taxes and the judicial system; coordinated the cultural policies of the monarchic state and inspired the plans for an absolutist symbolism of the sovereign. The expenses for the upkeep of the court and expansionist military policies, initially successful, burdened the nation with an increasing financial and economic crisis and consumed the prosperity generated under Colbert. Whole segments of the population abandoned F. after the abolition of the Edict of Tolerance in 1685, while hunger and high infant mortality intensified the demographic crisis at the turn of the century. Louis XV (1715–1774) inherited a bankrupt kingdom. ROMMEL, BETTINA

2. EDUCATION AND LEARNING
At the turn of the 17th cent., the pacification of the kingdom, divided by the Catholic League, and its reorganization by Henry IV created the basic conditions for the establishment of a new system of secondary education. Beginning in 1604, the Society of Jesus achieved a pedagogical monopoly in the kingdom by means of founding colleges throughout the country. For the first time, education was thereby unified, a development wholly in the interests of the formation of a monarchic, centralizing territorial state. With the accession to the throne of Louis XIII, the alliance with the Jesuit order became an official component of the monarchy's cultural policy, which set itself the primary task of overcoming feudal and confessional particularism.

The Jesuit curriculum was formulated with regard to F. in the *Ratio studiorum* of 1599, in which the emphasis of education was definitively shifted to a humanistic form of the *trivium* [28]. Rhetoric became the leading discipline of education. After covering the cycle of grammatical instruction and the reading of the Classics at the basic and intermediary stages, the teaching of poetic and rhetorical procedures at the advanced level aimed at a complete mastery of eloquence: 'ad perfectam eloquentiam informat'. This refined method of learning placed increasing emphasis on written tasks. In addition to translation and stylistic exercises, favourite exercises consisted in the imitation of passages from poets and orators, as well as excerpting Greek and Latin models, and the adaptation of rhetorical figures to various materials [52]. The results of this training in public speaking were presented at school celebrations. Students would display their proficiency in speeches they had composed themselves after the ancient model, or by the *declamatio* of poets. In the *classes rhetoricae*, they were additionally required to undertake independent, goal-directed readings. The resources of the Jesuit colleges, with libraries well-supplied with Classic texts, also provided a fundamental literary education. A model was thereby offered that enabled the rhetorical educational tradition of Antiquity to be joined to the demands of a modern school. As far as learning material and methodology are concerned, the *Ratio* discarded the learned humanism of the old educational elite. The canonization of Cicero as a simple school author, the reduction of themes and model authors and confining Latin language instruction to the final years of secondary education indicated a fundamental change in the determination of the function of rhetoric.

In subsequent times, the educational system of the Society of Jesus played a decisive role in the establishment, fundamental for the 17th cent., of rhetoric as the model of reference for culture as a whole. The great contribution of Jesuit school rhetoric consisted not least in the fact that it linked training in eloquence with the demands of courtly-secular civilization. A treatise on manners, Giovanni Della Casa's *Il Galateo*, was translated into French for the first time at the Collège de la Flèche in 1617. A large proportion of the kingdom's cultural standard-bearers received their education in the Jesuit colleges. Particularly outstanding in Paris was the Collège de Clermont, to which Louis XIV gave the name Louis-le-Grand in 1685. At this traditional training site for the court, a stylistic ideal of eloquence took shape that allied nobility and the golden mean, thereby laying the foundations for the French Classicism of the second half of the century. Use of the educational ideas of the later Cicero proved to be a bridge between humanistic education and courtly-aristocratic ideals of behaviour.

Of central importance for the adaptation of the ancient educational tradition and, in turn, the literarisation of courtly etiquette were the salons of the high aristocracy. Particularly influential in this regard was that of the Marquise de Rambouillet (1588–1665), frequented by Jean-Louis Guez de Balzac (1597–1654), who, in his *De la conversation des Romains* preached Roman *urbanitas*, embodied in an exemplary way in Terence and Horace, as the cultural index of the French *honnête homme*. In his romance *Aristippe* (1644), the symposiac culture of the Greeks forms the ideal milieu for the *bon-mot* culture of gallantry which he preached, marked as it was by → EPICUREANISM. In 1642, Madeleine de Scudéry (1607–1701), who nicknamed herself Sappho, wrote, together with her brother Georges, *Les Femmes Illustres ou Les Harangues de M. de Scudérie, avec les véritables portraits de ces héroïnes, tirés des Médailles antiques*, a collection of portraits dealing with great figures from the history of Antiquity. Scudéry praised women as the bearers of culture who spur men on to eloquence. For instance, Artemisia goads Isocrates into giving a flowery speech on Mausolos that would be appropriate to the funeral architecture she had designed. In the communicative environment of the salon, the 'éloquence d'une dame' permeated the criterion of proper conversation and hence of customary usage. In his widely-read treatise *L'honnête femme* (1632–1636), Jacques Du Bosc recommended that women read the ancient poets and philosophers in order to perfect feminine nature through *raison* and

usage against a background of a pragmatic-moralistic doctrine of life [24. 75–78]. Analogously, in his *L'honneste homme ou L'art de plaire à la Cour* (1630) Nicolas Faret recommended to courtiers the model of Alcibiades, who had built upon his natural advantages 'sur la connaissance des lettres et par les enseignements de Socrate ' ["on the knowledge of literature and by the teachings of Socrates" 7. 82].

The partially hedonistic conception of the conversational discourse of the salons stood in a tense relationship to the ideas of the monarchy. Under Louis XIII, the model of an *éloquence royale* took shape, which associated a stylistics geared towards clarity and order with the idea of *raison d'état* [32. 648 ff.]. Richelieu lent it an institutional status with the foundation of the *Académie Française* in 1634. This was a clever move, through which it proved possible to recruit a large number of authors for the cultural policies of the absolutist royal state. Among the first members, who made decisive contributions to the conceptual profile of French Classicism, were, in addition to Balzac and Faret (see above), the poets François de Boisrobert (1592–1662) and Jean Chapelain (1595–1674), the critics Jean Desmarets de Saint-Sorlin (1595–1676) and Claude de Vaugelas (1585–1650), as well as Nicolas Perrot d'Ablancourt (1606–1664), known above all for his elegant translations of Greek authors. By 1693, the illustrious society united such figures as the preacher Jacques-Bénigne Bossuet (1627–1704), Jean de la Fontaine (1621–1695), the author of *Fables* styled after Aesop (1686), the dramatist Jean Racine (1639–1699), and his friend Nicolas Boileau-Despréaux (1636–1711), the poet and literary theorist of the *doctrine classique*. Other members included Charles Perrault (1628–1703), who initiated the *Querelle* (see below) in 1687, Bernard de Fontenelle (1657–1757), who sought to popularise Cartesianism and, last but not least, Jean de la Bruyère (1645–1696), author of a free socio-critical adaptation of the *Charactères* of Theophrastus (1688), along with François de la Mothe-Fénelon (1651–1715), the educator of princes. The change in the function of rhetoric, universally observable and visible in the expansion of its influence, was also echoed in the Academy's activities centred around the care and preservation of language. Quintilian provided the standard for the Academy's institutionalised promotion of language. The concentration on *elocutio* was, moreover, striking in this context. Vaugelas set forth its stylistic principles in his *Remarques sur la Langue Française* (1645), in which he adapted the doctrine of the virtues of the *Institutio oratoria*. This was the source of his central requirements: first of all, 'clarté' or the concept of consistently speaking clearly; then, 'pureté' or linguistic correctness. Both of these postulates had already been mentioned by François de Malherbe (1555–1628) in his *Commentaire de Desportes* (1606). In Vaugelas too, however, one can also observe the latent loss of authority the ancient model had undergone in the process of inventing rules of style. Alongside the authority of the 'bons auteurs', that is, the classical models of literary style, there appears empirical linguistic usage, or 'bon usage', about which consensus reigns among the 'plus saine partie de la Cour '["the sound-minded part of the court" 63].

In view of the ideological and political dimension of the quest for norms in the Academy, its innovative impulses in the treatment of Antiquity have often been overlooked. In its activities, the Academy no longer emphasized the learned defence of tradition through the reproduction of the canon, but rather a discriminating codification of French as the speech of conversation, literature and diplomacy. It thereby supported the assimilation of Antiquity on a broad, non-scholarly basis. Examples of this were the translations of D'Ablancourt, which were adapted to worldly taste [65]. Through these versions, which were anything but true to the original upon which they explicitly sought to improve, as d'Ablancourt emphasizes in the preface to his widely-read translation of Lucian (1654–1655), Homer, Anacreon, Theocritus and Plutarch were made available to a secular audience. Ovid was the great favourite among Latin authors, followed by Horace, Lucretius, Persius and Juvenal. Among the key trends promoted by this process of appropriation was the preference for copies over originals in the long term. This process of familiarization is also shown clearly by the large number of travesties which arose around mid-century, such as *Le jugement de Pâris en vers burlesques* (1648) or *Ovide en belle humeur* (1650). Paul Scarron's (1610–1660) *Le Virgile travesti* (1648–1652) was a showcase for the author's talent, as was *Les murs de Troie* (1653), a collaborative work of the Perrault brothers which presupposed a precise knowledge of the *Aeneid*.

On the other hand, dressing up tradition in an appropriate worldly manner enabled criticism to be concealed in ancient garb, a possibility utilized above all by the high-aristocratic opposition against Louis XIV, for instance, by B. La Fontaine, La Bruyère and Fénelon. Fénelon set the wheels of censorship in motion with his educational novel *Les Aventures de Télémaque* (1699), which he declared to be a sequel to the *Odyssey*. Of course, turning Antiquity into a French court also provided the starting-points for pedagogical enlightenment as conceived by the monarchy. In his *Dialogues des Morts* (1683), Bernard de Fontenelle returned, following the example of Lucian, to the scheme of the contest (*synkrisis*) in order to elucidate the difference between ancient and modern science in dialogue form to a broad public, for instance, in a dialogue between the Greek physician Erasistratus and Harvey, the discoverer of the circulation of the blood. At the same time, signs of an increasingly distanced perception of Antiquity were gathering. Fontenelle contributed to this relativizing, insofar as he revealed ancient divination to be deceit on the part of priests in his *Histoire des oracles* (1686). In the realm of theory, the confrontation with the authority of tradition was exacerbated by the so-called → *Querelle des Anciens et des Modernes* [35].

The conflict was launched by Charles Perrault in 1687, when he had his poem *Le siècle de Louis le Grand* recited at a session of the Académie Française. In it the preeminent rank of Antiquity was decisively challenged through the negative example of Homer, whose epic is said to display poor taste. In his *Parallèle des Anciens et des Modernes* (1688–1697), Perrault then defended the superiority of the moderns, which he sought to prove by the example of contemporary architecture, sculpture, painting, rhetoric and poetry, science, philosophy and music. The debate over the value of one's own adaptive contribution found a literary-historical forerunner in the so-called contest between Homer and Virgil. Paradigmatic here was Julius Caesar Scaliger [11. 32–38]. The debate also found an echo in the *Querelle d'Homère* (18th cent., see below). Whereas the *Querelle* took place in a wholly public context and provoked the most important contemporaries to take a position on it [43], the questioning of the philosophical authority of Aristotle took place, owing to censorship, in secret. Pierre Gassendi (1592–1655) appealed to Epicurus to vouch for his criticism, and his *Syntagma philosophiae Epicuri* (1659) developed a methodology that called the official dogma of → ARISTOTELIANISM into question by concentrating on ancient natural philosophy. Learned advocates of libertinism such as François de La Mothe Le Vayer (1588–1672), who preached that the ethics of the ancients and those of Christianity were of equal value in his *La vertu des païens* (1642), remained without great influence.

3. POETRY AND LITERATURE

Aristotle and Horace supplied the poetological parameters for the theory of poetry [22]. The so-called '*doctrine classique*' developed out of the confrontation with the doctrines of poetry of the late 16th cent., above all, with that of Julius Caesar Scaliger. It gained theoretical prominence through readings of Aristotle's *Rhetoric*, translated into French (1624–1630) by Robert Estienne, as well as through the interplay with poets' actual practice, particularly in the contemporary theatre. In his *Lettre sur la règle des vingt-quatre heures* of 1630, Jean Chapelain postulated that the three unities (time, place, action) be observed. François Hédelin d'Aubignac (1604–1667) resumed the discussion in 1657 with his *La pratique du théâtre*. The establishment of generic conventions took place in a way that was anything but conflict-free, as is shown by the polemical reactions occasioned by the *Cid* (1637) by Pierre Corneille (1606–1684). Such poetological rules went through a trial phase with dramatists like Jean Mairet (1604–1686), who had brought the first classical tragedy to the stage with *La Sophonisbe* in 1634. Jean Rotrou (1609–1650) recast the verse of Plautus and, in *Les Ménechmes* (1630), *Les Sosies* (1637) and *Les Captifs* (1630), supplied the model for a comedy focused on comical effects. Molière (1622–1672) continued this trend with his adaptations from Plautus, *Amphitryon* and *L'Avare* (both from 1668). In Corneille, the emphasis on aesthetic effect stood clearly in tension with conformity to rules. After the so-called *Querelle du Cid*, in which the dramatist was accused of breaking the rules, such tragedies as *Horace* (1640), *Cinna* (1641), *Polyeucte* (1642) and *La mort de Pompée* (1643) now demonstrated mastery of the precepts. Nevertheless, the *Trois discours sur le poème dramatique* (1660), in which Corneille summarized his reflections on the theatre, show that the dramatist had not abandoned the orientation of his art towards popularity with the audience.

The complex approach to Antiquity in Corneille also manifests itself in the choice of themes. On the one hand, he drew his subjects from Roman history, for which purpose he used Livy, Lucan, Cassius Dio and Appian, alongside Tacitus and Suetonius. In *Médée* (1635) and *Œdipe* (1659), he took up themes from Greek tragedy transmitted via Seneca. His rival Jean Racine makes explicit reference to Greek models. He read Aeschylus, Sophocles, and Euripides in the original, using the critical editions by A. Turnèbe and H. Estienne [44]. His tragedies *Andromaque* (1667), *Iphigénie* (1674), *Phèdre et Hippolyte* (1677) and *Alexandre le Grand* (1665) show how willfully Racine developed room to manoeuvre, which the generally scant knowledge of Attic tragedy made possible, thus encouraging a productive transformation of the material. This sovereign interpretation lent classical theatre its peculiar physiognomy, as was also shown in its actual performances, in which the heroes appeared in contemporary dress. The Roman Empire provided material for *Britannicus* (1669), *Bérénice* (1670) and *Mithridate* (1673). The choice of themes itself points to the proximity of Classical French theatre to the ideas of absolutism. In their tragedies, Corneille and Racine dealt with the monarchy's rules of order, and depicted affairs of state and noble sentiments. In so doing, Corneille placed the conflict between emotion and reason as the ethical norm, as defined by the state, at the centre of interest. Racine, on the other hand, focused on the observation of the psychological effects of the absolutist power structure, depicting the perversion of sovereignty. His characterization of Nero as a monster in *Britannicus* is famous.

The 1670s were a high point of poetological reflection, stimulated not least by the translation of Aristotle's *Poetics* (1671). In 1674, René Rapin (1621–1687) reacted to this translation in his *Réflexions sur la Poétique d'Aristote, et sur les origines des poëtes anciens et modernes*. They attest the drive for assimilation that occurred during the 17th cent. in the course of the poetological debate. In his *Préface*, Rapin celebrates Aristotle's poetological authority as method personified, 'la nature mise en méthode, et le bon sens réduit en principe: on ne va à la perfection que par ces règles, et on s'égare dès qu'on ne les suit pas' ("nature requires method, and good sense boils down to the principle: one arrives at perfection only through rules, and one goes astray by not following them") [10]. The transformation into a proper system of reference was definitively accomplished in Boileau's *Art poétique* (1674). In its reference to the key poetological work of Augustan Classicism, namely, Horace's *Ars poetica*, this → DIDACTIC POEM already implicitly asserted a claim to a classical epoch of French poetry. Here, the mutual adaptation that had occurred in poetry and poetic theory since the beginning of the century becomes visible in a variety of ways. Malherbe, whom Boileau celebrated as the leading figure of the new conception of poetry, had already attacked the idolatry of Antiquity in the *Pléiade*. Similarly, Chapelain pleaded for a relaxation of the appeal to authority (1632): 'Homère et Virgile, qui sont des divinités pour moi, ont bien de la peine à être mes patrons, et vous vous souvenez bien que je vous ai fait remarquer en l'un et en l'autre des choses qu'ils pouvaient mieux ordonner. L'idée de l'art est mon seul exemplaire, sur lequel je me règle uniquement' ("Homer and Virgil, who are divinities for me, have a very hard time being my patrons, and you remember well that I have mentioned to you one or another of the matters which they might be able to prescribe better. The idea of art [however] is my sole model, according to which alone I set rules for myself") [4. I,18]. Consequently, Boileau too dictates no norms in his art of poetry, but transmits a methodology of poetry in pointed formulations that have often remained proverbial down to today. Here too he follows his model Horace, insofar as he places all his emphasis on the knowledge and mastery of rules, that is, of a literary conception of writing. Right at the beginning of the first section of his *Art poétique*, he confirmed the correspondence of poetological classicism and epistemological rationalism, following the principle that was to be taken to heart by the poet: 'Aimez donc la raison: que toujours vos écrits/Empruntent d'elle seule et leur lustre et leur prix' ("Therefore, love reason: that your writings always (should) make use of it alone, [reason being] both their splendour and their worth", verse 11 f.). At the same time, he probed the region beyond the prescribed rules, adding his version of the pseudo-Longinus, *Traité du sublime, ou Du Merveilleux dans le discours*, to his poetological didactic poem, thereby paving the way for the 18th-cent. aesthetics of genius.

4. FINE ARTS, ARCHITECTURE AND OTHER ARTS
Henry IV made the Louvre the permanent residence of the French kings. He took up the urbanizing projects of the Valois and had the Place Royale (now the Place des Vosges) built. Here, the urban palaces demonstrate the anti-Classical tendencies that also appeared in the new domed sacral buildings of the first third of the century. These were influenced by the Italian Church architecture of the Jesuits, above all by Il Gesù. A late example is the church of Val-de-Grâce by François Mansart (1598–1666). Also of Roman inspiration, albeit in clear rejection of the Mannerist interpretation, was the domed structure of the church of the Sorbonne, commissioned by Richelieu in 1635, whose court façade features a peristyle on the model of the → PANTHEON. Beginning with the mid-17th cent., architectural styles

once again linked up more decisively with the classicism of the High French Renaissance. When Louis XIV rejected Bernini's design for the layout of the entrance façade of the Louvre, the colonnades of this complex were erected under the direction of Claude Perrault (1613–1688), after a design by Louis Le Vau (1612–1670). As master builder, Le Vau represented a well-balanced grand style, which he first executed, for instance, in the plan of the Hôtel de Lambert (1641–1642). The regular division of the Louvre's façade, lined with Corinthian columns, together with the renunciation of heterogeneous building material, emphasize the unity of the building and bear witness to the return to Classical Attic forms that was proverbial for the reign of Louis XIV. On a conceptual level, this return was reflected in writings on architectural theory. François Blondel (1618–1686), who designed the Porte Saint-Denis (1672), established in his *Cours d'architecture* (1675) such principles of Classicism in architectural style as the symmetry and regularity of architectural form. His goal was:' [...] d'épouiller l'Architecture de ces ornemens vicieux [...] et [...] l'enrichir de ces beautez naturelles et de ces grâces qui l'ont rendüe si recommendable parmi les Anciens' ("[...] to rid architecture of its unsound ornaments [...] and [...] enrich its natural beauty and gracefulness which made it so commendable among the ancients") [35. 47].

The return to Roman Antiquity in architecture went hand-in-hand with a new reception of Vitruvius, newly translated and commented on by Claude Perrault in *Les dix livres d'architecture de Vitruve, corrigés et traduits nouvellement en français, avec des notes et figures* (1673), which determined the subsequent discussion of the doctrine of proportions. Perrault demonstrated the shift of focus that he advocated in Classical architecture toward a use-oriented aesthetics in his design for the Paris Observatory, in which the axis of the quadratic pavilion on the north side of the building coincides with the meridian of Paris. Similarly, the geometry of the ground plan and the clearly proportioned surface of the unadorned façade emphasize the function of the building, whose construction is, moreover, precisely related to the sun's position at the solstice and the equinox.

At the same time, on Colbert's initiative, the rebuilding of the capital along urban lines made further progress. Beginning in 1630, Paris received its first boulevards, which replaced the fortification walls, while the high towers were replaced by Roman-style triumphal arches as *Tropaia* of the *Roi-Soleil*. Preserved examples include Porte-St.-Denis (see above) and the Porte-St.-Martin (1674). State public welfare institutions such as the Hôpital de la Salpêtrière and the Hôtel des Invalides (1670–1674) with its Dôme des Invalides, whose central building, crowned by a dome, represents one of the most successful examples of French Classicism, show an extensive abandonment of decorative elements of an architecture as regular as it is massive. Jules Hardouin de Mansart (1646–1708), who also designed the great complex of the Place Vendôme in Paris, took over the

direction of construction at Versailles from Louis Le Vau. In collaboration with Charles Lebrun (1619–1690), who was responsible for the interior decoration, and the garden architect André Le Nôtre (1613–1700), a palace complex emerged that represented an extremely influential model for the elaboration of ruler-symbolism, based on ancient structural principles and the allegorizing of myths [23]. The model here was the metaphorical language of Augustus, referring to the sovereign. The decorative program of the palace and the → PARK complex were centred on the theme of Apollo. In the interplay between architecture and garden layout, water-games and sculptures, it created a semiotics of allusions whose reference point was the godlike existence of the Sun King. The absolutist claim unfolded in a narrative way in the famous sequence of the fountain of Apollo, which shows the god with his triumphal chariot, the fountain of the Sirens and the grottoes of Thetis [19]. The interplay of garden art and mythical codification was reflected in La Fontaine. In *Les amours de Psyché et de Cupidon* (1669), the novella from Apuleius was inserted into a contemporary atmosphere: friends tell one another the story while strolling in the park at Versailles, whose scenery is described in detail. This pleased the court.

Jean-Baptiste Lully (1632–1687) inaugurated the type of *tragédie lyrique*, to which he gave form in a series of operas for which the poet Philippe Quinault (1635–1688) composed the libretti. Such operas as *Cadmus et Hermione* (1673), *Alcestis* (1674) or *Thésée* (1675) provided variations on classical theatre by means of a characteristic mixture of drama and courtly display. Peculiarities, such as the rhetorically declamatory recitative and the frequent use of the chorus, underlined the pathos-laden and solemn conception of the genre. In just as magnificent a manner, Lully transfigured a beloved genre of courtly celebrations, the allegorical masque, into the theatrical type of the *ballet de cour* [48].

In painting, the framework was initially provided by the style of the papal court of Urban VIII, towards which the Classical conception of images was oriented. Its most important inspirer was Nicolas Poussin (1594–1665), who arrived in Rome in 1624 with the help of Giambattista Marino. Here he began to develop his own conception of painting while confronting a pictorial art that emphasized the rhetorical elements in the structural scheme. Crucial for him was the expression of emotion, which follows levels of style in a manner analogous to ancient music, which associated keys with emotional states [21]. The representation of emotions by the mimicry and gestures of actors was analysed and systematized in light of ancient → PHYSIOGNOMY, as imparted by Giovanni della Porta, in Charles Le Brun's *Méthode pour apprendre à dessiner les passions* (published posthumously in 1698), which took its material from the study of ancient works of art, as for instance, the → *Laocoon group* as an *exemplum doloris*. A new tendency to psychologize became visible here in the theatricality of painting. In the 1660s, this theory of expression became a central subject of discussion within the Academy. The influence of rhetoric on contemporary art theory can also be seen in C. A. Dufresnoy's (1611–1665) didactic poem *De arte graphica* (published posthumously in 1667), written on the model of Horace's *Ars poetica* and translated into French in 1668 by Roger de Piles.

C. 18TH CENTURY
1. HISTORY, POLITICAL, SOCIAL AND CULTURAL CONDITIONS 2. EDUCATION AND LEARNING 3. POETRY AND LITERATURE 4. FINE ARTS, ARCHITECTURE AND OTHER ARTS

1. HISTORY, POLITICAL, SOCIAL AND CULTURAL CONDITIONS

The situation of the *Ancien Régime* before the Revolution, which lasted barely ninety years and represented a phase of particular cultural wealth, was determined by the tensions resulting from the crown's loss of authority and an increase in the political strength of the bourgeoisie. Whereas under Louis XIV the monarchy had succeeded in establishing an absolutist organization of its sovereignty, the royal state fell into a lengthy crisis beginning with the accession to government of the regent Philippe d'Orléans (1715–1724). Louis XV (1724–1774) sought in vain to remedy the financial misery, which was worsened by the loss of the first French colonial empire in 1763. The reforms attempted by Louis XVI (1774–1793) with the help of the physiocrat Anne Robert Turgot (1721–1781) failed, among other reasons, because of the stability of the corporative structure of the administrative and tax system. The weakness of the crown led to a rebirth of feudal particularism, which went so far as to restore the aristocracy in the second half of the century. The class-system hindered any exchange between representatives of the multifaceted society, finely hierarchized from a social and cultural viewpoint. The crown's lack of power to integrate further was not the least important factor in the court's isolation at Versailles. The capital Paris, already the administrative and judicial centre of the realm, once again became the centre of literary life. The Parisian salons regained their cultural significance, providing the framework in which the Enlightenment took shape as a new and powerful intellectual force whose interpretative propositions were intended to bring new order and lucidity to the chaotic situation. Not until 1789, however, did this result in the political collapse of the *Ancien Régime*: seigneuries were abolished and the social revolution thereby ushered in proclaimed universal human rights in society. The Convention declared F. a republic in 1792; but, in 1799, a military putsch by the young revolutionary general Napoléon Bonaparte signaled the country's reorganization back into a class state.

2. EDUCATION AND LEARNING

The framework of educational institutions created in the 17th cent. remained initially intact. The teaching canon of the colleges continued to concentrate on the study of ancient authors. Cicero remained the most frequently read author, and his reputation as the key author for instruction in language, eloquence and the ancient philosophy of life was uncontested. Alongside him, Virgil, Ovid, Isocrates, Lucian, Homer, Horace, Demosthenes, Aesop, Plutarch, Sallust and Caesar formed the standard reading material [36. 103]. Nevertheless, Latin, and especially competence in written Latin, steadily lost importance as a goal of education. Beginning with the mid-century, scores of textbooks emerged that promised to produce, with the help of French, a knowledge of Latin 'without tears' and 'in a short time'. While the Jesuit colleges remained a stronghold of Latin, the colleges of the university of Paris had already switched to instruction in the vernacular at the beginning of the century. Here, moreover, exercises in the two-year-long class in rhetoric were adjusted to the demands of French eloquence. Racine, Bossuet and Boileau achieved the status of model authors; yet this did not yet call into doubt the preeminence of the ancient educational tradition. This is clearly shown in the role played by Charles Rollin (1661–1741), whose *Traité des études* (1726–1728) still authoritatively determined school education at the end of the century. In addition to the acquisition of linguistic-literary capabilities by employing stylistic models, he placed great emphasis on reading the ancient historians.

This educational standard was, however, losing its popularity. In the second half of the century, the Enlightenment criticized such elements of a thoroughly traditional conception of education as its low esteem of the vernacular, the predominance of the ancient tradition as a source of knowledge and the lack of a practical use for the rhetorical arts and for Latin literacy. The main reproaches were collected by Jean Le Rond d'Alembert (1717–1783) under the heading '*Collèges*' in the *Encyclopédie*. He complained that education in the *humanités* was restricted to composing more or less correct Latin essays, and that in the last years of secondary school, students became acquainted with rhetoric only in its most reprehensible form, namely, in its ornamental-elocutionary orientation. The speeches they fabricated were called *amplificatio*: 'nom très convenable en effet, puisqu'ils consistent pour l'ordinaire à noyer dans deux feuilles de verbiage, ce qu'on pourroit & ce qu'on devrait dire en deux lignes ('"a very convenient name indeed, since it consists, as a rule, in pouring forth in two pages of verbiage what one could and should say in two lines") [1. III, 653]. However, not until the educational-political program of an *enseignement national*, by which the members of parliament sought to impose a reform on the colleges through the institutionalization of a national educational system in the 1760s, was a higher-level purpose accorded such observations. It was above all the fashionable Jesuit colleges that came under fire as establishments whose *Ratio* did not suffice for the demands of political reason, since, among other things, they neglected the historical, geographical and planning knowledge necessary for the administration of the kingdom. In their own programs, the reformers placed value on the metaphysical sub-disciplines, especially mathematics, as the basis of the curriculum. Their considerations sketched a new scenario for social planning and organization. In the process, the rhetorical-literary orientation tended to yield its place to reason operating according to mathematical principles [51]. In 1762, the Parisian parliament resolved that the Jesuits be banned from teaching, and the order was expelled from the nation by royal edict in 1764.

The methodical introduction of the principle of reason was also reflected in oratory by a decisive turn away from *grande éloquence* and towards an ideal of speech that emphasized natural objectivity. Already Fénélon had complained of the neglect of the classical genres of rhetoric in contemporary oratory. In his famous treatise in the form of a letter to the French Academy *Lettre à l'Académie* (1716), he reminds his audience that the Greeks were constantly aware of the ethical and political significance of public speech and consequently did not reduce oratory to epideictic display-speeches and court sermons. The Encyclopedists picked up on the criticism, widespread in the 18th cent., of this hypertrophy of style, and made clarity and comprehensibility the highest priority of communication. Eloquence is not shown in *elocutio,* but is based on the art of discussion and the dialectical interplay of question and answer. Thus, in his Encyclopedia article, Voltaire emphasized Aristotle's contribution: 'Il fait voir que la dialectique est le fondement de l'art de persuader' (It is necessary to see that dialectic is the foundation of the art of persuasion") [12. V, 529]. The guiding figure for the investigation of truth that occurs in conversation was Socrates, whom Denis Diderot (1713–1784) celebrated as the epitome of naturalness and wisdom [59]. The Encyclopedists' ideal of discourse was placed against a background of the concept of a national language. Voltaire (François Marie Arouet, 1694–1778) identified French as the language of pure reason with clarity and order: 'Le génie de cette langue est la clarté et l'ordre' ("the genius of this language is clarity and order") [13. VII, 286]; while in his *Discours sur l'universalité de la langue française* (1784), Antoine Comte de Rivarol (1753–1801) deduced the primacy of French before all other languages of culture from its rational syntax, comparing its structure with elementary geometry. In the case of Greek and Latin, the theory of curves was arguably the primary inspiration.

In the French Revolution, public discourse found ideal communicative background conditions in the same revolutionary institutions (clubs, parliament, committees, tribunals and festivals), which lead to a flowering of oratory [55]. Busts of the great orators of Antiquity were exhibited in the *manège* of the Tuileries, which had been transformed into an assembly hall and meeting place for delegates. The legislative assembly, and especially later the National Convention, developed a new type of parliamentary rhetoric, whose stylistic syncretism competed with the laconic ideal, as well as the utilization of the ethos-pathos formula of individual revolutionaries [15]. Demosthenes achieved contemporary significance as a freedom fighter, yet the vehemence of his oratory met with little acceptance [56].

In the last third of the century, the political implementation of the Humanistic educational tradition was based on a broad knowledge of the ancient tradition. The example of Maximilien de Robespierre (1758–1794), a graduate of the Collège Louis-le-Grand, can stand for many. This lawyer, famed for his rhetorical brilliance, had already received royal commendations as a student for his extraordinary accomplishments, above all in oratory. This generation of students was familiar with the historical writings of Antiquity and had a definite outlook on antiquities. As a matter of fact, the course of the century witnessed a clear expansion of the cultured class. For the first time, groups that were traditionally hostile to culture opened themselves up to reading and the cultivation of linguistic and literary pursuits. In the first half of the century, the lower hereditary nobility, the merchant bourgeoisie and artisans were included in the general movement towards increased literacy. Among the classes that were the standard-bearers of the Enlightenment, written communication was henceforth a part of daily life. This expansion of the educated public took place in conjunction with the development of a literary market, in which need for information had recourse not only to the book trade, but above all to the new publication organs represented by the newspapers. The popularisation of the knowledge of Classical Studies, characteristic of the second half of the century, assumed the encyclopedic inventory of factual knowledge initially intended for the privileged cultural elite. Of outstanding importance in this regard was the publication of *L'antiquité expliquée et représentée en figures* (1719). In this ten-volume compendium, whose clarity and vividness was based on a comprehensive philological-antiquarian investigation of Antiquity, Bernard de Montfaucon (1655–1741) assembled all available illustrations of the antiquities of Italy and F., also making the holdings of the private collections of the time known to the educated public. This splendid, often-reprinted work with its approximately 40,000 copper engravings was followed in 1724 by five supplementary volumes. However, the Benedictine's erudition displayed definite methodological defects in the view of Anne Claude de Tubières Comte de Caylus (1692–1765), in that it was oriented toward the prestige value of ancient finds. He pleaded for a new procedure, namely, ordering antiquities by comparing archaeological finds. At the same time, his seven-volume *Recueil d'antiquités égyptiennes, étrusques, grec-*

ques et romaines (1752–1767) promoted a broad knowledge of the material culture of Antiquity, which, with the excavations of the Vesuvian towns beginning in 1738, brought about a correction in perception. This new view did not, however, become perceptible until after 1760, in the light of the main excavations at → HERCULANEUM and → POMPEII. Both these provincial towns of Magna Graecia offered the unusual spectacle of small-scale Antiquity, which was very surprising to travellers, as their travel reports show, who had been previously impressed by the monumental remains of Rome. Pompeii in particular offered detailed insights into daily life in Antiquity. The comfort and decorative fittings of the houses, especially the baths and gardens, were respectfully noted, and people thought they recognized in them a way of life and ideas about hygiene characteristic of their own time [36. 204–222].

Interest in the basic forms of ancient civilization increasingly turned towards Greece. M. G. F. Comte de Choiseul-Gouffier (1752–1817), whose journey to Greece was published in the famous report entitled *Voyage pittoresque de la Grèce* (1782), read the ancient sites as a legendary topography–Homer and Herodotus at hand. Jean Jacques Abbé Barthélemy's (1716–1795) novel based on Antiquity was aimed at a broad reading public: *Le voyage du jeune Anacharsis en Grèce* (1789) represents the high point of that kind of popular writing on Classical Studies that sought to make the state of knowledge of the specialists of the time generally accessible in as authentic a way as possible. The rediscovery of Greece was also reflected in the publication of many scholarly works. From 1760 on, the number publications on Greek history continued to increase, as did the number of translations of Greek authors, whereby the free French versions of the 17th cent. were to some extent revised. Editions of Homer were usually in French or, in a few cases, bilingual [36. 292 ff.].

The perception of Antiquity as a culturally distinct realm, that is, as a historical manifestation, came into its own only gradually in the course of a wider reception of the material culture in particular. The assimilation of Antiquity by French Classicism often proved in specific instances to be an obstacle. The translations published by Anne Dacier (1647–1720) of the *Iliad* (1711) and the *Odyssey* (1717) still met with a unanimously reserved reception on the part of contemporary critical taste, while the so-called '*Querelle d'Homère*' ended with the defeat of the proponents of the original Homer. Scholarly philological reception also failed to prevail in the '*Querelle d'Œdipe*' [36. 558 ff.].

The intellectual program of the Enlightenment nevertheless clearly promoted a proto-historical view of Antiquity. Ancient civilization occupied the central place in the scenario sketched by the Enlightenment's reflections on history, as it considered the pros and cons of various forms of social organization. In his *Considérations sur les causes de la grandeur des Romains et de leur décadence* (1734), Charles Louis de Secondat Baron de Montesquieu (1689–1755) departed from treating Roman rulers as models in the manner of Plutarch. He expanded his scope to include the history of the institutions and culture of the Romans. In contrast, Gabriel Bonnot de Mably (1709–1785) used Plutarch's model of presenting examples to imitate as the basis for his *Entretiens de Phocion* (1763) in which, following the example of Plato's student, he sketched a crude ideal portrait of civic and social virtues, surpassed only by that of Lycurgus, originator of the Spartan laws. Here, the Sparta-Athens antithesis, which had already been used by Jean Jacques Rousseau (1712–1778) in his famous *Discours sur les sciences et les arts* (1750), was developed typologically [50. 221–267]. Together with the Roman republic, → SPARTA formed the homeland of higher morality. From this mythical archetype all further social and cultural developments, in the sense of a logic of decline, were removed. A new standardization of thought became visible in attempts to sketch a new civic ethics, to which Rousseau lent an increasingly radical orientation. In a complementary way, *Émile* (1762) also reveals the limits of the social, where the body becomes the preferred object of social codifications, which manifest themselves in the way one leads one's life. One should practice self-control, moderation and naturalness, according to the motto taken from Seneca that nature helps free us from evils, since we are born to be healthy (De ira 2,13). In his *Lettres sur l'art de conserver la santé* (1738), Julien Offroy de la Mettrie (1709–1751) had already reminded his readers of ancient → DIETETICS [18. 252]. Physiocratism, furthered by François Quesnay (1694–1774), appealed to the ancient ideal of the acculturation of agriculture. In the 1770s, the new body economy also became apparent in aesthetic stylizations that made reference to Antiquity. The reversal of body semiotics was reflected, among other things, in the contemporary '*Mode à la grecque*', which imitated the loose garment of the Greek chlamys [17. 383–391]. Authenticity, noble plainness and refined simplicity entered as guiding concepts into an aesthetic anthropology which, in F., unlike in Germany, appealed equally to Greece and Rome as models of a better nature. They owed their attractive force, especially among the privileged cultural elite, to associating naturalness with social rationality.

3. POETRY AND LITERATURE

The system of Classical literature established in the 17th cent. formed a highly stable framework for literary production: poetry and poetics followed the rhetorical-poetic tradition in the form codified by the *doctrine classique*. The modifications and expansions characteristic of the 18th cent. did not at all question their validity [37]. This can be shown in an exemplary way by the development of the theatre, which, considered to be the loftiest literary genre, reacted with particular sensitivity to infractions against rules. Thus, the cultivation of tradition was predominant even as it was surpassed: In his horror-tragedy *Atrée et Thyeste* (1707), Prosper Joliot de Crébillon (1664–1762) took the stimulation of emotions to extremes. Voltaire had observed the dramatic conventions ever since his debut with *Œdipe* (1719) and became the most celebrated writer for the theatre of the century. When his attempt to add a chorus to tragedy on the model of Sophocles met with vehement rejection, he resorted to expanding his repertoire. However, even when he chose material which, like *Brutus* (1730), denounced despotism and preached a higher morality, he continued the practice of declamatory court drama.

In verse poetry, *imitatio* asserted its importance as the central component of poetic practice. In poetics, however, a shift can be observed in the conception of the principle of imitation. In the *Réflexions critiques sur la poésie et la peinture* (1719) by Jean Baptiste Abbé Dubos (1670–1742), the poet's natural talent gains greater importance as compared to his rhetorical skill, although *ingenium* here is not yet conceived as the opposite of rule-directed representation [39. 579 ff.]. In his encyclopedia article on 'imitation', Diderot explicitly stresses the author's awareness of his originality, insofar as he emphasizes *aemulatio*. Not only the *primus inventor* of a model genre deserves to be called a man of genius; the person whose imitation improves upon the model is also a genius: 'En effet, le plus originel génie a besoin de secours pour croître et se soutenir; il ne trouve pas tout dans son propre fonds' ["Indeed, the most innovative genius needs help to grow and to sustain himself; he does not find everything in his own being" 5. VIII, 567]. In fact, anticipating the new orientation among the Romantic poets, the domain of expression of subjective experience was increasingly assigned to the traditional poetic genres, as a complement to the strict orientation of prose, to the criterion of truth. In his *Principes abrégés de la littérature* (1764 and 1777), Charles Batteux (1713–1780) distinguished *belles lettres* from the *artes mechanicae*, as well as from the applied arts of architecture and eloquence, and saw the specific characteristic of literature in literary *imitatio* as a highly referential, intertextual process. The meaning of '*littérature*' was thereby narrowed down from the totality of the written tradition to the poetic text. Correspondingly, the followers of Boileau had to exclude non-fiction in verse form, which began to flourish around mid-century, from the repertoire of genres of poetry, as Aristotle had already done in his *Poetics*. Nevertheless, Jacques Delille (1738–1813), who published a metrical translation of the *Georgics* in 1770, enjoyed wide popularity with his versified list of the arts of the garden in *Les Jardins* (1786). In any case, Diderot's esteem was directed at the heterodox philosophy of nature, in the spirit of Epicurean materialism, which underlay the didactic poem, rather than at the usefulness of the didactic genre [33]. Jean François La Harpe (1739–1803), who in his *Cours de littérature* (1799–1805) laid the comprehensive foundations for a national classicism in school education later institutionalized in the Napoleonic era, codified the split between *belles lettres* on the one hand, and technical factual knowledge as well as the sciences on the other. He took

Lucretius as an example to show that poetic language is not appropriate for presenting either the contents of the natural sciences or the operations of the intellect characteristic of metaphysics [34. 162].

The development of prose took place in interaction with a rhetorical theory that gave more importance to the subjective disposition of the speaker, thus allowing more leeway for the independence of individual modes of expression [58]. César Chesneau Du Marsais (1676–1756) devoted a comprehensive investigation exclusively to modes of expression in his *Des tropes* (1729–30). The prose style of narrative literature was largely oriented towards Quintilian's precepts concerning the middle style, whose ideal Fénelon in his *Lettre à l'Académie* (1716) distinctly separated from a discourse rich in metaphors and figures as "simple, precise and unforced diction". Voltaire considered the novels of Pierre Carlet de Chamblain de Marivaux (1688–1736) to be the most successful examples of modern French eloquence. In the writers of the Enlightenment, the preference for the conversational genres of the essay, the dialogue, and the letter was based on their high esteem for the Socratic dialogue, which was considered the model of a mode of presentation capable of reproducing the process of thought itself. They thought that, unlike poetry, it satisfied the criterion of truth. The fictitious orality of Diderot's prose corresponded to the goal of mediation. He developed the fundamental dialogue structure in a multi-faceted literary prose that embraced both essay and novel. Voltaire, who critically exhausted the possibilities of unrestrained discourse in highly ingenious tales, considered Petronius' *Satyricon* to be the stylistic model of elegant ease and precision that he himself realized masterfully in *Candide* (1759) [26. 96ff.].

4. FINE ARTS, ARCHITECTURE AND OTHER ARTS

The principles of painting drawn up by Roger de Piles in his *Cours de peinture* (1708) bound it to the *imitatio* of *la belle nature* on the model of the ancients:' Un artiste qui laissera guider son esprit & sa main par la règle que les Grecs ont adoptée pour la nature, se trouvera sur le chemin qui le conduira directement à l'imitation de la Nature' ("An artist who would let his spirit and hand be guided by the rule which the Greeks adopted for nature would find himself on the road which would lead him directly to the imitation of nature") [9. 111]. When learning to draw, the eyes and hands of the young painters were trained on the canonical statues of the *Farnese Hercules*, the → BELVEDERE APOLLO and the → VENUS OF MILO in order to demonstrate their academic schooling in beautiful proportions and beautiful forms when drawing from nature. The emulative relation to models cannot be overlooked in painting at the beginning of the century. Antoine Watteau (1684–1721) shone with his Arcadian landscapes, in which myth was ambiguously superposed on modern *fêtes galantes*. François Boucher (1703–1770) preferred to choose subjects from ancient mythology that could be effortlessly translated into contemporary eroticism, as in the *Bathing Diana* or *Venus Dressing* [2]. Nevertheless, at the *Salon de 1761*, Diderot found Rococo painting rather insipid; above all, it lacked ancient austerity and unpretentiousness [6. 38–40]. Jacques Louis David (1748–1825), who became a celebrated defender of the new simplicity in the 1780s, freed himself only gradually from the painterly extravagances of his teacher Boucher. He received important inspiration during his stay at Rome from Joseph-Marie Vien (1716–1806), director of the French Academy of Art in that city. Vien experimented with the technique of encaustics and, inspired by archaeological publications of collections of ancient vases, made the reduction of decoration to basic ornamental forms into a program. David intensified the rhetorical effect of the stylised conception of the object, insofar as he preferred to choose speech acts as the theme of his paintings. Good examples of this are *The Oath of the Horatii* (1784), *The Death of Socrates* (1784) and *Brutus* (1789).

In architecture, the reduction to basic elements, which began to prevail in place of decorative variations of Classicism in the second half of the century, did not signify a return to the guiding idea of structures as harmonious wholes. As Julien-David Leroy soberly observed in 1758 in *Les ruines des plus beaux monuments de la Grèce*:' Les principes que Vitruve nous donne sur les Ordres, ne doivent pas nous suffire' ("The principles that Vitruvius gave us concerning the orders should not suffice for us") since they are not based on autopsy [personal examination], measurement and drawings that accurately reproduce the relations of magnitude [8. II, 5]. With that the symbolic language of Vitruvianism, foundational for French Classicism, was revised; conversely, Doric architecture could be integrated as a historical architectural form within ancient architectural history as a whole. The temple complex of Paestum, which was considered by classicistic taste as the epitome of clumsiness, was henceforth accepted, and the Odéon theatre building (1782) in Paris was even expressly modelled after it. It was not only Etienne Boullée (1728–1793) who indulged in the fascination of an architectural style reduced to basic geometrical forms in his project for the 'Temple of Reason'(never completed) and in the cenotaph for Newton [40]. Private master builders also opened themselves to its influence. Boullée, one of the most influential architects of the time, subordinated structural form to the goal of rhetorical efficacy, whereby he extended the Horatian simile → UT PICTURA POESIS to architecture. Another representative of so-called speaking architecture was Claude Nicolas Ledoux (1736–1806), who introduced new accents in public structures. In 1784, he was charged with the erection of toll houses on the outskirts of Paris, and he used this commission to build monumental gates which, as modern propylaea, were to symbolize the power of the central authority and the grandeur of the French capital. These buildings combined the formal repertoire of Antiquity with its renaissances. Ledoux mainly cited Italian architects such as Bramante

and Palladio. This master builder abandoned the criterion of appropriateness and used Doric columns without fluting or base, with triglyphs and metopes on functional buildings. Examples of his work include salt storage facilities in Compiègne, conceived as a temple, or the salt refineries at Chaux. The rhetorical goal sought in his buildings was the transmission of the conception of order in the sense of the monarchy. The highly influential justice building in Aix-en-Provence is a good example of this. The insurgents of 1789 quite reasonably directed their wrath against Ledoux's toll houses, which they saw as an expression of the fiscal tyranny of the Ancien Régime.

→ ARCHITECTURAL THEORY/VITRUVIANISM; → ENCYCLOPAEDIA; → GATES

SOURCES 1 J. LE ROND D'ALEMBERT, see Collège, in: Encyclopédie (1751–80) vol. 3, 1966 2 Exhibition catalogue François Boucher 1703–1770. Grand Palais 1986 3 J. DU BELLAY, Deffence et illustration de la langue francoyse, L. TERREAUX (ed.), 1972 4 J. CHAPELAIN, Lettres, TAMIZEY DE LARROQUE (ed.), Paris 1883 5 D. DIDEROT, see Imitation, in: Encyclopédie (1751–1780) vol. 8, 1967 6 Id., Salon de 1761, J. SEZNEC (ed.), 1960 7 N. FARET, L'honneste homme ou l'Art de plaire à la cour, M. MAGENDI (ed.), 1925 8 J. D. LEROY, Les ruines des plus beaux monuments de la Grèce, Paris 1758 9 R. DE PILES, Cours de peinture, Paris 1708 10 R. RAPIN, Préface to: Réflexions sur la poétique (1644), D. P. DUBOIS (ed.), 1970 11 J. C. SCALIGER, Poetics, vol. 4, G. VOGT-SPIRA (ed.), 1998 12 VOLTAIRE, see Éloquence, Encyclopédie (1751–1780) vol. 5, 1967 13 Id., see François, Encylopédie (1751–1780) vol. 7

LITERATURE 14 ANON., Étienne Pasquier et ses "Recherches de la France", (Cahiers V. L. Saulnier 8), 1991 15 F. A. AULARD, L'éloquence parlementaire pendant la Révolution française, Paris 1882 16 M. M.-L. AZIBERT, L'influence d'Horace et de Cicéron sur les arts de rhétorique première et seconde et sur les arts poétiques du seizième siècle en France, 1969 17 'M. BANDOLLE', L'abbé J. J. Barthélemy et l'hellénisme en France, 1928 18 K. BERGDOLT, Leib und Seele, 1999 19 R. W. BERGER, In the Garden of the Sun-King. Studies in the Parc of Versailles, 1985 20 A. BLUNT, Art and Architecture in France 1500–1700, 1957 21 Id., Nicolas Poussin, 1977 22 'R. BRAY', La Formation de la Doctrine Classique en France, 1963 23 P. BURKE, The Fabrication of Louis XIV, 1992 24 E. BURY, Littérature et politesse. L'invention de l'honnête homme 1580–1750, 1996 25 H. CHAMARD, s.v. Collège de France, Dictionnaire des lettres françaises, G. GRENTE (ed.), 1951, 186–192 26 A. COLLIGNON, Pétrone en France, 1905 27 J. COUSIN, Rhétorique latine et classicisme français, in: Revue des cours et conférences 34.2, 1933, 159–243 28 F. DE DAINVILLE, La naissance de l'humanisme moderne, 1969 29 G. DEMERSON, Dorat et son temps, 1983 30 A. DENIS, Charles VIII et les Italiens: histoire et mythe, 1979 31 J. DOLCH, Lehrplan des Abendlands, 1982³ 32 M. FUMAROLI, L'âge de l'éloquence, 1980 33 C.-A. FUSIL, La poésie scientifique de 1750 à nos jours, 1917 34 Id., Lucrèce et la littérature du XVIII e siècle, in: Revue d'histoire littéraire de la France 37, 1937, 161–76 35 H. GILLOT, La Querelle des anciens et des modernes en France, 1914 36 C. GRELL, Le dix-huitième siècle et l'antiquité en France 1680–1789, 1995 37 K. W. HEMP-

FER, A. KABLITZ, Französische Lyrik im 18. Jahrhundert, in: D. JANIK (ed.), Die französische Lyrik, 1987, 267–341 38 G. HUPPERT, Public Schools in Renaissance France, 1984 39 K. S. JAFFE, The Concept of Genius, in: Journal of the History of Ideas 41, 1980, 579–99 40 K. LANKHEIT, Der Tempel der Vernunft, 1968 41 C. LAUVERGNANT-GAGNIÈRE, Lucien de Samosate et le Lucianisme en France au XVIe siècle, 1988 42 A. M. LECOQ, François Ier imaginaire, 1987 43 J. M. LEVINE, The Battle of the Books, 1991 44 R. KNIGHT, Racine et la Grèce, 1950 45 H. J. MARTIN, Histoire de l'édition française, vol. 1, 1982 46 D. MURARASU, La poésie néo-latine et la Renaissance des lettres antiques en France (1500–1549), 1928 47 R. PFEIFFER, Die klassische Philologie von Petrarca bis Mommsen, 1982 48 H. PRUNIÈRES, Le ballet de cour en France avec Benserade et Lully, 1970 49 J. QUICHERAT, Histoire de Sainte-Barbe, Vol. 1, Paris 1860 50 E. RAWSON, The Spartan Tradition in European Thought, 1969 51 B. ROMMEL, Enseignement national, in: F. KITTLER, M. SCHNEIDER, S. WEBER (eds.), Diskursanalysen 2, 1990, 82–115 52 Id., s.v. Classe de Rhétorique, in: Historisches Wörterbuch der Rhetorik 2, 1994, 248–257 53 Id., Joachim Du Bellays Revision der Altertümer, in: G. VOGT-SPIRA, B. ROMMEL (eds.), Rezeption und Identität, 1999, 350–366 54 C. SAILLIÉREZ, François Ier et les artistes, 1992 55 T. SCHEERER, Peuple français écoute, in: H. KRAUSS (ed.), Literatur der französischen Revolution, 1988, 168–191 56 U. SCHINDEL, Demosthenes im 18. Jahrhundert, 1963 57 TH. SCHMITZ, Pindar in der französischen Renaissance, 1993 58 P. SERMAIN, Rhétorique et roman au XVIIIe siècle, 1985 59 R. TROUSSON, Socrate devant Voltaire, Diderot et Rousseau, 1967 60 A. VIDLER, Claude Nicolas Ledoux, 1988 61 J. VOSS, Geschichte Frankreichs, Vol. 2, 1980 62 CH. WANKE, Die französische Literatur, in: E. LEFÈVRE (ed.), Der Einfluß Senecas auf das europäischen Drama, 1978, 173–229 63 H. WEINRICH, Vaugelas und die Lehre vom guten Sprachgebrauch, in: Zeitschrift für romanische Philologie 76, 1960, 1–33 64 H. W. WITTSCHIER, Die Lyrik der Pléiade, 1971 65 R. ZUBER, Les "Belles Infidèles" et la formation du goût classique, 1968.

ADDITIONAL LITERATURE M. M. MCGOWAN, The Vision of Rome in Late Renaissance France, 2000; G. SANDY (ed.), The Classical Heritage in France, 2002.
                       BETTINA ROMMEL

IV. 19TH AND 20TH CENTURIES
A. HISTORY, POLITICAL, SOCIAL AND CULTURAL CONDITIONS   B. EDUCATION AND SCIENCE C. POETRY AND LITERATURE   D. MUSIC

A. HISTORY, POLITICAL, SOCIAL AND CULTURAL CONDITIONS

For long after the → REVOLUTION, F. experienced no peace in the sphere of internal politics. Years of disputes within the revolutionary parties, uprisings in the provinces (*chouanneries*) and the Reign of Terror (*Terreur*) were followed by the takeover of power by Napoleon Bonaparte (1769–1821), initially as 'First Consul' (19th Brumaire VIII = 10 November 1799), and from 1804 onwards as emperor. In foreign affairs, F. was able, after difficult battles against a coalition of anti-revolutionary states in the Napoleonic Wars, to gain control over broad areas of Europe, but the episode ended with defeats in the Battle of the Nations at Leipzig (October 1814) and at Waterloo (June 18, 1815, following the '100 days' of the return to F. of Napoleon, who had already been exiled). The Congress of Vienna reinstated the Bourbon monarchy in 1815, but the July Revolution of 1830 ended this restoration and brought the *roi citoyen* Louis Philippe (1773–1850) to the throne. The Second Republic, established in the 1848 Revolution, was of brief duration; Napoleon's nephew, Louis Napoleon (1808–1873) seized power in 1851, first as president and from 1852 as emperor. After defeat in the Franco-Prussian War, the workers revolted in Paris in 1871. The emperor, who had been taken prisoner of war, was toppled, and the (Third) Republic was proclaimed. Although it was again repeatedly shaken by scandals and incidents, this presidential republic, established after the bloody suppression of the uprising of the Paris Commune, long remained stable.

In foreign affairs, F. was able to regain, under the Restoration and the July Monarchy, the status of a major European power it had lost after the Napoleonic Wars. In the course of the 19th cent., it was able to conquer extensive colonial territories, particularly in West Africa and Southeast Asia. The First World War (1914–1918) brought the nation to the limits of its endurance, but F. and its allies ('Entente'), through great sacrifices, managed to defeat the Axis Powers. In the Second World War (1939–1945), the defeat at the hands of National Socialist Germany (June 22, 1940) and the transfer of power to Philippe Pétain (1856–1951) brought an end to the Republic. F. was first partially, then (in 1942) fully occupied by German troops. After Germany was defeated (liberation of Paris on August 25, 1944), a new French constitution was instituted in 1946; but the Fourth Republic thereby established lasted only until 1958, when a crisis broke out over the status of Algeria. The Fifth Republic (dating from Sept. 28, 1958) again provided for a stronger role for the presidency, held from 1958–1969 by Charles de Gaulle (1890–1970). During these years F. completed the process of decolonisation (1962, independence for Algeria); the initially hesitant integration into European supranational structures appeared at the end of the 20th cent. to be irreversible.

B. EDUCATION AND SCIENCE

The attempts of the Revolution to enable wider classes of society to gain access to a school education resulted, above all, in a spread of literacy but were unable fundamentally to reform the school system handed down by the *Ancien Régime*. Particularly its heterogeneity was retained down to the 20th cent. After the Restoration, private schools, in particular the Catholic schools, sometimes taught up to 50% of the pupils. Competing types also existed within the state schools: the *lycée* and *école primaire* were not coordinated in a complementary way, but both offered a full course of study from the beginning to the end of the period of compulsory education (the so-called *petites classes* of the *lycées*; *écoles primaires supérieures*). The syllabuses also remained problematical. Two models for higher education were available from the *Ancien Régime*: on the one hand, the humanistic model of the old *c olleges* with their emphasis on literature and ancient languages; on the other hand, the more science-oriented tradition of the → ENLIGHTENMENT, represented in an exemplary way by the *Encyclopédie* (1750–1772). It was long impossible to find a satisfactory compromise between the two ideals, and disputes regarding the correct emphasis to be given the two aspects determined debates over educational policy for long periods of the 19th and 20th cents. [26. 504–507]. The political restoration initially led to a re-establishment of the unlimited supremacy of ancient languages, particularly of Latin, in higher education, whereby the highest value was attributed to formal language training. In the 19th cent., instruction in ancient languages occupied up to 50% of the entire class time [26. 510–511]. It was in this period that political constellations developed that continued to have an influence even down to the 20th cent.: the reinvigorated Catholic clergy and politically conservative circles promoted the predominance of Latin in schools; progressives reacted to this with mistrust [3. 365]. As long as the *baccalauréat,* as the entry ticket to the world of the higher rungs of the bourgeoisie, remained the preserve of a small elite (at the end of the 19th cent., there were about 6,000–7,000 examination candidates per year [27. 145]), nothing much changed with respect to this predominance. Attempts made after the First World War to strengthen the position of the natural sciences in a preparatory school (*école unique*), uniform for all, proved unsuccessful; in 1941 the ancient historian Jérôme Carcopino (1881–1970), in his role as the Education Minister in the Vichy Regime, again confirmed Latin as a compulsory subject in all schools leading to the *baccalauréat.*

After the Second World War, the same development began in F. as in all other industrialized countries. For demographic and sociological reasons, masses of pupils crowded into preparatory schools. In 1930 there had been about 15,000 *bacheliers*, in 1979 almost 150,000 [32. 389]. Moreover, the overburdened system was faced with the demand to transmit to these masses, no longer an elite culture detached from the world, but one that directly provided a scientific training that would be immediately useful in the modern world. The fact that the conservative circles supporting ancient languages often opposed any reform of the education system and wanted to keep the university-entrance diploma socially exclusive proved damaging to their cause in the long term [34. 306–310]. The year 1968, in which the crisis in the French school and university system developed into a veritable national crisis, marked the turning-point: the teaching of Latin was abolished for pupils below the eighth grade; Latin was replaced by mathematics as a criterion of selection; and more and more students crowded into the mathematical and sci-

entific branches of the baccalaureate examinations [5. 232–234]. The ancient languages thereby lost the backing of precisely those strata of the population of the *haute bourgeoisie* that were most interested in their children's success at school, and in which knowledge of ancient culture was considered to be a self-evident component of the ideal of humanistic education [32. 525–526].

The → UNIVERSITIES had initially been dismantled by the Revolution in 1795; it was Napoleon who, in 1808, gave them the structure that endured into the 20th cent. They were initially small, corresponding with the low numbers of pupils in secondary schools. In contrast to the medical and legal faculties, the *facultés de lettres* did not consider themselves as preparation for specific professional careers but as a means of imparting a traditional humanistic education. Thus, aside from the certification of the *baccalauréat*, the main task of their professors was to give lectures to a broad, non-specialized audience; research was not of decisive importance in their self-understanding [20. 223]. Trends towards changing this situation on the model of Prussian universities, in which the specialisation and professionalisation of the professors were more advanced, became perceptible from the mid–19th cent. on; they intensified after the defeat in the war of 1870/71, which was attributed, among other reasons, to the superiority of German scholarship. The study of Antiquity, which was a leading discipline in Germany at the time, played an important role in this comparison between systems. Through a series of reforms, an attempt was made to raise the French university system to a higher level. Thus, in addition to the traditional universities, the *École pratique des hautes études* was founded in 1868, with the aim of facilitating specialized study; it was, however, initially unable to fulfil the expectations placed in it. French universities also suffered from competition from the elite *Grandes Écoles*, which deprived them of the most gifted part of the student body. Especially important for the study of Antiquity in F. was the *École normale supérieure*, re-founded in 1808. Almost all important researchers of the 19th cent. studied there [18].

As in the secondary schools, the explosion in student numbers after 1945 also produced constantly renewed plans for university reform, the need for which was brought dramatically to the attention of the entire nation in May 1968. A solution satisfactory to all, which, against the background of the social and technological developments of the 20th cent., could strike a balance between, on the one hand, the opening up the universities to broader circles of the population and, on the other, an elite education and the maintainence of scientific standards, has not yet been found in F. up to this day, so that attempts at reform persist.

Overall, the achievements of the French study of Antiquity in the 19th and 20th cents. are to be found more in the peripheral areas and ancillary sciences than in editing, commenting on and interpreting the canonical texts of ancient literature. Only the texts of the Church Fathers are an exception to this: since the colossal (together, the Latin and Greek series of *Patrologiae cursus completus* comprise almost 400 volumes), albeit scientifically problematic, edition of all texts from Antiquity to the Middle Ages by the Abbé Jacques-Paul Migne (1800–1875), this has been a particular strength of French research. It was continued at a high scholarly level in the 20th. cent. with the series *Sources chrétiennes*, established in 1942. Especially fruitful areas that should be mentioned include paleography, initiated in the 17th and 18th cents. in F. by scholars like Jean Mabillon (1632–1707) and Bernard de Montfaucon (1655–1741), codicology and epigraphy, in which fields French scholars have made outstanding contributions. Exemplary instances include the decipherment of the Rosetta Stone by Jean-François Champollion (1790–1832), which forms the basis of our knowledge of hieroglyphs, as well as the numerous works by Louis Robert (1904–1985). The works of such scholars as Jean-Pierre Vernant (born in 1914) and Pierre Vidal-Naquet (1930–2006), occasionally referred to as the 'Paris School', have been influential in the second half of the 20th. cent. They have sought an understanding, particularly of Greek Antiquity, by applying the methods of cultural anthropology and religious studies.

C. POETRY AND LITERATURE

The literary reception of Antiquity in the 19th cent. must be understood, in many respects, as a confrontation with the normative, often rigid image of Antiquity shaped by the Classicistic 17th cent. and passed down by the 18th cent. Further works appeared in this Classicistic style into the 2nd half of the 19th cent. Particularly in the theatre ancient mythological and historical materials were rearranged in the tradition of the great dramas of Corneille and Racine. Adherence to Aristotelian unities, the rules regarding social classes, a purified language achieved through the avoidance of 'ordinary' words, rhymed alexandrines and a plot unfolding over five acts are the rule in these works. With their rhetorically perfect recitations, figures from ancient myths or from (primarily Roman) history give the impression of courtiers of the *grand siècle*. Examples of these authors, most of whom have now been long forgotten, include Antoine-Vincent Arnault (1766–1834), *Scipion* (1804; Napoléon in ancient garb) and *Germanicus* (1817); Jean-Charles-Julien Luce de Lancival (1764–1810), *Hector* (1809; anticipates motifs from Giraudoux's *La Guerre de Troie*); Pierre Lebrun (1785–1873), *Ulysse* (1814); Jean-Pons-Guillaume Viennet (1777–1868), the opera *Aspasie et Périclès* (1820); Alexandre Soumet (1788–1845), *Clytemnestre* (1822) and *Cléopâtre* (1825); Alexandre Dumas Père (real name Alexandre Dumas Davy de la Pailletterie, 1802–1870), *Caligula* (1841); and François Ponsard (1814–1867), *Lucrèce* (1843). These works still enjoyed considerable prestige among critics in the Second Empire, although they often appear uninspired

and derivative to today's readers. Even epics continued to be written, for instance, Népomucène Louis Lemercier's (1771–1840) frigid poems *Homère* and *Alexandre* (1800). In contrast, the literary avant-garde soon turned away from this type of reception of Antiquity. → ROMANTICISM can thus be understood to a large extent as a rebellion against the norms of the poetics of rules, which were regarded as constricting. The cult of feeling and of the individual, the escape from the strict rules of linguistic respectability (*bienséance*) with its often-ridiculous periphrases, and the abolition of the traditional boundaries between the genres were deliberately anti-classical. It was already clear to the Romantic poets themselves that this battle against → CLASSICISM was not to be confused with a complete rejection of Antiquity. In his first *Lettre de Dupuis et Cotonet* (1836), Alfred de Musset (1810–1857) observed ironically that Aristophanes had already been a Romantic, 'si on le lisait davantage, on se dispenserait de beaucoup parler, et on pourrait savoir au juste d'où viennent bien des inventions nouvelles qui se font donner des brevets' ("if people read him more often, they could save themselves a lot of talk and know the exact origin of numerous new inventions that are now obtaining patents"). Although other areas were coming to the fore in the choice of subject matter (Christian subjects from 'national' history, particularly of the Middle Ages, the wave of enthusiasm for Shakespeare and the influence of German literature and philosophy), almost all the Romantics became thoroughly acquainted with ancient and particularly Latin literature in their school education, and they treated it repeatedly in their works as well. Thus, for instance, Victor Hugo (1802–1885) repeatedly confronted Virgil in his lyric works: in *À Virgile* (*Les Voix intérieures*, 1837) he addressed the ancient poet as 'mon maître divin' ("my divine master"); "Mugitusque boum" (in the 4th book of *Contemplations*, 1856) was a bow to the ancient model. Alfred de Vigny (1797–1863) inserted idylls influenced by Theocritus into his *Poèmes antiques et modernes* (1826). The extent to which a Romantic sense of life could be harmoniously combined with ancient material is also shown by the classicizing stories of Théophile Gautier (1811–1872: *Une Nuit de Cléopâtre* (1838), *Le Roi Candaule* (1844), *Arria Marcella, souvenir de Pompéi* (1852), as well as the *Roman de la momie* (1857). The effort to create some distance from the Classicist perspective is often clearly discernible in works that refer to Antiquity. This may occur through the choice of theme: François-René de Chateaubriand's (1768–1848) 24–book prose epic *Les Martyrs* (1809) is set in the world of the Christian persecutions in the early 4th cent., partly in Gaul, thus creating a bridge between typically Romantic and ancient themes. Vigny's novel *Daphné*, which remained in the form of a fragment, depicts, against the background of a vivid portrayal of the Parisian unrest of 1831, the discovery of ancient letters describing the last days of Emperor Julian the Apostate. Here the scene is not the Classical ancient world, but the exotic Middle East (Antioch), in which ancient philosophy, pagan religions and Christian sects come together. Familiar themes and motifs could also be given an unusual form. For instance, in *La Mort de Socrate* (1823), Alphonse de Lamartine (1790–1869) dramatizes the background story from Plato's *Phaedo* but has Socrates foretell, shortly before his death, the coming of Christ (a similar motif is already present in Guez de Balzac). This religious syncretism, especially between Christianity and Antiquity, was a popular Romantic theme that can also be found in Edgar Quinet's (1803–1875) *Prométhée* (1838), in which the archangels proclaim to Prometheus the arrival of the new god. Finally, the choice of a form can underline the anti-Classicistic trend of reception: it is true that Maurice de Guérin (1810–1839) expresses the Romantic themes of the experience of the proximity of death and religious enthusiasm in his *Le Centaure* and *La Bacchante* – published posthumously in 1840 – with the aid of ancient myth; but he uses the form of the prose poem, which had no place in Classicist poetics. Compared with the Classicistic authors of the same period, Romanticism thus managed to maintain a fresh view of Antiquity and to make it once again a source of poetic inspiration, though this was done at the cost of a certain distancing. Henceforth, Antiquity was no longer conceived exclusively as part of one's own tradition, but as an alien counterpart in which the present could be reflected. These two aspects, both the amalgamation of Antiquity into a timeless classicism represented especially by the French *grand siècle*, and a consciously unconventional, anti-Classicist perspective on Antiquity were to be found frequently over the next 100 years. This alienating reception achieved an initial aesthetic high point with Gérard de Nerval (real name Gérard Labrunie, 1808–1855), in whose cycle of 12 sonnets *Les Chimères* (in *Les Filles du feu*, 1854) – still enigmatic today – ancient, Biblical, Egyptian and occult elements are combined into an unresolvable knot.

Literary realism and naturalism, with their desire to depict contemporary society and their exclusive use of the prose novel and everyday language, also come across as emphatically unclassical; nevertheless, the thorough humanistic education received by almost all the authors at school is reflected again and again in their works. Thus, in his autobiographical novel fragment *Vie de Henry Brulard* (written between 1835 and 1836), Stendhal (real name Henri Beyle, 1783–1842) sketches a dismal portrait of the Latin instruction of his time [24] but shows how present ancient literature was to him by the numerous Latin epigraphs in *Le Rouge et le noir* (1830) [36]. Jules Vallès (real name Vallez, 1832–1885) begins his novel *Le Bachelier* (1879) with the ironic dedication 'A ceux qui nourris de grec et de latin sont morts de faim' ("To those who, nourished by Greek and Latin education, died of hunger"). With his *Salammbô* (1862), Gustave Flaubert (1821–1880) brought the genre of the historical novel to its culmination [33]. In a scene from the history of Carthage (the rebellion of the Carthaginian mercenaries after the First Punic War, bloodily repressed by Hamilcar), one finds the predilection for a decisively unclassical, exotic Antiquity, which takes particular pleasure in the representation of bloody and gruesome details (for instance, the meticulous description in the 15th chapter of the way Matho, the leader of the rebellion, is tortured to death). Although it received negative reviews from contemporary critics at first, the novel was to enjoy considerable influence on the reception of Antiquity over the subsequent decades. Flaubert's evocation of biblical Antiquity in *Hérodias* (in *Trois contes*, 1877) was similar in style. The anti-Classicistic view of Antiquity in Joris-Karl (real name Charles-Marie-Georges) Huysmans's (1848–1907) *À rebours* (1884) achieved programmatic status. Des Esseintes, the main character of the novel, became the model for a whole generation of 'decadent' dandies. His literary predilections are broadly portrayed in the novel's 3rd chapter: while he rejects such canonical authors as Cicero or Horace as dull, he enthuses over Petronius and Lucan, for instance, but especially over the Latin literature of late Antiquity and the time of the mass migrations.

In lyric verse, a counter-movement arose around the middle of the century against Romantic poetry, which was increasingly felt to be the formless expression of emotive exuberance. In contrast, the poets of the so-called Parnasse called for the careful polishing of verse and placed greater value on precisely calculated sound effects than on outbursts of pathos (*impassibilité*). The composition of small scenes or meticulous descriptions were preferred over epic breadth and dramatic action in a style reminiscent of the Alexandrian poetry of the 3rd cent. BC. The adherents of this movement of 'l'Art pour l'Art' preferred the unusual and the alien to an environment perceived as banal, utilitarian and ugly, whereby Antiquity played an important role as aesthetic model and nostalgically transfigured early age of mankind. Here, too, this was no mere return to classicistic patterns: reception again sought the unusual and changed the familiar image of Antiquity. Thus, in order to earn a living, Charles Leconte de Lisle (1818–1894) crafted influential translations of a series of canonical ancient authors (Homer, Hesiod, the Greek tragedians, Theocritus, the *Carmina Anacreontea*, Horace) but strove in his *Poèmes antiques* (1852) for immediate, fresh access to Greek Antiquity in particular. Although his style sometimes gives the impression of being affected and appears all too erudite, the tone of some of his poems, in its pessimism about the present, still speaks to today's readers, for instance, in *Hypatie*: 'Toujours des Dieux vaincus embrassant la fortune,/Un grand cœur les défend du sort injurieux:/L'aube des jours nouveaux le blesse et l'importune,/Il suit à l'horizon l'astre de ses aïeux '("A great heart sides with the defeated gods and defends them against hostile fate; the dawn of the new days wounds and annoys it, and on the horizon it follows the star of its forefathers"). Leconte de Lisle defamiliarizes Antiquity, not only by deliberately choosing exotic names and spellings ('Khirôn'; 'Bakkhos'), but also by including Indian Antiquity (the first French translation of the Vedic hymns had appeared in 1848–1851). Likewise, in the → OPERA *Bacchus*, (1909) set to music by Jules Massenet (1842–1912), Catulle Mendès (1841–1909) has Dionysus and Ariadne arrive in an already-Buddhist India, where he forces Queen Amahelli into his service. The motifs of Parnasse become superficial in *La Flûte de Pan* (1861) by André Lefèvre, the translator of Lucretius and Virgil. Here ancient mythology serves as a mere background for quite banal outpourings of emotion. José-Maria de Hérédia (1842–1905) brought Parnasse to a final culmination when, on the threshold of a new literary age in 1893, he published *Les Trophées*, a collection of 118 sonnets of perfect formal beauty, most of which had already been published individually. Taken together, they form a stroll through the history of mankind. The sections entitled 'La Grèce et la Sicile' and 'Rome et les barbares' make up more than half of the collection. One of the basic themes is the irreversible decline of the old world and the indifference of modernity, as in the introductory poem *L'Oubli*: 'Mais l'Homme indifférent au rêve des aïeux /Écoute sans frémir, du fond des nuits sereines, / La Mer qui se lamente en pleurant les Sirènes' ("But man, indifferent to the dream of his ancestors, listens unmoved, from the depth of serene nights, to the lamentation of the sea that weeps for the Sirens"). Meanwhile, the contemporary works of the Symbolists opened the way to poetic modernity but left very little room for Antiquity: Charles Baudelaire (1821–1867) already used Latin poem titles in his *Fleurs du mal* (1857) (*Sed non satiata, Mœsta et errabunda, Franciscæ meæ laudes* is written completely in Latin) and allusions to Antiquity (for instance, the allusion to Virgil 'Ce Simoïs menteur' in *Le Cygne*) only as intertextual highlights. In his youth, Stéphane Mallarmé (1842–1898) wrote several conventional poems imitating Classical Antiquity (*Rêve antique, Lœda* and the profession of paganism in *Pan*); in his mature works (above all, in *Hérodiade*, 1871, a scene from a drama that was never finished, and *L'Après-midi d'un Faune, Églogue*, 1876), the ancient elements are so deeply amalgamated with his own poetic style that concrete influences are barely perceptible [11]. The same holds true for the numerous classicizing poems of Paul Valéry (1871–1945): *Album de vers anciens* (1920); *La jeune Parque* (1917); and *La Pythie* and *Fragments de Narcisse*, in *Charmes* (1922). *Amphion* (1931) was set to music by Arthur Honegger (1892–1955).

As was already the case with the burlesque travesties of the 17th cent., the all-too-lofty pedestal upon which Antiquity was often placed in schools and in poetry also inspired the mockery of 19th-cent. authors. Félix-Auguste Duvert's (1795–1876) farce *Actéon et le centaure Chiron* (1835) transposes to mythology an erotic round dance in the style of Musset (Actéon introduces himself as 'Jean Actéon, petit-fils de Cadmus, qui a inventé les accents circonflexes' ("John Actaeon, grand-

son of Cadmus who invented the circumflex"). Théodore de Banville's (1823–1891) *Socrate et sa femme* (1885) is a charming little comedy that brought Socrates and Xanthippe to the stage as a bourgeois married couple of the present. Already in 1842, the same author had published a collection of lyric verse (*Les Cariatides*) that anticipated many of the aesthetic principles of the Parnasse. In the Second Empire, the burlesque *Orphée aux enfers* (1858/1874) by Hector Crémieux (1828–1892) and Ludovic Halévy (1834–1908), as well as *La Belle Hélène* (1864) by Henri Meilhac (1831–1897) and Halévy, became especially popular through the music of Jacques Offenbach (1819–1880). Here, the rollicking mockery, ranging from witty to platitudinous, of ancient myths and their Classicistic elaborations, often by means of burlesque anachronisms, is combined with satire on the social conditions of the time [28]. When in *Orphée*, for instance, Jupiter (who calls himself 'papa Piter') calls his chaotic royal household to order with the words 'Prenons pour mot d'ordre: Hexamètre et maintien' ("May our slogan be: hexameter and restraint!"; Act 3, Tableau 4, Scene 1), it is the Empire that is ridiculed along with semi-official Classicism. In 1900, Alfred Jarry (1873–1907) also wrote the operetta *Léda* in a similar vein.

Around the turn of the century, and particularly in the theatre, a series of works experimented with ancient, mainly mythological themes and sought to bring out new aspects from them, a tendency which reached its culmination in the decades after the First World War. Here ancient myth was viewed paradigmatically, while the situations and characters predetermined by tradition allowed attention to be fully focused on the human conflicts. In myth, as Marguerite Yourcenar (real name Marguerite de Crayencour, 1903–1987) expresses it in the *Avant-Propos* of her drama *Électre ou La chute des masques* (1954), one can see 'cette espèce d'admirable chèque en blanc sur lequel chaque poète, à tour de rôle, peut se permettre d'inscrire le chiffre qui lui convient'("that wonderful blank cheque on which each poet, in turn, is permitted to enter the sum of money that suits him"). If the authors often deal very freely with the ancient prescriptions, they were thus following not only the model of the French 17th cent., but ancient tragedy as well, in which innovations that do not affect the genuine core of the myth are likewise not infrequent. In almost all plays that will be discussed, intentional anachronisms underline the paradigmatic value of the mythical conflicts [16]. The use of everyday language (which can, however, for instance in Giraudoux, be intensified poetically) leaves no room for any idea of a lifeless and rigid Classicism. These stylistic means can also be understood as alienation effects of Antiquity.

Throughout the period of his creative activity, André Gide (1869–1951) had recourse to Greek myths [35], and his disrespectful treatment of this material was influential in F. but also exposed him to the justified reproach of playing frivolous games. One might mention the dramas *Philoctète ou Le traité des trois morales* (1898), *Le Roi Candaule* (1901), *Œdipe* (1931), and the opera *Perséphone* (1934), for which Igor Stravinsky (1882–1971) wrote the music. Mendès's *Médée* (1898) followed Euripides closely, but stressed, above all, the macabre and exalted elements of the myth, such as the conjuring of the spirits in Act 3. André Suarès's (1868–1948) *La Tragédie d'Élèktre et d'Oreste* (1905) is comparable in its stifling atmosphere and its ghostly apparitions. Émile Verhaeren's (1855–1916) passionate drama *Hélène de Sparte* (1912) introduces the motif of incest into the myth of Helen (Helen is desired by her brother Castor, who kills Menelaus and is in turn murdered by Electra). The short dramatic scenes by Francis Vielé-Griffin (1864–1937) in *La Lumière de la Grèce* (1912) are indebted to the Parnasse. Jean Cocteau (1889–1963) often turned to tragic material used by Sophocles. He adapted *Antigone* for the modern stage (1922) and dealt twice with the myth of Oedipus. His *Œdipe Roi* (published in 1928) was used by Stravinsky as the textual basis for his oratorio *Oedipus Rex* (1927). In *La Machine Infernale* (1934), the unstoppable nature of Oedipus's headlong rush to his destruction is depicted in haunting images. The 'Voix,' played by Cocteau himself at its first performance, explains the action as 'une des plus parfaites machines construites par les dieux infernaux pour l'anéantissement mathématique d'un mortel' ("one of the most perfect machines built by the gods of the underworld for the mathematical destruction of a mortal"; Act 1, Scene 1). *Orphée* (1926; not to be confused with the film of the same name of 1950) plays with motifs from the myth of Orpheus. From 1896–1920, Paul Claudel (1868–1955) published a translation of Aeschylus' *Oresteia* [25], which was set to music by Darius Milhaud (1892–1974). The traditional title *Proteus* of the lost satyr play that closed the tetralogy inspired Claudel to write his own satyr play *Protée* (1914/1927), which used motifs from Euripides' *Helen* and the 4th book of the *Odyssey*. *Sous le rempart d'Athènes* (1927) was a classicizing dialogue in honour of the chemist Marcellin Berthelot (1827–1907). Jean Giraudoux (1882–1944) provided what are the most impressive adaptations of ancient myths in this period. His primary aim was to give a vivid portrayal of the psychological life of the characters. In *Amphitryon 38* (1929) the focus of interest is not just Alcmene, who not only refuses the offer of immortality, but also rejects Jupiter: can a god inspire love or friendship in human beings? In *La Guerre de Troie n'aura pas lieu* (1935), all the desperate attempts by Hector and Ulysses cannot prevent the warmongers on both sides from ultimately causing the outbreak of the Trojan War, which had almost been prevented. In *Électre* (1937) the eponymous heroine is initially unaware of the crimes of her mother and Aegisthus; the play raises the question of whether Electra's fanatical love of justice, which accepts even the downfall of the city, can be justified in a world of compromise. Jean Anouilh (1910–1987) devises a similar conflict in his *Antigone*

(1942): even the pure and uncompromising Antigone is fanatically convinced of her duty, while Creon is the man of duty who makes every effort to save her but fails because of her intransigence. He cannot help but condemn her to death, yet he knows that life must go on: 'Il faut pourtant qu'il y en ait qui disent oui. Il faut pourtant qu'il y en ait qui mènent la barque' ("And yet there must be some who say yes. And yet there must be some to steer the boat") [1]. Other classicizing dramas by Anouilh include *Eurydice* (1941; the Orpheus myth is set in the present), *Œdipe ou Le roi boiteux* (1978) and the gloomily archaic *Médée* (1946). In his *Pasiphaé* (1938), Henry de Montherlant (1896–1972) presents the titular heroine as the symbol of guilty passion, while *La Guerre civile* (1965) dramatizes the situation of the battle of Dyrrhachium [12]. In Jean-Paul Sartre's (1905–1980) *Les Mouches* (1943) [23], Orestes' matricide becomes the symbol of the authentic act that founds the freedom of man. While Electra agrees to Jupiter's offer to deny responsibility for the deed, thereby returning to the world of compromises and half-measures she had previously disdained, Orestes refuses to take this escape; he is painfully free, for he has discovered the secret, 'le secret douloureux des Dieux et des rois: c'est que les hommes sont libres' ("the painful secret of the gods and kings: that men are free"; Act 2, Scene 5). Sartre once again returned to Greek tragedy in 1965 with an adaptation of Euripides' *The Trojan Women*. Albert Camus (1913–1960) gave similar meaning to the Sisyphus myth in *Le Mythe de Sisyphe* (1942); in his drama *Caligula* (1944) the titular hero becomes the symbol of the absurdity of human life. M. Yourcenar [31] dealt even more freely than Sartre with the traditions concerning Electra: in her *Électre ou La chute des masques* (1954) Orestes is the son of Aegisthus, who had already had an affair with Clytemnestra before Agamemnon's departure for Troy; Pylades is Aegisthus's agent. Electra kills her hated mother, but her deed is senseless: 'Ta mère, Électre, souffrait depuis deux ans d'un mal incurable. Tu lui as épargné quelques mois d'horrible agonie' ("Your mother, Electra, has been suffering for two years from an incurable disease. You have saved her several months of terrible agony"; Act 2, Scene 4). Although Orestes learns his true relation to Aegisthus, he kills him; as the latter dies, he helps Electra, Pylades and Orestes flee. *Le Mystère d'Alceste* (1963) is an adaptation of Euripides' *Alkestis*, while *Qui n'a pas son Minotaure?* (1963) portrays a vain and egotistical Theseus on Crete and Naxos. Working with sophisticated shifts in temporal perspective, Jacques Audiberti's (1899–1965) *Le Soldat Dioclès* (1961) presents Diocletian's rise to emperor and his persecution of the Christians.

Although less pronounced, a re-intensified interest in Antiquity can also be observed in other genres. In the novel, as in the psychologically-oriented interpretation of ancient myths in the theatre, one may speak of an alienation of Antiquity through proximity: the result of presenting ancient characters in a deliberately antiheroic manner and turning them into people 'like you and me', is the emergence of a likewise anti-Classicistic, emancipatory, but sometimes also banalizing view of Antiquity. This tendency is especially pronounced in the novels of Gide. *Le Prométhée mal enchaîné* (1899) displays a playful treatment of motifs from the myth: Prometheus comes to contemporary Paris together with his eagle, where he causes a scandal ('Mais nous ne le portons pas à Paris. À Paris c'est très mal porté. L'aigle gêne'; "But we do not carry something like that in Paris. In Paris it's unbearable. The eagle is a nuisance") [13] and gives lectures. In *Thésée* (1946), the mythical hero himself tells his life story: in spite of all his frailties and vanities, he has left behind him an immortal work in the city of Athens, which he founded. Around the turn of the century, Antiquity was often used as a backdrop for sultry and erotic novels, as for instance in Catulle Mendès's novella *Lesbia* (1887). More discreet is the eroticism in Anatole France's (real name Anatole-François Thibault, 1844–1924) novel *Thaïs* (1890), which, like Vigny's *Daphné*, introduces the reader to the world of late ancient Egypt, with its Christian ascetics and philosophical discussions. Graphic descriptions of what it meant at the end of the 19th cent. to lead the bourgeois life of a professor of Classical philology are provided by France's novel *Le Crime de Sylvestre Bonnard, membre de l'Institut* (1881) and the novels that make up the tetralogy *Histoire contemporaine*: *L'Orme du mail* (1897), *Le Mannequin d'Osier* (1897), *L'Anneau d'améthyste* (1899) and *M. Bergeret à Paris* (1901), whose hero Bergeret is working on a *Virgilius nauticus*. Hugues Rebell's (real name Georges Grassal, 1867–1905) novel *La Saison à Baïa* (1899) seems in parts like a parody of *Quo vadis*; thus, for instance, Paul appears as a pompous preacher. In his novel *Aphrodite* (1896), Pierre Louÿs (1870–1925) presents the tale of the hetaera Chrysis in Ptolemaic Alexandria; his collection of novellas *Le Crépuscule des nymphes* (1925) displays similar taste. His *Chansons de Bilitis* (1894) present themselves as translations of poems by a female pupil of Sappho. They caused a scandal in their time (Wilamowitz penned a narrow-minded review of *Bilitis*) and were bestsellers; they appear dull to today's readers. More interesting is Jarry's *Messaline* (1900), a tableau of the morals of 'decadent' Rome under Claudius, told from the perspective of Messalina. In his scholarly *Héliogabale ou L'anarchiste couronné* (1934), based on an exact study of sources, Antonin Artaud (1896–1948) also displayed his fascination with the violence, eroticism and religiosity of late ancient Rome. He rehabilitates Elagabalus as 'un esprit indiscipliné et fanatique, un vrai roi, un rebelle, un individualiste forcené' ("an undisciplined and fanatical spirit, a true king, a rebel, a raging individualist") [2]. Two novels offer a playful treatment of themes from the *Odyssey*: the main character of Giraudoux's *Elpénor* (1919) is Odysseus's companion, "not terribly capable of defending himself in battle nor quite right in the head" (Od. 10,552 f.; trans. Schadewaldt), who in the *Odyssey* falls to his

death when they are leaving Calypso's island (10,511–560) and asks Odysseus in the underworld to bury him (11,51–83). Around this character, 'le Charlot de l'Odyssée' ("the clown of the Odyssey") [15. 450], Giraudoux weaves a series of fantastic adventures, brings the dead man back to life and has him reach the Phaeacians, where he is mistaken for Odysseus. The style is precious and often even parodistic (for instance, the description in nonsense words of how Odysseus saves himself after the shipwreck: 'il arga une conasse dans le virempot, puis, la masure ayant soupié, bordina l'astifin: il était sauvé!' [15. 437]). In Jean Giono's (1895–1970) *Naissance de l'Odyssée* (1930), Odysseus is a humble farmer who, after taking part in the Trojan War, amuses himself for many years with a series of women in various port cities of the Greek islands. Seized by homesickness, he returns to Ithaca, where he learns that his wife Penelope is having an affair with the athletic Antinous. The mendacious stories he has invented precede his arrival, and he ultimately finds himself caught in their web: 'Ulysse! Ce ne serait plus désormais ce nez de goupil, ces minces lèvres, ces yeux que l'habitude du rêve mensonger creusait de regards insondables, mais un hétéroclite amalgame de géants, de déesses charnelles, d'océans battant la dentelle des îles perdues' ("Odysseus! From now on, there would no longer be this fox nose, these thin lips, these eyes, furrowed with unfathomable glances by the habit of mendacious dreams, but a strange amalgam of giants, carnal goddesses, and oceans that beat the lacy shores of lost islands") [14]. The story is captivating, not only in its sophisticated handling of Homeric motifs, but particularly because of its impressive depiction of nature in the Mediterranean. M. Yourcenar's *Mémoires d'Hadrien* (1951) is one of the high points of the reception of Antiquity in the novel: through Hadrian's resigned, self-questioning summary of his life story, the author succeeds in giving a historically defensible portrait of the empire in the 2nd cent.; yet, at the same time, she makes the magic of his personality and his period exert an immediate effect on the modern reader. Only in exceptional cases does Antiquity continue to influence the experimental prose of the *Nouveau Roman*. Claude Simon's (1913–2005) *La Bataille de Pharsale* (1969) dispenses with continuous narration; one strand of the multi-voice montage made up of the narrating parties, conversations and interior monologue describes a visit to the battlefield of Pharsalus, and passages describing the battle from Caesar's and Lucan's *Bellum ciuile* and Plutarch's life of Caesar are interspersed throughout it. In the three volumes of his romanesque *Histoire d'Alexandre* (*La Jeunesse d'Alexandre*, 1977; *Les Conquêtes d'Alexandre*, 1979; *Alexandre le Grand*, 1981), Roger Peyrefitte (1907–2000) uses a conventional narrative style. Henry Bauchau (born in 1913) has confronted the myth of Oedipus in several novels (*Œdipe sur la route*, 1990; *Antigone*, 1997). As far as broad influence is concerned, the phenomenon of reception in postwar F. certainly assumed unprecedented dimensions. The year

1959 saw the appearance in the youth magazine *Pilote* of the first issues of the → Comics *Astérix le Gaulois*, with texts by René Goscinny (1926–1977) and drawings by Albert Uderzo (born in 1927), which were published in 1961 as a collected volume. The volumes published in the following years of the adventures of the cunning Gallic warrior Asterix and his friend Obelix reached an audience of millions, not just in F. Again and again in these volumes, anachronistic side-swipes at modern F. are cleverly intertwined with allusions to Antiquity. Particularly successful installments include *Astérix légionnaire* (1967), *Astérix en Hispanie* (1969), *Les Lauriers de César* (1972) and *Astérix en Corse* (1973).

1 J. Anouilh, Nouvelles Pièces Noires, 1947, 184 2 A. Artaud, Œuvres complètes, vol. 7, 1967, 134 3 S. Ballestra-Puech, La Question du Latin en France dans la seconde moitié du XIXe siècle, in: [10. 235–244] 4 J.-J. Becker, S. Berstein, Victoire et frustrations 1914–1929, 1990 5 S. Berstein, J.-P. Rioux, La France de l'expansion, vol. 2: L'Apogée Pompidou 1969–1974, 1995 6 J. Bollack, Pour une histoire sociale de la critique, in: [8. 17–24] 7 Id., M. de W.-M. (en France), in: W. M. Calder, H. Flashar, T. Lindken (eds.), Wilamowitz nach 50 Jahren, 1985, 468–512 8 M. Bollack, H. Wismann (eds.), Philologie und Hermeneutik im 19. Jahrhundert II, 1983 9 M. Brix, Quelque chose d'énorme, de sauvage et de barbare. Le romantisme français et les tragédies d'Eschyle, in: Les Études classiques 60 (1992) 329–343 10 G. Crebron, L. Richer (eds.), La Réception du Latin au XIXe siècle, 1996 11 G. Cohn, Mallarmé and the Greeks, in: [22. 81–88] 12 P. Duroisin, Montherlant et l'antiquité, 1987 13 A. Gide, Romans, récits et soties, œuvres lyriques, 1958, 315 14 J. Giono, Œuvres romanesques complètes, vol. 1, 1971, 53 15 J. Giraudoux, Œuvres romanesques complètes, vol. 1, 1990 16 E. C. Hicks, Anachronism in the Modern Theater of Myth, in: [22. 175–192] 17 G. Highet, The Classical Tradition, 1949 18 P. Hummel, Humanités normaliennes, 1995 19 M. Jacob, Étude comparative des systèmes universitaires et place des études classiques au 19e siècle en Allemagne, en Belgique et en France, in: [8. 108–141] 20 A. Jardin, A. J. Tudesq, La France des notables, vol. 1: L'Évolution générale 1815–1848, 1973 21 P. Judet de la Combe, Champ universitaire et études homériques en France au 19ème siècle, in: [8. 25–61] 22 W. G. Langlois, ed., The Persistent Voice, 1971 23 L. W. Leadbeater, Greek Patterns in Sartre's 'Les Mouches', in: Classical and Modern Literature 16 (1995/96) 107–118 24 A. Léonard, La Formation au Latin dans le souvenir de Vallès (' *L'Enfant* ') et de Stendhal (' *Vie de Henry Brulard* '), in: [10. 143–153] 25 W. H. Matheson, Claudel and Aeschylus, 1965 26 F. Mayeur, De la révolution à l'école républicaine, 1981 27 J.-M. Mayeur, Les Débuts de la IIIe République 1871–1898, 1973 28 H.-J. Neuschäfer, Die Mythenparodie in 'La Belle Hélène', in: Romanistische Zeitschrift für Literaturgeschichte 5 (1981) 63–73 29 P. Petitmengin, Deux têtes de pont de la philologie allemande en France: le ' *Thesaurus Linguae Graecae* ' et la ' *Bibliothèque des auteurs grecs* ' (1830–1867), in: [8. 76–98] 30 H. Peyre, L'Influence des littératures antiques sur la littérature française moderne, 1941 31 R. Poignault, L'Antiquité dans l'œuvre de Marguerite Yourcenar, 1995 32 A. Prost, L'École et la famille dans une société en mutation, 1981 33 H. Riikonen, Die Antike im historischen Roman des 19. Jahrhunderts, 1978 34 J.-P. Rioux, La France de la Quatrième République, vol. 2: L'Expansion et l'impuissance, 1983 35 H. Watson-Williams, André Gide and the Greek Myth, 1967 36 G. de Wulf (ed.), Stendhal 1783–1842. Cultures antique et médiévale, 1992.

Additional Literature F. Letoublon, C. Volpilhac-Auger (eds.), Homère en France après la querelle (1715–1900), 1999; A. Prost, Histoire de l'enseignement en France, 1800–1967, [6]1986; F. Waquet, Le latin ou l'empire d'un signe, (Engl. J. Howe (trans.), Latin or the Empire of a Sign 2001) Thomas A. Schmitz

D. Music

1. Presuppositions 2. 19th and 20th Centuries

1. Presuppositions

Ancient subjects are conspicuous by their presence in French music, particularly after the Franco-Prussian War of 1870/71, a consequence of which was a return to the French classical tradition. Although compositions by R. Strauss, Nielsen, Mussorgsky, Tscherepnin and Respighi also took up subjects from Antiquity, the reception of ancient themes in European music was primarily a French phenomenon.

This development can, first of all, be traced back to the fact that Antiquity had deep roots in French culture since the Renaissance, and references back to ancient models had a fundamental influence on French self-understanding. The ancient themes treated in the fine arts, literature and music in the 17th and 18th cents. were repeatedly taken up once again in the 19th and 20th cents., achieving new prominence through this reception of a reception. In the process, thoroughly autonomous directions were set, and forms of musical expression were found that can be traced back to a reinterpretation of ancient material.

After 1870/71, French composers repeatedly took the *Tragédie lyrique* of Lully and Rameau, which adapted Greek myth, as their guide, thus deliberately tying in with the tradition of *Classicisme*. This marked the beginning of a return to the *Ars gallica*, which, down to the 20th cent., combined this form of French opera and its linguistic-musical declamation with ancient material. This reception ranges from Saint-Saëns and Fauré to Debussy and Séverac, Magnard and Mariotte.

An evaluation of the reception of Antiquity around 1900 should take cultural-historical factors into consideration: At the → Fin de siècle, their implications included the concepts of originality, primitiveness, humanity and decadence, so that it possessed a complex intellectual-historical background that can by no means be reduced to mere admiration of Antiquity as a Classical model. In music, the reception of Antiquity was to a large extent communicated by means of the theme; only in isolated cases did composers also attempt to imitate the form of ancient music, which was little known.

Fig. 1: Lucienne Bréval,
Stage set for G. Fauré's Pénélope, Act 2,
Théâtre des Champs-Elysées
(set: Ker-Xavier Roussel,
costumes: Henri-Gabriel Ibels) 1912

2. 19TH AND 20TH CENTURIES

At the beginning of the 19th cent., one first encounters ancient material in the works of Hector Berlioz (1803–1869). His cantata *La Mort d'Orphée* (1827) is an attempt to grasp the unification of man and nature by means of music, while his cantata *La Mort de Cléopâtre* (1829) presents a psychological profile of a dying person. With his grand opera *Les Troyens* (1856–1858), Berlioz succeeded in making an important contribution to the reception of Antiquity in music. As a musical epic with passages partly adopted from Virgil's *Aeneid*, it is, however, rather unusual in this period. Additional materials from ancient literature, for instance from Homer or Sappho, as well as from Classical myth, were occasionally taken up in compositions by Auber, Bizet, Delibes, Dubois, Gounod and Reicha; for the mid–19th cent., however, they appear to be less significant and have no effect on the musical language.

In contrast to painting and literature, ancient subjects receded into the background in French music in favour of exoticism until 1870/71. Before the presentation of non-European cultures at the world exhibition of 1889, the foreign was represented in F. and, above all, in Paris, in the Oriental opera. The pseudo-authenticity of local colour, enriched by the knowledge of travel reports, was in keeping with the taste of the times and enjoyed great popularity. As a consequence, ancient material that had until then only been rarely absorbed was ultimately interpreted according to the customary representations of the Orient. Even in the 20th cent., isolated works still took up themes from the Orient, which was seen as a living relic of Antiquity.

An important representative of opera stamped by local colour was Jules Massenet (1842–1912), who, however, turned to ancient material. In many of his mostly opulent operas, arranged in the style of Meyerbeer, he worked with musical contrasts in order to set off concurrent spheres and cultures against each other. In this process, Massenet oriented himself in his choice of

Fig. 2: Serge Lifar as Apollo with muses
in Stravinsky's Apollon musagète, 1928
Bibliothèque Nationale de France

material by a dramaturgy that made a strong impression on audiences. He achieved colouristic effects primarily by imitating Oriental or liturgical citations, which he used as melodic or rhythmic fragments, or integrated into the harmonic fabric. Massenet's historical operas, such as *Hérodiade* (1881), *Roma* (1912) and *Cléopâtre* (1912), his works based on French literature, such as the comédie lyrique *Thaïs* (1894), based on A. France, and *Phèdre* (1900) based on Racine, as well as such mythical material as the *idylle antique Narcisse* (1877) or the operas *Ariane* (1906) and *Bacchus* (1909) show the very different ways in which ancient themes were received.

Camille Saint-Saëns (1835–1921), who opposed the influence of Wagner predominant at that time, deliberately took up the maxims of French *Classicisme* of the 17th and 18th cents. In the operas of Saint-Saëns, the reception of ancient material was simultaneously associated with a return to the literary form of Greek tragedy. In *Antigone* (1893), based on Tiersot, he succeeded in creating a convergence in the treatment of melodics (monody) and rhythm. In the *tragédie lyrique Déjanire* (1898), Saint-Saëns undertook to imitate ancient tragedy through the simply spoken, prosodic passages of the choruses. He also sought to increase authenticity by premiering *Déjanire* and *Parysatis* (1902) in the ruins of the Roman amphitheatre at Béziers.

With his *tragédie lyrique Prométhée* (1900), Gabriel Fauré (1845–1924) initially continued the style of his teacher Saint-Saëns. He achieved a new form of

expression with the opera *Pénélope* (1912; fig. 1), in
which he attained a reduction of stylistic means by adjusting the singing voices to language, thus providing a
new formulation for modern times of the Classical,
ancient ideal of simplicity.

Claude Debussy (1862–1918), described by Rolland
as the renewer of French music, had given it a new form
of expression through his pantheistic, associative interpretation of Antiquity, which was one of his most
important sources of inspiration. His idea of a free
music also found its transposition through the choice of
mythical materials and characters, which could be
described as the incarnation of nature. The *Prélude à
l'après-midi d'un faune* (1894) based on Mallarmé,
Sirènes (1899) and *Syrinx* (1913) are examples of his
innovative treatment of musical parameters. In his
Trois Chansons de Bilitis (1898), a scoring of several
fictitious ancient songs by P. Louÿs, Debussy sought to
grasp the ancient atmosphere in music by treating melodics, rhythm and harmonics independently of each
other and placing them in a new relation to one another.
Through the medium of myth, he succeeded in developing an irrational compositional technique. Around
1900, nature's untamed violence was often characterised by the use of such modern compositional means as
polyrhythmics, bitonality, dissonant parallel chords
and pentatonics, as in Ravel's ballet *Daphnis et Chloé*
(1912), based on Longus, and in compositions by L.
Boulanger, Dukas, Koechlin, and Schmitt, as well as
later in the works of Roussel.

A trend that was typical of the *Fin de siècle* as a
whole was the interest in phenomena of ancient decadence, which also manifests itself in French music from
around 1900. In this context, one finds compositions of
the most varied subjects and musical genres. Popular
themes were primarily historical figures like the Roman
emperors, Salome or individual saints. Antiquity was
often confronted with early Christianity; here, too,
Oriental and liturgical stylistic citations made possible
the musical transposition of this opposition. Massenet's
Marie-Magdeleine (1873), Chabrier's *Briséïs* (1891),
Lalo's *Néron* (1891) and d'Indy's *La Légende de Saint
Christophe* (1915) are examples of this. Fauré had
already tried to evoke the decadent atmosphere in his
stage music *Caligula* (1888), based on Dumas, by combining two scales. This was continued by Debussy in
1911, when, in his *Martyre de Saint Sébastien*, based on
d'Annunzio, he characterised the fusion of the cult of
Adonis with Christian legends of the saints by the use of
chromatically influenced harmonics.

With Erik Satie (1866–1925), another type of reception of Antiquity began in the 20th cent. The radical
reduction of musical expression, motivated by ancient
subjects, is manifest in his *Socrate* (1918), which pays
homage to Socrates on the basis of dialogues from Plato's *Symposium*, *Phaedrus* and *Phaedo* in the dry translations by V. Cousin. Satie connoted Antiquity by
means of the colour 'white', which symbolizes purity
and simplicity. As a reconstruction of the Classical

ideal, the linear, recitative song is composed to a cubist-
structured piano accompaniment.

In Neo-Classicism, Antiquity acted as a medium on
whose projective surface traditional musical forms
were abstracted, defamiliarized and parodied. As
epochs, Greek myth and Antiquity offered a condition
of abstraction and a high degree of foreignness, which
produced sobriety and clarity as attributes of this aesthetic. As a ritual game, Igor Stravinsky's *Oedipus Rex*
(1927), based on Cocteau, is based on ancient tragedy
and caricatures traditional opera through its harsh articulation of the Latin language and its deliberate lack
of emotion.

Many compositions written in part for the Ballets
Russes show this abstraction and alienation, for
instance *Antigone* (1927) by Honegger, *Les Choépho-
res* (1915), *Plutus* and *Médée* (1938) by Milhaud, and
Apollon musagète (1928; fig. 2) and *Persephone* (1934)
by Stravinsky. In *Amphion* (1929), Honegger, following the myth, has the city of Thebes arise from a noise,
which slowly develops into music and intensifies until it
becomes a triple fugue.

In addition to the artistic analysis of Antiquity, an
intensive music-historical investigation of ancient
music also existed around 1900. Fauré's *Hymne à
Apollon* (1894) should be mentioned in this connection. Following the discovery of two Delphic hymns, it
was an attempt, in collaboration with archaeologists, at
a reconstruction of ancient hymns. The musicologist M.
Emmanuel was the author of various investigations into
Greek music and dance; at the same time, he composed
operas with ancient subject matter based on his scholarly knowledge. Louis Laloy's work on Aristoxenus of
Tarentum (1904) and an essay by Saint-Saëns on
ancient stringed instruments (1921) are further evidence of a genuine interest in authentic ancient music.
→ DANCE; → MUSIC; → OPERA; → ORIENT, RECEPTION
IN THE WEST

SOURCES   1 C. DEBUSSY, Monsieur Croche et autres
écrits, 1987   2 P. DUKAS, Les Écrits sur la musique, 1948
3 P. LOUŸS, Les Chansons de Bilitis, 1936   4 I. STRA-
VINSKY, Chroniques de ma vie, 1935
LITERATURE   5 'S. BAUD-GOVY', Maurice Emmanuel et
la Grèce, in: La Revue Musicale 410/411, 1988, 109–115
6 H. BECKER (ed.), Die Couleur locale in der Oper des 19.
Jahrhunderts, 1976   7 M. COOPER, French Music, 1951
8 M. FAURÉ, see Frankreich, in: MGG, vol. 3, 1995, 770–
776   9 T. HIRSBRUNNER, Debussy und seine Zeit, 22001
10 Id., Die Musik in Frankreich im 20. Jahrhundert, 1995
11 S. KUNZE, Die Antike in der Musik des 20. Jahrhunderts, 1987 (= Thyssen-Vorträge, Auseinandersetzungen
mit der Antike, vol. 6)   12 L. LALOY, La musique retrou-
vée, 1928   13 J.-M. NECTOUX, Gabriel Fauré: A Musical
Life, 1991   14 R. ROLLAND, Musiciens d'aujourd'hui,
1922   15 V. SCHERLIESS, Neoklassizismus, 1998   16 H.
SCHNEIDER, see Tragédie lyrique, in: MGG, vol. 9, 1998,
703–726   17 K. M. SCHNEIDER-SEIDEL, Antike Sujets
und moderne Musik, 2002   18 E. DE SOLENIÈRE, Massenet, 1897   19 J. TIERSOT, Un demi-siècle de Musique
française entre les deux guerres, 1918   20 O. VOLTA (ed.),
Erik Satie, Écrits, 1988.   KERSTIN M. SCHNEIDER-SEIDEL

V. History of the Teaching of Latin
A. Introduction B. The Monopoly
C. Kingdom D. From Norm to Choice
E. Pedagogical Practices F. Results
G. Pedagogical Arguments

A. Introduction

The name *Quartier latin*, used to designate the part of Paris situated on the left bank of the Seine where educational buildings have been located for centuries, transmits in an exemplary way the intimate and traditional connection that existed in F. between → EDUCATION/CULTURE and Latin. In modern times, three phases can be distinguished: the monopoly that coincides with the period of the *Ancien Régime;* the monarchy, characteristic of the 19th cent.; and, finally, a period of change, in which Latin, after having been the norm, becomes a matter of choice. The status of Latin in the educational system was not always defined by performance. In fact, the learning of Latin was increasingly characterized less by the goal of achieving linguistic competence than by a series of arguments, in conjunction with the humanistic model, claiming it belonged, more or less directly, to a liberal education.

B. The Monopoly

From the era of Humanism to the mid–18th cent., education was not determined primarily by the contents of Latin, but was rather an education in Latin. The 'first learning', or reading, was provided by Latin texts, in Paris until the 18th cent., and in provincial schools until the Revolution. The *collège*, or French secondary school, was a profoundly Latin world. Latin was the spoken language, in which the instructor taught and the child expressed himself, but also spoke when at play. It was not only the most important subject, it was also the key to all other knowledge. The student of the *collège* was prepared–even more in the 18th than in the 17th cent.–by an initial training that he received in a school or from a private tutor. He thus already possessed the rudiments of Latin and could then be introduced to a variety of exercises. These were divided into oral (explanation of texts, recitation, discussion) and written (composition in prose and verse, translation). With minimal changes, this plan of study was maintained until the 1750s and for the → JESUIT SCHOOLS until the expulsion of the Jesuits in 1762. The same education was dispensed in the Protestant *collèges* in the 17th cent., the only difference being that learning to read took place in French for reasons of religious instruction. At the same time, a mitigation of the monopoly over the Latin language occurred in some schools beginning with the 17th cent., for instance, in the monastery of Port-Royal, influenced by Jansenism, and in schools of the Oratorians, a congregation of secular priests. Moreover, in the 18th cent. a decline in spoken Latin can be observed.

On the one hand, the efforts of the *collèges* tended towards focusing exclusively on the written language.

This explains why translation from Latin into French occupied the most important place among school exercises. On the other hand, French gained ground as a language of instruction. Finally, and especially in the last third of the 18th cent., Latin became the occasional target of vehement attacks on the part of reformers (La Chalotais, Abbé Coyer, D'Alembert). Their goal was not so much to suppress Latin, but rather "to grant first place to the mother tongue"; however, no long-term changes were carried out. On the eve of the Revolution, Latin had maintained its strong position. It remained, far and away, the most important subject, so that students of the *collèges* spent a large part of their time learning Latin. Even at the → UNIVERSITY Latin dominated throughout the entire period of the Ancien Régime with regard both to instruction and to examinations. Only a few special courses, such as the one given by Buffon (1707–1788) in the *Jardin du Roi*, were given in French near the end of this period.

C. Kingdom

In the period after the Revolution, that is, after the dissolution of the central schools (1795–1802), where Latin was merely one subject among others, the schools once again became the 'land of Latin' they had been prior to 1789. Unlike the pre-revolutionary period, instruction was now carried on only in French: only from 1821 to 1830 was Latin re-introduced for the teaching of philosophy. Latin had a higher rank in advanced school education down to the 1880s. During this period, students of the sixth class had ten hours of Latin out of a total of 24 hours of instruction per week. Here, the ancient languages filled over one-third of instruction time throughout all classes. With the reforms of 1884 and 1890, this proportion rose to 40 per cent. The dominance of Latin in higher education can also be observed in final exams: it remained compulsory for all candidates until 1882; moreover, it was not until 1902 that the modern baccalaureate (without Latin) achieved legal equality with the classical baccalaureate. At the university level, Latin was required in exams until 1903. At the faculties of Catholic theology in Paris, it was compulsory until their dissolution in 1885 to write one's dissertation in Latin. Subjects considered most important were taught exclusively in Latin until 1838. This explains the large number of translation and composition exercises in Latin, as well as the intense production (201 new publications every ten years) of Latin textbooks (grammars, dictionaries, lexica, exercise books, anthologies, etc.).

The predominance of Latin was strengthened by the fifteen reforms that pedagogy underwent in the 19th cent. Each attempt by the younger generation to accord more importance to modern languages and the sciences was met not only with impassioned resistance, but with palpable reactions on the part of the traditionalists who, with their return to political power, sought to restore the supremacy of Classical humanism and, beyond that, to strengthen it to the greatest extent possible (1884 and 1890). This excessive elevation of Latin's significance was a reaction to the introduction of a continuing school education entirely without Latin between 1863 and 1865. As the 'basis of education', Latin continued to have a lasting influence on the pedagogy of the vernacular and on literature, so that written French was able be presented as a form of Latin (Michel Bréal).

D. FROM NORM TO CHOICE

Latin lost ground in the second half of the 19th cent. In 1872 versifying in Latin was ended, while in 1880 Latin essays and speeches were removed from the baccalaureate and from competitions, and in 1902 from the curriculum of the *lycées*. Translation into Latin had already receded around this time, with school exercises being limited to translation from Latin to French. With the reform of 1902, the old predominance of Latin in the last two years of secondary education came to an end. Branches without Latin were created in both newly-introduced cycles: B (from the sixth to the third class) and D (in the last two years of secondary education). This division was called into question in 1923 by the reform of Bérard, which abolished the modern branch of the first cycle. Latin once again became compulsory for all from the sixth class (seventh class in the German school system). One year later, the modern branch was reinstated, and in 1925 a new reform of further education ratified this regulation to the advantage of the natural sciences. An attempt in 1941 to return to a structure similar to that of 1902 failed. The 'Classical' was adjudged to be good and received even higher prestige through the devaluation of modern and technical education. When further education for girls was made equivalent to that for boys in 1924, it was regulated on the basis of the classical norm. Not until this time did girls receive the same education in Latin as boys.

Meanwhile, signs of a contrary direction became visible. About half the students who entered the sixth class in 1956–1957 chose the modern branch. The actual numbers of the Classical branch diminished throughout the entire time in school: in the baccalaureate, only about 30 per cent of students had had Latin since the sixth class. Although the curricula remained ambitious, hours were cut (750 hours for the total school time, as opposed to 1400 hours before the reform of 1902 and 1260 hours after it). The decisive change took place in 1968, when Latin disappeared from the sixth-class curricula (decree of October 9). In the following year, a new decree (of July 9) established the beginning of Latin instruction in the fourth class. The number of students dropped sharply: from 1975 on, there were three times fewer candidates for the baccalaureate exams than in 1968. Although the curricula remained ambitious, the hours dwindled–by two-thirds in the fourth and third class–and were often scheduled at highly unfavourable times. The consequences of the sagging importance of Latin are evident until today in

further education, which, in the 1990s, led to only 450 degrees per year in the Classical languages. In addition, Latin is no longer compulsory for the study of history and of French and Romance literatures. Since 1995, however, Latin may once again be taught beginning with the fifth class; one-third of students still chose this option in 1996. Since Latin is just an elective in the curriculum or in the baccalaureate, most students usually take no more than two or three years of Latin. To be more exact, one can mention that in the school year 1998/99 in public schools an average of barely more than one per cent of the students in their final year took Latin, and the vast majority of them took Latin as an (additional) elective.

E. PEDAGOGICAL PRACTICES

Under the *Ancien Régime*, the consolidation of pedagogy in Catholic education was achieved by the Jesuits. The teaching of Latin in French in the 19th and the first half of the 20th cent. displays some common features with teaching methods in other countries, such as recourse to the same texts or even extracts from texts, a moralizing role in school and the prevalence of teaching grammar under the influence of German philology, which led to the 'grammatical hypertrophy' of the 1960s.

This commonality in teaching practice should not conceal a certain number of peculiarities in French education, both in its methods and its exercises. In the 19th cent., these included the predominance of literature, far removed from the philological and grammatical method that was held in honour on the other side of the Rhine; the place of honour reserved for the Latin oration and hence the most precise investigation of relatively short texts; the importance attributed to questions of vocabulary and syntax; a limited interest in pronunciation; the banishment of the French translation of Latin texts from school usage; and the early and constant recourse to a dictionary (the famous *Gaffiot*, since the early 1930s).

The → PRONUNCIATION of Latin at school long remained French. The attempts in the last decade of the 19th cent. to introduce the Classical or restored pronunciation not only collided with routine but also kept the divergent opinions about what the correct pronunciation was alive even among the reformers. Some wished to implement the Classical pronunciation everywhere; others wished to restrict it to the upper grades of the *lycée*; others wished to allow active teachers to keep doing what they had been doing. Some wished to act out of conviction; others appealed to the authority of the state. There were also disputes about the content of imitation itself and, more precisely, about the problem of accent, or rather of accents. Whereas Classical Latin had two accents, of pitch and intensity, this caused great difficulty for French speakers, who were accustomed to place the accent on the last spoken syllable. There was therefore no shortage of debates between those who suggested its immediate abandonment, those who adhered only to the tonic accent and those who wished to emphasize both. The situation was further complicated by the fact that the great majority of French clergy abandoned French pronunciation and adopted the Latin one in the years between 1910 and 1930. It is therefore not surprising that, despite objective progress, the reform proceeded sluggishly, and the pronunciation of Latin in the mouths of French students often went awry, since they intermingled all three styles. In 1960, a circular letter from the Minister of Education stipulated the introduction of the Latin pronunciation.

F. Results

Little interest has been shown in the results of learning Latin, although it occupied an important part, even the greatest single amount of school time down to the 1960s. From the preserved exercises and from the reports of teachers or the reminiscences of students, one discovers that an elite achieved good, even splendid results, whereas the broad masses did not take particular pains with regard to their performance and, despite colossal expense, obtained only a very mediocre level in annual competitions. This was already the case in the 17th cent., when Antoine Arnaud wrote: "Out of 70 or 80 students, two or three might be such that you can get something out of them. The rest mope and struggle to accomplish nothing worthwhile". The same pessimistic observations recur throughout the entire period, and the words 'mediocrity' and 'worthlessness' became constant terms in the pedagogical literature.

Teachers, who knew what they were talking about from their twofold experience as pedagogues and as former students, noticed the children's problems and considered the learning of the Latin language to be very difficult, not very fruitful and too often doomed to failure. Subjects of complaints included pedantic teaching which, because it was long carried out in Latin, explained 'the unknown by the unknown', and made things even more difficult for the children because of the dry texts that had nothing to do with their lives. Changes were suggested in response to this diagnosis. The key words were simplicity and speed. Methods and textbooks were to facilitate learning, thereby guaranteeing at the same time lower costs and greater success. The mere repetition of this slogan might bear witness to the ongoing weakness of the results. Works were soon produced that were supposed to facilitate the study of Latin, and countless titles were adorned with the magic words 'simple', 'easy', 'quick' and their synonyms. Foremost among these was the famous Grammar of Port-Royal (1644), with its title *Nouvelle méthode pour apprendre facilement et en peu de temps le latin* ('New Method for Learning Latin Easily and in a Short time'). The most varied means were introduced to facilitate learning Latin: hence the use of the vernacular and of mnemonics for retaining the rules of grammar, as well as their presentation in the form of tables. Any means seemed valid to instill a little Latin in the student;

for instance, in the 1950s, the '*declinograph*', in which "a system of paragraphs, frames, arrows, parentheses, and circles produced signs in various colours" in order to help the student find his way in the declensions and conjugations.

The mediocre performance in Latin, despite continuing endeavours, was contrasted by pedagogues and other education theorists with the simple and successful acquisition of the mother tongue or of a living language, and they extolled learning through use. This method was condemned by the teachers of Port-Royal as a teaching that led to repeating the same thing a hundred times. Other 18th-cent. pedagogues, in contrast, were inclined, out of growing mistrust for rules, to preach an automatic learning of Latin through use rather than through a rational procedure. This was the origin of Du Marsais's method of 'routine' and of Pluche's 'mechanics'. They revitalized the debate over learning through rules or through use, a debate that was still alive in the 1950s. Whereas a grammatical method inherited from the 19th cent. reigned in the *lycées*, the fruitlessness of such a procedure was bemoaned: the "previous methodical study of theoretical grammar" at the expense of "a grammar [learned] through experience, studied in the texts" was condemned, and free commenting on texts was recommended as the preferred class exercise. The movement "for a living Latin" placed emphasis on the acquisition of vocabulary through oral use of the language and reading authors. Again, some were highly skeptical and even hostile towards methods that invited students to translate the text after a single reading, prior to any analysis. They condemned this 'intuitive' Latin on the grounds of the poverty of its results and the risks that had to be accepted as far as the education of the mind was concerned, and they extolled the return to explanation, analysis and grammar as opposed to the excesses of intuition. The centuries-long debate between rules and use may have found its solution in the newest educational methods, which have sacrificed linguistic knowledge in order to save Latin. More time is given to social studies of Classical times. Thus it is no longer primarily a question of linguistic results.

G. Pedagogical Arguments

As long as Latin was necessary for the practice of certain careers or, more precisely, as long as these careers could not be exercised without a mastery of the Latin language, the status of Latin in the educational system was unproblematic. All that was under discussion were the ways and means to learn it with the least expense and the greatest success. This changed when Latin was no longer seen as indispensable in civilized life, or when civilized life demanded knowledge that no longer presupposed a knowledge of Latin. The point was reached where whether one should learn Latin at all was called into question. Here again arguments justifying it were brought into play. The arguments produced in the last third of the 18th cent. no longer addressed problems of the transmission of language, but rather problems of intellectual and moral education through Latin. The stock of arguments scarcely changed in the following two centuries; however, the arguments gained added strength through the use made of them in the course of the controversies. This gave them, at various moments in history, an original coloration. They were thus always, sometimes more, sometimes less obviously, and without there necessarily being an awareness thereof, joined to the humanistic model, as it was conceived of in the 15th and 16th cents., namely, that Classical languages was the preferred path to a 'liberal' education.

Greatly summarizing and proceeding from the goal-directed to the goal-less, the following arguments were set forth: Latin provides help in learning one's mother tongue and other languages, particularly the Romance tongues; it contributes to the education of the mind in general, of the faculty of memory, and of logical thought; to the acquisition of strength of character; to intellectual growth; to the formation of taste through contact with the masterworks of Antiquity; and to the education of man on the basis of an ideal considered to be timeless. The opposition of the proponents of Classical education to a career-oriented and even specialized education becomes evident in the enumeration of these arguments. Latin is not 'technical knowledge', and the task of the *lycée* is not to train 'specialists' or 'Latinists', but *honnêtes hommes*, or well-rounded, educated human beings.

As background to these arguments, one must not forget the sociological presuppositions that made Latin into a 'bourgeois' subject. Limiting ourselves to the world of pedagogy alone, thereby simplifying a much more complex reality, we note that middle schools in the 18th cent., just like the *lycées* in the 19th cent., both of which required learning Latin, were elitist phenomena. Modern advanced education underlines this character still more. Latin-free institutions, originally created for children of the middle and lower bourgeoisie who received there an education appropriate for their social status, were long considered second-rate. Until not long ago, the social elites automatically gave their children over to a Classical education and considered being transferred to the modern one to be a step down; hence the sociologically highly eloquent expression 'descendre en moderne' ("to go down to the modern") to designate the transfer of a child with unsatisfactory results in the Classical track to the modern option. Although the school situation in 1968 was much more differentiated when the national Minister of Education abolished Latin, it was its bourgeois character that he offered as a justification: "It is accessible only to the heirs of culture [...] it is undeniable that it is an obstacle to democratisation". For a specific time, Latin thereby became the innocent victim of its own pedagogical history.

→ SCHOOL TEXT-BOOKS

1 A. SICARD, Les études classiques avant la Révolution. Paris, Librairie académique Didier, Perrin et Cien 1887

2 C. FALUCCI, L'humanisme dans l'enseignement secondaire en France au XIXe siècle, 1939   3 A. CHERVEL, M.-M. COMPÈRE (eds.), Les humanités classiques, monographic edition of the Revue Histoire de l'éducation, 1997   4 B. COLOMBAT, La grammaire latine en France de la Ren. à l'Âge classique. Théories et pédagogie, 1999   5 F. WAQUET, Le latin ou l'empire d'un signe, 1999, (Engl. J. HOWE (trans.), Latin or the Empire of a Sign, 2001)

ADDITIONAL BIBLIOGRAPHY A. PROST, Histoire de l'enseignement en France, 1800–1967, 6̇1986.

FRANÇOISE WAQUET

Frankfurt am Main, Liebieghaus; Museum of Ancient Sculpture.

The sculpture museum, organisationally linked with the *Städelsches Kunstinstitut*, which had been in existence since 1817, was opened in 1909 as part of the *Städtische Galerie*. The exhibition spaces comprise a historic villa, bequeathed to the city by the manufacturer Heinrich von Liebieg, and two gallery wings that flank a central entrance pavilion. One of those wings was not completed until after 1985, even though it had been planned since the foundation phase of the museum.

From the time of its inception the collection has included examples of sculpture from various cultures and historical periods. Its concept, which rejects the one-sided neo-classicistic norm, was developed by the art historian Georg Swarzenski, who, after several years at the Berlin *Kunstgewerbemuseum*, took over as director of the *Städel* and the *Städtische Galerie* in 1906. And yet the Liebieghaus does concentrate to some degree on ancient art. Approximately half of the present collection of large-scale ancient sculpture, primarily preserved as torsos and heads, was brought together between 1907 and 1909. One outstanding work acquired for Frankfurt at that time was a copy of Myron's statue of Athena from the early Imperial period (fig. 1). As purchases were for the most part made on the Roman art market, sculptures of Italian origin predominate, an example being a first-cent. satyr's head in the Hellenistic style (fig. 3). Original works of Greek art were initially represented by vases from the *Städelsches Kunstinstitut*, which now served to complement the display of ancient sculptural masterpieces in the Liebieghaus. While still in its early years, the museum's stock of small-scale objects was further broadened by the collection of the religious scholar C.M. Kaufmann, consisting of objects from the Early Christian sanctuary of Abu Mena and other items acquired in Egypt. The collection of the archaeologist A. Furtwängler was added in 1915.

As with other German museums, the means to make purchases were limited between the wars. The Liebieghaus nevertheless acquired some important original Greek items during those years. A lack of genuine items of Archaic art, however, did persist, and it was not until 1961 that this gap could be filled with a head from the Ionian Islands presumed to be that of a *kouros;* it was joined in 1982 by a bearded head from Cyprus. Another

Fig. 1: Inventory no. 195.
Copy of Myron's Athena, *Liebighaus Frankfurt*

Fig 2: Inventory no. 2608. Copy of Myron's
Discobolus, *Liebighaus Frankfurt*

Fig. 3: Inventory no. 13.
Head of a laughing satyr, *Liebighaus Frankfurt*

Fig. 4: Inventory no. 1528. Meleager
sarcophagus (detail), *Liebighaus Frankfurt*

key aspect since 1960 has been the museum's growing range of important small bronzes. The museum's original collection already contained fragments of Roman sarcophagi, but it was through new acquisitions including, above all, parts of a sarcophagus depicting the Meleager myth (fig. 4) that this particular form of art received more representative weight. The most significant acquisition of recent years has been the statue of a *discobolus* stepping up to his mark (fig. 2); it attests to a masterpiece of Classical sculpture, which also deserves our attention for its post-Antiquity history.

Owing to the relatively late date of its foundation, the sculpture collection in the Liebieghaus cannot compete in size with those museums in → BERLIN, → DRESDEN and other locations that grew out of princely collections. Instead, the opportunity to showcase the most important periods and genres of ancient sculpture by means of selected and for the most part artistically outstanding works was fully exploited. A distaste at the time for additions or reworkings also helped maintain the quality and integrity of the works on display. Indeed, the Liebieghaus stands comparison with other 'civic' museums such as the *Antikenmuseum* in → BASLE, not only in respect of the qualitative standards applied in the selection of its exhibits, but also in the combination of communal involvement and private patronage.

While Myron's Athena occupies a separate building, other objects representative of the history of ancient sculpture are at present assembled in the newly-constructed gallery tract. The presentation generally follows a chronological pattern without, however, resorting to schematic periodisation, this approach being aided by the architecture of the building. In the placement of individual sculptures attention has also been given to adequate, effect-free illumination in spaces lit from above. Forgoing any lengthy written commentaries that would exceed the minimum amount of necessary information, the sculptures are displayed purely as works of art.

In recent decades, alongside the reshaping of its permanent collection, the Liebieghaus has held a series of prestigious special exhibitions; to remain within the archaeological realm, the exhibitions on 'Late Antiquity and the Early Christian era' (1983–1984) and 'Polyclitus the Sculptor of Classical Greece' (1990–1991) are worthy of particular note.

1 E. BAYER-NIEMEIER, Liebieghaus – Museum alter Plastik. Wissenschaftliche Kataloge, Bildwerke der Sammlung Kaufmann I, 1988   2 P. C. BOL, Liebieghaus – Museum alter Plastik. Führer durch die Sammlungen. Antike Kunst, 1980 (Liebieghaus – Museum alter Plastik. Guide to the Collection. Ancient Art, 1981)   3 Id., Liebieghaus – Museum alter Plastik. Wissenschaftliche Kataloge. Antike Bildwerke I–III, 1983–1986   4 Id., Liebieghaus – Museum alter Plastik. Führer durch die Sammlungen. Griechische und römische Plastik, 1997   5 W. SELESNOW, Liebieghaus – Museum alter Plastik. Wissenschaftliche Kataloge. Bildwerke der Sammlung Kaufmann II, 1988   6 M. SONNABEND, Georg Swarzenski und das Liebieghaus, 1990.   DETLEV KREIKENBOM

Franz-Joseph-Dölger Institute
A. ORIGIN B. FRANZ JOSEPH DÖLGER AND HIS RESEARCH PROGRAM 'ANTIQUITY AND CHRISTIANITY' C. THE REALLEXIKON FÜR ANTIKE UND CHRISTENTUM D. RESULTS AND CURRENT STATE OF WORK

A. ORIGIN
The Franz-Joseph-Dölger (DI) is in charge for the publication of the *Reallexikon für Antike und Christentum* (RAC) and the *Jahrbuch für Antike und Christentum* (JbAC), as well as supplementary volumes and the series of monographs *Theophaneia*. It was planned by Theodor Klauser (1894–1984), who realized that completion of the *Lexikon* could not be achieved without institutionalizing the organizational and editorial work. The charter of the DI, which was to come into existence in connection with the University of Bonn, was authorized by the Ministry of Education of the federal state Nordrhein-Westfalen on April 13, 1955. Soon afterwards, the supporting organization which was provided by the charter came into existence, along with a scholarly advisory committee. In 1975, the editorship of the RAC and the JbAC was taken over by the former Rheinisch-Westfälische Akademie, now the Nordrhein-Westfälische Akademie, and the Institute was integrated within the University of Bonn. Scholarly responsibility was assumed by a committee of the Academy, while the administration of finance and personnel was taken over by the University, so that the supporting organization could be transformed into a purely promotional association and the advisory committee dissolved. The DI is headed by a director, named by the regional Ministry of Science upon recommendation of the Academy and the University senate. He must hold a university chair, and be suitable for directing the Institute on the basis of his research. The directors to date have been Theodor Klauser, founder of the Institute, from 1955–1973, Ernst Dassmann from 1973–2001 and Georg Schöllgen since 2001.

The DI does not carry out any teaching activities at the University, but devotes itself to the edition of the aforementioned publications. Manuscripts by specialists from throughout the world are first examined by the editors (see below); then their comments are collected by the Institute's scholarly collaborators and transmitted to the authors. Subsequently, the manuscripts, completed and corrected as the case may be, are translated and edited within the Institute, if necessary. Since the headings are intended to cover their subject in as comprehensive a way as possible, the additions and completions desired by the editors, whether they are of a geographical, chronological, archaeological, epigraphical, linguistic nature, and so forth, must, in view of the authors' specializations, often be elaborated within the Institute. Once edited in this way, the manuscript is once again returned to the author for revision and approval. Collaboration with the authors is usually excellent, since all parties share an interest in producing an article that treats its respective lemma in as comprehensive and reliable a manner as possible. An extensive specialized library, tailored to the needs of the editorial section, allows all the evidence to be checked against the best critical editions, thereby facilitating the work of the Institute's collaborators. The tendency is to provide camera-ready material to the press and printers, who concentrate on production and distribution.

B. Franz Joseph Dölger and his Research Program 'Antiquity and Christianity'

Dölger was born in Sulzbach in 1879, ordained a priest in 1902 and died in Schweinfurt in 1940. His studies in Catholic theology took place at a time when historical studies were extending their genetic approach to theology as well, when archaeological discoveries in the Near East sparked a debate over the originality of Old Testament narratives, and the comparative methods of the History of Religions school began to question the uniqueness of many New Testament traditions. Rigid fronts developed in both Christian confessions, so that it was a lucky accident that the Faculty of Catholic Theology in Würzburg was able to propose the theme of 'The Sacrament of Confirmation presented from a historical-dogmatic viewpoint' for its prize for the year 1901–1902. Dölger received the prize for his elaboration and was granted the doctorate on the basis of it in 1904. Dölger's work on this dissertation opened his eyes to the extent to which many forms of expression of Christian life are rooted in the traditions of their non-Christian environment, and he realized that the foundations for large-scale theoretical projects could only be provided by detailed investigations that were as comprehensive as possible. He took advantage of a study visit to Rome, in which he acquired the necessary familiarity with the monuments, to achieve a new orientation. His habilitation thesis of 1906 (published in 1909) was entitled *Der Exorzismus im altchristlichen Taufritual. Eine religionsgeschichtliche Studie* ('Exorcism in the ancient Christian baptismal ritual. A religious-historical study'), and he was granted the *venia legendi* in the History of Dogma. A further several-year-long stay at Rome, which also allowed him to avoid difficulties with his Church superiors, enabled the rapid publication of several monographs.

He was named Professor at Münster in 1912, at Breslau in 1927 and at Bonn in 1929. With his publications, including ΙΧΘΥΣ vols. 1–5 (Münster 1910–43; repr. 1999/2000), *Sol Salutis* (Münster ²1925) and others, he started the research program known as 'Antiquity and Christianity', which was also the title he gave to his journal, supported solely by his own contributions, the six volumes of which he published between 1929 and 1950. Unlike the research being done around him, oriented toward the intra-ecclesial history of dogma, Dölger recognized that the concrete form of early Christianity had taken shape through the adoption of pagan as well as Jewish influences, together with their philosophical and religious contents. Whereas his essay *Der Exorzismus im altchristlichen Taufritual* (1909) had met with a skeptical reception, he was able to win many colleagues in his discipline over to his new research orientation and methodology by his well-balanced and clearly-structured study *Sphragis. Eine altchristliche Taufbezeichnung in ihren Beziehungen zur profanen und religiösen Kultur des Altertums* (1911) ('Sphragis. An ancient Christian baptismal designation in its relations to the profane and religious culture of Antiquity').

While the process whereby Christianity took root was initially still considered as a "confrontation of Christianity with the ancient world" – this was the subtitle of the RAC – in which it took over contents, concepts and practices from the heathen and Jewish environment in an approbatory, corrective and transformative way, but also criticized and rejected them, the relationship was increasingly seen in a more differentiated way as Dölger's approach developed. Not least because of the adoption of 'Late Antiquity' as a term for this period, Christianity was no longer seen as the rival adversary of a culture that was heathen and, in many areas, also Jewish, but as a group that grew up in this late ancient culture, and was a part of it. Influences took place in both directions. It was important therefore not only to clarify how Church and community allowed themselves to be determined by the traditions of their environment in the development of their doctrines, organization, usages and behavioral norms, but also how the Christian message influenced the thinking, sensibility and behavior of the people of Late Antiquity as a whole.

C. The Reallexikon für Antike und Christentum

The RAC serves for the elaboration and presentation of this protracted, laborious, but also fascinating process of inculturation, elimination and fusion. Exactly when the plan for this lexicon emerged and from whom it derives can no longer be determined. It probably goes back only to a limited degree to Dölger himself, whose strength lay not in the systematic synthesis of the results of research, as is required for a lexicon, but in the meticulous pursuit of historical contexts, in which he could unfold his immense philological and historical knowledge without concern for formal limitations. It is also hard to imagine that Dölger should have yielded to the drudgery of a publishing obligation in alphabetical order. Although Dölger, as Th. Klauser notes in *Die Cathedra im Totenkult* (²1971) [p. V], had provided the impulse for a lexicon, the execution of the plan must have been carried out by Dölger's students, in particular Helmut Kruse, who as an unsalaried clerk at the Deutsche Bücherei in Leipzig was able to win the publisher and antiquarian Anton Hiersemann for the project. Three volumes were originally planned. With Dölger and Hans Lietzmann as the editors, Kruse, Theodor Klauser and Jan Hendrik Waszink were supposed to take over the preparation and editorial supervision of the lexicon. As is attested by the correspondence preserved at the DI, Kruse seems to have born the brunt of the work from 1937–1940. Partly because of the unfavorable circumstances of the time, which in particular made collaboration by foreign scholars increasingly difficult, it was not until the war year of 1941 that, after many delays, the first fascicle of the first volume could be printed. Five more fascicles appeared until 1943, while the completed copy of the seventh fascicle burned in an air raid on Leipzig and was reset. In 1945, two sheets were still lacking from fascicle eight, and hence for the completion of the first volume. Nevertheless, it then took until 1950 before the opening volume of the RAC was completed. It appeared "edited by Theodor Klauser in association with Franz Joseph Dölger (†) and Hans Lietzmann (†) and with the particular collaboration of Jan Hendrik Waszink and Leopold Wenger" in Hiersemann's publishing house, henceforth located in Stuttgart. These specifications document the changes that had taken place in the meantime. Dölger and Lietzmann had died, Kruse had left because his career had developed in a different direction, and the renowned Austrian legal historian Wenger was attracted as co-editor.

It was Klauser who became the editor-in-chief. Unfortunately, his share in the preparation of the lexicon in the first phase is hard to discern, since Klauser's files containing information on this point were destroyed at Bonn. After the end of his stay at Rome and his return to Bonn in 1934, he appears to have devoted himself more intensely to this task, once it had become clear to him that as a non-member of the NSDAP, he could not count on being named to a professor's chair in the foreseeable future. After the collapse of 1945, Klauser immediately began the continuation of the work, but he seems initially to have deluded himself about its difficulties. It was not only the external circumstances – lack of libraries, shortages of paper – that made the work more difficult, but Germany's intellectual and scholarly isolation as well. Foreign scholars hesitated to collaborate with a lexicon written in German, published by a German press and supervised by a German editor. A deep alienation had even set in between Dölger's students Klauser and Waszink, which was only slowly overcome. Klauser's personally irreproachable behavior during the Nazi past helped him to overcome initial aversions. He turned down requests to transfer the lexicon to a foreign press and to accept additional co-editors in order to win greater international prestige.

Once the first volume of the RAC was finally published in 1950, after a delay of nearly ten years, the work continued without interruption. Especially after the establishment of the DI, fascicles appeared in rapid succession, so that a volume could be completed every two to three years. Beginning with vol. 6 (1966), Carsten Colpe, Albrecht Dihle, Bernhard Kötting and Jan Hendrik Waszink supported Klauser in the responsibility for the scholarly quality of the Lexicon. Up to the present time (end of 2000), the only ones to withdraw from the editorial team have been Klauser, Kötting and Waszink, who died in the interval. New additions included Ernst Dassmann and Wolfgang Speyer with vol. 9 (1976), Josef Engemann and Klaus Thraede with vol. 13 (1986) and Heinzgerd Brakmann and Karl Hoheisel from vol. 17 on (1996). The decisive factor in the choice of the newly recruited editors was their knowledge of specialized disciplines. In addition to historians, philologists and theologians, it became increasingly important to recruit specialists in → CHRISTIAN ARCHAEOLOGY, Judaic studies and the Eastern churches, for since in view of increasing specialization no one can survey all scholarly fields pertaining to Antiquity, particular importance accrues to the knowledge of the editors, which must be as broad as possible, when it comes to editing contributions to the lexicon.

D. RESULTS AND CURRENT STATE OF WORK

The research enterprise of the RAC has now reached the headings of the letter K, and has therefore carried out half of the planned program. While the extent of the lexicon was given as three volumes in the initial invitation for collaboration, it was soon increased to six, and still later to 20 volumes; finally, the indication of volume numbers was abandoned. In the 19 volumes and one supplementary volume that have appeared so far (fascicle 167 of vol. 21 appeared on August 1, 2006), approximately 1300 key words have been dealt with in some 25,000 columns, in which more than 500 authors have participated; somewhat less than the same extent in length and above all in time will be required for the conclusion of the work. Since Christian doctrine, liturgy, history and archaeology were not to be investigated for their own sake, but only their share in the debate with ancient culture, and the latter, conversely, only in its effects on Christianity, it was initially thought that two or three columns per article would suffice. After restrictions in length were abandoned, many articles grew to undue length, sometimes achieving the dimensions of monographs. This development, which came to a head in the mid–1970s (cf. vol. 9) could, fortunately, be stopped. The varying length of the articles is, however, explained to some extent by the effort to attain a consistent quality of research. Space corresponding to the state of research continues to be allowed to authors, so that each collaborator may appropriately set forth the material, especially in the case of sources made available for the first time. The presentation of the material, rather than theories and speculation, constitute the main focus of the lexicon, which thus seeks to serve further research.

The fruitfulness of Dölger's research program and its continuation by the F. and the RAC (in 'Die Antike und ihre Vermittler', *Konstanzer Univ.-Reden* 9, 1969, 38, M. Fuhrmann names the RAC among "the few, therefore all the more laudable exceptions" that oppose "the orientationless treatment of infinitely fragmented details") is not only shown by the increasing number of relevant publications throughout the world. The founding of the Institute for Antiquity and Christianity in Claremont, California in 1969, as well as the choice of the combination 'Antiquity and Christianity', coined programmatically by Dölger, in the titles of books, essays and series, attest that Dölger's research orientation occupies an established position in studies of Antiquity.

As a complement to the RAC, the journal *Jahrbuch für Antike und Christentum* was founded after the model of Dölger's journal *Antike und Christentum*. It appeared for the first time in 1958; vol. 47 was published in 2004. To reduce the extent of their RAC articles, authors can publish in-depth studies on individual aspects in the JbAC, or research to accompany their contributions to the lexicon. In addition, the *Jahrbuch* preferentially contains contributions that make new historical and patristic sources available, or familiarize the public with unknown archaeological monuments. In order to publish more extensive works dealing with the subject area of the RAC, the series of Supplementary volumes to the JbAC came into existence in 1964, and since that time over 30 volumes have appeared. It is noteworthy that a recent volume, with its investigations on the theme of 'Cross-Cosmos-Jerusalem', takes up the studies of the history of the sign of the cross with which the first volume of the *Jahrbücher* opened. The series entitled *Theophaneia*,–37 volumes to date – has been open since its beginning to "contributions to the religious and ecclesiastical history of Antiquity". The informational work *Das Reallexikon* [2. 65–78] offers a survey of the contents of volumes 1–37 of the JbAC, as well as the titles taken up in the series of Supplementary volumes to the *Jahrbuch* and in *Theophaneia*. The *Reallexikon* replaced the homonymous work published in a second edition by Klauser in 1970 with *Berichte, Erwägungen, Richtlinien* for the RAC and the DI. A comparison of the two works documents the continuity and further development of the RAC project. The constraints of publishing in alphabetical order led in 1985 to the publication of the first volume of addenda, which contains articles that were not submitted on time, and appeared earlier in the JbAC, as well as headings that had been overlooked, or whose importance was realized only after the fact. In the latest volumes, the history of the reception of the Old Testament has been more intensely considered, along with the literature of the Early Judaic period. In the meantime, a volume of indices was completed, which is intended to make available the contents of the first fifteen volumes of the RAC for a more effective use in research. The usefulness of the Lexicon is attested by its broad utilization in scholarly literature; one may also point to the reviews, a selection of which is listed in the informational work *Das Reallexikon* [2. 51–54].

1 N. M. BORENGÄSSER, Briefwechsel Theodor Klauser – Jan Hendrik Waszink 1946–1951. Ein zeitgeschichtlicher Beitrag zur Fortführung des RAC nach dem 2. Weltkrieg, in: JbAC 40, 1997, 18–37   2 E. DASSMANN (ed.), Das Reallexikon für Antike und Christentum und das Franz-Joseph-Dölger-Institut in Bonn, 1994   3 Id., Theodor

Klauser. 1894–1984, in: JbAC 27/28, 1985, 5–23   4 Id., Dölger, LThK 3, 304 f. (third edition)   5 Id., Entstehung und Entwicklung des Reallexikons für Antike und Christentum und des Franz-Joseph-Dölger-Instituts in Bonn, in: JbAC 40, 1997, 5–17   6 F. W. DEICHMANN, Theodor Klauser, in: MDAI(R) 92, 1985, 1–8   7 A. DIHLE, Antike und Christentum, in: CHR. SCHNEIDER (ed. for the Deutsche Forschungsgemeinschaft), Forschung in der Bundesrepublik Deutschland: Beispiele, Kritik, Vorschläge, 1983, 31–37   8 J. FONTAINE, Christentum ist auch Antike, in: JbAC 25, 1982, 5–21   9 E. A. JUDGE, 'Antike und Christentum': Towards a Definition of the Field. A Bibliographical Survey, in: ANRW II 23.1, 3–58, 1979   10 TH. KLAUSER, Franz Joseph Dölger, 1879–1940. Sein Leben und sein Forschungsprogramm 'Antike und Christentum' (= JbAC Supplement vol. 7), 1980   11 G. SCHÖLLGEN, Franz Joseph Dölger und die Entstehung seines Forschungsprogramms 'Antike und Christentum', in: JbAC 36, 1993, 7–23   12 K. THRAEDE, Antike und Christentum, LThK 1, ³1993 (completed with vol. 11, 2001; special complete edition, 2006), 755–759

URL http://217.160.73.214/doelger/index.php?

ERNST DASSMANN

Fürstenschule

A. DEFINITION   B. HISTORY

A. DEFINITION

The term *Fürstenschule* designates the scholarly educational establishments founded by Protestant rulers in the course of the Reformation, which were intended to train gifted children of their domains for service in the Church, higher state offices, teaching careers and scholarly activity. These new institutions replaced the former → MONASTERY SCHOOLS and had the status of public state schools. They functioned as links between the municipal → LATIN SCHOOLS and the → UNIVERSITY. Their legal foundations were provided by school ordinances that regulated the German educational system beyond the municipal context for the first time, and can be seen as the forerunners of the present national school legislation.

B. HISTORY

The term *Fürstenschule* usually refers to the institutions founded by Duke Moritz, later Elector of Saxony (1541–1553), following the plan of Christoph von Carlowitz (1507–1578), the student of Erasmus and princely counsellor: St. Marien at Pforta (1543), also known as Schulpforta, St. Afra at Meißen (1543) and St. Augustin at Grimma (1550). The ruler expected from these new educational establishments, "that youth should be brought up to praise God and to be obedient, and they be taught and instructed in languages and arts, and then primarily in the Holy Scripture, so that, with time, there may be no lack of servants of the Church and other learned people in our lands" (Foundation Charter of May 21, 1543 *Von dreyen neuen Schulen* ('On three new schools'), cited in [1. 11]). These state schools were granted long-term financial security through the freehold of the three secularized monasteries. In addition, their pupils were aided by a generous system of scholarships. According to the foundation decree, the students were to "be maintained and taught therein free of charge for six years", and then "sent to the University of Leipzig" [1. 12]. The selection of students followed the merit principle. In case of equal merit, the socially weaker candidate was to be preferred, and no class was to be excluded. The age of acceptance was 12. In the first years, approximately 230 students attended the Saxon *Fürstenschulen*, 100 of whom went to Schulpforta alone.

These *Fürstenschulen* were the models for state schools in other Protestant areas of Germany [2. 290–371], as well as for foundations in the Baltic, Switzerland and Transylvania regions. Among the best known, for instance, were the Ilfeld monastery school in the county of Stolberg, founded in 1550 by Michael Neander (1525–1595), a student of Melanchthon; the institution founded in 1554 in a Cistercian convent in Rossleben on the river Unstrut; the state school at the Graue Kloster in Berlin, in existence since 1574; and the *Fürstenschule* at Joachimsthal near Eberswalde, founded by the Elector Joachim Friedrich von Brandenburg (1598–1608), which was transferred to Berlin in 1647, and from there, in 1912, to Templin [3].

The lifestyle of the *Fürstenschulen* continued the ascetic practices of the monastery. The daily routine was strictly regulated: students wore a uniform similar to the vestment of a religious order; a monastic discipline reigned; and celibacy was initially prescribed for the teachers. Collaboration by married teachers was first made possible by the Elector August I (1526–1586). The pedagogical spirit and organization of the *Fürstenschule* were essentially determined by the principle of self-initiative. The students carried out their own reading and versification in classical metrical forms, often from four in the morning. Valedictory compositions, voluntarily written, testify to the zeal for learning and intellectual capabilities. These compositions, together with debates and theatrical productions at festivities and celebrations, provided occasions for the students to develop their talents and their community life. A study-day, held regularly, offered students a free choice of themes for work, and promoted the spirit and methods of independent work. A system of helpers and supervision, in which older students, the so-called 'Uppers' (=upperclassmen), played an influential role, supported student learning and at the same time kept tabs on their social behavior. This system substantially marked the life of the institution. Toward the end of the 18th century, the normative pedagogy of supervision was relaxed under the influence of Basedow's philanthropism, and the cooperation of the student body in the formation and administration of the student government was expanded. In general, only those who had made a name for themselves in a scholarly discipline were appointed as → TEACHERS. Many a well-known professor of a neighboring university occupied the

sought-after position of Rector. No doubt, the teaching faculty played an important part in the high educational standards of the *Fürstenschule*; but the practice of visitation also made a substantial contribution. Almost annually until 1700, six or seven external visitors – members of the Consistory as well as professors of the universities of Leipzig and Wittenberg – inspected the performance and overall condition of the institutions. Their recommendations and the prizes they distributed regulated the pedagogical efforts of the teachers and stimulated the students' motivation to achieve high levels of performance.

The → CURRICULUM was focused on Classical philology. In addition to Latin, Greek was taught to a lesser extent, and Hebrew was a compulsory subject beginning in 1588. The state schools of Württemberg – in addition to Adelberg (later Hirsau, then Denkendorf), they included Blaubeuren, Bebenhausen, Maulbronn and, above all, the Tübinger Stift, founded in 1536 – concentrated more strongly on the subjects that were essential for the study of theology. Their political and legal foundation was the school ordinance enacted by Duke Christoph (1550–1568) in 1559 [4. vol. 1. 68–165]. Latin was the language of instruction in all *Fürstenschulen*, but the students were also to use Latin in the everyday life of the boarding school. The curriculum underwent appropriate modifications with the changing times. Mathematics received a relatively strong emphasis, and the inclusion of modern languages and "useful knowledge" was stipulated in the Elector's school regulations of 1773 [4. vol. 3. 618]. At the turn of the 19th cent., the concept of the *Fürstenschulen* was influenced by Humboldt's neo-Humanist educational ideas. Schulpforta's transfer to Prussia in 1815 led to adaptations to the Prussian *gymnasium* system.

The *Fürstenschulen* did not remain untouched by the spirit of their respective times: not, for instance in the 17th cent. by the decline in good manners, which accelerated as a result of the disorders of the Thirty Years' War, and expressed itself in educational institutions in the form of so-called pennalism. Nor were they free from the State's inclination to exert a transformative influence, as was attempted by Prussian educational policies after 1815 at Schulpforta. Until the 20th cent., however, their Christian-Humanist educational tradition had never been open to question. Structural interference first occurred in the wake of the political and social upheavals following the First World War. In 1924, after the abolition of the *Fürstenschulen's* preparatory *gymnasium*, the St. Augustin state school at Grimma became a reformed humanistic *gymnasium*. From 1945 to 1950/51, it had the status of a *gymnasium*, but maintained the title of state school. Both designations were then used alternately until 1953, after which point it was called the Grimma secondary school, and from 1963 the expanded Grimma secondary school. From 1943 to 1945, St. Afra at Meissen was a German boarding school under the direction of the SS.

After the Second World War, there was no chance in the Soviet Occupation Zone for the institution to start over again in the spirit of the old *Fürstenschulen*. In 1946, St. Afra housed an institution for normal school education, and from 1947 a state party school of the SED. In 1953 it became, in cooperation with the University of Leipzig, the School of Agriculture, which also served as the site for continuing education for the leaders of collective farms. In 1934, Schulpforta was transformed by the National Socialists into a national-political educational institution, and thereby separated from essential elements of its tradition. After its reopening in 1945, where the students, following tradition, pledged to be "God-fearing, diligent, obedient and grateful", the institution soon underwent another reorganization, this time in a thoroughly socialist direction. The foundation was abolished in 1950, and in 1951 the state school became a boarding school with the curriculum of an extended secondary school. The principle of promoting the gifted came into effect once again at the beginning of the 1980s, when special tracks for English and French were established in 1981, to which an emphasis on music was added in 1983.

Since the tradition of Saxon *Fürstenschulen* could not be continued in their original locations in the → GDR, in 1968 an alumni promotional association founded a successor establishment under Church sponsorship in Nordrhein-Westfalen, the *Evangelische Landesschule zur Pforte in Meinerzhagen* [5. 299–336]. It was dissolved at the end of 1991. Henceforth, the experience gained on the basis of the educational concept of the *Fürstenschulen* over 24 years in schools and boarding schools, albeit in a context of changed circumstances, could benefit the reconstruction of traditional institutions in the Saxon region. The archive of the alumni association of the *Fürstenschulen*, which had also been located at Meinerzhagen after the division of Germany, returned to its original site in 1992, and has since then been accessible for consultation at Grimma.

As early as 1991, Schulpforta, which now belonged to the Federal State of Saxony-Anhalt, once again received the status of a state school. Here, highly gifted students can choose music, foreign languages (English, Russian, Latin and Greek), or the natural sciences as the focus of their individual educational process. The prevailing set up is that of a coeducational boarding school, which is at the same time oriented toward principles of the *Fürstenschulen*. At the present time (as of 1997), 210 girls and 110 boys attend the school. The new foundation of St. Afra at Meissen as a state school was decreed by the cabinet of the Free State of Saxony on June 17, 1997. It was conceived as a secondary-level boarding school (*gymnasium*) for highly gifted students, that calls for a broad foundation of mathematical and language immersion in at least three languages, one of which must be Latin or Greek. In 2001 classes resumed for grades 7 and 12. The institution at Grimma now bears the name of the *Gymnasium St. Augustin zu Grimma*, which is intended as an allusion to its tradi-

tion. Educational work is focused on the languages, mathematical-scientific areas and the arts. The boarding school is supported by the Melanchthon Foundation. It is possible that the Grimma secondary school will also, at a later date, become a state school once again.

Many personages who have deeply marked German intellectual life have come out of the Saxon *Fürstenschulen*. From Schulpforta, for instance, came Klopstock, Fichte, Ranke, Nietzsche and Wilamowitz-Moellendorff [6. 31–46, 51–57, 96–104, 120–130]; from St. Afra at Meißen came Gellert, Rabener and Lessing, and from St. Augustin at Grimma came Pufendorf and Paul Gerhardt.

Valuable libraries were assembled at the *Fürstenschulen*. The library at Schulpforta, which has survived all sorts of vicissitudes and even the eventful 20th cent. almost undamaged, contains ca. 80,000 volumes. St. Afra's holdings are affiliated with other Saxon libraries, but have been decimated. The library of St. Augustin at Grimma, in contrast, which had remained intact throughout the war, was dispersed. Parts of it appeared on the used book market, but the rare books are nowhere to be found. A considerable portion of them were even destroyed.

→ LIBRARY; → EDUCATION / CULTURE; → HUMANIST GYMNASIUM; → NEO-HUMANISM; → SCHOOLS

SOURCES 1 Schulpforta, 1543–1993. Ein Lesebuch, 1993 2 F. PAULSEN, Geschichte des gelehrten Unterrichts auf den deutschen Schulen und Universitäten vom Ausgang des Mittelalters bis zur Gegenwart. Mit besonderer Rücksicht auf den klassischen Unterricht, vol. 1, Leipzig ²1896 3 S. JOOST, Das Joachimsthalsche Gymnasium, 1982 4 R. VORMBAUM, Die evangelischen Schulordnungen des 16.–18. Jahrhunderts, vol. 1, Gütersloh 1860; vol. 3, Gütersloh 1864 5 K. BOHNER, CH. ILGEN, Die Evangelische Landesschule zu Pforte in Meinerzhagen 1968 bis 1991, in: H. HEUMANN (ed.), Schulpforta. Tradition und Wandel einer Eliteschule, 1994 6 H. GEHRIG (ed.), Schulpforte und das deutsche Geistesleben: Lebensbilder alter Pförtner, 1943.
LITERATURE 7 J. A. ERNESTI, Erneuerte Schulordnung ... für die Kursächsischen drei Fürsten- und Landesschulen ..., Dresden 1773 (also in: [4] vol. 3, 613–699) 8 TH. FLATHE, Sanct Afra. Geschichte der königlich sächsischen Fürstenschule zu Meißen vom Jahre 1543 bis zu ihrem Neubau in den Jahren 1877–1879, 1879 9 H. GRÖGER, Fürsten- und Landesschule St. Afra 1543–1943. 400 Jahre der Bewährung, 1943 10 J. HEIDEMANN (ed.), Geschichte des Grauen Klosters, Berlin 1874 11 M. HOFFMANN (ed.), Pförtner Stammbuch 1543–1893. Zur 350jährigen Stiftungsfeier der königlichen Landesschule Pforta, 1893 12 H. PETER, Veröffentlichungen zur Geschichte des gelehrten Schulwesens im Albertinischen Sachsen, 4 vols., 1900–1913 13 K. J. ROESSLER, Geschichte der Königlich Sächsischen Fürsten- und Landesschule Grimma, 1891 14 E. SCHWABE, Das Gelehrtenschulwesen Kursachsens von seinen Anfängen bis zur Schulordnung von 1580, 1914 15 K. SCHWABE, Gesamtbestandsverzeichnis des Archivs des Vereins ehemaliger Fürstenschüler e.V., 1995 16 H.-A. STEMPEL, Melanchthons pädagogisches Wirken, 1979 17 T. WOODY, Fürstenschulen in Germany after the Reformation, 1920

ADDITIONAL BIBLIOGRAPHY K. GOEBEL, Luther in der Schule: Beiträge zur Erziehungs- und Schulgeschichte, Pädagogik und Theologie, 1985

URLs   http://www.sn.schule.de/~afragym/afrahomepage/index.php;   http://www.landesschule-pforta.de/index.php   LEONHARD FRIEDRICH

Funeral Oration

A. DEFINITION AND GENERAL CONSIDERATIONS
B. ORIGIN AND HISTORY

A. DEFINITION AND GENERAL CONSIDERATIONS

The funeral oration (FO) was a key element in the historically and culturally specific commemorative practices of the ancient European ruling classes. It represented the central speech act during a funeral ceremony and was therefore embedded in the strongly-normed performance routine of the ceremonial acts associated with burial. The allocution addressed to the deceased took place before his interment. It praised his person and accomplishments, whereby this commemoration of the deceased's exemplary life was simultaneously aimed at the strengthening of the social community made up of the survivors. In return, *polis*, *gens*, community, and family sought to keep the deceased materially and spiritually alive through ritual and speech. The FO was part of a demonstratively public communicative practice, whose validity was independent of the level of its artistry. Its gradual fall into disuse, beginning in the modern age and becoming manifest in the 18th cent. [35], is indicative of long-term transformations in the history of attitudes observable in the change in the conception–central for ancient European culture–that ties between the dead and survivors continue on [27. esp. 437]. A traditional form of self-assurance for traditional societies thereby lost its validity. The presence of the dead, which attributed a visibly high social and legal status to the deceased, disappeared more and more from the domain of public activity, while its linguistic-rhetorical confirmation was increasingly left to the discretion of subjective remembrance [26. 22 f.]. These assumed ties of the dead to the living resulted, especially in literature, in their demonisation.

B. ORIGIN AND HISTORY

1. 5TH CENTURY BC TO 5TH CENTURY AD   2. 4TH TO 15TH CENTURY   2.1 EASTERN ROMAN EMPIRE/BYZANTIUM   2.2. WESTERN EUROPE   3. 16TH TO 18TH CENTURY

1. 5TH CENTURY BC TO 5TH CENTURY AD

The FO was a conventionalised oratorical practice that displayed an extremely broad range of linguistic-rhetorical organisation. Two types, clearly distinct in their degree of conceptualisation, have been handed down from Antiquity and have been influential in the history of the FO. On the one hand, there is the *epitáphios logos*, a highly elaborate and artfully formed speech; this type is first attested literarily in Thuc. 2,40,4 ff. Here, Pericles' famous FO for those who fell for Athens in the Peloponnesian War (430–431) provides, at the same time, an example of state eloquence, aimed at the *polis* community. Since the Battle of Marathon, the centuries-old ceremony of funeral games and commemoration of heroes had become an instrument of political propaganda [21]. The epitaphs that have come down to us provide material for conceptualising the rhetoric in the FO of the later empire in connection with the theory of epideictic eloquence in Menander Rhetor and the pseudo-Dionysius of Halicarnassus.

In the Roman Republic, honouring the dead had also become, since the 4th cent. BC, the occasion for a public staging, whose sequence of events is documented by Polybius (6,53,1–54,3). The *laudatio funebris* was part of the *pompa funebris* and hence of an exclusive ceremony through which the aristocratic ruling class made an impressive display of its familial status, the prestige it had won from holding office and its political power. The theatrical effect relied essentially on the interplay between linguistic and visual means, and especially on the display, reserved for the *pompa*, of the masks of the ancestors [10]. At the climax of the funeral rites, a representative of the *gens*, as orator, delivered his FO from the rostrum to the people gathered in the marketplace and to the mourners. His *oratio* combined praise of the deceased with lament. The formal nature of the address, usually brief, together with such techniques as accumulation, assonance, repetition and rhythm, by which the Roman FO continued Italian oral traditions, lent it the look of a pre-literary oratorical exercise. Unlike the Greek epitaph, both the consolatory and the protreptical elements were foreign to it. Instead, it powerfully activated the non-linguistic and situational context. The collective weeping of all the mourners provided emotional support for the formation of an image of the deceased worth preserving. The FO produced this in the presence of the deceased through the enumeration of his physical qualities, his ancestors, his military deeds, his political merits and his *virtutes*, as they manifested themselves in the way he led his life. The speech ended with the enumeration of the deceased's *tituli* and those of the ancestors of the *gens*, conceived as present in the wax masks. The FO is an important witness for the character of political culture in Rome [13]. It maintained its eminent public significance until the Late Republic. Caesar used it for self-propaganda and to demonstrate his lofty ancestry (Plut. Caesar 5). The theatricality of Marcus Antonius's FO for Caesar (App. civ. 2,146,611) inspired Shakespeare's rendition of his speech (Julius Caesar III,2,57 f.; 73 ff.).

With the separation of politics and eloquence in the imperial age, the FO lost its intensely political function [18]. It was now used, as the codified form of ancient Roman oratorical practice, for the symbolic display of the imperial house in ceremonial acts. At the same time, it received a new value in the daily life of wider sectors of the population. The FOs for women from the time of the Principate (*Thuriae* and *Murdiae*) [9] exhibit highly stylised features, in conformity with Augustan ideology, which adapted central values from the time of the Republic.

The influence of rhetoric on oratorical practice can first be observed in the 1st cent. BC. and is reflected in a new format for the FO [18. 76]. The chronological enumeration of *honores* gives way to the abstract division *per species* according to the schema *per virtutes*. The FO nevertheless remained a borderline area of the literary canon at Rome, and its oratorical traditions were not dealt with in the theory of rhetoric. [34]. Cicero already judged it negatively because of its lack of form (ad Brut. 61). An orator could not gain glory through an FO (Cic. de orat. 2,84,341). Even in Quintilian's theory of forms, influenced by the Greek model, the successful transposition of the rules of Classical literary prose to the FO is not achieved. Rather, the FO is listed under the genre–unimportant for Rome–of epideictic speech (inst. 3,7,2).

A comprehensive rhetorical theory of the FO first occurs in the practice-oriented Greek rhetorical treatises of Late Antiquity. In Ch. 5 of the τέχνη ῥητωρική/ *téchnē rhētōrikē* of pseudo-Dionysius of Halicarnassus, the parts of the funeral eulogy are defined according to the model of the Attic *epitaphios*. Pseudo-Dionysius rejects mourning and focuses on praise, admonition and consolation. His division follows Classical rules: the *prooemium* is followed by the main body, with its *épainos*; then come the *protreptikós* and the *paramuthikós*, while a prayer occurs optionally at the end. Menander Rhetor deals with the FO in his work Περὶ ἐπιδεικτικῶν/*Perì epideiktikōn* as an example of the panegyric [31], and he distinguishes four basic forms of the *epitáphios*: the encomium, monody, consolation speech and funeral speech. He establishes both the emotions to be appealed to and the themes of this type of speech. Protreptic features and the consolatory portion of the FO demonstrate the development of the genre; the assimilation of the FO to the eulogy was particularly seminal for its further evolution, especially in the East. This process was accompanied by the differentiation of independent literary forms, such as that of → CONSOLATION LITERATURE [16], on the one hand, and praise of a city on the other [6].

2. 4TH TO 15TH CENTURY

2.1 EASTERN ROMAN EMPIRE/BYZANTIUM

The validity of the Late Greco-Hellenistic model of the FO remained practically intact in the Eastern Roman Empire in almost uninterrupted continuity until the fall of Constantinople in 1453. A retroactive effect of the practice-oriented rhetorical treatises on the Christian rhetoric of the Church Fathers is evident [32]. Gregory Nazianzen's FO for his brother Caesarius, who died in 379, follows the prescriptions of Menander Rhetor but, in the process, transforms the pagan *topos* of praise by means of biblical metaphors. In Gregory, the Christian reevaluation of these *topoi* is in any event

accompanied by a justification of the speech of praise in the service of parenesis [11]. As is affirmed in the FO for Basil, remembrance of the dead improves the living, whose improved life represents the true praise of the dead (PG 46, 816 C-D). The Church Fathers thus engage in competition with the Sophists, as well as with the pagan philosophy of life they represented [15].

The eminent validity of the instructions on the FO first formulated in the treatises of Late Antiquity on rhetoric is, moreover, reflected in the numerous epitaphs that emerged out of the rhetoricized court culture of the Eastern Roman Empire. Here, the FO developed into a variation of the dominant genre of epideictic speech [14]. Its characteristic feature is a refined technique of praise, through which the FO functions as a showpiece of courtly panegyric. Brilliant examples of the encomiastic FO at the imperial court are provided by Libanius, particularly in his speech for the emperor Julian (AD 362–363, Or. 18). Speeches in praise of the ruler flourished at the court of Byzantium. In addition to epitaphs for members of the imperial house, FOs are later also preserved for representatives of the imperial elite, such as clergymen and authors [30]. In Byzantium between the 11th and 14th cents., the FO became more and more detached from its originally pragmatic field of application. It was no longer given directly at the burial, but fictively prolonged the deceased's presence by addressing him. The FOs of Michael Psellos (1018 – ca. 1078) are good examples of this phenomenon. Private life also became increasingly the object of monodies. That the FO became a formal literary exercise is clear from the playful treatment of the formal repertoire, as is shown in monodies on pets, as well as by their parodies. A Humanistic reflection on this Byzantine formal variant of the FO is Leon Battista Alberti's ironic praise *Canis* (ca. 1438), on the loss of his dog [12].

2.2 WESTERN EUROPE

Already in Late Antiquity, the FO assumed a different path of development in the Latin West than in the Greek East. The transmission is significantly more complex, since in the Western Roman Empire the continuity of a rhetorical education, institutionally ensured through school and court, was, in general, no longer available. After the fall of the Roman administration, the sponsorship of literate culture passed, from the 6th cent. on in Western Europe, to the monasteries, which thus developed into the most important centres of transmission. As the intermediaries of the culture of Rome, they were then enrolled, above all by Charlemagne, in the translation projects of the kingdom of the Franks. (Medieval) Latin literature was deliberately promoted at the Carolingian court. For instance, collections of provincial Roman epitaphs were compiled, while the originally German elegy for fallen brothers-in-arms was transformed into the *planctus*, thereby obtaining a rudimentary rhetorical structure. Nevertheless, both structure (eulogy of the deceased, lament, intercession) as well as the range of emotions (*flete* as a command) point back to the Roman practice of the FO more than to the subdued Christian type. The *planctus* for Charlemagne offers impressive evidence of this connection [2]. Especially in the dynastic context, the *planctus* takes over the function of orientation and remembrance; its Middle-Latin form is found throughout Europe between the 9th and the 13th cent. [33].

The *planctus*, with its links between verses and stanzas, represents a variant of the FO that paved the way for a vernacular poetry of lament. Its emergence in the feudal courts, in its basic features, can be observed beginning with the 11th cent. In close exchange with the *planctus*, the Old Provençal [28] arises in the Occitan language area; in the Frankish area, the *dit, complainte,* and *déploration* [33. 29 ff.]. Old French variants were already firmly established in the literary canon by the mid–13th cent. Determined metrically and prosodically by the vernacular, the Old French poetry of lament was at the same time oriented towards the theory of figures (→ FIGURES, THEORY OF), by which contemporary poetics continued the rhetorical tradition at a rudimentary level and from an elocutionary perspective. In his *Poetria nova* (ca. 1210) Geoffroy de Vinsauf shows express interest in the poetry of lament, illustrating it with an elegy on Richard the Lionhearted [1. 208–210]. The poetry of lament found its way into all West European literatures and, as a supplement to funeral ceremonies and often complementary to funerary art, it formed an elementary component of the courtly memorial culture. The courtly centres formed the background for significant shifts noticeable in the profile of the poetry of lament, beginning in the 14th cent. It then developed into moralising-didactic poetry, whose orienting function tended to reach a broader lay audience as well; it also developed increasingly into historiographic narration. The example of Burgundian court poetry elucidates well this transformation [24]. Georges Chatelain (1405?–1475) provides a good example of the exchanges with the chronicles, while Jean Meschinot (ca. 1420–1491) masterfully practiced didacticism in association with allegorical discourse.

In addition to these examples, a type developed within the framework of Christian eloquence that was integrated into the sermon. The FOs by Ambrose of Milan formed an often-imitated model, whose influence can be observed down to the 13th cent. [25]: Radberg of Corbie, *Vita S. Adalhardi* (PL 120, 1507–52), William of St. Denis, *Vita Sugerii* (PL 186, 1194–1208), down to Vincent of Beauvais' *Consolatio* for Louis IX are all oriented according to this formal variant of the FO, to which Ambrose had lent the features of a consolatory work with particular emphasis on the idea of salvation. The goal of the Ambrosian FOs was the overcoming of grief [8]; instead of increasing emotion, they encouraged its attenuation [5]. In addition to the *Consolationes* handed down in writing, a rudimentary form of FO was transmitted orally in the monasteries. It was inserted into a sermon as an address to the monastic community. This formal variant of the FO ultimately represents a transitional form between situation-bound

usage and rhetorical structuring. The completed development of the FO, integrated into the liturgy, into an independent oratorical form first appears again in the 12th cent., via the *artes praedicandi*. The numerous collections of sermons of the 13th and 14th cents. give evidence of this form of oratory [4. 42–53]. The Dominicans Remigio de' Girolami and Giovanni da San Geminiano exercised a broad influence [36]. However, the ideal of the *sermo humilis* ('laudes parce, vitupera parcius') preached by the mendicant orders clearly stood in the way of the development of the encomiastic part of the FO. The re-emergence of encomia can be observed in the context of princely funeral ceremonies, where praising the deceased was allotted its own space outside the liturgy. On the occasion of the death of William the Conqueror in 1087, Gilbert of Evreux made an elaborate speech after the Mass for the Dead and in the presence of the corpse lying in state. In it he highlighted the ruler's accomplishments (PL 188, 553 C 14 – 554 A 9). The development of this formal type of the FO originated primarily in lower Italy, where Byzantine influence remained a lasting force. Beginning in the 13th cent., *sermones pro mortuis* came into existence through the joint influence of preachers and other speakers at the court; they seem to anticipate thematically the humanistic FO through their emphasis on ethical concerns [4. 118].

In the framework of this tradition of public speaking, limits were nevertheless fixed as to the rhetorical development of the FO into a formal genre of discourse, as is affirmed by Pier Paolo Vergerio the Elder. His *Oratio in funere Francisci senioris de Carraria Patavii principis* (1393) was the first example of an FO that once again sought to make use of a Classical format [22]. Vergerio displays a newly-sharpened awareness of rules. The model of Greek funeral orators plays a role in the further development of the Latin FO that should not be underestimated. Bessarion's FO for Manuel II (1419) was still considered exemplary in the second half of the century, while George of Trapezond, later secretary at the papal court, shone at Venice with a Latin FO (1437) before the Doge and the senate. How quickly the Humanistic FO established itself as a new genre of oratory is shown by the countless transcriptions in circulation from the beginning of the century, whereby the speeches of Leonardo Bruni, Gian Francesco Poggio Bracciolini, Giovanni Pontano and Cristoforo Landino in particular gained canonical status [23. 24]. The humanistic FO developed its profile from a peculiar symbiosis between the Byzantine Greek and Roman traditions. The speeches elaborated in writing, with their *prooemium, narratio,* and *peroratio,* were oriented in their structure after the Attic *epitaphios*, and stylistically after Classicistic literary prose. Poggio Bracciolini, who drew up a model FO in 1426 [3], particularly stresses the *claritas* of the *narratio* and reserves strong emotions for the introduction and conclusion. In fact, it was above all the city-republics that offered the communicative conditions in which the FO could develop into a leading genre of public speaking. The expense lavished by local authorities on on public burial ceremonies for members of the ruling class was considered justified by calling to mind the funeral processions of the Roman Republic. This is evident, for instance, in Florence, where the later chancellor Leonardo Bruni used his FO for Nanni Strozzi (1428) to propagate the political goal of *umanesimo civile*[37]. The Medici adopted this form of urban republican representation and were still using the FO for the public display of their power as a dynasty in the 16th cent. [23. 49 ff.].

3. 16TH TO 18TH CENTURY

Significant shifts and reformulations can be observed in early modern times in Europe. The development in France can well serve as an example. Here, the FO, which since time immemorial had occupied a solid place in how the ruling class presented itself to the public, was used increasingly as an instrument of propaganda in the monarchical state which was then establishing itself. It became customary for *oraisons funèbres* to be given after the ruler's death from all the pulpits in the realm [29]. This oratory, indebted to French oratorical traditions of the 15th cent., was thus gradually adapted to the formal-stylistic corpus of the Classical model down to Jacques Bénigne Bossuet's *Oraisons funèbres* (from 1655), which represent the brilliant synthesis of pulpit rhetoric and the sovereign eloquence of absolutism [37]. In Germany, a considerable transformation of the FO began with the Reformation when Luther incorporated it once again strictly into the liturgy. The highly influential Protestant formal variation replaced the *cura pro mortuis* with the consolation the community needed. Under Luther's motto: 'lerne den todten ansehen nicht im Grabe und sarck, sondern in Christo' ("learn to see the deceased not in the grave and coffin, but in Christ", Weimar edition 36, 244), the Protestant funeral sermon prepared the way for the modern transformation in the relationship between the living and the dead, characterised by a loss of proximity and visibility as well as by increasing abstractness. Nevertheless, this genre also underwent a strongly rhetorical formalisation process and took on artistic form because of the increased importance of rhetoric for the culture of the 17th cent. [38. 35 ff.]. Here, rhetorical art and edification went hand in hand. FOs were worked on, as though they were literary works and were often published in memorial editions, along with elegies, obituaries, sheet music of the songs sung at the burial, menus from the funeral meal, portraits of the deceased and his ancestors, illustrations of the funeral procession and so forth. The book thereby had an important function of remembrance, complementary to the memorial service. Such collections, typical of the Baroque Age and immensely widespread, represent important sources for intellectual history because of their biographical and historiographical details [19].

In the 18th cent., several signs pointed towards fundamental change. The rhetorical form was everywhere maintained, yet lay speakers usurped the field of spiritual edification, as is shown by J. Chr. Gottsched's Preface to Fléchier's funeral speeches and eulogies (1748). As burials took on a private character (to some extent even as night-burials, as a sign of the new invisibility of the dead), the FO was no longer a social event. Like all strongly-normed actions associated with burial, it lost its formality and was supposed to become a spontaneous expression: the speaker says what he feels at graveside [17. 90]. That the end of the formal oratorical tradition of the FO has passed is manifest at the burial of Fr. Schiller [17. 110 ff.]: at the poet's hushed interment on the night of May 11, 1805, speech was replaced by an eloquent silence.

→ Burial; → Epitaphios; → Laudatio funebris

SOURCES 1 Arts poétiques du XIIe et du XIIIe siècle, E. FARAL (ed.), 1923, 208–210   2 MGH Poet. lat. Aevi Caroli, vol. 1, 345   3 G. F. POGGIO BRACCIOLINI, Opera omnia, R. FUBINI (ed.), vol. 3, 1970, 224–258
LITERATURE 4 D. L. D'AVRAY, Death and the Prince, 1994   5 M. BIERMANN, Die Leichenreden des Ambrosius von Mailand, 1995   6 C. J. CLASSEN, Die Stadt im Spiegel der descriptiones und laudes urbium in der antiken und mittelalterlichen Literatur, 1986   7 S. DAUB, Leonardo Brunis Rede auf Nanni Strozzi, 1996   8 Y.-M. DUVAL, Formes profanes et formes bibliques dans les oraisons funèbres de Saint-Ambroise, in: Christianisme et formes littéraires 23), 1997, 235–291   9 D. FLACH, Die sogenannte Laudatio Turiae, 1991   10 E. FLAIG, Die pompa funebris, in: O. G. OEXLE (ed.), Memoria als Kultur, 1995, 115–148   11 U. GANTZ, Gregor von Nyssa: Oratio Consolatoria, 1999   12 C. GRAYSON, Il canis di Leon Battista Alberti, in: Umanesimo e rinascimento a Firenze e Venezia. Miscellanea V. Branca, Vol. 3, 1983, 193–204   13 K.-J. HÖLKESKAMP, Oratoris maxima scaena, in: M JEHNE (ed.), Demokratie in Rom?, 1995, 11–49   14 H. HUNGER, Die hochsprachliche, profane Literatur der Byzantiner, vol. 1, 1978   15 H.-TH. JOHANN, Trauer und Trost, 1968   16 R. KASSEL, Untersuchungen zur griechischen und römischen Konsolationsliteratur, 1958   17 M. KAZMEIER, Die deutsche Grabrede im 19. Jahrhundert, 1977   18 W. KIERDORF, Laudatio funebris, 1980   19 R. LENZ, Gedruckte Leichenpredigten (1550–1750), in: Id., Leichenrede als Quelle historischer Wissenschaft, 1975–1984, vol. 1, 36–51   20 B. LIER, Topica carminum sepulcralium latinorum. I–II, Philologus 62, 1903, 445–477; 563–603; III, Philologus 63, 1904, 54–65   21 N. LORAUX, L'invention d'Athènes. Histoire de l'oraison funèbre dans la "cité classique", 1981 (Engl,: The Invention of Athens, 1986)   22 J. M. MCMANAMON, S. J., Innovation in Early Humanist Rhetoric. The Oratory of P. P. Vergerio the Elder, Rinascimento 22, 1982, 3–32   23 Id., Funeral Oratory and the Cultural Ideals of Italian Humanism, 1989   24 C. MARTIENAU-GÉNIEYS, Le thème de la mort dans la poésie française de 1450 à 1550, 1978   25 P. VON MOOS, Consolatio. Studien zur mittellateinischen Trostliteratur, 4 vols., 1971   26 O. G. OEXLE, Die Gegenwart der Toten, in: H. BRAET, W. VERBEKE (eds.), Death in the Middle Ages, 1983, 19–77   27 Id., Memoria und Memorialbild, in: K. SCHMID, J. WOLLASCH (eds.), Memoria. Der geschichtliche Zeugniswert des liturgischen Gedenkens, 1984, 384–440   28 D. RIEGER, Klagelied, in: E. KÖHLER (ed.), Les genres lyriques, GRLMA 2/1, fasc. 4 Bii, 1980, 83–92   29 V. L. SAULNIER, L'oraison funèbre au XVIe siècle,

Bibliothèque d'Humansime et Renaissance 10, 1948, 124–157   30 A. SIDERAS, Byzantinische Leichenreden, in: R. LENZ (ed.), Leichenpredigten als Quelle historischer Wissenschaft, 1975–1984, Vol. 3, 17–49   31 J. SOFFEL, Die Regeln Menanders für die Leichenrede, 1974   32 A. SPIRA, Rhetorik und Theologie in den Grabreden Gregors von Nyssa, Studia Patristica 9, 1966, 106–114   33 C. THIRY, La plainte funèbre, 1978   34 G. VOGT-SPIRA, Rednergeschichte als Literaturgeschichte, in: W. RAECK (ed.), Bewertung und Darstellung von Rede und Redner in den antiken Kulturen, 2000, 207–226   35 M. VOVELLE, La mort et l'occident de 1300 à nos jours, 1983   36 E. WINKLER, Scholastische Leichenpredigten: Die sermones funebres des Johann von S. Geminiano, in: Kirche – Theologie – Frömmigkeit. Festschrift G. Holtz, 1965, 177–186   37 H. SCHOBEL, Die Trauerrede des Grand Siècle, 1949   38 E. WINKLER, Die Leichenpredigt im deutschen Luthertum bis Spener, 1967.   BETTINA ROMMEL

Furniture

A. THE EARLY AND HIGH MIDDLE AGES (500–1250)   B. LATE MIDDLE AGES (1250–1500)
C. RENAISSANCE (1450–1600)   D. BAROQUE (1600–1730) AND ROCOCO (1730–1770)
E. EARLY CLASSICISM (1760–1790), EMPIRE (1790–1820), BIEDERMEIER (1800–1850)
F. HISTORISM   G. DEVELOPMENTS FROM 1890 TO THE PRESENT

A. THE EARLY AND HIGH MIDDLE AGES (500–1250)

The majority of the few surviving examples of the art of furniture making from the Early and High Middle Ages are chairs. Besides their use as furniture for sitting, their predominant purpose was to indicate their owner's rank. The influence of ancient examples is evident in both design and usage. Their designs fall into three main types: the (Greek) *thrónos* or the (Roman) *solium*, the (Greek) *klismós* or the (Roman) *cathedra*, and the faldistory. An early medieval example of a *solium* is the *Cathedra Sancta Petri* (Rome, St. Peter), probably crafted in Metz between 870 and 875. It was not originally intended to be used as a papal throne, but had been commissioned by Emperor Charles the Bald for his own use. In Antiquity, the distinguishing features of the *solium* were its high straight back and armrests, in conjunction with its ceremonial appearance. The armrests are missing in the *Cathedra Sancta Petri*, but its overall appearance is a clear homage to its ancient model: its use as an imperial throne also complies with the ancient concept. Even though there are no other surviving thrones from this period, the existence of a great number of other such ceremonial chairs cannot be ruled out, as indicated by images of rulers in illuminated manuscripts.

In Antiquity, the *cathedra* was specifically a chair for women; in Late Antiquity, it was the characteristic seat of philosophers and rhetors. In this sense, it was also used during the Early and High Middle Ages, as evident in the *cathedra* of Archbishop Maximian of Ravenna

Fig. 1: Cathedra of Archbishop Maximian of Ravenna, wooden structure with ivory plates, Ravenna or Constantinople, mid-6th cent. Ravenna, Museo Arcivescovile

(546–556) (Ravenna, Museo Arcivescovile), dating from the mid–6th cent. (fig. 1). An ancient *cathedra* had a round back and no armrests; its front legs flared slightly outwards. The round back is still evident in the example dating from the 6th cent., but not the outward slanting legs; the armrests are only rudimentary. In that way, this throne represents a combination of *cathedra* and *solium*, appropriate to the office of an (arch)bishop, for whom according to ancient understanding a *cathedra* was the appropriate seat in his role as teacher and pastor, but a *solium* the fitting reflection of his standing as a dignitary of the Church. Simpler examples constructed from posts with wickerwork seats were used in Late Antiquity as seats for older people and for women. Images from the Romanesque period confirm this tradition for the Middle Ages, such as those of the enthroned Mother of God.

The faldistory, the folding chair, is the third type of chair; two examples of this from the Early and High Middle Ages are the *Throne of Dagobert* (Paris, Cabinet des Médailles de la Bibliothèque nationale), a bronze chair, manufactured at the end of the 8th cent., probably in Aachen (fitted with armrests and a backrest in the 12th cent.), and the folding chair in the Benedictine convent of Nonnberg (Salzburg, Benediktinerinnenstift Nonnberg), produced ca. 1242 in the Rhineland or in a workshop in Salzburg (fig. 2). In Roman Antiquity, folding chairs (the so-called *sella curulis*) were used as royal seats; this was later extended to high-

Fig. 2: Faldistorium, wood, bone, leather, Salzburg or Rhineland, 1242 (?) with later additions. Salzburg, Benedictine convent of Nonnberg

The development of the guild system furthered a refinement in the production technology, particularly evident in the construction of the furniture itself: load-bearing sides of items of furniture were constructed as a wooden frame filled with a panel. This not only reduced the weight of the furniture considerably, but also greatly increased the decorative options. Apart from painting, the main decorative element in the late Middle Ages was woodcarvings. While Romanesque furniture generally referred back to ancient patterns, albeit in a new Christian interpretation, it was the contemporary Gothic architecture which served as a model for the decorative motifs of late medieval furniture. Besides decorative vertical patterns, the decorated panels were dominated by tracery and pointed arches. Over time – in line with developments in architecture – the decor became increasingly more detailed. There was thus a departure from the ancient models in decorative styles, production technique and material.

The *cathedra* lost in importance compared with the *solium*. The *solium* was based on the construction principle outlined earlier (box chair), with the seat of the chair doubling as the lid of a storage chest; in this way, this type of furniture was both a seat and a storage unit. The many surviving examples show clearly that this kind of chair was no longer restricted to being used as a throne for ecclesiastical or secular dignitaries, but had become a status symbol in all social classes.

C. RENAISSANCE (1450–1600)

The rediscovery of Antiquity, which started in Italy, also affected the design of furniture. Excavations and the study of ancient texts systematically expanded the knowledge about Antiquity, and this knowledge was disseminated across all of Europe by means of printed texts and publication of pattern books with engravings of ancient images. Late medieval production methods still prevailed, but the artistic embellishment concealed the frame-based construction. One option used was to extend the decoration (carvings) beyond the filling to the frame itself, the other, particularly popular in Italy, to cover the entire body of the piece of furniture with colourful, shaped mouldings. A new technique, though already known in Antiquity, was intarsation, i.e. inlaying various differently-coloured wood cuttings into the base wood. Again starting in Italy, this technique became the standard decoration for representative furniture all over Europe. Some furniture styles were directly modelled on ancient examples, e.g. the chest, shaped like sarcophagi (*cassone a sarcofago*), with the body of the chest richly decorated with carvings, often antiquizing reliefs modelled on Roman stone sarcophagi. The emerging style of trestle tables (*Wangentisch*) was based on ancient marble designs. In Italy, the importance of the *solium* declined in favour of the folding chair; the scissor chair, not in common use during the Middle Ages, can be seen as a rediscovery from Antiquity. The construction of its body is based on several interlocking folding scissors, with the seat

ranking officials, whenever they had to be sitting in their official function. In the Church's partial adoption of the Roman official hierarchy, it also adopted this type of seat as a sign of rank; furthermore, manuscript illuminations point to a similar use in the secular sphere. These chairs complied with their ancient models not only in their actual usage, but also in the materials used, with preference given to ivory and bone in accordance with the ancient Biblical tradition. The decoration of these thrones was, at times, enhanced by Inlaid gems and cameos, metal, enamel or precious stones were used in. As in Antiquity, cushions and textile coverings are loosely fitted. Apart from thrones, hardly any other pieces of early and high medieval furniture have survived in their original forms.

Charlemagne's testament mentions three silver tables and a golden one, presumably ancient heirlooms or spoils, probably in the context of establishing an immediate link with Antiquity during the *renovatio imperii*. Gable-roofed chests from the Romanesque period are reminiscent of Hellenistic wooden sarcophagi as well as Roman stone ones; a similar style used in shrines for the worship of saints and relics points to a common ancient model. Cabinets with gable tops for general storage or as bookcases were also modelled on (late-) antique models.

B. LATE MIDDLE AGES (1250–1500)

With the rise of the cities to political, social, economic and artistic centres and a decrease in mobility within society, furniture gained new importance: first, it had become possible to produce more elaborate artistic styles in furniture; second, furniture became an important tool in the self-representation of the bourgeois elites; and third, more and more different types of furniture were produced.

formed from wooden slats and not from leather or textile coverings as in folding chairs. In this case, ancient
furniture designs had comparatively little influence on
construction and form, but significantly more on decoration which was based on ancient models. In the same
way as in the Gothic period, the decoration of furniture
took its lead from the trends in contemporary architecture. Tracery and pointed arches were replaced by antiquizing arcades and columns. In addition to architectural elements, figurative reliefs became increasingly
dominant. They were based on ancient stories; split into
individual scenes, these images could cover the entire
body of a piece of furniture; there were, however, also
images of individuals based on ancient examples. These
scenes are framed by antiquizing friezes. In the countries north of the Alps, furniture designs developed in
the late Middle Ages were retained longer, as e.g. the
box chair. New designs not based on ancient models
were the *Fassadenschrank* (a cabinet consisting of an
upper and a lower part, a style developed from the late
Middle Ages on and reaching its zenith in the Renaissance), the cabinet (a corpus resting on a trestle, with
internal shelves and compartments to store curiosity
items, documents or jewellery), and the chest of drawers. The latter two designs, in particular, were significant for subsequent developments in Baroque furniture.

D. BAROQUE (1600–1730) AND ROCOCO (1730–1770)

During the Baroque, the interior design of a room as
an entity gained increasing importance; programs of
images of antiquizing subjects or individual scenes were
presented generally in the form of paintings or tapestries. Equivalent scenes on furniture, therefore, became
less prevalent, and references restricted to antiquizing
structural elements (pilasters, half columns, columns)
and ornamental quotes. Decorative techniques became
increasingly refined, and intarsation was replaced by
marquetry, with a whole image composed of differently-coloured wooden veneers placed on the base wood.

Chair and seats continued as indicators of rank and
hierarchy. Firm upholstery, unknown in Antiquity,
played an increasingly important role. On the whole,
furniture design once again moved away from ancient
examples, both in production techniques and form, as
in the materials used. This development which began in
the Baroque reached its zenith in the Rococo: not even
individual ornaments were still based on ancient examples. The 18th cent. saw the development of a whole
range of new furniture types, mainly aimed at the comfort of the user, not only placing the emphasis on his
social position.

E. EARLY CLASSICISM (1760–1790), EMPIRE (1790–1820), BIEDERMEIER (1800–1850)

The excavations in → HERCULANEUM and → POM-
PEII rekindled the interest in Antiquity. As earlier in the
Renaissance, the newly acquired knowledge was disse-
minated in books of engravings, e.g. those by G. B. Pira-

Fig. 3: Pierre-Benoit Marcion (1769–1840),
Secretary desk, mahogany on oak, gilded bronze
fittings, marble top, Paris, ca. 1801

nesi. In consequence, furniture with antiquizing ornaments began to appear in Paris about 1760, seen as a
counter-movement to the Rococo style. However, the
types of furniture and the refined production techniques of the 18th cent. were retained, but ornamental
fittings, marquetries and carvings were now based on
ancient designs, mainly borrowed from architecture.
Straight lines dominated the silhouettes of this style of
furniture, and colourful marquetry pictures gave way to
the extensive use of mahogany. The contemporary
labels for these styles – *goût grec* and *goût étrusque* –
confirm that they were indeed based on the detailed and
scholarly study of ancient forms. This development was
subsequently continued in the Empire style. Whereas in
the period of early Classicism, ornaments were mainly
modelled on Hellenistic examples, the attention now
turned to Roman Antiquity. Corpus-style items of furniture, such as bureaus (fig. 3) and chests of drawers, no
longer had ornamental designs on three sides, as in early
Classicism, but only on one. In addition, the Empire
period saw the recourse to ancient furniture designs,
such as the daybed for the salon or the folding chair.
After 1790, Roman style elements were increasingly
joined by Egyptizing ones. This latter style spread
across all of Europe due to the books of engravings by
C. Percier and P. Fontaine. Similar outline etchings
were published in England by T. Hope.

Whereas after the Revolutionary Wars Napoleon
gave an increased stimulus to the French luxury goods
industry by state-funded orders, the other countries of

continental Europe soon found themselves economically exhausted by the financial burden of these wars. For
that reason, a new and much simpler furniture style
evolved, the *Biedermeier* style. The furniture corpus
was veneered with native woods without elaborate carvings or ornamental fittings. This could almost be seen
as the implementation of J. J. Winckelmann's postulate
of *edle Einfalt und stille Größe* ("noble simplicity and
calm greatness"). As in the Empire style, the design of
chairs and seats took a direct recourse to ancient examples. Based on images from Greek vase paintings, the
klismós style of chair with a curved back, flared legs and
without armrests became widely popular. Architects
such as K. F. Schinkel in Berlin or L. v. Klenze became
important designers of *Biedermeier* furniture. The Restoration after 1815 also brought with it a return of
wealth to the bourgeoisie, and as a result, furniture
design once again became more lavish. Ancient ornaments – lion's masks, sphinxes, antiquizing columns,
carved, painted or made from pressed metals – were in
evidence in addition to style elements borrowed from
the Gothic or the Baroque; in contrast with the Empire
style, *Biedermeier* did not take an exclusive recourse to
Antiquity.

F. Historism
From about 1840, furniture design was increasingly
modelled on historic styles, particularly Gothic, Renaissance and Baroque. Initially, this implied the application of individual style elements to the basic furniture
designs of the *Biedermeier* period. In the beginning,
Antiquity played but a minor role. Only with a more
systematic art-historical study of the different styles by
the craft industry (from ca. 1870) and the demand to be
true to the original down to the last detail, Antiquity,
too, began to exert a stylistic influence (without, however, any compromises on modern comforts, such as upholstery). The function of a room was associated with a
certain style: whereas the salon was the domain of
French royal styles of the Baroque or Rococo, the preferred style for the dining room was that of Neo-Renaissance. Rooms inspired by Antiquity were rarer,
mostly restricted to a study or an office. The Viennese
architect T. Hansen was an important proponent of this
development. However, ancient forms and designs
were mainly adopted indirectly via the Renaissance or
Early Classicism. ;

G. Developments from 1890 to the Present
With its floral, stylized-floral and geometric forms,
the Art Deco movement set itself apart from historical
furniture designs. Around 1900, references to Antiquity
once again gained some prevalence, but here, too,
mainly as a result of the influence of the Classicistic

furniture of a century earlier (Empire, Biedermeier); it
was very rare to find an entire room in antiquizing
decor, as in the villa of F. v. Stuck in Munich. This trend
continued in a limited way into the 1920s, with the
Egyptian elements once again increasing in furniture
design.

The types of chair and stool developed by L. Mies
van der Rohe for the German Pavilion at the Barcelona
World Exhibition of 1929, modelled on ancient folding
chairs, remain the exception. At the opening ceremony
of the exhibition, the Spanish royal couple was to take
their seat in these chairs, thus not only linking the chairs
to Antiquity in their design, but also very clearly in their
usage.

During the 1930s and 1940s, the design of the furniture in representative buildings of state and industry
was based on principles of architectural structure. The
severity of these designs with pilasters and ledges still
hinted at ancient (architectural) models.

Especially In the United States as well as in Scandinavia, new synthetic materials such as plastics, and new
techniques such as the three-dimensional moulding of
wood were discovered in the production of furniture,
opening the way to almost unlimited design options.
The decades after 1945 saw the development of a wide
range of different individual design trends, mostly seeking a style divorced from historical examples and the
past. Only the Post-Modern movement of the 1980s
referred back to ancient (architectural) forms, albeit
sometimes ironically; but this was only one brief phenomenon in a wide range of different developments and
trends.

→ Furniture

1 J. Bahns, Biedermeier-Möbel: Entstehung, Zentren,
Typen, 1979   2 R. G. Blakemore, History of Interior
Design and Furniture, 1997   3 M. Deschamps, Empire,
1994   4 O.v. Falke, H. Schmitz (eds.), Deutsche Möbel
vom Mittelater bis zum Anfang des 19. Jahrhunderts,
1923   5 H. Groth, Neoclassicism in the North, 1990
6 S. Hinz, Innenraum und Möbel, 1976   7 H. Kreisel,
G. Himmelheber, Die Kunst des deutschen Möbels :
Möbel und Vertäfelungen des deutschen Sprachraums von
den Anfängen bis zum Jugendstil, 1968, 1973   8 D.
Ledoux-Lebard, Les ébénistes du XIXe siècle, 1984
9 H. Ottomeyer, Zopf- und Biedermeiermöbel, 1991
10 P. Thornton, The Italian Renaissance Interior, 1991
11 F. Windisch-Graetz, Möbel Europas, 1982/1983
12 H. Whitehead, The French Interior in the Eighteenth
Century, 1992
Additional Bibliography R. Pressler, R. Straub,
Biedermeier Furniture, 1996; J. Morley, The History of
Furniture: Twenty-Five Centuries of Style and Design in
the Western Tradition, 1999   MARTIN EBERLE

G

Galenism Whereas between about AD 500 and 1100, Galen was almost unknown in Western Europe, the orthodox medicine of the Byzantine and Muslim world was substantially based on his concepts that were increasingly systemized and put into a logical order, with a particular focus on their theoretical content. Galen's monotheism and teleology commended his works also to an environment dominated by religion. From the 12th cent. on, Galenism reached Western Europe in an Arabic guise where it soon gained dominance in the medical schools of the newly founded universities. The rediscovery of Galen's writings themselves, albeit in translation, gave a new impetus to medical thinking in the early 14th cent.; among its effects were a revival of dissection and anatomy. The medical Humanists of the late 15th and early 16th cent. called for a return to Galen's texts in their original Greek. The *Aldina*, the *editio princeps* of his works dating from 1525, and the subsequent flood of newer Latin translations allowed access to long-forgotten works, particularly in the fields of anatomy and philosophy, as e.g. *De placitis Hippocratis et Platonis* and *Protreptikós*. In this way, physicians were able to preserve the authority of their medical doctrines and at the same time surpass their medieval predecessors. However, Galen's rediscovery also uncovered inconsistencies and errors within his work, not all of which could be explained away as errors by translators or copyists. In his *De humani corporis fabrica* (1543), Andreas Vesalius (1514–1564), who pursued an anatomical research programme in accordance with Galen's philosophy, concluded that Galen's results may contain errors, because his dissections had been limited to animals. William Harvey (1578–1657) employed both Galenic and Aristotelian concepts in his *Physiology* in order to prove the circular movement of the the the blood contrary to Galen (1628). By about 1700, Galenic theorems were restricted to just hygiene and semiotics. However, here, too, his categories, as e.g. the temperaments, were reinterpreted in very different ways. By about 1870, Galenism had degenerated into the epitome of everything perceived as bad in Classical medicine: a theory breaking with observation, a crude teleology, and a greater inclination towards excesses of logic rather than sickbed medicine.

→ Galen of Pergamum

→ ARABIC MEDICINE

1 O. TEMKIN, Galenism. Rise and Decline of a Medical Philosophy, 1973

ADDITIONAL BIBLIOGRAPHY V. NUTTON, The Unknown Galen, 2002   VIVIAN NUTTON

Games
A. GAME BOOKS FROM THE FIFTEENTH TO THE EIGHTEENTH CENTURY B. EDUCATIONAL GAMES FROM THE SIXTEENTH TO THE NINETEENTH CENTURY C. THE ANCIENT WORLD AS DISCOVERY ZONE: PARLOUR GAMES IN THE SECOND HALF OF THE TWENTIETH CENTURY

A. GAME BOOKS FROM THE FIFTEENTH TO THE EIGHTEENTH CENTURY
References to Antiquity were less concerned with the purpose of a game or its subject matter. Rather, Classical authorities served to legitimize the very concept of games and game-playing, to explain their rationale, origins and forms. Thus Pythagoras acts as the *Protos heuretes* of *Rhythmomachia*, the mathematical battle game of the Middle Ages; Dido and Aeneas are drawn on as the cultural model for courtly games in early modern times and Mercury is claimed as the inventor of the game of cards, for instance, by the *Poeta laureatus* Johannes Praetorius in the commentary to his game *Antiquiteten Karthe* of 1662. In the 18th cent., the most popular book of games in German-speaking areas also followed this tradition. Four editions appeared in Leipzig (1719–1755) under the title *Palamedes redivivus. Nothwendiger Unterricht, wie heutiges Tages gebräuchliche Spiele (...) nach künstlicher Wissenschaft recht und wohl zu spielen* ('Palamedes redivivus. Essential instruction, providing expert knowledge on how to play today's common games correctly and skilfully').

B. EDUCATIONAL GAMES FROM THE SIXTEENTH TO THE NINETEENTH CENTURY
In accordance with contemporary educational criteria, knowledge of the ancient world was vitally important in didactic games from the 16th to the 19th cent. The fields of law, history, mythology and literature were thematized in equal measure. In this respect, two types of games were especially important: card games including those similar to quartet games (the players have to collect sets of four cards of the same rank) and the so-called goose game, a board race game played with dice that was extremely popular in Early Modern Europe and continued to be far into the 19th cent.

The Franciscan monk Thomas Murner (1475–1537) who, with his *Chartiludium logicae* and the *Chartiludium institutae summariae*, sought to teach the basic concepts of logic and Justinian Law within the university curriculum, was the first to use playing cards for educational purposes. This principle is also found in the *Orbis sensualium pictus* of John Amos Comenius (1592–1670), and achieved its full flowering in 17th cent. France. Four card games that gained special significance were devised in 1644 by Jean Desmarets for the formal education of the young prince Louis XIV. In particular, the games *Les reines renommées* ('Famous Queens') and *Les Metamorphoses* were designed to convey knowledge of ancient history and mythology. These cards engrossed the whole of Europe and quickly found successors such as the *Antiquiteten Karthe* of Praetorius, in which Egyptian, Biblical, Greek and Roman subjects were depicted, or the *Vorstellung Für-trefflicher Maenner* ('Gallery of Famous Men'), publis-hed by Johann Stridbeck in Augsburg in 1685. Each card featured a medallion with the portrait of a figure from Greek or Roman Antiquity and gave a brief bio-graphical description. The purpose of the *Troisième jeu des cartes historiques* ('Third Game of Historical Cards') was to teach the history of Greece, and it was an obligatory part of the game to come up with the requi-red historical knowledge in order to win the respective trick. The genre of the history-based card game, par-ticularly in the shape of the historical quartet, was pres-ent well into the early 20th cent.

Classical motifs in the game of tarot and in other conventional card games are a special case. The prevail-ing Classicistic taste, more than any educational inten-tion, may account for the frequency of Classical, espe-cially mythological depictions. Paralleling the enthusi-asm for all things Classical and Greek that developed in the late 1770s, a marked increase – dominance even – of mythological subjects occurred in this area of bourgeois entertainment and game culture.

The spiral course of the goose game – made up, as a rule, of 63 squares – helps to visualize and graphically depict valuable and interesting information. From the 17th to the 19th cent., one theme in particular – alongs-ide religious and moral edification, military matters and geography – was history; its chronological course could conveniently be likened to the progression along the game's series of squares. The history-themed versions of the game included titles such as *Nouveau jeu d'his-toire universelle* ('New Game of World History') (Paris 1745), and *Tableau chronologique de l'histoire univer-selle en forme de jeu* ('Chronological Chart of World History in Game Formation') (Paris 1767), but we also find editions devoted specifically to ancient history, e.g. *L'histoire romaine depuis la fondation de Rome jusqu'à Constantin* ('Roman History from the Foundation of Rome to the Time of Constantine'), with a sequel con-tinuing to the time of Charlemagne (1773). A game published in Vienna around 1820 with the title *Die Weltgeschichte – Belehrendes und unterhaltendes Gesellschaftsspiel für die Jugend* ('World history – Edu-cational and Entertaining Parlour Game for Young People') could be cited as a German example of this type: it offered a detailed periodization of world history and presented problematic turning points in world his-tory rather pointedly as typical goose game hazard squares. Classical literature and its didactically valu-able themes were also taken up: in 1812 by the *Jeu des Fables d'Ésope* ('Game of Aesop's Fables'), and in 1814 by the *Jeu historique des avantures de Télémaque* ('His-torical Game of the Adventures of Telemachus'). Howe-ver, the change in cultural and social premises during the second half of the 19th cent. made itself felt on the game-board as well. Increasingly, themes from geo-graphy and journeys of discovery as well as technology (railways) and contemporary history were replacing Classical subjects on the illustrated advertisements of the game manufacturers.

C. The Ancient World as Discovery Zone: Parlour Games in the Second Half of the Twentieth Century

The boom in board games and parlour games of the late 1950s and early 1960s specifically recognized adults as a target group but rarely relied on Classical allusions. For one thing, this had to do with the fact that early examples of this new board game generation pres-ented abstract game mechanics in an abstract way and secondly, where thematic accoutrements were added reference was made mainly to the areas of commerce and sport. The exquisitely crafted game by the Hausser company, *Römer gegen Karthager* ('Romans vs Car-thaginians') from the mid–1960s was an isolated attempt to evoke Classical Antiquity. The game, which has as its theme the Battle of the Metaurus (207 BC), was part of a large project that was never realized: to present historic battles in game form. The tendency since the late 1970s and, above all, during the early 1980s to elaborate the parlour game around a theme and to allow the players to immerse themselves in an environment of discovery signaled a qualitative change in the games scene. Since the end of the 1980s, after initial domination of the market by the thriller, adven-ture and fantasy genres, historical subjects have been on the rise. Egypt, Greece and Rome are now frequently providing themes alongside the Middle Ages and early modern scenarios. An important starting point is marked here by *Civilization*, the complex game of de-velopment about ancient civilizations, which first appeared in the United States and Britain and came to Germany in 1988. Significant examples of this thematic reorientation are *Forum Romanum*, originally concei-ved by its author Wolfgang Kramer as a mayoral game, or the chariot race by Wolfgang Riedesser, published in 1989 as *Ave Caesar*, which, as the layout of the race track reveals, has its origins in a Formula One racing game. Historical themes, and particularly themes from Classical Antiquity, have since been a regular feature of the games scene, a fact illustrated by the presence of ca. 150 Antiquity-related titles on the German games mar-ket, from *Das große Troja-Spielbuch* (Robert Wolf, 1986) via *Ben Hur* (Jean du Poël, 1992) and the histori-cal scenarios to Klaus Teubner's *Die Siedler von Catan* (Settlers of Catan), culminating in Reiner Knizia's *Kampf der Gladiatoren* (Clash of the Gladiators) of 2002. Interdependencies with contemporary discussi-ons on Classical matters can occasionally be observed. It is no coincidence, therefore, that the presence of → Troy in the (German) media in 2001 was also reflec-ted in the titles of several games. A special case is *Troia*:

developed by Thomas Fackler, it was created in the context of the exhibition *Troia – Traum und Wirklichkeit* ('Troy – Dream and Reality') and presents the archaeological finds in a hands-on format.

Paralleling the development of the games market outlined above, there has been since the 1980s a growing interest in reviving ancient games for the modern market. Collections of games from the ancient world have been produced particularly as part of the range of didactic material offered by museums (→ ARCHAEOLOGICAL PARK). In addition to that, however, reproductions and new versions of the *Royal Game of Ur* and of the Egyptian game of *Senet*, as well the occasional edition of the Roman tactical game *Ludus Latrunculorum* and the fore-runner of backgammon *Duodecim Scripta* also appeared on the regular games market.

Since the 1970s, video, computer, and Internet-based games have greatly increased in popularity. While some are based on older board games, most rely on new content. Many of the most popular, including the "Prince of Persia," "Civilization," and "Legion Arena," have themes from Classical Antiquity and the ancient Near East. While a few of these games have varying degrees of historical accuracy, the vast majority of them either deal with alternate possible futures (what would the present be like if Rome had not fallen?), or combine elements of Antiquity with themes from fantasy or science fiction. In the final analysis, apart from the examples named in the preceding paragraph, the transfer of cultural knowledge about Antiquity does not play a major role in the current games market; the presence of ancient themes is above all a consequence of the post-modern appeal of the exotic-historic scenario.

1 PH. ARIÈS, Les jeux à la Renaissance, 1982   2 A. BORST, Das mittelalterliche Zahlenkampfspiel, 1986   3 H. D'ALLEMAGNE, Le noble jeu de l'oie en France, de 1640 à 1950, 1950   4 W. ENDREI, Spiele und Unterhaltung im alten Europa, 1988   5 J. FRITZ, Spiele als Spiegel ihrer Zeit, 1992   6 A. GIRARD, C. QUÊTEL, L'Histoire de France racontée par le jeu de l'oie, 1982   7 E. GLONEGGER, Das Spiele-Buch, 1988 (Das große Spiele-Buch, 1999)   8 D. HOFFMANN, Kultur- und Kunstgeschichte der Spielkarte, 1995   9 D. ILMER, N. GÄDECKE, Rhythmomachia, 1987   10 J.-M. LHÔTE, Histoire des jeux de société, 1994   11 J. MEHL, Les jeux au royaume de France du XIIIᵉ au debut du XVIᵉ siècle, 1990   12 H. J. R. MURRAY, A History of Board-Games other than Chess, 1952   13 D. PARLETT, A History of Card Games, 1990   14 R. REICHARDT, Das Revolutionsspiel von 1791, 1989   15 A. RIECHE, Römische Kinder- und Gesellschaftsspiele, 1984   16 Id., So spielten die alten Römer, 1991   17 K. WEBERPALS, Lehrkarten aus fünf Jahrhunderten, in: Spielbox 3, 1992, 26–29   18 Id., Die Religionen und das Kartenspiel. Die Götter Griechenlands und Roms, in: Spielbox 6, 1993, 42–46   19 C. ZANGS, H. HOLLÄNDER (eds.), Mit Glück und Verstand. Zur Kunst- und Kulturgeschichte der Brett- und Kartenspiele. 15.–17. Jahrhundert, 1994   20 M. ZOLLINGER, Bibliographie der Spielbücher des 15.–18. Jahrhunderts, vol. 1, 1996.

ADDITIONAL BIBLIOGRAPHY D. S. PARLETT, The Oxford History of Board Games, 1999; S. SACKSON, The Book of Classic Board Games, 1991.

URLS 21 www.uni-marburg.de/spiele-archiv (Deutsches Spielearchiv Marburg) 22 www.moz.ac.at/user/spiel/spielforschung (Institut für Spielforschung und Spielpädagogik, Universität Mozarteum Salzburg)   23 www.boardgamesstudies.org (International Society for Board Game Studies)

HELMUT KRASSER

Gandhara art see → PAKISTAN; GANDHARA ART

Gardens see → PARK

Gates/City Gates
A. ICONOGRAPHIC AND SYMBOLIC RECEPTION IN THE MIDDLE AGES   B. ARCHITECTURAL RECEPTION IN THE MIDDLE AGES   C. RENAISSANCE, BAROQUE   D. CLASSICISM, HISTORICISM

A. ICONOGRAPHIC AND SYMBOLIC RECEPTION IN THE MIDDLE AGES

Apart from their archaeological and architectural reception, town gates throughout the Middle Ages and beyond represented a symbolic and iconographic formula that was widespread as a sovereignty motif. In this way, gate iconography was an image of the imperial idea of Rome and the Christian concept of Jerusalem [8; 22]. Gates were also considered to be architectural representations of various towns. Beginning in Antiquity, this shorthand appeared on images of sovereignty such as coins, and later on coats-of-arms and seals. The most obvious examples of this type of gate image are the bulla of Charlemagne with the ideological inscription *Renovatio Romanorum Imperii* andthe golden bulla of Emperor Louis IV, reused by Emperor Sigismund in 1433 [8; 20]. Use of ancient gate monuments on town seals to represent the *communitas* by communal institutions was infrequent (Ravenna, Fano, Rimini) [9; 16] (fig. 1). More frequently, ancient gates were treated as monuments modelled on → TRIUMPHAL ARCHES when they were deliberately displayed on medieval fortifications (Verona, Fano, Nîmes, Rimini, Spello, Spoleto, Perugia) [13]. By contrast, the treatment of the Porta Nigra in Trier may be taken as an example of a building's loss of significance because neither St. Simeon as hermit nor the church dedicated to him inside the gate building (ca. 1040–1060) refer to this structure [14] (→ TRIER).

B. ARCHITECTURAL RECEPTION IN THE MIDDLE AGES

For medieval gates, the reception of the architecture of ancient city gates was not uniform. An outstanding example of an architectural *interpretatio christiana* is the gate of the monastery of Lorsch on the Rhine (767–774), whose basic form is derived from Roman municipal gates [18]. A whole series of High and Late Medieval twin-tower gates in Central Europe was apparently derived from Rome's Late Imperial two-tower gates with one or two arches and rows of windows. Note-

Fig. 1: Impression of a seal of the town of Fano with a picture of the ancient Porta Augustea (13th cent.)

worthy are the city gates of the late Staufen period in the Rhineland (Cologne, Aachen) [17], the Porta Soprana in Genoa (1155–1159) [11] as well as numerous Dutch, Flemish, Westphalian and Lower Saxon twin-tower gates of the 13th and 14th cents. (Gent, Bruges, Dortmund, Goslar), the Lübeck Holstentor with its Roman inscription formula (1467–1479) and the Danzig Krantor (1442) [21]. However, the bridge gate of Emperor Frederick II in Capua (c. 1234–1239) shows how unspecific the medieval reception of Antiquity could be. Due to partial cloaking with an artistic bossage and an extensive sculpture programme, it seems entirely non-Classical yet has a classicizing effect [27].

C. RENAISSANCE, BAROQUE

The growing tendency towards monumental gate architecture with artistic design during the 15th cent. took the richly decorated city gates of the Augustan and Tiberian period as models [9]. It peaked with the statement by L. B. Alberti that town gates were to be cloaked like triumphal arches (8,6 in: [1]). Alberti's identification of gates with triumphal arches, only rarely taken up by theoreticians (Serlio, Scamozzi) [4; 5], resulted, in the building practice of the 15th–18th cents., set against the background of bastion-style fortifications, to the establishment of town gates as works of construction in their own right [23]. The most telling examples, which are found overwhelmingly in Italy, link defence and civil representational architecture (Perugia: Porta S. Pietro by A. di Duccio, 1470 ff.; Naples: Porta Capuana by G. da Maiano, 1487 ff.; fig. 2). The extensive refortification work in most European towns beginning in the 16th cent. resulted in the construction of numerous new town gates whose debt to Antiquity is for the most part limited to → COLUMNIATION, triumphal motif and bossed facades and is primarily observable in Italy. The bossed facade as a

defence motif was erroneously derived from the Porta Maggiore in Rome which was not an ancient town gate [7]. Despite their military function, the buildings were understood as monuments and thus, illustrate the unspecific character of the reception of Antiquity (e.g., Padua: Porta Savonarola, Porta San Giovanni by G. M. Falconetto, 1528 ff.; Verona: Porta Nuova, Porta Palio by M. Samicheli 1533 ff.; Genoa: Porta Molo by G. G. Alessi, completed in 1553; Rome: Porta S. Giovanni by A. da Sangallo the Younger (1543–1546) [23].

The Italian Renaissance gates were models for all of Europe. The *Säulenbücher* ('books of columns') of the 16th and 17th cents. supported the spread of the triumphal bossed gate [12]. In the process Baroque architecture created gates, still remote from Antiquity, sometimes monumental, which can only be understood as triumphal arches, such as the Parisian Porte Saint Denis, built in 1671–1673 by F. Blondel.

D. CLASSICISM, HISTORICISM

C.-N. Ledoux found his way, in terms of his own understanding, to a 'more original' classicizing gate form in the Parisian toll gates (1784–1789). These buildings, which were for most part destroyed during the 19th cent., combined Classical architectural patterns with elementary forms such as circle, ball, cube and pyramid [25]. E.-L. Boullée pushed the town gate project to the limit with his megalomaniac designs and their theoretical reflection [2]. Nevertheless, these projects experienced a revival in the framework of the *Doric Revival* (→ GREEK REVIVAL) that was functionally modified by the defortifying of European towns (F. Gilly's 1799 design for a city gate; N. A. de Salins de Montfort's 1807 gate designs for Frankfurt; C. F. Hansen's 1808 design for an arsenal gate; G. Rossi's 1810 design for a toll gate) [19].

The reappropriation of Greek art resulted in an expanded architectural canon and more intense reception of the propylaea of the Acropolis (→ ATHENS). Popularized through the reproductions of J. Stuart and N. Revett [6], the propylaea with gable fronts and lateral wings were the model for C. G. Langhans in Berlin (Brandenburg Gate, 1788–1791), K. F. Weinbrenner in Karlsruhe (Ettlingen Gate, 1797), J. H. Jussow in Kassel (*Entwurf für Wilhelmshöher Tor* ('Design for the Wilhelmshöhe Gate'), 1803) and W. P. Stassow in Moscow (Petersburg Gate, 1833–1839). On the other hand, L. v. Klenze cites the Athenian model in Munich in the form of a wall at the Königsplatz (1854–1862) and its use in illustrating Greek architectural styles (→ ATHENS I, fig. 4) [26]. In historical train station architecture of the 19th cent., Euston station (1835–1839) in London constitutes an example of the reception of the Athenian propylaea.

By way of comparison, Roman gates, already reinterpreted as arcades by J. N. L. Durand in his influential treatise [3. vol. 2], became exemplary. Subsequently, train station facades with an arched entrance (two to five arches) and window rows flanked by towers were

Fig. 2: Perugia, Porta San Pietro,
Agostino di Duccio (1475)

created in Leipzig (Sächsisch-Bayerisch train station, 1842–1845), Berlin (Hamburg train station, 1845–1847), Stockholm (main train station, 1871) or, independently of Durand, the Liverpool Edge Hill Station (1830) in the style of a pylon gate with triumphal arches – the earliest train station that returned to this type of historical architecture. [10].

SOURCES   1 L. B. ALBERTI, De re aedificatoria, 1485 (Eng.: On the Art of Building in Ten Books, 1988)   2 E. L. BOULÉE, Architektur. Abhandlungen über die Kunst (1793 manuscript), B. WYSS (ed.), 1987   3 J. N. L. DURAND, Précis de leçons d'architecture données à l'École royale polytechnique, Paris 1802 (Engl. D. BRITT (trans.), Précis of the Lectures on Architecture, 2000)   4 S. SERLIO, Il libro dell'architettura, Venice 1584 (Engl. A. E. SANTANIELLO (ed.), The Book of Architecture, 1970, 1611)   5 V. SCAMOZZI, L'idea dell'architettura universale, Venice 1615 (Engl. The Mirror of Architecture, ⁴1693)   6 J. STUART, N. REVETT, Antiquities of Athens, vol. 2, London 1762

LITERATURE   7 J. ACKERMANN, The Tuscan/Rustic Order, in: Journal of the Society of Architectural Historians 42, 1983, 15–34   8 C. BOZZO DUFOUR, La porta urbana nel Medioevo: porta soprana di Sant'Andrea in Genova, immagine di una città, 1989   9 G. BRANDS, Architekturrezeption der Hochrenaissance am Beispiel römischer Stadttore, in: R. HARPRATH, H. WREDE (eds.), Antikenzeichnung und Antikenstudium in Renaissance und Frühbarock, 1989, 81–110   10 R. DAUBER, Stadtpalais, Landhaus und Stadttor, in: Architectura 1990, 77–90   11 E. FORSSMANN, Dorisch, Jonisch, Korinthisch. Studien über den Gebrauch der Säulenordnungen in den Architektur des 16.–18. Jahrhunderts, 1984   12 M. GREENHALGH, The Survival of Roman Antiquities in the Middle Ages, 1989   13 F.-J. HEYEN, Das Stift St. Simeon in Trier (= Germania Sacra 41,9), 2002   14 H. KÄHLER, Die römischen Torburgen in der frühen Kaiserzeit, in: JDAI 57, 1942, 1–108   15 Id., Die Porta Aurea in Ravenna, in: Römische Mitteilungen 50, 1935, 172–244   16 U. MAINZER, Stadttore im Rheinland, 1973   17 K. MERKEL, Die Antikenrezeption der sogenannten Lorscher Torhalle, in: Kunst in Hessen und am Mittelrhein, 32/33, 1992/93, 23–42   18 W. NERDINGER, K. J. PHILIPP,

HANS-PETER SCHWARZ (eds.), Revolutionsarchitektur: ein Aspekt der europäischen Architektur um 1800, 1990   19 Kunst und Kultur der Karolingerzeit: Karl der Grosse und Papst Leo III. in: C. STIEGEMANN, M. WEMHOFF (eds.), Paderborn (Exhibition catalogue), 1999   20 W. SCHADENDORF, Das Holstentor zu Lübeck: der Bau und seine Geschichte, 1978   21 N. SCHNEIDER, Civitas: Studien zur Stadttopik und zu den Prinzipien der Architekturdarstellung im frühen Mittelalter, 1972   22 ST. SCHWEIZER, Zwischen Repräsentation und Funktion: die Stadttore der Renaissance in Italien, 2002   23 E. B. SMITH, Architectural Symbolism of Imperial Rome and the Middle Ages, 1956   24 H. TROST, Norddeutsche Stadttore zwischen Elbe und Oder, 1959   25 A. VIDLER, C.-N. Ledoux: Architecture and Social Reform at the End of the Ancien Régime, 1990   26 U. WESTFEHLING, Der Triumphbogen im 19. und 20. Jahrhundert, 1977   27 C. A. WILLEMSEN, Kaiser Friedrichs II. Triumphtor zu Capua. Ein Denkmal hohenstaufischer Kunst in Süditalien, 1953.   STEFAN SCHWEIZER

Gem see → GEM CUTTING

Gem Cutting
A. RESEARCH HISTORY   B. THE CURRENT SITUATION

A. RESEARCH HISTORY
1. FROM THE MIDDLE AGES TO THE LATE RENAISSANCE   2. THE 17TH AND EARLY 18TH CENTURIES   3. THE AGE OF ENLIGHTENMENT   4. THE 19TH CENTURY   5. THE 20TH CENTURY

1. FROM THE MIDDLE AGES TO THE LATE RENAISSANCE
During the early Middle Ages interest in cut gems had declined rapidly. Colourful gemstones were indeed used to decorate objects, but generally without figurative motifs. In the Carolingian and the Hohenstaufen

Fig. 1: Pier Leone Ghezzi,
The antiquary Ficoroni
discussing gems, drawing.
*with permission of Albertina,
Vienna*

periods (9th cent.; 12th/13th cents.), the cutting of cameos was once again taken up [2; 11. 2. fn. 3, 375. fn. 2 und 6, 380. fn. 30]. In the Middle Ages, gems and cameos from Antiquity were held in high regard because of their quality and their age; despite their pagan motifs, some famous pieces were used to decorate reliquaries and crosses in churches [11. 2. fn. 2, 380. fn. 30] (Shrine of the Three Kings, Cologne Cathedral; Lotharkreuz, Aachen Cathedral; → RULER, FIG. 5). Because of Byzantine (→ BYZANTIUM) influence as well as, for example, Pliny's book on precious stones (Plin. HN 37), the focus was on the variety of the stones themselves, especially those which were associated with all kinds of significance; these met with renewed interest as a result of alchemist teachings (→ NATURAL SCIENCES VII. CHEMISTRY/ALCHEMY) and were dealt with in medieval lapidaries (*lapidarium* – e.g. Marbod, Albertus Magnus, 12th/13th cent.).

With the Renaissance came an increased interest in ancient gems, which were considered to be the best-preserved ancient works of art because of the hardness and preciousness of the gemstones. Glyptic art soon became sought after for the treasure chambers of royal courts all over Europe; alongside ancient works, the preserved gem collections also contained many contemporary pieces. The renewed interest in the ancient gems also resulted in a revival of the craft of gem-cutting: cf. Vasari's lists of contemporary gem cutters (1550) who attempted to engrave gemstones with *all' antica* images [11. 3. fn. 4, 388 ff., 440 f.]. Workshops for gem cutters were set up once again (cf. wood engraving in Jost Ammann's *Ständebuch* ('Book of Trades'), 1568 [11. 3; 13. IX]). With the advent of letterpress printing, copperplate engravings of 'ancient' gems began to be reproduced, on the basis of which it was possible to discuss the gems 'scientifically'; examples of this are the engravings by Enea Vico [13. 38]. In his *Imagines et*

elogia virorum illustrium (1570), Fulvio Orsini, the erudite *padre* of the *iconographia antica*, published portraits of ancient gems, and the famous *Dactyliotheca* (1601) by the Dutchman Abraham Gorlaeus as a collection record is also evidence of early scholarly ambitions [8. 68 f.; 11. 3f.; 13. 30 f.].

2. THE 17TH AND EARLY 18TH CENTURIES

By the beginning of the 17th cent., interest in ancient gem cutting had almost assumed feverish proportions. Not just royalty, but also wealthy burghers such as the Nuremburg trader P. Praun [7. 66 f.] and artists such as P. P. Rubens collected gems for their cabinets [11. 5f.; 13. 19. fn. 57]. Considerable collections of magnificently decorated gem-books offered commentaries, drawn from Antiquity, on rings and precious stones: Lungus (1615), Kirchmann (1623), Kornemann (1654) [11. 4f.; 13. 37 f.], later La Chausse, Stephanoni, Canini, Beger, Bellori, de Wilde, Cheron, Gronovius, Agostini, Maffei, *et. al.* [13. 5ff., 30 ff.]. Gems were collected in accordance with contemporary fashion, and lavish publications demonstrated both erudition and refinement (fig. 1: Ficoroni in discussion, on the table 4 volumes by Maffei). In the middle of the 17th cent., the 'scholars' J. Chiflet and J. Macarius ignited the debate over magical gems, a popular genre of the 2nd- 4th cents., with their treatises, which were published in a single volume and illustrated with copperplate engravings [8. 73 ff.; 11. 4; 13. 32f]. Chiflet's simplified copperplate engravings, in particular, were used by contemporary gem cutters as patterns to add motifs to one's collection or in order to circulate new amulets produced in the style of the ancient tradition [7. 348 ff.; 8. 73 ff.]. As part of the blossoming art trade, the Venetian Antonio Capello offered for sale a collection predominantly based on magical gems, which was acquired for Kassel in 1700 by Landgrave Karl I of Hesse [vol. 1, III. 179 f.; 12. 1ff.], even before Capello's *Pro-*

Fig. 2: Winckelmann's 'Tydeus', Etruscean scarab made of Carnelian, 5th cent. BC Museum of Greek and Roman Antiquities, Staatliche Museen zu Berlin, © *Bildarchiv Preußischer Kulturbesitz*

Fig. 4: Tablet from Monaldini, *Novus Thesaurus ...*, ca. 1797

Fig. 3: Winckelmann's 'Stosch'scher Stein', Etruscean scarab made of Carnelian, 5th cent. BC Museum of Greek and Roman Antiquities, Staatliche Museen zu Berlin, © *Bildarchiv Preußischer Kulturbesitz*

domus iconicus, with its promotionally effective frontispiece and prospectus-like picture plates came out in 1702. Such was the topicality of magical gems that in his famous encyclopaedia *L'antiquité expliquée* (1719), B. Montfaucon later reprinted both Chiflet's copperplate engravings as well as Capello's 'sales catalogue' [13. 33, 42 f.].

3. THE AGE OF ENLIGHTENMENT

In the belief that gems were the best-preserved works of art from Antiquity, there was a drive to subject them to scientific investigation. As it was hardly possible to ascertain the meaning of the stones and, in particular, the secrets of the gnostic 'Abraxas' stones (magical gems), attention turned to the aesthetic forms. The earliest scholarly treatise on ancient gems with comparatively faithful copperplate engravings was published in 1724: the *Gemmae antiquae caelatae* by Baron Philipp von Stosch, a prime example of the rationalism of the Enlightenment (figs. 2, 3). Winckelmann, for

whom Stosch was both a promoter and a model, took up Stosch's scholarly approach and continued it in his catalogue of the Stosch gem collection: *Description des pierres gravées du feu Baron de Stosch* (1760), a book that brought its author the *laudeat* of the Academy of Cortona, membership in the artists' academy of St. Luca in Rome, as well as honors from the Society of Antiquaries in London and helped him to a successful career [13. 77]. However, despite subsequent attempts to produce illustrated plates, Winckelmann's work, written in academic French, remained unillustrated [13. 181 ff.]. Schlichtegroll's (1775) ultimate failure with this reproduction technique resulted finally in the rejection of copperplate engravings [8. 81 ff.; 13. 145 ff.]. The glorification of images of ancient gems, conveyed on 'copper', gave way to skepticism regarding the faithfulness of their representation, especially as the imprint could not be checked because of the general unavailability of the originals. In the meantime, imaginative creations had appeared on the market, such as Monaldini's plates (fig. 4) and the allegories of the Duc d'Orleans, detracting from the authentic reception. As part of attempts to make images of gems more accessible three-dimensionally by making casts in wax, sealing wax or plaster, the plaster technique developed by D. Lippert in Dresden proved to be the most successful [7. 82 ff.; 13. 137ff]. After 1755, Lippert's casts introduced the age of the gem cast collections, which gradually eclipsed that of the copperplate engraving. The 'plaster casts' in the drawers of boxes in book form came to be valued even more than the originals themselves, and they were used as collections for study. The factory-like production of series of casts created an opening for the images of gems in general education, and indeed, made them into teaching aids in Prussian schools. Professor Klotz's well-intentioned book *Über den Nutzen und Gebrauch der geschnittenen Steine und ihrer Abdrücke* ('On the Benefits and Use of Cut Gems and their Castings', 1768) had this popularization as its goal, but met with extremely fierce criticism from Lessing, whose harsh review entered world literature as a classic example of damning critique and as an appeal for strict adherence to the demands of scholarship [13. 164 ff.]. Winckelmann's works, published at about the same time, signaled the birth of art history as an academic discipline based on stylistic arguments. Subsequent periods were dominated by a deep skepticism, deepened further by the problem of forgeries, which neither copperplate engravings nor gem cast collections could overcome [13. 186 ff.].

4. THE 19TH CENTURY

Even if framed boxes of gem-casts could be found on the walls of bourgeois parlours in the Biedermeier period and even edible sugar gem-pastes were all the rage, the actual study of gems was in decline. Rescue attempts such as the writings of Gurlitt and Roth, published at the turn of the 19th century and still advertising gems (1798, 1805) [8. 65, 82 f.; 13. 168 ff., 184 f.], remained unsuccessful, as did newly produced gem-cast collections, the largest of which was the plaster cast corpus by Tommaso Cades (1831–1868) in 78 folding boxes, initiated by Eduard Gerhard after the establishment of the German Archaeological Institute (1831; DAI – → DEUTSCHES ARCHÄOLOGISCHES INSTITUT) [13. 194 f.]. It was only after 1871 that the archaeologist Heinrich Brunn turned his attention back to the "very best sources from Antiquity" in his study of the signatures of master craftsmen found on gems [13. 199 ff.]. In England, C. W. King. with a few poor drawings in the text of his book *The Gnostics and their Remains* (1887), drew attention to the hidden messages within the genre of magical gems, but was unable to interpret the content of the images and inscriptions. In his monumental three-volume work *Die antiken Gemmen* ('Ancient Gems'), the Munich archaeologist A. Furtwängler – a pupil of Brunn [13. 203] – gave King's book a scathing review [13. 213], but just as did the former, he appealed to posterity to search for a broader understanding of Antiquity in these small and as yet insufficiently researched works of art. The appeals of the two scholars did not remain unheeded, as was to become evident half a century later.

5. THE 20TH CENTURY

After the two World Wars, the shift in focus of Classical Studies to a comprehensive study of Antiquity, comprising not only art, but all available documentary sources, led to a revival of interest in gems. The German papyrologist K. Preisendanz presented his work on *Papyri Graecae Magicae* immediately after the Second World War, and it soon after also became available in annotated translations [8; 10]. With the aid of the papyrus texts, it was now possible for the first time to decipher the images, inscriptions and magic formulas of the long known, but previously misinterpreted magical gems, and shed light on their syncretistic character. On this foundation, A. Delatte and Ph. Derchain then published the large Paris collection of magical gems for the first time from the perspective of Egyptologists [5]; it became evident that this genre of gems could only be dealt with by interdisciplinary research. However, the reproduction of the pieces as rather lifeless plaster casts which had to be viewed as mirror images continued to impede the deciphering of the magical inscriptions. In his essay on the J. Jantzen gem collection, the Hamburg archaeologist P. Zazoff pioneered the use of enlarged photographs of the originals in recto and verso; because of this innovative approach, the DAI commissioned him with the organization and publication of the AGD catalogues [Vol.1,. I.7 f.]. This series of catalogues was published between 1968 and 1975 – to date the only publication of a country's entire stock of gems. There was now a complete record of the gems in black and white photographs in recto and verso, with text commentary following a standard system. With photographs of the originals, supplemented by images of plaster casts and a clear systematic approach in the text, publication of Minoan and Mycenaean seals (CMS) was begun, and, in the end, numerous gem collections in Europe and the US were made public in the form of technically appropriate museum catalogues, monographs or essays for all areas of glyptic art. On the basis of a 'history of thought', emanating from the US, the subject of → MAGIC ARTS and its associated documents became a greater focus of scholarly interest, to the extent that towards the end of the 20th cent., a separate field of research was devoted to magical gems in particular [9; 15]; also, the world's largest collection, that of the British Museum, unpublished and hidden for centuries, was published in form of a 'Catalogue raisonné' [7].

B. THE CURRENT SITUATION

Parallel to research on gems, (re-)activated by technical innovations such as macro-photography, colour films, slides, video films and digital picture processing, interest on the part of the general public as well in gems and gem-cutting increased during the decades of economic growth in the second half of the 20th cent. In addition, globalization, an openness to ancient cultures, the boom in esoterism as well as a fashionable penchant for gold and jewellery brought gems and gem-cutting back into public view. The trade in surrogates, crudely worked gems and, in particular, shell cameos flourished. Whereas in the 1960s and 1970s, there were still some master gem-cutters such as R. Hahn, M. Seitz and I. Linskens [11. 396], the craft has almost died out by the present day. Occasionally, engravers of precious stones in Idar-Oberstein incorporate the content of ancient legends and pictorial motifs for their work in precious stones, frequently produced as cameos with laser technology, while intaglio cuts are almost completely restricted to family crests or seals. Ancient gems are sold in art or numismatic auctions and are generally sought after by collectors. Magical amulet gems, integrated into sophisticated gold creations, are treasured as rings, bracelets or necklaces, not only as works of art and precious jewellery, but also because of their original function as amulets or talismans [6. 18 f.].

After long years of neglect, it is only now that with the use of all available technical innovations, gems are being shown 'in their true light'; alongside the improvements in reproduction technology, more and more frequently, the originals themselves can be viewed in special exhibitions [6; 16]. In this way, through the medium of museums, can interest in ancient gems be rekindled, and current research into gems also be made accessible to a wider public. For academic research itself, the high quality and the increased quantity of currently published materials opens a wide range of new perspectives. Ancient gems await further clarification in questions of dating, workshop of origin, and iconography. Magical gems originating from the multicultural environment of the ancient metropolis of Alexandria and its surroundings open up new areas of research for inquiries in social history, the history of thought or religious history. In the end, the scholarly study of cut gems and the lives of gem-cutters in the modern period is still a culturally historical *desideratum* [8. 71 ff.; 11. 392 f.].

→ Gem cutting

1 AGD.   2 R. Becksmann et al. (eds.), Beiträge zur Kunst des Mittelalters. Festschrift für H. Wentzel, 1975   3 H. D. Betz (ed.), The Greek Magical Papyri in Translation. Including the Demotic Spells, 1986   4 C. Bonner, Studies in Magical Amulets, chiefly Graeco-Egyptian, 1950   5 A. Delatte, Ph. Derchain, Les intailles magiques Gréco-Égyptiennes, Bibliothèque Nationale, Cabinet des Médailles, 1964   6 S. Michel (ed), 'Bunte Steine – Dunkle Bilder: Magische Gemmen' (Exhibition catalogue), 2001   7 Id., Die magischen Gemmen im Britischen Museum, vols. I–II, P. Zazoff, H. Zazoff (eds.), 2001   8 Id., Nürnberg und die Glyptik. Steinschneider, Sammler und die Gemmenkunde im 17. und 18. Jahrhundert in: Nürnberger Beilagen zur Archäologie 16, 1999/2000, 65–91   9 H. Philipp, Mira et Magica. Gemmen im Ägyptischen Museum der Staatlichen Museen Preußischer Kulturbesitz. Berlin-Charlottenburg, 1986   10 K. Preisendanz, Papyri Graecae Magicae, II and III, 1941; Index (unpublished, 1944); I and II, A. Henrichs (ed.), ²1973/74   11 Zazoff, AG   12 Id., Gemmen in Kassel, in: AA 1965, 1–115   13 Zazoff, GuG   14 Id., Zur Geschichte des Stosch'schen Steines, in: AA, 1974, 466–484   15 E. Zwierlein-Diehl, Magische Amulette und andere Gemmen des Instituts für Altertumskunde der Universität zu Köln, 1992   16 Id. et al. (eds.), Siegel und Abdruck. Antike Gemmen in Bonn. Sonderausstellung Akademisches Kunstmuseum – Antikensammlung der Universität Bonn, 2002

Additional Bibliography S. Michel, Die Magischen Gemmen. Zu Bildern und Zauberformeln auf geschnittenen Steinen der Antike und Neuzeit, Studien aus dem Warburg-Haus, vol. 7, 2004   SIMONE MICHEL

Gender Studies

A. Definition, Concept and Conceptual History B. Gender Studies and Classical Studies

A. Definition, Concept and Conceptual History

Gender Studies (GS) is an interdisciplinary research approach to the role of sex or gender in culture, society and science. This discipline, which is particularly flourishing in Classical Studies within the Anglo-American sphere, differs from other forms of historical or literary gender research in its combination of methods developed in women's studies with those of post-structuralism.

In social and cultural sciences, the English term *gender* (originally 'grammatical gender') has been used since the 1970s in the sense of socially defined ('constructed') femaleness and (initially) maleness as opposed to sex, i.e. the biological gender. The concept has its roots in → CULTURAL ANTHROPOLOGY and ethnology, both highlighting the cultural diversity of male and female roles; an essay by Gayle Rubin [78] was particularly influential in its adoption by historians and literary specialists. In respect to Greco-Roman Antiquity, the call for gender to become one of the basic concepts in historical studies (summarized: [81; 62]) was first answered by Women's Studies (WS) at American universities. Using gender as an analytical category emphasizes the fact that neither femaleness nor maleness are biologically-determined, transhistorical constants, even if they are presented as innate and 'natural' in the studied societies and texts.

The distinction between sex and gender (in analogy to nature and culture) only gained academic acceptability with the establishment of WS as an academic discipline; from the late 1980s onwards, though, it has been critically discussed in conjunction with identity and subject autonomy, especially under the influence of post-structuralism and postmodern feminism. Since then, research has frequently included the body and sexuality as aspects of gender in its historical variability (gender: 'Konstruktion des Natürlichen als Text der Kultur' ("construct of the natural as a text of a culture") [40. 121]), and has revealed connections to other social structures.

B. Gender Studies and Classical Studies
1. Women's Studies

1. Women's Studies
1.1 Development 1.2 Trends 2. Changes in
Perspective 3. Michel Foucault's *Histoire de
la sexualité* 4. Current Approaches and
Topics 4.1 Men's Studies
4.2. (Homo)Sexualities Research 4.3. The
Body 5. Conclusion and Outlook

1.1 Development
The critical questioning of the naturally-predeter-
mined character of gender roles, and thus male dominance as well as male power of definition, led also to
questioning of the androcentric outlook of both history
and literature. The introduction of gender perspectives
revolutionized the study of literature, initially within
universities in the United States, and particularly within
the area of WS, which had become established both
institutionally and as a research field in the United
States starting in the 1970s. The questions which GS
and WS raised quickly affected the study of Classical
Antiquity as well [57]; the journals *Arethusa* and *Helios*
still retain their position as discussion forums for these
new approaches. Part of the reason why Classical Studies in the United States was so much more responsive
to the approaches and topics of WS, and later GS, than
their European (particularly German) counterparts also
lies in the political-academic foundation of both feminism and gender research [98; 99], as well as in the
integration of Classics as part of the Liberal Arts curriculum.

Trailblazers of WS in Antiquity were two special editions of *Arethusa* (6. 1, 1973 and 11, 1978; in book
form [66]), and particularly Sarah Pomeroy's monograph on women in Antiquity (1975, today a classic
[67]). In this work, she discussed the subject within the
limits of the discipline, without any potentially offensive emphasis on her feminist standpoint, thus paving
the way for a rapid new development (critical:
[92.11 f.]). Even prior to this, 'Women in Antiquity' had
already been the subject of research, for example, as a
complement to a universal or political history, but lak-
king any critical analysis of the 'female nature' (which
was assumed to be universal) and generally without
critically questioning the source material (summarized
in [3]) For examples of the lasting influence of central
19th-cent. topics, e.g., the 'oriental' seclusion of Athenian women, see [92; 93; 44. 35 f.].

Initially, the newly established WS focused mainly
on decoding the 'image of women' in ancient texts, with
the purpose of using the literary discourse in order to
discover the social reality. While this procedure seems
rather naive at times, from the current perspective, it is
explicable, however, when one considers the scarcity of
historical evidence on the history of women at that
time. This criticism of the images of women revealed
two aspects: on the one hand, the misogynist leanings in

the Graeco-Roman concept of women and the corresponding rhetorical conventions regarding their alterity, and, on the other, the difficulties of balancing literary constructs (such as the centrality of female characters in Greek tragedies) with the historical evidence.
These point to a fundamental dilemma of the correlation between representation and reality [11; 24; pointedly, 16]. In consequence, literary images were soon
criticized as nothing but 'male fantasies' that did not
provide any evidence on the reality of women in Antiquity [83; 3].

The next step was to look for evidence of the living
conditions of women in Antiquity beyond any male
constructs. New sources were utilized in order to fill the
substantial gaps in knowledge (such as vase paintings,
inscriptions, gravestones, papyri and artifacts). Medical, legal and religious documents [46; 29; 51], as well
as documents on everyday life [54] were among the
sources made accessible through the compilations of
documentary evidence in English translation, and their
scientific interpretation. This shed light even on women
who had never before crossed the perceptive boundary,
such as slaves and freedwomen. These sources are, at
least to some degree, less rhetorically alienated, or filtered, than literary images; however, one should compare with [30; 47]. The fundamental problem of representation and referentiality remained despite this effort.
In order to combat this, ancient women as subjects,
rather than objects of male representation, were the
focus of J. M. Snyder's compilation of the surviving
texts of 21 ancient women writers [84].

One aim of this compensatory programme of including the neglected knowledge about women was to
register the presence of women within the history of
ancient cultures; another was the generation of a separate history of women in Antiquity [22], as opposed to
an (only apparently) universal male history. These new
findings and approaches also laid important foundations for GS. Historical surveys (still largely without a
critical analysis of gender) have been published in many
languages, such as [12; 60; 79a; 80; 13]; alongside them
are publications on 'Women in Antiquity' (predominantly essay collections) with theoretical approaches
based on gender [1; 38; 4; 48. updated introduction:
14–25]. More recent collections of primary sources on
women's history with a sound knowledge of scientific
methods are [72; 23; 87].

Beginning in the 1980s and occurring in parallel to
the collection of raw gender data, texts of the classical
canon were analysed in respect of their gender perspective, and were read afresh with an approach sharpened
by theory ('Resisting Reader'). Thus it was asked whether the works of Ovid, Catullus or Euripides revealed a
'feminist' perspective, or rather violence against women
and misogyny [73]. The historical contextualization of
gender aspects provides a specific research framework
for such conundrums.

Classical archaeology became involved with WS and
GS much later than philology and ancient history had

done [8]; however, most of the 'Women in Antiquity' volumes, even the earliest ones, contain some articles on the interpretation of archaeological evidence. The 1990s saw numerous new publications in the fields of archaeology and history of art, particularly on the history of sexuality and that of the body (see below: 4).

1.2 TRENDS

In the light of the questions posed by literary and historical hermeneutics, the study of women in Antiquity and GS attempted to utilize a variety of analytical methods, in particular those employed in the cultural history, in structuralism [22], anthropology [56] (particularly in Europe), as well as in post-structuralism.

The main threads in earlier WS were, on the one hand, the topic of female oppression, and on the other, the (rarely verbalized) assumption of a common female identity: a transhistorical connection between the lives of all women, marked by experiences of repression in patriarchal society, or by female generativity. The female history of want – the lack of political and economical rights, their lack of (access to) education, the lack of women's right to have their voices heard, and their inability to possess their own subjectivity – was soon joined by a reconstruction of women's conditions of life and women's experiences. These constructions deliberately omitted heteronomy as a category and avoided any fixation on male domains [92]. Female spheres and their significance in ancient societies (particularly in connection with symbolic systems) were studied from the perspective of anthropology, cultural history or structuralism. The results highlighted a symmetry rather than an asymmetry in ancient gender relationships, such as male and female social spheres in the ancient city, or men's and women's functions as exercised during rituals [55; 92; 41]. Social history thus appeared as a history of structures, with sexuality as one of the categories structuring society; however, the analysis was not particularly focused on the gender aspects. For a detailed overview of the topic in the study of ancient women, see [79].

2. CHANGES IN PERSPECTIVE

Around 1990, there was a noticeable shift in the emphasis of WS towards GS; this should be considered an expansion rather than a change of paradigms.

Using gender as a research category was perceived to have the advantage of being relational, that is: (1) it incorporates 'maleness' as a socio-cultural construct to a greater degree than the earlier feminist approaches or WS, and clarifies the interconnections within the ever reciprocal gender relations; and (2) it focuses on correlations of gender patterns with other social structures, such as class, ethnicity, age, religion etc. The treatment of gender in ancient sources is linked to political, religious, literary, philosophical, moral, juridical and other thought patterns and is understood as representing additional, cultural rule systems. The division between 'male' and 'female' becomes evident as a principle of classification of social practices and discourses. Because of this integrative potential, GS proved more accessible to those Classical scholars who perceived WS as too particular or too biased. Calls were soon issued, warning of the danger of a retreat from a committed WS [73. 286], but WS retained its important critical position within GS (and also within the generally less theoretical gender history).

GS involves, like WS, various trends within this field of discussion [70; 43]. GS and WS generally "do not assume a fixed notion of gender, but investigate how such a notion is generated within its respective contexts ..., which importance is attached to it and what effect it has on the distribution of political power, social structures and the production of knowledge, culture and art" ('[setzen] keinen festen Begriff von Geschlecht voraus, sondern untersuchen, wie sich ein solcher Begriff in verschiedenen Zusammenhängen jeweils herstellt ..., welche Bed. ihm beigemessen wird und welche Auswirkungen er auf die Verteilung der polit. Macht, die sozialen Strukturen und die Produktion von Wissen, Kultur und Kunst hat') [6. 1].

Amongst the various trends within GS, the focus in this article will be on Anglo-American GS, since it has more or less come to dominate Anglo-American Classical studies. Also, it integrates various theoretical approaches, predominant among them those employed in feminist WS, post-structuralism and *New Historicism*. Under the influence of M. Foucault's works, scholars of GS take an interest in constructs of gender, sexuality, and the body, analysing gender as both a product and a model of social differentiation, especially within power structures. Studies published in the last decade lay claim to a high theoretical level (their academic vocabulary takes some getting used to and is often spurned by critics as mere jargon). Here, too, one sees that Foucault has alienated Antiquity from traditional Classical Studies by opening it up to postmodernism. In their epistemological interest and deconstructive tendencies, these forms of GS are essentially different from gender history, which maintains its historical-empirical orientation and focuses on the reconstruction and interpretation of the realities of life in Antiquity.

3. MICHEL FOUCAULT'S *Histoire de la sexualité*

M. Foucault's *Histoire de la sexualité*, whose 2nd and 3rd vols. (English editions 1985, 1986 [25]) deal with Classical Antiquity, triggered an explosive and sustained development of GS within the field of Classical Studies and opened the study of ancient history of sexuality, particularly Greek history, to a wider interdisciplinary interest in much the same way as WS had previously done regarding the history of women in Antiquity. Foucault gave a particular impetus to (homo-)sexual research. His criticism of the western models of knowledge, power and identity lead to the historical qualification of concepts of sexuality; modern concepts of sexuality were demonstrated to be products of 19th-cent. discursive and scientific practices and were not transferable to Antiquity. Because each period constructs its very own sexual categories, it is also possible to deconstruct them in scientific analysis. Sexuality and the body emerge as variables and as domains, where power manifests itself. The thesis that the sexual order in Antiquity had its roots in the contrast of sexual activity/dominance (maleness) and passivity/heteronomy (femaleness or effeminization) had already been advocated by K. J. Dover [20] and P. Veyne [90]. Foucault focuses thus on questions of male self-discipline. (On Foucault's interpretation of Antiquity, see [35] and the introduction to [63; 59; 53].) His works ran parallel to arguments by feminist historians and philosophers [75; 53], particularly in regard to the connections between language and power, or sexuality and power, to cite only two examples.

The critical analysis of Foucault's approach by Classical historians raised three main concerns (overview: introduction to [53]): the extreme constructivism and/or the radical relativism of his theories on history and sexuality [18; 75]; the lack of knowledge of Antiquity and the uncritical treatment of ancient texts, or his biased selection of sources [15; 32]; the neglect of women (and WS) and the resulting renewed suppression of the female subject and female desire [75]. Numerous studies in the 1990s tried to provide better scientific, philological, archaeological, philosophical etc. foundations for Foucault's framework, and thus to improve its differentiation and to further its development. Additionally, attempts were made to lessen his androcentric bias and to integrate his concepts into approaches of WS [95; 36]. All of this scholarship employed methods of literary theory and comparative cultural anthropology [49; 59; 33; 21].

4. Current Approaches and Topics

In addition to continuing scholarship in WS, current subdivisions within GS, which demonstrate overlapping subject matters, include the new Men's Studies (MS) as well as Sexualities and Homosexualities Studies (pluralized to emphasise their range and variety) [58. 13]. Note that there is a particular distinction between the Greek and the Roman spheres.

4.1 Men's Studies

Starting in the 1970s, patterns of maleness in Antiquity had essentially been taken into account by WS, due primarily to the nature of the available sources, in which, with a few exceptions, men define their own selves. Recent publications on Men's Studies (MS) function on the deliberate assumption that being a man is just as much a product of culture and just as politically charged as being a woman [26; 27]. Since the 1990s, there has been an increase in research into the male body; male sexuality in Antiquity, especially homosexuality, (see below 4.2); male codified behaviour, including homosociality and public display [31; 2]; as well as individual aspects such as fatherhood. Studies have frequently revealed the hierarchical claims as well as the instabilities of male identity [33], which find their expression in the sexual devaluation of alterity, with respect to class, nation, gender, political orientation etc. Within the Roman sphere, the dissociation from male pathic sexuality culminated in invectives against the

cinaedus, defined by M. Gleason as 'a sexual deviant, in its most specific sense referring to males who prefer to play a passive role in intercourse with other men' [31] and ultimately characterized as a negative anti-subject [94]. On the development of MS of Antiquity, see the introduction to [26].

Recent studies take account of the feminist criticism that MS of Antiquity should also involve women (and WS), based on the argument that, alongside male internal differentiations and matters of homosexuality (the initial focus of research after Foucault), an understanding of both genders can only be achieved in their relationship to each other [33; 86].

4.2 (Homo)Sexualities Research

Sexuality and the body are the main subjects in the current GS of Classical Antiquity. Foucault's sensational thesis that the modern dichotomy between the categories 'heterosexual' and 'homosexual' did not exist in Greek and Roman Antiquity (and thus can not be regarded as a universal or essential constant) – and must be replaced by the fundamental contrast between penetrating and being penetrated – has been widely discussed and academically implemented [91; 39; 35; 94; 63.3f.]. (On the controversy between 'constructivists' and 'essentialists' and an overview of research into ancient sexuality after Foucault, see: [33. 6–13; 53. 22–33].) Whereas ancient sources hold a wealth of evidence regarding male homosexuality, female homosexuality has to be reconstructed from sparse and generally hostile sources [7; 34; 85; 65].

At the same time, various aspects of ancient sexuality have been researched in individual studies, frequently in contributions to anthologies, drawing upon textual and visual sources [95; 36; 49; 38; 33; 42]. Methods used in feminist studies of pornography [74] and film theory [8; 76] have also been applied. Some of the most recent studies attempt to reconstruct female sexuality on the basis of visual evidence found on pottery [64], or, in the case of the Roman woman poet Sulpicia [45], or Sappho [85], by examining textual cues. The monopoly and inevitability of the gaze of the male observer (reader, interpreter) are being questioned: thus, arguments have been made that ancient images were also seen by women, for example, Aphrodite of Knidos, as demonstrated by [43. 198f.]. Ignoring women in the interpretation equates to misunderstandings of the gender system, as demonstrated by J. Clarke's interpretation of the sexual images in the Pompeii baths, which could be seen by both men and women [14]. A. Stähli's text appears noteworthy among the monographs dealing with ancient erotic art in a gender context [88].

4.3 The Body

Since the late 1980s, a wealth of Classical-historical studies, from a wide range of perspectives, such as philosophy, medicine [17], literature, politics, and particularly archaeology have been devoted to the *gendered body* and its reception in Post-Antiquity [61; 69; 96]. In the visual arts, where the symbolic gender order found its most obvious expression, the sociological setting and the context of both male and female observers has gained widespread consideration, particularly when interpreting aspects of nakedness and sexuality [42; 89; 14; 88; 97. introduction].

5. CONCLUSION AND OUTLOOK

Gender means neither just 'woman', nor just 'man' alone; the isolated view based only on biological sexual identity is of little historical or academic value. The fundamental assumptions of GS are: the double perspective and interdependence of maleness and femaleness; their historical internal differentiation; the contextualization within a wider framework of contemporary sources. The simple identification of gender ideologies by means of a close reading of an ancient text can only provide the preparatory work. Ideally, gender research should also take into account the interpreter's own historical-cultural background. GS's hermeneutic approaches, which are based on relationality and contextualization, can also avoid some of the problems associated with WS: a wide range of sources provide fragments of the communicative construct of ancient gender reality as transmitted in language, images and signs. However, the relationship between representation and reality remains as yet unclarified.

In recent years, GS has evolved from a controversial special discipline to a more widely accepted scientific approach, especially within Anglo-American Classical Studies. Among the providers of up-to-date bibliographies are the websites of *Diotima* [19] and the *Bryn Mawr Classical Review* [5], as well as [98; 99]. Within the context of German Classical Studies, GS, and especially WS, tend to focus currently on historical, historical-anthropological [93a] or text-analytical aspects [76a]. American GS and WS, however, have been met with a lack of interest rather than open rejection, and have hardly been embraced or academically debated within Classics [6. 347–357]. Some exceptions are worth mentioning: Th. Späth's analysis of the text is supplemented with a detailed theoretical discussion [86]; E. Meyer-Zwiffelhoger's study on the connections between Roman gender discourse and the political-social order [59]; A. Stähli's interpretation of Dionysian visual language as a cultural text [88]; and H.-P. Obermayer's detailed literary study and discourse analysis [63]. It remains to be seen whether the approaches of WS and GS will find greater acceptance within the German-speaking world: their delay in adopting WS and GS may offer German-speaking Classicists the opportunity to benefit by allowing them to profit from the Anglo-American head start in theory.

In spite of the many individual studies, there are still gaps that remain to be filled, such as the Post-Classical reception of ancient gender representations in textual and visual arts. Another important project yet to be undertaken is the adoption and integration of gender perspectives into the universal, literary, artistic, political, and philosophical histories of Antiquity.

GS has neither a uniform methodology nor a uniform ideology. The characteristic form of publication is an interdisciplinary anthology by various authors on a range of subjects and with a variety of approaches, sometimes with reference to a larger historical or geographical area (Mesopotamia, Egypt, Christian Antiquity and Byzantium) [97; 11; 1; 61; 42]. This pluralistic approach permits different, even divergent perspectives. The metaphor 'construction site' [36. 4f.] to describe the new discipline is not only a successful pun, but it also emphasizes the extent to which GS is still 'under construction' or in flux.

→ Gender roles; → Homosexuality; → Paederasty; → Sexuality; → Woman

→ MATRIARCHY

1 L. ARCHER, S. FISCHLER, M. WYKE (eds.), Women in Ancient Societies: 'An Illusion of the Night', 1994 2 K. BASSI, Acting Like Men: Gender, Drama, and Nostalgia in Ancient Greece, 1999 3 J. BLOK, Sexual Asymmetry. A Historiographical Essay, in: J. BLOK, P. MASON (eds.), Sexual Asymmetry. Studies in Ancient Society, 1987, 1–57 4 S. BLUNDELL, Women in Ancient Greece, 1995 5 BMCR: http://ccat.sas.upenn.edu/bmcr/ 6 C. VON BRAUN, I. STEPHAN (eds.), Gender Studien. Eine Einführung, ²2006 7 B. BROOTEN, Love between Women: Early Christian Responses to Female Homoeroticism, 1996 8 S. BROWN, 'Ways of Seeing' Women in Antiquity: An Introduction to Feminism in Classical Archeology and Ancient Art History, in: [49. 12–42] 9 P. BROWN, The Body and Society. Men, Women and Sexual Renunciation in Early Christianity, 1988 10 H. BUSSMANN, R. HOF (eds.), Genus. Zur Geschlechterdifferenz in den Kulturwissenschaften, ²2005 11 A. CAMERON, A. KUHRT (eds.), Images of Women in Antiquity, 1983; ²1993 12 E. CANTARELLA, L'ambiguo malanno. Condizione e immagine della donna nell'antichità greca e romana, 1981 (Engl.: Pandora's Daughters: the Role and Status of Women in Greek and Roman Antiquity, 1987) 13 G. CLARK, Women in the Ancient World, 1989, ²1993 14 J. CLARKE, Looking at Lovemaking. Constructions of Sexuality in Roman Art, 100 B.C. to A. D. 250, 1998, ²2001 15 D. COHEN, R. SALLER, Foucault on Sexuality in Greco-Roman Antiquity, in: J. GOLDSTEIN (ed.), Foucault and the Writing of History, 1994, 35–59 16 P. CULHAM, Ten Years after Pomeroy: Studies of the Image and Reality of Women in Antiquity, in: Helios 13, 1986, 9–30 17 L. DEAN-JONES, Women's Bodies in Classical Greek Science, 1994 18 W. DETEL, Macht, Moral, Wissen. Foucault und die klassische Antike, 1998 (Engl: D. WIGG-WOLF (trans.), Foucault and Classical Antiquity: Power, Ethics, and Knowledge, 2005 19 Diotima: http://www.stoa.org/diotima/ 20 K. J. DOVER, Greek Homosexuality, 1978, ²1989 21 P. DuBOIS, Sowing the Body: Psychoanalysis and Ancient Representations of Women, 1988 22 G. DUBY, M. PERROT (eds.), Histoire des femmes en occident, vol. 1: L'Antiquité, 1991 (Engl.: A History of Women in the West, vol. 1: From Ancient Goddesses to Christian Saints, 1992) 23 E. FANTHAM, H. FOLEY, N. KAMPEN, S. POMEROY, H. SHAPIRO, Women in the Classical World: Image and Text, 1994, ²1995 24 H. FOLEY (ed.), Reflections of Women in Antiquity, 1981 25 M. FOUCAULT, Histoire de la sexualité (Engl.: The History of Sexuality, vol 1: An Introduction, 1978); vol. 2: L'usage des plaisirs, 1984 (Engl.: The Use of

Pleasure, 1985); vol. 3: Le souci de soi, 1984 (Engl.: The Care of the Self, 1986) 26 L. FOXHALL, J. SALMON (eds.), Thinking Men: Masculinity and Its Self-Representation in the Classical Tradition, 1998 27 Id. (ed.), When Men Were Men: Masculinity, Power, and Identity in Classical Antiquity, 1998 28 V. FRENCH, What Is Central for the Study of Women in Antiquity?, in: Helios 17.2, 1990, 213–219 29 J. GARDNER, Women in Roman Law and Society, 1986 30 Id., Gender-Role Assumptions in Roman Law, in: Echos du Monde Classique/Classical Views 39 (N. S. 14), 1995, 377–400 31 M. GLEASON, Making Men: Sophists and Self-Presentation in Ancient Rome, 1995 32 S. GOLDHILL, Foucault's Virginity: Ancient Erotic Fiction and the History of Sexuality, 1995 33 J. HALLETT, M. SKINNER (eds.), Roman Sexualities, 1997 34 Id. Female Homoeroticism and the Denial of Roman Reality in Latin Literature, in: [33. 255–273] 35 D. HALPERIN, One Hundred Years of Homosexuality: and Other Essays on Greek Love, 1990 36 Id., J. WINKLER, F. ZEITLIN (eds.), Before Sexuality. The Construction of Erotic Experience in the Greek World, 1990 37 K. HAUSEN, H. WUNDER (eds.), Frauengeschichte – Geschlechtergeschichte, 1992 38 R. HAWLEY, B. LEVICK (eds.), Women in Antiquity. New Assessments, 1995 39 L. HERMANS, Bewust van andere lusten: Homoseksualiteit in het Romeinse keizerrijk, 1995 40 R. HOF, Die Grammatik der Geschlechter. Gender als Analysekategorie in der Literaturwissenschaft, 1995 41 S. HUMPHRIES, The Family, Women and Death. Comparative Studies, 1983 42 N. KAMPEN, B. BERGMANN (eds.), Sexuality in Ancient Art: Near East, Egypt, Greece, and Italy, 1996 43 Id, Gender Studies, in: A. BORBEIN, T. HÖLSCHER, P. ZANKER (eds.), Klassische Archäologie. Eine Einführung, 2000, 189–204 44 M. A. KATZ, Ideology and the 'Status of Women' in Ancient Greece, in: [38. 21–43] 45 A. KEITH, Tandem Venit Amor: A Roman Woman Speaks of Love, in: [33. 295–310] 46 E. KEULS, The Reign of the Phallus. Sexual Politics in Ancient Athens, 1985, ²1993 47 H. KING, Hippocrates' Woman: Reading the Female Body in Ancient Greece, 1998 48 D. KLEINER, S. MATHESON (eds.), I, Claudia: Women in Ancient Rome, vol. 1, 1996; I, Claudia II: Women in Roman Art and Society, vol. 2, 2000 49 A. KOLOSKI-OSTROW, C. LYONS (eds.), Naked Truths: Women, Sexuality and Gender in Classical Art and Archaeology, 1997 49a D. KONSTAN, M. NUSSBAUM (eds.), Sexuality in Greek and Roman Society (special issue: Differences 2.1), 1990 50 D. KONSTAN, (ed.), Documenting Gender: Women and Men in Non-Literary Classical Texts (special issue: Helios 19.1, 2), 1992 51 R. KRAEMER, Maenads, Martyrs, Matrons, Monastics: A Sourcebook on Women's Religions in the Greco-Roman World, 1988 52 T. LAQUEUR, Making Sex: Body and Gender from the Greeks to Freud, 1990, ²1992 53 D. LARMOUR, P. MILLER, C. PLATTER (eds.), Rethinking Sexuality: Foucault and Classical Antiquity, 1998 54 M. LEFKOWITZ, M. FANT (eds.), Women's Life in Greece and Rome: A Source Book in Translation, 1982, ³2005 55 N. LORAUX, Les enfants d'Athéna. Idées athéniennes sur la citoyenneté et la division des sexes, 1981 (Engl.: The Children of Athena: Athenian Ideas about Citizenship and the Division between the Sexes, 1993) 56 J. MARTIN, R. ZOEPFFEL (eds.), Aufgaben, Rollen und Räume von Mann und Frau, 1989 57 B. MCMANUS, Classics and Feminism: Gendering the Classics, 1997 58 K. HAUSEN, H. MEDICK, A.-C. TREPP (eds.), Geschlechtergeschichte und allgemeine Geschichte: Herausforderungen und Perspek-

tiven, 1998 59 E. MEYER-ZWIFFELHOFFER, Im Zeichen des Phallus: Die Ordnung des Geschlechtslebens im antiken Rom, 1995 60 C. MOSSÉ, La femme dans la Grèce antique, 1983 61 D. MONTSERRAT (ed.), Changing Bodies, Changing Meanings: Studies on the Human Body in Antiquity, 1997 62 H. NAGL-DOCEKAL, Für eine geschlechtergeschichtliche Perspektivierung der Historiographiegeschichte, in: W. KÜTTLER, J. RÜSEN, E. SCHULIN (eds.), Geschichtsdiskurs, vol. 1, 1993, 233–256 63 H.-P. OBERMAYER, Martial und der Diskurs über männliche "Homosexualität" in der Literatur der frühen Kaiserzeit, 1998 64 R. OSBORNE, Desiring Women on Athenian Pottery, in: [42. 65–80] 65 T. PASSMAN, Out of the Closet and into the Field: Matriculture, the Lesbian Perspective and Feminist Classics, in: [71. 181–208] 66 J. PERADOTTO, J. SULLIVAN (eds.), Women in the Ancient World: The Arethusa Papers, 1984 67 S. POMEROY, Goddesses, Whores, Wives and Slaves: Women in Classical Antiquity, 1975 68 Id., Women's History and Ancient History, 1991 69 J. PORTER (ed.), Constructions of the Classical Body, 1999 70 N. RABINOWITZ, Introduction, in: [71. 1–20] 71 Id., A. RICHLIN (eds.), Feminist Theory and the Classics, 1993 72 E. REEDER (ed.), Pandora: Women in Classical Greece, 1995 73 A. RICHLIN, The Ethnographer's Dilemma and the Dream of a Lost Golden Age, in: [71. 272–303] 74 Id. (ed.), Pornography and Representation in Greece and Rome, 1991 75 Id., Zeus and Metis: Foucault, Feminism, Classics, in: Helios 18.2, 1991, 160–180 76 D. ROBIN, Film Theory and the Gendered Voice in Seneca, in: [71. 102–124] 76a R. ROLLINGER, C. ULF (eds.), Geschlechterrollen und Frauenbild in der Perspektive antiker Autoren, 2000 77 A. ROUSSELLE, Porneia. de la maîtrise du corps à la privation sensorielle: IIe-IVe siècles de l'ère chrétienne, 1983 (English: Porneia: On Desire and the Body in Antiquity, 1988) 78 G. RUBIN, The Traffic in Women: Notes on the "Political Economy" of Sex, in: R. REITER (ed.), Toward an Anthropology of Women, 1975, 157–210 79 T. SCHEER, Forschungen über die Frau in der Antike. Ziele, Methoden, Perspektiven, in: Gymnasium 107, 2000, 143–172 79a W. SCHULLER, Frauen in der griechischen Geschichte, 1985 80 Id., Frauen in der römischen Geschichte, 1987 81 J. SCOTT, Gender. A Useful Category of Historical Analysis, in: Ibid, Gender and the Politics of History, 1988, 28–50 82 M. SKINNER, Classical Studies vs. Women's Studies: Duo moi ta noêmata, in: Helios 12.1, 1985, 3–16 83 Id. (ed.), Rescuing Creusa: New Methodological Approaches to Women in Antiquity (special issue: Helios 13.2), 1987 84 J. SNYDER, The Woman and the Lyre: Women Writers in Classical Greece and Rome, 1989 85 Id, Lesbian Desire in the Lyrics of Sappho, 1997 86 T. SPÄTH, Männlichkeit und Weiblichkeit bei Tacitus. Zur Konstruktion der Geschlechter in der römischen Kaiserzeit, 1994 87 Id., B. WAGNER-HASEL (eds.), Frauenwelten in der Antike. Geschlechterordnung und weibliche Lebenspraxis: mit 162 Quellentexten und Bildquellen, 2000 88 A. STÄHLI, Die Verweigerung der Lüste: Erotische Gruppen in der antiken Plastik, 1999 89 A. STEWART, Art, Desire and the Body in Ancient Greece, 1997 90 P. VEYNE, La famille et l'amour sous le Haut-Empire romain, in: Annales: Économies, Sociétés, Civilations 33, 1978, 35–63 91 Id., L'homosexualité à Rome, in: P. ARIÈS, A. BÉJIN (eds.), Sexualités occidentales, 1982, 41–51 (Engl.: Homosexuality in Ancient Rome, in: Western Sexuality: Practice and Precept in Past and Present Time, 1985, 26–

35) 92 B. WAGNER-HASEL, Das Private wird politisch. Die Perspektive »Geschlecht« in der Altertumswissenschaft, in: U. BECHER, J. RÜSEN (eds.), Weiblichkeit in geschichtlicher Perspektive: Fallstudien und Reflexionen zu Grundproblemen der historischen Frauenforschung, 1988, 11–50 93 Id., Frauenleben in orientalischer Abgeschlossenheit? Zur Geschichte und Nutzanwendung eines Topos, in: Der altsprachliche Unterricht 32.2, 1989, 18–29 93a K. WALDNER, Geburt und Hochzeit des Kriegers. Geschlechterdifferenz und Initiation in Mythos und Ritual der griechischen Polis, 2000 94 C. WILLIAMS, Roman Homosexuality: Ideologies of Masculinity in Classical Antiquity, 1999 95 J. WINKLER, The Constraints of Desire. The Anthropology of Sex and Gender in Ancient Greece, 1990 96 M. WYKE (ed.), Parchments of Gender: Deciphering the Bodies of Antiquity, 1998 97 Id. (ed.), Gender and the Body in Mediterranean Antiquity (special issue: Gender and History 9.3), 1997 98 Women's Classical Caucus: http://www.wccaucus.org/ 99 Lesbian and Gay Classical Caucus: http://www.lambdacc.org/
BRIGITTE EGGER

Geneva Declaration. One of the first official acts of the World Medical Association, founded in 1947, was drafting the Geneva Declaration (GD), a contemporary reformulation of the Hippocratic Oath; further improvements were made in 1968. The so-called abortion paragraph and the ban on surgery made way for more modern general provisions to respect human life from the moment of conception and always to use medical knowledge in harmony with the laws of humanity. It retained mention of a doctor's obligation to confidentiality and the status of the medical profession, however all religious overtones from the Hippocratic Oath were removed. The GD is supported by an international code of medical ethics which is meant to apply both in times of peace and of war.

→ HIPPOCRATIC OATH

1 C. BURNS, Legacies in Ethics and Medicine, 1977 2 P. CARRICK, Medical Ethics in Antiquity: Philosophical Perspectives on Abortion and Euthanasia, 1985.
VIVIAN NUTTON

Genre, Genre Theory
A. ANCIENT FOUNDATIONS B. THE MIDDLE AGES
C. THE RENAISSANCE D. THE 17TH CENTURY
E. THE 18TH/19TH CENTURIES

A. ANCIENT FOUNDATIONS

In Antiquity, the genre debate was largely determined by Aristotle's *Poetics* and Horace's *Ars poetica* (*Epistula ad Pisones*). The views expressed in these texts, albeit at times contradictory, affected the entire modern reception of the ancient genre debate. The trend towards a normative poetics, and thus a prescriptive understanding of ancient theorems, was generally dominant and already evident in Horace's thinking [18. 257]. In the modern debate, therefore, the actual reality of genres often took second place to their theory. The specific character of the Aristotelian 'normativity', which was largely congruent with 'descriptivity' due to

Aristotle's concept of entelechy, remained largely unrecognised in this context [6. 13]. Aristotle developed his genre theory with recourse to Plato's attempts at a differentiation of the genres. In Plato's view, the mode of representation of the respective texts (the so-called 'mode of speech') played a central role in the differentiation of 'genres' (for a critical discussion of this term [2. 11]). This resulted in a three-fold division of genres: 1. 'mimetic' art, using direct speech to emulate the actions of men (Pl. Resp. 10,603c), such as done in tragedy or comedy; 2. simple narrative spoken by the poet himself, as in the (older) dithyramb; 3. a mixture of both, as occurs, e.g., in the epic (Pl. Resp. 3,392d–394c). The focus on the mode of speech in this classification model went hand-in-hand with the omission of existing forms of lyrical poetry: 'lyric poetry' does not exist as a generic term in Plato's model [2. 10f.].

This notion of mimesis, already of importance to Plato [4], was elevated in Aristotle's model to become the central defining category for poetry (Aristot. Poet. 1–3): all forms of poetry (exemplified forms include: epic, tragedy, comedy, dithyramb or playing the flute or zither) are 'imitations', that is, *mimeseis*. They differ from each other in three aspects: according to the mimetic medium (rhythm, language, melody); the mimetic object (ethically qualifiable actions by human beings); and the mimetic mode, or the type of speech (narrative or dramatic mode of representation). This recourse to the Platonic mode of speech directed Aristotle towards a differentiation within the narrative mode of representation: the poet either spoke in 'different' roles, as Homer did, or always as himself, thus without altering the speaking authority (Aristot. Poet. 3). Inspired by Plato, Aristotle developed in this context a categorization model which was to prove greatly influential, even though it was incompatible with his general concept that *poiesis* equals mimesis (which general concept also included musical forms) [6. 19]. Privileging the criterion of mimesis led to a rejection of previously applied, external criteria (verse form) for 'poetry': didactic verse does not perform any mimesis, and thus does not meet the criteria for poetry (Aristot. Poet. 1). Neither did Aristotle deal with lyric poetry as an overall complex [2. 14f.]. Under the auspices of a movement from particular to universal subject matters, Aristotle distinguished two parallel lines of development with regard to the historical foundation of familiar poetic forms: serious poetry evolved from the hymn via the epic into tragedy; frivolous poetry evolved via defamatory and satirical poems into comedy (Aristot. Poet. 4–5).

In the first book of his *Poetics* that is extant, Aristotle combined his general genre-theoretical approach with an investigation of the genres of tragedy and epic, focusing mainly on poetical structure and aesthetic response. In the same text (Aristot. Poet. 26), he ranked tragedy above the epic because of its affective power, thus becoming the progenitor of all attempts to establish a hierarchical order of genres, attempts at which continued well into the 18th cent.

In contrast with the interrupted European reception of the *Poetics*, Horace's *Ars poetica* was studied without interruption since its first publication. Influenced by Hellenistic poetic theories (Neoptolemus of Parium was most probably a primary source) and a rhetorisation of poetics [7. 289 f., 296 f.], its essential feature was a poetics of styles; it gave a lot of space to categories pertaining to the aesthetics of the work and its production. The rhetorical *imitatio* of literary examples assumed an important role (Hor. Ars P. 134) [4. 215] alongside the Aristotelian mimesis (Hor. Ars P. 317 f.). The essentially rhetorical category of 'appropriateness' (*prepón, harmottón*; *decorum, aptum*), already evident in Aristotle's works (Aristot. Eth. Nic. 4,1128a 22–24) with reference to the comedy [6. 63], becomes fully significant in Horace. In a section on the appropriate stylistic pitch (Hor. Ars P. 73–118), Horace points out that certain metrics and styles are only suitable for certain subject matters (decorum of style); this is the context in which the literary genre theory was developed [18. 251 f.]. The criterion of probability, seen as objective by Aristotle, takes second place to the decorum of content, i.e. a content which the audience perceives as appropriate; if it is not 'appropriate', it will not be believed (Hor. Ars P. 188). Of the individual genres, Horace deals in detail with tragedy (Hor. Ars P. 189 f.: 5 act rule) and satirical comedy (Hor. Ars P. 220–250). The latter points to the problem of mixed genres which were to play an important part in the debates of the 16th to 18th cents. In general, however, Horace perpetuated the fixation on the three Platonic-Aristotelian genres of epic, tragedy, and comedy, even though they agreed neither with literary reality nor with his own literary output. A possible explanation for this may have been the influence of his model, Neoptolemus' *Poetics* [6. 149–151].

With a certain shift in emphasis, the *Tractatus Coislinianus* (1st cent. BC) and Diomedes' *Ars grammatica* (4th cent. AD) modified the strict Platonic-Aristotelian, tri-partite organization based on mimesis: both theories took into account non-imitative, didactic poetry [15. 11]. Diomedes' flexible three-category model (*genus dramaticum, narrativum, mixtum*) integrated new genres as well as sub-genres such as bucolic poetry, elegy, epod,e and satire [14. 31; 10. 44–46]. The refusal to consider both didactic and lyric poetry, as well as various mixed genres, by the Platonic-Aristotelian tradition on the one hand, and the abandonment of the same tradition's criterion (mode of speech) in favour of a rhetorically influenced poetics of styles (already evident in Horace), on the other, was to become the cause of much tension in subsequent debates [15. 10 f., 14 f.].

B. THE MIDDLE AGES

Aristotle's *Poetics*, which already met with little interest in Late Antiquity, remained largely unknown in medieval western Europe despite the existence of some adaptations [7. 290 f.; 1. 103–106]. In contrast, Hora-

ce's *Ars poetica*, together with Porphyrio's prescriptive commentaries and the *Scholia* of Pseudo-Acro, were widely read [17. 72–79; 10. 41–43]. The *Scholia* reenforced the rhetorical biases of the *Ars*: its guiding principles were appropriateness (*convenientia*) and consideration of the audience. This conformed with the dissolution of the concept of 'poetry', which was no longer theoretically distinguished from prose, and which, in the Middle Ages, was dealt with as part of the Seven Liberal Arts (→ ARTES LIBERALES), mostly in the form of an appendix to the subjects of rhetoric or grammar [2. 42]. 'Poetry' was but one particular form of linguistic expression, and 'writing poetry' was nothing but versification.

Despite this, medieval poetics, beginning with the *Ars versificatoria* by Matthew of Vendôme (ca. 1175), provided stylistic rules with a selection of rhetorical tropes and figures. The dominant doctrine was that of the three styles; it originally went back to Theophrastus and was known in the medieval period from rudiments in Horace (Hor. Ars P. 26–31, 86–107), as well as from Rhet. Her. (4,11 f.) and Servius' commentaries on Virgil. Servius employed Virgil's three works as paradigms for the three styles: *Aeneid* – *stylus gravis (high style)*, the *Georgics* – *stylus mediocris (middle style)*, the *Bucolics* (or *Eclogues*) – *stylus humilis (low style)*. In the Middle Ages, this led to the concept of the *stylus materiae*: the style is a mode of speech that is predetermined by the subject matter. In his *Rota Virgilii* (13th cent.), John of Garland assigned a hierarchy of social orders and subject matters to these three styles [5. 191 f.]. At the same time, the specific knowledge of genres in respect to ancient texts had already begun to decline by the early Middle Ages. Beginning with Isidore of Seville (ca. 560–636), the names of the poetic genres were increasingly muddled in spite of an awareness of Diomedes' model [2. 33–59]; literature was classified according to completely different categories such as content, metric, intention, stylistic pitch, and degree of fictionality [9]. In addition, the problem of applying traditional genre terms to contemporary literary production existed [11. 535 f.]. Toward the end of the Middle Ages, the conflict between Latin genres and those in the vernacular, as systemized in Italy by A. da Tempo in his *Summa artis rithmice* (1329/32) [2. 60–65], continued to increase.

C. THE RENAISSANCE

Prior to the reception of Aristotle's *Poetics*, the Early Renaissance was shaped by the medieval tradition. The blending of poetry and rhetoric continued; the *Rota Virgilii* was perfected through the integration of the poetic genres and metrics (thus, Jodocus Badius Ascensius's commentary on the *Ars poetica*, 1500). C. Landino's commentary on Horace (1482) forbade any mixing of styles or subjects under the postulate of *decorum* [17. 79–85; 5. 192–194]. Until the mid–16th cent., the *Ars poetica* retained its position as the seminal text, studied with an emphasis on rhetoric. Even around

1560 and later, the doctrine of the three styles, in conjunction with *decorum* and *convenientia,* was the main tool for the distinction of genres [17. 151, 197].

Following the 'rediscovery' of Aristotle's *Poetics* (1498, Latin translation by G. Valla; 1508, first printed edition of the original Greek in Aldus Manutius's *Rhetores Graeci*; 1536, Greek-Latin dual-language edition by A. de' Pazzi), it became the dominant text in the genre debate of the second half of the 16th cent. A normative-prescriptive reading of the text dominated, and there was also a tendency to interpret Aristotle in the light of the medieval Horatian rhetorical tradition [17. 476f.; 7. 297]. Due to these textual-interpretive conditions, the confrontation of the *Poetics* with contemporary forms of poetry, especially the vernacular and mixed genres, gave rise to a number of questions: (a) How did the Platonic-Aristotelian model relate to the actual range of contemporary literary genres? (b) How should the lyrical forms, which had been passed over by Plato and Aristotle, be classified, and how should the vernacular forms be included? (c) Can Aristotles' typification of the epic be applied to the contemporary form of the novel (*romanzo*)? (d) Does tragedy deserve to outrank the epic (as in Aristot. Poet. 26), or is the reverse true? The debate was always controversial; there was hardly ever an agreement on the outcome, and both sides referred to Aristotle and Horace to underpin their arguments.

To summarize in detail: (a) Aristotle's exclusion of didactic poetry challenged the Renaissance theoreticians to define their own positions in regard to two decisive questions: whether it was possible to define poetry by metrics (as stipulated by the medieval tradition in contradiction to Aristotle) and whether in a work of poetry, with regards to *Ars poetica* 333 ('aut prodesse volunt aut delectare poetae'), usefulness or delight was of greater importance. Depending on the answers to these questions, didactic poetry could either be completely excluded from the poetic genre (Castelvetro), or, within the framework of the three Diomedian categories, subsumed within the *genus narrativum* (Scaliger), or hailed as the most important of all poetic genres due to its philosophical content (Lambin) [2. 117, 207; 3. 122]. Contemporary to the Aristotelian triad of genres (epic, tragedy, and comedy), there were other Renaissance classifications, as e.g. in the *Lezioni della Poesia* by B. Varchi, who also considered vernacular forms of poetry [2. 81f.]. In contrast, fictional prose (novels and novellas) was largely ignored by the Renaissance genre theories [3. 158; 12. 69–72]. (b) The importance and status of Petrarch's *Canzoniere,* as well as the fashion for Petrarchism that followed, made it impossible to ignore the problem of the classification of lyrical forms. To that end, a decision was necessary as to whether, in accordance with the *Poetics,* lyric poetry was to be classified as poetry at all. In view of the Aristotelian postulate for mimesis, it was necessary to prove that lyric poetry was mimetic in order to classify it as poetry in the Aristotelian sense. An example appears in

J. Mazzoni's *Difesa della Comedia di Dante* (1587); his approach met with fierce rejection by the adamantly anti-Aristotelian F. Patrizi [2. 95 f.]. Using a tripartite system modelled on Diomedes, poetry could be classified as a *genus mixtum* (*imitando et narrando: as imitating and narrating*), as e.g. by A. S. Minturno in his *L'arte poetica* (1564) [2. 87]. An example of the wide diversity of these approaches is evident in *La poetica* by G. G. Trissino, who elevated lyric poetry to the sole representative of the *genus narrativum* [2. 73]. There were also attempts to add lyric poetry as a fourth genre, as an addendum to the Aristotelian triad [12. 90]. On the whole, the Aristotelian tradition proved to be rather a hindrance [3. 156] to a fixed definition of lyric poetry as a genre in its own right, as had been attempted as early as 1536 by B. Daniello in his *Poetica* [2. 76f.]. The Aristotelian tradition could even be used as a weapon in the battle against the theoretical establishment of new literary forms [12. 89]. (c) The so-called *romanzo* dispute [17. 954–1073] about the vernacular epic (Ariosto's *Orlando furioso* serves as a prime example) concerned two primary questions: the extent to which the fantastic subject of the *romanzo* could be compatible with the Aristotelian postulate of probability, and how its multifaceted and complex plot structure could be reconciled with the Aristotelian demand for a unity of action. There were three different answers to these questions: 1. The *romanzo* was a genre in its own right, which, due to diachrony, Aristotle could not have known about and taken into account; from which it followed that Aristotelian norms could not be applied to the *romanzo.* This was argued by G. B. Giraldi Cinthio in his *Discorso intorno al comporre dei romanzi* (1554); however, this position implies an historically oriented, non-normative understanding of the *Poetics.* 2. From the perspective of the *Poetics,* the *romanzo* is to be condemned, because it violates the postulates of probability and unity, a view purported in Minturno's *Arte poetica* (1564). 3. The *romanzo* is not a separate genre, as its criteria do not differ in essence from those of the epic. While the unity of action is to be maintained, *varietas* within this unity was permitted, an argument put forward by T. Tasso in his *Discorsi dell'arte poetica* (1570). Both the second and the third position assume a universal transhistorical validity of the *Poetics.* The other two great literary debates of the 16th cent. – on the definition of Dante's *Divina Commedia* [17. 819–911] and on the permissibility of the mixed genre of a tragicomical pastoral drama (Guarini's *Pastor fido*) [17. 1074–1105; 1. 360–369] – also highlighted the limited applicability of the Aristotelian theorems to literary reality. (d) In the debate on the primacy of epic or tragedy, although a highly respected theoretician such as Castelvetro supported tragedy, and thus the *Poetics,* the superiority of the epic, underpinned by the powerful example of the *Aeneid,* remained unassailable in the Renaissance view (Strozzi, Tasso, Scaliger *et. al.*); it was considered superior in diction and rhetorical ornament (*ornatus*), in its role as a moral example, in its wealth of moral teachings, and in its affective effectiveness and usefulness [3. 152 f.; 17. 684 f.]. This resulted in a distancing from the *Poetics*, which ascribed to the tragedy a greater unity of action than to the epic (Aristot. Poet. 26). Renaissance thinkers frequently subordinated the unity of action, which was the only important unity in Aristotle's view, to the unities of place and time (which unities had only been explicitly defined in the 16th cent.). In further contrast with Aristotle, the unity of action was not seen as the logical coherence of a continuous plot, rather it was diluted to a (theoretically largely unclarified) harmonizing of all parts of a poetic work into the central plot [7. 297 f.; 17. 803].

D. The 17th Century

In the 17th cent., the centre of the debate on genre theory shifted to France. There was no significant innovation in the diversification of genres; 'lyric poetry' as a genre was still not firmly established [2. 134]. In the division of genres, there were some attempts to integrate new forms into the traditional schemes: thus J. Chapelain (*Préface de l'Adone*, 1623) attempted to subsume Marino's mythological poem *Adone* into the traditional concept of the epic genre; while A. Dacier attempted to justify the modern prose novel with Aristotelian arguments in his annotated translation of the *Poetics* (1692) [2. 136, 145 f.]; and Ch. Perrault classified opera as one of Aristotle's forms of dramatic poetry [3. 204 f.]. Contemporary small lyrical forms were variously classified [2. 135–149]. The primary emphasis, however, remained on the Aristotelian genres of epic and, in particular, tragedy, which were accepted without question.

The Horatian *Ars poetica* lost considerably in importance, while the *Poetics* (under the influence of D. Heinsius's interpretation of Aristotle [3. 170–175]) broke free from the rhetorical tradition, into which it had been previously integrated by the Italian Renaissance. In a counter-movement to Baroque conceptism [3. 186–191], the rigorous French Aristotelism turned the *Poetics* into a reference point for a normative poetic with a strictly moral orientation. This prescription for a genre theory under the dictates of *raison*, augmented with genre rules derived from the *Ars poetica*, became influential enough to suppress mixed genres such as the pastoral drama, the tragicomedy, or the comic-heroic epic [5. 234 f.]. With regard to the genre of tragedy, classicist poetic theory (J. Chapelain, J. de la Mesnardière, G. de Scudéry, Abbé d'Aubignac) focused less on aspects of style and rhetoric (and thus quite in line with Aristotle) than on questions regarding the structure and principles governing the order of the dramatic plot with its demands for clarity, economy, and strict observance of form.

The preoccupation with conventions, so typical for that period, began to dominate the valency of appropriateness (*bienséance [decorum]*, *convenance [suitability]*), originally a central notion associated with rhetoric. The basic postulate of verisimilitude *[vraisemblance]* – though only somewhat vaguely defined in reference to the *opinion commune [public opinion]* – was derived from Aristotle (Aristot. Poet. 9), and was the precondition for achieving the desired moral effect of a tragedy (in the views of French Aristotelians, there was no doubt about the primacy of the didactic over entertaining) [5. 225–228]. The exemplary character of the represented actions and the strict application of poetic justice were supposed to achieve a moral improvement of the audience. In the opinion of the Aristotelians, verisimilitude could only be achieved by the strictest adherence to the 'Three Unities', which had been prefigured by the Italian Renaissance and were now elevated to absolute rules [5. 231–236]. The case of Corneille, however, demonstrates that there often existed a considerable gap between the demands of theory and poetic practice: after his tragicomedy *Le Cid* (*Querelle du Cid*) had been the subject of a fierce controversy, he declared his willingness to accept the corpus of Aristotelian rules, and then attempted, in his *Trois discours sur le poème dramatique* (1660), to expand his creative freedom of poetic practice as much as possible while remaining within those rules [16].

Thus, in France, the debate focused on a theoretically advanced discussion of individual genres; however, the poetics of genres elsewhere in Europe often stagnated on the level of Scaliger's Renaissance poetics; M. Opitz's *Buch von der Deutschen Poeterey* (1624) was geared towards this level. In a manner comparable to G. P. Harsdörffer in his *Poetischer Trichter*, Opitz treated genres in an unspecific, formalising manner according to their subject matter and their metric structure; however, he retained the Renaissance correspondences of genre with stylistic pitch and social standing of the people depicted (the so-called appropriate social status requirement) [11. 542 f.].

A work like A. Buchner's *Anleitung zur Deutschen Poeterey* (1665) appears as an exception: he was familiar with the Aristotelian differentiation of genres according to media, object, and representational mode; he classified the mode of speech as the most important category and approved of Aristotle's reservations regarding the classification of lyric verse [15. 19–21]. In the actual population of his system with specific individual genres, Buchner's approach is less stringent than that of Th. Hobbes. In 1650, Hobbes classified genres horizontally, according to the social rank of their subjects (court, town, country), and vertically, according to the mode of speech (*narrative* vs. dramatic *representation*). He thus arrives at the following structure: epic / tragedy (court); satire / comedy (town); epic idyll / dramatic idyll (country) [15. 23].

E. The 18th/19th Centuries

In the 18th cent., the *Poetics* still retained its dominant position in relation to the *Ars poetica*; in the conflict between traditional rule-based poetics and progressive poetic theories, Classical genre theory stood firmly on the side of tradition. Although in England and France, the traditional genre terms retained their validity, at least as pragmatic descriptors [15. 273]; the valency of the ancient genre tradition had already begun to crumble in the German-speaking area under the influence of such divergent movements as: the aesthetics of genius, the interest in the historical multitude of genres, and, from a Classicistic-idealistic perspective, the possibility of setting this variety into relationship with the 'true basic forms' as the very essences of an organic poetic entity [18. 279 f.], and finally, the positivistic desire for a detailed description of individual observations of the great variety in poetics [11. 549].

As part of a trans-European trend to move away from the traditional poetics of genres [15. 220–222], the Aristotelian principle of mimesis, and with it the concrete genre classifications, were increasingly abandoned: a distinction between various poetic forms, based on the mode of speech, appeared inadequate to an accentuated aesthesiology of poetics with a strong emphasis on the aesthetics of production. This approach does not perceive the wide range of possible poetic forms as reduceable to the rules of strictly defined generic concepts [15. 265 f.]; these critics of traditional rule-based poetics had no problems accepting those mixed genres which had always proved difficult to classify in the traditional model [18. 273–275].

The directly effective reception of ancient genre poetics, in correlation with the mimesis postulate and notions of normativity, had thus essentially come to an end in the 19th cent., even though variously associated generic concepts endured ('epic', 'drama', 'lyric poetry' or their corresponding adjectives), and in spite of the persistence into the 20th cent. of occasional theoretical reflections, such as that of the Neo-Aristotelian *Chicago critics* [7. 317; 8. 115–117], or the sporadic recourse to mode of speech as a category [8. 156–160]. From this point of view, two approaches represent themselves as the final culminations of the immediate influence of the Classical genre theory: J. Ch. Gottsched's *Versuch einer Critischen Dichtkunst* (1730, 4th ed. 1751) and Ch. Batteux's *Les beaux arts réduits à un même principe* (1746, later expanded in: *Cours de belles lettres*), with the latter also being widely read in Germany.

Gottsched rejected the poetics of rhyme and metrics, which dominated the German theoretical discussion, and vehemently supported the mimesis principle as the basis of all poetry [15. 29–32]. He distinguished between three mimetic genres [15. 32–39]: (a) mere description or vivid portrayal; (b) the assumption by the poet of an 'alternate' voice or the appearance of other characters; (c) the fable, defined, in analogy to Aristotle (Aristot. Poet. 6), as a blend of various elements, and also as a narrative tale of a possible event that contains a moral message. However, Gottsched intermingled rhetorical categories (description) and Aristotelian-poetological categories (myth) [5. 263]; he separated the action principle (fable) from the mimesis postulate

[15. 33]; he failed to apply the 'mode of speech' criterion consistently; and he failed to reconcile his theoretic 'mimetic genres' with his historical genres [18. 266 f.]. Nor did he formulate a coherent definition of 'lyric poetry' as a genre.

Batteux was the first to accomplish this goal. He firmly established 'lyric poetry' as a genre alongside epic and dramatic poetry using explicit recourse to Aristotle [2. 167]: this was successful due to the application of the mimesis principle to lyric poetry, where mimesis was understood as the imitation of emotions and sensations (rudiments of which were already evident in the Renaissance in P. Torelli [13. 409] and in A. S. Minturno's *L'arte poetica*). Didactic poetry, which had posed a problem since Antiquity, he simply defined as a fourth genre; however, it appeared as little more than an annex to the three main genres due to the inapplicability of the mimesis criterion [15. 57–82]. Batteux' system represents both a checkpoint and a turning point: though recognized by the traditional orthodox poetics until well into the 19th cent., it nevertheless marked the transition towards the rejection of the Classical genre theory (described earlier) which had lost any flexibility in application due to its inherent contempt for normativity. ;

→ Artes liberales; → Diomedes

→ ARTES LIBERALES

1 K.-H. BAREISS, Comoedia, 1982   2 I. BEHRENS, Die Lehre von der Einteilung der Dichtkunst, 1940   3 J. BESSIÈRE, et al., Histoire des poétiques, 1997   4 H. FLASHAR, Eidola, 1989, 201–219   5 M. FUHRMANN, Einführung in die antike Dichtungstheorie, 1973   6 Id., Die Dichtungstheorie der Antike, 1992   7 S. HALLIWELL, Aristotle's Poetics, 1986   8 K. W. HEMPFER, Gattungstheorie, 1973   9 U. KINDERMANN, Gattungssysteme im Mittelalter, in: W. ERZGRÄBER (ed.), Kontinuität und Transformation der Antike im Mittelalter, 1989, 303–313   10 P. KLOPSCH, Einführung in die Dichtungslehren des lateinischen Mittelalters 1980   11 S. KOMFORT-HEIN, Gattungslehre, HWbR 3,528–557   12 F. LECERCLE, Théoriciens français et italiens, in: G. DEMERSON (ed.), La notion de genre à la Renaissance, 1984, 67–100   13 G. REGN, Mimesis und autoreferentieller Diskurs, in: W.-D. STEMPEL, K. STIERLE (eds.), Die Pluralität der Welten, 1987, 387–414   14 W. V. RUTTKOWSKI, Die literarische Gattung, 1968   15 K. R. SCHERPE, Gattungspoetik im 18. Jahrhundert, 1968   16 P. THIERCY, La réception d'Aristote en France à l'époque de Corneille, in: Ant. Dramentheorien und ihre Rezeption, B. ZIMMERMANN (ed.), 1992, 169–190   17 B. WEINBERG, A History of Literary Criticism in the Italian Renaissance, (repr.) 1974   18 G. WILLEMS, Das Konzept der literarischen Gattung, 1981

ADDITIONAL BIBLIOGRAPHY F. CAIRNS, Generic Composition in Greek and Roman Poetry, 1972; R. L. COLIE, The Resources of Kind: Genre Theory in the Renaissance, 1973; A. FOWLER, Kinds of Literature: An Introduction to the Theory of Genres and Modes, 1982; JOURNAL Genre, 1– (1968–)   BERNHARD HUSS

Geography
A. Introduction B. Medieval Geography
C. Reception of Ptolemy D. Geography,
History and 'Climate'

A. Introduction
Geography belongs to those scientific disciplines in which the state of knowledge of Antiquity in the modern era has proven to be in need of a great deal of correction and expansion. The discovery of the 'New World' (1492) and the sea route to India (1498) exemplarize the beginning of the modern era [13]. Nevertheless, ancient geographical thought has influenced the practice of scientific geography until today [1. 57–58]. In terms of content and time, three main phases can be distinguished in the history of reception and influence: the period of only limited knowledge of Greek geography in Latin Christianity up to the end of the 14th cent.; the period of reception of Ptolemy's *Geographia* in the 15th and 16th cents.; and a third period (18th and 19th cents.) in which → HISTORICISM brought new awareness of the ancient ethnographically-historically oriented regional geography (Herodotus, Strabo), which significantly shaped scientific geography [17. 32–34, 86–88].

B. Medieval Geography
The ancient image of the world was only rudimentarily known to the Latin Middle Ages. The basis of the reception consisted of only a few works which reflected that image in excerpts (Mela, Plin. HN, Solin., Macr. In Somn., Oros., Mart. Cap.) [20. col. 1265; 21; 29. 14–15]. These were the sources of the authors who contributed to the spread of geographical knowledge in the Early Middle Ages (Isidorus Hispalensis, the Geographus Ravenna, Beda Venerabilis, Dicuil, Alcuin, Rabanus Maurus and Adam of Bremen, as well as Gervasius of Tilbury) [27. vol. 2. 286–295]. It was primarily mathematical geography, which had achieved a high standing in Greek Antiquity (with Eratosthenes and Ptolemy), which was lost to the Christian Middle Ages [8]. Its place was taken by a Christian cosmography, in which the description of the Earth was merged with Biblical and mythological concepts, and which thus scarcely shows the actual borders and locations of the world [14; 1. 63]. In the 12th and 13th cents., the geographical knowledge of the Arabs provided a correction and expansion of the picture of the world to Latin Christianity with [20. 1266–1267]. Of primary significance to this transmission was Muḥammad Ibn-Muḥammad al-Idrīsī, who worked at the court of Roger II in the 12th cent. [1. 74]. The new geographical knowledge found expression in Alexander Neckam, Roger Bacon and in the work *De natura locorum* by Albertus Magnus, among others [20. 1268; 25].

C. Reception of Ptolemy
The reception of Greek geography in the West before the 16th cent. is synonymous with the reception of Ptolemy's *Geographia*. Mathematical geography or the question of the size of the Earth, its position in the cosmos, the determination of a geographical coordinate system etc. continued only in the Islamic cultural sphere at first. The *Geographia* of Ptolemy had there been translated into Arabic in the 9th cent. [15. 10, 94–100]. The work reached the Christian West around 1400. The first Latin translation occurred in 1406 in Italy, following a Greek edition from Constantinople [33]; the map labels were first translated about 1415 [24]. The *Cosmographia* (as it is called in the Latin translation) had an extraordinary circulation (not least because of the cartography), which was promoted further by the invention of the printing press [17. 45]. The definitive influence of Ptolemy continued in the 16th cent. [23]. However, the new geographic discoveries at the end of the 15th cent. had clearly revealed the shortcomings of ancient geography. Up-to-date maps were increasingly added to Ptolemy's *Cosmographia*, and in 1570 the *Cosmographia* was finally replaced as the definitive representation of the contemporary geographical view of the world by the *Theatrum orbis terrarum* of Abraham Ortelius. Nevertheless, the ancient image of the earth has remained effective until today, at least to the extent that with Ptolemy – at the latest – an arrangement of geographical material had become standard in which Europe was treated first, followed by Africa and Asia. The 'New World' (North and South America, Australia) was later simply 'appended', and this order of representation is still common in atlases today.

D. Geography, History and 'Climate'
Although the ancient image of the earth became obsolete no later than the end of the 16th cent., the ancient concept of geography as a science asserted itself throughout the 18th and 19th cents. J. H. Zedler defined "geography" in the Ptolemaic sense as "mathematical geography", i.e. as a "science of the shape and size of the globe and its properties based thereon"; this was to be the "basis" of the other types of geography ("political description of the Earth, historical and physical description of the Earth" [34. vol. 10. 919]). Mathematical geography was viewed as part of geometry, astronomy and cosmology; the other types, on the other hand – because they dealt with specific things that can be encountered in individual countries – belonged to *historia* or *historiae naturalis* [34. vol. 10. 919–920]. (Physical) geography shared the breadth of its subjects and its predominantly descriptive character with the ancient *historia (naturalis)*: According to the French *Encyclopédie*, 'Géographie physique est la description raisoné des grands phänomenes de la terre' [9. vol. 7. 613]. Thus, the question of the origin and causes of the natural things described did not belong to physical geography (→ GEOLOGY). This methodical limitation of geography to observation and description resulted from its close connection to history and was essentially a legacy of the ancient historians (Herodotus, Thucydides, Polybius); according to which *historia* was to be

based on its own observations and was to provide a precise and accurate description of everything [27. vol. 1. 101–103, 171–172, 297–298]. Here, modern geography proves to be a successor to that ethnographically-historically oriented regional geography as conceived by Herodotus (on reception in the modern era [19]) and Strabo (textual history [6]). About the middle of the 18th cent., geography (to the extent that it was not mathematical or physical geography) was considered to be historical, and in particular 'ancient geography', i.e. the geography of the ancient world. In the French *Encyclopédie*, the headword *Géographie* deals primarily with an overview of the historical development of geographical knowledge, with almost half of the article dedicated to ancient geography alone (Thales, Pytheas of Massilia, Socrates, Aristotle, Theophrastus, Pomponius Mela and especially Ptolemy) [9. vol. 7. 608–610]. This corresponds to one of the common divisions of geography into *Géographie ancienne*, *Géographie du moyen âge* and *Géographie moderne* [9. vol. 7. 613; 18. 163]. The unity of geography and history was further manifested by the fact that most of the leading historians of the 18th cent. were also known as geographers, for example J. C. Gatterer (1727–1799) [1. 159] or A. L. Schlözer (1735–1809). Besides his famous *Universalhistorie* [32], the latter wrote a geography of America (A. L. Schlözer, *Neue Erdbeschreibung von ganz Amerika*, 2 vols., Göttingen 1777). These historians understood geography as an ancillary study to history or as the 'study of locations'. In this sense, J. G. Herder (1744–1803) wrote: "Geography and history… are the setting and the book of God's housekeeping in our world: history is the book, geography the setting" [16. 495] (cf. also [18. 163]). Herder emphasized primarily the educational value or the 'convenience' and 'utility' of geography. In addition, the latter contributes to the "search for truth, beauty, utility" and "sharpens" the "sensus humanitatis" [16. 492] (cf. also [18. 163]). A. F. Büsching (1724–1793) emphasized the significance of geography for the statesman. Above all, the "regent" must "necessarily know his own and foreign lands, especially neighbouring countries, because no one can become a statesman without the description of the world" [3. 6–7]. This 'postulate of utility' occurs frequently in the geographers of the 18th and 19th cents. and is, in turn, a legacy of ancient geography (and history). Strabo prefaced his description of the Earth with a section on the utility of geography for both the scholar and the statesman (Strab. 1,1,1 and 16), in which he drew primarily on Polybius [27. vol. 1. 295–296]. C. Ritter (1779–1859), one of the founders of modern geography and a distinguished expert on ancient history, came from this 'historical tradition' [5. 37–40; 30]. In his treatise *Über das historische Element in der geographischen Wissenschaft* (1833), the ancient historians and geographers (Thucydides, Strabo, Hecataeus, Dicaearchus, Herodotus, Ptolemy, among others) are placed on an equal footing with more modern authors [31. 153, 163 et passim] (cf. also

[31. 22–23]). Above all, Ritter's 'geographic determinism' refers to Antiquity. The objective of his geography – namely to show the "influence" which "nature has had on peoples" [31. 5], respectively the geographical factors which have determined the course of human history – traces back over medieval geography (Albertus Magnus) into Antiquity (Herodotus, Polybius, Strabo) [2; 27. vol. 1. 298–300; vol. 2. 360–362] (cf. also [31. 182–184, 205]). Another ancient line of tradition affected the 'geographical determinism' of the 19th cent., that is the doctrine of the relationship between humans and their physical environment or 'climate', which traces back to Hippocrates [28] (→ METEOROLOGY). In the 18th cent., the theory of climate was significant for the philosophy of history [11], and it can be found regularly in the geographic compendia [3. 64–70]. Climate theory developed its actual significance for geography as an ideo-historical background for the concept of 'interdependency' (between animate and inanimate nature) as a central term for 19th cent. geography [26]. But, above all, it formed the background for the central inquiry of modern geography into the regional distribution of natural things on the Earth (E. A. W. Zimmermann, J.-L. Giraud-Soulavie, A. von Humboldt, 1769–1859) [1. 168, 195, 223–227]. Even in the 20th cent., geographers tied in with ancient climate theory [10. 369–370].

→ METEOROLOGY, → GEOLOGY (AND MINERALOGY)

1 H. BECK, Geographie. Europäische Entwicklung in Texten und Erläuterungen, Orbis Academicus II/16, 1973 2 J. BERGEVIN, Déterminisme et géographie. Hérodote, Strabon, Albert le Grand et Sebastian Münster, Travaux du Département de Géographie de l'Université Laval 8, 1992 3 F. A. BÜSCHING, Erdbeschreibung, 1. Theil, welcher Dänemark, Norwegen, Schweden, und das ganze russische Reich enthält, Hamburg ⁸1787 4 M. BÜTTNER (ed.), Wandlungen im geographischen Denken von Aristoteles bis Kant, Abh. und Quellen zur Gesch. der G. und Kosmologie 1, 1979 5 Die Carl Ritter Bibliothek, E. PLEWE (ed.), Erdkundliches Wissen 50, 1978 6 A. DILLER, The Textual Tradition of Strabo's Geography, 1975 7 J. DÖRFLINGER, Die Geographie in der *Encyclopédie*. Eine wissenschaftsgeschichtliche Studie, Veröffentlichungen der *Kommission für Gesch. der Mathematik, Naturwiss. und Medizin* 17, 1976 8 G. DRAGONI, La misurazioni fisico-astronomiche di Eratostene, in: Cosmographica et Geographica, vol. 1, B. FRITSCHER, G. BREY, (eds.), Algorismus 13, 1994, 97–124 9 Encyclopédie, ou Dictionnaire raisonné des sciences, des arts et des métiers, par une société de gens de lettres, Paris 1751 ff. (repr. 1966) 10 R. FALTER, Prägung des Menschen durch die Landschaft. Umweltpsychologischer Forschungsansatz oder Rückfall in 'Blut- und Boden-Ideologie'?, in: B. FRITSCHER, G. BREY (eds.), Cosmographica et Geographica, vol. 2, Algorismus 13, 1994, 369–402 11 G.-L. FINK, Von Winckelmann bis Herder. Die deutsche Klimatheorie in europäischer Perspektive, in: G. SAUDER (ed.), Johann Gottfried Herder, 1744–1803, Stud. zum 18. Jh. 9, 1987, 156–176 12 P. GAUTIER DALCH, Géographie et culture. La représentation de l'espace du VIe au XIIe siècle, Variorum Collected Studies series 592, 1997 13 A. GRAFTON, New Worlds, Ancient Texts. The Power of Tradition and

the Shock of Discovery, 1992   14 J. Hamel, Die Vor-
stellung von der Kugelgestalt der Erde im europäischen
Mittelalter bis zum Ende des 13. Jahrhunderts, Abh. zur
Gesch. der Geowiss. und der Religion/ Umwelt-Forsch. 3,
1996   15 J. B. Harley, D. Woodward, History of Car-
tography, vol. 2/1, 1992   16 J. G. Herder, Von der
Annehmlichkeit, Nützlichkeit und Notwendigkeit der
Geographie. Schulrede Juli 1784, in: Werke, vol. 9/2, R.
Wisbert (ed.), 1997, 480–495   17 A. Hettner, Die
Geographie. Ihre Geschichte, ihr Wesen, ihre Methoden,
1927   18 I. Kant, Physische Geographie, F. T. Rink (ed),
in: Gesammelte Schriften, vol. 9, *Königlich Preußische
Akad. der Wiss.*, 1923, 151–436   19 S. Kipf, Herodot als
Schulautor. Ein Beitrag zur Geschichte des Griechischun-
terrichts in Deutschland vom 15. bis zum 20. Jahrhundert,
Studien und Dokumentationen zur deutschen Bildungsgeschichte 73, 1999   20 M. Kratochwill, H. Hunger,
s. v. Geographie, LMA 4, 1265–1269   21 G. Loose, Das
2. Buch der *Naturalis historia* von Plinius dem Älteren.
Eine kritische Analyse im Lichte moderner geowissen-
schaftlicher Erkenntnisse, 1995   22 W. McCrady, Isidore, the Antipodeans, and the Shape of the Earth, in: Isis
87, 1996, 108–127   23 M. Milanesi, Tolomeo sosti-
tuito. Studi di storia delle conoscenze geografiche nel XVI
secolo, Studi e ricerche sul territorio 14, 1984   24 Id.,
Geography and Cosmography in Italy from XV to XVII
century, Memorie della Società Astronomica Italiana 65,
1994, 443–468   25 P. Moraw (ed.), Das geographische
Weltbild um 1300. Politik im Spannungsfeld von Wissen,
Mythos und Fiktion, in: Zschr. für Histor. Forsch., Beih.
6, 1989   26 G. H. Müller, 'Wechselwirkung' in den Erd-
und Biowissenschaften von Kant bis zum Ende des
19. Jahrhunderts, in: W. Kreisel (ed.), Geisteshaltung
und Umwelt. Abhandlungen zur Geschichte der Geowis-
senschaften und Religion/ Umweltforschung 1, 1988,
125–141   27 K. E. Müller, Geschichte der antiken Ethnographie und ethnologischen Theoriebildung, 2 vols.,
Stud. zur Kulturgesch. 29 and 52, 1972 and 1980   28 M.
Pinna, La teoria dei climi. Una falsa dottrina che non
muta da Ippocrate a Hegel, in: Memorie della Società
Geografica Italiana 41, 1988   29 Pomponius Mela,
Kreuzfahrt durch die Alte Welt, K. Brodersen (ed.), 1994
30 C. Ritter, Die Vorhalle europäischer Völkergeschichte
vor Herodotus, um den Kaukasus und an den Gestaden
des Pontus, Berlin 1820   31 Id., Einleitung zur allgemeinen vergleichenden Geographie und Abhandlungen zur
Begründung einer mehr wissenschaftlichen Behandlung
der Erdkunde, Berlin 1852   32 A. L. Schlözer, Vorstellung seiner Universalhistorie, Göttingen 1772, (repr.
H. W. Blanke (ed.), 1997)   33 A. Stückelberger, Planudes und die *Geographia* des Ptolemäus, in: Museum
Helveticum 53, 1996, 197–205   34 J. H. Zedler,
Grosses vollständiges Universal-Lexicon aller Wissenschaften und Künste, Halle und Leipzig 1732 ff.

Additional Bibliography W. Hübner (ed.), Geographie und verwandte Wissenschaften, in: G. Wöhrle
(ed.), Geschichte der Mathematik und der Naturwissenschaften in der Antike, vol. 2, 2000; H. Inglebert, Interpretatio christiana: les mutations des savoirs (cosmogra-
phie, géographie, éthnographie, histoire) dans l'antiquité
chrétienne (30–630 aprčs J.-C.), in: Collection des études
augustiniennes, Série Antiquité, 166, 2001; J. M. Latti s,
Between Copernicus and Galileo, 1994; N. Lozovsky,
The Earth is our Book: Geographical Knowledge in the
Latin West ca. 400–1000, 2000 ; S. Tomasch, S. Gilles,

Text and Territory: Geographical Imagination in the European Middle Ages, 1998   BERNHARD FRITSCHER

Geology (and Mineralogy)

A. Introduction B. Middle Ages and Renaissance C. 17th and 18th Centuries
D. 19th Century

A. Introduction

The phenomena and questions with which geology
and mineralogy deal today were the subject of two
methodologically separate disciplines in Antiquity.
Meteorologia inquired into the causes of terrestrial phenomena; the description and classification of rocks and
minerals (and fossils) were the subject of *historia naturalis* (and, with regard to the medicinal benefits of minerals, of pharmacology and medicine). As the science of
the Earth's history, geology is, to be sure, a creation of
the modern era. To that effect, the reception history and
effective history of ancient geology and mineralogy
show three phases: the phase of resumption and continuation of the ancient teachings up until the development of an independent "science of the things below the
earth" (Middle Ages and Renaissance); the phase of development of the new historical geology (17th and
18th cents.); as well as a phase of the implicit after-ef-
fects of ancient mineralogy in the 19th cent.

B. Middle Ages and Renaissance

Into the middle of the 16th cent., the reception history and the impact history of ancient geology and mineralogy largely coincide with that of meteorology and
historia naturalis (and pharmacology). The primary
source for ancient knowledge of rocks and minerals in
the Latin Middle Ages was the *Naturalis historia* of
Pliny the Elder, which was based on Theophrastus,
among others [1. 19–21; 20. col. 1965]. The work *De
materia medica* by Dioscurides Pedanius had a certain
independent significance [1. 23–24]. The further
spread of mineralogical knowledge up to the middle of
the 13th cent. occurred primarily through Solinus and
Isidore of Seville – in addition to the medieval books of
stones [30] – and later through the Latin encyclopaedists [12. 15–30]. Ovid and Orosius were of significance specifically for the knowledge of fossils [6. 62–63,
73–75; 19. 517–520]. The thoughts concerning the
classification and formation of minerals (and metals)
set out in Plato, Aristotle, and Theophrastus are scarcely continued in these works (which are largely limited
to listing minerals and their properties). Definitive for
them was the differentiation between the metals which
can be smelted (composed of the element 'water') and
the rest of the minerals which do not become liquid in
fire (composed of the element 'earth'), as well as the
Aristotelian teaching of the two 'effluvia', of which the
moist was responsible for the genesis of metals (*metal-
leuta*), and the dry for the origin of the remaining minerals (*orykta*, Latin *fossilia*) [20. 1964–1965]. At first,
these approaches were perpetuated only in the Islamic

culture area (Ğābir Ibn-Ḥaiyān, *Book of Stones by Aristotle*) [32. 105–110, 140–141]. Definitive was the classification of Avicenna, who adopted the two main groups of Aristotle and Theophrastus (the ores and metals which can be smelted and the 'stones' which cannot) as *liquefactiva* and *lapides* and added the groups (at least implicitly set out in Theophrastus) of the combustible 'sulphur types' (*sulphura*) and the (water soluble) 'salts' (*salia*) [1. 18–19; 32. 142–143]. Albertus Magnus followed this classification, though he no longer differentiated strictly between *salia* and *sulphura*, but rather combined these two groups (which stood in the 'middle' between stones and metals) as *media* [2nd vol. 4. 7; 3.]. For Avicenna, heat and cold are the essential effective powers in the origin of minerals; according to Albertus, the 'stones' arise from the element 'earth' in connection with the quality of 'moisture' [19. 522–523]. The assumption of a petrifying force (*vis lapidificativa*), which was very influential in the early modern era, and the sulphur-mercury theory of the origin of metals, are primarily an Arab legacy [25. 28, 30; 32. 127–128]. However, with the further reception of Aristotle's *Meteorology*, his teaching of the two effluvia became the predominant theory for the origin of metals and minerals. G. Reisch summarized the conventional view for the beginning of the 16th cent. when he differentiated minerals as *lapides*, *sales* and *metalla* and had them arise from vapours and exhalations (*ex vapores et exhalationibus*) as well as through the effect of celestial heat (*calore celesti*) [29. lib. 9, cap. 24]. Ulrich Rülein of Calw formulated the customary theory of the origin of metals around 1500: the effect of celestial rays causes vapours to rise in the Earth's interior; by means of these vapours (which consist physically of sulphur and mercury) metals are formed or brought to 'ripeness' [1. 299–301]. The actual intermediary between ancient-medieval concepts and modern geology was Georgius Agricola. In *De ortu et causis subterraneorum libri V* ('On Origins and Causes under the Earth', Basel 1546), he deals with the origin of rocks and minerals and their deposits as well as the causes of other geological phenomena (earthquakes, water in the interior of the Earth, erosion, etc.) in the context of the ancient-medieval theories [1. 93–94]. His mineral classification, which he developed in *De natura fossilium libri X* (*De natura fossilium (Textbook of Mineralogy)*, Basel 1546), corresponds to that of Avicenna, except that Agricola segregates soils as 'earths' (*terrae*) and ores (because they consist of a metal and another substance) as 'mixtures' (*mixta*) [2. vol. 4. 39–43]. Agricola's sources were, in particular, Albertus Magnus, Alexandrus of Aphrodisias, Aristotle, Avicenna, Pliny the Elder, Seneca, Strabo, Theophrastus, Dioscorides, Galen and Hippocrates [2. vol. 4. 15–16]. To be sure, Agricola just as clearly abandoned this context in his new science of the "things below the earth" (*de rebus subterraneis*) when he merged the description of the minerals and the enquiry into their causes (which in Antiquity were separated as *historia*

naturalis and *meteorologia* respectively) into one science [11]. Thus, nowhere does he mention *meteorologia*; atmospheric phenomena appear merely as "disturbances or agitations of the atmosphere" (*de perturbationibus aeris*) [2. 17].

C. 17TH AND 18TH CENTURIES

The autonomy granted by Agricola to the "science of things below the earth" was carried on in the 17th cent., although the causes of terrestrial phenomena (earthquakes, volcanoes, origin of metals and minerals) were also often dealt with in the framework of meteorology. In 1662 J. Micraelius discerned (in addition to *Uranologia*, *Zoologia*, *Meteorologia*, among other disciplines) a separate *Nerterologia* (Greek *nerteros* = 'subterranean'), which was to deal with *de subterraneis* [24. col. 1004–1005]. The new science, also already occasionally called *Geologia* [6. 191; 12. 66, 84], found expression in A. Kircher's *Mundus subterraneus* (Amsterdam 1665), J. J. Becher's *Physica subterranea* (Frankfurt 1669), G. W. F. Leibniz' *Protogaea* (written 1691) [22], and W. Whiston's *New Theory of the Earth* (London 1696). The classification and theories of the origin of rocks and minerals themselves nevertheless remained closely bound to the ancient concepts. The (implicit) empirical basis of mineral classification was, as before (and as in Plato, Theophrastus and Aristotle), the behaviour of the minerals in fire. Until well into the 18th cent., the mineral classifications corresponded to the ancient/medieval division into salts, stones, 'combustible minerals' (*Brenzen*), and ores or metals [8. 543–544; 28. 508–9; 10. 24–26, 82–84]; this was still authoritative for J. G. Wallerius [33] and A. G. Werner [16. 52–53]. In the theories of the origin of metals and minerals, with the development of the new natural sciences in the 17th and 18th cents., the ancient doctrine of the elements increasingly gave way; in its place, the Aristotelian doctrine of effluvia became all the more definitive. In 1644 R. Descartes explained the origin of ore-bearing lodes by postulating a layer of heavy metals which is heated by the Earth's fiery interior, creating vapours which rise through cracks in the Earth and petrify there [6. 223]. In 1661 J. J. Becher traced the origin of metals back to lead-bearing water which seeps into the Earth and meets there salt and sulphur vapours which rise from the interior and then solidify under the influence of celestial rays [1. 288–299] (see also 1753 J. G. Lehmann [21. 178–179, 256–257; 1. 286–287]). A specific manifestation of the Aristotelian doctrine was 'weather', a type of "effluvium" from ore-bearing lodes, emitted when the lodes had reached their "maturity" [1. 301–304]. This notion of 'weather' was still scarcely challenged around the middle of the 18th cent. [35. vol. 57. 1876; 8. vol. 6. 254–255]. In a variety of ways, ancient mineralogy remained really rather current. J. H. Zedler defined "mineralogy" (with reference to Hippocrates and Galen) as "that doctrine in the Materia Medica which deals with minerals" [35. vol. 21. 346]. Further, in the descriptions of rocks and minerals and in the discussion of geologic processes, it was still customary, as before, to draw on the contributions of ancient authors [31. vol. 2. 47, 414 *et passim*]. J. Hutton, the founder of modern geology, referred to Polybius and Pliny in the discussion of coastal erosion by the waters of the sea [18. 299–300], and his authoritative *Theory of the Earth* [18] was developed generally in the intellectual climate of the Scottish Enlightenment, which was influenced in no small way by Antiquity [13. 222, 224–225].

D. 19TH CENTURY

In the 19th cent. the mineralogical-geological views of Antiquity were likewise still current in many cases [26. vol. 13. 24; vol. 21. 98], though from that point on, they developed a constitutive significance in natural philosophy. The "form" of the minerals was discussed, into the 18th cent., in the context of the philosophical question concerning the relationship of form and substance [7]. This legacy appears, for example, in G. W. F. Hegel's *Individueller Physik* and in his treatment of the geological development of rocks [17. 53–108, 114–116]. Furthermore, L. Oken made the ancient-medieval classification of rocks and minerals explicit as the basis of his treatment of geology and mineralogy, and thus offered a final testimonial to ancient mineralogy [14. 64–67].

→ METEOROLOGY

1 F. D. ADAMS, The Birth and Development of the Geological Sciences, 1954   2 G. AGRICOLA, Ausgewählte Werke, 10 vols., H. PRESCHER (ed.) 1955 ff.   3 ALBERTUS MAGNUS, Le monde minérale. Les pierres. De Mineralibus (livres I et II), présentation, traduction et commentaires par M. ANGEL (Sagesses chrétiennes), 1651, 1995 (Engl. D. WYCKOFF (trans.), Book of Minerals, 1967)   4 A. BORST, Das Buch der Naturgeschichte. Plinius und seine Leser im Zeitalter des Pergaments, AHAW 2, 1994   5 J. DÖRFLINGER, Die Geographie in der 'Encyclopédie'. Eine wissenschaftsgeschichtliche Studie, Veröffentlichungen der Kommission für Geschichte der Mathematik, Naturwissenschaft und Medizin 17, 1976   6 F. ELLENBERGER, Histoire de la géologie, vol. 1, 1988 (History of Geology, 1996 ff.)   7 N. E. EMERTON, The Scientific Reinterpretation of Form, 1984   8 Encyclopédie, ou Dictionnaire raisonné des sciences, des arts et des métiers, par une societé de gens de lettres, Paris, 1751 ff., (repr.1966)   9 H. FORS, Vetenskap i alkemins gränsland. Om J. G. Wallerius Wattu-riket, Svenska Linnésällskapets Årsskrift 1996/1997, 33–60   10 B. FRITSCHER, Vulkanismusstreit und Geochemie. Die Bedeutung der Chemie und des Experiments in der Vulkanismus-Neptunismus-Kontroverse, Boethius 25, 1991   11 Id., Wissenschaft vom Akzidentellen. Methodische Aspekte der Minerologie Georgius Agricolas, in: F. NAUMANN (ed.), Georgius Agricola – 500 Jahre, 1994, 82–89   12 Id., Tabellarische Übersicht der Geschichte der Geowissenschaft von Plinius bis auf Charles Lyell, 1996   13 Id., Volcanoes and the 'Wealth of Nations'. Relations between the Emerging Sciences of Political Economy and Geology in 18th-century Scotland, in: N. MORELLO (ed.), Volcanoes and History. Proceedings of the 20th INHIGEO Symposium Napoli-Eolie-Catania (Italy), 19–25, September 1995, 1998, 209–28

14 Id., Bemerkungen zu einer historischen Epistemologie der romantisch-idealistischen Erdwissenschaft am Beispiel der 'Geosophie' Lorenz Okens, Zeitschrift für geologische Wissenschaft 27, 1999, 61–69   15 C. GUILLEMIN, J.-C. ROUX, Mystères et réalités des eaux souterraines, La Vie des Sciences. Comptes Rendus de l'Académie des Sciences 11, 1994, 87–114   16 M. GUNTAU, Abraham Gottlob Werner, Biographien hervorragender Naturwissenschaftler, Techniker und Mediziner 75, 1984   17 G. W. F. HEGEL, Naturphilosophie, vol. 1, (ed.) M. GIES, 1982 (Engl. M. PETRY (trans.), Hegel's Philosophy of Nature, 1970)   18 J. HUTTON, Theory of the Earth; or an Investigation of the Laws observable in the Composition, Dissolution, and Restoration of Land Upon the Globe, Transactions of the Royal Society of Edinburgh 1, 1788, 209–304   19 U. KINDERMANN, Conchae marinae. Marine Fossilien in der Fachliteratur des frühen Mittelalters, Geologische Blätter für Nordostbayern 31, 1981, 515–30   20 F. KRAFFT, s. v. Mineralogie (and Geologie), LAW 2, 1963–1966   21 J. G. LEHMANN, Abhandlung von den Metall-Müttern und der Erzeugung der Metalle, Berlin 1753   22 G. W. LEIBNIZ, Protogaea, sive de prima facie telluris, et antiquissimae historiae vestigiis in ipsis naturae monumentis dissertatio, Göttingen 1749 (German edition in W. von Engelhardt's translation, 1949), English translation project with synopsis on World Wide Web at http://dibinst.mit.edu/DIBNER/Leibniz/   23 H. LÜSCHEN, Die Namen der Steine. Das Mineralreich im Spiegel der Sprache, 1968   24 J. MICRAELIUS, Lexicon philosophicum terminorum philosophis usitatorum, Stettin ²1662, L. GELDSETZER (ed.), 1966   25 H. M. NOBIS, Über die Bedeutung der geistigen Strömungen des Mittelalters für die Entwicklung der Erdwissenschaften, in: M. BÜTTNER (ed.), Zur Entwicklung der Geographie vom Mittelalter bis zu Carl Ritter. Abhandlungen und Quellen zur Geschichte der Geographie und Kosmologie 3, 1982, 21–41   26 Nouveau Dictionnaire d'Histoire naturelle, appliqué aux artes, à l'agriculture, à l'Économie rurale et domestique, à la Médecine, etc. Par une société de naturalistes et agriculturs, 36 vols., Paris 1816 ff.   27 D. R. OLDROYD, Some Neo-Platonic and Stoic Influences on Mineralogy in the Sixteenth and Seventeenth Centuries, Ambix 21, 1974, 128–156   28 Id., A Note on the Status of A. F. Cronstedt's Simple Earths and his Analytical Methods, Isis 65, 1974, 506–512   29 G. REISCH, Margarita philosophica, Basel ⁴1517, (ed.) L. GELDSETZER, Instrumenta Philosophica, series Thesauri 1, 1973   30 J. M. RIDDLE, Marbode of Rennes (1035–1123). Considered as a Medical Treatise with Text, Commentary and C. W. King's Translation, Sudhoffs Archiv, Beiheft 20, 1977   31 J. S. SCHRÖTER, Lithologisches Real- und Verballexikon, in welchem nicht nur die Synonymien der deutschen, lateinischen, französischen und holländischen Sprachen angeführt und erläutert, sondern auch alle Steine und Versteinerungen ausführlich beschrieben werden, 8 vols., Frankfurt/Main 1779 ff.   32 M. ULLMANN, Die Natur- und Geheimwissenschaften im Islam, Handbuch der Orientalistik I/6,2, B. SPULER (ed.), 1972   33 J. G. WALLERIUS, Mineralogia eller Mineral-Riket, Stockholm 1747   34 A. G. WERNER, Kurze Klassifikation und Beschreibung der verschiedenen Gebirgsarten, Dresden 1787 (Engl. A. OSPOVAT (trans.), Short Classification and Description of the Various Rocks, 1971)   35 J. H. ZEDLER, Grosses vollständiges Universal-Lexicon aller Wissenschafften und Künste, Halle und Leipzig, 1732 ff.   36 M. ZONTA, Mineralogy, Botany and Zoology in

Medieval Hebrew Encyclopedias. 'Descriptive' and 'Theoretical' Approaches to Arabic Sources, Arabic Sciences and Philosophy 6, 1996, 263–315

ADDITIONAL BIBLIOGRAPHY G. AGRICOLA, De natura fossilium (Textbook of mineralogy): M. C. BANDY, J. A. BANDY (trans.), 1955; G. A. GOOD (ed.), Sciences of the Earth: An Encyclopedia of Events, People, and Phenomena, 1998; M. T. GREENE, Natural Knowledge in Pre-classical Antiquity, 1992; A. DE VIVO, Le parole della scienza: sul trattato 'de terrae motu' di Seneca, in: Storia e scienze della terra 3, 1992   BERNHARD FRITSCHER

Geometry see → MATHEMATICS

Georgia

A. INTRODUCTION B. MIDDLE AGES C. PERIOD OF DECLINE (SECOND HALF OF THE 13TH CENTURY TO THE FIRST HALF OF THE 17TH CENTURY) D. RESTORATION (SECOND HALF OF THE 17TH CENTURY TO THE BEGINNING OF THE 19TH CENTURY) E. 19TH–20TH CENTURIES

A. INTRODUCTION

Besides the traditional interest in Graeco-Roman culture, there are a few factors in Georgia (G.) which determine the standards of scholarly study and the influence of Antiquity: 1. From the earliest times, G. (ancient Colchis and Iberia) had close relations with the ancient world. 2. There is much mythological, geographical and historical information about ancient G. in ancient mythology and literature. 3. Until the first written records in the Georgian language (4th–5th cent. AD), Greek, together with Aramaic, functioned as the official written language, which is also confirmed by a wealth of epigraphic material. 4. After the declaration of Christianity as the official religion (4th cent. AD), Georgian culture developed in close relationship with the Byzantine, which is also manifested in the particular attention paid to Greece. 5. In medieval G., in the 11th–12th cents., the characteristic tendencies of the Renaissance (an interest in ancient philosophy and science) took on a distinct form as a result of intense contact with the Arab world.

B. MIDDLE AGES

Interest in Antiquity grew in G., beginning primarily in the 8th cent. and becoming stronger in the 10th–11th cents. Georgian centres of learning played the most important role in this development. According to Themistius, a primarily Neo-Platonic, philosophical-rhetorical academy of Colchis already existed in Phasis (western G., modern Poti) in the 4th cent. AD. Georgian intellectuals became more and more active in famous Christian centres of the world. Among many others, the Lavra of Sabatsminda (near Jerusalem) must be pointed out, where Georgian monks had their own monastery beginning in 532 and where literary and translation work was carried out from the 8th–9th cents. on. The various Christian centres were particularly involved in

the growing scope of translation into Georgian: on Mt. Sinai, where the Georgian monastery colony existed starting in the 10th cent.; in the Iviron monastery on the Holy Mountain (Athos), which was built in 980–983; in the Georgian monastic colony on the Black Mountain near Antiochia, where 60 Georgians lived in the 11th cent.; in the Holy Cross monastery in Palestine, which was built in the 11th cent.; in the Petritsoni monastery in Bulgaria, which was built at the end of the 11th cent.; and in others. Many Georgian intellectuals received their education at the best schools in Byzantium. Even more important was the formation of universities or academies in G. itself, among which the academies of Iqalto (founded in the 11th cent.) and Gelati (founded 1106) are noteworthy. King Davit the Builder convened the most famous Georgian scholars in the latter. The program of the academies included the study of the following disciplines: geometry, arithmetic, music, philosophy, rhetoric, grammar and astronomy. G. was actively integrated into the process of the cultural life of the Byzantine empire and the Oriental world. Close contacts with Byzantine intellectual centres and intensive literary activity brought a systematic nature to the influence of both the Graeco-Christian and ancient cultures. In philosophy, particular mention must be made of Arsen Iqaltoeli (11th–12th cent.) and Ioane Petrizi (11th–12th cent.), who received their training from Michael Psellus and Johannes Italus. Italus considered Petrizi to be one of his closest associates and friends. Petrizi's work flourished in the academy of Gelati. Because of the religious and philosophical tolerance of the time his enthusiasm for ancient philosophy was not threatened by the battles against heresy. Like his teachers, Petrizi evinced particular interest in Plato, the Neo-Platonists and Aristotle, whose *Topics* and *On Interpretation* he translated into Georgian. He added extensive commentary to the translation of Proclus Diadochus' *Elements of Theology*, which is recognized as an independent philosophical work. Profound knowledge of ancient Greek philosophy, mythology and science are in evidence here. He considered his greatest authorities to be Socrates, Plato, Aristotle, Porphyrius and Iamblichus. Scholarly discussion continues until the present day as to how to qualify his philosophical thoughts. He appears to be a representative of developed scholasticism who uses philosophy positively and bases the wisdom of the phenomenon on rational arguments.

Many Georgian historiographic works extensively reflect Antiquity. From this point of view, *The Life of King Davit* (11th–12th cent.) is interesting. In the description of the deeds of the king who unified G., the historiographer, in a variety of contexts, mentions Homer and the figures in his epics (Achilles, Odysseus, Priam, Hector), Josephus Flavius, Alexander the Great and his historian Aristoboulus, the *Alexander Romance*, Ptolemaeus Philadelphus, Vespasian, Titus as well as Athens as a symbol of scholarship. In his *Istoriani da azmani scharavandedtani*, the first historian of King Tamar mentions not only more or less well-known ancient authorities – Homer, Socrates, Plato, Plutarch, Philodorus, Critias – but also derives Georgian adjectives from ancient personal names, e. g. *achiliani, alexandriani, apoloniani, aphroditiani, augustiani, ulimpiani*. The influence of Antiquity emerges particularly clearly in medieval secular poetry. In panygeric works, in Chakhrukhadze's *Tamariani* and Iohane Shavteli's *Abdulmesiani*, mention of ancient Greek poets, philosophers and authors is already common. Particularly important in this respect is the masterpiece of Georgian poetry, Shota Rustaveli's *The Knight in the Panther's Skin* (12th cent.), in which the influence of Antiquity already has a systematic character and is demonstrated in its principal philosophical aspects, which provide an interesting synthesis of Christian, Oriental and ancient Greek thought. He himself names the ideas which he 'learned' from Plato among the most important sources of wisdom for his own philosophy. For his lead figure Avtandil, philosophy is a philosophy of action; the rule of life is to live philosophically; one of the chief principles is the progression from the love of splendid things to the love of splendid deeds. His other important source is obviously Aristotle, particularly his ethics. Scholars' attention has also been drawn to the closeness of Rustaveli's 'true truth' and 'idleness', on the one hand, and ἐπιείκεια and σχολή in the teachings of Aristotle on the other. The question of Rustaveli's relationship to the Homeric epic deserves particular attention. Although no direct reference to Homeric epic can be found in *The Knight in the Panther's Skin*, some Homeric motifs are reflected in the Georgian poet which, in the opinion of a number of scholars, go far beyond the boundaries of typological similarity. In both cases, the abduction of the woman is the chief cause of conflict. In both cases, there is a central leading character, who is the strongest and in whom the emotional aspect predominates (Achilles/Tariel), and a second who is clever and skilful, in whom the rational aspect dominates, and who reaches his goal after long wanderings (Odysseus/Avtandil). In both the *Iliad* and *The Knight in the Panther's Skin*, the chief figure takes virtually no part in the action for a long period, but wins the main battle after returning. In Homer and Rustaveli, the war is fought to free the woman. In both authors, the skilled and clever hero wanders through the real and the fantastic world, and so on. Homer's influence on medieval Georgian literature is not coincidental. For Georgian thought in the 11th–12th cents., Homer was considered the greatest authority of all time among poets. His rather frequent mention, his quotation, the attempts to find a Georgian equivalent in some hexametric lines, and the appearance of the elements of the subject and figures from Homeric epic in the works of all genres of secular literature have caused some scholars to assume that Homer's epic could have existed in the Middle Ages, even if in abridged translation (*Iliad*).

Translated literature which included extensive information about Antiquity and, above all, Greek culture served as an important source for the spread of information about Antiquity. Special translation schools were founded, which offer us varying theories for the translation of Greek texts (exact translation, free translation, expository translation). Of course, the question of adopting ancient personal names was also treated. It is interesting that, although Greek onomastics correspond primarily to the pronunciation of the Byzantine era, the cases where we encounter Classical pronunciation are also not uncommon. Thus, for example, the Greek χ is primarily transliterated into Georgian with x, but we also have instances in which it is replaced by k. Greek υ is often transliterated with Georgian wi and not i, η with e and not i, δ with d, β with b, etc. Ekvtime Atoneli, Eprem Mzire, Arsen Iqaltoeli, Ioane Petrizi, and many others translated from Greek everything important, which in Byzantium was considered a necessary prerequisite to education for both secular and clerical society. Some collections of sayings in translation by Democritus, Socrates, Plato, Aristotle and the Neo-Platonists were important for information about Antiquity. According to the translation of the homilies of Gregory of Nazianzus, the mythological commentaries of Pseudo-Nonnus were translated twice in the 10th–11th cents. The translation of John of Damascus' *On the Orthodox Faith*, Georgius Hamartolus' *Chronicle*, the works of Proclus Diadochus, and many other authors which contain extensive information about Antiquity promoted the knowledge of numerous ancient names and historical events among Georgian-speaking readers. This, in turn, stimulated the reception of the ancient legacy through medieval Georgian culture. This comprehensive influence of Antiquity on Georgian thought and literature was accompanied by reinforcement of tendencies of the proto-Renaissance. The same processes occurred in G. which somewhat later in Europe would lead to the development of Humanism and the Renaissance.

C. Period of Decline (Second Half of the 13th Century to the First Half of the 17th Century)

In G., the second half of the 13th cent. began with the invasion of the Mongols and then of the Ottomans. With the fall of Byzantium, G. was separated for a long time from those processes, which were taking place in Europe from the 14th cent. on. There was less and less information about Antiquity in Georgian literature, although an anonymous historical work written in the 14th cent., which describes Georgian history of the previous 100 years, demonstrates solid knowledge of the Greek language, as well as some aspects of mythology (Trojan legend cycle), history (Astyages and Cyrus), and philosophy (Aristotle).

D. Restoration (Second Half of the 17th Century to the Beginning of the 19th Century)

Despite a difficult political situation, feudal fragmentation and endless bloody wars with powerful Oriental states, there began in the second half of the 17th cent. those processes in the development of Georgian culture which are frequently referred to in research as "restoration". Starting at this time, G. built new relationships with Europe, primarily through contact with Russia. The increasing interest in Antiquity became ever more evident. The names of Homer, Aristotle and Plato reappear in the poetry of King Arcil (1647–1713). In the fantasy epic *Rusudaniani*, Achilles and Alexander the Great are once again objects of comparison. In the work of the 18th cent. author Timote Gabashvili, *The Journey*, Proclus Diadochus is also mentioned among the translated authors, although the Orthodox reader is recommended to deal with him carefully. Other collections, this time translated from Russian, were added to the four collections of *Apophthegmata* that were popular in the Middle Ages. Another reason for the popularity of the *Apophthegmata* among Georgian readers was the fact that the famous author, publisher and king Vakhtang reworked it and gave it poetic form in the collection *Sibrdsne Malagobeli*. Here are represented famous wise sayings and episodes from the lives of Socrates, Plato, Aristotle, Aristophanes, Menander, Zeno, Antisthenes, Anaxagoras, Agathocles, Epicurus, Julian, Augustus, Cicero and Alexander the Great. Commissioned by Vakhtang, many books connected with Antiquity were also translated from Russian and other languages. Interest in theatre and dramaturgy became ever stronger. The technical term *theatron* had been found in many contexts starting in the 7th cent.; it denoted the arena, a place where something is exhibited. The questions of Greek tragedy and comedy have an important place in the literature, whether in the original or translated into Georgian. In the historical poem *The Battle at Rukhi* by the famous Georgian poet Besiki (1750–1791), Homer, the best poet, and Achilles, the bravest hero, appear again. In the 18th cent., Anton, the Catholicos of G., wrote two editions of Georgian grammar (1753, 1767). The author concludes that the methods of the ancient grammarians must be used as a foundation. In the most important work of Georgian lexicography *Georgian Lexicon*, compiled by Sulchan-Saba Orbeliani in 1685–1716, the author demonstrates and explains many words and technical expressions from Greek which are retained in Georgian. In the 18th and first half of the 19th cents., translation work became quite intensive. Both the language of the original and primarily Russian or European languages were used in translating. Of the numerous translations, I. Garsevanishvili's translations of the *Iliad* (finished 1826) and the *Odyssey* (by 1815) as well as of Aesop's *Fables* (second half of the 18th cent.) deserve particular interest. Besides medieval attempts at translation of the *Alexander Romance*, the Georgian poetic version *Alexandriani* was written in the 18th cent., taking the Serbian redaction of the life of Alexander into account. Works by Russian and European dramatists with ancient subjects were also intensively translated (V. Ozerov, P. Corneille, J. Racine). Antiquity is rather thoroughly represented in the encyclopaedic literature. Ancient mythology and culture have particular significance in I. Bagrationi's (1768–1830) *Kalmasoba*, where we are offered much information from every sphere of educated culture and scholarship in the form of dialogues. New mythological lexicons were prepared which used not merely old versions of the *Tales of the Hellenes*, but also new reference works as their basis. Of particular noteworthiness is *The Mythology* by D. Bagrationi, which was written at the end of the 18th cent. Interest in Antiquity became stronger once again in the works of historians. Of interest are attempts to connect the saga of the Argonauts with ancient periods of Georgian history, as in Teimuraz Bagrationi's (1782–1846) *Georgian History*, where the author is of the opinion that Medea did not murder her children.

E. 19th–20th Centuries

A few periods can be distinguished in the political history of G. since the 19th cent: 1801–1917: loss of statehood and union with Russia; 1918–1921: restoration of national independence; 1921–1991: sovietization after annexation; since 1991 restoration of national independence. Despite change in political systems and societal forms, the process of creative adoption and scholarly study of Antiquity continued to increase steadily.

1. Literature and Art   2. Classical Studies

1. Literature and Art

The use of Classical material in Georgian literature has a systematic character. Of course, the topic of the Argonauts and the legendary Colchis holds a special place. The classicist of Georgian literature, Akaki Tsereteli (1840–1915), wrote a five-act play *Media*, which was meant to be the first part of a trilogy. At first a prose work, the poet himself later put it into verse. He added explanations to his drama in which he attempted quite objectively to interpret all of the names connected with Colchis in the saga using the Georgian language. The names of the famous figures are accordingly Georgianized: Aeetes – Iata, Medea – Media, Apsyrtus – Isir, Circe – Tirta. The action takes place in Colchis. At the beginning, Jason fights only for Medea. The matter of the Golden Fleece only comes later. Medea does not participate in the murder of Apsyrtus; her brother is sacrificed to the god of the sea by the Greeks. The play *Medea* and the mythological novel *The Tale of the Colchian Princess* by the contemporary author and antiquarian L. Sanikidze were also dedicated to this subject. The play is set in Corinth, and in the novel, the story encompasses the complete legend of the Argonauts from the episode of Phrixus and Helle to Medea's homecoming. In both works, Medea's responsibility for the murder of the children is denied. The author shares the view of versions of the pre-Euripidean Greek tradition. In these works, Medea is represented as a wise and loving woman who is the victim of adultery and emigration from her homeland. The contemporary novelist Otar Chiladze shows the legend of the Argonauts from another view in his two-part work *A Man Went Down the Road* (1. Aeetes, 2. Ukheiro ("The Ne'er-do-well")). Here, the subject of the myth is more or less unchanged, without being concretized in time and space and to this extent without a search for any historical basis; however, it is conceived so that the author offers us the tragedy of not just one person, but of the entire generation. It is a novel full of political intrigue, in which drama, irony and parody are interlinked.

The second legend which draws the attention of Georgian authors is that of Prometheus, or, more properly said, that of his Caucasian prototype Amirani. In the 19th cent., Akaki Tsereteli wrote his poem *Amirani* (1895), in which the Georgian legend is enhanced with elements from Greek mythology. The author D. Gachechiladze wrote the drama *Amirani* (1963), in which a hero is depicted fighting against tyranny and for freedom, a theme which gained currency under the political conditions of the time.

Interest in ancient tradition extended throughout Georgian literature of the 20th cent. At the beginning of the century, some Georgian symbolists argued that the ancient material should be replaced in modern literature by new mythology, new symbols and masks. However, Antiquity is impressively represented in the works of the famed symbolist T. Tabidze (arrested and executed in 1937). In his drama *The Amazons*, he virtually wrote a new myth of the Amazons and their queen Tomiranda. In *The Created Myth*, he relates the love of Alexander the Great and the Amazon queen Isovela. He gives us his own version of the legend of the Argonauts in his poems *The Harbour of Rioni* and *Medea*. In *New Colchis*, he attempts to show the connection between the famous legend and the trials taking place in modern Colchis. Ancient subjects are presented in abundance in the works of the well-known German-language Georgian author Grigol Robakidze, who was forced to leave Soviet G. and died in emigration in 1962. The greatest Georgian poet of the 20th cent., Galaktion Tabidze, quite consciously considered ancient Hellas to be the home of eternal beauty and poetic inspiration. In his poem *The Conversation Regarding Lyric Poetry*, he offers a poetic overview of the development of ancient Greek lyric poetry and its contribution to world poetry. His poems *The Roses, The Marble, When Actaeon Son of Aristaus, The Muse, The Hetaera* and many others are heavily inspired by ancient Greek subject matter. In the poetry of Galaktion, some 150 symbols and figures, names or terms connected with Antiquity are used and included in the system of his poetic thought.

There is a rich tradition of performing ancient dramas and of their reception on the Georgian stage. Of note are the operas *Cleopatra* by F. Glonti (1976) and *The Daughter of Kolkheti* by B. Kvernadze (1997), and the ballet performances *Orpheus* by S. Nasidze (1972), *Medea* by R. Gabichvadze and *Medea* by A. Machavariani.

Ancient subjects are very popular in modern Georgian painting and sculpture. At the exhibit *Greece in Modern Georgian Art* (Tbilisi, 1998), 150 Georgian artists of the 20th cent. participated with 400 pieces reflecting nearly the whole of Greek myth and literature.

2. CLASSICAL STUDIES

After the Middle Ages, Classical studies in G. attained a particular standard in the 20th cent. once intensive research into and study of ancient culture and its relationship to G. had begun, first at the University of Tbilisi (1918) and then at other scholarly and educational facilities. Of many research centres, especially noteworthy are the Institute for Classical Philology, Byzantine Studies and Modern Greek Studies at Tbilisi State University (60 staff members, 250 students, its own specialized library and publishing house *Logos*) and the Archaeology Centre at the Academy of Sciences, which directs archaeological excavations in G. Gr. Tsereteli (1870–1938) and S. Kaukhchishvili (1895–1981) have played a major role in the development of Classical studies in G., establishing great authority for the subject both in G. and abroad.

The main directions of work are: a) the publication of information about G. in Greek and Roman authors (text in original language, translations, commentaries). Approximately 20 books have already appeared in this series. The encyclopaedia *Caucasus Antiquus* is in preparation; it extensively covers names and terms connected with the Caucasian region recorded in Greek and Roman sources in ca. 1000 headwords. b) Research into Graeco-Roman literature, mythology and civilization. The multi-volume academic edition *The History of Greek Literature* (Gr. Tsereteli) had its first publication in the former Soviet Union in the 1930s. In the 1950s, S. Kaukhchishvili's two-volume *History of Greek Literature* and later the one-volume *Ancient Literature* enjoyed several editions. Currently, publication of the three-volume *Ancient Literature* (R. Gordesiani) and the ten-volume *Greek Myths* is underway. Starting in 1998, *The Cultures of Antiquity* in six volumes has been in publication (two volumes have already appeared). Approximately 300 books and thousands of articles on Homerology, Greek lyric poetry, drama, novels, Hellenistic epic, ancient traditions, the history of Greece and Rome, Classical architecture, Graeco-Roman-Georgian relations, ancient philosophy, etc. have already appeared. c) Study of and research into Classical languages. Ancient Greek and Latin are taught in all university humanities departments. Since 1998, as a result of the reform of the educational system, the study of Classical languages has been introduced into the secondary schools. Several textbooks for ancient Greek and Latin are being prepared in Georgian. Individual works are devoted to the linguistic relationships between pre-Greek, Greek and Georgian, Greek inscriptions preserved in G., the history of the Greek language and questions of vocabulary of Greek origin in the Georgian language.

→ Alexander the Great; → Amazons; → Argonauts; → Aristoteles; → Byzantium; → Historiography; → Homerus; → Iberia; → Colchis; → Medea; → Prometheus → Renaissance; → Humanism

> 1 V. Asatiani, Classical and Byzantine Traditions in Georgian Literature, Tbilisi 1996 2 R. Gordeziani, S. Siamanidou, Ελληνικες Σπουδές στη Γεωργία (Greek Studies on Georgia), Tbilisi 1997 3 Η Ελλάδα στη σύγχρονη γεωργιανή τέχνη (Greece in Modern Georgian Art), Catalogue of the Exhibit, Tiblisi-Athens 1998.

RISMAG GORDESIANI

Georgics see → Bucolics

Geriatrics
A. Introduction B. Dietetics in the Gerocomias C. Examples of Longevity D. Pathology of Old Age

A. Introduction
Although the term 'geriatrics' is a 20th cent. creation (J. L. Nascher, 1909), diagnostic and dietetic elements of health care for the elderly were already recorded for ancient medicine. The main sources of its reception, which was very significant in practice until into the 18th cent., were, on one hand, sporadic references in the *Corpus Hippocraticum* (Aphorisms 3,31; De victu 1,33) to diseases of old age and the age dependence of various ailments, their progress and the recommended diet, and, on the other, Galen, who, influenced by speculations of the Roman imperial period on age and immortality (De mar. 2; De san. tuenda 5,4), devoted special attention to this topic. Especially in the 5th volume of his ' Hygiene ' (*De sanitate tuenda*), which was almost exclusively dedicated to the care of seniors as a branch of medicine ('μέρος τῆς τέχνης γηροκομικόν'), he not only provided the impulse for all later 'Gerocomias', but also elaborated on the Aristotelian imbalance of fluids in old age (cold and dry: Aristot. Gen. an. 784a 34). The Stagirite's concept of a *calor innatus* (θερμότης φυσική: Parv. nat. 469b 9) that extinguished with age was interpreted by Galen as a cold variant of marasmus (De mar. 3 f.; De temper. 2,2). Another important structural element of the reception of geriatrics of Antiquity was the definition of the phases of ageing: Galen admittedly rejected a chronological determination for the three phases of old age that he differentiated (De san. tuenda 5,12) while the *Corpus Hippocraticum* related a speculative division of the ages of life into seven to ten periods of seven years, of which two belong to old age (πρεσβύτης from the 50th year, γέρων from the 58th year; *Corpus Hippo-*

craticum, De hebdomadibus 5; cf. Isidore, *Etymologiae* 11,2,1 ff.; Thomas Cantimpratensis, *Liber de natura rerum* 1,82–83). The church fathers had a completely different approach to geriatrics when they transferred the topos of the sinful ageing of the world onto the human body. In contrast the soul does not age in as much as penitence and the Eucharist act as 'φάρμακον ἀθανασίας' (John Chrysostom, 5th cent., De paenitentia, MPG 60,766; Ignatius, 2nd cent., Epist. ad Ephesios 20,2).

B. Dietetics in the Gerocomias
Galen's realistic opinion of a more or less 'natural' (because unavoidable) ageing process that could be delayed by dietetics but in the end was unstoppable shapes medical perspective to this day because of a lack of therapeutic alternatives. Utopian hopes for an extension of longevity have always been present but remain speculative. Short extracts of Galenic dietetics for old age are found in Oribasius (4th cent., Synopsis ad Eusthatium 5,18), Aetius of Amida (6th cent., Libri medicinales 4,30) and Paulus of Aegina (7th cent., Epitomae medicae libri septem 1,23). Since both *De sanitate tuenda* and *De temperamentis* entered, as adaptations, the teaching canon of the *Summaria Alexandrinorum*, they were often adopted in Islamic medicine, most thoroughly by Avicenna (about 1000, Canon 1,3,3). The *Responsum* of Maimonides (12th cent.) on the question of a firmly predetermined date of death shows, on the other hand, a clearly expanded aetiology of old age [4]. In contrast to the Islamic healing arts, the Latin Middle Ages passed on, up until the middle of the 14th cent., biological theses on old age following Aristotle and Galen (Albertus Magnus, Commentary on the *Parva naturalia*, about 1250; Roger Bacon, *De retardatione accidentium senectutis*, about 1280; Arnald of Villanova, *De conservanda iuventute et retardanda senectute*, about 1300) but took no notice of the crucial fifth book of the *Hygiene*, which became accessible, at the latest, with Niccolòs da Reggio's translation (1308–1345). Only with Marsilio Ficino [1. pars 2] and Gabriele Zerbi (already recognizable from the title *Gerontocomia*, 1489: first printed monograph of the ' Geriatrics ') did the genre of special regimes for old age in dietetics founded by Bacon and Arnald take its direction from Galen's ' Gerocomia '. The organisation of Zerbi's work according to the *Sex res non naturales* (effects of air, nutrition, movement and rest, sleep and waking, filling and emptying and emotions) was a model for texts on health in old age over the next 300 years (Antonio Fumanelli, *De senium regimine*, 1540; Aurelio Anselmo, *Gerocomica*, 1606; Bernardinus Stainer, *Gerokomicon*, 1631; John Floyer, *Medicina gerocomica*, 1724; Gerard van Swieten, *Oratio de senum valetudine tuenda*, 1778), just as it had shaped Islamic dietetics according to ancient patterns. This main section is usually preceded by biological and diagnostic notes on old age while pharmacological notes complete the texts. Even critical voices such as Girolamo Car-

dano and religious authors such as Daniel Tossanus (*De senectute*, 1591) and Benedictus di Bacquere (*Senum medicus*, 1673) picked up on Galen's recommendations. Not until the clinical, pathology-based, and later scientifically influenced medicine of the 19th cent. would the universal concept of a pathology based on the humors or of mechanistic interpretations of the elderly constitution with their corresponding holistic strategies be rejected in favor of the treatment of individual symptoms or diseases.

C. EXAMPLES OF LONGEVITY

The fascination aroused by sprightly individuals or entire ethnic groups having advanced age was already reflected during Antiquity in relevant *memorabilia* or *paradoxa*. While the first collections of this type of *exempla* were created outside of medicine (Plin. HN 7,48ff; Valerius Maximus, De dictis factisque memorabilibus 8,13) – partially on the occasion of a birthday (Lucian Macrobii), a tradition, which the Early Modern period willingly took up (Tommaso Rangoni, *De vita hominis ultra CXX. annos protrahenda*, 1550; Heinrich Meibom, *Epistola de longaevis*, 1664) – the gerocomias made use of individual biographical notes to illustrate the benefits of a recommended diet or therapy. For this purpose, already Galen had chosen the example of a doctor (Antiochus; De san. tuenda 5,4); the Early Modern period liked mentioning Democritus and the gymnastics teacher Herodicus of Selymbria, whom Plato criticized (Rep. 406 a7b7 [1. pars 2,1; 8]), but increasingly also authors of dietetics such as the allegedly 140–year old Galen himself [2. 1,2]. Medical opponents, whose theoretical teachings did not match their personal longevity, were also cited as (negative) examples. Following Galen's example, who maligned an anonymous Egyptian sophist in this manner (De mar. 2; cf. Zerbi, Gerontocomia 8), Henry Cuffe (The differences of the ages of mans life, 1607, 71 f.) and many others after him argued against Paracelsus who died at the early age of 57. However, after 1600 the autobiographic example of the old Alvise Cornaro (*Discorsi alla vita sobria*, 1558–63) almost completely replaced the ancient *exempla* in medicine. The satire by Johann Heinrich Cohausen (*Hermippus redivivus*, 1742), often mistaken as personal conviction, of a supposedly ancient inscription that explained the advanced age of a teacher at a high school for girls as being caused by the breath of his pupils (a variant of so-called sunamitism) actually demonstrated a playful and at the same time critical treatment of the tradition.

D. PATHOLOGY OF OLD AGE

Apart from an altered constitution of the aged organism (*Kakochymia*), which is evident in various symptoms such as altered pulse (Galen, De causis pulsuum 3,5; cf. Avicenna 1), urine and respiration, but also in changes to the heart (according to Galen; cf. [3. 171]), Antiquity discussed diseases that mostly occurred with advanced age. The ailments mentioned in the *Corpus Hippocraticum* (Aphorisms 3,31) gave rise in the Early Modern period to numerous summary studies or monographs, which partially also followed dietetic treatises (David de Pomis, *Enarratio brevis de senum affectibus*, 1588). Independently or by comparison, doctors and theologians interpreted the ailments of old age represented allegorically in Eccl. 12 (John Hill, *The pourtract of old age*, 1666).

After 1600 a quote from Terence ('senectus ipsast morbu': Phormio 575) ignited a debate in scientific medicine between Galenists and Iatromechanics (Jakob Hutter, *Tractatio medica qua senectus ipsa morbus sistitur*, 1732; following Santorio Santorio, *De medicina statica*, 1614, 1,83; 5,35) regarding the interpretation of old age as a disease, which had already become proverbial in Antiquity with respect to the Aristotelian sentence 'τὸ δὲ γῆρας νόσον φυσικὴν' (Aristot. Gen. an. 784 b 34) but was decidedly rejected by Galen (De san. tuenda 5,4) and especially by his early modern followers [5. 541 f.]. Although the Hippocratic concept of diseases in old age (after 1800 conceived as organrelated) was established subsequently, the question of the biology and pathology of old age and their fundamental assessment remains unanswered to the present.
→ Aetius of Amida; → Aristoteles; → Galenus; → Herodicus; → Hippocrates; → Ignatius; → Oribasius; → Paulus of Aegina; → Summaria Alexandrinorum

SOURCES   1 MARSILIO FICINO, De triplice vita, 1489 2 LAURENT JOUBERT, Erreurs Populaires au Fait de la Médecine et Régime de Santé, 1578 (Engl. G. D. DE ROCHER (trans.), Popular Errors, 1989)   3 ANDRÉ DU LAURENS, A Discourse of the Preservation of the Sight, of Melancholike Diseases, of Rheumes, and of Old Age, 1599   4 MAIMONIDES, Über die Lebensdauer. Ein unediertes Responsum, G. WEIL (ed.), 1953   5 FRANCISCI RANCHINI, ΓΗΡΟΜΙΚΗ- De senum conservatione & senilium Morborum Curatione, in: FRANÇOIS RANCHI N, Opuscula medica, 1627, 456–592

LITERATURE   6 L. DEMAITRE, The Care and Extension of Old Age in Medieval Medicine, in: M. M. SHEEHAN (ed.), Aging and the Aged in Medieval Europe, 1990, 3–22 7 J. T. FREEMAN, Ageing. Its History and Literature, 1979 8 M. D. GRMEK, On Ageing and Old Age, 1958   9 P. LÜTH, Geschichte der Geriatrie, 1965   10 G. MINOIS, History of Old Age, 1989   11 H. ORTH, ΔΙΑΙΤΑ ΓΕΡΟΝΤΩΝ die Geschichte der griechischen Antike. Centaurus 8, 1963, 19–47   12 D. SCHÄFER, That Senescence Itself Is an Illness .... Concepts of Age and Ageing in Perspective. Medical History 46, 2002, 525–548   13 Id., Alter und Krankheit in der Frühen Neuzeit. Der ärztliche Blick auf die letzte Lebensphase, 2004   14 J. STEUDEL, Zur Geschichte der Lehre von den Greisenkrankheiten. Sudhoffs Archiv 35, 1942, 1–27   15 F. D. ZEMAN, Life's Later Years. Studies in the Medical History of Old Age (1944–51), repr. in: G. J. GRUMAN (ed.), Roots of Modern Gerontology and Geriatrics, 1979, 168   DANIEL SCHÄFER

German Democratic Republic (GDR)
I. CLASSICAL STUDIES   II. LITERATURE, MUSIC
AND THE FINE ARTS

I. CLASSICAL STUDIES
A. GENERAL   B. CONDITIONS   C. UNIVERSITIES
AND COLLEGES   D. ACADEMIES   E. MUSEUMS AND
LIBRARIES   F. SOCIETIES   G. CURRENT STATE OF
RESEARCH

A. GENERAL
On the whole, the development in all disciplines concerned with Antiquity in the Soviet Occupation Zone (SOZ) and, since 1949, in the GDR, was characterised, on the one hand, by efforts to preserve traditional areas of research and forms of work with a view to international scholarship, especially in the non-Socialist world and, in addition, to break new ground. On the other hand, ideological indoctrination continually increased and aimed, with varying degrees of success, at an understanding of history shaped by Marxist-Leninism. These transformations were incorporated into comprehensive 'reforms' in schools, universities and research institutes (see below, B, C, D). That fundamental differences of this kind were also reflected to a large degree in human relations should not be surprising when one considers the intention of the proponents of Marxist-Leninism to grasp the human being in his entirety. In research institutions and in the university sector, this split between those classical scholars concerned with traditional goals and those pursuing Marxist aims was hardened organizationally by the fact that ideologically induced prerequisites had to be fulfilled, both for promotion to so-called leadership functions as well as for obtaining a more or less permanent authorization to travel (designated by the ugly neologism *Reisekader*). Here, as always, exceptions proved the rule. It is in keeping with this picture that neither Classical Studies in the GDR as a whole nor individual disciplines within it were represented long-term by special → PROFESSIONAL ASSOCIATIONS. But if membership in the pan-German *Mommsen-Gesellschaft*, as could be still expected after its founding in 1950 in Jena (thus, on East German soil), was no longer possible after the construction of the Berlin Wall in 1961, there was resistance from the outset against any corresponding official membership in the *Deutsche Altphilologenverband*. And if the *Mommsen-Gesellschaft* was able to be maintained for a while by the members, it was without any effect. Attempts to establish a corresponding association solely for the territory of the GDR led to no visible results; here, too, personal rivalries among the leading representatives of the various disciplines were partly responsible. The result of the lack of such an association was that Classical Studies could not be represented in the *Fédération Internationale des Associations pour les Études classiques* , an outsider role, matched only by that of the USSR. This development clearly contributed to the relative isolation of East German Classical Studies in the international context. This isolation could not, of course, be compensated for by the GDR's membership in the *Eirene-Committee*, founded in 1957, which loosely connected Classical Studies in Socialist countries by, among other things, a journal published at Prague and regular conferences. The degree of isolation of Classical Studies as compared to developments in the Western world as a whole is difficult to determine. The denied or restrictively regulated participation in international organisations, together with the already-mentioned *Reisekader*-regulation, certainly had negative consequences, and not only for individuals. If, by contrast, the Corpus-Projects of the Berlin Academy (see below, D) continued, albeit under increasingly difficult circumstances, to be able to claim a place in international scholarship, this occurred, apart from contacts that existed more or less *sub secreto*, because the corresponding collaboration with scholars and institutions of other states represented a *condicio sine qua non*. This, however, also characterizes the exceptional status of the academy's projects and within Classical Studies in the GDR and, correspondingly, that of its great museums.

B. CONDITIONS
It is impossible to discuss training in the disciplines of Classical Studies without taking into account the constantly shrinking instruction in ancient languages (→ ANCIENT LANGUAGES, TEACHING OF) in the secondary schools of the GDR. Whereas in the SOZ and the early GDR a fairly dense network of classes with instruction in Greek and Latin still existed whose → CURRICULUM was still largely oriented towards that of the traditional grammar schools, in the period that followed, and definitively since the 'Law on Uniform Socialist Education' of 1965, "the ancient languages ... were starved half to death in a scandalous fashion" (H.-J. Meyer, Minister for Education and Science in the last government of the GDR). By 1989, although a four-year program in Latin still existed, Greek continued to be taught at only nine post-secondary institutions (Berlin, Dresden, Eisenach, Halle, Leipzig, Magdeburg, Potsdam, Rostock and Zwickau) at the rate of a mere three hours per week during the last three years before the final exams. An additional optional Latin course was also available, where necessary, at the other post-secondary schools (exact figures for 1989/90: [13]). Only in the case of theological studies were there provisions for Greek and Latin instruction in the preparatory schools of the two major religious denominations [14]. In any event, only a part of contemporary theology students were affected by this measure, so that the Protestant theological departments at the universities, as well as the Catholic philosophical-theological department at Erfurt, had to take action, where necessary, to improve matters with special curricula. The same holds true for the study of Latin in the colleges of arts and medicine. Basically, instruction in ancient languages not provided in the post-secondary schools had

to be made up later in the specialized fields, which was uneconomical.

C. Universities and Colleges

After the collapse, the traditional universities situated in the territory of the SOZ (Berlin, Greifswald, Halle, Jena, Leipzig, Rostock) were all able to reopen their doors, if not immediately, then at least after a relatively short pause. Regardless of their respective form of organisation, they each began with a full range of course offerings in Classical Studies. Although the pre-programmed ideological pressure on universities became increasingly acute on the whole (the foundation the Free Berlin University in 1948 in reaction to this pressure by former students and professors of the Berlin Humboldt University was symptomatic of this situation), Classical Studies organisations were initially able to escape it. Together with their universities, however, Classical Studies was drawn ever deeper over time into the consequences of the post-secondary educational policies of the GDR, which were marked by a total of three 'reforms of higher education' (1: 1945–50, 2: 1951, 3: 1967; the last of these was, apparently, disowned by its originators). The devastation wrought in the field of Classical Studies is best documented by the state of affairs in November 1989 (with ancient history being taught within the framework of general history, except in Jena): In Berlin the Chair of Latin studies was abolished and the Chair of Greek studies was filled again in 1988 after a long vacancy; in Greifswald Classical philology and Classical archaeology were abolished; in Leipzig Chairs were filled for Greek studies with specialization in modern Greek; in Rostock Chairs in Classical philology were left vacant or were transferred to the history department. Regardless of the available teaching staff, no enrolment was approved for any of these fields (modern Greek studies, however, was approved in Berlin and Leipzig). Only the University of Halle was allowed, on condition of full enrolment, to provide education in ancient languages with a limited contingent of teachers, while in Jena it proved possible, likewise on condition of full enrolment, to combine philology, archaeology and ancient history into one section of Classical Studies. Here, unlike in Halle, it was possible to receive a degree in (Classical) philology (roughly corresponding to studies leading to the Master of Arts). Archaeological training, with a similarly limited number of applicants, who were not accepted every year, was provided at all universities, with the exception of Greifswald. Ancient History, as represented by professorships at teachers' colleges, was less influential for Classical Studies.

D. Academies

In 1945, there were three scholarly academies (*Akademien der Wissenschaften*) in the territory of the SOZ, in Berlin, Leipzig and Erfurt. Although it was not disbanded, this last-named organization, the *Akademie gemeinnütziger Wissenschaften zu Erfurt*, founded in

1745, was not permitted to continue its work until 1989. The *Sächsische Akademie der Wissenschaften*, which came into being in 1846, was able to begin its work again in 1948. It did not set up its own projects in the field of Classical Studies, but, by means of financial grants, took part nominally and materially in inter-academic projects. The *Preußische Akademie der Wissenschaften*, founded in 1700, took up its work again as early as 1946, thereafter under the name *Deutsche Akademie der Wissenschaften*, with which an expression of a specific entitlement was also being made. It thereby largely pursued its traditional mandate and its corresponding structures in the field of Classical Studies; that is, it continued, as far as possible, the great corpora and the tasks associated with them: a) *Inscriptiones Graecae, Corpus Inscriptionum Latinarum, Prosopographia Imperii Romani, Polybios-Lexikon, Corpus Medicorum Graecorum* and *Latinorum, Die Griechischen Christlichen Schriftsteller* (including the associated *Texte und Untersuchungen zur Geschichte der altchristlichen Literatur*) and the *Mittellateinisches Wörterbuch*. Added to this was: b) an *Institut für Hellenistisch-römische Philosophie*, newly founded by Johannes Stroux; a working group for the study of papyri, later transferred to the papyrus collection of the *Staatliches Museum* (East); and a working group for the *Corpus Vasorum Antiquorum*, whose work was directed *de facto* by the Pergamon Museum, but which was affiliated, rather nominally, with the Academy. A re-established office for → Byzantine Studies was initially oriented largely towards internationally targeted publication activities, but it achieved a respectable research profile by the 1980s. A modern Greek dictionary, prepared in this framework over a period of several years at the cost of intense dedication on the part of many participants, was abandoned in 1990, due, no doubt, less to the internal and external academic processes after the political change than to the indolence of the people in positions of responsibility. In addition to these tasks, the Academy initiated a wide variety of publications, in which, on the one hand, it took up traditional material, which had, however, originally been housed elsewhere. Thus, the journals *Philologus* and *Klio* were revived; in the case of the *Biblioteca Teubneriana*, a scholarly editorial board was established in the Academy, insofar as it was published by the *Verlagsgesellschaft B.G. Teubner*, which had originated in Leipzig. However, steps were also taken toward new enterprises. One can mention the *Schriften der Sektion für Altertumswissenschaften*, a series of publications intended to replace the supplementary volumes of *Philologus*; the popular-scientific journal *Das Altertum*, modelled, *mutatis mutandis*, on Jaeger's *Antike*, flanked by the series *Lebendiges Altertum*, which was later discontinued. Finally, there was the *Bibliotheca Classica Orientalis*, a bibliographical guide to works from Socialist countries, whose significance was certainly disputed but which was, for many scholars behind the Iron Curtain, the only possibility to draw international attention to their work.

Prior to 1945 the undertakings listed under a) – as well as some others that were not continued after the war – had already been centralized into a *Kommission für griechisch-römische Altertumskunde*. In 1955 this trend was continued by the unification of all the above-mentioned projects into the *Institut für griechisch-römische Altertumskunde*. Later, the *Griechisches Münzwerk*, which had been taken up once again, together with a working group for Mycenology and one for the edition of the works of Ammianus Marcellinus were integrated with it, whereas the resumption of the *Corpus Inscriptionum Etruscorum* failed. As a result of the attempt to cooperate, above all, with Classical scholars from Socialist countries, an excavation at Kriwina (Bulgaria) undertaken jointly with the Bulgarian Academy of Sciences, which had begun as an instructional dig but was then expanded, was carried out over a period of several years. Whereas, until the foundation of the institute, the direction at least of the traditional ventures had been in the hands of committees made up of Academy members as well as non-academic experts, such commissions henceforth continued only as 'advisory' committees. The end of this structure, whose members had worked well together and which was quite productive under the existing conditions, but which was certainly capable of improvement in many respects, came in 1967 with the reform of the Academy. This reform centralized the Academy's undertakings according to the Soviet model, for the most part, in so-called central institutes, whereby the model of the large industrial conglomerates of the GDR certainly played a role and also occasionally led to unrealistic dreams. The entire organisation was henceforth known as the *Akademie der Wissenschaften der DDR*. The Institute of Classical Studies was divided into two branches (Greek-Roman History and Greek-Roman Cultural History), and these, together with Pre- and Protohistory and Ancient Oriental Studies, were incorporated into a *Zentralinstitut für Alte Geschichte und Archäologie*, whereby 'ancient history' also meant, in Soviet parlance, Classical philology. Traditional projects were continued, albeit sometimes on a reduced scale; only the *Griechische Christliche Schriftsteller* was removed from the organisation and ultimately absorbed by the *Akademie-Verlag Berlin*; strangely, the *Bibliotheca Classica Orientalis* also fell victim to the reform. The 'main tasks' were henceforth considered to be major projects like the *Kulturgeschichte der Antike*, joint work on ancient tragedy, the ancient novel, special problems in ancient history and other such matters, with the ultimate goal being 'theoretical generalizations', that is, the insertion of facts into an ideological Procrustean bed. If the prescribed ideas were often not realized, this was due to the steadfastness of individual collaborators. It must not be forgotten, however, that the consequences of the reform of Classical Studies in the Academy did a considerable amount of substantial damage.

E. Museums and Libraries

The museums in the GDR were also of considerable importance for research. Foremost among these are the Pergamon Museum and the Antiquities Collection on Museum Island in East Berlin, which, despite the fact that a large proportion of its holdings were located in West Berlin (Charlottenburg), were among the institutions that were highly respectable according to international standards. Only general indications can be provided here with regard to the rich publication activity of its collaborators, as consigned to such publications as the *Forschungen und Berichte der Staatlichen Museen zu Berlin* (enumerated for instance in [10; 11; 12]). The same holds true, in addition to the university institutions (Berlin, Humboldt University; Leipzig and Jena) for the antiquities collections in individual towns; for instance, the Palace Museum in Gotha (Friedenstein Palace), the Lindenau Museum in Altenburg and the museum in Schwerin. In these four museums in particular, intensive work was done on cataloging the vase holdings for the *Corpus Vasorum Antiquorum* (publications listed [15], although it should be noted that under pressure from the authorities of the GDR, different nationalities had to be indicated for the collections in the GDR and the Federal Republic of Germany. This verged on the grotesque in the case of the holdings of West and East Berlin). The Wincklemann Museum in Stendal, which was able to develop from a small memorial establishment into a functional body of international significance, proved to be increasingly important for work on the ancient world, particularly concerning reception. Mention should also be made, for instance, of the collection of ancient toys in the German Toy Museum at Sonneberg [16], not merely for curiosity's sake, but also because it showed that there was still ancient material to be discovered. Activities may well have been restricted in the museum sector in different degrees in the various institutions; here, however, economic considerations must sometimes have outweighed ideologically determined ones (or else both went hand in hand), as in shown, for instance, in the inability to carry out excavations at classical sites. The outside observer often gets the impression that the Ministry of Culture, to which the museums were subordinate, acted in a more 'cooperative' way than, for instance, the Ministry of Higher Education. Other research institutions to be mentioned in this context include, of course, the → LIBRARIES with larger holdings in medieval manuscripts (Berlin, Dresden, Gotha, Jena), as well as the papyrus collections of the State Museum and the Universty of Jena.

F. Societies

As was stated in the introduction, a professional association of representatives of Classical Studies, for whatever reasons, was unable to be founded in the GDR. The so-called sections of the *Historiker-Gesellschaft* of the GDR (originally called the *Deutsche Historiker-Gesellschaft*), one for ancient history and a much more active one for Byzantine studies, were unable to compensate for this lack. The *Winckelmann-Gesellschaft*, founded as early as 1941 with its headquarters in Stendal, was neither willing nor able to provide such an association, if only because it had the status of an international society. With its periodic, pan-German and internationally attended conferences, however, and its publishing activity–astonishingly broad for conditions in the GDR, it formed a reference point both for specialists and for wider circles of the population interested in more specific research on Winckelmann, on Antiquity in general and in the reception of the ancient world. To be sure, the society's work went far beyond what is generally circumscribed by the concept of the popularisation of research results. This was rather the responsibility of the Cultural Alliance of the GDR, founded shortly after the war as the Cultural Alliance for the Democratic Renewal of Germany. In Berlin, for instance, for twenty-five years this association supported a flourishing 'interest group in ancient culture', which turned out to be largely free from ideology for long periods. Similar groups were to be found in many towns of the GDR. The 'Urania' (East) also offered a forum for Classical Studies in Berlin, until it was almost completely eliminated in the last years before the political change because its lecturers did not feel obligated to adhere to the ideological maxims of the leadership of that society.

G. Current State of Research

The critical study of the development of Classical Studies in the GDR – ancient history, Classical philology, Classical archaeology – is only just beginning. Most progress has been made in ancient history, whose methods and results had already been determined before 1989 in individual points by authors from the Federal Republic [3. 311–330; 4. 325–346, 503] and had also been presented in a brief but trend-setting survey. The attempt at a general presentation based on rich material, originally a Marburg dissertation ([5]; summary in [6]), must be considered a failure because of its foreshortened definition of the discipline and its uncritical attitude toward attempts to indoctrinate ideologically. For Classical philology, matters have progressed no farther than brief critical surveys by observers from both East [8] and West [9] Germany from the time immediately after the political turn in the GDR. Precise bibliographies are available up to 1965 [10; 11], whereby it should be noted that all works published in the GDR are noted without consideration of the authors' place of residence or nationality. For the period from 1973 on, relatively complete bibliographical information is to be found in the volumes of reports [12] compiled under the auspices of the *Problemrat für Alte Geschichte und Archäologie* by the *Zentralinstitut für Alte Geschichte und Archäologie*. For the intermediary period, the only help provided are the catalogues of individual institutions and personal bibliographies (itemization: [5. 288f.]). Over the next few years, a spe-

cial task force of the *Akademie gemeinnütziger Wissenschaften zu Erfurt* will dedicate itself to the history of Classical Studies in the GDR.

→ Academy; → Berlin

1 B. Steinwachs (ed.), Geisteswissenschaften in der ehemaligen DDR, 1: Berichte; 2: Projekte, 1993   2 W. Schuller, Alte Geschichte in der DDR. Vorläufige Skizze, in: A. Fischer, G. Heidemann (eds.), Geschichtswissenschaft in der DDR, vol. 2, 1990, 37–58 (= in [1], vol. 1, 272–297 (with an epilogue on the period after the fall of the Wall, *Nachwende*)   3 Christ, RGG   4 Demandt   5 M. Willing, Althistorische Forschung in der DDR, 1991   6 Id., Die DDR – Althistorie im Rückblick, in: Geschichte in Wissenschaft und Unterricht 42, 1991, 489–497   7 K. J. Reinschke, Bolschewisierung der ost-deutschen Universität, dargestellt am Beispiel der Universität Leipzig und der Technischen Universität Dresden, in: K. Strobel (ed.), Die deutsche Universität im 20. Jahrhundert, 1994, 116–163   8 J. Dummer, G. Perl, Die Klassische Philologie in der ehemaligen DDR, in: [1], vol. 1, 256–265   9 M. Fuhrmann, Das Rinnsal war ein unterirdischer Strom, in: Frankfurter Allgemeine Zeitung vom 17.05.1991 (= [1]: vol. 1, 266–271)   10 H. Köpstein, Altertumskundliche Publikationen, erschienen in der DDR 1945–1955, 1957   11 Id., Altertumskundliche Publikationen in der DDR 1956–1965, in: Bibliotheca Classica Orientalis 10/6, 1965   12 Mitteilungen zur Alten Geschichte und Archäologie 1, 1973ff.   13 W. Kirsch, in: Fremdsprachenunterricht 34, 1990   14 J. Dummer, De linguae Graecae et Latinae studiis, quae in institutis praetheologicis Rei publicae Democraticae Germanicae exercentur, in: Latinitas 23, 1975, 181–188   15 M. G. Kanowski, Containers of Classical Greece, 1984, 155–200   16 E. Schmidt, Spielzeug und Spiele der Kinder im klassischen Altertum, 1971

URLs Akademie gemeinnütziger Wissenschaften zu Erfurt: http://www.akademie-erfurt.de/; Die Berlin-Brandenburgische Akademie der Wissenschaften: http://www.bbaw.de/bbaw/Akademie/; Staatliche Museen zu Berlin: http://www.smb.spk-berlin.de/smb/index.php; Winckelmann-Gesellschaft: http://www.winckelmann-gesellschaft.de/gesell/index.html

JÜRGEN DUMMER

II. Literature, Music and the Fine Arts
A. Reasons for the Reception of Antiquity
B. Areas of Influence   C. Artists and Their Works

A. Reasons for the Reception of Antiquity

The extent, diversity and quality of the reception of the art of Antiquity in the GDR are remarkable. This is particularly true for literature, but also for the fine arts, whereas in music, work with ancient texts and materials played a comparatively minor role. In view of the almost complete abolition of the → Humanist gymnasium and the drastic limitation of the study of Classical philology to the two universities of Halle and Jena, this fact must appear at first glance paradoxical. A series of reasons can, however, explain this surprising phenomenon:

The basis of all socialist reception of Antiquity is, to be sure, formed by the fact that the classics of socialism, the works of Marx and Engels, concerned themselves intensively with the history, myth and literature of Antiquity, whereby they emphasized again and again the importance, above all, of the Greeks for Western intellectual history and the development of socialist humanism. This holds true in modified form for Lenin as well, whose fourth thesis *On proletarian culture* is of central importance for the status of Antiquity in socialist cultural politics of the 20th cent.: "Marxism achieved its world-historical importance by the fact that it by no means rejected the most valuable achievements of the bourgeois period but, on the contrary, appropriated and elaborated all that was of value in the two-thousand year development of human thought and culture" [21]. This programmatic statement by Lenin was adopted by the founding fathers of the GDR, and further developed into the thesis of 'cultural legacy', which was henceforth constitutive for the cultural policy of the young state. "In view of the decadence of late capitalism, it is all the more necessary for us that, with the development of our socialist national culture, we carefully preserve the great traditions of the humanistic legacy, interpreting them correctly and making them available to contemporary man. For us, the humanistic legacy is neither a museum-style cultural element nor the playground of subjectivist interpretations. It is, rather, an indispensable component of the humanistic image of man of our socialist society". (Walter Ulbricht at the 9th Session of the Central Committee of the Socialist Unity Party of Germany). Literary studies in the GDR carried out these calls for a cultural policy through much scholarly work on Classical literature, whereby the ancient world, under the guiding idea of 'legacy' (or the 'inherited tradition'), was not forgotten [7;43].

That in practice the reception of Antiquity was "the most pressing and influential process of appropriation of our legacy" (Mittenzwei), did not depend only on official cultural politics and its scholarly underpinnings. It also depended, of course, on the influence of the all-powerful father figure Bertolt Brecht [22] and on the fact that, in addition to Brecht, an entire series of influential authors, such as Johannes R. Becher [27. 213–25], Georg Maurer, Anna Seghers [35] and Erich Arendt [27. 226–44; 11], as well as visual artists of the first generation, such as Wilhelm Höpfner und Günter Horlbeck, turned to Antiquity again and again. This tradition-forming continuity in the reception of Antiquity in socialist authors and artists since the Weimar Republic was to exert a considerable influence on the following generations.

However, legacy theory and tradition could scarcely have had so powerful an influence if the reception of Antiquity had not been attractive for authors and visual artists for three additional reasons. First, creative work on the ancient world made possible the avoidance, or at least a considerable modification, of socialist realism, which was long demanded and promoted by the party and by official critics (the 'Bitterfeld Way'), with its aesthetic and thematic restrictions [15. 50–158]. Second, myth not infrequently provided images for the intensive historical-philosophical analysis of both past and present so critical for civilization [8]. Third, with the help of the reception of Antiquity cloaked in discussions of legacy, delicate questions could be taken up, hopes could be expressed, utopias could be sketched, and social and political difficulties and contradictions could be addressed that could no doubt have scarcely been uttered or represented in unveiled form. "In the early 1960s, one could not write a piece about Stalinism, and one needed this kind of model (sc. the myth of Philoctetes) if one wanted to raise the right questions. People here are quick to understand this" [25]. Whereas Brecht had often utilised Antiquity for the critique of capitalism and → FASCISM, many authors and artists in the GDR used "Aesop's slave-language" (Lenin) for criticizing actually existing → SOCIALISM. The heated debates over Heiner Müller's *Philoctetus* as well as the fact that Christa Wolf's *Kassandra* could only appear in the GDR with substantial cuts show that, even so, the critical tones did not always remain unobserved. Nevertheless, they were ultimately tolerated.

B. AREAS OF INFLUENCE

Since the → CLASSICAL PERIOD, German reception of Antiquity has been oriented primarily towards Greek Antiquity. This also holds true for the reception of Antiquity in the GDR.

a) → MYTH was of central importance. The great symbols of basic human situations, Heracles and Prometheus, Sisyphus and Icarus, Orpheus and Cassandra, Medea, Antigone, Oedipus and Odysseus, also served the authors of the GDR to give form to problems of the individual and of society against the background of mythical models. Here, a significant change in leading figures may be observed. Whereas after the war it was initially the homecoming of Odysseus, then the 'workers' Heracles and Prometheus, that occupied the centre of attention, other figures alongside them came increasingly into the foreground who provided the occasion for critical reflection and commentary on the present. These included such ambivalent symbols as Icarus and Sisyphus, or the great seers and admonishers Tiresias, Laocoon and Cassandra. In the fine arts, one also found figures alongside them in which sensuality and *joie de vivre* could be reflected: Pan and the nymphs, Apollo and the muses, Aphrodite and the judgment of Paris [1]. However, the growing critical distance adopted by artists towards social and political developments and their dwindling hopes for the realisation of a humane socialism were not reflected only in this transformation of ancient models. They can be discerned even more clearly in the fact that, beginning in the 1960s, even the ancient figures that were initially presented as positive models, such as Odysseus, Heracles and Prometheus, were portrayed in an increasingly critical way. Overall, one observes an increase in the darkening and problematisation of the image of Antiquity.

b) Closely connected to the reception of mythic archetypes were the many-faceted adaptations of ancient literature. These ranged from allusions to a famous ancient text, through a citation or a poetic motif, to the imitation and recreation of entire works. Preferred objects of reception included Homer (Arendt, Fühmann, Wolf) and Greek drama (Müller, Hacks) as well as, with a clear distancing, Sappho, Plautus, Catullus and Horace [27.295–310]. It is significant in this context that the knowledge of ancient literature was promoted by readable and inexpensive translations (Schottlaender, Ebener, U. and K. Treu), and that the theatre of the GDR regularly presented ancient plays. High points included Benno Besson's productions of Sophocles' *Oedipus the King* (in the version by Heiner Müller) or of Aristophanes' *Peace* (in a free adaptation by Peter Hacks), the Schweriner Theaterprojekt (1985), and the long series of Stendal theatre festivals (beginning in 1981). That the visual arts were also inspired by ancient literature and its reception is demonstrated not only by Günter Horlbeck's illustrations for Hacks's *Peace* and Lucian's *Judgment of Paris*, or by those of Wieland Förster for Fühmann's *Odysseus und Kirke*, but also by the varied reactions of artists to Christa Wolf's *Kassandra*.

c) In ancient history, the third important field of reception, Roman material was clearly predominant [27]. Following Brecht, whose reception of Antiquity was nourished first and foremost from Roman sources, Heiner Müller and, above all, Peter Hacks repeatedly dramatised Roman subjects. Along with this came an entire series of historical and cultural-historical novels, whose choice of material and structure were more or less ideologically stamped, and a large quantity of poems (Braun, Hacks, Huche, etc.). For obvious reasons, ancient art and architecture, and the Mediterranean landscape, with its testimonies to the ancient past, played a subordinate a role, as did ancient philosophy and science.

C. Artists and Their Works
1. Literature   2. Music   3. Art

1. Literature

a) Drama: Brecht, who, after his return from exile, began his theatre work with the *Churer Antigone* (1946) continued his literary and dramaturgical work in the following period in the GDR with ancient plays and materials. He transposed the radio play *Das Verhör des Lukullus* (1939) into a libretto for Paul Dessau's opera *Die Verurteilung des Lukullus* (1951) and adapted Shakespeare's *Coriolanus*. His two most important students were also stimulated by the master's reception of Antiquity. The proportion of Roman materials in the works of Peter Hacks [34; 42; 28] is as great as it is in Brecht. In addition to *Omphale* (1971) and his free ad-

aptation of the Aristophanes' comedies, *Frieden* (1962), *Vögel* (1975) and *Plutus* (*Wealth*, 1993), there are no fewer than four plays that deal with Roman history and Latin literature. In *Numa* (1971), the protagonist, the head of a future socialist republic of Italy by the name of Numa Pompili, appears as the reincarnation of the legendary Roman king Numa Pompilius. *Senecas Tod* (1978) re-creates the famous suicide of the philosopher. *Rosie träumt* (1974) is Hacks's homage to Hrotswitha of Gandersheim. Scenes and motifs from her plays are elaborated into a jovial and clever game that Hacks backdates to the time of Diocletian. Finally, in addition to these three of his 'own' plays, there is Hacks's *Amphitryon* (1967), which, like many other adaptations of this material, goes back to Plautus' *Amphitruo*, but also draws life from an amusing confrontation, rich in ideas, with Molière, Dryden, Kleist and Giraudoux.

With his didactic play *Der Horatier* (1968), Heiner Müller [4; 10; 20; 13; 29; 40] ties in with the 'Roman Brecht' (H. Mayer); however, if one excepts his free adaptation of Shakespeare, *Anatomie Titus Fall of Rome* (1987), and the series of minor ancient elements he integrated into his play *Germania Tod in Berlin* (1971), this short text remains rather isolated within Müller's overall work compared to his rich reception of Greek plays and materials. The prelude was formed by the most important 'ancient' plays of German literature since 1945, *Philoktet* (1958/64) and the one-act *Herakles 5* (1964). The 1960s also witnessed versions of Sophocles' *Oedipus the King* (1967, based on Hölderlin) and of the *Prometheus*, attributed to Aeschylus (1969, based on an interlinear version by P. Witzmann). In the subsequent period, Müller wrote no further dramas based on an ancient text or subject; yet until his death he continued to integrate ancient material in his plays and stage productions in constantly new ways: *Lanzelot* (1969); *Germania Tod in Berlin* (1971); *Zement* (based on a novel by Gladkow, 1972), with intermezzi on Prometheus, Hercules, Oedipus and Medea; *Leben Gundlings Friedrich von Preußen Lessings Schlaf Traum Schrei* (1972); *Traktor* (1955/61; 1974); *Verkommenes Ufer Medeamaterial Landschaft mit Argonauten* (1982). Added to this was a series of tragic scenarios such as *Elektratext* (1969), *Medeaspiel* (1974) or *Bildbeschreibung* (Alcestis, 1989). At the end of his life, Müller's creations included, in addition to a series of poems and the autobiographical text *Mommsens Block*, a free adaptation of the messenger speech from Euripides' *Heracles* (*Herakles 13*), and a free translation of Aeschylus's *Persians* (based on an interlinear version by P. Witzmann).

The dramatic reception of Antiquity by Hacks and Müller inspired a whole series of younger authors: Karl Mikkel, *Nausikaa* (1963/64), *Halsgericht, 2. Teil: Der Angeklagte* (a comedy based on Apuleius's *Apology*, 1987); Stefan Schütz, *Odysseus' Heimkehr* (1979), *Antiope und Theseus* (1979), *Laokoon* (1980); Jochen Berg's tetralogy, *Niobe*, *Klytaimestra*, *Iphigeneia*,

Niobe am Sipylos (1983); Hans Köhler, *Der verwunschene Berg* (1983); Klaus Schönberg, *Minotauros oder Die glückseligen Inseln der Erfindungen* (1985) and Hartmut Lange, whose ancient plays *Herakles* (1968), *Die Ermordung des Aias oder Ein Exkurs über das Holzhacken* (1971) and *Staschek oder Das Leben des Ovid* (1973) did not appear until after he had resettled in the West (1965) but owe their origin to the influence of Hacks and Müller and are intended first and foremost for a GDR audience. If we also recall the radio plays by Peter Gosse (*Tadmor, Ostern 30, Orpheus,* all from 1986) and Franz Fühmann (*Die Schatten,* 1986), as well as his libretti, and add Hans Pfeiffer's *Begegnung mit Herakles* (1966) and the more or less free adaptations of Aristophanes and Plautus by Joachim Knauth, *Die Weibervolksversammlung* (based on Aristophanes' *Ecclesiazusae,* 1969), *Lysistrata* (based on Aristophanes, 1975), *Der Maulheld* (based on Plautus, *Miles Gloriosus,* 1973); Erika Wilde, *Der Weiberheld* (also based on *Miles Gloriosus,* 1973); Egon Günther, *Das gekaufte Mädchen* (based on Plautus, *Mercator,* 1965) and Arnim Stolper, *Amphitryon* (1974), then the picture of the reception of Antiquity in the drama of the GDR becomes even richer.

b) In prose there appeared, above all, historical and cultural-historical novels and stories that were more or less clearly in the tradition of Brecht and Feuchtwanger without achieving the quality of their great models. The choice of subject matter and type of treatment were more or less stamped by ideology; the focus was not on the Classical phases of ancient history but on periods of crisis and upheaval. Narration took place preferably 'from below' or from the perspective of the oppressed. Worthy of particular mention are the novels of Klaus Hermann, *Babylonischer Sommer* (1948, Alexander in Babylon), *Die ägyptische Hochzeit* (1953, Anthony and Cleopatra), *Der Brand von Byzanz* (1955, from the time of Justinian), *Die Zauberin von Ravenna* (1957, the Goths in Italy) and Volker Ebersbach, *Der Schatten eines Satyrs* (1985) and *Tiberius* (1991), as well as the trilogy of novels by Waldtraut Lewin, *Herr Lucius und sein Schwan* (1973), *Die Ärztin von Lakros* (1977) and *Die stillen Römer* (1979), which sketches a colourful picture of Augustan and early imperial society. Another area that served the purposes of entertainment and instruction was the re-telling of ancient myths and literature for children and adults. Important authors of the GDR took on this task: Franz Fühmann, *Das hölzerne Pferd* (1968); Stefan Hermlin, *Argonauten* (1974); Rolf Schneider, *Die Abenteuer des Herakles* (1978); Hans Hüttner, *Herakles, Die zwölf Abenteuer* (1979), and *Herakles, Der Dank der Götter* (1987); Gerhard Holtz-Baumert, *Daidalos & Ikaros* (1984) and Werner Heiduczek, *Orpheus und Eurydike* (1989). Also worthy of mention are Peter Hacks's children's book on Hercules, *Der Mann mit dem schwärzlichen Hintern* (1980) and *Die Kinder, Ein Theaterstück für Kinder über den Sturz des Kronos durch Zeus* (1983), as well as J. Bobrowski's adaptation of Schwab's *Sagen des klassischen Altertums* (1954).

Works with literary ambitions were also be found in the form of prose poems and short stories in the tradition of Brecht (e.g. *Berichtigung alter Mythen*): Volker Braun, *Höhlengleichnis,* the short prose texts of Heiner Müller, e.g. *Herakles 2*; Volker Brasch, *Marsyas*; and many short stories by Günter Kunert, e.g. *Der Traum des Sisyphos* and, of course, Franz Fühmann's political *König Ödipus* and mythological tales *Der Geliebte der Morgenröte* and *Das Ohr des Dionysios.* Among the 'mythological' novels, Fühmann's *Prometheus* occupies a special position (unfortunately, the author has not carried out the planned continuations) [27. 254–72]. The only works of equal significance are Christa Wolf's [30; 12] great stories *Kassandra* (1983, the greatest public success in post–1945 literary reception of Antiquity) and *Medea, Stimmen* (1996, which came into being after the reunification but is, in many respects, a play of GDR literature) [19]. Christa Wolf's Frankfurt poetry lectures on *Kassandra* are the best known but, by no means, only use of Antiquity in essay form. Pertinent essays were also penned by Arendt, Maurer, Hacks, Kunert, Ebersbach and Fühmann.

c) The rich reception of Antiquity in the → LYRIC POETRY of the GDR cannot be documented individually, as it can for drama and prose. At the beginning were Johannes R. Becher, with his frequently semi-unbearable mythologisation of socialism and its heroes, and Bertolt Brecht, both of whom built upon material from the 'quarry' of Antiquity as early as the Weimar period and in exile. From the 1950s onwards, all the important (and many of the less important) lyricists then worked, at least occasionally, with figures and motifs from ancient mythology, literature and history [39]. In the first generation, this is true of Erich Arendt, whose great cycle on Greece *Ägäis* adapted important ideas from the history, mythology and poetry of Antiquity, and of Georg Maurer, but also of Peter Huchel [14], whose masterly lyric journeys to Antiquity did not emerge until after he resettled in the West, but who had already previously used Antiquity as an ironic-critical weapon against his opponents (*Der Garten des Theophrast*), and of Johannes Bobrowski, who not only created impressive portrait poems on Sappho and Pindar but also mythical incantations of nature (e.g. *Dryade*), and who owed the wonderful musical form of his lyric poetry not least to his creative work with the metrical structures of Aeolian lyric poetry [32; 36]. Of the lyric poets of the next generation, one can mention Sarah Kirsch, Heinz Czechowski, Hans Cibulka, Karl Mickel, Volker Braun and Peter Gosse but, above all, Günter Kunert, whose rich lyric oeuvre is nourished by Antiquity to an astonishing degree. Finally, there are Peter Hacks and Heiner Müller (particularly at the start and end of his literary production), who absorbed Antiquity not only dramatically, but also lyrically. The reception of Antiquity also played an important role for the third and last generation of lyric poets of the GDR (Uwe Kolbe, Jochen Berg, Wilhelm Bartsch, Uwe Grüning and Durs Grünbein). It is therefore not surprising that among the 'German-German' parodies of Kurt Bartsch (*Die Hölderlinie*), no less than four are devoted to this phenomenon.

2. MUSIC

As in the Federal Republic of Germany, the musical reception of Antiquity in the GDR was not of great importance. In the field of → opera, however, one might mention, in addition to Paul Dessau's *Die Verurteilung des Lukullus* (libretto by B. Brecht, 1953), S. Matthus's *Die Heimkehr des Odysseus* (a musical adaptation of Cl. Monteverdi's *dramma per musica*, 1965) and *Omphale* (libretto by P. Hacks, 1971), as well as two operas by G. Katzer: *Gastmahl oder Über die Liebe* (1987) and *Antigone oder Die Stadt* (1990), both based on libretti by G. Müller. In addition to P. Hacks (*Vögel* and *Omphale*), F. Fühmann also tried his hand at the libretto form in *Alkestis, Stück mit Musik* (1989) and *Kirke und Odysseus. Ein Ballett* (1984). It is also worth mentioning that S. Matthus, in addition to operas, theatre music for *König Ödipus* and *Ödipus auf Kolonos* (Vienna, 1979) and a work for a children's choir in three parts and chamber orchestra entitled *Ikarus* (text by H. Baierl, 1978), also set Catullus to music: first, *Fünf Liebeslieder des Catull für zwölfstimmigen gemischten Chor* (1973); then, *Liebesqualen des Catull. Ein musikalisches Drama für Sopran, Baß (oder Bariton), gemischten Chor und Instrumente* (1986).

3. ART

Much richer than that of music was the reception of Antiquity in the fine arts of the GDR. Three of the 16 monumental murals that decorated the main foyer of the Palace of the Republic in former East Berlin worked with ancient figures and motifs: Werner Tübke's pentaptychon *Mensch – Maß aller Dinge* (war of the Lapiths and Centaurs as the victory of good over evil, torso of a Greek female sculpture), Walter Womacka, *Wenn Kommunisten träumen* (capital of an Ionian column, Icarus, Laocoon) and Bernhard Heisig, *Ikaros*. The astonishing presence of ancient motifs and themes in such a propagandistically prominent position is an impressive indication of the extensive and diverse reception of Antiquity in the fine arts of the GDR, which reached its pinnacle in the second half of the 1970s. A detailed investigation into the reception of Antiquity in the fine arts of the GDR lists no fewer than 351 artists with a total of about 1700 'myth-related' works [2]. Added to these are individual works that arose from encounters with Italian and Greek landscape and are, in many cases, reflections of ancient art. There are also a larger number of illustrations for translations of ancient and modern texts (for instance, the lively drawings by Günter Horlbeck for Peter Hacks's adaptation of Aristophanes' *Peace* or Lucian's *Judgment of Paris*). In general, the rich literary reception of Antiquity in the GDR repeatedly proved a fertile ground that influenced the fine arts. This is particularly true of Christa Wolf's *Kassandra* (e.g. N. Quevedo, 12 etchings, 1982/83; Cassandra cycles by A. Hampel, 1984, and K. Süß, 1984) and of Heiner Müller's adaptation of Sophocles' *Oidipus Tyrannos,* based on Höl-

derlin's version (the text performed in 1967 appeared in 1969, with nineteen graphic works by nine artists) and of Franz Fühmann's theoretical and practical work on the mythology and literature of Antiquity (e.g. Binder's illustrations for *Das hölzerne Pferd*, or R. Paris's panel *Marsyas und Apollon*, 1981). Barely represented, in contrast, was the field of ancient history, which played a considerable role in literary reception thanks to Bertolt Brecht. The reception of Antiquity so surprisingly extensive and diverse in the fine arts was not divided up evenly over the four decades of GDR history. Over the first 15 years, it receded completely behind the Socialist Realism demanded by the party. To be sure, there was also no small number of artists during these years who, in addition to the officially sanctioned line, also worked with ancient subjects and motifs (e.g. W. Höpfner, G. Horlbeck and W. Sitte, who was also later very influential as a government official); however, these works were not shown at the main art exhibitions of the districts and the state. A turning point did not come about until the party congresses of the 1960s that declared the victory of Socialist production methods and called upon all to work for the creation of a (fully) developed Socialist society. The narrow concept of realism gradually disappeared, and cultural policy and official art criticism increasingly accepted symbolic forms in the depiction of social themes and problems. The artistic reception of Antiquity thus increased steadily from the mid–1960s onwards; at the same time, the treatment of ancient myths, heretofore affirmative, became increasingly ambivalent and critical. After a brief delay, this trend, which has parallels in literature and in the theatre, also became visible in the official art exhibitions of the GDR and was intensively absorbed and discussed by the public (especially Mattheuer's Sisyphus paintings). The high point came around 1980, at about the same time as Franz Fühmann's and Christa Wolf's great literary successes, and certainly not independent of them. Individual exhibitions of important artists like Mattheuer, as well as special exhibitions on the theme of 'Icarus' in Magdeburg (1981) and Erfurt (1983), documented the importance of this phenomenon, as did the 9th Art Exhibition of the GDR 1982/83 in Berlin. Here the reception of Antiquity occupied considerable space for the first time. In the mid–1980s, there followed a whole range of exhibitions, some of which were quite comprehensive, on individual ancient topics: 'Parisurteil' (Gotha 1986 and Stendal 1987), 'Kassandra' (Halle 1987) and 'Ikaros' (Mühlhausen 1987) [6; 3; 44; 45; 16; 47; 17; 18]. Among the many artists who, in the heyday of the reception of Antiquity in the fine arts in the GDR, worked more or less intensively with ancient figures and materials, one may mention, in addition to W. Sitte and W. Tübke, particularly Bernhard Heisig, who from 1970 on consistently created new (initially rather optimistic and then increasingly gloomy and ominous) variations on the theme of Icarus. U. Mattheuer-Neustädt, M. Morgner, H. Lange, H. Metzkes, K. Süß, Ph. Oeser, A.T. Mörstedt, M. Pietsch,

W. Herzog, J. John, R. Paris and the poet-painter H. Zander also worked or continue to work intensively with ancient material. The Winckelmann Museum in Stendal contains a rich collection of over 600 works of graphic art. Particularly important is Wolfgang Mattheuer, who since the early 1970s has dealt with, first, the theme of Sisyphus and, then, that of Icarus in innovative 'memorials'. His three great paintings of Sisyphus brought together in the Dresden Gemäldegalerie (*Die Flucht des Sisyphos*, 1972; *Sisyphos behaut den Stein*, 1974; *Der übermütige Sisyphos und die Seinen*, 1976) are certainly the best known examples of the extensive and complex reception of Antiquity in the fine arts of the GDR.

→ MARXISM; → SOCIALISM

1 P. ARLT, Der Hirt und die schönen Göttinnen, 1982 2 Id., Antike-Rezeption in der bildenden Kunst der DDR, 1984 3 Das Urteil des Paris in der bildenden Kunst der DDR, Schloß-Museum Gotha (Exhibition catalogue), 1986 4 R. BERNHARDT, Antike-Rezeption im Werk H. Müllers, (diss. Berlin) 1979 (cf. also Weimarer Beiträge, 1976, No. 3, 83–122) 5 Id., Odysseus' Tod – Prometheus' Leben. Antiken Mythen in der Literatur der DDR, 1983 6 J.-H. BRUNS (ed.), Ikarus, Kunstgalerie Magdeburg (Exhibition catalogue), 1981 7 D.-D. DAHNKE, Erbe und Tradition in der Literatur, ²1981 8 W. EMMERICH, Das Erbe des Odysseus. Der zivilisationskritische Rekurs auf den Mythos in der neueren DDR-Literatur, in: Studies in DDR Culture and Society 5, 1985, 173–88 9 Id., Antike Mythen auf dem Theater der DDR, in: U. PROFITLICH (ed.), Dramatik der DDR, 1987, 223–65 10 Id., Der vernünftige, der schreckliche Mythos, in: Heiner Müller Material, 1988 11 D. GELBRICH, Antike-Rezeption in der sozialistischen deutschen Lyrik des 20. Jahrhundert, Diss. 1984 12 CHR. GLAU, Christa Wolfs Kassandra und Aischylos' Orestie. Zur Rezeption der griechischen Tragödie in der deutschen Literatur der Gegenwart, 1996 13 B. GRUBER, Mythen in den Dramen Heiner Müllers, 1989 14 P. HABERMEHL, Das Verstummen des Mythologen. Ein Versuch zu den drei Odysseus Gedichten Peter Huchels, A&A 42, 1996, 155–73 15 P. HACKS, Die Maßgaben der Kunst, 1977, 50–158 16 M. HEBECKER, Antikewandel. Mythos und Antike in der DDR-Karikatur, Schloßmuseum Gotha, 1989 17 Ikarus. Mythos als Realismus in Beispielen der Gegenwartskunst, Realismusstudio 33, 1986 18 Karikatur – Bildende Kunst. Antike(n) – auf die Schippe genommen. Bilder und Motive aus der antiken Welt in der Karikatur, Ausstellung (with a catalogue), 1998 19 Das klassische Altertum in der sozialistischen Kultur, Wissenschaftliche Zeitschrift der Friedrich Schiller-Universität, Jena, Reihe 18, No. 4, 1969 20 H. KRAUS, Heiner Müller und die griechische Tragödie, in: Poetica 17, 1985, 299–339 21 LENIN, Werke, vol. 31, 1970, 308 22 H. MAYER, Bertolt Brecht und die Tradition, 1961 23 W. MITTENZWEI, Brechts Verhältnis zur Tradition, 1972 24 Id., Die Antike-Rezeption des DDR-Theaters, in: Id., Kampf der Richtungen, 1978 25 H. MÜLLER, Rotwelsch, 1982, 308 26 V. RIEDEL, Antikerezeption in der Literatur der DDR, 1984 27 Id., Literatur. Literarische Antikerezeption. Aufsätze und Vorträge, 1996 28 Id., Facetten des Komischen in den Antikestücken von Peter Hacks, in: S. JÄKEL (ed.), Laughter down the Centuries III, 1997, 213–32 29 Id., Antikere- zeption in den Dramen Heiner Müllers, in: G. BINDER, B. EFFE (eds.), Das Antike Theater: Aspeke seiner Geschichte, Rezeption und Aktualität, 1997, 345–84 30 W. RIES, Bewundert viel und viel gescholten Aischylos, in: Wirkendes Wort 35, 1985, 5–17 31 E. G. SCHMIDT, Die Antike in Lyrik und Erzähl-Literatur der DDR, Wissenschaftliche Zeitschrift der Friedrich Schiller-Universität, Jena, Reihe 18, 1969, No. 4, 123–41 and 20, 1971, No. 5, 5–62 32 Id., Die Sapphogedichte Johannes Bobrowskis, in: Das Altertum 28, 1972, 49–61 33 Id., Die Antike in Lyrik und Erzähl-Literatur. Die letzten zehn Jahre (1969–78), in: H. GERICKE (ed.), Rezeption des Altertums in modernen literarischen Werken, 1980, 7–31 34 P. SCHÜTZE, Peter Hacks, 1976 35 A. SEGHERS, Gesammelte Werke in Einzelausgaben, 1961ff. (= Sagen vom klassischen Altertum, 1940, vol. 9, 231–58; Der Baum des Odysseus, 1940, vol. 9, 275f.; Das Argonautenschiff, 1948, vol. 10, 126–43) 36 B. SEIDENSTICKER, Antike-Rezeption in der deutschen Literatur nach 1945, in: Gymnasium 98, 1991, 420–53 37 Id., Römisches in der literarischen Antike-Rezeption nach 1945, in: Gymnasium 101, 1994, 7–42 38 Id., P. HABERMEHL, Antike-Rezeption in der deutschsprachigen Literatur der Gegenwart, in: AU 36, 1994, H. 2 39 Id., Unterm Sternbild des Hercules, 1996 40 F. SUÁREZ SÁNCHEZ, Individuum und Gesellschaft, Die Antike in Heiner Müllers Werk, 1998 41 CH. TRILSE, Antike und Theater heute, ²1979 42 Id., Peter Hacks, 1980 43 R. WEIMANN et al, Zur Tradition des Realismus und Humanismus, in: Weimarer Beiträge 16, 1970 Heft 10, 31–119 44 C. WIEG (ed.), Kassandra, Staatliche Galerie Moritzburg, (Exhibition catalogue) 1987 45 J. WINTER (ed.), Ikarus, Grafik von DDR-Künstlern zu einem antiken Mythos, Galerie am Entenbühl, Mühlhausen, (Exhibition catalogue) 1987 46 P. WITZMANN, AntikeTradition im Werk Bertolt Brechts, 1964 47 G.-H. ZUCHOLD, Das Erbe der Antike, Griechischer und römischer Mythos in der bildenden Kunst der DDR, Altes Museum Berlin, (Exhibition catalogue) 1980 48 Id., Kassandra, Janus, Ikarus. Antike Mythen in der bildenden Kunst der DDR, in: Deutschland Archiv 1985, 490–97   BERND SEIDENSTICKER

Germanic Languages
I. MIDDLE AGES II. MODERN ERA

I. MIDDLE AGES
A. INTRODUCTION B. INFLUENCE OF LATIN AND GREEK C. INFLUENCE OF ROMAN PHYSICAL CULTURE D. INFLUENCE OF CHRISTIANITY E. SCHOLARSHIP F. INTERNATIONAL VOCABULARY

A. INTRODUCTION
The Germanic Languages (GL) constitute a branch of the Indo-European family of languages; its members are related through a range of special linguistic developments such as the Germanic sound shift, the development of a dental preterite/past tense, a 'weak' adjective inflection and other matters. The GL consist of the following language groups: the North Germanic languages (with the modern standard languages Swedish, Danish, Norwegian in two variants and, further afield, the island languages of Icelandic and Faroese); English

in various manifestations and its derivative languages, the Frisian language (with West Frisian as a regionally limited standard language in the Netherlands); and Dutch and [modern standard] German, both with a historic base of dialect traditions. In the Low German area, attempts at establishing an independent standard language were abandoned in early modern times. Languages such as Gothic, recorded in the Early Middle Ages, Crimean Gothic (not closely related to Gothic), attested in Early Modern times in residual areas, Lombardic, evidence of which exists only in small pockets from the 7th cent., and West Frankish in France, which is difficult to associate with transmitted texts, as well as the languages of many Germanic tribes that left no language tradition, have all died out.

B. Influence of Latin and Greek

All modern GL have been substantially influenced by Latin culture and language, while the influence of Greek culture and language generally arrived via the medium of Latin. Only Gothic, which died out later, was directly influenced by Greek; isolated, attested cases of a direct influence on southeast German dialects (e.g. Bavarian *Pfinztag* 'Thursday' corresponding with Greek *pémptē hēmérā* with a translation of the second component, Bavarian *Er[ge]tag* 'Tuesday' corresponding with Greek *Áreōs hēmérā*) can probably be explained as having been transmitted via Gothic and are difficult to delineate [in terms of the area of contact].

C. Influence of Roman Physical Culture

The superior Roman physical culture in many fields must have deeply impressed the Germanic people, for they borrowed relevant terminology (probably together with the objects and techniques) very early, thus for example in house construction the terms *Mauer, Ziegel, Fenster, Mörtel* ['wall', 'tile', 'window', 'mortar']. Typically, at this early stage of borrowing, the words were fully assimilated into the host language. Many of these words are represented in all GL. Among the practical pursuits, commerce is particularly prominent (*kaufen, Münze, Pfund* ['to buy', 'coin', 'pound']), designations for containers (*Kessel, Schüssel, Kiste* ['kettle', 'dish', 'chest']), words for non-indigenous plants and food derived from them (*Wein, Birne, Kirsche, Pflaume* ['wine', 'pear', 'cherry', 'plum']). Frequently, the old Germanic objects or techniques were referred to by the Germanic word, the superior new Roman object or technique by the loan word (e.g. the native word *Wand* found its companion in the loan word *Mauer*). In such cases, it appears that German more frequently chose the loan word than the other GL where the native word was also applied to the foreign technology. Thus, German uses the loan word *schreiben* when dealing with Latin book script, but the borrowed meaning *lesen* (originally only *auflesen* ['to pick', 'gather up'], then extended in analogy to Lat. *legere* "auflesen" ['to gather'] and "Schrift lesen" ['to read writing']); in contrast, English and the Nordic languages have transferred the designa-tions of rune techniques to Latin script: compare English *to write*, cf. German "ritzen" ['to scratch'], and *to read*, cf. German "raten" ['to interpret', 'advise'], both expressions for dealing with runes.

D. Influence of Christianity

Christianity came to the various Germanic peoples in different ways, and this is reflected in their languages and the use of religious language, even though the terminology itself clearly had to be largely based on the native languages. One of the earliest layers of Christian terminology can be found in early borrowings which presumably were absorbed even before missionary activity and thus actually belong to the category 'physical culture'. The word that stands out in this (difficult to delineate) group is *Kirche* [=church], which must have existed very early (churches as objects of plunder by heathen Germanic tribes) so that the (Greco-) Latin word *ecclesia* could not establish itself during later missionary activity. Furthermore, the layer of replacement of Christian terms with pagan words of related meaning (*Hölle, Sünde, Gott, heilig* ['hell', 'sin', 'god', 'holy']) is quite common in general and possibly based on a process of substitution even in pagan times. In the period of missionary activity and early Christianity, masses of Christian terms had to be absorbed. This occurred only partly by borrowing (in particular for Church offices and the like: *Priester, Bischof, Papst, Mönch, Nonne* ['priest', 'bishop', 'pope', 'monk', 'nun']; Christian buildings such as *Kloster, Münster, Zelle, Kirche, Dom* ['monastery', 'minster', 'cell', 'church', 'cathedral']; parts of the religious service such as *Messe, Predigt* ['mass', 'sermon'] etc.); otherwise, terms are translated or newly formed, which, again, resulted in several different layers: The basic terms, relating to the faithful, such as *beten, Buße, Reue, Gnade, fasten, taufen, (Heiliger) Geist* ['pray', 'penance', 'repentance', 'grace', 'to fast', 'to baptise', '(Holy) Ghost'] are based on older words with similar meanings, which were adapted to religious practice – they usually have been retained and still occur in modern German. This only applies only in a very limited way to loan-translations: *Beichte* ['confession'] (from *confessio*); *Gewissen* ['conscience'] (from *conscientia*, this in turn from *syneídēsis*); *barmherzig* ['merciful'] (from *misericors*); *Mitleid* ['compassion'] (from *compassio*, this in turn from *sympátheia*) etc. Far more frequent were the loan-translations for less mainstream Christian concepts and Christian ethics. For those (as well as for some more central concepts), there were different attempts at rendering them, which were in competition for a long time. In only a few cases did one of the variants prevail. Eventually, it was mostly a later word that was preferred, which, not uncommonly, was also a borrowing from the source language. It was significant for the status and the extent of this terminology how widely the native language was used in religious instruction and church services. Among the Goths (as well as the Arians and Homoiousians in general), the use of the vernacular was quite common – hence the early translation of the Bible. To a certain extent, this also applies to the Angles and Saxons in Britain, to whom Christianity came peacefully in the 6th cent., arriving almost simultaneously with the Irish and from Rome, where Gregory the Great had commissioned missionaries with that special task. In Britain, translations into the vernacular occurred to an unusually large extent and, in later times (10th/11th cents.), there even were attempts of the School of Winchester to devise a systematic vernacular terminology (Old Engl. *þrowere* 'endurer' alongside *martir* 'martyr', in Winchester *cyðere* 'witness' occurs as an exact translation of the Greek word). After the Norman conquest, a large part of these achievements in the vernacular was abandoned. On the continent, Christianity was enforced to a large extent (even though by no means everywhere) in a warlike and aggressive manner. Therefore, pagan customs were largely eradicated and Christianity was mainly established in Latin form; here, the vernacular played a considerably lesser part. Moreover, there were various different missionizing movements on the continent: an early mission from the Romance area, then the also very early and continued Irish mission and finally the English mission (with the tendency to displace previous endeavours) – in the southeast, there are also Church-related borrowings from Greek, which are attributed to an otherwise unrecorded Gothic mission. Only in individual cases – but there is no certainty – can these activities be associated with particular linguistic terms; in these cases either; but it should be beyond doubt that they played a role in the development of vernacular terminology. In the northern countries, the mission arrived considerably later (influenced by England and Germany), concluding with the resolution of the Icelandic people's assembly, in the year 1000, to adopt Christianity in order to end internal disputes in this matter. As a result, the religious terminology was largely influenced by the mediating languages German and English; in Icelandic, there is the additional determining factor of an aversion to foreign words.

E. SCHOLARSHIP

Probably the most important influence of the ancient languages on the Germanic (and the modern cultural European languages in general) is due to the fact that in the early Middle Ages scholarship and related cultural pursuits were largely conducted in the Latin language and according to the Latin model (while this in turn was dependent to a great extent on the Greek model). The native languages took on this task only very slowly, while borrowing parts of Latin and Greco-Latin terminology and translating them frequently. It can generally be stated that attempts at carrying out scholarly work in the vernacular were made early (no later than the 10th/11th cents. in Germany, somewhat earlier in England), but these attempts did not really aim at replacing Latin-based scholarship, but rather to lead towards it. For this reason (and for others as well), these early

attempts to establish a scholarly terminology in the vernacular were not effective in the long run. It was not until the introduction of the printing press, at the earliest, that terminologies were established on a larger scale, with the timing varying according to language area and subject matter. Thus, it can be assumed for a period extending far into modern times that the needs of those areas that required form of language, such as scholarship (and liturgy), were covered by Latin; as a consequence the development of the vernacular languages in these areas was inadequate and could only achieve self-sufficiency with difficulty (and with extensive borrowings from Latin). To what extent Latin also influenced grammar and style of the native languages (e.g. through slavish translation), is subject to debate.

F. INTERNATIONAL VOCABULARY

As a result of this development the standard European languages to a large extent share the Greco-Latin scholarly and cultural terminology, i.e. a considerable part of their vocabulary is international (which need not be the same everywhere and it may vary in different languages). Furthermore: The need for new terms was, and still is filled from the pool of special terms and their constituents, be it via the correct formation according to the rules of the ancient languages, be it via modern modifications (abbreviations etc.), be it via hybrid forms (mixtures of different languages). The 'set pieces' [movable language parts] used here are frequently called confixes, the formation process configuring. The influence of Antiquity manifests itself in a different way in the so-called educated vocabulary, which often refers to ancient history and mythology (*Ariadnefaden*, *Tantalusqualen*, *Achillesferse* ['Ariadne's thread', 'suffering of Tantalus', 'Achilles' heel']). However, in many cases, in particular with translations, the original is no longer consciously perceived (*Labyrinth*, *Zankapfel* ['labyrinth', 'bone of contention']). This peculiarity of an international vocabulary alongside the native one has a fundamental effect on the language structure – although this obviously differs from one language to another.

→ GERMANIC LANGUAGES II; → INTERNATIONALISMS

(COMPREHENSIVE SURVEYS UNDER GL II) 1 W. BETZ, Der Einfluß des Lateinischen auf den althochdeutschen Wortschatz. 1. Der Abrogans, 1936 2 K. BÜCHNER (ed.), Latein und Europa. Tradition und Renaissance, 1978 3 E. GAMILLSCHEG, Zur Geschichte der lateinischen Lehrwörter im Westgermanischen, FS Marchand 1968, 82–92 4 O. LENDLE et al (eds.), Mediterrane Kulturen und ihre Ausstrahlung auf das Deutsche, 1986 5 F. MAURER, H. RUPP, Deutsche Wortgeschichte, ³1974 (esp. 55–164, 399–508) 6 M. PEI, The Influence of Latin-Romance on Western European Languages. In: Id., The Story of Latin and the Romance Languages, 1976, 187–206 7 A. SCHIRMER, W. MITZKA, Deutsche Wortkunde. Kulturgeschichte des deutschen Wortschatzes, 1969

ELMAR SEEBOLD

II. Modern Era
A. Introduction B. Developments in the
Modern Era C. Special Features of Individual Languages

A. Introduction
The influence of Latin and Greek, over centuries on
the GL of the modern era, – German, Dutch, Frisian,
English and the North Germanic languages (Swedish,
Danish, Norwegian, Icelandic and Faroese), – becomes
visible in the area of vocabulary, the different vocabulary levels and in word formation.

B. Developments in the Modern Era
1. Internationality of Loan Words
2. Formation of New Words from
Loan-Word Components 3. Educated Vocabulary

1. Internationality of Loan Words
All modern GL (with some reservations applying to
Icelandic) as well as the other European languages share
to a large extent the Greco-Latin scholarly and cultural
terminology. This can be traced back to the fact that the
ancient languages were determining for the academic
and related cultural areas from the early Middle Ages
on, far into the modern era, and had precedence here
over the vernacular languages. Depending on the field,
the results of academic work were presented in Latin
until the 20th cent. This is the reason that a considerable part of the vocabulary of these languages is international, even if to a varying degree and volume (*Allegorie, Dialog, Dynastie, Emblem, Horizont, Kilometer,
Kosmos, Logik, radioaktiv, Sphäre, Symbol, Theater*
etc.). Scholarly presentations and investigations dealing
with the different GL contain tables of Latin and Greek
loan-words, usually in alphabetical order [e.g. 3; 10;
18; 24; 31; 34]; in many cases they also contain details
regarding their chronology or periods (Renaissance,
Humanism, Reformation, Classicism) [7] as they relate
to the various fields (Church, school, university,
applied sciences, book printing, chancellory, court
system, etc.) [8; 36], as well as regarding their quantitative share in the overall vocabulary and word frequency
[19; 29]. Characteristic for all these languages is the
flood of Latin and Greek words coming in during the
era of Humanism when, as a result of studies of Antiquity, Greek is rediscovered and the use of Latin, informed by Classical authors, became the rule. Medieval
Latin forms were replaced by borrowings from Classical Latin. Academic treatises or documents not written
in Latin were nevertheless interspersed with inflected
Latin words. In oral communication, too, especially in
scholarly discourse, Latin was mixed with the vernacular (Luther). In the 16th cent., this led, on the one hand,
to a new type of dictionary for the explanation of such
unknown words: the dictionary of foreign words; but
on the other, there was an awakening of the desire to
liberate one's own language from foreign influences

and to help it achieve proper recognition. However, this
is more aimed at French than at Latin or Greek. This
striving for "purity of language" began as early as in the
16th cent., and was reinforced by the language societies
in the 17th cent. and, from the 18th – 20th cents. in part
rationally and systematically, in part nationalistically
and aggressively by individual persons and associations
A considerable portion of today's vocabulary owes its
existence to these endeavours. Here, we are dealing
with loan-translations or replacement words for Greco-Latin expressions, e.g. from the field of grammar (Lat.
casus – German *Fall*, Lat. *nomen* – Dutch *naamwoord*
etc.).

2. Formation of New Words from
Loan-Word Components
The need for new terms was filled by the vocabulary
of technical terms already established and its elements.
This occurred, on the one hand, via the correct [grammatical] formation according to the rules of the ancient
languages, and on the other, via modern modifications
(abbreviations etc.), and finally also via hybrid forms
where different languages are mixed. The 'set pieces'
used here, namely word stems from Greek and Latin,
which in the 'receiving languages' cannot stand on their
own, are frequently called confixes (*bio-, geo-, micro-,
thermo-*), the formation process configuring. By way of
example, quantitative data may be provided: The technical vocabulary of biology and medicine shows up to
1600 confixes within a total body of 30,000 terms.
Among the prefixes of Greek and Latin origin, whose
usage extends across different languages, more than 71
productive prefixes (Greek *a-, ana-, anti-, apo-, di-,
dia-, dys-, ekto-, en-, endo-, epi-, ex-, hyper-, hypo-,
kata-, meta-, para-, peri-, syn-* and Latin *ab-, ad-, con-,
de-, dis-, ex-, in-, inter-, ob-, per-, prae-, pro-, re-, sub-,
trans-* etc.) and 122 suffixes are recorded (Greek *-ía,
-iké, -ikós, -ismós, -istés* and Latin *-ant/-ent, -antia/-
entia, -ia, -ion, -mentum, -tor, -ura, -arius, -aris, -alis,
-ivus, -osus* etc.); detailed, comparative linguistic investigations are still needed here. The constant need for
new word coinages in the areas of science, technology,
culture, politics, ideology and commerce is filled to a
large extent from the Greco-Latin components since
they have international validity and can be used for the
extension of nomenclatures and terminological systems
according to certain rules.

3. Educated Vocabulary
Part of the intellectual heritage are not only individual words, but also expressions and phrases (*semper
idem, vice versa*), noun groupings (*alter ego, terminus
technicus*) or entire sentences (*suum cuique, quod erat
demonstrandum*), which often did not appear until the
Middle Ages. These not only provided forms (*autorisieren* corresponding to Middle Latin *auctorizare*) and
meanings (*Notar* corresponding to Middle Latin *notarius*: 'public scribe appointed by imperial power'),but
also conveyed borrowings from Greek (*Arzt* [=physician] via Middle Latin *archiater* from Greek *archiātrós*
['archphysician', 'court physician']), Arabic (*Ziffer*

['figure'/'number'] via Middle Latin *cifra* from Arabic *sifr* 'zero') and other languages. The special nature of an international vocabulary alongside the inherited vocabulary has a long-ranging influence down to the language structure, although this obviously differs amongst the individual languages. (see also GL I "International Vocabulary")

C. SPECIAL FEATURES OF INDIVIDUAL LANGUAGES

1. GERMAN 2. ENGLISH 3. NORTH GERMANIC LANGUAGES

1. GERMAN

In German, a foreign structure – with, preferably, a strong adherence to the foreign model (as a result of Humanistic endeavours) – can be detected when compared with the native one. This went so far that, in the early New High German period, Greco-Latin affixes were not only combined with Classical word stems, but also with words of German origin (*Grob-ian* ['boor', 'lout'], *Schlendr-ian* ['slackness'], *morgan-atisch* ['morganatic']). The Classical words, including their inflectional suffixes, were borrowed and inflected in accordance with the Latin and Greek rules, which is still reflected today in plural forms such as *Tempora* ['tenses'], *Themata* and *Themen* ['themes'] or *Kommata* and *Kommas* ['commas'] and, like a relic, in phrases such as *nach Christi Geburt* ['after the birth of Christ']. Literal translations of Latin expressions such as *minderjährig* ['under age'] from Middle Latin *minorennis*, *Völkerrecht* from Latin *ius gentium* or *Hauptsache* from Latin *causa principalis*. Furthermore, German borrowed a full range of prepositions from Latin (*ad, exklusive, inklusive, kontra, minus, per, plus, pro, qua, versus, via*), some of which are very productive (*per Bahn* ['by rail'], *per Anhalter* ['by hitch-hiking'], *per Gesetz* ['by law'], *per Anschreiben* ['by cover letter'] etc.). Finally, mention must be made of the phenomenon of re-Latinisation, in which borrowed words (preferably from Romance languages) were converted into Latin form, for example, *Animosität* ['animosity'] was borrowed from French *animosité* and relatinised according to Latin *animositas* (cf. also *äquivalent* from French *équivalent* ['equivalent'] from Middle Latin *aequivalens* or *Konservatorium* from Italian *conservatorio* ['conservatory'] etc.).

2. ENGLISH

In English, the original Germanic character was considerably repressed due to the Norman conquest of 1066 and the influx of French words; in this context, it is obvious that the Romance foreign influence was at least as strongly Latin as it was French. From the time of Humanism in the 16th cent., the fact that a related Romance-French element already existed, favoured the influx of scholarly Latin (and Greek) words in the form of borrowings or neologisms. In no other GL has the volume of the vocabulary increased to such an extent through Renaissance Latinisms as in English. Partly, the

borrowings were adopted without morphological change (*arena, status, extra*), partly, the foreign suffix was dropped (Lat. *critic-us* > Engl. 'critic', Lat. *extendere* > Engl. 'extend'), partly, it was substituted by an native suffix. From the 16th cent. on, but particularly since the 18th cent., the increased need for technical and scientific terms was met by new formations from Classical or neo-Classical vocabulary stock. While German frequently has a vernacular expression alongside a Latinism (or a Grecism) (*Geographie – Erdkunde, Computer – Rechner, synonym – bedeutungsgleich*), there is often only the word of foreign origin in English ('geography', 'computer', 'synonymous'). Where in English there are synonyms, the Latin usage is considered the more refined one; the inherited Germanic words are left to the vocabulary for everyday use. For ordinary speakers, the words of obvious Latin origin are often felt to be 'hard words', namely words that are difficult to use. These 'hard words' are not only characterised by fine differences in meaning in relation to their synonyms or by stylistic nuances, difficult spelling or pronunciation, they frequently are also dissociated, i.e. they cannot be connected, either formally or by content, with another basic word or with other, already-existing vocabulary: While for a German speaker, for example, the adjective *mündlich* is recognisably derived from the noun *Mund*, the English adjective *oral* is isolated from the noun *mouth*. These 'hard words' present a linguistic difficulty which, in the final analysis, results in a social separation of the speakers. Thus, the engagement with the Classical heritage in the English language in dictionaries and text books, has been taking place since the early 17th cent. with the primary aim to improve language competency in this area.

3. NORTH GERMANIC LANGUAGES

The North Germanic languages, in principle, behave in the same way as German when it comes to the continuation of Latin as the international language of scholars and the formation of new international words on a Latin or Greek basis in the area of scholarship, with German playing an intermediary role. Here, too, since the middle of the 18th cent., increasing efforts have been made to avoid foreign, in particular Latin and French words or to complement them with native synonyms (*musik* with Danish *tonekunst*, *medicin* with *lægekunst*) or to replace them (*gække* instead of *ridikulere*, *selskabelig* instead of *sociable*). Icelandic in particular is sensitive toward foreign words to an unusual degree. As one of the languages with the lowest number of speakers in Europe, it indulges in the luxury to consistently translate otherwise common → INTERNATIONALISMS, such as *hitabelti* for 'tropics' (literally 'hot belt'), or to replace them by artificial words. New words are formed with recourse to native lexemes and derivation elements such as *sími* 'telephone' [from *síma* 'wire'], *hreyf-ill* 'mover' for motor or *smá-sjá* 'small seeer' for microscope. Artificial words are formed by arbitrary, not a morphologically-based selection of parts of a foreign word (*berk-* out of *t uberkel*) and the extension with indigenous affixes (-*ill* as a suffix of agency) so that a word like *berk-ill* 'tubercle' can occur, which fits in well with the structure of the vocabulary. With the consistent formation of neologisms instead of borrowings, Icelandic is able to maintain the impression of diachronic uniformity, at least in its written form.

1 G. Ahrens, Medizinisches und naturwissenschaftliches Latein. Mit latinisiertem griechischem Wortschatz, ²1992   2 D. M. Ayers, English Words from Latin and Greek Elements, 1977   3 P. G. Aringström, Gunnar Ekelöf och antiken, 1992 (with a lexicon of Latin and Greek words, derivations, loanwords and quotations)   4 G. J. M. Bartelink, Uitgewiste Latijnse sporen in het Nederlands, in: Hermeneus 56 (1984), 262–266   5 P. Braun et al. (ed.), Internationalismen. Studien zur interlingualen Lexikologie und Lexikographie, 1990   6 M. Byrne, Eureka! A Dictionary of Latin and Greek Elements in English Words, 1997   7 Deutsches Fremdwörterbuch, ²1995f. (vol 5: 'Eau de Cologne'- 'Futurismus'–for missing volumes in the new edition, the volumes in the first edition may be consulted)   8 F. Dornseiff, Die griechischen Wörter im Deutschen, 1950   9 K. Ehlich, Greek and Latin as a Permanent Source for Scientific Terminology: The German Case, in: F. Coulmas (ed.), Language Adaptation, 1989, 135–157   10 P. Gessler, Griechische Fremd- und Lehnwörter im Deutschen, 1967   11 U. Groenke, Vom Kunstwort zum Wort. Eine Besonderheit der isländischen Neuwortproduktion, in: Festschrift H. Seiler, 1980, 287–291   12 Id., Isländische Kunstwörter – natürliche Wörter, in: K. Sroka (ed.), Kognitive Aspekte der Sprache, 1996, 93–96   13 H. Halldórsson, Icelandic Purism and its History, in: Word. Journal of the International Linguistic association 30 (1979), 76–87   14 P. Halleux, Le Purisme Islandais, in: Etudes Germaniques 20 (1965), 417–427   15 A. G. Hatcher, Modern English Word-Formation and Neo-Latin, 1951   16 E. Haugen, Die skandinavischen Sprachen, 1984   17 F. J. Hausmann, W. Seibicke, Das Internationalismen-Wörterbuch, in: Wörterbücher, Dictionaries, Dictionnaires II, 1990, 1179–1184   18 A. Hemme, Das lateinische Sprachmaterial im Wortschatze der deutschen, französischen und englischen Sprache, 1904 (Repr. 1979)   19 A. J. Hoof, Hoe klassiek in het Nederlands, in: Kleio 9 (1979), 25–35   20 G. Hoppe, Das Präfix ex-. Beiträge zur Lehnwortbildung. Mit einer Einführung in den Gegenstandsbereich, 1999   21 G. Hoppe et al.(eds.), Deutsche Lehnwortbildung. Beiträge zur Erforschung der Wortbildung mit entlehnten Wortbildungseinheiten im Deutschen, 1987   22 A. Kirkness, Das Fremdwörterbuch, in: Wörterbücher, Dictionaries. Dictionnaires II, 1990, 1168–1178   23 Id., Eurolatin and English Today: An Examination of the Nature, History and Roles of Classicisms in English and other European Languages, in: English today 13 (1997), 3–8   24 B. Kytzler, Unser tägliches Latein: Lexikon des lateinischen Spracherbes, ⁴1995   25 E. Leisi, C. Mair, Das heutige Englisch: Wesenszüge und Probleme, ⁸1999   26 B. Lindberg, De lärdes modersmål. Latin, humanism och vetenskap i 1700 talets Sverige, 1984   27 G. Lurquin, Elsevier's Dictionary of Greek and Latin Word Constituents: Greek and Latin Affixes, Words and Roots used in English, French, German, Dutch, Italian and Spanish, 1998   28 C. A. Luschnig, Etyma: An Introduction to Vocabulary Building from Latin and Greek, 1982   29 M. Mader, Latei-

nische Wortkunde für Alt- und Neusprachler, 1979   30 H. H. Munske, A. Kirkness (eds.), Eurolatein. Das griechische und lateinische Erbe in den europäischen Sprachen, 1996   31 F. Richter, Unser tägliches Griechisch: Deutsche Wörter griechischer Herkunft, 1981   32 H.-F. Rosenfeld, Klassische Sprachen und deutsche Gesamtsprache, in: Lexikon der Germanistischen Linguistik, ²1980, 653–660   33 M. Scheler, Der englische Wortschatz, 1977   34 K. A. Sinkovich, A Dictionary of English Words from Greek and Latin Roots, 1987   35 M. C. van den Toorn, Neoklassiek en postmodern: een morfolexicografische verkenning, in: Jaarboek van de Stichting Instituut voor Nederlandse Lexicologie, 1987 (1988), 66–100   36 J. Verheggen, Heureka: Grieske cultuur in Nederlandse woorden, 1996   37 A. Weijnen, Leenwoorden uit de Latinitas, stratigrafisch beschouwd, in: Id., Algemene en vergelijkende dialectologie, 1975, 189–299   38 E. C. Welskopf, Das Fortleben altgriechischer sozialer Typenbegriffe in der deutschen Sprache, 1981   39 C. Werner, Wortelemente lateinisch-griechischer Fachausdrücke in den biologischen Wissenschaften., ⁷1997   40 O. Wittstock (ed.), Latein und Griechisch im deutschen Wortschatz, ⁶1999.

BRIGITTE BULITTA

Germany

I. To 1600   II. The Baroque   III. Up to 1806
IV. The 19th Century to 1918   V. The 20th
Century (after 1918)

I. To 1600

A. History and Social Development under Carolingian Rule to 918   B. History and Social Development   C. History and Social Development from the Interregnum to the Reformation (1250–1519)   D. History and Social Development in the Age of Reformation and Early Counter-Reformation (1500 – ca. 1600)

A. History and Social Development under Carolingian Rule to 918

The coronation of Charlemagne as emperor (800) laid the foundation for the medieval German empire. In a lengthy process, the German people evolved from those Germanic tribes that had remained settled during the great migration of the peoples, together with some *foederati*, Rome's former allies. Larger communities developed around many *villae*, still evident in some place names, particularly in the Rhineland, but settlements also developed independently. Latin remained the language of the educated. → Medieval Latin combined elements from vulgar Latin with those of the developing national languages. The continuity of administration as well as in social order and care was largely retained, whereas the educational structure of Late Antiquity was taken over by institutions of the Church such as monasteries and → cathedral schools. The predominantly Germanic nobility made do with private tutors and was mainly interested in military education. With a few exceptions, this resulted in an increasing lack of education in the aristocracy, a trend only reversed with the rise of Humanism. The empire was weakened under Charlemagne's successor Louis the Pious (division of the empire in the Treaty of Verdun, 843). Louis the German received the lands east of the Rhine as the East-Franconian kingdom. After a temporary restoration of the Franconian empire as a whole, Conrad, formerly Duke of Franconia, was elected king of the East-Franconian kingdom, thus truly establishing it as the 'German kingdom' alongside those of → FRANCE, Burgundy and → ITALY .

The earliest evidence of the term 'deutsch' (*theodisce*), originally as 'belonging to the people' (*thiuda* = 'people' in Gothic), is found in records pertaining to the ceremonial oath of fealty in 786/788, referring to the language that was not Latin. The earliest use of *theutiscus*, latinized as *t(h)eutonicus*, as a noun is found in 9th cent. documents from Italy [1]. The term *Regnum Theutonicum* was in use from the early 11th cent., the descriptive title of 'Roman Empire of the German Nation' only prevailed at the time of Emperor Maximilian, towards the end of the 15th cent.

1. EDUCATION, ART AND LITERATURE 2. ROMANESQUE ARCHITECTURE

1. EDUCATION, ART AND LITERATURE

The rule of Charlemagne aimed for a revival of education which experienced a particular bloom at the palace school in Aachen. Eminent scholars such as Alcuin and Paulus Diaconus began to work on compiling all of the written records and emending the works of the Church Fathers as well as those by pagan authors. Their efforts have ensured the survival of large parts of classical and late-antique Latin literature. Much credit for the imparting of ancient culture and literature must go to monasteries such as those on the island of Reichenau and in St. Gall. The language was developed further, heroic songs were written down, and → HISTORIOGRAPHY was renewed. The new script of the Caroline minuscule, based on Roman models, was further developed in the scriptoria, alongside a distinctive style in art, encompassing not only architecture, but also mural paintings and book illustrations, gold work, and much more.

The most eminent individual of the Carolingian period was Einhard (ca. 770– 14 March 840), historiographer and director of building projects at the court of Charlemagne. Einhard's Arch, of which only a drawn copy has survived, is an example for the new iconographic programme of *renovatio*. This exquisitely designed base for a reliquary cross in the shape of a Roman → TRIUMPHAL ARCH combines the earthly sphere of the ruler with the salvatory. The triumphal arch of Roman emperors is 'translated' into Christian terminology: instead of the emperor, it is the figure of Christ on the cross who is the eternal victor, while the donor (Einhard) refers to himself as *peccator* (sinner). Though modelled on Suetonius' vita of Augustus, Einhard's biography of Charlemagne (*Vita Karoli Magni*) is an original work. The Franconian scholar Rabanus

Maurus (ca. 780–856) was an important mediator of ancient learning for the East- Franconian region, in particular through his work *De institutione clericorum*.

After the initial decline and a transitional period, medieval Latin literature experienced a first period of flourishing under Carolingian rule (→ CAROLINGIAN RENAISSANCE), still essentially linked to the same means of artistic expression as in Antiquity. In numerous genres, ancient tradition combined with medieval elements to create new entities, particularly in the fields of → BIOGRAPHY (Einhard, Notker) and historiography (Gregory of Tours, Paulus Diaconus). The Christian aspect was perceived as equal to the ancient one.

2. ROMANESQUE ARCHITECTURE

The new ideology found a particularly pertinent expression in architecture, with a conscious recourse to Roman models and also, at least at times, by deliberately distancing itself from Byzantine palaces. The use of bronze portals, round arches, pillars, columns, barrel vaults and domes point to Roman models, while octagonal central-plan buildings and crypts are more likely new creations. The term 'romanesque' was coined in around 1820 by French scholars to describe this style of round arches, highlighting its relationship with Roman architecture. This architectural style developed first in France and reached Germany some decades later. The 'cathedral' of Charlemagne's royal palace in Aachen, built between 796 and 805 as a central-plan building, was inspired by examples from Late Antiquity such as San Vitale in Ravenna. It is the manifestation of the Franconian king's adoption of the Roman notion of empire; it is also his burial place. In keeping with this, it served as the coronation church for all Franconian and German kings between 813–1531. Gernrode, St. Michael in Hildesheim and the cathedral in Speyer – the latter as the largest building (around 1030) after the end of Roman antiquity – should be named as outstanding examples of German → ROMANESQUE style. St. Pantaleon in Cologne is modelled on the palace chapel in Aachen. Romanesque church architecture is characterized by the introduction of vaulting across large spaces, initially of the side aisles, but increasing also of centre aisles and transepts.

B. HISTORY AND SOCIAL DEVELOPMENT

With Henry I (919–936), the first of the Saxon Ottonian dynasty of rulers, came a consolidation of the kingdom. He conquered Bohemia and the Slavic tribes east of the Elbe river and successfully repelled Hungarian incursions. His son Otto I further expanded the power of the monarchy (936–973). He relied on the support of the bishops, and deprived the tribal dukes of their power. He founded marches and bishoprics in the Slavic East. He gained supremacy over Italy, and was crowned Roman emperor by the pope in 962, thus laying the foundation for the future Roman-German emperorship. With the imperial title, he also adopted the ancient tradition of the universal claim to rule. Modelled on the ancient title, the empire was known from the early 11th cent. as *Imperium Romanum-Sacrum Imperium Romanum* (from mid–13th cent.). The title 'Holy Roman Empire of the German Nation' only referred to the German inhabited parts of the empire. It was first used under the rule of emperor Frederick III (1440–1493). Otto II (973–983) had to defend his rule in southern Italy in battles against Saracens and Byzantines. A major uprising by the Elbe Slavs resulted in the loss of German conquests in the east. In Italy, Otto adopted the same title as the Byzantine emperors: *Romanorum Imperator Augustus*. At a diet of German and Italian nobles in Verona, he had his young son elected king, who subsequently as Otto III (983–1002), supported by his mother, the former Byzantine princess Theophanou, adopted the notion of universal emperorship. Conrad II (1024–1039), the descendant of a daughter of Otto I, was the first of the Franconian or Salian dynasty to ascend to the throne. In 1034, the kingdom of Burgundy was joined with Germany (G.) in personal union. His son Henry III (1039–1056) appointed German bishops in Italy to consolidate his power there. Pope Gregory VII, however, aimed for the liberation of the church from any secular rule, resulting in the investiture Controversy. Henry V (1106–1125) was the last of the Franconian emperors. The power of the empire rose once again under Frederick I Barbarossa (1152–1190), the first Staufen emperor. His grandson Frederick II focused his interests in Italy. His death in 1250 marked the end of the great period of German medieval emperorship.

1. Education, Art and Literature 2. Gothic Architecture 3. Sepulchral Monuments and Inscriptions

1. Education, Art and Literature

Medieval Latin is the umbrella term for all forms of Latin used from the 6th cent. to Renaissance Humanism. Newly developed literary forms were sequence, trope, rhythmic poetry and rhyme, religious plays and animal epics. In quantity, these works far exceed that of the extant ancient literature. This is partly due to the direct transmission in quite a number of manuscripts, and partly due to the greater geographical spread, encompassing almost all of Europe. The Roman Church with its authors and its audience was the main champion of medieval Latin, which reached its golden age in the 12th/13th cent.

In several literary genres, ancient tradition blended with medieval characteristics to create new forms, particularly in historiography (exemplary are Thietmar von Merseburg's *Chronicon* (ca. 1000), the historical and contemporary annals by Lambert of Hersfeld (11th cent.), and Otto von Freising's historical-philosophical *Chronicon seu rerum ab initio mundi ad sua usque tempora* (12th cent., based on Augustine's doctrine of the two empires). The monasteries at Fulda, Hersfeld and Corvey played an outstanding role in the history of the transmission of Roman historians. A narrative literature developed from the anecdotes and legends surrounding the figure of Charlemagne. Into this category falls an 1170 translation of the *Chansons de Roland* at the behest of Henry the Lion, modernised around 1233. Widely known were the *Gesta Romanorum*, an anthology of unhistorical secular stories (early 14th cent.), totaling more than 300 stories, novellas, as well as fairy tales and legends of ancient, Christian and Oriental origin, often with a rather arbitrary link to Roman history. Nothing is known about the authors, compilers or the place of origin. The *Legenda aurea*, a collection of short biographies of the calendar saints by the Dominican friar Jacobus de Voragine (1226–1298), was very influential not only on legendary literature, but also on the visual arts.

Theological and philosophical tractates reached their zenith in the tradition of → scholasticism. The Dominican friar Albertus Magnus (d. 1280) systematized the teachings of Aristotle, under consideration of the Arabic commentaries which had by then become known to scholars. In his "Ethics", he combined ancient and Christian virtues. He supported the principle of free will which was later to assume a major role in the dispute between Humanism and Reformation. As a mystic and theologian, Meister Eckhart (d. 1328) stood in the (neo)-Platonic tradition.

One of the main representatives of medieval dramatic poetry, apart from Christmas and passion plays, was Rosvitha of Gandersheim (935–975). In addition to saintly legends and contemporary epics in hexameters or distichs, she wrote six plays in rhymed prose in order to replace Terence with Christian matter as reading material for clerics. Her language shows the influence of ancient poets such as Terence, Virgil, Prudentius and Boethius. Her plays, written for reading rather than performance, represent the most important reception of ancient → comedies in the Middle Ages. Her works were rediscovered by the Humanist Conrad Celtis in 1493 (*Editio princeps* 1501).

The secular epic continued in the form of heroic poetry. The *Waltharius* (9th cent.) is a Latin heroic epic in hexameters, telling the story of Walther of Aquitaine's flight from the court of King Attila the Hun and his subsequent battle with King Gundahar of Burgundy. Nowadays, the authorship of the St. Gall monk and poet Ekkehard I is a matter of dispute. Germanic heroic epics were refashioned in line with ancient examples (Virgil, Prudentius), but with Christian features.

Animal poetry as a vehicle for a satirical view on life at court and in monasteries reached a peak within the German-speaking world. *Ysengrimus* with the wolf representing an ignorant lecherous cleric is the most important medieval beast-epic, written in 6574 distichs by the German scholar Nivardus in Gent between 1146 and 1148; it style is modelled on Ovid. A remarkable example of a romance in Latin hexameters is *Ruodlieb*, the earliest medieval German novel, probably written by a cleric in Tegernsee in about 1050.

Lyric poetry, both secular and religious, was widely disseminated as goliardic poetry by travelling scholars.

With very few exceptions, such as the Archipoeta, the pseudonym of a (most likely German) knight at the court of Frederick Barbarossa, the anthologies remained anonymous. Filled with the joy of earthly life, he poems sang of nature, love, wine and playing dice. In addition, there were moral-satirical and also political poems against the decline in the moral standards of the clergy. Reminiscences of ancient authors – particularly Horace and Ovid – were common. Apart from the *Carmina Cantabrigiensia*, dating from 11th cent. G. and France, the *Carmina Burana* represents the most comprehensive anthology of goliardic poetry. Compiled around the mid–13th cent. in the Bavarian monastery of Benediktbeuren, it comprises about 250 poems mostly in medieval Latin, but also in German or in a mixture of the two. The *Carmina Burana* owes much to ancient examples, both in form and in content; there are numerous references to Augustan poets.

Didactic poetry, both religious and morally-didactic, took a variety of forms, as did chronicles and anthologies such as the *Disticha Catonis*; the latter was compiled around 300 and used in the Middle Ages and later by Humanists to practice reading and poetry. Humorous poems and riddles together with → EPIGRAMS modelled on ancient patterns on a wide range of topics and occasions had a lasting effect on vernacular authors across Europe.

2. GOTHIC ARCHITECTURE

The term 'Gothic' to describe European architecture from 1140 to 1520 dates back to L.B. Alberti's 1435 definition of *mani ... gotiche*, translated into Latin as *rusticanae* = 'rough'. A similar distinction was made by L. Valla in 1440 between Gothic (= bad) and Roman (= good) letters, while in 1550 G. Vasari expressed his disdain for northern art by referring to the *maniera tedesca* or *maniera dei Goti*. All of these were directed at the vertical and illusionistic elements of the Gothic style, in contrast with Romanesque architecture. Impulses from French models (from about 1140, St. Denis) were modified in G. in Trier, Marburg, Freiburg/Breisgau, Halberstadt, Magdeburg and Breslau/Wroclaw; only Cologne Cathedral after 1248 and the Cathedral of Strasbourg are examples of a direct adoption of the French style. The preference was for hall churches, with nave and aisles of approximately equal height; the translation of Gothic elements into brick architecture in St. Mary's church in Lübeck became the model for the sacral architecture in the entire Baltic region. The combined effect of the unification of space and the window facade was to allow light to flood the entire interior, a reference to the celestial → JERUSALEM and the cosmos. This again is evidence of ancient reminiscences. Gothic style elements and vaults are also found in the secular architecture of the 14th and 15th cent., in castles and palaces, in town halls and houses, as well as in town gates, particularly in northern G.

3. SEPULCHRAL MONUMENTS AND INSCRIPTIONS

In Late Antiquity, the image of Christ was developed on the model of the ancient ideal of the male youth, in particular after images of the gods Apollo and Dionysus. The raised hand of the ruler in an expression of dignity and power can be found on the images of Christ Pantocrator. Its prototypes were Alexander the Great, who had died in his youth, as well emperor Augustus with his notions of empire and visions of peace in addition to more general cosmic-messianic concepts [2; 3]. The birthday of Sol Invictus on 25 December was undoubtedly of influence for the liturgical development.

The development of sepulchral monuments is to be seen as a 'structural remembrance' linked both to the ancient concept of *memoria*, the preservation of the memory of a person after death, and the *memento mori* of Christianity. Following the example of Christ, sepulchral sculptures depict a person of about 30 years of age, i.e. in the prime of life and not disfigured by age or physical deterioration; the eyes are frequently open and hands folded in prayer in expectation of eternal life. Initially, only the name of the deceased was given alongside the dates of his birth and death, often rendered as a scratch drawing with very few symbols and abstract ornamentation. A classification according to various types and styles has been developed over time. Vertical and horizontal memorial slabs are evident throughout the ages. A special Romanesque feature was the wheel cross, as was the sarcophagus which emulated ancient examples, but often in form of an empty tomb over the actual grave, in the early period often in the crypt of a church. Memorial slabs were frequently placed side by side, isolated graves were placed in portal-shaped niches. The epitaph, a memorial plate of stone, marble or wood, fastened to a wall or a pillar, only appeared in the 14th and 15th cent. Formerly horizontal memorial slabs were put upright. The fully fashioned sepulchral sculpture became increasingly common in the 13th cent., even though the sepulchral image as *effigies* of the deceased had been one of the most important manifestations of medieval sculpture since the end of the 11th cent. [4; 5]. Dress attire according to office and social standing became increasingly important: clerics in liturgical robes, burghers in festive attire, scholars in academic gowns, knights in armour, founders with a model of the building, usually with the family crest and ancestral line. It also became increasingly common for animals to be depicted on tombs. The ancient notion of *vita activa* was reflected in the tombs for knights, that of the *vita contemplativa* on the graves of scholars or clerics. Modelled on ancient examples, the epitaphs of the 14th and 15th cent. tended to become realistic images rather than the often drastic representations of the late Gothic period.

Simple inscriptions in prose as in verse are evident from Antiquity onwards. Some epitaphs were of high literary standard and belonged to the epigrammatic genre. For prose and verse inscriptions, an inventory of stock motifs and formulae developed, gradually also adopted by Christians. The abbreviation for *obiit* (Ø = 'he died'), which developed in Late Antiquity, not only affected Latin texts, but also German ones well into the

Early Modern period. Compilations of Roman inscriptions existed quite early on in the Middle Ages and were of demonstrable influence. Epitaphs came in a wide variety of designs. The predominant metric structure was the elegiac distich; the use of the third person was common, but there are also examples of the reader being addressed directly – a common practice in Antiquity – as well as an address by the deceased himself. The *laudatio funebris* once again became common practice. However, the literary form of the epitaph was also used in schools as a poetical-rhetorical exercise for a lament, as well as for parody. In Renaissance Humanism, a clear distinction has to be made between the true epitaph, i.e. the inscription on a tomb, and the literary genre. Structures and forms from Classical Antiquity once again replaced medieval features. The epigraphic changes [6] in Humanist epitaphs are immediately obvious: Gothic majuscules and minuscules were replaced by Humanist lettering, at times even by Roman capitals in a deliberate imitation. The Humanist minuscule, a print font known as Antiqua, arose in the 16th cent. taken up from the Carolingian period.

C. History and Social Development from the Interregnum to the Reformation (1250–1519)

The rule of the Hohenstaufen was followed from about 1250 by the Great Interregnum, a period in which the strong regional princes expanded their own power. The seven Prince-Electors, the only ones after the mid–13th cent. with the right to elect the king, attempted to find a counterbalance to a strong monarchy. From 1347, the kingship of Charles IV of Luxembourg was generally acknowledged; his rule continued until his death in 1378. He abstained from a restoration of the German emperorship in Italy. With Albrecht II of Austria, son-in-law of the last of the Luxembourg kings, the crown passed to the Habsburg line. Frederick III (1440–1493) focused predominantly on the expansion of his power base. His son, the future Emperor Maximilian I (1493–1519), obtained Burgundy through his marriage to Mary of Burgundy (1477). Maximilian was the first to assume the imperial title without coronation, but with papal consent. Based on the example of Roman emperors, he assumed the title of *Imperator Caesar Maximilianus Pius Felix Augustus*. The period after the Hohenstaufen saw an economic rise of the cities which increasingly favoured a flourishing of education.

1. German Renaissance Humanism: Its Centres and Important Representatives 2. Willibald Pirckheimer and Classical Antiquity 3. Renaissance Humanism and Reformation: Martin Luther and Philipp Melanchthon 4. Renaissance Humanism and Art 5. Albrecht Dürer as a Representative of his Time

1. German Renaissance Humanism: Its Centres and Important Representatives

Renaissance Humanism (or, simply, → Humanism) as an epochal designation in the narrower sense refers to the first pan-European cultural movement between the Middle Ages and Modern Period (14th–16th cent.). It arose from the rediscovery, admiration and imitation of Classical Antiquity. Its ideal and role model was the *vir humanus et doctissimus* (Italian *umanista*), whose outlook and attitude was honed by his studies of Classical Antiquity and whose predominant focus was on the *studia humanitatis*. There was a deliberate emphasis on the the contrast with medieval scholars who had focused only on the *studia divina*. The transitory period from the 14th to the 16th cent. with its ambivalence between old traditional and new innovative elements makes it difficult to gain a clear understanding of the interrelations. Humanism can be seen as part of the much wider-reaching → Renaissance which, though predominantly an artistic movement, affected all areas of culture; however, education and culture are so closely intertwined that the term Renaissance Humanism increasingly prevails. With its reference to ancient literature and philosophy – especially Plato and Aristotle – and its fundamental challenge of the previous tradition, Renaissance Humanism became the basis and guide for modern ways of thinking and living. The battle cry *ad fontes* was decisive for a new way of dealing with source material. Centres of this Renaissance Humanism were the cities with their increasing economic and political powers, also secular and religious courts, but to a lesser extent the more conservative universities. The latter changed in G. only with the foundation of the first Protestant universities and the Catholic Counterreformation. The main aim of Humanists was the development of a Classical Latin style to replace the inelegant medieval Latin. The invention of the printing press by Johann Gutenberg in Mainz meant a great boost to the dissemination of knowledge. Greek Antiquity moved into focus after about 1400 and in particular after the conquest of Constantinople by the Turks in 1453, when Byzantine scholars such as Gemistos Plethon and Bessarion came to Italy.

In addition to epic and dramatic poetry, the latter a particular favourite as school plays or on special festive occasions, occasional poetry and love poems were cultivated, in form and content modelled on ancient examples but with clear references to the poet's contemporary period and personal experience. In addition, satire blossomed, as did epistolary literature and artful oratory. There were also advancements in historiography, biography and specialist literature. The astronomer and physician Nicolaus Copernicus developed his revolutionary heliocentric model of the universe in the course of a critical examination of Ptolemy. Humanism was introduced to G. by Petrarch and Cola di Rienzi with whom Johannes von Neumarkt, chancellor at the court of Charles IV in Prague, had contact. In the ambience of the Prague chancellery, *elegantia* was developed as the new style model. The disputation *Der Ackermann aus Böhmen (Ploughman from Bohemia)* by the Master Johann von Tepl, one of Neumarkt's pupils, was written in elaborate artistic prose in accordance with the new rules (published in 1410). While the form remained that of the medieval disputation, the new self-confidence expressed itself in the references to Plato, Aristotle, Seneca and Boethius. Vienna under the rule of emperor Frederick II was a further centre for Humanists. Of seminal importance was a speech delivered in 1445 at Vienna university by the secretary of the imperial chancellery, Enea Silvio Piccolomini, the future pope Pius II. Vienna retained its importance in later periods, particularly through Conrad Celtis, the 'German Archhumanist' (1459–1508). In 1487 he became the first German to receive the crown of *poeta laureatus,* an award initially revived in Italy in continuation of ancient tradition [7].

University teachers with traditional conservative views put up bitter resistance, as evident in the *Epistulae obscurorum virorum.* This collection of fictitious Latin letters addressed to Ortwin Gratius, spokesman of the Cologne theologians in the dispute with the Humanist Johannes Reuchlin (d. 1522) used a barbaric → DOG LATIN to caricature the dogmatic-scholastic attitude of their supposed authors. The dispute centred around the question of Jewish books which in the views of Johannes Pfefferkorn, a baptized Jew, were to be destroyed in order to keep the Biblical books 'clean'. His principal opponent was the Hebraist Reuchlin, soon joined by many of his Humanist friends. The satirical letters originated from this circle of friends, amongst them Ulrich von Hutten.

Initially, itinerant scholars such as Peter Luder (d. ca. 1470) were the ones who disseminated Humanist thinking. The foundation of → UNIVERSITIES in the German speaking areas took place comparatively late: Prague in 1348, Vienna in 1365, Heidelberg in 1386, Cologne in 1389, Erfurt in 1392, followed in the early 15th cent. by Würzburg, Leipzig, Rostock and Wittenberg, and in the second half of that century by Greifswald, Freiburg, Besançon, Basel, Mainz, Ingolstadt, Trier and Tübingen. After 1527, there were some Protestant foundations.

The canon of the Seven Liberal Arts (→ ARTES LIBERALES), at the heart of the university curriculum, was based on the ancient notion of intellectual activities deemed worthy of a free man. From the 9th cent. the language-based subjects grammar, rhetoric and dialectic were grouped together as *trivium,* whereas *quadrivium* was used from Late Antiquity to describe the mathematical-physical disciplines, i.e. arithmetic, geometry, astronomy and music [8; 9]. As a result of their systematic representation in late-Roman encyclopaedias, the *artes* with their supposed (and at times varied) founders became the basis of the medieval and (with some variation) early modern art faculties and thus also the foundation for specialist studies of theology, philosophy, jurisprudence and medicine. The religious revival movement of the *devotio moderna,* following from the mysticism of the High Middle Ages, was an important ally for Humanism in the dispute with medieval → SCHOLASTICISM. Latin and Greek technical terms found their way into German. Following the example of Italian academies, *sodalitates litterariae* were founded, particularly in the free cities of upper G. In the early phase of Humanism, Nuremberg was known for historiographers such as Hartmann Schedel (d. 1514), while other centres of early Humanism were Ulm and Strasbourg. At the peak of Renaissance Humanism, the free city of Augsburg rose to importance due to the patrician Konrad Peutinger (d. 1547) and that of Nuremberg due to the patrician Pirckheimer family. Major roles were also played by Tübingen with Johannes Reuchlin and Heidelberg with Rudolf Agricola (d. 1485). In Erfurt, critical neo-Latin poets began to gather around Mutianus Rufus, a religious critic rooted in the *devotio moderna.* Sebastian Brant und Beatus Rhenanus were the dominant representatives of Humanism in the upper Rhine valley. Even during his lifetime, Erasmus of Rotterdam (1466–1536) was acknowledged as the secret head of all Humanists, as master of the *bonae litterae.* Long years of study and travel had taken him to Holland, France, England, Italy, Switzerland and G. He spent some longer time periods in Basel and Freiburg. His aim was to reconcile Classical Antiquity with Christianity. His aesthetic-philological study of ancient literature is evident in his mastery of the Classical use of forms, e.g. in *Laus stultitiae (In Praise of Folly),* 1511. His return to the origins of Christianity found expression in the programmatic *Enchiridion militis christiani* (1504) and the edition of the purified original text of the New Testament (1516) which was to be used by Luther in his German bible translation.

An outstanding personality at the end of German Humanism was the knight Ulrich von Hutten (1488–1523); in Latin and German polemical writings, he attempted to reconcile Humanist ideals with national and contemporary political aims. The positive feature of Humanism was its potential for the development of a modern personality. Erasmus, in particular, defended the concepts of freedom of the will and self-determination, based on ancient conceptions, against the reformer Luther, who in this aspect remained attached to a more medieval point of view [10].

2. WILLIBALD PIRCKHEIMER AND CLASSICAL ANTIQUITY

As a representative of the Nuremberg patriciate, as city councillor and imperial councillor, patron of the arts and friend of Albrecht Dürer and as a learned correspondent with almost all of the personalities of his time, Willibald Pirckheimer is a contemporary witness of immeasurable value. As his ancestors before him, from 1489 to 1495 he studied the Humanities and law in Italy. In Padua, a Byzantine teacher taught him the basics of Greek, a language which was to fascinate him throughout his life. At that time, however, the study of Greek was still the exception rather than the rule. A clergyman from Freiburg, for example, warned in one of his sermons against the "newly invented language known as Greek; it was the mother of all heresies. Furthermore, a book in this language, entitled the New Testament, is now owned by many". Significantly, the "new book" in question was Erasmus's *Novum Testamentum Graece*, published in 1516 in G. as the first Greek edition. In the eyes of the traditional Church, the Byzantines were heretics and schismatics – a verdict that was also applied to their language. The philological analysis of Greek literature was thus seen as an attack against the previously undisputed authority of the clergy. For that reason, it is understandable that the study of Greek hardly prevailed, initially only at a small number of universities and → LATIN SCHOOLS. The first chair for Greek was established in Leipzig in 1515 for *professor publicus* Richard Crocus, followed by other universities in Wittenberg, Erfurt, Ingolstadt, Freiburg, Tübingen, Heidelberg, Vienna and Rostock.

It is to Pirckheimer's particular credit that he was one of the very few German Humanists to make a significant contribution towards a spread in the knowledge of Greek. In his letter of dedication for the German translation of Plutarch [11], he postulated as a principle for translations that each translator "should render only the meaning–clearly, purely and the like–into the language, regardless of the words". In his approval of a translation which conveys the gist of the source, Pirckheimer found himself largely in agreement with Luther's thoughts as expressed in the *Sendbrief vom Dolmetschen* ('Open letter on translating'). Pirckheimer mainly translated works by Plutarch and Lucian, but also Homer, Aristophanes, Plato, Ptolemy, Theophrastus, Xenophon, Isocrates, as well as Greek Christian authors such as Gregory of Nazianz, Fulgentius and Nilus. From Pirckheimer's workshop came an extant verbatim translation of the *Iliad* into Latin (bks. 1–3), based on the *editio princeps* of Homer (Florence, 1488) [12]. Under the guise of Antiquity, Pirckheimer cleverly commented on contemporary problems, e.g. on the Reuchlin dispute in his translation of Lucian's *Piscator* (1517) and by naming progressively-minded Humanists in his famous *Epistola apologetica*. In Pirckheimer's view, the new theologian should ideally have mastered the entire literature in Latin, Greek and Hebrew, in addition to dialectic and rhetoric, and furthermore have detailed knowledge of canon and civil law and philosophy, particularly Plato's, in addition to being schooled in the mathematical disciplines.

Plato was of particular significance to Pirckheimer; it is even possible to identify a 'Platonic period' (1500–1523) in his life. During his time in Italy, he had encountered the re-evaluation and restoration of the *divus Plato*. In order to avoid any possible accusation of heresy, Marsilio Ficino in Florence tried to bring Plato into line with Christian tradition ('Qui te ad Platonem vocat, ad ecclesiam vocat'; "he who calls you to Plato, calls you to the Church"). As a result of his work as a translator and editor, Pirckheimer had arrived at a more objective point of view and distanced himself from Ficino's notion of a Christian interpretation of the philosopher. He liked to quote Plato's thoughts in his own works and letters of dedication; in his (in parts–first) Latin translation of the eight *Pseudoplatonica*, published in Nuremberg in 1523 under the title of *Dialogi Platonis*, he separated the genuine from the spurious and recommended the study of Plato in order highlight him against Aristotle who had dominated medieval thinking (→ ARISTOTELIANISM). The most important of these dialogues is the one entitled *Axiochos*; its topic – overcoming the fear of death – makes it part of the *consolatio* genre. After an initially pessimistic tenor, further emphasized by Pirckheimer with a metric addition consisting of 21 distichs, it concludes by singing the praises of human potential, thus establishing a link to the Humanist credo of self-realization [13]. This optimistic addition is also reflected in his letter of dedication to this anthology.

3. RENAISSANCE HUMANISM AND REFORMATION: MARTIN LUTHER AND PHILIPP MELANCHTHON

Even the contemporary view was that the Reformation had arisen from Renaissance Humanism. At a time of burgeoning nationalism and self-confidence, the Humanists attempted to revive the traditions of Classical Antiquity, because they perceived the Classical ideal of humanity as the reflection of true humanity. The recourse to original Christian sources revealed the partial aberrations in the development of the Church and helped to uncover abuses. For Humanists, the battle against the Church was also a battle against the degradation of philosophy to a mere 'handmaiden of theology'. Initially it had seemed as if Martin Luther had aimed for a continuation or a revival of the old dispute, especially as he had recommended himself to Erasmus as a "little brother in Christo", and Ulrich von Hutten had hoped that he would achieve G.'s liberation from the "popish yoke". Luther's posting of his theses on 31 October 1517 rang in significant changes under the guise of religion. The break with the Roman Church marked the beginning of the development of Lutheran and Reformed regional churches and the dissolution of Europe's religious unity. Between 1517 and 1521, Luther found sympathy and support with the burghers, the lesser nobility and the peasants; after 1521 more that of regional dukes and princes. Because of this, the papal excommunication affected not only Luther, but also his Humanist sympathizers such as Pirckheimer. However, despite large areas of agreement, the call 'Redite ad fontes!' meant something different to the Humanists than to the reformers. The former understood it to encompass ancient literature and tradition, the latter, particularly Luther, as restricted to Holy Scripture. This explains why the number of Humanists who supported Luther in the long run remained very low, in particular, because they feared that the unrest caused by the peasants' revolt would result in a decline in education. These contrasting views became evident in the dispute between Erasmus (*De libero arbitrio*, 1524) and Luther (*De servo arbitrio*, 1525) about the freedom of will. Luther's thoroughly religious understanding with an emphasis on constant obedience was barely reconcilable with the basic Humanist aim of striving for a cosmopolitan outlook. To a large extent, the increasing inter-confessional dispute marked the end of Humanism, even though Philipp Melanchthon is an example of the possibility for a mutually beneficial diffusion.

The university in Wittenberg, residence of the prince-elector of Saxony, had been founded in 1502 and was soon to become the centre of the Reformation due to Luther and Melanchthon. It was through the latter that Luther who had received excellent schooling in Latin found access to the Greek language. However, his preference was for the *Disticha Catonis*, for Terence, Aesop in Latin translation and Virgil; he found Greek insufficiently "rich in sententiae". He saw the entire Humanist movement as an act of divine providence in order to prepare for the new revelation in the Gospel, the "discovery and destruction of the Antichrist's (sc. the pope's) rule". He attached great importance to languages, because "they are the sheath for the knife that is the mind." Luther's verdict on Aristotle was harsh: "the dead pagan without art", "the actor who had fooled the Church." It was the Aristotle in the scholastic interpretation, against whom Luther directed his anger. Plato and his teachings, which only became more widely known at that time, had become a source of new and better insights. This was further aided by the beauty of the Platonic language and the interesting form of the dialogue in contrast with Aristotle's sober tractates. The separation of paganism and revelation, of faith and knowledge remained Luther's basic reformatory principle throughout.

It was his great uncle Johannes Reuchlin who had recommended the young Philipp Melanchthon for the Greek chair at Wittenberg university's faculty of arts. Aged only 21, on 29.8.1518 he delivered his famous inaugural lecture entitled *De corrigendis adolescentiae studiis* ('On Improving the Studies for the Young'). Melanchthon propagated a truly Humanist programme: a return to the original Greek Aristotle, but also to the New Testament in its original language. It was only in the study of classical languages, and foremost that of Greek, that he saw a way to overcome the degenerate educational system. For the first time ever, he also foresaw a greater role to be given to the study of history alongside a better education in philosophy and the mathematical disciplines. Because of its high stylistic and rhetorical quality, this inaugural lecture with its wealth of original quotations in Greek and Hebrew became a very important Humanist manifesto and a print version was published in the same year. As a Humanist who supported the reformatory cause in Wittenberg, Melanchthon was closer in his thinking to Erasmus than to Luther. The responsibility of man as a result of his free will was an essential constituent in his new ideal of humanity. Melanchthon worked tirelessly as an academic organizer and reformer of Protestantism. In his role as *praeceptor Germaniae*, he wrote a great number of influential textbooks and treatises across almost the entire university curriculum, delivered numerous academic lectures and kept an enormous correspondence (ca. 10 000 letters are extant). His text editions, Latin translations of Greek authors, and his commentaries on the main authors of Classical Antiquity, written as teaching aids, extended his fame far beyond G.'s borders.

4. Renaissance Humanism and Art

The medieval view of the world was one in which every human being had his or her allocated place in a divinely-ordained whole, structured according to estate, and where the ultimate goal of all human striving was the afterlife depicted in the most alluring colours; by contrast, at the threshold to the modern age, Renaissance Humanism saw a vast array of other options for personal initiatives and responsibility opening up. There was an increasing awareness of human individuality. In G. during the transitional period from 1470 and 1530, all of the sociopolitical contradictions had come to a head, resulting in a crisis affecting the entire nation. The feudal system as a whole was shaken, also as a result of the discovery of the New World and its gold reserves; the Reformation had shattered the unity of the Church; and Humanism had secularized thinking. Science had been given a new impetus. All of these developments also had an effect on art. As a result of the liberation of the personality from its medieval bonds, self-assured, identifiable artists became well-known in the same way as their ancient counterparts had. The artist no longer saw himself as an anonymous creator of artifacts for the glorification of God, but signed his works with confidence and self-assurance. The influence of Classical Antiquity on Renaissance art must not be overestimated, though. In G. itself, Renaissance art only began to appear 1500. However, the principle guiding the use of ancient architectural elements such as columns or pilaster, cornices and profiles (as e.g. in the *Weserrenaissance*) was not *imitatio*, but to create something new. The Church remained the primary commissioner for building works, but secular themes for private buyers were on the increase. Modelled on the equestrian statue of Marcus Aurelius, freestanding sculptures were erected. Monuments, including sepulchral monuments, became much more lavish and ornate than in the Middle Ages, for the purpose of exemplifying the fame of the deceased. The bronze cenotaph for Emperor Maximilian I in Innsbruck, designed by the Humanist Konrad Peutinger, remained incomplete but is still impressive. The ancient form of the portrait bust was taken up again. Painting, however, once liberated from the supremacy of architecture, underwent the greatest expansion. Landscape painting emerged as a genre, as did early still lifes of animals and plants. New graphic genres such as wood cuts and copper plate engravings expressed Christian and mythological topics. The confidence in one's own strength and ability found its expression in the portrait, the image of a particular person with individual features. The newly discovered laws of perspective and geometric construction opened up the depth of space, and details of identifiable landscape were depicted.

5. ALBRECHT DÜRER AS A REPRESENTATIVE OF HIS TIME

In the wide range of his work, the genius of Albrecht Dürer had found the artistic expression that matched the trends of the age in which he lived. Ulrich von Hutten referred to him as the "Apelles of our time." Dürer's self-assurance is clearly evident in his Italian letters, in his famous monogram, and particularly in his self-portraits. No other artist of his time had produced as many self-portraits: from the earliest silverpoint drawing when he was only thirteen to the frontal view of a handsome man in a fur coat around 1500 and finally the drawing of his infirm, naked body in old age.

More than any other artist of his time, Dürer was influenced by Classical Antiquity. During his apprenticeship in Nuremberg, he used the images of ancient mythological scenes to perfect his technique and sharpen his own style. The cycle began with the *Death of Orpheus* (1494), spanning to *The Dream of the Doctor*, a preliminary study for his nude painting of Eva in 1504 – also interpreted as a depiction of Temptation. The engraving of the *Four Witches* turned the charming model of the three graces into an allegory of transience. Hercules was the topic of a number of Dürer's works, one of them depicting Nuremberg castle as a natural landscape. His proportional studies 'from measurements' culminated in the copper engraving of *Adam and Eve* (1504). The figure of Adam was clearly modelled on ancient examples, based on a drawing of the → BELVEDERE APOLLO, of Asclepius and Sol. The four humours are even recognizable in Dürer's animals. In the 1507 panel painting, the sensual attraction of the bodies became even more obvious. In line with the new Humanistic but also artistic view, the human body in its anatomical structure was seen as part of the cosmos as a whole. Man was seen as master of the universe. In recourse to the ancient beauty of the body, the 'Fall of Man' was reinterpreted as an affirmation of life. Dürer's masterpiece engravings *Knight, Death and Devil* (1513), *Melencolia* (1514) and *St. Hieronymus in his Study* (1514) had arisen from his familiarity with ancient and Humanistic topics: the theory of the four humours which also played a major role in Dürer's theoretical works in the *Großer ästhetischer Exkurs*. It is said that the flute player in the wood cut of *The Men's Bath* (ca. 1496) is a self-portrait of Dürer as a melancholic. The number 'I' found in his *Melencolia* suggests the representation of the four humours. According to the new view of Marsilio Ficino, transmitted to Dürer by Pirckheimer, melancholia was the hallmark of an artist. Dürer returned to this topic repeatedly until 1526. It is likely that Dürer who had attended a Latin School was able to read Vitruvius and Pliny the Elder in the original Latin. His friendship with Pirckheimer also proved very beneficial: he illustrated several of Pirckheimer's books, painted and drew him on a number occasions; in addition, both men were linked through their work for Emperor Maximilian. Pirckheimer also inspired him to study the theory of art; as a result, Dürer was the first German to develop a Renaissance aesthetics. It was Dürer's aim, as he wrote in the dedication of his book to Pirckheimer in 1528, "to keep, as in ancient times, a written record of my opinion and invention..., in order to restore the art of painting... to its previous perfection" [14].

D. HISTORY AND SOCIAL DEVELOPMENT IN THE AGE OF REFORMATION AND EARLY COUNTER-REFORMATION (1500 – CA. 1600)

For his oldest grandson Charles, the future emperor Charles V (1519–1556), Maximilian I had managed in 1516 to unite Aragon, Castile and Naples-Sicily with the Habsburg and Burgundy core lands. In 1515, he had secured the claim to Bohemia and Hungary of his second grandson Ferdinand, the future emperor Ferdinand I (1556–1564). Charles V was crowned by the pope in Bologna in 1530, but his successors assumed the title of 'emperor-elect' without coronation by the pope. From then on, the heirs to the throne bore the title 'rex Romanorum'. However, the call for a "reform from top to bottom" had not ceased. Martin Luther's action against the trade in letters of indulgence on 31 October 1517 signaled the start of the great political and religious movement of the Reformation, which was also influenced by the ideas of the Czech reformer Jan Hus. In G., the tensions between the people's desire for greater independence and the papal claim to supremacy came to a peak. The *Reichsacht* ('imperial ban') that Charles V imposed on Luther and his closest followers in 1521 at the Imperial Diet in Worms was ultimately ineffective. The spread of the 'new doctrine' was unstoppable. The papal intervention and the imperial interdict prevented the constitution of a general council. This was the beginning of G.'s religious division. The regional princes used their powers to their own advantage, while the attempt to turn the religious reformation into a social reform failed during the Knights' Revolt of 1523 and more significantly during the Great Peasant War of 1525. Charles V, preoccupied by his wars with France until 1529, was forced to consider the 'protestation' at Speyer by the followers of the 'new doctrine', initially through recognition of the *Confessio Augustana* of 1530. The Turkish and French threats forced the emperor to change his mind and to agree to a temporary religious peace. After peace agreements with France and Turkey, Charles V managed to win a victory in the Schmalkaldic War, but without gaining lasting supremacy. His brother Ferdinand, his successor in G. from from 1556–1564, could no longer deny religious tolerance to the Protestants. The Peace of Augsburg guaranteed equal standing to the Protestant religion. Regional princes were given the unlimited religious authority in their territories, i.e. the *ius refor-mandi* based on the principle of *cuius regio, eius religio*. After considerable early success, Protestantism became increasingly ground down by disputes about dogma. Catholic regions saw the beginning of the Counterreformation. The two Habsburg monarchs Ferdinand I and his reformation-minded son Maximilian II (1564–1576) tried to mediate. Rudolf II (1576–1612), himself educated by Jesuits, was the first openly to favour Catholicism. German Protestantism was split into two factions, Lutheran Electoral Saxony and Reformed Electoral Palatinate. In 1608, the Protestant Union was formed, countered in 1609 by the Catholic League under Bavarian leadership. The economic boom in G. had largely continued throughout the 16th cent., but internal progress had faltered in consequence of the religious division, finally resulting in the Thirty Year War.

1. RENAISSANCE HUMANISM: ART AND REFORMA-TION 2. WILLIBALD PIRCKHEIMER AND CLASSICAL ANTIQUITY

1. RENAISSANCE HUMANISM: ART AND REFORMATION

The Reformation opened new possibilities for artists as they took on Luther's Christocentrism. By focusing on Christ, the focus is on the Son of Man who rose to divine honours – that is man himself with all of his abilities and opportunities, but also limitations. Dürer's only self-portrait in a strict frontal pose exudes beauty, calm and majesty. It seems to be based on the proportional pattern of the religious image of Christ. As in Antiquity, Apollo was the god of arts, in the view of Neo-Platonists and Humanists the artist himself had divine qualities. Dürer's inclination towards the Reformation is evident in the two full-length panel paintings depicting the *Four Apostles* painted in 1526. He had added text from Luther's bible translation of 1522 to a plinth at the bottom of the two panels, one depicting John and Peter, the other Mark and Paul. The figure of John is suspected to be a crypto-portrait of Philipp Melanchthon. It remains controversial whether this expression of Reformation thinking was polemically directed at the papal church or against contemporary anabaptism and religious fanaticism in Nuremberg.

Lucas Cranach the Elder, a friend of Martin Luther, deliberately adopted the Reformation's artistic agenda. His 1547 altar in the town church of St. Mary, the church in which Luther delivered most of his sermons, is his last work in Wittenberg. The *predella* depicts Luther in the pulpit pointing to Christ on the cross, thus again taking up the new doctrine's main idea. The left side of the picture shows town folk, amongst them Cranach himself, but also Luther's wife and their son Hans. The central panel illustrates the three main sacraments of the Lutheran church, on the left Baptism with Philipp Melanchthon, on the right Confession with the theologian Johannes Bugenhagen, who had preached at Luther's wedding and funeral, and in the centre the Last Supper against the backdrop of a typical German landscape. The young man holding the cup is Cranach the Younger, offering it to Luther who, in the guise of 'Junker Jörg', takes it. The increased self-assurance of the artist and burgher, modelled on ancient examples, expressed itself in the appearance of contemporary historical figures. The artist and his fellow countrymen are equal participants in the biblical events. In paintings, the image of the Jew is often replaced by that of the Turk. Even in Cranach's early period, saints were integrated as human beings into contemporary life; however, this artistic emphasis on the 'here and now' lasted for only a few decades. Probably the last example of this is the Dessau altarpiece by Cranach the Younger of 1565. It depicts the leaders of the Reformation – with the exception of the traitor Judas – as Jesus' disciples. The founder of the church, Joachim of Anhalt, is shown kneeling in front of the panel, his brother, prince-elector Georg of Anhalt, sitting next to Jesus as John. The artist himself is the figure pouring the wine.

In architecture, ancient forms were used as → SPOLIA in secular buildings such as town halls (e.g. in Görlitz) and palaces as in Dresden, Wismar and Heidelberg. The earliest Protestant palace chapels were built in Torgau and in Augustusburg near Chemnitz. Renaissance decorations were increasingly used on implements and equipment, particularly on tiles.

2. WILLIBALD PIRCKHEIMER AND CLASSICAL ANTIQUITY

As councillor in his home city of Nuremberg and later as imperial councillor, the Humanist Willibald Pirckheimer tried to combine the *vita activa* with the *vita contemplativa*. Two of his works in particular, written as part of the controversy between the old system and the new Humanistic one, bear evidence to his adaptation of ancient philosophies. *Eccius dedolatus* as a targeted attack against some of Luther's prominent adversaries falls into the category of anonymously published dialogues. The name of the author is given as Johannesfranciscus Cottalembergius, and the work was published in 1520 'in Utopia'. It caricatures the theologian Johannes Eck from Ingolstadt, who had risen to fame in the disputation of theologians in Leipzig in July 1519 and who had boasted excessively about his alleged victory over the Wittenberg representatives Luther and Karlstadt. This Humanistic satire, which can, like a comedy, be divided into five acts, depicts and ridicules Eck as the anti-hero: even an operation, the *Enteckung* ('having his rough edges cut', the *dedolatio* of the title), cannot save him.

References to Lucian and particularly Aristophanes appear in form of numerous quotations and proverbial expressions. This familiarity with the Attic comic poet was very unusual for a German Humanist. In an decisive passage of the satirical dialogue, the author, most likely Pirckheimer, revealed himself with his main concern for the *bonae litterae*: 'nec Lutheranus neque Eckianus, sed Christianus sum.' In this mixture of prose and poetry, the ancient models provided a strong basis for Eck's caricature, in the same way as Aristophanes in the *Clouds* had once depicted Socrates as an arch-sophist. Appealing to the pope, Eck managed to have Pirckheimer and six other of his Nuremberg friends included in the 1521 papal letter of excommunication. Conscious of the need to preserve his reputation as a Nuremberg councillor, Pirckheimer did not admit to his authorship orally or in writing [15; 16].

In a further Latin satire, Pirckheimer took up another much debated topic of his time. With much humour and at times clear references to Erasmus' *Laus Stultitiae*, he paid his thanks in the *Apologia seu Laus Podagrae*, (Nuremberg 1522) to *Miss Podagra* for granting her followers *nolens volens* enough leisure to pursue their studies. From 1512, Pirckheimer had kept a diary recording his gout attacks and the various remedies that he had tried. In his satire, he – well versed in law – had Miss Podagra stand trial in an imaginary court of justice. However, thanks to the brilliance of the apology, the trial ends in an acquittal. The enforced sedentary activity, it is argued, results in an advancement of art and science, thus allowing man's better part, i.e. his soul, to strive for higher aims and thus to be led to the real purpose of human life. This is a clear reference to Plato's image in *Phaedrus* of the soul as charioteer, but even elsewhere, Pirckheimer stands in the tradition of the Greek orators. Apollonius of Tyana, Philostratus and Lucian had all treated gout as a subject for a parody, as had Petrach in 1360, but Pirckheimer created something unique with his fictitious plea at court: as Socrates once did, *Miss Podagra*, too, conducted her own defence, drawing on the rich treasure of ancient quotations. In the years to 1700, the work was reprinted ten times, and soon also translated into German, English, French and Czech. In free adaptations, it was used in other satirical works, e.g. by Hans Sachs.

Pirckheimer had written an → AUTOBIOGRAPHY; though probably not meant for publication, it is nonetheless, like Dürer's self-portraits, a further indication of the increased self-assurance of the individual and his awareness of his own worth. Unlike other Humanists, Pirckheimer never Latinized or Graecicized his name, but he always emphasized his predilection for the *studia humanitatis*. In the preface to his Latin translation of the first 15 characters of Theoprastus together with the Greek original in an *Editio princeps* (1527), dedicated to his artist friend Dürer, Pirckheimer compared the unleashed passions described by the Greek psychologist with the lack of restraint in his own time, with the radical fanatics among the supporters of the Reformation.

In the latter years of his life, he translated further speeches – altogether 38 of the total of 45 – by Gregory of Nazianz, who had only recently been rediscovered; however, apart from that he got caught up in day-to-day disputes with Protestant Nuremberg clerics. His choleric nature had turned pessimistic. The deaths of his wife and his only son, but also that of Dürer, the effect of the illness which ultimately forced his departure from office, combined with the increasingly bitter religious dispute resulted in his resignation. Like most other Humanists, Pirckheimer had initially actively supported Luther in his writings and private correspondence. But with the increasing radicalisation of the Reformation, he retreated into private life, disappointed also by the rigid attitudes of his Catholic friends. Erasmus was the only one with whom he kept in touch. 'Vivitur ingenio, caetera mortis erunt' ("His spirit will live on, the remainder is mortal"): this is the motto on Dürer's portrait of Pirckheimer, painted in 1524. Pirckheimer's *ingenium* ('talent') has made a valuable contribution, particularly for the understanding and continued importance of Classical Antiquity [17].

→ Apollo; → Aristophanes; → Aristoteles; → Augustinus; → Augustus; → Dionysus; → Epithalamion; → Homerus; → Horatius; → COMEDY; → Lucianus; → Ovidius; → PLATO; → Plinius; → Plutarchus; → Socrates; → Suetonius; → Terentius; → Theophrastus; → Virgilius; → Vitruvius;

→ MEDIEVAL LATIN; → SATIRE; → SEPTEM ARTES LIBERALES

1 C. VOSSEN, Mutter Latein und ihre Töchter. Europas Sprachen und ihre Herkunft, 1992   2 R. REISER, Götter und Kaiser. Antike Vorbilder Jesu, 1995   3 J. SEZNEC, Das Fortleben der antiken Götter. Die mythologische Tradition im Humanismus und in der Kunst der Renaissance, 1990 (Engl. B. F. SESSIONS (trans.), The Survival of the Pagan Gods: The Mythological Tradition and its Place in Renaissance Humanism and Art, 1981; Orig.: La survivance des dieux antiques; essai sur le rôle de la tradition mythologique dans l'humanisme et dans l'art de la Renaissance, ²1980)   4 H. KÖRNER, Grabmonumente des Mittelalters, 1997   5 A. ANGENEDT, Geschichte der Religiosität im Mittelalter, 1997   6 R. M. KLOOS, Einführung in die Epigraphik des Mittelalters und der frühen Neuzeit, 1980, 70–80   7 H. GÜNTHER, Die Renaissance der Antike, 1998   8 J. KOCH (ed.), Artes Liberales. Von der antiken Bildung zur Wissenschaft des Mittelalters, 1959   9 M. PICONE (ed.), L'enciclopedismo medievale, 1994   10 W. TRILLITZSCH, Der deutsche Renaissance-Humanismus, 1981   11 W. PIRCKHEIMER, Plutarch, Moralia 5 (German translation), Nürnberg 1519   12 N. HOLZBERG, Griechischer Humanismus in Deutschland, 1981   13 R. JOHNE, Willibald Pirckheimer und das Platonbild des deutschen Renaissance-Humanismus, (typescript, Diss. Berlin) 1981   14 Id., Dürers Studium nach der Antike, in: Das Alt. 17, 1971, 229–237   15 Id., Aristophanes-Studien im deutschen Renaissance-Humanismus. Zum *Eccius dedolatus* Willibald Pirckheimers, in: B. ZIMMERMANN (ed.), Antike Dramentheorie und ihre Rezeption, 1992, 159–168   16 Id., Albrecht Dürer und Willibald Pirckheimer auf den Spuren der Antike, in: J. DUMMER, MAX KUNZE (eds.), Antikerezeption, Antikeverhältnis, Antikebegegnung in Vergangenheit und Gegenwart, 1983, 169–186   17 W. P. ECKERT, CH. VON IMHOFF, Willibald Pirckheimer, Dürers Freund im Spiegel seines Lebens, seiner Werke und seiner Umwelt, 1971.

RENATE JOHNE

II. THE BAROQUE

A. INTRODUCTION B. EDUCATION C. LOSS IN
IMPORTANCE OF THE ANCIENT DISCIPLINES
D. POETRY E. MYTHOLOGY IN LITERATURE AND
FINE ARTS F. HISTORIOGRAPHY G. ANTIQ-
UITIES COLLECTIONS H. COURT ART I. ARCHI-
TECTURE

A. INTRODUCTION

At the beginning of the 17th cent., an epochal
change of taste took place in G., for which the term
Baroque has been adopted. While older research emphasized the anti-classical aspect of the period between
1600 and 1730, more recent research explains the phenomenon of Baroque specifically through the reception
and adaptation of ancient traditions. Empirical studies
into the history and reception of style have shown that
the transition from the classicism of the Renaissance to
the mannerism of the Baroque was accompanied by a
different understanding of *decorum* and a different concept of → *imitatio* : the stylistic means developed a
momentum of their own, and the aim was no longer to
imitate Classical patterns but to outdo them (*aemulatio*).

Even though after 1600 German schools, universities and the book market turned away from the 'dead'
languages and towards the national language, neo-
Latin rhetoric and late Humanistic poetic genres were
of significant influence in the protracted rise of the
German language to that of a competitive literary language. The Baroque period is still one of German-Latin
bilingualism, even though the ratio of Latin books continued to fall throughout the 17th cent. This process
sped up in the 1670s, but it was to take another two
decades before German-language book production
finally prevailed. This gradual displacement of Latin
differed for the various academic disciplines. While
German dominated Protestant theology and the historical disciplines even as early as the 17th cent., Latin prevailed in medicine, philosophy and, most importantly,
law until far into the 18th cent. [20. 626f.]. Poetry is
placed somewhere between these two extremes: it is
only toward the end of the 17th cent. that the poetic G.
was no longer a land of Latin. Even as late as the middle
of the 18th cent. about a quarter of the German book
production was still published in Latin; however, this
does not detract from the fact that between 1600 and
1750 the Classical languages successively lost in importance.

B. EDUCATION

The cultural-patriotic education reforms with the
aim of strengthening German at the expense of the Classical languages are part of the same trend. While the
order of languages (German, Hebrew, Greek, Latin)
suggested by the educational reformer Wolfgang Ratke
1617 (1571–1635) did not prevail, Classical languages
were–towards the end of the 17th cent.–increasingly
replaced by the modern foreign languages, French and

Italian, as they were more suited to the more practical
approach of modern education. The Strasbourg philologist Johann Heinrich Böckler, for example, reacted
to the crisis in the → TEACHING OF ANCIENT LANGUAGES
with his *Kurtze Anweisung/Wie man die Authores Clas-
sicos bey und mit der Jugend tractiren soll* ('Brief
Instruction on How to Treat the Classical Authors with
the Young', 1679). While Latin changed from a language of literature to an academic utility [20. 487],
Greek lost its former importance. It is indicative that
editions of works by Greek authors ceased almost entirely: between 1615 and 1715, there was no publication
of works by Demosthenes, Isocrates, Sophocles, Euripides, Pindar and Plato [20. 488].

C. LOSS IN IMPORTANCE OF THE ANCIENT
DISCIPLINES

The Thirty-Years War (1618–1648) paralyzed education and cultural life in Germany. In addition, the
interest of scholars shifted from poetry to theology, philosophy as well as to the practical sciences. Successes in
modern science outshone ancient achievements
[20. 489]. Experiment-based natural sciences, their
beginning exemplarily marked by William Harvey's
discovery of the circulatory system (*De motu cordis*,
Frankfurt/M. 1628), diminished the authority of eminent ancient scholars. In medicine, for example, experiments and autopsies replaced the authority (and thus
the guarantee of truth) of ancient physicians such as
Hippocrates (→ HIPPOCRATISM) or Galen (→ GALE-
NISM). However, the loss in importance not only affected medicine and the technical-practical sciences, but
the entire culture of ancient knowledge. During this
time of educational reform and the attempt to find textbooks and teaching aids fit for a contemporary education, the view that the present time was superior to antiquity found many prominent supporters (Caspar
Dornau the Elder, 1577–1632, Johann Balthasar
Schupp, 1610–1661, Christian Thomasius, 1655–
1728). Exemplary for the new self-confidence in dealing with ancient tradition was the change in the study
of law, where an "up-to-date practice of Roman law"
replaced its "theoretical reception". Hermann Conring
(1606–1681) was among the important protagonists of
the → USUS MODERNUS (GERMAN) which made it possible to define legal institutions without reference to
Roman texts [29. 204–215].

D. POETRY

1. POETICS 2. ANCIENT STROPHIC FORMS
2.1. HORATIAN ODES 2.2. PINDARIC ODE
3. GENRES 3.1. EPIC 3.2. TRAGEDY
3.3. PASTORAL 3.4. EPIGRAM 3.5. HEROIDES
4. OPERA 5. MORAL SATIRE

1. POETICS

The early phase of the German Baroque still dominated by late Humanism was bilingual, and its poetics
stood under ancient auspices. Ancient tradition was

particularly significant for the early-modern understanding of the poet's role. In order to enhance the status of poetry in the German language, references were made to the Platonic notion of the inspired poet and the poet who could defy the transitory nature of life (cf. Opitz's rendition of Hor. Carm. 3,30). Ancient examples were also used to engage the nobility into becoming patrons of the arts and to tie them to an 'alliance of pen and sword'.

It is significant that Latin was the language chosen by Martin Opitz (1597–1639) for his programmatic treatise *Aristarchus sive de contemptu linguae Teutonicae* (1617), in which he pleaded the case for poetry in German. His poetic reform in the *Buch von der Deutschen Poeterey* (1624), which turned German into a competitive literary language, consisted of preserving the taxonomy of the ancient metric, but to transform its quantifying prosody into an accent-based system: instead of long and short syllables, Opitz distinguished between stressed and unstressed ones. He established the Alexandrine, a rhymed verse with six iambic feet, as the German equivalent to the Classical hexameter.

2. Ancient Strophic Forms
2.1 Horatian Odes

Parallel to Opitz's verse reforms, attempts were made to imitate ancient verse forms, both in Latin and in German. The most prominent of the neo-Latin lyric poets who picked up on Horatian patterns, was Jacob Balde (1604–1668). His odes to Mary (*Odae partheniae*, Lyricorum libri IV, 1643) were so closely modelled on the ancient examples in metre as in diction that his contemporaries praised him as the 'German Horace'. Balde's synthesis of Christian and ancient poetry was not merely restricted to the form: he integrated Classical mythology into his veneration of Mary by praising the mother of God as 'Nympha' or 'Diana' [27. 40]. Many later paraphrases of Horace's works by Jesuits (Johannes Bisselius, 1601–1682, Adam Widl, 1639–1710, Nicolaus von Avancini, 1612–1686) were indebted to the works of their fellow Jesuit, Balde.

Protestant and German-language poetry, by contrast, oriented itself less on Balde's restoration of the Horatian ode than on the models of the *Pléiade*, nationalizing the ancient form of the ode in accordance with its French Renaissance version as a rhymed German strophic song. But for the broad expanse of Baroque poetry, intended for the upper strata of society, Horace was, at best, a standard in terms of content: the difference in quality between Latin and early German odes is reflected in the work of Paul Fleming (1609–1640), whose only German Horatian ode (*Teütsche Poemata*, 1646, ode 1,2) compares rather poorly with his Latin odes and epodes. The imitation of the ancient ode remained purely formal, as long as one adhered to the principle of alternation in addition to the rhyme and dispensed with the combination of di- and tri-syllabic metres that was typical for ancient odes. However, as early as in the 1630s, the Adonic verse is sometimes found in the final verse of a stanza, e.g. in the odes of Ernst Christoph Homburg (1605–1681) and the church hymns of Johann Heermann (1585–1647) (*Trost-Gesang*, 1638). The first truly Sapphic ode was written by Johann Plavius in Danzig as early as 1630: his *Deutsches Sapphicum*, a wedding poem, used the dactyl at the beginning of the verse, placed the caesura after the fifth syllable and used the Adonic verse at the end of each stanza [15. 34]. However, the metric principle of alternation was only finally overcome by the Nuremberg school of poets with reference to Augustus Buchner (1591–1661). The use of three-syllable metres such as dactyl and anapaest made it easier to translate the ancient form of the ode into German. Johann Klaj (Clajus) (1610–1656) and Sigmund von Birken (1626–1681) were important representatives of the *Pegnitzschäfer* ('Shepherds on the Pegnitz river'), a Nuremberg poetic association; both experimented with Sapphic odes (Johann Klaj, *Dem Aufferstandenen Siegsfürsten Christo*, 1644; cf. Georg Greflinger, 1620(?)–1677(?), *Zwey Sapphische Oden von Geburt und Leiden Jesu Christi*, 1644) as well as Anacreontic odes (Birken, Klaj), but still all rhymed. Georg Philipp Harsdörffer (1607–1658; *Alcaische Ode*) was the first in 1644 to achieve a perfect Alcaic ode, followed by Matthäus Apelles von Löwenstern (1594–1648, 1644) and Andreas Gryphius (1616–1664; *Manet unica virtus*, 1646).

2.2 Pindaric Ode

Martin Opitz's only stipulation for the Pindaric ode was its tripartite structure (strophe, anti-strophe, epode) with a range of possible combinations of two-syllable feet: as set out earlier by Georg Rodolf Weckherlin (1584–1653; 1618), strophe and anti-strophe should be identical in metre, number of stanzas and rhyme. Opitz' 'Pindarizing' was much copied. However, while the elevated style and serious content of the Pindaric ode was retained, stipulations regarding the mixture of verse forms and rhyme patterns were successively expanded, as in the case of the Horatian ode. Thus in 1645 Justus Georg Schottelius (1612–1676) was the first to use a mixture of dactyls and anapaests with trochees in the epodes and Andreas Gryphius varied the stanza pattern of the Pindaric ode for the purpose of forced dialectics. As a result, the Pindaric ode was a popular form for the 'Reyen', the interludes in the Baroque tragedy modelled on the ancient chorus.

3. Genres
3.1 Epic

The 17th cent. hierarchy considered the epic as the most noble of genres. The Roman epic poet Virgil enjoyed greater popularity as an exemplary model in keeping with the times than did Homer. Thus, Michael Schirmer the Younger (1606–1673) translated Virgil's *Aeneis* (1668, [2]1672) as a → Princes' mirror. However, in the need to make up for the scarcity of epic poetry in German literature, more attention was paid to Italian Renaissance chivalric epics. The ancient epic poets, though, rose to new honours towards the end of the 17th cent. when their authority was called upon to accredit the prose novel as a new genre (Daniel Georg Morhof, 1639–1691). Even before Veit Ludwig von Seckendorff's (1626–1692) translation of the *Pharsalia* (1695) [10. 69–78], Lucian had been among the venerated models. Johann Michael Moscherosch (1601–1669) adapted the Machiavellian *Pothinus speech* in the seventh of his *Gesichte Philanders von Sittewalt* ("Visions of Philander of Sittewald", 1640), while the Roman plays by Andreas Gryphius (*Papinianus*, 1659) and Daniel Casper von Lohenstein (1635–1683; *Epicharis* and *Agrippina*, both 1665) competed with Lucan's pathos [10. 61–68].

3.2 TRAGEDY

In the hierarchy of genres, Opitz and other 17th cent. poetics ranked the tragedy at the top alongside the epic poem. The German Baroque tragedy had arisen from the spirit of Antiquity. Catharsis was brought into line with the Christian-Stoic ideal virtue of *constantia*, as Martin Opitz stated in the preface to his translation of Seneca's *Troades* ('Women of Troy') (1625): 'Solche Beständigkeit aber wird uns durch beschawung der Mißligkeit deß Menschlichen Lebens in den Tragedien zu förderst eingepflantzet' ("Such constancy is implanted in us most of all through the observation of the misfortunes of human life in the tragedies."). In his adaptation of Seneca's play as in his translation of Sophocles' *Antigone* (1636), Opitz gave a Christian slant to the ancient material and dampened the passion. In fact, the Stoic concepts of *constantia* and *tr anquillitas animi* not only dominated 'pre-Baroque Classicism' [1], but also the representation of passion at the height of the Baroque and even the pompous exotism of the second Silesian school of poets (Daniel Casper von Lohenstein, Johann Christian Hallmann, 1640?–1704?) with its unexpected plot turns and forced scenes of blood and gore. It is worth pointing out that Seneca's stoicism – and also other ancient philosophies throughout this period of Baroque Classicism – was frequently only indirectly assimilated: through the Dutch Neostoicism of Justus Lispius (1547–1606; *De constantia*, 1584), Neolatinists such as Caspar Schoppe (1576–1649) or by way of translations (cf. Johann Peter Titz, 1619–1689, *Des Diogenes Rede an Alexander den Großen, aus Dan. Heinsii Oration von der Stoischen Philosophie, in Deutschen Versen abgesetzt*, 1640 ['Diogenes' address to Alexander the Great, from Daniel Heinsius' Oration on Stoic Philosophy, translated into German Verse']). In all of these, the attempt was made to overlay pagan Stoicism with Christian values, as e.g. Jacob Balde, who devised his *Jephtias* (1637) as a *parodia christiana* of Seneca's *Hercules Oetaeus*.

3.3 PASTORAL

The elegiac concept of the Baroque pastoral is based on the imitation and emulation of Virgil, to whom Opitz's praise of rural life owes as much as to Horace whose epode 2 was frequently imitated [19]. The effect of Virgil as a bucolic poet extended to the idyllic poetry of the Rococo.

3.4 EPIGRAM

Baroque epigrammatic poetry also drew richly from the ancient reservoir. Again and again, be it directly (*Anthologia Graeca*, Martial) or indirectly (Neolatinists such as John Owen, 1560(?)–1622, Maciej Kazimierz Sarbiewski, 1595–1640), epigrammatic and emblematic poets had recourse to ancient typology and topics, and attempted to attain the stylistic concept of satirical brevity [25]. Opitz had propagated the patterns in his *Florilegium Variorum Epigrammatum* (1639).

3.5 HEROIDES

Hoffmann von Hoffmannswaldau's *Heldenbrieffe* (1680) was a contemporary adaptation of ancient patterns. It transposed Ovid's *Heroides*, later translated by Caspar Abel (1704), into the highly stratified society of Early Absolutism. Its main topics are amorous liaisons from the 9th to the 16th cents., which break with the strictures imposed by status; the rhetoric of the amatory love poetry rivaled that of French models.

4. OPERA

Even new genres specific to this period were linked to ancient models. Thus, → OPERA was seen as a restoration of the Greek tragedy, and indeed, ancient mythology, later also ancient history, provided the main source for Baroque librettos: the first ever German opera (first performed in Torgau, 1627) by Martin Opitz (libretto) and Heinrich Schütz (1585–1672; music, lost) was based on the Daphne myth.

5. MORAL SATIRE

The early modern moral satire is also based ancient traditions. Its programme – poetic freedom for the purpose of moral improvement – is illustrated by the monstrous satyr on the copper title plate of Hans Jakob Christoffel von Grimmelshausen's *Der Abentheurliche Simplicissimus Teutsch* (1668): as the very personification of satire, he illustrated the *mixtum compositum* as developed by Horace in the introduction to his *Ars poetica*.

E. MYTHOLOGY IN LITERATURE AND FINE ARTS
1. LITERATURE   2. FINE ART

1. LITERATURE

Around the middle of the 17th cent., a fierce debate arose about the compatibility of ancient mythology and Christianity. Protestant theologians in particular polemicized against the adoption of ancient mythology. Balthasar Gockel, for example, condemned any imitation of "pagan idolatry"in his *Heidnische Poeterey/ Christlich corrigiert und verbessert* ['Pagan poetry corrected and emended in a Christian spirit'] (1647), and Paul Gerhardt (1607–1676), too, emphasized the primacy of the Bible above Classical Antiquity in respect of the transitory nature of human life: 'Aber wenn der Tod uns trifft | Was hilft da Homerus' Schrift?' ("But when death calls us, what avails us Homer's writ?"). The criticism of pagan poetry and mythology had some effect: in his *Poetischer Schauplatz* ['Poetic Stage'](1646),

Johann Rist (1607–1667), previously quite fond of ancient mythology, stated categorically: "No upright poet should use such riffraff pagan verse" (translated from quote in [5. 298]). And even Philipp von Zesen (1619–1689) finally added his voice to those who rejected the use of "pagan idolatrous names" in poetry. By qualifying the ancient myths as fictitious (*Der erdichteten Heidnischen Gottheiten/(...) Herkunft und Begäbnisse*, ['Origin and Characteristics of the Fictitious Pagan Gods'], 1688) and consistently replacing the ancient names of the gods with his own German creations (*Libinne* instead of *Venus*), he mediated between the disputing factions [3. 159–163].

2. FINE ART

The mythology controversy was almost entirely limited to literature and urban cultural life. In emblematic (→ EMBLEMS) and fine arts, especially courtly culture, ancient mythology remained the predominant source of artistic material. In addition to Cesare Ripa's *Iconologia* (German translation 1659), another work of importance for Baroque art was Joachim von Sandrart's (1606–1688) mythological handbook (*Iconologia deorum, oder, Abbildung der Götter, welche von den Alten verehrt worden*, ['Depiction of the gods that were venerated by the Ancients'] 1680). Artists were also the addressees of the descriptions by Samuel Bottschild, senior court painter at the Saxon court since 1677, of his mythological ceiling paintings in the main hall of the Palais im Grossen Garten in Dresden (*Opera varia Historica, Poetica et Iconologica*, 1693).

Amongst the most popular mythological subjects in German Baroque art were 'Narcissus at the Spring', 'Leda and the Swan', 'The Rape of Europe', 'Hercules and Omphale', 'Bathing Diana and Callisto', 'Diana and Actaeon' and 'The Liberation of Andromeda' [21]. Amatory subjects were almost exclusively based on episodes from Ovid's *Metamorphoses*; they also dominated the choice of motifs used in the craft industry. Ovid was the most influential Classical poet in the Baroque [18]; attempts were made to moralize his poetry and to employ allegoresis in order to turn his mythological stories into didactic ones. For that reason, the elegant illustrations to the metamorphoses by Johann Wilhelm Baur (first in 1640), painter at the imperial court, were even in their late editions (1709) accompanied by the moralizing tetrastichs of Johannes Posthius (1537–1597), dating back to 1563 (Horn in [28]). The threat of being accused of atheism also compelled later mythographers such as Magnus Daniel Omeis (1646–1708) to embrace allegorizations and moralizations, paving the way for the rational interpretation of myths and their critical comparative analysis in the → ENLIGHTENMENT.

F. HISTORIOGRAPHY

The reception of ancient historiography, as that of mythology, also stood for a long time under moral-pedagogic auspices. Thus, moralization and Christian allegoresis are characteristic of Peter Lauremberg's

Fig. 1: Gottfried Christian Leygebe, Equestrian statue of Friedrich Wilhelm of Brandenburg (The Great Elector)

Acerra philologica (first published in 1637), a popular anthology of historical and legendary stories from Classical Antiquity. With the rise of Early Absolutism, the historical-political interest shifted from the Roman Republic to the Imperial Age. Whereas Henning Arnisaeus (ca. 1575–1636) referred to Aristotle (→ ARISTOTELISM) in his deduction of the sovereign princely state and the raison d'etat [6], subsequent historians increasingly took guidance from Suetonius and even more so from Tacitus, both of whom conveyed a scientific and unprejudiced view of practical politics. Absolutism took the *arcana* of the Roman Imperial period as a mirror. The empirical approach of its historian, Tacitus; which was sometimes also denounced as Machiavellian, came close to modern political sciences. This → TACITISM also characterized the poetic adaptation of Roman history, a favourite source of material particularly for tragedies (Andreas Gryphius, *Papinian*, 1659, Daniel Casper von Lohenstein, *Agrippina*, based on the Annals of Tacitus,. *Cleopatra*) lyrical dramas (Johann Christian Hallmann, *Heraclius*, 1684) and courtly historical novels (Anton Ulrich von Braunschweig-Wolfenbüttel, *Octavia. Römische Geschichte*, 1677–1707, [2]1712–1714, 1762, Lohenstein, *Großmüthiger Feldherr Arminius*, 1689/90). Representative references to Roman history also prevailed in Baroque public art, possibly because ideals of community were easier to convey with historical material. The town halls of Nuremberg and Augsburg, for example, were decorated with images of the moderation of Scipio (Liv. 26,50) [21, vol. 2. 429].

Fig. 2: Gerard van Hoet, Allegory on Emperor Leopold I as victorious Hercules (c. 1670/1675)
© *Kunsthistorisches Museum Vienna*

Fig. 3: Georg Philipp Harsdörffer, *Porticus...*,
Nuremberg 1646. Duke August the Younger
of Braunschweig-Lüneburg as Apollo,
holding a caduceus in his right hand,
on the heraldic horse of Lower Saxony
depicted as Pegasus, inmidst of a hall of columns
decorated with stations from his life.

Fig. 4: Salomon de Caus, *Narcissus*.
Design of a grotto for the gardens of Heidelberg castle

G. Antiquities Collections

The artistic and literary taste of the ruling nobility remained largely unaffected by the debate about ancient mythology: the Baroque princes had themselves glorified – through the medium of Roman history and Classical mythology – in their palaces in so-called Imperial or Princes' Rooms. Imperial galleries like the Munich *Antiquarium,* however, are mostly of Humanist origin; during the Baroque, they were refashioned as *Kunstkammer* (art chambers) with a lesser emphasis on antiquities. There was less adherence to the figure of twelve based on Suetonius, but combinations were freer and the sometimes overbearing parallelization reduced. While in the Alabaster Hall (1681/85) of the Berlin palace, statues of Brandenburg prince-electors alternated with those of Roman emperors, Raymond Leplat was rebuked in 1733 for his planned opposition of the statues of August the Strong and emperor Augustus [24. 11] – exemplary for the attempts of the Early Classicism of the 1730s to reduce and regulate Baroque variety, The material itself also indicates a change in taste: the light-coloured marble heads of the Renaissance gave way to darker heads made from porphyry and bronze mounted on coloured marble busts. This new taste agreed more with newly fashioned copies than with ancient originals [24. 11]. The creative achievement of the Baroque in the heightened imitation of ancient sculptures has only recently been adequately recognized by art historians as a 'verlebendigende Formsteigerung' ("enlivening formal intensification") [17. 44f.] (→ Antiquities, collections of).

The historical awareness of the princes is evident in their purposeful enthusiasm for excavations and collections, e.g. in Berlin and Dresden. Archaeological finds and collections of coins from their own territories served the same purpose of underpinning the continuity and cultural tradition of their rule as did antiquizing genealogies. Frederick William of Prussia, the Great Elector, thus continued the tradition of the dynastic house of Jülich-Kleve-Berg, i.e. to collect coins found locally; he purchased a collection of ancient coins and compiled an archaeological collection mainly from Roman finds in Xanten. He purposefully acquired further collections, particularly one of marble sculptures, the sight of which would "gladden his heroic spirit" (J. Sandrart, *Teutsche Academie* II, Nuremberg 1679, 2,74). When the Palatinate inheritance of 1686 included a sizeable collection of coins, Lorenz Beger ensured the compilation of a systematic inventory and expanded the collection to become "the first complex museum of antiquities in the North" [11. 69]. The collecting of Roman coins fitted in particularly well with the Early Modern notions of princely education. The reasonably sized gallery of rulers' portraits and historical images was supposed to provide the prince with examples that would sharpen his mind for princely virtues (→ Peace). Among the most important coin collections of the 17th cent. are the *Thesaurus Palatinus* (1685) of Charles Louis, Elector Palatine, and his daughter Elisabeth Charlotte, and the *Thesaurus Brandenburgicus* (1696–1701) of the Great Elector [11].

H. Court Art

Early Absolutism utilized ancient mythology and the tradition of the Roman emperors for the exaltation of its own rule. Mythological portraits depicted princesses in the guise of Diana, while princes had their military victories glorified in mythological images produced by their court artists and poets. In 1680, for example, the Great Elector of Brandenburg commissioned the sculptor Gottfried Christian Leygebe to depict him as the dragon slayer Bellerophon [2. no. 88] (fig.1). At the end of the 17th cent., Gerard van Hoet (1648–1738) painted emperor Leopold I (fig. 2) after the latter's successful wars against the Turks as the victorious Hercules with the slain Hydra [14. 156]; Hercules was also the motif used by Balthasar Permoser (1651–1732) in his → apotheosis of Prince Eugen (1718/21) to depict the vanquisher of the Turks. The ceiling fresco in the Ancestral Hall of the palace in Rastatt depicts Hercules' admission to Olympus, a thinly veiled apotheosis of Ludwig Wilhelm, Margrave of Baden-Baden.

Encomiastic allegories, apotheoses and medals glorify the princes in mythological guise, as did ephemeral monuments (fireworks, triumphal portals, *castra dolorns*). As an expression of his absolute power, Johann Georg I Elector of Saxony organized the 1678 Hercules fireworks in Dresden, showing the deeds of Hercules [9. 121–124]. Even warning mythological examples were used to illustrate the ruler's sovereignty. In 1713/14, Giovanni Antonio Pellegrini thus painted a ceiling fresco for Johann Wilhelm von Pfalz-Neuburg's palace in Bensberg depicting the Fall of Phaeton, and Johann Zick (1702–1762) decorated the Marble Hall of Bruchsal Palace with the Fall of the Giants [21, vol. 1. 97]. The mythological imagery of Baroque residences, however, also celebrated the prince as a patron and sponsor of learning and art, preferably in the shape of Apollo. Georg Philipp Harsdörffer thus glorified Prince August the Younger of Braunschweig-Lüneburg as prince of the muses astride Pegasus and ruler of the Parnassus on a metaphorical-literary monumental arch (Porticus, 1646; Fig. 3), and Balthasar Permoser equipped the corner pavilion of the Dresden Zwinger programmatically with statues of Apollo and Minerva (1715/16). Apollo and the muses decorate the libraries of many Baroque residences and monasteries (Luca Antonio Colomba in Ludwigsburg, 1711/13; Jacopo Amigoni, 1682–1752: ceiling fresco in Schleissheim; Antoine Pesne, 1683–1757: ceiling painting in Schloß Charlottenburg; Daniel Gran, 1694–1757: lunette fresco Hofbibliothek, Vienna Bartolomeo Altomonte, 1694–1783: ceiling paintings in the monastic libraries of Admont and St. Florian).

I. Architecture

Architects and architectural theorists of the 17th cent. kept with Vitruvius' rules, transmitted through

Palladio (first German edition by Georg Andreas Böckler, 1693). Fortified by the study of ancient architecture in Italy, architects, as e.g. Joseph Furttenbach (1591–1667), also copied buildings from ancient Rome. The influence of Antiquity is particularly evident in the numerous books on columns published in the 17th and 18th cents. with classifications of ancient orders of architecture. Amongst the more curious products of the architectural reception of Antiquity is a design by Duke Karl Eusebius of Liechtenstein (1684) for a church whose façade bears all five architectural orders one above the other.

Garden architecture, too, took guidance from ancient mythology. The grotto of Orpheus, furnished in 1615 by the architect Salomon de Caus with automatons, was the highlight of the Heidelberg palace gardens (fig. 4). The pleasure garden (*Lustgarten*) at the Berlin Palace was modelled on ancient gardens and decorated with 47 antiquizing sculptures. In Kleve, the column made from the barrel of a field-gun at the centre of the garden laid out by Duke Johann Moritz of Nassau-Siegen (1604–1679) as governor for the Great Elector bore a sculpture of Cupid looking down on upturned bombards: an allegory of Amor's peaceful rule [23]. However, ancient mythology could also be used for a rather more aggressive glorification of rulership, as evident in the giant statue of Hercules in Kassel, crafted by Johann Jacob Anthoni (d. 1688) based on the Farnesian Hercules, which has crowned the park of Castle Wilhelmshöhe at the Karlsberg ever since 1717. It has a commanding view of the entire garden and dominates the group of fallen giants, one of which, Enceladus, spouts water towards the hero – a prime example for the way in which ancient forms were exaggerated and utilized for purposes of representation in German Baroque.

→ BAROQUE I. GERMANY

1 R. ALEWYN, Vorbarocker Klassizismus und griechische Tragödie, 1926   2 E. BERCKENHAGEN, Barock in Deutschland, 1966   3 TH. BLEICHER, Homer in der deutschen Literatur, 1972   4 R. BOLGAR (ed.), Classical Influences on European Culture, 1976   5 K. O. CONRADY, Lateinische Dichtungstradition und deutsche Lyrik des 17. Jahrhunderts, 1962   6 H. DREITZEL, Protestantischer Aristotelismus und absoluter Staat, 1970   7 J. DUMMER et al. (eds.), Antikerezeption, Antikeverhältnis, Antikebegegnung in Vergangenheit und Gegenwart, 1983   8 E.-L. ETTER, Tacitus in der Geistesgeschichte des 16. und 17. Jahrhunderts, 1966   9 E. FÄHLER, Feuerwerke des Barock, 1976   10 W. FISCHLI, Studien zum Fortleben der Pharsalia, 1944   11 H.-J. GIERSBERG et al., Der große Kurfürst: Sammler, Bauherr, Mäzen, Exhibition Catalogue, 1988   12 V. C. HABICHT, s.v. Architekturtheorie, Reallex. zur dt. Kunstgesch. 1, 1937, 959–992   13 N. HAMMERSTEIN (ed.), Handbuch der deutschen Bildungsgeschichte 1, 1996   14 G. HEINZ, K. SCHÜTZ, Porträtgalerie zur Geschichte Österreichs von 1400 bis 1800, 1976   15 R. HOSSFELD, Die deutsche horazische Ode von Opitz bis Klopstock, 1961   16 E. R. KEPPELER, Die Pindarische Ode in der deutschen Poesie, 1911   17 H. LADENDORF, Antikenstudium und Antikenkopie, in: Abh.

der Sächs. Akad. der Wiss. Phil.-histor. Kl., 46, 2, ²1958   18 H.-J. LANGE, Aemulatio Veterum, sive de optimo genere dicendi, 1974   19 A. M. LOHMEIER, Beatus ille, 1981   20 F. PAULSEN, Geschichte des gelehrten Unterrichts auf den deutschen Schulen und Universitäten, 1, ³1919   21 A. PIGLER, Barockthemen, 3 vols., ²1974   22 H. RADEMANN, Versuch eines Gesamtbildes über das Verhältnis von Martin Opitz zur Antike, 1926   23 P. O. RAVE, Gärten der Barockzeit, 1951   24 D. RÖSSLER (ed.), Antike und Barock, 1989   25 M. RUBENSOHN, Griechische Epigramme und andere kleinere Dichtungen in deutschen Übersetzungen des 16. und 17. Jahrhunderts, 1897   26 P. STACHEL, Seneca und das deutsche Renaissancedrama, 1907   27 K. VIËTOR, Geschichte der deutschen Ode, 1923   28 H. WALTER et al. (eds.), Die Rezeption der Metamorphosen des Ovid in der Neuzeit, 1995   29 F. WIEACKER, Privatrechtsgeschichte der Neuzeit, ²1967   30 TH. ZIELINSKI, Cicero im Wandel der Jahrhunderte, ³1912.   ACHIM AURNHAMMER

III. UP TO 1806

A. BETWEEN HUMANISM AND ENLIGHTENMENT
B. SCHOOL AND EDUCATION   C. GRAECOPHILIA
D. HOMER AND HERODOTUS   E. WINCKELMANN
AND HEYNE   F. STUDYING ANTIQUITY   G. UTOPIA
AND LITERARY GENRES

A. BETWEEN HUMANISM AND ENLIGHTENMENT

The Humanistic model of philology prevailed into the 18th cent.: philologists published text-critical editions of and commentaries on ancient authors, but without any historical evaluation. However, the period between → HUMANISM and → ENLIGHTENMENT saw the publication of an ever increasing number of editions, anthologies and resources. The *Bibliotheca Graeca* by Johann Albert Fabricius (1668–1736) can be seen as the zenith of this activity: the work comprised 14 vols. (published from 1705 to 1728) and can be considered the first history of Greek literature; it was revised by Gottlieb Christoph Harles (1790–1809) and published in 12 vols., and in 1827–1828 expanded by Chr.D. Beck (*Accessionum ad Fabricii bibl. Graec. specimina duo*). His near-namesake Johann Andreas Fabricius played an important role as organizer at Jena university and was significantly involved in the learned societies [37], particularly in the *Societas Latinae Jenensis* (1733–ca. 1848), which experienced its heyday between 1752–1778 under the direction of Johann Ernst Immanuel Walch (1734–1799); he was editor of the five volumes of *Acta* (1752–1756), comprising all areas of Antiquity.

The cultural and educational policies of the Saxon princes benefited the → UNIVERSITIES in particular. In the early 18th. cent., the universities of Leipzig ('the Athens of Saxony'), Jena, and Wittenberg were the best in Germany. From Hanover and Saxony hailed the most important representatives of → NEO-HUMANISM: not only Johann August Ernesti (1707–1781) and Johann Matthias Gesner (1691–1761), but also Johann Friedrich Christ (1701–1756), who in Leipzig pioneered the inclusion of archaeological monuments and ancient coins into his university teachings, thus laying the foundation for an 'archaeology of art'; other scholars worthy of mention are Gottfried Ephraim Müller, editor of an incomplete work entitled *Historische Einleitung zu nöthiger Kenntnis und nützlichen Gebrauch der alten lateinischen Schrifsteller* (['Historical Introduction to Necessary Knowledge and Profitable Use of the Ancient Latin Authors'], Dresden 1747–1751) and Johann Christian Wernsdorf (1723–1793), a pupil of the famous Pforta school and a student from Wittenberg, who became professor in Helmstedt and attempted to separate and distinguish philology from theology (cf. [12]). The first to produce a modern linguistic and factual commentary on ancient texts was Johann Matthias Gesner (1691–1761) [51. 18–24], professor for poetry and rhetoric in Göttingen (1734–1761). Gesner's main aim was to establish Classical Studies as an independent discipline. He was able to put his plans into reality at the University of Göttingen by liberating philology from its close ties with theology. In 1737, he established the *Seminarium philologicum*. This was the first attempt ever to concentrate the study of philology – previously spread across various academic disciplines such as Latin and Greek grammar, rhetoric, poetry, history etc. – within a single institute [42. 66]. The establishment of this seminar is also proof of the university's modernity: for the first time, the purpose of studying Classical Antiquity was not defined as the acquisition of rhetorical skills, but the education of taste, judgment, and reason. This started the gradual evolvement of a specific education for philologists, which until the end of the 18th cent. continued to be dominated by theology [20. 91]. Gesner's refoms were also reflected in the 1737 Braunschweig-Lüneburg *Schulordnung* (school rules and curriculum).

Ernesti's inaugural lecture at Leipzig university on 24.3.1742, entitled *De humanitatis disciplina*, can be seen as the manifesto of Neo-Humanism. Ernesti supported an encyclopaedic notion of knowledge: each aspect of knowledge was closely interconnected to another, required the support of the other, but also had an intrinsic value. The ideal of erudition – as evident in Quintilian and Cicero –, however, required knowledge in a range of disciplines. In Ernesti's view, the *studia humanitatis* were useful for medicine, law and theology. Philology, in particular, was the 'science of words and things' (*scientia et verborum et rerum*): of 'things', because, in Cicero's words, the beautiful form of speech was nothing without good thoughts. But to have good ideas required an understanding of the thoughts expressed by ancient authors, not just a mastery of their language. On the other hand, in order to be effective, 'truth' should be presented in an aesthetically pleasing form. This observation was aimed at the *nova philosophia* of Pietism. In Pietistic schools, foremost among them the *Paedagogium* in Halle founded by August Hermann Francke (1663–1727), Latin authors were studied in order to develop a fluent and elevated writing style;

Latin grammars were written for that same purpose (e.g. Joachim Lange, 1707). The Pietists opposed the study of Greek authors: they accused Humanists such as Melanchthon of having introduced the study of 'immoral' authors like Homer, Euripides and Aristotle into the school curriculum; instead, they wanted pupils to concentrate solely on the study of the sacred texts [12]. Ernesti set out to prove that it had been foremost the study of ancient authors which had enabled Luther to overcome Roman Catholicism. The ability to mount an effective opposition against the 'Barbaric philosophy' of scholasticism required knowledge of ancient philosophy. Similar thoughts had been expressed by the theologian Gottlieb Wernsdorf (1717–1774) in Wittenberg. Ernesti stressed in particular the role played by the university in Leipzig in the dissemination of Humanistic ideas and reminded his audience of Mosellanus and Camerarius, who had both taught at this university. Ernesti's successor in the polemic dispute with the Halle theologians was Johann Benedict Carpzow (*De damno, quod parit philosophia absque litteris humanioribus et arte critica* (['On the Damage that Philosophy Inflicts if Separated from Literary and Textual Criticism'] Leipzig 1748).

B. SCHOOL AND EDUCATION
Into the 18th cent. Latin, together with the teaching of Christian doctrine, remained at the core of the school curriculum: pupils were expected to be able to translate difficult texts from German into Latin and know by heart such Latin texts as Cornelius Nepos' *Vitae* or the *Disticha Catonis* in order to exercise their rhetorical and poetic abilities in the language. Reading and writing were learned through the study of Latin. An impressive contemporary record of this is found in Karl Philip Moritz's novel *Anton Reiser* (1785–1790): "Within a year, Reiser had thus progressed far enough to write in Latin without a single mistake and to express himself in that language better than in German. Because in Latin, he knew exactly when to use the accusative and when the dative. But in German, he had never thought about the fact that *mich* was accusative and *mir* dative and that one needed to be able to decline and conjugate in one's mother tongue as well as in Latin."

Schools paid no attention to the contents of the works by ancient authors, unless they had found recognition with the medieval, Christian tradition. The → LATIN SCHOOLS took their guidance first and foremost from the clergy. However, because they were also municipal schools, their educational objectives were somewhat contradictory: they educated future scholars as well as future craftsmen [34. 16]. The Latin schools met with fiercest opposition from the Philanthropines, who, however, did not call for the abolition of Latin as a subject either at all; in fact, they saw Latin as the global cultural language. Indeed, Latin at that time was the undisputed language of academia. In all faculties, lectures were delivered in Latin, even though the end of this tradition probably started in Halle in 1688, when

Thomasius allegedly was the first to lecture in German. Well into the 19th cent. Latin thus ensured the unity of scholarship across national borders and disciplines; however, it also meant a clear segregation of academic scholars from the rest of the population who had no knowledge of Latin (cf. [39. 419]), a segregation which also remained of importance for the Philanthropines. The Philanthropinist Johann Bernard Basedow (1723–1790) stipulated in his educational concept the need for two different kind of schools: one for the 'common rabble', for children who required less knowledge than others, and a smaller school for the 'children of well-mannered citizens', the target group for the *Gymnasium* (at the latter, pupils should converse and debate in Latin and not just be involved in mindless grammatical drill). This distinction was to influence future educational reforms. Basedow stipulated that state and education had to be closely linked, because it was to be the responsibility of the state to implement these reforms [34. 36].

Another opponent of the Latin School was Johann Gottfried Herder: "The philanthropist can but sigh when he sees how in these schools proudly displaying the name of 'Latin School' the first flush of enthusiasm is wilted, the first show of strength restrained, where talent is buried in dust and the genius held back, until all power is lost like that of a broken spring. ... Suppressed geniuses! Martyrs of a solely Latin education! O, if you could all voice your lament!" *(Über die neuere Deutsche Literatur*, in: *Sämtliche Werke* vol. IV, 380, quoted in [34. 20]). Herder saw the study of Greek language and culture as a means of attaining a higher level of humanity. Similarly, the credo of the German adoration of Greek culture, placed by Johann Joachim Winckelmann (1717–1768) at the centre of his manifesto entitled *Gedanken über die Nachahmung der griechischen Werke in der Malerei und Bildhauerkunst* ('Thoughts on the Imitation of Greek works of Art in Painting and Sculpture', 1755), was to determine a new direction in education, later termed → NEO-HUMANISM. Its first practical implementation was at the Friedrichs-Werdersche Gymnasium in Berlin, whose curriculum was significantly influenced by Friedrich Gedike (1754–1803) [36. 40]. The dispute between Philanthropinism and Neo-Humanism about the educational system was not merely a learned debate, as e.g. expressed in the theoretical thoughts of Karl Friedrich v. Zedlitz (*Vorschläge zur Verbesserung des Schulwesens in den Königlichen Landen*, ['Suggestions for the Improvement of Education in the Royal countries'] in the *Berliner Monatsschrift*, 1787), but also resulted in concrete reforms, initially in Prussia under Friedrich Wilhelm II with the establishment in 1787 of an 'Oberschulkollegium', a a school supervisory authority which also later played a role in the examination of teachers [34. 22–29], followed later by a similar establishment in Bavaria. But it was only in 1797, under the ministerial direction of Julius von Massow, that a systematic reform of the Prussian university system was attempted. Howe-

ver, the plan to establish a university in Berlin itself was not seriously considered until Halle, home to what had hitherto been the monarchy's most important university, was lost in the course of the catastrophic defeat in 1806/1807 [41. 314–15]

C. GRAECOPHILIA

Neo-Humanism and the 'verneration' of Greek culture and language stemmed from different political-historical and cultural roots: Germans perceived themselves as the people in the modern world with the closest spiritual affinity to ancient Greece. They saw it as their mission to restore Greek philosophy and Greek language to the modern world; in Klopstock's view, German alone among the modern languages was able to provide an adequate reproduction of the Greek. In this respect, Germans saw themselves as far superior to other nations, particularly to the French [24. 122]. Winckelmann and Goethe were described as 'Greeks'. The identification of Germans with Greeks thus became the principal medium to secure their own national identity. With Wilhelm von Humboldt, this affinity between the Greek and the German national character assumed almost axiomatic qualities (letter to Goethe on 30.5.1800): "In its language, variety of aspiration, simplicity of mind, in its federal constitution and its most recent fate, there is an undoubtable similarity between Germany and Greece" [24. 125]. The reference to recent events obviously referred to the Napoleonic occupation; the claim for similarity with the Greeks thus became an attempt to find compensation in the cultural sector for their political-military defeat. Because French → CLASSICISM took the Roman authors as its models, the German interest in the Greeks arose from a conscious attempt at distancing themselves from the French. This segregation also found its expression in the clichéd perception of the French national character and of the conventionality and superficiality of French intellectuals with their significant influence on German courts – a detrimental one which alienated the Germans from themselves, according to Herder [24. 121]. In Germany, too, both the Romano-centric view of Antiquity and French literary models prevailed until the appearance of Winckelmann, Lessings und Herder: the main protagonist of French Classicism in Germany was Johann Christoph Gottsched who in his *Versuch einer critischen Dichtkunst* (1729) ranked Virgil higher than Homer [15; 50. 160–161]. It was Gotthold Ephraim Lessing's (1729–1781) discovery of the Greek world that led to a real break with tradition, in this case the orientation on Classicistic French culture, which in turn was solely and exclusively shaped by the Latin culture. For that reason, Lessing's fight against the French theatre and its theoreticians can be considered as 'la lutte de l'Hellenisme contre l'esprit latin' (Ignàc Kont). However, Lessing's Latin studies should not be dismissed as mere 'early works' that had not achieved the same standard of his later works devoted to Greek culture [13; 48]. Undeniably, though, as a result of the Graecophaelia initiated by Winckelmann, the study of the Latin language and culture came to be seen as second-class. The first attempt of the Greeks in 1770 to free themselves from Turkish rule gave rise to the actual political → PHILHELLENISM. The first German work directly inspired by this movement was the novel *Ardinghello oder die glückselige Insel* (1787) by Wilhelm Heinse (1746–1803); the hero in Friedrich Hölderlin's *Hyperion oder der Eremit in Griechenland* (1797–1799), a contemporary Greek, participated in his country's struggle for freedom from the Turks, as did the protagonist of a later novel (*Phaethon*) by Wilhelm Waiblinger (1804–1830) [19]. Archaeological excavations and finds were a further stimulus for the reception of Classical Antiquity in German culture, particularly in the fields of art and architecture (foremost Friedrich Schinkel, 1781–1841). The publication of the Tablets of Heraclea (discovered in 1732) greatly impressed all of educated Europe; this led to the rediscovery of *Magna Graecia*. Early excavations in → HERCULANEUM (1738) and → POMPEII (1748) awakened a general interest in Antiquity. The discovery of → PAESTUM (1734–1740) established the Doric temple as an effective model in European culture and art [60; 16; 45].

D. HOMER AND HERODOTUS

A central role fell to the 'rediscovery' of Homer, initiated in particular by Johann Gottfried Herder. In his *Prolegomena ad Homerum* (1795), Friedrich August Wolf used only the tools of literary criticism to raise the question of the *Iliad's* historicity and unity; but in his conclusion, he emphasized the uniqueness of this work, a fact acknowledged also by other supporters of Wolf's theories, as e.g. the Schlegel brothers. The desire for a 'German Homer' was voiced, which was answered with the translations by Johann Heinrich Voss (*Odyssey* 1781, *Iliad* 1793). It also reflected an intensive translating activity; which had a considerable impact on literary theory and poetry. One only needs to point to Wilhelm von Humboldt's translations of Aeschylus (1816).

In addition to Homer, Herodotus was the pre-Romantic generation's model of the universal historian. In his *Allgemeine Historische Bibliothek* (1767), the Göttingen historian Johann Christoph Gatterer provided a detailed overview of Herodotus' writings and presented him to his contemporaries as a model historiographer. Indeed, Herodotus' point of view is a 'philosophical' one in the sense that the observation of the individual elements and components allowed him successfully to uncover their substantial, deeper connection. In the views of both Gatterer and Friedrich Creuzer (*Herodot und Thukydides*, 1797; [17]), the aesthetic unity of Herodotus' work was matched by a uniform and deliberate historiographical concept. Creuzer wrote that "it was only through Herodotus that historiography raised itself to become universal" [17. 123f.]. This was exactly what Gatterer and August Ludwig von Schlözer – i.e. the Göttingen historical

school – demanded of historiography: it should be an *historia universalis* of all peoples and in a systematic account reveal the overarching, general connection (*nexus universalis*). Arnold K.L. Heeren (1760–1842) – pupil, son-in-law and biographer of Christoph Gottlob Heyne, – attempted to turn this historiographical ideal into reality. In his *Ideen über die Politik, den Verkehr und den Handel der vornehmsten Völker der alten Welt* ('Ideas on Politics, Traffic and Trade of the Most Important Peoples of the Ancient World' 1793–1796) that which Heyne had prepared in his works on mythology and history of ancient art is carried out as a historiographical project. "The literature on ancient monuments thus truly transforms itself into the historiography of Antiquity" [42. 72–74]. On the other hand, there was the Thucydidean model of historiography which was concerned with individual states and peoples. The contrast between the two models was recognized as the conflict of German culture at that time, torn between the fascination of a 'universal history', a 'universal synthesis', and the more restrictive but safe sphere of 'historical criticism'.

E. WINCKELMANN AND HEYNE

In spite of outstanding individuals such as Ernesti and Gesner, German philology continued into the 18th cent. to lag behind its French, Dutch and English counterparts. It only came out the the shadows with Johann Heinrich Winckelmann (1717–1768) and Christoph Gottlob Heyne (1729–1812). Without Winckelmann, "the humanistic doctrine of Classical Germany" would be inconceivable" (E. Bergmann, translated from quote in [53. 122]). "Winckelmann perceived Greek art in its entirety as an *individuum*, clearly distinguished from everything that came before or after" [53. 85]. Winckelmann's understanding of art, projected onto Greek culture, "achieved, through its unparalleled dogmatic coherence, a maximum of normativity and is therefore as unhistorical as would be possible" [42. 56]. However, it should be pointed out that such an ahistorical Classicism did not entirely correspond to Winckelmann's intentions; he wanted a revival of ancient art not only with a view to the "essential nature of art", but also to its "external circumstances." This dichotomy, which he expressed in the introduction to his *Geschichte der Kunst*, was to have a significant influence on later historiography and is very similar to historiographical models in natural history which attempt to combine systematic-general and empirical research. This could be seen as the effect of Winckelmann's attempt to unite the two basic approaches to historiography, that of Herodotus and that of Thucydides. On the one hand, universal history is closer to Herodotus, Theopompus and Diodorus; on the other, the 'limited' history of 'external circumstances' together with the basic principle to range 'only among Greeks and Romans' is much closer to Thucydides' principle to tell of only one war.

In his works, from the *Gedanken über die Nachahmung der griechischen Werke* (1755) to the *Geschichte der Kunst des Altertums* (1764), Winckelmann endeavoured to point modern art to a way of liberating itself from decadence through a process of 'imitation' that could reach the true 'beauty' emanating from Greek art – a notion that can not deny its Platonic roots. Winckelmann saw as the ideal of Greek art and the characteristic feature of its masterpieces their 'edle Einfalt und stille Größe' ("noble simplicity and quiet grandeur"). The didactic function of Winckelmann's aesthetic ideal lay in the 'calm' and composure, which was not discarded even in the greatest pain (cf. → LAOCOON), and the Stoic mastery of passion. Wickelmann thus detected in the products of Greek art first and foremost a great ethical superiority. By contrast, Classicistic architecture looked for this same superiority in the architectural forms. The Temple of Olympian Zeus in Agrigentum became a model even for those artists and architects who had never set foot on Sicily. The collective dream of German Classicism was the (never built) monument to Frederick II, the design of which occupied a generation of architects in the attempt to link Classicism to the Gothic tradition, thus aiming for a synthesis which in itself was the characteristic feature of Romantic aesthetics. The main representative of this Neo-Classicist course was Friedrich Gilly [16; 49; 60].

To the present day, there is no comprehensive appraisal of Heyne, but his great significance needs to be pointed out emphatically: he is the one who established the *studia antiquitatis* as an independent academic discipline and who assigned to philology the task to contribute to the aesthetic and ethical education of mankind. In his speech *De genio saeculi Ptolemaerum*, delivered on the festive occasion of the 25th anniversary of the Georgia Augusta in Göttingen, Heyne stressed the importance of research and the patronage which made it possible. He wanted Göttingen to become the 'new Alexandria'. The modern study of mythology also started with Christian Gottlob Heyne. In his *Temporum mythicorum memoria a corruptelis nonnullis vindicta*, a lecture delivered at the Göttingen Royal Society of Sciences on 10 December 1763, Heyne spoke out against *corruptelae*, i.e. errors and misunderstandings of modern scholars in the interpretation of ancient myths. His polemics were directed against the attempt either to interpret the myths as a kind of secret knowledge (*res arcanas ac sacras*) or to dismiss them as silly fables (*fabulae*). In order to distance himself from these views also in his terminology, he coined the term 'Mythos' in the introduction to *Apollodors Bibliothek* (1782/3). Heyne's understanding of myths is distinctly historical in character. He denounced what he saw as a fundamental misconception, namely to let modern contemporary views guide the understanding of mythology; on the contrary, it was necessary to go back to the very origins of humanity. Mythology was not the product of a single people, but that of a general human imagination, as the many points of contact between in-

dividual nationals myths indicated more than one single source. In Heyne's view, 'symbol' and 'myth' had originally been one and the same. They were the original way in which humanity expressed itself, developed out of the limited intelligence and poverty of language ('ab ingenii humani imbecillitate a dictionis egestate: Sermonis mythici seu symbolici interpretatio ad caussas et rationes ductasque inde regulas revocata', 1807). This understanding of the role of symbols had a decisive influence on the symbolic interpretation of Greek mythology, an approach systematically applied in Friedrich Creuzer's *Symbolik und Mythologie der alten Völker, insbesondere der Griechen* (4 vols., 1810–1812, ^{2}1819, ^{3}1836). Heyne applied the same theories to mythology as then prevailed regarding the origin of languages (Condorcet; especially *De causis fabularum seu mythorum veterum physicis*, 1764). He based his proof of the existence of an original mime language on the comparison with such uncivilized peoples that he was aware of, e.g. the native peoples in America. He developed this concept further in his later works, with particular consideration of literature on travels to North America or India, which Heyne reviewed for the *Göttingischen Gelehrten Anzeigen* (*De vita antiquissimorum hominum, Graeciae maxime, ex ferociorum et barbarorum populorum comparatione illustrata*). Heyne's merit was also the attempt to study mythology with the help of artistic representations. In 1767 he gave the first of his successful lectures on 'mythology in art'; in this context, he also established the first German plaster → CAST COLLECTION. It was Heyne more than anyone else who gave the impetus to a comprehensive view of Antiquity. In his important laudatio for Winckelmann (*Lobschrift auf Winckelmann*, 1778), a clear and unrhetorical acknowledgement of Winckelmann's significance for the study of Classical Antiquity and at the same time a vademecum for the future of the discipline, he again stressed the need for a broad knowledge base in general history as well as the history of ideas, mythology, also every aspect of literature and art [23. 115f.]. Heyne's notion of *Altertumswissenschaft* (study of Classical Antiquity) was the result of his intensive philological work on ancient texts [28]; his edition of Virgil in particular is a clear example of his notion as to the form that a scientific commentary should ideally take: the appendix contains various digressions on the most important mythological and anthropological problems connected with Virgil's text [15]. One example for his methodical approach is his treatise on *Irrtümer in Erklärung alter Kunstwerke aus einer fehlerhaften Ergänzung* ('Mistaken interpretations of ancient works of art based on faulty completions') defining as archaeology's foremost task to assess, analogous to textual criticism, the genuineness of an object before making any attempt at interpretation. This is a precise reflection and expression of a fundamental requirement in historical-critical philology. [45. 60–61]. Heyne's seminar was attended by W. v. Humboldt, the Schlegel brothers, both von Stolbergs, J.H. Voss, F.A. Wolf (who later had to defend the originality of his *Prolegomena* against his teacher) but also the Danish archaeologist Georg Zoega (1775–1806). The latter was the author of *De origine et usu obeliscorum* and founder of a 'symbolic 'philology with a particular interest in the mythical and occult aspect of Antiquity and the Near East. This same direction, with various results, was later taken by F.G. Welcker, F. Creuzer, K.W. Solger, O.M. von Stackelberg und K. Ottfried Müller. In that way, Heyne's academic teaching thus had a decisive influence on the "change-over from a rationalistic interpretation of mythology, as represented by Ramler, Moritz, Voss and others, to a Romantic study of myths which turned its back on Olympian clarity and focused instead on the Chthonic, pre-Olympian and Oriental aspects of Greek mythology. Its new contemporary leaders soon after 1800 were Creuzer, Görres, and Kanne (later also Schelling and the aging Friedrich Schlegel)" (J. Wohlleben, translation of quote in: [62. 21f.]). However, in Winckelmann's works as well, it is possible to detect some Dionysian elements and notions that anticipated the Romantic understanding of mythology.

F. STUDYING ANTIQUITY

Heyne pioneered the historical analysis of Antiquity, i.e. a detailed evaluation according to ancient, not modern categories: F.A. Wolf elevated this hermeneutic principle to a didactic rule, not without polemics against that naiveté when reading ancient authors which J.J. Rousseau had advised as the way to "true wisdom". Instead, Wolf stipulated, one should "leave the present behind" and approach Antiquity historically with the aid of interdisciplinary studies [29. 426f.]. But apart from Wolf, and even predating him, the study of Classical Antiquity had its origin in Wilhelm von Humboldt's sketch *Über das Studium des Altertums und des griechischen inbesondere* ('On the study of Antiquity, especially of Greece', 1793): this essay was the first to emphasize that the study of Classical Antiquity was of intrinsic value, because Greek civilization was the historically realized model of an absolute humanity and not just one nation's step in the development towards this ultimate goal, as it had still been seen by Herder. In the conclusion to his essay, Humboldt spoke of the usefulness of Antiquity, thereby implicitly contradicting the usefulness which other disciplines had successfully claimed for themselves, while at the same time elevating this usefulness to a higher level, as it was both practical and ideal. In that way, he brought the debate on the value and importance of the study of the Humanities to an extreme point and at the same time transcended the enlightened view that the Humanities were only ancillary disciplines. It remained to be shown, however, to what extent they could become independent fields of academic pursuit in their own rights.

This then was the task that Wolf set himself in his *Darstellung der Altertumswissenschaft* (1807) [23], in which he emphasized one crucial difference in comparison with the Natural Sciences: because Ancient Studies represent not only an enrichment of mind and intellect, but are of practical use as well, it is not enough merely to have knowledge of ancient languages or of the ancillary disciplines such as palaeography and epigraphy; what was needed was the ability to imagine oneself in Antiquity, to empathize. Knowledge about Antiquity thus was most of all 'apperception', intuition. Indeed Winckelmann, the father of modern archaeology, had shown in his descriptions and assessments of ancient masterpieces that enthusiasm was an essential supplement to scholarship. This same direction was later pursued by Friedrich Creuzer, editor of Plotinus, in his essay *Über das Studium des Alterthums als Vorbereitung zur Philosophie* (1805); in Neo-Platonic diction and clearly influenced by Schelling, he emphasized that the main objective of studying Classical Antiquity was to gain knowledge about ideal beauty. He confirmed the same view in his tractate on *Das akademische Studium des Alterthums* (1807), a theoretical preliminary consideration regarding the establishment of a Philological Seminar at Heidelberg university. In Creuzer's view, to reach this ideal required more than just the knowledge of ancient languages or the dry scientific application of historical 'criticism', it required enthusiasm and intuition. Even Wilhelm von Humboldt supported enthusiasm as a legitimate approach to Antiquity: "Only enthusiasm can fuel further enthusiasm, and the only reason for the wonderful effect that the Greeks have upon us is that they are the living embodiment of this all-pervading heavenly yearning", (*Geschichte des Verfalls und Unterganges der griechischen Freistaaten*, 1807, in: *Werke in 5 Bänden*, vol. 2, 1969, 120). However, such enthusiasm was but the privilege of a few chosen ones: that community which saw as its foundation the idea of *symphilosophia* (of philosophizing together) and which was in different forms and with different results what the Schlegel brothers and Novalis yearned for. On the one hand, those years witnessed the development of a separation, but also a mutually influential exchange of ideas between a purely formal philology and a view of Antiquity that was largely based on intuition. These two approaches to Antiquity still exist today. They have not only influenced the history of Classical Philology, but every political-pedagogical project to model the education of youngster on ancient examples. To endow Ancient Studies with a didactic dimension also meant to endow them with the greatest possible degree of usefulness. In that way, the two faces of Ancient Studies which were to shape its future development had been defined in the early years of the 19th cent.: a specialist academic discipline but with a claim to a universal social role and significance.

G. UTOPIA AND LITERARY GENRES

The 18th and early 19th cent. perception of Antiquity was significantly shaped by an element of utopia associated with the notion of Antiquity, the 'metaphysics of Greekdom'. Antiquity provided the literary reference point that made it possible to escape from a difficult political situation – a unifying element in the face of G.'s political fragmentation. The Enlightenment poet Christoph Martin Wieland, one of the forerunners in the dissemination of Classical authors, especially through his journal *Attisches Musum* (1796–1801, continued as *Neues attisches Museum* (1802–1812)), saw Antiquity as the embodiment of the Platonic ideal of beauty, as did Shaftesbury. Goethe characterized Wieland's *Musarion oder die Philosophie der Grazie* thus: 'Hier war es, wo ich das Antike lebendig und neu wieder zu sehen glaubte' ("It was here that I felt I saw the ancient world alive and new"). Winckelmann, Goethe, Schiller and also Humboldt completely disregarded the social and political foundations of ancient culture, as they might have interfered or even destroyed this idealized notion of Antiquity. Goethe's *Iphigenie auf Tauris* thus searched for the distant Greeks with the soul, while Winckelmann in the final paragraph of his *Geschichte der Kunst* compared his feeling towards Antiquity with that of a lover whose beloved was sailing off across the sea, leaving him behind consumed with longing. In his poetological works, Schiller attributed only the authors of Classical Antiquity with 'naiveté', i.e. only they were at one with nature. It was not uncommon for educational travellers – as in Goethe's case – to make do with the reflection of Greek culture in Sicily without ever travelling to its source, to Greece itself. This attitude has been characterized – not without justification – as the 'faith' of the Germans in the world of the Greeks [47]. The contrast between Antiquity and Modernity was not only used to criticize the present and to indulge in a yearning for the past, but also to utilize this yearning in the creation of a new era that was to transcend Antiquity in a new all-encompassing unity. This idea is evident in Schiller's work (cf. [24. 117]), but most strikingly in that of F. Schlegel [59]. Schlegel studied the ancient poetic texts – emphatically contrasting 'study' to Winckelmann's 'imitation' – to define the nature of contemporary literature against this backdrop: he saw the poetry of Romanticism as the poetic form to embrace and transcend all other genres, forms and eras. Regarding the understanding of literary genres, Schlegel thus took a path that ran counter to the views of Goethe and Schiller, as expressed by the latter in their correspondence [27]. They developed a poetics of the epic genre on the basis of post-Homeric epic poetry, the idea of an epic poetry that was 'pure'; this poetry went quite deliberately against popular taste, it retreated almost aristocratically into the world of mythology and saw itself as an alternative to the confused poetry of the day. The intellectual elite thus wanted to rise above the interests of the masses; the poetry modelled on ancient examples represented a way, open only to a select few, into a sphere that lay outside of the historical process – and in that sense was truly utopian. Goethe's uncompleted *Achilleis* was an attempt to translate this utopia into reality. However, the work had to remain unfinished, because it proved

impossible to transpose the 'objectivity' of the Homeric epic and its lack of passion into a world dominated by tragic and pathetic situations, but also, because there was no room any more for the narrative element of retardation, so crucial to Homer's style, in a modern world and society, where progress advanced without impediment [27]. Epic poetry had its place, its purposeful function, only in the world of the past. The French Revolution, the roar of the cannons on the battlefield of Valmy marking the dawning of a new age, also forced the transformation of Homer's Achilles into a modern hero.

1 C. AMPOLO, Storie greche. La formazione della moderna storiografia sugli antichi Greci, 1997   2 O. BATLER, Wieland und die griechische Antike, 1952   3 A. BECK, Griechisch-deutsche Begegnung. Das deutsche Griechenerlebnis im Sturm und Drang, 1947   4 R. BENZ, Wandel des Bildes der Antike in Deutschland. Ein geistesgeschichtlicher Überblick, 1948   5 W. BINDER, Die Deutsche Klassik und die Antike – Goethe, Schiller, Hölderlin, in: M. SVILAR, S. KUNZE (eds.), Antike und europäische Welt. Aspekte der Auseinandersetzung mit der Antike, 1984, 121–143   6 R. R. BOLGAR (ed.), Classical Influences on European Culture A.D. 1500–1700, 1976   7 BOLGAR   8 F. BORNMANN, s.v. Germania. Fortuna letteraria, EV 2, 706–711   9 H. BUCHOLZ, Ursprungswelt. Die Gestalt des Mythos bei Christian Gottlob Heyne, in: Perspektiven der Neuen Mythologie. Mythos, Religion und Poesie im Schnittpunkt von Idealismus und Romantik um 1800, 1990, 33–40   10 E. M. BUTLER, The Tyranny of Greece over Germany, 1935   11 U. CARPI, Introduzione. La 'Antike' di Wilhelm von Humboldt, in: W. VON HUMBOLDT, Scritti sull' antichitá classica, 1994   12 G. CHIARINI, La nascita dell' *Altertumswiss.* 2. Germania, in: Lo spazio letterario della Grecia antica, II: La ricezione e l'attualizzazione del testo, 1995, 679–712   13 Id., Lessing e Plauto, 1983   14 Id., s.v. Germania. Studi filologici, EV 2, 701–706   15 Id., s.v. Heyne, Christian Gottlob, EV 2, 701–706   16 M. COMETA, Duplicità del classico. Il mito del Tempio di Giove olimpico da Winckelmann a Leo von Klenze, 1993   17 F. CREUZER, Erodoto e Tucidide – Herodot und Thukydides (dual-language ed.), S. FORNARO (ed.), 1994   18 W. DAHLHEIM, Die Antike, ⁴1995, 699–734   19 L. DROULIA, Philhellenisme. Ouvrages inspirés par la guerre de l'indipendence grecque 1821–1833, 1974   20 TH. ELLWEIN, Die deutsche Universität. Vom Mittelalter bis zur Gegenwart, 1985   21 C. EPHRAIM, Wandel des Griechenbildes im 18. Jahrhundert. (Winckelmann, Lessing, Herder), 1961   22 H. FLASHAR, Die methodisch-hermeneutischen Ansätze von Friedrich August Wolf und Friedrich Ast – Traditionelle und neue Begründungen, in: Philologie und Hermeneutik im 19. Jahrhundert, 1979, 21–31   23 S. FORNARO, Lo 'studio degli antichi' 1793–1807, in: Quaderni di storia 43, 1996, 109–155   24 M. FUHRMANN, 'Die Querelle des Anciens et des Modernes', der Nationalismus und die deutsche Klassik, in: BOLGAR, 107–129   25 Id., Von Wieland bis Voss: Wie verdeutscht man antike Autoren?, in: Jb. des Freien Dt. Hochstifts, 1987, 1–22   26 J. W. GOETHE, Nausicaa, S. FORNARO (ed.), 1994   27 Id., Achilleide, S. FORNARO (ed.), 1998   28 F. GRAF, Die Entstehung des Mythosbegriffs bei Christian Gottlob Heyne in: Id. (ed.), Mythos in mythenloser Gesellschaft. Das Paradigma Roms, 1993, 284–294   29 A. GRAFTON, Man

muß aus der Gegenwart heraufsteigen: History, Tradition und Traditions of Historical Thought in F.A.Wolf, in: H. E. Bödeker, G. G. Iggers, J. B. Knudsen, P. H. Reill (eds.), Aufklärung und Geschichte. Studien zur deutschen Geschichtswissenschaft im 18. Jahrhundert, 1986, 416–429   30 N. Hammerstein, Zur Geschichte der deutschen Universität im Zeitalter der Aufklärung, in: H. Rössler, G. Franz (eds.), Universität und Gelehrtenstand 1400–1800, 1970, 145–182   31 Id., Die Universitätsgründungen im Zeichen der Aufklärung, in: P. Baumgart, N. Hammerstein (eds.), Beiträge zu Problemen deutscher Universitätsgründungen der frühen Neuzeit, 1978, 263–298   32 A. Horstmann, Die Forschung in der Klassischen Philologie des 19. Jahrhunderts, in: A. Diemer (ed.), Konzeption und Begriff der Forschung in den Wissenschaften des 19. Jahrhunderts, 1978, 27–57   33 A. E. A. Horstmann, Mythologie und Altertumswissenschaft. Der Mythosbegriff bei Christian Gottlob Heyne, in: Archiv für Begriffgesch. 16, 1972, 60–85   34 M. Kraul, Das deutsche Gymnasium. 1780–1980, 1984   35 M. Kunze (ed.), Christoph Martin Wieland und die Antike. Eine Aufsatzsammlung, 1986   36 M. Landfester, Humanismus und Gesellschaft im 19. Jahrhundert, 1989   37 F. Marwinski, Johann Andreas Fabricius und die Jenaer gelehrten Gesellschaft des 18. Jahrhunderts, 1989   38 C. Menze, Wilhelm von Humboldts Lehre und Bild vom Menschen, 1965   39 J. Mittelstrass, Neuzeit und Aufklärung. Studien zur Entstehung der neuzeitlichen Wissenschaft und Philosophie, 1970   40 G. W. Most, From Logos to Mythos, in: From Myth to Reason? Studies in the Development of Greek Thought, 1999   41 U. Muhlack, Die Universität im Zeichen von Neuhumanismus und Idealismus: Berlin, in: P. Baumgart, N. Hammerstein (eds.), Beiträge zu Problemen deutscher Universitätsgründungen der frühen Neuzeit, 1978, 299–339   42 Id., Historie und Philologie, in: H. E. Bödeker, G. G. Iggers, J. B. Knudsen, P. H. Reill (eds.), Aufklärung und Geschichte. Studien zur deutschen Geschichtswissenschaft im 18. Jahrhundert, 1986, 49–81   43 Id., Klassische Philologie zwischen Humanismus und Neuhumanismus, in: R. Vierhaus (ed.), Wissenschaft im Zeitalter der Aufklärung. Aus Anlaß des 250jährigen Bestehens des Verlages Vandenhoeck & Ruprecht, 1985, 93–119   44 A. Pellegrini, Wieland e la classicità tedesca, 1968   45 M. Praz, Gusto neoclassico, 1974   46 G. Pucci, Il passato prossimo. La scienza dell' antichità alle origini della cultura moderna, 1993   47 W. Rehm, Griechentum und Goethezeit. Geschichte eines Glaubens, 1936   48 V. Riedl, Lessing und die römische Literatur, 1976   49 A. Rietdorf, Friedrich Gilly. Wiedergeburt der Architektur, 1943   50 H. Rüdiger, Wesen und Wandlung des Humanismus, 1966   51 U. Schindel, Johann Matthias Gesner, Professor der Poesie und Beredsamkeit 1734–1761, in: C. J. Classen (ed.), Die Klassische Altertumswissenschaft an der Georg-August-Universität Göttingen. Eine Ringvorlesung zu ihrer Geschichte, 1989, 9–26   52 W. Seidl, Das Land der Griechen mit der Seele suchend ... Über das Griechenlandbild der deutschen Klassik, in: E. Konstantinou, U. Wiedenmann (eds.), Europäischer Philhellenismus. Ursachen und Wirkungen, 1989, 15–36   53 H. Sichtermann, Kulturgeschichte der klassischen Architektur, 1996   54 E. Spranger, Wilhelm von Humboldt und die Humanitätsidee, 1909 (repr. 1928)   55 Id., Wilhelm von Humboldt und die Reform des Bildungswesens, 1910   56 H. Trevelyan, Goethe and the Greeks, 1941   57 F. Turato, Prometeo in Germania, 1988   58 L. Uhlig (ed.), Griechenland als Ideal. Winckelmann und seine Rezeption in Deutschland, 1988   59 F. Vercellone, Identità dell' antico. L'idea del classico nella cultura tedesca del primo Ottocento, 1988   60 D. Watkin, T. Mellinghoff, German Architecture and the Classical Ideal. 1740–1840, 1987   61 W. M. Calder III, A. Köhnken, W. Kullmann, G. Pflug (eds.), Friedrich Gottlieb Welcker: Werk und Wirkung, 1986.

Sotera Fornaro

IV. The 19th Century to 1918

A. Institutionalizing the Reception of Classical Antiquity   B. Social Consequences and Discourses   C. Areas of Tension and Attempted Solutions   D. Jurisprudence, Economics   E. Philhellenism and Travel to Greece   F. Literature, Theatre and Philosophy   G. Art and Architecture   H. Archaeology

A. Institutionalizing the Reception of Classical Antiquity

The great 19th cent. boom in the reception of Classical Antiquity in G. began with the reforms of the Prussian educational system (→ Prussia). It was Wilhelm von Humboldt who initiated the application of Neo-Humanist theories (→ Neo-Humanism) to public institutions. The aim was a general comprehensive education of the individual which should at the same time be a new national education to strengthen German identity in culture and science. This was to be based on the study of Classical Antiquity, in particular of Greek culture and civilization, because they had exemplarily mapped out the path that an individual had to take in order to attain a state of perfect humanity. A very similar Neo-Humanist concept had been developed earlier by Fr. Niethammer in → Bavaria, but (at least initially) without the success and impact associated with the name of Humboldt. However, despite some resistance, Humanistic education prevailed in all of the German states: the reception of Classical Antiquity, a long-lost culture, was prescribed by the state as the modern educational standard for the male elite who would go on to occupy important governmental and social functions; the newly evolving academic discipline of → Classical Philology played a central role in the German cultural landscape.

The success of this new educational concept was due to the fact that it provided an answer to a range of different contemporary requirements. Having the state provide for and guarantee the main aim of Humboldtian Humanism, namely the development of the individual, settled the question of the relationship between individual and state, a problem first highlighted in the → Enlightenment and then more recently in the Prussian War of Liberation: the transparent structure of the educational system provided the individual citizen with clear and – at least in principle – generally applicable criteria for an entry into the state's ruling elite (defeudalization; emancipation of the middle classes through education). The interest of the state was to gain access to the educational system which until then had largely been the domain of the Church; with ancient literature, the state could provide a curricular content unthreatened by any interdenominational dispute. The German enthusiasm for the Greeks in particular was at least in part a reaction against the culture of the dominant French nation with its clear focus on Rome. But its power was mainly due to the fact that this Graecophilia wanted "to reverse the alienation of the individual in the modern world through the link to Greek civilization" [9. 98]. To gain true humanity with the aid of the Greeks – seen as the ideal example of a synthesis of nature and culture – was the optimistic hope of Germans ever since Winckelmann; confirmed by Humboldt, it proved itself as the final – and ultimately utopian – consolation in the face of the crisis of modern humanity [11. 44–46].

Classical education was institutionalized in a number of ways: as the actual implementation of Humboldt's educational ideal, a university was founded in Berlin (and others elsewhere); very effective was the establishment of the → PHILOLOGICAL SEMINAR, the dominant institution within Philosophical faculties. In theory, it was to provide the didactic education of the new teaching profession, in practice, however, the focus was more on an introduction to scholarly methodology and linguistic-historic text interpretation. The increasing specialization led to the development of specific fields such as → EPIGRAPHY, → PAPYROLOGY and → ANCIENT HISTORY [8], but only → CLASSICAL ARCHAEOLOGY emancipated itself by the establishment of its own institutes. In addition to the universities, the → ACADEMIES of Sciences (Berlin, Munich, Göttingen) were transformed into centres for the study of Classical Antiquity, and new research institutions were established (→ DEUTSCHES ARCHÄOLOGISCHES INSTITUT, → RÖMISCH-GERMANISCHE KOMMISSION). To prepare students for academic university study was the main aim of the newly established → HUMANIST GYMNASIUM. The → CURRICULUM stipulated a great number of lessons to be devoted to the → TEACHING OF ANCIENT LANGUAGES (for the top class of a Prussian gymnasium of 1812: eight hours per week of Latin, seven of Greek), the Abitur was made compulsory and concentrated mainly on the ancient languages. For candidates of the teaching profession, the examen pro facultate docendi was introduced as an obligatory entrance exam with the main focus on philological knowledge. This institutionalization soon spread from Prussia to other German countries (for selected data see table below), but with strong regional variations: in Württemberg, for example, → MONASTERY SCHOOLS prevailed for a long time, as did the → Fürstenschulen in Saxony, and twice as much Latin as Greek was taught in Baden. Following the creation of the North German League and ultimately the foundation of the German Empire in 1871, the harmonization of the higher education system along

Prussian lines was accelerated. Apart from this institutionalization in the educational system, Classical Antiquity played an important role in public discourse through publicly accessible collections of ancient art works, newly established museums of antiquities and, above all, through → CAST COLLECTIONS (109 just in G. according to a survey of 1909) (see table).

B. SOCIAL CONSEQUENCES AND DISCOURSES

One of the consequences of this institutionalizaton was the creation of a well respected professorial class, defined by their ideal of a scholarly approach ('criticism') and by explicit access criteria (doctoral thesis), which saw its freedom, including in a political respect, guaranteed by the state; the professionalization of Ancient Studies and its career paths became the model for other disciplines [7]. Another was the evolvement of a class of teachers/philologists, formally defined by the teaching examination and intellectually shaped by their Humanist education (→ EDUCATION/CULTURE; 1837: foundation of the Verein deutscher Philologen und Schulmänner) [5], who were civil servants of the state and not any more of the Church. Only the Humanist gymnasium could bestow the right of access to university education and thus to leading positions within the state; this monopoly remained in place until 1900. Academies and research institutes not only expanded the freedom to conduct academic research without the obligation to teach, they were also instrumental in and essential for the major projects which are so typical for Ancient Studies in 19th cent. G. (collections of Greek and Latin inscriptions, corpora, collections of fragments, Thesaurus linguae latinae, excavations). Plaster cast collections, initially only intended as academic teaching aids, and museums of Antiquity provided a wider public with the opportunity of a visual reception of ancient works of art. For the first time, examples of Winckelmann's ideal art were thus directly accessible, mainly in the form of white, naked male statues.

Within and between these various groups of recipients, various discourses regarding the reception of Classical Antiquity developed: the professors praised their primacy of a purely scholarly approach and often looked down on any non-academic reception of Antiquity; on the other hand, they had to justify and defend their discipline to the general public. Indicative for the increasing intellectualization was the speedy emergence of academic journals for Ancient Studies (four journals before 1846), a vibrant system of academic reviews, the annual publication of a specialist bibliography (Bibliotheca classica from 1848), publisher's series of scientific text editions (Bibliotheca Teubneriana) and major reference works (Pauly-Wissowas Realencyklopädie der classischen Altertumswissenschaften). Philologists teaching at schools pursued a double legitimization of their position, evident particularly in the typical medium of the → SCHULPROGRAMME: on the one hand, by carrying out their own academic research and, on the other, by transmitting Humanist education to pupils and parents; they were the crucial mediators between the scholarly and non-scholarly reception. In later years, philologists themselves became the subject of literary portraits (Th. Mann, *Buddenbrooks*, ch. XI.2, 1901; H. Mann, *Professor Unrat*, 1905). The educated middle class, the product of Humanist *gymnasium*, developed a considerable interest in Classical Antiquity (reception of Classical Antiquity as a fashion); a veritable market developed for translations (with print runs of up to 20,000), popular historical works (Th. Mommsen, *Römische Geschichte*, from 1854, awarded the Nobel prize in 1901), mythological anthologies, also specifically adapted for a readership without Humanist education (G. Schwab, *Sagen des klassischen Altertums*, 1838–40), antiquarian and historical novels (F. Dahn, *Ein Kampf um Rom*, 30 editions between 1876 and 1900) as well as popular lectures and talks [9. 53]. Even non-specialized journals and newspapers contained reviews about text editions, commentaries, translations and philological interpretations of Classical texts in addition to essays about ancient history and the importance of Humanist education. But at the same time, more and more critical voices could be heard about the one-sidedness of school education and about the academic life and practices of Classical philologists (cf. satire by L. Hatvany, *Die Wissenschaft des Nichtwissenswerten*, 1908).

C. Areas of Tension and Attempted Solutions

The implementation of the Humanist educational reform and its adaptation to the social, cultural, and political conditions resulted in numerous areas of tension, which had a significant impact on the reception of Classical Antiquity in G. Neo-Humanists and their successors, for example, clearly focused on Greek as the more authentic, more harmonic and thus also more exemplary culture, while the Roman culture took second place (→ GRAECO-ROMAN CONTROVERSY). However, in schools, under the label of 'formal education', this new theory reverted back to the practices of the traditional Latin schools: the ratio of Latin lessons was noticeably higher than that of Greek ones – and was even increased in later revisions of the curriculum – and the analysis of content is restricted by the dominance of a grammatical-stylistic formalism. This presented the opponents of the Humanist gymnasium with significant targets, particularly the compulsory active mastery of Latin, an anachronism when Latin was no longer the *lingua franca* of scholars and academics. In addition, the historization of Classical Antiquity, which became more intense in the wake of the critical evaluation of Homer (F.A.Wolf: [6]), culminated in the opposition of → CLASSICISM and → HISTORISM [3. 21–33]. The ideal of *Altertumswissenschaft* (Ancient Studies) as a discipline taking into consideration the entire range of cultural phenomena necessitated almost inevitably a wealth of individual and specialized research, mainly into lesser known authors, non-literary sources

(inscriptions, papyri) and other material remains. However, this made it difficult to arrive at a uniform view of Antiquity, it undermined the normative validity of Greek fine art and literature, and rendered impossible the practical implementation of the broadest possible education of the individual. This contrast is still evident in the → NIETZSCHE-WILAMOWITZ-CONTROVERSY: Fr. Nietzsche, a philologist himself, preached a decidedly unhistorical, non-academic (but at the same time anti-Classicistic) reception of Classical Antiquity, which was vehemently rejected by Wilamowitz-Moellendorff with a defence of historical positivism. In addition, the increasingly scientific and academic nature of Ancient Studies furthered the rivalry of opposing methodological approaches, e.g. that between supporters of a 'philology of things' (*Sachphilologie*) as opposed to a 'philology of language' (*Sprachphilologie*) (→ BÖCKH-HERMANN dispute); different methods became associated with different geographical centres, and 'schools' developed. e.g. that of H. Usener on the history of religion (→ RELIGION, HISTORY OF, D. 2.1.). The latent contradiction between the general philanthropic education of the individual towards the ultimate goals of autonomy, freedom and emancipation, as put forward by the Neo-Humanists, and the educational aim of producing obedient citizens of the monarchy, as demanded by the state, resulted in a politicization of Antiquity in both action and reaction [3. 31–36]. Scholars of Classical Antiquity voiced their view on central political topics such as → DEMOCRACY, → MONARCHY and → SOCIALISM with reference to Classical Antiquity. The societal debate about the value of Classical education also broached the issue of the contrast between pagan culture and Christian tradition: externally, this conflict manifested itself in the resistance of religious circles against taking away the Church's educational monopoly, internally in the controversy about the content and morality of Classical education (mainly in the 1830s and 1840s). Furthermore, it should not be overlooked that the emancipation from theology and the programmatic rejection of Christianity also changed the way that philologists viewed Jews and Christians in Antiquity: at best, they no longer considered it their concern. Finally, in view of the increasing industrialization, Humanist education found itself the object of ever increasing doubts regarding its usefulness in a modern technical age. Ultimately, this controversy was to peak towards the end of the century in the so-called 'school war' (*Schulkrieg*) between supporters of the Humanist gymnasium and advocates of the → REALSCHULE

A variety of frequently-used strategies to deal with these conflicts can be distinguished in the reception of Classical Antiquity in 19th cent. G.: the demonstration of kinships (e.g. between the Greek and the German language) or analogies (e.g. between the 'patchwork' structure of the Greek and the German political world, between the Macedonian and the Prussian monarchy), the resolution of the contrast on a new and higher level [9. 91–93] (e.g., E. Curtius claimed that German culture represented the unification of ancient Greek and Christian culture), the reference to the primacy of a general and formal school education over an immediate practical relevance (this was to dominate the school debate in the second half of the 19th cent. in the context of the debate about Realism), as well as the instrumentalization, domestication and reduction of Antiquity, e.g. in the frequently political-propagandistic use of the reception of Classical Antiquity in the architecture and interior design of public buildings. This political dimension was also particularly evident in the school curriculum of the latter years of the *Kaiserreich* [1. 76–106], after Wilhelm II 1889/90 had declared that the educational aims of schools were to be patriotism and the fight against socialism: 'Wir sollen junge Deutsche erziehen, und nicht junge Griechen und Römer' ("Our task is to educate young Germans, not young Greeks or Romans"). The original concept of a Humboldtian general education of the individual had to give way to a nationalistic monopolization of Antiquity.

D. JURISPRUDENCE, ECONOMICS

Whereas in other European states Roman law had generally ceased to be an active element in legal practice and theory as a result of the legal codifications around 1800, it continued to be applied as *ius commune* in the civil law of almost all countries within the German Confederation. This only changed in 1900 with the introduction of the *Bürgerliches Gesetzbuch* as a uniform civil law code for the entire German Empire. However, its general legal principles and concepts are nonetheless very clearly of Roman origin, due to the influence of F.C. von Savigny's → HISTORISCHE RECHTSSCHULE. This had dominated jurisprudence at German faculties of law from about 1815 on, but its effect went far beyond G. and resulted in an impressive revival of the study and analysis of Roman law; its main focus was not so much simply historical reconstruction as pursued by Th. Mommsen (*Römisches Staatsrecht*, 1871–1888, *Römisches Strafrecht*, 1899), but the intention to derive legal concepts from Roman law for the contemporary legal reality through academic studies (→ PANDECTIST STUDIES).

The reception of Antiquity in the *Historische Schule der deutschen Nationalökonomie* ('historical school of German economics') was extensive, but has as yet been little researched. On the one hand, W. Roscher, B. Hildebrand and K. Bücher, mostly Classical philologists and historians by training, added an economic dimension to the ancient cultures through their historical research; the actual assessment of ancient economic structures was a matter of highly controversial debate, mainly in the → BÜCHER-MEYER CONTROVERSY. The other intention was to identify analogies between Classical Antiquity and the present and thereby to draw conclusions for contemporary economic theory and practice. In a similar way, ancient political theory was harnessed for the contemporary debate: in his *Politik, geschichtliche Naturlehre der Monarchie, Aristokratie*

und Demokratie (1892), W. Roscher not only debated these forms of government, but also modern phenomena such as → CAESARISM and socialism against the backdrop of Classical Antiquity, while R. v. Pöhlmann used his *Geschichte des antiken Kommunismus und Sozialismus* (1893–1901) to combat these same political movements in his own time.

E. PHILHELLENISM AND TRAVEL TO GREECE

In the course of the political → PHILHELLENISM, the involvement of the European states in the Greek wars of liberation opened a new, direct contact to → GREECE, which previously had only been accessible in spirit. For the German volunteers, the modern Greeks' struggle for independence became a substitute for their own repressed reform desires, but turned into a political and military disappointment. It was accompanied by numerous journalistic and poetic declarations of sympathy and calls for solidarity, foremost amongst them Wilhelm Müller's poetry, which gained him the epithet 'Griechen-Müller' (*Lieder der Griechen*, 1821–24): 'Ohne die Freiheit, was wärest du, Hellas?/Ohne dich, Hellas, was wäre die Welt?' ("Without freedom, what would you, Hellas, be? / Without you, Hellas, what would the world be?"). Encouraged by the subsequent Bavarian rule over Greece (1832–1863), it became fashionable to travel to Greece. However, the Classicistic image of Greece in the minds of German scholars, writers and painters was increasingly called into question as a consequence of these travels [2]: it was not uncommon for the landscape to be perceived as desolate; its inhabitants cared little about their Hellenic cultural heritage – in contrast with the Graecophile Germans –, and the physiognomy of modern Greeks conflicted with the ideal of the Greek profile gleaned from ancient statues. This contrast brought forth an awareness of the distance between the contemporary modern age and Classical Antiquity and in some way resulted in the perception of an end of the Humanist age up to the experience of a existential *Grenzsituation*, as evident in the German travel literature of the late 19th cent.

F. LITERATURE, THEATRE AND PHILOSOPHY

With its central position within the German world of thought, Greek and Roman culture provided a wealth of material for literary transformation, while also ensuring a common horizon of education and expectation for writers and readers. This resulted in an almost constant reception of Antiquity in a wide range of genres. The spectrum included an elitist Classicism fixated on formal structure (A. von Platen, E. Geibel), popularizations, especially in form of ancient historical novels, and the couching of contemporary criticism in an ancient-historical guise in order to circumvent censorship. However, the wide dissemination of the literary reception of Classical Antiquity was offset by an undeniable lack of literary innovation: the hope expressed by Goethe and Schiller that German literature would redefine itself through the recourse to that of ancient Rome and Greece remained unfilled, and the approaches by poets such as Hölderlin or Kleist found no true successors. When the philologist Th. Kock translated Goethes *Iphigenie* back into Greek in 1861, adding a Latin commentary, this was certainly eccentric, but nevertheless symptomatic. A possible productive revival of ancient literature was opposed by some important literary movements, e.g. → ROMANTICISM with its preference for the Middle Ages, Realism and Naturalism. But it was precisely the very standardization and regulation of Classical education in the Humanist gymnasium with its restricted focus on language and grammar that may have deterred some of the more unconventional writers from any further dealings with Antiquity.

This almost paradoxical situation is particularly evident in the development of the drama, which was, from Lessing on and especially in the wake of Hegel's influential theory, considered the noblest of literary genres. The 19th cent. saw a significant broadening in opportunity for the reception of Greek tragedies: a performance of Sophocles' *Antigone* in Potsdam in 1841 was the first ever modern staging of an ancient drama in an expressly historical production, i.e. for the most part without further additions or adaptations. Hegel's philosophical interpretation had assigned this tragedy an prominent dignity and a realizable political dimension. The production was a huge success [4. 60–76]. After that, Greek tragedies, especially *Antigone*, were staged by many municipal German theatres (seemingly a uniquely German phenomenon) [4. 91]. And "even if the share of ancient drama on 19th cent. German stages was still comparatively modest" [4. 97] – a veritable flourishing only set in after 1900 [4. 110–135] –, this was the first time that a broader public was given the opportunity of a direct visual experience of ancient drama. By contrast, the German tragedy ceased being a vibrant genre after the early 19th cent., despite or maybe because of various attempts of keeping it alive by choosing topics from ancient history. To some extent, the only productive reception of the Greek tragedy took place in → OPERA, particularly in the concept of the *Gesamtkunstwerk* developed by R. Wagner through intensive study of the ancient drama.

In the intellectual life of 19th cent. Germany, the tragedy itself was more or less replaced by the many philosophical theories about the nature of the tragic [12]. Greek tragedy was the starting point, but the search was for a clearly modern typical metaphysical category to describe the human condition within the world, with the result that from Schiller to Nietzsche, via Schelling, Hegel and Schopenhauer, the concept of what defined the tragic became more and more removed from tragedy itself. The locus of the tragic was life; it was no longer a literary genre. However, this gave also rise to the question to what extent Greek tragedies were truly 'tragic' in this new understanding of the term, a question which still occupies modern interpretations of tragedies.

In other respects, too, reflections on the theory of art were based on ancient art and literature. While a philologist wrote a history of literature, a 'real' philosopher of this period was supposed to write a work on aesthetics, which would be mainly concerned with the analysis of ancient genres. Hegel's pioneering combination of a historical approach and philosophical rigour had resulted in a cross-fertilization, but also to a degree of schematism. Philosophy as an academic discipline devoted a lot of space to the study and analysis of ancient philosophy, but mainly in the form of a *Philosophiegeschichte*, a 'history of philosophy' typical for German university philosophers. A reception of ancient philosophical positions in which the issues themselves were addressed, independently further developed or even transcended, is mainly found in philosophical outsiders such as Schopenhauer (Plato's theory of ideas), Marx (ancient → ATOMISM) and Nietzsche (→ APOLLONIAN/DIONYSIAN).

G. ART AND ARCHITECTURE

Similar trends in the reception of Antiquity to those in literature are also evident in painting. Here, too, 18th cent. (Neo-)Classicism still continued into the early decades of the 19th cent., but over the years, the interest in Antiquity declined noticeably (with the exception of the orbit of the Academies of Art). The reason for this may not just have been a German rejection of French Classicism, but also the increasing desire of artists/painters to liberate themselves from (court) commissions with their insistence on a propagandistic instrumentalization of Antiquity. Romanticism, Realism and Impressionism are thus united in their preference for modern subjects as opposed to Classical tradition. It is symptomatic that the Nazarenes revived the tradition of a German artists' colony in Rome, but one that turned its back on Antiquity and focused on the Middle Ages. By contrast, ancient sculpture continued to thrive in German sculptural art, possible because of this genre's greater public impact. Amongst its main representatives at the beginning of the century was H. Dannekker, a friend of Schiller and Goethe and sculptor at the Württemberg court. Dannecker established an important collection of antiquities in Stuttgart, but among his contemporaries, he was mainly famous for his antiquizing portrait busts and statues from Greek mythology. The work of J.G. Schadow, the most important Prussian sculptor (→ PRUSSIA), was continued by his pupil Chr. D. Rauch. Whereas these three artists were still firmly rooted in Neo-Classicism, R. Begas represented the art concept of a new era: art was no longer committed to Winckelmann's ideal of form and harmony, the ancient heritage was used more freely, but often also coarsened. Begas was instrumental in introducing ancient motifs to the Neo-Baroque; with his monumental statues, he became the most important sculptor of the new German empire. This trend was countered to some extent by the Munich artist A. Hildebrandt with his return to statues of male nudes.

However, in the eyes of the wider public, the greatest visual impact of ancient art was on architecture. G.'s great Classicistic architects gained national and international recognition. K. F. Schinkel shaped the appearance of Prussia's capital, Berlin, in a similar Classicist way as L. v. Klenze did that of Philhellenist Munich; the latter had also designed the Walhalla near Regensburg, the hall of fame for great German minds in imitation of the → PARTHENON. Architectural Classicism affected all of G. → ARCHITECTURAL COPIES/ CITATIONS from Antiquity (columns, → TEMPLES, → TRIUMPHAL ARCHES) continued to dominate the architectural style of public, representational buildings, but were also applied to bourgeois residences. Ancient motifs were used particularly lavishly and with an openly political message in the interior decoration and painting of many buildings (mostly in form of allegories or historical images).

H. ARCHAEOLOGY

In addition to Classical Philology with its dominant position in German culture throughout the century, Classical Archaeology entered into the awareness of a wider public during the last third of the 19th cent. From 1871, H. Schliemann's excavations in → MYCENA, Tiryns und → TROY, though sharply criticized by experts, had awakened a great enthusiasm for Classical Antiquity and its legends. By contrast, professional archaeology, which rejected Schliemann as an outsider, owed its rise as a 'major academic discipline' (*Großwissenschaft*) to the efforts of E. Curtius [10. 75–115], who, from 1852 on, had used his links to the Prussian court together with his public appeal to raise sponsorship for archaeological projects abroad. To that end, Curtius combined the ideal of a pure science with the anticipated gain in national prestige. Thus, Curtius did indeed successfully raise the required funds for the excavations which began in 1875, but he also laid archaeology open to the influence of the state. The German Empire used its cultural diplomacy to strengthen its positions in the Greek-Turkish region, archaeology thus became a 'science of conquest' (*Eroberungswissenschaft*). The aggressive excavation and museum policy was also used for the nation's self-representation and -affirmation: the superiority of German science and culture was to be demonstrated to the world, and the expected spectacular findings were to ensure that the Berlin museums ranked equal with those in → ROME, → PARIS and → LONDON.

However, the results of the excavations in → OLYMPIA (from 1875), → PERGAMUM (from 1878), → PRIENE (from 1895) and → MILETUS (from 1899) did not quite meet these high expectations. Instead of monumental statues from the Classical period, they unearthed mainly artifacts, deemed inferior, from lesser known periods such as the Archaic and the Hellenistic period. This forced archaeology to abandon its last ambitions for a primary aesthetic artistic analysis and to concentrate on trying to cope with the masses of finds through

an ever greater refinement of technical methods and the development of a appropriate → STYLISTIC ANALYSIS. This resulted in archaeology becoming more scientific, technical and bureaucratic. Even though archaeologists feared problems in presenting their results to a wider public, the latter's reaction was on the whole very positive, e.g. with regards to the → PERGAMUM ALTAR. Even Humanist education, threatened by school reforms, was revived by the grand-scale representation of the visual dimension of Classical Antiquity; there was an increasing demand for "visual instruction" (*Anschauungsunterricht*) about Classical Antiquity [10. 142–151].

The wave of enthusiasm even affected the highest social circles. Although, in his speech at the 1890 educational conference, Emperor Wilhelm II had radically denied any justification of Classical education, he insisted in 1911 on personally attending an excavation of the Artemis temple on Corfu, during which the impressive Gorgon-Medusa pediment was uncovered. The Greek island had become the emperor's favourite holiday residence after his purchase in 1908 of the Achilleum, previously the summer palace of the Austrian empress Elisabeth. Surrounded by numerous Classicist statues and frescos, he indulged in his adoration of Achilles, the greatest of Greek heroes, until this dream, too, was shattered by the outbreak of the First World War.

→ DEUTSCHES ARCHÄOLOGISCHES INSTITUT

1 H.-J. APEL, ST. BITTNER, Humanistische Schulbildung 1890–1945, 1994   2 R. BECHTLE, Wege nach Hellas. Studien zum Griechenlandbild deutscher Reisender, 1959   3 K. CHRIST, Aspekte der Antike-Rezeption in der deutschen Altertumswissenschaft des 19. Jahrhunderts, in: Id., A. MOMIGLIANO (eds.), L'Antichità nell'Ottocento in Italia e Germania, 1988, 21–37   4 FLASHAR   5 CH. FÜHR, Gelehrter Schulmann – Oberlehrer – Studienrat. Zum sozialen Aufstieg der Philologen, in: W. CONZE, J. KOCKA (eds.), Bildungsbürgertum im 19. Jahrhundert I, 1985, 417–457   6 M. FUHRMANN, Friedrich August Wolf, in: DVjS 33, 1959, 187–236   7 A. GRAFTON, Polyhistor into Philolog. Notes on the Transformation of German Classical Scholarship 1780–1850, in: History of Univ. 3, 1983, 159–192   8 A. HEUSS, Institutionalisierung der Alten Geschichte (1989), in: GS Bd. 3, 1938–1970   9 M. LANDFESTER, Humanismus und Gesellschaft im 19. Jahrhundert: Untersuchungen zur politischen und gesellschaftlichen Bedeutung der humanistischen Bildung in Deutschland, 1988   10 S. MARCHAND, Down from Olympus. Archaeology and Philhellenism in Germany 1750–1970, 1996   11 G. W. MOST, Vom Nutzen und Nachteil der Antike für das Leben. Zur modernen deutschen Selbstfindung anhand der alten Griechen, in: Human. Bildung 19, 1996, 35–52   12 Id., Il Tragico (planned)   13 F. PAULSEN, Geschichte des gelehrten Unterrichts II, ³1925   14 W. RÜEGG, Die Antike als Leitbild der deutschen Gesellschaft des 19. Jahrhunderts, in: Id., Bedrohte Lebensordnung, 1978, 93–105.

MARTIN HOLTERMANN

V. The 20th Century (after 1918)
A. 1918–1933 B. 1933–1945 C. The Federal
Republic of Germany

A. 1918–1933

The lost war, the revolutions of 1917 and 1918/19, and the political turmoil of the 1920s were experienced as a universal crisis, which also affected academia. The representatives of Ancient Studies felt particularly threatened by this crisis; they saw themselves challenged as much by Spengler's cultural pessimism as by the primacy of German culture, proclaimed by national völkisch circles with their emphasis on Germanic roots as well as the Prussian school reforms of 1925 (under the direction of H. Richert). The influence of the new workers' parties and their call for a comprehensive school boded hardly well for the traditional Humanist gymnasium with its already shaken position.

Against this backdrop, a new generation of philologists attempted to transcend → HISTORISM and to develop a new understanding of Classical Antiquity. P. Friedländer's 1921 letter to his teacher Wilamowitz can be read as a private manifesto for this new thinking, in which he rejected the historical ideal of science in favour of new idols such as Nietzsche, Wölfflin, Burckhardt and George [6]. The protagonist of this movement was W. Jaeger, a pupil of Wilamowitz and from 1921 his successor [5]. Inspired by Nietzsche, Jaeger's main focus was on the meaning of Antiquity for the present time, but in contrast with Nietzsche, he placed an increasing emphasis on its political and ethical force ('Paideia'). The Classicistic programme of this → THIRD HUMANISM with its obvious links to the educational concept of German Classicism (Herder, Schiller, W. von Humboldt) attempted to reconcile the idealizing Neo-Humanist view of Antiquity with 19th cent. scholarly positivism and to restore Ancient Studies to their traditional leading role within the Humanities as an influential cultural and social force. Furthermore, it wanted to make its contribution towards a renewal of the present against a modernity, seen as sick, which was to be healed with the aid of the Hellenic ideals. This elitist dream of such an existential encounter with Antiquity also found its followers among poets such as Hofmannsthal (e.g. Vermächtnis der Antike, ['Heritage of Antiquity'] in: Die Antike 4, 1928, 99–102).

Jaeger advanced his ideas with the help of societies and journals which he had brought into being, in particular the Gesellschaft für antike Kultur, founded in 1924 and its journal Die Antike (1925–44), also the journal Neue Philologische Untersuchungen (1926–37). In 1925, he initiated the Fachtagung der Klassischen Altertumswissenschaften, an association of German speaking representatives of Ancient Studies. The famous 4th Annual Congress, held in Naumburg in 1930 on the subject of 'Das Problem des Klassischen und die Antike' ('Antiquity and the Problem of the Classical') was completely dominated by Jaeger's programme and contributed significantly to Jaeger's suc-

cess, particularly among the younger generation of Greek scholars in G. The Deutsche Altphilologen-Verband, also founded in 1925 with Jaeger as vice-chairman, disseminated these ideas among the teaching profession.

Other than Jaeger, little heed was paid to other voices such as B. Snell or K. von Fritz, who argued for a historical understanding of ancient culture with a recognition not only of its timeless importance, but also of its historical dependence, its distance and its strangeness. Under the influence of R. Heinze, later also E. Fraenkel and F. Klingner, Latin Studies also developed a new view of its subject [28]. No longer did it view Roman culture as a mere transmitter of the Greek, but focused increasingly on the characteristics and originality of the Roman people, on Romanness. The 'renewal' of Rome and of the old Roman virtues of the Augustan age also galvanized poets and writers such as R. Borchardt and R.A. Schröder as well as scholars such as E.R. Curtius and L. Curtius. At least some of them responded positively to Mussolini's attempts at portraying himself as Augustus' political heir. This was reflected in the journalistic accompaniment to the German-Italian celebrations of Virgil's bimillennial birthday in 1930. ;

However, Jaeger remained the dominant force of that period. With their 'conservative-revolutionary' analysis of the contemporary political and cultural crisis and their almost blind hope in the healing forces of Antiquity and a new authoritarian order, Jaeger and his followers unwillingly lent a helping hand to the new National-Socialist ideology [15]. The same applied to Theodor Haecker's influential essay Vergil, Vater des Abendlandes ('Virgil, father of the Occident', 1931), a Catholic-conservative interpretation of the Augustan poet which detects in Virgil's imperial and Augustan theology the foundation of Constantine-Christian political theology. Despite his spiritual distance to → NATIONAL SOCIALISM, Haecker's interpretation further fuelled the apocalyptic mood of that era. A calamitous proximity to Third Reich ideology was particularly evident in his plea for an authoritarian corporative state and his vision of a 'clerico-fascist' empire [10].

The circle around the poet Stefan George, which despite its elitist behaviour gained influence at universities (particularly in Frankfurt), searched for an individual spiritual form of Greekness, its very essence (Gestalt), which transcended all historical explanation. The yearning for a spiritual-political leader found its expression in the adoration which George and his followers paid to Alexander, Caesar and foremost to Plato [18; 35]. In Nietzsche's footsteps, the George Circle conjured up the ecstatic force of the Dyonisiac (e.g. R. Borchardt, Bacchische Epiphanie; Th. Däubler, Päan und Dithyrambos, both 1924; R. Pannwitz, Meinungen des Gottes Dionysos, 1929) or proclaimed a Greek Christ who in his deepest soul was at one with Dionysus. W. F. Otto attempted to develop a scholarly foundation for this Dyonisiac spirit, initially in Die

Götter Griechenlands (1929), and later more so in *Dionysos* (1933), a missionary manifesto against the Christian world and in favour of Nietzsche's god [7].

Ancient Studies were also influenced by the study of folklore as pursued by scholars such as K. Meuli or O. Weinreich and publicized in the *Archiv für Religionswissenschaft* (1898–1941/42), in the 1920s and 1930s a journal of considerable impact and importance [8], and also by → PSYCHOANALYSIS with forged a link to the Humanities in the journal *Imago* (1912–37).

The Warburg Library, founded in Hamburg in 1919 by Aby Warburg and centering on cultural history, is unique as an institution in its international contribution towards research on the reception of Classical Antiquity. Scholars such as E. Panofsky and E. Wind were products of the Warburg school; its series of talks (*Vorträge der Bibliothek Warburg* (1921–31)) and studies (*Studien der Bibliothek Warburg* (1922–32)) were enormously influential. In 1933, the institute moved to its present location in London (*Warburg Institute*) [22].

The most important works in the 'musical' reception of Classical Antiquity of this period belonged to the music theatre, a genre which – after a break of almost a century – in the 1920s once again became intensely involved with ancient mythology and Greek tragedies. Richard Strauss continued his co-operation with Hugo Hofmannsthal which had begun with *Elektra* (first performed in 1909) and *Ariadne auf Naxos* (first performed in 1912): 1928 saw the premiere of the *Ägyptische Helena*. Other operatic composers were his Viennese contemporaries E.Wellesz (*Alkestis*, based on Euripides/Hofmannsthal, 1924; *Die Bakchantinnen*, after Euripides, 1931) and E. Krenek (*Orpheus und Eurydike*, based on Kokoschka, 1926; *Leben des Orest*, 1930). In 1924, W. Braunfels enjoyed considerable success with his musical version of Aristophanes' *The Birds*. The reception of ancient material was an important part of the musical avant-garde, as evident in the contemporary works of Strawinsky, Milhaud, Honegger, Satie and others.

In the fine arts, sculptors such as F. Klimsch, G. Kolbe, R. Scheibe and R. Sintenis named many of their female sculptures and torsos after female figures from ancient mythology (e.g. Demeter and Aphrodite, Daphne and maenad) or allegories (e.g. Flora, Aurora or Nike). G. Marcks began his lifelong productive involvement with ancient mythology and its characters [37]. Mythological, literary and historical subjects from Classical Antiquity are occasionally found in paintings by M. Slevogt and L. Corinth, but also by C. Rohlfs, P. Klee and M. Ernst. 'Modern Classicism', which after the end of World War One had risen to great importance in France, Spain and Italy, had but limited effect in G. [3].

In architecture, the Classicist style linked with the name of P. Behrens (→ CLASSICISM), which had dominated the early years of the century, initially continued after the war and then returned as early as the late 1920s as a conservative reaction again the modern avant-garde, only to be monopolized not much later by the monumental Neo-Classicism of the totalitarian regimes in G., Italy and the Soviet Union [36].

The theatre of the Weimar Republic saw significant productions of ancient plays such as M. Reinhardt's *Orestie* (1919), J. Tralow's *Orestie* (1920/23) and L. Jessner's *Ödipus* (1929). The rediscovery of Hölderlin's Sophocles adaptations for the stage was even more important from a theatrical-historical point of view.

The literature of the Weimar years was inspired by Antiquity in many different ways. There is hardly any among the leading writers of that age who did not either continue with his creative involvement with Antiquity (Rilke and George, Hofmannsthal and Hauptmann) or began to work with ancient material, thoughts, motifs and figures (Benn, Brecht). This is evident in the plays of that period which repeatedly took recourse to ancient myths or their literary adaptation in ancient Greek literature (e.g. O. Kokoschka, *Orpheus und Eurydike*, 1919; F. Werfel, *Bocksgesang*, 1921; K. Kraus, *Wolkenkuckucksheim*, 1923; Hofmannsthal, *Achilles auf Skyros*, 1925 and *Die ägyptische Helena*, 1928; H.H. Jahnn, *Medea*, 1926); the same also applies to → LYRIC POETRY, where thematic and formal influences of Antiquity abound (Brecht, George, Hofmannsthal, Rilke, R.A. Schröder, C. Spitteler and, above all, Benn). Somewhat erratically placed within the literary landscape of the era are three stories by Kafka, *Das Schweigen der Sirenen* (1917; Brechts reply in *Odysseus und die Sirenen*, ca. 1933), *Prometheus* (1918) and *Poseidon* (1920), which ironically and sometimes even grotesquely alienated and annihilated the myth.

The 'historical novel', originally a product of the 19th cent. to satisfy the Wilhelminian and post-Wilhelminian educated classes' desire for entertainment, bloomed during the Weimar years. However, historical accuracy, a principle held in such high regard by Victor Hugo and Walter Scott, increasingly gave way to political updating, in which an anachronistic Antiquity became a biased reflection of the present, sometimes from a Socialist point of view (e.g. Klaus Mann, *Alexander*, 1930), more often, though, from a conservative-national perspective (e.g. M. Jelusich, *Caesar*, 1929; H. Heyck, *Sulla*, 1931).

B. 1933–1945

Soon after Hitler's rise to power, his policy of *Gleichschaltung* ('forcing into line') also affected the Humanist gymnasium and the entire range of university disciplines involved in Ancient Studies. National-Socialist school curricula and research programmes had a particularly pronounced impact on Ancient History but also affected Archaeology and Classical Philology. Jaeger's academically sound 'Third Humanism' was joined by an image of Antiquity that was mainly based on the pseudo-scientific racial theories of A. Rosenberg (*Der Mythus des 20. Jahrhunderts* ['The myth of the 20th cent.']) and H.F.K. Günther (*Rassenkunde des hellenischen und römischen Volkes*)['Racial anthropology of the Greek and Roman people'] who aimed to develop in detail and underpin scientifically Hitler's much emphasized Aryan *Rassengemeinschaft* ('racial community') of Greeks and Germans [1].

However, neither this development nor further restrictions imposed on the traditional gymnasium, which after 1938 had been reduced to the status of a 'special school', had as much impact on science and academia as the personnel 'purges' at the universities. Many eminent scholars in Ancient Studies emigrated, mostly to Britain and the US, e.g. the archaeologist M. Bieber, ancient historians such as E. Bickermann, V. Ehrenberg and E. Stein (F. Münzer died in 1942 in the Theresienstadt concentration camp), the Classical philologists E. Fraenkel, H. Fränkel, P. Friedländer, K. von Fritz, F. Jacoby, P. Maas, E. Norden, R. Pfeiffer and F. Solmsen, to name but the most important. In 1936 W. Jaeger accepted the offer of a chair at the University of Chicago [26]. The great age of of Ancient Studies in German academia thus came to an irrevocable end.

Hitler's admiration for Greece (particularly Sparta) and Rome is much documented. It is evident in his written work, but also in the form and content of many of his public speeches. He held Greek architecture in high regard and was inspired by Pericles, who had commissioned the → PARTHENON, to develop his own plans for reshaping Berlin as the capital of the Reich. Both in architecture (e.g. A. Speer) [33] and sculpture (e.g. A. Breker; eminent sculptors of the Weimar era such as Klimsch, Kolbe or Scheibe also allowed themselves to the taken over by the new masters), Hitler's regime linked back to ancient forms, as it also did in the organization of the large party convention and the Olympic Games of 1936. The festival production was the *Orestie* in the translation by Wilamowitz directed by L. Müthel at the Staatliches Schauspielhaus Berlin (theatre director: G. Gründgens). The Hellenic *gymnasion* experienced a revival in the cult of the athletic body (e.g. L. Riefenstahl).

Among the visual artists, mention should be made of G. Marcks, who retreated into 'internal exile', and particularly Max Beckmann who created a number of important works on mythical subjects while in exile: *Mars und Venus* (1939), *Prometheus* (1942), *Odysseus und Kalypso* (1943) as well as the great triptych *Perseus* (1940/41).

Richard Strauss continued to work on ancient motifs and material: after Hofmannsthal's death (1929), J. Gregor wrote the libretti of his operas *Daphne* (first performed in 1938) and *Die Liebe der Danae* (first performed in 1944). However, the most influential event in the contemporary musical reception of Antiquity was the first performance of Carl Orff's *Carmina Burana* (1937), which rose to greater and greater success, especially after 1945. This success also benefited Orff's *Catulli Carmina* (1943).

In the literary reception of Antiquity, National-Socialist ideology is particularly evident in the historical novel, a genre of continued popularity (e.g. M. Jelusich,

Hannibal; G. Birkenfeld, *Leben und Taten des Caesar Augustus*, both 1934; H.F. Blunck, *König Geiserich* ('King Geiseric') 1936; H. Benrath, *Die Kaiserin Galla Placidia*, 1937; R. Kassner, *Der Gottmensch*, 1938), but also in drama (e.g. C. Langenbeck, *Alexander*, 1934; E. Bacmeister, *Kaiser Konstantins Taufe*, 1937; E.W. Müller, *Der Untergang Karthagos*, 1938; B. von Heiseler, *Caesar*, 1941; H. Baumann, *Alexander*, 1941). Benn's essay *Dorische Welt* (1934) evoked a distorted image of Sparta, hailing Apollo as a pre-Fascist god and Sparta as the prototype of the new National-Socialist state.

Travel literature about journeys to Greece took on a new face during World War Two (esp. E. Jünger, *Gärten und Straßen* 1942; Erhart Kästner, *Griechenland*, 1942; revised as *Ölberge, Weinberge*, 1953; F.G. Jünger, *Wanderungen auf Rhodos*, 1943). The reality of the war was firmly pushed aside by a strictly Classicistic view, which also glorified German soldiery against the backdrop of Homeric heroism. ;

Works with an outspoken democratic or socialist emphasis were mainly written by exiled authors: among them Feuchtwanger with his Hitler novel *Der falsche Nero* (1936) and his Josephus trilogy (*Der jüdische Krieg, Die Söhne, Der Tag wird kommen*, 1932–45) and Brecht with his didactic play *Die Horatier und die Kuriatier* (1936), his unfinished novel *Die Geschäfte des Herrn Julius Cäsar* (1937/39), his Lucullus plays (*Die Trophäen des Lukullus* and *Das Verhör des Lukullus*, 1939)m the planned *Pluto-Revue* (based on Aristophanes) as well as several of his poems. In his Demeter trilogy, H. Broch tried to counter the male-heroic National-Socialist *Blut und Boden* ('blood and soil') ideology with a female-humane myth inspired by Antiquity (*Die Verzauberung*, 1935/36). His later novel *Der Tod des Vergil* (*The Death of Virgil*, 1945) is a meditation on the role of the artist in a totalitarian system and on death. The novel's humane psychology links it to Th. Mann's tetralogy *Joseph und seine Brüder* (*Joseph and his Brothers*, 1933–43), a cathartic 'descent into hell' through the 'well of the past'. Ancient mythology was also the subject of two important philosophical outlines written in exile, Bloch's *Prinzip Hoffnung* (*The Principle of Hope*, 1936–47), and the *Dialektik der Aufklärung* (*Dialectic of Enlightenment*) by Horkheimer and Adorno (1944/47).

For authors (and visual artists) who remained and worked in G., mythological Antiquity was anything but a noncommittal retreat. Serious reflections on past values (e.g. Th. von Scheffer, *Kyprien*, 1934) was joined by thoughts on the role of art (e.g. G. Kaiser, *Pygmalion*, 1943/44); Christian hope for life after death (e.g. Ö. v. Horváth, *Pompeji*, 1937) was expressed alongside pacifist yearning (e.g. G. Kaiser, *Bellerophon*, 1944). A late rejection of the Third Reich is evident in some of G. Benn's wartime work (esp. *Kunst und Drittes Reich*, 1941) as well as in that of R. Borchardt (*Jamben*). A similar interpretation has been applied to Hauptmann's *Atridae* tetralogy *Iphigenie in Aulis, Agamemnons Tod, Elektra, Iphigenie in Delphi* (1941–48).

C. THE FEDERAL REPUBLIC OF GERMANY

In the divided G. after 1948, the fundamental differences between the two social systems and their intellectual foundations soon resulted in very different developments in all cultural areas, affecting the educational and academic importance of Antiquity as much as its artistic reception (→ GDR).

In spite of the loss of eminent scholars of Ancient Studies and the bitter realization of the ideological corruptibility during the Third Reich of quite a few of the discipline's representatives both at schools and at universities, Antiquity experienced a boom during the first two post-war decades. The return to the ancient and Christian roots of European culture in reaction to the ideology of National-Socialism resulted in a renaissance of the Humanist ideal of education (this spirit governed the journal *Antike und Abendland* started by B. Snell in 1945 or the *Bibliothek der Alten Welt*, set up in Switzerland in 1948), whose most influential representatives were still rooted in the Third Humanism (W. Schadewaldt). The rapid increase in student numbers resulted in a considerable expansion of Classical Philology departments; more pupils learned Greek and Latin at school than in any preceding period. With the foundation of the *Mommsen-Gesellschaft*, an association of scholars within the various fields of Ancient Studies (1950), and the re-establishment of the *Deutscher Altphilologen-Verband* (1952), academia and schools created important bodies to represent their interests.

The social and cultural development of the 1960s called into question Antiquity's long undisputed relevance for coping with contemporary issues. The significant expansion of the educational system and the student movement with its critical attitude towards any tradition threatened to marginalize all subjects within the umbrella of Ancient Studies at both schools and universities. The teaching and study of Greek was (and is) particularly hit by this development.

A fundamental discussion ensued about the modern role of Classical Philology, mainly voiced at the 1970 Freiburg conference of the *Mommsen-Gesellschaft* (M. Fuhrmann, H. Tränkle) [16; 21]. The controversy calmed down in the 1980s and 1990s; however, the influence of Anglo-American academic life, as well as the ongoing decline of Greek at schools and universities continued to cause disquiet. The noticeable increase in the interest in the history of 20th cent. Ancient Studies and related subjects may be taken as an indication for the seriousness with which the question is taken as to how and 'to what end' Antiquity is studied these days.

Compared with earlier periods, Antiquity and its creative appropriation in music, art and literature was of lesser importance in West German cultural life. Individual events such as Peter Stein's production of Aeschylus' *Orestie* (Berlin 1980) or the exhibition devoted to Emperor Augustus (Berlin 1988) generated passing excitement and took over the feature pages of the national press and the cultural programmes of

public service television and radio; however, nowadays one cannot speak of a profound impact of the world of ancient Greece and Rome on the public mind. The great extent to which the cultural landscape has changed since the early years of the 20th cent. can be gleaned from the fact that such an important analysis of Antiquity as H. Blumenberg's *Arbeit am Mythos* (1979; Engl. ed. *Work on Myth*, 1989) remains almost isolated within the current philosophical debate. This finding is not altered by the fact that non-fiction books on ancient topics or travel guides to the ruins of Rome and Greece can still count on an interested readership.

In music, R. Strauss' opera *Des Esels Schatten* (*The Donkey's Shadow*) from 1947/48 (first performed in 1964) and E. Krenek' two operas *Pallas Athene weint* (1955) and *Der goldene Bock* (1964) both took up their composer's earlier reception of Antiquity. In his *Penelope* of 1954, Rolf Liebermann composed an → OPERA on the then current topic of the return home; this was followed four decades later by *Freispruch für Medea*. Newer developments in music were reflected in the free musical adaptations of ancient tragedies by H.W. Henze (*Die Bassariden*, based on Euripides, 1966), A. Reimann (*Troades*, based on Euripides/Werfel, 1986) and, above all, by W. Rihm (*Ödipus*, a free adaptation based on Sophocles with texts by Nietzsche and Heiner Müller, 1987; his cello concert *Styx und Lethe* was first performed in 1998). Carl Orff's attempts to recreate the ancient → TRAGEDY out of the spirit of his music – *Antigonä* (Sophocles/Hölderlin, 1949), *Oedipus der Tyrann* (Sophocles/Hölderlin, 1959) and *Prometheus* (Aeschylos, Greek text, 1968) – are more interesting from a theatrical-historical point of view than a musical one [27]. Worthy of mention are also the ballets *Lysistrata* by B. Blacher (1960) and *Orpheus* by H.W. Henze (1976) and the musical settings of works of Sappho by W. Killmayer (1960) and of Horace by H. Vogt (1970). Already in 1951, Orff had written his third and last choral work *Trionfo di Afrodite* with ancient texts (Sappho, Euripides, Catullus) [9].

In the visual arts, the bond with ancient forms and subjects decreased further, not surprising in view of the developments in modern art. However, there are quite frequent (often indirect) thematic references to Antiquity in the works of sculptors like G. Marcks (latest in *Prometheus mit Adler*, 1981), H. Arp (e.g.. *Demeter*, 1960; *Die drei Grazien*, 1961), B. Heiliger (e.g. *Niobe*, 1959; *Auge der Nemesis*, 1981) or G. Seitz, who moved from Halle to Hamburg in 1958 as successor to G. Marcks at the Hamburg Academy of Art (e.g. *Der Wählerische*, 1956; *Paris*, 1965; *Entwurf zur Großen Danae*, 1967) as well as in that of well-known painters such as O. Kokoschka, HAP Grieshaber, J. Grützke, P. Wunderlich, M. Lüpertz, J. Beuys [38] and A. Kiefert. The modern architecture of the New Functionalism displays hardly any links to Graeco-Roman architecture; only postmodernist architects have started playing with citations from the ancient repository of forms again [20].

Greek tragedies, but also the classical plays of the European reception of Antiquity, are still regularly performed at German theatres. Productions such as H. Heyme's *König Ödipus* and *Ödipus auf Kolonos* (Köln 1968), K. Grubers *Bakchen* (Berlin 1974) or P. Stein's *Orestie* (Berlin 1980) have made theatrical history [13]. The reproduction of Greek sacrificial rites based on Wagner, Nietzsche, Freud and the history of ancient religion, staged since the 1960s by the Viennese 'happening artist' (*Aktionskünstler*) Hermann Nitsch and his *orgien mysterien theater*, are happenings in an antiquizing pose [34].

However, the modern reception of Antiquity had its most profound effect in literature. Post-war German authors were clearly concerned to re-establish a link to the international modern literary scene after the barbarism of National-Socialism; it is also likely that they registered far more sensitively the seducibility of Humanism than education and academia did. For a long time, the literary debate was dominated by 'ancient' works of foreign authors such as Anouilh's *Antigone* (translated into German in 1946), O'Neill's *Mourning Becomes Electra* (translated into German in 1947), Sartre's *Les Mouches* (translated into German in 1948) and Camus' *Le Mythe de Sisyphe* (translated into German in 1950). In German literature, ancient subjects and motifs at first appeared on a larger scale in the context of dealing with the traumatic experiences of war and home-coming, of personal guilt and collective crime. These contemporary events were mainly reflected in texts on the wider topic of the Trojan War (e.g. B. Heiseler, *Der Bogen des Philoktet*, R. Bayr, *Agamemnon*; H.E. Nossack, *Kassandra*; all 1948) and Odysseus, who had returned home a stranger (e.g. H.W. Geissler, *Odysseus und die Frauen*, 1947; L. Feuchtwanger, *Odysseus und die Schweine*, 1948; F. Mayröcker, *Die Sirenen des Odysseus* and *Nausikaa*, 1956; E. Schnabel, *Der sechste Gesang*, 1956; W. Jens, *Das Testament des Odysseus*, 1957).

Hades and the descent into hell are the topics of H. Kasack's *Die Stadt hinter dem Strom*, H.E. Nossack's *Nekyia* and Th. Mann's *Doktor Faustus* (all 1947). The distortion of young minds as a result of the 'Classical education' provided by the → HUMANIST GYMNASIUM of the post-Wilhelmian and National-Socialist era was highlighted by H. Böll (*Wanderer kommst du nach Spa ...,* [*Stranger Bring Word to the Spartans We...*], 1950) and later A. Andersch (*Der Vater eines Mörders*, 1980). Into this group also belong I.Bachmann's satire *Das Lächeln der Sphinx* (1949) or Arno Schmidt's Hellenic tales (*Gadir oder Erkenne dich selbst* and *Enthymesis oder W.I.E.H.*, both 1949; *Alexander oder Was ist Wahrheit*, 1959). The fate of artists during the years of Adenauer's chancellorship is the topic of Schmidt's Orpheus story *Caliban über Setebos* (1964).

For most of the well-known prose authors (such as Böll and Lenz, Grass and Walser) and playwrights (such as Frisch and Dürrenmatt, Bernhardt and Krötz, Kipphardt and Walser), Antiquity played but a marginal role in their early decades. Nonetheless, quite a number of successful texts were produced, some of which can be grouped thematically. The explosive power of the Greek tragedy is embodied in Sophocles' *Antigone*, and Brecht is not the only modern author to take this up. The famous first stasimon is parodied by Dürrenmatt (*Der Besuch der alten Dame* [*The Visit*], 1957) and Frisch (*Biedermann und die Brandstifter*, [*The Firebugs / The Fireraisers*] 1958); R. Hochhuth wrote a *Berliner Antigone* (1966/75); the sudden topicality of Sophocles' play during the years when the Baader-Meinhof Rote Armee Fraktion dominated the German political scene, is dealt with in Rainer Fassbinder's film *Deutschland im Herbst* (1977). Grete Weil grappled with the figure of Antigone in her autobiographical novel *Meine Schwester Antigone* (1980); the initial identification with the character was followed by a rejection of her humane credo: 'Nicht mitzulieben, mitzuhassen bin ich da' ("My nature is not to join in love but in hatred") – the mythical figure is lost for answers faced with the suffering of the Shoah. The story of a modern Oedipus is told in Frisch's *Homo faber* (1957). The peace movement and Pacifism of the 1970s and 1980s gave great popularity to Aristophanes' peace maker Lysistrate (R. Hochhuth, *Lysistrate und die Nato*, 1973; Ch. Brückner, *Du irrst, Lysistrate!*, 1983; E. Fried, *Lysistrate*, 1985; W. Jens, *Die Friedensfrau*, 1986).

In literary reception, Rome is generally overshadowed by Greece; at times, however, its history becomes a mirror for modern developments. The role of the political intellectual in inhospitable times is highlighted by M. Brod (*Armer Cicero*, 1955); Grass' play *Die Plebejer proben den Aufstand* ([*The Plebeians Rehearse the Uprising*], 1966) centres around a performance of Shakespeare's *Coriolanus*; Caesar's death is a topic of speculation for W. Jens (*Die Verschwörung*, 1969); P. Rühmkorf's *Was heißt hier Volsinii?* (1969) is a satirical view of capitalism. Later examples are R. Schneider's *Octavius und Kleopatra* (1972) and M. Walser's *Nero läßt grüßen* (1989). Late Antiquity as a a time of decline and destruction whetted historical curiosity, evident e.g. in Döblin's *Pilgerin Aetheria* (1947), Dürrenmatt's *Romulus der Große* (1950/57), Arno Schmidt's *Kosmas* (1959), H.E. Nossack's *Das Testament des Lucius Eurinus* (1964) or St. Andres' *Die Versuchung des Synesios* (1971).

In lyric poetry, Antiquity is constantly present, also and especially in the works of great poets such as C. Atabay, R. Ausländer, I. Bachmann, P. Celan, H. Domin, G. Eich, E. Fried, E. Jandl, M.L. Kaschnitz, K. Krolow, E. Meister or P. Rühmkorf [29]. During the 1980s and 1990s, the literary reception of Antiquity in prose and drama also gained noticeably in importance: in Peter Weiss's principal work *Die Ästhetik des Widerstands* (1975–81; *The Aesthetics of Resistance*, 2005), the mythical worker and hero Hercules represents the historical subject, the working class in general and its historical task of completing history in the resistance against Fascism regardless of its temporary failure. Botho Strauss developed ever new methods of integrating ancient subject and motifs into his plays: a modern Dionysus, who loses his intoxicating effect on humans, is the central figure in *Kalldewey, Farce* (1981); the fascination of Troy and the Atridae is evident in *Der Park* (1983) and *Die Fremdenführerin* (1986; *The Tourist Guide*, 1987); Medea appears in *Die Zeit und das Zimmer* ([*the Time and Place*], 1989); Odysseus' revenge is the subject of *Ithaka* (1996).

Various texts based on Sappho provide a female perspective on life (e.g. Ch. Brückner, *Vergeßt den Namen des Eisvogels nicht*, 1983; or H. Hegewisch, *Ich aber schlafe allein*, 1992). In her Demeter trilogy (*Herrin der Tiere, Über die Verhältnisse, Einander Kind*, 1986–90) B. Frischmuth transposed the myth of the mother goddess into contemporary Austria and examines it in its psychological, historical and mystical aspects. Several male and female authors tried to understand and exonerate Medea; the infanticide becomes a cipher for women's rebellion and struggle for self-determination (e.g. G. Tabori, *M*, 1985; W. Hilbig, *medium medea*, 1986; U. Haas, *Freispruch für Medea*, 1987, E. Jelinek, *Krankheit oder Moderne Frauen*, 1987; D. Nick, *Medea*, 1988; O. Rinne, *Medea*, 1988; Ch. Wolf, *Medea. Stimmen*, 1996) [11].

Several, only posthumously published texts show Hubert Fichte as an outstanding expert of Antiquity: a series of essays on ancient history and literature as well as the two plays *Ödipus auf Håknäss*, which deals with the tragic figure of Sophocles (*c.* 1960/61; published 1992), and *Ich bin ein Löwe. Und meine Eltern sind Eichen und Steine*, a cryptic homage to Empedocles (1985). The reception of ancient authors played an essential role in Peter Handke's literary works; his study of Lucretius is evident in *Langsame Heimkehr* (1979), of Pindar and Thucydides in *Kindergeschichte* (1981) and *Noch einmal für Thukydides* (1990), of Virgil's *Georgica* in *Der Chinese des Schmerzes* (1983) and of Greek tragedy in *Aischylos, Prometheus, gefesselt*, 1986.

The 1990s saw a renaissance of the historical novel, with G. Haef as its most sophisticated representative (*Hannibal*, 1989; *Alexander*, 1992/93; *Troja*, 1997). In addition, there were 'postmodern games' with mythology, whose lavish set-ups are often no more than facade (W. Wenger, *Die Manhattan Maschine*, 1992; S. Nadolny, *Ein Gott der Frechheit*; [1994; *God of Impertinence*, 1997] W. Schwab, *Troiluswahn und Cressidatheater*, 1994). Ch. Ransmayr's *Die letzte Welt* (1988; *The Last World*, 1990), an exercise in historical pessimism on the topic of Ovid's *Metamorphoses.*, is more likely to pass the test of time. The ancient hero that has attracted most modern reception- Odysseus – also invited similar interpretations, particularly evident in M. Köhlmeier's planned tetralogy on the hero (*Telemach*, 1995; *Kalypso*, 1997; *Tantalos*, 2000), but also in W. Grond's anthology entitled *Absolut Homer* (1995) with texts on the *Odyssey* by a number of authors. The enthusiastic reception for the books by Ransmayr, Köhlmeier oder Christa Wolf testifies to the myth's unbroken fascination.

1 H. J. APEL, S. BITTNER, Humanistische Schulbildung 1890–1945, 1994   2 G. BINDER, Altertumswissenschaft und altsprachlicher Unterricht in Deutschland 1933–1945, in: Id. (ed.), Saeculum Augustum I, 1987, 44–58   3 G. BOEHM et al. (eds.), Canto d'Amore. Klassizistische Moderne in Musik und bildender Kunst 1914–1935, 1996   4 E. BÖHRINGER, Der Caesar von Acireale, 1933   5 W. M. CALDER (ed.), Werner Jaeger Reconsidered: Illinois Class. Stud., Suppl. 3, 1992   6 Id., The Credo of a new generation, in: A&A 26, 1980, 90–102   7 H. CANCIK, Dionysos 1933, in: R. FABER, R. SCHLESIER (eds.), Die Restauration der Götter, 1986, 105–123   8 Id., Antike Volkskunde 1936, in: AU 25/3, 1982, 80–99   9 J. DRAHEIM, Vertonungen antiker Texte vom Barock bis zur Gegenwart, 1981   10 R. FABER, Roma aeterna, 1981   11 B. FEICHTINGER, Medea. Rehabilitation einer Kindsmörderin?, in: Grazer Beiträge 18, 1992, 205–234   12 La filologia greca e latina nel secolo XX. Atti del Congresso Internazionale, 3 Bde., 1989   13 FLASHAR   14 Id., (ed.), Altertumswissenschaft in den 20er Jahren, 1995 (bibliography)   15 A. FRITSCH, Dritter Humanismus und Drittes Reich, in: R. DITHMAR (ed.), Schule und Unterricht in der Endphase der Weimarer Republik, 1993, 152–175   16 M. FUHRMANN, H. TRÄNKLE, Wie klassisch ist die klassische Antike?, 1970   17 E. H. GOMBRICH, Aby Warburg, 1981   18 F. GUNDOLF, Caesar. Geschichte seines Ruhms, 1924   19 R. HERZOG, Antike-Usurpationen in der deutschen Belletristik seit 1866, in: A&A 23, 1977, 10–27   20 C. JENKS, Die Postmoderne. Der neue Klassizismus in Kunst und Architektur, 1987   21 W. JENS, Antiquierte Antike, 1971   22 R. KANY, Mnemosyne als Programm, 1987   23 S. KUNZE, Die Antike in der Musik des 20. Jahrhunderts (Thyssen-Vorträge 6), 1987   24 G. LOHSE, H. OHDE, Zum Verhältnis von Antike und deutscher Nachkriegsliteratur (...), in: Hephaistos 4, 1982, 139–170; 5/6, 1983/84, 163–226   25 V. LOSEMANN, Nationalsozialismus und Antike, 1977   26 W. LUDWIG, Amtsenthebung und Emigration klassischer Philologen: Würzburger Jbb. N.F. 12, 1986, 217–239   27 W. SCHADEWALDT, Carl Orff und die griechische Tragödie, in: Id., Hellas und Hesperien ²1970, 423–435   28 P. L. SCHMIDT, Die deutsche Latinistik vom Beginn bis in die 20er Jahre, in: H. FLASHAR (ed.), Altertumswissenschaften in den 20er Jahren, 1995, 115–182   29 B. SEIDENSTICKER, P. HABERMEHL (eds.), Unterm Sternbild des Hercules. Antikes in der Lyrik der Gegenwart, 1996   30 Id. (eds.), Antikerezeption in der deutschsprachigen Literatur der Gegenwart, in: AU 36/2, 1994   31 B. SEIDENSTICKER, Zur Antikerezeption in der deutschen Literatur nach 1945, in: Gymnasium 98, 1991, 420–453 (Lit.)   32 Id., Exempla. Römisches in der literarischen Antikerezeption nach 1945, in: Gymnasium 101, 1994, 7–42   33 A. SPEER, Architektur. Arbeiten 1933–42, 1978   34 E. STÄRK, Hermann Nitschs 'Orgien Mysterien Theater' und die 'Hysterie der Griechen', 1987   35 E. E. STARKE, Das Platonbild des George-Kreises, 1959   36 W. TEGETHOFF, Vom modernen Klassizismus zur klassischen Moderne, in: G. BOEHM et al. (eds.), Canto d'Amore. Klassizistische Moderne in Musik und bildender Kunst 1914–1935, 1996, 442–451   37 G. Marcks und die Antike (Exhibition catalogue), Bremen 1993   38 Beuys und die Antike, (Exhibition catalogue) Glyptothek München, 1993.

BERND PETER HABERMEHL SEIDENSTICKER

Getty-Museum see → MALIBU

Glossators
A. NAME B. GLOSSED TEXTS C. SCHOOLS
D. IMPORTANT AUTHORS E. WORKS F. HISTORY
OF RESEARCH

A. NAME

The name *glossator* is given to 12th and early 13th cent. law professors because they provided textbooks used for instruction with glosses as teaching aids. Law professors of the following period, however, are referred to by a different name: commentators. The name 'post-glossator' was also sometimes used because they were freed from the task of compiling their own glosses. By then, revised collections of instructional glosses with fixed texts had been published, and for each instructional text a certain collection of glosses had been established as standard (hence referred to as *glossa ordinaria*). At most, professors still wrote additional remarks (*additiones*) to the *glossa ordinaria* but no additional glosses.

B. GLOSSED TEXTS

Five groups of texts were used for instruction and therefore glossed: 1. The → DIGESTS and the other books of the *Corpus iuris civilis* of Emperor Justinian. 2. The *Decretum gratiani*, which consisted of a selection from canon law drawn from the Bible, works by ancient Church Fathers, conciliar decisions and papal letters. The first edition was compiled in the 1120s, the second was published in or shortly after 1139. The only facts known about the author are his name Gratianus, that he lived in central Italy and that he was sympathetic towards Roman church reform. 3. Various collections of excerpts from the *litterae decretales*. These were letters of popes about legal matters, among them especially the *Compilatio prima* (ca. 1190), the *secunda* (shortly after the *tertia*), the *tertia* (1210), the *quarta* (probably 1217), the *quinta* (1226) and the collection of decrees taken from it by Pope Gregory IX in 1234 (the *Liber extra*). 4. In northern Italy, the *Lombarda*, a collection of excerpts from laws of the Langobardic kingdom was glossed at the same time in independent, less famous schools. The *Libri feudorum* was glossed as well. This was a collection of laws and other legal texts along with commentaries on → FEUDAL LAW which had been revised numerous times. 5. In the Anglo-Norman-nic cultural realm, the *Corpus iuris civilis* was less well known; instead, three collections of excerpts from the latter were glossed there, namely, the *Liber pauperum* by Vacarius, an Italian emigré to England, the *Ordo iudiciorum* ('Olim edebatur actio ...'), attributed to a certain Otto (*Papiensis?*) and the *Brocarda* ('Dolum per subsequentia purgari ...'). We know nothing about its compilers.

In addition, commentators taught the text of further decretal collections, creating a *glossa ordinaria* for each of them: for the *Liber Sextus* (1298), the *Clementinae*

(texts to 1315) and the *Extravagantes* (1220s and 1230s). The totality of all canonical instructional texts was referred to as the *Corpus iuris canonici*. Incidentally, the term *corpus iuris* appears in the glosses from as early as the 12th cent. It did not originate in the 16th cent., as is often incorrectly stated. In the 13th cent., notarial skills were taught in Bologna with the aid of the *Ars notaria* by Rolandinus Passagerii, a text which had already been furnished with a *glossa ordinaria* by the author himself.

C. SCHOOLS

In the 12th cent., instruction in law was the same both north and west of the Alps; namely, clerics instructed other clerics in Church law. Since the Church relied on Roman law in cases where it lacked its own rules ('ecclesia vivit lege Romana'), Roman law was regarded as part of Church law and taught as well. This type of instruction can also be found in the Anglo-Norman cultural realm, in Paris, in the Rhône Valley, in Cologne and, more sporadically, in other cultural centres. Very likely it was found in Italy as well. In early 12th cent. Bologna, on the other hand, instructors were legally trained laymen who exclusively taught Justinian's *Corpus iuris civilis* for use in secular courts as well, since this was one of the regions of Europe where Roman law had remained in effect even outside Church jurisdiction. A second school tradition in which Church law was taught did not emerge in Bologna until after 1150. Both Bolognese schools of law were pre-eminent in their respective fields. The level, length and academic thoroughness of instruction rose steadily until 1220, with the result that all other law schools withered under the pressure of competition. Although new law schools emerged abroad in such places as Naples, Padua, Orleans (only Roman law) Paris (only canon law), Toulouse and later in many other towns, they all followed the Bolognese curriculum and separated the study of canon law from that of Roman law. However, outside of northern Italy and southern France, law as an academic discipline–canon law as well as Roman law (the two combined were referred to as 'common law', → (IUS COMMUNE)–remained almost exclusively restricted to clerics and was taught by clerics until the early 16th cent. Through the influence of learned cleric-jurists, scholarly law texts gradually became the standard for secular jurisdictions as well in the period between 1200 and 1600 (at different times in different regions of Europe), as long as local law did not have its own, diverging rules (→ MODES OF RECEPTION).

D. IMPORTANT AUTHORS

Wernerius (later cited as 'Irnerius') was the first to gloss the *Corpus iuris civilis* in the early 12th cent. in Bologna. He was followed there by Bulgarus de Bulgarinis, Martinus Gosia, Hugo de Porta Ravennata, Jacobus, Albericus, Johannes Bassianus (who glossed canon law as well), Placentinus (who emigrated to Montpellier), Henricus de Bayla, Otto Papiensis, Pilius de Medicina (who also taught in Modena), Azo Portius (ca. 1210), Hugolinus Presbyteri, Jacobus Balduini, Odofredus de Denariis (d. 1265), Accursius (d. 1263), and others. The collections of glosses by Accursius on the books of the *Corpus iuris civilis* became the *glossa ordinaria*. Rogerius taught about 1160, whether in the south of France or in northern Italy is unknown. Carolus de Tocco glossed the *Lombarda*. Jacobus de Ardizone, perhaps Jacobus Columbi, and certainly the previously mentioned authors Pilius und Accursius glossed the *Libri feudorum*. The *Decretum gratiani* and the decretal collections were glossed by the → CANONISTS Paucapalea (1150's), Rufinus, Stephanus Tornacensis (who returned to France), Simon de Bisignano, Rolandus (not identical with Rolandus Bandinelli, who became Pope Alexander III), Sicardus de Cremona, 'cardinalis' (Raimundus de Arenis), Johannes Faventinus, Gandulphus, Bernardus Papiensis (who authored the *Compilatio prima* in ca. 1190), Guilielmus Vascus, Damasus (Ungarus), Honorius, Alanus, Bernardus Compostellanus (senior), Tancredus, Laurentius Hispanus, Vincentius Hispanus, Huguccio (ca. 1210), Johannes Teutonicus and others. The glosses by the Johannes Teutonicus on the *Decretum Gratiani* (ca. 1216) became *glossa ordinaria*. The decretals cited in it were adapted to the *Liber extra* of 1234 by Bartholomaeus Brixiensis. The *glossa ordinaria* to the *Liber Extra* were written by Bernardus Parmensis de Botone. Regarding these it should be noted that the only glossators known by name are those from the Bolognese schools of law. Glosses and other works transmitted from the other law schools are almost exclusively anonymous.

E. WORKS

Gloss collections consist of *allegationes* (references to related passages) and various types of glosses explaining words or legal concepts. Older glosses also contain *notabilia* (headings and abstracted legal guidelines) and various types of signs.

Aside from glosses and commentaries, the glossators, as well as the commentators, published several other types of literature. *Summae* offered summaries of the material in a specific field of instruction organised according to topics. For example, the *summae* by Rogerius, Placentinus, Azo and two anonymous authors exist for the *Codex justinianus*. For the *Decretum gratiani*, about thirty different *summae* are extant, the most important among them by Huguccio; furthermore, numerous fragments of additional *summae* are extant. Lecture notes were referred to as *lectura*. In revised versions for publication, they were often called a *commentarius*. *Repetitiones* were detailed discussions of a selected passage from one area of instruction that took into careful consideration what other passages had to say on the topic. A comprehensive presentation on a given topic was called a *tra ctatus,* as long as it did not originate from a specific passage, which would make it a *repetitio*. However, the boundaries are not fixed. Frequently the same work is referred to in the manuscripts sometimes as a *tractatus* and other times as a *repetitio*. The terms *ordo iudiciorum, ordo iudiciarius* or *practica* referred to a treatise on procedural law. Directions for notaries are called an *ars notaria*. Collections of *notabilia*, also called *argumenta* or *regulae*, listed core legal pronouncements. In part they have been taken word for word and in part abstracted from passages. *Brocardum, brocardicum* ('biting') was the term for a rule for which an opposite rule existed. Collections of brocarda listed each rule and cited passages to support it, followed by the respective opposite rule, again with citations supporting it. This was usually followed by an explanation of the cases to which the rule applied. Then the same procedure was followed for the opposing rule. *Distinc tiones* treated a complex topic from various points of view and thus divided it into several groups of cases, each group requiring different legal treatment. In order to allow ready access to the works of other law professors while a student was studying under a rival professor, lists of differences in opinion were made available (*dissensiones*). *Consilia* developed expert solutions for cases in law practice. *Quaestiones* were used in academic instruction to challenge the students with a difficult legal problem which was often presented as a real-life case. Different ways of solving a legal problem are presented through disputations, in which the various arguments pro and con were given. The disputation ended with the professor giving his personal opinion. *Q uare* presented a brief inquiry into the reasons behind the wording of a law and answered it just as briefly. The expression *vocabularium iuris* referred to an alphabetical lexicon. Such works were also called *dictionaria, repertoria, directoria,* or *remissoria*. The earliest extant *dictionarium iuris* was written by Jacobus de Raveniaco (also called 'de Ravanis' or de Révigny, late 13th cent.).

F. HISTORY OF RESEARCH

The *glossa ordinaria* on the various textbooks remained well known and much used into modern times, since they were a part of almost all medieval manuscripts and almost all printed editions up to the early 17th cent. They enjoyed an authoritative status; thus the proverb *Quidquid non agnoscit glossa, non agnoscit curia*. The *Summae* by Azo Portius on various parts of the *Corpus iuris civilis* was also well known, leading to the proverb 'Che non ha Azzo, non va al palazzo', which could be taken two ways: 1. "What Azo does not have, does not work in the court palace"; 2. "Who does not have Azo, does not go to the palace". All other works by the glossators were consigned to oblivion after the 14th cent. However, many of them became available again in the 16th cent. through printed editions; but they failed to regain their influence on the practice of law. Scholarly research on the manuscript transmission of the glossators did not begin until the 19th cent. Especially Friedrich Carl von Savigny devoted himself to studying the glossators and commentators of the *Corpus iuris civilis*. Johann Friedrich von Schulte and Franz Gillmann studied those of the *Corpus iuris canonici*. Research on manuscripts containing the works of canonist glossators made a giant leap forward with Stephan Kuttner's publication of his *Repertorium der Kanonistik* in 1937. After a large number of the relevant manuscripts came to be known through his efforts, many scholars became interested in this field, which brought about a rapid increase in the body of knowledge. Similar progress was achieved regarding the literature on the *Corpus iuris civilis* in 1972 after the publication of a *List of MSS on Roman Law to 1600*. On the whole, it is important to point out that although there exists a large number of reliable studies about individual glossators, individual works and individual legal topics, the cautiously stated conjectures contained in them about, for example, biographical dates and circumstances, have been compiled rather uncritically in the summarising literature, which presents them as well-supported facts. At the present time, a multi-volume handbook on canon law is being produced, published by K. Pennington and W. Hartmann. Thus far, the lack of such a handbook has been compensated for by using information contained in J. F. von Schulte's work and in S. Kuttner's *Repertorium* as a starting point, and then by supplementing and improving upon these with the aid of bibliographical and biographical material found in the newer works about dogmatic law, for example, at present utilizing the material found in Zeliauskas, Chiodi and Maceratini. For supplementation, the material found in contributions to the *Bulletin of Medieval Canon Law* and in the *Proceedings of the International Congress of Medieval Canon Law*, which appears every four years, should be used.

One can employ a similar strategy regarding the medieval treatment of Roman law. First, one should consult F. C. von Savigny and H. Coing's handbook. Books by H. Lange and E. Schrage are good sources as well. However, the information found there must be checked and supplemented with the aid of the specialised literature found in the footnotes and the bibliographies of these sources as well as in the *Repertorium manuscriptorum veterum Codicis Justiniani* (p. 1 ff. and p. 34) and in the above-mentioned list of manuscripts. Since 1990, the *Rivista internazionale di diritto comune* offers a bibliographical survey of the most recent literature.

→ Glossography

SOURCES 1 W. C. BECKHAUS, (ed.), Bulgari ad Digestorum titulum De diversis regulis iuris antiqui commentarius et Placentini ad eum additiones sive exceptiones, 1856 (repr., 1967) 2 E. BESTA, L'opera d'Irnerio, 2 vols., Turin, 1896 3 S. CAPRIOLI, Bertrandi quaedam de regulis iuris, in: Annali di storia del diritto 8, 1964, 225–267; 10/11, 1966/67, 479–526 4 Id. (ed.), Bertrandus Metensis, de regulis iuris, 1981 5 S. CAPRIOLI, V. CRESCENZI, G. DIURNI, P. MARI (eds.), Glosse preaccursiane alle Istituzioni. Strato azzoniano, vol. 2 (schede unificate), 1978 6 Id. et al. (eds.), Glosse preaccursiane alle istituzioni. Strato azzoniano, vol. 3 (schede unificate), 1982 7 S. CAPRIOLI, Habemus et Ioannem, in: Annali di storia del diritto 5/6, 1961/62, 375–385 8 Id., Quem Cuiacius Iohanni tribuerat, in: Annali di storia del diritto 7, 1963, 131–248 9 G. DOLEZALEK, Azos Glossenapparat zum Infortiatum, in: Ius commune 3, 1970, 186–208 10 Id., Der Glossenapparat des Martinus Gosia zum Digestum Novum, in: Zeitschrift der Savigny-Stiftung für Rechtsgeschichte, Romanistische Abteilung 84, 1967, 245–349 11 Id., Repertorium manuscriptorum veterum Codicis Iustiniani, 1985, 515–853 12 A. GARCIA AND GARCIA (eds.), Constitutiones Concilii Quarti Lateranensis una cum Commentariis glossatorum, 1981 (Monumenta iuris canonici. Series A: Corpus Glossatorum 2) 13 H. U. KANTOROWICZ, W. W. BUCKLAND, Studies in the Glossators of the Roman Law. Newly Discovered Writings of the 12th Century, 1938 (repr., 1969 with additions by P. WEIMAR) 14 P. MARI AND P. PERUZZI, Glosse preaccursiane alle Istituzioni. Strato azzoniano. vol. I, 1984 (Fonti per la storia d'Italia, 107) 15 K. PENNINGTON (ed.), Iohannis Teutonici Apparatus glossarum in compilationem tertiam, vol. 1. Città del Vaticano 1981 (Monumenta iuris canonici. Series A: Corpus Glossatorum 3) (continued on the internet) 16 A. ROTA (ed.), L'apparato di Pillio alle Consuetudines feudorum, in: Studi e memorie per la storia dell'Università di Bologna 14, 1938, 1–170 17 E. SEKKEL, Distinctiones Glossatorum ..., in: Festschrift der Berliner Juristischen Fakultät für Ferdinand von Martitz, 1911, 277–436 (repr., 1956) 18 F. DE ZULUETA (ed.), The Liber Pauperum of Vacarius, 1927

LITERATURE 19 H. COING (ed.), Handbuch der Quellen und Literatur der neueren europäischen Privatrechtsgeschichte, vol. I, 1973 20 G. CHIODI, L'interpretazione del testamento nel pensiero dei glossatori, 1996 21 E. CORTESE, Il diritto nella storia medievale, I–II, 1995 22 G. DOLEZALEK, Repertorium manuscriptorum veterum Codicis Iustiniani, 1985 (complete bibliography on the glosses);; 23 Id., Research on Manuscripts of the Corpus iuris with Glosses ...: State of Affairs, in: Miscellanea Domenico Maffei dicata, vol. I, 1995, 143–171 (continuation of the bibliography) 24 G. DOLEZALEK, AND H. VAN DE WOUW, Verzeichnis der Handschriften zum römischen Recht bis 1600, 1972 25 G. DOLEZALEK AND R. WEIGAND, Das Geheimnis der roten Zeichen. Ein Beitrag zur Paläographie juristischer Handschriften des 12. Jahrhunderts, in: Zeitschrift der Savigny-Stiftung für Rechtsgeschichte, kanonistische Abteilung 100 (69), 1983, 143–199 26 F. GILLMANN, Gesammelte Schriften zur klassischen Kanonistik, vols. 1–3, 1988–1993 27 S. KUTTNER, E. RATHBONE, Anglo-Norman Canonists of the 12th Century, Traditio 7, 1949–51, 279–358 28 S. KUTTNER, Repertorium der Kanonistik (1140–1234). Prodromus Corporis Glossatorum I., 1937 (Studi e testi 71) 29 H. LANGE, Römisches Recht im Mittelalter, vol. I: Die Glossatoren, 1997 30 R. MACERATINI, Ricerche sullo status giuridico dell'eretico ... (da Graziano ad Uguccione), 1994 31 O. F. ROBINSON, T. D. FERGUS AND W. M. GORDON, European Legal History, ²1994; 32 F. C. v. SAVIGNY, Geschichte des römischen Rechts im Mittelalter, ²1834–1851 (repr., 1961) 33 E. J. H. SCHRAGE, Utrumque ius: eine Einführung in das Studium der Quellen des mittelalterlichen gelehrten Rechts, 1992 (Schriften zur Europäischen Rechts- und Verfassungsgeschichte 8) 34 J. FR. V. SCHULTE, Die Geschichte der Quellen und Literatur des Canonischen Rechts von Gratian bis auf die Gegenwart, 1875–1880 (repr., 1956) 35 R. WEIGAND, Die Glossen zum Dekret Gratians. Studien zu den frühen Glossen und Glossenkompositionen = Studia Gratiana

25-26, 1991; 36 Id., Glossatoren des Dekrets Gratians, 1996   37 J. ZELIAUSKAS, De excommunicatione vitiata apud glossatores (1140–1350), 1967.   GERO DOLEZALEK

Glyptothek see → MUNICH

Gnosis
A. INTRODUCTION B. MIDDLE AGES C. GNOSTIC SELF-AWARENESS DURING THE RENAISSANCE AND IN THE EARLY MODERN PERIOD D. FROM ENLIGHTENMENT TO ROMANTICISM
E. RECURRENCES OF GNOSTICISM IN THE 20TH CENTURY

A. INTRODUCTION
Western religious and intellectual history broadly adopted what the 1st cent. AD had described as gnosticism or, more generally and transcending its more specific forms of expression, as gnosis. There are difficulties surrounding the terminology [39]. Reception went along two different strands: on the one hand, a direct strand deriving from ancient religious communities (as in the case of the Cathars) and, on the other hand, gnosis as a religious, cultural and philosophical 'concept', which at times has been called the third basic component of occidental culture (along with reason and faith) [33] and which has, among others, the following basic characteristics: The primacy of experience (of the self or of God) over purely rational explanation or simple faith; the emphasis on man's 'self-empowerment' [32; 15] and his release from all constraints as opposed to subservience to God and fate; the dualistic intensification of the battle between the enlightened few and the ignorant masses, the few often caught in a conflict with ruling powers; the visionary development of philosophical and religious premises [27. 111–116]; and the metaphorical construct of the world as a prison from which only knowledge (*gnōsis*) can free one. Gnosis has accompanied European history–in close affinity to hermetics and esoterics–as a central counterpoint to ecclesiastical Christianity and scientism into the 20th cent.

B. MIDDLE AGES
At the end of Antiquity, the greater Roman-Byzantine Church had gained dominance over gnostic Christendom, which, nonetheless, proved, again and again, to be a threat to Christian identity. In late 7th cent. Armenia, for instance, the strongly dualistic movement of the Paulicians emerged which later spread to the Balkans where its existence can be verified until the 13th cent. [31. 46–53; 32]. Closely related in content was the gnosis of Bogomile, which gained ground in 10th cent. Macedonia and Bosnia and then also in Italy and France up to the 12th cent [30; 25; 31]. It prepared the ground for the most important challenge to the Catholic Church–the Cathars [13]. Pope Innocent III took up the fight against the Cathars in writing with his work *De miseria humanae conditionis* (1195) which, in contrast

to gnosis, laments the irreevocable sin and the calamity of the human condition in its captivity as a given [3. 45]. Innocent also attacked with the force of arms, which led to the extermination of the Cathars between 1209 and 1229 in the Albigensian Crusade. Gnostic traces appear later in German mysticism, as in Meister Eckhart, who repeats the myth of the divine spark and states in his sermons: "God and I, we are one. Through knowing I take God into myself; through love I enter into God" [4. 186]. Similar ideas appear in Jakob Böhme, although it is true for both thinkers that they do not follow the gnostic devaluation of reality or the idea of the biblical God as demiurge; instead, self-empowerment is regarded as the opposite of devotion and merging [32. 53–55].

C. GNOSTIC SELF-AWARENESS DURING THE RENAISSANCE AND IN THE EARLY MODERN PERIOD
Following Marsilio Ficino's translation of the ancient *Corpus Hermeticum* in 1471, the ideas about the (human) subject in these documents were strongly revitalised, ideas that matched the gnostic tendency towards a higher evaluation and even deification of man. Pico della Mirandola (1463–94) and Giordano Bruno (1548–1600) took them up again. Mirandola has the God of creation say to man: "You are to determine your own (nature) without any limits or restrictions and according to your own discretion which I have entrusted to you" [6. 7]; with the result that man was elevated and quasi deified: "Let us spurn earthly things, scorn heavenly things and, finally, by leaving all earthly things behind us, let us hurry towards the court beyond the world which is closest to exalted divinity" [6. 11]. Bruno, in turn, speaks of the bitter and confident fight of "extraordinary, heroic and godly men" [1. 118f.], who, as opposed to the ignorance of the majority and the deception of the rulers, "search for what is true and right apart from the masses" [1. 104] (s. [40. 194]). Altogether, despite some discrepancies in content, we can agree with Pauen: "a direct path can be traced from the gnostic insistence on the divine rank of the (human) subject through Pico's theory of human dignity to Ernst Bloch's apotheosis of the subject" [32. 64].

D. FROM ENLIGHTENMENT TO ROMANTICISM
In the 17th and 18th cents., philosophical discourse was fundamentally shaped by the concepts of reason and understanding. A close look at the way these concepts were understood reveals an interesting difference from their modern counterparts in that they often referred to a higher reason and an absolute understanding, ideas that show a gnostic element. If "one notices the concurrence between certain ways of thinking in the 18th cent. and the forms of syncretistic religiosity, the reason is not to be found in the unmediated adoption of Antiquity and even less in a sub rosa continuation of secret societies, but in esotericism alone" ('die Koinzidenz zwischen bestimmten Denkweisen des 18. Jahrhunderts und Formen synkretistischer Religiosität auf-

fällt, so ist dies nicht unvermittelte Antikenrezeption und schon gar nicht im geheimen fortwirkende Tradition von Mysterienbünden, sondern Esoterik' [29. 173 f.]). It is rooted in Renaissance philosophy with its interpretation of the *Corpus Hermeticum*. Two examples should be mentioned: In his translation of the Bible from 1735–the *Göttliche Schriften vor der Zeit des Messie Jesus* ('Divine Writings before the TIme of Jesus the Messiah'), confiscated in 1738 – the Enlightenment thinker Lorenz Schmidt directly refers to gnostic semantics when he has the snake say to Eve: "Oh no, you will not have to die. Rather, God knows that you will experience a great enlightenment when you eat of this fruit: yes, you will gain a divine intellect and an elevated understanding" (from [36. 88]). In a text published in 1787 for the recruitment of new members to the order of the Illuminata founded by Adam Weishaupt, it is advised that: "those who are to be recruited must show a disposition for enjoying the understanding of higher (...) truths" (from [29. 171]). Gnostic ideas also abound in the 're-founding' of the order by Theodor Reuß in the late 19th cent., in his eclectic reception of Weishaupt's works [28. 83–105] and in Reuß's own popularisation of the 'gnostic Mass' (designed by Aleister Crowley in 1913 for the Ordo Templi Orientis), in his membership in the gnostic Catholic Church and in his function as *Légate Gnostique de l'Église Gnostique Universelle de France pour la Suisse* [28. 224–236].

The strong influence of the gnostic-esoteric world view on Romanticism is apparent in motifs, such as the reunification with original wisdom, the search for understanding beyond mere knowledge and the introduction of a developmental model for human consciousness [8. 187–93]. This history of personal development and the notion that a maturing person can educate and form himself led to a kind of universal gnosis [22. 249]. The philosophical discussions of the time were well aware of this trend, as is evidenced in the analysis of Schelling, Schleiermacher and Hegel by the theologian Baur in Tübingen from 1835 [10]. The aftereffects of this discourse are still noticeable in the socalled 'New Age' movement, which frequently refers to gnosis in the sense of a fusion with an ultimate level of being and the realisation of man's higher self [21. 371; 20].

E. Recurrences of Gnosticism in the 20th Century

The 20th cent. saw a heightened interest in gnostic ideas, now however in the context of a critical stance toward scientism and the success of the Enlightenment. While, in 1907, Eugen Heinrich Schmitt declared that "there is nothing more sacred and greater, (...) nothing divine except the sacred light of reason", and "the veneration of the latter in the general consciousness (will) (...) be the great sign of the coming third age of the world" [7. 14], clearly pessimistic voices soon emerged that reversed the dramatic roles and articulated a longing for a truth that exists beyond reason. One example

is Ludwig Klages's poem *Vision*, that declares: 'Nimm mich auf und löse, du weite See,/Diesen Leib, den Kerker der Sonnenseele,/Daß befreit aus den staubgewordenen Fesseln/Glutentrunkensteige die Sonnenseele' ("O vast sea, take me inside you,/ free this body, the dungeon of the sunny soul,/ so that from shackles turned to dust/ the sunny soul may rise drunken with burning" [5. 168] s. [32. 135–198]). The gnostic ideology of the chosen few who have special knowledge led many to feel immunised in their own philosophical position, which isolated them from criticism. The most obvious example is found in Martin Heidegger, whose talk of man's 'Geworfensein' ('being thrown') into the world or of a special calling heard by the one who searches presents a direct reference to ancient gnosis. 'Geworfenheit' ('thrownness') means 'in seinem Woher und Wohin verhüllten, aber an ihm selbst um so unverhüllter erschlossenen Seinscharakter des Daseins' ("human existence's character of being which is veiled as to where from and where to, but which, in itself, is revealed in an ever so undisguised way") [2. 134 f.]. Heidegger's pre-metaphysical ontology presents itself as a dualism, wherein evil is linked to God and is understood as a dialectic necessity of development, and where what is horrible is a part of man insofar as it strives toward being [9. 172–175]. Heidegger's gnostic references were first noticed by his student Hans Jonas [23. 1. 107], who created an important new scholarly interpretation of gnosis on the basis of this philosophy. A political perspective of this gnostic ontology ultimately revealed itself in Heidegger's glorification of national socialism.

After World War II, a broad philosophical debate emerged about the legitimacy of modernity. After Eric Voegelin had 'rejected' modernity "as gnostic, since the gnostic aeons of light and darkness, truth and lie (...) had become dominant forms in political thinking" [38. 42 f.], Blumenberg offered a contrasting thesis in describing modernity as the second and final triumph over gnosis [11. 144 f.], the first having failed at the beginning of the Middle Ages. Compared to the past, the triumph of technology and science changed the way the burden of modern man should be viewed: 'sie ist Verantwortung für den Zustand der Welt als zukunftsbezogene Forderung, nicht als vergangene Urschuld' ("it lies in the responsibility for the state of the world as a challenge in relation to the future, not as an original sin of the past"); consequently, there no longer exists a vanishing point in the *Kósmos átheos* beyond the world or a gnostic escape from the world [12. 78]. The gnostic affirmation of removing oneself from the world, which one views negatively, is replaced by the opposite view, which leads to the neutralisation of the eschatological intensification in modernity: 'Dieser Neutralisierungsvorgang ist Aufklärung: durch sie werden die genannten Neuzeitpotenzen häresie-unfähig–ihre Probleme werden von heilserheblichen Entscheidungen entlastet–und dadurch pragmatisch ernüchtert: indem die Neuzeit–als zweite Überwindung der Gnosis: als Negativie-

rung der Weltfremdheit durch positivierung der Welt–
die Lebensverhältnisse pragmatisiert, wird sie die
bewahrenswerteste der uns historisch erreichbaren
Lebenswelten' [26.34]. ("This process of neutralisation
is a type of enlightenment: it renders the above mentioned modern potencies incapable of heresy. Their problems are relieved of matters of salvation and thus
become pragmatic and sober. In its pragmatic view of
the conditions of life, modernity–as the second triumph
over Gnosis through a negative interpretation of other-
worldliness and a positive view on the world–becomes
the most worthwhile of the historical realms accessible
to us".)
→ Gnosis, Gnostics, Gnosticism
→ Kabbala; → Magic; → Occultism

Sources 1 G. Bruno, Cena de le ceneri, (Engl. S. L. Jaki
(trans.), The Ash Wednesday Supper, 1975) 2 M. Hei-
degger, Sein und Zeit, 1927, ¹⁶1986 (Engl. J. Stam-
baugh (trans.), Being and Time, 1996) 3 Innocent III,
Two Views of Man: Pope Innocent III 'On the Misery of
Man'. Giannozzo Manetti 'On the Dignity of Man, B.
Murchland (trans.), 1966 4 Meister Eckehart,
Deutsche Predigten und Traktate, J. Quint (trans. and
ed.), 1963, repr., 1979 5 L. Klages, Rhythmen und
Runen. Nachlaß, 1944 6 G. Pico della Mirandola,
De hominis dignitate, (Engl. C. G. Wallis (trans.), On the
Dignity of Man, 1965) 7 E. H. Schmitt, Die Gnosis;
Grundlagen der Weltanschauung einer edleren Kultur, 2
vols., 1903/07
Sources 8 M. H. Abrams, Natural Supernaturalism.
Tradition and Revolution in Romantic Literature, 1971
9 W. Baum, Gnostische Elemente im Denken Martin Hei-
deggers? Eine Studie auf den Grundlagen der Religionsphilosophie von Hans Jonas, 1997 10 F. Chr. Baur, Die
Christliche Gnosis oder die Religionsphilosophie in ihrer
geschichtlichen Entwicklung, Tübingen 1835 11 H. Blumenberg, Säkularisierung und Selbstbehauptung, ²1983
12 Id., Die Legitimität der Neuzeit, 1966 (Engl. R. M.
Wallace (trans.), The Legitimacy of the Modern Age,
1983 13 A. Borst, Die Katharer, 1953, ²1991 14 R.
van den Broek, W. J. Hanegraaff (eds.), Gnosis and
Hermeticism from Antiquity to Modern Times, 1998
15 M. Brumlik, Die Gnostiker. Der Traum von der Selbst-
erlösung des Menschen, 1992 16 C. Colpe, W.
Schmidt-Biggemann (eds.), Das Böse. Eine historische
Phänomenologie des Unerklärlichen, 1993 17 K. R. H.
Frick, Die Erleuchteten. Gnostisch-theosophische und
alchemistisch-rosenkreuzerische Geheimgesellschaften
bis zum Ende des 18. Jahrhunderts. Ein Beitrag zur Geistesgeschichte der Neuzeit, 1973, 1988 18 Id., Licht und
Finsternis (= Die Erleuchteten II), 2 vols., 1975 19 C.
Gilly, F. A. Janssen (eds.), 500 Years of Gnosis in
Europe: Exhibit of Printed Books and Manuscripts from
the Gnostic Tradition, 1993 20 W. J. Hanegraaff, The
Problem of Post-Gnostic Gnosticism, in: U. Bianchi (ed.),
The Notion of Religion in Comparative Research. Selected Proceedings of the Sixteenth Congress of the International Association for the History of Religions, Rome,
3rd–8th Sept. 1990, 1994, 625–632 21 Id., The New
Age Movement and the Esoteric Tradition, in: R. van den
Broek, W. J. Hanegraaff (eds.), Gnosis and Hermeticism from Antiquity to Modern Times, 1998, 359–382
22 Id., Romanticism and the Esoteric Connection, in: R.
van den Broek, W. J. Hanegraaff (eds.), Gnosis and

Hermeticism from Antiquity to Modern Times, 1998,
237–268 23 H. Jonas, Gnosis und spätantiker Geist,
1934, ⁴1988 24 Chr. Graf v. Krockow, Die Entschei-
dung. Eine Untersuchung über Ernst Jünger, Carl Schmitt,
Martin Heidegger, 1958 25 R. Kutzli, Die Bogumilen:
Geschichte, Kunst, Kultur, 1977 26 O. Marquard, Das
gnostische Rezidiv als Gegenneuzeit. Ultrakurztheorem in
lockerem Anschluß an Blumenberg, [37. 31–36] 27 D.
Merkur, Gnosis. An Esoteric Tradition of Mystical Visions and Unions, 1993 28 H. Möller, E. Howe, Merlin
Peregrinus. Vom Untergrund des Abendlandes, 1986
29 M. Neugebauer-Wölk, Höhere Vernunft und höhe-
res Wissen als Leitbegriffe in der esoterischen Gesell-
schaftsbewegung. Vom Nachleben eines Renaissancekon-
zepts im Jahrhundert der Aufklärung, in: Id., H. Zaun-
stöck (eds.), Aufklärung und Esoterik, 1999, 170–210
30 D. Oblensky, The Bogomils. A Study in Balkan Neo-
Manichaeism, 1948 31 K. Papasov, Christen oder
Ketzer – Die Bogomilen, 1983 32 M. Pauen, Dithyram-
biker des Untergangs. Gnostizismus in Ästhetik und Philosophie der Moderne, 1994 33 G. Quispel (ed.), Gnosis: De derde component van de Europese cultuurtraditie,
1988 34 Id. (ed.), De Hermetische Gnosis in de loop der
eeuwen. Beschouwingen over de invloed van een Egypt.
religie op de cultuur van het Westen, 1992 35 St. Run-
ciman, The Medieval Manichee. A Study of the Christian
Dualist Heresy, ²1955 36 W. Schmidt-Biggemann,
Theodizee und Tatsachen. Das philosophische Profil der
deutschen Aufklärung, 1988 37 J. Taubes (ed.), Religi-
onstheorie und politische Theologie, vol. 2: Gnosis und
Politik, 1984 38 E. Voegelin, Philosophie der Politik in
Oxford, in: Philosophische Rundschau 1, 1953/54, 23–48
39 M. A. Williams, Rethinking Gnosticism. An Argument for Dismantling a Dubious Category, 1996
40 F. A. Yates, Giordano Bruno and the Hermetic Tradition, 1964. Kocku von Stuckrad

Gotha, Schloßmuseum
A. History of the Collection B. Exhibition
Concept

A. History of the Collection
The existence of ancient collectibles in Friedenstein
castle in the 17th and 18th cents. is confirmed by relevant entries in the oldest inventories of the cabinet of
curiosities and by other archival records, or can be assumed with a high degree of probability. Commensurate
with contemporary views on the encyclopaedic character of royal collections, antiquities appeared there as
individual items or as small collections on particular
topics. For example, the *Artificalia*, a collection of
about 1150 objects, which Duke Ernst I of Sachsen-
Gotha-Altenburg (1640–1675), the builder of Friedenstein castle, had brought to Gotha after the division of
Saxony in 1640, included among 'Allerhand Antiquitäten insgemein ein Idolum Aegyptiacum, dergleichen
bey den Mumys gefunden worden ...'("all kinds of antiquities an *idolum Aegyptiacum*, as commonly found
with mummies") also an 'urna cinerum, dabey die
Beschreibung, wo solche gefunden und außgegraben
worden'("*urna cinerum*, including a description of
where it was found and excavated") [5]. Without a

Fig. 1: Primato Painter, Bell krater. Third quarter of 4th cent. BC A gift from Pope Pius VII to Frederick IV of Saxony-Gotha-Altenburg Schloßmuseum Gotha (Photograph: Lutz Ebhardt)

doubt, this is the first reference to an ancient collectible within the Gotha *Kunstkammer* ('Cabinet of Curiosities'). The latter was set up in the western tower of the newly-built castle very shortly after Duke Ernst had moved into his new residence. Antiquities were also used as decorative showpieces, as e.g. in the Coin Cabinet or the ducal apartments. Subsequent *Kunstkammer* inventories also named objects of ancient character, as. e.g. in the 1721 list 'eine Römische Lampe aus dem Arnstädter Kabinett mit 110 bezeichnet (...), eine antike Lampe aus Bronze '("a Roman lamp from the Arnstadt cabinet as object number 110 (...), an ancient bronze lamp"), and the items listed in the 1764 inventory also included 'eine irdene Urna, eine gläserne Urna, 26 Lampen, 18 Tränengläser' ("an earthenware urn, a glass urn, 26 lamps, and 18 small vials") [7; 4].

In his travel journal of 1741, *Fortsetzung Neuester Reisen, durch Teutschland, Böhmen, Ungarn, die Schweitz, Italien und Lothringen* ..., ('Continuation of most recent travels through Germany, Bohemia, Hungary, Switzerland, Italy and Lorraine') Johann Georg Keyßler mentioned in the course of his detailed description of the Gotha collections 'etliche Heidnische Götzenbilder ... Urnen von Kupfer, Thon und Glas, deren letztern eine von dem verstorbenen Fürsten von Schwarzburg-Arnstadt mit 100 Ducaten bezahlet worden ist' ("several pagan idols, ... copper, earthenware and glass urns, one of the latter purchased by the late Duke of Schwarzburg-Anstadt for 100 ducats")[6].

Compared with the antiquities mentioned above, Friedenstein castle held a great number of gems and ancient coins in the 17th and 18th cents. Under minted objects, for instance, 893 were already listed in the Ludolph inventory of 1656. In subsequent centuries, as a result of the expertise of the dukes and collection directors, the holdings of the Gotha *Kunstkammer* were systematically extended, with definite peaks in the acquisition of antiquities. ;

Apart from purchases and gifts from art dealers and private individuals, the dukes themselves often returned to Gotha with antiquities from their travels to Italy or the Mediterranean. It also happened that objects previously on display in the *Kunstkammer* were returned to the private ducal apartments; i.e, 'drey Thränen Gläßer, und 1 ant. Lampe, welche am Eingang auf dem Schrank der Mumie befindlich waren' ("three small vials and one antique lamp which used to be on the mummy cabinet at the entrance") were transferred to Duke August von Sachsen-Gotha-Altenburg (1804–1822) on 21 January 1813 [10].

In his 1833 inventory of *Das Herzogliche Kunst- und Naturalien-Cabinet zu Gotha*, Johann Heinrich Möller was the first to list the "Etrurian and Roman" antiquities. These were: 12 ancient vases, six bowls and small bottles, five marble pieces, 59 earthenware lamps, 13 ornaments of burnt clay, several small vials and other vessels, fragments of ancient wall paintings and seven bronze objects [8]. His inventory also indicates that as early as 1808, five antique vessels had arrived in Gotha from Italy. They were given to Friedrich IV, Prince of Sachsen-Gotha-Altenburg (1822–1825), by two notable contemporaries, namely Pope Pius VII and Queen Caroline of Naples (fig. 1). From 1804 to 1810, Friedrich IV had stayed in Rome, Venice and Naples and had excavations carried out in various locations. As a result of these ventures, he had brought a number of antiquities back with him to Gotha, where most of them were included in the ducal art cabinet alongside his purchases. Among them were fragments of ancient wall paintings, earthenware vessels and urns, as well as sculptures and small artifacts [11].

In 1824, all the ducal art and scientific collections were combined in a single museum and thus made accessible to a wider public. There was a dedicated announcement informing the public about visiting the collections which is said to have been available in every inn. The museum was open from 1 April to 31 October; on Tuesdays 9:00–13:00, admission was free, on all other days (with the exception of Sundays and holidays) the admission price was one *Taler* and ten *Groschen*.

The antiquities collection grew considerably up to the end of the 1860s. Adolf Bube, Director of the *Kunstkammer*, listed in his inventory the *Herzogliche Kunstkabinet zu Gotha* 86 objects under the classification of painted vases and other vessels from southern Italy; Roman objects numbered 427 [3]. It is often very difficult or impossible to reconstruct the exact provenance of individual pieces. It is known that some

Fig. 2: Music room (1799) with cork model in the context of the later reception of Classical Antiquity (Photograph: Lutz Ebhardt), *Schloßmuseum, Gotha*

Fig. 3: Replica of a burial chamber in the Egyptian section (Photograph: Lutz Ebhardt), *Schloßmuseum, Gotha*

Fig. 4: Room with Roman portraits and statues, small artefacts and everyday objects (Photograph: Lutz Ebhardt), *Schloßmuseum, Gotha*

objects came to the collection in the 1850s and early 1860s from purchases and from the estate of the court sculptor Wolfgang, others were incorporated from the joint collection of Duke Ernst II of Sachsen-Coburg and Gotha (1844–1893) and of Prince Albert of Coburg, and there were also some from the Grassi collection, from individual purchases, or individual finds in Italy and also the German Rhine area.

In his 1866 essay on the collection in Friedenstein castle (*Ueber die Sammlungen von Alterthümern auf Schloß Friedenstein zu Gotha*), Wieseler wrote: 'Die Griechisch-Römischen Alterthümer nun stammen dem bei weitem grössten Theile nach aus Italien. Ausserdem hat auch Deutschland, namentlich Salzburg und die Rheinlande, ein wenn auch nur geringes Contingent gestellt. (...) Sie repräsentieren so gut wie alle Haupt-gattungen antiker Kunstübung' ("Most of the Graeco-Roman antiquities originate from Italy. In addition, Germany, namely Salzburg and the Rhineland, have also made a contribution, albeit a small one ... They represent almost the entire range of ancient artistic activities") [12].

The Graeco-Roman collection experienced its greatest expansion, both in quality and quantity, between 1870 and 1890, determining the future profile and structure of the antiquities collection. The inventory by Carl Aldenhoven, then director of the Gotha Ducal Museum, completed in 1890, lists 48 stone objects, 59 bronze objects, 330 ceramic vessels, 302 ceramic images, 36 glass items and 40 objects described as various [2]. This considerable expansion of the antiquities collection was mainly the result of a continuous policy of acquisitions and purchases implemented since the 1870s under Duke Ernst II of Sachsen-Coburg and Gotha. On behalf of this ruling family, Wolfgang Helbig, Second Secretary of the German Archaeological Institute in Rome, purchased several art objects in Italy and Greece for the Gotha collection. For the vessel collection alone, he was able to make more than 100 purchases in that period, among them several vases of outstanding quality [9]. The many years of good relations between the ruling house of Gotha and its representative Helbig with the Italian art trade not only helped with their purchases, but also resulted in a number of gifts, received by Duke Ernst II for the collection of antiquities.

From 1879 on, the Gotha antiquities formed a separate section among the art collections. Their separation from the ducal *Kunstkabinett* was directly linked to the construction of a dedicated multi-purpose museum (1864–1879) in the park of the Friedenstein castle by Duke Ernst II of Sachsen-Coburg and Gotha. The Neo-Renaissance building designed by the Viennese architect Franz von Neumann provided extensive exhibition areas, permitting a spacious presentation of the Graeco-Roman collections and its further expansion.

Between the end of the 19th cent. and the early 1920s, there was hardly a year without further acquisitions for the antiquities collection. Among the last purchases before 1945 was an ancient vessel, added to the collection in 1942.

The ducal family and the curators of their collections made increasing use of auctions; they also maintained relations with international art dealers as a source of further acquisitions. In addition, the museum received a considerable number of ancient objects, many glasses and vessels as well as terracottas and bronze objects from the estate of Duke Alfred (1893–1900) of Sachsen-Coburg and Gotha [1]. The duke, who took a keen interest in archaeology, had a penchant for purchasing ancient collectibles on his travels to the Mediterranean. Particular mention should be made of some Cypriot vessels that he had brought back from excavations on Cyprus. Under the curatorship of Karl Purgold, Director of the Gotha Art Collections from 1890 to 1934, the antiquities collection underwent a systematic expansion, benefiting from the director's archaeological training. He also played a major role in promoting variety in the make-up of the collection. This underlying policy of continuous acquisition is apparent, for example, in his purchases of 1905: in addition to five bronze items, one bronze statuette, an ancient portrait and a marble relief, the archaeological collection received three marble statues, various terracotta figures, an ancient vessel and an ancient glass. In 1934, the museum, the library and the coin collection were merged to become the *Herzog von Sachsen-Coburg und Gothaische Stiftung für Kunst und Wissenschaft,* under the supervision of the Thuringian Ministry of Education. This was to ensure that these institutions remained in Gotha and continued to be maintained for the benefit of the public. At that time, the antiquities collection was housed on the ground floor of the museum building of 1879 and followed, in line with the newly developed exhibition concept, the Egyptian exhibition.

World War II and the post-war period resulted in considerable losses for the Gotha collection, affecting all of its genres. The reorganization of the museum in the 1950s determined the current location of the Friedenstein art collections. The painting and sculpture collection, the antiquities and the Egyptian collections together with the East Asia collection and the engravings collection were moved back into Friedenstein castle, where visitors can now see them as complete exhibitions on particular topics or as partial collections.

In view of the number of its objects, the Gotha antiquities collection can be classified as a medium-sized collection, which in addition to its important collection of vessels, contains a number of culturally and art-historically significant small artifacts as well as marble objects. The collection has a clearly discernible art-historical profile. The collecting activity centred around the main genres of ancient art with a clear focus on vase painting. The sculptures and reliefs are of uniform dimensions, comparatively small due to the conditions at Gotha. These days, the objects in the Gotha antiquities collection are grouped as follows: about 300 vessels from the period of 2,500 BC to the Roman Imperial

Age, with the main emphasis on black- and red-figured vase paintings of the 6th and 5th cents. BC; 40 marble objects, among them individual objects representing Hellenistic portrait sculpture as well as mythological sculpture, portraits and decorative art from the Late Roman Republican and the Imperial periods, fragments of tomb reliefs and inscriptions; 650 bronze objects, jewellery and statuettes; 130 terracotta lamps, mainly of the Roman Imperial period; more than 100 glasses, predominantly from the 1st to 3rd cents. AD; about 300 terracottas and terracotta fragments; 25 objects of various genres, including fragments of ancient wall paintings.

B. Exhibition Concept

Since 1991, the antiquities collection in the Gotha Schlossmuseum presents itself in a modern setting. The conceptual remodelling formed part of a comprehensive revision of the permanent exhibitions housed in the Friedenstein castle's classicist west wing. After the permanent exhibition on 'Classicist sculpture', opened in 1990, and the Egyptian exposition, on show in its new form from April 1991, the reinstallation of the Graeco-Roman collection completed this project. The constraints imposed by the siting of the exhibition in historical rooms and settings, due to the lack of available neutral exhibition space, became a particular attraction in the design stage, as the overall change had made it possible to show the links between Antiquity and Classicism on a variety of levels. The basic idea behind this integration of the antiquities and Egyptian collections was to create – and allow visitors to experience – a content-related and visual synthesis of the historical rooms and the Egyptian and Graeco-Roman objects of the exhibition. It fitted in well with this overall concept that the onset of the systematic collection of antiquities by the dukes of Gotha coincided with and reflected the contemporary fashion of reminiscing. The exhibits provide visual evidence of the reception and stylistic adaptation of Graeco-Roman art within the various Classicist styles. A number of plaster casts of ancient sculptures and reliefs lead into the antiquities collection; they were originally part of the once important plaster cast collection, established in 1779 in the spirit of the Enlightenment by Duke Ernst II of Sachsen-Gotha-Altenburg. Three historical rooms form the conclusion of the antiquities exhibition, again showing various aspects of the reception of the Classical tradition. Among the exhibits are, for example, Gotha porcelain from the period around 1795, imitating Classical shapes and decoration, together with various drawings and paintings of landscapes and ruins with ancient motifs, and also cork models almost exclusively of Roman buildings made by the Italian cork sculptor Antonio Chichi, which had presumably come to Gotha soon after 1779. They were put on display in the music room and corresponded topically with the mythological wall decorations created in 1779 by the Gotha court sculptor Friedrich Wilhelm Eugen Doell (fig. 2). In addition to this

reference to Classicism which marks the opening and closing of the Antiquity and Egyptian collections, modern exhibition technology has been used to integrate reminiscences of ancient architecture and Egyptian tomb architecture into the exhibition (fig. 3). The room dedicated to Greek vases and vessels thus appears almost like a Greek temple. Small square display cabinets have become columns full of vessels; the central display cabinet is a treasure house of ancient culture. In addition to various marble objects, it contains a wide range of small artifacts – terracottas, bronze statuettes and everyday objects, glasses, gold jewellery – a veritable treasure indicating the wide range of ancient art and artists. In the area dedicated to Roman art and everyday objects, the design of the apse, the door and wainscoting bear witness to the Classicist ambience, into which the portraits and sculptures, on their plain pedestals, are harmoniously integrated (fig. 4).

1 Akten zur Antikensammlung, Archiv Schloßmuseum, 140   2 C. Aldenhoven, Katalog der griechisch-römischen Alterthümer des Herzoglichen Museums Gotha, 1890   3 A. Bube, Das Herzogliche Kunstkabinet zu Gotha, Gotha, ³1869, 6ff. (completely revised ed.) 4 Inventarium über die Herzogliche Kunst-Cammer auf Friedenstein, 1764, Intrade 68   5 Inventarium über die Kunst Cammer, aufgerichtet den 29. Februari 1659, Folio 27   6 J. G. Keyssler, Fortsetzung Neuester Reisen, durch Teutschland, Böhmen, Ungarn, die Schweiz, Italien und Lothringen, worinnen der Zustand und das merckwürdigste dieser Länder beschrieben wird, Hannover, 1741, 1137   7 Kunstkammer-Inventarium 1721, 182 8 J. H. Möller, Das Herzogliche Kunst- und Naturalien-Cabinet zu Gotha, Gotha, 1833, 7 f.   9 E. Rohde, Corpus Vasorum Antiquorum, Gotha Schloßmuseum, vols. 1 und 2, Berlin 1964, 1968   10 Thüringisches Staatsarchiv Gotha, Belege zur Kunstkammer 18./19. Jahrhundert   11 Thüringisches Staatsarchiv Gotha, Herzogliches Oberhofmarschallamt zu Gotha, 26. Acta die Uebergabe des Kunst- und Naturalien Cabinets von Archivrath Dr. Möller an den Oberkonsistorialsekretär Bube betreffend (1842–1843), 583h   12 F. Wieseler, Ueber die Sammlungen von Alterthümern auf Schloß Friedenstein zu Gotha, in: Jb. des Vereins von Alterthumsfreunden im Rheinlande, fasc. XLI, Bonn, 1866, 51.

UTA WALLENSTEIN

Gothic

A. Concept B. Genres C. Themes (iconography)

A. Concept

The stylistic designation 'Gothic' is founded upon the view, which arose in Italy and was primarily applied to architecture, that the Germanic Goths in the course of the folk-migration period brought to an end the 'golden age' of Classical Antiquity and imposed instead their barbaric style (see e.g. Vasari, *Le Vite de' più eccellenti pittori, scultori, ed architettori* (= *Lives of the Artists*) I,3 [2; 16; 20]). Even after the correction of this error and the re-evaluation and new dating of what continued to be termed 'Gothic' after the Romantic period, the term still retained its character, patent and underlined by the name, of a radical opposition to Classical Antiquity. However, in the context of art-historical differentiation, more emphasis was now laid upon the division between it and the Romanesque style, in which the cultural traditions of (Roman) Antiquity were present, not only in the name, but also (or perhaps once again) in material form. In this manner Gothic and Romanesque were treated as iconographic opposites – Christian modernity (*sub gratia*) versus Old Testament Antiquity (*sub lege*) – already in early Netherlandish painting [17]. Nevertheless, it is impossible to deny the Gothic mode, as the predominant artistic style in Europe in the 13th–15th cents., any connection to the Classical world.

In what follows we shall take account only of the specifically 'Gothic' aspects of the reception of the Classical world, not, however, features applicable to the whole of the Middle Ages, such as the use of → SPOLIA – a decreasing tendency (but cf. the bronze horses of → SAN MARCO, Venice) – or – a constant in this case – the use of ancient jewellery and gems for contemporary works of art (e.g. Shrine of the Three Kings, early 13th cent., Cologne Cathedral; Shrine of St Elisabeth, ca. 1235, Marburg, St Elisabeth Church; Bust of Charlemagne, ca. 1350, Aachen, Cathedral Treasury).

B. Genres

1. Architecture   2. Sculpture (Drawing)

1. Architecture

There are clear differences between individual artistic genres (and landscapes) and their attitudes towards Classical Antiquity. The break with the Classical tradition is seen most vividly in architecture, which may be ascribed above all to the momentous change from the Romanesque (originally 'Roman') rounded arch to the Gothic pointed arch. The associated gradual replacement of the massive, cubic construction resting in itself by an increasingly filigree skeletal building style led step by step to a completely new – Gothic – appearance in vaulted architecture. For all that, the basilica as the basic form of the early Christian church in Rome, lived on, and this was certainly deliberate. The continued use of individual forms in the Classical style for decorative elements (such as pillar-like supports, Attic bases) and pictorial motifs (such as centaurs, sirens and others) remained marginal; the acanthus pattern (on Corinthian capitals) became naturalistic foliage.

Furthermore, a distinction has to be made between the heartlands of the Gothic mode (France, Germany, England) and Italy, where the Gothic style established itself only in a limited and moderate manner, where the rounded arch was never completely abandoned, and where the changeover to the High Middle Ages was far less spectacular (Spain is a special case).

2. Sculpture (Drawing)

By contrast, sculpture presents an opposite picture, even though the loose 'wet' garment, often a Classical inheritance for Romanesque figures, disappeared and gave way to the Gothic clothed figure. But with the recovery at the same time of the 'beautiful' image of the human form there was a fundamental revision of the Christian ban on statues which had lasted well into the Romanesque period. It marked the return of independent statues no longer attached to any wall: as part of portals or other buildings and as free-standing sculptures ('Schönlebendigkeit' [16. 174]). One symptom of this was that now, in the 13th cent., the Classical and long-dismissed topos of the love for beautiful statues, which was linked originally with the → CNIDIAN APHRODITE of Praxiteles (cf. e.g. Plin. HN 36,20), was transferred to images of the Madonna and could thus redeem itself (Gautier de Coincy, *Miracles of Notre Dame*, begun 1218) [11. 149f.].

A relationship has often been suggested between Early and High Gothic and Classical sculpture; but this relationship is somewhat opaque and conceptual rather than material. More or less direct imitations are rare; cf. the reliefs on the façade of the cathedral at Auxerre (thematic and stylistic): Hercules, Sleeping Cupid, Dancing Satyr etc., Judgment of Solomon (before and after 1300) [14] (fig. 1). See also the stylistically related representations of Classical gods on the so-called imperial goblet in Osnabrück [18].

Instead more general connections are apparent. Especially Gothic clothed figures are often clearly modelled on Roman togati in contrapost: the most striking examples are the sculptures found at Reims cathedral, e.g. the prophet on the west central portal (5th figure from the left). Beside the free-standing nature of the statues, it was probably the adoption of 'formal recipes' [9. 179ff.] more than anything that was responsible for the Classical impression of the Reims group in particular (Master of the Visitation, Joseph Master, etc.), for which Julio-Claudian models have been proposed. From Reims, the new figural 'spirit' spread over large parts of Europe, without necessarily depending on any further contact with Classical material.

The restored balance in statuary manifested itself in a Classically-related contrapposto, which soon, beneath the now obligatory clothing, developed into the characteristic Gothic S-curve (and in so doing denied its genesis).

Nakedness was still frowned upon, and occurs only as an iconographic motif: for the (lost) innocence of Adam and Eve, or for debauchery, sin and mortality (in various allegorical and dogmatic representations). Significantly, the poses of the naked statues on Adam's Doorway at Bamberg Cathedral (ca. 1240) are far less 'Classical' than those of the clothed figures there (Emperor Heinrich and St Peter versus Adam and Eve). This is true too, *mutatis mutandis*, of some of the drawings in the pattern-book of Villard de Honnecourt (*c.* 1230/1240): inhibited by the unrestrained nakedness of

Fig. 1: Dancing Satyr, Hercules. portal relief, end of 13th cent. Auxerre, Cathedral

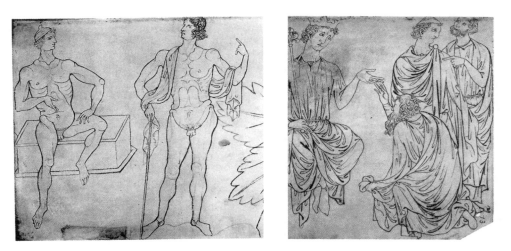

Fig. 2: Villard de Honnecourt, Two naked men (fol. 43), King and retinue (fol. 25).
Sketch book, ca. 1230/40, *Bibliothèque Nationale, Paris*

the Classical statues that he had in mind, the draughts-man reverted to the 'conceptual' (ultimately Roman-esque) patterns most familiar to him, while he had no problems with clothed figures in the Classical style [9. 193] (fig. 2).

More associations with Classical Antiquity, both in form and disposition, have at times been ascribed to Gothic funerary sculpture: the tomb of a married couple in Löwenberg in Silesia (ca. 1350) appears to be linked with Roman wedding sarcophagi through the *dextrarum junctio*. The elegiac postures of the deceased on the tomb of Cuno von Falkenstein and Anna von Nassau in Lich, Hesse (1329/1333) [15] are reminiscent of Attic funeral *stelae*.

A quite specific problem is that posed by the previously much-noticed affinity between 'Greek culture and the Gothic', which referred to the well-known and startling similarity in the smiles of figures from the early Gothic and Archaic periods. The heads of the prophets on the Bamberg rood screens (ca. 1235) and those of the pediment figures at Olympia (ca. 460 BC) and Aegina (ca. 480 BC) have also been seen as sibling phenomena. Since contact with Greek art as such may be ruled out, the relationship has been interpreted as a parallel phenomenon, as an analogy of historical development [9. 226–238].

Taken as a whole, sculpture in Italy remained more closely related to the Classical world than elsewhere in Europe. The cult of Antiquity, which emerged in the 13th cent. (first at the court of the Emperor Frederick II), and the fact that the Gothic style was adopted only to a reduced or partial extent permitted the rise of an artistic milieu in late medieval Italy (Niccolò and Giovanni Pisano, Giotto, Arnolfo di Cambio, Andrea Pisano), which, after a renewal of the Gothic mode, merged without clear borders into the early Renaissance: cf. the framing statuettes in the Classical style of the Gothic Porta della Mandorla at the Duomo in Florence (1391/1397), the portal reliefs of San Petronio in Bologna by Jacopo della Quercia (begun 1425) and other examples. One representative of this transition is Ghiberti (statues for the Or San Michele, Florence); his *Commentarii* also tell us about an instance of early enthusiasm for the Classical world: the public exhibition (and later demolition) of a Venus statue (before 1348) in Siena [11. 171–173]. Vasari's *Lives of the Artists* (1550 and 1568) focuses on demonstrating that the gradually advancing regeneration of the arts was brought about by a growing appreciation of Classical or natural standards (since Cimabue and Giotto), and it links the reception of the Classical world and 'naturalism' with the narrative of art-historical progress.

And yet, even in Italy figures like the naked Hercules (Fortitudo) and the reliefs on Niccolò Pisano's pulpit (Pisa, Baptistery, ca. 1260) are exceptions. Niccolò's quasi-Classical style depended upon local circumstances – the frequency in the Camposanto of Pisa of Roman sarcophagus reliefs. More striking still is the Venus by his son Giovanni as an allegorical caryatid for

Fig. 3: Giovanni Pisano, *Venus Pudica*. Pulpit support, prior to 1311. Pisa, Cathedral

the otherwise Gothic pulpit of Pisa Cathedral (before 1312): it is an almost literal repetition of a Hellenistic *Venus pudica* [11. 164–166] (fig. 3).

C. THEMES (ICONOGRAPHY)

Figures such as these lead us on to a particular modality in the Gothic awareness of Antiquity: iconographic reception. Classical themes and objects do not appear independently, but primarily as illustrations of texts. Nearly all of the Classical writings known today were transmitted and in some cases, more often during the Gothic period, illustrated by medieval scribes. However, only astronomical/astrological manuscripts (e.g. Zodiacus), of which there were growing numbers in the late Middle Ages, remained relatively faithful to Late Antique patterns because of pictorial stereotypes [19].

Fig. 4: Workshop of Diepold Lauber, *Paris hands the apple to Venus*.
Illustration in the War of the Trojans by Konrad of Würzburg (fol. 25r),
ca. 1440. Berlin, *Staatsbibliothek Preußischer Kulturbesitz*

As a general rule, Classical themes and figures, regardless of the genre of text involved, were anachronistically 'modernised', that is, they were furnished with contemporary clothes and placed in contemporary environments; this is especially noticeable with themes from Classical literature cultivated in a courtly context. Examples are the (vernacular) adaptations of the three 'classical' epics of Antiquity: the *Roman des Thèbes*, the *Roman d'Enéas* and the *Roman de Troie* of Benoît de Saint-Maure around the middle of the 12th cent. [6]. Here, undisguised reflections of medieval nobility can be found in the adventures, love-affairs and heroic deeds of Antiquity. In both text and image the lords and ladies involved in the *Aventiuren* follow those very same rules the high society had created for themselves to define their cultural identity and engage in social reproduction. In Gothic/late Gothic illustrations, Paris and Aeneas or Helen and Dido look no different from Tristan and Lancelot or Isolde and all the other courtly 'Dames', 'Frouwen', 'Madonne' and 'Ladies' (fig. 4). The same is also true for the representation of Classical gods and heroes in moralising and mythographical texts, such as the *Ovide moralisé* or the *Othea* of Christine de Pisan [12].

In this manner the Gothic view of Classical Antiquity reached well into the renaissance of Classical Antiquity, down to the wedding-chests and the gift *deschi* of Florentine society that Botticelli still catered to. Even for the elder Cranach, Paris, the hero of that fateful judgment, always remained a knight in armour.

Conversely, the (fairly rare) formal imitations, like Niccolò's Pisa Herkules, Giovanni's Pisa Venus or the gods on the Osnabrück goblet, were subject to the → INTERPRETATIO CHRISTIANA. Panofsky recognised that the modi of form and content were governed by the law of 'disjunction', the logic of either/or, creating the chiasmus by which Classical forms could only be articulated with contemporary content, and Classical content only in contemporary forms [18. chap. 2, sect. III].

Corresponding to this is the iconography of the idol in Gothic art: it preserves the echo of pagan statues, diminished in size and perched atop a pillar. Thus the idol, depending on the situation, might be profanely worshipped, or piously cast down from its pedestal [4]. Occasionally new themes and images were created in the Classical style, with pejorative intent: thus for example the story of the magician Virgil [5] or the legend of Aristotle and Phyllis. The latter arose in the context of 13th cent. anti-Aristotelean polemics, and remained a favourite subject in the canon of masculine follies and female wiles lasting into the Early Modern period [22].

A separate case is that of the (inset or relief) labyrinths found in and on Gothic cathedrals (Chartres, Amiens, Reims, Sens, Lucca, Bayeux and others). They represent the dangerous road taken by Christians ('Chemin de Jérusalem'), but also allowed the master builder to sign his work of ingenuity (Amiens, Reims) as a new Daedalus [3].

Taken as a whole, the reception of the Classical world in the Gothic period is not uniform, and in each case conditioned by particular circumstances. In the words of Panofsky: 'Die Gotik dagegen hat die Antike stets nur als etwas Fremdartiges, nicht aber als etwas Historisch-Distanziertes gesehen und daher immer nur einzelne Seiten ihres Wesens dem eigenen zu assimilieren versucht' ("The Gothic period, on the other hand, always viewed Classical Antiquity just as something foreign to itself, but not as something historically distanced, and therefore it tried always to assimilate to itself only individual aspects of its nature") [16. 175]. The Gothic era ended with the emergence of a decidedly antiquarian attitude, which crossed the gulf of the Middle Ages (and in doing so defined the Middle Ages as such) in order to approach Antiquity by deliberately distancing itself from Antiquity. It is an epoch-making process, prepared from the 14th cent. on by Humanists and Classical scholars, which triggered the renaissance of Classical art, and which continues in the modern (Euro-American) consciousness to the present day.

1 J. ADHÉMAR, Influences antiques dans l'art du Moyen Age français, 1939   2 E. S. DE BEER, Gothic: Origin and Diffusion of the Term, in: JWI 11, 1948, 143–162   3 H. BIRKHAN, s.v. Labyrinth, LCI, vol. 3, 2–4   4 M. CAMILLE, The Gothic Idol, 1989   5 D. COMPARETTI, Virgilio nel Medio Evo, 1–2, 1937–1941 (Engl. E. F. M. BENECKE (trans.), Vergil in the Middle Ages, 1966)   6 A. EBENBAUER, Antike Stoffe, in: V. MERTENS, U. MÜLLER (eds.), Epische Stoffe des Mittelalters, 1984, 247–289   7 P. FRANKL, Meinungen über Herkunft und Wesen der Gotik, in: W. TIMMLING, Kunstgeschichte und Kunstwissenschaft, 1923, 9–35   8 Id., The Gothic. Literary Sources and Interpretations through Eight Centuries, 1960   9 R. HAMANN-MACLEAN, Antikenstudium in der Kunst des Mittelalters, in: Marburger Jahrbuch für Kunstwissenschaft 15, 1949/50, 157–250   10 N. HIMMELMANN, Antike Götter im Mittelalter, 1986   11 B. HINZ, Aphro-

dite. Geschichte einer abendländischen Passion, 1998   12 C. LORD, Three Manuscripts of the Ovide moralisé, in: The Art Bulletin 57, 1975, 161–175   13 E. MÂLE, L'art religieux du XIIe siècle en France, 1928 (Engl. Religious Art in France, the Twelfth Century, 1978)   14 F. NORDSTRÖM, The Auxerre Reliefs, 1974   15 R. PROBST, Der Meister des Löwenberger Doppelgrabmals, in: H. TINTELNOT (ed.), Kunstgeschichtliche Studien, 1943, 201–217   16 E. PANOFSKY, Die Antike in der nordischen Gotik (lecture summary, 1928), in: Id., Deutschsprachige Aufsätze I, 1998, 74f.   17 Id., Early Netherlandish Painting, 1953, vol. I, chapt. V, sect. II   18 Id., Renaissance and Renascences in Western Art, 1960   19 Fr. SAXL, H. MEIER, Verzeichnis astrologischer und mythologischer illustrierter Handschriften des lateinischen Mittelalters I–IV, 1915, 1927, 1953, 1966   20 J. SCHLOSSER, Zur Geschichte der Kunsthistoriographie: Gotik, in: Id., Präludien, 1927, 270–295   21 J. SEZNEC, Das Fortleben der antiken Götter, 1990 (orig. La survivance des dieux antiques, 1940; B. F. SESSIONS (trans.), The Survival of the Pagan Gods, 1953)   22 W. STAMMLER, Der Philosoph als Liebhaber, in: Id. (ed.), Wort und Bild, 1962, 12–44   23 H. WENTZEL, Antiken-Imitationen des 12. und 13. Jahrhunderts in Italien, in: Zeitschrift für Kunstwissenschaft 9, 1955, 29–72.   BERTHOLD HINZ

Graeco-Roman Controversy

A. DEFINITION   B. EARLY HISTORY   C. ART-HISTORICAL AND THEORETICAL PREMISES AND CONTEXTS   D. EXPEDITIONS TO GREECE AND PUBLICATIONS BY STUART AND REVETT, AND LEROY   E. PIRANESI'S POLEMIC AGAINST LEROY   F. PIRANESI CONTRA MARIETTE AND THE END OF THE DEBATE

A. DEFINITION

The Graeco-Roman Controversy (GRC), also called 'Greek controversy' took place in the 1750s and 1760s. At its centre was the question whether Greek or Roman art was of greater historical and artistic significance, especially in the field of architecture. The immediate occasion for the most heated phase of the controversy was a publication by the French architect J.-D. LeRoy in 1758, the first publication on Greek architecture that was based on actual measurements. The Italian engraver, architect and archaeologist G. B. Piranesi reacted vehemently against it. His strong response may have been spurred on by the publication in 1755 of J. J. Winckelmann's *Gedancken über die Nachahmung der Griechischen Wercke in der Mahlerey und Bildhauer-Kunst* ('Thoughts on the Imitation of Greek Works in Painting and Sculpture') that had challenged the primacy of Roman art as upheld by Piranesi. Over the course of the debate Piranesi became less interested in arguing about historical and architectural priorities and focussed instead on the more fundamental question, as he saw it, of what was more important for the creative process: to be guided by the Greek 'belle et noble simplicité' or an imagination, unencumbered by rules, that could freely draw from a repository of all historical styles.

Fig. 1: Giuliano da Sangallo, *Parthenon, Rome* (drawing, ca. 1500). Cod. Barberini 4424, 28, © *Biblioteca Apostolica Vaticana*

B. EARLY HISTORY

The first publications of Greek architecture based on precise measurements caused a sensation in the late 1750s and early 1760s, especially since there had been complete ignorance in this area. In fact, any ideas about ancient architecture had been derived exclusively from monuments of the Roman world. In the 1430s and 1440s, Ciriaco di Filippo Pizzicolli (Ciriaco d' Ancona, from 1391 to after 1453), a humanist and merchant from Ancona [4; 16], in his quest for antiquities had extended his radius beyond Italy to Dalmatia, Greece, Byzantium and the Near East. From his travels he brought back sketches of inscriptions and architectural details as well as of front elevations of entire buildings, e.g. of the Parthenon (→ ATHENS III). However his impact was limited because the six volumes of his *Commentaria* probably were destroyed in the fire at the library of Pesaro in 1514 [17, 1–3]; a copy of Ciriaco by Giuliano da Sangallo from around 1500 (fig. 1) exemplifies the reinterpretation of Greek architecture in the 'Roman' style that was part of the reception process [5]. For a long time after the Turkish occupation under Mohammed II (1451–1481), Greece and Athens were far removed from the awareness of Europeans. Thus, in 1605 William Biddulph, who was on an extensive journey of the Near East and one of Athens' first western visitors, noticed with surprise that the city was still inhabited (*The Travels of certaine Englishmen into Africa, Asia, Troy*, 1609) [7. vol. I. 873; 6. 2].

The 'rediscovery of Greece' finally beginning in the 1670s, was mostly due to English and French travelers. In 1674 the French ambassador in Constantinople, Charles-François Ollier, Marquis de Nointel, visited Athens on an official mission and with the usual courtly pomp. In his entourage was Jacques Carrey, who drew the pediment sculptures of the Parthenon before they were destroyed by the devastating explosion of 1687 (→ ATHENS III, fig. 5; fig. 2) [7. vol. I. 881; 19. 19]. Sig-

nificant for the GRC of the 18th cent. is Nointel's comment that the antiquities of Athens would "surpass the most beautiful reliefs and statues of Rome" [3. 340].

In the same year (1674), Jacob Spon (1647–1685), a physician and antiquarian from Lyon published a text written two years earlier by the Jesuit priest Jacques Paul Babin, to which he added a preface, a brief history of the city of Athens and a view of the city (*Relation de l' état présent de la ville d' Athènes ancienne capitale de la Grèce, batie depuis 3400 ans avec un abrégé de son histoire et de ses antiquités*, Lyon 1674)). However, this first detailed description of Athens based on personal experience – the Jesuits had settled in Athens in 1645 – did not contribute to the knowledge of Greek architecture. In the same year Spon, himself, and the English botanist George Wheler (1650–1723) departed on a journey [8]. Their report (*Voyage d' Italie, de Dalmatie, de Grèce et du Levant, fait aux années 1675 & 1676 par Jacob Spon docteur médecin agregé à Lyon et George Wheler gentilhomme anglois*), published in 1678, contained a number of illustrations and although small and sketchy, they were the main source of information for Greek architecture for more than half a century. For instance, Johann Bernhard Fischer von Erlach relied on Spon for his rendering of the Parthenon (*Tempel Minervae zu Athen*) in his *Entwurff einer historischen Architektur* (1721) ('A Plan of Civil and Historical Architecture'); yet instead of Spon's west pediment that depicted the contest between Athena and Poseidon he chose the east pediment with the birth of Athena – portraying it, however, in a manner closer to Christian iconography (birth of Christ, death of Mary) than to Greek art (fig. 2).

A second phase (and a real wave) of journeys to Greece and Asia Minor followed in the 1730s and 1740s, mostly by English aristocrats, which showed an interesting development. While the first of these undertakings (Richard Pococke, 1736–40; John Montagu, Earl of Sandwich, 1738, with the painter Jean-Etienne Liotard in his entourage; as well as James Caulfield, Earl of Charlemont, 1749) had still been under the banner of the wide-ranging educational interests of the *Grand Tour* (which could, as in the case of the Earl of Sandwich, certainly include measuring the Parthenon), around 1750 the explicit study of Greek architecture came to the forefront. An example is Robert Wood, who had already been to the Greek islands in 1742 and 1743 in the sense of the above-mentioned general orientation, but who, after his third visit in 1750 with James Dawkins and John Bouverie, published a folio edition that was the first in what was to become a long series of great English archaeological and architectural publications: *The Ruins of Palmyra, otherwise Tedmor in the Desert*, London 1753 [7. II 497–498]. It was a response to a proposal, first published in 1748, that called for the exact recording and description of the buildings of Athens – and simultaneously promised them: the *Proposals for publishing a new and accurate Description of the Antiquities, &c. in the Province of*

Der Tempel Minervæ ʒü Athen.
Welcher biß auf die leʒte Belagerüng
noch gantʒ ʒü sehen gewesen.

Le Temple de Minerve à Athenes
Qui s'est conservé jusqu'au demier.
Siege.

Fig. 2: Johann Bernhard Fischer von Erlach, Entwurff einer historischen Architektur, 1721, vol. 1, pl. XIX (detail): 'The Temple of Minverva in Athens'

Attica by James Stuart (1713–1788; called 'Athenian') and Nicholas Revett (1720–1804). The authors justified such a project by claiming historical and artistic superiority of Greek over Roman art. They wrote (in a passage from the *Proposals* of 1751): 'There is perhaps no part of Europe more deservedly excites the Curiosity and Attention of lovers of Polite Literature than the Province of Attica, and in particular Athens its capital City; whether we reflect on the figure it makes in History (...), or whether we consider the number of Antiquities still remaining there, monuments of the good sense and elevated genius of the Athenians, and the most perfect Models of what is excellent in Sculpture and Architecture. (...) Rome, who borrowed her Arts and frequently her Artificers from Greece, has by means of Serlio, Palladio, Santo Bartoli, and other ingenious men, preserved the memory of the most excellent Sculptures, and magnificent Edifices which once adorned her (...). But Athens, the mother of Elegance and Politeness, whose magnificence scarce yielded to that of Rome, and who for the beauties of a correct style must be allowed to surpass her, as much as an original excels a copy, has been almost entirely neglected, and unless exact drawings from them be speedily made, all her beauteous Fabricks, her Temples, her Theatres, her Palaces will drop into oblivion (...)' [19. 77–78; 7. vol. II. 479–481].

C. Art-Historical and Theoretical Premises and Contexts

Of course the radical revaluation of traditional ideas as expressed in the previous sentences should not be considered as an isolated opinion of two Englishmen (who dabbled in painting and architecture), who had come to Rome in 1742 – one 29 years old, the other 22 –

where they probably made their living as *ciceroni* [13. 130]. Their opinions reflect theories that originated mostly in France where the idea of the primacy of Greek over Roman art allowed the claim of an artistic development independent of Rome (and thus of Italy) [19. 49; 14. 316–18]. In fact, in France after 1687, in connection with the → QUERELLE DES ANCIENS ET DES MODERNES, the question concerning the rank of modern vs. ancient artists had been raised (and answered in various ways), as well as the question concerning the relative significance of Greek and Roman Antiquity. Four decades earlier Roland Fréart de Chambray (1606–1676) in his *Parallèle de l' architecture antique et de la moderne* (Paris 1650; Engl. *A parallel of the antient architecture with the modern: in a collection of ten principal authors who have written upon the five orders (...) / written in French by Roland Freart (...); made English for the benefit of builders; to which is added An account of architects and architecture, in an (...) explanation of certain terms (...) affected by architects; with Leon Baptista Alberti's treatise Of statues by John Evelyn(...),*1664) had pleaded for the superiority of Greek architecture over Roman: "For the excellency and perfection of an art, consists not in the multiplicity of its principles; but contrarily, the more simple they are, and few in number, the more worthy they are of our admiration" [11. 140–142; 23. 8].

Anne Claude Philippe de Tubières, Comte de Caylus (1692–1765), by far the most important French antiquarian of his time, expressed the same opinion 100 years later in the context of his large and comprehensive, ambitious work *Recueil d' Antiquités Egyptiennes, Etrusques, Grecques et Romaines*. Although publication of the seven volumes started only in 1752 (and continued until 1767), their main thesis had undoubtedly been known before. In Caylus's cyclical view of history the gravitas of Egyptian hieratic architecture and sculpture stood at the beginning of all artistic development; art had come from Egypt via Etruria to Greece where it reached the highest degree of perfection (under Alexander the Great). In Rome, finally, it could shine a little longer "only with foreign help" and fight barbarism before its was finally buried with the decline of the empire. The Jesuit priest Marc-Antoine Laugier (1713–1769), who dabbled in architectural theory, expressed the same opinion in the introduction to his *Essai sur l' architecture* (English translation: London 1755, 1756) [9; 20. 534–535]. It was first published anonymously in 1753 and as the manifesto of a 'new simplicity' immediately caused a sensation beyond France. For Caylus 'simplicité' (not original but acquired over a long historical process) was the characteristic of Greek art that distinguished it from all previous and subsequent periods; it was synonymous with that particular quality which according to Winckelmann was 'das allgemeine vorzügliche Kennzeichen der Griechischen Meisterstücke: eine edle Einfalt, und eine stille Größe, so wohl in der Stellung als im Ausdruck' (*Gedancken über die Nachahmung der Griechischen Wercke in der Mahlerey und Bildhauer-Kunst*, 1755; *Reflections on the painting and sculpture of the Greeks: with Instructions for the connoisseur, and an essay On grace in works of art. Translated from the German original of the Abbé Winkelmann by Henry Fusseli*, [2]1767) ("The general and most distinctive characteristic of the Greek masterpieces is a noble simplicity and quiet grandeur, both in posture and expression.")

Fig. 3: Giovanni Battista Piranesi, Ostium, 'sive Emissarium Cloacae Maximae in Tiberim', in: *Della Magnificenza* (...), 1761, pl. II

D. Expeditions to Greece and Publications by Stuart and Revett, and LeRoy

In the effort to reach the purported highest stage of architecture again, Stuart's and Revett's announcement in 1748 of precise measurements and a multi-volume publication promised new standards for research and scholarly insights. The veritable race after 1750 to be the first to publish reliable data reveals a real need for such a work.

In January 1751 with support from members of the *Society of Dilettanti*, founded in London in 1732, Stuart and Revett set sail from Venice for Greece. For over two years, until the autumn of 1753, they stayed in Athens measuring and drawing any extant ancient buildings. In October 1755 they returned to England and started to work on their publication. The first volume of *The Antiquities of Athens, Measured and Delineated by James Stuart, F. R. S. and F. S. A., and Nicholas Revett, Painters and Architects* was published in 1762 in London; after Stuart's death and after Revett had already withdrawn from the project, three more volumes followed until 1816 [7. vol. II, 481–485]. However, when the first volume came out, *Antiquities* did not cause the sensation that had been envisioned

because a Frenchman had been faster than the two Englishmen.

In 1754, only a few months after Stuart's and Revett's return from Athens, the French architect Julien-David LeRoy (1724-1803) had departed for Greece from Rome, where he had stayed since 1751 with a scholarship from the French Academy. He had the same goal as the two Englishmen. After visiting the island of Delos he spent only a few months in Athens, travelled to Corinth and Sparta and returned via Rom to Paris in 1755 – the same year Stuart and Revett returned to London (and the year of Winckelmann's arrival in Rome). In Paris, assisted by Caylus and a team of draughtsmen and engravers, he started working on the publication of his notes from Greece. His book *Les Ruines des plus beaux monuments de la Grèce* was published in Paris in 1758 (Engl. *Ruins of Athens: with remains and other valuable antiquities in Greece*, 1759), four years before the first volume of *Antiquities* (→ Athens I, fig. 1; Athens III, fig. 9).

E. Piranesi's Polemic against LeRoy

LeRoy's *Ruines* was the first publication that claimed to provide the visual proof for the superiority

Fig. 4: J. D. LeRoy, Column bases
and capitals of the Erechtheum,
in: Julien-David LeRoy,
*Les Ruines des plus beaux
monuments de la Grèce*, 1758

of Greek over Roman architecture, a claim that up to that point had been rather abstract. With this assertion (and by reformulating old theses: "In short, the Greeks achieved a greater beauty and a larger wealth of ideas in architecture; and the Romans, who defeated the Greeks by force of arms, were obliged to recognize the superiority of their intellect, as they themselves confess" [20. 535]) LeRoy provoked the most vehement objection of that unconditionally Roman archaeologist who, from his first publication in 1743 (and during the 1750s in response to the increasingly louder voices that claimed the opposite) had not tired to invoke the *magnificenza* of the Romans and especially of their architecture: namely of the (as he called himself all his life) *Architetto Veneziano* Giovanni Battista Piranesi (1720–1778).

In 1756 Piranesi's four volumes of *Antichità Romane*, by then his longest and most ambitious work, were published. Undoubtedly the sometimes daring reconstructions, especially in the 4th volume (e.g. the monumental plates with the vision of the foundations of the Hadrian Mausoleum) were a reaction against the assertions of the 'Greek faction', which to a Roman must have seemed both scandalous and ridiculous. It was not until 1761, four years later, that Piranesi issued his first explicit statement in the schism: *Della Magnificenza ed Architettura de' Romani*. But he had apparently been working on his theses when LeRoy's book came out in 1758 when he wrote in a letter to the English architect George Dance the Younger that he found himself compelled to expand his ideas in light of the new situation [20. 536].

In fact, large parts of the text of *Della Magnificenza* [1], consisting of a hundred pages in Latin and just as many in Italian, could have been written shortly after 1755 – as a response to *Dialogue on Taste* [7. vol. II. 504], an anonymous publication of the same year by the Scottish painter Alan Ramsay (whom Piranesi had hon-

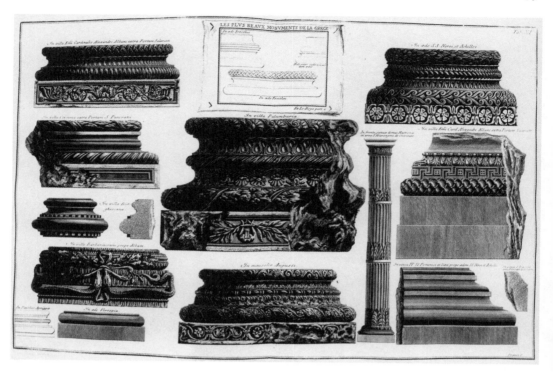

Fig. 5: Giovanni Battista Piranesi, A comparison of Various column bases
with those of the Erechtheum according to LeRoy, in: *Della Magnificenza (...)*, 1761, pl. II

Fig. 6: Giovanni Battista Piranesi, Comparison of Roman capitals, friezes and ornamental fragments
with a detail from LeRoy, in *Della Magnificenza...*, 1761, pl. XVII (left side)

oured in the frontispiece of the second volume of *Antichità...*). In this text, for which he probably had help, the author insisted on the superiority of the Etruscans and Romans, especially in their engineering structures – the example *par excellence* was the *Cloaca maxima* (fig. 3). In over two thirds of the plates – many of them covered two pages and could be unfolded to a width of over 120 cm – Piranesi blithely abandoned the first criterion of functional austerity. By quoting from LeRoy's plates he fully illustrated the paltry simplicity of Greek architectural ornamentation by comparing it to the products of Roman imagination – the boundaries between stringent visual argumentation and skillful visual polemic had become fluid (figs. 4–6).

F. Piranesi contra Mariette and the End of the Debate

In a *Lettre (...) sur un Ouvrage de M. Piranesi concernant les Antiquités Romaines*, printed in the *Gazette Littéraire de l' Europe* of 4 November, 1764, the French critic Jean Pierre Mariette responded to Piranesi's *Della Magnificenza*. Mariette argued that the Etruscans were of Greek origin, that Roman art had its origin in Greece and it was mostly executed by Greek slaves. The Greeks had "a beautiful and noble simplicity" and "good taste" for merely a brief period; but among the Romans art had become "ridiculous and barbaric" [11. 225]. – A year later Piranesi countered Mariette's 15 pages with a three-part book [1].

He designed the title page of the first part, *Osservazioni (...) sopra la Lettre de M. Mariette aux Auteurs de la Gazette Littéraire de l' Europe (...)*, as a scathing caricature of the artist at work aimed at the scribbler Mariette (fig. 7); the text of *Osservazioni* was arranged in two columns: in the narrow right column Mariette's letter was reprinted in its entirety, on the left side Piranesi, in caustic rage, inveighed against his adversary point by point. The second part, entitled *Parere su l'Architettura* is a dialogue – a *cicalata* ('playful conversation') [11. 225–226], whose substance and actual message is difficult to ascertain – between Protopiro, a follower of Marc-Antoine Laugier, and Didascalo, Piranesi's mouthpiece. In the final third part, entitled *Della introduzione e del progresso delle belle arti in Europa ne' tempi antichi* and presented as an introduction to a new (never published) book, Piranesi repeated his anti-Greek invectives.

But as it befitted a visual artist, Piranesi's last 'words' were five illustrations – etchings, to be precise – which he integrated into *Parere* after 1768. The five architectural sketches may be regarded a total affront to all theoretical rules and laws. On the uppermost ledge of the last of these sketches (fig. 8) is a line from Sallust's *Bellum Iugurthinum*: 'Novitatem meam contemnunt, ego illorum ignaviam' – "they despise my novelty, I their inactivity". But the façade Piranesi presented is "an inferno of the rules of Classical order" [11. 226].

The GRC ended in the final decades of the 18th cent. with the widespread acceptance of Classical tendencies

Fig. 7: *Osservazioni di Gio. Battista Piranesi sopra la Lettre de M. Mariette (...)*, 1764, title page

fashioned on Greek models – de facto a 'victory' for the 'Greek faction'. Maybe it was indeed more than a 'tempest in a tea-pot' (Miller) or merely 'paper-warfare' (Wilton-Ely). Its outcome led, on the one hand, to the "Tyranny of Greece over Germany" (E. M. Butler, 1935); the 'Greek' Winckelmann became – but only in the German-speaking countries – the one and only 'father of Classical archaeology'. In contrast, Piranesi, the Roman, fell into disregard as a serious archaeologist (which, in fact, he always was and continues to be).

Source 1 J. Wilton-Ely (ed.), G. B. Piranesi: The Polemical Works (Rome 1757, 1761, 1765, 1769), 1972
Literature 2 C. Bersani, I monumenti archeologici nelle opere degli artisti e dei viaggiatori stranieri dei secoli XVIII e XIX, in: L' immagine dell' antico fra settecento e ottocento, 1983, 73–120   3 L. Beschi, La scoperta dell' arte greca, in: S. Settis (ed.), Memoria dell' antico nell' arte italiana, vol. 3: Dalla tradizione all' archeologia, 1986, 295–372   4 E. W. Bodnar, Cyriacus of Ancona and Athens, 1960   5 B. L. Brown, D. E. Kleiner, Giuliano da Sangallo's Drawings after Ciriaco d' Ancona. Transformations of Greek and Roman Antiquities in Athens, in: JSAH 42, 1983, 321–335   6 J. M. Crook, The Greek Revival. Neo-Classical Attitudes in British Architecture 1760–1879, 1972   7 J. Dobai, Die Kunstliteratur des Klassizismus und der Romantik in England, vol. I, 1974, 867–920 (Travels abroad); vol. II, 1975, 476–526 (archaeological architecture publications)   8 R. Éti-

Fig. 8: Giovanni Battista Piranesi, Architectural design ('Novitatem meam contemnunt, ego illorum ignaviam'), Additional plate to *Parere su l'Architettura*, after 1768

ENNE, J.-C. MOSSIÈRE (eds.), Jacob Spon. Un humaniste Lyonnais du XVIIème siècle, 1993   9 W. HERRMANN, Laugier and Eighteenth Century French Theory, 1962   10 E. KAUFMANN, Piranesi, Algarotti and Lodoli. A Controversy in XVIII Century Venice, in: Gazette des Beaux-Arts 97, 1955, 21–28   11 H.-W. KRUFT, Geschichte der Architekturtheorie. Von der Antike bis zur Gegenwart, 1985, 218–244 (Engl. R. TAYLOR, E. CALLANDER, A. WOOD, (trans.), A History of Architectural Theory: From Vitruvius to the Present, 1994)   12 S. LANG, The Early Publications of the Temples at Paestum, in: Journal of the Warburg and Courtauld Institutes 13, 1950, 48–64   13 L. LAWRENCE, Stuart and Revett: Their Literary and Architectural Careers, in: JWI 2, 1938, 128–146   14 N. MILLER, Europäischer Philhellenismus zwischen Winckelmann und Byron, in: Aufklärung und Romantik 1700–1830 (Propyläen Gesch. der Lit.), 1983, 315–366   15 Id., Winckelmann und der Griechenstreit. Überlegungen zur Historisierung der Antike-Anschauung im 18. Jahrhundert, in: T. GAEHTGENS (ed.), J. J. Winckelmann 1717–1868, 1986, 239–264   16 G. PACI, S. SCONOCCHIA (eds.), Ciriaco d' Ancona e la cultura antiquaria dell' umanesimo, 1998   17 A. SCHMIDT, Antikenkopien und künstlerische Selbstverwirklichung in der Frührenaissance, in: R. HARPRATH, H. WREDE (eds.), Antikenzeichnung und Antikenstudium in Renaissance und Frühbarock, 1989, 1–20   18 D. WATKIN, Athenian Stuart, Pioneer of the Greek Revival, 1982   19 D. WIEBENSON, Sources of Greek Revival Architecture, 1969   20 J. WILTON-ELY, Vision and Design: Piranesi's Fantasia and the Graeco-Roman Controversy, in: G. BRUNEL (ed.), Piranèse et les français, 1978, 529–544   21 Id., The Art of Polemic: Piranesi and the Graeco-Roman Controversy, in: P. BOUTRY et al. (eds.), La Grecia antica. Mito e simbolo per l' età della Grande Rivoluzione, 1991, 121–130   22 R. WITTKOWER, Piranesi's Parere su l'architettura, in: JWI 2, 1938, 147–158

ADDITIONAL BIBLIOGRAPHY S. JONES, The Eighteenth Century, 1985.; J. RYKWERT, The First Moderns: The Architects of the Eighteenth Century, 1983; J. SUMMERSON, The Architecture of the Eighteenth Century, 1986

MARCEL BAUMGARTNER

Grammar see → LINGUISTICS

Great Britain see → UNITED KINGDOM

Greece
I. GENERAL   II. EDUCATION AND SCHOLARSHIP   III. MUSEUMS

I. GENERAL
A. CHRONOLOGY AND DELINEATION   B. POST-BYZANTINE ERA   C. ENLIGHTENMENT AND NATIONALISM   D. THE MODERN GREEK STATE

A. CHRONOLOGY AND DELINEATION
'Greece' (G.) can be understood in a dual sense: on the one hand, the term is used to refer to the modern Greek state since its foundation (1830); however, 'G.' can also – without immediate reference to questions of statehood – describe the territories of the former Byzantine empire in which the Greek-speaking culture found

expression after 1204 or 1453, whether in the context of the Ottoman Empire (OE) or within the area under Venetian rule. Although the modern Greek reception of Antiquity after 1830 is inconceivable without the preceding period, it is advisable that the two strands be separated, especially since the territorial congruence between ancient Hellas and modern G. is merely an apparent one. Therefore, we shall first deal with the period up to ca. 1700 which can be understood as the 'post-Byzantine' era. It is distinguished from the subsequent era of Enlightenment, which can be understood as a transitional phase, by drastic developments and events (Crete came under Turkish rule, permanently, in 1669; defeat of the OE at Vienna in 1683; decline of the Venetian and Turkish empires; rise of the Habsburg monarchy). Following that will be a description of the ca. 150 years of the modern Greek state.

B. POST-BYZANTINE ERA

Any investigation of the reception of Antiquity in the Byzantine and modern Greek areas must begin with one basic assumption [4. 11ff.]: despite historical discontinuities and ethnic displacements, despite numerous catastrophes such as the Fourth Crusade, the Byzantine élite never relinquished their claim to represent the continuation of the Roman state and the preservation of the Hellenistic legacy. After the decline in language skills in late Antiquity and prior to the 14th cent. the Byzantine empire was the only territory where ancient and Christian-Patristic Greek literature continued to be cultivated, and it was almost all-too conscious of this fact. Besides this indisputable continuity in the cultivation of literature, there is also that of language: modern Greek (and its dialects) is the direct and only descendant of ancient Greek. Late Byzantine scholars (such as G. Plethon) were also acutely aware of the resulting problems of descent that are today experienced by modern Greeks [18. 160ff.].

It is no longer possible to speak of a uniform development in the former Byzantine territories after 1204, and certainly no later than the end of the 13th cent.: aside from the steadily shrinking rump state, which disappeared in 1453, larger and larger territories came under Islamic (Seljuk, then Ottoman) or Venetian (Genoan, French) rule. While there was a revival of ancient studies in the Palaiologan empire, development in the areas ruled by the west were completely different: the massive Italian and French influence led to a flourishing of vernacular literature and, especially in Crete [1; 15], to a fusion of late Byzantine and Italian Humanism [19]. Not only were numerous copies of ancient manuscripts (especially the scientific writers of the 'Alexandrian School', ca. 300BC – 200 AD) made in 'Candia' in the second half of the 15th cent. (Michael Apostolis, ca. 1422 – ca. 1480 [8. 73ff.]), but a vibrant intellectual life modelled on the Italian Renaissance developed on the island, which included the production of works not only in Greek but also in Latin and Italian. However, true to the traditions of *umanesimo volgare*,

it was primarily the local Greek dialect, Cretan, that developed into the first fully valid literary variety of modern Greek. Translations and adaptations of the representative works of the Renaissance, Mannerism and the Baroque (such as *Pastor fido* by Guarini as Ὁ πιστικὸς βοσκός) meant that soon all the genres of Italian literature were represented on the island. A revival of ancient drama, therefore, took place not in a direct line of tradition but through the Cretan emulation of Western models: Jesuit drama, gothic play, idylls, religious theatre and comedy (the most important representative: G. Chortatsis) flourished. This output was printed almost exclusively in Venice [17]. Another centre of literary activity was Venetian Euboea (N. Sagundinos, ca. 1400–1462 [2]). This Greek branch of Venetian Humanism was sustained, on the one hand, by the old Byzantine nobility now serving the new rulers and, on the other hand, by Graecized Venetian settlers who had been present on the island since the 13th century.

This contact with the West also produced a Christian Humanism which sometimes culminated in Protestantism: Zacharias Gerganos [20. 160ff.] studied in Wittenberg and had the first Lutheran-inspired catechism in modern Greek printed there in 1622; Kyrillos Loukaris [10] of Crete, Patriarch of Constantinople, converted to Calvinism and had a modern Greek Bible printed in Geneva. This led to an accusation of heresy, which cost him his life (1638).

Circumstances in the OE [20] were completely different. Here late Byzantine trends toward a modern Greek national state (Empire of Nicaea) were subdued by the Ottoman *millet* system: in principle, as members and leading group of the Orthodox religious community (*Rūm milleti*), the Greeks lived there largely undisturbed; however, they were cut off from the Renaissance and subsequent developments because of the ban on printing and other restrictions. Intellectual life was centred around the Patriarchate of Constantinople and, to a large extent, moved along the traditional, late Byzantine theological lines; a certain degree of ossification was inevitable. The close symbiosis between the Ottoman state and the Orthodox Church persecuted any and all signs of Humanism, Reformation and the Renaissance and ultimately even the Enlightenment.

C. ENLIGHTENMENT AND NATIONALISM

The Ottoman conquest of Crete limited the Venetian possessions to the Ionian Islands; Greek Catholicism on the remaining islands declined. On the other hand, military crises and decentralization in the OE gave the Greeks an extraordinary starting basis compared to the other Balkan peoples: Phanariote dynasties ruled in the semi-autonomous principalities of Moldavia and Wallachia and as a trading people, the Greeks had colonies in almost all major western European cities. At the same time, they maintained close relations with Europeans who had settled in the Orient (Constantinople, Thessaloniki, Smyrna, Beirut, Alexandria) and whose schools they attended. As a result, they came into contact with the ideas of the Enlightenment, the beginnings of nationalism and revolutionary ideas that were circulating in the west [6]. While in the 18th and 19th cents. the Orthodox Church adopted a negative attitude toward these developments (evidence of a serious debate can only be found in E. Vulgaris, 1716–1806 [20. 344ff.]), the Greek bourgeoisie inside and outside of the OE followed the discussions in Europe intensely. Its most important representatives (such as A. Korais, 1748–1833 [16]) also adopted the Neo-Classicist concept of Antiquity and applied it to their concept of a Greek nation. Thus, at the time of the definitive defeat of the Ottomans by the Russians (1774, Küçük Kaynarcı), the Greek or Graecized educated classes (such as the Phanariotes in Constantinople) underwent a paradigm shift that was crucial for modern Greek history [7; 9] from their Byzantine/post-Byzantine identity (manifested in the Ottoman *millet* system) to an idealized image of their own past shaped by the European ideal of Antiquity [5; 13]. They believed that the Greek nation had been held in thrall since Roman times, and that the OE represented the worst excesses of this state of servitude. It was through education that they thought their nation could be freed from cultural and political decay. The most effective means to accomplish this task, they claimed, would be the creation of a nation state.

This radical step not only called into question the entire Byzantine legacy, but also the continuing power of the Orthodox Church, around whose centre – the Patriarchate – the majority of Greeks at that time and the other Orthodox Balkan Christians were organized. It was in this context also that the language question, which dominated the entire 19th cent. [11], erupted with severity: should Ancient Greek predominate in the new state, as demanded by the majority of Phanariotes, including P. Kodrikas (1762(?) – 1827) – or modern Greek, which was 'contaminated' by Turkisms and seemed less suited to represent the new-old Hellenic ideal, a solution nevertheless favoured by the reformers D. Katartzis (ca. 1730–1807) and Vilaras (1771–1823)? Or a compromise (thus Korais)? These ultimately insoluble tensions between western Neo-Humanism and the (post-) Byzantine tradition found expression in the anathema against the Greek revolutionaries of 1821 by the Orthodox Patriarch Gregorios V at the instigation of the Ottoman government. The hopeless situation of the Church is demonstrated by the fact that, regardless of this measure, the same Patriarch was hanged in his church on Easter by the Turks as a representative of the 'treasonous' *Rūm-millet* (10 April 1821).

D. THE MODERN GREEK STATE

The modern Greek state thus inherited a heavy ideological burden from the 18th cent., adding to its nearly hopeless internal and external problems [12; 22]: owing its very existence to a compromise between the Great Powers (England, France, Russia) and the OE, it was forced to accept a disagreeable form of government

(monarchy) and a foreign – Catholic – dynasty (Otto I of Wittelsbach), while the borders of 1830 included only a fraction of the population who felt themselves to be 'Greeks'. As a consequence, the irridenta problem determined Greek politics in its entirety until at least 1923 and essentially until 1974 (Cyprus conflict). The reception of Antiquity from a nationalist point of view that was handed down through the discourses of the 18th cent. continued and was reinterpreted in a chauvinist, revanchist fashion. As could be expected, the Greek sense of national identity, based on their descent from the ancient Hellenes, suffered a shock when an originally liberal → PHILHELLENISM and 19th cent. German Classical scholarship clashed with the reality of a country ravaged by war and civil war, and which was deeply marked by its Ottoman past: as the German enthusiasm for Antiquity failed utterly in face of the intellectual challenge posed by the existence of the contemporary Greek population (notable exceptions aside), the inhabitants of the tiny state on the southeastern periphery of Europe reacted with an even more passionate insistence on their ancient heritage. The apodictic and in effect racist verdict of J.P. Fallmerayer [23] (see also Meraklis in [5. 269ff.]), who disputed the 'biological' line of descent between ancient and modern Greeks, was countered by the former through a vigorous identification with the ideology of German Classical scholarship: for the most part, the Greek founders of Classical Studies, archaeology and ancient history, but also those of linguistics and folk studies, had studied in Germany – if they were not themselves Germans teaching at the newly established (1837) University of Athens. To the extent that German Classical Studies changed over the course of the 19th cent. from a liberal to an increasingly pre-Fascist discipline (F. Thiersch, 1784–1860, one of the first professors in Munich under whom young Greeks studied, not only wrote an account of the conditions in modern Greece in 1834 that is still worth reading today, but was also denounced by Metternich to his sovereign [22. 55f.]), the young country of G. followed this paradigm: studies concerned with 'Hellenism' also served to justify irredentist claims to the Ottoman heritage in the second half of the 19th cent. The founding manifesto for this ideology was the Ἱστορία τοῦ Ἑλληνικοῦ Ἔθνους (*History of the Greek Nation*, first published in 1860–1874) by K. Paparrigopulos (1815–1891) which is but one entire apologia against Fallmerayer. The reception of the Byzantine legacy, which began at the end of the 19th cent. and was at first suppressed, was incorporated into the framework of this concept of 'ethnos'.

The demand for the realization of the 'grand idea', the reestablishment of the Byzantine Empire with a strong Greek nationalist element, was the order of the day until the failed campaign in Asia Minor (1922–23) [12. vol. I. 305ff.]. Up to this point and even beyond, the country lapsed into a giant exercise in mimicry: place names were replaced (sometimes erroneously) with ancient names; Roman, Byzantine and especially Venetian and Ottoman historical buildings were destroyed under the assiduous leadership of European archaeologists in order to find antiquities; in place of the old 'Rhomaioi' word, the almost forgotten 'Hellenic' term was once again propagated, etc. The destruction of the past as part of the adopted Hellenic ideal reached its peak in the 'excavation' (more correctly: new construction) of the Athenian Acropolis [21]: after the clearance of all non-ancient monuments from this old castle, which had still served as a fortress in the war of 1821–1830, it can be said without exaggeration that the modern Acropolis of Athens is the most representative monumental ruin built by German Classical scholarship in the capital city of the new state.

The opening of this ideological edifice through various factors, which occurred after the First World War (foundation of the University of Thessalonika) but primarily after the end of the monarchy and dictatorship (1974), suffered a serious setback after the end of the Cold War in the Macedonian crisis, which demonstrated paradigmatically how even today the discourse on Greek nationalism remains entrenched in 19th cent. German patterns: in order to support Greek claims to Macedonia, O. Hofmann's book [14] from 1906, which sought to prove the Greek 'national character' of the ancient Macedonians, was translated in G. by the (rightfully) famous Cretan philologist G. Chatzidakis (1848–1941), who had studied in Germany. At the height of the new Macedonian crisis in the mid–1990s, it was precisely this old translation that was republished and furnished with a nationalistic foreword – again by a modern Greek linguist highly regarded in every respect, G. Babiniotis. He, too, had studied in Germany (Cologne) ([3. 259ff.]: 'Ψευδώνυμη γλῶσσα ψευδεπί-γραφου κράτους'. There is hardly a better illustration of the reflex of a German Classical scholarship with ethnic-nationalist overtones in Southeastern Europe. It remains an irony of history that its reception continued not only irrespective of any German political stance, e.g. on the dispute over Macedonia, but also that it was precisely this German school of Classical scholarship which has helped – and still does – determine the scholarly and political discourse in G. – a country with which it has been as incapable in the 20th cent. as it had been in the 19th of forming a meaningful relationship. Whether its present crisis will lead to the breakdown of existing barriers and unite both traditions in a comprehensive 'Hellenology' seems doubtful at the present time.

→ ARABIC-ISLAMIC CULTURAL SPHERE; → BAVARIA; → BAROQUE; → BYZANTIUM; → ENLIGHTENMENT; → GREEK; → MODERN GREEK LITERATURE; → RENAISSANCE

1 F. BABINGER, Veneto-kretische Geistesstrebungen um die Mitte des XV. Jahrhunderts, in: ByzZ 57, 1969, 62–77 2 Id., Nikolaos Sagoundinos, ein griechisch-venedischer Humanist des 15. Jahrhunderts, in: Id., Aufsätze und Abhandlungen zur Geschichte Südosteuropas und der Levante, vol. III, 1976, 242–256 3 G. BABINIOTIS (ed.), Η γλώσσα της Μακεδονίας. Η αρχαία Μακεδονική και η ψευδώνυμη γλῶσσα των Σκοπίων, 1993 ('The Language of Macedonia. Old Macedonian and the so-called Language of Skopje') 4 H.-G. BECK, Das byzantinische Jahrtausend, 1978 5 E. CHRYSOS (ed.), Ἕνας νέος κόσμος γεννιέται ..., 1996 ('A New World is Born: The Image of Greek Culture in 19th Century German Scholarship') 6 K. TH. DIMARAS, Νεοελληνικός Διαφωτισμός, Athens ⁶1993 ('Modern Greek Enlightenment') 7 H. EIDENEIER, Hellenen – Philhellenen: ein historisches Mißverständnis?, in: AKG 67.1, 1985, 137–159 8 D. J. GEANAKOPLOS, Greek Scholars in Venice, 1962 9 G. P. HENDERSON, The Revival of Greek Thought 1620–1830, 1971 10 G. HERING, Ökumenisches Patriarchat und europäische Politik 1620–1638, 1968 11 Id., Der Streit über die neugriechische Schriftsprache, in: Sprachen und Nationen im Balkanraum, in: CHR. HAMMICH, 1987, 125–194 12 Id., Die politischen Parteien in Griechenland 1821–1936, 2 vols., 1992 13 R. HEYDENREUTER et al. (eds.), Die erträumte Nation. Griechenlands Wiedergeburt im 19. Jahrhundert, 1995 14 O. HOFFMANN, Die Makedonen, ihre Sprache und ihr Volkstum, 1906 15 D. HOLTON (ed.), Literature and Society in Renaissance Crete, 1991 16 C. HOPF, Sprachnationalismus in Serbien und Griechenland. Theoretische Grundlagen sowie ein Vergleich von Vuk Stefanovic Karadžič und Adamantios Korais, 1997 17 E. LAYTON, The Sixteenth Century Greek Book in Italy, 1994 18 J. NIEHOFF-PANAGIOTIDIS, Koine und Diglossie, 1994 19 N. PANAGIOTAKIS, The Italian Background of Early Cretan Literature, in: Dumbarton Oaks Papers 49, 1995, 281–323 20 G. PODSKALSKY, Griechische Theologie in der Zeit der Türkenherrschaft, 1988 21 L. SCHNEIDER, CHR. HÖCKER, Die Akropolis von Athen. Antikes Heiligtum und modernes Reiseziel, 1990 22 W. SEIDL, Bayern in Griechenland. Die Geburt des griechischen Nationalstaats und die Regierung König Ottos, 1981 23 G. VELOUDIS: Jakob Philipp Fallmerayer und die Entstehung des neugriechischen Historismus, in: Südost-Forschungen 29, 1970, 43–90.   JOHANNES NIEHOFF

II. EDUCATION AND SCHOLARSHIP
A. TURKOCRACY AND DIASPORA   B. THE MODERN GREEK STATE

A. TURKOCRACY AND DIASPORA

1. Continuous conflicts between Byzantium and the Latin West, on the one hand, and the Slavic peoples of the Balkans (Serbs, Bulgars) on the other, strengthened the Greek consciousness of the Byzantines from the 13th cent. on. The conquest of Constantinople by the Crusaders (1204) and the disintegration of the ecumenical form of government were instrumental in the adaptation of Roman imperial ideology to the idea of a Greek monarchy (cf. the ideology of the kings of Nicaea: [23]). Increasing self-determination through the concept of 'Hellenes' (instead of 'Romans') [54. 17] was accompanied by the appropriation of ancient tradition by many scholars of the Palaeologan period (especially G. Gemistos-Plethon; for the revival of the term in the 19th cent. see [25]). Nevertheless, the influence of scholarly ideas on the spoken language and folk culture (i.e. on the linguistic and ideological foundations of modern Greek literature) remained minimal at first.

The advance of the Ottomans and the fall of Constantinople (1453) resulted in the dissolution of the educational centres of the late Byzantine period and an increase in the significance of the Church, because the new rulers regarded education as associated with the religion which they tolerated [22. 6]. While a programmatic 'Hellenisation' of education was delayed in Venetian-controlled areas (Chios: important trading and cultural centre until 1566; Crete; Cyprus; Ionian Islands) through the influence of the Italian Renaissance and restrictions on the authority of the Orthodox Church, the Patriarch of Constantinople, as the head of all Christians in the Ottoman Empire, remained the heir to the late-Byzantine, Hellenocentric traditions. However, the scarce material and intellectual resources did not permit a cultural breakthrough. Scholarly treatment of the ancient texts declined, the study of Greek literature served a conservative, Christian-oriented education (as a part of which it had never lost its position in the east), but only insofar as it did not compromise morality and faith. At first, philosophy also supported the true faith and, from this perspective, the continuing conflicts in the west between the Platonists (Michael Apostolis, Bessarion) and Aristotelians (Theodoros Gazis, Andronikos Kallistos) were discussed as well [39. vol. 1. 35–42]: in 1460 the *Laws* of Plethon were condemned by Patriarch Georgios (Gennadios) Scholarios. As a result, Plato was banished from Greek education for almost three centuries [2].

Despite the increasing divide between the Greeks in the Ottoman Empire and those in the diaspora, numerous Greeks in Italy worked towards the 'rebirth' of the genos, and Antiquity was now crucial for its definition. This was the aim, e.g., of Nikolaos Sofianos' editorial translation program [56]: in 1534, he wrote the first Greek grammar in the vernacular (published in 1870) and was the first to edit an ancient prose text, Plutarch's *On the Education of Children* in a modern Greek translation (1534), as well as a map (*Totius Graeciae descriptio*, 1536; reprint 1544: list of ancient and modern place names in the appendix); he also envisaged translating Classical authors into modern Greek, a plan that was doomed to failure in the face of insurmountable financial and practical difficulties. Translations and adaptations of ancient texts (especially popular among these was the *Iliad*, which can be explained, on the one hand, by the high regard in which this epic was held during in the Renaissance, and on the other it attests to an interest in a Greek heroic legend) rarely reached a broad audience in the East. One exception was the Alexander romance with ca. 50 editions from 1680 on.

Greek education in Italy was often indebted to the assistance of the Catholic Church (e.g. the Collegio Greco, founded by Pope Gregory XIII in Rome in 1577; a Greek *gymnasium* had been established in Rome in 1515) or depended on support from wealthy Greeks: in 1662, Thomas Flangines of Corfu created scholarships for the school (*frontisterion*) in Venice founded by him in 1655. In addition to Greek and Latin, the natural

sciences were also taught at these schools. During Ottoman rule, most Greek teachers were educated in Italy, and the most important modern Greek book editions, including those used for teaching, were published there.

The first attestations of a school in Constantinople are from 1556; except for a few schools in major cities (above all Ioannina), where instruction was heavily dependent upon the person and interests of the teachers who often had to move between locations, no public schools existed in the second half of the 16th cent.; only in 1593 did Patriarch Meletios Pigas demand that his bishops actively promote education. In the 17th cent., Patriarch Kyrillos Lukaris (1572–1638), a forerunner of the Greek Enlightenment who was in close contact with the Reformation, launched concrete educational initiatives: particularly worth mentioning are the purchase of a print shop (1627), the translation of the New Testament into modern Greek by Maximos Kallipolitis (Geneva, 1638) and the appointment of Theophilos Korydalleus to Constantinople (1574–1646; studies in Padua with Cremonini [50]) to head the Patriarchal Academy, which had, in the meantime, been reorganized (in 1663 it received a department of philosophy and in 1716 a theological school). In place of the dominant theological orientation, Korydalleus focused on the systematic teaching of philosophy (which had previously been restricted to logic and rhetoric) through interpretation and annotation of all Aristotelian works (and no longer through the commentaries of Alexander, Simplicius and Themistius). Korydalleus tied the revival of philosophy to the study of Classical authors. In the 17th cent., after initial hesitation, neo-Aristotelian 'Korydallism' became a fixed component of a religious Humanism that from ca. 1700 served as a shield for the Church against the new ideas and educational ideals flooding in from the West and culminating in the so-called Greek Enlightenment. The authority of Aristotle was first decisively questioned in the *Philotheou parerga* (edited posthumously, Moscow 1800) by Nikolaos Mavrokordatos (1680–1730); at the same time, Plato came to be regarded more highly and the concept of natural law was propagated. The high point of the Church's reaction to the introduction of modern thought came with the the condemnation of Methodios Anthrakitis, who in 1723 was said to have removed Peripatetic doctrine from his curriculum (in Siatista and Kastoria) and replaced it with geometry and physiology. Among the prominent exponents of European natural philosophy in the 18th cent. were Vikentios Damodos (1679–1757; taught in Kefallenia) and Eugenios Voulgaris (1716–1806; taught in Ioannina, Kozani, Athos, Constantinople), an eclectic who translated numerous contemporary European philosophical works and wrote theological, philological and philosophical treatises. European philosophy (influenced by Descartes, Locke, Voltare) is reflected in his *Logic* (1766). The severance from with dogmatic Aristotelianism reached its first peak in the *Apology* (1780) of Iosipos Moisiodax (ca. 1725–1800). Moisiodax attempted to steer a middle way between the conservative veneration of Antiquity and the tendency of many proponents of the Enlightenment towards a radical break with the past [27. 167–176].

In the 18th cent., the Church increasingly felt the competition from the emerging bourgeoisie (supported by the Greeks of the diaspora) and their ambitious educational initiatives (establishing of schools and libraries, translation of ancient and European authors). Trading centres in Epirus and Macedonia, in addition to Athens, Patmos and Constantinople, became centres of education; the treaty of Küçük Kaynarcı (1774), which granted the Greeks the right to free navigation through the Bosporus, further increased the prosperity of ports such as Chios, Smyrna and Kydoniai. Local communities in Thessaly and in the Peloponnese (under Turkish control from 1715) also flourished. Book production (Venice, later Vienna, Leipzig and other locations) increased. The proportion of theological literature became smaller, while the percentage of grammars rose from 9 to 14 per cent of all Greek books in the 18th century.

Moldavia and Wallachia represent a special case. From 1709 on, they were ruled by Greek princes (from the social milieu of the Phanariotes) who cultivated economic and cultural contacts with the West (Greek-Latin schools existed in Moldavia from ca. 1560). Prince N. Mavrokordatos actively supported the schools in Jasi and Bucharest. As early as the beginning of the 19th cent., Bucharest was an important cultural centre with print shops and a significant theatre life: the first performances of Greek tragedies were held there and in Odessa [40]. From 1620, there was also a Greek-Latin school in Kiev, in 1633 another one was opened in Moscow. In the 18th cent., the Greek communities in central Europe, especially in Vienna und Trieste, also increased in size. The rising level of education and the Greek awareness of life in the diaspora were an important prerequisite for the ideological and material preparation of the struggle for independence (for the Greek communities in Europe cf. [55. 115–131]).

The emergence of an educated reading public and contact with the philosophy of the Enlightenment and its humanistic ideals, with the liberal ideas of the French Revolution and the freedom movements in Italy, contributed to the formation of a new self-awareness among the bourgeoisie. The newly-felt need for freedom and human rights was understood as a renewal and rebirth of the nation. In this context, fresh approaches to Antiquity were sought. The focus was less on philosophical and/or scholarly knowledge than on a) Humanistic ideals and historical examples and b) the principles shaping Greek identity. In the rich protreptic literature from the so-called Greek Enlightenment [13; 28], knowledge and freedom stood side by side as equally valid goals; quotations from ancient authors were more numerous than those from the Church Fathers. According to the anonymous author of the *Hellenike Nomarchia* (1806), the Greek people's awareness of their descent and cultural identity was not compatible with the political situation in G. at the time. At the same time, he was confident about their ability to emulate their ancestors: "Greece still sires Leonidases and Themistocleses" (*Hellenike Nomarchia*, 43). Rigas Pheraios dreamed of a Greek republic that would unite all the peoples of the Balkans into a multi-cultural state founded on Greek education and modelled on the empire of Alexander.

In the context of a reawakened people, the language question arose with particular acuteness. The new bourgeoisie wished for a uniform codification of its national and cultural identity and saw language as a unifying instrument for all Greeks; further, it should be suitable for communicating modern Western ideology and science. Between the 'archaists' (P. Kodrikas, S. Kommetas), who understood Classical education as the rebirth of ancient G. [33. 55], and reformers such as A. Psalidas (1767–1829), headmaster in Ioannina (1796–1820), who wanted to replace historical with phonetic orthography (this was done, for example, by B.J. Vilaras in *Romeikia Glossa*, 1814), stood Adamantios Korais (1748–1835), probably the most influential scholar of the pre-revolutionary period [12]. In 1805, the philologist, who lived in Paris, initiated a series of modern Greek translations of ancient authors (*Hellenike Bibliotheke*; 16 vols. appeared between 1807 and 1826). His thoughts are reflected in the extensive *Prolegomena* of the works he edited [29]. His moderate language theory, which aimed at purifying the vernacular of foreign elements, seemed at first to offer an alternative to the indiscriminate adoption of a wide variety of dialect elements, and a means to facilitate communication with Europeans who were versed in ancient Greek. Because of the artificiality and vagueness of this concept, his followers (N. Doukas, K. Oikonomos) soon reached a rapprochement with the archaists. Korais' circle also included Anthimos Gazis, the first editor of the journal *Logios Hermes* (Vienna, 1811–1821), in which, among other things, the achievements of European Classical scholarship were for the first time presented in the Greek language, while Greek folk culture was presented as indicative of a 'national character' rooted in Antiquity.

The political and ideological messages associated with the veneration of Antiquity regularly encountered resistance from the Church. In the Patriarchal Encyclical of 1819, the teaching of grammar as opposed to mathematics and physics was strongly approved, but the fashion of replacing Christian names with ancient ones was condemned. In contrast to the Church's restrictive attitude, support for a public education was provided from the beginning of the 19th cent. by cultural societies established in several places (1810: Philological Society in Bucharest; 1813: the Philomousos Society in Athens, also promoted archaeology; 1814: Philomousos Society in Vienna). This tradition was also followed by the Association for the Dissemination of Greek Education (founded in 1869) and the Philological Society of Constantinople (founded in 1861), which in the 19th cent. promoted Greek education in the areas still controlled by the Ottomans (Macedonia, Thrace, Asia Minor) [43. vol. 3]. (The first Greek state held none of the important centres of education of the previous period.)

The economic and social strength of the Greeks resulted in a high regard for Greek education and made Greek the primary language throughout the Balkans. At the beginning of the 19th cent., Greek schools were preferred by a variety of ethnic groups (for example, Greek was the language of instruction in primary schools in Serbia around 1810 [1. 293]). From the mid–19th cent. onwards, an organized network of Greek primary schools were operating in Macedonia. In the 1860s, there were *hellenika scholeia* teaching Greek language and history throughout the Ottoman Empire [5. 47–48]. The national conflicts, which increased in the second half of the 19th cent., put up boundaries to halt the spread of Greek education; its reduced appeal (even among the the Greek-speaking population) [52. 123–147; 11 vol. 2. 133] was not least due to a strong orientation towards Antiquity and the use of an archaizing language of instruction. The monumental collection of epigraphical and archaeological material by M. Dimitsas with the significant title Ἡ Μακεδονία ἐν λίθοις φθεγγομένοις καὶ μνημείοις σῳζομένοις (1896; reprint 1988) was an attempt to document the Greek past of Macedonia (cf. Kofos in [5. 107]).

Until its destruction in 1922 and the subsequent exchange of population, Smyrna remained a flourishing cultural centre that rivaled Athens. Evidence of this can be found in the numerous associations, journals, print shops (there were 14 in 1904) and finally the plans of the government of E. Venizelos to establish a Greek university (1920) which would offer among its courses Oriental languages and ethnology. The Protestant School, independent of the Church and the Turkish authorities (established in 1733; its autonomy was guaranteed by the English Consulate), maintained an archaeological museum from 1747 (large numismatic collection with over 15,000 coins), a print shop and a library (35,000 vols., 180 manuscripts). The Philological Gymnasium, founded by Korais' pupil K. Koumas (1777–1836), included experimental science in its curriculum (on the educational system in Asia Minor cf. [43]).

While education declined dramatically on the islands of Cyprus and Crete, which were conquered by the Turks in 1571 and 1669 respectively (Cretan schools did not open until the 18th cent., because educated people fled to the west and to the Ionian Islands), public education was introduced in the Ionian islands under Venetian rule beginning in the mid–16th cent.. Both ancient and modern Greek as well as Latin were taught there by teachers trained in their subject [15. 191–233]. From 1803 (founding of the Ionian Republic, the first modern Greek state), Greek was the official language. History (ancient as well as modern) was

taught in the gymnasiums. The Ionian Academy (1824–1864) can be regarded as a precursor of the Greek universities. The desire to connect with the ancient tradition was obvious: the Academy's benefactor, Frederick North, Fifth Earl of Guildford (1766–1827), and the first seven professors appeared at the opening crowned with wreaths and clad in chiton, chlamys and sandals; the attire of the students of philology was similar. This first Greek university was of great importance, not least because it educated scholars who were later needed by the Greek state. Several lecturers like the Greek, Latin and history professor K. Asopios were later appointed to Athens.

2. The Greek school system in the Ottoman Empire was not uniform. There was a general distinction between two levels: primary schools (*koina*) and secondary schools (most often called *museia, frontisteria, gymnasia, scholai* etc.; the *akedemiai* were often more strongly oriented towards theology) [15. LXXXI]. The Patriarchal Academy (from 1691) and the schools of Athos (from 1753) and Patmos (18th cent.) had higher status (even though they were not actually universities).

The basis for instruction was grammar, mostly from the works of Theodoros Gazis (1496; more conservative, was used more in Constantinople and the Church-controlled schools) or Konst. Laskaris (1476; more widespread outside the Ottoman Empire) [51. 56f.]. The first school texts were the Psalms and hymns, followed by ecclesiastic and ancient texts selected for their linguistic form and their moral content: Aesopian fables, gnomai (e.g. from the *Gnomai monosticho*i by Manuel Chrysoloras), ruler pareneses; later came Plutarch, Xenophon, Lucian, rhetoric, epistolography, the *Batrachomyomachia*, the *Progymnasmata* of Aphthonios, Keves' *Pinax*, sermons of Basilius of Caesarea and Gregory of Nazianzus and more; finally poetry, often using the metrical work of Gerasimos Vlachos, which was also helpful for versification; the most popular texts were: epics (particularly the *Iliad* and *Erga*), dramas (*Hecuba, Orestes, Plutus, Clouds, Ajax,* Sophocles' *Electra*), Theocritus, and to a lesser extent Pindar. Plato did not reappear until the 18th cent. [41]. A gradual standardization occurred with the publication of textbooks: worth mentioning are Joh. Patousas' *Enkyklopaideia philologike* (Venice 1710, several reprints; Homer was missing, perhaps because of the aberrations from the Attic dialect [1]), and St. Kommetas's *Encyclopaedia of Greek Disciplines* (Vienna 1812). They were also used to some extent in the schools of the modern Greek state alongside the textbooks of Th. Pharmakides, *Chrestomatheia Hellenike* (from 1836) and A. Rangavis (from 1844).

The texts were translated word for word; often several synonyms were given for each word (so-called psychagogical method); grammatical phenomena were dealt with in detail (*technologia*). In the so-called *thematographia*, the translation was from modern Greek (*koine*) into ancient Greek. Interpretation was limited to the obvious. History was not taught systematically until the 19th century. It is reported that Neophytos Kavsokalyvitis (first director of the Athonite Academy 1749; d. 1774) was asked by his students in Bucharest to discuss Lysias' *Epitaphius*, but he replied that, regrettably, he was unable to oblige, as he did not have the necessary knowledge of history [14. 52f.]. However, the need that was felt for an encyclopaedic education coincided with the ideological framework of historicism and led to the perception of Greek history as an independent discipline (originally associated with geography [30]) at the beginning of the 19th cent. Neophytos's pupil Lambros Photiades was praised by Korais and Koumas because he "attached pragmatic scholarship to textual commentary" [41. 305]. The ten-volume edition of Thucydides by Neophytos Doukas (1805–6) signaled an awakening interest in ancient Greek history, and the first chronological, historical and historical-geographical overviews, as well as descriptions of the development of various disciplines, appeared in the years around 1820 [14. 52f.].

School instruction was often aided by the additional use of dictionaries. The first printed modern Greek dictionary, Gerasimos Vlachos's Θησαυρὸς τῆς ἐγκυκλο-παιδικῆς βάσεως τετράγλωσσος (1659, 21723, 31784; published by N. Glykys, Venice), was a compilation of existing dictionaries (four languages: the primary language is modern Greek, word explanations are provided in ancient Greek, Latin and Italian, in the third edition also French) [46]. Only in the quadrilingual lexicon of Georgios Konstantinou (1786) is the primary language ancient Greek. In 1816 a project for translating the *Thesaurus Linguae Graecae* was announced at the print shop of the Patriarchate (established in 1798), but the plan was never fully realized [20].

B. THE MODERN GREEK STATE

1. An enthusiastic tendency to modernize Classical education manifested itself in the first attempts to build an educational system in the modern Greek state (selected documents on Greek educational policy: [11]). The Second National Assembly (1824) already decided to unify the school system: the first cycle was to introduce instruction in the spoken language, while classes in ancient Greek, Latin and French were only planned from the second cycle on; furthermore, it was decided to collect the antiquities of each province in school museums to promote the knowledge of history and to facilitate research on the nation's forefathers. The first governor of the newly-founded republic, J. Capodistrias (1828–1831), undertook far-reaching initiatives in the organization of the schools. Archaeology, philosophy and palaeography were among the subjects to be taught in the curriculum of the teachers' college he founded. The pride and zeal of the 'reborn' nation soon coincided with the reverence for Antiquity during German Classicism. Under the Bavarian monarchy (1833–1864), a school system was introduced which consisted of the primary schools (*demotika scholeia*, 4 years; based on the French model) and, at the secondary

level, the 'Greek schools' (*hellenika scholeia*, based on the model of the 'Latin school') and the 'Gymnasiums' (defined in the Humboldtian sense; 3 + 4 years). A detailed curriculum for primary schools was not established until 1883 [16. 154f.]. At first, the subjects and methods remained largely committed to pre-revolutionary practice. Due to a shortage of school books and teacher training, modern Greek, introduced in 1833 to run parallel with instruction in ancient Greek, was soon abandoned as a language of instruction [3. vol. 3. 86]. Until 1897, 'Greek' in the Greek school system meant ancient Greek [15. 2]: a decree of 1856 ruled that only Attic grammar would be taught in Greek education – even in primary schools [19. 29] (cf. also [47]). In this way schools helped foster the ideal of imitating the ancient language. The resulting equation of Archaism with linguistic competence shaped a new view of education and contributed to the emergence of new hierarchies: the new 'educated' class won great respect and, after initial competition with the Phanariotes, went on to take leading positions in the administration and in political and social life. At the same time, the ideologically conditioned selection and interpretation of texts and the gearing of the teaching process towards the linguistic form of those texts were significant for the idealization of Antiquity and the instrumentalization of the textual message to support linguistic, moral or nationalistic intentions.

Primary school and Greek school were compulsory; schooling was free of charge at all levels. This was in keeping with the need to promote education in general, because an administrative system for the young country had to be created from a people who were largely illiterate. The number of school and university students remained correspondingly high throughout the 19th cent. (in 1885 G. was the leading nation in Europe in this respect). However, because the completion of a particular school level did not furnish students with any specific qualifications, but was meant to prepare them for the next level (and ultimately for university) [42. 145], the education system did not encourage a differentiation of social roles based technical or vocational competency; rather it sanctioned superficial knowledge and suggested a quantitative criterion by which the individual's qualifications for social and cultural integration were measured. The primary criterion was the acquisition of the archaistic language (*katharevousa*) and the social and national ideology associated with it. Fees were introduced in 1892, clearly marking an attempt by the ruling classes of the time, on the one hand, to secure their own privileges, and on the other to simplify the recruitment of a much-needed workforce for the growing industrial sector. Although the measure only applied for five years, it signaled the growing self-awareness of a new bourgeois class which no longer insisted on reproducing the ideology of the largely corrupt (and now bankrupt) state, but which was now the bearer of a new class consciousness, and ready for new roles. The archaizing language was no longer part of a utopian program to revive the past, but increasingly a symbol of the authority and ideology of a societal group. The language conflict ceased to be limited to supporters of different forms of an archaizing language, but now came to be waged between archaists and proponents of the vernacular (*demotike*). Among these were liberal intellectuals and protesters from the nationalist camp (cf. [44]) as well as members of the petit-bourgeoisie and of an organized working class, whose emergence at the same time reinforced the impression of a deep chasm between the inflexible official language and reality [49].

In spite of small reductions in teaching hours (1884, 1886, 1897), ancient Greek remained the strongest subject in all types of schools, while far more than half the lessons were devoted to theoretical disciplines. Modern Greek literature was added to the school program as late as 1884; however this meant almost exclusively literature of the 19th cent. written in an archaizing language. Modern Greek was not recognized as a major subject until 1927. A chair of Medieval and Modern Greek literature was not established at the University of Athens until 1925, about the same time as the founding of the University of Thessalonika, which was to focus on the study of modern Greek. The gymnasium retained its philological character throughout the 19th cent. The statement by the first major congress of Greek cultural associations from G. and other countries that school programs needed to "change their philological nature and acquire an encyclopaedic and reality-based character" had no effect [14. 354]. A comprehensive reform was presented to parliament in 1899 by the Minister for Church Affairs and Public Education, Athanasios Eutaxias (modern Greek to replace ancient Greek in primary schools, founding of practical gymnasiums to complement the philological gymnasiums, adaptation of the school system to the needs of the country's social and economic developments), but was rejected; even after the establishment of vocational schools (1959), 'Classical' gymnasiums were still attended by 74 percent of primary school graduates. The Humanistic school based on the German model was also introduced in the mid–19th cent. by the Greeks in Cyprus, where it held its ground even against the practically oriented Anglo-Saxon tradition preferred by the English colonial government (from 1878) [38].

The reforms of 1913–1917, which were made possible for the first time by the populist movement of 1909, (draft legislation by D. Glinos: archaizing school books were replaced by new ones; abolition of Greek schools; introduction of a 'six plus six' structure of primary and secondary education stipulating six years of each, introduction of a three-year vocational school), and the later ones from 1929 (introduction of the demotic language into the primary school classroom; Latin became optional outside the philological gymnasium; ancient Greek could also be taught from translations) and 1964 (draft legislation by E. Papanoutsos: the demotic language was now sanctioned in all grades, and

gymnasiums could freely teach and study ancient Greek literature from translations, and much more) were rescinded in 1920, 1932 and 1967 respectively. Only after the fall of the military dictatorship (1967–1974) was the Greek school system (following the principles of the 1964 reform) thoroughly reformed: in 1976 *demotike* was recognized as the only official state language. On the level of secondary education, the period at the gymnasium was reduced to three years, with the newly-established lyceum offering an additional three-year cycle. At the gymnasium, Ancient Greek literature was taught from translation, and only in the lyceum was it taught in the original language; Latin was limited to lyceums with a Classical orientation. In 1982 spelling was reformed through the introduction of the monotonic system, and since then questions regarding teaching methods and text books have been the focus of discussions and reform attempts.

At first, educational targets and the selection of texts were viewed narrowly: aside from imparting a humanistic ideal, the study of Antiquity was meant to prove the continuity of Greek language and culture and to contribute to the renewal of the intellectual life of the nation (case study in: [17]). In 1914 a new aspect was added: "The new lines of action of the nation after the successful outcome of the most recent events [sc. the Balkan Wars]". Accordingly, the two first books of Xenophon's *Hellenika* depicting wars in which Greeks fought against each other were replaced by texts referring to wars in which the Greeks were victorious against the Persians. A group of intellectuals who opposed this posture founded the 'Association for Education' (*Ekpaideutikos homilos*) in 1910. They initiated a wide-ranging discussion of the goals and methods of the educational system. Their chief representative was D. Glinos (1882–1943; 1924–1926 Director of the Pedagogical College, a resolute critic of formalism in Greek Classical Studies [18], who sought to reshape the relationship with Antiquity by means of 'creative historicism', a term of his own coinage. By this, he meant the critical examination and creative appropriation of the ancient heritage that is consistent with an enlightened, liberal lifestyle. Other members of the association were M. Triantafyllidis (1883–1959), a prominent philologist and later professor at the University of Thessalonika as well as the author of the first standard grammar of modern Greek, and the educationalist A. Delmouzos (1880–1950), who had founded an alternative girls' school in Volos in 1908. The school had to close following fierce attacks in 1911; there Delmouzos had introduced comparative methods for the study of ancient literature in order thereby to better familiarise the students with the world of the texts.

2. The University of Athens, founded in 1837 [34], was subject to the royal court and subsequent governments; in recognition of its political and social significance it was for a time represented by a member of parliament (1844–1862). The largest of the initial four faculties was Law, set up to produce a new generation

of well-educated administrators for the young state. The philosophical faculty, which also included the natural sciences until 1904, was given the task of developing a corresponding ideological framework. At the dedication ceremony [9. 11], the first Rector K. Schinas, professor of history and pupil of A. Boeckh, B.G. Niebuhr as well as Fr. K. von Savigny (whose daughter he had married), emphasized that the new university was to act as a bridge for the eastward transmission of modern knowledge; it was also to be instrumental in fostering the spiritual unity of the Greek world, even though (as in Antiquity) that world lacked political unity (Dimaras in [24. 48]). While the cultural life of the 19th cent. was primarily shaped by French influences, the German influence in the field of Classical Studies was a fact illustrated by the presence of German professors at the new university. These included the first professor of archaeology Ludwig Ross and the Latinist Heinrich Nikolaus Ulrichs, who compiled the first Latin-modern Greek dictionary (1843; this was revised by his successor S. Koumanoudis, who also distinguished himself as an epigraphist). Greek Classical philology [26] was unable and did not intend to compete with European scholarship. Apart from contributions of a textual critical nature (K. Kontos was particularly adept at this [8]) and sparse editions (e.g. Gr. Vernardakis), international recognition for Ancient Greek scholarship in Greece itself eventually came with J. Sykoutris (1901–1937), who died prematurely [45]. Only after the Second World War did Greek universities generally gain acceptance as centres of scholarship in the field of Classical Studies. Notable contributors were A. Skiadas in Athens and J.Th. Kakridis (1901–1992) as well as S. Kapsomenos (1907–1978) in Thessalonika. The philological work of the 19th cent. and the first decades of the 20th cent. was limited to the production of didactic material (especially commentaries), for the most part translated for school and university instruction (Ph. Kakridis in [10. 25–40]). The relationship with Antiquity fulfilled a crucial role in the formation of an identity in 19th cent. Greek scholarship. In accordance with the political and ideological postulates, history and language were the focus of academic and journalistic discussions of this period, in which the Athenian professors played a decisive role. The continuity of the Greek people from Antiquity to the present was the basic premise (contradicting the theory of J.Ph. Fallmerayer) of the monumental 'History of the Greek Nation' (1860–1877) by Konstantinos Paparrigopoulos (1815–1891), which was written in several stages (a shorter, one-volume edition already appeared in 1853). The significance of the long underestimated Byzantine Empire (depicted as a Greek monarchy [42. 179–183]) was also enhanced, earning the author no small amount of criticism from the admirers of Antiquity and from the circles of the Phanariotes, who no longer wanted to be identified with the policies of the Patriarchate [5. 12]. In the words of P. Kalligas, "[Paparrigopoulos] used history as evidence of a particular topic". Other ideologi-

cally motivated reservations were expressed by some of the leading intellectuals of the time, among them S. Koumanoudis, N. Saripolos and I. Rizos Neroulos [5. 12].

The ambition for a complete study Greek culture and history opened broad perspectives for the exploration of neglected periods, such as the late and post-Byzantine eras. Spyridon Lambros (1851–1919) and Konstantinos Sathas (1842–1914) were among the most productive editors of texts from these periods. The exploration of the national character (in Herder's sense) and efforts to verify the organic unity of modern and earlier G. led to further projects: Spyridon Zambelios published a collection of Greek folksongs (1852) and also coined the term 'Hellenochristian civilization' to describe the fusion of the ancient legacy with the Christian tradition in the national character of modern Greece. The associated examination of a specifically Greek character also remained a central task for the philosophical scholarship of the period [4. vol. 2. 57]; a simultaneous interest in Plato is no surprise in this context. In the last two decades of the 19th cent., folk culture finally gained a higher standing (Puchner in [10. 247–267]), not least because of Nikolaos Politis (1852–1921) and his works (among them collections of modern Greek proverbs and legends). His concern was to prove the continuity between ancient and modern Greek culture. The work of Politis inspired the circle of literati around the writer and critic K. Palamas and contributed significantly to the definition of the modern Greek cultural sphere. For an investigation of the traces of Hellenistic paganism and the ancient view of the world see in particular [53]; on Cyprus [32]; this direction has been followed up in recent works (especially by G. Megas; cf. also [33]), but there still remains much to explore; for the survival of Aesopian fables and the *Vita Aesopi* see [36].

Greek linguistics long remained in the grip of the debate about the modern Greek language. Typical of the consolidation of the conservative camp at the beginning of the 20th cent. is the case of the eminent philologist G.N. Hatzidakis (1848–1941; main work: *Einleitung in die neugriechische Grammatik*, Leipzig 1892). In contrast to the matter-of-fact approach he demonstrated early on in his career, when he still held relatively moderate scholarly positions [21], Hatzidakis later became a prime champion of archaism and opposed all reforms of the education system (above all, the separation of modern Greek studies from Classical Studies). After heated debates preceding the founding of the University of Thessalonika (1925), which had been envisaged and designed by liberal governments [31], he was finally appointed by the conservatives as its first Rector.

Although fierce resistance caused some of the original ambitious plans to fail (including the introduction of a diploma in Hebrew Studies and the development of Slavic Studies), the University of Thessalonika became a stronghold of the demotic language and offered a counterweight to the conservative University of Athens in the debates on the education system and the place of Classical Studies in the 20th cent. Today philosophical faculties also exist at the Universities of Ioannina and Crete; they were joined in 1989 by the University of Cyprus. In the 1990s, the universities of Thrace (Komotini) and Patras began offering degree programmes in Classical Studies.

The Academy of Athens (founded in 1926) has assumed responsibility for important projects such as the "Historical Lexicon of Modern Greek" (1933ff.), initiated in 1908, and the Hellenic Folklore Research Centre (formerly the Folklore Archive), established in 1918, this in addition to the series *Hellenike Bibliotheke* (named for the editorial programme of Korais), which began in 1955 with the editions of J. Sykoutris and is today published by the Academy's Centre for the Research of Greek and Latin Literature (K.E.E.L.G., formerly the Centre for the Edition of Works of Greek Authors). At the National Hellenic Research Institute, Classical Studies are represented by the Institute of Greek and Roman Antiquity. Among the activities of the Society for Macedonian Studies (Thessaloniki, founded in 1939) is the publication of the journal *Hellenika*. A Society of Greek Philologists has existed since 1948; also worthy of note is the Greek Humanistic Society (established in 1958).

1 A. K. ABDALI, Ἡ ῝Εγκυκλπαιδεία φιλολογικὴ᾽τοῦ Ἰωάννη Πατούσα. Συμβολὴ στὴν Ἱστ. τῆς Παιδείας τοῦ Νέου Ἑλληνισμοῦ (1710–1839), 1984 2 A. ANGHELOU, Πλάτωνος τύχαι. Ἡ λόγια παράδοση στὴν Τουρκοκρατία, 1963 3 D. ANTONIOU, Προγράμματα Μέσης Ἐκπαίδευσης (1833–1929), 3 vols., 1987–1989 4 R. D. ARGYROPOULOU (ed.), Ἡ φιλοσοφ. σκέψη στὴν Ἑλλ. ἀπὸ τὸ 1828 ὣς τὸ 1922, 2 vols., 1995–1998 5 M. BLINKHORN, TH. VEREMIS (eds.), Modern Greece: Nationalism & Nationality, 1990 6 V. CANDEA, Les intellectuels du sud-est européen au XVIIe siècle, in: Revue des études sud-est européennes 8 (1970) 181–230, 623–668 7 P. CHARIS (ed.), Ἡ δίκη τῶν τόνων, 1943 8 G. A. CHRISTODOULOU, Κωνσταντῖνος Στ. Κόντος, 1979 9 TH. CHRISTOU, Κωνσταντίνος Δημητρίου Σχινᾶς, 1998 10 E. CHRYSOS (ed.), ῝Ενας νέος κόσμος γεννιέται, 1996 11 A. DIMARAS (ed.), Ἡ μεταρρύθμιση ποὺ δὲν ἔγινε, 2 vols., 1973f. 12 K. TH. DIMARAS, Ὁ Κοραῆς καὶ ἡ εποχή του, 1953 13 Id., La Grèce au temps des Lumières, 1969 14 Id., K. Παπαρρηγόπουλος, 1986 15 T. EVANGELIDES, Ἡ παιδεία ἐπὶ Τουρκοκρατίας, 2 vols., 1936 16 R. FLETCHER, Cultural and Intellectual Development 1821–1911, in: J. KOUMOULIDES (ed.), Greece in Transition, 1977, 153–172 17 A. GARTZIOU-TATTI, Ὁ Ἐπιτάφιος τοῦ Περικλῆ (Θουκ. II, 35–46) στὴ μετεπαναστατικὴ Ἑλλ.: Ἰδεολογικές συνιστῶσες, Δωδώνη 28 (1999), 209–228 18 D. GLINOS, Μερικοὶ στοχασμοὶ γιὰ τὴ σημερινὴ θέση τῶν ἀνθρωπιστικῶν σπουδῶν στὴν Ἑλλάδα, in: Πλάτων, Σοφιστής, 1940, 4–63 19 A. E. GOTOVOS, Παράδοση και γλώσσα στο σχολείο. Προβλήματα νομμότητας των γλωσσικών μεταρρυθμίσεων στηνNE εκπαίδευση, 1991 20 T. A. GRITSOPOULOS, Ἡ Κιβωτὸς τῆς Ἑλλ. Γλώσσης, in: Ἀθηνᾶ 70 (1968), 223–252 21 G. N. HATZIDAKIS, (= CHATZIDAKIS), Περὶ τοῦ γλωσσικοῦ ζητήματος ἐν Ἑλλάδι, in: Ἀθηνᾶ 2 (1889), 169–235 22 G. P. HENDERSON, The Revival of Greek Thought 1620–1830, 1971 23 J. IRMSCHER, Nikäa als Zentrum des Griechischen Patriotismus,

in: Revue des études sud-est européennes 8 (1970), 33–47 24 Ιστ. Ἀρχείο Ελλ. Νεολαίας, Γεν. Γραμματεία Ν. Γενιάς, Πανεπιστήμιο: Ιδεολογία και Παιδεία. Ιστορική Διάσταση και προοπτικές, 2 vols., 1989 25 J. TH. KAKRIDIS, Alte Hellenen und Hellenen der Befreiungskriege, in: Gymnasium 68 (1961), 315–328 26 J. KALITSOUNAKIS, Ἡ ἀναβίωσις τῶν κλασσικῶν σπουδῶν ἐν Ἑλλάδι ἀπὸ τῆς ἀπελευθερώσεως καὶ ἐντεῦθεν, EEAth (1957/58), 325–450 27 P. KITROMILIDIS, Ἰ. Μοισιόδαξ, 1985 28 P. KONDYLIS, Ὁ Νεοελλ. Διαφωτισμός. Οἱ φιλοσοφ. ἰδέες, 1988 29 A. KORAIS, Προλεγόμενα στοὺς Ἀρχαίους ῝Ελλ. συγγραφεῖς, repr. 1986ff. 30 CH. KOULOURI, Ἱστορία καὶ Γεωγραφία στὰ Ἑλλ. σχολεῖα (1834–1914), 1988 31 B. L. KYRIAZOPOULOS et al., 1926–1976. Τὰ πενήντα χρόνια τοῦ Πανεπ. Θεσσαλονίκης, Thessaloniki 1976 32 G. LOUKAS, Φιλολογικαὶ ἐπισκέψεις τῶν ἐν τῷ βίῳ τῶν νεωτέρων Κυπρίων μνημείων τῶν ἀρχαίων, Athens 1874 (repr. 1974) 33 J. C. LAWSON, Modern Greek Folklore and Ancient Greek Religion, 1910 34 I. PANTAZIDIS, Χρονικὸν τῆς πεντηκονταετίας τοῦ ἑλλ. Πανεπ., Athens 1889 35 A. PAPADEROS, Metakenosis. Griechenlands kulturelle Herausforderung durch die Aufklärung in der Sicht des Korais und des Oikonomos, 1970 36 J.-TH. PAPADEMETRIOU, Αἰσώπεια καὶ αἰσωπικά, 1989 37 E. PAPANOUTSOS, Νεοελλ. Φιλοσοφία, 1953 38 P. PERSIANIS, Πτυχὲς τῆς ἐκπαίδευσης τῆς Κύπρου κατὰ τὸ τέλος τοῦ 19ου καὶ τὶς ἀρχὲς τοῦ 20 αἰ., Nicosia 1994 39 N. K. PSIMMENOS, Ἡ Ἑλλ. φιλοσοφία ἀπὸ τὸ 1453 ὥς τὸ 1821, 2 vols., 1988–89 40 J. SIDERIS, Τὸ ἀρχ. θέατρο στὴ νέα Ἑλλ. Σκηνή, 1817–1932, 1976 41 A. SKARVELI-NIKOLOPOULOU, Τὰ μαθηματάρια τῶν ἑλλ. σχολ. τῆς Τουρκοκρ., 1993 42 E. SKOPETEA, Τὸ πρότυπο βασίλειο᾽ καὶ ἡ μεγ. ἰδέα. ῝Οψεις τοῦ ἐθν. προβλ. στὴν Ἑλλ. (1830–1880), 1988 43 CH. S. SOLDATOS, Η εκπαιδευτική και πνευματική κίνηση του Ελληνισμού της Μ. Ασίας (1800–1922), 3 vols. 1989–1991 44 P. STAVRIDI-PATRIKIOU, Δημοτικισμός καὶ κοινωνικὸ πρόβλημα, 1976 45 J. SYKOUTRIS, Μελέται καὶ ῝Αρθρα, 1956 46 B. N. TATAKIS, Γεράσιμος Βλάχος ὁ Κρῆς (1605/7–1685). Φιλόσοφος, Θεολόγος, Φιλόσοφος, Venice 1973 47 D. TOMBAΪDIS, Le problème de la langue d'enseignement en Grèce, Diss. Paris 1975 48 M. TRIANTAFYLLIDIS, Νεοελληνικὴ Γραμματική. Ἱστορικὴ εἰσαγωγή, 1938 49 K. TSOUKALAS, Dépendance et reproduction. Le rôle sociale des appareils scolaires en Grèce, 1975 50 C. TSOURKAS, Les débuts de l'enseignement philosophique et de la libre pensée dans les Balkans. La vie et l'œuvre de Théophile Corydalée (1570–1646), Thessaloniki ²1967 51 N. D. VARMAZIS, HAE γλώσσα και γραμματεία ως πρόβλ. της NE εκπαίδευσης, Thessaloniki 1992 52 S. VOURI, Εκπαίδευση και εθνικισμός στα Βαλκάνια, 1992 53 C. WACHSMUTH, Das alte Griechenland im neuen, Bonn 1864 54 S. G. XYDIS, Medieval Origins of Modern Greek Nationalism, in: Balkan Studies 9 (1968) 1–20 55 D. A. ZAKYTHINOS, The Making of Modern Greece, 1976 56 P. CH. ZIOGAS, Μιὰ κίνηση πνευματικῆς ἀναγεννήσεως τοῦ ὑπόδουλου Ἑλληνισμοῦ κατὰ τὸν 16ο αἰ. (1540–1550), in: Ἑλληνικά 27 (1974) 50–78, 268–303 ANTONIS TSAKMAKIS

III. Museums
A. Subject B. History

A. Subject

The museums of the Republic of G. are state institutions or private museums with state registration.
They form a department of the Ministry of Culture,
which is responsible for the cultural heritage and the
arts in the country. The Ministry was established in September 1971.

B. History

The history of Greek museums is that of a cultural
phenomenon. Inseparable companions of G.'s national
and scholarly history, they have always contributed to
shaping the image of G. in the world since the modern
Greek state was created in 1833. To understand the
Greek museum system, it is important to recognize that
the country's museums have played multiple mediating
roles from the beginning: they act as intermediaries between the changing reality of the local material as it is
gradually discovered and the views of the visitors
which, in the western hemisphere, are based on a centuries-old, but deeply amodern, purely traditional
image of Antiquity.

This means that the museums of Hellas reflect a
peculiar level of knowledge in their technology and
presentation, which corresponds to the ideas and desires of a national cultural policy. On the one hand, this
policy was determined by the prevailing trends in domestic politics. On the other hand, the influential role of
foreign countries was still acknowledged, even as they
were being rejected. On the whole, Greek museums are
implicitly fulfilling a state mandate, so that political or
economic aims are able to push scientific goals and
enquiries into the background.

Over the millennia, first the Roman Empire and then
Christian Europe have quarried the cultural and artistic
achievements of this small nation. Their utilisation contributed significantly to the formulation of the intellectual framework of Europe since the Renaissance.
However, G. itself, being a part of the Sultanate of
Istanbul, remained excluded from the effect its heritage
was having until well into the 18th cent. When the
Greek state was created in 1830, after the War of Independence, the European Great Powers, acting as god-
parents, placed the Bavarian prince Otto (I) on the
throne. The repercussions of the once-close ties between Bavaria and G. are still perceptible in many
aspects of Greek life today, from the cityscape of Athens
to the organisation of the bureaucracy and the law [1;
8].

Under pressure from the Continent, the newly-constructed Greek state saw itself confronted by the necessity of developing its own cultural life that would meet
European demands [3]. Indeed in the 18th cent., a
small, western-oriented bourgeoisie emerged from the
economic upturn that was brought about by the Greek
merchant navy. However, this social class lost its fleet in

the war – and thus its source of income – and could not
offer a basis for the creation from scratch of a national
cultural policy [10]. The reality of G. around 1830,
with a population of under a million, left little room for
an independent cultural development, particularly
since an infrastructure which would allow the implementation of a general education had yet to be developed.

The European philhellenic movement (→ Philhellenism) and the European volunteers in the War of Independence represented an additional burden. The new
arrivals brought with them a conception of G. that was
not attuned to the historical, i.e. Byzantine and latent
Islamic realities of the new state. Their vision was then
projected onto the new/old G., with a certain missionary zeal determining the early decisions of the government.

The discovered Classical heritage, its preservation
and further exploration were at the centre of the activities that began with the Bavarian regency. Museums
were required for preservation and storage. The first
steps in setting up a central collection were taken in the
island city of Aegina in 1829; these antiquities were
moved to Athens, the new capital city, in 1834. Non-
state organisations also played an important role in
creating the systematic principles for the exploration of
local antiquities and their exhibition. One of these organisations was the Archaeological Society of Athens,
founded in 1837. Further contributions came from foreign archaeological institutes conducting excavations
at certain sites [12]. The → École française, founded
in 1846, was the first of these; the → Deutsches
Archäologisches Institut opened its Athenian
branch in 1875 [9]. The involvement of these currently
seventeen schools and institutes goes far beyond the respective local excavations, because, among other
things, they also maintain an important exchange of
knowledge through their own libraries and scholarships.

For central Europe, the Americas or Australia, antiquities museums are essentially 'foreign museums', i.e.
their exhibits are cultural assets imported into each of
these countries' individual sphere of every-day life and
experience. This 'exotic factor' that was originally attached to collections of antiquities and a basic reason for
the existence of ethnographic museums has largely receded from the western consciousness. Exposure over
generations to visual and linguistic records of the Classical era in education has made 'antiquities', in the
broadest sense of the word an integral component of the
modern cultural context. However, through the expansion of the educational system and the curtailment of
the traditional Humanistic education, awareness of this
situation has to a large extent been repressed. What
remains on the surface is a fascination for the 'adven-
ture' of archaeology and 'buried treasures'. However,
this in turn presents a general concept which applies
only partially to Greece.

The museums showed in concentrated form why G., alongside Italy, had for a long time been the classical destination of bourgeois educational journeys. Up until well into the 1960s, G. represented a relatively select destination in the travel history of the European bourgeoisie. Only the Europe-wide rise in tourists travelling to G. on the one hand, and the arrival of Greek 'guest workers' in Europe on the other, led Europeans to revise their idea of G. as one large open-air antiquities museum. As a result, tourism – based on the display of G.'s own ancient past coupled with Mediterranean summer pleasures – is today the most important source of revenue for the roughly ten million inhabitants of the Greek Republic.

The history of the museums in G. illustrates a continuous conflict: on the one side there is archaeological research, in which the museums participate. They are expected to construct, by scientific means, a Classical Antiquity that is believed to be lost. On the other side stands the Sisyphus task of cataloguing – in practical, archaeological and museological terms – the enormous amount of discovered material. In the early days of the modern Greek state, the country's inherited cultural burden was largely unknown; moreover, the country itself was still partly occupied. Only since the incorporation of the Dodecanese in 1947 does the Greek Republic cover a territory that includes more or less all of the islands in the Aegean.

Greek museums, therefore, have since their inception faced a difficult path which has not become any easier over the course of time. An unbroken chain of new discoveries and the constant refinement of archaeological methods regarding the collection and documentation of finds have proportionally increased the amount of material to be processed and displayed. At the time of the foundation of the Greek state, for instance, the cultures of the Bronze Age, the early Iron Age, the Archaic age, and certainly the Neolithic age were virtually unknown. Today this prehistoric period is itself a large and important field of research.

In modern G., antiquities museums are part of the entire cultural heritage in the sense that they constitute a 'homeland institution'. The Classical legacy collected in the museums is both a source of national pride and a binding obligation the maintenance of which makes great demands on the state finances and also has political repercussions, for example in the case of the Parthenon sculptures [5] (cf. also the petition for the return of the Parthenon sculptures before the European Parliament, 1999). A change has occurred to the extent that in recent decades Greek cultural history is increasingly understood as a continuum within the overall historical image of the nation. A more comprehensive image of G. is emerging, particularly through the greater attention that is now being paid to the post-Antiquity periods – a development that is also reflected by the museums.

The archaeological museums are part of the Greek Antiquities Service and thus legal repositories of all the remains of the material culture of the country, including excavation finds. This regulation reveals a problem which affects those countries with a rich ancient cultural heritage, especially in the eastern Mediterranean: the museums generally lack any freedom of choice, a fundamental condition for almost all western museums. Instead of pursuing a concentrated – i.e. self-limiting – acquisition policy, these museums are burdened with a largely passive duty to collect and secure everything, leaving little room for typical museum tasks such as selection and exhibition.

Under these at times adverse conditions, G. has produced a variety of museums over a period of almost two centuries. Approximately 250 in number, they are listed according to category on the Ministry of Culture's excellent 'Odysseus' web site: a) archaeological museums and collections, b) Byzantine museums and collections, c) historical and folklore museums, d) museums of Greek art (ancient, Byzantine, modern), e) museums of Asian art, f) art museums and galleries, g) theatrical museums, h) cinema museums, i) music museums, j) nautical museums, k) museums of natural history, l) museums of science and technology (cf. http://www.culture.gr). The Ministry of Culture also administers over 430 archaeological sites, some of which are the same as the listed museum locations, as well as approximately 330 registered monuments.

At the top level is a General Director of Antiquities, who oversees the Directorates of a) Prehistoric and Classical Antiquities, b) Byzantine and Post-Byzantine Monuments, c) Museums, Exhibitions and Educational Programmes, d) the National Archive of Monuments, e) Expropriations and Real Estate as well as f) Modern Cultural Heritage, which is of particular importance in the wider context of the European Union. Another General Directorate at the Ministry of Culture is concerned with Restoration, Museums and Technical Works, and it in turn oversees a number of sub-departments, including the Directorate of Museum Studies and Cultural Buildings. General policy questions are decided by the Central Archaeological Council.

The administration of the country's archaeological sites and institutions is further organised into districts (ephorates). 39 Ephorates of Prehistoric and Classical Antiquities carry out the archaeological fieldwork. There are also 28 Ephorates of Byzantine Antiquities and eight ephorates under the Directorate of Restoration of Modern and Contemporary Monuments. The ephorates of each Directorate are numbered from 1–n. In recognition of the Bavarian-centralist origin of the state administration, the numbering begins in Athens for all areas. Sometimes, the districts show boundaries which do not correspond with the geographical conditions, but rather with political spheres of influence.

The 147 archaeological museums comprise more than half of G.'s museums and are distributed throughout the country. They are divided into central, regional, local and excavation museums. As a national institute, the Archaeological Museum of Athens is in a category of its own. Covering large geographical areas, the museums in Thessalonika and Herakleion hold an intermediate status. Regional museums exhibiting items from a wider area include the Museum of Prehistoric Thera (cf. http://www.culture.gr/2/21/211/21121m/ e211um18.html) and the Chora Archaeological Museum, which presents the archaeology of Messenia along with finds from the excavations at the 'Palace of Nestor' in Pylos. The museum in Nauplion, situated in a historical Venetian building, exhibits finds from the surrounding area, e.g. Tiryns, Mycenae and Dendra. By contrast, the archaeology of nearby Argos is on display in that town's own museum.

Purely local museums are for the most part excavation museums, which are often maintained by one of the 17 foreign schools accredited by the Ministry of Culture. These include Olympia [7], Delphi, the Kerameikos in Athens [6], the Acropolis Museum in Athens and the Museums of Ancient Corinth and Nemea. All are closely associated with the excavation sites themselves, which in turn assume the character of open-air museums.

Greek archaeologists have enriched the museum landscape with an 'open museum' style of presentation: objects and structures that have come to light during the construction of the Athenian underground transport system are exhibited in situ at various stations, e.g. Syntagma, Omonoia and Evangelismos (cf. art. 'Das längste Museum Athens', Athener Zeitung 302 of 21 January 2000, p. 7). The project represents a new way of placing immovable monuments such as the Acropolis, the Temple of Zeus and similar structures in the public arena side by side with more human-scale, individual items, thus providing a direct link between ancient history and the modern present.

In recent years, more independence has been granted to local excavation sites and find spots, and archaeological museums anywhere are free to illustrate the country's past, irrespective of their location. Whenever discoveries of special artistic, archaeological or national importance are made, the principle of the central authority of the capital still applies. In 1875, therefore, the natural home for Schliemann's finds from Grave Circle A (Mycenae) was the Athenian National Museum. Similarly, the finds from the royal tombs in → VERGINA (1977) – certainly no less predominant in the national psyche – went to the archaeological museum in Thessaloniki, the Republic's second capital. At the tomb site itself, protective measures similar to those in → MYCENAE were put in place to cover the archaeological structures; these steps allow for a rewarding visit in touristic terms as well.

Aside from the state museums, the importance of the private sector is clearly growing. As early as 1931 the Benaki Museum was established by the Alexandrian family of the same name; it reopened in 2000, after a ten-year rebuilding phase. Among its exhibits are an important collection of ancient jewellery [11], late antique bone carvings and Hellenistic mummy portraits from the Fayum. After the Second World War, the ship-owning Goulandris family in particular made their name in museum endowments: the Museum of Cycladic Art (cf. http://www.cycladic-m.gr/) in the centre of Athens is a modern museum with a meticulously designed architecture. The same family is also committed to the – of modern art, both at the Athens museum and on the island of Andros. Remarkable for its extensive collection housed in an old villa in the Athenian Plaka is the Paul and Alexandra Kanellopoulos Museum (cf. http://www.culture.gr/2/21/211/21101m/e211am03.html). A fine example of the Greek endowment tradition is the collection of H. Stathatos – donated to the Athenian Museum in 1957 – which, like the Kanellopoulos Museum, includes an important collection of ancient jewellery (cf. http://www.culture.gr/2/21/214/21405m/e21405m8.html).

1 K. DICKOPF, Georg Ludwig von Maurer und die bayerische Regentschaft in Griechenland 1833–1835. Probleme einer Staatsgründung, in: [4. 83–95]   2 H.-J. HEKKER, Die bayerische Regentschaft und das griechische Recht, in: [4. 97–98]   3 M. HERZFELD, Ours Once More: Folklore, Ideology, and the Making of Modern Greece, 1982   4 R. HEYDENREUTER, J. MURKEN, R. WÜNSCHE (eds.), Die erträumte Nation. Griechenlands Wiedergeburt im 19. Jahrhundert, ²1995   5 C. HITCHENS, The Elgin Marbles: Should they be returned to Greece?, 1987   6 U. KNIGGE, Der Kerameikos von Athen. Führer durch Ausgrabungen und Geschichte, Athens 1988 (Engl. The Athenian Kerameikos. History, Monuments, Excavations, 1991)   7 A. MALLWITZ, H.-V. HERRMANN (eds.), Die Funde aus Olympia. Ergebnisse hundertjähriger Ausgrabungstätigkeit, 1980   8 J. MURKEN et al., König-Otto-von-Griechenland-Museum der Gemeinde Ottobrunn (= Bayerische Museen, Bd. 22), 1995   9 W. SCHIERING, Zur Geschichte der Archäologie, in: U. HAUSMANN (ed.), Allgemeine Grundlagen der Archäologie, 1969, 63ff., 118ff.   10 H. SCHMIDT, Die wirtschaftliche Entwicklung Griechenlands während der Herrschaft Ottos I., in: [4. 167–173]   11 B. SEGALL, Katalog der Goldschmiede-Arbeiten, Museum Benaki, 1938   12 M. SHANKS, Classical Archaeology of Greece (Experiences of the Discipline = Experience of Archaeology), 1996, chap. 1.   WOLF RUDOLPH

Greek

I. BYZANTINE MIDDLE AGES AND MODERN PERIOD   II. LATIN MIDDLE AGES

I. BYZANTINE MIDDLE AGES AND MODERN PERIOD
A. PREFATORY REMARKS ON METHOD
B. INTERNAL LINGUISTIC HISTORY   C. EXTERNAL LINGUISTIC HISTORY   D. THE ROLE OF GREEK FOR NON-GREEK LANGUAGES AFTER LATE ANTIQUITY

A. PREFATORY REMARKS ON METHOD
The terms 'Middle Greek' and 'Modern Greek' are adopted only as conventions. Their use in the literature is based upon an unreliable application of Western

European categories to entirely different practices in the Byzantine East [1]. Fundamental for the following outline is the dichotomy 'written' vs. 'oral' as well as that of 'external' vs. 'internal' linguistic history. While the former hardly needs any clarification, by 'internal linguistic history' is meant the phonological, morphological and syntactical changes that a language undergoes in the course of its history; the 'external linguistic history', on the other hand, encompasses all socially motivated judgments that apply to a given community with respect to a language. A concrete example: the disappearance of the optative in the Hellenistic period is part of the 'internal linguistic history' of *koiné* Greek; the manner and extent to which the disappearance is reflected in the written texts of the Hellenistic period and afterwards, whether, for example, an author also abandons the optative in writing (as do most of the New Testament writers) or tries to preserve it, are matters of the social norms in which a particular linguistic usage is embedded. Thus, this level also represents, in a methodological sense, the bridge between linguistics proper and related disciplines such as literary history, cultural history and social history. Long neglected by 'pure' linguistics, it will be in the foreground in the following material.

B. INTERNAL LINGUISTIC HISTORY

Because of the bilingualism of late Rome that was then continued by Byzantium, it is difficult to track changes in the spoken language through written texts. Where papyri from Egypt are sufficiently available (even after the Arab conquest and into the 8th cent.), this is easier than it is later on. It is precisely the transitional period until the introduction of a vernacular literature (8th–12th cents.) where sources are few and far between (with the exception of the writings of Constantine VII Porphyrogenitus (905–959) and the rhythmical acclamations of the demes). What is certain is that most of the changes typical of 'Modern Greek' had already made their appearance on this level towards the end of Late Antiquity (6th/7th cent.): itacism, loss of the dual and optative (in both cases as early as the Hellenistic period), loss of the dative, changes to the declensions (the third declension is limited to the neuter, loss of the feminine in –ος), loss of the synthetic perfect. Foreshadowed at least were the loss of the infinitive and its replacement by ἵνα and changes to the system of tenses and moods: modern Greek essentially continued the ancient tenses for the indicative present, imperfect and aorist, but the synthetic future is replaced by a periphrastic form with θέλω ἵνα, which modern Greek passed on to the Balkan languages (see below). From that a conditional was to be developed later. The whole process so closely resembles that of the Latin-Romance parallel development that a genetic connection seems irrefutable. J. Kramer quite rightly speaks of a 'Greek-Latin linguistic federation' in Late Antiquity [2]. The vocabulary of the vernacular, in contrast to the written language of Late Antiquity, is enriched with numerous Latinisms that are also of interest for Romance studies and have been partly continued into modern Greek. Further foreign influences are attested locally and are even partly verifiable in the case of Egypt and Syria/Palestine but, with the exception of the Hebrew/Aramaic vocabulary of the New Testament, they only rarely extended into the demotic Greek vernacular. From the High Middle Ages on, there was a marked penetration of Italian, and then also Turkish features. Likewise attested, even if difficult to demonstrate in detail, is the existence of dialects in the Greek-speaking world in Late Antiquity and the Byzantine period. Through a combination of several items of evidence it is, however, possible to show that the first dialectal boundaries must have existed as early as the end of Antiquity. Extensive written evidence, however, is available only after the Fourth Crusade (1204). Nevertheless, it is probable that today's 'peripheral dialects' of modern Greek in southern Italy, the southeastern Peloponnese (Tsakonian, continuing Doric), on the Black Sea (Pontic, with strong Ionian elements) and Cypriot had already started to take on separate identities. To what extent the dialect of the capital Constantinople gained any prominence and whether it existed at all is, on the other hand, a matter of contention. Modern Greek vernacular is, in any case, derived genetically from Peloponnesian dialects.

C. EXTERNAL LINGUISTIC HISTORY

The Romance languages are widely known to have been the daughters of Latin in two senses. First, they are genetically derived from local variants of spoken Latin; second, they were used for centuries as a written language alongside Latin, developed a standard form from its written traditions and borrowed from Latin most of the terms for intellectual life, scholarship, administration and technology. The case with modern Greek is similar. It was genetically derived from ancient Greek but, at the same time, the final standard form of ancient Greek was for centuries the model by which the vernacular was measured and which it ultimately replaced. These similarities with the Romance languages, however, should not mislead us as to the fundamental differences, precisely on the level of 'external linguistic history'. With the exception of Romanian, which developed separately out of the Latin-Catholic tradition, the Romance languages emancipated themselves gradually from Latin from the Middle Ages on; by the Early Modern Period they are full-fledged literary languages. Modern Greek did not become a recognized literary language until the 19th cent. and became an official language of administration only in the last quarter of the 20th cent. Thus, several Romance written languages form part of the Latin family, whereas modern Greek is the only written language linked to ancient Greek. Both departures from the Romance pattern have a common cause. Eastern Rome continued as Byzantium for a thousand years; the standard language and language of prestige in this empire was the ancient standard language, whether in its somewhat modified form (e.g., the New Testament) or the strictly Attic variation. From the period of the Macedonian dynasty, an increasingly strong tendency towards Classicism prevailed in Byzantium. Writers from the 14th cent. like Pachymeres wrote a more Classical, Thucydidean Greek than did John Malalas in the 6th cent. Thus, it was probably Western influences (Crusades) that caused some literati in Byzantium to use the vernacular in poetry (*p tocho-prodromika*). A development really comparable to that in Romance languages came about only in the two and a half centuries of Latin dominance following the Fourth Crusade. Venetians and Genoese, the French on the Peloponnese and the Lusignans on Cyprus used modern Greek dialects as written languages in their areas of control, just as they were used to doing in in their Romance homelands. These sometimes extensive texts include collections of laws, historiography and poetry and, for the most part, represent the first evidence of modern Greek dialects. This process was, however, delivered a setback by the Ottoman conquest. Admittedly Mehmed II's earliest state treaty was composed in modern Greek; but by appointing Orthodox patriarchs in the Byzantine fashion after the conquest of Constantinople (1453), by placing all Balkan orthodox Christians under his jurisdiction and forcing the Catholic powers out of southeastern Europe, the sultan and his followers gained dominion over all Greeks and over the Orthodox in the Balkans. In this way, the Ottoman Empire also became the executor of the Byzantine legacy: as *Rum millet* (Orthodox communities; literally: 'Roman nation'), the Orthodox enjoyed cultural and religious autonomy in that imperial system. However, the preferred medium of expression of the patriarchate, as the group's centre, was by far the ancient standard language. The tradition of the Crusades was pursued only on the Ionian islands and amongst the culturally very active Catholic minority. There, modern Greek was sometimes used in Roman script. As was the case elsewhere as well, the Ottoman regime thus had a conservative effect on a situation rooted ultimately in Late Antiquity. This situation did not become a problem until various ideas for a Greek national state were debated shortly before 1800. From the beginning, there was controversy as to what would be the national language of the state that was yet to be created. Intellectuals from the Ionian islands (like Solomos) and supporters of the French Revolution advocated the vernacular, while clerics and the elite surrounding the Constantine Patriarchate, on the other hand, advocated the traditional idiom. A. Korais sought a compromise, which he himself named Καθαρεύουσα/*kathareúousa*. It is therefore not, as is sometimes claimed, simply the continuation of the ancient standard language, but a middle way. The really traditional language was instead named αρχαίζουσα/*archaízousa*. Out of this combination arose the modern Greek language struggle that aroused passions into the 1970s. Only after the end of the dictatorship did the vernacular become an official state language. Debate still continues, though in muted form, over its character, especially over the extent of possible borrowings from ancient Greek.

D. THE ROLE OF GREEK FOR NON-GREEK LANGUAGES AFTER LATE ANTIQUITY

The early Church's decision essentially to adopt the ancient standard language and its literary ideals corresponds in its consequences to the significance of the Byzantine mission among the peoples of the Balkans. The loss of the Arabic eastern provinces and the constant threat via Bulgaria led to the resolute decision of the Byzantine elite in the 9th cent. to bind the southeastern European Slavs to them by conversion. This plan was thoroughly successful, initially through Cyril's creation of a Slavonic liturgical language, which, while not actually Greek, was in every respect entirely dependent on the Greek model (and indeed on all levels, from script form to literary genres, where foreign borrowings are rather rare). For its part, this *langue calque*, which is sometimes quite incomprehensible without a knowledge of the model, became in turn the model for most Slavonic languages. Just as with Latin for the Romance languages, Old Church Slavonic was for centuries the model of Slavic vernaculars, providing them with a large part of their vocabulary etc. until today. The Byzantine Church's liturgical language, however, was also for a long time the model for the Romance language, Romanian, that until the 19th cent. was written in Cyrillic script. Here, too, the Ottoman regime preserved what was already in existence and, indeed, after 1453, reversed processes: the new regime of Greek patriarchs allowed Greek to gain ground as a written language in the whole of southeastern Europe (the most important factor being the Greek school monopoly), and quite predominantly the scholarly variation. Bulgarians, Romanians, Macedonians and even the Serbs were subjected to a renewed Grecization that lasted into the 19th cent. Old Church Slavonic receded into the background, and entire languages like Albanian were used in writing almost only by the Catholics until the 18th cent. Greek, in both variations, was similarly influential on modern Balkan languages. A large number of loan-words, influences on syntax and phraseology, indeed on morphology ('Balkan language union'), and finally the existence of a pan-Balkan folk literature bear testimony even today to this cultural dominance of the Greeks over Orthodox adherents in the Balkans during the Ottoman period. Research into this, without nationalist prejudices, is only gradually being carried out.

1 J. NIEHOFF-PANAGIOTIDIS, Koine und Diglossie, 1994   2 J. KRAMER, Der kaiserzeitliche griechisch-lateinische Sprachbund, in: N. REITER (ed.), Ziele und Wege der Balkanlinguistik, 1983, 115–131   3 F. BABINGER, F. DÖLGER, Mehmeds II. frühester Staatsvertrag (1446), in: Orientalia Christiana Periodica 15, 1949, 225–258

JOHANNES NIEHOFF

II. Latin Middle Ages
A. Greek Script and Language B. Greek Literature

A. Greek Script and Language

The Greek alphabet is to be found in many medieval works, e. g. the *Etymologiae* of Isidore of Seville, Bede's *De temporum ratione*, Hrabanus Maurus's, *De computo* and Hugh of St. Victor's, *De grammatica*. Numerical values are often indicated. A knowledge of the numerical values of Greek letters of the alphabet was required for the *Epistola formata*, a Church letter of accreditation in which the numerical value of certain letters in the names of the sender, appointee, addressee and of the place of issue were added together with the amount of indiction and other items to form a total amount [20. 91–93]. The Greek alphabet was sometimes used as a secret script for the entry of subscriptions to documents and books, for writing down recipes and the formulae of blessings. While the Greek alphabet was put to such use, especially from the 9th to the 11th cent., this meant that for the whole of the High and Late Middle Ages each bishop had to be able to write the Greek alphabet correctly for the Roman rite of Church consecration. That is recalled in the 13th cent. by the sharp critic of foreign language learning in his time, Roger Bacon (d. 1294). He criticized the practice, on the part of bishops who were ignorant of Greek, of using the Greek alphabet for writing down the numerals 6, 90 and 900. "Since, for the sake of a great mystery, it has been laid down by the Church that Greek letters are to be used, some other symbols that are not letters of the alphabet must not be surreptitiously introduced; and, consequently, in the case of consecrations, one cannot write those symbols that are not letters, without doing an injustice to the Sacrament" [15. 83]. The form of Greek letters used in the Latin Middle Ages was entirely majuscule, in which a letter, the grammalogue *M* [21] (fig. 1), was used. The new Greek minuscule alphabet was used only in a few monuments of the 9th and 10th cents., and only sporadically in the High Middle Ages [2; 21; 48]. Bacon's Greek grammar teaches both alphabets; it belongs to the period of renewed Western activity in, and contact with the Greek Mediterranean.

Longer consecutive texts in Greek script or manuscripts entirely in Greek written by Western Europeans are rare. Characteristic of Greek studies in the Latin Middle Ages is the incidence of Greek texts transcribed into Roman script, generally in itacistically flavoured orthography. Greek liturgical texts, as they appeared in the *Missa graeca* in circulation from the 9th cent. on, were generally transcribed into Roman script in Europe and were more concerned with pronunciation than spelling. However, even bilingual biblical manuscripts recorded the Greek in Roman script, as was the case with the earliest extant Greek-Latin Psalter-manuscript in the Biblioteca Capitolare of Verona (cod. I [1], around 600) (fig. 2).

Fig. 1: *Formae litterarum secundum Graecos*:
Aphabetic tablet with Greek majuscules from 799, with graphic variations of Greek letters
(e.g. the alternative form of M as 'sigle M'), phonetic transliteration, Latin equivalents (left of the Greek letter as 'pro a', 'pro b', etc.), and the numerical value of the Greek letters. Vienna, Österreichische Nationalbibliothek Cod. 795, fol. 19 recte

The Latin Middle Ages had access to a considerable Greek vocabulary in the form of ancient school glossaries, which sometimes contained information on idiomatic usage. Such glossaries were still occasionally created in the early Middle Ages. In general, however, these glossaries declined in quality and finally disappeared in the course of the Middle Ages. From the 9th cent. on, routine dialogues in the old glossaries were already being used simply as lexical material. With school Greek in the High Middle Ages, there was a characteristic tendency of having Greek nouns end only in -*os* and -*on*, and verbs, in -*in* and -*on*. Latin lexicographers of the 13th cent. separated and analysed Greek compounds with a view to explaining them etymologically. The word parts circulated as independent 'Greek words' in the schools [30]. A reaction set in during the 13th cent. against corrupt 'school Greek', which was, nevertheless, to continue into the 15th cent.

Fig. 2: Oldest bilingual psalter (uncial script, ca. 600), Verona, Biblioteca Capitolare I (1), fol. 46 verso-47 recte. The Greek text (left) is written in Latin letters.

There was no manual in the Middle Ages for learning Greek like those of Donatus and Priscian for learning Latin. From Antiquity there was the grammar of Dositheus, in a parallel Latin-Greek version, that was originally conceived as a medium for teaching Latin to Greeks. Only a fraction of the grammatical material of Greek could be extracted from it, almost nothing on morphology. The most extensive evidence of efforts to attain a grammatical appreciation of Greek in the early Middle Ages is provided by Cod. 444 of the municipal library of Laon. This manuscript, which had its origins in the circle of Irishmen around Martinus of Laon (d. 875), contains, among other things, an outline of a Greek grammar [35]. In the Ottonian period, Froumund von Tegernsee [3; 18; 20. 47] started work on a Greek grammar.

It is surprising that we are not aware of any attempt at a Greek grammar from the productive and multifaceted 12th cent. Thus, John of Salisbury felt it a shortcoming not to know Greek, and he set about rectifying the situation – as it happens, virtually unsuccessfully – by taking Greek lessons from a Greek from southern Italy [20. 276f.]. A practical knowledge of Greek was not unusual in Italy in the 12th cent. We know the names of a number of Italians who, for the most part in Constantinople, translated documents and books from Greek. It is becoming increasingly clear that these West-erners in the eastern capital of the empire were directly involved in the emperor's splendid bilingual foreign correspondence [45. 49]. For Westerners who did not grow up in this bilingual milieu and who were interested in Greek, there was no alternative but to study bilinguals, e.g. Greek/Latin manuscripts of individual books of the Bible, a considerable number of which have survived from the Middle Ages [20; 50].

In the 13th cent., an attempt was made in England to make Greek accessible for students. Roger Bacon prepared a grammar suitable as an introduction for reading Greek [15]. Bacon dwelt in detail on the Greek alphabet, phonetics and orthography. Morphology is treated briefly but in compelling paradigms. Versions of current Latin texts, like the *Pater noster* and *Cantica*, are added as exercises. Bacon's work did not, however, gain any popularity.

Only when the early Humanists expressed their longing for sources in Greek had the time also come for a broader call for a Greek grammar. In his Ἐρωτήματα τῆς Ἑλληνικῆς γλώσσης/*Erōtémata tês Hellēnikês glôssēs*, Manuel Chrysoloras (d. 1415) composed a grammar in question and answer format that became the first widely disseminated work for teaching Greek in the Latin West. The work, which was composed in Greek, was intended for the private reader. Guarino of Verona (d. 1460) reworked the Chrysoloras grammar into a

Latin-Greek text that at last enabled self-study of Greek.

The new grammatical aids only slowly replaced the medieval techniques for learning Greek. Thus, the Humanist and Camaldulensian Prior-General Ambrogio Traversari (d. 1439), who later translated Diogenes Laertius and Dionysius Areopagita (pseudo-Dionysius), learned his Greek from bilingual biblical texts, starting with the familiar Psalter and progressing to more difficult texts [20. 47].

B. GREEK LITERATURE

'Graeca non leguntur' ("Greek is not read") – this motto applies to the Latin Middle Ages insofar as only few Europeans of this period acquired the ability to read and comprehend a fairly challenging Greek text in the original. However, the quantity of translations from Greek in the Middle Ages is usually underestimated, along with the role of Greek authors, especially the Church Fathers, in European intellectual life by virtue of those translations.

There are four periods in particular in which the stock of Greek literature in Europe was enlarged by translation: Late Antiquity, the Carolingian period, the High Middle Ages and Humanism.

1. LATE ANTIQUITY 2. THE 9TH AND 10TH CENTURIES 3. HIGH MIDDLE AGES 4. HUMANISM

1. LATE ANTIQUITY

In Late Antiquity, Neoplatonism represented the most enduring incentive for Greek studies for scholars of all persuasions. Vettius Agorius Praetextatus (d. 384) translated the Aristotelian commentaries of Themistius (d. 388), who worked in Constantinople; the philologist Macrobius explored the relationship between Latin and Greek in his work on *Differences and Similarities in the Greek and Latin Verb* and, with a commentary on Cicero's *Somnium Scipionis*, gave an introduction to Platonism that, together with Calcidius's *Timaeus* commentary and Boethius's *Consolation of Philosophy*, remained a basic philosophical text until Aristotelianism came into fashion in the High Middle Ages.

In the 4th and 5th cents. the Neoplatonism of Plotinus and Porphyry dominated the thinking even of Christians, like the Roman rhetor Marius Victorinus, the translator of the *Isagoge* of Porphyry, and the Milanese rhetor Manlius Theodorus. Thereafter, the translator and commentator of Plato's *Timaeus* in Late Antiquity, the Christian Calcidius, was likewise sought after in the circle of Milanese Platonism around 400. Until the middle of the 12th cent., Calcidius's *Timaeus* was the only Platonic dialogue that could be read in Europe in Latin translation.

For Christians of the the Latin-speaking part of the empire, Christianity's Holy Scriptures and their interpretation constituted a special incentive for studying Greek. The original language of the New Testament texts was almost exclusively Greek; that of the Old Testament was only to a small degree in Greek but, with respect to the Old Testament as a whole, the *Septuagint* was a Greek translation from the Hebrew regarded as authoritative. Of the ancient schools of textual analysis, the Alexandrian school excited the greatest interest, particularly the great exegetical work of Origen (d. 254).

In the last third of the 4th cent., two outstanding transmitters of Greek-Christian literature appeared–two clerics who knew each other in their youth: Rufinus of Aquileia (d. 410) and Jerome (Hieronymus) (d. 420). The most important translations by Rufinus are the *Ecclesiastical History* of Eusebius and Origen's dogmatic masterpiece *De principiis*. In both works Rufinus was at the same time both translator and reviser. The *Ecclesiastical History* of Eusebius, which covers the period to 324, was tightened, amended and expanded. His most valuable addition is its continuation up to the death of Theodosius the Great (395).

In his younger years, Jerome also devoted himself to transmitting the works of Eusebius and Origen. Around 380, he translated and revised the *Chronica* of Eusebius and extended it to 378. About the same time, Jerome met the strong demand for Origen's text by translating fourteen homilies each on Jeremiah und Ezekiel and announced his intention of translating a large part of Origen's work into Latin. After rejecting Origen's dogma, after about 394, Jerome translated only one other work of Origen: *De principiis*, as a rival translation to that by Rufinus. Under the aegis of Pope Damasus I (366–384), Jerome initially revised the New Testament and the Psalter from the Greek. He did not entirely dismiss the non-Classical linguistic form (which derives partly from the principle of literal translation) but changed it where the sense seemed to demand it. Later, when Jerome got to know Origen's *Hexapla* in Caesarea, he began to revise the Old Testament and translate it anew, but from the original Hebrew, and no longer from the *Septuagint*. 'Novum testamentum graecae fidei reddidi, vetus iuxta hebraicum transtuli', was Jerome's own self-appraisal at the end of his literary history *De viris illustribus*.

To a certain extent, Augustine's (d. 430) interest in Greek indicates the direction that can generally be observed in the following years. Augustine was no Hellenist; he did not like Homer. As a theologian, however, he wanted and was able to compare the Greek text of the Holy Scriptures. Augustine read the Greek exegetes in translation and he reverted to Greek symbolism whenever it was a linguistic issue that could not be translated directly into Latin, like interpreting the name of the first man AΔAM/ADAM from the initial letters of the four points of the compass in Greek [3; 20. 7; 32]

ANATOΛH/ANATOLĒ
ΔYΣIΣ/DUSIS
APKTOΣ/ARKTOS
MEΣHMBPIA/MESĒMBRIA

and the deciphering of the numerical value of the letters of the name AΔAM as 1+4+1+40=46. That was the Church Father's favourite Greek exercise, and it thereafter became the educational tool for the Christian Latin world.

In Late Antiquity, the councils [1], which almost without exception took place on Greek soil, brought Latin clergy into practical contact with Greek. The history of the council records in the Latin West, however, shows that no firm tradition took hold to assimilate and translate the Greek texts. For a fairly long time in the first half of the 6th cent., the Roman Church had a translator working from Greek: Dionysius Exiguus, who published several editions of Greek council records.

In Italy during the time of the Goths, Boethius appeared once more as a great representative of philosophical Hellenism. His ambition was to bring Roman world dominion to fruition by translating Greek wisdom for his fellow Roman citizens. To that end he planned first to translate all of Aristotle's works, comment on them and assemble them all in a concordance. Boethius realized only a fraction of this mighty enterprise. He translated and commented on sections of the parts of the Aristotelian corpus treating logic. As a preparatory guide to philosophy, Boethius designed a *quadrivium* of arithmetic, music, geometry and astronomy that imparted a great deal of Greek knowledge.

Cassiodorus (d. after 580) founded a formal school of translation in his monastery Vivarium. Epiphanius translated Didymus, Bellator translated some writings from Origen, Mutianus some from John Chrysostom and unidentified people translated Clement of Alexandria. The translators of Vivarium achieved significant results in the field of history. Cassiodorus, in earlier years the historian of the Gothic people, ensured that the Latin West, poorly served in terms of ecclesiastical history, received a fuller historical picture. "With much effort" (Institutiones I 17) he had the *Antiquitates Iudaicae* of Flavius Josephus translated into Latin; and, with the help of Epiphanius, he compiled the works of the ecclesiastical historians Theodoret, Sozomen and Socrates, who were linked to Eusebius, into the Latin *Historia tripartita*.

In Rome, the above-mentioned monk Dionysius, who gave himself the epithet Exiguus (d. middle of the 6th cent.), was active in the service of Church policy by translating Greek writings. Cassiodorus was associated with him and praised his translating ability. His most important translation was, together with his *Canones* collection, Gregory of Nyssa's work *De opificio hominis*. Dionysius Exiguus also translated hagiographical material like the *vitae* of Abbot Pachomius and the converted courtesan Thais.

The strong Byzantine presence in Italy from the middle of the 6th until well into the 8th cent. allows us to postulate an intensive series of exchanges between authors, including literature in translation [51]. However, there is little that we can be sure of. Thus, from the 'Byzantine period of the papacy' (ca. 537–752), the name of only one translator, Bonifatius Consiliarius, is clearly known to us so far, with the dates for his birth, death and work [24].

2. THE 9TH AND 10TH CENTURIES

Marriage plans in Charlemagne's court triggered the beginnings of a gradually regularized exchange of envoys between Constantinople and the Frankish court that was consolidated in 800 (the year of Charlemagne's coronation as emperor). From 810 to 817 there were even annual visits by envoys [29]. The decisive intellectual event in Greek-Latin relations in the 9th cent. was bound up with a Byzantine legation in 827. At that time Michael II, the Eastern Roman Emperor, handed over to the Carolingian King Louis in Compiègne the four theological texts and the ten letters of Dionysius the Areopagite (pseudo-Dionysius. The manuscript has survived: Paris, BN gr. 437). Emperor Louis passed the codex on to the monastery of St Denis in Paris, whose abbot Hilduin (d. 855/859) arranged for the first translation into Latin. John Scotus Eriugena undertook a new translation at the request of Charles the Bald. "It is in our view a very tortuous work that is remote from modern appreciation, is inaccessible to many and opens itself to few, not because of its age but because of the depths of heavenly mysteries" (MGH Epistolae 6, 159). Eriugena tried to avoid the errors and incomprehensibility of the Hilduin translation, while on the other hand remaining closer to the Greek text. He also composed a commentary on the *Celestial Hierarchies*. Again at the request of Charles the Bald, he translated a second great early Byzantine work, the *Ambiguae* of Maximus Confessor ([12] and [13]). Eriugena was not content with transmitting Eastern theology in translation and commentary. He himself wrote a large speculative work, *De divisione naturae*. The ambition of Carolingian Hellenists even found expression in writing poems in Greek [8].

Much better at Greek than Eriugena was Anastasius of S. Maria in Trastevere, antipope for a while and later librarian (d. 879). The papacy acquired in him, following Dionysius Exiguus another enthusiastic translator who was able to make himself indispensable as a Greek expert in Rome in spite of his compromised past. He honoured influential personalities by dedicating to them translations from Greek hagiography [16; 24, 38–40]. His translation of Leontius of Cyprus' biography of John the Almsgiver deserves special mention. [23. 2. 162–164]. It is the only early Byzantine biography that also became a biographical classic in the Latin West. For John the Deacon, who was working at the papal court with him as a historian, Anastasius translated and revised Greek texts of ecclesiastical history in a *Chronographia tripartita* (871–874) and in *Collectanea* (874). The most important of these are translations from the *Chronographia* of Theophanes (d. 818). With them Anastasius restored historical writing's links with the East, just as Eriugena had done in theology. The *Chronicle of Theophanes* is the last historical work of the Middle Ages to be read by both a Greek and a Latin readership. As a legate of Pope Hadrian II and Emperor Louis II, Anastasius participated in the Eighth Ecumenical Council in Constantinople (869/870) and translated the Greek records of the council into Latin.

The 'Ottonian era' can unhesitatingly be regarded as Greek-friendly. There was something of a Greek *anachoresis* in the West [20. 226–230]: a Greek woman did not just become the wife of an emperor but became herself *imperator* [sic]: Theophanu (d. 991). In view of the extensive speculation about the bridal dowry, patronage and Hellenizing influence of this remarkable woman, it must be stressed that not a single book, piece of ivory or goldsmith's work has ever been demonstrably linked to Theophanu [18; 40]. However high the emotional level of these Greek-Latin relations may have been, the intellectual level remained at studying the Greek alphabet, bilingual psalters [2; 34], the *Missa graeca* and other gestures of openness towards Greek as a holy language [33]. The great exception is Liudprand of Cremona, from an ambassadorial family. With his ΑΝΤΑΠΟΔΟΣΙΣ/ANTAPOLOSIS (begun in 958 in Frankfurt) and *Relatio de legatione Constantinopolitana* (968), he provided glittering examples of stylistic work, unique for centuries, in a Greek-Latin prose mix [5; 20. 214–222; 22; 44].

As early as the 9th cent. Naples had become, together with Rome, a focal point of Latin culture in Italy. What was translated from Greek in Naples was almost exclusively hagiography. The translators [23. 2. 167–171; 4/1. 22–30] were for the most part deacons. A deacon Paulus translated the famous *vita* of Maria Aegyptiaca and the equally famous *Poenitentia* of Theophilus, dedicating them to Charles the Bald. Deacon John (ca. 900), known as the historian of the Church of Naples, translated amongst other things the *vita* of St Nicholas. An important profane item among the Neapolitan translations was the Alexander novel of pseudo-Callisthenes. A certain archpriest Leo, as envoy of the Lombard princely house of Campania, got to know it on the journey to Constantinople in 942, when he was looking for 'books to read'. Leo wrote the story down and brought it to his lord's wife. A Latin translation was prepared later that marked the start of the extensive and complex Latin Alexander romance.

3. High Middle Ages

The productivity of Cardinal Humbert of Silva Candida (d. 1061) brings the previous era to a close. He was the first translator from Greek to interest himself exclusively in the controversy between East and West. He translated, for example, the letter that Leon of Achrida sent to Bishop Johannes of Trani in 1053 against Saturday feasts and the Latinist Azymites, which provoked a reaction from the papacy. That launched the ecclesiastical-dogmatic feud between Greek and Latin that lasted throughout the High and Late Middle Ages. With the battle over the addendum of *filioque* [41], which was pointedly adopted into the creed, the controversy continues to the present day.

At first, the theological dispute hardly affected the intellectual exchange between Byzantium and the Campanian coastal towns of Amalfi and Salerno. A whole series of Greek-Latin translations, especially of a hagiographical nature, was attributed in the last century to the translators' school of Amalfi that was active in the 11th cent. [4; 14; 26; 38]. These translators, however, might also have been active in Amalfi's overseas trading colonies. One such was in Constantinople, and even on the holy mountain of Athos there was a monastery of Amalfitani from about 985 to 1287. (The *Pirgos Amalfinon* on Athos is a vestige of it). Around the middle of the 11th cent. a monk named Leo translated the famous *Miraculum a S. Michaele Chonis patratum* there. The same Leo may have arranged for the translation of the Greek Barlaam and Josaphat tale (which corresponds in essence to the Buddha legend) by a Westerner in Constantinople in 1047. It was no less warmly received in the West than in the East [14].

The Comiti(s) Mauronis family, in particular, promoted Amalfi's cultural relations with Byzantium. Around 1080, a scion of the family named Lupinus arranged for a *vita* of Saint Irene to be translated by the priest and monk John, who was living in Constantinople. Pantaleo often encouraged the same John to translate into Latin things found in Greek books or tales. John responded to this request with his *Liber de miraculis*, which contains Greek ascetic tales, especially from the *Pratum spirituale* of John Moschus.

In Salerno, it was possible to see how Greek survived in a Latin environment, namely through the liturgy. Around 1100, a writing school was active there, producing deluxe manuscripts, apparently for the school's own use. That can be taken as an indication of the milieu from which the translators of specialist medical literature emerged, who worked for the school in Salerno which was rapidly becoming famous [27]. The Arabic influence is much slighter here than was earlier believed. Of the five parts of the *Articella* [46], Salerno's educational work that was in wide circulation from the 12th cent. on, at least three are translated from Greek. The best known Greek translator of Salerno is Bishop Alfanus of Salerno (d. 1085), who produced *Latinorum cogente penuria*, a translation of the anthropological-medical work *De natura hominis* of Nemesius of Emesa.

In the 12th cent., Constantinople was home to a group of Latinists who were gifted in language and engaged in literary work. Moses of Bergamo [38; 49] was in the service of the Byzantine court in Constantinople (around 1130–1140). He was the first Westerner to collect Greek manuscripts in Constantinople, but his collection was lost in a fire in the Venetian quarter. He seems only occasionally, and in response to a specific request, to have imparted anything from his profound knowledge of Greek, although he said of himself that he "had learned Greek especially so as to be able to translate it into our language, if I were to find something useful ...."(C. H. Haskins, Medieval Science ²1927,

201). Jacob of Venice, who called himself *Veneticus Grecus*, is probably the most important mediator of Aristotle's 'new logic' [37]. Jacob was the first to translate the *Analytica posteriora*, probably inspired to do so by his Aristotelian studies in Constantinople.

Burgundio of Pisa (d. 1193), the greatest translator of the 12th cent. [6; 33; 53], began around 1140 with a translation of juridical work, that of the Greek quotations in the digests of the *Corpus Iuris Civilis*. There followed theological translations, at the request of Pope Eugene III, who came from Pisa, of the 90 Matthew homilies of John Chrysostom in 1151 and the *In Isaiam* of Basil the Great in 1152, likewise dedicated to Eugene III. The same pope was also behind Burgundio's most important translation, the *Expositio fidei orthodoxae* of John of Damascus. He dedicated to Emperor Frederick I a new translation of *De natura hominis* of Nemesius of Emesa. During an ambassadorial assignment to Constantinople 1173, Burgundio lost his son and, 'pro redemptione animae eius', he translated the 88 homilies on John by John Chrysostom into Latin. Around 1185, Burgundio dedicated to a King Henry – probably the later Emperor Henry VI – the translation of a tract of Galen. In the last years of his long life he was preoccupied with Greek medicine.

It is impossible to sketch fully here the panorama of literature in translation that was being generated in the cosmopolitan city of Constantinople. We will instead just mention the names of the Western translators and the authors that they translated. Translators: Cerbanus, Hugo Etherianus, Leo Tuscus [11], Pascalis Romanus. Translations of Greek authors: John Chrysostom, John of Damascus, *Achmet's Book of Dreams*, the *Cyranides*, a book on the powers of animals, stones and plants, Epiphanius of Constantinople.

In Norman Sicily, Greek-Latin literature in translation in the Middle Ages began with the biography of a saint [17]. Then there appeared in the 12th cent. an Aristippus, who translated Plato's *Phaedo* und *Meno*. This Aristippus had links with the capital of the Eastern empire. He took away from there Ptolemy's Μεγίστη σύνταξις/*Megístē sýntaxis* (in the High and Late Middle Ages, generally called *Almagest*, after the Arabic) and had the work translated. A translation of Euclid's *Data* also seems to have been produced in this circle [10].

In France a mysterious John the Saracen worked at improving Eriugena's translation of pseudo-Dionysius. Literary interrelations in the crusader states were strikingly weak: so far we cannot name one single work translated from the Greek [20. 248 f.]. On the other hand, we know that around 1150 Pope Eugene III tried in vain to obtain via the patriarch of Antioch a Latin translation of the homilies on Matthew by John Chrysostom. The pope was sent a copy that was then translated in Pisa by Burgundio [20. 268].

Under Frederick II [52], Apulian Otranto was the centre of Greek-Latin contact. Homer's *Odyssey* was studied there [28]: the copy written in Otranto in 1201 is extant (Heidelberg Pal. gr. 45). The engaging figure of Nicholas-Nectarius of Otranto (d.1235) promoted Greek amongst Latinists with bilingual texts. An Italo-Greek school of poets defended the Hohenstaufen-Ghibelline cause in Greek verse [7], and Frederick II left behind the first national statute book in the West (*Liber Augustalis*, the *Constitutions of Melfi*) in Latin and Greek.

The best known and most significant translators of the 13th cent. are the Englishman Robert Grosseteste (d.1253), Bishop of Lincoln [36], and the Flemish Dominican William of Moerbeke [31], who died as the missionary Bishop of Corinth (before 1286). They are the linguistic representatives of the age that undertook the Herculean task of understanding and mediating Aristotle, Aristotelianism and Greek scholarship in general. In the process, they created the presupposition that this state of knowledge would someday be surpassed.

4. Humanism

Petrarch aroused amongst Humanists the desire to acquire a better understanding of Greek than that of a language based on alphabet tablets and bilingual texts and studied after a fashion–of Greek as the 'holy language' honoured in complicated ceremonies and embedded in theology and philosophy. In the 14th cent., some early Humanists tried to make headway with the help of Italo-Greeks. Petrarch took Greek lessons from the Calabrian Barlaam (d. 1350), probably without much success, for when in 1353/54 Petrarch finally held in his arms a Homer codex (Milan, Ambros. gr. I 98 inf.) delivered by an a Byzantine emissary, he said with a sigh: "O great man, how I wish I could hear you". His longed-for Homer remained mute.

Boccaccio made somewhat better progress than Petrarch, again with the help of an Italo-Greek, Leontius Pilatus (d.1365). Finally there appeared, in the form of the Byzantine envoy Manuel Chrysoloras (d. 1415 during the Council of Constance and buried in the Dominican monastery in Constance = 'Inselhotel'), a great teacher of Greek (from 1397 in Florence), at whose feet the Humanists sat to learn Greek grammar.

From then on, medieval translations from Greek were denounced as barbaric and replaced with new translations more attuned to the rhetorical sensitivity of the time (more elegant but not always more accurate). The focus of interest changed. Whereas scholasticism and the Middle Ages had been predominantly interested in Greek theology, philosophy, medicine and science, it was now poetry, historical writing, drama and *belles lettres* in general that became the focal point. At the same time, period perspectives changed as well. From Humanism onwards, it was taken for granted in the West that a very distant period of Greek, Classical Antiquity, would be studied. Being able to read Homer was the aim of studying Greek. Humanism finally created a readership able to read Greek literature in the original. After the catastrophe of 1453, there was for centuries no intellectually-alive Greek counterpart, but Greek studies and Greek literature had at least to some extent survived in the West.

SOURCES 1 Acta Conciliorum Oecumenicorum, series 1, E. SCHWARTZ et.al. (eds.), t. 1–4, 1922–1984; series 2, R. RIEDINGER (ed.), 1–2, 1984–1995 (the acts of all Ecumenical Councils in English are available on the World Wide Web at http://www.piar.hu/councils/~index.htm) 2 W. BERSCHIN, Drei griechische Majestas-Tituli in der Trier-Echternacher Buchmalerei, in: W. NYSSEN (ed.), Begegnung zwischen Rom und Byzanz um das Jahr 1000, 1991, 37, 52 3 Id., Eine griechische-althochdeutsche-lateinische Windrose von Froumund von Tegernsee im Berlin-Krakauer Codex latinus 4°939, in: Mittellateinische Studien, 2005, 285–291 4 P. CHIESA, Vita e morte di Giovanni Calibita e Giovanni l'Elemosiniere. Due testi amalfitani inediti, 1995 5 Id., Liutprandi Cremonensis opera omnia, 1998 6 R. J. DURLING, Burgundio of Pisa's Translation of Galen's ... De interioribus, 1–2, 1992 7 M. GIGANTE, Poeti bizantini di terra d'Otranto nel secolo XIII, ²1979 8 M. W. HERREN, Iohannis Scotti Eriugenae carmina, 1993 9 J. HOECK, R. J. LOENERTZ, Nikolaos-Nektarios von Otranto, Abt von Casole, 1965 10 S. ITO, The Medieval Latin Translation of The Data of Euclid, 1980 11 A. JACOB, La traduction de la Liturgie de saint Jean Chrysostome par Léon Toscan, Orientalia Christiana Periodica 32, 1966, 111–162 12 E. JEAUNEAU, Maximi Confessoris Ambigua ad Iohannem iuxta Iohannis Scotti ... interpretationem, 1988 13 C. LAGA, C. STEEL, Maximi Confessoris quaestiones ad Thalassium ... una cum ... interpretatione Iohannis Scotti 1–2, 1980–1990 14 J. MARTÍNEZ GÁZQUEZ (ed.), Historia Barlae et Iosaphat, 1997 15 E. NOLAN, S. A. HIRSCH, The Greek Grammar of Roger Bacon, 1902 16 E. PERELS, G. LAEHR, Anastasii Bibliothecarii epistolae sive praefatione, MGH Epistolae 7, 1912–1928, 395–442 17 M. V. STRAZZERI, Una traduzione dal greco ad uso dei Normanni. La vita latina di Sant'Elia lo Speleota, in: Archivio Storico per la Calabria e la Lucania 59, 1992, 1–108Lit LITERATURE 18 W. J. AERTS, The Knowledge of Greek in Western Europe at the Time of Theophano and the Greek Grammar Fragment in ms. Vindobona 114, in: Byzantium and the Low Countries in the 10th Century, 1985, 78–103 19 C. M. ATKINSON, Zur Entstehung und Überlieferung der Missa Graeca, in: Archiv für Musikwissenschaft 39, 1982, 113–145 20 W. BERSCHIN, Griechisch-lateinisches Mittelalter, 1980 (Engl. J. C. FRAKES (trans.), Greek Letters and the Latin Middle Ages, 1988) 21 Id., Griechisch bei den Iren, in: Die Iren und Europa im früheren Mittelater 1, 1982, 501–510 22 Id., Liudprands Griechisch und das Problem einer überlieferungsgerechten Edition, in: MLatJb. 20, 1985, 112–115 23 Id., Biographie und Epochenstil im lateinischen Mittelalter, parts1–4/1, 1986–1999 24 Id., Bonifatius Consiliarius. Ein römischer Übersetzer in der byzantinischen Epoche des Papsttums, in: Mittellateinische Studien, 2005, 65–78 25 Id., Griechisch in der Klosterschule des alten St. Gallen, in: Mittellateinische Studien 2005, 179–192 26 Id., I traduttori d'Amalfi nell' 11. secolo, in: Mittellateinische Studien, 305–315 27 Id., Salerno um 1100. Die Übersetzungen aus dem Griechischen und ihr byzantinisch-liturgischer Hintergrund, in: Mittellateinische Studien, 2005, 317–322 28 Id., Homer im Reich Friedrichs II. von Hohenstaufen, in: Mittellateinische Studien, 351–355 29 Id., Die Ost-West-Gesandtschaften am Hof Karls des Großen und Ludwigs des Frommen (768–840), in: Mittellateinische Studien, 2005, 105–117 30 B. BISCHOFF, Das griechische Element in der abendländischen Bildung des Mittelalters, in: Id., Mittelalterliche Studien 2, 1967, 246–275 31 J. BRAMS, W. VANHAMEL (eds.), Guillaume de Moerbeke, 1989 32 D. CERBELAUD, Le nom d'Adam et les points cardinaux, in: Vigiliae Christianae 38, 1984, 285–301 33 P. CLASSEN, Burgundio von Pisa, 1974 34 J. L. VAN DIETEN, Plastes ke piitis. Die "versiculi greci" des Bischofs Reginold von Eichstätt, in: Studi Medievali III 31, 1990, 357–416 35 A. C. DIONISOTTI, Greek Grammars and Dictionaries in Carolingian Europe, in: M. W. HERREN (ed.), The Sacred Nectar of the Greeks, 1988, 1–56 36 Id., On the Greek Studies of Robert Grosseteste, in: The Uses of Greek and Latin, 1988, 19–39 37 B. G. DOD, Aristoteles latinus, in: The Cambridge History of Later Medieval Philosophy, 1982, 45–79 38 F. DOLBEAU, Une liste ancienne d'apôtres et de disciples, traduite du grec par Moïse de Bergame, Anal. Boll. 104, 1986, 299–314 39 Id., Le rôle des interprètes dans les traductions hagiographiques d'Italie du Sud, in: Traduction et traducteurs au moyen âge, 1989, 146–162 40 A.VON EUW, P. SCHREINER (eds.), Kaiserin Theophanu. Begegnung des Ostens und Westens um die Wende des ersten Jahrtausends 1–2, 1991 41 J. M. GARRIGUES, L'esprit qui dit Père et le problème du filioque, 1982 42 E. JEAUNEAU, Etudes Erigéniennes, 1987 43 B. M. KACZYNSKI, Greek in the Carolingian Age. The St. Gall Manuscripts, 1988 44 J. KODER, T. WEBER, Liutprand von Cremona in Konstantinopel, 1980 45 O. KRESTEN, A. E. MÜLLER, Die Auslandsschreiben der byzantinischen Kaiser des 11. und 12. Jahrhunderts, in: ByzZ 86/87, 1993/1994, 402–429 46 P. O. KRISTELLER, Studi sulla Scuola medica salernitana, 1986 47 D. LUSCOMBE, Denis the Pseudo-Areopagite in the Middle Ages from Hilduin to Lorenzo Valla, in: Fälschungen im Mittelalter 1, 1988, 133–152 48 A. PARAVICINI BAGLIANI, La provenienza "angioina" dei codici greci della biblioteca di Bonifacio VIII, in: Italia medioevale e umanistica 26, 1983, 27–69 49 F. PONTANI, Mosè del Brolo e la sua lettera da Costantinopoli, in: Aevum 72, 1998, 143–175 50 P. RADICIOTTI, Manoscritti digrafici grecolatini e latinogreci nell'alto medioevo, in: Römisch-Historische Mitteilungen 40, 1998, 49–118 51 J.-M. SANSTERRE, Les moines grecs et orientaux à Rome 1–2, 1983 52 M. B. WELLAS, Griechisch aus dem Umkreis Kaiser Friedrichs II., 1983 53 N. G. WILSON, Ioannikios and Burgundio, in: G. CAVALLO et al. (eds.), Scritture, libri e testi nelle aree provinciali di Bisanzio, 1991, 447–455

WALTER BERSCHIN

Greek Comedy

A. ANTIQUITY AND MIDDLE AGES   B. 17TH–19TH CENTURY   C. THE 20TH CENTURY

A. ANTIQUITY AND MIDDLE AGES

In contrast to Greek tragedies, where repeat performances had been officially permitted since 386 BC, there is no epigraphical evidence of any repeat performances of 'ancient' comedies prior to 339 BC. It appears, though, that not the 5th cent.-comedies, but those by contemporary authors or by poets of the immediate past, i.e. those from the periods of the Middle and New Comedy, were performed again. The Old Comedy of the 5th cent., embedded in its own period with its typical contemporary references–in particular the naming and mocking of well-known personalities (*onomastí komodeín*)–could not expect a very positive reception by Hellenistic audiences. The exceptions might be plays with a more general and less political topic. Aristophanes' *Thesmophoriazusae* thus seems to have enjoyed a certain popularity because it dealt with Euripides, one of the most popular tragedians of the 4th cent. The Würzburg Telephos vase (Martin von Wagner Museum of Würzburg University, H 5697), originating from Apulia, is probably less a reflection of a farcical performance by *phlyakes* (mimes) than a direct response to the Aristophanian comedy [7. 38 ff.]. The fact that, of the extensive 5th-cent. comedy production, at least eleven plays by Aristophanes are extant as manuscripts is due to the Atticist movement during Rome's imperial age, which saw the language of Aristophanes as the manifestation of pure Attic [13. 9 ff.].

Inscriptions confirm that the works of Menander, the most important writer of comedies in the Hellenistic period, were put on stage again in the 2nd and 1st cent. BC. His popularity is evident in numerous images depicting scenes from his plays (e.g. the mosaics of Mytilene). With the prevalence of a strict Atticism since the 2nd cent. AD, Menander declined in importance and disappeared from school reading lists. This ultimately resulted in Menander's disappearance from the manuscript tradition during the Dark Ages in Byzantium (AD 726–842). Only aphorisms from his comedies (*Menandru Gnomai*) have been directly transmitted to modern times; the comedies only became known again towards the end of the 19th cent. and in the 20th cent. after extensive papyrus finds.

As in the case of the three Greek tragedians, the philologists of the 13th/14th cent. also edited and annotated Aristophanes' comedies, with a particular focus on three of his plays ('Byzantine Triad'): *Plutus* (*Wealth*), the *Clouds* and the *Frogs*, i.e., those plays that were suitable reading material for schools because of their moralizing and universal tone (*Plutus*), their philosophical (*Clouds*) or their literary-historical content (*Frogs*).

B. 17TH–19TH CENTURY

Aristophanes made his first appearance on a European stage in Strasbourg's Theatrum Academicum in 1613 with a performance in Greek of the *Clouds*. The moralizing tenor of the production is evident in Isaak Fröreisen's instructive epilogue to the German translation: the audience was to learn strength of character from Socrates, whose "thinking-place" ('phronistérion') was set on fire at the end of the comedy [8. 464]. There is little doubt that the way for the performance in Strasbourg was paved by the Humanist Nicodemus Frischlin's Latin translation of the *Clouds* (1586); he had also produced Latin translations of *Plutus*, *Frogs*, *Knights* and *Acharnians*.

After this short run in Strasbourg, Aristophanes disappeared once again from the European stage. The references in his plays to his own time, and especially the sometimes crude, even obscene content of the plays

(already denounced by Plutarch in his comparison of Menander and Aristophanes), hindered the reception of this writer of Attic comedies. Only *Plutus* was translated (Chr. Mylius, 1744), followed in 1783 by a translation of the *Frogs* by Goethe's brother-in-law J. G. Schlosser, who emphasized the political character of Aristophanes' comedy [8. 469]. However, it was not until after 1794 that public awareness of Aristophanes increased as a result of Chr. M. Wieland's translations into German of the *Acharnians*, *Knights*, *Clouds* and *Birds*.

A new appraisal of Aristophanes began in the early 19th cent., even though in Weimar, J. W. von Goethe had already staged his own adaptation of the *Birds* as early as 1780: "This was definitely not an attempt to restore the ancient drama to the stage, but a merry masquerade using ancient forms" [2. 50]. Goethe was quite appreciative of Aristophanes' dramatic art (letter to F. Schiller, 08.04.1794); however, his characterization of Aristophanes as a 'buffoon' (diary entry of 22.11.1831) indicated that he still followed the tradition, established by Plutarch, of rejecting the Attic comic poet. Only the Romantics were to discover Aristophanes as a literary challenge, and the authors of the pre-revolutionary *Vormärz* took him as a political example. In the same way that the return of the Greek tragedy was preceded by the critical analysis of its theory (Aristotle's *Poetics*; Hegel), it was a theoretical study which opened the doors for Aristophanes' comedies to return to literary awareness and ultimately to the stage: in his treatise *Vom ästhetischen Wert der griechischen Komödie* ('On the Aesthetic Value of Greek Comedy', 1794), F. Schlegel proclaimed Aristophanes to be the embodiment of the comic ideal. Inspired by Schlegel's work, the Romantics made an attempt, albeit short-lived, to revive Aristophanes' comedy (L. Tieck, *Der gestiefelte Kater*) (*Puss in Boots* 1794). Of greater influence was the role of people's poet which Schlegel had ascribed to Aristophanes. The explosive political nature of Aristophanes' comedy is particularly evident in the foreword to L. Seeger's translation (1845–1848), which introduced to his contemporaries both Aeschylus and Aristophanes as true patriots, as men "of enthusiastic words and enthusiastic deeds" [5/1. 18 f.]. Heinrich Heine also praised Aristophanes' true, i.e. radical-political character (*Germany. A Winter's Tale*, Ch. 27): 'For the real Aristophanes,/ It would have been a disaster;/ Poor chap, we'd soon see him going,/ With a chorus of gendarmes after!' (translation by J. Massaad)

C. THE 20TH CENTURY

The political, critical and even subversive character of Aristophanes' comedies prevented them from enjoying stage successes similar to the Greek tragedies until after World War II. M. Reinhardt's production of *Lysistrata* in the adaptation by L. Greiner and with a prologue by H. von Hofmannsthal (Berlin, Kleines Theater, 27.02.1908) was an enormous box-office success, but did not find favour with U. von Wilamowitz-Moel-

Aristophanes, The Clouds, 1988; Photograph Maltese, Siracusa, © *Foto Maltese/Dramma Antico*

lendorff [10. 91; 11. 7] and remained very much the exception. Productions of Aristophanes' plays experienced a short period of popularity in Switzerland in the 1930s and 1940s in productions by Reinhardt's pupil G. Kachler. Kachler hailed from Basle and, undoubtedly inspired both by K. Meuli's studies and the carnival customs of his home town, was fascinated by the cultic character of Greek drama. In his productions (Aristophanes, *Frogs* 1936, *Acharnians* 1938, *Peace* 1945, *Birds* 1946; Sophocles, *Electra* 1939, *Antigone* 1944; Euripides, *Cyclops*, *Iphigenia in Taurus* 1943/44) he tried to break the rigidity of the ancient theatrical masks "by turning them in all directions in the light and though shifts in perspective, thus enabling an extraordinary range in mood variations. The same mask could laugh, express joy, cry, or be angry" [2. 168]. This tradition was continued by Kachler in the Roman theatre in Augst (near Basle) (*Wealth or Money Rules the World : Plutus* 1965; *The Acharnians or How to Enjoy a Better Life* 1974) and was carried on even more recently (*Birds* 1983, Director: J. Hatz; *Peace* 1989, Director: J. Hatz).

After 1945, Aristophanes' peace plays (*Acharnians*, *Peace*, *Lysistrata*) experienced a stage renaissance; however, the topicality of Aristophanes' comedy had already been recognized in the aftermath of World War

I: simultaneously, and obviously independently from each other, both L. Feuchtwanger and H. Blümner had combined the *Acharnians* and *Peace* into a single play (L. Feuchtwanger, *Friede. Ein burleskes Spiel. Nach den Acharnern und der Eirene des Aristophanes*), 1918; H. Blümner, *Krieg und Frieden. Mit einem Nachspiel: Die Befreiung der Friedensgöttin. Nach den Acharnern und der Eirene des Aristophanes für die heutige Bühne frei bearbeitet von H. B.*, 1918). The new beginning in 1945 was marked by a little-known, and to my knowledge never-performed, adaptation of the *Acharnians* 'by E. Kästner (in: *Die kleine Freiheit. Chansons und Prosa 1949–1952*). In Kästner's style of 'occasional verse', the choir sings the praises of peace in the exodos: 'Reicht euch die Hände, seid eine Gemeinde!/Frieden, Frieden heiße der Sieg. / Glaubt nicht, ihr hättet Millionen Feinde./Euer einziger Feind heißt – Krieg! /.../Schön sein, schön sein könnte die Erde,/wenn ihr nur wolltet, wenn ihr nur wollt!' ("Hold hands, be one with each other!/ Peace, peace be the victory./ Believe not your foes to be millions. / Your only enemy is – war./ ... / How beautiful, how beautiful earth could be,/ if only you want it, if only you want it") [3. 285 f.]. Following on from *Lysistrata* in the adaptation by C. Bremer, directed by U. Brecht and set to music by A. Asviel (Kassel, 2 October 1966) [2. 207], P. Hacks's adaptation of *Peace*

(Berlin, Deutsches Theater, October 14,1962) [2. 209 f.] unleashed a veritable flood of Aristophanes productions. Hacks's *Peace* was an incredible success: in Berlin alone it was performed more than 250 times, followed by guest performances all over Europe. In his adaptation of *Peace*, Hacks was the "first to take seriously on stage the political dimension of the Old Comedy without destroying the character of the comedy" [2. 210]. He avoided a crude updating of the plot but elaborated on the basic poetic structure. The political dimension and direction became even more obvious in the production of the rarely staged *Knights* by the Greek director St. Doufexis (Nuremberg, 14 October 1967). The play was aimed at the Greek Junta with references to the contemporary political situation (student revolts, extra-parliamentary opposition) [2. 211 f.]. However, this obvious attempt at relevance required very few changes to the text. K. Koun's production of the *Birds* in the Herodes Atticus Theatre in Athens (1959) ended in a theatre scandal [2. 213 f.], because Koun staged Aristophanes' parodies of prayer and sacrifice according to the rites of the Greek Orthodox Church. The *Birds* is the play that, as a result of the discussion on utopia in the wake of E. Bloch's *The Principle of Hope* (1959), not only occupied philosophical studies [12] but was also seen in frequent stage productions. The political dimension of the comedy was particularly apparent in H. Heyme's Stuttgart production (18.4.1980) [2. 257 f.; 11]. In recent years, greater emphasis has been placed on the fantastic, fairy-tale character of the play (Konstanz, 24 February 1988 in the adaptation by D. Dorn and E. Wendt, Director: O. Schnelling). The production by the Istituto Nazionale del Dramma Antico (INDA) in the Greek theatre of Syracuse emphasized the comic-fantastic elements of Aristophanes' comedy (*Clouds* 1988, see fig. 1, Director: G. Sammartano. Music: S. Marucci; *Acharnians* 1994, Director: E. Marucci. Music: G. Gregori) [4].

In contrast to Aristophanes, Menander has not yet found his way back into the major theatres. The German première of *Dyskolus* took place in the Roman Theatre of Augst (Switzerland) to mark the 500th anniversary of Basle University, directed by Kachler (repeated in 1967).

→ Aristophanes; → Menander; → Plutarch; → Euripides
→ Greek Tragedy

1 M. Brauneck, Die Welt als Bühne. Geschichte des europäischen Theaters, 3 vols., 1993–1999   2 H. Flashar, Inszenierung der Antike. Das griechische Drama auf der Bühne der Neuzeit, 1991   3 E. Kästner, Vermischte Beiträge, Gesammelte Werke, vol. 5, 3rd ed., no date   4 T. Leto, Ombra della parola. Ottanta anni di teatro nella Siracusa del novecento 1914–1918, 1994   5 L. Seeger, Aristophanes, 3 vols., 1845–1848   5 W. Süss, Aristophanes und die Nachwelt, 1911   6 O. Taplin, Comic Angels and other Approaches to Greek Drama through Vase-Paintings, 1993   7 O. Werner, Aristophanes-Übersetzungen und Aristophanes-Bearbeitungen in Deutschland, in: H.-J. Newiger (ed.), Aristophanes und

die alte Komödie, 1975, 459–485   8 U. v. Wilamowitz-Moellendorff, Die griechische Literatur des Altertums, ³1912 (1995)   9 Id., Aristophanes, Lysistrate, 1927   10 Württembergisches Staatstheater Stuttgart (ed.), Die Vögel. Komödie des Aristophanes, Stuttgarter Hefte 12, 1980   11 B. Zimmermann, Utopisches und Utopie in den Komödien des Aristophanes, in: Würzburger Jahrbücher, Neue Folge 9, 1983, 57–77   12 Id., Die griechische Komödie, 1998.

I. Stark, Die Hämische Muse: Spott als Soziale und Mentale Kontrolle in der Griechischen Komödie, 2004 ; B. Zimmermann, Die griechische Tragödie, 1986 (Engl. T. Marier (trans.), Greek Tragedy, 1991)

BERNHARD ZIMMERMANN

Greek Philology see → Philology

Greek Revival
A. General B. Important Greek Revival Architects and their Major Works (Selection)

A. General
In architectural history the technical term Greek Revival (GR) refers to the copying and imitating of ancient Greek architectural patterns that took place in the late 18th and 19th cents. The term was coined after 1900 in the English-speaking world and usually only applies to Great Britain and the United States; there is no compelling reason, however, to exclude similar examples of Classicist architecture in other countries, especially in the German-speaking world. The relationship between American and British GR is controversial. For a long time most scholars thought that the style transfer from Europe to North America was unilateral (the architect Benjamin H. Latrobe, 1764–1820, was a key figure; he emigrated to the US from England where he was already well-known), but recently American GR has been recognized for its considerable eclecticism, implying that there was a typical home-grown style. As one among many building and decorating options in the late 19th cent., GR became part of the formal repertoire of → Historicism. The emergence of GR architecture coincided with the rediscovery of the monuments of Greek Antiquity and their appreciation. Important impulses came from the rediscovery of the Greek Doric order in its architecturally correct form (temple of Paestum; Parthenon on the Athenian Acropolis). It was a form unencumbered by Hellenistic or Roman interpretation or any Vitruvian description, which in its turn dominated the reception of ancient architecture in both the Renaissance (Alberti, Palladio) and Baroque eras (e.g. 'Palladianism' à la Inigo Jones in England; French 'Académisme'). Equating 'GR' with the technical term Doric Revival, as is common in the scholarly literature, is wrong since GR adopts not only Doric models but Ionic and Corinthian elements as well, and it copies them directly from the rediscovered archaeological monuments.

GR also reflects the association between the general appreciation of Greek Antiquity and the leading anti-absolutist ideas of the Enlightenment; not surprisingly this connection first emerged in English architecture and soon afterwards in the American architectural landscape – each time in the context of 'freedom'/'republicanism'. Ancient Greek building types were interpreted as ennobling forms, but as such they were no longer reserved for the magnificent buildings of nobility and clergy: they could be used in bourgeois and early industrial settings (villas, town homes, factory buildings), on the public buildings of the modern infrastructure (train stations) and for the representational architecture of an increasingly pluralistic state system (parliament and court buildings).

Publications of ancient architecture played a crucial role in the transmission of ancient architectural models to an increasingly fascinated group of European and American architects and their clients; tracings and more or less detailed copies were soon available in pattern books and architectural compendia. Julien David LeRoy's monograph *Les Ruines des plus beaux monuments de la Grèce* (first edition, Paris 1758), translated into many languages and republished many times, was widely consulted in architectural circles. Art historians and archaeologists consider as pivotal the work of the English architects James Stuart and Nicholas Revett *Antiquities of Athens*, written in the 1750s and commissioned by the → SOCIETY OF DILETTANTI. Wealthy property owners and developers appreciated the *de luxe* editions, but because of their exorbitant price, the small print run and the unpredictably slow publication schedule (4 volumes, published in London between 1762 and 1816, supplementary volume in 1830), they were initially available to architectural circles in excerpts only and as sketchy copies. The wide impact and significance of the work came only with the publication of abbreviated reprints, which circulated from the middle of the 19th cent. in various languages (in Germany especially in the compact edition by C. Gurlitt). In the 18th cent. more important impulses came from various publications on the temples of Paestum, among them Winckelmann's carefully illustrated *Anmerkungen über die Baukunst der Alten* ('Observations on the Architecture of the Ancients') of 1762. Because the geographical distance to the original architecture was nearly insurmountable, American architects depended on secondary compilations of these primary publications. With Asher Benjamin's bestseller *The American Builder's Companion* (first edition, Boston 1806), reprinted several times, began a series of pattern books that made ancient Greek architectural forms a feasible option not only for the technologically advanced New England States in the East but for the remote towns of the gold rush in Alaska as well as for the outposts of Oregon and the agrarian states of the colonial South. The highpoints of these pattern books were the works of Minard Lafever from the middle of the century.

This very peculiar situation regarding sources and their transmission explains the limited scope of ancient architectural forms that were copied: models were based entirely on what was available in the form of printed illustrations. The meticulous drawings of buildings from Athens and Attica reproduced in LeRoy and Stuart/Revett were of the greatest significance. The Parthenon (with an impressive eight-columned portico) and the Hephaesteion on the Athenian Agora (a hexastyle 'canonical temple' of classical proportions) exemplified the Doric order in its detail and variety. The prototype of the Ionic order was the Erechtheion, both in the execution of individual elements and with regard to possible combinations of elements; along with the representative Doric pediment, the window motif framed by Ionic half columns (as seen on the west wall of the Erechtheion) became a topos of the GR. The choregic monument of Lysicrates on the east slope of the Acropolis in Athens, dating to the late 4th cent. BC, expanded the repertoire of the Corinthian order which was well known since the Renaissance through architectural patterns from Rome and Italy. In the decades around 1800 Lysicrates' monument became a very popular motif for the towers of capitol and court buildings, churches, country estates and in the villa and garden architecture of the period.

Art historians and archaeologists have argued again and again that the selection of architectural types from the few existing patterns depended on the socio-economic context; however, a closer inspection of GR buildings – the majority of which remain to this day unpublished – calls this assumption into question: not only 'official' buildings, such as train stations or banks, but villas and apartment buildings as well make use of the Doric order, characterized by the symbolic attributes 'severe' and 'formal'. On the other hand the 'embellishing' and 'decorative' Ionic and Corinthian orders, supposedly the almost exclusive reserve of private architecture, often appear in a prominent position on public and semi-official architecture which is generally described as 'severe' and 'formal'. In light of the normative → ARCHITECTURAL THEORY of the Renaissance or the *architecture parlante* of the 16th, 17th and early 18th cent. it is still disputed in how far meaning was associated with the various architectural orders of GR and their elements. An interesting phenomenon – and a double anachronism – of American GR is the translation of ancient Doric stone architecture into contemporary wooden buildings. Also remarkable is the fusion of ancient Greek, ancient Roman and Renaissance architectural motifs that began in the late 18th cent. and prepared the way for Historicism – e.g. capitol buildings with façades that resemble a Greek peripteros, but in their overall design are modelled after a Roman temple raised on a podium with steps across the front; these are often combined with a steep central dome in the style of the High Renaissance and various other Palladian characteristics. Such buildings exemplify the core dilemma of Classicist architecture: they display a grand exterior but are of little utilitarian value. In the United States, too, architects were unable to reconcile ancient architectural types with modern technical and rational requirements, such as the placement of windows.

B. Important Greek Revival Architects and their Major Works (Selection)
1. Great Britain 2. United States

1. Great Britain
Joseph Bonomi the Elder (Great Packington: St James Church). Decimus Burton (London, Regent's Park: Coliseum; London, Hyde Park Corner: Constitution Arch; London, Whitehall: Athenaeum Club). Charles R. Cockerell (Oxford: Ashmolean Museum; Cambridge: Fitzwilliam Museum). Thomas Hamilton (Edinburgh: Royal High School). Thomas Harrison (Chester Castle). Henry Holland (Woburn Abbey, Bedfordshire). William Inwood and Henry William Inwood (London: St Pancras Church; London, Camden: All Saints Church). James Milne (Edinburgh: St Bernard's Crescent). John Nash (London, Regent Street; London, Regent's Park: Terraces). William Playfair (Edinburgh: Scottish Academy; Edinburgh: Carlton Hill Monument, with C.R. Cockerell). Sir Robert Smirke (London: Covent Garden Theatre; London: British Museum; London: Canada Building). Sir John Soane (London: Bank of England, collaboration). James Stuart (London: Lichfield House; Greenwich: Hospital Chapel, collaboration; Hagley Park and Shugborough Park: garden architecture). Alexander Thomson (Glasgow: United Presbyterian Church).

2. United States
Charles Bulfinch (Washington: United States Capitol, collaboration; Massachusetts: State House). James H. Dakin (Mobile: Barton Academy; Louisville: Bank of Louisville). Alexander J. Davis, Ithiel Town (New York: Lafayette Street; New York: Customs House/Treasury; Raleigh: North Carolina State Capitol). George Hadfield (Arlington: Arlington House). John Haviland (Philadelphia: First Presbyterian Church; Portsmouth: Naval Hospital). Benjamin H. Latrobe (Philadelphia: Bank of Pennsylvania; Baltimore: Cathedral; Charlottesville: University of Virginia, collaboration). Robert Mills (Charleston: Records Office; Washington: Washington Monument, original design; Washington: Old Patent Office). William Strickland (Nashville: State Capitol; Philadelphia: Second Bank of the United States; Philadelphia: Merchants' Exchange). Thomas U. Walter (Philadelphia: Girard College). Ammi B. Young (Boston: Custom House).
→ Athens; → Paestum

1 H. Colvin, A Biographical Dictionary of British Architects 1600–1840, ³1995   2 T. Hamlin, Greek Revival Architecture in America, 1944   3 E. Harris, British Architectural Books and Writers, 1990   4 H. R. Hitchcock, American Architectural Books, ³1976   5 C. Hökker, Greek Revival America? Reflections on Uses and Functions of Antique Architectural Patterns in American Architecture, in: Hephaistos 15, 1997, 197–240   6 R. G. Kennedy, Greek Revival America, 1989   7 J. Mordaunt Crook, The Greek Revival. Neo-Classical Attitudes in British Architecture 1760–1870, ²1995   8 W. H. Pierson, Jr., American Buildings and their Architects I: The Colonial and Neo-Classical Styles, 1970   9 J. Raspi Serra (ed.), Paestum and the Doric Revival, catalogue of the exhibition New York 1976   10 L. Schneider, Antike ohne Archäologie. Ein Blick auf griechisch inspirierte Architektur des 19. Jahrhunderts in den USA, in: Veröffentlichungen der Joachim Jungius-Gesellschaft 87 (dedicated to H.G. Niemeyer), 1999, 859–868   11 D. Stillman, English Neo-Classical Architecture, 1988   12 R. K. Sutton, Americans interpret the Parthenon. The Progression of Greek Revival Architecture from the East Coast to Oregon 1800–1860, 1992   13 P. Tournikiotis, The Place of the Parthenon in the History and Theory of Modern Architecture, in: Id. (ed.), The Parthenon and its Impact in Modern Times, 1994, 200–229   14 D. Watkin, Athenian Stuart: Pioneer of the Greek Revival, 1982   15 D. Wiebenson, Sources of Greek Revival Architecture, 1969

Additional Bibliography J. M. Crook, The Greek Revival: Neo-Classical Attitudes in British Architecture 1760–1870, 1995; R. G. Kennedy, J. M. Hall, Greek Revival America, 1989   Christoph Höcker

Greek Tragedy
A. Antiquity and Middle Ages B. The Renaissance C. 1700–1832 D. The 19th Century
E. 1900–1945 F. 1945–2000 G. Conclusion

A. Antiquity and Middle Ages
The following article is only concerned with the performance of plays by the three main Greek tragedians and the various tendencies of their productions in modern times. It is not possible in this context to deal with adaptations, new arrangements or reworkings, nor with the reception of Greek tragedy as a whole in the history of European cultural and intellectual history.

The seminal year marking a decisive change in the practice of performing dramatic plays in Athens was 386 BC, because it was then that repeat performances of 'old' plays were officially permitted. Before that, repeat performances had only been permitted under exceptional circumstances and outside the city of Athens. The decree of 386 BC opened the door to a repertoire theatre in the modern sense. Dramatic plays, which in the 5th cent. had only been permitted to be staged once as spiritual sacrificial gifts to the god Dionysus, thus became mere theatrical pieces. Plato reflected on this radical change in his Laws (700a); he criticized the fact that from then on, after the various poetic genres had lost their traditional 'place in life', the only guidance that poets could take was from popular taste. The secularization of the theatre went hand-in-hand with a professionalization of the actors and a dissemination of theatres across the whole the Greek-speaking world, especially in Hellenistic times, and then in the Roman imperial age across the entire Imperium Romanum [9].

This development was due in particular to the Artists of Dionysus, guilds that flourished into Late Antiquity, not only of actors, but also of authors, chorists, musicians, and rhapsodes [12. 279 ff.]. These groups had to have a certain repertoire of plays which, in addition to the selectivity caused by choosing what was suitable for schools, may well have been a further reason for the loss of texts of numerous plays. The performance of highlights from popular plays, particularly plays by Euripides, influenced the orally transmitted Greek folk songs of the Middle Ages (*Tragúdia*).

Whereas the Latin-speaking medieval world had no access to the Greek tragedies, the extant texts of the tragedians and of Aristophanes were revised and re-edited, their texts and metrics having been carefully examined by the Byzantine philologists Maximus Planudes (ca. 1250–1310), Thomas Magister (ca. 1270–1325), Manuel Moschopoulos (ca. 1265–1315) and Demetrius Triclinius (ca. 1280–1340). They mainly concentrated on three plays each by the three tragedians ('Byzantine Triad': Aeschylus: *Prometheus, Seven against Thebes, Persians*; Sophocles: *Ajax, Electra, Oedipus the King*; Euripides: *Hecabe, Orestes, Phoenissae*). Their editions largely determined the print versions of the 15th cent., thus forming the most important prerequisite for the renewed performances of Greek tragedians in modern times.

B. THE RENAISSANCE

Serious study of ancient poetry by Italian Humanists resulted in the rediscovery of the *Poetics* of Aristotle (*editio princeps* 1508 by Aldus Manutius; 1498 first translation into Latin by G. Valla, superseded by that of A. Pazzi in 1536) and led to an intensive involvement with the text, especially by devoting to it commentaries (F. Robertello, 1548; V. Maggi and B. Lombardi 1550; P. Vettori 1560; L. Castelvetro, 1576) and poetological reflections (J. C. Scaliger, *Poetices libri septem*, 1561) [17]. The high regard in which Aristotle held Sophocles' *Oedipus the King* smoothed the way for Greek tragedy to return to the stage. Undoubtedly, the increased interest in Greek musical theory and ancient architecture (Vitruvius [3/1. 450 ff.]) was also beneficial, as was the establishment of academies devoted to ancient literature.

The Accademia Olimpica in Vicenza, founded in 1555 with 21 members, was probably inspired by the performance of G. Trissino's archaized tragedy *Sofonisba*, based on Livy (30, 12–16) (published in 1524 and performed under the direction A. Palladio, academy member and architect), in its decision to commission A. Palladio with the planning and construction of a theatre [10. 3 ff.]. While the plays under consideration for the inaugural performance initially included Terence's *Andria* or F. Pace's pastoral drama *Eugenio*, the final decision was for Sophocles' *Oedipus the King*. The text was translated by Orsatto Giustiniani, and the chorus parts set to music by Andrea Gabrieli – except for the 3rd stasimon (1086–1109) and the exodus. The

play was directed by Angelo Ingenieri, in line with the contemporary understanding of Aristotle's *Poetics*, thus placing particular emphasis on the the fall of the tragic hero. The stage set by V. Scamozzi was inspired and guided by Vitruvius. The performance on 3 March 1585 was 'das Resultat einer Verbindung von griechischer Tragödie, römischem Prinzipatsdenken, Überhöhung der Antike ins Idealische und Anwendung all dieser Ideen auf eine idealisierte Gegenwart' ("the result of a combination of Greek tragedy, Roman Principate thought, an idealistic elevation of Antiquity, and the application of all these notions to an idealized image of the present")[5. 33].

C. 1700–1832

After its dazzling return, Greek tragedy never completely disappeared again from public awareness, but it did so from the public stage and eked out a shadowy existence in school theatres (especially in Strasbourg [5. 35]). These theatres were dominated by plays inspired by Seneca and by→ OPERA with subjects drawn from Antiquity [5. 41]. In Weimar, J. W. von Goethe paved the way for the second revival of the Greek tragedy [5. 49 ff.] with the production at his behest of Euripides' *Ion* in the translation by A. W. Schlegel (2 January 1802), albeit without resounding success. Sophocles' *Antigone* in an arrangement by J. F. Böttiger was performed on 30 January 1809, followed in 1813 by *Oedipus und Iocaste*, a tragedy by Klingemann loosely based on Sophocles. It is obvious that Greek tragedy hardly thrived on the theatre stages in Goethe's time; however, his theoretical analysis and study of Greek literature, in particular his *Iphigenie in Tauris*, combined with F. Schiller's practical and theoretical pursuit of Greek drama, in particular, the role of the chorus (in his preface to *Braut von Messina*, 1803), prepared the ground to be built on during the second half of the 19th cent.

D. THE 19TH CENTURY

(Overview [5. 60 ff.]). In the same way as the performance of *Oedipus the King* in Vicenza was significantly aided by the theoretical debate, i.e. the reception of Aristotle's *Poetics*, it was G. W. F. Hegel's analysis of Sophocles' *Antigone*, particularly in his lectures on aesthetics, which acted as a catalyst for the 1841 Berlin and Potsdam production of this tragedy in the translation by L. Tieck. In order to ensure a stage setting that recreated ancient conditions as authentically and realistically as possible, A. Böckh in his role as philological advisor insisted on having the choral songs set to music, a task assigned to F. Mendelssohn Bartholdy. The Potsdam Court Theatre in the New Palace was set up in accordance with the concepts developed by the architect and archaeologist H. C. Genelli (*Das Theater von Athen*, 1818). Because of the great success of this performance, Friedrich Wilhelm IV instructed L. Tieck to translate additional tragedies; as a result, Euripides' *Medea* with incidental music by G. W. Taubert was performed in 1843, Sophocles' *Oedipus at Colonus* in 1845 – again with music by Mendelssohn – and, finally, in 1851, Euripides' *Hippolytus* with music by A. Schulz. A production of Aeschylus's *Eumenides* failed. The deaths of Mendelssohn und Tieck and the growing disinterest of the Prussian king brought a close to this short golden age.

The success of the Potsdam *Antigone* production also opened the door for productions outside Prussia (1844 Paris). In Munich, *Antigone* was staged in 1851 with Mendelssohn's music with a set designed by L. von Klenze. This was followed by *Oedipus the King* (1852) and *Oedipus at Colonus* (1854), both directed by F. Dingelstedt. Inspired by the Munich productions, A. Wilbrandt produced in Meiningen in his own translation *Oedipus the King*, *Oedipus at Colonus* and *Antigone* as a trilogy (1867). The aim of his production was historical authenticity; he placed particular importance on mass scenes, in which he split the chorus into individual voices. At Vienna's *Burgtheater*, Wilbrandt produced Sophocles' *Electra* and Euripides' *Cyclops* (1882), as well as *Oedipus the King* (1886) and *Oedipus at Colonus* (1887). As for what was actually performed on stage, the 19th cent. was predominantly a Sophoclean age. The interest in Aeschylus was mainly awakened by R. Wagner, but did not take effect on the theatre until the 20th cent.

E. 1900–1945

[5. 110 ff.] As the collaboration of Tieck, Böckh and Mendelssohn in the 1840s was extremely fruitful for Greek tragedy, the new impulses emanating from the collaboration of U. von Wilamowitz-Moellendorff and M. Reinhardt in the early years of the 20th cent. proved to be even more so. Wilamowitz, who had been teaching at the University of Berlin since 1897 and whose translations of Greek tragedies were published from 1899 onwards, was engaged by Reinhardt as the academic advisor for the production of *Oedipus the King* (28 February 1900). Wilamowitz gave the introductory lecture *Die Aufführbarkeit der griechischen Tragödie* ('Can Greek Tragedy Be Put on Stage?'). As pioneered by Wilbrandt, chorus scenes were staged as mass scenes and chorus parts recited in unison. This was followed on 24 November 1900 by the *Oresteia* translated by Wilamowitz and arranged for the stage by H. Oberländer. The musical setting by M. von Schilling was the first to develop a new form of the chorus melodrama, and gestures were used to interpret the words. M. Reinhardt directed the *Oresteia* (without the *Eumenides*) in K. Vollmoeller's translation in Munich and Berlin in 1912, and the complete version in Berlin in 1919. A thousand walk-ons were employed, and special light and sound effects together with the stage set produced a splendidly enhanced theatrical experience [5. 129]. The influence of Wagner's notion of the *Gesamtkunstwerk*, 'total art work', was also evident in the performance of Aeschylus's *Agamemnon* in Syracuse (1914) in the translation and musical setting by E.

Romagnoli [11]. In the years leading up to World War I, the Dionysian aspect of the Greek tragedy was emphasized by H. von Hofmannsthal in his *Electra* (1903), while F. Werfel combined the Dionysian with the notion of Christian salvation in his adaptation of Euripides' *Trojan Women* (1915) [18. 179 ff.]. The splendid enhancement of the theatrical experience was increased even more in the wake of the 'rediscovery' of F. Hölderlin's Sophocles translations (1919 performance of Hölderlin's *Antigonae* in Zurich). The archaic, ritualistic and alien elements of Greek tragedy were the focus in J. Cocteau's *Oedipus Rex*, set to music by I. Strawinsky; the alien character was emphasized even further by the Latin libretto in the translation by the Jesuit J. Danielou [5. 147 ff.]. The notion of Greek tragedy as a ceremonial play in conjunction with the concept of salvation and a focus on the alien and distant, the dark and gruesome, characterized the production of Aeschylus' *Oresteia* on the occasion of the Berlin Olympics (2 August 1936, Director: L. Müthel); the new order, created in the *Eumenides*, was intended as a reference to the National-Socialist regime [5. 164 ff.].

F. 1945–2000

The opportunity to relate Greek tragedy to the contemporary political situation, which had already been done after World War I by F. Werfel (*Trojan Women*, 1915) and W. Hasenclever (*Antigone*, 1917), dominated the productions in the second half of the 20th cent. The first to do so was B. Brecht with his adaptation of *Antigone* (Chur, 15 February 1948). The main aim of C. Orff's *Antigonae* (in Hölderlin's translation) was to restore the unity of music, words and gestures, and emphasize the hieratic-ritualistic character of the tragedy [5. 181 ff.]. In his production of the *Oresteia* (Syracuse 1960, translated by P. P. Pasolini), V. Gassmann used the clash of the old and the new order in the *Eumenides* to illustrate the contrast between Italy's industrialized North and the backward archaic South. A blend of Marxist theory and S. Freud's psychology formed the backdrop to P. P. Pasolini's filming of Greek tragedies (*Edipo Re*, 1967; *Medea*, 1969; *Appunti per un' Orestiade Africana*, 1975) [6]. An archaic-alien past and the present intermingle; the action seems distant and at the same time familiar and ever repeatable. Ancient myths serve to interpret the present. The desire to make the symbolic meaning of the Greek myths relevant and to have them serve as a critical view on current events dominated various productions of the modern interpretive theatre. Particular mention should be made of H. Heyme's preoccupation with Greek tragedies [5. 225 ff.] and H. Müller's adaptations of Sophocles' *Philoctetes* (1968) and *Prometheus* (1978) [5. 241 ff.]. In his Berliner Schaubühne production of the *Oresteia* (18 October 1980), P. Stein wanted to recreate the ancient theatre experience (by the length of the production alone – nine-and-a-half hours). In the same way as Tieck and Böckh, Reinhardt and Wilamowitz had engaged in a fruitful dialogue between

Sophocles, Ajax, 1988; Photograph Maltese, Siracusa, © *Foto Maltese/Dramma Antico*

philological research and practical directorship, Stein, too, incorporated controversial scholarly opinions into his translation. Like Wilbrandt, Stein dissolved the chorus into individual voices in order to create a 'choric debate' and thus to further the integration of the chorus into the action [5. 263 ff.; 14]. A similar direction was taken by S. Schoenbohm's production of Euripides' *Bacchae* (Athens 1996, Music: A. Kounadis). It was not Schoenbohm's intention to provide complete renditions of the chorus parts, but to reduce them to essentials, so that they might express and emphasize the prevailing 'mood' in any particular scene. Dance, song, and pantomime were conceived as a single unit [13. 271 ff.]. Influenced by M. Foucault's theories, A. Mnouchkine's tetralogy *Les Atrides* in a far-eastern setting (Paris, concluded 1992) emphasized the anthropological-ritualistic dimensions and the ecstatic-Dionysian substrate of Greek tragedy [2. 54 ff.]. The most recent production of the *Oresteia* (G. Ladavaunt, Paris 1999) once again stressed the political message of the *Eumenides*. H. Heyme's recent work as a director at the 2000 Ruhrfestspiele can be seen as a critical involvement with the ancient form of the trilogy (*Imera – Der Tag – Medea, Alcestis, Ion*). A similar direction was taken by the 'Theban Trilogy' (Sophocles, *King Oedipus, Antigone, Oedipus at Colonus*) staged by INDA in the Colosseum in Rome in July/August 2000.

G. CONCLUSION

Looking back to the Greek tragedy's 415 years of stage performances in modern times from the first performance of Sophocles' *King Oedipus* in Vicenza on 3 March 1585 to the year 2000, four consistent trends in interpretation are evident.

1. The desire for authenticity characterized the performance in Vicenza and the 19th cent. productions. P. Stein's *Oresteia* also takes its place within this tradition. Typical features of this trend are a musical setting of the lyric sections, the treatment of the chorus and the fact that classical philologists are consulted as advisors. The Istituto Nazionale del Dramma Antico (INDA) in Syracuse is particularly strong in its support for the collaboration of directors, philologists, actors and composers (see fig. 1).

2. The close interconnection between various theories and actual productions of Greek tragedies has been a dominant factor in productions from the earliest one in 1585 to the present. In contrast to Antiquity, when the theory, i.e. Aristotle's *Poetics*, followed the practical experience, in modern times, theory has paved the way for the return to the stage of Greek tragedy and has continued to add new stimuli (Aristotle, Hegel, Freud, Marxist theory) [2; 6].

3. In the 20th cent. the political dimensions of the Greek tragedy became ever more central in the wake of the experience of two world wars and a number of other military conflicts, of social tensions, tyrannical regimes

and inhuman ideologies. Tragedies become the counter images or the distorted images of reality; myth – in conjunction with the intensive debate on mythology after World War II – becomes a cipher, a symbol, by which we reflect and interpret reality.

4. Influenced by F. Nietzsche (*The Birth of Tragedy*, 1872), E. Rohde (*Psyche*, [2]1898) and other literary tendencies at the turn of the 19th to the 20th cent. (e.g. Th. Mann, *Death in Venice*, 1912), there was a growing interest in Greek tragedy's cultic-ritualistic, Dionysian-ecstatic roots [15; 18. 179 ff.]. Productions in this tradition emphasize the alien, archaic and sometimes even the violent and dark side of the Greek tragedy.

→ Aristotle; → Aeschylus; → Euripides; → Sophocles; → Tragedy

→ GREEK COMEDY; → LATIN TRAGEDY

1 P. AMOROSO, A. KARAPANOU, A Stage for Dionysos. Theatrical Space and Ancient Drama, 1997 (= Mia skene gia ton Dionuso: theatrikos choros & archaio drama) 2 A. BIERL, Die Orestie des Aischylos auf der modernen Bühne. Theoretische Konzeptionen und ihre szenische Realisierung, 1997 3 M. BRAUNECK, Die Welt als Bühne. Geschichte des europäischen Theaters, 3 vols., 1993–1999 4 F. DUNN (ed.), Sophocles' Electra in performance, 1996 5 H. FLASHAR, Inszenierung der Antike. Das griechische Drama auf der Bühne der Neuzeit, 1991 6 M. FUSILLO, La Grecia secondo Pasolini. Mito e cinema, 1996 7 V. GREISENEGGER-GEORGILA, H. J. JANS (eds.), Was ist die Antike wert? Griechen und Römer auf der Bühne von Caspar Neher, 1995 8 Memoria del futuro. I teatri greci e romani – censimento, 1992 9 M. MCDONALD, Ancient Sun, Modern Light. Greek Drama on the Modern Stage, 1992 10 G. NOGARO, Cronache degli spettacoli nel Teatro Olimpico di Vicenza dal 1585 al 1970, 1972 11 Ombra della parola. Ottanta anni di teatro antico nella Siracusa del Novecento 1914–1994, 1994 12 A. PIK-KARD-CAMBRIDGE, The Dramatic Festivals of Athens, [2]1968 (1988) 13 P. RIEMER, B. ZIMMERMANN (eds.), Der Chor im antiken und modernen Drama, 1999 14 B. SEIDENSTICKER (ed.), Die Orestie des Aischylos. Übersetzung von Peter Stein, 1997 15 E. STÄRK, Hermann Nitschs 'Orgien Mysterien Theater' und die 'Hysterie der Griechen'. Quellen und Tradition im Wiener Antikebild seit 1900, 1987 16 A. STEFANI, Cronache degli spettacoli nel Teatro Olimpico di Vicenza dal 1971 al 1991, 1992 17 B. ZIMMERMANN (ed.), Antike Dramentheorien und ihre Rezeption, 1992 18 Id., Europa und die griechische Tragödie Vom kultischen Spiel zum Theater der Gegenwart, 2000

ADDITIONAL BIBLIOGRAPHY W. J. DOMINIK, Africa, in C. W. KALLENDORF (ed.), Companion to the Classical Tradition, 2007, 117–31; A. S. GREEN, The Revisionist Stage: American Directors Reinvent the Classics, 1994; E. HALL & F. MACINTOSH, Greek Tragedy and the British Theatre 1660–1914, 2005; E. HALL, F. MACINTOSH, O. TAPLIN (eds.), Medea in Performance 1500–2000, 2000; E. HALL, F. MACINTOSH, A. WRIGLEY (eds.), Dionysus since 69, 2004; L. HARDWICK, Remodelling Reception: Greek Drama as Diasporic Performance, in C. MARTINDALE, R. THOMAS (eds.), Classics and the Uses of Reception, 2006, 204–15; K. HARTIGAN, Greek Tragedy on the American Stage: Ancient Drama in the Commercial Theatre, 1882–1994, 1995; P. MAVROMOUSTAKOS (ed.), Productions of Ancient Greek Drama in Europe during Modern Times, 1999; M. MCDONALD, Ancient Sun, Modern Light: Greek Drama on the Modern Stage, 1992; M. MCDONALD & J. M. WALTON (eds.), Amid Our Troubles: Irish Versions of Greek Tragedy, 2002; S. MERCOURIS (ed.), A Stage for Dionysus: Theatrical Space and Ancient Drama, 1998; S. PATSALIDIS AND E. SAKELLARIDOU (eds.), (Dis)placing Classical Greek Theatre, 1999; K. J. WETMORE, JR., The Athenian Sun in an African Sky, 2002; K. J. WETMORE, JR., Black Dionysus: Greek Tragedy and African American Theatre, 2003

URLS Open University Reception of Classical Texts Research Project: http://www2.open.ac.uk/ClassicalStudies/ GreekPlays; Oxford University Archive of Performances of Greek and Roman Drama: http://www.apgrd.ox.ac.uk

BERNHARD ZIMMERMANN

Greek, pronounciation see→ PRONOUNCIATION

Grotesque

A. INTRODUCTION B. MIDDLE AGES C. REDISCOVERY AND RECEPTION DURING THE RENAISSANCE D. DEBATES IN ART THEORY E. RECEPTION IN THE MODERN PERIOD

A. INTRODUCTION

Many stately and magnificent buildings of Antiquity contained paintings and stucco work covering walls and vaults. The most important examples for later reception, the grotesques in the *Domus Aurea* of the Roman emperor Nero, thought to be the baths of Titus at the time of their discovery, were stylistically equivalent to the 3rd and 4th Pompeian style: They consisted of thread-like and thread-shaped plants, animals and monsters. The grotesque decoration in the *Domus Aurea* used a system based on a geometric order into which small images were inserted and which represents, in itself, a reception of Hellenistic art by this graecophile emperor. The *Domus Aurea* received its name from an abundant use of gold. Through numerous architectural changes that essentially began under the emperor Titus (79–81), the rooms were blocked up and only rediscovered about 1470/1480. The paintings and gilded stucco found in the palace rooms that had become grottoes ('grotesques') fascinated artists of the Renaissance, Mannerism and later centuries, but then were forgotten in the 19th cent. Terminologically, the grotesque is difficult to capture and a dispute over the correct designation erupted with their discovery: In the 16th cent. the grotesques were called *mostri* (B. Cellini, *Vita*, first published in 1728 in Naples), generally *ogni di pittori* or *più specifico del "capriccio" manirista*, which also included arabesque and mau(o)resque. Beyond these the term was also applied to literature and dance. However, in practice these different art genres are barely distinguishable in the 15th–18th cents.

B. MIDDLE AGES

The grotesques of the *Domus Aurea* were unknown in the Middle Ages but their fantastic world of forms

Fig. 1: Luca Signorelli, Dado decorated with grotesques (detail). 1501/04. Orvieto, Cathedral (San Brizio Chapel)

Fig. 2: Giovanni da Udine, Acanthus leaf in the Loggia. Completed 1519. Rome, Vatican

already existed to a significant extent in manuscripts, sculptural decoration of capitals and other parts of mediaeval churches [2]. Their models were ancient sarcophagi, lesene decoration, stucco sculpture and paintings (e.g., in crypts: [9]), as they are later found in ceiling paintings of the *Libreria Piccolomini*, Siena cathedral, (School of Pinturicchio, 15th cent.), in which only the scheme is derived from the *Domus Aurea*.

C. Rediscovery and Reception during the Renaissance

After the rediscovery of the *Domus Aurea*, the grotesques caused great excitement among Renaissance artists. As if in an artistic competition they spread in ever-new variants – they covered churches and palaces in an enormous number. Just to name a few examples: Ghirlandaio used them as pilaster filler in his *Birth of Mary* (*Tornabuoni* Chapel, *S. Maria Novella*, Florence 1488; in the *Codex Escurialensis* from Ghirlandaio's workshop there are numerous drawings of grotesques that were used as templates). The artists who could study them on location also attempted to imitate them stylistically: Pinturicchio attempted to copy the fast brush strokes of the *Domus Aurea* in his paintings in the Chapel *San Gerolamo* (*S. Maria del popolo*, Rome 1488). Filippino Lippi's grotesques in the *Carafa* Chapel (*S. Maria sopra Minerva*, Rome, 1488–92) are 'more plastic'; he also used them to show off his ar-

chaeological knowledge. The same applies to the *Strozzi* Chapel (*S. Maria Novella*, Florence, from 1489), while Perugino's grotesques on the ceiling vault of the *Collegio del cambio* in Perugia (1499/1500) are reminiscent of Pinturicchio's but are more traditional than those of Lippi. In Signorelli's frescoes in the *Brizio* Chapel (cathedral, Orvieto, 1501–1504; fig. 1) we find in the artist's hybrid world of shapes a quasi-demonic version of the 'normal' grotesque. His grotesques do not conform any longer to the composition principles of, for example, 'classical monsters' but vibrate with vitality. Early in the 16th cent. regular specialists like Amico Aspertini, a student of Pinturicchio, emerged: He was the first to insert fantastic architecture borrowed from Antiquity. With Giovanni da Udine, who, according to a legend by G. Vasari, discovered the grotesques of the *Domus Aurea* together with Raphael, a break with the 15th-cent. tradition occurred. Giovanni took his lead again from the original patterns of Nero's age (examples: *stufetta,* finished in 1516; *loggetta,* finished in 1519, of Cardinal Bibbiena, Rome, Vatican). The painter completely covered the walls with a network of grotesques and developed a new decorative scheme that later became important for the Mannerists. Finally, Cesare Baglione's *Salon des jongleurs* in the castle *Torrechiara* (1525–1590) should be noted. The most famous example and brilliant high point are the loggias by Giovanni da Udine and Raphael (finished in 1519) (fig. 2); the latter had already been active in the *Chigi Chapel* (*S. Maria del popolo*, Rome). He also originally studied the technique of the Romans, possibly in the *porticati* of the Colosseum, and was able to use it for his white stucco work in the Vatican. Immediately after their creation, the loggias of Raphael aroused unanimous enthusiasm and were celebrated as *decorazione alla antica* (Castiglione). They were considered perfect at the time because they seemed refined but not scholarly and displayed a naturalism combined with gaiety. The grotesques that frame the Biblical scenes in the loggias consist of simple pagan creatures such as sphinxes, sirens, nymphs, satyrs, fauns, centaurs etc. There are also depictions of nature such as various plants drawn with great love for detail. Using the same system that he had developed for the loggias, Raphael and his helpers also worked in the *Villa Madama* (Rome, interrupted in 1525). Many artists saw and imitated the loggias even during Raphael's life time [6], e.g., Correggio (*Camera di San Paolo*, Parma, 1519), Parmigianino (*castello* of Sanvitale in Fontanellato near Parma, ca. 1523) and Beccafumi (former *Palazzo Bindi Sergardi*, today *Palazzo Casini Casunicci*, Siena, 1524–25 or 1528–30). Raphael's students spread them over all Italy, e.g., Perin del Vaga (*Palazzo Doria Pamphili*, Genoa, 1529), Giulio Romano (*Palazzo del Tè*, Mantua; 1527–29; 1530–35) – his grotesques are disproportionally massive–, Peruzzi (*Villa Belcaro* near Siena, before 1523) and Bronzino (chapel of Eleonora of Toledo, *Palazzo Vecchio*, Florence, 1540/41). The grotesques of Raphael's loggias were subsequently distributed in engravings and drawings outside of Italy, especially in France, Germany and the Netherlands. These imitations are partially free interpretations and partially exact copies. Grotesques, in general, were distributed like those of Raphael's loggias as engravings during the 16th cent., e.g., by Nicoletto da Modena, A. Veneziano or Enea Vico, and entered the decorative arts. They are found on grave monuments (example: tomb of Julius II by Michelangelo in *S. Pietro in Vincoli*, ca.1514–16) or as applied art such as *graffiti* on palace façades (Florence: Andrea di Cosimo Feltrini; Rome: Polidoro da Caravaggio). They also decorated tapestry in Florence (A. Aspertini, Giovanni da Udine, Bachiacca; ca. 1550), ceramics and goldsmith work, armour and weapons. In the religious area, the grotesque fashion runs out after 1580. In secular surroundings grotesques only begin to fade early in the 17th cent. and later are only used as decorative additions, e.g., in the decoration of the *galleria* of the *Palazzo Ruccellai*, Florence, by Jacopo Zucchi 1586/87 (door and window openings), although Zucchi no longer used them in the Chapel *Orsini-Tolfa* in *Santo Spirito in Sassia* (Rome 1588). The same applies to grotesques in Federico Zuccari's home (1590–1600), the modern *Bibliotheca Hertziana*, where they are only decorative additions, while in the 16th cent. they were understood, in part, as 'demonic hieroglyphs' (see below). The grotesques in the *Uffizia* represent a late example (1st Galleria 1581; 2nd Gal-

leria from 1658). Finally, the export of grotesques to the Netherlands should be noted, where they, for instance, are found in the work of Cornelis Floris (1514–1575); to Germany, especially with Peter Flötner (ca. 1485–1546); and to France, where Primaticcio decorated after 1540 the Odysseus Gallery in Paris with painted and stuccoed grotesques and where, through the publication of the *Livre des Grotesques* (1550, republished in 1562 and 1566) by Jacques Androuet du Cerceau, they aroused great interest. In the 16th cent. they also made their way to Latin America, specifically to the Spanish-occupied part of Mexico, where grotesques decorated manuscripts (Diego Duràn, *Historia de las Indias de Nueva España*, 1579–81 and *Codice Magliabecchiano*, before 1566) and 16th-cent monasteries (Acolman, Puebla and Ixmiquilpan [12]).

D. DEBATES IN ART THEORY

Especially in the mid 16th cent., grotesques enflamed a lively debate in art theory regarding their admissibility and meaning: Their opponents usually referred to Vitruvius (*De architectura*) and Horace (*De arte poetica*). The grotesques were viewed by many artists with enthusiasm as expressions of artistic freedom (e.g., Michelangelo) but later encountered heavy criticism, especially in the context of the Counter-Reformation. Serlio (*Sette libri sull'archittetura*, Venice 1537), Francisco de Hollanda (*I quatro dialogos da pintura antigua*, 1548, published in Porto 1896, in Portuguese translation), Vasari, whose interest in grotesques grew noticeably between the publication of the first and second editions of his *Vite* (Florence 1551: 41 occurrences; Florence 1568: 104), R. Borghini (*Il Riposo*, Florence 1584), B. Cellini (*Vita*, published in Naples in 1728) and others were occupied with the grotesques and welcomed them. They were considered to be central concepts of the Renaissance transformed into an image, i.e., that of the metamorphosis (Ovid) and the concept of the factually existing but invisible analogy of diverse things, as in the sense of Foucault [14]. Lomazzo (*Trattato dell'arte della pittura, scultura e archittetura*, Milan 1584, and *Rime di Gio. Paolo Lomazzo Milanese pittore, divise in sette libri, nelle quali ad imitatione de' grotteschi usati dai pittori ...*, Milan 1587) agreed to their limited use – he considered them to be emblems or hieroglyphs of an as-yet undeciphered writing. Pirro Ligorio (*Libro dell'antichità*, Venice 1553) spoke against the grotesques, and commentators on Vitruvius such as D. Barbaro (*Traduzione di Vitruvio*, Venice 1556) polemicized explicitly against them. Similar considerations applied to the so-called moralists such as G. A. Gilio, *Errori ed abusi dei pittori nei quadri storici*, Camerino 1564, and G. B. Armenini, who spoke of the "terrible uninhabited places" where the grotesques were found and would have preferred to "extinguish" them (*De veri concetti della pittura libri III*, Ravenna 1587). However, their worst opponent was Cardinal G. Paleotti (*Discorso intorno alle imagini sacre e profane*, Bologna 1582). He thought the grotesques unacceptable because they did not observe the difference between truth and fiction and because the difference between fiction (possible) and the fantastic (impossible) was transgressed. Moreover, he viewed their origin from underground, lightless rooms filled with horror that were dedicated to infernal deities. 'Modern' painters only imitated the grotesques because knowledge of their original function was lacking and, therefore, they misused them.

E. RECEPTION IN THE MODERN PERIOD

The history of reception of grotesques was dependent on their distribution in 'media' such as drawings, engravings etc. This applies specifically to those of the *Domus Aurea* and of Raphael's loggias as their most extensive 'copy'. Both represent a decoration system that required a detailed publication. Therefore, studying the grotesques on site was initially reserved for artists residing in Rome who, as a result, were the first to understand them as a whole decoration system even though reception initially was limited to individual elements of this system. When over time the grotesques also became known outside of Italy, the artistic use of individual elements early in the 17th cent. resulted in the formation of genres. On the one hand, there were figurative compositions (fig. 3), which were also often heirs to the medieval world of monsters; on the other, there were the ornaments. Primarily in the north of Europe large series of engravings were created that became full-fledged (model) books (examples: *Grotesco, in diversche manieren*, in the style of Hans Vredemann de Vries, 1565, or *Neuw Grottesken Buch* with engravings by Christoph Jamnitzer, 1610), though some of those were far removed from ancient models. Several isolated motifs of the pilasters and garlands aroused great interest. When creating its own stone and shell work, the Rococo used these books for developing forms. Simultaneously, a dissolution of the strict separation of genres and its hierarchy set in during the early 18th cent. -the overall impression was appreciated then, but often 'only' as an inspiration, not as a 'copy'. It could be taken home: that was the tone of travel reports such as the *Lettres historiques et critiques sur l'Italie* of 1739/40 (published in 3 vols., Paris 1798) by Charles De Brosses or Montesquieu's *Voyages* of 1729 (published in Bordeaux 1894). In the history of reception, Raphael's loggias in the Vatican were for a long time considered to be the grotesques *par example*. They were considered faithful copies of the ancient originals and spared travellers to Rome (artists and educated art lovers) the discomfort of the foray into the 'grottoes' – see Vasari. When → HERCULANEUM (after 1739) and → POMPEII (after 1748) were excavated, their wall paintings were initially not made available in their entirety; consequently Raphael's grotesques were those that fuelled a new wave of enthusiasm. Cardinal Valentin Gonzaga, the state secretary of Benedict XIV, ordered in 1745 a complete copy from the Spanish painter and engineer Francisco La Vega. From about 1760

Fig. 3: Luigi and Maria Augusta Cavaliere, *The green Fisher*. Illustration for: C. Collodi, *Le avventure di Pinocchio*, Florenz (Salani) 1924

Raphael's grotesques were distributed throughout Europe as engravings such as those by Teseo, Volpato and Ottaviani (ca. 1775), and in 1768 they were copied by the draughtsmen Savorelli and Camporesi. After their distribution in various prints, inquiries for prices appeared, e.g., for decorating a new house in Milan (1776). With the broader distribution of the engravings in the 18th cent., a new possibility opened up, namely that of a copy of the entire ambience which could thus be restored to its original context of meaning – namely to that of a palatial decoration system: Copies of the loggia grotesques decorated the palace in Dresden which was reconstructed in 1783 for Prince Maximilian; the chateau at Pillnitz (near Dresden), which was built by the architect Weinling (1739–1799) starting in 1760 and decorated in 1768 by Salvorelli and Camporesi, the copyists of Raphael's loggias; and the chateau and a pavilion of Prince Johann Georg. In Sweden the grotesques are to be found in the 'Blue Anteroom' in the Pavilion of Gustav III in the Park at Haga (near Stockholm). In France they decorate, e.g., the Hotel Hostein or Véfour, where they are mixed with vegetative elements from the *Domus Aurea*. The chateau of Bagatelle contains the most direct copy (1777–1787).

The grotesques of the loggias also influenced the style of Louis XVI and the Directorate (1795–1799) in France (e.g., the jewellery box furniture of Marie Antoinette). Painted copies are also found in the library of the

French king. But perhaps the most famous example outside Italy is found in Russia: Enthused in September of 1778 by an engraving, Catherine II also wanted to own the loggias of Raphael. In Rome the president of the Russian Academy, Reiffenstein, commissioned Unterberger, one of the best students of Mengs, to assemble a group of painters that could work as copyists. In 1787 the *panelli* sent to St. Petersburg were mounted. The copies only made slight changes but they aroused such enthusiasm that a *sala degli arabeschi* (a common term for Raphael's loggias in the 18th cent.), a *salottino raffaellesco* and a *gabinetto d'argento* were created in other rooms of the residence at Tsarskoye Selo. In 1776 the works of the *Domus Aurea* (still confused with the baths of Titus) were published through the engravings of Mirri and Carletti, followed in 1786 by Ponce. While the success of the loggias was initially due to the finds at Herculaneum and Pompeii, the excavations of the *Domus Aurea* and their publication began to displace the interest in the loggias. The comparison of the ancient grotesques of the *Domus Aurea* and Raphael's increasingly resulted in criticism of the latter, which were relegated as 'arabesques' to the realm of *bizzarerie* (F. Milizia, *Dell'arte di vedere nelle belle arti del disegno secondo i principi di Suzer e di Mengs*, Venice 1781). Catharine II switched to copies in the style of Mirri during further palace decoration work, and Napoleon also preferred the grotesques of the *Domus Aurea*. During English Neo-Classicism there were hardly any traces of the loggias because taste was more in line with Etruscan and Egyptian styles and those of Pompeii and Herculaneum. At the beginning of the 19th cent. some elements of the grotesque entered into furniture design (lamp stands) but otherwise interest in the loggias vanished with a few exceptions (e.g., Biblical scenes): Because of Ingres' veneration of Raphael, a form of the grotesque arose in 1835 that combined the Bible and arabesques with approval from the government (painters: P. and R. Balze, Flandrin, Comairas, Jourdy and Rousseau): 52 images were created and exhibited with great success in 1847 in the Paris Pantheon, which inspired, for example, T. Gauthier and R. Delacroix. Later, they went to the church *Petits Augustins*, and then to the gallery of the *Ecole des Beaux Arts*. Then the history of the loggias' reception broke off. They were only of interest in Rome: Pius IX

(1922–1939) had the third *braccio* of the loggias painted. Possibly the last example of an 'imperial' reception of the loggias is found in the decoration of the Capitol in Washington, D.C., which was built in a classicizing style. Its interior was painted between 1855 and 1880 with decorations by the Greco-Italian artist Constantino Brumidi, who was born in Rome. When Gregory XVI (1831–1846) began to show interest in the loggias, he had restored their third floor. The pilaster decorations and stucco medallions of the loggias were transposed in the Capitol as flat painting on an ochre background; also, there are numerous variants in the repertoire of the birds and plants.

In the 20th cent. echoes of the grotesque are found in the paintings of the surrealists, in the work of Paul Klee and as illustrations of popular works such as C. Collodi's children's book *Pinocchio* in the figure of the green fisher, a truly grotesque 'sea monster' (fig. 4).
→ Eroticism

SOURCE 1 A. PARÉ, Des monstres et prodiges, 1575 (critical ed. by J. CÉARD, 1971) Bibliography
LITERATURE 2 J. BALTRUSAITIS, Le Moyen Age fantastique. Antiquités et exotismes dans l'art gothique, 1973 3 F. K. BARASCH, The Grotesque. A Study in Meaning, 1971 4 M. CAMILLE, Image on the Edge. The Margins of Medieval Art, 1992 5 A. CHASTEL, La grottesque. Essai sur l'ornament sans nom, 1988 6 N. DACOS, s. v. grottesche, in: Dizionario della pittura e dei pittori, vol. 2, 1990, 711–713 7 Id., Le logge di Raffaello. Maestro e bottega di fronte all'antico, 1986 8 Id., La Découverte de la Domus Aurea et la Formation des grotesques à la Renaissance, 1969 9 M. DE VOS, La ricezione della pittura antica fino alla scoperta di Ercolaneo e Pompei, in: Memoria dell'antico nell'arte italiana, vol. II, 1985, 351–377 10 J. EVANS, Pattern. A Study of Ornament in Western Europe. From 1180–1900, 1975 11 J. W. GOETHE, Von den Arabesken, in: Der Teutsche Merkur, Februar 1789 12 S. GRUZINSKI, La pensée métisse, 1999 13 G. G. HARPHAM, On the Grotesque. Strategies of Contradiction in Art and Literature, 1982 14 PH. MOREL, Il funzionamento simbolico e la critica delle grottesche nella seconda metà del Cinquecento, in: Roma e l'antico nell'arte e nella cultura del Cinquecento, 1985, 149–178 15 F. PIEL, Die Ornament-Groteske in der italienischen Renaissance. Zu ihrer kategorialen Struktur und Entstehung, 1962 16 C.-P. WARNCKE, Die ornamentale Groteske in Deutschland 1500–1650, 1979.
GABRIELE HUBER

H

Halicarnassus. The earliest information about the origin of the city is provided by Herodotus, its native son. According to Herodotus, Halicarnassus (H.) was founded on the Peloponnese by Doric settlers from Troezen. While a member of the Doric Hexapolis, it formed a cultic community with Lindus, Camirus, Ialysus, Cos and Cnidos (Hdt. 1,144; 7,99).

The name of H. was first made famous by Artemisia, ruler of the city, who fought with surprising vigour in the naval battle of Salamis in 480 BC on the Persian side, eliciting the High King's proverbial comment that "my men have become women and my women men" (Hdt. 8,88). Herodotus claims that Artemisia had taken over the rule of H. from her deceased husband (Hdt. 7,99). The *Suda* (s.v. Πίγρης/Pigres) records that Maussolus was the husband of "that Artemisia who had excelled in warfare". This is without doubt a reference to the heroine of the naval battle and not the younger Artemisia who is credited with building the Mausoleum. By the same token, there is no reason to identify the Maussolus mentioned in the *Suda* with the later king of the same name. It is much more likely there were two ruling couples with identical names – an earlier and a later one.

The only clues as to the city's 5th cent. appearance – before it was redesigned by the Hecadomnides – may be found in its later development (figs. 1, 2). The point from where it expanded was without doubt the harbour and the strategically advantageous clifftop next to it which was connected to the coast by a promontory. The site that would eventually be occupied by the Mausoleum was a necropolis, the tombs of which were razed in the building of the monument. Presumably this area was located in the open space between H. and Salmacis.

A 5th cent. inscription mentions an Apollo sanctuary (Apollonion) from the Archaic or High Classical period as one of the monumental buildings in H. (SGDI 5726, 45). Single stones have been built into the walls of modern residences and particularly in the medieval clifftop castle of the Knights of Rhodes: Early Classical capitals, trachelia drums decorated with reliefs [12] and Ionic column bases are strongly influenced by Samian models (Temple of Polycrates) [16. 27f.].

Halicarnassus was a member of the Delian League and appears to have sympathised with Athens almost until the end of the Peloponnesian War in 404 BC [3. 28]. Mylasa, the capital of Caria, had to pay taxes to the Delian League as well (IGI3 263.I.12; 272.II.76) but because of its location was also forced to get along with the Persians in the interior. This became even more crucial the harder Athens fought to maintain its position of power in the Aegean. An influential citizen of Mylasa by the name of Hecatomnus appears to have risen to the top of a pro-Persian movement, thus gaining the trust of Great King Artaxerxes II who installed him as the first satrap of a new Carian satrapy in ca. 392/1 BC.

Of Hecatomnus' three sons and two daughters, the oldest son Maussolus married the older daughter Artemisia. The children probably received their names as a demonstration of loyalty towards the High King. In doing so, Hecatomnus may have anticipated the future marriage of the siblings as well as the later transfer of the capital to Halicarnassus.

In 377/6 BC, Maussolus succeeded his father (Diod. Sic.16,36,2). The city was expanded to include Salmacis and the area in-between. The location of Salmacis directly across from H. at the other side of the harbour is attested in an inscription first published in 1998 [9]. The new, enlarged city area was enclosed by a wall of ca. 7 kilometres in length, which ran from Salmacis in the west to the cliff in the east, thus encircling the entire harbour (fig. 1: 1). Within the wall circuit, the new city was crisscrossed by an orthogonal system of streets still recognisable in the present-day road network [14. 98–103]. The main street, 15 metres wide and connecting the Myndus Gate in the west with the road to Mylasa, crossed the market square and ran along the Mausoleum (fig. 1: 9). It can still be distinguished in the path of the present Turgut Reis Caddesi. In this sense, the new layout of the city appears to have been the model for Priene which was built not much later (cf. fig. 140 in [2. 145]).

In the course of the city's expansion by fusion (Gk. *synoikismos*), six smaller villages on the H. peninsula were vacated and their inhabitants moved to H., apparently at Maussolus' instigation (Str. 13,611). Probably in recognition of his role as the founder of the new city, an enormous tomb and memorial was built for Maussolus on the market square [6]. After his death, his widow Artemisia took over the position of satrap [3. 40]. Vitruvius, who might have been informed by a guide in H., reports that she successfully employed a war stratagem to ward off an attack by the Rhodians (Vitr. De arch. 2,8,14–15). Theopompus of Chios, winner of the arts competition organised by Artemisia on the occasion of her husband's funeral, wrote that she "died from a wasting disease over the grief for her husband and brother Maussolus" (Harpocration, s.v. Artemisia). Later, this report impressed even Cicero (Cic. Tusc. 3,31). According to Pliny the Elder (Plin. HN 36,30–31), Artemisia oversaw the building of the tomb, but it was not fully completed when she died. Gellius (Gell. NA 10,18) also knew of other accounts about her passionate love for her husband. The artists of the → RENAISSANCE presented her as a paragon of marital devotion (fig. 3).

Scattered remains attest to the existence of other monumental buildings from the Hecatomnid period in H., such as kalupter (imbrex) tiles from a marble roof and fragments of column drums and capitals from an Ionic temple found in the present-day district of Türkkuyusu (fig. 1: 7; cf. figs. 3–8 in [13. 361f.]). A terrace as

Fig. 1   **Map of Halicarnassus (Bodrum), including the results
of the Danish excavations since 1966**

1   City wall
2   Myndus Gate
3   Approximate location of the Mylasa Gate
4   Terrace of the Sanctuary of Ares
5   Stadium
6   Hellenistic stoa in Doric style
7   Building remains in the Türkkuyusu area
8   Theatre
9   Main Street
10   Maussolleion terrace
11   Hellenistic house with mosaics
12   Late Roman villa
13   Agora
14   House façades on the north side of the Main Street
15   Sanctuary of Demeter
16   Ancient mole
17   Palace of Mausolus on the Castle peninsula
18   Salmacis inscription
19   Tomb of the 'Carian princess'
20   Fortification tower

Altitude (in metres):

0   50   100   150   200   250

0   500 m

Fig. 2: Model of Halicarnassus, Principal features of the town at the time of the Hecatomids in the mid-4th cent. BC (K. Jeppesen, P. Pedersen)

wide as that of the Mausoleum has been preserved; it held a large Ionic temple of which only column fragments remain. Presumably this temple is to be identified with the the Ares sanctuary Vitruvius located above the city's main street (Vitr. De arch. 2,8,11) (fig. 1: 4) [13. 360f.]. It is unclear whether the old theatre stood in the same location as the later one (fig. 1: 8) or whether perhaps the stadium from Late Antiquity (fig. 1: 5) had a Classical precursor as well. Both may have served as venues for the artistic and hippic contests that were staged during Maussolus' funeral. The remnants of Mausollos' palace mentioned by Vitruvius have not yet been found on the clifftop by the harbour (Vitr. De arch. 2,8,10) (fig. 1: 18), neither have those of the secret harbour next to it (Vitr. De arch. 2,8,13). The emporium must have been located outside the city wall on the shore of the bay east of the harbour (Vitr. 2,8,11) [4. 85f.]. The city wall still stretches today from Salmacis to a point ca. 800 metres from the coast east of the harbour clifftop. Particularly well maintained is the tower of the Myndus Gate (fig. 1: 2) which has recently been restored with support from Ericsson/Turkcell. According to Vitruvius, the market square was immediately above the harbour, thus on the east side of the Mausoleum terrace. Aside from the main street and another one running parallel to it along the north side of the villa from Late Antiquity (fig. 1: 12) and the south side of the Mausoleum terrace, no other trace of the ancient street grid has as yet been identified.

Following Artemisia's death in 351/0 BC, the younger pair of siblings Idrieus and Ada took over the satrapy. When Idrieus died as early as 344/3 BC, Ada became the sole ruler until she was banished by her brother Pixodarus in 341/0 BC and forced to seek shelter in Alinda in the mountainous Carian hinterland. After Pixodarus' death in ca. 336 BC the city was ruled by the Persian Orontobates who had married Ada, the daughter of Pixodarus. In 334 BC Alexander the Great besieged the city before capturing it and then arranged for the older Ada to adopt him [3. 41–51].

Idrieus erected a striking number of lavish buildings in the precinct of the Mylasian sanctuary of Zeus at Labraunda. In the inscribed dedications he refers to himself as "son of Hecatomnus, from Mylasa" [22. 117], while Maussolus referred to himself on his banquetting house simply as "son of Hecatomnus", without mentioning his place of origin [1. 64f.]. Apparently he was trying to avoid a clear declaration of loyalty either to Mylasa or Halicarnassus.

Following the death of Alexander, Caria was first ruled by several of his descendants, then became a Roman province in 129 BC. By the 3rd cent. BC, the Mausoleum had come to be regarded as one of the seven → WONDERS OF THE WORLD (Anth. Pal. 9,58, epigram

Fig. 3: Artemisia during the building of the Mausoleum, Painting by Simon Vouet (1590–1649), court painter at the court of Louis XIII. *Nationalmuseum Stockholm*

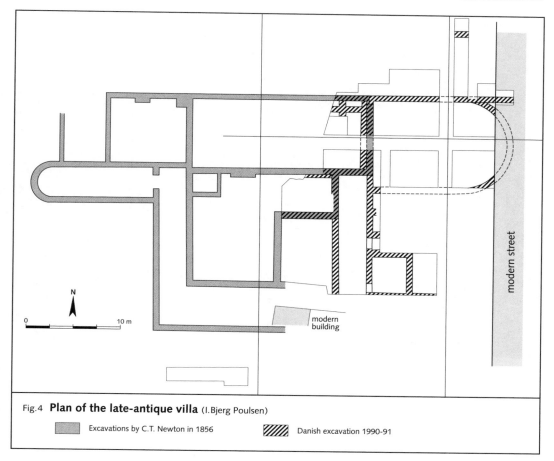

N

0 —————— 10 m

modern
building

modern street

Fig.4 Plan of the late-antique villa (I.Bjerg Poulsen)

▨ Excavations by C.T. Newton in 1856　　　▨ Danish excavation 1990-91

of Antipater of Sidon). A long poem from the 2nd half of the 2nd cent. BC engraved in a wall block has recently been found on a beach in the Salmacis area, thus confirming its location. Retrospective in character, the poem glorifies the magnificent past of H. in hexameters [9]. From the Hellenistic Period, ruins of a private residence have recently been excavated; the discoveries included beautiful mosaics (fig. 1: 11) and a Doric column hall, of which only few remnants are left *in situ*. A gymnasium approved by King Ptolemaeus and a column hall dedicated to Apollo and Ptolemaeus are attested in inscriptions.

In the 1st cent. BC, pirates repeatedly laid waste to H. Cicero writes that after it was "ruined and almost deserted", the city was "restored" by his brother who at the time was the governor of the Roman province of Asia (Cic. Ad Q. fr. 1,1,25). Vitruvius' comprehensive description of the city (Vitr. De arch. 2,8,10–15) appears to be based on his own observations. He participated as a siege engineer in Caesar's last campaigns against political enemies. The victory at Zela in the Pontus in 47 BC (*veni, vidi, vici*) may have afforded him the opportunity to visit H. on his return to Rome. His participation in the last military action of the following year in Africa is documented [4. 96f.].

In the time of Tiberius, H. was one of the cities that applied for permission to build a temple for the emperor – H. with the assertion that the city had not suffered an earthquake in 1,200 years (Tac. Ann. 4,55). A late peak of the ancient city is evidenced by the discovery of a large villa richly paved with mosaics. It was already partially excavated by C.T. Newton [18] (figs. 4 + 5). The impressive mosaics are praised in a verse inscription in the apsidal central room, also praising a certain Charidemus as the originator. The poem is similar in style to the work of the epic poet Nonnus of Panopolis who lived in the 5th century AD.

Almost an entire millennium passed until H. rose again from obscurity. In the meantime, Turkish nomads had occupied almost all of Asia Minor, and Constantinople was captured in 1453. At the beginning of that cent., the Knights of Rhodes built a small fort on the harbour clifftop, which constantly had to be enlarged and consolidated in the ensuing period in order to forestall attacks from the Turkish side [10. 117–214, 219–222]. From about 1494, stones from the Mausoleum were used in the walls of the fort. In 1522, the last remnants of the monument were dismantled under the direction of a group of Knights. Soon afterwards, however, the Knights were forced to hand over their strong-

Fig. 5: Mosaics with inscription from the apsidal main room of the late-antique villa

hold in Rhodes, and the fort in H. was vacated. One of the knights later reported the discovery of a magnificent tomb in the foundations of the dismantled monument [5. 67f.; 8].

Before the 18th cent., H. was rarely visited by European foreigners [20. 379]. All the more important were the reports by ancient authors who had become accessible to lay-persons as well as experts since the invention of the printing press [10. 165]. The archaeological investigation of H. was initiated by C.T. Newton [11]. Newton correctly identified the stone blocks with friezes and lion figures built into the Knight of Rhodes' fort as belonging to the Mausoleum, and he was later able to demonstrate the location of the monument as well as several main features of its ground plan. Of the aboveground fragments of the building, Newton had all pieces of friezes and freestanding sculpture shipped to England. However, the selection of architectural fragments proved too small: it soon became evident that these finds were insufficient as a basis for reconstructing the monument. Additional digs undertaken by A. Biliotti in the vicinity of the foundation excavations have not yielded any further insights [15. pt. 1. 117–173]. Newton also explored other ancient ruins in the city area and the necropoleis east and west of the city wall (fig. 1: 4, 11, 12, 14) [11. 280–341].

At the start of the British excavations, the short descriptions in the *Natural History* of Pliny the Elder (Plin. HN 36,30–31) were all that was known about the Mausoleum. And even after the Danish re-excavation,

Pliny's report remains an important and in part indispensable testimony. When it was not yet possible to compare Pliny's descriptions transmitted in manuscript form to any concrete archaeological finds, interpretation of the text was open to all manner of speculation about the lost tomb, and people felt compelled to add their own supplements and extensions. Contradictory or nonsensical sentence constructions gave rise to the speculation that it must have been a fantastic building such as the skyward-reaching tomb of King Porsenna in Etruria. Contributing to this were probably the fame of the Mausoleum as one of the Wonders of the World and Vitruvius' exuberant praise of the two architects (Vitr. De arch. 7, praef. 12–13). Freemasons, in particular, considered the Mausoleum an architectural model to emulate. Others were convinced that its uniqueness was due to secret building codes.

Newton's excavations prompted a closer analysis of the ground in the location indicated by Pliny, although for a long time the lack of comparable material prevented any positive results. However, in conjunction with a careful textual interpretation of Pliny (Plin. HN 36,30–31), they did reveal a circumference of 440 feet (ca. 140 metres) for the building, with a height of 140 feet (ca. 45 metres).

In the new excavations carried out by Danish archaeologists between 1966 and 1977 archaeologists found that the great terrace on which the monument stood measured 242 x 105 metres [15]. This archaeological activity also brought to light the original exca-

Fig. 6: **Plan of Halicarnassus (Bodrum) including the results of the British excavations,**
according to: C. T. Newton, A History of Discoveries at Halicarnassus etc (1862) pl. 1

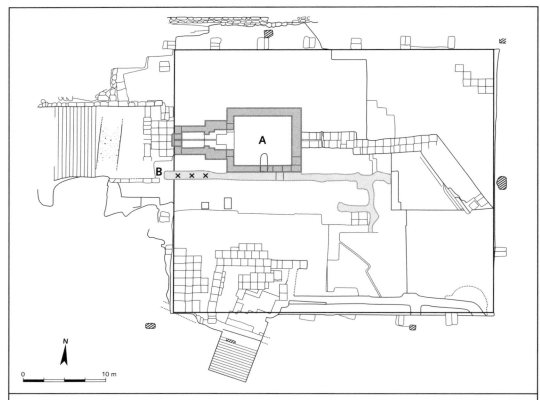

Fig. 7:   Spolia left by grave robbers were found between the burial chamber (A) and the entrance (B)
          at the western (left) side of the Mausoleum to the multi-branched tunnel, marked by crosses (K. Jeppesen)

vations for the foundation of the Mausoleum, thereby uncovering the burial chamber that had so far been missing and a tunnel carved into the rock through which robbers had entered the chamber (fig. 7) [5. 63f.]. In both locations, remnants of burial gifts of gold and semi-precious stones were found. In addition, the burial chamber yielded glass and ivory objects as well as broken pieces of alabaster vessels and Attic vases from the 4th cent. BC [19. 66–72].

Fragments have made it possible to complete the marble double door which allowed access from the corridor to the antechamber of the burial chamber. Remains of a marble lid presumably belong to the casket which the Knights of Rhodes found in the antechamber when they were about to dismantle the last ruins of the Mausoleum. Since Maussolus' body was cremated [4. 102f.] and his bones were probably deposited in a box of ashes within the burial chamber, this might be Artemesia's casket.

New finds of fragments from still unknown parts of the architectural structure [5. 72–96; 7. 161–203] along with G. Waywell's publication and systematic organisation of all the fragments of freestanding sculpture in the British Museum [21] that had been brought to England by Newton have contributed much towards solving the

problems of reconstruction (fig. 8). It was not a building in the traditional sense that contained rooms: the interior was compact and consisted of different layers of lava rock. Only one cavity existed in this cube for the burial site of Maussolus. The exterior was sided with white marble blocks and bluish limestone. This construction gave the appearance of a free combination of traditional building elements culminating in a column hall in the Ionic style. Above it rose an innovation in architectural history: a roof pyramid of 12 steps with a quadriga on top, probably for the purpose of glorifying the deceased dynast and his queen. The base of the group was covered by the so-called Centaur frieze. Lion figures stood along the edge of the roof, and the corners were adorned with acroteria; remnants of their pedestals have been documented (cf. plate 22.3 in [5. 81]).

Behind the column hall was no cella; instead, portrait statues of the members of the Hecatomnid dynasty and other sculptures were placed on a limestone ledge along the back wall. Above them ran the so-called Chariot frieze [7. 176]. The transition between the column hall and the high podium of the lower structure was marked by the so-called Amazon frieze.

Fig. 8: Experimental model of the Mausoleum, front view. On the very bottom of the base: Scene of an audience with Mausolus at the cente (colossal seated statue in the British Museum). Made from wood and cardboard. Fecit K. Jeppesen 1987

Surrounding the podium were two additional steps of which the upper, limestone one carried life-size battle groups. The lower one carried compositions of colossal free-standing sculptures with depictions of a hunting party and an audience assembly – typical themes from the rich life of the deceased satrap. Thus, the exterior of the building must be regarded as a proud memorial of enormous splendour commemorating his life and mighty deeds. Its relation to the tomb hidden in the interior was merely suggested by the fatalistic stance of the guard sculptures placed between the columns.

After completing the excavations of the Mausoleum, Poul Pedersen continued his investigation of the ancient city with new observations and excavations. Now the focus is on the city wall, of which only the main segments have been studied so far. As the best-preserved structure from the ancient city's peak period it finally receives its due attention [17].
→ Halicarnassus; → Mausoleum

1 P. Hellström, Th. Thieme, The Androns at Labraunda. A Preliminary Account of their Architecture, in: Medelhavsmuseet 16, 1981, 58–74   2 W. Hoepfner, E.-L. Schwandner, Haus und Stadt im klassischen Griechenland, 1986   3 S. Hornblower, Mausolus, 1982   4 K. Jeppesen, The Ancient Greek and Latin Writers, in: Id., A. Luttrell (ed.), The Maussolleion at Halikarnassos 2,1, 1986   5 Id., Tot Operum Opus. Ergebnisse der dänischen Forschungen zum Maussolleion von Halikarnass seit 1966, in: JDAI 107, 1992, 59–102   6 Id., Founder Cult and Maussolleion, in: J. Isager (ed.), Halicar-

nassian Studies 1, 1994, 73–84   7 Id., Das Maussolleion von Halikarnass. Forschungsbericht 1997, in: S. Dietz, S. Isager (eds.), Proceedings of the Danish Institute at Athens 2, 1998, 161–231   8 Id., The Maussolleion at Halikarnassoss 4: The Quadrangle. The Foundations of the Mausolleion and its Sepulchral Compartments, 2000, appendix 3   9 S. Isager, The Pride of Halikarnassos, Editio princeps of an inscription from Salmakis, in: ZPE 123, 1998, 1–23   10 A. Luttrell, The Later History of the Maussolleion and and its Utilisation in the Hospitaller Castle at Bodrum (= Id., K. Jeppesen (eds.), The Maussolleion at Halikarnassos 2,2), 1986   11 C. T. Newton, A History of Discoveries at Halicarnassus, Cnidus and Branchidae, London 1862   12 P. Pedersen, Zwei ornamentierte Säulenhälse aus Halikarnassos, in: JDAI 98, 1983, 87–121   13 Id., Two Ionic Buildings in Halicarnassus, in: V. Araştırma Sonuçları Toplantısı 1987, 259–363 (published in 1988)   14 Id., Town-planning in Halicarnassus and Rhodes, in: S. Dietz, I. Papachristodoulou (eds.), Archaeology in the Dodecanese, 1988   15 Id., The Maussolleion Terrace and Accessory Structures (= The Maussolleion at Halikarnassos 3, 1–2), 1991   16 Id., The Ionian Renaissance and some Aspects of its Origin within the Field of Architecture and Planing, in: J. Isager (ed.), Halicarnassian Studies 1, 1994, 11–35   17 Id., The Fortifications of Halikarnassos, in: REA 96, 1994, 215–235   18 B. Poulsen, S. Isager, Patron and Pavements in Late Antiquity (= Halicarnassian Studies 2), 1997, 9–29   19 B. B. Rasmussen, Gold Ornaments from the Mausoleum at Halikarnassos in the British Museum, in: D. Williams (ed.), The Art of the Greek Goldsmith, 1998, 66–72   20 H. Riemann, s.v. Pytheos, RE 24, 371–513   21 G. Waywell, The Free-Standing Sculptures of the Mausoleum at Halicarnassus in the British Museum. A Catalogue, 1978   22 A. Westholm, Labraunda, vol. 1,2: The Architecture of the Hieron, 1963

Additional Bibliography B. F. Cook, Relief Sculpture of the Mausoleum at Halicarnassus, 2005
KRISTIAN JEPPESEN

Hebraic Studies see → Semitic Studies

Hellenism see → Epochs, concept of

Herculaneum
A. The Excavations in the 18th Century
B. The Excavations in the 19th and 20th Century   C. Organisation, Conception and Critique of the Excavations in the 18th Century   D. Evaluation and Influence

A. The Excavations in the 18th Century
In contrast to → Pompeii, Herculaneum (H.) was buried so deeply and massively that no plundering of the ruins was possible after the eruption of Vesuvius in AD 79. The eruption of 1631 increased these layers to a thickness of 25 metres. However, when wells were drilled in the area of the town of Resina (known as Ercolano since 1969), ancient remains repeatedly came to light. The first tunnel excavations were carried out by Prince d'Elbœuf between 1709 and 1716. This led to the salvaging of numerous statues in the area of the

Fig. 1: *Theseus and Minotaurus*. Herculaneum
Basilica. C.-N. Cochin had drawn these pictures of
paintings in Herculaneum (published in 1754) from
memory, even though this was forbidden. His mainly
negative assessment of their artistic value prevailed
for a long time.

theatre of H., among these being the so-called Herculaneum Matron and Maiden (now in Dresden). Official
excavations began at the same spot in 1738, at the
behest of Charles of Bourbon (King of Naples, 1734–
1759). All the finds were initially preserved and restored in the summer palace at Portici, which was built at
the same time, and in 1758 a *Herculanense Museum*
was established especially for them (closed in 1799)
[14]. An inscription discovered in 1740 confirmed the
naming of the ruins. The engineering officer Roque
Joachim de Alcubierre was the nominal director of the
operations, with interruptions (Pierre Bardet de Villeneuve was director from 1741–1745), until his death.
The actual excavation work, however, was in the hands
of the Swiss military engineer Karl Jakob (Carlo) Weber
from 1750 to 1764, and was subsequently directed by
the architect Francesco La Vega until 1776. From central entrance shafts, extensive parts of the city were
explored by means of narrow tunnels: first the theatre
(with numerous statues, equestrian statues of the Balbi,
inscriptions, and structural elements), then the area
around the so-called Basilica (in 1739, with statues and
wall paintings) and finally, from 1750–1761, the Villa

dei Papiri (a large number of marble and bronze statues
as well as portrait busts; discovery of the papyri in October 1752). The last investigations in the theatre were
completed in 1776.

B. The Excavations in the 19th and 20th Century

Excavations were resumed In 1828, with the additional goal of uncovering the ruins. By 1838 it was thus
possible, under the leadership of Carlo Bonucci, to
excavate the Case del Argo, del Genio and dello Sche-
letro, and from 1869 to 1875 to unearth additional
house façades and parts of the thermal baths. An
attempt by the Anglo-American archaeologist, Charles
Waldstein, to tackle the uncovering of the city once
again as a international research project failed in 1905,
not least because of national (sc. Italian) reservations
[32]. Not until 1927 was Amedeo Maiuri, with the
express support of Benito Mussolini, able to begin large-scale excavations in H., which he continued until
1960 (with an interruption between 1942 and 52) [24].
The excavations were accompanied by the extensive
restoration of all the buildings. Eight insulae inside the
city and the suburban thermal baths were henceforth
accessible. Minor investigations followed after 1960,
above all in the area of the Cardo Maximus and beneath
the city walls. Since 1980, numerous skeletons were discovered of people who had attempted in vain to escape
during the eruption by sea [23]. Purchases of land between the excavated part of the city and the suburban
Villa dei Papiri have facilitated far more extensive excavations since the end of the 1980s, and parts of this villa
have now come to light for the first time [20]. A conclusion to this work is not yet foreseen.

C. Organisation, Conception and Critique of the Excavations in the 18th Century

King Charles of Bourbon, and, later, the regent Bernardo Tanucci, promoted the excavations because of
their interest in art, and in order to provide cultural
legitimation for their young kingdom, which had existed since 1734 [13]. The finds from the towns of Vesuvius were thus equated with achievements in war. Charles reserved for himself unrestricted control over the
new antiquities, which were sometimes unique, as in the
case of the paintings. In addition to the surveyors Alcubierre, Weber and La Vega, the sculptor Joseph Canart
was appointed from 1739 to restore the sculptures and
remove the wall paintings, and the painter Camillo
Paderni from 1751 as director of the collections, while
Antonio Piaggio was placed in charge of the papyri
from 1753. In 1746, Ottavio Antonio Bayardi was
given the task of publishing the finds [3; 4]. The establishment of a fifteen-member *Reale Accademia Ercolanese di Archeologia,* chaired by Tanucci, in 1755 led
to the publication of the *Antichità di Ercolano esposte*
from 1757. The eight volumes that appeared by 1792
(40 were planned) were published, to be sure, in a large

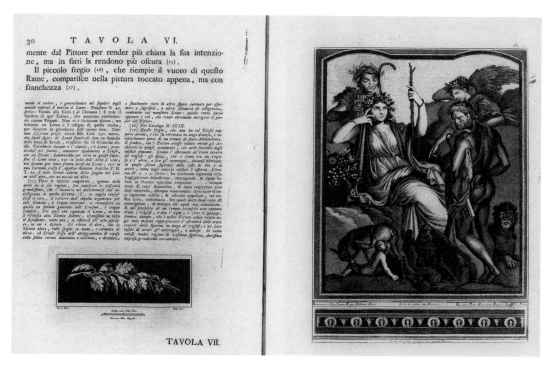

Fig. 2: *Hercules and Telephus*. Herculaneum, Basilica.
The copper plate engravings in the official publication were accompanied by learned commentaries.
Illegal copies generally dispensed with the commentaries and only disseminated the images.

edition, but were initially solely distributed as a gift of the king and were therefore accessible only with difficulty [1; 33].

From both a technical and an intellectual perspective, the excavations were a completely new endeavour. The tunnel excavations and the conservation, especially of the paintings, brought with them enormous problems [27; 31]. Nevertheless, fine plans of the underground discoveries, which although unpublished had already, in part, been praised by Winckelmann, were drawn up (city plan by Bardet [29. 52 f.]; Villa dei Papiri [29. 100 f.] by Weber, theatre by Weber and La Vega [29. 233–263; 28]). Weekly work reports enable the precise reconstruction of the excavations [8; 2; 7]. The unique opportunity to understand a city as a context of ancient life had not yet been grasped, despite the initial reflections of C. Weber [29. 264–281]. In the forefront of all the efforts was the recovery of treasures for the museum, which were classified by genre, exhibited, and published. Wall paintings were cut out and hung like panel paintings, and statues were restored. Unusable materials might be destroyed or melted down. Since the publication of the finds was initially delayed and later proved disappointing, travellers and scholars were extremely critical of the work. The king's absolute claim to ownership was diametrically opposed to demands for rapid and comprehensive information [13; 33]. Reports such as those of Winckelmann, who for obvious reasons of self-interest was not sparing in his

disparaging remarks, were immediately translated and greeted with enormous interest ([12], with commentaries). They are partly responsible, even today, for the lopsided image of the administration in Naples as for the most part incompetent and marred by internal squabbles.

A visit to the excavations themselves was not without risks, and involved considerable efforts (fig. 3); this explains why most travellers toured only → Pompeii and the *Herculanense Museum*, the "A and Ω of all antiquities collections" (Goethe). Access was granted only by special permit, and sketches were prohibited [14]. As a result, complaints about these restrictions, and stories of attempts to bypass them, are among the topoi of travel reports from the 18th cent. [21].

D. Evaluation and Influence

Right from the beginning, interest in the finds from H., whose name stood for all the Vesuvius towns, was enormous throughout the whole of Europe. As a result of a lack of authentic descriptions and above all of illustrations, bizarre rumours spread from time to time [22]. The first reproductions of the paintings from the basilica by Charles-Nicolas Cochin, which were drawn from memory, led to a primarily negative evaluation of the paintings found at H., which were regarded as stiff, inept and unnatural in their colouring ([5] and fig. 1). This assessment scarcely changed, even with the publication of the *Antichità* (fig. 2). With the exception of *La*

Fig. 3: Anonymous. *A visit to the theatre* in *Herculaneum*. Early 19th cent. Steep steps, smoking torches and a lack of fresh air added to the difficulties of visiting the underground ruins of Herculaneum. The extant views emphasize the daring and adventurous nature of these excavations.

marchande d'amours from → STABIAE, which enjoyed great success in the adaptation by Joseph-Marie Vien, exhibited at the salon of 1762, the paintings played no part in the contemporary artistic debate, the *Querelles des Anciens et des Modernes*. On the other hand, the influence of the finds from H. on the applied arts was considerable [15; 30]. Even if the *à la grecque* fashion in Paris was not triggered by the finds, it was nourished by them. However, not until the reprints and excerpts from the *Antichità*, which appeared in several languages beginning in 1773, usually scaled down and partially reduced to etchings [25. 571–573 No. 8. 55–56; 8. 58; 8. 63], was the pictorial world of H. brought into general circulation. Decorative motifs in particular, such as the floating figures, were reproduced in countless copies in wall paintings, as gouaches, on porcelain and on furniture; utilitarian objects were copied, and sculptures were transposed to biscuit porcelain [16. 504f., 509–522]. The architecture, largely invisible, naturally had the least influence. The completely preserved theatre, on whose plans Weber, La Vega and Giovanni Battista Piranesi worked intensively, was published too late for it to play a role in the discussion concerning theatre construction in the 18th cent. [28]. In contrast, the effect of the J. Paul Getty Museum in Malibu, California [18] (fig. 4), built as a copy of the Villa dei Papiri, is spectacular. It was developed from Weber's plan of 1756 [18. 34], and dedicated in 1974.

SOURCES 1 Le Antichità di Ercolano esposte con qualche spiegazione, 8 vols., Naples 1757–1792 (vol. 1–4, 7: Pitture; 5, 6: Bronzi; 8: Lucerne e candelabri) 2 ARCHIVIO DI STATO DI NAPOLI (ed.): Fonti documentarie per la storia degli scavi di Pompei, Ercolano e Stabia, 1979 3 A. BAYARDI, Prodromo delle Antichità d'Ercolano, 5 vols., Naples 1752 4 Id., Catalogo degli antichi monumenti dissotterrati dalla discoperta città di Ercolano, Naples 1754 5 CH.-N. COCHIN, J. CH. BELLICARD, Observations sur les antiquités d'Herculaneum, Paris 1754 (²1755/1757, Engl. 1753/55) 6 A. D. FOUGEROUX DE BONDAROY, Recherches sur les ruines d'Herculaneum, Paris 1770 7 U. PANNUTI, Il 'Giornale degli scavi' di Ercolano (1738–1756). Atti della Accademia Nazionale dei Lincei, Memorie, Ser. VIII vol. 26, fasc. 3, 1983. 8 M. RUGGIERO, Storia degli scavi di Ercolano ricomposta su' documenti superstiti, Napoli 1885 9 M. DE VENUTI, Descrizione dell prime scoperte dell'antica città d'Ercolano, ritrovato vicino a Portici, Villa della Maestà del Re delle Due Sicilie ..., Rome 1748, Venice 1749, (Engl. A Description of the First Discoveries of the Ancient City of Herculaneum. Found near Portici, a Seat of His Majesty the King of the Two Sicilies, London 1750) 10 J. J. WINCKELMANN, Sendschreiben von den Herculanischen Entdeckungen, Dresden 1762 (French 1764, Engl. 1765 and 1771) 11 Id., Nachrichten von den neuesten Herculanischen Entdeckungen, Dresden 1764 (French 1784) 12 Id., Schriften und Nachlaß. St.-G. Bruer, M. Kunze (eds.), 1997
LITERATURE 13 A. ALLROGGEN-BEDEL, Winckelmann und die Archäeologie im Königreich Neapel, in: Winckelmann-Gesellschaft Stendal (ed.), Johann Joachim Winckelmann. Neue Forschungen, 1990, 27–46 14 Id., H. KAMMERER-GROTHAUS, Das Museo Ercolanese in Portici, in: Cronache Ercolanesi 10, 1980, 175–217 15 F. BOLOGNA, Le scoperte di Ercolano e Pompei nella cultura del XVIII secolo, in: La Parola del Passato, 188/89, 1979, 377–404 16 A. CARÓLA-PERROTTI, Le porcellane dei Borbone di Napoli. Exhibition catalogue, Naples 1986 17 E. C. CORTI, Untergang und Auferstehung von Pompeji und H.,1940 (9th enlarged ed. 1978), (Engl. The Destruction and Resurrection of Pompeii and Herculaneum, London 1951) 18 M. TRUE, J. SILVETTI (eds.), The Getty Villa, 2006 19 M. GIGANTE, I papiri ercolanesi in: Le antichità di Ercolano, 1988, 63–80 20 A. DE SIMONE, Ercolano e la Villa dei Papiri alla luce dei nuovi scavi, in: Cronache Ercolanesi 33, 2003, 279–311 21 C. GRELL, Herculaneum et Pompéi dans les récits des voyageurs français du XVIIIe siècle, 1982 22 Id., CHR. MICHEL, Erudits, hommes de lettres et artistes en France au XVIIIe siècle face aux découvertes d'Herculaneum, in: L. Franchi dell'Orto (ed.), Ercolano 1738–1988, 1993, 133–144 23 V. KOCKEL, Funde und Forschungen in den Vesuvstädten II, in: AA 1986, 523–532 24 A. MAIURI, Ercolano. I nuovi Scavi 1927–1958, 1958 25 C. MCILWAINE, Herculaneum: A Guide to Printed Sources, 2 vol., 1988 26 Id., Supplement, in: Cronache Ercolanesi 20, 1990, 87–128 27 M. PAGANO, Metodologia dei restauri borbonici a Pompei ed Ercolano, in: Rivista di Studi Pompeiani 5, 1991/92, 169–191 28 Id., Il teatro di Ercolano, in: Cronache Ercolanesi 23, 1993, 121–156 29 CHR. C. PARSLOW, Rediscovering Antiquity. Karl Weber and the Excavation of H., Pompeii, and Stabiae, 1995 30 M. PRAZ, Il Gusto neoclassico, 1940,1974, (Engl. A. Davidson, On Neoclassicism, London, 1969) 31 L. A. SCATOZZA HÖRICHT, Restauri alle collezioni del Museo

Fig. 4: J. Paul Getty Museum, Malibu/California. The building is a copy of the Villa dei Papiri, lavishly furnished with replicas of Greek statues; its owner is generally assumed to be C. Calpurnius Piso. As a collector, J. Paul Getty thus linked himself to ancient tradition, with California becoming the new Rome.

Ercolanese di Portici alla luce di documenti inediti, in: Atti della Accademia Pontaniana N. S. 31, 1982, 495–540 32 C. WALDSTEIN, L. SHOOBRIDGE, Herculaneum. Past, Present and Future, 1908   33 F. ZEVI, Gli Scavi di Ercolano e le Antichità, in: Le Antichità di Ercolano, 1988, 9–38
URLs   34 The Friends of Herculaneum Society: www.herculaneum.ox.ac.uk/   35 Herculaneum: Destruction and Re-Discovery: www.romanherculaneum.com/   36 Soprintendenza archeologica di Pompei: www2.pompeiisites.org/   37 Le Antichità di Ercolano Esposte (online version of Sources 1 above): www.picure.l.u-tokyo.ac.jp/arc/ercolano/index.html

ADDITIONAL BIBLIOGRAPHY C. C. MATTUSCH, The Villa dei Papiri at Herculaneum, 2005; J. MUEHLENBROCK, D. RICHTER (eds.), Verschuettet vom Vesuv. Die letzten Stunden von Herculaneum, 2005; C. PADERNI, Monumenti antichi rinvenuti ne reali scavi di Ercolano e Pompei e delineati e spiegati. Trascrizione e nota da U. Pannuti, 2000; M. PAGANO (ed.), I diari di scavo di Pompei, Ercolano e Stabia di Francesco e Pietro La Vega 1764–1810, 1997   VALENTIN KOCKEL

Hermetics see → OCCULTISM

Heroic poetry see → EPIC

Hippocratic Oath. Documentary evidence for a use of the HO in Late Antiquity is ambiguous. Gregory of Nazianzus (Greg. Naz. Or. 7,10) reported that his brother Caesarius did not have to swear the oath as a medical student in Alexandria, thus implying that others probably had to. However, there is no record for the Byzantine or Muslim world to confirm any official obligation to swear this oath, even though it was evidently well-known. In practice, it was superseded by the Galenic concept equating ethically sound medicine with efficient therapy, and it was assumed that the legends surrounding Hippocrates, together with his 'will', provided guidance for physicians regarding their professional conduct. Even though translations and versions of the oath existed in numerous medieval languages, thus attesting to a certain demand, most oaths sworn by physicians took the form of loyalty declarations to rulers or → UNIVERSITIES, with specific regulations regarding

medical practice and remuneration. During the → RE-
NAISSANCE, excerpts of the HO appeared in university
oaths, e.g. in Wittenberg in 1508 and Basel in 1570. In
Heidelberg, the dean of the medical faculty had to
swear it publicly within a month of assuming office,
while Jena graduates from 1558 into the 19th cent. had
to commit to all of the stipulations set out by Hippocrates in his oath and in *De medico*. In 17th cent. Leiden, medical graduates had to agree to a Latin version
of the oath, and so did students in Edinburgh between
1705 and 1731, before this version was replaced by a
shorter and less clearly defined one. From 1804, as part
of the academic graduation ceremony, each successful
medical candidate in Montpellier had to recite the oath
in front of a bust of Hippocrates donated by the French
government. From 1840 onwards, the call to swear the
HO became especially strident in the United States, as
adherence in particular to its prohibition of abortion
served to distinguish the true physician from the quack.
However, it was still thought that a new code for medical practitioners would be more appropriate for the
new country. By about 1880, the enthusiasm for the
HO had died down, with the result that universities
which still insisted on it being sworn, such as McGill,
were considered old-fashioned. Where medical oaths
continued to be sworn, they generally took the form of
loyalty oaths. This applies for example to the oath for
Prussian physicians of 1810, drafted by C.W. Hufe-
land, which specified obligations both towards the state
and to the patient. WWII was a turning point in that it
renewed interest in medical oaths and codes, following
the revelations of the Nuremberg Trials. The 1948
→ GENEVA DECLARATION placed the oath into a
modern context, while in the US and Canada the
number of medical faculties requiring the HO – or a
variant thereof – rose from 20 in 1928 to 69 in 1965,
108 in 1977, and 119 in 1989. A similar development
took place in the United Kingdom, where an updated
version of the HO for the 21st cent. was published by
the British Medical Association in 1996. In order to
take account of changing social circumstances, it has
been common practice since Late Antiquity to leave out
or amend certain paragraphs of the HO (e.g. the invocation of the gods, or in the 1960s the paragraph dealing with abortion) without abrogating the symbolic
importance of the oath in general. Some medical ethi-
cists, particularly those from a conservative background, still maintain their loyalty to the principles
which they see immortalized in the HO – even though
the following rule applies: the more general the principles, the less Hippocratic in the truest sense their content. Others, by contrast, consider the HO to be no
more than a stage in the developmental history of
modern medical ethics that has long since been overcome.
→ Hippocrates [6] H. of Cos

1 Auctores varii, The Hippocratic Oath, in: JHM 51/4,
1996, 401–500   2 D. CANTOR (ed.), Reinventing Hippocrates, 2002   3 C. LICHTENTHAELER, Der Eid des Hippokrates. Ursprung und Bedeutung, 1984   4 V. NUTTON,
Hippocratic Medicine and Modern Morality, in: Médecine et morale dans l'Antiquité (= Entretiens 43), 1997,
31–63   5 T. RÜTTEN, Hippokrates im Gespräch, 1993,
50–63.   VIVIAN NUTTON

Hippocratism. Even though in Byzantium and the
medieval Christian Occident Hippocrates was seen as
the founder of medicine and given legendary status, his
teachings, as compiled in the *Corpus Hippocraticum*,
were studied only on a very narrow textual basis, and
the few available texts were known only through
Galen's interpretation or from the lemmata of the Galenic commentaries on Hippocrates. In the Western medicine of the Middle Ages, pseudonymous treatises were
at least as influential as those contained in the modern
edition of Hippocrates' texts, with the exception of the
Aphorisms, the *Prognostikon* and the treatise on the
regimen in acute diseases *De diaeta acutorum*. The
corpus only became commonly available with the first
Latin translation in 1525. This was followed in 1526 by
the Aldine edition – the first in Greek. From 1550
onwards, the teaching of medicine, esp. in Paris, came
to be based on Hippocratic rather than Galenic texts.
The vast array (and sometimes the incomprehensibility)
of the doctrines contained in the corpus invited a multitude of interpretations, and with that came an interpretative freedom that the more logical structure of
→ GALENISM did not offer. Hippocrates was regarded
as the inventor of detailed procedures for clinical medicine, with special emphasis on observation, and physicians such as Pieter van Foreest (1521–1597) in Holl-
and, Guillaume de Baillou (1538–1616) in France and
Thomas Sydenham (1624–1689) in England were
hailed as the 'Hippocrates' of their respective countries.
Paracelsists such as Petrus Severinus (1540–1602) and
iatrochemists such as Friedrich Hoffmann (1660–1742)
could each invoke the authority of Hippocrates for their
respective ideas by referring to different texts in the corpus. Other scholars believed that Hippocrates had anticipated Harvey's discovery of the circulation of the
blood. In the 18th cent., Herman Boerhaave (1668–
1738), whose numerous pupils spread his teachings
across the world, argued that Hippocrates had been the
first to conduct proper clinical observations. Hippocratic notions of environmental medicine and surgery
as well as disease were widely held into the late 19th
cent., particularly in France. J.P.E. Pétrequin's edition
of Hippocrates' treatises on surgery, published in 1877–
78, and above all M.P.E. Littré's monumental complete
edition of the *Corpus Hippocraticum* (1839–1861)
were to contribute to the medical debates and practices
of the day. Furthermore, Littré's edition consolidated
the modern image of Hippocrates as a practical observer, unburdened by theory, who with his works *De
vetere medicina* and *De morbo sacro* liberated medicine
from its entanglement with philosophy and religion.
(Littré's confidence in the importance and the authenticity of these two works was not shared by every one of

Hippocrates' earlier supporters.) Even though the Hippocratic Oath was seen as the foundation charter of medical ethics, its relevance for the contemporary medicine of a given period was often questioned. Only in the 1920s, and notably in the 1950s, did a growing number of medical schools, primarily in the US, demand that the Oath be taken. In the 1920s and 1930s, Hippocratism experienced a renaissance among Europe's leading medical practitioners. They claimed that only the physician, not the medical scientist or his instruments, could successfully diagnose a patient and treat the whole individual. This positive view of Hippocratism can still be found in medical circles today.
→ Galen of Pergamum; → Hippocrates [6] H. of Cos
→ Hippocratic Oath

1 G. Baader, R. Winau (eds.), Die hippokratischen Epidemien, 1989   2 J. R. Pinault, Hippocratic Lives and Legends, 1992   3 T. Rütten, Demokrit – lachender Philosoph und sanguinischer Melancholiker. Eine pseudohippokratische Geschichte, 1992   4 Id., Hippokrates im Gespräch, 1993   5 W. D. Smith, The Hippocratic Tradition, 1979   6 O. Temkin, Hippocrates in a World of Pagans and Christians, 1992.   VIVIAN NUTTON

Historical demography see → Population

Historical Geography
A. Definition   B. Origins   C. Laying the Foundations   D. Ancient Historical Geography after Polybius   E. Middle Ages   F. Modern Period   G. Methods

A. Definition
Historical geography (HG) is a branch of geography or, to be precise, → historiography and is concerned with the ever changing relationship between human beings and the landscape. As well as verbal (literary, epigraphic, numismatic) and representational (archaeological) evidence of the past, its main source is the topographical framework of historical events. Nowadays, HG is essentially characterized by two different paths of scholarly research; one path derives from the cultural geographer Otto Schlüter (1872–1959) and sees itself as applied HG, whose primary concern is the origin and derivation in history of present-day topographical and settlement planning from the spatial conditions, structures and relationships of different historical periods [2; 13]. The other path of HG, which is the subject of this entry, goes back to the beginnings of Western scholarship, where the questions and the methods used in both the natural sciences and the humanities were still seen as having a unitary character.

B. Origins
History and geography were still closely bound together in the scholarly work of Hecataeus (ca. 560–480 BC). His geographical knowledge, drawn from the teaching tradition of Anaximander (early 6th cent BC; cf. Str. 14,1,7) and acquired in his own numerous tra-

vels (Hdt. 2,143; Agatharchides geogr. 1,1), is reflected in his revision of Anaximander's map of the world (*Gês Períhodos*), and similarly in his two prose works, a commentary on this map (*Perihégesis*), oriented towards the sub-literary genre of the logbook, and the *Genealogíai*, in which he arranged the Greek world of the gods genealogically. How both fields of knowledge combined to have a practical application was illustrated in 500 BC, when, aware of the inexhaustible power of the Persian Empire, he warned against any uprising against the Great King and then, when the Ionians did not follow his counsel, advised them to build a fleet so that they might at least stand up to the Great King at sea (Hdt. 5,36; cf. also his advice to withdraw to the island of Leros in an emergency, in Hdt. 5,126). It can also be seen in his two literary works (cf. FGrH 1 F 129; 266; 275 and. 6 f.; 18a; 27), that show with the greatest possible clarity that history, ethnography and geography form an organic unity for him. His contemporaries called this scholarly discipline *historíe*. The epic reports that Hecataeus tackled in the *Genealogíai* were for him error-riddled representations of historical reality that he subjected to rationalist criticism – and this unquestionably marks him as the first Western historian in the modern understanding of the term. In its methodology and manner of representation, Hecataeus' literary work became a model of scholarship. That is evidenced, for example, by the *Genealogíai* of Acusilaus of Argos (end of the 6th/1st half of the 5th cent. BC; FGrH 2), whose interest did not just cover gods and heroes but also the people of the early age and, in the framework of Trojan War-related stories of return, the geography of Greece and the Aegean area as well. The *Genealogíai* of Pherecydes of Athens (1st half of the 5th cent. BC; FGrH 3) started off with a depiction of the Heroic Age and likewise contained a large number of geographic elements. When Pherecydes traces the genealogical lines of development down into his own time (FGrH 3 F 2), he is showing the beginnings of the writing of contemporary history. While, from a modern perspective, historical aspects seem to be in foreground over against geographical ones in the above-mentioned writings of early Greek scholarship, in works, on the other hand, in which primarily geographical concerns have moved the author to literary activity, historical aspects were initially never ignored. The work of Democles from Phygela (first half of the 5th cent. BC; [3rd vol. 2. 71 Note 45]) serves as an example here; he attempts to offer a natural explanation for phenomena that have a moral basis in myth – thus, for example, the destruction of Sipylus, home town of Tantalus: in its mythical conception this catastrophe was divine punishment; for Democles, however, it was the natural consequence of a region-wide earthquake (Str. 1,3,17). Consequently, a piece of expert writing, decidedly geographical, has clearly dissociated itself from descriptive geography and historical writing and, in the framework of cartography, has enquired into specifically geographic (also mathematical-astronomical) problems – a development that had been foreshadowed as early as Hecataeus and that culminated as late as Eratosthenes (3rd cent. BC), who regarded cartography, incorporating mathematical and astronomical methods, as the real focus of geography (cf. Hipparchus of Nicaea, middle of the 2nd cent. BC, Marinus of Tyre, 2nd cent. AD), in contrast to merely literary regional studies as Homer, for example, had practised it (Poseidonius, Strabo, Pliny the Elder, Pomponius Mela). Historians, on the other hand, never lost the link with descriptive geography. Thus, geography and ethnography are the determining background for historical events in the historiography of Herodotus (ca. 485–424 BC), whether he gives them voice in relatively long or relatively short digressions or fits them into the event's unfolding (cf. [14. 41 f.]). By concerning himself principally with politico-military actions, Thucydides (ca. 455–400 BC) joins this historical-geographical tradition only in those places where the links are drawn to individual events in the war. In Xenophon's (ca. 430–350) historical writings, the event is highlighted by geography which is familiar to the author through first-hand experience.

C. LAYING THE FOUNDATIONS

Not until Polybius (ca. 200–120 BC) did anyone offer a theoretical justification for the need to provide historical accounts with a geographical context. According to him, three qualities distinguish a historian; in third place, knowledge of the written sources (12,25i,2; unranked 12,25e,1; 4), in second place, practical life-experience (12,25e,1; 4; 25g,1; 20,12,8), but most important for him is geographical knowledge acquired first-hand (12,25e,1; 25f,5). His acquaintance with geography as a science did not extend beyond what was fitting for a practising *strategos*: he therefore did not concern himself in principle with questions of general and mathematical-astronomical geography, even if he regarded such considerations as sensible (cf. e.g. the hydrography of the Sea of Azov, the Black Sea and the Sea of Marmara: Pol. 4,39–42). In the 34th book – lost to us – of his History, he gave an overview, detached from the course of history, of the geography of the Ancient World (announced in 3,37,11; 57,5; 59,6; cf. Str. 8,1,1). A perfect example of an historical-geographic line of argument embedded in his historical account is the characterization of Byzantium's location, given by Polybius on the occasion of the war that the Rhodians waged against the city of Byzantium in 220 (4,38–46; [18. 486–507; 19. 469–479]). If Thucydides is regarded as the founder of modern historical scholarship, Polybius can justifiably be named the founder of modern HG.

D. ANCIENT HISTORICAL GEOGRAPHY AFTER POLYBIUS

As in other fields of cultural history, even with the exemplary nature of Polybius' objectives, no steady development can be traced in the area of HG. With all the interest in the ethnography and geography encountered

in his writings, Caesar (100–44 BC) is hardly likely to be sought among the ranks of historiographers, though his *commentarii* have a quite distinct, even if not historiographic character. Quite different, on the other hand, is Sallust (86–34 BC), who follows the Hellenistic tradition of historical writing. Most of that tradition is lost to us – only the historical work of Polybius is partly extant – and this with all its thematic and stylistic dissimilarity; as far as historical-geographical commentary on historical events is concerned, Sallust follows Polybius closely (cf. [14. 57 f.]). The same can be said of Pompeius Trogus (Augustan period), whose *Historiae Philippicae* is available to us only in Justin's epitome (3rd cent AD) and in the abridgement of prologues to individual books, but still shows how essential the geographical background of an event was to this historian (cf. [14. 54 f.]). Livy (59 BC – 17 AD), who certainly was not much travelled, nevertheless understood how to frame the geographical setting of various passages in his historical narrative so dramatically that he can be regarded as an epigone of Polybius in terms of the historical-geographical side of his work (cf. [14. 47–49]). In his predominantly historical works, Tacitus (born. ca. AD 55), on the other hand, placed less importance on the geographical education of his readership, and this is perhaps connected to his observance of rhetorical principles. The situation is different in his *Germania*, which is structured as an ethnographic rather than a historiographic work, with geographical passages as appropriate to the genre. Even Arrian (85/90 – after AD 146) was bothered with geography only when it was necessary for the understanding of a military campaign (cf. Arr. Anab. 5,5 f.). The fact that Xenophon was his literary model did not change anything. Like him, Herodian (born ca. AD 178/180) and Cassius Dio (ca. 164 – after AD 229) were sparing with geographic detail, which was provided solely to clarify military actions. At the end of this list of historians of Antiquity stand, along with Ammianus Marcellinus (ca. AD 330–400) and Procopius (490/507 – after AD 555; cf. [14. 55–57]), authors who – as far as consideration of historical-geographical features in their work is concerned – adhere to Polybian standards. Indeed, Ammianus wrote an imperial history on the basis of geography [1. 19].

E. MIDDLE AGES

As Christianity, with its exclusive focus on the Holy Scriptures and their interpretation, repressed interest in the scientific exploration of the world in late Antiquity, the level of geographic scholarship correspondingly reached a particularly low point for HG, in the East as much as in the West (cf. Kosmas Indikopleustes). All the same, → CONSTANTINOPLE still exercised in this regard the effective preservative function which it had for other areas as well (cf. Stephanus of Byzantium; copies of Strabo and Ptolemy from the 9th cent.). Even → CARTOGRAPHY had entered the service of ecclesiastical culture. While ancient cartography was, however, fundamentally at pains to record the present world, the medieval *mappae mundi*, with their concentration on the salvific events in Jerusalem, acquired in part a backward-looking perspective and thus, in the end, took the first steps towards HG. On the other hand, the portolan charts that possibly derived from Byzantine cartographic material featured no geographic names in the interior regions, and historical motifs served mainly decorative purposes.

F. Modern Period

The debate over the main geographic work by Ptolemy (2nd cent AD), whose works had first become known Europe-wide in their original Greek version in connection with the wave of refugee scholars and their → LIBRARIES from Constantinople before the city was conquered by the Turks in 1453 – furthered by advances in printing technology – gave a huge stimulus to scholarship in geography and cartography. In the wake of the discovery of America, the euphoria of tracking down more and more new countries was likewise a contributing factor. Taking part in this activity were such scholars as Gerhard Mercator (1512–1594), Abraham Ortelius (1527–1598), G. Delisle (1675–1726), Jean Baptiste Bourguignon d'Anville (1697–1782) and Eberhard David Hauber (1695–1765). By any modern measurement, these geographers did, however, repeatedly turn to the affairs of the ancient world.

1. Ph. Clüver 2. C. Ritter 3. K. J. H. Neumann

1. Ph. Clüver

It should come as no surprise, therefore, that the first real impetus towards the study of HG in the modern period should have come from Classical Studies. Philipp Clüver (1580–1622) revived this tradition which originated with Hecataeus and was founded by Polybius. During his legal studies in Leiden, under the influence of the Classical philologist Joseph Justus Scaliger (1540–1609), he studied Classical Antiquity, and ancient geography in particular. Between 1607 and 1613, he undertook several journeys throughout the whole of Europe and in the process, in England made the acquaintance of the Classical philologist Isaac Casaubon (1559–1614), who particularly impressed Clüver because of his deep familiarity with Strabo. Clüver's *Germania Antiqua*, a pictorial of German antiquarianism, opened up a position for him as Geographicus Academicus [6] at the university in Leiden in 1616. In 1617/18 he travelled through Italy and Sicily; in the last years of his life, he incorporated the knowledge accumulated on this journey in various publications on the ancient geography of Sicily and Italy [9; 8]. Of these, his introduction into ancient and contemporary geography [7] gained a particularly wide readership. Clüver's writings stimulated interest across a broad readership in historical-geographical issues – but almost exclusively still in the area of Greco-Roman

Antiquity. Thus, while the rise of HG in Antiquity had its main impetus from historiography (Polybius), the stimuli for the discipline's modern revival came primarily from ancient geography (Strabo, Ptolemy).

2. C. Ritter

Carl Ritter (1779–1859) did not commit himself in his schooling to studies in Classical Antiquity; history and geography were his favourite subjects. When he gained recognition for his skills at drawing maps, he was directed to the craft of copperplate engraving. The studies to which he dedicated himself in Halle, however, were aimed at a general education with the goal of an encyclopedic approach to teaching. At that time he was also attending lectures by Friedrich August Wolf on the history of Greek and Roman literature, but did not have occasion to learn Greek until he was between 26 and 29 years old, by which time he had long been earning his livelihood as a private teacher. His interest in history and geography then found expression in an essay on *Die Ruinen am Rhein. Über die Alterthümer in Cölln* ('The Ruins on the Rhine: On Antiquities in Cologne') [17]. Already evident in this first publication was something that became a characteristic of his later scholarly, pedagogical and journalistic work: the view that geography and history ought not be considered separately and can lead to meaningful results only when taken together. It comes to the fore in his work *Vorhalle europäischer Völkergeschichte vor Herodotos, um den Kaukasus und an den Gestaden des Pontus. Eine Abhandlung zur Alterthumskunde* ('Portico of the History of European Peoples before Herodotus, around the Caucasus and on the Shores of the Black Sea. A treatise on Classical Antiquity'), published in Berlin in 1820, and is the overriding concern of his main work *Die Erdkunde im Verhältnis zur Natur und Geschichte des Menschen* ('Geography and its Relationship to Nature and Human History') [16]. As a lecturer at the university in Berlin (from 1820), he gained further recognition for this view, which was very substantially influenced by his conversations with Alexander von Humboldt, whom he accompanied for ten years. Ritter is thus regarded today as a pioneer of general HG, who, notwithstanding the traditional focus on Antiquity in this field of study, opened up horizons to other regions of the world and to later periods of history.

3. K. J. H. Neumann

Just as little as the history of scholarly research can basically be represented as a series of thoughts which build upon each other in a seamless and unchallenged manner, as similar but independent thinking can lead to similar results in different locations, so must Karl Johann Heinrich Neumann (1823–1880) of Königsberg be understood as a scholar who extended the HG of his time beyond Antiquity, but not [merely] as a successor of Ritter. He studied history in Königsberg, where Walter Drumann was one of his teachers. Neumann gained his doctorate with a thesis on the history of Olbia [11] and in 1855 published the first (and ultimately only) volume of Black Sea studies *Die Hellenen im Skythenlande* ('The Hellenes in Scythia') [10]. This work made his academic reputation, on the basis of which he received a full professorship at the University of Breslau in 1865. Especially in his teaching but also in his research he continued to express his conviction about the fertile partnership of geography and history. That he also gave due attention to physical geography is evident in his work, revised by his student J. Partsch, on the *Allgemeine Physikalische Geographie von Griechenland* ('General Physical Geography of Greece') [12].

Since the end of the 18th cent., increasing numbers of travellers from all over the world, especially from England, France and Germany, have, with a view to the remains of ancient cultures, been improving our knowledge of the material culture as well as of the geography of the ancient world. It is to ancient topography in particular that serious thought has been given. Capturing the ancient world on maps has been a predominant concern. Helping to achieve this objective were the studies of geographers and classical philologists like Heinrich Kiepert (1818–1899), Conrad Bursian (1830–1883), Alfred Kirchhoff (1838–1907), Wilhelm Sieglin (1855–1935), Joseph Partsch (1851–1925), Eugen Oberhummer (1859–1944), Wilhelm Tomaschek (1841–1901), Johann Sölch (1883–1951), Heinrich Nissen (1839–1912), Gustav Hirschfeld (1847–1895), Alfred Philippson (1864–1953) and Hugo Hassinger (18771952). Friedrich Ratzel (1844–1904), under whom, among others, Ellen Churchill Semple (1863–1932) studied, lectured, following the historian and political scientist R. Kjellén (1864–1922), in favor of a topographically fixed determinism – a view of HG that did not survive for long [4; 15]. Historical geography's evolution, beginning with Polybius, is expanding today into a large international world of scholars, representative of whom is Ernst Kirsten (1911–1987), who in his comprehensive research strongly emphasised HG's far-reaching interdisciplinarity.

G. Methods

As important as it was for Polybius to incorporate geography into historical studies, he did not explicitly offer any ideas about the application of specific methods in HG. HG did not develop as an independent scientific discipline until during the 19th cent. and it is only from that time that one can talk of the development of an independent methodology for HG. HG is basically defined not by the objects of its interest (as for example canonical disciplines like historical studies or biology) but by the questions asked in investigating historical developments. It is therefore a discipline that fixes its attention on a distinct, namely geographical, aspect of historical studies. The common denominator of historical-geographical scholarship is in this sense the changing relationship between human beings and environment. Two main issues can be discerned in this: on the one hand, historical developments in which the environment has had a definite effect on people and

their actions, or on the other, historical developments in which people have had a definite effect on the environment in which they live. According to the topographical dimension of a given historical issue, either geographic or chorographic, or ultimately, topographic techniques can be applied [5]; aimed at macro-developments is the geography-based cognitive interest in problems of the interplay of relationships between man and environment, i.e. principally in problems of social geography (as in describing areas of differing social forms of living and and behaving) and of geosystem studies (as in the investigation of short- and middle-term developments, of possibilities for controlling the ecosystem and of concrete design problems in certain regions): we are speaking here of HG. Such questions can also be interesting for particular landscapes; they can, therefore, also take on chorographic relevance. Historical chorography, however, can also, in some areas, approach historical topography, under whose jurisdiction come sets of problems restricted to small regions within topographical areas. Here it is an issue of micro-analysis and micro-reconstruction of historical landscape features, with the help of literary, archaeological, palaeographical, palaeobotanical and palaeozoological finds, and thus microidentification of the geographic provenance of certain objects. By this is meant, for example, the working out of contemporary and historic geographic qualities, the location of a geographic phenomenon, as e.g. a place in the surrounding countryside; also meant is the description of its geological-geographical-physical qualities, such as, for instance, the soil, the flora and fauna, the climate and also the analysis and depiction of the technical administrative structures, of the inhabitants and of the effects of human artifice on the landscape through the construction of streets, dams, terraces, canals, and the like. Historical-geographical procedures such as retrogression and progression are applied in connection with chorographic and topographic problems in particular. The former involves a past-focused, reductive process with the help of which certain features of the historical landscape are reconstructed from their later stage of development (retrogression). Here the focus of scholarly interest is a landscape's past, the appearance of which is reconstructed with the help of its modern condition. The latter uses an evolutionary method (progression) to explain certain features of the landscape from their origin by taking the historical conditions of a landscape and proceeding step by step from the older to the more recent period.

As HG is by definition a form of applied multidisciplinary scholarship, it avails itself of the methods of various scientific disciplines. Just a selection of scholarly fields will be mentioned here to demonstrate the methodological variety of historical-geographic scholarship. Some of these fields must be consulted on a case by case basis, others more frequently or even fundamentally. Where it is a matter of human beings and their nature as individuals and as members of society, one turns to anthropology, anthropogeography, demography, ethnology and ethnography; if the available linguistic material can furnish information, then to comparative linguistics, linguistic geography and toponymy; cultural points of reference are offered generally by agrarian geography, architecture, astronomy, geodesy, philosophy, religious geography, theology and economic geography. Archaeology opens up the material legacy of human cultures; for the culture and nature of particular countries or regional groupings, one might consult African studies, Egyptology, Germanic antiquity, Indology, Judaic studies, Celtic studies, Classical philology, ancient history and Oriental studies; for natural phenomena, botany, geology, geophysics, climatology, marine science and zoology are the relevant fields.

SOURCES 1 W. ENSSLIN, Zur Geschichtsschreibung und Weltanschauung des Ammianus Marcellinus (Klio Beiheft 16), 1923. 2 K. FEHN, Stand und Aufgaben der historischen Geographie, in: Blätter für Deutsche Landesgeschichte 111, 1975, 31–53. 3 K. v. FRITZ, Die griechische Geschichtsschreibung, 2 vols., 1967. 4 C. HEUCKE, Von Strabon zu Haushofer? in: Orbis Terrarum 1, 1995, 203–211. 5 E. KIRSTEN, Möglichkeiten und Aufgaben der historischen Geographie des Altertums in der Gegenwart, in: Stuttgarter Kolloquium zur historischen Geographie des Altertums 1, 1980 (Geographica Historica 4), 1987, 1–50. 6 PH. CLÜWER, Germaniae Antiquae libri III, adiectae sunt Vindelicia et Noricum, 1616, microfiche, 1992. 7 Id., Introductionis in universam geographiam tam veterem quam novam libri VI, Amsterdam 1659. 8 Id., Italia antiqua, 2 vols., 1624, microfiche, 1998. 9 Id., Sicilia antiqua cum minoribus insulis adiacentibus, item Sardinia et Corsica, 1619, 1994. 10 C. J. H. NEUMANN, Die Hellenen im Skythenlande. Ein Beitrag zur alten Geographie, Ethnographie und Handelsgeschichte 1, Berlin 1855. 11 Id., De rebus Olbiopolitanorum, dissertation, Königsberg 1852. 12 Id., J. PARTSCH, Physikalische Geographie von Griechenland mit besonderer Rücksicht auf das Alterthum, Breslau 1885. 13 H.-J. NITZ, Historische Geographie, in: Siedlungsforschung 10, 1992, 211–237. 14 E. OLSHAUSEN, Einführung in die historische Geographie der Alten Welt, 1991. 15 Id., Gebirgsland als Lebensraum, in: Id., (ed.) Stuttgarter Kolloquium zur historischen Geographie des Altertums 5, 1993 (Geographica Historica 8), 1996, 1–11. 16 C. R. RITTER, Die Erdkunde im Verhältnis zur Natur und Geschichte des Menschen, 2 vols., 1817/18 (later complete revised version by the author: vol. 1, Afrika, Berlin 1822, further treatment is found in Die Erdkunde von Asien, 19 vols., Berlin 1832/59). 17 Id., Die Ruinen am Rhein. Über die Alterthümer in Cölln, in: Rheinisches Archiv für Geschichte und Litteratur 1, 1810, 199–220. 18 F. W. WALBANK, A Historical Commentary on Polybius, vol. 1, 1957. 19 Id., Polybius on the Pontus and the Bosphorus (IV. 39–42), in: G. E. MYLONAS (ed.), Studies Presented to David Moore Robinson on His Seventieth Birthday, 1951.
LITERATURE 20 P. PÉDECH, La méthode historique de Polybe, 1964, 517–597. 21 J. G. TEXIER, Polybe géographe: Dialogues d'Histoire ancienne 2, 1976, 385–411. 22 F. W. WALBANK, The Geography of Polybius: CeM 9, 1948, 155–182. 23 K. ZIEGLER, s. v. Polybios 1, RE 21, 1567–1569.
ECKHART OLSHAUSEN

Historicism
I. GENERAL II. ART HISTORY

I. GENERAL
A. IN LIEU OF A DEFINITION
B. ORIGINS AND HISTORY OF THE TERM
C. THE 'CRISIS OF HISTORICISM'
D. MODERN INVESTIGATIONS INTO THE HISTORY OF HISTORIOGRAPHY
E. HISTORICISM AND CLASSICAL STUDIES

A. IN LIEU OF A DEFINITION
The term 'historicism', which describes a central scientific paradigm of modernity, is the subject of numerous studies in the history and philosophy of science. Occasionally, it is also used as a polemical catchphrase for the ethical relativism and estrangement from reality that is associated with historical studies. There is no consensus regarding its meaning. Thus, not only do the various academic disciplines each have a specific understanding of 'historicism', but within the disciplines themselves, especially in philosophy, macroeconomics, Protestant theology, law, fine arts and history, varying definitions have been and are still being suggested (surveys: [55; 57; 88; 89; 116]). In German historical studies, which will be the focus of this article, historicism is equated with efforts since about 1800 to elevate history to the rank of a systematic scholarly field. This concept of historical studies as a scholarly field is said to have contributed to the singular rise of the historical disciplines at German universities and, after they had diversified into different schools and tendencies in the second half of the 19th cent., to have entered a 'crisis' during the first third of the 20th cent. [32. 3; 78. 81]. However, controversial discussions were not limited to the German language area but took place in England [25; 65; 106], France [3] and Spain [90] as well. Italy had a lively debate on the possibilities and limits of a complete historicization of reality following the examination of historicism by Benedetto Croce [26] (cf. [103. 55–101]). In literary studies, New Historicism is a familiar term developed in the United States. In an effort to distinguish itself from structuralist and post-structuralist theories, it calls for the historical and cultural contextualization of texts [6; 39] (cf. [103. 13–54]). There is also the term 'historicism' as used by Karl Popper for various schools of thought (especially → MARXISM) that attempt to derive theories from history, which take on the force of rules, which, in turn, permit the making of prognoses for the future [92].

B. ORIGINS AND HISTORY OF THE TERM
The word 'historicism' first appeared at the turn of the 18th to the 19th cent. with Friederich Schlegel and Novalis [52; 102], but only became more frequent in philosophical discourses of the first half of the 19th century. Interpretations differed. Ludwig Feuerbach (1839) polemicized against "religious materialism and historicism" ('religiöse[r] Materialismus und Historis-

mus'), meaning the backward-looking theology of his age. One decade later, Christlieb Julius Braniß and Carl Prantl re-coined the term in treatises on the philosophy of history probing function and methodology of historical studies [101]. For Prantl historicism aimed at recognizing individuality in its "specific time and space" ('konkrete[n] Zeit und Räumlichkeit') [93]. Subsequently, the relationship of past and present is at the centre of the debate over Historicism, amid ongoing reflections on German idealistic philosophy and the experience of the French Revolution. At the same time, historicism is used to characterize the German Historical School of Law (→ HISTORISCHE RECHTSSCHULE), which came into being in Prussia after the Wars of Liberation and emphasized the historical conditionality of institutional law while turning away from the natural law concept of the Enlightenment. Its main representatives were Friedrich Carl von Savigny, Carl Friedrich Eichhorn, Barthold Georg Niebuhr and Jacob Grimm.

Of critical importance for the development of the term is the theory of historical knowledge developed by historical scholars during the 19th cent., which resulted in a fundamental historicization of man and the world. An interpretation of tradition based on a thorough recording of the sources was presented as the decisive cognitive process in historical research. The effort to achieve full objectivity became the signature of the 'historicistic' period. In terms of methodology, the consensus was to proceed with the critical philological method that had been developed in the centuries from → HUMANISM to the → ENLIGHTENMENT [77]. The historico-philosophical concepts of Fichte, Schleiermacher and Hegel provided significant theoretic stimulation. Contemporary ideas were characterized by a deep-rooted belief in the essential purposefulness of historical events and emphasized the role of the individual through which reason progressively revealed itself in historical reality.

Leopold von Ranke was of outstanding importance in the establishment of history as an academic discipline. His struggle for objectivity culminated in the maxim that the historian reconstructs the past "as it actually was" ('wie es eigentlich gewesen'); cf. Thuc. 1,22,2 [94. VII]. According to Ranke, it is the duty of the historian to recognize the conditions and interrelationships beyond the individual that are not explicitly stated in the sources and, consequently, to present the reader with the shaping forces of history [110]. Deeply rooted in Protestantism, he optimistically had confidence in the economy of the divine will, which reveals itself anew with each new period. The rather casually expressed ideas of Ranke on a theory of history were taken up and continued by Johann Gustav Droysen [22. 50–67]. His lectures on the 'Enzyklopädie und Methodologie der Geschichte' ('Encyclopaedia and Methodology of History'), which he repeatedly revised between 1857 and 1881 and which were not published until 1937 (as Historik), reflected the research practices of his age and defined the standards of historical research:

'Das Wesen der geschichtlichen Interpretation ist forschend zu verstehen, ist die Interpretation' ("The nature of historical interpretation is to understand through research, it is interpretation") [29. 22]. It marked the beginning of history as a hermeneutic science [35. 162–205] that must prove progress in historical change. While Ranke claimed to objectively detect the workings of God and Droysen "moral forces" ('moralische Mächte'), for Wilhelm von Humboldt 'ideas', following the categories of idealistic philosophy, were the significant forces shaping history. The objectivity claim of historical studies was thus justified metaphysically and not in terms of cognitive logic [47]. However, neither the exponents of the mainstream of modern historiography nor their most important critics used the word 'historicism'. It only came to be employed retrospectively for historical studies of the 19th cent. in discussions since the turn of the 20th cent. and increasingly in the 1920s.

The rise of historicism in German historical studies went hand-in-hand with the professionalization, institutionalization and differentiation of history as a subject at the universities. The 'Historical School' profoundly shaped historical research and had an influential publishing organ in the journal Historische Zeitschrift, founded by Heinrich von Sybel in 1859. The 19th cent. experienced the predominance of the historical method and historical thinking. The nation state and the creative energy of 'great men' were at the centre of historiographical interest. Historical hermeneutics affected philosophy, legal and political sciences, macroeconomics and Protestant theology. Subject-specific methodologies emerged and distinguished themselves in particular through efficient source criticism. However, in historical studies the willingness to reflect on philosophical and epistemological matters declined. Instead, historians dedicated themselves to highly specialized research that by no means precluded a political instrumentalization of bourgeois historiography. After 1848, younger historians (e.g., Droysen, Sybel and Treitschke) advocated a political historiography and campaigned for the so-called 'Kleindeutsche Lösung' ('Small German Solution', i.e. German unification without Austria) of the 'national question' (i.e. unification) under Prussian hegemony [58. 120–162; 59. 86–92].

C. THE 'CRISIS OF HISTORICISM'

The explosive increase of knowledge and the pluralization of values led to a deeply-felt sense of insecurity in the second half of the 19th cent. Critical voices were increasingly denouncing the 'positivism' of a self-absorbed factual research and the relativism of an analytical and empirical science that historicized all values without differentiation and could only insufficiently describe complex social structures. Historicism was equated with the sterile, hostile-to-life objectives of antiquarian research. According to an often heard reproach, an abundance of material was accumulated without accounting for the necessity and function of such collections. The Basel historian and cultural pessimist Jacob Burckhardt in his *Weltgeschichtliche Betrachtungen* (Engl. *Force and Freedom. Reflections on History*) criticized the life-denying consequences of a historical science founded on an individualizing interpretation that is detached from real life, and he railed against the "brash anticipation of a world plan" ('kekke[s] Antizipieren eines Weltplanes'). In 1874, Friederich Nietzsche in his *Unzeitgemässe Betrachtungen. Zweites Stück: Vom Nutzen und Nachtheil der Historie für das Leben* (*Untimely Meditations. Second Part: Of the Use and Disadvantage of History for Life*) attacked the optimistic belief in progress of his colleagues who wished to understand the present based on the past [78; 88. 73–94; 116. 42–55]. In his view, because of the destruction of all historical norms, historical studies could no longer offer any concrete help for the proper conduct of one's life. Therefore, against the theoretical and methodological standards of contemporary Classical and historical studies, Nietzsche created the concept of a history serving life,. The question of the correlation between historical research and living reality, which Nietzsche clearly formulated but by no means answered convincingly, subsequently became a central problem in the fields of epistemology and the philosophy of history. However, this discourse did not initially affect historiographical practice. Historical scholars refused to engage in a discussion of theory and stubbornly insisted on the objectivity postulate while renewing its claim to cultural and educational leadership. 'Non-partisanship' became the ideal in both scientific and political writing. Even the Lamprecht controversy of the late 1880s only briefly cast doubt on the traditional methodological approach of professional historians. Karl Lamprecht's model of an integral cultural history that, analogous to the natural sciences, was to establish general contexts conforming to rules went virtually unheeded [8. 439–474; 9; 59. 141–136].

The many social, political and cultural upheavals of the late 19th and early 20th cents. shook the confidence in scientifically-founded and historically-deduced standards of general applicability. The question of how scholarship and life could be reconciled was asked more and more frequently. Macroeconomics, jurisprudence, philosophy and theology all participated in this debate [116. 61–125]. Wilhelm Dilthey and the Neo-Kantians Wilhelm Windelband and Heinrich Rickert set out to establish historical studies as a 'human' science, clearly distinct from the natural sciences [59. 148–156]. Dilthey attempted to overcome the relativity necessarily inherent in all historical convictions, which resulted from historical comparison, with the fundamental philosophical concept 'life', replacing Humboldt's 'ideas' and Droysen's 'moral forces': 'Leben ist das erste und immer Gegenwärtige, die Abstraktionen des Erkennens sind das zweite und beziehen sich nur auf das Leben' ("Life is what is first and always present, the abstractions of cognition are secondary and relate only to life") [27. 148]. The historian as the cognitive subject

is part of this 'real world' relationship of cause and effect and therefore capable of 'intuitive' understanding.

During the first decades of the 20th cent. the discourse in the philosophy of history regarding the intrinsic scientific and life-related function of historical studies and its epistemological axiomatic was significantly shaped by Ernst Troeltsch and Max Weber. However, the latter never used the central term 'historicism' [116. 213 n. 5].

In a number of studies published between 1897 and 1922, Troeltsch presents a convincing analysis of the problem of relativism in historicism [107; 108; 109] (cf. [38; 40; 42; 43]). Furthermore, in his later publications Troeltsch sought to give a new direction to the debate on the term 'historicism', which had by now acquired negative connotations. Troeltsch proposed an – as it were – neutral definition: the "fundamental historization of all our thinking about human beings, their culture and values" ('grundsätzliche Historisierung alles unseres Denkens über den Menschen, seine Kultur und seine Werte') [107. 102]. To Troeltsch historicism was – in addition to Naturalism – one of the "two great scholarly creations of the modern world" ('[eine der] beiden großen Wissenschaftsschöpfungen der modernen Welt') [107. 104 ff.]. It describes a historical way of thinking that aims for the "construction of a contemporary cultural system which derives from history and determines the next future trend" ('[die] Konstruktion eines gegenwärtigen und die nächste Zukunftsrichtung bestimmenden Kultursystems aus der Historie heraus') [107. 82]. His efforts to create a new beginning entirely in the European-Western tradition culminated in the postulate to "overcome history with history" ('Geschichte durch Geschichte überwinden') [107. 772]. Troeltsch believed that the contemporary relativism of historical studies could be mastered through a 'cultural synthesis' with the aim to establish a system of objective values legitimized by science and philosophy through the study of European-Western history.

Weber did not share this belief in the harmonization of historical and scientific knowledge with normative, real-world insight: because science is only composed of the individual values of the scientist, it cannot establish objective values. It can only be a forum for rational discourse over diverging interpretations [37; 60; 87; 88. 73–94]. The historian as the subject of historiography is incapable of recognizing 'what actually happened': 'Das Schicksal einer Kulturepoche, die vom Baum der Erkenntnis gegessen hat, ist es, wissen zu müssen, daß wir den Sinn des Weltgeschehens nicht aus dem noch so vervollkommneten Ergebnis seiner Durchforstung ablesen können, sondern ihn selbst zu schaffen imstande sein müssen' ("The fate of a cultural epoch that has tasted from the Tree of Knowledge is to know that we cannot glean the meaning of world affairs from examining them, however minutely; we must be able to generate it for ourselves") [113. 154]. Because of its real-world conditioning, science is not oriented towards absolute knowledge but is part of a continuous process of revision and progress: 'Wissenschaftlich – überholt zu werden, ist – nicht nur unser aller Schicksal, sondern unser aller Zweck' ("For all of us, to become scientifically obsolete is not only inevitable, it is our purpose") [113. 592]. The historian no longer imparts normative values to guide our conduct; rather, he is an expert performing drudge work. His scientific work becomes a form of innerworldly asceticism [47].

In engaging with Nietzsche, Dilthey, Troeltsch and Weber, various disciplines attempted to solve the historicism problem during the 1920s and 1930s [5; 7]. The historian Otto Hintze wanted to dissociate historical and ethical knowledge to cancel out the relativizing effect of historicism on individual value standards [31]. In philosophy, Max Scheler paralleled historicism with Albert Einstein's theory of relativity. Martin Heidegger recognized in historicism only the "helplessness" ('Ratlosigkeit') of an "ahistorical" ('ungeschichtliche') historical science. Rather than enquire into the objectivity of historical knowledge, he raised the question of historical being [4; 116. 161–184]. In 1932 the ecclesiastical historian Karl Heussi, boldly summing up the discussion in Germany [52], defined historicism without recognizable reference to the history of the term as "the historiography of the period around 1900" ('die Geschichtsschreibung der Zeit um 1900') [52. 20]. Under the heading 'Krisis des Historismus' ("Crisis of Historicism"), he lamented that in Germany the belief in the possibility of objective historical research had been lost in the years after the First World War.

Several studies by Friedrich Meinecke [70] are of central importance for the historical field, especially his 1936 work on Die Entstehung des Historismus (Historism. The Rise of a New Historical Outlook) [69] (cf. [30; 58. 253–294; 88. 17–40, 95–136; 104]). Meinecke propagated a positive understanding of historicism that was to overcome the crisis of historical knowledge. He considered historicism to be a Weltanschauung, rather than a scientific concept: 'die Anwendung der in der großen deutschen Bewegung von Leibniz bis zu Goethes Tode gewonnenen neuen Lebensprinzipien auf das geschichtliche Leben' ("the application to historical life of the new principles of life gained in the great German movement from Leibniz to Goethe's death") [69. 2]. The rejection of static natural law, Meinecke claimed, the secularisation of medieval historiography based on theology and the reception of Neo-Platonic thought in the age of German Classicism shaped the development of a historical thought which clearly distanced itself from the Enlightenment and which initiated "one of the greatest intellectual revolutions ever experienced in Western thought" ('eine der größten geistigen Revolutionen, die das abendländische Denken erlebt hat') [69. 1]. Moreover, he continues, the emergence of historicism had been a genuinely German phenomenon, one of the "mighty deeds" ('Großtaten') of German intellect

[69. 2]. The specific achievement of historicism, according to Meinecke, was to link the concept of development with "individualising observation" ('individualisierende[r] Betrachtung'). Here, as in his classical work on the Idee der Staatsräson (Machiavellism. The Doctrine of raison d'état and its Place in Modern History), Meinecke produced a synthesis of intellectual and political history. He did not address the issue of the relativization of values, preferring instead to observe, 'Wir sehen in ihm die höchste bisher erreichte Stufe in dem Verständnis menschlicher Dinge und trauen ihm eine echte Entwicklungsfähigkeit auch für die um uns und vor uns liegenden Probleme der Menschheitsgeschichte zu' ("We see in it [i.e. Historicism] the highest stage of understanding of human affairs achieved so far and consider it capable also of a potential for development regarding the problems of humanity's history around and before us" [69. 4].

The detailed discussions surrounding the 'crisis of historicism' since the late 19th cent. by no means resulted in a clarification of the concept or its content. On the one hand, historicism was a synonym for relativism, objectivism, nihilism and positivism; on the other hand it was used to characterize modern historical sciences, their methods and achievements.

D. MODERN INVESTIGATIONS INTO THE HISTORY OF HISTORIOGRAPHY

German historical studies after 1945 focused, above all, on Meinecke's concept of historicism. Hardly any notice was taken of discussions in other countries. In the 1960s and 1970s a new generation of historians distanced themselves from a historicism they viewed as a continuation of the tradition of historical studies in Germany, that had defended the Bismarckian national state. But even those critics who were calling for a 'historical discipline beyond historicism' that would seek contemporary relevance, and who were championing a historical social science, dealt with Meinecke's historicism ex negativo [58; 74; 115]. Historicism for them became a cipher for the methodological innovations of German historical studies in the 19th cent. and its political entanglements in the politics of the time. In their view, a critical history of historiography has the function, therefore, of finding those ideological components of historicism that in the 19th and 20th cents. helped bring about the political instrumentalization of historical studies. In his 1975 essay [84], Thomas Nipperdey answered the political and methodological objections that historians leaning towards social sciences raised against historicism. He noted that historicism, liberated from the specific political and philosophical conditions of its origins, could indeed be the basis for a modern form of historical studies. According to Nipperdey, historicism is "a new method in the cognitive handling of the past that reveals its uniqueness, 'individuality', 'development' and interactive conditionality. For this purpose, it makes use of source criticism and access through 'understanding'" ('eine neue Methode im erkennenden Umgang mit Vergangenem, die das Eigen-recht und die tiefe Andersartigkeit des Vergangenen, seine 'Individualität', seine 'Entwicklung', seine wech-selseitige Bedingtheit ans Licht stellt und sich dazu der Quellenkritik und des Zugriffs des 'Verstehens' bedient') [85. 498].

Beginning in the 1980s, scholars in the history of historiography have increasingly turned to the phenom-enon of historicism. The sometimes polemical debates (cf. *Rechtshistorisches Journal* 11, 1992, 54–66; 12, 1993, 585–597) have repeatedly questioned the role of historicism in laying the groundwork for 'modern' his-torical studies: is it an obsolete or an innovative scien-tific paradigm? Based on Thomas S. Kuhn's [61] reflec-tions on the philosophy of science, Jörn Rüsen devel-oped the model of the 'disciplinary matrix' and applied it to historicism. The actual contribution of historicism in establishing historical studies as an independent dis-cipline, he claims, lies in the "view of the historical method as a system of rules for research" ('[die] Auf-fassung von der historischen Methode als Regelsystem der Forschung'). Method, in historicism, is "a form of presentation that combines facts gained through source criticism into historical contexts" ('eine Form der Dar-stellung, die die quellenkritisch ermittelten Tatsachen zu historischen Zusammenhängen verbindet') [59. 48f.] (cf. [98]), i.e. a method that "understands [his-tory] through research" ('forschend versteht'), as Droy-sen had put it earlier. Horst Walter Blanke, building on Rüsen, sought to separate the age of historicism from neighbouring periods by demonstrating its structural homogeneity; the last 250 years of the history of histo-riography in his view were characterized by the three successive periods of 'Enlightenment history', 'histori-cism' and 'historical social sciences' [8]. For Rüsen and Blanke historicism is an antiquated paradigm. By con-trast, Ulrich Muhlack was inspired by Nipperdey and Croce. He believed "that the genesis of modern histori-cal studies in Germany coincides with the emergence of what has been termed historicism since the turn of the 18th to the 19th cent." ('daß die Entstehung der moder-nen Geschichtswissenschaft in Deutschland mit der Entstehung des sogenannten Historismus seit der Wende vom 18. zum 19. Jahrhundert zusammenfällt') [78; 79. 7]. Historicism, according to Muhlack, ought to be clearly distinguished from the historiography of Humanism and the Enlightenment; it led to the auto-nomy of historical cognition, the complete seculariza-tion of the study of historical causes and the loss of the distinction between general and individual insight.

It is obvious that the current discussion is still colou-red by Meinecke's concept of historicism [89; 103]. Controversy surrounds not the fact that historicism represents a deep caesura in the development of modern historical studies, but the evaluation of this phenom-enon. In terms of its theoretical and problem-historical aspects, this overflowing debate has hardly been settled but certainly expanded by three diverging approaches: with good reason the importance of Enlightenment his-toriography for the creation of modern historical stu-dies has been pointed out. Not only has a series of stu-dies shown multiple lines of continuity [8; 11; 12], it also discovered among the achievements of the Enlight-enment the autonomization of history as a discipline, its methodological understanding and the presence of 'his-torical' categories such as 'individuality' and 'develop-ment' [15; 67; 98]. Secondly, Otto Gerhard Oexle and Anette Wittkau have examined the historicism debates in other cultural disciplines largely neglected by histori-cal scholars. Referring back to Max Weber, they were able to provide a new transdisciplinary and problem-historical perspective [88; 116] (cf. [99; 105]). Oexle moreover suggests two separate phases of historicism: 'Historicism I', which describes the philosophical and epistemological debates in the late 19th and first third of the 20th cent. regarding historical knowledge and the cognitive formation of values, and 'Historicism II', which refers to the "idealistic foundation of historical studies" ('[die] idealistische Begründung der Geschichtswissenschaft') in the 19th cent. [88. 31]. Lastly, Wolfgang Hardtwig questioned historicism's claim to objectivity and noted the religious and theo-logical components in the concept of history [47] (cf. also [54; 88]). The recent attempt by Frank R. Ankers-mit to re-define, through the function of language, the role of historicism in the contemporary discourse on the theory of history has not been received without criti-cism [1; 2; 89. 389–410] (cf. [56]).

E. HISTORICISM AND CLASSICAL STUDIES

Within the history of historiography, the importance of Classical Studies for the creation of a critical histori-cal discipline that was termed 'historicism' (after Fried-rich Meinecke) cannot be over-stated. Given the pro-minent role Antiquity played in forming the self-image of the academically trained élites of German Classicism and → NEO-HUMANISM, it is no wonder that many his-torians and Classical scholars sought to find in Classical subjects answers to the question of possible conditions for objective knowledge in history. In doing so, they applied the principles of hermeneutics – a discipline newly established by them – to the philosophical and historical analysis of ancient texts [16; 34]. Under the impression of the French Revolution, Greek Antiquity became the most exalted historical showcase for reason-based individuality. In this context, the 'histori-cal hiatus' is negligible because Classical Studies in many ways, both in terms of content and methodology, relied on the work accomplished by scholars of Anti-quity during Humanism and the Enlightenment [12. 167–186; 71; 73; 76; 79; 82; 118] (cf. also [45; 48; 100]). The critical historical method of historical stu-dies was especially shaped by critical biblical studies and Classical philology. Classical scholars described their methodology and philological criticism in count-less lectures. The contribution of Classical Studies to the development of a modern understanding of history and to a scientific methodology is no less significant than the contribution of contemporary philosophy, especially that of Friedrich Schleiermacher [35].

Christian Gottlob Heyne and Friedrich August Wolf are considered the *heros ktistes* (founder- heroes) of a new type of Classical Studies committed to understanding and explaining the ancient world. The aestheticizing enthusiasm for, particularly Greek Antiquity, rational criticism as already developed by the Enlightenment, the apotheosis of the creative individual and an educational concept borrowed from New Humanism, all formed the basis for a theory of the philological method and the interpretation of the ancient tradition. Friedrich August Wolf practised source criticism in his *Prolegomena ad Homerum* (Halle 1795), in which the unity of the Homeric text was radically questioned. In his lectures and then in his essay *Darstellung der Althertums-Wissenschaft nach Begriff, Umfang, Zweck und Werth* ('Outline of Classical Studies According to Definition, Extent, Purpose and Value') (= Id., *Kleine Schriften*, vol. 2, Halle 1869, 808–895), he also developed the beginnings of a comprehensive concept of Classical Studies, integrating a number of related fields. At the same time, Wolf contributed to the emergence of Classical philology as a historical study of Antiquity interested in a historical understanding of its subjects [117]. Following Wolf's model, Barthold Georg Niebuhr, in his *Römische Geschichte* (vol. 1–2: 1811/12; 21827–1830; vol. 3: 1832), reconstructed Rome's early history from literary fragments. He fused "all the common, hardly 'original' views of his age into a new systematic whole" ('all die gängigen, an sich alles andere als 'originellen' Ansichten seiner Zeit zu einem neuen, systematischen Ganzen') [112. 18] (cf. [22. 26–49; 51; 72]) and founded an autonomous historical science based on epistemological insight [49. 65–96; 77]. In his lecture Encyklopädie und Methodologie der philologischen Wissenschaften (abridged trans: *On Interpretation and Criticism*), given 26 times and edited posthumously [14; 53], Wolf's pupil August Boeckh redefined the scope of the material eligible for scrutiny: no longer was it to be solely a matter of textual evidence; instead the entirety of Greek and Roman remains were now eligible to be examined by the historical discipline of philology. Its objective was "the recognition of that which the human spirit has produced, i.e., that which has been recognized" ('das Erkennen des vom menschlichen Geist Producierten, d.h. des Erkannten') [14. 10]. Thus, Boeckh with the support of the Preußische Akademie der Wissenschaften turned to collecting Greek inscriptions (*Corpus Inscriptionum Graecarum*, 1825ff.) and used them to examine the national economy of the Athenians (2 vols., Berlin 1817; 3 vols., Berlin ²1851; ³1886). His pupil Karl Otfried Müller wrote a *Prolegomena zu einer wissenschaftlichen Mythologie* (Göttingen 1825; Engl. *Introduction to a Scientific System of Mythology*) to demonstrate the link between religion and art [20]. The new ideal of totality provided access to new resources and demanded new methods. A canon of ancillary historical disciplines was formed to serve historical understanding rather than antiquarian preferences. The scientification of 'antiquities' went hand-in-hand with the polemic against older compilations and with the systematic recording of material remains under key aspects [36].

Boeckh's doctrine of science, which aimed to permanently restructure Classical philology, strongly influenced historical studies including the theoretical discussion within the discipline, as is evident in Droysen's *Historik* (*Outline of the Principles of History*). This pupil of Boeckh understood history to be that which his teacher defined as philology: historical knowledge *per se*. Boeckh was also of great significance for Droysen in methodological terms. This is demonstrated by Droysen's *Materialien zur Geschichte Alexanders des Großen* ('Resources on the History of Alexander the Great') in the appendix of the second edition of *Geschichte des Hellenismus* ('History of Hellenism') (Gotha 1877): the critical analysis of the sources is dependent on the historical interests that guide it.

The historistic age of Classical Studies brought about internal differentiation and specialization. Ancient history split from both universal history and Classical philology. Archaeology was founded as an independent discipline [44; 66. 36–115]. However, this development was not without opposition. Initially, Gottfried Hermann, Karl Lachmann, August Immanuel Becker and Friedrich Ritschl initially voiced their general criticism of the rather broad scope of Classical philology as defined by Boeckh [53. 101–114; 83; 111]. The conflict between the 'philology of words' and the 'philology of objects' was ignited by a fundamental difference in their understanding of language. While 'Textphilologen' propagated the concept of a formal science focussing on linguistic aspects, 'Sachphilologen' felt responsible for the "totality of facts" ('Totalität der Thatsachen)' [14. 263f.]. The dispute about the *cognitio totius antiquitatis* would continue throughout the history of Classical Studies under the sign of historicism. However, efforts to develop a scientific theory and a universal methodology died down after the 1840s [13]. Classical scholars increasingly confined themselves to the highly specialized operations of source criticism and hermeneutic understanding. Formidable results were in fact achieved in this area. Colossal cooperative enterprises – *corpora*, *monumenta* and *thesauri* – made the legacy of the ancient word accessible and set the standard for other fields [95] (→ ACADEMY). An analytical historical empiricism proudly raised its head. Belief in progress and scientific optimism were the characteristic features of professionalized Classical Studies at universities and academies. The exemplary work of Theodor Mommsen institutionalized the totality ideal and the philological method for historical studies. It followed his programmatic call, "to put the archives of the past in order" ('die Archive der Vergangenheit zu ordnen') [75. 37]. Activity within the field of Classical Studies rose to an almost industrial scale and impressively confirmed the effectiveness of the critical historical method. Heuristics and interpretation, however, parted company, and the scholar became a labourer and drudge [75. 196]. This function of the researcher was established in academic practice by Theodor Mommsen before Max Weber legitimized it in theory. The author of the *Römische Geschichte* (3 vols., Leipzig; Berlin 1854–1856), which reflected the political experience of the 1848 Revolution, would later declare that the historian was an artist rather than a scientist [75. 11] (cf. [50; 68; 119]). The rapid historicization of Classical Studies necessarily resulted in a departure from the earlier normative and aestheticizing perspective. The privileged position of – especially Greek – Antiquity was given up and the ancient world became an equal among other historical formations.

As in other disciplines, a sense of crisis also spread through the various fields of Classical Studies at the end of the 19th and early in the 20th century. Critical voices denounced a science that in their eyes only produced epigones and was in danger of fragmentation. Jacob Burckhardt's and Friedrich Nietzsche's influence [66. 124–133], in conjunction with older concepts, led to discussions about the problem of the relativism of values and the correlation between science and life. Critics were severely questioning the legitimacy of a Classical discipline that saw its purpose in positivistic productivity, and whose self-declared scientific approach undermined the normative function of Antiquity. Calls for comprehensive reconstruction and contemporary synthesis grew louder. Within Classical Studies itself, Hermann Usener outlined the new model of a comparative type of cultural studies that was to advance from historical facts to insights of universal validity, while Ulrich von Wilamowitz-Moellendorff defined philology as a historical discipline that must understand and bring to life Greek and Roman culture in its true nature and all its expressions. This required the double effort not only to collect sources but to interpret them as well [62] (cf. [19; 72]). Eduard Meyer presented ancient history as an integral part of universal history [18; 21. 45–60; 22. 286–333]. In historical theology, another crowning achievement of historicism, a broad movement arose early in the 20th cent. against the historicization of the Gospel, of Church history and of the history of Church doctrine – to which Adolf von Harnack dedicated his life's work [96]. Rather than a historical cultural study of Christianity, the call was for a systematic normative discipline [41; 86]. In numerous publications, Classical scholars sought to entrench Antiquity as relevant medium of education and to give clear guidance to a society shaken by political, social and cultural changes [63; 66. 133–142]. And yet, scholarship was in fact barely affected by the 'crisis of historicism'. An abundance of dissertations in Classical Studies remained dedicated exclusively to source criticism [28]. The scientific community continued to applaud finely detailed work on texts and monuments.

The First World War intensified the identity crisis of Classical Studies. A number of new approaches attempted to overcome this historicism or 'historical positivism' [33]. Although the term 'historicism' never received any theoretical foundation, even the various disciplines of Classical Studies were forced to confront the urgent question of how to bridge the gap between science and life. The majority of the concepts developed under this Leitmotiv shared a desire to re-establish Antiquity as a meaningful historical epoch but rejected a return to historicism. Adepts of the Stefan George Circle, who glorified 'monumentalistic history' and turned against the 'historical malaise', sought their salvation in the scienza nuova ideology [46]. Classical philologists remembered Friedrich Nietzsche's 'philology of the future' and defended him against Wilamowitz' verdict. Models borrowed from New Humanism took the place of historical Classical Studies. The term Klassik ('Classicism') was intensely debated. For example, Werner Jaeger founded with his Third Humanism a concept of Classicism 'beyond historicism' that focussed on Greek Antiquity. Its content was determined by the term paideia, and it defined history as a teleological process [17]. Archaeology observed and analyzed style and together with Classical philology searched for 'inner form' and 'spiritual' substance. Historical understanding of individuality and the 'spirit' was also demanded in ancient historical studies. The criticism levelled against a supposedly degenerate historicism, against the epigonal character of purely positivistic scholarly research and the absolutization of individualistic subjectivity increased in the 1920s and 1930s. A deep-rooted sense of crisis, the rivalry between the prevailing scientific and political, anti-democratic and anti-parliamentarian ideologies, the declining significance of Antiquity and – last, but not least – an anti-historistic reflex caused some scholars to absorb fascist and national socialist ideologemes in their search for a new image of Antiquity [64; 80; 81; 114]. Classical Studies, with its historical orientation, demanding strict objectivity and rationality (at least in theory), did not conform to the irrationalistic cultural criticism of National Socialist historical theory. The undertaking to restructure the content and methods of the Classical disciplines and to demonstrate the cultural and educational relevance of Antiquity was terminated rather abruptly by National Socialism and the Second World War.

Since 1945 Classical scholars in Europe and North America have been engaged in efforts to define their position between 'historistic' factual research and (post-) structuralist models of interpretation, between contemporary relevance, adherence to scientific methods and a sense of crisis. In this way, the second half of the 20th cent. has experienced both the vindication and condemnation of historicism. Appeals for the reconciliation of historicism and Humanism have also abounded. For the self-image and reassurance of Classical Studies, it is essential that the phenomenon of historicism be addressed from the perspective of Classical Studies, in terms of the history of the discipline and its issues. This is a desideratum.

→ ACADEMY; → BÖCKH-HERMANN DISPUTE; → HISTORISCHE RECHTSSCHULE; → HISTORIOGRAPHICAL METHODS; → PHILOLOGICAL METHODS; → UNIVERSITY

1 F. R. ANKERSMIT, Historiography and Postmodernism, in: History and Theory 28, 1989, 137–153   2 Id., Historicism: An Attempt at Synthesis, in: History and Theory 34, 1995, 143–161   3 R. ARON, Introduction à la philosophie de l'histoire. Essai sur les limites de l'objectivité historique, 1938 (repr. 1986), (Engl. G. J. IRWIN (trans.), Introduction to the Philosophy of History, 1976, 1961)   4 CH. R. BAMBACH, Heidegger, Dilthey, and the Crisis of Historicism, 1995   5 P. BAHNERS, Kritik und Erneuerung – Der Historismus bei Franz Schnabel, in: Tel Aviver Jahrbuch für deutsche Geschichte 25, 1996, 117–153   6 M. BASSLER (ed.), New Historicism. Literaturgeschichte als Poetik der Kultur, 1995   7 W. BIALAS, G. RAULET (eds.), Die Historismusdebatte in der Weimarer Republik, 1996   8 H. W. BLANKE, Historiographiegeschichte als Historik, 1991   9 Id. (ed.), Transformation des Historismus. Wissenschaftsorganisation und Bildungspolitik vor dem Ersten Weltkrieg, 1994   10 Id., Die Kritik der Alexanderhistoriker bei Heyne, Heeren, Niebuhr und Droysen, in: Storia della storiografia 13, 1988, 106–127   11 H. W. BLANKE, D. FLEISCHER (eds.), Theoretiker der deutschen Aufklärungshistorie, 2 vols., 1990   12 H. W. BLANKE, J. RÜSEN (eds.), Von der Aufklärung zum Historismus. Zum Strukturwandel des historischen Denkens, 1984   13 H. W. BLANKE, D. FLEISCHER, J. RÜSEN, Historik als akademische Praxis, in: Dilthey-Jahrbuch 1, 1983, 182–255   14 A. BOECKH, Encyklopädie und Methodologie der philologischen Wissenschaften, Leipzig 1877 (²1886 = Darmstadt 1966) (Engl. J. P. PRITCHARD (trans.), On Interpretation and Criticism, 1968)   15 H. E. BÖDEKER, G. G. IGGERS, J. B. KNUDSEN, P. H. REILL (eds.), Aufklärung und Geschichte. Studien zur deutschen Geschichtswissenschaft im 18. Jahrhundert, 1986   16 M. BOLLACK, H. WISMANN (eds.), Philologie und Hermeneutik im 19. Jahrhundert. Philologie et herméneutique en 19ème siècle, vol. 2, 1983   17 W. M. CALDER III (ed.), Werner Jaeger Reconsidered, 1990   18 W. M. CALDER III, A. DEMANDT (eds.), Eduard Meyer. Leben und Leistung eines Universalhistorikers, 1990   19 W. M. CALDER III, H. FLASHAR, TH. LINDKEN, Wilamowitz nach 50 Jahren, 1985   20 W. M. CALDER III, R. SCHLESIER (eds.), Zwischen Rationalismus und Romantik. Karl Otfried Müller und die antike Kultur, 1998   21 L. CANFORA, Politische Philologie. Altertumswissenschaften und moderne Staatsideologien, 1995   22 K. CHRIST, Von Gibbon zu Rostovtzeff. Leben und Werk führender Althistoriker der Neuzeit, ³1989   23 Id., Römische Geschichte und deutsche Geschichtswissenschaft, 1982   24 Id., Hellas. Griechische Geschichte und deutsche Geschichtswissenschaft, 1999   25 R. G. COLLINGWOOD, The Idea of History, 1946 (rev. ed. by J. VAN DER DUSSEN, 1993)   26 B. CROCE, La storia come pensiero e come azione, 1938, ⁶1954 (Engl. SYLVIA SPRIGGE (trans.), History as the Story of Liberty)   27 W. DILTHEY, Einleitung in die Geisteswissenschaften (1883), Gesammelte Schriften, vol. 1, ²1922 (Engl. R. A. MAKKREEL, F. RODI (eds.), Introduction to the Human Sciences, 1989)   28 H.-J. DREXHAGE, Deutschsprachige Dissertationen zur Alten Geschichte 1844–1978, 1980   29 J. G. DROYSEN, Historik, P. LEYH (ed.), 1977   30 M. ERBE (ed.), Friedrich Meinecke heute, 1981   31 Id., Das Problem des Historismus bei Ernst Troeltsch, Otto Hintze und Friedrich Meinecke, in: [43. 73–91]   32 K.-G. FABER, Ausprägungen des Historismus, in: HZ 228, 1979, 1–22   33 H. FLASHAR (ed.), Altertumswissenschaft in den 20er Jahren. Neue Fragen und Impulse, 1995   34 Id., K. GRÜNDER, A. HORSTMANN (eds.), Philologie und Hermeneutik im 19. Jahrhundert. Zur Geschichte und Methodologie der Geisteswissenschaften, vol. 1, 1979   35 H.-G. GADAMER, Wahrheit und Methode, ⁴1975 (Engl. J. WEINSHEIMER, D. G. MARSHALL (trans. & eds.), Truth and Method, ²1995)   36 W. GAWANTKA, Die Monumente reden. Realien, reales Leben, Wirklichkeit in der deutschen Alten Geschichte und Altertumskunde des 19. Jahrhunderts, in: W. M. CALDER III, J. COBET (eds.), Heinrich Schliemann nach 100 Jahren, 1990, 56–117   37 A. GERMER, Wissenschaft und Leben. Max Webers Antwort auf eine Frage Friedrich Nietzsches, 1994   38 P. GISEL (ed.), Historicisme et théologie chez Ernst Troeltsch, 1992   39 J. GLAUSER, A. HEITMANN (eds.), Verhandlungen mit dem New Historicism. Das Text-Kontext-Problem in der Literaturwissenschaft, 1999   40 F. W. GRAF, Ernst Troeltsch. Kulturgeschichte des Christentums, in: N. HAMMERSTEIN (ed.), Deutsche Geschichtswissenschaft um 1900, 1988, 131–152   41 Id., Geschichte durch Übergeschichte überwinden. Antihistorisches Geschichtsdenken in der protestantischen Theologie der 1920er Jahre, in: W. KÜTTLER et al. (eds.), Geschichtsdiskurs 4, 1997, 217–244   42 Id., H. RUDDIES (eds.), Ernst Troeltsch Bibliographie, 1982   43 Id. (eds.), Umstrittene Moderne. Die Zukunft der Neuzeit im Urteil der Epoche Ernst Troeltschs, 1987   44 A. GRAFTON, Polyhistor into Philolog. Notes on the Transformation of German Classical Scholarship 1780–1850, in: History of Universities 3, 1983, 159–192   45 Id., Defenders of Text. The Traditions of Scholarship in an Age of Science 1450–1800, 1991   46 C. GROPPE, Die Macht der Bildung. Das deutsche Bürgertum und der George-Kreis 1890–1933, 1997   47 W. HARDTWIG, Geschichtsreligion – Wissenschaft als Arbeit – Objektivität. Der Historismus in neuer Sicht, in: HZ 252, 1991, 1–32   48 F. HASKELL, History and its Images, 1994   49 A. HENTSCHKE, U. MUHLACK, Einführung in die Geschichte der Klassischen Philologie, 1972   50 A. HEUSS, Theodor Mommsen und das 19. Jahrhundert, 1956 (Repr. 1998)   51 Id., Barthold Georg Niebuhrs wissenschaftliche Anfänge, 1981   52 K. HEUSSI, Die Krisis des Historismus, 1932   53 A. HORSTMANN, Antike Theoria und moderne Wissenschaft. August Boeckhs Konzeption der Philologie, 1992   54 G. G. IGGERS, Ist es in der Tat in Deutschland früher zur Verwissenschaftlichung der Geschichte gekommen als in anderen europäischen Ländern?, in: W. KÜTTLER et al., Geschichtsdiskurs 2, 1994, 73–86   55 Id., Historicism: The History and Meaning of the Term, in: Journal of the History of Ideas 56, 1995, 129–152   56 Id., Comments on F.R. Ankersmit's Paper, 'Historicism: An Attempt at Synthesis', in: History and Theory 34, 1995, 162–167   57 Id., Historismus – Geschichte und Bedeutung eines Begriffs. Eine kritische Übersicht der neuesten Literatur, in: [103. 102–126]   58 Id., Deutsche Geschichtswissenschaft. Eine Kritik der traditionellen Geschichtsauffassung von Herder bis in die Gegenwart, ²1997 (Engl. The German Conception of History. The National Tradition of Historical Thought from Herder to the Present, 1968, rev. ed. 1983)   59 F. JAEGER, J. RÜSEN, Geschichte des Historismus. Eine Einführung,

1992   60 J. Kocka (ed.), Max Weber, der Historiker, 1986   61 Th. S. Kuhn, The Structure of Scientific Revolutions, ²1970   62 M. Landfester, Ulrich von Wilamowitz-Moellendorff und die hermeneutische Tradition des 19. Jahrhunderts, in: [34. 156–180]   63 Id., Humanismus und Gesellschaft im 19. Jahrhundert, 1988   64 V. Losemann, Nationalsozialismus und Antike. Studien zur Entwicklung des Faches Alte Geschichte 1933–1945, 1977   65 M. Mandelbaum, The Anatomy of Historical Knowledge, 1979   66 S. L. Marchand, Down from Olympus. Archaeology and Philhellenism in Germany 1750–1970, 1996   67 L. Marino, I Maestri della Germania, Göttingen 1770–1820, 1975   68 Chr. Meier, Das Begreifen des Notwendigen. Zu Theodor Mommsens 'Römischer Geschichte', in: R. Koselleck, H. Lutz, J. Rüsen (eds.), Formen der Geschichtsschreibung, 1982, 201–244   69 F. Meinecke, Entstehung des Historismus, Werke, vol. 3, ⁴1965 (Engl. J. E. Anderson (trans.), Historism. The Rise of a New Historical Outlook, 1972) 70 Id., Zur Theorie und Philosophie der Geschichte, Werke, vol. 4, ²1965   71 A. Momigliano, Ancient History and the Antiquarian (1950), in: Id., Studies in Historiography, 1966, 1–39 (= Contributo alla storia degli studi classici, 1955, 67–106)   72 Id., New Paths of Classicism in the Nineteenth Century, in: History and Theory, suppl. 21, 1982, 1–64   73 Id., The Classical Foundations of Modern Historiography, 1990   74 W. J. Mommsen, Die Geschichtswissenschaft jenseits des Historismus, ²1972 75 Th. Mommsen, Reden und Aufsätze, 1905 (repr. 1976)   76 U. Muhlack, Klassische Philologie zwischen Humanismus und Neuhumanismus, in: R. Vierhaus (ed.), Wissenschaft im Zeitalter der Aufklärung, 1985, 93–119   77 Id., Von der philologischen zu historischen Methode, in: Chr. Meier, J. Rüsen (eds.), Historische Methode (= Beiträge zur Historik 5), 1988, 154–180 78 Id., Bildung zwischen Neuhumanismus und Historismus, in: R. Koselleck (ed.), Bildungsbürgertum im 19. Jahrhundert, Teil II: Bildungsgüter und Bildungswissen (= Industrielle Welt 4), 1990, 80–105   79 Id., Geschichtswissenschaft im Humanismus und in der Aufklärung. Die Vorgeschichte des Historismus, 1991   80 B. Näf, Von Perikles zu Hitler? Die athenische Demokratie und die deutsche Althistorie bis 1945, 1986   81 Id. (ed.), Antike und Altertumswissenschaft in der Zeit von Nationalsozialismus und Faschismus, 2001   82 W. Nippel, 'Geschichte' und 'Altertümer'. Zur Periodisierung in der Althistorie, in: W. Küttler et al. (eds.), Geschichtsdiskurs 1, 1993, 307–316   83 Id., Philologenstreit und Schulpolitik. Zur Kontroverse zwischen Gottfried Hermann und August Böckh, in: W. Küttler et al. (eds.), Geschichtsdiskurs 3, 1997, 244–253   84 Th. Nipperdey, Historismus und Historismuskritik heute (1975), in: Id., Gesellschaft, Kultur, Theorie. Gesammelte Aufsätze zur neueren Geschichte, 1976, 59–73   85 Id., Deutsche Geschichte 1800–1866, 1983 (Engl. D. Nolan (trans.), Germany from Napoleon to Bismarck: 1800–1866, 1996) 86 K. Nowak, Historische oder dogmatische Methode? Protestantische Theologie im Jahrhundert des Historismus, in: W. Küttler et al. (eds.), Geschichtsdiskurs 3, 1997, 282–297   87 O. G. Oexle, 'Wissenschaft' und 'Leben'. Historische Reflexionen über Tragweite und Grenzen moderner Wissenschaft, in: Geschichte in Wissenschaft und Unterricht 41, 1990, 145–161   88 Id., Geschichtswissenschaft im Zeichen des Historismus. Studien zu Problemgeschichten der Moderne, 1996   89 Id., J. Rüsen (eds.), Historismus in den Kulturwissenschaften.

Geschichtskonzepte, historische Einschätzungen, Grundlagenprobleme, 1996   90 J. Ortega y Gasset, Sobre la razón histórica (1944), 1979 (Engl. P. W. Silver (trans.), Historical Reason, 1984)   91 R. Pfeiffer, Die Klassische Philologie von Petrarca bis Mommsen, 1982 (Engl. History of Classical Scholarship from 1300 to 1850, 1976)   92 K. R. Popper, The Poverty of Historicism, 1957 (²1960)   93 C. Prantl, Die gegenwärtige Aufgabe der Philosophie, Munich 1852   94 L. v. Ranke, Geschichte der romanischen und germanischen Völker von 1494–1514. Vorrede zur ersten Ausgabe (1824), Sämtliche Werke, vol. 33, Leipzig ²1874 (Engl. G. R. Dennis (trans.), History of the Latin and Teutonic nations (1494 to 1514), 1909)   95 St. Rebenich, Die Altertumswissenschaften und die Kirchenväterkommission an der Akademie: Theodor Mommsen und Adolf Harnack, in: J. Kocka (ed.), Die Königlich Preußische Akademie der Wissenschaften zu Berlin im Kaiserreich, 1999, 199–233 96 Id., Der alte Meergreis, die Rose von Jericho und ein höchst vortrefflicher Schwiegersohn: Mommsen, Harnack und Wilamowitz, in: K. Nowak, O. G. Oexle (eds.), Adolf von Harnack. Theologe, Historiker, Wissenschaftspolitiker, 2001, 39–69 (= Veröffentlichungen des Max-Planck-Institutes für Geschichte 161)   97 P. H. Reill, The German Enlightenment and the Rise of Historicism, 1971   98 J. Rüsen, Konfigurationen des Historismus. Studien zur deutschen Wissenschaftskultur, 1993   99 H. Schnädelbach, Geschichtsphilosophie nach Hegel. Die Probleme des Historismus, 1974   100 A. Schnapp, La conquête du passé, 1993 (Engl. The Discovery of the Past, 1996)   101 G. Scholtz, Historismus als spekulative Geschichtsphilosophie: Christlieb Julius Braniß (1792–1873), 1973   102 Id., s.v. Historismus, Historizismus, in: HWPh 3, 1974, 1141–1147   103 Id. (ed.), Historismus am Ende des 20. Jahrhunderts. Eine internationale Diskussion, 1997   104 E. Schulin, Das Problem der Individualität. Eine kritische Betrachtung des Historismuswerkes von Friedrich Meinecke, in: HZ 197, 1963, 102–133 (= Id., Traditionskritik und Rekonstruktionsversuch. Studien zur Entwicklung von Geschichtswissenschaft und historischem Denken, 1979, 97–116)   105 V. Steenblock, Transformationen des Historismus, 1991   106 H. Stuart, Consciousness and Society, 1979   107 E. Troeltsch, Der Historismus und seine Probleme, 1922 (Repr. 1961) (Engl. Historicism and its Problems: Selections, 1922)   108 Id., Die Krisis des Historismus, in: Die Neue Rundschau 33,1, 1922, 572–590   109 Id., Der Historismus und seine Überwindung. Fünf Vorträge, F. v. Hügel (ed.), 1924 (Engl. Christian Thought, Its History and Application, 1957)   110 R. Vierhaus, Rankes Begriff der historischen Objektivität, in: R. Koselleck et al. (eds.), Objektivität und Parteilichkeit in der Geschichtswissenschaft (= Beiträge zur Historik 1), 1977, 63–76   111 E. Vogt, Der Methodenstreit zwischen Hermann und Böckh und seine Bedeutung für die Geschichte der Philologie, in: [34. 103–121]   112 G. Walther, Niebuhrs Forschung, 1993   113 M. Weber, Gesammelte Aufsätze zur Wissenschaftslehre, ³1968 (⁶1985)   114 C. Wegeler, '... wir sagen ab der internationalen Gelehrtenrepublik'. Altertumswissenschaft und Nationalsozialismus, 1996   115 H.-U. Wehler, Geschichte als Historische Sozialwissenschaft, ³1983   116 A. Wittkau, Historismus. Zur Geschichte des Begriffs und des Problems, ²1994   117 F. A. Wolf, Studien. Dokumente. Bibliographie, 1999   118 H. Wrede, Die Entstehung der Archäologie und das Einsetzen der neuzeitlichen Geschichtsbetrachtung, in: W. Küttler et al. (eds.), Geschichtsdiskurs 2, 1994, 95–119   119 A. Wucher, Theodor Mommsen. Geschichtsschreibung und Politik, ²1968.

STEFAN REBENICH

II. Art History
A. Introduction B. Definitions, Assessments C. Painting D. Architecture E. Sculpture

A. Introduction
In Art History, historicism is not precisely defined in terms of period and content. The relationship to other chronological and stylistic phases such as Classicism and Realism can only be imprecisely stated because of multiple overlaps.

B. Definitions, Assessments
As a term, historicism entered the historiography of art at a later date though important aspects were already mentioned in the late 18th cent. (imitation of past periods, dependence on Antiquity, pluralism of styles, longing for creative novelty). After contemporary art historians each time acknowledged the fundamental dependence of the diversity of art on history while initially proclaiming the superiority of Antiquity (J.J. Winckelmann, 1755 [12]); A. Hirt, 1809 [5] and 1822 [6]; Chr.L. Stieglitz, 1792 [9] and 1801 [10]), a broad acceptance of reference to past ages, a "free and independent browsing and emotional identification" ('freies, selbstständiges Umschauen und Hineinfühlen)' took place (F.Th. Vischer, 1854 [11. 482]). Cornelius Gurlitt in his overview of the 19th cent. still looked favourably on its variety but emphasized the turn away from Antiquity: 'Das Wort Marathon regt uns nicht mehr auf' ("The word Marathon no longer excites us") [33. 185]. Max Schmid's art history [61] and M. Osborn in A. Springer's handbook of 1907 were already negative towards this development, though the latter did not speak of historicism but, taking up an older usage, of *Historienkunst* ('historical art') [52. 226]. Eduard Hildebrandt's 1931 critique was harsher: 'Auflösung', 'Abstieg', 'Zerfall', 'Verdorren' ("dissolution", "decline", "decay", "withering") [42]. In 1938, H. Beenken, when attempting a first comprehensive definition of historicism in architecture, used the term *Krankheit* ('malaise') because he saw it as an inability to detach oneself from the past [13]. Nikolaus Pevsner also adhered to this judgement in 1961 [55]. In 1970 W. Götz developed a new definition. Parts of his specifications were taken from historical studies (F. Meinecke), such as the description of historicism as a *Gesinnung* ('disposition') and *Eklektismus* ('eclecticism') as its method. He differentiated historicism from *Nachleben* (roughly, 'influence') and tradition and proclaimed: 'Historismus in der Kunstgeschichte heißt: Kunst im Dienste einer Weltordnung, einer Staatsidee, einer Weltanschauung, die aus der Geschichte programmatisch ihre Denkmodelle und Formmodelle beziehen' ("historicism in art history means: art in the service of a

world order, a state idea, a world view – all of which programmatically derive their conceptual and formal models from history") [31. 211]. Especially W. Hardtwig attributed the generality of this definition to the concreteness of the late 18th and 19th cents. Following R. Koselleck, he again pointed to the period's fundamentally new understanding of this historical concreteness: the loss of the normative force of exempla, permanent reversibility of history, relativization through history, optimization of its patterns, arbitrariness of the reversions [38]. Otto Gerhard Oexle, referring to W. Hofmann, emphasized historicism as a period term in art history [51]. Recently, the term has come to be used in art history for the period from about 1770 to 1914, and the pluralism of styles is viewed as its decisive feature, as for example at the major exhibition in Vienna in 1996 [27]. The apparently unambiguous phenomenon of → Classicism is largely treated as an independent concept. Classicism only became part of historicism with the loss of its dominance around 1840.

C. Painting
In France, the scene was dominated by the École des Beaux Arts, with its training in drawing based on Ancient sculptures, and the Academie à Rome. At the annual competition for the Grand Prix de Rome, Antiquity-related tasks were often posed but not preferred over religious topics [32]. Recipients of the Rome Scholarship had to submit only few ancient topics as mandatory works. Thus, a reconstruction of the inventory of the Musée du Luxembourg in Paris, with its collection of works by accredited contemporary painters, shows that in 1874, out of a total of 240 works, only 29 are listed as having a Classical reference [50]. Painters could have success with depictions of the decline of Rome (Th. Couture, 1847), and with the dramatically touching (L. Gerôme, *The Death of Caesar*, 1867), erotic (A. Cabanel, *The Birth of Venus*, 1863) or ancient genre scenes (L. Gerôme, *The Slave Market in Rome*, 1884) [60]. Stylistic orientation was drawn from Italian and Flemish models of the 16th and 17th cents. or from new realistic techniques. The criticism of Antiquity in → Caricatures could be harsh (H. Daumier, after 1841). Classical themes taken from Greek mythology, Roman history and allegory were widespread in murals – especially at cultural institutions. Works by P. Puvis de Chavannes in the museums of Marseilles (1869), Amiens (1882), Lyon (1886), Rouen (1891) and in Boston (Public Library, 1861) are worthy of note [28]. Eugène Delacroix was commissioned to paint allegorical and literary scenes from Antiquity in politically important buildings (Paris, Palais Bourbon, 1833/1847; Paris, City Hall, Hercules cycle, 1851). The large number of American painters in Paris led to Antiquity-themed allegorical murals in American public buildings, but in non-commissioned painting Antiquity played a subordinate role [68].

In Germany lengthy phases of drawing according to ancient models (→ Cast; Cast collections) [14] no

Fig. 1: Karl Theodor v. Piloty, *The Assassination of Caesar*. Painting, 1865.
Niedersächsisches Landesmuseum Hannover

Fig. 2: Arnold Böcklin, *Triton and Nereid*. Painting, 1874.
Bayerische Staatsgemäldesammlungen, Schack-Galerie, Munich

longer served to copy those models; they were a general means of practising drawing skills. After 1840, the representation of history was one of the most important tasks [35], with a preference for national and religious history, e.g., at the Academies in Munich and Düsseldorf, where Antiquity played no major role in large historical paintings, as a genre or as a stylistic pattern (E. Bendemann, *Sacrifice of Iphigenia*, 1867). Theoreticians like Vischer supported these developments with ideas that sought to justify these tendencies from within the realm of art itself, claiming that "the materials of ancient history are less picturesque than those of the Middle and Modern Ages" ('die Stoffe der alten Geschichte [sind] weniger malerisch als die der mittleren und neueren Zeit') and that the Near East was especially well suited [11. 398]. Karl von Piloty, Munich, was a master of the empathetic, dramatizing, personalizing painting of highly distinguished historical subjects. Antiquity took a backseat to representations of recent history (*Death of Caesar*, 1865, fig. 1; *Death of Alexander the Great*). Piloty's pupil H. Makart replaced emotion with a Baroque-style staging that suggested fullness of life, even in death (*Triumph of Ariadne*, 1873; *Death of Cleopatra*, 1876). By contrast, A. Böcklin found in the concentration on the lower castes of Greek mythology an area in which gender conflicts, freedom and obligation could be presented in a playfully ambiguous manner (*Triton and Nereid*, 1874, fig. 2; *Playing in the Waves*, 1883) [46]. Max Klinger took over Böcklin's cast of characters, articulated certain aspects more explicitly (*Triton and Nereid*, 1895) and with his graphic cycles offered sometimes ironic-critical manipulations of the fixed structures of ancient mythology and literature (*Deliverances of Sacrificial Victims Told in Ovid and Brahms-Phantasie*, 1879; *Amor and Psyche*, 1880). Otto Greiner and F. von Stuck with their fauns and centaurs showed seemingly untroubled images of Antiquity but were also able to depict ambiguity pregnant with meaning (F. von Stuck, *The Sphinx*, 1895). As early as 1914 R. Hamann characterized as 'high life painters' artists such as A. von Keller, who refined ancient myths into coquettish images rife with sexual allusions (*Empress Faustina*, 1882; *Judgment of Paris*, 1891 and 1905) [36]. A wholly different approach had already been evident in A. Feuerbach's treatment of ancient themes: pathos, severity in structure, restrained and veiled colours, encryption of persons and themes all characterized his paintings, some of which were executed in large format (*Iphigenia*, 1862 and 1871; *Medea*, 1870; *The Symposium of Plato*, in various details following Roman antiquities, 1869 and 1873). Historical subjects with a Christian theme set in Antiquity often received a medieval mood through accompanying cast (angels) and costumes (E. von Gebhardt, *Lazarus Raised from Death*, 1896). In Germany, Antiquity also held an important position in mural painting. Museums, academies, universities and *Gymnasien* were furnished with literary and historical cycles. Personifications and allegories mostly appeared in an ancient guise, while depictions of contemporary history in ancient costume declined. The *Life of Emperor Wilhelm I* on the occasion of his 90th birthday on the Academy building in Berlin, painted as a frieze, showed everyone in ancient costume (F. Geselschap, 1886). Schinkel's illustrations of the development of culture in the Old Museum in Berlin (begun 1841) worked with specific mythological themes (*Kronos and the Stars*) but especially with allegories. Both were criticized because of the barely discernible reference to the present time [67]. Wilhelm von Kaulbach's gigantic murals with themes from world history in the stairwell of the New Museum in Berlin (1847/1865) reacted to this. *Homer and the Greeks* was only one of six pictures, though the only one offering an allegorization which eluded the concreteness of the historical moment depicted in the others. The *Destruction of Jerusalem* was declassicized by a Christianization of the iconographic apparatus [48]. Sequences with ancient references in the Kunstmuseum Düsseldorf (C. Gehrts, 1887/1897) and the Breslau Museum (H. Prell, 1894) are noteworthy. Representations of Antiquity were often a feature of the interior design of bourgeois private homes, such as the salons of the apartment palaces along Ringstraße in Vienna [45].

For Italy, the reader is directed to the large frescoes of exempla from Roman history by C. Maccari for the Senate in the Palazzo Madama, Rome (1881/1888) [26]. Antiquity assumed a special position in the paintings of the English Pre-Raphaelites and Symbolists. Especially women from the artists' personal environment were subjected to a demonization and in some cases eroticization when portrayed in ancient roles (D.G. Rossetti, *Proserpina*, 1877; *Venus Verticordia*, 1868; G.F. Watts, *Daphne*, 1870). The cycles of E. Burne-Jones (*Pygmalion*, 1868/1878; *Perseus*, 1875/1895) delivered psychologizing versions of the myth that were detached from traditional iconographic templates. However, no stylistic proximity to Antiquity was sought. Emerging in France in the 1860 and later in other European countries as well, open-air painting (Impressionism) rejected themes from the past almost completely (E. Degas, *Young Spartans Exercising*, 1860; A. Renoir, *Diana*, 1867; P. Cezanne, *Bathers*). Influenced by F. Nietzsche, L. Corinth in Germany created an often exuberant, tumultuous Antiquity (*The Childhood of Zeus*, 1905), which particularly served to enhance the effect of certain painterly problems (colour, composition). Irony served to break the authority of the myth.

D. ARCHITECTURE

The multiplicity of styles in landscape gardening since the 2nd half of the 18th cent. and the early appreciation of the Gothic provided a conspicuous stylistic pluralism which was combined with historical interpretative depth. In French architecture, the works on architectural history by Percier/Fontaine (1798) [8] and by Gailhabaud (1839) [3], and the instruction and pattern

Fig. 3: Gottfried Semper, Picture gallery (detail).
1847/56. Dresden. Picture Library Foto Marburg

books of J.N.L. Durand (after 1800) [1] offered a comprehensive set of patterns from almost all periods, which contrasted with the strictly Classical teaching of the École des Beaux Arts. Its new building (1834/1840) by F. Duban offered an astonishing example of historicism [70]. The style of a Renaissance palace of about 1480 was defended by Duban as a model of modern development since Antiquity. He illustrated this route in the courtyard with large spolia from the → GOTHIC period and the early and high French Renaissance, while original casts from Antiquity were set up in the inner courtyard of the new Palais d'Etudes. This concentrated display of architectural history, was rounded off in 1869 by Ch. Garnier's panegyric praising the optimizing role of stylistic pluralism [4]. He singled out Greek and Roman architecture as the ultimate models, as did the architects of the *Neo Grec* (H. Labrouste, L. Duc, L. Vaudoyer), who from 1830, together with Duban, were looking for new solutions that showed no formal link with Antiquity (Labrouste, Bibliothèque Sainte Geneviève, Paris, 1843/1850) [25]. Hector-Martin Lefuel's new Baroque parts of the Louvre and Garnier's Opera (Paris, 1861/1875) matched this overlying dynamic idea of an *architecture classique*. Training at the École des Beaux-Arts [49] and its Rome branch, with its required reconstruction drawings, encouraged the rehearsal of Roman models [57]. By contrast, Greek architecture was viewed with mistrust until the 1830s because of the irregularities in the temples at Paestum. Extensive borrowing from ancient architecture was rare in France. The many churches with columned porticoes that were built until 1850 fol-

lowed J. Chalgrin's Saint-Philippe-du-Roule in Paris (1768/1784) and, therefore, had a conservative appearance. Jacques-Ignace Hittorf's attempt to transfer the newly discovered ancient polychromy to ecclesiastical architecture (Saint-Vincent-de-Paul in Paris, 1830/1846) was successful only in isolated cases [71]. The various Palaces of Justice were among the few buildings that consistently exhibited ancient forms such as temple façades.

Unlike their French counterparts, the large group of American architects trained in Paris began to apply Classical forms with increasing frequency from the late 19th cent. onwards. The representational buildings of the Chicago World's Fair (1893) formed the starting point, and the native tradition since the late 18th cent. served as the foil (→ GREEK REVIVAL). This resulted in copies of ancient temples, such as the Parthenon for the exhibition building in Nashville (1896 and 1920), including the sculptures. In New York, the Public Library (J.M. Carrere, 1897/1911) displayed Antiquity in a Baroque mode, Pennsylvania Station (McKim, Mead, White, 1906/1910) followed Roman temples on the outside and thermal baths on the inside. The polychromy debate was reflected in a few isolated works (Madison Square Presbyterian Church in New York, McKim, Mead, White, 1906). Buildings such as the Philadelphia Museum of Art (Ch. Zantzinger, 1916/1928) and the Jefferson Memorial in Washington (J.R. Pope, 1924/1935) demonstrate how far Antiquity reached into the 20th cent. and how widely native models of the early Greek Revival were used alongside Roman ones [44].

Apart from Washington only Athens is probably as densely populated with ancient – here Greek – models among its public buildings. In this context, it is remarkable that H. Schliemann, of all people, had his Athens home built in the style of the Venetian Renaissance (E. Ziller, 1879). Earlier than in France, ancient architecture in Germany found a rival in Gothic architecture through the assertions that were being made in the fields of philosophy (Herder) and the philosophy of art (Schlegel, Hegel) regarding e.g. the validity of different periods and cultures. Gothic architecture was ranked highly for being organic, living and striving for 'infinity'; moreover it was national and Christian. The possibility of selecting styles was available from an early point in time. In 1815 L. von Klenze presented designs in Greek, Roman and Italian (Renaissance) styles for the → GLYPTOTHEK in Munich. It was eventually executed in Greek style (1816/1830), incorporating Renaissance forms. Schinkel's stylistic variations on the Werdersche Kirche in Berlin (1821/1830) are noteworthy. As in France, the Renaissance was perceived as a Classical style up to the 1820s. This was part of a synthetic way of thinking, which included the Gothic mode and especially occupied Schinkel, who in his designs for a national monument (1814) had a Gothic tower rise from a Doric temple. Even around 1835, he still thought that the best achievements of the Middle

Fig. 4:
J. Hibbert, Harris
Museum and Art
Gallery. 1882/93.
Preston

Ages should be called Greek, while Roman architecture should be seen as an impure style [56]. Schinkel's Academy of Architecture in Berlin (1831/1835) was a solution in which the vault inside could only be combined with the skeleton-like pillar construction through the massive use of covered iron anchors. The rejection of Antiquity by H. Hübsch (1828) provided an alternative that pointed towards the future [7]. For structural, material, climatic and social reasons Hüsch rejected the Greek model and, instead, demanded and built a vaulted architecture based on Roman, Romanesque and Renaissance models [6]. Gottfried Semper had similar reasons for his preference of the Renaissance, which he fused with strong ancient Roman traits (Dresden, Opera, 1838/1841). Despite the general proliferation of Neo-Renaissance, Neo-Gothic and Neo-Romanesque styles, displaced ancient forms such as aedicules, columned porticoes and caryatids still played a role (in Prussia as the so-called Schinkel School) [17]. From the middle of the century ancient temples clearly inspired the design of the National Gallery in Berlin (F. Stüler, H. Strack, 1865/1875), the Königsbau in Stuttgart (hall structure, arcades, Chr.F. Leins, 1855/1859), the theatre in Breslau (K.F. Langhans, 1864/1867) and the Alte Oper in Frankfurt am Main (R. Lucae, 1873/1880). Colonnades were used for the front sides of the stock exchange (F. Hitzig, 1859/1863) and the Reichsbank (Id., 1869/1876) in Berlin. Large buildings were fitted with imposing columned porticoes, resulting in Classical motifs being incorporated into Renaissance contexts, e.g. on the Reichstag in Berlin (P. Wallot, 1884/1894) and the Reichsgericht in Leipzig (L. Hoffmann, 1887/1896). The integration of Roman-style tri-

umphal arcs as a monumental façade motif, e.g. on G. Semper's Picture Gallery Old Masters in Dresden (1847/1856) [69] should also be noted (fig. 3). While the influential Deutsche Bauzeitung (1872, p. 183) categorically ruled out a strictly Hellenistic epistylar structure for the Berlin Reichstag, with the Parliament in Vienna (Th. von Hansen, 1874/1883), a structure came into being, which, with its central temple serving as an Austrian Hall of Fame, incorporated the Walhalla, and whose general architecture was intended to suggest self-determination after the Greek model. Even before 1900 (Munich, Villa Stuck, 1898; O. Wagner's plans in Vienna), a new tendency towards ancient models can be observed that by 1914 had developed into a broad reform movement. Paul Mebes's book Um 1800 [47] inspired buildings such as the Stadttheater in Dortmund (M. Dülfer, 1902/1904), Peter Behrens's German embassy in St. Petersburg (1911/12), the Pergamon Museum in Berlin (A. Messel, begun 1909), the Festival Building in Dresden-Hellerau (H. Tessenow, 1912) and the Austrian Pavilion at the Cologne exhibition of the Werkbund Exhibition in Cologne (J. Hoffmann, 1914).

The development in England and Scotland can be briefly summarized with reference to the Greek Revival. The flexibility of ancient building forms was limited in structural terms (vaults, spans), limiting their representational effect – despite the use of cast iron for the British Museum (R. Smirke, 1823/1847) and the spectacular Doric propylaea at Euston Station in London (P. Hardwick, 1835/1837). Thus, after 1830 London Clubs began using the Italian High Renaissance, which over the course of the decades became the main style for public buildings. In Scotland A. Thomson developed in

Fig. 5: Max Klinger, Cassandra. Marble, 1895.
Leipzig, *Museum der Bildenden Künste*

the 1850s to the 1870s a fairly independent Classicizing architecture; his aim – very much like Schinkel's – was to bring the ancient models to perfection rather than to copy them, to build as the Greeks would if they were building today [21]. His three imaginatively composed churches in Glasgow (United Presbyterian Churches, 1857, 1859, 1867) testify to this. The Egyptian Halls in Glasgow (1871/1873), a commercial building, is a first class design because of its incorporation of Ionic, Corinthian and Egyptian forms in conjunction with a façade consisting only of supports and glass. The mixture of Classicizing components and Renaissance elements is common. An extreme case is the Birmingham Town Hall (J.A. Hanson, 1832/1861), where a Corinthian peripteral temple stands on a round-arched Renaissance basement. For museums, columned porticoes of various orders were used more than once in a Baroque mode, thus at Oxford, Ashmolean Museum (C.R. Cockerell, 1841/1845). A late example the Harris Free Library, Museum and Art Gallery in Preston (J. Hibbert, 1882/1893, fig. 4), while the Mapping Art Gallery in Sheffield presents a more severe version (Flockton and Gibbs, 1887).

In Italian historicist architecture, borrowings from Antiquity only played a minor role while the Neo-Renaissance prevailed. In Rome the tobacco factory (A. Sarti, 1859/1863) and the church S. Antonio da Padova in Via Merulana (L. Carimini, 1888) can be named. In

particular, the use of monumental triumphal arches for façades should be noted, e.g. on the Galleria Vittorio Emanuele II in Milan (G. Mengoni, 1863/1867), the Aquarium in Rome (E. Bernich, 1885) and as a component of urban architecture in the Piazza Vittorio Emanuele II (today: della Repubblica) in Florence (1893/1895), each within a Neo-Renaissance context. In Rome the large-scale monument for Victor Emanuel II was built with a strongly Classicizing design in 1885/1911 (G. Sacconi) [8].

An interesting phenomenon deserves to be mentioned here: in Germany, and to some extent in Italy as well, crematoria were mostly built in Classical forms, while in Italy, and less often in Germany, cemetery buildings were erected in the shape of Classicizing temples and colonnades. Examples of crematoria: Gotha (Ionic, 1878), Heidelberg (Doric, 1891), Chemnitz (Doric, 1906) and Milan (Doric, 1876/80). Cemetery buildings: Genua (Doric, begun 1840), Messina (ionic, 1872), Bologna (Doric, 1880) and Munich, East Cemetery (Doric, 1894/1900). Reasons for this may have been associations with rest, relaxation and timelessness.

E. SCULPTURE

In contrast to painting, sculptors had not only Roman works but also an abundance of Greek models to work from. In France the École des Beaux Arts remained attached to ancient models until after 1900. Despite strict principles (imitation of Antiquity, allegory, themes from mythology and history, the primacy of Greece), a tendency towards an individualizing style of representation is noticeable as early as the 1830s. Formerly strict Classicists like J. Pradier introduced this type of individualization, as well as a greater degree of realism and an empathetic perception even into works with Classical themes around 1850, so that for instance Pradier's *Chloris Caressed by Zephyr* (1849) exhibits an emotionally rich eroticism in the posture of a *Venus pudica* (Capitoline Venus). Marble from Paros, a Greek inscription on the base and a tender polychromy linked the work to Greek models. Eugene Guillaume almost copied Roman forms, yet gave his figures an empathetic presence in both physiognomy and posture while depicting them in perfect period costume (fig 5: *Cenotaph of the Gracchi*, 1853; *Roman Couple*, 1877). Assignments for the Prix de Rome increasingly included 'lower' history. Louis-Ernest Barrias, for instance, won in 1865 with the relief *The Founding of Marseilles* whereas A. Falguière had been heavily criticized in 1864 for sending his statue of a *Contemporary Neapolitan Woman* from Rome [66]. A renewed interest in Roman history and a stylistic orientation towards the Italian and French Renaissance and Baroque began to emerge around 1850. Thus, L.-E. Barrias modelled *The Oath of Spartacus* (1871) in form and style on works by Michelangelo; J. Dalou based his *Processsion of Silenus* (1884) on Rubens. Classical themes presented in a pleasing genre-like manner or in a highly dramatic rage found a broad market as small bronzes (A.-E. Carrière-Belleuse, *Abduction of Hippodamia*, 1871) [64]. At the time the Academy gave up its strict adherence to Antiquity (ca. 1905), artists like A. Maillol were already following a trend towards monumental, calm, voluminous sculptures that was comparable to the new Classicism of A. Hildebrand in Germany.

Generally speaking, a similar development took place in Germany: ancient sculptures were available as study objects in major cast collections and as originals [14]. The groundwork for the rejection of Classical themes and their constraints – but not of the Classical ideal of beauty – was broadly laid out by F.Th. Vischer in his *Aesthetik* (1853) [11]. Popular critical assessments of the use of Classical themes in contemporary sculpture greeted the figures of the Schloßbrücke in Berlin (begun 1842), for example, with derision and expressed a lack of understanding for the monument's allegorical content and gratuitous nudity. A tendency towards individualization can also be observed at an early point in Germany: it offered the possibility of presenting the statues of the generals at the Neue Wache in Berlin in contemporary costume, whereas the plinth reliefs were decorated in Classical relief style. Forming the basis for each statue, these reliefs lent validity to the individual depicted (Ch.D. Rauch, 1816/1822). The costume question was yet to be resolved definitively: Rauch's monument for Max I Joseph in Munich still showed the ruler in a heavily Classicizing cloak (1826/1835) [65]. His design for the Goethe and Schiller statues in Weimar (1848/1849) showed the poets in ancient dress, but the objection of the patron, Ludwig I of Bavaria, secured the commission for E. Rietschel and contemporary clothes (1853/1856). Sculptures depicting Classical themes were particularly in demand for the decoration of buildings having to do with the fine arts; almost all of them were executed in a Baroque style as was, for example, the colossal group of *Dionysus and Ariadne with Panther* quadriga on the Semperoper in Dresden (J. Schilling, 1876) and the *Muse on a Panther* quadriga in the theatre in Wiesbaden (G. Eberlein, 1893). There was a broad demand for the Classical genre in small-scale sculpture; erotically appealing themes were especially popular. However, Th. Kalide's *Bacchante on a Panther* (1844/1848) ended in scandal whereas, e.g., A. Clesinger's *Woman Bitten by a Snake* (1847) was able to combine notoriety with success in Paris. Classically inspired polychromatic sculpture was rare (L. von Schwanthaler, Walhalla caryatids, 1842). M. Klinger was admired for his sculptures made of differently coloured types of stone (*Cassandra*, 1895, fig. 6) and B. Elkan for his painted figures (*Persephone*, 1908) [16]. The lower deities also found entrance into contemporary sculpture on a monumental scale; this was no doubt prepared by Böcklin's paintings and Vischer's justification of such subjects in his theory of art (1. § 631). The Neptune fountain in Berlin (R. Begas, 1888/1891), the Triton fountain in Vienna (E. Hofmann, 1890) and the Teichmann fountain in

Bremen (R. Maison, 1899) must be mentioned here. Their figures are characterized by an opulent Baroque and contemporary realism in their interpretation of Antiquity that is partially tempered with irony (as required by Vischer). A stark contrast was presented by A. Hildebrand's Wittelsbach fountain in Munich (1891/1895). It was executed in the new calm, planar style that was pursued by a group of sculptors including H. Hahn, H. Lederer and, especially, L. Tuaillon. The latter's monument for Friedrich III in Bremen showed the emperor in a tight cuirass that suggested ancient nudity, and thus a return to ancient costume (1905).

→ Nudity in art

Sources 1 J. N. L. Durand, Recueil et parallèle des édifices de tout genre, anciens et modernes, Paris 1800 2 Id., Précis des leçons d'architecture, 2 vols., Paris 1802–1805 (Engl. D. Britt (trans.), Précis of the Lectures on Architecture, A. Picon (Intro.), 2000) 3 J. Gailhabaud, Monuments anciens et modernes, collection formant une histoire de l'larchitecture des différents peuples a toutes les époques, Paris 1839 4 Ch. Garnier, A travers les arts, Paris 1869, 67–90 5 A. Hirt, Die Baukunst nach den Grundsätzen der Alten, Berlin 1809 6 Id., Die Geschichte der Baukunst bei den Alten, Berlin 1821 7 H. Hübsch, In welchem Style sollen wir bauen?, Karlsruhe 1828 (Engl. W. Herrmann (trans.), In What Style Should We Build?, 1992) 8 Ch. Percier, P. F. L. Fontaine, Palais, maisons et autres édifices modernes dessinés à Rome, Paris 1798 9 Ch. L. Stieglitz, Geschichte der Baukunst der Alten, Leipzig 1792 10 Id., Archaeologie der Baukunst der Griechen und Römer, Weimar 1801 11 F. Th. Vischer, Aesthetik oder Wissenschaft des Schönen (1854), vol. 3, ²1923 12 J. J. Winckelmann, Gedanken über die Nachahmung der griechischen Werke in der Malerei und Bildhauerkunst, Dresden 1755 (Engl. Reflections on the Painting and Sculpture of the Greeks, (repr. of 1765 ed.), 1999)

Literature 13 H. Beenken, Der Historismus in der Baukunst, in: HZ, 157, 1938, 27–68 14 M. Berchtold, Gipsabguß und Original, (Diss.) Stuttgart 1987 15 W. Arenhövel, Ch. Schreiber (eds.), Berlin und die Antike. Architektur, Kunstgewerbe, Malerei, Skulptur, Theater und Wissenschaft vom 16. Jarhundert bis heute, 2 vols., 1979 16 A. Blühm, The Colour of Sculpture 1840–1910, 1996 17 E. Börsch-Supan, Berliner Baukunst nach Schinkel 1840–1870, 1977 18 H. Börsch-Supan, Die deutsche Malerei von Anton Graff bis Hans von Marées, 1988 19 A. Boime, The Academy and French Painting in the Nineteenth Century, 1971 20 M. Brix, M. Steinhauser (eds.), Geschichte allein ist zeitgemäß. Historismus in Deutschland, 1978 21 J. M. Crook, The Dilemma of Style. Architectural Ideas from the Picturesque to the Post-Modern, 1987 22 Id., The Greek Revival. Neoclassical Attitudes in British Architecture 1760–1870, 1972 23 K. Döhmer, 'In welchem Style sollen wir bauen?' Architekturtheorie zwischen Klassizismus und Jugendstil, 1976 24 D. Dolgner, Historismus. Deutsche Baukunst 1815–1900, 1993 25 A. Drexler (ed.), The Architecture of the École des Beaux-Arts, 1977 26 S. v. Falkenhausen, Italienische Monumentalmalerei im Risorgiomento 1830–1890, 1993 27 H. Fillitz (ed.), Der Traum vom Glück. Die Kunst des Historismus in Europa, 2 vols., 1996 28 S. Germer, Historizität und Autonomie. Studien zu Wandbildern im

Frankreich des 19. Jahrhunderts, 1988 29 W. H. GERDTS, American Neo-Classical Sculpture, 1973 30 W. GÖTZ, Historismus. Ein Versuch zur Definition des Begriffs, in: Zeitschrift des Deutschen Vereins für Kunstwissenschaft 24, 1970, 196–212 31 H. GOLLWITZER, Zum Fragenkreis Architekturhistorismus und politische Ideologie, in: Zeitschrift für Kunstgeschichte 42, 1979, 1–14 32 P. GRUNCHEC, La peinture à l'École des Beaux-Arts. Les Concours des Prix de Rome 1797–1863, 2 vols., 1986 33 C. GURLITT, Die deutsche Kunst des 19. Jahrhunderts. Ihre Taten und Ziele, Berlin 1899 34 W. HAGER (ed.), Beiträge zum Problem des Stilpluralismus, 1977 35 Id., Geschichte in Bildern. Studien zur Historienmalerei des 19. Jahrhunderts, 1989 36 R. HAMANN, Die deutsche Malerei im 19. Jahrhundert, 1914 37 W. HAMMERSCHMIDT, Anspruch und Ausdruck in der Architektur des Historismus in Deutschland 1860–1914, 1985 38 W. HARDTWIG, Kunst und Geschichte im Revolutionszeitalter. Historismus in der Kunst und der Historismusbegriff der Kunstwissenschaft, in: Archiv für Kulturgeschichte 61, 1979, 154–190 39 J. HARGROVE (ed.), The French Academy. Classicism and its Antagonists, 1990 40 L. HAUTECOEUR, Histoire de l'architecture classique en France, vol. 7: La Fin de l'architecture classique 1848–1900, 1957 41 M. HELLENTHAL, Eklektizismus. Zur Ambivalenz einer Geisteshaltung und eines künstlerischen Konzepts, 1993 42 H. HILDEBRANDT, Die Kunst des 19. und 20. Jahrhunderts, 1931 43 S. JORDAN, Geschichtstheorie in der ersten Hälfte des 19. Jahrhunderts, 1999 44 W. C. KIDNEY, The Architecture of Choice. Eclecticism in America 1880–1930, 1974 45 W. KITLITSCHKA, Die Malerei der Wiener Ringstraße, 1981 46 A. LINNEBACH, Arnold Böcklin und die Antike. Mythos, Geschichte, Gegenwart, 1991 47 P. MEBES, Um 1800. Architektur und Handwerk im letzten Jahrhundert ihrer traditionellen Entwicklung, 1908 48 A. MENKE-SCHWINGHAMMER, Weltgeschichte als Nationalepos. Wilhelm von Kaulbachs kulturhistorischer Zyklus im Treppenhaus des Neuen Museums in Berlin, 1994 49 R. MIDDLETON (ed.), The Beaux-Arts and Nineteenth Century French Architecture, 1982 50 G. LACAMBRE (ed.), Le Musée du Luxembourg en 1874. Peintures, 1974 51 O. G. OEXLE, Geschichtswissenschaft im Zeichen des Historismus. Studien zur Problemgeschichte der Moderne, 1996 52 M. OSBORN, Das 19. Jahrhundert, 1907 (= A. SPRINGER (ed.), Handbuch der Kunstgeschichte, vol. 5) 53 M.-L. CAZALAS et al. (eds.), Paris – Rome – Athènes. Le voyage en Grèce des architectes français aux 19e et 20e siècles. (Exhibition catalogue), 1982 54 N. PEVSNER, Academies of Art. Past and Present, 1940 55 Id., Die Wiederkehr des Historismus (1961), in: L. GROTE (ed.), Historismus und bildende Kunst, 1965, 116–117 56 G. PESCHKEN et al. (eds.). Karl Friedrich Schinkel. Lebenswerk, vol. 14: Das architektonische Lehrbuch, 1979 57 L. MASCOLI et al. (eds.), Pompéi. Travaux et envois des architectes français au 19e siècle (Exhibition catalogue), 1981 58 P. PORTOGHESI, L'eclettismo a Roma 1870–1922, 1968 59 A. D. POTTS, Political Attitudes and the Rise of Historicism in Art Theory, in: Art History 1, 1978, 191–213 60 C. RITZENTHALER, L'École des Beaux-Arts du 19e siècle. Les pompiers, 1987 61 M. SCHMID, Kunstgeschichte des 19. Jahrhunderts, 2 vols., 1904–1906 62 G. SCHOLTZ (ed.), Historismus am Ende des 20. Jahrhunderts, 1997 63 M. SCHWARZER, German Architectural Theory and the Search for Modern Identity, 1995 64 CHR. GERMANAZ et al. (eds.), La sculpture française au 19e siècle (Exhibi-

tion catalogue), 1986 65 J. V. SIMSON, Wie man die Helden anzog, in: Zeitschrift des Deutschen Vereins für Kunstwissenschaft 43, 1989, 47–63 66 K. TÜRR, Zur Antikenrezeption in der französischen Skulptur des 19. und 20. Jahrhunderts, 1979 67 M. WAGNER, Allegorie und Geschichte. Ausstattungsprogramme öffentlicher Gebäude des 19. Jahrhunderts in Deutschland. Von der Cornelius-Schule zur Malerei der Wilhelminischen Ära, 1989 68 H. B. WEINBERG, The Lure of Paris. Nineteenth Century American Painters and their French Teachers, 1991 69 U. WESTFEHLING, Triumphbogen im 19. und 20. Jahrhundert, 1977 70 D. V. ZANTEN, Felix Duban and the Buildings of the École des Beaux-Arts, 1832–1840, in: Journal of the Society of Architectural Historians 37, 1978, 161–174 71 Id., The Architectural Polychromy of the 1830's, 1977. HAROLD HAMMER-SCHENK

Historiographical Methods
A. INTRODUCTION B. DEVELOPMENT C. LATEST DEVELOPMENTS

A. INTRODUCTION

The meaning of the term 'historiographical methods' (HM) ranges from descriptions of certain techniques and work methods, almost in the sense of a craft, to discussions of fundamental (methodological) questions about the possibilities and modes of historical understanding. In the field of ancient history, which is both a historical discipline as well as the study of Antiquity in general, in addition to HM those of the two most closely related areas, archaeology and philology, must also be considered.

B. DEVELOPMENT
1. HUMANISM AND ENLIGHTENMENT 2. THE TURN TO HISTORICISM 3. THE 'HISTORICAL' CENTURY 4. THE CRISIS IN HISTORICISM 5. BETWEEN THE WARS 6. DEVELOPMENTS AFTER 1945

1. HUMANISM AND ENLIGHTENMENT

Humanism, a movement characterised by a new appreciation of Antiquity that began with Petrarch and gained much greater momentum in the 15th cent., was oriented primarily toward aesthetic and practical (i.e., ethical-political and educational) goals. The same held true for historiography. It served political purposes and took its cues from ancient historiography [2. 48 on L. Bruni and G. Poggio Bracciolini]. Two elements characteristic of Humanism proved especially important for the method and the understanding of history. First, a return to the sources (ad fontes), as propagated above all by Melanchthon [35. 26], promoted access to documents regarded as original and unadulterated, that is, to the oldest documents and thus closest to the events. Second, the ancient authorities could not only be imitated and applied to modern situations; they were also to lead to an improved understanding of Antiquity itself, as postulated already by Lorenzo Valla in his debate with Poggio about the latter's translation of Cyropaedy [36. 42 f.]. The 'tension' between model and the difference to its modern counterpart, the closeness and yet distance between them, articulated especially in Erasmus' *Ciceronianus*, opened up the possibility of viewing Antiquity from a distanced, that is historical perspective. [2. 132f.; 29. 614f.]. To be sure, orientation of a practical-political nature as well as normative instruction continued to be prevalent in historiography and the recourse to history itself [2. 94; 35. 43; 18. 10].

This tendency continued into the historiography of the Enlightenment. Philosophical and programmatic models clearly dominated the field with much attention given to literary form. However, in the 18th cent. there emerged an obvious interest in historical development and in human progress. This led to the posing of new questions relating to historical material and to new assertions about the character and the value of historical epochs. The Classical authors were no longer the 'masters'; instead, lessons were learned from history itself [35. 461]. Classics of this genre, such as Montesquieu's *Considérations sur les causes de la grandeur des Romains et de leur décadence* (1734) and Gibbon's *History of the Decline and Fall of the Roman Empire* (1776–1788), offered important historical insights but were not based on a detailed analysis of the source material.

Even so, it was precisely in this area that important achievements resulted. The use of sources for orientation and the effort to comprehend Antiquity adequately led to the development of rational methods of understanding, editing and interpreting ancient texts. Essential aspects were formulated by Joseph Justus Scaliger and, regarding history, by Jean Bodin. Descartes's methodical rationalism in particular influenced the development of a scholarly-philological way of dealing with the texts, especially in textual criticism. Furthermore, various non-literary documents and fragments were increasingly collected and made accessible in large corpora (inscriptions, coins, etc.) out of antiquarian interest as well as for the better understanding of Classical authors [29. 615f.; 18. 62f.].

2. THE TURN TO HISTORICISM

Baldly put, modern historiography is the treatment of important historical themes, combined with philological methods of source research. Thus it applies the method of textual criticism to all historical materials, contents and statements. This definition describes historiography in the sense that it is a craft. It did not become effective, however, until a specific constellation was achieved in which several elements could interact: 1. The dramatic consequences of the French Revolution and the subsequent experience of enormously rapid developments [29. 611f. with a reference to B. Croce; 20. 1973f.; 23]; 2. A new understanding of science formulated by Kant precisely for the Natural Sciences, according to which the researcher is to understand the object of his study as the 'issue' (*Sachverhalt*), thereby rendering it 'objective' and thus ready for methodical analysis (*legis arte*) [20. 2107ff.; 31. 32ff.]; 3. An uneasiness with Enlightenment historiography combined

with the desire–characteristic of Romanticism, Classicism and, above all, of German Idealism–to form an inner connection with the past with which one feels a spiritual affinity [18. 65ff.; 31. 37f.; 22. 62ff.].

The idea that this constellation came about by coincidence is supported by the almost simultaneous emergence and rapid spread of this new perspective. Relying on the Humanistic-philological tradition of research that provided the basis for their methodical analysis, the first examples for a new historiography can be found in the study of Antiquity–in B. G. Niebuhr's analysis of the *lex agraria* and of the early Roman Republic, in the 'philology of objects/thing philology' (*Sachphilologie*) by A. Boeckh, whose first large work about the Athenian state budget (1817) was dedicated to Niebuhr, and in the founding of the → HISTORISCHE RECHTS-SCHULE by F. C. de Savigny [19; 38; 6; 21. 34ff.].

Notwithstanding both the distance to the past and its 'reification', this newly found access to the past consisted in vividly imagining and understanding not only actions by individuals or groups [8. 128ff.] but situations and structures as well, i.e., the "impersonal forces determining existence" [20. 2121]. The object of interest was the human being or humanity in an all-encompassing sense [32. 177] and in all its human manifestations seen from a historical perspective or 'historicised'. This perspective is therefore also referred to as → HISTORICISM, a term which expresses not only this specific approach in the field of history but encompasses the "fundamental tendency to historicize thinking and knowledge" (E. Troeltsch) in the comprehensive sense so characteristic for the 19th cent., the 'historical century' [31. 17, 40; 32].

3. THE 'HISTORICAL' CENTURY

The process of turning history into a scholarly discipline by adopting philological methods had an immediate effect on the treatment of the period of Post-Antiquity. One example of this is the *Gesellschaft für Deutschlands ältere Geschichtskunde* ('Society (for the Study) of Germany's Older History'), founded by K. vom Stein in 1819 to organise the scholarly edition, collection and the recording of medieval sources (*Monumenta Germaniae Historica*). A preeminent role was played by L. von Ranke, who is still regarded as the founder of modern historical scholarship and historicism [22. 86ff.; 7. 25ff.]. Ranke completely rejected the practice of judging a historical period from the point of view of a later time and emphasised its value in itself: a period must always be understood in itself. The purpose of history is not to teach lessons; rather, it is there to "show how it really was" [33. VII]. This can only be achieved by referring to the sources using philological methodology.

The triumph of this new approach became evident in the study of Antiquity, promoted in Germany in particular through the reform of secondary schools and universities [20. 1941, 1950f., 1978, 2108; 24]. Furthermore, this historical approach opened up fresh perspectives on epochs that had fallen victim to the

Humanist-Classicist verdict and on previously neglected areas. In this manner, J. G. Droysen instituted the modern study of Hellenism [14], and K. O. Müller, another student of Boeckh, strongly supported the study of regional historical geography. In so doing, he left his mark on his student E. Curtius, one of the most influential ancient historians of the second half of the century [13].

Similar developments manifested themselves in Roman history, too, where Niebuhr's influence, combined with a juristic orientation, led especially to a discussion of issues concerning law with all their economical, administrative and social implications. This approach led to the study of sources other than legal texts and to studies in the history of language. For the latter, Th. Mommsen can serve as representative. His approach to philology was, in turn, influenced by O. Jahn [21].

Along with the philological criticism of known texts, regardless of the type, the discovery, publication and interpretation of new texts became a major preoccupation. The essential aim of research consisted in gaining more and more insights on the basis of such texts. In this context, Mommsen considered the task of organising the "Archives of the past as laying the foundation of historical scholarship" [30. 165]. In this way, special 'ancillary disciplines' emerged, such as epigraphy (→ THE STUDY OF INSCRIPTIONS), → NUMISMATICS, and, later, → PAPYROLOGY, all providing the first presentation of material in the sense of a scholarly division of labour. Through a → DECIPHERING of previously unknown languages such as Egyptian, Assyrian and Old-Persian, new access to completely different cultures was gained. The idea that research means, or is based upon, skillfully working through the sources remains a fundamental element of HM, especially in view of the fact that history as that which is past presents itself exclusively in such traces.

On the other hand, past events are not mirrored or reflected photographically in the sources. Their reconstruction, while necessary, does not yet amount to a scientific and methical treatment of history. History is both the reconstruction and its presentation by the historian. Regarding this aspect in particular we encounter considerable methodological problems. One can ask to what extent scientific objectivity can be achieved on this level. Mommsen is a good example of this problem. He is a master of scholarship in the above sense and, at the same time, the author of a dramatic and biased *Roman History*, which was awarded the Nobel Prize for Literature. Mommsen himself underlined this problem when he declared in his speech, on becoming university rector in 1874, that true historians were "not trained but born" [7. 69]. In other words, the methodological problem lies in correctly placing the historian between the roles of 'recorder', on the one hand, and 'poet', on the other [20. 2286].

The idealistic basis of historicism at first kept this problem from becoming virulent because its adherents offered a plausible explanation. Droysen in his *Historik* [4] gives this explanation in justifying to his audience and to himself his methodological basis. He discusses at length the principles of reconstructing, criticising and interpreting the sources. Most of these principles remain standard today. (The distinction between 'tradition' and 'remnant' is now referred to in a more neutral way as primary and secondary, or as 'original' and 'derived' sources [28. 112]; also standard is his distinguishing between forms of criticism according to genuineness, place in time, correctness and differentiated criticism of the sources). However, the essential thing for Droysen was inner coherence: not the events in themselves, but the 'knowledge of the events' [4. 397]. The historian has access to this because he is a human being dealing with human beings. They are therefore accessible to him because he can understand their plans, actions and milieus: "The essence of the historical method is through study to understand" [4. 398]. The object of the historian is accessible to him from this inner, ideational proximity, just as the historian himself is "involved in his object (namely, history)" [31. 43].

4. THE CRISIS IN HISTORICISM

Informed by the principles outlined above, historical research was able to produce impressive results by the end of the 19th cent. The organisation of scholarly studies, which had been funneled more and more into → ACADEMIES, universities (→ UNIVERSITY) and other such institutions, had led to the formation of large organisations and to 'large-scale research' with a high degree of international cooperation. Many editions had appeared or were in the process of appearing, new materials, such as papyri, were being collected, bought and published; explorations of Greek landscapes were to be tackled internationally. The various research activities were reflected in numerous collections of material as well as in important syntheses. An example of the latter was E. Meyer's great success–an true *Geschichte des Altertums* ('History of Antiquity') which not only considered the Classical sources but Egyptian and ancient Oriental sources as well and, from this basis, proceeded from a historical point of view that was decidedly universal.

However, controversies going on both in Germany and in France immediately before and after the turn of the century [34] signaled a crisis in historicism. It resulted from the comparable and ever more obvious triumph of the Natural Sciences and found an ally in the cultural pessimism of the Fin de siècle (fed, in part, by Nietzsche). The scientific challenge was very acute because, based on A. Comte's philosophical positivism, it championed the objective character of empirically observed reality and thus the knowledge of nature attainable through observation. An explicitly religious character was therefore bestowed on Natural Science [31. 22 f.]. Scientific dignity was found to consist in the knowledge of things and especially in the discovery and postulation of laws. This notion spread (essentially via W. Wundt's psychology) to history as well, with K. Lamprecht demanding the search for "general laws of development" and, at the same time, postulating a change in orientation from political history to cultural history in the larger sense [22. 256 ff.; 34]. Especially in the realm of economic history, the historicist school had made much of the analysis of steps of development. The controversy between E. Meyer and the national economist K. Bücher concerning the comparability of ancient and modern economies must be understood in this context [37. 1 ff.].

The 'historians' controversy' was, however, not limited to academic historians (where Lamprecht had little chance); instead, it led to a fundamental methodological discussion about the status of what were now regarded as the 'Humanities' and their differentiation from the Natural Sciences. This discussion was carried on primarily in philosophy. Like Droysen, W. Dilthey remained essentially committed to idealist hermeneutics, pointing to the spiritual connection between object (history) and subject (the first-person perspective of the historian) as providing the basis for understanding and insight [22. 175 ff.]. The Neo-Kantians W. Windelband, who created the distinction between Natural Sciences and the historical discipline as 'nomothetic' and 'idiographic', and H. Rickert also believed in inner, supra-temporal connections and in a *logos* that reigned over all historical events and manifested itself at the very least in the realm of cultural values [22. 192 ff.].

The fact that this debate was not restricted to laws and generalities in history but concerned itself more generally with the relationship of historical scholarship to the more systematic and scientific neighbouring fields of geography, psychology, economics and sociology became more evident in the controversy going on simultaneously in France. Sociology, which was still based on philosophy, was placed in close proximity to history by E. Durkheim. In fact, he saw the two as identical. For Durkheim the key to historical explanations is found in the comparison and, therefore, in the connection between a special plane of individual phenomena and a plane of general assertions about social phenomena [10. 348].

M. Weber is of particular importance in this context. In his thought many things converged. His ideas were influenced by his study of Romance law and the teachings of the historicist school on national economics, by the philosophical debate concerning method, by his vast knowledge of history and by a historically relativistic view of the empirical world. Without referring to idealist contexts, he found a category for relating empirical-historical details to general statements; namely, in the 'ideal type'. This category refers to a historical phenomenon, such as nobility, state or feudalism, as a conceptual entity which was abstracted from empirical reality through logical operations. It does not exist in the empirical world in its 'pure state', but it allows comparisons and therefore an explanation and an understanding that transcends epochs and cultural realms. In this way, sociology and universal history ultimately coincide [20. 1835 ff., 1863 ff.; 22. 208 ff.].

5. BETWEEN THE WARS

World War I not only inflicted lasting damage on the international cooperation so important for historical 'grand research', it also brought the 'crisis of purpose' outlined above to the fore. Reactions within the historical disciplines varied widely. In France, for instance, the direction inspired by Durkheim began to dominate in the 1920s, aided by the circle around the journal *Annales* (especially L. Febvre and M. Bloch). In this group history was understood as knowledge about humanity with geography and a strongly anthropological and ethnological sociology as the most important neighbouring disciplines. The combination of anthropology and history had an effect on the study of Antiquity as well (L. Gernet) [9; 5].

In Germany, on the other hand, the study of Antiquity was clearly influenced by the critique of historicism and by the 'objective' (*wertneutral*) research on all ancient expressions of life, a critique that became evident in its emphasis on the classical heritage in the so-called → THIRD HUMANISM by W. Jaeger [18. 128 ff.]. This approach also influenced history where the perspective was directed toward inner forces and principles, for example, on the significance of the Greek tribes and their nature (H. Berve) or on the intellectual trends of a period This was also a tendency common in studies on later historical periods (W. Weber) [20. 787 ff.; 34. 356]. This approach, with its focus on 'great men' and 'ethnic-national' identities was easy to reconcile with the ideology of National Socialism, which was thus able to gain a foothold in the study of ancient history where it brought pseudo-scientific methods and concepts of racism to bear to its advantage (F. Altheim, F. Schachermeyer, J. Vogt). M. Weber's influence, on the other hand, remained limited (J. Hasebroek).

Weber's concepts, however, and, along with them, important positions filled by those of the historical school of national economy were wide spread internationally, especially in socio-anthropological research and conceptualizing, as in American Functionalism (T. Parsons) and in economic anthropology (K. Polanyi, M. Finley). at the same time, France saw the advance of similar concepts thanks to the close relationship between the Durkheim school (M. Halbwachs, M. Mauss) and the *Annales* circle (supported by mutual exchanges).

6. DEVELOPMENTS AFTER 1945

The isolation of Germany caused by dictatorship and war was an intellectual one as well and could be felt into the 1960s. Because of the continuity prevailing of those holding positions before and after 1945 and the general trend to restore the *status quo ante,* the above-mentioned concepts and methods being employed more and more internationally were slow to be adopted in Germany. Instead, the division of Germany was reflected in controversies between 'bourgeois' and Marxist historiography, especially concerning the differing assessments of ancient slavery. Historical materialism was countered with the objectivist postulate of a value-neutral interpretation of sources.

The 1960s saw the emergence, cautious at first, of a theoretically founded methods debate which introduced socio-politological concepts and quickly emphasised the importance of M. Weber (A. Heuß, Ch. Meier) [20. 1835 ff., 1863 ff.; 27; 8]. This movement was intensified by the effects of the so-called student revolts of 1968. Although they were an international phenomenon, in Germany they led specifically to the adoption of 'newer' Western approaches in the historical disciplines. The special attention paid to the *Annales* school may be taken as *pars pro toto*. In a very short time the 1970s saw a paradigm shift which was especially noticeable in Germany. Even today, the historical disciplines and the state of HM are marked by it. Accompanied by theoretical reflections and debates, a social history, which was focused on structures and stratifications and which used, at times, quantifying methods, was the first to gain acceptance was [7. 44 ff.]. Since the 1980s, the latter has been joined increasingly by micro-historical research and studies of everyday life, which also analyse collective mentalities and concepts. The discrepancy between the study of structures and interpretation seems to have been 'abolished' in the new focus on cultural history that is found in the historical disciplines as well.

As a result, highly specific research fields have established themselves based primarily on turn-of-the-century concepts (E. Durkheim, M. Weber) and therefore clearly show their anthropological and sociological roots. However, because they focus on the *humanum*, they are actually related to the orientation of early historicism, as found in A. Boeckh and K. O. Müller, although this dependency has thus far not been acknowledged.

Within this framework, a new understanding of the function of history has developed in the context of a 'mémoire collective' (M. Halbwachs). The distinction between practices and discourses, that is, between ways of thinking and viewing (M. Foucault, P. Bourdieu [1]), has strongly furthered the use of anthropological concepts as well as comparative history. Regional historical studies and studies of settlements and regional archaeology have enjoyed a remarkable rise. Due largely to the work of M. Finley, economic history has been able capture and elaborate on the specific nature of ancient economies. Traditional endeavours, such as the history of terminology, have also been newly strengthened in an atmosphere that promotes theoretical reflection [15].

C. LATEST DEVELOPMENTS

The current situation in HM is characterised by a controversy which is on a par with the *Fin de siécle* debates. The post-modern challenge to HM is often referred to as a *linguistic turn*. This term refers to the theories of the French (post-)structuralists (especially R. Barthes and J. Derrida), according to which there is

no reality outside of texts. These theories have been given much weight in literary criticism, of course, but in ethnology as well, where rites and practices are read like a text in C. Geertz' 'thick description'. In this manner, history and historiography can also be regarded as a literary genre which is no longer distinguished from fictional literature (H. White) [12; 39]. History dissolves into arbitrary constructions by different historians.

This challenge is particularly grave because it touches on points that are especially problematic in historical methodology. What is the role of the (re-) constructing historian with his powers of understanding and imagination, and how far can his object be conceived as independent from him? Post-structuralist theory is therefore able not only to use Gadamer's hermeneutics; it can also refer to works as fundamental for historicism as Droysen's *Historik*. The challenge and the debates of the 1990s that have resulted from it (survey in [7]) have therefore proven fruitful and have led to new or newly reconsidered reflections about HM, especially about the relationship between the historian and his object [32; 7; 10; 25]. In the process, the roles of empathy, experience; fantasy and imagination have been elucidated as legitimate elements necessary for constructing the coherence of historical events, elements that are expressed in historiography [11; 20. 2250 ff.; 8. 137 ff.]. Evidence of this can be found in the literary and artistic character of historical presentation (or at least in some historical presentations), which doubtlessly exists, and, furthermore, it promotes a dialogue with a sub-field of literary criticism (*New Historicism*) which works toward the reconstruction of historical contexts from literary works [17. 7ff.].

On the other hand, the argument that objects of historical knowledge do indeed exist outside of texts and that events and situations (contexts) have left their traces in the sources has been strongly emphasised. Although the historical state of affairs is defined only by the historian (regarding this, one should refer to Kant and Droysen [31; 7. 86 f.]), the resulting presentation is by no means arbitrary but subject to a rational and inter-subjectively comprehensible process that includes the formation of types [8. 93 ff.]. Simply said, it is a case of controlled imagination, similar to the method of "reflexive anthropology" represented by P. Bourdieu [10. 355; 1].

Thus it follows that sources alone neither constitute the historical object itself, as suggested by certain 'positivist' ideas, nor directly reflect history. Still, the expert reconstruction, presentation, and analysis of the material along with the continuous production of new and refined interpretations and reconstructions remain central elements of historical research. The traditional related and complementary disciplines, such as philology, epigraphy, papyrology, and numismatics, therefore, have not lost any of their value. This holds true as well for the fields of ancient Oriental and ancient Egyptian studies because of the increasingly comparative and universal orientation of history. Ultimately, however, as emphasised already by L. Febvre [9. 18], textual materials cannot be counted as sources. The historian must rely, as always, not only on archaeological research but increasingly on methods from the Natural Sciences as well, through which additional material is uncovered and prepared or which improve the interpretation and the dating of known remnants (C–14 method, dendrochronology, palaeobotanical pollen diagrams, thermoluminiscence method) [26; 16]. Each historical construction must be confronted with these and other materials again and again and can be proven false through a new interpretation or through new finds at any time. If nothing else, it is that practice that provides HM with their scholarly validity [7. 120; 3. 26].

1 P. BOURDIEU, Le sens pratique, 1980, (Engl. R. NICE (trans.), The Logic of Practice, 1990) 2 P. BURKE, The European Renaissance, 1998 3 R. CHARTIER, On the Edge of the Cliff. History, Language and Practices, 1997 4 J. G. DROYSEN, Historik. Rekonstruktion der ersten vollständigen Fassung der Vorlesungen (1857), Grundriß der Historik in der ersten handschriftlichen (1857/58) und in der letzten gedruckten Fassung (1882), P. LEYH (ed.), 1977 (Engl. E. B. ANDREWS (trans.), Outline of the Principles of History, 1967, 1893) 5 G. DUBY, Über einige Grundtendenzen der modernen französischen Geschichtswissenschaft, in: HZ 241, 1985, 543–554 6 F. EBEL, Friedrich Carl von Savigny, in: M. ERBE (ed.), Berlinische Lebensbilder. Geisteswissenschaftler, 1989, 21–36 7 R. J. EVANS, Fakten und Fiktionen. Über die Grundlagen historischer Erkenntnis, 1998 8 K.-G. FABER, Theorie der Geschichtswissenschaft, 1972 9 L. FEBVRE, Das Gewissen des Historikers, 1988 10 E. FLAIG, Geschichte ist kein Text, in: M. W. BLANKE, F. JAEGER, TH. SANDKÜHLER (eds.), Dimensionen der Historik, 1998, 345–360 11 J. FRIED, Wissenschaft und Phantasie, in: HZ 263, 1996, 291–316 12 C. GEERTZ, Works and Lives: The Anthropologist as Author, 1988 13 H.-J. GEHRKE, Carl Otfried Müller und das Land der Griechen, in: MDAI(A) 106, 1991, 9–35 14 Id., Johann Gustav Droysen, in: M. ERBE (ed.), Berlinische Lebensbilder. Geisteswissenschaftler, 1989, 127–142 15 Id., Zwischen Altertumswissenschaft und Geschichte. Zur Standortbestimmung der Alten Geschichte am Ende des 20. Jahrhunderts, in: E.-R. SCHWINGE (ed.), Die Wissenschaft vom Altertum am Ende des 2. Jahrtausends nach Christus, 1995, 160–196 16 Id., Historische Landeskunde, in: A. H. BORBEIN, T. HÖLSCHER, P. ZANKER (eds.), Klassische Archäologie, 2000, 39–51 17 S. GREENBLATT, Learning to Curse: Essays in Early Modern Culture, 1990 18 A. HENTSCHKE, U. MUHLACK, Einführung in die Geschichte der Klassischen Philologie, 1972 19 A. HEUSS, Barthold Georg Niebuhrs wissenschaftliche Anfänge, 1981 20 Id., Gesammelte Schriften in 3 Bänden, 1995 21 Id., Theodor Mommsen und das 19. Jahrhundert, 1956, (repr. 1996) 22 G. G. IGGERS, Deutsche Geschichtswissenschaft. Eine Kritik der traditionellen Geschichtsauffassung von Herder bis zur Gegenwart, 1971 (Engl. The German Conception of History: The National Tradition of Historical Thought from Herder to the Present, 1968; rev. ed. 1983) 23 R. KOSELLECK, Vergangene Zukunft. Zur Semantik geschichtlicher Zeiten, 1979 (Engl. K. TRIBE (trans.), Futures Past: On the Semantics of Historical Time, 2004, 1985) 24 M. LANDFESTER, Humanismus und Gesellschaft im 19. Jahrhundert. Untersuchun-

gen zur politischen und gesellschaftlichen Bedeutung der humanistischen Bildung in Deutschland, 1988 25 CH. LORENZ, Konstruktion der Vergangenheit. Eine Einführung in die Geschichtstheorie, 1997 26 F. G. MAIER, Neue Wege in die alte Welt. Moderne Methoden der Archäologie, 1977 27 CH. MEIER, Entstehung des Begriffs 'Demokratie'. Vier Prolegomena zu einer historischen Theorie, 1970 28 A. MOMIGLIANO, Wege in die Alte Welt, 1995 29 U. MUHLACK, Empirisch-rationaler Historismus, in: HZ 232, 1981, 605–616 30 W. NIPPEL (ed.), Über das Studium der Alten Geschichte, 1993 31 O. G. OEXLE, Die Geschichtswissenschaft im Zeichen des Historismus. Bemerkungen zum Standort der Geschichtsforschung, in: HZ 238, 1984, 17–55 32 O. G. OEXLE, J. RÜSEN (eds.), Historismus in den Kulturwissenschaften. Geschichtskonzepte, historische Einschätzungen, Grundlagenprobleme, 1996 33 L. VON RANKE, Sämtliche Werke. Zweite Gesamtausgabe, vol. 33/34, Leipzig 1874 34 L. RAPHAEL, Historikerkontroversen im Spannungsfeld zwischen Berufshabitus, Fächerkonkurrenz und sozialen Deutungsmustern. Lamprecht-Streit und französischer Methodenstreit der Jahrhundertwende in vergleichender Perspektive, in: HZ 251, 1990, 325–363 35 W. RÜEGG (ed.), Geschichte der Universität in Europa, vol. II, 1996 (Engl. H. DE RIDDER-SYMOENS (ed.), History of the University in Europe: Universities in Early Modern Europe (1500–1800), 1996) 36 H. SANCISI-WEERDENBURG, Cyrus in Italy, in: Id., Achaemenid History V. The Roots of the European Tradition, 1990, 31–52 37 H. SCHNEIDER (ed.), Sozial- und Wirtschaftsgeschichte der römischen Kaiserzeit, 1981 38 Id., August Boeckh, in: M. ERBE (ed.), Berlinische Lebensbilder. Geisteswissenschaftler, 1989, 37–54 39 H. WHITE, Metahistory: The Historical Imagination in Nineteenth-Century Europe, 1973 HANS-JOACHIM GEHRKE

Historiographical Models

A. INTRODUCTION AND TERMS B. ANTIQUITY C. LATIN MIDDLE AGES D. RENAISSANCE AND PROTESTANTISM E. BAROQUE AND ENLIGHTENMENT F. THE 19TH CENTURY G. VIEW OF THE 20TH CENTURY

A. INTRODUCTION AND TERMS

Historical thinking and historiography have roots in Antiquity. Models were developed at the time that shaped later historiography as well as later historical thinking. The word 'history' first appears in Herodotus (ca. 484 – after ca. 430 BC) (Hdt. pr. 1: histories apodexis, ἱστορίης ἀπόδεξις) in the sense of the result of research. According to him, history is the acquisition of knowledge through the questioning of witnesses or through witnessing events oneself. This definition has shaped historical studies until today. The relationship to philosophy, religion, theology and to learning in general, as well as to poetry, has become constitutive for historiography beginning with Greek Antiquity. In Aristotle (384–322 BC), the reporting of events as the recounting of details contrasts with the more general character of poetry (Aristot. poet. 9, 1451a 36–1451b 1/11). Historiography is the collecting and, possibly the explaining as well, of past events; this explanation determines the interpretation of history. Biography should not be included in historiography because it is a specialised genre dealing exclusively with individuals instead of processes. Political theory, on the other hand, is related through close interaction with historiography, since politics exerts an obvious influence on historiography.

B. ANTIQUITY

1. ANCIENT ORIENT 2. JEWS 3. GREECE 3.1. UNIVERSAL HISTORY 3.2 LOCAL AND REGIONAL HISTORY 3.3 HISTORY OF FOREIGN NATIONS AND CULTURES 3.4. RHETORICAL HISTORIOGRAPHY 3.5. TRAGIC HISTORIOGRAPHY 3.6 POLITICAL, ECONOMIC, AND SOCIAL HISTORIOGRAPHY 3.7 METHODOLOGY 3.8 EVOLUTION, PROGRESS, AND DECLINE 3.9 MYTH OF AGES 3.10. SUCCESSION OF EMPIRES 3.11. CYCLICAL THEORIES 3.12. LAWS OF HISTORY 4. ROME 4.1. CHARACTERISTICS OF ROMAN HISTORIOGRAPHY AND THEIR INFLUENCE 4.2. ROMAN HISTORY AS A HISTORY OF THE CITY AND THE EMPERORS 4.3. COMPARISONS TO THE STAGES IN HUMAN LIFE 4.4. HISTORICAL MONOGRAPHS 5. CHRISTIANS; LATE ANTIQUITY; EARLY BYZANTINE PERIOD 5.1. NEW HISTORICAL DIVISIONS 5.2. CHRONOLOGY AND CHRONICLES 5.3 CHURCH HISTORY 5.4. HAGIOGRAPHY 5.5. EUSEBIUS, JEROME, AUGUSTINE, OROSIUS 5.6. LATE ROMAN PAGAN HISTORIOGRAPHY 5.7. PECULIARITIES OF THE LATE ROMAN PAGAN INTEREST IN HISTORY 5.8. EFFECTS OF THE MIGRATION PERIOD 5.9. EARLY BYZANTINE PERIOD

1. ANCIENT ORIENT

Fundamental differences exist between modern historiographical models (HM) and those found in the ancient Orient (Egypt, Hittites, Iran, Mesopotamia). There historiography was conceived of as a list of events and rulers. Oriental historiography was made obsolete by the Greeks and transformed into a presentation of events concerning all, not just certain individuals. Written on scrolls and designed for an audience, this new form of HM is very different from ancient Oriental monumental inscriptions. Nonetheless, monumental inscriptions continued to play a role as a type of historiography.

2. JEWS

In contrast to Herodotus's concept of history as research, the Jews regarded history as a presentation of the events of the chosen people. The history of the chosen people is a national history and a history of salvation at the same time, since the chosen people is led by God. Jews as well as Christians have a linear view of the course of history. In the Old Testament, the Book of Daniel contains the theory of a sequence of world empires (Dan 2,31–34; 7,2–27; 8,2–26). This theory of successive empires has exerted a tremendous influence on

the philosophy of history as a sequential model of historical events.

3. GREECE

3.1 UNIVERSAL HISTORY

Universal historiography is one of the most significant developments in ancient historiography. It did not deal with the entire inhabited world, but rather only with the peoples known in Antiquity. The foundation for world historiography in a cultural-historical and ethnographical sense was laid by Herodotus with his *Historiae* as well as by Ephorus' (ca. 405–330 BC) *Historiae*. The founder of universal historiography is Polybius (ca. 200–ca. 118 BC) who strove to explain Rome's rise to a world empire in his *Historiae*. This work is politically and geographically oriented and regards world history as contemporary history. The conquest of the known world by the Romans thus provided the final impetus for a crystallisation of universal historiography. Polybius regarded the history of his time as a coherent whole wherein actions and events in different parts of the world are tied together with Rome as the centre of history. Polybius' historical work is a universal history of the Mediterranean realm from 264 to 144 BC. The universalist philosophy of Stoicism inspired the idea of world history in the *Historiae* of Poseidonius (ca.135–ca. 51 BC), the first philosopher to write history. The universal historical compilation by Diodorus (ca. 90–30 BC) was published at the end of the Roman Republic in the spirit of Stoicism. Universal historiography is even more prevalent in the period of Augustus, when a large part of the known world was joined together in political unity. This is expressed in the *Historiae* by Strabo (64/63 BC-after AD 23) or in Nicolas of Damascus (ca.. 63 BC- after AD 4) and in the *Historiae Philippicae* by Pompey Trogus (mid–1st cent. BC-after AD 14), a work written in Latin following Hellenistic models which was later epitomised by Justin and which was to exert great influence in the Middle Ages.

3.2 LOCAL AND REGIONAL HISTORY

Local history begins with the Atthidographers, or local historians of Attica. The predecessor is Hellanicus of Lesbos (ca. 480–395 BC), but the most important figure is Philochorus of Athens (ca. 340–260 BC). Regional history–the history of a larger area–is found in the works of Sicily's historians: Antioch of Syracuse (5th cent. BC) and Timaeus of Tauromenion (ca. 350–260 BC), historian of the western Greeks who discovered the importance of the western Mediterranean. His work was continued by Polybius. Local and regional historiography has influenced many works up to modern times.

3.3 HISTORY OF FOREIGN NATIONS AND CULTURES

Some Greek historians, among them Ktesias (2nd half of the 5th cent.–1st half of the 4th cent.) on Persia and Megasthenes (ca. 350–290 BC) on India, focused on foreign cultures in their works. Both works are the result of the writers' own experiences and contributed to broadening the Greeks' horizon. They also served as building blocks for the development of universal historiography. Specialised genres distinct from historiography are ethnography and geography, which have obviously been fundamental for medieval as well as modern historiography.

3.4 RHETORICAL HISTORIOGRAPHY

In every period rhetoric has been a determining factor in the narrative modelling of historiography. It first became excessively dominant in the *Hellenika* and *Philippikai historiai* of Theopompus of Chios (378/377–320 BC), who had been strongly influenced by his teacher, the orator Isocrates (436–338 BC).

3.5 TRAGIC HISTORIOGRAPHY

In the Hellenistic period, the historical works of Duris of Samos (ca. 340–260 BC) and Phylarchus of Athens (2nd half of the 3rd cent. BC) emphasized regarding a work of history as tragedy. The tragic view of history has frequently been found attractive. The earliest historical indications appear in the Greek tragedies, especially in the *Persians* by Aeschylus.

3.6 POLITICAL, ECONOMIC, AND SOCIAL HISTORIOGRAPHY

Thucydides (ca. 460–ca. 400 BC) is the founder of political historiography, which he closely linked to other factors, especially from the realm of economic history. The study of constitutions by Aristotle and his school has left traces in the 6th book of the *Historiae* of Polybius (ca. 200–120 BC), where history is presented as a sequence of forms of government guided by natural law: monarchy, aristocracy and democracy. According to Polybius, the Roman constitution combined the three elements and was therefore an ideal constitution–a mixed constitution. At the same time, Polybius offers an in-depth analysis of the causal and factual relationships of events, which he refers to as "pragmatic historiography". Polybius is the first to discover links between events, carrying on Thucydides' interest in political history. A strong interest in social problems arising from the slave revolts in Sicily can be found in the fragments of the *Historiae* by Poseidonius (ca.135–50 BC).

3.7 METHODOLOGY

The only extant example of a text about historical methodology is Lucian's (ca. AD 120–after 180) work *How Should History Be Written?* Lucian had famous predecessors: Thucydides in the so-called 'Methods Chapter' (Thuc. 1,20–23) and Polybius in the 12th book of his *Historiae*. The preoccupation with methods in history has become especially common in our time. After the early beginnings in the Humanist *ars historica* and after scholars of Antiquity (above all Johann Gustav Droysen) wrote fundamental works on historical methodology in the 19th cent., statements about such issues are again being made on a regular basis in the seminal publications of recent times (thus: F. G. Maier, Ch. Meier, A. Momigliano, H.-I. Marrou or P. Veyne).

3.8 EVOLUTION, PROGRESS, AND DECLINE

Antiquity held a notion of evolution which can be regarded as the antithesis of the pessimistic myth of ages. This notion of evolution is found in materialist Greek philosophy–in Democritus, Diodorus (Diod. 1,8), the Sophists Gorgias and Protagoras, Epicurus and in Rome in Lucretius, who talks about progress. Lucretius (ca. 94–55 BC) divides prehistory into the periods of the Stone, Bronze, and Iron Ages based on material culture, just as Hesiod had done before him. Horace (65 BC- AD 8) reflects on the past from the point of view of evolution (Carm. 3,6,46–48). Manilius (early 1st cent. AD, Astronomica, 1,95–117) and Seneca the Younger (d. 65 AD, Nat. 6,5,3 and Epist. 64,7) show the beginnings of a notion of progress as well as evolution (Nat. 7,30,5). The idea of progress, which in Antiquity is understood culturally and technically rather than morally, appears as early as in the *Archaeology* of Thucydides (1,2–19). This concept was echoed in the idea of progress in 18th-cent. France, as represented by Turgot and Condorcet. Evolutionary thinking was given a biological foundation by Darwin in 19th-cent. England.

3.9 MYTH OF AGES

Hesiod (ca. 700 BC) presents the myth of ages (erg. 106–201), according to which human history runs its course over five ages: the Golden, Silver and Bronze Ages, the Age of the Heroes and the Iron Age. In this first attempt to divide history into periods, Hesiod adopted the core of a Babylonian myth and added to it the Heroic Period, which corresponds to the Mycenaean Age. In the modern period this interpretation has at times been mentioned along with other ancient pieces of evidence in the interpretation of archaeological finds and in the development of the three-period system (Stone Age, Bronze Age, Iron Age). It is important to note the frequent adoption or the citing of the pessimistic view of history, according to which humanity is said to have degenerated step by step after the Golden Age. In Antiquity, Hesiod's division into periods hardly found resonance because it was replaced by simpler systems. Claudian (ca. AD 370–404) was its last adherent. In Plato's philosophy (ca. 429–348 BC) the idea of a lost Golden Age plays a role. Plato also compares types of people with types of metal (Plat. Rep. 416a-c). Traces of the myth of ages can be found in the Orphics. In Rome, also, the notion of world ages was often employed.

3.10 SUCCESSION OF EMPIRES

Closely related to political history is the theory of the succession of empires which divides the course of history into periods of world monarchies. This theory of history remained vital up to Bossuet in the 17th cent. It was first employed by Herodotus, who formulated the following succession of world empires: Assyria, Media, Persia (Hdt. 1,95.130). For the universal historian Polybius, they are: Persia, the Spartan hegemony, Macedonia, Rome (Polyb. 1,2,2–7). Demetrius of Phaleron (2nd half of the 4th cent. BC) was the first to introduce

Macedonia (Polyb. 29,21) and Aemilius Sura (1st half of the 2nd cent. BC) the first to introduce Rome (Vell. 1,6,6). For Dionysius of Halicarnassus, the historical process was brought to completion by the Roman Empire (Dion. Hal. Ant. 1,95.130). The theory of the succession of empires was used in accordance with the different goals of historians. It is the basis for the popular medieval idea of the *translatio imperii*.

3.11 Cyclical Theories

Theories of cyclical eras are linked to the idea of a return of the same and belong to the realm of philosophy. Cyclical theories resurface in the idea of a systematic succession of constitutions and of types of states (especially Polyb. 6,4,11–13). Cyclical concepts of human history have continued to be vital, especially through Vico, up to the present, as shown by O. Spengler or A. Toynbee.

3.12 Laws of History

Theories of historical laws in the sense of anthropological constants or laws derived from the nature of politics can be found especially in Thucydides and Polybius. Polybius was not held in very high esteem during Antiquity, even though he exerted a strong influence on later Roman and Greek historiography. Byzantine historians, however, avidly referred to him. Following his rediscovery in Florence, he became the most influential ancient historian for a long time until Thucydides took his place in the 19th cent.

4. Rome

4.1 Characteristics of Roman Historiography and Their Influence

During the period of Fabius Pictor (ca. 270– after 216 BC), the first Roman historiographer, Rome was drawn more and more into the Greek world; Fabius Pictor himself therefore wrote in Greek. For a long time thereafter, Greek historiography and its principles guided the course of Roman historiography. The earliest Roman sources, the annual chronicles of the highest priests, already seemed inadequate to Cato (Cato Orig. 77). What Roman historiography itself was still unable to provide–that is, a reconstruction of early Roman history not based on myth–became an important criterion for the emergence of a modern historiography critical of its sources. Nonetheless, the Roman mythological glorification of early history, as documented classically by Titus Livius (or Livy, 59– AD 17) in his work *Ab urbe condita*, remained of fundamental importance for all later views of history.

The same holds true for the strong interest of Roman historians in the ethical substance of historical actions. It reveals itself not only in the great histories written by such figures as Sallust, Tacitus, or Ammianus Marcellinus. It is also expressed in the highly effective *exempla* of Roman history, as they were documented by Valerius Maximus, among others.

Romans, too, found that history was not its own simple field. Important statements about the nature of historiography can be found in the rhetorical works of Cicero or Quintilian, works which have been quoted regularly in modern times when the nature of historiography was debated; note, for example, the famous topos of history as *magistra vitae* (Cic. de Orat. 2,36).

An important model for dealing with the past is the collection of antiquarian knowledge about the most varied fields. By continuing this tradition, antiquarians of the early modern period laid the foundation for a historiography that includes cultural history and that goes beyond a narrow focus on the history of political events.

4.2 Roman History as a History of the City and the Emperors

Later a national and patriotic trend became central in historiography. The city of Rome as the main object of a historical work first appears in Livy. The epitome of Rome is, however, not only the city, but its emperors as well. A history of emperors was written by Tacitus in his *Historiae* and *Annales*. The concept of Roman history as a history determined by the city of Rome as well as by individual emperors was solidified and disseminated by numerous historical summaries during the imperial period and Late Antiquity. Handbooks of this type spread basic historical knowledge in the Middle Ages as well as in the Early Modern period.

4.3 Comparisons to the Stages in Human Life

The premise of this theory is the similarity of the development of a state with the stages in human life. In Rome, the development of the Roman state is interpreted by comparing it to the different human ages. In the *Origines* of Cato (234–149 BC), for example, the Roman Republic goes through four stages. Comparisons to life stages such as these continue to reappear in modern theories of society.

4.4 Historical Monographs

A historical monograph deals with a temporally limited topic. Roman historiography in particular cultivated the genre, which still exists today. The first example is the *Punic War* by L. Coelius Antipater (ca. 175– after 121 BC). In the Late Republic, Sallust's (ca. 86–35 BC) *Coniuratio Catilinae* appeared, as well as his *Bellum Iugurthinum*. Both presented the moral and political decay of the state. The *Commentarii* by Caesar (100–44 BC) also belong to this genre. The *Commentarii* have been imitated in many different epochs.

5. Christians; Late Antiquity; Early Byzantine Period

5.1 New Historical Divisions

Like the Jews, Christians have a linear conception of history which starts from a beginning and proceeds in a straight line, guided by Providence, to an end. Time is divided into the pre-messianic and messianic periods. In Christianity we find the following model: paradise, fall and salvation divided into two periods: Adam to Christ and Christ to the Last Judgment. History thus becomes historical theology. God's actions in history are based on his plan of salvation. The notion that the course of history is influenced by Providence (*providentia*) shapes the entire medieval interpretation of history.

The works of the Apostle Paul present history as divided into three sections: the period of natural law (from Adam to Moses), the period of Mosaic law (from Moses to Christ), and the period of the Gospel (since the coming of Christ). According to chiliastic doctrine (*chilioi* = thousand), the entire duration of the world spans six creation days of a 1000 years each, thus 6000 years. 7000 years or eras will pass between creation and the second coming of Christ; the seventh day is the 'sabbath of the world'; the Last Judgment will follow thereafter and a new world will begin as the eighth day. Millenarianism appears in the Epistle of Barnabas (written between 70 and 130). Again and again, Christianity was interpreted as the return of the Golden Age (Lact. Inst. 5,7,1; Eusebius HE 9,9,4; 9,9,11; 10,1,1).

The stages in life in a Christian sense occur in Origen (ca. 184–252): they correspond to Adam, Noah, Abraham, Moses and Christ. In this scheme, the history of the world can be divided into ages *(aetates)* just like human life. This is the preferred structure of history in medieval historiography. The Roman Empire was viewed as the last empire of history and afetr it, on believed, the end of the world would take place. Tertullian (ca. AD 160–ca. 225, Apol. 32,1) as well as Cyprian (ca. AD 205–258) interpreted the last of the four world empires mentioned in the Book of Daniel in this sense, with Rome as an aging organism.

5.2 Chronology and Chronicles

Christian chronography begins with Judas (Eusebius HE 6,7), whose work is not extant. After 221, the first Christian chronicle of the world is published by Sextus Julius Africanus. It is a chronographic compilation from Adam to AD 217; the birth of Christ is set in the year 5500 after the creation of the world. The chronicle by Eusebius of Caesaria (ca. 260–339), later to be continued by Jerome (ca. 345–420) to the year 378, introduced a chronology of world history which had a determining influence on future works.

5.3 Church History

Christian Church historiography, which began with Eusebius and was soon continued by other important authors, introduced new topics and criteria for evaluation into historiography and also brought a methodological innovation: For the first time, documents quoted word for word are inserted into historical works.

5.4 Hagiography

Hagiography also emerged in Christian Late Antiquity. It is similar to biography in that it technically does not belong to the genre of historiography, yet had an enormous influence on the way history was understood in Late Antiquity and in other periods that adopted models from Late Antiquity, such as the *Vita* of Saint Martin of Tours.

5.5 Eusebius, Jerome, Augustine, Orosius

These four authors definitively shaped the development of historiography in their time as well as the contemporary view of history, and their works continued to be of fundamental importance in the Middle Ages

and in the modern period. Eusebius of Caesaria is not only the author, among other things, of a chronicle and a Church history. His *Life of Constantine* was the foundation of imperial theology which creates a connection between the emergence of the *Imperium Romanum* and the spread of Christianity. His world chronicle passed the Old Testament interpretation of history stressing God's saving grace on to the Middle Ages. The commentary on the Book of Daniel by Jerome (ca. 347–419/20) introduced the Hellenistic model of the four world monarchies into the medieval Christian view of history.

The looting of Rome by the Goths in the year 410 demanded a Christian response to the pagan accusation blaming it on Christians. In this context, Augustine (354–430) wrote his *De civitate Dei* (413–426). In it history is interpreted in a theological sense. There is a *civitas terrena* and a *civitas Dei* which fight against each other and which will be separated at the end of time. Augustine argues against a cyclical concept of history. Influenced by Varro (116–27 BC) and Lactantius (ca. AD 250–ca. 325, Inst. 7,14,9), he divides world history into six ages: *infantia* from Adam to Noah, *pueritia* to Abraham, *adolescentia* to David, *iuventus* to the Babylonian Captivity, *senior aetas* to Christ and *senectus* from the time of Christ to the Last Judgment (Questionum sexaginta quinque, 26; Sermo 91).

This historical theology was expressed historiographically in the *Historiae adversum paganos libri VII* (418) by Paulus Orosius (late 4th cent.–418). It can be regarded as the first attempt to write a universal history based on Christian thought.

5.6 Late Roman Pagan Historiography

Corresponding to the two parts of the empire, one can find Greek as well as Latin historiography. The chronicle by Dexippus (3rd cent.), an example for the tradition focused on world history, covers history up to 269/70 and was continued in Byzantine historiography. The greatest personality, however, is Ammianus Marcellinus (2nd half of the 4th cent.), who in his *Res gestae* takes up and continues the work of Tacitus to 378, the year of the Battle of Adrianople. His objectivity sets him apart from the other authors. Ammianus Marcellinus deeply influenced the historical work of Gibbon (18th cent.).

5.7 Peculiarities of the Late Roman Pagan Interest in History

In the second half of the 4th cent., *brevaria* or summaries of Roman history became highly popular: for instance, those by Ampelius, Eutropius, Exuperantius, Iulius Obsequens, Festus Rufius or the *Historiae abbreviatae* by Aurelius Victor, which is divided into an *Origo gentis romanae*, a *De viris illustribus urbis romae* and an *Epitome de caesaribus* to form the *Corpus aurelianum*. The tendency to write summaries such as these is also prevalent in the Middle Ages. In the late 4th cent., the senatorial circles of the city of Rome took an interest in the Roman past, inspired by Symmachus among others. As a result, new editions of classics such as Livy appeared. The historiography of Late Antiquity borrowed excerpts from the collection of *exempla* by Valerius Maximus.

5.8 Effects of the Migration Period

The Germanic peoples that had penetrated the Roman Empire created a new historical genre: the history of Germanic tribes. The first representative is the Roman Cassiodorus (485–490) with his no longer extant *Historia Gothorum*. An excerpt from it is contained in the *Getica* (ca. 551) of Jordanes (6th cent.). The identification of the Germanic concept of a people with an area led to a national historiography.

5.9 Early Byzantine Period

The tradition of Greek historiography was continued in Byzantium. Latin historiographical texts translated into Greek, such as the *Breviarium* by Eutropius, are the exception. Zosimus (late 5th-early 6th cent.) is the last pagan representative of contemporary history with his *Historia Nea*, written in ca. 501. An author of great historiography was Procopius (ca. 500–after 551), historian of the emperor Justinian. Johannes Malalas (ca. 490–ca. 570) is the author of the first Byzantine world chronicle, which begins with the creation of the world and ends in 563. Johannes Xiphilinus (11th cent.) used excerpts from Dio Cassius. We also find Church history, annals, chronicles and presentations of contemporary history. The Byzantine chronicles were influential in Russia.

C. Latin Middle Ages

In contrast to Byzantine historiography, which ended with the fall of Constantinople (1453), it is difficult to delineate the chronological boundaries of historiography written in Western Europe. The roots of medieval historiography are found in Late Antiquity and in the period of the migrations. Medieval historiography consists of several genres: universal history with political and theological interpretations, Church history, historiography of Germanic and Slavic tribes, annals, chronicles, *gesta*, *exempla* and *specula* with predominantly political content. The Bible plays a large role in medieval historiography.

1. World History   2. Chronology and Ideology   3. The Chronicles   4. History of Tribes   5. Trojan Descent   6. Story of Alexander   7. Local History   8. Church History   9. Annals   10. Crusade history   11. *Gesta*   12. *Exempla*   13. *Specula*   14. Effect of Rhetoric on Historiography   15. Methodology   16. Basic Traits of Medieval Historiography   17. Reception of Historiographers from Classical Antiquity

1. World History

The most important representatives regarding the interpretation of world history in the Middle Ages are Otto von Freising (ca. 1112–1159) and Joachim of Fiore (ca. 1136–1202). Otto von Freising takes up Augustine's two *civitates* in his *Historia de duabus civitatibus*. He interprets history as a battle between the earthly and divine realms. He employs the theory of the four world empires and takes Babylon as the origin of civilisation. The *translatio imperii* appears in connection with the theory of world empires found in the Book of Daniel. Otto is a defender of the *Sacrum Imperium Romanum* held by the Hohenstaufens during his time. The *Historia* by Otto von Freising relates back to the *Historiae philippicae* by Pompeius Trogus in its universal tendency. Otto's predecessors are Fechulf of Lisieux (9th cent.), Frutolf von Michelsberg (d. 1103), and Hugo of Saint-Victor (d. 1141). Sigebert of Gembloux (ca. 1028/9–1112) wrote a *Chronica universalis* which included Byzantium. The theory of three eras, which views the world and world history as a product of the Trinity and organises it accordingly, appears in Ruppert von Deutz (ca. 1075/80–1129/30) and in Joachim of Fiore (ca. 1135–1202), who speaks of three eras: 1. the era of the Father and the Old Testament, 2. the era of the Son and the New Testament, 3. the era of the Holy Spirit. His interpretation of history is in line with the Bible and is understood to be linear, as in Otto von Freising and the medieval historiographers, as opposed to the concept of history as cyclical, as in pagan philosophers against whom Augustine had already written polemics. The idea of a third empire was the force behind the political attempt by Cola di Rienzo (d. 1354) to revive the Roman Republic. Revivals of the three-part models would again occur much later, for instance, in the terms 'Third Reich' in national-socialist Germany or 'Third International' in the communist notion of an empire of peace on earth.

2. Chronology and Ideology

The Julian calendar introduced by Caesar in 46 BC usually served as the basis. It is part of the Gregorian Reform (1582) still valid today. Augustine's theory of eras, which assigns each day of the week to a certain era, was adopted by Isidor and Bede. Dionysius Exiguus (d. between 526 and 556) determined that the year 754 after the founding of Rome is the year of Christ's birth in *Ab incarnatione domini*, thus creating a point of departure for chronology which gains acceptance only slowly. Bede took it up in *Historia ecclesiastica gentis anglorum*. Bede wrote the most important chronographic work of the Middle Ages: *De temporum ratione*. The dating 'Anno Domini' has been retained into modern times. However, a Christian term for the period before Christ was first introduced much later by D. Petavius (1583–1652). The chronology of medieval historiography is determined by Christianity. Jesus Christ is the centre of history, a history oriented towards the hereafter. Medieval historians regard history as the work of God according to his plan of salvation, as explained by Orosius.

3. The Chronicles

The material of medieval chronicles is taken from Roman historiography with the intention of presenting a chronological sequence of events in world history.

The model was Cornelius Nepos (ca. 100–ca. 25 BC). The founders of this genre, however, were Eusebius (ca. AD 260/64–ca. 339/40) and Jerome (AD 347/78–419/20). The chronicle of Jerome was continued by Prosper of Tiro (ca. 390–after 445) to 445. Marius of Avenches (530/31–594) continued it from 445 to 581. For his part, Hydatius (5th cent.) continued his *Continuatio chronicorum hieronymianorum* to 468. Medieval chronicles are primarily interested in political and military history. The genre was popular in all European countries. One of the reasons for the importance of Anglo-Saxon chronicles is the fact that they were among the first to be written in the mother tongue.

4. History of Tribes

Tribal history, which describes the history of one tribe and turns into an early form of national historiography, was written in the tradition of Cassiodorus and Jordanes. This genre is represented by: Gregory of Tours (538/39–after 593) with his *Historiae francorum* for the Franks, Isidor of Seville (ca. 560–636) with *Historiae gothorum, vandalorum et sueborum* for the West Goths and the Venerable Bede (673/4–735), with his *Historia ecclesiastica gentis anglorum* for the Anglo-Saxons. Paulus Diaconus (ca. 720/30–ca. 799) was the author of a *Historia langobardorum* for the Langobards. Widukind of Corvey (ca. 925–ca. 1004) wrote *Res gestae saxonicae* for the Saxons. Dudo of St. Quentin (ca. 960–1020) wrote *De moribus et actibus primorum normanniae ducum* for the Normans and Adam of Bremen (d. ca. 1085) wrote *Gesta hammaburgensis ecclesiae pontificum* for the Scandinavians. William of Malmesbury (ca. 1090–1143) wrote *De rebus gestis regum anglorum* along the lines of Bede. Geoffrey of Monmouth (ca. 1090/1100–1155) wrote *Historia regum britanniae* as Bede's successor and the founder of the British view of history. Cosmas of Prague (ca. 1045–1125) created a *Chronica boemorum* about Bohemia. Anonymus Gallus (late 11th cent.-early 12th cent.) wrote the *Chronica et gesta ducum sive principum polonorum* about Poland. The Nestor Chronicle (early 12th cent.) reports about the Russians. Helmond of Bosaus (ca. 1120–after 1177) wrote the *Chronica slaworum* about the Slavs and Saxo Grammaticus (ca. 1150–ca. 1220) reports about the Danes in *Gesta danorum*.

5. Trojan Descent

In *Antiquitates romanae*, Dionysius of Halicarnassus tried to show that the Romans descended from the Trojans in an effort to reconcile Greeks and Romans during the period of Emperor Augustus. The Fredegar Chronicle (6th cent.) tried to reveal a Trojan origin (*origo*) for the Franconian region. This genre continued to have an effect throughout the Middle Ages in all of Europe.

6. Story of Alexander

The historians of Alexander the Great have, above all, shaped the legend of Alexander from Late Antiquity and throughout the Middle Ages. It was taken up in all European countries, as well as in Hebrew and Islamic literature. Quintus Curtius Rufus (1st cent. AD) wrote the version preferred in the West with his *Historiae alexandri magni*. This work served as a model for the *Vita caroli magni* by Einhard in the 9th cent. Curtius' work gave a new impetus to the genre in the 12th cent., as shown by Walter of Châtillon.

7. Local History

Ancient local history had an important influence on the almost countless city chronicles of the Middle Ages. The chronicles of the leading families, which cannot be named individually here, are connected to them as well in a specific way. The historiography of dynasties increased parallel to the development of the territorial state. City chronicles are closely linked to the increasing autonomy of the bourgeoisie. The Villiani, several authors from the same family, wrote a history of Florence to 1360 in Italian. They are the precursors of the Humanist historiographers.

8. Church History

Church history continued in the tradition of Eusebius, with Bede as the first important representative of medieval Church historiography. In the Middle Ages, however, a new genre gains ground: monastery history, which in the modern period transforms itself into the history of religious orders. Closely related to this is the *Liber pontificalis*, a title denoting the *Gesta pontificum romanorum* based on the papal lists of Antiquity.

9. Annals

The *Annales* are a peculiar form of medieval historiography in that they practically function as its backbone. They begin in the 8th cent. and are rooted the *Annales* of Roman historiography. Like the *Annales* of Tacitus, medieval annals refer to a relatively distant past, a past that Tacitus had already distinguished from contemporary history. In the Middle Ages, annals are records of events year by year.

10. Crusade History

The historiography of the Crusades is a typical historiographical genre of the Middle Ages. The most important historiographer is William of Tyre (ca. 1130–ca. 1185), who based his work largely on what he himself saw. The Spanish *Reconquista* and the German capture of the regions beyond the river Elbe are also presented as crusades. The idea of a Crusade had an influence on modern historiography at various times. A core element is the concept of a *bellum iustum*, which one finds already in Augustine.

11. Gesta

The *gesta* or history of deeds have their origin in the *res gestae* of Roman historiography. Such is, for instance, the title of the historical work by Ammianus Marcellinus. In the Middle Ages, *gesta* are closely related to the reports of deeds by Church personalities. There are also *gesta* of secular personalities.

12. Exempla

The *exempla* are a highly popular genre in medieval historiography modelled after the *exempla* of Roman literature, especially those by Valerius Maximus, whose *Facta et dicta memorabilia* was read as a historical work.

13. Specula

The term *speculum* goes back to Augustine and, in this context, can be understood as a model. *Specula* were intended for theological and political purposes but contained historical summaries as well. The most important *Speculum* was written by Vincentius of Beauvais (ca. 1190–1264). Although the *Specula* enjoyed their peak in the Middle Ages, they continued to have an effect on political theory up to the modern period.

14. Effect of Rhetoric on Historiography

According to the rhetoricians, history (*historia*) is a literary genre. Cicero's (106–43 BC) *De inventione* and the *Rhetorica ad herennium* (mid 1st cent. BC) as well as the *Institutio oratoria* by Quintilian (ca. 35–after 96) have exerted a great influence on medieval historiography.

15. Methodology

The *Historiae* by Paulus Orosius contain principles of a historical methodology. Medieval historiography clearly distinguishes between *res gestae* and *historia*, the latter being a comprehensive concept for all kinds of historiography. The moralising character of history is revealed in the fact that its goal is the *exemplum*. It is based on Latin sources along with oral tradition and the personal experiences of the author. Medieval historians copied documents and included them in their reports. Ordericus Vitalis (ca. 1075–1142) was the first to research archives and use inscriptions, which makes him a precursor of modern historical research.

16. Basic Traits of Medieval Historiography

Isidorus of Sevilla defined *historia* as 'narratio rei gestae, per quam ea, quae in praeterito facta sunt, dinoscuntur' ("a recounting of a thing carried out, through which things done in the past are recognized as different",Isid. Orig. 1,41,1). The goal of history was to give a true report of the past. History was also *magistra vitae*, a teacher who undertook the moral orientation of Roman historiography. The belief in *providentia Dei* resulted in a providentialist interpretation of history. The theory of empires regarded the Roman Empire as the last in a sequence of empires and claimed that it would continue to exist until the arrival of the Antichrist. The *Imperium Romanum* was an empire like the earlier empires before it, but the Church was the agent of universal unity. Here, one can detect Orosius' influence.

17. Reception of Historiographers from Classical Antiquity

Before the 15th cent., Greek texts were hardly known in the Latin Middle Ages. Pagan Greek historiography simply was not translated into Latin. The Jewish historian Flavius Josephus was an exception. In the 4th cent., the *Bellum iudaicum* was translated into Latin and in the 6th cent., the *Antiquitates iudaicae* as well. Hence Josephus was known in the Middle Ages. Latin models were Sallust, Vergil's *Aeneid* (regarded, however, not as literature but as a historical work), Livy, Pompeius Trogus in the excerpt by Iustinius and Florus, whose historical work was a summary of Livy and therefore very influential. Tacitus had less influence, indirectly through the *Historiae* by Orosius. Eutropius (4th cent.) was important because of the summarising character and the brevity of his historical work. Furthermore, Ammianus Marcellinus and the *Historia augusta* were read as well. The *Historiae* by Orosius were well known and remained influential. They form the basis of Latin world chronicles. Orosius was translated into Anglo-Saxon and Arabic. Caesar was used almost exclusively by historians interested in the history of warfare. Suetonius strongly influenced the authors of biographies.

D. Renaissance and Protestantism

During the Renaissance, the HM of Antiquity were rediscovered and valued highly. Humanists of the Reformation period used these models for theological as well as political purposes. The invention of printing contributed to the spread of historiography. Modern historical criticism began in the 15th cent. During the Renaissance the idea that there is a difference between knowledge and belief gained strength. History was newly regarded as a process for detecting causes and effects, similar to Thucydides' analyses.

1. Trends in Humanist Historiography
2. Protestantism   3. Division of History
into Periods   4. Historical Methodology
5. Discovery of the Classics and Their Use

1. Trends in Humanist Historiography

The idealisation of Antiquity during the Renaissance led to a strong interest in ancient historiography, which, however, did not exclude a critical attitude. In contrast to the Middle Ages, history became a secular field. Petrarch (1304–1374) discovered Livy. Historiography followed the rules of ancient rhetoric. The Florentine Leonardo Bruni (ca. 1370–1444) is the founder of Humanist historiography. Along with Humanist historiography, we see the emergence of a national historiography first in Italy, then in the rest of Europe, focusing on the regions of the national states under formation. It is modelled on tribal history going back to Cassiodorus and Jordanes. In this way, England in the period of Queen Elisabeth I was searching for its Anglo-Saxon roots. W. Camden (1551–1623) wrote *Britannia* (1586). A critical study of the sources began in the 15th cent. with Flavio Biondo (1392–1463). In 1453 he completed a work dealing with the history of southern Europe from 410 to 1442. This work was based on chronicles as well as documents such as letters. He influenced Beatus Rhenanus (1486–1547), who dealt critically with the sources of ancient Germanic history. As early as 1440, Lorenzo Valla (1405 or 1407–1457) expressed doubts regarding the Donation of Constantine. In the mid 16th cent., L. V. de la Popelinière questioned the Trojan descent of the Franks. Political historiography following Thucydides's model begins in the 15th cent. with Niccolò Machiavelli (1469–1527) and Francesco Guicciardini (1483–1540). Both authors used ancient history as a model for the presentation of the political history of Italian states. The *Discorsi* by Machiavelli and the *Ricordi* by Guicciardini also take into consideration the laws to explain human behaviour and politics formulated by Thucydides and Polybius. Machiavelli showed a special interest in Livy in his *Discorsi sulla prima deca di Tito Livio* (1531). He regarded the *exempla* of the old historians as the essence of history and the Romans as masters of politics. The *Istorie Fiorentine* (1532) shows that Machiavelli believed in the political realism of power whose goal was the political unity of Italy. However, Machiavelli largely neglected source research. Guicciardini's *Storia d'Italia* (written between 1537 and 1540; published between 1561 and 1564) is influenced by Thucydides and Polybius. His work deals with the time from 1492 to 1532 and the beginnings of the European system of states. This author refers to documents in his work, as did Thucydides and Polybius. The study of Roman law influenced historiography as well. The writings of Guillaume Budé (1467–1540) are an example.

2. PROTESTANTISM

The Protestant view held that history is the work of God. Luther influenced the Humanists, and, as a consequence, Church history, established by Eusebius, was rediscovered. The historiography of the religious battles began with the *Vitae romanorum pontificum* by the Englishman Robert Barnes (1495–1540) who published this work in 1535. The publication of Johannes Sleidanus's (1506–1566) work *Commentarii de statu religionis et rei publicae, carolo quinto caesare* in 1555 marked the beginning of journalistic imperial historiography. Protestant ecclesiastical historiography emerged with the *Magdeburger Zenturien* (1559–1574), published by Matthias Flacius Illyricus. The Catholic response was provided by the *Annales ecclesiastici* (1588–1607) of Caesar Baronius (1538–1607).

3. DIVISION OF HISTORY INTO PERIODS

The model 'Antiquity', 'Middle Ages', 'Modernity' was created during the Renaissance–an age which idealised Antiquity and despised the Middle Ages. Lorenzo Valla used this structure as early as 1440, with preference given to Antiquity. He claimed that Antiquity was followed by an intermediate period, a *medium tempus*, i.e., the Middle Ages, which lasted up to the Renaissance. Protestantism revived the old theory of the four world monarchies. This theory was represented by the Englishman Johannes Carion (1499–1537). The edition of the *Chronicon carionis* by Philipp Melanchthon (1497–1560) presented the four world empires of which each was claimed to have lasted 2000 years. Johannes Sleidanus presented a description of the four world monarchies as well in his world chronicle *De quattuor summis imperiis*, published in 1556.

4. HISTORICAL METHODOLOGY

Jean Bodin (ca. 1530–1596) is one of the founders of modern historical methodology with his *Methodus ad facilem historiarum cognitionem* (1566). He elaborates on certain ideas found, for instance, in Lucian's work *How History Should be Written*. Along with Hippocrates and Poseidonius, he represents the theory that climate influences human behaviour. Bodin also offers ideas about empires that are connected to the theory of the *translatio imperii*. However, Bodin's concept that the history of humanity is a universal whole did not find favour with subsequent authors.

5. DISCOVERY OF THE CLASSICS AND THEIR USE

Thucydides was rediscovered in 1452 thanks to Lorenzo Valla's Latin translation. He was a model for Machiavelli's *Il Principe* (1513). This work was influenced by Aristotle's *Politics* as well as by Tacitus. A large number of these texts was disseminated beginning in 1473 through the printing press. The work of Fabius Pictor was one of the models for Renaissance national historiography. Cicero's ideal of the state had a tremendous effect. The Renaissance view of Rome goes back to Livy. The work of Valerius Maximus was one of the most widely known ancient Latin prose works. The story of Alexander in Quintus Curtius Rufus' version became known thanks to the Humanists Coluccio Salutati (1331–1406) and Lorenzo Valla (1407–1457). As early as the 14th cent., Giovanni Boccaccio (1313–1375) studied Tacitus, whose *Germania* and *Agricola* spread thanks to Enea Silvio Piccolomini (1405–1464, who became Pope Pius II in 1458). In Germany, the tendency to glorify one's own past began in ca.1500. Jakob Wimpfeling (1450–1528) strove to prove in his *Germania* that Alsace was a Germanic settlement. Konrad Celtis's (1459–1508) *Germania illustrata* (1518) was published posthumously, and Ulrich of Hutten (1488–1523) began what became a cultic worship of the title figure in his *Arminius* (1519–1520, published in 1529). The historian Florus influenced Petrarch. With the spread of Tacitus' historical works emerged the political phenomenon of → TACITISM, a movement (1580–1680) that justified the introduction of absolute monarchies. The historical works of Xenophon were valued highly in the Renaissance.

E. BAROQUE AND ENLIGHTENMENT

In contrast to the Renaissance and Protestantism, we now detect the beginnings of a direct study of history, a history much less influenced by the texts of Classical Antiquity. The 17th and 18th cents. saw the development of a critical stance towards history. There was a transition from theological to philosophical ways of viewing historical processes. Rationalism and the Enlightenment separated historiography from theology, morality and rhetoric. As a consequence, the historical dimensions of human actions were actually discovered. Historical learning became increasingly important.

1. Division of History into Periods

The Humanist model 'Antiquity', 'Middle Ages', 'Modernity' receives new importance in the 17th cent., although traces of the older theory of world empires still remain in the periodization of history. Justus Lipsius (1547–1606) divided *historia humana* into four periods in his *Epistolarum selectarum chilias* (Leiden, posthumously published, 1611): *Orientalis, Graeca, Romana* and *Barbarica*. G. Voetius (1589–1676) divided Church history into three epochs: *antiqua ecclesia, intermedia aetas* and *novitates ecclesiasticae*. J. A. Bose (1626–1674) differentiates the following three epochs: *antiquitas, media aetas* and *nostrum saeculum*. Beginning with Christoph Cellarius (1638–1707), the division into Antiquity (up to Constantine), Middle Ages (up to the capture of Constantinople) and Modernity becomes prevalent, although even Cellarius himself did not completely rid himself of Christian-theological patterns of interpretation. J. W. Jan published a text *De IV monarchiis* as late as 1712, in which he defends the old system of four monarchies.

2. Theological History

The last great representative of the idea that history is guided by Divine Providence is Jacques-Bénigne Bossuet (1627–1704). His *Discours sur l'Histoire universelle* (1681) is strongly influenced by the interpretation of history found in Augustine's *De civitate dei*. Bossuet used the Augustinian division of time for his own epochal divisions. The interpretation of history is used by him to legitimise the present: The French monarchy is regarded as the heir to the Roman Empire.

3. History as a New Science

With his *scienza nuova*, Giovanni Battista Vico (1668–1744) became the father of modern historiography and a precursor of historicism. Vico created a view of history that ties histories or stories together into the collective singular 'history' as a comprehensive term for evaluating human actions in time and space. Vico favoured the idea of cyclical processes in history (*corsi* and *ricorsi*) which are rooted in ancient designs. According to Vico, there are the three eras (*corsi*) of gods, heroes and humans, after which the different peoples developed. At the end we have barbarism and thus another *ricorso*. Vico set up a sequence of spiritual epochs which all peoples go through in all cultural realms in a way governed by law. He believed in Providence. He considered the rise and fall of peoples to be guided by a basic law that runs a spiral course, as it were. Vico defended the validity of historical knowledge. He is convinced that human nature is unchanging, an idea already expressed by Thucydides. This search for reasonable rules to explain historical processes was a strong force in the history of historiography. The term 'historical science' was first used in 1752 by J. M. Chladenius; this marked its conceptual separation from rhetoric and jurisprudence.

4. Philosophy of History, Universal History, World History

The replacement of theological patterns of interpretation by rational explanations was largely due to Voltaire (1694–1778). His *Essai sur les moeurs et l'esprit des nations* (1769) makes him the founder of philosophy of history (*philosophie de l'histoire*) in a cultural sense. The philosophical view of history puts an end to theological interpretation. The new genre of world history from a philosophical standpoint also included the Orient. History is no longer Eurocentric but universal. Johann Gottfried Herder (1744–1803) combined providential thinking and the idea of progress in *Auch eine Philosophie der Geschichte zur Bildung der Menschheit* (*This Too a Philosophy of History for the Formation of Humanity,*1774) and *Ideen zur Philosophie der Geschichte der Menschheit* (*Ideas for the Philosophy of History of Humanity,*1784–1791); with these works, he deepened the philosophy of history. He shared Voltaire's linear understanding of the course of history. For Herder the goal of historical development was the realisation of an ideal humanity. Herder distinguished between man and nature. He contributed much to the foundation of historicism. In this context, Immanuel Kant's (1724–1804) *Ideen zu einer allgemeinen Geschichte in weltbürgerlicher Absicht* (*Idea for a Universal History with a Cosmopolitan Purpose,*1784) must be mentioned as well, a work in which history is subsumed under nature. In *Was heißt und zu welchem Ende studiert man Universalgeschichte?* (*What Is, and to What End Do We Study, Universal History?*, 1789), Friedrich Schiller (1759–1805) combined the ideas of Herder and Kant regarding world history. An interest in universal history as such can be found in the 18th cent. in the academic context of the historical school at the University of Göttingen, in particular, in its most prominent representative, August Ludwig Schlözer (1735–1809).

5. Idea of Progress

The → Querelle des Anciens et des Modernes in 17th-cent. France is one of the conditions under which the idea of progress was developed. The idea is Christian in origin but was later secularised. The term itself does not appear until the 18th cent. Its roots can be found in literary history, particularly in Bernhard Fontenelle (1657–1757). The main representatives of the idea of progress are Turgot (1727–1781) and Condorcet (1743–1794), who regard the perfection of humanity as a process guided by natural law. They are the precursors of positivism.

6. History, Politics, Society, and Education

Similar to Caesar and Machiavelli, Friedrich II (the Great, 1712–1786, King of Prussia from 1740) concerned himself with contemporary history. Montesquieu (1689–1755) examined the influence of climate and environment on peoples and states in *De l'Esprit des lois* (1748); Poseidonius was a precursor of this theory in Classical Antiquity. The approach reveals a deterministic view. Governmental situations are subject to laws. The *Considérations sur les causes de la grandeur des Romains et de leur décadence* (1738) was written from this perspective as well. A. Ferguson (1723–1816) contemplated progress and decline in the framework of examining society in *An Essay on the History of Civil Society* (1767). G. E. Lessing (1729–1781) also believed in a gradual perfection of humanity through education in *Education of Humankind* (1780). In opposition to the idea of progress, J. J. Rousseau (1712–1778) regarded the decline of peoples as the result of civilisation, which he juxtaposed to the natural state of primitive man. These thoughts are developed in greater detail in *Discours sur les Sciences et les Arts* (1750) and in *Discours sur l'origine et les fondaments de l'inégalité parmi les hommes* (1755).

7. Historical Criticism

The scientific revolution of the Early Modern Period brought an end to old authorities. This process stimulated the development of historical criticism, which can be found especially in the various disciplines within ancient studies and ancient sciences. F. A. Wolf practiced such criticism excessively in his *Prolegomena ad Homerum,* his introductory remarks to an edition of the *Iliad* (1794–1795). Important for the development of historical criticism were the works on the history of the Catholic Church and its orders popular among Jesuit Bollandists and the Benedictines of St. Maurs. From 1643 the Jesuits published the *Acta Sanctorum* in connection with J. Bolland (1596–1665). On the basis of a critical study of the sources, the lives of saints were published. The Benedictines of St. Maur published the *Acta* of Benedictine saints (1668), and J. Mabillon (1632–1707), the founder of diplomatics, published the *Annales ordinis sancti benedicti* (1703). The criticism voiced by I. Perizonius (1651–1715) about the sources of early Roman history in the *Animadversiones historicae* (1685) was far ahead of its time. In the 17th cent., P. Bayle (1647–1706) further enforced historical skepticism and rationalism in his *Dictionnaire historique et critique* (1697). Between 1751 and 1780, the *Encyclopédie ou Dictionnaire raisonné des sciences, des arts et des métiers* appeared under the guidance of Diderot and d'Alembert. This monumental work contains ample skepticism and criticism regarding the traditional understanding of history. The 18th. cent. saw the development of an interest in concrete historical details, as well as in the Late Roman Republic, an interest which led to an increased appreciation of the fundamental work of antiquarians. The interest in natural history further stimulated the historical disciplines.

8. Historiographical Development

The historiography of partisan political battles, such as those in Caesar's *Bellum civile,* is represented in England in the Restoration period by Lord Clarendon (1609–1674). Besides a *Histoire des Empereurs* (1690–1739), the Jansenist Louis-Sébastien Le Nain de Tillemont (1637–1698) wrote the authoritative *Mémoires pour servir à l'histoire ecclésiastique des six premières siècles* (1693–1712), modelled after Eusebius. Edward Gibbon (1783–1794), influenced by Ammianus Marcellinus and the use of many ancient sources, wrote *The History of the Decline and Fall of the Roman Empire* (1766–1788), the greatest historiographical work of the century. In this work, Gibbon deals with the history of the Roman Empire beginning with the period of Antoninus Pius (117–138), a golden age according to Gibbon, and follows the continuation of the Roman Empire in the East to 1453. In the examination of the causes for Rome's decline, Christianity appears as an important factor. The *History of Scotland* (1759) by W. Robertson (1793) was written following the less popular model of tribal history. Very important also is David Hume's (1711–1776) *History of England, from the Invasion of Julius Caesar to the Revolution of 1688* (1754–1763). Local history was represented by J. Möser (1720–1794). Antiquarian research was continued in art history. Of fundamental importance here is Johann Joachim Winckelmann (1717–1768) with his *Geschichte der Kunst des Altertums* (1764).

9. Reception of the Classics

The interest in the Classics of Antiquity remained unbroken during the Baroque and the Enlightenment.Thucydides was a model for *Leviathan* by Thomas Hobbes. Absolutism brought with it an interest in Suetonius. Duris of Samos can be regarded as a precursor of the historical novel and the Baroque style of the 17th cent. In the 17th cent. the interest in Polybius reached its peak.

F. The 19th Century

The 19th cent. can be regarded as the period in which the scholarly disciplines were developed and therefore as the peak of the historical sciences. History is no longer viewed as the result of actions by individuals but as the result of the dynamism of social forces. The natural sciences enjoy an enormous upsurge. A historical method is developed as the basis for historical scholarship with the critical study of sources and heuristic at its core. The Classical authors are studied according to these principles in the 19th cent. The many critical editions of ancient authors are an important legacy of the 19th cent.

1. Trends in the Philosophy of History
2. The Beginnning of a Critical Study of Ancient History and of Modern Historical Scholarship

1. Trends in the Philosophy of History

Romanticism left traces in the philosophy of history, as is apparent in the work of Friedrich von Schlegel

(1772–1829). Schlegel regards primitive peoples as the result of the decline from a golden age. This view echoes the theory of the Golden Age found in Classical Antiquity. The great philosophers of idealism are J. G. Fichte (1762–1814), F. W. J. Schelling (1775–1854) and W. G. F. Hegel (1770–1831). For Fichte history is an element of a universal plan. He distinguishes five periods in the development of humanity, in the course of which humanity is claimed to have attained greater rationality. This amounts to a revival of Classical ideas. In the *Reden an die deutsche Nation* (*Addresses to the German Nation*, 1807–1809), the old Germanic patriotism which had been described by Tacitus in his *Germania* is discernible. Schelling presents the Classical theory of epochs. In 1830 Hegel gave lectures at the University of Berlin about the philosophy of history which were published after his death (1831). In these lectures Hegel uses Herder's model and discusses the Orient, Greece, Rome and Germania, where the world spirit is claimed to unfold and humanity gradually attains freedom. According to Hegel's division of history into periods, the Orient corresponds to humanity's childhood, Greece and Rome form its youth, and the Germanic world achieves maturity. History is understood as the progress of consciousness towards freedom. The last period, the Germanic period, is also the time of the origin of the state. Historical dialectics is the principle that determines the course of the progressive self-realisation of the world spirit. The succession of empires appears as a pattern of history which unfolds towards freedom.

Historical dialectics forms the basis for the historical-economic theory of Karl Marx (1813–1883) and Friedrich Engels (1820–1895). History is considered to be the result of the economic conditions of production and of class struggle. The goal of history is the dictatorship of the proletariat. This served as the basis for historical materialism, which frequently used ancient historians and especially Diodorus for its arguments.

For Auguste Comte (1798–1857), history is a system of general sociological laws with three developmental stages: a theological, a metaphysical and a positive stage. Positivism, as expressed by Comte or Herbert Spencer (1820–1903), is rooted in the idea of progress.

Evolutionism, which also can be traced back to Antiquity, has deeply influenced historical thinking. It was formulated in detail by Charles R. Darwin (1809–1882). For evolutionism there exists a progressive development of humanity in stages: wildness, barbarism, civilisation.

The Classical authors exerted a deep influence on the philosophy of Friedrich Nietzsche (1844–1900). And yet Nietzsche presents a crisis and a criticism of philosophical thinking about history as well as a break from the idea that historical material has a value in itself, an idea cultivated by Jacob Burckhardt (1818–1897), who saw that value as a counterbalance to the relativism of his time. In Nietzsche's *Zweite Unzeitgemäße Betrachtung über Nutzen und Nachteil der Historie für das Leben* ("Second Untimely Meditation On the Use and Abuse of History for Life", 1874), this break is final. Nietzsche is an irrationalist. He presents the old pagan idea of the eternal return of the same. His writings contain racist notions as well.

2. The Beginning of a Critical Study of Ancient History and of Modern Historical Scholarship

Contemporary theories of history gained entrance into academic life not least through Wilhelm von Humboldt (1767–1835) and the founding of the new university in Berlin. Critical research on ancient history begins with Barthold Georg Niebuhr's (1776–1831) *Römische Geschichte* (1811). Niebuhr researches the first decade of Livy from a critical point of view. In 1824 the edition of the *Monumenta Germaniae Historica* began, which also included authors of Late Antiquity. The most important personality is Theodor Mommsen (1817–1901). Mommsen was an organiser of scholarship and master of the ancillary sciences who wrote countless authoritative works, of which the unfinished *Römische Geschichte* –the only work to be named here–earned him the Nobel Prize for Literature in 1902.

The founder of historicism was Leopold von Ranke (1795–1886). Among his numerous works, the *Weltgeschichte* (1881–1888) must be mentioned, where he develops a scholarly foundation for historical accounts. Ranke evaluates all historical forces. Although primarily an expert in modern history, his goal is universal history. Ranke is the founder of modern historical methodology. In his view of history, a strict methodical approach is more important than literary qualities. In a certain sense, he introduces positivism into history. The core of his method is the critical study of sources as well as philology. States are regarded by him as individuals.

The basic principles of historical understanding are explicitly described in the *Historik* by Johann Gustav Droysen (1808–1884). This work could not have been written without Droysen's study of Antiquity, especially of Alexander and Hellenism.

The 19th cent. saw the beginning of massive historical specialisation. Added to traditional historiography (political, diplomatic and military) are constitutional history with its two branches, history of law and history of institutions and economic and social history, as well as cultural history (founder: Jacob Burckhardt).

In his *Einleitung in die Geisteswissenschaften* (*Introduction to the Human Sciences*, 1883), Wilhelm Dilthey (1833–1911) offered a theory of historical understanding which presents historical science and natural science as different areas. In contrast, 18th-cent. thinkers regarded nature and history as a unified field. Historicism began with Dilthey. According to him, a human being is not a substance in itself, but becomes such through the historical process.

The 19th cent. also saw the emergence of a biologically oriented cultural morphology, a movement to which Vico's theory of the rise and fall of peoples and Hegel's theory of world epochs had contributed.

G. VIEW OF THE 20TH CENTURY

At first and in general, the 20th cent. followed the scientific trends of the previous century. concerning the study of history. Historical science expanded into more new fields. It is now closely related to the social sciences as well.

HM, as they were developed in Antiquity, maintain considerable influence in the various movements within the philosophy of history, as in Oswald Spengler's work (1880–1936), *Untergang des Abendlandes* (*Decline of the West*, 1918–1922). This work takes up Vico's theory of cultural cycles and reveals Herder's influence. Spengler distinguishes eight societies, each passing through three phases, just like biological life: early culture, high culture, and late culture. This theory of cultural cycles is rooted in Antiquity, as is that of Arnold Toynbee (1889–1975), who discusses twenty one civilizations in *A Study of History* (1934–1961) that are independent cultural realms. In *Ursprung und Ziel der Geschichte* (*The Origin and Goal of History*, 1949), Karl Jaspers (1883–1969) offers an existentialist interpretation of history in which he regards a so-called axial time from 800 BC to AD 200 as the turning point.

The study of Antiquity received productive impulses from Max Weber (1864–1920). He introduced sociology and economics into universal history and presented economic and social history in a systematic way.

There are no HM that did not find some use in later periods. Many factors play a role in their adoption, not least among them the prevailing ideologies and aesthetic preferences. Although the historiographical genres of Antiquity are different in many ways from those of modern times, they are still very important for the self-assurance of historical studies. And, of course, ancient historiography will remain a major source for all studies of Antiquity.

SOURCES 1 G. J. VOSSIUS, De historicis grecis libri IV, ²1651, repr. 1970) 2 Id., De historicis latinis libri III, ²1651, repr. 1970)
LITERATURE 3 J. M. ALONSO-NÚÑEZ, El pensamiento historiológico alemán en el siglo XVIII. Investigaciones sobre Herder y los origenes de la Filosofía de la Historia, 1971 4 Id. (ed.), Geschichtsbild und Geschichtsdenken im Altertum, 1991 5 Id., El concepto de historia universal en el pensamiento contemporaneo. Indagaciones sobre la historiografia universal en el siglo XX, 1994 6 R. R. BOLGAR, The Classical Heritage and its Beneficiaries, 1954 7 A. D. V. DEN BRINCKEN, Studien zur lateinischen Weltchronistik bis in das Zeitalter Ottos von Freising, 1957 8 P. BURKE, A Survey of the Popularity of Ancient Historians, 1450–1700, History and Theory 5, 1966, 135–152 9 B. CROCE, Teoria e storia della storiografia, 1913 (⁸1963) 10 A. DEMPF, Sacrum Imperium. Geschichts- und Staatsphilosophie des Mittelalters und der polititschen Renaissance, ³1962 11 E. FUETER, Geschichte der neueren Historiographie, 1911, (new ed., 1985) 12 B. GATZ, Weltalter, goldene Zeit und sinnverwandte Vorstellungen, 1967 13 H.-W. GOETZ, Von der res gesta zur narratio rerum gestarum. Anmerkungen zu Methoden und Hilfswissenschaften des mittelalterlichen Geschichtsschreibers, in: Revue Belge de Philologie et d'Histoire 67, 1989, 695–713 14 W. GOEZ, Translatio imperii. Ein Beitrag zur Geschichte des Geschichtsdenkens und der politischen Theorien im Mittelalter und in der frühen Neuzeit, 1958 15 G. P. GOOCH, Geschichte und Geschichtsschreiber im 19. Jahrhundert, 1964 16 H. GRUNDMANN, Geschichtsschreibung im Mittelalter. Gattungen, Epochen, Eigenart, 1987 17 B. GUENÉE, Histoires, annales, chroniques. Essai sur les genres historiques au moyen âge, in: Annales ESC 28, 1973, 997–1016 18 Id., Histoire et culture historique dans l'occident médiéval, 1980 19 D. HAY, Annalists and Historians. Western Historiography from the 8th to the 10th Centuries, 1977 20 G. G. IGGERS, Geschichtswissenschaft im 20. Jahrhundert. Ein kritischer Überblick im internationalen Vergleich, ²1996 21 W. KAMLAH, Utopie, Eschatologie, Geschichte-Theologie: Kritische Untersuchungen zum Ursprung und zum futuristischen Denken der Neuzeit, 1969 22 N. KERSKEN, Geschichtsschreibung im Europa der 'nationes'. Nationalgeschichtliche Gesamtdarstellungen im Mittelalter, 1995 23 A. KLEMPT, Die Säkularisierung der universalhistorischen Auffassung. Zum Wandel des Geschichtsdenkens im 16. und 17. Jahrhundert, 1960 24 J. KNAPE, Historie im Mittelalter und früher Neuzeit. Begriffs- und gattungsgeschichtlichen Untersuchungen im interdiziplinären Kontext, 1984 25 K. H. KRÜGER, Die Universalchroniken, 1975 26 B. LACROIX, L'historian au Moyen Age, 1971 27 W. LAMMERS (ed.), Geschichtsdenken und Geschichtsbild im Mittelalter, 1961 28 K. LÖWITH, Meaning in History, 1949 29 S. MAZZARINO, Il pensiero storico classico, 1966 (⁵1974) 3 vols. 30 F. G. MAIER, Der Historiker und die Texte, in: HZ 238, 1984, 83–94 31 G. MELVILLE, System und Diachronie. Untersuchungen zur theoretischen Grundlegung geschichtsschreibender Praxis im Mittelalter, in: Histor. Jahrbuch 95, 1975, 33–67 u. 308–341 32 A. MOMIGLIANO, Contributi alla Storia degli Studi Classici e del Mondo Antico, 1955–1992 33 Id., Studies in Historiography, 1966 34 Id., Essays in Ancient and Modern Historiography, 1977 35 Id., The Classical Foundations of Modern Historiography, 1990 36 K. E. MÜLLER, Geschichte der antiken Ethnographie und ethnologischen Theoriebildung, 2 vols., Studien zur Kulturkunde 29 and 52, 1972 and 1980 37 U. MUHLACK, Geschichtswissenschaft im Humanismus und in der Aufklärung. Die Vorgeschichte des Historismus, 1991 38 J. H. J. VAN DER POT, De periodisering der geschiedenis. Een overzicht der theorien, 1951 39 V. REINHARDT (ed.), Hauptwerke der Geschichtsschreibung, 1997 40 M. RITTER, Die Entwicklung der Geschichtswissenschaft an den führenden Persönlichkeiten betrachtet, 1919 41 H. RUPP u. O. KÖHLER, Historia – Geschichte, in: Saeculum 2, 1951, 627–638 42 F. J. SCHMALE, Funktion und Form mittalterlicher Geschichtsschreibung, 1985 43 R. SCHMIDT, Aetates mundi. Die Weltalter als Gliederungsprinzip der Geschichte, ZKG 67 1955/56, 288–317 44 V. W. SCHOLZ, Annales und Historia(e), in: Hermes 127, 1994, 64–79 45 A. SEIFERT, Historia im Mittelalter, Archiv für Begriffsgeschichte 21, 1977, 226–284 46 B. SMALLEY, Historians of the Middle Ages, 1974 47 G. SPITZLBERGER, C. D. KERNIG, Periodisierung, Sowjetsystem und demokratische Gesellschaft IV, 1971, 1135–1160 48 R. STADELMANN (ed.), Große Geschichtsdenker. Ein Zyklus Tübinger Vorlesungen, 1949 49 H. STRASBURGER, Die Wesenbestimmung der Geschichte durch die antike Geschichtsschreibung, in: M. SCHMITTHENNER, R. ZOEPFEL II (eds.), Studien zur Alten Geschichte, 1982, 963–1016 50 G. W. TROMPF, The

Idea of Historical Recurrence in Western Thought. From Antiquity to Reformation, 1979   51 F. Wagner, Geschichtswissenschaft, ²1966
Additional Bibliography G. Forsythe, Livy and Early Rome: A Study in Historical Method and Judgment, 1999 G. Marasco, Greek and Roman Historiography in Late Antiquity: Fourth to Sixth Century A.D., 2003 D. Rohrbacher, The Historians of Late Antiquity, 2002 F. Santoro L'Hoir, Tragedy, Rhetoric, and the Historiography of Tacitus' *Annales*, 2006

José Miguel Alonso-Núñez

Historiography
I. General   II. Greek History   III. Roman History   IV. Late Antiquity

I. General
A. Introduction   B. Authors, Formal Types, Genres   C. Terms, Metaphors, Temporal Structures   D. Rhetoric   E. History of the Discipline

A. Introduction
History and historiography are terms that can be used in a variety of ways. Not only are they frequently used synonymously, but depending on the context they refer to such different activities as the study of the past and the presentation of research results. This difference is reflected in the words *historíēs apódexis*, with which Herodotus began his accounts. In Herodotus' usage, the Greek noun *historíē*, which still defines 'historical knowledge' as distinct from other types of knowledge, refers to the process of exploration and investigation, while the noun *apódexis* is used for the (written or oral) presentation of one's findings. Even a strictly academic definition of these terms still implies the ancient distinction between *res gestae*, as actions that have taken place (i.e. 'history'), and *historia*, as a narrative account of those (historical) actions. Keeping in mind that the past is part of the present, we shall consider first certain authors and genres (B), then the instrumentalization of ancient concepts and metaphors as general guidelines for interpreting history (C), followed by rhetorical aspects of the production of historiographic texts (D) and finally certain implications of the reception of Antiquity for the formation of the discipline (E).

B. Authors, Formal Types, Genres
Herodotus, Thucydides and Xenophon are in the vanguard of a Classical canon that was compiled over a period of centuries. As this influential tradition was taking hold, the works of Herodotus became a model for a type of historiography that used imagination and embellishment to synthesize military, contemporary and cultural history. Since the Renaissance, however, Thucydides' work, which opens with a meta-historical reflection, has become the prototype for a monographic historiography associated with the pathos of a search for the truth, i.e. with a claim to 'scientificality'. Moreover, the names of both of these historians have become

the hallmarks of but complementary communicative functions of historiography: Herodotus stands for historical memory, Thucydides for the prognostic use of historiography.

The most important names in the canon of ancient history, whose works were avidly studied up to the 19th cent., are those of Polybius, Livy, Tacitus and Plutarch. During the 16th and 17th cents., a substantial portion of the Classical canon was used as a 'thesaurus' of political ideas by thinkers ranging from Machiavelli (1469–1528) and Jean Bodin (1530–1596) to Thomas Hobbes (1588–1679). In the further course of historiographic reception, however, each of the authors mentioned came to be regarded as a model worthy of imitation and emulation. Polybius was viewed as a model for the pragmatic, Livy for the dramatic, Tacitus for the revelatory and Plutarch for the biographical school of historiography.

The various formal types were roughly matched with the three main historiographic genres *annales* (history as chronicle), *historiae* (contemporary history) and *vitae* (stories of individual lives), which are still in use today, although there were semantic changes, as in the case of the French *École des Annales*.

C. Terms, Metaphors, Temporal Structures
Specific terms and verbal images are not merely a superficial aspect of historical thinking; they govern the techniques used in shaping historiographical compositions. Among the familiar concepts providing temporal structuring are the originally Greek terms 'epoch' and 'period', both of which were – in Antiquity -borrowed from astronomy and then applied to history [3. 127, 129]. The pattern believed in ancient mythological and historical thinking to underlie changes in genre, power relationships and epochs is still widely accepted today: a biomorphic, life-cycle structure organized according to 'childhood', 'youth' and 'old age' (decadence), perhaps also 'rebirth' (renaissance). The ancient images of a rise and fall, often in combination with the metaphor of a healthy or sick organism, have promoted the kind of historical thinking which, as the 'tragic', flirts with the idea of decay and downfall. Other ancient verbal images that were later rediscovered and elaborated upon mark the direction of the course of time: the images of the 'wheel', 'disk' or 'cycle' show recurrence (a cyclical view of history); the concepts of the 'current' and 'arrow' emphasize progress towards a goal (a linear view of history). Christian historiography, which presumed a beginning and an end, was at odds with Greco-Roman chronologies, going back instead to the periods posited in the Old Testament (four kingdoms, six ages etc.). Traces of this imagery have survived into the modern philosophy of history.

Particularly influential was Cicero's personification of history as a teacher (*historia magistra vitae*, De or. 2,9,36). This concept has found an important place in modern scholarship as an emblem of the historiography of the ancient world and the early modern era [9. 38ff.]. The *magistra* topos evokes a question that still invites controversy to this day: whether or not history provides lessons for the future.

D. RHETORIC

In ancient Rome, historiography was considered to be the province of the orator and was counted among the genres of oratory, with a strong emphasis placed on teaching (*docere*). With Herodotus it became common to have historical figures comment upon events in freely invented speeches. Barthold Georg Niebuhr (1776–1831), one of the founders of scientific historiography, still adhered to this method. However, historiography did not depend on this formal device for its rhetoric value; it had long been regarded as a collection of examples, an 'aggregate' of stories from which the orator could choose the appropriate one for his purpose, for example to demonstrate the limited applicability of political, military and other rules of conduct. As rhetorical handbooks pointed out, an orator might therefore use a story from history as an example, illustration or argument, while the historian was expected to combine both aspects – *narratio* and *argumentatio* – with artistry but without deceit. Oratory and historiography went together, and were closely related to the techniques of poetry. Particularly the *artes historicae* (historiographic arts) of the Renaissance, in harking back to the Classics, attached supreme importance to these ties between rhetoric, poetics and history [7].

Rhetoric has been and still is sometimes reduced to a set of stylistic rules (*elocutio*) or even equated with an underhand partiality on the part of the orator/historian. For even in its conventional form, it still played a part in the systematic establishment of history as a discipline, e.g. in the 'Heuristik' (*inventio*) and 'Topik' of Johann Gustav Droysen (1808–1886) [5. 867f.]. If rhetoric is not reduced to mere formalisms, but is conceived as an organon of textual and communicative pragmatics, it continues to have a place in the theory of historiography. To the degree that analysis concerns itself with what is constructed in historical texts and images, whether they are of popular or scholarly origin, the ancient dialectics of the study of the past and skilled eloquence – whose genealogy can certainly be traced – again finds itself the focus of historical criticism [10].   HARTH, DIETRICH

E. HISTORY OF THE DISCIPLINE

A number of important paired concepts whose precarious connections have repeatedly caused disagreement in modern Historical Studies are more or less loosely related to Greco-Roman Antiquity: art and science, partiality and objectivity, as well as – and not least – Antiquity and the modern era. If the critical examination of the 'testimonials' and 'sources' of a historical text – two metaphors bearing the scientific seal of approval – is a touchstone of its scientific dignity, then proto-scientific historiography was born in the era

of Humanism. Paradoxically, that period reinforced the literary authority of the ancient Classics of historiography, while at the same time undertaking the first steps toward their doxographic demystification. During the reign of → TACITISM throughout Europe in the late Humanistic period, Antiquarian Studies created a distinction between the Classical texts and the archaeological remains of ancient civilizations. At the same time, scholars gained a new perception of their own time from the dispute over the authority and validity of the ancient canon that was being conducted in the → QUERELLE DES ANCIENS ET DES MODERNES. In this discussion, the modern era learned to distinguish between its own unique characteristics and those of Antiquity, and under the banner of → CLASSICISM it began the museological and aesthetic restoration of the preserved structures and monuments (→ CLASSICISM AFTER CLASSICAL ANTIQUITY).

The consequence was an ambivalent attitude towards the past: on the one hand, Antiquity was historicized, while on the other it was idolized. In the course of this process, historiography also dissociated itself from the literary style of the Classics, developing instead the professional norms of research and text production that distinguish it, as an academic discipline, from novelistic versions of historiography. As Leopold Ranke (1795–1886) observed with reference to the ancient Classics, 'Wir unsers Orts haben einen andern Begriff von Geschichte' ("For our part, [we] have a different concept of history") [14. 24].

Whether historiography should be considered an art or science, a hybrid of the two, an autonomous kind of discourse or a literary, i.e. audience-pleasing late descendant of the muse Clio remained a hotly disputed topic of debate, both within the discipline and between it and other fields, until well into the 20th cent. [6. 224ff.]. However, the ancient Classics are quoted not only in the context of these stylistic and formal issues: even the minimal theoretical characterization of historical activity, "to make true statements", or "to give true descriptions" of events in the past seems to require a reference to Thucydides [2. 25]. The discipline of ancient history, by contrast, is actively resisting the presumption of closeness between the late modern era and Antiquity that various theoretical models are still trying to imply in this manner, even if it is only in a minor detail. It opposes the false affinity between the ancient and the modern periods that is based on idealization and myth, and favours a historiography aimed at discovering that which is alien and unfamiliar in the Greco-Roman world [15].

→ Historiography

1 R. CHEVALLIER, R. POIGNAULT (eds.), Présence de Tacite, 1992   2 A. DANTO, Analytical Philosophy of History, 1965   3 A. DEMANDT, Metaphern für Geschichte, 1978   4 D. FULDA, Wissenschaft aus Kunst, 1996   5 D. HARTH, s.v. Geschichtswissenschaft, in: HWdR III 1996, 832–870   6 J. KENYON, The History Men, 1993   7 E. KESSLER, Theoretiker humanistischer Geschichtsschreibung, 1971   8 R. KOSELLECK, W.-D. STEMPEL (eds.),

Geschichte – Ereignis und Erzählung, 1973   9 R. KOSEL-
LECK, Vergangene Zukunft, 1979 (Engl. K. TRIBE (trans.),
Futures Past, 1985)   10 D. LACAPRA, History and Criti-
cism, 1985   11 J. LE GOFF, Histoire et mémoire, 1986
(Engl. S. RENDALL, E. CLAMAN (trans.) History and
Memory, 1992)   12 N. LORAUX, Thucydide n'est pas un
collègue, in: Quaderni di Storia 12, 1980, 55–81   13 A.
MOMIGLIANO, Storia e storiografia antica, 1987   14 L. V.
RANKE, Sämtliche Werke, vol. 33/34, Leipzig 1874   15 P.
VEYNE, L'inventaire des différences, 1976   16 P. VIDAL-
NAQUET, La démocratie grecque vue d'ailleurs, 1990
(Engl. J. LLOYD (trans.), Politics Ancient and
Modern, 1995).   DIETRICH HARTH

II. GREEK HISTORY

A. SOURCES   B. MULTI-VOLUME NARRATIVE
HISTORIES   C. THE 'STUDY OF ANTIQUITIES'
D. CULTURAL HISTORY   E. OTHER GENRES AND
THEMES   F. BASIC PROBLEMS AND TENDENCIES IN
SCHOLARSHIP   G. ENVOI

A. SOURCES

1. A lively survey by Carmine Ampolo [2b] is the first
study of the history of Greek history. The periodic surveys once carried by Conrad Bursian's *Jahresberichte*
and *Revue historique* focused on the detailed reportage
and critique of publications rather than on the shape of
the subject, and lapsed after 1942 and 1983 respectively. More useful are the longer-range surveys of Adolf
Bauer [3] and Max Hoffmann [42], supplemented by
the standard histories of Classical philology and the
biographical compilations of Conrad Bursian and John
Edwin Sandys [10; 65]. The more detailed biographical
studies of Arnaldo Momigliano and Karl Christ have
changed perspectives [17–19b; 50–53]. Until recently,
19th cent. reception was better mapped than 20th cent.
reception, but the balance is being redressed [18; 55].

2. However, the study of individual scholars cannot
by itself plot the reception (or, better, the changing conceptions) of Greek history: the growth of institutions,
the changing patterns of school and university teaching
[69], the interests of the wider reading public, the
reading of the present into the past, and the growing
complexities and interpenetrations of older and newer
academic fields of study, have all helped to transform
the *Zeitgeist*. Moreover, the main themes of the reception of Greek history, from spiritual identification ('We
are all Greeks') and the idealisation of Athens, through
study of the *polis* and its 'failure' to the complexities of
response to Greek democracy, slavery, Athenian or
Spartan imperialism, and Graeco-Macedonian monarchy, have all had political resonances.

B. MULTI-VOLUME NARRATIVE HISTORIES

1. As a serious intellectual construct, Greek history is
much younger than her Roman sister. True, the Greek
historians had attracted editors and translators from
Lorenzo Valla onwards, Pope Nicholas V being a major
patron, while the antiquarians had been active since the
early Renaissance [50. 1–39; 52. 54–79]. Plutarch's

Lives had kindled interest in personalities, but Greeks
attracted less attention than Romans Poussin's two
paintings of 1648 depicting the death of Phocion are
exceptional. The most significant contribution, uncritical though it was, was that of Charles Rollin [63],
mostly concerned with Greek history in spite of its title,
which found a receptive public both in French and
English.

2. In comparison, the work of William Mitford [49]
and John Gillies [33] in the 1780s marked a new epoch.
Larger in scale, using a greater range of source-materi-
als, and more closely focused on political and military
affairs, they broke away from the antiquarian tradition
to offer a more overtly political tone and impetus which
attracted mainstream European attention and translation. Their new start was followed by Niebuhr's emu-
lator Connop Thirlwall [70] and above all by George
Grote [37; 53. 15–31], whose 12 volumes both defined
the subject chronologically and set the agenda of debate
for over fifty years.

3. It is a real question why 'Greek history' crystallised when and where it did. The influence of the Scottish
Enlightenment will have been at best indirect, even for
Gillies, while none of the Anglo-Scottish quartet ever
visited Greece, more accessible though it was after the
1750s. The intrinsic difficulties of separating myth
from reality and of integrating fragmentary mini-narra-
tives played a part, as the prefaces of Gillies and Mitford reveal. So did the practical and theoretical challenge, more intractable for Greek history than for
Roman, of separating the study of history from the
study of historians. The impulse to confront such technical difficulties was primarily political. Though the use
of Graeco-Roman exempla in the French and American
→ REVOLUTIONS [61; 71. 82–169] was more rhetorical
than structural, the issues of monarchy and democracy
which had been raised in and after the 1770s preoccupied all four pioneers, for all their deep ideological
divergences. However briefly, Greek history was seen,
both by authors and readers, as having contemporary
resonance, whether as an ideal or as a horrifying example.

4. In this way the multi-volume narrative 'history of
Greece' was the first literary form to treat its source-
material critically, to interact with contemporary political themes and social developments, and to wield
influence internationally in wider intellectual circles. It
became, and long remained, the backbone of the subject, though its Anglo-Scottish founding fathers were
superseded by two brilliant generations of German
scholarship. Supplemented outside Germany by Victor
Duruy [24], Evelyn Abbott [1], Eugène Cavaignac [15]
and Gaetano De Sanctis [21], the sequence began in the
1850s with Johann Friedrich Christoph Kortüm [46],
Maximilian Duncker [23], and Ernst Curtius [19a. 123–
143; 20], to continue with Adolf Holm [43] and to cul-
minate in the works of Georg Busolt [12; 16], the Greek
volumes of Eduard Meyer [13; 48; 53. 209–222], and
Julius Beloch [4; 53. 97–120]. It also became the prin-

cipal vehicle through which contemporary attitudes and preoccupations, in all their variety, could be applied to the events, institutions, and personalities of the past. It is striking how many historians of ancient Greece have been politically active.

5. The *Geschichten* of Busolt, Beloch and Meyer, each the masterpiece products of single minds, represented the culmination of the multi-volume monograph tradition. Gustave Glotz needed two collaborators in the 1920s–1930s [35; 35a], while the general post–1918 response (Helmut Berve apart [6]) was to recognise that the growth of knowledge and the proliferation of published scholarship made Busolt's ideal of perfection – to cite every text and contribution relevant to the topic under discussion – impossible to sustain. Practice developed instead in three alternative directions. One was the one-volume summary monograph as represented by J.B. Bury [11], Hermann Bengtson [5], Wolfgang Schuller [67] and others. A second was to create a new artform of collective history, where an editorial team commissioned chapters from individual specialists to fit within a still largely diachronic format the *Cambridge Ancient History* led the way, followed by *Storia e Civiltà*, *Hellenische Poleis* [72], and *I Greci*. Third, more recent, has been the growth of monograph series such as those of Methuen, Nouvelle Clio, and Fontana/dtv

6. Grote's influential decision to treat pre–776 BC material as unhistorical made the subject manageable but created a barrier which has become a handicap. Likewise, his decision to end in 301 BC typified a growing consensus to focus only on the Greece of the 'free' states: Beloch alone went on till 217, De Sanctis not even continuing past 404. Indeed, the history of the Greece of the Successor kingdoms had already become a separate sub-genre with Gillies's later book [34]. It received definitive form in Johann Gustav Droysen's new term *Hellenismus* of 1836 [7; 22; 53. 147–161], and was taken forward by Gustav Friedrich Hertzberg [41], Benedikt Niese [56], Julius Kaerst [45], Carl Schneider [66] and Éduoard Will [73].

7. The split between 'Classical' and 'Hellenistic', later mirrored by the emergence of 'Archaic' as a third category, has deeply influenced the reception of Greek history. It has perpetuated notions of rise, zenith and decadence, has hindered wider views of Greece as part of the Balkan-Mediterranean Iron Age, and has left entrenched the prejudice that military power and the quality of art and literature are what define 'central' periods.

C. The 'Study of Antiquities'

1. The second form to emerge was that of a systematic synchronic description of the public and private antiquities of ancient Greece. First formulated by Friedrich August Wolf from the 1780s onwards, and first committed to print in 1807 [59. 76–103], it crystallised in May 1817 with August Boeckh's *Staatshaushaltung der Athener* [8]. Dedicated to Niebuhr, but owing its

title as much to Hume as to Wolf, its publication, together with his later work on Greek inscriptions, made him the other founding father of Greek history. Indeed, the first words of his preface, 'Die Kunde der Hellenischen Altertümer steht noch in ihren Anfängen: großer Stoff ist vorhanden, die meisten wissen ihn nicht zu gebrauchen' ("The study of Hellenic antiquities is still in its infancy: impressive material abounds, yet few know how to make use of it") [59. 106f.], were at once programmatic and prophetic.

2. A generation later his vision had become reality, represented above all via the common format of the volumes of Karl Friedrich Hermann's *Lehrbuch der griechischen Antiquitäten* [40], in its various editions. They came to include public, legal, military, stage- and private antiquities, and were in their turn succeeded by Iwan von Müller's *Handbuch der Altertumswissenschaft*, whose all-embracing structure saw Greek history as merely one topic and one volume among many.

3. Even the *Lehrbuch/Handbuch* format did not include everything. Work on the topography and geography of Greece, stimulated by the Napoleonic Wars, has remained a specialist area. So, regrettably, have numismatic study and papyrology. So, above all, has the study of Greek inscriptions. Boeckh led the way with his *Corpus Inscriptionum Graecarum*, as much by energy and organising ability as by specifically epigraphical acumen, creating a format followed but much expanded by *Inscriptiones Graecae* and *Supplementum Epigraphicum Graecum* and by a steady stream of specific titles. The reception of these specialist areas presents a paradox within the sociology of knowledge. While they – particularly epigraphy – have become the prime source of new evidence for the political, administrative, social, and cultic history of ancient Greece, those attuned to the literary narrative tradition, whether in texts or in textbooks, still find them, as a bridge into a new and untidy semantic world, hard to cross.

D. Cultural History

1. As a form of reception, the *Handbuch* format was an extreme form of professionalization, systematizing knowledge within an outward uniformity at the cost of fragmentation, impersonality, and a forbidding level of detail. Its necessary complement was a response which resurrected the individual person of Greek antiquity and attempted to reconstruct his values and his psychological world within a static or slow-changing environment of rituals, institutions, and representations.

2. This was cultural history. Though already foreshadowed in Boeckh's unwritten 'Hellen' and named by 1857–8 in Hermann's *Lehrbuch*, it owes its centrality, and the basic distinction between it and life-and-manners accounts, to two pioneers, Numa Denis Fustel de Coulanges and Jacob Burckhardt. Fustel's *La cité antique* of 1864 [19a. 114–122; 27; 28; 53. 162–178] was one of a number of works of the 1850s and 1860s which reflected the discovery of Indo-Europeans and of collective property-ownership [53. 236–251]. It offered a

complex interwoven reading of the origins, via the *gens/genos* and the cult of the dead, of society, property, and the state which lost none of its influence for being simplistically linear, not being finally dismantled until the 1970s. It stimulated a distinguished tradition of (largely French) scholarship which has run through Émile Durkheim, Marcel Mauss, Louis Gernet, and Henri Jeanmaire to Jean-Pierre Vernant and the present day [44. 76–106], both owing and contributing much to general historical sociology and social anthropology.

3. The lectures which posthumously became Burckhardt's *Griechische Kulturgeschichte* [9; 53. 44–53] complemented Fustel by 'reading' Greek society through its representations and the *mentalités* which they consciously or unconsciously reflected. By exploring conflicts of values and the relationships between politics, religion and culture, it showed how the evidence of Greek literary and philosophical texts could be constructively used in a non-narrative, non-antiquarian way. Its influence, though slow, diffuse, and indirect, has made the cultural history of Greece into a very broad church, in part untheoretical [60] but also warmly receptive to interpretative approaches drawn from a variety of newer disciplines. These have ranged from Freudian psychoanalysis through legal sociology and Lévi-Straussian structural anthropology [44; 58] to the deconstructionism of current literary criticism: Michel Foucault and Philippe Ariès can fairly be seen as heirs of the tradition.

E. OTHER GENRES AND THEMES

1. These can be more briefly and straightforwardly surveyed. They can of course reflect teaching needs [75], or national prestige projects at major sites, as much as 'reception' in the strict sense. Some, such as editions of texts or historiographical work [36], are as much philological as historical, but even here contrasts reflect selective reception: Athenian inscriptions attract attention while those of Boeotia are neglected, Thucydides has a second full-scale commentary while Diodorus or Demosthenes do without.

2. Among the simpler genres are chronology, a core service to scholars from Joseph Justus Scaliger and later Henry Fynes Clinton to the more recent specialists in the field, transformed by epigraphy and far more intricate in the polycentric Greek context than in the Roman. Equally intricate is the making of collections of fragments (notably Felix Jacoby's *Fragmente der griechischen Historiker*), which alone have allowed some estimate of lost historians, orators and biographers. A third is biography itself, not just of major individuals but also of élite groups such as Alexander's commanders or even, as prosopography, of whole societies. Histories of individual states and regions have been ubiquitous, more obviously of Sparta and of less prominent polities than of Athens, whose history tends to be seen as coterminous with that of Greece. Likewise, military history has always been a core component, along with its close relation *Landeskunde*.

3. Other genres are more ideologically complex. Throughout the twentieth cent. social and economic history, exemplified at its most ambitious by Michael Rostovtzeff [64], has been a prime battleground for the reception and reconciliation of competing ideas, ranging from neo-Classical economics through the embeddedness (of ancient economics within societies and their institutions) of Karl Polanyi and Moses Finley [25] to the geographers' locational analysis. Even historiography, long a matter primarily of studying source materials, has come to embrace genre-analysis and narratology as well as the classic 'historical commentary'. Work on Greek law, long conditioned (or hampered) by the categories of Roman law, by the mirage of a Greek constitutional law, and by the comparative uniformity of law in Ptolemaic Egypt [74], has had not only to acknowledge the kaleidoscopic range of Greek legal systems [26] but also to grapple with notions of 'prelaw' [32. 175–321] and of law as discourse rather than as a system of statutes and precedents [60]. A similar complex shift is affecting work on Greek religion, long pursued as a quasi-autonomous study through traditions such as the Scandinavian school magisterially represented by Martin P. Nilsson [57], but now increasingly being steered by Durkheim's insistence that religion is above all a social act into rejoining the mainstream as an aspect of cultural history. More complex still is site excavation and publication, where conceptual or institutional boundary disputes with → CLASSICAL ARCHAEOLOGY interact with common-sense perceptions that if Greek history is not also about the history of Delos or Olympia or the Athenian Agora, it has no serious *raison d'être*. Most complex of all is the history of political ideas and of their relationship with events and institutions.

F. BASIC PROBLEMS AND TENDENCIES IN SCHOLARSHIP

1. The title of this section borrows that of Schuller's invaluable survey [67], to which the reader is referred. However, a few salient themes of the current reception of Greek history need emphasis as a supplement. They can all be defined in terms of boundaries. Topographically, the explosion of recent work on Thessaly, Epirus, and Macedonia has extended *das dritte Griechenland* (the German term for the Greek world outside Athens and Sparta) [30] still further north and is allowing Macedonia to be seen from the inside rather than through a Demosthenic distorting mirror. To the east, Louis Robert's lifetime work on Asia Minor [62], plus the growing epigraphical harvest from the *Inschriften griechischer Städte aus Kleinasien* series (1972ff.) and elsewhere, are allowing a *viertes Griechenland* to take shape. Further east still, ever more intensive work on the Achaemenid empire, on Perso-Greek relations, and on the Seleucid empire is at last replacing a Hellenocentric image of autonomous Greek development by a more realistic discourse which treats Greek and Eastern Mediterranean history as a continuum. To the south, in

contrast, in proportion as more demotic documents are deciphered and more is understood about Egypt, both pre- and post-Alexander, the less abnormal, the less uniformly governed, and the less Greek it appears: a prime example of the decolonization of 'Greek' history. Lastly, Magna Graecia and the west, once seen in Greek terms as classically colonial, are re-emerging from the Taranto *Atti dei Convegni di studi sulla Magna Grecia* and the rapid progress of Italian and Spanish archaeology as the venue of a very complex cultural inter-penetration which has yet to be properly mapped.

2. Professional subject boundaries are also under pressure. The decipherment of Linear B as Greek both turned much pre-history into 'Greek history' and made the Dark Ages into territory contested between Classical archaeologists, with their own (by now autonomous) agendas of social action [54], and Greek historians who sought therein the roots of their own 'Archaic Greece'. Greek history is therefore not merely caught between two stools (sc. Classical Studies and history) [31] but awkwardly between three stools. Since information from intensive surface surveys [2a] is impinging on other periods and areas too, this contestation will undoubtedly spread.

3. Lastly, four ideological issues are live and urgent. First, surveys have helped to give work on rural settlement, land-use, crop-yields, demography, and land-ownership a much enhanced role in analysing social action. Such work tends to ignore political boundaries and to highlight country rather than town. It has thereby reinforced the post-war, partly Marxist- or feminist-inspired, concern to re-orientate scholarship round the invisible and the dispossessed – metics, women, slaves, serfs, or peasants. Second, and closely linked thereto, is the 'polis-debate'. Nineteenth-century historiography treated Athens, Sparta, Thebes etc. straightforwardly as 'states', even if interest concentrated on the unified urbanized states, not the poorly attested rural cantons and leagues. However, the 20th cent. tendency has been, with Aristotle but against recent scepticism [29], to see the *polis* as a specific form of government and as a precise juridical category [39]. The unresolved issues are whether historians of Greece must follow the analytical terminology used by the Greeks themselves or should devise their own, and whether study of the trajectory of Greek *polis* development can be separated from that of other regions of Mediterranean urbanization.

4. A third issue involves *alterité*, a term of complex paternity [14. 2–7] now used to emphasise the immense distance – especially in values, mind-sets, and rationality – between Ancient Greece and ourselves, and thereby to challenge cozy emotional identifications. Fourthly, the very word 'Greek' itself, together with other ethnic identifiers such as 'Dorian' or 'Pelasgian' and with group-labels such as 'tribe', is caught up in a debate about ethnicity and ethnogenesis, the argument being that 'Dorians', 'Geleontes', etc. denoted not primordial human groups but recent, artificial, fluid social constructs [38]. It is too early to judge what effect these two last issues will have.

G. Envoi

'Greek history' should not be over-reified. For 200 years it has consisted of an ever-changing field of four-way interaction between (a) ancient texts, landscapes and artifacts; (b) a small network of professional scholars; (c) a disarticulated clientele of students and the lay interested public; and (d) the general world-wide flux of ideas, issues and values. Throughout that period the focuses of reception have moved continually. They are currently moving very rapidly, and will continue to do so. Momigliano's famous diagnosis, that 'Greek history is passing through a crisis' [53. 16], was true in 1952: it no longer is, though Greek history has lost the wider 'relevance' it had until Eduard Meyer.

1 E. Abbott, A History of Greece, I–III, London, New York 1888–1900   2a S. Alcock, Breaking up the Hellenistic world: Survey and Society, in: [54. 171–190]   2b C. Ampolo, Storie greche. La formazione della moderna storiografia sugli antichi Greci, 1997   3 A. Bauer, Die Forschungen zur griechischen Geschichte 1888–1898, Munich 1899   4 K. J. Beloch, Griechische Geschichte, I/1–IV/2, Berlin et al. ¹1893–1904, ²1912–1927   5 H. Bengtson, Griechische Geschichte von den Anfängen bis in die römische Kaiserzeit, ¹1950, ⁵1977 (Engl. E. F. Bloedow (trans.), History of Greece from the Beginnings to the Byzantine Era, 1988)   6 H. Berve, Griechische Geschichte, I–II, 1930   7 R. Bichler, Hellenismus. Geschichte und Problematik eines Epochenbegriffs, 1983   8 A. Boeckh, Staatshaushaltung der Athener, I–II, Berlin ¹1817, ²1851, ³1886 (Engl. E. C. Lewis (trans.), The Public Economy of Athens, London 1828 and later)   9 J. Burckhardt, Griechische Kulturgeschichte, Berlin 1898–1902 (Engl. S. Stern (trans.), The Greeks and Greek civilization, 1998)   10 C. Bursian, Geschichte der classischen Philologie in Deutschland, von den Anfängen bis zur Gegenwart, Munich, Leipzig 1883   11 J. B. Bury, A History of Greece to the Death of Alexander the Great, ¹1900, ²1913, ³1951 (rev. R. Meiggs), ⁴1975   12 G. Busolt, Griechische Geschichte bis zur Schlacht bei Chaeronea I–III/2, Gotha ¹1885–88, ²1893–1904   13 W. M. Calder III, A. Demandt (eds.), Eduard Meyer. Leben und Leistung eines Universalhistorikers, 1990   14 P. Cartledge, The Greeks, 1993   15 E. Cavaignac, Histoire de l'antiquité, I–IV, 1913–1920   16 M. H. Chambers, Georg Busolt. His career in his letters, 1990   17 K. Christ, Von Gibbon zu Rostovtzeff, ¹1972, ²1979   18 Id., Neue Profile der alten Geschichte, 1990   19a Id., Griechische Geschichte und Wissenschaftsgeschichte, 1996   19b Id., Hellas. Griechische Geschichte und deutsche Geschichtswissenschaft, 1999   20 E. Curtius, Griechische Geschichte, I–III, Berlin ¹1857–1867, ⁶1887–1889 (Engl. A. W. Ward (trans.), History of Greece, 1883)   21 G. De Sanctis, Storia dei Greci, dalle origini alla fine del secolo v, I–II, 1939   22 G. Droysen, Geschichte des Hellenismus, I–II, Hamburg 1836–1843; I–III, Gotha ²1877–1878   23 M. Duncker, Geschichte des Altertums, I–IV, Berlin 1855–1857, ⁴1874–1886   24 V. Duruy, Histoire grecque, Paris 1851   25 M. I. Finley, The Ancient Economy, ¹1973, ²1985   26 Id., The Problem of the Unity of Greek Law, in: La storia del diritto nel quadro delle scienze storiche, 1966, 129–142   27 Id.,

The Ancient City: From Fustel de Coulanges to Max Weber and Beyond, in: Comparative Studies in Society and History 19, 1977, 305–327 28 N.-D. FUSTEL DE COULANGES, La cité antique, Paris 1864 (Engl. W. SMALL (trans., 1874), The Ancient City, 1956; with a new foreword by A. MOMIGLIANO, S. C. HUMPHREYS, 1980) 29 W. GAWANTKA, Die sogenannte Polis, 1985 30 H.-J. GEHRKE, Jenseits von Athen und Sparta. Das dritte Griechenland und sein Staatenwelt, 1986 31 Id., Zwischen Altertumswissenschaft und Geschichte. Zur Standortbestimmung der Alten Geschichte am Ende des 20. Jahrhunderts, in: E.-R. SCHWINGE (ed.), Die Wissenschaft vom Altertum am Ende des 2. Jahrtausends n. Chr., 1995, 160–196 32 L. GERNET, Anthropologie de la Grèce antique, 1968 (Engl. J. HAMILTON (trans.), The Anthropology of Ancient Greece, 1981) 33 J. GILLIES, The History of Ancient Greece: Its Colonies, and Conquests; From the Earliest Accounts till the Division of the Macedonian Empire in the East, I–II, London 1786 34 Id., The History of the World from the Reign of Alexander to that of Augustus ..., I–II, London 1807 35 G. GLOTZ, R. COHEN, P. ROUSSEL, Histoire grecque, I–IV/1, 1925–1938 36 G. T. GRIFFITH, The Greek Historians, in: M. PLATNAUER (ed.), Fifty Years of Classical Scholarship, 1954, 150–192 37 G. GROTE, A History of Greece I–XII, London 1846–1856 38 J. M. HALL, Ethnic Identity in Greek Antiquity, 1997 39 M. H. HANSEN (ed.), The Ancient Greek City-State, 1993 40 K. F. HERMANN (ed.), Lehrbuch der griechischen Antiquitäten, I–IV, Heidelberg 1831–1852 41 G. F. HERTZBERG, Die Geschichte Griechenlands unter der Herrschaft der Römer, I–IV, Halle 1866–1875 42 M. HOFFMANN, August Boeckh. Lebensbeschreibung und Auswahl aus seinem wissenschaftlichen Briefwechsel, 1901 43 A. HOLM, Griechische Geschichte von ihrem Ursprunge bis zum Untergange der Selbständigkeit des griechischen Volkes, Berlin 1886–1894 (Engl. The History of Greece from its Commencement to the Close of the Independence of the Greek Nation, F. CLARKE (trans.), London 1894–1898) 44 S. C. HUMPHREYS, Anthropology and the Greeks, 1978 45 J. KAERST, Geschichte des Hellenismus, I–II, ²1916f. 46 J. F. CH. KORTÜM, Geschichte Griechenlands ... bis zum Untergang des Achaischen Bundes, I–III, Heidelberg 1854 47 S. L. MARCHAND, Down from Olympus. Archaeology and Philhellenism in Germany 1750–1970, 1996 48 ED. MEYER, Geschichte des Altertums, I–V, Stuttgart ¹1884–1902, ²1907–1939 49 W. MITFORD, The History of Greece, I–V, London 1784–1810 50 A. MOMIGLIANO, Studies in Historiography, 1966 51 Id., Essays in Ancient and Modern Historiography, 1977 52 Id., The Classical Foundations of Modern Historiography, 1990 53 Id., Studies on Modern Scholarship, G. W. BOWERSOCK, T. J. CORNELL (eds.), 1994 54 I. MORRIS (ed.), Classical Greece. Ancient Histories and Modern Archaeologies, 1994 55 B. NÄF, Von Perikles zu Hitler? Die athenische Demokratie und die deutsche Althistorie bis 1945, 1986 56 B. NIESE, Geschichte der griechischen und makedonischen Staaten seit der Schlacht bei Chaeronea, I–III, Gotha 1893–1903 57 M. NILSSON, Geschichte der griechischen Religion, I–II, 1941–1950 (Engl. F. J. FIELDEN (trans.), History of Greek Religion, ²1949) 58 W. NIPPEL, Griechen, Barbaren und 'Wilde'. Alte Geschichte und Anthropologie, 1990 59 Id. (ed.), Über das Studium der Alten Geschichte, 1993 60 R. OSBORNE, Law in Action in Classical Athens, in: JHS 105, 1985, 40–58 61 P. A.

RAHE, Republics Ancient and Modern. Classical Republicanism and the American Revolution, 1992 62 L. ROBERT, Hellenica, I–XIII, 1940–1965 63 CH. ROLLIN, Histoire ancienne des Egyptiens, des Carthaginois, des Assyriens, des Babyloniens, des Medes et des Perses, des Macedoniens, des Grecs, Paris 1730–1738 (Engl. The ancient history of the Egyptians, Carthaginians, Assyrians, Babylonians, Medes & Persians, Macedonians and Grecians, London 1738 and later) 64 M. I. ROSTOVTZEFF, The Social and Economic History of the Hellenistic World, I–III, ¹1941, ²1953 65 J. E. SANDYS, A History of Classical Scholarship, I–III, 1903–1908 (I ²1906, I ³1921) 66 C. SCHNEIDER, Kulturgeschichte des Hellenismus, I–II, 1967–1969 67 W. SCHULLER, Griechische Geschichte, ¹1980, ³1991 68 H. E. STIER, Grundlagen und Sinn der griechischen Geschichte, 1945 69 CH. STRAY, Classics Transformed. Schools, Universities, and Society in England 1830–1960, 1998 70 C. THIRLWALL, A History of Greece, I–VIII, London 1835–1847 71 P. VIDAL-NAQUET, Politics Ancient and Modern, 1995 (orig. La démocratie greque vue d'ailleurs, 1990) 72 E. C. WELSKOPF (ed.), Hellenische Poleis, I–IV, 1974 73 ÉD. WILL, Histoire politique du monde hellenistique, I–II, ¹1966–1967, ²1979–1982 74 H. J. WOLFF, Das Recht der griechischen Papyri Ägyptens in der Zeit der Ptolemäer und des Prinzipats, vol. 2: Organisation und Kontrolle des privaten Rechtsverkehrs, 1978 75 D. VOLLMER et al., Alte Geschichte in Studium und Unterricht, 1994.

JOHN K. DAVIES

III. ROMAN HISTORY

A. OVERALL SIGNIFICANCE OF ROMAN HISTORY BEFORE 1800 B. FORMS C. OUTLOOK

A. OVERALL SIGNIFICANCE OF ROMAN HISTORY BEFORE 1800

By 1500 Roman history had attained such a central position within universal history, it had almost come to be identified with it. One important reason for this development was the Christian notion of universal history as the history of salvation. At the height of Rome's power, it was thought, Jesus Christ had appeared on earth, and as a consequence Church and papacy had emerged. As the fourth and last world empire before the Last Judgement, the Roman Empire was the culmination of the biblical history of salvation. For this reason, it had never perished in the eyes of contemporary observers. Instead, it had been transferred through a process of the *translatio imperii* to the Franks, and their political succession had been a source of dispute between the Emperors of the Holy Roman Empire and the French kings ever since.

The duration of its greatness and power was a second reason for Rome's prestige. Not only were the cities and the titles of many institutions it had created still flourishing, but the significance of → ROMAN LAW was steadily increasing all over Europe with the rise of modern principalities in the 15th century. Having served as the basis of the most remarkable empire ever, it could not be anything less than perfect. Prudence and judiciousness could therefore be learned from the

Romans. Anyone curious about the best constitution, about maxims for maintaining power, but also about the causes of revolutions and processes of decay, could be sure to find the best, most instructive examples in Roman History. All these factors allowed Roman Antiquity to influence the concepts, models, ideas, institutions, stereotypes and symbols which defined and organized contemporary politics. In this respect, Roman history was not a thing of the past; it was a powerful component of the political present.

And yet the fact remained that the Roman Empire, despite its grandeur and its many virtues, had been destroyed. Even those who believed in its *translatio* – and this belief lasted well into the 17th cent. [80] – felt obliged to determine the date of its occurrence (and thus the end of ancient Rome) as precisely as possible. The Rome euphoria of the Italian Humanists in particular arose from the realization that a deep chasm existed between their own time and Classical Antiquity, which those who truly sought to imitate the Romans could only bridge through scholarly research [76. 27–43]. Rome therefore appeared as a contemporary and at the same time thoroughly historical phenomenon. It presented an ideal study case, exemplifying the apparent rule that every state is subject to the law of rise and fall.

Finally, Roman history became a paradigm in formal and aesthetic terms: from the Humanistic age to the beginning of the 19th cent. the Classical authors, which had taught ancient history to every educated man from his schooldays onwards, were considered unsurpassable models of the historical style. It would have been seen as absurd for anyone to try to compete with Caesar, Cicero, Livy, Sallust or Tacitus. Where Roman History had to be retold – e.g. as part of universal histories – modern authors were content to paraphrase these authorities, to copy their style as closely as possible and to fill gaps in the transmission with material from other Classical sources that were altered stylistically to match the prevailing text. Some Humanists were so good at this, that their emendations – for example on Livy in the *Annales Romanorum* of Stephanus Vinandus Pighius [39] – were read as originals by later editors (→ FORGERY). Edward Gibbon was the first who dared to write about Roman history in a modern voice.

Generally speaking, until the early 19th cent. the depiction of Roman history remained principally a moral and aesthetic task. It was only after 1810 – and first in Germany – that it came to be governed by the modern 'research' principle: the pragmatic, moralistic perspective was replaced by a historical and systematic treatment that emphasized the uniqueness and individuality of the epoch, no longer viewing ancient authors as authorities but as 'sources' of information, the reality of which had to be ascertained and reconstructed synthetically through modern critical methods [76. 412–435]. As a consequence, all attempts by subsequent scholars to write a comprehensive Roman history based on their own research have remained unfinished. More strongly than → ANTIQUARIA-

NISM, Roman historiography before 1800 was bound up in traditions and conventions.

B. FORMS
1. COMPREHENSIVE HISTORIES 2. SPECIFIC STUDIES 2.1. COMMENTARIES AND STUDIES UP TO THE EIGHTEENTH CENTURY 2.2. TOWARDS GIBBON: ENLIGHTENED ROMAN HISTORIOGRAPHY 2.3. GERMAN CLASSICAL SCHOLARSHIP: NIEBUHR AND MOMMSEN 2.4. ROMAN ECONOMIC AND SOCIAL HISTORY FROM PÖHLMANN TO FINLEY 2.5. PROSOPOGRAPHY 2.6. FROM THE HISTORY OF RELIGION TO ANTHROPOLOGY

1. COMPREHENSIVE HISTORIES
This is generally the case with comprehensive histories. Since the time of the Church Fathers, Roman history had been presented within the framework of the four successive world empires as the history of the formation and dissemination of Christianity, which is why the main focus was always on the Imperial period. Even Protestant texts like the world chronicle of Johannes Carion (an edition revised by Philipp Melanchthon and Caspar Peucer appeared in 1558/1560) or *De quatuor summis imperiis* (1566) by Johannes Sleidans followed this pattern [28; 43; 70; 83. 19–27]. However, in the wake of the Protestant Reformation this form of Roman history became a medium for bitter confessional controversies: 1559 saw the publication of the first volume of the *Magdeburg Centuries*, a collective effort providing a universal history of the world, divided into centuries, and beginning with the birth of Christ. Headed by the orthodox Lutheran acolyte Matthias Flacius Illyricus, it attempted to prove that the Early Church was in complete accord with Luther's teachings, before the papacy came to power through fraudulent means in the seventh century [14]. This provoked Catholic authors from Caesar Baronius (*Annales ecclesiastici*, Rome 1588–1607) to Jacques-Bénigne Bossuet (*Discours sur l'histoire universelle*, Paris 1681 [76. 197–199; 283–289]) and Louis-Sébastien Le Nain de Tillemont to compose voluminous works on the same subject, defending the opposite theory of the original and sole authority of St Peter's successors.

In the late 17th cent. these teleological models were secularized. In his *Historia antiqua* (Jena 1685) Christoph Cellarius abandoned the concept of the successive world empires: his Roman history no longer simply comprised the rise of the Church, it also included the expansion of the Empire, and it meant cultural progress as well [6; 70]. In Voltaire's *Siecle de Louis XIV* (1751) Roman history reached a pinnacle of world culture in the Augustan period [45]. Hegel's *Philosophie der Weltgeschichte* saw it as an age where the state asserted itself against all particularities. Against the "abstract universality of authority" ('abstrakte Allgemeinheit der Herrschaft'), though, to which "the individual in his own moral life [had been] sacrificed" ('[der] die Individuen in ihrem sittlichen Leben aufgeopfert [worden seien]'), Christianity had arisen as a necessary antithesis, a "universality in and of itself" ('an und für sich seiende Allgemeinheit'), which had led to the Empire being transferred into the Germanic world [21. 659–719; 49]. Leopold von Ranke, in his Weltgeschichte of 1883 considered it crucial that in the course of Roman history, "a universal power [had] reached the highest authority" ('[daß] eine einheitliche Macht zur höchsten Autorität [gelangt sei]'), while at the same time the "idea of a universal religion" ('Idee einer allgemeinen Religion') had become predominant [41]. Theodor Mommsen and his modern successors, on the other hand, saw the world-historical significance of Rome in the founding of a common European civilization. Comprehensive histories in the 20th cent. prefer to express such interpretations implicitly: more variety rather than uniformity, and more summing-up of specialized research rather than over-arching interpretation are at the heart of these collaborative efforts originally devised by British and French scholars (*The Cambridge Ancient History*, vols. 7–10, 1928–1934; *Histoire générale: Histoire romaine*, 1925–1947; *Histoire générale des civilisations*, vol. 2, 1954).

2. SPECIFIC STUDIES

2.1 COMMENTARIES AND STUDIES UP TO THE EIGHTEENTH CENTURY

Specific studies presented a different picture. Up to the 18th cent. these were only conducted in the context of philological [76. 347–411] or antiquarian research, with the purpose of elucidating cryptic passages in Classical texts or to legitimize political institutions by proving their Roman origins. Because the first efforts of this kind took place in Rome itself, Humanists loyal to the Pope initially monopolized this field. Soon, however, topography, genealogy, numismatics, chronology and legal history evolved into independent branches of scholarly interest. Early reconstructions of the fasti were attempted by the Augustan monk Onuphrius Panvinius from Verona in 1557/58, while Carolus Sigonius from Modena began his in 1550 [36; 37; 69]. Sigonius also wrote the first monograph on the late Roman Empire (*Historiarum de occidentali imperio libri XX*, Bologna 1578) and pioneered Roman and Italic constitutional history (*De antiquo iure civium Romanorum libri II*; *De antiquo iure Italiae libri III*, both Venice 1560) [69]. Following the Reformation, Roman legal history became the domain of Calvinistic scholars. In France, Jacques Cujas (Cujacius), François Douaren (Duarenus), Hugues Doneau (Donellus), François Hotman (Hotomannus) and Denis and Jacques Godefroy (Gothofredus) developed philological-antiquarian methods (*mos Gallicus*) to reconstruct the pre-Justinian forms of Roman law down to the legendary Twelve Tables [68; 76. 368–374]. In the 1570s, these projects were primarily pursued at Dutch universities. One of their political aims was to demonstrate that even though it was being used by popes, emperors, kings and princes to centralize government, Roman law was by its very nature a republican institution and could thus be made to serve the States General and their libertarian cause.

The typical form of Roman Studies during this epoch were textual commentaries (on the *Corpus Juris*, the *Codex Theodosianus* or on historians like Livy or Tacitus; → COMMENTARY). This also applies to the *Discorsi sopra la prima deca di Tito Livio* (1513/1519, printed in 1531), in which Niccolò Machiavelli explored the actual principles of Roman politics as opposed to the topical praise of Roman virtue, as well as for the works of late Humanistic → TACITISM. Justus Lipsius published his political maxims as commentaries on Tacitus (1575/1581) and his treatise *De militia Romana libri V* (1596), which set the direction for the Dutch army reforms of the 16th cent., as *Commentarius ad Polybium*. Unlike the comprehensive histories, these pragmatic studies were less interested in the Imperial period than in Rome's rise to world power. In Machiavelli's *Discorsi*, this rise was for the first time explained in purely rational terms: as the positive consequence of an open and balanced form of mixed government, the absolute authority of the law, the chance to rise through the ranks for those willing to work, the channelling of internal conflicts into external wars and the appropriation of religion as an instrument of power. Rome became a model for the modern age, because its might and splendour appeared to be founded on reason alone.

In the meantime, the endeavour to reconstruct a rational history of Rome and to arrange the ever-increasing source material supplied by the archaeological finds into a chronological, systematic order raised radical doubts in the 17th cent. about the Classical accounts of Rome's early history. In 1684 the Leiden head of this school of thought, Jacobus Gronovius, disputed the existence of Romulus; in 1701 Henry Dodwell voiced his scepticism about of the Kings of Alba Longa [8; 20]. Since this provided welcome arguments for those who completely opposed the concept of a Classical education (→ QUERELLE DES ANCIENS ET DES MODERNES), it was at times paramount for Roman scholars to find criteria for the credibility of early Roman sources. The Leiden scholar Jacob Perizonius adopted an optimistic position in 1685 with the theory that, in Livy's work, family legends from the time before the Gallic invasion ('Sack of Rome', 387 BC) had been preserved [38]. Writing from his exile in the Netherlands, the Huguenot historian Louis de Beaufort rejected Perizonius' argument in 1738, claiming that the Romans had been late in developing a sense of history, and thus had never been in possession of authentic accounts detailing their early history [2; 77]. In 1766 he nevertheless included it in a voluminous constitutional history [3], thus making an important contribution to those collections 'public antiquities' whose prototype had been created by Flavio Biondo (1471) and the Regensburg antiquarian Johannes Rosinus (1583).

2.2 Towards Gibbon: Enlightened Roman Historiography

Contemporary histories of Rome were affected in a variety of ways by the debates of the antiquarians (cf. [77] on each of the following). Some simply ignored the source (credibility) problem, thus for instance the *Roman History* (1699) by the English clergyman Laurence Echard, narrated in the style of Tacitus [10], the Livian *Histoire des révolutions arrivées dans le gouvernement de la République Romaine* (1719) of René Auber de Vertot [44] that was held in high regard by Voltaire, or the popular, uncritical *Histoire romaine* by the Paris Jansenist Charles Rollin (16 vols., 1738–1748) [42]. A more ambitious project was the monumental *Histoire Romaine depuis la fondation de Rome* (20 vols., 1725–1737) by the Jesuits François Catrou and Pierre-Julien Rouillé. While it rejected the antiquarian attention to detail, their traditional moralistic and monarchist account nevertheless sought to conform to scholarly standards with supplements comprising sources, images and maps [5]. All these works ended roughly with the Battle of Actium, but an ambitious scholarly continuation was already on hand: the *Histoire des empereurs* (5 vols., Paris 1690–1697, vol. 6 posthumously in 1738) by the Jansenist Sébastien Le Nain de Tillemont [25]. Listing the entire source material for each of its biographies, this chain of Imperial lives up to Anastasius, together with Catrou/Rouillé, provided the basis for all subsequent work on the subject.

The conceptual achievement of all these efforts was surpassed by the *Considérations sur les causes de la grandeur des Romains et de leur décadence* (1734) by Charles de Secondat, Baron de Montesquieu, who was also a member of the Parlement of Bordeaux [33]. Montesquieu once again looked at Roman history from Machiavelli's practical-political point of view, without however assuming human nature to be immutable. Instead, his work displayed an enlightened awareness of the interdependencies between physical, natural, moral and political circumstances. It showed how an ingenious legislation had helped the Roman national character to reach its fullest potential, and how this exact same development had – with the inevitability of a law of nature – destroyed precisely those virtues and principles of Roman political life that had rendered it possible in the first place. The further the Empire had spread across Italy, the more Rome had lost that national unity, morality and force for dynamic constitutional reforms, which had been the cornerstones of its power [56; 76].

If Montesquieu's brief sketch had already paid more attention to the decline rather than the rise of Rome, it was the central theme of the most famous Roman history of the → Enlightenment: Edward Gibbon's *History of the Decline and Fall of the Roman Empire* (6 vols., 1776–1788) [19]. A self-educated *philosophe*, Gibbon nevertheless built his monumental panorama stretching to the fall of Constantinople on the fruits of antiquarian research. Despite his reliance on Tille-

mont's work in this regard [71; 72], he parodied the ecclesiastical historian's narration of the Church's progress in the spirit of Voltaire when aside from the moral decay, the abuse of power by the ruling classes and the barbarian invasions, he singled out Christianity as the reason for Rome's decline. Its aggressive intolerance, he claimed, had paralysed the state and corroded it from the inside [50; 55; 59]. This provocative assertion, the use of all known sources, the witty-ironic voice, the wealth of colours and perspectives within the narrative have earned the work its rank as a classic of the genre, which long retained its reputation as the supreme account of the Imperial period [73]. Not even Mommsen dared to compete with Gibbon in historiographical terms. Scholarly interest, therefore, already sensitized following the political upheavals of the French → Revolution, shifted once more to the Republican period. A particularly lively political discussion had previously taken place in England [81]. In 1741 the Whig historian Conyers Middleton had praised Cicero in a two-volume biography as a champion of liberty, while the Catholic writer Nathaniel Hooke had glorified the Gracchi and Caesar as the true saviours of Rome [23] – a credit the Scottish historian Adam Ferguson sought in 1783 to grant exclusively to the Senate [11].

2.3 German Classical Scholarship: Niebuhr and Mommsen

The one work, however, that was seen all over Europe as the harbinger of a new era in Roman scholarship, was dedicated to the depiction of Rome's early history. Like Montesquieu and Gibbon before him, the Prussian reform politician Barthold Georg Niebuhr was an autodidact [63], when in 1811 he was invited to give lectures on Roman history at the newly opened university in Berlin. The hastily published print version of his lectures (2 vols., 1811/12), which he virtually spent rewriting up to his early death (3 vols., 1827–1832), sought to chronicle events leading up to Gibbon's *Decline and Fall*, but it never reached beyond the Phyrric War. In a manner similar to Gibbon's (but lacking the latter's literary brilliance), Niebuhr fused detailed antiquarian analyses with bold political judgements, but also with a revival of Perizonius' theory of an 'oral tradition'. In contrast to the predecessor he admired, Niebuhr read the Classics with the practical knowledge of the fiscal and financial expert, ignoring the scholarly literature. This allowed him to bridge gaps in the transmission with strikingly plausible 'divinations' (especially concerning constitutional questions and land legislation). Niebuhr praised Rome not only for its mixed constitution, but also for its ability to permanently reform its own legal system. In a provocative break with tradition, he no longer viewed the plebeians as clients of the patricians but as a distinct ethnic group and, together with the office of the people's tribune, as the source of Rome's greatness [49; 82]. Despite being written in a difficult scholarly style, Niebuhr's *Römische Geschichte* caught the imagination of contemporary audiences. In Germany it inspired Karl Ottfried Müller's *Die Etrusker* (1828) and Albert Schwegler's *Römische Geschichte* (3 vols., 1853–1858, down to the laws of Licinius), as well as the property theory of a young Karl Marx [49. 82–86] and handbooks such as those by Becker and Marquard (3 parts, 1843–1853) [4] or Ludwig Lange (3 vols., 1856–1871) [24]. In France it stimulated Jules Michelet's *Histoire romaine* (2 vols., 1830) [30], in England Thomas Babington Macaulay's *Lays of Ancient Rome* (1842) and George Grote's *History of Greece* (12 vols., 1846–1856). The old discussion about early Roman sources was being repeated on a new level.

Embodying the ideal of the autonomous 'scholar', Niebuhr (who was never a professor) became a symbolic figure for the renewal of the German university in the spirit of Kant and Humboldt. Their main scholarly disciplines had been philosophy and history; the new academic paradigm was a universal, systematic study of Antiquity, which soon attracted world-wide attention. Ancient history, which was at first still being taught within the larger framework of Classical philology or as a component of universal history, now received its own chairs (first in Göttingen in 1856; the first professorship especially for Roman history was that of Mommsen in Berlin) [57. 341; 64]. This association with the historical disciplines was what separated German academic research on Roman history from that of other countries; in the Anglo-American world it was, for instance, located within the 'Classics'. For this reason, the study of Roman history in Germany was for the most part conducted in a more systematic, more scientific manner, but it was also more focused on the state, and more prosaic than in neighbouring scholarly cultures.

The most important representative of this modern historistic, universal Roman history was Theodor Mommsen [67]. His *Römische Geschichte* (3 vols., 1854–1856), which the 1848 liberal wrote in his Swiss exile, rapidly eclipsed all previous works on the subject. In a dramatic and suggestive, often trenchant, ironic style, provocative through political judgements that were both confident and exposed, it depicted the growth of Italy's nationhood from the beginnings to the triumph of Caesar in 46 BC. Even though Mommsen rejected hypotheses regarding the early history as "fantasies" ('Phantasien'), he made an effort to present the Latins as an autochthonous people, whose "ingenious receptiveness" ('geniale Rezeptivität') for external ideas had revealed their moral force and made them, over time, the most powerful people in Italy. World dominance, by contrast, had fallen to Rome not through its active pursuit thereof but through the failure of its ruling class to evolve the city's constitution into a representative system. As a result, it became necessary to install a "military monarchy" ('Militärmonarchie'). Prefigured in C. Gracchus and founded by Sulla, it reached its highest perfection with Caesar. Cato and Cicero, on the other hand, the heroes of the Classicist tradition, were derided by him as two smug, small-minded old ham actors [66].

Despite its eminent success, Mommsen did not continue with his early work, deciding instead to dedicate the rest of his long, productive scholarly life to the study of legal history and major international projects such as the collection of Roman inscriptions, Roman provincial archaeology and late Roman prosopography [79]. It was to these projects that Mommsen owed his worldwide fame. The work delivered by the 68–year old in the fifth volume of his *Römische Geschichte* (1885) was a highly specialized economic and administrative history of the Roman provinces that remained authoritative until Rostovtzeff. Mommsen's new view of the Republic informed his most significant work, *Römisches Staatsrecht* (3 vols., 1871–1888) [32], in which he exponentiated the old theory, previously revived by Carl von Savigny's → HISTORISCHE RECHTSSCHULE*, that the Roman state had been a closed system of rational law: Mommsen no longer looked at clan systems, classes, the magistrates' and other offices individually, but as forces of varying 'intensity' within a state organism that he understood as a dynamic, interactive network. The sharp, abstract, contemporary language seemed ahistorical, yet the emerging structure so compelling, it was not until recently that critical voices and new approaches have made a mark.

2.4 ROMAN ECONOMIC AND SOCIAL HISTORY FROM PÖHLMANN TO FINLEY

Mommsen's late work reflected the growing tendency of the late 19th cent. to concentrate on the building of theoretical models. In doing so, German Classical Studies reacted to the challenge posed by new, statistical disciplines (economics, demography and sociology) and social problems of the time, characterized by the experience of industrialization and urbanization. The boldest ideas in this regard were expressed by Robert von Pöhlmann, who in his *Geschichte des antiken Kommunismus und Sozialismus* (2 vols., 1893–1901) [40] projected contemporary urban problems onto the ancient city of Rome, denounced Roman capitalism and sought to establish communist forms of property – against Mommsen's *gens* theory – not as an ancient Italic tradition but as a symptom of Roman decadence [53. 201–247]. Greater scholarly consensus existed over Karl Julius Beloch, who employed modern demographic methods in a systematic exploration of the structure and density of the population of ancient Italy (*Die Bevölkerung der griechisch-römischen Welt*, Leipzig 1886) [53. 248–285]. However, it was Beloch's pupil Max Weber who presented the most ambitious – and most successful – continuation of Mommsen's ideas [65]. In his *Habilitationsschrift Die römische Agrargeschichte in ihrer Bedeutung für das Staats- und Privatrecht* (1891) [46], as in his handbook contribution "Agrarverhältnisse im Altertum" (1897) [47], he analysed the political and economic relations between urban and rural areas and how they affected ancient culture – which he defined as 'urban', 'coastal' and 'slave-based'. According to Weber's theory, by the end of the Roman wars of conquest this culture had ceased to exist: the slaves had become unfree peasants, and the peasants villeins of the large landowners. These had taken their (trade) capital with them to the countryside, and in abandoning the cities to the lower classes and thus to gradual decay, had caused the demise of the Roman civilization.

Particularly in the newly unified Italy, which enjoyed a rich local tradition of Roman scholarship and where questions of agrarian policy were followed closely, the German discussions excited a lively interest [75]. They inspired works like the highly speculative, much-revised *Storia di Roma* (1898) of the Mommsen pupil Ettore Pais [35; 35a] and the solid *Storia dei Romani* by the Beloch pupil Gaetano De Sanctis, which only extended to 133 BC. In 1902, seven years after Mommsen's most avid pupil Otto Seeck published his *Geschichte des Untergangs der antiken Welt* (6 vols., 1895–1921), Guglielmo Ferrero presented a poetic, energetic narrative on the same subject [12].

Until 1914 the German tradition was also present in American Classical Studies. While the First and certainly the Second World War resulted in a radical break with this tradition, it was often the work of European emigrées that gave Roman scholarship in the United States its formidable (post-war) reputation. The most famous among them was Michael Rostovtzeff, who left Russia for the United States during the Revolution and accepted a position at the University of Wisconsin (1920–1925). In 1925 he was appointed Sterling Professor of Ancient History and Archaeology at Yale, a position he held until his retirement in 1918 and from 1920 taught at Yale [53. 334–349; 22. 526–528]. His positivistic, universal approach to scholarship allowed him to display a never-before-seen versatility in consulting papyri as well as archaeological material, some of which he himself had prepared before 1914, for his *Social and Economic History of the Roman Empire* (1926). Combining a detailed description of the property and social structures with political evaluations coloured by the shock of the Russian Revolution, he expanded on Weber's theory of a city-countryside tension by depicting Roman small-scale peasants as ancient Bolsheviks, whose victory over the urban bourgeoisie had destroyed the Roman Empire.

This was a direct challenge to his Soviet colleagues – who were in fact drawing similar parallels. Following a directive from Stalin, however, they equated the Roman lower classes with those of their own age, and celebrated Rome's downfall as the successful outcome of a 'slave revolution' on the way to the proletarian world revolution [62] (extensive bibliography in [78]). And yet, in the ensuing period, the most prominent Marxist scholars carefully distanced themselves from this model by subjecting it to a growing amount of specialized scrutiny: N.A. Maskin rejected it as early as 1949; in 1965 S.L. Utcenko found it could not be applied to the civil war period. Elena M. Staerman asserted in 1957 that the real revolutionaries in the third century AD had not been the slaves but the estate owners in the provinces, and that the inequality in the different forms of property ownership had indeed led via a crisis of production to a general crisis, but that it had not been a revolution [62. 208–212, 308–310]. The collective *Vsemirnaja istoija* ('World History', vol. 2, 1956) shared this view. Studies of ancient Italic economic types and property ownership (e.g. by M.E. Sergeenko, 1958, and V.I. Kuziscin, 3 vols., 1966–1976 [62. 224–230]) have since been the domain of socialist historians. As late as 1979/80 the Italian Marxist F. de Martino, author of a comprehensive *Storia della costituzione romana* (6 vols., 1951–1972) created a *Storia economica di Roma antica*.

Rostovtzeff's work also prompted a series of related studies in the United States. One monument to this legacy is the *Economic Survey of Ancient Rome* (6 vols., 1933–1940), headed by the Johns Hopkins professor Tenney Frank. A distinct anthropological colouring was brought to the field of comprehensive economic surveys in 1973 by the US-educated Cambridge scholar Moses I. Finley [51. 295–337]. In *The Ancient Economy* he returned to Max Weber's assertion that people in Antiquity did not act according to the principles of a modern market economy in order to maximize profit. Rather, their concern was with returns and the maintenance of their social status. In another nod to Weber, Finley sought to characterize ancient economic activity in typological terms, while Geza Alföldy found guidance for his *Römische Sozialgeschichte* (1975) in the models of contemporary sociology.

2.5 PROSOPOGRAPHY

Unlike their colleagues in the history of economics, political historians were somewhat slow in detaching themselves from the larger-than-life figure of Theodor Mommsen. The first major criticism came in 1907 from Eduard Meyer, the last German representative of a universal *Altertumswissenschaft* [53. 286–333]. In the second edition of his *Geschichte des Altertums* he discarded Mommsen's view of the Roman state as being derived from the family-like structures of the early village community. In 1918, against Mommsen's apotheosis of Caesar, he praised Pompey as the superior statesman because his policies had prefigured the Principate, whereas Caesar had planned to erect a monarchy based on the Hellenistic model, following not the ideal of the Gracchi but that of Alexander the Great [29]. Up until the 1960s the question of the political concepts held by Caesar and his opponents remained a popular subject among scholars of Roman history in Germany. These debates (e.g. between Matthias Gelzer and Hermann Strasburger, 1953/54) ultimately did not stray very far from Mommsen's path. The spell of his suggestive systematic method was not really broken until historiography discovered prosopography.

Already in the 1830s Wilhelm Drumann had split his *Geschichte Roms in seinem Übergange von der republikanischen zur monarchischen Verfassung* (6 vols., 1834–1844) into individual biographies, claiming that in times of "great disquiet" ('großer Gärung') everything depended on the actions of those who acted alone. In 1912 Matthias Gelzer analysed the nobility of the Roman Republic (*Die Nobilität der römischen Republik*) not in terms of their powers or their legal position but with regard to their social structure [18]. However, it was Friedrich Münzer who in his *Römische Adelsparteien und Adelsfamilien* (1920) and in numerous articles for Pauly-Wissowa's Real-Encyclopädie refined the prosopographical method to perfection, so that in 1937 Anton von Premerstein could use it in his *Vom Werden und Wesen des Prinzipats* to prove that the bond between clients and patrons was at the heart of all socio-political relationships in Rome [52.164–165, 128–133].

Ronald Syme was referring back to Münzer and Premerstein when in 1939 he gave a provocative description of the transition from the Republic to the Principate – already burdened with a long theoretical tradition – as a struggle between 'persons, not programs'. Not economics, constitutional or ideological matters formed the centre of *The Roman Revolution*, an analysis of the period between 60 BC and 14 AD [51.188–247], but the concrete representatives of the ruling classes, in whose careers Syme, with a high degree of literary artistry, traced the development of their parties. At the same time he shared with Mommsen not only a common concept of 'revolution', but also the latter's admiration for Ceasar and antipathy for Augustus, who had organized his followers into a 'national party' and thus appeared as an ancient mirror image of Adolf Hitler. With an irony reminiscent of Gibbon, Syme undermined the Classicistic ideal of the Augustan Age. As a worthy successor to *Decline and Fall* his brilliant work still inspires scholarly interest in prosopography today.

The National Socialist regime destroyed the international standing of German scholarship [52. 164–260] (→ NATIONAL SOCIALISM). In both Germany and the United Kingdom, the decline of the Classical languages, compounded by the education reforms of the late 1960s, eradicated the basis for any public interest in the professional study of Classical Antiquity. In many places, this development has since 1968 led to a 'second emigration' of leading European scholars to the United States. The best German-language publications continued to focus on political aspects and constitutional history; a sober, matter-of-face style prevailed, thus for instance in the works of the Swiss historian Matthias Gelzer, in his biography of Caesar (six editions, 1921–1960) [48; 52. 120–128], or in the best comprehensive history published in Germany after 1945, *Römische Geschichte* by Alfred Heuß, [22; 52. 275–282]. The maverick Heuß, moreover, pioneered a modern approach toward the study of historiography with his monographs on Mommsen [66] and Niebuhr [63]. The world's foremost expert on the history of historiography, the Italian cosmopolitan scholar Arnoldo Momigliani, meanwhile, who taught in London from 1938, worked on all periods of ancient history, including Roman history [51. 248–294].

2.6 FROM THE HISTORY OF RELIGION TO ANTHROPOLOGY

One other strand of tradition has also shaped today's international scholarly interests: those who deliberately distanced themselves from the modern 'German' political historiography by emphasizing the religious and cultural dimension of Roman history. Johan Jakob Bachofen sought the explanation for Rome's rise not in political intelligence, expedient laws or constitutional reforms. In *Geschichte der Römer* (Basel 1851) [1] – which he co-wrote with his teacher Franz D. Gerlach – he found it in a religious piety permeating all areas of life and in the moral purity of a peasant people that had been lost in the course of the Republic [58]. Similarly, in *La cité antique* (1864), Numa Denis Fustel de Coulanges developed Roman statehood not from rational foundations but from an ubiquitous cult of the dead and the Romans' veneration of their ancestors [17; 61; 74].

Even though both works eschewed source criticism and preached a flawless Antiquity in the Humanistic spirit, they found successors especially in France and in the United Kingdom, where colonial contacts with non-European cultures had. fostered a comparative ethnological view of history from the 18th cent. on. In the United Kingdom, for instance, works were written on the family, law and consciousness of archaic societies, e.g. Henry Maine's *Ancient Law* (1861), J.F. McLennan's *Primitive Marriage* (1865), E.B. Taylor's *Primitive Culture* (1871) and James Frazer's *The Golden Bough* (1890) [75]. While these studies often examined the 'primitive mentality' as exemplified by the early Greeks, W. Warde Fowler – aside from Ludwig Deubler – attempted early on to apply ideas articulated by the Cambridge Ritualists to the reconstruction of Rome's origins [15]. By contrast, the German standard work on the subject, Georg Wissowa's *Religion und Kultus der Römer* (1902, new ed. 1912), brought Mommsen's systematic approach and a sober rationality to his explanation of the Roman religion as a purely political state cult. Ecclesiastical historians like Adolf von Harnack and Ernst Troeltsch focused on the Christian period. The leading study of the cults of the Imperial period was written in 1906 by the Belgian scholar Franz Cumont [7]. Beginning in the 1930s, these positions were being outmoded by the work of Andreas Alföldi and others [51. 8–59].

The combination of political and cultural history with anthropological concepts became a characteristic especially of French Roman studies in the 20th century. The leading French representative was Jérôme Carcopino [60]; Ludwig Friedländer's *Sittengeschichte Roms* [16] formed the German equivalent. André Piganiol, a member of the *Annales* founding group in Strasbourg, who in 1939 published a much-consulted *Histoire de Rome* [51. 348], analysed the Roman circus games using Durkheim's categories (*Recherches sur les jeux romains*, 1923) – a subject revisited by Paul Veyne in *Le pain et le cirque* (1976), who used it to describe municipal patronage as a ritual 'gift' and 'expenditure' in the sense of Marcel Mauss and Georges Bataille. Seemingly extravagant, these experiments did in reality follow the Classicistic tradition to which Roman history owes its vital importance for European intellectual, cultural and educational history, and the history of ideas and sciences as well: its ability to serve as an experimental field for the study of current ideas, ideals and problems, new political models and scholarly methods.

C. Outlook

The development of Roman Studies in the last 150 years has seen an increasing differentiation and academic professionalization; the resulting competitive and innovative pressure is on the one hand fuelled by a plethora of archaeological finds and at the same time hampered by the growing difficulty of producing fundamentally new interpretations and conclusions in profoundly traditional fields. Collectively, these factors encouraged the high specialization of individual scholars, a predilection for quantitative methods and a concentration on the margins of the Roman (living) environment. This was beneficial in particular for the study of Roman everyday life, its provinces, neighbours and enemies, but it also forced the discipline into self-isolation. Thus it seems the fate of Roman history at the beginning of the third millennium depends more than ever on the ability of its representatives to accomplish what their enlightened antiquarian predecessors achieved in the 18th cent.: to convince a sceptical public of the intrinsic political and practical value of Roman studies for the present age.

→ Historicism

Sources   1 J. J. Bachofen Gesammelte Werke, K. Meuli (ed.), vol. 1, 1943   2 L. de Beaufort, Dissertation sur l'incertitude des cinq premiers siècles de l'histoire romaine. Nouvelle édition. Revue, corrigée & considérablément augmentée, The Hague 1750 (Engl. A Dissertation upon the Uncertainty of the Roman History during the First Five Hundred Years, London, 1740)   3 Id., La republique romaine ou plan général de l'ancien gouvernement de Rome, où l'on develope des différents ressorts de de gouvernement, l'influence qu'y avait la religion; la souveraineté du peuple, la maniére, dont il l'exerçcoit; quelle étoit l'autorité du sénat & celle des magistrats, l'administration de la justice, les prérogatives du citoyen romain, & les différentes conditions des sujets de ce vaste empire, The Hague 1766   4 W. A. Becker, Handbuch der römischen Alterthümer. Nach den Quellen bearbeitet, Erster und Zweiter Theil, 2 and 3 vols., Leipzig 1843 f.; Dritter Theil (by J. Marquardt), Leipzig 1853   5 F. Catrou, P.-J. Rouillé, Histoire romaine, depuis la fondation de Rome. Avec des notes historiques, géographiques et critiques; des gravûres en taille-douce; des cartes géographiques, et plusieurs médailles authentiques, 21 vols., Paris 1725–1732, vol. 21 by B. Routh (Engl. Mr. Ozell (trans.), The Roman History: Complete from the Foundation of Rome, Down to Charlemain, London, 1725)   6 Ch. Cellarius, Historia universalis breviter ac perspicue exposita, in antiquam, et medii aevi ac novam divisa, Jena 1708 (complete edition of the parts previously published in 1685, 1688, 1698)   7 F. Cumont, Les reli-

gions orientales dans le paganisme romain, 1906 (Engl. The Oriental Religions in Roman Paganism, 'authorized trans.', 1911)   8 H. Dodwell, De veteribus Graecorum Romanorumque cyclis, obiterque de cyclo Judaeorum aetate Christi dissertationes decem, cum tabulis necessariis. Inseruntur tabulis fragmenta veterum inedita, ad rem spectantia chronologicam. Opus historiae veteri, tam Graece, quam Romanae, quam et sacrae quoque, necessarium, Oxford 1701   9 W. Drumann, Geschichte Roms in seinem Übergange von der republikanischen zur monarchischen Verfassung oder Pompeius, Caesar, Cicero und ihre Zeitgenossen nach Geschlechtern und mit genealogischen Tabellen, 6 vols., Königsberg 1834–1844 (a reprint of the 2nd edition 1899–1929 was published in 1964)   10 L. Echard, The Roman History, vol. 1: From the Building of the City to the Perfect Settlement of the Empire by Augustus Caesar; vol. 2: From the Settlement of the Empire by Augustus Caesar to the Removal of the Imperial Seat by Constantine the Great, London ⁴1699   11 A. Ferguson, The History of the Progress and Termination of the Roman Republic, 4 vols., London 1783 (revised edition: 5 vols. 1799)   12 G. Ferrero, Grandezza e decadenza di Roma, 5 vols., 1902–1907 (Engl. The Greatness and Decline of Rome, A. E. Zimmern et al. (trans.), 1907–1909)   13 M. I. Finley, The Ancient Economy, 1973   14 M. Flacius Illyricus et al., Ecclesiastica Historia, integram Ecclesiae Christi ideam ... secundum singulas centurias perspicuo ordine complectens, 13 vols., Basel 1559–1574   15 W. Warde Fowler, The Religious Experience of the Roman People, 1911   16 L. Friedländer, Darstellungen aus der Sittengeschichte Roms in der Zeit von Augustus bis zum Ausgang der Antonine, 4 vols., Leipzig 1862–1871   17 N. D. Fustel de Coulanges, La Cité antique, Paris 1996 (Engl. W. Small (trans., 1874), The Ancient City, 1956; with a new foreword by A. Momigliano, S. C. Humphreys, 1980)   18 M. Gelzer, Die Nobilität der römischen Republik (1912), in: Id., Kleine Schriften 1, 1962, 17–135 (Engl. R. Seager (trans.), The Roman Nobility, 1969)   19 E. Gibbon, The History of the Decline and Fall of the Roman Empire, J. B. Bury (ed.), 7 vols., London 1909–1914   20 J. Gronovius, Dissertatio de origine Romuli, Leiden 1684   21 G. W. F. Hegel, Vorlesungen über die Philosophie der Weltgeschichte. Vollständig neue Ausgabe von G. Lasson (= Philosophische Bibliothek 171), vol. 3, ⁴1944 (Engl. H. B. Nisbet (most recent trans.), Lectures on the Philosophy of History, 1975   22 A. Heuss, Römische Geschichte, herausgegeben, eingeleitet und mit einem neuen Forschungsteil versehen von J. Bleicken, W. Dahlheim und H.-J. Gehrke, ⁶1998   23 N. Hooke, The Roman History. From the Building of Rome to the Ruin of the Commonwealth. Illustrated with Maps and other Plates, vols., London 1738–1771   24 L. Lange, Römische Altertümer, 3 vols., Berlin 1856–1871   25 S. Le Nain de Tillemont, Histoire des empereurs et des autres princes qui ont régné durant les six premiers siècles de l'Église ..., 16 vols., Brussels 1707–1739   26 N. Machiavelli, Discorsi sopra la prima deca di Tito Livio, ed. by C. Vivanti, 1983 (Engl. Discourses on Livy, J. Conaway Bondanella, P. Bondanella, (most recent trans.), 1997)   27 J. Marquardt, Die römische Staatsverwaltung, 3 vols., Leipzig ²1881–1885 (Part of Handbuch der römischen Altherthümer, cf. [4])   28 Ph. Melanchthon, Caspar Peucer (eds.), Chronicon Carionis, latine expositum et auctum multis et veteribus et recentibus historiis in descriptionibus regnorum et gentium antiquarum et narrationibus rerum ecclesiasticarum et politicarum Graecarum, Romanarum, Germanicarum et aliarum, ab exordio mundi usque ad Carolum Quintum, Wittenberg 1572 29 E. Meyer, Caesars Monarchie und das Prinzipat des Pompejus, 1918   30 J. Michelet, Histoire romaine, in: Id., Oevres complètes, vol. 2: 1828–1831, P. Viallaneix (ed.), 1972   31 Th. Mommsen, Römische Geschichte, 3 vols., Berlin 1854–1856, vol. 5, Berlin 1885 (new edition by K. Christ, 8 vols., 1976) (Engl. W. Purdie Dickson (trans.), The History of Rome, 5 vols., London 1862–1866 and later. New editions by D. A. Saunders, J. H. Collins, 1958 and Th. Wiedemann, 1996)   32 Id., Römisches Staatsrecht, 3 in 5 vols., Leipzig 1871–1888 (repr. 1971; summary: Abriß des römischen Staatsrechts, Leipzig 1893, repr. 1974) (Part of Handbuch der römischen Alterthümer, cf. [4])   33 Ch.-L. de Secondat, Baron de la Brède et de Montesquieu, Considérations sur les causes de la grandeur des romains et de leur décadence, ed. by J. Ehrard, 1968, 1990 (Engl. D. Lowenthal (trans.), Considerations on the Causes of the Greatness of the Romans and their Decline, 1965, repr. with corrections 1999)   34 B. G. Niebuhr, Römische Geschichte, 2 vols., Berlin 1811/12 (revised edition: Berlin 1827–1830, vol. 3 posthumously 1832) (first Engl. trans. by F. A. Walter, London 1827; then by J. C. Hare, C. Thirlwall, Cambridge 1828–1842, completed by W. Smith, L. Schmitz, London 1844)   35 E. Pais, Storia di Roma, vol. 1, Rome 1898–1899   35a Id., Storia critica di Roma durante i primi cinque secoli, 5 vols., 1913–1920   36 O. Panvinius, Fasti et triumphi Romanorum, Venice 1557   37 Id., Fastorum libri V, eiusdem in Fastorum librorum commentarii, Venice 1558   38 J. Perizonius, Animadversiones historicae, Amsterdam 1685   39 St. Vinandus Pighius, Annales magistratuum et provinciarum SPQR ab urbe condita opera et studio Andreae Schottii, 3 vols. Antwerp 1599–1615   40 R. v. Pöhlmann, Geschichte des antiken Kommunismus und Sozialismus, 2 vols., 1893–1901 (2nd edition published as Geschichte der sozialen Frage und des Sozialismus in der antiken Welt, 1912)   41 L. v. Ranke, Weltgeschichte, parts II and III, 3 vols., Leipzig 1883 (Engl. G. W. Prothero, D. C. Tovey (trans.), Universal History. The Oldest Historical Group of Nations and the Greeks, London 1884)   42 Ch. Rollin, Histoire romaine, depuis la fondation de Rome jusqu'à la bataille d'Actium, c'est-à-dire jusqu'à la fin de la république, 16 vols., Paris 1738–1748 (vols. 8–9 revised and completed by J. B. L. Crevier, vols. 10–16 written by Crevier) 43 J. Sleidanus, De quatuor summis imperiis libri tres, in gratiam iuventutis confecti, Strasbourg 1556   44 R. Auber, Abbé de Vertot, Histoire des révolutions arrivées dans le gouvernement de la république romaine, 3 vols., Paris 1719   45 Voltaire, Le siècle de Louis XIV, in: Œuvres historiques, René Pomeau (ed.), 1957, 603–1274   46 M. Weber, Die römische Agrargeschichte in ihrer Bedeutung für das Staats- und Privatrecht, Stuttgart 1891 (= Max Weber Gesamtausgabe, J. Deininger (ed.), I,2, 1986)   47 Id., Art. Agrarverhältnisse im Altertum, in: Handbuch der Staatswiss., Bd. 1, ³1909, 52–188, (M. Weber, Gesamtausgabe I, 6) (Engl. R. I. Frank (trans.), The Agrarian Sociology of Ancient Civilizations, 1976)

Literature   48 J. Bleicken, C. Meier, H. Strasburger (eds.), Matthias Gelzer und die römische Geschichte, 1977   49 G. Bonacina, Hegel, il mondo romano e la storiografia (= Pubblicazioni della Facoltà di lettere e filosofia dell'Università di Milano 19), 1991   50 G. W.

Bowersock, J. Clive, S. R. Graubard (eds.), Edward Gibbon and the Decline and Fall of the Roman Empire, 1977   51 K. Christ, Neue Profile der Alten Geschichte, 1990   52 Id.., Römische Geschichte und deutsche Geschichtswissenschaft, 1982   53 Id., Von Gibbon zu Rostovtzeff, 1972   54 P. B. Craddock, Edward Gibbon. A Reference Guide, 1987   55 Id., Edward Gibbon, 1989   56 L. Desgraves, Répertoire des ouvrages et des articles sur Montesquieu, 1988   57 J. Engel, Die deutsche Universität und die Geschichtswissenschaft, in: HZ, 189, 1959, 223–378   58 L. Gossman, Orpheus Philologus. Bachofen versus Mommsen on the Study of Antiquity (= Transactions of the American Philosophical Society 73,5), 1983   59 Id., The Empire Unpossess'd. An Essay on Gibbon's Decline and Fall, 1981   60 P. Grimal, Jérôme Carcopino, 1981   61 F. Hartog, Le XIXᵉ siècle et l'histoire. Le cas Fustel de Coulanges, 1988 62 H. Heinen (ed.), Die Geschichte des Altertums im Spiegel der sowjetischen Forschung, 1980   63 A. Heuss, Barthold Georg Niebuhrs wissenschaftliche Anfänge (= AAWG, Dritte Folge, 114), 1981   64 Id., Institutionalisierung der Alten Geschichte, in: Id., Gesammelte Schriften 3, 1995, 1938–1970   65 Id., Max Webers Bedeutung für die Geschichte des griechisch-römischen Altertums, in: Id., Gesammelte Schriften 3, 1995, 1835–1862   66 Id., Theodor Mommsen als Geschichtsschreiber, in: N. Hammerstein (ed.), Deutsche Geschichtswissenschaft um 1900, 1988, 37–95   67 Id., Theodor Mommsen und das 19. Jahrhundert, 1956   68 D. R. Kelley, Civil Science in the Renaissance: Jurisprudence in the French Manner, in: Id., History, Law and the Human Sciences. Medieval and Renaissance Perspectives, 1984, 261–276   69 W. McCuaig, Carlo Sigonio, 1989   70 E. Meyer-Zwiffelhoffer, Alte Geschichte in der Universalgeschichtsschreibung der Frühen Neuzeit, in: Saeculum 46, 1995, 249–273 71 A. Momigliano, Eighteenth-Century Prelude to Mr. Gibbon, in: Id., Sesto contributo, 1980, 249–263   72 Id., Gibbon's Contribution to Historical Method, in: Id., Contributo alla storia degli studi classici, 1955, 195–211 73 Id., After Gibbon's Decline and Fall, in: Id., Sesto contributo, 1980, 265–284   74 Id., Foreword to N.D. Fustel de Coulanges, The Ancient City, in: Id., Settimo contributo, 1984, 171–177   75 Id., From Mommsen to Max Weber, in: Id., New Paths of Classicism in the Nineteenth Century (= History & Theory 21, suppl. 21), 1982, 16–32 76 U. Muhlack, Geschichtswissenschaft im Humanismus und in der Aufklärung, 1991   77 M. Raskolnikova , Histoire romaine et critique historique dans l'Europe des lumières, 1992   78 Id., La recherche en Union Soviétique et l'histoire économique et sociale du monde hellénistique et romain, 1975   79 S. Rebenich, Theodor Mommsen und Adolf Harnack, 1997   80 A. Seifert, Der Rückzug der biblischen Prophetie von der neueren Gesch. Studien zur Gesch. der Reichstheologie des frühneuzeitlichen dt. Protestantismus (= Beihefte zum Archiv für Kulturgeschichte 31), 1990   81 F. M. Turner, British Politics and the Demise of the Roman Republic: 1700–1939, in: Historical Journal 29, 1986, 577–599   82 G. Walther, Niebuhrs Forschung, 1993   83 G. Wirth, Die Entwicklung der Alten Geschichte an der Philipps-Universität Marburg, 1977.

Gerrit Walther

IV. Late Antiquity
A. History of Research B. Interpretation

A. History of Research

Scholarly interest in Late Antiquity began with Humanism, which called into question the continuity of the Imperial tradition as postulated by the Roman Pope, the German Emperor and the Byzantine Basileus. Ever since Petrarch's melancholy admiration for the ruins of Rome an explanation was required for the demise of Roman glory; it was sought, in general terms, in the turnings of the Wheel of Fortune, and specifically in Roman history. In 1358 Giovanni Boccaccio identified its cause in the collapse of Roman morality; his contemporary Givonanni Villani held the Germanic barbarians responsible.

Leonardo Bruni (1429/1475) identified both internal and external causes for Rome's decline; subsequently, Flavio Biondo (d. 1463) devoted a serious study to the *Historiarum ab inclinatione Romanorum Imperii*, which he saw as beginning with Alaric. Lorenzo Valla was a pupil of both of the above. In 1440 he completed his treatise *On the Forgery of the Alleged Donation of Constantine*, in which he demonstrated that this document, actually written at the Curia in the late 8th cent., was not authentic. Valla, for instance, disproved its claim that Constantine had retreated to the East and handed over worldly power over the West to the Pope, by pointing out that the Western Empire had continued under Constantine's sons and their successors. Late Antiquity continued to be a topic of discussion during the 16th cent. Aside from Ioannes Baptista Egnatius and Pomponius Laetus, Machiavelli also studied the decline of Rome. He identified as its causes the change of the capital, religious strife and the Germanization of the army. In 1558 Onuphrius Panvinius explained the survival of the Eastern Empire with the path of the migratory peoples which had led them to invade the West instead. In his *Historiae de occidentali imperio* (1579) Carolus Sigonius traced the history of the Western Empire between 285 and 565 – two dates which have remained significant cornerstones for the late ancient period. The first work devoted exclusively to the reasons for Rome's decline was the eleventh *Discorso politico* of Paolo Paruta (d. 1598).

Humanists in Germany and France studied the late ancient period because of their interest in the Germanic tribes. In 1492 Konrad Celtis reminded the academic youth of Ingolstadt of the victory of the 'courageous Germanic peoples' over the 'depleted Romans'. Similar observations were made by Jakob Wimpfeling (1505) and Albert Krantz (d. 1517); anti-Roman accents are also found in the writings of the Protestant scholars Caspar Hedio of Strasbourg, François Hotman of Bourges and Johannes Magnus of Uppsala. The dazzling image that had now emerged of Constantine was in keeping with a positive assessment of Julian and the pagan historiography of Johannes Leunclavius (also called Löwenklau, 'Lion's Claw') in 1576.

Editions of the sources came to be of vital importance for the study of Late Antiquity: Ammianus Marcellinus 1474, Claudian 1482, Aurelius Victor 1579, Zosimos 1581 (Latin already in 1576) and Procopius (1531, 1607, 1623). Gothofredus – father and son – edited the *Corpus Juris Civilis* and the *Codex Theodosianus*. A copy of the *Speyer Codex* that was later lost in the Thirty Years' War and which included the *Notitia Dignitatum* appeared in Basel in 1552. The gathering of data on late antique Church history began on the Protestant side with the *Ecclesiastica Historia* of the Magdeburg Centuriators (Vol. V in 1562), on the Catholic side with the *Annales ecclesiastici* of Caesar Baronius (d. 1607). The Jansenist Sébastien Le Nain de Tillemont (d. 1698) then compiled his well-documented account of the late Roman and early Christian eras. These works formed the basis for Charles Le Beau's *Histoire du Bas Empire* (1752) and Edward Gibbon's (d. 1794) *History of the Decline and Fall of the Roman Empire*, which Mommsen regarded as the best work ever written on the subject of Roman history. From the 19th cent. onwards, studies of the late ancient period began to exhibit more scholarly precision, but also more relevance to current events, as Late Antiquity was viewed as mirroring contemporary crises. Examples of these new scholarly approaches are *Die Zeit Konstantins des Großen* (Engl. *The Age of Constantine the Great*, trans. M. Hadas, ca. 1949) by Jacob Burckhardt, which was published in 1853 and revised in 1880, and in which the adjective *spätantik* ('Late Ancient') appeared for the first time, and the monumental *Geschichte des Untergangs der antiken Welt* (1895–1922) by Mommsen's pupil Otto Seeck who, in his turn, inspired Oswald Spengler's *Untergang des Abendlandes* (1917; Engl. *The Decline of the West*, trans. C.F. Atkinson, 1926).

Of the series of sources published during the 19th cent., the following must be mentioned: the *Corpus Scriptorum Historiae Byzantinae*, begun in 1828 by Niebuhr; the Church Fathers, published by J.P. Migne: the *PL* beginning in 1844, the *PG* beginning in 1857; the *Auctores Antiquissimi* of the *MGH* (1877–1919), for many years under the supervision of Theodor Mommsen, who was also involved in the new editions of the *Corpus Juris Civilis* (1892) and the *Codex Theodosianus* (1904). Work continues on the *Corpus Ecclesiasticorum Latinorum*, begun in Vienna in 1866, as well as on *Die Griechischen Christlichen Schriftsteller der ersten Jahrhunderte*, which was begun in Leipzig in 1897, and has been appearing in Berlin since 1953, and in Paris the *Sources Chrétiennes* have been appearing since 1942. Very useful working tools are Otto Seeck's *Regesten* (1919), the *RAC* (1950ff.) and the *PLRE* of A.H.M. Jones, J. Morris and J.R. Martindale (vol. I in 1971; vol. II in 1980; vol. III in 1992).

B. Interpretation

Late Antiquity calls into question three widely-held assumptions: that a well-ordered state should survive forever, that a civilized people is superior to its barbaric neighbours and that civilization develops in an uninterrupted process of advancement. Five questions arise in this context: 1. The essential question is this: What actually occurred during this period? A minimalist approach confines itself to the interruption of the Imperial succession in the West in 476; a maximal approach underscores the transformation from a pagan to a Christian world. Between those approaches are mixtures of the two: the end of the Western Roman Empire, the decline of the slave-based economy, the end of Greco-Roman paganism, the birth of Europe and its family of nations, the emergence of the West, the metamorphosis or transformation of the Mediterranean region. There is frequent mention of 'crisis', sometimes of 'revolution' (of the Christians, Germanic tribes, slaves, feudal lords, soldier-emperors etc.), as well as of debacles or catastrophes. The term 'late antique' itself, in referring to a past age, implies that an end is imminent; as a noun (*Spätantike*, 'Late Antiquity') it was first used by Max Weber in 1909 (*Handwörterbuch der Staatswissenschaften*, 3rd edition, I, 182, s.v. Agrargeschichte I 7). The French term is *antiquité tardive*; Italian: *basso impero*.

The second interpretative problem concerns periodization. The question is, which year and which event marked the entry into the Middle Ages. The following have been proposed: the era of Constantine, his accession to power in 306, his victory at the Milvian Bridge in 312 or the beginning of his autocratic rule in 324, as well as the onslaught of the Huns (no doubt earlier than 375) and the crossing of the Danube by the Goths in 376, along with the Battle of Adrianople in 378 and the settlement of the Goths in 382; also the 395 'division of the Empire' by Theodosius among his sons, and the sakking of Rome by Alaric in 410, but most frequently the overthrow of Romulus Augustulus in 476; even contemporary observers such as Eugippius, Marcellinus Comes and Procopius recognized that event as a turning point. Through Bede the epochal year 476 entered medieval literature; through the Humanists (Machiavelli, Hedio, Melanchthon) and the thinkers of the Enlightenment (Johann Christoph Gatterer, Edward Gibbon, Arnold Hermann Ludwig Heeren) it became part of the Historicist tradition (Leopold v. Ranke, Seeck, Ernst Stein). Later models favoured the era of Justinian or even the founding of Islam.

The third problem, namely how deep was the gap between Antiquity and the Middle Ages, addresses the question of continuity. Ancient traditions continued to exist, and not only in Byzantium: Roman cities, their written language and monetary system survived in the West as well, albeit in rudimentary form. The Church, the monasteries and the royal court replaced the state and its citizens as the bearers of culture. For the socio-economic sphere, Alfons Dopsch underscored the continuity of traditions. In this light, the Germanic tribes did not destroy the ancient civilization, but preserved and renewed it.

The fourth issue, however, remains untouched by this: the decadence that is supposed to have caused the disintegration of the Empire. Its onset has been variously assigned to Constantine, the soldier-emperors, or even Augustus, and it is seen as a continuation of the declining Republic. The Romans themselves attributed the moral decay to prosperity, believing that the prolonged period of peace had undermined their ability to wage war. Other explanations included the loss of freedom, of patriotism, of a healthy rustic live. Aside from the theory of a general 'cultural regression' or 'return to primitivity', symptoms of decline have been identified in the art of Late Antiquity, in the agriculture of the period, its cities, the construction of roads and bridges, in the educational sphere, in the state and the army. These phenomena are being interpreted in terms of a cyclical pattern of cultural or fatalistic inevitability or as culpable failures.

The fifth and most extensive controversy focuses on the question of culpability: who – or what – is to blame for the demise of the Empire? More than 200 internal factors have been cited. Depending on the viewpoint of the respective author, the following have been held responsible: Christians, who directed all their hopes towards the afterlife; the supposedly ever-growing discrepancy between the (good) poor and the (evil) rich; the depletion of living resources (climate deterioration, karst formation, depopulation, miscegenation), corruption in the state and the army, resulting in an inability to resist external pressure at the borders.

As a rule, these explanations tend to overlook the fact that this external pressure had increased as a result of developments in the *barbaricum*. There is no indication that the Empire would have disintegrated of its own accord – voluntarily abandoning the level of of civilization it had attained – without extraneous causes.
→ CONSTANTINOPLE; → EPOCHS, CONCEPT OF

1 Av. CAMERON, P. GARNSEY (eds.), The Late Empire, AD 337–425 (= CAH 13), 1998 2 K. CHRIST (ed.), Der Untergang des römischen Reiches, 1970 3 A. DEMANDT, Der Fall Roms. Die Auflösung des römischen Reiches im Urteil der Nachwelt, 1984 4 Id., Die Spätantike. Römische Geschichte von Diocletian bis Justinian 234–565 n. Chr. (= HdbA 3,6), 1989 5 S. D'ELIA, Il Basso impero nella cultura moderna dal Quattrocento ad oggi, 1967 6 M. FUHRMANN, Rom in der Spätantike, 1994 7 P. E. HÜBINGER (ed.), Kulturbruch oder Kulturkontinuität im Übergang von der Antike zum Mittelalter (= Wege der Forschung 201), 1968 8 Id. (ed.), Zur Frage der Periodengrenze zwischen Altertum und Mittelalter (= Wege der Forschung 51), 1969 9 J. P. ISAAC, Factors in the Ruin of Antiquity, 1971 10 A. H. M. JONES, The Later Roman Empire 284–602, 3 vols., 1964 11 S. MAZZARINO, La fine del mondo antico, 1959 (Engl. The End of the Ancient World, G. HOLMES (trans.), 1966 12 W. REHM, Der Untergang Roms im abendländischen Denken, 1930 13 O. SEECK, Regesten der Kaiser und Päpste für die Jahre 311 bis 476 n. Chr., 1919 14 Id., Geschichte des Untergangs der antiken Welt, 6 vols., 1895–1921.

ALEXANDER DEMANDT

Historische Rechtsschule
A. Name B. Origin C. Core Ideas
D. Position in its Time E. Scholarship
F. New Juridical Principles G. Achieve-
ments H. Criticism

A. Name
The name *Historische Rechtsschule* (HR)–literally
'Historical School of Jurisprudence'–first referred to a
small group of jurists, associated with Friedrich Carl
von Savigny (1779–1861) and Karl Friedrich Eichhorn
(1781–1854), which proclaimed itself a 'historical
school' in 1815. A secular flourishing of achievements
in the history of law, in the broadest sense, subsequently
marked the 19th cent. The methodological substance of
the school, however, became more and more obscure.
The essence of the movement is best understood from
its inception.

B. Origin
The HR had its roots in private law which was still
clearly predominant the 19th cent. It was involved with
the contemporary preservation and advancement of
European-continental jurisprudence. Socially, this
affected the class of university-trained jurists (especially
in Germany); in terms of legal content, it affected the
tradition of *Ius commune* primarily regarding the sources and developments of the Late Roman *Corpus iuris
civilis* of 533, as well as local traditions particularly in
the areas of family and inheritance law, e.g. from the
time of the *Sachsenspiegel* (ca. 1230). Since the late
18th cent., this pluralistic heritage had come under
pressure from the codification movement, that is, a
movement toward comprehensive and centralised
systems of justice that were either monarchic (Bavaria
1750ff., Prussia 1794, Austria 1811) or revolutionary
(*Cinq Codes* in France 1804–1810). The establishment
of this French law also in the German area after 1806
increased the pressure as did the new freedom after
1813. The social issue was a renewal of the role of the
university in competition with the new French conception of professional schools and the → Fürstenschule
Savigny's famous rejection of the *Beruf unsrer Zeit
für Gesetzgebung und Rechtswissenschaft* ('avocation
of our time for legislation and jurisprudence') in October 1814 cannot yet be regarded as the moment of the
school's formation, but rather, the first issue of the new
journal *Zeitschrift für geschichtliche Rechtswissen-
schaften* in March 1815. Berlin and its new university
formed the context. Savigny's poignant introduction
Über den Zweck dieser Zeitschrift [2. 1–17] contains
the program, while Eichhorn's essay *Über das
geschichtliche Studium des Deutschen Rechts* [2. 124–
146] serve to exemplify it. Explicitly, it was not a HR
that was founded, but rather a 'historical school'. Its
"unhistorical" opponents were not only "philosophy
and natural law" but the representatives of "common
sense" as well [2. 2]. The French as well as the Rhine
Confederation- Bavarian polemic of a N. Th. Gönner

(1764–1827) and others, which, since 1815 had finally
been overcome, was now confidently turned into
something positive. Since 1808 Gönner had been railing
against 'unsere neuesten Civilisten–berühmt unter dem
Namen der historischen Schule' ("our newest civilists–
well known by the name of the historical school")
[6. 82–86 und 73 f.] because they clung to Roman Law
against all reason and against the philosophy of law.
His main target was Gustav Hugo (1764–1844) law
professor at Göttingen. After 1815, the name 'historical school' was no longer used in a derogatory way but
instead became a commendation. With the deliberate
use of German terms and a new focus, a "historical
jurisprudence" was demanded that went beyond the
usual "proper history of law" [2. 14].
This meant: It was not a school of law, but a school
for the study of law, not the history of law as such, but
historical jurisprudence, not a debate between experts,
but a vital political-social process, not legislation or
even civil law or Roman law alone, but the concept of
law in its entirety. For a significant period of time thereafter, the events of 1815 would decide a debate about
jurists and law, university and scholarship, a debate
that had been continuing since the 1790s.

C. Core Ideas
The precise meaning of this movement remained surprisingly controversial. Accordingly, there are no clear
statements about who belonged to the school, when it
began and was completed etc. An example is the immediate complaint by Hugo in 1816, who certainly belonged to it in some respect, about "the historical
school as it is now unfortunately called". He criticised
the combination "historical-scholarly" as unclear: on
the one hand it meant simply "scholarly and learned",
but on the other, the term "historical" excluded "present-day applicable law" even though it belonged to it.
The name created a false antagonism, according to
Hugo, since the essential issue was to rescue scholarship
from the law books [6. 74, 330]. For Hugo, law scholarship had not yet been subsumed under the term 'historical'. His statement of the problem was a striking
prophecy still valid today–except for the fact that Savigny's diction, which is authoritative here, has become
even more alien to us.
Savigny himself often found occasion to distinguish
his "truly historical" concept from merely historical or
narrow-minded versions (compiled in [6. 331 f.]). His
criticism was directed at the outdated *cognitio ex datis*
as well as at the 'pragmatic' method which, with
various means, organized history causally and psychologically etc. with a focus on actions and in a clearly
structured way, a method noticeable in Hugo and Eichhorn. Savigny, by contrast, stressed the natural and
organic nature of processes as a "developing whole"
[2. 4] and the constant "continuation and development
of all periods of the past" [2. 3]. He thus organizes history according to natural continuities and autonomous
processes, not according to human posits and actions.

The action here takes its direction from the "true under-standing" of the process and no longer from a "moral-political collection of examples" [2. 4]. A path was forged between the positions of, for instance, a lawgi-ver's sheer arbitrariness and the "blind overestimation of the past" [2. 11] and was proven to be scholarly pas-sable. The great heritage was removed from mere "human hands" [1. 43] and entrusted to the scholarly insight into the "inevitable" [2. 4] historical processes, an appealing solution both thematically and socially. The effects were felt on at least three levels: on a general, a scholarly and on the specialized legal level.

D. Position in its Time

In a remarkably bold statement, Savigny claims that the difference between the schools "will be most notice-able in all things that concern the constitution and the government of countries", that is, in politics and law. However, it can only be understood through the "oppo-sition...of a completely general nature", the relation-ship between "past and present, becoming and being, freedom and necessity" [all 2. 2f.]. He therefore addres-ses the importance of history, ontology, of what should be and what is. The different elements are no longer methodically separated but firmly joined as an "indis-soluble union" and as " simultaneously necessary and free", a union as the concrete idea of a "higher nature of the people as a constantly becoming, developing whole" [2. 3f.]. The HR can thus essentially be regarded as a variation of and as in basic alignment to the ideal-istic Post-Kantian trend of its generation. It was guided not so much by "a hidden necessity", "revelation of the absolute" (Schelling 1802) or the comprehensible unfolding of reason (Hegel 1802/03: 'Es geht vernünftig zu';"things are handled reasonably"), but by the cor-rectly understood self-development of the conceived natural-organic substance of the people (*Volk*) and its awareness. Politically this entails, in a negative sense, clearly anti-revolutionary attitudes, and in a positive sense, a spectrum from conservative to liberal-con-servative views on reform [6. 208ff., 376ff.; 11. 98ff.]. The challenging generality of this approach explains the fame, complexity and attraction of the HR that have lasted into present times.

E. Scholarship

The most important goal was to gain a scholarly understanding of the ambivalence inherent in the idea of this necessary yet free process of development. This was supposed to be accomplished by a "twofold scho-larly sense" [2. 48]: the historical and the systematical. Either one in itself was not new in its time. The impor-tant point lay in the new combination and in the two-fold orientation that manifested itself in all the word combinations. "Truly historical" was more than 'his-torical'. The old *cognitio ex datis* was newly combined with the *cognitio ex principiis* in a different concept of history and scholarship. The principles arose from the right observation, or rather 'view', of history itself—thus

resulting in a new concept of history that followed Kant. The past could therefore be unified with the pres-ent and the study of law was able to avoid two 'errors' prone to arbitrariness: the non-scholarly, merely his-torical jurisprudence with actions guided only by "common sense" [1. 2] as well as the merely philo-sophical juristic inventions of "natural law" and "normal law" [3. I 52.f.; VIII 533], both of which failed to arrive at "real law" [1. 17]. The work of jurists was elevated to a scholarly perception from a spectrum spanning the knowledge of laws, the ability to judge or to argue. The challenge was no longer to compile his-torical-factual processes according to an exterior or-ganization (antiquarian, scholarly), but to recognize the real law that had manifested itself in its "unity" which is "inherent" (1812, 1815) and "concealed in its diversi-ty" (thus 1827–1842) [8. 39 along with [5]]. This his-torical approach to the study law came to be regarded as the medium for revealing an inner system. It found an "organised whole" according to its own "principles" (Kant) and therein a connection to the most demanding concept of scholarship in its time. This type of percep-tion logically became the "only way" [1. 4]. The his-torical 'material' must be seen here as "given through inner necessity" [2. 6]. Consequently, an "organic prin-ciple" could result and even "from that, which still con-tains life" [1. 117f.], if one were to undertake–as was famously expressed–"to pursue each given material to its root in a strictly historical way (...) and thus reveal its organic principle" [1. 117]; "to clearly understand this material, given through inner necessity, and to reju-venate it and to keep it fresh" [2. 2], or "in a truly his-torical sense (...) to pursue that which has been given upwards through all its transformations, to trace it back to its inner unity", thus "transforming and spiri-tualising it" (Rev. Gönner 1815, in [4. V 141]). Simple historicism was never the point. What was demanded was a constant connection or double orientation: his-torical-systematical, methodical as well as material, empirical as well as normative. The decisive belief held that on this basis, principles would emerge on their own, yet how this can happen could hardly be explai-ned in an abstract way. The premise was that of an "inner unity". The following comparison was used as an illustration: The process of finding guiding princi-ples from individual determinations or, conversely, the process of an organic supplementation from principles [1. 74] resembles the geometric analysis of a triangle from "two sides and the angles between them" [1, 22] or the mathematical "construct" [1. 128, 134; 3. I 8] of unknown from known elements.

F. New Juridical Principles

In civil law it made sense to imagine the development of law in the same way as the development of language: it neither developed arbitrarily nor was planned contin-gently, but rather still open. An example offered by Savigny is the law governing currency rates and exchan-ges which he claims to have emerged unintentionally "through the inner need of global commerce") [unprinted, 8. 59]. This institutional, functional and non-intentional view was also held by David Hume and Adam Smith ('invisible hand') as well as G. Hugo (1812). Here, it was no longer a utilitarian approach but instead was embedded in idealism (especially with Schelling) [8. 61 f.]. Legal dogma and methods "in a historical sense" [2. 14] did therefore not mean the perfection of law but the search for principles in the given material, not in that of legal clauses but that of the law. Law, in turn, did have a "independent existence", but no mere "existence for its own sake" [1. 30; 3. I 54, 322]. Basic concepts such as the methods, terms, origin, sources and interpretation of the law, legal relationships, legal institutions, subjective law, the role of law-makers, judges and lawyers, and any others had to be reconsidered—"everything is changing radically, depending on one or the other opinion" [2. 7]. Revolutionizing clauses in this sense were created especially in 1814/15 [1; 2] and in 1840–49 [3]. In the realm of criminal law and national law, this approach collided with the stronger need for secure and fixed legal clauses, "for an external factum that determines the rights of the citizens" [1802, unprinted, 6. 126]. Consequently, Savigny was an advocate for penal legislation from early on, as was recently discovered [1816/17, unprinted 6. 164; 8. 57] and definitely after 1842 in his role as minister. In national law, he rejected the predominant theories of contracts and sovereignty. According to him, the nation was a "natural whole" (not a machine), a "bodily form of the living community of a people" (not an instrument) [1840, 1814/15, 6. 312, 328]; the nation is where a people and law emerge in "visible and organic appearance" [6. 313]; "a people" is an organic substance, not a political subject. The monarch, people, legislation and jurists became "organs" of "true law"– in radical terms, they only needed to "recognize and articulate the law that exists independent of them" [6. 177]. In criminal and national law, the HR thus stood in opposition to the stronger movement towards codification and the creation of a constitution. Compared to its influence on civil law, the HR–although adding a greater focus on history–has contributed less "historical jurisprudence" in this area up to the present time in the sense of a positive development of principles and a 'natural' dogmatism [10. 97].

G. Achievements

The HR's achievements in historical research extend from editions and source histories, literary histories, histories of scholarship and histories of dogma to large handbooks, stimulating histories of development and expansive designs of history; and, systematically, from in-depth monographs to grand systems and extremely compact 'textbooks'. Prime examples are editions such as *Gaius* (1817–1820), that of the *Monumenta Germaniae Historica* (1817 ff.) and Homeyer's *Sachsenspiegel* (1827 ff.), indices such as Homeyer's *Rechtsbücher* (1836), Eichhorn's comprehensive *Deutsche*

Staats- und Rechtsgeschichte (1808–23), Savigny's unsurpassed *Geschichte des römischen Rechts im Mittelalter* (1815–31), his monograph *Recht des Besitzes* (1803), his *System des heutigen römischen Rechts* and *Obligationenrecht* (1840–51) and Eichhorn's *Einleitung in das deutsche Privatrecht* (1823), Puchta's *Pandekten* (1838), along with a large number of monographs (e.g. by Hasse, Rudorff, Albrecht, Beseler). However, whoever claims to see the real "discovery of the history of law" [12. 416 ff.] not until ca. 1880, has yet another perspective. At that time, the past and the present, history and dogmatics were again separated out with a strong belief in the laws, albeit in the relativistic historical spirit of historicism. An interpretation of the past according to principles and in the sense of Savigny's double orientation was difficult to achieve and therefore was accused of micrology etc. It easily led to different interpretations of the principles as in the debate about codification up to the *Bürgerliches Gesetzbuch* and in the discussion about national law versus juridical law with the younger generation of Germanists (Reyscher, Wilda, Beseler).

H. Criticism

The program and the practice of the HR were bold and contained multiple fronts; hence, it became the target of a correspondingly fierce criticism which continues up to the present day [9. 325 ff.]: principles cannot be dug up, the school is antiquarian, reactionary, formalistic, positivist (in parts from critics as early as Feuerbach, Gönner; then Hegel, Gans, Marx, Ruge, Lorenz von Stein; in part Reyscher, Beseler, Gierke, Kantorowicz, Wilhelm, Wiethölter). Inversely, it was regarded as unhistorical in its focus on philosophy (Welcker, Reyscher, Bergbohm, Wieacker, Böckenförde). The idea of the nation, especially the German nation, was seen as running dry and as inconsistent, elitist, unhistorical (Reyscher, Beseler, Gierke, Böckenförde). Its approach to civil law was regarded as too Kantian and individualistic (Gierke, Wieacker, Larenz, Wiethölter) or–from an opposite point of view, as too weak (K. W. Nörr). However, it was less a matter of objections than alternatives to the highly successful and coherent proposition of the HR, based on its approach.

Sources 1 F. C. von Savigny, Vom Beruf unserer Zeit für Gesetzgebung und Rechtswissenschaft, Heidelberg 1814 2 Zeitschrift für geschichtliche Rechtswissenschaft, vol. 1, F. C.von Savigny et al (eds.), Berlin 1815 3 F. C.von Savigny, System des heutigen römischen Rechts, vols. 1–8, Berlin 1840–49 4 Id., Vermischte Schriften, vols. 1–5, Berlin 1850 5 Id., Vorlesungen über juristische Methodologie 1802–1842, A. Mazzacane (ed.) (= Savignyana, vol. 2, J. Rückert (ed.), 1995) Literature 6 J. Rückert, Idealismus, Jurisprudenz und Politik bei Friedrich Carl von Savigny, 1984 (essentially complete bibliography of sources and literature) 7 Id., Savignys Konzeption von Jurisprudenz und Recht, ihre Folgen und Bedeutung bis heute, in: TRG 61, 1993, 65–95 (bibliography to 1992) 8 Id., Der Methodenklassiker Savigny (1779–1881), in: Fälle und Fallen in der neueren Methodik des Zivilrechts seit Savigny, 1997, 29 f. (bibliography to 1997)   9 Id., A. L. Reyschers Leben und Rechtstheorie. 1802–1880, 1974   10 M. Stolleis, Geschichte des öffentlichen Rechts, vol. 2, 1992   11 J. Q. Whitman, The Legacy of Roman Law in the German Romantic Era, 1990   12 F. Wieacker, Privatrechtsgeschichte der Neuzeit, ²1967.   Joachim Rückert

History Painting see → Paintings on historical subjects

Hittite Studies
A. Name, Field of Work   B. History
C. Structure of the Discipline

A. Name, Field of Work
The discipline of Hittite Studies (HS) in the narrow sense deals with the language, history and culture of the Hittites–the people who built a great empire in Anatolia and Syria in the course of the 2nd millennium BC, originating from a homeland in central Anatolia. In the broadest sense, however, the field of work of HS also includes the languages of the other Indo-European (Palaic, Cuneiform Luwian) and non Indo-European languages (Hattic, Hurrian) recorded in Hittite archives as well as Hieroglyphic Luwian used by the Hittites in stone inscriptions and seals, and furthermore includes the Anatolian languages of the 1st millennium (Lydian, Lycian etc.). In the broad sense of the term used here, HS is synonymous with the designation 'Ancient Anatolian Studies', which is, however, less common.

Strictly speaking, the terms 'HS' and 'Hittite' are not accurate. The term 'Hittites' originates from the early years of HS and is based on the Biblical *Hittim* (this word actually refers to the Syrians of the 1st cent. BC, not the Anatolians of the 2nd mill. BC), on the Akkadian 'Land of Ḫatti' and the Egyptian 'Land of Ḫata'. The Hittites themselves named their language after the earlier Anatolian royal seat of Neša (or Kaneš) – 'Nešili' (or 'Kanešic') and named themselves after the capital city of their kingdom and that of their kingdom in general – 'people of Ḫattusa'. But despite the anachronism of the word 'Hittite' and despite the fact that it is based in part on false premises, it has firmly established itself and should therefore be retained as the traditional term.

HS are first of all a sub-discipline of → Ancient Near Eastern Philology and History because Hittite literary culture was shaped by the Mesopotamian cultural realm through its borrowing of cuneiform script. On the other hand, the Anatolian languages are counted among the oldest historical representatives of the Indo-European language family and HS can therefore be regarded as part of Indo-European Studies.

B. History
1. Beginnings (1834–1915)   2. The 'Deciphering': Structure and Development of Hittite Philology (beginning in 1915)

1. Beginnings (1834–1915)
In 1834, Ḫattusa (with the rock sanctuary Yazılıkaya) was discovered by Charles Texier near the Turkish village of Boğazköy. The ruins were first identified as the cities of Pteria and Tavium known from the ancient sources but could not yet be connected to the Hittites (whose most probable home was thought to be Syria, based on hieroglyphic inscriptions found there). It took several more decades before the connection between the Syrian hieroglyphic texts and the stone monuments in Anatolia was recognized. In the 1880's, the identification of the ruins near Boğazköy with the Hittite capital was finally accepted. Here, in 1893, E. Chantre found several fragments of a clay tablet in an unknown language, the same language used in the two so-called Arzawa letters from the Amarna Archive (found in 1887). As a result, archaeological interests strongly focused on Boğazköy. As in Mesopotamia, international competition existed here as well. The British archaeologist John Garstang had requested an excavation permit for Boğazköy. Due to an intervention by the Turkish Sultan, instigated by the German Emperor Wilhelm II, who was fascinated by archaeology, the permit was given not to him but to a German: Hugo Winckler. His excavations between 1906–1912 yielded great results: many texts in the already known Akkadian language were uncovered, but the majority of texts were in the language of the Arzawa letters. The texts in this language were readable – cuneiform script had been deciphered in the mid 19th cent. primarily through the efforts by G. F. Grotefend, H. C. Rawlinson, E. Hincks and J. Oppert – but it was not yet possible to interpret the texts in this new language. In cooperation with S. Bugge and A. Torp, J. A. Knudtzon had surmised in 1902 that the language in the Arzawa letters was Indo-European, but this hypothesis failed to gain recognition and was not taken up for the time being.

2. The 'Deciphering': Structure and Development of Hittite Philology (beginning in 1915)
In 1915, the Czech Assyriologist B. Hrozný was able to offer convincing proof that with Hittite, one was dealing with an Indo-European language. His results were first published in the MDOG LXVI of 1915 along with a first brief historical evaluation by E. Meyer. This marked the beginning of Hittite philology. In the following decades, the new discipline was quickly developed and expanded. The texts from Winckler's excavations that had been brought to the Vorderasiatisches Museum in Berlin were edited by a group of scholars; the lion's share of the editorial work was by H. EheIolf, from 1927 curator of the Near Eastern Department of the Staatliches Museum in Berlin. The young Swiss

E. O. Forrer, who was also working in Berlin, was quick to recognize the different languages written in Ḫattusa and presented a detailed list of characters. A foundation for the understanding of Hittite grammar and lexicon was laid above all by the German philologists H. Ehelolf, J. Friedrich, A. Goetze and F. Sommer. Beginning in 1931, excavation at Ḫattusa was resumed under the direction of K. Bittel.

In the 1930's and 1940's, Germany, which up to that time had been the uncontested centre of the discipline, was deprived of several of its best minds. A. Goetze and H. G. Güterbock, a student of H. Ehelolf and of the Leipzig Assyriologist B. Landsberger, were forced to leave the country under the Nazi regime. Goetze went to Denmark in 1933 and to Yale in 1934; Güterbock worked in Ankara from 1936 to 1948, then one year in Sweden, after which he was offered a position in Chicago. In 1939, Ehelolf died from blood poisoning at the age of 47. Forrer left Berlin as well as HS in April of 1945, discouraged by vicious attacks on his position in the so-called Aḫḫiyawa debate, a debate in which, by current standards, he turned out to be on the correct side.

Germany's division after World War II had serious consequences for HS. The clay plates from Winckler's excavations, which were kept in East Berlin, were edited in the GDR while the texts from Bittel's excavations were edited in West Germany. The result of this 'division of labour' was that, beginning in the 1950's, Hittite cuneiform texts appeared in two separate series: in East Germany, the series *Keilschrifturkunden aus Boghazköi* (*KUB*) ('Cuneiform Documents from Boğazköy'), to which especially Ehelolf and his team had contributed, was continued by H. Otten, H. Freydank, H. Klengel and L. Jakob-Rost, while in West Germany, the series *Keilschrifttexte aus Boghazköi* (*KBo*), ('Cuneiform Texts from Boğazköy') of which six issues had appeared between 1916 to 1923, was revived beginning in 1954, largely by H. Otten. *KUB* and *KBo* were and continue to be the most important series of editions for HS.

The post war development of HS until the present has especially been shaped by four scholars: H. G. Güterbock, A. Kammenhuber, E. Laroche and H. Otten. Güterbock's (1908–2000) early works on historiography, myth and seals (especially the royal seals) have in many ways pointed the direction for the further development in philology. In Turkey in the 30' and 40's, he accomplished much essential work towards the creation of HS there. Following his appointment at the Oriental Institute of the University of Chicago, he influenced the further development of HS in the USA to a high degree. A. Kammenhuber (1922–1995) provided many insights into Hittite and the other Anatolian languages in numerous publications. She was largely responsible for promoting a methodology for dating Hittite texts based on linguistic arguments. The present state of Hittite lexicography would be unthinkable without her dictionary (see below) and thesaurus.

Among other things, HS owes the French linguist Laroche (1914–1991), working in Strasbourg and Paris, a compilation of Hittite names of gods as well as one of personal names and, above all, an organised catalogue of Hittite texts with all their known representations (*Catalogue des textes hittites*, 1971). Laroche also published authoritative works for other languages: a Hurritic glossary, a dictionary with a grammar of Cuneiform Luwian, a Hieroglyphic Luwian character list and many articles on Lycian. Otten (1913–), excavation philologist of Ḫattusa for many years, is the author of many volumes in both the *KBo* and the *KUB* series. A very extensive project is in progress under his direction: a comprehensive thesaurus of Hittite vocabulary at the *Akademie der Wissenschaften* in Mainz. He is primarily to thank for advancements in the area of Hittite palaeography (see below). Many Hittologists now working in Germany and other countries have studied under him.

The excavation in Ḫattusa is still under way. Bittel [3] directed it until 1977 with an interruption from 1939 to 1952; his successors have been P. Neve [7] and, since 1993, J. Seeher [9]. Their annual studies have contributed much to the clarification of the city's topography and have greatly enriched the corpus of Hittite texts. In the last few decades, larger finds of tablets have also been made outside of Ḫattusa. In the 70's and 80's, T. Özgüç excavated an extensive archive, especially of letters, on the Maşat-Höyük [1]. Since 1990, A. and M. Süel have uncovered more and more clay tablets at Ortaköy. In 1993, A. Müller-Karpe began a successful dig in Kuşakli (near Sivas) [11].

The constant increase of edited texts has provided new insights in many areas. Beginning in the late 60's, an often rather polemic discussion was held in HS concerning palaeography as an aid in the dating of texts; in the meantime, a consensus has been reached here. It is now possible to roughly date the copy of a text on the basis of the form of its characters. The picture has gradually come into focus in geography as well. This is largely due to the work of S. Alp and M. Forlanini. Furthermore, text materials found outside of Ḫattusa have ensured that many Hittite toponyms can now be localized with greater certainty.

For a long time J. Friedrich's *Hethitisches Wörterbuch* (HW, 1952, with supplemental issues from 1957, 1961 and 1966) was rightly regarded as the highpoint of Hittite lexicography. However, research advancements created the need for a new lexicon. Up until her death, Kammenhuber worked on a second edition of Friedrich's dictionary; since 1975, the letters A, E and the first third of Ḫ have appeared The second edition has a broader scope than Friedrich's concisely formulated first edition. For some lemmata, the circumstances surrounding their discovery is described in great detail; etymology receives much attention as well. A second comprehensive dictionary project was begun in 1976 at the Oriental Institute of the University of Chicago under the direction of H. A. Hoffner and H.-G. Güterbock: the *Chicago Hittite Dictionary* (CHD). The project was inspired by the *Chicago Assyrian Dictionary* (CAD) from the same university. From 1981 until the present, the letters L to P have appeared. The *CHD* is organized more tightly than the second edition of *HW*. It is more philologically oriented and does not include etymologies. Aside from these two general dictionary projects, two etymological dictionaries are also currently in progress: the *Hittite Etymological Dictionary* by J. Puhvel (since 1984) and the *Hethitisches Etymologisches Glossar* by J. Tischler (since 1983).

Friedrich had set the standard not only with his dictionary but also with his *Hethitisches Elementarbuch Erster Teil: Kurzgefaßte Grammatik* ('Elementary Hittite, Part One: Grammar Summary', 1940, ²1966). Kammenhuber has taken more recent research results into account in a later publication (in a comprehensive article in the 1969 volume *Altkleinasiatische Sprachen* ('Languages of Ancient Asia Minor') of the *Handbuch des Orients*). Many grammatical studies have appeared since then, but still needed is a new comprehensive Hittite grammar that does justice to newly discovered insights about the stages of the Hittite language and to descriptive methods of linguistics developed in the last few decades.

Two works have long been regarded as authoritative general Hittite histories: *Kleinasien* (1957) by Goetze (first published in 1933 as *Kulturgeschichte Kleinasiens*) and *The Hittites* by O. R. Gurney (1952, reprinted numerous times). Both monographs offer a broad survey of Hittite culture and have had a stimulating effect on scholarship. They are, however, somewhat dated. A general Hittite cultural history is therefore greatly to be desired. Fortunately, in recent years two excellent books about political and military history [4; 5] and two about religious history [5; 8] have appeared, so that these two sub-disciplines now have up-to-date descriptions.

C. Structure of the Discipline

After the Hittite language was deciphered, HS were established in German universities and soon thereafter in other Western and Eastern European countries as well as in the USA. This situation could continue after World War II. Although HS are represented academically in many countries, their continued existence is uncertain in many places. This is due, on the one hand, to the almost global trend at universities to 'clear away' the study of the so-called smaller disciplines, and on the other hand, to the fact that it is difficult for HS, as a sub-discipline of both Ancient Oriental Studies and Indo-European Studies, to develop an independent presence.

Outside of the European/North American sphere, HS are also conducted today in Israel, Japan and recently in China as well. In Turkey, the 'home' of HS, where the study of the Hittite language was strongly stimulated by Kemal Atatürk, many scholars of HS are active; this is owed largely to the foundational work of Güterbock and the leading Turkish Hittite scholar S. Alp.

The *Rencontre Assyriologique Internationale*, the general conference of Ancient Oriental Studies, has always served as an important forum for HS. In 1990, the First International Congress of HS took place in Çorum. Since then, it has been organised every three years and has proven itself to be a firmly established meeting of the discipline.

→ Akkadian; → Amarna Letters; → Hattic; → Hurritic; → Indo-European languages; → Hieroglyphic texts; → Lydian; → Luvian; → Hattusa; → Tavium

1 S. Alp, Maşat-Höyükte bulunan çivi yazili Hitit tabletleri (Hittite Cuneiform Tablets from Maşat-Höyük), 1991 2 Id., Hethitische Briefe aus Maşat-Höyük, 1991 3 K. Bittel, Hattuscha: Hauptstadt der Hethiter: Geschichte und Kultur einer altorientalischen Großmacht, 1983 4 T. Bryce, The Kingdom of the Hittites, 1998 5 V. Haas, Geschichte der hethitischen Religion, 1994 6 H. Klengel, F. Imparati, V. Haas, Geschichte des hethitischen Reiches, 1999 7 P. Neve, Hattuša – Stadt der Götter und Tempel: neue Ausgrabungen in der Hauptstadt der Hethiter, 1992 8 M. Popko, Religions of Asia Minor, 1995 9 J. Seeher, Hattuscha-Führer: ein Tag in der Hethitischen Hauptstadt, 1999 10 V. Souvek, J. Siegelová, Systematische Bibliographie der Hethitischen Studien, 1915-1995, 1996 11 G. Wilhelm, Kuşakli-Sarissa, vol. 1: A. Müller-Karpe, Keilschrifttexte, fasc. 1, 1997.
Additional Bibliography S. Alp, Song, Music, and Dance of Hittites, 2000 G. M. Beckman, H. A. Hoffner, Hittite Diplomatic Texts, ²1999 T. Bryce, Life and Society in the Hittite world, 2002; C. A. Burney, Historical Dictionary of the Hittites, 2004 JOOST HAZENBOS

Hohenstaufen Renaissance

A. Concept and the 12th Century Renaissance B. Early Hohenstaufen Era C. The Later Hohenstaufen

A. Concept and the 12th Century Renaissance

The Hohenstaufen Renaissance (HR) should only be seen as part of the so-called 12th century Renaissance. Unlike the → Carolingian Renaissance, the HR did not emanate from the ruler but grew out of a European awakening that the Hohenstaufen kings and emperors used to good effect. In fact, this awakening encompassed almost every sphere of society and learning and came along with an increased reception of Antiquity. Therefore, the term '12th century Renaissance' was coined. C. H. Haskins turned this already current term into a epochal designation in 1927, which largely does justice to the general awakening since the last third of the 11th cent. even though the reception of Antiquity was only of partial significance. The presumable cause was the changing attitude of humans towards themselves, which is clearly evident in the writings of Bernard of Clairvaux (1090–1153), which followed traditional doctrine; likewise in the writings of Peter Abelard (1079–1142), who in the *Historia calamitatum* and his letters to Heloise related his personal setbacks; and in

Fig. 1: Augustus (skin type, fringe in the shape of 'fork and pincer', 27 BC–16 BC, probably soon after the conferment of the cognomen Augustus in 27 BC) Rome, Palazzo dei Conservatori Inv. 2394

Fig. 2: Head from Lanuvio/southern Italy, 2nd quarter of the 13th cent.
Deutsches Archäologisches Institut Rome, Inst. Neg. 54.1

the *Metalogicon* (1159) of John of Salisbury (about 1115/1120–1180), in which he commented upon his times.

Toward the end of the 11th cent., (Early) Scholasticism became a part of academic activity. It repudiated authority as the only principle of teaching, and then as High Scholasticism received primarily through Thomas Aquinas its essential impulses from the reception of Aristotle's philosophical writings.

The art of writing letters (→ LETTER-WRITING/ARS DICTAMINIS) was again carried on more actively and Cicero, whose catalogue of virtues was largely considered compatible with Christian ideals, was its major model.

After the Norman sack of Rome in 1087, there were tremendous efforts in art, beginning with papal building activity. Then, ancient forms or concepts of ancient forms, such as the small coloured mosaics of the artist family of the Cosmati in Rome, were implemented to a larger degree and also → SPOLIA from ancient art were more often visibly incorporated in architecture [11. 88 f.].

About the turn of the 12th cent., the new communes of northern Italy also employed ancient reminiscences to do justice to the novelty of urban self-governance, e.g., by calling the highest officeholders consuls.

Of special significance was the renewal of jurisprudence, which likewise began in the late 11th cent. It was initially supported by the Church and soon used by jurists in the imperial service; it finally became a matter of importance in the communes. In Bologna, the

Corpus Iuris Civilis (→ ROMAN LAW) became a subject of learned study in the twelfth cent.

B. EARLY HOHENSTAUFEN ERA
1. ORGANIZATION OF THE RECEPTION 2. ROMAN LAW AND THE IMPERIAL IDEA 3. LITERATURE 4. ART

1. ORGANIZATION OF THE RECEPTION
The HR of Antiquity drew on the 12th century Renaissance in several ways. Its protagonists at court, above all the bishop Otto of Freising (ca. 1112–1158), was familiar with the scholastic method and had a solid knowledge of ancient literature. Among these highly educated clerics around Emperor Frederick I Barbarossa was Wibald of Stablo and Corvey (1098–1158), whose education and knowledge of ancient literature is reflected, for example, in his extensive correspondence ([2. No. 167, 207 f.] the latter on the books of Cicero).

In the confrontation with the communes of Northern Italy and the Roman Church, the Hohenstaufen increasingly emphasized the ancient heritage of the imperial office. This was initially reflected in the reception of articles of Roman law relating to the emperor and empire as well as in panegyric literature (→ PANEGYRICS). The Hohenstaufen emperors' claim to the Classical inheritance of the Caesars found its justification and shape only through a slow process, so that an increased reception of Antiquity remained an exception in early Hohenstaufen art. The preoccupation with ancient philosophy and natural sciences was not

Fig. 3: Jupiter's eagle delivering the victor's palm and the *corona civica*
(cameo, after 27 BC) © *Kunsthistorisches Museum Vienna*, Inv.-No. IX A 26

directly encouraged by the early Hohenstaufen court. Therefore, intensive reception of Antiquity at the Hohenstaufen court essentially depended on the initiative of scholars close to it. Several genealogies of rulers leading from Caesar and Augustus directly to the Hohenstaufen were created in this period.

2. ROMAN LAW AND THE IMPERIAL IDEA

The reception of Roman law was taken up by Emperor Frederick I Barbarossa because he expected the Justinian codification to promote the imperial idea. Thus, already in 1158 at Roncaglia he received four Bolognese legal scholars who suggested to him the desired promotion of the imperial idea by addressing him, for instance as the 'Living Law' (*lex viva*) in a free translation of the term νόμος ἔμψυχος from Justinian's Nov. 105 (the emperor as law with a soul). The reception of Roman law by Barbarossa provided the only basis of imperial law but did not alter judicial practice. Imperial law contained several provisions that made the emperor the supreme legislator (e.g., 'princeps legibus solutus est', Dig. 1,3,31; Inst. 2,17,8), whose rule was grounded independent of other contemporary powers (e.g., the *lex regia* regarding the origin of imperial power through delegation by the Roman Senate and people, quoted in Dig. 1,4,1 and Inst. 1,2,6). Through the scholarly revival of Roman law, the jurists enabled the Hohenstaufen to expand their claim to the heritage of

the Caesars in political terms and to counter the papal claim to superiority.

Even before his imperial coronation in 1152, Frederick Barbarossa referred to himself in his notification of election to Pope Eugene III as the father of the fatherland (*pater patriae*) (MGH DF I 5), thereby announcing the significance of the political reception of Antiquity for his later imperial idea. Otto of Freising recorded the dismissive answer of Frederick Barbarossa to the repeated offer of being crowned by the Roman Senate and people; whereby Frederick made clear how much his political ideas were formulated in ancient forms and showed that he believed that continuity with ancient Rome was already given in his rule. Despite the harsh rejection of the city of Rome's plan, it is probable that the Hohenstaufen imperial idea was inspired by the concepts of the contemporary Romans [6], possibly to expanding the empire's title *Sacrum Imperium* with 'Romanum' (according to [42. 376 f.], in detail [28]), perhaps even by the usage of the ancient imperial epithet *sacer* for the empire; this usage was soon introduced in the imperial chancellery [6]. It is no longer seriously disputed [32; 36] that Frederick and his court took seriously the Roman ideas of the validity of the renovation of the ancient Senate held by the citizens of Rome (*Renovatio Senatus*, 1143) and of their claim to participation in the elevation of the emperor with reference to the *lex regia*.

3. LITERATURE

As with the Hohenstaufen manner of dealing with matters of jurisprudence, so also authors of Latin literature in the second half of the 12th cent. considered it a matter of course to deal with ancient culture, even if pagan. Particularly Bishop Otto von Freising showed a comprehensive knowledge of ancient history and ancient authors, of whom he used, for example, Orosius, Plato, Aristotle, Cicero, Virgil, Horace, Ovid, Iuvenal, Lucan, Statius, Pindar, Sallust and perhaps Suetonius. The *Gesta Frederici* of Otto and his continuator Rahewin of Freising, in which the latter also exhibited considerable knowledge, was written under the impression of Italian affairs, the imperial coronation and the conflict of Barbarossa with the federation of Lombard communes [30]. Anonymous epics such as the *Ligurinus* and the *Carmen de Gestis Frederici I imperatoris in Lombardia*, which celebrates the hero Barbarossa with consistently ancient-like words, also deal with Italian affairs, though the authors of either poem did not belong to the immediate personal circle of the emperor; the same applies to the verses of the Archipoeta. The court chaplain Gottfried of Viterbo (ca. 1125 to ca. 1192/1200) stood out with historical works. His writings (especially *Pantheon*, last version 1190) served the Hohenstaufen idea of a hereditary emperorship by inserting the Hohenstaufen rule into the context of world history, in which history and fable are knowledgeably interwoven.

4. ART

12th cent. art found new forms, but an explicit reception of Antiquity is only rarely recognizable in Hohenstaufen art. In the case of the imperial golden bulls the reference to the city of Rome was not new and also in other areas a strong continuity with imperial predecessors is recognizable. Possibly, the intensive construction activity and building of imperial palaces in the age of Barbarossa was inspired by an image of Antiquity, but, nevertheless, references to Antiquity are not discernible in the execution. It is very different with the Barbarossa head of Cappenberg, which the emperor gave to his godfather Otto of Cappenberg. The head was possibly later redesigned as a reliquary of John the Evangelist. The similarity of the sculpture, supposedly modelled on the emperor's natural appearance, with Sassanian portraits is striking [37]. The emperor is represented as an ancient *imperator*, he wears the imperial headband but the imperial wreath representing the ruler's victoriousness is lost. The picture also seems to be designed as an *imago clipeata*, i.e., modelled after the ancient medallions of rulers wreathed by the Victories, which originally symbolized the imperial apotheosis and later a sanctification in the Christian sense when the emperor was elevated by angels rather than the Victories (→ APOTHEOSIS). The production of sculpted portraits was new and classicizing forms are also recognizable in the reliquary of Pope Alexander I from Stavelot (1145, produced at the initiative of Wibald of Stavelo (= Stablo) and (since 1146) Corvei, now in Brussels, Musées royaux d'Art et d'Histoire, No. 1031 [19. No. 542, fig. 333]).

C. THE LATER HOHENSTAUFEN

1. TRANSITION PERIOD AND ORGANIZATION OF THE RECEPTION 2. ROMAN LAW AND THE IMPERIAL IDEA 3. ART

1. TRANSITION PERIOD AND ORGANIZATION OF THE RECEPTION

The age of Emperor Henry VI brought a new intensive reception of Antiquity in the literary field. It was partly still in continuity with the period of Barbarossa but benefited from the better organization of the Sicilian royal court, where reception of Antiquity was a tradition. The richly illustrated *Liber ad honorem Augusti* of Petrus de Ebulo displays the cult of the ruler that characterized the age of Emperor Frederick II, i.e., a theologically daring mixture of the reception of ancient mythology and ruler worship as well as the Biblical idea of the ruler. It describes Emperor Henry as the ruler of peace at the end of times, in whose empire wild animals live in harmony with each other and, freely after Virgil, the age of Saturn and the peaceful reign of Jupiter ('regna quieta Iovis') returned (particula (III) 48). His young son, the later Frederick II, is virtually praised as the prophesied boy and receives the attributes of the sun and the son of Jupiter (particula (II) 44 [3]).

The core of the organization of Frederick II's realm was his kingdom of Sicily. There he created the basis for a pronounced cult of the ruler by expanding the existing forms of rule using all the means available to him, so that one can justifiably speak of his Sicilian state. This provided him with the means, more strongly than his imperial predecessors, to promote art and culture and place them in his service. He founded the → UNIVERSITY of Naples (1224) as a rival of Bologna with the primary objective of training scholars for service in his empire. Frederick gathered scholars at his court from the most diverse disciplines whom he presented with questions and then was capable of competently discussing them.

In this he was not interested in Antiquity as a model, but rather in the problems and issues themselves. For their solution and formulation the commissioned scholars and the emperor himself repeatedly turned to ancient observations, experiences and theories that were often transmitted by Jewish and Arab scholars. The intensive reception of Aristotle falls precisely into this age and was nourished by the translation of additional works. Aristotle was transmitted in this period via Arab culture and, with him, contemporary works of Arabic Aristotle commentators such as Avicenna (Ibn Sīna, 973/980–1037) and Averroës (Ibn Rushd, 1126–1192) entered the Latin world (→ ARABIC-ISLAMIC CULTURAL SPHERE). Frederick's special interest lay with the natural sciences, which he discussed especially with Michael Scotus, who was also a translator.

2. ROMAN LAW AND THE IMPERIAL IDEA

Apart from his interest in the natural sciences and humanities, questions concerning law and legislation were of particular importance to Frederick. In the organization of his empire and propagation of his imperial grandeur, Frederick particularly relied on legislation for which he used, in addition to existing legal conventions, which in Sicily included also relics of Roman law, extensive borrowings from Roman law. With the *Constitutions of Melfi*, he issued a regular code of law in which he revealed himself as an heir to Justinian [34. II. 194 ff.]. His model can be recognized, among others, in the laws against heresy, which consistently shaped the imperial role as *lex animata* and *alter Christus*. The imperial majesty was representative of the *maiestas Domini*; trespasses against the emperor were considered trespasses against Christ ([4. I. 1], cf. [25. 42]).

Apart from the imperial self-designation as animate law on earth (*lex animata in terris*), following the νόμος ἔμψυχος in Nov. 105 ([40. 336 f.] with examples) and the reception of the *lex regia* [4. I.31], the institution of the *defensa* is noteworthy. Anywhere in the kingdom of Sicily unjustly threatened persons should have the right to make their matter an imperial matter by invoking the emperor's name. If it was ignored, the persecutor would be treated as a persecutor of the emperor. This custom already existed in Sicily for invoking local powers, but only Frederick turned it into a legal institution with the *Constitutions of Melfi* [4. I.16–19]. However, its origins probably lie in Hellenistic legal concepts, which continued in the Roman imperial period with the imperial omnipresence in its statues [22]. Decreeing the emperor's birthday a public holiday in 1233 undoubtedly also had ancient roots [34. II. 349]. It is exceptionally difficult to reconstruct in detail along which routes ancient ideals were transmitted in Frederick's case because, apart from the traditional *latinitas*, Sicilian customs, Byzantine influences and Arabic transmissions of Antiquity must also be considered.

Frederick sponsored literature – especially in the vernacular. For this reason, and because of his distinctive concept of the ruler, he was a favourite addressee of panegyric poems, which were sometimes also addressed to members of his court such as his chancellor Petrus de Vinea, whose extensive collection of letters preserved some otherwise lost letters of Frederick. The emperor's letters rank next to the skillful letters of Petrus, possibly with the latter's input. In them, especially in the letters to the Romans, the emperor's concept of Rome and emperorship is expressed with considerable linguistic agility and, consequently, his nuanced reception of Antiquity, as it continued to be found in the manifesto of his illegitimate son king Manfred of Sicily to the Romans when he was a supplicant for the imperial crown (ed. [1. 216–229]).

3. ART

In assessing the reception of Antiquity in the art surrounding Frederick II, it becomes obvious how unclear Antiquity's role is in the emperor's self-presentation.

For a long period many presumably ancient portraits were ascribed to the age of Frederick II. However, even those are now doubted, which despite all their similarities with images of Augustus only exhibit few characteristics of Classical portraiture (fig. 1), as for example the head of Lanuvio (fig. 2; thus [12. 195 f.] and [13. 219], but differing [18. 385 ff.]), whose similarity with Augustus – if it really represents Frederick II – fits well with the *augustales*, the gold coins of Frederick, which in addition to their name in their later coinages also exhibit significant similarities with images of Augustus, especially on the coin portraits of the *denari* and *aurei* (→ COINS, MINTING, fig. 2). Iconographic similarities exist in some issues of the *augustales* and also with the coin portraits of Constantine [23. 90].

That the emperor was portrayed as Augustus becomes more probable if his political reception of Antiquity in the letters to the Romans is considered. These present the emperor as the successor and heir of Caesar and Augustus and, apart from emphasizing the titles *caesar* and *augustus,* depict the emperor himself as the new Caesar or Augustus [33].

This is contrasted by the visible lack of a reception of Antiquity in architecture, which was limited to emphasizing *Iustitia*, for example, in figurative decoration and possibly adopting the ancient ruler's *adventus*, as with the bridge gate of Capua.

Almost all traditional forms of art in the service of the ruler show no special reception of Antiquity. However, it is very different with one new form of imperial art. Gems and cameos originated in large numbers in the circles around Frederick II (→ GEM CUTTING). Their designs ranged from those approximating early impe-

Fig. 4: Eagle carrying a snake in its talons (Sardonyx, southern Italy, ca. 1250). Wittelsbacher Ausgleichsfonds, Munich, *Residenz-Schatzkammer*, WAF, Cat.-No. 11

rial models to ones strikingly similar to Augustan pieces. Frederick II himself collected ancient cut stones, which explains why some stones of his time are so similar to ancient pieces that they could pass for genuinely ancient ones [13. 216 f.]. Here, too, there appear to have been Augustan pieces among the artistic models in the art surrounding Frederick II (fig. 3), for example the numerous representations of eagles (fig. 4), e.g., on the reverse of the *augustales*.

→ Augustus [1]; → Pater patriae
→ Glossators; → Imperium; → Portrait; → Ruler;
→ Sacrum Imperium; → Translation

Sources 1 E. Dupré Theseider, L'idea imperiale di Roma nella tradizione del medioevo, 1942
2 Monumenta Corbeiensia, Ph. Jaffé (ed.), 1964, 76–622
3 Petrus de Ebulo, Liber ad honorem Augusti sive de rebus Siculis, Th. Kölzer, M. Stähli (eds.), 1994   4 W. Stürner (ed.), Die Konstitutionen Friedrichs II. für das Königreich Sizilien, 1996
Literature 5 R. L. Benson, G. Constable (eds.), Renaissance and Renewal in the Twelfth Century, 1982
6 R. L. Benson, Political renovatio, in: [5. 339–386]
7 K. Bosl, Europa im Aufbruch, 1980   8 Ch. Brooke, The Twelfth Century Renaissance, 1969   9 Th. Lieck-Buyken Das Römische Recht in den Constitutionen von Melfi, 1960   10 M. S. Calò Mariani, R. Cassano (eds.), Federico II. Immagine e Potere, 1995   11 P. C. Claussen, Renovatio Romae, in: B. Schimmelpfennig, L. Schmugge (eds.), Rom im hohen Mittelalter. Festschrift R. Elze, 1992, 87–125   12 Id., Die Erschaffung und Zerstörung des Bildes Friedrichs II. durch die Kunstgeschichte, in: K. Kappel, D. Kemper, A. Knaak (eds.), Kunst im Reich Kaiser Friedrichs II. von Hohenstaufen, 1996, 195–209   13 A. Esch, Friedrich II. und die Antike, in: Id., N. Kamp (eds.), Friedrich II., 1996, 201–234   14 St. Ferruolo, The Twelfth Century Renaissance, in: R. Treadgold (ed.), Renaissances before the Renaissance, 1984, 114–143   15 A. Giuliano, Il ritratto di Federico II: gli elementi antichi, in: Xenia 5, 1983, 63–70   16 H.-W. Goetz, Das Geschichtsbild Ottos von Freising, 1984   17 Ch. H. Haskins, The Renaissance of the 12th Century, 1927   18 U. Hausmann, Zur Bedeutung des römischen Kaiserbildes im Mittelalter, in: MDAI, Rom. Abt. 97, 1990, 383–393   19 R. Haussherr (ed.), Die Zeit der Staufer. Geschichte – Kunst – Kultur. Exhibition catalogue, 5 vols., 1977   20 P. Johanek, Kultur und Bildung im Umkreis Friedrich Barbarossas, in: A. Haverkamp (ed.), Friedrich Barbarossa, 1992, 651–677   21 E. H. Kantorowicz, Kaiser Friedrich II., 1927/1931 (repr., 1993), (Engl.) Frederick the Second, 1194–1250, E. O. Lorimer (trans.)   22 Id., Kaiser Friedrich II. und das Königsbild des Hellenismus (1952), in: G. G. Wolf (ed.), Stupor Mundi, 1966, 296–330   23 H. Kowalski, Die Augustalen Kaiser Friedrichs II., in: Schweizerische Numismatische Rundschau 55, 1976, 77–150   24 D. E. Luscombe, G. R. Evans, The Twelfth Century Renaissance, in: The Cambridge History of Medieval Political Thought c. 350–c. 1450, (1988) 1995, 306–338   25 M. Macconi, Federico II – Sacralità et potere, 1994   26 L. B. Mortensen, The Texts and Contexts of Ancient Roman History in Twelfth-Century Western Scholarship, in: P. Magdalino (ed.), The Perception of the Past in Twelfth-Century Europe, 1992, 99–116   27 E. Panofsky, Renaissance and Renascences in Western Art,

1960   28 J. Petersohn, Rom und der Reichstitel 'Sacrum Romanum Imperium', 1994   29 M. Pomtow, Über den Einfluß der altrömischen Vorstellungen vom Staat auf die Politik Kaiser Friedrichs I. und die Anschauungen seiner Zeit, (Diss.) Halle 1885   30 S. Reisner, Form und Funktion der Imitatio bei Rahewin. Die Verwendung antiker Vorbilder in seinem Anteil an den Gesta Frederici I. imperatoris, in: Mitt. des Österreichischen Inst. für Geschichtsforsch. 104, 1996, 266–285   31 T. Stiefel, The Intellectual Revolution in Twelfth Century Europe, 1985   32 J. Strothmann, Kaiser und Senat, 1998   33 Id., Caesar und Augustus im Mittelalter. Zwei komplementäre Bilder des Herrschers in der staufischen Kaiseridee, in: M. Baumbach (ed.), Tradita et Inventa, 2000, 59–72   34 W. Stürner, Friedrich II., 2 vols., 1992, 2000   35 Th. Szabo, Römischrechtliche Einflüsse auf die Beziehung des Herrschers zum Recht, in: Quellen und Forsch. aus it. Archiven und Bibl. 53, 1973, 34–48   36 M. Thumser, Die frühe römische Kommune und die staufischen Herrscher in der Briefsammlung Wibalds von Stablo, in: Dt. Archiv für Erforsch. des MA 58, 2001, 111–147   37 R. Tölle-Kastenbein, Der Cappenberger Barbarossa-Kopf und sassanidische Porträts, in: A&A 21, 1975, 111–139   38 P. Toubert, A. Paravicini Bagliani (eds.), Federico II, 3 vols., 1994   39 H. Wentzel, Antiken-Imitationen des 12. und 13. Jahrhunderts in Italien, in: Zschr. für Kunst-Wiss. 9, 1955, 29 ff.   40 G. Wolf, Kaiser Friedrich II. und das Recht, in: ZRG, Rom. Abt. 102, 1985, 327–343   41 Id., Imperator und Caesar. Zu den Anfängen des staufischen Erbreichsgedankens, in: Id. (ed.), Friedrich Barbarossa, 1975, 360–374   42 K. Zeillinger, Kaiseridee, Rom und Rompolitik bei Friedrich I. Barbarossa, in: I. Lori Sanfilippo (ed.), Federico I Barbarossa e l'Italia, 1990, 367–419.

JÜRGEN STROTHMANN

Homeric Question
I. General II. Literary Theory around 1800

I. General
A. Definition and Scope of the Problem
B. History C. Significance for the Study of Classical Antiquity and the Humanities

A. Definition and Scope of the Problem
The Homeric Question (HQ) can be divided into a question in the narrower and in the wider sense. In its most simple form, the HQ in its narrower sense reads: "are the *Iliad* and the *Odyssey* the works of one (possibly one and the same) poet or those of several poets?" Phrased like this, the HQ represented a specialist philological problem, mainly of the 19th cent., but with offshoots into the 1960s. – In its wider sense, the HQ asks: "what is the genesis of the two ancient Greek epics transmitted under the titles of *Iliad* and *Odyssey* and the author's name of Homer"? This umbrella question, which also encompasses the HQ proper, is a systematic question, independent of time; it includes a number of subquestions that can only be answered in form of probability assessments (hypotheses) because of the absence of any object-related documents dating from the time of origin of these epics other than the epics

themselves. The most important of these subquestions are: 1. Who or what is contained in 'Homer'? 2. Did 'Homer' write both epics or just one of them? 3. Did 'Homer' create the *Iliad* (and possibly the *Odyssey*) entirely by himself, from the first to the last verse? 4. Did 'Homer' work a) orally or b) in writing or c) in a combination of both? – Depending on how they are answered, each one of these (and other) subquestions becomes an umbrella question for a host of further individual questions. If, for example, the answer to 1. is "a particular and real poet by the name of Homer", it gives rise to subsequent questions such as: was Homer "a creative spirit, a skillful adapter, a superb reciter, a diligent scribe – or perhaps only the last editor?" [11. 7]. However, if the answer to question 1. is: "no more than a collective term for the members of a poets' guild" [4; 55] or "the epitome of epic poetry in general as represented in the *Iliad* and the *Odyssey*" [11. 7], then subsequent questions are: when and how did these two epics become the integrated wholes that we know today? By a process of successive inclusions and additions to an existing core [14]? By a "poetic *Volksgeist*" [21]? In which form were these epics conceived and disseminated (orally – in writing – a combination of both)? How were they passed on (initially only orally and only written down centuries later, or in a written form from their very beginning)? With this approach, the HQ is a tangle of interdependent individual questions with innumerable Yes/No options and a corresponding number of subsequent questions. Because of the complexity of factors that need to be taken into account combined with the absence of objective control options, it has not yet been possible and might never be achievable to combine these into a generally accepted structure of hypotheses. However, the enduring fascination with this enigma prompts attempts at more detailed and deeper analyses, thus opening ever more comprehensive perspectives and leading to deeper insights into the poetic essence of the *Iliad* and the *Odyssey*. In this way, the HQ is an exemplary field for system-orientated, strictly logical interdisciplinary literary and humanistic research.

B. HISTORY
1. ANTIQUITY 2. MODERN TIMES 2.1 PRIOR TO F. A. WOLF 2.2 F. A. WOLF 2.3. FROM F. A. WOLF TO M. PARRY 2.4 M. PARRY 2.5 AFTER M. PARRY

1. ANTIQUITY
Reflections on the genesis of the two epics manifested itself in three, possibly four, debates: 1. the debate between the Alexandrian Homer philologists Zenodotus, Aristophanes of Byzantium and Aristarchus (3rd/2nd cent. BC) on the authenticity or not of individual verses or groups of verses, resulting in the deletion or the questioning of numerous passages (overview in [28. 835–838]). The background to this was the insight (gained from the comparison of divergent manuscripts

of the epics) that the original version of the epics was no longer extant in the 3rd cent. BC. 2. The debate mainly between Aristarchus and Hellanicus/Xenon – all 2nd cent. BC – on the question whether the *Iliad* and the *Odyssey* were the works of the same or of different authors. 3. The debate on a possible influence exerted by the Athenian tyrannic dynasty of the Peisistratidae (6th cent. BC) on the transmission or even the constitution of the epics; this debate culminated in doubts cast on the general belief that the structure of both epics dated back to Homer (Cic. Orat. 3,137): "(Peisistratus) who was the first to place Homer's previously jumbled books in the order that we know today". 4. In his treatise *On the Antiquity of the Jews* (= *Contra Apionem*), the Jewish historian Flavius Josephus (1st cent. AD) argued that the Greeks had learned to read and write much later than the Jews: their oldest written record was by Homer who had not lived until after the Trojan War, and "it is said that not even he had transmitted his poetry in written form, but from memory; it was only assembled from the [individual] songs at a later date which is the reason for its many inconsistencies" (1,2). As this treatise was addressed to Apion, a well-known (anti-Jewish) Alexandrian Homer expert and grammarian, Josephus would not have done himself any favours by inventing this *on-dit*. For that reason, it may well refer to a further Alexandrian debate on Homer, used here as a weapon. Conclusion: even in Antiquity, the possibility of 'orality' had been considered as a factor in the genesis and transmission of the epics. However, it was never doubted that both epics were created by a single author – albeit in the initial form of individual songs – (the unquestioning acceptance of this assumption is illustrated, for example, in Aristotle's *Poetics*). There was, though, a small minority who questioned whether Homer was the author of both epics (Chorizontes).

2. MODERN TIMES
2.1 PRIOR TO F. A. WOLF
The modern treatment of this problem from about 1700 on is characterized by an ever increasing awareness of the historicity of poetry: Homer has moved out of the virtual, timeless poets' gallery, which in the Middle Ages he had shared with Dante and Virgil, and moved back centuries away from his original position next to Virgil. This gave rise to the questions regarding which period Homer belonged to exactly and which influence this period had had on poetry. This change in the angle of questioning threw new light on the ancient debates and once again made them worthy of discussion. The first to resume and combine them (mainly nos. 3 and 4) was the Dutch historian Perizonius (= Jacob Voorbrock) in 1685 [36. 203 f.], who widened his research into the oral tradition of the early Roman history also to encompass that of Greece. According to him, Homer orally created individual songs that were written down at a later date, then taken to Athens, where at Peisistratus' behest they were combined to form the *Iliad* und *Odyssey*. Wolf had no knowledge of

this work. Instead, he obtained of a copy of the pamphlet by the far less reputable François Hédelin, Abbé d' Aubignac, written prior to 1670, but kept from publication by friends until 1715, in which Hédelin turned against his contemporaries' adoration of Homer, disputing the very existence of a man called Homer and describing the two epics as cobbled combinations "from tragedies and a motley of street songs by beggars and street artists, in the nature of the Chansons du Pontneuf" ([13] in [60. ch. 26, fn. 84]). With its crude polemic dilettantism, this book which Wolf read several times [60. ch. 26, fn. 84] very nearly led him to abandon the work on his own theory with a similar thrust that he had been working on since about 1780 (it was only after the publication of his Prolegomena that Wolf came across the hypothesis of Giambattista Vico from Naples, published in 1725 [51], which was almost identical to Josephus' comment [61]). On the other hand, Wolf felt confirmed by remarks such as those by the eminent critic Richard Bentley [1. 18] that Homer had written "a sequel of songs and rhapsodies to be sung by himself, for small comings and good cheer, at festivals and other days of merriment. (...) These loose songs were not collected together, in the form of an epic poem, till about Peisistratus' time, about five hundred years after".

A new impetus was given to these older speculations by the books of the English authors Thomas Blackwell [2] and Robert Wood [62], who were the first to make a stringent attempt of looking at Homer in the context of the area where he lived, i.e. Ionia in Asia Minor, and of the suggested period of his life (supported by Wood's own travel experiences). Both (Wood in combination with the ancient debates) saw Homer as an orally improvising rhapsodist in an era before written records. This view was then positively received in Germany by influential contemporary scholars such as Herder, Heyne, Tiedemann, Köppen (in [54. 27–31]), in book reviews, essays, lectures and so on; by the time that F. A. Wolf, a student of Heyne at Göttingen since 1777, set out on his studies of Homer, it had become the generally accepted view on Homer.

2.2 F. A. Wolf

(seminal [54]; cf. [12; 26. 402–407]) It had not been Wolf's intention to deal with the HQ – this term was only coined after him (he referred to it consistently as quaestio = 'question') –, but to compile a complete edition of the Homeric epics. As is still customary today, he began with a Latin preface (praefatio), the first part of which was to set out the history of the text from its earliest written record to Wolf's edition (the idea for this approach came from biblical research, cf. [12. 18–26]) and the second part was to contain the explanations of Wolf's textual presentation; the combined title that he gave to his work was Prolegomena ad Homerum [60]. The first part (published in Halle in March 1795) was to retrace the tradition of the text in six periods (1: From the genesis of the epic in ca. 950 BC to Peisistratus; 2: From Peisistratus to Zenodotus; 3: From Zenodotus to

Apion; 4: From Apion to Longinus and Porphyrius; 5. From Porphyrius to the first printed edition in 1488; 6: From the first printed edition to Wolf); however, he only completed it up to the third period (Crates of Mallus, an opponent of Aristarchus, 2nd cent. BC); the second part was never published.

In order to reconstruct the first period, Wolf took into consideration all of the ancient and modern Homer debates, as far as he was aware of them, and used them to construct a system of hypotheses; though its individual components were well known, his system was entirely new not only in content but also in methodology, both in view of the completeness of the material covered and the stringent logic in the structure and linkage of his arguments, so that this slim volume defined the standards of (not only Classical) → Philology as a scholarly discipline. His main thesis was: because Homer lived at a time in which texts were not yet recorded in writing, but only preserved by oral tradition, his original songs could have only contained the basic outline and certain core parts of the epics' stories (which they were, would still need to be identified by further detailled research); later, rhapsodists passed them on (learning them by heart, but with slight changes in the actual wording due to the very nature of oral presentation [60. ch. 24/25]), continually embellishing it in the spirit of the manifest basic structure, until the 6th cent. BC, when Peisistratus in Athens ordered them each to be compiled into a single written work; the Iliad and Odyssey are thus not creations of a single poet, but of many. In this way, Wolf had a) theoretically identified the three (still valid) main characteristics of early Greek bardic poetry: 1. orality, 2. traditionality, 3. instability of the actual wording; and b) deduced from the orality of the work due to the absence of script that it would have been impossible for a single individual poet to have written one or both of these epics: "This seems to lead to the inevitable conclusion, however, that the shape of continuously running works of such length could not have been conceived and elaborated in the mind of a single poet – without an appropriate memory aid" [60. ch. 26].

Only about six weeks after the publication, Herder wrote to Heyne: "It seems to me everyone will agree with his main and basic points; they have generally not been in doubt since Blackwell and Wood" (in [24. 43 fn. 9]; cf. [54. 90f.]). It was thus recognized from the beginning that Wolf's real achievement had been the systematization of known facts.

2.3 From F. A. Wolf to M. Parry

Today, this period – in which the HQ in the narrower sense reached its zenith – largely appears as a methodological aberration ("The treatment of the HQ since Fr. A. Wolf can be described as the most questionable chapter of philological research", A. Lesky, 1954, in [24. 297]): Wolf had arrived at the fundamental assumption of his theory (the absence of script, thus the oral creation) only by external deduction, not based on an internal study of the design of the epics themselves.

However, instead of confirming this basis, i.e. the assumption of a plurality of authors, through the analysis of the internal diction, it was accepted as self-evident (cf. [24. 32 f.]) and, using contemporary improvisational epic poetry as a parallel, set aside as 'proven' (cf. [24; 37]), even though good arguments against this assumption had been put forward very early in the debate (Hug 1801 [18]; Nitzsch 1830 [34]). Instead, scholars pounced on Wolf's deduction of the plurality of authors: Karl Lachmann [21] who divided the *Iliad* into 10–14 individual 'songs' (*Liedertheorie*) initiated a dogged scholarly debate which was to continue for decades on whether the *Iliad* (and after Kirchhoff in 1859 [20] also the *Odyssey*) had been created by several authors or, after all, by only a single one; supporters of the former view (the 'analysts') sought to identify different authors ('hands') through the analysis of language and style ('older = good, younger = bad'), sometimes supported by a structural analysis of the epics, while the latter faction (the 'unitarians') attempted to find counterarguments to prove each epic's internal unity. Neither faction noted the cardinal flaw in their logic, i.e. while assuming the oral genesis of the epics, in their argumentation, they presumed a modern text form together with a modern approach to producing a text ("desk, scissors, glue": Lesky in [24. 299]); they thus applied (at times in a rather subjective manner) standards of logic, structure, aesthetics and originality, derived from written poetry, to early works characterized by their orality. Locked in their dispute, neither the analysts (peak: Wilamowitz 1916 [57]; latecomers: Theiler 1947/1954/1962 [47–49]; Von der Mühll 1952 [31]) nor the unitarians (peak: Rothe 1910/1914 [40; 41]; latecomer: Reinhardt 1961 [39]) achieved their final goal of providing indisputable proof. For that reason, the conclusion was justified that this dispute was fruitless (Lesky [24. 297]), even more so, as the foundation of Wolf's theories had finally crumbled with the discovery in 1871, and publication in 1880 of the hexametric inscription on the Dipylon jug, dating back to ca. 740 BC [17. 116 fn. 631].

As a by-product, this dispute did, however, provide valuable partial insights into the nature of the epics' internal structure. This was used in 1938 by Wolfgang Schadewaldt in his excellent outline of an 'X-ray image' of the *Iliad* [43], which transcended and overcame the original dispute. Using categories developed for the study of narrative forms in neighbouring philologies ('foreshadowing', 'regression', 'retardation' and others, later systematized by [22]), as well as those for general comparative epic studies (including research on Serbo-Croatian popular epic [43. 24–28]; Schadewaldt encountered – and appreciated – Parry's theory only at a later date [44]), he was able to reveal the highly elaborate large-scale architecture of the *Iliad*, thus suggesting more strongly than ever that it was the planned creation of a single poet.

While the main battle between analysts and unitarians raged, a new field of research developed, ignored

by both combatants, which was both methodologically and thematically appropriate: the analysis of the epics' linguistic and metric structure. In 1840, Gottfried Hermann [15] demonstrated the essential orality of the epic diction from the text's structure, in particular its essential dependence on the verse structure, resulting in his recognition of the padding function of the epic epithets (*epitheta ornantia*). From these internal indications, he inferred the improvisational technique (which Wolf and others had but claimed [24. 43 fn. 10]), which forced singers to comply with this particular form of diction with its characteristic repetition of set phrases, entire verses or even scenes (formularity; typicality). The study of epic diction, which began with this first cohesive theory of orality, continued, with the methodologically clear and most comprehensive works by J. H. Ellendt [7], H. Düntzer [5], J. Meylan-Faure [30] and K. Witte [58], culminating in the studies of M. Parry.

2.4 M. PARRY

The American scholar Milman Parry studied the European research on Homer in Paris in the 1920s under the linguist and metrics expert Antoine Meillet; in his doctoral thesis of 1928, written in French and entitled *L'Epithète traditionnelle dans Homère* [38], he explicitly took up from Ellendt, Düntzer, Witte and other researchers on Homer's formulaic diction (catalogue: [24. 574–583]). Like Hermann before him (the only one among his forerunners whose works Parry unfortunately does not seem to have studied), his starting point was the diction conditioned by verse, but in contrast to Hermann and his successors, Parry concentrated on a single phenomenon resulting from the metrical requirements, i.e. the padding function of stereotypical epithets (*epitheta ornantia*). This concentration on a single aspect allowed him to massively increase not only the material which he studied, but also the aspects under which he investigated it. His microscopic analysis of the material produced convincing proof that the formulaic noun-epithet combinations ('round ships', 'leader of men'; 'clever Odysseus', if required expandable to 'forbearing, divine Odysseus' etc.) were determined by metrical conditions and requirements and that the epithets in these combinations ('round', 'leader', 'clever', 'forbearing, divine') are frequently (though not always) meaningless in the actual context (Hermann 1840: "words that, as it were, fill gaps in the sentences", [24. 49]; modern: 'context-semantic zero-valency'). Applying an exact statistic analysis of the relations between the noun-epithet formulas and their position within the verse, he arrived at a 'law of epic economy' (or 'thrift'): to denote a particular character or object (Agamemnon, Achilles; sword, ship), the epic diction uses a number of semantically and metrically different epithet-noun combinations, but limited in such a way (obviously to make their memorization easier) that for any particular verse position, there is only one expression available (even though a range of other metrically equivalent but semantically different expressions would be possible). From this perfectionist economy of formulaic expressions, Parry inferred the traditionality of epic diction (such a technique and such a rich repertoire of formulas could only have developed over many generations), and from the traditionality in turn the inherent pressure of producing an oral improvisation in front of an expectant audience. As an external confirmation of his results gained from internal investigations, he also took into consideration contemporary improvisational epic its then – and since the early 19th cent. – most well-known form: the Serbo-Croatian popular epic, at Parry's time last studied by M. Murko [32; 33]. Together with his assistant Albert Lord, Parry spent the next few years recording and evaluating these works; his early death in 1935 prevented him from an evaluation of his results with with regard to reformulating the HQ.

2.5 AFTER M. PARRY

The same statement as for F. A. Wolf is also true for M. Parry 'that each of the specific tenets which make up Parry's view of Homer had been held by some former scholar' [37. XXII]. However, as for Wolf, it is equally justified to state that his 'work began a new era in Homeric studies' [37. LX]. In both instances, the preceding developments were ripe to be summarized. Parry's achievement in this (continuing and expanding the work of predecessors) was to turn post-Wolf research on Homer back onto its feet by finally providing an answer to the research problem originally posed by Wolf, but skipped by his successors – i.e. the finding of proof within the epic diction itself for the claim regarding its traditionality and orality. In this way, as his son rightly stated in 1971, 'Parry's Homeric theory (...) made the whole Unitarian-Analyst controversy, at least in its older and best-known form, obsolete' [37. LI]. If each representative of the poetic tradition reconstructed by Parry could make use of the entire range of formulaic expressions regardless of whether they were recent or ancient – thus turning the repetition of formulaic elements into a style-defining element, even in aesthetically or logically less appropriate contexts –, it is not possible to use criteria of language and style to distinguish various layers within the epic.

The period following Parry's work – albeit with a delay of about 30 years due to World War Two – was one of reception and extension, at times also modification, of the theory pioneered by Parry and further developed by Albert B. Lord [29] (oral poetry theory; see [9]) in two areas of research: 1. research on the formulaic expressions, 2. research on current contemporary oral poetry across the globe. Regarding further work on the HQ, this phase of Parryism (in the same way as Wolfianism earlier) meant a further stagnation (outlined and referenced to the most important original research in [24]; cf. also the research report in [16]). Real progress beyond Parry did not set in until the 1980s, when 1. linguistic research could establish that tradition and traditionality of epic diction were much older than even Parry had assumed – dating at least as far back as the 16th cent. BC, and 2. a study by Edzard Visser in 1987

[52] on the epic versification technique finally liberated Parry's theory from its limitation to one minute aspect, i.e. the phenomenon of the noun-epithet formulas, by providing an insight into the entire process of generating improvisational hexametric verse: the singer does not form the hexameter, as Parry had assumed, by assembling a number of formulaic building blocks, but verse by verse in new combinations of a set number of determinants, complemented by variables and free additions to fill those gaps left deliberately for this purpose; formulaic building blocks, which originally were themselves the result of this technique, can be be used in this way, but this method also allows verses to be generated from scratch ([52; 53]; summary in [26]; "significant advance": [6. 266]; "new impulse": [42. 254–257]). This technique avoids the danger of any rapid ossification of the diction which would have been a risk under the assumptions of Parry's theory; Visser's theory provides a rational foundation for the creativity of the singers and the ability of epic diction to remain vibrant over centuries and thus also for its actual life span.

On the basis of this research, the current state of the HQ can be summarized in the following widely accepted working hypothesis: using contemporary and as well as much older linguistic-stylistic elements from a tradition of oral improvisation of poetry in the form of set hexameters, which at his time was already at least 850 years old, about 700 BC an individual singer by the name of Homer, whose talents far exceeded mere craftsmanship, created with the aid of writing (which had become available from about 800 BC on), which he used for the structuring of his poetic material, one (or, presuming the author to be the same, two) thematically and structurally unified, individually formed and shaped composition(s) based on episodes from the old and popular tale of Troy: 1. the retardation of the capture of Troy in a 51–day narration about 'Achilles' wrath' (= *Iliad*), 2. in a 40–day narration the 'return of Odysseus' (= *Odyssey*) against all odds, 20 years after he had fought at Troy. Both epics are the products of a brief transitional period from orality to literacy, exceptional in European cultural history. This explains their formal and qualitative singularity within European literature [25]. While both epics were conceived with the aid of script and written down immediately, they continued to be disseminated orally by rhapsodists until the complete textualization of Greek culture in the 5th cent. BC. Thanks to the parallel transmission of written records, rhapsodic changes in wording and textual structure remained very limited, thus preserving the overall structure [56]. Scholars across the world are currently working on a validation of this hypothesis.

C. SIGNIFICANCE FOR THE STUDY OF CLASSICAL ANTIQUITY AND THE HUMANITIES

The HQ is the collective focus of all of the questions from the point of view of literary aesthetics, scholarship and scholarly history in conjunction with these two earliest works of European literature.

In its Early Modern phase, as the HQ in the narrower sense, it acted both as a gathering point and as an innovative force for the pan-European debate on Homer which, emerging from the → QUERELLE DES ANCIENS ET DES MODERNES dominated literary life in the 18th cent. [45; 59]. In the form given it by F. A. Wolf, positing an original core Iliad, it had three immediate effects: 1. The historical perspective definitively replaced the previous view of Homer and of ancient literature in general, which had been determined by literary aesthetics, admiration, even enthusiasm; 2. it laid the foundations for philology as a critical scholarly discipline with 'enlightening' potential as against the traditional transmission of knowledge in general, thereby also establishing it as a serious counterforce against religion and the Church [23. 65f; 50. 141–144]; 3. as proof of the efficiency and strength of the philological method, it provided the neo-Humanist movement of the 19th cent. and, in particular, the general reform of Prussian education through Wilhelm von Humboldt with decisive arguments for basing the new German national education on Graeco(-Roman) Antiquity [23. 37–39; 50. 131]; in that way, it played a part in the dominance of the teaching of → ANCIENT LANGUAGES and Classical education in general in the German Gymnasium as well as the dominant role of (initially Classical) philology at 19th cent. German universities, which contributed to their worldwide reputation and indeed in some cases role model status.

In its renewed form, M. Parry's oral poetry theory, the HQ in the 20th cent. has given impulse not only to the global expansion of research on orality and literacy [8] but also to modern media and communication studies linked foremost to the name of Marshall McLuhan [37. XLIII fn. 2]. The HQ is thus (and has been for more than 250 years) an effective and influential intellectual stimulus within the modern European and European-influenced intellectual and cultural history.

→ Chorizontes; → Epic (Greek); → Homerus; → NEO-HUMANISM

1 R. BENTLEY, Remarks upon a late Discourse of Free-Thinking, in a Letter to F. H. D.D. by Phileleutherus Lipsiensis, London/Cambridge (1713) ⁵1716   2 TH. BLACK-WELL, An Enquiry into the Life and Writings of Homer, London 1735   3 A New Companion to Homer, I. MORRIS, B. POWELL (eds.), 1997   4 G. CURTIUS, De nomine Homeri, Kiliae 1855   5 H. DÜNTZER, Homerische Abhandlungen, Leipzig 1872   6 M. EDWARDS, Homeric Style and 'Oral Poetics', in [3. 261–283]   7 J. H. ELLENDT, Drei homerische Abhandlungen, Leipzig 1864   8 J. M. FOLEY, Oral-Formulaic Theory and Research. An Introduction and Annotated Bibliography, 1985   9 Id., The Theory of Oral Composition: History and Methodology, 1988   10 Id., Oral Tradition and its Implications, in: [3. 146–173]   11 H. FRÄNKEL, Dichtung und Philosophie des frühen Griechentums, ²1962   12 A. GRAFTON, G. W. MOST, J. E. G. ZETZEL, Prolegomena to Homer 1795 (translation with introduction and notes), 1985   13 F. HÉDELIN, Abbé d'Aubignac, Conjectures académiques ou Dissertation sur l'Iliade, Paris 1715   14 G. HERMANN, Über die Behandlung der griechischen Dichter bei den Engländern, nebst Bemerkungen über Homer und die Fragmente der Sappho (1831), in: Id., Opuscula, vol. VI, Leipzig 1835, 70–141 (esp. 88) and De interpolationibus Homeri dissertatio (1832), Ibid, vol. V, Leipzig 1834, 52–77 (esp. 70)   15 Id., De iteratis apud Homerum, Leipzig 1840 (German in [24. 47–59])   16 A. HEUBECK, Die Homerische Frage, 1974   17 Id., Schrift, 1979 (= Archaeologia Homerica, fasc. X)   18 J. L. HUG, Die Erfindung der Buchstabenschrift, Ulm 1801   19 V. S. KARAŽIĆ, Srpske narodne pjesme, Leipzig 1823   20 A. KIRCHHOFF, Die homerische Odyssee, Berlin (1859) ²1879   21 K. LACHMANN, Betrachtungen über Homers Ilias, mit Zusätzen von M. HAUPT, Berlin 1847   22 E. LÄMMERT, Bauformen des Erzählens, 1955   23 M. LANDFESTER, Humanismus und Gesellschaft im 19. Jahrhundert, 1988   24 J. LATACZ (ed.), Homer. Tradition und Neuerung, 1979   25 Id., Hauptfunktionen des antiken Epos in Antike und Moderne, in: Der Altsprachliche Unterricht 34/3, 1991, 8–17   26 Id., Erschließung der Antike. Kleine Schriften zur Literatur der Griechen und Römer, 1994   27 A. LESKY, Mündlichkeit und Schriftlichkeit im Homerischen Epos, in: [24. 297–307]   28 Id., s. v. Homeros, RE Suppl.-vol. 11, 687–846   29 A. B. LORD, The Singer of Tales, 1960   30 J. MEYLAN-FAURE, Les Epithètes dans Homer, Lausanne 1899   31 P. VON DER MÜHLL, Kritisches Hypomnema zur Ilias, 1952   32 M. MURKO, Neues über Südslavische Volksepik, in: [24. 118–152]   33 Id., La poésie épique en Yougoslavie au début du XXième siècle, 1929   34 G. W. NITZSCH, De historia Homeri maximeque de scriptorum carminum aetate meletemata, Hannover 1830   35 Oralità. Cultura, Letteratura, Discorso. Atti del Convegno Internazionale Urbino 1980, a cura di B. GENTILI e G. PAIONI, 1985   36 J. PERISONII (sic), Animadversiones historicae, Amsterdam 1685   37 A. PARRY (ed.), The Making of Homeric Verse: The Collected Papers of Milman Parry, 1971   38 M. PARRY, L'Epithète traditionnelle dans Homère, 1928   39 K. REINHARDT, Die Ilias und ihr Dichter, 1961   40 C. ROTHE, Die Ilias als Dichtung, 1910   41 Id., Die Odyssee als Dichtung, 1914   42 J. RUSSO, The Formula, in: [3. 238–260]   43 W. SCHADEWALDT, Iliasstudien (1938) ³1966   44 Id., Die epische Tradition, in: [24. 529–539]   45 K. SIMONSUURI, Homer's Original Genius: Eigtheenth-Century Notions of the Early Greek Epic, 1979   46 TALVJ, Volkslieder der Serben, metrisch übersetzt und historisch eingeleitet by TALVJ, Leipzig 1824 (²1835)   47 W. THEILER, Die Dichter der Ilias, in: Festschrift E. Tièche, 1947, 125–167   48 Id., Noch einmal die Dichter der Ilias, in: Thesaurismata, Festschrift I. Kapp, 1954, 113–146   49 Id., Ilias und Odyssee in der Verflechtung ihres Entstehens, in: MH 19, 1962, 1–27   50 F. TURNER, The Homeric Question, in: [3. 123–145]   51 G. VICO, Principi di scienza nuova d'intorno alla commune natura delle nazioni, Milano 1725   52 E. VISSER, Homerische Versifikationstechnik, 1987   53 Id., Formulae or Single Words? in: WJA 14, 1988, 21–37   54 R. VOLKMANN, Geschichte und Kritik der Wolfschen Prolegomena zu Homer, Leipzig 1874   55 M. L. WEST, The Date of the Iliad, in: MH 52, 1995, 203–219   56 Id., Geschichte des Textes, in: J. LATACZ (ed.), Homers Ilias: Gesamtkommentar. I: Prolegomena, ²2002   57 U. v. WILAMOWITZ-MOELLENDORFF, Die Ilias und Homer, 1916   58 K. WITTE, s. v. Homeros (language), RE 8.2, 2213–2247   59 J. WOHLLEBEN, Die Sonne Homers, 1990   60 FR. A. WOLF, Prolegomena ad Homerum sive de operum Homericorum prisca et genuina forma variisque mutationibus et

probabili ratione emendandi, Halis Saxonum 1795
61 Id., Giambattista Vico über den Homer, in: Museum
der Alterthums-Wiss. 1, 1807, 555–570   62 R. WOOD,
Essays on the Original Genius of Homer, London (1769)
²1775   JOACHIM LATACZ

II. LITERARY THEORY AROUND 1800
A. INTRODUCTION   B. WOLF's *Prolegomena ad
Homerum* AND GERMAN PHILOLOGY
C. AUTHORS' REACTIONS   D. ORIGINS OF POETRY,
NEW MYTHOLOGY   E. ROMANTIC EPIC THEORY,
GOETHE'S FAUST

A. INTRODUCTION

The reception of Homer played a central role in the
aesthetic discussion, in fine arts and literary practice in
Germany since the middle of the 18th cent. [7]. The
fascination with Homer produced literary and aesthetic
innovations. The development of a German literary
language around 1800 was largely due to the Homer
translations of Johann Jacob Bodmer (1698–1783),
Gottfried August Bürger (1747–1794) and, above all,
Johann Heinrich Voss (1751–1826) [3]. The explosive
and shocking impact of Friedrich August Wolf's *Prolegomena ad Homerum* (1795) on the literary scene
becomes clear against this backdrop of Homer reception and contemporary aesthetic developments and
constellations. The aesthetic debate was determined by
opposing sides such as nature – art, natural poetry/folk
poetry (*Naturpoesie/Volkspoesie*) – literary poetry
(*Kunstpoesie*), Antiquity-Modern Age, Classicism –
Romanticism, orality – literacy, homogeneity – heterogeneity. The opposites sensuality – intellectuality
became the motivating force for the projects linked to a
'New Mythology'. These intellectual concepts were
affected by Wolf's 'destruction' of Homer (Goethe,
Conversation with Eckermann, 1 Feb. 1827: "Wolf has
destroyed Homer, but could not do harm to the poem")
both a challenge and a response. The debate surrounding the HQ had an immediate effect on literary theory.
The dissolution of the notion of the one poet Homer
into a heterogeneous process of development and transmission, but still with an inherent normative Classical
context and validity, required rethinking the relationship of Antiquity and Modernity, Classicism and Romanticism, the author, his work(s) and his listeners/
readers.

B. WOLF's *Prolegomena ad Homerum* AND
GERMAN PHILOLOGY

The HQ also proved influential for German philology which was only just in the process of establishing
itself as an academic discipline. Wolf's hypotheses inspired the understanding and also the edition of the *Nibelungenlied* (*Song of the Nibelungs*), the topic of intense
debates around 1800 [1]. In 1816, Karl Lachmann
(1793–1851) published his *Untersuchung über die
ursprüngliche Gestalt des Gedichtes von der Nibelunge
Noth*. As early as 1815, Wolf's pupil Wilhelm Müller

(1794–1827) had applied Wolf's hypotheses to Old
German 'Dichtkunst' ('poetry') in the preface to his
Blumenlese aus den Minnesingern ('Anthology of
German Minnesingers') (1816). Lachmann held the
view that the *Nibelungenlied* developed from a compilation of individual and still identifiable ballad-style
songs. He argued that the various, orally transmitted
songs had been collected by 'diaskeuasts'. 1826 saw the
publication of Lachmann's seminal edition *Der Nibelunge Noth mit der Klage*, widely seen as the first reliable edition of the *Nibelungenlied*. A new complete edition was published in 1841. As in the HQ, the debate on
Lachmann's *Liedertheorie* ('song theory') centred on
the contrast and the relationship between traditional
literature ('natural poetry') and literature written by a
particular author ('literary poetry'), the relationship
between the genesis of a literary work and its aesthetic
unity and finally on the validity of the aesthetic norm of
homogeneity. The 'natural poetry' ('folk poetry',
'national poetry') of the Grimm brothers also took
inspiration from Wolf's hypotheses as well as from Herder's theories on popular poetry. In the view of the
Grimm brothers, an anonymous and collective authorship was the characteristic feature of folk songs, myths,
fairy tales as well as epics such as the *Nibelungenlied*. In
his controversy with Achim von Arnim, in 1811, who
challenged this contrast, Jacob Grimm defined *Kunstpoesie* ('artistic poetry') as a "creation", but *Naturpoe-
sie* ('natural poetry') as a "something that created
itself". To him it seemed "inconceivable that there ever
was a Homer or an author of the Song of the Nibelungs"(letter to A. von Arnim, 20 May 1811).

C. AUTHORS' REACTIONS

Wolf's *Prolegomena* split the literary scene into
enraged opponents and convinced supporters [8]. Some
changed sides, such as Goethe, who initially rejected
Wolf's hypotheses (letter to Schiller 17 May 1795), but
later saw them as a liberation from Homer's aesthetic
authority, enabling him to write *Hermann und Dorothea* (1797), an epic for his time. In his own words,
Goethe felt deterred by the "elevated concept of unity
and indivisibility" of Homer's works. Because these
"wonderful works" were now assigned to a "family"
and not to an individual author, it took "less boldness
to venture onto a wider stage" (letter to Wolf, 26 Dec.
1796; cf. also his poem *Hermann und Dorothea*, in
which he expressed his gratitude to Wolf). However,
after repeated and detailed studies of the *Iliad*, Goethe
once more tended toward the view of "the poem's unity
and indivisibility" (letter to Schiller, 16 May 1798; cf.
his 1821 poem *Homer wieder Homer* ('Homer, always
Homer') and the *Tag- und Jahreshefte zum Jahr 1820*).

Among those who rejected Wolf's theses were Chri-
stoph Martin Wieland, Johann Heinrich Voss, Jean
Paul, Friedrich Hölderlin, Novalis and Friedrich Schil-
ler. Much of the correspondence between Goethe and
Schiller was given over to the discussion of the HQ.
Schiller thought that the assumption "that these works

were strung together by rhapsodists and of diverse origin was an essentially barbarian notion", because "the wonderful continuity and reciprocity of the whole and its parts is one of its most effective beauties" (letter to Goethe, 27 Apr. 1798). Without actually naming Wolf, Hölderlin refers indirectly to the HQ. He called Homer explicitly "this extraordinary man " (letter to Böhlendorff, 4 Dec. 1801) and chose the character of Achilles to illustrate the unity of the *Iliad*, the very same which Wolf had taken as proof for the epic's composition from various pieces (Prolegomena ad Homerum, ch. 27): "People have often expressed astonishment why Homer who had wanted to sing about Achilles' wrath had let him appear so rarely. He did not want to profane the gods' favourite in the turmoil outside of Troy" (on Achilles). Hölderlin's reflections on Homer were finally to result in his *Briefe über Homer* ('Letters on Homer'). Wilhelm von Humboldt took a more conciliatory view. Johann Gottfried Herder took Wolf's hypotheses, particularly the concept of a 'family' of authors, as long-held insights (*Homer, ein Günstling der Zeit*, 1795, ch. 8; similarly in *Adrastea*, 9th piece, 1803). Wolf, who in this treatise was only mentioned in passing, subsequently accused Herder of plagiarism (*Ankündigung eines deutschen Auszugs aus Professor Wolfs Prolegomena ad Homerum und Erklärung über einen Aufsatz im IX. Stück der Horen*, in: Intelligenzblatt der Allgemeinen Literaturzeitung, 24 Oct. 1795) [2].

Among the Romantic poets, Novalis and Jean Paul rejected Wolf's hypotheses, while they were accepted by Friedrich and August Wilhelm Schlegel, Friedrich Wilhelm Schelling as well as by Jacob and Wilhelm Grimm. Both Friedrich Schlegel (*Über die homerische Poesie. Mit Rücksicht auf die Wolfischen Untersuchungen*, 1796, a preliminary study for his *Geschichte der Poesie der Griechen und Römer*, first and only part published in 1798) and subsequently August Wilhelm Schlegel (review of Goethe's *Hermann und Dorothea*, 1796; Berlin lecture *Geschichte der klassischen Literatur*, 1802) formulated a new theory following the *Prolegomena* regarding the origins of poetry as well as a new theory on the epic. In speculative exaggeration, Schelling finally employed Wolf's theories in his 'New Mythology' project with contributions by Herder, F. Schlegel, Hölderlin, Hegel, Novalis and others.

D. ORIGINS OF POETRY, NEW MYTHOLOGY

In his *Gespräch über die Poesie* (1800), Friedrich Schlegel saw in the "living growth" of Homeric poetry "the genesis, as it were, of all poetry". His imagery, of the "spring", the "river", the "fluid form", the "erudite chaos" of Homeric poetry, based on Quintilian (inst. 2,10,1,46), contrasts the classicistic ideal of an opus defined and completed by a single artist with the notion that in the origin of poetry both the formation and the dissolution of artistic forms merge [5]. Schelling's *System des transzendentalen Idealismus* (1800) concludes with the prospect of a 'New Mythology': once it is achieved, philosophy and science are to flow back

"into the general ocean of poetry", whence they had originated. In his lecture on *Philosophie der Kunst* (1802/03), this new mythology is conceived as a work of humankind, "provided that it is itself an individual". Schelling "with this apodictic statement wants to claim the same for mythology that Wolf had claimed for Homer". That allowed him to arrive at the conclusion that "mythology and Homer are one and the same". [6]. Homer became the by-word for a new, poetically created unity in the history of humankind.

E. ROMANTIC EPIC THEORY, GOETHE'S FAUST

The *Prolegomena* inspired a new theory of the epic. Because of its synthesis of nature and history, Schelling (*Philosophie der Kunst, Ausgewählte Schriften* 2, 285) proclaimed the "Homeric epic (according to its literal meaning as the unifying force, the identity)" as both origin and goal, as the "alpha" and "omega" of all art. In his essay *Über die Homerische Poesie. Mit Rücksicht auf die Wolfischen Untersuchungen*, Schlegel viewed the → EPIC as defined by an "indefinite number of episodic events", each event "a link in an endless chain". Unlike the drama, characterized by a "complete poetic plot", the epic was in Schlegel's view nothing but an "undefined mass of events", creating "an infinite expectation of mere abundance". The image chosen by Schlegel to illustrate the typical structure of the epic was that of the octopus (polyp), an animal much discussed by 18th cent. natural scientists: "the epic poem is (...) a poetic polyp where every small or larger limb (...) has a life of its own, indeed as much of the same harmony as the whole". The parts of the polyp are both a (divisible and increasable) whole and also parts of a whole. In the same way as contemporary scientists placed the polyp somewhere between animals and plants, the Homeric epic (in Schlegel's view) had its place between nature and art. This imagery transferred poetic productivity from the author to the history of the work regarding its genesis, transmission and reception.

Schlegel's treatise agreed with Goethe's own thoughts, formulated in his correspondence with Schiller. In contrast with Schlegel, Goethe insisted on the individual parts tending towards unity (letter to Schiller, 28 Apr. 1797. Schlegel would not have disagreed!). Goethe also used Schlegel's thoughts in the conception of his drama *Faust*: "the whole, which will always remain but a fragment, may benefit from the new theory about epic poetry" (letter to Schiller, 27 June 1797). Because of the fragmentary structure of this play, whose "small worlds (...), complete in themselves, may affect, though not really concern each other" (conversation with Eckermann, 13 Feb. 1831), Goethe referred to his work as a "rhapsodic drama" (letter to Schiller, 11 Apr. 1798). This dramatic concept, inspired by the Romantic interpretation of Wolf's hypotheses, transcends the aesthetic boundaries of Classicism and Romanticism [4].

→ Homer

→ EPIC

1 O. Ehrismann, Das Nibelungenlied in Deutschland, 1975   2 O. Fambach, Ein Jahrhundert deutscher Literaturkritik, vol. 3: Der Aufstieg zur Klassik, 1959, 664–685   3 G. Häntzschel, Johann Heinrich Voß. Seine Homer-Übersetzung als sprachschöpferische Leistung, 1977   4 G. Kurz, Das Drama als Ragout. Zur Metaphorik des Essens und Trinkens in Goethes Faust, in: Interpreting Goethe's Faust Today, J. K. Brown, M. Lee, Th. P. Saine (eds.), 1994, 172–186   5 S. Matuschek, Homer als unentbehrliches 'Kunstwort'. Von Wolfs *Prolegomena ad Homerum* zur 'Neuen Mythologie', in: D. Burdorf, W. Schweickard (eds.), Die schöne Verwirrung der Phantasie. Antike Mythen in Literatur und Kunst um 1800, 1998, 15–28   6 F. W. J. von Schelling, Ausgewählte Schriften, M. Frank (ed.), 1985, vol. 2, 244   7 M. Kunze (ed.), Wiedergeburt griechischer Götter und Helden – Homer in der Kunst der Goethezeit. Eine Ausstellung der Winckelmann-Gesellschaft im Winckelmann-Museum Stendal (6 November 1999 to 9 January 2000) (Exhibition Catalogue), 1999   8 J. Wohlleben, Die Sonne Homers. Zehn Kapitel deutscher Homer-Begeisterung. Von Winckelmann bis Schliemann, 1990.
Additional Bibliography M. S. Jensen, The Homeric Question and the Oral-Formulaic Theory, 1980; G. Nagy, Homeric Questions, 1996   GERHARD KURZ

Homer-Virgil Comparison

A. Subject and Significance   B. Classical
Antiquity   C. Renaissance   D. 17th und
18th Centuries

A. Subject and Significance

The Homer-Virgil comparison is the conflict – sometimes pursued with considerable passion – about the relative position of the two greatest Classical poets. Because it provided a platform for the debate about central aesthetic concepts from the Roman Empire down to the end of the 18th cent., it represents one of the constants of European literary criticism. In the argument about precedence, which has its roots in the system of syncrisis in Classical grammar, there is more at issue than the decision of whether the Greek or the Roman poet is the greater; rather, the question gives rise to strategies of argumentation which lead well beyond its original literary-stylistic boundaries. This is especially the case from the 16th. to the 18th.cent., the period in which the debate reached its high point, and is, in a complex manner, taken up into the process of self-definition for the Early Modern period in its confrontation with the Classical world. The lines taken can be very different: 'Homère et Virgile deviennent (...) les acteurs allégoriques d'un débat entre le 'sublime sans art' et le 'sublime régulier' des âges classiques' [11. 452]. Alternatively: 'controversy about Homer's merits and vices becomes one of the dominant modes of public discussion of literary and, beyond that, cultural values' [15. 56]. Beyond this, the comparison forms a parallel to what is known (after its main phase in France) as the → Querelle des Anciens et des Modernes, with which, in view of the paradigmatic nature of its two sides, it often overlaps; it might almost be seen as a

'Querelle within the Classical world'. There are two points in time when a reversal in judgment occurs about who holds the first place. While the Classical judgment on Homer's precedence retains its force down to the time around 1500, from the 16th. cent. the first place is overwhelmingly given to Virgil. The second reversal to Homer's favour in the 18th. cent. is an indicator of the passing of the imitatio-oriented 'age of rhetoric', and also runs parallel with a radical change in the concept of literature.

B. Classical Antiquity

The origins and processes of the Homer-Virgil comparison are closely tied in with the premises of the Classical view of literature. A limit is set by the doctrine of literary → *imitatio* , which not only serves as a model in the highest literary levels, but is found also in the more elementary levels of text-production in the study of grammar and rhetoric. On the basis of the premise that one should accommodate oneself to figures who are recognised as models, and even set oneself up against them, in order, if possible, to surpass their achievements, Homer and Virgil, as the representatives of the genre of poetry with the highest level of excellence, are afforded the status of paradigms, in the very practical sense of how to write. Although nowadays it has largely disappeared from view, this pragmatic aspect, which is expressly stressed by the most prominent proponents of the Homer-Virgil comparison, such as Macrobius, Vida or Scaliger, permits us to understand the peculiarities of the way in which the comparison is pursued. The process is decontextualised and specific, and is pursued, above all, without temporal parameters: thus authors from entirely different epochs find themselves subjected to a unified and normative judgment, in which the actual circumstances of production are ignored. If Homer and Virgil are thus compared within a framework of timelessness, this does not, however, stem from the inability to distinguish differences in periods. The regular attempts at the composition of literary histories in the Classical and Early Modern periods testify sufficiently to the contrary. It may be explained rather from its set aim, since within the context of the *imitatio*-doctrine, especially within a teaching context, historical difference has no real role, and it is possible therefore to distance oneself from it.

In the conflict about the order of precedence between Homer and Virgil, a second factor comes into play, namely that the creative-aesthetic principle of mimesis is applied not only to the comparison as such, but also to the objects of comparison. This is shown in an exemplary manner in the case of Virgil, 'who in his *Aeneid* pursues and indeed achieves a 'complete' imitation of Homer' [23. 478; 13]. Evidence of this is provided by the contemporary assumption that a greater work is being created than the *Iliad* (Prop. 2,34,65f). Literary criticism also reacts within the framework provided by the doctrine. The Donatus-Vita (44–46) provides the information that a Perellius Faustus published a catalogue of Virgil's *furta*, a Q. Octavius Avitus an eight-volume compilation of Virgilian passage-overlaps with earlier writers and, finally, that a certain Q. Asconius Pedianus compiled a *Liber contra obtrectatores Vergilii* – all standard sources for later Virgil commentaries and used to Late Antiquity. In spite of any hostility, Virgil is still seen from the 1st cent. AD on as the pinnacle of Roman epic writing and is thus placed immediately beside Homer, as the comparison demands. A standard judgment is that of Quintilian (Inst. 10,1,85 f.), who grants Homer the first and Virgil the second place among all poets, adding that he is nearer to the first place than he is to the third. Nor is the Homer-Virgil comparison restricted to professional literary discussion; it becomes a popular theme in the dinner-table symposium, too. In the distorting mirror of Juvenal's satire we encounter a representative of the female sex, "who, as soon as she had taken her seat, praises Virgil, feels for Dido's suicide, makes comparisons between poets, and weighs up Virgil against Homer" (Sat. 6,434-7; reference to the habit of including the comparison in symposia also in Sat. 11,180f.). Although references are limited, Gellius does provide some indication of how that comparison was carried out in practice both in conversation and in the schools.

The principal reference in the Classical period is provided by Macrobius's *Saturnalia*, practically speaking a compendium of Late Classical poetics, which offers in its fifth book the most extensive comparison from Classical times, and is therefore the standard transmitter of the Homer-Virgil comparison to the Early Modern period [23]. After first referring on several occasions to the *imitatio* as such (2–10), the central part is so arranged as to show first the superiority, then the equality, and finally the subordination of Virgil to Homer (11–13). The long-term effect of this chapter is visible in various stages. When it says, for example, that Virgil attempted not only to compete with Homer's greatness, but also with his *simplicitas*, with the effectiveness of his oratory and finally with his *tacita maiestas*, then it is clear that Winckelmann's celebrated formula 'edle Einfalt und stille Größe' ("noble simplicity and quiet greatness") is a literal translation in which the straightforward notion of simplicity has merely been augmented by the epithet 'noble' [9. 81; 20. 21; 24. 11–14].

C. RENAISSANCE

The conditions of the comparison in the Early Modern period are first determined by the inequality of the two protagonists. Homer is, to be sure, present as a great name during the Middle Ages, but the reading of Greek texts only starts again in the 15th. cent., after the point when Petrarch, in his *Letter to Homer* (1360), declares that the question of which of the two poets is the greater is unresolved. He does so only on the basis of Macrobius. Interest in Homer is determined by the superior position of Virgil; his re-discovery by way of commentaries on the *Aeneid*, where the parallels noted in Servius commentary are copied out and expanded

[13. 62], leads to a distorted view, so that the early Humanist attempt to make Homer accessible again may be described as the history of a failure [19]. For all that, the precedence of Homer is not radically questioned in the most significant treatises on the Homer-Virgil comparison in the 15th. cent. by Angelus Decembrius, Angelus Politianus and Ioannes Iovianus Pontanus. The real turning point, in fact, is the *Poetices libri tres* of Marcus Hieronymus Vida (1527; written ca. 1516 at the court of Leo X), in which for the first time a clear and elaborately circumscribed argument for the precedence of Virgil is made. Vida's verse poetics is confirmed in this epochal role by its reception history. With over 100 printings to the early 19th. cent. it became a standard work in Europe. The actual novelty in Vida's *Poetics*, apart from reversing the relative evaluation, is, however, that the work opened up a path away from the Classical concept of a model poet as an authority and led to an examination of methods. It represents the first reasonably large-scale attempt to derive from the Latin poet the rules of poetry [21]. Often the implicit central point of this process is a comparison between Homer and Virgil in which, following each individual rule, there is a negative example from Homer, to which is attached either a positive one from Virgil or the comment that the Latin poet would never have done that. In Vida's criticism of Homer what is at issue are frequently features which nowadays are described as features of an early literary form strongly influenced by orality, seen in connection with the situation in which the Homeric epics developed. The methodology is consistent insofar as Virgil, as the representative of a highly developed written culture and as the best model for correct writing within the paradigm of imitation, no longer shows these features or indeed lets it be seen in his Homer-imitation how such 'oral' stylistic features are eliminated.

The strongest defender of Virgil's superiority over Homer is Julius Caesar Scaliger, who, in the fifth book of his *Poetices libri septem* (1561), offers the second-longest Homer-Virgil comparison that had ever been presented [7. 64–307], overtaken only a little later by Fulvius Ursinus [8], who provides, however, simply a collection of parallels with no attempt at literary evaluation. Scaliger's comparison was extraordinarily influential, and had an influence even down to school-level (in the curriculum of the Jesuit schools, for example). Evidence of his influence is shown by the overblown criticism that he obscured knowledge of Homer for centuries, and had indeed kept back the study of Greek as opposed to Latin literature for generations [18. 72f.]. Scaliger's unrestrained polemics do indeed border at times on the grotesque; Joannes Ludovicus de La Cerda makes the judgment that he seems to be railing not so much at Homer as at an enemy [3]. The argumentation proceeds, on the one hand, within the framework of a Renaissance social ideal. If Homeric verse is shown as so far below Virgilian as a shepherd's meal is below a royal banquet [7. 142], or if the distance between the two poets is so great as that between a woman of the people and a noble lady [7. 48], then the social implication of the old antithesis between 'raw nature' und 'artistic embellishment' is evident. Also of significance is the effort to exploit historical difference as an additional strand of the argument, in that the attempt is made to raise this difference, which has been determined upon literary-critical grounds, to the status of an historical-developmental model. Scaliger formulates the model of a gradual optimisation very clearly indeed: "The material that Homer takes from nature as if it were dictated to a schoolboy is improved by Virgil as if by a teacher" [7. 238].

A further potential for the Homer-Virgil comparison becomes apparent in the *Recherches de la France* by Estienne Pasquier (written before 1565; reworked down to 1607), in which Macrobius's und Scaliger's comparisons are explicitly taken up and placed into the 'ancient-modern' antithesis, so that the *translatio-* und *Querelle*-schemes overlap. Virgil takes over the role of Homer and Ronsard that of Virgil in this book [5. 719 ff.]. Furthermore, at the start of the 17th cent. a direct interlinking of the *Querelle*-scheme with the Homer-Virgil comparison is offered by Paolo Beni, whose *Comparazione di Homero, Virgilio e Torquato* (1607) is ultimately extended also to Ariosto.

More strongly than in the 'Querelle between the ancients and the moderns' there begin to appear from the 15th cent. on historically oriented patterns of argumentation with the conventional aim of justifying the respective literary evaluations. In this new context old lines of argument develop a different dynamic: in contrast to Classical discussions, what is completely new here is that the chronological distance between Homer and Virgil has significance in the debate. This idea, even if it is only tentatively pursued in the initial stages, provides the basis for a decisive change from the 18th cent. in the perception of a literary beginning, in that the protagonist, Homer, is no longer viewed, as in Classical times, simply as a literary pinnacle of excellence and an unsurpassable rhetorical model, but can be discovered rather to be an archaic poet distinguished by a specific cultural individuality [22]. In this context the Homer-Virgil comparison allows, on the basis of the paradoxical structure of Renaissance recourse to the *auctores veteres*, for a division of the functions 'ancient' and 'new or modern' within Classical Antiquity as such: taking Homer as a representative of the past calls for a differentiation in the perception of 'ancient'; in Virgil, who stands for an aspect of Antiquity in which modernity is implied, the exemplary function is subordinate to a process of abstraction, which may be located within the need to establish a pattern of norms. The different directions within the antithesis are not on the same plane: from this arise movements which give the Homer-Virgil debate an inherent dynamic, which, unlike the Ciceronianus debate, for example, allows it to remain current throughout the gradually changing circumstances of the 17th and 18th cents.

D. 17TH UND 18TH CENTURIES

One indication of the move away from the Renaissance view of the problem is an increasing criticism of the comparative method by which only individual passages are taken into consideration. After J. L. de La Cerda, in the introduction to his monumental Virgil-edition (1608), had provided a systematic overview of the individual positions and their representatives from Classical times onward [3], René Rapin made the complaint in the middle of the 17th cent. that Macrobius und Scaliger had looked at Homer and Virgil simply from the point of view of grammarians, and thus had remained superficial instead of looking at the essential nature of their work [6. 12 f.; 10. 171 f.]. This criticism, which became a standard one (as late as the 19th cent. Ch. Nisard proclaimed heatedly that Scaliger's criticism was like that of a man judging a whole building on the basis of its capitals [16.375]), is an indication of the gradual loss of the poetical-rhetorical paradigm, in which the newly discovered original genius of Homer is an important feature. This paradigm shift was a European phenomenon, which has as its starting point A. Pope's Homer-translation (1726). All the same, the debate was still carried on along the lines of argumentation which had been established since Quintilian by a comparison of the Greek with the Roman poet. This is true in particular of German aesthetics, which focused with special intensity upon Homer, and which from Herder down to the Schlegels used standpoints and concepts which are largely comparable with those of Renaissance poetics, differing from them only in evaluative terms [25. 21]. That the roots remain within the older rhetorical-poetical discourse in clear in the dominant concepts, which are set against the doctrine of *ars*.

One key idea in the context of which Homer again takes precedence over Virgil is the emphatically stressed notion of simplicity. Winckelmann's formula, noted above, is not just an example of the reception of Classical ideas, but a direct reversal of the Renaissance view according to which Homer's 'unpolished simplicity' is seen as a negative quality, whilst Virgil is perceived as having elevated to the heights of perfection what had come to him in the form of raw material [7. 46]. The beginning of this turn-about are seen in Diderot's judgment in his *De la poésie dramatique*, which made an impact in Germany by way of Lessing's translation (1760): "Nature has given me a taste for simplicity, and I strive to make this taste more complete by reading the Classical authors. (...) Whoever reads Homer with a little bit of genius will find with greater confidence the source which nourishes me. Oh, my friend, how beautiful is simplicity! How badly have we acted in continuing to draw away from it!" [1. 165]. What follows, after declaring that genius may be felt but not imitated, is the second central concept: places in which Virgil's *imitatio Homeri* are interpreted as a lack of originality, which are declared lacking in true genius, and where his *ars* is just artifice, are legion. There is a prominent example of this in the 18th section of Lessing's *Laokoon* [17. 74–

78]; the 19th.-cent. German view of Virgil is also thoroughly characterised by this. However, this is nothing more than a recourse to the dual concepts in terms of which Homer and Virgil have been compared since Quintilian. In Quintilian, to be sure, reference is made to *natura,* which is there taken to be synonymous with *ingenium* (Inst. 10,1,86). Nature, the third of the key concepts to be set against *ars*, changes significantly as a concept. Herder's statement may stand as a paradigm when he says that Homer "is at the precise point where nature places the complete work of her hands on the boundary of her domain, so that from this point on art might begin; but the work itself (...) is the essence of its perfection. With Homer everything is still nature" [2. 165; 24. 15–26]. According to older views of the relationship between *ars* and *natura*, nature is both the origin and the aim of poetic production. In the Renaissance view Homer, as the first poet, had no option but to imitate nature, while the later poet was in the happy situation of having rough sketches at hand which he could use as patterns and polish up; at the same time, that process of reworking did not betoken any loss of originality, but rather takes *natura* as its goal. Thus the Roman poet succeeds, for example, in creating things with words and does not allow the words to emerge from things as much as the things from the words, where Homer merely narrates.

Independent of any continuity in the area of categorisation, the question of the conflict itself about which of the two poets is the greater is increasingly seen as obsolete after the middle of the 18th cent. In his epoch-making Virgil commentary (1771), Christian Gottlob Heyne raises the objection that many had made comparisons between Virgil and Homer, but that it is irritating to see how learned men approached this with anger towards one of the two poets and went on to damn one of them and praise the other excessively without having any sensitivity in terms of judgment, since they focus only on individual words and verses. By ignoring the whole and the interplay of the different parts, they disregard precisely what they should be looking at [4. 36; 20. 29]. From the third edition on (1797–1800) this aesthetic argument is augmented with reference to chronological, social and linguistic differences, prompted by Friedrich August Wolf's *Prolegomena ad Homerum* (1795), which introduces to Homer-criticism the basic idea of the historical viewpoint, and in Chapter 12 explicitly condemns the customary practice of reading 'Homer, Kallimachus, Vergil, Nonnus und Milton mit derselben Auffassung' ('in the same frame of mind') [14. 29–31]. With this, the pairing of two representative Classical authors, separated from one another by three-quarters of a millennium, comes to the same historicising conclusion as the 'Querelle des anciens et des modernes' [12], in that the concept of the incomparability of the two that were compared wins the day. However, the price of this historical hermeneutic is the loss of meaning of the models [14. 1]. If Homer and Virgil are no longer comparable with one another, then

they are also no longer comparable with regard to their respective times.

SOURCES   1 D. DIDEROT, Œuvres esthétiques, P. VER-NIÈRE (ed.),1968   2 J. G. HERDER, Fragen über die Bildung einer Sprache, in: Werke, W. PROSS (ed.), vol. 1, 1984   3 I. L. DE LA CERDA, Vergilii opera, 3 vols., 1642–1663, vol. 1 'Elogia' (without page numbers)   4 Virgilii opera, ed., CH. G. HEYNE, 3 vols., ²1787–1788, vol. 2 5 E. PASQUIER, Recherches de la France, in: Œuvres, 1723, vol. 1   6 R. RAPIN, Comparaison des poèmes d'Homère et de Virgile (later published as: Observations sur les poèmes d'Homère et de Virgile), 1669   7 I. C. SCALIGER, Poetices libri septem Vol. 4, 1998   8 F. URSINUS, Virgilius collatione scriptorum Graecorum illustratus, 1568 9 J. J. WINCKELMANN, Kunst Studien und Briefe, H. UHDE-BERNAYS (ed.), 1925, vol. 1

LITERATURE   10 G. FINSLER, Homer in der Neuzeit, 1912 11 M. FUMAROLI, L'âge de l'éloquence, 1980   12 H. R. JAUSS, s.v. Antiqui/moderni, in: Historisches Wörterbuch der Philosophie. 1, 1971, 410–414   13 G. N. KNAUER, Die *Aeneis* und Homer, ²1979   14 J. LATACZ, Tradition und Neuerung in der Homerforschung, in: Id. (ed.), Homer: Tradition und Neuerung, 1979, 26–44   15 G. MOST, The Second Homeric Renaissance, in: P. MURRAY (ed.), Genius, 1989, 54–75   16 CH. NISARD, Les gladiateurs de la république des lettres, 1860   17 J. SCHMIDT, Geschichte des Geniegedankens, 2 vols., 1988   18 E. STEMPLINGER, Horaz im Urteil der Jahrhundert, 1920 19 R. SOWERBY, Early Humanist Failure with Homer (I), in: International Journal of the Classical Tradition 4, 1997, 37–63   20 G. VOGT-SPIRA, Ars oder Ingenium, Literaturwissenschaftliches Jahrbuch, 35, 1994, 9–31 21 Id., Von Auctoritas zu Methode, in: U. ECKER, C. ZINTZEN (eds.), Saeculum tamquam aureum, 1997, 149–163 22 Id., Warum Vergil statt Homer? Der frühneuzeitliche Vorzugsstreit zwischen Homer und Vergil im Spannungsfeld von Autorität und Historisierung, Poetica 34 (2002), 323–344   23 A. WLOSOK, Zur Geltung und Beurteilung Vergils und Homers in Spätantike und früher Neuzeit, in: E. HECK, E. A. SCHMIDT (eds.), Res humanae – Res divinae, 1990, 476–498   24 J. WOHLLEBEN, Die Sonne Homers, 1990   25 F. J. WORSTBROCK, Elemente einer Poetik der Aeneis, 1963

ADDITIONAL BIBLIOGRAPHY D. S. FERRIS, Silent Urns: Romanticism, Hellenism, Modernity, 2000; T. VAN NORT-WICK, Somewhere I Have Never Travelled: The Second Self and the Hero's Journey in Ancient Epic, 1992; S. L. WOFFORD, The Choice of Achilles: The Ideology of Figure in the Epic, 1992   GREGOR VOGT-SPIRA

Homiletics/*Ars praedicandi*
A. DEFINITION   B. ANTIQUITY   C. INFLUENCE

A. DEFINITION
As a special form of public speech, the Christian sermon is often regarded as a genre of rhetoric. The history of its theory reflects both the sermon's roots in ancient rhetoric and a critical examination of the tradition with the goal of establishing it as a distinct and autonomous form as well as retaining a constructive use of the tradition. In its medieval form–the *ars praedicandi* or homiletics (AP) is formally still a branch of rhetoric; it does not develop its character as an inde-

pendent art form of practical theology until the modern period. While the medieval term for the theory of sermons (Latin: *praedicare*, 'to declare publicly'; the meaning in ecclesiastical Latin is 'to preach') refers to an oratorical technique, the modern term (first documented in the 17th cent. as *cursus homileticus*) refers more to the social and ethical role of preaching (Greek *homilía*, 'togetherness', 'social discourse', 'conversation' in the sense of ecclesiastical oration in Iustinus and Flavius Josephus).

B. Antiquity

Already in the New Testament what the early Christian preacher has in common with the ancient orator is to appear in front of the public with the goal of persuasion (Apg 17,16–34; 18,4). He thus needs the instruments of argumentation and delivery developed by ancient rhetoric, especially when faced with pagan competitors, such as the contemporaneous diatribes of popular philosophy. A poignant example for the influence of rhetorical style is found in the antitheses used in the Epistles of Paul [33]. The development of a "practical sermon rhetoric" [14. 308] in the early era of Christianity was accompanied by the emergence of important hermeneutic and ethical foundations for the later theoretical development. The 'father' of allegorical Bible interpretation, which directly shaped medieval exegesis and was practiced up into the modern period, was Origen (AD 185–254) with his neo-Platonic theory of a threefold meaning of scripture (historical, moral and allegorical, as analogous to the human body, soul, and spirit). The reasons why the form of Christian sermons in the Greek cultural realm followed contemporary rhetoric can be found, first, in the rhetorical education of most Church Fathers, which followed the usual educational canon and, second, in the realisation that a sermon shaped according to rhetorical standards would better serve to spread Christianity in a society influenced by pagan educational traditions. The sermon style of the three Cappadocians (Gregory of Nyssa, Gregory Nazianzine and Basil the Great) is representative of 4th cent. rhetorical homiletics. The demand that the preacher serve as an ethical role model is a central topic in the works of John Chrysostom (AD 349–407), whose *Homilia* are regarded as impressive examples of the combination of sermon and rhetorical stylistics. He emphasises the need for teaching through the word and propagates through his style the ideal of simplicity by renouncing superfluous embellishments (De sacerdotio 4,3 ff.).

Rhetorical ethos and the question of appropriate expression (preference for a clear and modest style) are also central elements in the sermon theory of his contemporary Augustine (AD 354–430), who in his treatise *De doctrina Christiana* created a Christian sermon rhetoric that follows Cicero in particular and is based on the ancient system of rhetoric, a rhetoric which became the foundation and the model for the entire homiletic discipline of the Middle Ages. Augustine regards rhetoric as a 'maidservant' that follows wisdom (4,6,10); in dealing with Sacred Scripture, he distinguishes–according to the Classical organisation of rhetoric–between *inventio* (finding thoughts and arguments) and *elocutio* (linguistic expression), the *modus inveniendi* having to do with the comprehension of the content and the *modus proferendi* with its linguistic expression and delivery (1,1,1; 4,1,1). While it was no longer necessary to adjust the level of style according to the importance of the material, because the subject matter was always exalted, the three functions of ancient speech were still in effect: *delectare* (to delight), *movere* (to move) and–most importantly–*docere* (to teach). The fulfillment of these functions was to be supported by stylistic variations ('ut veritas pateat, placeat, moveat', "so that the truth lies open, pleases and moves", 4,28,61). The adoption of the Classical functions into sermon theory is based on a consideration of the audience's composition (4, 12,27), which, in turn, is a central category of the medieval AP. On the one hand, Augustine utilises ancient Classical rhetoric for his theory of the Christian sermon; on the other hand, however, his effort to legitimise this approach reveals the tension-filled and often-conflicting relationship between theology and rhetoric that has characterised the history of homiletics up to the present day. The origin of the tension lies in the necessity–recognised as early as in late Antiquity–of a distinction based on fundamental differences between secular rhetoric and Christian sermons both as to application and goals. While secular rhetoric serves to bring contested issues to a decision and to create (individual) moods and opinions, Christian rhetoric sees itself in the service of the propagation and the spread of (universally valid) Christian truths. The primary goal of the sermon is not the success of the orator but the salvation of the audience–a view that becomes decisive for the Middle Ages [28. 282]. Since rhetoric as an art of persuasion is not necessarily tied to truth, Augustine must confront the question of whether a technique for creating plausibility can ever serve to proclaim the truth. He answers in the affirmative by regarding rightful use of it as the decisive criterion: eloquence in itself is not responsible for its possible abuse ('non est facultas ipsa culpabilis, sed ea male utentium perversitas', "not the faculty itself but the corruption of those who would abuse it is reprehensible": 2,36,54). Indeed, the preacher needs a rhetorical education in order to defend against secular orators who master the art of guiding the audience (4,2,3); this view of rhetoric as an instrument to do battle becomes more important in the Protestant sermons of the Reformation period.

C. Influence
1. Middle Ages   2. Modern Period
3. The 19th and 20th Centuries

1. Middle Ages
The tradition of ancient rhetoric remained influential in medieval sermons and for the theory of rhetoric

both through adaptation and reinterpretation. Until ca. 120, homiletics was essentially shaped by Augustine's view of the preacher's office and by Gregory the Great's (ca. 540–604) pastoral ethics, and was rarely examined in any systematic way: Hrabanus Maurus's (780–856) *De institutione clericorum* is based on Augustine and Gregory and integrates the → ARTES LIBERALES into clerical training. Guibert of Nogent, *Liber quo modo sermo fieri debeat* (1084), sets up rules for the structure, style and delivery of sermons that are based on rhetorical tradition. As an aid, especially for less educated clerics, who were required to preach on Sundays and holidays–a rule introduced by Charlemagne in 801–collections of sermons were produced (homiliaries) which contain both contemporary texts (Hrabanus Maurus) as well as sermons by the Church Fathers of Late Antiquity (especially Augustine, Leo the Great and Gregory the Great), whose authority was thereby further strengthened.

Gregory the Great's largely pastoral *Regula pastoralis* emphasises that a preacher must be revered in order to be heard (2, 8: 'difficile est, ... ut praedicator, qui non diligitur, libenter audiatur', "one hardly likes to listen to a preacher whom one does not love"), a demand that shows the Christian version of a rhetorical means of persuasion already defined as an ethos by Aristotle (Rhet. 1,2,4), who characterized the orator as one who is likeable, credible and accepted as a human role model in his self-presentation. The essential matter of concern for medieval sermons as articulated by Gregory was to find an appropriate way to address various types and various financial classes of listeners. In the medieval world, marked by fixed social ranks, the issue of finding the proper (*aptum*) delivery led to a shift of focus from the topic of the speech to the social position of the audience, a change of interpretation which influences medieval poetics and especially → LETTER-WRITING/ARS DICTAMINIS. In principle, ancient rhetorical theory had already considered this aspect (Quint. inst. 10,1, 43 ff.). Gregory's typology of listeners divided as to age, gender, social status, temperament or character (Book 3) refers to a problem also addressed by ancient rhetoric, in that it included psycho-social analysis (Aristot. rhet. 2,2 ff.) or postulated that orators ought to be trained in psychology (Cic. orat. 1,12,53).

In ca. 1200, Alan of Lille shifted to a typology of audience that was exclusively based on rank, thus founding the genre of class sermons. His *Summa de arte praedicatoria* marks the beginning of a systematic medieval AP that is evidenced in the production of large numbers of tracts. From the 13th cent. on, sermons became increasingly important as a tool for public instruction (Alan refers to them as *publica instructio*). The influence of scholastic logic and argumentation underlined the need for works addressing the rules of homiletics and the development of more artful sermon forms; for instance, theme sermons that employ extended methods of reasoning reminiscent of Roman judicial rhetoric, or university sermons that follow ancient rhetorical systems and logic. The main emphasis of the usually rhetorically structured AP are the preacher's ethos; the structure and form of the sermon, including stylistic considerations such as clauses and figures of speech; and the manner of delivery. Numerous elements of ancient rhetorical theory can be found; the 13th cent. was particularly influenced by the *Rhetorica ad Herennium*, attributed to Cicero in the Middle Ages, and by Cicero's *De inventione*. The orator's task to move his audience in three ways was a demand placed on the preacher as well by Alexander of Ashby in *De modo praedicandi* (ca. 1200) ('ut ... auditores reddat dociles, benivolos et attentos', "that he will make his audience ready to learn, benevolent, and attentive"; cf. Rhet. Her. 1,6). Thomas of Salisbury's *Summa de arte praedicandi* (early 13th cent.) specifically deals with Roman rhetoric and cites from the *Rhetorica ad Herennium*. A rhetoric of prayer [32. 45] modelled on ancient structural schemata was designed by Wilhelm of Auvergne (d. 1249) in his *De rhetorica divina*; in another homiletic tract, his *De arte praedicandi*, the structure is based on questions about circumstances ('quis, quibus, ubi, quando, quomodo, quid', "who, with what, where, when, how, what"), a method that had been developed as early as in the 2nd cent. BC by Hermagoras of Temnos and had become a tool, especially for Roman judicial rhetoric (cf. Quint. inst. 3,6) [21. 99 ff.]. A work influential up to the early modern period was Robert of Basevorn's *Forma praedicandi* (1322), which was based on ancient structures and Augustine's authority (also on Cicero's rhetoric in some matters). The 24th chapter places special emphasis on various introductory forms that are to elicit the audience's attention and benevolence. The importance of delivery is stressed by Thomas Waley in *De modo componendi sermones* (mid 14th cent.); he advises preachers to practice at first away from people, in front of trees or rocks–a method borrowed from rhetorical practice. The question remains as to what extent theoretical reflections and rules were employed in the homiletic practice of the Middle Ages. Aside from the training of the individual preacher, one must consider the differences between sermons for simple folk and sermons for a clerically trained or courtly audience.

2. MODERN PERIOD

The significance of ancient rhetoric for modern homiletics is apparent, first, because the Humanist theory of sermons is strongly influenced by ancient models; however, the formalism of Baroque sermons was also based on the knowledge of rhetoric; and even after the Enlightenment a Classical education in rhetoric still served as a basis for training preachers. In the 16th cent., an education in rhetoric based on Cicero and Quintilian became the established general preparation in Protestant school programs (Melanchthon, J. Sturm), while the Jesuit *Ratio studiorum* (1599) established rhetoric as a component in the training of Catholic priests with far-reaching effects.

Humanism's theory of homiletics is based on ancient rhetoric; Erasmus's *Ecclesiastes* (1534), in particular, shows a structural as well as thematic connection to ancient tradition. Especially valued was the *Institutio oratoria* by Quintilian, which was rediscovered in 1415 and which influenced Martin Luther's sermon style [36. 474]. Sermons received a new and more central importance for Church services in the wake of the Reformation, which was closely tied to Humanism in spirit, and also because of the notion, emphasized by Luther, that divine revelation occurs through the word. For Protestant sermons, this meant delivering them in the vernacular, but the Catholic Church preserved Latin as a cultic and institutional language until the Second Vatican Council (1962–65). Augustine's theory of the sermon was revived in the modest and simple style of Protestant orthodoxy (rejection of any superfluous and pointless speech embellishments) and in the idea of rhetoric as a weapon to be used in the controversies of the Reformation, especially in polemic and argumentative sermons. The adoption of ancient rhetorical theory was characterised in this period, on the one hand, by efforts to apply the orator's traditional tasks to preaching and, on the other hand, by the search for new rhetorical genres that could serve the aims of Christian teaching better than the ancient models. Melanchthon first regarded homiletics as a sub-discipline of rhetoric; he demanded that theologians study rhetoric and dialectics (*Encomium*, 1523) and, in his *Elementa rhetorices* (1531,) added to the ancient genres of judicial speech, counsel, and panegyrics the *didascalicum* as a genre, which focused on the sermon. Later, he restricted himself to the rhetoric of sermons alone and expanded the homiletic genre with the didactic *genus epitrepticum* and the morally admonishing *genus paraeneticum* (*De officiis concionatoris*, 1535). The determination of the Christian sermon as a genre follows the structural paths of ancient rhetoric. Modern theology regards Andreas Hyperius as "the liberator of homiletics from the shackles of rhetoric" [12. 104] and as the founder of an independent Protestant theory of the sermon. In his work *De formandis concionibus sacris* (1552/1562), he identified precisely the fundamental differences between secular rhetoric and Christian sermons and analysed the extent to which rhetoric is useful for homiletics. Although this resulted in an increased thematic separation, the schematics of disposition continued to follow the ancient and Humanist tradition. First, in the earlier version of 1552, he divided sermons into the categories of didactic, polemic, moral, punitive and consoling, while allowing the *genus mixtum*. Then, in a later version, he reduced the categories to three–those that are related to the three aims adopted from rhetoric (*docere, delectare, flectere*). The different stages of production (*inventio, dispositio, elocutio, memoria, pronuntiatio*, finding the ideas, organisation, linguistic rendering, memorisation, delivery) are kept, with special importance placed on *inventio* (choice of material).

Baroque sermons show a trend towards expansion (*amplificatio*) and a fixed structure similar to the parts of ancient orations [20. 131]. The influence of the literary style of Baroque and the Classical Ciceronic rhetoric of the Jesuits led to increased formalism, the use of speech embellishments (especially metaphors and emblems) and the choice of an elevated style. Ancient elements of style were used particularly in funeral sermons, panegyrics on the saints or court sermons, which show similarities to the ancient epideictic genre (encomiastic and affirming functions).

A counterweight to the artfully rhetorical sermon can be found in Pietism with what is often referred to as hostility towards rhetoric (H. A. Francke, J. Lange, J. J. Rambach) ("to teach someone an understanding of Sacred Scripture per oratoriam/is wasted effort / like striking the water with a rod". P. J. Spener, *Theologische Bedencken. Dritter Teil. Das sechste Kapitel, Artic. II, Sect. XXIII*, 1700, 752). Here, an emotional experience of faith and its effect on a person's heart are of highest importance, mediated through the preacher's piety (in rhetorical terms: the ethos); correspondingly, the desired style is simple and natural.

Homiletics marked by the intellectual trends of the Enlightenment again follows primarily the intention of *docere* in the effort to direct the sermon to a particular audience. Coherent and factually logical argumentation and proofs are necessary to convince reason to create a will (L. v. Mosheim, *Anweisung erbaulich zu predigen*, posthumously, 1763). Influenced by Platonism and the early Christian sermon of the Church Fathers, Fénelon (*Dialogues sur l'éloquence en général et celle de la chair en particulier*, posthumously, 1718) placed homiletics once again in the context of ancient rhetoric. All in all, it appears that ancient rhetorical intentions are retained in the sermons of the modern period, albeit with changes in emphasis that reflect various developments in intellectual history. For instance, J. J. Spalding, *Vertraute Briefe die Religion betreffend* (1784), again focused on the importance of moving the audience emotionally (*movere*) in order to bestow binding power on a rational presentation (7th Letter).

Since the steady decline in importance of political and public speeches (since the mid–18th cent.) led to a general decline of rhetoric, Church sermons are regarded as the last publicly effective form of oratory. In his work *Sollen wir Ciceronen auf den Kanzeln haben?* (in: *Sämmtliche Werke. Zur Schönen Literatur und Kunst. Zweiter Teil*), J. G. Herder (1744–1803) discussed the question–following the statement that eloquence "had fled into the temple"–whether contemporary sermons can be measured according to the norms of ancient rhetoric. Referring to the differences in goals and cultural conditions, he rejected the imitation of ancient patterns and pleaded for a new, independent sermon rhetoric. A defence of ancient models, on the other hand, can be found in F. V. Reinhard (*Geständnisse seine Predigten und seine Bildung zum Prediger betreffend in Briefen an einen Freund*, ²1811), who, educated in the works of Demosthenes and Cicero as representatives of "true eloquence", demanded rules like those of ancient rhetoric, so that a sermon might "be clear for reason, graspable for memory, inspiring for emotions, stirring for the heart" (53 ff.).

3. The 19th and 20th Centuries

Despite various convergences and efforts at mediation over the course of history, the distance from Classical rhetoric continued to grow to the extent that homiletics developed into an independent theological discipline. An essential contributor to its establishment in the context of practical theology was F. Schleiermacher (1768–1834), who gave the sermon a new function. As a communicative element in worship it was to awaken a religious consciousness. The notion of Christianity as a religion of the word is also reflected in A. Vinet (1797–1847), whose work is based on a rhetoric that can be either secular or Christian depending on its subject matter (Ausgewählte Werke, E. Staehelin, ed., Vol. 3, 1944, 80). Like Schleiermacher, Vinet's sermon structure was based on the schema of ancient oratory. Along with examples of openness towards rhetoric in 19th cent. sermon theory (H. A. Schott, F. Theremin, A. Schweizer), one also finds anti-rhetorical (pietistic) trends that continued up into the 20th cent.: 'Wo Gott verkündigt wird, da ersterben die armseligen Versuche menschlicher Redekunst'. "Where God is preached, the pitiful attempts of human oratory die away" (E. Thurneysen, Die Aufgabe der Predigt, 1929, 112).

Principles of ancient rhetoric are called to mind, on the one hand, by historical research within modern homiletics and, on the other hand, are newly debated in the context of general rhetorical issues. Rhetoric is now one aspect within an interdisciplinary realm that includes communication, sociology and psychology. Rhetorical elements are applied to special homiletic matters such as argumentative strategies (as early as in the 19th cent.: F. L. Steinmeyer, *Die Topik im Dienste der Predigt*, 1847). The current view holds that the work of the preacher can be divided, as in Augustine, into the processes of finding and communicating the truth, and can therefore be regarded as rhetorical (G. Otto, Predigt als rhetorische Aufgabe, 1987, 14), although the ancient division between *inventio* and *elocutio* as the thematic and formal core of rhetoric is less important here.

Sources 1 Alanus ab Insulis, Summa de arte praedicatoria, PL 210, 111–195   2 Erasmi v. Rotterdam, Ecclesiastes, in: Desiderii Erasmi Roterodami Opera omnia, J. Clericus (ed.), repr. 1961/62, 5, 767–1100 (Engl. Ecclesiastes: or, The Preacher, 1979, 1797) 3 Gregory the Great, Regula pastoralis, PL 77 (Engl. H. Davis (trans.), Pastoral Care, 1978, 1950) 4 Guibert von Nogent, Liber quo modo sermo fieri debeat, PL 156, 11–21   5 Rabanus Maurus, De institutione clericorum, A. Knöpfer, (ed.), 1900   6 A. Hyperius, De formandis concionibus sacris libri 2, H. B. Wagnitz (ed.), Halle 1781 (Engl. I. Ludham, The Practise (sic) of Preaching, 1577)   7 P. Melanchthon, Elementorum rhetorices libri duo, 1519 (Ger. J. Knape

(trans.), Philipp Melanchthons "Rhetorik,' 1993)   8 Id., Encomium, in: Werke in Auswahl, R. Stupperich (ed.), ²1978–83, vol. 3   9 Robert von Basevorn, Forma praedicandi, T.-M. Charland (ed.), Artes praedicandi, Paris/Ottawa 1936, 233–323 (Engl. J. J. Murphy, Three Medieval Rhetorical Arts, 1971, 114–215)   10 Thomas Waleys, De modo componendi sermones, T.-M. Charland (ed.), [9], 328–403   11 Wilhelm von Auvergne, Opera omnia, 2 vols., Paris/Orléans 1674–75, repr.,1963   Literature   12 E. Ch. Achelis, Lehrbuch der praktischen Theologie, vol. 2, 61912   13 T. E. Ameringer, Stylistic Influence of the Second Sophistic on the Panegyrical Sermons, 1921   14 E. Auerbach, Sermo humilis, Romanische Forschungen 64, 1952, 304–364   15 W. Barner, Barockrhetorik, 1970   16 B. Bauer, Jesuitische ars rhetorica im Zeitalter der Glaubenskämpfe, 1986   17 B. Bohne, R. G. Bogner (eds.), Oratio funebris. Die katholische Leichenpredigt der frühen Neuzeit, 1999   18 H. Caplan, Classical Rhetoric and the Medieval Theory of Preaching, in: A. King, H. North (eds.), Of Eloquence, 1970, 105–134   19 J. Dyck, Ornatus und Decorum im protestantischen Predigstil des 17. Jahrhunderts, Zeitschrift für deutsches Altertum und deutsche Literatur 94, 1965, 225–236   20 L. Fendt, Grundriß der praktischen Theologie, vol. 1, 1938   21 M. Fuhrmann, Die antike Rhetorik, 1984   22 W. Grünberg, Humanismus und Rhetorik, 1973   23 M. Hansen, Der Aufbau der mittelalterlichen Predigt, 1972   24 M. Jossutis, Rhetorik und Theologie in der Predigtarbeit, 1986   25 G. A. Kennedy, Classical Rhetoric and Its Christian and Secular Traditions from Ancient to Modern Times, 1980   26 H.-I. Marrou, Augustinus und das Ende der antiken Bildung, 1982   27 H. M. Müller, Humanismus. Eine evangelische Predigtlehre, 1996   28 J. J. Murphy, Rhetoric in the Middle Ages, 1974   29 U. Nembach, Predigt des Evangeliums. Luther als Pädagoge, Prediger und Rhetoriker, 1972   30 P. Prestel, Die Rezeption der ciceronianischen Rhetorik durch Augustinus in De doctrina christiana, 1992   31 F. Quadlbauer, Die antike Theorie der genera dicendi im Mittelalter, 1962   32 D. Roth, Die mittelalterliche Predigttheorie und das Manuale Curatorum des J. U. Surgant, 1956   33 N. Schneider, Die rhetorische Eigenart der paulinischen Antithesen, 1970   34 U. Schnell, Die homiletische Theorie Melanchthons, 1968   35 W. Schütz, Geschichte der christlichen Predigt, 1972   36 B. Stolt, Docere, delectare und movere bei Luther, DVjS 44, 1970, 433–474   37 P. Wehrle, Orientierung am Hörer: die Predigtlehre unter dem Einfluß des Aufklärungsprozesses, 1975.   Sylvia Usener

Horoscopes
I. History   II. Present Perspectives

I. History
A. Introduction B. Middle Ages C. Renaissance D. Early Modern Period E. Modern Period

A. Introduction

The term *Horoskópos*, 'hour observer', originally referred to the ascendant (zodiacal sign rising on the eastern horizon), later to the first 30° segment of the dodecatropus (twelve hour circle), and finally to the position of all the stars at a particular point in time. The ca. nine Egyptian and over 180 extant Greek horoscopes have been transmitted mostly on papyrus but also on ostracon or as graffito [1; 17], further in → didactic poetry (in Manethon as sphragis) or in specialized literature, such as the only Latin horoscope in Firmicus Maternus. Horoscopes were cast for individuals, cities, countries and even for the entire world. A special form of the horoscope asks for the most favourable moment to undertake certain actions (*katarchaí*). Most post-ancient sources are still hidden in manuscripts. The Warburg Institute in London specializes in their maintenance. The time has not yet come for a conclusive overview.

B. MIDDLE AGES

In the Middle Ages, astrology was enjoyed a great flourishing in the Arab world as evidenced by the presence of numerous horoscopes. The sources, several of which collected by D. Pingree, must still be analysed: two horoscopes from 281 and 381 [24. XV], five from Māshāǎllāh between 766 and 768 [25. 135], eleven from al-Qaṣrānī between 531 and 884 [25. 135], furthermore, the birth horoscope of the famous astrologist Abū Maʿšar [20. 487] and another in Kunitzsch [14. 109 Note 60]. Historical Sassanide horoscopes based on Indian methods were integrated into an astrological work of history by an Arab astrologist (Abū Maʿšar?), from which 79 horoscopes are preserved as an excerpt [20].

Horoscope technique reached the Latin West by two routes: the first through India and Persia and the Greek East, the other along with the Arabs through Sicily and southern Spain. Although various attempts were made in the West to adapt this pagan practice to Christianity [9], few traditional horoscopes can be found due to the condemnation of the lore by the Church. Māshāǎllāh, Abū Maʿšar, Cecco d'Ascoli, Albertus Magnus, Roger Bacon, Pierre D'Ailly, Lucas Gauricus (with Papal approval), Girolamo Cardano, Johann Valentin Andreae, Johannes Kepler and others speculatively sought to produce Christ's horoscope [9. 127 Note 21 b], and G. Voss [31. 143–155] attempted to cast a horoscope for the hour of Christ's death as late as in 1980.

The practice remained stronger in the Byzantine East than in the Lat. West, with the MSS revealing that the ancient circle was gradually replaced by a square (see Fig. 1). Horoscopes were cast for cities as well. While Alexandria was founded under the expansive summer sign of Leo, the chosen sign for Constantinople–and for Venice as its temporary successor–was the amphibian Cancer [26; 27]. D. Pingree published and calculated several Byzantine horoscopes: three of them from between 475 and 483–the reign of emperor Zeno [25]–, one from 601 [24. XII], the horoscope of Constantine VII Porphyrogenitus from 905 [23], two from 984 and 1011 [24. XIIIsq.], others from between 1003 and 1162 [22. IX; XIX–XXII]. Political and private horoscopes

from between 1345 and 1396 were produced by the school of Johannes Abramius [21]. A later one from 18 October 1626 is contained in A. Delatte, CCAG X (1924), 251. The *Corpus des Astronomes Byzantins* appearing since 1983 promises further material.

C. RENAISSANCE

The → RENAISSANCE referred to Greek ideas directly–not through Arab transmission–and became a high point for astrology which now was especially valued for its cosmological and universal character. Court astrologers cast horoscopes for rulers and popes. Astrologers were used by Pope Julius II to determine the date of his enthronement and by Paul III to find the most favourable moment for laying the foundation stone of St. Peter's [30. V 259]. The position of the stars was also consulted for the founding and the re-founding of the University of Wittenberg. Horoscopes for cities were cast by the German astrologers Peter Johannes Hensel (for Berlin) and Andreas Goldmayer. The astronomer Regiomontanus cast horoscopes as well [11], and Lucas Gauricus collected 200 nativities of famous contemporaries and falsified Luther's horoscope in the service of the Church [32]. In Berlin, he cast horoscopes for Brandenburg princes that are still extant [32. 210 Note 15]. The horoscope collections by Carion and de Scheppers essentially refer back to Gauricus. Horoscopes were also collected by Erasmus Reinhold, cf. the MSS kept in Munich and Leipzig [32. 13] as well as in Stuttgart: cod. math. 4° 22 (written in 1602 by Conradus Haegaeus Cellarius) [28. I 464 Fig. G 48] and cod. math. 4° 24 (with horoscopes for six members of the House of Württemberg between 1588 and 1643). In scholarly correspondence, people informed each other of horoscopes of outstanding figures as well as of infants. People studied the horoscopes of → RULERS but were particularly interested in their own horoscopes: Cardano included his horoscope in his autobiography *De vita propria*, later to appear as part of a collection of horoscopes of 112 well known figures from the past and present [4]. Joseph Justus Scaliger published his horoscope in his first edition of Manilius (in 1579, no further editions), and later it was printed in *Epistola de vetustate et splendore gentis Scaligerae*. Similar to the didactic poet Manethon who had written his own horoscope as sphragis at the end of the sixth book, Konrad Celtis wrote his own horoscope in verse form (1459) in the first poem of *Amores* (1,1) while Petrus Lotichius cast his own horoscope (in 1528) in the elegy *De natali suo* (2,8) as well as Melanchthon's (1497) in the elegy upon his teacher's death (4,4).

D. EARLY MODERN PERIOD

In the 17th cent., the most important astrologer in Rome was Morandi [5], in England, it was William Lilly who effectively used astrology as a political weapon [6]. Kepler cast horoscopes for money, created a more sophisticated aspect theory [8] and calculated the horoscope of Emperor Augustus in order to find out which role Capricorn–the sign of rulership–played therein since Rudolf II had his ascendant in Capricorn. His most famous horoscope is of Wallenstein (1609) [8. 93; 15], which was corrected numerous times.

The Copernican revolution and the Enlightenment suppressed astrology to such a degree that Romanticism, which was actually affine to its spirit, no longer found anything it could have tied up to in a technical sense. Horoscopes were no longer taken seriously as science. Goethe used an excerpt from the Manilius verse 4,197 'hic et scriptor erit velox' in order to create a spurious connection between the Mercury sign of Virgo–on the meridian at the time of his birth–and his calling as a poet (Manilius, however, referred to the vocation of tachygraphers as favoured by the god of scribes, Thot) [10. 265 Note 441]. F. Boll [3. 67–71, regarding this: 160–164] jokingly interpreted Goethe's horoscope in detail based on Pearce's *Textbook of Astrology* and was criticized for it. Others tried to correct it later [3. 161]. The birth signs of King Emmanuel III and Czar Nicholas II were still known in the 19th cent. [33. 207–210].

E. Modern Period

Modern horoscopes are based on ancient methods which have been improved [12]: They take into consideration the planets discovered since the 18th cent., the precession of the boundaries of the zodiacal signs, the exact point in time which is now usually known, and especially the precise geographical latitudes of the places of birth. Now there is a clear distinction between the abstract ecliptic twelfth of 30° and the constellation, which–although it no longer corresponds–still underlies the symbolism. For the most part, the general awareness is limited to the seasonal location of the sun at the time of birth and the position of the ascendant, while other details of the theory are reserved for the experts. Print media disseminate horoscopes and new electronic tools make the necessary calculations much easier.

Horoscopes continue to appear in literature as well: In his novel *Joseph und seine Brüder,* Th. Mann includes a horoscope [9. 35 f.] cast for him by an astrologer from Munich [7. 71 Note 2]. In Thomas Mann's horoscope, Mercury plays a special role as it did for Goethe. → Natural sciences

1 D. Baccani, Oroscopi greci. Documentazione papirologica, 1992   2 F. Boll, Die Erforschung der antiken Astrologie, in: Neue Jahrbücher für das Klassische Altertum 21, 1908, 103–126   3 Id., C. Bezold, W. Gundel, Sternglaube und Sterndeutung, ⁷1977 (¹1918)   4 A. Buck, Cardanos Wissenschaftsverständnis in seiner Autobiographie 'De vita propria', in: Sudhoffs Archiv 60, 1976, 1–12   5 B. Dooley, Morandi's Last Prophecy and the End of Renaissance Politics, 2002   6 A. Geneva, Astrology and the Seventeenth Century Mind, 1995   7 A. Heimann, Thomas Mann's 'Hermesnatur', in: Publications of the English Goethe Society, N. F. 27, 1957/58, 46–72   8 N. Herz, Keplers Astrologie, Vienna 1895   9 W. Hübner, Zodiacus Christianus, 1983   10 Id., Manilius als Astrologe und Dichter, ANRW II 32.1, 1984, 126–320   11 W. Knappich, Regiomontanus als Astro-

loge, in: Zenit 7, 1936, 137–144   12 Id., Die Astrologie im Weltbild der Gegenwart, 1948   13 Id., Geschichte der Astrologie, 1967   14 P. Kunitzsch, The Description of the Night in Gurgānī's *Vīs u Rāmīn*, in: Der Islam 59, 1982, 93–110   15 M. List, Das Wallenstein-Horoskop von Johannes Kepler, in: Katalog zur Kepler-Ausstellung in Linz, 1971, 127–136   16 O. Mazal, Die Sternenwelt des Mittelalters, 1993   17 O. Neugebauer, H. B. van Hoesen, Greek Horoscopes, 1959   18 J. D. North, Astrology and the Fortunes of Churches, in: Centaurus 24, 1980, 181–211   19 Id., Horoscopes and History, 1986   20 D. Pingree, Historical Horoscopes, in: Journal of the American Oriental Society 82, 1962, 487–502   21 Id., The Astrological School of John Abramius, in: Dumbarton Oaks Papers 25, 1971, 189–215   22 Id. (ed.), Hephaestio Thebanus, Apotelesmatica II, 1974   23 Id., The Horoscope of Constantine VII Porphyrogenitus, in: Dumbarton Oaks Papers 27, 1973, 217–231   24 Id. (ed.), Dorotheus Sidonius, Carmen astrologicum, 1976   25 Id., Political Horoscopes from the Reign of Zeno, in: Dumbarton Oaks Papers 30, 1976, 133–150   26 Id., The Horoscope of Constantinople, in: Y. Maeyama, W. G. Saltzer (eds.), Πρίσματα: Naturwissenschaftsgeschichtliche Studien. Festschrift für Willy Hartner, 1977, 305–315   27 Th. Preger, Das Gründungsdatum von Konstantinopel, in: Hermes 36, 1901, 336–342   28 Die Renaissance im deutschen Südwesten (Exhibition catalogue), Karlsruhe 1986   29 R. Reisinger, Historische Horoskopie. Das iudicium magnum des Johannes Carion für Albrecht Dürers Patenkind, 1997   30 L. Thorndike, A History of Magic and Experimental Science, 1923–1958   31 G. Voss OSB, Astrologie – christlich, 1980   32 A. Warburg, Heidnisch-antike Weissagung in Wort und Bild zu Luthers Zeiten, 1920   33 O. Zanotti Bianco, Astrologia e Astronomia, 1905.

Additional Bibliography   1 S. Heilen, Hadirani Genitura: Die astrologischen Fragmente des Antigonos van Nikaia, Edition, Übersetzung und Kommentar, 2007   2 W. Huebner, Sulla's Horoscope? (Firm. math. 6, 31, 1), in: G. Oestmann, H. Darrel Rutkin, K. von Stuckrad (eds.), Religion and Society 42, 2005, 13–35
WOLFGANG HÜBNER

II. Present Perspectives
A. Overview   B. Trends and Schools

A. Overview

In Germany as in most European countries, astrology was almost completely non-existent by the first half of the 19th cent.; efforts by the astronomer J. W. A. Pfaff (1774–1835) and the natural philosopher Gotthilf Heinrich Schubert (1780–1860) to rebuild its reputation in academic circles were ignored or rejected. Late 18th cent. England, however, saw a noticeable revival of astrological ideas. The Ebenezer brothers and Manoah Sibly published an astrological compendium in 1784/90 and arranged for the republication of the English translation of Ptolemaeus' *Tetrabiblion* [6. 189 f.], first published in 1701 by John Whalley. The discovery of Uranus by Wilhelm Herschel (1781) initially created barely a stir among astrologers even though it meant that all the traditional allocation patterns based on seven planets and twelve signs of the zodiac had to be expanded. The same holds true for the discovery of the first asteroids at the beginning of the 19th cent. and of Neptune, discovered in 1846 as a consequence of disruptions in Uranus' orbit.

In the course of the 19th cent., a number of very popular manuals and tables appeared in England under pseudonyms like "Zadkiel" and "Raphael". The incorporation of theosophical ideas (the Theosophical Society was founded in 1875 in New York, gaining influence in England as well after 1884) led to the development of an esoteric astrology with Alan Leo (William Frederick Allen, 1860–1917) as its best known representative. Leo, enthusiastic author as well as businessman, operated a virtual 'horoscope factory' and, thanks to his numerous books that are still available today he created a revival of interest in astrology [8. 84 ff.]. Other astrologers worth mentioning in Germany are Karl Brandler-Pracht (1864–1945) who published an astrology textbook in 1905 [1] as well as Otto Pöllner, Albert Kniepf and Ernst Tiede as representatives of theosophical astrology [8. 114 ff.]. English textbooks set the tone as far as the mathematical-technical premises are concerned. The division into houses according to Placidus from the 17th cent., still common today, owes its popularity less to its proclaimed superiority over other systems and more to the fact that it was the preferred method in England and that it was accessible through numerous printed tables [14].

During the period of economic crisis after the end of the First World War, astrology became highly popular in Germany where the production of astrological texts after 1920 by far exceeded that in other European countries. This period also witnessed the first connections between astrology and psychology, based especially on the works of C. G. Jung and E. Kretschmer. As probably the most important pioneer of this trend, Herbert Freiherr von Klöckler (1896–1950) sought to formulate an astrology in keeping with the needs of the 20th cent., also providing statistical analyses [10; 11]. Aside from this erudite form of astrology claiming to be scientific, the trend of publishing general predictions based on signs in relation to the position of the sun in daily newspapers began to emerge from England.

B. TRENDS AND SCHOOLS

A much debated and contentious question among astrologers is how best to classify the twelve houses [7]. In the first third of the 20th cent., a controversy began which led, on the one hand, to the creation of new systems, and on the other, to a rediscovery or variation of 'classical methods' (for instance the 'equal manner' attributed to Ptolemaeus or the classification systems associated with Regiomontan and Campanus) [12; 14]. A group of astrologers interested in science and mathematics, most of them academics, wrote articles for the journal *Zenit*, established in 1930 and banned by the Nazis eight years later. This publication not only offers insights into the debate about the 'correct' method of classification of houses but also contains important historical material [8. 144].

Of special significance was the 'Hamburg School' founded by Alfred Witte (1878–1941), which practiced a complex interpretation system and assumed the existence of eight 'Transneptunian' planets [6. 242 f.]. In any case, the discovery of the planet Pluto by Clyde Tombaugh in 1930 added another heavenly body for which ephemerides along with astrological interpretations of its influence were soon produced [6. 244 f.]. While the new planet's name selected by astronomers was admittedly mythological, it also immortalized–through the abbreviation PL–its intellectual discoverer Percival Lowell who had long dedicated himself to the calculation of the new planet [20. 24]. Considered from a historian's perspective, astrology fell prey to what art scholar Aby Warburg termed "simple name fetishism": Pluto stood for the hidden, destructive powers that were claimed to have resulted in the 'Third Reich' and in the atomic bomb during the Second World War. From the perspective of astrologers, however, for whom such occurrences are no coincidence, there exists a connection between the discovery, the names and the effects of new planets

The discovery of the asteroid Chiron (1977) gave rise to the publication of a large number of essays, books and ephemerides. With the alleged discovery of the 'Dark Moon', also called 'Lilith', in 1897, earth was supposed to gain an additional satellite–a hypothesis discussed by the English astrologer Sepharial (Walter Richard (Gorn) Old, 1864–1929). However, current astrology regards 'Lilith' as a geometric point (the second focal point of the ellipse of the moon).

A further trend that sharply contrasts with classic astrological thought such as aspect theory is cosmobiology founded by Reinhold Ebertin (1901–1988). While this trend rejects Transneptunian planets, it does employ the 'half-distance points' (mid-point on the ecliptic between the positions of two planets or between planet and ascendant or heavenly median) in the interpretation of horoscopes which were used also by the 'Hamburg School'. Statistical methods to verify astrology were first applied by the French artillery officer Paul Choisnard (1867–1930). Extensive investigations of this type were also conducted by the French psychologist Michel Gauquelin (1928–1991) and his wife Françoise who looked for correlations between professions and planets in various positions in the sky [1. 236–238] and raised the hypothesis that parents pass certain planetary positions on to their children – given a normal birth process [4; 5].

Due to the great diversity of approaches, it is impossible to characterize current astrology in any uniform manner. Four trends can roughly be distinguished (with many overlapping areas): 1. horoscope interpretation and prediction of the future according to traditional techniques (this term can be understood in many different ways but it essentially includes Hellenistic doctrines and their continuation into the Renaissance); 2. psychologically oriented astrology that refrains from predictions and regards horoscopes more as a form of meditation and a vehicle of psychoanalysis or psychotherapy; 3. esoteric astrology interwoven with religious, mythological and philosophical thoughts of most varied provenance; 4. hour astrology, i.e. the production of horoscopes for special times and events. Astrometeorology and astrological medicine, practiced into the 17th cent., play only a marginal role today.

Despite all 20th cent. innovations in astrology, the classic models continue to be revered. A group of American astrologers has been working for several years on translating and commenting the entire corpus of Latin, Greek, Arabic, Hebrew and Sanskrit sources and has already produced numerous texts. The core idea of this venture, termed 'Project Hindsight', is the notion that the 'pure source' of astrological wisdom, if not submerged, has at least been misinterpreted or completely misunderstood. This return *ad fontes* is close to the efforts of Humanist authors of the 16th cent. with astrological inclinations, and many astrologers regard the reconstruction and practical application of Hellenistic interpretations and prediction techniques as a genuine improvement of the theory.

Astrology has always experienced a boom during periods of radical change and crisis. The present revival is based, for one thing, on the need for meaningful order in the world, a need that is obviously not satisfied by political ideologies or by the traditional religious communities and that is often connected to a critical attitude towards the mechanistic world view shaped by science. For another thing, astrology may promise some sense of direction in an age that is centred around the personal development of the individual. In spite of all efforts to substantiate astrology scientifically, to verify it statistically or to expand it through psychology, its real attraction has always been the idea of the cosmos in the ancient Greek sense, a cosmos in which man is part of a larger order.

→ Astrology

1 K. Brandler-Pracht, Mathematisch-instruktives Lehrbuch der Astrologie, 1905,³⁻⁵1921   2 A. Fankhauser, Das wahre Gesicht der Astrologie, 1932   3 Id., Horoskopie, 1939   4 M. Gauquelin, Les hommes et les astres, 1960 (English in: Written in the Stars, 1988)   5 Id., L'Heredité Planetaire, 1966 (Planetary Heredity, 1988)   6 J. H. Holden, A History of Horoscopic Astrology from the Babylonian Period to the Modern Age, 1996   7 R. W. Holden, The Elements of House Division, 1977   8 E. Howe, Uranias Kinder: Die seltsame Welt der Astrologen und das Dritte Reich, 1995 (Astrology and the Third Reich, 1984)   9 W. Hübner, Antike in der Astrologie der Gegenwart, in: W. Ludwig (ed.), Die Antike in der europäischen Gegenwart (= Veröffentlichung der Joachim-Jungius-Gesellschaft Hamburg, 72), 1993, 103–124   10 H. Frhr. v. Klöckler, Grundlagen für die astrologische Deutung, 1926   11 Id., Astrologie als Erfahrungswissenschaft, 1927   12 W. Knappich, Entwicklung der Horoskop-Technik vom Altertum bis zur Gegenwart (= Qualität der Zeit: Tradition und Fortschritt der klassischen Astrologie, Nr. 38/39), 1978   13 Id., Geschichte

der Astrologie, ²1988   14 Id., Das Häuserproblem in England, in: Zenit: Zentralblatt für astrologische Forsch. 7, 1936, 19–22, 42–46   15 Id., Die Astrologie im Weltbild der Gegenwart: Eine kritische Untersuchung, 1948   16 H. Korsch, Geschichte der Astrologie, 1935   17 F. Riemann, Psychoanalyse und Astrologie, 1972   18 Id., Lebenshilfe Astrologie, 1976   19 Th. Ring, Astrologische Menschenkunde, 1956–1969   20 D. Wattenberg, Die Namen der Planeten und ihrer Satelliten (= Archenhold-Sternwarte Berlin-Treptow: Vorträge und Schriften, Nr. 18), 1964.

Additional Bibliography T. Barton, Power and Knowledge: Astrology, Physiognomics, and Medicine under the Roman Empire, 2002; W. Newman, A. Granton, Secrets of Nature: Astrology and Alchemy in Early Modern Europe, 2001; S. Tester, A History of Western Astrology, 1987, 1996. ; P. Whitfield, Astrology: A History, 2001
GÜNTHER OESTMANN

Hospital. In Late Antiquity, a hospital was a place within an environment of religious character, where one cared for people in need including old and sick ones. In the early MA, along the great routes of pilgrimage, chains of small inns developed. Many Benedictine monasteries had their own hospital wards, which may also have catered for the needs of a large part of the public. As of the 11th cent., hospitals were constructed in cities, again under the influence of eastern Mediterranean culture – but without a connection to religious institutions. Most of these buildings were small – most rarely had more than 20 beds – and only a few could offer medical services themselves. But in the larger cities of northern Italy, such as in Florence, Sienna and Milan, as well as later in Paris, large hospitals were erected using the models of Constantinople or Jerusalem, which could serve as a central port of call for a health service provided to the entire population of a city [3]. The modern hospital developed from such institutions, but in the 20th cent., especially regarding the treatment of older patients or the dying, thinking returned to the older model of small 'hospices'.

In the larger cities of the Byzantine Empire, hospitals could reach an enormous size and offer a full range of medical services. In 550 AD, the hospital of St. Sabas in Jerusalem had more than 200 beds, that of St. Samson in Constantinople nearly twice as many. Signs of an increasing specialisation also start to appear: in hospitals in Antioch and Constantinople, women's and men's wards were separated; around 650 AD at St. Samson's in Constantinople, there was a special ward for eye diseases and probably a further one for surgical cases [6; 8; 5]. The foundation charter of the Pantocrator Hospital (1087) reflects a complex organisational structure, with a whole range of special wards and health care personnel being on duty around the clock in order to care for a maximum of 55 patients; to what extent this charter was actually implemented in practice, is debatable [6; 2; 4]. Similar hospitals of the same general size were founded by Muslims since the 7th cent. They were meant to overshadow the then smaller Christian hospitals in the Near East, if not replace them completely, and to be advanced to the centre of medical activities, the training of doctors and medical specialisation within an urban community [1]. With the support of religious endowments, such medical centres survived up to the present day in cities such as Damascus, Cairo and Baghdad. The encounters with hospitals of the Near East – be it with those in Constantinople or others in the Arab world, is debatable [7] – gave the impetus for founding the hospitaler orders during the crusades and explains the growing spread of hospitals in medieval western Europe.

→ Hospital

1 M. W. DOLS, The Origin of the Islamic Hospital. Myth and Reality, in: BHM 61, 1987, 367–390 2 P. GAUTIER, Le Typikon du Christ Sauveur Pantocrator, in: REByz 32, 1974, 1–145 3 D. JETTER, Geschichte des Hospitals, vol. 1, 1966 4 E. KISLINGER, Der Pantokrator-Xenon, ein trügerisches Ideal, in: Jb. des österreichischen byz. Instituts 37, 1987, 173–186 5 Id., Xenon und Nosokomeion – Hospitäler in Byzanz, in: Historia Hospitalum, 1986–1988, 1–10 6 T. S. MILLER, The Birth of the Hospital in the Byzantine Empire, ²1997 7 Id., The Knights of Saint John and the Hospitals of the Latin West, in: Speculum 53, 1978, 709–733 8 Id., The Sampson Hospital of Constantinople, in: ByzF 15, 1990, 101–135. VIVIAN NUTTON

Human Rights

A. CLARIFICATION OF TERM B. THE QUESTION OF THE ORIGINS OF HUMAN RIGHTS IN SCHOLARSHIP C. SCHOLARLY EVIDENCE OF THE ROOTS OF HUMAN RIGHTS IN ANTIQUITY D. ANCIENT RECEPTION IN THE PREHISTORY OF HUMAN RIGHTS E. ANCIENT RECEPTION IN THE CONTEXT OF THE AMERICAN DECLARATION OF RIGHTS F. ANCIENT RECEPTION IN THE CONTEXT OF THE FRENCH DECLARATION OF HUMAN AND CITIZEN'S RIGHTS

A. CLARIFICATION OF TERM

Since the great human rights (HR) declarations of the 18th cent., HR have been understood to mean those individual legal claims to protection of basic freedoms and necessities of life that everyone is entitled to by virtue of one's humanity. By their focus on individual human beings, HR extend to all humans equally, and thus universally (cf. Art. 2, UN Declaration of Human Rights of 1948). Linked to the idea of HR as innate, inalienable and irrevocable natural rights of humankind is a further claim to their having a pre- and suprastatal validity: guaranteeing HR should thus be a normative measure, from which the law and the state draw their own legitimacy. Even if a claim for substantiation of HR based on a philosophical-natural law and transcending positive law is endorsed, HR only achieve their full potential as basic laws when they are institutionally or constitutionally guaranteed and legally enforceable.

B. THE QUESTION OF THE ORIGINS OF HUMAN RIGHTS IN SCHOLARSHIP

If one were to search for evidence of an ancient reception of the history of HR thinking and its realization, one would first have to address the question whether there is any evidence of HR in Antiquity. Scholars have adopted various points of view on this issue. Some Classical scholars favour the theory that, depending on the issue in question, HR or basic rights can be demonstrated in Antiquity, e.g. in terms of the history of ideas [8] or even of legal practice [21; 20]. This stands in stark contrast with the *o pinio communis* of historical and legal historical researchers into the HR declarations of the 18th cent. and their prehistory. There is general agreement here that HR should be seen as a product of the revolutionary upheavals of the modern period. For their prehistory, any roots going back to antiquity are at best evidenced in the context of the history of ideas, while the political prehistory only begins, in the most extreme scenario, with the corporative attestations of freedoms and the contracts of rule from the Middle Ages (*Magna Charta* of 1215 and *Joyeuse Entrée* of Brabant of 1356) and the Early Modern Period (Tübingen Agreement of 1514) [16; 7]. These demonstrate a tradition, important for the later Middle Ages, of legal restrictions on power, as well as the "written recording and cataloguing of basic rights" [7. 242]. This is probably particularly true of the Anglo-Saxon legal tradition, in which, through the early reduction of corporative privileges, a universalization may conditionally be said to have taken place with rights and freedoms originally thought of as corporative [14]. Even in continental European legal history, the view has recently been espoused that, in institutions providing for individual protection, for 'basic economic necessities' or in the early domestic forms of religious freedom, there developed, even in ancient social orders based on privilege, "a zone of quasi-individual entitlements, which went beyond corporative freedom of action, heading in the direction of human rights freedoms" [7. 243].

Regarding the evolution of HR thinking, the influence of natural law teaching from the 16th to the 18th cent., as well as the political philosophy and propagation of the Enlightenment (Salamanca School, Hugo Grotius, the so-called Prussian natural law from Samuel Pufendorf to Christian Wolff, John Locke), has been thoroughly researched and validated [4; 5]. That the evolution of HR thinking had drawn on ancient, principally Stoic philosophy and elements of the Christian tradition has been especially highlighted in the dated, but still authoritative general account by Gerhard Oestreich [16. 14] and has meanwhile become almost established as a commonplace in specialised literature. Nevertheless, evidence for this thesis, in the form of a systematic review of concrete traces of reception, is still largely lacking. Consequently, it is appropriate to discuss the most important items of evidence that have been cited in scholarly research for the existence of HR in Antiquity and their later reception.

C. Scholarly Evidence of the Roots of Human Rights in Antiquity

Even if infrequent, the use of terms like *ius hominum* or *ius humanum* is cited to illustrate the place of Antiquity in the conceptual evolution [20. 1258]. The problem with such allusions lies in the fact that these phrases mostly stand in conceptual opposition to natural or divine law and refer to human statute (e.g. Cic. Off. 1, 26). In other sources often cited as evidence (Cic. Tusc. 1, 64, 2: 'ius hominum, quod situm est in genere humani societate'; Sen. benef. 3, 18, 2), it is still questionable whether the term *ius* is intended to cover the aspect, central to HR, of subjective law rather than its objective-legal meaning in the sense of *lex* (the latter unambiguous in Gai. Inst. 1, 2, 1: 'communi omnium hominum iure'). Even reference to Tertullian's expression, coming closest to the modern concept of HR (ad Scapulam 2, 2: 'humani iuris et naturalis potestatis est unicuique, quod putaverit, colere') cannot by itself suffice to demonstrate the presence of HR thinking in Antiquity. Therefore, it is not without reason that it is ignored in relevant conceptual research of Antiquity [13]. These items of evidence point instead to the phrase 'rights of mankind/humanity' (or their equivalents in other languages) not becoming a key concept of political-philosophical discourse until the 18th cent. By contrast, broader conceptual research into the genealogy of HR comes up with terms like *ius naturale, potestas* or *facultas moralis, ius connatum, natural rights, droits naturels*, which have been shown to have had the meaning of natural rights from no earlier than the Middle Ages [22; 11].

When, in terms of HR, scholarly literature talks of parallels. correspondences, traces or roots in Antiquity, this generally refers to the concrete substance of rights in actual legal practice, as distinct from claims justified in terms of natural law and the universal applicability of HR [21; 20]. Or else the focus is on ethical, anthropological or philosophical-legal reflections in philosophical [8] or pagan and Christian literature [19]. A framework for such questions – especially if non-European societies of Antiquity are included – is offered by the *Revue internationale des droits de l'antiquité* (RIDA) der *Société internationale Fernand de Visscher pour l'histoire des droits de l'antiquité* (SIHDA), which recently devoted its 50th session (Brussesl 16.–19.9.1996) specifically to the subject of 'Le monde antique et les droits de l'homme' [12].

As far as the significance of Antiquity and its reception for the later development of HR is concerned, Hubert Cancik has in the end gained acceptance for the view that too little attention has been paid so far to the ancient roots of modern thinking on HR [8]. He has rightly pointed out that central concepts and lines of argument in modern discussion on HR, such as the recourse to "Nature" and "natural law", "natural state" or "social contract", are encountered in Antiquity [8. 312]. Whether we can then go so far as to assume the direct influence of Classical natural law or

of Stoic anthropology for particular phrases in the French declaration of HR [8. ibid.], however, seems open to question.

However justified it may be to dismiss the bald assertion that HR thinking has its origin in Christianity alone, it is no more valid to derive the entire substance of modern HR thinking solely from ancient pagan roots. It is also not a matter of denying Christianity any importance in the history of HR. A suitably differential evaluation in this context would have to take into account that, as Hans Meier tellingly phrased it, HR 'ebenso im Bund mit christlichen Überlieferungen wie im Widerspruch gegen konkrete zeitgeschichtliche Ausprägungen des Christentums erkämpft worden sind' ("have been fought for as much in concert with Christian traditions as in opposition to concrete contemporary characteristics of Christianity") [15. 48 f.].

D. Ancient Reception in the Prehistory of Human Rights

It should not be overlooked that key points of the declaration of rights of individual American states, such as Massachusetts and Virginia, for example, and of the *Declaration of Independence* (1776) and the *Déclaration des droits de l'homme et du citoyen* (1789) draw on natural law as part of their justifying argument. However, even if natural law has its roots in Cicero and the Stoa, the HR claims of American and French revolutionaries were linked to contemporary teachings of natural law. These were based on the tradition of modern Protestant natural law, as established by Hugo Grotius in the 17th cent., disseminated throughout Europe principally by the works of Samuel Pufendorf and radicalised by Enlightenment thinkers like John Locke, Jean-Jacques Rousseau or Immanuel Kant in moving towards the notion of the inalienability of personal as well as political freedom. That this modern natural law itself drew impetus, in turn, from Antiquity is indisputable. Thus, for example, neo-Epicurean influences took effect in the natural law of Thomas Hobbes or John Locke, probably imparted through Pierre Gassendi's circle, while the natural law teachings of Grotius (concept of self-preservation, *appetitus societatis*) and Pufendorf (teaching of *socialitas*) display distinct influences of the Stoa, in particular its *oikeiosis* teaching. Though here the HR question at issue, namely the human being as an individual enjoying subjective natural laws, does not seem to have its roots in Antiquity. The advocates of 'secular' natural law derived it from the Christian-scholastic natural law of the Middle Ages, from which they were more sharply independent than may superficially seem to be the case in the light of the polemic on 'Aristotelian-Scholastic dogmatism'. Natural laws can be found in a distinctly developed form even in Spanish late Scholastics like Francisco Suarez (*De legibus ac Deo legislatore*, 1612), Fernando Vasquez y Menchaca (*Controversiae illustres*, praef., 1559), Bartolomé de las Casas or Francisco de Vitoria (*Relectio de Indis*, 1539), but also in even earlier Scholastic philosophers like Jean Gerson and William of Ockham [22]. Moreover, the medievalist Brian Tierney advanced the theory that the early scholastic theories of natural laws were themselves influenced by the decretists of the 12th and 13th cents., who, he argued, had conceived the concept of subjective law when glossing the *Decretum Gratiani*. Tierney attaches particular importance to the decretists. Should it in the meantime be proven, and there are indications that this may be the case [9], that the same process took place in the preparation of commentaries on the *Corpus iuris civilis* by the legists, that could in itself be seen as evidence of a contribution from ancient reception, albeit extremely indirect, to the development of HR.

E. ANCIENT RECEPTION IN THE CONTEXT OF THE AMERICAN DECLARATION OF RIGHTS

Scholarly research has not thus far evinced any direct and defining influence that the reception of ancient traditions may have exercised on the great declarations of HR of the 18th cent.: the declarations of rights by individual American states, the *Declaration of Independence* and the *Déclaration des droits de l'homme et du citoyen*. Certainly, Classical authors were a staple fare in the education of the intellectual elite among American colonists, and references to Antiquity abound in the writings of leading revolutionaries, as in the pamphlet literature of the revolutionary period in general, even if they may have served purely rhetorical-illustrative purposes [3. 26; 18]. Moreover, there is evidence of the decisive influence of 'Classical republicanism' on the Founding Fathers' constitutional debate [3; 18]. The *spiritus rector* of the Declaration of Independence, Thomas Jefferson, was undoubtedly influenced by ancient thinkers. Thus, he once described himself as an 'Epicurean' (Letter to William Short of 31. 10. 1819) [2. 1430]. On another occasion, he cited as the 'elementary books of public right' that he regarded as significant for the the Declaration of Independence the works of Aristotle and Cicero, as well as those of Locke and Algernon Sidney (Letter to Henry Lee of 8. 5. 1825) [2. 1501]. Nevertheless, the characteristic appeal, in the American Declaration of Independence and the Declaration of Rights of many individual American states, like the *Virginia Declaration of Rights*, to the individual's 'unalienable and inherent rights' did not derive from the ancient authors who were otherwise important for the natural law thinking of American revolutionaries. Its sources are to be found elsewhere. The historiography of the American *Bill of Rights* points to the influence of the English legal tradition and the awareness of the colonists to be claiming for themselves the 'Rights of an Englishman'. In contrast to the English influences, the first step towards a constitution based on individual rights evolving from the *Common Law* can be discerned, even in the early colonial period, in the charters and basic laws of individual colonies (New Plymouth, West New Jersey). On top of that is the overwhelming influence of European natural law that, at the moment of separation from the motherland, was elevated to being the decisive basis for legitimizing these rights. As far as the rights of the individual are concerned, the 'common sense' that the the the leading protagonists of the American Revolution repeatedly invoked, showed the influence of Blackstone's *Commentaries on the Law of England* and the natural law teachings of Jean-Jacques Burlamaqui, Emer de Vattel, Pufendorf and Grotius, together with Locke, whose influence in this respect cannot be overestimated. Although the colonists were familiar with the thoughts of these authors right from their schooldays, natural law was part of the curriculum of American colleges, whether for private reading or in the form of explanatory textbooks [11. 323 ff.]. Also, the Founding Fathers' esteem for these authors is explicitly attested. Thus, for example, James Otis consistently quoted John Locke as an authority in matters of natural law, while Alexander Hamilton described the works of Grotius, Pufendorf, Locke, Montesquieu and Burlamaqui as required reading [23. 79].

F. ANCIENT RECEPTION IN THE CONTEXT OF THE FRENCH DECLARATION OF HUMAN AND CITIZEN'S RIGHTS

As in America, Roman Classical authors were a fixed feature in the educational canon of French *collèges* [17. 14 f.]. References to ancient authors can therefore be found in the speeches that were delivered in debates of the constituent national assembly [17. 18 f.]. Ancient orators served as a model at a historical moment when the written word and free speech were gaining an increasingly powerful political significance. The political history of the Roman Republic and its institutions acquired a thematic-conceptual relevance going beyond the rhetorical realm, as the introduction of a republican form of government became the subject of debate. It is nevertheless scarcely surprising that no evidence can be found of Antiquity's placing any comparable value on the discussion of a declaration of HR. Isolated evidence can indeed be found, such as Durand de Maillane's reference in the debate of 1. 8. 1789 [19. 235] to Ulpian's naturalistic definition of natural law (Dig. 1, 1,3), but no decisive influence of ancient thinking on natural law can be deduced from that. Even if Art. 1 of the French declaration of human and citizens' rights asserts that 'les hommes naissent et demeurent libres et égaux en droits', this is only ostensibly in keeping with ancient thinking on natural law. For, on the one hand, Classical natural law did not recognize any innate individual rights, and on the other, at the very point where the idea of original freedom and human equality is articulated, there is lacking among the Roman jurists (Institutiones 1,2,2 and 1,5 praef.; Dig. 50,17,32), that element of their inalienability ('demeurent'; cf. by contrast Dig. 1,5,4) that was so essential for the drafters of the *Déclaration*. The intellectual foundations of the *Déclaration* are, on the contrary, of modern provenance. It (the *Déclaration*)

Fig. 1: Picture of the 'Déclaration' - this one dating
from 1791/92 - with the allegorical figure of France
(top left) together with antiquizing motifs such as
the Phrygian cap and fasces (Musée Carnavalet, Paris)
© *Photothèque des Musées de la Ville de Paris*

Fig. 2: Minerva in charge at the 'Déclaration':
Jean-Baptiste Regnault (1754–1829),
Allégori relative à la Déclaration des droits de
l'homme, 1790 (Musée Lambinet, Versailles)

reflects English constitutional thinking, as transmitted,
among others, by Montesquieu and Voltaire, modern
natural law and the political and philosophical attitudes of the encyclopedists and physiocrats, as well as,
ultimately, the concrete model of the American Declaration of Rights [19].

The *Déclaration* itself does not explicitly situate
itself in any intellectual evolutionary tradition – not
even that of Antiquity. Contemporary political iconography, however, is another matter. It abounds in Classical allusions. Motifs from Antiquity have found their
way into the representations of the *Déclaration*. These
are sometimes depicted in the shape of stone tablets of
law, adorned with, among other things, *fasces* and
Phrygian cap (fig. 1). The motifs with an ancient flavour
are here scarcely more than decorative accretions. In
one painting by Jean-Baptiste Regnault, however, it is
Minerva, the goddess of wisdom who is represented as
being the author of the declaration on HR (fig. 2). Insofar as Antiquity in the contemporary milieu of the
French Revolution become the focus of historical considerations on HR, as in Sylvain Maréchal (*Déclaration
des droits de l'homme et du citoyen décrétée par l'As-
semblée nationale, comparée avec les lois des peuples
anciens et modernes et principalement avec les décla-
rations des États-Unis d'Amérique*, 1791) and Marie
Jean Antoine Nicolas de Condorcet (*Esquisse d'un
tableau historique des progrès de l'esprit humain*,
1794), it is thoroughly incorporated in these representations of human history – in the case of Maréchal in an
idealizing manner [10. 57] – into the prehistory of HR.
If in Condorcet it is not accorded the status of an ideal
model, this comes about not just because of his paradigm of progress as the basis for his blueprint of history
but also because of his awareness of the limits, for
example, of freedom and equality in Attic democracy.
Thus, he points out that these were entitlements of only
a small proportion of the actual population and that
neither reason nor 'les droits que tous les hommes ont
également réçus de la nature' had been the foundation
on which the legislators based their laws [1. 114–120].
→ Human rights; → Human dignity

SOURCES 1 A. DE CONDORCET, Esquisse d'un tableau
historique des progrès de l'esprit humain (1794)/Entwurf
einer historischen Darstellung der Fortschritte des
menschlichen Geistes, W. ALFF (ed.), 1963   2 TH. JEF-
FERSON, Writings, M. D. PETERSON (ed.), 1984
LITERATURE 3 B. BAILYN, The Ideological Origins of the
American Revolution, 1967   3a R. A. BAUMAN, Human
Rights in Ancient Rome, 2000   4 G. BIRTSCH (ed.),
Grund- und Freiheitsrechte im Wandel von Gesellschaft
und Geschichte, 1981   5 Id. (ed.), Grund- und Freiheitsrechte von der ständischen zur spätbürgerlichen Gesell-
schaft, 1987   6 Id., M. TRAUTH, I. MEENKEN (eds.),
Grundfreiheiten, Menschenrechte 1500–1850. Eine inter-

nationale Bibliographie, 5 vols., 1992   7 Id., s.v. Rechte des Menschen, Menschenrechte, in: Historisches Wörterbuch der Philosophie, J. RITTER (ed.), vol. 8, 1992, 241–251   8 H. CANCIK, Gleichheit und Freiheit, Die antiken Grundlagen der Menschenrechte, in: Id., Antik – Modern, Beiträge zur römischen und deutschen Kulturgeschichte, 1998   9 H. COING, Zur Geschichte des Begriffs subjektives Recht (1958), in: Id., Zur Geschichte des Privatrechtssystems, 1962   10 M. GAUCHET, La Révolution des droits de l'homme, 1989   11 K. HAAKONSSEN, Natural Law and Moral Philosophy. From Grotius to the Scottish Enlightenment, 1996   12 H. JONES (ed.), Le monde antique et les droits de l'homme, 1998   13 G. KLEINHEYER, s.v. Grundrechte, in: Geschichtliche Grundbegriffe. Historisches Lexikon zur politisch-sozialen Sprache in Deutschland, O. BRUNNER, W. CONZE, R. KOSELLECK (eds.), vol. 2, 1975, 1047–1082   14 M. KRIELE, Zur Geschichte der Grund- und Menschenrechte, in: Öffentliches Recht und Politik, Festschrift for H. U. Scupin, N. ACHTERBERG (ed.), 1973, 187–211   15 H. MAIER, Überlegungen zu einer Geschichte der Menschenrechte, in: Wege und Verfahren des Verfassungslebens, Festschrift for Peter Lerche zum 65. Geburtstag, P. BADURA, R. SCHOLZ (eds.), 1993, 43–50   16 G. OESTREICH, Geschichte der Menschenrechte und Grundfreiheiten im Umriss, ²1978 (1966)   17 H. T. PARKER, The Cult of Antiquity and the French Revolutionaries, 1937   18 C. J. RICHARD, The Founders and the Classics. Greece, Rome, and the American Enlightenment, 1994   19 S.-J. SAMWER, Die französische Erklärung der Menschenrechte von 1789/91, 1970   20 P. SIEWERT, s.v. Menschenrechte, in: Der Neue Pauly, vol. 7, 1999, cols. 1258–1260 (Engl.: Brill's New Pauly, vol. 6, 2005, cols. 563–565)   21 G. TÉNÉKIDÈS, La cité d'Athènes et les droits de l'homme, in: F. MATSCHER, H. PETZOLD (eds.), Protecting Human Rights. The European Dimension, 1988, 605–37   22 B. TIERNEY, The Idea of Natural Rights, Studies on Natural Rights, Natural Law, and Church Law, 1150–1625, 1997   23 M. WHITE, The Philosophy of the American Revolution, 1978   24 S. F. WILTSHIRE, Greece, Rome and the Bill of Rights, 1992   TIM SCHWARZ, STEFAN KAMMASCH

Humanism
I. RENAISSANCE   II. LAW   III. MEDICAL
IV. MUSIC

I. RENAISSANCE
A. DEFINITION   B. 14TH CENTURY
C. 15TH CENTURY   D. 16TH CENTURY

A. DEFINITION
Renaissance Humanism (RH) is understood as a literary and philological movement which first established itself with Petrarch in the courts and city oligarchies of Italy (and to a lesser extent in the universities). Its objective was to imitate and restore Classical Latin (essentially Cicero's for prose and Vergil's for metric texts), in view of a newly arisen, non-clerical, urban bourgeois educated class for both production and reception. In its focus on and, in part, rediscovery of the rhetorical doctrine of Antiquity and Sophism, RH is at the same time the continuation of the *ars dictaminis* of the 13th cent.

and relates to the same social classes: notaries, secretaries of princes and cities, teachers in the schools and sometimes universities, and, from the end of the 15th cent. on, increasingly to the nobility and merchants. The Humanistic 'Wiederbelebung des classischen Alterthums' ('Revival of Classical Antiquity'; G. Voigt 1859) presupposes the awareness that Antiquity and its academic and political institutions are past and not immediately capable of being continued. Therefore, the reorientation to the *usus* or the *consuetudo* of the *aurea latinitas* means an epochal break with both the tradition of medieval scholastic Latin and with the vernacular languages and literatures. In contrast to the latter, Humanistic Latin remained a purely male language. From the middle of the 16th cent. on, Latin lost its exclusive position of authority, and Greek and Hebrew gained in importance. Not least, the vernacular languages benefited from this through the transmission of the Latin norms which had since been adopted by them; the result was the so-called vernacular Humanism (*umanesimo volgare*). In the same period and in the wake of the same development, Humanism radiated outward from Italy to other European countries, and non-Italians (such as Erasmus) were even able to take a leading role. In general, RH can be limited to the period between ca. 1350–1520.

The term 'Humanist' (like 'Renaissance') is a modern invention. The expression *studia humanitatis* had been current since Petrarch and especially since Leonardo Bruni, and comprises the subjects of the *trivium*. The word *humanista* (in analogy to *jurista, canonista, legista* etc.) first appeared in student jargon at the end of the 15th cent., and entered official university language in the following century to designate teachers of Greek and Latin. The word 'Humanism' is even more recent, being used for the first time in 1808 by the Jena professor Friedrich Immanuel Niethammer in a defence of Classical philology.

B. 14TH CENTURY
1. PRE-HUMANISM   2. PETRARCH AND BOCCACCIO

1. PRE-HUMANISM
In the *Commedia*, Dante presents himself still as the direct successor to Vergil and uses the legal language of the *dictatores* in his Latin writings. Politically, he assumes the continued existence of the Empire (*De Monarchia*); linguistically, the perpetuity and incorruptibility of Latin under the name *grammatica* (*De vulgari eloquentia*). His poetological terminology is not Classical (*Epist. a Candgrande*). The *Commedia* is not written for the Latin *litterati*, whom Dante accuses of not being interested in literature, but rather for the 'volgari e non letterati' (Il Convivio 1,9,2–4), that is, for the urban bourgeoisie of the higher guilds without a university education, the *popolo grasso*. Although Dante – in contrast to the vernacular tradition of the Middle Ages – clearly conceived his lyric poetry and the *Commedia* as written texts (cf. e.g. the acrostics in Purg. 12,25–72

and Par. 19,115–141), he nevertheless took their oral transmission into account (in Purg. 2,112, Dante's canzone *Amor che ne la mente mi ragiona* is sung), and he guards against interpolations by the use of *terza rima*. For these reasons, Dante, who is granted a special position, is not considered a pre-Humanist; however, his Latin-speaking opponents are. Giovanni del Virgilio, who read Ovid at the University of Bologna, reproached Dante in an eclogue of 1318/19 with betraying philosophical knowledge to the *gens idiota*: 'Clarus vulgaria temnit' (1,15). Dante did not respond. Besides Bologna, the starting point of the *ars dictaminis*, Padua was a centre of Pre-Humanism in Dante's time. Following the model of Lovato de' Lovati (1262–1309), Albertino Mussato (1262–1329) there, in 18 verse epistles, defended the study of the Latin poets against philosophical and theological criticism, thus anticipating a subject which would enjoy extraordinary popularity after Petrarch. He used Livy as a model in his historical work (*De gestis Italicorum post mortem Henrici VII*) and Seneca in his (rather macabre) scholastic tragedy *Ecerinus*. Both Lovati and Mussato had enjoyed an education in the legal faculty, where, unlike in the medical faculty, the *ars dictaminis* had established itself. In 1315, Mussato was crowned poet in Padua following the ancient model.

2. Petrarch and Boccaccio

However, RH in the narrower sense only begins with Petrarch (1304–74); G. Voigt's work *Die Wiederbelebung des classischen Alterthums oder das erste Jahrhundert des Humanismus* ('The Revival of Classical Antiquity, or the First Century of Humanism', 1859) also started with him. No longer was it only characterized by the return to a lost *aetas aurea*, but also by critical distancing from contemporary cultural, political and religious conditions. Independent of Petrarch's chiliastic tendencies, in his epistle to Cola di Rienzo from 1347 [13.73–81] (Epist. fam. ed. Rossi, 103),– too strongly emphasized by K. Burdach– a coincidence can be found in his work between the *renascentia studiorum*, the return to Classical Latin, and attempts at restoring the Empire, which had ensured cultural flourishing and should do so again. After the political hopes placed on Cola quickly collapsed, Petrarch spoke out more and more in polemical works against the Aristotelian establishment of the *scholae*, against the *logici recentiores*, i.e. *britanni*, who based their instruction on unreliable and thus incomprehensible texts, and even produced a corrupt Latin themselves. The attacks focused primarily on the Aristotelian-oriented medical faculties, which had also incorporated rhetoric as a component of the affect theory (*Invectiva contra medicum quendam, Invectiva contra quendam magni status hominem sed nullius scientie et virtutis*, 1355). This polemic is most radical in the explicitly anti-Averroistic, but implicitly anti-Aristotelian invective *De sui ipsius et multorum ignorantia* (1367–1371). This polemic comes down to a fundamental incompatibility of pagan, ancient philosophy and Christianity, which is better argued based on the methods of rhetorical argumentation and the *sensus communis*. In a passage in his *Rerum memorandarum libri* (following the model of Valerius Maximus' *Factorum et dictorum memorabilium libri*, which was widely known in the Middle Ages), Petrarch presents his own work as the last bastion of *civilitas* in the *aetas tenebrarum* [43. 19]. Petrarch owned the most comprehensive private library of his age, consisting exclusively of Latin Classics and the Church Fathers (apart from a copy of the *Commedia* which Boccaccio had had produced for him in 1351), and which he was able to enrich with his own finds. Among the most important were Cicero's oration *Pro Archia poeta* (1333), which would become significant for Humanistic poetry, and the Ciceronian *Epistulae ad familiares* (1350), which he imitated in the 350 pieces of his *Rerum familiarum libri*. The most famous of these letters (4.1, from 1351 or 1352) describes his ascent of Mont Ventoux near Avignon and ends in a thoroughly traditional reflection on *vanitas mundi* with reference to Augustine's *Confessiones*: 'Et eunt homines admirari alta montium et ingentes fluctus maris et latissimos lapsus fluminum et oceani ambitum et giros siderum, et relinquunt se ipsos'("men go to marvel at the summits of mountains and mighty waves of the sea, the broadest flows of rivers and the circuit of the ocean and the motions of the stars, and they forsake themselves"). Greek literature did not play a role for Petrarch. Thus, he was not in a position to read Homer in the original. Rather, he had a Latin version of the *Iliad* and parts of the *Odyssey* produced by Leonzio Pilato in 1366, thanks to the mediation of Boccaccio. In any case, the search for transmitted codices of ancient texts, which is characteristic of Humanism, began with Petrarch; in the 15th cent., Poggio Bracciolini would become the unsurpassed master of this search.

Petrarch's younger contemporary and admirer Giovanni Boccaccio (1313–1375) was just as avid in the rediscovery of Classical texts. While Petrarch was a cleric, though he never assumed an ecclesiastical office, RH now crossed over into the urban bourgeois circles. During his stay in Naples (1327–1340), Boccaccio was able to access the library of Montecassino, where he discovered, among other things, the complete Ausonius, *De lingua latina* of Varro, the Statius commentary of Placidus, *Ibis* by Ovid, a collection of 80 *priapea* and the possibly complete corpus of the Ciceronian *Verrinae*. His most significant find was probably the historical works of Tacitus, which formed the textual basis of Tacitism in the second half of the 16th cent. Like Petrarch, Boccaccio also used late ancient and early medieval sources on an equal footing (e.g. Paulus Diaconus) and did not limit himself to the Augustan *aurea latinitas*. Boccaccio's poetic production in Latin is, on the other hand, very limited (*Bucolicum carmen*, 1367). However, his encyclopaedic works are that much more comprehensive: *De casibus virorum illustrium* (1373) with the corresponding *De mulieribus claris* (1362), *De montibus, silvis, fontibus* etc. (1355–1374) and above all the *Genealogia deorum gentilium* (1350–1375) in 14 books, the final two of which are dedicated to the defence of poetry. There, Boccaccio invokes the Platonic *furor*, but does not draw on Plato himself, but rather Cicero's *Pro Archia*. All of these works are in the tradition of medieval encyclopaedism, but strive for a (partly effected) standard Latin. Unlike Petrarch, Boccaccio was tied strongly enough to the Florentine tradition to have to deal with the city's vernacular tradition. He rose to Dante's defence both in Latin (*De origine, vita, studiis et moribus viri clarissimi Dantis Aligerii florentini*, 1351–1355) and in the vernacular (*Esposizioni sopra la Comedia*, 1374). Here poetry derives its claim to leadership among the disciplines in that it communicated not only *eloquentia*, but also *doctrina* and, if possible, *sapientia* and was capable of the highest rhetorical virtue of *movere*. As in the final books of the *Genealogia deorum*, that Ciceronian identity of rhetoric and philosophy, which would become central for the Humanism of the following century, again makes itself known. At the same time, doubts begin to appear in Boccaccio about Dante's decision to use the vernacular, doubts which were to increase decidedly in the following generation. The legend of an originally Latin version of the *Commedia* goes back to the observations of Boccaccio. Due to these doubts, which likewise affected Boccaccio's own vernacular work, and due to the growing pressure of the Latin elite, he appears to have broken off his public readings of Dante after *Inf.* XVII. From this perspective, Boccaccio's defence of poetic *obscuritas* in *Genealogia deorum* XIV,12, which is meant to serve as protection against incompetent readers, becomes relevant: 'Damnanda non est obscuritas poetarum'. Through his decision to use the vernacular, Dante was guilty of crossing a critical boundary, which the following Humanistic generation no longer understood.

C. 15TH CENTURY
1. THE FLORENTINE CHANCELLORY 2. DIALOGUE LITERATURE 3. RHETORIC 4. HISTORIOGRAPHY 5. LYRIC POETRY

1. THE FLORENTINE CHANCELLORY

With Coluccio Salutati, chancellor of the republic of Florence from 1375 to 1406, and his circle of students, Humanism found its undisputed centre in Florence. The regular Greek lessons by Manuel Chrysoloras, instituted by Salutati in 1396, were a crucial contribution. Petrarch and Boccaccio had been bilingual, inasmuch as they cultivated vernacular literature alongside Latin, albeit on a lower level. Petrarch himself described his *Rerum vulgarium fragmenta*, later called the *Canzoniere*, as 'nugae' ('trifles'). The following centuries confirmed this estimation, for Petrarch's Latin works were, as their edition and translation history clearly show, disproportionately more successful. In Salutati's generation, this diglossia was increasingly replaced by Latin-Greek. The vernacular disappeared almost completely from the Humanist horizon in the 15th cent., surviving in the lower genres such as the burlesque, chivalric epic etc. Salutati's *De laboribus Herculis* takes up the *Genealogia deorum* of his friend and teacher Boccaccio. However, it places the defence of poetry in first place. In his *Invectiva* against the Humanist Antonio Loschi, who was employed in Milan, Salutati introduced the model of the Ciceronian oration, also politically, for the first time in diplomatic correspondence. In his criticism of the contemporary educational system (*De nobilitate legum et medicinae*), he stood on the shoulders of Petrarch, though he spared the polemic against Aristotle, which presaged the attempt by his student Leonardo Bruni to pit a new text of Aristotle against that used in schools.

2. DIALOGUE LITERATURE

In Leonardo Bruni, Salutati's successor as Florentine chancellor (1410/1411, 1427–1444), the full rigour of Humanistic distancing from both vernacular literature and scholastic Latin is revealed. In this respect, his *Ad Petrum Paulum Histrum Dialogus* (1401/1416) represents an important break, when he stages a dispute conducted according to Ciceronian rules *in utramque partem*, thus departing from the Augustinian genre of *soliloquia* (which Petrarch had still cultivated). Bruni placed the introductory praise of the *disputatio* in the mouth of his teacher Salutati, under whose supervision the dialogue takes place: 'Nam quid est (...) quod ad res subtiles cognoscendas atque discutiendas plus valere possit quam disputatio? (...) Quid est quod animum fessum atque labefactum (...) magis reparet (...) quam sermones in corona coetuque agitati, ubi vel gloria, si alios superaveris, vel pudore, si superatus sis, ad legendum atque perdiscendum vehementer incenderis? Quid est quod ingenium magis acuat, (...) quam disputatio? '[18. 46f.]. Here, Bruni assigns the dialogue a threefold function: under the cognitive aspect, it is the only possible guarantee for the completeness and reliability of the statements gained; it serves to incite tired minds through *aemulatio;* and ultimately it hones ingenuity. Subsequently, the speaker Salutati laments at length the decline of culture and the unattainability of the Classical texts; however, he sees the first signs of a rebirth in the poets since Dante. Niccolò Niccoli, who like Bruni belonged to the younger Humanist generation, protests against this opinion. Dante in particular (he said) is unworthy of being called a Humanist and belongs to the horizon of the 'lanarii, pistores atque eiusmodi turba' [22. 70]. In his praise of the three poets, the elderly Salutati referred to the *consensus omnium*, thus expressing his agreement with the society surrounding him. Contrarily, the young Niccoli emphasizes quite decisively the break introduced by the Humanistic elite in the literary tradition of Florence. In the second part of the dialogue, however (*Dialogus II*), Niccoli retracts his attack, declaring that he only wanted to provoke his listeners, especially Salutati, and henceforth places Dante above Homer and Vergil. The dialogue thus contains an irreconcilable ambiguity: the

Niccoli of *Dialogus I* first appears as genuine and the retraction in *Dialogus II* as a fictitious palinode; on the other hand, Niccoli declares that *Dialogus II* reflects his actual opinion and *Dialogus I* is fictitious. Niccoli is thus shown as a rhetor who can speak equally convincingly in accordance with the Ciceronian model *in utramque partem* and whose authentic opinion remains open. With this, the Humanist claims a purely technical, rhetorical competence for himself, which can be wielded against princely patrons. The analogies to Cicero's rhetoric go even further, because the relationship between Salutati and Niccoli reflects that of Crassus and Antonius in *De oratore*. There, Crassus refuses to continue the discussion, which he began himself, on the scholarly status of rhetoric; Crassus does not want to continue *de dicendo dicere* (1,24,112), and Salutati likewise does not want to continue with the *de disputando disputatio* [22. 62]. They leave not only the further development of rhetorical theory to Antonius and Niccoli, respectively, but also demonstrate it in exemplary fashion at the same time. Since Bruni the crucial Ciceronian legacy for Humanism lay in this interlacing of *rhetorica docens* and *rhetorica utens*.

The introduction of the ambivalent dialogue form without a conclusion is, at the same time, an implicit protest against Augustine's subjugation of dispute to the written word in *Contra Academicos*. It became quite popular in Humanism; for the following ca. 150 years, the dialogue remained the leading genre by far, still being used even by such heterodox vernacular Humanist authors as Machiavelli (*Arte della guerra*, 1521). In the generation following Bruni, above all Lorenzo Valla in *De vero falsoque bono* (1441, in the first version *De voluptate*) exploited the paradoxical possibilities of this form most radically. In the first book of the dialogue, Catone Sacco supports the theory of virtues of the Stoa. In the second, and by far the longest book, the poet Maffeo Vegio refutes this opinion, and demonstrates from an Epicurean perspective that even the most rigorous ataraxia aims only for an ultimately earthly *voluptas*. In the third and shortest book, the preacher Antonio da Rho rises to speak, expressly admitting the correctness of the Epicurean refutation of the Stoa; however he refers sensual *voluptas* to celestial bliss. In conclusion, the Christian preacher declares that he allowed the two opponents to speak only to practice their ingenuity. The question of the correct theory of virtue is thus reduced to a mere rhetorical exercise. In any case, the Stoic doctrine is much farther removed from the Christian doctrine than the Epicurean, and even the brief palinode in the third book can only represent a 'salvation clause' to fall back on in the event of ecclesiastic or philosophical attacks. In this dialogue, Valla responds not only, like Bruni, to Augustine's *Contra academicos*, but also to Cicero's *De finibus bonorum et malorum*. There, Cicero began with Epicurean teaching, since it was easiest to understand (1,5,13), in order to then ascend to the Stoic. Valla reverses this order, thus allocating the central and dominant position to Epicurus. Valla is in agreement with Augustine in his attack on the Stoa; however, he refutes the latter's opinion that the search for the *summum bonum* proceeds from worldly to heavenly goods (Conf. 7,17,23). On the contrary, Valla disputes precisely the consistency of the Stoic notions of virtue.

3. RHETORIC

All of these dialogues initially present themselves as rhetorical practice of inventiveness, e.g. *De avaritia*, *De nobilitate* and *De varietate fortunae* by Poggio Bracciolini, *De libero arbitrio* and *De professione religiosorum* by Valla, *I libri della famiglia* (1433–40) by Leon Battista Alberti, the numerous dialogues by Giovanni Pontano (*Charon*, *Antonius*, *Actius*, *Aegidius*, *Asinus*), up to the *Libro del Cortegiano* (1528) by Baldassarre Castiglione. Classical rhetoric, based on an increasingly reliable textual foundation primarily since the rediscovery of Quintilian's *Institutio oratoria* by Poggio Bracciolini (1417), was thus the central discipline of Humanism. The ideal of RH remained the universally employable, perfect orator of the Ciceronian tradition, who was now, however, largely limited to the production of written texts. A clear indication of this revaluation of rhetoric is also Valla's *Elegantiae*, in which, according to a formulation by Carlo Dionisotti, the only elegant feature is the title. In this stylistic handbook overloaded with educational material, the intent of withdrawing the practice of style from the *grammataci* and assigning it to the teachers of rhetoric is continuously apparent. The *praefatio* to book IV notes: 'Ego sic ago, tanquam eloquentiae contra calumniantes patrocinium praestem, quod est maius propositio meo' [52. 120]. From this primacy of rhetoric it follows that positions of content can be very easily changed. A well-known extreme example of this is, once again, Lorenzo Valla, who had disproved the authenticity of the Donation of Constantine in *De falso credita et ementita Constantini donatione* (1440) with philological – not political – arguments, because his employer, Alfonso d'Aragón, King of Naples, at the time happened to be conflict with the Papal States. This did not prevent him, however, from going to the Curia as a papal secretary beginning in 1448. The career of Poggio Bracciolini was similarly changeable. Therefore, it is possible, at the most, to speak of a republican 'civic Humanism' (Hans Baron) for the Florentine early Humanism, especially with regard to L. Bruni. However, just as in the (nominal) Republic of Florence, Humanists found positions as secretaries with the *signorie* or lesser city rulers, and thoroughly mastered the art of the sudden volte-face. Thus, in Milan, we find Antonio Loschi, Pier Candido Decembrio, Gasparino Barzizza, Francesco Filelfo, Giorgio Merula, Maffeo Vegio and occasionally Valla; in Naples, Antonio Beccadelli (Panormita), Giovanni Pontano and Jacopo Sannazaro; in Rome, Poggio Bracciolini, Pomponio Leto, Flavio Biondo, Giorgio Gemisto Pleton (Cardinal Bessarion) and so on.

On the other hand, the Humanists only had little influence on the university curriculum. Because they focused on rhetoric, they did not even cover the complete *trivium*. In any case, in status they remained below the academic disciplines (medicine, jurisprudence, theology). As a rule, chairs of Humanism at the universities did not have the right to grant doctorates and were also not as well remunerated. Therefore, top-rank Humanists were only rarely found at the universities, preferring instead the lucrative courts and civic schools. Around the middle of the 15th cent., chairs of Latin and Greek, largely held by the medical faculty, where rhetoric was treated in connection with the theory of affects, shifted to the legal faculty, where they could be connected to the tradition of the *ars dictaminis*. Moreover, chairs at the universities did not appeal primarily to Italian students, who had already gone through the Humanistic *trivium* before entering the university, but rather to a northern and central European demand, which demonstrated a need to catch up in this respect. Scholastic philosophy and Humanism regarded each other with disapproval; the Humanist attempt to place rhetoric above philosophy can only be understood in this context. According to Valla, ancient rhetoric is compatible with Christianity, while the speculations of Aristotelianism are not: 'Cur non potius Ciceronis philosophia nocuisse putanda Hieronymo est, quam ars dicendi? Nolo hoc in loco comparationem facere inter philosophiam et eloquentiam, utra magis obesse possit, de quo multi dixerunt, ostendentes philosophiam cum religione vix coherere, omnesque haereses ex philosophiae fontibus profluxuisse '(Opera 119). Here, Valla also takes an extreme position, for he even rejects Bruni's attempt to adopt some Aristotelian works into the Humanistic canon. However, Bruni's translation of the *Nicomachean Ethics* is only a stylistic reworking of the medieval version by Grosseteste. Valla's *Dialecticae disputationes* (1439) simplifies Aristotelian logic by reducing it to the level of rhetoric, based on Quintilian's recently rediscovered *Institutio*. While rhetoric and poetics were considered part of moral philosophy in the medieval curriculum and were dealt with by the medical faculty (in Aristotle, they are placed between politics and economics, on the one hand, and ethics and politics, on the other), Humanism sought to free them from their function as ancillary disciplines and to raise them to leading ones. This primacy of rhetoric also explains the philosophical and religious syncretism of Humanism from the second half of the 16th cent. on. Since Francesco Filelfo, Humanists sought not only a balance between Platonic and Aristotelian philosophy, but also between religions and denominations, based on general, naturally evident principles. This is most evident in the *Oratio de hominis dignitate* (1486) by Giovanni Pico della Mirandola. But even speculative Neoplatonism, which was primarily in demand at the court of the Medici in Florence (Marsilio Ficino, *Theologia platonica de immortalitate animae*, 1482; Cristoforo Landino, *Disputationes Camaldulenses*, 1480), initially had

very little influence on the universities. From the side of scholastic philosophy, it immediately incurred the energetic resistance of the Aristotelian Pietro Pomponazzi from Padua, who, as a philosophy professor opposing the philological arguments of the Humanists, always boasted that he did not know Greek, and also wrote an almost 'macaronic' Latin which was strongly coloured by the vernacular (*De immortalitate animae*). Then as now, the conclusion of P. O. Kristeller concerning all attempts to grant Humanism 'philosophical' dignity applies: 'I should like to suggest that the Italian Humanists on the whole were neither good nor bad philosophers, but no philosophers at all' [28. 51]. This situation at the universities only changed to a certain degree in the first decades of the 16th cent., when Francesco Patrizi da Cherso taught Platonic philosophy in Ferrara.

4. HISTORIOGRAPHY

The works of Pietro Pomponazzi are a good example of the kind of non-Classical Latin that was used still at the universities. In contrast, the Humanists gave Leonardo Bruni the credit for restoring the Classical language in diplomatic communication. Thus, it says in Gianozzo Manetti's *Oratio funebris in Leonardi Historici* (1444): 'Quibus quidem in magistratibus quantum primum litteras, cum ad diversos Italiae populos, tum ad varios principes, reges, imperatores, pontefices Florentini populi nomine elegantissime scriptas profecerit, difficile dictu est' [10. 97]. Such a caesura was associated with a more precise determination of the *medium aevum* between Antiquity and the modern era, which, among other things, the comprehensive historiography of the epoch sought to accomplish. Bruni limited it to the 700 years before 1404 in *Historicarum florentini populi libri* and *Commentarii rerum suo temporum gestarum*; those were precisely the years in which knowledge of Greek was said to have been lost: 'Septingentis iam annis nemo per Italiam graecas litteras tenuit; atque tamen doctrinas omnes ab illis esse confitemur' [11. 403 f.]. In 1457, Flavio Biondo dated the Middle Ages to exactly 410–1412 in *Historiarum ab inclinatio Romanorum Imperio decades tres* [6. 393]. Thus, Humanistic historiography determined the epochal coordinates which essentially still apply today.

5. LYRIC POETRY

Humanistic poetic production was less comprehensive than Humanistic treatise and dialogue literature as well as historiography. For the most part it was commissioned by princes and focused largely on lesser and open genres (epigrammatic writings, pastoral poetry and *silvae*). The first Christian-Humanistic epic – after Petrarch's fragmentary *Africa* (1341) – was *De partu virginis* (1526) by Jacopo Sannazaro. Naturally, Humanist lyric poetry required ancient models, although it avoided overly literal borrowings. Even Petrarch asked his friend Boccaccio to emend two verses from Eclogue X of his *Bucolicum carmen*, which too obviously used a model from Vergil and Ovid (Epist. Fam. XXII,2). It is known of Panormita (Antonio Beccadelli) that he had originally written 'accedant capiti cornua, Bacchus eris' in Epigram II, 3, 4 of his *Hermaphroditus* (1425), but then emended the verse to avoid quoting Ovid, Epist. 15,24 (Herm. ed. Coppini, 90). Occasionally, an ironic use of ancient models is found in Panormita. Thus, in *Hermaphroditus* II,1, *Laus Aldae*, he renders an elegy of Ovid (Epist. 15,23–24) in a decidedly obscene epigram: 'Si tibi sint pharetrae atque arcus, eris, Alda, Diana;/si tibi sit manibus fax, eris, Alda, Venus./Sume lyram et plectrum:fies quasi verus Apollo;/si tibi sit cornu et thyrsus, Iacchus eris./Si desint haec et mea sit tibi mentula cunno,/pulchrior, Alda, deis atque deabus eris'. Similar virtuoso use of ancient models is found even in the countless occasional poems to princes, ladies and other patrons, which almost all Humanists, even of second and third rank, produced.

Agnolo Poliziano (1454–1494) occupied an outstanding position in Humanistic lyric poetry and left a legacy of Greek, Latin and vernacular (*Stanze, Favola d'Orfeo*, 1480) works. The most notable of these are the *Sylvae* (1482–86), which followed the model of Statius, forming a kind of versified *praelectiones* to literary history and poetry. Poliziano completely disregarded here the Christian poetry of Late Antiquity and the Middle Ages and joined his own time to Antiquity. Particularly relevant in this collection is the balance between an understanding of rhetoric and poetry as *téchnai* in the Aristotelian-Horatian tradition and the Neoplatonic *enthousiasmós* of Ficino and his students in the *Nutricia* (ed. Del Lungo 369 ff.). Both poetic theories had existed side by side unreconciled since Boccaccio's *Genealogia* XIV. Referring to *Ion* 533d, Poliziano assumes a transferability of the *furor*, i.e. the poet virtually passes on the spark of inspiration: 'Deque aliis alios idem proseminat ardor/ Pectoris instinctu vates; ceu ferreus olim/Anulus, arcana quem vi magnesia cautes/ Sustulerit, longam nexu pendente catenam/Implicat et caecis inter se conserit hamis' (5,192 ff.). Thus, reading, imitation and textual work became a necessary preparation for inspiration, which was now historically communicated. The medieval theory of the fourfold meaning of the text, which had still served Boccaccio and Salutati for the ethical justification of poetry, no longer appears in Poliziano and his contemporaries.

Besides writing their own texts, Humanists were also involved in publishing and annotating the Classics, not least the long-neglected Greek works. Lorenzo Valla, for example, oversaw editions of Herodotus, Aesop, Thucydides, Homer and the Gospels. While Humanists such as Filelfo and Guarino still had to travel to Byzantium in order to learn Greek, more and more Greek scholars came to Italy, especially after the fall of the city to the Ottoman Turks in 1453. In 1468, the most famous of them, G. G. Pleton (*Bessarion*, 1403–72), gave his valuable collection of books to the city of Venice. Also among these immigrants was Georgius Trapezuntius, who introduced the *Téchne Rhetoriké* of Hermogenes of Tarsus and the Byzantine rhetorical tradition to the West with his *Rhetoricorum libri V* (1433). Thus, a Humanist could avail himself of an expressly Sophistic alternative to the Ciceronian-Quintilian tradition; it was not able to establish itself due to Trapezuntius's separation of *eloquentia* and *philosophia*, but it did reappear sporadically (e.g. in G. G. Trissino in the 16th cent.).

D. 16TH CENTURY
1. DE IMITATIONE 2. ERASMISM 3. VERNACULAR HUMANISM 4. ARISTOTELIAN POETICS

1. DE IMITATIONE
From the outset, the Neo-Latin literature of Humanism faced the question of exactly which authors should be imitated. The Florentine Humanists, who never completely lost their connection with vernacular poetry, represented an eclectic position. On the other hand, the Curia was committed to a strict Ciceronianism, in which the *Ecclesia* appears as a legitimate successor to the *Imperium*. The dispute first became public in 1494, in a correspondence between Paolo Cortesi (1465–1510) and Agnolo Poliziano. Poliziano had written: 'Quid tum? non enim sum Cicero, me tamen, ut opinor, exprimo' [22. 902]. However, according to Poliziano, this is precisely what could be learned from Cicero. Thus, Ciceronianism is unmistakable evidence for the lack of understanding of Cicero. As spokesman for the Curia, Cortesi, who also wrote the treatise *De cardinalatu* (1509), stood by the necessity of a single model for imitation, which could be used to measure the perfection of a speech or written work: 'Eloquentia una est ars, una forma, una imago' [22.908]. In 1502, this dispute was continued in the correspondence of the same name between Pietro Bembo (1470–1547), the future cardinal, historiographer of Venice and papal secretary, and Gian Francesco Pico (1469–1533), the nephew of the philosopher Giovanni Pico. Pico invoked the primacy of the rhetorical *inventio*, which makes any strict imitation theory impossible given the disparity of *ingenia*. For Bembo, on the other hand, the immediacy of the *inventio* is only an illusion, behind which hide years of accumulated reading. Thus, Bembo took up Cortesi's focus on Ciceronian models; even more, he also succeeded in promoting it in Italian.

2. ERASMISM
Naturally, such claims of cultural hegemony by the Church had to be repudiated by the Humanism which had since developed outside of Italy. The undisputed leading figure here was Erasmus of Rotterdam (1466–1536), who accused the now-strict Classical Church Latin of neopagan aberration in his *Ciceronianus sive de optimo genere dicendi dialogus* (1528). Erasmus continued Valla's philology-based line and focused on rhetorical genres such as the paradoxical *laudatio* (*Moriae Encomion*, 1511), collections of proverbs (*Adagia*, 1508), lessons from letter writers' guides (*De conscribendis epistolis*, 1522) and the like. In Italy, Erasmus was fiercely fought, primarily by Alberto Pio

da Carpi, and suspected of heresy from the beginning. On the other hand, Humanists from northern Europe and Spain gathered around the Dutchman, as shown by his extensive correspondence. Erasmism was particularly successful at the court of Charles V, which sought to reconcile the confessions, represented there by Alfonso de Valdés (1490–1532). In the Spanish Netherlands, Juan Luis Vives (1492–1540) and Fadrique Furió Ceriol (Ceriolanus) continued Erasmus's approaches. In France, he was followed by G. Budé and J. Dorat, among others. Here, Humanism also encroached heavily on the academic curriculum. The Erasmian simplifications of the Classical *trivium* (which, in turn, were based on Valla's work) led, through the mediation of Johannes Sturm in Strasbourg, to the reorganization of the *trivium* by Petrus Ramus (Pierre de La Ramée), whose reform in the following century would determine the curriculum, especially in Protestant countries. However, in Germany, Melanchthon permitted both the Ramistic and the Classical, Aristotelian program of study. In Catholic countries, the Jesuit *Ratio studiorum* (1599) maintained the Classical *trivium* with relatively few alterations and, accordingly, the Ciceronian style model as well.

3. VERNACULAR HUMANISM

At the beginning of the 16th cent., Italy lost its leading position in Europe and began to play a special role. Similar to the way in which he implemented strict imitation guidelines in the field of Latin, Pietro Bembo also succeeded in committing the newly developed vernacular Humanism, for which he provided the first example himself in the dialogue *Gli Asolani* (1506), to the imitation of Petrarch for lyric poetry and Boccaccio for prose–that is, to an archaic language model (*Prose della volgar lingua*, 1525). This imitation theory did what other positions could not: prescribing the language with a fixed and therefore learnable grammar. Thus, the Italian vernacular Humanism of the 16th cent. transferred the rules developed for Latin to vernacular literature. For example, Castiglione's *Libro del Cortegiano* (1528), which was successful across Europe, introduced the model of a Ciceronian dialogue with countless literal borrowings in a vernacular work. Even the first sentence of the book is nothing more than a translation of the first sentence of Cicero's *Orator*. The Vicentine Gian Giorgio Trissino (1478–1550) presented all Classical genres in proper form in the vernacular: the tragedy *Sophonisba* (1529), the epic *Italia liberata dai Goti* (1547), the comedy *I Simillimi* (1548). He was not able to establish himself in the market against Ariosto's fully non-classical romance *Orlando furioso* (1532), or his (rule-abiding) comedies. From the middle of the 16th cent. on, knowledge of the ancient Classics was no longer required in order to be considered a Humanist. Rather, knowledge of the vernacular authors who had become canonical, above all Petrarch and Boccaccio, was sufficient. This, at any rate, was the position of the most important Italian-language society, the *Accademia della Crusca*, and its spokesman, Lionardo Salviati.

In vernacular Humanism, Latin suffered a loss of authority, which had been furthered by the rise of Greek and, around the turn of the century, Hebrew (Pico della Mirandola, Johannes Reuchlin). However, it cannot be said that Latin Humanism was simply displaced by vernacular Humanism; rather, the two existed side by side. The production of Latin literature and treatises even increased sharply, thanks not least to printing. This generation of Latin Humanists in Italy fled, without exception, to the Curia. The members of the still fully secular noble society, which Castiglione described in 1528 in his *Libro del Cortegiano*, reappeared a few years later, all as cardinals or at least as bishops. After Florence also entered the orbit of the Curia with the Medici Popes (Leo X and Clement VII), Italy could no longer show an alternative cultural centre.

4. ARISTOTELIAN POETICS

The Renaissance is usually considered to have ended with the Reformation (1519), the *Sacco di Roma* (1527) or the opening of the Council of Trent (1545). The major philological achievements of the 16th cent., such as the Tacitus and Seneca editions by the Dutchman Justus Lipsius, are thus outside its boundaries. The same is true of the very extensive Jesuit production of epigrams and Jesuit theatre. In only one area did Italian Humanism still play a leading role which would be seminal for the Classical literature of other countries: in the publication and annotation of the Aristotelian *Poetics*. This was first translated into Latin in 1498 by Giorgio Valla, but only experienced its real upsurge, together with Horace's *Ars poetica*, after Girolamo Vida's *De arte poetica* (1527). Countless commentaries on Aristotelian poetics were written in Italy in the 16th cent. They range from efforts to bring it into accord with the psychomachia of the Counter-Reformation by Minturno (*De Poeta libri VI*, 1559; *L'arte poetica*, 1563) to the complex body of rules by the Protestant Lodovico Castelvetro (*Poetica volgarizzata et sposta*, 1570). However, especially Giulio Cesare Scaliger's *Poetices libri septem* (1561) became a model for Europe, especially for French Classicism.

→ PHILOLOGY

1 R. AVESANI, La professione dell'umanista nel Cinquecento, in: Italia medioevale ed umanistica, 13, 1970, 205–232   2 C. S. BALDWIN, Renaissance Literary Theory and Practice, 1939   3 H. BARON, The Crisis of Early Italian Renaissance Civic Humanism and Republican Liberty in an Age of Classicism and Tyranny, 1966   4 CH. BEC, Les marchands écrivains, 1967   5 G. BILLANOVICH, Petrarca letterato, 1947   6 F. BIONDO, Italia illustrata, historiarum ab inclinatio imperio decades II, 1531   7 G. BREITENBÜRGER, Metaphora, 1975   8 P. B. BROWN, A Significant Sixteenth Century Use of the Word 'Umanista', in: Modern Language Review, 64, 1969, 565–575   9 F. BRUNI, L'invenzione della letteratura mezzana, 1990   10 L. BRUNI, Epistolarum libri octo, L. MEHUS (ed.), 1741   11 Id., Historiarium Florentini Populi libri XII et Rerum suo tempore gestarum commentarius, E. SANTINI, C. DI PIERRO (eds.), 1914   12 K. BURDACH, Rienzo und die geistige Wandlung seiner Zeit, 1913–28   13 Id., P. PIUR

(eds.), Briefwechsel des Cola di Rienzo, 1929 14 A. CAM-PANA, The Origin of the Word Humanist, in: Journal of the Warburg and Courtauld Institutes, 9, 1946, 60–73 15 D. L. CLARK, Rhetoric and Poetry in the Renaissance, 1922 16 L. D'ASCIA, Erasmo e l'umanesimo romano, 1991 17 C. DIONISOTTI, Gli umanisti e il volgare fra Quattro e Cinquecento, 1968 18 C. DIONISOTTI, Geografia e storia della letteratura italiana, 1967 19 R. FUBINI, Ricerche sul De voluptate di Lorenzo Valla, in: Medioevo e Rinascimento, 1, 1987, 189–239 20 E. GARIN (ed.), Filosofi italiani del Quattrocento, 1942 21 Id., Der italienische Humanismus, 1947 22 Id. (ed.), Prosatori latini del Quattrocento, 1952 23 H. H. GRAY, Renaissance Humanism: The Pursuit of Eloquence, in: Journal of the History of Ideas, 24, 1963, 497–514 24 M. GUGLIELMINETTI, Memoria e scrittura, 1977 25 CH. H. HASKINS, The Renaissance of the 12th Century, 1928 26 B. HATHAWAY, The Age of Criticism, 1962 27 M. T. HERRICK, The Fusion of Horatian and Aristotelian Literary Criticism 1531–1555, 1946 28 R. HIRZEL, Der Dialog, 1895 29 J. HUTTON, The Greek Anthology in Italy, 1935 30 W. J. KENNEDY, Rhetorical Norms in Renaissance Literature, 1978 31 P. O. KRISTELLER, La tradizione classica nel pensiero del Rinascimento, 1965 (trans. of The Classics and Renaissance Thought, 1955) 32 Id., Studies in Renaissance Thought and Letters, 1969 33 J. LINHARDT, Rhetor, Poeta, Historicus, 1979 34 D. MARSH, The Quattrocento Dialogue, 1980 35 A. v. MARTIN, Soziologie der Renaissance, 1974 36 L. MARTINES, The Social World of the Italian Humanists 1390–1460, 1963 37 G. MAZZACURATI, Misure del classicismo rinascimentale, 1967 38 A. MICHEL, La parole et la beauté. Rhétorique et esthétique dans la tradition occidentale, 1982 39 J. MONFASANI, George of Trebisond, 1976 40 J. J. MURPHY (ed.), Renaissance Eloquence, 1983 41 W. A. ONG S. J., Ramus, 1958 42 PANORMITA (A. BECCADELLI), Hermaphroditus, D. COPPINI (ed.), 1990 43 F. PETRARCA, Rerum memorandarum libri, G. BILLANOVICH (ed.), 1943 44 A. POLIZIANO, Nutricia, G. BOCCUTO (ed.), 1990 (Engl. J. S. VAN WHY (trans.), A Critical Translation of Angelus Politianus Nutricia, 1951) 45 N. A. ROBBS, Neoplatonism of the Italian Renaissance, 1935 46 C. SEGRE, Studi sulla storia della prosa italiana, 1963 47 R. SABBADINI, Le scoperte dei codici latini e greci ne'secoli XIV e XV, 1905–14 48 S. SEIDEL-MENCHI, Erasmo in Italia, 1987 49 J. E. SEIGEL, Rhetoric and Philosophy in Renaissance Humanism, 1968 50 J. E. A. SPINGARN, A History of Literary Criticism in the Renaissance, 1924 51 F. TATEO, Umanesimo etico di G. Pontano, 1972 52 L. VALLA, Opera omnia, 1540 (repr. 1962) 53 C. VASOLI, La dialettica e la retorica dell'Umanesimo, 1968 54 TH. ZIELINSKI, Cicero im Wandel der Jahrhunderte, 1912 55 G. ZONTA, Rinascimento, Aristotelismo, Barocco, in: Giornale Storico della Letteratura Italiana, 104, 1934, 1–63, 185–240

ADDITIONAL BIBLIOGRAPHY R. L. BENSON, G. CONSTABLE (eds.), Renaissance and Renewal in the Twelfth Century, 1982; A. GRAFTON, L. JARDINE, From Humanism to the Humanities: Education and the Liberal Arts in Fifteenth- and Sixteenth-Century Europe, 1986; C. KALLENDORF, In Praise of Aeneas: Virgil and Epideictic Rhetoric in the Early Italian Renaissance, 1989; C. KALLENDORF (ed.), Humanist Educational Treatises, 2002; J. KRAYE (ed.), The Cambridge Companion to Renaissance Humanism, 1996; A. RABIL, JR. (ed.), Renaissance Humanism, 3 vols., 1988; B. THOMPSON, Humanists and Reformers: A History of the Renaissance and Reformation, 1996; C. TRINKAUS, In Our Image and Likeness: Humanity and Divinity in Italian Humanist Thought, 2 vols., 1970, rpt. 1995   MANFRED HINZ

II. LAW

A. DEFINITION B. DEVELOPMENT AND DISSEMINATION C. CONTENT D. EFFECTS E. ELEGANT JURISPRUDENCE F. DUTCH ELEGANCE

A. DEFINITION

Legal Humanism (LH) describes the period in the history of law from around 1510/20 to 1530/40, which contrasted the 'ancient' analytical-exegetic methods of the *mos italicus*, developed in Bologna, with the newly created *mos gallicus*, developed in France under the influence of Humanism, in order to draw conclusions from this for the teaching of jurisprudence and a systematic method.

B. DEVELOPMENT AND DISSEMINATION

The transition from the late Middle Ages to the modern era is characterized by the Renaissance, the 'rebirth' of Antiquity, particularly in art, and by Humanism, which in the Humanities confronted the ecclesiastic traditions with a new world view, focused on humanity and emphasizing the individual, as realized in the ancient Classics. 'Reformations' were introduced in all areas of life (Church, state, law) from the ancient sources, prompted by the call *ad fontes*. While this movement was effective earlier and more extensively south of the Alps through the 'grammarians' Petrarch, Filelfo, Valla or Poliziano, it did not aspire to a reorganization of jurisprudence. In Germany, however, Humanism was ideologically charged with the ideas of ecclesiastic reformation and criticism of papal and imperial universalism, and assumed polemic features. LH gained in significance as a program of reform, because it coincided with the practical reception of Roman law.

Humanist reform of jurisprudence began at the French university of Bourges (est. 1464). Its founders were Guillaume Budé (1467–1540) [25], Andrea Alciato (1492–1550) [7], who taught in Avignon and Bourges, and Ulrich Zasius (1461–1535) in Freiburg [29; 10]. Humanism strongly criticised the entire profession, which tended towards a monopoly of jurists, and found broad agreement among the populace ("lawyers, bad Christians" [16]). One lamented a lack of professional ethics, greed and sophistry and suspected the application of a foreign law, opposed to ancient tradition, in the service of the sovereigns. In his *Praise of Folly*, Erasmus denounces the jurists in an exemplary fashion, which, on the other hand, also must have led alert minds among them to self-reflection. With that, LH was withdrawn from the grammarians and became a matter for jurists. However, here recourse was made to the arguments of the Humanists. In Germany, since around 1520 LH spread from Louvain (L. Vives) to the Upper Rhine; it gained a foothold in Basle (C. Cantiuncula, J. Sichardus, B. Amerbach), where Erasmus [21] also relocated at the same time. The movement spread to Heidelberg (J. Wimpfeling, J. Spiegel), Tübingen (Spiegel), Vienna (Brassican) [9] and Wittenberg (Ph. Melanchthon, J. Apel among others). In contrast, Leipzig in particular remained a centre of the traditional *mos italicus*.

C. CONTENT

LH began with the criticism of the *mos italicus* in the works of the Italians, and turned against the scholastic form of instruction, absolute faith in authority, lack of language culture and ignorance in historical understanding. The studies of the ancients required by the Italians declined. Nevertheless, an increased study of Tacitus' *Germania* promoted a newly-emerging interest in legal history. J. Sichardus, a student of Zasius, edited the Visigothic *Breviarium Alarici* (Basle 1528) and the Germanic *Leges* (Basle 1530).

LH became primarily a paedagogical concern. Its primary target was the strong faith in authorities which characterized the scholastic method. The demand for a return to the sources could not be made compatible with the traditional teaching of Roman law by means of the *Glossa ordinaria* of Accursius and even more so via the commentaries of the postglossators Bartolus and Baldus. However, while the *mos gallicus* discarded the medieval tradition in France, German LH adhered to it out of practical considerations.

The criticism of the reformers focused not least on the inadequate transmission of written records. Textual criticism gained in importance for instruction, with Greek texts now also being included [34]. Gregor Haloander created the first complete critical edition of the *Corpus iuris civilis* (1529/31).

The call for a system which would overcome the legal order, or rather disorder, of the *Corpus iuris civilis* was also unmistakable. In place of the common analytical-exegetic method, the systematic method was to appear as it had been implemented, according to the conviction of the reformers, by Cicero in the lost work *De iure civili in artem redigendo*. The goal of finding or reconstructing this work led to many different attempts to set up a legal system (Apel, Derrer, Lagus, Donellus, among others).

Both paedagogic concerns (reduced use of commentaries, curtailment of the subject matter, independent use of reason) and the required fashioning of the system aimed at gaining time: the citation of '1000 leges' and 'totidem glossas' [38] and the usual citing of an enormous number of commentaries made the material unmanageable. Students were burdened with much useless material; and "while they learn one thing", say the 'Heidelberg Statutes', "they have forgotten the other, and if we do not have the book, the art is also lost" [5]. The total reception of Roman law, the establishment of

the Imperial Chamber Court (*Reichskammergericht*) and numerous princely courts of law, the development of territorial rule based on a modern civil service system, the development of the *Constitutio Criminalis Carolina* of Charles V–in short, the realization of the emerging juristic monopoly required a large number of jurists with scholarly training in a short time. However, a shortening of the course of study could only be achieved by a corresponding reform. Another factor which led to the shortening of the period of study was the shifting of the previous emphasis on canon law to civil (Roman) law or an even greater reduction of Church law in the course of the Reformation.

The reform programme also sought to realize stylistic matters. Apart from the traditional doubts of the old school, 'neminem posse et latine scire et iurisconsultum agere', followers of the reform programme (B. Amerbach, J. Hattstedt, A. Gentilis) were also of the opinion that the jurist should not become irrelevantly dependent on philologists. In this sense, Sichardus also provoked criticism within the reform movement when he interpreted the *Digests* in the same way as Terence or Plautus. In Vienna, such an approach was even codified by the statutes of 1537, by enjoining the Pandectists also to impart 'elegantiam et castitatem linguae Latinae' to young jurists [9]. The even more rigorous demand to adapt medieval legal terms to the style of a Cicero or Livy must have been counterproductive, because this would merely have created new confusion for students, while seeking precisely to reduce it.

KARL HEINZ BURMEISTER

D. EFFECTS

Notwithstanding the many criticisms levelled by LH, the *mos italicus* was able to maintain its position in practice. Even in 1562 the preface to an edition of Bartolus which appeared in Basle maintained "that any jurist who sticks to Bartolus is to be preferred to all others, because Bartolus represents the greatest authority". In judging the effects of the reform programme, it must be borne in mind that it was a paedagogical matter oriented toward beginners. Here, something was indeed achieved. Thus, study guides were used in an attempt to lead students toward independent reasoning. Steering beginners to the institutions and familiarizing them with the system of Gaius complied with the demand for "system instead of exegesis". At the same time, parallel lectures on codices and digests were established in accordance with *more gallico*, and thus not only presented the material in abbreviated form, but also focused on specific parts of the system (e.g. contract law, inheritance law). In instruction, the rejection of the legal order became fully established through the introduction of systematic lectures after the middle of the 16th cent. The holders of the chairs of codices, digests and amendments arranged which of them would read *materia iuris personarum, materia contractuum* or *materia testamentorum et successionis*, while the *materia actionum iuris civilis* fell to the canonists [8. 107–

111]. Thus the curriculum was based on the institution system of Gaius (*personae, res, actiones*).

E. Elegant Jurisprudence

The *mos gallicus*, which originated in Bourge,s continued to be developed there from the middle of the 16th cent. Unlike in the Empire, in France the *Corpus iuris civilis* was not accepted based on imperial order *ratione imperii*, but rather *imperio rationis*, i.e. based on its inherent qualities. While in Italy and Germany the historical authorities were followed for practical considerations ('nemo iurista nisi Bartolista'), a looser attitude toward the *Corpus iuris civilis* could be taken in France: the 'wrong track' of doctrines was left behind, and the text itself became the focus in order to interpret it by reason alone. Because of the clarity of the system and the Classically-oriented language, this approach was described as 'elegant jurisprudence'.

The philological direction of elegant jurisprudence found its zenith in J. Cujas (1522–1590), the master of the historical-exegetic method. The systematic direction was represented above all by H. Donellus (1527–1591). D. Godefroy (1549–1622), the publisher of the *Corpus iuris civilis* (1583), made a name for himself as the most important textual critic. Pioneering for the future codification movement of the 18th cent. was F. Hotman (1524–1590), who in his *Antitribonianus* (1574) presented the *Corpus iuris civilis* as a deficient, shoddy effort which required that a new beginning had to be found. Calvinist Bourges had replaced papal Bologna as the leading legal school in Europe [13; 15; 17; 36; 37].

The violent suppression of the Huguenots forced numerous representatives of elegant jurisprudence into exile in, among other places, Germany (Dumoulin in Tübingen, Hotman in Strasbourg, Donellus in Heidelberg and Altdorf, Godefroy in Strasbourg and Heidelberg) and Switzerland (Donellus, Hotman, Bonnefoy and Godefroy in Geneva, Hotman in Basle). The frequent exchange between universities worked against the foundation of new schools. Elegant jurisprudence reached its crowning conclusion in Geneva with J. Godefroy (1587–1652), the son of D. Godefroy, who superbly edited and annotated the *Codex Theodosianus* (Lyon 1665).

F. Dutch Elegance

In the 17th and 18th cents., the legacy of elegant jurisprudence passed to the Calvinist Netherlands. In the Netherlands, too, Roman law did apply not because of the medieval imperial concept, but because of the power of the exemplariness of Antiquity. The goal of the Dutch elegance school was to free Classical law from medieval falsifications through the use of philological and historical antiquarian methods. Representatives of Dutch elegance include A. Vinnius (1588–1657), G. Noodt (1647–1725), A. Schultingh (1659–1734), C. von Bynkershoek (1673–1743), H. Brenkman (1680–1736), J. O. Westenberg (1667–1737) and–

with reservations– U. Huber (1636–1694) and J. Voet (1647–1713) [26; 36; 37].

In the 17th and 18th cents., German jurisprudence was strongly influenced by the Dutch; Voet taught in Herborn, and Noodt was appointed to Duisburg and Heidelberg. A connection can be made from Holland to the rise of German jurisprudence of the 19. cent.: Holland passed the torch of the great jurists – which had been ignited in Italy and from there migrated to France and then to the Netherlands – on to Germany [37. 169].

Sources 1 A. Alciato, Opera omnia, Basel 1582　2 G. Budé, Opera omnia, Basel 1557　3 J. Cujas, Opera, Prati 1859/71　4 H. Donellus, Opera, Firenze 1840/47　5 A. Thorbecke, Statuten und Reformationen der Universität Heidelberg vom 16. bis 18. Jahrhundert, Leipzig 1891　6 U. Zasius, Opera omnia, Lyon 1550, (repr. 1964)

Literature 7 R. Abbondanza, s.v. Alciato Andrea, Dizionario Biografico degli Italiani 2, 1960, 69–77　8 K. H. Burmeister, Das Studium der Rechte im Zeitalter des Humanismus im deutschen Rechtsbereich, 1974　9 Id., Einflüsse des Humanismus auf das Rechtsstudium am Beispiel der Wiener Juristenfakultät, in: Acta humaniora 1987, 136–145　10 Id., Ulrich Zasius (1461–1535), Humanist und Jurist, in: Humanismus im deutschen Südwesten, Biographische Profile, 1993, 105–123　11 A. M. M. Canoy-Olthoff, P. L. Nève, Holländische Eleganz gegenüber deutschem Usus modernus Pandectarum? Ein Vergleich des privatrechtlichen Unterrichts in Leiden und an einigen deutschen Universitäten anhand einiger holländischer und deutscher juristischer Dissertationen über locatio-conductio (1650–1750), 1990　12 H. Coing, Die juristische Fakultät und ihr Lehrprogramm, in: H. Coing (ed.), Handbuch der Quellen und Literatur der neueren europäischen Privatrechtsgeschichte II/1, 1977, 3–102　13 H. Conrad, Deutsche Rechtsgeschichte, 2, 1966　14 F. Elsener, Die Schweizer Rechtsschulen vom 16. bis zum 19. Jahrhundert, 1975　15 H. Hattenhauer, Europäische Rechtsgeschichte, ²1994　16 M. Herberger, s.v. Juristen, böse Christen, HWB zur dt. Rechtsgesch. 2, 1978, 481–484　17 R. Hoke, Österreichische und deutsche Rechtsgeschichte, 1992　18 G. Kisch, Johannes Sichardus als Basler Rechtshistoriker, 1952　19 Id., Humanismus und Jurisprudenz: Der Kampf zwischen mos italicus und mos gallicus an der Universität Basel, 1955　20 Id., Bartolus und Basel, 1960　21 Id., Erasmus und die Jurisprudenz seiner Zeit, 1960　22 Id., Die humanistische Jurisprudenz, in: La storia del diritto nel quadro delle scienze storiche, 1966, 469–490　23 Id., Claudius Cantiuncula, 1970　24 Id., Stud. zur humananistischen Jurisprudenz, 1970　25 D. R. Kelley, Guillaume Budé and the First Historical School of Law, in: American Historical Review 72, 1967, 807–834　26 G. Kleinheyer, J. Schröder, Deutsche und Europäische Juristen aus neun Jahrhunderten, 1996　27 K. Luig, s.v. Mos gallicus, mos italicus, HWB zur dt. Rechtsgesch. 3, 1984, 691–698　28 D. Maffei, Gli inizi dell' umanesimo giuridico, ³1972　29 St. Rowan, Ulrich Zasius. A Jurist in the German Renaissance, 1987　30 M. Senn, Rechtsgeschichte – ein kulturhistorischer Grundriss, 1997　31 H. E. Troje, Die europäische Rechtsliteratur unter dem Einfluß des Humanismus, in: Ius Commune 3, 1970, 33–63　32 Id., Arbeitshypothesen zum Thema Humanistische Jurisprudenz, in: Tijdschrift voor rechtsgeschiede-

nis 38, 1970, 519–563   33 Id., Zur humanistischen Jurisprudenz, in: Festschrift H. Heimpel 2, 1972, 110–139
34 Id., Graeca leguntur, 1971   35 Id., Die Literatur des
gemeinen Rechts unter dem Einfluß des Humanismus, in:
Coing (ed.), Handbuch der Quellen und Literatur der
neueren europäischen Privatrechtsgeschichte, II/1, 1977,
615–795   36 G. Wesenberg, G. Wesener, Neuere deutsche Privatrechtsgeschichte, 1985   37 F. Wieacker, Privatrechtsgeschichte der Neuzeit, ²1967   38 Id., Humanismus und Rezeption. Eine Studie zu Johannes Apel Dialogus, in: Gründer und Bewahrer, 1959, 44–91.

III. Medical

Medical Humanism (MH) is the name given by
modern historians to the movement in medicine that,
from the 1490s on, demanded a return to the original
Greek sources of learned medicine [5]. It rejected both
Classical Latin intermediaries such as Cornelius Celsus
and Pliny the Elder, who had become prominent again
in the 15th cent., and Arabic authors such as Avicenna
and Rhazes, who in Latin translation had been the
mainstay of medieval academic medicine. Niccolò Leoniceno (1428–1524), professor of medicine at Ferrara
and the owner of the finest contemporary library of
Greek medical and scientific writings, showed in his *De
Plinii et aliorum in medicina erroribus* (1492) that confusion abounded through ignorance or misunderstanding of the Greek of Galen, Pedanius Dioscurides, Hippocrates and the like [3]. His prescription was a return
to Greek directly, or, since only a handful knew both
Greek and medicine, and had access to Greek manuscripts, in new Latin translations based on the Greek.

Until 1525, when the *Aldine* Galen appeared in
Greek (and Hippocrates in 1526), most new translations were of the standard university texts, e.g. Hippocrates, *Aphorisms*, but between 1526 and 1560 there
was a veritable flood of translations of all ancient medical texts into Latin, and occasionally into the vernacular [1]. After 1540 interest shifted to developing ancient
ideas either newly reinterpreted or rediscovered. Particularly in Paris, commentaries on Hippocrates could
range widely, grounding new ideas on e.g. the influence
of climate on Classical precedent [2]. By 1600, the editing and translating of Classical texts had almost ceased, and the philological methods of the earlier medical
Humanists now formed part of the past of a medicine
still largely based on Classical authorities.

The achievements of MH are: (1) the rediscovery of
ancient texts, notably Dioscurides (editio princeps
1499), Galen (editio princeps 1525) and Hippocrates
(editio princeps 1526; Latin trans. 1525); (2) the introduction of new techniques and ideas deriving from
ancient writers, e.g. the importance of anatomy (promoted by Humanists such as Matteo Corti (1475–
1544), Jacobus Sylvius (1478–1555) and John Caius),
of botany (Leoniceno, P.A. Matthioli (1501–1577)),
and of surgery (Vidus Vidius (d. 1569)); (3) the development of new clinical methods of observation and
classification (G.B. Da Monte (1498–1552)).

Above all, the medical Humanists imposed a new,
Galenic conception of orthodox medicine, especially
through their dominance of medical colleges, rejecting
uroscopy and astrology as quackery, and setting higher
educational standards for the orthodox physician (especially involving a knowledge of Greek) that widened
the gap between him and other providers of health care
[4].

→ Celsus; → Galen of Pergamum; → Hippocrates;
→ Plinius
→ Arabic-Islamic Cultural Sphere; → Arabic
Medicine; → Medicine

1 R. J. Durling, A Chronological Census of Renaissance
Editions and Translations of Galen, in: JWI 24, 1961, 230–
305   2 I. M. Lonie, The 'Paris Hippocratics': Teaching
and Research in Paris in the Second Half of the Sixteenth
Century, in: A. Wear, K. French, I. M. Lonie (eds.), The
Medical Renaissance of the Sixteenth Century, 1985, 155–
174   3 D. Mugnai Carrara, La Biblioteca di Nicolò
Leoniceno, 1991   4 V. Nutton, Pieter van Foreest on
Quackery, in: H. A. Bosman-Jelgersma (ed.), Petrus
Forestus Medicus, 1997, 245–258   5 W. Pagel, Medical
Humanism, in: F. Maddison, M. Pelling, C. Webster
(eds.), Essays on the Life and Work of Thomas Linacre,
1977, 375–386

Additional Bibliography D. Biow, Doctors,
Ambassadors, Secretaries: Humanism and Professions in
Renaissance, Italy, 2002, 47–98

IV. Music

The attitude inherent in the Western mentality to
establish the origin of culture and its associated ways of
thinking in Antiquity emanated, as did Scholasticism,
from Italy. Besides the term *studia humanitatis*, which
was coined by Cicero and initially covered mainly
grammar, rhetoric, poetics, history and moral philosophy, it later also included the → artes liberales, that
is the *trivium* (grammar, rhetoric, dialectic) and the
quadrivium (arithmetic, geometry, music, astronomy),
through the expansion of the *curriculum* disseminated
at the → universities. Thus, musical Humanism as
understood through ancient music theory (*musica theorica*) and contemporary practice (*musica practica*;
→ Musica) was perceived as a branch discipline of
Humanism oriented towards interdisciplinary studies.
Because in music, unlike in the applied arts (architecture, sculpture, painting, poetry and literature), it was
not possible to revive Antiquity due to the lack of musical examples, research in the fields of music aesthetics
and music theory was accorded a main role in academic
disputes. Despite this lack of practical reference to Antiquity, questions of composition techniques and performance were nevertheless of importance, particularly
in a broader concept of Humanism.

1.The *scientia musicae*, which in Boethius belongs
primarily to the *quadrivium*, referred, on the one hand,
to the classification system developed by him of *musica
mundana*, *musica humana* and *musica instrumentalis*;
and, on the other, essentially to the discussion of the
Greek scale system (*systema teleion*), the octave species

and the modes (*tonoi*; → Music II.C.1); this was based on the Pythagorean number theory transmitted by Nicomachus of Gerasa. The first effects of the *scientia musicae* on the *ars musica*, in this case in the discussion of scales and modes in Gregorian chant with reference to Boethius, can be seen in Hucbald of Saint-Amand (9th cent.), whose theory together with that of St. Augustine provided the foundations of knowledge of ancient music theory in the early Middle Ages. However, the theoreticians of the 13th and 14th cents. (Johannes de Garlandia, Hieronymus de Moravia, Johannes de Muris and Walter Odington) increasingly devoted themselves to questions of mensural notation, but without neglecting abstract *musica theorica* (cf. Jacobus Leodiensis, *Speculum musicae*). However, even in the late 14th and 15th cents., the *auctoritas* thinking of Boethius was widespread in works of music theory, for example in Prosdocimus de Beldemandis, Marchettus de Padua and Ugolino de Orvieto. The full scale of Humanistic influences is especially noticeable in Franchino Gaffurio, above all in his *Theorica musice* (1492). In this work, his treatment of *enconium musicae*, music classification, physics, arithmetic, theory of intervals (as part of Greek *harmonia*) and finally in the problematic comparison of the *systema teleion* and the *solmisation* of Guido of Arezzo – based on a serious misunderstanding in the equating of Latin Church keys and Greek *tonoi*, which was only clarified in his *De harmonia musicorum instrumentorum opus* (1518) – refers to over 150 sources, some mentioned for the first time. The latter include encyclopaedic works (Isidore of Seville, Martianus Capella), relevant Latin works (Guido of Arezzo, Giorgio Anselmi, Ugolino de Orvieto, Johannes Gallicus) as well as specially commissioned translations of Greek texts (Ermolao Barbaro's translation of the Themistius paraphrases of Aristotle's *De anima*, Marsilio Ficino's translation of Plato's works, Giovanni Francesco Burana's translation of the *Introductio artis musicae* of Bacchius). Gaffurio's contemporary Johannes Tinctoris was well-known through his specialized Humanist dictionary (*Terminorum musicae diffinitorium*, around 1473/74). Furthermore, in his *Libri contrapuncti* (1477), he developed a method of Humanist textual criticism and its application to contemporary composition practice (explained with on numerous examples) with reference to the technique of movements, i.e. the principle of *varietas*, drawing support from ancient poetics. Such Humanist tendencies, and an occupation with rhetoric (in accordance with the *Institutio oratoria* of Fabius Quintilianus) led to a new musical classification system formulated by Nicolaus Listenius (1533), including *musica poetica* as the highest, most comprehensive concept of musical practice. In the 16th cent., the mathematic-physical concept of music as vocal number (*numerus sonorus*) experienced a fundamental expansion. Thus in Lodovico Fogliano, the champion of musical ethics theory (→ Music–section II, C 3), thirds, sixths and their multiples were determined by using Euclidian geometry, together with the traditional consonances of Pythagorean theory (octave, fifth, fourth). This trend introduced a gradual turning away from the musical theory of Boethius. The new orientation also brought a progressive avoidance of the Pythagorean tuning apostrophized in the 15th cent. (Ramos de Pareja) and at the beginning of the 16th cent. (Giovanni Spataro). While the dissociation from ancient traditions also occurred in the mode theory of Gioseffo Zarlino, Heinrich Glareanus in his theory of twelve modes (similar to Gaffurio in his reflections) still held to a division of the seven octave species into twelve, into fifths and fourths.

2. Personal encounters between Humanists and musicians at the princely courts (e.g. Heinrich Isaac and Lorenzo de Medici) were vital to understanding Humanistic tendencies in contemporary composition. The works of the 'Burgundian School' and the 'Dutch School' (before 1530) were still fully polyphonic vocal arrangements, based on the *cantus prius factus*, and thus also obligated to the text declamation inherent in Gregorian chant. Here a melisma-based declamation of the chant, with the metre falling on unaccented syllables, was also adopted in polyphony. However, in the course of a gradual dissociation from the techniques of *cantus firmus*, there was a change from the imitating, linear counterpoint with its vocalising melismatics, oriented to the *cantus firmus* and characterized by the independent introduction of melodies in the individual voices, and an often differentiated mensuration to an increased homophonic structure; this was based on simple tone progressions and metric uniformity (often in *tempus imperfectum diminutum*), with accentuated declamation of syllabic text accompaniment. At first, both techniques appeared alongside each other in individual works (e.g. in the motet *Tu solus* by Josquin Desprez). This assimilation of musical metre oriented toward natural text declamation and polyphonic arrangement with occasionally occurring chromatics for the augmentation of the emotional content of texts (presumably as conscious imitation of the soft character of the Greek tone system) is encountered primarily in the verbose ordinary movement of choral-free *cantus firmus* masses; here *cantus firmus* movements are designed as *soggetti cavati* (e.g. in Josquin's *Missa Hercules Dux Ferrarie*), in psalm settings and also in *carmina congratulatoria*, epitaphs (e.g. *Epitaphium Lutheri* by Caspar Othmayr), panegyrics, *intermedii*, laments (e.g. for Johannes Ockeghem), hymns and mourning odes as well as in those works utilized for purely didactic purposes (namely for testing the principle of equating the quantities in poetry with corresponding note values), primarily in Humanist odes which, based on setting poetry to music (e.g. Conrad Celtis), were often suitable for ancient metres (e.g. *Glogauer Liederbuch*). In the course of the progressive adaptation of texts, copyists and printers made use of the idem sign for the completely syllabic texting of passages which were previously declaimed on one syllable; a like-

wise accent-related metrification of the text is not excluded for melismatics, which still occasionally appeared (cf. e.g. Giovanni Pierluigi Palestrina's *Missa Papae Marcelli*). The urge for greater comprehensibility of larger texts probably also explains the flourishing of solos usually accompanied by a lyre in the late 15thcent. as a rediscovery of ancient musical performance practices; here the resulting monodic style finds its continuation in → OPERA, the genre which combines the ancient unity of poetry, music and dance with the rhetorical figure theory into an *opus perfectum*.

1 H. ALBRECHT, s.v. Humanismus und Musik, MGG¹, 6, 1957, 895–918   2 Id., s.v. Humanismus, Riemann Musiklexikon, Sachteil, W. GURLITT, H. H. EGGEBRECHT (eds.), 1967, 380–381   3 J. HAAR, s.v. Humanismus, MGG², 4, 1996, 440–454   4 W. K. KREYSZIG, Francio Gaffurio, The Theory of Music (= Music Theory Translation Ser.), 1993   5 C. V. PALISCA, Humanism in Italian Renaissance Musical Thought, 1985.   WALTER KREYSZIG

Humanist Gymnasium
A. CONCEPT   B. HISTORY   C. PRESENT-DAY
UNDERSTANDING

A. CONCEPT

The humanist gymnasium (HG) is a type of secondary school intended to foster the education of young people in the sense of a "thorough intellectual development" through the "analysis of literarily formed humanity" [6. 312]. Traditionally, the curriculum of the HG includes the study of the ancient languages–Latin and Greek. The institution is regarded as 'humanistic' because the education of young people is based on the instruction in Classical languages and is made complete by further studies in modern languages, mathematics, social and natural sciences, as well as in the arts and sports. The core subjects are the ancient languages along with German and mathematics. This traditional concept has recently been modified through a new interpretation of the term 'humanist'.' Overall, gymnasiums are regarded as humanist schools because their primary goal is an education that enables young people to act responsibly in historical-social situations.

B. HISTORY

The HG was a result of the Prussian educational reform, which was instigated in 1809 by Wilhelm von Humboldt, who was the leader of the section for education and the arts in Berlin. Within the general educational system, it constituted the second level between elementary school and the → UNIVERSITY. The didactic focus on "ancient languages, native language and mathematics" was intended to generate a well-rounded education. Humboldt assumed that learning Classical languages helped in the development of grammatical, rhetorical and dialectical abilities. Further, they enabled access to the foreign world of Antiquity as an advanced culture, and through that conveyed examples of rational actions. Combined with the study of the native lang-

uage and mathematics, Classical languages offered the foundation for the development of 'Persönlichkeit' as a 'selbständige[r] Individualität, die sich auch unter widrigen Bedingungen in Freiheit entschließen und handeln kann' ("personality as an independent individuality that is able to decide and act in freedom even under adverse circumstances") [5. 353].

The HG was intended to be the institutional realisation of these ideas. Furthermore, it was 'die Reaktion auf einen Umbruch in der Zeit' ("the reaction to a radical change of the times") [4. 13] and a solution for the reformers, who wanted neither another elite school nor another professional training institution. Instead, they preferred a general secondary school whose curriculum would reflect the premise of humanistic education: 'daß sich in Sprache, Kunst, Mathematik jene Welten darstellen, durch die reine Menschenbildung erwirkt werden kann' ("that language, the arts and mathematics represent those worlds through which a pure education of humanity can be achieved") [5. 352]. This type of school had been under development since 1809, and was initially established in Prussia by J. W. Süvern in 1816. It originally comprised ten grades and was divided into lower, middle and upper levels. Altogether, 320 hours of classroom instruction were planned: 78 of them for Latin, 50 for Greek, 44 for German, 60 for mathematics, and the remaining 88 hours were divided among the other subjects. Thus, ancient studies alone comprised 40% of classroom instruction; together with the core subjects of languages and mathematics, they accounted for 70% of instruction time. Contrary to Humboldt's intentions, this plan required all students aiming for the 'Abitur' to learn both Classical languages. The conclusion of gymnasium instruction was the Abitur examination, which (in Prussia) was an absolute prerequisite for university attendance from 1834 on, thus creating the so-called 'monopoly of the gymnasium'. The HG was firmly established in Bavaria after 1830 by F. Thiersch.

After a short time, serious problems began to appear with this type of school, primarily because the urban middle class rejected the requirement of Greek as outdated. The attempt to convince the interested public of the advantages of such studies for a well founded general education remained unsuccessful. The increasing focus on philology in Classical language instruction–translations from Greek and Latin, Abitur essays and poems composed in Latin–resulted in an exaggerated 'Latin training' and obstructed the original intentions of cultivating the ideals of truth, beauty and the good based on ancient texts. The problems with this trend were underscored by complaints about excessive demands on the students. Education through the study of ancient languages degenerated into an acquisition of knowledge and skills whose display became a status symbol. Education thus became the means to distinguish oneself from the uneducated. This development occurred in a social environment of growing industrialisation, in which science and technology were constantly growing in importance. With their insistence on the extreme importance of studying the Classical languages, the representatives of the HG increasingly found themselves in a defensive position, opposing representatives of 'realistic concepts', whose acceptance, along with their corresponding curricula, was demanded as an instrument for general education. In this situation, the survival of the HG was ensured only by the 'Abitur monopoly'. An additional aid appeared in the second half of the 19th cent. with the establishment of two further gymnasial school forms: the 'Realgymnasium', which maintained instruction in Latin, but with a stronger focus on modern languages, mathematics and science; and the 'Oberrealschule', which dropped instruction in the Classical languages entirely. When, in 1900, the three school types were officially declared to have an equal rank regarding university admission, the representatives of the HG had no choice but to recognise that their previously claimed superiority could no longer be legitimised. The same effort failed again during the so-called → THIRD HUMANISM, whose representatives strove for a renewal of the HG after 1920. This movement lacked political force in the tense atmosphere of the Weimar Republic. The HG was regarded as outmoded and inappropriate for the current social developments, a relic from an earlier period. The representatives of the HG were especially disturbed by the following situation: 'Weiten politischen Kreisen, hauptsächlich den Vertretern der Arbeiterschaft, gilt der Geist des Gymnasiums als reaktionär' ("The spirit of the gymnasium was regarded as reactionary in broad political circles") [3. 2]. German nationalist factions deemed the HG to be representative of an un-German mind-set. Studies in youth psychology also seemed to disavow these schools, and the HG had to hold its ground once again in the face of 'realistic forms of education'. It became increasingly difficult to legitimise the importance of ancient subjects as educational models.

Following 1933, the HG was also drawn into Nazi ideology. First, content changes were made, in many cases resulting in a different focus on Classical language instruction [1]. In 1938, the traditional gymnasium was replaced by a German secondary school with eight grade levels, with English as the first and Latin as the second foreign language. This, however, no longer had anything to do with with the concept of a humanistic education. In those HG that were retained, the teaching material in the Classical languages was geared towards German national interests. Politicising the school's function was nothing new: during the German empire, the HG had already been used as an aid for fostering German nationalism. During that period, ancient texts were selected in a biased manner and interpreted in relation to current political issues, at times even chauvinistically. Ancient literature as well as ancient history were used to educate with patriotic intentions. The original intention, of an education based on the study of the wealth of ideas in these works, was renounced in favour of nationalist and patriotic instruction. This same tendency, that of serving the current, dominant political force, was again highly apparent after 1933. However, it must be noted that not all of the teachers of the HG succumbed to the temptation: the reading of ancient texts also offered the possibility of political distancing.

After 1945, the HG, in its traditional form, could once again be established in the Western sectors, although the Americans in particular were skeptical about the German gymnasium and strove for a different form for German re-education. In the Eastern sector (from 1949, the GDR), the traditional gymnasium was abolished following a fundamental educational reform. Soon thereafter, in the West, complaints about the HG's out-of-datedness grew louder again. While the 'Düsseldorf Agreement', ratified in 1955 at the Conference of the Ministry of Education and the Arts (*Kultusministerkonferenz–KMK*) by the federal states, confirmed the three gymnasial types (Classical, Modern Language, and Science and Mathematics), the social position of this type of school become increasingly problematic due to debates about early Latin instruction, the social selectivity of the HG and the purpose of Classical language studies. A further decline was influenced by several factors: the introduction of new core areas, the popularity of the new gymnasial forms, and the new option of elective subjects in the upper level. The 'Latinum', still required for university admittance, could be attained as early as in the 10th grade. The 'Graecum' retained importance only for future theologians or scholars of Antiquity. The reaction to these problems was the implementation of a method that had been tried and proven already circa 1900: the attraction of a HG was expanded by the introduction of various gymnasial branches in a single school. Thus, the HG was able to hold its own among other, more modern gymnasial types in a period when previously strict educational curricula were loosened.

C. PRESENT-DAY UNDERSTANDING

The different types of gymnasiums–with or without ancient language instruction–all see themselves as humanistic educational institutions in the sense of a broad humanistic education. Their particular pedagogical task is understood as helping children and adolescents develop the ability to judge and act through a large variety of learning opportunities and specific situational stimulation in languages, mathematics, in the physical and social sciences and in the arts. Although the Classical languages and instruction in ancient history have become less important now, Latin is again emphasised and appreciated as a core subject. The basis of the HG is, when, for instance, Latin remains the first foreign language, English is required from grade seven on, and in grade nine students can choose among the possibilities: Classical or modern languages and mathematics and science. Today, the HG regards itself as a cosmopolitan school which conveys the right balance between tradition, the contemporary world and progress.

The core subjects are German, Latin and mathematics, complemented by English as the first modern language. Latin is offered as the fundamental, European base language, the learning of which can impart system and order–sentence structures based on clear logic–without causing added difficulties with spelling and pronunciation. It is more difficult to legitimise instruction in Greek; it is carried out with reference to the importance of ancient texts. Humanistic school education today also aims for a historically-oriented general education, in which, however, the tradition of our social tradition is to be linked with a well-founded understanding of reality. The latter is served by a stronger focus on the social and physical sciences, which, along with art and music, are to ensure a broad educational program. The HG is meant to provide students with the opportunity to develop their abilities through specific linguistic challenges, and to allow them to practice the ability to decide and to act.

→ ANCIENT LANGUAGES, INSTRUCTION OF; → Curriculum; → EDUCATION

SOURCES 1 H. APEL, S. BITTNER, Humanistische Schulbildung 1890–1945: Anspruch und Wirklichkeit der altertumskundlichen Unterrichtsfächer, 1994 2 W. v. HUMBOLDT, Der Königsberger und der litauische Schulplan. Werke, vol. 13, 1920 3 M. KRÜGER, Methodik des altsprachlichen Unterrichts, 1930 4 C. MENZE, Die Bildungsreform Wilhelm von Humboldts, 1975 5 Id., see article: Bildung, in: D. LENZEN, K. MOLLENHAUER (eds.), Enzyklopädie Erziehungswissenschaft: Handbuch und Lexikon der Erziehung in 11 Bänden und einem Registerband. vol. 1, 1983, ²1992, 350–356 6 W. RÜEGG, Prolegomena zu einer Theorie der humanistischen Bildung, in: Gymnasium 92.4, 1985, 306–328
LITERATURE 7 K. E. JEISMANN, Das preußische Gymnasium in Staat und Gesellschaft, vol. 1 1974, vol. 2 1996 8 M. LANDFESTER, Humanismus und Gesellschaft im 19. Jahrhundert: Untersuchungen zur politischen und gesellschaftlichen Bedeutung der humanistischen Bildung in Deutschland, 1988 9 F. PAULSEN, Geschichte des gelehrten Unterrichts: auf den deutschen Schulen und Universitäten vom Ausgang des Mittelalters bis zur Gegenwart; mit besonderer Rücksicht auf den klassischen Unterricht, vol. 2 1921, ²1965   HANS JÜRGEN APEL

Humoral Theory. The doctrine that the human body was made up of four humours, blood, phlegm, bile and black bile, and that health consisted in their being in balance, was accepted as the creation of Hippocrates well before the 2nd cent. AD. Galen's authority, buttressed by his logical and rhetorical skills, ensured that it became for centuries the dominant theory in Western medicine and in its oriental siblings. It was expounded in short (often pseudonymous) tracts like the ps.-Galenic *Perì chymôn* [16] or the *Epistula Yppocratis de quattuor humoribus* [1], as well as in large compendia, like the *Canon* of Ibn Sina (Avicenna) (→ ARABIC MEDICINE), and in the lectures of medieval university professors, discussing the precise way in which the four humours were mixed together in the individual [6].

Its foundations were part empirical, based on the human body's tendency to homoeostasis, and part theoretical. Its combination of Hippocratic and Aristotelian doctrines (→ Melancholy) made it particularly attractive to an intellectual community used to explaining the universe in terms of elements and qualities. It was also a valuable means of classifying and organising data. Its circularity, with the balance of humours changing throughout the year in an orderly manner, could be easily adapted to explain e.g. the colours of urine on a medieval urine chart [8].

Galen's strong insistence on the interaction between body and soul, especially in *Quod animi mores*, IV, 767–822 K., was subsequently developed in Late Antiquity and the Middle Ages into a theory of temperament that divided mankind into four main psychological as well as physical types [7; 15]. The two reinforced each other. The *homo phlegmaticus* was white, flabby, and slow-witted; an angry man showed by his anger that he was naturally choleric, with an excess of bile and hence a tendency to choleric diseases. Visual representations stressed the psychological aspect of the four temperaments at least as much as they did the physical [4], and poets, playwrights, and essayists based the characterisations of their heroes and villains on this understanding of the four humours [7].

The classification system of the four humours also was extended in the Middle Ages to cover far more than the elements, qualities and seasons of Galen. The link with the mind also explained the physical effects of the four main tonalities, the seasonal rhythm fitted easily into the constellations of astrology. Similarly, organs that were thought to be under the influence of a particular sign could thus be assigned to one of the four humours. Other tetrads, like the four Evangelists, could also be adapted to this scheme [17].

Until the Paracelsian revolution of the 16th cent., the doctrine of humours was unchallenged. Academic debate refined the categories, e.g. the different types of melancholy or phlegm, rather than rejecting them [19; 21]. Even Paracelsianism, at Basle or Montpellier, could be taught as explaining the differences between the body's major fluids in terms of their chemistry [11].

William Harvey's *De motu cordis et sanquinis*, 1628, challenged but did not overthrow this humoralism. While asserting the primacy of blood, circulating throughout the body, Harvey in his therapeutics continued to talk in terms of the four humours, which could be seen as constituents of his supreme blood [12]. Others, more radical, saw temperaments and humours as at best secondary features. E.g. Friedrich Hoffmann (1660–1742) saw the temperaments as the result of the relationship in the body between solids and fluids; they were an index of the health of the systems by which the fluids circulated around the body or in each organ [10]. Fifty years later, William Brownrigg, a typical English doctor, talked about phlegmatic or sanguine constitutions, but without invoking humours as an explanation [22]. In literature, music, and especially in figurative art, the four temperaments continued to inspire artists to depict the changes and contrasts between the four ideal types [3]. The melancholic genius flourished into the 19th cent. [14].

By 1850, humours and temperaments had largely disappeared from formal Western medicine, although in many Muslim countries today there are officially backed attempts to relate these traditional concepts of 'Yunani' (Greek) medicine to the findings of modern medical science, although with varied results (see, e.g., the many publications of the Hamdard Institute, Pakistan). The four temperaments survive as popular psychological descriptions, just as patients find it easier to understand and accept a doctor's advice when they can interpret it for themselves in humoral terms [5]. The resurgence of alternative medicine after 1970 frequently champions a holistic approach to the patient that goes back, sometimes overtly, to the humoral theories of Greece and Rome. Humoralism is a long time dying.

→ Aristoteles [6] Aristotle, son of Nicomachus, of Stagira; → Astrology; → Galen of Pergamum; → Hippocrates [6] H. of Cos; → Melancholy; → Humoral theory

1 A. Beccaria, I codici di medicina del periodo presalernitano, 1956, 169   2 C. M. Brooks, J. L. Gilbert, H. A. Levey, D. R. Curtis, Humors, Hormones, and Neurosecretions, 1962   3 Z. Z. Filipczak, Hot Dry Men, Cold Wet Women. The Theory of Humours in Western Art, 1575-1700, 1997   4 H.-M. Gross, Illustrationen in medizinischen Sammelhandschriften, in: G. Keil (ed.), Ein teutsch puech machen. Untersuchungen zur landessprachlichen Vermittlung medizinischen Wissens, 1993, 191-193   5 C. G. Helman, 'Feed a Cold and Starve a Fever', in: Medicine and Society 2, 1978, 107-137   6 D. Jaquart, La science médicale occidentale entre deux renaissances (XIIe s. - XVe s.), 1997, vi, 71-76   7 R. Klibansky, E. Panowsky, F. Saxl, Saturn und Melancholie, 1990   8 L. C. Mackinney, Medical Illustrations in Medieval Manuscripts, 1965, fig. 6   9 I. W. Müller, Humoralmedizin. Physiologische, pathologische und therapeutische Grundlagen der galenistischen Heilkunst, 1993   10 Id., Iatromechanische Theorie und ärztliche Praxis, 1991, 138-142   11 W. Pagel, From Paracelsus to Van Helmont, 1986, XII, 440-441   12 Id., William Harvey's Biological Ideas, 1967   13 K. E. Rothschuh, Konzepte der Medizin in Vergangenheit und Gegenwart, 1972   14 T. Rütten, Demokrit, lachender Philosoph & sanguinischer Melancholiker, 1992   15 H. Schipperges, Der Garten der Gesundheit, 1985, 64-71   16 A. Schmidt (ed.), Ps.-Galeni liber de humoribus, Diss. Göttingen 1964   17 E. Schöner, Das Viererschema in der antiken Humoralpathologie, 1964   18 K. Schönfeldt, Die Temperamentenlehre in deutschsprachigen Texten des 15. Jahrhunderts, Diss. Heidelberg 1962   19 Chr. J. Schweickardt, Theoretische Grundlagen galenistischer Therapie im Werk des Gießener Arztes und Professors Gregor Horst (1578-1636), Diss. Gießen 1996   20 R. E. Siegel, Galen's System of Physiology and Medicine, 1968   21 N. G. Sirasi, Avicenna in Renaissance Italy, 1987, 24-27, 290-306   22 J. E. Ward, J. Yell, The Medical Casebook of William Brownrigg, M.D., F.R.S. (1712-1800), 1993.   VIVIAN NUTTON

Hungary
I. Classical Influence on the Culture of Hungary   II. History of Classical Studies

I. Classical Influence on the Culture of Hungary
A. Middle Ages (11th–14th Centuries)
B. Humanism and Reformation   C. 17th and 18th Centuries   D. 19th and 20th Centuries

A. Middle Ages (11th–14th Centuries)
As everywhere in medieval Europe, Latin authors made up a definitive element of higher culture in Hungary (H.) too. Traces of acquaintance with these authors (especially Horace and Vergil) can be detected in the oldest written Latin texts (11th cent.). Besides factual knowledge, turns of phrase and moral → dicta were of primary significance. This did not necessarily imply knowledge of complete works; they could also be acquired from *florilegia*. Because of its language, ancient culture affected primarily scholars; however, some components were assimilated by broader circles: e.g., the existence of a Hungarian Troy novel can be verified. Some elements were folklorized.

B. Humanism and Reformation
1. Beginnings   2. The Age of Matthias Corvinus (1458-1490)   2.1. To the First Half of the 1470s   2.2. From the Second Half of the 1470s   2.3. The Period after the Death of Matthias (to about the End of the 16th Century)

1. Beginnings
Beginning in the 14th cent. with the Angevin kings and later, at the time of King Sigismund of Luxemburg (1387-1437), H. had active contact with → Italy. Many humanists came to H. from Italy; some Hungarians studied in Italy. Since no native-language court culture developed in H. (the language of higher culture was Latin), Latin language-based Italian → Humanism was quickly received. Its pioneer was P.P. Vergerio, who was in service to King Sigismund from 1417 and died in Buda in 1444. For a brief period several Humanists gathered at the court.

2. The Age of Matthias Corvinus (1458-1490)

2.1 To the First Half of the 1470s
J. Vitéz (after 1400-1472) helped these hopeful beginnings come to fruition. He had a good Humanistic education, studied in Vienna, then became bishop at Várad and royal chancellor (1445); as such, he was also an orator and diplomat and ultimately became Archbishop of Gran. He was friends with Vergerio, later also with Bessarion, and had a large library. He was responsible for the founding of the University of Bratislava (Academia Istropolitana, 1465), where foreign Humanists were also active (among others, J. Regiomontanus,

G. Gatti, M. de Bylica). Vitéz also prepared the foundation of a printing house in Buda though he did not live to see its opening in 1473. In order to allow gifted young people a modern Humanistic education, he sent them to Italian universities, a practice which other princes of the Church would later follow. Among these young people was his nephew, the famous poet Janus Pannonius. As a 13–year-old prodigy, he was a student of Guarino in Ferrara, where he also acquired a thorough knowledge of Greek. Later, he studied in Padua, where he received his doctorate in 1458. He was friends with Galeotto and Mantegna. In 1459, he became bishop of Pécs, chancellor to the queen and a diplomat. He wrote elegant, witty epigrams, large-scale panegyrics suited to the taste of the times and deeply-moving elegies in exemplary Latin; and he brilliantly translated passages from the *Iliad* and other Greek texts.

The ideal of the age was the '*poeta et orator*', who increased the lustre of the royal court. His tasks also included diplomatic activities (possibly diplomatic notes in the form of a poem) and sophisticated correspondence, which would be compiled in a corpus. Until the end of the 16th cent., epistolary literature ($\rightarrow$ LETTER-WRITING/ARS DICTAMINIS) remained the most characteristic genre of Hungarian Humanism. The fall of the two intellectuals J. Vitéz and Janus Pannonius as a result of their participation in a violently suppressed political conspiracy against the king meant the end of an important era.

2.2 FROM THE SECOND HALF OF THE 1470S

Although King Matthias, who had been greatly deceived in his Hungarian Humanists, looked more to Italian Humanists, whose role was generally definitive, the development of a humanistically-educated Hungarian class progressed.

The most important features of the epoch are: a) the reception of whole works, authors and genres (also from the Greek); knowledge of Roman philology (Servius) and astrology; the reception was linguistic (though not Ciceronianism) and rhetorical (orations, panegyric poetry), political (the speeches of Demosthenes against Philipp were recast to refer to the struggle against the Turks) and philosophical (emphasis on the individual, emotions, poetic self-awareness as opposed to the pride of feudal nobility); b) the flourishing of the $\rightarrow$ BIBLIOTHECA CORVINIANA, founded in the 1480s; c) the beginning of Humanistic historiography (M. Galeotto, A. Bonfini, P. Ransanus): Matthias was represented not only as the successor of the Romans, as the new Alexander, but also as the new Attila/Etzel – in a positive sense in Bonfini's works, in a negative one by Callimachus Experiens; d) the strong impact of Florentine $\rightarrow$ NEOPLATONISM. To be sure, Neoplatonism was known earlier – J. Vitéz and Janus Pannonius maintained relationships with Bessarion and Ficino – but now a small Platonic circle developed in Buda, the most important members of which – P. Garázda, P. Váradi and N. Báthory – studied in Italy. In 1476, Ficino's friend F. Bandi came to Buda, and not only Ficino, but

also several of his students (A. Poliziano, N. Naldi) were in contact with the king, who was inclined to Platonism. After the death of Matthias, this circle fell apart, but its ideas continued to have an effect and prepared the way for Erasmianism; e) the beginnings of Classical Studies in H., the collection of inscriptions, at first by Italians. Almost nothing has been preserved of the Hungarian poets who, taking Janus as their model, wrote in Latin.

2.3 THE PERIOD AFTER THE DEATH OF MATTHIAS (TO ABOUT THE END OF THE 16TH CENTURY)

After the death of Matthias, central power weakened under the Jagiellonian kings (1490–1526); after the disastrous battle of Mohács (1526), the country had two kings, Ferdinand of Habsburg and János Zápolya. After the Turks had conquered Buda and the centre of the country (1541) and occupied them for a year and a half, H. dissolved into three parts: in western and northern H., so-called Royal H., the Habsburg kings ruled, while Transylvania became now a loosely, now a more closely dependent principality of the Turkish Empire, ruled by the members of various Hungarian noble families.

The significance of the royal court declined, and the episcopal courts (chapters), or, in the 2nd half of the 16th cent., the court of the Transylvanian princes, became centres of humanistic culture. Humanistic culture also reached broader classes through the schools. (The influence of Erasmus and Melanchthon also contributed to this.) Besides relations with Italy, contacts with Humanists in German-speaking countries became ever more important. The practice of sending young people to study abroad continued – but with an increasing number of secular patrons. The Bibliotheca Corviniana was dismembered shortly after the death of Matthias; however, smaller Humanistic libraries formed. Platonism was replaced by Erasmianism and the Reformation. The near-Humanist trend of the latter (Melanchthon) gained many adherents. Stimulus for translation of the Bible and of Greek tragedies came from both directions (in part adapted to the moral and political demands of the time, as with the Hungarian reworking of *Electra* by P. Bornemissza).

$\rightarrow$ EPIGRAPHY and philology developed without interruption from the 15th cent. on, but now also cultivated by Hungarians. In the 16th cent., also promoted by the requirements of the schools, Greek and Latin grammar and text editions were also included. The first Hungarian grammars appeared, still in Latin, but also taking Hebrew grammar into consideration.

The historiography genre was adopted by Hungarians, partly in the form of commemorative works by the Erasmians St. Brodarics (on the Battle of Mohács) and N. Oláh (on the erstwhile glamour and glory of H. with integration of the Attila tradition), partly in comprehensive works, as with A. Verancsics, F. Forgách, St. Szamosközy, N. Istvánffy, particularly inspired by Livy and Tacitus. Almost all of them wrote poems, none of which attained great significance. The remaining Latin poetry of the period, such as the five books of the *Stauromachia* by St. Taurinus (1519) about the Hungarian Peasants' War of 1514 or the twelve books of the *Ruinae Pannoniae* by Chr. Schesaeus on the history of H. from 1540 to 1571, are more of historical than aesthetic interest. Belles-lettres were already making use of the native language at the time. The reception of Antiquity in fact stimulated the development of a higher culture in the native language, invoking Cicero's opinion in favour of Latin as a native language over Greek. Following the model of Latin, a purely quantitative Hungarian metre (→ → METRICS) was developed, the only one of its kind in modern Europe.

As for philosophy, an → ARISTOTELIANISM developed toward the end of the 16th cent. in Transylvania. This was spread by young nobles who had been educated in Padua around 1570 in the spirit of Pomponazzi, in antitrinitarian or religiously indifferent circles, and interpreted the Stagirite in a materialistic sense. At the beginning of the 1590s, after the death of Aristotelianism's adherents, Neostoicism gained significance under the influence of J. Lipsius, who brought the ancient Stoics Seneca, Plutarch and Epictetus back to the fore.   ÁGNES RITOÓK-SZALAY

C. 17TH AND 18TH CENTURIES

In the 17th and 18th cents., it was primarily the epic poetry of the ancients that was adopted The more scholastic Latin epics of the Jesuits about the king of the Huns Attila/Etzel harkened back to medieval and Humanistic traditions. In his magnificent Hungarian epic on the Turkish siege of the fortress Szigetvár, the poet and politician N. Zrínyi adapted Vergil, Ovid and also Tasso in a confident, topical manner, similar to his major Baroque contemporaries. On the other hand, in the epic of I. Gyöngyösi, which focused on love, Ovid was the primary model. Gyöngyösi also reworked Heliodorus' novel of love. In political thought, Tacitus (*virtus* versus *otium*) exercised major influence. At the end of the 18th cent., this impact received a different emphasis among the Hungarian Jacobins. They fought as republicans against imperial absolutism and saw in Tacitus, misunderstanding him to their own benefit, a like-minded thinker. (This interpretation returned for similar reasons after defeat in the war of independence in 1848/49, when Lucan was also much read.)

Because Latin was the language of instruction outside of primary school (Latin was the official language in H. until 1844), Latin culture (to a lesser extent Greek) was part of the education of nobles and commoners, although to very differing degrees. Until the end of the 19th cent. it was also common for landed nobility to read ancient authors regularly and cite them from memory in speeches.

D. 19TH AND 20TH CENTURIES

The pursuit of civic-progressive modernization at the end of the 18th and beginning of the 19th cent. also fostered the aspiration for the 'purification of the nation' (development of a contemporary culture), a fertile reception of the French → ENLIGHTENMENT and German → CLASSICISM as well as a novel reception of ancient culture.

Numerous → TRANSLATIONS – primarily of the works of Vergil and Horace, but also of Homer – were produced; Greek tragedies and Anacreontea were translated, partly with the goal of 'polishing' the Hungarian language (linguistic renewal), partly because of the ideas they applied (moderation, Rococo or pastoral-idyllic, anti-tyrant, depending on the attitude of the translator).

Classical influence had a strong effect on poetry. Lyric poetry was particularly influenced by the reception of Horace, as in one of the major poets of the period D. Berzsenyi, who even expressed romantic feelings in Classical Horatian forms and phrases. Vergil and Claudian influenced the epic. The awakening of the civil national feeling brought with it the expectation of a Hungarian national epic, the theme of which was to have stemmed from early Hungarian history, which also meant a certain connection to the Attila tradition. This expectation was fulfilled by M. Vörösmarty, who in turn wrote an epic in Classical Vergilian form, but in enchanting romantic language. However, this did not settle the question of the epic. From the beginning of the 19th cent., folk poetry, the 'naive' (folk) epic, had been gaining ever-greater significance, in part under the influence of Herder. The poet J. Arany, who produced magnificent work in this type of epic, dealt with the situation of the Homeric poet in ancient society, his relationship to tradition and the audience and with the difference between the status of ancient and modern epic poets. In his studies he worked out not only important aesthetic ideas, but also thoughts which anticipated the results of modern comparative Homeric scholarship and the Parry school. Unlike his contemporaries, he saw in Homer not merely a trouble-free, harmonious world, but also the tragic ("the epic hero fights against fate, although he knows that he cannot defeat it"). Thus, he prepared a new understanding of Homer and Antiquity, which was first initiated at the end of the 19th cent. by 'lay' critics and developed in the literature of the 20th cent. No longer were quiet grandeur, the Classical-harmonious, seen in Homer and Antiquity, to say nothing of childlike naiveté; but rather much more often the problematic and disturbing. Instead of the *Iliad*, the restless wanderer Odysseus was interpreted as a symbol of a contemporary attitude towards life in M. Babits' novella, in Zs. Móricz' drama or in S. Márai's novel. Babits translated the Oedipus dramas, but not, for instance, the *Antigone*. D. Kosztolányi wrote a novel about Nero and a poem about Marcus Aurelius. Poets adopted figures and situations from mythology and ancient history, in which the time of crisis through which they found self-understanding could be recognized. Literary works were more often analysed as such by non-philologists (cf. e.g. the essays of L. Németh).

Although Latin was still considered as the basis of higher education, interest shifted to Greek. This was encouraged starting in the middle of the 19th cent. by the Classical *Gymnasien,* although other school types also developed over time. Being a 'Latinist' meant belonging to a special class – which gave occasion to much criticism of Classical education in general.

It was also this criticism that played a role in the transformation of the → SCHOOLS after 1945. In the post-war era, Greek was no longer taught in the schools at all, Latin only a little; thus, the language element was forced out. Instead, a wealth of literature in translation developed to which the best poets also contributed. At all times, translation has been considered as the work of poets in H. These translations made ancient literature more accessible than ever to broader societal classes. From the 1960s on, Greek dramas (in translation, not adaptation) were frequently performed in the theatre and on radio; a fruitful collaboration between philologists and theatre people developed.

Because even texts from the ancient Orient were accessible in translation, interest shifted in this direction from the 1980s on. In recent decades, the type of reception has reappeared in which authors adopt the mask of an ancient poet (or write him poetic letters), but present problems connected with the end of the millennium.

ISTVÁN RITOÓK, ZSIGMOND BORZSÁK

II. History of Classical Studies

A. 15TH–16TH CENTURIES B. 17TH–18TH
CENTURIES C. 19TH CENTURY D. TURN OF THE
CENTURY E. BETWEEN THE WORLD WARS
F. WORLD WAR II AND THE POST-WAR ERA

A. 15TH–16TH CENTURIES

Roman authors were also known to scholars in medieval H.; however, the scholarly study of Antiquity did not begin until the 15th cent., when Italian → HUMANISM (P.P. Vergerio) reached H. and quickly had a major impact. At first, Italians came to collect Roman inscriptions–e.g. F. Giustiniani (1464) and F. Feliciano (1479, who has been able to be identified with the epigrapher whom Mommsen called only 'Antiquus' in CIL). Almost at the same time, there were also Hungarians working on Roman authors (J. Vitéz), translating Greek authors into Latin (Janus Pannonius) and somewhat later also collecting Roman inscriptions (J. Megyericsei's collection was prepared for print by Aldus). In 1522, the edition of Seneca's *Quaestiones naturales* by Matthaeus Fortunatus appeared, which even Erasmus recognized. The revival lost some strength in the 16th cent.: political events on one hand and the Reformation on the other steered interest in other directions (struggle for survival or in some cases development of a native-language high culture, theological and philosophical matters). Nevertheless, around the middle of the century, although not in H., J. Sambucus began to occupy himself extensively with collecting ancient manuscripts. The collection of

Roman inscriptions also continued (A. Verancsics, St. Szamosközy), and in Bratislava, the capital of the so-called Kingdom of H. at the time, a small circle of Humanists developed around the Dutch Humanist N. Ellebodius, who, though only having published Nemesius' writing *De natura hominis* (1565), was also extensively occupied with other Greek authors, especially Aristotle.

B. 17TH–18TH CENTURIES

The 17th and 18th cents. brought no significant new insights. Inscriptions continued to be collected, a Latin-Hungarian / Hungarian-Latin dictionary was published by the reformer A. Szenci Molnár (three greatly expanded editions one after another: 1604, 1611, 1621) as was a Latin-Hungarian / Hungarian-Latin-German dictionary by the doctor and reformed theologian F. Pápai Páriz (1708, revised by the pastor P. Bod). After the expulsion of the Turks (1686–1699), the entire country, including Transylvania, came under the rule of the Habsburg kings. In the devastated country, questions of Classical Studies did not seem to be the most important one (as, for example, in → GERMANY after the Thirty Years War); the impact of the utilitarian spirit of the → ENLIGHTENMENT was all the greater. The first stimulus for the development of Classical scholarship in the modern sense came from Göttingen, where many Hungarians studied, among others É. Budai and L. Schedius. After his return home, Budai published some useful school editions (Cicero, Terence) with annotations and a Graeco-Roman literary history. Although as active as both he and Schedius were in the schools, neither of them became the founder of Hungarian Classical Studies. Reforms dealing with backward economic and social conditions seemed to be of primary importance, and for enlightened and philanthropic educational utilitarianism philology was something of no use. Its position was very unfavourable even in the university system (→ UNIVERSITY). While knowledge of Latin was taken for granted, there was no chair for philology. On the other hand, → PROVINCIAL ROMAN ARCHAEOLOGY was represented at the University of Pest by renowned scholars (St. Schönvisner, P. Katanchich). Under the influence of German → NEO-HUMANISM, an intellectual lay elite turned strongly towards Greek culture, which bore fruit in its work with poetry and philosophy and became the basis of a competent Classical philology.

C. 19TH CENTURY

The actual development of Classical Studies in the 19th cent. began with university reform (1848–1850), which, following the Prussian model, proclaimed academic freedom and changed the philosophical faculty from a kind of introductory, preparatory entity to a proper faculty. Classical philology became an independent subject. Expertise replaced Enlightenment encyclopaedism, and the scholarly replaced the scholastic. The strictly absolutist government following the revolution and war of independence in 1848/49 gradually relaxed from the beginning of the 1860s on, so that, in 1867, reconciliation between Austria and H. could be achieved. Among other things, this reconciliation also gave a boost to scholarship and helped to develop modern Classical Studies. In tune with the times, the Humanities saw the assertion of the historical approach, and philology saw the assertion of Lachmann's method, or, more exactly, comparative and historical linguistics. Both were advanced by E. Thewrewk von Ponor, who had been Vahlen's student in Vienna, both in his demanding school commentaries and in his scholarly and teaching activities. Through this and through his organizational activity (philological society, periodical, publication series), he is considered the founder of Hungarian Classical philology. His students, who also studied at German universities and in part surpassed their teacher in scholarship, continued to work in a variety of directions: E. Ábel (late Greek poetry, Pindar scholia, Hungarian humanism), W. Petz (comparative trope scholarship, founder of Hungarian → BYZANTINE STUDIES), G. Némethy (Euhemerus, Roman poetry, criticism of divinatory texts), Gy. Czebe, and J. Révay (late Antiquity, Silver Age Latin). Starting in 1883, the Hungarian Academy of Sciences, founded in 1825, had its own commission for Classical philology, which published critical and bilingual editions and translations, as well as supporting the general periodical for linguistic and literature studies *Egyetemes Philologiai Közlöny* and the Budapest Philological Society.

D. TURN OF THE CENTURY

However, the adoption of the methods of German Classical philology was not without its problems. The enormous accumulation of sources and knowledge brought increasing professional specialization throughout Europe. The crisis of perception at the turn of the century and the looming crisis of → HISTORICISM allowed for scepticism toward methods that had previously been considered completely correct and made detailed research more advisable. Classical philology thus was threatened with the loss of the major legacy of neo-humanistic Classical Studies, the comprehensive view of Antiquity and the relevance of Classical Studies. Classical Studies took very little notice of the new, non-historical, structuralist, systematic methods. In addition, the radical bourgeoisie and the workers' movement objected that Classical philology was useless for modern life; extreme nationalists accused it of being irrelevant to the national culture. Thus at the end of the 19th cent., Hungarian Classical Studies were in the paradoxical position of having to overhaul and modernize that which had just been recovered. Solutions were sought in a variety of directions: a) in a 'linear' extension of Classical Studies to connect it with the modern era, i.e., by including Middle and Modern Greek and Latin studies (W. Petz); b) in a convergence with political science (J. Schvarcz); c) in the reception of the results and methods of French sociology and psychol-

ogy or the British ethnological school (Gy. Hornyánszky, K. Marót); d) in convergence with current events, i.e., in emphasis on the significance of Classical Studies for the exploration of the national culture (R. Vári).

The latter three shifted the focus toward 'real philology' at the expense of textual philology, which flourished only in Byzantine and Middle Latin studies. Among the traditional areas of research, provincial archaeology continued to be cultivated (B. Kuzsinszky). Research into ancient art also increased (N. Láng, A. Hekler).

E. BETWEEN THE WORLD WARS

In the very critical economic, social and political situation after World War I (H. had lost two-thirds of its previous territory), a polarization of pre-war trends could be observed: on the one hand, there was the tendency to represent Classical Studies as national scholarship or to recast it through setting appropriate goals (provincial archaeology, Middle Greek and Latin studies, problems of reception, etc.; J. Huszti, Gy. Moravcsik); on the other hand, the concept of a uniform, no longer simply 'Classical' studies developed, which, in addition to the whole culture of the Graeco-Roman world, also included the Ancient Orient and peripheral peoples, as well as all related disciplines. This concept was a logical step due to the increased knowledge of the 19th cent. and aspired to realize the overall neo-humanistic view on a higher level. At the time, this aspiration was completely new; something similar in an earlier period could be found only in the historiography of Ed. Meyer and in the programme of the *Cambridge Ancient History*. This concept took shape from the 1920s on in the scholarly practice of K. Marót and A. Alföldi and was formulated programmatically in the 1930s by K. Kerényi.

F. WORLD WAR II AND THE POST-WAR ERA

The generation whose scholarly career began in the 1930s was affected by these stimuli. Admittedly, everyone went his own way: I. Trencsényi-Waldapfel (Greek literature, history of religion, Old Testament, Humanism research), Á. Szabó (student of K. Reinhardt, Greek literature and history, history of philosophy, history of mathematical thought and astronomy), I. Borzsák (Roman literature, history of Alexander, textual criticism, humanistic scholarship), I. Hahn (ancient history, history of religion), J. Harmatta (Greek historiography, Indo-European linguistics in the framework of cultural history, especially Iranian studies, Indian studies, Hungarian prehistory), J. Gy. Szilágyi (Greek art, Etrusco-Corinthian vase painting, Roman literature). Scholarship thus realized the principle of totality. In addition to the 'real philological' approach, which had become somewhat one-sided, textual philology reappeared after World War II. Middle Greek and Middle Latin flourished; from the 1930s on, an important series of Middle Latin texts was published (J. Juhász). In the post-war era, an orthodox form of → MARXISM dominated at first, which meant, in terms of world-view, certain philosophical limitations (abrupt rejection of ahistorical, formal principles, as well as of the new structuralist methods, which caused great damage particularly in literary studies; constantly referring phenomena back to the productive forces). However, it also had a positive impact, primarily in the inclusion of previously overlooked questions of economic and social history and sociological points of view. The activity of the latter generation developed in the decades after the war; a large part of the results fall in this period. A particular upturn in scholarship of the Ancient Orient can be observed. Provincial archaeology flourished, and young scholars appeared alongside the older (A. Mócsy, J. Fitz). When the ideological atmosphere became more liberalized from the 1960s on, both the younger and older generations adopted structuralist methods, which advanced the inherent analysis of works of art without disregarding the historical contexts. In Middle Greek studies, instead of the issue of Hungarian-Byzantine relations, other questions of Byzantine culture have come to the fore. The publication of the great dictionary of medieval Hungarian Latinity (→ MIDDLE LATIN) has already begun; new critical text editions are also appearing. The focus of modern scholarship is on the following areas: a) the results of a Hungarian excavation in Egypt; questions of economic and social history in the ancient Near East; b) Mycenaean scholarship, early Greek epic, history of the Athenian democracy, Greek drama, Roman comedy, Roman epic, especially in the post-Augustan period, Roman historians and their textual criticism; aesthetic thought in Antiquity, ancient rhetoric, the ancient novel, history of philosophy (especially logic) and science in Antiquity, late antique culture, Greek vase painting; Pannonian scholarship. c) early Byzantine historiography; Humanistic scholarship. Part of this work is overseen by the Hungarian Academy of Sciences, which, among other things, also publishes the journals *Acta Archaeologica* and *Acta Antiqua* (in foreign languages) and (in place of *Egyetemes Philologiai Közlöny* which stopped in 1948) *Antik Tanulmányok* (in Hungarian) since 1950 and 1954 respectively.

1 J. BALÁZS (ed.), Klasszikus álmok a magyar költészet klasszikus hagyatéka; anthológia, Introduction: D. KERESZTURY, Budapest 1943   2 I. BORZSÁK, Az antikvitás XVI. századi képe, Budapest 1960   3 A. FÖRSTER, A Magyar Tudományos Akadémia és a klasszikus ókor, Budapest 1927   4 J. HARMATTA, The Study of the Ancient World, in: T. ERDEY-GRUZ, K. KULCSÁR (eds.), Science and Scholarship in Hungary, Budapest 1975   5 D. HEGYI, Zs. RITOÓK, 25 Jahre Indogermanistik in Ungarn, in: Acta Linguistica Academiae Scientiarum Hungaricae 22, 1972, 401–417   6 J. HORVÁTH, Az irodalmi müveltség megoszlása. Magyar humanizmus, Budapest ²1944   7 J. HUSZTI, Tendenze platonizzanti alla corte di Mattia Corvino, in: Giornale critico della filosofia italiana, 1930, 1–37, 135–162, 220–236   8 Id., Klassi-

sche Philologie, in: Z. MAGYARY (ed.), Die Entstehung einer internationalen Wissenschaftspolitik: die Grundlagen der ungarischen Wissenschaftspolitik, Leipzig 1932, 68–72   9 Id., Pier Paolo Vergerio és a magyar humanizmus kezdete, in: Filológiai Közlöny 1, 1955, 521–533   10 G. ISTVÁNYI, Die mittellateinische Philologie in Ungarn, in: Deutsches Archiv für Geschichte des Mittelalters 4, 1940, 206–223   11 T. KARDOS, La tradizione classica in Ungheria, Budapest 1944   12 Id., La Hongrie latine, Paris 1944   13 Id., A magyarországi humanizmus kora, Budapest 1955   14 K. KERÉNYI, Klasszika-filológiánk és a nemzeti tudományok, in: Egyetemes Philológiai Közlöny 54, 1930, 20–35 (cf. PhW 50, 1930, 947 f.)   15 T. KLANICZAY, La Renaissance hongroise. Les nouvelles recherches et l'état de la question, in: Bibliothèque d'Humanisme et Renaissance 26, 1964, 439–475   16 Id., Das Contubernium von Johannes Vitéz. Die erste ungarische 'Akademie', in: K. BENDA, TH. V. BOGYAY, H. GLASSL, Zs. K. LENGYEL (eds.), Forschungen über Siebenbürgen und seine Nachbarn: Festschrift für Attila T. Szabó und Zsigmund Jakó, Vol. 2, 1988, 227–243   17 J. KORNIS, Ungarische Kulturideale 1777–1848, Leipzig 1930   18 Gy. MORAVCSIK, Stand und Aufgaben der klassischen Philologie in Ungarn, Berlin 1955   19 Id., Dix années de philologie classique hongroise (1945–1955), in: Acta Antiqua Academiae Scientiarum Hungaricae 3, 1955, 191–206   20 Zs. RITOÓK, Emil Thewrewk von Ponor und die Klassische Philologie in Ungarn bis zum Ende des I. Weltkrieges, in: E. KLUWE, Zs. RITOÓK, J. SLIWA (eds.), Zur Geschichte der klassischen Altertumswissenschaft: der Universitäten Jena, Budapest, Kraków, Jena 1990, 13–39   21 Id., Die Alten Sprachen in Ungarn, in: Gymnasium 100, 1993, 163–166   22 Id., The Contribution of Hungary to International Classical Scholarship, in: Hungarian Studies 12, 1997, 5–15   23 Id., L'enseignement du Latin dans les écoles secondaires de Hongrie (1945–1995), in: Acta Antiqua Academiae Scientiarum Hungaricae 38, 1998, 275–296   24 Id., Ein Kampf um das Griechische, in: Acta Antiqua Academiae Scientarum Hungaricae 41, 2001, 225–230   25 A. RITOÓK-SZALAY, Der Kult der römischen Epigraphik in Ungarn zur Zeit der Renaissance, in: A. BUCK, T. KLANICZAY, S. K. NÉMETH (eds.), Geschichtsbewußtsein und Geschichtsschreibung in der Renaissance, Budapest 1989, 65–75   26 G. STANGLER (ed.), Matthias Corvinus und die Renaissance in Ungarn, 1458–1541: Schallaburg '82. Exhibition Catalogue, Vienna 1982   27 R. VÁRI, A classica-philologia encyclopaediájia, Budapest 1906, 436–456

ADDITIONAL BIBLIOGRAPHY I. BARTOK, Companion to the History of the Neo-Latin Studies in Hungary, 2005; L. SZÖRÉNYI (ed.), Camoenae Hungaricae 1, 2004–present (Yearbook of Hungarian and Middle European Neo-Latin Studies)   ZSIGMOND RITOÓK

Hymnos. The Greek hymnos (Latin *h ymnus*, English hymn) was originally a song of praise in honour of a deity performed in connection with religious festivals and accompanied by instruments. The basic elements recall the ancient 'Sitz im Leben': exaltation, invocation, praise and petition. The exaltation is manifested in the enthusiastic tone, the invocation (epiclesis) in formulaic-sacral attributions and predications, the praise (aretology) in the mythic tale of the being and deeds of the god invoked, the petition in the evocation of mutual sympathy. The invocation entails a particular height of style (of the sublime). By addressing the deity as a representative of the community, the hymnal poet assumes an intermediary position: on the one hand, he reveals the divine lore to the audience; on the other hand, he increases the esteem of the deity with his song. This median position grants him a particular authority (cf. the Roman Odes of Horace), but it also exposes him to great danger (cf. Hölderlin's *Feiertagshymne*).

While in Antiquity and in Christianity (until the Renaissance), the liturgical use of the hymn predominated and purely literary hymns developed on the fringes, since the Renaissance, this relationship has been reversed: Latin hymnal poetry lost its vitality; at the same time, a versatile hymnody in national languages arose. With its release from the religious framework (profanation), the hymn opened up to profane topics which it enhanced sacrally (sacralization). This dialectic of sacralization shapes the history of the modern hymn. General ideas (such as harmony, freedom) also became the object of hymnic invocation. The enthusiastic tone became more important than the religious moment of referring to God and prayer. The distinctive profile of the genre faded in favour of a conceptually blurred 'hymn-like' style. Because there is no specific metric form for hymns, a broad spectrum of preferred forms has developed. It includes choral lyrics, hexameter, odic measures, rhymed verse, prose and free verse. Since the hymn is defined only thematically, there is frequent terminological overlap (particularly with the ode).

The development of the hymn is closely connected with the reception of Pindar [4] and Horace [11]. The poetics of Humanism and the Baroque recommended emulating Pindar for the sake of the magnificent praise. Thus Trissino and Alamanni developed *canzones* and hymns with characteristics of Pindaric form and style; in France, under the influence of Ronsard (*Odes*, 1550, *Hymnes*, 1555/56), it became the fashion of the *pindariser* in the circle of the Pléiade [7]. Stimulated by this, the powerful tradition of the *Pindaricks* developed in England, ranging from Milton, Jonson, Cowley (*Pindarique Odes*, 1656), Dryden (*A Song for St. Cecilia's Day*, 1687, *Alexander's Feast*, 1697), Congreve, Th. Gray and Wordsworth into the present [5]. In German literature [1], Klopstock established lyric poetry in free verse with recourse to Pindar and the psalms. His *Gesänge* (1757/59) dispensed with identical stanzaic forms, metre and rhyme in favour of a strong rhythmicity. They offered archaisms, new word compositions, declamatory repetitions, confusing inversions, 'hard constructions,' caesuras, laconisms and strophic enjambments [3]. Appearing alongside the free verses were smaller hymnal forms such as the dithyrambic poetry following Willamov (1763), prose hymns (Goethe's *Von Deutscher Baukunst*, 1775), hexameter rhymes following the model of the Homeric and Orphic hymns (Stäudlin, Stolberg) and finally the great rhymed hymns of Schiller and Hölderlin, which drew on Antiquity – not metrically, but thematically [10]. In contrast, the *Hymnen an die Nacht* (1799/1800) use traditional Christian hymnody and song composition. Novalis used changing metres and forms of expression for the composition of his profound, religious-speculative cycle. Platen's *Festgesänge* (ca. 1830) were a classicistic attempt to faithfully imitate the metres of Pindar. He likewise had no successors, while Klopstock's free verse prevailed: Goethe's *Sturm und Drang* hymns (after 1772) [6], Hölderlin's *Vaterländische Gesänge* (after 1800) [8], Heine's *Nordsee* cycle (1825/26), Nietzsche's *Dionysos-Dithyramben* (1884) [2] and the free verse poetry of Naturalism (Dehmel, Bierbaum) appeared. Following Nietzsche, Whitman (*Leaves of Grass*, after 1855) and Verhaeren (*Les heures claires*, 1896), Expressionism (Stadler, Mombert, Trakl, Heym) brought a renewal of hymnic poetry, which tended toward political panegyric in Becher, sacerdotal solemnity in the George Circle and ideological reflection in Rilke, Weinheber, Werfel [9]. The Christian tradition was also taken up (Le Fort) or 'converted' (Brecht, *Psalmen*, 1920). In hymnic poetry after 1945, Hölderlin with his prosaic pathos offered a starting point for Celan, Meister, Sachs and Bachmann. With his national history cycle *To Axion Esti* (1959), Elytis harkens back to the hymnal liturgy of Greek Orthodoxy. Noteworthy parodies are offered by Enzensberger, Rühmkorf, Benn (*Eine Hymne*, 1951), Brinkmann (*Hymne auf einen italienischen Platz*, 1975),and Henscheid (*Hymne auf Bum Kun Cha*, 1979).
→ Homer, → Horatius, → Orpheus, → Pindarus

1 N. GABRIEL, Studien zur Geschichte der deutschen Hymne, 1992   2 W. GRODDECK, Friedrich Nietzsche, Dionysos-Dithyramben, 2 vols., 1991   3 K. M. KOHL, Rhetoric, the Bible and the Origins of Free Verse. The Early 'Hymns' of Friedrich Gottlieb Klopstock, 1990 4 S. LEMPICKI, Pindar im literarischen Urteil des 17. und 18. Jahrhunderts, in: Eos 33, 1930/31, 419–474   5 K. SCHLÜTER, Die englische Ode. Studien zu ihrer Entwicklung unter dem Einfluß der antiken Hymne, 1964   6 J. SCHMIDT, Die Geschichte des Genie-Gedankens in der deutschen Literatur, Philosophie und Politik 1750–1945, vol. 1, 1985, 179–309   7 T. SCHMITZ, Pindar in der französischen Renaissance. Studien zu seiner Rezeption in Philologie, Dichtungstheorie und Dichtung, 1993   8 P. SZONDI, Hölderlin-Studien, 1967   9 H. THOMKE, Hymnische Dichtung im Expressionismus, 1972   10 M. VÖHLER, 'Danken möcht' ich, aber wofür?' Zur Tradition und Komposition von Hölderlins Hymnik, 1997 11 Zeitgenosse Horaz, H. KRASSER, E. A. SCHMIDT (eds.), 1996

ADDITIONAL BIBLIOGRAPHY J. T. HAMILTON, Soliciting Darkness: Pindar, Obscurity and the Classical Tradition, 2004; P. ROLLINSON, Hymn, in: A. PREMINGER, T. V. F. BROGAN (eds.), The New Princeton Encyclopedia of Poetry and Poetics, 1993, 542–44.   MARTIN VÖHLER

Hymnus. Broadly defined in Antiquity, the term *hymnus* was increasingly limited in the Middle Ages to metric or rhythmic spiritual strophic songs in praise of God. Notwithstanding all the revisions, recompilations and comprehensive expansions to the repertoire of the medieval collection of liturgical hymns, the core is composed of hymns of Patristic origin, such as those by Ambrosius, which took a fixed place in the Roman liturgy of the Hours beginning in the 12th cent. The hymnal of Late Antiquity – which was compiled and fixed in the 6th and 7th cents., primarily in the Gallic monastic rules for liturgical use in the Divine Office as the so-called Old Hymnal – continued to be passed down into the 9th cent. In the 9th cent., possibly in the surroundings of the imperial court chapel, a significant reshaping of hymnal practice occurred through the so-called New Hymnal, which would form the basis for the later Roman hymnal practice in the *Breviarium Romanum*. However, Patristic hymns remained, as before, an important base of liturgical hymnody. Even more than the comparably small body of authentic texts from Late Antiquity – only 14 hymns, for example, are ascribed to Ambrosius – the metric-rhythmic verse models from early Christian hymns have a particular after-effect. The traditional schemata, primarily the Ambrosian hymn strophe, the Sapphic and the Asclepiadic strophes, form the basis for a majority of the newly written medieval hymns. In the course of the Middle Ages, the range of strophes apparently increasingly narrowed to iambic dimeter and the Sapphic strophe. A partial reorientation of the entire corpus of liturgical hymns on the ancient strophic models is clear in the liturgical reforms of the 16th and 17th cents., leading to the first authoritative Roman hymnal in 1643. The musical notation of hymns can be demonstrated beginning in the 10th cent. The extent to which ancient melodies and musical elements find expression in medieval hymns can scarcely be resolved due to the lack of ancient melodic notation. Thanks to its strophic form, the Latin hymn lent itself particularly to translation. Beginning in the 14th cent., texts in the vernacular gained their first access to the Latin liturgy through translation of hymns and prepared the ground for the vernacular strophic church song of the 16th cent. Beginning in the 15th cent., hymns were composed for several voices by, among others, Guillaume Dufay, primarily for use in vespers.

SOURCES 1 G. M. DREVES, C. BLUME, H. M. BANNISTER, Annalecta hymnica medii aevi, 55 vols., 1886–1922 2 B. STÄBLEIN, Hymnen I. Die mittelalterlichen Hymnenmelodien des Abendlandes, 1956
ADDITIONAL BIBLIOGRAPHY J. M. ZIOLKOWSKI, Nota Bene: Reading Classics and Writing Songs in the Early Middle Ages (forthcoming).   VOLKER SCHIER

Hysteria. On a wall in his treatment rooms, Sigmund Freud had an engraving showing one of J.-M. Charcot's female patients during an hysterical attack. Even though from modern knowledge of ancient medical diagnosis, nothing is known which could compare with such depiction of a grand four-phase hysterical attack with an *arc de cercle* gesture, repeated attempts have been made in Western medicine to authoritatively corroborate this diagnosis by tracing it back to Hippocratic medicine [3]. Regardless of this, Hippocratic works do not use the category 'hysteria' as a summary term in their descriptions of symptoms caused by a 'wandering womb', but associated the various clinical pictures with the location in the body at which the uterus supposedly interrupted its travels.

Whereas in modern terms, hysteria describes a range of conditions "without associated physical findings" [2], ancient descriptions of *hysterikê pnix* invariably traced such manifestations of 'uterine suffocation' back to physical causes; the uterus was unanimously identified as the cause, irrespective of whether it was assumed to move freely around the body or not. Views on uterine suffocation and various concepts of therapy drew on Hippocratic works as on those by Pliny, Celsus and Galen. In Late Antiquity, these amalgams were transmitted in the works of encyclopaedists such as Oreibasius, Aetius and Paulus of Aegina. In the course of the incorporation of Greek medicine into Arabic medicine, an ongoing process since the 9th cent., Galen's view that retained menstrual blood or retained 'female sperm' poisoned the body interlinks with the belief that the uterus was mobile and the source of rising 'vapours' which could even affect the head.

In Western medicine, most authors still believed into the 17th cent. that the uterus was the cause of potentially serious symptoms, unless the excess of blood in the female organism was reduced by diet, bloodletting or menstruation. However, in the 1680s, Thomas Sydenham, the 'English Hippocrates', claimed that hysteria made use of the body's nervous system and was thus able to imitate the symptoms of all other diseases. In that way, he made it possible to expand the diagnosis to men who pursued a sedentary occupation or excessive bookish studies.

The belief in the 18th cent., however, was that the female nerve tracts were ensconced in much finer membranes and that an excess of blood was one of the major causes of nervous irritation, thus restoring hysteria to its 'ancient right' as a female disease.

The 19th cent., by contrast, produced a whole series of theories. While the neurologist Jean-Martin Charcot (1825–1893) believed that men, too, could suffer from hysteria, he still thought that the disease in his female patients was triggered by emotional experiences, whereas in his (much rarer) male patients he blamed past physical traumas for the genesis of hysteria. General practitioners considered their hysteria patients as little worthy of trust and were quite hostile towards them in their attitudes, as shown in Freud's discussion of the case of Dora, which marks the beginning of psychoanalysis [1]. Nowadays, the term is also used to describe the 'hysterical personality disorder', characterized by manipulative, deceitful and sexually provocative behaviour. It is also used to describe epidemic outbreaks of 'mass hysteria'.

SOURCES 1 C. BERNHEIMER, C. KAHANE (eds.), In Dora's Case, 1985   2 E. SLATER, Diagnosis of 'hysteria', British Medical Journal 1965, 1395–1399   3 I. VEITH, Hysteria, 1965
LITERATURE 4 S. GILMAN et al., Hysteria Beyond Freud, 1993   5 M. MICALE, Approaching Hysteria, 1995 6 Id., Hysteria and its Historiography, in: History of Science 27, 1989, 223–261 and 319–351
ADDITIONAL BIBLIOGRAPHY L. B. COATES, Female Disorders, 2005; G. DIDI-HUBERMAN, J. -M. CHARCOT, The Invention of Hysteria, 2004 (orig. 2003)

HELEN KING

I

Iceland. Only after its relatively late Christianization in 1000, and the founding of bishoprics (Skálholt in 1056, Hólar in 1106) and monasteries (Þingeyrar in 1112, Munkaþverá in 1155, etc.) [7] did Iceland seek and obtain access to the ancient-Christian tradition of education, with its Latin-speaking written culture as transmitted by Church and scholarship [8; 13]. Thus the first original works (primarily historiographical and hagiographical in content) were composed in Latin; however, as soon as they had been written most of them were translated into the vernacular, which gained ground, as Latin's peer as a language of writing and literature, in Iceland faster than in countries on the continent. That, and the recording and revision of indigenous material that started in the early 12th cent., on the basis of older oral transmissions (especially legal texts, sagas, Eddas and skaldic poetry), strongly curtailed Latin's share. Nevertheless, the very scant number of extant Latin manuscripts, or Old Norse manuscripts with a Latin glossary, probably provides an incomplete picture of the book-holdings of the Catholic period, since religious works in Latin had lost their appeal after the Reformation and others had become superfluous through translations. In Iceland, too, Latin and the vernacular co-existed for a long time, in that Latin had to fill its function as the language of clerics and scholars but also as the language of instruction for those attending cathedral schools, monastery schools (that up until the 13th cent. admittedly played a minor role in the school system) and private schools (in particular Haukadalr and Oddi) – together with future clerics, other members of the upper class. The sources provide evidence not only of education in Icelandic schools but also of of periods of study undertaken overseas quite early on by Icelandic clerics and scholars [3].

Even if we have no direct sources for the book-holdings for the first Christian centuries on Iceland, later, indirect evidence allows one to conclude that the most important works, either known in Latin or written in Latin during the Middle Ages (Greek culture was accessed only through transmission in Latin), reached Iceland in entirety or in part: Donatus and Priscian as textbooks, Sallust (*Catilina* and *Bellum Iugurthinum*) and Lucan (*Pharsalia*), who both had great significance for indigenous historical writing, works of Ovid [11], Augustine and Gregory the Great, the *Etymologiae* of Isidore of Seville, the *Historia scholastica* of Peter Comestor, the *Speculum historiale* of Vincent of Beauvais, among others. The *Physiologus*, Prosper's *Epigrams* and the *Elucidarius* of Honorius Augustodunensis were translated into Old Icelandic as early as around 1200. Patristic literature was apparently well known; scholastic literature, on the other hand, was little known.

In translating Latin literature (e.g. Dares Phrygius: *De excidio belli Troiani*), the Icelanders dealt quite in-dependently with their sources and adapted them linguistically to the indigenous oral narrative tradition, regularly translating verse into prose [14].

With the Reformation, monasteries were closed as traditional educational institutions. Economic and social conditions for new institutions were lacking. In 1552, the Danish king, in whom the monopoly for education had been vested, authorized the establishment of Latin schools in the two dioceses. Because of scanty material and personnel resources, they were, however, unable to satisfy the need for pastors, and as a result men had to be consecrated who spoke only their native language [6]. Nevertheless, the Latin schools produced a succession of graduates who, with a good knowledge of Latin and Greek, left with all the prerequisites for successful study overseas (especially in Copenhagen and Rostock) [1]. Arngrímur Jónsson inn lærði (the Learned, 1568–1648), Rector of the Latin school of Hólar and a most significant Icelandic humanist, translated excerpts from the Old Norse historiographical literature into Latin and composed a series of Latin geographical works. From the 17th cent. on, a large number of ancient works were translated from Latin (Ovid, Horace, Virgil *inter alia*), as well as some from Greek, into Icelandic, and Old Icelandic works were translated into Latin. Scholarly treatises and dictionaries used Latin, and verse compositions were occasionally produced in Latin in Iceland [4; 5; 9; 10].

After the unification of the two dioceses in 1801, the Latin schools of Skálholt and Hólar were merged into one Latin school at Reykjavík, which survives today as Menntaskóli (Classical high school or gymnasium). At the University of Iceland it is possible to study Latin and Greek as a minor or major (1 or 2 years) for the B. A. degree.

1 S. BAGGE, Nordic Students at Foreign Universities until 1660, in: Scandinavian Journal of History 9, 1984, 1–29　2 J. BENEDIKTSSON, Skole, Island, in: Kulturhistorisk Leksikon for Nordisk Middelalder 15, 1970, 640　3 Id., Studieresor, Island, in: Kulturhistorisk Leksikon for Nordisk Middelalder 17, 1970, 341–342　4 H. HERMANNSSON (ed.), The Hólar Cato. An Icelandic Schoolbook of the Seventeenth Century, 1958　5 G.Á. HARDARSON, Latin philosophy in 17th-Century Iceland, in: M. S. JENSEN (ed.), A History of Nordic Neo-Latin Literature, 1995, 302–308　6 V. A. ÍSLEIFSDÓTTIR-BICKEL, Die Einführung der Reformation in Island. 1537–1565, 1996　7 M. L. LÁRUSSON, Kloster, in: Kulturhistorisk Leksikon for Nordisk Middelalder 8, 1963, 544–546　8 P. LEHMANN, Skandinaviens Anteil an der lateinischen Literatur und Wissenschaft des Mittelalters, (=Sitzungsberichte der Bayerischen Akademie der Wissenschaften. Philosophisch-historische Abteilung, 1936, issue 2; 1937, issue 7. 1937)　9 S. PÉTURSSON, Iceland, in: M. S. JENSEN (ed.), A History of Nordic Neo-Latin Literature, 1995, 96–128　10 Id., Latin Teaching in Iceland after the Reformation, in: I. EKREM, et al (eds.), Reformation and Latin Literature in Northern Europe, 1996　11 Id., Ovid in Iceland, in: Cul-

tura classica e cultura germanica settentrionale. Atti del Convegno internazionale di studi, Universitá di Macerata, 1988, 53–63   12 S. H. SVAVARSSON, Að hugsa á latínu, in: Skírnir 171, 1997, 518–525   13 E. WALTER, Die lateinische Sprache und Literatur auf Island und in Norwegen bis zum Beginn des 13. Jahrhunderts. Ein Orientierungsversuch, in: Nordeuropa Studien 4, 1971, 195–229   14 S. WÜRTH (ed.), Isländische Antikensagas, 1996.

ADDITIONAL BIBLIOGRAPY G. JENSSON, Puritas Nostrae Linguae: Upphaf íslenskrar málhreinsunar í latneskum húmanisma, in: Skírnir 177, 2003, 37–67; G. JENSSON, The Lost Latin Literature of Medieval Iceland: The Fragments of the Vita Sancti Thorlaci and Other Evidence, in: Symbolae Osloenses 79, 2003, 150–170; S. PÉTURSSON, Studiet af latinsk Grammatik i Island, in: Studies in the Development of Linguistics in Denmark, Finland, Iceland, Norway and Sweden, 1996, 274–296; S. PÉTURSSON, Latínurit Íslendinga frá lokum 16. aldar fram á 19. öld, in: Milli himins og jarðar. Maður, guð og menning í hnotskurn hugvísinda, 1997, 113–24; S. PÉTURSSON, Da, musa, modos! (Gef þú, sönggyðja, ljóð!) Um latínukveðskap tengdan Þórði Þorlákssyni og Skálholti. Frumkvöðull vísinda og mennta. Þórður; Þorláksson biskup í Skálholti, 1998, 197–219; S. PÉTURSSON, Voru til lærðar konur, feminae doctae, á Íslandi?, in: Skírnir 175, 2001, 67–82; S PÉTURSSON, Fire latinske digte og deres betydning i en trængselstid, in: Norden och Europa 1700–1830, Synvinklar på ömsesidigt kulturellt inflytande, 2003, 155–196; S. H. SVAVARSSON, The Latinity of Neo-Latin Historiography in Iceland ca. 1600–1800, in: O. MERISALO, R. SARASTI-WILENIUS (eds.), Erudition and Eloquence, The Use of Latin in the Countries of the Baltic Sea (1500–1800), Acts of a Colloquium Held in Tartu, 23–26 August, 1999, Annales Academiae Scientiarum Fennicae, Humaniora 325, 2003, 66–85; S. H. SVAVARSSON, Greatness Revived: The Latin Dissemination of the Icelandic Past, in: E. KESSLER, H. C. KUHN (eds.), Germania Latina – Latinitas teutonica, vol. 1, 2003, 553–62
GERT KREUTZER

Idyll see → BUCOLICS

Igel Column see → TRIER

Imagination
A. INTRODUCTION B. MIDDLE AGES C. RENAISSANCE D. 18TH, 19TH AND 20TH CENTURIES

A. INTRODUCTION
Imagination is the English translation of the Greek *phantasía* ('idea, image'). The term *phantasía* was initially shaped by Greek philosophy, where it was also evaluated and critiqued. In medieval philosophy, the Latin term *imaginatio* appears alongside the Greek *phantasía*, where imagination in the sense of *phantasía* was first discussed in connection with epistemology. Imagination subsequently entered the context of debate on aesthetics, art and poetic theory, primarily through the philosophy of the → RENAISSANCE. It was during this period that the word imagination entered into German through Jan Amos Comenius (1592–1670). In the philosophy of the 18th and 19th cents., imagination

became a key term for creative invention and action and in the 20th cent. for the design or creation of new social conditions as well.

B. MIDDLE AGES
Reality, in the medieval sense, appeared as an ensemble of possibility, facticity and necessity, guaranteed by God. Only after embracing Modern concepts of perception – by freeing themselves of the idea that humanity is sustained and borne by God, by reducing the actual to the simply factual and by disassociating the possible from the merely real – could imagination be discovered by Renaissance thinkers as a 'world-creating power'. Medieval philosophers inherited both Classical and Christian views on imagination. Augustine of Hippo (354–430) already recognized three types of visions: the vision of the senses, the vision of the fantasy and the vision of the *intellectus*. He perceived an abyss between the spiritual vision of the fantasy and the intellectual vision of reason. Under reasonable conditions, the fantasy provides the reason with important conditions for perception; under unreasonable conditions, it hides the danger of excess (letter to Nebridius = Aug. Epist. 3, No. 7, p. 12, ed. Hoffmann). Pseudo-Dionysius Areopagita (ca. 500) considered the significance of the fantasy to lie in connection with gnosis. The images of fantasy, which introduce the divine into poetry and art, are signs, disguises and mystical revelations of the divine (De coel. hierarch. 2,3 = PG 3,12 col. 140). While Thomas Aquinas (1225–1274) regarded the fantasy in an Aristotelian manner in the process of perception [2. 299], Bonaventura (1221–1274) remained Platonically-NeoPlatonically reserved. For him. the imaginative powers belonged more to carnality than the spirit. The fantasy can disturb the freedom of the will and even become a point of contact for demonic influence [5].

C. RENAISSANCE
In the course of reducing the concept of reality to the factual, imagination was given the opportunity to conceive possibilities arbitrarily (cf. [23]). Nicolaus of Cusa (1401–1461) conceived the creative modern human being in his *Idiota* dialogues. The layman, a craftsman, an *idiota* compared to the scholars of the time, emphasizes, for example, that a spoon has "no other archetype besides the idea in our mind" [8. 213]. The human being is given the title of a 'second God' or a 'microcosm', not in an absolute sense, but rather merely as an 'analogue' (*De conjecturis* 2,14). Such thoughts provide the keywords for interpreting the imagination in the Renaissance as a creative, godlike instance. It is no coincidence that reflection on the creativity of fantasy is found as part of the reflection on art in this period. The anticipation of the scope of artistic freedom, of the infinity of the possible as compared to the finiteness of the factual, can be perceived in Renaissance philosophy. Lorenzo Valla (1415–1457), the author of *Elegantiae linguae Latinae* (*c.* 1435–44), emphasized the independence of the Renaissance as a

period and the originality of the author in his foreword. Marsilio Ficino (1433–1499) speaks – in the Platonic sense – of the inspiration of the poet, which makes him godlike (*Commentarium in Convivium* 7,13). Leonardo da Vinci (1452–1519) writes: "If the painter wishes to see beauties which will enamour him, he is the master of their production, and if he wishes to see monstrous things which frighten or those which are buffoonish and laughable or truly compassionate, he is their lord and God" [21. 14]. However, Leonardo also remained devoted to nature, to the established reality as the revelation of the divine: fantasy anticipates that which lies as a possibility in nature itself. Julius Caesar Scaliger (1484–1558) is considered one of the theoreticians of modern artistry. When confronted with the term *imitatio*, he articulates the creative artistic ability: "Poetry represents existing things more beautifully and gives form to that which does not exist" (*Poetices libri septem*, 1,1). In this case, poetry appears creative like a 'second God' (*alter deus*). Poets themselves also reflected on creative ability in the 16th cent.: Torquato Tasso (1544–1595) explains that "the power of art can, to a certain degree, do violence to the nature of matter (*materia*) so that things appear probable which, in and of themselves, are not (...)" [20]. Giovan Pietro Bellori (1615–1696) stressed that art should not be mere imitation, but should take its starting point from the 'idea'. The Creator, Bellori continues, has expressed "every type" (*specie*) through a 'first idea'. Following Plato, he says that artists imitate "that first Craftsman," design an "archetype" of the highest beauty in their minds and improve nature. This idea is "marked off by the compass of the intellect", transformed into the "measure of the hand," and "animated by imagination, it gives life to the images" [3. 3–11].

D. 18TH, 19TH AND 20TH CENTURIES

Renaissance thought pointed the way for interpreting the creative ability of the imagination: it was discussed primarily in connection with artistic, though not technical, production. In art (especially in poetry and visual arts), it was exemplary of human creation. The imagination appeared independently alongside the divine power of the Creator. Shaftesbury (1671–1713) compares the artist to the 'creating God': 'Such a poet is indeed a second Maker: a just Prometheus under Iove' [8. 07]. Joseph Addison (1672–1719) emphasized the significance of the imagination for creating art and claims the right of the genius to violate the established rules [1. No. 291]. According to him, the 'imaginative' gains in significance [1. No. 339]. DuBos (1679–1742) appreciated the inventive talent of the poet and the painter. Such talent is able to arouse the feelings of the viewer and reader, and art depends on this arousal alone [10]. The Swiss theoreticians Bodmer (1701–1776) and Breitinger (1701–1776) declared that the creative imagination is capable of granting the colour of probability to the 'wonderful' [6; 7]. For David Hume (1711–1776), imagination was the ability to go far

beyond the area of familiar experience, 'even beyond the universe, into the unbounded chaos, where nature is supposed to lie in total confusion' [13. 14].

Kant (1724–1804) systematized the transformations in regard to and appreciation of the imagination from the beginning of the modern era and gave them a 'transcendental' foundation. The imagination was discussed within the philosophy of art and within the framework of epistemology. The 'transcendental imagination' synthesized the *a priori* views and the *a priori* terms of reason and constituted the conditions of 'actual' experience in contrast to the merely 'possible'. From the aesthetic point of view, the imagination is the prerequisite for the possibility of seeing and creating beauty: while the reason can think that 'ideas' are nonsensical, beauty refers to the representation in the sensual. 'Das Vermögen der Darstellung aber ist Einbildungskraft' ("the faculty of presentation being the imagination") [15. § 17]. 'Genius' is the outstanding ability of this imagination 'zu einem gegebenen Begriffe Ideen aufzufinden und andererseits zu diesen den Ausdruck zu treffen' ("to find out ideas for a given concept, and, besides, to hit upon the expression for them (...)") [15. § 49]. According to Schelling (1775–1854), the 'productive' imagination was influenced by the unity of unconscious activity and free, conscious invention and design. Nature and mind appear reconciled in art [19. 628]. Jean Paul (1763–1825) viewed 'fantasy or imagination' as the intermediary between the finite and the infinite: it is the only capacity of the consciousness able to comprehend the 'infinite' in ever-new visions and make it visible in works of art [17. 18]. For Hegel (1770–1831), fantasy was the *innere Werkstätte der Kunst* 'inner workshop of art' [12. § 457, 267]. Fantasy gives the general ideas of the 'intelligence' a 'sensible existence' in the specifics of a concrete image. "While the intelligence (...) is productive imagination", it forms 'das Formelle der Kunst, denn die Kunst stellt das wahrhaft Allgemeine oder die Idee in der Form des sinnlichen Daseins, des Bildes dar' ("the formal element of art; for art represents the veritable general, or the idea in the form of sensual existence, of the image") [12. § 456, 266]. According to Nietzsche, imagination can be seen as the *good will of illusoriness*: life succeeds only because the consciousness covers over the terribleness of existence with images, and thus overcomes it. Even scientific terms come exclusively from the imagination, or rather from the original ability of life to deceive and lie [16. 316]. Baudelaire (1821–1867) viewed nature as the 'living book', from which the artist takes his material and transforms it according to his creative ability. The artist creates a new world in the metaphors of poetry, the colours of painting and the tones of music: he is a 'second nature', as it were. In the possibilities of the ugly, the offensive and of evil, Baudelaire saw new dimensions for the imagination; evil opens up – for the painter Delacroix, for example – a "nightmare full of unknown things" [3. 760].

In the 20th cent., the pendulum of interest in the imagination swung again towards epistemology: the major period of art philosophy was over. E. Husserl (1859–1938) conceived the ideas of the fantasy as 'intentional acts', as sensible, viewable images, both of which cause individual objects to appear. The fantasy has the possibility of creating a 'virtual world' [14. 535f.]. M. Scheler (1874–1928) declared that the fantasy in the human consciousness is always the First, which differentiates perception and imagining: imagination is an 'original energy of the vital soul.' Life determined which images of the imagination were used and which were not. The fantasy in the 'waking life' of the highly-civilized person is only the miserable remains of spontaneous fantasy [18. 349]. Bloch (1885–1977), H. Marcuse (1898–1979) and Adorno (1903–1969) gave imagination a Marxist interpretation, in terms of social theory, as that instance which was able to overtake an unsatisfactory reality. Nietzsche's idea, that creative thought in the sciences had an aesthetic character, returned in the work of Paul Feyerabend (1924–1994): he emphasized the significance of the quasi-artistic imagination in the formation of theories in science [11].

→ Creatio; → Demonology
→ Imitatio; → Mimesis

SOURCES   1 J. ADDISON, Essays from the Spectator, 1830, ²1894   2 THOMAS AQUINAS, Summa theologica 1,78,4, in: Opera omnia, R. BUSA, S. J. (ed.), vol. 2, 1980, 299   3 C. BAUDELAIRE, La vie et l'œuvre d'Eugène Delacroix, in: Œuvres complètes, vol. 2, 1976 (Engl. J. M. BERNSTEIN (trans.), Eugene Delacroix: His Life and Work, 1947, ²1979   4 G. P. BELLORI, Le vite de' pittori, scultori e architetti moderni, 1672 (Engl. L'idea: The Introduction to the Lives of Modern Painters, Sculptors and Architects, 1960)   5 BONAVENTURA, Librum Sententiarum 2,25,1,6, in: Opera Omnia, 10 vols., 1882–1892   6 J. J. BODMER, Die Discourse der Mahlern I–IV, 1721–23   7 J. J. BREITINGER, Critische Dichtkunst, 1740, facsimile ed., 1966 8 A. A. COOPER (3RD EARL OF SHAFTESBURY), Characteristicks of Men, Manners, Opinions, Times, 1711, facsimile ed. 1999   9 NICHOLAS OF CUSA (NICOLAUS CUSANUS), Liber de mente, in: E. CASSIRER (ed.), Individuum und Kosmos in der Philosophie der Renaissance, 1927 (Engl. M. DOMANDI (trans.), The Individual and the Cosmos in Renaissance Philosophy, 2000)   10 JEAN BAPTISTE ABBÉ DUBOS, Réflexions critiques sur la poésie et sur la peinture, vols. 1–2, Paris 1719, 1770, repr. 1993 11 P. FEYERABEND, Wissenschaft als Kunst, 1984 12 G. W. F. HEGEL, Enzyklopädie der philosophischen Wissenschaften im Grundrisse 3 § 455, Theorie-Werkausgabe, 1970 (Engl. Philosophy of Nature. [Part three of the Encyclopedia of the Philosophical Sciences], 1970) 13 D. HUME, An Enquiry Concerning Human Understanding, in: D. HUME, TH. H. GREEN, TH. H. GROSE (eds.), The Philosophical Work, Part I, Vol. 4, 1886   14 E. HUSSERL, Phantasie, Bildbewußtsein, Erinnerung: zur Phänomenolgoe der anschaulichen Vergegenwärtigungen. Texte aus dem Nachlaß (1898–1925), E. MARBACH (ed.), 1980 (Engl. J. B. BROUGH (trans,) Phantasy, Image Consciousness, and Memory (1898–1925) 2005)   15 I. KANT, Kritik der Urtheilskraft, Akademie-Ausgabe, 1968 (Engl. J. C. MEREDITH (trans.), The Critique of Judgment, 1790)   16 F. NIETZSCHE, Über Wahrheit und Lüge im außermoralischen Sinne, in: Werke in drei Bänden, K. SCHLECHTA (ed), vol. 3, 1966   17 JEAN PAUL, Vorschule der Ästhetik, § 4, in: Werke, N. MILLER (ed.), vol. 5, ³1973   18 MAX SCHELER, Erkenntnis und Arbeit. Eine Studie über Wert und Grenzen des pragmatischem Motivs in der Erkenntnis der Welt, in: Gesammelte Werke, MARIA SCHELER (ed.), vol. 8, 1960   19 F. W. J. SCHELLING, System des transzendentalen Idealismus, in: Werke, nach der Originalausgabe. In neuer Anordnung, M. SCHRÖTER (ed.), vol. 2, 1965   20 TORQUATO TASSO, Discorsi dell'arte poetica 4, A. SOLERTI (ed.), 1901 (Engl. M. CAVALCHINI, I. SAMUEL (trans.), Discourses on the Heroic Poem, 1973)   21 LEONARDO DA VINCI, Traktat von der Malerei, H. LUDWIG (trans.), M. HERZFELD (ed.), ²1925, 14, Fasz. 3, Nr. 19 (Italian: Trattato della pittura de Leonardo da Vinci, 1913; Engl. J. F. RIGAUD (trans.), A Treatise on Painting, 2002)

LITERATURE   22 G. BLAMBERGER, Das Geheimnis des Schöpferischen, oder, Ingenium est ineffabile? Studien zur Literaturgeschichte der Kreativität zwischen Goethezeit und Moderne, 1991   23 H. BLUMENBERG, Die Legitimität der Neuzeit, 1966, 489, 503, 535 (Engl. R. M. WALLACE (trans.), The Legitimacy of the Modern Age, 1983) 24 H. UND G. BÖHME, Das Andere der Vernunft. Zur Entwicklung von Rationalitätsstrukturen am Beispiel Kants, 1983   25 M. W. BUNDY, The Theory of Imagination in Classical and Mediaeval Thought, 1927   26 D. KAMPER, Zur Geschichte der Einbildungskraft, 1981   27 G. POCHAT, Geschichte der Ästhetik und Kunsttheorie: von der Antike bis zum 19. Jahrhundert, 1986   28 B. RÄNSCH-TRILL, Phantasie – Welterkenntnis und Welterschaffung. Zur philosophischen Theorie der Einbildungskraft, 1996 29 W. SZILASI, Phantasie und Erkenntnis, 1969   30 W. TATARKIEWICZ, Geschichte der Ästhetik, 3 vols., 1979–1987   31 W. WAETZOLDT, Schöpferische Phantasie, 1950.

ADDITIONAL BIBLIOGRAPHY J. P. BARTH, J. L. MAHONEY, (eds.), Coleridge, Keats and the Imagination, 1989; W. J. BATE, Sympathetic Imagination in 18th-Century English Criticism, ELH, 12 (1945); D. BOND, Neoclassical Psychology of the Imagination, ELH, 4 (1937); E. S. CASEY, Imagining: A Phenomenological Study, ²2000; J. ENGELL, Imagination, in A. PREMINGER, T. V. F. BROGAN (eds.), The New Princeton Encyclopedia of Poetry and Poetics, 1993, 566–74; M. H. NICOLSON, Science and Imagination, 1956; I. A. RICHARDS, Coleridge on Imagination, 1934; D. P. VERENE, Vico's Science of Imagination, 1981.   BARBARA RÄNSCH-TRILL

Imitatio

A. GENERAL   B. HISTORY

A. GENERAL

In the post-Classical tradition, the term *imitatio* refers to various, very different aesthetic, rhetorical and sometimes even ethical phenomena or standards. The ethically or religiously motivated imitation of exemplary lives (e.g. *Imitatio Christi*) should be distinguished from *imitatio* as an aesthetic and rhetorical concept. In an aesthetic and literary context, *imitatio* refers to the specific characteristic of the arts to give concrete expressions to abstract ideas, or to represent reality in a more or less idealizing way (*imitatio natu-*

rae). In that sense, *imitatio* usually corresponds to the Platonic or Aristotelian concept of mimesis. At times, however, this form of *imitatio* can also refer to the ability of the arts to imitate the creative productivity of nature. From the Renaissance and Humanism up to the end of Classicism, the concept of *imitatio auctorum* remained the centre of normative aesthetics and poetics, originating in rhetoric and referring to the imitation of one or more canonized models. In general, *imitatio auctorum* was not presented in opposition to *imitatio naturae*, which was based directly on the fact, among others, that the model authors were credited with an exemplary imitation of nature. Aside from the diverse functions that are connected with the poetological norm of *imitatio auctorum*, and the diverse objectives of practical imitation (which can consist of a mere linguistic and stylistic *exercitatio*, an artistic *aemulatio* of the model, or an adoption of specific conventions of style or genre derived from model texts, for example), the relationship between 'imitating' text and 'imitated' texts, in structural terms, is twofold:

1) System actualisation using the relation of *langue-parole*, i.e. employing one or more semiotic systems (abstracted from the texts of one or more authors); these systems consist of elements and structures (some necessary, some arbitrary), and, by applying these systems, new texts are produced according to the inherent rules of the system.

2) Intertextuality, i.e. references between texts (one hypertext and one or more hypotexts) in the sense of *parole* acts, based on syntactic, semantic, lexical or pragmatic structural similarities. The textual characteristics of the updated system may be independent of the genre or go beyond the genre boundaries; or the updated system could consist of elements and structures which necessarily define the genre, or are typical of the genre. The latter appears in terms of *inventio (res), dispositio* and *elocutio (verba)*. Intertextuality can apply to the *res* (subject matter) or to the *verba* (language) of the text. In addition, there are diverse degrees, types and functions of the transformation of the hypotext (marking the system, parody, etc.).

B. HISTORY
1. MIDDLE AGES   2. RENAISSANCE   3. 17TH AND 18TH CENTURIES

1. MIDDLE AGES
The relationship between the Middle Ages and Antiquity has been understood, on the one hand, as characterized by an essentially uncomplicated continuity, which implies an extensive integration of Classical knowledge and culture. On the other hand, the same relationship appears characterized by a medieval consciousness of fundamental difference from and superiority to Antiquity, which is based upon the privileged access to the revealed [Christian] truth. Although the study and imitation of Antiquity were still practiced, they were no longer required and were often subordi-

nated to higher goals, such as the didactic conveying of truth.

This implies, for the concept of *imitatio naturae*, that, while it was possible to portray the manifest reality in art and literature, it was not required: truths could also be presented in allegorical and fictional guise. *Imitatio auctorum*, in the sense of applying Classical linguistic or stylistic models to contemporary literature, did not play a significant role in the theory and practice of literature in the Middle Ages; a few rare exceptions exist, such as the verse letters by Baudri de Bourgueil that imitate Ovid's *Heroides*. The phenomenon that appears to be more characteristic of the period was the 'principle of disjunction', as proposed by E. Panofsky for visual art [1. 84]: i.e. the material of the Classical authors was treated in modern genres (e.g. the Old French Eneas romance). When medieval authors returned to Classical genres, the topic and/or its treatment were modern (e.g. in the *Waltharius*, an epic, written in hexameter, about a topic from Germanic Mythology; or in the allegorical and philosophical epics composed at the School of Chartres).

In vernacular literature, the models for *imitatio* were almost exclusively vernacular *auctores* and genres (e.g the lyric poetry of the troubadours). Throughout the Middle Ages *imitatio* in the sense of intertextuality predominated: i.e. individual elements (topoi, comparisons, aphorisms or poignant expressions) and/or structures of the hypotexts were integrated into new structural relationships (e.g. Walter of Châtillon employs quotations from Classical Latin authors in his Goliardic stanzas *cum auctoritate*, or the descent to the underworld from the *Aeneid* as it is integrated in Dante's *Commedia*). Accordingly, the contemporary *ars versificatoria* was mostly concerned with novel rhetorical techniques for *variatio* when working with pre-existing material.

2. RENAISSANCE
The self-understanding of the Renaissance is marked by a recognition of historical discontinuity, which implied, on the one hand, a deliberate break with the Middle Ages and, on the other, a new cognizance of the distance from Antiquity. This newly defined relationship to Antiquity – which understood the Classical as superior to the modern epoch – resulted in a humanistic programme of comprehensive renewal, modeled on Antiquity, affecting all scientific and artistic disciplines and all areas of cultural praxis; only the selection of the models, their application and the degree and extent to which they were binding, came under discussion.

Imitatio naturae became the norm, influenced by Aristotle's newly rediscovered *Poetics* and ancient literary models, wherein *imitatio naturae* was partially understood, in a narrow sense, as the scenic-dramatic representation of persons on stage. Discussions about *imitatio naturae* focused on the potential of lyric poetry and narrative texts for mimesis, as well as the specific techniques through which mimesis could be achieved (e.g. dialogues, the rhetorical device of *evidentia*). *Imi-*

tatio naturae, however, never came into conflict with *imitatio auctorum*. Rather, starting with the Renaissance, *imitatio naturae* and *imitatio auctorum* were at the foundation of a conception of literature (inspired by canonized models) that was simultaneously mimetic and imitative. Only at the end of the 18th cent., and especially in the Romantic period, was this concept of literature replaced by an aesthetic of genius focused on expressivity and absolute originality.

In the Renaissance, Petrarch was the first to thoroughly consider the rhetorical concept of systemic actualising of imitative literary models and to incorporate his reflections into his own literary practice. He deliberately followed Classical Roman models of style and genre (Cicero, Livy, Seneca, Virgil), particularly in his Latin prose and poetry, and, indeed, applied these models to all structural levels of the text. Thus, Petrarch was able to resolve the principle of disjunction that had become characteristic of medieval literature (e.g. in his unfinished epic *Africa*). He understood the comprehensive *imitatio* of Latin Classics as innovative in relation to contemporary literature. Two ideas stand at the centre of Petrarch's imitation theory (formulated especially in the Epistulae familiares XXII,2; XXIII,6 and XXIII,19), which was primarily concerned with the intertextual relationship to the hypotexts being considered:

1) *Imitatio* aspires to *similitudo* not to *identitas*, i.e. it deals with a similarity, which is difficult to specify (like that between father and son), and which, in its similarity, makes the dissimilar stand out even more. Paradoxically, the objective of *imitatio* is to produce something new and unique. Yet, the goal is not total individuality, but rather an individuality that formulates the *res* (subject matter) of the hypotext – according to the medieval notion of literature – through new *verba* (language), or by concealing alterations to the *verba* of the hypotext.

2) In the spirit of Seneca's bee simile, *imitatio* is eclectic and transformative, and simultaneously implies *aemulatio* of the hypotexts.

In the 15th and 16th cents., there was an exhaustive theoretical discussion about the various concepts of *imitatio* in Classical rhetoric and poetics and how they interrelated, primarily in Italy (e.g. B. Ricci, *De imitatione*, 1541). *Imitatio auctorum* was the subject of several controversies (especially between Paolo Cortesi and A. Poliziano, later between P. Bembo and G. Pico della Mirandola). *Imitatio* was consistently perceived as a means of actualising the entire system, while intertextuality was defined as the arbitrary integration of select elements or structures of a text, with terms like *sumere* (select), *mutuari* (borrow), or *excerpere* (pick out). In the beginning, the discussion focused on what would constitute an obligatory linguistic and stylistic model (across genres or genre specific), particularly in Latin literature. The eclectic position, wherein several authors or historical periods of Latin literature could serve as reference models, was opposed by the purist position, which insisted on a single linguistic model, i.e. Cicero for prose (→ Ciceronianism) and Virgil for poetry.

For vernacular literature, the discussion proceeded along similar lines: P. Bembo postulated 14th-cent. Tuscan as the standard language of literature (Boccaccio for prose, Petrarch for poetry), while others proposed the language spoken in contemporary Florence (e.g. Machiavelli) or a *lingua cortigiana*, a language based on several regional and historical traditions (e.g. B. Castiglione). *Imitatio auctorum* played an essential role in the programmatic renewal of Latin and vernacular literature, in so far as Classical, and sometimes even modern, authors became obligatory, or at least optional, models for genres. Thus, alternative systems could coexist (e.g. lyric poetry informed by Petrarch as well as Classical Latin or Hellenistic love poetry). Intertextual references generally took on the function of marking systems actualised by *imitatio,* especially texts, to which artistic *aemulatio* aspired, or texts and/or systems treated with irony, thereby highlighting them for the recipient. The normative character of Classical models was not beyond dispute. For example, by invoking the rhetorical standard of *aptum* (suitability), which, among other things, demanded that all speech should be appropriate to the situation, Erasmus of Rotterdam (*Ciceronianus*, 1528) criticised the historically indifferent usage of Ciceronian language. In genre poetics, the question of new genres not legitimised by Classical models was extensively discussed with regard to modern genres such as the *Romanzo* (Ariost's *Orlando furioso*) and the pastoral drama (Guarino's *Pastor fido*).

3. 17th and 18th Centuries

Within the aesthetics of the 17th and 18th cents., the trend increased in which the conception of *imitatio naturae* appears less as an imitative relationship between reality and art. Instead, it appears primarily as a mode of illusionist representation: either with the objective of establishing an autonomous poetic discourse, not bound by truth (Baroque Period), or with the intention of fostering identification with the represented subject, thereby subordinating the poetic discourse to didactic purposes (e.g. Diderot). With regard to *imitatio auctorum,* there was a sometimes-radical revaluation of *ingenium* (genius), which led, in the → Baroque Period, to a surprising *novitas*. Within the aesthetic of genius, as it originated in England, this revaluation led to a point where the *ingenium* and *ars* or *imitatio* components of aesthetic production that had previously been viewed as complementary, were perceived as diametrically opposed. *Imitatio auctorum,* based on rational reflection and guided by critical *iudicium*, nevertheless continued to be the predominant model for an artistically idealizing *imitation de la belle nature* (Batteux), especially in the Romance countries.

However, starting with the → Querelle des anciens et des modernes, the exclusive canonization of Classical models was called into question. Modern models were justified, in particular, by invoking the difference between essential and invariable norms of literature or individual genres, and the historically variable taste of the public, which is subject to changing mores (absolute beauty vs. relative beauty in Claude Perrault). This differentiation already existed in a similar form in the poetological writings of T. Tasso. The essential norms of Classical genres (e.g. *decorum*) remained valid, even though Antiquity had relinquished its status as a role model, especially in the representation of the details of the world. Additionally, in so far as there had been some progress, in comparison to Antiquity, in the manner in which the abstract standards of beauty were expressed in concrete forms, modern literary models often replaced Classical ones (thus, e.g., the tragedy of the French Classical period became the model for the tragedy of the 18th cent.).

SOURCES 1 E. PANOFSKY, Renaissance and Renascences in Western Art, 1960
LITERATURE 2 H. GMELIN, Das Prinzip der *Imitatio* in den romanischen Literatur der Renaissance, in: Romanische Forschung 46 (1932), 83–360 3 P. GODMAN, O. MURRAY (eds.), Latin Poetry and the Classical Tradition. Essays in Medieval and Renaissance Literature, 1990 4 B. HATHAWAY, The Age of Criticism. The Late Renaissance in Italy, 1962 5 M. L. McLAUGHLIN, Literary Imitation in the Italian Renaissance: The Theory and Practice of Literary Imitation in Italy from Dante to Bembo, 1995 6 G.-W. PIGMAN, Versions of Imitation in the Renaissance, in: Renaissance Quarterly 33 (1980), 1–32 7 B. WEINBERG, A History of Literary Criticism in the Italian Renaissance, 1961

ADDITIONAL BIBLIOGRAPHY S. AGACINSKI et al. (eds.), Mimesis, 1975; E. AUERBACH, Mimesis: The Representation of Reality in Western Literature, W. R. TRASK (trans.), 1953; G. B. CONTE, The Rhetoric of Imitation, C. SEGAL (ed. & trans.), 1986; T. M. GREENE, The Light in Troy: Imitation and Discovery in Renaissance Poetry, 1982; R. McKEON, Literary Criticism and the Concept of Imitation in Antiquity, in Modern Philology 34 (1936–37), 1–35; V. F. ULIVI, L'imitazione nella poetica del Rinascimento, 1959; D. WEST AND A. WOODMAN (eds.), Creative Imitation and Latin Literature, 1979

FRANZ PENZENSTADLER

Imitation see → IMITATIO, → MIMESIS

Imperator see → RULER

Imperialism see → CAESARISM; → IMPERIUM

Imperium
A. ANTIQUITY B. MIGRATION OF THE GERMANIC PEOPLES C. MIDDLE AGES D. BRITISH ISLES E. FRANCE; ITALY (MODERN PERIOD)

A. ANTIQUITY
Dealing with the concept of *imperium* in terms of its reception began in the Roman Republic [22; 37]. To its original meaning (authority of Roman magistrates) was added first of all the element of *dominion* (*imperium populi Romani*: Cic. Rep. 3,24), which soon acquired a Roman notion of world domination (*imperium sine fine*: Verg. Aen. 1,279ff; 6,851 ff.). In the Principate the range of meaning extended to *area of domination*. From roughly the middle of the 1st cent., the expression *imperium Romanum* (initially Sall. Catil. 10,1) corresponded in meaning to *Roman Empire* (Plin. HN 6,120; Tac. Germ. 29,1; Tac. Ann 2,61,2), which increasingly came to be seen as synonymous with *orbis terrarum* [49. 5f.]. The use of *imperium* for non-Roman empires, on the other hand, is to be found mainly in writings on universal history. In the Principate, *imperium* progressed to become the central concept for *rule by the Emperors* (Cass. Dio 53,32,5; Dig. 4,1), who had borne the title of *Imperator* ever since Nero. Modern scholarship, therefore, frequently uses *imperium Romanum* as a synonym for the historical period of the emperors [28].

As a matrix of political and historical self-description, the geographical-political structure of the *imperium Romanum* exercised a long-enduring power of suggestion on the post-classical world, heightened by the prestige of the Byzantine Empire that survived until 1452 as its generally acknowledged successor. For their part, the Byzantines maintained the claim of being the bearers of the only divinely sanctioned empire and universal imperial rule. In the 6th cent. Justinian was the last to attempt to bestow practical political form once more on the identity of *orbis terrarum* and *imperium Romanum* by restoring imperial unity. In a programmatical sense, this found expression in the *Corpus Iuris Civilis* that was compiled at his order, with *imperium* standing for imperial dominion and *orbis terrarum/Romanus,* for empire. Only the breakdown of Byzantine autonomy after 1204 meant a concrete loss of prestige for the Eastern *imperium*. The concept of empire itself, on the other hand, survived the downfall of the Eastern Empire. At the beginning of the 16th cent., the Turkish Sultan Suleiman the Magnificent laid claim against Charles V for the title of *Imperator*. Similarly, the Czarist Russian concept of *Roman* was based on the political succession to Byzantium, even if it had initially been imported to Russia in order to gain an ally in the struggle against the Ottomans [30].

B. MIGRATION OF THE GERMANIC PEOPLES
The Goths [18] accepted the Byzantine *imperium Romanum* as *unicum imperium* (epist. Theoderici to Byzantium: Cassiod. Var. 1,1,3) and foil for their *imperium Italiae/nostrum* (ibid. 1,18,2; 12,22,5; 2,2,2), which in diplomatic relations remained a *regnum* (ibid. 10,1,2). The Franks continued the practice of using *imperium* (*Romanum*) only for Byzantium (Fredegar 2,56d; 4,33). Although they called the Persian leaders *imperatores* (ibid. 4,64), they did not refer to the Persian empire as *imperium*. Moreover, sacral influences played an incalculable role in the concept of one single empire in terms of Christian prayer formulae (1. Clement's epistle 61) for *the* empire and *the* emperor.

C. Middle Ages

Up until the Renaissance, two major directions of thought characterised the tradition of the Roman notion of *imperium* in the West. First, the legalistic idea of *translatio imperii*, i.e., the notion that the new emperors were successors to the ancient *imperatores*, and secondly, the more starkly political idea of a *renovatio Romae* that looked to a renewal or a restoration of the ancient Roman Empire. Both ideas had their roots in Antiquity. *Renovatio* was linked to the ancient conception of Rome, that, alongside the notion of world domination stemming from the Augustan period, also included the notion of the city as eternal and revived (*Roma aeterna*) [14; 24]. Even the founding of Constantinople (330) by a Christian emperor served as a model of an ancient political revival of Rome (δευτέρα Ῥώμη; νέα Ῥώμη) [1; 21], especially as it was geographically removed from Rome. An ancient *translatio* concept, on the other hand, deriving in part from the legal transfer of Roman governance, without fundamentally calling into question the continued existence of the idea of a universal empire, is to be found to some extent in the regional movements of rebellion during the Principate (e. g. 68/69 *imperium Galliarum*: Tac. Hist. 4,59,2; 67,1; 69,2). In their local separate kingdoms, the usurpers of the 3rd cent. formally set up miniature empires on the soil of the *imperium* that nevertheless were oriented towards the political catchwords *Roma aeterna*, *renovat(or) Roma(m/e)*, *renovatio Romana* and *restitutor/conservator orbis/Galliarum* (RIC V,2, No. 36ff; 387ff). This development was highlighted by a lack of alternative, legitimizing frames of reference for governance as well as, from the 3rd cent., the increasingly frequent recognition of the divisibility of the imperial office. As a concrete political theory with various constitutional implications, on the other hand, the *translatio imperii* emerged only after the end of the 11th cent. and was then a reference to the transfer of rule from the Byzantines to the Franks through Charlemagne's coronation. [17. 104]. This more modern notion of *translatio imperii* was supported in part by Biblical concepts of *translatio*. Already the early Christian authors had drawn the connection between Christian salvation history (Lk 2) and the geographical establishment of the *imperium Romanum* (Oros. 6,1,8) and thus interpreted its significance from the perspective of world history. This overlapping of Roman imperial history and Christian salvation history fitted in with the four world kingdoms in the Book of Daniel (2,21), which for its part linked the Greek concept of a succession of world empires with Jewish Messianic concepts [29]. Drawing support from Paul (Romans 9–11), Tertullian (Apol. 32,1; Ad nat. 2,17,18–19; de resurrectione mortuorum 24,17f.; ad Scapulam 2,6) was the first to develop, out of a teleological Christian view of history, the thesis that the Roman Empire was to be the last before the Final Judgement [13]. This adapted a Roman historiographical way of thinking that had initially coined the term *imperium transferre* in the context of universal

history (Pomp. Trog./Just. 1,3; Vell. Pat. 1,6), and likewise described the transfer of primacy from one people to another as abrupt internal shifts of power within a state (Sall. Catil. 2,6). In the process, admittedly, it adapted the Greek concept, present in the Book of Daniel, of a succession of kingdoms, by converting it into a succession of rule. This theory of *translatio imperii* underwent transmission to the Middle Ages through Jerome's [45. 97–110] Vulgate and commentary on Daniel [17. 16ff. 37ff. 49ff], as well as through a translation of the chronicle of Eusebius, who had drawn the connection between monarchical imposition of peace and divine revelation (Hist. ecl. 1,2,17–23; Demonstratio evangelica 3,6) [33. 71–82; 10].

1. The Papacy   2. The Franks   3. The Ottonians   4. Salians and Hohenstaufens

1. The Papacy

Most clearly indebted to Antiquity was the Curial concept of *imperium*, which was derived from Curial claims to imperial power and exercised considerable influence on the development of secular concepts of *imperium* in the Middle Ages. It relied on a juristically-based claim (Clement's epistle) to Peter's succession and thus the claim of the Bishop of Rome to be Christ's representative on earth (Mt 16:18f.). Adapted in the 4th cent. by drawing on Tertullian and Cyprian, this primacy was finally formulated in the 5th cent. by Pope Leo I (440–461) [47]. While Peter's succession served in particular to keep a distance from the bishopric of Constantinople, founded by the Roman emperor (as new Roman church), it implicitly claimed to dispute the spiritual functions of the office of the emperor (Council of Rome in 382), made concrete in Gelasius I (epist. 12: doctrine on the duality of power). It was given expression in the assumption of the title of *pontifex maximus* (from Leo I onwards), which until 382 had been an exclusive part of the emperor's title. The monarchical character of the Curia as an institution, modelled on the Roman emperorship [48. cp. 5; 20. 23–71], likewise fashioned an imperial role for the Papacy, without *imperium* itself being applied to Papal power [15]. By way of example, Leo I used the term *principatus* or *princeps apostolorum* for the primacy of the Pope; Gelasius I articulated the notion of a *sacrata auctoritas*. Notwithstanding Constantine's original deference to the Bishop of Rome, the Empire rejected this claim in the 4th cent. and sought to set up a patriarchate of equal ranking in Constantinople, legitimised by the city's public-judicial civil status (Council of Constantinople in 381); this encountered bitter resistance from the Roman Church.

Not until Charlemagne's coronation as Emperor in 800 did the Curial concept of *imperium* have any chance to take on concrete political shape. In keeping with his primacy over the whole of Christianity, which was identical to the old *imperium Romanum*, Pope Leo III had claimed the right to call into being a new Roman emperor, proclaimed by the army, the Senate and the people. A prerequisite was that the Pope declare vacant the (eastern) Roman Imperial throne that was occupied by Empress Irene, and that Charlemagne, whom Byzantium had acknowledged in 785 and 798 as *patricius Romanorum,* ascend the throne – from a constitutional perspective – as a Roman. Shortly thereafter, drawing upon the *constitutio Constantini* (→ DONATION OF CONSTANTINE) [34] of ca. 750, Leo III formulated his claim to have a supra-imperial status vis-a-vis the new emperor. In spite of Charlemagne's express rebuttal of Constantine's alleged testament, the Curia succeeded after 816 in making Papal coronation an integral part of imperial appointment, thereby giving lasting currency to the Curial *imperium* theory that the Pope appoints emperors.

2. THE FRANKS

Charlemagne's Frankish concept of *imperium* [2], on the other hand, was based principally on a revaluation of the *imperium Francorum* and its equal status, as *imperium,* with the Roman *imperium,* which is why Charlemagne, in questions of title, largely dispensed with the additional Roman title and took pains to gain Byzantine recognition. Only when his plans failed in the face of opposition from Emperor Nicephorus I, did he resort to a systematic heralding of his own imperial role. The notion of restoring the *imperium Romanum* (*renovatio imperii*), essentially anticipated by the Pope, now came to the forefront in the West. In 803 there appeared *Romanum gubernans imperium* in a bull (MGH DD 1, 265 Nr. 197). The formula *renovatio Romani imperii,* on the other hand, was shortened, after the emperor's title had been recognized in Byzantium in 812 without the additional Roman title (Einhard MGH SS 1, 199: *imperator [autokrator] et basileus*), as *renovatio regni Franc[orum]* and reflected in the emperor's title simply as *imperator Augustus.* An expression of equal imperial ranking was Charlemagne's elevation of his son to co-emperor in 814 on the Roman/Byzantine model (since 364/7). The Pope, for his part, revived the Curial concept of *imperium* in 816, when he repeated the coronation in Reims with the putative crowning of Constantine and with the addition of anointing.

While the dual emperorship represented an ongoing constitutional problem for the Eastern Empire and led, in terms of title, to the introduction of βασιλεὺς τῶν Ῥωμαίων as early as the 7th cent. [38. 12 f.], any deeper sensitivity was lacking in the West. Here, on the contrary, the problem evened itself out, as the Eastern emperor came to be seen, following up on the traditional genteel state policy, as the holder of a *regnum* with an exaggerated title. Moreover, in the West, the notion of the duality of *imperium* and *sacerdotium* became established from the 9th cent. on, and found its symbolic expression in the imperial coronation. In a ceremonial sense, for the time being, it imitated the Byzantine imperial coronation, as the Pope from the end of the 9th until into the 12th cent. had adopted the emperor as *filius ecclesiae* before the coronation proper, by analogy with the elevation of the heir to the throne as co-emperor [8. 40–223].

3. THE OTTONIANS

The Ottonian concept of *imperium* was characterized by the universal extension of a conception of emperor that was originally particular to the Franks. The kings of the East Franconian empire, Otto I and Otto II, were still aiming only at achieving parity with Constantinople and were sparing with their use of the term *imperium Romanorum.* They nevertheless pressed ahead with developing the Empire institutionally on the model of the Eastern Empire. Otto III, son of a Byzantine princess, went further and lodged an exclusive claim for the Western Empire to be the Roman *imperium,* in which Rome was entitled to the role of head (contra constitutio Const. 18) and the Western Emperor to universal authority. He adopted the title *imperator Romanorum.* Using the slogan *renovatio imperii Romanorum,* he ordered a large number of measures for this program. This included the building of a palace on the Palatine, the place of residence for the pre-Constantine emperors, the reform of court ceremonial as well as official titles according to the ancient model, and a revival of a patriciate for the city of Rome. Over against the Pope, Otto declared the *constitutio Constantini* to be a forgery and granted him lands and rights of dominion out of his own absolute power as *imperator* (MGH DD 2/2, 820 No. 389). Admittedly, Otto's *renovatio*-ideology may well have been prompted by much shorter-term political goals, as academic scholarship, following P. E. Schramm [16. 267 ff.], has assumed. As *defensor ecclesiae,* Otto, exercising his imperial office, intervened in those of Rome's relationships which had gotten out of control. On the other hand, the return to imperial tradition has to be seen as an attempt to bracket integration for the Western Empire, which, as always, consisted of a great number of competing *gentes,* among whom the Saxons were never able to achieve a leading role as an imperial people, similar to the one the Franks had once had. Unlike any other Western emperor, Otto III had gained the broadest concessions in Byzantium with respect to a possible affiliation with the council of Eastern Roman rulers, which was prevented by his early death [32. 145 f.]. Instead, the conflict of the dual empires took the foreground once again in the 11th and 12th cents. In their formal documents, the Ottonians continued describing the Empire as *imperium* without further amplification.

4. SALIANS AND HOHENSTAUFENS

The Salian Konrad II was the first to adopt *imperium Romanum* as imperial title in 1034. In a phase of expansionist imperial policy under Manuel II, with the goal of restoring imperial unity on the model of Justinian, *imperium* came to be re-defined. Frederick Barbarossa now sought to ensure the integrity of a Western Empire as an independent *imperium Romanum* (Treaty of Constance in 1153) and tried hard, by reviving the co-emperorship principle (appointing his son Heinrich VI as Caesar), to bring about an hereditary *imperium,* independent of the Papacy, whose essential legitimacy of rule would be based on law, and thus take up the *imperium* concepts of late Antiquity. The smouldering conflict between Emperor and Pope, exploited by Byzantium, further fuelled this new understanding of *imperium*, which took root with the catchphrase *sacrum imperium*.

D. British Isles

For England, various phases of *imperium*-reception can be pointed out as exemplary. By the end of the 8th cent. an *imperator*-concept had already taken hold there that was closely linked to the meaning of *imperator* as "general" and, while disclaiming any universal claim of leadership, developed the notion of a local military emperorship (Bede: *Anglorum imperium*) which would exercise leadership over various *gentes* (*regna*). For this idea the Old English term *Bretwalda* has been passed down to us from the 9th and 10th cents. [42]. To a certain extent, this construction was based on the Roman view that Britain formed its own *orbis* (Verg. Ecl. 1,66). The influential *historia ecclesiastica Anglorum* of Bede, who used a Romance language, sought as starting point the Roman notion of empire and pointed out Britain's special significance in connection with a number of imperial elevations, of which, however, only Constantine's was recognised throughout the Empire.

In the 12th cent., in the politico-constitutional domain of Henry II in England, a local concept of *imperium* was developed under the influence of John of Salisbury (Opera omnia 2, 1848, No. 239, S. 114: (...) *qui* (Heinrich) *in terra sua erat rex, legatus apostolicus, patriarcha, imperator et omnia, quae volebat*), who first coined the formula *imperator in regno suo*, for which Pope Innocent III found a new use in the context of the rejection of the imperial claims of the Hohenstaufen Emperor Friedrich II. This interpretation must be seen in connection with a wide-ranging Continental as well as Irish imperial view of a king who was trying to strengthen his right to rule. Again, in the 16th cent., King Henry VIII made use of the concept of *imperium* in his separation from Rome. The decisive *Act in Restraint of Appeals* (1533) provided a detailed basis for a concept of *imperium* which encompassed an independent British *imperium* and for which the term *empire* was now current. This came under an imperial crown that, by virtue of its being a state, unified spiritual and temporal power, the traditional domains of a Roman *imperator*. The Britannic *imperium*-status was quite consciously kept separate from the *sacrum imperium Romanum*, which was consecrated by the Pope. Britain's imperial status, by contrast, was considered genuine and not additive. British history, in its link to the ancient world, provided the key argument. Henry's claim, therefore, stood in direct reference to the imperial role of Constantine, who had initially been a British *imperator* [27. 157ff]. In the dispute between Crown and Parliament in the 17th cent., this construction then served as a basis for monarchical prerogatives.

A final phase is linked to the British Empire of the 19th cent. In imperialistic discussion of that time [11] concerning governing world empires, people believed themselves to be playing the role of successors to Rome and its world empire. While imperialism was discussed on the Continent in the context of French continental-European expansion as militaristic despotism, in Britain the catchphrase of *true imperialism* was coined (Lord Carnavon), which was seen as an obligation to look after the welfare of the colonies and the cohesion of the Empire. The *imperium Romanum* seemed a suitable foil for solving the problems of one's own world empire (from 1870) [5]. For those uneasy at their own imperial role, which ran counter to the prevailing independence ideology of the Whigs, the Ciceronian concept of *patrocinium* appeared very attractive. That involved the conviction that in the long term the colonies would have to free themselves from the motherland, and this clearly implied a long period of educative preparation. This principle of educating for self-government competed at times with the belief in the mission of *pax Britannica* (analogous to the *pax Romana*), according to which chaos and anarchy would follow a British withdrawal. By contrast, the French *imperium* in North Africa, which likewise saw itself as a direct successor to the *imperium Romanum*, adapted the notion of assimilation/Romanization as Gallicization. British identification with Rome in the search for a political solution to the problems in governing a world empire was facilitated by the presence of Classical literature as an essential ingredient in the education [31] of the ruling classes up until the First World War.

E. France; Italy (Modern Period)

Links to the *imperium Romanum* can be found in the modern period in a great number of other countries, in Austria, Portugal, Spain or the USA. Even the idea of a united Europe has often been legitimized by comparisons with the *imperium Romanum*.

Reception in → France had an especially distinctive role. It reached its peak with Napoleon I and his *Grand Empire* [7. 53 ff.]. That Napoleon governed Europe in close parallel to a Roman emperor was entirely promoted by Napoleon after the Consular constitution was rescinded with popular approval. The *Code Civil* of 1804, the Imperial coronation of 1806 or the *pax Napoleonica* fit the picture of a revived Roman *imperium*. The Napoleonic form of exercising power has thus also been criticised as → Caesarism in the modern period. The classicism of the empire-style can likewise be understand in this context, even if the objection might be raised that it was at the same time all about aesthetic preferences, as they began to be established throughout Europe from about 1760 on. Associations between Rome and Napoleonic France supported the new regime in a propagandist sense, although, at the same time, the emotional substance of other historical periods had been similarly exploited. Napoleon I was compared with Caesar; he himself dictated the *Précis de guerre de César* while on St. Helena.

Characteristic of the links to Roman emperors are certain buildings in Paris: in 1806, after the victory at Austerlitz, Napoleon had the *Arc de Triomphe* erected in honour of the French army. In memory of the victorious battle, he erected a column, modelled on that of Trajan in Rome, in the centre of the *Place Vendôme* in 1810. Spiral-shaped bronze reliefs, cast from captured cannons, coil around it and display battle scenes, while Napoleon stands atop the 44 metre-high column as *imperator*. The monument was considerably damaged in 1814 but was restored. In 1809, Napoleon had declared Rome to be the second capital of the Empire and launched a comprehensive program of excavation there. In Germany, as a reaction to French claims on the Roman past, people turned more markedly to Greek history as a source of inspiration. In France, on the other hand, reception of Antiquity focusing on the *imperium Romanum* continued, with another highpoint in the *Second Empire* under Napoleon III.

In the 20th century, ideological returns to Rome's imperial greatness were most striking in Fascist Italy (→ FASCISM). The opening of the *Via dell'Impero* (today's Via dei Fori Imperiali) on the occasion of the tenth anniversary of Mussolini's 'March on Rome' in 1932 or the *Mostra Augustea della Romanità* in 1937, on the 2000th anniversary of Augustus' birthday, represented particularly blatant dramatic productions in the service of Fascist Italy.

→ Imperium; → Patrocinium

1 H.-G. Beck, Konstantinopel, das neue Rom, in: Gymnasium 71, 1964, 166–174 2 H. Beumann, Nomen imperatoris. Studien zur Kaiseridee Karls des Großen, in: HZ 185, 1958, 515–549 3 Id., Der deutsche König als 'Romanorum rex', Sitzungsberichte der Wissenschaftlichen Gesellschaft an der J. W. Goethe-Universität Frankfurt a.M. 18,2, 1981 4 A.-D. v. den Brincken, Von den Studien zur lateinischen Weltchronistik bis in das Zeitalter Ottos von Freising, 1957 5 P. Brunt, Reflections on British and Roman Imperialism, in: Comparative Studies in Society and History 7, 1965, 267–288 6 E. Dupré Theseider, L'idea imperiale di Roma, 1942 7 Ch. Edwards (ed.), Roman Presences: Receptions of Rome in European Culture, 1789–1945, 1999 8 E. Eichmann, Die Kaiserkrönung im Abendland, vol. 1, 1942 9 C. Erdmann, Das ottonische Reich als Imperium Romanum, in: Deutsches Archiv für Erforschung des Mittelalters 6, 1943, 412–441 10 R. Farina, L'impero e l'imperatore cristiano in Eusebio di Cesarea, 1966 11 D. Flach, Der sogenannte römische Imperialismus: Sein Verständnis im Wandel der neuzeitlichen Erfahrungswelt, in: HZ 222, 1976, 1–42 12 R. Folz, L'Idée d'Empire en Occident du Ve au XIVe siècle, Collection Historique, 1953 13 R. Frick, Die Geschichte des Reich-Gottes-Gedankens in der alten Kirche bis zu Origines und Augustin, 1928 14 M. Fuhrmann, Die Romidee in der Spätantike, in: HZ 207, 1968, 529–561 15 J. Gaudemet, La formation du droit séculier et du droit de l'église dans l'empire romain aux 4ᵉ–5ᵉ siècles, 1959 16 K. Görich, Otto III. Romanus Saxonicus et Italicus, 1993 17 W. Goez, Translatio Imperii. Ein Beitrag zur Geschichte des Geschichtsdenkens und der politischen Theorien im Mittelalter und in der frühen Neuzeit, 1958 18 F. Haens-

sler, Byzanz und die Byzantiner. Ihr Bild im Spiegel der Überlieferung der germanischen Reiche im frühen Mittelalter, Diss. 1960 19 F. Hardegen, Die Imperialpolitik König Heinrichs II. von England, in: Heidelberger Abhandlungen zur mittleren und neueren Geschichte 12, 1905 20 E. Herrmann, Ecclesia in re publica, 1980 21 J. Irmscher, Neurom oder zweites Rom, in: Klio 65, 1983, 431–439 22 D. Kienast, Corpus Imperii. Überlegungen zum Reichsgedanken der Römer, in: G. Wirth (ed.), Romanitas-Christianitas, Festgabe J. Straub, 1982, 1–17 23 G. Klingenberg, s.v. Imperium, in: RAC 17, 1996, 1121–1142 24 C. Koch, Roma aeterna, in: R. Klein (ed.), Prinzipat und Freiheit, Wege der Forschung, vol. 135, 1982, 23–67 25 K. Koch, Europa, Rom und der Kaiser vor dem Hintergrund von zwei Jahrtausenden Rezeption des Buches Daniel, Bericht aus den Sitzungen der Joachim-Jungius Gesellschaft der Wissenschaften, Hamburg, Jahrgang 15,1, 1997 26 R. Koebner, Empire, 1961 27 Ch. Kunst, Römische Tradition und englische Politik, Spudasmata 55, 1994 28 A. Momigliano, La formazione della moderna storiografia sull'impero romano (1936), in: Id., Primo Contributo, 1955, 107–164 29 Id., Daniel und die griechische Theorie von der Abfolge der Weltreiche (1980), in: Id., Die Juden in der Alten Welt, 1988, 49–56 30 P. Nitsche, Moskau – das Dritte Rom? in: Geschichte in Wissenschaft und Unterricht 42, 1991, 341–354 31 R. M. Ogilvie, Latin and Greek: A History of the Influence of the Classics on English Life from 1600–1918, 1964 32 W. Ohnsorge, s.v. Abendland und Byzanz, Reallexikon der Byzantinistik 1, 1968, 126–170 33 E. Peterson, Monotheismus als politisches Problem. Ein Beitrag zur politischen Theologie im Imperium Romanum (1935), repr. in: Theologische Traktate, 1951, 45–147 34 W. Pohlkamp, Privilegium ecclesiae Romanae pontifici contulit. Zur Vorgeschichte der Konstantinischen Schenkung, in: Fälschungen im Mittelalter, Schriften der MGH 33/2, 1988, 413–490 35 N. Reitter, Der Glaube an die Fortdauer des römischen Reiches im Abendlande während des 5. und 6. Jahrhunderts, dargestellt nach den Stimmen der Zeit, Diss. 1910 36 Renovatio Imperii, Società di Studi Romagnoli, 1963 37 J. Richardson, Imperium Romanum. Empire and the Language of Power, in: JRS 81, 1991, 1–9 38 G. Rösch, ΟΝΟΜΑ ΒΑΣΙΛΕΙΑΣ. Studien zum offiziellen Gebrauch der Kaisertitel in spätantiker und frühbyzantischer Zeit, Byzantina Vindobonensia 10, 1978 39 H. M. Schaller, Die Kaiseridee Friedrichs II., 1974 40 P. E. Schramm, Kaiser, Rom und Renovatio. Studien zur Geschichte des römischen Erneuerungsgedankens vom Ende des antiken bis zum karolingischen Reiches bis zum Investiturstreit, Studien der Bibliothek Warburg 17, 1929, repr. 1984 41 A. Graf Schenk v. Stauffenberg, Das Imperium und die Völkerwanderung, 1947 42 E. Stengel, Imperator und Imperium bei den Angelsachsen (1960), in: Id., Abhandlungen und Untersuchungen zur Geschichte des Kaisergedankens im Mittelalters 1965, 287–342 43 J. Straub, Vom Herrscherideal in der Spätantike, 1964 44 W. Suerbaum, Vom antiken zum frühmittelalterlichen Staatsbegriff. Über Verwendung und Bedeutung von res publica, regnum, imperium und status von Cicero bis Jordanis, orbis antiquus 16/17, 1961 45 K. Sugano, Das Rombild des Hieronymus, 1983 46 M. Uhlirz, Das Werden des Gedankens der renovatio imperii Romanorum bei Otto III., in: Settimane di studio del centro italiano di studi sull' alto medioevo 2, 1955, 201–219 47 W. Ullmann, Leo I and the Theme of Papal

Primacy, in: Journal of Theological Studies N.S. 11, 1960, 25 ff.   48 Id., Papal Growth of Authority, 1966   49 J. VOGT, Vom Reichsgedanken der Römer, 1942   50 H. ZIMMERMANN, Imperatores Italiae, in: H. BEUMANN (ed.), Historische Forschungen für Walter Schlesinger, 1974, 379–399

ADDITIONAL BIBLIOGRAPHY M. TANNER, The Last Descendant of Aeneas: The Hapsburgs and the Mythic Image of the Emperor, 1993   CHRISTIANE KUNST

India. That India has, to a large extent, escaped the dialectic of ancient and modern has been shown by L. Dumont. Even before him, however, others had pointed out India's inability to make use of its own past, other than in mythical form. There is some truth to this, yet some instances of programmatic archaism should be studied further (e.g. the resumption of models taken from the Maurya in the Gupta period) and more recent movements which aim at a 'national' art should also be more closely examined.

Classical Antiquity is foreign to modern India in two respects: it is distant both in time and in geographical-cultural space. In the past, however – between the 4th cent. BC and the 6th cent. AD – India was in intensive communication with the Greek world and the Roman empire. The art of Gandhara was the most striking product of these relations, but the art of the Gupta period also received a variety of stimuli from the major Greek centres of the Near East. This Greek past had been completely forgotten when the Europeans brought neo-Classical models of architecture to India for their residential and, even more, for the public buildings of the imperial power. Already in the period around 1780, Madras and Calcutta could appear as 'Greek' cities.

At first, planning was mostly entrusted to military architects, but the English soon made sure that their planners received good architectural training. The contribution to the discussion by European amateurs was also significant: J. P. Parker and the Frenchman Claude Martin come to mind in this context. The latter is responsible for the magnificent palace built in Lucknow at the end of the 18th cent., known as *La Martinière*.

As opposed to purely neo-Classical or even – through explicit citation of the Parthenon – expressly 'Greek' buildings such as the Town Hall of Calcutta (J. Garstin, 1807–13) or even more the Town Hall of Bombay (Th. Cowper and others, completed in 1833), *La Martinière* represents one of the most committed attempts to combine the rules of Classical architecture with a traditional plan from Moghul architecture. Many other examples of syncretism from the end of the 18th and beginning of the 19th cents. are attested in the area of public, private and religious construction activity in British Bengal, with sometimes surprising results. The most striking and influential of these may be the Viceroy's House by Sir Edwin Lutyens in New Delhi. At the beginning of the 19th cent., the adoption of Greek architectural models represented a means of social advancement for wealthy Indians. The investiga-

tion of many city plans, which use Classical approaches to urban development in a variety of ways, is interesting in this regard.

To Indians, these neo-Classical structures must have seemed no less alien to their own tradition than the neo-Gothic structures from the second half of the 19th cent. However, for cultivated Indians the progressive discovery of the art of Gandhara in the course of the 19th cent., contributed to the understanding of these Classical buildings in their difference from, or better said, their opposition to the Gothic. It is no accident that Mountstuart Elphinstone in his *Account of the Kingdom of Caubul* (1815) describes the stupa of Manikyala as 'imitating the Grecian style, in just such a way as any building that the Europeans could construct today, if they employed inexperienced local artisans'. As is well known, the 'Graeco-Buddhist' (or 'Romano-Buddhist') art of Gandhara was described by western experts – inter alia for obvious ideological motives – as the only truly great art produced by India. Those scholars who, in contrast, saw India as the creative birthplace of an illustrious tradition of arts and crafts also gave voice to similar views. The reaction of such Indian intellectuals as A. K. Coomaraswamy was understandably dismissive, and this attitude was also shared by Englishmen such as E. B. Havell, who described the Buddha and Bodhisattva figures of Gandhara art as 'dolls without souls' (1908). It is not difficult to recognize the underlying ideological motives behind this aesthetic confrontation: the Hellenism of the art of Gandhara was rejected, because it contradicted the norms of a tradition represented as purely Indian, and at the same time appeared as an anticipation of that neo-Classical architecture which was equated with British colonialism.

The debate became even more significant when the time came to establish curricula for the art academies. The decision in favour of the Classical model seemed self-evident to the administration in the mid–19th cent., and had its analogue in the study of the texts of Classical Greek and Roman literature, which was compulsory in the schools. Yet this attitude was also shared by some Indian intellectuals: in his handbook *Chitravidya* (1874), Charuchandra Nag affirms that the best-proportioned forms of the human body are those of ancient Greece, which therefore ought to serve as a model for all. Objections were raised by men such as John Lockwood Kipling (superintendent of the Mayo School of Art in Lahore from 1875–95), who was associated with the Pre-Raphaelites and the *Arts and Crafts* movement, or by E. B. Havell (Superintendent of the School of Arts in Madras from 1884 on, and from 1896 on principal of the School in Calcutta). They did not hesitate to separate themselves from Graeco-Roman models, and instead imparted to their students those from the Indian tradition which was more familiar to them. In this way, they, like Rabindranath Tagore, Ananda K. Coomaraswamy and others, contributed to the development of the debate over 'New Indian art'.

Only in recent years have Indian cultural circles begun to turn to the Greek and Roman west as a scholarly subject. Thus, it is significant that in 1991 an *Indian Society for Greek and Roman Studies* was founded (Bareilly).

→ UNITED KINGDOM; → PAKISTAN; GANDHARA ART

1 S. K. ABE, Inside the Wonder House: Buddhist Art and the West, in: D. S. LOPEZ, JR. (ed.), Curators of the Buddha: The Study of Buddhism under Colonialism, 1995, 63–106   2 M. ARCHER, Lockwood Kipling: Champion of Indian Arts and Crafts, in: L. CHANDRA-J. JAIN (ed.), Dimensions of Indian Art: Pupul Jayakar Seventy, 1986, 7–12   3 M. BENCE-JONES, Palaces of the Raj, 1973   4 S. CROSS, E. B. Havell and the Art of India, in: Temenos 10, 1989, 224–243   5 PH. DAVIES, Splendours of the Raj: British Architecture in India 1660–1947, 1985   6 L. DUMONT, La civilisation indienne et nous, 1964   7 T. GUHA-THAKURTA, The Making of New 'Indian' Art, 1992   8 A. D. KING, The Westernisation of Domestic Architecture in India, in: Art and Archaeology Research Papers 11, 1977, 32–41   9 G. MICHELL, Neo-Classicism in Bengali Temple Architecture, in: Art and Archaeology Research Papers 11, 1977, 28–31   10 P. MITTER, Artistic Responses to Colonialism in India, in: C. A. BAYLY (ed.), The Raj. India and the British 1600–1947, 1990   11 Id., Art and Nationalism in Colonial India 1850–1922: Occidental Orientations, 1994   12 S. NILSSON, European Architecture in India 1750–1850, 1968   13 G. STAMP, British Architecture in India 1857–1947, in: Journal of the Royal Society of Arts, 1981

ADDITIONAL BIBLIOGRAPHY K. KARTTUNEN, India and the Hellenistic World, 1997   MAURIZIO TADDEI (†)

Indo-European Studies see → HITTITE STUDIES; → LINGUISTICS

Industry and Trade
A. DEFINITION B. RENAISSANCE C. 18TH–19TH CENTURY D. 20TH CENTURY

A. DEFINITION
The categories of 'art craftwork' or 'art handicrafts' appear as sub-headings under the larger topic of 'Industry and Trade'. These first two terms are understood to include utilitarian, decorative and ornamental objects produced or designed by visual artists. They also indicate a multifaceted array of objects of cultural value formed from glass, ceramics, textiles, carpets, metals etc. In addition to the general understanding of 'art craftwork' or 'art handicrafts', which have no temporal or material-based limitations, the terms also refer in their narrow sense to the deliberately executed artistic conception and crafted production of these objects This latter sense arose during the industrialization of the 19th cent. as a response to the aesthetic insufficiency of machine production. As opposed to 'free' art, this type of art is described as 'applied' or 'decorative'. Primary in this development was the desire for a unity of artistically demanding, aesthetically constructed objects of daily use and modern living styles, which

would then lead to *Industrial Design* by way of *Art Nouveau*, *Wiener Werkstätte*, *Deutscher Werkbund* and the *Bauhaus*, which Gropius established in Weimar in 1919.

Antiquity's role as a model for applied art has varied from epoch to epoch. In the → RENAISSANCE, Antiquity had an comprehensive function as a model that included the entire range of life. In 18th cent. → HISTORICISM one found the absorption of images either directly from originals or indirectly from engravings and architectural publications. Antiquity was understood as an ethical authority. In the 19th cent., other model epochs and styles become available. Characterized by practicality, the 20th cent. viewed Antiquity as one possibility among many. It referred rarely to Antiquity and then only eclectically and without reliance on the moral emphasis of earlier epochs.

B. RENAISSANCE
Renaissance Man saw himself in all respects as a part of a continuing tradition with the ancients; he connected the present with the past in order to secure it. The reception of Antiquity extended from faithful copying through adaptation and on to the transfer of ancient forms for individual purposes. The small bronze statues created in 16th cent. Italy reproduced in miniature well-known art works that had been found and preserved in → ROME, for example, the → BELVEDERE APOLLO, the Venus Felix, the → LAOCOON GROUP, the Belvedere Torso, the Belvedere Antinous, the busts of Marcus Aurelius, Antonius Pius, Lucius Verus, Hadrian, Alexander the Great and Caesar, the Lupa Romana, the *Spinario* (Boy Removing a Thorn) or the → EQUESTRIAN STATUES of Marcus Aurelius [12. 322–359]. Various types of ancient reliefs, Roman candelabra, and sarcophagi provided stylistic models for utilitarian objects, lamps, porcelain, oil lamps, candle sticks, incense burners, inkwells and writing cases [17. 157–189; 12. 494–533]. The murals discovered in the Domus Aurea in Rome were greeted with enthusiasm. They were used as → GROTESQUES in painting and also transferred to other genres [17. 193–273].

C. 18TH–19TH CENTURY
In the 18th cent., sensational architectural discoveries and their publication exercised a great influence on artistic creation. Preserved in the royal palace in Portici, the finds of → HERCULANEUM were published in eight volumes between 1757 and 1792 in the *Antichità di Ercolano* [20]. Goethe was allowed to see these images only after promising not to make any sketches. Under the influence of François Anne David's (1741–1824) engravings in his *Antiquités Etrusques, Grècques et Romaines*, Herculanean designs were transferred onto plates made by the Electoral Mainz Porcelain Factory [22].

In the second half of the 18th cent., Josiah Wedgewood (1730–1795) began a business fashioning ceramic products that fulfilled both artistic and industrial demands [23; 30; 33; 36]. From 1750 on, Antiquity served as the aesthetic guide for various product lines. This move began as early as 1760 for *Cream/Queen's Ware*, which was stoneware with the color effect of ivory, and for *Black Basalt*, a fine-grained, unglazed black stoneware with a very smooth surface. In 1767 Wedgewood joined with Thomas Bentley, who brought both scientific background and a library. As form guidelines, the factory employed the work of Comte de Caylus (1752–1767) [1] and the publication of the 'Etruscan' vases gathered in the Campagne by William Hamilton [21], who was the English ambassador in the Kingdom of Both → SICILYS. This publication is illustrated with engravings by D'Hancarville (1766–1767) [3]. In these depictions the vases are rolled out and in part framed and colored with motifs that dfiffer from the originals (→ ETRUSCANS: LATER RECEPTION).

On 13 June 1769, Wedgewood and Thomas Bentley founded a factory and a factory town in Barlaston/Stoke on Trent with the name *Etruria*, a term indicative of things to come. Greek vase forms were chosen for the six *First Day Vases* that were produced for this occasion. The painting of these vases was done after the models of the Hamilton/D'Hancarville publication, and each vase carried the motto ARTES ETRURIAE RENASCUNTUR.

In 1774 the factory introduced 'Jasper Ware', which was a predominantly light blue stoneware decorated with extremely thin white reliefs, which in appearance was similar to that of ancient gems. Jasper Ware was used originally for small decorative items and then later for larger vessels and statuettes. For this material and on the basis of engravings, the sculptor and draftsman John Flaxman (1755–1826) designed the much beloved motifs of *The Six Muses, Apollo and the Nine Muses*, and *The Apotheosis of Homer* (→ ETRUSCANS: LATER RECEPTION, fig. 2). As its trademark the company used the Portland Vase [18]; the exact date of discovery of the vase is uncertain with suggestions ranging from the last quarter of the 16th cent. to the first quarter of the 17th cent. It came into the hands of the Dowager Duchess of Portland in 1784 and was deposited in the British Museum in 1810 by the fourth Duke of Portland. (The vase had been intermittently in the possession of Hamilton.) A faithful copy of this vase exists in *Jasper Ware*. Further copies produced in the 19th cent. show the Portland Vase in various sizes and color variations.

Along with portrait busts of Homer, Virgil and the Roman Emperors done in *Black Basalt*, there are also extremely rare 'ancient' vases done in *Cane Ware*. These Hamilton/D'Hancarville are painted encaustically in a red-figure style. [36. 69].

An important collection of Wedgewood products is located in Castle Wörlitz (→ PARK V.) where for decades Prince Leopold III Friedrich Franz von Anhalt Dessau constantly acquired Wedgewood products. The motif of 'Apollo and the Nine Muses' is again found on the fireplace of the classicistic pavilion 'Villa Hamilton' [36. 21]. The Wedgewood-bust of the poet Homer ap-

pears in a mural in Castle Wörlitz. [35.25, Cat. No. 21]. A copy of the Portland Vase also appears in the Wörlitz mural [36. 29, fig. 30]. A mural by Johann Fischer (1797) in the Wörlitz *Floratempel* depicts a *Black Basalt* vase from the princely collection [36. Cat. No. 64].. So-called archeological classicism, which was strictly oriented on ancient models, was mixed in with variations and new designs from Wedgewood's product palette.

Friedrich Böttger invented the manufacture of porcelain (1707–09). It was only in the last two decades of the 18th cent. that the idea of Antiquity as defining form and content established itself in the porcelain production of Sèvres, in the Royal Porcelain Factory in Berlin and in the Real Fabbrica delle Porcellane di Napoli [9; 30. Cat. No. 452–455, 460, 447].

Imitations and counterfeits of Wedgewood were produced in porcelain by the factories of Meissen, Sèvres, Vienna, Berlin, Petersburg, Fulda and Ilmenau. From 1808 on there were Wedgewood imitations by Christian Georg Frick, Berlin, for the factory of Rotbert, Gotha [36. Cat. Nr. 163–165]. Beginning in 1790, Meissen worked in the Wedgewood style and actually obtained officially the corresponding relief forms from Wedgewood. [27. 51, 55; 14. 114]. Meissen employed ancient forms of vessels from the beginning of the 19th cent. on [27. figs. 116, 122, 124; 14. 123, 139].

Along with individual ancient-appearing artistic inventions of classicistic sculptors, a series of twelve small-format ancient replicas [12. Cat. No. 338–343] shows how the spread of copies of ancient works made a decisive contribution to the development of → CLASSICISM as the dominant style around 1800. Primarily Roman art and classicistic forms from France and England took on a leading role. Here one can distinguish among copies, imitations of individual forms and combinations. Much loved decorative elements included bead and reel, acanthus, architectural elements, sphinxes, griffins, dolphins and the lyre. The lyre, the instrument of *Apollon musagetes*, the divine leader of the choir of the Muses, provided an aesthetic appearance as a decorative trim for upright pianos. The lyraflügel was an important Berlin invention of the first half of the 19th cent. It was developed by Johann Christian Schleip and was copied in the period between 1820 and 1850 by at least twelve firms [25].

At the beginning of the 19th cent., Germany's Applied Arts movement (=‘Arts and Crafts’, as understood in the British sense) received impulses from France and England. In 1821–1837 Karl Friedrich Schinkel and Christian Peter Wilhelm Beuth published their *Vorbilder für Fabrikanten und Handwerker* in Berlin. This work, illustrated with tables, was was designed for their Berlin *Gewerbeschule* ('applied arts school'), an institution founded in 1821, as pedagogical material to cultivate students' artistic taste. In the manner of Historicism, Applied Arts also relied stylistically upon past epochs of art history (Gothic, Renaissance, Baroque etc). With reference to Antiquity, architecture in particular (columns, capitals, cornices, friezes) along with bronze utensils, ceramic vessels and pottery reliefs–partly faithful to Antiquity and partially classicistically oriented–were all adopted. In the first half of the 19th cent, zinc and iron casting were popular processes for the production of 'ancient bronzes' [9]. The cast iron Bacchanalia Vase appeared in 1832 as an imitation of a marble vase dating from the first cent. AD. This vase, which was known to Hamilton, was found in Lanuvium, and arrived in the British Museum in London in 1805 [9. Cat. No. 409]. Produced in 1840, the zinc-cast Warwick Vase was modeled after a much larger marble crater, which was discovered in Hadrian's Villa in 1771 [9. Cat. No. 469]. Both vases are presented as models in *Vorbilder für Fabrikanten und Handwerker*.

In 1851 at the first World's Fair in London the aesthetic insufficiency of industrial production became clear; as a result, Applied Arts museums were opened. On the basis of the model established by the South Kensington Museum (Victoria and Albert Museum), which was founded in 1852, the Viennese *Kunstgewerbemuseum* was founded in 1864. German institutions were founded in 1867 in Berlin and in 1888 in Cologne. Further establishments followed in Frankfurt, Hamburg, Cologne, Dresden and Leipzig. The goal of these institutions was the development of taste and a sense for beauty. They set up model collections with exemplary pieces for artists and added libraries and schools. Their emphases differed; the spectrum reached, for example, from linen materials of the 8th to the 9th cents. from → BYZANTIUM and Syria to contemporary materials that were made accessible to the public by means of exhibits. In 1864 Owen Jones introduced a *Grammar of Ornament* in several sheets that presented all available stylistic directions and geographic characteristics: Medieval, Moorish, Indian, Chinese, Japanese and Greco-Roman. The last was represented by Pompeian murals, Cupids, griffins, tendrils, masks and elements of Greek vase decoration and architectural ornaments, which he colored according to his own ideas.

The taste preferences of the bourgeois Biedermeier society were matched well with pottery figurines of small-figured dancing maidens wrapped in richly folded garments–the so-called Tanagra figures–some of which were in their original colors. Franz Winter had found huge numbers of these figurines in Boeotia as early as 1873. → FORGERIES were able to satisfy the great demand. These can be recognized presently either through a scientific age determination or stylistically by mannered details or completeness [13; 24; 31]. Tanagras were also converted into other materials, for example, into faience by Théodore Deck [14].

D. 20TH CENTURY
Whereas the playful *Art Noveau* adapted forms from Minoan art [11; 28], *Bauhaus* and *Werkbund* treasured clear lines. Abandonment of pattern and Minimalism left little room for ancient forms and

models. Ever since Marinetti in his 1909 "Manifesto of Futurism" praised the beauty of a racing car above that of the Nike of Samothrace, the tradition of Antiquity's exemplary role–in the sense of the sublime bearer of dignity, value and ethics–has been broken. In addition to the availability of all historical stylistic forms, there was an interest in the creativity of primitives, of the uneducated child and in banality. While Neoclassicism asserted itself in architecture during the time of the World Wars, in the applied arts the functional, clear and geometric forms created by the banned *Bauhaus* and *Werkbund* were preferred. The incorporation of ancient forms in the 20th cent. wavered between individual adoptions in a classicistic manner and a new practicality. Exemplary for the first case were the designs of the 1920s and 1930s by Gio Ponti, a porcelain vessel in the form of a bronze Etruscan cist from the 4th cent. BC and a fabric design in silk with a column motif [32. 124. fig. 3, 387. fig. 4]. Also corresponding to a traditional classicistic sensibility was the seating furniture that was produced in Athens in the 1960s by Terence Robsjohn-Gibbings (1905–1976) in cooperation with the firm Saridis. This furniture closely resembled that found on Classic Attic tomb steles [15].

Picasso's production of pottery figures, faience and pots occupied a special position. Their inspiration and associative relationship depended upon archaic terracottas from Boeotia and pots from Cyprus and Crete [26]. For Picasso these models contained both a strong basis and original creative force.

In the 1960s eclecticism, pluralism, pattern and ornament reasserted themselves, in part under the influence of American Pop Art, giving rise to a new post-modern Classicism that unhesitatingly drew upon the past unhindered by the ballast of learning or knowledge. Transformations of ancient forms no longer had to be appropriate to function and material, nor to be practical or harmonious. In 1979–1980 Trix and Robert Hausmann introduced a column cabinet, 'Formalismo funzionale' [7. fig. 60]. In 1979 the metal wares manufacturer Alessi In Crusinallo, Milan challenged eleven international architects to design a tea and coffee service made of solid silver. The American Charles A. Jencks (born 1939) included classical → COLUMNS in his designs [16. 10, 82–83]. Also in his other creations Jencks reverted to Greco-Roman architecture for items of everyday use, as his Coliseum arm-chair and stool of 1984 clearly show [16. 139, 141, 143]. In the designs he completed in 1982–1985 for seating furniture, another American, Stanley Tigerman (born in 1931), used Doric, Ionic and Corinthian columns [16.168]. The form of Ionic capitals reappeared in the jewelry made for Cleto Munari in 1986–1987 [16. 176]. In his fabric designs of 1984–1985 for Hamano, Tigerman presented models with allusions to ancient coffered ceilings and colorful ornamental strips with meander and cyma [16. 177]

Gianni Versace's Medusa-emblem and trademark may be loosely connected with the relief heads of

Medusa from the Imperial period and with Goethe's beloved Medusa Rondanini. This emblem was repeated as a basic element on dinner services and textiles [5]. From the 1920s to the 1960s, the so-called Ars Arentina Wares were fashioned as → SOUVENIRS in Italy in the vicinity of → POMPEII as were an imitation of the full-blooded red terra-sigllata table-services. In 1979 in a similar allusion to a terra-sigillata serving plate that had been found in Pompeii, the house-articles designer Alessi reissued just this sort of tray in a red-colored metal [6]. Swatch watches, produced in Switzerland since 1983 as an answer to cheap Asian competition, allow merely a vague perception of late-ancient mosaics, steer-killing Nikes, griffins, ancient architecture and borrowings from Classical statues and vase painting. These traits are particularly noticeable in items produced for the occasion of the Olympic Games [19. 97, 107–108, 120, 123–124, 292–295, 526].

SOURCES 1 A. C. P. COMTE DE CAYLUS, Recueil d'Antiquité Egyptiennes, Etrusques, Grecques, Romaines et Gauloises, 7 vols., Paris 1752–1767 2 M. GRAVES, Officina Alessi. Tea and Coffee Piazza, 1983 3 P. H. D'HANCARVILLE, Collection of Etruscan, Greek and Roman Antiquities from the Cabinet of the Hon. William Hamilton, His Britannic Majesty's Envoy Extraordinary and Plenipotentiary at the Court of Naples, 4 vols., Naples/Paris 1766–67 4 O. JONES, One Thousand and One. Initial Letters, London 1864 5 'Gianni Versace': Rosenthal. studio-linie. Das Originale unserer Zeit (Werbebroschüre der Firma Rosenthal für die Produktlinie 'Gianni Versace', n.d.) 6 www.alessi.it/special/anonymous/index.htm

LITERATURE 7 S. ANNA (ed.), Global Fun, 1999, fig. 60 8 W. ARENHÖVEL, C. SCHREIBER (eds.), Berlin und die Antike. Exhibition Catalogue (I); Supplementary Volume (II), Berlin 1979 9 Id., Manufaktur und Kunsthandwerk im 19. Jahrhundert, in: [8. vol. I. 209–250] 10 W. BAER, Der Einfluß der Antike auf das Erscheinungsbild der Berliner Porzellanmanufaktur, in: [8. vol. I. 251–270] 11 A. BAMMER, Wien und Kreta: Jugendstil und minoische Kunst, in: JÖAI 60, 1990, 129–151 12 H. BECK, P. C. BOL (eds.), Natur und Antike in der Renaissance. Exhibition Catalogue. Liebieghaus, Frankfurt a.M., 1985 13 K. BRAUN, Katalog der Antikensammlung des Instituts für Klassische Archäologie der Universität des Saarlandes, 1998, 87 14 R. BUSZ, P. GERCKE (eds.), Türkis und Azur: Quarzkeramik im Orient und Okzident, Exhibition Catalogue. Kassel 1999, Number 297 15 M. BYARS, Design Encyclopedia 1880 to the Present, 1994, fig. 94 16 M. COLLINS, Design und Postmoderne, 1990 17 A. GRUBER, The History of Decorative Arts. The Renaissance and Mannerism in Europe, 1993 18 W. GUDENRATH, K. PAINTER, D. WHITEHOUSE, The Portland Vase, in: Journ. of Glass Stud. 32, 1990, 14–23 19 A. HENNEL, M. STRAUSS, J. BERG (eds.), Bonello's Swatch Collector 2000, 1999 20 N. HIMMELMANN, Minima Archaeologica. Utopie und Wirklichkeit der Antike, 1996, 277–291 21 I. JENKINS, K. SLOAN, Vases and Volcanoes. Sir William Hamilton and His Collection, 1996 22 H. KOMNICK, Höchster Porzellan und pompeianische Wandmalerei, in: M. HERFORT-KOCH, U. MANDEL, U. SCHÄDLER (eds.), Begegnungen. Frankfurt und die Antike, 1994, 45–54, table 3 23 I. KRAUSKOPF, Servizi etruschi – 'griechische'

Vasen aus Porzellan, in: R. STUPPERICH (ed.), Lebendige Antike. Rezeptionen der Antike in Politik, Kunst und Wissenschaft der Neuzeit. Kolloquium für W. Schiering, 1995, 125–134 24 I. KRISELEIT (ed.), Bürgerwelten Hellenistische Tonfiguren und Nachschöpfungen im 19.Jahrhundert, Exhibition Catalogue, Berlin 1994 25 W. D. KÜHNELT, Antikenrezeption im Berliner Musikinstrumentenbau der 1. Hälfte des 19. Jahrhunderts, in: [8.vol. II. 473–480. figs. 4–11; vol. I. 289–291] 26 M. MCCULLY (ed.), Picasso. Scolpire e dipingere. La ceramica. Exhibition catalogue, Ferrara 2000, 85–111 27 R. MÖLLER, Porzellan von Meißen bis zur Gegenwart, 1995 28 B. MUNDT, Ein Institut für den technischen Fortschritt fördert den klassizistischen Stil im Kunstgewerbe, in: [8. vol. II. 455–472] 29 W. D. NIEMEYER, Die Utopie eines verlorenen Paradieses: Die minoische Kultur Kretas als neuzeitliche Mythenschöpfung, in: R. STUPPERICH (ed.), Lebendige Antike. Rezeptionen der Antike in Politik, Kunst und Wissenschaft der Neuzeit. Kolloquium für W. Schiering, 1995, 195–206 30 M. PALLOTTINO (ed.), Die Etrusker und Europa, Exhibition Catalogue, Paris 1992, Berlin 1993, 272–482 31 C. PEEGE, Die Terrakotten aus Böotien der archäologischen Sammlung der Universität Zürich, 1997, 43–59 32 C. PIROVANO (ed.), History of Industrial Design 1919–1990, 1991 33 R. REILLY, Wedgwood, 1989 34 C. W. SCHÜMANN, Antikisierende Tendenzen im Berliner Silber, in: [8. vol. I. 271–284] 35 B. SCHUSTER, Meissen, 1993 36 T. WEISS (ed.), 1795-1995 Wedgwood. Englische Keramik in Wörlitz, 1995.

EVA CHRISTOF

Infrastructure see→ ROADS, ROAD CONSTRUCTION; → Water pipes

Inheritance Law
A. UNIVERSAL SUCCESSION B. SELECTION OF HEIRS BY MEANS OF A TESTAMENT C. TESTAMENTARY RULES D. LEGAL SUCCESSION E. TAKING POSSESSION OF THE ESTATE F. STATUTORY SHARE

A. UNIVERSAL SUCCESSION
Roman inheritance law assumes general succession to the sum total of the assets (including debts: *successio in omne ius defuncti*). Because it is creditor-friendly ("the creditor is the first heir, ranking above all others"), all modern codifications have incorporated it (§ 1922 German Civil Code (BGB): "assets as a whole"). According to article 732 of the French Code civil (1804), and in contrast to the vulgar-law rule *paterna paternis, materna maternis*, the origin (*l'origine*) of the goods and their function are irrelevant (*la nature*: among the German tribes weapons passed in the male line = sword kin (*Schwertmagen*), household goods in the female line = distaff kin (*Spindelmagen*). As in modern times, the Romans also did not differentiate between real estate and movable goods (the Germanic peoples originally did; the English even until 1925). Singular succession was an exception (e.g., in the *droit domanial*). Individual bequests (legacy) are not material according to § 2174 BGB; but not so in Roman

vindication legacy, which Italy followed with article 649 of the *Codice civile* (1942). Among the grounds for appealing succession, deliberate succession based on a revocable testament derives from Roman Antiquity, while the binding inheritance agreement dates from the Middle Ages. 'Statutory' succession (intestate, in Rome also according to praetorian law) always existed.

B. Selection of Heirs by Means of a Testament

Voluntary succession was alien to the Germanic peoples, who only knew heirs by birth, not by selection (*nullum testamentum*). Childless benefactors could use adoption as a substitute (affatomy). Among the propertied classes, the testament, which had been used in Rome since the earliest period, permitted childless persons to select heirs, and those with many children to select an heir for the main estate. This included compensation for other offspring through bequests, thus avoiding an existence-threatening splitting of the estate. Ancillary provisions (conditions, requirements) also provided the testament with creative flexibility for planning the post-mortem future. The existing testament law rested on a healthy compromise between strict formality according to the ancient *ius civile* and the excessively liberal freedom of form visible in trusts, which were recognized from the time of Augustus and the soldiers' wills which were permitted from the time of Trajan. A *libripens* and a trustee (*familiae emptor*, functioning more or less as the precursor of the executor) participated together with 5 adult male witnesses in the civil mancipation or free testament. After the *libripens* and trustee ceased to be formal witnesses, a document sealed by seven witnesses became sufficient as the basis for a praetorian succession (*bonorum possessio*). The seven-sealed testament was received in the Imperial Notary Ordinance of 1512. However, following the canonical example, the number of witnesses was often reduced to two or three. For (individual or universal) trusts, which were recognized in early imperial law, a formless, clear statement of intent (not just a recommendation) in any language (even verbal or mere gestures) towards the beneficiary was sufficient. The practice of having the testament recorded by courts, governors or municipal authorities (*testatio apud acta conditum*) or transferred to the emperor (*testatio principi oblatum*) was the precursor of notarised testaments in the 4th cent. AD. Although terminologically the testament was an act of the last will recorded before witnesses (*testatio mentis*), establishing a proper testament today only requires the participation of witnesses in exceptional cases (e.g., in the case of blind or mute persons; otherwise only if requested by the testator). Valentinian III introduced a form of testament in the testator's own hand (holographic) in AD 446 in the western empire that was virtually without witnesses. Though it was not incorporated in Justinian's imperial law, it survived among the Visigoths and Franks. In modern Central Europe, it was revived despite an unsecured continuity

(§ 2247 BGB). Joint testaments of spouses have also been permitted since AD 446. Gifts from one parent to children, appointed intestate heirs, did not require a testamentary form. Binding inheritance agreements were not permitted in Antiquity, just as they are not currently allowed in most Romance-speaking countries ('divieto di patti successori': Art. 458 of the Italian *Codice civile*).

C. Testamentary Rules

A Roman testament had to start by instating one or more heirs as universal successors (*heredis institutio est caput et fundamentum totius testamenti*). Though not taken up in the German Civil Code (BGB), § 2087 differentiates a universal bequest of the estate (instating heirs) from individual bequests of certain objects (legacies). Mere legate testaments were already reinterpreted as trusts in Antiquity, instating heirs to particular objects (*ex re certa*, e.g., properties) as inheritance shares. According to the *favor testamenti*, which was retained, testaments must be interpreted so that the testator's intent can succeed (*ut magis valeat quam pereat*, § 2084 BGB). Bequests under a delaying potestative condition were reinterpreted as dissolving conditions (§ 2075 BGB, according to the old *cautio Muciana*). As per the ambulatory character of the last will, testaments can now be revoked at any time without cause. In Rome, a new testament completely destroyed an earlier one (*nemo cum duobus testamentis decedere potest*), but according to § 2258 BGB, only to the extent that it contradicted the earlier one. A pure revocation resulted in the presumed rightful statutory succession and, therefore, is simpler in form (destruction of the intent of revocation or annulment record, § 2255 BGB). After dissolving the seals in the intent of revocation, the praetor also granted the legal heirs the *bonorum possessio contra tabulas* (*cum re*). Legal and testamentary succession can now exist parallel to each other (§ 2088 BGB), but could not exist in Rome (*nemo pro parte testatus, pro parte intestatus decedere potest*). When releasing a share, accrescence to the instate heir's or heirs' benefit was mandatory in Rome, but according to § 2089 BGB only in cases of an accidental release, otherwise for the remainder only in case of a legal succession. Instatement as a substitute heir (§ 2096 BGB) conforms to Roman law but not post factum according to §§ 2100ff. BGB, because of the rule *semel heres semper heres* (which was softened in Rome by the entail).

D. Legal Succession

Differences between male and female relatives regarding legal succession were abolished under Justinian (Roman *ab intestato*). The existing parental systems (each *parens* forms a branch) are derived from natural law (J.G.Darjes, 1740). The degree of relationship only decides the appointment of the next parental (order) to a secondary degree. The intestate right of inheritance of direct relatives no longer depends on the continuation of patriarchal powers (*patria potestas*) (no setting back of emancipated persons). The right of entry of descendants of predeceased children and lateral relatives only developed slowly. Today, inheritance follows lines (*pro stirpe*), not principals (*pro capite*: However, "children's children inherit by principal" in a legal decision of 1529 supported by U. Zasius), so that accidents of pre- and post-deceasing are ruled out. Conceived, but as yet unborn children were already equal to those born for the same reason in Antiquity (*nasciturus pro iam nato habetur*, § 1923 II BGB). Until 1969 illegitimate children were not considered as related to their father (§ 1589 II BGB aF). Instead of the right to inheritance, they only had an inheritable right to sustenance. Since then they only receive a double statutory portion next to legitimate heirs or a wife as a substitute to an inheritance claim. However, in inheritance law they are equal since 1975 in Italy, since 1978 in Spain, and since 1998 also in Germany. A succession from mother to child was recognized in the 2nd cent. AD in two senate resolutions; today it is completely equal. Widows were primarily sustained by having their dowry returned; in the course of the contraction from the extended to the nuclear family, the surviving spouse's right to inherit was increasingly strengthened at the expense of the children.

WACKE, ANDREAS

E. Taking Possession of the Estate

Regarding this type of estate acquisition, § 1942 BGB took over the principle of automatic inheritance with a retroactive entitlement of refusal, which applied in Rome to dependent heirs (equivalent to the praetorian *beneficium abstinendi*). By contrast, Austria received inheritance by acceptance, which applied to heirs (with interim official administration of the resting inheritance, *hereditas iacens*) from outside the household. The deceased (*defunctus*) is also called *de cuius* after the Latin *is, de cuius hereditate queratur*, in Romance legal areas. Multiple co-heirs are liable as collective debtors for debts in the German legal area (§§ 1967, 2058 BGB). In those countries whose legal systems are based on Roman law, they are liable according to their share in the inheritance as partial debtors according to the Roman model (*nomina sunt ipso iure divisa*. Nevertheless, debts secured by collateral or mortgaging are undivided: *pignoris causa est indivisa*). Recording the inventory is not a means for limiting liability (deviating from the Justinian *beneficium inventarii*) according to the German Civil Code (§§ 1993ff.; cf. instead §§ 1970ff., 1975ff., but also § 2005). Transfers *inter vivos* must be compensated according to §§ 2050ff. BGB equivalent to the Roman collation. A suit for a division of the inheritance in court (*actio familiae erciscundae*) was not incorporated in the liberal-minded German Civil Code. A claim to releasing the inheritance according to §§ 2018ff. BGB is equivalent to the Roman *hereditatis petitio*. An inheritance tax of five percent was introduced by Augustus.

F. Statutory Share

The unreceived formal material statutory succession right required the explicit disinheritance of unconsidered descendants. Its elevation to a material statutory share right is based on a contamination of an appeal against the will due to lovelessness (*querella inofficiosi testamenti*) with the *quarta Falcidia*, which guaranteed testamentary heirs a quarter of the inheritance share and a proportionally reduced excess. If the intestate heir received less than a quarter, they had a claim to supplementing their statutory share (*actio ad supplendam legitimam*, similar § 2305 BGB). The statutory share (including that of the spouse) was increased by the German Civil Code to half the value of the legal portion (§ 2303). Reasons for withdrawing the statutory portion are equivalent to those received for ineligibility (especially: "The bloody hand does not inherit", *indigno aufertur hereditas*: §§ 2333, 2346 BGB). Benevolent disinheritance or withdrawal of the statutory share of an overindebted descendant is permissible (*exheredatio bona mente*, according to § 2338 BGB).

→ Succession, law of; → Inheritance, division of; → Fideicommissum; → Legatum; → Testament
→ Marriage; → Roman Law

1 H. Coing, Europäisches Privatrecht I 1985, §§ 117ff.; II 1989, §§ 122ff. 2 HWB zur dt. Rechtsgesch., s.v. Erbengemeinschaft, Erbfolgeordnung, Erbrecht, Erbvertrag, Noterben, Parentelenordnung, Pflichtteilsrecht, Verzicht 3 A. Sanguinetti, Dalla querela alla portio legitima, 1996 4 A. Wacke, Die Entwicklung der Testamente in Antike und Mittelalter, in: Orbis Iuris Romani (OIR) 2, 1996, 113–120 5 Id., Ungeteilte Pfandhaftung, in: Index 3, 1972, 454, 463ff. 6 G. Wesener, Geschichte des Erbrechtes in Österreich seit der Rezeption, 1957 7 Id., Einflüsse und Geltung des römisch-gemeinen Rechts in den altösterreichischen Ländern, 1989, 79ff. 8 Id., Sondervermögen und Sondererbfolge im nachklassischen römischen Recht (bona materna etc.), in: H.-P. Benöhr, K. Hackl, R. Knütel, A. Wacke (eds.), Iuris professio: Festschrift M.Kaser zum 80. Geburtstag, 1986, 331–346 9 G. Wesener, Remedia der Noterben bei Glossatoren etc., in: D. Medicus, H.-J. Mertens, K. W. Nörr, W. Zöllner (eds.), Festschrift Hermann Lange, 1992, 285–300 10 G. Wesener, Beschränkung der Erbenhaftung im römischen Recht, in: M. J. Schermaier, Z. Végh (eds.), Ars boni et aequi: Festschrift W. Waldstein, 1993, 401–416 11 B. Windscheid, Th. Kipp, Pandekten III, ⁹1906, §§ 527ff.

ANDREAS WACKE

Inscriptions, study of see → Epigraphy, Greek

International Law
A. Introduction B. Natural Law/Law of Nations C. Laws of War
D. Institutions of International Law
E. Private-Law Institutions

A. Introduction

The modern concept of International Law (IL), which began to emerge in the 13th cent. as a consensus-based legal order of the international society of states, has adopted a great deal from the ancient world: legal concepts and institutions, philosophy, historiographic representations of legally relevant events and literature in general–the doctrines of → NATURAL LAW and *ius gentium*, the concept of the 'just war', institutions of ancient IL that have influenced modern IL, and institutions of Roman civil law. However, all of these underwent a steady process of change in content as they were received by successive generations. They were legally normative, in so far as legists and canonists of the Middle Ages adopted Roman law as current law, and historically normative in the sense that – particularly in the doctrine of humanistic natural law that became part of IL in the Early Modern period – the natural-law based doctrine of IL, that began to develop in the 16th cent., drew upon the authority and evidence provided by ancient philosophers, historiographers, legal scholars and writers in establishing itself as bound to a tradition.

The significance and influence of these ancient sources for modern IL have been noted and recorded, elaborated on in parts or at least mentioned, ever since the historiography of IL commenced in the 19th cent. [58. 26; 42. 7; 46. 43; 47. 121; 31. 4; 45. 9, 177; 27. 108; 59; 48. 100; 61. 40, 62]. However, there has been no thorough examination of their reception. Assessments of the importance of Antiquity for modern IL range from identifying merely an "indirect effect" [41. 13] to the assertion of an "uninterrupted historical continuity" in IL from the time of the Roman Republic [59. 1]. Modern IL still shows elements of its ancient origin, but they tend not to be recognized as such, but rather to be viewed in more general terms.

B. NATURAL LAW/LAW OF NATIONS

It was in Cicero and Livius [14; 35; 37] and the Digests [1,1,1,3; 1,1,9] that the initially separate concepts of philosophical-legal and historical-legal *ius gentium* were first linked. This association, which was incorporated via Isidore (nat. orig. 5,4,6) into the *Decretum Gratiani* [I, C VI–VIII], shaped the formulation of international-law doctrine by theologians, philosophers and legal practitioners from the Middle Ages to the Early Modern era [47. vol. 1. 54]. The former concept was always general in nature, while the latter was more specific [48. 104]. The point of departure was Ulpian's definition of *ius naturale* as the law of all living creatures and of *ius gentium* as the law of all human beings [Dig. 1,1,1,3²; 4]. As time went by, however, the contents of both concepts underwent considerable change. It was not until the 16th cent. that the concept of *ius gentium* as 'IL' and as the "law of or existing among all peoples" or the "law between human beings" [35. 10], which until the Middle Ages was a two-dimensional concept encompassing both international and civil law, came to have the single meaning of 'IL' [48. 108]. Thomas Aquinas appears to have largely followed the reasoning of Ulpian and Gaius [13. vol. 18. 10]. In late Scholasticism, however, F. de Vitoria

replaced, in Gaius' definition of *ius gentium* – "That which has been determined by natural reason between all human beings is known as law among all nations"-, the words "between all human beings" with "between all nations" [15. 460]. According to F. de Vitoria, therefore, *ius gentium* should be translated as IL. For his part, F. Suarez, following Soto, rejected Ulpian's position that natural law also applied to animals [12. 180]. He was joined in this view by Grotius, Pufendorf and others [5. 52; 11. vol. 1. 304]. In his further analysis, Suarez defined *ius gentium* in both senses as positive human law. As the doctrine of IL in the context of natural law became ever more sophisticated, it came to be defined as natural law applicable to the relations among states, which were treated as individuals [12. 390; 16. 4; 14. VI]. However, since these authors derived natural law philosophically from reason-based insight, the principles contained in the Digests lost their normative significance and, in accordance with their fundamentally Humanist character, were used as arguments, evidence and supporting materials alongside the Bible, the Church fathers, Greek and Roman philosophers, historiographers and writers. In the title of his book, Grotius borrowed wording from Cicero [Balb. VI 15] and employed a dense network of citations and examples from ancient authors to back up nearly every aspect of his formulation of natural law and IL [5. 633]. In his book on IL, the English author Richard Zouche made reference to fetial law, i. e. Roman law which was practised by a priesthood specifically dedicated to that purpose and which governed Rome's relations with other polities [60. 99] [17]. This Humanism-based reception of ancient IL ended in the course of the 17th cent., however. The basic structure of natural law and IL that had been handed down took on other content in the 18th cent., independent of ancient presuppositions [53. 112]. Along with the liberal IL doctrine that emerged in the mid–19th cent., the doctrine of IL that was shaped by positivistic law distanced itself from the model based on natural law [37. 11] and, thus, from its ancient premises. Nonetheless, a natural-law tradition was preserved in the philosophical doctrine of IL [49] and continues to the present [55. 13].

C. LAWS OF WAR

The laws of war in the Middle Ages and the Early Modern era also adopted Roman traditions [2. vol. 1. 8; 27. 144]. These laws were shaped by the concept of the "just and pious war" that had its origin in the fetial rite [60. 102] (→ War). As a result of the process of Christianization that took place between the time of Augustine [21] and Thomas Aquinas [13. vol. 17B. 82], however, there was a fundamental change in the substance of Roman legal grounds for war. These grounds were now provided by a just cause, which was not limited to a violation of the law, but during the Middle Ages and up to the time of the Reformation might include such things as a grave sin, unbelief or heresy [30. 17]. Up to the 18th cent., theologians, philosophers and legal scholars affirmed that war was basically permissible, pointing to the Holy Scriptures but also, particularly in the Humanist literature of the 16th and 17th cents., to philosophical, historical and literary writings of the ancient world [9. 229; 1. 7; 4. 42; 5. 28]. Gradually, however, the inherent difficulty of determining the soundness of a just cause led to a loss of its legitimizing effect in favour of formal legitimacy. Ever since Augustine, the official requirement was that a just war be waged by an authority of the polity or by a sovereign. According to Bartolus, only the Emperor, as ruler of all the Roman people, i.e. of Latin Christendom, was permitted *de jure* to wage a permissible war; kings and princes could do so only *de facto*, if there was no mutually-accepted superordinate authority to rule on their conflicts [2. vol. 4. 236v]. But even in the late Middle Ages, this doctrine was disputed [9. 234]. According to the natural-law based IL of the Early Modern era, all rulers and states which were autonomous in their dealings with external entities were entitled to wage war [51. 116]. Thus war became a ceremonial [5. 439] or formal matter [14. vol. 1. 46]. The formal declaration of war which was required under Roman fetial law and according to Cicero, was introduced by Isidore (orig. XVIII, 1) into the Decretum (II,XIII,II,C.1). Up to the time of natural-law based IL, legal literature continued to hold that a declaration of war was necessary, referring to Roman law and historical practice [1. 1; 4. 209; 5. 441; 14. vol. 2. 46]. Even today, Article 1 of the Hague Convention of 1907, concerning the commencement of hostilities, requires a declaration of war. Provisions concerning the acquisition of ownership of the spoils of war and the rights over prisoners of war were based on the Digests, although it should be noted that slavery among Christians had been abolished [9. 270; 52]. The right of return under Roman law, termed *postliminium,* was a topic for discussion until well into the 19th cent., albeit with substantially altered content [1. 42v; 4. vol. 2. 236; 4. 90; 14. vol. 2. 185; 10. 278; 39. 296]. Grotius believed that under natural law or internal IL the victor should have comprehensive rights over the vanquished, making reference to ancient authors [5. 447], but at the same time in citing those authors he restricted such rights in accordance with the principles of justice, equity and mercy [5. 502]. According to Vattel, such restrictions were an inherent component of natural law [14. vol. 2. 104].

D. INSTITUTIONS OF INTERNATIONAL LAW

In the IL of the Early Modern era, the reception of the Roman concept of trust (*fides* [40]) came to be of central importance, first for the binding nature of treaties [5. 236; 3, 251; 16, 30, 550; 14. vol. 1. 433; 22. 234], second as an obligation towards one's enemies [1. 54v; 5. 549; 16. 651; 14. vol. 2. 145]. A wide variety of Roman sources were cited in both contexts. According to Bynkershoek, trust was the very foundation of IL. Today, under Art. 2 Para. 2 of the Charter of the United Nations (CUN), 'good faith' is the guiding

principle governing the behaviour of states in their dealings with one another, and under Art. 31 of the Vienna Convention on the Law of Treaties it is central to the interpretation and application of treaties. This principle is discussed in detail in the literature on IL [56. 24].

The Roman concept of *amicitia*, a usually informal bond of peaceful relations [44. 296; 61. 47], is even today the fundamental component of IL, although its content continues to change. On the one hand, it was seen as a pact based on a treaty [4. 632; 44. 239; 18]; on the other, modern translations have included it as a fixed part of the wording of peace formulas in peace treaties [38; 50. 205]. According to Art. 1 Para. 1 of the CUN, the resulting order is based on "friendship between nations". The → TREATY, which is the central legal instrument governing relations between polities, has generally been referred to as *foedus*. Other terms have been used as well: *conventio,* as an all-encompassing concept [5. II, XV. 2]; *contractus* [5. II, XII] and *pactionum* for more temporary commitments [16. 297]; and *pax* for peace treaties [4. 286]. Furthermore, while the term *foedus* retained its more general meaning [5. 276; 16. 297], it was used with increasing frequency for closer and more specific ties, although not exclusively for war alliances [1. 73v; 4. 649]. The older, informal Roman *sponsio,* which referred to a simple promise, was also used, along with the distinction between a *foedus aequum* and a treaty between unequal partners [1. 77; 16. 376; 14. vol. 1. 416]. Historical examples, legal arguments based on civil law as well as philosophical arguments from ancient authors, played a part not only in general discussions of treaties and treaty law, but also in more specific analyses, for example in questions of interpretation [1. 74; 5. 289; 14. vol. 1. 433, 462]. In modern IL, however, guidelines derived from Roman law for interpreting civil-law agreements play only a limited role [20. 759]. In the case of particularly well-developed organizational and institutional bonds forming connections, of varying cohesion, between states, *foedus* has retained its meaning of 'alliance' in the terms of *foederatio, confoederatio* and in the corresponding Latinisms that have become part of the modern European languages. In both the Middle Ages and the Early Modern era, doctrine followed the Roman view contained in the Digests (50,7,17) that the law governing emissaries was part of the law of all nations and thus also of IL, albeit, since Grotius, this has been viewed as a voluntary kind of IL [1. 86v; 5. 309]. This thinking echoed that of ancient authors, concluding that emissaries could only be exchanged between politically organized polities, and that they must, as a matter of principle, be received [7. 5; 1. 87v; 5. 309; 14. vol. 2. 293]. The necessary guarantee of such emissaries' personal safety, in particular, was based on Roman law [60. 100], historiographers and other ancient authors [1. 86v; 5. 311; 14. vol. 2. 315].

E. Private-Law Institutions

Among other things, legists adopted the provisions of Roman law that addressed the acquisition of territorial rights related to changes in the course of a river, alluvial land and bank erosion, the formation of new islands, etc. [35. 112; 27. 155]. In natural-law based IL, these legal issues were, of course, decided on the basis of natural law, but also with reference to Roman jurists [5. 159; 14. vol. 1. 236]. During the Middle Ages, it was held that the ocean belonged to all people under natural law, and that there should be free access to its shores, provided that no harbour facilities or other structures had been erected [27. 157; 35. 107]. Those who upheld the fundamental principle of the freedom of the seas invoked that argument in rejecting Portuguese and Spanish claims to sovereignty [6. 23]. Later on, a basis for this principle was established through natural law [14. vol. 1. 243], then positivist law. The right of European nations to take possession of newly discovered territories was seen as rooted in the concept of *occupatio* found in Roman law, as developed from Roman civil law, notably by Bartolus in his treatise *De Insula*. Unclaimed regions could be occupied as *res nullius* [16. 226; 14. vol. 1. 192; 10. 41; 39. 98; 26. 405]. The question of whether a region inhabited by heathens, non-believers, schismatics or heretics was unclaimed was addressed not from the perspective of Roman law, but in terms of theology, natural law and canonic law. For the acquisition of territorial property and sovereignty thereof (→ PROPERTY), the institutions of Roman law of adverse possession, i.e. statute of limitations, were also of relevance [5. 166; 16. 285; 14. vol. 1. 357]. This is a controversial matter in the positivistic tradition of IL [10. 75; 39. 159; 25]. The same holds true for easement or servitude rights as set down in Roman civil law [24]. In the general context of the reception of Roman law, the various statements on *aequitas* and *aequum et bonum* were adopted, particularly in the context of international arbitration [5. 572]. Under Art. 38 Para. 2 of its Statute, the International Court of Justice has since 1920 had the authority, with the consent of the respective parties, to rule *ex aequo et bono* [34]. This is a matter of legal principle rather than of extra-legal grounds for decision.

To sum up, ancient and particularly Roman institutions, concepts, theories, ideas and authors appear to have had a profound impact on modern IL, and they remain influential today. However, only by more closely analyzing the reception of these influences, historical conditions and changes over time will we be able to determine their degree and manner of continuity and discontinuity.

→ International law

SOURCES 1 B. AYALA, De iure et officiis Bellicis et disciplina militari, libri III, Duaci 1582, (repr. lat./engl. 2 vols.,1912)   2 BARTOLUS DE SASSOFERATO, Commentaria digesti novi et veteri, in: Opera, 9 vols., Lyon 1547   3 C.v. BYNKERSHOEK, Quaestionum Juris Publici Libri Duo, Leiden 1737, (repr. lat./engl. 2 vols., 1930)   4 A. GENTILIS, De iure belli Libri III, Hannover 1612, (repr. lat./engl. 2 vols., 1933)   5 H. GROTIUS, De Jure Belli ac Pacis Libri tres, in quibus Jus Naturae et Gentium, item Juris Publici praecipua explicantur, Paris 1625 (Engl. The Law of War and Peace, 1925, repr. 1984)   6 Id., De mare libero, 1608, (repr. lat./engl., 1916)   7 V. E. HRABAR, De Legatis et Legationibus Tractatus varii, B. ROSAGIERO, M. G. LAUDENSIS (eds.), 1905   8 ISIDOR V. SEVILLA, Etymologiae (Engl. The Etymologies of Isidore of Seville, S. A. BARNEY, W. J. LEWIS, J. A. BEACH, O. BERGHOF (trans), 2006)   9 J. LEGNANO, Tractatus De Bello, De Represaliis et de Duello, Mss., (repr. lat./engl. 2. vols., 1917)   10 G. F. MARTENS, A compendium of the law of nations, founded on the treaties and customs of the modern nations of Europe: to which is added, a complete list of all the treaties, conventions, compacts, declarations, &c. from the year 1731 to 1788, inclusive, indicating the several works in which they are to be found and the list of treaties, &c. brought down to June, 1802, W. Cobbett (trans.), 1802 (Summary of the Law of nations, founded on the treaties and customs of the modern nations of Europe, by Mr. Martens; translated from the French by William Cobbett, 1986)   11 S. PUFENDORF, De iure naturae et gentium libri octo, Lund 1672; Engl. 1934 (repr. 1995)   12 F. SUAREZ, De legibus ac deo legislatore, 1612, De triplici virtute theologica, fide, spe, et charitate, 1621, (repr. lat./engl. 2 vols., 1944)   13 THOMAS V. AQUIN, Summa Theologica   14 E. DE VATTEL, Le droit des Gens ou Principes de la Loi naturelle, London 1758, (repr. fr./engl. 3 vols., 1983)   15 F. DE VITORIA, Relectio de Indis, Relectio de iure belli, in: U. HORST, H. G. JUSTENHOVEN, J. STÜBEN (eds.), Vorlesungen II, 1997, 370–541, 542–605   16 C. WOLFF, Jus gentium, Halle 1749, 1972   17 R. ZOUCHE, Iuris et iudicii fecialis, sive iuris inter gentes et quaestionum de eodem explicatio, Oxford 1650, (repr. lat./engl. 2 vols., 1911)

LITERATURE 18 G. ALTHOFF, Amicitiae et pacta, 1992   19 A. D'AMATO, s. v. Good Faith, in: R. BERNHARDT (ed.), Encyclopedia of Public International Law 2, 1995, 599–601   20 C. BALDUS, Regelhafte Vertragsauslegung nach Parteirollen im klassischen römischen Recht und in der modernen Völkerrechtswissenschaft, 2 vols., 1998   21 M.-F. BEROUARD, s. v. Bellum, in: C. MAYER (ed.), Augustinus-Lexikon, vol. 1, 1986–1994, cols. 638–646   22 J. C. BLUNTSCHLI, Das moderne Völkerrecht der civilisirten Staaten als Rechtsbuch dargestellt, Nördlingen 1868   23 U. EISENHARDT, Deutsche Rechtsgeschichte 3, 1999   24 U. FASTENRATH, s. v. Servitudes, in: R. BERNHARDT (ed.), Encyclopedia of Public International Law, vol. 4, 2000, 387   25 C. A. FLEISCHHAUER, s. v. Prescription, in: R. BERNHARDT (ed.), Encyclopedia of Public International Law, vol. 3, 1997, 1105   26 W. GRAF VITZTHUM (ed.), Völkerrecht, Berlin 1996   27 W. G. GREWE, Epochen der Völkerrechtsgeschichte, 1984   28 P. GUGGENHEIM, Jus gentium, Jus naturale, Jus civile et la Communauté internationale issue de la diviso regnorum intervenue au cours des 12e et 13e siècles, in: Comunicazioni e studi dell'istituto di diritto internazionale 5, 1956, 1–31   29 A. W. HEFFTER, Das Europäische Völkerrecht der Gegenwart, Berlin ⁵1867   30 E.-D. HEHL, Kirche, Krieg und Staatlichkeit im hohen Mittelalter, in: W. RÖSENER (ed.), Staat und Krieg – Vom Mittelalter bis zur Moderne, 2000, 17–36   31 V. E. HRABAR, Esquisse d'une histoire littéraire du Droit International au Moyen-âge du IVe au XIIIe siècle, In: Revue de Droit International 1936, 1–101   32 A. HEUSS, Die völkerrechtlichen Grundlagen der römi-

schen Außenpolitik in republikanischer Zeit, 1933, (repr.
1968)   33 F. A. V.D. HEYDTE, Die Geburtsstunde des
souveränen Staates, 1952   34 M. V. JANIS, Equity in
International Law, in: Bernhardt 24, vol. 2, 1995, 109–
113   35 M. KASER, Ius Gentium, 1993   36 H. KIPP,
Völkerordnung und Völkerrecht im Mittelalter, 1950
37 M. KOSKENNIEMI, The Gentle Civilizer of Nations: The
Rise and Fall of International Law 1870–1960, 2001
38 R. LESAFFER, Amicitia in Renaissance Peace and Alli-
ance Treaties (1450–1530), in: Journal of the History of
International Law 4, 2002, 77–99   39 F. v. LISZT, Das
Völkerrecht systematisch dargestellt, ⁹1913   40 D.
NÖRR, Die fides im römischen Völkerrecht, 1991   41 A.
NUSSBAUM, Geschichte des Völkerrecht in gedrängter
Darstellung, 1960   42 E. NYS, Les origines de Droit
International, Brüssel/Paris 1894   43 B. PARADISI, Storia
del Diritto Internazionale nel Medio Evo I, 1940   44 Id.,
Civitas Maxima – Studi di storia del Diritto Internazio-
nale, 1974   45 W. PREISER, Macht und Norm in der
Völkerrechtsgeschichte, 1978   46 R. REDSLOB, Histoire
des Grands Principes du Droit des Gens depuis l'Antiquité
jusqu'à la Veille de La Grande Guerre, 1923   47 E. REIB-
STEIN, Völkerrecht – Eine Geschichte seiner Ideen in Lehre
und Praxis, 2 vols., 1958, 1963   48 H. STEIGER, s. v.
Völkerrecht, in: O. BRUNNER, W. CONZE, R. KOSELLECK
(eds.), Geschichtliche Grundbegriffe, Historisches Lexikon zur politisch-sozialen Sprache in Deutschland,
⁷1992, 97–140   49 Id., Völkerrecht und Naturrecht zwischen Christian Wolff und Adolf Lasson, in: D. KLIPPEL
(ed.), Naturrecht im 19. Jahrhundert. Kontinuität – Inhalt
– Funktion – Wirkung, 1997, 45–74   50 Id., Die Frie-
denskonzeption der Verträge von Münster und Osnabrück vom 24. Oktober 1648, Rechtstheorie 29, 191–209
51 Id., Die Träger des ius belli ac pacis 1648–1806, in:
[30. 115–135]   52 Id., 'Occupatio bellica' in der Literatur der Völkerrechts der Christenheit (Spätmittelalter bis
18. Jahrhundert),in: M. MEUMANN, J. ROGGE (eds.), Die
besetzte Res publica: zum Verhältnis von ziviler Obrigkeit
und militärischer Herrschaft in besetzten Gebieten vom
Spätmittelalter bis zum 18. Jahrhundert, 2006, 201–240
53 M. STOLLEIS, Geschichte des öffentlichen Rechts in
Deutschland, vol. 1., 1988   54 A. TRUYOL Y SERRA,
Histoire du droit international public, 1995   55 A. VER-
DROSS, Völkerrecht, ⁵1964   56 Id., s. v. Bona fides, in:
H. J. SCHLOCHAUER (ed.), Wörterbuch des Völkerrechts,
begr. von Karl Strupp, vol. 1, 1960, 223–224   57 Id., Die
Quellen des universellen Völkerrechts, 1973   58 H.
WHEATON, Histoire des progrès du Droit des gens en
Europe et en Amérique depuis la Paix de Westphalie jus-
qu'à nos jours, Leipzig ³1853   59 K.-H. ZIEGLER, Die
römischen Grundlagen des europäischen Völkerrechts, in:
Ius Commune 4, 1973, 1–27   60 Id., Das Völkerrecht der
römischen Republik, in: H. TEMPORINI-VITZTHUM (ed.),
Aufstieg und Niedergang der römischen Welt, vol. 1 part
2, 172, 68–114   61 Id., Völkerrechtsgeschichte, 1994
62 Id., Zum Völkerrecht in der römischen Antike, in: M. J.
SCHERMAIER, J. M. RAINER, L. C. WINKEL (eds.), Iuris-
prudentia universalis, Festschrift Theo Mayer-Maly,
2002, 933–944.   HEINHARD STEIGER

Internationalisms

A. DEFINITION B. ORIGINS C. DISSEMINATION
D. WORDS AND WORD FORMATION ELEMENTS OF
GREEK AND LATIN ORIGIN IN MODERN LAN-
GUAGES

A. DEFINITION

Internationalisms are words that occur in the same
or in similar form in several languages with the same or
similar meaning. In terms of expression, they are congruent in orthography, pronunciation and/or on the
structural level; the Latin *definitio* ('delimitation',
'definition of a term') appears in English as *definition*,
and, with lexical convergence, in other languages:
German *Definition*, French *définition*, Dutch *definitie*,
Danish/Swedish *definition*, Norwegian *definisjon*, Italian *definizione*, Spanish *definición*, Portuguese *defini-
çaõ*, Czech *definice*, Polish *definicja*, Croatian *defini-
cija*, Romanian *definiție*, Hungarian *definíció*, or also
Indonesian *definisi* etc. Internationalisms are identified
by words' cores. In complex internationalisms these
remain significantly more stable than the word formation elements, which are generally adapted to the graphemic and morphemic requirements of the individual
language (compare, for example, the Greek suffix –ισμός
with Latin -*ismus*, English -*ism*, German -*ismus*, Italian/
Spanish -*ismo*, French -*isme*, Romanian -*izm*, Polish
-*yzm*, Croatian -*izam*, or Finnish -*ismi*, etc.). In their
(greater or lesser) integration into the various subsys-
tems of the individual languages, internationalisms
differ from international quotations (quoted words or
syntagms such as e.g. *cum grano salis* 'with a grain of
salt') that are adapted unchanged from their original
language. In terms of content, complete semantic equivalence can only be observed in those internationalisms
that are used as technical terms in scholarship, technology and commerce. Internationalisms adopted into
everyday language are as a rule congruent in one or
more parts of their meaning: English *concept*, French
concept, Spanish *concepto* and Italian *concetto* (related
to Latin *conceptus*) have the same meaning as the
German *Konzept* in the sense of 'term' or 'idea' but not
in the sense of 'draft' or 'sketch'. Because meanings can
frequently not be separated clearly from one other (cf.
German *ökonomisch* 'cost-effective', 'energy-saving'-
from Latin *oeconomicus* by way of Greek οἰκονομικός –
and English "economic"), the border with 'false
friends' ('falsche Freunde', 'fauxamis'; formal congruence with different meanings) is rather fluid [1]. Internationalisms in the widest sense also include complex
words without equivalence of expression, but with
semantic congruence and an equivalent word formation structure, foremost among them 'loan translations' (cf. Latin *influere* – *influentia*, German *Einfluß*,
Polish *wpływ*, Czech *vliv* and Russian *vlijanie*, with
translation of the preposition and the stem). Volmert
has projected an expansion of the term to embrace
almost all linguistic levels with his distinction between
'intermorphemes' and 'interlexemes' on the word level,

'intersyntagms' and 'interphraseologisms' on the level of syntagms or rather units fossilized as phrases, as well as 'intersentences' or respectively 'intertexts' on the level of sentences and texts [2]. In view of the strong emphasis given to the criteria of formal congruence and content equivalence, the central focus of research on internationalisms is found at the morpheme level with word formation, and at the lexeme level.

B. Origins

According to Hausmann/Seibicke, internationalisms originate from "etymologically related words (cognates) within the Indo-European language family" as well as from "the Latin cultural superstratum" for one, and for the other, from "borrowing, especially from English" [5. 1179]. However, the main focus is not on words that are congruent on the basis of common inheritance (e.g. English *ship*, German *Schiff*), but rather on common features on the basis of loan words or neologisms: internationalisms with Greek or Latin roots can, on one hand, be loan words from Classical, Medieval or Modern Latin, or on the other hand they can be words in the modern languages that have been modelled on Greek or Latin patterns. In many cases, the origin and path of borrowing via modern mediator languages remain unclear. Here, the insufficient study of the vocabularies of Medieval and Modern Latin, particularly with respect to technical terminology, is a complicating factor.

C. Dissemination

There is a wide fluctuation in statements regarding the number and nature of languages said to contain internationalisms: under discussion are at least two or more, usually genetically related or, more precisely, European languages; only occasionally have non-European languages come under investigation. Because of the dissemination into several European languages, or languages with a European origin, the term 'Europism' also occurs as a hyponym for 'internationalism'. The range of internationalisms extends from occurences in more than one language to their dissemination into languages of different continents [1].

D. Words and Word Formation Elements of Greek and Latin Origin in Modern Languages

Most internationalisms with Greek or Latin roots occur in educated and technical vocabularies. In addition, numerous 'cultural terms' have been created out of the shared Graeco-Latin fundus, such as *democracy* (Greek δημοκρατία), *imagination* (lat. *imaginatio*) or *humour* (related to Latin *humor* 'humidity'); the semantic development of these terms through various time periods has often involved several speech communities. In the creation of educated or technical neologisms on a neo-Classicist basis, several Greek and Latin suffixes have been used in German and English nouns, for example. Greek suffixes are –ία, –ική, –ισμός, –ιστής,

and Latin ones are -and-/-end-, -ant/-ent, -antia/-entia, -atus, -ia, -ion, -mentum, -tat-, -tor, -ura. They are exceeded by the large number of serializing prefixes of Greek (ἀ-, ἀνα-, ἀντ(ι)-, ἀπ(ο)-, δι-, δι(α)-, δυς-, ἐκτο-, ἐν-, ἐνδο-/ἐντο-, ἐπ(ι)-, ἐξ-, ὑπερ-, ὑπο-, κατ(α)-, μετ(α)-, παρ(α)-, περι-, συν-) and Latin origin (ab-, ad-, con-, de-, dis-, ex-, in- 'in, into' in- (negative), inter-, ob-, per-, prae-, pro-, re-, sub-, trans-) [3]. However, the central building blocks in the formation of neologisms are 'confixes' or 'combinemes' which in Greek or Latin have either free or bound stems, and which in the modern languages only occur as bound morphemes with a lexical-conceptual meaning (cf. *therm-* from Greek θερμ-ός 'warm, hot' or *loc-* related to Latin *loc-us* 'place, site'). The international specialized terminology for anatomy, botany and zoology alone is based on more than 2000 of such Greek and Latin stems [7]. Confixes are apparent in derivations and/or compounds with *therm-*, for example, found in *therm-al*, *therm-o-phile*, *therm-o-stat* or *idio-therm-ic*, but also in everyday hybrid formations (e.g. *therm-o-harden*). Hybrid neologisms consisting of a combination of classical elements with (usually productive) word formation elements from modern languages become internationalisms particularly if they are rooted in languages of a highly mixed character, such as French or English; cf. Latin *tranquillus* – Medieval Latin *tranquillisare* – English *tranquillize* – English *tranquillizer*) [8].

Within the context of international communication, internationalisms – whether inherited, newly created or still to be coined – constitute a framework which can be regarded as a kind of second *koine* alongside the dominant global language English.

→ Germanic Languages; → Romance Languages

1 R. Bergmann, Europäismus und Internationalismus. Zur lexikologischen Terminologie, in: Sprachwissenschaft 20, 1995, 239–277 2 P. Braun, B. Schaeder, J. Volmert (eds.), Internationalismen. Studien zur interlingualen Lexikologie und Lexikographie, 1990 (Reihe Germanistische Linguistik 102) 3 K. Ehlich, Greek and Latin as a Permanent Source of Scientific Terminology: The German Case, in: F. Coulmas (ed.), Language Adaptation, 1989, 135–157 4 R. Geysen, Dictionnaire des formes analogues en 7 langues, 1985 5 F. J. Hausmann, W. Seibicke, Das Internationalismenwörterbuch, in: F. J. Hausmann, O. Reichmann, H. E. Wiegand, L. Zgusta (eds.), Wörterbücher. Ein internationales Handbuch zur Lexikographie, vol. 2, 1990 (Handbuch zur Sprach- und Kommunikationswissenschaft 5.2), 1179–1184 6 H. H. Munske, A. Kirkness (eds.), Eurolateinisch. Das griechische und lateinische Erbe in den europäischen Sprachen, 1996 (Reihe Germanistische Linguistik 169) 7 F. Cl. Werner, Wortelemente lateinisch-griechischer Fachausdrücke in den biologischen Wissenschaften, 1972 (suhrkamp-taschenbuch-wissenschaft 64) 8 F. Wolff, O. Wittstock, Lateinisch und griechisch im deutschen Wortschatz. Lehn- und Fremdwörter, ⁶1990

Additional Bibliography L. Bauer, Is There a Class of Neoclassical Compounds, and if so, is it Productive?, in: Linguistics 36, 1998, 403–422; P. Braun, B. Schaeder, J. Volmert (eds.), Internationalismen II. Studien zur interlingualen Lexikologie und Lexikographie, in: Reihe Germanistische Linguistik 246, 2003; M. GOERLACH (ed.), A Dictionary of European Anglicisms. A Usage Dictionary of Anglicisms in Sixteen European Languages, 2001; A. KIRKNESS, Word-formation: Neo-Classical Combinations, in: R. E. ASHER, J. M. Y. SIMSON (eds.), The Encyclopedia of Language and Linguistics, Vol. 9, 1994, 5026–5028; A. KIRKNESS, Europäismen. Internationalismen im heutigen deutschen Wortschatz, Eine lexikografischen Pilotstudie, in: G. STICKEL (ed.), Neues und Fremdes im deutschen Wortschatz, Aktueller lexikalischer Wandel, 2001, 105–130; A. LUEDELING, Neoclassical Compounding, in K. BROWN (ed.), Encyclopedia of Language & Linguistics, vol. 8, ²2006, 580–582; A. LUEDELING, T. SCHMID, S. KIOKPASOGLOU, Neoclassical Word Formation in German, in: Yearbook of Morphology 2001, 2002, 253–283; P. O. MUELLER (ed.), Fremdwortbildung: Theorie und Praxis in Geschichte und Gegenwart. Dokumentation germanistischer Forschung 6, 2005

MECHTHILD HABERMANN

Interpolation, Study of

A. CONCEPT B. DEVELOPMENT C. PRESENT SITUATION D. METHODS

A. CONCEPT

Interpolations are later changes to a given source made by intentionally adding or removing material and which are not indicated as such. The aim of the study of interpolations in legal history is to establish the presence of such alterations within the sources of Roman law. The pre-Classical and Classical juridical writings preserved in Justinian's Corpus Iuris (1st cent. BC to ca. 240 AD) are the principal focus of interest in this area.

B. DEVELOPMENT

Leaving aside the Humanist forerunners (Cujaz, Faber), the study of interpolation established itself towards the end of the 19th cent., when, in view of modern codifications, the Corpus Iuris lost its status as a legal source-work and thus became a potential object for historical investigation. Building upon the palingenetic studies of O. Lenel (on their significance: [1. 170–182]), the first generation of textual investigators (on which, see [11. 856 f.]) established a methodology for the study of interpolation. In the first half of the 20th cent. the number of assumed interpolations grew on a massive scale (just see the indices to [3] and [9]). This radical textual criticism (paradigmatic example: G. Beseler [2]) neglected the individuality of the Classical lawyers (see, for example, [14. 181]) and postulated a unified and strictly subject-oriented Classical style. In substance, they demanded from Classical law a purity of principle which cannot be expected from a legal system which is problem-oriented and characterised by controversy and casuistry (see: [8. 150]); moreover, the philosophical influences to which the legal system was subject in the Late Republic were also neglected (on this and on the connection with the nationalistic-romantic basis for this radical text-critical phase, see: [1. 203 ff.]). Texts which did not match up to this idea were regarded as interpolations. Especially after the Second World War, this radical textual criticism gave way to a less prejudicial approach to the sources, which gave greater credibility to the transmitted texts (see further C, D).

C. PRESENT SITUATION

→ 'TEXTSTUFENFORSCHUNG' has made clear that Classical writings were subject to alterations even before Justinian (see the basic study [12]); they resemble a "picture which has been painted over several times"' [14. 165]. However, it is clear that we may only assume influences from common law in the western Roman Empire (4th and 5th cents. AD) or direct textual interventions from the law schools of the eastern empire (5th cent. AD) on rare occasions (see [7. 71 ff.; 14. 170, note 72] for divergent opinions). The emphasis of the pre-Justinian textual changes is increasingly seen as falling in the period between 250 und 300 AD, although there is still no complete clarity as regards the form (expansion by glosses or rather an abridgement for the sake of simplification?), extent and intention (deliberate abridgement or unintentional loss of text?) (see [7. 60 ff.; 13. 10 f.; 14. 169 f. with references, note 68]). We are on slightly firmer ground with Justinian's interpolations. It may be regarded as certain that he removed outdated legal institutions, such as mancipatio and fiducia, took into account the change in procedural rules and accommodated legal writings to the new imperial law (such as making the text of D.19.2.25 pr. correspond to C.4.38.15.1), that furthermore he adapted texts to give them a more general meaning (such as the generalisation of the concept princeps legibus solutus in D.1.3.31) and that he radically removed the numerous controversies in the Classical writings (a comparison between Vat. 75.3/5 and D.7.2.1.2 is instructive [see 12. 294 ff.]) [7. 31, 80 ff.; 8. 134 ff.; 14. 157 f.]. Whether beyond this Justinian changed Classical resolutions to any real extent is increasingly being questioned ([7. 30 f.; 13. 5] but see also [6. 485 ff.]). The extent to which he incorporated school tractates from the eastern empire into the Digests remains a matter of debate (affirmative [7. 93 f.]; negative [14. 171 f.]).

D. METHODS

It is sometimes possible to point directly to Justinian's interpolations through references in Basilica scholia, editorial comments that have mistakenly not been removed, to contradictions and, above all, to parallel transmissions [14. 159]. In the absence of such direct evidence, the study of interpolations has to be based upon indications resting only upon probability. Such cases are either linked with formal criteria, such as syntactic or logical inconsistencies in the text, or are passages which stand out in stylistic terms [14. 160 ff.]. In the latter cases, however, care must be taken: Graecisms, didactic and rhetorical style-elements may also be expected of Classical lawyers.

[14. 161; 7. 53 ff.]. Only very broadly based examinations of the stylistic features of Classical lawyers, on the one hand, and of Justinian, on the other, can promise results having any real validity [4; 5]. In particular, passages contradicting the Classical legal position can – beside the palingenesis of the passage – provide an objective indication of an interpolation. However, in view of Justinian's Classical outlook [7. 16 ff.; variant view: 6. 486 ff.], consideration must always be given to the possibility that we may be faced with what remains of a deleted Classical controversy [7. 27; 8. 140] or an adaptation by Justinian of Classical material [7. 31].

1 O. BEHRENDS, Das Werk Otto Lenels und die Kontinuität der romanistischen Fragestellungen. Zugleich ein Beitrag zur Überwindung der interpolationistischen Methode." Index 19, 1991, 169–213 2 G. VON BESELER, Beiträge zur Kritik der römischen Rechtsquellen. 5 vols. 1910–1931 3 G. BROGGINI, Index Interpolationum, quae in Iustiniani Codice inesse dicuntur, 1969 4 T. HONORÉ, Tribonian, 1978 5 Id. Ulpian, 1982 6 A. GUARINO, Sulla credibilità della scienza romanistica moderna. vol. 1,1973, 479–502 7 M. KASER, Zur Methodologie der römischen Rechtsquellenforschung, 1972 8 Id. Ein Jahrhundert Interpolationenforschung an den römischen Rechtsquellen. Römische Rechtsquellen und angewandte Juristenmethode. 1986, 112–154 9 E. LEVY, E. RABEL, Index Interpolationum, quae in Iustiniani Digestis inesse dicuntur, 1929 10 K.-H. SCHINDLER, Justinians Haltung zur Klassik, 1966 11 L. WENGER, Die Quellen des römischen Rechts, 1953, 853–877 12 F. WIEACKER, Textstufen klassischer Juristen, 1960 13 Id. Textkritik und Sachforschung, SZ 91 (1974): 1–40 14 Id. Römische Rechtsgeschichte. Erster Abschnitt, 1988, 154–182.   RALPH BACKHAUS

Interpretatio Christiana
A. INTRODUCTION B. EARLY HISTORY C. LATE ANTIQUITY D. KEMP'S THESIS E. THE MIDDLE AGES F. MODERN AESTHETICS G. HEIDEGGER AND AFTER

A. INTRODUCTION
By *Interpretatio Christiana* (IC) is meant in the most general sense the reception of a non-Christian cultural element or historical fact with a view to adapting it to Christianity by means of appropriate interpretation. Since such a method implies a philosophical and philological basis of the kind that would not be expected in the new religion before the end of the 2nd cent., the idea of the IC is embedded in a complex intellectual history, the premises and components of which have to be taken into consideration [1].

B. EARLY HISTORY
The basis for the IC is the notion of interpretation as such, something which is ascertainable from the 6th cent. BC onwards. Theagenes of Rhegion (late 6th cent. BC) is regarded as the first to try by his interpretation to save the Homeric epics from attacks by critics of mythology. Similar efforts are recorded for orphic poetry. The

methodology of semantic encoding and solution was naturally familiar to the mystery religions; in addition to Eleusis and Delphi, mention must be made in this context above all of the Pythagoreans [7]. The Homeric apologists assumed the belief in a deeper truth to be found behind the veil of poetry, a distinction between two levels which matched most closely the Platonic doctrine of ideas. Plato himself, however, was as critical about the interpretation of poetical works as he was about the works themselves. The interpreters of passages which had become incomprehensible or repugnant used primarily physical or ethical-moral patterns to resolve the problems (according to [31. 35] also psychological ones). From the 4th cent. on interpretation turned, because of the connection with the respective philosophies of those carrying it out, into a form of reflexive apologetics. Poetic allegorical interpretation was continued by the Stoics with special reference to the etymological method of interpretation, and also by Neoplatonism, the starting point for which was metaphysical ([4]: 'substitutive' and 'dihairetic' allegorical method). By the end of the Hellenic period a thoroughly scholastic practice of interpretation with a pedagogical direction had established itself, and it would not be without effect on Jewish and, eventually, Christian theology. Nor should one overlook the Classical interpretation of dreams, the roots of which go back perhaps even further than the allegorical interpretation of Homer, and which had an established place beside the interpretation of poetic works. Modern psychology is its heir [19, 84–86].

It was not until late that the interpreting process was subsumed under the concept of allegorical interpretation. *Allegoria* as a rhetorical term is first attested in Philodemus of Gadara (1st cent. BC), where it indicates (as with *metaphora*) a stylistic form of expression, the content of which goes beyond the literal meaning. *Allegoria* is used in this way by Pseudo-Heraclitus (1st cent. AD) in his Homer-interpretations. Plutarch (ca. 45–125) offers the explanation that the word had displaced the earlier *hyponoia*. Behind this exchange it is possible to suspect a change in perspective, from that of the interpreter's viewpoint to that of the author, by which *allegoria* actually became the concept in communication theory used to the present day in literary and artistic reception in the West [19].

Classical allegorical interpretation was adapted by Jewish scholars at first also with an apologetic intention for the interpretation of the Old Testament. The first witnesses to this are Aristobulus (ca. 150 BC) und Pseudo-Aristeas (Epistle of A., between 127–118). The most important representative of this line of interpretation was Philo of Alexandria, however (Philo Judaeus; 15/10 BC. – ca. 45/50). Philo, who was a Platonist, attempted by applying the allegorical interpretation of poetical works to the Bible, to take the latter to the pagans, and to demonstrate how the Pentateuch could be reconciled with the pagan philosophy of religion. He made use of the concepts of *allegoria* and *allegorein*; his methodologies were the usual ones of physical and ethical allegorical interpretation. Since he was convinced that Moses had received divine inspiration and that therefore the Scriptures were in the nature of a revelation, he theologised his interpretations and placed them in a hierarchical order. He was the first to look at the Scriptures according to four aspects, which existed side-by side: the historical, the legislative, the liturgical and the prophetic [5].

Philo had considerable influence upon early Christianity, especially on Clement, Origen, Ambrose and Augustine. In the New Testament itself, however, the reflection of Jewish allegorical interpretation of the Bible is less prominent than the notion of typology. The term typology, current since the 18th cent. and derived from Latin *typologia*, has its philological basis in Greek *typos*, from *typto* = strike or *typoo* = imprint. What is meant is the making of an impression in the active as well as the passive sense, the image (*eikon* and *mimema*), therefore, in the sense of a model and of a copy, just as the coiner's die and hammer give a coin its impression with a single blow. A related concept is that of *paradeigma*, and in post-Classical times *archetypos* or *prototypos* were used in preference to *typos* [2]. By typology is understood the pattern of interpretation according to which the foreshadowing in the Old Testament of one of the factors of the Christian salvation story is hidden in a specific image or event, the *typos,* the revelation and fulfillment of which is set against it in the New Testament as the antitype. This system has its roots in Judaism. Already in the Old Testament the Kingdom of God at the end of the world is described in terms of paradise (Am 9: 13; Is 11: 6–8); there is a repetition of events during the wanderings in the desert (Ho 2: 16; Is 40: 3) and the prediction of a new covenant (Jr 31: 31) or of a new creation (Is 65: 17). In the same way in the frescoes of the Dura Europos synagogue the tent of the covenant and the temple, that is, the old and the new covenants, are made parallel. In the New Testament, that typology is introduced by Christ himself, when applying the types of Jonah (Mt 12: 40) and the bronze serpent (Jn 3: 14) to the resurrection and the cross, and thus to himself. In the case of the bronze serpent of Numbers 21 a plastic symbol from the Old Testament, a work of art, becomes the object of interpretation, taking an important step beyond the literary object of interpretation. Paul interprets Adam as Christ (Rm 5: 14) and the crossing of the Red Sea as a type of baptism (I Co 10: 1ff.). In 1 Peter the flood is compared with baptism (3: 21). The most important passage is in the Epistle to the Galatians (4: 24), where Paul places two far-reaching series of comparisons, one from the Old and the other from the New Testament, typologically side-by-side. Paul uses for this, however, the term *allegorein*, which is not otherwise attested in the New Testament – possibly to refute specific opponents [19, 121].

Pauline allegorical interpretation is determined by the belief that Christ had ushered in the eschatological age, and that the Old Testament contains testimony to its reality which are now visible, just as the lamb in Revelations 5 opens the book with seven seals. But what was intended on the original level of meaning as a juxtaposition in historical-factual terms also offered the possibility of moving on to an evaluative differentiation. The passing of time between the type and the antitype, and the presumption that in a kind of circular argument [5, 141] only the belief in Christ makes the recognition of the connection possible, automatically move the authority in the interpretation toward Christianity. From the non-evaluative connection with Jewish transmission there emerged a methodology which placed that Jewish transmission into a secondary role. Future anti-Semitic connotations are also foreshadowed in the New Testament. For Paul a veil lies over the Old Testament, indicated already in the covering of the face of Moses (Ex 34: 33–35), which was only moved aside for Christians (see II Co 3: 13 and 15). As in Galatians, in Ephesians 1 the fulfillment and revelation of the truth of the Old Testament is ascribed to the Christians. In Hebrews the rending of the veil at the crucifixion is taken as a symbol of the new hermeneutic possibilities. The apocryphal Epistle of Barnabas strengthens the anti-Jewish line; similarly (see 6: 11 of that text), Justin (d. ca.165) perceives in the Christian claims of the possibility of interpretation a justification of Christian belief and a new quality in its adherents. These, then, are the premises upon which paganism, too, could be made subordinate to the interpretative authority of Christianity.

Typology initially plays rather a minor role in the visual arts. Conditions for transferring it were certainly made more favourable by the constant increase in the availability of types found in the Scriptures. According to the Barnabas Epistle the sacrifice of Isaac as well as Joshua were also prefigurations of Christ. Through the medium of the Mass, Abel, Abraham and Melchisedech became types of the priest celebrating the Eucharist. Even sacraments, such as baptism or the eucharist were taken as antitypes. In reliefs, Jonah is joined as a symbol of the resurrection by Daniel, the three youths in the fiery furnace and Noah's ark. The spread of typology away from the strict linking of Old and New Testaments as in early Christianity blurred the distinction between this and Classical allegorical interpretation. This is reflected in the visual arts: Jonah, whose typological position is clear (see above) appears on late Classical sarcophagus reliefs as a single figure, like pagan allegorical figures such as Ariadne or Proserpine. A figure such as a shepherd carrying a lamb can no longer be assigned exclusively to one methodology or context. Not only was the boundary between literary and visual objects of interpretation laid open by such themes, but they also blurred that between allegorical interpretation as the act of an interpreter and the element which is to be subjected to that allegorisation. The representation can in itself imply an interpretation. The method of interpretation in images seems to have taken on such a dominant function that it was reflected in a literary form in collections of *tituli,* without ever actually being realised as works of art (Prudentius).

C. LATE ANTIQUITY

Christian writers were hesitant in using pagan allegorical interpretations, however, because they seemed to offer support for polytheism. Homer-interpretations were adopted when they could be used paradigmatically. Rm I: 19f. gave a basis for the Christian adaptation of pagan cultural or historical elements in saying that traces of divine truth may be found also in the pagan world. Further impetus was provided by the conflict about the priority of religions or cultures, which was developed with Moses and Homer as the protagonists. Thus allegorical interpretation in the form of IC finally became a means of coming to terms with a dominant pagan culture, which at specific points – as with Old Testament typology – could be read as conveying concealed Christian prophecy. The decisive historical step for this method of drawing the inheritance of the pagan world into Christian thought was taken by Clement.

Clement of Alexandria (Titus Flavius Clemens Alexandrinus, ca. 150 – before 215) was influenced by Philo, whose allegorical method he adopted and Christianised [5. 152]. His interpretation of the Sarah-Hagar-episode is in accord, for example, with Philo's, rather than with that of Paul in Ga 4: 24. Like Philo, he assumed a fourfold meaning of text and not a consolidated one, and distinguished between historical, legal, liturgical and theological sections of the Bible. Clement did not only link his allegorical interpretations with typology [5. 269], but applied them also to pagan philosophers as much as to the Bible. The IC was for him a means of reconciling pagan culture with Christianity. Thus he interpreted Odysseus tied to the mast of the ship as a pre-figuration of the crucified Christ (Protrepticus 12,118,4) [23. 395f.]. In the *Paidagogos* he commended to the Christians signet-rings with familiar contemporary motifs that could be interpreted in a Christian manner (Paidagogos 3, 11). He showed the way, and many followed. Origen (ca. 185–254) separated himself more clearly than Clement from the model of Philo. He took up the possibility of a threefold interpretation of any biblical passage, dividing his meanings into different levels, namely the somatic (literal, historical-grammatical), the psychic (moralising) and the pneumatic (allegorical or mystical). Eusebius (ca. 260–339) provides, beside an extensive typological allegorisation of the building of a new church (Hist. eccl. X, 44 and 66–68), the most famous of all Christian reinterpretations: the exegesis of the new-born child in the 4th Eclogue of Virgil, with which the poet celebrated the birth of the Roman Republic under Augustus, as Christ, an IC, which was allegedly used by Constantine himself in an address to the Gathering of the Saints in 313. Eusebius conveys it in an appendix to his *Vita Constantini* in Greek. (Oratio ad Sanctorum coetum XIX). In this way

many deities and events of Classical culture (which have sometimes only been preserved by this method), were given a Christian reinterpretation, a technique of appropriation which, within the conflicts between religions and cultures in Late Antiquity [12], did not go unnoticed in the pagan world, which stressed, for example, its own morality in a number of images. One practical special form of the IC was the substitution of a Christian dedication in place of pagan deities, as in the construction of churches (Minerva – Maria). The development passed through Ambrose (ca. 340–397), who couched his own interpretations in allegorical form [16], Augustine (354–430), who turned away from an allegorical interpretation of pagan texts and was closer to Jewish hermeneutics, and Orosius (early 5th cent.), who based his universal history on a Christian interpretation, and finally to Gregory the Great (Pope 590–604), who established a fixed allegorical method for the Middle Ages which merged all the interpretative processes so far considered. [14]. He also institutionalised the parallelism between word and image as potentially revelatory, something which remains valid to the present day [9]. All this contributed to the Romanisation of Christianity, which became a political objective under the Carolingians.

A clarification of the concept of IC, therefore, is confronted with the problem that it affects the basic intention of Christian hermeneutics, but that in actual scholarly practice, for the sake of a more precise definition, the following limitations have become accepted: allegorical interpretation in the case of given, especially written evidence of past events; typology for the written or iconographic juxtaposition of an Old Testament type and a New Testament antitype indicating its Christian fulfillment; and IC for the Christian reinterpretation of pagan elements. Whenever during the High Middle Ages typology strongly emphasises the juxtaposition of Old and New Testament times, the description *concordantia veteris et novi testamenti* lends itself as a useful designation. This sketch has already shown that the methodology of IC is a component of an ideological complex which affects the Christian world view as such. The scholarly interpretation of early Christian art in particular needs to take account of the problems inherent in all this. The most significant recent overview of the theme is that by Kemp [17].

D. KEMP'S THESIS

Kemp makes the attempt to read the relational elements of representation in early Christian art, that is, connections between themes and individual image motifs which have become commonplace, as Christian narrative style from the standpoint of a philologically oriented 'narrative technique'. The model for this narrative style was provided, according to Kemp, by the Bible, the dissemination of which in the 2nd and 3rd cents. was supported also by the visual arts, which in turn adopted from it their mediatory structure. Sequential representation as an expression of the historically determined direction of the Bible became the most important formal sign of differentiation from pagan representations of the cycle of existence. The irregularity of biblical narrative has not, for the believer, diminished its value as a revelatory message, but in fact it became a characteristic of the 'Great Code' (W. Blake). Various strategies emerged for coming to terms with the problems which nevertheless came about in the reception of the biblical story: typology, which provided a deeper sense for the individual element, and the gap-filling narratives of the Jewish and Christian apocrypha (and pseudepigrapha), which provided for further elucidation of the content, and thereby continued the irregular pattern of the narrative. With this orientation towards typologies and verbal expansions there was from the beginning a parallelism between Judaism and Christianity, just as there was in the reluctant use of visual images. The Jewish art from Dura Europos is seen by Kemp, who follows Kessler in this [34. 157], already as reflecting Christianity within the context of the competition between religions in Late Antiquity, although he goes beyond Kessler in doubting whether there was ever an independent tradition of Jewish art. The discussed structural principle is for him specific to Christian art, something not found in the Mithraei, for example, and only fully developed in the confrontation with Roman art after Constantine. IC is, therefore, for him always also an *interpretatio romana*. The immediate narrative through the visual arts in Roman forms is read by him as being provided with an historical dimension which led from de-Judaising on to Christianisation. Overall he remains convinced that the artistic media, divided basically into the narrative mode with the histories and the thematic mode with individual images, followed the "historical credo" [17. 256] of the great narrative. Individual motifs are given meaning, therefore, only by their ordering: 'Das Bildschema ist also das Primäre, die Füllung das Sekundäre – zuerst kommt der Beziehungssinn, dann der geistige Sinn, erst die Relation, dann die Identifikation. Der identifikatorische Modus, der die Textexegese beherrscht, lebt davon, Entitäten ineinander aufgehen zu lassen; der relationale Modus, der die Kunst regiert, hält sie auseinander, um ihren relativen und ihren phänomenalen Wert auszubauen' ("the schematic pattern of images is therefore primary, fulfillment secondary – first comes the denotative sense, then the spiritual sense, first the relation, then the identification. The identificatory mode, which dominates in textual exegesis, depends upon allowing separate entities to merge into one another; the relational mode, which dominates art, keeps them apart in order to maintain and develop their relative and phenomenological values") [17. 256]. This tendency, according to Kemp, is changed and finally brought to an end by the theologians, at whose head he sets Origen, and then, in the West, Hilary of Poitiers (ca. 315–ca. 367). According to Kemp, the development that began in the second half of the 4th cent. led eventually around 1150 to the formation of the great cycles

in which two or more individual images are linked to one another typologically [18].

Kemp's concept is implicitly directed against the art-historical scholarly method of iconology, which first of all considers the content of an image and then interprets it with recourse to written sources. Rather he moves the content of an image onto its framework to a certain extent, and thus views a practical determination, as that of typology, as a formal structural principle, which, in pattern-like fashion, links the books of the Bible with one another. Future discussions will show whether or not we may accept the thesis that the questionable elements in the biblical narrative, which according to Kemp, typology and allegorical interpretation served to resolve, were indeed consciously reproduced in the visual arts. As far as the opposition which has been set up between the narrative and the thematic mode is concerned, one might well ask, as does Pochat, who considered the same works in his sketch for a history of art on a time-referenced basis, whether the narrative animation of the thematically condensed pictures actually has to be seen in contrast with the pictures as such [25. 188]. The controlling role of the theologians, who, according to Kemp, put an end to the reflection in art of biblical narrative style, was viewed by Eberlein in connection with the problem of adapting the reservoir of motifs in Classical art to the new religion [11]. A further point for discussion is that Kemp's postulation of a meaningfully determined mode of representation affects the question of a work's graphic impression, and that of the hard-to-establish appropriate observer.

E. The Middle Ages
The further historical development is determined by the fact that in Christian custom the allegorical interpretation, whether it is orientated towards Judaism in the form of typology, or towards paganism as IC, established itself institutionally as an all-embracing method of providing a world view. Truth was, in this context, the result of conclusions based upon a fixed history, where the ability, claimed by Christianity, of establishing the truth determined in advance the nature and direction of the results insofar as the system in which it was to be placed already existed. Certainty could therefore be achieved by a process which is independent of rational thought. The clarity of recognition became a means of proving the truth. This ideological claim may be grasped iconologically through the development of the motif of the curtain. It was depicted in the form of the curtain in post-Constantine court ceremonials, opened and divided symmetrically into two halves. The form was then transferred to the curtain which in Jewish art distinguished the shrine of the Torah (see the title of the so-called Ashburnham Pentateuch: Paris, Bibl. Nat. Nouv. acq. lat. 2334, f. 2r, probably 7th cent..). In the pre- and in the early Carolingian period the motif is shifted to the image of the Evangelist, who takes the place of the Pentateuch. The content basis of this change is the parallelism, already noted, of the cur-

tains in the Epistle to the Hebrews with the rending of the veil of the temple at the death of Christ, which in patristic exegesis became a symbol for the overcoming of Jewish blindness by Christianity, and thus a symbol for allegorical interpretation as such. This basic meaning may be assumed too in pictures of the Evangelists in which, instead of the opened halves of the curtain, no curtain at all is now visible [8]. With this the revelatory character of the image in the west, and its theological basis, become clear: since then the image has become a message, since then it can have the quality of a revelation of the truth: 'Hoc visibile imaginatum figurat illud invisibile verum, cuius splendor penetrat mundum', as it says on the page opposite the Majestas-miniature in the so-called Hitda-Codex (Darmstadt, HLB Cod. 1640, f. 6v; early 11th cent.).

In late Classical art there are no couplings of images in which the type and the antitype would have been related to one another. Most frequently the nature of the antitype is indicated by clarifying features in the type. Only from the 7th cent. onwards do we find references in the sources to the typological pairing of images [28]. The increasing schematic development proceeds with an extension of the range of types which may be taken from Classical sources far beyond the Old Testament (cf. Sulpicius Severus, Vita of St Martin: Old Testament kings = Julian [23, 393]) and natural history (Physiologus), so that typology eventually merges completely with IC [18. 107]. At the same time the differentiation of a fourfold sense of Scripture becomes the norm, by which the allegorical interpretation itself, which goes beyond the historical-literal sense, subdivides into three (allegorical, moral, anagogical). The typological method of hermeneutics leaves its imprint on the great sequences of images, the best example of which is the Klosterneuburg Altar, which shows the Classical division (see Ambrose, Expos. in Psalm 38: 25) into ante legem, sub lege, sub gratia. In the course of the development the distance between the points of contact was necessarily affirmed. A consolidation of the anti-Judaistic tendency can be perceived from the end of Late Antiquity. Ecclesia and Synagoga can be understood until that time as the pagan and the Christian church, and appear only since Carolingian times with the customary medieval interpretations of blind Judaism and Christianity now seeing, under the Cross. The typological cycles after the 12th cent. take into account contemporary heresies.

In the wake of the IC a formal degeneration of Classical images came about in art. Since the Christians saw pagan gods in Classical statuary, there occurred in Late Antiquity the greatest programme of destruction of the plastic arts in the history of civilisation. Whenever later in the Middle Ages Classical gods were portrayed in plastic form, it was always in a distorted form as devils, or in places where they could do no harm, such as on column capitals, eaves or as gargoyles etc. This negative interpretation was founded not only upon theological, but also upon moral considerations, thus in the case of

the so-called Spinario it was on account of the unself-conscious way the youth is holding his leg. The denunciation of pagan deities came about in the High and Late Middle Ages according to the principle of disjunction formulated by Panofsky: Classical forms were Christianised, that is, adapted to Christian themes, while Classical themes were treated in an anachronistic, that is a modern manner: the Virgin appeared in Classical form, Venus in a medieval one. In this context the significance of the Renaissance is that it did away with this distinction and treated Classical themes in truly Classical forms, so that this become the norm [24].

With this change, however, which also removed the offensive character of the IC within the visual arts, the history of the idea was not yet complete. The Reformation, of course, worked against the practice of allegorical interpretation in theology [22]. According to Melanchthon no dogmatic decisions were possible on this basis, although allegories could still be accepted as picturae. The criticism of the reformers matched in this point that of Judaism. In the period which followed, attempts were made to separate 'Christian' typology from 'Jewish' or 'Alexandrian' allegorisation, and to preserve the method by those means. At the same time an increasing number of comparisons were made between Protestants and the Children of Israel in the Old Testament, in which Judaism was seen positively. The Protestant provinces of the Low Countries compared themselves with the Children of Israel, protected by God; the Pilgrim Fathers saw their emigration as an Exodus; in the 'Third Reich' Protestant theologians used the concept of typology against the 'German Christians' loyal to the regime as a proof that the Old Testament belonged to Christianity [2].

F. MODERN AESTHETICS
The most important results of the development of the thought-processes sketched above came in the area of the appreciation of art. The equation of Old Testament/ Jews with shadows and Christians with image seemed secure for centuries on the basis of the fact that there was no Jewish art. Hence the significance of the excavation in the 1920s of the synagogue in Dura Europos, and of its assessment. The old arguments of typology and IC were then introduced once again in the most prominent place in the history of western aesthetics as a justification for the superiority of Christian art, namely in Hegel's lectures on aesthetics (1820–1829). The demand that the content of the highest form of art should not be an 'abstractum' was fulfilled, according to Hegel, solely in Christian art, in 'romantic art'. He demonstrates this by means of the usual separation of Judaism and paganism, using, in this case, 'Turks' to embody the latter: 'Sagen wir z.B. von Gott, er sei der einfach Eine, das höchste Wesen als solches, so haben wir damit nur eine tote Abstraktion des unvernünftigen Verstandes ausgesprochen. Solch ein Gott, wie er selbst nicht in seiner konkreten Wahrheit gefaßt ist, wird auch für die Kunst, bes. für die bildende, keinen Inhalt abge-

ben. Die Juden und Türken haben deshalb ihren Gott, der nicht einmal nur solche Verstandesabstraktion ist, nicht durch die Kunst in der positiven Weise darstellen können wie die Christen. Denn im Christentum ist Gott in seiner Wahrheit und deshalb als in sich durchaus konkret, als Person, als Subjekt und in näherer Bestimmtheit als Geist vorgestellt. Was er als Geist ist, expliziert sich für die religiöse Auffassung als Dreiheit der Personen, die für sich zugleich als Eine ist. Hier ist Wesenheit, Allgemeinheit und Besonderung sowie deren versöhnte Einheit, und solche Einheit erst ist das Konkrete ' ("If we say, for example, of God that he is the One, the highest being as such, then all we have done is to express a dead abstraction from an understanding devoid of reason. Such a God, who is himself not to be grasped in his concrete truth, will also provide for art, especially the visual arts, no real content. The Jews and the Turks have therefore not been able in art to portray their god, who is not even such a rational abstraction, in the same positive manner as have the Christians. For in Christianity god is in his truth and therefore is represented as entirely concrete in himself, as a person, as a subject, and in closer detail as a spirit. What he is as a spirit is explained in the religious concept of the trinity, which are at the same time one. Here is essence, generality and singularity, as well as the reconciled unity of all three, and only such unity is concrete", Hegel, Werke. Moldenhauer edition, Vol. 13, 100f.). In his discussion of 'sublimity' Hegel takes up the argument that Judaism has left behind a vast amount of evidence for the glory of God. But since it does not use the image, it has to take the whole world as an image, which is thus forced into a functional role: 'Das negative Verhältnis dagegen der eigentlichen Erhabenheit müssen wir in der hebräischen Poesie aufsuchen, in dieser Poesie des Herrlichen, welche den bildlosen Herrn des Himmels und der Erden nur dadurch zu feiern und zu erheben weiß, daß sie seine gesamte Schöpfung nur als Akzidens seiner Macht, als Boten seiner Herrlichkeit, als Preis und Schmuck seiner Größe verwendet und in diesem Dienste das Prächtigste selbst als negativ setzt, weil sie keinen für die Gewalt und Herrschaft des Höchsten adäquaten und affirmativ zureichenden Ausdruck zu finden imstande ist und eine positive Befriedigung nur durch die Dienstbarkeit der Kreatur erlangt, die im Gefühl und Gesetztsein der Unwürdigkeit allein sich selbst und ihrer Bedeutung gemäß wird' ("We must seek in Hebrew poetry the negative relationship of sublimity as such, in this poetry of the majestic, which is able to celebrate and glorify the image-less lord of the heavens and the earth only by using his entire creation as the access to his greatness, the heralds of his majesty and the crown and glory of his greatness, and in service of this sees the noblest itself as a negative, because it is unable to find an appropriately fulfilling and affirmative expression for the power and majesty of the all-highest, and reaches a positive satisfaction only through the subjection of creation, which is true to itself and to its significance only in the feeling and steadfastness of unworthiness", Hegel, Werke. Moldenhauer edition, Vol. 13, 416). It is through Hegel that the old basic connection of western art with revealed truth, which for him could be nothing more than Christian truth, was placed on record. Thus it was only in European culture that there came about a development of the 'history of art' as a science of hermeneutics, which tries to establish with the aid of the hidden levels of meaning the truth' of a picture, a process that receives additional legitimisation from the concept of 'depth' [30].

In his aesthetics (Meditationes 1735; Aesthetica 1–2 1750–1758), Alexander Gottlieb Baumgarten (1714–1762) laid the foundation of the notion of 'aesthetic rationality' (Martin Seel), that is, he placed alongside the logical-rational method, as an equally valid approach, the recognition of sense-perceptions as a path to 'aesthetic truth' instead of the hitherto rationally founded one. These were not seen as contradictory, but represented equally the one objective truth. Baumgarten – like all his predecessors – sees God as its axiomatic point of reference. He also adopts the traditional criterion of 'clarity' as gauge for the aesthetic recognition of truth [33]. With respect to the present theme, Baumgarten's aesthetics meant in effect a step back, away from the all-determining rationalism of his time, to bases of recognition which are once again more readily accessible to religion and metaphysics.

G. HEIDEGGER AND AFTER

The extreme and radical nature of the suggestion made by Martin Heidegger (1889–1976) in a lecture, first delivered in Freiburg in 1935 and later much repeated, on Der Ursprung des Kunstwerks, becomes clear when seen against this background. Heidegger ruled out all theological connections and merged art and truth in such a way that the latter became a self-evident quality of the former: art is the revelation of truth. The power of this idea, by which Heidegger banished metaphysics from the tradition, was, to be sure, vitiated by the fact that its author brought in, for the practical clarification of the possibilities of aesthetic judgments, assessments of art in the style of the National Socialists. The thesis was, in the supplementary material in the afterword to the 1950 publication, tied to the time of its origin. At this point Heidegger was at pains to include the concept of beauty, which had rightly been viewed before as not fundamental, and to refer to art as a "metaphysical concept". This pointer was taken up by a group of his adherents, and led to the identification of Heidegger's ontologically intended truth with conservative central concepts like 'God, centrality, wholeness' (Sedlmayr [29]) or 'celebration' (Kuhn [20]).

It hardly needs mentioning that Marxist aesthetics, with their socially determined concept of truth, distanced themselves from this definition [21]. However, the largest of the counter-movements was that of 'iconology', the now internationally-known art-historical methodology established by Warburg and Panofsky, which attempts to base its work not upon the authority of the interpreter, but upon an historically and critically verified source-base. Members of the Warburg school, driven out by the Nazis, established in the USA something like a humanistic alternative to the barbarism of Nazi Germany [10]. The contrast can be substantiated less by their own statements than by the attacks of their opponents, who applied the topos of the blindness of Judaism to 'Jewish' iconology. In 1935 there appeared in the *Völkischer Beobachter* a review of the *Kulturwissenschaftliche Bibliographie zum Nachleben der Antike*, published in 1934 by the Warburg library. After a – frequently capricious – designation of most of the contributors as 'Jewish' there follows beneath the declaration that "we, however, have become able to see ..." the rejection of the collection as an undertaking inimical to the new Germanness [26]. After the Second World War, IC changed into an ideological model in which the iconologists could take the place of the Jews, the Protestants the place of the pagans and Catholicism that of Christianity. In 1949 the painter and publicist Schlichter, who was not without influence on the Munich school of art history, published a polemical piece against abstract art, in which he derived it from the Jewish prohibition of images, and Protestant disapproval of them [27], a thesis which would be propounded thereafter in modified form at regular intervals, as for example by Sedlmayr. Thus it is no surprise that in the *Kunsthistorik* of Sedlmayr's student Bauer, iconologists are compared with iconoclasts [3. 99]. The basis of their criticism is: "art history as the history of symbols (= iconology, author) distorts access to the truth of art and at the same time conceals the truth of art" (Dittmann [6. 139]). The vitality of this tradition is confirmed by attempts to assert that there was from the start a division between Church/image and heretic/image-rejection [13]. Finally, in a kind of 'IC, 'the Renaissance was declared a Catholic age that had been wrongly designated as a pagan epoch by Protestants and Jews (meaning the 'iconologists') on account of their approval of the Old Testament proscription against images [32. 23–24]. The explosive effect of the iconological concept, which avoids any orientation towards the traditional notion of truth in the interpretation of art, can be gauged indirectly through such reactions. The avoidance of the support of the interpreting authority by the depth of the interpretation, that is, basically the attempt to de-allegorise the interpretation and to de-mystify the interpreter, need not in the context of critical studies of the history of civilisation imply also the loss of the category of 'depth' as an indication of the quality of the artistic product, as the division made by the 'Frankfurt School' between the creations of the culture industry and works of art as such has made clear [15]. The appearance of the concept of 'truth' in hermeneutic programmes (Sedlmayr, Gadamer) will always have to be tested against the connection with the relevant tradition. Ultimately it is a question of the very basis of the Western view of the world, and consequently, of the

problem of the Eurocentric view. It is a matter for the scholarship of cultural heritage to what extent it will or can reach a point where its interpretations can or cannot separate themselves from the historical starting-point of the IC.

SOURCES   1 J. K. EBERLEIN, C. MIRWALD-JAKOBI, Grundlagen der mittelalterlichen Kunst. Eine Quellenkunde, Berlin 1996   2 B. STRENGE, H.-U. LESSING, s. v. Typos; Typologie, Historisches Wörterbuch der Philosophie 10, 1587–1607
LITERATURE   3 H. BAUER, Kunsthistorik. Eine kritische Einführung in das Studium der Kunstgeschichte, ²1979   4 W. BERNARD, Spätantike Dichtungstheorien. Untersuchungen zu Proklos, Herakleitos und Plutarch, 1990 (Beiträge zur Altertumskunde, vol. 3)   5 C. BLÖNNINGEN, Der griechische Ursprung der jüdisch-hellenistischen Allegorese und ihre Rezeption in der alexandrinischen Patristik, 1992 (Europäische Hochschulschriften Reihe XV Klass. Sprachen und Lit. vol. 59)   6 L. DITTMANN, Stil, Symbol, Struktur. Studien zu Kategorien der Kunstgeschichte, 1967   7 H. DÖRRIE, Spätantike Symbolik und Allegorese, in: Frühma. Studien 3, 1969, 1–12   8 J. K. EBERLEIN, Apparitio regis – revelatio veritatis. Studien zur Darstellung des Vorhangs in der bildenden Kunst von der Spätantike bis zum Ende des Mittelalters, 1982   9 Id., Die Selbstreferenzialität der abendländischen Kunst (Hans Belting zum 60. Geburtstag), in: CHRISTOPH BERTSCH et al (eds.), Diskurs der Systeme (z. B.): Kunst als Schnittstellenmultiplikator; Dokumentation der gleichlautenden Ausstellungs- und Vortragsreihe an der Geisteswiss. Fakultät Univ. Innsbruck 1995/96, 1997 (Exhibition catalogue/ Institut für Kunstgeschichte der Universität Innsbruck; No. 9), 54–63   10 Id., Inhalt und Gehalt: Die ikonographisch-ikonologische Methode, in: H. BELTING et al (eds.), Kunstgeschichte. Eine Einführung, 1985, 164–186 (²1986, enlarged ed. ³1988, ⁴1991, enlarged ed. ⁵1996)   11 Id., Miniatur und Arbeit. Das Medium Buchmalerei, 1995   12 M. FUHRMANN, Die antiken Mythen im christlich-heidnischen Weltanschauungskampf der Spätantike, in: A&A 36, 1990, 138–151   13 C. HECHT, Katholische Bildertheologie im Zeitalter von Gegenreformation und Barock. Studien zu Traktaten von Johannes Molanus, Gabriele Paleotti und anderen Autoren, 1997   14 D. HOFMANN, Die geistige Auslegung der Schrift bei Gregor dem Großen, 1968 (Münsterschwarzacher Studien. 6)   15 M. HORKHEIMER, T. W. ADORNO, Dialektik der Aufklärung, 1947 (G. NOERR (ed.), E. JEPHCOTT (trans.), Dialectic of Enlightenment, 2002)   16 C. JACOB, 'Arkandisziplin', Allegorese, Mystagogie. Ein neuer Zugang zur Theologie des Ambrosius von Mailand, 1991 (athenäum monografien. Theologie. Theophaneia. Beiträge zur Religions- und Kirchengesch. des Alt., vol. 32)   17 W. KEMP, Christliche Kunst: ihre Anfänge, ihre Strukturen, 1994   18 Id., Sermo corporeus. Die Erzählung der mittelalterlichen Glasfenster, 1987 (Engl. C. SALTZWEDEL (trans.), The Narratives of Gothic Stained Glass, 1997)   19 H.-J. KLAUCK, Allegorie und Allegorese in synoptischen Gleichnistexten, ²1986 (¹1978) (Neutestamentliche Abhandlungen NF, vol. 13)   20 H. KUHN, Die Ontogenese der Kunst, in: Festschrift für Hans Sedlmayr, 1962, 13–55   21 G. LUKÁCS, Kunst und objektive Wahrheit. Essays zur Literaturtheorie und -geschichte, W. MITTENZWEI (ed.), 1977   22 F. OHLY, Gesetz und Evangelium. Zur Typologie bei Luther und Lucas Cranach. Zum Blutstrahl der Gnade in der Kunst, 1985 (Schriftenreihe der Westfäli-

schen Wilhems-Universität Münster NF, No. 1) 23 Id., Schriften zur mittelalterlichen Bedeutungsforschung, 1977 24 E. Panofsky, Renaissance and Renascences in Western Art, 1972 25 G. Pochat, Bild – Zeit. Zeitgestalt und Erzählstruktur in der bildenden Kunst von den Anfängen bis zur frühen Neuzeit, 1996 (Ars viva. 3) 26 M. Rasch, Juden und Emigranten machen deutsche Wissenschaft, in: Völkischer Beobachter Nr. 5, Jan. 1935, S. 5 u. Nr. 23, 23. Jan. 1935, S. 6; repr. in: D. Wuttke (ed.), Kosmopolis der Wissenschaft. E. R. Curtius und das Warburg Institute. Briefe 1928 bis 1952 und andere Dokumente, 1989, 295–299 (Saecula Spiritalia. 20) 27 R. Schlichter, Das Abenteuer der Kunst und andere Texte, Dirk Heisserer (ed.), 1998 (enlarged ed. of the 1949 first edition: Das Abenteuer der Kunst) 28 S. Schrenk, Typos und Antitypos in der frühchristlichen Kunst, 1995 (Jahrbuch für Antike und Christentum Supplement vol. 21) 29 H. Sedlmayr, Kunst und Wahrheit. Zur Theorie und Methode der Kunstgeschichte, 1958 30 Red., s. v. Tiefe, HWdPh 10, 1102–1194 31 S. Tochtermann, Der allegorisch gedeutete Kirke-Mythos. Studien zur Entwicklungs- und Rezeptionsgeschichte, 1992 (Studien zur klass. Philol. vol. 74) 32 J. Traeger, Renaissance und Religion. Die Kunst des Glaubens im Zeitalter Raphaels, 1997 33 T. Trummer, Die Herausbildung der Ästhetik im historischen Rationalismus. Studien zum metaphysischen und epistemologischen Begründungshorizont des Schönen und der Kunst bei Leibniz, Wolff, Gottsched, Bodmer und Breitinger und Baumgarten (Diplomarbeit Graz, 1993, typescript) 34 K. Weitzmann, H. L. Kessler, The Frescoes of the Dura Synagogue and Christian Art, 1990 (Dumbarton Oaks Studies 28)

Additional Bibliography J. Chance, Medieval Mythography, 1994; K. Heinrichs, The Myths of Love: Classical Lovers in Medieval Literature, 1990 ; C. Baswell, Virgil in Medieval England, 1995 ; M. L. Stapleton, Harmful Eloquence: Ovid's Amores from Antiquity to Shakespeare, 1996 ; A. S. Bernardo, S. Levin (eds.), The Classics in the Middle Ages: Papers of the Twentieth Annual Conference of the Center for Medieval and Early Renaissance Studies, 1990; F. Fajardo-Acosta (ed.), The Influence of the Classical World on Medieval Literature, Architecture, Music, and Culture: A Collection of Interdisciplinary Studies, 1992

JOHANN KONRAD EBERLEIN

Intertextuality see → Intertextuality

Initiation see → Occultism

Iranian Studies
A. Name, Concept and Object   B. The 'Rediscovery' of Persia   C. Scholarly Pioneers   D. The First Archaeological Missions and the *Grundriß*   E. Iranian Studies in the 20th Century   F. Turfan Research and Its Effects

A. Name, Concept and Object
In German-speaking areas, Iranian Studies (IS) are, for historical reasons having to do with their pioneering role in these areas, primarily linguistically and philologically oriented. Elsewhere, the terms 'Iranian stu-

dies/études iraniennes' – meaning approximately 'expertise or research on Iran' – are conceived much more inclusively as the intellectual and, to some extent, sociological study of the cultural area inhabited by an Iranian-speaking population from prehistory to the present. In the investigation of the Islamic age, IS touch upon Islamic studies, while for the most recent period there are also overlaps with such disciplines of the social sciences as ethnology, geography, political science, sociology and so forth. Important in the present context are the linguistic-philological, historical (in the broadest sense) and archaeological studies on the pre-Islamic period, since it is above all here that one naturally finds closer links with Indo-European studies, ancient Oriental studies, ancient history and Byzantine studies. Obviously, the Iranian cultural area extends far beyond the borders of today's Islamic Republic of Iran (known as Persia until 1934). Ethnic Iranian-speaking groups also inhabit Afghanistan, Pakistan and several Trans-Causcasian and Central Asian republics that have in the meantime become independent from the former Soviet Union, as well as some other states of the Orient. Before the great migrations of the Turkish tribes, they were to be found over a far larger area, since Iranian Scythians and Sarmatians settled along the northern and western coast of the Black Sea in Antiquity. To the east, the presence of Sakas and Sogdians in east Turkestan and as far as Mongolia and China is attested until approximately AD 1000. In addition, many words that were borrowed from an early stage of proto-Iranian and adopted into the Slavic and → Finno-Ugric languages allow the assumption that Iranian tribes advanced as far as Europe in the pre-Achaemenid period. Within the Indo-European language family, the 'Iranian' languages (the term was used for the first time around 1840 by August Friedrich Pott and Christian Lassen) are closely related to those Indo-Aryan languages designated as 'Indo-Iranian'. It is generally assumed that the Indian and Iranian peoples went their separate ways approximately at the beginning of the 2nd millennium BC. The Indians were presumably the first to leave the common homeland region in the central Asian steppes on the lower course of the Volga in Kazakhstan (Sogdia, Khwarezmia and Bactria) and crossed the passes of the Hindu Kush. The Iranians, in contrast, are not thought to have migrated to the Iranian highlands, which they did in several successive waves, until around the turn of the 2nd to the 1st millennium BC.

B. The 'Rediscovery' of Persia
If the interest of the West was still limited to the Levant at the time of the Crusades, the Mongolian conquests at the beginning of the 13th cent. once again provided the opportunity for contact between the Occident and Persia. The Europeans decided to send delegations to the Mongols, consisting primarily of merchants – a typical example was the Venetian Marco Polo (1254–1324) – as well as Franciscan and Dominican missionaries, who naturally also visited Persia on their

way. It was in this context, for instance, that the *Codex Cumanicus* (dated 1303, but going back to a 13th cent. original) came into being, which, in its first part, contains a late Latin-Persian-Turkish (i.e. Cuman) word list. Persian must have been used by the Turkish interpreters of the Italian merchants as the lingua franca for trade in the East. Similarly, it is probably no coincidence that we owe what is probably the oldest, albeit very brief, information about Persepolis ('Comerun') in European literature to the Franciscan monk Odoric de Pordenone (ca. 1325), who stayed there for a short time on the way to China in 1318. The first German to give an eye-witness account of Persia was the Bavarian mercenary Hans Schiltberger, whose report on his trip to the Orient at the beginning of the 15th cent. was not published until 1473. Almost two centuries were to pass before the Silesian nobleman Heinrich von Poser (1599–1661) reported on Persepolis, the first German to do so. Among the most important European travellers of this early phase (dates are those of their journeys) were the Venetian envoy Iosafat Barbaro (1474), whose travel report was included in the oldest 'overall presentation' of Iranian history, in twelve volumes, by the Umbrian historian Petrus Bizarus (1525–after 1586), *Rerum Persicarum Historia, initia gentis, mores, instituta, resque gestas ad haec usque tempora complectens* (1583, ²1601); Don Garcias de Silva y Figueroa (1618); the Roman Patrician Pietro della Valle (1616–23), who brought back to Europe the first illustration of a cuneiform fragment; Adam Olearius (1637–38) and Johann Albrecht von Mandelslo (1638–40); Sir Thomas Herbert (1627–28); Jean Baptiste Tavernier (1629–75); Jean de Thévenot (1664–67); and Jean Chardin (1665–77), whose report contains a detailed description of the 'Guebres', i.e. the Zoroastrian Parsis; and, finally, the Westphalian doctor and secretary of a Swedish royal delegation, Engelbert Kaempfer (1684–88). The latter four derived much of their knowledge from the French Capuchin priest Raphael du Mans, who lived in Isfahān for almost four decades (1656–96). None of these early travellers, however, connected what he was able to see in Persepolis with the Achaemenids. They made inquiries among the locals, but these had lost all knowledge of their own history. Thus, they were told that Persepolis (or: Čihilminār 'with 40 columns', as it is called in the travel reports) had been built by Ĵamšīd, the maternal grandfather of Alexander the Great (*taxt-i Ĵamšīd*, 'Throne of Ĵamšīd'); the tomb of Cyrus at Pasargadae was considered to be the *qabr-i mādar-i Sulaimān* ('tomb of Solomon's mother'); and the Sassanid cliff reliefs at Naqš-i Rustam to be the depiction of the Kayānid hero Rustam. Until the beginning of the 17th cent., 'knowledge' of the Iranian languages in the West was still limited to occasional remarks on Modern Persian, as well as a couple of Persian-Latin glossaries (e.g. by Jacob Golius, 1596–1667) and, from the end of the 16th cent., to the compilation of lists of word similarities between Dutch and German, on the one hand, and (Latin and) Persian, on the other. The first brief modern

Persian grammars by Ludovicus (Lodewijk) de Dieu (1628), Johannes (John) Greaves (1649) and Ignazio di Gesù (1661) appeared at short intervals in the mid–17th cent. They were still very strongly oriented towards the Latin models of Donatus (4th cent. AD) and Priscian (5th/6th cent.); to a lesser degree, they were also influenced by the contemporary terminology of Hebrew and Arabic grammarians.

C. Scholarly Pioneers

The rediscovery of Persia by European travellers continued into the beginning of the 18th cent. The exploration of Persia had now become the specific goal of these journeys, rather than an accidental by-product. After the fall of the Safavids (1500–1736), the stream of travellers on journeys of discovery decreased slightly, but they now had better preliminary information and, at the same time, were more precise in their graphic reproductions. Thus, the pictures by the Dutch artist Cornelis de Bruijn (1652–1726/27) are highly accurate. His *Reizen over Moskovie, door Persie en Indie ...* (1711) also include a detailed history of Persia by an otherwise unknown scholar named Praetorius, based on the reports of ancient authors. The precise description of Persepolis by Carsten Niebuhr (1733–1815), father of the ancient historian Barthold Georg Niebuhr (1776–1831), in his *Beschreibung von Arabien aus eigenen Beobachtungen und im Lande selbst gesammelten Nachrichte n* (1772) is generally considered to be the first scholarly treatise on Persepolis (see below). Other travellers (dates refer to their journeys) from this period include Robert Ker Porter (1818–20), James Justinian Morier (1808, 1811–15), William Ouseley (1811–12), James B. Fraser (1821–34), Charles Texier (1839–40, who produced the first colour illustrations of Persian monuments), the British officer and diplomat Henry Creswicke Rawlinson (1834–60), who, at risk of his life, copied and made accessible the trilingual inscription of Darius I (522/1) at Bīsutūn; and the painter Eugène Flandin and his travel companion, the architect Pascal Coste (1839–41), who published a two-volume monumental work with accurate drawings of outstanding quality. Until then, travellers had been interested primarily in Persepolis (and Pasargadae). However, in their desire to find the palace of the biblical Esther in Shushan, the English, and specifically William Kennett Loftus (1820–58), began the first 'excavations' in Susa (1849–52). These were certainly not much more than digs, and by no means measure up to today's scientific standards. Loftus's efforts nevertheless signified the beginning of archaeological activity in Persia. Archaeological research had also begun in Afghanistan with the campaign of Charles Masson, who had several primarily Buddhist sites around Kabul surveyed from 1833 to 1836, and who investigated Kapisa, the main city of Kušān during the period from the 1st to the 3rd cent. AD. In general, cultivated circles toward the end of the 17th cent. and during the 18th cent. Enlightenment seemed very open to Persian themes. In 1674 Pierre

Corneille (1606–84) wrote his last tragedy *Suréna*; in 1721 Montesquieu (1699–1755) published a philosophical novel in the form of the *Lettres persanes*. For the cultural philosopher Johann Gottfried Herder (1744–1803), Niebuhr's above-mentioned work was the immediate occasion for his work *Persepolis. Eine Muthmaßung* (1787). In England, the opera *Xerxes* (1738) by Georg Friedrich Händel and *Artaxerxes* (1762) by Thomas Arne were devoted to Achaemenid figures. It is therefore not surprising that several historical works were published at precisely this time, such as Thomas Hyde's *Veterum Persarum et Parthorum et Medorum religionis historia* (²1790) and Arnold Hermann Ludwig Heeren's (1760–1842) *Ideen über die Politik, den Verkehr und den Handel der vornehmsten Völker der alten Welt, 1. Theil. Asiatische Völker, 1. Abt. Einleitung. Perser* (1793–1812; ⁴1824). The *Geschichte Alexanders des Großen* (1833), Johann Gustav Droysen's (1808–84) strongly Hellenocentrically-oriented biography of Alexander also appeared shortly afterwards. The knowledge of Iranian languages also made immense progress during this period. In 1762 Abraham Hyacinthe Anquetil-Duperron (1731–1805) brought back 180 Avestan manuscripts with him from India. These he deposited at the Bibliothèque Nationale in Paris (his *Zend Avesta*, with a translation, appeared in 1771). With his *A Grammar of the Persian Language* (1771), Sir William Jones (1746–94), regarded as the forerunner of comparative Indo-European studies on the basis of a famous speech to the Asiatic Society in London on February 2, 1786, produced the first grammar of modern Persian written in a language other than Latin. A few years later, in 1787, Antoine Isaac Silvestre de Sacy (1758–1838), holder of the Chair for Persian and Arabic at the Collège de France and founder of Arabic studies, was the first to succeed in deciphering Middle Persian and Parthian inscriptions. Subsequently, in 1802, Georg Friedrich Grotefend (1775–1853), while still a student, succeeded, on the basis of preliminary work by the Danish researchers Olaf Gerhard Tychsen und Fredrik Münter, in deciphering (→ DECIPHERMENT) Old Persian cuneiform. Both accomplishments took place primarily on the basis of the sketches by Niebuhr (see above). Franz Bopp of Mainz (1791–1867) is regarded as the actual founder of Indo-European studies. Only a few years after the publication of his *Vergleichende Grammatik ...* (1833), Johann August Vuller published his *Institutiones linguae Persicae cum Sanscrita et Zendica lingua comparata* (1840–50; ²1870), the first detailed historical and comparative grammar of Persian. He is also the author of the first etymological dictionary of Persian, the *Lexicon Persico-Latinum etymologicum* (1855–64). In the first half of the 19th cent., the first descriptions of Paštō by M. Elphinstone (1815) and the Russian privy counsellor Boris Andreevich Dorn (1805–81) also appeared. Down into the second half of the 19th cent., however, this East Iranian language, indigenous to Afghanistan, was still erroneously considered to be one of the Indo-Aryan languages (for instance, by Ernst Trumpp, 1828–1885, the father of modern Indian philology in Germany).

D. The First Archaeological Missions and the *Grundriß*

Travel reports were also produced in the second half of the 19th cent., but their goal was less to increase previous knowledge about Persia than to transmit personal opinions and experiences. Travellers of this period who deserve special mention include Friedrich Stolze and Friedrich Carl Andreas (1846–1930), who, after a long journey to Persia (1874–1881), published two impressive volumes with the first photographs of Persepolis and Pasargadae (1882); however, the drawings by E. Flandin (cf. above) were sharper. Andreas also used his time in Persia for dialectological records. His valuable notes were published after his death by his students (including Arthur Christensen, see below) and friends. Because the couple Jane (1851–1916) and Marcel-Auguste Dieulafoy (1844–1920) had been particularly impressed by Susa when they travelled in Persia 1881–1882, they applied for and received permission from the Persian government in 1884 to conduct excavations there under the auspices of the Louvre. Dieulafoy, a trained civil engineer, was interested less in fine 'museum artifacts' than in construction methods and architecture. Thanks to the great success of this archaeological mission, which brought a rich collection of artworks to the Louvre, the French received in 1897 a monopoly on excavations in Persia for a lengthy period (until 1927). The first head of the excavations (1897–1912) of the French 'Délégation Archéologique Scientifique en Perse' at Susa was Jacques de Morgan (1857–1924). The monumental work by George Rawlinson, brother of the above-mentioned Henry Creswick, *The Five Great Monarchies of the Ancient Eastern World ...*, 4 vols. (1862–67), later supplemented by two additional chapters on the Parthians and Sassanids to become *The Seven ...*, 3 vols. (1889), was a turning-point in historical research on pre-Islamic Persia. Here, for the first time, not only Greek and Latin texts were consulted, but also Oriental sources, for instance, Armenian and Arabic authors in the section on the Sassanid (or: 'neo-Persian') Empire. The 'School' of neo-grammarians had developed in the 1870s in Germany around Karl Brugmann (1849–1919) and Hermann Osthoff (1847–1909), which through its strict methodology (the regularity principle of 'sound laws') brought 19th cent. historical and comparative Indo-European linguistics to a kind of completion. In IS, this movement culminated in the realization of Wilhelm Geiger and Ernst Kuhn's *Grundriß der iranischen Philologie* (2 vols., 1895–1904), with its sections on 'linguistic history' [vol. I. 1], 'literature' [vol. I. 2], and 'history and culture' [vol. II], as well as important contributions by Friedrich Carl Andreas, Christian Bartholomae, Karl Friedrich Geldner, Paul Horn, Heinrich Hübschmann, Ferdinand Justi, Carl Salemann, Theodor Nöldeke and several others. Working independently in Paris, James Darmesteter (1849–1894) produced both an English (1879–82, 3 vols.) and a French (1892–93, 3 vols.) translation of the text of the *Avesta*. Until today, the fundamental scholarly edition of the text remains that of K. F. Geldner, *Avesta. The Sacred Books of the Parsis* (3 vols., 1886–96). Chr. Bartholomae's *Altiranisches Wörterbuch* (1904) has also not been superseded. Darmesteter's *Études iraniennes* (2 vols., 1883) and his *Chants populaires des Afghans* (2 vols., 1888–90), in whose introduction Paštō was first classified as an Iranian language, also represented an important stage in Iranian linguistics. Also published in the 19th cent. was Julius Mohl, *Le livre des rois …*, 7 vols. (1838–78), long the standard textual edition (with a French translation) of the *Shānāmeh*, whose existence had first been noted by W. Jones. Like Geldner's edition of the *Avesta*, it was based on a wealth of manuscript material.

E. IRANIAN STUDIES IN THE 20TH CENTURY

With the abolition of the French monopoly on archaeological activities in Persia in 1927, the path was free for others. The first to profit from the abrogation of this privilege was Ernst Herzfeld (1879–1948), who, after working for six months in Pasargadae in 1928, directed the excavations in Persepolis for the Oriental Institute of Chicago from 1931 to 1934, when he was replaced by Erich Friedrich Schmidt. Upon his return to his professorial position in Berlin at the beginning of 1935, Herzfeld fell victim to the persecution of Jews by the growing → NATIONAL SOCIALISM movement. As early as the 1930s, and until 1941, the Germans also had a delegation stationed in Isfahān headed by Wilhelm Eiler (1906–89); however, it was not until 1961 that the → DEUTSCHES ARCHÄOLOGISCHES INSTITUT founded its Teheran division, which has since closed. Further foreign (including Belgian, British, Italian and Japanese) and domestic expeditions followed over the years. Since the Islamic Revolution in 1979, archaeological activity in Iran has come to an almost complete standstill, not least because of the withdrawal of the foreign archaeological institutes, once so numerous. In Afghanistan, the 'Délégation Archéologique Française en Afghanistan' (DAFA) was established in 1922, with Alfred Foucher as its first director. Even before the outbreak of the Second World War, the Americans became the second nation to conduct excavations in Afghanistan; Britons, Germans, Italians, Indians and the Soviets followed. Shortly after the beginning of the Soviet military intervention in 1979, field research was interrupted here as well, and has not been resumed since. Excavations in central Asia have been conducted seriously only since the end of the 1920s and were, until a few decades ago (in the 1980s), an almost exclusively Russian affair.

In the first half of the 20th cent., a series of comprehensive presentations of individual pre-Islamic periods appeared, such as: Albert TenEyck Olmstead, *History of the Persian Empire* (1948), Neilson C. Debevoise, *A*

Political History of Parthia (1938), and Arthur Christensen, *L'Iran sous les Sassanides* (1936, ²1944). All, however, are now outdated and have been superseded, except for the work on the Sassanids. The quality of these three works is seriously compromised because they attribute relatively too much weight to Western sources. In National Socialist terminology, the term 'Aryan' was misused, with well-known consequences, and was initially equated with 'Indo-European'. Further strengthened by the tendency of Indo-European studies (called Indo-Germanic at that time) to seek the 'original homeland' of the Indo-Europeans in northern Europe, 'Aryan' and 'Jewish' quickly became antonyms for the National Socialist ideologues. One of the worst outgrowths of this tendency was the *Indogermanisches Bekenntnis* (1941, ²1943) by the Munich Professor of 'Aryan Culture and Linguistics' (*Arische Kultur- und Sprachwissenschaft*) Walther Wüst, who, as head of the 'German Ancestral Heritage Association' (*Deutsche Ahnenerbe*), founded in 1935 by Heinrich Himmler, *Reichsführer* of the SS among others, had rapidly risen to become one of the most powerful linguists of the National Socialist era.

F. TURFAN RESEARCH AND ITS EFFECTS

The most positive and far-reaching change in the picture of Iranian philology and linguistics was brought about by competition among several nations (Great Britain, Germany, Japan, France, Russia etc.) in the first quarter of the 20th cent. regarding the oases at the edge of the huge Taklamakan Desert, from Kāšγar in the west to Tun-huang and Karachoto in the east. The archaeological race for the art treasures in these places had already begun a few years earlier with the Swede Sven Hedin (1865–1952) and the Briton of Hungarian extraction, Sir Mark Aurel Stein (1862–1943). Numerous finds of Iranian texts (ca. 40, 000), were made primarily, but not exclusively, in the Turfan oasis (Chinese Turkestan) by four Prussian expeditions from 1902 to 1914 under the leadership of Albert Grünwedel (1856–1935), director of the Ethnological Museum in Berlin, and his 'assistant' Albert von Le Coq (1860–1930). These finds greatly increased, if not completely revolutionized, our knowledge of the Middle Iranian languages. IS were suddenly enriched by this new branch of Turfan research, and the 'looted' (or 'rescued'?) manuscripts are now stored and studied at the former Prussian (now the Berlin-Brandenburg) Academy of Science in Berlin. However, they constitute only a fraction of the manuscripts found along the Silk Road; further material is located at the British Library in London and elsewhere.

Whereas, at the beginning of the century, only Parthian and Middle Persian inscriptions in addition to the Middle Persian 'Pahlavī' of the Zoroastrian books were known, all at once, through the discoveries in the oases of Turfan, Khotan and Tumšuq, half a dozen new Iranian scripts and languages suddenly came to light: Manichaean Parthian and Middle Persian; Buddhist,

Manichaean and Christian-Nestorian Sogdian; Hephtalite literature; Khotanese Saka and Tumšuq Saka. As early as 1904, the linguistic genius Friedrich Wilhelm Karl Müller succeeded in deciphering the first manuscript remnants in the Estrangela script from Turfan, Chinese Turkestan (I. SPrAW 1904, 348–52; II. *Anhang zu Abhandlungen der Preußischen Akademie der Wissenschaften*, 1904). His achievements may be less well-known than those of A. I. Silvestre de Sacy and G. F. Grotefend, but are by no means less significant. Bactrian, an additional Middle Iranian language, did not become known until the beginning of the 1950s, and numerous other documents in this language were not unearthed until the course of the 1990s. Their imminent publication is awaited with great anticipation. Overall, in the quarter century of expeditions along the northern and southern routes of the Silk Road (until the Chinese in 1925 finally put a stop to the constant exporting of art treasures and manuscripts), 17 new languages and 13 new scripts were discovered. Also for religious history, the importance of the Silk Road on which so many different communities of believers (Buddhists, Manichaeans, Christian Nestorians, Zoroastrians and Muslims) lived together, can scarcely be overestimated.

→ Ai Khanum; → Persepolis; → Sacae; → Sarmatae; → Scythians

→ Ancient Near Eastern philology and history (Assyriology); → Byzantine studies; → Historiography; → Linguistics; → Zoroastrianism

1 T. Benfey, Geschichte der Sprachwissenschaften und orientalischen Philologie in Deutschland seit dem Anfange des 19. Jahrhunderts mit einem Rückblick auf die früheren Zeiten, Munich 1869 (repr. 1965)   2 R. N. Frye, The History of Ancient Iran, 1984   3 A. Gabriel, Die Erforschung Persiens, 1952   4 P. Hopkirk, Foreign Devils on the Silk Road. 1980   5 D. Metzler, Die Achämeniden im Geschichtsbewusstsein des 15. und 16. Jahrhunderts. Kunst, Kultur und Geschichte der Achämenidenzeit und ihr Fortleben, 1983, 289–303   6 H. Sancisi-Weerdenburg, Introduction. Through Travellers' Eyes: The Persian Monuments as Seen by European Travellers, in: Achaemenid History 7, 1991, 1–35   7 D. Stronach, W. Ball, B. A. Litvinskii, Excavations i.-iv., EncIr 9, 88–113   8 R. Schmitt (ed.), Compendium Linguarum Iranicarum, 1989   9 U. Weber, J. Wiesehöfer, Das Reich der Achaimeniden: eine Bibliographie, 1996   10 J. Wiesehöfer, Das antike Persien, 1994

Bibliographies and Reference Works:
11 Abstracta Iranica, 1978 ff.   12 Archäologische Bibliographie, in: AMI, 1973 ff.   13 Bibliographie Linguistique, 1939 ff.   14 The Cambridge History of Iran, vols. 2–3, 1983–85   15 The Cambridge Ancient History, vols. 4–10 and 13, 1984–87   16 Encyclopaedia Iranica. 1982 ff.

Additional Bibliography M. Brosius, Women in Ancient Persia, 559–331 BC, 1996; N. Sims-Williams, J. Cribb, A New Bactrian Inscription of Kanishka the Great, in: Silk Road Art and Archaeology 4, 1995/96; J. D. Pearson, A Bibliography of Pre-Islamic Persia, 1975; J. Wiesehöfer, Ancient Persia: From 550 BC to 650 AD, 2001

URLs   http://www.gengo.l.u-tokyo.ac.jp/~hkum/bactrian.html;   http://depts.washington.edu/silkroad/index.html

PHILIP HUYSE

Iraq Museum, Baghdad. The world's most significant collection of Mesopotamian antiquities, the Iraq Museum (IM) in Baghdad, owes its origin to the initiative of Gertrude Bell, Director of Antiquities, who established the first permanent exhibition with finds from C.L. Wooley's excavations at Ur in a modest room in the Serail on the East bank of the River Tigris in 1923. As a result of the first Iraqi antiquities law (1924), which guaranteed the most important finds from foreign excavations in the country for the IM, its inventory grew rapidly and was able, in 1932, to be moved into its own building in the Ma'moun Street. With the founding of the *Iraqi Directorate General of Antiquities* and the resulting increase in excavation activity, particularly in connection with dam projects (with active international participation), the repositories filled rapidly. In 1963, the IM moved into a generous new building in the Salhiya district of western Baghdad. There was a considerable expansion in 1984–at which time 20 halls were available as exhibition space. As a national museum, the IM has branches with their own display collections at several locations in the country. At the end of the 1970s, an archaeological children's museum was opened in Baghdad as part of the IM. Touring exhibitions with finds from the IM could be seen in Europe and Japan in 1964–1967, at the end of the 1970s and the middle of the 1980s. A large exhibition in the USA was planned for 1991. With the outbreak of the Kuwait crisis in 1990, the exhibition in the IM was closed and its contents placed in a secret storage. In 1991, several provincial museums were plundered and ravaged (loss of more than 4,000 objects). The IM was partly reopened in 2000 and closed again in 2003, at the dawn of Gulf War II. In the aftermath of that war, from April 10–12, 2003, the museum was looted. Some 15 000 objects were lost, mainly from the storerooms, many more were damaged. With the help of the Iraqi people and the Iraqi authorities, supported by the international community half of this number has been returned (2006). The rehabilitation of the museum complex included the building of a new high security store and a new lighting and security system for the public galleries. To date (2006) the IM has not reopened.

The inventory of the IM (more than 250,000 registered objects) encompasses the entire spectrum of Mesopotamian history, from the Palaeolithic to the modern era. It consists of objects recovered in the territory of the state of Iraq after 1923. At first, only half of the objects discovered in foreign excavations went to the IM (in accordance with the antiquities law, the excavators were entitled to the other half, and thus material went to → London, British Museum, Oxford (Ashmolean Museum), → Paris, Louvre, → Berlin (Vorderasiatisches Museum), Heidelberg (Uruk-Warka Collection), → Philadelphia, Univer-

sity of Pennsylvania Museum of Archaeology
and Anthropology, Ancient Near Eastern Section (University Museum), and → Chicago, Oriental Institute Museum (also in the Field Museum of
Natural History); until 1917, the share of finds allotted
to the host country was sent to Istanbul (Eski šark Eser-
leri Müzesi). Since 1974, the IM has a claim to all archaeological finds recovered in Iraq. Finds from other
countries have also come to the IM through purchase,
gifts and exchanges. The display collection is laid out
chronologically and begins in the Prehistoric Hall with
Palaeolithic stone implements and skeletal finds
(Neanderthals) from the Šhanidar cave in northern
Iraq, and material from Neolithic agricultural settlements. In the Sumerian Hall, finds from the early Sumerian culture of the Uruk period, including from Uruk
itself, are displayed. These include the oldest written
documents (clay tablets with pictographic script, end of
the 4th millennium), stone sculptures, cylinder seals
(likewise the oldest representatives of their kind), and
stone vessels (fig. 2). Among the materials from the
early dynastic city states in the south of the country are
goods from the royal tombs of Ur (middle of the 3rd
millennium): jewelery, implements and weapons of precious metal and valuable stones (fig. 4), as well as
mosaic inlays from wooden musical instruments. In the
Akkadian and Babylonian Hall are life-size copper
sculptures from the period of the Akkadian empire,
including the copper head of an Akkadian king from
Niniveh (fig. 1) and the cult statue of Bassetki, with
dedicatory inscription of King Naramsin (3rd millennium). Old Babylonian clay tablets from Tell Harmal,
Eshnunna, and other cities come from the early 2nd
millennium BC. Displayed finds from the Middle Babylonian (Kassite) period include the moulded-brick
façade of the Karaindash temple in Uruk, with life-size
water and mountain gods. The Assyrian Hall contains
monumental stone sculptures and orthostat reliefs from
the Neo-Assyrian palaces in northern Iraq (Kalkhu =
Nimrud, Khorsabad, and Niniveh). Two newly furnished halls house the rich goods from the tombs of Neo-
Assyrian queens of the 9th and 8th cents. BC, discovered untouched in Kalkhu. In two more halls, items
from the same period found in other locations (e.g.,
Phoenician ivory from Kalkhu: fig. 3) can be seen. The
Late Babylonian Hall holds, for instance, material from
the new excavations in → Babylon and from Kiš. In
three Hatra Halls, finds from the Seleucid and Parthian
eras are exhibited, including a bronze statuette of Hercules from Seleucia (fig. 5), and life-size stone sculptures
and reliefs from the Parthian desert city of Hatra (fig.
6), as well as early Christian artefacts from al-Qusair,
Dakakin and Tikrit. In the Taha Baqir Hall, Arabic
manuscripts, including significant editions of the
Qur'an, are displayed. Finally, four additional halls
contain finds from the Islamic era, including stone and
stucco building ornamentation, glazed tiles, and
wooden sarcophagi.
→ Hatra; → Kalḫu; → Naramsin; → Ninive; → Ur;
→ Uruk

→ Ancient Near Eastern Philology and History;
→ Near Eastern Archaeology

1 Anon., Guide-Book to the Iraq Museum ([1]1966; [2]1973)
2 F. Basmachi, Treasures of the Iraq Museum (1975–76)
3 M. S. Damerji, Das Kindermuseum-Baghdad. Idee und
Experiment (arab.), in: Sumer 38, 1982 (arab. Teil 25–39)
4 Sumer, Assur, Babylon: 7000 Jahre Kunst und Kultur
zwischen Euphrat und Tigris, (Exhibition catalogue) Berlin, 1978   5 The Land Between Two Rivers: Twenty years
of Italian Archaeology in the Middle East. The Treasures
of Mesopotamia, (Exhibition catalogue) Turin, 1985
6 The Grand Exhibition of Silk Road Civilizations: The
Oasis and Steppe Routes, (Exhibition catalogue) Nara,
1988   7 Lost Heritage, vol. 1, 1992; vol. 2, 1993; vol. 3,
1996

ADDITIONAL BIBLIOGRAPHY M. Bogdanos, W.
Patrick, Thieves of Baghdad: One Marine's Passion for
Ancient Civilizations and the Journey to Recover the
World's Greatest Stolen Treasures, 2005; M. Polk and A.
Schuster (eds.), The Looting of the Iraq Museum, Bagh-
dad: The Lost Legacy of Ancient Mesopotamia, 2005.
                    MICHAEL MÜLLER-KARPE, DONNY GEORGE YOUKHANNA

Ireland. 'Gens igitur Hibernica, a primo aduentus sui
tempore (...), usque ad Gurmundi et Turgesii tempora
(...), iterumque ab eorum obitu usque ad hec nostra
tempora, ab omni alienarum gentium incursu libera
mansit et inconcussa', Giraldus Cambrensis, *Topogra-
phia Hibernie* (ca. 1188; "The Irish, therefore, from the
earliest time of their arrival to the times of Gurmundus
and Turgesius (...), and again from their passing on up
until these times of ours, have remained free and uns-
haken by an incursion of foreign tribes").

A. Early Contacts with the Roman Empire
B. Middle Ages   C. Renaissance and Modern
Times

A. Early Contacts with the Roman Empire
Ireland (I.) was never actually conquered by the
Romans. This fact is of less significance for the development of I.'s cultural history than for the image that
the Irish developed of themselves and of foreigners,
because I. was actually shaped and influenced by the
material and intellectual culture of Antiquity and late
Antiquity. From the 1st. cent. onwards (with a gap in
the 3rd cent.), archaeological finds attest to early contacts with the Roman Empire, in particular with the
province of Britannia, through traders and returning
Irish mercenaries and plunderers. Votive offerings in the
passage grave of Newgrange point to a rather isolated,
comparatively long-term Romano-British influence on
cult practices. The Christianisation in the 5th cent., associated with the figure of St. Patrick, who was of British origin, most likely started out from centres of royal
power with long-term contacts with Romano-British
areas. Ogham, a writing system probably developed in
the late 4th cent., was inspired by a knowledge of the
Latin alphabet and, with regard to its internal organization, the classification of speech sounds by late Anti-

que grammarians. The use of Ogham stones as tomb-stones on graves has been linked to contemporary Christian practice on the Continent and in Britain.

B. MIDDLE AGES
1. LATIN SCHOLARSHIP 2. CRAFTS AND ARCHITECTURE

1. LATIN SCHOLARSHIP

The extent of the knowledge of Greek by Irish scholars up to 900 (none is assumed for the period after that) is a matter of debate. It is probable that Latin-Greek glossaries and elementary didactic works were available. The Greek alphabet was used for special purposes, for example, for a Latin version of the Lord's Prayer in the *Book of Armagh* (ca. 807). As one of the three sacred languages, Greek was held in high regard by scholars, as was Hebrew. A further indication is the typical predilection of these scholars for listing individual words in all three holy languages.

Latin scholarship in I. reached its zenith in the 7th and 8th cents. The outstanding Hiberno-Latin authors of the 9th cent., such as Sedulius and Eriugena, were already active on the Continent. For the period from 850 to 1050, no Latin hagiographies written in I. are transmitted. It was only from late 11th cent. onwards, in the context of Church reform, that Latin erudition became stronger again. The Hiberno-Latin text culture encompasses all of the genres relevant to Christian education and culture: fundamental texts (grammars, glossaries, reckoning the Church calendar), theology (commentaries on the Bible, exegesis, speculative theology), hagiography, liturgy, legal texts and documents, inscriptions and poetry. The Late Classical-medieval concept of *grammatica*, aimed at assisting in the exploration of a textual culture in its entirety, also shaped and dominated the approach taken by Hiberno-Latin authors as well as those writing in the vernacular. One can gain an impression of the didactic methods and curriculum goals of the early medieval monastic schools, which provided an education both in Latin and in the vernacular, from the glossaries, the commentaries (some in the form of question-and- answer sequences) and the illustrated aids for Latin constructions found in Latin manuscripts.

The two extant works of St. Patrick attest to a good knowledge of the Bible and of Patristic authors. Some of the outstanding hagiographers known by name are Tírechán (ca. 670), Cogitosus (ca. 680) and Adomnán (d. 704), who wrote about the lives of the monastery-founders Patrick, Brigit and Columba (Colum Cille) respectively. Two high-medieval catalogues of the library of Gerald FitzGerald, 9th Earl of Kildare (d. 1534), provide evidence that in the 16th cent., too, Latin texts were in the private possession of the nobility. The older catalogue lists 21 Latin works (as opposed to 11 works in French, 7 in English, and 20 in Irish), and the later catalogue contains 34 Latin works (as opposed to 36 French and 22 English, with the page for the Irish entries left blank).

Historiographic-annalistic works were initially written only in Latin, but from ca. 820 at the latest we also find them in the vernacular. Latin and the vernacular were also used side by side in other types of texts. Latin legal documents date from the 11th and 12th cents., while older vernacular phrases point to the existence of a much longer but lost tradition. The culture of Latin texts was actively appropriated through the compilation of vernacular glossaries, translations or paraphrases into the vernacular. The use of the vernacular gradually displaced Latin between the 9th and 11th cents. Outstanding examples of multilingual Irish-Latin glossaries, which are the most important documents for the linguistic period of Old Irish, are the Würzburg glosses on the Epistles of St. Paul and the Epistle to the Hebrews (up to Chap. 12; three glossators, *prima manus* ca. 700, main glossator 8th cent.), the Milan glosses on a commentary on the psalms (lst quarter of the 9th cent.), and the St. Gallen glosses on the first 16 books of Priscian's *Institutiones Grammaticae* (9th cent., a total of 9412 glosses, of which about 37% are in Old Irish). They contain explanations on lexicology and syntax as well as interpretations of the original texts. The Würzburg glosses contain competent, albeit brief translations of Latin bible exegeses (Ambrosiaster, Pelagius). These show that perhaps even as early as the 7th cent., Irish exegetes were not using Latin exclusively. Latin quotes from the Bible or from canon law with their Irish translations are also found in medieval legal texts, which remain very difficult to date exactly because of their multiple textual layers. Particularly instructive is the legal text *Bretha Nemed toísech* ('The First Judgments respecting Privileged Persons', 2nd quarter of the 8th cent.) containing a paraphrase of a passage from the *Collectio canonum Hibernensis* in both Old Irish prose and *rosc*, as well as a further passage only in *rosc*. *Rosc* is a highly stylised form of medieval epigrammatic poetry characterized by rhythm, cadence and alliteration – probably an Irish advance on late Antique art forms. There was also a close and productive interconnection between Hiberno-Latin grammars and the Irish treatise *Auraicept na nÉces* ("The Scholars' Primer") and also between metrical analyses of Late Antiquity and the native categorizations of poetic forms in the so-called Middle Irish metrics.

The St. Gallen glosses also afford some insight into the degree to which (late) ancient authors were known in the 9th cent. Virgil is the only ancient poet to be mentioned, together with late Ancient Virgil commentators, late Ancient scholars such as Boethius and Martianus Capella and Christian authors such as Orosius, Augustine, Ambrose, Cassian and Cassiodorus. Other texts point to the conclusion that Horace was known, and there are a number of allusions to Classical mythology in the Hiberno-Latin hymns. Not only the Bible and the liturgy have been identified as likely sources of Adomnan's exegetic work *De locis sanctis*, but also writings by Jerome, Sulpicius Severus, Gregory, Juvencus, Josephus, Augustine, Cassiodorus, Isidor and pseudo-

Eucherius. A list of (late) Ancient authors known to medieval scholars remains a desideratum. The extent to which Latin literary models influenced the Irish-language literature is still a matter of controversy. Its supporters not only point to the narrative genre of *Táin Bó Cúailnge* ("The Cattle Raid of Cooley") itself, but also to the identification of the war goddess Mórrígan with the Fury Allechtu/Allecto, the reference to the coat that Simon the Magician gave Darius and the attribution of one of Hercules' heroic acts to Cú Chulainn, the hero of *Táin*. Middle Irish poems compared the heroes in the local tradition with the heroes of Troy, and prominent Irish places such as Cruachán and Emain Macha with the city of Troy. Scholars also debate whether it is possible that the large-scale vernacular narratives pertaining to historiography and the pseudo-national historical tradition (ca. AD 1000) may have also been inspired by late Ancient historical works and their Irish adaptations. The oldest Irish version of Dares Phrygius' *Historia de excidio Troiae* (*Togail Troi*), of which three later versions, two in prose, one in verse, are still extant, and the biography of Alexander based on Orosius' depiction in the *Historia adversus paganos* as well as the *Epistola ad Aristotelem* and the *Collatio Alexandri* probably date to the 10th/11th cent. The adaptations of Lucan's *Bellum Civile* (*In Cath Catharda*), of Statius' *Thebais* (*Togail na Tebe*) and *Achilleis* (a prose version as part of the third revision of *Togail Troi* and also as an autonomous prose version), and of Virgil's *Aeneid* probably date from the 12th cent. There are also a number of texts whose sources cannot be clearly identified and that are not based on adaptations of traditional models; for example, texts about Odysseus, with an idiosyncratic combination of Homeric and international folkloric motifs (*Merugud Uilix Maicc Leirtis*), about Atreus, Oedipus and about the Minotaur. Irish versions of (late) Ancient subject matter are free adaptations with close adherence to local stylistic conventions. Just as with respect to subjects from their own history, the interest of the revisers of these stories was action-centred, synthesizing and historiographic. One of the extant copies of *Togail Troi* is a manuscript of monastic origin dating from the 12th cent.; otherwise, the texts mentioned here are contained in later manuscripts belonging to secular scholarly families who continued the tradition of monastic erudition under the patronage of members of the nobility. These adaptations also influenced the local literature. *In Cath Catharda* was thus the model for the accounts in *Cogad Gáededel re Gallaib* (12th cent.) and *Caithréim Thoirdhealbhaigh* (14th cent.), describing the disputes between Irish and Scandinavians as well as disputes within the O'Brien family. Classical allusions and comparisons are also evident in early modern Irish bardic poetry.

2. Crafts and Architecture

Even after the Norman Conquest (1169) and the Church reform of the 12th cent., Irish scribes continued to use characteristic insular adaptations of late Ancient forms of writing, probably based on provincial British models of the 5th and 6th cents. In the arts, Graeco-Roman naturalism did not prove influential. Liturgical vessels such as the *Chalice of Ardagh* (8th cent.) adopted a Byzantine formal vocabulary into the local arts and crafts tradition. Also of likely Byzantine origin were the iconographic elements in the *Gospels of Kells*, probably transmitted through Italian, Greek or Coptic models. Metal and stone-working in the 9th and 10th cents. drew partly on Carolingian and Ottonian sources, while English influences remained pertinent until well into the 15th cent. The first and only purely Romanesque building is Cormac's Chapel in Cashel (dedicated in 1134). Many monasteries were built in the 12th cent. based on the routine building plans of their continental counterparts. In the 13th cent., master builders from the West of England built Gothic cathedrals in such cities as Dublin, Kilkenny and Waterford that were under Norman rule; it was not until the 15th cent. that a local late Gothic style developed.

C. Renaissance and Modern Times
1. Institutions 2. Classical Education
3. Literary Reception of Antiquity 4. Art and Architecture

1. Institutions

Grammar schools funded by private endowments were established from 1538 onwards. The educational focus was on Classical languages. The only schools available to Catholics after their exclusion from official secondary education with the enactment of the *Penal Laws* in 1695 and the ban on Catholic schools were the 'hedge schools'. Latin was regularly taught in these schools, so that into the early 19th cent. travellers repeatedly reported with amazement on the Classical erudition of the rural population: 'they speake Latine like a vulgar language' (Campion 1571, [6. 562]). In the late 18th and in the 19th cent., Catholic and Non-Conformist secondary schools established after the *Relief Act* of 1782 also placed great emphasis on Classical languages, as well as on English language and literature. The first university, Trinity College in Dublin, was founded in 1592; under the influence of Cambridge, its initial orientation was Ramist, changing to conservative and Aristotelian after 1633. Between 1637 and 1793, non-Protestant students were barred from sitting for any examinations; for that reason, they tended to attend Scottish and continental universities. The establishment in 1734 of a print shop owned by the university provided the impetus for editing and publishing Classical texts. In 1795, St. Patrick's College in Maynooth was established to train Catholic priests; the college also provided for the study of Classical languages and literatures. In 1845, three non-denominational colleges were established in Cork, Galway and Belfast; they joined to form Queen's University in 1850 and in 1879 joined with the Catholic University in Dublin (founded in 1854) and the Presbyterian Magee College in Londonderry (founded in 1865) to become the Royal

University of I. It was closed in 1908 and replaced by the state-financed National University of I. (with colleges in Dublin, Cork and Galway) and Queen's College, Belfast. In the course of the 20th cent., institutional interest in Classical languages waned significantly. In 1974, Ancient Greek was taught in only eight schools in the Republic of I. Latin is no longer a prerequisite to matriculate at a university, and its importance as a school subject is decreasing accordingly.

In the 1930s, the works of Ovid were placed on the index of banned books by the Irish Censorship Board, prompting the poet Austin Clarke to react with an ironic and biting four-liner entitled *Penal Law*:

'Burn Ovid with the rest. Lovers will find'
'A hedge-school for themselves and learn by heart'
'All that the clergy banish from the mind,'
'When hands are joined and head bows in the dark.'

2. CLASSICAL EDUCATION

For the period from 1550 to 1700, Latin remained an important medium of written culture and contemporary critical analysis. Authors in I. and Catholic exiles on the Continent wrote a great number of works in Latin, primarily dealing with theology, historiography and, in the broadest sense, politics. These writings were a consequence of the cultural and political situation resulting from the Reformation and Counter-Reformation, and the conflicts between the various sections within the population. Translations are an immediate reflection of the involvement with Latin literature. An early example of a rare translation into Irish is Riocard do Búrc's poem *Fir na Fódla ar ndul d'éag* ('Are the Men of Ireland Dead'), a free translation of Ovid's *Amores* II.4, probably transmitted via John Harrington's English translation of 1618. Between 1707 and 1721, Lucas Smyth translated a selection of Greek and Latin authors. The first Irish translator to translate into English was Richard Stanihurst (1547–1618), who rendered the first four books of the *Aeneid* in a very idiosyncratic linguistic form (1582). When success eluded him, he wrote historiographical works in Latin. In I. the controversy concerning the comparative value of ancient and modern literature was debated around 1700, at least in part in conjunction with the question of the authenticity of the letters of Phalaris. Jonathan Swift contributed to this debate with his *Battle of the Books* (1704).

The earliest Classical philologist whose editorial work also proved influential outside of I. was Thomas Leland with his editions of Demosthenes' *Philippian* and *Olynthiac Orations* (1754). An important early contribution to the study of Homer was Robert Wood's *Essay on the Original Genius and Writing of Homer* (1769), which sought to interpret Homer against the historical backdrop of his time as an oral poet. This interpretation was received positively by, among others, Goethe, Heyne and Wolf. The academic analysis of ancient literature and history reached its zenith at Trinity College Dublin in the second half of the 19th cent., and is associated with such scholars as J.P.

Mahaffy, A. Palmer, R.Y. Tyrrell, L.C. Purser and J.B. Bury. An outstanding 20th cent. scholar was W. B. Stanford (1910–1984), whose contributions on the reception of ancient culture in I. were fundamental. In the 20th cent., medieval Hiberno-Latin texts have become a focal point of Irish scholarship.

3. LITERARY RECEPTION OF ANTIQUITY

Anglo-Irish literature was an important medium in the reception of Antiquity. Well into the 19th cent., the treatment of Classical themes and motifs tended to be rather traditional and in keeping with the taste of the times (e.g. Nahum Tate's classicist libretto for Henry Purcell's *Dido and Aeneas* (1689), Aubrey de Vere's *Search after Proserpine* (1843) in the style of neo-Hellenistic English poets such as Shelley). However, the intellectual and emotional analysis of Antiquity by authors such as Oscar Wilde (1854–1900), William Butler Yeats (1865–1939) and James Joyce (1882–1941) took a more unconventional and idiosyncratic form. Wilde received a good Classical education both at school and at university, and collaborated with Mahaffy on the latter's *Social Life in Greece* (1874), in which Mahaffy also provided a detailed description of the Greek attitude to homosexuality. Wilde translated Greek texts and used Greek themes and figures in his poems in order to accentuate the contrast between sensual Hellenism and ascetic Christianity. Yeats's writings were also influenced by Greek literature and philosophy, particularly by Plato and neo-Platonism, alongside occultism and the vernacular Irish tradition. In his *Autobiographies*, he referred to the Classical authors as the 'builders of my soul' [10. 59]. Yeats perceived a particular affinity between Greek and Irish literature with regard to their emotional points of departure. His *King Oedipus* (1926) and *Oedipus at Colonus* (1927) are free adaptations of Sophocles' play. The works of James Joyce were also significantly influenced by Greek and Latin authors, particularly in their aesthetics and structure. In his autobiographical novel *Portrait of the Artist as a Young Man* (1916), this is evident, for example, in the choice of the name Stephen Daedalus for the hero, the reference to Ovid's treatment of the Daedalus theme and the influence of Aristotle and Thomas Aquinas on the theory of aesthetic perception as purported in this novel; it is also evident in the many Classical allusions in *Finnegans Wake* (1939). *Ulysses* (1922) describes the experiences of the main characters on a single day in Dublin in a multi-faceted and complex refraction of Homer's *Odyssey*. To varying degrees, Classical motifs have also been adopted by more recent authors. In his poem *Epic*, Patrick Kavanagh (1904–1967) juxtaposes Irish local events with the *Iliad*: 'I am inclined / To lose my faith in Ballyrush and Gortin/Till Homer's ghost came whispering to my mind/He said: I made the Iliad from such/A local row' [3. 136], thus assuring himself of the significance of his own experiences. Ovid's *Metamorphoses* was the source of motifs in Austin Clarke's (1896–1974) late volumes of poetry *The Dilemma of Iphis* (1970) and *Tiresias* (1971). References to Classical myths in Seamus Heaney's (1939 –) works can be found, for example, in *The Haw Lantern* (1987) and in *Seeing Things* (1991). The latter volume begins and ends with translations of descriptions by Virgil and Dante of the descent into the underworld; Hermes, the messenger of the gods, is a central figure in the poem *Crossings xxvii*.

4. ART AND ARCHITECTURE

Painting was of little importance in I. until after 1660. The two outstanding Irish painters in the classicist style who sought to imitate the effect of ancient sculptures in their art were James Barry (1741–1806) and Hugh Douglas Hamilton (1739–1808); both had stayed in Italy for lengthy periods. From the early 17th cent. on, Classical influences are evident in the architectural details of fortified manor houses; in a parallel development, Renaissance-style ornamental gardens with fountains and terraces were created (e.g. Portumna Castle in County Galway before 1618). Classicist models were influential on a grander scale in the designs of Sir William Robinson (ca. 1643–1712), whose Royal Hospital of Kilmainham, Dublin (1680–87) was the first great classicist building in I. The most important architects in Palladio's footsteps were Sir Edward Lovett Pearce (ca. 1699–1733), the designer of Parliament House Dublin (now the Bank of I.) who had travelled throughout Italy to study architecture, and Richard Castle (ca. 1690–1751), whose designs included the plans for a number of grand country houses. At the end of the 18th cent., important examples of classicist architecture were built in Dublin (Custom House, Four Courts, King's Inns), based on designs by James Gandon (1743–1823).

1 A. AHLQVIST, Notes on the Greek Materials in the St. Gall Priscian (Codex 904), in: M. W. HERREN, S. A. BROWN (eds.), The Sacred Nectar of the Greeks, 1988, 195–214　　2 R. HOFMAN, The Sankt Gall Priscian Commentary, 1996　　3 P. KAVANAGH, Collected Poems, 1964　　4 M. LAPIDGE, R. SHARPE, Celtic-Latin Literature 400–1200, 1985　　5 M. MAC CRAITH, Gaelic Ireland and the Renaissance., in: G. WILLIAMS, R. O. JONES (eds.), The Celts and the Renaissance, 1990, 57–89　　6 B. MILLET, Irish Literature in Latin, 1550–1700, in: T. W. MOODY, F. X. MARTIN, F. J. BYRNE (eds.), A New History of Ireland, vol. 3, Early Modern Ireland 1534–1691, 1991, 561–586　　7 W. B. STANFORD, Towards a History of Classical Influences in Ireland, Proceedings of the Royal Irish Academy 70 C 3, 1970　　8 W. B. STANFORD, Ireland and the Classical Tradition, 1976　　9 H. L. C. TRISTRAM, Der insulare Alexander, in: W. ERZGRÄBER (ed.), Kontinuität und Transformation der Antike im Mittelalter, 1989, 129–155　　10 W. B. YEATS, Autobiographies, 1955.

ADDITIONAL BIBLIOGRAPHY B. ARKINS, Hellenising Ireland: Greek and Roman Themes in Modern Irish Literature, 2005; U. MAC GEARAILT, Togail Troí: An Example of Translating and Editing in Medieval Ireland, in: Studia Hibernica 31, 2000–2001, 71–85; L. D. MYRICK, From the De Excidio Troiae Historia to the Togail Troí: Literary-Cultural Synthesis in a Medieval Irish Adaptation of Dares' Troy Tale, 1993; N. Ní SHÉAGHDHA, Trans-

lations and Adaptations into Irish, in: Celtica 16, 1984, 107–24; E. POPPE, Imtheachta Aeniasa, The Irish Aeneid: The Classical Epic from an Irish Perspective, (=Irish Texts Society, Subsidiary Series 3), 1995; G. SERPILLO, D. BADIN (eds.) The Classical World and the Mediterranean, 1996; O. SZERWINIACK, l' Irlande médiéval et la culture antique, in: P. LARDET (ed.), La tradition vive, Mélanges d' histoire des textes en l' honneur de Louis Holtz, 2002, 85–105　　　　　　　　　　　　　　　ERICH POPPE

Irony

A. INTRODUCTION　B. ROMANTICISM
C. POST-ROMANTIC RECEPTION

A. INTRODUCTION

Irony (Latin, from the Greek *eirôneía*, 'feigned ignorance') is traditionally understood as a figure of speech related to euphemism, with which one implies the opposite of what one says, while the illusoriness incarnated in the ironic discursive gesture must remain perceptible from the viewpoint of the addressee. This understanding of irony, designated as *dissimulatio*, which places the intentional deceptiveness of the ironic speaker in the foreground, was subsequently influential above all in Classical rhetoric, for instance in Quintilian. It finds its reference-point in the irony practiced by Socrates, whose maieutic procedure of ironic dialogicity, just as important as the doctrine of *dissimulatio* from the viewpoint of the history of reception, already documents the functional recourse to irony in the context of epistemological questions. In Socrates, ironic deceptiveness manifests itself in the performatively contradictory principle of ignorance that is aware of itself as such, in contrast with which the illusory knowledge of his respective interlocutors is again revealed as illusion. To this extent, irony in the Socratic model of maieutics regulates as it were *ex negativo* the process of the search for truth, which is set in motion thanks to the intentional deceptiveness of the *eirôn*. The understanding of irony as *dissimulatio* subsequently remained predominant down to the 18th cent.

B. ROMANTICISM

The term 'irony' underwent an uncommon semantic broadening in the early Romantic sketches of the concept of irony dating from around 1800, and particularly in F. Schlegel's conception of "Romantic irony". The basis of the new early Romantic conception of irony nevertheless remained the ancient doctrine of *dissimulatio*, which Schlegel, in his Lyceum-fragment (1797), sought to develop according to the fundamental type of "Socratic irony" [1. 160]. At the same time, however, this type bursts apart at a decisive point through Schlegel's resolutely philosophical interest in the term of 'irony', which means more than a simple, non-literal way of speaking. In Schlegel's conception, Socratic irony becomes perceptible as an antagonistic attitude which, as such, refers to the fundamentally antagonistic mutual relations of our epistemic self-view. In the same fragment on Socrates, we read further: "it [irony] contains and arouses a feeling of the irresolvable contradiction of the unconditioned and the conditional" [1 160] – with the result that "we feel ourselves to be simultaneously finite and infinite" [2. 333]. In this way, Romantic irony becomes explicitly apparent as an aesthetic response to an epistemological problem. Whereas antagonism in the medium of philosophical reflection can always be designated only discursively, irony, as a means for structuring poetic texts, can make tension visible qua tension, and hence portray the accomplishment of our insufficient self-mediation as such. This is achieved through the fact that irony simultaneously gives positive, finite form to what is represented, and shows it to be allegorically that which is not meant (thus, once again denying the 'finite' form of concretisation). The 'infinite', equally inaccessible both to epistemological reflection and to the concrete act of representation, can thereby be inscribed structurally within the representative process as unrepresentable. Irony thus manifests itself in Schlegel in the repetitive exchange between contradictory modes of representation, whose synthesis, achieved in a manner immanent to representation, always succeeds only temporarily, so that the dialectical process of the progression of ironic reification leads structurally to infinity. Schlegel's considerations on the 'transcendental-poetic' nature of ironic art are also situated in the context of this conception. The divergent modes of representation are synthetically merged, insofar as the author, by accomplishing the representation, co-reflects the conditions of possibility of the ironic retraction of what has already been said, thereby making the artistic mode of production itself into the object of poetry within poetry, a procedure that C. M. Wieland, Jean Paul and L. Tieck had already practiced in the German-speaking world before Schlegel. Among those who later strove to systematise the utterances on irony scattered rhapsodically throughout Schlegel's works was K. W. F. Solger. To the extent that irony also functions as a possible aesthetic solution to an epistemological problem in Solger's later theory of Romantic irony, the departure from the ancient and medieval understanding of irony can be regarded as definitively accomplished by 1815.

C. Post-Romantic Reception

The technique of ironic disillusionment, already wielded with virtuosity by L. Tieck, was then developed further by H. Heine, both theoretically (in the literary-theoretical work *Die romantische Schule*, 1835) and practically (in his own poems). In contrast, S. Kierkegaard, in his 1841 dissertation, assumed a critical distance from Romanticism, and returned to the concept of Socratic irony, which is apologetically defined as a victory over the self and an existential mode of self-domination. The most lasting, albeit indirect, reception of irony is, however, found in the creations of modern poets. Thus, the 'transcendental-poetic' nature of ironic art, which goes back to F. Schlegel, could be classified as

a characteristic property of the modern novel. The ironic play with representation, which discloses the structural conditions immanent in its origins, thus aesthetically undercutting the boundaries between fictionality and reality, has subsequently been elevated to the status of a formal principle of writing by authors as different as J. Cortazar, F. O'Brien, G. Perec or I. Calvino.

→ Maieutic method; → Rhetoric; → Socrates
→ Allegory; → Figures, theory of

Sources 1 F. Schlegel, Kritische Ausgabe (KA) vol. 2, Ernst Behler (ed.), 1967 2 Id., Kritische Ausgabe (KA) vol. 12, Ernst Behler (ed.), 1964
Literature 3 E. Behler, Ironie und literarische Moderne, 1997 4 M. Frank, Einführung in die frühromantische Ästhetik, 1989 5 U. Japp, Theorie der Ironie, 1983 6 M. Müller, Die Ironie. Kulturgeschichte und Textgestalt, 1995 7 I. Strohschneider-Kohrs, Die romantische Ironie in Theorie und Gestaltung, 1960

Additional Bibliography W. Booth, A Rhetoric of Irony, ²1982; C. Brooks, The Well Wrought Urn, 1947; L. R. Furst, Fictions of Romantic Irony, 1984; D. Knox, Ironia, 1990; W. V. O'Connor, E. Behler, Irony, in: A. Preminger, T. V. F. Brogan (eds.), The New Princeton Encyclopedia of Poetry and Poetics, 1993, 633–35
ANDREAS BARTH

Istituto (Nazionale) di Studi Romani
A. Foundation (1923–1925) B. Period of Flourishing (1924–1944) C. Programme and Objective D. Development after 1944

A. Foundation (1923–1925)
The foundation of the *Istituto di Studi Romani* (ISR) in 1925 was inextricably linked with contemporary Fascist cultural policies. In his plans, C. Galassi-Paluzzi (1893–1972), founder of the ISR and later its president (1934–1944), followed the views of the philosopher G. Gentile, Minister for *Pubblica Istruzione* (1922–1924) and Fascist Italy's leading intellectual. Gentile's policy can be described as a 'nationalization' of instruction, culture and science. His aim was an extensive modernization and centralization of the Italian system in these areas; however, this was achieved at the expense of regional cultural traditions and the autonomy of local academic and cultural institutions. At the same time, Fascist Italy propagated a new cultural vigour, claiming a forerunner position in a wide range of areas within Western culture. This claim was linked to the belief in the uniqueness and continuity of Roman-Italian history and culture within Western culture, largely based on the continuation of Roman antiquity – the *Romanità* (represented above all by the eras of Caesar and Augustus and also the 'Goldenen Latinity'). History and culture of the *Romanità* had to be studied and taught in a 'typically Italian fashion': only Italians, as the modern 'Romans', had an 'innate' intuition of *Romanità* and its contemporary importance within the Fascist revolution.

The plan for establishing the ISR was closely linked to the journal *Roma*, set up in 1923 by Galassi-Paluzzi, which propagating a 'typically Italian' view of *Romanità*. The following clerical-nationalist intellectuals involved in this journal and whose views were to have a fundamental impact and set the tone for the cultural climate within the ISR, were: the journalist G. Ceccarelli (alias Ceccarius), C. Cecchelli, the archaeologist of early Christian Rome, G. Giovannoni, city planner and architectural historian, the medievalist P. Fedele and the Jesuit P. Tacchi Venturi. They set out the objective of the ISR: to promote any possible way of researching and reflecting on the history of the city of Rome *ab urbe condita* and its influence on the history of Western civilization. This was to be achieved by a three-prong approach: research and scholarly production; the methodical organization of Roman Studies; and popularization of this academic discipline.

B. PERIOD OF FLOURISHING (1924–1944)

Between 1925 and 1944, the presidents of the ISR were: P. Fedele, L. Federzoni, V. Scialoja, and, after the latter's death in 1933, C. Galassi-Paluzzi (appointed *ad vitam*). Supported by O. Morra, who prior to his retirement in 1974 successively held the offices of Secretary (1925), Secretary-General (1938) and Director (1952), Galassi-Paluzzi set the course of the ISR. The ISR also had a steering committee, the *Giunta direttiva;* apart from those already mentioned, seats on this committee were given to influential academic specialists and (Fascist) executive members, such as E. Bodrero, G. Bottai, P. de Francisci, G. Q. Giglioli and R. Paribeni. The ISR's good relationship with the regime was underscored in 1929, when King Victor Emanuel III agreed to become its patron (*alto patronato*) and Mussolini its honorary president.

The ISR was an independent foundation (*ente morale*), but starting with the academic year of 1933/34, the payment of an annual subsidy by the *Ministero della Educazione Nazionale* (MEN) turned it into a semi-official institution. In this latter role, the ISR operated as an equal partner within Rome's (inter)national scholarly and cultural institutions. Galassi-Paluzzi, for example, was a member of the *Giunta centrale per gli studi storici*, and it was debated whether to award the ISR an official status comparable to the various other national research institutes for archaeology, history and art history. Mussolini himself supported Galassi-Paluzzi's plan of setting up a research institute, the *Scuola Storica di Studi Romani* (SSSR). Even though this plan was the reason for the subsidies paid by the MEN to the ISR, the SSSR itself was never established. The existing research institutes feared that Galassi-Paluzzi's plans would weaken their own positions. However, Galassi-Paluzzi succeeded from 1935 in establishing local ISR sections in Italy's most important cultural centres. With this he hoped to be able to match the successful model of the *Società Dante Alighieri*. Though some ISR sections were set up outside of Italy – e.g. in Stockholm and Paris –, Galassi-Paluzzi never managed to equal the international success of the *Società Dante Alighieri*.

Mussolini recognized the benefits of Galassi-Paluzzi's programme and its ideological potential for the regime's imperialist policies, which from 1931 on determined the political propaganda. Galassi-Paluzzi's plans were closely linked to the ambitions of radical ancient historians such as De Francisci und Giglioli, views expressed, for example, in the national celebrations of the *bimillenario augusteo* (1937–1938) as well as in the associated events of the *Mostra Augustea della Romanità*, and the ISR organized International Augustus Convention (*Convegno Augusteo*) of 1938, the latter attended by leading scholars from home and abroad. In this context, the *Romanità* cult, as proclaimed by the ISR, reached its zenith: the *bimillenario augusteo* coincided with the first celebration to commemorate the foundation of the Second Empire in 1936, a fact hailed as confirmation of the vital importance of *Romanità* for modern Italy.

National commemorations for Virgil, Horace, Augustus and Livy, together with numerous conventions and exhibitions on Papal Rome and Rome 'reborn' after Italy's unification in 1870 produced an impressive corpus of publications. In addition, the ISR invested considerable effort in the *Corsi superiori di studi romani*. These series of lectures, conducted from 1926 on in Borromini's Oratory of the Chiesa Nuova, acted as a kind of 'salon', a meeting place for the city's cultural elite with high-ranking representatives of the regime, the aristocracy and the clergy. The lectures were regularly published in the journal *Roma* and also as individual brochures, if they were deemed to be of ideological importance.

Beginning in 1928, the ISR also organized the biennial national conventions for the *Studi Romani*, to which prominent experts were invited depending on the topic of debate. The success of these various activities in the field of popular science was largely determined by the pronounced imperialism of the 1930s and the cult of *Romanità* as proclaimed by the ISR. This gave rise to the impression that the ISR had developed into a semi-official propaganda office in the service of the regime. However, this impression does not do justice to the academic ambitions which Galassi-Paluzzi had for the ISR.

C. PROGRAMME AND OBJECTIVE

The programme of the ISR was aimed at promoting Italian research in the following areas: archaeology and topography of Rome through the centuries, ancient history and Latin philology, the history and architecture of Christian Rome, the culture and history of Papal Rome, history of morals, learning and culture of Rome through the centuries, as well as architecture and urban development in contemporary Rome. The ISR was strongly involved in the urban building programmes ordered by the *Governatorato di Roma*, which also provided financial support for the ISR. The integral approach of the *Studi Romani* was not only evident in the systematic establishment of the *Corsi superiori*, but also in the publication of the monumental series *Storia di Roma*. The first parts of this series were published in 1938; they developed into an impressive series of reference books in Italian on the history and culture of the city of Rome, with contributions by many prominent Italian experts. This ambitious project survived the fall of Fascism.

The propaganda success of the *bimillenario augusteo* and the *Mostra Augustea della Romanità* (1937–1938) with significant contributions by the ISR gave new impetus to Galassi-Paluzzi's scholarly ambitions. In 1940, Mussolini forced the MEN to agree to a drastic raise in the subsidies paid to the ISR in view of the planned *Centro Internazionale di Studi Romani* (CISR) and the role of the ISR in organizing the public demonstration *Roma nel Ventennale* and the 1942 World Fair (both events were cancelled because of the war). Even though the CISR, an international version of the SSSR project, did not survive Mussolini's fall, it provided an ideal platform for all of the ISR scholarly ambitions: (inter)national coordination, promotion and popularization of research on the history and culture of the city of Rome *a.u.c.* and their influence on Western civilization, as well as the training of national and international scholars working in this field. The recognition of these ambitions by the regime was not only evident in the planned increase in subsidies, but also in the award of the royal seal of approval, the allocation of suitable accommodation on the Aventine in 1941, and the fact that Galassi-Paluzzi was nominated in this period to become a minister of state. The intention was that within the envisaged European Fascist system, the CISR and its staff were to play a leading role in the field of Roman Studies.

In order to achieve these aims, Galassi-Paluzzi designed his projects as prominent expressions of Fascist cultural policy. He realized that the only way to secure a leading role for the CISR was to establish it within an (inter)national framework. As the position desired by the CISR was to be at the expense of the MEN's established national scholarly institutions, G. Bottai, the then Minister of Education (1936 to 1943), was somewhat reluctant in his support of Galassi-Paluzzi's ambitions. Even though Bottai was an *ex officio* member of the *Giunta direttiva* and had given lectures at the ISR, his support for Galassi-Paluzzi's plans was qualified by the condition that they were not to be implemented at the expense of either the MEN's regular budget or his own ambitions in cultural policy, which brought him into conflict with Mussolini after 1940. Although Galassi-Paluzzi maintained good relations with Bottai, his relationship with Mussolini was cordial and close, because he realized that the Duce's personal patronage was essential for the success of the CISR. For this loyalty to the Duce, both the ISR and Paluzzi were to pay a heavy price after 1944.

D. DEVELOPMENT AFTER 1944

The fall of the regime in 1943 and the Allied occupation of Rome in 1944 resulted in the temporary termination of the ISR; for Galassi-Paluzzi's presidency, they spelled the final end. Q. Tossati was appointed administrator in 1944, with the intention of restoring the ISR. Although the ISR was reopened in 1945, its activities remained very limited until 1950. In that year, Tossati was made president, and a new *Giunta direttiva* appointed with the task of adjusting the statutes. In 1953, the 1944 ban on *Roma* was lifted and the journal was allowed to be published under the new title of *Studi Romani*; the ISR could thus function as a de facto local historical society with a modest national and international impact.

Even though after 1944, many (personnel) changes were implemented on the board level and the institute's most radical aims, sullied by their association with the Fascist regime, removed, there was still talk of a greater continuity of those ideas and activities. This continuity was largely promoted by O. Morra, formally appointed as the ISR's director in 1952, who had, however, behind the scenes in the intervening years and in close cooperation with Galassi-Paluzzi, guarded the ISR's intellectual heritage of the Fascist period.

Even though prominent politicians of the *Democrazia Cristiana* – such as G. Andreotti and his successors as state presidents – followed the activities of the Institute with interest and maybe even provided financial support, the ISR could no longer count on as generous a funding as it had enjoyed between 1934 and 1944. In parts, this was compensated by the appointment of prominent cultural scholars who – often linked to the *Sapienza* – had already actively participated in ISR activities during the Fascist period, and had successfully risen to the top of their respective disciplines after World War II. One exponent of this generation, the archaeologist P. Romanelli, succeeded Tossati in the presidency of the ISR after the latter's death – a position which he was to hold until 1980.

In 1955, the *Premio Cultore di Roma* was set up to be awarded annually to a scholar who had made a major contribution to the research on *Romanità*. Among the prizewinners was a great number of (inter)nationally renowned scholars, a fact used by the ISR as an additional benefit to underscore its own academic standing. The prize winners include: G. De Sanctis, S. Riccobono, P. de Francisci, V. Arangio-Ruiz, M. Pallottino, J. Carcopino, R. Syme and R. Krautheimer. Although the prize was initially mainly awarded to ancient historians, further nurturing the misconception that the main focus of the ISR was on Classical Antiquity in Rome, the roll of honour does reflect the all-encompassing character of the *Romanità* cult.

Despite the attribute 'national' in its title since 1983 and its ensured membership of Rome specialists from home and abroad, the ISR currently ekes out a meagre existence due to the lack of funds. Apart from the publications under the auspices of the ISR and the administration of the library, of the archive and documentation systems, the primary focus of the ISR is on the organization of the *Corsi superiori di studi romani*, once the basis for its initial successes. The Institute also organizes a highly regarded annual translation competition, the *Certamen Capitoleum*. In addition, the ISR continues to be active in promoting the study of Latin, in close cooperation with the *Centro di Studi Ciceroniani* and the *Academia Latinitati Fovendae*.

Romanelli's resignation in 1980 signified the end of the generation of radical *cultori della romanità* who between 1925 and 1944 had given the ISR a Fascist face and who subsequently ensured the continuity of a clerical-nationalistic view of Rome's history. In spite of its ambitious claims during the first fifteen years of its existence, the ISR never attained an undisputed scholarly status, and its success was limited to the popularization of the history of the *Aeterna Urbs*. The current role of the the ISR cannot be seen in isolation from its position within the *Unione Internazionale degli Istituti d'Archeleogia, Storia e Storia dell'Arte in Roma*. In this context, the ISR functions as but one of the Italian institutes in this field, distinguished by its primary focus on Roman urban history, but in scholarship in no way competing with the nationally and internationally renowned institutes for archaeology, history and art history.

1 P. BREZZI, L'Istituto Nazionale di Studi Romani, in: Speculum Mundi. Roma centro internazionale di ricerche umanistiche, 1992, 708–728   2 F. SCRIBA, Augustus im Schwarzhemd? Die *Mostra Augustea della Romanità* in Rom 1937/38, 1995   3 R. VISSER, Storia di un progetto mai realizzato: il Centro Internazionale di Studi Romani, in: Mededelingen van het Nederlands Instituut te Rome, Historical Studies 53, 1994, 44–80.   ROMKE VISSER

Italy

I. FROM LATE ANTIQUITY TO THE 12TH CENTURY

A. GOTHIC RULE

The fall of the Western Roman Empire in Italy (I.) did not result in any perceptible 'decline' in cultural level as compared to the previous decades. However, there was a decisive change in the public perception of the system of government and the role and function of the state. After a break in continuity during the reign of Odoacer (476–493), the Gothic kingdom of Theoderic followed late-antique tradition, which continued to exist through the preservation and perhaps even the strengthening of schools and the education system. The initial aim was the political and cultural integration of

the Roman population and the 'Barbarian' aristocracy; however, the implementation of this policy proved to be utopian. Outstanding scholars of the time, particularly Boethius (480–524) and Cassiodorus (ca. 490–580), strove on the one hand to preserve the ancient cultural legacy, but on the other were convinced that the new political context also demanded a new confrontation with the past. Boethius, who can be considered the last representative of the ancient philosophical tradition in the West, was at the origin of the ambitious but only partially realized project of translating the works of Plato and Aristotle into Latin. In any case, it is likely that the intellectuals in I. who could still understand Greek were few and far between. The translations took place not so much for the sake of the Roman nobility as for that of the up-and-coming church elites; apparently, only the existence of texts in Latin could strengthen their legitimacy. Cassiodorus' activity in the last decades of his life, which he carried out in the monastery he founded at Vivarium in Calabria, was a response to this same need for preserving the legacy of the Roman past and making it accessible in the transformed circumstances of his time. At Vivarium, Cassiodorus assembled a valuable → LIBRARY attached to a *scriptorium* and recommended a canon of reading, which he justified in detail in his *Institutiones*. Alongside the Bible and the works of the Church Fathers, the most important texts read in late antique schools, from manuals to poetic anthologies, found their way into this Canon, divided according to the various disciplines. The *Institutiones* represent one of the most significant testimonies to the cultural interests and demands of 6th-cent. I., particularly with regard to the choices made in the selection of ancient texts. Alongside Boethius and Cassiodorus, the most important personalities, other authors who had acquired their → EDUCATION (*Bildung*) in the schools of this period also demonstrated a high standard of education and a sound knowledge of the ancient Classics. This is particularly evident in the poetic works of such authors as Arator, Maximianus and Venantius Fortunatus, but also in the rhetorical training of Pope Gregory the Great, as it can be deduced from his literary production.

B. LOMBARD RULE

The crisis of ancient education in I. is attributable to a number of different events: the devastating war between the Goths and Byzantines (535–553); the subsequent general impoverishment, which also marked the period of the Imperial reconquest; and finally the Lombard migration (568), resulting in the loss of I.'s geopolitical unity. Unlike the Goths, the new Lombard rulers did not seek integration with the remnants of the traditional Latin-speaking aristocratic elite. Moreover, they made no effort to appropriate for themselves the linguistic and literary tradition of these classes. The result of this development was a period of cultural decline, which continued until the first half of the 8th cent. With the exception of Rome, where a literary production oriented towards rhetorical models of Late Antiquity continued to exist for the needs of the Papal bureaucracy, interest in Antiquity seems to have been reduced to a minimum in the I. of these centuries. Information on teaching activity, which must have continued to exist in some form or another, is extremely sparse. Outside of Rome, there is sporadic but reliable evidence for the teaching of grammar and possibly also of law at Pavia. Other schools may have existed in Verona, Ravenna, Naples, and perhaps even in Milan, the site of one of I.'s most renowned schools in the 6th cent. The depopulation of the cities may ultimately have played a part in the preservation of architectural monuments which, though neglected, were not systematically destroyed. There were even examples of pagan buildings being reused or rededicated, as in the case of the Pantheon, which was consecrated as the Church of Sancta Maria ad Martyres at the instigation of Pope Boniface VIII in 609. Libraries, in contrast, suffered massive destruction. The only library whose holdings are attested from Late Antiquity down to the Carolingian period was the Roman library of the Lateran, which, at any rate, suffered considerable losses because, among other reasons, many of its volumes were taken over the Alps, particularly to England, either as spiritual support in the course of the missionary campaigns, or as presents for abbots, bishops or sovereigns. Little or nothing remains of the other libraries. The contents of the most famous one, at Vivarium, were probably dispersed throughout the world shortly after Cassiodorus' death. It is assumed that some volumes were taken to Bobbio or the Lateran. Remnants of libraries from Late Antiquity later appeared in Verona and in Campania, while other material, mostly of Padanian origin, was taken to Bobbio, the monastery founded in 612 by the Irishman Colombanus in the Emilian Appennines, where the books were preserved, but seldom read. Despite the undoubted reduction in the number and efficacy of schools, however, it cannot be said a priori that ancient tradition disappeared completely during the Lombard period. Relations with Rome and Ravenna, often conflictual but never severed, kept a channel open for cultural exchange. Down to the beginning of the 7th cent., the credit for this was due above all to skilled Byzantine artisans, who ensured the presence of a characteristic orientation toward Antiquity in Lombard art (for instance, in the frescoes of Castelseprio, the palace of Liutprand at Corteolona, the chapel at Cividale). Inscriptions, obviously modelled on exemplars from Late Antiquity, make up the little that is known of the literary production of the period. Continuity with the Roman tradition is clearly evident in the legal system, especially in its protocolar and formal aspects; it can be observed in Rothar's Edict (643) as well as in the structure of documents issued by the Lombard chancellery.

C. Carolingian and Ottonian Italy

With the conquest of the Lombard kingdom by Charlemagne (774), central and northern I. became part of the Carolingian state. The cultural transformation which occurred north of the Alps between the late 8th and the first half of the 9th cent. met with little echo in I. Only in the school of Pavia are grammatical studies of Classical origin supposed to have continued. In the mid–8th cent., the education provided by this school was of unquestionably high quality, as is attested by the literary production of such scholars as Petrus of Pisa, Paulus Diaconus and Paulinus of Aquileia. They were summoned to the court of Charlemagne and made a significant contribution to the elaboration of a project of Carolingian cultural reform, which, however, was implemented not in I. but in France and Germany. We have only limited information about the way public schools operated in I. (cf. the capitulary of the city of Olona, recorded by Lothar in 825). In addition to public schools, the → MONASTERY SCHOOLS and local churches exercised a tremendous influence on education. They gradually became increasingly important in the centres in which urban life developed once again. An increase in the number of schools can be taken as certain, primarily in those towns that were more immediately connected with the Frankish kingdom and/or the cultural and political centres south of the Alps (Pavia and Verona). This was the most important prerequisite for the resumption of the activity of scribes. The works copied in northern I. in the 9th cent. were of predominantly Christian religious content.

Rome and southern I. did not become part of the Carolingian state. In these areas, European cultural development had even less impact than in northern I. Nevertheless, thanks to the political continuity these regions enjoyed in the preceding centuries, and to the better state of preservation of their late-antique libraries, a cultural tradition, never completely interrupted, continued to exist. In the Benevento-Cassino region, where numerous texts of ancient authors were still available, Paulus Diaconus found the material for compiling his *Historia Romana*, as did Festus for his *Epitome*. In Montecassino, Paulus' pupil Hilderich wrote a grammar rich with Classical examples. Anastasius Bibliothecarius, a legal scholar and translator from the Greek, was active in Rome around 870. On the orders of Charles the Bald, he studied the works of Pseudo-Dionysius and translated the commentaries by Maximus Confessor and Johannes Scythopolitanus. The tradition of the Church Fathers is omnipresent in his writings.

At Naples towards the end of the cent., we find Eugenius Vulgarius, author of works on the Formosan controversy. He is probably the only Italian writer whose works contain explicit references to Classical models, not only to Virgil and Horace, but also to Seneca's tragedies, seldom cited at the time. His works, together with the contemporary Neapolitan hagiographic literature, show the existence of a functioning school system in which rhetorical education played a major part. The importance of the *scriptoria* and libraries of the Greek monasteries should not be underestimated, either: they were crucially important for the preservation of various works by the Church Fathers.

Among the reasons for the belatedness of the development of Italian culture in the 9th cent. were the lack of political stability and the geographical remoteness from contemporary centres of power. The overall situation deteriorated still further with the end of the Carolingian dynasty, which plunged I. into an anarchy from which even the papacy was unable to save itself. During the 10th cent., the centres of book culture and of the preservation of book holdings remained primarily isolated. Just as isolated were contemporary intellectuals, the most important of whom made use of the education they had partly acquired north of the Alps. This was the case with Ratherius (887–974), Bishop of Verona, who hailed from Liège, where he had received his training, or with Liutprand (ca. 920–972), a deacon at Pavia and then Bishop of Cremona, who had spent at least ten years of his life as an exile in Germany.

These personages brought the cultural trends that had developed in the rest of Europe to northern I. In the wake of this development, Italian intellectuals of the 10th cent. paid greater attention than previous generations of scholars to Classical authors, so that works by ancient writers, including Terence, Quintilian, and Livy, began to be copied in northern I. as well. Verona in particular, the city that was most closely linked to the German cultural centres, featured a Classically-oriented literary production, culminating in the *Gesta Berengarii*, an epic encomium to the Italian king Berengarius I which attests to a broad knowledge of the ancient poets (above all Virgil, Statius and Lucan). Great interest in the ancient classics can also be observed in the western Po valley, perhaps because of the influence of the school of Pavia. In addition to Liutprand, who knew Virgil and Horace, among others, and used Juvenal, Persius and above all Terence with particular predilection, this region also produced such authors as Gunzone, who went to Germany along with parts of his library, containing Martianus Capella and some translations of Plato and Aristotle from Late Antiquity. Stephen of Novara was so renowned for his erudition that the Saxon emperors called him to their court as a teacher. In general, not until the end of the 10th cent. did references to ancient Classics increase, both in literary production and in the fine arts. This development was promoted by the fact that I. had regained a central role in the context of Ottonian politics, as well as by the new imperial ideology which enhanced the status of Rome.

Southern I. was a special case, where the tradition of Classical studies, promoted by the preservation and copying of ancient manuscripts, had obviously continued without interruption. Around the mid–10th cent., Giovanni, Duke of Naples, owned a library which included authors like Ps.-Dionysius and Livy. It was in this cultural environment that the Pseudo-Callisthenes' *Historia Alexandri*, which was to become one of the most successful texts in the entire Middle Ages, was translated into Latin. The medical school at Salerno is already attested at the end of the century. It went back to Classical tradition, perhaps by way of Arabic transmission, and was to experience a great upsurge in the following century.

D. 11TH CENTURY

The particular attention paid by the Saxon emperors to I. culminated in the plan to restore the Roman Empire. It was initiated by Otto III, who took up residence in Rome and made ample use of ancient literature and symbolism for ideological and propagandistic purposes. Two great scholars were closely associated with Otto III: Gerbert of Aurillac and Johannes Philagathus. After having been abbot of Bobbio and then archbishop of Reims and Ravenna, Gerbert, a great enthusiast for ancient authors, became pope under the name of Silvester II. Philagathus came from Calabria, where he had benefited from a Greek education. He became abbot of Nonantola and bishop of Piacenza, and presented the emperor with an important collection of manuscripts of Classical authors.

The intellectual attitude and works of Gerbert and Philagathus show that although I. stood rather on the margins of the major developments of European culture in the 9th and 10th cents., it had maintained its function as the intermediary between Antiquity and the Middle Ages and still remained the most important site for the preservation of manuscripts of ancient authors. Although the anachronistic Ottonian restoration project proved to be short-lived, it left behind clear traces, particularly in Rome, where it favoured the return to Classical models in the fine arts, a trend which was not abandoned in subsequent periods (for instance, in the frescoes of San Clemente, the paintings in Santa Maria in Cosmedin, and the architecture of Santa Maria in Trastevere).

The dynastic crisis that followed the death of Otto III (1002) and the shift of the centre of imperial power back to the imperial territories north of the Alps had considerable consequences in I.. It accelerated the independent development of the Padanian cities, where the bishops, who in the preceding decades had enjoyed strong support by the Ottonians, suppressed the influence of the aristocracy. The boom experienced by the towns during this period, together with the developing dispute between the papacy and the empire (as in the Investiture Contest), which formed the main political problem dominating the second half of the 11th cent., formed the preconditions for the renewal of jurisprudence, which was henceforth to become a longstanding characteristic of Italian schools. At first, canon law studies were taken up with increased intensity. They had in any case never been completely abandoned since late Antiquity, but were only little practiced in I. between the 9th and 11th cent., as a consequence, among other reasons, of the credibility crisis of the papacy. The reforms initiated by Pope Gregory VII (1073–1085), which were certainly not bereft of political intentions, resulted in a new organization of the subject, in which

Bishop Anselm of Lucca played an important role. Towards the end of the century, studies in civil law appeared alongside those in canon law and were granted the same status. The most important school was the one in Bologna, the foundation of which was supposed to be associated with Irnerius, who was active between the end of the 11th and the early decades of the 12th cent. In fact, however, this foundation is to be attributed to a number of scholars, who continued the interest in Roman law which had already been manifested elsewhere.

An important precondition for the development of the Italian judiciary was the improvement in the educational system within the context of the → ARTES LIBERALES. Here, increasing importance accrued to → RHETORIC and dialectic, which were based on ancient material. Among the most important works stemming from these schools are the *Rhetorimachia* by Anselm of Besate, a moralizing praise of rhetoric against a cousin named Rotilandus, in which there are many borrowings from Cicero and the *Rhetorica ad Herennium,* and Papia's *Elementarium*, the prototype and model for numerous later dictionaries, which sought to assemble the vocabulary of Classical and Christian writers, providing contemporary scholars with a standard reference work.

In southern I., the most important event that contributed to the preservation of the ancient Classics was the resumption of cultural activity at Montecassino, an abbey that had been destroyed by the Saracens in 883 and rebuilt in 950. In the course of the century, Montecassino became a cultural centre of outstanding significance, primarily under Abbot Desiderius (1058–1086; later Pope Victor III) who considerably enriched its library. He also had many Classical authors copied from locally available texts, some of which still dated back to Late Antiquity. The abbey's library contained both works by well-known authors who were part of the reading canon, such as Cicero, Ovid, Terence, Virgil, Horace and Seneca, and such less-common works as those of Apuleius, Varro and Tacitus.

Associated with Montecassino were also literary figures such as Guaiferio, Giovanni of Gaeta and, particularly, Alfano of Salerno, the writer who was more receptive than other authors of this century to ancient influences. His polished poetic works manifest a thorough knowledge of Juvenal, Sedulius, Ovid and, above all, Horace, many of whose metrical forms he adopted and practiced masterfully. In the course of the century, and particularly since the Renaissance initiated by Desiderius, Montecassino became the hub for the reading, study and reception of ancient writers. Like many other European monasteries of the time, its role went beyond that of pure preservation of the Classical legacy. The medical school at Salerno also stood under the influence of this development: it was closely associated with Montecassino and reached its greatest importance in the course of this century. Outstanding personages included Guarimpoto (or Garioponto), author of a *Pas-*

sionarius (medical handbook) that went back to Hellenistic and Roman medicine. The development of the medical school of Salerno was probably also connected with the first translations of medical and philosophical texts from the Arabic and the Greek, which, according to common view, were connected with the name of Constantinus Africanus.

E. 12TH CENTURY

Translation activity from Greek and Arabic became gradually more intensive in 12th-cent. I. In Arabo-Norman southern I., Ptolemy and Aristotle were translated by such scholars as Eugene of Palermo and Henricus Aristippus, while translators such as Moses of Bergamo, James of Venice and Burgundio of Pisa worked in Constantinople, translating not only Aristotle but also medical and theological treatises. Other Italians, such as Gerard of Cremona and Plato of Tivoli, were active as translators from the Arabic in Spain and in the kingdoms founded by the Crusaders. These translations, which were intended to promote the study of ancient thinkers and scientists, foremost amongst them Aristotle, were linked to the development of the → SCHOOLS and the emergence of the first → UNIVERSITIES. The first Italian university was that of Bologna, attested from 1158, which maintained a strongly juridical orientation until the end of the century. In these institutions, the study of dialectics, based on Aristotle, played an important role. The emergence of the universities considerably encouraged the mobility of intellectuals, and Italian culture soon found itself connected with the rest of Europe in scholarly exchange. It was above all the translation activity in the south that granted I. an outstanding role as an intermediary between Antiquity and the Middle Ages.

In addition to the rediscovery of the Greek philosophical and scientific tradition, which shows itself in the translations, a further important contribution of I. to the preservation of the Classical tradition in the 12th cent. was connected to the development of the law school at Bologna. The way in which Roman law was applied in favour of imperial claims during the disputes between Frederick Barbarossa and the Italian communes is a good example of how ancient material was studied and interpreted by means of dialectics, and thereby also used for practical purposes. Bologna became the European focal point for the study of canon and Roman law. A large number of students from beyond the Alps attended the university, and famous teachers from Bologna were appointed to positions throughout Europe, where they founded their own new schools. The parallel studies of Roman and canon law led to the application of new methods of advanced study which were primarily analogical, as is shown by the use of dialectics in the most important and systematic canonical collection, compiled by the monk Graziano of Bologna.

The link between I. and Europe also became closer for political reasons, above all because of the renewed interest in I. shown by the Hohenstaufen emperors. The resumption and reutilisation of ancient models can be observed in varying degrees of intensity both in the field of literary creation – in northern I., in the *Gesta Friderici imperatoris* (*Deeds of Frederick Barbarossa*) or in the poem *De destructione Mediolani* ("On the Destruction of Milan"), and in central and south I., in the work of Gottfried of Viterbo, Arrigo of Settimello and Peter of Eboli – as well as in the fine arts and in architecture, where the Romanesque style was now clearly prevailing. In art and architecture, the return to late-antique models in I. was characterized by a pronounced Classical impact, which can be traced to the strong influence of Byzantine art. Similarly, the dissemination of ancient literature can no longer be called sporadic. Many items of evidence, among the most important of which is the catalogue of the abbey library at Pomposa, compiled toward the end of the century, indicate that ancient legacy had now become an essential component of contemporary culture, monastic and clerical as well as lay.

→ Boethius; → Cassiodorus

→ Arabic-Islamic cultural sphere; → Carolingian Renaissance

1 G. Bertelli, Traccia allo studio delle fondazioni medievali dell'arte italiana, in: Storia dell'arte italiana V: Dal Medioevo al Quattrocento, 1983, 3–163   2 F. Bertini, Letteratura latina medievale in Italia, 1988   3 G. Billanovich, M. Ferrari, La trasmissione di testi nell'Italia nord-occidentale, in: La cultura antica nell'Occidente latino dal VII all'XI secolo, 1975, 303–352   4 G. Cavallo, La trasmissione dei testi nell'area beneventano-cassinese, in: La cultura antica nell'Occidente latino dal VII all'XI secolo, 1975, 357–424   5 La cultura in Italia fra tardo antico e alto medioevo, 1981 (no editor)   6 H. Bloch, Monte Cassino's Teachers and Library in the High Middle Ages, in: La scuola nell'Occidente latino nell'Alto Medioevo, 1972, 563–605   7 N. Christie (ed.), From Constantine to Charlemagne: An Archaeology of Italy, AD 300–800, 2006   8 J. Irigoin, L'Italie méridionale et la tradition des textes antiques, in: Jahrbuch der Österreichischen Byzantinistik 18, 1969, 37–55   9 W. V. Harris, The Transformations of Vrbs Roma in Late Antiquity, 1999   10 C. W. Hedrick, History and Silence: Purge and Rehabilitation of Memory in Late Antiquity, 2000   11 C. La Rocca (ed.), Italy in the Early Middle Ages, 2002   12 B. Lançon, Rome in Late Antiquity: Everyday Life and Urban Change, AD 312–609, 2000   13 C. Leonardi, L'eredità medievale, in: Storia della letteratura italiana I, 1995, 45–136   14 A. M. Romanini, Il concetto di classico e l'Alto Medioevo, in: Magistra Barbaritas. I barbari in Italia, 1984, 665–678   15 C. Villa, Die Horazüberlieferung und die Bibliothek Karls des Großen. Zum Werkverzeichnis der Handschrift Berlin Diez B. 66, in: Deutsches Archiv für Erforschung des Mittelalters 51, 1995, 29–52.   PAOLO CHIESA

II. 13th and 14th Century
A. Duecento (13th Century)   B. Trecento (14th Century)

A. Duecento (13th Century)

Virgil's appearance in the first canto of the *Inferno* to lead the wanderer Dante through the dark forest to the summit of the Mountain of Purgatory marks a pivotal moment in the reception of Antiquity in medieval I. Indeed, the spring of 1300, date of the journey into the Beyond as narrated in the *Commedia*, seems to mark the break between two centuries and the beginning of a new era. The 13th cent., a period of apparent decline of Classical culture, during which Virgil was condemned to silence, had come to an end, and the 14th cent., in which the value of the Classics was to flourish again, thanks precisely to the poetry of Dante, had begun. By subjecting himself to Virgil's *auctoritas*, Dante inaugurated a period of cultural renewal. He revealed himself as the new Virgil of the modern world and the author of the new Christian epic. Strictly speaking, however, a more specific statement is made in the first canto of Dante's masterpiece, which functions as a prologue. Already in his youth, when he composed the *Vita Nuova* ('The new life') and the allegorical *Canzone*, which were later incorporated into the philosophical encyclopedia of the *Convivio* ('The banquet'), Dante had studied Virgil's 'volume', that is, the *Aeneid*. He had derived his 'bello stile', the beautiful style that had brought him 'onore' ('honour') and now justifies his privilege of a redemptive journey to the Beyond, from Virgil alone. Virgil is his 'maestro', his teacher, and his 'autore', or literary model. Yet this obviously corresponds to a distortion of Dante's literary career, since the *Vita Nuova* stood clearly under the influence of Ovid, while the *Convivio* expressly alluded to Cicero's *De amicitia* ('On Friendship') and Boethius' *Consolatio Philosophiae* (*The Consolation of Philosophy*). The reason for this manipulation is to be sought in the new orientation Dante wished to give to his poetry, or in the alternation of literary genres. By writing down his 'poema sacro,' or epic poem, he moved from didactic and autobiographical poetry to the heroic epic, and hence from the Ovidian model, which he had followed in the *Vita Nova*, to the Virgilian one that takes over in the *Commedia*. The *aetas Ovidiana* had come to an end, while on the horizon the *aetas Virgiliana* was clearly dawning.

In this context, mention should be made of the controversy that took place at the beginning of the 20th cent., particularly in America, between defenders of the theory of a decline of the ancient Classics in the course of the 13th cent. (especially Ch. H. Haskins [9]), and the contrary view, which defended a continuity between the revival of the ancient Classics in the 12th cent. and Humanism (E. K. Rand [17], H. Wieruszowski [20]). In I., G. Toffanin [18], in particular, championed discontinuity by characterizing the *Duecento* (13th cent.) as the 'secolo senza Roma', the 'century without Rome'. The continuity theory was defended by most scholars, from F. Novati [13] to G. Billanovich [2]. The second theory is dominant at the present time, although not without modifications and corrections. Whereas all of them accept the importance of ancient Classical authors for the development of an Italian literary tradition, at the same time investigations are being conducted on how Classical authors were actually read in the 13th cent., and on the processes of adaptation and alteration to which they were subjected. The elements that emerge from these investigations testify, if not to a break, then certainly to a differentiation between ancient Classical and more modern literature. Philological studies, concerned to demonstrate the presence of the ancient Classics, are complimented by hermeneutic analyses to determine the function of this presence and the new cultural value that results from it.

The Italian Duecento opened with a statement extolling the cultural divide by Boncompagno da Signa, Professor of Rhetoric at the University of Bologna during the early decades of the century. In his treatise *Palma*, he boasted never to have read 'Tullius', that is, that he did not base his teaching on Cicero's rhetorical writings, although he mentions shortly afterwards that he has not 'debased' Tullius, nor has he prevented his students from imitating Cicero. His polemic was directed at the absolute authority enjoyed in the rhetoric schools by Cicero's *De inventione* (*On the Discovery of Material*) and the *Rhetorica ad Herennium,* considered to be genuine in the Middle Ages. His concern was not the elimination of ancient rhetoric but its renewal. Boncompagno intended to replace the *rhetorica vetus*, or old rhetoric, with his *Rhetorica Nova* – hence the title of one of his treatises, also known as the *Boncompagnus* – and the *Novissima*, the final version of his treatise on rhetoric. Boncompagno also displays the same attitude in one of his other works that found favour in the Middle Ages, the *Rota Veneris* ('Wheel of Venus'), in which he plays through a series of erotic themes and situations that clearly derive from Ovid's love poems.

In the Duecento, teaching in schools and universities was based on ancient and modern rhetoric, on grammar (reading and commenting on ancient and medieval *auctores*, from Ovid's *Remedia amoris* to Arrigo da Settimello's *Elegia*), as well as on dialectics, which practically consisted of Boethius' translation of Aristotle's *Logic*. The study of these three → ARTES LIBERALES, which belonged to the *trivium*, opened the door to higher and more lucrative disciplines, such as jurisprudence, medicine and theology. These, together with the disciplines that made up the *trivium*, constituted the four faculties of the medieval university system. Whereas theology was founded on the Bible and patristic exegesis, jurisprudence and medicine were based on ancient culture, on Justinian's *Corpus iuris* and the scientific treatises of Aristotle and Galen, which were provided with medieval glosses and commentaries.

Significantly, the first Italian school of poets was formed at the court of Frederick II, who not only reorganized his state from a legal and administrative viewpoint on the model of ancient Rome (first the kingdom of Sicily and then, from 1220, the empire itself), but also founded a university in Naples that was to offer a worldly, non-religious education to train the officials who were to push forward his program of political and cultural renewal [11]. Indeed, the poets of the Sicilian School themselves also were officials and advisers to Frederick II; that is, they were notaries (like Giacomo da Lentini, who was *protonotarius*, or senior notary of the empire) and judges (like Guido delle Colonne, who was *iudex* or judge of Messina) who translated the cultural fund of knowledge they required in the exercise of their professions into their artistic works. Thus, they wrote their *canzone* and sonnets with the same stylistic technique they used in writing their documents and letters dealing with administrative matters in Latin. It was their very rhetorical competence and their argumentative skills that allowed them to further develop the traditional erotic themes that had already been treated by Provençal troubadours and French authors of romances, in a way that was more artistically conscious and conceptually more convincing.

The most outstanding figure at the court of Frederick II was undoubtedly Petrus de Vinea, who was *logoteta* ('treasurer') of the empire and a highly sophisticated writer both in Latin, in his numerous *Epistole* ('Letters'), one of the literary masterpieces of the century, and in the vernacular, in his concise but valuable collection of poems. Comparative analysis of both his productive currents shows that except for a certain thematic proximity, the Latin epistles are characterized by a higher pleasure in experimentation and a greater cultural openness. In the most famous of them, the so-called *epistola amatoria* ('Love Letter'), Petrus demonstrates his thorough knowledge not only of the Medieval literary tradition (particularly of Pamphilus) and of the Provençal tradition (especially with regard to the genre of the *salut* – an amorous salutation or love letter in verse), but also of the Classical ancient literary tradition. Every prose segment of this letter, which the author sends to the woman he loves in his imagination, ends with the citation of a verse, most of which derive from Ovid's love poems, but also partly from his *Metamorphoses* and *Tristia* [10].

After the death of Frederick II (1250) and the decline of the Hohenstaufen family line, the cultural centre shifted from southern to central I. (Tuscany) and the north (Venice). Whereas Tuscany maintained the poetic tradition in the vernacular, together with rhetorical studies, Venice concentrated on the philological study of the Classics and on literary production in Latin, whereby the first step towards Italian Humanism was fulfilled. In Tuscany, the key figure in this mediation activity, the *translatio studii*, was undoubtedly Dante's teacher Brunetto Latini. To him we owe the rediscovery of Classical rhetoric (he translated Cicero's *De inventione* into the vernacular and added a commentary), a discipline which he already understood in a humanistic and no longer in the utilitarian sense, viz. as an instrument of civic education and good political guidance, rather than as a means to win *piatora* ('trials'). Brunetto also wrote an allegorical poem entitled *Tesoretto* ('The Little Treasure'), which was important not only because it anticipated Dante's *Commedia*, but above all because it founded a new relationship with the *dictator* of the previous poetic tradition, Ovid. Thus, in the realm of love the protagonist encounters 'Ovidio maggiore', that is, the Ovid of the *Metamorphoses*, which 12th-cent. commentators such as Arnulf d'Orléans had interpreted in a moralistic sense. Thanks to Ovid's intervention, the protagonist escapes the love affair and is able to embark on the path of *penitenza* ('penitence'), the transformation of worldly love into virtuous love. Here we see a clear change in the reception of Ovid: he is no longer the master of eros but of ethos, and thus he is no longer the playful, frivolous poet of the *Ars amandi*, but the earnest author of the *Metamorphoses*, which are understood as the poetry of man's spiritual transformations (*mutationes*). This had a significant effect on subsequent poetic production. One of the most obvious consequences was bipartite books of songs (*canzonieri*) in the style of Guittone d'Arezzo, divided up into courtly and moralising poems, or later poems of Petrarch.

The writers of the *Stilnuovo* (from Guido Guinizelli to Dante and Cino da Pistoia) sought to unite this dichotomy. Their main concern was to integrate eros itself, which brings man from earth to heaven and from woman to God, into the educational process. This is the origin of the literary masterpiece of the Italian Duecento: the *Vita Nuova* by the young Dante. It is no accident that this work cites Ovid and *il libro di Remedio d'Amore* ('The Book of Remedies for Love') as its models, not only from an ideological but also from a formal perspective. Indeed, Dante's prosimetrum was inspired not by Boethius' *Consolatio*, as the most eminent interpreters believe, but by the *Liber Ovidii* in the form in which it was then circulating, i.e. by a book that reproduced the literary text by the ancient author in the middle of each page, but arranged around it the prose interpretation by the Christian commentator. In chapter 25 of his *libello* ('booklet'), Dante names, alongside Ovid, the other *auctores* of the Classical canon: the Virgil of the *Aeneid*, Lucan of the *Bellum civile*, and Horace of the *Ars poetica* (who in turn quotes Homer, insofar as he translates the first verse of the *Odyssey* into Latin). We find the same canon, with only slight variations (here, for instance, Horace appears as a satirical poet) in the fourth canto of the *Inferno*, at the point when the wanderer Dante meets the poets who form the *bella scuola* ('beautiful school') of poets under Homer's leadership in the noble palace of *Limbus*, on the edge of the deep abyss. Dante even joins the five ancient poets to become *sesto fra cotanto senno*, or the sixth among so much intellect. However, the *Commedia* allows for an important extension of the canon of the five *auctores,*in the person of Statius, whom Dante

meets near the summit of the Mountain of Purgatory (*Purgatorio* 21 f.). The author of the *Thebaid* thus becomes the only ancient poet who was able to save himself and had found the light of Christian truth even in pagan poetry, more precisely in Virgil's *Fourth Eclogue*. Statius therefore assumes the role of an additional guide on this journey to the Beyond. He accompanies the wanderer Dante where Virgil cannot go, namely to the earthly paradise, the place of man's original beatitude, from which all those who do not know the gospel are categorically excluded (as shown by the exemplary case of Odysseus in *Inferno* 26).

Statius' conversion represents a decisive event in the economy of the *poema sacro*, whereby Dante creates an intimate connection between ancient and medieval culture. Statius acts as a link in the chain that binds the ancient pagan *auctor* (Virgil) to the new Christian *auctor* (Dante himself). Insofar as Dante redeemed Statius, however, he clearly infringed against the medieval reception of the ancient world, for legends had circulated in the preceding centuries about the Christianity of Virgil [7] or Ovid, according to the narration in *De vetula* ('On the Old Woman', an apocryphal autobiography of Ovid, which the Middle Ages and Dante considered authentic), but not the narrator of the Theban war. The strategic value of this cashing in on Statius must be sought at the macrostructural level. In the *Commedia*, Dante imitated both Virgil's *Aeneid* – the wanderer is a new Aeneas on the journey to the celestial Rome – and Ovid's *Metamorphoses*, since the Beyond is to be seen as the realm of the spiritual transformation of man. At the same time, however, Dante wished to compete with these absolute paradigms of the poetic canon and even to surpass them (cf. *Inferno* 25, 97–102). To convey this notion of his actual overcoming of ancient poetry, Dante invented the figure of the converted Statius, entrusted with the task of showing the way to Christian redemption not just to Virgil, but also to Ovid and the other *auctores* – a path of which they may have have had a premonition, but which they never actually took [15].

In addition to the Tuscan towns, the culture of the Hohenstaufian period also left traces behind in the plane of the Po, and particularly in Padua, where the jurists trained by Petrus de Vinea were active. Here, toward the end of the 12th cent. and the first decades of the 13th cent., a pre-humanist movement formed, led by the notary Lovato Lovati, who had undertaken a serious study of the ancient authors in order to bring about a revival of the literary genres of Antiquity [4]. Lovato's discovery of the tragedies of Seneca (in the Cod. *Etruscus* of the abbey of Pomposa) paved the way for his student Albertino Mussato to write the *Ecerinis*, the first modern tragedy in hexameters. In imitation of Seneca, Albertino was thus able to deal with the bloody reality of such historical events of recent times as the unbridled attack on the cities of Veneto by the tyrant Ezzelino da Romano, and the current political situation, such as Cangrande della Scala's plans to expand to

Padua; the latter topic was treated in the poem *De obsidione ... Paduane civitatis* ('On the Siege ... of the City of Padua'). Likewise, the philological attention paid to the tradition of the Latin elegy (from Catullus to Propertius and Statius) motivated Lovati and Albertino to experiment with this genre's typical tones and themes in their own *Epistole metrice* ('Verse Epistles'). Lovato later even attempted to translate the moving story of the love and death of Tristan and Isolde into Latin verse; a short six-hexameter fragment of this attempt has survived in a *Zibaldone* ('Mixed Contributions') by Boccaccio.

Directly linked to Padua's cultural ambience was the correspondence in Latin hexameters between Dante, then in exile in Ravenna, and the Bolognese grammarian Giovanni del Virgilio, who had assumed this name because of his admiration for the Classical author. Giovanni began this correspondence by reproaching Dante for having written the *Commedia* in the Italian vernacular, a language unsuitable for such sublime philosophical material of high cultural significance. In addition, he encourged Dante to write an epic Latin poem in the style of Mussato on a contemporary historical theme. This would bring him fame among scholars, and bring him nomination as *poeta laureatus* of the city of Bologna. Dante replied with two eclogues in perfect Virgilian style, in which he posed as the shepherd Titiro, who had been banished from his homeland but was satisfied with the protection assured to him by the new Augustus, Guido Novello, Lord of Ravenna. Insofar as he described his stay at Ravenna in idyllic turns of phrase and refused to move to Bologna in order to be crowned with the promised laurel wreath, he not only substantiated the validity of his linguistic and stylistic choice, but also provided brilliant proof of poetic expressive power in Latin as well, not, indeed, in the elevated style of the epic, as Giovanni had wished, but in the more lowly style of the bucolic. Dante thus initiated a new literary tradition – none other than the bucolic – that was immediately taken up by Petrarch (a student of Giovanni del Virgilio in Bologna) and by Boccaccio (who reproduced the entire correspondence between Giovanni and Dante in one of his *Zibaldoni*), then perfected and disseminated by Italian Humanism throughout the whole of Renaissance and Modern Europe [8].

B. TRECENTO (14TH CENTURY)

The efforts by Humanistic circles of northern I. toward a revival of the Classical epic were partly satisfied by Francesco Petrarca (or Petrarch), who worked between 1338 and 1341 on a hexametric poem entitled *Africa*, albeit without finishing it. His subject was not contemporary, but ancient history (it celebrated Scipio Africanus, the hero of the Second Punic War), and the 'imitatio' was modelled not only on Virgil's *Aeneid*, but also extended to Cicero's *Somnium Scipionis*, which was all that was known at the time of the *De republica*, Ovid's elegies and, above all, the historical work of Titus Livius, of whom Petrarch prepared a complete

edition, the most philologically reliable of his time [1]. For this work, Petrarch received the poet's crown, which Dante had hoped for but had never achieved: he was crowned with the laurel wreath on the Capitol by Robert d'Anjou, King of Naples, in 1341. Petrarch wrote most of his works in Latin, the language of his beloved Classical *auctores* and his admired Christian *patres* ('Church Fathers'). Latin was also the official language of the papal court at Avignon, where Petrarch was active during the most important years of his intellectual formation. His literary production developed in parallel with his philological interests [3]. Thus, the study he devoted to the text of Livy led to his *De viris illustribus*, a series of biographies of the outstanding figures of Roman history, with additional portraits of mythological and Biblical figures, while his interest in Valerius Maximus inspired the *Rerum memorandarum*, a collection of ancient and modern *exempla* illustrating the cardinal virtues. If, on the other hand, the discovery of Cicero's correspondence inspired Petrarch to renew the ancient 'ars dictaminis' (rules for composing prose works) of the medieval rhetoricians and create a new, more personal genre of letter-writing, as is shown by his variegated collections of letters, ranging over many years, from the *Familiares* to the *Seniles*, it was the reading of Seneca, together with the doctrine of Augustine, that led to his most ambitious philosophical creations, such as the *De remediis utriusque fortunae*, or 'Remedy against Both Kinds of Fate', and his other ascetic and moral treatises. Petrarch wrote both works in the vernacular – the verse collection entitled *Rerum vulgarium fragmenta* ('Fragments of Popular Things') and the allegorical poem *Triumphi* are characterized by a more pervasive presence of the ancient world. The song book, in particular, resounds throughout with echoes from Classical mythology and from his *auctor* Ovid, to an extent never seen before in the lyric tradition, but only in Dante's epic. In fact, the love story of Petrarch's lyrical alter ego for Laura is told and analysed in a series of myths of transformations, ranging from the myth of Apollo and Daphne, in which poetry represents a kind of sublimated eros, to the myth of Actaeon and Diana, in which eros meets with a tragic end [14]. Myth, together with Ovid's *Metamorphoses*, is used to describe the dark side of love, or the human pole of an *iter amoris* ('path of love') that strives to rise up to the divine pole without ever being able to reach it definitively. The gap between eros and *caritas* (Christian love neighbour), Classical mythology and Christian truth, which the poets of the *Stilnuovo* (the 'New Style') and Dante had sought to bridge, once again became evident.

The literary career of Giovanni Boccaccio, the last of the three 'laureates', was marked by the tension, dominating the 14th cent., between the Classicism pursued by Dante and that of Petrarch. Although the literary output of his younger years, written primarily in the vernacular, was influenced by Dante, his mature works, written predominantly in Latin, followed Petrarch. In fact, his meeting with Petrarch in Florence in 1350 marks the transition in Boccaccio's life from a period oriented toward multifarious literary activity to a new period dominated by philological interests and scholarly, encyclopedic research. This contrast is not, of course, always clear-cut. If we analyse Boccaccio's creativity in detail, neither are encyclopedic tendencies absent from his early works, nor does his narrative vein become exhausted later. Nevertheless, the direction this writer imposed upon his own artistic 'curriculum' is clearly recognisable as the one just described. It was thus not only Petrarch who heralded the great age of Florentine and Italian humanism, but Boccaccio as well: the former worked on a higher level, while the latter, in contrast, was active on the plane of a 'middle culture', which nevertheless left behind deeper traces and was more enduring.

The young Boccaccio, who had received his education at the splendid court of Anjou and among the poor merchant bourgeoisie of Florence, made it his goal to achieve acknowledgement of Classical status for the genres inherited from the Romance narrative tradition, particularly French and Italian. It is obvious, however, that the works of his Neapolitan period adapted material from the French *romans antiques*. His first work, the prose adventure romance *Filocolo*, takes up the love story of Floire and Blancheflor, set in Rome at the time of the transition from paganism to Christianity. *Filostrato* develops an episode from the *Roman de Troie*, while the *Teseida* continues the *Roman de Thèbes*. At the same time, however, Boccaccio attempted to restore to these tales their original rhetorical and stylistic dimension, which had gone lost; this is the reason for the Greek-sounding titles, which are intended to emphasize the recovery of Classical *auctoritas*: the ancient novel in the case of the *Filocolo*, Ovid's elegy for the *Filostrato*, and Statius' epic for the *Teseida*.

The works of his Florentine period sought to unite the Classicism of the Latin models of the distant past (Ovid, but Seneca as well) with the recent Classicism of the new Italian *auctor* (Dante). The result was the *Comedia delle ninfe fiorentine* ('Comedy of the Florentine Nymphs'), a *prosimetrum* with mythological content clearly inspired by the *Vita Nuova*, and the *Elegia di madonna Fiammetta* ('Elegy of Lady Fiametta'), in which the modern heroine tells of her disappointment in love in lengthy, romance-style prose. Even the masterpiece of this period, the *Decamerone*, responded to the same need for a modern Classicism. Boccaccio constructed his book of a hundred novellas after the model of the hundred songs of the *Commedia*, in order to offer the equivalent, in the narrative field, of what Dante's poem had provided in the field of the epic. Of course, Boccaccio drew mainly on Romance and Middle Latin sources for this literary operation, but Classical predecessors are not completely absent, either. In addition to the familiar Ovid (who was the source of inspiration for the tragic love stories of the fourth day), we find the ancient novel, along with Apu-

leius, as the source of the themes and action for the novellas of the second and fifth days, dedicated to the complications of love and various cases of luck. Two novellas of the *Decamerone* (5, 10 and 7, 2) are based directly on two *fabulae* of Apuleius' *Metamorphoses* [16].

The other Boccaccio, the Humanist, did not employ the vernacular, but preferred Latin, thanks to which he could communicate with scholars of all ages and latitudes. He frequented neither courts nor urban circles, but chose instead the solitude and tranquility of his home in Certaldo, so well-suited for meditation and study. He wrote no books of entertaining tales, but collections of educational *exempla*, from the *De casibus virorum illustrium* ('On the Fall of Famous Men') to the *De claris mulieribus* ('On Famous Women'). These works were not intended to entertain, but to provide moral education to their readers; and Boccaccio placed himself not under Dante's protection, but sought recognition from Petrarch, his new *praeceptor*, model and master [19; 5]. By translating *Griseldis*, the final novella of the *Decamerone*, into Latin, Petrarch paved the way for this masterpiece to achieve lasting influence throughout Europe. Boccaccio, for his part, did not forget the author of his youth, and prepared for the latter's future reception by writing his biography (in this case in the vernacular) and publishing a commentary on the *Commedia*, whereby he revealed the depth of philosophical and moral content of a work written in the vernacular. The most important work of this period was certainly the *Genealogia deorum gentilium* ('Genealogy of the Heathen Gods'), a genuine cultural testament, bequeathed by Boccaccio and the entire Middle Ages to European culture. Here, Boccaccio collected and compared not only the Classical versions of the myths, but also their medieval allegorical interpretations. For him, mythology is the fusion of human invention with historical truth and moral-religious doctrine. Thus, entire generations of artists (men of letters and philosophers, poets and storytellers, but also painters, sculptors and musicians, etc.) consulted this annotated encyclopedia of myth, in order to gain a more solid foundation for their own creations and acquire a deeper knowledge of their own cultural genealogy.

→ Prosimetrum

1 G. BILLANOVICH, La tradizione del testo di Livio e le origini dell' Umanesimo, 1981   2 Id., Lo scrittoio di Petrarca, 1947   3 Id., Petrarca e il primo Umanesimo, 1996   4 Id., Il preumanesimo padovano, in: Storia della cultura veneta, vol. 2, 1976, 19–110   5 F. BRUNI, Boccaccio, 1990   6 Id., Boncompagno da Signa, Guido delle Colonne, Jean de Meung: metamorfosi dei classici nel Duecento, in: Medioevo romanzo, 1987   7 D. COMPARETTI, Virgilio nel Medioevo, ²1946 (Engl. E. F. M. BENECKE (trans.) with a new introduction by J. ZIOLKOWSKI, Vergil in the Middle Ages, 1997)   8 M. FEO, Tradizione latina, in: A. ASOR ROSA (ed.), Letteratura italiana, vol. 5, 1986, 311–378   9 CH. HASKINS, The Renaissance of the 12th Century, 1958   10 Id., Studies in

Medieval Culture, 1965, 124–147 11 E. KANTORO-WICZ, Kaiser Friedrich der Zweite, 1938 (Engl. E. O. LORIMER (trans.), Frederick the Second, 1194–1250, 1957) 12 P. O. KRISTELLER, The Classics and Renaissance Thought, 1955 13 F. NOVATI, L' influsso del pensiero latino sopra la civiltà italiana del Medioevo, 1897 14 A. NOYER-WEIDNER, Umgang mit Texten, vol. 1, 1986, 221–242 15 M. PICONE, Dante and the Classics, in: A. A. IANNUCCI (ed.), Dante, 1995, 51–73 16 Id., B. ZIMMERMANN (eds.), Der antike Roman und seine mittelalterliche Rezeption, 1997 17 E. RAND, The Classics in the 13th Century, in: Speculum, 1929, 249–269 18 G. TOFFANIN, Il secolo senza Roma, 1942 19 G. VELLI, Petrarca e Boccaccio, 1979, 61–211 20 H. WIERUSZOWSKI, Politics and Culture in Medieval Spain and Italy, 1971, 589–627

ADDITIONAL BIBLIOGRAPHY V. BRANCA, Boccaccio, the Man and His Works, R. MONGES (trans.), 1976; R. HOLLANDER, Il Virgilio dantesco: tragedia nella "Commedia," 1983; R. JACOFF, J. T. SCHNAPP (eds.), The Poetry of Allusion: Virgil and Ovid in Dante's Commedia, 1991; E. MOORE, Studies in Dante. First Series, Scripture and Classical Authors in Dante, 1968; M. SOWELL, (ed.), Dante and Ovid: Essays in Intertextuality, 1991; E. H. WILKINS, Life of Petrarch, 1961; R. G. WITT, 'In the Footsteps of the Ancients': The Origins of Humanism from Lovato to Bruni, 2000

III. 15TH AND 16TH CENTURY
A. EXPLANATION OF THE TERM B. THE 15TH CENTURY C. THE 16TH CENTURY

A. EXPLANATION OF THE TERM

The term 'Renaissance', coined in the 19th cent. to designate a historical period (Burckhardt [12]; Michelet [29]), signifies the renewal of intellectual and cultural life on the basis of a return to Antiquity. The reception of Antiquity affected almost all areas: from poetry, both in Latin and in the vernacular, by way of historiography, philosophy, painting, sculpture, architecture and the decorative arts, to theatre, music and the culture of festivals.

A transformed image of history was decisive for the new relation to Antiquity, whose reception had not been interrupted during the Middle Ages. The Humanists no longer assumed a continuity between Antiquity and their own times (*translatio studii et imperii*), but attributed epochal significance to the end of the Roman empire (or the end of the Roman Republic), since it marked the beginning of the 'dark' Middle Ages. Not until seven or eight centuries later did the 'rebirth' of intellectual and cultural life began with Petrarch; a thesis argued, for example, by the Florentine Humanist Leonardo Bruni in his biographies of Dante and Petrarch (1436). This model, put forth by the Humanists, sprang from their need for a polemical differentiation from the preceding period. Modern research has shown, however, that the cultural bloom of the Italian Renaissance would not have been conceivable without the political and economic upturn and the great cultural achievements of the preceding centuries.

B. THE 15TH CENTURY
1. HISTORICAL OVERVIEW 2. THE FOUNDATIONS OF CULTURE 3. LANGUAGE AND LITERATURE 4. MUSIC (15TH AND 16TH CENTURY) 5. FINE ARTS AND ARCHITECTURE 5.1 ARCHITECTURE 5.2 SCULPTURE 5.3 PAINTING 6. PHILOSOPHY 7. AUXILIARY DISCIPLINES 8. RELIGION

1. HISTORICAL OVERVIEW

The transition from the Age of the Communes (the free towns of the Middle Ages) to that of the 'signorie' (small states ruled by an individual, later elevated to the status of hereditary duchies or principalities) was largely complete by around 1400. Only a few towns were able to maintain their freedom, including Florence, which, however, was being threatened by the expansionist efforts of the Duchy of Milan. In view of the danger to its communal freedom from the 'tyrant' Gian Galeazzo Visconti, Florentine scholars recalled the civic virtues and values previously molded in Republican Rome. The consciousness of their special political situation also contributed to the development of a new concept of history [2]. The promotors of this 'civic humanism' were not clerics, but laymen who played an active part in the political life of their commune, that is, notaries, secretaries or high officials such as Coluccio Salutati (1331–1406), Leonardo Bruni (ca. 1370–1444) and Matteo Palmieri (1406–75). If one asks why the Renaissance arose and why Florence played a leading role in this regard, reference to the special historical experience of the period around 1400 is undoubtedly essential, but not sufficient for an explanation. Social, economic and artistic factors also need to be taken into consideration.

The social and political situation in 15th-cent. I. was characterized by the juxtaposition of various types of states. These included the republics of Florence and Venice (the former developed under the Medici into a state comparable to the 'signorie' while largely preserving its communal structures, whereas the latter expanded its dominion far into the mainland in the course of the 15th cent.), principalities and duchies (the most important, but by no means the only ones, were Milan under the Visconti, then the Sforza, Ferrara under the Este, Mantua under the Gonzaga, Urbino under the Montefeltro and Rimini under the Malatesta), a monarchy (the Kingdom of Naples, ruled by the Aragonese) and the Papal States, which had also become a significant territorial and political player. The most important Italian powers, which had been entangled in frequent conflicts, achieved a political balance with the Peace of Lodi (9. 4. 1454), thus making the second half of the 15th cent. a period of relative peace.

The rivalry between small states, all striving for the greatest possible display of power and splendour; their alliances, created and confirmed by a sophisticated politics of marriages; and the strong need for princely self-promotion – all of these factors favoured the exchange and dissemination of new ideas, and contributed towards the creation of further fields of activity for scholars and artists. It was not only the princely courts, however, but also republics, municipal corporations and institutions, popes, cardinals, business people and bankers that played an important role in commissioning works of art.

2. THE FOUNDATIONS OF CULTURE

The new Humanist culture was first and foremost a lay culture. Interaction with ancient knowledge shifted away from monastic libraries, churches and universities into the political and cultural life of the communes and, above all, the courts. The popes of the second half of the century often had Humanistic interests themselves and were important clients and patrons of the arts (especially Nicholas V, 1447–55, and Pius II, 1458–64). Recourse to Antiquity, which underlay the plans for the architectural reorganization of Rome (undertaken on a grander scale only in subsequent centuries), as well as commissions to painters and sculptors, also served the project of restoring Rome to its status as the capital city of Christendom after the end of the great Western Schism.

The focal points of Humanist culture were not the universities, still marked by the scholastic educational system, but newly founded schools, which were connected to the courts (Mantua: Vittorino da Feltre; Ferrara: Guarino Veronese), or served for the education of the urban elite. The Humanists' activities, based on the ancient authors, were focused on the fields of grammar, → RHETORIC, poetry, history and moral philosophy, the five subjects of the 'studia humanitatis' (whence the term *umanista* derived in the 15th cent. to designate one who teaches or pursues the 'studia humanitatis'). The new educational goals were oriented towards the practical needs of Humanists as teachers, educators of princes, chancellors, secretaries or historiographers, and they aimed at the perfection of man in his life on earth.

Alongside the schools, an important role in the reception and dissemination of ancient knowledge was played by early forms of the → ACADEMIES, such as the Platonic Academy in Florence, the Roman Academy of Pomponio Leto, 1428–97 and that of Antonio Beccadelli, known as Il Panormita, 1394–1471, in Naples. The monastic libraries and private collections of scholars and princes, which sometimes assumed considerable proportions, were reinforced by the first public → LIBRARIES, such as the Biblioteca di San Marco in Florence and the Biblioteca Vaticana, founded by Nicholas V. In 1468, Cardinal Bessarion's gift of his collection of manuscripts provided the basis of the Biblioteca Marciana, which did not become a reality until decades later. 'Discoveries' of ancient manuscripts in monastic libraries, both in I. and north of the Alps, of texts that had previously been either inaccessible or little disseminated, provided the impetus for the study and dissemination of works by ancient authors. Increasing numbers of Greek manuscripts arrived in I., through the traditionally close relationships of various Italian cities with the East, and through cultural travel by Italian Humanists as well as by Byzantine scholars to I. The importance of this increase in ancient knowledge as a result of manuscript discoveries was certainly not negligible: thus, the discovery of twelve 'new' comedies of Plautus by Nicholas of Cusa in 1429 provided the crucial impetus for the development of the Humanistic and later of the vernacular theatre. Yet it should not be overestimated, either, as has often occurred, on the basis of the enthusiastic reports by Humanist travellers concerning their finds of books. It represents only one aspect among the many that contributed to the reception of Antiquity in the Italian Renaissance.

An important contribution was provided by new forms of reproduction and dissemination of texts. This took place, on the one hand, through an 'industrially' organized reproduction of manuscripts, by means of which Vespasiano da Bisticci supplied the library of Federico da Montefeltro in Urbino, and on the other hand, to a rapidly increasing degree, through the printing of books. The latter was first introduced at Subiaco near Rome by two German printers in 1465, and it soon led to a significant book production in the towns.

3. LANGUAGE AND LITERATURE

The foundation of Humanist education was the cultivation of the Latin language, which, through the use of ancient authors as models, was to be returned to the purity it had lost in the Middle Ages (Lorenzo Valla, 1405–57, *Elegantiarum latinae linguae libri VI*). Correct, cultivated expression was linked inseparably to content. From the study of language and textual tradition emerged the beginnings of a critical text-philological method, which already in the 15th cent. found two important representatives in Valla, who used philological methods to uncover the document of the Donation of Constantine (→ CONSTANTINE, DONATION OF) as a → FORGERY, and Angelo Poliziano (1454–94). The restoration of texts to the most authentic form possible (in association with studies of the orthography, grammar, rhetoric and metrics of Antiquity) and explanatory commentary (studies of ancient history, culture and myth) formed the basis for the utilisation of ancient knowledge, as well as for original literary production based on ancient authors taken as models.

Greek was less important to the Italian Renaissance than Latin, which could rely on the continuity of Latin studies throughout the Middle Ages and had an active utility value in many areas of life. Nevertheless, the Humanists made a decisive contribution to the study of Greek as well. Already before the fall of Constantinople (1453), which resulted in an increased influx of Byzantine scholars into I., the elements needed to continue the efforts of Petrarch and Boccaccio toward institutionalising the teaching of Greek were in place. The Council of Ferrara and Florence (1438–45) promoted west-east contacts, and was reflected in the fine arts by numerous representations of Greek dignitaries and scholars. Texts by Greek scientists, philosophers, orators, historians and poets also became the subject of study by philologists and historians and found their way into libraries through new editions. The comparatively small number of poems in Modern Greek contrasted with a flood of Latin translations from the Greek (new translations of texts already known in the Middle Ages as well as texts translated for the first time); these provided decisive stimuli to philosophy, the sciences and literature.

A wealth of neo-Latin poetry, dependent on Antiquity, arose in the 15th cent. The effort to imitate ancient genres and to achieve linguistic and stylistic perfection gave rise to a wide range of occasional and technical literature (including epithalamia, epicedia, eulogies, diplomatic speeches and so on), lyrical works such as elegies, → EPIGRAMS, and bucolic poetry; dramatic texts, vitae, centones and books of → LOCI COMMUNES), as well as the typically Humanist genres of → DIALOGUE, letters (epistles), and essays.

The → IMITATIO practiced by neo-Latin poets should not be understood as mere slavish imitation, for it was inseparable from *aemulatio*, or creative rivalry with ancient models. The 15th cent witnessed a lively debate over the right kind of imitation. The Ciceronian Paolo Cortese championed a restrictive concept of *imitatio*, whereas Poliziano expressed his opposition to the limitation to Cicero as the only valid linguistic and stylistic model (or rather Cicero for prose and Virgil for poetry) and spoke out in favour of an eclectic selection and original creation based on a wide range of model authors, including some from 'Silver Latinity'. This debate was continued in the 16th cent. by Giovan Francesco Pico and by Pietro Bembo (1470–1547), the latter in support of → CICERONIANISM.

In view of the dominant position of Humanism, with its concentration on Latin and neo-Latin poetry, the vernacular literature of the 15th cent. seems unimportant. Closely connected to independent literary production was translation activity, which, after the great age of *volgarizzamenti* (translations from Latin into the Italian *volgare*) in the 14th cent., now focused primarily on the translation of Greek texts into Latin. There were, however, also early indications of a reevaluation of the vernacular in the 15th cent., particularly in Florence, where the great tradition of the 'three crowns' Dante, Petrarch and Boccaccio was continued. The polymath Leon Battista Alberti (1404–72) played an important part in this process, as did the statesman and poet Lorenzo de' Medici (1449–92), whose promotion of all things Florentine went hand in hand with claims to political power. The great Humanist and philologist Poliziano, a close friend of Lorenzo, was also the author of an epic mythological poem in Italian (*Stanze per la giostra*, 1475–78), which was to find imitators well into the 16th cent, and of the *Fabula di Orfeo* (around 1480?), the most important example of a mythological festival play.

Vernacular poetry also had recourse to Antiquity, as becomes especially clear from the reception of mythological themes and motifs. A brief glance at the history of the theatre will provide an example of the actualisation and utilisation of Antiquity. Towards the end of the century, alongside Latin Humanist drama, which played a major part in schools and academies as well as at court, translations of ancient, mainly Plautine, comedies appeared (beginning with the performance of the *Menaechmi* (→ LATIN COMEDY) at the court of Ferrara in 1486), as well as performances of mythological or mythological-allegorical festival plays in the vernacular. Here, alongside the spoken text, such visual elements as pantomime, costumes, props, and so on played an important role, as they did in the mythical intermezzi of performances of comedy. The visual aspect became determinant in the primarily pantomimic genus of the Venetian 'mumaria', which also drew from the reservoir of motifs from (Ovidian) myths.

In the courtly festivals of the 15th and especially the 16th cent., Humanist erudition (Humanists were active as the authors of designs for programs, texts for recitation and inscriptions and descriptions of festivals), vernacular culture and the fine arts were blended into a total work of art, for which the organizers spared no expense. Themes borrowed from Antiquity were found in the entry procession, inspired both by the ancient triumphal procession and by Petrarch's allegorical *Trionfi*; in songs, eulogies and dance performances; in banquets with mythological figures or mythological 'entrements' made out of sugar; in tournaments with ancient-style costumes and erudite mottos; and not least in various kinds of scenic or dramatic performances. In these festivals, held by both courts and city republics, forms and contents derived from Antiquity were placed in the service of contemporary political and cultural demands, and exerted an influence that went far beyond the small circle of the humanistically educated.

4. MUSIC (15TH AND 16TH CENTURY)

In the 15th cent., Humanist endeavours to edit, translate and comment on ancient sources and to make them accessible for praxis also extended to ancient texts on musical theory, primarily Greek. Only indirect sources were known until the end of the 16th cent. Elements of ancient musical theory that were influential on the Renaissance included the notion of the harmony of the spheres (→ SPHERES, HARMONY OF) and the belief that music could influence human feeling and behaviour. In Ficino, music was linked to magical practices, and his 'Orphic songs' were intended to bring about a favourable influence from the planets. The Humanist Giorgio Valla was an important collector and translator of Greek works on musical theory. His encyclopedia *De expetendis et fugiendis rebus opus*, published in 1501, is a summary of Greek musical theory, based on original texts. The tendency toward the practical application of knowledge of ancient music, which became stronger in the 16th cent., began with the musician Franchino Gaffurio (1451–1522), who had numerous Greek sources translated for his studies and concerned himself with the reconstruction of ancient music. The academies, or comparable meeting places of scholars such as Giovanni Bardi's (1534–ca. 1614) *Camerata* in Florence, were centres of debates and research on these themes.

It was above all in the second half of the 16th cent. that reflection on ancient musical theory and corresponding attempts at reconstruction provided impulses toward the reform of musical practice. The research of Girolamo Mei (1519–94) was taken up by Bardi and the Venetian Gioseffo Zarlino, both of whom advocated rather moderate positions, while Vincenzo Galilei (ca. 1520–91) aimed at a thorough-going reform of musical practice, in close dependence on Antiquity (*Dialogo della musica antica e moderna*, 1581). The reflections inspired by ancient musical theory, particularly on the question of how to obtain the emotional effects of music attested in the sources, together with the idea that ancient tragedies were performed entirely in song, contributed to the development of a theory of the recitative. This new style was first implemented in the *Euridice* by Jacopo Peri and Ottavio Rinuccini, performed in Florence on October 6, 1600, which marked the beginning of the great history of the → OPERA.

5. FINE ARTS AND ARCHITECTURE

In the field of fine arts and architecture, the influence of Antiquity was apparent in the transition from the Gothic style (which 15th- and 16th-cent. theoreticians dismissed as the 'Barbarian style') to the stylistic and formal repertoire of the Renaissance. In the 15th cent., in conjunction with the emancipation of the mechanical arts, then beginning but still not complete by the 16th cent., the endeavour to place painting, sculpture and architecture on a new theoretical foundation became apparent. This could only occur through recourse to ancient writings and models, since the exemplary nature of Antiquity was generally acknowledged in the wake of Humanism. The connection between Humanism and the fine arts was personified in the polymath Leon Battista Alberti, who wrote treatises on painting, sculpture and architecture (*De pictura*, 1435, translated by Alberti himself into Italian; *De statua*; *De re aedificatoria*, 1455) and who was himself active as an architect. Dance was also included in the reorganization of art as legitimized by Antiquity (treatises by Domenico da Piacenza, Guglielmo Ebreo and Antonio Cornazzaro).

5.1 ARCHITECTURE

The remains of Roman buildings, which were measured and sketched, provided a wealth of illustrative material for architects and, increasingly, for sculptors as well. Filippo Brunelleschi (1377–1446) and Donatello (1382/83–1466) may be taken as representative of early Renaissance students of Antiquity in both of these fields. Along with interest in ancient architecture, the awareness gradually developed of the need to preserve and protect the ancient ruins, which even in the 15th cent. were still being used for building material. In architectural drawings, one can detect a drive to supplement the ancient remains, most of them incompletely preserved or only partly visible, and to create from them something new and individual.

In the Renaissance, the confrontation with the architecture of Antiquity took place to a substantial extent by way of the reception of Vitruvius' *De architectura*. A central theme, for the elaboration of which the ancient tradition was exploited in the 15th cent., was the hierarchy of building types, with sacred buildings at the summit. The ideal form of the 'temple', as described in Vitruvius and in the theoretical writings of the Renaissance, was the domed central building after the model of the Pantheon. Examples of the implementation of this type are found not only in actual architecture, but also in painting, in the form of idealised city views and stage backdrops. A second significant theme was that of proportion. Pythagorean-Platonic and medieval number symbolism were included in designs for church buildings, which were to reflect the divine harmony of the world in the clarity and harmony of their parts. Since perfect mathematical proportions were also found in music, it was possible to base a building on musical proportions (as in the expert opinion rendered by Fra Francesco Zorzi in 1535 on Jacopo Sansovino's design for the church of San Francesco della Vigna in Venice, or in the architecture of Palladius). The ideal human body also corresponded to the harmony and perfect proportion of the universe, and could therefore become the basic unit of measurement of architectural layouts, as was already the case in Antiquity, in the view of Renaissance theoreticians.

Ancient writings and ideas had an important influence not only on individual buildings, but also on town planning. The Humanist pope Pius II (1458–64) undertook the (only partially realised) remodelling of his home town, which he renamed 'Pienza', while in Ferrara, Duke Ercole I d'Este had the extension of the city, which was named after him, carried out on the basis of Humanistic plans. However, large-scale urban planning, realised according to the methods of contemporary knowledge, was not implemented, as at Sabbioneta, until the 16th cent.

5.2 SCULPTURE

In sculpture, the study of Antiquity and observations of nature led to a further development of the medieval tradition, and above all to new forms of representing the human body (proportions, 'contrapposto', nudity). Many decorative elements were also derived from Antiquity. Added to these was the revival of techniques (bronze casting: Donatello's *David*, about 1435) and types (as in the portrait medallion and the freestanding monumental sculpture).

5.3 PAINTING

Unlike architecture and sculpture, painting was confronted with the problem of a virtually complete lack of ancient models to imitate. Only a few frescoes, mosaics and decorations (such as the grotesques of the *Domus aurea*) were known. Painters therefore sought guidance, on the one hand, from ancient reliefs, sculptures and buildings, and on the other from literary sources. Following the motto adopted from Horace → UT PICTURA POESIS (now understood as meaning that painting imitates poetry and rivals it), painting and writing became closely interconnected in the Renaissance, for instance through the transposition into paintings of famous descriptions of ancient pictures (Botticelli: *Calumny of Apelles*, 1495). The fact that categories and terminology were borrowed from ancient rhetoric is further evidence of the new convergence of painting (and the theory of painting) and poetry.

Secular painting, and therefore mythological subjects, became increasingly important in the Renaissance. To be sure, Ovidian myths were depicted in a variety of ways, for instance in book illustrations, throughout the Middle Ages, but they were always represented in contemporary dress. The courtly knights and ladies who populated medieval representations of myths were henceforth replaced by figures depicted as either naked or dressed 'all'antica'.

Despite the recourse to Antiquity typical of the Renaissance, the continuity of the medieval tradition remained unbroken. Since most painters did not know Latin, they often did not use the original texts but went back to writings, paraphrases, compendia or translations that were either medieval or belonged to the medieval tradition. Thus, for instance, the translation of Ovid's *Metamorphoses* by Giovanni de' Bonsignori, based on a medieval university lecture and first published at Venice in 1497, was still used as a source for mythological representations until well into the 16th cent., as can be seen e.g. in Giulio Romano's *Sala dei Giganti* in the Palazzo del Te at Mantua. It was sometimes precisely these deviations from the ancient sources, conditioned by the history of transmission, that led to the invention of apparently new images.

6. PHILOSOPHY

Renaissance Platonism developed outside of the university curriculum, which was marked by an Aristotelian emphasis. Its main representative was Marsilio Ficino (1433–99), who founded the Platonic Academy in 1462 and was the first to translate the Platonic dialogues in their entirety into Latin. Central themes of Ficino's philosophy included the position of the human soul in the universe, the contemplative life, the immortality of the soul, the Neoplatonic conception of love as connecting the elements of the universe and enabling man's ascent to the divine, as well as the fundamental agreement between Platonism and Christianity. Ficino, a priest, doctor and scholar, based his theories not only on Plato's writings but also on their commentators from Antiquity, Late Antiquity and the Middle Ages, as well as on the corpus of Hermetic writings (Hermes Trismegistus, Zoroaster, Orpheus and Pythagoras), a group of texts from Late Antiquity, which, in Renaissance understanding, reflected a universal wisdom that pre-dated Antiquity.

Giovanni Pico della Mirandola (1463–94) stood close to the Platonic Academy in his outlook. On the basis of his extensive studies (Plato and the associated Greek, Latin and Arabic texts, Aristotle, Hermetic writings, the → KABBALA, and medieval philosophers), he strove, even more than Ficino, for a syncretistic unity between all known philosophical doctrines and religions. In his speech *De hominis dignitate*, he defended the concept, characteristic of early Renaissance philosophy, of the dignity and freedom of man, who shapes his destiny through his own force.

From the two outstanding figures of Ficino and Pico, it becomes clear that in its desire to return to the sources, the Renaissance did not stop with Greco-Roman Antiquity. Ancient Jewish and Egyptian wisdom (or what was regarded as such) also served as the objects of study and as sources of inspiration for scholars and artists. The Hermetic tradition can be traced right to the end of the period presented here (Giordano Bruno, 1548–1600), and made its contribution to the renewal of scientific thought in the 17th cent.

7. AUXILIARY DISCIPLINES

The Humanists' interest was not directed exclusively toward the written sources of Antiquity, but ancient coins, inscriptions, buildings and sculptures were also investigated, documented and used as sources. This led to the emergence of the basic principles of → NUMISMATICS, epigraphy and architecture (Ciriaco d'Ancona, 1391–1452). Two examples of the creative utilisation of archaeological studies are the paintings by Andrea Mantegna (1431–1506) and the *Hypnerotomachia Poliphili*, an allegorical romance published at Venice in 1499. With its language made up of Italian, Latin and Greek elements, and its masterly antique-style illustrations, the latter is one of the most enigmatic Renaissance texts. Collections of ancient coins, medallions, gems, vases, small bronzes and their imitations adorned the *studioli* of scholars (the *studioli* of Federico da Montefeltro in Urbino and of Isabella d'Este in Mantua) and royal libraries, and became the nuclei of modern museums.

8. RELIGION

The intensive interest in the language and culture of Antiquity, and the admiration felt by many Humanists for everything ancient, did not signify a renunciation of Christianity. On the contrary, Humanism contributed towards a deepening and a reform of theology. Humanists such as Valla and Manetti also extended their philological work and translation activities to include the Bible, the Latin Church Fathers and Greek patristic texts, thus preparing the way for the textual studies and translations of the Reformation.

C. THE 16TH CENTURY

1. HISTORICAL OVERVIEW 2. CULTURE
3. LANGUAGE AND LITERATURE 4. FINE ARTS AND ARCHITECTURE 5. PHILOSOPHY 6. ANTICHI E MODERNI

1. HISTORICAL OVERVIEW

Since the Italian campaigns of the French kings Charles VIII (1494) and Louis XII (1499), I. had become the 'plaything' of the European superpowers. The first half of the 16th cent. was marked by repeated wars over sovereignty between the French king and the emperor Charles V. The *Sacco di Roma*, or sack of Rome by Habsburg troops in May 1527, signified a radical turning-point, often regarded, particularly in art history, as the end of the Renaissance. The Peace of Cateau-Cambrésis (3. 4. 1559) sanctioned Habsburg-Spanish sovereignty over I. Thus began a period of peace, but in many respects also one of stagnation. There can be no question, however, of an overall decline in the 16th cent. After 1530, the economy experienced a recovery; alongside the Republic of Venice, important principalities persisted (Ferrara, Mantua, Urbino, the duchy of Savoie). As the centre of the duchy or grand duchy of Tuscany, Florence was able to play the role of an autonomous power broker. Genoa and Livorno profited from new trade relations, and new principalities emerged, such as that of the Farnese in Parma and Piacenza.

After the popes of the first two decades of the 16th cent. who were enormously important as patrons and commissioners of works of art and architecture, Paul III (1534–49) turned increasingly toward reforms within the Church (Council of Trent: 1545–63). In the second half of the cent., the Index, censorship and the Inquisition inhibited scientific and intellectual progress. Nevertheless, decisive new impulses emanating from I. affected European art and culture of the following century, including the Baroque, the emergence of the opera and the reception of the Aristotelian *Poetics*, later developed further by French Classicism.

2. CULTURE

The academies that flourished in many towns in the 16th cent. played a leading role in cultural and artistic development. In addition to Classical culture, they also devoted themselves particularly to the cultivation of Italian language and literature (e.g. the Florentine Accademia della Crusca). Other academies specialised in the fine arts (the Accademia del Disegno in Florence), music, or theatrical performances (the Accademia Olimpica in Vicenza).

Since the end of the 15th cent., book printing had played a leading role in the reception and dissemination of ancient texts, with Venice its most important Italian centre. The Venetian publisher Aldo Manuzio (ca. 1450–1515) specialised in editions of Greek texts, but also included fundamental Latin and vernacular works in his program. Connected with this editorial activity was the philological revision of texts, and the preparation of translations, prefaces and commentaries. Centres of erudite discussion therefore arose in the ambit of these publishing houses, along with new fields of work for intellectuals, some of whom also wrote their own works for the growing reading public (Ludovico Dolce, 1508–68). Book production had to adapt to the needs of a market that was no longer determined by a small elite of scholars with a solid humanist education, but increasingly also by people who knew no Latin, such as women, merchants or artisans.

3. LANGUAGE AND LITERATURE

The achievements of Humanism (methods of textual criticism, concept of 'imitatio'), the political situation, and factors related to the expansion of the reading public and the demands of the publishing houses contributed to the intensification and ultimately to the solution of a problem that had been repeatedly discussed since the time of Dante: the so-called "questione della lingua", or the search for a uniform literary language capable of forging a cultural identity. The eventually successful rule was formulated by Pietro Bembo, the Humanist and member of the circle around Manuzio, for whom he prepared editions of Dante and Petrarch, among others. Influenced by Ciceronianism, Bembo (*Prose della volgar lingua*, 1525) recommended the imitation of Petrarch for lyric verse and of Boccaccio for prose. The success of 14th cent. Tuscan as a literary language took place gradually. The question of whether one should write in this archaising language, in modern Tuscan, or in Latin, remained basically unresolved down to the mid–16th cent., and Latin remained the language of universities, of law, and of the Church even after this. The newly found self-awareness of vernacular literature after about 1540 found expression in, among other fields, the theory and practice of translation. Italian translations came to compete with the Latin originals, and the ancient authorities were replaced by the 'classics' of national literature. The veneration felt for the ancient original gave way to a freedom which in many respects paved the way for the *belles infidèles* of the 17th cent.

The literature of the 16th cent. took up both the vernacular tradition of the 14th cent. (and, to a lesser extent, of the 15th cent.) and certain trends in the Humanist reception of Antiquity. Petrarch's lyricism and elements of Ficino's Neoplatonism combined to make up the Petrarchan lyric verse of the 16th cent. (Bembo, *Rime*, 1530). Like his predecessor Boiardo (*Orlando Innamorato*, 1506) before him, Ludovico Ariosto made use of numerous mythological themes and motifs in his *Orlando Furioso* (1532), in order to present material borrowed from the medieval Charlemagne-epics (→ CHANSON DE GESTE) to his courtly audience and to the reading public in a way that was both sophisticated and appealing. That knowledge of ancient literature and history had already become part of a general cultural canon by this time is shown by Castigione's demand that the perfect courtier have a "more than mediocre" training in the Humanistic disciplines and acquire knowledge of Greek, so as to improve his eloquence, compose his own literary works (in Italian) and be able to pronounce competent judgments on literature (*Il libro del Cortegiano*, 1528, I, 44). There was no call for exaggerated specialization in the trend-setting courtly culture of the 16th cent. Humanistic erudition that was merely reproductive and had degenerated to the level of being a goal in itself was attacked in the figure of the pedant spouting Latin jargon, who is to be found in many Renaissance comedies.

The use of ancient mythology in the Christian epics of Ariosto and Tasso (*La Gerusalemme liberata*, 1581) was far more successful than the attempts at writing mythological epic poems by authors, who are now almost forgotten, such as Battista Caracini, Andrea Stagi, and Giovanni Filoteo Achillini. More successful than the reception granted to such scholarly works was that obtained by the mythological *cantari*, *popular* adaptations performed in streets and squares and disseminated in unassuming prints. The fact that ancient material was no longer treated with Humanist reverence is also shown by the vernacular mythological burlesques (→ BURLESQUE) that arose around the middle of the century.

The field of theatre witnessed the emergence of vernacular comedies (→ COMEDY), composed after ancient models, and based on translations of the Classics, as well as on 15th cent. performative practice. Here, the court of Ferrara once again took centre stage (Ariosto, *La Cassaria*, 1508). This was followed in 1524 by Giangiorgio Trissino's *Sofonisba*, the first → tragedy to be written under the inspiration of the Aristotelian *Poetics*. Added to this was the pastoral drama, particularly popular at the courts (Tasso, *Aminta*, 1573), which harked back to Latin eclogic verse as well as to *volgare* precursors (Poliziano's *Orfeo*, Sannazaro's *Arcadia*, 1504, already written 1481–86). In these plays, ancient → ARCADIA became a place of evasion, but also of the self-representation of courtly society. The pastoral play was important for the development of musical theatre, in that it was here that sung dialogues were first introduced. According to the contemporary view, this did not contradict the Aristotelian requirement for believability, since singing was, as it were, the natural form of expression for Arcadian shepherds and nymphs.

The literature of the late 16th cent. was characterised by an increasingly need for normative parameters, division and theoretical reflection. This took place in close conjunction with the reception of the Aristotelian *Poetics* (Latin translation by Giorgio Valla in 1498 and by Alessandro Pazzi in 1536; Latin commentary by F. Robortello in 1548; Italian commentary by L. Castelvetro in 1570). Ancient texts were commented and interpreted in a way that enabled the derivation of a fixed system of rules. This led, for instance, to the formulation of the rules of the three unities (→ TRAGEDY/ THEORY OF TRAGEDY), which were to spark heated debates down to the 19th cent. The importance of this system derived from Antiquity was shown by the attempts of Renaissance theoreticians to use it to classify and evaluate genres that were not of ancient origin, such as the *romanzo*.

4. FINE ARTS AND ARCHITECTURE

The architecture of the 16th cent. was marked by a stronger reception of Vitruvius than had been the case in the 15th cent. The phenomenon was decisively advanced by the editions, translations, commentaries and illustrations of this ancient treatise (illustrated editions include those by Fra Giocondo in 1511 by Cesa-

riano in 1521). Modern treatises (Serlio, Palladio, Vignola) continued the Vitruvian tradition.

Rome became the centre of the arts in the High Renaissance. Popes Julius II (1503–13), Leo X (1513–21) and Clement VII (1523–34) summoned important artists to their court, and commissioned projects that were to correspond to Rome's recovered grandeur and power as the capital city of Christianity. Reference to ancient Rome was obligatory in this process. Real space and pictorial space merged in the Vatican's Stanza della Segnatura (1509–11) painted by Raphael, where ancient and biblical themes were juxtaposed with equal justification, documenting the continuity of ancient philosophy (*The School of Athens*) and Christianity (*La Disputa*). The immense dome of St. Peter's, designed by Bramante and then by Michelangelo, cited the Pantheon and became the symbol of the reconciliation of Antiquity and Christianity.

A rather strictly Classicising style continued to exist in parallel to the further development of the Renaissance style in the architecture of → Mannerism and the early → BAROQUE. Its most important exponent was Andrea Palladio (1508–80), who, in his architecture shaped by intensive study of Antiquity and theoretical reflection, found solutions which became exemplary in their turn, such as the colossal order, the temple-fronted villa, and the church façades of Il Redentore and San Giorgio Maggiore in Venice, with its two superimposed temple fronts. Palladio's *Teatro Olimpico* in Vicenza (opened in 1585), built by order of the Accademia Olimpica, was based on the reconstruction of the Roman theatre. This building, completed by Palladio's pupil Scamozzi (1522–1616), features a fixed *frons scaenae* with illusionist perspectives (→ GREEK TRAGEDY).

Mythological themes and motifs found their way into all fields of arts and craft, from architectonic decoration and sculptures integrated into architecture, through panel paintings, fresco cycles, small and monumental sculptures, graphic illustrations, gold work, porcelain, coats of arms and emblems, to marquetry and veneering, decorations for festive occasions, garden design, weapons, suits of armour, and stove tiles.

Important finds of ancient sculptures (→ BELVEDERE APOLLO; → LAOCOON GROUP) gave fresh stimulus to sculpture and painting, while collections of sculptures and 'Gardens of Antiquities' served aesthetic as well as didactic and representative-political purposes.

Beginning in the late 1520s, the 'Classical' formal language of the Renaissance which had emerged since the 15th cent. from the encounter with Antiquity, among other factors, was superseded by Mannerism and then by the Baroque. In the process, ancient history and mythology retained their absolute validity as reservoirs of subjects and motifs for the arts, literature, and festive culture. They served as a means for decoration and entertainment, as the starting point for learned discussion, and as the vehicles for philosophical, scientific, art-theoretical or political statements. The dissemination of ancient and particularly mythological subjects and motifs increased decisively in the 16th cent. as a result of book printing, especially through emblem books and mythographical handbooks (Lilio Gregorio Giraldi, 1548; Natale Conti, 1551; Vincenzo Cartari, 1556), one of whose goals was to provide models for artists. Like their precursor, Boccaccio's *Genealogia deorum*, these handbooks did not renounce the allegorical interpretation of ancient myths. Although the Council of Trent prohibited the Christian typological interpretation of myths, this had no affect on their interpretation in a moral, physical or euhemeristic sense.

5. PHILOSOPHY

The Neo-Platonism of the 15th cent. was broadly diffused in the 16th cent., but also became more superficial. Ficino's concept of love was particularly influential, and was absorbed by Petrarchan lyric verse as well as in numerous works on the theory of love (Bembo, *Gli Asolani*, 1505).

Pietro Pomponazzi (1462–1525; *De immortalitate anima e*, 1516) represented the → ARISTOTELIANISM that remained associated with the university tradition (Bologna, Padua). The replacement of Aristotelian-influenced natural philosophy by the 'modern' sciences, which took place in the 17th cent., was foreshadowed in the writings of important natural philosophers of the second half of the 16th cent. (Bernardino Telesio, 1509–88; Francesco Patrizi, 1529–97; Giordano Bruno, 1548–1600).

6. ANTICHI E MODERNI

To understand the reception of Antiquity in any particular period, it is of central importance to see how that period itself defined its relationship with Antiquity. At the beginning of the period presented here, examples of a feeling of inferiority can be detected in Humanist utterances: the ancient models were considered unattainable in their perfection. With time, a growing self-awareness can be observed on the part of the 'moderni', whereby architecture, the fine arts and science, which could appeal to technical progress and new discoveries, clearly freed themselves from the oppressive weight of ancient tradition earlier than philology and literature. Already in the dedication to his treatise on painting (1435), Alberti referred to the dome of the Florence cathedral built by Brunelleschi as an example of the ancients being surpassed by the moderns. It is not possible, however, to discern a uniform development in the relation to Antiquity. In the 15th as in the 16th cent., various positions and historical models coexisted. The debate over the superiority of the ancients or of one's own time was to be continued at the end of French Classicism in the → QUERELLE DES ANCIENS ET DES MODERNES.

→ Corpus Hermeticum; → Hermetic writings

→ ALLEGORESIS; → ARCHAEOLOGICAL METHODS AND THEORIES; → ARCHITECTURAL THEORY/VITRUVIANISM; → Education / Culture; → EMBLEMS; → FESTIVE PROCESSIONS/TRIONFI; → FÜRSTENSCHULE; → OCCASIONAL POETRY; → MUSIC AND ARCHITECTURE; → PHI-

LOLOGICAL METHODS; → PLATONISM; → SCHOLASTICISM; → TRANSMISSION

1 Antiquarische Gelehrsamkeit und Bildende Kunst. Die Gegenwart der Antike in der Renaisssance, 1996   2 H. BARON, In Search of Florentine Civic Humanism, 2 vols., 1988   3 H. BECK, P. C. BOL (eds.), Natur und Antike in der Renaissance, 1985   4 Bibliographie internationale de l'Humanisme et de la Renaissance, I, 1965 ff.   5 P. BOBER, R. RUBINSTEIN, Renaissance Artists and Antique Sculpture. A Handbook of Visual Sources, 1986   6 E. R. BOLGAR, Classical Influences on European Culture AD 1500–1700, 1976   7 A. BUCK (ed.), Zu Begriff und Problem der Renaissance, 1969   8 Id. (ed.), Renaissance und Barock (Part), 1972 (Neues Handbuch der Literaturwissenschaft, 9)   9 Id., Die Rezeption der Antike in den romanischen Literaturen der Renaissance, 1976   10 Id., Zum Selbstverständnis der Renaissance, in: Wolfenbütteler Renaissance Mitteilungen 21, 1997, 49–57   11 A. BUCK, K. HEITMANN (eds.), Die Antike-Rezeption in den Wissenschaften während der Renaissance, 1983   12 J. BURCKHARDT, Die Cultur der Renaissance in Italien, 1860 (Engl. S. G. C. MIDDLEMORE (trans.), The Civilization of the Renaissance in Italy, 1954)   13 P. BURKE, The Italian Renaissance: Culture and Society in Italy, 1999   14 D. R. COFFIN (ed.), The Italian Garden, 1972   15 M. DE PANIZZA LORCH (ed.), Il teatro italiano del Rinascimento, 1980   16 F. A. GALLO, R. GROTH, C. V. PALISCA, F. REMPP, Italienische Musiktheorie im 16. und 17. Jahrhundert, 1989   17 E. GARIN, Die Kultur der Renaissance, in: Propyläen Weltgeschichte, 6, 1991 (¹1960–64), 429–534   18 Id., La Cultura filosofica del Rinascimento italiano, 1961   19 E. H. GOMBRICH, Norm and Form. Studies in the Art of the Renaissance, 1966   20 E. GRASSI, Einführung in die humanistische Philosophie, ²1991   21 P. F. GRENDLER, Schooling in Renaissance Italy: Literacy and Learning, 1300–1600, 1989   22 H. GÜNTHER, Das Studium der antiken Architektur in den Zeichnungen der Hochrenaissance, 1988   23 B. GUTHMÜLLER, Ovidio Metamorphoseos Vulgare. Formen und Funktionen der volkssprachlichen Wiedergabe klassischer Dichtung in der italienischen Renaissance, 1981   24 Id., Studien zur antiken Mythologie in der italienischen Renaissance, 1986   25 J. HALE, Die Kultur der Renaissance in Europa, 1994   26 P. O. KRISTELLER, Renaissance Thought and the Arts, 1990   27 L. LÜTTEKEN, s. v. Renaissance, MGG, Sachteil, vol. 8, ²1998, col. 143–156   28 C. LAZZARO, The Italian Renaissance Garden, 1990   29 J. MICHELET, Histoire de France, 7 (Ren.), Paris 1855 (Engl. G. H. SMITH (trans.), History of France, 1978)   30 CH. G. NAUERT, Humanism and the Culture of Renaissance Europe, 1995   31 E. PANOFSKY, Stud. in Iconology. Humanistic Themes in the Art of the Renaissance, 1939   32 Id., Renaissance and Renascences in Western Art, 2 vols., 1960   33 N. PIRROTTA, Li due Orfei. Da Poliziano a Monteverdi, 1975   34 J. POESCHKEM, Die Skulptur der Renaissance in Italien, 1990   35 A. RABIL JR (ed.), Renaissance Humanism. Foundations, Forms and Legacy, 1: Humanism in Italy, 1988   36 R. SCHUMANN, Geschichte Italiens, 1983   37 S. SETTIS (ed.), Memoria dell'antico nell'arte italiana, 3 vols., 1984–86   38 J. SEZNEC, The Survival of the Pagan God: The Mythological Tradition and its Place in Renaissance Humanism and art, 1995 (¹1940)   39 R. STILLERS, Humanistische Deutung. Studien zu Kommentar und Literaturtheorie in der italienischen Renaissance, 1988   40 Id., Drama und Dramen-

theorie der Antike in der Poetik des italienischen Humanismus, in: B. ZIMMERMANN (ed.), Antike Dramentheorien und ihre Rezeption, 1992   41 L. THORNDIKE, Science and Thought in the Fifteenth Century, 1963   42 W. TOTOK, Handbuch der Geschichte der Philosophie, 3 (Renaissance), 1980   43 CH. TRINKAUS, In our Image and Likeness. Humanity and Divinity in Italian Humanist Thought, 2 vols., 1970   44 C. VASOLI, Umanesimo e Rinascimento, 1976   45 G. VOIGT, Die Wiederbelebung des classischen Altertums oder Das erste Jahrhundert des Humanismus, 2 vols., Berlin ³1859   46 A. WARBURG, Sandro Botticellis 'Geburt der Venus' und 'Frühling'. Eine Untersuchung über die Vorstellungen von der Antike in der italienischen Frührenaissance, 1893, in: Gesammelte Schriften, 1, 1969, 1–60   47 R. WEISS, The Renaissance Discovery of Classical Antiquity, 1969   48 N. G. WILSON, From Byzantium to Italy: Greek Studies in the Italian Renaissance, 1992   49 E. WIND, Pagan Mysteries in the Renaissance, 1968 (¹1958)   50 R. WITTKOWER, Architectural Principles in the Age of Humanism, 1998 (¹1949)   51 F. A. YATES, Giordano Bruno and the Hermetic Tradition, 1964

ADDITIONAL BIBLIOGRAPHY L. BARKAN, Unearthing the Past: Archaeology and Aesthetics in the Making of Renaissance Culture, 1999; H. BARON, The Crisis of the Early Italian Renaissance, (rev. ed.), 1966; M. BAXANDALL, Giotto and the Orators: Humanist Observers of Painting in Italy and the Discovery of Pictorial Composition 1350–1450, 1971; R. BLACK, Humanism and Education in Medieval and Renaissance Italy, 2001; J. CUNNALLY, Images of the Illustrious: The Numismatic Presence in the Renaissance, 1999; M. FELDMAN, City Culture and the Madrigal at Venice, 1995; E. GARIN, Italian Humanism: Philosophy and Civic Life in the Renaissance, P. MUNZ (trans.), 1965; A. GRAFTON, Leon Battista Alberti, Master Builder of the Italian Renaissance, 2000; T. M. GREENE, The Light in Troy: Imitation and Discovery in Renaissance Poetry, 1982; P. F. GRENDLER, The Universities of the Italian Renaissance, 2002; C. KALLENDORF (ed.), Humanist Educational Treatises, 2002

SUSANNE TICHY

IV. THE 17TH AND 18TH CENTURY
A. THE 17TH CENTURY   B. THE 18TH CENTURY

A. THE 17TH CENTURY

While the entire literary production of the 17th cent. was marked by the reception of Classical Antiquity, the approach to it fluctuated between the modernity of the Baroque and Classicistic severity. For Giambattista Marino's (1569–1625) poetics of imitation, the Classical heritage represented a storehouse of topoi that could be freely shaped according to the rhetorical categories of astuteness (*argutia*), exaggeration (hyperbole, *superlatio*) and obscurity (*obscurum*). For the opposing camp, especially the Roman circle around Maffeo Barberini (1568–1644, who became Pope Urban VIII in 1623), Antiquity was a treasury of wisdom, dignity and heroic vigour – values upon which a moral and rationalist literary program could be constructed.

The Classicist faction, whose best known exponents were Gabriello Chiabrera (1552–1638) and Fulvio Testi (1593–1646), was distinguished by its literary experiments, such as the eclectic adoption of the metres, stylistic features and poetic norms of Greek and Latin authors (especially Anacreon, Pindar, Horace and Propertius). In the process, they made frequent attempts to approach the models of the Classical authors, although such approximation was often in open contradiction to the Classicist program. Chiabrera's prolific lyrical output (he also wrote epic poems and tragedies, in which allusions to Classical myth alternate with references to the work of Ariosto and Tasso) culminated in the collection of *Poesie* ('Poems', 1605–6), whereby he established a tradition that was to extend into the 'Arcadian' 18th cent. The *Canzoni* ('Songs'), subdivided into *Eroiche* ('Heroic Songs'), *Sacre* ('Sacred Songs'), *Lugubri* ('Songs of Mourning') and *Morali* ('Moral Songs'), contain echoes of Pindar and Horace. The *Canzonette* ('Little Songs'), subdivided into *Amorose* ('Love Songs'), *Morali* and *Sacre*, reflect his confrontation with the Greek lyric poets, primarily Anacreon. They are often reduced to a simple tone and diluted by affected playfulness, in which rhythm and form are always central. The *Sermoni* ('Conversations') in free hendecasyllables, which remained unpublished until the 18th cent., were modelled after Horace's *Epistles*. By appealing to Pindar and Horace in his *Poesi liriche* ('Lyric Poems', definitive edition 1645–1646), and in the encomiastic stanzas known as *Il pianto d'Italia* (*Lament of Italy*, 1617), dedicated to Carlo Emanuele I of Savoy, Fulvio Testi sketched a model of sublimity for his age. The rhetorical vigour that appears alongside the Horatian ideal of moderation *(medietas)*, even in the gnomic sections, indicates a longing for a heroic past. It is also worth mentioning that Chiabrera's interest in Greek → MUSIC provided a new understanding of the relation between music and poetry, thereby making an essential contribution to the 'birth of the'' → OPERA ' in the Florentine circle.

Whereas the reference to the ancient Classics in lyric poetry was primarily aimed at a revival of style in the context of the polemics directed against Marino, the real field of confrontation with ancient literature was represented especially by → Tragedy and the epic, which the Aristotelian-influenced poetics of the 16th cent. acknowledged as the genres *par excellence*. To be sure, these genres were present in the cultural consciousness as literary ideals, but they were, for various reasons, undergoing a period of crisis. The strict form of tragedy struggled to find a position between the extremes of the *commedia dell'arte* and the melodrama (*melodramma*), which, moreover, drew upon Greek myth with the lack of inhibition characteristic of the Baroque. Thus, in the 1649 libretto *Giasone* by Giacinto Andrea Cicognini, the tragic material of the *Medea* was transformed into an inextricable burlesque. The replacement of the Classical motif of fate by the problem of the reason of state dictated the choice of political and military subjects, while the hegemony of Catholicism and the Jesuit theatre demanded a Christian interpretation and accentuation of the play's conclusion. The eclecticism that was habitual at this time encouraged the transition from historical to mythological and from Biblical to contemporary themes. Prospero Bonarelli wrote the historical tragedy *Solimano* (1620), while in Giovanni Delfino's plays *Cleopatra*, *Lucrezia*, *Creso*, and *Medoro,* references to ancient history alternate with courtly tradition.

In the works of the two greatest Italian tragedians of the 17th cent., Federico Della Valle (1560–1628) and Carlo De' Dottori (1618–1688), the representation of the negative exercise of power and the inevitable march of fate bear witness to the strong influence of Seneca's tragedies. Della Valle was the author of *Adelonda di Frigia* (1595), a drama with musical intermezzi which was a modern version of Euripides' *Iphigenia in Taurus*. He also wrote two tragedies with happy endings and Biblical themes, *Esther* and *Judith* (1627), and one whose subject was taken from contemporary history, *Reina di Scotia* ('the queen of Scotland', 1595, ²1628). Unlike more traditionally-oriented plays of intrigue, the emphasis in these works was on the emphatic opposition between the corrupt court and a heroic female figure, with the contrast being underlined by the unity of place and time. Carlo De' Dottori's *Aristodemo* (1657), on the other hand, was constructed according to the standard pattern of a play of intrigue, characterised by a complicated plot and dramatic tension. In a letter to Ciro di Pers of March 16, 1624, he cited as his models Euripides and above all Seneca, whose mistrust of the sublimity of human sacrifice and whose perception of the irrationality of fate and the meaninglessness of suffering he adopted with pathetic exaggeration. Seneca's *Oedipus* was the model for the *Edipo* (1661) by Emanuele Tesauro (1592–1675). Tesauro, an extremely versatile author, adopted the central conceit of Seneca's play and strengthened it by emphasising the theme of unconscious sin and the irrational feeling of guilt associated with power as a source of evil. In addition, he made a striking departure from the original by hinting at Antigone's hidden passion for Oedipus prior to the revelation of the actual incest of Oedipus and Iocaste. He thus exhibited the tendency, typical of the → Baroque, of doubling motifs and of establishing the same motif in different contexts.

In the epic, reference to ancient generic paradigms was more of an ambitious claim than it was an actual source of inspiration. After the failed attempt of the 16th cent. to establish a programmatic link to Homer in Giangiorgio Trissino's (1478–1550) *Italia liberata dai Goti* ('Italy Liberated from the Goths'), 17th cent. poetry tended, once the author's moral and pedagogical intentions and his scrupulous observance of Aristotelian prescripts concerning the unity of action had been announced in the prooemium, toward variegated courses of action that ignored the rules. These plots derived from a mixture of allusions to the ancient Classics

and from the repertoire of the courtly romance, which, although quite controversial, was still present. Compared to their Greek and Latin models, the topic of love became increasingly common. In the *Iliad*, Helena and Briseis appeared rather on the margins of the story, and even the conjugal love of Hector and Andromache was granted little space, while in Virgil's *Aeneid* the Dido episode was more of a self-contained tragedy than a developmental phase of the overall story. In the epics of the 16th–17th cent., by contrast, the interweaving of amorous relations and the themes of war became a constant feature of the content. Thus, for instance, there was room for the hero's seduction by pagan sorceresses, or the love between the members of hostile parties, or even the simultaneous heroic death of pairs of lovers on the field of battle.

Modern elements were also to be found alongside the appeal to the ancient Classics. The characters' behaviour was determined both by contemporary moral concepts and the rules of verisimilitude; in other words, Homeric 'excess' was pruned back in every respect. Contemporary political topics, modern military technology and geographical discoveries found their place, with the Classicist program of seriousness being combined with pride in the achievements of modernity. The supernatural elements of pagan mythology were replaced by Christian ones. The pagan gods, who, guided by their emotions, had intervened in the action and taken sides, gave way to the less overt, but lasting and unfailing supervision by God, as the symbol of the Catholic world order and of Christian providence. The emphasis on scenes of struggle and death, which echoed Lucan, can be considered signs of the instability of contemporary values. The blending of various sources and models was almost unavoidable: even in poems such as Francesco Bracciolini's *La croce riacquistata* ('The Reconquered Cross", 1611), Lucrezia Marinella's *L'Enrico o Bisanzio acquistato* ('Henry or Byzantium Conquered', 1635) and Nicola Villani's *La Fiorenza difesa* ('Florence Defended', 1641), in which contamination by motifs from the romance was rejected, noble deeds of war were eulogised, and a lofty style was maintained, one finds lapses into the lyric-pathetic or the extraordinary-bizarre, albeit to a lesser extent, in correspondence with contemporary taste. Their quotes from Homer and Virgil, even when they occasionally represent a verbatim resumption, were further complicated by the fact that they must always be read in conjunction with the model of the modern epic, Torquato Tasso's (1544–1595) *La Gerusalemme liberata* ('Jerusalem Liberated').

However, the weakening of the epic tradition as a result of this interference of literary models also sparked some innovations, such as Giambattista Marino's eccentric text *Adone*, and even the emergence of the new genre of the comic-heroic poem, based on the dismantling of the epic. Yet even these new developments also partially continued the Classical legacy, in order to demonstrate that modernity could assert itself in the face of Antiquity, which it had no need to constantly emulate, imitate, or appropriate. This gave rise to an impatience that has rightly been qualified as Oedipal, which pushed for the overcoming of Antiquity, while at the same time insisting on independence from it. Marino's *Adone* (1623), a poem that was not only antiheroic but also anti-narrative, showed that there could be no reduction to the canonical authors in its new relation to Antiquity. It enriched the individual songs with the insertion of difficult citations, which represented a challenge to the reader. Above all, it referred back to authors who could not be considered among the classics of the epic genre: Nonnus and Ovid were preferred to Homer or Virgil. The entire work was influenced by Ovid's *Metamorphoses*. The mythological narratives, in particular, stem from Ovid; they interrupt the plot and have as their content a tragic metamorphosis or a sudden reversal from joy to sorrow. The comic-heroic poems, which continued the ancient model of the pseudo-Homeric *Batrachomyomachia*, referred explicitly to the models chosen by the epic genre, exposing its topics and formulas to their derision. Francesco Bracciolini's (1566–1645) *Lo scherno degli dei* ('The Mockery of the Gods, 1618) does not so much mock the Classic authors, as it does their excessive recourse to ancient mythology. Although the heroic values in Alessandro Tassoni's (1556–1635) *Secchia rapita* ('The Stolen Bukket, 1622) are derisively qualified as no longer current, the epic model still represented a solid structural basis for his work; the *Iliad* is alluded to at the beginning, with Helen being replaced by the bucket. Alongside the comic-heroic poem was the travesty, a more or less playful adaptation of the Classics. The most famous Italian example, Giovan Battista Lalli's (1572–1637) *L'Eneide travestita* ('The Aeneid in Disguise', 1634, which gave its name to the travesty), weakens the solemnity of Virgil's epic through anachronisms and the distortion of language, yet by stopping short of aggressive derision, it achieves a balance between clever variations and the undisputed prestige of the Classical work.

The Baroque romance, with its tendency to replace the epic by the narration of heroic deeds and the declaration of its elevated intentions, had particular recourse to the ancient imperial romance, insofar as it hybridised various models. Giovan Francesco Biondi's (1572–1644) *L'Eromena* (1624), *La donzella desterrada* (1627), *Il Coralbo* (1632), and Giovanni Ambrosio Marini's (1594–1650) *Il Calloandro fedele* (1653) provided more complicated and convoluted versions of the sentimental-adventurous model of Achilles Tatius' *Leucippe and Clitophon* and Heliodorus' *Aethiopica*. To illustrate the increasingly more frequent blends of genres, with their clear deviations from poetological norms, it is interesting to note that Marini's novel itself was rewritten in verse by Giambattista Basile under the title *Il Teagene* (1637). While this work seemed to appropriate the outward characteristics of the epic, it still preserved the polyphonic form of the original.

B. The 18th Century

Reference to the Classics remained a constant feature throughout the 18th cent. in I., assuming a variety of forms. The literary → ACADEMY of Arcadia, founded in 1690 with the declared aim of practicing poetry modelled on Greek → Bucolics and the Latin → ELEGY, preached a restoration of Classical formal and intellectual clarity, as a reaction to the experimental boldness and inventiveness of the Baroque. It was manifested in various forms, for instance in the moderate program of Giovan Mario Crescimbeni (1663–1728), or the strict adherence to rules recommended by Gian Vincenzo Gravina (1664–1718). The latter had first attempted to lend the *favole antiche* a noble ethical-civic function, but had subsequently retreated to a Classicism that was contemptuous of its own time. With its glamorous form and its flight into fictive idyllic landscapes, the allegorical pastoral poetry of Giovan Battista Zappi (1667–1719), Faustina Maratti Zappi (1680–1745) and Carlo Innocenzo Frugoni (1692–1786), a representative of Anacreontic verse (→ ANACREONTIC POETRY, ANACREONTICA) who produced several variations on the models established by Chiabrera, reflected the stability of the courtly society of the time. The Enlightenment thought that subsequently prevailed, usually in the form of a dichotomy between dialectics and rhetoric or practical eloquence, tended towards a careful compromise between enthusiasm for new contents and the elegance of lofty and erudite forms. Neo-Classicism, which became dominant in the second half of the 18th cent., beginning with Winckelmann's archaeological discoveries and reflections, inclined more toward the restoration of a sublime and superior culture than to a strict imitation of Antiquity, and was laden with moral ideals that were often associated with plans for social reforms.

With their moralising tone, Gasparo Gozzi's (1720–1806) *Sermoni* ('Conversations', 1763) followed Horace's *Satires* (*Sermones*). The balance between Classical culture and interest in the natural sciences and useful information, evident in the works of Saverio Bettinelli (1718–1808) and Francesco Algarotti (1712–1764), led to the joint publication with Carlo Innocenzo Frugoni of the *Versi sciolti di tre moderni eccellenti autori* ('Loose Verses by Three Outstanding Modern Poets', 1757). The renunciation of rhyme was an expression of the abandonment of the artificial, musical character of poetry in favour of greater communicative potential, which nevertheless gained in prestige through its pedagogical claims. In contrast, Ludovico Savioli Fontana (1729–1804), who produced Rococo-style variations on Classicism, turned away from the poetics of *utile dulci*, or the conveying of useful ideas in a pleasant form. He returned to Ovid's *Amores* in his own *Amori* (1758), a collection of odes with a mythological glossary, while in his drama *Achille* (1761), he added a tender, humane dimension to the ancient myth by having Achilles' love for Polyxena returned by a hidden, timid longing on the part of the girl. The best-known example of the attempt to create a balance between enthusiasm for contemporary themes and a polished poetic language is clearly offered in the works of Giuseppe Parini (1729–1799), especially the two published parts of his epic *Il Giorno* ('The Day'), entitled *Il Mattino* ('The Morning", 1763) and *Il Mezzogiorno* ('Noon', 1765). Here, Virgil was clearly the model, in two respects. The poem is based primarily on the genre of the didactic poem founded by Virgil's *Georgica*. Parini altered his model in a parodic way, but alluded to it clearly, through such techniques as learned syntax, rich in anastrophes and hyperbata, mythological periphrases, aetiological myths, apostrophes, and pareneses. In addition to the Latin paradigm, he also alluded to modern forms of → Didactic poetry, from the 16th-cent. verse of Alamanni and Rucellai to such 18th-cent. works as Zaccaria Betti's *Il baco da seta* ('The Silkworm', 1756) and Gian Battista Spolverini's *La coltivazione del riso* ('The Cultivation of Rice', 1758). Parini's metre, the free hendecasyllable, also conformed to the norms of the genre. There were also elements taken from the comic-heroic poem, reminiscent of anti-aristocratic satire in their clever and paradoxical distortions of the solemn iterata, anaphora, and addresses of Virgil's *Aeneid*, often influenced by Antonio Conti's translation of Alexander Pope's (1688–1744) *Rape of the Lock* (1712).

Although the demand for new contents and subjects often contributed towards the creation of new disciplines, the tradition of scholarly treatises nevertheless continued. They included the comprehensive works by Crescimbeni, Gravina and Quadrio, which conformed to the Aristotelian system in their division into genres according to a strict hierarchy. Many writers of the time adhered to the genres that had been legitimised by tradition. The gap left by the henceforth definitive weakness of epic poetry was filled by the rediscovery of the great Classics, above all Homer, who became a focal point of interest. In his *Scienza nuova* ('New Science', 1725), Giambattista Vico (1668–1744) made him a symbol of the heroic, original dawn of time. Various translations were made, of which Melchiorre Cesarotti's (1730–1808) two versions of a translation of the *Iliad* are worthy of mention. The first was literal and in prose, the second, entitled *La morte di Ettore* ('The Death of Hector', 1795), was a free verse translation.

Since the epic no longer represented a poetic challenge, tragedy became the area in which the will to reclaim Antiquity, as advocated by the poetology of Arcadia, showed its effects. The imitation of 17th-cent. French theatre yielded to a direct resumption of Greek models. However, the goal of reviving tragic emphasis, tragic pathos and the tragic claim to absoluteness stood in clear contradiction to the increasing tendency toward *medietas*, that is, toward milder, more moderate tones, or to a sentimental-maudlin pathos which would eventually help bourgeois drama to achieve its breakthrough. The ever-increasing difficulty of actualising in a plausible way the conception of the inevitability of fate that was inherent in Greek tragedy ran the risk of making catastrophe fail to appear as the logical consequence of the course of action, thereby destroying the canonical structure of tragedy. The tension between veneration of Antiquity and the gradual emergence of modernity resulted in various reactions, ranging from a complete retreat to tradition to attempts at compromise. Gian Vincenzo Gravina's (1664–1718) five tragedies of 1712 (*Palamede*, *Andromeda*, *Appio Claudio*, *Papiniano*, *Servio Tullio*), though not highly successful, attest to the period of his strictest Classicism. Such pre-Enlightenment themes as the exposure of clerical hypocrisy were clad in an archaising, dignified style, characterised by a plethora of Latinisms. The attempts by extreme Aristotelians at a revival of Antiquity proved not only unsuccessful, but also downright ridiculous; they sought to compensate for the catastrophe's lack of logical necessity by a multiplication of its consequences and a strong emphasis on cruelty. In his *L'Ulisse il Giovane* ('Young Odysseus', 1720), Domenico Lazzarini (1668–1734), a professor of Greek and Latin, completely transformed the story of Oedipus: the hero kills his son and marries his own daughter. This strange adaptation of the myth, already condemned by his contemporaries, inspired Zaccaria Valaresso to produce a witty parody, *Rutzvanscad il Giovine* ('Young Rutzvanscad', 1724) whose paradoxical plot – the hero marries his grandmother – showcased the risk of exclusive fixation on familiar ancient material. Pier Jacopo Martello (1665–1727) was more innovative. He began by replacing the hendecasyllable with a distich consisting of four septenarii in rhyming couplets, an imitation of the Alexandrine which was called the *martelliano* after him. In his view, it was impossible to fall back exclusively on the prescriptions of the Aristotelian *Poetics*. He assimilated mythological subjects to the criteria of logic and verisimilitude. His preference for the rare tragic material that features a happy ending was notable. Like their Euripidean models, *Ifigenia in Tauris* ('Iphigenia in Taurus') and *Elena casta* ('Chaste Helen') oscillate between tragedy and tragicomedy. The sobriety of the events represented allows concentration on psychological interpretation, enabling a sympathetic and at the same time sobering view of human modes of behaviour, and finally making room for a modest comic realism. In *L'Edipo tiranno* ('King Oedipus', 1720) one finds alongside the emphasis on a just and dignified reign, which can be traced back to Sophocles, an equally justified interest in the emotional dimension: the passion that joins Oedipus to Jocaste, and the feelings of guilt that torment them from the beginning, but which are not explained until the end. Martello's attempt to revive literary tragedy and make it accessible to his contemporaries is expressed in colloquial escapades, and ultimately stands in blatant contradiction to his claim of recapturing Classical solemnity and sublimity.

Much greater was the success achieved by Scipione Maffei (1675–1755) with his *Merope* (1713), inspired by the material of Euripides' *Cresphontes*, extant only in fragments. Long considered as the masterpiece of 18th-cent. tragic theatre, it was imitated by Voltaire, among others. The play is a successful reconciliation between the demand for preserving the sublime nature of ancient drama and making allowances for modern feelings.

Vittorio Alfieri (1749–1803) distinguished himself among 18th-cent. Italian playwrights by the most original confrontation with the ancient Classics, which he knew through the French translation by Brumoy, *Théâtre des Grecs*, through Routro and from Voltaire's plays and Seneca's tragedies. Direct contact with Greek theatre came only very late in his career. In addition to a new *Merope* (1782), he also wrote two diptychs inspired by well-known ancient myths, *Polinice* and *Antigone* (1775/76), as well as *Agamennone* and *Oreste* (1778/1781). Alfieri translated Euripides' *Alcestis* (*Alceste prima*) from Latin, making use of the knowledge of the Greek texts he had acquired in the meantime, and then adapted the play in his *Alceste seconda* (1797/98), which, however, ranks among his weakest works. His best-known tragedy, *Mirra* (1784–1786), is based on the story told in Ovid's *Metamorphoses* (10, 298–514). Alfieri was not primarily concerned by the intricacies of the plot. Instead, he used a variety of means to focus attention on the tension between an individual and the forces governing him in the configurations known from myths. The conflict could take the form of passionate love or an insatiable lust for power, in which both tyrant and rebel are subject to the same agonizing logic of power. This tension, overcome by reality which it nevertheless attempts to overcome in its turn, is internalised by the hero and ultimately destroys him, thereby contributing at least partially to a restoration of ancient Greek tragedy's claim to absoluteness. Alfieri traced the feeling of hopelessness and of defencelessness, which in Greek tragedy stems from the relationship between man and the divinity, back to the darkest and deepest roots of the soul. The thoughts and impressions sometimes anticipate 20th-cent. psychoanalytical discoveries and reinterpretations of Greek mythology. In the *Agamennone*, both Clytemnestra and Aegisthus are obsessed and overcome by injustices suffered in the past. Their crime cannot eradicate these feelings, as becomes clear from the helplessness and distress that torments them at the end of the tragedy, thus foreshadowing the gloomy conclusion of the *Oreste*. In *Polinice* and *Antigone*, the usual confrontation between a tyrant and a heroic martyr of freedom conceals more secret driving forces: Eteocles' profound hatred for his brother appears to stem from his perception of Polynices as a disturbing double. Antigone's steadfast insistence on her right to bury her brother contains erotic undertones, and it is no coincidence that instead of Ismene, as in Sophocles' play, it is Polynices' widow Argia, a character familiar from Statius' *Thebaid*, who stands beside the heroine. In his *Mirra*, Alfieri adopts only the incest motif from Ovid's *Metamorphoses*,

stopping short of its actual realisation, and concentrates the action on the heroine's all-consuming but unsuccessful attempt to suppress her feelings, which has led to comparisons with Racine's *Phèdre*. This can be cited as strong evidence of Alfieri's tendency to characterise his tragic world by the same insularity and inevitability that is featured in Greek tragedies, although he replaced fate with an inescapable psychological drive.

This use of the mythical repertoire, which must be called downright obsessive, lasted until the end of the century. Melodrama drew upon it as well, insofar as it undertook reinterpretations of ancient myths that corresponded to the dominant erotic theme of the genre, as for instance in Pietro Metastasio's *Didone abbandonata* (1724) and *Orfeo ed Euridice* (1762), or in Ranieri Calzabigi's *Alceste* (1767) and *Paride ed Elena* (1770). The last adaptations of ancient tragedies include, in addition to such insipid works such as Carlo Alberghetti Forciroli's (1797) *Edipo*, the early works of Ugo Foscolo (1778–1827) dating from 1796, *Tieste* and *Edippo*. The latter is a still-unpublished version of Sophocles' *Oedipus at Colonus*, only recently attributed to Foscolo, in which early signs of the Romantic historical drama can already be detected within the Classical framework.

The Neo-Classical fashion also infected the novel, a genre that followed no fixed poetological rules, and whose development in 18th-cent. I. progressed only slowly, and not without borrowings from other genres. After a youthful phase of uncompromising, nonconformist thinking under the influence of Enlightenment thought, Alessandro Verri (1741–1816) turned to the Classical tradition, with such works as a prose version of the *Iliad* (1770/71). Against the clumsy, contemporary imitations of successful new English and French novels, he opposed his own works, rooted in Antiquity: *Le avventure di Saffo, poetessa di Mitilene* ('The Adventures of Sappho, Poetess of Mytilene', 1782), *Le notti romane al sepolcro degli Scipioni* ('Roman Nights at the Tomb of the Scipios', 1792–1804) and *La vita di Erostrato* ('The Life of Herostratus', 1815). *Le avventure di Saffo* is marked by a hybridisation with pre-Romantic ideas, as is typical of Neo-Classicism. The plot is based on the story of the hopeless and unrequited love of the poetess Sappho for Phaon; the literary model is the 15th letter of Ovid's *Heroides*. The themes of disappointed passion, of the empathy between the heroine and the landscape, as well as of suicide, are also present in a similar way in other contemporary works, primarily in Rousseau's *Nouvelle Héloïse* and in Goethe's *Werther*. This can be regarded as further proof that the link with Antiquity had emancipated itself from the restrictive fetters of sets of rules and prescriptions for literary genres. It was thus no longer understood as an educational program of learned imitation, but as a combination of heterogeneous approaches and as a free search for 'original' beauty, clarity and greatness.

→ Arcadianism; → Epic; → Imitatio
→ Lucanus; → Nonnus; → Seneca

1 A. Buck, Forschungen zur romanischen Barockliteratur, 1980 2 M. Hardt, Geschichte der italienischen Literatur, 1996 3 V. Kapp (ed.), Italienische Literaturgeschichte, 1992 4 K. D. Schreiber, Untersuchungen zur italienischen Literatur- und Kulturgeschichtsschreibung in der zweiten Hälfte des Settecento, 1968

Additional Bibliography W. Heller, Emblems of Eloquence: Opera and Women's Voices in Seventeenth-Century Venice, 2003 CLOTILDE BERTONI

V. 1800 TO THE PRESENT
A. The 19th Century B. The 20th Century

A. The 19th Century

Italian culture of the beginning of the 19th cent. was dominated by a strict Classicism with antiquarian tendencies, which was opposed by a moderate and relatively undeveloped Romantic movement. The polemic between Classicists and Romantics, which dominated academic and intellectual life at every level, turned primarily around the validity of the Aristotelian poetological rules and the use of ancient myths, which the Romantics regarded as superfluous, irreligious and irrational. This polemic could scarcely have occurred in the context of European → Romanticism, where it was precisely the investigation of ancient → Myth that played an important role. Neo-Classicism as the cult of the poetic word and of mythological ornamentation was particularly represented by Vincenzo Monti (1754–1828), whose works included *Sermone sulla mitologia* ('Discourse on Mythology', 1825). Of his extensive and many-sided occasional writings, the translation of the *Iliad* in free hendecasyllables (*Iliade*, 1810, in several revisions) is still known today. Together with Ippolito Pindemonte's translation of the *Odyssey* (*Odissea*, 1822), it remained a fixture of Italian school education until a few decades ago.

The most important figure of this transitional period was Ugo Foscolo (1778–1827). He laid claim to a direct relationship with Classical Antiquity by frequently bringing up the biographical datum that he was born of a Greek mother on the Greek island of Zakynthos, then under Venetian rule. In one of his earliest critical works, *Commento alla Chioma di Berenice* ('Commentary on the Lock of Berenice', 1803), Foscolo defined poetry as the conjunction of contemporary passions and mythical dimensions. In fact, his entire work oscillated between a strong autobiographical orientation and its transfiguration into the ideal of Classical beauty. From his earliest poetic attempts, Foscolo's poetry developed in an intensive, creative intertextual dialogue with the ancient models. The lyrical tone of the sonnets was permeated with allusions to Virgil, Tibullus and Propertius, while the new versions of Greek poems (for instance of Callimachus, in the *Inno alla nave delle Muse*, 'Hymn to the Ship of the Muses') are even more obviously indebted to their models. In his best known work, the poem *Dei sepolcri* ('From the Graves', 1807), Foscolo takes up the deeper tones of the *Iliad* that run counter to the theme of war: the undifferentiated equality of victors and losers in the face of the common fate of death. Although he failed in his attempt at a political revival of Greek tragedy – the fiasco of his *Aiace* at the Milan Scala in 1811 is well known – his last unfinished work, the hymns *Le Grazie* ('The Graces', 1803–1822, published in 1848), mark the zenith of an Alexandrine poetics which attributes the power of bestowing immortality to poetic recollection or to literary memory. The fragmentary and unsystematic sequence is reminiscent of both Callimachus and L. Sterne. The *Sepolcri* also contain a remarkably erudite reference to the Hellenistic poet and philologist Lycophron of Chalcis.

Antonio Canova (1757–1822), to whom Foscolo dedicated his *Grazie*, was the most important representative of Neo-Classicism in the field of the fine arts. After beginning with sculptures indebted to ancient mythology and to Bernini, he strove increasingly for an ever-greater geometrical and symmetrical simplification of forms by specialising in themes of mourning, influenced in their turn by Foscolo. The high point of his Neo-Classicism were the statues of Napoleon as *Marte pacificatore* (1803–1806) and of Paolina Borghese Bonaparte as *Venere vincitrice* (1804–1808), and most of all the sensual, sophisticated arabesque of the group of the Graces (1812–1816). His encounter with the marble works of Pheidias in the → Parthenon in 1815 provided the occasion for a revision and reorientation of his own poetics toward greater archaisation. Also noteworthy is his commitment to the preservation of the Italian cultural heritage, as manifested *inter alia* in his role as Inspector for 'Antiquities and Fine Arts' (1802). In the context of Roman Neo-Classicism, mention should also be made of the painter Vincenzo Camuccini and the architect, town planner and archaeologist Giuseppe Valadier, while from the field of Milanese Neo-Classicism, the extensive urbanistic activity of the architect Luigi Cagnola should be emphasised.

The relationship with Classical sculpture is a consistent theme throughout the poetics of the most important 19th-cent. Italian author, Giacomo Leopardi (1798–1837). He is even more difficult than Foscolo to assign to a literary movement, although he had adopted a clearly anti-Romantic stance. According to one scholarly view, his poetry belonged to genuine European Romanticism, whereas others see his work as marked by an Enlightenment or materialistic Classicism, which still remained alive throughout 19th-cent. Italian culture. Leopardi grew up in the provincial atmosphere of the small, central Italian town of Recanati, part of the Papal States, and was educated in the good-sized library of his father Monaldo, which was rich in scholarly works. Even in the first poetic attempts of his childhood, at about the same time that he translated Hesiod, Moschus, the first song of the *Odyssey* and the *Batrachomyomachia*, he busied himself with imitations of the Greek and Latin Classics, above all Virgil. These playful attempts rapidly developed into a complex, intertextual engagement with ancient literature, which ran parallel to his philological, erudite work and to the theoretical reflections of his work entitled *Zibaldone*, an unsystematic collection of ideas. Leopardi's aesthetic was shaped by the 18th cent., above all by Rousseau. He had a particular penchant for Homer's originality, which he considered to be perfectly natural and prior to any kind of poetic rules, while he prized Alexandrine poetry for its pithyness and refinement of expression. He also admired these same traits in the Augustan poets, although he criticised their entanglement with power. His favourite among these poets was Virgil. In Horace, he admired the poetic technique, which nevertheless lacked genuine inspiration, while he rejected Ovid's overly analytical and descriptive style. In his own poetry, these judgments found expression in a preference for those literary techniques which convey an impression of indeterminacy and infinity, such as difficult junctures, enjambment and polysemy, often taken directly from ancient and modern classics. After an initial phase under the influence of Rousseau, in which he praised Antiquity as the happy childhood of a humanity still close to its natural condition, and contrasted it with the disaster of modernity, Leopardi's view transformed into a radical nihilism which saw nature as a negative factor, opposing man like a hostile stepmother. This second phase, usually designated as 'cosmic pessimism', was represented in literature by the satirical dialogues *Operette morali* ('Little Moral Works'), which had their immediate model in the work of Lucian of Samosata. Moreover, Leopardi always had a satirical and parodic streak, clearly evident in his three translations of the *Batrachomyomachia* and in the *Paralipomeni alla Batracomiomachia* ('Supplements to the Batrachomyomachia'), a heroic-comic poem rich in political satire.

Italian Romanticism found its fullest and most popular expression in → Music, in the → Operas by Donizetti, Bellini and above all Verdi. Romantic melodrama dealt only with Biblical or historical themes (especially of the Middle Ages). Noteworthy among the last neoclassical mythological works are *Medea in Corinto* (1813) and *Fedra* (1820) by Simone Mayr (Donizetti's Italo-German teacher). By contrast, an anti-classicist and anti-mythological choice of themes are found in the two most flourishing literary genres of the 19th cent., → Tragedy and the historical novel. Alessandro Manzoni (1785–1873), the second great literary personality of the 19th cent. alongside Leopardi, concerned himself both theoretically and practically with both these fields. The plot structure of the Greek novel is still discernible behind his masterpiece, *I promessi sposi* ('The Betrothed', 1825/26), albeit through the intermediary of the Baroque novel. The historical atmosphere did not, however, imply 'a priori' the complete exclusion of Greco-Roman Antiquity. One might point, for instance, to the homoerotic novel *I neoplatonici* ('The Neoplatonists', published posthumously in 1977) by Luigi Settembrini (1813–1876), a patriot and man of letters who also wrote a literarily successful translation of Lucian

(1861), or to the tragedies of Pietro Cossa (*Nerone*, 1871; *Messalina*, 1876).

Parallel developments can be observed in Romantic painting, which in I. experienced a delayed and modest dissemination in comparison to literature. The career of Francesco Hayez (1791–1882) is significant in this regard. From a late Neo-Classicism under the aegis of Canova (*Ulisse alla corte di Alcinoo*, 'Odysseus at the Court of Alcinous', 1816), he became the most important representative of historical Romantic painting, in strong agreement with the world of Manzoni.

The second generation of Romantic writers abandoned any kind of polemic against Classicism. They now dedicated themselves to a maudlin and mawkish poetry in which mythological figures could also reappear as an expression of pure escapism, as for instance in Giovanni Prati's (1814–1884) collections *Psiche* ('Psyche', 1876) and *Iside* ('Isis', 1878). It was just such a mawkish, degrading view of Romanticism that inspired the fulminations of Giosuè Carducci (1835–1907), the most important poet of young, united I. The first phase of his literary production, emphatically Jacobin and Republican, returned to the model, created by Tyrtaeus, of the poet as seer and culminated in the collection of *Giambi ed Epodi* ('Iambs and Epodes'), reminiscent of Horace, in which Classical Antiquity was instrumentalised as a means in the fight against tyranny. After his committment to the monarchy and his full integration into the political system as a senator in Crispi's I., he followed a concept, stemming from Winckelmann, of → Greece as a place of of cheerful, perfect beauty, which culminated in his *Primavere elleniche* ('Greek Springs', in *Rime nuove*, 1887). The work is rich with echoes of German poetry (Goethe, Schiller, Heine and also Hölderlin. whose *Griechenland* he translated in 1874) and of ancient lyric poetry. Carducci wanted to go back directly to ancient Greece (Sappho and Alcaeus), but was of course under the intermediary influence of Horace and Latin poetry. Also noteworthy are his two collections of *Odi barbare* ('Barbaric Songs', 1877 and 1889), in which he attempted to reconstitute the rhythm of ancient lyric verse.

Carducci, who taught Italian rhetoric and literature at the University of Bologna almost all his adult life, was also active as a critic and disseminator of Classical authors, at a time when Casati's reform of 1859 had turned Classical education into one of the focal points of the state educational system. Not until the second half of the 19th cent. can one speak of Classical philology as a unified historical discipline in I., which, following in the footsteps of German studies of Antiquity, began to develop with a considerable interest in Greek literature. Suffice it here to point to the many-sided activity of Domenico Comparetti (1835–1927). For the beginning of the 19th cent., one can adduce only Amedeo Peyron, a papyrologist and Thucydides scholar. After centuries of glorification of Latin-Roman culture, there now began in I. as well a tendency to acknowledge and investigate pre-Roman civilisations, above all the Etruscans, as for instance in the studies of Giuseppe Micali.

Between the end of the 19th and the beginning of the 20th cent., a pagan mode of approaching the ancient world was opened up by the aesthetics of → DÉCA-DENCE, in which Greek culture assumed a prominent role. Strongly influenced by Nietzsche's idea of the Dionysian and of the *Übermensch*, the prolific literary output of Gabriele D'Annunzio (1863–1938) was permeated by references to Classical mythology and literature. Pan in particular played a prominent role as the symbol of an all-embracing sensuality, as did Odysseus as the symbol of perfect vitality. The poetry collections *Maia*, *Elettra* and *Alcyone* (1903), in particular, as well as the tragedy *Fedra* (1909) are interwoven with intertextual references to Antiquity. In *Fedra*, the 'barbarian', wild passion of the heroine is brought, together with other mythical figures also borrowed from Euripidean tragedy, into a complex dramatic context. D'Annunzio also collaborated on Giovanni Pastrone's film *Cabiria* (1914), one of the first historical films on Rome, in which history was mixed with fantastic elements and the language was pompous and rich in neologisms.

It is precisely the myth of Odysseus that makes it possible to identify the clear differences between the poetics of D'Annunzio and that of Giovanni Pascoli (1855–1912), another great writer of the Italian *Décadence*. In his *Poemi conviviali* ('Dinner Poems', 1904) Pascoli gives a negative representation of this mythic figure, as the embodiment of the agonising impossibility of a perfect experience. After a collection of poems with the Virgilian title *Myricae* (1891), which turned on the subjects of nature and landscape, Pascoli later experimented with different registers, characterised by a regression to childhood (as in the well known poem *Fanciullino*, 'Boy') and a playful approach to language, which in turn contained many onomatopoetic expressions, technical terms and Latinisms. His sophisticated works inspired by the late ancient world and written in Latin (including *Centurio*, 1901; *Pomponia Graecina*, 1909; *Thalussa*, 1911) tend in a comparable direction. Two anthologies with commentaries were also dedicated to Latin poetry (*Lyra*, 1895; *Epos*, 1897), in which he displayed a critical sensitivity for the texts which must be called virtually impressionistic.

B. THE 20TH CENTURY

Italian poetry of the early 20th cent. stood in marked opposition to the aesthetics of *Décadence*, with which it nevertheless maintained a twofold connection. In the search for the essential and the fragmentary, which dominated Hermeticism and its associated currents, recourse to the Classical tradition could only occur through cryptic allusions. In the works of Eugenio Montale (1896–1981), the most important Italian poet of this century, one can observe such Classical topoi as the *recusatio* and echoes of Horace, e.g. of his Ode to Leuconoe 1,11 in *La casa dei doganieri* ('The House of

the Customs Officers', 1930). These, however, must always be interpreted conversely, as a reference to Montale's poetics of the irretrievability of memory. In the late phase of his lyric poetry, by contrast, beginning with *Satura* (1971), Montale employed a satiric register directly reminiscent of diatribe. Similar observations hold true of Giuseppe Ungaretti (1888–1970), the other great literary personality of this time, who continued Vergilian themes via a detour into the investigation of the emotional expressive force of the word in *Terra promessa* ('Promised Land', 1950). Virgil was also taken up once again by authors of the following generations, such as Andrea Zanzotto (1921–), who dared to undertake remarkable linguistic experiments (*IX Ecloghe*, 1962). In contrast, Greece was important in the literary creativity of Salvatore Quasimodo (1901–1968), both in relation to the mythology of his birthplace Sicily and particularly in his masterpiece, the 1940 translation of Greek lyric poets. He also translated Homer, the tragedians and Virgil.

After Romantic and Naturalistic painting, which rejected Classical subjects, and the Futurist avant-garde, which denied even the idea of tradition, a more in-depth dialogue with Classical Antiquity first recommenced in Italian art with the phase of trepresented by the journal *Valori plastici*, published by Mario Broglio, on which Giorgio De Chirico (1888–1978) also collaborated. References to ancient myth are already found in his earliest works, still under the influence of Böcklin, and later above all in his metaphysical phase (*Le Muse inquietanti*, 'The Disconcerting Muses', 1916; *Ettore e Andromaca*, 'Hector and Andromache', 1917). Ancient mythology is also very much present in the works of De Chirico's brother, Alberto Savinio, who was born in Greece and educated in Munich. He showed a clear preference for the playful and grotesque handling of mythical themes, which can be discerned both in his theatrical (*Il capitan Ulisse*, 1934; *Alcesti di Samuele*; *Emma B. vedova*; *Giocasta*, 1949) and his musical productions (*Orfeo vedovo*, 1950).

Whereas reference to ancient tradition was only marginal in the avant-gardists' revolutionary frame of mind of the 1970s and 1980s (*conceptual art*, *body art*, *arte povera*), somewhat like an archetypal trace of memory, it once again became a focal point in the context of the de-familiarised return to figurativeness of the 1980s and 1990s, primarily of the Transavanguardia (Enzo Cucchi, Sandro Chia, Mimmo Palladino), which fell back upon archaic stylistic elements.

20th-cent. Italian music, in its various phases and trends, was permeated with resumptions of Antiquity. The beginning can be seen in the generation of the 1880s, who had made it their goal to reestablish Italian music in the European context by entering into dialogue with Stravinsky's Neo-Classicism and returning to Renaissance and Gregorian stylistic elements. Among the most important names in this context are Ildebrando Pizzetti, a friend of D'Annunzio, who made a musical adaptation of *Fedra* (1915) for him, and wrote a *Clitennestra*

(1965); he also set Leopardi's version of Sappho fragment 94 (Diehl) to music. In his trilogy *Orfeide* (1923), Gian Francesco Malipiero made clear references to Antiquity; he also wrote *Ecuba* (1941). Giorgio Federico Ghedini was the author of *Le Baccanti* (1948). There were also other composers who were more interested in instrumental music, such as Alfredo Casella (*La favola di Orfeo*, 1932) or Ottorino Respighi, who continued German romanticism (*I Persiani*, 1900; *La fiamma*, 1934, which takes place in a Byzantine setting). Ancient mythology, brought back into public awareness in this century thanks to Freud, also appeared in the last posthumously published work of a protagonist of the period of Verismo (*Edipo re* by Ruggero Leoncavallo, 1916), while Vittorio Gnecchi's *Cassandra* (1905) is remembered primarily because of the plagiarism controversy with Hofmannsthal-Strauss.

The music of the second half of the 20th cent., which followed Weber and tended toward experimentation, showed a strong intertextual link with the Classics. Between 1942 and 1945, Luigi Dallapiccola, the master of Italian twelve-tone music, set to music the poetry of Sappho, Alcaeus and Anacreon, and dedicated one of his operas to a myth that has been important in this century (*Odyssee*, 1968, with texts by Homer, Aeschylus, Ovid, Dante, Pascoli, Thomas Mann and others), turning Odysseus into a symbol of the human drive for freedom and man's rebellion against the divine. Recently, Luciano Berio also adapted the same myth into an opera, albeit with a very different meaning (*Outis*, 1996, after a libretto by the Milanese Hellenist Dario del Corno). It features a metatheatrical character and a plot influenced by James Joyce, whose structure includes Odysseus' death at the hand of his son. A playful, polyphonic structure, with a text constantly based on quotations from the *Cena Trimalchionis*, underlies Bruno Maderna's *Satyricon* (1973). A completely different, speculative approximation to Antiquity is found in the work of Luigi Nono, a further protagonist of the Italian avant-garde, whose *Prometeo* (1978, compiled by Massimo Cacciari from various texts) can be described as a tragedy of listening and of silence. Also belonging to this spectrum are such representatives of the younger generation as Salvatore Sciarrino (*Amore e Psiche*, 1972; *Perseo e Andromeda*, 1991) and Adriano Guarnieri with his film opera *Medea*, 1988.

In the second half of the 20th cent., the engagement with Antiquity gained more serious poetic and ideological gravity. On the one hand, this was the result of the influence of the sciences which had been unable to develop in the years of → FASCISM (psychology, anthropology, → MARXISM), and on the other hand, of the development of such modern approaches as structuralism and semiotics. Theatre engaged Freud's Oedipus myth in various forms, and with a different critical grasp, which ranged from Roberto Zerboni's (1946) neo-realist *Edipo* to the de-familiarising transfer of the Oedipus material to a concentration camp in Alberto Moravia's *Il dio Kurt* ('Kurt the God', 1968); from Giovanni

Testori's (1977) exhilarated, Dionysian and linguistically sumptuous *Edipus* to Renzo Rosso's *Edipo. Ambigui paesaggi disadorni e senza profumo* ('Oedipus. Ambiguous Landscapes without Adornment and Fragrance', 1990). Corrado Alvaro subjected the myth of Medea to an anthropological interpretation in his *La lunga notte di Medea* ('The Long Night of Medea', 1949), in which the heroine embodies the magical culture of the south, while her infanticide is represented as an act of self-defence against the threat of lynch justice from a racist mob. Alvaro thus offered a reinterpretation of the myth that anticipated Christa Wolf's revolutionary reinterpretation. At the same time, Greek tragedies were increasingly staged in innovative ways: among many other examples, one may cite the *Orestee* by Luca Ronconi (1972) and the Societas Raffaello Sanzio (1995).

In I., Pier Paolo Pasolini (1922–1975) was the artist who most sought a dialogue with Antiquity, first as the translator of the *Oresteia*, which he interpreted as a conflict between the magico-sacral archaic civilisation and rationalist-pragmatic modern one, and later as a film director. Pasolini's interpretation of the *Oresteia* was repeated in *Orestea di Gibellina* (1983–1985) by Emilio Isgrò, a protagonist of visual poetry. The image of Antiquity that emerges from Pasolini's films, which were mythical, non-literary and highly imagistic (*Edipo re*, 1967; *Medea*, 1969; *Appunti per un'Orestiade africana*, 'Notes for an African Oresteia', 1970), is anti-Classicist and barbarian, in line with a poetics developed in the same years by Elsa Morante, who wrote an adaptation of Sophocles' *Oedipus at Colonos* (*La serata a Colono*, 'Evening at Colonos', 1968), in a manner comparable to Pasolini. Greece became the metaphor of an agrarian civilisation, the symbol of a millennia-old way of life, which was shattered by the savage modernisation of neo-capitalism, whereas a more balanced development should have worked towards harmonious assimilation. Pasolini's plays, which unlike his films have clear ideological and didactic orientation, are modelled in their structure after Greek tragedies. He adopts many of their themes, which he incorporates directly into the contemporary context, as in *Affabulazione*, a new version of the Oedipus myth from the viewpoint of Oedipus' father Laius (1966); or *Pilade*, a fictive continuation of the *Oresteia* set in contemporary I. (1967). In the final years of his life, Pasolini once again turned to the novel: in *Petronio* (the incomplete fragments of which were not published until 1992), which he himself designated as a modern *Satyricon*, he took from Petronius the fluidity of the form, the polyphonic mixture of stylistic and linguistic levels, and the prosimetric form. He also intended to include into this novel *Argonautiche*, inspired by Apollonius of Rhodes, in modern Greek; the Argonauts' voyage to the east was to symbolise colonialism and the exploitation of the Third World by the West.

Petronius' novel experienced a many-sided reception in I., if one thinks of its translation and adaptation by

Edoardo Sanguineti, a protagonist of the neo-avant-garde Gruppo '63 (Il gioco del Satyricon, 1968), or Federico Fellini's 1969 film Satyricon, which was influenced by C. G. Jung. More generally, Petronius played the role of a model for a free, playful 'Menippean' narrative art, as for instance in Alberto Arbasino's extensive works (Fratelli d'Italia, 1963; Super-Eliogabalo, 1969). In contrast, the modern revisions of the Odysseus myth, associated with the archetypal concept of a journey, point to a return to a more traditional narrative technique. In Vincenzo Consolo's L'olivo e l'olivastro ('The Cultivated and the Wild Olive Tree', 1994), Odysseus' homecoming provides the model for the narration of a journey in contemporary Sicily. In Luigi Malerba's Itaca per sempre ('Ithaca forever', 1997), the ancient myth is seen entirely from Penelope's perspective, as it is in Silvana de Santi's Penelope (1998).

In addition to Pasolini and Fellini, other representatives of the modern Italian → FILM have also taken up ancient themes in their works. Examples include Liliana Cavani in I cannibali (1969), a contemporary political adaptation of the myth of Antigone, or Paolo Benvenuti in Medea (1973) who filmed a popular production of Niccolino's 1816 play by the Maggio di Buti theatre, or recently Mario Martone's Teatro di guerra (1998), the story of a Neapolitan theatre group trying to stage Aeschylus' Seven against Thebes in Sarajevo, to represent the conflict of our time in a ritual and emotional form.

→ Diatribe; → Callimachus; → Lucian of Samosata; → Lycophron of Chalcis; → Phidias; → Tyrtaeus → ANCIENT LANGUAGES, TEACHING OF

LITERATURE   1 V. DI BENEDETTO, Lo scrittoio di Foscolo, 1990   2 R. BERTAZZOLI, Ulisse in D'Annunzio e Pascoli, in: Humanitas, 1996   3 A. BIERL, Die Orestie auf der modernen Bühne, 1997   4 M. FUSILLO, La Grecia secondo Pasolini, 1996   5 A. LA PENNA, La tradizione classica nella cultura italiana, in Storia d'Italia 5.2, 1973 6 Id., Tersite censurato, 1991   7 Leopardi e il mondo antico, 1987   8 G. PADUANO, Lunga storia di Edipo re, 1994   9 S. TIMPANARO, Classicismo e illuminismo nell'Ottocento italiano, 1969   10 Id., La filologia di Giacomo Leopardi, 1977

ADDITIONAL BIBLIOGRAPHY J. T. KIRBY, Secrets of the Muses Retold: Classical Influences on Italian Authors of the Twentieth Century, 2000   MASSIMO FUSILLO

VI. MUSEUMS
A. OVERVIEW   B. ARCHITECTURE   C. HISTORY
D. INFORMATION ON SELECTED MUSEUMS

A. OVERVIEW
It is probably true to say that every Italian town with a major archaeological excavation has a collection of antiquities. So far, however, an overall presentation of public museums and, in particular, their recent history is completely lacking. The present article considers museums of antiquities and/or museums with an important department of antiquities, which possess Italian,

Etruscan, Greek and Roman antiquities or, more rarely, Egyptian, Punic-Phoenician or didactic collections.

B. ARCHITECTURE
Once antiquities came to be preserved in a small study ('studiolo'), the latter was transformed in the 15th cent. into a cabinet of antiquities, comparable to the use, often encountered later, of libraries for expositions of finds. At the same time, large-scale stone sculptures were exhibited in villas and gardens of antiquities (e.g. by Poggio Bracciolini in the 'Academia Valdarnina' near Terranuova in 1438; Palazzo Medici, Florence 1444–92). Other varieties included the portico or the loggia as a lapidarium (e.g. the Palazzo dei Conservatori, Rome, for large bronzes, 1471), the courtyard of antiquities (e.g. the Cortile delle Statue, Vatican, from 1506, and the Palazzo Capranica della Valle, Rome, 1532/39), followed somewhat later by the façade with antiquities (e.g. the Villa Medici in the 16th cent., and in the 17th cent. the Villa Borghese, the Palazzo Mattei, Villa Pamphili, all in Rome, and, as late as ca. 1715, the Palazzo Riccardi in Florence). The Galleria degli Uffizi in Florence, founded in 1588, can be considered the prototype for the popular museum galleries of later times (cf. e.g. the Gonzagas' galleries: Sabbioneta, 1580–84; Palazzo Ducale in Mantua, 1595–1612). An enclosed building was more suitable for the protected exhibition of antiquities than an open loggia, and the loggia of the Palazzo Farnese in Rome was converted into a gallery from 1568/93. In the 17th cent., the term 'gallery' became synonymous with an art collection. However, none of these buildings was originally planned as a museum. A specialised museum architecture, implying a decisive step away from villa decoration, did not develop until the latter half of the 18th cent. (e.g. → ROME, VILLA ALBANI, 1760; Museo Pio Clementino and Museo Braccio Nuovo, Vatican, 1770–1822; extension of the → UFFIZI, Florence, 1787). Unlike the rest of Europe, the numerous museum foundations of the 19th cent. scarcely resulted in new construction: almost without exception, older buildings were fitted out appropriately for this new purpose. Not until the 20th cent. did several new buildings arise: Cagliari and the Barracco Museum, Rome, 1904; Fiesole, 1912; Reggio/Calabria, 1932; Paestum, 1952; Museo della Civiltà Romana, EUR, 1951–55; Adria, 1961; Museo Paolino, Vatican, 1963; Agrigento, Syracuse and Policoro, 1967–69.

C. HISTORY
1. PRIVATE COLLECTIONS   2. THE CREATION OF THE FIRST MUSEUMS   3. MUSEUMS SINCE THE 18TH CENTURY   4. THE CONCEPT OF COLLECTIONS AND DISPLAYS

1. PRIVATE COLLECTIONS
The history of Italian museums is inextricably interwoven with that of the early private collections. They formed the origin of many public museums; moreover,

older private collections were incorporated into museums. Most private collections arose in Rome, and popes, cardinals, princes, Humanists and artists were active as collectors from the 15th cent. The importance of private collections becomes clear from the descriptions by Aldrovandi (1550) and Bellori (1665), who counted more than 150 collections in Rome alone. The largest and most important of them, until its dispersal in 1720, can be considered the collection of Vincenzo Giustiniani. The Albani collection, established in 1734, the last old-style, large private collection, showed the way for future museum architecture. The opening of these collections to visitors was left up to the benevolence and generosity of their owners. Today, new research and publications on *collezionismo* provide a good overview of the history of private collections.

2. THE CREATION OF THE FIRST MUSEUMS

The collection of large-scale ancient bronzes founded in 1471 by Pope Sixtus IV and set up in the Palazzo dei Conservatori in Rome, must be considered the world's first public museum and the precursor of the Capitoline museums. Collections of inscriptions and statues of interest for municipal history, that is, which had historical-political significance like those on the Capitol in Rome, were also set up in other cities in the Palazzi Comunali or Pubblici (e.g. Brescia, 1480/85; Pesaro, 2nd half of the 15th cent.; Rimini, 1542/45). Even the Courtyard of Statues in the Vatican, which was set up beginning in 1506 at the instigation of pope Julius II, and soon became renowned for the quality of its works of art, served the purpose of the pope's self-representation. As the foundation of the Grimani collections had already brought the Statuario Pubblico to life at Venice in 1523/96, so several other private collections that had arisen in the 17th cent. became public institutions, often by bequest after their owner's death. Henceforth, an often-attested designation for these institutions is *Musaeum* or *Museo* (e.g. Museo Aldrovandi in the Palazzo Pubblico, Bologna, 1603/48; Musaeum Septalianum, Milan, 1664; Museo Cospiano, Bologna, 1667/77; and Museo Kircheriano in the Collegio Romano, Rome, 1678). One may compare the catalogue-style publications that appeared even more frequently under this title (e.g. Musaeum: Borromeo, Cat. Pinacoteca Ambrosiana, Milan, after 1618 f.; Musaeum Metallicum, U. Aldrovandi, Bologna, 1648; Musaeum Chartaceum: Cassiano dal Pozzo, Rome, before 1657; Musaeum Etruscum: A. F. Gori, Florence, 1736-43; Musaeum Veronense: S. Maffei, Cat. Verona, 1749).

3. MUSEUMS SINCE THE 18TH CENTURY

The 18th cent. saw the creation of state and municipal museums, which, as public institutions, were now provided with a director, curators, regular opening hours and catalogues. Particular mention should be made of the museums in Rome sponsored by the popes (Museo Ecclesiastico, Vatican, 1703-16; Musei Capitolini, 1734/1838; Museo Pio Clementino, 1769/84) and the Uffizi in Florence (1737/89). As far as the collections of the Bourbons in Naples were concerned (Capodimonte, 1738; Portici, 1750), it is true to a certain extent that interested visitors were denied access as far as possible. In the rest of Europe, one cannot speak of an 'Age of Museums' until the 19th century. As a result of the growing interest in antiquities abroad and under the influence of the Napoleonic art theft after the Treaty of Tolentino in 1797, there were increasing efforts in I. to control the export of antiquities. The "Chirografo", of 1802, promulgated by Pope Pius VII and probably drafted by Antonio Canova, was influential on future antiquities legislation. Finds from the many new excavations and the return of many art works from the Louvre in 1815 brought about the creation or expansion of many museums in I. The great national museums arose in Rome after the Italian unification of 1870 (Museo delle Terme, Villa Giulia, Museo Paletnologico) and in Florence (Archaeological Museum). Beginning in 1874, the state's solicitude also resulted in the formation of supervisory committees, from the *Consiglio centrale* and the *Direzione generale* under Giuseppe Fiorelli to the creation of individual *Sopraintendenze* in 1907. Increasing excavation activity throughout I. resulted in an increasing number of creations of new museums around the end of the 19th cent. and the beginning of the 20th cent. Excavation finds no longer migrated into the central museums, but a decentralisation was introduced, particularly in Etruria and South I., with the finds remaining in the new local museums. Unlike other European museums, Italian museums continued to receive unrestricted input from excavations in the 20th cent., which led to the establishment of numerous collections of antiquities at the locations of finds.

4. THE CONCEPT OF COLLECTIONS AND DISPLAYS

Until the 16th cent., it was primarily minor arts that were collected; in addition, there were also lapidaria and collections of paintings. The encyclopedic interest of the 16th cent., which also embraced natural history, manifested itself in the 'curiosity cabinets' that were widespread particularly in northern Europe (*guardaroba, camerino, studiolo*; e.g. the Aldrovandi collection, 2nd half of the 16th. cent., the Cospi collection, mid–17th cent., both in Bologna; the Kircher collection, 17th cent., Rome). In the 18th cent., the material was sorted, classified and displayed according to chronological or aesthetic criteria (following Winckelmann). In the 19th cent., attempts were often made to display the finds in an historicising setting (Pompeian red walls, Egyptianising decor). From the end of the 19th cent., the goal was to create thematically classified exhibitions (Villa Giulia, Rome; Archaeological Museum, Florence); finally, didactic museums were instituted (E. Löwy, Plaster Cast Museum/Museo dei Gessi, 1892; R. Lanciani, exhibition of ancient Rome, 1911; both at Rome). The current situation reflects the respective period of a museum's origin, which is taken into account in all renovation and restoration projects.

Thus, historical collections/villa decorations subsist alongside chronological arrangements, aesthetic exhibits and thematic museums. In addition to the displays in the new buildings mentioned above, some Roman museums have recently undergone a complete overhaul of their displays (e.g. the Palazzo Massimo and Palazzo Altemps, 1995–97).

1 M. BARBANERA, L'archeologia degli Italiani, 1998
2 H. BECK et al. (eds.), Antikensammlungen im 18. Jahrhundert, 1981   3 D. BOSCHUNG, H. v. HESBERG (eds.), Antikensammlungen des europäischen Adels im 18. Jahrhundert, Kongreß Düsseldorf 1996, 1999   4 Capire l'Italia. I musei. Touring Club Italiano, 1980   5 Documenti inediti per servire alla storia dei musei italiani pubblicati per cura del Ministero della pubblica istruzione 1–4, 1878–80   6 H. DÜTSCHKE, Antike Bildwerke in Oberitalien 1–5, 1874–82   7 A. EMILIANI, Leggi, bandi e provvedimenti per la tutela dei beni artistici e culturali negli antichi stati italiani 1571–1860, 1978   8 Enciclopedia Italiana 5. App. 1979–92, 1993, 589–597 s. v. Museo   9 Enciclopedia Universale dell'Arte 9, 1963, 738–772 s. v. Musei e collezioni   10 C. GASPARRI, s. v. Collezioni archeologiche, in: EAA 2. Suppl. II, 1994, 192–225   11 R. FRANCOVICH, A. ZIFFERERO (eds.), Musei e parchi archeologici, 1999   12 R. FRANCOVICH, D. MANACORDA (eds.), Dizionario di archeologia, 2000, 196–199 s. v. Musei   13 W. LIEBENWEIN, in: H. BECK, P. C. BOL (eds.), Forschungen zur Villa Albani. Antike Kunst und die Epoche der Aufklärung, 1982, 464–496   14 Musei e Gallerie d'Italia 1–25, 1956–80. N. S. 1–10, 1982–86   15 F. NUVOLARI, V. PAVAN (eds.), Archeologia, Museo, Architettura, 1987   16 F. PELLATI, I musei e le gallerie d'Italia, 1922   17 C. PIETRANGELI, in: Museo perchè – Museo come, 1980, 11–20   18 N. THOMPSON DE GRUMMOND (ed.), An Encyclopedia of the History of Classical Archaeology, 1996, s. v. esp. Collecting, Museum.

D. INFORMATION ON SELECTED MUSEUMS

The following catalogue makes no claim to completeness; it attempts to offer a cross-section of the many-sided spectrum of Italian museums, and in the process to present some of the most important institutions. The 'great' museums are dealt with under their own headings.

1. BOLOGNA, MUSEO CIVICO ARCHEOLOGICO
2. BRESCIA, MUSEO CIVICO ROMANO
3. FERRARA, MUSEO ARCHEOLOGICO NAZIONALE
4. FLORENCE, MUSEO ARCHEOLOGICO
5. MOZIA, MUSEO WHITAKER 6. PALESTRINA, MUSEO ARCHEOLOGICO NAZIONALE PRENESTINO
7. PARMA, MUSEO NAZIONALE DI ANTICHITÀ
8. REGGIO CALABRIA, MUSEO NAZIONALE
9. ROME, MUSEO BARRACCO 10. ROME, MUSEO E GALLERIA BORGHESE 11. ROME, MUSEO DELLA CIVILTÀ ROMANA 12. SPERLONGA, MUSEO ARCHEOLOGICO NAZIONALE 13. SYRACUSE, MUSEO ARCHEOLOGICO REGIONALE PAOLO ORSI
14. TARANTO, MUSEO ARCHEOLOGICO NAZIONALE 15. TURIN, MUSEO EGIZIO
16. VENICE, MUSEO ARCHEOLOGICO
17. VERONA, MUSEO LAPIDARIO MAFFEIANO

1. BOLOGNA, MUSEO CIVICO ARCHEOLOGICO

The Aldrovandi collection was bequeathed to the city in 1603, and opened in 1617 in the Palazzo Pubblico as the Museo Aldrovandi; the Cospi collection was added to it in 1660. In 1711, the University Museum was founded on the basis of the Marsili collection. The Aldrovandi and Cospi collections were ceded to this museum in 1743, and it enjoyed the patronage of Pope Benedict XIV from 1740 to 1758. In the 19th cent., it received acquisitions from excavations (e.g. from Certosa in 1869), in addition to a collection of coins in 1857, and the creation of the Palagi collection in 1860 (head of Athena Lemnia). The Museo Civico was founded in 1871; from 1878/81, it united the existing museums at its present location in the Palazzo Galvani. In addition to Italian-Etruscan antiquities (Felsina steles, bronze situlas), it has Roman and Egyptian sections.

19 A. M. BRIZZOLARA, Le sculture del Mus. Civico Archeologico di Bologna. La Collezione Marsili, 1986   20 Id., Ocnus 1, 1993, 53–61   21 P. DUCATI, Guida del Mus. Civico di Bologna, 1923   22 G. GUALANDI, Carrobbio 5, 1979, 243–260; 14, 1988, 309–321   23 C. MORIGI GOVI, D. VITALI, Il Mus. Civico Archeologico di Bologna, 1982/1988²   24 C. MORIGI GOVI, G. SASSATELLI, Dalla Stanza delle Antichità al Mus. Civico, 1984   25 Museu Civico Archeologico on the World Wide Web: www.comune.bologna.it/museoarcheologico

2. BRESCIA, MUSEO CIVICO ROMANO

By a decree of 1480, a public lapidarium was established in the Piazza della Loggia as early as 1485. After excavations at the Roman Capitol in 1823–26, the Museo Patrio was opened in 1830, and renamed the Museo dell'Età Romana following its separation from the medieval collection in 1882. The Capitol was dismantled from 1939 to 1943, and the museum it housed was renovated between 1948 and 1956. Outstanding in the collection of Roman antiquities are the bronze Victoria and bronze portraits. Plans for a new display of the antiquities resulted in the opening of the Museo della Città at the San Giulia monastery in 1999.

26 Brescia romana. Materiali per un Museo II, 1979   27 M. MIRABELLA ROBERTI, Il Civico Museo Romano di Brescia, 1959/1981²   28 G. PANAZZA, La Pinacoteca e i Musei di Brescia, 1961/1968², 7–42   29 C. STELLA, Guida del Museo Romano di Brescia, 1987   30 C. STELLA, F. MORANDINI, Quaderni di Archeologia del Veneto 14, 1998, 164–167   31 Museo Santa Giulia on the World Wide Web: www.santagiulia.info/museo_di_santa_giulia, www.numerica.it/santagiulia

3. FERRARA, MUSEO ARCHEOLOGICO NAZIONALE

The Este collection in the Palazzo dei Diamanti was dispersed as early as 1598 (some of it to Modena). After the creation of the Museo Atestiniano by Andrea Vico and Pirro Ligorio, a lapidarium arose in the Palazzo dell'Università in 1735, which was united with several other collections (Riminaldi collection, 1750; Bellini

collection, 1758; Ugolini vase collection, 1846), to become the Museo Civico di Schifanoia in 1898. In 1935, the Museo Archeologico Nazionale was created in the Palazzo Ludovico il Moro, to house the rich finds from the Etruscan necropoleis of Spina (Greek vases, particularly Attic red-figured vases of the 5th–3rd cent. BC, jewellery, bronzes). Spina was excavated between 1922 and 1935 and then again from 1954 onwards.
→ UFFIZI GALLERY, FLORENCE

32 N. ALFIERI, Spina. Museo Archeologico Nazionale di Ferrara 1, 1979   33 N. ALFIERI, P. E. ARIAS, Guida al Museo Archeologico di Ferrara, 1960   34 S. AURI-GEMMA, Il R. Museo di Spina, 1935/²1936   35 D. BALDONI, Guida al Museo Archeologico Nazionale di Ferrara (n.d.)   36 F. BERTI, P. G. GUZZO (eds.), Spina. Storia di una città tra Greci ed Etruschi, Exhibition Ferrara, 1993   37 F. BERTI, M. HARARI (eds.), Spina tra archeologia e storia, 2004   38 Museo Archeologico Nazionale on the World Wide Web: www.archeobo.arti.beniculturali.it/ferrara, www.archeologia.beniculturali.it/pages/atlante/S45.html

4. FLORENCE, MUSEO ARCHEOLOGICO

Material from the collections of the Medici and the Lorenas constitutes the nucleus of the museum; several pieces stem from the earliest collections of Cosimo the Elder and Lorenzo il Magnifico (bronze horse head), and many from the Palazzo Vecchio and the Uffizi. The Nizzoli Egyptian collection was separated from the Uffizi and stored in the Cenacolo di Foligno in 1824, followed by the Etruscan antiquities in 1832. The Museo Etrusco was created In 1870, moving in 1881 to its current seat in the Palazzo della Crocetta. In 1897/98, L. A. Milani reorganised the material, and the museum was henceforth named Museo Topografico Centrale dell'Etruria; a section for Etruscan painting was set up in 1928. The floods of 1966 forced extensive renovations. The museum possesses the largest Italo-Etruscan collection outside of the Villa Giulia (bronzes: chimaeras, the Arringatore, the Idolino, the Minerva; the François vase and other Greek vases; the Milani kouroi; the most important Egyptian collection after Turin).

39 A. DE AGOSTINO, Il Museo Archeologico centrale dell'Etruria, 1959/68   40 P. BOCCI PACINI, Bollettino d'arte 68, 6. Ser. 17, 1983, 93–108   41 Id., in: C. MORIGI GOVI, G. SASSATELLI, Dalla Stanza delle Antichità al Museo Civico, 1984, 565–570   42 G. CAPUTO, Il Museo Archeologico di Firenze, 1967   43 L. A. MILANI, Il Museo Topografico dell'Etruria, Florence and Rome 1898   44 Id., Il R. Museo Archeologico di Firenze, 1912/1923²   45 Id., Origine e sviluppo. Studi e materiali N. S. 5, 1982, 35–175   46 A. MINTO, Il Museo Archeologico dell'Etruria, 1950

5. MOZIA, MUSEO WHITAKER

Giuseppe Whitaker founded a small museum on Mozia, an island situated off the coast of Marsala, to house the finds from his 1906–1929 excavations. It possesses the only collection of Punic-Phoenician antiquities in I. outside of Cagliari. The materials discovered in various campaigns since 1960 in the sanctuary and necropoleis (stelae, inscriptions, ceramics, jewellery) made necessary the addition of a new wing to the building. The best-known piece is the "Giovinetto di Mozia", found in 1979.
→ NAPLES, MUSEO NAZIONALE ARCHEOLOGICO

47 M. DENTI, RA 1997, 107–128   48 EAA 2. Suppl. 1971–1994, 1995, 827–832 s.v. Mozia, 1989, 62–92   49 C. O. PAVESE, L'auriga di Mozia, 1996   50 J. I S. WHITAKER, Motya, a Phoenician Colony in Sicily, 1921 (It. 1991)

6. PALESTRINA, MUSEO ARCHEOLOGICO NAZIONALE PRENESTINO

The antiquities in the Barberini collection came from Praeneste to Rome, where most of them went to the Villa Giulia in 1908. A small collection was set up in a hall of the episcopal seminary in Palestrina in 1905/13. In 1956, the Museo Nazionale was opened in the Palazzo Barberini, built on the site of the Roman sanctuary of Fortuna. Its displays include the Nile Mosaic (found before 1588 and returned from Rome), a fragmentary statue of Fortuna, and the Capitoline Triad, seized by the Carabinieri in 1994, along with other finds from the sanctuary and the surrounding countryside.

51 S. GATTI, Il Museo Archeologico di Palestrina, 1996   52 S. GATTI, N. AGNOLI, Palestrina: Santuario della Fortuna Primigenia, 2001   53 G. JACOPI, Il Santuario della Fortuna Primigenia e il Museo Archeologico Prenestino, 1959/⁴1973   54 P. G. P. MEYBOOM, The Nile Mosaic of Palestrina, 1995   55 J. F. MOFFITT, Zeitschrift für Kunstgeschichte 60, 1997, 227–247   56 Palestrina: Il Museo Archeologico Nazionale, 1999   57 G. QUATTROCCHI, Il Museo Archeologico Prenestino, 1956   58 P. ROMANELLI, Palestrina, 1967, 83–93

7. PARMA, MUSEO NAZIONALE DI ANTICHITÀ

The Farnese collection was transferred from Parma to Naples at the instigation of the Bourbon king Charles III in 1734/36; only a few antiquities from this collection remained at the Palazzo del Giardino or, from 1752, in the *Accademia delle Belle Arti* (colossal head of Zeus, Praxitelean Eros, basalt torso). On the other hand, antiquities from the Gonzaga collection came to Parma from Mantua in 1587. In 1760, Philip I of Bourbon founded the Palazzo Reale Museo di Antichità to house the finds from his excavations at Velleia (from 1760–63; cycle of statues of the Julio-Claudian imperial family; discovery of the *tabula alimentaria* as early as 1747). The museum was augmented down to 1828/33 by several other collections (Canonici collection, 1768; Cattaneo collection, 1773; vases, Egyptian artifacts). As director from 1867 to 1870/75, Luigi Pigorini placed particular emphasis on the prehistoric collection.

59 A. FROVA, R. SCARANI, Parma. Museo Nazionale di Antichità, 1965   60 H. JUCKER, JDAI 92, 1977, 204–240   61 M. MARINI CALVANI, Museo Archeologico Nazionale di Parma, 2001   62 M. MARINI CALVANI, Veleia, 1975   63 Id., in: C. MORIGI GOVI, G. SASSATELLI, Dalla Stanza delle Antichità al Museo Civico, 1984, 483–492   64 Id., Ocnus 3, 1995, 125–153

8. Reggio Calabria, Museo Nazionale

In 1882, the Museo Civico was established in the bishop's palace, which was severely damaged in the 1908 earthquake. At the instigation of the Soprintendenza created in 1907, under the direction of Paolo Orsi, the municipal and state collections were to be joined, and construction of a new building for the Museo Nazionale di Reggio Calabria began in 1932. The museum, intended to house finds from all of Calabria, was not opened until 1958; several branch museums arose from 1967–1971. The bronze statues salvaged in 1972 from the sea off Riace and restored in Florence, have been in the museum since 1981. Also noteworthy are a bronze portrait of a philosopher, excavation finds from Locri, and the prehistoric collection.

65 D. Da Empoli, Klearchos 4, 1962, 99–105   66 A. De Franciscis, Il Museo Nazionale di Reggio Calabria, 1959 67 G. Foti, Il Museo Nazionale di Reggio Calabria, 1972 68 E. Lattanzi, Il Museo Nazionale di Reggio Calabria, 1987   69 Id., in: F. Mazza (ed.), Reggio Calabria. Storia, cultura, economia, 1993, 65–90   70 V. Spinazzola, Delle antichità e dell'ordinamento del Museo di Reggio, 1905/1907

9. Rome, Museo Barracco

The Giovanni Barracco collection, established on the advice of W. Helbig in 1860, was donated to the city in 1902. The Museo di Scultura Antica, under the direction of L. Pollak, opened in 1904 in a specially-constructed building. It continued to register new accessions until 1914, but was demolished in 1938, reopening in 1948 as the Museo Barracco in the Palazzo Farnesina dei Baullari. Its ca. 380 pieces provide an overview of all ancient Mediterranean cultures: particularly noteworthy are the Greek originals and good Roman copies (head of Marsyas, head of Pericles, Diadumenos fragment, Caesar Barracco).

76 G. Barracco, W. Helbig, La Collection Barracco, 1893/1907 ital.   77 G. Barracco, L. Pollak, Catalogo del Museo di Scultura Antica, 1910   78 M. Nota Santi, M. G. Cimino, Museo Barracco, 1991   79 Il 'Nuovo' Museo Barracco. Mostra storica e documentaria, 1982 80 C. Pietrangeli, Museo Barracco di scultura antica, ⁴1973

10. Rome, Museo e Galleria Borghese

The Scipione Borghese collection, with its ancient and contemporary sculptures and paintings, came into being beginning in 1605. The antiquities were displayed until 1628 in the villa and garden of the Villa Pinciana, built 1612–1615. At the same time, the sculpture collection increased rapidly in size, incorporating the Ceoli collection by 1607, and the della Porta collection, by way of Scipione's uncle Giovanni Battista, in 1609. Marcantonio Borghese continued to enlarge the collection down to the late 18th cent. (finds from excavations at Gabii, 1792). With the sale of almost the entire holdings (523 items) by Camillo Borghese and Paolina Bonaparte to Napoleon and the Louvre in 1807, the collection lost its importance, which it was unable to regain despite the partial return of pieces for which payment had not been received, and the attempted restoration, until 1828/1832, by Francesco Borghese. The museum, under public administration since 1902, was completely renovated in 1997, and its antiquities were restored (Trajanic Frieze, sarcophagus with battle scene, relief of a horseback rider).

81 H. Herdejürgen, AA 1997, 479–503   82 K. Kalveram, Die Antikensammlung des Kardinals Scipione Borghese, 1995   83 L. de Lachenal, Xenia 4, 1982, 49–117   84 P. Moreno, Museo e Galleria Borghese. La collezione archeologica, 1980   85 P. Moreno, C. Sforzini, Scienze dell'Antichità 1, 1987, 339–371

11. Rome, Museo della Civiltà Romana

The items on display at the 1911 Mostra Archeologica, organised by Rodolfo Lanciani and preserved in the Museo dell'Impero Romano from 1927, along with those from the 1937 Mostra Augustea della Romanità, were to be presented at the World Exhibition of 1942, which did not take place owing to the Second World War. Construction of the new building on the site of the Esposizione Universale di Roma (EUR) did not begin until 1951. The didactic museum, with some 50 sections, was able to open in 1955 (plaster casts, models, model of Constantinian Rome by I. Gismondi; objects of everyday Roman life; building technique, transport, industry, religion).
→ Rome, Capitoline Museums; → Rome, National Museum; → Rome, Villa Albani; → Rome, Villa Giulia; → Rome, Vatican Museums

86 A. M. Colini, G. Q. Giglioli, Il Museo della Civiltà Romana, 1955   87 Dalla Mostra al Museo. Dalla mostra archeologica del 1911 al Museo della Civiltà Romana, 1983   88 Esposizione internazionale di Roma. Catalogo della Mostra Archeologica nelle Terme di Diocleziano, 1911   89 M. Guicciardino, Il Museo della Civiltà Romana, Bollettino dei Musei Comunali di Roma 2, 1988, 81–93   90 A. M. Liberati Silverio, Il Palazzo della Civiltà Romana e il Museo della Civiltà Romana in EUR. Guida degli istituti culturali, 1995, 56ff. and 109ff. 91 A. M. Liberati Silverio (ed.), Museo della Civiltà Romana. Guida, 1987   92 Mostra Augustea della Romanità. Catalogo, ⁴1938   93 Museo della Civiltà Romana. Catalogo, 1976/²1982

12. Sperlonga, Museo Archeologico Nazionale

About 7,000 fragments of marble sculptures were found during the excavation of the Grotto of Tiberius in 1957. A new museum building was opened directly on the find spot in 1963, to house the large statue groups portraying adventures from the Iliad and Odyssey (Scylla, Polyphemus; restorations 1967–71) as well as smaller finds.

94 B. Andreae, Praetorium Speluncae, 1994/1995² it. 95 Id., Odysseus. Mythos und Erinnerung, Exhibition catalogue, 1999/²2000, 177–223   96 N. Cassieri, Il Museo Archeologico di Sperlonga, 1996   97 F. Coarelli,

Tiberio e Sperlonga, 1973   98 B. CONTICELLO, B. ANDREAE, Die Skulpturen von Sperlonga, AntPl 14, 1974   99 G. JACOPI, L'Antro di Tiberio a Sperlonga. I Monumenti Romani, 1963

13. SYRACUSE, MUSEO ARCHEOLOGICO REGIONALE PAOLO ORSI

The episcopal Alagona collection, housed in the library at the end of the 18th cent., was combined with the Trigona, Landolina and Iudica collections to create the Museo Civico in 1804/1811. The National Museum was created in the Convent on the Piazza del Duomo in 1886, with Paolo Orsi as the director from 1891. The museum was able to open in 1988, in the new building erected in 1968 on the grounds of the Villa Landolina. It holds primarily excavation finds from eastern and central Sicily (prehistoric, Greek, terracotta architecture: Megara Hyblaea, Camarina, Gela; Hellenistic ceramics from Centuripe; Aphrodite Landolina).

100 G. AGNELLO, Siculorum Gymnasium 21, 1968, 38–53   101 B. DAIX WESCOAT (ed.), Syracuse, the Fairest Greek City. Exhibition Atlanta, 1989   102 B. DE MARTINEZ LA RESTIA, Archivio Storico per la Sicilia Orientale 4. Ser. 8–9, 1955–56, 94–111   103 G. LIBERTINI, Il Regio Museo Archeologico, 1929   104 G. VOZA, Museo Archeologico Regionale Paolo Orsi, 1987

14. TARANTO, MUSEO ARCHEOLOGICO NAZIONALE

After the rich finds from L. Viola's first excavations from 1881 on, the creation of a museum was decided in 1887. In was not until 1906 that, with the extension of the convent of San Pasquale, a museum arose from the existent antiquities depot. Through the large quantities of finds from the necropoleis of Tarentum (vases, terracottas, gold jewellery; especially 4th cent. BC and Hellenistic) and antiquities from throughout Apulia, it soon developed into the most important museum in the south, outside of Naples. Despite the addition of a new wing (1939–1952), there was not enough room for the archaeological materials, which grew rapidly, particularly after the Second World War–a problem which still persists, even after the construction of an underground depot in 1972. The art-historical arrangement of the exhibition, newly created in 1954–63, broke up many of the grave contexts, which today are once again highly valued.

105 Catalogo del Museo Nazionale Archeologico di Taranto I–IV, 1990–95   106 D. GRAEPLER, Tonfiguren im Grab, 1997, 23–30   107 E. DE JULIIS, D. LOIACONO, Taranto. Il Museo Archeologico, 1985   108 E. LIPPOLIS (ed.), Arte e artigianato in Magna Grecia, Exhibition Taranto, 1996   109 Il Museo di Taranto. Cento anni di archeologia, Exhibition Taranto, 1987, 1988   110 Il Museo Nazionale di Taranto e i suoi protagonisti, 1992

15. TURIN, MUSEO EGIZIO

The Museo d'Antichità, created in 1724 from the 16th-/17th-cent. collection of the kings of Savoy, already contained Egyptian antiquities (Mensa Isiaca from Rome, ca. 1630, statues of V. Donati, 1760). The acquisition of some 5,300 Egyptian antiquities from the Drovetti collection (New Kingdom and later, particularly from Thebes) led in 1824 to the creation of the Museo Egizio by Carlo Felice of Savoy, and in 1831 to the unification of the museums in the Palazzo dell'Accademia delle Scienze, which had been under public administration since 1880. The separation of Egyptian from Egyptianising antiquities was undertaken in 1882. The Graeco-Roman section was separated from the Egyptian section in 1939/40, and relocated in 1982. The holdings of the Museo Egizio were increased considerably through the excavations of its directors Ernesto Schiaparelli (1894–1928) and Giulio Farina (1928–1947); in 1965, the Egyptian government donated the cliff temple of Thutmosis III of Nubia to the museum.

111 S. CURTO, Storia del Museo Egizio di Torino, 1976   112 Id., L'antico Egitto nel Museo Egizio di Torino, 1984   113 A. M. DONADONI ROVERI et al., Il Museo Egizio di Torino, 1988   114 S. DONADONI et al., L'Egitto dal mito all'Egittologia, 1990   115 A. ROCCATI, Museo Egizio Torino, 1988   116 E. VASSILIKA, Tesori d'Arte del Museo Egizio, 2006

16. VENICE, MUSEO ARCHEOLOGICO

As early as 1460, Cardinal Pietro Barbo (later Pope Paul II) owned a collection of ancient minor arts, which was soon dispersed. The collection compiled at Rome by Cardinal Domenico Grimani ca. 1505 (statues, Grimani Library) was bequeathed to the city of Venice in 1523. The donation of the collection of his nephew Giovanni (130 sculptures, gem collection) in 1586/93 led to the establishment in 1596 of the Statuario Pubblico of the Republic of Venice in the Libreria del Sansovino. Inventories prepared in 1528 and 1593 provide information about the extent of the collection. The museum, transferred to the Palazzo Ducale in 1811, grew constantly through the amalgamation of other collections (Contarini, before 1713; Zulian, 1795; Molin, 1816; Cernazai of Udine, 1900). After the museum's war-time evacuation, it reopened in 1926 in the Palazzo Reale, its current location. In 1939, antiquities from the Museo Correr were added to its collection. Among the numerous marble sculptures (Ara Grimani, Agrippa) are a few Greek originals.

117 C. ANTI, Il R. Museo Archeologico nel Palazzo Reale di Venezia, 1930   118 I. FAVORETTO, G. TRAVERSARI, Tesori di scultura greca a Venezia. Raccolte private del '500, 1993   119 I. FAVORETTO, G. L. RAVAGNAN (eds.), Lo Statuario Pubblico della Serenissima. Due secoli di collezionismo, exhibition Venice, 1997   120 B. FORLATI TAMARO, Il Museo Archeologico del Palazzo Reale di Venezia, 1953/²1969

17. VERONA, MUSEO LAPIDARIO MAFFEIANO

The Bevilacqua sculpture collection, which arose 1536–1593, was dispersed at an early stage (to Munich in 1811). Scipione Maffei collected some 200 antiquities for the museum he had founded in 1714, 30 of which came from the Roman Nichesola collection. The lapidarium in the vestibule of the Teatro Filarmonico, consisting primarily of Roman inscriptions, grew rapidly (some 600 inscriptions, as well as Greek reliefs). A portico was built to house the collection between 1744 and 1749. Maffei's publication *Museum Veronense*, arranged by sections, was published in 1749. The original exhibition was not fundamentally changed, even after the renovation completed in 1982. The Museo Archeologico del Teatro, installed in the San Gerolamo Convent in 1920, goes back to the Museo Civico of 1812 (finds of Roman theatrical equipment).

121 L. FRANZONI, A. RUDI, in: F. NUVOLARI, V. PAVAN (eds.), Archeologia, Museo, Architettura, 1987, 26–34; 56–59; 96–103   122 D. MODONESI, Museo Maffeiano. Iscrizioni e rilievi sacri latini, 1995   123 Il Museo Maffeiano riaperto al pubblico, 1982/1986²   124 Nuovi Studi Maffeiani, colloquium Verona 1983, 1985   125 G. ROMANELLI, in: L. PUPPI (ed.), Ritratto di Verona, 1978, 397–427.   JENS KÖHLER

Ius commune see → CODIFICATION